Goldmine™

STANDARD CATALOG OF®

Rhythm & Blues Records

Tim Neely

Published by

krause publications
An F&W Publications Company

700 East State Street • Iola, WI 54990-0001
715-445-2214 • 888-457-2873
www.krause.com

Please call or write for our free catalog of music publications.
Our toll-free number to place an order or obtain a free catalog is 800-258-0929
or please use our regular business telephone 715-445-2214
for editorial comment and further information.

Library of Congress Catalog Number: 2002105776
ISBN: 0-87349-435-0
Printed in the United States of America

Contents

Introduction

At last, the wait is over.

Welcome to the *Goldmine* Standard Catalog of ® Rhythm & Blues Records. This book has been many years in the making; collectors and dealers alike have sought a comprehensive and up-to-date guide to "the sound of the city" for over two decades. Several attempts at a new R&B guide were made in the interim, but were marred by poor distribution, among other problems.

Inside, you'll find more R&B, soul and other related records listed in one place than in any other price guide. We also have thoroughly revised the pricing for those artists who appeared in earlier *Goldmine* price guides to reflect the growing demand for this music. Many of the increases are a result in the growing demand for 1970s soul and "old school" hip-hop and rap. Some of the values for early 12-inch singles are catching up to the values of some 1950s vocal group 45s.

When we started work on this book, we figured that the book's emphasis would be on the "classic" R&B and soul period from 1946-71. Basically, 1946 corresponds with the end of World War II and the beginning of the independent record labels that would spread "blues and rhythm" music to the masses, and 1971 is the year that Motown Records, one of the greatest of all the indie labels, moved its operations from Detroit to Los Angeles.

As the book developed, though, we found that we could not limit our focus on those years. Indeed, you'll find records by at least a couple artists whose first recordings were not issued until 2001!

But we're getting a bit ahead of ourselves here. As with all our *Goldmine* price guides, we consider the *Standard Catalog of ® Rhythm & Blues Records* a work in progress. Later, we'll tell you how you can make a second edition of this book even better. Let's first tell you what to expect from this edition.

What's included

Let's start at the end of the book's title – *Records*. This book consists of records, and only records. No tapes or compact discs are included. Even with all the listings from the years when vinyl was supposed to be dead, they are all records.

Included are the standard formats found in other *Goldmine* price guides – LPs, 45s, EPs and picture sleeves. Also, we've included thousands of 78s by artists who had success in the 1940s and 1950s and thousands of 12-inch singles by more recent artists.

We've been somewhat selective as to whose 78-rpm listings we've included this time. Generally, we've focused our 78-rpm research on those artists whose careers began before their labels started to make LPs and/or 45s. Unlike our past efforts in listing 78s, we've chosen to include *all* of an artist's 78s, even those that have a 45-rpm counterpart. You'll be able to see at a glance the difference in value between a 78 and a 45 of the same record. In general, the 45 is more valuable than the 78 – sometimes a *lot* more valuable – through about 1954 or 1955. Then the 78's value catches up to the 45. Around 1957, almost all 78s are worth more than the 45 version, with a huge difference by the end of 1958 and into 1959.

Twelve-inch singles were introduced in the United States in 1976 and are still being made today; you'll find a decent number of 2002 releases on 12-inch single in here.

Also, just because we set an arbitrary start date of 1946 doesn't mean there aren't older records in here. Many of the most successful R&B pioneers of the late 40s began recording before World War II, and in several cases, as early as the 1920s. When we chose to include those artists, we did not cut off their discographies; we went as far back as we could.

In sum, if it's meant to be played by a stylus gliding through a groove, it's listed.

The next part of the title – *Rhythm & Blues* – is more of a problem. We have chosen not to strictly define "rhythm & blues." No definition we could come up with really worked that well, and even the *Billboard* music charts have had a hard time with it.

Both the name of the charts, and the kind of music that appeared on them, have changed many times over the years. Some of the names used over the years include "Harlem Hit Parade," "Race Records," "Rhythm & Blues," "Soul" and, controversially in the 1980s, "Black." Today the charts are called "R&B/Hip-Hop."

Unlike when we did a country & western price guide, we could not in good conscience use the charts as a guide to whom to include. In the early 1960s, the R&B charts were looking more and more like the pop charts; *Billboard* even discontinued the R&B charts from late 1963 to early 1965 because they appeared redundant. In retrospect, this was a really bad time to do so, because 1964 is one of the pivotal years in R&B music history. That's the year that the Supremes, Temptations and Four Tops had their first major hits and Motown truly became "the sound of young America," at

least to those not completely infatuated with the sound of young England.

All this is a roundabout way of saying that, in addition to R&B/soul, you'll find other related genres when we felt it was appropriate. You'll find some pure blues, some jazz, some pop and some rock.

We also did not discriminate on the basis of race. There are many white performers mixed in with the predominantly black listings, most notably white doo-wop groups, "blue-eyed soul" performers and dance artists. We've also included Elvis Presley; after all, he did have six Number 1 records on the R&B charts, including one song that didn't get to the top of any other *Billboard* chart ("Wear My Ring Around Your Neck"), and he remains one of the top 50 R&B artists of all time according to chart data.

For more on the subject, please check Chuck Miller's preface on the subject and also his selection of the 50 essential R&B albums.

Finally, we reach the start of the book's title – *Standard Catalog of ®*. Our *American Records* titles strive toward completeness, and so does this book. We have not intentionally omitted any records by any artist listed in this book, except in the cases of some 78s and 12-inch singles where we didn't have enough time to finish the research. But we will get back to them.

For those for whom we do list 78s and 12-inch singles, all those we were able to confirm are included. If you have something we didn't list, and it was made in the United States, we want to know about it.

What's not included

As we implied earlier, *imports are not included, nor will they be in the future.* Even more than with other forms of music, collectors worldwide seek the United States pressings of the vast majority of the records and artists included in here.

Some artists who belong in a book such as this, but who have long and/or complicated discographies, didn't make the cut this time because of our deadlines. We have not forgotten them, and we will return to them.

For the most part, we did not include 78s by artists whose singles all exist on 45s. Most artists for whom we included 78s have at least one title in the format that was never released officially on 45. We plan to change that in the future.

Speaking of that, we don't include reproductions, or "repros" as they are known. They first started to

surface in the 1970s, when the prices of many R&B (especially vocal group) records started to creep into the hundreds of dollars. They were a way of making the music available to collectors who wanted it, and at a fraction of the going rate. The justification for what they were doing was the common belief that this rare music would otherwise be lost forever, as the owners of the rights to these records showed no interest in ever re-releasing them legitimately. The argument then falls apart because many of the reproductions were made to appear similar to, if not exactly like, the rare originals! In some cases, colored vinyl was used to add to the desirability. If the idea was to simply make the music available, why were the efforts at authenticity made? Of course, today, most of the music is available on compact disc for those who just want to hear it.

This has created a problem now, as many of these repros start to fall into hands other than those who originally owned them. People who don't know better think these are rare originals!

We'd like to add some information on repros in the future. For now, be alert that they exist, and unless you really trust your source, if a rare record looks too good to be true, it probably is. As a rule, a repro tends to sell in the $5-$8 range, about the same as a 1960s oldies reissue.

Grading your records

When it comes to records, and how much you'll get for them, remember this above all:

Condition is (almost) everything!

Yes, it's possible to get a high price for a beat-up record, if it's exceptionally rare. But for common material, if it's not in at least Very Good condition – and preferably closer to Near Mint – you won't get many buyers. Or at least you won't the second time around. So accurately grading your discs is important, whether you're selling your records to a dealer or selling them to another collector.

Visual or play grading? In an ideal world, every record would be played before it is graded. But the time involved makes it impractical for most dealers, and anyway, it's rare that you get a chance to hear a record before you buy through the mail. Some advertisers play-grade everything and say so. But unless otherwise noted, records are visually graded.

How to grade. Look at everything about a record – its playing surface, its label, its edges – under a strong light. Then, based on your overall

impression, give it a grade based on the following criteria:

Mint (M): Absolutely perfect in every way – certainly never played, possibly even still sealed. (More on still sealed under "Other considerations.") Should be used sparingly as a grade, if at all.

Near Mint (NM or M-): A nearly perfect record. Many dealers won't give a grade higher than this, implying (perhaps correctly) that no record is ever truly perfect.

The record should show no obvious signs of wear. A 45 RPM or EP sleeve should have no more than the most minor defects, such as almost invisible ring wear or other signs of slight handling.

An LP jacket should have no creases, folds, seam splits or any other noticeable similar defect. No cut-out holes, either. And of course, the same should be true of any other inserts, such as posters, lyric sleeves and the like.

Basically, an LP in Near Mint condition looks as if you just got it home from a new record store and removed the shrink wrap.

Near Mint is the highest price listed in all *Goldmine* price guides. Anything that exceeds this grade, in the opinion of both buyer and seller, is worth significantly more than the highest *Goldmine* book value.

Very Good Plus (VG+): Generally worth 50 percent of the Near Mint value.

A Very Good Plus record will show some signs that it was played and otherwise handled by a previous owner who took good care of it.

Record surfaces may show some slight signs of wear and may have slight scuffs or very light scratches that don't affect one's listening experience. Slight warps that do not affect the sound are OK.

The label may have some ring wear or discoloration, but it should be barely noticeable. The center hole will not have been misshapen by repeated play.

Picture sleeves and LP inner sleeves will have some slight ring wear, lightly turned-up corners, or a slight seam split. An LP jacket may have slight signs of wear also and may be marred by a cut-out hole, indentation or corner indicating it was taken out of print and sold at a discount.

In general, if not for a couple minor things wrong with it, this would be Near Mint. All but the most mint-crazy collectors will find a Very Good Plus record highly acceptable.

A synonym used by some collectors and dealers for "Very Good Plus" is "Excellent."

Very Good (VG): Generally worth 25 percent of the Near Mint value.

Many of the defects found in a VG+ record will be more pronounced in a VG disc.

Surface noise will be evident upon playing, especially in soft passages and during a song's intro and fade, but will not overpower the music otherwise. Groove wear will start to be noticeable, as will light scratches (deep enough to feel with a fingernail) that will affect the sound.

Labels may be marred by writing, or have tape or stickers (or their residue) attached. The same will be true of picture sleeves or LP covers. However, it will not have all of these problems at the same time, only two or three of them.

This *Goldmine* price guide lists Very Good as the lowest price. This, *not* the Near Mint price, should be your guide when determining how much a record is worth, as that is the price a dealer will normally pay you for a Near Mint record.

Good (G), Good Plus (G+): Generally worth 10-15 percent of the Near Mint value.

Good does not mean Bad! A record in Good or Good Plus condition can be put onto a turntable and will play through without skipping. But it will have significant surface noise and scratches and visible groove wear (on a styrene record, the groove will be starting to turn white).

A jacket or sleeve will have seam splits, especially at the bottom or on the spine. Tape, writing, ring wear or other defects will start to overwhelm the object.

If it's a common item, you'll probably find another copy in better shape eventually. Pass it up. But if it's something you have been seeking for years, and the price is right, get it... but keep looking to upgrade.

Poor (P), Fair (F): Generally worth 0-5 percent of the Near Mint price.

The record is cracked, badly warped, and won't play through without skipping or repeating. The picture sleeve is water damaged, split on all three seams and heavily marred by wear and writing. The LP jacket barely keeps the LP inside it. Inner sleeves are fully seam split, crinkled, and written upon.

Except for impossibly rare records otherwise unattainable, records in this condition should be bought or sold for no more than a few cents each.

Other grading considerations. Most dealers give a separate grade to the record and its sleeve or cover. In an ad, a record's grade is listed first, followed by that of the sleeve or jacket.

With **Still Sealed (SS)** records, let the buyer beware, unless it's a U.S. pressing from the last 10-15 years or so. It's too easy to re-seal one. Yes, some legitimately never-opened LPs from the 1960s still exist. But if you're looking for a specific pressing, the only way you can know for sure is to open the record. Also, European imports are not factory-sealed, so if you see them advertised as sealed, someone other than the manufacturer sealed them.

Grading scale for 78s

Most dealers in 78s have a slightly different grading system than the *Goldmine* system. The system uses only single-letter abbreviations and a series of pluses and minuses as follows:

N – New. Exactly that. This is a 78 that obviously has never been played and is in its original company paper sleeve. This grade is almost never used except for unplayed store stock. In this book, the "NM" value would be the "N" value for a 78, and should only be used for truly new 78s.

E – Excellent. The highest grade used by most 78 rpm dealers, with the occasional "+" to designate a really strong record. It's equivalent to "VG+" in this book. (If this book was all 78s, this is the highest price we'd list.)

V – Very Good. Most 78 rpm collectors are happy with a V record. It's roughly equivalent to a VG record for LPs and 45s. It's been played a bit and shows some obvious wear, but it is far from being abused.

G – Good. Here's where things start to get dicey. A record may have been played enough to cause some enlargement of the center hole, or the groove may be turning white, or some chips that don't affect the play have flaked off the edges.

F – Fair. See Good, except that the record has probably got an audible crack in it, too.

P – Poor. A truly unpleasant listening experience. Only acceptable for extremely rare, one-of-a-kind discs.

Common collecting abbreviations

In addition to the letters used to designate a record's grade, it's not uncommon to see other abbreviations used in dealer advertisements. Knowing the more common ones helps to prevent confusion. Here are some:

boot: bootleg (illegal pressing)
cc: cut corner
co: cutout
coh: cut-out hole
cov, cv, cvr: cover
demo: demonstration record (synonym for promo, this is the more common term overseas)
dh: drill hole
dj: disc jockey (promotional) record
ep: extended play (can be used for both 45s and LPs)
gf: gatefold (cover)
imp: import
ins: insert
lbl: label
m, mo: monaural (mono)
m/s: mono/stereo (usually used to describe a promo single that has the same song on both sides, with the only difference in the type of sound)
nap: (does) not affect play
noc: number on cover
nol: number on label
obi: not actually an abbreviation, "obi" is the Japanese word for "sash" and is used to describe the strip of paper usually wrapped around Japanese (and occasional US) pressings of LPs
orig: original
pr, pro, promo: promotional record
ps: picture sleeve (the cover that appears with some 45s and most 7-inch extended play singles)
q: quadraphonic
re: reissue
rec: record
repro: reproduction
ri: reissue
rw: ring wear
s: stereo
sl: slight
sm: saw mark
soc: sticker on cover
sol: sticker on label
ss: still sealed
s/t: self-titled
st: stereo
sw: shrink wrap
toc: tape on cover
tol: tape on label
ts: taped seam
w/: with
wlp: white label promo

wobc: writing on back cover
woc: writing on cover
wofc: writing on front cover
wol: writing on label
wr: wear
wrp: warp
xol: "x" on label

Some notes on the pricing

The prices listed in this book were determined from many sources.

The more common items reflect a consensus of used record shops and collectors, plus prices in ads over the past few months. In some ways, these items are more difficult to get a handle on; they sell without much publicity because of their low value, thus they aren't reported as often.

The rarer items are often the matter of conjecture because they so rarely come up for public sale. A high auction price for a truly rare piece can be the only way such an item's "worth" can be gauged, no matter what someone says about the value being inflated. Records, as with all collectibles, are only worth what someone will pay for them.

Because of the inexact nature of this undertaking, that's why we always urge you to use a book such as this as a guide and not as the final word on pricing.

We, too, can always use more input on the subject. See the **How you can help** section for more information.

And by the way, the publisher of the book does not engage in the buying and selling of records. So the prices listed in here should not be construed as "offers to buy" or "offers to sell" from Krause Publications.

Some notes on promotional records

To list every promotional version of every record in this book would be a consumption of space better used for unique listings. It would come close to doubling the length of the book. Some selected promos are listed, either because they are unique – in other words, the only version of the record is promotional or because it was pressed on a different color of wax than the stock copies – or because there is a significant, verifiable price difference between the promo and stock copies.

Obviously, not all promos are created equal.

It's probably easier to say which promotional copies are *not* going to fetch a premium. Those are copies that are otherwise identical to stock copies – the same label, the same number, the same everything – but are merely stamped on the front or back cover with (usually) a gold "For Promotion Only" indicator. There's nothing special about these records for the most part; any time the record company wants to create a promo, it can take a stock copy and gold-stamp it!

These are known as "designate promos" and rarely get more than 10 percent above the price of a regular stock copy, if that. For some sought-after rare items, such as Tori Amos' early album *Y Kant Tori Read,* designate promos go for much, much *less* than copies not so designated.

Some albums that appear to be "designate promos" do have collector value. These are copies pressed on special "audiophile vinyl," the most notable of which are the "Quiex II" pressings from the Warner-Reprise-Geffen family. Some of these fetch as much as 4-5 times the regular editions! These will *always* be marked on the cover with a sticker advertising the "Quiex II" record within.

Other promos of little collector value are those with a hole punch in the corner. This was Capitol's preferred method of creating promos during much of the 1970s. These are never worth more than the stock copy, and usually go for less.

Also, Columbia for a time merely used a "timing strip" on the front or back cover to designate a promo; these, too, also have little extra value above the stock copy. There is a major exception, though: The earliest promos for Bruce Springsteen's *Greetings From Asbury Park, N.J.* included both an attached timing strip *and* a glossy 8 1/2 x 11 "Bruce Springsteen Fact Sheet" glued to the back cover along the top. By the way, no white-label promos were ever pressed of this title.

Promos that *do* attract interest are those with custom promotional labels. Most of the time, these are white versions of the regular label, thus the term "white label promo." Of course, the label isn't always white; sometimes it's yellow or blue or pink or some other color. But it will always have as part of the label typesetting, "Promotional Copy" or "Audition Copy" or "Demonstration" or some other such term. Sometimes, the label will be almost identical to the stock versions, but some sort of words alluding to the promotional nature of the record will have been added to the typeset copy.

What makes these promos special? They are far more likely to have been mastered from the actual master mixdown tape, rather than a several-

generations-removed copy, thus making them of higher sonic quality than later editions. They are among the first to come off the presses – after all, promos get sent out before stock copies Sometimes they are specially mastered to sound better over the air or through a store's loudspeakers. Regardless, they are sought after, and their value ranges from the same as a stock copy to as much as twice that of a stock copy.

Another rule of thumb when it comes to promos: In most cases, the more valuable a stock copy is, the *less* valuable the promo is. That's because in these instances, there are fewer stock copies known to exist than the promos.

Making sense of the listings

The artists' names are in bold capital letters. They are alphabetized, for the most part, the way our computer did, so blame anything that seems way out of line on that. We've programmed in some "fudge factors" – artists who have numbers in their names are listed as if they spelled out the name; artists with "Mr." are listed as if their name was "Mister," and the same with "St." and "Saint."

On the next line under some artists are cross-references or other information we feel is helpful. In some cases, you'll see a number after an artist in parentheses. That means we have more than one different artist by that name in our database. If you have records by, say, Sylvia or Shorty Long and they are not listed in here, then they are most likely not by the R&B singer we list.

You'll also note that there are countless examples of groups with the same names. In some cases, we know that they are different groups and have broken up the listings accordingly. If we knew a group was *not* R&B-related, we omitted them. If we weren't sure, we erred on the side of inclusion.

Records are listed in five formats, in this order: "12-Inch Singles"; "45s"; "78s"; "7-Inch Extended Plays"; "Albums."

These are defined for the purposes of this book as follows:

A **12-inch single** is meant to promote or make available one particular song. These rarely have a name other than that of the song being promoted. Album-sized records with three or four songs on them that are not meant to specifically "sell" one song are 12-inch extended plays, and are listed under "Albums." Sometimes we had to make a judgment call as to where to put some of these.

A **45** is a seven-inch record, usually with one song on each side. It need not have a big hole. It need not even play at 45 rpm – for simplicity's sake, we've included Columbia Microgroove 33 1/3 rpm singles of the late 1940s and early 1950s in this category. They always have a note attached to them explaining what they are. Sometimes we list a 45 with more than one song on a side; either that's because the record was sold as a 45 or it was part of a record company's regular numbering system for 45s.

A **78** is usually a 10-inch record (larger than a 45, smaller than most LPs), usually with one song on each side. They are usually heavy, thick and brittle compared to newer records, and require a special stylus for best playback results, which are a couple reasons why they are not as avidly collected as 45s and LPs.

A **7-Inch Extended Play**, a product of the 1950s and early 1960s, is a hybrid. Most of the time they contain two songs on each side and had big holes, like 45s. But they almost always came with cardboard sleeves, like albums. Again, until only a few years ago, price guides always treated these items as inseparable. Consumers, however, often treated EPs like 45s – they threw out the covers. Reflecting that, all EP listings here have separate lines, and values, for the cover and the record.

An **album** is defined here as a 10- or 12-inch record (never 7 inches) that has a small hole and isn't a 12-inch single. Defining it any more than that is problematical. Some albums have only one song on a side, others have over a dozen; some play for 15 minutes, others for over an hour; some albums even play at 45 rpm rather than the standard 33 1/3 rpm. Unless noted, however, all albums are assumed to be 33 1/3s. No 78s are listed under albums.

Under each format listing, the records are sorted alphabetically by label, which are printed in all capital letters, then numerically within each label, ignoring prefixes. The one exception is with RCA Victor 45s, which are arranged with APBO issues first, then PB issues, then 447- series reissues, then other issues in order of prefix.

After many of the numbers is a number or letter in brackets. These designate something special about the listing as follows:

DJ: some sort of promotional copy, usually for radio stations and not meant for public sale

EP: extended play album (only used with album listings for 12-inch releases with 4 to 6 tracks and not as long as a regular album)

M: mono record

P: partially stereo record (rarely are records advertised as such; the determination has been made by careful listening)

PD: picture disc (the artwork is actually part of the record; these proliferated in the late 1970s and early 1980s and tend to have inferior sound quality)

PS: picture sleeve (this is the value for the sleeve *alone*; combine the record and sleeve value to get an estimated worth for the two together)

Q: quadraphonic record

R: rechanneled stereo record (these will usually be labeled with such terms as "Electronically Re-Channeled for Stereo"; "Enhanced for Stereo"; "Simulated Stereo"; or "Duophonic," but sometimes they aren't labeled as rechanneled)

S: stereo record

10: a 10-inch LP

(x) where x is a number: the number of records in a set (this is in parentheses inside the brackets so that in those rare instances where they exist, 10-record sets won't be confused with 10-inch LPs)

Most albums after 1968 do not have a stereo content designation. After 1968, if no designation is listed, it's probably stereo, though not necessarily. More importantly, it means that there was only one purchasing option available (except for the quadraphonic years of 1972-1977).

In the next, widest, column, we list the titles.

In the 12-inch single listings, we mention whether the version is extended, or how long it is, or something to identify it. We also mention, when known, whether a record has the same version on both sides.

For 45s, we list both the A- and B-side.

Each EP has two listings, one with its contents in order, one with the title of the EP as listed on the cover. In many cases, the title of the EP is found nowhere on the actual label – another reason to list the record and its sleeve separately.

If an asterisk (*) precedes the contents of the EP, we know that these are the songs on this record, but we're not sure this is the correct order. Readers with this information are welcome to supply confirmation.

As most albums are almost worthless without a cover, they have one listing with the title as shown on the cover (assuming a title is shown on the cover). Most album listings have a prefix, usually from one to five letters. These prefixes often tell you whether your album is a first pressing and can have a considerable effect on an album's value.

The next column lists the year of release. Please note that the year of release and the year of recording are not necessarily the same! For example, if an album had several singles taken from it, the later singles may not have come out until another year, even though all of the singles have the same year on them. Also note that many archival recordings are reissued many times. Just because an album claims to be "recorded in 1941" doesn't mean that it actually came out in 1941. It's far more likely to be a more modern release.

That said, some of these dates might be off by a year; sometimes a record is released in December of the year before or January of the year after. Other years we can only guess the decade, and the year will have a question mark in it.

The next three columns are the values in Very Good (VG), Very Good Plus (VG+), and Near Mint (NM) condition. For all but the rarest pieces, the Very Good Plus value is twice the Very Good value, and the Near Mint value is twice the VG+ listing or four times the VG listing.

In some cases, dashes appear in the pricing column. That means that the VG or VG+ value is under $2 (bargain bin, yard sale, thrift shop material). If all three columns have dashes, there is some other reason, and we mention that in the explanatory notes below the listing. Every item with no value listed in any column is explained. If not, it's our error.

Finally, many items have a descriptive line in italics under the entry. This often conveys important information that plays a role in the above record's value, such as label design, cover design or colored vinyl. Sometimes, relatively insignificant differences can make a huge difference in value. Just look at the Elvis Presley listings for proof.

Selling your records

At some point, perhaps after looking through this book, you may decide that you want to sell your collection. Good for you! And you want to take them to your local used record store with the idea that you'll get the prices you see in this book. Bad for you!

What the values in here reflect are *retail* prices – what a collector might pay for the item from a dealer, and *not* what a dealer will pay a collector for resale. Too many non-collectors (and even some collectors) don't understand that.

I know one dealer who has told me that he won't buy records from someone who tells him they consulted a price guide first. While that is extreme, it shows the distrust some dealers have for books like this and how the public uses (and abuses) them.

Just as importantly, the highest values are for records in the best condition (re-read the section on "Grading your records"). And there is a reason for that: Truly pristine records are very difficult to find! Many collectors are willing to pay handsomely for them – but for many of the records in this book, Near Mint examples aren't even known to exist!

One reason we've expanded the price listing to three grades of condition is to reflect that. There's a tendency to look at the highest price listed for something and assume that's what your record is worth. More realistically, though, such a small percentage of records are truly Near Mint – especially from the 1950s and 1960s and earlier – that your own records, if you were a typical accumulator and not a collector, are considerably less than Near Mint.

Even if you do end up trying to sell to a dealer, choose him or her carefully. Many dealers want nothing to do with country music because they have no clientele for it. It's always best to find someone who has a customer base for your kind of records.

There is only one way you'll be able to get anything close to the prices listed for most items, and that's to sell them direct to the collector.

The "old-fashioned" way is through record collecting magazines. The oldest and most widely read remains *Goldmine,* which was founded in 1974. Published every two weeks, the magazine is loaded with ads from people selling records of all kinds and from all eras. *Goldmine* has advertising salespeople who will help you put your ad together for maximum impact. To see what *Goldmine* is about, pick up a copy. It is available at all Tower Records stores in the U.S., most Barnes and Noble and Borders bookstores and hundreds of independent record dealers. If you still can't find a copy, call 1-800-258-0929.

The "new" way to sell records and other memorabilia is over the Internet. The most popular method is through the online auction, and the most popular of these sites is eBay (www.ebay.com).

Online selling seems to draw two widely different audiences. One is very much the same audience as a stand-alone record store, except on a global scale rather than a regional one. Browsers who know next to nothing about record collecting and the relative scarcity of the listed pieces are common. These are people who can sometimes be fooled into paying too much for a common piece, especially certain million-selling compact discs, because of three magic letters: "OOP," short for "out of print." Just because something's out of print doesn't mean it has vanished off the face of the earth!

The other audience drawn to online sales is the hyper-specialist, and this is often where items can justifiably go for much larger sums than in a retail store. Thanks to search engines on most of the better sites, a fan of, say, Aretha Franklin can type in the words "Aretha Franklin" and find nothing but the Aretha Franklin-related material. People who specialize in one artist will usually pay more – sometimes a *lot* more – than someone who collects a more broad range of artists. But because they are specialists, they also know which items are common, so they don't get taken on the easy stuff.

I have bought records over the web, and have yet to have significant problems. It's faster than "snail mail" and less expensive than a long-distance telephone call. But it's not perfect. Just as in real life, it pays to be wary.

As a seller, you are reaching a larger audience than you would in a record collecting magazine, but also a much less targeted one. The Internet seems to be a good place to sell lower-priced items that might take up valuable space in an expensive print ad. But many more valuable pieces sit or fetch less than they might through more traditional means.

Also, many sellers have found that eBay overreacts if you say you are selling a promo. Promos are an accepted part of record collecting; there's even been an entire book on collecting promotional records and CDs. Despite that, eBay can, and does, remove these items, almost at random, for no good reason. (It's one thing if you're selling an advance copy of a CD that hasn't been issued to the general public yet. It's another to try to sell a 25-year-old vinyl promo.) So if you're selling promos, be aware of this.

As a buyer, you have to watch out for overgraded, under-described items. Photos of the items help. Also, buying from someone who deals in records as a primary area rather than as an obvious sideline to his/her Beanie Baby business is recommended. Look for dealers with strong feedback ratings; that is a sign of satisfied customers. Also, check for use of something resembling the *Goldmine* grading system. People who say their albums

are in "good condition" don't know record collecting, because "good" is a low grade in the world of records (as it is in some other collecting areas, such as coins).

Also as a buyer, don't be afraid to e-mail the seller if you have any questions about the item. If you don't get a satisfactory answer, or get no answer at all, don't bid.

Remember, though, that even with the growth of buying and selling over the Internet, it's still far from eclipsed other proven selling methods.

How you can help

Within this book, we have well over 40,000 listings of rhythm & blues and related records – 12-inch singles, 45s, 78s, LPs and picture sleeves. All the information is located in a growing database of records, which will make both our future price guides and *Goldmine* magazine better products over time.

But as you look through this book, you may see holes large enough to drive a fully loaded mothership through. Certain parts of the book aren't as good as they could be. Readers have helped tremendously with other *Goldmine* projects; we know you can lend a hand with this one.

While any information is helpful, here are some areas where the most help is needed:

78s. This is the second book that we've compiled with information on 78-rpm records. In some cases we have detailed and accurate data, and in others, we don't. I'm sure we're missing many of these discs from the pre-1949 era.

You'll also see that we're missing some B-sides, and in a few cases we only know the number, but neither of the songs that appeared on the disc. Again, any good information will be appreciated.

We also want to know if we're missing any 78s from 1958-59. These usually bring a lot more than their 45-rpm counterparts. We only listed those that we know exist; some later ones have shown up on collectors' and dealers' want lists, but we don't know if those listings are based on reality or wishful thinking. So if you know, for example, that there are U.S. Drifters 78s after "There Goes My Baby" and can prove it with solid evidence, we'd like to know.

Missing B-sides; repeated A-sides. Some records are listed as "(B-side unknown)." In some cases, it's because the record never was issued with a different B-side. Some of the independent labels issued the same version of the same song on both sides, even on stock copies! We figure that many of these unknown B-sides actually are the A-side repeated, but we could not confirm this with certainty. If you have any of these discs, we'd like to know for sure about B-sides.

Picture sleeves. R&B music generally has had fewer 45 rpm picture sleeves than pop or rock music. Several major artists are only known to have one sleeve! Certainly there must be more R&B picture sleeves than we have listed.

Extended plays. Hundreds of extended play 7-inch singles are listed in this book. Most of them are certainly collectible, and many fetch healthy sums. But some of them we don't yet know about.

Anywhere you see the words "(contents unknown)," we'd like to know exactly what's on the record. What we need is side 1 and side 2, plus sleeve variations. As the titles of extended plays are often not listed on the records, we feel that actually listing the songs will be of greater help to the collector.

For the best results, follow these guidelines:
- Use the *record*, not the jacket, to determine the exact order of songs. Often, the titles on the sleeve are arranged to look better and don't necessarily correspond to the playing order.
- Not all EPs list Side 1 and Side 2 explicitly. So how do you tell? Look for the master numbers, which are usually found below the main number. On most EPs, the master number for Side 1 is one smaller than the master number for Side 2. For example, one of the Elvis Presley EPs has a Side 1 master number of "G2WH-7209" and a Side 2 number of "G2WH-7210."

Also, on those EP listings with an asterisk before the contents, we need confirmation of the exact order of tracks.

So if you're an EP collector, you can play a big role in helping us.

Albums. We're sure there are many missing albums from the listings. Most of these probably fall into two categories:
- Reissues of older material on different labels.
- Albums from small independent labels.

If you have albums that don't appear in the book, let us know. Please note, though, that we're only interested in albums on American labels. We don't intentionally list imports in here, nor do we plan to in the future.

Tupac Shakur. Known on record as "2Pac" and "Makaveli," the rap artist of the 1990s is highly collectible. But for some reason, concrete information

on his vinyl releases – especially 12-inch singles – is scarce. We're almost 100 percent sure there are no U.S. 7-inch singles of his material. But we know that there are more 12-inch singles than we have listed. If you're a collector of 2Pac's vinyl material, we can use your help

Any incorrect information. In a book such as this, typographical errors are bound to happen, regardless of how hard we try to prevent them. If your record number or prefix doesn't match what's listed in here, let us know.

Missing artists. We think we have as broad a listing of rhythm & blues artists as you'll find in one book. That said, I'm sure someone of importance is not listed.

Some artists aren't in here because, as of press time, none of their music has come out on vinyl. Others aren't in here because of deadlines.

Make your case for an artist who belongs in the book, preferably one who had releases on either 45 or LP, and who knows, we may include them in the second edition!

Basically, any information you have on any R&B artist's U.S. record releases that isn't in the book is welcome. We receive many contributions and suggestions, so not everyone can be acknowledged. But rest assured that even your one little correction helps in the long run.

You can contact me by mail:
**Tim Neely
Goldmine Standard Catalog of
   Rhythm & Blues Records
700 E. State St.
Iola, WI 54990**

or by telephone:
(715) 445-2214 or 4612, ext. 782

or by e-mail:
neelyt@krause.com

If you write or e-mail, please include a *daytime* telephone number where I can contact you in case I have any questions.

Acknowledgments

Thanks first to Chuck Miller for his overview of the music and for his list of essential LPs (yes, all 50 he lists are available on vinyl, even the more recent ones).

Thanks to those at Krause Publications who believed in the project and who patiently shepherded it through its growing pains: Greg Loescher, Paul Kennedy and Debbie Bradley.

Thanks to Good Rockin' Tonight for many of the photos of rarely-seen R&B 45s, 78s and LPs scattered throughout the book. Though now largely inactive, the auction site, which helped to spur a surge in collecting interest – and prices – in the late 1990s, has not officially closed its doors. It ran an auction in 2002, and it will probably have others as conditions warrant. Check out www.collectors.com for more information.

Thanks to Fast Hits Music for some of the other photos. The company specializes in selling newer 45s, but has plenty of older material available at www.fasthits.com.

Thanks to the hundreds of people who, in contributing information to our other price guides, have made an impact on this one as well.

Finally, thanks to all the artists and labels who have made this music available to all of us for all these years.

Tim Neely
October 2002

Preface by Chuck Miller

It goes by many names. Rhythm and Blues. Hip-hop. Urban sound. Motown. Quiet Storm. It was also called "race" music, "colored" music, and other assorted euphemisms that family magazines and books don't use any more. It grew from various major metropolitan areas – Chicago, Detroit, New Orleans, Memphis, Philadelphia, New York City, Los Angeles, St. Louis, and hundreds of other places where soul music absorbed the local influences of music and culture and life, to become the soundtrack of generations. Arthur Conley said it as clearly as anyone could. "Do you like good music, that sweet soul music? As long as it's swinging, oh yeah, oh yeah."

We call it "soul" music – melodies and lyrics and orchestrations that pull and stir your soul. The singers' vocal emoting and lyrical gymnastics raise powerful emotions in the listener. You can see the tears streaming down Jackie Wilson's face as he sings "My heart is crying, crying…" You can feel the passion in James Brown's voice as he begs her to "please, please, please don't go…"

Soul music is empowerment, as Aretha Franklin asks only for a little respect when she comes home. Soul music is also music of social consciousness – you can hear it in the call to arms of Marvin Gaye, asking us to look at our world and consider what's going on; or in the rallying cry of the Isley Brothers, imploring us to battle oppression and fight the powers that be.

Soul music is also the music of passion, nestled in the candlelight dinners and candlelight-dimmed bedrooms. You can hear it in the smoldering sensuality of Teddy Pendergrass as he beckons an ingénue to turn off the lights. Soul music is also about breakups and their residual aftermath, whether all that was left was a band of gold, or a lonely man at the park asking strangers, "have you seen her... tell me have you seen her?" Or about a man who caught his woman with him, with him... walking in the rain... they were holding hands and he would never be the same.

One can listen to a Scott Joplin ragtime piece, or to the gospel compositions of Thomas A. Dorsey, and hear the earliest fragments of soul. Or listen to some of the best jazz and big band groups – Duke Ellington and John Coltrane, Count Basie and Louis Armstrong and Coleman Hawkins and Charlie Parker, to name only a few. By the 1940's, "rhythm and blues" music combined gospel, jazz and an uptempo big band sound called "jump blues" into an exciting new sound. R&B artists like Louis Jordan, Ruth Brown and LaVern Baker took the blues, added horns and drums, and sang over the instruments with fire and thrust, as if they were shouting above the music to the audience in the back rows.

Eventually R&B groups like the Ravens, the Dominoes, the Royals, the Crows and the Orioles blended their gospel-edged melodies with intricate choruses, creating doo-wop music. By the mid-1950s, R&B music (along with rockabilly and doo-wop) formed the holy trinity of rock and roll. Rock and roll also afforded artists such as Chuck Berry, Little Richard and Sam Cooke a new avenue to spread rhythm & blues music to previously untapped audiences. Groups such as the Drifters, the Platters and the Coasters achieved massive popularity with both white and black audiences; their songs were played on every radio station; they performed on every major TV variety show.

Many other R&B vocal groups made inroads into the pop music field, before their songs were "covered" by white vocal groups and artists. It was not unusual for an R&B artist or group to discover that their own song had been re-recorded by a white artist or group, and was racing up the charts while their own version struggled to find airplay. Many white artists recorded these "cover" records, which essentially allowed a songwriter to have his or her composition played on more radio stations and in more jukeboxes. Cover songs were not an uncommon occurrence; in fact, up until the 1950s the same song could be recorded and released by several artists, in many cases the competing versions would appear on the pop charts simultaneously. But in the 1950s, with more teenagers listening to R&B and rock 'n' roll music, the idea of clean-cut Pat Boone covering Little Richard's "Tutti-Frutti", or Georgia Gibbs' version of the Royals' "Work With Me Annie" as a sanitized "Dance With Me Henry" was too much to take.

That being said, many R&B artists were able to "cross over" the unwritten yet enforced musical color barrier, as teenagers eventually eschewed the pale imitations and purchased instead the soulful originators. Some of these artists that were able to establish themselves to both black and white audiences eventually earned nicknames like "The

Genius," "Mr. Excitement," "The Godfather of Soul" and "The Queen of Soul."

Ray Charles, "The Genius," recorded a series of R&B classics for Atlantic, including "Hallelujah I Love Her So" and "Rockhouse," as well as his soul-meets-gospel call-and-response classic "What'd I Say." Charles would later move to ABC Records and continue his soul classics with "Hit The Road Jack" and "Unchain My Heart." His album *Modern Sounds in Country and Western Music* became one of the biggest-selling albums of 1962, as Charles took classic country songs like "I Can't Stop Loving You" and "You Don't Know Me," and brought them to life with his own soulful arrangements.

James Brown, "The Godfather of Soul," started his career as a gospel singer. The gospel group Brown joined, the Flames, was signed by Federal Records, and recorded the heart-wrenching "Please, Please, Please" as "James Brown and the Famous Flames." A series of soul ballads and uptempo numbers followed, including "Try Me," "Think" and "Night Train." One of the crowning achievements in Brown's career was the release of a 1962 live album that captured all the energy and excitement of a James Brown concert. The album, *Live at the Apollo,* sold millions of copies and inspired a generation of performers, who listened to that album every night and tried to replicate Brown's dance steps and moves.

A record company – in this case, Columbia Records, who had her singing soulless songs like "Rock-A-Bye Your Baby With A Dixie Melody" – musically handcuffed the "Queen of Soul," Aretha Franklin. But when she signed with Atlantic Records, producer Jerry Wexler took Franklin to Muscle Shoals, Alabama, where she recorded with the legendary Muscle Shoals Rhythm Section, a group of white musicians that played R&B with an intense fervor. The collaborations between Franklin and the Muscle Shoals band produced hits like "Respect," "I Never Loved A Man (The Way I Love You)," and "Chain of Fools."

The story of Jackie Wilson's career is both bitter and sweet. After initial hits with "Reet Petite" and "Lonely Teardrops," Wilson spent the next ten years recording in every musical style from pop to opera, at the request of his record company Brunswick. He earned the nickname "Mr. Excitement," as his talent and charisma would create pop hits like "Doggin' Around," "Baby Workout" and "(Your Love Keeps Lifting Me) Higher and Higher," despite all the overly lush orchestrations and banal background singers fostered upon him by Brunswick. Sadly, while on stage in a New Jersey club in 1975, Wilson was felled by a stroke, and died in a nursing home eight years later. His musical legacy, however, lives on in such singer-dancer-entertainers as Michael Jackson and Al Green.

Jackie Wilson also provided a struggling songwriter's first big break. Berry Gordy penned "Lonely Teardrops" and "Reet Petite" for Wilson; both songs would become huge hits. Gordy parlayed his songwriting success into one of the most successful independent record companies in history – Motown Records. With a house band capable of creating stellar soul and dance grooves, hit songwriting teams like Eddie Holland-Lamont Dozier-Brian Holland, Norman Whitfield-Barrett Strong, and Nickolas Ashford-Valerie Simpson, Motown became a consistent and powerful force in the music world, beginning with their first million-selling single, the Miracles' "Shop Around."

Led by singer William "Smokey" Robinson, the Miracles evolved from a successful doo-wop group to a pop-soul band that brought Gordy his own label's hits. Songs like "Shop Around," "Mickey's Monkey," "You Really Got A Hold On Me" and "What's So Good About Good-By" established the Miracles as Gordy's first superstars. Eventually Gordy moved his record company into a house at 2648 West Grand Boulevard. For the next decade, the greatest singers and musicians in the Detroit area converged on this small house, recording the most dominant hits of an era.

By the early 1960s, the Tamla/Motown/ Gordy conglomerate created a series of pop and soul smashes, including songs by the Marvelettes, the Contours, Martha and the Vandellas, Marvin Gaye and Stevie Wonder. By the mid-1960s, Motown groups like the Temptations, the Supremes and the Four Tops dominated the R&B and pop charts. The Supremes would have five straight #1 songs and 12 #1 songs overall. But whether the vocalists were the Supremes or the Vandellas, the Temptations or the Miracles, the Motown house band provided top-of-the-line musicianship for all of them. Led by keyboardist Earl Van Dyke, the house band consisted of bassist James Jamerson, guitarists Robert White and Joe Messina, and drummer Benny Benjamin. It's their orchestrations that can be heard on nearly every Motown record during the 1960s. And their ability to tailor their musical style

for each artist –- whether the party-dance sound of Martha Reeves and the Vandellas, the icy roughness of Marvin Gaye, or the emotional cries of the Four Tops – provided their artists with a flexibility previously unheard of in studio bands.

Motown could also take pride in its songwriting teams. The Holland-Dozier-Holland triumvirate composed chart-topping smashes for Diana Ross and the Supremes, while Whitfield and Strong gave the Temptations some of their greatest hits. Ashford and Simpson wrote their first big hits for the duo of Marvin Gaye and Tammi Terrell.

While the Motown musical hit factory was working overtime in Detroit, another record company proved that soul music could still be made in the Deep South. Originally formed in the early 1960s as Satellite Records, Stax/Volt Records was the home of Otis Redding, the Staple Singers, Rufus Thomas, Sam & Dave and the Dramatics, all of whom had hits for the label. Backing up the singers at Stax/Volt was its house band, Booker T. and the M.G.'s, creating the "Memphis Soul" sound – heavy on horns, with plenty of jazz and blues mixed in.

By the early 1970s, soul music found a new epicenter in Philadelphia. Songwriter-producers Kenny Gamble and Leon Huff created a new sound that mixed soul music with funk and classical overtones. Dubbed "The Sound of Philadelphia," Gamble and Huff's Philadelphia International Records made superstars out of the O'Jays, Harold Melvin and the Blue Notes, the Intruders, the Three Degrees, Billy Paul and the People's Choice. Philadelphia International's house band, MFSB, even had hits of their own with "Love is the Message" and the theme from Soul Train, "TSOP (The Sound of Philadelphia)."

Also in Philadelphia, producer-songwriter Thom Bell created aural soul symphonies for the Delfonics, the Stylistics, Blue Magic and the Spinners. In Los Angeles, Barry White turned his sensual bass voice into a series of love ballads and dance grooves. Artists like Curtis Mayfield and Isaac Hayes created funky soundtracks for films like "Superfly" and "Shaft," which became radio hits of their own.

Other cities produced groups with soulful sounds – the Tavares brothers from Boston; the Chi-Lites from Chicago, the Commodores from Alabama and the Gap Band from Atlanta. In these cities, the sound of soul music represented the strengths and struggles of the urban communities. Tavares sang

sweet ballads like "Check It Out," and dance tracks like "Heaven Must Be Missing An Angel." Though the Chi-Lites sang sweet soul ballads like "Oh Girl" and "Have You Seen Her," they also sang "(For God's Sake) Give More Power to the People."

Dance and disco music reigned on the charts in the mid-to-late 1970s, and whether the music was fused with rock (Earth Wind & Fire, the Isley Brothers), or with dance (Chic, the Brothers Johnson, McFadden and Whitehead), soul music reigned supreme. Groups like Chic and Instant Funk had songs that topped the dance and soul charts; singers like Donna Summer, Gloria Gaynor and Thelma Houston became queens of disco. Other vocal harmony soul groups, such as Sister Sledge, the Pointer Sisters and Stargard, also found popularity in disco.

Those dance beats also provided a basis for another soulful evolution – rap and hip-hop music. Rap music grew from the hard streets of New York City, as lyrical poets would recite intricate poems about power and prowess. They would "rap" over the instrumental portions of records, as a disc jockey, using two turntables and an electric sound mixer, stretched 20-second instrumental breaks into 5-minute jam sessions. Fueled by the commercial success of the Sugarhill Gang's 15-minute rap opus, "Rapper's Delight," rap groups such as Grandmaster Flash and the Furious Five, Run-D.M.C., Afrika Bambaataa and the Soul Sonic Force, began to dominate the soul music scene. By the late 1980s, rap music had evolved into its own genre, with artists like Public Enemy, De La Soul, N.W.A. and the Beastie Boys taking their metered anthems of power and oppression and party and pop culture to a whole new level of exposure and popularity.

During the 1960s, soul music merged with rock and roll to create funk music. Funk is hard-edged dance music designed to get your rump off the couch and boogie. With its thick, jumpy baselines, rhythmic drums, trumpet blasts and call-and-response vocals, funk has become a harder-edged version of soul music – or a danceable version of rock, take your pick.

James Brown may be the "Godfather of Soul," but he also helped popularize funk. Brown's biggest hits of the 1960s included "Papa's Got A Brand New Bag," "I Got You (I Feel Good)," "Cold Sweat" and "Mother Popcorn," songs which catapulted Brown across all radio and racial barri-

ers. He brought funk music to black and white fans alike, and Brown's Famous Flames backup band laid down such a funky beat that the concert theaters they performed in became dance clubs that night.

By 1971, many of Brown's Famous Flames band members joined up with George Clinton's Parliament/Funkadelic operation. Clinton's funk band evolved from a doo-wop group called the Parliaments, to two separate but distinct bands (Parliament and Funkadelic), providing the world with "Tear The Roof Off the Sucker (Give Up the Funk)", "Up for the Down Stroke," "(not just) Knee Deep", "Flash Light" and "One Nation Under a Groove."

More than any other musical genre, funk music brought the electric bass guitar to the forefront of the band. Bass guitarists, who formerly plucked their instruments in virtual anonymity, now slapped and thumped and pounded those strings with reckless abandon and fervor. By the 1970s, the next generation of funk-based artists would now layer their musical compositions around their bass player's thick, bouncing instrumental riffs.

Some of these groups mixed funk with a Latin beat (War), while others expanded on the call-and-response vocals of James Brown and Parliament-Funkadelic (the Ohio Players, Con Funk Shun). Bands like Sly and the Family Stone, Tower of Power and Charles Wright and the Watts 103rd Street Rhythm Band brought West Coast urban funk to radio; groups like the Brothers Johnson, the Gap Band and Cameo incorporated funk into slick, polished productions that captured millions of fans. Funk music charged into the 1980s, as performers like Rick James and Prince mixed their funk beats with salacious, double-entendre lyrics and booty-shaking beats that would keep people dancing all night.

Soul music in the 1980s was now influenced by other musical styles, including funk, rap, and dance. Sexy male singers like Luther Vandross, Teddy Pendergrass, Babyface and Kashif could melt hearts like ice in July. Meanwhile, singers like Anita Baker, Phyllis Hyman, Jennifer Holliday and Whitney Houston showed they could also use every inch of their vocal cords to create powerful recordings like "Sweet Love," "And I Am Telling You I'm Not Going" and "Don't Wanna Change the World." Today's soul artists continue to mine the musical gems of the past, to create their own masterpieces. Alicia Keys mixes soul music with classi-

cal themes of Chopin and Bach. Lauryn Hill and India.Arie take their inspirations from the soul hits of the 70s and 80s. Rappers continually mine classic R&B/soul grooves for rhythm tracks – James Brown's "Funky Drummer," for example, has arguably been sampled by more up-and-coming rappers than has any other classic track, with Funkadelic's "(not just) Knee Deep" and the Incredible Bongo Band's "Apache" neck-in-neck for second place.

So why are soul records so collectible? Why is there an entire book devoted to collecting these classic songs and stacks o' wax?

One reason why soul records are so collectible is their musical content. These were the recordings that inspired hundreds of singers and musicians to chart their own musical course. How much different would the Beatles' music be if they had not heard groups like the Marvelettes, Little Richard, Wilbert Harrison and the Shirelles (all of whose music appears on the Beatles' early albums). How much different would the Rolling Stones sound if they never heard Chuck Berry or Muddy Waters or any of the other stars from the Chess Records label.

Another factor in the collectible nature of soul music is that because the music was originally targeted toward the African-American community, the print runs are much lower than the runs for records pressed for Caucasian music lovers. Many soul recordings were pressed on independent record labels, which did not have the built-in distribution network that major companies like RCA, Columbia, Decca and Capitol employed. For example, blues 78's are one of the few 78 RPM records that has dramatically increased in collectible value – records by Robert Johnson and Charley Patton have sold at auction for thousands of dollars; 78s by Muddy Waters and Chuck Berry and Tampa Red have only increased in value on the collectible market.

These records are also a reflection of our musical and life history. They detail the musical and socioeconomic culture of America – songs like "The Message," "Fight the Power," "A Change Is Gonna Come," "What's Goin' On," and "Say it Loud, I'm Black And I'm Proud," are both music and social commentary. Songs like "Super Freak," "Let's Get It On" and "Juicy Fruit" encompass unbridled passion behind closed doors. And songs like "I'll Always Love My Mama," "Respect," and "People Get Ready" show the importance of family and

religion in soul music, and in the listeners who are part of it.

And one more important thing – soul music is just plain great to listen to. Just think about these names: Aretha. The Godfather. Sly. Diana. Marvin. Prince. Ray. The music and the memories return like long-lost friends. The grooves match our heartbeats; the lyrics tug at our heartstrings; the vocals melt our hearts.

Soul music is influence, it is culture, and it's just plain great music to listen to. So take a moment to go through this book with your own personal record collection; maybe even place a record or two on the turntable and hear for yourself why this music truly deserves its own collector's guide.

Chuck Miller is a regular writer and columnist for Goldmine *magazine. He also is the author of* Warman's American Records, *a great novice's guide to collecting records.*

50 Albums No R&B/Soul Music Collector Should Be Without

Chosen by Chuck Miller

1. James Brown, *Live at the Apollo* (King 826)
2. Marvin Gaye, *What's Going On* (Tamla 310)
3. Stevie Wonder, *Songs in the Key of Life* (Tamla 340)
4. Al Green, *Let's Stay Together* (Hi 32070)
5. Grandmaster Flash and the Furious Five, *The Message* (Sugarhill 268)
6. Michael Jackson, *Off the Wall* (Epic 35745)
7. Sly and the Family Stone, *Greatest Hits* (Epic 30325)
8. Isaac Hayes, *Hot Buttered Soul* (Enterprise 1001)
9. The Impressions, *People Get Ready* (ABC-Paramount 505)
10. Earth Wind & Fire, *The Best of Earth, Wind & Fire, Volume 1* (ARC/Columbia 35647)
11. The Four Tops, *Reach Out* (Motown 650)
12. Aretha Franklin, *Aretha's Gold* (Atlantic 8227)
13. Funkadelic, *One Nation Under a Groove* (Warner Bros. 3209)
14. Lauryn Hill, *The Miseducation of Lauryn Hill* (Ruffhouse 69035)
15. Rick James, *Street Songs* (Gordy 1002)
16. Quincy Jones, *The Dude* (A&M 3721)
17. Kool and the Gang, *Ladies' Night* (De-Lite 9513)
18. The 2 Live Crew, *As Nasty As They Wanna Be* (Luke Skyywalker 107)
19. Curtis Mayfield, *Superfly* (Curtom 8014)
20. Harold Melvin and the Blue Notes, *Harold Melvin and the Blue Notes* (Philadelphia International 31648)
21. Smokey Robinson and the Miracles, *Greatest Hits, Volume 2* (Tamla 280)
22. Ohio Players, *Ohio Players Gold* (Mercury 1122)
23. The O'Jays, *Ship Ahoy* (Philadelphia International 32480)
24. Parliament, *Mothership Connection* (Casablanca 7022)
25. Teddy Pendergrass, *Teddy* (Philadelphia International 36003)
26. Wilson Pickett, *The Exciting Wilson Pickett* (Atlantic 8129)
27. Prince, *1999* (Warner Bros. 3601)
28. Public Enemy, *It Takes a Nation of Millions to Hold Us Back* (Def Jam 44303)
29. Otis Redding, *History of Otis Redding* (Volt 418)
30. Diana Ross, *Touch Me in the Morning* (Motown 772)
31. Run-D.M.C., *Raising Hell* (Profile 1217)
32. B.B. King and Bobby Bland, *Together for the First Time... Live* (ABC/Dunhill 50190)
33. Ray Charles, *Modern Sounds in Country and Western Music* (ABC-Paramount 410)
34. Billy Ward and His Dominoes, *Billy Ward and His Dominoes* (Federal 548)
35. The Five Keys, *The Best of the Five Keys* (Aladdin 806)
36. The Midnighters, *Their Greatest Hits* (Federal 395-541)
37. The Platters, *Encore of Golden Hits* (Mercury 20472)
38. Dee Dee Sharp, *It's Mashed Potato Time* (Cameo 1018)
39. Chic, *C'est Chic* (Atlantic 19209)
40. The Chi-Lites, *The Chi-Lites' Greatest Hits* (Brunswick 754184)
41. The Staple Singers, *Bealtitude: Respect Yourself* (Stax 3002)
42. The Stylistics, *The Stylistics* (Avco 33023)
43. Donna Summer, *On the Radio – Greatest Hits Vols. 1 and 2* (Casablanca 7191)
44. The Supremes, *Where Did Our Love Go* (Motown 621)
45. The Temptations, *The Temptations' Greatest Hits* (Gordy 919)
46. War, *Greatest Hits* (United Artists 648)
47. Booker T and the MG's, *Best of Booker T and the MG's* (Atlantic 8202)
48. Jackie Wilson, *Jackie Wilson's Greatest Hits* (Brunswick 754140)
49. Jr. Walker and the All-Stars, *Shotgun* (Soul 701)
50. Janet Jackson, *Control* (A&M 5106)

Number	Title (A Side/B Side)	Yr	VG	VG+	NM

A

A.L.T. AND THE LOST CIVILIZATION
12-Inch Singles
ATCO

Number	Title (A Side/B Side)	Yr	VG	VG+	NM
❑ 1850 [DJ]	Tequila (Club 12") (LP Version) (Instrumental)	1992	2.50	5.00	10.00
❑ 1905 [DJ]	Summer Breeze (Extended Version) (LP Version) (Remix) (Instrumental)/In Between the Sheets	1992	2.00	4.00	8.00

45s
ATCO

Number	Title (A Side/B Side)	Yr	VG	VG+	NM
❑ 98533	Tequila/Refried Beans	1992	—	2.00	4.00

AALIYAH
12-Inch Singles
BLACKGROUND

Number	Title (A Side/B Side)	Yr	VG	VG+	NM
❑ DMD 2404 [DJ]	One in a Million (4 versions)	1996	2.50	5.00	10.00
❑ DMD 2405 [(2) DJ]	One in a Million (Nitebreed Mongolodic Mix) (Incredible B-boy Orchestra) (Geoffrey's House Mix) (Armand's Drum-n-Bass Mix) (Wolf-D's Big Bass Mix) (Nitebreed Mongolodic Dub) (Nitebreed Bootleg Mix)	1997	3.75	7.50	15.00
❑ DMD 2449 [DJ]	The One I Gave My Heart To (Soul Solution Club Mix) (Soul Solution Dub) (Bonus Beats)	1997	2.00	4.00	8.00
❑ PR 6818 [DJ]	If Your Girl Only Knew (LP Version) (Extended Version) (Beat-A-Pella) (Instrumental) (Acappella)	1996	2.00	4.00	8.00
❑ PR 6909 [DJ]	If Your Girl Only Knew (Remix) (4 versions)	1996	2.50	5.00	10.00
❑ PR 6936 [DJ]	One in a Million (3 versions)	1996	2.50	5.00	10.00
❑ PR 8058 [DJ]	4 Page Letter (4 versions)	1997	3.00	6.00	12.00
❑ PR 8219 [DJ]	Hot Like Fire (LP Version) (Timbaland's Groove) (Feel My Horns Mix)/(LP Instrumental) (Timbaland's Groove Instrumental) (Feel My Horns Mix Instrumental)	1997	2.00	4.00	8.00
❑ SPRO 16164 [DJ]	We Need a Resolution (Featuring Timbaland 4:02) (Instrumental 4:02) (No Rap 3:54) (Acappella 4:03)	2001	3.00	6.00	12.00
❑ 38722	Try Again (Album Version) (Timbaland Remix)/(D'Jam Hassan Club Mix) (Instrumental)	2000	2.00	4.00	8.00
❑ 38781	We Need a Resolution (LP Version) (Instrumental)/(No Rap Version) (A Cappella Version)	2001	2.00	4.00	8.00
❑ 95534 [(2)]	The One I Gave My Heart To (Soul Solution Club Mix) (Soul Solution Dub) (Bonus Beats)/One in a Million (Nitebreed Mongolodic Mix) (Armand's Drum n Bass Mix) (Wolf-D's Big Bass Mix) (Geoffrey's House Mix)	1998	3.00	6.00	12.00
❑ 95644	If Your Girl Only Knew (Album Mix) (Extended Mix)/(Remix) (Beat-a-Pella) (Instrumental)	1996	2.50	5.00	10.00

45s
BLACKGROUND

Number	Title (A Side/B Side)	Yr	VG	VG+	NM
❑ 38722	Try Again/Come Back in One Piece	2000	—	2.00	4.00
—B-side "featuring DMX"					
❑ 38781	We Need a Resolution/(Instrumental)	2001	—	2.00	4.00
❑ 38814	Rock the Boat/More Than a Woman	2001	—	2.00	4.00

Albums
BLACKGROUND

Number	Title (A Side/B Side)	Yr	VG	VG+	NM
❑ 10082 [(2)]	Aaliyah	2001	3.75	7.50	15.00

JIVE

Number	Title (A Side/B Side)	Yr	VG	VG+	NM
❑ 41533	Age Ain't Nothing But a Number	1994	3.00	6.00	12.00

AALON
45s
ARISTA

Number	Title (A Side/B Side)	Yr	VG	VG+	NM
❑ 0249	Cream City/Midnight Man	1977	—	2.50	5.00
❑ 0297	Rock and Roll Gangster/(B-side unknown)	1977	—	2.50	5.00

ABBOTT, GREGORY
12-Inch Singles
COLUMBIA

Number	Title (A Side/B Side)	Yr	VG	VG+	NM
❑ 44-05959	Shake You Down (Extended Club Mix) (Instrumental Mix) (Radio Edit)	1986	3.00	6.00	12.00
❑ 44-06710	I Got the Feelin' (It's Over) (3 versions)	1987	—	3.00	6.00
❑ 44-07809	I'll Prove It to You (Extended Mix)/(Radio Edit) (Instrumental)	1988	—	3.00	6.00
❑ 44-07891	Let Me Be Your Hero (Extended Single Version) (Single Version) (Dub Mix)	1988	2.00	4.00	8.00

45s
COLUMBIA

Number	Title (A Side/B Side)	Yr	VG	VG+	NM
❑ 38-06191	Shake You Down/Wait Until Tomorrow	1986	—	—	3.00
❑ 38-06191 [PS]	Shake You Down/Wait Until Tomorrow	1986	—	—	3.00
❑ 38-06632	I Got the Feelin' (It's Over)/Rhyme and Reason	1987	—	—	3.00
❑ 38-06632 [PS]	I Got the Feelin' (It's Over)/Rhyme and Reason	1987	—	—	3.00
❑ 38-07774	I'll Prove It to You/Two of a Kind	1988	—	—	3.00
❑ 38-07774 [PS]	I'll Prove It to You/Two of a Kind	1988	—	—	3.00
❑ 38-08027	Let Me Be Your Hero/She's an Entertainer	1988	—	—	3.00
❑ 38-08027 [PS]	Let Me Be Your Hero/She's an Entertainer	1988	—	—	3.00

Albums
COLUMBIA

Number	Title (A Side/B Side)	Yr	VG	VG+	NM
❑ BFC 40437	Shake You Down	1986	2.50	5.00	10.00
❑ FC 44087	I'll Prove It to You	1988	2.50	5.00	10.00

ABDUL, PAULA
12-Inch Singles
VIRGIN

Number	Title (A Side/B Side)	Yr	VG	VG+	NM
❑ DMD 1171 [DJ]	Knocked Out (7:03) (3:43) (4:58) (6:31)	1988	3.00	6.00	12.00
❑ 1239 [DJ]	(It's Just) The Way That You Love Me (12" Remix) (Radio Edit) (Dub) (Houseafire Mix)	1988	2.50	5.00	10.00
❑ 1262 [DJ]	Straight Up (6:52) (4:57) (7:10) (6:38)	1988	2.50	5.00	10.00
❑ DMD 1300 [DJ]	Forever Your Girl (3 versions)/Next to You/Straight Up (Kevin Saunderson Club Mix)	1989	2.50	5.00	10.00
❑ 1352 [DJ]	Cold Hearted (Extended Version 6:50) (House Mix 6:41)//(Dubstramental 5:41) (Percappella 4:00)/One or the Other	1989	2.50	5.00	10.00
❑ DMD 1370 [DJ]	Cold Hearted (Quiverin' 12") (7" Edit) (Chillin' Bass Dub) (Acapella) (Instrumental)	1989	2.00	4.00	8.00
❑ 1398 [DJ]	Opposites Attract (6 versions)	1989	2.50	5.00	10.00
❑ 1687 [(2) DJ]	Vibeology (8 versions)/The Promise of a New Day (12" Mix)	1991	3.75	7.50	15.00
❑ 1768 [DJ]	Vibeology (House 12") (Underground Mix) (Silky Sax Dub) (Underground Sax Dub)	1991	2.50	5.00	10.00
❑ SPRO-11016 [(2) DJ]	Crazy Cool (Deep Dish's Crazy Cool Remix) (Strike Vocal Mix) (Dub Fire Cool Dub) (Bad Boy Bill House Mix) (Bad Boy Dub) (Sharam Crazy Journey)	1995	5.00	10.00	20.00
❑ 38493	My Love Is for Real (3 versions)/Didn't I Say I Love You	1995	2.00	4.00	8.00
❑ 38497 [(2)]	My Love Is for Real (9 versions)	1995	3.75	7.50	15.00
❑ 38510	Crazy Cool (Bad Boy Bill House Mix) (Strike's Dub) (Deep Dish's Crazy Cool Remix)/The Choice Is Yours (Edit)	1995	2.50	5.00	10.00
❑ 96107	Vibeology (Hurley's House 7:04) (Hurley's Underground 5:27) (Silky Sax Dub 5:42) (Underground Sax Dub 4:58)	1991	2.50	5.00	10.00
❑ 96546	Cold Hearted (Extended Version) (House Mix) (Dubstramental) (Percappella)/One or the Other	1989	2.50	5.00	10.00
❑ 96565	Forever Your Girl (3 versions)/Next to You/Straight Up	1989	2.00	4.00	8.00
❑ 96594	Straight Up (6:52) (4:57) (7:10)	1988	2.00	4.00	8.00
❑ 96614	(It's Just) The Way That You Love Me (12" Remix)/(7" Dub) (Houseafire Mix)	1988	2.50	5.00	10.00
❑ 96661	Knocked Out (Extended) (Instrumental) (Radio Edit) (TKO Dub)	1988	3.00	6.00	12.00

45s
VIRGIN

Number	Title (A Side/B Side)	Yr	VG	VG+	NM
❑ S7-18850	Crazy Cool/The Choice Is Yours	1995	—	—	3.00
❑ S7-18877	Forever Your Girl/(It's Just) The Way That You Love You	1995	—	—	3.00
❑ 38493	My Love Is for Real/Didn't I Say I Love You	1995	—	—	2.00
❑ 38493 [PS]	My Love Is for Real/Didn't I Say I Love You	1995	—	—	2.00
❑ 98584	Will You Marry Me/Goodnight, My Love	1992	—	2.00	4.00
❑ 98683	Blowing Kisses in the Wind/Spellbound	1991	—	2.00	4.00
❑ 98737	Vibeology/Vibeology (House Mix)	1991	—	2.00	4.00
❑ 98752	The Promise of a New Day/The Promise of a New Day (West Coast 12")	1991	—	2.00	4.00
❑ 98828	Rush, Rush/Rush, Rush (Dub Mix)	1991	—	2.00	4.00
❑ 99158	Opposites Attract/One or the Other	1989	—	—	2.00
❑ 99158 [PS]	Opposites Attract/One or the Other	1989	—	—	2.00
❑ 99196	Cold Hearted/One or the Other	1989	—	—	2.00
❑ 99196 [PS]	Cold Hearted/One or the Other	1989	—	—	2.00
❑ 99230	Forever Your Girl/Next to You	1989	—	—	2.00
❑ 99230 [PS]	Forever Your Girl/Next to You	1989	—	—	2.00
❑ 99256	Straight Up/Straight Up (Power Mix)	1988	—	—	3.00
❑ 99256	Straight Up/Cold Hearted	1988	—	2.00	4.00
❑ 99282	(It's Just) The Way That You Love Me/(It's Just) The Way That You Love Me (Dub)	1988	—	2.00	4.00
—Originals on black labels					
❑ 99282	(It's Just) The Way That You Love Me/(It's Just) The Way That You Love Me (Dub)	1988	—	—	3.00
—Second pressing on orange labels					
❑ 99282 [PS]	(It's Just) The Way That You Love Me/(It's Just) The Way That You Love Me (Dub)	1988	—	2.00	4.00
❑ 99329	Knocked Out/(Instrumental)	1988	—	—	3.00
❑ 99329 [PS]	Knocked Out/(Instrumental)	1988	—	—	3.00

Albums
VIRGIN

Number	Title (A Side/B Side)	Yr	VG	VG+	NM
❑ 90943	Forever Your Girl	1988	2.50	5.00	10.00
❑ 91362	Shut Up and Dance	1990	3.00	6.00	12.00
—Red print on cover					
❑ 91362	Shut Up and Dance	1990	3.00	6.00	12.00
—Yellow print on cover					
❑ 91362	Shut Up and Dance	1990	3.00	6.00	12.00
—Purple print on cover					
❑ 91362	Shut Up and Dance	1990	3.00	6.00	12.00
—Blue print on cover					
❑ A1-91611	Spellbound	1991	6.25	12.50	25.00
—Columbia House edition; the only U.S. vinyl of this LP					

ABDULLAH
45s
SOUL

Number	Title (A Side/B Side)	Yr	VG	VG+	NM
❑ 35051	I Coma Zimba Zio (Here I Stand, The Mighty One)/Why Them, Why Me	1968	—	3.00	6.00

Number	Title (A Side/B Side)	Yr	VG	VG+	NM

ABOVE THE LAW
12-Inch Singles
RUTHLESS
❏ 0290	Black Superman (3 versions)	1994	2.50	5.00	10.00
❏ 88561-6324-1	Kalifornia (2 versions)/Ashes to Ashes, Dust to Dust (2 versions)/Pimp Clinic Anthem (2 versions)	1995	3.00	6.00	12.00

RUTHLESS/EPIC
❏ 49-73369	Untouchable/What Cha Can Do (Mega Mix)/Menace to Society/What Cha Can Prove (Instrumental)	1990	3.00	6.00	12.00
❏ 49-73951	4 the Funk of It (Radio Edit Clean)/(EP Version Dirty)	1991	3.00	6.00	12.00

RUTHLESS/GIANT
❏ PRO-A-5706 [DJ]	V.S.O.P. (4 versions)	1992	5.00	10.00	20.00
❏ 40837	Call It What U Want (4 versions)	1993	3.00	6.00	12.00

TOMMY BOY
❏ TB 460	Streets (3 versions)/Be About Yo Bizniz (2 versions)/Deep at the Root (2 versions)	1998	2.00	4.00	8.00
❏ TB 739	100 Spokes (3 versions)/Killaz in the Park (4 versions)	1996	2.00	4.00	8.00
❏ TB 742	100 Spokes (Clean Radio) (Fresh On D's Extended Clean Radio Remix) (LP Instrumental) (Cold 187um Remix) (LP Version) (Freshstrumental)	1996	2.00	4.00	8.00
❏ TB 747	City of Angels (Vocal) (Instrumental) (Acappella)	1996	2.00	4.00	8.00
❏ TB 767	Endonesia (Clean) (Instrumental) (Acappella)	1996	2.00	4.00	8.00

Albums
RUTHLESS/EPIC
❏ E 47934 [EP]	Vocally Pimpin'	1991	2.50	5.00	10.00

RUTHLESS/GIANT
❏ 24477	Black Mafia Life	1992	3.00	6.00	12.00

TOMMY BOY
❏ TB 1154	Time Will Reveal	1996	3.00	6.00	12.00
❏ TB 1233 [(2)]	Legends	1998	3.75	7.50	15.00

ABRAMS, COLONEL
12-Inch Singles
ACID JAZZ/SCOTTI BROTHERS
❏ 75294	You Don't Know (Somebody Tell Me) (Bass Tone Club Mix) (Instrumental) (Colonel's Mix) (Radio Mix) (Papa's Club Mix) (Papa's Club Mix)	1992	2.00	4.00	8.00
❏ 75322	Never Be Another One (Club Dub Mix) (Club Mix) (Techno Mix) (Single Mix) (Acid Jazz Mix) (Acapella)	1992	2.00	4.00	8.00

BASSLINE
❏ 022 [(2)]	I'm Not Gonna Let (9 versions)	1996	3.00	6.00	12.00

COLONEL
❏ CR 002	Heartbreaker (Dance Vocal Mix) (Mama's Children Overseas Mix)/(Ruff Flow Mix) (Original Mix)	1996	3.00	6.00	12.00

GREAT JONES
❏ 530630-1	So Confused (4 versions)	1994	2.50	5.00	10.00

HORUS
❏ VR 1252	Bad Timing (6 versions)	1990	3.00	6.00	12.00

MCA
❏ L33-17094 [DJ]	I'm Not Gonna Let (same on both sides)	1986	2.00	4.00	8.00
❏ L33-17138 [DJ]	Over and Over (same on both sides)	1986	—	3.00	6.00
❏ L33-17417 [DJ]	Nameless (Extended) (Radio Edit) (Instrumental) (Dub)	1987	2.00	4.00	8.00
❏ L33-17418 [DJ]	Nameless (Extended) (Edit) (Dub)	1987	2.00	4.00	8.00
❏ L33-17521 [DJ]	Soon You'll Be Gone (same on both sides?)	1988	—	3.00	6.00
❏ 23568	Trapped (Extended Vocal Version) (Dub 6:44) (Dub 4:06) (Acappella) (Vocal Version 4:13)	1985	2.50	5.00	10.00
❏ 23600	The Truth (7:50) (Radio Edit) (Instrumental) (Acappella)	1985	2.00	4.00	8.00
❏ 23612	I'm Not Gonna Let (4 versions)	1986	2.00	4.00	8.00
❏ 23636	Over and Over (Extended) (Edit) (Instrumental) (Bonus Beats)	1986	2.00	4.00	8.00
❏ 23670	Speculation (Extended) (Radio Edit) (Instrumental) (Woo Woo Version)	1986	2.00	4.00	8.00
❏ 23763	How Soon We Forget (Extended) (Radio Edit) (Dub Version)	1987	2.00	4.00	8.00
❏ 23806	Nameless (2 versions)	1987	—	3.00	6.00

MIC MAC
❏ 302	I'm Caught Up (6 versions)	199?	2.50	5.00	10.00
❏ 306	Get with You (4 versions)	199?	2.00	4.00	8.00

STREETWISE
❏ 2235	Music Is the Answer/Music Is the Answer (Dub)/Leave the Message Behind the Door	1984	3.75	7.50	15.00

45s
MCA
❏ 52638	Trapped/Trapped (Acappella)	1985	—	—	3.00
❏ 52638 [PS]	Trapped/Trapped (Acappella)	1985	—	—	3.00
❏ 52728	The Truth/(Instrumental)	1985	—	—	3.00
❏ 52728 [PS]	The Truth/(Instrumental)	1985	—	—	3.00
❏ 52773	I'm Not Gonna Let/(Instrumental)	1986	—	—	3.00
❏ 52773 [PS]	I'm Not Gonna Let/(Instrumental)	1986	—	—	3.00
❏ 52847	Over and Over/Margaux	1986	—	—	3.00
❏ 52927	Speculation/Picture Me in Love with You	1986	—	—	3.00
❏ 53121	How Soon We Forget/(Dub Version)	1987	—	—	3.00
❏ 53121 [PS]	How Soon We Forget/(Dub Version)	1987	—	—	3.00
❏ 53208	Nameless/(Dub Version)	1987	—	—	3.00
❏ 53282	Soon You'll Be Gone/When a Man Loves	1988	—	—	3.00

STREETWISE
❏ 1123	Leave the Message Behind the Door/(Instrumental)	1984	—	2.50	5.00
❏ 1135	Music Is the Answer/Music Is the Answer (Dub)	1984	—	2.50	5.00

Albums
ACID JAZZ/SCOTTI BROTHERS
❏ 75232	About Romance	1992	3.75	7.50	15.00

—Promo-only vinyl; white label, generic cover

MCA
❏ 5682	Colonel Abrams	1986	2.00	4.00	8.00
❏ 42029	You and Me Equals Us	1987	2.00	4.00	8.00

ABSTRAC'
12-Inch Singles
REPRISE
❏ 21278	Right and Hype (5 versions)	1989	—	3.00	6.00

45s
REPRISE
❏ 7-22872	Right and Hype/Right and Hype (Acappella Version)	1989	—	2.00	4.00
❏ 7-22872 [PS]	Right and Hype/Right and Hype (Acappella Version)	1989	—	2.50	5.00

Albums
REPRISE
❏ 25997	Abstrac'	1990	3.00	6.00	12.00

ACE, JOHNNY
45s
DUKE
❏ 102	My Song/Follow the Rule	1952	20.00	40.00	80.00
❏ 107	Cross My Heart/Angel	1953	15.00	30.00	60.00
❏ 112	The Clock/Ace's Wild	1953	15.00	30.00	60.00
❏ 118	Saving My Love for You/Yes Baby	1953	10.00	20.00	40.00
❏ 128	Please Forgive Me/You've Been Gone So Long	1954	10.00	20.00	40.00
❏ 132	Never Let Me Go/Burley Cutie	1954	10.00	20.00	40.00
❏ 136	Pledging My Love/No Money	1954	10.00	20.00	40.00
❏ 136	Pledging My Love/Anymore	1954	10.00	20.00	40.00
❏ 144	Anymore/How Can You Be So Mean	1955	10.00	20.00	40.00
❏ 148	So Lonely/I'm Crazy	1956	7.50	15.00	30.00
❏ 154	Still Love You So/Don't You Know	1956	7.50	15.00	30.00

FLAIR
❏ 1015	Midnight Hours Journey/Trouble and Me	1953	37.50	75.00	150.00

—B-side by Earl Forrest

78s
DUKE
❏ 102	My Song/Follow the Rule	1952	17.50	35.00	70.00
❏ 107	Cross My Heart/Angel	1953	12.50	25.00	50.00
❏ 112	The Clock/Ace's Wild	1953	10.00	20.00	40.00
❏ 118	Saving My Love for You/Yes Baby	1953	7.50	15.00	30.00
❏ 128	Please Forgive Me/You've Been Gone So Long	1954	6.25	12.50	25.00
❏ 132	Never Let Me Go/Burley Cutie	1954	6.25	12.50	25.00
❏ 136	Pledging My Love/No Money	1954	10.00	20.00	40.00
❏ 144	Anymore/How Can You Be So Mean	1955	7.50	15.00	30.00
❏ 148	So Lonely/I'm Crazy	1956	7.50	15.00	30.00
❏ 154	Still Love You So/Don't You Know	1956	7.50	15.00	30.00

7-Inch Extended Plays
DUKE
❏ 80	(contents unknown)	1955	37.50	75.00	150.00
❏ 80 [PS]	Memorial Album	1955	37.50	75.00	150.00
❏ 81	(contents unknown)	1955	37.50	75.00	150.00
❏ 81 [PS]	Tribute to Johnny Ace	1955	37.50	75.00	150.00

Albums
ABC DUKE
❏ DLPX-71	Memorial Album	1974	5.00	10.00	20.00

DUKE
❏ DLP-70 [10]	Memorial Album for Johnny Ace	1955	400.00	800.00	1200.
❏ DLP-71 [M]	Memorial Album for Johnny Ace	1956	125.00	250.00	500.00

—With no playing card on front cover
❏ DLP-71 [M]	Memorial Album for Johnny Ace	1961	50.00	100.00	200.00

—With playing card on front cover
❏ DLP-71 [M]	Memorial Album for Johnny Ace	1961	2000.	3000.	4000.

—Playing card cover; red vinyl

MCA
❏ 27014	Memorial Album	1983	2.00	4.00	8.00

ACE JUICE
12-Inch Singles
CAPITOL
❏ V-15469	Go Go (D.C. Mix)/(Cali Mix)	1989	2.00	4.00	8.00

45s
CAPITOL
❏ B-44370	Go Go/(Dub Version)	1989	—	2.00	4.00

ACE SPECTRUM
45s
ATLANTIC
❏ 3012	Don't Send Nobody Else/Don't Let Me Be Lonely Tonight	1974	—	2.50	5.00
❏ 3281	I Just Want to Spend the Night with You/Trust Me	1975	—	2.50	5.00
❏ 3296	Without You/Keep Holding On	1975	—	2.50	5.00
❏ 3353	Live and Learn/Just Like in the Movies	1976	—	2.50	5.00

Number	Title (A Side/B Side)	Yr	VG	VG+	NM
Albums					
ATLANTIC					
❑ SD 7299	Inner Spectrum	1974	3.00	6.00	12.00
❑ SD 18143	Low Rent Rendezvous	1975	3.00	6.00	12.00
❑ SD 18185	Just Like in the Movies	1976	3.00	6.00	12.00

ACKLIN, BARBARA
45s
BRUNSWICK

Number	Title (A Side/B Side)	Yr	VG	VG+	NM
❑ 55319	Fool, Fool, Fool (Look in the Mirror)/Your Sweet Loving	1967	2.00	4.00	8.00
❑ 55355	I've Got You Baby/Old Matchmaker	1967	2.00	4.00	8.00
❑ 55379	Love Makes a Woman/Come and See My Baby	1968	2.00	4.00	8.00
❑ 55388	Just Ain't No Love/Please Sunrise Please	1968	2.00	4.00	8.00
❑ 55388 [PS]	Just Ain't No Love/Please Sunrise Please	1968	3.75	7.50	15.00
❑ 55399	Am I the Same Girl/Be By My Side	1969	2.00	4.00	8.00
❑ 55412	Seven Days of Night/Raggedy Ride	1969	2.00	4.00	8.00
❑ 55421	After You/More Ways Than One	1969	2.00	4.00	8.00
❑ 55433	Is It Me/Someone Else's Arms	1970	2.00	4.00	8.00
❑ 55440	I Did It/I'm Living with a Memory	1970	2.00	4.00	8.00
❑ 55447	I Can't Do My Thing/Make the Man Love You	1971	2.00	4.00	8.00
❑ 55465	Lady, Lady, Lady/Stop, Look and Listen	1971	2.00	4.00	8.00
❑ 55486	I Call It Trouble/Love You Are Mine Today	1972	2.00	4.00	8.00
❑ 55501	I'm Gonna Bake a Man/I Call It Trouble	1973	—	3.00	6.00
CAPITOL					
❑ 3892	Raindrops/Here You Come Again	1974	—	2.50	5.00
❑ 4013	Special Loving/You Gave Him Everything, But I Gave Him Love	1974	—	2.50	5.00
❑ 4061	Give Me Some of Your Sweet Love/Fire Love	1975	—	2.50	5.00
SPECIAL AGENT					
❑ 203	I'm Not Mad Anymore/(B-side unknown)	196?	300.00	600.00	1200.
Albums					
BRUNSWICK					
❑ BL 754129	Great Soul Hits	1967	6.25	12.50	25.00
❑ BL 754137	Love Makes a Woman	1968	5.00	10.00	20.00
❑ BL 754148	Seven Days of Night	1969	5.00	10.00	20.00
❑ BL 754156	Someone Else's Arms	1970	5.00	10.00	20.00
❑ BL 754166	I Did It	1971	5.00	10.00	20.00
❑ BL 754187	I Call It Trouble	1972	5.00	10.00	20.00
CAPITOL					
❑ ST-11377	A Place in the Sun	1975	3.00	6.00	12.00

AD LIBS, THE
45s
AGP

Number	Title (A Side/B Side)	Yr	VG	VG+	NM
❑ 101	New York in the Dark/Human	1968	25.00	50.00	100.00
BLUE CAT					
❑ 102	The Boy from New York City/Kicked Around	1965	3.75	7.50	15.00
❑ 114	Ask Anybody/He Ain't No Angel	1965	2.50	5.00	10.00
❑ 119	On the Corner/Oo-Wee Oh Me Oh My	1965	2.50	5.00	10.00
❑ 123	Just a Down Home Girl/Johnny My Boy	1966	2.50	5.00	10.00
CAPITOL					
❑ 2944	Love Me/Know All About You	1970	—	3.00	6.00
JOHNNIE BOY					
❑ 01	Santa's On His Way/I Stayed Home (New Year's Eve)	19??	2.00	4.00	8.00
KAREN					
❑ 1527	Think of Me/Every Boy and Girl	1966	5.00	10.00	20.00
PHILIPS					
❑ 40461	Don't Ever Leave Me/You're in Love	1967	2.00	4.00	8.00
SHARE					
❑ 101	You're Just a Rolling Stone/Show a Little Appreciation	1969	2.00	4.00	8.00
❑ 104	Giving Up/Appreciation	1969	2.00	4.00	8.00
❑ 106	The Boy from New York City/Nothing Worse Than Being Alone	1969	2.00	4.00	8.00

ADAMS, FAYE
45s
ATLANTIC

Number	Title (A Side/B Side)	Yr	VG	VG+	NM
❑ 1007	Sweet Talk/Watch Out, I Told You	1953	12.50	25.00	50.00
HERALD					
❑ 416	Shake a Hand/I've Got to Leave You	1953	7.50	15.00	30.00
—Black vinyl					
❑ 416	Shake a Hand/I've Got to Leave You	1953	25.00	50.00	100.00
—Red vinyl					
❑ 419	I'll Be True/Happiness to My Soul	1953	6.25	12.50	25.00
❑ 423	Say a Prayer/Every Day	1954	6.25	12.50	25.00
❑ 429	Somebody, Somewhere, Someday/Crazy Mixed-Up World	1954	6.25	12.50	25.00
❑ 434	Hurts Me to My Heart/Ain't Gonna Tell	1954	6.25	12.50	25.00
❑ 439	I Owe My Heart to You/Love Ain't Nothin' to Play With	1954	6.25	12.50	25.00
❑ 444	Anything for a Friend/Your Love Has My Heart Burning	1955	6.25	12.50	25.00
❑ 450	You Ain't Been True/My Greatest Desire	1955	6.25	12.50	25.00
❑ 457	Angels Tell Me/Tag Along	1955	6.25	12.50	25.00
❑ 462	No Way Out/Same Old Me	1955	6.25	12.50	25.00
❑ 470	Teen-Age Heart/Witness to the Crime	1956	6.25	12.50	25.00
❑ 480	Takin' You Back/Don't Forget to Smile	1956	6.25	12.50	25.00
❑ 489	Anytime, Anyplace, Anywhere/The Hammer Keeps Knockin'	1956	6.25	12.50	25.00
❑ 512	Shake a Hand/I'll Be True	1958	5.00	10.00	20.00

Number	Title (A Side/B Side)	Yr	VG	VG+	NM
IMPERIAL					
❑ 5443	Keeper of My Heart/So Much	1957	5.00	10.00	20.00
❑ 5456	Johnny Lee/You're Crazy	1957	5.00	10.00	20.00
❑ 5471	I Have a Twinkle in My Eye/Someone Like You	1957	5.00	10.00	20.00
❑ 5525	When We Kiss/Everything	1958	5.00	10.00	20.00
LIDO					
❑ 603	That's All Right/It Made Me Cry	1960	3.00	6.00	12.00
❑ 606	It Can't Be Wrong/I Waited So Long	1960	3.00	6.00	12.00
SAVOY					
❑ 1606	Cry, You Crazy Heart/Step Up and Rescue Me	1960	3.00	6.00	12.00
❑ 4357	Sinner Man/God	197?	—	2.50	5.00
WARWICK					
❑ 590	Shake a Hand/It Hurts to My Heart	1960	3.00	6.00	12.00
❑ 620	Johnny, Don't/Obey My Rules	1961	3.00	6.00	12.00
❑ 638	It Can't Be Wrong/It's Nice to Know	1961	3.00	6.00	12.00
Albums					
COLLECTABLES					
❑ COL-5122	Golden Classics	1988	2.50	5.00	10.00
WARWICK					
❑ W 2031 [M]	Shake a Hand	1961	150.00	300.00	600.00

ADAMS, OLETA
12-Inch Singles
FONTANA

Number	Title (A Side/B Side)	Yr	VG	VG+	NM
❑ 868163-1	Circle of One (Full Circle 12" 6:25) (Hot Mix 12" 4:15) (Yvonne's Circle Club Mix 6:03) (Circle Dub 5:23)	1991	2.50	5.00	10.00
45s					
FONTANA					
❑ 876018-7	Rhythm of Life/Don't Look Too Closely	1990	—	2.00	4.00
MERCURY					
❑ 862376-7	I Just Had to Hear Your Voice/Get Here	1993	—	2.00	4.00
❑ 878476-7	Get Here/Watch What Happens	1991	—	2.00	4.00
Albums					
FONTANA					
❑ 846346-1	Circle of One	1990	3.00	6.00	12.00

ADAMS, YOLANDA
12-Inch Singles
ELEKTRA

Number	Title (A Side/B Side)	Yr	VG	VG+	NM
❑ ED 6178 [DJ]	Yeah (Digital Black N Groove Mix) (Digital Black N Groove Mix Dub Beats) (Digital Black N Groove Mix Acappella) (Digital Black N Groove Mix Instrumental)/(Maurice & Yolanda's Inspirational Club Mix) (Maurice & Yolanda's Inspirational Club Mix Acappella) (Maurice & Yolanda's Inspirational Club Mix Instrumental)	1999	2.50	5.00	10.00
❑ ED 6238 [DJ]	Open My Heart (unknown number of versions)	2000	2.50	5.00	10.00
❑ ED 6261 [(2) DJ]	Open My Heart (unknown number of versions)	2000	3.75	7.50	15.00
❑ 67118	Open My Heart (Album Version) (Live Version)/ (Newly Recorded Extended Version) (Instrumental) (Acappella)	2000	2.00	4.00	8.00

ADVENTURES OF STEVIE V
12-Inch Singles
MERCURY

Number	Title (A Side/B Side)	Yr	VG	VG+	NM
❑ 868357-1	That's the Way It Is (4 versions)	1991	—	3.50	7.00
❑ 875803-1	Dirty Cash (Money Talks) (5 versions)	1990	2.50	5.00	10.00
45s					
COLLECTABLES					
❑ 4867	Dirty Cash (Money Talks)/Jealousy (With Rap)	199?	—	—	3.00
—First U.S. 45 release of A-side					
MERCURY					
❑ 878662-7	Jealousy (Without Rap)/Jealousy (With Rap)	1990	—	2.00	4.00
Albums					
MERCURY					
❑ 846966-1	Adventures of Stevie V	1990	3.00	6.00	12.00

AFRIQUE
45s
MAINSTREAM

Number	Title (A Side/B Side)	Yr	VG	VG+	NM
❑ 5542	Soul Makossa/Hot Mud	1973	—	2.50	5.00
❑ 5547	Kumbo Coming/Hot Mud	1973	—	2.50	5.00
Albums					
MAINSTREAM					
❑ S-394	Soul Makossa	1973	3.00	6.00	12.00

AFROMAN
12-Inch Singles
UNIVERSAL

Number	Title (A Side/B Side)	Yr	VG	VG+	NM
❑ 440 015310-1	Because I Got High (Afropulco Gold & Dirty 3:18) (Original Afromix 5:10) (Afrolicious 3:18)/She Won't Let Me F**k 6:00/Tall Cans 7:09	2001	—	3.50	7.00
❑ 20657-1 [DJ]	Crazy Rap (Radio Edit With Effects) (Radio Edit Without Effects) (LP Version With Effects) (LP Version Without Effects) (Dirty Radio Edit) (LP Version)/Tall Cans 7:10	2001	2.00	4.00	8.00
45s					
UNIVERSAL					
❑ 440 015282-7	Because I Got High (same on both sides)	2001	—	—	3.00
—Black vinyl, large hole					
❑ 20587-7 [DJ]	Because I Got High (same on both sides)	2001	—	3.00	6.00
—Green vinyl, small hole; promo only					

Number	Title (A Side/B Side)	Yr	VG	VG+	NM

A

AFTER 7
12-Inch Singles
VIRGIN

Number	Title (A Side/B Side)	Yr	VG	VG+	NM
❑ DMD 1345 [DJ]Heat of the Moment (Extended Heat) (Radio Heat) (Heated Dub) (Percuss-a-pella) (Instrumental)		1989	2.00	4.00	8.00
❑ 1417 [DJ]	Don't Cha Think (Club) (LP) (Extended) (Dub)	1989	2.00	4.00	8.00
❑ 1494 [DJ]	Can't Stop (Extended Fun Mix 6:15) (Instrumental 4:38) (Clap-a-pella 4:08) (LP version 4:07) (One World 12" 6:25) (One World Instrumental 6:25)/ Ready or Not	1990	2.00	4.00	8.00
❑ DMD 1538 [DJ]My Only Woman (12") (New 7") (Percapella) (12" Dub) (Instrumental)		1990	—	3.00	6.00
❑ DMD 1572 [DJ]Heat of the Moment (4 versions)/My Only Woman (12" Version) (Instrumental)		1989	—	3.00	6.00
❑ 96429	My Only Woman (5 versions)	1990	2.00	4.00	8.00
❑ 96470	Can't Stop (Extended Version) (Instrumental) (Clap-a-pella) (LP Version)/(One World 12") (One World Instrumental)/	1990	2.00	4.00	8.00
❑ 96515	Don't Cha' Think (4 versions)	1989	2.00	4.00	8.00
❑ 96553	Heat of the Moment (5 versions)	1989	2.00	4.00	8.00

45s
VIRGIN

Number	Title (A Side/B Side)	Yr	VG	VG+	NM
❑ S7-17444	Truly Something Special/G.S.T.	1993	—	2.00	4.00
❑ S7-18587	'Til You Do Me Right/Gonna Love You Right	1995	—	2.00	4.00
❑ S7-56954	Baby I'm For Real/Natural High//Can He Love U Like This	1993	—	2.00	4.00
❑ 98961	Can't Stop/(Instrumental)	1990	—	2.00	4.00
❑ 98995	Ready or Not/(Instrumental)	1990	—	2.00	4.00
❑ 99143	Don't Cha Think/(Dub)	1989	—	2.00	4.00
❑ 99204	Heat of the Moment/(Instrumental)	1989	—	—	3.00
❑ 99204 [PS]	Heat of the Moment/(Instrumental)	1989	—	—	3.00

Albums
VIRGIN

Number	Title (A Side/B Side)	Yr	VG	VG+	NM
❑ 91061	After 7	1989	2.50	5.00	10.00

AFTERNOON DELIGHTS, THE
12-Inch Singles
MCA

Number	Title (A Side/B Side)	Yr	VG	VG+	NM
❑ L33-1746 [DJ] Dancing for Pennies (Vocal)/(Instrumental)		1982	2.00	4.00	8.00
❑ 13955	General Hospi-Tale (Extended Mix)/(Extended Instrumental)	1981	2.00	4.00	8.00

45s
MCA

Number	Title (A Side/B Side)	Yr	VG	VG+	NM
❑ 51148	General Hospi-Tale/(Instrumental)	1981	—	2.00	4.00
❑ 51206	Dancing for Pennies/Love on the Islands	1982	—	2.00	4.00

Albums
MCA

Number	Title (A Side/B Side)	Yr	VG	VG+	NM
❑ 5257	General Hospi-Tale	1981	2.50	5.00	10.00

ALEEM FEATURING LEROY BURGESS
12-Inch Singles
ATLANTIC

Number	Title (A Side/B Side)	Yr	VG	VG+	NM
❑ DMD 897 [DJ] Confusion/(Dub)		1985	5.00	10.00	20.00
❑ DMD 924 [DJ] Love's on Fire (3 versions)		1986	2.00	4.00	8.00
❑ DMD 947 [DJ] Fine Young Tender (Long Remix)/(Dub)		1986	2.00	4.00	8.00
❑ DMD 1091 [DJ]Love Shock (5:57) (Radio Mix) (Drumapella Mix) (Edit Version)		1987	2.00	4.00	8.00
❑ 86661	Love Shock (unknown versions)	1987	2.00	4.00	8.00
❑ 86804	Fine Young Tender (Long Remix 5:40)/(Dub 6:20)	1986	2.00	4.00	8.00
❑ 86825	Love's on Fire (Club) (Dub) (Edit)	1986	2.00	4.00	8.00

NIA

Number	Title (A Side/B Side)	Yr	VG	VG+	NM
❑ 1241	Release Yourself/(Dub)	1984	5.00	10.00	20.00
❑ 1243	Get Loose/(B-side unknown)	1984	6.25	12.50	25.00
❑ 1245 (?)	Confusion/(Dub)	1985	5.00	10.00	20.00

45s
ATLANTIC

Number	Title (A Side/B Side)	Yr	VG	VG+	NM
❑ 89113	Lonely Tears/Love Shock	1987	—	—	3.00
❑ 89206	Love Shock/Lonely Tears	1987	—	—	3.00
❑ 89401	Fine Young Tender/Two Faces	1986	—	—	3.00
❑ 89439	Love's on Fire/Dance to the Groove	1986	—	—	3.00

Albums
ATLANTIC

Number	Title (A Side/B Side)	Yr	VG	VG+	NM
❑ 81622	Casually Formal	1986	2.00	4.00	8.00
❑ 81784	Shock!	1987	2.00	4.00	8.00

ALEXANDER, ARTHUR
45s
BUDDAH

Number	Title (A Side/B Side)	Yr	VG	VG+	NM
❑ 492	Every Day I Have to Cry Some/Everybody Needs Somebody to Love	1975	—	2.50	5.00
❑ 522	Sharing the Night Together/She'll Throw Stones at You	1976	—	2.50	5.00
❑ 602	Sharing the Night Together/She'll Throw Stones at You	1978	—	2.00	4.00

DOT

Number	Title (A Side/B Side)	Yr	VG	VG+	NM
❑ 16309	You Better Move On/A Shot of Rhythm and Blues	1962	5.00	10.00	20.00
❑ 16357	Where Have You Been (All My Life)/Soldier of Love	1962	5.00	10.00	20.00
❑ 16387	Anna/I Hang My Head and Cry	1962	5.00	10.00	20.00
❑ 16425	You're the Reason/Go Home Girl	1963	3.75	7.50	15.00
❑ 16454	I Wonder Where You Are Tonight/Dream Girl	1963	3.75	7.50	15.00

Number	Title (A Side/B Side)	Yr	VG	VG+	NM
❑ 16509	Pretty Girls Everywhere/Baby Baby	1963	3.75	7.50	15.00
❑ 16554	Where Did Sally Go/Keep Her Guessin'	1963	3.75	7.50	15.00
❑ 16616	Black Knight/Ole John Amos	1964	3.00	6.00	12.00
❑ 16737	Detroit City/You Don't Care	1965	3.00	6.00	12.00

JUDD

Number	Title (A Side/B Side)	Yr	VG	VG+	NM
❑ 1020	Sally Sue Brown/The Girl That Radiates That Charm	1960	12.50	25.00	50.00

—As "June Alexander"
MONUMENT

Number	Title (A Side/B Side)	Yr	VG	VG+	NM
❑ 1060	I Need You Baby/Spanish Harlem	1968	2.00	4.00	8.00

MUSIC MILL

Number	Title (A Side/B Side)	Yr	VG	VG+	NM
❑ 1012	Hound Dog Man's Gone/So Long Baby	1977	—	3.00	6.00

SOUND STAGE 7

Number	Title (A Side/B Side)	Yr	VG	VG+	NM
❑ 2556	The Other Woman/(Baby) For You	1965	2.50	5.00	10.00
❑ 2572	Turn Around (And Try Me)/Show Me the Road	1966	2.50	5.00	10.00
❑ 2619	Set Me Free/Love's Where Life Begins	1968	2.00	4.00	8.00
❑ 2626	Bye Bye Love/Another	1969	2.00	4.00	8.00
❑ 2652	Glory Road/Cry Like a Baby	1970	2.00	4.00	8.00

WARNER BROS.

Number	Title (A Side/B Side)	Yr	VG	VG+	NM
❑ 7571	I'm Comin' Home/It Hurts to Want It So Bad	1972	—	3.00	6.00
❑ 7633	Mr. John/You Got Me Knockin'	1972	—	3.00	6.00
❑ 7658	Burning Love/It Hurts to Want It So Bad	1972	—	3.00	6.00

Albums
DOT

Number	Title (A Side/B Side)	Yr	VG	VG+	NM
❑ DLP 3434 [M]	You Better Move On	1962	25.00	50.00	100.00
❑ DLP 25434 [S]You Better Move On		1962	40.00	80.00	160.00

WARNER BROS.

Number	Title (A Side/B Side)	Yr	VG	VG+	NM
❑ BS 2592	Arthur Alexander	1972	6.25	12.50	25.00

ALEXANDER, JOE, AND THE CUBANS
45s
BALLAD

Number	Title (A Side/B Side)	Yr	VG	VG+	NM
❑ 1008	Oh Maria/I Hope These Words Will Find You Well	1954	500.00	1000.	1500.

ALISHA
12-Inch Singles
CRITIQUE

Number	Title (A Side/B Side)	Yr	VG	VG+	NM
❑ 15587	Wherever the Rhythm Takes Me (Extended Dance Mix) (Euro Dance Mix) (Progressive Soul Remix) (Lost Soul Instrumental) (Radio Edit)	1996	—	3.00	6.00

MCA

Number	Title (A Side/B Side)	Yr	VG	VG+	NM
❑ 24018	Bounce Back (LP Version) (7" Radio Remix) (12" Vocal Remix) (12" Techno-Bounce Dub)	1990	2.00	4.00	8.00
❑ 24051	Wrong Number (12" Extended Dance Mix) (7" Radio Edit) (Club Dub Mix)	1990	2.00	4.00	8.00

RCA

Number	Title (A Side/B Side)	Yr	VG	VG+	NM
❑ 6432-1-RD	Into My Secret (3 versions)/Do You Dream About Me	1987	2.00	4.00	8.00
❑ 6432-1-RDX	Into My Secret (New Brooklyn Remix)//Into My Dub/Secret Beats	1987	—	3.00	6.00
❑ 6821-1-RD	Let Your Heart Make Up Your Mind (6 versions)	1987	2.00	4.00	8.00

VANGUARD

Number	Title (A Side/B Side)	Yr	VG	VG+	NM
❑ SPV 72	All Night Passion/Beat All Night//Dub All Night	1984	2.50	5.00	10.00

—Stock copies have three tracks

Number	Title (A Side/B Side)	Yr	VG	VG+	NM
❑ SPV 72 [DJ]	All Night Passion (2 versions)/Beat All Night/Dub All Night	1984	3.00	6.00	12.00

—Promo copies have four tracks

Number	Title (A Side/B Side)	Yr	VG	VG+	NM
❑ SPV 82	Too Turned On (6:17)/(Dub)	1985	2.50	5.00	10.00
❑ SPV 89	Baby Talk (3 versions)	1985	2.50	5.00	10.00
❑ SPV 90	Stargazing (5:45)/(Dub)	1986	2.00	4.00	8.00

—Stock copies have two tracks

Number	Title (A Side/B Side)	Yr	VG	VG+	NM
❑ SPV 90 [DJ]	Stargazing (5:45) (Radio Edit) (Dub 7:11)	1986	2.50	5.00	10.00

—Promo copies have three tracks

45s
MCA

Number	Title (A Side/B Side)	Yr	VG	VG+	NM
❑ 79021	Bounce Back/I Need Forever	1990	—	2.00	4.00
❑ 79064	Wrong Number/Kiss Me Quick	1990	—	2.00	4.00

RCA

Number	Title (A Side/B Side)	Yr	VG	VG+	NM
❑ 5219-7-R	Into My Secret/Do You Dream About Me	1987	—	—	3.00
❑ 5219-7-R [PS] Into My Secret/Do You Dream About Me		1987	—	2.00	4.00
❑ 5278-7-R	Into My Secret (Remix)/(B-side unknown)	1987	—	2.00	4.00

VANGUARD

Number	Title (A Side/B Side)	Yr	VG	VG+	NM
❑ 35249	All Night Passion/Dub All Night	1984	—	2.00	4.00
❑ 35254	Too Turned On/(B-side unknown)	1985	—	2.00	4.00
❑ 35262	Baby Talk/One Little Lie	1985	—	2.00	4.00
❑ 35263	Stargazing/Boys Will Be Boys	1986	—	2.00	4.00

Albums
MCA

Number	Title (A Side/B Side)	Yr	VG	VG+	NM
❑ 6378	Bounce Back	1990	2.50	5.00	10.00

RCA

Number	Title (A Side/B Side)	Yr	VG	VG+	NM
❑ 6248-1-R	Nightwalkin'	1987	2.50	5.00	10.00

VANGUARD

Number	Title (A Side/B Side)	Yr	VG	VG+	NM
❑ VSD-79456	Alisha	1985	3.00	6.00	12.00

ALLEN, DEBBIE
12-Inch Singles
MCA

Number	Title (A Side/B Side)	Yr	VG	VG+	NM
❑ L33-17845 [DJ]Special Look (Extended Version) (Radio Edit) (Instrumental) (Dub Version) (Bonus Beats)		1989	2.50	5.00	10.00
❑ L33-18066 [DJ]Holdin' On to Love (same on both sides)		1989	—	3.00	6.00
❑ 23841	Special Look (Extended Version 8:21) (Instrumental 8:21)	1989	2.00	4.00	8.00

Number	Title (A Side/B Side)	Yr	VG	VG+	NM

45s
MCA
❏ 53281   Special Look/(Instrumental)   1989   —   —   3.00
Albums
MCA
❏ 6317   Special Look   1989   2.50   5.00   10.00

ALLEN, DONNA
12-Inch Singles
21 RECORDS
❏ DMD 1038 [DJ]Satisfied (Edit Version Remix) (Short Version Remix) (Long Version Remix) (Dub) (Acappella)   1987   2.00   4.00   8.00
❏ DMD 1088 [DJ]Sweet Somebody (3 versions)   1987   2.00   4.00   8.00
❏ 96745   Sweet Somebody (Dance Mix 4:50)/(Dub Mix 7:10)   1987   2.00   4.00   8.00
❏ 96775   Satisfied (unknown versions)   1987   2.50   5.00   10.00
❏ 96794   Serious (2 versions)/Bad Love   1986   2.50   5.00   10.00
ATLANTIC
❏ DMD 1114 [DJ]Make It My Night (Edit) (LP Version)   1988   2.00   4.00   8.00
❏ 86631   Make It My Night (LP Version 4:11)/Red Hot (LP Version 3:51)   1988   2.50   5.00   10.00
—B-side by Debbie Gibson
EPIC
❏ 49-77702   Real (5 versions)   1994   2.00   4.00   8.00
❏ 49-77707   Love Is the Thing (Spike Boys Club) (Dub)/ Jambalaya (Main Mix) (Eu-Topia Mix)   1994   2.00   4.00   8.00
—B-side by Miami Sound Machine
OCEANA
❏ DMD 1326 [DJ]Can We Talk (Club) (Edit Radio) (LP Version) (Dub)   1989   2.00   4.00   8.00
❏ 96575   Joy and Pain (Edited Remix) (LP Version)/(Dance Version) (Edited Dance Version)   1989   2.00   4.00   8.00
45s
21 RECORDS
❏ 99418   Sweet Somebody/Bit by Bit   1987   —   —   3.00
❏ 99459   Satisfied/Another Affair   1987   —   —   3.00
❏ 99497   Serious/Bad Love   1986   —   —   3.00
ATLANTIC
❏ 89152   Make It My Night/Red Hot   1988   —   —   3.00
—B-side by Debbie Gibson
❏ 89152 [PS]   Make It My Night/Red Hot   1988   —   —   3.00
—Picture sleeve promotes the movie "Fatal Beauty"
OCEANA
❏ 99213   Can We Talk/Come for Me   1989   —   —   3.00
❏ 99213 [PS]   Can We Talk/Come for Me   1989   —   —   3.00
❏ 99244   Joy and Pain/Wild Nights   1988   —   —   3.00
❏ 99244 [PS]   Joy and Pain/Wild Nights   1988   —   —   3.00
❏ 99265   Heaven on Earth/Renew the Love   1988   —   —   3.00
❏ 99265 [PS]   Heaven on Earth/Renew the Love   1988   —   —   3.00
Albums
21 RECORDS
❏ 90548   Perfect Timing   1987   2.50   5.00   10.00
OCEANA
❏ 91028   Heaven on Earth   1988   2.00   4.00   8.00

ALLEN, LEE
45s
ALADDIN
❏ 3334   Shimmy/Rockin' at Cosmos   1956   6.25   12.50   25.00
EMBER
❏ 1027   Walkin' with Mr. Lee/Promenade   1957   6.25   12.50   25.00
❏ 1031   Strollin' with Mr. Lee/Boppin' at the Hop   1958   5.00   10.00   20.00
❏ 1039   Tic Toc/Chuggin'   1958   5.00   10.00   20.00
❏ 1047   Jim Jam/Short Circuit   1958   5.00   10.00   20.00
❏ 1057   Cat Walk/Creole Alley   1959   5.00   10.00   20.00
❏ 1082   Twistin' with Mr. Lee/Twist Around the Clock   1962   3.75   7.50   15.00
7-Inch Extended Plays
EMBER
❏ 103   Walkin' with Mr. Lee/Teen Dream//Promenade/ Big Horn Special   1958   50.00   100.00   200.00
❏ 103 [PS]   Walkin' with Mr. Lee   1958   50.00   100.00   200.00
Albums
EMBER
❏ ELP-200 [M]   Walkin' with Mr. Lee   1958   125.00   250.00   500.00
—Red label
❏ ELP-200 [M]   Walkin' with Mr. Lee   1959   50.00   100.00   200.00
—White "logs" label
❏ ELP-200 [M]   Walkin' with Mr. Lee   1961   25.00   50.00   100.00
—Red and black label

ALLEN, PHYLICIA
45s
CASABLANCA
❏ 946   Colors/Josephine Superstar   1978   2.00   4.00   8.00
Albums
CASABLANCA
❏ NBLP-7108   Josephine Superstar   1978   6.25   12.50   25.00

ALLISON, LUTHER
45s
GORDY
❏ 7128   The Little Red Rooster/Raggedy and Dirty   1973   —   2.50   5.00
❏ 7137   Part Time Love/Now You Got It   1974   —   2.50   5.00

Albums
DELMARK
❏ DS-625   Love Me, Mama   1969   6.25   12.50   25.00
GORDY
❏ G-964   Bad News Is Coming   1973   2.50   5.00   10.00
❏ G-967   Luther's Blues   1974   2.50   5.00   10.00
❏ G-974   Night Life   1976   2.50   5.00   10.00

ALSTON, GERALD
12-Inch Singles
MOTOWN
❏ 3746310651 [DJ]Hell of a Situation (3 versions)   1992   2.50   5.00   10.00
❏ L33-17644 [DJ]Take Me Where You Want To (versions unknown)   1988   2.50   5.00   10.00
❏ L33-17765 [DJ]You Laid Your Love on Me (4 versions)   1989   2.00   4.00   8.00
❏ L33-17859 [DJ]I Can't Tell You Why/(Instrumental)   1989   2.50   5.00   10.00
45s
MOTOWN
❏ 935   Slow Motion/(Instrumental)   1990   —   2.50   5.00
❏ 1951   Take Me Where You Want To/Still in Love with Loving You   1988   —   —   3.00
❏ 1951 [PS]   Take Me Where You Want To/Still in Love with Loving You   1988   —   2.50   5.00
❏ 1957   You Laid Your Love on Me/(Album Version)   1989   —   —   3.00
❏ 1969   I Can't Tell You Why/(Instrumental)   1989   —   —   3.00
❏ 1997   Stay a Little While/(LP Version)   1989   —   —   3.00
Albums
MOTOWN
❏ 6265   Gerald Alston   1988   2.50   5.00   10.00
❏ 6298   Open Invitation   1990   3.75   7.50   15.00

AMBASSADORS, THE (1)
45s
ARCTIC
❏ 147   I Can't Believe You Love Me/I Really Love You   1969   3.00   6.00   12.00
❏ 150   Ain't Got the Love of One Girl/Music Makes You Wanna Dance   1969   2.50   5.00   10.00
❏ 153   Storm Warning/I Dig You Baby   1969   2.50   5.00   10.00
❏ 156   Can't Take My Eyes Off You/A.W.O.L.   1969   2.50   5.00   10.00
ATLANTIC
❏ 2442   (I've Got to Find) Happiness)/I'm So Proud of My Baby   1967   2.50   5.00   10.00
❏ 2491   Good Love Gone Bad/Happiness   1968   2.50   5.00   10.00
❏ 2547   We Got Love/Never Get Tired of Loving You   1968   2.50   5.00   10.00
Albums
ARCTIC
❏ ALPS-1005   Soul Summit   1969   6.25   12.50   25.00

AMBER
12-Inch Singles
TOMMY BOY
❏ 396   Sexual (Li Da Di) (unknown versions)   1999   2.00   4.00   8.00
❏ 735   This Is Your Night (unknown mixes)   1996   2.00   4.00   8.00
❏ 748   Colour of Love (Spike Club) (Spike Dub) (Berman 12") (Cibola Mix) (Cibola Dub)   1996   —   3.00   6.00
❏ 788   One More Night (Hani's Num Club Mix 9:53) (Hani's One More Beat 2:46) (Hani's Club Mix 6:57) (Hani's One More Dub 6:02)   1997   2.00   4.00   8.00
❏ 2053   Above the Clouds (unknown versions)   1999   2.00   4.00   8.00
❏ 2064   Above the Clouds (unknown versions)   1999   2.00   4.00   8.00
❏ 2098   Above the Clouds (unknown versions)   1999   2.00   4.00   8.00
❏ 2145   Love One Another (Rosabel Anthem Mix 7:38) (Ralphi Rosario Classic Mix 7:46) (Mystica Trance Mix 5:16) (Junior Extended Club Mix 8:26)   2000   2.00   4.00   8.00
Albums
TOMMY BOY
❏ 1424 [(3)]   The Hits Remixed   2000   5.00   10.00   20.00

ANA
12-Inch Singles
PARC
❏ 4Z9-06771   Shy Boys (12" Version) (Dub Version)   1987   2.00   4.00   8.00
❏ 4Z9-07801   Before I Jump (4 versions)   1988   2.00   4.00   8.00
❏ 4Z9-73183   Got to Tell Me Something (Dance Mix) (Radio Edit) (Red Zone Mix) (Piano Beats)   1990   2.00   4.00   8.00
45s
PARC
❏ ZS4-07056   Shy Boys/Love Is the Winner   1987   —   2.00   4.00
❏ ZS4-07056 [PS]Shy Boys/Love Is the Winner   1987   —   2.00   4.00
❏ ZS4-07767   Before I Jump/The Boy Next Door   1988   —   2.00   4.00
Albums
PARC
❏ FZ 40668   Ana   1987   2.50   5.00   10.00

ANACOSTIA
12-Inch Singles
TABU
❏ 494   Ain't Nothing To It (5:39)/Anything for You (7:55)   1978   6.25   12.50   25.00
45s
MCA
❏ 40838   I Can't Stop Loving Her/What Kind of Love   1977   —   3.00   6.00

After Johnny Ace's untimely death in 1954, Duke Records put together this compilation of his hits. The original cover features his photo and a list of songs.

The second cover took the photo of Johnny Ace and put it into a playing card. This one is more common, but neither is exactly easy to find in an original pressing.

Joe Alexander and the Cubans was an obscure St. Louis band in the early 1950s. But this record has become collectible because Chuck Berry makes his first recorded appearance on it.

Donna Allen, a former NFL cheerleader, had six R&B chart hits in the late 1980s. This is the 45-rpm picture sleeve from her top-20 hit "Heaven on Earth," from 1988.

Lee Allen's only hit single, "Walkin' with Mr. Lee," spawned this album release, which was around long enough to be issued on three different Ember labels. Still, all three variations are scarce today.

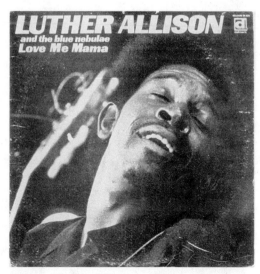

Bluesman Luther Allison recorded his debut album for the Chicago jazz and blues label Delmark in 1969. It is now his most collectible LP.

Number	Title (A Side/B Side)	Yr	VG	VG+	NM
ROULETTE					
❏ 7300	Love Is Never Wrong//(B-side unknown)	1980	2.00	4.00	8.00
TABU					
❏ 5506	Ain't Nothing To It/Anything for You	1978	—	2.50	5.00
Albums					
MCA					
❏ 2269	Anacostia	1977	3.00	6.00	12.00
TABU					
❏ JZ 35570	Anacostia	1978	2.50	5.00	10.00

ANASTACIA
12-Inch Singles
EPIC

Number	Title (A Side/B Side)	Yr	VG	VG+	NM
❏ 49-79354	I'm Outta Love (unknown versions)	2000	2.00	4.00	8.00
45s					
EPIC					
❏ 34-79343	I'm Outta Love/Baptize My Soul	2000	—	—	3.00

ANDANTES, THE
45s
DOT

Number	Title (A Side/B Side)	Yr	VG	VG+	NM
❏ 16495	My Baby's Gone/No Yo Ru	1963	6.25	12.50	25.00
V.I.P.					
❏ 25006	If You Were Mine//(Like a) Nightmare	1964	2000.	3000.	4000.
—One of the rarest of all Motown-related 45s					

ANDERSON, VICKI
45s
BROWNSTONE

Number	Title (A Side/B Side)	Yr	VG	VG+	NM
❏ 4202	I'm Too Tough for Mr. Big Stuff/Sound Funky	1971	—	3.00	6.00
❏ 4204	I'll Work It Out/In the Land of Milk and Honey	1971	—	3.00	6.00
❏ 4307	Don't Throw Your Love in the Garbage Can/In the Land of Milk and Honey	1972	—	3.00	6.00
DELUXE					
❏ 6201	Wide Awake in a Dream/Nobody Cares	1966	2.00	4.00	8.00
FONTANA					
❏ 1527	Never, Never Let You Go (Part 1)/Never, Never Let You Go (Part 2)	1965	3.00	6.00	12.00
KING					
❏ 6066	You Send Me/Unchain My Heart	1967	2.00	4.00	8.00
❏ 6091	Think/Nobody Cares	1967	2.50	5.00	10.00
—A-side: With James Brown					
❏ 6109	Tears of Joy/If You Don't Give Me	1967	2.00	4.00	8.00
❏ 6138	That Feelin' Is Real/Baby Don't You Know	1967	2.00	4.00	8.00
❏ 6152	You've Got the Power/What the World Needs Now Is Love	1968	2.50	5.00	10.00
—A-side: With James Brown					
❏ 6221	What the World Needs Now Is Love/I'll Work It Out	1969	2.00	4.00	8.00
❏ 6251	The Answer to Mother Popcorn (I Got a Mother for You)/I'll Work It Out	1969	2.00	4.00	8.00
❏ 6274	Wide Awake in a Dream/I Want to Be in the Land of Milk and Honey	1969	2.00	4.00	8.00
❏ 6293	Let It Be Me/Baby, Don't You Know	1970	2.50	5.00	10.00
—A-side: With James Brown					
❏ 6314	Never Find a Love Like Mine/No More Heartaches, No More Pain	1970	2.00	4.00	8.00
❏ 6377	Message from the Soul Sisters Part 1/Yesterday	1971	2.00	4.00	8.00
SMASH					
❏ 1985	I Love You/Nobody Cares	1965	2.50	5.00	10.00
TUFF					
❏ 420	I Can't Stop Loving You/I Lost a Good Man	1964	2.50	5.00	10.00

ANDREWS, LEE, AND THE HEARTS
45s
ARGO

Number	Title (A Side/B Side)	Yr	VG	VG+	NM
❏ 1000	Tear Drops/The Girl Around the Corner	1957	12.50	25.00	50.00
CASINO					
❏ 110	Baby, Come Back/I Wonder	1958	7.50	15.00	30.00
❏ 452	Try the Impossible/Nobody's Home	1958	200.00	400.00	600.00
—With playing cards on label					
❏ 452	Try the Impossible/Nobody's Home	1958	50.00	100.00	200.00
—All-black label					
CHESS					
❏ 1665	Long Lonely Nights/The Clock	1957	10.00	20.00	40.00
—Silver-top "chess pieces" label					
❏ 1665	Long Lonely Nights/The Clock	1957	3.75	7.50	15.00
—All-blue label					
❏ 1675	Tear Drops/The Girl Around the Corner	1957	5.00	10.00	20.00
—All-blue label (if a "chess pieces" label exists, we aren't aware of it)					
CRIMSON					
❏ 1002	Oh My Love/Island of Love	1967	2.00	4.00	8.00
❏ 1009	Nevertheless/Island of Love	1967	2.00	4.00	8.00
❏ 1015	I've Had It/Little Bird	1968	2.00	4.00	8.00
GOTHAM					
❏ 318	Bluebird of Happiness/Show Me the Meringue	1956	50.00	100.00	200.00
❏ 320	Lonely Room/Leona	1956	75.00	150.00	300.00
❏ 321	Just Suppose/It's Me!	1956	75.00	150.00	300.00
GRAND					
❏ 156	Teardrops/The Girl Around the Corner	1962	3.00	6.00	12.00
❏ 157	Long Lonely Nights/The Clock	1962	3.00	6.00	12.00
LANA					
❏ 110	Long Lonely Nights/The Clock	196?	—	3.00	6.00
❏ 111	Try the Impossible/Nobody's Home	196?	—	3.00	6.00

Number	Title (A Side/B Side)	Yr	VG	VG+	NM
❏ 112	Teardrops/The Girl Around the Corner	196?	—	3.00	6.00
—Lana records are reissues					
LOST-NITE					
❏ 104	The Fairest/Much Too Much	196?	—	3.00	6.00
❏ 106	The Bells of St. Mary/Much Too Much	196?	—	3.00	6.00
❏ 108	The White Cliffs of Dover/Much Too Much	196?	—	3.00	6.00
❏ 110	Maybe You'll Be There/Baby Come Back	196?	—	3.00	6.00
❏ 135	The Bluebird of Happiness/Show Me the Meringue	196?	—	3.00	6.00
❏ 136	Lonely Room/Leona	196?	—	3.00	6.00
❏ 137	Just Suppose/It's Me	196?	—	3.00	6.00
❏ 176	Teardrops/The Girl Around the Corner	196?	—	3.00	6.00
❏ 190	Long Lonely Nights/The Clock	196?	—	3.00	6.00
❏ 193	Try the Impossible/Nobody's Home	196?	—	3.00	6.00
❏ 216	All I Ask Is Love/Maybe You'll Be There	196?	—	3.00	6.00
❏ 234	Glad to Be Here/Why Do I	196?	—	3.00	6.00
—All the above Lost-Nite records (three-digit numbers) are reissues					
❏ 1001	Cold Gray Dawn/All You Can Do	1968	2.00	4.00	8.00
❏ 1004	Oh My Love/Can't Do Without You	1968	2.00	4.00	8.00
❏ 1005	Quiet As It's Kept/Island of Love	1968	2.00	4.00	8.00
—The above three are NOT reissues					
MAIN LINE					
❏ 102	Long Lonely Nights/The Clock	1957	100.00	200.00	400.00
—Green label, no address					
❏ 102	Long Lonely Nights/The Clock	1957	50.00	100.00	200.00
—Black label, Philadelphia address on label					
❏ 102	Long Lonely Nights/The Clock	1962	7.50	15.00	30.00
—Black label, no address					
❏ 105	Teardrops/The Girl Around the Corner	1962	3.00	6.00	12.00
PARKWAY					
❏ 860	I'm Sorry, Pillow/Gee, But I'm Lonesome	1962	3.75	7.50	15.00
❏ 866	Looking Back/Operator	1963	3.75	7.50	15.00
RAINBOW					
❏ 252	Maybe You'll Be There/Baby Come Back	1954	100.00	200.00	400.00
—Black vinyl					
❏ 252	Maybe You'll Be There/Baby Come Back	1954	200.00	400.00	800.00
—Red vinyl					
❏ 252	Maybe You'll Be There/Baby Come Back	1962	2.50	5.00	10.00
—Reissue with large print					
❏ 256	White Cliffs of Dover/Much Too Much	1954	375.00	750.00	1500.
—Yellow label original					
❏ 256	White Cliffs of Dover/Much Too Much	1962	2.50	5.00	10.00
—Blue label reissue					
❏ 259	The Bells of St. Mary's/The Fairest	1954	150.00	300.00	600.00
—Yellow label original					
❏ 259	The Bells of St. Mary's/The Fairest	1962	2.50	5.00	10.00
—Blue label reissue					
RCA VICTOR					
❏ 47-8929	Quiet As It's Kept/You're Taking a Long Time Coming Back	1966	2.50	5.00	10.00
SWAN					
❏ 4065	I Miss You So/I've Got to Cry	1960	25.00	50.00	100.00
❏ 4076	A Night Like This/You Gave to Me	1961	37.50	75.00	150.00
❏ 4087	P.S. I Love You/I Cried	1961	50.00	100.00	200.00
UNITED ARTISTS					
❏ 123	Try the Impossible/Nobody's Home	1958	6.25	12.50	25.00
❏ 136	Why Do I/Glad to Be Here	1958	5.00	10.00	20.00
❏ 151	Maybe You'll Be There/All I Ask Is Love	1958	5.00	10.00	20.00
❏ 162	Boom/Just Suppose	1959	5.00	10.00	20.00
❏ 592	Try the Impossible/Nobody's Home	1963	3.75	7.50	15.00
Albums					
COLLECTABLES					
❏ COL-5003	Gotham Recording Sessions	1982	3.00	6.00	12.00
❏ COL-5028	Biggest Hits	198?	3.00	6.00	12.00
LOST-NITE					
❏ LLP-1 [10]	The Best of Lee Andrews and the Hearts, Volume 1	1981	3.00	6.00	12.00
—Red vinyl; in die-cut cover with sticker					
❏ LLP-2 [10]	The Best of Lee Andrews and the Hearts, Volume 2	1981	3.00	6.00	12.00
—Red vinyl; in die-cut cover with sticker					
❏ LP-101 [M]	Biggest Hits	1964	25.00	50.00	100.00
—Yellow vinyl					
❏ LP-101 [M]	Biggest Hits	1964	12.50	25.00	50.00
—Black vinyl					
❏ LP-113 [M]	Lee Andrews and the Hearts Live	1965	12.50	25.00	50.00

ANGELOU, MAYA
Albums
LIBERTY

Number	Title (A Side/B Side)	Yr	VG	VG+	NM
❏ LRP-3028 [M]	Miss Calypso	1958	12.50	25.00	50.00

ANOTHER BAD CREATION
12-Inch Singles
MOTOWN

Number	Title (A Side/B Side)	Yr	VG	VG+	NM
❏ 37463 1109 1 [DJ]	Where's Ya Little Sista? (Remix Version 4:20) (Dr. Jam Mix 4:04) (Smooth Mix 5:20) (Street Mix 4:27) (LP Version 4:35)	1993	2.00	4.00	8.00
❏ 37463 1135 1 [DJ]	I Don't Wanna Be Grown Up (4 versions)	1993	2.00	4.00	8.00
❏ 37463 1138 1 [DJ]	I Don't Wanna Be Grown Up (Remix Edit) (Remix Edit w/o Rap) (The Maddness Remix)/(Yo Don't Sleep The Remix) (Instrumental Version) (LP Version)		2.00	4.00	8.00

Number	Title (A Side/B Side)	Yr	VG	VG+	NM
❏ 37463 1151 1 [DJ]Where's Ya Little Sista? (LP Version) (Remix Version) (Smooth Mix) (Dr. Jam Mix) (Street Mix) (Acapella Version)		1993	2.00	4.00	8.00
❏ 37463 1166 1 [DJ]Where's Ya Little Sista? (Chris & Ray's Phat Remix) (LP Version) (Chris & Ray's Phat Remix Instrumental) (Remix Version) (Smooth Mix) (Acapella)		1994	2.00	4.00	8.00
❏ 1360 [DJ]	Playground (7" Mix) (12" Mix) (Dub Mix) (Acappella) (Mo Beats)	1991	2.50	5.00	10.00
❏ 1577 [DJ]	Jealous Girl (4 versions)	1991	2.00	4.00	8.00
❏ 4747	Iesha (Mental Mix) (Stupid Club 12")	1991	2.00	4.00	8.00
❏ 4765	Playground (7" Version) (Acappella)	1991	2.00	4.00	8.00
❏ 4845	I Don't Wanna Be Grown Up (3 versions)	1993	—	3.00	6.00

45s
MOTOWN

Number	Title (A Side/B Side)	Yr	VG	VG+	NM
❏ 2132	Playground/Iesha	1991	—	2.50	5.00

Albums
MOTOWN

Number	Title (A Side/B Side)	Yr	VG	VG+	NM
❏ MOT-6318	Coolin' at the Playground Ya' Know!	1991	3.75	7.50	15.00
—Columbia House edition; only U.S. vinyl version of this record					
❏ 37463 6363-1 [DJ]It Ain't What U Wear, It's How U Play It		1993	3.75	7.50	15.00
—Vinyl is promo only; in black company sleeve					

ANQUETTE
12-Inch Singles
LUKE SKYYWALKER

Number	Title (A Side/B Side)	Yr	VG	VG+	NM
❏ 102	Throw the P/Miami	1986	3.75	7.50	15.00
❏ 107	Ghetto Style/Shake It	1986	3.75	7.50	15.00
❏ 122	Janet Reno (5 versions)	1988	3.00	6.00	12.00
❏ 124	I Will Always Be There for You/Get Off Your Ass and Jam	1989	2.50	5.00	10.00
❏ 129	Let's Rock & Roll Y'All/Funky Stuff/Material Girl	1989	2.50	5.00	10.00

45s
LUKE SKYYWALKER

Number	Title (A Side/B Side)	Yr	VG	VG+	NM
❏ (# unknown)	Ghetto Style/(B-side unknown)	1986	2.50	5.00	10.00

Albums
LUKE SKYYWALKER

Number	Title (A Side/B Side)	Yr	VG	VG+	NM
❏ 103	Respect	1988	2.50	5.00	10.00

ANTHONY AND THE SOPHOMORES
45s
ABC

Number	Title (A Side/B Side)	Yr	VG	VG+	NM
❏ 10844	Heartbreak/I'll Go Through Life Loving You	1966	5.00	10.00	20.00

ABC-PARAMOUNT

Number	Title (A Side/B Side)	Yr	VG	VG+	NM
❏ 10737	Gee (But I'd Give the World)/It Depends On You	1965	5.00	10.00	20.00
❏ 10770	Get Back to You/Wild for Her	1966	5.00	10.00	20.00

GRAND

Number	Title (A Side/B Side)	Yr	VG	VG+	NM
❏ 163	Embraceable You/Beautiful Dreamer	1963	15.00	30.00	60.00

JAMIE

Number	Title (A Side/B Side)	Yr	VG	VG+	NM
❏ 1330	Serenade (From The Student Prince)/Work Out	1967	3.75	7.50	15.00
❏ 1340	One Summer Night/Work Out	1967	3.75	7.50	15.00

JASON SCOTT

Number	Title (A Side/B Side)	Yr	VG	VG+	NM
❏ 18	Embraceable You/Beautiful Dreamer	1978	—	2.00	4.00

MERCURY

Number	Title (A Side/B Side)	Yr	VG	VG+	NM
❏ 72103	Play Those Oldies Mr. D.J./Clap Your Hands	1963	15.00	30.00	60.00
❏ 72168	Swingin' at the Chariot/Better Late Than Never	1963	7.50	15.00	30.00

ANTUAN AND RAY RAY
12-Inch Singles
BIV 10

Number	Title (A Side/B Side)	Yr	VG	VG+	NM
❏ 860833-1	Dance Wit Me (6 versions)	1998	—	3.00	6.00

APACHE
12-Inch Singles
TOMMY BOY

Number	Title (A Side/B Side)	Yr	VG	VG+	NM
❏ 541	Gangsta Bitch (4 versions)/Apache Ain't Shit	1993	2.50	5.00	10.00
❏ 566	Do Fa Self (3 versions)/Hey Girl (3 versions)	1993	2.50	5.00	10.00

45s
TOMMY BOY/COLLECTABLES

Number	Title (A Side/B Side)	Yr	VG	VG+	NM
❏ 541	Gangsta Bitch (same on both sides)	1993	—	2.00	4.00

Albums
TOMMY BOY

Number	Title (A Side/B Side)	Yr	VG	VG+	NM
❏ 1068	Apache	1993	3.75	7.50	15.00

APOLLONIA
12-Inch Singles
WARNER BROS.

Number	Title (A Side/B Side)	Yr	VG	VG+	NM
❏ PRO-A-3291 [DJ]Since I Fell for You (3 versions)		1988	2.50	5.00	10.00
❏ PRO-A-3394 [DJ]Mismatch (5 versions)		1988	2.00	4.00	8.00
❏ 20855	Since I Fell for You (3 versions) (These Boots Were Made for Walkin'	1988	2.00	4.00	8.00
❏ 21143	Mismatch (3 versions)/You Can't Win	1989	—	3.00	6.00
❏ 21253	Same Dream (3 versions)/Since I Fell for You	1989	—	3.00	6.00

45s
WARNER BROS.

Number	Title (A Side/B Side)	Yr	VG	VG+	NM
❏ 7-22903	The Same Dream/Since I Fell for You	1989	—	2.00	4.00
❏ 7-27589	Mismatch/You Can't Win	1989	—	—	3.00
❏ 7-27589 [PS]	Mismatch/You Can't Win	1989	—	2.00	4.00
❏ 7-29092	Blue Limousine/Some Kind of Lover	1985	—	2.00	4.00
❏ 7-29182	Sex Shooter/In a Spanish Villa	1984	—	2.00	4.00
❏ 7-29182 [PS]	Sex Shooter/In a Spanish Villa	1984	—	2.50	5.00

Albums
WARNER BROS.

Number	Title (A Side/B Side)	Yr	VG	VG+	NM
❏ 25108	Apollonia 6	1984	2.00	4.00	8.00
❏ 25594	Apollonia	1988	2.00	4.00	8.00

AQUATONES, THE
45s
FARGO

Number	Title (A Side/B Side)	Yr	VG	VG+	NM
❏ 1001	You/She's the One for Me	1958	6.25	12.50	25.00
❏ 1002	Say You'll Be Mine/So Fine	1958	6.25	12.50	25.00
❏ 1003	Our First Kiss/The Drive-In	1958	6.25	12.50	25.00
❏ 1005	My Treasure/My One Desire	1959	6.25	12.50	25.00
❏ 1015	Every Time/There's a Long, Long Trail	1960	6.25	12.50	25.00
❏ 1016	Wanted/Crazy for You	1961	6.25	12.50	25.00
❏ 1022	My Treasure/Say You'll Be Mine	1962	6.25	12.50	25.00
❏ 1111	My Darling/For You, For You	1960	5.00	10.00	20.00

Albums
FARGO

Number	Title (A Side/B Side)	Yr	VG	VG+	NM
❏ 3001 [M]	The Aquatones Sing	1964	125.00	250.00	500.00

RELIC/FARGO

Number	Title (A Side/B Side)	Yr	VG	VG+	NM
❏ 5033 [M]	The Aquatones Sing	198?	2.00	4.00	8.00

ARCHIBALD
45s
IMPERIAL

Number	Title (A Side/B Side)	Yr	VG	VG+	NM
❏ 5212	Early Morning Blues/Great Big Eyes	1953	750.00	1125.	1500.
❏ 5358	Stack-O-Lee (Part 1)/Stack-O-Lee (Part 2)	1955	25.00	50.00	100.00
❏ 5563	Stack-A-Lee/Whispering Hope	1959	12.50	25.00	50.00

78s
COLONY

Number	Title (A Side/B Side)	Yr	VG	VG+	NM
❏ 105	Crescent City Bounce/Little Miss Muffet	1951	100.00	200.00	400.00

IMPERIAL

Number	Title (A Side/B Side)	Yr	VG	VG+	NM
❏ 5068	Stack-A-Lee, Part 1/Part 2	1950	50.00	100.00	200.00
❏ 5082	Shake Shake Baby/Ballin' with Archie	1950	37.50	75.00	150.00
❏ 5101	My Gal/She's Scattered Everywhere	1950	37.50	75.00	150.00
❏ 5212	Early Morning Blues/Great Big Eyes	1953	62.50	125.00	250.00
❏ 5358	Stack-O-Lee (Part 1)/Stack-O-Lee (Part 2)	1955	25.00	50.00	100.00

ARIE, INDIA
See INDIA.ARIE under I.

ARMSTRONG, VANESSA BELL
12-Inch Singles
JIVE

Number	Title (A Side/B Side)	Yr	VG	VG+	NM
❏ 1115-1-J	Pressing On (Extended Remix) (Single Edit) (Instrumental)	1988	2.50	5.00	10.00
❏ 1304-1-JD	I'm Coming Back (Extended) (7" Version) (Instrumental)/Tell the World	1989	2.00	4.00	8.00

45s
JIVE

Number	Title (A Side/B Side)	Yr	VG	VG+	NM
❏ 1051-7-J	You Bring Out the Best in Me/Always	1987	—	—	3.00
❏ 1051-7-J [PS]	You Bring Out the Best in Me/Always	1987	—	—	3.00
❏ 1104-7-J	Pressing On/Don't Turn Your Back	1988	—	—	3.00
❏ 1248-7-J	Something Inside So Strong/Living for You	1989	—	—	3.00

ARRESTED DEVELOPMENT
12-Inch Singles
CHRYSALIS

Number	Title (A Side/B Side)	Yr	VG	VG+	NM
❏ SPRO-4674 [DJ]Mr. Wendal (4 versions?)		1992	3.75	7.50	15.00
❏ Y-24806	Mr. Wendal (5 versions)	1992	2.50	5.00	10.00
❏ SPRO-24809 [DJ]Revolution (5 versions)		1992	3.75	7.50	15.00
❏ 58199	United Front (3 versions)/Southern Fried Funk (2 versions)	1994	2.50	5.00	10.00

45s
CHRYSALIS

Number	Title (A Side/B Side)	Yr	VG	VG+	NM
❏ S7-17321	Natural/Fishin' for Religion	1993	—	—	3.00
❏ S7-17931	Ease My Mind/Shell	1994	—	—	3.00
❏ S7-18087	United Front/Southern Fried Funk	1994	—	—	3.00
❏ S7-56800	Mr. Wendal/Revolution	1993	—	2.00	4.00
❏ S7-57882	Tennessee/People Everyday	1992	—	2.00	4.00

Albums
CHRYSALIS

Number	Title (A Side/B Side)	Yr	VG	VG+	NM
❏ F1-21929	3 Years, 5 Months, & 2 Days in the Life of...	1992	2.50	5.00	10.00
❏ F1-29274 [(2)] Zingalamaduni		1994	3.00	6.00	12.00

ARTISTICS, THE
45s
BRUNSWICK

Number	Title (A Side/B Side)	Yr	VG	VG+	NM
❏ 55301	I'm Gonna Miss You/Hope We Have	1966	2.00	4.00	8.00
❏ 55315	Girl I Need You/Glad I Met You	1967	2.00	4.00	8.00
❏ 55326	Love Song/I'll Always Love You	1967	2.00	4.00	8.00
❏ 55342	The Chase Is On/One Last Chance	1967	2.00	4.00	8.00
❏ 55353	You Make Me Happy/Nothing But Heartaches	1967	2.00	4.00	8.00
❏ 55370	Hard to Carry On/Trouble, Heartaches and Pain	1968	2.00	4.00	8.00
❏ 55384	Lonely Old World/You Left Me	1968	2.00	4.00	8.00
❏ 55404	Walking Tall/What Happened	1969	2.00	4.00	8.00
❏ 55416	Price of Love/Yesterday's Girl	1969	2.00	4.00	8.00
❏ 55431	Just Another Heartache/Ain't It Strange	1970	2.00	4.00	8.00
❏ 55444	(I Want You To) Make My Life Over/Sugar Cane	1971	2.00	4.00	8.00
❏ 55477	Being in Love/It's Those Little Things That Count	1972	2.00	4.00	8.00
❏ 55493	She's Heaven/Look Out I'm Gonna Get You	1973	2.00	4.00	8.00

OKEH

Number	Title (A Side/B Side)	Yr	VG	VG+	NM
❏ 7177	I Need Your Love/What'll I Do	1963	2.50	5.00	10.00

Number	Title (A Side/B Side)	Yr	VG	VG+	NM
❑ 7193	Get My Hands on Some Lovin'/I'll Leave It Up to You	1964	2.50	5.00	10.00
❑ 7217	In Another Man's Arms/Patty Cake	1965	2.50	5.00	10.00
❑ 7232	This Heart of Mine/I'll Come Running	1965	2.50	5.00	10.00
❑ 7243	Loveland/So Much Love in My Heart	1966	2.50	5.00	10.00

Albums

BRUNSWICK

Number	Title (A Side/B Side)	Yr	VG	VG+	NM
❑ BL 54123 [M]	I'm Gonna Miss You	1967	6.25	12.50	25.00
❑ BL 754123 [S]	I'm Gonna Miss You	1967	6.25	12.50	25.00
❑ BL 754139	The Articulate Artistics	1968	6.25	12.50	25.00
❑ BL 754153	What Happened	1969	6.25	12.50	25.00
❑ BL 754168	I Want You to Make My Life Over	1970	6.25	12.50	25.00
❑ BL 754195	Look Out	1973	5.00	10.00	20.00

OKEH

Number	Title (A Side/B Side)	Yr	VG	VG+	NM
❑ OKM-12119 [M]	Get My Hands on Some Lovin'	1967	20.00	40.00	80.00
❑ OKS-14119 [S]	Get My Hands on Some Lovin'	1967	20.00	40.00	80.00

ASHFORD, NICK

45s

ABC

Number	Title (A Side/B Side)	Yr	VG	VG+	NM
❑ 11260	Let's Go Get Stoned/Dead End Kids	1970	—	3.00	6.00

VERVE

Number	Title (A Side/B Side)	Yr	VG	VG+	NM
❑ 10463	I Don't Need No Doctor/Young Emotions	1966	2.50	5.00	10.00
❑ 10493	When I Feel the Need/Young Emotions	1967	2.50	5.00	10.00
❑ 10599	California Soul/Young Emotions	1968	2.00	4.00	8.00

ASHFORD AND SIMPSON

12-Inch Singles

CAPITOL

Number	Title (A Side/B Side)	Yr	VG	VG+	NM
❑ V-8528	Street Corner/Make It Work Again	1982	2.50	5.00	10.00
❑ V-8558	High Rise (6:05)/(Instrumental)	1983	2.00	4.00	8.00
❑ V-8570	It's Much Deeper (3:47) (6:30)	1983	2.00	4.00	8.00
❑ V-8612	Solid (Special Club Mix 6:12)/(Dub Version 5:51)	1984	2.50	5.00	10.00
❑ V-8623	Outta the World (6:05)/(6:16)	1985	2.00	4.00	8.00
❑ V-8641	Babies (unknown versions)	1985	2.00	4.00	8.00
❑ SPRO-9020/1 [DJ]	It's Much Deeper (3:47) (6:30)	1983	2.50	5.00	10.00
❑ SPRO-9951 [DJ]	Nobody Walks in L.A. (same on both sides?)	1986	2.50	5.00	10.00
❑ V-15243	Count Your Blessings/Side Effect	1986	2.00	4.00	8.00
❑ V-15259	What Becomes of Love (Edit) (LP)/It's a Rush	1986	2.00	4.00	8.00
❑ V-15272	Nobody Walks in L.A. (3 versions)/Way Ahead	1986	2.00	4.00	8.00
❑ V-15448	I'll Be There for You/Way Ahead	1989	2.00	4.00	8.00
❑ V-15487	Cookies and Cake (5 versions)	1989	—	3.50	7.00

ORPHEUS

Number	Title (A Side/B Side)	Yr	VG	VG+	NM
❑ V-72289	Hungry for Me Again (Edit) (LP) (Instrumental)	1990	2.50	5.00	10.00

WARNER BROS.

Number	Title (A Side/B Side)	Yr	VG	VG+	NM
❑ PRO-A-837 [DJ]	Nobody Knows (6:35) (same on both sides)	1979	5.00	10.00	20.00
❑ DWBS 8874	Found a Cure (7:00)/You Always Could	1979	3.00	6.00	12.00

45s

CAPITOL

Number	Title (A Side/B Side)	Yr	VG	VG+	NM
❑ B-5109	Street Corner/Make It Work Again	1982	—	—	3.00
❑ B-5109 [PS]	Street Corner/Make It Work Again	1982	—	—	3.00
❑ B-5146	Love It Away/Street Opera (Part 2)	1982	—	—	3.00
❑ B-5190	I'll Take the Whole World On/Mighty Mighty Love	1982	—	—	3.00
❑ B-5250	High-Rise/(Instrumental)	1983	—	—	3.00
❑ B-5250 [PS]	High-Rise/(Instrumental)	1983	—	—	3.00
❑ B-5284	It's Much Deeper/Working Man	1983	—	—	3.00
❑ B-5284 [PS]	It's Much Deeper/Working Man	1983	—	—	3.00
❑ B-5310	I'm Not That Tough/Side Effect	1984	—	—	3.00
❑ B-5310 [PS]	I'm Not That Tough/Side Effect	1984	—	—	3.00
❑ B-5397	Solid/Solid (Dub Version)	1984	—	—	3.00
❑ B-5397 [PS]	Solid/Solid (Dub Version)	1984	—	—	3.00
❑ B-5435	Outta the World/Outta the World (Dub)	1985	—	—	3.00
❑ B-5435 [PS]	Outta the World/Outta the World (Dub)	1985	—	—	3.00
❑ B-5468	Babies/Street Corner	1985	—	—	3.00
❑ B-5468 [PS]	Babies/Street Corner	1985	—	—	3.00
❑ B-5598	Count Your Blessings/Side Effect	1986	—	—	3.00
❑ B-5598 [PS]	Count Your Blessings/Side Effect	1986	—	—	3.00
❑ B-5637	What Becomes of Love/It's a Rush	1986	—	—	3.00
❑ B-5666	Nobody Walks in L.A./Way Ah Way Ahead	1987	—	—	3.00
❑ B-44326	I'll Be There for You/Way Ahead	1989	—	—	3.00
❑ B-44326 [PS]	I'll Be There for You/Way Ahead	1989	—	—	3.00
❑ B-44404	Cookies and Cake/(B-side unknown)	1989	—	2.00	4.00

HOPSACK & SILK

Number	Title (A Side/B Side)	Yr	VG	VG+	NM
❑ 96-398	Been Found/I Remember All	1996	—	—	3.00

—With Maya Angelou

WARNER BROS.

Number	Title (A Side/B Side)	Yr	VG	VG+	NM
❑ 7745	(I'd Know You) Anywhere/I'm Determined	1973	—	2.00	4.00
❑ 7781	Have You Ever Tried It/Time	1974	—	2.00	4.00
❑ 7811	Main Line/Don't Fight It	1974	—	2.00	4.00
❑ 8030	Everybody's Got to Give It Up/Over to Where You Are	1974	—	2.00	4.00
❑ 8070	Bend Me/Ain't Nothin' But a Name	1975	—	2.00	4.00
❑ 8179	It'll Come, It'll Come, It'll Come/Caretaker	1976	—	2.00	4.00
❑ 8216	Somebody Told a Lie/It Came to Me	1976	—	2.00	4.00
❑ 8286	Tried, Tested and Found True/Believe in Me	1976	—	2.00	4.00
❑ 8337	So So Satisfied/Maybe I Can Find It	1977	—	2.00	4.00
❑ 8391	Over and Over/It's You	1977	—	2.00	4.00
❑ 8453	Send It/Couldn't Get Enough	1977	—	2.00	4.00
❑ 8514	Don't Cost You Nothing/Let Love Use Me	1978	—	2.00	4.00
❑ 8571	By Way of Love's Express/Too Bad	1978	—	2.00	4.00
❑ 8651	It Seems to Hang On/Too Bad	1978	—	2.00	4.00
❑ 8710	Is It Still Good to Ya/As Long As It Holds You	1978	—	2.00	4.00
❑ 8775	Flashback/Ain't It a Shame	1979	—	2.00	4.00
❑ 8870	Found a Cure/You Always Could	1979	—	2.00	4.00
❑ 49099	Nobody Knows/Crazy	1979	—	2.00	4.00
❑ 49269	Love Don't Make It Right/Finally Got to Me	1980	—	2.00	4.00
❑ 49269 [PS]	Love Don't Make It Right/Finally Got to Me	1980	—	2.50	5.00
❑ 49594	Happy Endings/Make It to the Sky	1980	—	2.00	4.00
❑ 49646	Get Out Your Handkerchief/You Never Left Me Alone	1980	—	2.00	4.00
❑ 49805	It Shows in the Eyes/Enough	1981	—	2.00	4.00
❑ 49867	I Need Your Light/It's the Long Run	1981	—	2.00	4.00

Albums

CAPITOL

Number	Title (A Side/B Side)	Yr	VG	VG+	NM
❑ ST-12207	Street Opera	1982	2.00	4.00	8.00
❑ ST-12282	High Rise	1983	2.00	4.00	8.00
❑ ST-12366	Solid	1984	2.00	4.00	8.00
❑ ST-12469	Real Love	1986	2.00	4.00	8.00
❑ C1-46946	Love Or Physical	1989	2.50	5.00	10.00

WARNER BROS.

Number	Title (A Side/B Side)	Yr	VG	VG+	NM
❑ BS 2739	Gimme Something Real	1973	2.50	5.00	10.00
❑ BS 2789	I Wanna Be Selfish	1974	2.50	5.00	10.00
❑ BS 2858	Come As You Are	1976	2.50	5.00	10.00
❑ BS 2992	So So Satisfied	1977	2.50	5.00	10.00
❑ BS 3088	Send It	1977	2.50	5.00	10.00
❑ BSK 3219	Is It Still Good to Ya	1978	2.50	5.00	10.00
❑ BSK 3357	Stay Free	1979	2.50	5.00	10.00
❑ HS 3458	A Musical Affair	1980	2.50	5.00	10.00
❑ 2BS 3524 [(2)]	Performance	1981	3.00	6.00	12.00

ATLANTIC STARR

12-Inch Singles

A&M

Number	Title (A Side/B Side)	Yr	VG	VG+	NM
❑ SP-12026	Kissin' Power (6:23)/Straight to the Point	1979	3.00	6.00	12.00
❑ SP-12126	Freak-A-Ristic (Extended Dance Mix) (Dub Remix)	1985	2.00	4.00	8.00
❑ SP-12134	Cool, Calm, Collected (Remix) (Dub)	1985	2.00	4.00	8.00
❑ SP-12148	Silver Shadow/Cool, Calm, Collected	1985	—	3.00	6.00
❑ SP-12189	In the Heat of Passion (6:58)/Silver Shadow (6:54)	1986	2.50	5.00	10.00
❑ SP-17031 [DJ]	Stand Up (Extended Disco Mix 6:24)/(LP Mix 4:29)	1978	2.50	5.00	10.00
❑ SP-17079 [DJ]	(Let's) Rock 'N' Roll (Disco) (Album Version)	1979	2.50	5.00	10.00
❑ SP-17168 [DJ]	Think About That (5:02) (3:42)	1981	2.50	5.00	10.00

MANHATTAN

Number	Title (A Side/B Side)	Yr	VG	VG+	NM
❑ V-56029	Armed and Dangerous (3 versions)	1986	2.00	4.00	8.00

REPRISE

Number	Title (A Side/B Side)	Yr	VG	VG+	NM
❑ PRO-A-5156 [DJ]	Unconditional Love (With Dialogue)/(Without Dialogue)	1992	2.00	4.00	8.00
❑ 40203	Love Crazy (Hardcore Mix) (Without Rap) (Without Piano) (12" Remix) (String Mix)/Under Your Spell	1991	—	3.00	6.00

WARNER BROS.

Number	Title (A Side/B Side)	Yr	VG	VG+	NM
❑ PRO-A-2949 [DJ]	Thankful (2 versions)/Let the Sun Shine In	1987	—	3.00	6.00
❑ PRO-A-3460 [DJ]	My First Love (7" Edit) (7" Edit with Dialogue)	1989	2.00	4.00	8.00
❑ 20699	One Lover at a Time (3 versions)/I'm in Love	1987	—	3.00	6.00
❑ 21168	My First Love (Extended Mix 6:30) (Instrumental Mix 5:10) (7" Edit 4:15)	1989	—	3.00	6.00
❑ 21406	Bring It Back Home Again (4 versions)/I Can't Wait	1989	2.00	4.00	8.00

45s

A&M

Number	Title (A Side/B Side)	Yr	VG	VG+	NM
❑ 2065	Stand Up/Don't Abuse My Love	1978	—	2.00	4.00
❑ 2101	Keep It Comin'/Being in Love with You Is So Much Fun	1978	—	2.00	4.00
❑ 2135	(Let's) Rock and Roll/Gimme Your Lovin'	1979	—	2.00	4.00
❑ 2164	Kissin' Power/Straight to the Point	1979	—	2.00	4.00
❑ 2198	Losin' You/Straight to the Point	1979	—	2.00	4.00
❑ 2312	When Love Calls/Mystery Girl	1981	—	2.00	4.00
❑ 2340	Send for Me/Does It Matter	1981	—	2.00	4.00
❑ 2364	Think About That/Does It Matter	1981	—	2.00	4.00
❑ 2392	Circles/Does It Matter	1982	—	2.00	4.00
❑ 2392 [PS]	Circles/Does It Matter	1982	—	2.00	4.00

—Not really a picture sleeve, but a blue sleeve with a large hole and the words "Atlantic Starr"

Number	Title (A Side/B Side)	Yr	VG	VG+	NM
❑ 2420	Love Me Down/Does It Matter	1982	—	2.00	4.00
❑ 2435	Perfect Love/Love Moves	1982	—	2.00	4.00
❑ 2435 [PS]	Perfect Love/Love Moves	1982	—	2.00	4.00

—Sleeve similar in format to the "Circles" sleeve

Number	Title (A Side/B Side)	Yr	VG	VG+	NM
❑ 2512	Sexy Dancer/Your Love Finally Ran Out	1982	—	2.00	4.00
❑ 2580	Touch a Four Leaf Clover/Circles	1983	—	2.00	4.00
❑ 2580 [PS]	Touch a Four Leaf Clover/Circles	1983	—	2.00	4.00
❑ 2607	Yours Forever/Love Me Down	1983	—	2.00	4.00
❑ 2619	More, More, More/Love Me Down	1984	—	2.00	4.00
❑ 2638	Second to None/I Want Your Love	1984	—	2.00	4.00
❑ 2718	Freak-a-Ristic/Island Dream	1985	—	—	3.00
❑ 2718 [PS]	Freak-a-Ristic/Island Dream	1985	—	2.00	4.00
❑ 2742	Cool, Calm, Collected/Island Dream	1985	—	—	3.00
❑ 2742 [PS]	Cool, Calm, Collected/Island Dream	1985	—	—	3.00
❑ 2766	Silver Shadow/(Remix)	1985	—	—	3.00
❑ 2766 [PS]	Silver Shadow/(Remix)	1985	—	2.00	4.00
❑ 2788	Secret Lovers/Thank You	1985	—	—	3.00
❑ 2808	In the Heat of Passion/Thank You	1986	—	—	3.00
❑ 2822	If Your Heart Isn't In It/One Love	1986	—	—	3.00
❑ 2822 [PS]	If Your Heart Isn't In It/One Love	1986	—	—	3.00
❑ 2849	In the Heat of Passion/Silver Shadow	1986	—	—	3.00

MANHATTAN

Number	Title (A Side/B Side)	Yr	VG	VG+	NM
❑ B-50043	Armed and Dangerous/(Instrumental)	1986	—	—	3.00

Number	Title (A Side/B Side)	Yr	VG	VG+	NM
REPRISE					
❏ 19076	Masterpiece/Bring It Back Home Again	1992	—	—	3.00
WARNER BROS.					
❏ PRO-S-2663 [DJ]Always (same on both sides)		1987	2.50	5.00	10.00

—Heart-shaped red vinyl record in large sleeve; record plays as if it were a 7-inch single

Number	Title (A Side/B Side)	Yr	VG	VG+	NM
❏ 22772	Bring It Back Home Again/I Can't Wait	1989	—	—	3.00
❏ 22896	My Sugar/I Can't Wait	1989	—	—	3.00
❏ 27525	My First Love (7' Edit)/My First Love (7" Edit with Dialogue)	1989	—	—	3.00
❏ 27525 [PS]	My First Love (7' Edit)/My First Love (7" Edit with Dialogue)	1989	—	2.00	4.00
❏ 27916	Let the Sun In/My Mistake	1988	—	—	3.00
❏ 28100	Thankful/Let the Sun In	1988	—	—	3.00
❏ 28215	All in the Name of Love/I'm in Love	1987	—	—	3.00
❏ 28215 [PS]	All in the Name of Love/I'm in Love	1987	—	—	3.00
❏ 28327	One Lover at a Time/I'm in Love	1987	—	—	3.00
❏ 28327 [PS]	One Lover at a Time/I'm in Love	1987	—	—	3.00
❏ 28455	Always/(Instrumental)	1987	—	—	3.00
❏ 28455 [PS]	Always/(Instrumental)	1987	—	—	3.00
Albums					
A&M					
❏ SP-3166	Atlantic Starr	198?	2.00	4.00	8.00

—Budget-line reissue of 4711

Number	Title (A Side/B Side)	Yr	VG	VG+	NM
❏ SP-3167	Straight to the Point	198?	2.00	4.00	8.00

—Budget-line reissue of 4764

Number	Title (A Side/B Side)	Yr	VG	VG+	NM
❏ SP-4711	Atlantic Starr	1978	2.50	5.00	10.00
❏ SP-4764	Straight to the Point	1979	2.50	5.00	10.00
❏ SP-4833	Radiant	1981	2.00	4.00	8.00
❏ SP-4883	Brilliance	1982	2.00	4.00	8.00
❏ SP-4948	Yours Forever	1983	2.00	4.00	8.00
❏ SP-5019	As the Band Turns	1985	2.00	4.00	8.00
❏ SP-5141	Secret Lovers: The Best of Atlantic Starr	1986	2.00	4.00	8.00
WARNER BROS.					
❏ 25660	All in the Name of Love	1987	2.00	4.00	8.00
❏ 25849	We're Movin' Up	1989	2.50	5.00	10.00

AURRA
12-Inch Singles

Number	Title (A Side/B Side)	Yr	VG	VG+	NM
DREAM					
❏ DG 704	In the Mood (To Groove) (8:12)/When I Come Home (5:22)	1980	3.75	7.50	15.00
❏ DG 705	When I Come Home (7:03)/Who Are You	1980	3.75	7.50	15.00
SALSOUL					
❏ SG 346	Are You Single (6:30)/Living Too Fast (4:55)	1981	3.75	7.50	15.00
❏ SG 352	Keep Doin' It/Nasty Disposition	1981	3.00	6.00	12.00
❏ SG 360	Make Up Your Mind (2 versions)	1981	3.00	6.00	12.00
❏ SG 369	Checking You Out/It's You	1982	3.75	7.50	15.00
❏ SG 394	Baby Love (5:48)/(Instrumental 6:15)	1983	3.00	6.00	12.00
45s					
DREAM					
❏ 0355	In the Mood (To Groove)/You're the Only One	1980	—	2.50	5.00
SALSOUL					
❏ 2139	Are You Single/Living Too Fast	1981	—	2.00	4.00
❏ 2148	Keep Doin' It/Nasty Disposition	1981	—	2.00	4.00
❏ 7017	Make Up Your Mind/(Instrumental)	1981	—	2.00	4.00
❏ 7023	A Little Love/In My Arms	1982	—	2.00	4.00
❏ 7027	Checking You Out/It's You	1982	—	2.00	4.00
❏ 7043	Such a Feeling/One More Time	1982	—	2.00	4.00
❏ 7049	Baby Love/Positive	1983	—	2.00	4.00
Albums					
DREAM					
❏ DA-3503	Aurra	1980	3.75	7.50	15.00
SALSOUL					
❏ SA-8538	Send Your Love	1981	3.00	6.00	12.00
❏ SA-8551	A Little Love	1982	3.00	6.00	12.00
❏ SA-8559	Live and Let Live	1983	3.00	6.00	12.00

AUSTIN, PATTI
12-Inch Singles

Number	Title (A Side/B Side)	Yr	VG	VG+	NM
CTI					
❏ OJL-4	Love Me by Name (same om both sides?)	1979	3.75	7.50	15.00
GRP					
❏ 4010	Through the Test of Time (4 versions)	1990	2.00	4.00	8.00
❏ 4013	Soldier Boy (3 versions)	1991	2.00	4.00	8.00
❏ 4019	Reach (7:41) (3:48) (9:48)	1992	—	3.00	6.00
QWEST					
❏ PRO-A-2076 [DJ]It's Gonna Be Special (Dance Remix 6:30)/ (Single Edit 4:14)		1984	2.00	4.00	8.00
❏ PRO-A-2144 [DJ]Rhythm of the Street (Edit) (LP Version)		1984	—	3.00	6.00
❏ PRO-A-2339 [DJ]The Heat of Heat (Edit)		1986	—	3.00	6.00
❏ PRO-A-2516 [DJ]Gettin' Away with Murder (Edit) (LP Version)		1986	2.50	5.00	10.00
❏ PRO-A-3271 [DJ]Smoke Gets in Your Eyes (same on both sides?)		1988	2.50	5.00	10.00
❏ 20222	Rhythm of the Street (6:09)/It's Gonna Be Special (6:30)	1984	2.00	4.00	8.00
❏ 20235	Shoot the Moon/Rhythm of the Street	1984	2.00	4.00	8.00
❏ 20361	Honey for the Bees (2 versions)/Hot! In the Flames of Love	1985	2.00	4.00	8.00
❏ 20462	The Heat of Heat (4 versions)	1986	—	3.00	6.00
45s					
ABC					
❏ 11104	Music to My Heart/Love 'Em and Leave 'Em Kind of Love	1968	3.75	7.50	15.00

Number	Title (A Side/B Side)	Yr	VG	VG+	NM
COLUMBIA					
❏ 45337	Are We Ready for Love/Now That I Know What Loneliness Is	1971	—	2.50	5.00
❏ 45410	Black California/All Good Gifts-Day by Day	1971	—	2.50	5.00
❏ 45499	God Only Knows/Can't Forget the One I Love	1971	—	2.50	5.00
❏ 45592	Day by Day/Didn't Say a Word	1972	—	2.50	5.00
❏ 45785	Come to Him/Turn On the Music	1973	—	2.50	5.00
❏ 45906	Being with You/Take a Closer Look	1973	—	2.50	5.00
CORAL					
❏ 62455	He's Good Enough for Me/Earl	1965	5.00	10.00	20.00
❏ 62471	I Wanna Be Loved/A Most Unusual Boy	1965	5.00	10.00	20.00
❏ 62478	Someone's Gonna Cry/You'd Better Know What You're Getting	1966	25.00	50.00	100.00
❏ 62491	Take Your Time/Take Away the Pain Stain	1966	5.00	10.00	20.00
❏ 62500	Leave a Little Love/My Lovelight Ain't Gonna Shine	1966	5.00	10.00	20.00
❏ 62511	Got to Check You Out/What a Difference a Day Makes	1967	5.00	10.00	20.00
❏ 62518	Only All the Time/Oh How I Need You Joe	1967	5.00	10.00	20.00
❏ 62541	I'll Keep Loving You/You're Too Much a Part of Me	1967	5.00	10.00	20.00
❏ 62548	(I've Given) All My Love/Why Can't We Try It Again	1968	5.00	10.00	20.00
CTI					
❏ 7	In My Life (Part 1)/In My Life (Part 2)	1973	—	2.50	5.00

—With Jerry Butler

Number	Title (A Side/B Side)	Yr	VG	VG+	NM
❏ 33	Say You Love Me/In My Life	1976	—	2.00	4.00
❏ 41	We're in Love/Golden Oldies	1977	—	2.00	4.00
❏ 51	Love Me by Name/You Fooled Me	1978	—	2.00	4.00
❏ 59	What's at the End of the Rainbow/In My Life	1978	—	2.00	4.00
❏ 9600	Body Language/People in Love	1980	—	2.00	4.00
❏ 9601	I Want You Tonight/Love Me Again	1980	—	2.00	4.00
QWEST					
❏ 27718	Smoke Gets In Your Eyes/How Long Has This Been Goin' On?	1988	—	—	3.00
❏ 27718 [PS]	Smoke Gets In Your Eyes/How Long Has This Been Goin' On?	1988	—	—	3.00
❏ 28573	Only a Breath Away/Summer Is the Coldest Time of Year	1986	—	—	3.00
❏ 28659	Gettin' Away with Murder/Anything Can Happen Here	1986	—	—	3.00
❏ 28788	The Heat of Heat/Hot in the Flames of Love	1986	—	—	3.00
❏ 28935	Honey for the Bees/Hot in the Flames of Love	1985	—	—	3.00
❏ 29136	All Behind Us Now/Fine Fine Fella (Got to Have You)	1984	—	2.00	4.00
❏ 29234	Shoot the Moon/Change Your Attitude	1984	—	2.00	4.00
❏ 29305	Rhythm of the Street/Solero	1984	—	2.00	4.00
❏ 29373	It's Gonna Be Special/Solero	1984	—	2.00	4.00
❏ 29618	How Do You Keep the Music Playing/same (Long Version)	1983	—	2.00	4.00
❏ 29727	Every Home Should Have One/Solero	1983	—	2.00	4.00
❏ 49754	Do You Love Me/Solero	1981	—	2.00	4.00
❏ 49854	Every Home Should Have One/Solero	1981	—	2.50	5.00
❏ 50036	Baby, Come to Me/Solero	1982	—	2.00	4.00

—With James Ingram

Number	Title (A Side/B Side)	Yr	VG	VG+	NM
UNITED ARTISTS					
❏ 50520	The Family Tree/Magical Boy	1969	2.00	4.00	8.00
❏ 50588	I Will Wait for You/Big Mouth	1969	2.00	4.00	8.00
❏ 50640	Your Love Made a Difference in Me/It's Easier to Laugh Than Cry	1970	2.00	4.00	8.00
Albums					
CTI					
❏ 5001	End of a Rainbow	1976	2.50	5.00	10.00
❏ 5006	Havana Candy	1977	2.50	5.00	10.00
❏ 7086	Live at the Bottom Line	1979	2.50	5.00	10.00
❏ JZ 36503	Body Language	1980	2.50	5.00	10.00
❏ PZ 36503	Body Language	198?	2.00	4.00	8.00

—Budget-line reissue

Number	Title (A Side/B Side)	Yr	VG	VG+	NM
GRP					
❏ GR-9603	Love Is Gonna Getcha	1990	2.50	5.00	10.00
QWEST					
❏ QWS 3591	Every Home Should Have One	1981	2.00	4.00	8.00
❏ 23974	Patti Austin	1984	2.00	4.00	8.00
❏ 25276	Gettin' Away with Murder	1985	2.00	4.00	8.00
❏ 25698	The Real Me	1988	2.00	4.00	8.00

AVERAGE WHITE BAND
12-Inch Singles

Number	Title (A Side/B Side)	Yr	VG	VG+	NM
TRACK					
❏ 58831	The Spirit of Love (5 versions)	1988	2.00	4.00	8.00
45s					
ARISTA					
❏ 0515	Let's Go Round Again/Shine	1980	—	2.00	4.00
❏ 0553	For You, For Love/Whatcha 'Gonna Do for Me	1980	—	2.00	4.00
❏ 0580	Into the Night/(B-side unknown)	1980	—	2.00	4.00
❏ 0679	Easier Said Than Done/(B-side unknown)	1982	—	2.00	4.00
❏ 1022	Cupid's in Fashion/(B-side unknown)	1982	—	2.00	4.00
ATLANTIC					
❏ 3044	Nothing You Can Do/I Just Can't Give You Up	1974	—	2.00	4.00
❏ 3229	Pick Up the Pieces/Work to Do	1974	—	2.50	5.00
❏ 3261	Cut the Cake/Person to Person	1975	—	2.00	4.00
❏ 3285	If I Ever Lose This Heaven/High Flyin' Woman	1975	—	2.00	4.00
❏ 3304	School Boy Crush/Groovin' the Night Away	1975	—	2.00	4.00
❏ 3354	Queen of My Soul/Would You Stay	1976	—	2.00	4.00
❏ 3363	Soul Searching/Love of Your Own	1976	—	2.00	4.00

Number	Title (A Side/B Side)	Yr	VG	VG+	NM
❑ 3388	Cloudy/Love Your Life	1977	—	2.00	4.00
❑ 3402	Get It Up/Keepin' It To Myself	1977	—	2.00	4.00
—With Ben E. King					
❑ 3427	A Star in the Ghetto/What Is Soul?	1977	—	2.00	4.00
—With Ben E. King					
❑ 3444	Fool for You Anyway/The Message	1977	—	2.00	4.00
—With Ben E. King					
❑ 3481	Your Love Is a Miracle/One Look	1978	—	2.00	4.00
❑ 3500	Big City Lights/She's a Dream	1978	—	2.00	4.00
❑ 3563	Walk On By/Too Late to Cry	1979	—	2.00	4.00
❑ 3581	Feel No Fret/Fire Burning	1979	—	2.00	4.00
❑ 3614 [DJ]	When Will You Be Mine (same on both sides)	1979	—	2.00	4.00
—May be promo only					
MCA					
❑ 40168	This World Has Music/The Jugglers	1973	—	2.50	5.00
❑ 40196	Twilight Zone/How Can You Go Home	1974	—	2.50	5.00
Albums					
ARISTA					
❑ AB 9523	Shine	1980	2.50	5.00	10.00
❑ AB 9594	Cupid's in Fashion	1981	2.50	5.00	10.00
ATLANTIC					
❑ SD 2-1002 [(2)]	Person to Person	1977	3.00	6.00	12.00
❑ QD 7308 [Q]	Average White Band	1975	5.00	10.00	20.00
❑ SD 7308	Average White Band	1974	2.50	5.00	10.00
❑ SD 18140	Cut the Cake	1975	2.50	5.00	10.00
❑ SD 18179	Soul Searching	1976	2.50	5.00	10.00
❑ SD 19105	Benny and Us	1977	2.50	5.00	10.00
—With Ben E. King					
❑ SD 19116	Average White Band	1977	2.00	4.00	8.00
—Reissue					
❑ SD 19162	Warmer Communications	1978	2.50	5.00	10.00
❑ SD 19207	Feel No Fret	1979	2.50	5.00	10.00
❑ SD 19266	Volume VIII	1980	2.50	5.00	10.00
MCA					
❑ 345	Show Your Hands	1973	6.25	12.50	25.00
❑ 475	Put It Where You Want It	1975	2.50	5.00	10.00
—Reissue of MCA 345					
MOBILE FIDELITY					
❑ 1-245	Average White Band	1996	5.00	10.00	20.00
—Audiophile vinyl					
TRACK					
❑ 58830	Aftershock	1988	2.50	5.00	10.00

AVONS, THE (1)
45s
ASTRA

Number	Title (A Side/B Side)	Yr	VG	VG+	NM
❑ 1023	Baby/Whisper (Softly)	1966	7.50	15.00	30.00
—Reissue of Hull material					
HULL					
❑ 717	Our Love Will Never End/I'm Sending S.O.S.	1956	50.00	100.00	200.00
—Black label					
❑ 717	Our Love Will Never End/I'm Sending S.O.S.	1956	12.50	25.00	50.00
—Red label					
❑ 722	Baby/Bonnie	1957	37.50	75.00	150.00
❑ 726	You Are So Close to Me/Gonna Catch You Nappin'	1958	30.00	60.00	120.00
❑ 728	What Will I Do/Please Come Back to Me	1958	30.00	60.00	120.00
❑ 731	What Love Can Do/On the Island	1958	30.00	60.00	120.00
❑ 744	Whisper (Softly)/If I Just (Had My Way)	1961	25.00	50.00	100.00
—White label					
❑ 744	Whisper (Softly)/If I Just (Had My Way)	1961	25.00	50.00	100.00
—Pink label					
❑ 744	Whisper (Softly)/If I Just (Had My Way)	196?	20.00	40.00	80.00
—Brown label					
❑ 754	A Girl to Call My Own/The Grass Is Greener on the Other Side	1962	37.50	75.00	150.00
—White label					
❑ 754	A Girl to Call My Own/The Grass Is Greener on the Other Side	1962	20.00	40.00	80.00
—Brown label					
Albums					
HULL					
❑ HLP-1000 [M]	The Avons	1960	175.00	350.00	700.00

AVONS, THE (U)
45s
ABET

Number	Title (A Side/B Side)	Yr	VG	VG+	NM
❑ 9419	Talk to Me/Got to Get Used to You	1967	2.00	4.00	8.00
EXCELLO					
❑ 2296	Since I Met You Baby/He's My Hero	1968	2.00	4.00	8.00
GROOVE					
❑ 58-0022	Oh, Gee Baby/Push a Little Harder	1963	3.75	7.50	15.00
❑ 58-0022 [PS]	Oh, Gee Baby/Push a Little Harder	1963	7.50	15.00	30.00
❑ 58-0033	Words Written on Water/Rolling Stone	1964	3.00	6.00	12.00
❑ 58-0039	Whatever Happened to Our Love/Tonight Kiss Your Baby Goodbye	1964	3.00	6.00	12.00
MERCURY					
❑ 71618	We Fell in Love/Pickin' Petals	1960	3.75	7.50	15.00
REF-O-REE					
❑ 700	Tell Me Baby/A Sample of My Love	196?	5.00	10.00	20.00
SOUND STAGE 7					
❑ 2561	Be Good to Your Baby/Just As Long As I Live	1966	2.50	5.00	10.00

AYERS, ROY
12-Inch Singles
COLUMBIA

Number	Title (A Side/B Side)	Yr	VG	VG+	NM
❑ CAS 2804 [DJ]	I'm the One (Extended Version 7:18) (Extended Radio 5:35) (Instrumental 8:23)	1987	—	3.00	6.00
❑ 44-05115	In the Dark (5:51)/Love Is in the Feel	1984	2.00	4.00	8.00
❑ 44-05330	Hot (6:03)/(Dub)	1985	2.00	4.00	8.00
GROOVETOWN					
❑ 64361	Naste (5 versions)	1995	—	3.00	6.00
ICHIBAN					
❑ 12 PO 14 [DJ]	Fast Money (same on both sides)	1989	—	3.00	6.00
❑ 12 PO 23 [DJ]	Suave/And Then We Were One	198?	2.50	5.00	10.00
45s					
COLUMBIA					
❑ 38-04653	In the Dark/Love Is in the Feel	1984	—	—	3.00
❑ 38-04821	Poo Poo La La/Sexy Sexy Sexy	1985	—	—	3.00
❑ 38-05613	Slip n' Slide/Can I See You	1985	—	—	3.00
❑ 38-05752	Hot/Virgo	1985	—	—	3.00
❑ 38-05874	Programmed for Love/For You	1986	—	—	3.00
ICHIBAN					
❑ 149	Fast Money/(Instrumental)	1987	—	2.00	4.00
❑ 157	D.C. City/(Instrumental)	1987	—	2.00	4.00
POLYDOR					
❑ 2020	Fever/I Wanna Feel It	1979	—	2.00	4.00
❑ 2037	Don't Stop the Feeling/Don't Hide Your Love	1979	—	2.00	4.00
❑ 2066	What You Won't Do for Love/Shack Up, Pack Up, It's Up (When I'm Gone)_	1980	—	2.00	4.00
❑ 2138	Rock Your Roll/Sigh & Feel the Vibration	1981	—	2.00	4.00
❑ 2154	Love Fantasy/Baby Bubba	1981	—	2.00	4.00
❑ 2185	There's a Master Plan/Land of Fruit and Honey	1981	—	2.00	4.00
❑ 2198	Turn Me Loose/Ooh	1982	—	2.00	4.00
❑ 2204	Fire Up the Funk/Let's Stay Together	1982	—	2.00	4.00
❑ 14078	Pretty Brown Skin/He Gives Us All His Love	1971	—	2.50	5.00
❑ 14111	He's a Superstar (Part 1)/He's a Superstar (Part 2)	1972	—	2.50	5.00
❑ 14165	Will Your Soul Be Free (Henceforth)/Rhythms of Your Mind	1973	—	2.50	5.00
❑ 14171	Red, Black and Green/Will Your Soul Be Free (Henceforth)	1973	—	2.50	5.00
❑ 14275	Magic Lady/No Question	1975	—	2.00	4.00
❑ 14294	Way of the World/2000 Black	1975	—	2.00	4.00
❑ 14316	Mystic Voyage/(B-side unknown)	1976	—	2.00	4.00
❑ 14337	The Golden Rod/Tongue Power	1976	—	2.00	4.00
❑ 14349	You and Me My Love/Hey-Uh-What You Say Come On	1976	—	2.00	4.00
❑ 14370	Vibrations/Domelo (Give It to Me)	1977	—	2.00	4.00
❑ 14379	Searching/Come Out and Play	1977	—	2.00	4.00
❑ 14415	Running Away/Cincinnati Growl	1977	—	2.00	4.00
❑ 14451	Freaky Deaky/You Came Into My Life	1978	—	2.00	4.00
❑ 14477	Let's Do It/Melody Maker	1978	—	2.00	4.00
❑ 14509	Get On Up, Get On Down/And Don't You Say No	1978	—	2.00	4.00
❑ 14573	Love Will Bring Us Back Together/Leo	1979	—	2.00	4.00
Albums					
ATLANTIC					
❑ 1488 [M]	Virgo Vibes	1967	5.00	10.00	20.00
❑ SD 1488 [S]	Virgo Vibes	1967	3.75	7.50	15.00
❑ SD 1514	Stoned Soul Picnic	1968	5.00	10.00	20.00
❑ SD 1538	Daddy Bug	1969	5.00	10.00	20.00
COLUMBIA					
❑ FC 39422	In the Dark	1984	2.50	5.00	10.00
ICHIBAN					
❑ ICH-1028	Drive	198?	2.50	5.00	10.00
❑ ICH-1040	Wake Up	198?	2.50	5.00	10.00
POLYDOR					
❑ PD 5022	He's Coming	1972	3.00	6.00	12.00
❑ PD 5045	Red, Black and Green	1973	3.00	6.00	12.00
❑ PD 6016	Virgo Red	1973	3.00	6.00	12.00
❑ PD 6032	Change Up the Groove	1974	2.50	5.00	10.00
❑ PD 6046	A Tear to a Smile	1975	2.50	5.00	10.00
❑ PD 6057	Mystic Voyage	1976	2.50	5.00	10.00
❑ PD-1-6070	Everybody Loves the Sunshine	1976	2.50	5.00	10.00
❑ PD-1-6078	Red, Black and Green	1976	2.50	5.00	10.00
—Reissue of 5045					
❑ PD-1-6091	Vibrations	1977	2.50	5.00	10.00
❑ PD-1-6108	Lifeline	1977	2.50	5.00	10.00
❑ PD-1-6126	Let's Do It	1978	2.50	5.00	10.00
❑ PD-1-6159	You Send Me	1978	2.50	5.00	10.00
❑ PD-1-6204	Fever	1979	2.50	5.00	10.00
❑ PD-1-6246	No Stranger to Love	1979	2.50	5.00	10.00
❑ PD-1-6301	Love Fantasy	1980	2.50	5.00	10.00
❑ PD-1-6327	Africa, Center of the World	1981	2.50	5.00	10.00
❑ PD-1-6348	Feeling Good	1982	2.50	5.00	10.00
UNITED ARTISTS					
❑ UAL-3325 [M]	West Coast Vibes	1964	5.00	10.00	20.00
❑ UAS-6325 [S]	West Coast Vibes	1964	6.25	12.50	25.00

AYERS, ROY, AND WAYNE HENDERSON
Albums
POLYDOR

Number	Title (A Side/B Side)	Yr	VG	VG+	NM
❑ PD-1-6179	Step Into Our Life	1978	2.50	5.00	10.00
❑ PD-1-6276	Prine Time	1980	2.50	5.00	10.00

Number	Title (A Side/B Side)	Yr	VG	VG+	NM

AZ
12-Inch Singles
EMI
| ❏ Y-58655 | Hey Az (4 versions)/Sosa (2 versions) | 1997 | — | 3.00 | 6.00 |

Albums
NOO TRYBE
| ❏ 56715 [(2)] | Pieces of a Man | 1998 | 3.75 | 7.50 | 15.00 |

AZ YET
12-Inch Singles
LAFACE
| ❏ 4198 | Last Night (LP Version) (LP Acapella) (LP Instrumental) (Kenny Smoove Remix) (Remix Instrumental) | 1996 | 2.00 | 4.00 | 8.00 |
| ❏ 24238 | Hard to Say I'm Sorry (5 versions) | 1997 | 2.50 | 5.00 | 10.00 |

45s
LAFACE
| ❏ 24181 | Last Night/(Instrumental) | 1996 | — | — | 3.00 |
| ❏ 24223 | Hard to Say I'm Sorry/Last Night | 1997 | — | — | 3.00 |

Number	Title (A Side/B Side)	Yr	VG	VG+	NM

B

B ANGIE B
12-Inch Singles
BUST IT
| ❏ 74001 | It's My Life (6 versions) | 1995 | — | 3.00 | 6.00 |

—As "Angie B"
CAPITOL
❏ V-15656	I Don't Want to Lose Your Love (4 versions)	1991	—	3.00	6.00
❏ V-15721	So Much Love (3 versions)	1991	—	3.00	6.00
❏ V-15759	Sweet Thang/I Am Angie B	1991	—	3.00	6.00

GIANT
| ❏ 40407 | Class Act 1 (3 versions) | 1992 | — | 3.00 | 6.00 |

Albums
CAPITOL
| ❏ C1-95236 | B Angie B | 1990 | 3.00 | 6.00 | 12.00 |

B.M.U.
45s
MERCURY
| ❏ 856272-7 | U Will Know (same on both sides) | 1994 | — | 2.00 | 4.00 |

B.T. EXPRESS
12-Inch Singles
COAST TO COAST
❏ AS 1494 [DJ]	Keep It Up (Long) (Short)	1982	3.75	7.50	15.00
❏ 4Z9-02631	Let Yourself Go/Cowboy Dancer	1981	2.00	4.00	8.00
❏ 4Z9-03247	Star Child (Spirit of the Night) (7:26)/This Must Be the Night for Love (7:26)	1982	3.75	7.50	15.00

COLUMBIA
| ❏ AS 403 [DJ] | Shout It Out (stereo/mono) | 1977 | 3.75 | 7.50 | 15.00 |
| ❏ 43-60518 | Let Me Be the One/Midnight Beat | 1981 | 3.75 | 7.50 | 15.00 |

KING DAVIS
| ❏ 3661 | Cover Girl (Radio Version) (Club Version) | 1985 | 3.00 | 6.00 | 12.00 |

ROADSHOW
| ❏ 233 [DJ] | Can't Stop Groovin' Now, Wanna Do It Some More (5:54) (stereo/mono) | 1976 | 12.50 | 25.00 | 50.00 |

45s
COAST TO COAST
❏ ZS5-02630	Let Yourself Go/Cowboy Dancer	1981	—	2.00	4.00
❏ ZS5-02994	Keep It Up/Dancin' Dreams	1982	—	2.00	4.00
❏ ZS4-03246	Star Child (Spirit of the Night)/This Must Be the Night for Love	1982	—	2.00	4.00

COLUMBIA
❏ 3-10346	Can't Stop Groovin' Now, Wanna Do It Some More/Herbs	1976	—	2.00	4.00
❏ 3-10399	Energy to Burn/Make Your Body Move	1976	—	2.00	4.00
❏ 3-10582	Funky Music (Don't Laugh at My Funk)/We Got It Together	1977	—	2.00	4.00
❏ 3-10649	Shout It Out/Ride On B.T.	1977	—	2.00	4.00
❏ 3-10752	You Got Something/What You Do in the Dark	1978	—	2.00	4.00
❏ 1-11200	Heart of Fire/Better Late Than Never	1980	—	2.00	4.00
❏ 1-11249	Give Up the Funk (Let's Dance)/Better Late Than Never	1980	—	2.00	4.00
❏ 1-11336	Does It Feel Good/Have Some Fun	1980	—	2.00	4.00
❏ 11400	Stretch/Just Want to Hold You	1980	—	2.00	4.00

ROADSHOW
❏ 7001	Express/Express (Disco Mix)	1975	—	2.00	4.00
❏ 7003	Give It What You Got/Peace Pipe	1975	—	2.00	4.00
❏ 7005	Close to You/(B-side unknown)	1975	—	2.00	4.00

SCEPTER
| ❏ 12395 | Do It ('Til You're Satisfied)/(Long Version) | 1974 | — | 2.50 | 5.00 |

Albums
COAST TO COAST
| ❏ FZ 38001 | Keep It Up | 1982 | 2.50 | 5.00 | 10.00 |

COLLECTABLES
| ❏ COL-5190 | Golden Classics: Express | 198? | 2.50 | 5.00 | 10.00 |

COLUMBIA
❏ PC 34178	Energy to Burn	1976	2.50	5.00	10.00
❏ PCQ 34178 [Q]	Energy to Burn	1976	3.75	7.50	15.00
❏ PC 34702	Function at the Junction	1977	2.50	5.00	10.00
❏ JC 35078	Shout!	1978	2.50	5.00	10.00
❏ JC 36333	B.T. Express 1980	1980	2.50	5.00	10.00
❏ JC 36923	Greatest Hits	1980	2.50	5.00	10.00

ROADSHOW
| ❏ 41001 | Non-Stop | 1975 | 3.00 | 6.00 | 12.00 |

ROADSHOW/SCEPTER
| ❏ 5117 | Do It ('Til You're Satisfied) | 1974 | 3.00 | 6.00 | 12.00 |

BABY FACE LEROY
Those credited to the "Baby Face Leroy Trio" featured backing by LITTLE WALTER and MUDDY WATERS.
45s
SAVOY
| ❏ 1122 | Moonshine Baby/Red Headed Woman | 1954 | 30.00 | 60.00 | 120.00 |
| ❏ 1501 | Moonshine Baby/Red Headed Woman | 1956 | 20.00 | 40.00 | 80.00 |

—Reissue of 1122

Number	Title (A Side/B Side)	Yr	VG	VG+	NM

78s
CHESS

Number	Title (A Side/B Side)	Yr	VG	VG+	NM
❏ 1447	My Head Can't Rest Anymore/Take a Little Walk with Me	1951	37.50	75.00	150.00

—*Reissue of J.O.B. 100*

J.O.B.

❏ 100	My Head Can't Rest Anymore/Take a Little Walk with Me	1949	100.00	200.00	400.00
❏ 1002	Pet Rabbit/Louella	1952	50.00	100.00	200.00

PARKWAY

❏ 104	Boll Weevil/Red Headed Woman	1950	100.00	200.00	400.00
❏ 501	Rollin' and Tumblin' Part 1/Part 2	1950	2000.	3000.	4000.
❏ 502	I Just Keep Loving Her/Moonshine Blues	1950	250.00	500.00	1000.

SAVOY

❏ 1122	Moonshine Baby/Red Headed Woman	1954	15.00	30.00	60.00

BABY RAY
45s
IMPERIAL

❏ 66216	There's Something On Your Mind/House on Soul Hill	1966	3.75	7.50	15.00
❏ 66232	Elvira/Just Because	1967	3.75	7.50	15.00
❏ 66256	Your Sweet Love/Yours Until Tomorrow	1967	3.75	7.50	15.00

BABYFACE
12-Inch Singles
ARISTA

❏ ARDP-3942 [DJ]	There She Goes (Main Mix 4:21) (Instrumental 4:29) (Acapella 4:34)	2001	3.75	7.50	15.00
❏ ARDP-3953 RE1 [DJ]	There She Goes (Main Mix 4:21) (Instrumental 4:29) (Acapella 4:34)	2001	—	3.50	7.00
❏ ARDP-3953 [DJ]	There She Goes (Club Mix) (Instrumental) (Acappella)	2001	2.00	4.00	8.00
❏ 13593	There She Goes (Main Mix)/(Instrumental) (Acappella)	2001	—	3.00	6.00
❏ 15034	What If (Main) (Instrumental)	2001	—	3.00	6.00

EPIC

❏ EAS 8668 [DJ]	This Is for the Lover in You (4 versions)	1996	2.50	5.00	10.00
❏ EAS 8888 [DJ]	This Is for the Lover in You (6 versions)	1996	2.50	5.00	10.00
❏ EAS 8894 [DJ]	Every Time I Close My Eyes (Radio Edit) (Instrumental) (LP Version) (Acappella)	1996	2.50	5.00	10.00
❏ EAS 9180 [DJ]	Every Time I Close My Eyes (6 versions)	1997	2.50	5.00	10.00
❏ 49-77151	For the Cool in You (6 versions)	1993	2.50	5.00	10.00
❏ 49-77599	When Can I See You (7 versions)	1994	2.50	5.00	10.00
❏ 49-78444	This Is for the Lover in You (4 versions)	1996	2.00	4.00	8.00

—*With L.L. Cool J, Howard Hewett, Jody Watley and Jeffrey Daniels*

SOLAR

❏ 4Z9-68832	It's No Crime (Extended Mix) (Single Mix)/ (Extended Radio Mix) (Cussapella) (Instrumental)	1989	2.00	4.00	8.00
❏ V-71156	I Love You Babe (4 versions)	1987	2.00	4.00	8.00
❏ V-71159	Mary Mack (Club Mix) (Radio Edit) (Instrumental) (Yodel Dub Mix) (Bass-a-Pella)	1987	2.00	4.00	8.00
❏ 4Z9-74502	Tender Lover (The Long Mix) (Radio Version) (Instrumental)	1989	2.00	4.00	8.00
❏ 4Z9-74510	My Kinda Girl (Scratch Mix) (Radio Mix) (Racquet Gass Dub) (L.A. Face Bonus Beats) (Single Version) (Instrumental) (Dope Duff Dub Mix)	1990	2.00	4.00	8.00

45s
EPIC

❏ 34-77109	For the Cool in You/For the Cool in You (Remix)	1993	—	—	3.00
❏ 34-77264	Never Keeping Secrets/For the Cool in You	1993	—	—	3.00
❏ 34-77394	And Our Feelings/Never Keeping Secrets	1994	—	—	3.00
❏ 34-77608	When Can I See You/When Can I See You (R&B Remix)	1994	—	2.00	4.00
❏ 34-78443	This Is for the Lover in You (2 versions)	1996	—	—	3.00

—*With L.L. Cool J, Howard Hewett, Jody Watley and Jeffrey Daniels*

❏ 34-78485	Every Time I Close My Eyes/Lady, Lady	1996	—	—	3.00

SOLAR

❏ ZS4-68966	It's No Crime/(Instrumental)	1989	—	—	3.00
❏ B-70002	You Make Me Feel Brand New/Faithful	1987	—	2.50	5.00
❏ B-70004	Lovers/Take Your Time	1987	—	—	3.00
❏ B-70009	I Love You Babe/(Instrumental)	1987	—	—	3.00
❏ B-70016	Mary Mack/(Instrumental)	1987	—	—	3.00
❏ B-70022	If We Try/(Instrumental)	1988	—	—	3.00
❏ ZS4-74003	Tender Lover/(Instrumental)	1989	—	—	3.00
❏ ZS4-74007	Whip Appeal/(Instrumental)	1989	—	—	3.00
❏ 35-74515	My Kinda Girl/(Instrumental)	1990	—	—	3.00

Albums
ARISTA

❏ 12667 [(2)]	Face2Face	2001	3.75	7.50	15.00

EPIC

❏ E 53558	For the Cool in You	1993	3.00	6.00	12.00
❏ E 67293	The Day	1996	2.50	5.00	10.00

SOLAR

❏ FZ 45288	Tender Lover	1989	2.50	5.00	10.00
❏ ST-72552	Lovers by Babyface	1987	3.00	6.00	12.00

BACHELORS, THE (2)
American male vocal group.
45s
ALADDIN

❏ 3210	Pretty Baby/Can't Help Loving You	1953	625.00	1250.	2500.

ROYAL ROOST

❏ 620	I Found Love/You've Lied	1952	75.00	150.00	300.00

BADU, ERYKAH
12-Inch Singles
MOTOWN

❏ 1587 [DJ]	Southern Gul (Radio Mix) (Acapella Mix)	1999	2.00	4.00	8.00
❏ 20099 [DJ]	Bag Lady (Cheeba Sac Main 5:09) (Cheeba Sac Radio 4:04) (Main Radio Edit 4:06) (Cheeba Instrumental 4:57) (Main Instrumental 5:50) (Main Acapella 5:40)	2000	2.50	5.00	10.00
❏ 156360	Southern Gul (unknown versions)	1999	—	3.00	6.00
❏ 012-158274-1	Bag Lady (4 versions)	2000	—	3.00	6.00

UNIVERSAL/KEDAR

❏ 1075 [DJ]	On & On (4 versions)	1997	2.50	5.00	10.00
❏ 1150 [DJ]	On & On (Dance 3:50) (Dance 6:44) (Instrumental)/Certainly Flipped It	1997	2.50	5.00	10.00
❏ 1218 [DJ]	Tyrone (6 versions)	1997	3.00	6.00	12.00
❏ 56002	On & On (Album Version 3:47) (Clean Version 3:47) (Acapella 3:47) (Instrumental 3:47)	1997	2.00	4.00	8.00

45s
UNIVERSAL/KEDAR

❏ US7-56189	Tyrone/On & On	1998	—	2.50	5.00

Albums
MOTOWN

❏ 012-153287-1 [(2)]	Mama's Gun	2000	3.75	7.50	15.00

—*Comes in generic sleeve with large center hole; red vinyl*

UNIVERSAL/KEDAR

❏ 53027	Baduizm	1997	2.50	5.00	10.00

—*Comes in generic sleeve with large center hole*

❏ 53109	Live	1997	3.75	7.50	15.00

—*Comes in generic sleeve with large center hole*

BAHA MEN
12-Inch Singles
BIG BEAT

❏ DMD 1864 [DJ]	Back to the Island (Coconut Club Mix) (Original Island Mix) (Da Hub Dub) (Cheesy Organ Dub) (Yeah in the House Dub)	1992	2.00	4.00	8.00
❏ 2131 [DJ]	Dancing in the Moonlight (Classic Vocal Remix) (Tribal Island Dub) (Remix Edit)	1994	2.00	4.00	8.00
❏ 10061	Back to the Island (Coconut Club Mix) (Original Island Mix) (Da Hub Dub) (Cheesy Organ Dub) (Yeah in the House Dub)	1992	2.50	5.00	10.00

MERCURY

❏ 1970 [DJ]	Living on Sunshine (28th Street Club Mix) (28th Street Dub Mix) (28th Street Radio Edit)	199?	2.00	4.00	8.00

S-CURVE

❏ 51000	Who Let the Dogs Out? (Doggy Style 6:35) (Instrumental 3:07) (Barking Mad Mix Radio Edit 3:11)/(Barking Mad Mix Extended 5:19) (LP Version 3:17)	2000	2.50	5.00	10.00

45s
S-CURVE

❏ 77687	Move It Like This (Radio Edit)/Move It Like This - Shake It Like That Mix (Radio Edit)	2002	—	—	3.00

BAILEY, PHILIP
Also see EARTH, WIND AND FIRE.
12-Inch Singles
COLUMBIA

❏ AS 1786 [DJ]	Trapped (Single Version)/(Album Version)	1983	2.00	4.00	8.00
❏ 44-04027	I Know/The Good Guy's Supposed to Get the Girls	1983	2.00	4.00	8.00
❏ 44-05093	Photogenic Memory/Children of the Ghetto	1984	2.00	4.00	8.00
❏ 44-05160	Easy Lover (6:18)/Woman	1984	2.50	5.00	10.00
❏ 44-05372	State of the Heart (4:15) (5:10)	1986	—	3.00	6.00

HORIZON

❏ SP-12205	Thank You (Extended) (A Cappella) (Instrumental)/All Soldiers	1986	2.50	5.00	10.00

WTG

❏ 41-08169	Twins (4 versions)	1988	2.50	5.00	10.00

—*With Little Richard*

ZOO

❏ 14133	Here with Me (5 versions)	1991	2.50	5.00	10.00

45s
COLUMBIA

❏ 38-03968	I Know/The Good Guy's Supposed to Get the Girls	1983	—	2.00	4.00
❏ 38-03968 [PS]	I Know/The Good Guy's Supposed to Get the Girls	1983	—	2.50	5.00
❏ 38-04241	Trapped/Vaya (Go with Love)	1983	—	2.00	4.00
❏ 38-04607	Photogenic Memory/Children of the Ghetto	1984	—	2.00	4.00
❏ 38-04679	Easy Lover/Women	1984	—	—	3.00

—*A-side with Phil Collins*

❏ 38-04679 [PS]	Easy Lover/Women	1984	—	2.00	4.00
❏ 38-04826	Walking on the Chinese Wall/Children of the Ghetto	1985	—	—	3.00
❏ 38-04826 [PS]	Walking on the Chinese Wall/Children of the Ghetto	1985	—	2.00	4.00
❏ 38-05861	State of the Heart/Take This With You	1986	—	—	3.00
❏ 38-05861 [PS]	State of the Heart/Take This With You	1986	—	2.00	4.00
❏ 38-06216	Echo My Heart/Special Effect	1986	—	—	3.00

B

Number	Title (A Side/B Side)	Yr	VG	VG+	NM
❏ 38-73797	Easy Lover/Woman	1991	—	—	3.00

—A-side with Phil Collins; reissue

MYRRH

| ❏ 9016 [DJ] | Love of God (same on both sides) | 1986 | — | 2.50 | 5.00 |

MYRRH/A&M

| ❏ 2725 | I Want to Know You/The Wonders of His Love | 1985 | — | 2.00 | 4.00 |
| ❏ 2876 | Thank You/All Soldiers | 1986 | — | 2.00 | 4.00 |

WTG

| ❏ 31-08492 | Twins (Long)/Twins (Short) | 1988 | — | 2.00 | 4.00 |

—With Little Richard

Albums

COLUMBIA

| ❏ FC 38725 | Continuation | 1983 | 2.50 | 5.00 | 10.00 |
| ❏ PC 38725 | Continuation | 198? | 2.00 | 4.00 | 8.00 |

—Budget-line reissue with new prefix

| ❏ FC 39542 | Chinese Wall | 1984 | 2.50 | 5.00 | 10.00 |
| ❏ FC 40209 | Inside Out | 1986 | 2.50 | 5.00 | 10.00 |

HORIZON

| ❏ SP-754 | Triumph | 1986 | 2.50 | 5.00 | 10.00 |

MYRRH

| ❏ 7-01-679606-X | Wonders of His Love | 1984 | 3.00 | 6.00 | 12.00 |
| ❏ 7-01-683406 | Triumph | 1986 | 3.75 | 7.50 | 15.00 |

—Released simultaneously with the Horizon issue, this version was found in Christian bookstores

MYRRH/A&M

| ❏ WR-8448 | Family Affair | 1989 | 3.00 | 6.00 | 12.00 |

BAKER, ANITA

12-Inch Singles

ELEKTRA

❏ ED 5131 [DJ]	Sweet Love (same on both sides)	1986	2.00	4.00	8.00
❏ ED 5180 [DJ]	Caught Up in the Rapture (same on both sides?)	1986	2.00	4.00	8.00
❏ ED 5213 [DJ]	Same Ole Love (365 Days a Year) (same on both sides)	1987	2.00	4.00	8.00
❏ ED 5238 [DJ]	No One in the World (same on both sides)	1987	2.00	4.00	8.00
❏ ED 5331 [DJ]	Giving You the Best That I Got (Extended Version) (LP Version) (Edited Version)	1988	2.50	5.00	10.00
❏ ED 5375 [DJ]	Lead Me Into Love (Edit) (same on both sides)	1989	2.00	4.00	8.00
❏ ED 5730 [DJ]	I Apologize (same on both sides?)	1994	2.50	5.00	10.00

45s

BEVERLY GLEN

❏ 2005	No More Tears/Will You Be Mine	1983	—	2.50	5.00
❏ 2010	Angel/Do You Believe Me	1983	—	2.50	5.00
❏ 2011	You're the Best Thing Yet/Squeeze Me	1983	—	2.50	5.00
❏ 2013	Feel the Need/Sometimes	1984	—	2.50	5.00

ELEKTRA

❏ 64910	Fairy Tales/Watch Your Step	1991	—	—	3.00
❏ 64935	Soul Inspiration/Good Enough	1990	—	—	3.00
❏ 64964	Talk to Me/Good Enough	1990	—	—	3.00
❏ 69299	Lead Me Into Love/Good Enough	1989	—	—	3.00
❏ 69299 [PS]	Lead Me Into Love/Good Enough	1989	—	2.00	4.00
❏ 69327	Just Because/Good Enough	1988	—	—	3.00
❏ 69327 [PS]	Just Because/Good Enough	1988	—	—	3.00
❏ 69371	Giving You the Best That I Got/Good Enough	1988	—	—	3.00
❏ 69371 [PS]	Giving You the Best That I Got/Good Enough	1988	—	—	3.00
❏ 69456	No One in the World/Watch Your Step	1987	—	—	3.00
❏ 69456 [PS]	No One in the World/Watch Your Step	1987	—	2.00	4.00
❏ 69484	Same Ole Love (365 Days a Year)/(Live Version)	1987	—	—	3.00
❏ 69484 [PS]	Same Ole Love (365 Days a Year)/(Live Version)	1987	—	2.00	4.00
❏ 69511	Caught Up in the Rapture/Mystery	1986	—	—	3.00
❏ 69511 [PS]	Caught Up in the Rapture/Mystery	1986	—	2.00	4.00
❏ 69554	Watch Your Step/Mystery	1986	—	—	3.00
❏ 69557	Sweet Love/Watch Your Step	1986	—	—	3.00

Albums

BEVERLY GLEN

| ❏ 10002 | The Songstress | 1983 | 3.00 | 6.00 | 12.00 |

ELEKTRA

❏ 60444	Rapture	1986	2.00	4.00	8.00
❏ 60827	Giving You the Best That I Got	1988	2.00	4.00	8.00
❏ 60922	Compositions	1990	2.50	5.00	10.00

BAKER, LAVERN

45s

ATLANTIC

❏ 1004	How Can You Leave a Man Like This/Soul on Fire	1953	12.50	25.00	50.00
❏ 1030	I Can't Hold Out Any Longer/I'm Living My Life for You	1954	10.00	20.00	40.00
❏ 1047	Tweedlee Dee/Tomorrow Night	1954	10.00	20.00	40.00
❏ 1057	Bop-Ting-a-Ling/That's All I Need	1955	10.00	20.00	40.00
❏ 1075	Play It Fair/That Lucky Old Sun	1955	10.00	20.00	40.00
❏ 1087	Get Up Get Up (You Sleepyhead)/My Happiness Forever	1956	6.25	12.50	25.00
❏ 1093	Fee Fee Fi Fo Fum/I'll Do the Same for You	1956	6.25	12.50	25.00
❏ 1104	I Can't Love You Enough/Still	1956	6.25	12.50	25.00
❏ 1116	Jim Dandy/Tra La La	1956	6.25	12.50	25.00
❏ 1136	Jim Dandy Got Married/The Game of Love	1957	6.25	12.50	25.00
❏ 1150	Humpty Dumpty Heart/Love Me Right	1957	6.25	12.50	25.00
❏ 1163	St.Louis Blues/Miracles	1957	6.25	12.50	25.00
❏ 1176	Substitute/Learning to Love	1958	6.25	12.50	25.00
❏ 1189	Harbor Lights/Whipper Snapper	1958	6.25	12.50	25.00
❏ 2001	It's So Fine/Why Baby Why	1958	6.25	12.50	25.00
❏ 2007	I Cried a Tear/Dix-A-Billy	1958	6.25	12.50	25.00
❏ 2021	I Waited Too Long/You're Teasing Me	1959	5.00	10.00	20.00
❏ 2033	So High So Low/If You Love Me	1959	5.00	10.00	20.00
❏ 2041	Tiny Tim/For Love of You	1959	5.00	10.00	20.00

Number	Title (A Side/B Side)	Yr	VG	VG+	NM
❏ 2048	Shake a Hand/Manana	1960	5.00	10.00	20.00
❏ 2059	Wheel of Fortune/Shadows of Love	1960	3.75	7.50	15.00
❏ 2067	A Help-Each-Other Romance/How Often	1960	3.75	7.50	15.00

—With Ben E. King

| ❏ 2077 | Bumble Bee/My Time Will Come | 1960 | 3.75 | 7.50 | 15.00 |
| ❏ 2090 | You're the Boss/I'll Never Be Free | 1961 | 3.75 | 7.50 | 15.00 |

—With Jimmy Ricks

❏ 2099	Saved/Don Juan	1961	3.75	7.50	15.00
❏ 2109	I Didn't Know I Was Crying/Hurtin' Inside	1961	3.75	7.50	15.00
❏ 2119	Hey, Memphis/Voodoo Voodoo	1961	3.75	7.50	15.00
❏ 2137	Must I Cry Again/No Love So True	1962	3.00	6.00	12.00
❏ 2167	See See Rider/The Story of My Love	1962	3.00	6.00	12.00
❏ 2186	Trouble in Mind/Half of Your Love	1963	3.00	6.00	12.00
❏ 2203	Itty Bitty Girl/Oh, Johnny Oh, Johnny	1963	3.00	6.00	12.00
❏ 2234	You'd Better Find Yourself Another Fool/Go Away	1964	2.50	5.00	10.00
❏ 2267	Fly Me to the Moon/Ain't Gonna Cry No More	1965	2.50	5.00	10.00

ATLANTIC OLDIES SERIES

| ❏ 13001 | See See Rider/Jim Dandy | 196? | — | 2.50 | 5.00 |

—Originals have gold and black labels

| ❏ 13002 | I Cried a Tear/Saved | 196? | — | 2.50 | 5.00 |

—Originals have gold and black labels

BRUNSWICK

| ❏ 55285 | Let Me Belong to You/Pledging My Love | 1965 | 2.00 | 4.00 | 8.00 |
| ❏ 55287 | Think Twice/Please Don't Hurt Me | 1965 | 2.00 | 4.00 | 8.00 |

—With Jackie Wilson

❏ 55291	One Monkey (Don't Stop the Show)/Baby	1966	2.00	4.00	8.00
❏ 55297	Batman to the Rescue/Call Me Darling	1966	2.50	5.00	10.00
❏ 55311	Nothing Like Being in Love/Wrapped, Tied and Tangled	1967	2.00	4.00	8.00
❏ 55341	Born to Lose/I Need You So	1967	2.00	4.00	8.00
❏ 55408	I'm the One to Do It/Baby	1969	—	3.00	6.00

KING

| ❏ 4556 | Trying/Snuff Dipper | 1952 | 12.50 | 25.00 | 50.00 |

—B-side by Todd Rhodes

| ❏ 4583 | Must I Cry Again/Hog Maw and Cabbage Slaw | 1952 | 12.50 | 25.00 | 50.00 |

—B-side by Todd Rhodes

| ❏ 4601 | Lost Child/Thunderball Boogie | 1953 | 12.50 | 25.00 | 50.00 |

—B-side by Todd Rhodes

7-Inch Extended Plays

ATLANTIC

❏ 566	(contents unknown)	1956	50.00	100.00	200.00
❏ 566 [PS]	LaVern Baker: Tweedle Dee	1956	25.00	50.00	100.00
❏ 588	*Jim Dandy/Still/Play It Fair/Tra La La	1957	20.00	40.00	80.00
❏ 588 [PS]	LaVern Baker: Jim Dandy	1957	37.50	75.00	150.00
❏ 617	(contents unknown)	1958	20.00	40.00	80.00
❏ 617 [PS]	LaVern Baker: I Cried a Tear	1958	37.50	75.00	150.00

Albums

ATCO

| ❏ SD 33-372 | Her Greatest Recordings | 1971 | 3.00 | 6.00 | 12.00 |

ATLANTIC

| ❏ 1281 [M] | LaVern Baker Sings Bessie Smith | 1958 | 30.00 | 60.00 | 120.00 |

—Black label

| ❏ 1281 [M] | LaVern Baker Sings Bessie Smith | 1960 | 7.50 | 15.00 | 30.00 |

—Red and purple label, "fan" logo in white

| ❏ 1281 [M] | LaVern Baker Sings Bessie Smith | 1963 | 5.00 | 10.00 | 20.00 |

—Red and purple label, "fan" logo in black

| ❏ SD 1281 [S] | LaVern Baker Sings Bessie Smith | 1959 | 37.50 | 75.00 | 150.00 |

—Green label

| ❏ SD 1281 [S] | LaVern Baker Sings Bessie Smith | 1960 | 10.00 | 20.00 | 40.00 |

—Green and blue label, "fan" logo in white

| ❏ SD 1281 [S] | LaVern Baker Sings Bessie Smith | 1963 | 6.25 | 12.50 | 25.00 |

—Green and blue label, "fan" logo in black

| ❏ 8002 [M] | LaVern | 1956 | 62.50 | 125.00 | 250.00 |

—Black label

| ❏ 8002 [M] | LaVern | 1960 | 7.50 | 15.00 | 30.00 |

—Red and purple label, "fan" logo in white

| ❏ 8002 [M] | LaVern | 1963 | 5.00 | 10.00 | 20.00 |

—Red and purple label, "fan" logo in black

| ❏ 8007 [M] | LaVern Baker | 1957 | 62.50 | 125.00 | 250.00 |

—Black label

| ❏ 8007 [M] | LaVern Baker | 1960 | 7.50 | 15.00 | 30.00 |

—Red and purple label, "fan" logo in white

| ❏ 8007 [M] | LaVern Baker | 1963 | 5.00 | 10.00 | 20.00 |

—Red and purple label, "fan" logo in black

| ❏ 8030 [M] | Blues Ballads | 1959 | 50.00 | 100.00 | 200.00 |

—Black label

| ❏ 8030 [M] | Blues Ballads | 1960 | 37.50 | 75.00 | 150.00 |

—White "bullseye" label

| ❏ 8030 [M] | Blues Ballads | 1960 | 7.50 | 15.00 | 30.00 |

—Red and purple label, "fan" logo in white

| ❏ 8030 [M] | Blues Ballads | 1963 | 5.00 | 10.00 | 20.00 |

—Red and purple label, "fan" logo in black

| ❏ 8036 [M] | Precious Memories | 1959 | 50.00 | 100.00 | 200.00 |

—Black label

| ❏ 8036 [M] | Precious Memories | 1960 | 37.50 | 75.00 | 150.00 |

—White "bullseye" label

| ❏ 8036 [M] | Precious Memories | 1960 | 7.50 | 15.00 | 30.00 |

—Red and purple label, "fan" logo in white

| ❏ 8036 [M] | Precious Memories | 1963 | 5.00 | 10.00 | 20.00 |

—Red and purple label, "fan" logo in black

| ❏ SD 8036 [S] | Precious Memories | 1959 | 75.00 | 150.00 | 300.00 |

—Green label

| ❏ SD 8036 [S] | Precious Memories | 1960 | 50.00 | 100.00 | 200.00 |

—White "bullseye" label

Number	Title (A Side/B Side)	Yr	VG	VG+	NM
❑ SD 8036 [S]	Precious Memories	1960	10.00	20.00	40.00
—Green and blue label, "fan" logo in white					
❑ SD 8036 [S]	Precious Memories	1963	6.25	12.50	25.00
—Green and blue label, "fan" logo in black					
❑ 8050 [M]	Saved	1961	25.00	50.00	100.00
—Red and purple label, "fan" logo in white					
❑ 8050 [M]	Saved	1963	5.00	10.00	20.00
—Red and purple label, "fan" logo in black					
❑ SD 8050 [S]	Saved	1961	37.50	75.00	150.00
—Green and blue label, "fan" logo in white					
❑ SD 8050 [S]	Saved	1963	6.25	12.50	25.00
—Green and blue label, "fan" logo in black					
❑ 8071 [M]	See See Rider	1962	25.00	50.00	100.00
—Red and purple label, "fan" logo in white					
❑ 8071 [M]	See See Rider	1963	5.00	10.00	20.00
—Red and purple label, "fan" logo in black					
❑ SD 8071 [S]	See See Rider	1962	37.50	75.00	150.00
—Green and blue label, "fan" logo in white					
❑ SD 8071 [S]	See See Rider	1963	6.25	12.50	25.00
—Green and blue label, "fan" logo in black					
❑ 8078 [M]	The Best of LaVern Baker	1963	37.50	75.00	150.00
—Red and purple label, "fan" logo in black					
❑ 90980	LaVern Baker Sings Bessie Smith	1989	3.00	6.00	12.00
—Reissue of SD 1281					
BRUNSWICK					
❑ BL 754160	Let Me Belong to You	1970	5.00	10.00	20.00

BAKER, MICKEY "GUITAR"
Also see MICKEY AND SYLVIA.
45s
ATLANTIC

Number	Title (A Side/B Side)	Yr	VG	VG+	NM
❑ 2042	Third Man Theme/Baia	1959	3.00	6.00	12.00
KING					
❑ 5951	Side Show/Steam Roller	1964	2.50	5.00	10.00
❑ 5979	Do What You Do/Night Blue	1965	2.50	5.00	10.00
MGM					
❑ 12418	Spinnin' Rock Boogie/Tricky	1957	5.00	10.00	20.00
RAINBOW					
❑ 288	Shake Walkin'/Greasy Spoon	1955	7.50	15.00	30.00
❑ 299	Bandstand Stomp/Rock with a Sock	1955	7.50	15.00	30.00
❑ 303	Old Devil Moon/Guitarambo	1955	7.50	15.00	30.00
SAVOY					
❑ 867	Guitar Mambo/Riverboat	1952	12.50	25.00	50.00
❑ 874	Love Me Baby/Oh Happy Day	1953	12.50	25.00	50.00

Albums
ATLANTIC

Number	Title (A Side/B Side)	Yr	VG	VG+	NM
❑ 8035 [M]	The Wildest Guitar	1959	37.50	75.00	150.00
—Black label					
❑ 8035 [M]	The Wildest Guitar	1960	12.50	25.00	50.00
—Red and purple label, "fan" logo in white					
❑ SD 8035 [S]	The Wildest Guitar	1959	62.50	125.00	250.00
—Green label					
❑ SD 8035 [S]	The Wildest Guitar	1960	20.00	40.00	80.00
—Green and blue label, "fan" logo in white					
KICKING MULE					
❑ 140	The Jazz Rock Guitar of Mickey Baker	1978	3.00	6.00	12.00
❑ 142	The Blues and Jazz Guitar of Mickey Baker	1978	3.00	6.00	12.00
KING					
❑ 839 [M]	But Wild	1963	100.00	200.00	400.00
—Black label, no crown					
❑ 839 [M]	But Wild	196?	20.00	40.00	80.00
—Blue label with crown					
❑ S-839 [R]	But Wild	196?	10.00	20.00	40.00

BAKER, YVONNE
Also see THE SENSATIONS.
45s
JAMIE

Number	Title (A Side/B Side)	Yr	VG	VG+	NM
❑ 1290	What a Difference Love Makes/Funny What Time Can Do	1965	3.00	6.00	12.00
MODERN					
❑ 1055	A Woman Needs a Man/My Baby Needs Me	196?	2.50	5.00	10.00
PARKWAY					
❑ 140	You Didn't Say a Word/To Prove My Love Is True	1967	25.00	50.00	100.00

BALLARD, FLORENCE
Former member of THE SUPREMES.
45s
ABC

Number	Title (A Side/B Side)	Yr	VG	VG+	NM
❑ 11074	Goin' Out of My Head/It Doesn't Matter How I Say It	1968	7.50	15.00	30.00
❑ 11144	Love Ain't Love/Forever Faithful	1968	7.50	15.00	30.00
❑ 11144 [PS]	Love Ain't Love/Forever Faithful	1968	20.00	40.00	80.00

BALLARD, HANK, AND THE MIDNIGHTERS
Includes records credited only to Hank Ballard. Also see THE MIDNIGHTERS; THE ROYALS (1).
45s
CHESS

Number	Title (A Side/B Side)	Yr	VG	VG+	NM
❑ 2111	Love, Why Is It Taking You So Long/I'm a Junkie for My Baby's Love	1971	—	3.00	6.00
KING					
❑ 5171	Teardrops on Your Letter/The Twist	1959	7.50	15.00	30.00
❑ 5195 [M]	Kansas City/I'll Keep You Happy	1959	6.25	12.50	25.00
❑ S-5195 [S]	Kansas City/I'll Keep You Happy	1959	12.50	25.00	50.00

Number	Title (A Side/B Side)	Yr	VG	VG+	NM
❑ 5215 [M]	Sugaree/Rain Down Tears	1959	6.25	12.50	25.00
❑ S-5215 [S]	Sugaree/Rain Down Tears	1959	12.50	25.00	50.00
❑ 5245	Cute Little Ways/A House with No Windows	1959	6.25	12.50	25.00
❑ 5275	I Could Love You/Never Knew	1959	6.25	12.50	25.00
❑ 5289	Look at Little Sister/I Said I Wouldn't Beg You	1959	6.25	12.50	25.00
❑ 5312	The Coffee Grind/Waiting	1960	6.25	12.50	25.00
❑ 5341	Finger Poppin' Time/I Love You, I Love You So-o-o	1960	6.25	12.50	25.00
❑ 5400	Let's Go, Let's Go, Let's Go/If You'd Forgive Me	1960	6.25	12.50	25.00
❑ 5430	The Hoochi Coochi Coo/I'm Thinking of You	1960	5.00	10.00	20.00
❑ 5459	Let's Go Again (Where We Went Last Night)/Deep Blue Sea	1961	5.00	10.00	20.00
❑ 5491	The Continental Walk/What Is This I See	1961	5.00	10.00	20.00
❑ 5491 [PS]	The Continental Walk/What Is This I See	1961	20.00	40.00	80.00
❑ 5510	The Switch-A-Roo/The Float	1961	3.75	7.50	15.00
❑ 5513	The Big Frog/Doin' Everything	1961	3.75	7.50	15.00
—B-side by Henry Moore					
❑ 5535	Nothing But Good/Keep On Dancing	1961	3.75	7.50	15.00
❑ 5550	Big Red Sunset/Can't You See — I Need a Friend	1961	3.75	7.50	15.00
❑ 5578	Do You Remember/I'm Gonna Miss You	1961	3.75	7.50	15.00
❑ 5593	Do You Know How to Twist/Broadway	1962	3.75	7.50	15.00
❑ 5601	It's Twistin' Time/Autumn Breeze	1962	3.75	7.50	15.00
❑ 5635	Good Twistin' Tonight/I'm Young	1962	3.75	7.50	15.00
❑ 5655	I Want to Thank You/Excuse Me	1962	3.75	7.50	15.00
❑ 5677	Dream World/When I Need You	1962	3.75	7.50	15.00
❑ 5693	Shaky Mae/I Love and Care for You	1962	3.75	7.50	15.00
❑ 5703	Bring Me Your Love/She's the One	1962	3.75	7.50	15.00
❑ 5713	All the Things in Life That Please You/The Rising Tide	1963	3.75	7.50	15.00
❑ 5719	The House on the Hill/That Low-Down Move	1963	3.75	7.50	15.00
❑ 5729	Christmas Time for Everyone But Me/Santa Claus Is Coming	1963	3.75	7.50	15.00
❑ 5746	How Could You Leave Your Man Alone/Walkin' and Talkin'	1963	3.75	7.50	15.00
❑ 5798	Those Lonely, Lonely Feelings/It's Love, Baby	1963	3.75	7.50	15.00
❑ 5821	Buttin' In/I'm Leavin'	1963	3.75	7.50	15.00
❑ 5835	Don't Let Temptation Turn You Around/Have Mercy, Have a Little Pity	1964	3.75	7.50	15.00
❑ 5860	Don't Fall in Love with Me/I'm So Mad with You	1964	3.75	7.50	15.00
❑ 5884	I Don't Know How to Do But One Thing/These Young Girls	1964	3.75	7.50	15.00
❑ 5901	Stay Away from My Baby/She's Got a Whole Lot of Soul	1964	3.75	7.50	15.00
❑ 5931	Daddy Rolling Stone/What's Your Name	1964	3.75	7.50	15.00
❑ 5954	Let's Get the Show on the Road/A Winner Never Quits	1964	3.75	7.50	15.00
❑ 5963	One Monkey Don't Stop No Show/What Can I Tell You	1964	3.75	7.50	15.00
❑ 5974	The Handwriting on the Wall/I Done It	1964	3.75	7.50	15.00
❑ 5996	Poppin' the Whip/You, Just You	1965	3.00	6.00	12.00
❑ 6001	I'm Just a Fool and Everybody Knows/Do It Zulu Style	1965	3.00	6.00	12.00
❑ 6018	Sloop and Slide/My Sun Is Going Down	1966	3.00	6.00	12.00
❑ 6031	I'm Ready/Togetherness	1966	3.00	6.00	12.00
❑ 6055	I Was Born to Move/He Came Alone	1966	3.00	6.00	12.00
❑ 6092	Here Comes the Hurt/Dance Till It Hurt Cha	1967	3.00	6.00	12.00
❑ 6119	You're in Real Good Hands/Unwind Yourself	1967	3.00	6.00	12.00
❑ 6131	Funky's Soul Train/Which Way Should I Turn	1967	3.00	6.00	12.00
❑ 6177	I'm Back to Stay/Come On Wit' It	1968	3.00	6.00	12.00
❑ 6196	How You Gonna Get Respect (When You Haven't Cut Your Process Yet)/Teardrops on Your Letter	1968	2.50	5.00	10.00
—As "Hank Ballard Along With The Dapps"					
❑ 6215	You're So Sexy/Thrill on the Hill	1969	2.50	5.00	10.00
—As "Hank Ballard Along With The Dapps"					
❑ 6228	Are You Lonely for Me Baby/With Our Sweet Lovin' Self	1969	2.50	5.00	10.00
❑ 6244	Butter Your Popcorn/Funky Soul Train	1969	3.75	7.50	15.00
❑ 6246	Come On with It/Blackenized	1969	3.75	7.50	15.00
❑ 6332	Work With Me Annie/Sexy Ways	1970	2.50	5.00	10.00
PEOPLE					
❑ 604	Teardrops on Your Letter/Annie Had a Baby	1972	—	2.50	5.00
❑ 606	With Your Sweet Lovin' Self/Finger Poppin' Time	1972	—	2.50	5.00
POLYDOR					
❑ 14128	Finger Poppin' Time/From the Love Side	1972	—	2.50	5.00
❑ 14166	Going to Get a Thrill/(B-side unknown)	1973	—	—	—
—Canceled?					
SILVER FOX					
❑ 23	Sunday Morning Coming Down/Love Made a Fool of Me	1970	—	3.00	6.00
STANG					
❑ 5053	Let's Go Streaking/Let's Go Streaking (Part 2)	1974	—	2.50	5.00
❑ 5058	Hey There Sexy Lady/(Instrumental)	1975	—	2.50	5.00
❑ 5061	Let's Go Skinny Dipping/Love On Love	1975	—	2.50	5.00

7-Inch Extended Plays
KING

Number	Title (A Side/B Side)	Yr	VG	VG+	NM
❑ 435	Teardrops on Your Letter/The Twist//Cute Little Ways/House with No Windows	1959	30.00	60.00	120.00
❑ 435 [PS]	Singin' and Swingin', Vol. 1	1959	30.00	60.00	120.00
❑ 436	(contents unknown)	1959	30.00	60.00	120.00
❑ 436 [PS]	Singin' and Swingin', Vol. 2	1959	30.00	60.00	120.00

Albums
KING

Number	Title (A Side/B Side)	Yr	VG	VG+	NM
❑ 618 [M]	Singin' and Swingin'	1959	62.50	125.00	250.00
❑ 674 [M]	The One and Only Hank Ballard	1959	62.50	125.00	250.00
—Brown cover					

Before they had their biggest hits, Lee Andrews and the Hearts made some hard-to-find singles for Philadelphia-based labels, including this one for Gotham.

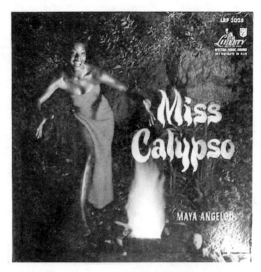

Best known as a poet, long before that Maya Angelou tried a singing career. This intriguing album, issued in 1957, was the result.

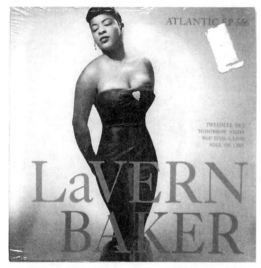

LaVern Baker had 11 top 10 hits on the R&B charts. Her first two, "Tweedlee Dee" and "Bop-Ting-a-Ling," were compiled onto this rare Atlantic EP.

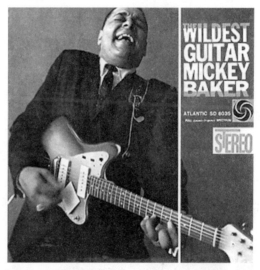

Mickey "Guitar" Baker, best known as half of the hit duo Mickey and Sylvia, was popular enough as a session musician that he gained his nickname. This is his solo album from 1959.

This EP contains selections from the Hank Ballard LP, *Singin' and Swingin'*. Among the songs on this record are his first two hits with his name prominent on the record, "The Twist" and "Teardrops on Your Letter."

Hank Ballard and the Midnighters were popular enough in the early 1960s that King began to compile LPs quickly. *Let's Go Again* was Ballard's fifth King LP, in 1961.

Number	Title (A Side/B Side)	Yr	VG	VG+	NM
❑ 674 [M]	The One and Only Hank Ballard	1960	37.50	75.00	150.00
—Green cover					
❑ 700 [M]	Mr. Rhythm and Blues	1960	37.50	75.00	150.00
❑ 740 [M]	Spotlight on Hank Ballard	1961	37.50	75.00	150.00
❑ KS-740 [S]	Spotlight on Hank Ballard	1961	75.00	150.00	300.00
❑ 748 [M]	Let's Go Again	1961	30.00	60.00	120.00
❑ 759 [M]	Dance Along	1961	30.00	60.00	120.00
❑ 781 [M]	The Twistin' Fools	1962	25.00	50.00	100.00
❑ 793 [M]	Jumpin' Hank Ballard	1962	25.00	50.00	100.00
❑ 815 [M]	The 1963 Sound of Hank Ballard	1963	25.00	50.00	100.00
❑ 867 [M]	Biggest Hits	1963	25.00	50.00	100.00
❑ 896 [M]	A Star in Your Eyes	1964	25.00	50.00	100.00
❑ 913 [M]	Those Lazy, Lazy Days	1965	17.50	35.00	70.00
❑ 927 [M]	Glad Songs, Sad Songs	1965	17.50	35.00	70.00
❑ 950 [M]	24 Hit Tunes	1966	15.00	30.00	60.00
❑ 981 [M]	24 Great Songs	1968	10.00	20.00	40.00
❑ KSD-1052	You Can't Keep a Good Man Down	1969	12.50	25.00	50.00

BALTINEERS, THE
45s
TEENAGE

Number	Title (A Side/B Side)	Yr	VG	VG+	NM
❑ 1000	Moments Like This/New Love	1956	75.00	150.00	300.00
❑ 1002	Tears in My Eyes/Joe's Calypso	1956	75.00	150.00	300.00

BAMBAATAA, AFRIKA, AND THE SOUL SONIC FORCE
12-Inch Singles
CAPITOL

Number	Title (A Side/B Side)	Yr	VG	VG+	NM
❑ V-15379	Reckless (2 versions)/Mind, Body & Soul (3 versions)	1988	2.00	4.00	8.00
—With UB40					
❑ V-15385	Shout It Out (C&C Club Vocal) (Jazzy Dub) (Done Properly Dub)/Tell Me When You Need It Again	1988	—	3.00	6.00
EMI					
❑ V-56225	Just Get Up and Dance (12" Club Mix) (Doom Doom Mix) (Detroit Remix) (Stomp Remix) (Trumpet Mix) (A Cappella Mix)	1991	2.00	4.00	8.00
❑ V-56241	Power Boy Power (Techno Paradise) (Ecstasy Mix) (Club Heaven) (Soca Fever)	1991	2.50	5.00	10.00
HOT					
❑ 2293	Planet Rock (6 versions)	1996	2.00	4.00	8.00
TOMMY BOY					
❑ TB 330	Looking For the Perfect Beat (Brutal Bill Extended Version) (Original Version) (Brutal Hard Tribal Dub) (Brutal Perfect Dub)	1998	2.50	5.00	10.00
❑ TB 821	Jazzy Sensation (3 versions)	1983	15.00	30.00	60.00
❑ TB 823	Planet Rock (Vocal) (Bonus Beats I) (Instrumental)	1983	12.50	25.00	50.00
—Original with orange labels					
❑ TB 831	Looking for the Perfect Beat (Vocal) (Bonus Beats II) (Instrumental)	1982	10.00	20.00	40.00
❑ TB 839	Renegades of Funk/(Renegade Chant) (Instrumental)	1984	7.50	15.00	30.00
❑ TB 847	Unity (Part 1, The Third Coming) (Part2, Because It's Coming) (Part 3, Nuclear Wild Style) (Part 4, Can You See It) (Part 5, The Light) (Part 6, World III)	1984	7.50	15.00	30.00
—With James Brown					
❑ TB 870	Funk You! (Radio Mix) (Club Mix) (All the Way Live) (Dub Instrumental)	1985	10.00	20.00	40.00
❑ TB 879	Bambaataa's Theme (Assault on Precinct 13)/Tension	1986	10.00	20.00	40.00
WINLEY					
❑ (# unknown)	Zulu Nation Breakdown (2 versions)	1980	50.00	100.00	200.00
YORK					
❑ 786	The Return to Planet Rock (3 versions)/Inside Looking Out (3 versions)	1989	2.00	4.00	8.00
—Green vinyl					

45s
CAPITOL

Number	Title (A Side/B Side)	Yr	VG	VG+	NM
❑ B-44163 [DJ]	Reckless (same on both sides)	1988	—	2.00	4.00
—With UB40					
❑ B-44163 [PS]	Reckless	1988	—	2.00	4.00
—With UB40					
TOMMY BOY					
❑ 823	Planet Rock/(Instrumental)	1982	3.00	6.00	12.00
—Original has orange labels					
❑ 823	Planet Rock/(Instrumental)	1982	—	3.00	6.00
—Second edition has light blue labels					
❑ 831	Looking for the Perfect Beat/(Instrumental)	1982	—	3.00	6.00
❑ 839	Renegades of Funk/(Instrumental)	1984	—	3.00	6.00
❑ 847	Unity (Part 1)/Unity (Part 2)	1984	—	3.00	6.00
—With James Brown					

Albums
CAPITOL

Number	Title (A Side/B Side)	Yr	VG	VG+	NM
❑ C1-90157	The Light	1988	3.00	6.00	12.00
TOMMY BOY					
❑ TBLP-1007	Planet Rock — The Album	1986	3.75	7.50	15.00
❑ TBLP-1008	Beware (The Funk Is Everywhere)	1986	3.75	7.50	15.00
❑ TBEP-1052 [EP]	Don't Stop...Planet Rock (The Remix EP)	1992	2.50	5.00	10.00
❑ TBLP-1457 [(2)]	Looking for the Perfect Beat 1980-1985	2001	3.75	7.50	15.00

BAND OF GOLD
12-Inch Singles
RCA

Number	Title (A Side/B Side)	Yr	VG	VG+	NM
❑ PW-13867	Medley: Love Songs Are Back Again (Vocal) (Instrumental) (Accapella)	1984	2.50	5.00	10.00
❑ PW-14018	In Love Again (Medley) (Vocal Theme) (Instrumental)	1985	2.50	5.00	10.00
❑ PW-14130	Medley: This Is Our Time/Never Let You Go	1985	2.50	5.00	10.00

45s
RCA

Number	Title (A Side/B Side)	Yr	VG	VG+	NM
❑ PB-13866	Medley: Love Songs Are Back Again (Edited)/Medley: Love Songs Are Back Again	1984	—	2.00	4.00
❑ PB-13933	Love Songs Are Back Again (Edited)/(Instrumental)	1984	—	2.00	4.00
—This is the actual song without the interwoven medley					
❑ PB-14019	In Love Again (Medley)/(Vocal Theme)	1985	—	2.00	4.00
❑ PB-14129	Medley: This Is Our Time/Never Let You Go	1985	—	2.00	4.00

Albums
RCA VICTOR

Number	Title (A Side/B Side)	Yr	VG	VG+	NM
❑ AFL1-5360	Love Songs Are Back Again	1984	2.50	5.00	10.00

BANDWAGON, THE
Also includes records credited to "Johnny Johnson and the Bandwagon."
45s
BELL

Number	Title (A Side/B Side)	Yr	VG	VG+	NM
❑ 902	Sweet Inspiration/Pride Comes Before Fall	1970	—	3.00	6.00
❑ 953	(Blame It) On the Pony Express/Never Let Her Go	1971	—	3.00	6.00
EPIC					
❑ 10255	Baby Make Your Own Sweet Music/On the Day We Fell in Love	1967	2.00	4.00	8.00
❑ 10352	Breakin' Down the Walls of Heartache/Dancin' Master	1968	2.00	4.00	8.00
❑ 10412	I Ain't Lying/You	1968	2.00	4.00	8.00
—Artist credit: "Johnny Johnson and the Bandwagon"					
❑ 10442	Don't Let It In/When Love Has Gone Away	1969	2.00	4.00	8.00
❑ 10473	You Blew Your Cool (And Lost Your Fool)/Let's Hang On	1969	2.00	4.00	8.00
—Artist credit: "Johnny Johnson and the Bandwagon"					

Albums
EPIC

Number	Title (A Side/B Side)	Yr	VG	VG+	NM
❑ BN 26426	Johnny Johnson and the Bandwagon	1969	5.00	10.00	20.00

BANKS, BESSIE
45s
BLUE CAT

Number	Title (A Side/B Side)	Yr	VG	VG+	NM
❑ 106	Go Now/It Sounds Like My Baby	1965	2.50	5.00	10.00
SPOKANE					
❑ 4009	Do It Now/(You Should Have Been a) Doctor	1963	3.75	7.50	15.00
TIGER					
❑ 102	Go Now/It Sounds Like My Baby	1964	5.00	10.00	20.00
VERVE					
❑ 10519	I Can't Make It (Without You Baby)/Need You	1967	2.00	4.00	8.00
VOLT					
❑ 4112	Ain't No Easy Way/Try to Leave Me If You Can	1974	—	3.00	6.00
WAND					
❑ 163	Do It Now/(You Should Have Been a) Doctor	1964	3.00	6.00	12.00

BANKS, DARRELL
45s
ATCO

Number	Title (A Side/B Side)	Yr	VG	VG+	NM
❑ 6471	Here Come the Tears/I've Got That Feeling	1967	6.25	12.50	25.00
❑ 6484	Angel Baby Don't You Leave Me/Look Into the Eyes of a Fool	1967	6.25	12.50	25.00
COTILLION					
❑ 44006	I Wanna Go Home/Love of My Woman	1968	2.50	5.00	10.00
REVILOT					
❑ 201	Open the Door to Your Heart/Our Love Is In the Pocket	1966	3.75	7.50	15.00
❑ 203	Somebody (Somewhere) Needs You/Baby Whatcha Got (For Me)	1966	3.75	7.50	15.00
VOLT					
❑ 4014	Just Because Your Love Has Gone/I'm the One Who Loves You	1969	2.50	5.00	10.00
❑ 4026	Beautiful Feeling/No One Blinder	1969	2.50	5.00	10.00

Albums
ATCO

Number	Title (A Side/B Side)	Yr	VG	VG+	NM
❑ 33-216 [M]	Darrell Banks Is Here	1967	6.25	12.50	25.00
❑ SD 33-216 [S]	Darrell Banks Is Here	1967	7.50	15.00	30.00
VOLT					
❑ VOS-6002	Here to Stay	1969	6.25	12.50	25.00

BANKS, PATRYCE "CHOC'LET"
45s
T-ELECTRIC

Number	Title (A Side/B Side)	Yr	VG	VG+	NM
❑ 41308	I Waited for Love/Sunshine Love	1980	—	2.50	5.00

Albums
T-ELECTRIC

Number	Title (A Side/B Side)	Yr	VG	VG+	NM
❑ 3243	She's Back and Ready...	1980	3.75	7.50	15.00

BAR-KAYS, THE

12-Inch Singles

BASIX

Number	Title (A Side/B Side)	Yr	VG	VG+	NM
❑ 1309	Old School Mega Mix/Out of My Mind	1994	2.00	4.00	8.00

MERCURY

Number	Title (A Side/B Side)	Yr	VG	VG+	NM
❑ PRO 296-1 [DJ]	Dirty Dancer (same on both sides)	1984	—	3.00	6.00
❑ MDS-4024	Do It (Let Me See You Shake) (Original Mix) (Instrumental)	1982	2.00	4.00	8.00
❑ 818631-1	Freakshow on the Dance Floor/Lovers Should Never Fall in Love	1984	2.00	4.00	8.00
❑ 870018-1	Don't Hang Up (4 versions)	1987	2.00	4.00	8.00
❑ 872103-1	Struck by You (Extended 12-Inch Mix) (Dub Mix) (Acapella) (7-Inch Mix)/Your Place or Mine	1989	—	3.50	7.00
❑ 872955-1	Animal (4 versions)/Time Out	1989	—	3.50	7.00
❑ 880255-1	Sexomatic (3 versions)	1984	2.00	4.00	8.00
❑ 880966-1	Your Place or Mine (Club Version) (Dub Version)	1985	2.00	4.00	8.00
❑ 884232-1	Banging the Walls (2 versions)/Gina	1985	2.00	4.00	8.00
❑ 888837-1	Certified True (3 versions)/It Be That Way Sometimes	1987	—	3.50	7.00

45s

HIGH STACKS

Number	Title (A Side/B Side)	Yr	VG	VG+	NM
❑ 9801	Body Fine/Hey Rufus!	1999	—	—	3.00

—B-side by Rufus Thomas; artist listed as "The Barkays"

MERCURY

Number	Title (A Side/B Side)	Yr	VG	VG+	NM
❑ 73833	Shake Your Rump to the Funk/Summer of Our Love	1976	—	2.00	4.00
❑ 73888	Too Hot to Stop (Pt. 1)/Bang Bang (Stick 'Em Up)	1977	—	2.00	4.00
❑ 73915	Spellbound/You're So Sexy	1977	—	2.00	4.00
❑ 73971	Let's Have Some Fun/Cozy	1977	—	2.00	4.00
❑ 73994	Attitudes/Can't Keep My Hands Off You	1978	—	2.00	4.00
❑ 74039	I'll Dance/Angel Eyes	1978	—	2.00	4.00
❑ 74048	Shine/Are You Being Real	1979	—	2.00	4.00
❑ 76015	Move Your Boogie Body/Love's What It's All About	1979	—	2.00	4.00
❑ 76036	Today is the Day/Loving You Is My Occupation	1980	—	2.00	4.00
❑ 76088	Boogie Body Land/Running In and Out of My Life	1980	—	2.00	4.00
❑ 76097	Body Fever/Deliver Us	1981	—	2.00	4.00
❑ 76123	Hit and Run/Say It Through Love	1981	—	2.00	4.00
❑ 76143	Freaky Behavior/Backseat Driver	1982	—	2.00	4.00
❑ 76187	Do It (Let Me See You Shake)/Feels Like I'm Falling in Love	1982	—	2.00	4.00
❑ 810435-7	She Talks to Me with Her Body/Anticipation	1983	—	2.00	4.00
❑ 818631-7	Freakshow on the Dance Floor/Lovers Should Never Fall in Love	1984	—	2.00	4.00
❑ 870018-7	Don't Hang Up/Contagious	1988	—	—	3.00
❑ 870018-7 [PS]	Don't Hang Up/Contagious	1988	—	—	3.00
❑ 870214-7	Many Mistakes/Contagious	1988	—	—	3.00
❑ 872102-7	Struck by You/Your Place or Mine	1989	—	—	3.00
❑ 872102-7 [PS]	Struck by You/Your Place or Mine	1989	—	—	3.00
❑ 872954-7	Animal/Time Out	1989	—	—	3.00
❑ 872954-7 [PS]	Animal/Time Out	1989	—	—	3.00
❑ 880045-7	Dirty Dancer/(Instrumental)	1984	—	—	3.00
❑ 880255-7	Sexomatic/Sexomatic (Bonus Beats)	1984	—	—	3.00
❑ 880966-7	Your Place or Mine/(Instrumental)	1985	—	—	3.00
❑ 884232-7	Banging the Walls/Gina	1985	—	—	3.00
❑ 888837-7	Certified True/It Be That Way Sometimes	1987	—	—	3.00

STAX

Number	Title (A Side/B Side)	Yr	VG	VG+	NM
❑ 3216	Holy Ghost/Monster	1978	—	2.50	5.00

VOLT

Number	Title (A Side/B Side)	Yr	VG	VG+	NM
❑ 148	Soul Finger/Knucklehead	1967	2.00	4.00	8.00
❑ 154	Give Everybody Some/Don't Do That	1967	—	3.00	6.00
❑ 158	A Hard Day's Night/I Want Someone	1968	—	3.00	6.00
❑ 4007	Copy Cat/In the Middle	1968	—	3.00	6.00
❑ 4011	Don't Stop Dancing/Don't Stop Dancing (Part 2)	1969	—	3.00	6.00
❑ 4019	Midnight Cowboy/A.J. The Housefly	1969	—	3.00	6.00
❑ 4033	Song and Dance/I Thank You	1970	—	3.00	6.00
❑ 4050	Montego Bay/Humpin'	1971	—	2.50	5.00
❑ 4073	Son of Shaft/Song and Dance	1972	—	2.50	5.00
❑ 4081	Dance, Dance, Dance/Memphis at Sunrise	1972	—	2.50	5.00
❑ 4092	You're the Best Thing That Ever Happened to Me/You're Still My Brother	1973	—	2.50	5.00
❑ 4097	God Is Watching/It Ain't Easy	1973	—	2.50	5.00

Albums

ATCO

Number	Title (A Side/B Side)	Yr	VG	VG+	NM
❑ SD 33-289	Soul Finger	1968	6.25	12.50	25.00

MERCURY

Number	Title (A Side/B Side)	Yr	VG	VG+	NM
❑ SRM-1-1099	Too Hot to Stop	1976	2.50	5.00	10.00
❑ SRM-1-1181	Flying High on Your Love	1977	2.50	5.00	10.00
❑ SRM-1-3732	Light of Life	1978	2.50	5.00	10.00
❑ SRM-1-3781	Injoy	1979	2.50	5.00	10.00
❑ SRM-1-3844	As One	1980	2.50	5.00	10.00
❑ SRM-1-4028	Nightcruising	1981	2.50	5.00	10.00
❑ SRM-1-4065	Propositions	1982	2.50	5.00	10.00
❑ 818478-1	Dangerous	1984	2.50	5.00	10.00
❑ 824727-1	Banging the Wall	1985	2.50	5.00	10.00
❑ 830305-1	Contagious	1987	2.50	5.00	10.00
❑ 836774-1	Animal	1989	2.50	5.00	10.00

STAX

Number	Title (A Side/B Side)	Yr	VG	VG+	NM
❑ 4106	Money Talks	1978	2.50	5.00	10.00
❑ 4130	Gotta Groove	1979	2.50	5.00	10.00
❑ MPS-8510	Cold Blooded	1981	2.50	5.00	10.00
❑ MPS-8542	The Best of the Bar-Kays	1988	2.50	5.00	10.00

VOLT

Number	Title (A Side/B Side)	Yr	VG	VG+	NM
❑ 417 [M]	Soul Finger	1967	10.00	20.00	40.00
❑ S-417 [S]	Soul Finger	1967	10.00	20.00	40.00
❑ 6004	Gotta Groove	1969	7.50	15.00	30.00
❑ 6011	Black Rock	1971	6.25	12.50	25.00
❑ VOS-8001	Do You See What I See	1972	6.25	12.50	25.00
❑ 9504	Cold Blooded	1974	6.25	12.50	25.00

BARBARA AND THE BROWNS

45s

STAX

Number	Title (A Side/B Side)	Yr	VG	VG+	NM
❑ 150	Big Party/You Belong to Her	1964	5.00	10.00	20.00
❑ 158	Please Be Honest with Me/In My Heart	1964	3.75	7.50	15.00
❑ 164	I Don't Want Trouble/My Lover	1965	3.75	7.50	15.00

BARGE, GENE

45s

CHECKER

Number	Title (A Side/B Side)	Yr	VG	VG+	NM
❑ 839	Way Down Home/Country	1954	7.50	15.00	30.00
❑ 1110	Fine Twine/The "In" Crowd	1965	2.50	5.00	10.00

LEGRAND

Number	Title (A Side/B Side)	Yr	VG	VG+	NM
❑ 1006	Thinking of You/Autumn Leaves	1961	10.00	20.00	40.00

PARAMOUNT

Number	Title (A Side/B Side)	Yr	VG	VG+	NM
❑ 0160	Love Theme from "The Godfather"/Gina	1972	—	2.50	5.00

Albums

CHECKER

Number	Title (A Side/B Side)	Yr	VG	VG+	NM
❑ LP-2994 [M]	Dance with Daddy G	1965	12.50	25.00	50.00

BARNES, J.J.

45s

BUDDAH

Number	Title (A Side/B Side)	Yr	VG	VG+	NM
❑ 120	Evidence/I'll Keep Coming Back	1969	3.75	7.50	15.00

CONTEMPO

Number	Title (A Side/B Side)	Yr	VG	VG+	NM
❑ 7003	How Long/The Erroll Flynn	1977	—	2.50	5.00

GROOVESVILLE

Number	Title (A Side/B Side)	Yr	VG	VG+	NM
❑ 1006	Baby Please Come Back Home/Chains of Love	1967	3.75	7.50	15.00
❑ 1008	Now That I Got You Back/Forgive Me	1967	3.75	7.50	15.00
❑ 1009	Easy Living/(B-side unknown)	1967	4.00	8.00	16.00

INVASION

Number	Title (A Side/B Side)	Yr	VG	VG+	NM
❑ 1001	My Baby/(You Still) My Baby	1970	2.50	5.00	10.00

KABLE

Number	Title (A Side/B Side)	Yr	VG	VG+	NM
❑ 437	Won't You Let Me Know/My Love Came Tumbling Down	1960	12.50	25.00	50.00

MAGIC TOUCH

Number	Title (A Side/B Side)	Yr	VG	VG+	NM
❑ 1000	To An Early Grave/Cloudy Days	1970	2.50	5.00	10.00

MICKAY'S

Number	Title (A Side/B Side)	Yr	VG	VG+	NM
❑ 3004	Just One More Time/Hey Child, I Love You	1963	20.00	40.00	80.00
❑ 4472	Get a Hold of Yourself/Lonely No More	1964	20.00	40.00	80.00

PERCEPTION

Number	Title (A Side/B Side)	Yr	VG	VG+	NM
❑ 546	Just a Living Doll/Touching You	1974	—	3.00	6.00

REVILOT

Number	Title (A Side/B Side)	Yr	VG	VG+	NM
❑ 216	Hold On to It/Now She's Gone	1968	3.75	7.50	15.00
❑ 218	I'll Keep Coming Back/Sad Day a-Comin'	1968	3.75	7.50	15.00
❑ 222	Our Love Is in the Pocket/All Your Goodies Are Gone	1968	20.00	40.00	80.00
❑ 225	So-Called Friends/Now She's Gone	1968	3.75	7.50	15.00

RIC-TIC

Number	Title (A Side/B Side)	Yr	VG	VG+	NM
❑ 106	Please Let Me In/I Think I Found a Love	1965	3.75	7.50	15.00
❑ 110	Real Humdinger/I Ain't Gonna Do It	1966	3.75	7.50	15.00
❑ 115	Day Tripper/Don't Bring Me Bad News	1966	3.75	7.50	15.00
❑ 117	Deeper in Love/Say It	1966	3.75	7.50	15.00

RICH

Number	Title (A Side/B Side)	Yr	VG	VG+	NM
❑ 1005	Won't You Let Me Know/My Love Came Tumbling Down	1960	25.00	50.00	100.00
❑ 1737	Won't You Let Me Know/My Love Came Tumbling Down	1962	6.25	12.50	25.00

RING

Number	Title (A Side/B Side)	Yr	VG	VG+	NM
❑ 101	She Ain't Ready/Poor-Unfortunate Me	1964	6.25	12.50	25.00

SCEPTER

Number	Title (A Side/B Side)	Yr	VG	VG+	NM
❑ 1266	Just One More Time/Hey Child, I Love You	1964	7.50	15.00	30.00

VOLT

Number	Title (A Side/B Side)	Yr	VG	VG+	NM
❑ 4027	Got to Get Rid of You/Snowflakes	1969	3.75	7.50	15.00

Albums

VOLT

Number	Title (A Side/B Side)	Yr	VG	VG+	NM
❑ VOS-6001	Rare Stamps	1969	7.50	15.00	30.00

—With Steve Mancha

BARRY, CLAUDJA

12-Inch Singles

CHRYSALIS

Number	Title (A Side/B Side)	Yr	VG	VG+	NM
❑ CDS 2316	Boogie Woogie Dancin' Shoes/(B-side unknown)	1979	3.75	7.50	15.00
❑ CDS 2389	You Make Me Feel the Fire/Everybody Needs Love	1980	2.50	5.00	10.00

EPIC

Number	Title (A Side/B Side)	Yr	VG	VG+	NM
❑ EAS 2508 [DJ]	Down and Counting (2 versions)/On the Edge (Dub)	1986	2.50	5.00	10.00
❑ EAS 02885 [DJ]	Hot to the Touch (Houseboy Mix) (Houseboy Dub) (Towering Inferno Dub) (Mellow Mix)	1987	2.50	5.00	10.00
❑ 49-05926	Down and Counting (Extended Version)/(Emulator Dub)	1986	—	3.50	7.00
❑ 49-06718	Can't You Feel My Heart Beat (3 versions)	1987	—	3.50	7.00
❑ 49-06837	Secret Affair (4 versions)	1987	—	3.50	7.00
❑ 49-07496	Hot to the Touch (5 versions)	1987	—	3.50	7.00

MIRAGE

Number	Title (A Side/B Side)	Yr	VG	VG+	NM
❑ 336 [DJ]	If I Do It to You (Long)/(Short)	1982	2.00	4.00	8.00

BARRY, LEN

Number	Title (A Side/B Side)	Yr	VG	VG+	NM
PERSONAL					
❏ 49808	Tripping on the Moon (4 versions)	1984	2.00	4.00	8.00
❏ 49815	Born to Love/Your Sweet Touch	1984	2.00	4.00	8.00
❏ PRO 59801 [DJ]	For Your Love/Beat My Drum	198?	2.00	4.00	8.00
RADIKAL					
❏ 12325	Summer of Love (4 versions)	1992	—	3.00	6.00
RCA					
❏ 2850-1-RD	Love Is an Island (Tropical Heat Mix) (Island Instrumental) + 3 more	1991	2.00	4.00	8.00
❏ 62022	Love Is an Island (6 versions)	1991	2.00	4.00	8.00
SALSOUL					
❏ 12D 2032	Sweet Dynamite//(B-side unknown)	1977	2.50	5.00	10.00
❏ 12D 2050	Dancin' Fever/Johnny, Johnny, Please Come Home	1977	3.00	6.00	12.00
❏ 2062	It Takes Two/Dance, Dance, Dance	1978	3.75	7.50	15.00
—With Ronnie Jones					
45s					
CHRYSALIS					
❏ 2313	Boogie Woogie Dancin' Shoes/Love of the Hurtin' Kind	1979	—	2.50	5.00
❏ 2391	You Make Me Feel the Fire/(B-side unknown)	1980	—	2.50	5.00
EPIC					
❏ 34-06308	Down and Counting//(Dub)	1986	—	2.00	4.00
❏ 34-06669	Can You Feel My Heartbeat//(Percapella)	1987	—	2.00	4.00
❏ 34-07198	Secret Affair/Dance for Your Life	1987	—	2.00	4.00
MIRAGE					
❏ 4050	If I Do It to You/Up All Night	1982	—	2.50	5.00
SALSOUL					
❏ 2023	Sweet Dynamite/Taste of Love	1977	—	3.00	6.00
❏ 2046	Dance, Dance, Dance/Why Must a Girl Like Me	1977	—	3.00	6.00
❏ 2058	Dancin' Fever/Long Lost Friend	1978	—	3.00	6.00
❏ 2065	Take It Easy/Johnny, Johnny, Please Come Home	1978	—	3.00	6.00
Albums					
CHRYSALIS					
❏ CHR 1232	Boogie Woogie Dancin' Shoes	1979	3.00	6.00	12.00
❏ CHR 1251	Feel the Fire	1980	3.00	6.00	12.00
EPIC					
❏ FE 40622	I, Claudja	1987	2.50	5.00	10.00
PERSONAL					
❏ 59801 [EP]	No La De Da Part 2	1983	3.00	6.00	12.00
SALSOUL					
❏ SA 5512	Sweet Dynamite	1977	3.00	6.00	12.00
❏ SA 5525	Claudja	1977	3.00	6.00	12.00

BARRY, LEN

Former member of THE DOVELLS.

Number	Title (A Side/B Side)	Yr	VG	VG+	NM
45s					
AMY					
❏ 11026	4-5-6 (Now I'm Alone)/Funky Night	1968	—	3.00	6.00
❏ 11037	You're My Picasso, Baby/Christopher Columbus	1968	—	3.00	6.00
❏ 11047	The Child Is Born/Wouldn't It Be Beautiful	1968	—	3.00	6.00
BUDDAH					
❏ 284	Just the Two of Us/Diggin' Life	1972	—	2.50	5.00
❏ 284 [PS]	Just the Two of Us/Diggin' Life	1972	—	3.00	6.00
CAMEO					
❏ 303	Jim Dandy/Don't Come Back	1964	3.00	6.00	12.00
❏ 318	Little White House/Hearts Are Trump	1964	3.00	6.00	12.00
DECCA					
❏ 31788	Lip Sync (To the Tongue Twisters)/At the Hop '65	1965	2.50	5.00	10.00
❏ 31827	1-2-3/Bullseye	1965	3.75	7.50	15.00
❏ 31889	Like a Baby/Happiness (Is a Girl Like You)	1966	2.50	5.00	10.00
❏ 31923	Somewhere/It's a Crying Shame	1966	2.50	5.00	10.00
❏ 31969	It's That Time of the Year/Happily Ever After	1966	2.50	5.00	10.00
❏ 32011	I Struck It Rich/Love Is	1966	2.50	5.00	10.00
❏ 32054	Would I Love You/You Baby	1966	2.50	5.00	10.00
MERCURY					
❏ 72299	Let's Do It Again/Happy Days	1964	3.00	6.00	12.00
PARAMOUNT					
❏ 0206	Heaven Plus Earth/I'm Marching to the Music	1973	—	2.50	5.00
PARKWAY					
❏ 969	Little White House/Hearts Are Trump	1966	2.00	4.00	8.00
RCA VICTOR					
❏ 47-9150	Our Song/The Moving Finger Writes	1967	2.00	4.00	8.00
❏ 47-9275	All Those Memories/Rainy Side of the Street	1967	2.00	4.00	8.00
❏ 47-9348	The ABC's of Love/Come Rain or Shine	1967	2.00	4.00	8.00
❏ 47-9464	Sweet and Funny/I Like the Way	1968	2.00	4.00	8.00
SCEPTER					
❏ 12251	Put Out the Fire/Spread It On Like Butter	1969	2.00	4.00	8.00
❏ 12263	Keem-O-Sabe/This Old World	1969	2.00	4.00	8.00
❏ 12284	Bob & Carol & Ted & Alice/In My Present State of Mind	1970	—	3.00	6.00
Albums					
BUDDAH					
❏ BDS-5105	Ups & Downs	1972	3.75	7.50	15.00
DECCA					
❏ DL 4720 [M]	1-2-3	1965	7.50	15.00	30.00
❏ DL 74720 [P]	1-2-3	1965	10.00	20.00	40.00
—"Lip Sync" is rechanneled					
RCA VICTOR					
❏ LPM-3823 [M]	My Kind of Soul	1967	6.25	12.50	25.00
❏ LSP-3823 [S]	My Kind of Soul	1967	5.00	10.00	20.00

BARTHOLOMEW, DAVE

Number	Title (A Side/B Side)	Yr	VG	VG+	NM
45s					
DECCA					
❏ 48216	Tra La La/Teejim	1951	30.00	60.00	120.00
IMPERIAL					
❏ 5210	Who Drank the Beer While I Was in the Rear/The Rest of My Life	1952	30.00	60.00	120.00
—Dave Bartholomew records on Imperial before 5210 are unconfirmed on 45 rpm					
❏ 5249	No More Black Nights/Air Tight	1953	30.00	60.00	120.00
❏ 5273	Texas Hop/When the Saints Go Marchin' In Boogie	1954	37.50	75.00	150.00
❏ 5308	Cat Music/Jump Children	1954	30.00	60.00	120.00
❏ 5322	Another Mule/I Want to Be with Her	1955	12.50	25.00	50.00
❏ 5350	Every Night, Every Day/Four Winds	1955	12.50	25.00	50.00
❏ 5373	Shrimp and Gumbo/An Old Cowhand from a Blues Band	1956	10.00	20.00	40.00
❏ 5390	Would You/Turn Your Lamp Down Low	1956	10.00	20.00	40.00
❏ 5408	Lovin' You/Three Time Loser	1956	7.50	15.00	30.00
❏ 5438	The Monkey/The Shuffling	1957	6.25	12.50	25.00
❏ 5460	How Could You/Barrel House	1957	6.25	12.50	25.00
❏ 5481	Hard Times (The Slop)/Cinderella	1957	6.25	12.50	25.00
❏ 5560	Button Blues/Short Subjects	1959	5.00	10.00	20.00
❏ 5702	I Cried/Somebody New	1960	5.00	10.00	20.00
❏ 5714	People Are Talking/Yeah, Yeah	1961	5.00	10.00	20.00
❏ 5803	I'm Walkin'/Going to the River	1962	3.75	7.50	15.00
❏ 5835	A Sunday Kind of Love/Honky Tonk Trumpet	1962	3.75	7.50	15.00
KING					
❏ 4482	Sweet Home Blues/Twins	1951	37.50	75.00	150.00
❏ 4508	In the Alley/I'll Never Be the Same	1952	50.00	100.00	200.00
❏ 4523	Lawdy, Lawdy, Lawd (Part 1)/Lawdy, Lawdy, Lawd (Part 2)	1952	37.50	75.00	150.00
❏ 4544	My Ding-a-Ling/Bad Habit	1952	62.50	125.00	250.00
❏ 4559	The Golden Rule/Mother Knows Best	1952	25.00	50.00	100.00
❏ 4585	High Flying Woman/Stormy Weather	1953	25.00	50.00	100.00
78s					
IMPERIAL					
❏ 5064	Carnival Day/That's How You Got Killed Before	1950	7.50	15.00	30.00
❏ 5069	Country Boy Goes Home/Ain't Gonna Do It	1950	7.50	15.00	30.00
❏ 5089	Messy Bessie/Frantic Chick	1950	7.50	15.00	30.00
❏ 5096	Oh Cubanas/Going to Town	1950	7.50	15.00	30.00
KING					
❏ 4482	Sweet Home Blues/Twins	1951	7.50	15.00	30.00
❏ 4508	In the Alley/I'll Never Be the Same	1952	12.50	25.00	50.00
❏ 4523	Lawdy, Lawdy, Lawd (Part 1)/Lawdy, Lawdy, Lawd (Part 2)	1952	10.00	20.00	40.00
❏ 4544	My Ding-a-Ling/Bad Habit	1952	25.00	50.00	100.00
❏ 4559	The Golden Rule/Mother Knows Best	1952	7.50	15.00	30.00
❏ 4585	High Flying Woman/Stormy Weather	1953	7.50	15.00	30.00
Albums					
IMPERIAL					
❏ LP-9162 [M]	Fats Domino Presents Dave Bartholomew	1961	25.00	50.00	100.00
❏ LP-9217 [M]	New Orleans House Party	1963	25.00	50.00	100.00
❏ LP-12076 [S]	Fats Domino Presents Dave Bartholomew	1961	37.50	75.00	150.00
❏ LP-12217 [S]	New Orleans House Party	1963	37.50	75.00	150.00

BASE, ROB, AND D.J. E-Z ROCK

Number	Title (A Side/B Side)	Yr	VG	VG+	NM
12-Inch Singles					
PROFILE					
❏ 7186	It Takes Two/(Instrumental)	1988	3.75	7.50	15.00
❏ 7239	Get On the Dance Floor (4 versions)/Keep It Going Now (Hardcore Remix)	1988	—	3.50	7.00
❏ 7247	Joy and Pain (4 versions)	1989	2.00	4.00	8.00
❏ 7275	Turn It Out (Go Base) (Sky King Remix) (Percapella)/(Sky King Dub) (Album Version)	1989	2.00	4.00	8.00
❏ 7292	Get Up and Have a Good Time (3 versions)/Turn It Out (Of Control) (2 versions)	1990	2.00	4.00	8.00
❏ 7300	Outstanding/More Outstanding	1990	2.00	4.00	8.00
RAMPAGE					
❏ 670168	Diamonds (unknown versions)	2000	—	3.00	6.00
45s					
PROFILE					
❏ 5186	It Takes Two/(Instrumental)	1988	—	3.00	6.00
❏ 5239	Get On the Dance Floor/Keep It Going Now	1988	—	—	3.00
❏ 5247	Joy and Pain/Times Are Gettin' Ill	1989	—	—	3.00
❏ 5247 [PS]	Joy and Pain/Times Are Gettin' Ill	1989	—	—	3.00
❏ 5275	Turn It Out (Go Base)/Crush	1989	—	2.50	5.00
Albums					
PROFILE					
❏ PRO-1267	It Takes Two	1988	3.00	6.00	12.00
❏ PRO-1285	The Incredible Base	1989	3.00	6.00	12.00

BASS, FONTELLA

Number	Title (A Side/B Side)	Yr	VG	VG+	NM
45s					
BOBBIN					
❏ 134	I Don't Hurt Anymore/Brand New Love	1962	3.75	7.50	15.00
❏ 140	Honey Bee/Bad Boy	1963	3.75	7.50	15.00
CHECKER					
❏ 1097	Don't Mess Up a Good Thing/Baby, What You Want Me to Do	1965	2.50	5.00	10.00
—With Bobby McClure					
❏ 1111	You'll Miss Me (When I'm Gone)/Don't Jump	1965	2.50	5.00	10.00
—With Bobby McClure					
❏ 1120	Rescue Me/Soul of the Man	1965	5.00	10.00	20.00
—Red label with "Checker" vertically on left					

Number	Title (A Side/B Side)	Yr	VG	VG+	NM
❏ 1120	Rescue Me/Soul of the Man	1965	3.75	7.50	15.00
—Light blue label with red and black checkers					
❏ 1120	Rescue Me/Soul of the Man	1966	2.50	5.00	10.00
—Fading light blue label, no checkers					
❏ 1131	Recovery/Leave It in the Hands of Love	1965	2.50	5.00	10.00
❏ 1137	I Surrender/I Can't Rest	1966	2.50	5.00	10.00
❏ 1147	Safe and Sound/You'll Never Ever Know	1966	2.50	5.00	10.00
❏ 1183	Lucky in Love/Sweet Lovin' Daddy	1967	2.50	5.00	10.00
EPIC					
❏ 50341	Soon as I Touched Him/You Can Betcha in Love	1977	—	2.00	4.00
PAULA					
❏ 360	Who You Gonna Blame/Hold On This Time	1972	—	2.50	5.00
❏ 367	I Need to Be Loved/I Want Everyone to Know	1972	—	2.50	5.00
❏ 376	It Sure Is Good/I'm Leaving the Choice to You	1973	—	2.50	5.00
❏ 389	Home Wrecker/Now That I've Found a Good Thing	1973	—	2.50	5.00
❏ 393	Talking About Freedom/It's Hard to Get Back In	1974	—	2.50	5.00
Albums					
CHECKER					
❏ LP-2997 [M]	The "New" Look	1966	15.00	30.00	60.00
—Blue label with red and black checkers					
❏ LP-2997 [M]	The "New" Look	1967	7.50	15.00	30.00
—Blue and white label					
❏ LPS-2997 [S]	The "New" Look	1966	20.00	40.00	80.00
—Blue label with red and black checkers					
❏ LPS-2997 [S]	The "New" Look	1967	10.00	20.00	40.00
—Blue and white label					
PAULA					
❏ LPS-2203	Free	1971	3.00	6.00	12.00

BASS, FONTELLA, AND TINA TURNER
Also see each artist's individual listings.
45s
VESUVIUS

Number	Title (A Side/B Side)	Yr	VG	VG+	NM
❏ 1002	This Would Make Me Happy/Poor Little Fool	1963	6.25	12.50	25.00

BASS, MARTHA AND FONTELLA
Albums
SOUL NOTE

Number	Title (A Side/B Side)	Yr	VG	VG+	NM
❏ SN-1006	From the Root to the Source	197?	3.00	6.00	12.00

BAZUKA, TONY CAMILLO'S
45s
A&M

Number	Title (A Side/B Side)	Yr	VG	VG+	NM
❏ 1666	Dynomite Part 1/Dynomite Part 2	1975	—	2.00	4.00
❏ 1744	Bazuka Limited/Love Explosion	1975	—	2.00	4.00
❏ 1840	Theme from "Policeman"/Walkin' Tall	1976	—	2.00	4.00
VENTURE					
❏ 110	(C'est) Le Rock/Rock the Night Away	1979	—	2.00	4.00

BEES, THE
45s
IMPERIAL

Number	Title (A Side/B Side)	Yr	VG	VG+	NM
❏ 5314	Toy Bell/Snatchin' Back	1954	50.00	100.00	200.00
❏ 5320	I Want to Be Loved/Get Away Baby	1954	75.00	150.00	300.00
78s					
IMPERIAL					
❏ 5314	Toy Bell/Snatchin' Back	1954	20.00	40.00	80.00
❏ 5320	I Want to Be Loved/Get Away Baby	1954	20.00	40.00	80.00

BELL, ARCHIE, AND THE DRELLS
12-Inch Singles
BECKET

Number	Title (A Side/B Side)	Yr	VG	VG+	NM
❏ BKD-501	Any Time Is Right (5:25)/Why Didja Do Me (5:05)	1981	3.00	6.00	12.00
PHILADELPHIA INT'L					
❏ ASD 375 [DJ]	Glad You Could Make It (5:36)/There's No Other Like You (4:45)	1977	5.00	10.00	20.00
PHILADELPHIA INT'L.					
❏ 4Z8 3701	Strategy/We Got 'Um Dancin'	1979	3.00	6.00	12.00
45s					
ATLANTIC					
❏ 2478	Tighten Up/Tighten Up — Part 2	1968	2.00	4.00	8.00
❏ 2478	Tighten Up/Dog Eat Dog	1968	3.00	6.00	12.00
❏ 2534	I Can't Stop Dancing/You're Such a Beautiful Child	1968	—	3.50	7.00
❏ 2559	Do the Choo Choo/Love Will Rain on You	1968	—	3.50	7.00
❏ 2583	(There's Gonna Be A) Showdown/Go for What You Know	1968	—	3.50	7.00
❏ 2612	I Love My Baby/Just a Little Closer	1969	—	3.50	7.00
❏ 2644	Girl You're Too Young/Do the Hand Jive	1969	—	3.50	7.00
❏ 2663	My Balloon's Going Up/Giving Up Dancing	1969	—	3.50	7.00
❏ 2693	A World Without Music/Here I Go Again	1969	—	3.50	7.00
❏ 2721	Don't Let the Music Slip Away/Houston, Texas	1970	—	3.50	7.00
❏ 2744	I Wish/Get from the Bottom	1970	—	3.50	7.00
❏ 2769	Wrap It Up/Deal with Him	1970	—	3.50	7.00
❏ 2793	I Just Want to Fall in Love/Love at First Sight	1971	—	3.00	6.00
❏ 2829	Let the World Know/Archie's in Love	1971	—	3.00	6.00
❏ 2855	Green Power/I Can't Face You Baby	1972	—	3.00	6.00
BECKET					
❏ 45-4	Any Time Is Right/(B-side unknown)	1981	—	2.00	4.00
EAST WEST					
❏ 2048	She's My Woman/The Yankee Dance	1968	—	3.50	7.00

GLADES

Number	Title (A Side/B Side)	Yr	VG	VG+	NM
❏ 1707	Dancing to Your Music/Count the Ways	1973	—	3.00	6.00
❏ 1711	Ain't Nothing for a Man in Love/You Never Know What's On a Woman's Mind	1973	—	3.00	6.00
❏ 1718	Girls Grow Up Faster Than Boys/Love's Gonna Rain on You	1973	—	3.00	6.00
OVIDE					
❏ 228	Tighten Up/Dog Eat Dog	1967	7.50	15.00	30.00
PHILADELPHIA INT'L					
❏ 3605	Nothing Comes Easy/Right Here Is Where I Want to Be	1976	—	2.50	5.00
❏ 3615	Everybody Have a Good Time/I Bet I Can Do That Dance You're Doin'	1977	—	2.50	5.00
❏ 3632	Glad You Could Make It/There's No Other Like You	1977	—	2.50	5.00
❏ 3637	I've Been Missing You/It's Hard Not to Love You	1977	—	2.50	5.00
❏ 3651	Old People/On the Radio	1978	—	2.50	5.00
PHILADELPHIA INT'L.					
❏ 3710	Strategy/We Got 'Um Dancin'	1979	—	2.50	5.00
TSOP					
❏ 4767	I Could Dance All Night/King of the Castle	1975	—	2.50	5.00
❏ 4774	The Soul City Walk/King of the Castle	1975	—	2.50	5.00
❏ 4775	Let's Groove (Part 1)/Let's Groove (Part 2)	1976	—	2.50	5.00
WMOT					
❏ 03057	Touchin' You/(Instrumental)	1982	—	2.50	5.00
Albums					
ATLANTIC					
❏ 8181 [M]	Tighten Up	1968	12.50	25.00	50.00
❏ SD 8181 [S]	Tighten Up	1968	7.50	15.00	30.00
❏ SD 8204	I Can't Stop Dancing	1968	7.50	15.00	30.00
❏ SD 8226	There's Gonna Be a Showdown	1969	7.50	15.00	30.00
PHILADELPHIA INT'L.					
❏ PZ 34323	Where Will You Go When the Party's Over	1976	2.50	5.00	10.00
❏ PZ 34855	Hard Not to Like It	1977	2.50	5.00	10.00
❏ JZ 36096	Strategy	1979	2.50	5.00	10.00
TSOP					
❏ PZ 33844	Dance Your Troubles Away	1975	2.50	5.00	10.00

BELL, WILLIAM
12-Inch Singles
WRC

Number	Title (A Side/B Side)	Yr	VG	VG+	NM
❏ 12204	Headline News/Let Him Pay the Band	1986	2.50	5.00	10.00
45s					
ATLANTIC					
❏ 13154	Everyday Will Be Like A Holiday/Winner	197?	—	2.00	4.00
—Oldies Series reissue					
KAT FAMILY					
❏ 03502	Bad Time to Break Off/The Truth in Your Eyes	1983	—	2.00	4.00
❏ 03995	Playing Hard to Get/The Truth in Your Eyes	1983	—	2.00	4.00
MERCURY					
❏ 73839	Tryin' to Love Two/If Sex Was All We Had	1976	—	2.50	5.00
❏ 73922	Coming Back for More/You I Absolutely Positively Love	1977	—	2.00	4.00
❏ 73961	Your Love Keeps Me Goin'/Easy Comin' Out	1977	—	2.00	4.00
STAX					
❏ 0005	Private Number/Love-Eye-Tis	1968	—	2.50	5.00
—With Judy Clay					
❏ 0015	I Forgot to Be Your Lover/Bring the Curtains Down	1968	—	3.00	6.00
❏ 0017	Left-Over Love/My Baby Specializes	1968	—	2.50	5.00
—With Judy Clay					
❏ 0032	My Whole World Is Falling Down/All God's Children Got Soul	1969	—	2.50	5.00
❏ 0038	My Kind of Girl/Happy	1969	—	2.50	5.00
❏ 0043	Love's Sweet Sensation/Strung Out	1969	—	2.50	5.00
—With Mavis Staples					
❏ 0044	I Can't Stop/I Need You Woman	1969	—	2.50	5.00
—With Carla Thomas					
❏ 0054	Born Under a Bad Sign/A Smile Can't Hide a Broken Heart	1969	—	2.50	5.00
❏ 0067	All I Have to Do Is Dream/Leave the Girl Alone	1970	—	2.50	5.00
—With Carla Thomas					
❏ 0070	Lonely Soldier/Let Me Ride	1970	—	2.50	5.00
❏ 0092	A Penny for Your Thoughts/Till My Back Ain't Got No Bone	1971	—	2.50	5.00
❏ 0106	All for the Love of a Woman/I'll Be Home	1971	—	2.50	5.00
❏ 116	You Don't Miss Your Water/Formula of Love	1961	5.00	10.00	20.00
❏ 128	Any Other Way/Please Help Me I'm Falling	1962	5.00	10.00	20.00
❏ 0128	If You Really Love Him/Save Us	1972	—	2.50	5.00
❏ 132	I Told You So/What'Cha Gonna Do	1963	3.75	7.50	15.00
❏ 135	Just As I Thought/I'm Waiting on You	1963	3.75	7.50	15.00
❏ 138	Somebody Mentioned Your Name/What Can I Do to Forget	1963	3.75	7.50	15.00
❏ 141	I'll Show You/Monkeying Around	1963	3.75	7.50	15.00
❏ 146	Don't Make Something Out of Nothing/Who Will It Be Tomorrow	1964	3.00	6.00	12.00
❏ 0157	Livin' on Borrowed Time/The Man in the Street	1973	—	2.50	5.00
❏ 174	Crying All By Myself/Don't Stop Now	1965	3.00	6.00	12.00
❏ 0175	You've Got the Kind of Love I Need/I've Got to Go On Without You	1973	—	2.50	5.00
❏ 191	Share What You Got/Marching Off to War	1966	2.50	5.00	10.00
❏ 0198	All I Need Is Your Love/Gettin' What You Want	1974	—	2.50	5.00
❏ 199	Soldier's Goodbye/Never Like This Before	1966	2.50	5.00	10.00

Number	Title (A Side/B Side)	Yr	VG	VG+	NM
❑ 212	Everybody Loves a Winner/You're Such a Sweet Thing	1967	2.00	4.00	8.00
❑ 0221	Get It While It's Hot/Nobody Walks Away from Love Unhurt	1974	—	2.50	5.00
❑ 227	One Plus One/Eloise (Hang On In There)	1967	2.00	4.00	8.00
❑ 237	Everyday Will Be Like a Holiday/Ain't Got No Girl	1967	2.00	4.00	8.00
❑ 248	A Tribute to a King (Otis Redding)/Every Man Oughta Have a Woman	1968	—	3.00	6.00
WRC					
❑ 202	I Don't Want to Wake Up (Feelin' Guilty)/Whatever You Want (You Got It)	1986	—	2.50	5.00
—With Janice Bulluck					
❑ 204	Headline News/Let Him Pay the Band	1986	—	2.50	5.00
Albums					
KAT FAMILY					
❑ FZ 38643	Survivor	1983	2.50	5.00	10.00
MERCURY					
❑ SRM-1-1146	Coming Back for More	1977	2.50	5.00	10.00
❑ SRM-1-1193	It's Time You Took Another Listen	1978	2.50	5.00	10.00
STAX					
❑ 719 [M]	Soul of a Bell	1967	10.00	20.00	40.00
❑ S-719 [S]	Soul of a Bell	1967	12.50	25.00	50.00
❑ ST-2014 [M]	Bound to Happen	1969	12.50	25.00	50.00
—Mono is promo only					
❑ STS-2014 [S]	Bound to Happen	1969	7.50	15.00	30.00
❑ STS-2037	Wow…	1971	7.50	15.00	30.00
❑ STS-3005	Phases of Reality	1973	5.00	10.00	20.00
❑ STS-5502	Relating	1974	5.00	10.00	20.00
❑ MPS-8541	The Best of William Bell	1988	2.50	5.00	10.00
WRC					
❑ WL-3007	On a Roll	1986	3.00	6.00	12.00

BELL & JAMES
12-Inch Singles

Number	Title (A Side/B Side)	Yr	VG	VG+	NM
A&M					
❑ SP-12012	Livin' It Up (Friday Night) (7:03)/Don't Let the Man Get You	1978	3.00	6.00	12.00
❑ SP-12029	Shakedown/I Love the Music	1979	3.00	6.00	12.00
❑ SP-12305	Livin' It Up (Friday Night)/Say It, Say It	1989	2.00	4.00	8.00
—B-side by E.G. Daily; reissue					
❑ SP-17052	I Love the Music (same on both sides?)	1978	2.50	5.00	10.00
❑ SP-17104	Shakedown (same on both sides?)	1979	2.50	5.00	10.00
45s					
A&M					
❑ 2069	Livin' It Up (Friday Night)/Don't Let the Man Get You	1978	—	3.00	6.00
❑ 2137	You Never Know What You've Got/Just Can't Get Enough of Your Love	1979	—	2.50	5.00
❑ 2185	Shakedown/Nobody Knows It	1979	—	2.50	5.00
❑ 2204	Only Make Believe/Stay	1979	—	2.50	5.00
❑ 2347	In Spanish Harlem/Lover Call My Name	1981	—	2.50	5.00
Albums					
A&M					
❑ SP-4728	Bell & James	1978	2.50	5.00	10.00
❑ SP-4784	Only Make Believe	1979	2.50	5.00	10.00
❑ SP-4834	In Black & White	1981	2.50	5.00	10.00

BELL BIV DEVOE
Splinter group from NEW EDITION.
12-Inch Singles

Number	Title (A Side/B Side)	Yr	VG	VG+	NM
MCA					
❑ L33-1022 [DJ]	B.B.D. (I Thought It Was Me)? (same on both sides)	1990	—	3.50	7.00
❑ L33-1288 [DJ]	When Will I See You Smile Again? (6 versions)	1990	2.50	5.00	10.00
❑ MCA8P-1345 [DJ]	She's Dope! (EPOD Mix) (EPOD Radio Mix) (EPOD Instrumental)	1991	2.50	5.00	10.00
❑ MCA8P-1435 [DJ]	Let Me Know Something (7 versions)	1991	2.50	5.00	10.00
❑ MCA8P-2490 [DJ]	Gangsta (Without Rap) (Instrumental) (Suite)	1993	2.50	5.00	10.00
❑ MCA8P-2537 [DJ]	Gangsta (Extended) (Edit) (Short) (Suite)	1993	2.50	5.00	10.00
❑ MCA8P-2624 [DJ]	Above the Rim (same on both sides)	1993	—	3.00	6.00
❑ MCA8P-2900 [DJ]	Show Me the Way (Album Version) (Album Version Without Rap) (Instrumental)/(same on both sides)	1993	2.50	5.00	10.00
❑ L33-18488 [DJ]	Do Me! (5 versions)	1990	2.50	5.00	10.00
❑ L33-18489 [DJ]	Do Me! (East Coast Mental Mix)/(Instrumental)	1990	2.50	5.00	10.00
❑ 24003	Poison (4 versions)	1990	2.00	4.00	8.00
❑ 24037	Do Me! (3 versions)	1990	2.50	5.00	10.00
❑ 53999	When Will I See You Smile Again? (Remixed Club Version)/(Instrumental)	1991	—	3.00	6.00
❑ 54056	She's Dope! (EPOD Mix)/(EPOD Instrumental)	1991	2.00	4.00	8.00
❑ 54556	Gangsta (Extended Version)/(Remix) (Suite)	1993	2.00	4.00	8.00
45s					
MCA					
❑ 53772	Poison/(Instrumental)	1990	—	—	3.00
❑ 53897	B.B.D.(I Thought It Was Me)?/(Instrumental)	1990	—	—	3.00
❑ 54555	Gangsta/(Instrumental)	1993	—	—	3.00
❑ 54620	Above the Rim/(Instrumental)	1993	—	—	3.00
❑ 54725	Something in Your Eyes/(Instrumental)	1993	—	—	3.00
❑ 79045	Do Me!/(Instrumental)	1990	—	—	3.00
Albums					
MCA					
❑ 6387	Poison	1990	3.00	6.00	12.00
❑ 10345	WBBD — Bootcity! The Remix Album	1991	3.00	6.00	12.00
❑ 10682	Hootie Mack	1993	3.00	6.00	12.00

BELLE, REGINA
12-Inch Singles

Number	Title (A Side/B Side)	Yr	VG	VG+	NM
COLUMBIA					
❑ 44-07587	How Could You Do It to Me (Remix) (Remix Edit)/(same on both sides?)	1988	2.00	4.00	8.00
MCA					
❑ MCA8P-4235 [DJ]	Don't Let Go (unknown versions)	1998	2.00	4.00	8.00
❑ MCA8P-4300 [DJ]	I've Had Enough (Intimate Room Mix) (Intimate Room Instrumental) (Large Venue Mix) (Belle-Apella)	1998	2.00	4.00	8.00
❑ 55526	I've Had Enough (unknown versions)	1998	—	3.00	6.00
45s					
COLUMBIA					
❑ 38-07080	Show Me the Way/(Instrumental)	1987	—	—	3.00
❑ 38-07388	So Many Tears/Gotta Give It Up	1987	—	—	3.00
❑ 38-07388 [PS]	So Many Tears/Gotta Give It Up	1987	—	—	3.00
❑ 38-07735	How Could You Do It to Me/Intimate Relations	1988	—	—	3.00
❑ 38-08075	After the Love Has Lost Its Shine/Please Be Mine	1988	—	—	3.00
❑ 38-68969	Baby Come to Me/This Is Love	1989	—	—	3.00
❑ 38-73022	Make It Like It Was/Special Part of Me	1989	—	—	3.00
❑ 38-73201	What Goes Around/Intimate Relations	1990	—	2.00	4.00
❑ 38-74864	If I Could/Love	1993	—	2.00	4.00
❑ 38-77965	Love T.K.O./Could It Be I'm Falling in Love	1995	—	2.00	4.00
Albums					
COLUMBIA					
❑ BFC 40537	All By Myself	1987	2.00	4.00	8.00
❑ FC 44367	Stay with Me	1989	2.50	5.00	10.00

BELLS, THE (2)
45s

Number	Title (A Side/B Side)	Yr	VG	VG+	NM
RAMA					
❑ 166	What Can I Tell Her Now/Let Me Love You, You	1955	125.00	250.00	500.00

BELLTONES, THE
45s

Number	Title (A Side/B Side)	Yr	VG	VG+	NM
GRAND					
❑ 102	Estelle/Promise Love	1954	2000.	3000.	4000.
78s					
GRAND					
❑ 102	Estelle/Promise Love	1954	1000.	1500.	2000.

BELVIN, JESSE
Also see THE CLIQUES; JESSE AND MARVIN.
45s

Number	Title (A Side/B Side)	Yr	VG	VG+	NM
ALADDIN					
❑ 3431	Let Me Dream/Sugar Doll	1958	10.00	20.00	40.00
CASH					
❑ 1056	Dry Your Tears/Beware	1957	25.00	50.00	100.00
—Black and silver label					
❑ 1056	Dry Your Tears/Beware	1957	6.25	12.50	25.00
—Orange and black label					
CLASS					
❑ 267	I'm Confessin'/Deep in My Heart	1960	6.25	12.50	25.00
HOLLYWOOD					
❑ 1059	Betty My Darling/Dear Heart	1956	100.00	200.00	400.00
IMPACT					
❑ 23	Tonight My Love/Looking for Love	1962	3.75	7.50	15.00
JAMIE					
❑ 1145	Goodnight My Love (Pleasant Dreams)/My Desire	1959	5.00	10.00	20.00
KENT					
❑ 326	Sentimental Reasons/Senorita	1959	6.25	12.50	25.00
KNIGHT					
❑ 2012	Little Darling/Deacon Dan Tucker	1959	10.00	20.00	40.00
MODERN					
❑ 45x1005	Goodnight My Love (Pleasant Dreams)/Let Me Love You Tonight	1956	10.00	20.00	40.00
❑ 45x1005	Goodnight My Love (Pleasant Dreams)/I Want You With Me Xmas	1956	12.50	25.00	50.00
❑ 1013	I Need You So/Senorita	1957	7.50	15.00	30.00
❑ 1015	By My Side/Don't Close the Door	1957	7.50	15.00	30.00
❑ 1020	Sad and Lonesome/I'm Not Free	1957	7.50	15.00	30.00
❑ 1025	You Send Me/Summertime	1957	7.50	15.00	30.00
❑ 1027	My Satellite/Just to Say Hello	1957	7.50	15.00	30.00
MONEY					
❑ 208	I'm Only a Fool/Trouble and Misery	1955	15.00	30.00	60.00
RCA VICTOR					
❑ 47-7310	Volare/Ever Since We Met	1958	5.00	10.00	20.00
❑ 47-7387	Funny/Pledging My Love	1958	5.00	10.00	20.00
❑ 47-7469	Guess Who/My Girl Is Just Enough Woman for Me	1959	5.00	10.00	20.00
❑ 47-7543	Here's a Heart/It Could've Been Worse	1959	5.00	10.00	20.00
❑ 47-7596	Give Me Love/I'll Never Be Lonely Again	1959	5.00	10.00	20.00
❑ 47-7675	Something Happens to Me/The Door Is Always Open	1960	5.00	10.00	20.00
❑ 47-8040	Guess Who/Funny	1962	3.75	7.50	15.00
❑ 61-7469	Guess Who/My Girl Is Just Enough Woman for Me	1959	12.50	25.00	50.00
—"Living Stereo" (large hole, plays at 45 rpm)					
RECORDED IN HOLLYWOOD					
❑ 120	Dream Girl/Hang Your Tears Out to Dry	1951	150.00	300.00	600.00
❑ 412	Love Comes Tumbling Down/(B-side unknown)	1953	100.00	200.00	400.00

Number	Title (A Side/B Side)	Yr	VG	VG+	NM
SPECIALTY					
❏ 435	Confusin' Blues/Baby Don't Go	1952	20.00	40.00	80.00
❏ 550	Gone/One Little Blessing	1955	12.50	25.00	50.00
❏ 559	Where's My Girl/Love, Love of My Life	1955	12.50	25.00	50.00
Albums					
CROWN					
❏ CLP-5145 [M]	The Casual Jesse Belvin	1959	17.50	35.00	70.00
—Black label					
❏ CLP-5145 [M]	The Casual Jesse Belvin	196?	3.75	7.50	15.00
—Gray label					
❏ CLP-5187 [M]	The Unforgettable Jesse Belvin	1959	17.50	35.00	70.00
—Black label					
❏ CLP-5187 [M]	The Unforgettable Jesse Belvin	196?	3.75	7.50	15.00
—Gray label					
RCA CAMDEN					
❏ CAL-960 [M]	Jesse Belvin's Best	1966	3.00	6.00	12.00
❏ CAS-960 [S]	Jesse Belvin's Best	1966	3.75	7.50	15.00
RCA VICTOR					
❏ LPM-2089 [M]	Just Jesse Belvin	1959	10.00	20.00	40.00
❏ LSP-2089 [S]	Just Jesse Belvin	1959	15.00	30.00	60.00
❏ LPM-2105 [M]	Mr. Easy	1960	7.50	15.00	30.00
❏ LSP-2105 [S]	Mr. Easy	1960	10.00	20.00	40.00
SPECIALTY					
❏ SP-7003	The Blues Balladeer	1990	3.75	7.50	15.00

BEN, LA BRENDA
45s
Number	Title (A Side/B Side)	Yr	VG	VG+	NM
GORDY					
❏ 7009	Camel Walk/The Chaperone	1962	12.50	25.00	50.00
❏ 7021	I Can't Help It, I Gotta Dance/Just Be Yourself	1963	12.50	25.00	50.00
MOTOWN					
❏ 1033	Camel Walk/Chaperone	1962	100.00	200.00	400.00

BENET, ERIC
12-Inch Singles
Number	Title (A Side/B Side)	Yr	VG	VG+	NM
WARNER BROS.					
❏ PRO-A-8357	[DJ]Femininity (LP Version) (Instrumental) (Acappella)/(same on both sides)	1996	2.00	4.00	8.00
❏ PRO-A-8871	[DJ]True to Myself (8 versions)	1997	2.00	4.00	8.00
❏ PRO-A-9625	[DJ]Georgy Porgy (Featuring Faith Evans) (4 versions)	1999	2.50	5.00	10.00
❏ PRO-A-9721	[(2) DJ]Georgy Porgy (unknown versions)	1999	3.75	7.50	15.00
❏ PRO-A-9943	[DJ]Spend My Life with You (Buttered Soul Remix 4:36) (Buttered Soul A Capella 4:22)	1999	2.00	4.00	8.00
45s					
WARNER BROS.					
❏ 16958	Spend My Life with You (Featuring Tamia)/ Georgy Porgy (Featuring Faith Evans)	1999	—	—	3.00
❏ 17498	Spiritual Thang/(Instrumental)	1996	—	—	3.00
❏ 17571	Femininity/While You Were Here	1997	—	—	3.00

BENSON, GEORGE
12-Inch Singles
Number	Title (A Side/B Side)	Yr	VG	VG+	NM
VERVE					
❏ 01028 [DJ]	El Barrio (Maw Mix 7:14) (Instrumental 5:02) (LP Version 8:29) (+1 more?)	2000	3.00	6.00	12.00
❏ 561788-1	The Ghetto (El Barrio) (4 versions)	2000	2.00	4.00	8.00
WARNER BROS.					
❏ PRO-A-2026	[DJ]Inside Love (So Personal) (5:13) (7:03) (4:08)	1983	2.50	5.00	10.00
❏ PRO-A-2251	[DJ]20/20 (Extended Dance Mix 6:32) (same on both sides)	1984	2.00	4.00	8.00
❏ PRO-A-2617	[DJ]Shiver (Extended) (7" Version) (Dub)/Love Is Here Tonight	1986	2.00	4.00	8.00
❏ PRO-A-3454	[DJ]Good Habit (Remix) (Radio Version)	1988	—	3.50	7.00
❏ PRO-A-3722	[DJ]Here, There and Everywhere (Edit) (Instrumental Edit)	1989	2.50	5.00	10.00
❏ PRO-A-6237	[DJ]Love of My Life (same on both sides)	1993	2.50	5.00	10.00
❏ PRO-A-6242	[DJ]Kiss and Make Up/My Heart Is Dancing/Got to Be There/I'll Be Good to You	1993	2.50	5.00	10.00
❏ PRO-A-6365	[DJ]I'll Be Good to You (Edit) (LP Version)	1993	2.00	4.00	8.00
❏ 20110	Inside Love (So Personal) (2 versions)/In Search of a Dream	1983	—	3.00	6.00
❏ 20572	Shiver (3 versions)/Love Is Here Tonight	1986	—	3.50	7.00
❏ 20640	Teaser (3 versions)/Did You Hear Thunder	1987	—	3.50	7.00
❏ 21115	Twice the Love (Guitar Love Mix) (Guitar Love Edit) (Club Love Edit) (Club Love Dub)	1988	2.00	4.00	8.00
45s					
ARISTA					
❏ 0251	The Greatest Love of All/Ali's Theme	1977	—	2.00	4.00
—B-side by Michael Masser					
❏ 0251 [PS]	The Greatest Love of All/Ali's Theme	1977	—	3.00	6.00
A&M					
❏ 1003	Chattanooga Choo Choo/The Shape of Things to Come	1968	—	3.00	6.00
❏ 1057	Don't Let Me Lose This Dream Part 1/Part 2	1969	—	3.00	6.00
❏ 1076	Jackie All/My Woman's Good to Me	1969	—	3.00	6.00
❏ 1124	My Cherie Amour/Tell It Like It Is	1969	—	3.00	6.00
❏ 1128	I Got a Woman Part 1/I Got a Woman Part 2	1969	—	3.00	6.00
❏ 8395	Golden Slumbers-You Never Give Me Your Money (Medley)/(B-side unknown)	1971	—	3.00	6.00
—May be promo only					
COLUMBIA					
❏ 43684	Summertime/Ain't That Peculiar	1966	2.50	5.00	10.00
❏ 43998	The Man from Toledo/Georgia Stick	1967	2.50	5.00	10.00

Number	Title (A Side/B Side)	Yr	VG	VG+	NM
CTI					
❏ 25	Supership/My Latin Brother	1975	—	3.00	6.00
❏ 30	Summertime & 2001 (Part 1)/Summertime & 2001 (Part 2)	1977	—	2.50	5.00
❏ 47	Hold On, I'm Comin'/Gone	1978	—	2.50	5.00
GROOVE					
❏ 0024	It Should Have Been Me #2/She Makes Me Mad	1954	10.00	20.00	40.00
PRESTIGE					
❏ 317	Just Another Sunday/Shadow Dancers	1964	3.00	6.00	12.00
WARNER BROS.					
❏ 8209	This Masquerade/Lady	1976	—	2.50	5.00
❏ 8268	Breezin'/Six to Four	1976	—	2.00	4.00
❏ 8360	Everything Must Change/The Wind and I	1977	—	2.00	4.00
❏ 8377	Gonna Love You More/Valdez in the Country	1977	—	2.00	4.00
❏ 8542	On Broadway/We As Love	1978	—	2.00	4.00
❏ 8542 [PS]	On Broadway/We As Love	1978	—	2.50	5.00
❏ 8604	Lady Blue/California P.M.	1978	—	2.00	4.00
❏ 8604 [PS]	Lady Blue/California P.M.	1978	—	2.50	5.00
❏ 8759	Love Ballad/You're Never Too Far from Me	1979	—	2.00	4.00
❏ 8759 [PS]	Love Ballad/You're Never Too Far from Me	1979	—	2.50	5.00
❏ 8843	Unchained Melody/Before You Go	1979	—	2.00	4.00
❏ 27537	Good Habit/Stephanie	1989	—	—	3.00
❏ 27658	Twice the Love/(Instrumental)	1989	—	—	3.00
❏ 27658 [PS]	Twice the Love/(Instrumental)	1989	—	—	3.00
❏ 27780	Let's Do It Again/Let Go	1988	—	—	3.00
❏ 27780 [PS]	Let's Do It Again/Let Go	1988	—	—	3.00
❏ 28410	Did You Hear Thunder/Teaser	1987	—	—	3.00
❏ 28523	Shiver/Love Is Here Tonight	1986	—	—	3.00
❏ 28640	Kisses in the Moonlight/Open Your Eyes (Instrumental)	1986	—	—	3.00
❏ 28640 [PS]	Kisses in the Moonlight/Open Your Eyes (Instrumental)	1986	—	—	3.00
❏ 28969	New Day/No One Emotion	1985	—	—	3.00
❏ 29042	I Just Wanna Hang Around You/Beyond the Sea (La Mer)	1985	—	—	3.00
❏ 29120	20-20/Shark Bite	1984	—	2.00	4.00
❏ 29120 [PS]	20-20/Shark Bite	1984	—	2.00	4.00
❏ 29442	In Your Eyes/Never Too Far to Fall	1983	—	2.00	4.00
❏ 29563	Lady Love Me (One More Time)/Being with You	1983	—	2.00	4.00
❏ 29649	Inside Love (So Personal)/In Search of a Dream	1983	—	2.00	4.00
❏ 29649 [PS]	Inside Love (So Personal)/In Search of a Dream	1983	—	2.00	4.00
❏ 49051	Hey Girl/Welcome Into My World	1979	—	2.00	4.00
❏ 49505	Give Me the Night/Dinorah, Dinorah	1980	—	2.00	4.00
❏ 49505 [PS]	Give Me the Night/Dinorah, Dinorah	1980	—	2.50	5.00
❏ 49570	Love Dance/Love X Love	1980	—	2.00	4.00
❏ 49637	Midnight Love Affair/Turn Off the Lamplight	1980	—	2.00	4.00
❏ 49846	Turn Your Love Around/Nature Boy	1981	—	2.00	4.00
❏ 49846 [PS]	Turn Your Love Around/Nature Boy	1981	—	2.00	4.00
❏ 50005	Never Give Up on a Good Thing/Livin' Inside Your Love	1982	—	2.00	4.00
❏ 50005 [PS]	Never Give Up on a Good Thing/Livin' Inside Your Love	1982	—	2.00	4.00
Albums					
A&M					
❏ SP-3014	Shape of Things to Come	1969	5.00	10.00	20.00
—Brown label					
❏ SP-3014	Shape of Things to Come	1976	3.00	6.00	12.00
—Silvery label					
❏ SP-3014	Shape of Things to Come	198?	3.75	7.50	15.00
—Audiophile reissue					
❏ SP-3020	Tell It Like It Is	1969	5.00	10.00	20.00
—Brown label					
❏ SP-3020	Tell It Like It Is	1976	3.00	6.00	12.00
—Silvery label					
❏ SP-3020	Tell It Like It Is	198?	3.75	7.50	15.00
—Audiophile reissue					
❏ SP-3028	The Other Side of Abbey Road	1970	6.25	12.50	25.00
—Brown label					
❏ SP-3028	The Other Side of Abbey Road	1976	3.00	6.00	12.00
—Silvery label					
❏ SP-3028	The Other Side of Abbey Road	198?	3.75	7.50	15.00
—Audiophile reissue					
❏ SP-3203	The Best of George Benson	1983	2.50	5.00	10.00
COLUMBIA					
❏ CL 2525 [M]	The Most Exciting New Guitarist on the Jazz Scene Today — It's Uptown	1966	5.00	10.00	20.00
❏ CL 2613 [M]	The George Benson Cook Book	1967	5.00	10.00	20.00
❏ CS 9325	The Most Exciting New Guitarist on the Jazz Scene Today — It's Uptown	1976	2.50	5.00	10.00
—Orange label					
❏ CS 9325 [S]	The Most Exciting New Guitarist on the Jazz Scene Today — It's Uptown	1966	5.00	10.00	20.00
—Red "360 Sound" label					
❏ PC 9325	The Most Exciting New Guitarist on the Jazz Scene Today — It's Uptown	198?	2.00	4.00	8.00
—Reissue with new prefix					
❏ CS 9413	The George Benson Cook Book	1976	2.50	5.00	10.00
—Orange label					
❏ CS 9413 [S]	The George Benson Cook Book	1967	5.00	10.00	20.00
—Red "360 Sound" label					
❏ PC 9413	The George Benson Cook Book	198?	2.00	4.00	8.00
—Reissue with new prefix					
❏ CG 33569 [(2)]	Benson Burner	1976	3.00	6.00	12.00
CTI					
❏ 6009	Beyond the Blue Horizon	1971	3.00	6.00	12.00

B

Number	Title (A Side/B Side)	Yr	VG	VG+	NM
❏ 6015	White Rabbit	1972	3.00	6.00	12.00
❏ 6033	Body Talk	1973	3.00	6.00	12.00
❏ 6045	Bad Benson	1974	3.00	6.00	12.00
❏ 6062	Good King Bad	1976	3.00	6.00	12.00
❏ 6069	Benson & Farrell	1976	3.00	6.00	12.00
❏ 6072	George Benson In Concert — Carnegie Hall	1976	3.00	6.00	12.00
❏ 8009	White Rabbit	198?	2.50	5.00	10.00
❏ 8014	Take Five	198?	2.50	5.00	10.00
❏ 8030	Cast Your Fate to the Wind	1982	2.50	5.00	10.00
❏ 8031	Summertime: In Concert	198?	2.50	5.00	10.00

FANTASY

❏ OJC-461	New Boss Guitar	1990	3.00	6.00	12.00

—Reissue of Prestige 7310

MOBILE FIDELITY

❏ 1-011	Breezin'	1979	15.00	30.00	60.00

—Audiophile vinyl

POLYDOR

❏ PD-1-6084	Blue Benson	1976	2.50	5.00	10.00

PRESTIGE

❏ PRLP-7310 [M]	The New Boss Guitar of George Benson	1964	6.25	12.50	25.00
❏ PRST-7310 [S]	The New Boss Guitar of George Benson	1964	7.50	15.00	30.00
❏ 24072 [(2)]	George Benson & Jack McDuff	1976	3.75	7.50	15.00

VERVE

❏ V6-8749	Giblet Gravy	1968	5.00	10.00	20.00
❏ V6-8771	Goodies	1969	5.00	10.00	20.00

WARNER BROS.

❏ BS 2919	Breezin'	1976	3.75	7.50	15.00

—With no mention of "This Masquerade" on front cover

❏ BS 2919	Breezin'	1976	2.50	5.00	10.00

—With "Contains This Masquerade" on front cover

❏ BSK 2983	In Flight	1977	2.50	5.00	10.00
❏ BSK 3111	Breezin'	1977	2.00	4.00	8.00

—Reissue of 2919

❏ 2WS 3139 [(2)]	Weekend in L.A.	1978	3.00	6.00	12.00
❏ 2BSK 3277	Livin' Inside Your Love	1979	3.00	6.00	12.00
❏ HS 3453	Give Me the Night	1980	2.50	5.00	10.00
❏ 2HS 3577 [(2)]	The George Benson Collection	1981	3.00	6.00	12.00
❏ 23744	In Your Eyes	1983	2.50	5.00	10.00
❏ 25178	20/20	1985	2.50	5.00	10.00
❏ 25475	While the City Sleeps…	1986	2.50	5.00	10.00
❏ 25705	Twice the Love	1988	2.50	5.00	10.00
❏ 25907	Tenderly	1989	3.00	6.00	12.00
❏ 26295	Big Boss Band	1990	3.75	7.50	15.00

BENSON, GEORGE, AND EARL KLUGH

45s

WARNER BROS.

❏ 27975	Since You're Gone/Love Theme from "Romeo and Juliet"	1988	—	—	3.00
❏ 27975 [PS]	Since You're Gone/Love Theme from "Romeo and Juliet"	1988	—	2.00	4.00
❏ 28244	Dreamin'/Love Theme from "Romeo and Juliet"	1987	—	—	3.00

Albums

WARNER BROS.

❏ 25580	Collaboration	1987	2.50	5.00	10.00

BENTON, BROOK

45s

ALL PLATINUM

❏ 2364	Can't Take My Eyes Off You/Weekend with Feathers	1976	—	2.50	5.00

BRUT

❏ 810	Lay Lady Lay/A Touch of Class	1973	—	2.50	5.00
❏ 816	South Carolina/(B-side unknown)	1973	—	2.50	5.00

COTILLION

❏ 13107	Rainy Night in Georgia/Nothing Takes the Place of You	197?	—	2.00	4.00

—Part of "Atlantic Oldies Series"

❏ 44007	I Just Don't Know What to Do with Myself/Do Your Own Thing	1968	2.00	4.00	8.00
❏ 44031	She Knows What to Do with 'Em/Touch 'Em with Love	1969	2.00	4.00	8.00
❏ 44034	Nothing Can Take the Place of You/Woman Without Love	1969	2.00	4.00	8.00
❏ 44057	Rainy Night in Georgia/Where Do You Go from Here	1969	2.50	5.00	10.00
❏ 44072	My Way/A Little Bit of Soap	1970	—	3.00	6.00
❏ 44078	Don't It Make You Want to Go Home/I've Gotta Be Me	1970	—	3.00	6.00
❏ 44093	Shoes/Let Me Fix It	1970	—	3.00	6.00
❏ 44110	Whoever Finds This, I Love You/Heaven Help Us All	1971	—	3.00	6.00
❏ 44119	Take a Look at Your Hands/If You Think God Is Dead	1971	—	3.00	6.00
❏ 44130	Please Send Me Someone to Love/She Even Woke Me Up to Say Goodbye	1971	—	3.00	6.00
❏ 44138	A Black Child Can't Smile/If You Think God Is Dead	1971	—	3.00	6.00
❏ 44141	Soul Santa/Let Us All Get Together with the Lord	1971	2.00	4.00	8.00
❏ 44152	Movin' Day/Poor Make Believer	1972	—	3.00	6.00

EPIC

❏ 9177	Love Made Me Your Fool/Give Me a Sign	1956	6.25	12.50	25.00
❏ 9199	The Wall/All My Love Belongs to You	1957	6.25	12.50	25.00

Number	Title (A Side/B Side)	Yr	VG	VG+	NM
MERCURY					
❏ 30101	Merry Christmas, Happy New Year/This Time Of The Year	196?	2.00	4.00	8.00
—Reissue					
❏ 71394	It's Just a Matter of Time/Hurtin' Inside	1959	3.75	7.50	15.00
❏ 71443	Endlessly/So Close	1959	3.75	7.50	15.00
❏ 71478	Thank You Pretty Baby/With All of My Heart	1959	3.75	7.50	15.00
❏ 71512	So Many Ways/I Want You Forever	1959	3.75	7.50	15.00
❏ 71554	This Time of the Year/Nothing in the World	1959	3.75	7.50	15.00
❏ 71558	This Time of the Year/How Many Times	1959	3.75	7.50	15.00
❏ 71566	The Ties That Bind/Hither, Thither and Yon	1960	3.00	6.00	12.00
❏ 71566 [PS]	The Ties That Bind/Hither, Thither and Yon	1960	5.00	10.00	20.00
❏ 71652	Kiddio/The Same One	1960	3.00	6.00	12.00
❏ 71652 [PS]	Kiddio/The Same One	1960	5.00	10.00	20.00
❏ 71722	Fools Rush In (Where Angels Fear to Tread)/Someday You'll Want Me to Want You	1960	3.00	6.00	12.00
❏ 71722 [PS]	Fools Rush In (Where Angels Fear to Tread)/Someday You'll Want Me to Want You	1960	5.00	10.00	20.00
❏ 71730	This Time of the Year/Merry Christmas, Happy New Year	1960	3.00	6.00	12.00
❏ 71774	Think Twice/For My Baby	1961	3.00	6.00	12.00
❏ 71774 [PS]	Think Twice/For My Baby	1961	5.00	10.00	20.00
❏ 71820	The Boll Weevil Song/Your Eyes	1961	3.00	6.00	12.00
❏ 71820 [PS]	The Boll Weevil Song/Your Eyes	1961	5.00	10.00	20.00
❏ 71859	Frankie and Johnny/It's Just a House Without You	1961	3.00	6.00	12.00
❏ 71859 [PS]	Frankie and Johnny/It's Just a House Without You	1961	5.00	10.00	20.00
❏ 71903	Revenge/Really Really	1961	3.00	6.00	12.00
❏ 71903 [PS]	Revenge/Really Really	1961	5.00	10.00	20.00
❏ 71912	Shadrack/The Lost Penny	1961	3.00	6.00	12.00
❏ 71912 [PS]	Shadrack/The Lost Penny	1961	5.00	10.00	20.00
❏ 71925	Walk on the Wild Side/Somewhere in the Used to Be	1962	2.50	5.00	10.00
❏ 71925 [PS]	Walk on the Wild Side/Somewhere in the Used to Be	1962	5.00	10.00	20.00
❏ 71962	Hit Record/Thanks to the Fool	1962	2.50	5.00	10.00
❏ 71962 [PS]	Hit Record/Thanks to the Fool	1962	5.00	10.00	20.00
—Blue background with orange title banner					
❏ 71962 [PS]	Hit Record/Thanks to the Fool	1962	7.50	15.00	30.00
—All-orange background with different photo					
❏ 72009	Two Tickets to Paradise/It's Alright	1962	—	—	—
—Unreleased					
❏ 72024	Lie to Me/With the Touch of Your Hand	1962	2.50	5.00	10.00
❏ 72024 [PS]	Lie to Me/With the Touch of Your Hand	1962	5.00	10.00	20.00
❏ 72055	Hotel Happiness/Still Waters Run Deep	1962	2.50	5.00	10.00
❏ 72055 [PS]	Hotel Happiness/Still Waters Run Deep	1962	5.00	10.00	20.00
❏ 72099	I Got What I Wanted/Dearer Than Life	1963	2.50	5.00	10.00
❏ 72099 [PS]	I Got What I Wanted/Dearer Than Life	1963	5.00	10.00	20.00
❏ 72135	My True Confession/Tender Years	1963	2.50	5.00	10.00
❏ 72135 [PS]	My True Confession/Tender Years	1963	5.00	10.00	20.00
❏ 72177	Two Tickets to Paradise/Don't Hate Me	1963	2.50	5.00	10.00
❏ 72177 [PS]	Two Tickets to Paradise/Don't Hate Me	1963	5.00	10.00	20.00
❏ 72214	This Time of the Year/You're All I Want for Christmas	1963	2.50	5.00	10.00
❏ 72214 [DJ]	You're All I Want For Christmas/This Time Of The Year	1963	2.50	5.00	10.00
❏ 72230	Going, Going, Gone/After Midnight	1963	2.50	5.00	10.00
❏ 72230 [PS]	Going, Going, Gone/After Midnight	1963	5.00	10.00	20.00
❏ 72266	Too Late to Turn Back Now/Another Cup of Coffee	1964	2.50	5.00	10.00
❏ 72266 [PS]	Too Late to Turn Back Now/Another Cup of Coffee	1964	5.00	10.00	20.00
❏ 72303	A House Is not a Home/Come On Back	1964	2.50	5.00	10.00
❏ 72303 [PS]	A House Is not a Home/Come On Back	1964	5.00	10.00	20.00
❏ 72333	Lumberjack/Don't Do What I Did (Do What I Say)	1964	2.50	5.00	10.00
❏ 72333 [PS]	Lumberjack/Don't Do What I Did (Do What I Say)	1964	5.00	10.00	20.00
❏ 72365	Do It Right/Please, Please Make It Easy	1964	2.50	5.00	10.00
❏ 72365 [PS]	Do It Right/Please, Please Make It Easy	1964	5.00	10.00	20.00
❏ 72398	Special Years/Where There's a Will (There's a Way)	1965	2.50	5.00	10.00
❏ 72446	Love Me Now/A-Sleepin' at the End of the Bed	1965	2.50	5.00	10.00
❏ 872796-7	It's Just a Matter of Time/Hurtin' Inside	1989	—	2.00	4.00
❏ 872798-7	Endlessly/So Many Ways	1989	—	2.00	4.00
MGM					
❏ 14440	If You've Got the Time/You Take Me Home Honey	1972	—	2.50	5.00
OKEH					
❏ 7058	The Kentuckian Song/Ooh	1955	6.25	12.50	25.00
❏ 7065	Bring Me Love/Some of My Best Friends	1956	6.25	12.50	25.00
OLDE WORLD					
❏ 1100	Makin' Love Is Good for You/Better Times	1977	—	2.50	5.00
❏ 1107	Soft/Glow Love	1978	—	2.50	5.00
POLYDOR					
❏ 2015	I Cried for You/Love Me a Little	1979	—	2.00	4.00
RCA VICTOR					
❏ 47-7489	Only Your Love/(B-side unknown)	1959	—	—	—
—Unreleased?					
❏ 47-8693	Mother Nature, Father Time/You're Mine	1965	2.50	5.00	10.00
❏ 47-8693 [PS]	Mother Nature, Father Time/You're Mine	1965	5.00	10.00	20.00
❏ 47-8768	Where There's Life/Only a Girl Like You	1965	2.50	5.00	10.00
❏ 47-8830	Too Much Good Lovin'/A Sailor Boy's Love Song	1966	2.50	5.00	10.00
❏ 47-8879	Break Her Heart/In the Evening in the Moonlight	1966	2.50	5.00	10.00
❏ 47-8944	Where Does a Man Go to Cry/The Roach Song	1966	2.50	5.00	10.00
❏ 47-8995	So True in Life, So True in Love/If You Only Knew	1966	2.50	5.00	10.00
❏ 47-9031	Our First Christmas Together/Silent Night	1966	3.00	6.00	12.00
❏ 47-9096	Wake Up!/All My Love Belongs to You	1967	2.00	4.00	8.00
❏ 47-9105	Keep the Faith Baby/Going to Soulsville	1967	2.00	4.00	8.00

B

Number	Title (A Side/B Side)	Yr	VG	VG+	NM
REPRISE					
❏ 0611	You're the Reason I'm Living/Laura (Tell Me What He's Got That I Ain't Got)	1967	2.00	4.00	8.00
❏ 0649	Glory of Love/Weakness in a Man	1967	2.00	4.00	8.00
❏ 0676	Instead (Of Loving You)/Lonely Street	1968	2.00	4.00	8.00
STAX					
❏ 0231	Winds of Change/I Keep Thinking to Myself	1974	—	2.50	5.00
VIK					
❏ 0285	I Wanna Do Everything for You/Come On Be Nice	1957	5.00	10.00	20.00
❏ 0311	A Million Miles from Nowhere/Devoted	1957	5.00	10.00	20.00
❏ 0325	Because You Love Me/Crinoline Skirt	1958	5.00	10.00	20.00
❏ 0336	Crazy in Love with You/I'm Coming Back to You	1958	5.00	10.00	20.00
78s					
MERCURY					
❏ 71394	It's Just a Matter of Time/Hurtin' Inside	1959	25.00	50.00	100.00
Albums					
ALL PLATINUM					
❏ 3015	This Is Brook Benton	1976	3.00	6.00	12.00
ALLEGIANCE					
❏ AV-5033	Memories Are Made of This	1986	2.50	5.00	10.00
COTILLION					
❏ SD 9002	Do Your Own Thing	1969	3.00	6.00	12.00
❏ SD 9018	Brook Benton Today	1970	3.00	6.00	12.00
❏ SD 9028	Home Style	1970	3.00	6.00	12.00
❏ SD 9050	Story Teller	1971	3.00	6.00	12.00
❏ SD 9058	The Gospel Truth	1972	3.00	6.00	12.00
EPIC					
❏ LN 3573 [M]	Brook Benton At His Best	1959	12.50	25.00	50.00
HARMONY					
❏ HL 7346 [M]	The Soul of Brook Benton	196?	3.00	6.00	12.00
❏ HS 11146 [R]	The Soul of Brook Benton	196?	3.00	6.00	12.00
HMC					
❏ 830724	Beautiful Memories of Christmas	1983	3.00	6.00	12.00
MERCURY					
❏ MG-20421 [M]	It's Just a Matter of Time	1959	10.00	20.00	40.00
❏ MG-20464 [M]	Endlessly	1959	7.50	15.00	30.00
❏ MG-20565 [M]	So Many Ways I Love You	1960	7.50	15.00	30.00
❏ MG-20602 [M]	Songs I Love to Sing	1960	7.50	15.00	30.00
❏ MG-20607 [M]	Golden Hits	1961	5.00	10.00	20.00
❏ MG-20619 [M]	If You Believe	1961	5.00	10.00	20.00
❏ MG-20641 [M]	The Boll Weevil Song and 11 Other Great Hits	1961	5.00	10.00	20.00
❏ MG-20673 [M]	There Goes That Song Again	1962	5.00	10.00	20.00
❏ MG-20740 [M]	Singing the Blues — Lie to Me	1962	5.00	10.00	20.00
❏ MG-20774 [M]	Golden Hits, Volume 2	1963	5.00	10.00	20.00
❏ MG-20830 [M]	Best Ballads of Broadway	1963	5.00	10.00	20.00
❏ MG-20886 [M]	Born to Sing the Blues	1964	5.00	10.00	20.00
❏ MG-20918 [M]	On the Country Side	1964	3.75	7.50	15.00
❏ MG-20934 [M]	This Bitter Earth	1964	3.75	7.50	15.00
❏ SR-60077 [S]	It's Just a Matter of Time	1959	12.50	25.00	50.00
❏ SR-60146 [S]	Endlessly	1959	10.00	20.00	40.00
❏ SR-60225 [S]	So Many Ways I Love You	1960	10.00	2.00	40.00
❏ SR-60602 [S]	Songs I Love to Sing	1960	10.00	20.00	40.00
❏ SR-60607 [S]	Golden Hits	1961	7.50	15.00	30.00
❏ SR-60619 [S]	If You Believe	1961	7.50	15.00	30.00
❏ SR-60641 [S]	The Boll Weevil Song and 11 Other Great Hits	1961	7.50	15.00	30.00
❏ SR-60673 [S]	There Goes That Song Again	1962	7.50	15.00	30.00
❏ SR-60740 [S]	Singing the Blues — Lie to Me	1962	7.50	15.00	30.00
❏ SR-60774 [S]	Golden Hits, Volume 2	1963	7.50	15.00	30.00
❏ SR-60830 [S]	Best Ballads of Broadway	1963	6.25	12.50	25.00
❏ SR-60886 [S]	Born to Sing the Blues	1964	6.25	12.50	25.00
❏ SR-60918 [S]	On the Country Side	1964	5.00	10.00	20.00
❏ SR-60934 [S]	This Bitter Earth	1964	5.00	10.00	20.00
❏ 822321-1	It's Just a Matter of Time: His Greatest Hits	1984	2.50	5.00	10.00
MGM					
❏ SE-4874	Something for Everyone	1973	3.00	6.00	12.00
MUSICOR					
❏ 4603 [(2)]	The Best of Brook Benton	1977	3.00	6.00	12.00
PAIR					
❏ PDL2-1100 [(2)]	Brook Benton's Best	1986	3.00	6.00	12.00
RCA CAMDEN					
❏ CAL-564 [M]	Brook Benton	1960	3.75	7.50	15.00
❏ CAS-2431	I Wanna Be with You	1970	3.00	6.00	12.00
RCA VICTOR					
❏ APL1-1044	Book Benton Sings a Love Story	1975	2.50	5.00	10.00
❏ LPM-3514 [M]	That Old Feeling	1966	3.75	7.50	15.00
❏ LSP-3514 [S]	That Old Feeling	1966	5.00	10.00	20.00
❏ LPM-3526 [M]	Mother Nature, Father Time	1965	3.75	7.50	15.00
❏ LSP-3526 [S]	Mother Nature, Father Time	1965	5.00	10.00	20.00
❏ LPM-3590 [M]	My Country	1966	3.75	7.50	15.00
❏ LSP-3590 [S]	My Country	1966	5.00	10.00	20.00
REPRISE					
❏ R-6268 [M]	Laura (What's He Got That I Ain't Got)	1967	5.00	10.00	20.00
❏ RS-6268 [S]	Laura (What's He Got That I Ain't Got)	1967	3.75	7.50	15.00
RHINO					
❏ RNFP 71497 [(2)]	The Brook Benton Anthology (1959-1970)	1986	3.00	6.00	12.00
WING					
❏ MGW-12314 [M]	Brook Benton	1966	3.00	6.00	12.00
❏ SRW-16314 [S]	Brook Benton	1966	3.00	6.00	12.00

Number	Title (A Side/B Side)	Yr	VG	VG+	NM
BENTON, BROOK, AND DAMITA JO					
45s					
MERCURY					
❏ 72196	Yaba-Taba-Do/Almost Persuaded	1963	—	—	—
—Unreleased					
❏ 72207	Baby, You've Got It Made/Stop Foolin'	1963	2.50	5.00	10.00
BERRY, CHUCK					
Also see JOE ALEXANDER AND THE CUBANS; BO DIDDLEY/CHUCK BERRY.					
45s					
ATCO					
❏ 7203	Oh What a Thrill/California	1979	—	2.00	4.00
CHESS					
❏ 1604	Maybellene/Wee Wee Hours	1955	12.50	25.00	50.00
❏ 1610	Thirty Days (To Come Back Home)/Together	1955	12.50	25.00	50.00
❏ 1615	No Money Down/Down Bound Train	1956	12.50	25.00	50.00
❏ 1626	Roll Over Beethoven/Drifting Heart	1956	12.50	25.00	50.00
❏ 1635	Too Much Monkey Business/Brown Eyed Handsome Man	1956	12.50	25.00	50.00
❏ 1645	You Can't Catch Me/Havana Moon	1956	12.50	25.00	50.00
❏ 1653	School Day (Ring! Ring! Goes the Bell)/Deep Feeling	1957	12.50	25.00	50.00
❏ 1664	Oh Baby Doll/La Jaunda	1957	12.50	25.00	50.00
❏ 1671	Rock & Roll Music/Blue Feeling	1957	7.50	15.00	30.00
❏ 1683	Sweet Little Sixteen/Reelin' and Rockin'	1958	7.50	15.00	30.00
❏ 1691	Johnny B. Goode/Around and Around	1958	7.50	15.00	30.00
❏ 1697	Beautiful Delilah/Vacation Time	1958	7.50	15.00	30.00
❏ 1700	Carol/Hey Pedro	1958	7.50	15.00	30.00
❏ 1709	Sweet Little Rock and Roll/Joe Joe Gun	1958	7.50	15.00	30.00
❏ 1714	Run Rudolph Run/Merry Christmas Baby	1958	10.00	20.00	40.00
❏ 1716	Anthony Boy/That's My Desire	1959	7.50	15.00	30.00
❏ 1722	Almost Grown/Little Queenie	1959	7.50	15.00	30.00
❏ 1729	Back in the U.S.A./Memphis Tennessee	1959	7.50	15.00	30.00
❏ 1737	Broken Arrow/Childhood Sweetheart	1959	10.00	20.00	40.00
❏ 1747	Too Pooped to Pop ("Casey")/Let It Rock	1960	6.25	12.50	25.00
❏ 1754	Bye Bye Johnny/Worried Life Blues	1960	6.25	12.50	25.00
❏ 1763	I Got to Find My Baby/Mad Lad	1960	6.25	12.50	25.00
❏ 1767	Our Little Rendezvous/Jaguar and Thunderbird	1960	6.25	12.50	25.00
❏ 1779	I'm Talking About You/Little Star	1961	6.25	12.50	25.00
❏ 1799	Come On/Go-Go-Go	1961	5.00	10.00	20.00
❏ 1853	I'm Talking About You/Diploma for Two	1963	5.00	10.00	20.00
❏ 1866	Memphis/Sweet Little Sixteen	1963	5.00	10.00	20.00
❏ 1883	Nadine (Is It You?)/O Rangutang	1964	5.00	10.00	20.00
❏ 1898	No Particular Place to Go/You Two	1964	5.00	10.00	20.00
❏ 1898 [PS]	No Particular Place to Go/You Two	1964	12.50	25.00	50.00
❏ 1906	You Never Can Tell/Brenda Lee	1964	5.00	10.00	20.00
❏ 1906 [PS]	You Never Can Tell/Brenda Lee	1964	10.00	20.00	40.00
❏ 1912	Little Marie/Go Bobby Soxer	1964	3.75	7.50	15.00
❏ 1912 [PS]	Little Marie/Go Bobby Soxer	1964	10.00	20.00	40.00
❏ 1916	Promised Land/Things I Used to Do	1964	3.75	7.50	15.00
❏ 1916 [PS]	Promised Land/Things I Used to Do	1964	12.50	25.00	50.00
❏ 1926	Dear Dad/Lonely School Days	1965	3.75	7.50	15.00
❏ 1943	It Wasn't Me/Welcome Back Pretty Girl	1965	3.75	7.50	15.00
❏ 1943 [PS]	It Wasn't Me/Welcome Back Pretty Girl	1965	7.50	15.00	30.00
❏ 1963	Ramona Say Yes/Lonely School Days	1966	3.75	7.50	15.00
❏ 1963	Ramona Say Yes/Havana Moon	1966	3.75	7.50	15.00
❏ 2090	Tulane/Have Mercy Judge	1970	—	3.00	6.00
❏ 2131	My Ding-a-Ling/Johnny B. Goode	1972	—	3.00	6.00
—All-blue label					
❏ 2131	My Ding-a-Ling/Johnny B. Goode	1972	—	2.00	4.00
—Orange and blue label					
❏ 2136	Reelin' & Rockin'/Let's Boogie	1972	—	2.00	4.00
❏ 2140	Roll 'Em Pete/Bio	1973	—	2.00	4.00
❏ 2169	Baby What You Want Me to Do/Shake, Rattle and Roll	1975	—	2.00	4.00
COLLECTABLES					
❏ 3437	Run Rudolph Run/Merry Christmas Baby	199?	—	—	3.00
MERCURY					
❏ 30143	Maybellene/Sweet Little Sixteen	196?	—	3.00	6.00
❏ 30144	Memphis/School Day (Ring, Ring Goes the Bell)	196?	—	3.00	6.00
❏ 30145	Back in the U.S.A./Roll Over Beethoven	196?	—	3.00	6.00
❏ 30146	Johnny B. Goode/Rock and Roll Music	196?	—	3.00	6.00
—The Mercury 30000 series are re-recordings of the Chess hits					
❏ 72643	Club Nitty Gritty/Laugh and Cry	1966	2.50	5.00	10.00
❏ 72680	Back to Memphis/I Do Really Love You	1967	2.50	5.00	10.00
❏ 72748	It Hurts Me Too/Feelin' It	1967	2.50	5.00	10.00
❏ 72840	Louie to Frisco/Ma Dear	1968	2.50	5.00	10.00
❏ 72963	It's Too Dark in There/Good Looking Woman	1969	5.00	10.00	20.00
❏ 72963 [PS]	It's Too Dark in There/Good Looking Woman	1969	7.50	15.00	30.00
PHILCO-FORD					
❏ HP-34	Maybellene/Roll Over Beethoven	1969	5.00	10.00	20.00
—4-inch plastic "Hip Pocket Record" with color sleeve					
7-Inch Extended Plays					
CHESS					
❏ CH-5118	School Day (Ring, Ring Goes the Bell)/Wee Wee Hours//Brown Eyed Handsome Man/Too Much Monkey Business	1957	30.00	60.00	120.00
❏ CH-5118 [PS]	After School Session	1957	50.00	100.00	200.00
❏ CH-5119	Rock & Roll Music/Blue Feeling//Oh Baby Doll/La Jaunda (Espanol)	1957	25.00	50.00	100.00
❏ CH-5119 [PS]	Rock and Roll Music	1957	50.00	100.00	200.00
❏ CH-5121	Sweet Little Sixteen/Rockin' at the Philharmonic//Reelin' and Rockin'/Guitar Boogie	1958	25.00	50.00	100.00
❏ CH-5121 [PS]	Sweet Little Sixteen	1958	50.00	100.00	200.00

Number	Title (A Side/B Side)	Yr	VG	VG+	NM
❏ CH-5124	(contents unknown)	1958	25.00	50.00	100.00
❏ CH-5124 [PS]	Pickin' Berries	1958	50.00	100.00	200.00
❏ EP-5126	Jo Jo Gun/Sweet Little Rock and Roller//Johnny B. Goode/Around and Around	1958	25.00	50.00	100.00
❏ EP-5126 [PS]	Sweet Little Rock and Roller	1958	50.00	100.00	200.00

Albums

ACCORD

| ❏ SN-7171 | Toronto Rock 'N' Roll Revival, Vol. 2 | 1982 | 2.50 | 5.00 | 10.00 |
| ❏ SN-7172 | Toronto Rock 'N' Roll Revival, Vol. 3 | 1982 | 2.50 | 5.00 | 10.00 |

ARCHIVE OF FOLK AND JAZZ

| ❏ 321 | Chuck Berry's Greatest Hits | 197? | 2.50 | 5.00 | 10.00 |

ATCO

| SD 38-118 | Rockit | 1979 | 3.00 | 6.00 | 12.00 |

CHESS

❏ LP-1426 [M]	After School Session	1958	50.00	100.00	200.00
❏ LPS-1426 [R]	After School Session	196?	3.00	6.00	12.00
❏ LP-1432 [M]	One Dozen Berrys	1958	50.00	100.00	200.00
❏ LPS-1432 [R]	One Dozen Berrys	196?	3.00	6.00	12.00
❏ LP-1435 [M]	Chuck Berry Is On Top	1959	45.00	90.00	180.00
❏ LPS-1435 [R]	Chuck Berry Is On Top	196?	3.00	6.00	12.00
❏ LP-1448 [M]	Rockin' at the Hops	1960	45.00	90.00	180.00
❏ LP-1456 [M]	New Juke Box Hits	1961	45.00	90.00	180.00
❏ LP-1465 [M]	Chuck Berry Twist	1962	25.00	50.00	100.00
❏ LP-1465 [M]	More Chuck Berry	1963	30.00	60.00	120.00
—Retitled version of above					
❏ LPS-1465 [R]	More Chuck Berry	196?	3.00	6.00	12.00
❏ LP-1480 [M]	Chuck Berry On Stage	1963	30.00	60.00	120.00
❏ LPS-1480 [R]	Chuck Berry On Stage	196?	3.00	6.00	12.00
❏ LP-1485 [M]	Chuck Berry's Greatest Hits	1964	30.00	60.00	120.00
❏ LPS-1485 [R]	Chuck Berry's Greatest Hits	196?	3.00	6.00	12.00
❏ LP-1488 [M]	St. Louis to Liverpool	1964	15.00	30.00	60.00
❏ LPS-1488 [S]	St. Louis to Liverpool	1964	20.00	40.00	80.00
❏ LP-1495 [M]	Chuck Berry in London	1965	7.50	15.00	30.00
❏ LPS-1495 [S]	Chuck Berry in London	1965	10.00	20.00	40.00
❏ LP-1498 [M]	Fresh Berry's	1965	7.50	15.00	30.00
❏ LPS-1498 [S]	Fresh Berry's	1965	10.00	20.00	40.00
❏ 2CH-1514 [(2) R]	Chuck Berry's Golden Decade	1972	3.75	7.50	15.00
—New cover has a pink radio					
❏ LP-1514 [(2) M]	Chuck Berry's Golden Decade	1967	10.00	20.00	40.00
❏ LPS-1514 [(2) R]	Chuck Berry's Golden Decade	1967	5.00	10.00	20.00
—Old cover does not have a pink radio					
❏ LPS-1550	Back Home	1970	5.00	10.00	20.00
❏ CH-9171	New Juke Box Hits	1986	2.50	5.00	10.00
—Reissue of 1456					
❏ CH-9186	St. Louis to Liverpool	1988	2.50	5.00	10.00
—Reissue of 1488					
❏ CH-9190	More Rock 'n' Roll Rarities	1986	2.50	5.00	10.00
❏ CH-9256	Chuck Berry Is On Top	1987	2.50	5.00	10.00
—Reissue of 1435					
❏ CH-9259	Rockin' at the Hop	1987	2.50	5.00	10.00
—Reissue of 1448					
❏ CH-9284	After School Session	1989	2.50	5.00	10.00
—Reissue of 1426					
❏ CH-9295	The London Chuck Berry Sessions	1989	2.50	5.00	10.00
—Reissue of 60020					
❏ CH-9318	Missing Berries: Rarities, Volume 3	1990	2.50	5.00	10.00
❏ CH-50008	San Fransisco Dues	1971	5.00	10.00	20.00
❏ CH-50043	Chuck Berry/Bio	1973	5.00	10.00	20.00
❏ CH-60020	The London Chuck Berry Sessions	1972	5.00	10.00	20.00
❏ 2CH-60023 [(2)]	Chuck Berry's Golden Decade, Vol. 2	1973	6.25	12.50	25.00
❏ 2CH-60028 [(2)]	Chuck Berry's Golden Decade, Vol. 3	1974	6.25	12.50	25.00
❏ CH6-80001 [(6)]	The Chess Box	1989	12.50	25.00	50.00
❏ CH2-92500 [(2)]	The Great Twenty-Eight	1983	3.00	6.00	12.00
❏ CH2-92521 [(2)]	Rock 'n' Roll Rarities	1986	3.75	7.50	15.00

GUSTO

| ❏ 0004 | The Best of the Best of Chuck Berry | 198? | 2.50 | 5.00 | 10.00 |

MERCURY

❏ SRM-2-6501 [(2)]	St. Louis to Frisco to Memphis	1972	5.00	10.00	20.00
❏ MG-21103 [M]	Chuck Berry's Golden Hits	1967	3.75	7.50	15.00
❏ MG-21123 [M]	Chuck Berry in Memphis	1967	3.75	7.50	15.00
❏ MG-21138 [M]	Love at the Fillmore Auditorium	1967	5.00	10.00	20.00
❏ SR-61103 [S]	Chuck Berry's Golden Hits	1967	3.75	7.50	15.00
❏ SR-61123 [S]	Chuck Berry in Memphis	1967	3.75	7.50	15.00
❏ SR-61138 [S]	Love at the Fillmore Auditorium	1967	5.00	10.00	20.00
❏ SR-61176	From St. Louie to Frisco	1968	5.00	10.00	20.00
❏ SR-61223	Concerto in B Goode	1969	5.00	10.00	20.00
❏ 826256-1	Chuck Berry's Golden Hits	1985	2.00	4.00	8.00
—Reissue					

PICKWICK

❏ PTP-2061 [(2)]	Flashback	1975	3.00	6.00	12.00
❏ SPC-3327	Johnny B. Goode	1973	2.50	5.00	10.00
❏ SPC-3345	Sweet Little Rock and Roller	1974	2.50	5.00	10.00
❏ SPC-3392	Wild Berrys	1974	2.50	5.00	10.00

QUICKSILVER

| ❏ QS-1017 | Live Hits | 198? | 2.50 | 5.00 | 10.00 |

SSS INTERNATIONAL

| ❏ 36 | Chuck Berry Live | 1981 | 2.50 | 5.00 | 10.00 |

BERRY, RICHARD

45s

FLAIR

❏ 1016	I'm Still in Love with You/One Little Prayer	1953	20.00	40.00	80.00
❏ 1052	Bye Bye/At Last	1954	15.00	30.00	60.00
—With the Dreamers					

Number	Title (A Side/B Side)	Yr	VG	VG+	NM
❏ 1055	What You Do to Me/The Big Break	1954	15.00	30.00	60.00
❏ 1058	Daddy Daddy/Baby Darling	1954	15.00	30.00	60.00
—With the Dreamers					
❏ 1064	Please Tell Me/Oh Oh Get Out of the Car	1955	12.50	25.00	50.00
❏ 1068	God Gave Me You/Doncha Go	1955	12.50	25.00	50.00
❏ 1071	Next Time/Crazy Lover	1955	12.50	25.00	50.00
❏ 1075	Together/Jelly Roll	1955	12.50	25.00	50.00

FLIP

❏ 318	Take the Key/No Kissin' and Huggin'	1956	10.00	20.00	40.00
❏ 321	Louie, Louie/You Are My Sunshine	1957	15.00	30.00	60.00
❏ 321	Louie, Louie/Rock, Rock, Rock	1957	10.00	20.00	40.00
❏ 327	Sweet Sugar You/Rock, Rock, Rock	1957	10.00	20.00	40.00
❏ 331	You're the Girl/You Look So Good	1958	10.00	20.00	40.00
❏ 336	Heaven on Wheels/The Mess Around	1958	10.00	20.00	40.00
❏ 339	Besame Mucho/Do I, Do I	1958	7.50	15.00	30.00
❏ 349	Have Love, Will Travel/No Room	1960	7.50	15.00	30.00
❏ 352	I'll Never Ever Love Again/Somewhere There's a Rainbow	1961	7.50	15.00	30.00
❏ 360	You Look So Good/You Are My Sunshine	1962	7.50	15.00	30.00

HAPPY TIGER

| ❏ 5063 | Louie Louie/Rock Rock Rock | 1972 | 2.00 | 4.00 | 8.00 |

K&G

| ❏ 9001 | I'm Your Fool/In a Really Big Way | 1961 | 7.50 | 15.00 | 30.00 |

RPM

❏ 448	Rockin' Man/Big John	1955	25.00	50.00	100.00
❏ 452	Pretty Brown Eyes/I Am Bewildered	1956	7.50	15.00	30.00
❏ 465	Angel of My Life/Yama Yama Pretty Mama	1956	25.00	50.00	100.00
❏ 477	Wait for Me/Good Love	1956	7.50	15.00	30.00

SMASH

| ❏ 1789 | What Good Is a Heart/Everybody's Got a Lover But Me | 1963 | 3.00 | 6.00 | 12.00 |
| ❏ 1811 | I'm Learning/Empty Chair | 1963 | 3.00 | 6.00 | 12.00 |

WARNER BROS.

| ❏ 5164 | Walk Right In/It's All Right | 1960 | 12.50 | 25.00 | 50.00 |

Albums

CROWN

| ❏ CST-371 [R] | Richard Berry and the Dreamers | 1963 | 7.50 | 15.00 | 30.00 |
| ❏ CLP-5371 [M] | Richard Berry and the Dreamers | 1963 | 15.00 | 30.00 | 60.00 |

PAM

| ❏ 1001 | Live at the Century Restaurant | 1968 | 10.00 | 20.00 | 40.00 |
| ❏ 1002 | Wild Berry | 196? | 10.00 | 20.00 | 40.00 |

BIG MAYBELLE

45s

BRUNSWICK

❏ 55234	Candy/Cry	1962	3.00	6.00	12.00
❏ 55242	Cold, Cold Heart/Why Was I Born	1963	3.00	6.00	12.00
❏ 55256	Everybody's Got a Home But Me/How Deep Is the Ocean	1963	3.00	6.00	12.00

CHESS

| ❏ 1967 | It's a Man's Man's Man's World/Big Maybelle Sings the Blues | 1966 | 2.50 | 5.00 | 10.00 |

OKEH

❏ 6931	Gabbin' Blues/Rain Down Rain	1953	10.00	20.00	40.00
❏ 6955	Way Back Home/Just Want Your Love	1953	10.00	20.00	40.00
❏ 6998	Send for Me/Jimmy Mule	1953	10.00	20.00	40.00
❏ 7009	My Country Man/Maybelle's Blues	1953	10.00	20.00	40.00
❏ 7026	I've Got a Feelin'/You'll Never Know	1954	7.50	15.00	30.00
❏ 7042	My Big Mistake/I'm Gettin' 'Long Alright	1954	7.50	15.00	30.00
❏ 7053	Ain't No Use/Don't Leave Poor Me	1955	7.50	15.00	30.00
❏ 7060	Whole Lotta Shakin' Goin' On/One Monkey Don't Stop No Show	1955	7.50	15.00	30.00
❏ 7066	Such a Cutie/The Other Night	1956	7.50	15.00	30.00
❏ 7069	Gabbin' Blues/New Kind of Mambo	1956	7.50	15.00	30.00

PARAMOUNT

| ❏ 0237 | Blame It on Your Love/See See Rider | 1973 | — | 3.00 | 6.00 |

PORT

| ❏ 3002 | Let Me Go/No Better for You | 1965 | 3.00 | 6.00 | 12.00 |

ROJAC

❏ 112	96 Tears/That's Life	1966	2.50	5.00	10.00
❏ 115	I Can't Wait Any Longer/Turn the World Around the Other Way	1967	2.00	4.00	8.00
❏ 116	Mama (He Treats Your Daughter Mean)/Keep That Man	1967	2.00	4.00	8.00
❏ 118	Quittin' Time/I Can't Wait Any Longer	1967	2.00	4.00	8.00
❏ 121	Heaven Will Welcome You, Dr. King/Eleanor Rigby	1968	2.50	5.00	10.00
❏ 124	How It Lies/Old Love Never Dies	1968	2.00	4.00	8.00
❏ 1003	Careless Love/My Mother's Eyes	196?	2.00	4.00	8.00
❏ 1003	Don't Pass Me By/It's Been Raining	1966	2.50	5.00	10.00

SAVOY

❏ 1195	Candy/That's a Pretty Good Love	1956	5.00	10.00	20.00
❏ 1500	Mean to Me/Tell Me Who	1956	3.75	7.50	15.00
❏ 1512	I Don't Want to Cry/All of Me	1957	3.75	7.50	15.00
❏ 1519	Rock House/Jim	1957	3.75	7.50	15.00
❏ 1527	So Long/Ring Dang Dilly	1957	3.75	7.50	15.00
❏ 1536	Blues Early, Early (Part 1)/Blues Early, Early (Part 2)	1958	3.75	7.50	15.00
❏ 1541	White Christmas/Silent Night	1958	3.75	7.50	15.00
❏ 1558	Baby Won't You Please Come Home/Say It Isn't Do	1959	3.75	7.50	15.00
❏ 1572	A Good Man Is Hard to Find/Pitiful	1959	3.75	7.50	15.00
❏ 1576	Some of These Days/I Understand	1959	3.75	7.50	15.00
❏ 1583	I Got It Bad and That Ain't Good/Ramblin' Blues	1960	3.75	7.50	15.00

Number	Title (A Side/B Side)	Yr	VG	VG+	NM
❏ 1583	I Got It Bad and That Ain't Good/Until the Real Thing Comes Along	1960	3.75	7.50	15.00
❏ 1595	I Ain't Got Nobody/Going Home Baby	1961	3.75	7.50	15.00

SCEPTER

Number	Title (A Side/B Side)	Yr	VG	VG+	NM
❏ 1288	I Don't Want to Cry/Yesterday's Kisses	1965	3.00	6.00	12.00

Albums

BRUNSWICK

Number	Title (A Side/B Side)	Yr	VG	VG+	NM
❏ BL 54107 [M]	What More Can a Woman Do	1962	12.50	25.00	50.00
❏ BL 754107 [S]	What More Can a Woman Do	1962	17.50	35.00	70.00
❏ BL 754142	The Gospel Soul of Big Maybelle	1968	10.00	20.00	40.00

EPIC

Number	Title (A Side/B Side)	Yr	VG	VG+	NM
❏ EE 22011 [M]	Gabbin' Blues	196?	7.50	15.00	30.00

—Reissue of Okeh recordings

PARAMOUNT

Number	Title (A Side/B Side)	Yr	VG	VG+	NM
❏ PAS-1011 [(2)]	The Last of Big Maybelle	1973	6.25	12.50	25.00

ROJAC

Number	Title (A Side/B Side)	Yr	VG	VG+	NM
❏ RS 123	Saga of the Good Life and Hard Times	196?	10.00	20.00	40.00
❏ R 522 [M]	Got a Brand New Bag	1967	10.00	20.00	40.00
❏ RS 522 [S]	Got a Brand New Bag	1967	10.00	20.00	40.00

SAVOY

Number	Title (A Side/B Side)	Yr	VG	VG+	NM
❏ MG-14005 [M]	Big Maybelle Sings	1957	75.00	150.00	300.00
❏ MG-14011 [M]	Blues, Candy and Big Maybelle	1958	75.00	150.00	300.00

SAVOY JAZZ

Number	Title (A Side/B Side)	Yr	VG	VG+	NM
❏ SJL-1143	Roots of Rock 'n' Roll Vol. 13: Blues & Early Soul	1985	2.50	5.00	10.00
❏ SJL-1168	Blues, Candy and Big Maybelle	1986	2.50	5.00	10.00

—Reissue of 14011

SCEPTER

Number	Title (A Side/B Side)	Yr	VG	VG+	NM
❏ S-522 [M]	The Soul of Big Maybelle	1964	10.00	20.00	40.00
❏ SS-522 [S]	The Soul of Big Maybelle	1964	12.50	25.00	50.00

BIG PUNISHER
12-Inch Singles

FLYTE TYME

Number	Title (A Side/B Side)	Yr	VG	VG+	NM
❏ MCA8P-4267 [DJ]	Makes Me Sweat (4 versions)	1998	3.00	6.00	12.00

—With Beenie Man

LOUD

Number	Title (A Side/B Side)	Yr	VG	VG+	NM
❏ 1979	How We Roll (4 versions)	2001	—	3.00	6.00
❏ LPROLP-4394 [DJ]	It's So Hard (Clean Version) (Main Version)/ (Instrumental) (Clean Acappella)	2000	2.50	5.00	10.00
❏ 65390	Twinz (4 versions)	1998	3.00	6.00	12.00
❏ 65478	Still Not a Player (2 versions)/Twinz (Deep Cover 98)	1998	3.75	7.50	15.00
❏ 65547	You Came Up (Clean Version) (Album Version) (Instrumental)	1998	2.50	5.00	10.00

—Featuring Noreaga

Number	Title (A Side/B Side)	Yr	VG	VG+	NM
❏ 44-79350	It's So Hard (4 versions)/Leatherface (3 versions)	2000	2.00	4.00	8.00

WHITEBOYS

Number	Title (A Side/B Side)	Yr	VG	VG+	NM
❏ TVT 8314	Who Is a Thug (4 versions)/Wanna Be's	1999	2.50	5.00	10.00

—Featuring 6430

Albums

LOUD

Number	Title (A Side/B Side)	Yr	VG	VG+	NM
❏ 1963 [(2)]	Endangered Species	2001	3.00	6.00	12.00
❏ C2 63843 [(2)]	Yeeeah Baby	2000	3.75	7.50	15.00
❏ 67512 [(2)]	Capital Punishment	1998	3.75	7.50	15.00

BILLY AND THE ESSENTIALS
45s

CAMEO

Number	Title (A Side/B Side)	Yr	VG	VG+	NM
❏ 344	Remember Me Baby/The Actor	1965	100.00	200.00	400.00

JAMIE

Number	Title (A Side/B Side)	Yr	VG	VG+	NM
❏ 1229	The Dance Is Over/Steady Girl	1962	7.50	15.00	30.00
❏ 1239	Over the Weekend/Maybe You'll Be There	1962	7.50	15.00	30.00

LANDA

Number	Title (A Side/B Side)	Yr	VG	VG+	NM
❏ 691	The Dance Is Over/Steady Girl	1962	12.50	25.00	50.00

MERCURY

Number	Title (A Side/B Side)	Yr	VG	VG+	NM
❏ 72127	Young at Heart/Lonely Weekend	1963	6.25	12.50	25.00
❏ 72210	Last Dance/Yes Sir, That's My Baby	1963	6.25	12.50	25.00

SMASH

Number	Title (A Side/B Side)	Yr	VG	VG+	NM
❏ 2045	Babalu's Wedding Day/My Way of Saying	1966	3.75	7.50	15.00
❏ 2071	Don't Cry (Sing Along with the Music)/Baby Go Away	1966	3.00	6.00	12.00

SSS INTERNATIONAL

Number	Title (A Side/B Side)	Yr	VG	VG+	NM
❏ 706	I Wrote a Song/Oh What a Feeling	1967	3.00	6.00	12.00

BILLY BOY
45s

COOL

Number	Title (A Side/B Side)	Yr	VG	VG+	NM
❏ 103	I Ain't Got No Money/Hello Stranger	1953	250.00	500.00	1000.

—As "Billy Boy Arnold"

VEE JAY

Number	Title (A Side/B Side)	Yr	VG	VG+	NM
❏ 146	I Wish You Would/I Was Fooled	1955	20.00	40.00	80.00
❏ 171	I Ain't Got You/Don't Stay Out All Night	1956	20.00	40.00	80.00

—Label lists artist as "Billy Boy Arnold"

Number	Title (A Side/B Side)	Yr	VG	VG+	NM
❏ 192	Here's My Picture/You've Got Me Wrong	1956	10.00	20.00	40.00
❏ 238	Kissing at Midnight/My Heart Is Crying	1957	10.00	20.00	40.00
❏ 260	Rockinitis/Prisoner's Plea	1957	10.00	20.00	40.00

VIVID

Number	Title (A Side/B Side)	Yr	VG	VG+	NM
❏ 109	Prisoner's Plea/I Wish You Would	1964	6.25	12.50	25.00

78s

COOL

Number	Title (A Side/B Side)	Yr	VG	VG+	NM
❏ 103	I Ain't Got No Money/Hello Stranger	1953	125.00	250.00	500.00

—As "Billy Boy Arnold"

VEE JAY

Number	Title (A Side/B Side)	Yr	VG	VG+	NM
❏ 146	I Wish You Would/I Was Fooled	1955	10.00	20.00	40.00
❏ 171	I Ain't Got You/Don't Stay Out All Night	1956	10.00	20.00	40.00

—Label lists artist as "Billy Boy Arnold"

Number	Title (A Side/B Side)	Yr	VG	VG+	NM
❏ 192	Here's My Picture/You've Got Me Wrong	1956	10.00	20.00	40.00
❏ 238	Kissing at Midnight/My Heart Is Crying	1957	10.00	20.00	40.00
❏ 260	Rockinitis/Prisoner's Plea	1957	10.00	20.00	40.00

Albums

PRESTIGE

Number	Title (A Side/B Side)	Yr	VG	VG+	NM
❏ PRLP-7389 [M]	Blues on the South Side	1965	7.50	15.00	30.00

—As "Billy Boy Arnold"

Number	Title (A Side/B Side)	Yr	VG	VG+	NM
❏ PRST-7389 [S]	Blues on the South Side	1965	10.00	20.00	40.00

—As "Billy Boy Arnold"

BIRDSONG, EDWIN
12-Inch Singles

PHILADELPHIA INT'L.

Number	Title (A Side/B Side)	Yr	VG	VG+	NM
❏ 2Z8 3671	Phiss-Phizz (8:38)/Goldmine (10:43)	1979	3.75	7.50	15.00
❏ 4Z8 3709 [DJ]	Lollipop (5:59) (2:52)	1979	3.75	7.50	15.00

SALSOUL

Number	Title (A Side/B Side)	Yr	VG	VG+	NM
❏ SG 363 [DJ]	Funtaztik/Win Tonight	1982	2.50	5.00	10.00

45s

PHILADELPHIA INT'L

Number	Title (A Side/B Side)	Yr	VG	VG+	NM
❏ 3659	Kunta Dance Part 1/Kunta Dance Part 2	1978	—	2.00	4.00
❏ 3670	Phiss-Phizz/Goldmine	1979	—	2.00	4.00

POLYDOR

Number	Title (A Side/B Side)	Yr	VG	VG+	NM
❏ 14058	The Old Messiah/Use What You Got	1970	—	2.50	5.00

—With Doug McClure

Number	Title (A Side/B Side)	Yr	VG	VG+	NM
❏ 14095	It Ain't No Fun Being a Welfare Recipient/Uncle Tom Game	1971	—	2.50	5.00
❏ 14118	My Father Preaches That God Is the Father of Us All/The Spirit of Do Do	1972	—	2.50	5.00
❏ 14186	Rising Sign/Rising Sign Climax	1973	—	2.50	5.00
❏ 14192	Rising Sign/Grow Some Flowers, You Will Learn to Love the Rain	1973	—	2.50	5.00
❏ 14224	Turn Around Hate (Communicate)/Down on the Beat	1974	—	2.50	5.00

SALSOUL

Number	Title (A Side/B Side)	Yr	VG	VG+	NM
❏ 2135	Rapper Dapper Snapper/(Instrumental)	1981	—	2.00	4.00
❏ 7019	Funtaztik/Win Tonight	1982	—	2.00	4.00
❏ 7024	She's Wrapped Too Tight (She's a Button Buster)/ (Instrumental)	1982	—	2.00	4.00

Albums

ABC DUNHILL

Number	Title (A Side/B Side)	Yr	VG	VG+	NM
❏ DSX-51036	Can't Stop the Madness	1974	3.75	7.50	15.00

PHILADELPHIA INT'L.

Number	Title (A Side/B Side)	Yr	VG	VG+	NM
❏ JZ 35758	Edwin Birdsong	1978	2.50	5.00	10.00

POLYDOR

Number	Title (A Side/B Side)	Yr	VG	VG+	NM
❏ 24-4071	What It Is	1971	3.00	6.00	12.00
❏ PD-5057	Super Natural	1973	3.00	6.00	12.00

SALSOUL

Number	Title (A Side/B Side)	Yr	VG	VG+	NM
❏ SA-8550	Funktaztic	1981	2.50	5.00	10.00

BIRMINGHAM SAM AND HIS MAGIC GUITAR
See JOHN LEE HOOKER.

BLACK BOX
12-Inch Singles

RCA

Number	Title (A Side/B Side)	Yr	VG	VG+	NM
❏ 2628-1-RD	Everybody Everybody (5 versions)	1990	2.00	4.00	8.00
❏ 2735-1-RD	I Don't Know Anybody Else (6 versions)	1990	2.00	4.00	8.00
❏ 2792-1-RD	Strike It Up (DJ Lelewell Remix 5:00) (Sensitive Mix 3:33) (Trainapella 2:22) (Original Remix 5:58) (Hard Core Remix 3:18)	1991	2.00	4.00	8.00
❏ 62003	Ride On Time (Massive Mix) (LP Version) (Ascot Mix) (Bright On Mix)	1991	2.50	5.00	10.00
❏ 62091	Fantasy (Album Edit)/Greatest Hits Snippets	1991	2.50	5.00	10.00
❏ 62118 [DJ]	Ride On Time (Bright On Mix) (same on both sides)	1992	2.00	4.00	8.00
❏ 62160	Open Your Eyes (Mirko's Mix) (Mirko's Instrumental)/(Valerio's Mix) (Daniele's Mix)	1992	2.50	5.00	10.00

45s

COLLECTABLES

Number	Title (A Side/B Side)	Yr	VG	VG+	NM
❏ 4704	Everybody Everybody (Le Freak Mix)/Ride On Time	1996	—	—	3.00

—First U.S. 45 release of 1990 hit

Number	Title (A Side/B Side)	Yr	VG	VG+	NM
❏ 04776	Strike It Up/I Don't Know Anybody Else	1997	—	—	3.00

—First U.S. 45 release of 1990 hit

Albums

RCA

Number	Title (A Side/B Side)	Yr	VG	VG+	NM
❏ 2221-1-R	Dreamland	1990	3.00	6.00	12.00

BLACK IVORY
45s

BUDDAH

Number	Title (A Side/B Side)	Yr	VG	VG+	NM
❏ 443	Will We Ever Come Together/Warm Inside	1975	—	2.00	4.00
❏ 489	Feel It/Daily News	1975	—	2.00	4.00
❏ 506	Love Won't You Stay/Daily News	1975	—	2.00	4.00
❏ 561	You Mean Everything to Me/White Wind	1977	—	2.00	4.00
❏ 610	Mainline/(B-side unknown)	1979	—	2.00	4.00
❏ 616	You Turned My Whole World Around/(B-side unknown)	1979	—	2.00	4.00

Number	Title (A Side/B Side)	Yr	VG	VG+	NM
KWANZA/WB					
❑ 7800	No One Else Will Do/What Goes Around	1974	—	2.50	5.00
PANORAMIC					
❑ 200	You Are My Lover/(B-side unknown)	1984	—	2.00	4.00
PERCEPTION					
❑ 508	You and I/Our Future	1972	—	3.00	6.00
TODAY					
❑ 1501	Don't Turn Around/I Keep Asking You Questions	1971	—	2.50	5.00
❑ 1508	You and I/Our Future	1972	—	2.50	5.00
❑ 1511	I'll Find A Way (Loneliest Man in Town)/Surrender	1972	—	2.50	5.00
❑ 1516	Time Is Love/Got to Be There	1972	—	2.50	5.00
❑ 1520	Spinning Around/Find the One Who Loves You	1973	—	2.50	5.00
❑ 1524	We Made It/Just Leave Me Some	1973	—	2.50	5.00
Albums					
BUDDAH					
❑ BDS-5644	Feel It	1975	2.50	5.00	10.00
❑ BDS-5658	Black Ivory	1976	2.50	5.00	10.00
❑ BDS-5722	Hangin' Heavy	1979	2.50	5.00	10.00
TODAY					
❑ 1005	Don't Turn Around	1972	3.00	6.00	12.00
❑ 1008	Baby, Won't You Change Your Mind	1972	3.00	6.00	12.00

BLACK ROB
12-Inch Singles
BAD BOY

Number	Title	Yr	VG	VG+	NM
❑ 9210	Lookin' at Us (LP Version) (Instrumental)/Thug Story (LP Version) (Instrumental) (Acapella)	1999	2.50	5.00	10.00
❑ 9228	You Don't Know Me (Club Mix) (Radio Mix) (Instrumental)	1999	2.50	5.00	10.00
❑ 9297	Whoa! (Club Mix) (Instrumental)/(Radio Mix) (Acappella)	2000	2.50	5.00	10.00
❑ 9328	Espacio (Club Mix 4:07) (Radio 3:45) (Instrumental)/Lookin' at Us (Club 4:53) (Radio 4:37) (Instrumental 4:53)	2000	2.50	5.00	10.00
IMMORTAL					
❑ (# unknown)	[DJ]I Dare You (4 versions)/Ain't No Stoppin' (4 versions)	1998	2.50	5.00	10.00
Albums					
BAD BOY					
❑ 73026 [(2)]	Life Story	2000	3.75	7.50	15.00

BLACK SATIN
See THE FIVE SATINS.

BLACK SHEEP (1)
12-Inch Singles
MERCURY

Number	Title	Yr	VG	VG+	NM
❑ PRO 983-1	[DJ]Strobelite Honey (Street Mix) (same on both sides)	1992	3.75	7.50	15.00
❑ PRO 1173-1	[DJ]North, South, East, West (Remix) (Clean Radio Edit)/(Remix Instrumental)/Only If You're Live (Clean)	1994	2.50	5.00	10.00
❑ 856171-1	Without a Doubt (3 versions)/We Boys	1994	2.50	5.00	10.00
❑ 864191-1	Strobelite Honey (Hot Mix) (Dance Radio Mix)/(Def Version) (Momo Beats)	1992	3.00	6.00	12.00
❑ 866087-1	The Choice Is Yours (unknown versions)	1992	3.00	6.00	12.00
Albums					
MERCURY					
❑ 522685-1 [(2)]	Non-Fiction	1994	3.75	7.50	15.00
—May be promo only					
❑ 848368-1	A Wolf in Sheep's Clothing	1991	3.75	7.50	15.00

BLACKBYRDS, THE
Also see DONALD BYRD.
45s
FANTASY

Number	Title	Yr	VG	VG+	NM
❑ 729	Do It, Fluid/Summer Love	1974	—	2.50	5.00
❑ 736	Walking in Rhythm/The Baby	1975	—	2.00	4.00
❑ 747	Flyin' High/All I Ask	1975	—	2.00	4.00
❑ 762	Happy Music/Love So Fine	1976	—	2.00	4.00
❑ 771	Rock Creek Park/Thankful 'Bout Yourself	1976	—	2.00	4.00
❑ 787	Time Is Movin'/Lady	1977	—	2.00	4.00
❑ 794	Party Land/In Life	1977	—	2.00	4.00
❑ 809	Soft and Easy/Something Special	1977	—	2.00	4.00
❑ 819	Supernatural Feeling/Looking Ahead	1978	—	2.00	4.00
❑ 904	What We Have Is Right/What's On Your Mind	1980	—	2.00	4.00
❑ 910	Love Don't Strike Twice/Don't Know What to Say	1981	—	2.00	4.00
❑ 914	Dancin' Dancin'/Lonelies for Your Love	1981	—	2.00	4.00
Albums					
FANTASY					
❑ FPM-4004 [Q]	Flying Start	1975	6.25	12.50	25.00
❑ F-9444	The Blackbyrds	1974	3.75	7.50	15.00
❑ F-9472	Flying Start	1974	3.75	7.50	15.00
❑ F-9490	City Life	1975	3.75	7.50	15.00
❑ F-9518	Unfinished Business	1976	3.75	7.50	15.00
❑ F-9535	Action	1977	3.00	6.00	12.00
❑ F-9570	Night Grooves	1978	3.00	6.00	12.00
❑ F-9602	Better Days	1980	3.00	6.00	12.00

BLACKGIRL
12-Inch Singles
RCA

Number	Title	Yr	VG	VG+	NM
❑ 62664	Krazy (Radio Edit) (LP Version) (Acapella) (Instrumental)	1994	2.50	5.00	10.00
❑ 62882	90's Girl (5 versions)	1994	2.50	5.00	10.00
❑ 64275	Let's Do It Again (LP Version) (Instrumental) (Radio) (Acapella)	1995	2.50	5.00	10.00
45s					
RCA					
❑ 64227	Give Love on Christmas Day/Where Did We Go Wrong	1994	—	2.00	4.00

BLACKSTREET
12-Inch Singles
INTERSCOPE

Number	Title	Yr	VG	VG+	NM
❑ INT8P-6481	[DJ]Take Me There (Album Version) (Want U Back Mix) (Radio Version)	1998	2.50	5.00	10.00
—With Mya featuring Mase & Blinky Blink					
❑ INT8P-6495	[DJ]Take Me There (Want U Back Mix) (Album Version) (Want U Back Instrumental) (Want U Back No Rap Version)	1998	2.50	5.00	10.00
—With Mya featuring Mase & Blinky Blink					
❑ INT8P-6524	[DJ]Girlfriend/Boyfriend (6 versions)	1999	3.00	6.00	12.00
—With Janet (Jackson)					
❑ INT8P-6588	[DJ]Think About You (Tunnel Clean) (All I Do) (Quiet Storm) (Club Mix) (Tunnel Instrumental) (All I Do Instrumental) (Quiet Storm Instrumental) (Club Mix Instrumental)	1999	3.75	7.50	15.00
❑ INT8P-6632	[DJ]Think About You (Album Version)/(Album Instrumental)	1999	2.50	5.00	10.00
❑ 95012	Fix (5 versions)/The Man Behind the Music	1997	2.50	5.00	10.00
—Featuring Ol' Dirty Bastard and Slash					
❑ 95043	Girlfriend/Boyfriend (3 versions)/Take Me There (3 versions)	1999	2.50	5.00	10.00
—With Janet (Jackson)					
❑ 95769	Joy (6 versions)	1995	3.75	7.50	15.00
❑ 95805	Before I Let You Go (7 versions)	1994	3.75	7.50	15.00
❑ 95863	Booti Call (6 versions)/I Like the Way You Work (4 versions)	1994	3.75	7.50	15.00
MCA					
❑ MCA8P-2590	[DJ]Baby Be Mine (Vocal) (Percapella) (Dub 1)/(Instrumental) (Bonus Beats) (Acapella)	1993	3.75	7.50	15.00
—Featuring Teddy Riley					
❑ 54634	Baby Be Mine (12" Remix) (Hip Hop Mix) (Club Mix)	1993	3.00	6.00	12.00
—Featuring Teddy Riley					
Albums					
INTERSCOPE					
❑ INT-90071 [(2)]	Another Level	1996	5.00	10.00	20.00
❑ INT2-90274 [(2)]	Finally	1999	3.75	7.50	15.00

BLACKWELL, OTIS
45s
ATLANTIC

Number	Title	Yr	VG	VG+	NM
❑ 1165	Make Ready for Love/When You're Around	1957	10.00	20.00	40.00
❑ 1178	Turtle Dove/What a Coincidence	1958	10.00	20.00	40.00
CUB					
❑ 9092	Jeannie's Wedding/I'd Rather Kiss You Than Eat	1961	5.00	10.00	20.00
❑ 9107	Sister Twister/Ga Ga	1962	5.00	10.00	20.00
DATE					
❑ 1006	Don't Run Away/Handle with Care	1958	7.50	15.00	30.00
EPIC					
❑ 10654	Just Keep It Up/It's All Over Me	1970	6.25	12.50	25.00
GROOVE					
❑ 0034	Oh, What a Babe/Here I Am	1954	10.00	20.00	40.00
JAY-DEE					
❑ 784	Daddy Rolling Stone/Tears! Tears! Tears!	1953	12.50	25.00	50.00
❑ 787	You're My Love/Bartender Fill It Up Again	1954	12.50	25.00	50.00
❑ 791	On That Power Line/Don't You Know How I Love You	1954	12.50	25.00	50.00
❑ 792	I'm Standing at the Doorway/Nobody Met the Train	1954	12.50	25.00	50.00
❑ 794	My Josephine/Ain't Got No Time	1954	12.50	25.00	50.00
❑ 798	Go Away Mr. Blues/I'm Comin' Back Baby	1955	12.50	25.00	50.00
❑ 802	You Move Me Baby/My Poor Broken Heart	1955	12.50	25.00	50.00
❑ 808	Oh What a Wonderful Time/Let the Daddy Hold You	1955	12.50	25.00	50.00
MGM					
❑ 13090	Kiss Away/Grandaddy of Them All	1962	5.00	10.00	20.00
RCA VICTOR					
❑ 47-5069	Wake You Fool/Please Help Me Find	1952	12.50	25.00	50.00
❑ 47-5225	The Fool That I Be/Number 000	1953	12.50	25.00	50.00
Albums					
DAVIS					
❑ 109 [M]	Singin' the Blues	1956	125.00	250.00	500.00
INNER CITY					
❑ 1032	These Are My Songs	1977	5.00	10.00	20.00

BLAND, BOBBY
Includes records by "Bobby 'Blue' Bland."
12-Inch Singles
MCA

Number	Title	Yr	VG	VG+	NM
❑ L33-1835	[DJ]I Feel Good, I Feel Fine/Tit for Tat/Come Fly with Me/Love to See You Smile	1979	3.75	7.50	15.00
45s					
ABC					
❑ 12105	Yolanda/When You Come to the End of Your Road	1975	—	2.00	4.00

Number	Title (A Side/B Side)	Yr	VG	VG+	NM
❑ 12134	I Take It On Home/You've Never Been This Far Before	1975	—	2.00	4.00
❑ 12156	Today I Started Loving You Again/Too Far Gone	1976	—	2.00	4.00
❑ 12189	It Ain't the Real Thing/Who's Foolin' Who	1976	—	2.00	4.00
❑ 12280	The Soul of a Man/If I Weren't a Gambler	1977	—	2.00	4.00
❑ 12330	Sittin' on a Poor Man's Throne/I Intend to Take Your Place	1978	—	2.00	4.00
❑ 12360	Love to See You Smile/I'm Just Your Man	1978	—	2.00	4.00
❑ 12405	Come Fly with Me/Ain't God Something	1978	—	2.00	4.00
ABC DUNHILL					
❑ 4369	This Time I'm Gone for Good/Where Baby Went	1973	—	2.50	5.00
❑ 4379	Goin' Down Slow/Up and Down World	1974	—	2.50	5.00
❑ 15003	Ain't No Love in the Heart of the City/Twenty-Four Hour Blues	1974	—	2.50	5.00
❑ 15015	I Wouldn't Treat a Dog (The Way You Treated Me)/I Ain't Gonna Be the First to Cry	1974	—	2.50	5.00
DUKE					
❑ 105	Lovin' Blues/I.O.U. Blues	1952	75.00	150.00	300.00
❑ 115	Army Blues/No Blow, No Show	1953	50.00	100.00	200.00
❑ 141	Time Out/It's My Life Baby	1955	15.00	30.00	60.00
❑ 146	You or None/Woke Up Screaming	1955	15.00	30.00	60.00
❑ 153	I Can't Put You Down/You've Got Bad Intentions	1956	12.50	25.00	50.00
❑ 160	I Learned My Lesson/I Don't Believe	1956	10.00	20.00	40.00
❑ 160	I Learned My Lesson/Lead Us On	1956	10.00	20.00	40.00
❑ 167	Don't Want No Woman/I Smell Trouble	1957	7.50	15.00	30.00
❑ 170	Farther Up the Road/Sometime Tomorrow	1957	7.50	15.00	30.00
❑ 182	Teach Me/Bobby's Blues	1957	6.25	12.50	25.00
❑ 185	You Got Me Where You Want Me/Loan a Helping Hand	1958	6.25	12.50	25.00
❑ 196	Little Boy Blue/Last Night	1958	6.25	12.50	25.00
❑ 300	You Did Me Wrong/I Lost Sight of the World	1959	6.25	12.50	25.00
❑ 303	Wishing Well/I'm Not Ashamed	1959	6.25	12.50	25.00
❑ 310	Is It Real/Someday	1959	6.25	12.50	25.00
❑ 314	I'll Take Care of You/That's Why	1959	6.25	12.50	25.00
❑ 318	Lead Me On/Hold Me Tenderly	1960	6.25	12.50	25.00
❑ 327	Cry Cry Cry/I've Been Wrong So Long	1960	6.25	12.50	25.00
❑ 332	I Pity the Fool/Close to You	1961	5.00	10.00	20.00
❑ 336	Don't Cry No More/How Does a Cheating Woman Feel	1961	5.00	10.00	20.00
❑ 338	Ain't That Loving You/Jelly, Jelly, Jelly	1961	5.00	10.00	20.00
❑ 340	Don't Cry No More/Saint James Infirmary	1961	5.00	10.00	20.00
❑ 344	Turn On Your Love Light/You're the One (That I Need)	1961	5.00	10.00	20.00
❑ 347	Who Will the Next Fool Be/Blue Moon	1962	5.00	10.00	20.00
❑ 352	Yield Not to Temptation/How Does a Cheating Woman Feel	1962	5.00	10.00	20.00
❑ 355	Stormy Monday Blues/Your Friends	1962	5.00	10.00	20.00
❑ 360	That's the Way Love Is/Call On Me	1962	5.00	10.00	20.00
❑ 366	Sometimes You Gotta Cry a Little/You're Worth It All	1963	3.75	7.50	15.00
❑ 369	Ain't It a Good Thing/Queen for a Day	1963	3.75	7.50	15.00
❑ 370	The Feeling Is Gone/I Can't Stop Singing	1963	3.75	7.50	15.00
❑ 375	Ain't Nothing You Can Do/Honey Child	1964	3.75	7.50	15.00
❑ 377	Share Your Love with Me/After It's Too Late	1964	2.50	5.00	10.00
❑ 383	Ain't Doing Too Bad (Part 1)/Ain't Doing Too Bad (Part 2)	1964	2.50	5.00	10.00
❑ 385	These Hands (Small But Mighty)/Today	1965	2.50	5.00	10.00
❑ 386	Blind Man/Black Night	1965	2.50	5.00	10.00
❑ 390	Dust Got in Daddy's Eyes/Ain't No Telling	1965	2.50	5.00	10.00
❑ 393	I'm Too Far Gone (To Turn Around)/If You Could Read My Mind	1965	2.50	5.00	10.00
❑ 402	Good Time Charlie/Good Time Charlie (Part 2)	1966	2.00	4.00	8.00
❑ 407	Poverty/Building a Fire with Hair	1966	2.00	4.00	8.00
❑ 412	Back in the Same Old Bag Again/I Ain't Myself Anymore	1966	2.00	4.00	8.00
❑ 416	You're All I Need/Deep in My Soul	1967	2.00	4.00	8.00
❑ 421	That Did It/Getting Used to the Blues	1967	2.00	4.00	8.00
❑ 426	A Touch of the Blues/Shoes	1967	2.00	4.00	8.00
❑ 432	Driftin' Blues/You Could Read My Mind	1968	2.00	4.00	8.00
❑ 433	Honey Child/A Piece of Gold	1968	2.00	4.00	8.00
❑ 435	Save Your Love for Me/Share Your Love with Me	1968	2.00	4.00	8.00
❑ 440	Rockin' in the Same Old Boat/Wouldn't You Rather Have Me	1968	2.00	4.00	8.00
❑ 447	Gotta Get to Know You/Baby I'm On My Way	1969	2.00	4.00	8.00
❑ 449	Chains of Love/Ask Me 'Bout Nothing (But the Blues)	1969	2.00	4.00	8.00
❑ 458	If You've Got a Heart/Sad Feeling	1970	2.00	4.00	8.00
❑ 460	Lover with a Reputation/If Love Ruled the World	1970	2.00	4.00	8.00
❑ 464	Keep On Loving Me (You'll See the Change)/I Just Got to Forget About You	1970	2.00	4.00	8.00
❑ 466	I'm Sorry/Yum Yum Tree	1971	2.00	4.00	8.00
❑ 471	Shape Up or Ship Out/The Love That We Share (Is True)	1971	2.00	4.00	8.00
❑ 472	Do What You Set Out to Do/Ain't Nothing You Can Do	1972	2.00	4.00	8.00
❑ 477	I'm So Tired/If You Could Read My Mind	1972	2.00	4.00	8.00
❑ 480	That's All There Is/I Don't Want Another Mountain to Climb	1973	2.00	4.00	8.00
KENT					
❑ 378	Love You Baby/Drifting	1962	2.50	5.00	10.00
—With Ike Turner					
MALACO					
❑ 2122	Members Only/I Just Got to Know	1985	—	—	3.00
❑ 2126	Can We Make Love Tonight/In the Ghetto	1986	—	—	3.00
❑ 2133	Angel/I Hear You Thinkin'	1986	—	—	3.00

Number	Title (A Side/B Side)	Yr	VG	VG+	NM
MCA					
❑ 41140	Tit for Tat/Come Fly with Me	1979	—	2.00	4.00
❑ 41197	Soon as the Weather Breaks/To Be Friends	1980	—	2.00	4.00
❑ 51068	You'd Be a Millionaire/Swat Vibrator	1981	—	—	3.00
❑ 51181	What a Difference A Day Makes/Givin' Up the Streets for Love	1982	—	—	3.00
❑ 52085	Recess in Heaven/Exactly, Where It's At	1982	—	—	3.00
❑ 52136	Here We Go Again/You're About to Win	1982	—	—	3.00
❑ 52180	Is This the Blues/You're About to Win	1983	—	—	3.00
❑ 52270	If It Ain't One Thing/Tell Mr. Bland	1983	—	—	3.00
❑ 52436	Looking Back/You Got Me Loving You	1984	—	—	3.00
❑ 52482	Get Real Clean/It's Too Bad	1984	—	—	3.00
❑ 52508	You Are My Christmas/New Merry Christmas Baby	1984	—	—	3.00
WAND					
❑ 1102	Honey, You've Been On My Mind/You've Got Time	1965	3.75	7.50	15.00
78s					
CHESS					
❑ 1489	Crying/A Letter from a Trench in Korea	1951	37.50	75.00	150.00
—As "Robert Bland"					
DUKE					
❑ 105	Lovin' Blues/I.O.U. Blues	1952	15.00	30.00	60.00
❑ 115	Army Blues/No Blow, No Show	1953	12.50	25.00	50.00
❑ 141	Time Out/It's My Life Baby	1955	10.00	20.00	40.00
❑ 146	You or None/Woke Up Screaming	1955	7.50	15.00	30.00
❑ 153	I Can't Put You Down/You've Got Bad Intentions	1956	7.50	15.00	30.00
❑ 160	I Learned My Lesson/I Don't Believe	1956	7.50	15.00	30.00
❑ 160	I Learned My Lesson/Lead Us On	1956	7.50	15.00	30.00
❑ 167	Don't Want No Woman/I Smell Trouble	1957	7.50	15.00	30.00
❑ 170	Farther Up the Road/Sometime Tomorrow	1957	7.50	15.00	30.00
❑ 182	Teach Me/Bobby's Blues	1957	7.50	15.00	30.00
❑ 185	You Got Me Where You Want Me/Loan a Helping Hand	1958	7.50	15.00	30.00
❑ 196	Little Boy Blue/Last Night	1958	10.00	20.00	40.00
❑ 300	You Did Me Wrong/I Lost Sight of the World	1959	25.00	50.00	100.00
❑ 303	Wishing Well/I'm Not Ashamed	1959	62.50	125.00	250.00
MODERN					
❑ 848	Crying All Night Long/Dry Up Baby	1952	50.00	100.00	200.00
—As "Robert Bland"					
❑ 868	Good Lovin'/Drifting from Town to Town	1952	50.00	100.00	200.00
—As "Robert Bland"					
Albums					
ABC					
❑ D-895	Get On Down with Bobby Bland	1975	3.00	6.00	12.00
❑ AB-1018	Reflections in Blue	1977	2.50	5.00	10.00
❑ AA-1075	Come Fly with Me	1978	2.50	5.00	10.00
ABC DUKE					
❑ DLPS-74	Two Steps from the Blues	197?	3.00	6.00	12.00
❑ DLP-75	Here's the Man!!!	1974	3.00	6.00	12.00
❑ DLP-77	Call On Me/That's the Way Love Is	1974	3.00	6.00	12.00
❑ DLP-78	Ain't Nothing You Can Do	1974	3.00	6.00	12.00
❑ DLP-79	The Soul of the Man	1974	3.00	6.00	12.00
❑ DLP-84	The Best of Bobby Bland	1974	3.00	6.00	12.00
❑ DLP-86	The Best of Bobby Bland, Volume 2	1974	3.00	6.00	12.00
❑ DLP-88	A Touch of the Blues	1974	3.00	6.00	12.00
❑ DLP-89	Spotlighting the Man	1974	3.00	6.00	12.00
❑ DLP 92-2 [(2)]	Introspective of the Early Years	1974	5.00	10.00	20.00
ABC DUNHILL					
❑ DSX-50163	His California Album	1973	3.75	7.50	15.00
❑ DSX-50169	Dreamer	1974	3.75	7.50	15.00
BLUESWAY					
❑ BLS-6065	Call On Me	197?	3.75	7.50	15.00
DUKE					
❑ DLP-74 [M]	Two Steps from the Blues	1961	62.50	125.00	250.00
—Purple and yellow label					
❑ DLP-74 [M]	Two Steps from the Blues	1962	62.50	125.00	250.00
—Orange label, red vinyl					
❑ DLP-74 [M]	Two Steps from the Blues	1962	25.00	50.00	100.00
—Orange label, black vinyl					
❑ DLPS-74 [R]	Two Steps from the Blues	196?	15.00	30.00	60.00
❑ DLP-75 [M]	Here's the Man!!!	1962	50.00	100.00	200.00
—Purple and yellow label					
❑ DLP-75 [M]	Here's the Man!!!	1962	25.00	50.00	100.00
—Orange label					
❑ DLPS-75 [S]	Here's the Man!!!	1962	50.00	100.00	200.00
—With spoken intro to "36-22-36"					
❑ DLPS-75 [S]	Here's the Man!!!	196?	25.00	50.00	100.00
—Without spoken intro to "36-22-36"					
❑ DLP-77 [M]	Call On Me/That's the Way Love Is	1963	25.00	50.00	100.00
❑ DLPS-77 [S]	Call On Me/That's the Way Love Is	1963	37.50	75.00	150.00
❑ DLP-78 [M]	Ain't Nothing You Can Do	1964	20.00	40.00	80.00
❑ DLPS-78 [S]	Ain't Nothing You Can Do	1964	30.00	60.00	120.00
❑ DLP-79 [M]	The Soul of the Man	1966	20.00	40.00	80.00
❑ DLPS-79 [S]	The Soul of the Man	1966	30.00	60.00	120.00
❑ DLP-84 [M]	The Best of Bobby Bland	1967	5.00	10.00	20.00
❑ DLPS-84 [P]	The Best of Bobby Bland	1967	6.25	12.50	25.00
❑ DLP-86 [M]	The Best of Bobby Bland, Volume 2	1968	6.25	12.50	25.00
❑ DLPS-86 [P]	The Best of Bobby Bland, Volume 2	1968	5.00	10.00	20.00
❑ DLP-88 [M]	A Touch of the Blues	1968	6.25	12.50	25.00
❑ DLPS-88 [S]	A Touch of the Blues	1968	5.00	10.00	20.00
❑ DLPS-89	Spotlighting the Man	1969	5.00	10.00	20.00
❑ DLPS-90	If Loving You Is Wrong	1970	5.00	10.00	20.00

Number	Title (A Side/B Side)	Yr	VG	VG+	NM
MCA					
❑ 3157	I Feel Good, I Feel Fine	1979	2.50	5.00	10.00
❑ 4172 [(2)]	Introspective of the Early Years	198?	2.50	5.00	10.00
—Reissue of Duke 92					
❑ 5145	Sweet Vibrations	1980	2.50	5.00	10.00
❑ 5233	Try Me, I'm Real	1981	2.50	5.00	10.00
❑ 5297	Here We Go Again	1982	2.50	5.00	10.00
❑ 5425	Tell Mr. Bland	1983	2.50	5.00	10.00
❑ 5503	You've Got Me Loving You	1984	2.50	5.00	10.00
❑ 27013	The Best of Bobby Bland	198?	2.00	4.00	8.00
—Reissue of Duke 84					
❑ 27036	Two Steps from the Blues	198?	2.00	4.00	8.00
—Reissue of Duke 74					
❑ 27038	Here's the Man!!!	198?	2.00	4.00	8.00
—Reissue of Duke 75					
❑ 27040	Ain't Nothing You Can Do	198?	2.00	4.00	8.00
—Reissue of Duke 78					
❑ 27041	The Soul of the Man	1984	2.00	4.00	8.00
—Reissue of Duke 79					
❑ 27042	Call On Me/That's the Way Love Is	1984	2.00	4.00	8.00
—Reissue of Duke 77					
❑ 27043	Reflections in Blue	1984	2.00	4.00	8.00
—Reissue of ABC 1018					
❑ 27044	Come Fly with Me	1984	2.00	4.00	8.00
—Reissue of ABC 1075					
❑ 27045	The Best of Bobby Bland, Volume 2	1984	2.00	4.00	8.00
—Reissue of Duke 86					
❑ 27047	A Touch of the Blues	1984	2.00	4.00	8.00
—Reissue of Duke 88					
❑ 27048	Spotlighting the Man	1984	2.00	4.00	8.00
—Reissue of Duke 89					
❑ 27073	I Feel Good, I Feel Fine	1985	2.00	4.00	8.00
—Reissue of MCA 3157					
❑ 27076	Sweet Vibrations	198?	2.00	4.00	8.00
—Reissue of 5145					

BLAND, BOBBY, AND B.B. KING
45s

Number	Title (A Side/B Side)	Yr	VG	VG+	NM
ABC IMPULSE					
❑ 31006	Let the Good Times Roll/Strange Things	1976	—	2.00	4.00
❑ 31009	Everyday I Have the Blues/The Thrill Is Gone	1976	—	2.00	4.00
Albums					
ABC DUNHILL					
❑ DSY-50190 [(2)]	Together for the First Time...Live	1974	3.75	7.50	15.00
ABC IMPULSE!					
❑ 9317	Together Again...Live	1976	3.00	6.00	12.00
COMMAND					
❑ CQDY-40012 [(2) Q]	Together for the First Time...Live	1974	6.25	12.50	25.00
MCA					
❑ 4160 [(2)]	Together for the First Time...Live	198?	2.50	5.00	10.00
—Reissue of ABC Dunhill 50190					
❑ 27012	Together Again...Live	198?	2.00	4.00	8.00
—Reissue of ABC Impulse! 9317					

BLIGE, MARY J.
12-Inch Singles

Number	Title (A Side/B Side)	Yr	VG	VG+	NM
ARISTA					
❑ 2989 [DJ]	Not Gon' Cry/(Instrumental)	1996	2.50	5.00	10.00
MCA					
❑ MCA8P-4358 [DJ]	All That I Can Say (Radio Edit) (Instrumental) (LP Version)	1999	2.50	5.00	10.00
❑ MCA8P-4458 [DJ]	Deep Inside (5 versions)	1999	2.50	5.00	10.00
❑ MCA8P-4472 [(2) DJ]	Deep Inside (3 versions)/Let No Man Put Asunder (3 versions)/As (3 versions)	1999	5.00	10.00	20.00
❑ 25032 [DJ]	Give Me You (Nino Remix Edit) (Nino Extended Remix) (Radio Edit) (Instrumental)	2000	3.00	6.00	12.00
❑ 25127 [DJ]	Your Child (Radio Edit) (LP Version) (Acapella) (Instrumental)	2000	2.50	5.00	10.00
❑ 25265 [DJ]	No Happy Holidays (Intro) (Radio Edit) (LP Version)	2000	2.50	5.00	10.00
❑ MCAR-25619-1 [(2) DJ]	No More Drama (8 versions)	2002	5.00	10.00	20.00
❑ MCAR-25663-1 [DJ]	No More Drama (4 versions)	2002	2.50	5.00	10.00
❑ 155708	Give Me You (unknown versions)	2000	—	3.00	6.00
❑ 155859	Family Affair (4 versions)	2001	2.00	4.00	8.00
UPTOWN					
❑ L33-2097 [DJ]	You Remind Me (4 versions)	1992	2.50	5.00	10.00
❑ UPT8P-2308 [DJ]	Real Love (unknown versions)	1992	2.00	4.00	8.00
❑ UPT8P-3394 [DJ]	You Bring Me Joy (E-Smoove's Joyous Club Mix) (E-Smoove's Joyous Club Dub)	1995	3.00	6.00	12.00
❑ UPT8P-3397 [DJ]	You Bring Me Joy (E-Smoove's Soul Mix) (LP Version) (E-Smoove's Dub) (E-Smoove's Funk Mix)	1995	3.00	6.00	12.00
❑ 54447	You Remind Me (Daddy Hip Hop) (Ad's Radio) (Bentley's)	1992	3.00	6.00	12.00
❑ 54456	Real Love (Hip-Hop Mix) (Album Version) (Hip-Hop Club Mix) (Acapella Version)	1992	2.50	5.00	10.00
❑ 54525	Reminisce (Bad Boy Remix) (Bad Boy Instrumental) (Audio 2 Remix) (Milky Mix) (Stringapella)	1992	2.50	5.00	10.00
❑ 54640	Love No Limit (Puff Daddy Mix) (Jazz) (Hip Hop)	1993	2.50	5.00	10.00
❑ 54702	You Don't Have to Worry (Album Radio Remix) (Radio Remix w/Clean Rap) (Remix)	1993	3.00	6.00	12.00
❑ 54724	I Don't Want to Do Anything (Hip Hop Radio Version) (Quiet Storm Version)	1993	3.00	6.00	12.00
—With K-Ci Hailey					

Number	Title (A Side/B Side)	Yr	VG	VG+	NM
❑ 54841	My Love (Hip Hop with Rap) (TR and Mary Mix) (Acapella)	1994	—	—	—
❑ 54928	Be Happy (3 versions)	1994	2.00	4.00	8.00
45s					
ARISTA					
❑ 12957	Not Gon' Cry/My Funny Valentine	1996	—	—	3.00
—B-side by Chaka Khan					
UPTOWN					
❑ 54455	Real Love/(Hip-Hop Version)	1992	—	—	3.00
❑ 54526	Reminisce/(Instrumental)	1992	—	—	3.00
❑ 54586	Sweet Thing/Slow Down	1993	—	2.00	4.00
❑ 54639	Love No Limit/(Instrumental)	1993	—	2.00	4.00
Albums					
MCA					
❑ 11606 [(2)]	Share My World	1997	3.75	7.50	15.00
❑ 111929 [(2)]	Mary	1999	3.75	7.50	15.00
❑ 112616 [(2)]	No More Drama	2001	3.75	7.50	15.00
—Original edition					
❑ 112808 [(2)]	No More Drama (2002)	2002	3.00	6.00	12.00
—Revised edition					
UPTOWN					
❑ 10681	What's the 411?	1992	3.75	7.50	15.00
❑ 11156	My Life	1994	3.75	7.50	15.00

BLOODSTONE
12-Inch Singles

Number	Title (A Side/B Side)	Yr	VG	VG+	NM
MOTOWN					
❑ M00017D1	Just Wanna Get the Feel of It (Vocal) (Instrumental)	1979	2.00	4.00	8.00
T-NECK					
❑ AS 1888 [DJ]	Instant Love (5:23) (same on both sides)	1984	2.00	4.00	8.00
❑ 4Z9-02863	We Go a Long Way Back/Nite Time Fun	1982	2.00	4.00	8.00
❑ 4Z9-03403	My Love Grows Stronger (Part 1 6:16) (Part 2 4:50)	1982	2.50	5.00	10.00
❑ 4Z9-05085	Bloodstone's Party (5:00) (7:03) (1:30)	1984	2.00	4.00	8.00
45s					
EPIC					
❑ 50437	Got to Find Myself Another Baby/Weeping Willow Tree	1977	—	2.00	4.00
LONDON					
❑ 1038	Girl/Judy, Judy	1972	—	2.50	5.00
❑ 1042	That's the Way We Make Our Music/This Thing Is Heavy	1972	—	2.50	5.00
❑ 1046	Natural High/Peter's Jones	1973	—	2.50	5.00
❑ 1051	Never Let You Go/You Know We've Learned	1973	—	2.50	5.00
❑ 1052	Outside Woman/Dumb Dude	1974	—	2.50	5.00
❑ 1055	That's Not How It Goes/Everybody Needs Love	1974	—	2.50	5.00
❑ 1059	I Believe You Now/I Need Time	1974	—	2.50	5.00
❑ 1061	My Little Lady/Loving You Is Just a Pastime	1975	—	2.50	5.00
❑ 1062	Give Me Your Heart/Something's Missing	1975	—	2.50	5.00
❑ 1062 [PS]	Give Me Your Heart/Something's Missing	1975	2.50	5.00	10.00
❑ 1064	Do You Wanna Do a Thing/Save Me	1976	—	2.50	5.00
❑ 1067	Just Like in the Movies/Little Linda	1976	—	2.50	5.00
MOTOWN					
❑ 1458	Just Wanna Get the Feel of It/It's Been a Long Time	1978	—	2.00	4.00
T-NECK					
❑ ZS5-02825	We Go a Long Way Back/Nite Time Fun	1982	—	2.00	4.00
❑ ZS5-03049	Go On and Cry/(Instrumental)	1982	—	2.00	4.00
❑ ZS4-03394	My Love Grows Stronger (Part 1)/(Part 2)	1982	—	2.00	4.00
❑ ZS4-04465	Instant Love/It Feels So Good	1984	—	2.00	4.00
❑ ZS4-04592	Bloodstone's Party/Feel the Heat	1984	—	2.00	4.00
Albums					
LONDON					
❑ XPS 620	Natural High	1973	5.00	10.00	20.00
❑ XPS 634	Unreal	1973	5.00	10.00	20.00
❑ APS 647	I Need Time	1974	5.00	10.00	20.00
❑ PS 654	Riddle of the Sphinx	1975	3.75	7.50	15.00
❑ PS 671	Do a Thing?	1976	3.75	7.50	15.00
MOTOWN					
❑ M7-909	Don't Stop!	1978	3.00	6.00	12.00
T-NECK					
❑ FZ 38115	We Go a Long Way Back	1982	2.50	5.00	10.00
❑ FZ 39146	Bloodstone's Party	1984	2.50	5.00	10.00
❑ PZ 40016	Greatest Hits	1985	2.00	4.00	8.00
❑ PZ 40042	Lullaby of Broadway	1985	2.00	4.00	8.00

BLOSSOMS, THE
45s

Number	Title (A Side/B Side)	Yr	VG	VG+	NM
BELL					
❑ 780	You've Lost That Lovin' Feeling/Something So Wrong	1969	2.00	4.00	8.00
❑ 797	(You're My) Soul and Inspiration/Stand By	1969	2.00	4.00	8.00
❑ 857	I Ain't Got to Love Nobody Else/Don't Take Your Love	1970	2.00	4.00	8.00
❑ 937	One Step Away/Break Your Promise	1970	2.00	4.00	8.00
CAPITOL					
❑ F3822	Move On/He Promised Me	1957	7.50	15.00	30.00
❑ F3878	Little Louie/Have Faith in Me	1958	6.25	12.50	25.00
❑ F4072	Baby Daddy-O/No Other Love	1958	6.25	12.50	25.00
CHALLENGE					
❑ 9109	Son-In-Law/I'll Wait	1961	5.00	10.00	20.00
—B-side by the Coeds					

Number	Title (A Side/B Side)	Yr	VG	VG+	NM
❑ 9122	Hard to Get/Write Me a Letter	1961	5.00	10.00	20.00
❑ 9138	The Search Is Over/Big Talking Jim	1962	5.00	10.00	20.00
EEOC					
❑ 8172	Things Are Changing (same on both sides)	1965	37.50	75.00	150.00
❑ 8172 [PS]	Things Are Changing (same on both sides)	1965	37.50	75.00	150.00
—Promotional item for the Equal Employment Opportunity Commission					
EPIC					
❑ 50434	There's No Greater Love (Than Mine for You My Love)/Walking on Air	1977	—	2.50	5.00
LION					
❑ 108	Touchdown/It's All Up to You	1972	—	3.00	6.00
❑ 125	Grandma's Hands/Cherish What Is Dear to You	1972	—	3.00	6.00
MGM					
❑ 13964	Tweedlee Dee/You Got Me Hummin'	1968	2.50	5.00	10.00
ODE					
❑ 101	Stoney End/Wonderful	1967	3.00	6.00	12.00
❑ 106	Cry Like a Baby/Wonderful	1968	3.00	6.00	12.00
❑ 125	Stoney End/Wonderful	1969	3.00	6.00	12.00
OKEH					
❑ 7162	I'm in Love/What Makes Love	1963	5.00	10.00	20.00
REPRISE					
❑ 0436	Good, Good Lovin'/That's When the Tears Start	1965	3.75	7.50	15.00
❑ 0475	Lover Boy/My Love, Come Home	1966	3.75	7.50	15.00
❑ 0522	Let Your Love Shine on Me/Deep Into My Heart	1966	3.75	7.50	15.00
❑ 0639	Deep Into My Heart/Good, Good Lovin'	1967	3.75	7.50	15.00
Albums					
LION					
❑ 1007	Shockwave	1972	3.75	7.50	15.00

BLOW, KURTIS
12-Inch Singles
MERCURY

Number	Title (A Side/B Side)	Yr	VG	VG+	NM
❑ MK 213 [DJ]	Tough (2 versions)	1982	3.00	6.00	12.00
❑ PRO 476-1 [DJ]	The Bronx (3 versions)/Unity Party Jam	1987	2.50	5.00	10.00
❑ MDS-4009	Christmas Rappin'/Christmas Rappin' (Do It Yourself)	1979	5.00	10.00	20.00
—Original issues came in a company sleeve					
❑ MDS-4009	Christmas Rappin'/Christmas Rappin' (Do It Yourself)	1981	5.00	10.00	20.00
—Reissues came in a picture cover					
❑ MDS-4010	The Breaks (Vocal 7:14) (Instrumental 5:52)	1980	5.00	10.00	20.00
❑ MDS-4012	Starlife/(B-side unknown)	1981	3.00	6.00	12.00
❑ MDS-4020	Tough (Vocal) (Instrumental)	1982	3.75	7.50	15.00
❑ 562559-1	Christmas Rappin'/Christmas Rappin' (Do It Yourself Version)	1999	—	3.00	6.00
—20th anniversary reissue					
❑ 812688-1	Party Time (2 versions?)	1983	3.00	6.00	12.00
❑ 814484-1	Nervous (Vocal) (Instrumental)	1983	3.00	6.00	12.00
❑ 870328-1	Back by Popular Demand (4 versions)	1988	2.50	5.00	10.00
❑ 870992-1	Only the Strong Survive (3 versions)/Still on the Scene (2 versions)	1988	2.50	5.00	10.00
❑ 880170-1	8 Million Stories/A.J. Scratch	1984	3.75	7.50	15.00
❑ 884079-1	America/A.J. Meets Davy DMX	1985	3.00	6.00	12.00
❑ 884269-1	If I Ruled the World (3 versions)	1985	2.50	5.00	10.00
❑ 884547-1	A.J. Is Cool (5:51) (3:53)/Respect to the King	1986	3.75	7.50	15.00
❑ 888004-1	I'm Chillin' (3 versions)/Don't Cha Feel Like Making Love	1986	3.00	6.00	12.00
❑ 888282-1	The Bronx (3 versions)/Unity Party Jam	1987	2.00	4.00	8.00
45s					
MERCURY					
❑ DJ 562 [DJ]	Christmas Rappin' Part 1/Christmas Rappin' Part 2	1979	2.50	5.00	10.00
❑ 76075	The Breaks (Part 1)/(Part 2)	1980	—	3.00	6.00
❑ 76083	Throughout Your Years (Part 1)/(Part 2)	1980	—	3.00	6.00
❑ 76093	Hard Times/Takin' Care of Business	1981	—	2.50	5.00
❑ 76112	Starlife/Way Out West	1981	—	3.00	6.00
❑ 76116	It's Gettin' Hot/All I Want in the World	1981	—	3.00	6.00
❑ 76170	Tough (Vocal)/(Instrumental)	1982	—	3.00	6.00
❑ 76194	Daydreamin'/Christmas Rappin' Part 1	1982	—	2.50	5.00
❑ 562559-7	Christmas Rappin'/Christmas Rappin' (Do It Yourself Version)	1999	—	2.00	4.00
—Reissue with full 8:11 version on A-side					
❑ 810324-7	The Breaks/Christmas Rappin' Part 2	1983	—	2.50	5.00
❑ 812687-7	Party Time/(Instrumental)	1983	—	2.50	5.00
❑ 814484-7	Nervous/(Instrumental)	1983	—	2.50	5.00
❑ 870328-7	Back by Popular Demand/(Dub)	1988	—	2.50	5.00
❑ 870992-7	Only the Strong Survive/Still on the Scene	1988	—	2.00	4.00
❑ 880170-7	8 Million Stories/A.J. Scratch	1984	—	2.50	5.00
❑ 880408-7	Basketball/One-Two-Five	1984	—	3.00	6.00
❑ 884079-7	America/(Dub)	1985	—	2.50	5.00
❑ 884269-7	If I Ruled the World/(Dub)	1985	—	2.50	5.00
❑ 884547-7	A.J. Is Cool/Respect to the King	1986	—	2.50	5.00
❑ 888004-7	I'm Chillin'/Don't Cha Feel Like Making Love	1986	—	2.50	5.00
❑ 888282-7	The Bronx/Unity Party Jam	1987	—	2.00	4.00
POLYDOR					
❑ 881529-1	Basketball/(B-side unknown)	1985	5.00	10.00	20.00
❑ 881529-7	Basketball/(It's) The Game	1985	—	3.00	6.00
—B-side by Ralph MacDonald					
Albums					
MERCURY					
❑ MX-1-505 [EP]	Tough	1982	2.50	5.00	10.00
❑ SRM-1-3854	Kurtis Blow	1980	3.00	6.00	12.00
❑ SRM-1-4020	Deuce	1981	2.50	5.00	10.00
❑ 812757-1	Party Time?	1983	2.50	5.00	10.00

Number	Title (A Side/B Side)	Yr	VG	VG+	NM
❑ 822420-1	Ego Trip	1984	2.50	5.00	10.00
❑ 826141-1	America	1985	2.50	5.00	10.00
❑ 830215-1	Kingdom Blow	1986	2.50	5.00	10.00
❑ 834692-1	Back by Popular Demand	1988	2.50	5.00	10.00

BLOWFLY
12-Inch Singles
T.K. DISCO

Number	Title (A Side/B Side)	Yr	VG	VG+	NM
❑ 453	Blowfly's Christmas Party/Blowfly's New Year's Party	1980	2.00	4.00	8.00
45s					
COLLECTABLES					
❑ 363	Christmas Party/New Years Party	199?	—	—	3.00
—Reissue					

BLUE DIAMONDS, THE
45s
SAVOY

Number	Title (A Side/B Side)	Yr	VG	VG+	NM
❑ 1134	Honey Baby/No Money	1954	15.00	30.00	60.00

BLUE JAYS, THE (1)
Los Angeles-based male vocal group.
45s
MILESTONE

Number	Title (A Side/B Side)	Yr	VG	VG+	NM
❑ 2008	Lover's Island/You're Gonna Cry	1961	10.00	20.00	40.00
—Dark blue label					
❑ 2008	Lover's Island/You're Gonna Cry	1961	7.50	15.00	30.00
—Light blue and white label					
❑ 2008	Lover's Island/You're Gonna Cry	1961	7.50	15.00	30.00
—Green label					
❑ 2009	Tears Are Falling/Tree Tall Men	1961	7.50	15.00	30.00
❑ 2010	Let's Make Love/Rock, Rock, Rock	1962	5.00	10.00	20.00
❑ 2012	The Right to Love/Rock, Rock, Rock	1962	5.00	10.00	20.00
❑ 2014	Venus, My Love/Tall Len	1962	15.00	30.00	60.00

BLUE MAGIC
12-Inch Singles
COLUMBIA

Number	Title (A Side/B Side)	Yr	VG	VG+	NM
❑ 44-68789	It's Like Magic/(B-side unknown)	1989	2.00	4.00	8.00
❑ 44-68849	Secret Lover/There's a Song in My Head	1989	2.00	4.00	8.00
DEF JAM					
❑ 44-68197	Romeo and Juliet (Vocal) (Instrumental)/Couldn't Get to Sleep Last Night	1989	2.00	4.00	8.00
MIRAGE					
❑ PR 398 [DJ]	Magic # (5:00) (4:26)	1983	2.50	5.00	10.00
45s					
ATCO					
❑ 6910	Spell/Guess Who	1972	—	3.00	6.00
❑ 6930	Look Me Up/What's Come Over Me	1973	—	3.00	6.00
❑ 6949	Stop to Start/Where Have You Been	1973	—	3.00	6.00
❑ 6961	Sideshow/Just Don't Want to Be Lonely	1974	—	3.00	6.00
❑ 7004	Three Ring Circus/Welcome to the Club	1974	—	3.00	6.00
❑ 7014	Love Has Found Its Way to Me/When Ya Coming Home	1975	—	3.00	6.00
❑ 7031	Chasing Rainbows/You Won't Have to Tell Me Goodbye	1975	—	2.50	5.00
❑ 7046	Grateful Part 1/Grateful Part 2	1976	—	2.50	5.00
❑ 7052	Freak-N-Stein/Stop and Get a Hold of Yourself	1976	—	2.50	5.00
❑ 7061	Teach Me (It's Something About Love)/Spark of Love	1976	—	2.50	5.00
❑ 7090	I Waited/Can't Get You Out of My Mind	1978	—	2.00	4.00
CAPITOL					
❑ 4977	Land of Make Believe/Remember November	1981	—	3.00	6.00
COLUMBIA					
❑ 38-68900	It's Like Magic/Couldn't Get to Sleep Last Night	1989	—	2.00	4.00
❑ 38-69017	Secret Lover/There's a Song in My Head	1989	—	2.00	4.00
DEF JAM					
❑ 38-68566	Romeo and Juliet/Couldn't Get to Sleep Last Night	1989	—	2.00	4.00
LIBERTY					
❑ 56146	Can I Say I Love You/One, Two, Three	1969	2.50	5.00	10.00
MIRAGE					
❑ 99843	See Through/(B-side unknown)	1983	—	2.00	4.00
❑ 99866	Since You Been Gone/If You Move You Lose	1983	—	2.00	4.00
❑ 99914	Magic #/See Through	1983	2.00	4.00	8.00
WMOT					
❑ 4003	Summer Snow/Spark of Love	1976	—	2.50	5.00
Albums					
ATCO					
❑ SD 36-103	The Magic of the Blue	1974	3.00	6.00	12.00
❑ SD 38-104	The Message	1977	3.00	6.00	12.00
❑ SD 36-120	Thirteen Blue Magic Lane	1975	3.00	6.00	12.00
❑ SD 36-140	Mystic Dragons	1976	3.00	6.00	12.00
❑ SD 7038	Blue Magic	1974	3.00	6.00	12.00
CAPITOL					
❑ ST-12143	Welcome Back	1981	2.50	5.00	10.00
COLLECTABLES					
❑ COL-5031	The Magic of the Blue: Greatest Hits	198?	2.50	5.00	10.00
COLUMBIA					
❑ C 45092	From Out of the Blue	1989	3.00	6.00	12.00
MIRAGE					
❑ 90074	Magic #	1983	2.50	5.00	10.00

B

Number	Title (A Side/B Side)	Yr	VG	VG+	NM
OMNI					
❑ 90527	Greatest Hits	1986	2.50	5.00	10.00

BLUE NOTES, THE (1)
This group evolved into HAROLD MELVIN AND THE BLUE NOTES.
45s

Number	Title (A Side/B Side)	Yr	VG	VG+	NM
3 SONS					
❑ 103	WPLJ/While I'm Away	1962	7.50	15.00	30.00
COLLECTABLES					
❑ 1113	Winter Wonderland/O Holy Night	198?	—	2.00	4.00
—Reissue					
JOSIE					
❑ 800	If You Love Me/There's Something in Your Eyes, Eloise	1956	50.00	100.00	200.00
❑ 814	Letters/With This Pen	1957	30.00	60.00	120.00
—As "Todd Randall and the Blue Notes"					
❑ 823	The Retribution Blues/Wagon Wheels	1957	37.50	75.00	150.00
PORT					
❑ 70021	If You Love Me/There's Something in Your Eyes, Eloise	1958	15.00	30.00	60.00
RED TOP					
❑ 135	My Hero/A Good Woman	1963	7.50	15.00	30.00
UNI					
❑ 55132	Got Chills and Cold Thrills/Never Gonna Leave You	1969	3.00	6.00	12.00
❑ 55201	This Time Will Be Different/Lucky Me	1970	3.00	6.00	12.00
VAL-UE					
❑ 213	My Hero/A Good Woman	1960	20.00	40.00	80.00
❑ 215	Winter Wonderland/O Holy Night	1960	20.00	40.00	80.00

BLUE NOTES, THE (2)
Earlier male vocal group, no relation to (1).
45s

Number	Title (A Side/B Side)	Yr	VG	VG+	NM
RAMA					
❑ 25	If You'll Be Mine/Too Hot to Handle	1953	50.00	100.00	200.00

BLUES BOY WILLIE
45s

Number	Title (A Side/B Side)	Yr	VG	VG+	NM
ICHIBAN					
❑ 166	Let's Go, Let's Go, Let's Go/One More Mile	1989	—	2.00	4.00
❑ 90-221	Be-Who/Let Me Funk with You	1990	—	2.00	4.00
❑ 90-227	Why Are You Cheatin' on Me/Crack Up	1990	—	2.00	4.00
❑ 91-244	Be-Who 2/Where Is Leroy	1991	—	2.00	4.00
❑ 92-265	Be-Who 3/Hard Headed Woman	1992	—	2.00	4.00
❑ 93-288	Better Not Look Down/Injustice	1993	—	2.00	4.00
Albums					
ICHIBAN					
❑ 1038	Strange Things Happening	1989	2.50	5.00	10.00
❑ 1064	Be-Who?	1990	2.50	5.00	10.00

BOB AND EARL
45s

Number	Title (A Side/B Side)	Yr	VG	VG+	NM
CHENE					
❑ 103	The Sissy/(B-side unknown)	1964	2.50	5.00	10.00
CLASS					
❑ 213	That's My Desire/You Made a Boo-Boo	1957	10.00	20.00	40.00
❑ 231	Gee Whiz/When She Walks	1958	7.50	15.00	30.00
❑ 232	Chains of Love/Sweet Pea	1958	7.50	15.00	30.00
❑ 247	That's My Desire/You Made a Boo-Boo	1959	6.25	12.50	25.00
LOMA					
❑ 2004	Everybody Jerk/Just One Look in Your Eyes	1964	2.50	5.00	10.00
MARC					
❑ 104	Harlem Shuffle/I'll Come Running	1963	5.00	10.00	20.00
❑ 105	Puppet on a String/My Woman	1964	5.00	10.00	20.00
MIRWOOD					
❑ 5517	Baby It's Over/Dancin' Everywhere	1966	2.00	4.00	8.00
❑ 5526	I'll Keep Running Back/Baby, Your Time Is My Time	1966	2.00	4.00	8.00
TEMPE					
❑ 102	Don't Ever Leave Me/Oh Baby Doll	1962	3.75	7.50	15.00
UNI					
❑ 55196	Uh Uh No No/(Pickin' Up) Love's Vibrations	1970	—	3.00	6.00
❑ 55248	Get Ready for the New Day/Honey, Sugar, My Sweet Thing	1970	—	3.00	6.00
WHITE WHALE					
❑ 310	Harlem Shuffle/I'll Come Running	1969	3.00	6.00	12.00
Albums					
CRESTVIEW					
❑ CRS-3055	Bob & Earl	1969	6.25	12.50	25.00
TIP					
❑ TLP-1011 [M]	Harlem Shuffle	1964	7.50	15.00	30.00
❑ TLS-9011 [S]	Harlem Shuffle	1964	12.50	25.00	50.00

BOB B. SOXX AND THE BLUE JEANS
45s

Number	Title (A Side/B Side)	Yr	VG	VG+	NM
PHILLES					
❑ 107	Zip-a-Dee-Doo-Dah/Flip and Nitty	1962	5.00	10.00	20.00
❑ 110	Why Do Lovers Break Each Other's Heart?/Dr. Kaplan's Office	1963	5.00	10.00	20.00
❑ 113	Not Too Young to Get Married/Annette	1963	5.00	10.00	20.00

Number	Title (A Side/B Side)	Yr	VG	VG+	NM
PHILLES/COLLECTABLES					
❑ 3207	Not Too Young to Get Married/There's No Other (Like My Baby)	1985	—	3.00	6.00
—Gold vinyl; part of box set "Phil Spector Wall of Sound Series Vol. 1"; B-side by the Crystals					
❑ 3207	Not Too Young to Get Married/There's No Other (Like My Baby)	1986	—	2.50	5.00
—Black vinyl; B-side by the Crystals					
❑ 3209	Why Do Lovers Break Each Other's Heart/Zip-a-Dee Doo-Dah	1985	—	3.00	6.00
—Gold vinyl					
❑ 3209	Why Do Lovers Break Each Other's Heart/Zip-a-Dee Doo-Dah	1985	—	2.50	5.00
—Black vinyl					
Albums					
PHILLIES					
❑ PHLP-4002 [M]	Zip-a-Dee Doo-Dah	1963	125.00	250.00	500.00

BOBBETTES, THE
45s

Number	Title (A Side/B Side)	Yr	VG	VG+	NM
ATLANTIC					
❑ 1144	Mr. Lee/Look at the Stars	1957	6.25	12.50	25.00
❑ 1159	Speedy/Come-a Come-a	1957	5.00	10.00	20.00
❑ 1181	Zoomy/Rock and Ree-Ah-Zole	1958	5.00	10.00	20.00
❑ 1194	The Dream/Um Bow Bow	1958	5.00	10.00	20.00
❑ 2027	Don't Say Goodnight/You Are My Sweetheart	1959	5.00	10.00	20.00
❑ 2069	I Shot Mr. Lee/Untrue Love	1960	7.50	15.00	30.00
DIAMOND					
❑ 133	Row, Row, Row/Teddy	1963	3.00	6.00	12.00
❑ 142	Close Your Eyes/Somebody Bad Stole De Wedding Bell	1963	3.00	6.00	12.00
❑ 156	My Mamma Said/Sandman	1964	3.00	6.00	12.00
❑ 166	I'm Climbing a Mountain/In Paradise	1964	3.00	6.00	12.00
❑ 181	You Ain't Seen Nothing Yet/I'm Climbing a Mountain	1965	3.00	6.00	12.00
❑ 189	Love Is Blind/Teddy	1965	3.00	6.00	12.00
END					
❑ 1093	Mr. Johnny Q/Teach Me Tonight	1961	5.00	10.00	20.00
❑ 1095	I Don't Like It Like That (Part 1)/I Don't Like It Like That (Part 2)	1961	5.00	10.00	20.00
GALLANT					
❑ 1006	Oh, My Papa/I Cried	1960	5.00	10.00	20.00
GONE					
❑ 5112	I Don't Like It Like That (Part 1)/Mr. Johnny Q	1961	3.75	7.50	15.00
JUBILEE					
❑ 5427	Over There/Loneliness	1962	3.00	6.00	12.00
❑ 5442	The Broken Heart/Mama, Papa	1962	3.00	6.00	12.00
KING					
❑ 5490	Oh My Papa/Dance With Me Georgie	1961	3.75	7.50	15.00
❑ 5551	Are You Satisfied/Looking for a Lover	1961	3.75	7.50	15.00
❑ 5623	I'm Stepping Out Tonight/My Dearest	1962	3.75	7.50	15.00
RCA VICTOR					
❑ 47-8832	I've Gotta Face the World/Having Fun	1966	3.75	7.50	15.00
❑ 47-8983	It's All Over/Happy-Go-Lucky Me	1966	3.75	7.50	15.00
TRIPLE-X					
❑ 104	I Shot Mr. Lee/Billy	1960	5.00	10.00	20.00
❑ 106	Have Mercy Baby/Dance with Me Georgie	1960	5.00	10.00	20.00

BODY
12-Inch Singles

Number	Title (A Side/B Side)	Yr	VG	VG+	NM
MCA					
❑ L33-1081 [DJ]	Body (4 versions)	1990	2.50	5.00	10.00
❑ L33-18397 [DJ]	Touch Me Up (same on both sides)	1990	2.50	5.00	10.00
❑ L33-18433 [DJ]	Touch Me Up (2 versions)	1990	2.50	5.00	10.00
❑ 23759	Middle of the Night (5 versions)	1987	2.00	4.00	8.00
❑ 23832	Possession (2 versions?)	1988	2.00	4.00	8.00
❑ 53929	Body (Get Busy Club Version)/(Instrumental)	1990	2.00	4.00	8.00
45s					
MCA					
❑ 53111	Middle of the Night (Edit)/(Instrumental)	1987	—	—	3.00
❑ 53111 [PS]	Middle of the Night (Edit)/(Instrumental)	1987	—	—	3.00
❑ 53265	Possession/Possession (Suite)	1988	—	—	3.00
❑ 53265 [PS]	Possession/Possession (Suite)	1988	—	—	3.00
❑ 53768	Footsteps in the Dark/(Instrumental)	1989	—	2.00	4.00
❑ 79056	Touch Me Up/(Instrumental)	1990	—	2.00	4.00
Albums					
MCA					
❑ 42058	Body	1987	2.50	5.00	10.00

BODY COUNT
Also see ICE-T.
12-Inch Singles

Number	Title (A Side/B Side)	Yr	VG	VG+	NM
SIRE					
❑ PRO-A-5680 [DJ]	The Winner Loses/Fly By/Escape from the Killing Fields	1991	2.50	5.00	10.00
Albums					
VIRGIN					
❑ 39802	Born Dead	1994	3.75	7.50	15.00

BOFILL, ANGELA
12-Inch Singles

Number	Title (A Side/B Side)	Yr	VG	VG+	NM
ARISTA					
❑ SP-148 [DJ]	Too Tough/(Instrumental)	1982	2.00	4.00	8.00
❑ CP 729	Too Tough (3 versions)	1982	2.50	5.00	10.00

Number	Title (A Side/B Side)	Yr	VG	VG+	NM
❑ 9186	Special Delivery (Extended Dance Mix 6:01)/(Instrumental) (LP Version 4:29)	1984	2.00	4.00	8.00
❑ 9277	Can't Slow Down (Extended Remix Version 5:54)/(Instrumental Version 4:46)	1984	—	3.50	7.00

CAPITOL

Number	Title (A Side/B Side)	Yr	VG	VG+	NM
❑ V-15441	Love Is In Your Eyes (2 versions)/I Just Wanna Stop	1989	—	3.00	6.00

45s

ARISTA

Number	Title (A Side/B Side)	Yr	VG	VG+	NM
❑ 0636	Something About You/Time to Say Goodbye	1981	—	—	3.00
❑ 0662	Holdin' Out for Love/Only Love	1982	—	—	3.00
❑ 0666	Only Love/Estory Esperando Por El Amor	1982	—	3.00	6.00
❑ 0688	Break It to Me Gently/(B-side unknown)	1982	—	2.50	5.00
—May be promo only					
❑ 1031	Too Tough/Rainbow Inside My Heart	1983	—	—	3.00
❑ 1060	Tonight I Give In/Song for a Rainy Day	1983	—	3.00	6.00
❑ 9015	Tonight I Give In/Song for a Rainy Day	1983	—	—	3.00
❑ 9109	I'm On Your Side/Gotta Make It Up to You	1983	—	—	3.00
❑ 9156	Special Delivery/Gotta Make It Up to You	1984	—	—	3.00
❑ 9270	Can't Slow Down/No Love in Sight	1984	—	—	3.00
❑ 9312	Let Me Be the One/Love Me for Today	1984	—	—	3.00
❑ 9339	Who Knows You Better/No Love in Sight	1985	—	—	3.00
❑ 9414	Tell Me Tomorrow/(If You Wanna Love Me) You're On	1985	—	—	3.00
❑ 9452	I Don't Wanna Come Down from Love/(B-side unknown)	1985	—	2.00	4.00

ARISTA/GRP

Number	Title (A Side/B Side)	Yr	VG	VG+	NM
❑ 2500	This Time I'll Be Sweeter/Baby I Need Your Love	1979	—	2.00	4.00
❑ 2503	What I Wouldn't Do (For the Love of You)/Rainbow Child	1979	—	2.00	4.00
❑ 2504	Angel of the Night/Rainbow Child	1980	—	2.00	4.00

CAPITOL

Number	Title (A Side/B Side)	Yr	VG	VG+	NM
❑ B-44169	I Just Wanna Stop/Everlasting Love	1988	—	—	3.00
❑ B-44169 [PS]	I Just Wanna Stop/Everlasting Love	1988	—	—	3.00
❑ B-44298	Love Is In Your Eyes/I Just Wanna Stop	1989	—	—	3.00

Albums

ARISTA

Number	Title (A Side/B Side)	Yr	VG	VG+	NM
❑ AL8-8000	Too Tough	198?	2.00	4.00	8.00
—Reissue of 9616					
❑ AL8-8125	Something About You	198?	2.00	4.00	8.00
—Reissue of 9576					
❑ AL8-8198	Teaser	1983	2.50	5.00	10.00
❑ AL8-8258	Let Me Be the One	1984	2.50	5.00	10.00
❑ AL8-8396	Tell Me Tomorrow	1985	2.50	5.00	10.00
❑ AL8-8425	The Best of Angela Bofill	1986	2.50	5.00	10.00
❑ AL 9576	Something About You	1981	2.50	5.00	10.00
❑ AL 9616	Too Tough	1983	2.50	5.00	10.00

ARISTA/GRP

Number	Title (A Side/B Side)	Yr	VG	VG+	NM
❑ GL 5000	Angie	1978	3.00	6.00	12.00
❑ GL 5501	Angel of the Night	1979	3.00	6.00	12.00
❑ GL8-8060	Angel of the Night	198?	2.00	4.00	8.00
—Reissue of 5501					
❑ GLB-8302	Angie	198?	2.00	4.00	8.00
—Reissue of 5000					

CAPITOL

Number	Title (A Side/B Side)	Yr	VG	VG+	NM
❑ C1-48335	Intuition	1988	2.50	5.00	10.00

BOHANNON

12-Inch Singles

COMPLEAT

Number	Title (A Side/B Side)	Yr	VG	VG+	NM
❑ CK 101 [DJ]	Rock Your Body (Part 1 and 2)	1983	2.00	4.00	8.00
❑ CPD 201	Make Your Body Move/Come Back My Love	1983	—	3.50	7.00
❑ CPD 203	Don't Leave Me (same on both sides?)	1983	2.50	5.00	10.00
❑ CPD 204	Let's Start the Dance III (2 versions)	1983	2.00	4.00	8.00
❑ CPD 207	South Africa (2 versions)	1984	2.00	4.00	8.00

MCA

Number	Title (A Side/B Side)	Yr	VG	VG+	NM
❑ L33-17946 [DJ]	House Train (Extended 7:15) (Radio Edit 5:28) (Instrumental 6:48) (Bonus Beats 6:37)	1989	2.00	4.00	8.00
❑ L33-18106 [DJ]	The Gang's All Here (Vocal) (Dub)/Over the Rainbow	1990	2.50	5.00	10.00
❑ 23522	Motions (Vocal)/(Instrumental)	1984	2.50	5.00	10.00
❑ 23967	House Train (2 versions)	1989	—	3.00	6.00
❑ 23997	The Gang's All Here/Over the Rainbow	1990	2.50	5.00	10.00

MERCURY

Number	Title (A Side/B Side)	Yr	VG	VG+	NM
❑ MK 49 [DJ]	Maybe You Can Dance (12:42)/I Found My Love	1977	3.75	7.50	15.00
❑ MK 77 [DJ]	Cut Loose (7:44)/The Beat Part 2 (6:14)	1979	2.50	5.00	10.00
❑ MK 128 [DJ]	Feel Like Dancin' (7:24)/The Funk Walk (6:02)	1980	2.50	5.00	10.00
❑ DS 2001	Bohannon Disco Symphony/Andrea	1977	3.75	7.50	15.00
❑ MDS 3002	Cut Loose (7:44)/The Beat Part 2 (6:14)	1979	3.00	6.00	12.00
❑ 888143-1	Jammin' in the Street (Part 1 6:02) (Part 2 5:12)	1986	2.00	4.00	8.00

PHASE II

Number	Title (A Side/B Side)	Yr	VG	VG+	NM
❑ AS 857 [DJ]	Throw Down the Groove (Part 1 and 2)	1980	3.00	6.00	12.00
❑ AS 961 [DJ]	Goin' for Another One/The Happy Dance	1981	3.00	6.00	12.00
❑ AS 1357 [DJ]	Take the Country to New York City (5:49)/(Instrumental 4:31)	1982	3.00	6.00	12.00
❑ AS 1497 [DJ]	The Party Train (Parts 1 and 2)	1982	2.00	4.00	8.00
❑ 4W8-02133	Goin' for Another One/The Happy Dance	1981	3.00	6.00	12.00
❑ 4W8-02146	Foot Stompin' in the Summertime/(Instrumental)	1981	3.00	6.00	12.00
❑ 4Z9-02876	I've Got the Dance Fever (With Rap Intro)/(Without Intro)	1982	2.50	5.00	10.00
❑ 4W8 5652	Dance, Dance, Dance All Night/April My Love (Part 1)	1980	2.00	4.00	8.00

45s

COMPLEAT

Number	Title (A Side/B Side)	Yr	VG	VG+	NM
❑ 103	Make Your Body Move/Come Back My Love	1983	—	2.00	4.00
❑ 107	Don't Leave Me/Funkville	1983	—	2.00	4.00
❑ 114	Wake Up/Enjoy Your Day	1983	—	2.00	4.00
❑ 118	Rock Your Body/(Instrumental)	1983	—	2.00	4.00
❑ 148	South Africa/South Africa (Special Mix)	1984	—	2.00	4.00

DAKAR

Number	Title (A Side/B Side)	Yr	VG	VG+	NM
❑ 4518	Save Their Souls/Stop and Go	1973	—	3.00	6.00
❑ 4521	The Pimpwalk/Happiness	1973	—	3.00	6.00
❑ 4525	Run It On Down Mr. DJ (Part 1)/Run It On Down Mr. DJ (Part 2)	1973	—	3.00	6.00
❑ 4528	Fat Man/Red Bone	1974	—	3.00	6.00
❑ 4534	Happiness/Truck Stop	1974	—	3.00	6.00
❑ 4535	Keep On Dancin' (Part 1)/Keep On Dancin' (Part 2)	1974	—	3.00	6.00
❑ 4539	South African Music (Pt. 1)/Have a Good Day	1974	—	2.50	5.00
❑ 4544	Foot Stompin' Music/Dance with Your Partner	1975	—	2.50	5.00
❑ 4549	Disco Stomp (Part 1)/Disco Stomp (Part 2)	1975	—	2.50	5.00
❑ 4551	Bohannon's Beat (Pt. 1)/East Coast Groove	1975	—	2.50	5.00
❑ 4554	Dance Your Ass Off/Happy Feeling	1976	—	2.50	5.00
❑ 4560	Gittin' Off/Come Winter	1976	—	2.50	5.00

MCA

Number	Title (A Side/B Side)	Yr	VG	VG+	NM
❑ 53685	House Train/(Instrumental)	1989	—	—	3.00
❑ 53766	The Gang's All Here/Over the Rainbow	1989	—	—	3.00

MERCURY

Number	Title (A Side/B Side)	Yr	VG	VG+	NM
❑ 73939	Bohannon Disco Symphony/Moving Fast	1977	—	2.00	4.00
❑ 73946	Just Doing My Thing/Andrea	1977	—	2.00	4.00
❑ 74015	Let's Start the Dance/I Wonder Why	1978	—	2.00	4.00
❑ 74035	Me and the Gang/Summertime Groove	1978	—	2.00	4.00
❑ 74044	Cut Loose/Listen to the Children Play	1979	—	2.00	4.00
❑ 74085	The Groove Machine/Love Floats	1979	—	2.00	4.00
❑ 76040	Feel Like Dancin'/Funk Walk	1980	—	2.00	4.00
❑ 76054	Baby I'm for Real/Hurry Mr. Sunshine	1980	—	2.00	4.00
❑ 888143-7	Jammin' in the Street/(B-side unknown)	1986	—	—	3.00

PHASE II

Number	Title (A Side/B Side)	Yr	VG	VG+	NM
❑ WS8-02062	Goin' for Another One/The Happy Dance	1981	—	2.00	4.00
❑ WS8-02145	Foot Stompin' in the Summertime/(Instrumental)	1981	—	2.00	4.00
❑ WS9-02573	Let's Start II Dance Again/Let's Start the Dance	1981	—	2.00	4.00
❑ ZS5-02682	Take the Country to New York City (Part 1 and 2)	1982	—	2.00	4.00
❑ ZS5-02897	I've Got the Dance Fever (With Rap Intro)/(Without Intro)	1982	—	2.00	4.00
❑ ZS5-02998	The Party Train (Parts I & II)/Thoughts and Wishes	1982	—	2.00	4.00
❑ 5650	Throw Down the Groove (Part I)/Throw Down the Groove (Part II)	1980	—	2.00	4.00
❑ 5651	Dance, Dance, Dance All Night/April My Love (Part 1)	1980	—	2.00	4.00
❑ 5654	Don't Be Ashame to Call My Name/(B-side unknown)	1981	—	2.00	4.00

Albums

COMPLEAT

Number	Title (A Side/B Side)	Yr	VG	VG+	NM
❑ CPL-1-1003	Make Your Body Move	1983	2.50	5.00	10.00
❑ CPL-1-1005	The Bohannon Drive	1984	2.50	5.00	10.00

DAKAR

Number	Title (A Side/B Side)	Yr	VG	VG+	NM
❑ 6910	Keep On Dancing	1973	3.00	6.00	12.00
❑ 76916	Insides Out	1974	3.00	6.00	12.00
❑ 76917	Bohannon	1975	3.00	6.00	12.00
❑ 76919	Dance Your Ass Off	1976	3.00	6.00	12.00

MCA

Number	Title (A Side/B Side)	Yr	VG	VG+	NM
❑ 42310	Here Comes Bohannon	1989	3.00	6.00	12.00

MERCURY

Number	Title (A Side/B Side)	Yr	VG	VG+	NM
❑ SRM-1-1159	Phase II	1977	2.50	5.00	10.00
❑ SRM-1-3710	On My Way	1978	2.50	5.00	10.00
❑ SRM-1-3728	Summertime Groove	1978	2.50	5.00	10.00
❑ SRM-1-3762	Cut Loose	1979	2.50	5.00	10.00
❑ SRM-1-3778	Too Hot to Hold	1979	2.50	5.00	10.00
❑ SRM-1-3813	Music in the Air	1980	2.50	5.00	10.00

PHASE II

Number	Title (A Side/B Side)	Yr	VG	VG+	NM
❑ JW 36867	One Step Ahead	1980	2.50	5.00	10.00
❑ FZ 37695	Alive	1981	2.50	5.00	10.00
❑ FZ 38113	Bohannon Fever	1982	2.50	5.00	10.00

BONDS, GARY U.S.

45s

ATCO

Number	Title (A Side/B Side)	Yr	VG	VG+	NM
❑ 6689	The Star/You Need a Personal Manager	1969	—	3.00	6.00

BLUFF CITY

Number	Title (A Side/B Side)	Yr	VG	VG+	NM
❑ 221	My Love Song/Blue Grass	1974	—	2.50	5.00

BOTANIC

Number	Title (A Side/B Side)	Yr	VG	VG+	NM
❑ 1002	I'm Glad You're Back/Funky Lies	1968	2.00	4.00	8.00

EMI AMERICA

Number	Title (A Side/B Side)	Yr	VG	VG+	NM
❑ 8079	This Little Girl/Way Back When	1981	—	2.00	4.00
❑ 8079 [PS]	This Little Girl/Way Back When	1981	—	2.50	5.00
❑ 8089	Jole Blon/Just Like a Child	1981	—	2.00	4.00
❑ 8099	Your Love/Just Like a Child	1981	—	2.00	4.00
❑ 8117	Out of Work/Bring Her Back	1982	—	2.00	4.00
❑ 8117 [PS]	Out of Work/Bring Her Back	1982	—	2.50	5.00
❑ 8133	Love's on the Line/Way Back When	1982	—	2.00	4.00
❑ 8145	Turn the Music Down/Way Back When	1982	—	2.00	4.00

LEGRAND

Number	Title (A Side/B Side)	Yr	VG	VG+	NM
❑ 1003	New Orleans/Please Forgive Me	1960	5.00	10.00	20.00
—Original lists artist as "By-U.S. Bonds"; purple label					

B

Number	Title (A Side/B Side)	Yr	VG	VG+	NM
❑ 1003	New Orleans/Please Forgive Me	1960	3.75	7.50	15.00
—Gold and red label					
❑ 1005	Not Me/Give Me One More Chance	1961	5.00	10.00	20.00
—Artist listed as "U.S. Bonds"; purple label					
❑ 1005	Not Me/Give Me One More Chance	1961	3.75	7.50	15.00
—Gold and red label					
❑ 1008	Quarter to Three/Time Ole Story	1961	10.00	20.00	40.00
—Artist listed as "U.S. Bonds"; purple label					
❑ 1008	Quarter to Three/Time Ole Story	1961	3.75	7.50	15.00
—Artist listed as "U.S. Bonds"; gold and red label					
❑ 1008 [PS]	Quarter to Three/Time Ole Story	1961	10.00	20.00	40.00
❑ 1009	School Is Out/One Million Years	1961	5.00	10.00	20.00
—Artist listed as "U.S. Bonds"					
❑ 1009	School Is Out/One Million Years	1961	3.75	7.50	15.00
—Artist listed as "Gary (U.S.) Bonds" as are all later Legrand singles					
❑ 1009 [PS]	School Is Out/One Million Years	1961	10.00	20.00	40.00
❑ 1012	School Is In/Trip to the Moon	1961	3.75	7.50	15.00
❑ 1012	School Is In/Trip to the Moon	1971	2.00	4.00	8.00
—Red label reissue					
❑ 1015	Dear Lady/Havin' So Much Fun	1961	5.00	10.00	20.00
—Original title of A-side					
❑ 1015	Dear Lady Twist/Havin' So Much Fun	1962	3.75	7.50	15.00
❑ 1018	Twist, Twist Senora/Food of Love	1962	3.75	7.50	15.00
❑ 1019	Seven Day Weekend/Gettin' a Groove	1962	3.75	7.50	15.00
❑ 1020	Copy Cat/I'll Change That Too	1962	3.75	7.50	15.00
❑ 1022	Mixed Up Faculty/I Dig This Station	1962	3.75	7.50	15.00
❑ 1025	Do the Limbo with Me/Where Did That Naughty Little Girl Go	1962	3.75	7.50	15.00
❑ 1027	I Don't Wanta Wait/What a Dream	1963	3.00	6.00	12.00
❑ 1029	No More Homework/She's Alright	1963	3.00	6.00	12.00
❑ 1030	Perdido Part 1/Perdido Part 2	1963	3.00	6.00	12.00
❑ 1031	King Kong's Monkey/My Sweet Ruby Rose	1964	3.00	6.00	12.00
❑ 1032	The Music Goes Round and Round/Ella Is Yella	1964	3.00	6.00	12.00
❑ 1034	You Little Angel You/My Little Miss America	1964	3.00	6.00	12.00
❑ 1035	Oh Yeah, Oh Yeah/Let ❑ Oh Yeah, Oh Yeah/Let Me Go Lover	1965	2.50	5.00	10.00
❑ 1039	Beaches U.S.A./Do the Bumpsie	1965	2.50	5.00	10.00
❑ 1040	Take Me Back to New Orleans/I'm That Kind of Guy	1966	2.50	5.00	10.00
❑ 1041	Due to Circumstances Under My Control/Slow Motion	1966	2.50	5.00	10.00
❑ 1043	Send Her Back to Me/Workin' for My Baby	1967	2.50	5.00	10.00
❑ 1045	Call Me for Christmas/Mixed Up Faculty	1967	3.00	6.00	12.00
❑ 1046	Sarah Jane/What a Crazy World	1967	2.50	5.00	10.00
MCA					
❑ 52335	One More Time Around the Block, Ophelia/Deadline U.S.A.	1984	—	2.00	4.00
—B-side by Shalamar					
❑ 52400	New Orleans/Rhythm of the Rain	1984	—	2.00	4.00
—With Neil Sedaka					
PRODIGAL					
❑ 0612	Grandma's Washboard/Believing You	1975	—	2.50	5.00
SUE					
❑ 17	One Broken Heart/Can't Use You in My Business	1970	—	3.00	6.00
Albums					
EMI AMERICA					
❑ SPRO-9666 [EP]	Dedication Sampler	1981	3.75	7.50	15.00
—Promo-only sampler with limited-edition number on pink sticker					
❑ SO-17051	Dedication	1981	2.50	5.00	10.00
❑ SO-17068	On the Line	1982	2.50	5.00	10.00
LEGRAND					
❑ LLP-3001 [M]	Dance 'Til Quarter to Three	1961	25.00	50.00	100.00
❑ LLP-3002 [M]	Twist Up Calypso	1962	17.50	35.00	70.00
❑ LLP-3003 [M]	Greatest Hits of Gary U.S. Bonds	1962	17.50	35.00	70.00
MCA					
❑ 905	The Best of Gary U.S. Bonds	1984	2.50	5.00	10.00
RHINO					
❑ RNLP-805	Certified Soul	1981	2.50	5.00	10.00

BONE THUGS-N-HARMONY
12-Inch Singles
DREAMWORKS

Number	Title (A Side/B Side)	Yr	VG	VG+	NM
❑ PRO-A-5073 [DJ]	War (4 versions)	1998	3.75	7.50	15.00
EASTWEST					
❑ ED 5871 [DJ]	Days of Our Livez (Soundtrack Album Version) (Soundtrack Album Version Edit)/(Instrumental) (Acappella)	1996	3.00	6.00	12.00
RUTHLESS					
❑ (# unknown)	Thuggish-Ruggish-Bone (unknown versions)	1994	5.00	10.00	20.00
❑ 0415 [DJ]	East 1999 (LP Version 4:21) (U-Neek's Last Dayz Remix 4:26)/1st of Tha Month (DJ Premier's Phat Bonus Remix 5:07)//East 1999 (Acappella)/Buddah Loverz	1995	3.75	7.50	15.00
❑ 0663 [DJ]	If I Could Teach the World (Clean Version) (LP Version) (Instrumental) (Accapella)/Body Rott (LP Version) (Instrumental) (Accapela)	1997	3.75	7.50	15.00
❑ 5540	Foe Tha Love of $ (LP Dirty Mix) (Tha Yella 9 Minutes Uv Funk Mix)//Moe Cheese (Instrumental)/Thuggish Ruggish Bone (DJ Uneek's Remix)/Moe $ (Instrumental)	1995	3.75	7.50	15.00
—Featuring Eazy-E					
❑ 6335	Tha Crossroads (4 versions)	1996	3.00	6.00	12.00
❑ 6343	Look Into My Eyes/(Instrumental)	1997	2.50	5.00	10.00
❑ EAS 12757 [DJ]	Can't Give It Up (6 versions)	2000	3.00	6.00	12.00
❑ EAS 15221 [DJ]	Change the World (Radio Edit) (Clean Accapella) (Instrumental)/(Extended Mix) (Extended Accapella) (Instrumental)	2000	3.00	6.00	12.00
❑ EAS 45794 [DJ]	Resurrection (Paper, Paper) (Radio Version) (Extended Radio Version) (Instrumental)/ (Album Version) (Album Version Instrumental) (Album Version Acappella)	2000	3.00	6.00	12.00
Albums					
RUTHLESS					
❑ 5539	E. 1999 Eternal	1995	3.75	7.50	15.00
❑ 6340 [(2)]	The Art of War	1997	3.75	7.50	15.00
❑ C2 63581 [(2)]	BTNH Resurrection	2000	3.75	7.50	15.00
❑ C 69715	The Collection: Volume One	1998	3.00	6.00	12.00
❑ C2 85172 [(2)]	The Collection: Volume Two	2000	3.75	7.50	15.00

BOOGIE BOYS, THE
12-Inch Singles
CAPITOL

Number	Title (A Side/B Side)	Yr	VG	VG+	NM
❑ V-8578	Break Dancer (Radio Mix)/Zodiac//Shake a Break/Break Dancer (Club Mix) (Bonus Beats)	1984	10.00	20.00	40.00
❑ V-8645	City Life (3 versions)/A Fly Girl (2 versions)	1985	2.50	5.00	10.00
❑ SPRO-9596/7	[DJ] Party Asteroid (Remix) (Edit) (Dub)	1985	3.75	7.50	15.00
❑ V-15207	You Ain't Fresh (Morning Dew Mix) (7" Sunrise Mix)/(High Noon Mix) (Midnight Mix)	1985	3.75	7.50	15.00
❑ V-15214	Runnin' from Your Love (Remix) (Dub)/Party Asteroid (Edit) (Dub)	1985	3.00	6.00	12.00
❑ V-15230	Girl Talk (4 versions)	1986	2.50	5.00	10.00
❑ V-15245	Dealin' with Life (The Mix of Life) (LP Edit)/ (Diamond Dub) (Instrumental)	1986	3.00	6.00	12.00
❑ V-15265	Share My World (Remix) (Dub)/Run It (Remix) (Dub)	1986	3.00	6.00	12.00
❑ V-15338	I'm Comin' (Extended) (Instrumental) (Edit)/ Romeo Knight (Extended) (Instrumental)	1987	3.75	7.50	15.00
❑ V-15371	Body (12" Version) (Dub)/KMD Step Off (12" Version) (Dub)	1988	2.00	4.00	8.00
45s					
CAPITOL					
❑ B-5325	Break Dancer/Zodiac	1984	2.00	4.00	8.00
❑ B-5498	A Fly Girl/(Dub)	1985	—	2.00	4.00
❑ B-5522	You Ain't Fresh/(Sunrise Mix)	1985	—	2.00	4.00
❑ B-5522 [PS]	You Ain't Fresh/(Sunrise Mix)	1985	—	2.00	4.00
❑ B-5546	Party Asteroid/Runnin' from Your Love	1986	—	2.00	4.00
❑ B-5594	Girl Talk/(Instrumental)	1986	—	2.00	4.00
❑ B-5594 [PS]	Girl Talk/(Instrumental)	1986	—	2.00	4.00
❑ B-5622	Dealin' with Life/(Instrumental)	1986	—	2.00	4.00
❑ B-5649	Share My World/Run It	1986	—	2.00	4.00
❑ B-5649 [PS]	Share My World/Run It	1986	—	2.00	4.00
❑ B-44076	I'm Comin'/(Instrumental)	1987	—	2.00	4.00
❑ B-44146	Body/I'm Comin'	1988	—	2.00	4.00
Albums					
CAPITOL					
❑ ST-12409	City Life	1985	3.00	6.00	12.00
❑ ST-12488	Survival of the Freshest	1986	3.00	6.00	12.00
❑ C1-46917	Romeo Knight	1988	2.50	5.00	10.00

BOOGIE DOWN PRODUCTIONS
12-Inch Singles
B BOY

Number	Title (A Side/B Side)	Yr	VG	VG+	NM
❑ BB 1002	South Bronx (Vocal Mix) (Instrumental)/The P Is Free (Vocal Mix) (Instrumental)	1987	3.75	7.50	15.00
❑ BB 1200	My 9MM Goes Bang/Criminal Minded	1987	3.75	7.50	15.00
❑ BB 1300	The Bridge Is Over/A Word from Our Sponsors	1987	3.75	7.50	15.00
❑ BB 1400	Poetry/Elementary	1987	3.75	7.50	15.00
❑ BB 1600	Super Hoe/Scott LaRock Megamix	1998	2.50	5.00	10.00
JIVE					
❑ 1096-1-JD	My Philosophy (Album Mix) (Extended Remix) (Single Edit) (Instrumental)	1988	2.50	5.00	10.00
❑ 1169-1-JD	Jack of Spades (BDP Movie Mix 4:49) (Extended Remix 5:46) (Instrumental 4:13)/Necessary//I'm Still #1 (Extended Remix 5:25) (Single Edit 4:50) (Numero Uno Re-Recording 5:23)	1989	2.50	5.00	10.00
❑ 1231-1-JD	Why Is That (Extended Edit) (Single Edit) (Instrumental)/Who Protects Us From You?	1989	2.50	5.00	10.00
❑ 1367-1-JD	Love's Gonna Get'cha (Material Love Version) (Extended Hard Version) (Extended Soft Version)//(7" Radio Edit) (Instrumental)/The Kenny Parker Show	1990	2.50	5.00	10.00
❑ 42486	Jack of Spades/You Must Learn	1997	2.00	4.00	8.00
❑ 42487	Love's Gonna Get'cha (2 versions)//The Kenny Parker Show/Ya Know the Rules/100 Guns	1997	2.00	4.00	8.00
45s					
JIVE					
❑ 1098-7-J	My Philosophy//(Instrumental)	1988	—	—	3.00
❑ 1120-7-J	Stop the Violence/(Instrumental)	1988	—	—	3.00
❑ 1120-7-J [PS]	Stop the Violence/(Instrumental)	1988	—	—	3.00
❑ 1168-7-J	Jack of Spades/I'm Still #1	1989	—	2.00	4.00
Albums					
B BOY					
❑ BB 2000 [(2)]	A Man and His Music	1997	3.75	7.50	15.00
❑ BB 4787	Criminal Minded	1987	3.00	6.00	12.00
—Reissued in 1997 with the same number					
❑ BB 5787	Criminal Minded Instrumental	1987	3.00	6.00	12.00
—Reissued in 1997 with the same number					

Number	Title (A Side/B Side)	Yr	VG	VG+	NM
JIVE					
❏ 1097-1-J	By All Means Necessary	1988	2.50	5.00	10.00
❏ 1187-1-J	Ghetto Music: The Blueprint of Hip-Hop	1989	2.50	5.00	10.00
❏ 1358-1-J	Edutainment	1990	3.75	7.50	15.00
LANDSPEED					
❏ LSR 8806 [(3)]	Best of B-Boy Records	2000	5.00	10.00	20.00

BOOGIE MAN, THE
See JOHN LEE HOOKER.

BOOKER, CHUCKII
12-Inch Singles
ATLANTIC

Number	Title (A Side/B Side)	Yr	VG	VG+	NM
❏ 86312	Touch (3 versions)	1989	2.00	4.00	8.00
45s					
ATLANTIC					
❏ DMD 1478 [DJ]	That's My Honey (3 versions)	1989	3.00	6.00	12.00
❏ 88841	Touch/(Dub Edit)	1989	—	—	3.00
❏ 88917	Turned Away/Keep Your Guard Up	1989	—	—	3.00
Albums					
ATLANTIC					
❏ 81947	Chuckii	1989	2.50	5.00	10.00

BOOKER, JOHN LEE
See JOHN LEE HOOKER.

BOOKER T. AND PRISCILLA
Also see BOOKER T. AND THE MG'S.
45s
A&M

Number	Title (A Side/B Side)	Yr	VG	VG+	NM
❏ 1298	The Wedding Song/She	1971	—	2.50	5.00
❏ 1487	Crippled Crow/Wild Fox	1973	—	2.50	5.00
Albums					
A&M					
❏ SP-3504 [(2)]	Booker T. and Priscilla	1971	3.75	7.50	15.00
❏ SP-4351	Home Grown	1972	2.50	5.00	10.00
❏ SP-4413	Chronicles	1973	2.50	5.00	10.00

BOOKER T. AND THE MG'S
Also see BOOKER T. AND PRISCILLA; STEVE CROPPER.
12-Inch Singles
A&M

Number	Title (A Side/B Side)	Yr	VG	VG+	NM
❏ SP-12046 [DJ]	Don't Stop Your Love/I Came to Love You	1981	3.75	7.50	15.00
—As "Booker T. Jones"					
❏ SP-17043 [DJ]	Let's Go Dancing (2 versions?)	1978	3.75	7.50	15.00
—As "Booker T. Jones"					
❏ SP-17188 [DJ]	Don't Stop Your Love (same on both sides?)	1981	3.75	7.50	15.00
—As "Booker T. Jones"					
❏ SP-20011	Don't Stop Your Love (unknown versions)	1981	3.00	6.00	12.00
—As "Booker T. Jones"					
45s					
ASYLUM					
❏ 45392	Sticky Stuff/The Stick	1977	—	2.00	4.00
❏ 45424	Grab Bag/Reincarnation	1977	—	2.00	4.00
A&M					
❏ 2100	Knockin' on Heaven's Door/Let's Go Dancin'	1978	—	2.00	4.00
—As "Booker T. Jones"					
❏ 2234	The Best of You/Let's Go Dancin'	1980	—	2.00	4.00
—As "Booker T. Jones"					
❏ 2279	Will You Be the One/Cookie	1980	—	2.00	4.00
—As "Booker T. Jones"					
❏ 2374	I Want You/You're the Best	1981	—	2.00	4.00
❏ 2394	Don't Stop Your Love/I Came to Love You	1982	—	2.00	4.00
COLUMBIA					
❏ 38-77526	Cruisin'/Just My Imagination	1994	—	2.00	4.00
EPIC					
❏ 50031	Evergreen/Song for Casey	1974	—	2.00	4.00
❏ 50078	Front Street Rag/Mama Stewart	1975	—	2.00	4.00
❏ 50149	Life Is Funny/Tennessee Voodoo	1975	—	2.00	4.00
STAX					
❏ 0001	Soul-Limbo/Heads Or Tails	1968	2.00	4.00	8.00
❏ 0013	Hang 'Em High/Over Easy	1968	2.00	4.00	8.00
❏ 0028	Time Is Tight/Johnny I Love You	1969	2.00	4.00	8.00
❏ 0037	Mrs. Robinson/Soul Clap '69	1969	2.00	4.00	8.00
❏ 0049	Slum Baby/Meditation	1969	2.00	4.00	8.00
❏ 0073	Something/Sunday Sermon	1970	—	3.00	6.00
❏ 0082	Melting Pot/Kinda Easy Like	1970	—	3.00	6.00
❏ 127	Green Onions/Behave Yourself	1962	5.00	10.00	20.00
—Gray label					
❏ 127	Green Onions/Behave Yourself	1962	4.00	8.00	16.00
—Blue label					
❏ 131	Jellybread/Aw' Mercy	1963	3.00	6.00	12.00
❏ 134	Big Train/Home Grown	1963	3.00	6.00	12.00
❏ 134	Big Train/Burnt Biscuits	1963	3.00	6.00	12.00
❏ 137	Chinese Checkers/Plum Nellie	1963	3.00	6.00	12.00
❏ 142	Mo' Onions/Tic Tac Toe	1963	3.00	6.00	12.00
❏ 142	Mo' Onions/Fannie Mae	1963	3.00	6.00	12.00
❏ 153	Soul Dressing/MG Party	1964	2.50	5.00	10.00
❏ 161	Can't Be Still/Terrible Thing	1964	2.50	5.00	10.00
❏ 169	Boot-Leg/Outrage	1965	2.50	5.00	10.00
❏ 0169	Sugarcane/Blackride	1973	—	2.50	5.00
—As "The MG's"					
❏ 182	Red Beans and Rice/Be My Lady	1965	2.50	5.00	10.00
❏ 196	Booker-Loo/My Sweet Potato	1966	2.50	5.00	10.00

Number	Title (A Side/B Side)	Yr	VG	VG+	NM
❏ 0200	Breezy/Neckbone	1974	—	2.50	5.00
—As "The MG's"					
❏ 203	Jingle Bells/Winter Wonderland	1966	3.00	6.00	12.00
❏ 211	Hip-Hug-Her/Summertime	1967	2.50	5.00	10.00
❏ 224	Groovin'/Slim Jenkin's Place	1967	2.50	5.00	10.00
❏ 236	Silver Bells/Winter Snow	1967	3.00	6.00	12.00
VOLT					
❏ 102	Green Onions/Behave Yourself	1962	7.50	15.00	30.00
Albums					
ASYLUM					
❏ 7E-1093	Universal Language	1977	2.50	5.00	10.00
ATLANTIC					
❏ 8202 [M]	The Best of Booker T. and the MG's	1968	12.50	25.00	50.00
—Mono is white label promo only					
❏ SD 8202 [S]	The Best of Booker T. and the MG's	1968	5.00	10.00	20.00
❏ 81285	The Best of Booker T. and the MG's	1985	2.00	4.00	8.00
A&M					
❏ SP-4720	Try and Love Again	1978	2.50	5.00	10.00
—As "Booker T. Jones"					
❏ SP-4798	The Best of You	1979	2.50	5.00	10.00
—As "Booker T. Jones"					
❏ SP-4874	I Want You	1981	2.50	5.00	10.00
—As "Booker T. Jones"					
EPIC					
❏ KE 33143	Evergreen	1974	3.00	6.00	12.00
MCA					
❏ 6282	The Runaway	1989	3.00	6.00	12.00
—As "Booker T. Jones"					
STAX					
❏ ST-701 [M]	Green Onions	1962	17.50	35.00	70.00
❏ STS-701 [R]	Green Onions	1966	12.50	25.00	50.00
❏ ST-705 [M]	Soul Dressing	1965	17.50	35.00	70.00
❏ STS-705 [R]	Soul Dressing	1966	12.50	25.00	50.00
❏ ST-711 [M]	And Now…Booker T. and the MG's	1966	12.50	25.00	50.00
❏ STS-711 [S]	And Now…Booker T. and the MG's	1966	20.00	40.00	80.00
❏ ST-713 [M]	In the Christmas Spirit	1966	100.00	200.00	400.00
—Fingers and piano keys cover					
❏ ST-713 [M]	In the Christmas Spirit	1967	50.00	100.00	200.00
—Same as above; Santa Claus cover					
❏ STS-713 [S]	In the Christmas Spirit	1966	100.00	200.00	400.00
—Fingers and piano keys cover					
❏ STS-713 [S]	In the Christmas Spirit	1967	50.00	100.00	200.00
—Santa Claus cover					
❏ ST-717 [M]	Hip Hug-Her	1967	10.00	20.00	40.00
❏ STS-717 [S]	Hip Hug-Her	1967	12.50	25.00	50.00
❏ STS-724	Doin' Our Thing	1968	12.50	25.00	50.00
❏ STS-2001	Soul Limbo	1968	6.25	12.50	25.00
❏ STS-2006	Uptight	1969	6.25	12.50	25.00
❏ STS-2009	The Booker T. Set	1969	6.25	12.50	25.00
❏ STS-2027	McLemore Avenue	1970	6.25	12.50	25.00
❏ STS-2033	Booker T. and the MG's Greatest Hits	1970	3.75	7.50	15.00
❏ STS-2035	Melting Pot	1971	3.75	7.50	15.00
❏ STX-4104	Free Ride	1978	2.50	5.00	10.00
❏ STX-4113	Soul Limbo	198?	2.50	5.00	10.00
—Reissue of 2001					
❏ MPS-8505	Booker T. and the MG's Greatest Hits	1981	2.50	5.00	10.00
❏ MPS-8521	Melting Pot	198?	2.50	5.00	10.00
—Reissue of 2035					
❏ MPS-8531	The Booker T. Set	1987	2.50	5.00	10.00
—Reissue of 2009					
❏ MPS-8552	McLemore Avenue	1990	3.00	6.00	12.00
—Reissue of 2027					
SUNDAZED					
❏ LP 5042	Soul Dressing	2000	3.75	7.50	15.00
—Reissue on 180-gram vinyl					
❏ LP 5043	And Now! Booker T. and the MG's	2000	3.75	7.50	15.00
—Reissue on 180-gram vinyl					
❏ LP 5053	In the Christmas Spirit	2000	3.75	7.50	15.00
—Reissue on 180-gram vinyl					
❏ LP 5079	Green Onions	2002	3.00	6.00	12.00
—Reissue on 180-gram vinyl					
❏ LP 5080	Hip Hug-Her	2002	3.00	6.00	12.00
—Reissue on 180-gram vinyl					

BOOTSY'S RUBBER BAND
Also see BOOTSY COLLINS.
12-Inch Singles
4TH & B'WAY

Number	Title (A Side/B Side)	Yr	VG	VG+	NM
❏ PRO 512-1 [DJ]	Jungle Bass (3 versions)/Disciples of Funk	1990	3.75	7.50	15.00
❏ 444023-1	Jungle Bass (2 versions)//Disciples of Funk/Interzone	1990	2.50	5.00	10.00
WARNER BROS.					
❏ 29919	Body Slam/I'd Rather Be With You	1982	3.75	7.50	15.00
45s					
WARNER BROS.					
❏ 8246	I'd Rather Be with You/Vanish in Our Sleep	1976	—	3.00	6.00
❏ 8291	Psychoticbumpschool/Vanish in Our Sleep	1976	—	3.00	6.00
❏ 8328	The Pinocchio Theory/Rubber Duckie	1977	—	3.00	6.00
❏ 8403	Can't Stay Away/Another Point of View	1977	—	3.00	6.00
❏ 8512	Bootzilla/Hollywood Squares	1978	—	3.00	6.00
❏ 8575	Hollywood Squares/What's a Telephone Bill	1978	—	2.50	5.00
❏ 8575 [PS]	Hollywood Squares/What's a Telephone Bill	1978	2.00	4.00	8.00
❏ 8818	Jam Fan (Hot)/She Jam (Almost Bootsy Show)	1979	—	2.50	5.00
❏ 29889	Body Slam!/I'd Rather Be With You	1982	—	2.00	4.00

Number	Title (A Side/B Side)	Yr	VG	VG+	NM
❑ 49013	Bootsy Get Live Part 1/Part 2	1979	—	2.50	5.00
❑ 49073	Under the Influence of a Groove/(Disco Version)	1979	—	2.50	5.00
❑ 49599	Mug Push/Scenery	1980	—	2.50	5.00
—As "Bootsy"					
❑ 49599 [PS]	Mug Push/Scenery	1980	—	3.00	6.00
—As "Bootsy"					
❑ 49661	F-Encounter/(Instrumental)	1981	—	2.50	5.00
—As "Bootsy"					
❑ 49708	Is That My Song?/It's a Musical	1981	—	2.50	5.00
—As "Bootsy"					

Albums

WARNER BROS.

Number	Title (A Side/B Side)	Yr	VG	VG+	NM
❑ BS 2920	Stretchin' Out in Bootsy's Rubber Band	1976	3.75	7.50	15.00
❑ BS 2972	Ahh... The Name Is Bootsy, Baby!	1977	3.75	7.50	15.00
❑ BSK 3093	Bootsy? Player of the Year	1978	3.75	7.50	15.00
—With perforated punch-out glasses intact					
❑ BSK 3093	Bootsy? Player of the Year	1978	2.50	5.00	10.00
—Without punch-out glasses					
❑ BSK 3295	This Boot Is Make for Fonk-n	1979	3.75	7.50	15.00
—With 8-page coloring book					
❑ BSK 3295	This Boot Is Make for Fonk-n	1979	2.50	5.00	10.00
—Without coloring book					
❑ BSK 3433	Ultra Wave	1980	3.75	7.50	15.00
—As "Bootsy"					

BOSTIC, EARL

45s

KING

Number	Title (A Side/B Side)	Yr	VG	VG+	NM
❑ 4444	Sleep/September Song	1951	7.50	15.00	30.00
❑ 4454	Always/How Could It Have Been You and I	1951	7.50	15.00	30.00
❑ 4475	Flamingo/I'm Getting Sentimental Over You	1951	7.50	15.00	30.00
❑ 4491	I Got Loaded/Chains of Love	1951	10.00	20.00	40.00
❑ 4511	The Moon Is Low/Lover Come Back to Me	1952	6.25	12.50	25.00
❑ 4536	Linger Awhile/Velvet Sunset	1952	6.25	12.50	25.00
❑ 4550	Moonglow/Ain't Misbehavin'	1952	6.25	12.50	25.00
❑ 4570	For You/Smoke Gets In Your Eyes	1952	6.25	12.50	25.00
❑ 4586	You Go to My Head/Hour of Parting	1953	6.25	12.50	25.00
❑ 4603	The Sheik of Araby/Steamwhistle Jump	1953	6.25	12.50	25.00
❑ 4623	Cherokee/The Song Is Ended	1953	6.25	12.50	25.00
❑ 4644	Melancholy Serenade/What, No Pearls?	1953	6.25	12.50	25.00
❑ 4653	The Very Thought of You/Memories	1953	6.25	12.50	25.00
❑ 4674	Deep Purple/Smoke Rings	1953	6.25	12.50	25.00
❑ 4683	Off Shore/Don't You Do It	1953	6.25	12.50	25.00
❑ 4699	My Heart at Thy Sweet Voice/Cracked Ice	1954	5.00	10.00	20.00
❑ 4708	Jungle Drums/Danube Waves	1954	5.00	10.00	20.00
❑ 4723	Blue Skies/Mambolino	1954	5.00	10.00	20.00
❑ 4730	These Foolish Things/Mambostic	1954	5.00	10.00	20.00
❑ 4741	Ubangi Stomp/Time on My Hands	1954	5.00	10.00	20.00
❑ 4754	Song of the Islands/Liebestraum	1954	5.00	10.00	20.00
❑ 4765	Embraceable You/Night and Day	1955	5.00	10.00	20.00
❑ 4776	Melody of Love/Sweet Lorraine	1955	5.00	10.00	20.00
❑ 4790	Cocktails for Two/When Your Lover Has Gone	1955	5.00	10.00	20.00
❑ 4799	Remember/Cherry Bean	1955	5.00	10.00	20.00
❑ 4815	East of the Sun/Dream	1955	5.00	10.00	20.00
❑ 4829	For All We Know/Beyond the Blue Horizon	1955	5.00	10.00	20.00
❑ 4845	O Solo Mio/Poeme	1955	5.00	10.00	20.00
❑ 4883	I Love You Truly/'Cause You're My Lover	1956	3.75	7.50	15.00
❑ 4905	Bugle Call Rag/I'll String Along with You	1956	3.75	7.50	15.00
❑ 4943	Roses of Picardy/Where or When	1956	3.75	7.50	15.00
❑ 4978	Harlem Nocturne/I Hear a Rhapsody	1956	3.75	7.50	15.00
❑ 5025	Too Fine for Crying/Avalon	1957	3.75	7.50	15.00
❑ 5041	Temptation/September Song	1957	3.75	7.50	15.00
❑ 5056	She's Funny That Way/Exercise	1957	3.75	7.50	15.00
❑ 5071	Vienna, City of My Dreams/Just Too Shy	1957	3.75	7.50	15.00
❑ 5081	A Gay Day/Answer Me	1957	3.75	7.50	15.00
❑ 5092	Josephine/Jeannie I Dream of Lilac Time	1957	3.75	7.50	15.00
❑ 5106	Southern Fried/No Name Jive	1958	3.75	7.50	15.00
❑ 5120	Lester Leaps In/Pompton Turnpike	1958	3.75	7.50	15.00
❑ 5127	Honeysuckle Rose/Back Beat	1958	3.75	7.50	15.00
❑ 5133	Woodchopper's Ball/John's Idea	1958	3.75	7.50	15.00
❑ 5136	Twilight Time/Over Waves Rock	1958	3.75	7.50	15.00
❑ 5144	Pinkie/Home Sweet Home Rock	1958	3.75	7.50	15.00
❑ 5152	Goodnight Sweetheart/Indian Boogie Woogie	1958	3.75	7.50	15.00
❑ 5161	Red Skin Cha Cha/Rockin' with Richard	1958	3.75	7.50	15.00
❑ 5175	My Reverie Cha Cha/Barcarole	1959	3.00	6.00	12.00
❑ 5190	Up There in Orbit/Sweet Pea	1959	3.00	6.00	12.00
❑ 5203	Up There in Orbit (Part 1)/Up There in Orbit (Part 2)	1959	3.00	6.00	12.00
❑ 5209	La Cucaracha Cha Cha/Dancing in the Dark	1959	3.00	6.00	12.00
❑ 5229	Who Cares/Feeling Cool	1959	3.00	6.00	12.00
❑ 5252	White Horse/Dark Eyes	1959	3.00	6.00	12.00
❑ 5263	Gondola/Once in a While	1959	3.00	6.00	12.00
❑ 5290	Tut-Strut/All the Things You Are	1959	3.00	6.00	12.00
❑ 5301	Ebb Tide/Hildegarde	1959	3.00	6.00	12.00
❑ 5309	Let's Move Out/I Burned Your Letter	1960	3.00	6.00	12.00
❑ 5314	Off Shore/Hello '60	1960	3.00	6.00	12.00
❑ 5317	Elegie/Out of Nowhere	1960	3.00	6.00	12.00
❑ 5345	Make Believe/A Gay Day	1960	3.00	6.00	12.00
❑ 5362	Tuxedo Junction/Polonaise	1960	3.00	6.00	12.00
❑ 5402	720 in the Books/Just in Time	1960	3.00	6.00	12.00
❑ 5454	That Old Black Magic/Full Moon and Empty Arms	1961	2.50	5.00	10.00
❑ 5477	Jersey Bounce/Because of You	1961	2.50	5.00	10.00
❑ 5564	The Thrill Is Gone/April in Portugal	1961	2.50	5.00	10.00
❑ 5600	How Deep Is the Ocean/Wrap It	1962	2.50	5.00	10.00
❑ 5636	Dark Eyes/People Will Say We're in Love	1962	2.50	5.00	10.00
❑ 5661	More Than You Know/Don't Blame Me	1962	2.50	5.00	10.00
❑ 5683	Ducky/Deep in My Heart	1962	2.50	5.00	10.00
❑ 5699	Autumn Leaves/Anita's Theme	1962	2.50	5.00	10.00
❑ 5711	El Choclo Bossa Nova/My Reverie	1963	2.50	5.00	10.00
❑ 5742	Cherry Pink (And Apple Blossom White)/Your Cheatin' Heart	1963	2.50	5.00	10.00
❑ 5776	Love Letters in the Sand/Tammy	1963	2.50	5.00	10.00
❑ 5819	Apple Cake/Don't Do It Please	1963	2.50	5.00	10.00
❑ 5839	Telstar Drive/Fast Track	1964	2.00	4.00	8.00
❑ 5861	Let's Dance Little Girl/Summertime	1964	2.00	4.00	8.00
❑ 5900	Make Believe/Star Gazer	1964	2.00	4.00	8.00
❑ 5925	The Pink Panther/Lawrence of Arabia	1964	2.00	4.00	8.00
❑ 5944	From Russia with Love/My Special Dream	1964	2.00	4.00	8.00
❑ 5955	Theme from The Unforgiven/Dominique	1964	2.00	4.00	8.00
❑ 5961	Hello Dolly/Walk on the Wild Side	1964	2.00	4.00	8.00
❑ 5977	More/Charade	1965	2.00	4.00	8.00
❑ 6254	September Song/Harlem Nocturne	1969	—	2.50	5.00

7-Inch Extended Plays

KING

Number	Title (A Side/B Side)	Yr	VG	VG+	NM
❑ EP-200	Flamingo/Swing Low Sweet Boogie//I Can't Give You Anything But Love/The Moon Is Low	195?	6.25	12.50	25.00
❑ EP-200 [PS]	Earl Bostic and His Alto Sax, Vol. 1	195?	6.25	12.50	25.00
❑ EP 201	*Sleep/Earl's Imagination/Lover Come Back to Me/I'm Gettin' Sentimental Over You	1953	6.25	12.50	25.00
❑ EP 201 [PS]	Earl Bostic and His Alto Sax, Vol. 2	1953	6.25	12.50	25.00
❑ EP 202	*Always/Linger Awhile/Merry Widow/Earl Blows a Fuse	1953	6.25	12.50	25.00
❑ EP 202 [PS]	Earl Bostic and His Alto Sax, Vol. 3	1953	6.25	12.50	25.00
❑ EP 203	*Deep Purple/Velvet Sunset/Choppin' It Down/You Go to My Head	1953	6.25	12.50	25.00
❑ EP 203 [PS]	Earl Bostic and His Alto Sax, Vol. 4	1953	6.25	12.50	25.00
❑ EP 204	*Cherokee/Seven Steps/No Name Blues/Don't You Do It	1953	6.25	12.50	25.00
❑ EP 204 [PS]	Earl Bostic and His Alto Sax, Vol. 5	1953	6.25	12.50	25.00
❑ EP 205	*Moonglow/For You/Blip Boogie/Wrap It Up	1953	6.25	12.50	25.00
❑ EP 205 [PS]	Earl Bostic and His Alto Sax, Vol. 6	1953	6.25	12.50	25.00
❑ EP 206	*Filibuster/The Sheik of Araby/Smoke Gets in Your Eyes/The Hour of Parting	1953	6.25	12.50	25.00
❑ EP 206 [PS]	Earl Bostic and His Alto Sax, Vol. 7	1953	6.25	12.50	25.00
❑ EP 207	*Serenade/Ain't Misbehavin'/Smoke Rings/Steamwhistle Jump	1953	6.25	12.50	25.00
❑ EP 207 [PS]	Earl Bostic and His Alto Sax, Vol. 8	1953	6.25	12.50	25.00
❑ EP 245	Melancholy Serenade/What! No Pearls//The Very Thought of You/Memories	1954	5.00	10.00	20.00
❑ EP 245 [PS]	Earl Bostic and His Alto Sax, Vol. 9	1954	5.00	10.00	20.00
❑ EP 284	*Jungle Drums/The Song Is Ended/Off Shore/Cracked Ice	1954	5.00	10.00	20.00
❑ EP 284 [PS]	Earl Bostic and His Alto Sax, Vol. 10	1954	5.00	10.00	20.00
❑ EP 285	*Danube Waves/My Heart at Thy Sweet Voice/Poeme/O Sole Mio	1954	5.00	10.00	20.00
❑ EP 285 [PS]	Earl Bostic and His Alto Sax, Vol. 11	1954	5.00	10.00	20.00
❑ EP 347	*Mambostic/Time on My Hands/Mambolino/Ven-A-Mi	1955	5.00	10.00	20.00
❑ EP 347 [PS]	Earl Bostic and His Alto Sax, Vol. 12	1955	5.00	10.00	20.00
❑ KEP 350	Blue Skies/Ubangi Stomp//Song of the Islands/These Foolish Things	1955	5.00	10.00	20.00
❑ KEP 350 [PS]	The Artistry of Earl Bostic, Vol. 13	1955	5.00	10.00	20.00
❑ EP 355	*Cherry Bean/Liebestraum/Night and Day/Embraceable You	1955	5.00	10.00	20.00
❑ EP 355 [PS]	Earl Bostic and His Alto Sax, Vol. 14	1955	5.00	10.00	20.00
❑ EP 363	*Melody of Love/Cocktails for Two/Blue Moon/Remember	1955	5.00	10.00	20.00
❑ EP 363 [PS]	Earl Bostic and His Alto Sax, Vol. 15	1955	5.00	10.00	20.00
❑ EP 375	*Dream/Beyond the Blue Horizon/East of the Sun/For All We Know	1956	5.00	10.00	20.00
❑ EP 375 [PS]	Earl Bostic with Strings, Vol. 16	1956	5.00	10.00	20.00
❑ EP 381	*Bugle Call Rag/I'll String Along with You/I Love You Truly/'Cause You're My Lover	1956	5.00	10.00	20.00
❑ EP 381 [PS]	Bostic Blows, Vol. 17	1956	5.00	10.00	20.00
❑ KEP 398	Harlem Nocturne/I Hear a Rhapsody//Roses of Picardy/Where or When	1957	5.00	10.00	20.00
❑ KEP 398 [PS]	Earl Bostic, Vol. 18	1957	5.00	10.00	20.00
❑ EP-405	*She's Funny That Way/How Deep Is the Ocean/Avalon/September Song	1958	5.00	10.00	20.00
❑ EP-405 [PS]	Earl Bostic Dance Time	1958	5.00	10.00	20.00
❑ EP-406	*Temptation/Sweet Lorraine/Away/Exercise	1958	5.00	10.00	20.00
❑ EP-406 [PS]	Alto-Tude	1958	5.00	10.00	20.00
❑ EP-409	*Just Too Shy/Laura/Josephine/A Gay Day	1958	5.00	10.00	20.00
❑ EP-409 [PS]	Earl Bostic for Listening and Dancing	1958	5.00	10.00	20.00
❑ EP-410	*Jeannine I Dream of Lilac Time/Answer Me/Vienna, My City of Dreams/Make Believe	1958	5.00	10.00	20.00
❑ EP-410 [PS]	Bostic Plays	1958	5.00	10.00	20.00
❑ EP-414	*Southern Fried/Jersey Bounce/Jumpin' at the Woodside/Tuxedo Junction	1958	5.00	10.00	20.00
❑ EP-414 [PS]	Hits of the Swing Age, Vol. 1	1958	5.00	10.00	20.00
❑ EP-415	*720 in the Books/Air Mail Special/Pompton Turnpike/Woodchopper's Ball	1958	5.00	10.00	20.00
❑ EP-415 [PS]	Hits of the Swing Age, Vol. 2	1958	5.00	10.00	20.00
❑ EP-416	*Night Train/Stompin' at the Savoy/Honeysuckle Rose/No Name Jive	1958	5.00	10.00	20.00
❑ EP-416 [PS]	Hits of the Swing Age, Vol. 3	1958	5.00	10.00	20.00
❑ EP-417	(contents unknown)	1958	5.00	10.00	20.00
❑ EP-417 [PS]	Showcase of Swinging Dance Hits, Vol. 1	1958	5.00	10.00	20.00
❑ EP-418	Two O'Clock Jump/Back Beat//John's Idea/Royal Garden Blues	1958	5.00	10.00	20.00
❑ EP-418 [PS]	Showcase of Swinging Dance Hits, Vol. 2	1958	5.00	10.00	20.00

"Toy Bell" by the Bees (1954) was a direct inspiration, if you want to call it that, for Chuck Berry's only #1 pop hit, "My Ding-a-Ling."

Chuck Berry's Chess EPs are quite hard to find today, especially with their covers intact. Here's one for his *After School Session* release.

Early albums on the Philles label are quite collectible. Here is the only LP for Bob B. Soxx and the Blue Jeans, *Zip-a-Dee Doo Dah.*

Here's an unusual reissue of the Gary U.S. Bonds hit, "School Is In." A careful reading of the master number indicates that RCA pressed this in 1971!

In the early days of King Records, no one sold more consistently than Earl Bostic, based on the number of LPs and EPs the label issued. This 10-inch LP was his first.

When the EP single was introduced in the early 1950s, the first eight that King issued were by Earl Bostic. This is the seventh of those EPs.

Number	Title (A Side/B Side)	Yr	VG	VG+	NM
❑ EP-419	(contents unknown)	1958	5.00	10.00	20.00
❑ EP-419 [PS]	Showcase of Swinging Dance Hits, Vol. 3	1958	5.00	10.00	20.00
❑ EP-420	Twilight Time/Stairway to the Stars//Rockin' with Richard/Be My Love	1958	5.00	10.00	20.00
❑ EP-420 [PS]	Alto Magic in Hi Fi, Vol. 1	1958	5.00	10.00	20.00
❑ EP-421	(contents unknown)	1958	5.00	10.00	20.00
❑ EP-421 [PS]	Alto Magic in Hi Fi, Vol. 2	1958	5.00	10.00	20.00
❑ EP-422	C Jam Blues/Wee-Gee Board//The Wrecking Rock/Home Sweet Home Rock	1958	5.00	10.00	20.00
❑ EP-422 [PS]	Alto Magic in Hi Fi, Vol. 3	1958	5.00	10.00	20.00

ROYALE

Number	Title (A Side/B Side)	Yr	VG	VG+	NM
❑ EP 367	The Man I Love/All On//Hurricane Blues/The Major and the Minor	195?	3.75	7.50	15.00
❑ EP 367 [PS]	His Saxophone and Orchestra	195?	3.75	7.50	15.00

Albums

GRAND PRIX

Number	Title	Yr	VG	VG+	NM
❑ K-404 [M]	The Grand Prix Series	196?	3.75	7.50	15.00
❑ KS-404 [R]	The Grand Prix Series	196?	3.00	6.00	12.00
❑ K-416 [M]	Wild Man	196?	3.75	7.50	15.00
❑ KS-416 [R]	Wild Man	196?	3.00	6.00	12.00

KING

Number	Title	Yr	VG	VG+	NM
❑ 295-64 [10]	Earl Bostic and His Alto Sax	1951	50.00	100.00	200.00
—Black vinyl					
❑ 295-64 [10]	Earl Bostic and His Alto Sax	1951	100.00	200.00	400.00
—Red vinyl					
❑ 295-65 [10]	Earl Bostic and His Alto Sax	1951	50.00	100.00	200.00
—Black vinyl					
❑ 295-65 [10]	Earl Bostic and His Alto Sax	1951	100.00	200.00	400.00
—Red vinyl					
❑ 295-66 [10]	Earl Bostic and His Alto Sax	1951	50.00	100.00	200.00
—Black vinyl					
❑ 295-66 [10]	Earl Bostic and His Alto Sax	1951	100.00	200.00	400.00
—Red vinyl					
❑ 295-72 [10]	Earl Bostic and His Alto Sax	1952	50.00	100.00	200.00
❑ 295-76 [10]	Earl Bostic and His Alto Sax	1952	50.00	100.00	200.00
❑ 295-77 [10]	Earl Bostic and His Alto Sax	1952	50.00	100.00	200.00
❑ 295-78 [10]	Earl Bostic and His Alto Sax	1952	50.00	100.00	200.00
❑ 295-79 [10]	Earl Bostic and His Alto Sax	1952	50.00	100.00	200.00
❑ 295-95 [10]	Earl Bostic Plays the Old Standards	1954	50.00	100.00	200.00
❑ 295-103 [10]	Earl Bostic and His Alto Sax	1954	50.00	100.00	200.00
❑ 395-500 [M]	Dance to the Best of Bostic	1956	25.00	50.00	100.00
—Original cover with Earl Bostic pictured					
❑ 395-500 [M]	Dance to the Best of Bostic	195?	20.00	40.00	80.00
—Second cover with girl in a swimsuit pictured					
❑ 395-503 [M]	Bostic for You	1956	25.00	50.00	100.00
❑ 395-515 [M]	Alto-Tude	1956	25.00	50.00	100.00
❑ 395-525 [M]	Dance Time	1956	20.00	40.00	80.00
❑ 395-529 [M]	Let's Dance with Earl Bostic	1956	20.00	40.00	80.00
❑ 395-547 [M]	Invitation to Dance	1956	20.00	40.00	80.00
❑ 558 [M]	C'mon and Dance with Earl Bostic	1956	20.00	40.00	80.00
❑ KS-558 [S]	C'mon and Dance with Earl Bostic	1959	37.50	75.00	150.00
❑ 571 [M]	Hits of the Swing Age	1957	20.00	40.00	80.00
❑ 583 [M]	Showcase of Swinging Dance Hits	1958	20.00	40.00	80.00
❑ 597 [M]	Alto Magic in Hi-Fi	1958	20.00	40.00	80.00
❑ KS-597 [S]	Alto Magic in Hi-Fi	1959	37.50	75.00	150.00
❑ 602 [M]	Sweet Tunes of the Fantastic Fifties	1959	12.50	25.00	50.00
❑ KS-602 [S]	Sweet Tunes of the Fantastic Fifties	1959	25.00	50.00	100.00
❑ 613 [M]	Bostic Workshop	1959	12.50	25.00	50.00
❑ KS-613 [S]	Bostic Workshop	1959	25.00	50.00	100.00
❑ 620 [M]	Sweet Tunes from the Roaring Twenties	1959	12.50	25.00	50.00
❑ KS-620 [S]	Sweet Tunes from the Roaring Twenties	1959	25.00	50.00	100.00
❑ 632 [M]	Sweet Tunes of the Swinging Thirties	1959	12.50	25.00	50.00
❑ KS-632 [S]	Sweet Tunes of the Swinging Thirties	1959	25.00	50.00	100.00
❑ 640 [M]	Sweet Tunes of the Sentimental Forties	1960	12.50	25.00	50.00
❑ KS-640 [S]	Sweet Tunes of the Sentimental Forties	1960	20.00	40.00	80.00
❑ 662 [M]	Musical Pearls	1960	12.50	25.00	50.00
❑ KS-662 [S]	Musical Pearls	1960	20.00	40.00	80.00
❑ 705 [M]	Hit Tunes of Big Broadway Shows	1960	12.50	25.00	50.00
❑ KS-705 [S]	Hit Tunes of Big Broadway Shows	1960	20.00	40.00	80.00
❑ 786 [M]	By Popular Demand	1961	12.50	25.00	50.00
❑ 827 [M]	Earl Bostic Plays Bossa Nova	1963	12.50	25.00	50.00
❑ 838 [M]	Songs of the Fantastic Fifties, Volume 2	1963	12.50	25.00	50.00
❑ 846 [M]	Jazz As I Feel It	1963	12.50	25.00	50.00
❑ 881 [M]	The Best of Earl Bostic, Volume 2	1964	12.50	25.00	50.00
❑ 900 [M]	The New Sound	1964	12.50	25.00	50.00
❑ 921 [M]	The Great Hits of 1964	1964	12.50	25.00	50.00
❑ 947 [M]	24 Songs That Earl Loved the Most	1966	10.00	20.00	40.00
❑ KS-1048 [S]	Harlem Nocturne	1969	6.25	12.50	25.00
❑ K-5010X	14 Original Greatest Hits	1977	3.00	6.00	12.00

PHILIPS

Number	Title	Yr	VG	VG+	NM
❑ PHM 200262 [M]	The Song Is Not Ended	1967	6.25	12.50	25.00
❑ PHS 600262 [S]	The Song Is Not Ended	1967	6.25	12.50	25.00

BOSTIC, EARL, AND BILL DOGGETT

45s

KING

Number	Title (A Side/B Side)	Yr	VG	VG+	NM
❑ 4930	Mean to Me/Bo-Do Rock	1956	3.75	7.50	15.00
❑ 4954	Indiana/Bubbins Rock	1956	3.75	7.50	15.00
❑ 5427	Special Delivery Stomp/Earl's Dog	1960	2.50	5.00	10.00

7-Inch Extended Plays

KING

Number	Title (A Side/B Side)	Yr	VG	VG+	NM
❑ EP-397	*Bubbins Rock/Indiana/The Bo-Do Rock/Mean to Me	1957	5.00	10.00	20.00
❑ EP-397 [PS]	Bill Doggett — Earl Bostic	1957	5.00	10.00	20.00

BOSTIC, EARL/JIMMY LUNCEFORD

Albums

ALLEGRO ELITE

Number	Title	Yr	VG	VG+	NM
❑ 4053 [10]	Earl Bostic/Jimmy Lunceford Orchestras	195?	10.00	20.00	40.00

BOUNTY KILLER

12-Inch Singles

PROFILE

Number	Title (A Side/B Side)	Yr	VG	VG+	NM
❑ 74410	Scare Him (unknown versions)	1995	2.00	4.00	8.00

TOMMY BOY

Number	Title (A Side/B Side)	Yr	VG	VG+	NM
❑ TB 763	Eyes a Bleed (RZA Remix) (Tom LaRock Remix) (Dancehall Version)	1996	2.50	5.00	10.00

TVT

Number	Title (A Side/B Side)	Yr	VG	VG+	NM
❑ 1464	Hip-Opera (unknown versions)	1997	—	3.00	6.00
—Featuring The Fugees					
❑ 8215	Deadly Zone (4 versions)	1998	—	3.00	6.00

Albums

TVT

Number	Title	Yr	VG	VG+	NM
❑ 6370	Next Millennium	1998	3.00	6.00	12.00
❑ 6420	5th Element	1999	3.00	6.00	12.00

BOYS, THE

12-Inch Singles

MOTOWN

Number	Title (A Side/B Side)	Yr	VG	VG+	NM
❑ 37463 1044 1	The Saga Continues... (5 versions)	1992	2.50	5.00	10.00
❑ L33-1045 [DJ]	Thing Called Love (2 versions)	1990	2.00	4.00	8.00
❑ 37463 1059 1	Doin' It with the B (5 versions)	1992	—	3.50	7.00
❑ L33-1110 [DJ]	Thing Called Love (7 versions)	1990	2.50	5.00	10.00
❑ L33-1147 [DJ]	Thanx 4 the Funk (6 versions)	1991	2.50	5.00	10.00
❑ 4614	Dial My Heart (3 versions)	1988	—	3.50	7.00
❑ 4625	Lucky Charm (4 versions)	1988	—	3.50	7.00
❑ 4640	A Little Romance (3 versions)	1989	—	3.50	7.00
❑ 4730	Crazy (2 versions?)	1990	2.00	4.00	8.00
❑ 4758	Thanx 4 the Funk (4 versions)	1990	2.00	4.00	8.00
❑ 10322	Thing Called Love (Radio Version) (LP Version)	1990	2.50	5.00	10.00
❑ L33-17740 [DJ]	Lucky Charm (Extended) (Radio Edit) (Instrumental) (Cussapella)	1988	2.50	5.00	10.00
❑ L33-17826 [DJ]	A Little Romance (4 versions)	1989	2.50	5.00	10.00
❑ L33-17933 [DJ]	Happy (4 versions)	1989	2.50	5.00	10.00
❑ L33-18423 [DJ]	Crazy (2 versions?)	1990	2.50	5.00	10.00

45s

MOTOWN

Number	Title (A Side/B Side)	Yr	VG	VG+	NM
❑ 924	Crazy (Radio Edit)/Crazy (Radio Mix)	1990	—	2.00	4.00
❑ 1952	Lucky Charm/(instrumental)	1988	—	—	3.00
❑ 1952 [PS]	Lucky Charm/(instrumental)	1988	—	—	3.00
❑ 1965	A Little Romance/(instrumental)	1989	—	—	3.00
❑ 1965 [PS]	A Little Romance/(instrumental)	1989	—	—	3.00
❑ 1993	Happy (With Rap)/(Without Rap)	1989	—	—	3.00
❑ 53301	Dial My Heart/(Instrumental)	1988	—	—	3.00
❑ 53301 [PS]	Dial My Heart/(Instrumental)	1988	—	—	3.00

Albums

MOTOWN

Number	Title	Yr	VG	VG+	NM
❑ 6260	Messages from the Boys	1988	2.50	5.00	10.00
❑ 6302	The Boys	1990	3.75	7.50	15.00

BOYS DON'T CRY

12-Inch Singles

ATLANTIC

Number	Title (A Side/B Side)	Yr	VG	VG+	NM
❑ PR 2099 [DJ]	Who the Am Dam Do You Think You Am? (same on both sides?)	1987	2.00	4.00	8.00
❑ PR 2301 [DJ]	We Got the Magic (same on both sides?)	1987	2.50	5.00	10.00

PROFILE

Number	Title (A Side/B Side)	Yr	VG	VG+	NM
❑ 7084	I Wanna Be a Cowboy (6:05)/(Instrumental)	1986	2.00	4.00	8.00
❑ 7114	Cities on Fire/(Instrumental)	1986	2.00	4.00	8.00

45s

ATLANTIC

Number	Title (A Side/B Side)	Yr	VG	VG+	NM
❑ 89085	We Got the Magic/Love Talk	1987	—	—	3.00
❑ 89085 [PS]	We Got the Magic/Love Talk	1987	—	—	3.00
❑ 89196	Who the Am Dam Do You Think You Am/The Cure	1987	—	—	3.00
❑ 89196 [PS]	Who the Am Dam Do You Think You Am/The Cure	1987	—	—	3.00

PROFILE

Number	Title (A Side/B Side)	Yr	VG	VG+	NM
❑ 5084	I Wanna Be a Cowboy/(Instrumental)	1986	—	2.00	4.00
❑ 5114	Cities on Fire/Lipstick	1986	—	2.00	4.00

Albums

ATLANTIC

Number	Title	Yr	VG	VG+	NM
❑ 81795	Boys Don't Cry	1987	2.00	4.00	8.00

PROFILE

Number	Title	Yr	VG	VG+	NM
❑ PRO 1219	Boys Don't Cry	1986	2.50	5.00	10.00

BOYZ II MEN

12-Inch Singles

MOTOWN

Number	Title (A Side/B Side)	Yr	VG	VG+	NM
❑ P12-1006 [DJ]	Uhh Ahh (Vocal) (Instrumental)	1991	2.00	4.00	8.00
❑ P12-1019 [DJ]	Uhh Ahh (unknown versions)	1991	2.00	4.00	8.00
❑ 37463 1045 1 [DJ]	Sympin' (Remix Radio Edit Without Rap) (Remix Radio Edit) (LP Version) (Remix Version) (Instrumental)	1992	3.00	6.00	12.00
❑ 37463 1061 1 [DJ]	End of the Road (4 versions?)	1992	2.00	4.00	8.00
❑ 37463 1129 1 [DJ]	Let It Snow (LP Version) (Instrumental)	1993	2.00	4.00	8.00
❑ 37463 1191 1 [DJ]	I'll Make Love to You (4 versions)	1994	2.50	5.00	10.00

Number	Title (A Side/B Side)	Yr	VG	VG+	NM
❏ 37463 1251 1 [DJ]	On Bended Knee (Human Rhythm Remix) (Human Rhythm Remix Edit) (Swingamix) (Swingamix Edit)	1994	2.00	4.00	8.00
❏ 37463 1270 1 [DJ]	Thank You (Remix) (unknown versions)	1995	2.00	4.00	8.00
❏ 37463 1304 1 [DJ]	Brokenhearted (3 versions)/I'll Make Love to You (3 versions)	1995	2.50	5.00	10.00
❏ 37463 1382 1 [DJ]	I Remember (LP Version) (Extended Version) (Instrumental) (TV Track)	1992	2.00	4.00	8.00
❏ L33-1640 [DJ]	It's So Hard to Say Goodbye to Yesterday (same on both sides?)	1991	2.00	4.00	8.00
❏ 37463 2007 1 [DJ]	You're Not Alone (4 versions)	1996	2.50	5.00	10.00
❏ 37463 2091 1 [DJ]	Can't Let Her Go (2 versions)//Baby C'mon/All Night Long	1998	—	3.00	6.00
❏ 860481-1	I Remember (4 versions)	1995	2.50	5.00	10.00

45s
MOTOWN

Number	Title (A Side/B Side)	Yr	VG	VG+	NM
❏ 2090	Motownphilly/Under Pressure	1991	—	2.50	5.00
❏ 2162	Please Don't Go/Uhh Ahh	1992	—	—	3.00
❏ 2168	It's So Hard to Say Goodbye to Yesterday/Sympin'	1992	—	2.50	5.00
❏ 2178	End of the Road/1-4-All-4-1	1992	—	2.00	4.00

—B-side by East Coast All-Stars

| ❏ 2193 | In the Still of the Night (I'll Remember)/Who's Lovin' You | 1992 | — | 2.00 | 4.00 |

—B-side by The Jackson Five

❏ 2218	Let It Snow/Silent Night	1993	—	2.00	4.00
❏ 2257	I'll Make Love to You/Thank You	1994	—	—	3.00
❏ 860284-7	On Bended Knee/I'll Make Love to You (Sexy Version)	1994	—	—	3.00
❏ 860422-7	Water Runs Dry/Vibin'	1995	—	—	3.00
❏ 860714-7	4 Seasons of Loneliness (LP Version)/(B II M Version)	1997	—	—	3.00
❏ 860744-7	A Song for Mama/(Instrumental)	1997	—	—	3.00

UNIVERSAL

| ❏ 012 158183-7 | Pass You By (same on both sides) | 2000 | — | — | 3.00 |

Albums
MOTOWN

| ❏ 31453 0323-1 [DJ] | II | 1994 | 6.25 | 12.50 | 25.00 |

—Vinyl is promo only; in Motown company cover

| ❏ 31453 0819-1 [(2)] | Evolution | 1997 | 3.00 | 6.00 | 12.00 |

BOZE, CALVIN
45s
ALADDIN

Number	Title (A Side/B Side)	Yr	VG	VG+	NM
❏ 3045	Waiting and Drinking/If You Ever Had the Blues	1950	37.50	75.00	150.00
❏ 3055	Safronia Blues/Angel City Blues	1950	37.50	75.00	150.00
❏ 3065	Lizzie Lou/Lizzie Lou (Part 2)	1950	37.50	75.00	150.00
❏ 3072	Stinkin' from Drinkin'/Look Out for Tomorrow Today	1950	25.00	50.00	100.00
❏ 3079	Beat Street on Saturday Night/Choo Choo Ch'Boogieing My Baby Back Home	1951	25.00	50.00	100.00
❏ 3086	Slippin' and Slidin'/Baby, You're Tops with Me	1951	25.00	50.00	100.00
❏ 3100	I've Got News for You/I Can't Stop Crying	1951	20.00	40.00	80.00
❏ 3110	I'm Gonna Steam Off the Stamp/Fish Tail	1952	20.00	40.00	80.00
❏ 3122	Hey, Lawdy Miss Clawdy/My Friend Told Me	1952	20.00	40.00	80.00
❏ 3132	Good Time Sue/Keep Your Nose Out of My Business	1952	15.00	30.00	60.00
❏ 3142	The Blue Tango/The Glory of Love	1952	15.00	30.00	60.00
❏ 3143	Blue Shuffle/Popside	1952	15.00	30.00	60.00
❏ 3147	Looped/Blow Man Blow	1952	15.00	30.00	60.00
❏ 3160	Havin' a Time/Shamrock	1953	12.50	25.00	50.00
❏ 3181	That Other Woman/Shoot De Pistol	1953	12.50	25.00	50.00

IMPERIAL

| ❏ 5844 | Shamrock/Safronia B | 1962 | 3.00 | 6.00 | 12.00 |

BRADLEY, JAMES
12-Inch Singles
T.K. DISCO

Number	Title (A Side/B Side)	Yr	VG	VG+	NM
❏ TKD (# unk)	I'm In Too Deep/I Can't Get Enough of Your Love	1979	3.75	7.50	15.00
❏ TKD 418	Let's Paint the Town/Wrapped Up in Your Love	1979	3.00	6.00	12.00

45s
MALACO

| ❏ 1056 | I'm In Too Deep/I Can't Get Enough of Your Love | 1979 | — | 2.50 | 5.00 |
| ❏ 2063 | Let's Do It Together/Knowing You're My Everything | 1979 | — | 2.50 | 5.00 |

Albums
MALACO

| ❏ 6358 | James Bradley | 1979 | 3.75 | 7.50 | 15.00 |

BRADSHAW, TINY
45s
KING

Number	Title (A Side/B Side)	Yr	VG	VG+	NM
❏ 4357	I Hate You/Well Oh Well	1950	15.00	30.00	60.00
❏ 4376	After You've Gone/Boogie Green	1950	15.00	30.00	60.00
❏ 4397	Butterfly/I'm Going to Have Myself a Ball	1950	15.00	30.00	60.00
❏ 4417	Breaking Up the House/If You Don't Love Me, Tell Me So	1950	15.00	30.00	60.00
❏ 4427	Walk That Mess/One, Two, Three, Kick Blues	1951	15.00	30.00	60.00
❏ 4447	Brad's Blues/Two Dry Bones on the Pantry Shelf	1951	15.00	30.00	60.00
❏ 4457	Bradshaw Boogie/Walkin' the Chalk Line	1951	15.00	30.00	60.00
❏ 4467	I'm a High Ballin' Daddy/You Came By	1951	15.00	30.00	60.00
❏ 4477	T-99/Long Time Baby	1951	50.00	100.00	200.00
❏ 4497	The Train Kept a-Rollin'/Knockin' Blues	1951	50.00	100.00	200.00
❏ 4537	Mailman's Sack/Newspaper Boy Blues	1952	50.00	100.00	200.00
❏ 4547	Rippin' and Runnin'/Lay It on the Line	1952	50.00	100.00	200.00
❏ 4577	Strange/Soft	1952	12.50	25.00	50.00
❏ 4621	The Blues Came Pouring In/Heavy Juice	1953	12.50	25.00	50.00
❏ 4664	South of the Orient/Later	1953	12.50	25.00	50.00
❏ 4687	Powder Puff/Ping Pong	1953	12.50	25.00	50.00
❏ 4713	Don't Worry 'Bout Me/Overflow	1954	10.00	20.00	40.00
❏ 4727	Spider Web/The Gypsey	1954	10.00	20.00	40.00
❏ 4747	A Stack of Dollars/Cat Fruit	1954	10.00	20.00	40.00
❏ 4757	Light/Choice	1954	10.00	20.00	40.00
❏ 4777	Cat Nap/Stomping Room Only	1955	10.00	20.00	40.00
❏ 4787	Phantom Turnpike/Come On	1955	10.00	20.00	40.00
❏ 5114	Short Shorts/Bushes	1958	6.25	12.50	25.00

7-Inch Extended Plays
KING

❏ EP 208	*Soft/Well Oh Well/Heavy Juice/The Train Kept a-Rollin'	195?	10.00	20.00	40.00
❏ EP 208 [PS]	Tiny Bradshaw	195?	10.00	20.00	40.00
❏ EP 248	Off and On/Free for All//South of the Orient/Later	195?	10.00	20.00	40.00
❏ EP 248 [PS]	Tiny Bradshaw, Vol. 2	195?	10.00	20.00	40.00
❏ EP 307	*Ping Pong/Powder Puff/Spider Web/Overflow	195?	10.00	20.00	40.00
❏ EP 307 [PS]	Tiny Bradshaw Plays, Vol. 4	195?	10.00	20.00	40.00

Albums
KING

❏ 295-74 [10]	Off and On	1955	250.00	500.00	1000.
❏ 395-501 [M]	Selections	1956	175.00	350.00	700.00
❏ 653 [M]	Great Composer	1960	75.00	150.00	300.00
❏ 953 [M]	24 Great Songs	1966	10.00	20.00	40.00

BRAND NEW HEAVIES, THE
12-Inch Singles
DELICIOUS VINYL

Number	Title (A Side/B Side)	Yr	VG	VG+	NM
❏ 1232 [(2)]	You Can Do It (11 versions)	1997	3.00	6.00	12.00
❏ DMD 1881 [DJ]	Dream Come True (DMC Remix)/Opus III — It's a Fine Day (DMC Remix)	199?	2.50	5.00	10.00
❏ PRO 2004 [DJ]	HRE Theme (Vocal) (Instrumental)	199?	2.50	5.00	10.00
❏ DMD 2146 [DJ]	Brother Sister (5 versions)	1994	2.50	5.00	10.00
❏ 4009 [(2)]	Sometimes (6 versions?)	1997	2.50	5.00	10.00
❏ SPRO-10257 [DJ]	Mind Trips (4 versions)/Bang	1995	3.00	6.00	12.00
❏ 58491	Mind Trips (4 versions)/Bang	1995	2.50	5.00	10.00

Albums
DELICIOUS VINYL

| ❏ 14243 [(2)] | Brother Sister | 1994 | 3.75 | 7.50 | 15.00 |
| ❏ 71806 | The Brand New Heavies | 1998 | 3.00 | 6.00 | 12.00 |

—Originally issued in 1991

| ❏ 71807 [(2)] | Heavy Rhyme Experience — Vol. 1 | 1998 | 3.00 | 6.00 | 12.00 |

—Originally issued in 1992

| ❏ 846874-1 | The Brand New Heavies | 1991 | 3.75 | 7.50 | 15.00 |

BRAND NUBIAN
12-Inch Singles
ARISTA

Number	Title (A Side/B Side)	Yr	VG	VG+	NM
❏ 3585 [DJ]	Take It to the Head (3 versions)/Back Up Off the Wall	1998	2.50	5.00	10.00
❏ 3599 [DJ]	Back Up Off the Wall (4 versions)	1998	2.50	5.00	10.00
❏ 3636 [DJ]	Let's Dance (Censored Version) (Instrumental)/(Street Version) (Acappella)	1999	3.00	6.00	12.00

—Featuring Busta Rhymes

| ❏ 3661 [DJ] | Come On and Get Down (4 versions)/Let's Dance | 1999 | 2.50 | 5.00 | 10.00 |

ELEKTRA

❏ ED 5703 [DJ]	Word Is Bond (LP Version) (Clean Edit) (LP Instrumental)	1994	2.50	5.00	10.00
❏ ED 5723 [DJ]	Hold On (4 versions)/Step Into Da Cipher/Alladat	1995	3.00	6.00	12.00
❏ 66191	Word Is Bond (4 versions)/Straight Off Da Head (2 versions)	1994	—	3.00	6.00
❏ 66320	Allah U Akbar (3 versions)/Steal Ya 'Ho (3 versions)	1993	2.50	5.00	10.00

LOUD

| ❏ 64952 | A Child Is Born (Album Version) (Clean Version) | 1997 | 3.00 | 6.00 | 12.00 |

45s
ELEKTRA

| ❏ 69285 | Brand Nubian/Feel So Good | 1989 | 2.00 | 4.00 | 8.00 |

Albums
ARISTA

| ❏ 19024 [(2)] | Foundation | 1998 | 3.75 | 7.50 | 15.00 |

ELEKTRA

❏ 60946	One for All	1990	3.75	7.50	15.00
❏ 61381	In God We Trust	1993	3.75	7.50	15.00
❏ 61682 [(2)]	Everything Is Everything	1994	3.75	7.50	15.00

BRANDY
12-Inch Singles
ARISTA

Number	Title (A Side/B Side)	Yr	VG	VG+	NM
❏ 12974	Sittin' Up in My Room (6 versions)	1996	3.75	7.50	15.00

ATLANTIC

❏ DMD 2173 [DJ]	I Wanna Be Down (Carson CA Edit) (Carson CA Instrumental)/(3 Boyz Dub) (Accapella)	1994	3.75	7.50	15.00
❏ DMD 2195 [DJ]	Baby (unknown versions)	1994	2.00	4.00	8.00
❏ DMD 2206 [DJ]	Baby (unknown versions)	1995	2.50	5.00	10.00
❏ DMD 2220 [DJ]	Best Friend (5 versions)	1995	2.50	5.00	10.00
❏ DMD 2469 [DJ]	The Boy Is Mine (4 versions)	1998	3.00	6.00	12.00

—With Monica

| ❏ DMD 2478 [DJ] | Top of the World (Radio Edit) (Instrumental)/(Album Version) (Acapella) | 1998 | 3.75 | 7.50 | 15.00 |

—Featuring Mase

Number	Title (A Side/B Side)	Yr	VG	VG+	NM
❏ DMD 2497 [DJ]	Angel in Disguise (Album Mix) (Percapella)/ (Instrumental) (Acapella)	1998	3.75	7.50	15.00
❏ DMD 2502 [DJ]	Almost Doesn't Count (DJ Premier Mix) (Album Version) (DJ Premier Instrumental)/(Club Remix) (Radio Remix) (Acapella Premier)	1999	3.75	7.50	15.00
❏ DMD 2515 [DJ]	U Don't Know Me (Like U Used To) (Remix) (Remix Clean Radio Mix) (Remix Acapella)/ (Album Version) (Album Version Instrumental) (Remix Instrumental Dub)	1999	3.00	6.00	12.00
—Featuring Shaunta & Da Brat					
❏ PR 6177 [DJ]	Brokenhearted (Soulpower Groove Mix) (Soulpower Mix) (Acoustic Mix)/(LP Version) (Soulpower Groove Instrumental)	1995	2.50	5.00	10.00
❏ 84118	The Boy Is Mine (4 versions)	1998	2.50	5.00	10.00
—With Monica					
❏ 84192	The Boy Is Mine (2 versions?)/Top of the World Part II	1998	2.50	5.00	10.00
—With Monica					
❏ 84508	U Don't Know Me (Like U Used To) (6 versions)	1999	—	3.50	7.00
—Featuring Shaunta & Da Brat					
❏ 85217	What About Us? (unknown versions)	2002	—	3.00	6.00
❏ 85551	Brokenhearted (unknown versions)	1995	2.00	4.00	8.00
❏ 85577	Best Friend (7 versions)	1995	2.00	4.00	8.00
❏ 85593	Baby (5 versions)/I Wanna Be Down	1995	2.00	4.00	8.00
❏ 85640	I Wanna Be Down (unknown versions)	1994	2.50	5.00	10.00
❏ PR 300725 [DJ]	What About Us? (LP Mix 4:12) (Instrumental 4:09) (Radio Mix 3:56) (Acapella 4:12)	2001	2.00	4.00	8.00
❏ PR 300806 [DJ]	Full Moon (LP Version 3:57) (Instrumental 3:58) (TV Track 3:58) (Acapella 3:58)	2002	—	3.00	6.00
❏ PR 300812 [(2) DJ]	What About Us? (7 versions)	2002	3.00	6.00	12.00
❏ PR 300817 [DJ]	What About Us? (Felix Da Housecat's Glitz Mix 5:52) (Felix Da Housecat's Instrumental 6:07) (Thee Electro Beat Dub 4:11)	2002	—	3.00	6.00
❏ PR 300884 [(2) DJ]	Full Moon (6 versions)	2002	5.00	10.00	20.00

45s
ARISTA

Number	Title (A Side/B Side)	Yr	VG	VG+	NM
❏ 12929	Sittin' Up in My Room/My Love, Sweet Love	1996	—	—	3.00
—B-side by Patti LaBelle					

ATLANTIC

Number	Title (A Side/B Side)	Yr	VG	VG+	NM
❏ 84089	The Boy Is Mine (Radio Edit with Intro)/ (Instrumental)	1998	—	2.00	4.00
—With Monica					
❏ 84198	Have You Ever?/Top of the World Remix	1999	—	—	3.00
❏ 85267	What About Us?/Full Moon	2002	—	—	3.00
❏ 87173	Baby/I Wanna Be Down	1995	—	2.00	4.00

Albums
ATLANTIC

Number	Title (A Side/B Side)	Yr	VG	VG+	NM
❏ PR 5970 [DJ]	Brandy	1994	3.75	7.50	15.00
—Vinyl is promo only					
❏ 83039 [(2)]	Never S-a-y Never	1998	3.75	7.50	15.00
❏ 83493 [(2)]	Full Moon	2002	3.75	7.50	15.00

BRANDY, TAMIA, GLADYS KNIGHT & CHAKA KHAN
45s
EASTWEST

Number	Title (A Side/B Side)	Yr	VG	VG+	NM
❏ 64262	Missing You/So Right, For Life	1996	—	2.50	5.00
—B-side by Michael Speaks					

BRASS CONSTRUCTION
12-Inch Singles
CAPITOL

Number	Title (A Side/B Side)	Yr	VG	VG+	NM
❏ V-8549	Walkin' the Line (4:50)/Forever Love (4:05)	1983	2.50	5.00	10.00
❏ V-8553	Walkin' the Line (LP Version) (Brassy Version)	1983	2.50	5.00	10.00
❏ V-8598	Never Had a Girl (4:43)/Breakdown (4:30)	1984	2.00	4.00	8.00
❏ V-8608	Partyline (Partymix) (Dub) (Single Version)	1984	2.00	4.00	8.00
❏ V-8618	International (Special Mix)/What Is the Law	1984	2.50	5.00	10.00
❏ V-8652	Give and Take (6:00) (Dub 5:00)/My Place	1985	2.00	4.00	8.00
❏ SPRO-9277/8 [DJ]	International (3:57) (7:29)	1984	2.50	5.00	10.00
❏ SPRO-9914/5 [DJ]	Walkin' the Line (LP Version) (Single Version)	1983	3.00	6.00	12.00
❏ SPRO-9954/5 [DJ]	Walkin' the Line (LP Version) (Brassy Version)	1983	3.00	6.00	12.00
❏ V-15208	Zig Zag (Extended) (Instrumental)	1985	2.00	4.00	8.00

LIBERTY

Number	Title (A Side/B Side)	Yr	VG	VG+	NM
❏ SP-205	How Do You Do (What You Do to Me) (6:38)/Do Ya (6:17)	1980	3.75	7.50	15.00
❏ SP-213	Can You See the Light (Vocal) (Instrumental)	1982	2.00	4.00	8.00
❏ SP-223	Attitude (same on both sides?)	1982	2.50	5.00	10.00

UNITED ARTISTS

Number	Title (A Side/B Side)	Yr	VG	VG+	NM
❏ SP-190	Get Up (8:01)/Starting Tomorrow (4:56)	1978	5.00	10.00	20.00

45s
CAPITOL

Number	Title (A Side/B Side)	Yr	VG	VG+	NM
❏ B-5219	Walkin' the Line/Forever Love	1983	—	—	3.00
❏ B-5219 [PS]	Walkin' the Line/Forever Love	1983	—	—	3.00
❏ B-5252	We Can Work It Out/Easy	1983	—	—	3.00
❏ B-5347	Breakdown/We Can Work It Out	1984	—	—	3.00
❏ B-5361	Never Had a Girl/Breakdown	1984	—	—	3.00
❏ B-5382	Partyline/We Can Bring It Back	1984	—	—	3.00
❏ B-5382 [PS]	Partyline/We Can Bring It Back	1984	—	—	3.00
❏ B-5425	International/What Is the Law	1984	—	—	3.00
❏ B-5500	Give and Take/My Place	1985	—	—	3.00

LIBERTY

Number	Title (A Side/B Side)	Yr	VG	VG+	NM
❏ 1387	How Do You Do (What You Do to Me)/Don't Try to Change Me	1980	—	2.00	4.00
❏ B-1453	Can You See the Light/E.T.C.	1982	—	2.00	4.00
❏ B-1473	Attitude/Hotdog	1982	—	2.00	4.00

UNITED ARTISTS

Number	Title (A Side/B Side)	Yr	VG	VG+	NM
❏ XW775	Movin'/Talkin'	1976	—	2.00	4.00
❏ XW837	Changin'/Love	1976	—	2.50	5.00
❏ XW921	Ha Cha Cha (Funktion)/Sambo (Conditions)	1976	—	2.50	5.00
❏ XW957	The Message (Inspiration)/What's On Your Mind (Expression)	1977	—	2.50	5.00
❏ XW1120	L-O-V-E-U/Get It Together	1978	—	2.50	5.00
❏ XW1160	Movin'/Changin'	1978	—	—	3.00
—Reissue					
❏ XW1204	Celebrate/Top of the World	1978	—	2.50	5.00
❏ XW1242	Help Yourself/Pick Yourself Up	1978	—	2.50	5.00
❏ X1262	Get Up/Perceptions (What's the Right Direction)	1978	—	2.50	5.00
❏ X1332	Right Place/It's Alright	1980	—	2.50	5.00
❏ X1346	Music Makes You Feel Like Dancing/I Want Some Action	1980	—	2.50	5.00
❏ X1371	We Are Brass/I'm Not Gonna Stop	1980	—	2.50	5.00

Albums
CAPITOL

Number	Title (A Side/B Side)	Yr	VG	VG+	NM
❏ ST-12268	Conversations	1983	2.00	4.00	8.00
❏ ST-12324	Renegades	1984	2.00	4.00	8.00
❏ ST-12423	Conquest	1985	2.00	4.00	8.00

LIBERTY

Number	Title (A Side/B Side)	Yr	VG	VG+	NM
❏ LT-1060	Brass Construction 6	1981	2.00	4.00	8.00
—Reissue of United Artists 1060					
❏ LT-51121	Attitudes	1982	2.50	5.00	10.00

UNITED ARTISTS

Number	Title (A Side/B Side)	Yr	VG	VG+	NM
❏ UA-LA545-G	Brass Construction	1976	2.50	5.00	10.00
❏ UA-LA677-G	Brass Construction II	1976	2.50	5.00	10.00
❏ UA-LA775-H	Brass Construction III	1977	2.50	5.00	10.00
❏ UA-LA916-H	Brass Construction IV	1978	2.50	5.00	10.00
❏ LT-977	Brass Construction 5	1979	2.50	5.00	10.00
❏ LT-1060	Brass Construction 6	1980	3.00	6.00	12.00

BRAXTON, TONI
Also see THE BRAXTONS.
12-Inch Singles
LAFACE

Number	Title (A Side/B Side)	Yr	VG	VG+	NM
❏ LFDP 4054 [DJ]	Breathe Again (LP Version) (Instrumental)	1993	2.50	5.00	10.00
❏ LFDP 4081 [DJ]	How Many Ways (4 versions)	1994	3.00	6.00	12.00
❏ LFDP 4201 [DJ]	Un-Break My Heart (4 versions)	1996	5.00	10.00	20.00
❏ LFDP 4213 [DJ]	Un-Break My Heart (Soul Hex Anthem Vocal) (Soul Hex No Sleep Beats) (Acapella) (Frankie Knuckles Franktidrama Club Mix) (Frankie Knuckles Classic Radio Mix)	1996	2.00	4.00	8.00
❏ LFDP 4241 [(2) DJ]	I Don't Want To (Classic Club Mix)/ (Franktified Club Mix)//Un-Break My Heart (Frankie Knuckles Director's Cut)/I Don't Want To (Deepjay's Delight) (Acappella Reprise)	1997	3.75	7.50	15.00
❏ LFDP 4468 [DJ]	He Wasn't Man Enough (Junior Marathon Mix 12:06) (Junior Instrumental 8:18)	2000	3.75	7.50	15.00
❏ LFDP 4482 [(2) DJ]	Spanish Guitar (3 versions)/He Wasn't Man Enough (Peter Rauhofer NYC Trance Mix)	2000	3.75	7.50	15.00
❏ LFDP 4512 [DJ]	Spanish Guitar (Mixshow Edit) (one more unknown version)	2000	3.00	6.00	12.00
❏ LFDP 4522 [DJ]	Spanish Guitar (Radio Edit) (JC Modulated Dub) (Joe Claussell Main Mix)	2000	3.00	6.00	12.00
❏ LFDP 4540 [DJ]	Maybe (HQ2 Club Mix 8:30) (HQ2 Radio Mix 3:33) (Dynamix NYC Club Mix 8:07)	2001	3.00	6.00	12.00
❏ 24041	Love Shoulda Brought You Home (unknown versions)	1992	2.00	4.00	8.00
❏ 24056	Breathe Again (5 versions)	1993	2.50	5.00	10.00
❏ 24063 [DJ]	Seven Whole Days (Ghetto Vibe 6:35) (Ghetto Vibe Instrumental 6:36)/(Album Version 6:22) (Live Version 6:15)/The Christmas Song	1993	7.50	15.00	30.00
❏ 24213	Un-Break My Heart (Soul Hex Anthem Vocal) (Soul Hex No Sleep Beats) (Acapella) (Frankie Knuckles Franktidrama Club Mix) (Frankie Knuckles Classic Radio Mix)	1996	2.00	4.00	8.00
❏ 24230	I Don't Want To (3 versions)//I Love Me Some Him/Un-Break My Heart	1997	2.00	4.00	8.00
❏ 24499 [(2)]	Spanish Guitar (HQ Mix) (HQ Radio Edit)/ (Mousse T's Deep Vocal Mix) (Mousse T's Radio Edit)//(Eiffel 65 Extended Mix) (Eiffel 65 TV Edit)/ (Mousse T's Extended Mix) (Royal Garden Flamenco Mix) (Album Version)	2000	2.50	5.00	10.00

45s
LAFACE

Number	Title (A Side/B Side)	Yr	VG	VG+	NM
❏ 24064	You Mean the World to Me/Seven Whole Days	1994	—	2.00	4.00
❏ 24160	You're Makin' Me High/Let It Flow	1996	—	2.00	4.00
❏ 24200	Un-Break My Heart/(Spanish Version)	1996	—	2.00	4.00

Albums
LAFACE

Number	Title (A Side/B Side)	Yr	VG	VG+	NM
❏ 26069 [(2)]	The Heat	2000	5.00	10.00	20.00

BRAXTONS, THE
When the group was on Arista, TONI BRAXTON was a member.
12-Inch Singles
ARISTA

Number	Title (A Side/B Side)	Yr	VG	VG+	NM
❏ ADP 2066	Good Life (unknown versions)	1990	2.50	5.00	10.00

ATLANTIC

Number	Title (A Side/B Side)	Yr	VG	VG+	NM
❏ DMD 2322 [DJ]	So Many Ways (5 versions)	1996	2.50	5.00	10.00
❏ DMD 2328 [(2) DJ]	Boss (7 versions)	1997	3.75	7.50	15.00

Number	Title (A Side/B Side)	Yr	VG	VG+	NM

BRENDA AND THE TABULATIONS
12-Inch Singles
CHOCOLATE CITY
| ❏ CCD 20006 | (I'm a) Superstar (unknown versions) | 1977 | 3.75 | 7.50 | 15.00 |

45s
CHOCOLATE CITY
❏ 004	Home to Myself/Leave Me Alone	1976	—	2.00	4.00
❏ 009	(I'm a) Superstar/Take It or Leave It	1977	—	2.00	4.00
❏ 012	Let's Go All the Way (Down)/I Keep Coming Back for More	1977	—	2.00	4.00

DIONN
❏ 500	Dry Your Eyes/The Wash	1967	2.50	5.00	10.00
❏ 501	Who's Lovin' You/Stay Together Young Lovers	1967	2.50	5.00	10.00
❏ 503	Just Once in a Lifetime/Hey Boy	1967	2.50	5.00	10.00
❏ 504	When You're Gone/Hey Boy	1967	2.50	5.00	10.00
❏ 507	To the One I Love/Baby You're So Right	1968	2.50	5.00	10.00
❏ 509	I Can't Get Over You/That's in the Past	1968	2.50	5.00	10.00
❏ 511	Reason to Live/Hey Boy	1968	2.50	5.00	10.00
❏ 512	That's the Price You Have to Pay/I Wish I Hadn't Done What I Did	1969	2.50	5.00	10.00

EPIC
❏ 10898	Little Bit of Love/Let Me Be Happy	1972	—	3.00	6.00
❏ 10954	One Girl Too Late/The Magic of Your Love	1973	—	3.00	6.00
❏ 11000	Key to My Heart/Love Is Just a Carnival	1973	—	3.00	6.00
❏ 11059	I'm in Love/Walk On In	1973	—	3.00	6.00
❏ 50081	Let Me Be Happy/Little Bit of Love	1975	—	2.00	4.00

PHILCO-FORD
| ❏ HP-40 | Dry Your Eyes/When You're Gone | 1969 | 5.00 | 10.00 | 20.00 |
—4-inch plastic "Hip Pocket Record" with color sleeve

TOP & BOTTOM
❏ 401	The Touch of You/Stop Sneaking Around	1969	2.00	4.00	8.00
❏ 403	And My Heart Sang (Tra La La)/Lies, Lies, Lies	1970	2.00	4.00	8.00
❏ 404	Don't Make Me Over/You've Changed	1970	2.00	4.00	8.00
❏ 406	A Child No One Wanted/Scuse Us All	1970	2.00	4.00	8.00
❏ 407	Right on the Tip of My Tongue/Always and Forever	1971	2.00	4.00	8.00
❏ 408	A Part of You/Where There's a Will	1971	2.00	4.00	8.00
❏ 411	Why Didn't I Think of That/A Love You Can Depend On	1971	2.00	4.00	8.00

Albums
CHOCOLATE CITY
| ❏ 2002 | I Keep Coming Back for More | 1977 | 2.50 | 5.00 | 10.00 |

DIONN
| ❏ LPM-2000 [M] | Dry Your Eyes | 1967 | 10.00 | 20.00 | 40.00 |
| ❏ LPS-2000 [S] | Dry Your Eyes | 1967 | 12.50 | 25.00 | 50.00 |

TOP & BOTTOM
| ❏ 100 | Brenda and the Tabulations | 1970 | 5.00 | 10.00 | 20.00 |

BRENSTON, JACKIE
45s
CHESS
| ❏ 1458 | Rocket "88"/Come Back Where You Belong | 1951 | 5000. | 7500. | 10000. |
—Early rockabilly classic; obscenely rare, even though the 45s were pressed later
❏ 1469	In My Real Gone Rocket/Tuckered Out	1951	500.00	750.00	1000.
❏ 1472	Juiced/Independent Woman	1951	500.00	750.00	1000.
❏ 1496	Leo the Louse/Hi-Ho Baby	1952	125.00	250.00	500.00
❏ 1532	Blues Got Me Again/Starvation	1953	62.50	125.00	250.00

FEDERAL
| ❏ 12283 | What Can It Be/Gonna Wait for My Chance | 1956 | 12.50 | 25.00 | 50.00 |
| ❏ 12291 | Much Later/The Mistreater | 1957 | 12.50 | 25.00 | 50.00 |

SUE
| ❏ 736 | Trouble Up the Road/You Ain't the One | 1961 | 5.00 | 10.00 | 20.00 |

78s
CHESS
❏ 1458	Rocket "88"/Come Back Where You Belong	1951	75.00	150.00	300.00
❏ 1469	In My Real Gone Rocket/Tuckered Out	1951	50.00	100.00	200.00
❏ 1472	Juiced/Independent Woman	1951	50.00	100.00	200.00
❏ 1496	Leo the Louse/Hi-Ho Baby	1952	37.50	75.00	150.00
❏ 1532	Blues Got Me Again/Starvation	1953	25.00	50.00	100.00

FEDERAL
| ❏ 12283 | What Can It Be/Gonna Wait for My Chance | 1956 | 12.50 | 25.00 | 50.00 |
| ❏ 12291 | Much Later/The Mistreater | 1957 | 12.50 | 25.00 | 50.00 |

BRICK
12-Inch Singles
BANG
❏ 4Z9-02253	Sweat (Til You Get Wet)/Seaside Vibes	1981	3.00	6.00	12.00
❏ 4Z9-03158	Free Dancer (6:44)/Stick By You	1982	3.00	6.00	12.00
❏ 4805	Dancin' Man/We'll Love	1979	2.50	5.00	10.00

MAGIC CITY
| ❏ MCR 002 | Kum Danz (Vocal 5:30)/(Instrumental 6:00) | 1987 | — | 3.00 | 6.00 |

45s
BANG
| ❏ 723 | Music Matic/Good High | 1976 | — | 2.50 | 5.00 |
—Reissue of Main Street 119
❏ 727	Dazz/Southern Sunset	1976	—	2.50	5.00
❏ 732	That's What It's All About/Can't Wait (Tick Tock)	1977	—	2.50	5.00
❏ 734	Dusic/Happy	1977	—	2.50	5.00
❏ 735	Ain't Gonna Hurt Nobody/Honey Chile	1977	—	2.50	5.00
❏ ZS5-02246	Sweat (Til You Get Wet)/Seaside Vibes	1981	—	2.00	4.00
❏ ZS5-02599	Wide Open/Seaside Vibes	1981	—	2.00	4.00
❏ ZS5-03157	Free Dancer/Stick By You	1982	—	2.00	4.00
❏ 4802	Raise Your Hands/Life Is What You Make It	1979	—	2.00	4.00

| ❏ 4804 | Dancin' Man/We'll Love | 1979 | — | 2.00 | 4.00 |
| ❏ 4810 | All the Way/Spread Love | 1980 | — | 2.00 | 4.00 |
MAIN STREET
| ❏ 119 | Music Matic/Good High | 1975 | 2.50 | 5.00 | 10.00 |
Albums
BANG
| ❏ BLP-408 | Good High | 1976 | 3.00 | 6.00 | 12.00 |
—Beware of sealed copies -- this album has been "reissued" to look exactly like the original
❏ BLP-409	Brick	1977	3.00	6.00	12.00
❏ JZ 35969	Stoneheart	1979	2.50	5.00	10.00
❏ JZ 36262	Waiting on You	1980	2.50	5.00	10.00
❏ FZ 37471	Summer Heat	1981	2.50	5.00	10.00
❏ FZ 38170	After 5	1982	2.50	5.00	10.00
MAGIC CITY
| ❏ MCR 1001 | Too Tuff | 1988 | 2.50 | 5.00 | 10.00 |

BRIDES OF FUNKENSTEIN, THE
Splinter group from PARLIAMENT/FUNKADELIC.
12-Inch Singles
ATLANTIC
| ❏ DSKO 129 | Disco to Go (5:06)/When You're Gone | 1978 | 3.00 | 6.00 | 12.00 |
45s
ATLANTIC
❏ 3498	Disco to Go/When You're Gone	1978	—	2.50	5.00
❏ 3556	Amorous/War Ship Touchante	1979	—	2.50	5.00
❏ 3640	Never Buy Texas from a Cowboy (Part 1)/(Part 2)	1979	—	2.50	5.00
❏ 3658	Mother May I/Didn't Mean to Fall in Love	1980	2.00	4.00	8.00
Albums
ATLANTIC
| ❏ SD 19201 | Funk or Walk | 1978 | 3.75 | 7.50 | 15.00 |
| ❏ SD 19261 | Never Buy Texas from a Cowboy | 1980 | 3.75 | 7.50 | 15.00 |

BRIDGES, ALICIA
12-Inch Singles
POLYDOR
❏ PRO 080 [DJ]	Body Heat (Mixed by James Burgess) (same on both sides)	1979	2.00	4.00	8.00
❏ PDD 503	I Love the Nightlife (Disco 'Round) (5:37)/City Rhythm	1978	2.50	5.00	10.00
❏ PDD 506	Body Heat/We Are One	1979	2.50	5.00	10.00
❏ PR-12-6851 [DJ]	I Love the Nightlife (Disco 'Round) (Original Version 3:25) (Rapino Bros. Night of the Disco Trash 12" Mix 4:47)/(Trash Europe Express 12" Mix 5:18) (Phillip Damien Extended Vox 6:20)	1994	2.50	5.00	10.00
❏ 853705-1	I Love the Nightlife (Disco 'Round) (Original Version 3:25) (Rapino Bros. Night of the Disco Trash 12" Mix 4:47)/(Trash Europe Express 12" Mix 5:18) (Phillip Damien Extended Vox 6:20)	1994	3.00	6.00	12.00
—Pink vinyl
| ❏ 871201-1 | I Love the Nightlife (Disco 'Round)/Body Heat | 1989 | 2.00 | 4.00 | 8.00 |
—Reissue of 12-inch versions
SECOND WAVE
| ❏ 22005 | Under the Cover of Darkness (2 versions)/Not Ready Yet (2 versions) | 1984 | 2.50 | 5.00 | 10.00 |
45s
AVI
| ❏ 339 | If You Only Knew/Picture of Success | 198? | — | 2.00 | 4.00 |
POLYDOR
❏ 2044	Starchild/Rex the Robot	1979	—	2.50	5.00
❏ 14483	I Love the Nightlife (Disco 'Round)/Self Applause	1978	—	2.00	4.00
❏ 14539	Body Heat/We Are One	1979	—	2.00	4.00
Albums
POLYDOR
| ❏ PD-1-6158 | Alicia Bridges | 1978 | 2.50 | 5.00 | 10.00 |
| ❏ PD-1-6219 | Play It As It Lays | 1979 | 2.50 | 5.00 | 10.00 |
SECOND WAVE
| ❏ 22007 | Hocus Pocus | 1984 | 3.00 | 6.00 | 12.00 |

BRIDGEWATER, DEE DEE
45s
ATLANTIC
| ❏ 3357 | Goin' Through the Motions/Every Man Wants Another Man's Woman | 1976 | — | 3.00 | 6.00 |
ELEKTRA
❏ 45466	Just Family/Thank the Day	1978	—	2.50	5.00
❏ 46031	Bad for Me/Back of Your Mind	1979	—	2.50	5.00
❏ 47046	One in a Million (Guy)/Give	1980	—	2.50	5.00
Albums
ATLANTIC
| ❏ SD 18188 | Dee Dee Bridgewater | 1976 | 3.00 | 6.00 | 12.00 |
ELEKTRA
❏ 6E-119	Just Family	1978	2.50	5.00	10.00
❏ 6E-188	Bad for Me	1979	2.50	5.00	10.00
❏ 6E-306	Dee Dee Bridgewater	1980	2.50	5.00	10.00
MCA/IMPULSE
| ❏ MCA-6331 | Live in Paris | 1989 | 3.00 | 6.00 | 12.00 |

BRISTOL, JOHNNY
45s
ATLANTIC
| ❏ 3360 | Do It to My Mind/Love to Take a Chance to Taste the Wine | 1976 | — | 2.00 | 4.00 |

B

Number	Title (A Side/B Side)	Yr	VG	VG+	NM
❏ 3391	You Turned Me On to Love/I Sho Like Groovin' with You	1977	—	2.00	4.00
❏ 3421	Waiting on Love/She's So Amazing	1977	—	2.00	4.00
❏ 3501	When He Comes (You Will Know)/Strangers in the Dark Corners	1978	—	2.00	4.00
❏ 3526	Why Stop Now/When He Comes (You Will Know)	1978	—	2.00	4.00

HANDSHAKE

❏ 02594	Take Me Down/Loving and Free	1981	—	2.00	4.00
❏ 5300	My Guy/My Girl//Now	1980	—	2.00	4.00
—A-side with Amii Stewart					
❏ 5304	Love No Longer Has a Hold on Me/Until I See You Again	1981	—	2.00	4.00

MGM

❏ 14715	Hang On In There Baby/Take Care of You for Me	1974	—	2.50	5.00
❏ 14762	You and I/It Don't Hurt No More	1974	—	2.50	5.00
❏ 14792	Leave My World/All Goodbyes Aren't Good	1975	—	2.50	5.00
❏ 14814	Love Takes Tears/Go On and Dream	1975	—	2.50	5.00

POLYDOR

❏ 813982-7	Hang On In There Baby/Stand By Me	1983	—	—	3.00
—Reissue					

Albums

ATLANTIC

❏ SD 18197	Bristol's Creme	1976	2.50	5.00	10.00
❏ SD 19184	Strangers	1978	2.50	5.00	10.00

HANDSHAKE

❏ FW 37666	Free to Be Me	1981	2.50	5.00	10.00

MGM

❏ M3G-4959	Hang On In There Baby	1974	3.00	6.00	12.00
❏ M3G-4983	Feeling the Magic	1975	3.00	6.00	12.00

BROOKLYN BRIDGE, THE
Also see JOHNNY MAESTRO.
45s
BUDDAH

Number	Title (A Side/B Side)	Yr	VG	VG+	NM
❏ 60	Little Red Boat by the River/From My Window	1968	—	3.00	6.00
❏ 75	Worst That Could Happen/Your Kite, My Kite	1968	2.00	4.00	8.00
❏ 95	Welcome Me Love/Blessed Is the Rain	1969	—	3.00	6.00
❏ 126	Your Husband, My Wife/Upside Down	1969	—	3.00	6.00
❏ 139	You'll Never Walk Alone/Minstrel Sunday	1969	—	3.00	6.00
❏ 162	Free as the Wind/He's Not a Happy Man	1970	—	3.00	6.00
❏ 179	Down by the River/Look Again	1970	—	3.00	6.00
❏ 193	Day Is Done/Opposites	1970	—	3.00	6.00
❏ 193	Day Is Done/Easy Way	1970	—	3.00	6.00
❏ 199	Nights in White Satin/Cynthia	1971	2.00	4.00	8.00
❏ 230	Wednesday in Your Garden (mono/stereo)	1971	2.00	4.00	8.00
—Stock copy unknown					
❏ 293	Man in a Band/Bruno's Place	1972	2.00	4.00	8.00
❏ 317	I Feel Free (mono/stereo)	1972	2.50	5.00	10.00
—As "The Bridge"; stock copy unknown					

COLLECTABLES

❏ 3997	Have Yourself A Merry Little Christmas/A Christmas Long Ago (Jingle Jingle)	199?	—	—	3.00
—As "Johnny Maestro and the Brooklyn Bridge"; B-side by the Echelons					

Albums

BUDDAH

❏ BDS-5034	Brooklyn Bridge	1969	5.00	10.00	20.00
❏ BDS-5042	The Second Brooklyn Bridge	1969	5.00	10.00	20.00
❏ BDS-5065	The Brooklyn Bridge	1970	5.00	10.00	20.00
❏ BDS-5107	Bridge in Blue	1972	5.00	10.00	20.00

COLLECTABLES

❏ COL-5015	The Greatest Hits	198?	3.00	6.00	12.00
—As "Johnny Maestro and the Brooklyn Bridge"					

BROOKLYN DREAMS
12-Inch Singles
MILLENNIUM

Number	Title (A Side/B Side)	Yr	VG	VG+	NM
❏ MND-20610	Street Dance/Music, Harmony and Rhythm///(B-side blank)	1978	5.00	10.00	20.00
❏ MND-20613	Street Man (7:55)/(B-side blank)	1978	5.00	10.00	20.00
❏ MND-20620	Street Man (Disco Remix 7:14)/(B-side blank)	1978	6.25	12.50	25.00

45s
CASABLANCA

❏ 962	Make It Last/Long Distance	1979	—	2.50	5.00
❏ 994	Hot Lovin' (Summer in the City)/(B-side unknown)	1979	—	2.50	5.00
❏ 2209	Your Love's So Good to Me/Take Me Back	1979	—	2.50	5.00
❏ 2272	The Hollywood Knights//(B-side unknown)	1980	—	2.50	5.00
❏ 2289	Lover in the Night/Moment in Time	1981	—	2.00	4.00
❏ 2313	I Won't Let Go/Beautiful Dreamer	1981	—	—	2.50

MILLENNIUM

❏ 606	Sad Eyes/Hollywood Circles	1977	—	2.50	5.00
❏ 610	Music, Harmony and Rhythm/Old Fashioned Girl	1978	—	2.50	5.00

Albums

CASABLANCA

❏ NBLP-7135	Sleepless Nights	1979	3.00	6.00	12.00
❏ NBLP-7165	Joy Ride	1979	3.00	6.00	12.00
❏ NBLP-7226	Won't Let Go	1980	2.50	5.00	10.00

MILLENNIUM

❏ MNLP-8002	Brooklyn Dreams	1977	3.00	6.00	12.00

BROTHER TO BROTHER
12-Inch Singles
SUGAR HILL

Number	Title (A Side/B Side)	Yr	VG	VG+	NM
❏ SH 560	Monster Jam (I Want to Funk With You)/Let Me Be for Real	1981	2.00	4.00	8.00

45s
SUGAR HILL

❏ 765	Monster Jam (I Want to Funk With You)/(B-side unknown)	1981	2.00	4.00	8.00

TURBO

❏ 039	In the Bottle/The Affair	1974	2.00	4.00	8.00
❏ 040	Every Nigger Is a Star/Mother Earth	1974	2.00	4.00	8.00
❏ 045	Let Your Mind Be Free/(Instrumental)	1976	2.00	4.00	8.00
❏ 048	Chance with You/Joni	1976	2.00	4.00	8.00
❏ 049	Leavin' Me/Phattenin'	1976	2.00	4.00	8.00

WIN OR LOSE

❏ 224	You're About to Love the One Who Loves You/I Gotta Situation	1972	2.50	5.00	10.00

Albums

SUGAR HILL

❏ SH 259	Brother to Brother 2	1981	3.00	6.00	12.00

TURBO

❏ 7013	In the Bottle	1974	3.75	7.50	15.00
❏ 7015	Let Your Mind Be Free	1976	3.75	7.50	15.00
❏ 7018	Shades in Creation	1977	3.75	7.50	15.00

BROTHERS JOHNSON, THE
12-Inch Singles
A&M

Number	Title (A Side/B Side)	Yr	VG	VG+	NM
❏ SP-12003	Strawberry Letter 23/Get the Funk Out Ma Face	1977	5.00	10.00	20.00
—Red vinyl					
❏ SP-12011	Ain't We Funkin' Now/(B-side unknown)	1978	3.75	7.50	15.00
❏ SP-12102	You Keep Me Comin' Back (Remix Version) (Dub Version)	1984	2.00	4.00	8.00
❏ SP-12262	Kick It to the Curb (5:47) (6:32)/P.O. Box 2000	1988	2.00	4.00	8.00
❏ SP-12281	Party Avenue (Dope Dance Mix) (Radio Edit) (Bonus Beats)	1988	2.00	4.00	8.00
❏ SP-12304	Strawberry Letter 23/Stomp!	1989	2.50	5.00	10.00
—Reissue of 12-inch mixes					
❏ SP-17046 [DJ]	Ride-O-Rocket/Streetwave	1978	3.75	7.50	15.00
❏ SP-17111 [DJ]	Stomp! (3:58) (6:22)	1980	3.75	7.50	15.00
❏ SP-17119 [DJ]	Light Up the Night (Extended Version) (LP Version)	1980	3.00	6.00	12.00
❏ SP-17160 [DJ]	The Real Thing (unknown versions)	1981	3.00	6.00	12.00
❏ SP-17170 [DJ]	Dancin' Free (same on both sides)	1981	2.00	4.00	8.00
❏ SP-17214 [DJ]	Welcome to the Club (2 versions)	1982	2.00	4.00	8.00

45s
A&M

❏ 1229	Party Avenue/Ball of Fire	1988	—	—	3.00
❏ 1806	I'll Be Good to You/The Devil	1976	—	2.00	4.00
❏ 1806 [PS]	I'll Be Good to You/The Devil	1976	—	3.00	6.00
❏ 1851	Get the Funk Out Ma Face/Tomorrow	1976	—	2.00	4.00
❏ 1851 [PS]	Get the Funk Out Ma Face/Tomorrow	1976	—	3.00	6.00
❏ 1881	Free and Single/Thunder Thumbs and Lightning Licks	1976	—	2.00	4.00
❏ 1949	Strawberry Letter 23/Dancin' and Prancin'	1977	—	2.00	4.00
❏ 1949 [DJ]	Strawberry Letter 23 (mono/stereo)	1977	3.75	7.50	15.00
—Promo only on red vinyl					
❏ 1949 [PS]	Strawberry Letter 23/Dancin' and Prancin'	1977	—	3.00	6.00
❏ 1982	Runnin' for Your Lovin'/Q	1977	—	2.00	4.00
❏ 1982 [PS]	Runnin' for Your Lovin'/Q	1977	—	3.00	6.00
❏ 2015	Love Is/Right On Time	1978	—	2.00	4.00
❏ 2086	Ride-O-Rocket/Dancin' and Prancin'	1978	—	2.00	4.00
❏ 2098	Ain't We Funkin' Now/Dancin' and Prancin'	1978	—	2.00	4.00
❏ 2216	Stomp!/Let's Swing	1980	—	2.00	4.00
❏ 2238	Light Up the Night/Street Wave	1980	—	2.00	4.00
❏ 2254	Treasure/Celebrations	1980	—	2.00	4.00
❏ 2280	Smilin' On Ya (mono/stereo)	1980	—	2.50	5.00
—Promo only					
❏ 2343	The Real Thing/I Want You	1981	—	2.00	4.00
❏ 2368	Dancin' Free/Do It for Love	1981	—	2.00	4.00
❏ 2506	Welcome to the Club/The End of an Era	1982	—	2.00	4.00
❏ 2527	I'm Giving You All My Love/The Real Thing	1983	—	2.00	4.00
❏ 2654	You Keep Me Coming Back/Deceiver	1984	—	2.00	4.00
❏ 2689	Lovers Forever/Hot Mama	1984	—	2.00	4.00
❏ 3013	Kick It to the Curb/P.O. Box 2000 (Instrumental)	1988	—	—	3.00
❏ 3013 [PS]	Kick It to the Curb/P.O. Box 2000 (Instrumental)	1988	—	—	3.00

QWEST

❏ 28877	Back Against the Wall Part 1/Part 2	1985	—	—	3.00

Albums

A&M

❏ SP-3716	Light Up the Night	1980	2.50	5.00	10.00
❏ SP-3724	Winners	1981	2.50	5.00	10.00
❏ SP-4567	Look Out for #1	1976	2.50	5.00	10.00
❏ SP-4644	Right on Time	1977	2.50	5.00	10.00
❏ PR-4714 [DJ]	Blam!!	1978	5.00	10.00	20.00
—Promo-only picture disc					
❏ SP-4714	Blam!!	1978	2.50	5.00	10.00
❏ SP-4927	Blast! (The Latest and the Greatest)	1982	2.50	5.00	10.00
❏ SP-4965	Out of Control	1984	2.50	5.00	10.00
❏ SP-5162	Kickin'	1988	2.50	5.00	10.00
❏ SP-17049 [DJ]	Blam!! Radio Special	1978	5.00	10.00	20.00
—Promo-only music and interview record					

BROWN, BOBBY

Includes "B. Brown Posse." Also see NEW EDITION.

12-Inch Singles

MCA

Number	Title (A Side/B Side)	Yr	VG	VG+	NM
❑ MCA8P-2134	[DJ]Humpin' Around (With Rap) (Without Rap) (Instrumental)	1992	2.50	5.00	10.00
❑ MCA8P-2349	[DJ]Humpin' Around (Extended Club Mix) (Humpapella) (Radio Edit) (Extended Humpstrumental) (Suite Humpin')	1992	3.00	6.00	12.00
❑ MCA8P-2430	[DJ]Get Away (5 versions)	1992	3.00	6.00	12.00
❑ MCA8P-2438	[DJ]Good Enough (4 versions)	1992	2.50	5.00	10.00
❑ MCA8P-2523	[DJ]Drop It on the One (3 versions)	1993	3.00	6.00	12.00
—As "B. Brown Posse"					
❑ MCA8P-2550	[DJ]Get Away (6 versions?)	1993	3.00	6.00	12.00
❑ MCA8P-2622	[DJ]That's the Way Love Is (unknown versions)	1993	3.00	6.00	12.00
❑ MCA8P-2661	[DJ]That's the Way Love Is (5 versions?)	1993	2.50	5.00	10.00
❑ MCA8P-4078	[(2) DJ]Feelin' Inside (12 versions)	1997	3.75	7.50	15.00
❑ L33-17272	[DJ]Girl Next Door (same on both sides)	1987	2.50	5.00	10.00
❑ L33-17538	[DJ]Don't Be Cruel (4 versions)	1988	3.75	7.50	15.00
❑ L33-17719	[DJ]Roni (2 versions)	1988	2.50	5.00	10.00
❑ L33-17791	[DJ]Every Little Step (Extended Version) (Instrumental) (Radio Edit) (Uptown Mix)	1989	2.50	5.00	10.00
❑ L33-17843	[DJ]Rock Wit'cha (3 versions)	1989	2.50	5.00	10.00
❑ L33-17892	[DJ]On Our Own (4 versions)	1989	2.00	4.00	8.00
❑ L33-18116	[DJ]Every Little Hit Megamix (Club Mix)/(Radio Edit)	1989	3.75	7.50	15.00
❑ 23643	Girlfriend (12" Version 6:13) (Instrumental 6:11)	1986	2.00	4.00	8.00
❑ 23720	Girl Next Door (5 versions)	1987	3.00	6.00	12.00
❑ 23772	Seventeen (Extended Club Version)/(Radio Edit) (Instrumental) (Bonus Beats)	1987	2.50	5.00	10.00
❑ 23861	Don't Be Cruel (3 versions)	1988	—	3.50	7.00
❑ 23888	My Prerogative (Extended Remix) (Radio Edit) (Instrumental) (Dub)	1988	—	3.50	7.00
❑ 23921	Roni (5 versions)	1988	2.00	4.00	8.00
❑ 23933	Every Little Step (unknown versions)	1989	2.00	4.00	8.00
❑ 23951	Rock Wit'cha (Extended Version 5:36)/ (Instrumental 4:47) (Suite 4:47)	1989	2.00	4.00	8.00
❑ 23957	On Our Own (Extended Club Version) (Radio Edit) (Instrumental)	1989	2.00	4.00	8.00
❑ 54343	Humpin Around (Extended Club Version)// (Humparella) (Ext. Humpstrumental)	1992	2.00	4.00	8.00
❑ 54512	Get Away (Teddy's Club Version) (Chris Stone's Extended) (MK Club Extended)	1992	2.00	4.00	8.00
❑ 54521	Good Enough (Extended Jeep Mix) (4 Deep in a Jeep) (2 Deep in Da Backseat)	1992	2.00	4.00	8.00
❑ 54571	Drop It on the One (5 versions)	1993	2.00	4.00	8.00
—As "B. Brown Posse"					
❑ 54619	That's the Way Love Is (12" Extended Club Version) (Ragamuffin Dub) (Guitarapella)	1993	2.00	4.00	8.00
❑ 54631	Drop It on the One (Extended Remix) (Radio Edit) (Instrumental)	1993	2.00	4.00	8.00
—As "B. Brown Posse"					

45s

COLLECTABLES

Number	Title (A Side/B Side)	Yr	VG	VG+	NM
❑ 90185	My Prerogative/Every Little Step	199?	—	—	3.00

MCA

Number	Title (A Side/B Side)	Yr	VG	VG+	NM
❑ 52866	Girlfriend/(Sing-a-Long Version)	1986	—	2.00	4.00
❑ 52866 [PS]	Girlfriend/(Sing-a-Long Version)	1986	—	2.00	4.00
❑ 53022	Girl Next Door/(Instrumental)	1987	—	2.00	4.00
❑ 53022 [PS]	Girl Next Door/(Instrumental)	1987	—	2.00	4.00
❑ 53135	Seventeen/(Instrumental)	1987	—	2.00	4.00
❑ 53327	Don't Be Cruel/(Instrumental)	1988	—	—	3.00
❑ 53327 [PS]	Don't Be Cruel/(Instrumental)	1988	—	—	3.00
❑ 53383	My Prerogative/(Instrumental)	1988	—	—	3.00
❑ 53383 [PS]	My Prerogative/(Instrumental)	1988	—	—	3.00
❑ 53463	Roni/(Instrumental)	1988	—	—	3.00
❑ 53463 [PS]	Roni/(Instrumental)	1988	—	—	3.00
❑ 53618	Every Little Step/Every Little Step (With Rap)	1989	—	—	3.00
❑ 53618 [PS]	Every Little Step/Every Little Step (With Rap)	1989	—	—	3.00
❑ 53652	Rock Wit'cha/(Instrumental)	1989	—	—	3.00
❑ 53662	On Our Own (With Rap)/On Our Own (Without Rap)	1989	—	—	3.00
❑ 54342	Humpin' Around (With Rap)/(Instrumental)	1992	—	—	3.00
❑ 54511	Get Away (With Rap)/Get Away (Without Rap)	1992	—	—	3.00
❑ 54517	Good Enough/(Instrumental)	1992	—	—	3.00
❑ 54570	Drop It on the One (Radio Edit)/(Album Version)	1993	—	—	3.00
—As "B. Brown Posse"					
❑ 54618	That's the Way Love Is/(Instrumental)	1993	—	—	3.00

Albums

MCA

Number	Title (A Side/B Side)	Yr	VG	VG+	NM
❑ 5827	King of Stage	1986	2.00	4.00	8.00
❑ 6342	Dance! ... Ya Know It!	1989	3.00	6.00	12.00
❑ 10417	Bobby	1992	3.75	7.50	15.00
❑ 10974	Remixes N the Key of B	1993	3.75	7.50	15.00
—Issued in generic black cardboard sleeve					
❑ 11691 [(2)]	Forever	1997	3.75	7.50	15.00
❑ 42185	Don't Be Cruel	1988	2.00	4.00	8.00

BROWN, BUSTER

45s

FIRE

Number	Title (A Side/B Side)	Yr	VG	VG+	NM
❑ 507	Sugar Babe/I'm Going — But I'll Be Back	1962	5.00	10.00	20.00
❑ 516	Raise a Rucks Tonight/Gonna Love My Baby	1962	5.00	10.00	20.00
❑ 1008	Fannie Mae/Lost in a Dream	1959	6.25	12.50	25.00
❑ 1020	The Madison Shuffle/John Henry	1960	5.00	10.00	20.00
❑ 1023	Is You Is or Is You Ain't My Baby/Don't Dog Your Woman	1960	5.00	10.00	20.00
❑ 1032	Sincerely/Doctor Brown	1960	5.00	10.00	20.00
❑ 1040	Blues When It Rains/Good News	1961	5.00	10.00	20.00
❑ 2021	Sugar Babe/Don't Dog Your Woman	1962	3.75	7.50	15.00

RCA VICTOR

Number	Title (A Side/B Side)	Yr	VG	VG+	NM
❑ PB-10023	Eloise/Fallin' Out of Love	1974	—	2.50	5.00

WHITE WHALE

Number	Title (A Side/B Side)	Yr	VG	VG+	NM
❑ 316	The Proud One/I've Got It Made	1969	2.50	5.00	10.00

78s

FIRE

Number	Title (A Side/B Side)	Yr	VG	VG+	NM
❑ 1008	Fannie Mae/Lost in a Dream	1959	150.00	300.00	600.00

Albums

COLLECTABLES

Number	Title (A Side/B Side)	Yr	VG	VG+	NM
❑ COL-5110	Golden Classics: The New King of the Blues	198?	2.50	5.00	10.00

FIRE

Number	Title (A Side/B Side)	Yr	VG	VG+	NM
❑ FLP-102 [M]	The New King of the Blues	1961	175.00	350.00	700.00
—White and red label					
❑ FLP-102 [M]	The New King of the Blues	1961	100.00	200.00	400.00
—Red and black label, purple cover					
❑ FLP-102 [M]	The New King of the Blues	1961	75.00	150.00	300.00
—Red and black label, white cover					

SOUFFLE

Number	Title (A Side/B Side)	Yr	VG	VG+	NM
❑ 2014	Get Down	1973	3.00	6.00	12.00

BROWN, CHARLES

45s

ACE

Number	Title (A Side/B Side)	Yr	VG	VG+	NM
❑ 561	Educated Fool/I Want to Go Back Home	1959	3.00	6.00	12.00
—With Amos Milburn					
❑ 599	Love's Like a River/Boys Will Be Boys	1960	3.00	6.00	12.00
❑ 599	Love's Like a River/Sing My Blues Tonight	1960	3.00	6.00	12.00

ALADDIN

Number	Title (A Side/B Side)	Yr	VG	VG+	NM
❑ 3076	Black Night/Once There Was a Fool	1951	37.50	75.00	150.00
—Charles Brown records on Aladdin prior to 3076 are unconfirmed on 45 rpm					
❑ 3091	I'll Always Be in Love with You/The Message	1951	20.00	40.00	80.00
❑ 3092	Seven Long Days/Don't Fool with My Heart	1951	20.00	40.00	80.00
❑ 3116	Hard Times/Tender Heart	1952	20.00	40.00	80.00
❑ 3120	Still Water/My Last Affair	1952	20.00	40.00	80.00
❑ 3138	See/Without Your Love	1952	20.00	40.00	80.00
❑ 3157	Rollin' Like a Pebble in the Sand/Alley Batting	1952	20.00	40.00	80.00
❑ 3163	Evening Shadows/Moonrise	1953	15.00	30.00	60.00
❑ 3176	Take Me/Rising Sun	1953	15.00	30.00	60.00
❑ 3191	Lonesome Feeling/I Lost Everything	1953	15.00	30.00	60.00
❑ 3200	All My Life/Don't Leave Me Poor	1953	15.00	30.00	60.00
❑ 3209	P.S. I Love You/Cryin' and Driftin' Blues	1953	15.00	30.00	60.00
❑ 3220	Everybody's Got Trouble/I Fool Around with You	1954	10.00	20.00	40.00
❑ 3235	Let's Walk/Crying Mercy	1954	10.00	20.00	40.00
❑ 3254	My Silent Love/Foolish	1954	10.00	20.00	40.00
❑ 3272	By the Bend of the River/Honey Slipper	1955	7.50	15.00	30.00
❑ 3284	Night After Night/Walk with Me	1955	7.50	15.00	30.00
❑ 3290	Hot Lips and Seven Kisses/Fools' Paradise	1955	7.50	15.00	30.00
❑ 3296	My Heart Is Mended/Trees, Trees	1955	7.50	15.00	30.00
❑ 3316	Please Don't Drive Me Away/One Minute to One	1956	6.25	12.50	25.00
❑ 3342	Soothe Me/I'll Always Be in Love with You	1956	6.25	12.50	25.00
❑ 3348	Merry Christmas, Baby/Black Night	1956	6.25	12.50	25.00
❑ 3366	Please Believe Me/It's a Sin to Tell a Lie	1957	5.00	10.00	20.00
❑ 3423	Hard Times/Ooh, Ooh Sugar	1958	5.00	10.00	20.00

BLUES SPECTRUM

Number	Title (A Side/B Side)	Yr	VG	VG+	NM
❑ 17	Merry Christmas, Baby/Rockin' Blues	197?	—	3.00	6.00

BLUESWAY

Number	Title (A Side/B Side)	Yr	VG	VG+	NM
❑ 61031	Merry Christmas, Baby/Rainy, Rainy Day	1969	—	3.00	6.00

CASH

Number	Title (A Side/B Side)	Yr	VG	VG+	NM
❑ 1052	Lost in the Night/I Sold My Heart to the Junkman	1957	7.50	15.00	30.00
—B-side by the Basin Street Boys					

CHARLENA

Number	Title (A Side/B Side)	Yr	VG	VG+	NM
❑ 001	Please Come Home For Christmas/Santa Claus Santa Claus	197?	—	2.00	4.00
❑ 001 [PS]	Please Come Home For Christmas/Santa Claus Santa Claus	197?	—	2.50	5.00

EASTWEST

Number	Title (A Side/B Side)	Yr	VG	VG+	NM
❑ 106	When Did You Leave Heaven/We've Got a Lot in Common	1958	5.00	10.00	20.00

EMI

Number	Title (A Side/B Side)	Yr	VG	VG+	NM
❑ S7-18213	Please Come Home for Christmas/Merry Christmas Baby	1994	—	2.00	4.00
—Green vinyl					

GALAXY

Number	Title (A Side/B Side)	Yr	VG	VG+	NM
❑ 762	I'm Gonna Push On/Cry No More	1968	2.50	5.00	10.00
❑ 766	Abraham, Martin, and John/(B-side unknown)	1968	2.50	5.00	10.00

HOLLYWOOD

Number	Title (A Side/B Side)	Yr	VG	VG+	NM
❑ 1006	Pleading for Your Love/The Best I Can Do	1954	10.00	20.00	40.00
❑ 1021	Merry Christmas Baby/Sleigh Ride	1954	5.00	10.00	20.00
—Charles Brown's first recording of the A-side, released on 78 on Exclusive 254 (1946); B-side by Lloyd Glenn; maroon label					
❑ 1021	Merry Christmas Baby/Sleigh Ride	196?	2.00	4.00	8.00
—B-side by Lloyd Glenn; color label					
❑ 1021	Merry Christmas Baby/Sleigh Ride	197?	—	2.50	5.00
—B-side by Lloyd Glenn; black label					

IMPERIAL

Number	Title (A Side/B Side)	Yr	VG	VG+	NM
❑ 5830	Fool's Paradise/Lonesome Feeling	1962	2.50	5.00	10.00
❑ 5902	Merry Christmas Baby/I Lost Everything	1962	2.50	5.00	10.00
❑ 5905	Black Night/Drifting Blues	1963	2.50	5.00	10.00

Number	Title (A Side/B Side)	Yr	VG	VG+	NM
❑ 5961	I'm Savin' My Love for You/Please Don't Drive Me Away	1963	2.50	5.00	10.00
JEWEL					
❑ 814	Christmas in Heaven/Just a Blessing	1970	—	3.00	6.00
❑ 815	Merry Christmas Baby/Please Come Home for Christmas	1970	—	3.00	6.00
❑ 830	I Don't Know/For You	1972	—	2.50	5.00
❑ 838	I've Got Your Love/I Just Can't Get Over You	1973	—	2.50	5.00
❑ 847	Please Come Home for Christmas/Christmas in Heaven	1974	—	2.50	5.00
KENT					
❑ 501	Merry Christmas Baby/3 O'Clock Blues	1968	2.50	5.00	10.00
KING					
❑ 5405	Please Come Home for Christmas/Christmas (Comes But Once a Year)	1960	3.00	6.00	12.00
—B-side by Amos Milburn; original blue label					
❑ 5405	Please Come Home for Christmas/Christmas (Comes But Once a Year)	1970	—	3.00	6.00
—B-side by Amos Milburn; black label					
❑ 5439	Angel Baby/Baby Oh Baby	1961	3.00	6.00	12.00
❑ 5464	I Wanna Go Back Home/My Little Baby	1961	3.00	6.00	12.00
—With Amos Milburn					
❑ 5523	Butterfly/This Fool Has Learned	1961	·3.00	6.00	12.00
❑ 5530	Christmas in Heaven/It's Christmas All Year 'Round	1961	3.00	6.00	12.00
❑ 5570	Without a Friend/If You Play with Cats	1961	3.00	6.00	12.00
❑ 5722	I'm Just a Drifter/I Don't Want Your Rambling Letters	1963	2.50	5.00	10.00
❑ 5726	It's Christmas Time/Christmas Finds Me Lonely	1963	2.50	5.00	10.00
❑ 5731	Christmas Questions/Wrap Yourself in a Christmas Package	1963	2.50	5.00	10.00
❑ 5802	If You Don't Believe I'm Crying/I Wanna Be Close	1963	2.50	5.00	10.00
❑ 5825	Lucky Dreamer/Too Fine for Crying	1963	2.50	5.00	10.00
❑ 5852	Blow Out All the Candles/Come Home	1964	2.50	5.00	10.00
❑ 5946	Christmas Blues/My Most Miserable Christmas	1964	2.50	5.00	10.00
❑ 5947	Christmas Comes (But Once a Year)/Bringin' In a Brand New Year	1964	2.50	5.00	10.00
❑ 6094	Regardless/The Plan	1967	2.00	4.00	8.00
❑ 6192	Hang On a Little Longer/Black Night	1968	2.00	4.00	8.00
❑ 6194	Merry Christmas, Baby/Let's Make Every Day Christmas	1968	2.00	4.00	8.00
❑ 6420	For the Good Times/Lonesome and Driftin'	1973	—	2.50	5.00
LIBERTY					
❑ 1393	Merry Christmas, Baby/Silent Night	1980	—	2.50	5.00
—B-side by Baby Washington					
❑ 5902	Merry Christmas, Baby/I Lost Everything	196?	2.00	4.00	8.00
—Reissue of Imperial 5902					
LILLY					
❑ 506	Bon Voyage/Bye and Bye	1962	2.50	5.00	10.00
MAINSTREAM					
❑ 607	Pledging My Love/Tomorrow Night	1965	2.00	4.00	8.00
NOLA					
❑ 702	Standing on the Outside/I'll Love You (If You Let Me)	1965	2.00	4.00	8.00
SWING TIME					
❑ 238	Merry Christmas, Baby/Lost In The Night	195?	25.00	50.00	100.00
—Originally released on 78, but a 45 does exist					
❑ 253	I'll Miss You/New Orleans Blues	1952	30.00	60.00	120.00
❑ 259	Be Fair with Me/Sunny Road	1952	30.00	60.00	120.00
TEEM					
❑ 1008	Merry Christmas Baby/Christmas Finds Me Oh So Sad	19??	—	3.00	6.00
UNITED ARTISTS					
❑ 0085	Drifting Blues/Black Night	1973	—	2.00	4.00
—Silver Spotlight Series issue					
❑ 0086	I Lost Everything/Lonesome Feeling	1973	—	2.00	4.00
—Silver Spotlight Series issue					
❑ XW582	Merry Christmas Baby/(B-side unknown)	1974	—	2.50	5.00
UPSIDE					
❑ PRO 002	Santa Claus Boogie (one-sided)	1986	—	2.00	4.00
—Flexidisc					
❑ PRO 002 [PS]	Santa Claus Boogie	1986	—	2.00	4.00
78s					
ALADDIN					
❑ 3020	Get Yourself Another Fool/Ooh Ooh Sugar	1949	6.25	12.50	25.00
❑ 3021	Long Time/It's Nothing	1949	6.25	12.50	25.00
❑ 3024	Trouble Blues/Honey Keep Your Mind on Me	1949	7.50	15.00	30.00
❑ 3030	In the Evening When the Sun Goes Down/Please Be Kind	1949	6.25	12.50	25.00
❑ 3039	Homesick Blues/Let's Have a Ball	1950	6.25	12.50	25.00
❑ 3044	Tormented/Did You Ever Love a Woman	1950	6.25	12.50	25.00
❑ 3051	My Baby's Gone/I Wonder When My Baby's Coming Home	1950	6.25	12.50	25.00
❑ 3060	Repentance Blues/I Got a Feeling	1950	6.25	12.50	25.00
❑ 3066	I've Made Up My Mind/Again	1950	6.25	12.50	25.00
❑ 3071	How High the Moon/Texas Blues	1950	6.25	12.50	25.00
❑ 3076	Black Night/Once There Was a Fool	1951	7.50	15.00	30.00
❑ 3091	I'll Always Be in Love with You/The Message	1951	6.25	12.50	25.00
❑ 3092	Seven Long Days/Don't Fool with My Heart	1951	6.25	12.50	25.00
❑ 3116	Hard Times/Tender Heart	1952	6.25	12.50	25.00
❑ 3120	Still Water/My Last Affair	1952	6.25	12.50	25.00
❑ 3138	See/Without Your Love	1952	6.25	12.50	25.00
❑ 3157	Rollin' Like a Pebble in the Sand/Alley Batting	1952	6.25	12.50	25.00
❑ 3163	Evening Shadows/Moonrise	1953	6.25	12.50	25.00
❑ 3176	Take Me/Rising Sun	1953	6.25	12.50	25.00

Number	Title (A Side/B Side)	Yr	VG	VG+	NM
❑ 3191	Lonesome Feeling/I Lost Everything	1953	6.25	12.50	25.00
❑ 3200	All My Life/Don't Leave Me Poor	1953	6.25	12.50	25.00
❑ 3209	P.S. I Love You/Cryin' and Driftin' Blues	1953	6.25	12.50	25.00
❑ 3220	Everybody's Got Trouble/I Fool Around with You	1954	6.25	12.50	25.00
❑ 3235	Let's Walk/Crying Mercy	1954	6.25	12.50	25.00
❑ 3254	My SIlent Love/Foolish	1954	6.25	12.50	25.00
❑ 3272	By the Bend of the River/Honey Slipper	1955	6.25	12.50	25.00
❑ 3284	Night After Night/Walk with Me	1955	6.25	12.50	25.00
❑ 3290	Hot Lips and Seven Kisses/Fools' Paradise	1955	6.25	12.50	25.00
❑ 3296	My Heart Is Mended/Trees, Trees	1955	6.25	12.50	25.00
❑ 3316	Please Don't Drive Me Away/One Minute to One	1956	6.25	12.50	25.00
❑ 3342	Soothe Me/I'll Always Be in Love with You	1956	6.25	12.50	25.00
❑ 3348	Merry Christmas, Baby/Black Night	1956	6.25	12.50	25.00
❑ 3366	Please Believe Me/It's a Sin to Tell a Lie	1957	7.50	15.00	30.00
❑ 3423	Hard Times/Ooh, Ooh Sugar	1958	10.00	20.00	40.00
CASH					
❑ 1052	Lost in the Night/I Sold My Heart to the Junkman	1957	7.50	15.00	30.00
—B-side by the Basin Street Boys					
HOLLYWOOD					
❑ 1006	Pleading for Your Love/The Best I Can Do	1954	6.25	12.50	25.00
❑ 1021	Merry Christmas Baby/Sleigh Ride	1954	5.00	10.00	20.00
—Charles Brown's first recording of the A-side, released by "Johnny Moore's Three Blazers" on Exclusive 254 (1946); B-side by Lloyd Glenn					
SWING TIME					
❑ 238	Merry Christmas, Baby/Lost In The Night	195?	7.50	15.00	30.00
❑ 253	I'll Miss You/New Orleans Blues	1952	7.50	15.00	30.00
❑ 259	Be Fair with Me/Sunny Road	1952	7.50	15.00	30.00
Albums					
ALADDIN					
❑ LP-702 [10]	Mood Music	1953	3000.	5250.	7500.
—Red vinyl					
❑ LP-702 [10]	Mood Music	1953	1500.	2750.	4000.
—Black vinyl					
❑ LP-809 [M]	Mood Music	1956	—	—	—
—Unreleased?					
ALLIGATOR					
❑ AL-4771	One More for the Road	1989	3.00	6.00	12.00
BIG TOWN					
❑ 1003	Merry Christmas Baby	1977	3.00	6.00	12.00
❑ 1005	Music Maestro Please	1978	2.50	5.00	10.00
BLUESWAY					
❑ BLS-6039	Charles Brown — Legend	1970	6.25	12.50	25.00
BULLSEYE BLUES					
❑ BB-9501	All My Life	1990	5.00	10.00	20.00
IMPERIAL					
❑ LP-9178 [M]	Charles Brown Sings Million Sellers	1961	100.00	200.00	400.00
JEWEL					
❑ 5006	Blues 'N' Brown	1972	3.00	6.00	12.00
KING					
❑ 775 [M]	Charles Brown Sings Christmas Songs	1961	37.50	75.00	150.00
❑ KS-775 [S]	Charles Brown Sings Christmas Songs	1963	75.00	150.00	300.00
—Stereo copies (whether true stereo or rechanneled, we don't know) exist on blue labels with "King" in block letters (no crown)					
❑ 878 [M]	The Great Charles Brown	1963	50.00	100.00	200.00
MAINSTREAM					
❑ S-6007 [S]	Boss of the Blues	1965	7.50	15.00	30.00
❑ S-6035 [S]	Ballads My Way	1965	7.50	15.00	30.00
❑ 56007 [M]	Boss of the Blues	1965	5.00	10.00	20.00
❑ 56035 [M]	Ballads My Way	1965	5.00	10.00	20.00
MOSAIC					
❑ MQ7-153 [(7)]	The Complete Aladdin Recordings of Charles Brown	199?	37.50	75.00	150.00
SCORE					
❑ SLP-4011 [M]	Driftin' Blues	1958	100.00	200.00	400.00
❑ SLP-4036 [M]	More Blues with Charles Brown	1959	—	—	—
—Unreleased					

BROWN, CHUCK AND THE SOUL SEARCHERS

12-Inch Singles

Number	Title (A Side/B Side)	Yr	VG	VG+	NM
FUTURE					
❑ F 0007	Go-Go Swing/Here We Go Again	1987	—	3.00	6.00
❑ F 0037	Hoochie Coochie Man (Extended) (Radio) (Instrumental)	1989	2.00	4.00	8.00
I HEAR YA!					
❑ IHY 1003	That'll Work 2001 (3 versions)	1988	—	3.00	6.00
SOURCE					
❑ L33-1839 [DJ]	Never Gonna Give You Up (5:43)/Could It Be Love (5:22)	1979	3.75	7.50	15.00
❑ 13910	Bustin' Loose (unknown version)	1979	3.75	7.50	15.00
❑ 13915	Game Seven (8:28)/If It Ain't Funky (6:00)	1979	3.75	7.50	15.00
T.T.E.D.					
❑ TDE 3004	We Need Some Money (8:24) (Radio Version I 4:28) (Radio Version II 4:53)	1984	2.50	5.00	10.00
45s					
SOURCE					
❑ 40967	Bustin' Loose Part 1/Bustin' Loose Part 2	1978	—	2.50	5.00
❑ 41013	Game Seven Part 1/Game Seven Part 2	1979	—	2.50	5.00
❑ 41226	Sticks and Stones (But the Funk Will Never Hurt You) Part 1/Part 2	1980	—	2.50	5.00
❑ 41279	Come On and Boogie Part 1/Come On and Boogie Part 2	1980	—	2.50	5.00

Number	Title (A Side/B Side)	Yr	VG	VG+	NM

Albums

SOURCE

| ❑ SOR-3076 | Bustin' Loose | 1979 | 3.00 | 6.00 | 12.00 |
| ❑ SOR-3234 | Funk Express | 1980 | 3.75 | 7.50 | 15.00 |

BROWN, CLARENCE "GATEMOUTH"

45s

PEACOCK

❑ 1600	Baby Take It Easy/Just Got Lucky	1952	100.00	200.00	400.00
❑ 1607	Dirty Work at the Crossroads/You Got Money	1952	62.50	125.00	250.00
❑ 1617	Boogie Uproar/Hurry Back Good News	1953	50.00	100.00	200.00
❑ 1619	Please Tell Me Baby/Gate Walks to Board	1953	50.00	100.00	200.00
❑ 1633	Midnight Hour/For Now So Long	1954	37.50	75.00	150.00
❑ 1637	Okie Dokie Stomp/Depression Blues	1954	37.50	75.00	150.00
❑ 1653	Gate's Salty Blues/Rock My Blues Away	1955	25.00	50.00	100.00
❑ 1662	Ain't That Dandy/September Song	1956	20.00	40.00	80.00
❑ 1692	Just Before Dawn/Swinging the Gate	1958	10.00	20.00	40.00

BROWN, FOXY (1)

Female rapper.

12-Inch Singles

DEF JAM

❑ 312 [DJ]	Job (Radio Edit) (LP Version) (Instrumental)/A Dog and a Fox (Radio Edit) (LP Version) (Instrumental)	1999	2.00	4.00	8.00
❑ 324 [DJ]	I Can't (Featuring Total Radio Edit) (Radio Edit)/Ride (Down South) (Radio Edit)//I Can't (Instrumental)/My Life (Instrumental)/Ride (Down South) (Instrumental)	1999	2.50	5.00	10.00
❑ 572836-1	Oh Yeah (Radio Edit) (LP Version) (Instrumental)/BK Anthem (Radio Edit) (LP Version) (Instrumental)	2001	—	3.00	6.00
❑ 870801-1	I Can't (Featuring Total) (Instrumental)/My Life/Ride (Down South)	1999	2.00	4.00	8.00

VIOLATOR

❑ 140 [DJ]	I'll Be (house mixes)	1997	2.50	5.00	10.00
❑ 165 [DJ]	Big Bad Mamma (3 versions)/Ill Na Na	1997	2.00	4.00	8.00
❑ 286 [DJ]	Hot Spot (4 versions)	1999	2.00	4.00	8.00
❑ 297 [DJ]	BWA (Radio Edit) (LP Version) (Instrumental)/Paper Chase (Radio Edit) (LP Version) (Instrumental)	1998	2.50	5.00	10.00
❑ 566499-1	Hot Spot (3 versions)/BWA	1998	2.00	4.00	8.00
❑ 571441-1	Big Bad Mamma (3 versions)	1997	2.00	4.00	8.00
❑ 574029-1	I'll Be (2 versions)/La Familia	1997	2.00	4.00	8.00

Albums

DEF JAM

| ❑ 558933-1 [(2)] | Chyna Doll | 1999 | 3.75 | 7.50 | 15.00 |

VIOLATOR

| ❑ 533684-1 [(2)] | Ill Na Na | 1996 | 3.75 | 7.50 | 15.00 |

BROWN, FOXY (2)

Female reggae singer.

12-Inch Singles

POW WOW

| ❑ PW 452 | Sorry (Baby Can I Hold You) (3 versions) | 1989 | — | 3.50 | 7.00 |

Albums

RAS

| ❑ 3059 | Foxy | 198? | 3.00 | 6.00 | 12.00 |
| ❑ 3070 | My Kind of Girl | 198? | 2.50 | 5.00 | 10.00 |

BROWN, JAMES

Also see VICKI ANDERSON; BOBBY BYRD; LYN COLLINS; FRED WESLEY AND THE JB'S.

12-Inch Singles

POLYDOR

❑ PRO 040 [DJ]	Eyesight/The Spank	1978	3.75	7.50	15.00
❑ PRO 059 [DJ]	For Goodness Sake, Look at Those Cakes (11:04) (same on both sides)	1978	6.25	12.50	25.00
❑ PRO 086 [DJ]	It's Too Funky in Here (6:33) (same on both sides)	1979	5.00	10.00	20.00
❑ PRO 100 [DJ]	Star Generation (8:07) (4:21)	1979	5.00	10.00	20.00
❑ PD-510	It's Too Funky in Here (6:33)/Are We Really Dancing	1979	3.75	7.50	15.00

SCOTTI BROTHERS

❑ 4Z9-05310	Living in America (LP Version) (Dance Mix) (Instrumental)	1985	2.00	4.00	8.00
❑ 4Z9-05943	Gravity (Extended Dance Mix) (7" Edit) (12" Dub Mix)/The Big G (Dig This Mess)	1986	2.00	4.00	8.00
❑ 4Z9-05990	How Do You Stop (Special Extended Remix)/Goliath (Special Extended Remix)	1986	2.50	5.00	10.00
❑ 4Z9-07805	I'm Real/Tribute	1988	2.00	4.00	8.00
❑ 4Z9-07863	Static (3 versions)/Godfather Runnin' the Joint	1988	2.50	5.00	10.00
❑ 4Z9-08130	Time to Get Busy (Full Force Remix) (Single Version)/Busy J.B. (Full Force Remix) (Single Version)	1988	2.00	4.00	8.00
❑ 75286	(So Tired of Standing Still We Got to) Move On (5 versions)	1991	2.50	5.00	10.00
❑ 75352 [(2)]	Can't Get Any Harder (4 versions)	1993	3.00	6.00	12.00
❑ 78034	Respect Me (6 versions)	1995	2.50	5.00	10.00
❑ 78094	Hooked on Brown (Long) (Radio Edit 1) (Radio Edit 2)	1996	3.75	7.50	15.00

T.K. DISCO

| ❑ TKD 452 | Rapp Payback (Where Iz Moses) (Part 1 7:00)/(Part 2 3:28) | 1980 | 3.00 | 6.00 | 12.00 |

45s

AUGUSTA SOUND

| ❑ 94023 | Bring It On ... Bring It On/The Night Time Is the Right Time (To Be With the One That You Love) | 1983 | — | 2.00 | 4.00 |

A&M

| ❑ 3022 | I Got You (I Feel Good)/Nowhere to Run | 1988 | — | 2.00 | 4.00 |

—B-side by Martha and the Vandellas

| ❑ 3022 [PS] | I Got You (I Feel Good)/Nowhere to Run | 1988 | — | 2.00 | 4.00 |

—"Good Morning Vietnam" sleeve

BACKSTREET

| ❑ 52215 | King of Soul/Theme from Doctor Detroit | 1983 | — | — | 3.00 |

—B-side by Devo

BETHLEHEM

| ❑ 3089 | I Loves You Porgy/Yours and Mine | 1969 | 3.75 | 7.50 | 15.00 |
| ❑ 3098 | A Man Has to Go Back to the Crossroads/The Drunk | 1969 | 3.75 | 7.50 | 15.00 |

FEDERAL

❑ 12258	Please, Please, Please/Why Do You Do Me?	1956	10.00	20.00	40.00
❑ 12264	I Don't Know/I Feel That Old Feeling Coming On	1956	6.25	12.50	25.00
❑ 12277	No, No, No, No/Hold My Baby's Hand	1956	6.25	12.50	25.00
❑ 12289	Just Won't Do Right/Let's Make It	1957	6.25	12.50	25.00
❑ 12290	I Won't Plead No More/Chonnie On Chon	1957	6.25	12.50	25.00
❑ 12292	Gonna Try/Can't Be the Same	1957	6.25	12.50	25.00
❑ 12295	Love or a Game/Messing with the Blues	1957	6.25	12.50	25.00
❑ 12300	I Walked Alone/You're Mine, You're Mine	1957	6.25	12.50	25.00
❑ 12311	Baby Cries Over the Ocean/That Dood It	1957	6.25	12.50	25.00
❑ 12316	Begging, Begging/That's When I Lost My Heart	1958	6.25	12.50	25.00
❑ 12316	Begging, Begging/That's When I Lost My Heart	1958	15.00	30.00	60.00
❑ 12337	Try Me/Tell Me What I Did Wrong	1958	7.50	15.00	30.00
❑ 12348	I Want You So Bad/There Must Be a Reason	1959	5.00	10.00	20.00
❑ 12352 [M]	I've Got to Change/It Hurts to Tell You	1959	5.00	10.00	20.00
❑ S-12352 [S]	I've Got to Change/It Hurts to Tell You	1959	12.50	25.00	50.00
❑ 12361 [M]	Don't Let It Happen to Me/Good Good Lovin'	1959	5.00	10.00	20.00
❑ S-12361 [S]	Don't Let It Happen to Me/Good Good Lovin'	1959	12.50	25.00	50.00
❑ 12364	It Was You/Got to Cry	1959	5.00	10.00	20.00
❑ 12369	I'll Go Crazy/I Know It's True	1960	5.00	10.00	20.00
❑ 12370	Think/You've Got the Power	1960	5.00	10.00	20.00
❑ 12378	This Old Heart/I Wonder When You're Coming Home	1960	5.00	10.00	20.00

KING

❑ 5423	The Bells/And I Do Just What I Want	1960	3.75	7.50	15.00
❑ 5438	The Scratch/Hold It	1961	3.75	7.50	15.00
❑ 5442	Bewildered/If You Want Me	1961	3.75	7.50	15.00
❑ 5466	I Don't Mind/Love Don't Love Nobody	1961	3.75	7.50	15.00
❑ 5485	Sticky/Suds	1961	3.75	7.50	15.00
❑ 5519	Night Flying/Cross Firing	1961	3.75	7.50	15.00
❑ 5524	Baby You're Right/I'll Never, Never Let You Go	1961	3.75	7.50	15.00
❑ 5547	Just You and Me, Darling/I Love You, Yes I Do	1961	3.75	7.50	15.00
❑ 5573	Lost Someone/Cross Firing	1961	3.75	7.50	15.00
❑ 5614	Night Train/Why Does Everything Happen to Me	1962	3.75	7.50	15.00
❑ 5654	Tell Me Why/Say So Long	1962	3.75	7.50	15.00

—With Yvonne Fair

❑ 5657	Shout and Shimmy/Come Over Here	1962	3.75	7.50	15.00
❑ 5672	Mashed Potatoes U.S.A./You Don't Have to Go	1962	3.75	7.50	15.00
❑ 5687	It Hurts to Be in Love/You Can Make It If You Try	1962	3.75	7.50	15.00

—With Yvonne Fair

❑ 5698	(Can You) Feel It Part 1/(Can You) Feel It Part 2	1962	3.75	7.50	15.00
❑ 5701	Three Hearts in a Tangle/I've Got Money	1962	3.75	7.50	15.00
❑ 5710	Like a Baby/Every Beat of My Heart	1963	3.75	7.50	15.00
❑ 5739	Prisoner of Love/Choo Choo	1963	3.75	7.50	15.00
❑ 5767	These Foolish Things/Can You Feel It — Part 1	1963	3.75	7.50	15.00
❑ 5803	Signed, Sealed and Delivered/Waiting in Vain	1963	3.75	7.50	15.00
❑ 5829	The Bells/I've Got to Change	1963	3.75	7.50	15.00
❑ 5842	Oh Baby Don't You Weep (Part 1)/Oh Baby Don't You Weep (Part 2)	1964	3.75	7.50	15.00
❑ 5842 [PS]	Oh Baby Don't You Weep (Part 1)/Oh Baby Don't You Weep (Part 2)	1964	6.25	12.50	25.00
❑ 5853	Please, Please, Please/In the Wee Wee Hours	1964	3.75	7.50	15.00
❑ 5876	How Long Darling/Again	1964	3.75	7.50	15.00
❑ 5899	So Long/Dancin' Little Thing	1964	3.75	7.50	15.00
❑ 5922	Tell Me What You're Gonna Do/I Don't Care	1964	3.75	7.50	15.00
❑ 5952	Think/Try Me	1964	3.75	7.50	15.00
❑ 5956	Fine Old Foxy Self/Medley	1964	3.75	7.50	15.00
❑ 5968	Have Mercy Baby/Just Won't Do Right	1964	3.75	7.50	15.00
❑ 5995	This Old Heart/It Was You	1965	3.00	6.00	12.00
❑ 5999	Papa's Got a Brand New Bag Part I/Papa's Got a Brand New Bag Part II	1965	3.75	7.50	15.00
❑ 6015	I Got You (I Feel Good)/I Can't Help It (I Just Do, Do, Do)	1965	3.75	7.50	15.00
❑ 6020	I'll Go Crazy/Lost Someone	1966	3.00	6.00	12.00
❑ 6025	Ain't That a Groove Part I/Ain't That a Groove Part II	1966	3.00	6.00	12.00
❑ 6029	Prisoner of Love/I've Got to Change	1966	3.00	6.00	12.00
❑ 6033	Come Over Here/Tell Me What You're Gonna Do	1966	3.00	6.00	12.00
❑ 6035	It's a Man's Man's Man's World/Is It Yes Or Is It No?	1966	3.00	6.00	12.00
❑ 6037	I've Got Money/Just Won't Do Right	1966	3.00	6.00	12.00
❑ 6040	I Don't Care/It Was You	1966	3.00	6.00	12.00
❑ 6044	This Old Heart/How Long Darling	1966	3.00	6.00	12.00
❑ 6048	Money Won't Change You Part 1/Money Won't Change You Part 2	1966	3.00	6.00	12.00
❑ 6056	Don't Be a Drop-Out/Tell Me That You Love Me	1966	3.00	6.00	12.00
❑ 6064	The Christmas Song (Version 1)/The Christmas Song (Version 2)	1966	3.75	7.50	15.00

Number	Title (A Side/B Side)	Yr	VG	VG+	NM
❏ 6065	Sweet Little Baby Boy (Part 1)/Sweet Little Baby Boy (Part 2)	1966	3.00	6.00	12.00
❏ 6071	Bring It Up/Nobody Knows	1967	3.00	6.00	12.00
❏ 6072	Let's Make Christmas Mean Something This Year (Part 1)/Let's Make Christmas Mean Something This Year (Part 2)	1967	3.00	6.00	12.00
❏ 6086	Kansas City/Stone Fox	1967	3.00	6.00	12.00
❏ 6091	Think/Nobody Cares	1967	3.00	6.00	12.00
—A-side: With Vicki Anderson; B-side: Vicki Anderson solo					
❏ 6100	Let Yourself Go/Good Rockin' Tonight	1967	3.00	6.00	12.00
❏ 6110	Cold Sweat — Part 1/Cold Sweat — Part 2	1967	3.00	6.00	12.00
❏ 6111	Mona Lisa/It Won't Be Me	1967	15.00	30.00	60.00
—Evidently not released or pulled shortly after release					
❏ 6112	America Is My Home — Part 1/America Is My Home — Part 2	1967	3.00	6.00	12.00
❏ 6122	Get It Together (Part 1)/Get It Together (Part 2)	1967	3.00	6.00	12.00
❏ 6133	The Soul of J.B./Funky Soul #1	1967	3.00	6.00	12.00
❏ 6141	I Guess I'll Have to Cry, Cry, Cry/Just Plain Funk	1967	3.00	6.00	12.00
❏ 6144	I Can't Stand Myself (When You Touch Me)/There Was a Time	1967	3.00	6.00	12.00
❏ 6151	You've Got to Change Your Mind/I'll Lose My Mind	1968	3.00	6.00	12.00
—A-side: With Bobby Byrd; B-side: Bobby Byrd solo					
❏ 6152	You've Got the Power/What the World Needs Now Is Love	1968	3.00	6.00	12.00
—A-side: With Vicki Anderson; B-side: Vicki Anderson solo					
❏ 6155	I Got the Feelin'/If I Ruled the World	1968	3.00	6.00	12.00
❏ 6159	Maybe Good, Maybe Bad (Part 1)/(Part 2)	1968	3.75	7.50	15.00
❏ 6164	Here I Go/Shhhh	1968	3.00	6.00	12.00
❏ 6166	Licking Stick — Licking Stick (Part 1)/Licking Stick — Licking Stick (Part 2)	1968	3.00	6.00	12.00
❏ 6187	Say It Loud — I'm Black and I'm Proud (Part 1)/Say It Loud — I'm Black and I'm Proud (Part 2)	1968	2.50	5.00	10.00
❏ 6187	Say It Loud — I'm Black But I'm Proud (Part 1)/Say It Loud — I'm Black But I'm Proud (Part 2)	1968	6.25	12.50	25.00
—Some copies have the above erroneous title on both sides					
❏ 6198	Goodbye My Love/Shades of Brown	1968	2.50	5.00	10.00
❏ 6203	Santa Claus Go Straight to the Ghetto/You Know It	1968	2.50	5.00	10.00
❏ 6204	Believers Shall Enjoy/Tit for Tat (Ain't No Turning Back)	1968	2.50	5.00	10.00
❏ 6205	Let's Unite the World at Christmas/In the Middle (Part 1)	1968	2.50	5.00	10.00
❏ 6206	In the Middle (Part 2)/Tit for Tat (Ain't No Turning Back)	1969	2.50	5.00	10.00
—A-side: With Marva Whitney					
❏ 6213	Give It Up or Turnit A Loose/I'll Lose My Mind	1969	2.50	5.00	10.00
❏ 6216	Shades of Brown (Part 2)/A Talk with the News	1969	2.50	5.00	10.00
—B-side by Steve Soul					
❏ 6218	You Got to Have a Job/I'm Tired, I'm Tired, I'm Tired	1969	2.50	5.00	10.00
—A-side with Marva Whitney; B-side: Marva Whitney solo					
❏ 6222	Soul Pride (Part 1)/Soul Pride (Part 2)	1969	2.50	5.00	10.00
❏ 6223	You've Got to Have a Mother for Me (Part 1)/You've Got to Have a Mother for Me (Part 2)	1969	2.50	5.00	10.00
❏ 6224	I Don't Want Nobody to Give Me Nothing (Open Up the Door, I'll Get It Myself) Part 1/Part 2	1969	2.50	5.00	10.00
❏ 6235	Little Groove Maker (Part 1)/Any Day Now	1969	2.50	5.00	10.00
❏ 6235	Little Groove Maker (Part 1)/I'm Shook	1969	2.50	5.00	10.00
❏ 6240	The Popcorn/The Chicken	1969	2.50	5.00	10.00
❏ 6245	Mother Popcorn (You Got to Have a Mother for Me) Part 1/Mother Popcorn (You Got to Have a Mother for Me) Part 2	1969	2.50	5.00	10.00
❏ 6250	Lowdown Popcorn/Top of the Stack	1969	2.50	5.00	10.00
❏ 6255	Let a Man Come In and Do the Popcorn Part One/Sometime	1969	2.50	5.00	10.00
❏ 6258	World (Part 1)/World (Part 2)	1969	2.50	5.00	10.00
❏ 6273	I'm Not Demanding (Part 1)/I'm Not Demanding (Part 2)	1969	2.50	5.00	10.00
❏ 6275	Part Two (Let a Man Come In and Do the Popcorn)/Get a Little Hipper	1969	2.50	5.00	10.00
❏ 6277	It's Christmas Time (Part 1)/It's Christmas Time (Part 2)	1969	2.50	5.00	10.00
❏ 6280	Ain't It Funky Now (Part 1)/Ain't It Funky Now (Part 2)	1970	2.00	4.00	8.00
❏ 6290	Funky Drummer (Part 1)/Funky Drummer (Part 2)	1970	2.00	4.00	8.00
❏ 6292	It's a New Day (Part 1)/It's a New Day (Part 2)	1970	2.00	4.00	8.00
❏ 6293	Let It Be Me/No More Heartaches, No More Pain	1970	2.00	4.00	8.00
—A-side: With Vicki Anderson; B-side: Vicki Anderson solo					
❏ 6300	Talkin' Loud and Sayin' Nothing (Part 1)/Talkin' Loud and Sayin' Nothing (Part 2)	1970	2.00	4.00	8.00
❏ 6310	Brother Rapp (Part 1) & (Part 2)/Bewildered	1970	2.00	4.00	8.00
❏ 6318	Get Up (I Feel Like Being A) Sex Machine (Part 1)/Get Up (I Feel Like Being A) Sex Machine (Part 2)	1970	2.00	4.00	8.00
❏ 6322	I'm Not Demanding (Part 1)/I'm Not Demanding (Part 2)	1970	2.00	4.00	8.00
❏ 6329	Call Me Super Bad (Part 1 & Part 2)/Call Me Super Bad (Part 3)	1970	5.00	10.00	20.00
—First pressing: Note longer title					
❏ 6329	Super Bad (Part 1 & Part 2)/Super Bad (Part 3)	1970	2.00	4.00	8.00
❏ 6339	Hey America/(Instrumental)	1970	2.00	4.00	8.00
❏ 6339 [PS]	Hey America/(Instrumental)	1970	3.75	7.50	15.00
❏ 6340	Santa Claus Is Definitely Here to Stay/(Instrumental)	1970	2.00	4.00	8.00

Number	Title (A Side/B Side)	Yr	VG	VG+	NM
❏ 6340 [PS]	Santa Claus Is Definitely Here to Stay/(Instrumental)	1970	7.50	15.00	30.00
❏ 6347	Get Up, Get Into It, Get Involved Pt. 1/Get Up, Get Into It, Get Involved Pt. 2	1971	2.00	4.00	8.00
❏ 6359	Talking Loud and Saying Nothing — Part 1/Talking Loud and Saying Nothing — Part 2	1971	2.00	4.00	8.00
❏ 6363	I Cried/World (Part 2)	1971	2.00	4.00	8.00
❏ 6366	Spinning Wheel (Part 1)/Spinning Wheel (Part 2)	1971	2.00	4.00	8.00
❏ 6368	Soul Power Pt. 1/Soul Power Pt 2 & Pt. 3	1971	2.00	4.00	8.00
MERCURY					
❏ 885190-7	Prisoner of Love/Please, Please, Please	1986	—	2.00	4.00
—Reissue					
❏ 885194-7	Get on the Good Foot/Give It Up or Turnit A Loose	1986	—	2.00	4.00
—Reissue					
PEOPLE					
❏ 664	Everybody Wanna Be Funky One More Time Pt. 1/Everybody Wanna Be Funky One More Time Pt. 2	1976	—	2.50	5.00
❏ 2500	Escape-ism (Part 1)/Escape-ism (Parts 2 & 3)	1971	—	3.00	6.00
❏ 2501	Hot Pants Pt. 1 (She Got to Use What She Got to Get What She Wants)/Hot Pants Pt. 2	1971	—	3.00	6.00
POLYDOR					
❏ 2005	Star Generation/Women Are Something Else	1979	—	2.50	5.00
❏ 2034	The Original Disco Man/Let the Boogie Do the Rest	1979	—	2.50	5.00
❏ 2054	Regrets/Stone Cold Drag	1979	—	2.50	5.00
❏ 2078	Let the Funk Flow/Sometimes That's All There Is	1980	—	2.50	5.00
❏ 2129	Get Up Offa That Thing/It's Too Funky in Here	1980	—	2.50	5.00
❏ 2167	Give the Bass Player Some Part 1/Part 2	1981	—	2.50	5.00
❏ 14088	Make It Funky Part 1/Make It Funky Part 2	1971	—	3.00	6.00
❏ 14098	My Part/Make It Funky, Part 3//Make It Funky, Part 4	1971	—	3.00	6.00
❏ 14100	I'm a Greedy Man Part 1/I'm a Greedy Man Part 2	1971	—	3.00	6.00
❏ 14109	Talking Loud and Saying Nothing Part 1/Part 2	1972	—	3.00	6.00
❏ 14110	Nothing Beats a Try But a Fail/Hot Pants Road	1972	—	—	—
—Unreleased					
❏ 14116	King Heroin/Theme from King Heroin	1972	—	3.00	6.00
❏ 14116 [PS]	King Heroin/Theme from King Heroin	1972	2.50	5.00	10.00
❏ 14125	There It Is Part 1/There It Is Part 2	1972	—	3.00	6.00
❏ 14129	Honky Tonk Part 1/Honky Tonk Part 2	1972	—	3.00	6.00
—Artist credit: "James Brown Soul Train"					
❏ 14139	Get On the Good Foot Part 1/Get On the Good Foot Part 2	1972	—	3.00	6.00
❏ 14153	I Got a Bag of My Own/Public Enemy #1	1972	—	3.00	6.00
❏ 14155	I Got a Bag of My Own/I Know It's True	1972	7.50	15.00	30.00
—Manufactured in U.S. for export					
❏ 14157	What My Baby Needs Now Is a Little More Lovin'/This Guy-This Girl's in Love	1972	—	3.00	6.00
—With Lyn Collins					
❏ 14161	Santa Claus Goes Straight to the Ghetto/Sweet Little Baby Boy	1972	—	3.00	6.00
❏ 14162	I Got Ants in My Pants (and I want to dance) Part 1/Part 15 and 16	1973	—	2.50	5.00
❏ 14168	Down and Out in New York City/Mama's Dead	1973	—	2.50	5.00
❏ 14169	The Boss/Like It Is, Like It Was	1973	—	2.50	5.00
❏ 14177	Think/Something	1973	—	2.50	5.00
❏ 14185	Think/Something	1973	—	2.50	5.00
❏ 14193	Woman Part 1/Woman Part 2	1973	—	2.50	5.00
❏ 14194	Sexy, Sexy, Sexy/Slaughter Theme	1973	—	2.50	5.00
❏ 14199	Let It Be Me/It's All Right	1973	—	—	—
—With Lyn Collins; canceled?					
❏ 14206	I Got a Good Thing Part 1/I Got a Good Thing Part 2	1973	—	—	—
—Canceled?					
❏ 14210	Stoned to the Bone Part 1/Stoned to the Bone Part 2	1973	—	2.50	5.00
—Notice corrected title					
❏ 14210	Stone to the Bone Part 1/Stone to the Bone Part 2	1973	2.50	5.00	10.00
❏ 14223	The Payback Part 1/The Payback Part 2	1974	—	2.50	5.00
❏ 14223 [PS]	The Payback Part 1/The Payback Part 2	1974	2.50	5.00	10.00
❏ 14244	My Thang/Public Enemy No. 1	1974	—	2.50	5.00
❏ 14255	Papa Don't Take No Mess Part 1/Part 2	1974	—	2.50	5.00
❏ 14258	Funky President (People It's Bad)/Coldblooded	1974	—	2.50	5.00
❏ 14268	Reality/I Need Your Love So Bad	1975	—	2.50	5.00
❏ 14270	Sex Machine Part 1/Sex Machine Part 2	1975	—	2.50	5.00
❏ 14274	Thank You For Letting Me Be Myself And... Part 1/Part 2	1975	—	2.50	5.00
❏ 14279	Dead On It Part 1/Dead On It Part 2	1975	—	—	—
—Unreleased					
❏ 14281	Hustle (Dead On It) Part 1/Hustle (Dead On It) Part 2	1975	—	2.50	5.00
❏ 14295	Superbad, Superslick Part 1/Superbad, Superslick Part 2	1975	—	2.50	5.00
❏ 14301	Hot (I Need to Be Loved, Loved, Loved, Loved)/Superbad, Superslick	1975	—	2.50	5.00
❏ 14302	Dooley's Junkyard Dogs Part 1/Part 2	1975	—	2.50	5.00
❏ 14304	(I Love You) For Sentimental Reasons/Goodnight My Love	1976	—	2.50	5.00
❏ 14326	Get Up Offa That Thing/Release the Pressure	1976	—	2.50	5.00
❏ 14354	I Refuse to Lose/Home Again	1976	—	2.50	5.00
❏ 14360	Bodyheat Part 1/Bodyheat Part 2	1976	—	2.50	5.00
❏ 14388	Kiss in 77/Woman	1977	—	2.50	5.00
❏ 14409	Give Me Some Skin/People Wake Up and Live	1977	—	2.50	5.00
—With the J.B.'s					
❏ 14433	Take Me Higher and Groove Me/Summertime	1977	—	2.50	5.00
—B-side by Martha and James					

B

James Brown, known as "The Godfather of Soul" and a host of other nicknames, is the #1 singles artist and #3 album artist in the history of the R&B charts. And if the R&B album charts had begun before 1965, no doubt he'd be atop that one, too. *Please Please Please* was his first LP, and it is exceedingly rare with this "legs" cover.

The second album of James Brown material, *Try Me*, featured this evocative cover of a woman with a cigarette and gun. It also is quite hard to find.

Think!, the third JB album, featured a baby on the cover of original editions.

Sometimes considered the greatest live album ever, *Live at the Apollo*, as it is generally known, was a consistent seller for years.

In the wake of the *Live at the Apollo* album, King issued this very rare 7-inch single to the jukebox trade.

One of JB's biggest crossover hits was "Super Bad." Not as well known is that some copies of the 45 called this song "Call Me Super Bad."

Number	Title (A Side/B Side)	Yr	VG	VG+	NM
❏ 14438	If You Don't Give a Doggone About It/People Who Criticize	1977	—	2.50	5.00
—With the New J.B.'s					
❏ 14460	Love Me Tender/Have a Happy Day	1978	—	2.50	5.00
—With the New J.B.'s					
❏ 14465	Eyesight/I Never Never Never Will Forget	1978	—	2.50	5.00
❏ 14487	The Spank/Love Me Tender	1978	—	2.50	5.00
❏ 14512	Nature Part 1/Nature Part 2	1978	—	2.50	5.00
❏ 14522	For Goodness Sakes, Look at Those Cakes Part 1/Part 2	1979	—	2.50	5.00
❏ 14540	Someone to Talk To Part 1/Someone to Talk To Part 2	1979	—	2.50	5.00
❏ 14557	It's Too Funky in Here/Are We Really Dancing	1979	—	2.50	5.00
❏ 871804-7	Think/Lost Someone	1989	—	—	3.00
—Reissue					
❏ 871808-7	Out of Sight/Maybe the Last Time	1989	—	—	3.00
—Reissue					
❏ 871810-7	I Got You (I Feel Good)/Papa's Got a Brand New Bag	1989	—	—	3.00
—Reissue					
❏ 887500-7	(Get Up I Feel Like Being a) Sex Machine/Vincent's Theme	1988	—	—	3.00
—B-side by Ethan James					
❏ 887500-7 [PS]	(Get Up I Feel Like Being a) Sex Machine/Vincent's Theme	1988	—	2.00	4.00
—B-side by Ethan James					

SCOTTI BROTHERS

Number	Title (A Side/B Side)	Yr	VG	VG+	NM
❏ ZS4-05682	Living in America/Farewell	1985	—	—	3.00
—B-side by Vince Di Cola					
❏ ZS4-05682 [PS]	Living in America/Farewell	1985	—	—	3.00
❏ ZS4-06275	Gravity/Gravity (Dub Mix)	1986	—	—	3.00
❏ ZS4-06275 [PS]	Gravity/Gravity (Dub Mix)	1986	—	—	3.00
❏ ZS4-06568	How Do You Stop/House of Rock	1987	—	—	3.00
❏ ZS4-06568 [PS]	How Do You Stop/House of Rock	1987	—	—	3.00
❏ ZS4-07090	Let's Get Personal/Repeat the Beat	1987	—	—	3.00
❏ ZS4-07783	I'm Real/Tribute	1988	—	—	3.00
❏ ZS4-07783 [PS]	I'm Real/Tribute	1988	—	—	3.00
❏ ZS4-07975	Static/Godfather Runnin' the Joint	1988	—	—	3.00
❏ ZS4-08088	Time to Get Busy/Busy J.B.	1988	—	—	3.00
❏ ZS4-68559	It's Your Money $/You and Me	1989	—	—	3.00
❏ 75286	(So Tired of Standing Still We Got to) Move On/You Are My Everything	1991	—	2.00	4.00

SMASH

Number	Title (A Side/B Side)	Yr	VG	VG+	NM
❏ 1898	Caledonia/Evil	1964	3.00	6.00	12.00
❏ 1898	Caldonia/Evil	1964	3.00	6.00	12.00
❏ 1898 [PS]	Caledonia/Evil	1964	6.25	12.50	25.00
❏ 1908	The Things That I Used to Do/Out of the Blue	1964	3.00	6.00	12.00
❏ 1908 [PS]	The Things That I Used to Do/Out of the Blue	1964	10.00	20.00	40.00
❏ 1919	Out of Sight/Maybe the Last Time	1964	3.00	6.00	12.00
❏ 1919 [PS]	Out of Sight/Maybe the Last Time	1964	10.00	20.00	40.00
❏ 1949	Who's Afraid of Virginia Woolf? Part 1/Part 2	1964	—	—	—
—Unreleased					
❏ 1975	Devil's Hideaway/Who's Afraid of Virginia Woolf?	1965	2.50	5.00	10.00
❏ 1989	I Got You/Only You	1965	12.50	25.00	50.00
—Withdrawn					
❏ 2008	Try Me/Papa's Got a Brand New Bag	1965	2.50	5.00	10.00
❏ 2028	New Breed Part 1/New Breed Part 2	1966	2.50	5.00	10.00
❏ 2042	James Brown's Boo-Ga-Loo/Lost in the Mood of Changes	1966	2.50	5.00	10.00
❏ 2064	Let's Go Get Stoned/Our Day Will Come	1966	2.50	5.00	10.00
❏ 2093	Jimmy Mack/What Do You Like	1967	2.50	5.00	10.00

T.K.

Number	Title (A Side/B Side)	Yr	VG	VG+	NM
❏ 1039	Rapp Payback (Where Iz Moses) Part 1/Part 2	1980	—	2.00	4.00
❏ 1042	Stay with Me/Smokin' and Drinkin'	1981	—	2.00	4.00

78s
FEDERAL

Number	Title (A Side/B Side)	Yr	VG	VG+	NM
❏ 12258	Please, Please, Please/Why Do You Do Me?	1956	15.00	30.00	60.00
❏ 12264	I Don't Know/I Feel That Old Feeling Coming On	1956	12.50	25.00	50.00
❏ 12277	No, No, No, No/Hold My Baby's Hand	1956	12.50	25.00	50.00
❏ 12289	Just Won't Do Right/Let's Make It	1957	12.50	25.00	50.00
❏ 12290	I Won't Plead No More/Chonnie On Chon	1957	12.50	25.00	50.00
❏ 12292	Gonna Try/Can't Be the Same	1957	12.50	25.00	50.00
❏ 12295	Love or a Game/Messing with the Blues	1957	12.50	25.00	50.00
❏ 12300	I Walked Alone/You're Mine, You're Mine	1957	12.50	25.00	50.00
❏ 12311	Baby Cries Over the Ocean/That Dood It	1957	12.50	25.00	50.00
❏ 12337	Try Me/Tell Me What I Did Wrong	1958	17.50	35.00	70.00
—Note: Later 78s on Federal may exist					

7-Inch Extended Plays
KING

Number	Title (A Side/B Side)	Yr	VG	VG+	NM
❏ EP-430	*Please, Please, Please/That's When I Lost My Heart/Try Me/Tell Me What I Did Wrong	1959	50.00	100.00	200.00
❏ EP-430 [PS]	Please, Please, Please	1959	100.00	200.00	400.00
❏ 826	(contents unknown)	1963	20.00	40.00	80.00
❏ 826 [PS]	Live at the Apollo	1963	30.00	60.00	120.00

SMASH

Number	Title (A Side/B Side)	Yr	VG	VG+	NM
❏ SRS 707-C	New Breed/Lost in the Mood of Changes/Hooks//Jabo/Fat Bag (Part 1)/Fat Bag❏ (Part 2)	196?	12.50	25.00	50.00
—Jukebox issue; small hole, plays at 33 1/3 rpm					
❏ SRS 707-C [PS]	James Brown Plays New Breed (The Boo-Ga-Loo)	196?	12.50	25.00	50.00
—Jukebox issue; small hole, plays at 33 1/3 rpm					

Albums
HRB

Number	Title (A Side/B Side)	Yr	VG	VG+	NM
❏ 1004 [(2)]	The Fabulous James Brown	1974	6.25	12.50	25.00

KING

Number	Title (A Side/B Side)	Yr	VG	VG+	NM
❏ 610 [M]	Please Please Please	1958	300.00	600.00	1200.
—"Woman's and man's legs" cover; "King" on label is two inches wide					
❏ 610 [M]	Please Please Please	1961	250.00	500.00	1000.
—"Woman's and man's legs" cover; "King" on label is three inches wide					
❏ 635 [M]	Try Me!	1959	225.00	450.00	900.00
—"Woman with cigarette and gun" cover; "King" on label is two inches wide					
❏ 635 [M]	Try Me!	1961	150.00	300.00	600.00
—"Woman with cigarette and gun" cover; "King" on label is three inches wide					
❏ 683 [M]	Think!	1960	225.00	450.00	900.00
—"Baby" cover; "King" on label is two inches wide					
❏ 683 [M]	Think!	1961	150.00	300.00	600.00
—"Baby" cover; "King" on label is three inches wide					
❏ 683 [M]	Think!	1963	25.00	50.00	100.00
—James Brown photo cover; "crownless" King label					
❏ 683 [M]	Think!	1966	12.50	25.00	50.00
—James Brown photo cover; "crown" King label					
❏ 743 [M]	The Amazing James Brown	1961	125.00	250.00	500.00
—"James Brown in suit" cover					
❏ 743 [M]	The Amazing James Brown	1963	37.50	75.00	150.00
—White title cover; "crownless" King label					
❏ 743 [M]	The Amazing James Brown	1966	125.00	250.00	500.00
—White title cover with "James Brown" in huge letters; "crown" King label					
❏ 771 [M]	Night Train	1961	75.00	150.00	300.00
—Original title					
❏ 771 [M]	Twist Around	1962	62.50	125.00	250.00
—Second title					
❏ 771 [M]	Jump Around	1963	50.00	100.00	200.00
—Third title					
❏ KS-771 [S]	Jump Around	1963	75.00	150.00	300.00
—Stereo copies of King 771 only exist with this title					
❏ 780 [M]	Shout and Shimmy	1962	62.50	125.00	250.00
—"Shout and Shimmy" on both cover and label					
❏ 780 [M]	Good Good Twistin'	1962	50.00	100.00	200.00
—"Good Good Twistin' " on either label or cover, or both					
❏ 780 [M]	Excitement	1963	37.50	75.00	150.00
—Third title; "crownless" King label					
❏ 780 [M]	Excitement	1966	12.50	25.00	50.00
—Third title; "crown" King label					
❏ 804 [M]	James Brown & His Famous Flames Tour the U.S.A.	1962	37.50	125.00	250.00
—"Crownless" King label					
❏ 804 [M]	James Brown & His Famous Flames Tour the U.S.A.	1966	12.50	25.00	50.00
—"Crown" King label					
❏ 826 [M]	Live at the Apollo	1963	50.00	100.00	200.00
—Custom back cover; "crownless" King label					
❏ 826 [M]	Live at the Apollo	1963	37.50	75.00	150.00
—Other King albums on back cover; "crownless" King label					
❏ 826 [M]	Live at the Apollo	1963	200.00	400.00	800.00
—White label promo, banded for airplay					
❏ 826 [M]	Live at the Apollo	1966	12.50	25.00	50.00
—"Crown" King label					
❏ KS-826 [S]	Live at the Apollo	1963	75.00	150.00	300.00
—Custom back cover; "crownless" King label					
❏ KS-826 [S]	Live at the Apollo	1963	50.00	100.00	200.00
—Other King albums on back cover; "crownless" King label					
❏ KS-826 [S]	Live at the Apollo	1966	17.50	35.00	70.00
—"Crown" King label					
❏ 851 [M]	Prisoner of Love	1963	50.00	100.00	200.00
—Custom back cover; "crownless" King label					
❏ 851 [M]	Prisoner of Love	1963	25.00	50.00	100.00
—Other King albums on back cover; "crownless" King label					
❏ 851 [M]	Prisoner of Love	1966	12.50	25.00	50.00
—"Crown" King label					
❏ 883 [M]	Pure Dynamite! Live at the Royal	1964	200.00	400.00	800.00
—White label promo; banded for airplay					
❏ 883 [M]	Pure Dynamite! Live at the Royal	1964	50.00	100.00	200.00
—"Crownless" King label					
❏ 883 [M]	Pure Dynamite! Live at the Royal	1966	12.50	25.00	50.00
—"Crown" King label					
❏ 909 [M]	Please Please Please	1964	25.00	50.00	100.00
—Reissue of 610; "crownless" King label					
❏ 909 [M]	Please Please Please	1966	12.50	25.00	50.00
—"Crown" King label					
❏ 919 [M]	The Unbeatable James Brown — 16 Hits	1964	25.00	50.00	100.00
—Reissue of 635; "crownless" King label					
❏ 919 [M]	The Unbeatable James Brown — 16 Hits	1966	12.50	25.00	50.00
—"Crown" King label					
❏ 938 [M]	Papa's Got a Brand New Bag	1965	20.00	40.00	80.00
—Red cover; "crownless" King label					
❏ 938 [M]	Papa's Got a Brand New Bag	1966	12.50	25.00	50.00
—Green cover; "crownless" King label					
❏ 938 [M]	Papa's Got a Brand New Bag	1966	10.00	20.00	40.00
—"Crown" King label					
❏ LPS-938 [P]	Papa's Got a Brand New Bag	1965	25.00	50.00	100.00
—Red cover; "crownless" King label					
❏ LPS-938 [P]	Papa's Got a Brand New Bag	1966	15.00	30.00	60.00
—Green cover; "crownless" King label					
❏ LPS-938 [P]	Papa's Got a Brand New Bag	1966	12.50	25.00	50.00
—"Crown" King label					
❏ 946 [M]	I Got You (I Feel Good)	1966	25.00	50.00	100.00
—"Crownless" King label					
❏ 946 [M]	I Got You (I Feel Good)	1966	10.00	20.00	40.00
—"Crown" King label					
❏ LPS-946 [S]	I Got You (I Feel Good)	1966	37.50	75.00	150.00
—"Crownless" King label					

Number	Title (A Side/B Side)	Yr	VG	VG+	NM
❑ LPS-946 [S]	I Got You (I Feel Good)	1966	12.50	25.00	50.00
—"Crown" King label					
❑ 961 [M]	Mighty Instrumentals	1966	25.00	50.00	100.00
❑ LPS-961 [S]	Mighty Instrumentals	1966	37.50	75.00	150.00
❑ 985 [M]	It's a Man's Man's Man's World	1966	12.50	25.00	50.00
❑ KS-985 [S]	It's a Man's Man's Man's World	1966	17.50	35.00	70.00
❑ 1010 [M]	Christmas Songs	1966	25.00	50.00	100.00
—Wreath on gray wall, no song titles on back					
❑ 1010 [M]	Christmas Songs	1967	20.00	40.00	80.00
—Wreath on white wall, song titles are on back					
❑ KS-1010 [S]	Christmas Songs	1966	37.50	75.00	150.00
—Wreath on gray wall, no song titles on back					
❑ KS-1010 [S]	Christmas Songs	1967	25.00	50.00	100.00
—Wreath on white wall, song titles are on back					
❑ 1016 [M]	Raw Soul	1967	12.50	25.00	50.00
❑ KS-1016 [P]	Raw Soul	1967	17.50	35.00	70.00
❑ 1018 [M]	Live at the Garden	1967	100.00	200.00	400.00
—Black label promo; banded for airplay					
❑ 1018 [M]	Live at the Garden	1967	20.00	40.00	80.00
❑ KS-1018 [S]	Live at the Garden	1967	25.00	50.00	100.00
❑ 1020 [M]	Cold Sweat	1967	12.50	25.00	50.00
❑ KS-1020 [S]	Cold Sweat	1967	17.50	35.00	70.00
❑ LPS-1022 [(2)]	Live at the Apollo, Volume II	1968	17.50	35.00	70.00
❑ LPS-1024	James Brown Presents His Show of Tomorrow	1968	12.50	25.00	50.00
—Various-artists album					
❑ LPS-1030	I Can't Stand Myself (When You Touch Me)	1968	12.50	25.00	50.00
❑ LPS-1031	I Got the Feelin'	1968	12.50	25.00	50.00
❑ LPS-1034	James Brown Plays Nothing But Soul	1968	12.50	25.00	50.00
❑ LPS-1038	Thinking About Little Willie John and a Few Nice Things	1968	12.50	25.00	50.00
❑ KS-1040	A Soulful Christmas	1968	20.00	40.00	80.00
❑ KS-1047	Say It Loud — I'm Black and I'm Proud	1969	12.50	25.00	50.00
❑ KS-1051	Gettin' Down To It	1969	12.50	25.00	50.00
❑ KSD-1055	James Brown Plays & Directs The Popcorn	1969	10.00	20.00	40.00
❑ KSD-1063	It's a Mother	1969	10.00	20.00	40.00
❑ KSD-1092	Ain't It Funky	1970	10.00	20.00	40.00
❑ KSD-1095	It's a New Day So Let a Man Come In	1970	10.00	20.00	40.00
❑ KSD-1100	Soul on Top	1970	10.00	20.00	40.00
❑ KSD-1110	Sho Is Funky Down Here	1971	10.00	20.00	40.00
❑ KSD-1115 [(2)]	Sex Machine	1970	12.50	25.00	50.00
❑ KSD-1124	Hey America!	1970	10.00	20.00	40.00
❑ KSD-1127	Super Bad	1971	10.00	20.00	40.00
POLYDOR					
❑ 25-3003 [(2)]	Revolution of the Mind — Live at the Apollo, Volume III	1971	15.00	30.00	60.00
❑ PD2-3004 [(2)]	Get On the Good Foot	1972	15.00	30.00	60.00
❑ PD2-3007 [(2)]	The Payback	1973	12.50	25.00	50.00
❑ 24-4054	Hot Pants	1971	10.00	20.00	40.00
❑ PD-5028	There It Is	1972	10.00	20.00	40.00
❑ SC-5401	James Brown Soul Classics	1972	6.25	12.50	25.00
❑ SC-5402	Soul Classics, Volume 2	1973	6.25	12.50	25.00
❑ PD-6014	Black Caesar	1973	12.50	25.00	50.00
❑ PD-6015	Slaughter's Big Rip-Off	1973	12.50	25.00	50.00
❑ PD-1-6039	Reality	1975	10.00	20.00	40.00
❑ PD-1-6042	Sex Machine Today	1975	10.00	20.00	40.00
❑ PD-1-6054	Everybody's Doin' the Hustle & Dead On the Double Bump	1975	10.00	20.00	40.00
❑ PD-1-6059	Hot	1976	10.00	20.00	40.00
❑ PD-1-6071	Get Up Offa That Thing	1976	10.00	20.00	40.00
❑ PD-1-6093	Bodyheat	1976	10.00	20.00	40.00
❑ PD-1-6111	Mutha's Nature	1977	10.00	20.00	40.00
❑ PD-1-6140	Jam/1980s	1978	10.00	20.00	40.00
❑ PD-1-6181	Take a Look at Those Cakes	1978	7.50	15.00	30.00
❑ PD-1-6212	The Original Disco Man	1979	7.50	15.00	30.00
❑ PD-1-6258	People	1980	7.50	15.00	30.00
❑ PD-2-6290 [(2)]	James Brown…Live/Hot on the One	1980	12.50	25.00	50.00
❑ PD-1-6318	Nonstop!	1981	7.50	15.00	30.00
❑ PD-1-6340	The Best of James Brown	1981	5.00	10.00	20.00
❑ PD-2-9001 [(2)]	Hell	1974	20.00	40.00	80.00
❑ PD-2-9004 [(2)]	Sex Machine Live	1976	12.50	25.00	50.00
❑ 821231-1	Ain't That a Groove: The James Brown Story 1966-1969	1984	3.75	7.50	15.00
❑ 821232-1	Doing It to Death: The James Brown Story 1970-1973	1984	3.75	7.50	15.00
❑ 823275-1	The Best of James Brown	1984	3.00	6.00	12.00
—Reissue of 6340					
❑ 827439-1	Dead on the Heavy Funk: The James Brown Story 1974-1978	1985	3.75	7.50	15.00
❑ 829254-1 [(2)]	Solid Gold: 30 Golden Hits	1985	5.00	10.00	20.00
❑ 829417-1	James Brown's Funky People	1986	3.75	7.50	15.00
—Various-artists LP					
❑ 829624-1	In the Jungle Groove	1986	3.75	7.50	15.00
❑ 835857-1	James Brown's Funky People 2	1988	3.75	7.50	15.00
—Various-artists compilation					
❑ 837126-1	Motherlode	1988	3.75	7.50	15.00
RHINO					
❑ RNLP-217	Live at the Apollo, Volume 2, Part 1	1985	3.75	7.50	15.00
❑ RNLP-218	Live at the Apollo, Volume 2, Part 2	1985	3.75	7.50	15.00
❑ RNLP-219	Greatest Hits (1964-1968)	1986	3.75	7.50	15.00
❑ R1 70194	Santa's Got a Brand New Bag	1986	2.50	5.00	10.00
—Reissue of King material					
❑ R1-70217	Live at the Apollo, Volume 2, Part 1	1988	3.00	6.00	12.00
—Reissue of 217					
❑ R1-70218	Live at the Apollo, Volume 2, Part 2	1988	3.00	6.00	12.00
—Reissue of 218					

Number	Title (A Side/B Side)	Yr	VG	VG+	NM
❑ R1-70219	Greatest Hits (1964-1968)	1988	3.00	6.00	12.00
—Reissue of 219					
SCOTTI BROTHERS					
❑ FZ 40380	Gravity	1986	3.00	6.00	12.00
❑ FZ 44241	I'm Real	1988	3.00	6.00	12.00
❑ FZ 45164	Soul Session Live	1989	3.75	7.50	15.00
❑ 75225-1	Love Overdue	1991	5.00	10.00	20.00
SMASH					
❑ MGS-27054 [M]	Showtime	1964	7.50	15.00	30.00
❑ MGS-27057 [M]	Grits & Soul	1965	7.50	15.00	30.00
❑ MGS-27058 [M]	Out of Sight	1965	25.00	50.00	100.00
❑ MGS-27072 [M]	James Brown Plays James Brown — Today & Yesterday	1965	7.50	15.00	30.00
❑ MGS-27080 [M]	James Brown Plays New Breed	1966	7.50	15.00	30.00
❑ MGS-27084 [M]	Handful of Soul	1966	7.50	15.00	30.00
❑ MGS-27087 [M]	The James Brown Show	1967	7.50	15.00	30.00
—Various-artists LP					
❑ MGS-27093 [M]	James Brown Plays the Real Thing	1967	7.50	15.00	30.00
❑ SRS-67054 [S]	Showtime	1964	10.00	2.00	40.00
❑ SRS-67057 [S]	Grits & Soul	1965	10.00	20.00	40.00
❑ SRS-67058 [S]	Out of Sight	1965	37.50	75.00	150.00
❑ SRS-67072 [S]	James Brown Plays James Brown — Today & Yesterday	1965	10.00	20.00	40.00
❑ SRS-67080 [S]	James Brown Plays New Breed	1966	10.00	2.00	40.00
❑ SRS-67084 [S]	Handful of Soul	1966	10.00	20.00	40.00
❑ SRS-67087 [S]	The James Brown Show	1967	10.00	2.00	40.00
—Various-artists LP					
❑ SRS-67093 [S]	James Brown Plays the Real Thing	1967	10.00	20.00	40.00
❑ SRS-67109	James Brown Sings Out of Sight	1968	7.50	15.00	30.00
—Abridged reissue of 67058					
SOLID SMOKE					
❑ SS-8006	Live and Lowdown at the Apollo, Vol. 1	1980	3.00	6.00	12.00
❑ SS-8013	Can Your Heart Stand It	1981	3.00	6.00	12.00
❑ SS-8023	The Federal Years, Part 1	198?	3.00	6.00	12.00
❑ SS-8024	The Federal Years, Part 2	198?	3.00	6.00	12.00
T.K.					
❑ 615	Soul Syndrome	1980	7.50	15.00	30.00

BROWN, MAXINE
45s
ABC-PARAMOUNT

Number	Title (A Side/B Side)	Yr	VG	VG+	NM
❑ 10235	I Don't Need You No More/Think of Me	1961	3.00	6.00	12.00
❑ 10255	After All We've Been Through Together/My Life	1961	3.00	6.00	12.00
❑ 10290	I Got a Funny Kind of Feeling/What I Don't Know	1962	3.00	6.00	12.00
❑ 10315	Forget Him/A Man	1962	3.00	6.00	12.00
❑ 10327	No Time for Cryin'/Wanting You	1962	3.00	6.00	12.00
❑ 10343	I Kneel at Your Throne/If I Knew Then	1962	3.00	6.00	12.00
❑ 10370	Promise Me Anything/Am I Falling in Love	1962	3.00	6.00	12.00
❑ 10388	Life Goes On Just the Same/If You Have No Real Objections	1962	3.00	6.00	12.00
AVCO					
❑ 4585	Always and Forever/Make Love to Me	1971	—	2.50	5.00
❑ 4604	Treat Me Like a Lady/I.O.U.	1972	—	2.50	5.00
❑ 4612	Picked Up, Packed and Went Away/(B-side unknown)	1972	—	2.50	5.00
COMMONWEALTH UNITED					
❑ 3001	We'll Cry Together/Darling Be Home Soon	1969	—	3.00	6.00
❑ 3008	I Can't Get Along Without You/Reason to Believe	1970	—	3.00	6.00
EPIC					
❑ 10334	Seems You've Forsaken My Love/Plum Outa Sight	1968	2.50	5.00	10.00
❑ 10424	Love in Them There Hills/From Loving You	1968	2.50	5.00	10.00
NOMAR					
❑ 103	All in My Mind/Harry, Let's Marry	1960	3.75	7.50	15.00
❑ 106	Funny/Now That You've Gone	1961	3.75	7.50	15.00
❑ 107	Heaven in Your Arms/Maxine's Place	1961	3.75	7.50	15.00
—B-side by Frankie and the Flips					
WAND					
❑ 135	Ask Me/Yesterday's Kisses	1963	2.50	5.00	10.00
❑ 135 [PS]	Ask Me/Yesterday's Kisses	1963	12.50	25.00	50.00
❑ 142	Coming Back to You/Since I Found You	1963	2.50	5.00	10.00
❑ 152	Little Girl Lost/You Upset My Soul	1964	2.00	4.00	8.00
❑ 158	I Cry Alone/Put Yourself in My Place	1964	2.00	4.00	8.00
❑ 162	Oh No Not My Baby/You Upset My Soul	1964	3.00	6.00	12.00
❑ 173	It's Gonna Be Alright/You Do Something to Me	1965	2.00	4.00	8.00
❑ 185	Anything for a Laugh/One Step at a Time	1965	2.00	4.00	8.00
❑ 1104	If You Gotta Make a Fool of Somebody/You're in Love	1965	2.00	4.00	8.00
❑ 1117	One in a Million/Anything You Do Is Alright	1966	2.00	4.00	8.00
❑ 1128	We Can Work It Out/Let Me Give You My Lovin'	1966	2.00	4.00	8.00
❑ 1145	I Don't Need Anything/The Secret of Livin'	1967	2.00	4.00	8.00
❑ 1179	Soul Serenade/He's the Only Guy I'll Ever Love	1968	2.00	4.00	8.00
Albums					
COLLECTABLES					
❑ COL-5116	Golden Classics	198?	3.00	6.00	12.00
COMMONWEALTH UNITED					
❑ CU-6001	We'll Cry Together	1969	5.00	10.00	20.00
GUEST STAR					
❑ GS-1911 [M]	Maxine Brown	1964	3.00	6.00	12.00
WAND					
❑ LP-656 [M]	The Fabulous Sound of Maxine Brown	1963	12.50	25.00	50.00
❑ WDS-656 [S]	The Fabulous Sound of Maxine Brown	1963	15.00	30.00	60.00
❑ WD-663 [M]	Spotlight on Maxine Brown	1965	7.50	15.00	30.00
❑ WDS-663 [S]	Spotlight on Maxine Brown	1965	10.00	20.00	40.00

Number	Title (A Side/B Side)	Yr	VG	VG+	NM
❑ WD-684 [M]	Maxine Brown's Greatest Hits	1967	5.00	10.00	20.00
❑ WDS-684 [S]	Maxine Brown's Greatest Hits	1967	6.25	12.50	25.00

BROWN, NAPPY

45s

ICHIBAN

Number	Title (A Side/B Side)	Yr	VG	VG+	NM
❑ 206	Lemon Squeezin' Daddy/Small Red Apples	1989	—	2.50	5.00

SAVOY

Number	Title (A Side/B Side)	Yr	VG	VG+	NM
❑ 1129	That Man/I Wonder	1954	7.50	15.00	30.00
❑ 1135	Is It True, Is It True/Two-Faced Woman	1954	7.50	15.00	30.00
❑ 1155	Don't Be Angry/It's Really You	1955	6.25	12.50	25.00
❑ 1162	Piddly Patter Patter/There'll Come a Day	1955	6.25	12.50	25.00
❑ 1176	Doodle I Love You/Sittin' in the Dark	1955	6.25	12.50	25.00
❑ 1187	Open Up That Door/Pleasing You	1956	6.25	12.50	25.00
❑ 1196	Am I/Love Baby	1956	6.25	12.50	25.00
❑ 1506	Little by Little/I'm Getting Lonesome	1956	5.00	10.00	20.00
❑ 1511	Pretty Girl (Yea Yea Yea)/I'm Gonna Get You	1957	5.00	10.00	20.00
❑ 1514	Goody Goody Gum Drops/Bye Bye Baby	1957	5.00	10.00	20.00
❑ 1525	The Right Time/Oh You Don't Know	1957	5.00	10.00	20.00
❑ 1530	If You Need Some Lovin'/I'm in the Mood	1958	5.00	10.00	20.00
❑ 1547	Skidy Wo/I Cried Like a Baby	1958	5.00	10.00	20.00
❑ 1551	It Don't Hurt No More/My Baby	1958	5.00	10.00	20.00
❑ 1555	You're Going to Need Someone/Skiddy Woe	1958	5.00	10.00	20.00
❑ 1562	A Long Time/All Right Now	1959	5.00	10.00	20.00
❑ 1569	This Is My Confession/For Those Who Love	1959	5.00	10.00	20.00
❑ 1575	I Cried Like a Baby/So Deep	1959	5.00	10.00	20.00
❑ 1579	Give Me Your Love/Too Shy	1959	5.00	10.00	20.00
❑ 1582	Down in the Alley/My Baby Knows	1960	3.75	7.50	15.00
❑ 1587	Baby, Cry, Cry, Cry, Baby/What's Come Over You	1960	3.75	7.50	15.00
❑ 1588	Apple of My Eye/Baby I Got News for You	1960	3.75	7.50	15.00
❑ 1592	The Hole I'm In/Nobody Can Say	1960	3.75	7.50	15.00
❑ 1594	Coal Miner/Honnie-Bonnie	1961	3.75	7.50	15.00
❑ 1598	Don't Be Angry/Any Time Is the Right Time	1961	3.75	7.50	15.00
❑ 1616	Didn't You Know/I've Had My Fun	1962	3.75	7.50	15.00
❑ 1621	Lock on the Door/So Glad I Don't Have to Cry No More	1963	3.75	7.50	15.00

Albums

BLACK TOP

Number	Title (A Side/B Side)	Yr	VG	VG+	NM
❑ BT-1039	Something Gonna Jump Out the Bushes	1987	3.75	7.50	15.00

ICHIBAN

Number	Title (A Side/B Side)	Yr	VG	VG+	NM
❑ ICH-1056	Apples and Lemons	1990	3.00	6.00	12.00

KING SNAKE/ICHIBAN

Number	Title (A Side/B Side)	Yr	VG	VG+	NM
❑ ICH-9006	Aw! Shucks	1991	3.75	7.50	15.00

LANDSLIDE

Number	Title (A Side/B Side)	Yr	VG	VG+	NM
❑ LD 1008	Tore Up	1984	3.75	7.50	15.00

MELTONE

Number	Title (A Side/B Side)	Yr	VG	VG+	NM
❑ 1502	Deep Sea Diver	1989	3.75	7.50	15.00

SAVOY

Number	Title (A Side/B Side)	Yr	VG	VG+	NM
❑ MG-14002 [M]	Nappy Brown Sings	1958	100.00	200.00	400.00
❑ MG-14025 [M]	The Right Time	1960	62.50	125.00	250.00
❑ 14427	Nappy Brown	1977	3.00	6.00	12.00

SAVOY JAZZ

Number	Title (A Side/B Side)	Yr	VG	VG+	NM
❑ SJL-1149	Don't Be Angry	1984	2.50	5.00	10.00

BROWN, PETER

12-Inch Singles

COLUMBIA

Number	Title (A Side/B Side)	Yr	VG	VG+	NM
❑ 44-04957	They Only Come Out at Night (6:15) (Instrumental 4:46)	1984	2.00	4.00	8.00
❑ 44-05102	(Love Is Just) The Game/Hot Flash	1984	2.50	5.00	10.00
❑ 44-05175	Zie Zie Won't Dance (2 versions)	1985	2.00	4.00	8.00

RCA

Number	Title (A Side/B Side)	Yr	VG	VG+	NM
❑ PD-13357	Baby Gets High/Shall We Dance	1982	2.50	5.00	10.00
❑ PD-13518	Overnight Sensation (5:20) (Instrumental)	1983	2.50	5.00	10.00

T.K. DISCO

Number	Title (A Side/B Side)	Yr	VG	VG+	NM
❑ TKD-35	Do Ya Wanna Get Funky with Me (8:30)/Burning Love Breakdown (5:26)	1977	3.75	7.50	15.00
❑ TKD-151	Crank It Up (Funk Town) (10:31) (8:00)	1979	3.00	6.00	12.00
❑ TKD-441	Can't Be Love-Do It to Me Anyway (8:30) (7:20)	1980	2.50	5.00	10.00

45s

COLUMBIA

Number	Title (A Side/B Side)	Yr	VG	VG+	NM
❑ 38-04381	They Only Come Out at Night/(Instrumental)	1984	—	—	3.00
❑ 38-04381 [PS]	They Only Come Out at Night/(Instrumental)	1984	—	2.00	4.00
❑ 38-04622	(Love Is Just) The Game/Hot Flash	1984	—	2.00	4.00
❑ 38-04832	Zie Zie Won't Dance/Hot Flash	1985	—	2.00	4.00

DRIVE

Number	Title (A Side/B Side)	Yr	VG	VG+	NM
❑ 6258	Do Ya Wanna Get Funky with Me/Burning Love Breakdown	1977	—	3.00	6.00
❑ 6269	Dance with Me/For Your Love	1978	—	3.00	6.00
❑ 6272	You Should Do It/Without Love	1978	—	3.00	6.00
❑ 6274	Fantasy Love Affair/It's True What They Say	1978	—	3.00	6.00
❑ 6278	Crank It Up (Funk Town) Pt. 1/Pt. 2	1979	—	2.50	5.00
❑ 6281	Stargazer/Penguin	1979	—	2.50	5.00
❑ 6286	Can't Be Love-Do It to Me Anyway/West of the North Star	1980	—	2.50	5.00

RCA

Number	Title (A Side/B Side)	Yr	VG	VG+	NM
❑ PB-13335	Give Me Up/The Love Game	1982	—	—	—
—Canceled					
❑ PB-13413	Baby Gets High/The Love Game	1982	—	2.00	4.00

Albums

DRIVE

Number	Title (A Side/B Side)	Yr	VG	VG+	NM
❑ 104	Do Ya Wanna Get Funky with Me? (A Fantasy Love Affair)	1977	2.50	5.00	10.00
—The actual title is "A Fantasy Love Affair," but the placement of the words "Do Ya Wanna Get Funky with Me?" along the upper edge of the front cover makes it seem as if that is the title					
❑ 108	Stargazer	1979	2.50	5.00	10.00

RCA VICTOR

Number	Title (A Side/B Side)	Yr	VG	VG+	NM
❑ AFL1-4604	Back to the Front	1983	2.50	5.00	10.00

BROWN, RANDY

12-Inch Singles

CHOCOLATE CITY

Number	Title (A Side/B Side)	Yr	VG	VG+	NM
❑ 20019	We Ought to Be Doin' It (4:49)/You're So Good (6:39)	1980	3.00	6.00	12.00

45s

CHOCOLATE CITY

Number	Title (A Side/B Side)	Yr	VG	VG+	NM
❑ 3204	You Ought to Be Doin' It/Things That I Could Do to You	1980	—	2.00	4.00
❑ 3209	The Next Best Thing to Being There/(B-side unknown)	1980	—	2.00	4.00
❑ 3224	If I Don't Love You/Looking for the Real Thing	1981	—	2.00	4.00

PARACHUTE

Number	Title (A Side/B Side)	Yr	VG	VG+	NM
❑ 506	I'd Rather Hurt Myself (Than to Hurt You)/I'm Always in the Mood	1978	—	2.50	5.00
❑ 517	I Wanna Make Love to You/Sweet, Sweet Darling	1978	—	2.50	5.00
❑ 523	You Says It All/Crazy 'Bout You Baby	1979	—	2.50	5.00
❑ 526	I Thought of You Today/Use It	1979	—	2.50	5.00

SHARP MOUTH

Number	Title (A Side/B Side)	Yr	VG	VG+	NM
❑ HW 004	Move Me (Part 1)/(Part 2)	197?	5.00	10.00	20.00

STAX

Number	Title (A Side/B Side)	Yr	VG	VG+	NM
❑ 3227	If I Had It to Do All Over/Smoking Room	1980	—	2.50	5.00

Albums

CHOCOLATE CITY

Number	Title (A Side/B Side)	Yr	VG	VG+	NM
❑ CCLP-2010	Midnight Desire	1980	3.75	7.50	15.00

PARACHUTE

Number	Title (A Side/B Side)	Yr	VG	VG+	NM
❑ RRLP-9005	Welcome to My Room	1978	3.75	7.50	15.00
❑ RRLP-9012	Intimately	1979	2.50	5.00	10.00

STAX

Number	Title (A Side/B Side)	Yr	VG	VG+	NM
❑ MPS-8512	Check It Out	1981	3.75	7.50	15.00

BROWN, ROY

45s

BLUESWAY

Number	Title (A Side/B Side)	Yr	VG	VG+	NM
❑ 61002	New Orleans Women/Standing on Broadway (Watching the Girls)	1967	2.00	4.00	8.00

DELUXE

Number	Title (A Side/B Side)	Yr	VG	VG+	NM
❑ 3318	Big Town/Train Time Blues	1951	50.00	100.00	200.00
—Roy Brown singles on DeLuxe before 3318 are unconfirmed on 45 rpm					
❑ 3318	Big Town/Train Time Blues	1951	100.00	200.00	400.00
—Blue vinyl					
❑ 3319	Bar Room Blues/Good Rockin' Man	1951	50.00	100.00	200.00
—Black vinyl					
❑ 3319	Bar Room Blues/Good Rockin' Man	1951	100.00	200.00	400.00
—Blue vinyl					
❑ 3323	I've Got the Last Laugh Now/Brown Angel	1951	50.00	100.00	200.00
—Black vinyl					
❑ 3323	I've Got the Last Laugh Now/Brown Angel	1951	100.00	200.00	400.00
—Blue vinyl					

HOME OF THE BLUES

Number	Title (A Side/B Side)	Yr	VG	VG+	NM
❑ 107	Don't Break My Heart/A Man with the Blues	1960	6.25	12.50	25.00
❑ 110	Tired of Being Alone/Rocking All the Time	1960	6.25	12.50	25.00
❑ 115	Oh So Wonderful/Sugar Baby	1961	6.25	12.50	25.00
❑ 122	Rock and Roll Jamboree/I Need a Friend	1961	6.25	12.50	25.00

IMPERIAL

Number	Title (A Side/B Side)	Yr	VG	VG+	NM
❑ 5422	Everybody/Saturday Night	1957	7.50	15.00	30.00
❑ 5427	Party Doll/I'm Sticking with You	1957	7.50	15.00	30.00
❑ 5439	Let the Four Winds Blow/Diddy-Y-Diddy-O	1957	7.50	15.00	30.00
❑ 5455	I'm Convicted of Love/I'm Ready to Play	1957	7.50	15.00	30.00
❑ 5469	Tick of the Clock/Slow Down Little Eva	1957	7.50	15.00	30.00
❑ 5489	Ain't Gonna Do It/Sail On Little Girl	1958	7.50	15.00	30.00
❑ 5510	Hip Shakin' Baby/Be My Love Tonight	1958	7.50	15.00	30.00
❑ 5969	Let the Four Winds Blow/Diddy-Yi-Diddy-Yo	1963	5.00	10.00	20.00

KING

Number	Title (A Side/B Side)	Yr	VG	VG+	NM
❑ 4602	Travelin' Man/Hurry, Hurry Baby	1953	15.00	30.00	60.00
❑ 4609	Grandpa Stole My Baby/Money Can't Buy Love	1953	15.00	30.00	60.00
❑ 4704	Trouble at Midnight/Bootlegging Baby	1954	15.00	30.00	60.00
❑ 4715	Up Jumped the Devil/This Is My Last Goodbye	1954	15.00	30.00	60.00
❑ 4722	No Love at All/Don't Let It Rain	1954	15.00	30.00	60.00
❑ 4731	Ain't It a Shame/Gal from Kokomo	1954	15.00	30.00	60.00
❑ 4743	Worried Life Blues/Black Diamond	1954	15.00	30.00	60.00
❑ 4761	Fannie Brown Got Married/Queen of Diamonds	1955	12.50	25.00	50.00
❑ 4816	Shake 'Em Up Baby/Letter to Baby	1955	12.50	25.00	50.00
❑ 4834	My Little Angel Child/She's Gone Too Long	1955	12.50	25.00	50.00
❑ 5178	La-Dee-Dah-Dee/Melinda	1959	5.00	10.00	20.00
❑ 5207	I Never Had It So Good/Rinky Dinky Doo	1959	5.00	10.00	20.00
❑ 5218	Hard Luck Blues/Good Looking and Forty	1959	5.00	10.00	20.00
❑ 5247	School Bell Rock/Ain't No Rocking No More	1959	5.00	10.00	20.00
❑ 5333	Ain't Got No Blues Today/Adorable One	1960	5.00	10.00	20.00
❑ 5521	Mighty Mighty Man/Good Man Blues	1961	5.00	10.00	20.00

MERCURY

Number	Title (A Side/B Side)	Yr	VG	VG+	NM
❑ 73166	It's My Fault Darling/Love for Sale	1970	—	3.00	6.00
❑ 73219	Mail Man Blues/Hunky Funky Woman	1971	—	3.00	6.00

78s

DELUXE

Number	Title (A Side/B Side)	Yr	VG	VG+	NM
❑ 1093	Good Rockin' Tonight/Lolly Pop Mama	1947	20.00	40.00	80.00
❑ 1098	Special Lesson No. 1/Woman's a Wonderful Thing	1947	17.50	35.00	70.00
❑ 1107	Roy Brown Boogie/Please Don't Go	1948	17.50	35.00	70.00
❑ 1128	Miss Fanny Brown/Mighty, Mighty Man	1948	17.50	35.00	70.00
❑ 1154	'Long About Midnight/Whose Hat Is That	1948	17.50	35.00	70.00
❑ 1166	All My Love Belongs to You/Ebony Rhapsody	1948	17.50	35.00	70.00
—With Ethel Morris					
❑ 3093	Good Rockin' Tonight/Lolly Pop Mama	1948	10.00	20.00	40.00
—Reissue of 1093					
❑ 3128	Miss Fanny Brown/Mighty, Mighty Man	1948	10.00	20.00	40.00
—Reissue of 1128					
❑ 3154	'Long About Midnight/Whose Hat Is That	1948	10.00	20.00	40.00
—Reissue of 1154					
❑ 3166	All My Love Belongs to You/Ebony Rhapsody	1948	10.00	20.00	40.00
—With Ethel Morris; reissue of 1166					
❑ 3189	Miss Fanny Brown Returns/Roy Brown Boogie	1948	15.00	30.00	60.00
❑ 3198	'Fore Day in the Morning/Rainy Weather Blues	1948	12.50	25.00	50.00
❑ 3212	Rockin' at Midnight/Judgment Day Blues	1949	15.00	30.00	60.00
❑ 3226	Please Don't Go (Come Back Baby)/Riding High	1949	15.00	30.00	60.00
❑ 3300	Boogie at Midnight/The Blues Got Me Again	1949	15.00	30.00	60.00
❑ 3301	Butcher Pete (Part 1)/Butcher Pete (Part 2)	1949	15.00	30.00	60.00
❑ 3302	I Feel That Young Man's Rhythm/The End of My Journey	1950	15.00	30.00	60.00
❑ 3304	Hard Luck Blues/New Rebecca	1950	15.00	30.00	60.00
❑ 3306	Love Don't Love Nobody/Dreaming Blues	1950	15.00	30.00	60.00
❑ 3308	Cadillac Baby/Long About Sundown	1950	15.00	30.00	60.00
❑ 3311	Teenage Jamboree/Double Crossin' Woman	1950	15.00	30.00	60.00
❑ 3312	Sweet Peach/Good Man Blues	1951	15.00	30.00	60.00
❑ 3313	Beautician Blues/Wrong Woman Blues	1951	15.00	30.00	60.00
❑ 3318	Big Town/Train Time Blues	1951	15.00	30.00	60.00
❑ 3319	Bar Room Blues/Good Rockin' Man	1951	15.00	30.00	60.00
❑ 3323	I've Got the Last Laugh Now/Brown Angel	1951	15.00	30.00	60.00

IMPERIAL

Number	Title (A Side/B Side)	Yr	VG	VG+	NM
❑ 5422	Everybody/Saturday Night	1957	7.50	15.00	30.00
❑ 5427	Party Doll/I'm Sticking with You	1957	7.50	15.00	30.00
❑ 5439	Let the Four Winds Blow/Diddy-Y-Diddy-O	1957	7.50	15.00	30.00
❑ 5455	I'm Convicted of Love/I'm Ready to Play	1957	7.50	15.00	30.00
❑ 5469	Tick of the Clock/Slow Down Little Eva	1957	7.50	15.00	30.00
❑ 5489	Ain't Gonna Do It/Sail On Little Girl	1958	7.50	15.00	40.00
❑ 5510	Hip Shakin' Baby/Be My Love Tonight	1958	12.50	25.00	50.00

KING

Number	Title (A Side/B Side)	Yr	VG	VG+	NM
❑ 4602	Travelin' Man/Hurry, Hurry Baby	1953	7.50	15.00	30.00
❑ 4609	Grandpa Stole My Baby/Money Can't Buy Love	1953	7.50	15.00	30.00
❑ 4704	Trouble at Midnight/Bootlegging Baby	1954	7.50	15.00	30.00
❑ 4715	Up Jumped the Devil/This Is My Last Goodbye	1954	7.50	15.00	30.00
❑ 4722	No Love at All/Don't Let It Rain	1954	7.50	15.00	30.00
❑ 4731	Ain't It a Shame/Gal from Kokomo	1954	7.50	15.00	30.00
❑ 4743	Worried Life Blues/Black Diamond	1954	7.50	15.00	30.00
❑ 4761	Fannie Brown Got Married/Queen of Diamonds	1955	7.50	15.00	30.00
❑ 4816	Shake 'Em Up Baby/Letter to Baby	1955	7.50	15.00	30.00
❑ 4834	My Little Angel Child/She's Gone Too Long	1955	7.50	15.00	30.00

Albums

BLUESWAY

Number	Title (A Side/B Side)	Yr	VG	VG+	NM
❑ BLS-6019	The Blues Are Brown	1968	6.25	12.50	25.00
❑ BLS-6056	Hard Times	1973	6.25	12.50	25.00

EPIC

Number	Title (A Side/B Side)	Yr	VG	VG+	NM
❑ E 30473	Live at Monterey	1971	6.25	12.50	25.00

INTERMEDIA

Number	Title (A Side/B Side)	Yr	VG	VG+	NM
❑ QS-5027	Good Rockin' Tonight	198?	2.50	5.00	10.00

KING

Number	Title (A Side/B Side)	Yr	VG	VG+	NM
❑ 956 [M]	Roy Brown Sings 24 Hits	1966	12.50	25.00	50.00
❑ KS-956 [R]	Roy Brown Sings 24 Hits	1966	12.50	25.00	50.00
❑ KS-1130	Hard Luck Blues	1971	6.25	12.50	25.00

BROWN, ROY / WYNONIE HARRIS

Albums

KING

Number	Title (A Side/B Side)	Yr	VG	VG+	NM
❑ 607 [M]	Battle of the Blues	1958	150.00	300.00	600.00
❑ 627 [M]	Battle of the Blues, Volume 2	1959	200.00	400.00	800.00

BROWN, ROY / WYNONIE HARRIS / EDDIE VINSON

Albums

KING

Number	Title (A Side/B Side)	Yr	VG	VG+	NM
❑ 668 [M]	Battle of the Blues, Volume 4	1960	625.00	1250.	2500.

BROWN, RUTH

45s

ATLANTIC

Number	Title (A Side/B Side)	Yr	VG	VG+	NM
❑ 893	Happiness Is a Thing Called Joe/Love Me Baby	197?	2.50	5.00	10.00
—Reissue 45 on glossy yellow label with black "fan" logo (there was no 45 of this in the 1950s)					
❑ 919	Teardrops from My Eyes/Am I Making the Same Mistake	1950	100.00	200.00	400.00
—This and Atlantic 914 were the label's first two 45s.					
❑ 948	Shine On—Big Bright Moon Shine On/Without My Love	1951	15.00	30.00	60.00
—Ruth Brown records on Atlantic before 948 (except as listed) are unconfirmed on 45 rpm					
❑ 962	5-10-15 Hours/Be Anything But Be Mine	1952	12.50	25.00	50.00
❑ 973	Daddy Daddy/Have a Good Time	1952	12.50	25.00	50.00
❑ 978	Three Letters/Good for Nothing Joe	1952	12.50	25.00	50.00
❑ 986	(Mama) He Treats Your Daughter Mean/R.B. Blues	1953	15.00	30.00	60.00
❑ 993	Wild Wild Young Men/Mend Your Ways	1953	10.00	20.00	40.00
❑ 1005	The Tears Keep Tumblin' Down/I Would If I Could	1953	7.50	15.00	30.00
❑ 1018	Love Contest/If You Don't Want Me	1954	7.50	15.00	30.00
❑ 1023	Sentimental Journey/It's All in Your Mind	1954	7.50	15.00	30.00
❑ 1027	If I Had Any Sense/Hello Little Boy	1954	7.50	15.00	30.00
❑ 1036	Oh What a Dream/Please Don't Freeze	1954	7.50	15.00	30.00
❑ 1044	Somebody Touch Me/Mambo Baby	1954	7.50	15.00	30.00
❑ 1051	Ever Since My Baby's Been Gone/Bye Bye Young Men	1955	7.50	15.00	30.00
❑ 1059	I Can See Everybody's Baby/As Long As I'm Moving	1955	7.50	15.00	30.00
❑ 1072	What'd I Say/It's Love Baby (24 Hours of the Day)	1955	7.50	15.00	30.00
❑ 1077	Love Has Joined Us Together/I Gotta Have You	1955	7.50	15.00	30.00
—With Clyde McPhatter					
❑ 1082	Old Man River/I Want to Do More	1956	6.25	12.50	25.00
❑ 1091	Sweet Baby of Mine/I'm Getting Right	1956	6.25	12.50	25.00
❑ 1102	I Want to Be Loved/Mom, Oh Mom	1956	6.25	12.50	25.00
❑ 1113	Smooth Operator/I Still Love You	1956	6.25	12.50	25.00
❑ 1125	Lucky Lips/My Heart Is Breaking Over You	1957	6.25	12.50	25.00
❑ 1140	When I Get You Baby/One More Time	1957	6.25	12.50	25.00
❑ 1153	Show Me/I Hope We Meet	1957	6.25	12.50	25.00
❑ 1166	A New Love/Look Me Up	1957	6.25	12.50	25.00
❑ 1177	Book of Lies/Just Too Much	1958	6.25	12.50	25.00
❑ 1197	This Little Girl's Gone Rockin'/Why Me	1958	6.25	12.50	25.00
❑ 2008	Mama, He Treats Your Daughter Mean/I'll Step Aside	1958	5.00	10.00	20.00
❑ 2015	5-10-15 Hours/Itty Bitty Girl	1959	5.00	10.00	20.00
❑ 2026	Jack O'Diamonds/I Can't Hear a Word You Say	1959	5.00	10.00	20.00
❑ 2035	I Don't Know/Papa Daddy	1959	5.00	10.00	20.00
❑ 2052	Don't Deceive Me/I Burned Your Letter	1960	5.00	10.00	20.00
❑ 2064	The Door Is Still Open/What I Wouldn't Give	1960	5.00	10.00	20.00
❑ 2075	Taking Care of Business/Honey Boy	1960	5.00	10.00	20.00
❑ 2088	Sure 'Nuff/Here He Comes	1961	3.75	7.50	15.00
❑ 2104	It Tears Me All to Pieces/Anyone But You	1961	3.75	7.50	15.00

DECCA

Number	Title (A Side/B Side)	Yr	VG	VG+	NM
❑ 31598	What Happened to You/Yes Sir That's My Baby	1964	2.50	5.00	10.00
❑ 31640	Come a Little Closer/I Love Him and I Know It	1964	2.50	5.00	10.00

MAINSTREAM

Number	Title (A Side/B Side)	Yr	VG	VG+	NM
❑ 611	On the Good Ship Lollipop/Hurry On Down	1965	2.50	5.00	10.00

PHILIPS

Number	Title (A Side/B Side)	Yr	VG	VG+	NM
❑ 40028	Shake a Hand/Say It Again	1962	3.00	6.00	12.00
❑ 40056	Mama (He Treats Your Daughter Mean)/Hold My Hand	1962	3.00	6.00	12.00
❑ 40086	He Tells Me with His Eyes/If You Don't Tell Nobody	1963	3.00	6.00	12.00
❑ 40119	Satisfied/If You Don't Tell Nobody	1963	3.00	6.00	12.00

78s

ATLANTIC

Number	Title (A Side/B Side)	Yr	VG	VG+	NM
❑ 879	It's Raining/So Long	1949	12.50	25.00	50.00
❑ 879 [DJ]	It's Raining/So Long	1949	125.00	250.00	500.00
—Red wax promo; label is white with red print					
❑ 887	I'll Get Along Somehow Part 1/I'll Get Along Somehow Part 2	1949	12.50	25.00	50.00
❑ 887	I'll Get Along Somehow/Rocking Blues	1949	12.50	25.00	50.00
❑ 893	Happiness Is a Thing Called Joe/Love Me Baby	1950	12.50	25.00	50.00
❑ 899	(I'll Come Back) Someday/Why	1950	12.50	25.00	50.00
❑ 905	I Can Dream, Can't I?/Sentimental Journey	1950	12.50	25.00	50.00
❑ 907	Where Can I Go?/Dear Little Boy of Mine	1950	12.50	25.00	50.00
❑ 919	Teardrops from My Eyes/Am I Making the Same Mistake	1950	15.00	30.00	60.00
❑ 930	I'll Wait for You/Standin' on the Corner	1951	12.50	25.00	50.00
❑ 941	I Know/I Don't Want Anybody at All	1951	12.50	25.00	50.00
❑ 948	Shine On—Big Bright Moon Shine On/Without My Love	1951	10.00	20.00	40.00
❑ 962	5-10-15 Hours/Be Anything But Be Mine	1952	10.00	20.00	40.00
❑ 973	Daddy Daddy/Have a Good Time	1952	10.00	20.00	40.00
❑ 978	Three Letters/Good for Nothing Joe	1952	10.00	20.00	40.00
❑ 986	(Mama) He Treats Your Daughter Mean/R.B. Blues	1953	10.00	20.00	40.00
❑ 993	Wild Wild Young Men/Mend Your Ways	1953	7.50	15.00	30.00
❑ 1005	The Tears Keep Tumblin' Down/I Would If I Could	1953	6.25	12.50	25.00
❑ 1018	Love Contest/If You Don't Want Me	1954	6.25	12.50	25.00
❑ 1023	Sentimental Journey/It's All in Your Mind	1954	6.25	12.50	25.00
❑ 1027	If I Had Any Sense/Hello Little Boy	1954	6.25	12.50	25.00
❑ 1036	Oh What a Dream/Please Don't Freeze	1954	6.25	12.50	25.00
❑ 1044	Somebody Touch Me/Mambo Baby	1954	6.25	12.50	25.00
❑ 1051	Ever Since My Baby's Been Gone/Bye Bye Young Men	1955	6.25	12.50	25.00
❑ 1059	I Can See Everybody's Baby/As Long As I'm Moving	1955	6.25	12.50	25.00
❑ 1072	What'd I Say/It's Love Baby (24 Hours of the Day)	1955	6.25	12.50	25.00
❑ 1077	Love Has Joined Us Together/I Gotta Have You	1955	6.25	12.50	25.00
—With Clyde McPhatter					
❑ 1082	Old Man River/I Want to Do More	1956	7.50	15.00	30.00
❑ 1091	Sweet Baby of Mine/I'm Getting Right	1956	7.50	15.00	30.00
❑ 1102	I Want to Be Loved/Mom, Oh Mom	1956	7.50	15.00	30.00
❑ 1113	Smooth Operator/I Still Love You	1956	7.50	15.00	30.00
❑ 1125	Lucky Lips/My Heart Is Breaking Over You	1957	7.50	15.00	30.00
❑ 1140	When I Get You Baby/One More Time	1957	10.00	20.00	40.00
❑ 1153	Show Me/I Hope We Meet	1957	10.00	20.00	40.00
❑ 1166	A New Love/Look Me Up	1957	10.00	20.00	40.00
❑ 1177	Book of Lies/Just Too Much	1958	12.50	25.00	50.00
❑ 1197	This Little Girl's Gone Rockin'/Why Me	1958	12.50	25.00	50.00

Number	Title (A Side/B Side)	Yr	VG	VG+	NM

7-Inch Extended Plays
ATLANTIC

Number	Title (A Side/B Side)	Yr	VG	VG+	NM
❑ 505	Teardrops from My Eyes/5-10-15//Mama He Treats Your Daughter Mean/So Long	1953	25.00	50.00	100.00
❑ 505 [PS]	Ruth Brown Sings	1953	37.50	75.00	150.00
❑ 585	*Lucky Lips/Mambo Baby/Smooth Operator/Oh What a Dream	1957	15.00	30.00	60.00
❑ 585 [PS]	Ruth Brown	1957	30.00	60.00	120.00

Albums
ATLANTIC

Number	Title	Yr	VG	VG+	NM
❑ 1308 [M]	Last Date with Ruth Brown	1959	50.00	100.00	200.00
—Black label					
❑ 1308 [M]	Last Date with Ruth Brown	1961	12.50	25.00	50.00
—Red and purple label, "fan" logo in white					
❑ SD 1308 [S]	Last Date with Ruth Brown	1959	75.00	150.00	300.00
—Green label					
❑ SD 1308 [S]	Last Date with Ruth Brown	1961	15.00	30.00	60.00
—Blue and green label, "fan" logo in white					
❑ 8004 [M]	Ruth Brown	1957	50.00	100.00	200.00
—Black label					
❑ 8004 [M]	Ruth Brown	1960	37.50	75.00	150.00
—White "bullseye" label					
❑ 8004 [M]	Ruth Brown	1961	12.50	25.00	50.00
—Red and purple label, "fan" logo in white					
❑ 8026 [M]	Miss Rhythm	1959	50.00	100.00	200.00
—Black label					
❑ 8026 [M]	Miss Rhythm	1960	37.50	75.00	150.00
—White "bullseye" label					
❑ 8026 [M]	Miss Rhythm	1961	12.50	25.00	50.00
—Red and purple label, "fan" logo in white					
❑ 8080 [M]	The Best of Ruth Brown	1963	10.00	20.00	40.00

DOBRE

Number	Title	Yr	VG	VG+	NM
❑ 1041	You Don't Know Me	1978	3.00	6.00	12.00

FANTASY

Number	Title	Yr	VG	VG+	NM
❑ F-9661	Have a Good Time	1988	3.00	6.00	12.00
❑ F-9662	Blues on Broadway	1989	3.00	6.00	12.00

ICHIBAN

Number	Title	Yr	VG	VG+	NM
❑ SPEG-4023	Brown, Black and Beautiful	198?	3.00	6.00	12.00

MAINSTREAM

Number	Title	Yr	VG	VG+	NM
❑ 369	Softly	1972	3.00	6.00	12.00
❑ S-6034 [S]	Ruth Brown '65	1965	7.50	15.00	30.00
❑ 56034 [M]	Ruth Brown '65	1965	6.25	12.50	25.00

PHILIPS

Number	Title	Yr	VG	VG+	NM
❑ PHM 200028 [M]	Along Comes Ruth	1962	10.00	20.00	40.00
❑ PHM 200055 [M]	Gospel Time	1962	7.50	15.00	30.00
❑ PHS 600028 [S]	Along Comes Ruth	1962	12.50	25.00	50.00
❑ PHS 600055 [S]	Gospel Time	1962	10.00	20.00	40.00

SKYE

Number	Title	Yr	VG	VG+	NM
❑ SK-13	Black Is Brown and Brown Is Beautiful	1970	3.75	7.50	15.00

BROWN, SHIRLEY
12-Inch Singles
20TH CENTURY

Number	Title	Yr	VG	VG+	NM
❑ TCD-116	You've Got to Like What You Do (5:50) (same on both sides?)	1980	5.00	10.00	20.00
❑ TCD-124	Same Time, Same Place (5:02)/You've Got to Like What You Do	1980	3.75	7.50	15.00

45s
20TH CENTURY

Number	Title	Yr	VG	VG+	NM
❑ 2473	You've Got to Like What You Do/Same Time, Same Place	1980	—	2.50	5.00

ABET

Number	Title	Yr	VG	VG+	NM
❑ 9444	I Ain't Gonna Tell Nobody/Love Is Built on a Strong Foundation	1974	3.00	6.00	12.00

ARISTA

Number	Title	Yr	VG	VG+	NM
❑ 0231	Blessed Is the Woman (With a Man Like Mine)/Lowdown, Dirty, Good Lover	1977	—	2.50	5.00
❑ 0254	I Need Somebody to Love Me/Givin' Up	1977	—	2.50	5.00
❑ 0270	Long on Lovin'/Mighty Good Feeling	1977	—	2.50	5.00
❑ 0334	I Can't Move No Mountains/Honey Babe	1978	—	2.50	5.00

MALACO

Number	Title	Yr	VG	VG+	NM
❑ 2157	Ain't Nothin' Like the Lovin' We Got/If This Is Goodbye	1989	—	2.50	5.00
—With Johnnie Taylor					
❑ 2160	Take Me to Your Heart/King Size Love	1990	—	2.50	5.00
❑ 2171	Still in Love/Lovin' Too Soon	1991	—	2.50	5.00

SOUND TOWN

Number	Title	Yr	VG	VG+	NM
❑ 0005	Leave the Bridges Standing/Looking for the Real Thing	1984	—	2.00	4.00
❑ 0007	I Don't Play That/Looking for the Real Thing	1984	—	2.00	4.00
❑ 0009	This Used to Be Your House/I Don't Play That	1984	—	2.00	4.00
❑ 0010	At Christmas Time/(Instrumental)	1984	—	2.50	5.00
❑ 0012	Boyfriend/I Don't Play That	1985	—	2.00	4.00

STAX

Number	Title	Yr	VG	VG+	NM
❑ 3222	After a Night Like This/Crowding In On My Mind	1979	—	2.50	5.00
❑ 3224	Dirty Feelin'/Eyes Can't See	1979	—	2.50	5.00

TRUTH

Number	Title	Yr	VG	VG+	NM
❑ 3206	Woman to Woman/Yes Sir, Brother	1974	—	3.00	6.00
❑ 3223	It Ain't No Fun/I've Got to Go On Without You	1975	—	3.00	6.00
❑ 3231	It's Worth a Whisper/Between You and Me	1975	—	3.00	6.00

Albums
ARISTA

Number	Title	Yr	VG	VG+	NM
❑ AL 4129	Shirley Brown	1977	5.00	10.00	20.00

MALACO

Number	Title	Yr	VG	VG+	NM
❑ 7451	Fire & Ice	1989	3.00	6.00	12.00
❑ 7459	Timeless	1991	3.00	6.00	12.00
❑ 7467	Joy & Pain	1993	3.75	7.50	15.00

SOUND TOWN

Number	Title	Yr	VG	VG+	NM
❑ ST 8008	Intimate Storm	1984	3.75	7.50	15.00

STAX

Number	Title	Yr	VG	VG+	NM
❑ STX-4126	For the Real Feeling	1979	3.00	6.00	12.00

TRUTH

Number	Title	Yr	VG	VG+	NM
❑ 4206	Woman to Woman	1975	3.75	7.50	15.00

BROWN SUGAR
45s
CAPITOL

Number	Title	Yr	VG	VG+	NM
❑ 4198	The Game Is Over (What's the Matter with You)/I'm Going Through Changes Now	1976	—	2.50	5.00
❑ 4367	Lay Some Lovin' on Me/Don't Tie Me Down	1976	—	2.50	5.00

CHELSEA

Number	Title	Yr	VG	VG+	NM
❑ 78-0125	Loneliness (Will Bring Us Together Again)/Don't Hold Back	1973	2.50	5.00	10.00
❑ BCBO-0149	Didn't I/Moonlight and Taming You	1973	2.50	5.00	10.00
❑ BCBO-0239	Dance to the Music/Love Can Bring You Down	1974	2.50	5.00	10.00

Albums
CHELSEA

Number	Title	Yr	VG	VG+	NM
❑ BCL1-0368	Brown Sugar Featuring Clydie King	1973	5.00	10.00	20.00

BROWNE, TOM
12-Inch Singles
ARISTA

Number	Title	Yr	VG	VG+	NM
❑ 9089	Rockin' Radio (2 versions)/Angeline (Special Mix)	1983	2.50	5.00	10.00
❑ 9140	Cruisin' (6:22) (Dub 6:08) (Short Version 4:10)	1984	2.00	4.00	8.00

ARISTA/GRP

Number	Title	Yr	VG	VG+	NM
❑ GP 05	Fungi Mama/Bebopafunkadiscolypso (2 versions?)	1981	2.00	4.00	8.00

45s
ARISTA

Number	Title	Yr	VG	VG+	NM
❑ 9088	Rockin' Radio/Angeline	1983	—	—	3.00
❑ 9144	Cruisin'/Mr. Business	1984	—	—	3.00
❑ 9272	Secret Fantasy/Hit Man	1984	—	—	3.00

ARISTA/GRP

Number	Title	Yr	VG	VG+	NM
❑ 2501	Brother, Brother/Throw Down	1979	—	2.50	5.00
❑ 2502	The Closer I Get to You/I Never Was a Cowboy	1979	—	2.50	5.00
❑ 2506	Funkin' for Jamaica (N.Y.)/Dreams of Lovin' You	1980	—	2.00	4.00
❑ 2510	Thighs High (Grip Your Hips and Move)/Midnight Interlude	1980	—	2.00	4.00
❑ 2513	Let's Dance/I Know	1981	—	2.00	4.00
❑ 2518	Fungi Mama/Bebopafunkadiscolypso//Come for the Ride	1981	—	2.00	4.00
❑ 2519	Bye Gones/A Message (Pride and Pity)	1982	—	2.00	4.00

MALACO

Number	Title	Yr	VG	VG+	NM
❑ 100	Ain't No Need to Worry/Happy Song	1989	—	2.00	4.00

Albums
ARISTA

Number	Title	Yr	VG	VG+	NM
❑ AL 8107	Rockin' Radio	1983	2.00	4.00	8.00
❑ AL8-8249	Tommy Gun	1984	2.00	4.00	8.00

ARISTA/GRP

Number	Title	Yr	VG	VG+	NM
❑ GL 5003	Browne Sugar	1979	2.50	5.00	10.00
❑ GL 5008	Love Approach	1980	2.50	5.00	10.00
❑ GL 5502	Love Approach	1981	2.00	4.00	8.00
—Reissue of 5008					
❑ GL 5503	Magic	1981	2.50	5.00	10.00
❑ GL 5507	Yours Truly	1981	2.50	5.00	10.00

MALACO

Number	Title	Yr	VG	VG+	NM
❑ MJ-1500	No Longer I	1989	3.00	6.00	12.00

BROWNMARK
12-Inch Singles
MOTOWN

Number	Title	Yr	VG	VG+	NM
❑ 4601	Next Time (5 versions)/Stakeout	1988	2.00	4.00	8.00
❑ 4609	I Can't Get Enough of Your Love (3 versions)/Stakeout	1988	—	3.50	7.00
❑ 4655	Bang Bang (LP Version) (7" Version) (Instrumental)	1989	2.00	4.00	8.00
❑ 4705	Through a Friend of Mine (Radio Edit) (Album Version) (Instrumental)	1990	2.50	5.00	10.00
❑ L33-17913 [DJ]	Bang Bang (7" Version) (LP Version) (Instrumental)	1989	2.50	5.00	10.00
❑ L33-18059 [DJ]	Bang Bang (Raw Mix) (Raw Mix Radio Edit)/(El-Virus Mix)	1989	2.00	4.00	8.00
❑ L33-18082 [DJ]	Luv Touch (3 versions)	1989	2.00	4.00	8.00

45s
MOTOWN

Number	Title	Yr	VG	VG+	NM
❑ 1923	Next Time/Stakeout	1988	—	—	3.00
❑ 1923 [PS]	Next Time/Stakeout	1988	—	2.00	4.00
❑ 1980	Bang Bang/(instrumental)	1989	—	—	3.00

Albums
MOTOWN

Number	Title	Yr	VG	VG+	NM
❑ MOT-6251	Just Like That	1988	2.50	5.00	10.00
❑ MOT-6277	Good Feeling	1989	3.00	6.00	12.00

Number	Title (A Side/B Side)	Yr	VG	VG+	NM

BROWNSTONE
12-Inch Singles
EPIC

Number	Title (A Side/B Side)	Yr	VG	VG+	NM
❑ 49-77575	Pass the Lovin' (7 versions)	1994	2.00	4.00	8.00
❑ 49-77865	I Can't Tell You Why (4 versions)/If You Love Me (2 versions)	1995	2.00	4.00	8.00

MJJ MUSIC/WORK

❑ AS 3213 [DJ]	Kiss and Tell (Bogeystone Remix) (Cutfather and Joe Remix) (Cycle Remix Extended) (Paco Extended Mix)	1997	3.75	7.50	15.00
—Clear vinyl					
❑ AS 8659 [DJ]	Kiss and Tell (Paco Extended Mix) (Acapella) (Cycle Extended Remix) (Cycle Instrumental)	1997	3.00	6.00	12.00
❑ AS 9327 [DJ]	5 Miles to Empty (Radio Edit) (LP Version) (Instrumental) (Acapella)	1997	3.00	6.00	12.00
❑ 42-78495	5 Miles to Empty (Dark Child Remix) (Do Me Remix) (Acappella) (LP Version) (Dark Child Instrumental) (Do Me Instrumental)	1997	2.50	5.00	10.00
❑ 42-78633	5 Miles to Empty (4 versions)	1997	2.00	4.00	8.00

45s
EPIC

❑ 34-77848	I Can't Tell You Why/If You Love Me	1995	—	—	3.00
❑ 34-77864	Grapevyne/If You Love Me	1995	—	—	3.00

MJJ MUSIC/WORK

❑ 32-78413	Kiss and Tell (Radio Edit)/(Cycle Remix)	1997	—	—	3.00
❑ 32-78496	5 Miles to Empty/Revenge	1997	—	—	3.00

BRUNSON, TYRONE
12-Inch Singles
BELIEVE IN A DREAM

❑ 4Z9-03166	The Smurf/I Need Love	1982	2.50	5.00	10.00
❑ 4Z9-03512	Sticky Situation/(Instrumental)	1983	2.50	5.00	10.00
❑ 4Z9-03938	Hot Line (4:44) (Instrumental 5:36)	1983	2.50	5.00	10.00
❑ 4Z9-04951	Fresh (2 versions)	1984	2.50	5.00	10.00
❑ 4Z9-05007	In Love with You (same on both sides?)	1984	2.00	4.00	8.00

JAM

❑ 1062	Say Yeah (5:50) (4:00)	1988	2.00	4.00	8.00

MCA

❑ L33-17214 [DJ]	The Method (7:00) (same on both sides)	1986	2.00	4.00	8.00
❑ 23657	The Method (Dance Version) (Dub Version) (7" Version)	1986	2.50	5.00	10.00
❑ 23712	Love Triangle (4 versions)	1987	2.50	5.00	10.00

45s
BELIEVE IN A DREAM

❑ ZS4-03163	The Smurf/I Need Love	1982	—	2.00	4.00
❑ ZS4-03511	Sticky Situation/(Instrumental)	1983	—	2.00	4.00
—As "Tyrone 'Tystick' Brunson"					
❑ ZS4-03937	Hot Line/(Instrumental)	1983	—	2.00	4.00
❑ ZS4-04330	Fresh/(Club Mix)	1983	—	2.00	4.00

MCA

❑ 52892	The Method/(B-side unknown)	1986	—	2.00	4.00
❑ 53000	Love Triangle/Freebee	1987	—	2.00	4.00

Albums
BELIEVE IN A DREAM

❑ FZ 39197	Fresh	1984	2.50	5.00	10.00

MCA

❑ 5810	The Method	1986	2.50	5.00	10.00
❑ 5968	Love Triangle	1987	2.50	5.00	10.00

BRYANT, SHARON
12-Inch Singles
WING

❑ 871723-1	Let Go (5 versions)	1989	2.00	4.00	8.00
❑ 873599-1	Body Talk (6 versions)	1990	2.50	5.00	10.00
❑ 889879-1	Foolish Heart (2 versions)/Saturday Nite	1989	2.00	4.00	8.00

45s
WING

❑ 871722-7	Let Go/Saturday Nite	1989	—	—	3.00
❑ 871722-7 [PS]	Let Go/Saturday Nite	1989	—	—	3.00
❑ 889878-7	Foolish Heart/Saturday Nite	1989	—	—	3.00

Albums
WING

❑ 837313-1	Here I Am	1989	2.50	5.00	10.00

BRYSON, PEABO
12-Inch Singles
ELEKTRA

❑ ED 5007 [DJ]	Slow Dancin' (same on both sides)	1984	2.00	4.00	8.00
❑ ED 5022 [DJ]	Learning the Ways of Love (same on both sides)	1984	2.50	5.00	10.00
❑ ED 5063 [DJ]	Take No Prisoners (In the Game of Love) (same on both sides)	1985	2.00	4.00	8.00
❑ ED 5072 [DJ]	There's Nothin' Out There/When You Talk to Me/Love Always Finds a Way	1985	3.00	6.00	12.00
❑ ED 5082 [DJ]	There's Nothin' Out There (3 versions)/When You Talk to Me	1985	2.50	5.00	10.00
❑ ED 5171 [DJ]	Good Combination (edit) (LP Version)	1986	2.00	4.00	8.00
❑ ED 5201 [DJ]	Catch 22 (same on both sides)	1987	—	3.00	6.00
❑ ED 5293 [DJ]	Come On Over Tonight (same on both sides)	1988	2.00	4.00	8.00
❑ 66901	Take No Prisoners (In the Game of Love) (2 versions)/Love Means Forever	1985	2.50	5.00	10.00

45s
ANGEL

❑ S7-19772	This Christmas/I'll Be Home for Christmas	1997	—	2.00	4.00

BULLET

❑ 01	Underground Music/It's Just a Matter of Time	1976	2.00	4.00	8.00
❑ 02	Just Another Day//(B-side unknown)	1976	2.00	4.00	8.00
❑ 03	I Can Make It Better/Smile	1977	2.00	4.00	8.00

CAPITOL

❑ 4522	Reaching for the Sky/You Haven't Learned About Love	1977	—	2.00	4.00
❑ 4573	Feel the Fire/A Fool Already Knows	1978	—	2.00	4.00
❑ 4656	I'm So Into You/Smile	1978	—	2.00	4.00
❑ 4694	Crosswinds/Don't Touch Me	1979	—	2.00	4.00
❑ 4729	She's a Woman/Spread Your Wings	1979	—	2.00	4.00
❑ 4844	Minute by Minute/Life Is a Child	1980	—	2.00	4.00
❑ 4887	I Love the Way You Love/When Will I Learn	1980	—	2.00	4.00
❑ 4989	Turn the Hands of Time/Friction	1981	—	2.00	4.00
❑ 4989 [PS]	Turn the Hands of Time/Friction	1981	—	2.50	5.00
❑ A-5065	Let the Feeling Flow/Move Your Body	1981	—	2.00	4.00
❑ B-5098	There's No Guarantee/Love Is on the Rise	1982	—	2.00	4.00
❑ B-5098 [PS]	There's No Guarantee/Love Is on the Rise	1982	—	2.00	4.00
❑ B-5157	Give Me Your Love/You	1982	—	2.00	4.00
❑ B-5188	We Don't Have to Talk (About Love)/Turn It On	1982	—	2.00	4.00
❑ B-5210	Remember When (So Much in Love)/Don't Play with Fire	1983	—	2.00	4.00
❑ B-44347	Show and Tell/Meant to Be	1989	—	—	3.00
❑ B-44347 [PS]	Show and Tell/Meant to Be	1989	—	—	3.00
❑ B-44429	All My Love/Show and Tell	1989	—	—	3.00
❑ 7PRO-79852	Lover's Paradise (Edited Version)/(LP Version)	1989	2.00	4.00	8.00
—Vinyl is promo only					

COLUMBIA

❑ 38-73745	Can You Stop the Rain/I Wish You Love	1991	—	2.00	4.00
❑ 38-73990	Lost in the Night/You Don't Have to Beg	1992	—	2.00	4.00

ELEKTRA

❑ 69404	Come On Over Tonight/The Higher You Climb	1988	—	—	—
❑ 69492	Catch 22/Only at Night	1987	—	—	3.00
❑ 69517	Good Combination/Only at Night	1986	—	—	3.00
❑ 69612	There's Nothin' Out There/She's Over Me	1985	—	—	3.00
❑ 69632	Take No Prisoners (In the Game of Love)/Love Means Forever	1985	—	—	3.00
❑ 69632 [PS]	Take No Prisoners (In the Game of Love)/Love Means Forever	1985	—	—	3.00
❑ 69679	Learning the Ways of Love/Real Deal	1984	—	—	—
❑ 69685	Love Always Finds a Way//(B-side unknown)	1984	—	2.00	4.00
❑ 69699	Slow Dancin'/Love Means Forever	1984	—	—	—
❑ 69728	If Ever You're In My Arms Again/There's No Getting Over You	1984	—	1.00	3.00

MCA

❑ 52344	D.C. Cab/Knock Me On My Feet	1984	—	2.00	4.00
—B-side by Giorgio Moroder					

SHOUT

❑ 309	Disco Queen/(Instrumental)	1975	2.50	5.00	10.00

Albums
CAPITOL

❑ ST-11875	Crosswinds	1978	2.50	5.00	10.00
❑ SOO-12063	Paradise	1980	2.50	5.00	10.00
❑ ST-12138	Turn the Hands of Time	1981	2.50	5.00	10.00
❑ ST-12179	I Am Love	1981	2.50	5.00	10.00
❑ ST-12241	Don't Play with Fire	1982	2.00	4.00	8.00
❑ SJ-12348	The Peabo Bryson Collection	1984	2.50	5.00	10.00
❑ C1-90461	All My Love	1989	2.50	5.00	10.00

COLUMBIA

❑ C 46823	Can You Stop the Rain	1991	3.75	7.50	15.00

ELEKTRA

❑ 60362	Straight from the Heart	1983	2.00	4.00	8.00
❑ 60427	Take No Prisoners	1985	2.00	4.00	8.00
❑ 60484	Quiet Storm	1986	2.00	4.00	8.00
❑ 60753	Positive	1988	2.00	4.00	8.00

BRYSON, PEABO, AND REGINA BELLE
45s
COLUMBIA

❑ 38-74751	A Whole New World (Aladdin's Theme)/After the Kiss	1992	—	2.50	5.00

ELEKTRA

❑ ED 5275 [DJ]	Without You (Edit Version) (LP Version)	1987	—	3.50	7.00
❑ 69426	Without You/The Higher You Climb	1987	—	—	3.00
—B-side by Bryson solo					
❑ 69426 [PS]	Without You/The Higher You Climb	1987	—	—	3.00
—B-side by Bryson solo					

BRYSON, PEABO, AND ROBERTA FLACK
45s
ATLANTIC

❑ 3775	Make the World Stand Still/Only Heaven Can Wait (For Love)	1980	—	2.00	4.00
—As "Roberta Flack and Peabo Bryson"					
❑ 3803	Love Is a Waiting Game/More Than Everything	1981	—	2.00	4.00
—As "Roberta Flack and Peabo Bryson"					

CAPITOL

❑ B-5242	Tonight, I Celebrate My Love/Born to Love	1983	—	—	3.00
❑ B-5242 [PS]	Tonight, I Celebrate My Love/Born to Love	1983	—	2.50	5.00
❑ B-5283	Maybe/Can We Find Love Again	1983	—	—	3.00
❑ B-5283 [PS]	Maybe/Can We Find Love Again	1983	—	—	3.00
❑ B-5307	You're Looking Like Love to Me/Let Me Be the One You Need	1983	—	—	3.00

Number	Title (A Side/B Side)	Yr	VG	VG+	NM
❑ B-5307 [PS]	You're Looking Like Love to Me/Let Me Be the One You Need	1983	—	—	3.00
❑ B-5353	I Just Came Here to Dance/Can We Find Love Again	1984	—	—	3.00

Albums

ATLANTIC

Number	Title (A Side/B Side)	Yr	VG	VG+	NM
❑ SD 7000 [(2)]	Live and More	1980	3.00	6.00	12.00

—As "Roberta Flack and Peabo Bryson"

CAPITOL

Number	Title (A Side/B Side)	Yr	VG	VG+	NM
❑ ST-12284	Born to Love	1983	2.00	4.00	8.00

BURCH, VERNON

12-Inch Singles

CHOCOLATE CITY

Number	Title (A Side/B Side)	Yr	VG	VG+	NM
❑ CCD 20015	Brighter Days (5:52)/(B-side blank)	1979	3.75	7.50	15.00
❑ CCD 20026	Fun City (4:54)/Steppin' Out (3:59)	1980	3.75	7.50	15.00

SRI

Number	Title (A Side/B Side)	Yr	VG	VG+	NM
❑ 00018	Do It to Me/There's Always Sometime for Love	1981	3.00	6.00	12.00
❑ 1001	Playing Hard to Get (5:30) (same on both sides?)	1982	3.75	7.50	15.00

45s

CHOCOLATE CITY

Number	Title (A Side/B Side)	Yr	VG	VG+	NM
❑ 015	Love Is/When the Summer's Over	1978	—	2.50	5.00
❑ 017	Brighter Days/Love-a-Thon	1979	—	2.50	5.00
❑ 3201	Never Can Find a Way (Hot Love)/Mr. Do It Good	1979	—	2.50	5.00
❑ 3203	Get Up/Sammy Jo Anne-One Half Woman, One Half Man	1979	—	2.50	5.00
❑ 3205	Once Again in My Life/For You	1980	—	2.50	5.00
❑ 3211	Fun City/Stiffin, Stuffin, Ain't Sho Nuffin	1980	—	2.50	5.00

COLUMBIA

Number	Title (A Side/B Side)	Yr	VG	VG+	NM
❑ 3-10564	Leaving You Is Killing Me/Bye, Bye, Baby	1977	—	2.50	5.00
❑ 3-10609	Sexsonic/Mr. Sin	1977	—	2.50	5.00

SRI

Number	Title (A Side/B Side)	Yr	VG	VG+	NM
❑ 00019	Do It to Me/There's Always Sometime for Love	1981	—	2.50	5.00
❑ 00021	Playing Hard to Get/Simply Love	1982	—	2.50	5.00

UNITED ARTISTS

Number	Title (A Side/B Side)	Yr	VG	VG+	NM
❑ XW587	Changes (Messin' with My Mind)/(Long Version)	1975	—	2.50	5.00
❑ XW647	Ain't Gonna Tell Nobody/Loving You Gets Better with Time	1975	—	2.50	5.00
❑ XW705	Frame of Mind/Loving You Gets Better With Time	1975	—	2.50	5.00

Albums

CHOCOLATE CITY

Number	Title (A Side/B Side)	Yr	VG	VG+	NM
❑ CCLP-2005	Love-a-Thon	1978	3.75	7.50	15.00
❑ CCLP-2009	Get Up	1979	3.75	7.50	15.00
❑ CCLP-2014	Steppin' Out	1980	3.75	7.50	15.00

COLUMBIA

Number	Title (A Side/B Side)	Yr	VG	VG+	NM
❑ PC 34701	When I Get Back Home	1977	3.75	7.50	15.00

SRI

Number	Title (A Side/B Side)	Yr	VG	VG+	NM
❑ SW-70005	Playing Hard to Get	1982	3.00	6.00	12.00

UNITED ARTISTS

Number	Title (A Side/B Side)	Yr	VG	VG+	NM
❑ UA-LA342-G	I'll Be Your Sunshine	1975	3.75	7.50	15.00

BURDON, ERIC, AND WAR

Also see WAR.

45s

ABC

Number	Title (A Side/B Side)	Yr	VG	VG+	NM
❑ 12244	Magic Mountain/Home Dream	1977	—	2.50	5.00

MGM

Number	Title (A Side/B Side)	Yr	VG	VG+	NM
❑ 14118	Spill the Wine/Magic Mountain	1970	—	3.00	6.00
❑ 14118 [PS]	Spill the Wine/Magic Mountain	1970	3.00	6.00	12.00
❑ 14196	They Can't Take Away Our Music/Home Cookin'	1970	—	2.50	5.00

Albums

ABC

Number	Title (A Side/B Side)	Yr	VG	VG+	NM
❑ D-988	Love Is All Around	1976	3.00	6.00	12.00

—As "War Featuring Eric Burdon"

LAX

Number	Title (A Side/B Side)	Yr	VG	VG+	NM
❑ PW 37109	Spill the Wine	1981	2.50	5.00	10.00

—Reissue of MGM 4663 with new title

MGM

Number	Title (A Side/B Side)	Yr	VG	VG+	NM
❑ SE-4663	Eric Burdon Declares "War"	1970	3.75	7.50	15.00
❑ SE-4710-2 [(2)]	The Black Man's Burdon	1970	5.00	10.00	20.00

—Add 50% if the package includes an "Official War Bond," entlitling the bearer to $1 off any Eric Burdon and War concert before December 31, 1973

BURKE, SOLOMON

12-Inch Singles

INFINITY

Number	Title (A Side/B Side)	Yr	VG	VG+	NM
❑ L33-1023 [DJ]	Sidewalks, Fences and Walls (3:39) (5:15)	1979	3.00	6.00	12.00

OUTPOST

Number	Title (A Side/B Side)	Yr	VG	VG+	NM
❑ 30001	Power (5 versions)	198?	2.00	4.00	8.00

45s

ABC DUNHILL

Number	Title (A Side/B Side)	Yr	VG	VG+	NM
❑ 4388	Midnight and You/I Have a Dream	1974	—	2.50	5.00
❑ 15009	Midnight and You/I Have a Dream	1974	—	2.00	4.00

AMHERST

Number	Title (A Side/B Side)	Yr	VG	VG+	NM
❑ 736	Please Don't You Say Goodbye to Me/See That Girl	1978	—	2.00	4.00

APOLLO

Number	Title (A Side/B Side)	Yr	VG	VG+	NM
❑ 485	Christmas Presents/When I'm All Alone	1955	7.50	15.00	30.00
❑ 487	I'm in Love/Why Do Me That Way	1956	6.25	12.50	25.00
❑ 491	I'm All Alone/To Thee	1956	6.25	12.50	25.00
❑ 500	No Man Walks Alone/Walking in a Dream	1956	6.25	12.50	25.00
❑ 505	A Picture of You/You Can Run But You Can't Hide	1957	6.25	12.50	25.00
❑ 511	I Need You Tonight/This Is It	1957	6.25	12.50	25.00
❑ 512	For You and You Alone/You Are My One Love	1957	6.25	12.50	25.00
❑ 522	They Always Say/Don't Cry	1958	6.25	12.50	25.00
❑ 527	My Heart Is a Chapel/This Is It	1958	6.25	12.50	25.00

ATLANTIC

Number	Title (A Side/B Side)	Yr	VG	VG+	NM
❑ 2089	Keep the Magic Working/How Many Times	1961	5.00	10.00	20.00
❑ 2114	Just Out of Reach (Of My Two Open Arms)/Be-Bop Grandma	1961	5.00	10.00	20.00
❑ 2131	Cry to Me/I Almost Lost My Mind	1962	5.00	10.00	20.00
❑ 2147	Down in the Valley/I'm Hanging Up My Heart for You	1962	3.75	7.50	15.00
❑ 2157	I Really Don't Want to Know/Tonight My Heart She Is Crying (Love Is a Bird)	1962	3.75	7.50	15.00
❑ 2170	Go On Back to Him/I Said I Was Sorry	1962	3.75	7.50	15.00
❑ 2180	Words/Home in Your Heart	1963	3.75	7.50	15.00
❑ 2185	If You Need Me/You Can Make It If You Try	1963	3.75	7.50	15.00
❑ 2196	Can't Nobody Love You/Stupidity	1963	3.75	7.50	15.00
❑ 2205	You're Good for Me/Beautiful Brown Eyes	1963	3.75	7.50	15.00
❑ 2218	He'll Have to Go/Rockin' Soul	1964	3.75	7.50	15.00
❑ 2226	Goodbye Baby (Baby Goodbye)/Someone to Love Me	1964	3.75	7.50	15.00
❑ 2241	Everybody Needs Somebody to Love/Looking for My Baby	1964	3.75	7.50	15.00
❑ 2254	Yes I Do/Won't You Give Him (One More Chance)	1964	3.75	7.50	15.00
❑ 2259	The Price/More Rockin' Soul	1964	3.75	7.50	15.00
❑ 2276	Got to Get You Off My Mind/Peepin'	1965	3.75	7.50	15.00
❑ 2288	Tonight's the Night/Maggie's Farm	1965	3.75	7.50	15.00
❑ 2299	Someone Is Watching/Dance, Dance, Dance	1965	3.00	6.00	12.00
❑ 2308	Only Love (Can Save Me Now)/A Little Girl That Loves Me	1965	3.00	6.00	12.00
❑ 2314	Baby Come On Home/(No, No, No) Can't Stop Lovin' You Now	1965	3.00	6.00	12.00
❑ 2327	I Feel a Sin Coming On/Mountain of Pride	1966	2.50	5.00	10.00
❑ 2345	Suddenly/Lawdy Miss Clawdy	1966	2.50	5.00	10.00
❑ 2349	Keep Looking/Don't Want You No More	1966	2.50	5.00	10.00
❑ 2359	When She Touches Me/Woman How Do You Make Me Love You Like I Do	1966	2.50	5.00	10.00
❑ 2369	Presents for Christmas/A Tear Fell	1966	3.00	6.00	12.00
❑ 2378	Keep a Light in the Window Till I Come Home/ Time Is a Thief	1967	2.50	5.00	10.00
❑ 2416	Take Me (Just As I Am)/Stayed Away Too Long	1967	2.50	5.00	10.00
❑ 2459	It's Been a Change/Detroit City	1967	2.50	5.00	10.00
❑ 2483	Party People/Need Your Love So Bad	1968	2.50	5.00	10.00
❑ 2507	I Wish I Knew (How It Would Feel to Be Free)/It's Just a Matter of Time Baby	1968	2.50	5.00	10.00
❑ 2527	Save it/Meet Me in Church	1968	2.50	5.00	10.00
❑ 2566	Get Out of My Life Woman/What'd I Say	1968	2.50	5.00	10.00

BELL

Number	Title (A Side/B Side)	Yr	VG	VG+	NM
❑ 759	Up Tight Good Woman/I Can't Stop	1969	2.00	4.00	8.00
❑ 783	Proud Mary/What Am I Living For	1969	2.00	4.00	8.00
❑ 806	That Lucky Old Sun/How Big a Fool	1969	2.00	4.00	8.00
❑ 829	I'm Gonna Stay Right Here/Generation of Revelations	1969	2.00	4.00	8.00
❑ 891	God Knows I Love You/In the Ghetto	1970	—	3.00	6.00

CHESS

Number	Title (A Side/B Side)	Yr	VG	VG+	NM
❑ 2159	You and Your Baby Blues/I'm Leaving on That Late, Late Train	1975	—	2.00	4.00
❑ 2172	Let Me Wrap My Arms Around You/Everlasting Love	1975	—	2.00	4.00

INFINITY

Number	Title (A Side/B Side)	Yr	VG	VG+	NM
❑ 50046	Sidewalks, Fences and Walls/Boo-Hoo-Hoo (Cra-Cra-Craya)	1979	—	2.50	5.00

MALA

Number	Title (A Side/B Side)	Yr	VG	VG+	NM
❑ 420	This Little Ring/I'm Not Afraid	1960	5.00	10.00	20.00

MCI

Number	Title (A Side/B Side)	Yr	VG	VG+	NM
❑ 712842	You're All I Want for Christmas/No Place Like Home	198?	2.00	4.00	8.00

—B-side by Rayne

MGM

Number	Title (A Side/B Side)	Yr	VG	VG+	NM
❑ 14185	Lookin' Out My Back Door/All for the Love of Sunshine	1970	—	3.00	6.00
❑ 14221	The Electronic Magnetism (That's Heavy, Baby)/ Bridge of Life	1971	—	3.00	6.00
❑ 14279	J.C. I Know Who You Are/The Things Love Will Make You Do	1971	—	3.00	6.00
❑ 14302	The Night They Drove Old Dixie Down/PSR 1983	1971	—	3.00	6.00
❑ 14353	Love's Street and Fool's Road/I Got to Tell It	1972	—	3.00	6.00
❑ 14402	We're Almost Home/Fight Back	1972	—	3.00	6.00
❑ 14402 [PS]	We're Almost Home/Fight Back	1972	3.00	6.00	12.00
❑ 14425	Get Up and Do Something for Yourself/We're Almost Home	1972	—	3.00	6.00
❑ 14571	Shambala/Love Thy Neighbor	1973	—	3.00	6.00
❑ 14651	Georgia Up North/Here Comes the Train	1973	—	3.00	6.00

POINTBLANK

Number	Title (A Side/B Side)	Yr	VG	VG+	NM
❑ S7-19520	Ooooooyou/Today Is Your Birthday	1997	—	2.00	4.00

PRIDE

Number	Title (A Side/B Side)	Yr	VG	VG+	NM
❑ 1017	I Can't Stop Loving You (Part 1)/I Can't Stop Loving You (Part 2)	1972	—	3.00	6.00
❑ 1022	All I Want for Christmas/I Can't Stop Loving You (Part 1)	1972	—	3.00	6.00
❑ 1028	My Prayer/Ookie Bookie Man	1973	—	3.00	6.00
❑ 1038	Sentimental Journey/Vaya Con Dios	1973	—	3.00	6.00

—With Lady Lee

Albums

ABC DUNHILL

Number	Title (A Side/B Side)	Yr	VG	VG+	NM
❑ DSX-50161	I Have a Dream	1974	3.00	6.00	12.00

Number	Title (A Side/B Side)	Yr	VG	VG+	NM
AMHERST					
❑ AMH-1018	Please Don't You Say Goodbye to Me	1978	3.00	6.00	12.00
APOLLO					
❑ ALP-498 [M]	Solomon Burke	1962	125.00	250.00	500.00
ATLANTIC					
❑ 8067 [M]	Solomon Burke's Greatest Hits	1962	12.50	25.00	50.00
❑ SD 8067 [S]	Solomon Burke's Greatest Hits	1962	20.00	40.00	80.00
❑ 8085 [M]	If You Need Me	1963	12.50	25.00	50.00
❑ SD 8085 [S]	If You Need Me	1963	20.00	40.00	80.00
❑ 8096 [M]	Rock N' Soul	1964	12.50	25.00	50.00
❑ SD 8096 [S]	Rock N' Soul	1964	20.00	40.00	80.00
❑ 8109 [M]	The Best of Solomon Burke	1965	7.50	15.00	30.00
❑ SD 8109 [S]	The Best of Solomon Burke	1965	10.00	20.00	40.00
❑ SD 8158	King Solomon	1968	6.25	12.50	25.00
❑ 8185	I Wish I Knew	1968	6.25	12.50	25.00
BELL					
❑ 6033	Proud Mary	1969	5.00	10.00	20.00
CHESS					
❑ CH-19002	Back to My Roots	1976	3.00	6.00	12.00
❑ CH-60042	Music to Make Love By	1975	3.00	6.00	12.00
CLARION					
❑ 607 [M]	I Almost Lost My Mind	1966	5.00	10.00	20.00
❑ SD 607 [S]	I Almost Lost My Mind	1966	6.25	12.50	25.00
INFINITY					
❑ INF-9024	Sidewalks, Fences and Walls	1979	3.00	6.00	12.00
KENWOOD					
❑ LP-498 [M]	Solomon Burke	1964	50.00	100.00	200.00
—Reissue of Apollo 498					
MGM					
❑ SE-4767	Electronic Magnetism	1971	3.75	7.50	15.00
❑ SE-4830	King Heavy	1972	3.75	7.50	15.00
PRIDE					
❑ 0011	The History of Solomon Burke	1972	3.75	7.50	15.00
ROUNDER					
❑ 2042/3 [(2)]	Soul Alive!	1984	3.00	6.00	12.00
❑ 2053	A Change Is Gonna Come	1986	2.50	5.00	10.00
SAVOY					
❑ 14660	Solomon Burke	1981	2.50	5.00	10.00
❑ 14679	Into My Life	1982	2.50	5.00	10.00
❑ 14717	Take Me, Shake Me	1983	2.50	5.00	10.00

BUSTA RHYMES
12-Inch Singles
EASTWEST

Number	Title (A Side/B Side)	Yr	VG	VG+	NM
❑ ED 5882 [DJ]	Live to Regret (Soundtrack Version Dirty) (Soundtrack Version Instrumental) (Soundtrack Version Clean)	1996	5.00	10.00	20.00
ELEKTRA					
❑ ED 5820 [DJ]	Woo-Hah!! Got You All in Check (4 versions)/ Everything Remains Raw	1996	3.75	7.50	15.00
❑ ED 5852 [DJ]	Ill Vibe (4 versions)	1996	5.00	10.00	20.00
❑ ED 5854 [DJ]	It's a Party (6 versions)	1996	5.00	10.00	20.00
❑ ED 5873 [DJ]	Do My Thing (4 versions)/Abandon Ship (4 versions)	1996	5.00	10.00	20.00
❑ ED 6065 [DJ]	Turn It Up/Fire It Up (4 versions?)	1998	3.75	7.50	15.00
❑ ED 6076 [DJ]	Turn It Up/Fire It Up (3 versions)//Rhymes Galore (3 versions)	1998	3.75	7.50	15.00
❑ ED 6123 [DJ]	What's It Gonna Be?! (4 versions)	1998	3.75	7.50	15.00
❑ ED 6124 [DJ]	Gimme Some More (2 versions)/Tear Da Roof Off (2 versions)	1998	3.75	7.50	15.00
❑ ED 6126 [DJ]	Tear Da Roof Off (2 versions)/Gimme Some More (2 versions)	1998	3.75	7.50	15.00
❑ ED 6135 [DJ]	Party Is Goin' On Over Here (LP Version Clean) (LP Version Dirty) (Instrumental)//Everybody Rise (LP Version Clean)/Tear Da Roof Off (LP Version Clean) (LP Version Dirty)	1999	3.75	7.50	15.00
❑ ED 6141 [DJ]	Do the Bus a Bus (LP Version Clean) (LP Version) (Instrumental)//Do It Like Never Before (LP Version Clean) (LP Version) (Instrumental)	1999	3.75	7.50	15.00
❑ ED 6162 [DJ]	What's It Gonna Be?! (4 versions)	1999	3.75	7.50	15.00
❑ ED 6165 [DJ]	Do the Bus a Bus (Remix Clean) (Remix Instrumental) (LP Version Clean) (Remix Instrumental)//(Remix Dirty) (LP Version Dirty) (Remix Instrumental)/Do It Like Never Before (LP Version Dirty)	1999	3.75	7.50	15.00
❑ ED 6225 [DJ]	Get Out (7 versions)	2000	2.50	5.00	10.00
❑ ED 6235 [DJ]	Fire (Amended Version) (LP Version) (Instrumental)/(same on both sides?)	2000	2.50	5.00	10.00
❑ 63769	What's It Gonna Be?! (LP Version 5:28) (LP Version Clean 5:28) (Instrumental 5:28)/Tear Da Roof Off (LP Version Clean 3:36) (Instrumental 3:36)	1999	2.00	4.00	8.00
❑ 63844	Turn It Up/Fire It Up//Rhymes Galore	1998	2.00	4.00	8.00
❑ 66023	It's a Party (unknown versions)	1996	2.00	4.00	8.00
❑ 66050	Woo-Hah!! Got You All in Check (unknown versions)	1996	2.00	4.00	8.00
❑ 67087	Fire (Amended Version) (Album Version) (Instrumental)/Bladow (Amended Version) (Album Version) (Instrumental)	2000	2.00	4.00	8.00
J					
❑ 21061	Break Ya Neck (4 versions)	2001	2.00	4.00	8.00
❑ 21118	As I Come Back (unknown versions)	2001	2.00	4.00	8.00
❑ J1PV-21144	Pass the Courvoisier Part II (6 versions)	2002	2.00	4.00	8.00
❑ J1PV-21188	Pass the Courvoisier Part II (unknown versions)	2002	2.00	4.00	8.00

Number	Title (A Side/B Side)	Yr	VG	VG+	NM
Albums					
ELEKTRA					
❑ ED 6052 [(2) DJ]	When Disaster Strikes	1997	5.00	10.00	20.00
—Promo-only version					
❑ 61742 [(2)]	The Coming	1996	3.75	7.50	15.00
❑ 62064 [(2)]	When Disaster Strikes	1997	3.75	7.50	15.00
❑ 62211 [(2)]	E.L.E. (Extinction Level Event)	1998	3.75	7.50	15.00
❑ 62517 [(2)]	Anarchy	2000	3.75	7.50	15.00
J					
❑ 20009 [(2)]	Genesis	2001	5.00	10.00	20.00

BUTLER, JERRY
Also see GENE CHANDLER; BETTY EVERETT; THE IMPRESSIONS.
12-Inch Singles
MOTOWN

Number	Title (A Side/B Side)	Yr	VG	VG+	NM
❑ M00004D1	Chalk It Up/Vitamin U	1977	5.00	10.00	20.00
—B-side by Smokey Robinson					
PHILADELPHIA INT'L					
❑ 3664	(I'm Just Thinking About) Cooling Out/Are You Lonely Tonight	1978	2.50	5.00	10.00

45s
ABNER

Number	Title (A Side/B Side)	Yr	VG	VG+	NM
❑ 1024	Lost/One by One	1959	7.50	15.00	30.00
❑ 1028	Hold Me Darling/Rainbow Valley	1959	7.50	15.00	30.00
❑ 1030	I Was Wrong/Couldn't Go to Sleep	1959	7.50	15.00	30.00
❑ 1035	A Lonely Soldier/I Found a Love	1960	7.50	15.00	30.00
FOUNTAIN					
❑ 400	No Love Without Changes/All the Way	1982	—	3.00	6.00
ICHIBAN					
❑ 269	Angel Flying Too Close to the Ground/You're the Only One	1992	—	—	3.00
❑ 290	Need to Belong/Sure Feels Good	1993	—	—	3.00
MCA					
❑ 52177	Let's Talk It Over/Especially You	1983	—	2.00	4.00
—With Stix Hooper; B-side by Stix Hooper solo					
MERCURY					
❑ 72592	Love (Oh How Sweet It Is)/Loneliness	1966	2.50	5.00	10.00
❑ 72625	You Make Me Feel Like Someone/For What You Made of Me	1966	2.50	5.00	10.00
❑ 72648	I Dig You Baby/Some Kinda Magic	1966	2.50	5.00	10.00
❑ 72676	Why Do I Lose You/You Walked Into My Life	1967	2.50	5.00	10.00
❑ 72698	You Don't Know What You've Got Until You Lose It/The Way I Love You	1967	2.50	5.00	10.00
❑ 72721	Mr. Dream Merchant/'Cause I Love You So	1967	2.50	5.00	10.00
❑ 72764	Lost/You Don't Know What You've Got Until You Lose It	1968	2.00	4.00	8.00
❑ 72798	Never Give You Up/Beside You	1968	2.00	4.00	8.00
❑ 72850	Hey, Western Union Man/Just Can't Forget About You	1968	2.00	4.00	8.00
❑ 72876	Are You Happy/I Still Love You	1968	2.00	4.00	8.00
❑ 72898	Only the Strong Survive/Just Because I Really Love You	1969	2.00	4.00	8.00
❑ 72929	Moody Woman/Go Away — Find Yourself	1969	2.00	4.00	8.00
❑ 72960	What's the Use of Breaking Up/Brand New Me	1969	2.00	4.00	8.00
❑ 72991	Don't Let Love Hang You Up/Walking Around in Teardrops	1969	2.00	4.00	8.00
❑ 73015	Got to See If I Can't Get Mommy (To Come Back Home)/I Forgot to Remember	1970	2.00	4.00	8.00
❑ 73045	I Could Write a Book/Since I Lost You, Baby	1970	2.00	4.00	8.00
❑ 73101	Where Are You Going/You Can Fly	1970	2.00	4.00	8.00
❑ 73131	How Does It Feel/Special Memory	1970	2.00	4.00	8.00
❑ 73169	If It's Real What I Feel/Why Are You Leaving Me	1971	—	3.00	6.00
❑ 73210	How Did We Lose It baby/Do You Finally Need a Friend	1971	—	3.00	6.00
❑ 73241	Walk Easy My Son/Let Me Be	1971	—	3.00	6.00
❑ 73290	I Only Have Eyes for You/A Prayer	1972	—	3.00	6.00
❑ 73335	One Night Affair/Life's Unfortunate Song	1972	—	3.00	6.00
❑ 73443	Power of Love/What Do You Do on a Sunday Afternoon	1973	—	3.00	6.00
❑ 73459	That's How Heartaches Are Made/Too Many Danger Signs	1974	—	3.00	6.00
❑ 73495	Take the Time to Tell Her/High Stepper	1974	—	3.00	6.00
❑ 73629	You and Me Against the World/Playing on You	1974	—	3.00	6.00
❑ 872914-7	Only the Strong Survive/Lost	1989	—	—	3.00
—Reissue					
❑ 872916-7	Never Give You Up/Hey, Western Union Man	1989	—	—	3.00
—Reissue					
MISTLETOE					
❑ 803	Silent Night/O Holy Night	1974	—	2.50	5.00
MOTOWN					
❑ 1403	The Devil in Mrs. Jones/Don't Wanna Be Reminded	1976	—	2.50	5.00
❑ 1403 [PS]	The Devil in Mrs. Jones/Don't Wanna Be Reminded	1976	2.50	5.00	10.00
❑ 1414	I Wanna Do It to You/I Don't Wanna Be Reminded	1977	—	2.50	5.00
❑ 1421	Chalk It Up/I Don't Want Nobody to Know	1977	—	2.50	5.00
❑ 1422	It's a Lifetime Thing/Kiss Me Now	1977	—	2.50	5.00
—With Thelma Houston					
PHILADELPHIA INT'L					
❑ 3113	Don't Be Ashamed/Best Love I Ever Had	1980	—	2.00	4.00
❑ 3117	Tell Me Girl (Why It Has to End)/We've Got This Feeling Again	1980	—	2.00	4.00
❑ 3656	(I'm Just Thinking About) Cooling Out/Are You Lonely Tonight	1978	—	2.00	4.00

Number	Title (A Side/B Side)	Yr	VG	VG+	NM
❏ 3673	I'm Glad to Be Back/Nothing Says I Love You Like I Love You	1979	—	2.00	4.00
❏ 3683	Let's Make Love/Dream World	1979	—	2.00	4.00

VEE JAY

Number	Title (A Side/B Side)	Yr	VG	VG+	NM
❏ 354	He Will Break Your Heart/Thanks to You	1960	5.00	10.00	20.00
❏ 371	Silent Night/O Holy Night	1960	5.00	10.00	20.00
❏ 375	Find Another Girl/When Trouble Calls	1961	3.75	7.50	15.00
❏ 390	I See a Fool/I'm a Telling You	1961	3.75	7.50	15.00
❏ 396	For Your Precious Love/Sweet Was the Wine	1961	3.75	7.50	15.00
❏ 405	Moon River/Aware of Love	1961	3.75	7.50	15.00
❏ 405	Moon River/Aware of Love	1961	3.75	7.50	15.00
❏ 405	Moon River/Aware of Love	1961	3.75	7.50	15.00
❏ 405	Moon River/Aware of Love	1961	3.75	7.50	15.00
❏ 426	Isle of Sirens/Chi Town	1962	3.75	7.50	15.00
❏ 451	Make It Easy on Yourself/It's Too Late	1962	3.75	7.50	15.00
❏ 463	You Can Run/I'm the One	1962	3.75	7.50	15.00
❏ 475	Theme from Taras Bulba (Wishing Star)/You Go Right Through Me	1963	3.00	6.00	12.00
❏ 475 [PS]	Theme from Taras Bulba (Wishing Star)/You Go Right Through Me	1963	10.00	20.00	40.00
❏ 486	You Won't Be Sorry/Whatever You Want	1963	3.00	6.00	12.00
❏ 526	Strawberries/I Almost Lost My Head	1963	3.00	6.00	12.00
❏ 534	Where's the Girl?/How Beautifully You Lie	1963	3.00	6.00	12.00
❏ 556	Just a Little Bit/A Woman with Soul	1963	3.00	6.00	12.00
❏ 567	Need to Belong/Give Me Your Love	1963	3.00	6.00	12.00
❏ 588	Giving Up on Love/I've Been Trying	1964	3.00	6.00	12.00
❏ 598	I Stand Accused/I Don't Want to Hear Anymore	1964	3.00	6.00	12.00
❏ 598 [PS]	I Stand Accused/I Don't Want to Hear Anymore	1964	7.50	15.00	30.00
❏ 651	Good Times/I've Grown Accustomed to Her Face	1965	3.00	6.00	12.00
❏ 696	I Can't Stand to See You Cry/Nobody Needs Your Love	1965	3.00	6.00	12.00
❏ 707	Believe in Me/Just for You	1965	3.00	6.00	12.00
❏ 711	Moon River/Make It Easy on Yourself	1966	3.00	6.00	12.00
❏ 715	For Your Precious Love/Give It Up	1966	3.00	6.00	12.00

Albums

ABNER

Number	Title	Yr	VG	VG+	NM
❏ R-2001 [M]	Jerry Butler, Esquire	1959	100.00	200.00	400.00

BUDDAH

❏ BDS-4001	The Very Best of Jerry Butler	1969	3.75	7.50	15.00

FOUNTAIN

❏ FR 2-82-1	Ice 'n Hot	1982	2.50	5.00	10.00

MERCURY

❏ SRM-1-689	The Power of Love	1973	3.75	7.50	15.00
❏ SRM-1-1006	Sweet Sixteen	1974	3.75	7.50	15.00
❏ SRM-2-7502 [(2)]	The Spice of Life	1972	5.00	10.00	20.00
❏ MG-21005 [M]	The Soul Artistry of Jerry Butler	1967	5.00	10.00	20.00
❏ MG-21146 [M]	Mr. Dream Merchant	1967	5.00	10.00	20.00
❏ SR-61005 [S]	The Soul Artistry of Jerry Butler	1967	3.75	7.50	15.00
❏ SR-61146 [S]	Mr. Dream Merchant	1967	3.75	7.50	15.00
❏ SR-61151	Jerry Butler's Golden Hits Live	1968	3.75	7.50	15.00
❏ SR-61171	The Soul Goes On	1968	3.75	7.50	15.00
❏ SR-61198	The Ice Man Cometh	1968	3.75	7.50	15.00
❏ SR-61234	Ice On Ice	1969	3.75	7.50	15.00
❏ SR-61269	You & Me	1970	3.75	7.50	15.00
❏ SR-61281	The Best of Jerry Butler	1970	3.75	7.50	15.00
❏ SR-61320	Jerry Butler Sings Assorted Sounds	1971	3.75	7.50	15.00
❏ SR-61347	The Sagittarius Movement	1971	3.75	7.50	15.00
❏ 810369-1	The Best of Jerry Butler	1983	2.50	5.00	10.00
❏ 822212-1	Only the Strong Survive: The Great Philadelphia Hits	1984	2.50	5.00	10.00

MOTOWN

❏ M6-850	Love's on the Menu	1976	3.00	6.00	12.00
❏ M6-878	Suite for the Single Girl	1977	2.50	5.00	10.00
❏ M6-892	It All Comes Out in My Songs	1977	2.50	5.00	10.00

PHILADELPHIA INT'L.

❏ JZ 35510	Nothing Says I Love You Like I Love You	1978	2.50	5.00	10.00
❏ JZ 36413	The Best Love I Ever Had	1979	2.50	5.00	10.00

RHINO

❏ RNLP-216	The Best of Jerry Butler (1958-1969)	1984	2.50	5.00	10.00

TRADITION

❏ TLP-2068	Starring Jerry Butler	1969	3.75	7.50	15.00

TRIP

❏ 8011 [(2)]	All Time Hits	1972	3.75	7.50	15.00

UNITED ARTISTS

❏ UA-LA498-E	The Very Best of Jerry Butler	1975	2.50	5.00	10.00

VEE JAY

❏ VJLP2-1003 [(2)]	Jerry Butler Gold	198?	3.75	7.50	15.00
❏ LP-1027 [M]	Jerry Butler, Esquire	1960	37.50	75.00	150.00

—Reissue of Abner 2001

❏ LP-1029 [M]	He Will Break Your Heart	1960	20.00	40.00	80.00
❏ LP-1034 [M]	Love Me	1961	12.50	25.00	50.00

—Reissue of 1027

❏ LP-1038 [M]	Aware of Love	1961	10.00	20.00	40.00
❏ SR-1038 [S]	Aware of Love	1961	12.50	25.00	50.00
❏ LP-1046 [M]	Moon River	1962	10.00	20.00	40.00
❏ SR-1046 [S]	Moon River	1962	12.50	25.00	50.00
❏ VJLP-1046	Moon River	1985	2.50	5.00	10.00

—Reissue of original 1046; has softer vinyl

❏ LP-1048 [M]	The Best of Jerry Butler	1962	6.25	12.50	25.00
❏ SR-1048 [P]	The Best of Jerry Butler	1962	7.50	15.00	30.00
❏ VJLP-1048	The Best of Jerry Butler	1985	2.50	5.00	10.00

—Reissue of original 1048; has softer vinyl

❏ LP-1057 [M]	Folk Songs	1963	6.25	12.50	25.00
❏ SR-1057 [S]	Folk Songs	1963	7.50	15.00	30.00
❏ LP-1075 [M]	For Your Precious Love	1963	6.25	12.50	25.00
❏ SR-1075 [S]	For Your Precious Love	1963	7.50	15.00	30.00
❏ LP-1076 [M]	Giving Up On Love/Need to Belong	1963	6.25	12.50	25.00
❏ VJS-1076 [S]	Giving Up On Love/Need to Belong	1963	7.50	15.00	30.00
❏ LP-1119 [M]	More of the Best of Jerry Butler	1965	6.25	12.50	25.00
❏ VJS-1119 [S]	More of the Best of Jerry Butler	1965	7.50	15.00	30.00
❏ D1-74807	He Will Break Your Heart	1989	3.00	6.00	12.00

BUTLER, JERRY, AND BRENDA LEE EAGER
Also see each artist's individual listings.

45s

MERCURY

Number	Title (A Side/B Side)	Yr	VG	VG+	NM
❏ 73255	Ain't Understanding Mellow/Windy City Soul	1971	—	3.00	6.00
❏ 73301	(They Long to Be) Close to You/You Can't Always Tell	1972	—	3.00	6.00
❏ 73395	Can't Understand It/How Long Will It Last	1973	—	3.00	6.00
❏ 73422	We Were Lovers, We Were Friends/The Love We Had Stays On My Mind	1973	—	3.00	6.00

Albums

MERCURY

❏ SRM-1-660	The Love We Have	1973	3.75	7.50	15.00

BUTLER, JERRY, AND THE IMPRESSIONS
See THE IMPRESSIONS.

BUTLER, JONATHAN
12-Inch Singles

JIVE

Number	Title (A Side/B Side)	Yr	VG	VG+	NM
❏ 1043-1-JD	Lies (Extended) (Edit) (LP Version)	1987	—	3.50	7.00
❏ 1064-1-JD	Holding On (Extended Version 6:21) (7" Version 4:23) (Instrumental 5:43)/Seventh Avenue Song	1987	—	3.50	7.00
❏ 1144-1-JD	There's One Born Every Minute (I'm a Sucker for You) (2 versions)//Going Home/Barenese	1988	—	3.50	7.00
❏ 1329-1-JD	Welcome Home/Deliverance	1990	2.00	4.00	8.00

JIVE/ARISTA

❏ 9458 [DJ]	Baby Please Don't Take It (I Need Your Love) (same on both sides?)	1986	2.50	5.00	10.00

45s

JIVE

❏ 1038-7-J	Lies/Haunted by Your Love	1987	—	—	3.00
❏ 1038-7-J [PS]	Lies/Haunted by Your Love	1987	—	—	3.00
❏ 1063-7-J	Holding On/Seventh Avenue Song	1987	—	—	3.00
❏ 1063-7-J [PS]	Holding On/Seventh Avenue Song	1987	—	—	3.00
❏ 1083-7-J	Take Good Care of Me/Barenese	1987	—	—	3.00
❏ 1083-7-J [PS]	Take Good Care of Me/Barenese	1987	—	—	3.00
❏ 1143-7-J	There's One Born Every Minute (I'm a Sucker for You)/Going Home	1988	—	—	3.00
❏ 1143-7-J [PS]	There's One Born Every Minute (I'm a Sucker for You)/Going Home	1988	—	—	3.00
❏ 1174-7-J	More Than Friends/Melodie	1988	—	—	3.00
❏ 1174-7-J [PS]	More Than Friends/Melodie	1988	—	—	3.00
❏ 1216-7-J	Sarah, Sarah/Sekona	1989	—	—	3.00
❏ 1216-7-J [PS]	Sarah, Sarah/Sekona	1989	—	—	3.00

JIVE/ARISTA

❏ 9500	Baby Please Don't Take It (I Need Your Love)/The Calm Before the Storm	1986	—	2.50	5.00

MERCURY

❏ 858968-7	I'm on My Knees/Grace	1994	—	2.00	4.00

Albums

JIVE

❏ 1032-1-J [(2)]	Jonathan Butler	1987	3.00	6.00	12.00
❏ 1136-1-J	More Than Friends	1988	2.50	5.00	10.00
❏ 1361-1-J	Heal Our Land	1990	3.00	6.00	12.00

JIVE/ARISTA

❏ JL8-8408	Introducing Jonathan Butler	1986	2.50	5.00	10.00

BWP
12-Inch Singles

NO FACE

❏ 44-73574	Two Minute Brother (XXX Uncensored Version)/We Want Money (The Pay The Bitch Mix)/Two Minute Brother (Radio Friendly Edit)	1990	2.50	5.00	10.00

Albums

NO FACE

❏ C 47068	The Bytches	1991	3.75	7.50	15.00

BYRD, BOBBY
Two different artists have this name. For records on the Cash, Jamie and Sage & Sand labels, see BOBBY DAY.

45s

ABC

Number	Title (A Side/B Side)	Yr	VG	VG+	NM
❏ 11134	Here Is My Everything/Loving You	1968	2.50	5.00	10.00

—With Vicki Anderson

BANG

❏ 562	Whatcha Gonna Do About It/If She's There	1968	—	3.00	6.00

BROWNSTONE

❏ 4203	Hot Pants - I'm Coming, Coming, I'm Coming	1971	—	3.00	6.00
❏ 4205	Keep On Doin' What You're Doin'/Let Me Know	1971	—	3.00	6.00
❏ 4206	If You Got a Love You Better (Hold On to It)/You Have Got to Change Your Mind	1972	—	3.00	6.00
❏ 4208	Never Get Enough/My Concerto	1972	—	3.00	6.00
❏ 4209	Sayin' It and Doin' It Are Two Different Things/Never Get Enough	1972	—	3.00	6.00

B

Singer-pianist Tiny Bradshaw had five Top 10 R&B hits in the early 1950s. His compiled albums for King can be quite hard to find, including this one.

Jackie Brenston is best known for "Rocket 88," which is tough to find on 78 and almost impossible on 45. He also issued some follow-ups, none of which had the same impact. One of these is "Leo the Louse."

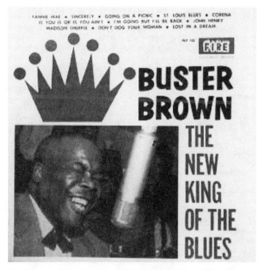

Best known for the #1 R&B hit "Fannie Mae," Buster Brown also had an album on the Fire label. Three different variations are known to exist; all are hard to find.

One of the world's most valuable albums of any genre is this Charles Brown compilation, *Mood Music*, which is extremely difficult to find in its original 10-inch configuration.

When Atlantic Records made its first 45s in 1951, one of the two titles it chose to issue first was Ruth Brown's "Teardrops From My Eyes." And for good reason: It spent 11 weeks at #1 on the R&B charts. Today, original 45s are a lot more rare than the 78s of the same record.

Here is a copy of Jerry Butler's first album, which appeared on the Vee Jay subsidiary label Abner in 1959.

Number	Title (A Side/B Side)	Yr	VG	VG+	NM
❑ 4210	Signed, Sealed and Delivered/I Need Help (I Can't Do It Alone)	1973	—	3.00	6.00
FEDERAL					
❑ 12486	They Are Sayin'/I Found Out	1963	3.75	7.50	15.00
INTERNATIONAL BROTHERS					
❑ 901	Back from the Dead/The Way to Get Down	1975	—	3.00	6.00
KING					
❑ 6069	I Found Out/I'll Keep Pressing On	1967	—	3.00	6.00
❑ 6126	Funky Soul #1 (Part 1)/Funky Soul #1 (Part 2)	1967	—	3.00	6.00
❑ 6151	You've Got to Change Your Mind/I'll Lose My Mind	1968	2.50	5.00	10.00
—A-side with James Brown					
❑ 6165	You Gave My Heart a Brand New Song/Concerto	1968	—	3.00	6.00
❑ 6289	You Gave My Heart a New Song/Hang-Ups We Don't Need	1970	—	3.00	6.00
❑ 6308	I'm Not to Blame/It's I Who Loves You (It's Not Him Anymore)	1970	—	3.00	6.00
❑ 6323	I Need Help (Part 1)/I Need Help (Part 2)	1970	—	3.00	6.00
❑ 6342	You've Got to Change Your Mind/You Got to Have a Job (If You Don't Work You Can't Eat)	1970	—	3.00	6.00
❑ 6378	I Know You Got Soul/It's I Who Love You (It's Not Him Anymore)	1971	—	3.00	6.00
KWANZA/WB					
❑ 7703	On the Move/Try It Again	1973	—	3.00	6.00
SMASH					
❑ 1903	Write Me a Letter/I Love You So	1964	2.00	4.00	8.00
❑ 1928	I'm Lonely/I've Got a Girl	1964	2.00	4.00	8.00
❑ 1964	No One Like My Baby/We Are In Love	1965	2.00	4.00	8.00
❑ 1984	Time Will Make a Change/The Way I Feel	1965	2.00	4.00	8.00
❑ 2003	You're Gonna Need My Lovin'/Let Me Know	1965	2.00	4.00	8.00
❑ 2018	Lost in the Mood of Changes/Oh, What a Nite	1966	2.00	4.00	8.00
❑ 2052	Ain't No Use/Let Me Know	1966	2.00	4.00	8.00
Albums					
KING					
❑ KS-1118	I Need Help	1970	50.00	100.00	200.00

BYRD, BOBBY, AND THE IMPALAS
See BOBBY DAY.

BYRD, DONALD
Also see THE BLACKBYRDS.

12-Inch Singles

ELEKTRA

Number	Title (A Side/B Side)	Yr	VG	VG+	NM
❑ AS 11400 [DJ]	Thank You for Funking Up My Life (4:43)/Loving You (7:20)	1978	3.75	7.50	15.00
❑ AS 11533 [DJ]	I Feel Like Loving You Today/I Love Your Love	1981	3.00	6.00	12.00
❑ 67985	Sexy Dancer/Moonlight	1982	3.00	6.00	12.00
45s					
BLUE NOTE					
❑ XW212	Black Byrd/Slop Jar Blues	1973	—	2.50	5.00
❑ XW309	Flight Time/Mr. Thomas	1973	—	2.50	5.00
❑ XW445	Witch Hunt/Woman of the World	1974	—	2.50	5.00
❑ XW510	Cristo Redentor/Black Byrd	1974	—	2.50	5.00
❑ XW650	Think Twice/We're Together	1975	—	2.50	5.00
❑ XW726	Change (Makes You Want to Hustle) Part 1/Part 2	1975	—	2.50	5.00
❑ XW783	(Fallin' Like) Dominoes/Just My Imagination (Runnin' Away with Me)	1976	—	2.50	5.00
❑ XW965	Dancing in the Street/Onward 'Til Morning	1977	—	2.50	5.00
❑ 1763	Here Am I (Part 1)/Here Am I (Part 2)	196?	2.00	4.00	8.00
❑ 1764	Amen/Fuego	196?	2.00	4.00	8.00
❑ 1798	Gate City/Little Boy Blue	196?	2.00	4.00	8.00
❑ 1799	Bo-Blue/Ghana	196?	2.00	4.00	8.00
❑ 1853	Hush/6 M's	196?	2.00	4.00	8.00
❑ 1854	Jorgie's (Part 1)/Jorgie's (Part 2)	196?	2.00	4.00	8.00
❑ 1916	Brother Isaac/I've Longed and Searched for My Mother	196?	2.00	4.00	8.00
❑ 1973	The Emperor (Part 1)/The Emperor (Part 2)	196?	2.00	4.00	8.00
ELEKTRA					
❑ 45545	Thank You for Funking Up My Life/Loving You	1978	—	2.00	4.00
❑ 46019	Loving You/Cristo Redentor	1979	—	2.00	4.00
❑ 46601	Veronica/Pretty Baby	1980	—	2.00	4.00
❑ 47168	Love Has Come Around/Love for Sale	1981	—	2.00	4.00
❑ 47241	I Love Your Love/Falling	1981	—	2.00	4.00
❑ 47419	I Feel Like Lovin' You Today/Butterfly	1982	—	2.00	4.00
❑ 69972	Sexy Dancer/Midnight	1982	—	2.00	4.00
VERVE					
❑ 10344	Blind Man, Blind Man/You've Been Talkin' 'Bout My Baby	1965	2.00	4.00	8.00
Albums					
AMERICAN RECORDING SOCIETY					
❑ G-437 [M]	Modern Jazz	1957	10.00	20.00	40.00
BLUE NOTE					
❑ BN-LA047-F	Black Byrd	1973	3.75	7.50	15.00
❑ LO-047	Black Byrd	1981	2.00	4.00	8.00
—Reissue of LA047					
❑ BN-LA140-G	Street Lady	1974	3.75	7.50	15.00
❑ BN-LA368-G	Sleeping Into Tomorrow	1975	3.75	7.50	15.00
❑ BN-LA549-G	Places and Spaces	1975	3.75	7.50	15.00
❑ LW-549	Places and Spaces	1981	2.00	4.00	8.00
—Reissue of LA549					
❑ BN-LA633-G	Caricatures	1976	3.75	7.50	15.00
❑ BN-LA700-G	Donald Byrd's Best	1976	3.75	7.50	15.00
❑ LT-991	Chant	1980	3.00	6.00	12.00
❑ LT-1096	Creeper	1981	3.00	6.00	12.00

Number	Title (A Side/B Side)	Yr	VG	VG+	NM
❑ BLP-4007 [M]	Off to the Races	1959	30.00	60.00	120.00
—"Deep groove" version (deep indentation under label on both sides)					
❑ BLP-4007 [M]	Off to the Races	1959	20.00	40.00	80.00
—W. 63rd St., NYC address on label					
❑ BLP-4007 [M]	Off to the Races	1963	6.25	12.50	25.00
—"New York, USA" address on label					
❑ BST-4007 [S]	Off to the Races	1959	20.00	40.00	80.00
—"Deep groove" version (deep indentation under label on both sides)					
❑ BST-4007 [S]	Off to the Races	1959	15.00	30.00	60.00
—W. 63rd St., NYC address on label					
❑ BST-4007 [S]	Off to the Races	1963	6.25	12.50	25.00
—"New York, USA" address on label					
❑ BLP-4019 [M]	Byrd in Hand	1959	30.00	60.00	120.00
—"Deep groove" version (deep indentation under label on both sides)					
❑ BLP-4019 [M]	Byrd in Hand	1959	20.00	40.00	80.00
—W. 63rd St., NYC address on label					
❑ BLP-4019 [M]	Byrd in Hand	1963	6.25	12.50	25.00
—"New York, USA" address on label					
❑ BLP-4026 [M]	Fuego	1960	30.00	60.00	120.00
—"Deep groove" version (deep indentation under label on both sides)					
❑ BLP-4026 [M]	Fuego	1960	20.00	40.00	80.00
—W. 63rd St., NYC address on label					
❑ BLP-4026 [M]	Fuego	1963	6.25	12.50	25.00
—"New York, USA" address on label					
❑ BLP-4048 [M]	Byrd in Flight	1960	30.00	60.00	120.00
—"Deep groove" version (deep indentation under label on both sides)					
❑ BLP-4048 [M]	Byrd in Flight	1960	20.00	40.00	80.00
—W. 63rd St., NYC address on label					
❑ BLP-4048 [M]	Byrd in Flight	1963	6.25	12.50	25.00
—"New York, USA" address on label					
❑ BLP-4060 [M]	Donald Byrd at the Half Note Café, Volume 1	1961	20.00	40.00	80.00
—W. 63rd St., NYC address on label					
❑ BLP-4060 [M]	Donald Byrd at the Half Note Café, Volume 1	1963	6.25	12.50	25.00
—"New York, USA" address on label					
❑ BLP-4061 [M]	Donald Byrd at the Half Note Café, Volume 2	1961	20.00	40.00	80.00
—W. 63rd St., NYC address on label					
❑ BLP-4061 [M]	Donald Byrd at the Half Note Café, Volume 2	1963	6.25	12.50	25.00
—"New York, USA" address on label					
❑ BLP-4075 [M]	The Cat Walk	1961	20.00	40.00	80.00
—61st St, New York address on label					
❑ BLP-4075 [M]	The Cat Walk	1963	6.25	12.50	25.00
—"New York, USA" address on label					
❑ BLP-4101 [M]	Royal Flush	1962	5.00	10.00	20.00
❑ BLP-4118 [M]	Free Form	1963	5.00	10.00	20.00
❑ BLP-4124 [M]	A New Perspective	1964	5.00	10.00	20.00
❑ BLP-4188 [M]	I'm Tryin' to Get Home	1965	5.00	10.00	20.00
❑ BLP-4238 [M]	Mustang!	1966	5.00	10.00	20.00
❑ BLP-4259 [M]	Blackjack	1967	6.25	12.50	25.00
❑ LN-10054	Street Lady	1981	2.00	4.00	8.00
—Budget-line reissue					
❑ B1-31875	Kofi	1995	3.75	7.50	15.00
❑ B1-36195	Electric Byrd	1996	3.75	7.50	15.00
❑ BST-84007 [S]	Byrd in Hand	1967	3.00	6.00	12.00
—"A Division of Liberty Records" on label					
❑ BST-84019	Byrd in Hand	198?	2.50	5.00	10.00
—"The Finest in Jazz Since 1939" reissue					
❑ BST-84019 [S]	Byrd in Hand	1959	15.00	30.00	60.00
—W. 63rd St., NYC address on label					
❑ BST-84019 [S]	Byrd in Hand	1963	6.25	12.50	25.00
—"New York, USA" address on label					
❑ BST-84019 [S]	Byrd in Hand	1967	3.00	6.00	12.00
—"A Division of Liberty Records" on label					
❑ BST-84026 [S]	Fuego	1959	15.00	30.00	60.00
—W. 63rd St., NYC address on label					
❑ BST-84026 [S]	Fuego	1963	6.25	12.50	25.00
—"New York, USA" address on label					
❑ BST-84026 [S]	Fuego	1967	3.00	6.00	12.00
—"A Division of Liberty Records" on label					
❑ BST-84048 [S]	Byrd in Flight	1960	15.00	30.00	60.00
—W. 63rd St., NYC address on label					
❑ BST-84048 [S]	Byrd in Flight	1963	6.25	12.50	25.00
—"New York, USA" address on label					
❑ BST-84048 [S]	Byrd in Flight	1967	3.00	6.00	12.00
—"A Division of Liberty Records" on label					
❑ BST-84060 [S]	Donald Byrd at the Half Note Café, Volume 1	1961	15.00	30.00	60.00
—W. 63rd St., NYC address on label					
❑ BST-84060 [S]	Donald Byrd at the Half Note Café, Volume 1	1963	6.25	12.50	25.00
—"New York, USA" address on label					
❑ BST-84060 [S]	Donald Byrd at the Half Note Café, Volume 1	1967	3.00	6.00	12.00
—"A Division of Liberty Records" on label					
❑ BST-84061 [S]	Donald Byrd at the Half Note Café, Volume 2	1961	15.00	30.00	60.00
—W. 63rd St., NYC address on label					
❑ BST-84061 [S]	Donald Byrd at the Half Note Café, Volume 2	1963	6.25	12.50	25.00
—"New York, USA" address on label					
❑ BST-84061 [S]	Donald Byrd at the Half Note Café, Volume 2	1967	3.00	6.00	12.00
—"A Division of Liberty Records" on label					
❑ BST-84075 [S]	The Cat Walk	1961	15.00	30.00	60.00
—61st St, New York address on label					
❑ BST-84075 [S]	The Cat Walk	1963	6.25	12.50	25.00
—"New York, USA" address on label					
❑ BST-84075 [S]	The Cat Walk	1967	3.00	6.00	12.00
—"A Division of Liberty Records" on label					
❑ BST-84101 [S]	Royal Flush	1962	6.25	12.50	25.00
—"New York, USA" address on label					
❑ BST-84101 [S]	Royal Flush	1967	3.00	6.00	12.00
—"A Division of Liberty Records" on label					

Number	Title (A Side/B Side)	Yr	VG	VG+	NM
❏ BST-84118 Free Form		1986	2.50	5.00	10.00
—"The Finest in Jazz Since 1939" reissue					
❏ BST-84118 [S]Free Form		1963	6.25	12.50	25.00
—"New York, USA" address on label					
❏ BST-84118 [S]Free Form		1967	3.00	6.00	12.00
—"A Division of Liberty Records" on label					
❏ BST-84124 A New Perspective		198?	2.50	5.00	10.00
—"The Finest in Jazz Since 1939" reissue					
❏ BST-84124 [S]A New Perspective		1964	6.25	12.50	25.00
—"New York, USA" address on label					
❏ BST-84124 [S]A New Perspective		1967	3.00	6.00	12.00
—"A Division of Liberty Records" on label					
❏ BST-84124 [S]A New Perspective		1973	2.50	5.00	10.00
—"A Division of United Artists Records Inc." on label					
❏ BST-84188 I'm Tryin' to Get Home		1986	2.50	5.00	10.00
—"The Finest in Jazz Since 1939" reissue					
❏ BST-84188 [S]I'm Tryin' to Get Home		1965	6.25	12.50	25.00
—"New York, USA" address on label					
❏ BST-84188 [S]I'm Tryin' to Get Home		1967	3.00	6.00	12.00
—"A Division of Liberty Records" on label					
❏ BST-84238 [S]Mustang!		1966	6.25	12.50	25.00
—"New York, USA" address on label					
❏ BST-84238 [S]Mustang!		1967	3.00	6.00	12.00
—"A Division of Liberty Records" on label					
❏ BST-84259 [S]Blackjack		1967	5.00	10.00	20.00
❏ BST-84292 Slow Drag		1968	5.00	10.00	20.00
❏ BST-84319 Fancy Free		1969	5.00	10.00	20.00
❏ BST-84349 Electric		1970	5.00	10.00	20.00
❏ BST-84380 Ethiopian Nights		1972	5.00	10.00	20.00
❏ B1-89796 Fancy Free		1993	3.75	7.50	15.00
DELMARK					
❏ DS-407 First Flight		1990	3.00	6.00	12.00
DISCOVERY					
❏ 869 September Afternoon		198?	2.50	5.00	10.00
ELEKTRA					
❏ 6E-144 Thank You for F.U.M.L. (Funking Up My Life)		1978	2.50	5.00	10.00
❏ 6E-247 Donald Byrd and 125th St., N.Y.C.		1980	2.50	5.00	10.00
❏ 5E-531 Love Byrd		1981	2.50	5.00	10.00
❏ 60188 Words, Sounds, Colors and Shapes		1982	2.50	5.00	10.00
LANDMARK					
❏ LLP-1516 Harlem Blues		1988	2.50	5.00	10.00
❏ LLP-1523 Getting Down to Business		1990	3.00	6.00	12.00
SAVOY					
❏ MG-12032 [M] Byrd's Word		1956	25.00	50.00	100.00
❏ MG-12064 [M] The Jazz Message of Donald Byrd		1956	30.00	60.00	120.00
SAVOY JAZZ					
❏ SJL-1101 Long Green		198?	2.50	5.00	10.00
❏ SJL-1114 Star Eyes		198?	2.50	5.00	10.00
TRANSITION					
❏ TRLP-4 [M] Byrd's Eye View		1956	150.00	300.00	600.00
❏ TRLP-5 [M] Byrd Jazz		1956	150.00	300.00	600.00
❏ TRLP-17 [M] Byrd Blows on Beacon Hill		1956	150.00	300.00	600.00
TRIP					
❏ 5000 [(2)] Two Sides of Donald Byrd		1974	3.75	7.50	15.00
VERVE					
❏ V-8609 [M] Up with Donald Byrd		1965	5.00	10.00	20.00
❏ V6-8609 [S] Up with Donald Byrd		1965	6.25	12.50	25.00

C

Number	Title (A Side/B Side)	Yr	VG	VG+	NM
C.O.D.'S, THE					
45s					
KELLMAC					
❏ 1003	Michael/Cry No More	1965	3.00	6.00	12.00
❏ 1005	Pretty Baby/I'm a Good Guy	1965	5.00	10.00	20.00
❏ 1008	I'm Looking Out for Me/I'll Come Running Back to You	1966	5.00	10.00	20.00
❏ 1010	She's Fire/It Must Be You	1966	375.00	750.00	1500.
❏ 1012	Coming Back Girl/It Must Be Love	1966	25.00	50.00	100.00
CADETS, THE					
Also see THE JACKS.					
45s					
JAN-LAR					
❏ 102	Don't/Car Crash	1960	15.00	30.00	60.00
MODERN					
❏ 956	Don't Be Angry/I Cried	1955	12.50	25.00	50.00
❏ 960	Rollin' Stone/Fine Lookin' Baby	1955	12.50	25.00	50.00
❏ 963	I Cried/Fine Lookin' Baby	1955	10.00	20.00	40.00
❏ 969	Annie Met Henry/So Will I	1955	10.00	20.00	40.00
❏ 971	Do You Wanna Rock/If It Is Wrong	1956	25.00	50.00	100.00
❏ 985	Church Bells May Ring/Heartbreak Hotel	1956	10.00	20.00	40.00
❏ 994	Stranded in the Jungle/I Want You	1956	10.00	20.00	40.00
❏ 1000	I Got Loaded/Dancin' Dan	1956	10.00	20.00	40.00
❏ 1006	Fools Rush In/I'll Be Spinning	1956	10.00	20.00	40.00
❏ 1012	Heaven Help Me/Love Bandit	1957	10.00	20.00	40.00
❏ 1017	Wiggle Waggle Woo/You Belong to Me	1957	10.00	20.00	40.00
❏ 1019	Pretty Evey/Rum, Jamaica Rum	1957	12.50	25.00	50.00
—As "Aaron Collins and the Cadets"					
❏ 1024	Hands Across the Table/Love Can Do Most Anything	1957	10.00	20.00	40.00
—As "Will Jones and the Cadets"					
❏ 1026	Ring Chimes/Baby Ya Know	1957	10.00	20.00	40.00
SHERWOOD					
❏ 211	One More Chance/I'm Looking for a Job	1960	12.50	25.00	50.00
Albums					
CROWN					
❏ CST-370 [R]	The Cadets	1963	25.00	50.00	100.00
❏ CLP-5015 [M]	Rockin' 'n' Reelin'	1957	62.50	125.00	250.00
—Black label					
❏ CLP-5370 [M]	The Cadets	1963	37.50	75.00	150.00
MODERN					
❏ LPM-1215 [M]	Rockin' 'n' Reelin'	1956	—	—	—
—Canceled					
RELIC					
❏ 5025	The Cadets' Greatest Hits	197?	3.00	6.00	12.00
CADILLACS, THE					
45s					
ARTIC					
❏ 101	Fool/The Right Kind of Lovin'	1964	25.00	50.00	100.00
CAPITOL					
❏ 4825	Groovy, Groovy Love/White Gardenia	1962	5.00	10.00	20.00
❏ 4935	La Bomba/I Saw You	1963	5.00	10.00	20.00
—As "Bobby Ray and the Cadillacs"					
JOSIE					
❏ 765	Gloria/I Wonder Why	1954	175.00	350.00	700.00
—Original with "joz" logo at top					
❏ 765	Gloria/I Wonder Why	196?	6.25	12.50	25.00
—Reissue with 1960s label					
❏ 769	Wishing Well/I Want to Know About Love	1954	125.00	250.00	500.00
❏ 773	Sympathy/No Chance	1955	25.00	50.00	100.00
❏ 778	Widow Lady/Down the Road	1955	50.00	100.00	200.00
❏ 785	Speedoo/Let Me Explain	1955	15.00	30.00	60.00
❏ 792	Zoom/You Are	1956	12.50	25.00	50.00
❏ 798	Woe Is Me/Betty My Love	1956	12.50	25.00	50.00
❏ 805	The Girl I Love/That's All I Need	1956	25.00	50.00	100.00
❏ 807	Rudolph the Red-Nosed Reindeer/Shack-a Doo	1956	10.00	20.00	40.00
❏ 812	Sugar Sugar/About That Girl Named Lou	1957	10.00	20.00	40.00
❏ 820	My Girl Friend/Broken Heart	1957	12.50	25.00	50.00
❏ 821	Lucy/Hurry Home	1957	10.00	20.00	40.00
—As "The Original Cadillacs"					
❏ 829	Buzz-Buzz-Buzz/Yes, Yes Baby	1957	10.00	20.00	40.00
—As "The Original Cadillacs"					
❏ 836	Speedo Is Back/A' Looka Here	1958	7.50	15.00	30.00
❏ 842	Holy Smoke Baby/I Want to Know	1958	7.50	15.00	30.00
❏ 846	Peek-a-Book/Oh, Oh Lolita	1958	7.50	15.00	30.00
❏ 857	Copy Cat/Jay Walker	1959	7.50	15.00	30.00
❏ 861	Cool It Fool/Please Mr. Johnson	1959	7.50	15.00	30.00
❏ 866 [M]	Romeo/Always My Darling	1959	7.50	15.00	30.00
❏ 870	Dumbell/Bad Dan McGoon	1959	7.50	15.00	30.00
❏ 876	Tell Me Today/It's Love	1960	7.50	15.00	30.00
❏ 883	That's Why/The Boogie Man	1960	7.50	15.00	30.00
❏ 915	Wayward Wanderer/I'll Never Let You Go	1963	5.00	10.00	20.00
—As "The Original Cadillacs"					
JUBILEE					
❏ 8010 [S]	Romeo/Always My Darling	1959	15.00	30.00	60.00
LANA					
❏ 118	Speedo/Baby It's All Right	196?	—	3.00	6.00
—Reissue					

Number	Title (A Side/B Side)	Yr	VG	VG+	NM
❑ 119	Gloria/Hey Bob E Re Bob	196?	—	3.00	6.00
—Reissue					
MERCURY					
❑ 71738	I'm Willing/Thrill Me So	1961	25.00	50.00	100.00
POLYDOR					
❑ 14031	Deep in the Heart of the Ghetto (Part 1)/Deep in the Heart of the Ghetto (Part 2)	1969	3.75	7.50	15.00
—As "The Original Cadillacs"					
ROULETTE					
❑ 4654	Let's Get Together/She's My Connection	1965	5.00	10.00	20.00
SMASH					
❑ 1712	You Are to Blame/What to Bet	1961	6.25	12.50	25.00
Albums					
HARLEM HIT PARADE					
❑ 5009	Cruisin' with the Cadillacs	197?	2.50	5.00	10.00
JUBILEE					
❑ JGM-1045 [M]	The Fabulous Cadillacs	1957	100.00	200.00	400.00
—Blue label					
❑ JGM-1045 [M]	The Fabulous Cadillacs	1959	62.50	125.00	250.00
—Flat black label					
❑ JGM-1045 [M]	The Fabulous Cadillacs	1960	25.00	50.00	100.00
—Glossy black label					
❑ JGM-1089 [M]	The Crazy Cadillacs	1959	75.00	150.00	300.00
—Flat black label					
❑ JGM-1089 [M]	The Crazy Cadillacs	1960	25.00	50.00	100.00
—Glossy black label					
❑ JGM-5009 [M]	Twisting with the Cadillacs	1962	50.00	100.00	200.00
MURRAY HILL					
❑ 1195	The Very Best of the Cadillacs	198?	3.75	7.50	15.00
❑ 1285 [(5)]	The Cadillacs	198?	10.00	20.00	40.00
—Box set					

CADILLACS, THE/ THE ORIOLES
Also see each artist's individual listings.
Albums
JUBILEE

Number	Title (A Side/B Side)	Yr	VG	VG+	NM
❑ JGM-1117 [M]	The Cadillacs Meet the Orioles	1961	50.00	100.00	200.00

CAMELOTS, THE
45s
AANKO

Number	Title (A Side/B Side)	Yr	VG	VG+	NM
❑ 1001	Your Way/Don't Leave Me Baby	1963	20.00	40.00	80.00
❑ 1004	Sunday Kind of Love/My Imagination	1963	20.00	40.00	80.00
CAMEO					
❑ 334	Don't Leave Me Baby/Love Call	1964	7.50	15.00	30.00
—B-side by the Ebonaires					
COMET					
❑ 930	Scratch/Charge	1962	3.75	7.50	15.00
CRIMSON					
❑ 1001	Don't Leave Me Baby/The Letter	1963	7.50	15.00	30.00
DREAM					
❑ 1001	Your Way/I Wonder	1967	2.00	4.00	8.00
EMBER					
❑ 1108	Pocahontas/Searching for My Baby	1964	5.00	10.00	20.00
LAURIE					
❑ 3239	Marie/Daddy's Going Away Again	1964	5.00	10.00	20.00
—As "The Harps"					
NIX					
❑ 101	Lulu/Never Been in Love Before	1961	5.00	10.00	20.00
RELIC					
❑ 530	Chain of Broken Hearts/Rat Race	196?	2.00	4.00	8.00
—B-side by the Bootleggers					
❑ 541	Dance Girl/That's My Baby	1965	2.00	4.00	8.00
—B-side by the Suns					
TIMES SQUARE					
❑ 32	Dance Girl/That's My Baby	1964	2.50	5.00	10.00
—B-side by the Suns					

7-Inch Extended Plays
CLIFTON/UGHA

Number	Title (A Side/B Side)	Yr	VG	VG+	NM
❑ EP 507/1	Music to My Ears/Daddy's Going Away// Pocahontas/Don't Leave Me Baby	1981	—	2.50	5.00
❑ EP 507/1 [PS]	(title unknown)	1981	—	2.50	5.00

CAMEO
12-Inch Singles
ATLANTA ARTISTA

Number	Title (A Side/B Side)	Yr	VG	VG+	NM
❑ PRO 282-1 [DJ]	Talkin' Out the Side of Your Neck (same on both sides)	1984	5.00	10.00	20.00
ATLANTA ARTISTS					
❑ PRO 217-1 [DJ]	Slow Movin' (2 versions?)	1983	5.00	10.00	20.00
❑ PRO 291-1 [DJ]	Hangin' Downtown (same on both sides)	1984	2.50	5.00	10.00
❑ PRO 543-1 [DJ]	She's Mine (2 versions)	1986	2.50	5.00	10.00
❑ PRO 839-1 [DJ]	I Want It Now (same on both sides)	1990	3.75	7.50	15.00
❑ PRO 868-1 [DJ]	Close Quarters (2 versions) (same on both sides)	1990	3.00	6.00	12.00
❑ 812053-1	Style (5:08) (5:19)	1983	3.00	6.00	12.00
❑ 818384-1	She's Strange (Club Mix 6:42) (LP Version 7:21)	1984	2.50	5.00	10.00
❑ 870587-1	You Make Me Work (3 versions)/DKWIG	1988	2.00	4.00	8.00
❑ 872315-1	Skin I'm In (3 versions)/Honey	1988	2.50	5.00	10.00
❑ 874051-1	Pretty Girls (12" Remix) (12" Dub) (7" Remix) (7" Dub)	1989	2.50	5.00	10.00
❑ 875589-1	I Want It Now (12" Edit) (Rough Mix) (Then Dub) (Now Dub)	1990	2.50	5.00	10.00

Number	Title (A Side/B Side)	Yr	VG	VG+	NM
❑ 878199-1	Close Quarters (4 versions)/Honey	1990	2.00	4.00	8.00
❑ 880038-1	Talkin' Out the Side of Your Neck/She's Strange (Rap Version)	1984	3.75	7.50	15.00
❑ 880744-1	Attack Me with Your Love (Extended Version 6:31) (7" Dance Remix 4:15)	1985	3.00	6.00	12.00
❑ 884010-1	Single Life (6:30)/I've Got Your Image	1985	2.50	5.00	10.00
❑ 884270-1	A Good-Bye (5:41)/Little Boys-Dangerous Toys	1985	3.00	6.00	12.00
❑ 884933-1	Word Up (3 versions)/Urban Warrior	1986	2.50	5.00	10.00
❑ 888193-1	Candy/She's Strange	1986	2.50	5.00	10.00
❑ 888385-1	Back and Forth (12" Club Remix 6:30) (Dub Mix 6:01) (7" Version 3:47)/You Can Have the World	1987	2.50	5.00	10.00
CHOCOLATE CITY					
❑ CCD 20005 [DJ]	Rigor Mortis (Disco Mix 6:14)/(Mono Mix 3:12)	1977	10.00	20.00	40.00
❑ CCD 20007 [DJ]	Post Mortem/(B-side blank)	1977	6.25	12.50	25.00
❑ CCD 20013 [DJ]	It's Serious/(B-side blank)	1978	7.50	15.00	30.00
❑ CCD 20014 [DJ]	Find My Way/Rigor Mortis///(B-side blank)	1978	7.50	15.00	30.00
❑ CCD 20016 [DJ]	I Just Want to Be/(B-side blank)	1979	7.50	15.00	30.00
❑ CCD 20020 [DJ]	We're Goin' Out Tonight (4:41)/(B-side blank)	1980	6.25	12.50	25.00
❑ CCD 20022	Shake Your Pants (5:59) (4:01)	1980	5.00	10.00	20.00
❑ CCD 20028	Keep It Hot/Your Love Takes Me Out	1980	5.00	10.00	20.00
❑ CCD 20034	Don't Be So Cool (4:23)/I Never Knew (4:34)	1981	5.00	10.00	20.00
❑ CCD 20035 [DJ]	Just Be Yourself (4:20) (same on both sides)	1982	5.00	10.00	20.00
❑ CCD 20037	Alligator Woman/(B-side blank?)	1982	3.75	7.50	15.00
❑ CCD 20038	Flirt (2 versions)	1982	5.00	10.00	20.00
❑ CCD 20039	Flirt (3 versions)	1982	5.00	10.00	20.00
REPRISE					
❑ PRO-A-5224 [DJ]	Emotional Violence (Edit) (LP Version)	1992	5.00	10.00	20.00
❑ PRO-A-5625 [DJ]	Raw But Tasty (Funk Mix) (Raw Remix) (Dub) (Ronnie's Mix)	1992	3.75	7.50	15.00
❑ 40392	Money (Reese Revamp Mix) (Reese Hardcore Instrumental) (Hardsell Mix)/Front Street	1992	7.50	15.00	30.00

45s
ATLANTA ARTISTS

Number	Title (A Side/B Side)	Yr	VG	VG+	NM
❑ PRO 272-7 [DJ]	She's Strange (Rap)/(Edit)	1984	2.50	5.00	10.00
❑ 812054-7	Style/Enjoy Your Life	1983	—	—	3.00
❑ 812472-7	Can't Help Falling in Love/For You	1983	—	—	3.00
❑ 814077-7	Slow Movin'/For You	1983	—	—	3.00
❑ 818384-7	She's Strange/Tribute to Bob Marley	1984	—	—	3.00
❑ 818870-7	Talkin' Out the Side of Your Neck/Leve-Toi	1984	—	—	3.00
❑ 870587-7	You Make Me Work/DKWIG	1988	—	—	3.00
❑ 870587-7 [PS]	You Make Me Work/DKWIG	1988	—	—	3.00
❑ 872314-7	Skin I'm In/Honey	1988	—	—	3.00
❑ 872314-7 [PS]	Skin I'm In/Honey	1988	—	—	3.00
❑ 872918-7	Single Life/She's Strange	1989	—	—	3.00
—Reissue					
❑ 874050-7	Pretty Girls/Pretty Girls (Dub)	1989	—	—	3.00
❑ 874050-7 [PS]	Pretty Girls/Pretty Girls (Dub)	1989	—	—	3.00
❑ 875588-7	I Want It Now/DKWIG	1990	—	—	3.00
❑ 878198-7	Close Quarters/Honey	1990	—	—	3.00
❑ 880169-7	Hangin' Downtown/Cameo's Dance	1984	—	—	3.00
❑ 880744-7	Attack Me With Your Love/Love You Anyway	1985	—	—	3.00
❑ 884010-7	Single Life/I've Got Your Image	1985	—	—	3.00
❑ 884270-7	A Good-Bye/Little Boys-Dangerous Toys	1985	—	—	3.00
❑ 884933-7	Word Up/Urban Warrior	1986	—	—	3.00
❑ 884933-7 [PS]	Word Up/Urban Warrior	1986	—	—	3.00
❑ 888193-7	Candy/She's Strange	1986	—	—	3.00
❑ 888193-7 [PS]	Candy/She's Strange	1986	—	—	3.00
❑ 888385-7	Back and Forth/You Can Have the World	1987	—	—	3.00
❑ 888385-7 [PS]	Back and Forth/You Can Have the World	1987	—	—	3.00
❑ 888711-7	Don't Be Lonely/I've Got Your Image	1987	—	—	3.00
❑ 888876-7	She's Mine/I've Got Your Image	1987	—	—	3.00
CHOCOLATE CITY					
❑ 001	Find My Way/Good Company	1975	—	2.50	5.00
❑ 005	Rigor Mortis/Stand By My Side	1976	—	2.50	5.00
❑ 008	Find My Way/Rigor Mortis	1977	—	2.00	4.00
❑ 010	Post Mortem/Smile	1977	—	2.00	4.00
❑ 011	Funk Funk/Good Time	1977	—	2.00	4.00
❑ 013	It's Serious/Inflation	1978	—	2.00	4.00
❑ 014	It's Over/Inflation	1978	—	2.00	4.00
❑ 016	Insane/I Want You	1978	—	2.00	4.00
❑ 018	Give Love a Chance/Two of Us	1979	—	2.00	4.00
❑ 019	I Just Want to Be/The Rock	1979	—	2.00	4.00
❑ 3202	Sparkle/Macho	1979	—	2.00	4.00
❑ 3206	We're Goin' Out Tonight/One the One	1980	—	2.00	4.00
❑ 3210	Shake Your Pants/I Came for You	1980	—	2.00	4.00
❑ 3219	Keep It Hot/I Came for You	1980	—	2.00	4.00
❑ 3222	Feel Me/Is This the Way	1981	—	2.00	4.00
❑ 3225	Freaky Dancin'/Better Days	1981	—	2.00	4.00
❑ 3227	I Like It/The Sound Table	1981	—	2.00	4.00
❑ 3231	Just Be Yourself/Use It or Lose It	1982	—	2.00	4.00
❑ 3233	Flirt/Owe It All to You	1982	—	2.00	4.00
❑ 3235	Alligator Woman/Soul Away	1982	—	2.00	4.00
Albums					
ATLANTA ARTISTS					
❑ 811072-1	Style	1983	2.50	5.00	10.00
❑ 814984-1	She's Strange	1984	2.50	5.00	10.00
❑ 824546-1	Single Life	1985	2.50	5.00	10.00
❑ 830265-1	Word Up!	1986	2.50	5.00	10.00
❑ 836002-1	Machismo	1988	2.50	5.00	10.00
❑ 846297-1	Real Men..Wear Black	1990	3.00	6.00	12.00
CHOCOLATE CITY					
❑ CCLP 2003	Cardiac Arrest	1977	3.00	6.00	12.00
❑ CCLP 2004	We All Know Who We Are	1978	3.00	6.00	12.00
❑ CCLP 2006	Ugly Ego	1978	3.00	6.00	12.00

Number	Title (A Side/B Side)	Yr	VG	VG+	NM
❏ CCLP 2008	Secret Omen	1979	3.00	6.00	12.00
❏ CCLP 2011	Cameosis	1980	3.00	6.00	12.00
❏ CCLP 2016	Feel Me	1980	3.00	6.00	12.00
❏ CCLP 2019	Knights of the Sound Table	1981	3.00	6.00	12.00
❏ CCLP 2021	Alligator Woman	1982	3.00	6.00	12.00

CAMPBELL, CHOKER
45s
APT
| ❏ 25011 | Walk Awhile/Walking on Thin-Soled Shoes | 1958 | 15.00 | 30.00 | 60.00 |

ATLANTIC
| ❏ 1014 | Last Call for Whiskey/How Could You Do This | 1953 | 10.00 | 20.00 | 40.00 |
| ❏ 1038 | Have You Seen My Baby/Jackie Mambo | 1954 | 10.00 | 20.00 | 40.00 |

FORTUNE
| ❏ 808 | Frankie and Johnny/Rocking and Jumping | 1953 | 15.00 | 30.00 | 60.00 |

MOTOWN
| ❏ 1072 | Come See About Me/Pride and Joy | 1964 | 6.25 | 12.50 | 25.00 |

Albums
MOTOWN
| ❏ M-620 [M] | Hits of the Sixties | 1964 | 25.00 | 50.00 | 100.00 |
| ❏ MS-620 [S] | Hits of the Sixties | 1964 | 37.50 | 75.00 | 150.00 |

CAPITOLS, THE (1)
Detroit-based R&B vocal group.
45s
KAREN
❏ 1524	Cool Jerk/Hello Stranger	1966	3.75	7.50	15.00
❏ 1525	I Got to Handle It/Zig Zagging	1966	2.50	5.00	10.00
❏ 1526	We Got a Thing That's In the Groove/Tired Running from You	1966	2.50	5.00	10.00
❏ 1534	Patty Cake/Take a Chance on Me Baby	1967	2.50	5.00	10.00
❏ 1536	Cool Pearl/Don't Say Maybe Baby	1967	2.50	5.00	10.00
❏ 1537	Cool Jerk '68/Afro Twist	1968	2.50	5.00	10.00
❏ 1543	Soul Brother, Soul Sister/Ain't That Terrible	1968	2.50	5.00	10.00
❏ 1546	Soul Soul/When You're in Trouble	1969	2.50	5.00	10.00

Albums
ATCO
❏ 33-190 [M]	Dance the Cool Jerk	1966	10.00	20.00	40.00
❏ SD 33-190 [S]	Dance the Cool Jerk	1966	12.50	25.00	50.00
❏ 33-201 [M]	We Got a Thing That's In the Groove	1966	10.00	20.00	40.00
❏ SD 33-201 [S]	We Got a Thing That's In the Groove	1966	12.50	25.00	50.00

COLLECTABLES
| ❏ COL-5105 | Golden Classics | 1988 | 2.50 | 5.00 | 10.00 |

SOLID SMOKE
| ❏ 8019 | The Capitols: Their Greatest Hits | 1983 | 3.00 | 6.00 | 12.00 |

CAPRIS, THE (1)
Italian male vocal group from New York.
45s
20TH CENTURY
| ❏ 1201 | My Weakness/Yes, My Baby, Please! | 1957 | 15.00 | 30.00 | 60.00 |

AMBIENT SOUND
| ❏ ZS5-02697 | There's a Moon Out Again/Morse Code of Love | 1982 | — | 3.00 | 6.00 |

CANDLELITE
| ❏ 422 | Oh, My Darling/Rock Pretty Baby | 196? | 3.00 | 6.00 | 12.00 |

LIFETIME
| ❏ 1001/2 | Oh My Darling/Rock Pretty Baby | 1961 | 25.00 | 50.00 | 100.00 |

LOST-NITE
| ❏ 101 | There's a Moon Out Tonight/Indian Girl | 1961 | 17.50 | 35.00 | 70.00 |
—Pink label original
| ❏ 101 | There's a Moon Out Tonight/Indian Girl | 196? | 2.00 | 4.00 | 8.00 |
—Yellow label reissue
| ❏ 148 | Little Girl/When | 196? | 2.00 | 4.00 | 8.00 |

MR. PEEKE
| ❏ 118 | Limbo/From the Vine Came the Grape | 1963 | 5.00 | 10.00 | 20.00 |

OLD TOWN
| ❏ 1094 | There's a Moon Out Tonight/Indian Girl | 1961 | 7.50 | 15.00 | 30.00 |
—Light blue label
| ❏ 1094 | There's a Moon Out Tonight/Indian Girl | 1962 | 5.00 | 10.00 | 20.00 |
—Mostly black label
❏ 1099	Where I Fell in Love/Some People Think	1961	7.50	15.00	30.00
❏ 1103	Tears in My Eyes/Why Do I Cry	1961	7.50	15.00	30.00
❏ 1107	Girl in My Dreams/My Island in the Sun	1961	7.50	15.00	30.00

PLANET
| ❏ 1010 | There's a Moon Out Tonight/Indian Girl | 1958 | 400.00 | 800.00 | 1200. |

SABRE
| ❏ 201/2 | My Promise to You/Bop! Bop! Bop! | 1959 | 37.50 | 75.00 | 150.00 |

TROMMERS
| ❏ 101 | There's a Moon Out Tonight/Indian Girl | 1961 | 6.25 | 12.50 | 25.00 |
—Red label
| ❏ 101 | There's a Moon Out Tonight/Indian Girl | 1961 | 6.25 | 12.50 | 25.00 |
—White label (not a promo)

Albums
AMBIENT SOUND
| ❏ FW 37714 | There's a Moon Out Again | 1982 | 3.75 | 7.50 | 15.00 |

COLLECTABLES
| ❏ COL-5016 | There's a Moon Out Tonight | 198? | 3.00 | 6.00 | 12.00 |

CAPRIS, THE (2)
Different male vocal group than (1).
45s
GOTHAM
| ❏ 304 | God Only Knows/That's What You're Doing to Me | 1954 | 150.00 | 300.00 | 600.00 |
—Blue label
| ❏ 304 | God Only Knows/That's What You're Doing to Me | 1954 | 30.00 | 60.00 | 120.00 |
—Red label
| ❏ 304 | God Only Knows/That's What You're Doing to Me | 1956 | 20.00 | 40.00 | 80.00 |
—Yellow label
| ❏ 306 | It Was Moonglow/Too Poor to Love | 1955 | 50.00 | 100.00 | 200.00 |
| ❏ 308 | It's a Miracle/Let's Linger Awhile | 1956 | 30.00 | 60.00 | 120.00 |

Albums
COLLECTABLES
| ❏ COL-5000 | Gotham Recording Stars | 198? | 3.00 | 6.00 | 12.00 |

CARA, IRENE
12-Inch Singles
CASABLANCA
| ❏ NBD 20248 | Flashdance... What a Feeling (Remix 7:16) (Instrumental) | 1983 | 6.25 | 12.50 | 25.00 |
| ❏ 812353-1 | Flashdance... What a Feeling (Remix 7:16)/ Found It (4:20) | 1983 | 3.75 | 7.50 | 15.00 |

GEFFEN
❏ PRO-A-2110 [DJ]	The Dream (Hold On to Your Dream) (Remix) (Single Edit)	1983	3.75	7.50	15.00
❏ PRO-A-2132 [DJ]	Breakdance (Extended Remix) (Extended Dub)	1984	2.50	5.00	10.00
❏ 20156	Why Me? (Extended Remix 7:02) (Instrumental Dubb)	1983	3.00	6.00	12.00
❏ 20196	Breakdance (Extended Remix 5:24) (Dub)	1984	—	3.50	7.00

45s
CASABLANCA
| ❏ 811440-7 | Flashdance... What a Feeling/Love Theme from Flashdance | 1983 | — | 2.00 | 4.00 |
—B-side by Helen St. John

ELEKTRA
| ❏ 69486 | Girlfriends/Dying for Your Love | 1987 | — | — | 3.00 |

GEFFEN
❏ 29328	Breakdance/Cue Me Up	1984	—	2.00	4.00
❏ 29396	The Dream (Hold On to Your Dream)/Receiving	1983	—	2.00	4.00
❏ 29464	Why Me?/Talk Too Much	1983	—	2.00	4.00
❏ 29464 [PS]	Why Me?/Talk Too Much	1983	—	2.00	4.00

NETWORK
| ❏ 47950 | Anyone Can See/Why | 1981 | — | 2.00 | 4.00 |
| ❏ 48011 | My Baby (He's Something Else)/Slow Down | 1982 | — | 2.00 | 4.00 |

RSO
| ❏ 1034 | Fame/Never Alone | 1980 | — | 2.00 | 4.00 |
| ❏ 1048 | Out Here On My Own (Piano Vocal)/(Orchestral Vocal) | 1980 | — | 2.50 | 5.00 |
—Tan label
| ❏ 1048 | Out Here On My Own (Piano Vocal)/(Orchestral Vocal) | 1980 | — | 2.00 | 4.00 |
—Silver label

Albums
ELEKTRA
| ❏ 60724 | Carasmatic | 1987 | 2.50 | 5.00 | 10.00 |

GEFFEN
| ❏ GHS 4021 | What a Feelin' | 1983 | 2.00 | 4.00 | 8.00 |

NETWORK
| ❏ E1-60003 | Anyone Can See | 1982 | 2.50 | 5.00 | 10.00 |

CARDINALS, THE (1)
Baltimore-based male vocal group.
45s
ATLANTIC
| ❏ 952 | I'll Always Love You/Pretty Baby Blues | 1952 | 100.00 | 200.00 | 400.00 |
—Cardinals records on Atlantic before 952 are unconfirmed on 45 rpm
❏ 958	Wheel of Fortune/Kiss Me Baby	1952	150.00	300.00	600.00
❏ 972	The Bump/She Rocks	1952	75.00	150.00	300.00
❏ 995	You Are My Only Love/Lovie Darling	1953	100.00	200.00	400.00
❏ 1025	Please Baby/Under a Blanket of Blue	1954	50.00	100.00	200.00
❏ 1054	The Door Is Still Open/Misirlou	1955	20.00	40.00	80.00
❏ 1067	Come Back My Love/Two Things I Love	1955	25.00	50.00	100.00
❏ 1079	Lovely Girl/There Goes My Heart to You	1955	25.00	50.00	100.00
❏ 1090	Choo Choo/Off Shore	1956	12.50	25.00	50.00
❏ 1103	The End of the Story/I Won't Make You Cry Anymore	1956	12.50	25.00	50.00
❏ 1126	Near You/One Love	1957	10.00	20.00	40.00

78s
ATLANTIC
❏ 938	Shouldn't I Know/Please Don't Leave Me	1951	50.00	100.00	200.00
❏ 952	I'll Always Love You/Pretty Baby Blues	1952	25.00	50.00	100.00
❏ 958	Wheel of Fortune/Kiss Me Baby	1952	25.00	50.00	100.00
❏ 972	The Bump/She Rocks	1952	25.00	50.00	100.00
❏ 995	You Are My Only Love/Lovie Darling	1953	20.00	40.00	80.00
❏ 1025	Please Baby/Under a Blanket of Blue	1954	15.00	30.00	60.00
❏ 1054	The Door Is Still Open/Misirlou	1955	10.00	20.00	40.00
❏ 1067	Come Back My Love/Two Things I Love	1955	12.50	25.00	50.00
❏ 1079	Lovely Girl/There Goes My Heart to You	1955	12.50	25.00	50.00
❏ 1090	Choo Choo/Off Shore	1956	12.50	25.00	50.00
❏ 1103	The End of the Story/I Won't Make You Cry Anymore	1956	12.50	25.00	50.00
❏ 1126	Near You/One Love	1957	12.50	25.00	50.00

Number	Title (A Side/B Side)	Yr	VG	VG+	NM

CAREY, MARIAH

Also see JD & MARIAH; LUTHER VANDROSS.

12-Inch Singles
COLUMBIA

Number	Title (A Side/B Side)	Yr	VG	VG+	NM
❑ CAS 3311 [DJ]	Honey (Def Rascal Anthem) (Def Rascal Dub)	1997	3.75	7.50	15.00
❑ CAS 4228 [DJ]	Fly Away (Butterfly Reprise) (Fly Away Club Mix) (Def B Fly Mix)/Honey (Def Rascal Dub) (Def Rascal Anthem)	1997	2.50	5.00	10.00
❑ CAS 6646 [DJ]	Joy to the World (Celebration Mix) (Flava Mix)/(Club Mix) (Crash Dub Crash) (LP Version)	1994	6.25	12.50	25.00
—Promo only on red vinyl					
❑ CAS 41886 [DJ]	I Still Believe (Stevie J. Remix) (Stevie J. Remix Instrumental) (Stevie J. Remix A Cappella)/I Still Believe-Pure Imagination (Damizza Reemix) (Damizza Reemix Instrumental) (Damizza Reemix A Cappella)	1998	3.75	7.50	15.00
❑ CAS 41887 [DJ]	I Still Believe (Morales Classic Club Mix) (The Eve of Souls Mix) (The Kings Mix) (The Kings Mix Instrumental)	1998	3.75	7.50	15.00
❑ CAS 42813 [DJ]	Heartbreaker-If You Should Ever Be Lonely (Junior's Heartbreaker Club Mix) (Junior's Heartbreaker Club Dub) (Junior's Heartbreaker Hard Mix)/Ain't No Fun (Remix)	1999	3.75	7.50	15.00
❑ 44-73560	Someday (New 12" House) (Pianoapercaloopapella) (New 12" Jackswing) (New 7" Straight)/Alone in Love	1991	3.00	6.00	12.00
❑ 44-74037	Emotions (12" Club Mix) (12" Instrumental) (LP Version)/There's Got to Be a Way (12" Mix)	1991	3.00	6.00	12.00
❑ 44-74189	Make It Happen (Extended Version) (Dub Version)/(C&C Classic Mix) (LP Version)	1992	5.00	10.00	20.00
❑ 44-77079	Dreamlover (Def Club Mix) (Def Instrumental) (USA Love Dub) (Eclipse Dub) (Def Tribal Mix)	1993	3.00	6.00	12.00
❑ 44-77418	Never Forget You (Extended) (Radio Edit) (Instrumental) (LP Version)/Without You	1994	2.00	4.00	8.00
❑ 44X-77528 [(2)]	Anytime You Need a Friend (All That and More Mix) (Ministry of Sound Mix) (Boriqua Tribe Mix) (C&C Dub) (LP Version)	1994	3.75	7.50	15.00
❑ 44X-78044 [(2)]	Fantasy (Album Version) (Def Club Mix) (MC Mix)/(Puffy's Mix) (Bad Boy with Ol' Dirty Bastard)//(The Boss Mix) (Sweet Dub Mix)/(Puffy's Club Mix) (Bad Boy Mix)	1995	3.75	7.50	15.00
❑ 44-78075	One Sweet Day (Album Version) (Sweet A Cappella) (A Cappella) (Chucky's Remix) (Live Version)/Fantasy (Def Drums Mix)	1995	2.50	5.00	10.00
—With Boyz II Men					
❑ 44-78277	Always Be My Baby (Reggae Soul Dub Featuring Lil' Vicious) (Mr. Dupri Extended Mix Featuring Da Brat and Xscape) (Reggae Soul Acapella Featuring Lil' Vicious) (Album Version)	1996	2.50	5.00	10.00
❑ 44-78313	Always Be My Baby (Always Club Mix) (Dub-a-Baby) (Groove-a-Pella) (St Dub)	1996	2.00	4.00	8.00
❑ 44X-78665 [(2)]	Honey (Album Version) (Bad Boy Remix) (So So Def Mix) (Morales Club Dub) (Classic Mix) (Morales Dub) (Mo' Honey Dub) (Classic Instrumental) (So So Def Radio Mix)	1997	3.75	7.50	15.00
❑ 44-78822	My All (Classic Club Mix)/The Roof (Mobb Deep Mix)/Breakdown (The Mo Thugs Remix) Fly Away (Butterfly Reprise) (Fly Away Club Mix)	1998	2.00	4.00	8.00
❑ 44-78981	My All-Stay Awhile (So So Def Remix) (So So Def Remix Without Rap) (Morales 'My' Club Mix) (Morales 'Def' Club Mix)/The Roof	1998	2.00	4.00	8.00
❑ 44X-79104 [(2)]	I Still Believe (Stevie J. Remix) (Stevie J. Clean Remix) (Stevie J. Remix Instrumental) (Stevie J. Remix A Cappella) (Morales Classic Club Mix) (The Eve of Souls Mix) (The Kings Mix) (The Kings Mix Instrumental)/I Still Believe-Pure Imagination (Damizza Reemix) (Damizza Reemix Instrumental) (Damizza Reemix A Cappella)	1998	3.00	6.00	12.00
❑ 44-79261	Heartbreaker (Featuring Jay-Z) (Featuring Da Brat and Missy Elliott)/Heartbreaker-If You Should Ever Be Lonely (Junior's Heartbreaker Club Mix) (Junior's Heartbreaker Hard Mix)	1999	2.00	4.00	8.00
❑ 44-79339	Thank God I Found You (Make It Last Remix Featuring Joe and Nas) (Make It Last Remix Instrumental) (Celebratory Remix Featuring Joe and 98)/Fantasy (Featuring O.D.B)	2000	2.00	4.00	8.00
❑ 44-79399	Can't Take That Away (Mariah's Theme) (Morales Club Mix) (Morales Instrumental) (Album Version) (Morales Revival Triumphant Mix)/Crybaby	2000	2.00	4.00	8.00

VIRGIN

Number	Title (A Side/B Side)	Yr	VG	VG+	NM
❑ SPRO-16193 [(2) DJ]	Loverboy (7 versions)	2001	3.75	7.50	15.00
❑ SPRO-16406 [DJ]	Loverboy (Remix Featuring Da Brat and Ludacris) (Instrumental Remix)/(Cameo Version) (Instrumental Mix)	2001	3.00	6.00	12.00
❑ 38791	Loverboy (Remix) (Instrumental Remix) (Album Version) (Instrumental Mix)	2001	—	3.00	6.00
❑ 38793 [(2)]	Loverboy (MJ Cole Remix) (MJ Cole Instrumental) (MJ Cole London Dub) (MJ Cole Radio Edit) (Club of Love Remix) (Dub Love Mix) (Drums of Love)	2001	2.00	4.00	8.00

45s
COLUMBIA

Number	Title (A Side/B Side)	Yr	VG	VG+	NM
❑ 38-73348	Vision of Love//Prisoner/All In Your Mind/Someday (album snippets)	1990	—	—	3.00
❑ 38-73455	Love Takes Time/Sent from Up Above	1990	—	—	3.00

Number	Title (A Side/B Side)	Yr	VG	VG+	NM
❑ 38-73561	Someday (Album Version)/Alone in Love	1990	—	2.50	5.00
❑ 38-73561	Someday (New 7" Jackswing)/Alone in Love	1991	—	—	3.00
❑ 38-73743	I Don't Wanna Cry/You Need Me	1991	—	—	3.00
❑ 38-73977	Emotions/Vanishing	1991	—	—	3.00
❑ 38-74088	Can't Let Go/To Be Around You	1991	—	—	3.00
❑ 38-74239	Make It Happen/Emotions (Special Motion Edit)	1992	—	—	3.00
❑ 38-74330	I'll Be There/So Blessed	1992	—	—	3.00
❑ 38-77080	Dreamlover/Do You Think of Me	1993	—	—	3.00
❑ 38-77224	Hero/Everything Fades Away	1993	—	—	3.00
❑ 38-77358	Without You/Never Forget You	1994	—	—	3.00
❑ 38-77499	Anytime You Need a Friend/Music Box	1994	—	—	3.00
❑ 38-77629	Endless Love/(Instrumental)	1994	—	—	3.00
—With Luther Vandross					
❑ 38-78043	Fantasy//(Bad Boy with O.D.B.)	1995	—	—	3.00
❑ 38-78072	One Sweet Day/I Am Free	1995	2.00	4.00	8.00
—With Boyz II Men; deleted on day of issue					
❑ 38-78276	Always Be My Baby/Long Ago	1996	—	—	3.00
❑ 38-78276 [PS]	Always Be My Baby/Long Ago	1996	—	—	3.00
❑ 38-78648	Honey (LP Version)/(Bad Boy Remix)	1997	—	—	3.00
❑ 38-78648 [PS]	Honey (LP Version)/(Bad Boy Remix)	1997	—	—	3.00
❑ 38-78821	My All/Breakdown	1998	—	—	3.00
❑ 38-78821 [PS]	My All/Breakdown	1998	—	—	3.00
❑ 38-79093	I Still Believe-Pure Imagination/I Still Believe	1999	—	—	3.00
❑ 38-79093 [PS]	I Still Believe-Pure Imagination/I Still Believe	1999	—	—	3.00
❑ 38-79260	Heartbreaker (Featuring Jay-Z)/(Featuring Da Brat and Missy Elliott)	1999	—	—	3.00
❑ 38-79338	Thank God I Found You (Album Version)/(Celebratory Mix)	2000	—	—	3.00
❑ 38-79348	Can't Take That Away (Mariah's Theme)/Crybaby	2000	—	—	3.00

VIRGIN

Number	Title (A Side/B Side)	Yr	VG	VG+	NM
❑ 38808	Loverboy/Never Too Far	2001	—	—	3.00

Albums
COLUMBIA

Number	Title (A Side/B Side)	Yr	VG	VG+	NM
❑ C 45202	Mariah Carey	1990	5.00	10.00	20.00
❑ C 47980	Emotions	1991	3.75	7.50	15.00
❑ C 53205	Music Box	1993	3.75	7.50	15.00
❑ C2 63800 [(2)]	Rainbow	1999	3.75	7.50	15.00
❑ C2 69670 [(2)]	#1's	1998	5.00	10.00	20.00

VIRGIN

Number	Title (A Side/B Side)	Yr	VG	VG+	NM
❑ 10797 [(2)]	Glitter	2001	3.75	7.50	15.00
❑ SPRO-16452 [(2) DJ]	Glitter	2001	5.00	10.00	20.00
—Promo-only version					

CARLTON, CARL

12-Inch Singles
20TH CENTURY

Number	Title (A Side/B Side)	Yr	VG	VG+	NM
❑ TCD-129	She's a Bad Mama Jama (She's Built, She's Stacked)/This Feeling's Rated X-Tra	1981	5.00	10.00	20.00

CASABLANCA

Number	Title (A Side/B Side)	Yr	VG	VG+	NM
❑ 880949-1	Private Property (Club Mix 6:43) (Dub Version 6:23)	1985	2.50	5.00	10.00
❑ 884274-1	Slipped, Tripped (Fooled Around and Fell in Love) (Special Club Remix) (Dub Version)/Hot	1986	3.00	6.00	12.00

RCA

Number	Title (A Side/B Side)	Yr	VG	VG+	NM
❑ PD-13314	Baby I Need Your Loving (5:56)/Everyone Can Be a Star	1982	2.50	5.00	10.00
❑ PD-13407	Swing That Sexy Thang/Just One Kiss	1982	2.50	5.00	10.00

45s
20TH CENTURY

Number	Title (A Side/B Side)	Yr	VG	VG+	NM
❑ 2459	This Feeling's Rated X-Tra/Fighting in the Name of Love	1980	—	2.00	4.00
❑ 2488	She's a Bad Mama Jama (She's Built, She's Stacked)/This Feeling's Rated X-Tra	1981	—	2.00	4.00
❑ 2513	Let Me Love You Till the Morning Comes/Sexy Lady	1982	—	2.00	4.00
❑ 2601	I Think It's Gonna Be Alright/Let Me Love You Till the Morning Comes	1982	—	2.00	4.00

ABC

Number	Title (A Side/B Side)	Yr	VG	VG+	NM
❑ 11378	You Can't Stop a Man in Love/You Times Me Plus Love	1973	—	2.50	5.00
❑ 12059	Smokin' Room/Signed, Sealed, Delivered, I'm Yours	1974	—	2.50	5.00
❑ 12089	Morning, Noon and Nightime/Our Day Will Come	1975	—	2.50	5.00
❑ 12166	Ain't Gonna Tell Nobody (About You)/Live for Today, Not for Tomorrow	1976	—	2.50	5.00
❑ 12226	Let's Groove/Live for Today, Not for Tomorrow	1976	—	2.50	5.00

BACK BEAT

Number	Title (A Side/B Side)	Yr	VG	VG+	NM
❑ 588	Competition Ain't Nothin'/Three Way Love	1968	—	3.00	6.00
—As "Little Carl Carlton"					
❑ 598	46 Drums — 1 Guitar/Why Don't They Leave Us Alone	1968	—	3.00	6.00
—As "Little Carl Carlton"					
❑ 603	Look at Mary Wonder (How I Got Over)/Bad for Each Other	1969	—	3.00	6.00
—As "Little Carl Carlton"					
❑ 610	Don't Walk Away/Hold On a Little Longer	1969	—	3.00	6.00
❑ 613	Drop By My Place/Two Timer	1970	—	3.00	6.00
—As "Little Carl Carlton"					
❑ 617	I Can Feel It/You've Got So Much (To Learn About Love)	1970	—	3.00	6.00
❑ 619	Sure Miss Loving You/Wild Child	1970	—	3.00	6.00
❑ 621	Wild Child/Look at Mary Wonder (How I Got Over)	1971	—	3.00	6.00
❑ 624	The Generation Gap/Where Have You Been	1972	—	3.00	6.00
❑ 627	I Won't Let That Chump Break Your Heart/Why Don't They Leave Us Alone	1972	—	3.00	6.00

C

Number	Title (A Side/B Side)	Yr	VG	VG+	NM
❏ 629	It Ain't Been Easy/I Wanna Be Your Main Squeeze	1973	—	3.00	6.00
❏ 630	Everlasting Love/I Wanna Be Your Main Squeeze	1974	2.00	4.00	8.00
❏ 27001	Everlasting Love/I Wanna Be Your Main Squeeze	1974	—	2.50	5.00

CASABLANCA

Number	Title (A Side/B Side)	Yr	VG	VG+	NM
❏ 880949-7	Private Property/Mama's Boy	1985	—	—	3.00
❏ 884274-7	Slipped, Tripped (Fooled Around and Fell in Love)/Hot	1986	—	—	3.00

GOLDEN WORLD

❏ 23	Nothin' No Sweeter Than Love/I Love True Love	1965	6.25	12.50	25.00

LANDO

❏ 8527	So What/(B-side unknown)	1965	12.50	25.00	50.00

MERCURY

❏ 73969	Something's Wrong/You, You	1977	—	2.00	4.00

RCA

❏ PB-13313	Baby I Need Your Loving/Everyone Can Be a Star	1982	—	2.00	4.00
❏ PB-13406	Swing That Sexy Thang/Just One Kiss	1982	—	2.00	4.00

Albums

20TH CENTURY

❏ T-628	Carl Carlton	1981	2.50	5.00	10.00

ABC

❏ D-857	Everlasting Love	1974	3.00	6.00	12.00
❏ D-910	I Wanna Be with You	1975	3.00	6.00	12.00

BACK BEAT

❏ BBLX-71	Can't Stop a Man in Love	1973	3.75	7.50	15.00

CASABLANCA

❏ 822705-1	Private Property	1985	2.50	5.00	10.00

RCA VICTOR

❏ AFL1-4425	The Bad C.C.	1982	2.50	5.00	10.00

CARR, GUNTER LEE
See CECIL GANT.

CARR, JAMES
45s

ATLANTIC

❏ 2803	Hold On/I'll Put It to You	1971	3.00	6.00	12.00

GOLDWAX

❏ 108	You Don't Want Me/Only Fools Run Away	1965	7.50	15.00	30.00
❏ 112	I Can't Make It/Lovers' Competition	1965	7.50	15.00	30.00
❏ 119	He's Better Than You/Talk Talk	1965	7.50	15.00	30.00
❏ 302	You've Got My Mind Messed Up/That's What I Want to Know	1966	5.00	10.00	20.00
❏ 309	Love Attack/Come Back to Me Baby	1966	3.75	7.50	15.00
❏ 311	Pouring Water on a Drowning Man/Forgetting You	1966	3.75	7.50	15.00
❏ 317	The Dark End of the Street/Lovable Girl	1967	4.00	8.00	16.00
❏ 323	Let It Happen/A Losing Game	1967	3.75	7.50	15.00
❏ 328	I'm a Fool for You/Gonna Send You Back to Georgia	1967	3.75	7.50	15.00
❏ 332	A Man Needs a Woman/Stronger Than Love	1968	3.75	7.50	15.00
❏ 335	Life Turned Her That Way/A Message to Young Lovers	1968	3.75	7.50	15.00
❏ 338	Freedom Train/That's the Way Love Turned Out for Me	1968	3.75	7.50	15.00
❏ 340	To Love Somebody/These Ain't Teardrops	1969	3.75	7.50	15.00
❏ 343	Everybody Needs Somebody/Row, Row Your Boat	1969	3.75	7.50	15.00

Albums

GOLDWAX

❏ 3001S	You Got My Mind Messed Up	1968	37.50	75.00	150.00
❏ 3002S	A Man Needs a Woman	1968	37.50	75.00	150.00

CARROLL, DELORES, AND THE FOUR TOPS
Also see THE FOUR TOPS.
45s

CHATEAU

❏ 2002	Everybody Knows/I Just Can't Keep the Tears from Tumblin' Down	1956	75.00	150.00	300.00

CARTER, CALVIN
45s

VEE JAY

❏ 419	The Roach/What'd I Say	1962	3.75	7.50	15.00
❏ 436	Twisting Bones/Crazy Little Mama Twist	1962	3.75	7.50	15.00

—As "The Cal Carter Singers"

❏ 439	Mashed Potatoes/Wimoweh	1962	3.75	7.50	15.00

Albums

VEE JAY

❏ LP-1041 [M]	Twist with Calvin Carter	1962	25.00	50.00	100.00
❏ SR-1041 [S]	Twist with Calvin Carter	1962	37.50	75.00	150.00

CARTER, CLARENCE
45s

ABC

❏ 12058	Warning/On Your Way Down	1974	—	2.00	4.00
❏ 12094	Everything Comes Up Roses/A Very Special Love Song	1975	—	2.00	4.00
❏ 12130	I Got Caught/Take It All Off	1975	—	2.00	4.00
❏ 12162	Dear Abby/Love Ain't Here No More	1976	—	2.00	4.00
❏ 12224	Heart Full of Song/All Messed Up	1976	—	2.00	4.00

ATLANTIC

❏ 2461	I Can't See Myself/Looking for a Fox	1967	—	3.00	6.00
❏ 2508	Slip Away/Funky Fever	1968	2.00	4.00	8.00
❏ 2569	Too Weak to Fight/Let Me Comfort You	1968	—	3.00	6.00
❏ 2576	Back Door Santa/That Old Time Feeling	1968	2.00	4.00	8.00
❏ 2605	Snatching It Back/Making Love	1969	—	3.00	6.00
❏ 2642	The Feeling Is Right/You Can't Miss What You Can't Measure	1969	—	3.00	6.00
❏ 2660	Doin' Our Thing/I Smell a Rat	1969	—	3.00	6.00
❏ 2702	Take It Off Him and Put It On Me/A Few Troubles I've Had	1970	—	3.00	6.00
❏ 2726	I Can't Leave Your Love Alone/Devil Woman	1970	—	3.00	6.00
❏ 2748	Patches/Say It One More Time	1970	—	3.00	6.00
❏ 2774	It's All in Your Mind/Till I Can't Take It Anymore	1970	—	3.00	6.00
❏ 2801	The Court Room/Getting the Bills	1971	—	3.00	6.00
❏ 2818	Slipped, Tripped, and Fell in Love/I Hate to Love and Run	1971	—	3.00	6.00
❏ 2842	I'm the One/Scratch My Back	1971	—	3.00	6.00
❏ 2875	If You Can't Beat 'Em/Lonesomest Lonesome	1972	—	3.00	6.00

—With Candi Carter

FAME

❏ XW179	Put On Your Shoes and Walk/I Found Somebody New	1973	—	2.50	5.00
❏ XW250	Sixty Minute Man/Mother-in-Law	1973	—	2.50	5.00
❏ XW330	I'm the Midnight Special/I Got Another Woman	1973	—	2.50	5.00
❏ XW415	Love's Trying to Come to You/Heartbreak Woman	1974	—	2.50	5.00
❏ 1010	Tell Daddy/I Stayed Away Too Long	1966	3.00	6.00	12.00
❏ 1013	Thread the Needle/Don't Make My Baby Cry	1967	3.00	6.00	12.00
❏ 1016	Road of Love/She Ain't Gonna Do Right	1967	3.00	6.00	12.00
❏ 91006	Back in Your Arms/Holdin' Out	1972	—	2.50	5.00

ICHIBAN

❏ 101	Messin' with My Mind/I Was in the Neighborhood	1986	—	—	3.00
❏ 106	If You Let Me Take You Home/So You're Leaving Me	1986	—	—	3.00
❏ 108	Strokin'/Love Me with Feelin'	1987	2.00	4.00	8.00
❏ 116	Doctor C.C./I Stayed Away Too Long	1987	—	—	3.00
❏ 131	Grandpa Can't Find His Kate/What'd I Say	1988	—	—	3.00
❏ 135	Trying to Sleep Tonight/(B-side unknown)	1988	—	—	3.00
❏ 158	I'm Just Not Good/I'm the Best	1989	—	—	3.00
❏ 164	Why Do I Stay Here and Take This Shit fro You/It's a Man Down There	1989	—	—	3.00
❏ 213	In Between a Rock and a Hard Place/Dance to the Blues	1990	—	—	3.00
❏ 222	Things Ain't Like They Used to Be/Pickin' 'Em Up, Layin' 'Em Down	1990	—	—	3.00
❏ 238	I Ain't Leaving, Girl/If You See My Lady	1991	—	—	3.00
❏ 262	"G" Spot/Hot Dog	1992	—	—	3.00
❏ 275	Hand Me Down Love/Let's Get a Quickie	1992	—	—	3.00

RONN

❏ 90	I Couldn't Refuse Your Love/What Was I Supposed to Do?	1977	—	2.50	5.00

VENTURE

❏ 130	Jimmy's Disco/Searching	1980	—	2.00	4.00
❏ 141	Let's Burn/If I Stay	1980	—	2.00	4.00
❏ 145	It's a Monster Thang/If I Were Yours	1981	—	2.00	4.00
❏ 147	Can We Slip Away Again/If I Were Yours	1981	—	2.00	4.00

7-Inch Extended Plays

ATLANTIC

❏ EP 1021 [DJ]	Bad News/Soul Deep//I Can't Do Without You/I Smell a Rat	1969	3.75	7.50	15.00

—Promo only; white label, large hole

❏ EP 1021 [PS]	Testifyin'	1969	5.00	10.00	20.00

—Promo only; white label, large hole

Albums

ABC

❏ X-833	Real	1974	3.75	7.50	15.00
❏ X-896	Loneliness & Temptation	1975	3.75	7.50	15.00
❏ X-943	A Heart Full of Song	1976	3.75	7.50	15.00

ATLANTIC

❏ SD 8192	This Is Clarence Carter	1968	7.50	15.00	30.00
❏ SD 8199	The Dynamic Clarence Carter	1969	7.50	15.00	30.00
❏ SD 8238	Testifyin'	1969	7.50	15.00	30.00
❏ SD 8267	Patches	1970	7.50	15.00	30.00
❏ SD 8282	The Best of Clarence Carter	1971	5.00	10.00	20.00

FAME

❏ FM-LA186-F	Sixty Minutes	1973	3.75	7.50	15.00

ICHIBAN

❏ ICH-1001	Messin' with My Mind	1986	3.00	6.00	12.00
❏ ICH-1003	Dr. C.C.	1986	3.00	6.00	12.00
❏ ICH-1016	Hooked on Love	1987	3.00	6.00	12.00
❏ ICH-1032	Touch of Blues	1988	3.00	6.00	12.00
❏ ICH-1068	Between a Rock and a Hard Place	1989	3.00	6.00	12.00
❏ ICH-1116	The Best of Clarence Carter: The Dr.'s Greatest Prescriptions	1991	3.00	6.00	12.00

VENTURE

❏ VL 1005	Let's Burn	1980	2.50	5.00	10.00
❏ VL 1009	Mr. Clarence Carter In Person	1981	2.50	5.00	10.00

CARTER, JAMES "SWEET LUCY"
78s

20TH CENTURY

❏ 20-51	Mean Red Spider/(B-side unknown)	1947	1000.	3000.	5000.

—Muddy Waters plays guitar on this record, his first released performance

Number	Title (A Side/B Side)	Yr	VG	VG+	NM

CARTER, MEL
45s
AMOS
| 132 | Everything Stops for a Little While/This Is My Life | 1970 | — | 3.00 | 6.00 |
| 139 | Kiss Tomorrow Goodbye/This Is My Life | 1970 | — | 3.00 | 6.00 |
ARWIN
| 123 | Sugar/I'm Coming Home | 1960 | 3.75 | 7.50 | 15.00 |
BELL
| 743 | Didn't We/I Pretend | 1968 | — | 3.00 | 6.00 |
| 775 | Another Saturday Night/Coming From You | 1969 | — | 3.00 | 6.00 |
CREAM
| 8041 | You Changed My Life Again/(B-side unknown) | 1980 | — | 2.00 | 4.00 |
| 8143 | Who's Right, Who's Wrong/I Don't Wanna Get Over You | 1981 | — | 2.00 | 4.00 |
DERBY
1003	When a Boy Falls in Love/So Wonderful	1963	3.00	6.00	12.00
1005	Time of Young Love/Wonderful Love	1963	3.00	6.00	12.00
1008	Why I Call Her Mine/After the Party, the Meeting Is Sweeter	1964	3.00	6.00	12.00
IMPERIAL
66052	'Deed I Do/What's On Your Mind	1964	2.00	4.00	8.00
66078	I'll Never Be Free/The Richest Man Alive	1964	2.00	4.00	8.00
66101	High Noon/I Just Can't Imagine	1965	2.00	4.00	8.00
66113	Hold Me, Thrill Me, Kiss Me/Sweet Little Girl	1965	2.50	5.00	10.00
66138	(All of a Sudden) My Heart Sings/When I Hold the Hand of the One I Love	1965	2.00	4.00	8.00
66148	Love Is All We Need/I Wish I Didn't Love You So	1965	2.00	4.00	8.00
66165	Band of Gold/Detour	1966	2.00	4.00	8.00
66183	You You You/If You Lose Her	1966	2.00	4.00	8.00
66208	Take Good Care of Her/Tar and Cement	1966	2.00	4.00	8.00
66228	As Time Goes By/Look to the Rainbow	1966	2.00	4.00	8.00
LIBERTY
| MLC-1 [DJ] | The Star Spangled Banner (same on both sides) | 196? | 3.00 | 6.00 | 12.00 |
| —Promo only; "This record is issued by Liberty Records as a Public Service" on label |
55970	Edelweiss/For Once in My Life	1968	—	3.00	6.00
55987	Star Dust/Enter Laughing	1967	—	3.00	6.00
56000	Be My Love/Look Into My Love	1967	—	3.00	6.00
56015	Excuse Me/The Other Woman	1968	—	3.00	6.00
PRIVATE STOCK
| 45057 | Put a Little Love Away/Dancing for Dimes | 1975 | — | 2.00 | 4.00 |
| 45087 | My Coloring Book | 1976 | — | 2.00 | 4.00 |
ROMAR
711	She Is Me/Do Me Wrong, But Do Me	1973	—	2.00	4.00
714	Treasure of Love/Do Me Wrong, But Do Me	1973	—	2.00	4.00
716	I Only Have Eyes for You/Treasure of Love	1974	—	2.00	4.00
Albums
AMOS
| 7010 | This Is My Life | 1971 | 3.00 | 6.00 | 12.00 |
DERBY
| LPM-702 [M] | When a Boy Falls in Love | 1963 | 75.00 | 150.00 | 300.00 |
IMPERIAL
LP-9289 [M]	Hold Me, Thrill Me, Kiss Me	1965	3.75	7.50	15.00
LP-9300 [M]	All of a Sudden My Heart Sings	1966	3.75	7.50	15.00
LP-9319 [M]	Easy Listening	1966	3.75	7.50	15.00
LP-12289 [S]	Hold Me, Thrill Me, Kiss Me	1965	5.00	10.00	20.00
LP-12300 [S]	All of a Sudden My Heart Sings	1966	5.00	10.00	20.00
LP-12319 [S]	Easy Listening	1966	5.00	10.00	20.00
SUNSET
| SUS-5227 | Mel Carter | 1968 | 2.50 | 5.00 | 10.00 |
| SUS-5295 | Easy Goin' | 1970 | 2.50 | 5.00 | 10.00 |

CASTELLES, THE
45s
ATCO
| 6069 | Happy and Gay/Hey Baby Baby | 1956 | 25.00 | 50.00 | 100.00 |
CLASSIC ARTISTS
| 114 | At Christmas Time/One Little Teardrop | 1989 | — | 2.00 | 4.00 |
GRAND
| 101 | My Girl Awaits Me/Sweetness | 1954 | 500.00 | 1000. | 2000. |
| —Blue label original |
| 103 | This Silver Ring/Wonder Why | 1954 | 500.00 | 1000. | 2000. |
| —Glossy yellow label original |
| 105 | Do You Remember/If You Were the Only Girl | 1954 | 375.00 | 750.00 | 1500. |
| —Glossy yellow label original |
| 109 | Baby Can't You See/Over a Cup of Coffee | 1954 | 500.00 | 1000. | 2000. |
| —Blue label original |
| 114 | Marcella/I'm a Fool to Care | 1955 | 400.00 | 800.00 | 1200. |
| —Cream label original |
| 122 | My Wedding Day/Heavenly Father | 1955 | 1750. | 3500. | 7000. |
| —Cream label original |
Albums
COLLECTABLES
| COL-5002 | The Sweet Sounds of the Castelles | 198? | 3.00 | 6.00 | 12.00 |

CASTELLS, THE
45s
BLACK GOLD
| 306 | Save a Chance/Children Who Dream | 196? | 2.00 | 4.00 | 8.00 |
DECCA
| 31834 | Just Walk Away/An Angel Cried | 1965 | 3.75 | 7.50 | 15.00 |
| 31967 | Life Goes On/I Thought You'd Like That | 1966 | 3.75 | 7.50 | 15.00 |
ERA
3038	Little Sad Eyes/Romeo	1961	6.25	12.50	25.00
3048	Sacred/I Get Dreamy	1961	6.25	12.50	25.00
3057	My Miracle/Make Believe Wedding	1961	5.00	10.00	20.00
3064	The Vision of You/Stiki De Boom Boom	1961	5.00	10.00	20.00
3073	So This Is Love/On the Street of Tears	1962	5.00	10.00	20.00
3083	Oh, What It Seemed to Be/Stand There, Mountain	1962	5.00	10.00	20.00
3089	Echoes in the Night/The Only One	1962	5.00	10.00	20.00
3098	Clown Prince/Eternal Spring, Eternal Love	1962	5.00	10.00	20.00
3102	Little Sad Eyes/Initials	1963	5.00	10.00	20.00
3107	Some Enchanted Evening/What Do Little Girls Dream Of	1963	5.00	10.00	20.00
LAURIE
| 3444 | I'd Like to Know/Rocky Ridges | 1968 | 2.50 | 5.00 | 10.00 |
UNITED ARTISTS
| 50324 | Two Lovers/Jerusalem | 1968 | 2.50 | 5.00 | 10.00 |
WARNER BROS.
| 5421 | I Do/Teardrops | 1964 | 20.00 | 40.00 | 80.00 |
| —A-side written and produced by Brian Wilson |
| 5445 | Could This Be Magic/Shinny Up Your Own Side | 1964 | 7.50 | 15.00 | 30.00 |
| 5486 | Love Finds a Way/Tell Her If I Could | 1964 | 5.00 | 10.00 | 20.00 |
Albums
ERA
| EL-109 [M] | So This Is Love | 1962 | 30.00 | 60.00 | 120.00 |
| ES-109 [S] | So This Is Love | 1962 | 100.00 | 200.00 | 400.00 |

CASTOR, JIMMY, BUNCH
12-Inch Singles
CATAWBA
| 4Z9-05299 | Godzilla (Vocal 4:28) (Instrumental) | 1985 | 2.00 | 4.00 | 8.00 |
COTILLION
DSKO 183 [DJ]	Don't Do That! (7:08) (same on both sides)	1979	3.75	7.50	15.00
DSKO 206 [DJ]	Party People (6:30) (same on both sides)	1979	5.00	10.00	20.00
DK 4731	Don't Do That! (7:08)/Psych-Out (6:55)	1979	5.00	10.00	20.00
DREAM
| DG 707 | Amazon (Long Version 5:45) (Short Version 3:45) (Dub 7:30) (Bonus Acapella 1:45) | 1984 | 5.00 | 10.00 | 20.00 |
| DG 708 | It Gets to Me (Vocal 6:33) (Short Version 3:45) (Dub 6:30) (Bonus Beats Acapella 2:15) | 1984 | 3.75 | 7.50 | 15.00 |
SALSOUL
| SG 361 | E-Man Boogie/Any Way, Any Where, Any Time | 1982 | 3.75 | 7.50 | 15.00 |
45s
ATLANTIC
3011	Maggie (Part 1)/Maggie (Part 2)	1974	—	2.50	5.00
3045	Everything Man (E-Man)/Heaven Kissed	1974	—	2.50	5.00
3232	The Bertha Butt Boogie (Part 1)/The Bertha Butt Boogie (Part 2)	1975	—	2.50	5.00
3270	Potential/Daniel	1975	—	2.50	5.00
3295	King Kong (Part 1)/King Kong (Part 2)	1975	—	2.50	5.00
3302	The Christmas Song (Chestnuts Roasting on an Open Fire)/Merry Christmas	1975	—	3.50	7.00
3316	Supersound/Drifting	1976	—	2.00	4.00
3331	Bom Bom/What's Best	1976	—	2.00	4.00
3362	Everything Is Beautiful to Me/The Magic Is in the Music	1976	—	2.00	4.00
3369 [DJ]	I Don't Wanna Lose You (mono/stereo)	1976	—	2.50	5.00
—May be promo-only
3375	Space Age/Dracula	1976	—	2.00	4.00
3396	I Love a Mellow Groove/I Don't Want to Lose You	1977	—	2.00	4.00
3424	The Return of Leroy (Part 1)/The Return of Leroy (Part 2)	1977	—	2.00	4.00
3451	Magnolia/TR-7	1978	—	2.00	4.00
3455	Maximum Stimulation/It Was You	1978	—	2.00	4.00
ATOMIC
| 100 | Somebody Mentioned Your Name/This Girl of Mine | 1957 | 125.00 | 250.00 | 500.00 |
CAPITOL
2358	Hey Shorty (Part 1)/Hey Shorty (Part 2)	1968	2.00	4.00	8.00
2487	Psycho Man/The Real McCoy	1969	2.00	4.00	8.00
2634	Helpless/Make Me	1969	2.00	4.00	8.00
CATAWBA
| ZS4-05676 | Godzilla/(Instrumental) | 1985 | — | 2.00 | 4.00 |
COMPASS
| 7019 | Soul Sister/Rattlesnake | 1968 | 2.00 | 4.00 | 8.00 |
COTILLION
| 44253 | Don't Do That!/Don't Do That! (Part 2) | 1979 | — | 2.00 | 4.00 |
| 45004 | Party People/I Just Wanna Stop | 1979 | — | 2.00 | 4.00 |
DECCA
| 31963 | In a Boogaloo Bag (Part 1)/In a Boogaloo Bag (Part 2) | 1966 | 2.50 | 5.00 | 10.00 |
DREAM
D7-0359	Don't Cry Out Loud/(Instrumental)	1983	—	2.50	5.00
D7-0360	Amazon/She's an Amazon	1984	—	2.50	5.00
D 70361	It Gets to Me/(Instrumental)	1984	—	2.50	5.00
DRIVE
| 6271 | Bertha Butt Encounters Vadar/Mystery of Me | 1978 | — | 2.00 | 4.00 |
| 6276 | You Light Up My Life/Let It Out | 1978 | — | 2.00 | 4.00 |
HULL
| 758 | Poor Loser/Oh Suzzana | 1963 | 5.00 | 10.00 | 20.00 |
LONG DISTANCE
| 702 | Can't Help Falling in Love with You/Stay with Me (Spend the Night) | 1980 | — | 2.50 | 5.00 |
RCA VICTOR
| 48-1024 | Say Leroy (The Creature from the Black Lagoon Is Your Father) (Parts 1 & 2) | 1972 | — | 2.50 | 5.00 |

Number	Title (A Side/B Side)	Yr	VG	VG+	NM
❏ 48-1029	Troglodyte (Cave Man)/I Promise to Remember	1972	—	3.00	6.00
❏ 74-0583	My Brightest Day/You Better Be Good	1971	—	2.50	5.00
❏ 74-0763	Luther the Anthropod/Party Life	1972	—	2.50	5.00
❏ 74-0836	Paradise/The First Time Ever I Saw Your Face	1972	—	2.50	5.00
❏ 74-0953	Soul Serenade/Purple Haze-Foxey Lady (Tribute to Jimi Hendrix)	1973		2.50	5.00
❏ APBO-0047	How Beautiful You Are/I'm Not a Child Anymore	1973	—	2.50	5.00
❏ AMBO-0120	Troglodyte (Cave Man)/Luther the Anthropod	1973	—	2.00	4.00
—*Gold Standard Series*					

SALSOUL

❏ 7018	E-Man Boogie/Any Way, Any Where, Any Time	1982	—	2.00	4.00
❏ 7058	E-Man Boogie '83/It's Just Begun	1983	—	2.00	4.00

SMASH

❏ 2069	Hey, Leroy, Your Mama's Calling You/Ham Hocks Espanol	1966	2.00	4.00	8.00
❏ 2085	Just You Girl/Magic Saxophone	1967	2.00	4.00	8.00
❏ 2099	Leroy Is In the Army/Dry	1967	2.00	4.00	8.00
❏ 2120	Jamaica Farewell/Mini-Sonata	1967	2.00	4.00	8.00

WING

❏ 90078	I Promise/I Know the Meaning of Love	1956	30.00	60.00	120.00

Albums

ATLANTIC

❏ SD 7305	The Everything Man	1974	2.50	5.00	10.00
❏ SD 18124	Butt Of Course	1975	2.50	5.00	10.00
❏ SD 18150	Supersound	1975	2.50	5.00	10.00
❏ SD 18186	E-Man Groovin'	1976	2.50	5.00	10.00
❏ SD 19111	Maximum Stimulation	1977	2.50	5.00	10.00

COTILLION

❏ SD 5215	The Jimmy Castor Bunch	1979	3.00	6.00	12.00

DRIVE

❏ 407	Let It Out	1978	3.00	6.00	12.00

LONG DISTANCE

❏ 1201	C	1980	3.00	6.00	12.00

RCA VICTOR

❏ APD1-0103	[Q]Dimension III	1973	5.00	10.00	20.00
❏ APL1-0103	Dimension III	1973	3.75	7.50	15.00
❏ APL1-0313	The Everything Man	1974	3.75	7.50	15.00
❏ LSP-4640	It's Just Begun	1972	3.75	7.50	15.00
❏ LSP-4783	Phase Two	1972	3.75	7.50	15.00

SMASH

❏ MGS-27091	[M]Hey Leroy!	1967	10.00	20.00	40.00
❏ SRS-67091	[S]Hey Leroy!	1967	10.00	20.00	40.00

CATHY JEAN AND THE ROOMATES
Also see THE ROOMATES.

45s

PHILIPS

❏ 40106	My Heart Belongs to Only You/I Only Want You	1963	5.00	10.00	20.00
—*As "Cathy Jean"*					
❏ 40143	Double Trouble/Believe Me	1963	5.00	10.00	20.00
—*As "Cathy Jean"*					

VALMOR

❏ 007	Please Love Me Forever/Canadian Sunset	1961	6.25	12.50	25.00
—*Red label*					
❏ 007	Please Love Me Forever/Canadian Sunset	1961	3.75	7.50	15.00
—*Black label*					
❏ 007 [PS]	Please Love Me Forever/Canadian Sunset	1961	17.50	35.00	70.00
—*Sleeve is promo only*					
❏ 009	Make Me Smile Again/Sugar Cake	1961	6.25	12.50	25.00
❏ 011	I Only Want You/One Love	1961	5.00	10.00	20.00
❏ 016	Please Tell Me/Sugar Cake	1962	5.00	10.00	20.00

Albums

VALMOR

❏ 78 [M]	Great Oldies	1962	200.00	400.00	800.00
—*Reissue of 789 with titles on cover and no group shot*					
❏ 789 [M]	At the Hop!	1961	225.00	450.00	900.00

CHAIRMEN OF THE BOARD

45s

INVICTUS

❏ 1251	Finder's Keepers/Finder's Keepers (Part 2)	1973	—	2.50	5.00
❏ 1263	Life & Death/Love with Me, Love with Me	1974	—	2.50	5.00
❏ 1268	Everybody Party All Night/Morning Glory	1974	—	2.50	5.00
❏ 1271	Let's Have Some Fun/Love at First Sight	1974	—	2.50	5.00
❏ 1276	The Skin I'm In/Love at First Sight	1975	—	2.50	5.00
❏ 1278	You've Got Extra Added Power in Your Love/Someone Just Like You	1975	—	2.50	5.00
❏ 9074	Give Me Just a Little More Time/Since the Days of Pigtails	1970	—	3.00	6.00
❏ 9078	(You've Got Me) Dangling on a String/I'll Come Crawling	1970	—	2.50	5.00
❏ 9079	Everything's Tuesday/Patches	1970	—	2.50	5.00
❏ 9081	Pay to the Piper/Bless You	1970	—	2.50	5.00
❏ 9081 [PS]	Pay to the Piper/Bless You	1970	2.50	5.00	10.00
❏ 9086	Chairman of the Board/When Will She Tell Me She Needs Me	1971	—	2.50	5.00
❏ 9089	Hanging On (To) A Memory/Tracked and Trapped	1971	—	2.50	5.00
❏ 9099	Try On My Love for Size/Working on a Building of Love	1971	—	2.50	5.00
❏ 9103	Men Are Getting Scarce/Bravo! Hurray!	1971	—	2.50	5.00
❏ 9106	Bittersweet/Elmo James	1972	—	2.50	5.00
❏ 9122	Everybody's Got a Song to Sing/Working on a Building of Love	1972	—	2.50	5.00
❏ 9126	Let Me Down Easy/I Can't Find Myself	1972	—	2.50	5.00

Albums

INVICTUS

❏ ST-7300	Chairmen of the Board (Featuring "Give Me Just a Little More Time")	1970	10.00	20.00	40.00
❏ SKAO-7304	In Session	1970	10.00	20.00	40.00
❏ ST-9801	Bittersweet	1972	10.00	20.00	40.00
❏ KZ 32526	The Skin I'm In	1974	10.00	20.00	40.00

CHAMBERLAIN, WILT "THE STILT"

45s

END

❏ 1066	By the River/That's Easy to Say	1960	6.25	12.50	25.00

CHAMBERS BROTHERS, THE

45s

AVCO

❏ 4632	Let's Go, Let's Go, Let's Go/Do You Believe in Magic	1974	—	2.00	4.00
❏ 4638	1-2-3/Looking Back	1974	—	2.00	4.00
❏ 4657	Miss Lady Brown/Stealin' Watermelons	1975	—	2.00	4.00

COLUMBIA

❏ 4-43816	Time Has Come Today (2:37)/Dinah	1966	3.00	6.00	12.00
—*A-side is a different recording than the later hit, both vocally and instrumentally*					
❏ 43957	All Strung Out Over You/Falling in Love	1967	—	3.00	6.00
❏ 44080	Please Don't Leave Me/I Can't Stand It	1967	—	3.00	6.00
❏ 44296	Uptown/Love Me Like the Rain	1967	—	3.00	6.00
❏ 4-44414	Time Has Come Today (4:45)/People Get Ready	1968	2.00	4.00	8.00
—*Hit version; label refers to the album "The Time Has Come"*					
❏ 4-44414	Time Has Come Today (3:05)/People Get Ready	1968	2.50	5.00	10.00
—*No reference to the album "The Time Has Come"; despite the listed time, this plays the 4:45 hit version (master number in trail-off ends in "3B"); we're not sure if stock copies list 3:05 and play 3:05, too*					
❏ 4-44414 [DJ]	Time Has Come Today (3:05) (same on both sides)	1968	3.75	7.50	15.00
—*"Special Rush Reservice" on label; this plays a 3:05 edit of the long LP version (master numbers in trail-off end in "1B" on one side and "1F" on the other)*					
❏ 44679	I Can't Turn You Loose/Do Your Thing	1968	—	3.00	6.00
❏ 44679 [PS]	I Can't Turn You Loose/Do Your Thing	1968	2.50	5.00	10.00
❏ 44779	Are You Ready/You Got the Power to Turn Me On	1969	—	3.00	6.00
❏ 44890	Wake Up/Everybody Needs Someone	1969	—	3.00	6.00
❏ 44986	Have a Little Faith/Baby Takes Care of Business	1969	—	2.50	5.00
❏ 4-45055	Merry Christmas, Happy New Year/Did You Stop to Pray This Morning	1969	—	3.00	6.00
❏ 45088	Love, Peace and Happiness/If You Want Me To	1970	—	2.50	5.00
❏ 45146	To Love Somebody/Let's Do It	1970	—	2.50	5.00
❏ 45277	Love, Peace and Happiness/Funky	1970	—	2.50	5.00
❏ 45394	When the Evening Comes/New Generation	1971	—	2.50	5.00
❏ 45488	Heaven/(By the Hair on) My Chinny Chin Chin	1971	—	3.00	6.00
❏ 45518	Merry Christmas, Happy New Year/Did You Stop to Pray This Morning	1971	—	3.00	6.00
❏ 45837	Boogie Children/You Make the Magic	1973	—	3.00	6.00

ROXBURY

❏ 2034	Bring It On Down Front Pretty Mama/Midnight Blue	1976	—	2.50	5.00

VAULT

❏ 920	Call Me/Seventeen	1965	3.75	7.50	15.00
❏ 923	Pretty Girls Everywhere/Love Me Like the Rain	1966	3.00	6.00	12.00
❏ 945	Shout Part 1/Shout Part 2	1968	2.00	4.00	8.00
❏ 955	Just a Closer Walk with Thee/Girls We Love You	1969	—	3.00	6.00
❏ 967	House of the Rising Sun/Blues Get Off My Shoulder	1970	—	3.00	6.00

Albums

AVCO

❏ 11013	Unbonded	1974	3.00	6.00	12.00
❏ 69003	Night Move	1975	5.00	10.00	20.00

COLUMBIA

❏ KGP 20 [(2)]	Love, Peace and Happiness	1969	6.25	12.50	25.00
❏ CL 2722 [M]	The Time Has Come	1967	7.50	15.00	30.00
❏ CS 9522	The Time Has Come	1971	3.00	6.00	12.00
—*Orange label*					
❏ CS 9522 [S]	The Time Has Come	1967	5.00	10.00	20.00
—*Red "360 Sound" label*					
❏ PC 9522	The Time Has Come	198?	2.00	4.00	8.00
—*Reissue with new prefix*					
❏ CS 9671	A New Time — A New Day	1968	5.00	10.00	20.00
❏ C 30032	New Generation	1970	3.75	7.50	15.00
❏ C 30871	The Chambers Brothers' Greatest Hits	1971	3.75	7.50	15.00
❏ PC 30871	The Chambers Brothers' Greatest Hits	198?	2.00	4.00	8.00
—*Reissue with new prefix*					
❏ KC 31158	Oh My God	1972	—	—	—
—*Canceled*					
❏ CG 33642 [(2)]	The Time Has Come/A New Time — A New Day	1975	3.75	7.50	15.00

FANTASY

❏ 24718 [(2)]	The Best of the Chambers Brothers	1973	3.75	7.50	15.00

FOLKWAYS

❏ 31008	Groovin' Time	1968	3.75	7.50	15.00

ROXBURY

❏ RLX-106	Live In Concert on Mars	1976	7.50	15.00	30.00

VAULT

❏ LP-115 [M]	The Chambers Brothers Now	1967	3.75	7.50	15.00
❏ VS-115 [S]	The Chambers Brothers Now	1967	3.75	7.50	15.00
❏ VS-120	The Chambers Brothers Shout	1968	3.75	7.50	15.00
❏ VS-128	Feelin' the Blues	1969	3.75	7.50	15.00

C

Number	Title (A Side/B Side)	Yr	VG	VG+	NM
❑ VS-135 [(2)]	The Chambers Brothers Greatest Hits	1970	5.00	10.00	20.00
❑ LP-9003 [M]	People Get Ready	1966	5.00	10.00	20.00
❑ LPS-9003 [S]	People Get Ready	1966	6.25	12.50	25.00

CHAMPLAINS, THE
FRED PARRIS of THE FIVE SATINS is the lead voice.
45s
UNITED ARTISTS

❑ 346	Ding Dong/Have You Changed Your Mind	1961	10.00	20.00	40.00

CHANCE, NOLAN
45s
BUNKY

❑ 161	Just Like the Weather/(B-side unknown)	1965	300.00	600.00	1200.
CONSTELLATION
❑ 144	She's Gone/If He Makes You	1965	6.25	12.50	25.00
❑ 161	Don't Use Me/Just Like the Weather	1965	30.00	60.00	120.00

CHANDLER, DENIECE
See DENIECE WILLIAMS.

CHANDLER, GENE
Includes records as "The Duke of Earl." Also see THE DUKAYS.
12-Inch Singles
20TH CENTURY

❑ TCD 80	When You're #1 (8:59)/I'll Remember You	1979	5.00	10.00	20.00
❑ TCD 98	Do What Comes So Natural (5:00)/That Funky Disco Rhythm (5:39)	1979	3.75	7.50	15.00
CHI-SOUND
❑ TCD 68	Get Down (8:14) (same on both sides)	1978	3.75	7.50	15.00
❑ TCD 73	Get Down/Contact	1979	3.75	7.50	15.00
—B-side by Edwin Starr					
❑ TCD 110	Does She Have a Friend?/Let Me Make Love to You	1980	2.50	5.00	10.00
❑ CH-2001	I'll Make the Living If You Make the Loving Worthwhile (Disco Version 6:10)/Time Is a Thief	1982	3.75	7.50	15.00

45s
20TH CENTURY

❑ 2411	When You're #1/I'll Remember You	1979	—	2.00	4.00
❑ 2428	Do What Comes So Natural/That Funky Disco Rhythm	1979	—	2.00	4.00
BRUNSWICK
❑ 55312	Girl Don't Care/My Love	1967	2.00	4.00	8.00
❑ 55339	There Goes the Lover/Tell Me What I Can Do	1967	2.00	4.00	8.00
❑ 55383	There Was a Time/Those Were the Good Old Days	1968	2.00	4.00	8.00
❑ 55394	Teacher, Teacher/Pit of Loneliness	1968	2.00	4.00	8.00
❑ 55413	Eleanor Rigby/Familiar Footsteps	1969	2.00	4.00	8.00
❑ 55425	This Bitter Earth/Suicide	1969	2.00	4.00	8.00
CHECKER
❑ 1155	I Fooled You This Time/Such a Pretty Thing	1966	2.00	4.00	8.00
❑ 1165	To Be a Lover/After the Laughter	1967	2.00	4.00	8.00
❑ 1190	I Won't Need You/No Peace, No Satisfaction	1967	2.00	4.00	8.00
❑ 1199	River of Tears/It's Time to Settle Down	1968	2.00	4.00	8.00
❑ 1220	Go Back Home/In My Baby's House	1969	2.00	4.00	8.00
CHI-SOUND
❑ 1001	I'll Make the Living If You Make the Loving Worthwhile/(B-side unknown)	1982	—	2.50	5.00
❑ 1168	Give Me the Cue/Tomorrow We May Not Feel the Same	1978	—	2.00	4.00
❑ 2386	Get Down/I'm the Traveling Kind	1978	—	2.00	4.00
❑ 2404	Please Sunrise/Greatest Love Ever Known	1979	—	2.00	4.00
❑ 2411	When You're #1/I'll Remember You	1979	—	2.50	5.00
❑ 2451	Does She Have a Friend?/Let Me Make Love to You	1980	—	2.00	4.00
❑ 2468	Lay Me Gently/You've Been So Good to Me	1980	—	2.00	4.00
❑ 2480	Rainbow '80/I'll Be There	1980	—	2.00	4.00
❑ 2494	I'm Attracted to You/I've Got to Meet You	1981	—	2.00	4.00
❑ 2507	Love Is the Answer/Godsend	1981	—	2.00	4.00
CONSTELLATION
❑ 104	From Day to Day/It's No Good for Me	1963	2.50	5.00	10.00
❑ 110	Pretty Little Girl/A Little Like Lovin'	1963	2.50	5.00	10.00
❑ 112	Think Nothing About It/Wish You Were Here	1964	2.50	5.00	10.00
❑ 114	Soul Hootenanny (Part 1)/Soul Hootenanny (Part 2)	1964	2.50	5.00	10.00
❑ 124	A Song Called Soul/You Left Me	1964	2.50	5.00	10.00
❑ 130	Just Be True/A Song Called Soul	1964	2.50	5.00	10.00
❑ 136	Bless Our Love/London Town	1964	2.50	5.00	10.00
❑ 141	What Now/If You Can't Help It	1964	2.50	5.00	10.00
❑ 146	You Can't Hurt Me No More/Everybody Let's Dance	1965	2.00	4.00	8.00
❑ 149	Nothing Can Stop Me/The Big Lie	1965	2.00	4.00	8.00
❑ 158	Rainbow '65 (Part 1)/Rainbow '65 (Part 2)	1965	2.00	4.00	8.00
❑ 160	Good Times/No One Can Love You	1965	2.00	4.00	8.00
❑ 164	Here Come the Tears/Soul Hootenanny (Part 2)	1965	2.00	4.00	8.00
❑ 166	Baby That's Love/Bet You Never Thought	1966	2.00	4.00	8.00
❑ 167	(I'm Just a) Fool for You/Buddy Ain't It a Shame	1966	2.00	4.00	8.00
❑ 169	I Can Take Care of Myself/If I Can't Save It	1966	2.00	4.00	8.00
❑ 172	Mr. Big Shot/I Hate to Be the One to Say	1966	2.00	4.00	8.00
CURTOM
❑ 1979	Don't Have to Be Lyin' Babe (Part 1)/Don't Have to Be Lyin' Babe (Part 2)	1973	—	2.50	5.00
❑ 1986	Baby I Still Love You/I Understand	1973	—	2.50	5.00
❑ 1992	Without You Here/Just Be There	1973	—	2.50	5.00

FASTFIRE

❑ 7003	Haven't I Heard That Line Before/You'll Never Be Free of Me	1985	—	2.50	5.00
❑ 7005	Lucy/Please You Tonight	1986	—	2.50	5.00
MERCURY
❑ 73083	Groovy Situation/Not the Marrying Kind	1970	—	3.00	6.00
❑ 73121	Simply Call It Love/Give Me a Chance	1970	—	3.00	6.00
❑ 73206	You're a Lady/Stone Cold Feeling	1971	—	3.00	6.00
❑ 73258	Yes I'm Ready (If I Don't Get to Go)/Pillars of Glass	1971	—	3.00	6.00
SALSOUL
❑ 7051	You're the One/I Keep Comin' Back for More	1983	—	2.00	4.00
—With Jaime Lynn					
VEE JAY
❑ 416	Duke of Earl/Kissin' in the Kitchen	1961	6.25	12.50	25.00
❑ 416	Duke of Earl/Kissin' in the Kitchen	1962	5.00	10.00	20.00
—Some later pressings as "The Duke of Earl"					
❑ 440	Walk On with the Duke/London Town	1962	3.75	7.50	15.00
—As "The Duke of Earl"					
❑ 450	Daddy's Home/The Big Lie	1962	3.75	7.50	15.00
—As "The Duke of Earl"					
❑ 455	I'll Follow You/You Left Me	1962	3.75	7.50	15.00
—As "The Duke of Earl"					
❑ 461	Tear for Tear/Miracle After Miracle	1962	3.75	7.50	15.00
❑ 468	You Threw a Lucky Punch/Rainbow	1962	3.75	7.50	15.00
❑ 511	Check Yourself/Forgive Me	1963	3.75	7.50	15.00
❑ 536	Baby, That's Love/Man's Temptation	1963	3.75	7.50	15.00
Albums
20TH CENTURY
❑ T-598	When You're #1	1979	2.50	5.00	10.00
❑ T-605	Gene Chandler '80	1980	2.50	5.00	10.00
❑ T-625	Ear Candy	1980	2.50	5.00	10.00
❑ T-629	Here's to Love	1981	2.50	5.00	10.00
BRUNSWICK
❑ BL 54124 [M]	The Girl Don't Care	1967	6.25	12.50	25.00
❑ BL 754124 [S]	The Girl Don't Care	1967	5.00	10.00	20.00
❑ BL 754131	There Was a Time	1968	5.00	10.00	20.00
❑ BL 754149	The Two Sides of Gene Chandler	1969	5.00	10.00	20.00
CHECKER
❑ LP-3003 [M]	The Duke of Soul	1967	12.50	25.00	50.00
❑ LPS-3003 [R]	The Duke of Soul	1967	7.50	15.00	30.00
CHI-SOUND
❑ T-578	Get Down	1978	2.50	5.00	10.00
CONSTELLATION
❑ LP 1421 [M]	Greatest Hits by Gene Chandler	1964	12.50	25.00	50.00
❑ LP 1423 [M]	Just Be True	1964	12.50	25.00	50.00
❑ LP 1425 [M]	Gene Chandler — Live On Stage in '65	1965	12.50	25.00	50.00
MERCURY
❑ SR-61304	The Gene Chandler Situation	1970	3.75	7.50	15.00
SOLID SMOKE
❑ SS-8027	Stroll On with the Duke	198?	2.50	5.00	10.00
VEE JAY
❑ LP-1040 [M]	The Duke of Earl	1962	30.00	60.00	120.00
❑ SR-1040 [M]	The Duke of Earl	196?	12.50	25.00	50.00
—"Stereophonic" on front; no "Important Notice..." on back; record plays mono. Most labels are all-black with "VJ" in brackets. This was a semi-authorized reissue after ex-Vee Jay executives bought the company's remnants in bankruptcy court in 1966.					
❑ SR-1040 [S]	The Duke of Earl	1962	200.00	400.00	800.00
—"Stereophonic" on front cover; top back cover contains note that begins: "Important Notice...This is a Stereophonic Record"; "Stereo" on record labels					
❑ SR-1040 [S]	The Duke of Earl	1962	62.50	125.00	250.00
—"Stereo" sticker on mono cover; "Stereo" on record labels					
❑ VJLP-1040	The Duke of Earl	198?	2.50	5.00	10.00
—Mid-1980s authorized reissue					

CHANDLER, GENE, AND BARBARA ACKLIN
Also see each artist's individual listings.
45s
BRUNSWICK

❑ 55366	Love Won't Start/Show Me the Way to Go	1968	2.00	4.00	8.00
❑ 55387	From the Teacher to the Preacher/Anywhere But Nowhere	1968	2.00	4.00	8.00
❑ 55405	Little Green Apples/Will I Find You	1969	2.00	4.00	8.00

CHANDLER, GENE, AND JERRY BUTLER
Also see each artist's individual listings.
45s
MERCURY

❑ 73163	You Just Can't Win (By Making the Same Mistake)/The Show Is Grooving	1971	—	3.00	6.00
❑ 73195	Two and Two (Take This Woman Off the Corner)/Everybody Is Waiting	1971	—	3.00	6.00
Albums
MERCURY
| ❑ SR-61330 | Gene & Jerry — One & One | 1971 | 3.75 | 7.50 | 15.00 |

CHANNELS, THE (1)
Group led by Earl Lewis.
45s
CHANNEL

❑ 1000	Gloria/You Said You Loved Me	1971	2.50	5.00	10.00
❑ 1001	We Belong Together/Hey Girl, I'm in Love with You	1972	2.50	5.00	10.00
❑ 1002	You Got What It Takes/Crazy Mixed-Up World	1972	2.50	5.00	10.00

Number	Title (A Side/B Side)	Yr	VG	VG+	NM
❑ 1003	Close Your Eyes/Work with Me Annie	1973	2.50	5.00	10.00
❑ 1004	Over Again/In My Arms to Stay	1973	2.50	5.00	10.00
❑ 1006	A Thousand Miles Away/Don't Let the Green Grass Fool You	1974	2.50	5.00	10.00
FIRE					
❑ 1001	My Heart Is Sad/The Girl Next Door	1959	12.50	25.00	50.00
—As "Earl Lewis and the Channels"					
FURY					
❑ 1021	Bye Bye Baby/My Love Will Never Die	1959	12.50	25.00	50.00
❑ 1071	Bye Bye Baby/My Love Will Never Die	1963	10.00	20.00	40.00
GONE					
❑ 5012	That's My Desire/Stay As You Are	1957	15.00	30.00	60.00
❑ 5019	Altar of Love/All Alone	1957	15.00	30.00	60.00
PORT					
❑ 70014	The Closer You Are/Now You Know	1960	6.25	12.50	25.00
—Reissue of Whirlin' Disc 100					
❑ 70017	The Gleam in Your Eyes/Stars in the Sky	1960	6.25	12.50	25.00
—Reissue of Whirlin' Disc 102					
❑ 70022	Flames in My Heart/My Lovin' Baby	1961	6.25	12.50	25.00
—Reissue of Whirlin' Disc 109					
❑ 70023	I Really Love You/What Do You Do	1961	6.25	12.50	25.00
—Reissue of Whirlin' Disc 107					
RARE BIRD					
❑ 5017	She Blew My Mind/Breaking Up Is Hard to Do	1971	2.50	5.00	10.00
WHIRLIN' DISC					
❑ 100	The Closer You Are/Now You Know	1956	62.50	125.00	250.00
—Block-letter label name; publisher listed as "Bob-Dan Music"					
❑ 100	The Closer You Are/Now You Know	1956	50.00	100.00	200.00
—Block-letter label name; publisher listed as "Spinning Wheel Music"					
❑ 100	The Closer You Are/Now You Know	1956	25.00	50.00	100.00
—Label name is all caps, but not in block letters					
❑ 102	The Gleam in Your Eyes/Stars in the Sky	1956	50.00	100.00	200.00
❑ 107	I Really Love You/What Do You Do	1957	50.00	100.00	200.00
❑ 109	Flames in My Heart/My Lovin' Baby	1957	50.00	100.00	200.00
Albums					
COLLECTABLES					
❑ COL-5012	New York's Finest: The Best of Earl Lewis and the Channels	198?	3.00	6.00	12.00
LOST-NITE					
❑ LLP-15 [10]	The Channels	1981	3.00	6.00	12.00
—Red vinyl					
❑ LLP-16 [10]	The Channels	1981	3.00	6.00	12.00
—Red vinyl					

CHANTELS, THE

Also see ARLENE SMITH; THE VENEERS.

45s

Number	Title (A Side/B Side)	Yr	VG	VG+	NM
CARLTON					
❑ 555	Look in My Eyes/Glad to Be Back	1961	5.00	10.00	20.00
❑ 564	Still/Well, I Told You	1961	5.00	10.00	20.00
❑ 569	Summertime/Here It Comes Again	1962	5.00	10.00	20.00
END					
❑ 1001	He's Gone/The Plea	1957	20.00	40.00	80.00
—Black label					
❑ 1005	Maybe/Come My Little Baby	1957	20.00	40.00	80.00
—Black label					
❑ 1005	Maybe/Come My Little Baby	1958	10.00	20.00	40.00
—Gray (white) label					
❑ 1005	Maybe/Come My Little Baby	1959	5.00	10.00	20.00
—Multi-color label					
❑ 1015	Every Night/Whoever You Are	1958	7.50	15.00	30.00
—Gray (white) label					
❑ 1015	Every Night/Whoever You Are	1959	5.00	10.00	20.00
—Multi-color label					
❑ 1020	I Love You So/How Could You Call It Off	1958	10.00	20.00	40.00
❑ 1026	Prayer/Sure of Love	1958	6.25	12.50	25.00
❑ 1030	If You Try/Congratulations	1958	6.25	12.50	25.00
❑ 1037	Never Let Go/I Can't Take It	1959	6.25	12.50	25.00
❑ 1048	I'm Confessin'/Goodbye to Love	1959	6.25	12.50	25.00
❑ 1069	Whoever You Are/How Could You Call It Off	1960	6.25	12.50	25.00
❑ 1103	Believe Me (My Angel)/I	1961	15.00	30.00	60.00
—Originally released on Princeton 102 as "The Veneers"					
❑ 1105	There's Our Song Again/I'm the Girl	1961	6.25	12.50	25.00
LUDIX					
❑ 101	Eternally/Swamp Water	1963	5.00	10.00	20.00
❑ 106	That's Why I'm Happy/Some Tears Fall Dry	1963	5.00	10.00	20.00
RCA VICTOR					
❑ 74-0347	I'm Gonna Win Him Back/Love Makes All the Difference in the World	1970	2.50	5.00	10.00
ROULETTE					
❑ 7064	Maybe/He's Gone	1969	2.50	5.00	10.00
TCF HALL					
❑ 123	Take Me As I Am/There's No Forgetting Me	1965	3.75	7.50	15.00
VERVE					
❑ 10387	You're Welcome to My Heart/Soul of a Soldier	1966	3.75	7.50	15.00
❑ 10435	Indian Giver/It's Just Me	1966	3.75	7.50	15.00

7-Inch Extended Plays

Number	Title (A Side/B Side)	Yr	VG	VG+	NM
END					
❑ 201	(contents unknown)	1958	37.50	75.00	150.00
❑ 201 [PS]	I Love You So	1958	62.50	125.00	250.00
❑ 202	(contents unknown)	1958	25.00	50.00	100.00
❑ 202 [PS]	C'est Si Bon	1958	50.00	100.00	200.00

C

Number	Title (A Side/B Side)	Yr	VG	VG+	NM
Albums					
CARLTON					
❑ LP-144 [M]	The Chantels On Tour/Look in My Eyes	1962	50.00	100.00	200.00
❑ STLP-144 [P]	The Chantels On Tour/Look in My Eyes	1962	100.00	200.00	400.00
—Eight tracks are true stereo, two are mono, two are rechanneled					
END					
❑ LP-301 [M]	We Are the Chantels	1958	500.00	1000.	1500.
—Group photo on front cover; gray label with "11-17-58" in trail-off wax					
❑ LP-301 [M]	We Are the Chantels	1959	100.00	200.00	400.00
—Jukebox on front cover; gray label, "11-17-58" in trail-off wax					
❑ LP-301 [M]	We Are the Chantels	1962	50.00	100.00	200.00
—Jukebox on front cover; gray label, "1962" in trail-off wax					
❑ LP-301 [M]	We Are the Chantels	1965	25.00	50.00	100.00
—Jukebox on front cover; gray label, "8-65" in trail-off wax					
❑ LP-301 [M]	We Are the Chantels	1965	20.00	40.00	80.00
—Jukebox on front cover; multicolor label, "8-65" in trail-off wax					
❑ LP-312 [M]	There's Our Song Again	1962	30.00	60.00	120.00
FORUM					
❑ F-9104 [M]	The Chantels Sing Their Favorites	1964	12.50	25.00	50.00
❑ FS-9104 [R]	The Chantels Sing Their Favorites	1964	6.25	12.50	25.00

CHANTERS, THE (1)

45s

Number	Title (A Side/B Side)	Yr	VG	VG+	NM
COMBO					
❑ 78	Why/Watts	1954	125.00	250.00	500.00
❑ 92	I Love You/Hot Mamma	1955	100.00	200.00	400.00
DELUXE					
❑ 6162	My My Darling/I Need Your Tenderness (I Love You Darling)	1958	12.50	25.00	50.00
❑ 6166	Row Your Boat/Stars in the Skies	1958	10.00	20.00	40.00
—Black label					
❑ 6166	Row Your Boat/Stars in the Skies	1958	5.00	10.00	20.00
—Yellow label					
❑ 6172	Angel Darling/Five Little Kisses	1958	12.50	25.00	50.00
❑ 6177	No, No, No/Over the Rainbow	1958	10.00	20.00	40.00
❑ 6191	No, No, No/I Make This Pledge (To You)	1961	7.50	15.00	30.00
❑ 6194	My My Darling/At My Door	1961	10.00	20.00	40.00
❑ 6200	Row Your Boat/No, No, No	1963	7.50	15.00	30.00
KEM					
❑ 2740	Lonesome Me/Golden Apple	1955	75.00	150.00	300.00
RPM					
❑ 415	Tell Me, Thrill Me/She Wants to Mambo	1954	75.00	150.00	300.00

CHANTEURS, THE

With Eugene Record, later of THE CHI-LITES.

45s

Number	Title (A Side/B Side)	Yr	VG	VG+	NM
VEE JAY					
❑ 519	You've Got a Great Love/The Grizzly Bear	1963	5.00	10.00	20.00

CHANTS, THE (1)

British soul group.

45s

Number	Title (A Side/B Side)	Yr	VG	VG+	NM
CAMEO					
❑ 277	I Don't Care/Come Go with Me	1963	5.00	10.00	20.00
❑ 297	I Could Write a Book/A Thousand Stars	1964	5.00	10.00	20.00
INTERPHON					
❑ 7703	She's Mine/Then I'll Be Home	1964	3.75	7.50	15.00

CHANTS, THE (U)

None of these are by group (1), but we doubt all of them are by the same group.

45s

Number	Title (A Side/B Side)	Yr	VG	VG+	NM
CAPITOL					
❑ F3949	Lost and Found/Close Friends	1958	5.00	10.00	20.00
CHECKER					
❑ 1209	Surfside/Chicken 'N' Gravy	1968	2.00	4.00	8.00
EKO					
❑ 3567/77	Respectable/Kiss Me Goodbye	1961	7.50	15.00	30.00
MGM					
❑ 13008	Respectable/Kiss Me Goodbye	1961	5.00	10.00	20.00
NITE OWL					
❑ 40	Heaven and Paradise/When I'm With You	1960	75.00	150.00	300.00
—Maroon label original					
❑ 40	Heaven and Paradise/When I'm With You	1960	10.00	20.00	40.00
—Black label, black vinyl					
❑ 40	Heaven and Paradise/When I'm With You	196?	5.00	10.00	20.00
—Red vinyl					
❑ 40	Heaven and Paradise/When I'm With You	196?	5.00	10.00	20.00
—Blue vinyl					
❑ 40	Heaven and Paradise/When I'm With You	196?	5.00	10.00	20.00
—Yellow vinyl					
U.W.R.					
❑ 4243	Rockin' Santa/Respectable	1962	6.25	12.50	25.00
VERVE					
❑ 10244	Dick Tracy/Choo Choo	1961	5.00	10.00	20.00

CHAPERONES, THE

45s

Number	Title (A Side/B Side)	Yr	VG	VG+	NM
JOSIE					
❑ 880	Dance with Me/Cruise to the Moon	1960	37.50	75.00	150.00
—With typographical error listing group as "The Cahperones"					
❑ 880	Dance with Me/Cruise to the Moon	1960	6.25	12.50	25.00
—With correct group name on label					
❑ 885	Shining Star/My Shadow and Me	1960	6.25	12.50	25.00
❑ 891	Man from the Moon/Blueberry Sweet	1961	12.50	25.00	50.00

Number	Title (A Side/B Side)	Yr	VG	VG+	NM

CHARIOTEERS, THE
Also see BILLY WILLIAMS.
45s
COLUMBIA

Number	Title (A Side/B Side)	Yr	VG	VG+	NM
❏ 1-168	A Kiss and a Rose/A Cottage in Old Donegal	1949	150.00	300.00	600.00
—Microgroove 7-inch, 33 1/3 rpm single					
❏ 1-363	This Side of Heaven/Hawaiian Sunset	1949	150.00	300.00	600.00
—Microgroove 7-inch, 33 1/3 rpm single					
JOSIE					
❏ 787	I've Got My Heart on My Sleeve/Don't Play No Mambo	1955	20.00	40.00	80.00
MGM					
❏ 12569	The Candles/I Didn't Mean to Be Mean to You	1957	20.00	40.00	80.00
RCA VICTOR					
❏ 47-6098	Easy Does It/Tremble, Tremble, Tremble	1955	20.00	40.00	80.00

Albums
COLUMBIA

Number	Title (A Side/B Side)	Yr	VG	VG+	NM
❏ CL 6014 [10]	Sweet and Low	1949	75.00	150.00	300.00
HARMONY					
❏ HL 7089 [M]	The Charioteers with Billy Williams	1957	25.00	50.00	100.00

CHARLENE
45s
ARIOLA AMERICA

Number	Title (A Side/B Side)	Yr	VG	VG+	NM
❏ 7696	Are You Free/We Know	1977	—	2.50	5.00
MOTOWN					
❏ 1262	Give It One More Try/Relove	1973	2.00	4.00	8.00
❏ 1285	All That Love Went to Waste/Give It One More Try	1973	2.00	4.00	8.00
❏ 1492	Hungry/I Won't Remember Ever Loving You	1980	—	2.00	4.00
❏ 1611	I've Never Been to Me/Somewhere in My Life	1982	—	—	3.00
❏ 1621	Nunca He Ido A Mi/If I Could See Myself	1982	—	2.00	4.00
❏ 1650	Used to Be/I Want to Come Back As A Song	1982	—	—	3.00
—A-side with Stevie Wonder					
❏ 1650 [PS]	Used to Be/I Want to Come Back As A Song	1982	—	—	3.00
❏ 1663	I Want to Go Back There Again/Richie's Song	1983	—	—	3.00
❏ 1734	We're Both in Love with You/I Want the World to Know He's Mine	1984	—	—	3.00
❏ 1761	Hit and Run Lover/Last Song	1984	—	—	3.00
PRODIGAL					
❏ 0632	It Ain't Easy Coming Down/On My Way to You	1977	—	2.50	5.00
❏ 0633	Freddie/(B-side unknown)	1977	—	2.50	5.00
❏ 0633 [PS]	Freddie/(B-side unknown)	1977	2.00	5.00	10.00
❏ 0636	I've Never Been to Me/It's Really Nice to Be in Love Again	1977	5.00	10.00	20.00

Albums
MOTOWN

Number	Title (A Side/B Side)	Yr	VG	VG+	NM
❏ 6007 ML	Charlene	1981	2.50	5.00	10.00
❏ 6027 ML	Used to Be	1982	2.50	5.00	10.00
❏ 6090 ML	Hit and Run Lover	1985	2.50	5.00	10.00
PRODIGAL					
❏ P6-10015	Charlene	1976	5.00	10.00	20.00
❏ P6-10018	Songs of Love	1977	5.00	10.00	20.00

CHARLENE WITH STEVIE WONDER
Also see each artist's individual listings.
45s
MOTOWN

Number	Title (A Side/B Side)	Yr	VG	VG+	NM
❏ 1650	Used to Be/I Want to Come Back As A Song	1982	—	—	3.00
❏ 1650 [PS]	Used to Be/I Want to Come Back As A Song	1982	—	—	3.00

CHARLES, BOBBY
45s
BEARSVILLE

Number	Title (A Side/B Side)	Yr	VG	VG+	NM
❏ 0010	Small Town Talk/Save Me Jesus	1973	—	2.00	4.00
CHESS					
❏ 1609	Later Alligator/On Bended Knee	1955	12.50	25.00	50.00
❏ 1617	Why Did You Leave/Don't You Know I Love You	1956	12.50	25.00	50.00
❏ 1628	Only Time Will Tell/Take It Easy. Greasy	1956	12.50	25.00	50.00
❏ 1638	Laura Lee/No Use Knocking	1956	12.50	25.00	50.00
❏ 1647	Put Your Arms Around Me/Why Can't You, Honey	1957	10.00	20.00	40.00
❏ 1658	No More/You Can Suit Yourself	1957	10.00	20.00	40.00
❏ 1670	One Eyed Jack/Yea Yea Baby	1957	10.00	20.00	40.00
IMPERIAL					
❏ 5542	Since She's Gone/At the Jamboree	1958	5.00	10.00	20.00
❏ 5557	Oh Yeah/Since I Lost You	1958	5.00	10.00	20.00
❏ 5579	The Town Is Talking/What Can I Do	1959	5.00	10.00	20.00
❏ 5642	Bye Bye Baby/Those Eyes	1960	5.00	10.00	20.00
❏ 5681	What a Party/I Just Want You	1960	5.00	10.00	20.00
❏ 5691	Four Winds/Nothing Sweet As You	1960	5.00	10.00	20.00
JEWEL					
❏ 728	Everybody's Laughing/Everybody Knows	1964	2.50	5.00	10.00
❏ 729	Goodnight Irene/I Hope	1964	2.50	5.00	10.00
❏ 735	Ain't Misbehavin'/Preacher's Daughter	1964	2.50	5.00	10.00
❏ 740	Oh Lonesome Me/One More Glass of Wine	1964	2.50	5.00	10.00
PAULA					
❏ 226	The Walk/Worrying Over You	1965	2.50	5.00	10.00

Albums
CHESS

Number	Title (A Side/B Side)	Yr	VG	VG+	NM
❏ CH 9175	Chess Masters	1984	3.75	7.50	15.00

CHARLES, RAY
Also see THE MAXIM TRIO.
12-Inch Singles
COLUMBIA

Number	Title (A Side/B Side)	Yr	VG	VG+	NM
❏ CAS 1421 [DJ]	I Wish I'd Never Loved You at All (same on both sides?)	1988	3.00	6.00	12.00
WARNER BROS.					
❏ PRO-A-4425 [DJ]	I'll Take Care of You (same on both sides)	1990	3.75	7.50	15.00
❏ PRO-A-4696 [DJ]	Living Without You (same on both sides)	1990	3.00	6.00	12.00
❏ PRO-A-5977 [DJ]	A Song for You (same on both sides)	1993	2.50	5.00	10.00

45s
ABC

Number	Title (A Side/B Side)	Yr	VG	VG+	NM
❏ 10808	Let's Go Get Stoned/At the Train	1966	2.00	4.00	8.00
❏ 10840	I Chose to Sing the Blues/Hopelessly	1966	2.00	4.00	8.00
❏ 10865	Please Say You're Fooling/I Don't Need No Doctor	1966	2.00	4.00	8.00
❏ 10901	I Want to Talk About You/Something Inside Me	1967	2.00	4.00	8.00
❏ 10938	Here We Go Again/Somebody Ought to Write a Book About It	1967	2.00	4.00	8.00
❏ 10970	In the Heat of the Night/Somebody's Got to Change	1967	2.00	4.00	8.00
❏ 11009	Yesterday/Never Had Enough of Nothing Yet	1967	2.00	4.00	8.00
❏ 11045	That's a Lie/Go On Home	1968	2.00	4.00	8.00
❏ 11045 [PS]	That's a Lie/Go On Home	1968	3.75	7.50	15.00
❏ 11090	Eleanor Rigby/Understanding	1968	2.00	4.00	8.00
❏ 11133	Sweet Young Thing Like You/Listen, They're Playing Our Song	1968	2.00	4.00	8.00
❏ 11170	If It Wasn't for Bad Luck/When I Stop Dreaming	1969	2.00	4.00	8.00
—With Jimmy Lewis					
❏ 11193	I'll Be Your Servant/I Don't Know What Time It Was	1969	2.00	4.00	8.00
❏ 11213	Let Me Love You/I'm Satisfied	1969	2.00	4.00	8.00
❏ 11239	We Can Make It/I Can't Stop Loving You Baby	1969	2.00	4.00	8.00
❏ 11251	Someone to Watch Over Me/Claudie Mae	1969	2.00	4.00	8.00
❏ 11259	Laughin' and Clownin'/That Thing Called Love	1970	2.00	4.00	8.00
❏ 11271	If You Were Mine/Till I Can't Take It Anymore	1970	2.00	4.00	8.00
❏ 11291	Don't Change on Me/Sweet Memories	1971	2.00	4.00	8.00
❏ 11308	Feel So Bad/Your Love Is So Doggone Good	1971	—	3.00	6.00
❏ 11317	What Am I Living For/Tired of My Tears	1971	—	3.00	6.00
❏ 11329	Look What They've Done to My Song, Ma/America the Beautiful	1972	2.50	5.00	10.00
❏ 11337	Hey Mister/There'll Be No Peace Without All Men as One	1972	—	3.00	6.00
❏ 11344	Every Saturday Night/Take Me Home, Country Roads	1973	—	3.00	6.00
❏ 11351	I Can Make It Through the Days (But Oh Those Lonely Nights)/Ring of Fire	1973	—	3.00	6.00

ABC-PARAMOUNT

Number	Title (A Side/B Side)	Yr	VG	VG+	NM
❏ 4801 [S]	Don't Cry Baby/Teardrops from My Eyes	1964	5.00	10.00	20.00
❏ 4802 [S]	Baby, Don't You Cry/Cry Me a River	1964	5.00	10.00	20.00
❏ 4803 [S]	I Cried for You/Cry	1964	5.00	10.00	20.00
❏ 4804 [S]	A Tear Fell/No One to Cry To	1964	5.00	10.00	20.00
❏ 4805 [S]	You've Got Me Crying Again/After My Laughter Came Tears	1964	5.00	10.00	20.00
—The above five are 33 1/3 rpm, small hole jukebox singles excerpted from the LP "Sweet and Sour Tears"					
❏ 10081	My Baby/Who You Gonna Love	1960	3.75	7.50	15.00
❏ 10118	Sticks and Stones/Worried Life Blues	1960	3.00	6.00	12.00
❏ 10135	Georgia on My Mind/Carry Me Back to Old Virginny	1960	3.75	7.50	15.00
❏ 10141	Them That Got/I Wonder	1960	3.00	6.00	12.00
❏ 10164	Ruby/Heard Hearted Woman	1960	3.00	6.00	12.00
❏ 10244	Hit the Road Jack/The Danger Zone	1961	3.75	7.50	15.00
❏ 10266	Unchain My Heart/But on the Other Hand, Baby	1961	3.75	7.50	15.00
❏ 10314	Hide 'Nor Hair/At the Club	1962	3.00	6.00	12.00
❏ 10330	I Can't Stop Loving You/Born to Lose	1962	3.75	7.50	15.00
❏ 10345	You Don't Know Me/Careless Love	1962	3.75	7.50	15.00
❏ 10375	You Are My Sunshine/Your Cheating Heart	1962	3.00	6.00	12.00
❏ 10405	Don't Set Me Free/The Brightest Smile in Town	1963	3.00	6.00	12.00
❏ 10435	Take These Chains from My Heart/No Letter Today	1963	3.75	7.50	15.00
❏ 10453	No One/Without Love (There Is Nothing)	1963	3.00	6.00	12.00
❏ 10481	Busted/Making Believe	1963	3.75	7.50	15.00
❏ 10509	That Lucky Old Sun/Ol' Man Time	1963	3.00	6.00	12.00
❏ 10530	Baby Don't You Cry/My Heart Cries for You	1964	3.00	6.00	12.00
❏ 10557	My Baby Don't Dig Me/Something's Wrong	1964	3.00	6.00	12.00
❏ 10571	No One to Cry To/A Tear Fell	1964	3.00	6.00	12.00
❏ 10588	Smack Dab in the Middle/I Wake Up Crying	1964	3.00	6.00	12.00
❏ 10609	Makin' Whoopee/(Instrumental)	1964	3.00	6.00	12.00
❏ 10615	Cry/Teardrops from My Eyes	1965	3.00	6.00	12.00
❏ 10649	I Gotta Woman (Part 1)/I Gotta Woman (Part 2)	1965	3.00	6.00	12.00
❏ 10663	Without a Song (Part 1)/Without a Song (Part 2)	1965	3.00	6.00	12.00
❏ 10700	I'm a Fool to Care/Love's Gonna Live Here	1965	3.00	6.00	12.00
❏ 10720	The Cincinnati Kid/That's All I Am to You	1965	3.00	6.00	12.00
❏ 10739	Crying Time/When My Dreamboat Comes Home	1965	3.75	7.50	15.00
❏ 10785	Together Again/You're Just About to Lose Your Clown	1966	3.00	6.00	12.00

ATLANTIC

Number	Title (A Side/B Side)	Yr	VG	VG+	NM
❏ 976	Roll with Me Baby/The Midnight Hour	1952	125.00	250.00	500.00
❏ 984	The Sun's Gonna Shine Again/Jumpin' in the Morning	1953	100.00	200.00	400.00
❏ 999	Mess Around/Funny (But I Still Love You)	1953	50.00	100.00	200.00
❏ 1008	Feelin' Sad/Heartbreaker	1953	25.00	50.00	100.00
❏ 1021	It Should've Been Me/Sinner's Prayer	1954	12.50	25.00	50.00
❏ 1037	Don't You Know/Losing Hand	1954	7.50	15.00	30.00

Number	Title (A Side/B Side)	Yr	VG	VG+	NM
❏ 1050	I've Got a Woman/Come Back	1954	12.50	25.00	50.00
❏ 1063	This Little Girl of Mine/A Fool for You	1955	7.50	15.00	30.00
❏ 1076	Blackjack/Greenbacks	1955	7.50	15.00	30.00
❏ 1085	Drown in My Own Tears/Mary Ann	1956	6.25	12.50	25.00
❏ 1096	Hallelujah, I Love Her So/What Would I Do Without You	1956	5.00	10.00	20.00
❏ 1108	Lonely Avenue/Leave My Woman Alone	1956	5.00	10.00	20.00
❏ 1124	I Want to Know/Ain't That Love	1957	5.00	10.00	20.00
❏ 1143	It's All Right/Get On the Right Track Baby	1957	5.00	10.00	20.00
❏ 1154	Swanee River Rock (Talkin' 'Bout That River)/I Want a Little Girl	1957	5.00	10.00	20.00
❏ 1172	Talkin' 'Bout You/What Kind of a Man Are You	1958	3.75	7.50	15.00
❏ 1180	Yes Indeed/I Had a Dream	1958	3.75	7.50	15.00
—With the Cookies					
❏ 1196	My Bonnie/You Be My Baby	1958	3.75	7.50	15.00
❏ 2006	Rockhouse (Part 1)/Rockhouse (Part 2)	1958	3.75	7.50	15.00
❏ 2006	Rockhouse (Part 1)/Rockhouse (Part 2)	1958	12.50	25.00	50.00
❏ 2010	(Night Time Is) The Right Time/Tell All the World About You	1959	3.75	7.50	15.00
❏ 2022	Tell Me How Do You Feel/That's Enough	1959	3.75	7.50	15.00
❏ 2031	What'd I Say (Part I)/What'd I Say (Part II)	1959	5.00	10.00	20.00
❏ 2043	I'm Movin' On/I Believe to My Soul	1959	3.00	6.00	12.00
❏ 2047	Let the Good Times Roll/Don't Let the Sun Catch You Cryin'	1960	3.00	6.00	12.00
❏ 2055	Heartbreaker/Just for a Thrill	1960	3.00	6.00	12.00
❏ 2068	Tell the Truth/Sweet Sixteen Bars	1960	3.00	6.00	12.00
❏ 2084	Come Rain or Come Shine/Tell Me You'll Wait for Me	1960	3.00	6.00	12.00
❏ 2094	Early in the Morning/A Bit of Soul	1961	3.00	6.00	12.00
❏ 2106	Am I Blue/It Should've Been Me	1961	3.00	6.00	12.00
❏ 2118	I Wonder Who/Hard Times (No One Knows Better Than I)	1961	3.00	6.00	12.00
❏ 2174	Carryin' That Load/Feelin' Sad	1963	2.50	5.00	10.00
❏ 2239	Talkin' 'Bout You/In a Little Spanish Town	1964	2.50	5.00	10.00
❏ 2470	Come Rain or Come Shine/Tell Me You'll Wait for Me	1968	2.50	5.00	10.00
❏ 3443	I Can See Clearly Now/Anonymous Love	1977	—	2.50	5.00
❏ 3473	A Peace That We Never Could Enjoy/Game Number Nine	1978	—	2.50	5.00
❏ 3527	Riding Thumb/You Forgot Your Memories	1978	—	2.50	5.00
❏ 3549 [DJ]	Christmas Time (same on both sides)	1978	—	3.00	6.00
—May be promo-only					
❏ 3611	Some Enchanted Evening/20th Century Fox	1979	—	2.50	5.00
❏ 3634	Just Because/Love Me or Set Me Free	1979	—	2.50	5.00
❏ 3762	Compared To What/Now That We've Found Each Other	1980	—	2.50	5.00
❏ 5005	Doodlin' (Part 1)/Doodlin' (Part 2)	1960	3.75	7.50	15.00
BARONET					
❏ 7111	See See Rider/I Used to be So Happy	1960	3.00	6.00	12.00
❏ 7111 [PS]	See See Rider/I Used to be So Happy	1960	6.25	12.50	25.00
COLUMBIA					
❏ 38-03429	String Bean/Born to Love Me	1982	—	2.00	4.00
❏ 38-03810	You Feel Good All Over/ 3/4 Time	1983	—	—	3.00
❏ 38-04083	Ain't Your Memory Got No Pride at All/I Don't Want No Strangers Sleeping in My Bed	1983	—	—	3.00
❏ 38-04297	We Didn't See a Thing/I Wish You Were Here Tonight	1983	—	—	3.00
—A-side with George Jones and Chet Atkins					
❏ 38-04420	Do I Ever Cross Your Mind/They Call It Love	1984	—	—	3.00
❏ 38-04500	Woman (Sensuous Woman)/I Was On Georgia Time	1984	—	—	3.00
❏ 38-04531	Rock and Roll Shoes/Then I'll Be Over You	1984	—	—	3.00
—Ray Charles and B.J. Thomas					
❏ 38-04715	Seven Spanish Angels/Who Cares	1984	—	—	3.00
—A-side with Willie Nelson; B-side with Janie Frickie					
❏ 38-04860	It Ain't Gonna Worry My Mind/Crazy Old Soldier	1985	—	—	3.00
—A-side with Mickey Gilley; B-side with Johnny Cash					
❏ 38-05575	Two Old Cats Like Us/Little Hotel Room	1985	—	—	3.00
—A-side with Hank Williams, Jr.; B-side with Merle Haggard					
❏ 38-06172	Pages of My Mind/Slip Away	1986	—	—	3.00
❏ 38-06370	Dixie Moon/A Little Bit of Heaven	1986	—	—	3.00
❏ 38-08393	Seven Spanish Angels/It Ain't Gonna Worry My Mind	1988	—	—	3.00
—Reissue; A-side with Willie Nelson, B-side with Mickey Gilley					
CROSSOVER					
❏ 973	Come Live with Me/Everybody Sing	1973	—	2.50	5.00
❏ 974	Louise/Somebody	1974	—	2.50	5.00
❏ 981	Living for the City/Then We'll Be Home	1975	—	2.50	5.00
❏ 985	America the Beautiful/Sunshine	1976	—	3.00	6.00
—A-side is a different recording than that on the B-side of ABC 11329					
IMPULSE!					
❏ 200	One Mint Julep/Let's Go	1961	2.50	5.00	10.00
❏ 202	I've Got News for You/I'm Gonna Move to the Outskirts of Town	1961	2.50	5.00	10.00
RCA					
❏ PB-10800	Oh Lawd, I'm On My Way/Oh Bess, Where's My Bess	1976	—	2.50	5.00
ROCKIN'					
❏ 504	Walkin' and Talkin' (To Myself)/I'm Wonderin' and Wonderin'	1952	75.00	150.00	300.00
SITTIN' IN WITH					
❏ 641	Baby Let Me Hear You Call My Name/Guitar Blues	1952	75.00	150.00	300.00

Number	Title (A Side/B Side)	Yr	VG	VG+	NM
SWING TIME					
❏ 250	Baby, Let Me Hold Your Hand/Lonely Boy	1951	125.00	250.00	500.00
—Ray Charles records on Swing Time before 250 are unconfirmed on 45 rpm					
❏ 274	Kissa Me Baby/I'm Glad for Your Sake	1952	125.00	250.00	500.00
❏ 300	Baby Let Me Hear You Call My Name/Guitar Blues	1952	125.00	250.00	500.00
❏ 326	The Snow Is Falling/Misery in My Heart	1953	125.00	250.00	500.00
TANGERINE					
❏ 1015	Booty Butt/Sidewinder	1971	—	3.00	6.00
TIME					
❏ 1026	I Found My Baby/Guitar Blues	1960	3.75	7.50	15.00
❏ 1054	Why Did You Go/Back Home	1962	3.00	6.00	12.00
WARNER BROS.					
❏ 18611	A Song for You/I Can't Get Enough	1993	—	—	3.00
❏ 49608	Beers to You/Cotton-Eyed Clint	1980	—	2.50	5.00
—A-side with Clint Eastwood; B-side by Texas Opera Company					
78s					
ATLANTIC					
❏ 976	Roll with Me Baby/The Midnight Hour	1952	17.50	35.00	70.00
❏ 984	The Sun's Gonna Shine Again/Jumpin' in the Morning	1953	12.50	25.00	50.00
❏ 999	Mess Around/Funny (But I Still Love You)	1953	12.50	25.00	50.00
❏ 1008	Feelin' Sad/Heartbreaker	1953	7.50	15.00	30.00
❏ 1021	It Should've Been Me/Sinner's Prayer	1954	7.50	15.00	30.00
❏ 1037	Don't You Know/Losing Hand	1954	7.50	15.00	30.00
❏ 1050	I've Got a Woman/Come Back	1954	12.50	25.00	50.00
❏ 1063	This Little Girl of Mine/A Fool for You	1955	7.50	15.00	30.00
❏ 1076	Blackjack/Greenbacks	1955	7.50	15.00	30.00
❏ 1085	Drown in My Own Tears/Mary Ann	1956	7.50	15.00	30.00
❏ 1096	Hallelujah, I Love Her So/What Would I Do Without You	1956	7.50	15.00	30.00
❏ 1108	Lonely Avenue/Leave My Woman Alone	1956	7.50	15.00	30.00
❏ 1124	I Want to Know/Ain't That Love	1957	7.50	15.00	30.00
❏ 1143	It's All Right/Get On the Right Track Baby	1957	7.50	15.00	30.00
❏ 1154	Swanee River Rock (Talkin' 'Bout That River)/I Want a Little Girl	1957	7.50	15.00	30.00
❏ 1172	Talkin' 'Bout You/What Kind of a Man Are You	1958	10.00	20.00	40.00
❏ 1180	Yes Indeed/I Had a Dream	1958	10.00	20.00	40.00
—With the Cookies					
❏ 1196	My Bonnie/You Be My Baby	1958	10.00	20.00	40.00
❏ 2010	(Night Time Is) The Right Time/Tell All the World About You	1959	25.00	50.00	100.00
❏ 2022	Tell Me How Do You Feel/That's Enough	1959	37.50	75.00	150.00
❏ 2031	What'd I Say (Part I)/What'd I Say (Part II)	1959	100.00	200.00	400.00
ROCKIN'					
❏ 504	Walkin' and Talkin' (To Myself)/I'm Wonderin' and Wonderin'	1952	12.50	25.00	50.00
SITTIN' IN WITH					
❏ 641	Baby Let Me Hear You Call My Name/Guitar Blues	1952	12.50	25.00	50.00
❏ 651	I Can't Do No More/Roly Poly	1952	20.00	40.00	80.00
SWING TIME					
❏ 215	I've Had My Fun/Sittin' on Top of the World	1949	12.50	25.00	50.00
—As "Ray Charles Trio"					
❏ 216	Ain't That Fine/Don't Put All Your Dreams in One Basket	1949	10.00	20.00	40.00
❏ 217	See See Rider/What Have I Done	1949	10.00	20.00	40.00
❏ 218	She's On the Ball/Honey Honey	1949	10.00	20.00	40.00
❏ 228	Late in the Evening Blues/The Echo Song	1950	10.00	20.00	40.00
❏ 229	I'll Do Anything But Work/Someday	1950	10.00	20.00	40.00
❏ 249	All to Myself/I Wonder Who's Kissing Her Now	1951	10.00	20.00	40.00
❏ 250	Baby, Let Me Hold Your Hand/Lonely Boy	1951	10.00	20.00	40.00
❏ 274	Kissa Me Baby/I'm Glad for Your Sake	1952	10.00	20.00	40.00
❏ 297	Baby Won't You Please Come Home/Hey Now	1952	10.00	20.00	40.00
❏ 300	Baby Let Me Hear You Call My Name/Guitar Blues	1952	10.00	20.00	40.00
❏ 326	The Snow Is Falling/Misery in My Heart	1953	10.00	20.00	40.00
7-Inch Extended Plays					
ABC-PARAMOUNT					
❏ EP 410	Half As Much/I Love You So Much It Hurts//You Win Again/It Makes No Difference Now	196?	7.50	15.00	30.00
—Jukebox issue; small hole, plays at 33 1/3 rpm					
❏ EP 410 [PS]	Modern Sounds in Country and Western	196?	7.50	15.00	30.00
❏ EP A-410	I Can't Stop Loving You/Born to Lose//You Don't Know Me/Careless Love	1962	6.25	12.50	25.00
❏ EP A-410 [PS]	(title unknown)	1962	6.25	12.50	25.00
❏ EP 415	Them That Got/Unchain My Heart/Hit the Road Jack//Sticks and Stones/I Wonder/The Danger Zone	1962	7.50	15.00	30.00
—Jukebox issue; small hole, plays at 33 1/3 rpm					
❏ EP 415 [PS]	Greatest Hits	1962	7.50	15.00	30.00
ATLANTIC					
❏ EP 587	*Ain't That Love/Greenbacks/Drown in My Own Tears/Hallelujah I Love Her So	1956	25.00	50.00	100.00
❏ EP 587 [PS]	Ray Charles	1956	25.00	50.00	100.00
❏ EP 597	(contents unknown)	1957	25.00	50.00	100.00
❏ EP 597 [PS]	The Great Ray Charles	1957	25.00	50.00	100.00
❏ EP 607	*A Fool for You/Mary Ann/Blackjack/Lonely Avenue	1958	25.00	50.00	100.00
❏ EP 607 [PS]	Rock with Ray Charles	1958	25.00	50.00	100.00
❏ EP 619	*Let the Good Times Roll/Come Rain or Come Shine/Don't Let the Sun Catch You Cryin'/Alexander's Ragtime Band	1959	25.00	50.00	100.00
❏ EP 619 [PS]	The Genius of Ray Charles	1959	25.00	50.00	100.00

Albums

ABC

Number	Title (A Side/B Side)	Yr	VG	VG+	NM
❑ S-335 [S]	The Genius Hits the Road	1967	3.00	6.00	12.00
❑ S-355 [S]	Dedicated to You	1967	3.00	6.00	12.00
❑ S-410 [S]	Modern Sounds in Country and Western Music	1967	3.00	6.00	12.00
❑ S-415 [S]	Ray Charles' Greatest Hits	1967	3.00	6.00	12.00
❑ S-435 [S]	Modern Sounds in Country and Western Music (Volume Two)	1967	3.00	6.00	12.00
❑ S-465 [S]	Ingredients in a Recipe for Soul	1967	3.00	6.00	12.00
❑ S-480 [S]	Sweet & Sour Tears	1967	3.00	6.00	12.00
❑ S-495 [S]	Have a Smile with Me	1967	3.00	6.00	12.00
❑ S-500 [S]	Ray Charles Live in Concert	1967	3.00	6.00	12.00
❑ S-520 [S]	Together Again	1967	3.00	6.00	12.00
❑ S-544 [S]	Crying Time	1967	3.00	6.00	12.00
❑ S-550 [S]	Ray's Moods	1967	3.00	6.00	12.00
❑ 590X [(2) M]	A Man and His Soul	1967	3.75	7.50	15.00
❑ S-590X [(2) S]	A Man and His Soul	1967	5.00	10.00	20.00
❑ 595 [M]	Ray Charles Invites You to Listen	1967	5.00	10.00	20.00
❑ S-595 [S]	Ray Charles Invites You to Listen	1967	3.75	7.50	15.00
❑ S-625	A Portrait of Ray	1968	3.00	6.00	12.00
❑ S-675	I'm All Yours — Baby!	1969	3.00	6.00	12.00
❑ S-695	Doing His Thing	1969	3.00	6.00	12.00
❑ S-707	Love Country Style	1971	3.00	6.00	12.00
❑ S-726	Volcanic Action of My Soul	1971	3.00	6.00	12.00
❑ H-731 [(2)]	A 25th Anniversary in Show Business Salute to Ray Charles	1971	3.75	7.50	15.00
❑ X-755	A Message from the People	1972	3.00	6.00	12.00
❑ X-765	Through the Eyes of Love	1972	3.00	6.00	12.00
❑ X-781/2 [(2)]	All-Time Great Country & Western Hits	1973	3.75	7.50	15.00
❑ QBO-91036 [(2) M]	The Ray Charles Story	1967	7.50	15.00	30.00
—Capitol Record Club exclusive					
❑ SQBO-91036 [(2) S]	The Ray Charles Story	1967	6.25	12.50	25.00
—Capitol Record Club exclusive					
❑ ST-91233 [S]	Ray Charles Invites You to Listen	1967	3.75	7.50	15.00
—Capitol Record Club edition					

ABC-PARAMOUNT

Number	Title (A Side/B Side)	Yr	VG	VG+	NM
❑ 335 [M]	The Genius Hits the Road	1960	5.00	10.00	20.00
❑ S-335 [S]	The Genius Hits the Road	1960	7.50	15.00	30.00
❑ 355 [M]	Dedicated to You	1961	5.00	10.00	20.00
❑ S-355 [S]	Dedicated to You	1961	7.50	15.00	30.00
❑ 410 [M]	Modern Sounds in Country and Western Music	1962	6.25	12.50	25.00
❑ S-410 [S]	Modern Sounds in Country and Western Music	1962	7.50	15.00	30.00
❑ 415 [M]	Ray Charles' Greatest Hits	1962	5.00	10.00	20.00
❑ S-415 [S]	Ray Charles' Greatest Hits	1962	6.25	12.50	25.00
❑ 435 [M]	Modern Sounds in Country and Western Music (Volume Two)	1962	5.00	10.00	20.00
❑ S-435 [S]	Modern Sounds in Country and Western Music (Volume Two)	1962	6.25	12.50	25.00
❑ 465 [M]	Ingredients in a Recipe for Soul	1963	5.00	10.00	20.00
❑ S-465 [S]	Ingredients in a Recipe for Soul	1963	6.25	12.50	25.00
❑ 480 [M]	Sweet & Sour Tears	1964	5.00	10.00	20.00
❑ S-480 [S]	Sweet & Sour Tears	1964	6.25	12.50	25.00
❑ 495 [M]	Have a Smile with Me	1964	5.00	10.00	20.00
❑ S-495 [S]	Have a Smile with Me	1964	6.25	12.50	25.00
❑ 500 [M]	Ray Charles Live in Concert	1965	3.75	7.50	15.00
❑ S-500 [S]	Ray Charles Live in Concert	1965	5.00	10.00	20.00
❑ 520 [M]	Country & Western Meets Rhythm & Blues	1965	3.75	7.50	15.00
❑ 520 [M]	Together Again	196?	3.75	7.50	15.00
—Retitled version of "Country and Western Meets Rhythm and Blues"					
❑ S-520 [S]	Country & Western Meets Rhythm & Blues	1965	5.00	10.00	20.00
❑ S-520 [S]	Together Again	196?	5.00	10.00	20.00
—Retitled version of "Country and Western Meets Rhythm and Blues"					
❑ 544 [M]	Crying Time	1966	3.75	7.50	15.00
❑ S-544 [S]	Crying Time	1966	5.00	10.00	20.00
❑ 550 [M]	Ray's Moods	1966	3.75	7.50	15.00
❑ S-550 [S]	Ray's Moods	1966	5.00	10.00	20.00
❑ ST-90144 [S]	Ray Charles Live in Concert	1965	5.00	10.00	20.00
—Capitol Record Club edition					
❑ T-90144 [M]	Ray Charles Live in Concert	1965	5.00	10.00	20.00
—Capitol Record Club edition					
❑ ST-90625 [S]	Crying Time	1966	5.00	10.00	20.00
—Capitol Record Club edition					
❑ T-90625 [M]	Crying Time	1966	5.00	10.00	20.00
—Capitol Record Club edition					
❑ ST-90847 [S]	Together Again	196?	6.25	12.50	25.00
—Capitol Record Club edition					

ABC IMPULSE!

Number	Title (A Side/B Side)	Yr	VG	VG+	NM
❑ AS-2 [S]	Genius + Soul = Jazz	1968	3.00	6.00	12.00

ARCHIVE OF FOLK AND JAZZ

Number	Title (A Side/B Side)	Yr	VG	VG+	NM
❑ 244	Ray Charles	1970	3.00	6.00	12.00
❑ 292	Ray Charles, Vol. 2	197?	2.50	5.00	10.00
❑ 358	Rockin' with Ray	1979	2.50	5.00	10.00

ATLANTIC

Number	Title (A Side/B Side)	Yr	VG	VG+	NM
❑ SD 2-503 [(2)]	Ray Charles Live	1973	3.75	7.50	15.00
❑ 2-900 [(2) M]	The Ray Charles Story	1962	10.00	20.00	40.00
❑ 1259 [M]	The Great Ray Charles	1957	12.50	25.00	50.00
—Black label					
❑ 1259 [M]	The Great Ray Charles	1960	6.25	12.50	25.00
—Red and white label, white fan logo on right					
❑ 1259 [M]	The Great Ray Charles	1962	5.00	10.00	20.00
—Red and white label, black fan logo on right					
❑ SD 1259 [S]	The Great Ray Charles	1959	12.50	25.00	50.00
—Green label					
❑ SD 1259 [S]	The Great Ray Charles	1960	6.25	12.50	25.00
—Blue and green label, white fan logo on right					
❑ SD 1259 [S]	The Great Ray Charles	1962	5.00	10.00	20.00
—Blue and green label, black fan logo on right					
❑ 1289 [M]	Ray Charles at Newport	1958	12.50	25.00	50.00
—Black label					
❑ 1289 [M]	Ray Charles at Newport	1960	6.25	12.50	25.00
—Red and white label, white fan logo on right					
❑ 1289 [M]	Ray Charles at Newport	1962	5.00	10.00	20.00
—Red and white label, black fan logo on right					
❑ SD 1289 [S]	Ray Charles at Newport	1959	12.50	25.00	50.00
—Green label					
❑ SD 1289 [S]	Ray Charles at Newport	1960	6.25	12.50	25.00
—Blue and green label, white fan logo on right					
❑ SD 1289 [S]	Ray Charles at Newport	1962	5.00	10.00	20.00
—Blue and green label, black fan logo on right					
❑ 1312 [M]	The Genius of Ray Charles	1960	10.00	20.00	40.00
—Black label					
❑ 1312 [M]	The Genius of Ray Charles	1960	10.00	20.00	40.00
—White "bullseye" label					
❑ 1312 [M]	The Genius of Ray Charles	1960	6.25	12.50	25.00
—Red and white label, white fan logo on right					
❑ 1312 [M]	The Genius of Ray Charles	1962	5.00	10.00	20.00
—Red and white label, black fan logo on right					
❑ SD 1312 [S]	The Genius of Ray Charles	1960	12.50	25.00	50.00
—Green label					
❑ SD 1312 [S]	The Genius of Ray Charles	1960	12.50	25.00	50.00
—White "bullseye" label					
❑ SD 1312 [S]	The Genius of Ray Charles	1960	6.25	12.50	25.00
—Blue and green label, white fan logo on right					
❑ SD 1312 [S]	The Genius of Ray Charles	1962	5.00	10.00	20.00
—Blue and green label, black fan logo on right					
❑ SD 1312 [S]	The Genius of Ray Charles	1968	5.00	10.00	20.00
—Brown and purple label					
❑ 1369 [M]	The Genius After Hours	1961	6.25	12.50	25.00
—Red and white label, white fan logo on right					
❑ 1369 [M]	The Genius After Hours	1962	5.00	10.00	20.00
—Red and white label, black fan logo on right					
❑ SD 1369 [S]	The Genius After Hours	1961	7.50	15.00	30.00
—Blue and green label, white fan logo on right					
❑ SD 1369 [S]	The Genius After Hours	1962	6.25	12.50	25.00
—Blue and green label, black fan logo on right					
❑ SD 1543	The Best of Ray Charles	1970	3.00	6.00	12.00
❑ 3700 [(6)]	Ray Charles: A Life in Music	198?	12.50	25.00	50.00
❑ SD 7101 [S]	The Great Hits of Ray Charles Recorded on 8-Track Stereo	1966	6.25	12.50	25.00
❑ 8006 [M]	Ray Charles (Rock and Roll)	1957	22.50	45.00	90.00
—Black label					
❑ 8006 [M]	Ray Charles (Rock and Roll)	1960	6.25	12.50	25.00
—Red and white label, white fan logo on right					
❑ 8006 [M]	Hallelujah! I Love Her So	1962	5.00	10.00	20.00
—Red and white label, black fan logo on right; retitled version					
❑ 8025 [M]	Yes, Indeed!	1958	12.50	25.00	50.00
—Black label; cover has screaming girls					
❑ 8025 [M]	Yes, Indeed!	1960	6.25	12.50	25.00
—Red and white label, white fan logo on right; cover has screaming girls					
❑ 8025 [M]	Yes, Indeed!	1962	5.00	10.00	20.00
—Red and white label, black fan logo on right; cover has Ray on it					
❑ 8029 [M]	What'd I Say	1959	12.50	25.00	50.00
—Black label					
❑ 8029 [M]	What'd I Say	1960	10.00	20.00	40.00
—White "bullseye" label					
❑ 8029 [M]	What'd I Say	1960	6.25	12.50	25.00
—Red and white label, white fan logo on right					
❑ 8029 [M]	What'd I Say	1962	5.00	10.00	20.00
—Red and white label, black fan logo on right					
❑ 8039 [M]	Ray Charles In Person	1960	10.00	20.00	40.00
—Black label					
❑ 8039 [M]	Ray Charles In Person	1960	6.25	12.50	25.00
—Red and white label, white fan logo on right					
❑ 8039 [M]	Ray Charles In Person	1962	5.00	10.00	20.00
—Red and white label, black fan logo on right					
❑ 8052 [M]	The Genius Sings the Blues	1961	6.25	12.50	25.00
—Red and white label, white fan logo on right					
❑ 8052 [M]	The Genius Sings the Blues	1962	5.00	10.00	20.00
—Red and white label, black fan logo on right					
❑ 8054 [M]	Do the Twist!	1961	6.25	12.50	25.00
—Red and white label, white fan logo on right					
❑ 8054 [M]	Do the Twist!	1962	5.00	10.00	20.00
—Red and white label, black fan logo on right					
❑ 8063 [M]	The Ray Charles Story, Volume 1	1962	5.00	10.00	20.00
❑ 8064 [M]	The Ray Charles Story, Volume 2	1962	5.00	10.00	20.00
❑ 8083 [M]	The Ray Charles Story, Volume 3	1963	5.00	10.00	20.00
❑ 8094 [M]	The Ray Charles Story, Volume 4	1964	5.00	10.00	20.00
❑ SD 8094 [S]	The Ray Charles Story, Volume 4	1964	6.25	12.50	25.00
❑ SD 19142	True to Life	1977	3.00	6.00	12.00
❑ SD 19199	Love and Peace	1978	3.00	6.00	12.00
❑ SD 19251	Ain't It So	1979	3.00	6.00	12.00
❑ SD 19281	Brother Ray Is At It Again	1980	3.00	6.00	12.00
❑ 90464	The Genius After Hours	1986	2.50	5.00	10.00
—Reissue					

BARONET

Number	Title (A Side/B Side)	Yr	VG	VG+	NM
❑ B-111 [M]	The Artistry of Ray Charles	196?	3.00	6.00	12.00
❑ BS-111 [R]	The Artistry of Ray Charles	196?	2.50	5.00	10.00
❑ B-117 [M]	The Great Ray Charles	196?	3.00	6.00	12.00
❑ BS-117 [R]	The Great Ray Charles	196?	2.50	5.00	10.00

BLUESWAY

Number	Title (A Side/B Side)	Yr	VG	VG+	NM
❑ 6053	The Genius Live	1973	3.00	6.00	12.00

Number	Title (A Side/B Side)	Yr	VG	VG+	NM
COLUMBIA					
❏ AS 1920 [DJ]	Friendship Radio Show	1984	5.00	10.00	20.00
❏ FC 38293	Wish You Were Here Tonight	1983	2.50	5.00	10.00
❏ PC 38293	Wish You Were Here Tonight	1985	2.00	4.00	8.00
—Budget-line reissue					
❏ FC 38990	Do I Ever Cross Your Mind	1984	2.50	5.00	10.00
❏ FC 39415	Friendship	1985	2.50	5.00	10.00
❏ FC 40125	The Spirit of Christmas	1985	2.50	5.00	10.00
❏ FC 40338	From the Pages of My Mind	1986	2.50	5.00	10.00
❏ FC 45062	Seven Spanish Angels and Other Hits (1982-1986)	1989	3.00	6.00	12.00
CORONET					
❏ CX-173 [M]	Ray Charles	196?	3.00	6.00	12.00
❏ CXS-173 [R]	Ray Charles	196?	2.50	5.00	10.00
CROSSOVER					
❏ 9000	Come Live with Me	1974	3.00	6.00	12.00
❏ 9005	Renaissance	1975	3.00	6.00	12.00
❏ 9007	My Kind of Jazz, Part 3	1976	3.00	6.00	12.00
DCC COMPACT CLASSICS					
❏ LPZ-2012	Greatest Country and Western Hits	1995	25.00	50.00	100.00
—Audiophile vinyl					
DUNHILL COMPACT CLASSICS					
❏ DZL-038	Genius + Soul = Jazz	1988	3.75	7.50	15.00
—Clear vinyl reissue					
HOLLYWOOD					
❏ 504 [M]	The Original Ray Charles	1959	37.50	75.00	150.00
❏ 505 [M]	The Fabuolus Ray Charles	1959	37.50	75.00	150.00
IMPULSE!					
❏ A-2 [M]	Genius + Soul = Jazz	1961	6.25	12.50	25.00
❏ AS-2 [S]	Genius + Soul = Jazz	1961	7.50	15.00	30.00
INTERMEDIA					
❏ QS-5013	Goin' Down Slow	198?	2.50	5.00	10.00
LONGINES SYMPHONETTE					
❏ 95647 [(5)]	The Greatest Hits of Ray Charles	1974	10.00	20.00	40.00
PAIR					
❏ PDL2-1139 [(2)]	The Real Ray Charles	1986	3.00	6.00	12.00
PREMIER					
❏ PM 2004 [M]	The Great Ray Charles	196?	3.00	6.00	12.00
❏ PS 2004 [R]	The Great Ray Charles	196?	2.50	5.00	10.00
❏ PS-6001 [R]	Fantastic Ray Charles	196?	2.50	5.00	10.00
RHINO					
❏ R1-70097	Greatest Hits, Volume 1	1988	2.50	5.00	10.00
❏ R1-70098	Greatest Hits, Volume 2	1988	2.50	5.00	10.00
❏ R1-70099	Modern Sounds in Country and Western Music	1988	2.50	5.00	10.00
TANGERINE					
❏ 1512	My Kind of Jazz	1970	3.00	6.00	12.00
❏ 1516	My Kind of Jazz No. II	1973	3.00	6.00	12.00
WARNER BROS.					
❏ 26343	Would You Believe?	1990	3.75	7.50	15.00

CHARLES, RAY / HARRY BELAFONTE
Also see each artist's individual listings.
Albums

Number	Title (A Side/B Side)	Yr	VG	VG+	NM
CORONET					
❏ CX-203 [M]	The Greatest Ever	196?	3.00	6.00	12.00
❏ CXS-203 [R]	The Greatest Ever	196?	2.50	5.00	10.00

CHARLES, RAY, AND BETTY CARTER
45s

Number	Title (A Side/B Side)	Yr	VG	VG+	NM
ABC-PARAMOUNT					
❏ 10298	Baby It's Cold Outside/We'll Be Together Again	1962	2.50	5.00	10.00
Albums					
ABC					
❏ S-385 [S]	Ray Charles and Betty Carter	1967	5.00	10.00	20.00
—Reissue of ABC-Paramount ABCS-385					
ABC-PARAMOUNT					
❏ ABC-385 [M]	Ray Charles and Betty Carter	1961	10.00	20.00	40.00
❏ ABCS-385 [S]	Ray Charles and Betty Carter	1961	15.00	30.00	60.00
DCC COMPACT CLASSICS					
❏ LPZ-2005	Ray Charles and Betty Carter	1995	37.50	75.00	150.00
—Audiophile vinyl					
DUNHILL COMPACT CLASSICS					
❏ DZL-039	Ray Charles and Betty Carter	1988	3.75	7.50	15.00
—Clear vinyl reissue					

CHARLES, RAY/IVORY JOE HUNTER/JIMMY RUSHING
Also see RAY CHARLES; IVORY JOE HUNTER.
Albums

Number	Title (A Side/B Side)	Yr	VG	VG+	NM
DESIGN					
❏ DLP-909 [M]	Three of a Kind	196?	3.00	6.00	12.00
❏ DLS-909 [R]	Three of a Kind	196?	2.50	5.00	10.00

CHARLES, RAY, AND MILT JACKSON
Albums

Number	Title (A Side/B Side)	Yr	VG	VG+	NM
ATLANTIC					
❏ 1279 [M]	Soul Brothers	1958	12.50	25.00	50.00
—Black label					
❏ 1279 [M]	Soul Brothers	1960	6.25	12.50	25.00
—Red and white label, white fan logo on right					
❏ 1279 [M]	Soul Brothers	1962	5.00	10.00	20.00
—Red and white label, black fan logo on right					
❏ SD 1279 [S]	Soul Brothers	1959	12.50	25.00	50.00
—Green label					
❏ SD 1279 [S]	Soul Brothers	1960	6.25	12.50	25.00
—Blue and green label, white fan logo on right					
❏ SD 1279 [S]	Soul Brothers	1962	5.00	10.00	20.00
—Blue and green label, black fan logo on right					
❏ 1360 [M]	Soul Meeting	1961	6.25	12.50	25.00
—Red and white label, white fan logo on right					
❏ 1360 [M]	Soul Meeting	1962	5.00	10.00	20.00
—Red and white label, black fan logo on right					
❏ SD 1360 [S]	Soul Meeting	1961	7.50	15.00	30.00
—Blue and green label, white fan logo on right					
❏ SD 1360 [S]	Soul Meeting	1962	6.25	12.50	25.00
—Blue and green label, black fan logo on right					

CHARLES, RAY, AND CLEO LAINE
Albums

Number	Title (A Side/B Side)	Yr	VG	VG+	NM
RCA VICTOR					
❏ CPL2-1831 [(2)]	Porgy & Bess	1976	3.75	7.50	15.00
❏ DJL1-2163	Porgy & Bess	1976	5.00	10.00	20.00
—Promo-only excerpts from 2-record set					

CHARMS, THE
45s

Number	Title (A Side/B Side)	Yr	VG	VG+	NM
CHART					
❏ 608	Love's Our Inspiration/Love, Love Stick Stov	1956	10.00	20.00	40.00
❏ 613	Heart of a Rose/I Offer You	1956	10.00	20.00	40.00
❏ 623	I'll Be True/Boom Diddy Boom Boom	1956	10.00	20.00	40.00
DELUXE					
❏ 6000	Heaven Only Knows/Loving Baby	1953	125.00	250.00	500.00
❏ 6014	Happy Are We/What Do You Know About That	1953	100.00	200.00	400.00
❏ 6034	Bye Bye Baby/Please Believe in Me	1954	100.00	200.00	400.00
❏ 6050	Quiet Please/55 Seconds	1954	100.00	200.00	400.00
❏ 6056	Come to Me Baby/My Baby, Dearest Darling	1954	50.00	100.00	200.00
❏ 6062	Hearts of Stone/Who Knows	1954	12.50	25.00	50.00
❏ 6065	Two Hearts/The First Time We Met	1954	12.50	25.00	50.00
❏ 6072	Crazy, Crazy Love/Mambo Sh-Mambo	1955	12.50	25.00	50.00
❏ 6076	Ling, Ting, Tong/Bazoom (I Need Your Lovin')	1955	12.50	25.00	50.00
❏ 6080	Ko Ko Mo (I Love You So)/Whadya Want?	1955	12.50	25.00	50.00
❏ 6082	Whadya Want?/Crazy, Crazy Love	1955	10.00	20.00	40.00
❏ 6087	When We Get Married/Let the Happenings Happen	1955	10.00	20.00	40.00
❏ 6089	One Fine Day/It's You, You, You	1955	10.00	20.00	40.00
ROCKIN'					
❏ 516	Heaven Only Knows/Loving Baby	1953	200.00	400.00	800.00
7-Inch Extended Plays					
DELUXE					
❏ EP-357	*Hearts of Stone/Bazoom (I Need Your Lovin')/ Ling Ting Tong/Crazy, Crazy Love	1955	100.00	200.00	400.00
❏ EP-357 [PS]	Hits by the Charms	1955	100.00	200.00	400.00

CHARTS, THE
45s

Number	Title (A Side/B Side)	Yr	VG	VG+	NM
EVERLAST					
❏ 5001	Deserie/Zoop	1957	20.00	40.00	80.00
❏ 5002	Dance Girl/Why Do You Cry	1957	20.00	40.00	80.00
❏ 5006	You're the Reason (I'm in Love)/I've Been Wondering	1958	15.00	30.00	60.00
❏ 5008	I Told You So/All Because of Love	1958	15.00	30.00	60.00
❏ 5010	My Diane/All Because of You	1958	17.50	35.00	70.00
❏ 5026	Deserie/Zoop	1963	6.25	12.50	25.00
GUYDEN					
❏ 2021	For the Birds/Ooba-Gooba	1959	5.00	10.00	20.00
WAND					
❏ 1112	Deserie/Fell in Love with Your Baby	1966	6.25	12.50	25.00
❏ 1124	Livin' the Night Life/Nobody Made You Love Me	1966	15.00	30.00	60.00
Albums					
COLLECTABLES					
❏ COL-5029	Greatest Hits	1986	3.00	6.00	12.00
LOST-NITE					
❏ LLP-10 [10]	The Charts	1981	3.00	6.00	12.00
—Red vinyl					

CHECKER, CHUBBY
12-Inch Singles

Number	Title (A Side/B Side)	Yr	VG	VG+	NM
AMHERST					
❏ AMH-D-4	The Rub (5:02)/Move It (4:45)	1976	5.00	10.00	20.00
SEA BRIGHT					
❏ 7128	Read You Like a Book (Extended Version) (Radio Version)	1986	2.00	4.00	8.00
45s					
20TH CENTURY					
❏ 2040	Reggae My Way/Gypsy	1973	—	2.50	5.00
❏ 2075	She's a Bad Woman/Happiness Is a Girl Like You	1974	—	2.50	5.00
ABKCO					
❏ 4001	The Twist/Loddy Lo	1972	—	2.50	5.00
❏ 4002	The Hucklebuck/Pony Time	1972	—	2.50	5.00
❏ 4003	Limbo Rock/Let's Twist Again	1972	—	2.50	5.00
❏ 4004	Hey Bobba Needle/Hooka Tooka	1972	—	2.50	5.00
❏ 4027	Slow Twistin'/Birdland	1973	—	2.50	5.00
AMHERST					
❏ 716	The Rub/Move It	1976	—	2.00	4.00
BUDDAH					
❏ 100	Back in the U.S.S.R./Windy Cream	1969	3.00	6.00	12.00

C

Number	Title (A Side/B Side)	Yr	VG	VG+	NM
MCA					
❑ 51233	Running/Is Tonight the Night	1982	—	2.50	5.00
❑ 52015	Running/Is Tonight the Night	1982	—	2.00	4.00
❑ 52043	Harder Than Diamond/Your Love	1982	—	2.00	4.00
PARKWAY					
❑ 003 [DJ]	Never on Sunday/Alouette	1962	10.00	20.00	40.00
—Yellow label, black print, promo only					
❑ 004 [DJ]	Love Is Like a Twist/Peppermint Twist	1962	10.00	20.00	40.00
—Yellow label, black print, promo only					
❑ 005 [DJ]	Your Lips and Mine/Dear Lady Twist	1962	10.00	20.00	40.00
—Yellow label, black print, promo only					
❑ 006 [DJ]	The Jet/The Ray Charles-ton	1962	7.50	15.00	30.00
❑ 105	You Got the Power/Looking at Tomorrow	1966	3.75	7.50	15.00
❑ 112	Karate Monkey/Her Heart	1966	3.75	7.50	15.00
❑ 804	The Class/Schooldays, Oh Schooldays	1959	7.50	15.00	30.00
❑ 808	Samson and Delilah/Whole Lotta Laughin'	1959	6.25	12.50	25.00
❑ 810	Dancing Dinosaur/Those Private Eyes (Keep Watchin' Me)	1960	6.25	12.50	25.00
—The existence of both 808 and 810 has been confirmed					
❑ 811	The Twist/Toot	1960	7.50	15.00	30.00
—First pressings have white label with blue print					
❑ 811	The Twist/Toot	1960	5.00	10.00	20.00
—Second pressings have orange label with black print					
❑ 811	The Twist/Twistin' U.S.A.	1961	3.75	7.50	15.00
❑ 811 [DJ]	The Twist/Twistin' U.S.A.	1961	50.00	100.00	200.00
—Promo copy on red vinyl					
❑ 811 [DJ]	The Twist/Twistin' U.S.A.	1961	37.50	75.00	150.00
—Promo copy on yellow vinyl					
❑ 811 [PS]	The Twist/Twistin' U.S.A.	1961	6.25	12.50	25.00
❑ 813	The Hucklebuck/Whole Lotta Shakin' Goin' On	1960	3.75	7.50	15.00
❑ 818	Pony Time/Oh, Susannah	1960	3.75	7.50	15.00
❑ 822	Dance the Mess Around/Good, Good Lovin'	1961	3.75	7.50	15.00
❑ 824	Let's Twist Again/Everything's Gonna Be Alright	1961	3.75	7.50	15.00
❑ 824	Let's Twist Again/Everything's Gonna Be Alright	1961	50.00	100.00	200.00
—Orange vinyl					
❑ 824 [PS]	Let's Twist Again/Everything's Gonna Be Alright	1961	6.25	12.50	25.00
❑ 830	The Fly/That's the Way It Goes	1961	3.75	7.50	15.00
❑ 830 [PS]	The Fly/That's the Way It Goes	1961	6.25	12.50	25.00
❑ 835	Slow Twistin'/La Paloma Twist	1962	3.75	7.50	15.00
—Features female vocal by Dee Dee Sharp					
❑ 835 [PS]	Slow Twistin'/La Paloma Twist	1962	6.25	12.50	25.00
❑ 842	Dancin' Party/Gotta Get Myself Together	1962	3.75	7.50	15.00
❑ 842 [PS]	Dancin' Party/Gotta Get Myself Together	1962	6.25	12.50	25.00
❑ 849	Limbo Rock/Popeye The Hitch-Hiker	1962	3.75	7.50	15.00
❑ 849 [PS]	Limbo Rock/Popeye The Hitch-Hiker	1962	6.25	12.50	25.00
❑ 862	Twenty Miles/Let's Limbo Some More	1963	3.75	7.50	15.00
❑ 862 [PS]	Twenty Miles/Let's Limbo Some More	1963	6.25	12.50	25.00
❑ 873	Birdland/Black Cloud	1963	3.75	7.50	15.00
❑ 873 [PS]	Birdland/Black Cloud	1963	6.25	12.50	25.00
❑ 879	Surf Party/Twist It Up	1963	3.75	7.50	15.00
❑ 879 [PS]	Surf Party/Twist It Up	1963	6.25	12.50	25.00
❑ 890	Loddy Lo/Everything's Gonna Be Alright	1963	4.00	8.00	16.00
❑ 890	Loddy Lo/Hooka Tooka	1963	3.75	7.50	15.00
❑ 890 [PS]	Loddy Lo/Everything's Gonna Be Alright	1963	7.00	14.00	28.00
❑ 890 [PS]	Loddy Lo/Hooka Tooka	1963	6.25	12.50	25.00
❑ 907	Hey Bobba Needle/Spread Joy	1964	3.75	7.50	15.00
❑ 907 [PS]	Hey Bobba Needle/Spread Joy	1964	6.25	12.50	25.00
❑ 920	Lazy Elsie Molly/Rosie	1964	3.75	7.50	15.00
❑ 920 [PS]	Lazy Elsie Molly/Rosie	1964	6.25	12.50	25.00
❑ 922	She Wants T'Swim/You Better Believe It, Baby	1964	3.00	6.00	12.00
❑ 922 [PS]	She Wants T'Swim/You Better Believe It, Baby	1964	6.25	12.50	25.00
❑ 936	Lovely, Lovely (Loverly, Loverly)/The Weekend's Here	1964	3.00	6.00	12.00
❑ 936 [PS]	Lovely, Lovely (Loverly, Loverly)/The Weekend's Here	1964	6.25	12.50	25.00
❑ 949	Let's Do the Freddie/(At the) Discotheque	1965	3.00	6.00	12.00
—Original A-side title (number is P-949-A) and probably correct B-side title					
❑ 949	Do the Freddie/(Do the) Discotheque	1965	5.00	10.00	20.00
—Reissue with new A-side title (number is P-949-C) and probably incorrect B-side title					
❑ 959	Everything's Wrong/Cu Me La Be-Stay	1965	3.00	6.00	12.00
❑ 965	You Just Don't Know/Two Hearts Make One Love	1965	100.00	200.00	400.00
❑ 989	Hey You! Little Boo-Ga-Loo/Pussy Cat	1966	3.00	6.00	12.00
SEA BRIGHT					
❑ 5128	Read You Like a Book/(B-side unknown)	1986	—	2.00	4.00

7-Inch Extended Plays

Number	Title (A Side/B Side)	Yr	VG	VG+	NM
PARKWAY					
❑ 5001	The Ray Charles-ton/The Mess Around//The Jet/The Continental Walk	1961	15.00	30.00	60.00
—Small hole, plays at 33 1/3 rpm					
❑ 5001 [PS]	Chubby Checker	1961	15.00	30.00	60.00
—Paper die-cut sleeve					

Albums

Number	Title (A Side/B Side)	Yr	VG	VG+	NM
ABKCO					
❑ 4219 [(2)]	Chubby Checker's Greatest Hits	1972	5.00	10.00	20.00
EVEREST					
❑ 4111	Chubby Checker's Greatest Hits	1981	3.00	6.00	12.00
MCA					
❑ 5291	The Change Has Come	1982	2.50	5.00	10.00
PARKWAY					
❑ P 7001 [M]	Twist with Chubby Checker	1960	10.00	20.00	40.00
—All-orange label					
❑ P 7001 [M]	Twist with Chubby Checker	1962	7.50	15.00	30.00
—Orange and yellow label					
❑ P 7002 [M]	For Twisters Only	1960	10.00	20.00	40.00
—All-orange label					
❑ P 7002 [M]	For Twisters Only	1962	7.50	15.00	30.00
—Orange and yellow label					
❑ P 7003 [M]	It's Pony Time	1961	10.00	20.00	40.00
—All-orange label					
❑ P 7003 [M]	It's Pony Time	1962	7.50	15.00	30.00
—Orange and yellow label					
❑ P 7004 [M]	Let's Twist Again	1961	10.00	20.00	40.00
—All-orange label					
❑ P 7004 [M]	Let's Twist Again	1962	7.50	15.00	30.00
—Orange and yellow label					
❑ P 7007 [M]	Your Twist Party	1961	10.00	20.00	40.00
—All-orange label					
❑ P 7007 [M]	Your Twist Party	1962	7.50	15.00	30.00
—Orange and yellow label					
❑ P 7008 [M]	Twistin' Round the World	1962	7.50	15.00	30.00
❑ SP 7008 [B]	Twistin' Round the World	1962	10.00	20.00	40.00
❑ P 7009 [M]	For Teen Twisters Only	1962	7.50	15.00	30.00
❑ SP 7009 [S]	For Teen Twisters Only	1962	10.00	20.00	40.00
❑ P 7014 [M]	All the Hits (For Your Dancin' Party)	1962	7.50	15.00	30.00
❑ P 7020 [M]	Limbo Party	1962	7.50	15.00	30.00
❑ SP 7020 [S]	Limbo Party	1962	10.00	20.00	40.00
❑ P 7022 [M]	Chubby Checker's Biggest Hits	1962	7.50	15.00	30.00
❑ SP 7022 [R]	Chubby Checker's Biggest Hits	1962	7.50	15.00	30.00
❑ P 7026 [M]	Chubby Checker In Person	1963	7.50	15.00	30.00
❑ SP 7026 [S]	Chubby Checker In Person	1963	10.00	20.00	40.00
—The above record is labeled "Twist It Up"					
❑ P 7027 [M]	Let's Limbo Some More	1963	7.50	15.00	30.00
❑ SP 7027 [S]	Let's Limbo Some More	1963	10.00	20.00	40.00
❑ P 7030 [M]	Beach Party	1963	7.50	15.00	30.00
❑ SP 7030 [S]	Beach Party	1963	10.00	20.00	40.00
❑ P 7036 [M]	Chubby Checker With Sy Oliver and His Orchestra	1964	7.50	15.00	30.00
❑ SP 7036 [S]	Chubby Checker With Sy Oliver and His Orchestra	1964	10.00	20.00	40.00
❑ P 7040 [M]	Folk Album	1964	7.50	15.00	30.00
❑ SP 7040 [S]	Folk Album	1964	10.00	20.00	40.00
❑ P 7045 [M]	Discotheque	1965	7.50	15.00	30.00
❑ SP 7045 [S]	Discotheque	1965	10.00	20.00	40.00
❑ P 7048 [M]	Chubby Checker's Eighteen Golden Hits	1966	7.50	15.00	30.00
❑ SP 7048 [P]	Chubby Checker's Eighteen Golden Hits	1966	10.00	20.00	40.00

CHECKERS, THE (1)

45s

Number	Title (A Side/B Side)	Yr	VG	VG+	NM
FEDERAL					
❑ 12355	So Fine/Sentimental Heart	1959	12.50	25.00	50.00
❑ 12375	White Cliffs of Dover/Let Me Come Back	1960	12.50	25.00	50.00
KING					
❑ 4558	Flame in My Heart/Oh, Oh, Oh Baby	1952	250.00	500.00	1000.
❑ 4581	Night's Curtains/Let Me Come Back	1952	250.00	500.00	1000.
❑ 4596	My Prayer Tonight/Love Wasn't There	1953	250.00	500.00	1000.
❑ 4626	Ghost of My Baby/I Wanna Know	1953	200.00	400.00	800.00
❑ 4673	I Promise You/You Never Had It So Good	1953	125.00	250.00	500.00
❑ 4675	White Cliffs of Dover/Without a Song	1953	125.00	250.00	500.00
❑ 4710	House with No Windows/Don't Stop Dan	1954	125.00	250.00	500.00
❑ 4719	Over the Rainbow/You've Been Fooling Around	1954	100.00	200.00	400.00
❑ 4751	I Wasn't Thinking, I Was Drinking/Mama's Daughter	1954	125.00	250.00	500.00
❑ 4764	Trying to Hold My Girl/Can't Find My Sadie	1955	125.00	250.00	500.00
❑ 5156	Heaven Only Knows/Nine More Miles	1958	100.00	200.00	400.00
❑ 5592	Over the Rainbow/Love Wasn't There	1962	5.00	10.00	20.00
—As "The Original Checkers"					

CHEROKEES, THE (5)

FRED PARRIS of THE FIVE SATINS was a member.

45s

Number	Title (A Side/B Side)	Yr	VG	VG+	NM
UNITED ARTISTS					
❑ 367	My Heavenly Angel/Bed Bug	1961	25.00	50.00	100.00

CHERRY, NENEH

12-Inch Singles

Number	Title (A Side/B Side)	Yr	VG	VG+	NM
VIRGIN					
❑ DMD 1296 [DJ]	Buffalo Stance (4 versions)	1989	3.00	6.00	12.00
❑ DMD 1378 [DJ]	Kisses on the Wind (English 12" Mix) (Spanish 12" Mix) (House Dub)//(Street Mix) (Moody Mix) (Bass Dub)/Buffalo Blues	1989	2.50	5.00	10.00
❑ DMD 1403 [DJ]	Manchild (4 versions)/Buffalo Stance (Sukka Mix II)	1989	2.50	5.00	10.00
❑ SPRO 12709 [DJ]	Money Love (Extended Version) (Perfecto Mix)/Twisted	1992	2.00	4.00	8.00
❑ SPRO 12734 [DJ]	Sassy/I Ain't Gone Under Yet/Red Paint//Somebody/Peace in Mind	1992	5.00	10.00	20.00
❑ SPRO 12776 [DJ]	Buddy X (6 versions)	1992	2.50	5.00	10.00
❑ 96532	Kisses on the Wind (English 12" Mix) (Spanish 12" Mix) (House Dub)//(Street Mix) (Moody Mix) (Bass Dub)/Buffalo Blues	1989	2.00	4.00	8.00
❑ 96573	Buffalo Stance (5 versions)	1988	2.00	4.00	8.00

45s

Number	Title (A Side/B Side)	Yr	VG	VG+	NM
VIRGIN					
❑ S7-56975	Buddy X/Trout	1993	—	2.50	5.00
—B-side with Michael Stipe (of R.E.M.)					
❑ 99154	Manchild/Phoney Ladies	1989	—	—	3.00
❑ 99154 [PS]	Manchild/Phoney Ladies	1989	—	—	3.00
❑ 99183	Kisses on the Wind/Buffalo Blues	1989	—	—	3.00
❑ 99183 [PS]	Kisses on the Wind/Buffalo Blues	1989	—	—	3.00
❑ 99231	Buffalo Stance/(Electro Ski Mix)	1989	—	—	3.00
❑ 99231 [PS]	Buffalo Stance/(Electro Ski Mix)	1989	—	—	3.00

This scarce LP, which appeared on the budget Crown label, features the Cadets' best-known record, a cover of "Stranded in the Jungle."

The Crazy Cadillacs, issued in 1959, is hard enough to find on a reissue Jubilee black label. Even more difficult is an original on the blue Jubilee label.

Released in the wake of the big hit single, *The Duke of Earl,* Gene Chandler's first album, is tough to find in the pictured mono and even tougher in stereo.

The original cover of the End album *We Are the Chantels* featured a photo of the group dressed in plantation-style dresses. Reissue covers feature kids at a jukebox.

Before Otis Williams affixed his name to the group, fired all the original members and brought in replacements, the Charms had the R&B hit (though not the original version) of "Hearts of Stone." It can be found on this scarce EP on the DeLuxe label.

The last time Chubby Checker's hits were available on 45s was on a series of reissues put out by Abkco Records in 1973. "Let's Twist Again" was one of these. Today, these reissues are sought-after in their own right, though not as much as the originals on Parkway.

Albums

VIRGIN

Number	Title (A Side/B Side)	Yr	VG	VG+	NM
❑ 91252	Raw Like Sushi	1989	2.50	5.00	10.00
❑ R 174031	Raw Like Sushi	1989	3.00	6.00	12.00

—BMG Direct Marketing edition

CHI-LITES, THE

12-Inch Singles

CHI-SOUND

Number	Title (A Side/B Side)	Yr	VG	VG+	NM
❑ TCD 121 [DJ]	Have You Seen Her (Long Version 5:28) (Short Version 3:39)	1981	3.75	7.50	15.00
❑ TCD 122	Have You Seen Her/Super Mad (About You Baby)	1981	3.00	6.00	12.00
❑ TCD 132 [DJ]	Me and You (stereo/mono)	1981	2.50	5.00	10.00
❑ TCD 136	Hot on a Thing (Called Love) (6:16)/Whole Lot of Good, Good Lovin'	1981	3.00	6.00	12.00
❑ TCD 138	Try My Side (Of Love)/Get Down with Me	1982	3.00	6.00	12.00

ICHIBAN

Number	Title (A Side/B Side)	Yr	VG	VG+	NM
❑ 12 PO 46	There's a Change (same on both sides)	1990	—	3.50	7.00
❑ 12 PO 55	Eternity (3 versions)	199?	—	3.50	7.00
❑ 12 PO 61	Solid Love Affair/Happy Music	199?	—	3.50	7.00

NUANCE

Number	Title (A Side/B Side)	Yr	VG	VG+	NM
❑ NU 1252	Hard Act to Follow (Vocal 5:24) (House Mix 6:57) (Vocal Edit 4:04)	1985	—	3.50	7.00

PRIVATE I

Number	Title (A Side/B Side)	Yr	VG	VG+	NM
❑ 4Z9-04962	Stop What You're Doin' (Club Version 6:17) (Instrumental 3:32)	1984	2.50	5.00	10.00
❑ 4Z9-05016	Gimme Whatcha Got (Club Version 6:20) (Dub Mix)	1984	2.50	5.00	10.00

T.K. DISCO

Number	Title (A Side/B Side)	Yr	VG	VG+	NM
❑ TKD-414	Higher (8:14)/Stay a Little Longer	1979	3.00	6.00	12.00

45s

BLUE ROCK

Number	Title (A Side/B Side)	Yr	VG	VG+	NM
❑ 4007	I'm So Jealous/The Mix-Mix Song	1965	6.25	12.50	25.00
❑ 4020	Doing the Snatch/Bassology	1965	6.25	12.50	25.00
❑ 4037	Never No More/She's Mine	1965	12.50	25.00	50.00

BRUNSWICK

Number	Title (A Side/B Side)	Yr	VG	VG+	NM
❑ 55398	Give It Away/What Do I Wish For	1969	2.00	4.00	8.00
❑ 55414	Let Me Be the Man My Daddy Was/The Twelfth of Never	1969	2.00	4.00	8.00
❑ 55422	I'm Gonna Make You Love Me/To Change My Love	1969	2.00	4.00	8.00
❑ 55426	24 Hours of Sadness/You're No Longer Part of My Heart	1970	2.00	4.00	8.00
❑ 55438	I Like Your Lovin' (Do You Like Mine)/You're No Longer Part of My Heart	1970	2.00	4.00	8.00
❑ 55442	Are You My Woman (Tell Me So)/Troubles A-Comin'	1970	2.00	4.00	8.00
❑ 55450	(For God's Sake) Give More Power to the People/Troubles A-Comin'	1971	2.00	4.00	8.00
❑ 55455	We Are Neighbors/What Do I Wish For	1971	2.00	4.00	8.00
❑ 55458	I Want to Pay You back (For Loving Me)/Love Uprising	1971	2.00	4.00	8.00
❑ 55462	Have You Seen Her/Yes I'm Ready	1971	—	3.00	6.00
❑ 55471	Oh Girl/Being in Love	1972	—	3.00	6.00
❑ 55478	The Coldest Days of My Life (Part 1)/The Coldest Days of My Life (Part 2)	1972	—	3.00	6.00
❑ 55483	A Lonely Man/The Man and the Woman (The Boy and the Girl)	1972	—	3.00	6.00
❑ 55489	We Need Order/Living in the Footsteps of Another Man	1972	—	3.00	6.00
❑ 55491	A Letter to Myself/Sally	1973	—	3.00	6.00
❑ 55496	My Heart Just Keeps On Breakin'/Just Two Teenage Kids	1973	—	3.00	6.00
❑ 55500	Stoned Out of My Mind/Someone Else's Arms	1973	—	3.00	6.00
❑ 55502	I Found Someone/Marriage License	1973	—	3.00	6.00
❑ 55505	Homely Girl/Never Had It So Good and Felt So Bad	1974	—	3.00	6.00
❑ 55512	There Will Never Be Any Peace (Until God Is Seated at the Conference Table)/Too Good	1974	—	3.00	6.00
❑ 55514	You Got to Be the One/Happiness Is Your Middle Name	1974	—	3.00	6.00
❑ 55515	Toby/That's How Long	1974	—	3.00	6.00
❑ 55520	It's Time for Love/Here I Am	1975	—	3.00	6.00
❑ 55522	Don't Burn No Bridges/(Instrumental)	1975	—	3.00	6.00
—With Jackie Wilson					
❑ 55525	The Devil Is Doing His Work/I'm Not a Gambler	1976	—	3.00	6.00
❑ 55528	You Don't Have to Go/(Instrumental)	1976	—	3.00	6.00
❑ 55546	First Time/Marriage License	1978	—	2.50	5.00

CHI-SOUND

Number	Title (A Side/B Side)	Yr	VG	VG+	NM
❑ 2472	Heavenly Body/Strung Out	1980	—	2.00	4.00
❑ 2481	Have You Seen Her/Super Mad (About You Baby)	1981	—	2.00	4.00
❑ 2495	All I Wanna Do Is Make Love to You/Round and Round	1981	—	2.00	4.00
❑ 2503	Me and You/Tell Me Where It Hurts	1981	—	2.00	4.00
❑ 2600	Hot on a Thing (Called Love)/Whole Lot of Good Lovin'	1982	—	2.00	4.00
❑ 2604	Try My Side (Of Love)/Get Down with Me	1982	—	2.00	4.00

DAKAR

Number	Title (A Side/B Side)	Yr	VG	VG+	NM
❑ 600	Baby It's Time/Price of Love	1968	3.00	6.00	12.00
—As "Marshall and the Chi-Lites"					

DARAN

Number	Title (A Side/B Side)	Yr	VG	VG+	NM
❑ 011	One by One/You Did That to Me	1964	25.00	50.00	100.00
—As "The Hi-Lites"					
❑ 0111	Pretty Girl/Love Bandit	1966	12.50	25.00	50.00
—As "Marshall and the Chi-Lites"					
❑ 222	I'm So Jealous/The Mix-Mix Song	1964	25.00	50.00	100.00
—As "The Hi-Lites"					

ICHIBAN

Number	Title (A Side/B Side)	Yr	VG	VG+	NM
❑ 90-205	There's a Change/Happy Music	1990	—	2.00	4.00

INPHASION

Number	Title (A Side/B Side)	Yr	VG	VG+	NM
❑ 7205	Higher/Stay a Little Longer	1979	—	2.50	5.00
❑ 7208	The Only One for Me (One in a Million)/You Won't Be Lonely Too Long	1979	—	2.50	5.00

JA-WES

Number	Title (A Side/B Side)	Yr	VG	VG+	NM
❑ 0888	You Did That to Me/I Won't Care About You	1966	3.75	7.50	15.00

LARC

Number	Title (A Side/B Side)	Yr	VG	VG+	NM
❑ 81015	Bottom's Up/Bottom's Up Groove	1983	—	2.00	4.00
❑ 81023	Bad Motor Scooter/I Just Wanna Hold You	1983	—	2.00	4.00

MERCURY

Number	Title (A Side/B Side)	Yr	VG	VG+	NM
❑ 73844	Happy Being Lonely/Love Can Be Dangerous	1976	—	2.50	5.00
❑ 73886	Vanishing Love/I Turn Away	1977	—	2.50	5.00
❑ 73934	My First Mistake/Stop Still	1977	—	2.50	5.00
❑ 73954	If I Had a Girl/I've Got Love on My Mind	1977	—	2.50	5.00

NUANCE

Number	Title (A Side/B Side)	Yr	VG	VG+	NM
❑ 752	Hard Act to Follow/(Instrumental)	1985	—	2.00	4.00

PRIVATE I

Number	Title (A Side/B Side)	Yr	VG	VG+	NM
❑ ZS4-04365	Stop What You're Doin'/Little Girl	1984	—	—	3.00
❑ ZS4-04484	Gimme Whatcha Got/Let Today Come Back Tomorrow	1984	—	—	3.00

REVUE

Number	Title (A Side/B Side)	Yr	VG	VG+	NM
❑ 11005	Love Is Gone/Love Me	1967	3.00	6.00	12.00
❑ 11018	(Um, Um) My Baby Loves Me/That's My Baby for You	1968	3.00	6.00	12.00

Albums

BRUNSWICK

Number	Title (A Side/B Side)	Yr	VG	VG+	NM
❑ BL 754152	Give It Away	1969	6.25	12.50	25.00
❑ BL 754165	I Like Your Lovin', Do You Like Mine?	1970	6.25	12.50	25.00
❑ BL 754170	(For God's Sake) Give More Power to the People	1971	6.25	12.50	25.00
❑ BL 754179	A Lonely Man	1972	6.25	12.50	25.00
❑ BL 754184	The Chi-Lites Greatest Hits	1972	6.25	12.50	25.00
❑ BL 754188	A Letter to Myself	1973	6.25	12.50	25.00
❑ BL 754197	Chi-Lites	1973	6.25	12.50	25.00
❑ BL 754200	Toby	1974	6.25	12.50	25.00
❑ BL 754204	Half a Love	1975	6.25	12.50	25.00
❑ BL 754208	The Chi-Lites Greatest Hits, Volume 2	1976	6.25	12.50	25.00

CHI-SOUND

Number	Title (A Side/B Side)	Yr	VG	VG+	NM
❑ T-619	Heavenly Body	1980	3.75	7.50	15.00
❑ T-635	Me and You	1982	3.75	7.50	15.00

EPIC

Number	Title (A Side/B Side)	Yr	VG	VG+	NM
❑ PE 38627	Greatest Hits	1983	2.50	5.00	10.00

ICHIBAN

Number	Title (A Side/B Side)	Yr	VG	VG+	NM
❑ ICH-1057	Just Say You Love Me	198?	2.50	5.00	10.00

LARC

Number	Title (A Side/B Side)	Yr	VG	VG+	NM
❑ 8103	Bottom's Up	1983	3.00	6.00	12.00

MERCURY

Number	Title (A Side/B Side)	Yr	VG	VG+	NM
❑ SRM-1-1118	Happy Being Lonely	1976	3.75	7.50	15.00
❑ SRM-1-1147	Fantastic	1977	3.75	7.50	15.00

PRIVATE I

Number	Title (A Side/B Side)	Yr	VG	VG+	NM
❑ FZ 39316	Steppin' Out	1984	2.50	5.00	10.00
❑ PZ 39316	Steppin' Out	1985	2.00	4.00	8.00

—Budget-line reissue

CHIC

12-Inch Singles

ATLANTIC

Number	Title (A Side/B Side)	Yr	VG	VG+	NM
❑ DSKO 101 [DJ]	Dance, Dance, Dance (Yowsah, Yowsah, Yowsah) (8:21) (3:45)	1977	5.00	10.00	20.00
❑ DSKO 109 [DJ]	Everybody Dance (8:25)/You Can Get By (5:20)	1978	3.75	7.50	15.00
❑ DSKO 131 [DJ]	Le Freak (5:30)/Savoir Faire (5:02)	1978	10.00	20.00	40.00
—Promo-only picture disc					
❑ DSKO 146 [DJ]	I Want Your Love/(Funny) Bone	1979	3.00	6.00	12.00
❑ DSKO 178 [DJ]	Le Freak (5:24)/You Can Get By (5:20)	1979	3.00	6.00	12.00
—Disco oldies reissue					
❑ DSKO 179 [DJ]	Dance, Dance, Dance (Yowsah, Yowsah, Yowsah) (8:21)/Everybody Dance (8:25)	1979	3.00	6.00	12.00
—Disco oldies reissue					
❑ DSKO 192 [DJ]	Good Times (8:13) (3:42)	1979	7.50	15.00	30.00
❑ DSKO 207 [DJ]	My Forbidden Lover (6:29)/What About Me (4:10)	1979	5.00	10.00	20.00
❑ DSKO 220 [DJ]	My Feet Keep Dancing (Disco Mix 6:44) (same on both sides)	1979	3.75	7.50	15.00
❑ DMD 241 [DJ]	Rebels Are We (4:55) (same on both sides)	1980	3.75	7.50	15.00
❑ DMD 247 [DJ]	Real People (5:28) (same on both sides)	1980	3.75	7.50	15.00
❑ DMD 306 [DJ]	Stage Fright (3:55)/So Fine (4:10)	1981	2.50	5.00	10.00
❑ DMD 371 [DJ]	Hangin' (unknown versions)	1982	2.50	5.00	10.00
❑ DMD 693 [DJ]	Give Me the Lovin' (Long Version) (Short Version)	1983	3.00	6.00	12.00
❑ DMD 1115 [DJ]	Jack Le Freak (Vocal Long Version 8:22) (same on both sides)	1987	3.00	6.00	12.00
❑ DK 4600	Dance, Dance, Dance (Yowsah, Yowsah, Yowsah) (8:21)/Sao Paulo (4:45)	1977	3.75	7.50	15.00
❑ DK 4621	Dance, Dance, Dance (Yowsah, Yowsah, Yowsah) (8:21)/Everybody Dance (8:25)	1979	3.00	6.00	12.00
—Disco oldies reissue					
❑ DK 4700	Le Freak (5:24)/Savoir Faire (4:53)	1978	5.00	10.00	20.00

C

Number	Title (A Side/B Side)	Yr	VG	VG+	NM
❑ DK 4712	I Want Your Love (6:53)/(Funny) Bone	1979	10.00	20.00	40.00
—Pink vinyl					
❑ DK 4801	Good Times (8:13)/A Warm Summer Night	1979	7.50	15.00	30.00
❑ 86606	Dance, Dance, Dance (Yowsah, Yowsah, Yowsah)/Only in My Dreams (2 versions)	1988	2.50	5.00	10.00
—B-side by Debbie Gibson; "Twin Winners" reissue					
❑ 86634	Jack Le Freak (Vocal Long Version 8:22)/Savoir Faire	1987	3.00	6.00	12.00
❑ 86919	Chic Cheer (unknown versions)	1984	3.00	6.00	12.00
BUDDAH					
❑ DSC 121	Dance, Dance, Dance (Yowsah, Yowsah, Yowsah) (8:30)/Sao Paulo (4:58)	1977	10.00	20.00	40.00
MIRAGE					
❑ DM 4827	Soup for One (7:58)/Bum Hard (5:12)	1982	3.75	7.50	15.00
WARNER BROS.					
❑ PRO-A-5069 [DJ]Chic Mystique (6 versions)		1992	3.00	6.00	12.00
❑ PRO-A-5457 [DJ]Your Love (Hank's Mix) (LP Edit)		1992	2.50	5.00	10.00
❑ 40225	Chic Mystique (7 versions)	1992	—	3.50	7.00
❑ 40393	Your Love (5 versions)/M.M.F.T.C.F.	1992	—	3.50	7.00
45s					
ATLANTIC					
❑ 3435	Dance, Dance, Dance (Yowsah, Yowsah, Yowsah)/Sao Paulo	1977	—	2.00	4.00
❑ 3469	Everybody Dance/You Can Get By	1978	—	2.00	4.00
❑ 3519	Le Freak/Savoir Faire	1978	—	2.00	4.00
❑ 3519 [PS]	Le Freak/Savoir Faire	1978	—	2.50	5.00
❑ 3557	I Want Your Love/(Funny) Bone	1979	—	2.00	4.00
❑ 3557 [PS]	I Want Your Love/(Funny) Bone	1979	—	2.50	5.00
❑ 3584	Good Times/A Warm Summer Night	1979	—	2.00	4.00
❑ 3584 [PS]	Good Times/A Warm Summer Night	1979	—	2.50	5.00
❑ 3620	My Forbidden Lover/What About Me	1979	—	2.00	4.00
❑ 3638	My Feet Keep Dancing/Will You Cry (When You Hear This Song)	1979	—	2.00	4.00
❑ 3665	Rebels Are We/Open Up	1980	—	2.00	4.00
❑ 3768	Real People/Chip Off the Old Block	1980	—	2.00	4.00
❑ 3887	Stage Fright/So Fine	1982	—	2.00	4.00
❑ 89725	Give Me the Lovin'/You Got Some Love for Me	1983	—	—	3.00
❑ 89954	Hangin'/Chic (Everybody Say)	1982	—	—	3.00
ATLANTIC OLDIES SERIES					
❑ OS 13211	Dance, Dance, Dance (Yowsah, Yowsah, Yowsah)/Everybody Dance	1979	—	—	3.00
—Reissue					
❑ OS 13215	Le Freak/I Want Your Love	1980	—	—	3.00
—Reissue					
❑ OS 13216	Good Times/My Forbidden Lover	1980	—	—	3.00
—Reissue					
BUDDAH					
❑ 583	Dance, Dance, Dance (Yowsah, Yowsah, Yowsah)/Sao Paulo	1977	5.00	10.00	20.00
MIRAGE					
❑ 4032	Soup for One/Burn Hard	1982	—	2.00	4.00
❑ 4051	Why/Why	1982	—	2.00	4.00
—B-side by Carly Simon					
Albums					
ATLANTIC					
❑ SD 16003	Risque	1979	2.00	4.00	8.00
❑ SD 16011	Les Plus Grands Succes de Chic — Chic's Greatest Hits	1979	2.00	4.00	8.00
❑ SD 16016	Real People	1980	2.00	4.00	8.00
❑ SD 19153	Chic	1977	2.00	4.00	8.00
❑ SD 19209	C'est Chic	1978	2.00	4.00	8.00
❑ SD 19323	Take It Off	1981	2.00	4.00	8.00
❑ 80031	Tongue in Chic	1982	2.00	4.00	8.00
❑ 80107	Believer	1983	2.00	4.00	8.00

CHICAGO BEARS SHUFFLIN' CREW, THE
12-Inch Singles
RED LABEL

Number	Title (A Side/B Side)	Yr	VG	VG+	NM
❑ V-70060	Superbowl Shuffle (3 versions)	1985	5.00	10.00	20.00
45s					
RED LABEL					
❑ B-71012	Superbowl Shuffle/(Instrumental)	1985	—	2.50	5.00
❑ B-71012 [PS]	Superbowl Shuffle/(Instrumental)	1985	—	2.50	5.00

CHIFFONS, THE
45s
BIG DEAL

Number	Title (A Side/B Side)	Yr	VG	VG+	NM
❑ 6003	Tonight's the Night/Do You Know	1960	20.00	40.00	80.00
BUDDAH					
❑ 171	So Much in Love/Strange, Strange Feeling	1970	2.50	5.00	10.00
B.T. PUPPY					
❑ 558	Secret Love/Strange, Strange Feeling	1970	2.50	5.00	10.00
LAURIE					
❑ 3152	He's So Fine/Oh My Love	1963	5.00	10.00	20.00
❑ 3152	He's So Fine/Oh My Lover	1963	5.00	10.00	20.00
—Both B-side titles have been confirmed; we're not sure which came first					
❑ 3166	Lucky Me/Why Am I So Shy?	1963	3.75	7.50	15.00
❑ 3179	One Fine Day/Why Am I So Shy	1963	5.00	10.00	20.00
❑ 3195	A Love So Fine/Only My Friend	1963	3.00	6.00	12.00
❑ 3212	I Have a Boyfriend/I'm Gonna Dry My Eyes	1963	3.00	6.00	12.00
❑ 3224	Tonight I Met an Angel/Easy to Love	1964	3.00	6.00	12.00
❑ 3262	Sailor Boy/When the Summer Is Through	1964	3.00	6.00	12.00
❑ 3275	What Am I Gonna Do with You/Strange, Strange Feeling	1964	3.00	6.00	12.00

Number	Title (A Side/B Side)	Yr	VG	VG+	NM
❑ 3301	Nobody Knows What's Going On (In My Mind But Me)/Did You Ever Go Steady	1965	3.00	6.00	12.00
❑ 3301	Nobody Knows What's Going On (In My Mind But Me)/The Real Thing	1965	3.00	6.00	12.00
❑ 3318	Tonight I'm Gonna Dream/Heavenly Place	1965	3.00	6.00	12.00
❑ 3340	Sweet Talkin' Guy/Did You Ever Go Steady	1966	3.75	7.50	15.00
❑ 3350	Out of This World/Just a Boy	1966	2.50	5.00	10.00
❑ 3357	Stop, Look, Listen/March	1966	2.50	5.00	10.00
❑ 3364	My Boyfriend's Back/I Got Plenty of Nuttin'	1966	2.50	5.00	10.00
❑ 3377	If I Knew Then/Keep the Boy Happy	1967	2.50	5.00	10.00
❑ 3423	Just for Tonight/Teach Me How	1968	2.50	5.00	10.00
❑ 3423	Just for Tonight/Keep the Boy Happy	1968	2.50	5.00	10.00
❑ 3460	Up on the Bridge/March	1968	2.50	5.00	10.00
❑ 3497	Love Me Like You're Gonna Lose Me/Three Dips of Ice Cream	1969	2.50	5.00	10.00
❑ 3630	My Sweet Lord/Main Nerve	1975	2.50	5.00	10.00
❑ 3648	Dream, Dream, Dream/Oh My Lover	1976	2.50	5.00	10.00
REPRISE					
❑ 20103	After Last Night/Doctor of Hearts	1962	5.00	10.00	20.00
RUST					
❑ 5070	When the Boy's Happy (The Girl's Happy Too)/Hockaday, Part 1	1963	6.25	12.50	25.00
—As "The Four Pennies"					
❑ 5071	Dry Your Eyes/My Block	1963	6.25	12.50	25.00
—As "The Four Pennies"					
WILDCAT					
❑ 601	Never Never/No More Tomorrows	1961	6.25	12.50	25.00
Albums					
B.T. PUPPY					
❑ S-1011	My Secret Love	1970	100.00	200.00	400.00
COLLECTABLES					
❑ COL-5042	Golden Classics	198?	3.00	6.00	12.00
LAURIE					
❑ LLP-2018 [M]	He's So Fine	1963	30.00	60.00	120.00
❑ LLP-2020 [M]	One Fine Day	1963	50.00	100.00	200.00
❑ LLP-2036 [M]	Sweet Talkin' Guy	1966	25.00	50.00	100.00
❑ SLP-2036 [S]	Sweet Talkin' Guy	1966	37.50	75.00	150.00
❑ 4001	Everything You Always Wanted to Hear by the Chiffons	1975	5.00	10.00	20.00
❑ DT-90075 [R]	He's So Fine	1965	50.00	100.00	200.00
—Capitol Record Club edition					
❑ ST-90779 [S]	Sweet Talkin' Guy	1966	50.00	100.00	200.00
—Capitol Record Club edition					

CHIMES, THE (1)
45s
LAURIE

Number	Title (A Side/B Side)	Yr	VG	VG+	NM
❑ 3211	Whose Heart Are You Breaking Now/Baby's Coming Home	1963	3.75	7.50	15.00
METRO					
❑ 1	Whose Heart Are You Breaking Now/Baby's Coming Home	1963	10.00	20.00	40.00
TAG					
❑ 444	Once in Awhile/Summer Night	1960	10.00	20.00	40.00
—Maroon label					
❑ 444	Once in Awhile/Summer Night	1960	10.00	20.00	40.00
—Light blue label					
❑ 444	Once in Awhile/Oh, How I Love You So	1960	12.50	25.00	50.00
—B-side is actually by a group called the Bi-Tones, though credited to the Chimes					
❑ 445	I'm in the Mood for Love/Only Love	1961	7.50	15.00	30.00
❑ 447	Let's Fall in Love/Dream Girl	1961	6.25	12.50	25.00
❑ 450	Paradise/My Love	1961	7.50	15.00	30.00

CHORDCATS, THE
See THE CHORDS.

CHORDS, THE
45s
ATCO

Number	Title (A Side/B Side)	Yr	VG	VG+	NM
❑ 6213	Sh-Boom/Little Maiden	1961	3.75	7.50	15.00
—As "The Sh-Booms"					
ATLANTIC					
❑ 2074	Blue Moon/Short Skirts	1960	5.00	10.00	20.00
—As "The Sh-Booms"					
CASINO					
❑ 451	Tears in Your Eyes/Don't Be a Jumpin' Jack	1958	7.50	15.00	30.00
CAT					
❑ 104	Sh-Boom/Cross Over the Bridge	1954	30.00	60.00	120.00
❑ 104	Sh-Boom/Little Maiden	1954	15.00	30.00	60.00
❑ 109	Zippety Zum (I'm in Love)/Bless You (For Being an Angel)	1954	10.00	20.00	40.00
❑ 112	A Girl to Love/Hold Me Baby	1955	10.00	20.00	40.00
—As "The Chordcats"					
❑ 117	Could It Be/Pretty Wild	1955	10.00	20.00	40.00
—As "The Sh-Booms"					
METRO					
❑ 20015	Elephant Walk/Pretty Face	1959	5.00	10.00	20.00
VIK					
❑ 0295	I Don't Want to Set the World on Fire/Lu Lu	1957	7.50	15.00	30.00
—As "The Sh-Booms"					
78s					
CAT					
❑ 104	Sh-Boom/Cross Over the Bridge	1954	15.00	30.00	60.00
❑ 104	Sh-Boom/Little Maiden	1954	7.50	15.00	30.00

Number	Title (A Side/B Side)	Yr	VG	VG+	NM
❏ 109	Zippety Zum (I'm in Love)/Bless You (For Being an Angel)	1954	7.50	15.00	30.00
❏ 112	A Girl to Love/Hold Me Baby	1955	7.50	15.00	30.00
—As "The Chordcats"					
❏ 117	Could It Be/Pretty Wild	1955	7.50	15.00	30.00
—As "The Sh-Booms"					

CHUBBY AND THE TURNPIKES
Some members later were in TAVARES.
45s
CAPITOL

Number	Title (A Side/B Side)	Yr	VG	VG+	NM
❏ 5840	I Didn't Try/I Know the Inside Story	1967	7.50	15.00	30.00

CHUCK-A-LUCKS, THE
45s
BOW

Number	Title (A Side/B Side)	Yr	VG	VG+	NM
❏ 305	Heaven Knows/Chuck-a-Luck	1957	12.50	25.00	50.00
CANDLELITE					
❏ 424	Heaven Knows/Chuck-a-Luck	196?	3.00	6.00	12.00
JUBILEE					
❏ 5415	Tarzan's Date/Unconditional Surrender	1961	5.00	10.00	20.00
LIN					
❏ 5010	Who Am I?/The Devil's Train	1958	6.25	12.50	25.00
❏ 5014	The Magic of First Love/Disc Jockey Fever	1958	12.50	25.00	50.00
MEL-O-DY					
❏ 106	Sugar Cane Curtain/Dingbat Diller	1963	6.25	12.50	25.00
WARNER BROS.					
❏ 5198	Long John/Pick Up and Deliver	1961	5.00	10.00	20.00
❏ 5234	Cotton Pickin' Love/I'm Hospitalized Over You	1961	5.00	10.00	20.00

CHURCH, EUGENE
Also see THE CLIQUES.
45s
CLASS

Number	Title (A Side/B Side)	Yr	VG	VG+	NM
❏ 235	Pretty Girls Everywhere/For the Rest of My Life	1958	6.25	12.50	25.00
❏ 254	Miami/I Ain't Goin' for That	1959	3.00	6.00	12.00
❏ 261	Jack of All Trades/Without Soul	1959	3.00	6.00	12.00
❏ 266	The Struttin' Kind/That's What's Happenin'	1960	3.00	6.00	12.00
KING					
❏ 5545	Mind Your Own Business/You Got the Right Idea	1961	3.00	6.00	12.00
❏ 5589	That's All I Need/Geneva	1962	2.50	5.00	10.00
❏ 5610	Light of the Moon/I'm Your Taboo Man	1962	2.50	5.00	10.00
❏ 5659	The Right Girl, the Right Time/Pretty Baby Won't You Come On Home	1962	2.50	5.00	10.00
❏ 5715	Sixteen Tons/Time Has Brought About a Change	1963	2.50	5.00	10.00
RENDEZVOUS					
❏ 132	Good News/Polly	1960	3.00	6.00	12.00
SPECIALTY					
❏ 604	How Long/Open Up Your Heart	1957	5.00	10.00	20.00
WORLD PACIFIC					
❏ 77866	Dollar Bill/U Maka Hanna	1967	3.75	7.50	15.00

78s
CLASS

Number	Title (A Side/B Side)	Yr	VG	VG+	NM
❏ 235	Pretty Girls Everywhere/For the Rest of My Life	1958	17.50	35.00	70.00

CHURCH STREET FIVE, THE
45s
LEGRAND

Number	Title (A Side/B Side)	Yr	VG	VG+	NM
❏ 1004	A Night with Daddy "G" Part 1/Part 2	1961	6.25	12.50	25.00
—Purple label original					
❏ 1004	A Night with Daddy G (Part 1)/A Night with Daddy G (Part 2)	1961	3.75	7.50	15.00
—Red, gold and white "shield" label					
❏ 1010	Fallen Arches/Everybody's Happy	1961	5.00	10.00	20.00
❏ 1014	Church Street Walk/I'm Gonna Sue	1961	5.00	10.00	20.00
❏ 1021	Daddy G Rides Again/Hey Now	1962	5.00	10.00	20.00
❏ 1026	Moonlight in Vermont/Sing a Song Children	1963	5.00	10.00	20.00

CLARK, DEE
Also see THE DELEGATES (3); KOOL GENTS.
45s
ABNER

Number	Title (A Side/B Side)	Yr	VG	VG+	NM
❏ (no #) [DJ]	Blues Get Off My Shoulder (B-side blank)	1959	25.00	50.00	100.00
—White label; noted as "Special D.J. Release from Latest E.P."					
❏ 1019	Nobody But You/When I Call on You	1958	6.25	12.50	25.00
❏ 1026	Just Keep It Up/Whispering Grass	1959	6.25	12.50	25.00
❏ 1029	Hey Little Girl/If It Wasn't for Love	1959	6.25	12.50	25.00
❏ 1029 [PS]	Hey Little Girl/If It Wasn't for Love	1959	10.00	20.00	40.00
❏ 1032	How About That/Blues Get Off My Shoulder	1959	6.25	12.50	25.00
❏ 1037	At My Front Door/Cling-a-Ling	1960	6.25	12.50	25.00
CHELSEA					
❏ 3025	Ride a Wild Horse/(Instrumental)	1975	—	2.50	5.00
COLUMBIA					
❏ 44200	In These Very Tender Moments/Lost Girl	1967	2.00	4.00	8.00
CONSTELLATION					
❏ 108	Crossfire Time/I'm Going Home	1963	3.00	6.00	12.00
❏ 113	It's Raining/That's My Girl	1964	3.00	6.00	12.00
❏ 120	Come Closer/That's My Girl	1964	3.00	6.00	12.00
❏ 132	Warm Summer Breeze/Heartbreak	1964	3.00	6.00	12.00
❏ 142	Ain't Gonna Be Your Fool/In My Apartment	1964	3.00	6.00	12.00
❏ 147	T.C.B./It's Impossible	1965	3.00	6.00	12.00
❏ 155	I Can't Run Away/She's My Baby	1965	3.00	6.00	12.00
❏ 165	I Don't Need (Nobody Like You)/Hot Potatoe	1966	3.00	6.00	12.00

Number	Title (A Side/B Side)	Yr	VG	VG+	NM
❏ 173	Old Fashion Love/I'm Goin' Home	1966	3.00	6.00	12.00
FALCON					
❏ 1002	Gloria/Kangaroo Hop	1957	7.50	15.00	30.00
❏ 1005	Seven Nights/24 Boy Friends	1957	10.00	20.00	40.00
❏ 1009	Oh Little Girl/Wondering	1958	10.00	20.00	40.00
LIBERTY					
❏ 56152	24 Hours of Loneliness/Where Did All the Good Times Go	1970	—	2.50	5.00
UNITED ARTISTS					
❏ 50759	You Can Make Me Feel So Good/Old Time Religion	1971	—	2.50	5.00
VEE JAY					
❏ 355	You're Looking Good/Gloria	1960	3.75	7.50	15.00
❏ 372	Your Friends/Because I Love You	1961	3.75	7.50	15.00
❏ 383	Raindrops/I Want to Love You	1961	5.00	10.00	20.00
❏ 394	Gotos Delluvia (Raindrops)/Livin' with Vivian	1961	3.75	7.50	15.00
—B-side by Al Smith					
❏ 409	Don't Walk Away from Me/You're Telling Our Secrets	1961	3.75	7.50	15.00
❏ 428	You Are Like the Wind/Drums in My Heart	1962	3.75	7.50	15.00
❏ 443	Dance On Little Girl/Fever	1962	3.75	7.50	15.00
❏ 462	I'm Going Back to School/Nobody But You	1962	3.75	7.50	15.00
❏ 487	I'm a Soldier Boy/Shook Up Over You	1963	3.75	7.50	15.00
❏ 532	How Is He Treating You/The Jones Boy	1963	3.75	7.50	15.00
❏ 548	Walking My Dog/Nobody But Me	1963	3.75	7.50	15.00
WAND					
❏ 1177	Nobody But You (Part 1)/Nobody But You (Part 2)	1968	2.00	4.00	8.00
WARNER BROS.					
❏ 7720	Raindrops '73/I'm a Happy Man	1973	—	2.50	5.00

7-Inch Extended Plays
ABNER

Number	Title (A Side/B Side)	Yr	VG	VG+	NM
❏ 900	(contents unknown)	1959	30.00	60.00	120.00
❏ 900 [PS]	Dee Clark	1959	30.00	60.00	120.00

Albums
ABNER

Number	Title (A Side/B Side)	Yr	VG	VG+	NM
❏ LP-2000 [M]	Dee Clark	1959	30.00	60.00	120.00
❏ SR-2000 [S]	Dee Clark	1959	87.50	175.00	350.00
❏ LP-2002 [M]	How About That	1960	20.00	40.00	80.00
❏ SR-2002 [S]	How About That	1960	30.00	60.00	120.00
SOLID SMOKE					
❏ 8026	His Best Recordings	1983	2.50	5.00	10.00
SUNSET					
❏ SUS-5217	Wondering	1968	3.00	6.00	12.00
VEE JAY					
❏ LP-1019 [M]	You're Looking Good	1960	12.50	25.00	50.00
❏ LP-1037 [M]	Hold On, It's Dee Clark	1961	12.50	25.00	50.00
❏ SR-1037 [S]	Hold On, It's Dee Clark	1961	25.00	50.00	100.00
❏ LP-1047 [M]	The Best of Dee Clark	1964	12.50	25.00	50.00
❏ SR-1047 [S]	The Best of Dee Clark	1964	25.00	50.00	100.00
❏ VJLP-1047	The Best of Dee Clark	1986	3.00	6.00	12.00
—Authorized reissue					

CLARKE, STANLEY
12-Inch Singles
EPIC

Number	Title (A Side/B Side)	Yr	VG	VG+	NM
❏ AS 779 [DJ]	You-Me Together/We Supply	1980	2.50	5.00	10.00
❏ EAS 2528 [DJ]	I'm Here to Stay (Edit) (LP Version)	1986	2.00	4.00	8.00
❏ 49-04792 [DJ]	Are You Ready (same on both sides)	1984	2.00	4.00	8.00
❏ 49-05015	Heaven Sent You (5:57) (6:00)	1984	2.00	4.00	8.00
❏ 49-05120	Spacerunner/Future	1984	2.00	4.00	8.00
❏ 49-05210	Born in the U.S.A. (5:10) (3:48)/Campo Americano	1985	2.00	4.00	8.00
❏ 49-05993	Listen to the Beat of Your Heart (3 versions)/Where Do We Go	1986	2.00	4.00	8.00
—With Angela Bofill					
NEMPEROR					
❏ ASD 450 [DJ]	More Hot Fun/Slow Dance	1978	3.75	7.50	15.00
❏ ASD 456 [DJ]	Rock 'n' Roll Jelly (same on both sides?)	1978	2.50	5.00	10.00
❏ 4Z8-7522	Just a Feeling (Special Disco Version)/The Streets of Philadelphia	1979	3.75	7.50	15.00
PORTRAIT					
❏ RAS 1226 [DJ]	Funny How Time Flies (When You're Having Fun) (same on both sides)	1988	2.50	5.00	10.00

45s
EPIC

Number	Title (A Side/B Side)	Yr	VG	VG+	NM
❏ 14-03038	Straight to the Top/The Force of Love	1982	—	—	3.00
❏ 34-03388	You Are the One for Me/Play the Bass	1982	—	—	3.00
❏ 34-04485	Heaven Sent You/Speedball	1984	—	—	3.00
❏ 34-04914	Born in the U.S.A./Camp Americano	1985	—	—	3.00
❏ 34-05584	What If I Should Fall in Love/Stereotypica	1985	—	—	3.00
❏ 34-06388	I'm Here to Stay/The Boys of Johnson Street	1986	—	—	3.00
❏ 34-06591	Listen to the Beat of Your Heart/Where Do We Go	1986	—	—	3.00
—With Angela Bofill					
❏ 9-50890	We Supply/Underestimation	1980	—	—	3.00
❏ 9-50924	You-Me Together/Rocks, Pebbles and Sand	1980	—	—	3.00
NEMPEROR					
❏ 001	Lopsy Lu/Vulcan Princess	1974	—	2.00	4.00
❏ 002	Silly Putty/Hello Jeff	1975	—	2.00	4.00
❏ 009	Hot Fun/Life Is Just a Game	1976	—	2.00	4.00
❏ 7518	Slow Dance/Rock 'n' Roll Jelly	1978	—	2.00	4.00
❏ 7521	Jamaican Boy/Rock 'n' Roll Jelly	1979	—	2.00	4.00
❏ 7523	Together Again (Part 1)/Together Again (Part 2)	1980	—	2.00	4.00

Number	Title (A Side/B Side)	Yr	VG	VG+	NM
PORTRAIT					
❏ 37-08051	Funny How Time Flies (When You're Having Fun)/If This Bass Could Only Talk	1988	—	2.00	4.00
Albums					
EPIC					
❏ JE 36506	Rocks, Pebbles and Sand	1980	2.50	5.00	10.00
❏ PE 36973	Stanley Clarke	1981	2.00	4.00	8.00
—Reissue of Nemperor 431					
❏ PE 36974	Journey to Love	1981	2.00	4.00	8.00
—Reissue of Nemperor 433					
❏ PE 36975	School Days	1981	2.00	4.00	8.00
—Reissue of Nemperor 900					
❏ FE 38386	Let Me Know You	1982	2.50	5.00	10.00
❏ FE 38688	Time Exposure	1984	2.50	5.00	10.00
❏ FE 40040	Find Out!	1985	2.50	5.00	10.00
❏ FE 40275	Hideaway	1986	2.50	5.00	10.00
NEMPEROR					
❏ SD 431	Stanley Clarke	1974	3.00	6.00	12.00
❏ SD 433	Journey to Love	1975	3.00	6.00	12.00
❏ SD 439	School Days	1976	3.00	6.00	12.00
❏ SD 900	School Days	1978	2.50	5.00	10.00
—Reissue of 439					
❏ JZ 35303	Modern Man	1978	2.50	5.00	10.00
❏ PZ 35305	Modern Man	1985	2.00	4.00	8.00
—Reissue with new prefix					
❏ KZ2 35680 [(2)]	I Wanna Play for You	1979	3.00	6.00	12.00
POLYDOR					
❏ PD-5531	Children of Forever	1973	3.00	6.00	12.00
❏ 827559-1	Children of Forever	1985	2.00	4.00	8.00
—Reissue					
PORTRAIT					
❏ OR 40923	If This Bass Could Only Talk	1988	2.50	5.00	10.00

CLARKE, STANLEY, AND GEORGE DUKE
Also see each artist's individual listings.

Number	Title (A Side/B Side)	Yr	VG	VG+	NM
12-Inch Singles					
EPIC					
❏ AS 1808 [DJ]	Trip You in Love/The Good Times	1983	2.50	5.00	10.00
❏ 49-04156	Heroes (Vocal) (Instrumental)	1983	2.50	5.00	10.00
❏ 49-73553	Mothership Connection (4 versions)	1990	2.00	4.00	8.00
45s					
EPIC					
❏ 19-01052	Sweet Baby/Never Judge a Cover By Its Book	1981	—	—	3.00
❏ 14-02397	I Just Want to Love You/Finding My Way	1981	—	—	3.00
❏ 14-02568	Touch and Go/Wild Dog	1981	—	—	3.00
❏ 34-04155	Heroes/Atlanta	1983	—	—	3.00
❏ 34-04322	Good Times/Great Danes	1984	—	—	3.00
❏ 34-73422	Lady/Find Out Who You Are	1990	—	2.00	4.00
Albums					
EPIC					
❏ FE 36918	The Clarke/Duke Project	1981	2.50	5.00	10.00
❏ PE 36918	The Clarke/Duke Project	198?	2.00	4.00	8.00
—Budget-line reissue					
❏ FE 38934	The Clarke/Duke Project II	1983	2.50	5.00	10.00

CLASSICS, THE (1)

Number	Title (A Side/B Side)	Yr	VG	VG+	NM
45s					
BED-STUY					
❏ 222	Again/The Way You Look Tonight	196?	2.50	5.00	10.00
DART					
❏ 1015	So in Love/Cinderella	1960	7.50	15.00	30.00
❏ 1024	Life Is But a Dream, Sweetheart/That's the Way	1961	50.00	100.00	200.00
❏ 1032	Angel Angela/Eenie Minie Mo	1961	12.50	25.00	50.00
MERCURY					
❏ 71829	Life Is But a Dream, Sweetheart/That's the Way	1961	6.25	12.50	25.00
MUSICNOTE					
❏ 118	P.S. I Love You/Wrap Your Troubles in Dreams	1963	6.25	12.50	25.00
❏ 1116	Till Then/Eenie Minie Mo	1963	6.25	12.50	25.00
—Black vinyl, blue label					
❏ 1116	Till Then/Eenie Minie Mo	1963	25.00	50.00	100.00
—Gold vinyl					
❏ 1116	Till Then/Eenie Minie Mo	1963	37.50	75.00	150.00
—Multi-color vinyl					
❏ 1116	Till Then/Eenie Minie Mo	1963	7.50	15.00	30.00
—Black vinyl, yellow label					
MUSICTONE					
❏ 1114	So in Love/Cinderella	1963	5.00	10.00	20.00
❏ 6131	Too Young/Who's Laughing, Who's Crying	1964	5.00	10.00	20.00
PICCOLO					
❏ 500	I Apologize/Love for Today	1965	6.25	12.50	25.00
STORK					
❏ 2	You'll Never Know/Dancing with You	1964	6.25	12.50	25.00
STREAM LINE					
❏ 1028	Life Is But a Dream, Sweetheart/Nuttin' in the Noggin	1961	6.25	12.50	25.00

CLAY, CASSIUS

Number	Title (A Side/B Side)	Yr	VG	VG+	NM
45s					
COLUMBIA					
❏ 43007	Stand By Me/I Am the Greatest	1964	6.25	12.50	25.00
❏ 43007 [PS]	Stand By Me/I Am the Greatest	1964	12.50	25.00	50.00
❏ ZSP 75717/77185 [DJ]	The Prediction/Will the Real Sonny Liston Please Fall Down	1964	10.00	20.00	40.00

Number	Title (A Side/B Side)	Yr	VG	VG+	NM
❏ ZSP 75717/77185 [PS]	The Prediction/Will the Real Sonny Liston Please Fall Down	1964	20.00	40.00	80.00
Albums					
COLUMBIA					
❏ CL 2093 [M]	I Am the Greatest!	1963	10.00	20.00	40.00
❏ CS 8893 [S]	I Am the Greatest!	1963	12.50	25.00	50.00

CLAY, JUDY

Number	Title (A Side/B Side)	Yr	VG	VG+	NM
45s					
ATLANTIC					
❏ 2669	Get Together/Sister Pitiful	1969	—	3.00	6.00
❏ 2697	Greatest Love/Saving All for You	1969	—	3.00	6.00
EMBER					
❏ 1080	More Than You Know/I Thought I'd Gotten Over You	1961	3.00	6.00	12.00
❏ 1085	Stormy Weather/Do You Think That's Right	1962	3.00	6.00	12.00
SCEPTER					
❏ 1273	My Arms Aren't Strong Enough/That's All	1964	2.00	4.00	8.00
❏ 1281	Lonely People Do Foolish Things/I'm Comin' Home	1964	2.00	4.00	8.00
❏ 12135	The Way You Look Tonight/Haven't You Got What It Takes	1966	2.00	4.00	8.00
❏ 12157	He's the Kind of Guy/You Busted My Mind	1966	2.00	4.00	8.00
❏ 12218	I Want You/He's the Kind of Guy	1968	2.00	4.00	8.00
STAX					
❏ 0006	Bed of Roses/Remove the Clouds	1968	—	3.00	6.00
❏ 0026	It Ain't Long Enough/Give Love to Save Love	1969	—	3.00	6.00
❏ 230	You Can't Run Away from Your Heart/It Takes a Lot of Good Love	1967	2.00	4.00	8.00

CLAY, OTIS

Number	Title (A Side/B Side)	Yr	VG	VG+	NM
45s					
COTILLION					
❏ 44001	She's About a Mover/You Don't Miss Your Water	1968	2.00	4.00	8.00
❏ 44009	Do Right Woman, Do Right Man/That Kind of Lovin'	1968	—	3.50	7.00
❏ 44068	Pouring Water on a Drowning Man/Hard Working Women	1970	—	3.50	7.00
❏ 44101	Is It Over/I'm Qualified	1970	—	3.50	7.00
DAKAR					
❏ 610	Baby Jane/You Hurt Me for the Last Time	1969	—	3.50	7.00
ECHO					
❏ 2002	Check It Out/Messing with My Mind	1975	2.50	5.00	10.00
ELKA					
❏ 301	Turn Back the Hands of Time/Good Lovin'	197?	2.00	4.00	8.00
GLADES					
❏ 1736	All I Need Is You/Special Kind of Soul	1976	2.50	5.00	10.00
HI					
❏ 2206	Home Is Where the Heart Is/Brand New Thing	1972	—	3.00	6.00
❏ 2214	Precious Precious/Too Many Hands	1972	—	3.00	6.00
❏ 2226	Trying to Live My Life Without You/Let Me Be the One	1972	—	3.50	7.00
❏ 2239	I Can't Make It Alone/I Didn't Know the Meaning of Pain	1973	—	3.00	6.00
❏ 2252	If I Could Reach Out/I Die a Little Bit Each Day	1973	—	3.00	6.00
❏ 2266	Woman Don't Live Here No More/You Can't Escape the Hands of Love	1974	—	3.00	6.00
❏ 2270	You Did Something to Me/I Was Jealous	1974	—	3.00	6.00
KAYVETTE					
❏ 5130	All Because of Your Love/Today My World Fell	1977	—	2.50	5.00
❏ 5133	Let Me In/Sweet Woman's Love	1977	—	2.50	5.00
ONE-DERFUL!					
❏ 4834	Three Is a Crowd/Flame in Your Heart	1965	2.50	5.00	10.00
❏ 4837	I Paid the Price/Tired of Falling In (And Out of) Love	1966	2.50	5.00	10.00
❏ 4841	I Testify/I'm Satisfied	1966	2.50	5.00	10.00
❏ 4846	Flame in Your Heart/It's Easier Said, Than Done	1967	2.00	4.00	8.00
❏ 4848	That's How It Is (When You're in Love)/Show Place	1967	2.00	4.00	8.00
❏ 4850	A Lasting Love/Got to Find a Way	1967	2.00	4.00	8.00
❏ 4852	Don't Pass Me By/That'll Get You What You Want	1968	2.00	4.00	8.00
Albums					
HI					
❏ HLP 6003	I Can't Take It	1977	3.75	7.50	15.00
❏ SHL 32075	Trying to Live My Life Without You	1972	5.00	10.00	20.00
ROOSTER BLUES					
❏ R-7609 [(2)]	Soul Man: Live in Japan	1985	3.75	7.50	15.00

CLEFTONES, THE

Number	Title (A Side/B Side)	Yr	VG	VG+	NM
45s					
CLASSIC ARTISTS					
❏ 121	She's So Fine/Trudy	1990	—	2.00	4.00
GEE					
❏ 1000	You Baby You/I Was Dreaming	1955	15.00	30.00	60.00
❏ 1011	Little Girl of Mine/You're Driving Me Mad	1956	10.00	20.00	40.00
❏ 1016	Can't We Be Sweethearts/Niki-Hoeky	1956	10.00	20.00	40.00
❏ 1025	String Around My Heart/Happy Memories	1956	10.00	20.00	40.00
❏ 1031	Why Do You Do Me Like You Do/I Like Your Style of Making Love	1957	10.00	20.00	40.00
❏ 1038	See You Next Year/Ten Pairs of Shoes	1957	10.00	20.00	40.00
❏ 1041	Hey Babe/What Did I Do That Was Wrong	1957	10.00	20.00	40.00
❏ 1048	Lover Boy/Beginners in Love	1958	7.50	15.00	30.00
❏ 1064	Heart and Soul/How Do You Feel	1961	6.25	12.50	25.00

CLEMONS, CLARENCE

Number	Title (A Side/B Side)	Yr	VG	VG+	NM
❏ 1067	(I Love You) For Sentimental Reasons/'Deed I Do	1961	5.00	10.00	20.00
❏ 1074	Earth Angel/Blues in the Night	1961	5.00	10.00	20.00
❏ 1077	Again/Do You	1961	5.00	10.00	20.00
❏ 1079	Lover Come Back to Me/There She Goes	1962	5.00	10.00	20.00
❏ 1080	How Deep Is the Ocean/Some Kinda Blue	1962	5.00	10.00	20.00

OLD TOWN

❏ 1011	The Masquerade Is Over/My Dearest Darling	1955	125.00	250.00	500.00

ROULETTE

❏ 4094	Trudy/She's So Fine	1958	6.25	12.50	25.00
❏ 4161	Mish Mash Baby/Cuzin Casanova	1959	6.25	12.50	25.00
❏ 4302	She's Gone/Shadows on the Very Last Row	1960	6.25	12.50	25.00

WARE

❏ 6001	She's Forgotten You/Right from the Git Go	1964	3.75	7.50	15.00

Albums

GEE

❏ GLP-705 [M]	Heart and Soul	1961	50.00	100.00	200.00
❏ SGLP-705 [S]	Heart and Soul	1961	125.00	250.00	500.00
❏ GLP-707 [M]	For Sentimental Reasons	1961	62.50	125.00	250.00
❏ SGLP-707 [S]	For Sentimental Reasons	1961	300.00	600.00	1200.

CLEMONS, CLARENCE

12-Inch Singles

COLUMBIA

❏ CAS 2200 [DJ]	You're a Friend of Mine (same on both sides)	1985	2.50	5.00	10.00

—With Jackson Browne

❏ CAS 2290 [DJ]	I Wanna Be Your Hero (Single Version) (Album Version)	1986	2.50	5.00	10.00

45s

COLUMBIA

❏ 38-04359	A Woman's Got the Power/Summer on Signal Hill	1984	—	2.50	5.00
❏ 38-05660	You're a Friend of Mine/Let the Music Say It	1985	—	—	3.00

—A-side with Jackson Browne

❏ 38-05660 [PS]	You're a Friend of Mine/Let the Music Say It	1985	—	2.00	4.00
❏ 38-05795	I Wanna Be Your Hero/Summer on Signal Hill	1986	—	2.00	4.00
❏ 38-68932	Quarter to Three/Something Always Happens	1989	—	2.00	4.00
❏ 38-73937	You're a Friend of Mine/Let the Music Say It	1991	—	—	3.00

—Reissue; A-side with Jackson Browne

CLINTON, GEORGE

Also see FUNKADELIC; PARLIAMENT; THE PARLIAMENTS.

12-Inch Singles

550 MUSIC

❏ BAS 7697 [DJ]	If Anybody Gets Funked Up (It's Gonna Be You) (4 versions)	1996	3.75	7.50	15.00
❏ BAS 7906 [DJ]	If Anybody Gets Funked Up (It's Gonna Be You) (6 versions)	1996	2.50	5.00	10.00
❏ BAS 8309 [DJ]	Summer Swim (LP Version) (Edit Version) (Instrumental) (Acappella)	1996	3.75	7.50	15.00
❏ 46-78391	Summer Swim	1996	2.50	5.00	10.00

CAPITOL

❏ V-8538	Loopzilla (5:58) (8:48)	1982	3.75	7.50	15.00
❏ V-8544	Atomic Dog (Album Version) (Single Version)	1982	6.25	12.50	25.00
❏ V-8572	Nubian Nut (LP Version 5:59)/Free Alterations	1983	2.50	5.00	10.00
❏ V-8580	Quickie/Last Dance	1984	3.00	6.00	12.00
❏ V-8581	Last Dance/Get Dressed	1984	2.50	5.00	10.00
❏ V-8603	Atomic Dog (Atomic Mix Long Version) (Instrumental)	1984	3.75	7.50	15.00
❏ V-8642	Double Oh-Oh (For Your Ears Only Mashed Mix) (LP Version) (Mixing Parts)	1985	2.50	5.00	10.00
❏ V-8653	Bullet Proof (Extended)/Silly Millameter	1985	3.00	6.00	12.00
❏ SPRO-9038/9 [DJ]	Nubian Nut (LP Version) (Single Version)	1983	2.50	5.00	10.00
❏ SPRO-9065/70 [DJ]	Last Dance (LP Version) (Single Version)	1984	3.00	6.00	12.00
❏ SPRO-9136 [DJ]	Quickie (same on both sides?)	1984	3.75	7.50	15.00
❏ SPRO-9628 [DJ]	Do Fries Go with That Shake (Thick Mix) (same on both sides)	1986	3.75	7.50	15.00
❏ SPRO-9728/9 [DJ]	Hey Good Lookin' (Rush This Mix 7:52) (Mirror Mix 4:33) (Marvelous Mix 5:35)	1986	2.50	5.00	10.00
❏ SPRO-9825/6 [DJ]	Loopzilla (Single Mix 4:13) (Broadcast Version 6:36)	1982	7.50	15.00	30.00
❏ V-15219	Do Fries Go with That Shake (10:15)/Scratch Medley: Do Fries Go with That Shake-Pleasures of Exhaustion (12:36)	1986	3.00	6.00	12.00
❏ V-15241	Hey Good Lookin' (Rush This Mix) (Mirror Mix) (Marvelous Mix)	1986	3.00	6.00	12.00
❏ V-15263	R&B Skeletons (In the Closet)/Nubian Nut	1986	2.50	5.00	10.00
❏ V-15562	Atomic Dog (Special Atomic Mix) (LP Version) (Instrumental)	1990	2.50	5.00	10.00
❏ 53576	Atomic Dog (2 versions)/Knee Deep/Hey Good Lookin'/Do Fries Go with That Shake	2000	2.00	4.00	8.00

—Red vinyl

❏ SPRO-79901 [DJ]	Atomic Dog (Special Atomic Mix) (same on both sides)	1990	3.00	6.00	12.00

FOX

❏ 10013	Erotic City (Extended Sweat Mix) (Groovestramental)/Stomp (LP Version) (Sir Nose Goes On)	1994	3.00	6.00	12.00

INTERSOUND

❏ 9284	Ain't Nuthin' But a Jam Y'All (4:02) (Instrumental)	1997	3.00	6.00	12.00

—With the Dazz Band

PAISLEY PARK

❏ PRO-A-3717 [DJ]	Tweakin' (Edit) (LP Version)	1989	2.00	4.00	8.00
❏ PRO-A-5995 [DJ]	Martial Law (Hey Man... Smell My Finger) (Single Version 4:14) (LP Version 7:13)	1993	2.50	5.00	10.00
❏ PRO-A-5998 [(2) DJ]	Martial Law (Hey Man... Smell My Finger) (Scratch & Sniff Mix 7:37) (Where's Your Finger Been Mix 7:28) (Smell My Finger Mix 9:05) (Stank Finger Mix) (2 Phunky Finger Mix) (Middle Finger Instrumental Mix) (Somethin' Stinks and I Want Some Bonus Beats Mix) (Single Version Edit)	1993	3.75	7.50	15.00

—One record is red vinyl, the other is green

❏ 21157	Why Should I Dog U Out? (4 versions)	1989	2.50	5.00	10.00
❏ 21337	Tweakin' (A-Mix) (Dub Mix) (C-Mixapella) (Radio Remix) (Hysterical Remix)	1989	2.50	5.00	10.00
❏ 41057	Paint the White House Black (3 versions)/Picture This/Booty	1993	2.50	5.00	10.00

45s

ABC

❏ 12040	Hold On to Your Lady/Nothing in This Whole World	1974	—	3.50	7.00

CAPITOL

❏ B-5160	Loopzilla/Pot Sharing Tots	1982	—	2.00	4.00
❏ B-5201	Atomic Dog/(Instrumental)	1983	—	2.00	4.00
❏ B-5201 [PS]	Atomic Dog/(Instrumental)	1983	—	3.00	6.00
❏ B-5222	Get Dressed/Free Alterations	1983	—	2.00	4.00
❏ B-5222 [PS]	Get Dressed/Free Alterations	1983	—	2.00	4.00
❏ B-5296	Nubian Nut/Free Alterations	1983	—	2.00	4.00
❏ B-5296 [PS]	Nubian Nut/Free Alterations	1983	—	2.00	4.00
❏ B-5324	Quickie/Last Dance	1984	—	2.00	4.00
❏ B-5324 [PS]	Quickie/Last Dance	1984	—	2.00	4.00
❏ B-5332	Last Dance/Get Dressed	1984	—	2.00	4.00
❏ B-5332 [PS]	Last Dance/Get Dressed	1984	—	2.00	4.00
❏ B-5473	Double Oh-Oh/Bangladesh	1985	—	2.00	4.00
❏ B-5473 [PS]	Double Oh-Oh/Bangladesh	1985	—	2.00	4.00
❏ B-5504	Bullet Proof/Silly Millimeter	1985	—	2.00	4.00
❏ B-5558	Do Fries Go With That Shake/Pleasure of Exhaustion (Do It Till I Drop)	1986	—	2.00	4.00
❏ B-5602	Hey Good Lookin' (Remix)/Hey Good Lookin' (Mirror Mix)	1986	—	2.00	4.00
❏ B-5642	R&B Skeletons (In the Closet)/Nubian Nut	1986	—	2.00	4.00

FOX

❏ 10012	Stomp/Pump It Up	1994	—	2.50	5.00

—B-side by Mudhoney

❏ 10012 [PS]	Stomp/Pump It Up	1994	—	2.50	5.00

PAISLEY PARK

❏ PRO-S-3438 [DJ]	Why Should I Dog U Out? (same on both sides?)	1989	—	3.00	6.00
❏ 22790	Tweakin'/French Kiss	1989	—	2.00	4.00
❏ 27557	Why Should I Dog U Out?/(Instrumental)	1989	—	—	3.00
❏ 27557 [PS]	Why Should I Dog U Out?/(Instrumental)	1989	—	—	3.00

Albums

550 MUSIC

❏ B2 67144 [(2)]	T.A.P.O.A.F.O.M. — The Awesome Power of a Fully Operational Mothership	1996	3.75	7.50	15.00

—Red vinyl

ABC

❏ D-831	The George Clinton Band Arrives	1974	3.75	7.50	15.00

CAPITOL

❏ ST-12246	Computer Games	1982	2.50	5.00	10.00
❏ ST-12308	You Shouldn't-Nuf Bit Fish	1984	2.50	5.00	10.00
❏ ST-12417	Some of My Best Jokes Are Friends	1985	2.50	5.00	10.00
❏ ST-12481	R&B Skeletons in the Closet	1986	2.50	5.00	10.00
❏ MLP-15021 [EP]	The Mothership Connection Live from Houston, Texas	1986	3.75	7.50	15.00
❏ C1-33911 [(2)]	Greatest Funkin' Hits	1996	3.00	6.00	12.00

—Red vinyl

❏ CJ-48424	The Best of George Clinton	1987	2.50	5.00	10.00

INVICTUS

❏ ST-9815	Black Vampire	1973	5.00	10.00	20.00

PAISLEY PARK

❏ PRO-A-6537 [(2) DJ]	Hey Man... Smell My Finger	1993	6.25	12.50	25.00

—Promo-only vinyl issue

❏ 25994	The Cinderella Theory	1989	3.00	6.00	12.00

WARNER BROS.

❏ 25887	George Clinton Presents Our Gang Funky	1988	2.50	5.00	10.00
❏ 25991	Under a Nouveau Groove	1989	2.50	5.00	10.00

CLINTONIAN CUBS, THE

JIMMY CASTOR was a member.

45s

MY BROTHERS

❏ 508	She's Just My Size/Confusion	1960	75.00	150.00	300.00

CLIQUES, THE

Also see JESSE BELVIN; EUGENE CHURCH.

45s

MODERN

❏ 987	Girl in My Dreams/I Wanna Know Why	1956	12.50	25.00	50.00

—Blue label

❏ 987	Girl in My Dreams/I Wanna Know Why	1956	7.50	15.00	30.00

—Black label

❏ 995	My Desire/I'm in Love with a Gal	1956	7.50	15.00	30.00

CLOVERS, THE

45s

ATLANTIC

❏ 934	Don't You Know I Love You/Skylark	1951	250.00	500.00	1000.

Stereo versions of most 1950s and 1960s albums are more sought after than the mono editions. *Sweet Talkin' Guy,* the Chiffons' 1966 release, is no exception.

Speaking of tough albums to find in stereo, here's the first release by Dee Clark. Abner, the Vee Jay subsidiary, issued it in 1959.

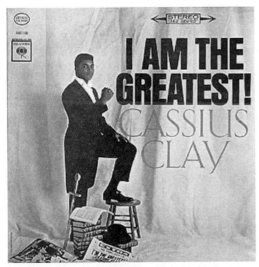

Cassius Clay, today known as Muhammad Ali, recorded a bunch of his poetry before a live audience in 1963, before his epic heavyweight title fight with Sonny Liston. The result, *I Am the Greatest!*, is sought after by collectors of several genres.

The Cleftones, a vocal group from Queens, had two R&B hits five years apart. The stereo edition of this, their second LP for the Gee label, is much more rare than its mono counterpart.

A very early 45 on the Atlantic label was "Fool, Fool, Fool" by the Clovers, which came out in 1951 and spent six weeks at #1.

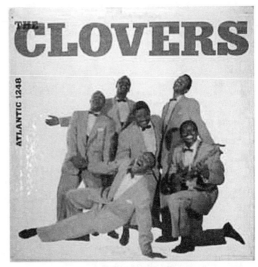

The first, self-titled, album by the Clovers was, perhaps inadvertently, originally issued in Atlantic's 1200-series jazz series. It was quickly reissued in the 8000 regular series.

Number	Title (A Side/B Side)	Yr	VG	VG+	NM
❑ 944	Fool, Fool, Fool/Needless	1951	62.50	125.00	250.00
❑ 963	One Mint Julep/Middle of the Night	1952	25.00	50.00	100.00
❑ 969	Ting-A-Ling/Wonder Where My Baby's Gone	1952	25.00	50.00	100.00
❑ 977	I Played the Fool/Hey, Miss Fannie	1952	62.50	125.00	250.00
❑ 989	Yes, It's You/Crawlin'	1953	15.00	30.00	60.00
❑ 1000	Good Lovin'/Here Goes a Fool	1953	20.00	40.00	80.00
❑ 1010	Comin' On/The Feeling Is So Good	1953	37.50	75.00	150.00
❑ 1022	Lovey Dovey/Little Mama	1954	12.50	25.00	50.00
❑ 1035	Your Cash Ain't Nothin' But Trash/I've Got My Eyes on You	1954	12.50	25.00	50.00
❑ 1046	I Confess/Alrighty, Oh Sweetie	1954	12.50	25.00	50.00
❑ 1052	Blue Velvet/If You Love Me (Why Don't You Tell Me So)	1955	15.00	30.00	60.00
❑ 1060	Love Bug/In the Morning Time	1955	12.50	25.00	50.00
❑ 1073	Nip Sip/If I Could Be Loved By You	1955	12.50	25.00	50.00
❑ 1083	Devil or Angel/Hey, Doll Baby	1956	50.00	100.00	200.00
—Yellow label, no spinner					
❑ 1083	Devil or Angel/Hey, Doll Baby	1956	10.00	20.00	40.00
—Red label, no spinner					
❑ 1083	Devil or Angel/Hey, Doll Baby	1956	2000.	3000.	4000.
—Red label, no spinner; red vinyl; value is conjecture					
❑ 1094	Love, Love, Love/Your Tender Lips	1956	10.00	20.00	40.00
❑ 1107	From the Bottom of My Heart/Bring Me Love	1956	7.50	15.00	30.00
❑ 1118	A Lonely Fool/Baby, Baby, Oh My Darling	1956	7.50	15.00	30.00
❑ 1129	Here Comes Romance/You Good-Looking Woman	1957	7.50	15.00	30.00
❑ 1139	I-I-I Love You/So Young	1957	7.50	15.00	30.00
❑ 1152	There's No Tomorrow/Down in the Alley	1957	7.50	15.00	30.00
❑ 1175	Wishing for Your Love/All About You	1958	7.50	15.00	30.00
❑ 2129	Drive It Home/The Bootie Green	1961	5.00	10.00	20.00
BRUNSWICK					
❑ 55249	Love! Love! Love!/The Kickapoo	1963	3.00	6.00	12.00
JOSIE					
❑ 992	For Days/Too Long Without Some Loving	1968	2.50	5.00	10.00
❑ 997	Try My Lovin' On You/Sweet Side of a Soulful Woman	1968	2.50	5.00	10.00
POPLAR					
❑ 110	The Gossip Wheel/Please Come On to Me	1958	6.25	12.50	25.00
❑ 111	The Good Old Summertime/Idaho	1958	6.25	12.50	25.00
PORT					
❑ 3004	Poor Baby/He Sure Could Hypnotize	1965	2.50	5.00	10.00
PORWIN					
❑ 1001/2	Stop Pretending/One More Time	1963	3.75	7.50	15.00
—As "Buddy Bailey and the Clovers"					
❑ 1004	It's All in the Game/That's What I Will Be	1963	3.75	7.50	15.00
—As "Buddy Bailey and the Clovers"					
STENTON					
❑ 7001	Please Mr. Sun/Gimme, Gimme, Gimme	1961	20.00	40.00	80.00
—As "Tippie and the Clovermen"					
TIGER					
❑ 201	Bossa Nova Baby/The Bossa Nova (My Heart Said)	1962	3.75	7.50	15.00
—As "Tippie and the Clovers"					
UNITED ARTISTS					
❑ 0133	Love Potion #9/Stay Awhile	1973	—	2.00	4.00
—"Silver Spotlight Series" reissue					
❑ 174	Rock and Roll Tango/That Old Black Magic	1959	6.25	12.50	25.00
❑ 180	Love Potion #9/Stay Awhile	1959	6.25	12.50	25.00
❑ 209	One Mint Julep/Lovey	1960	6.25	12.50	25.00
❑ 227	Easy Lovin'/I'm Confessin' That I Love You	1960	6.25	12.50	25.00
❑ 263	Yes It's You/Burning Fire	1960	6.25	12.50	25.00
❑ 307	The Honeydripper/Have Gun	1961	6.25	12.50	25.00
WINLEY					
❑ 255	Let Me Hold You/Wrapped Up in a Dream	1961	3.75	7.50	15.00
❑ 265	I Need You Now/Gotta Quit You	1962	3.75	7.50	15.00
❑ 265	They're Rockin' Down the Street/Be My Baby	1962	3.75	7.50	15.00
—As "The Fabulous Clovers"					
78s					
ATLANTIC					
❑ 934	Don't You Know I Love You/Skylark	1951	25.00	50.00	100.00
❑ 944	Fool, Fool, Fool/Needless	1951	20.00	40.00	80.00
❑ 963	One Mint Julep/Middle of the Night	1952	7.50	15.00	30.00
❑ 969	Ting-A-Ling/Wonder Where My Baby's Gone	1952	7.50	15.00	30.00
❑ 977	I Played the Fool/Hey, Miss Fannie	1952	7.50	15.00	30.00
❑ 989	Yes, It's You/Crawlin'	1953	7.50	15.00	30.00
❑ 1000	Good Lovin'/Here Goes a Fool	1953	7.50	15.00	30.00
❑ 1010	Comin' On/The Feeling Is So Good	1953	7.50	15.00	30.00
❑ 1022	Lovey Dovey/Little Mama	1954	7.50	15.00	30.00
❑ 1035	Your Cash Ain't Nothin' But Trash/I've Got My Eyes on You	1954	7.50	15.00	30.00
❑ 1046	I Confess/Alrighty, Oh Sweetie	1954	7.50	15.00	30.00
❑ 1052	Blue Velvet/If You Love Me (Why Don't You Tell Me So)	1955	7.50	15.00	30.00
❑ 1060	Love Bug/In the Morning Time	1955	7.50	15.00	30.00
❑ 1073	Nip Sip/If I Could Be Loved By You	1955	7.50	15.00	30.00
❑ 1083	Devil or Angel/Hey, Doll Baby	1956	10.00	20.00	40.00
❑ 1094	Love, Love, Love/Your Tender Lips	1956	10.00	20.00	40.00
❑ 1107	From the Bottom of My Heart/Bring Me Love	1956	10.00	20.00	40.00
❑ 1118	A Lonely Fool/Baby, Baby, Oh My Darling	1956	10.00	20.00	40.00
❑ 1129	Here Comes Romance/You Good-Looking Woman	1957	10.00	20.00	40.00
❑ 1139	I-I-I Love You/So Young	1957	10.00	20.00	40.00
❑ 1152	There's No Tomorrow/Down in the Alley	1957	10.00	20.00	40.00
❑ 1175	Wishing for Your Love/All About You	1958	12.50	25.00	50.00

Number	Title (A Side/B Side)	Yr	VG	VG+	NM
RAINBOW					
❑ 122	Yes Sir, That's My Baby/When You Come	1950	500.00	1000.	1500.
7-Inch Extended Plays					
ATLANTIC					
❑ 504	One Mint Julep/Fool, Fool, Fool//Hey, Miss Fannie/I Played the Fool	1953	50.00	100.00	200.00
❑ 504 [PS]	The Clovers Sing	1953	50.00	100.00	200.00
❑ 537	(contents unknown)	1954	37.50	75.00	150.00
❑ 537 [PS]	The Clovers Sing	1954	50.00	100.00	200.00
❑ 590	*Love, Love, Love/Devil or Angel/Blue Velvet/From the Bottom of My Heart	1955	37.50	75.00	150.00
❑ 590 [PS]	The Clovers	1955	50.00	100.00	200.00
Albums					
ATCO					
❑ SD 33-374	Their Greatest Recordings/The Early Years	1971	3.00	6.00	12.00
ATLANTIC					
❑ 1248 [M]	The Clovers	1956	150.00	300.00	600.00
❑ 8009 [M]	The Clovers	1957	100.00	200.00	400.00
—Reissue of 1248 on the "pop" series; black label					
❑ 8009 [M]	The Clovers	1960	75.00	150.00	300.00
—White "bullseye" label					
❑ 8009 [M]	The Clovers	1961	50.00	100.00	200.00
—Red and white label					
❑ 8034 [M]	Dance Party	1959	100.00	200.00	400.00
—Black label					
❑ 8034 [M]	Dance Party	1960	75.00	150.00	300.00
—White "bullseye" label					
❑ 8034 [M]	Dance Party	1961	50.00	100.00	200.00
—Red and white label					
GRAND PRIX					
❑ K-428 [M]	The Original Love Potion Number Nine	1964	7.50	15.00	30.00
❑ KS-428 [R]	The Original Love Potion Number Nine	1964	3.00	6.00	12.00
POPLAR					
❑ 1001 [M]	The Clovers In Clover	1958	100.00	200.00	400.00
UNITED ARTISTS					
❑ UAL-3033 [M]	The Clovers In Clover	1959	75.00	150.00	300.00
❑ UAL-3099 [M]	Love Potion Number Nine	1959	62.50	125.00	250.00
❑ UAS-6033 [R]	The Clovers In Clover	196?	50.00	100.00	200.00
❑ UAS-6099 [S]	Love Potion Number Nine	1959	125.00	250.00	500.00

COASTERS, THE

Also see THE ROBINS.

45s

Number	Title (A Side/B Side)	Yr	VG	VG+	NM
AMERICAN INT'L.					
❑ 1122	If I Had a Hammer/If I Had a Hammer (Disco Version)	1976	—	2.50	5.00
—As "The World Famous Coasters"					
ATCO					
❑ 6064	Down in Mexico/Turtle Dovin'	1956	20.00	40.00	80.00
❑ 6073	One Kiss Led to Another/Brazil	1956	15.00	30.00	60.00
❑ 6087	Searchin'/Young Blood	1957	17.50	35.00	70.00
—Maroon label (first pressing)					
❑ 6087	Searchin'/Young Blood	1957	6.25	12.50	25.00
—White and yellow label					
❑ 6098	Idol with the Golden Head/(When She Wants Good Lovin') My Baby Comes to Me	1957	10.00	20.00	40.00
❑ 6104	Sweet Georgia Brown/What Is the Secret of Your Success	1957	10.00	20.00	40.00
❑ 6111	Dance!/Gee, Golly	1958	10.00	20.00	40.00
❑ 6116	Yakety Yak/Zing Went the Strings of My Heart	1958	6.25	12.50	25.00
❑ 6126	The Shadow Knows/Sorry But I'm Gonna Have to Pass	1958	6.25	12.50	25.00
❑ 6132	Charlie Brown/Three Cool Cats	1959	6.25	12.50	25.00
❑ 6141	Along Came Jones/That Is Rock and Roll	1959	5.00	10.00	20.00
❑ 6146	Poison Ivy/I'm a Hog for You	1959	5.00	10.00	20.00
❑ 6153	Run Red Run/What About Us	1959	5.00	10.00	20.00
❑ 6163	Besame Mucho (Part 1)/Besame Mucho (Part 2)	1960	6.25	12.50	25.00
❑ 6168	Wake Me, Shake Me/Stewball	1960	6.25	12.50	25.00
❑ 6178	Shoppin' for Clothes/The Snake and the Book Worm	1960	6.25	12.50	25.00
❑ 6186	Thumbin' a Ride/Wait a Minute	1961	5.00	10.00	20.00
❑ 6192	Little Egypt (Ying-Yang)/Keep On Rolling	1961	5.00	10.00	20.00
❑ 6204	Girls, Girls, Girls (Part 1)/Girls, Girls, Girls (Part 2)	1961	5.00	10.00	20.00
❑ 6210	Bad Blood/(Ain't That) Just Like Me	1961	5.00	10.00	20.00
❑ 6219	Teach Me How to Shimmy/Ridin' Hood	1962	5.00	10.00	20.00
❑ 6234	The Climb/(Instrumental)	1962	5.00	10.00	20.00
❑ 6251	The P.T.A./Bull Tick Waltz	1962	5.00	10.00	20.00
❑ 6287	Speedo's Back in Town/T'Ain't Nothin' to Me	1964	3.75	7.50	15.00
❑ 6300	Lovey Dovey/Bad Detective	1964	3.75	7.50	15.00
❑ 6321	Wild One/I Must Be Dreaming	1964	3.75	7.50	15.00
❑ 6341	Hungry/Lady Like	1965	3.75	7.50	15.00
❑ 6356	Money Honey/Let's Go Get Stoned	1965	3.75	7.50	15.00
❑ 6379	Bell Bottom Slacks and a Chinese Kimono (She's My Little Spodee-O)/Crazy Baby	1965	6.25	12.50	25.00
❑ 6407	Saturday Night Fish Fry/She's a Yum Yum	1966	3.75	7.50	15.00
ATLANTIC					
❑ 89361	Yakety Yak/Stand By Me	1986	—	—	3.00
❑ 89361 [PS]	Yakety Yak/Stand By Me	1986	—	—	3.00
—B-side by Ben E. King. See listing of this record under "King, Ben E." for more information.					
CHELAN					
❑ 2000	Searchin' '75/Young BLood	1975	—	2.50	5.00
—As "The Coasters 2+2"					
DATE					
❑ 1552	Soul Pad/Down Home Girl	1967	5.00	10.00	20.00

C

Number	Title (A Side/B Side)	Yr	VG	VG+	NM
❑ 1607	Everybody's Woman/She Can	1968	5.00	10.00	20.00
❑ 1617	D.W. Washburn/Everybody's Woman	1968	5.00	10.00	20.00

KING

Number	Title (A Side/B Side)	Yr	VG	VG+	NM
❑ 6385	Love Potion #9/D.W. Washburn	1972	—	3.00	6.00
❑ 6389	Cool Jerk/Talkin' 'Bout a Woman	1972	—	3.00	6.00
❑ 6404	Soul Pad/D.W. Washburn	1972	—	3.00	6.00

SAL WA

❑ 1001	Take It Easy, Greasy/You Move Me	1975	—	2.50	5.00

TURNTABLE

❑ 504	Act Right/The World Is Changing	1969	2.50	5.00	10.00

7-Inch Extended Plays

ATCO

Number	Title (A Side/B Side)	Yr	VG	VG+	NM
❑ 4501	Searchin'/Young Blood///(When She Wants Good Lovin') My Baby Comes to Me/Idol with the Golden Head	1958	37.50	75.00	150.00
❑ 4501 [PS]	Rock and Roll	1958	50.00	100.00	200.00
❑ 4503	Yakety Yak/Framed//Loop De Loop Mambo/Riot in Cell Block Number Nine	1959	50.00	100.00	200.00
❑ 4503 [PS]	Keep Rockin' with the Coasters	1959	50.00	100.00	200.00
❑ 4506	*Charlie Brown/Three Cool Cats/The Shadow Knows/Sorry But I'm Gonna Have to Pass	1959	37.50	75.00	150.00
❑ 4506 [PS]	The Coasters	1959	37.50	75.00	150.00
❑ 4507	Along Came Jones/That Is Rock & Roll//Dance!/Gee, Golly	1959	37.50	75.00	150.00
❑ 4507 [PS]	The Coasters' Top Hits	1959	37.50	75.00	150.00

Albums

ATCO

Number	Title (A Side/B Side)	Yr	VG	VG+	NM
❑ 33-101 [M]	The Coasters	1958	75.00	150.00	300.00
—Yellow "harp" label					
❑ 33-101 [M]	The Coasters	196?	15.00	30.00	60.00
—Gold and dark blue label					
❑ 33-111 [M]	The Coasters' Greatest Hits	1959	37.50	75.00	150.00
—Yellow "harp" label					
❑ 33-111 [M]	The Coasters' Greatest Hits	196?	15.00	30.00	60.00
—Gold and gray label					
❑ 33-123 [M]	One By One	1960	37.50	75.00	150.00
—Yellow "harp" label					
❑ 33-123 [M]	One By One	196?	15.00	30.00	60.00
—Gold and gray label					
❑ SD 33-123 [S]	One By One	1960	100.00	200.00	400.00
—Yellow "harp" label					
❑ SD 33-123 [S]	One By One	196?	37.50	75.00	150.00
—Purple and brown label					
❑ 33-135 [M]	Coast Along with the Coasters	1962	25.00	50.00	100.00
—Gold and gray label					
❑ SD 33-135 [P]	Coast Along with the Coasters	1962	37.50	75.00	150.00
—Purple and brown label; "Wait a Minute" is rechanneled					
❑ SD 33-371	Their Greatest Recordings/The Early Years	1971	5.00	10.00	20.00

CLARION

❑ 605 [M]	That Is Rock and Roll	1965	10.00	20.00	40.00
❑ SD 605 [S]	That Is Rock and Roll	1965	12.50	25.00	50.00

KING

❑ KS-1146	The Coasters On Broadway	1971	6.25	12.50	25.00

POWER PAK

❑ 310	Greatest Hits	198?	2.50	5.00	10.00

TRIP

❑ 8028	It Ain't Sanitary	197?	3.00	6.00	12.00

COFFEY, DENNIS

12-Inch Singles

WESTBOUND

Number	Title (A Side/B Side)	Yr	VG	VG+	NM
❑ DSKO 117 [DJ]	Calling Planet Earth (5:06) (same on both sides)	1978	3.00	6.00	12.00

45s

SUSSEX

❑ 208	Getting It On/Summertime Girl	1970	—	2.50	5.00
❑ 226	Scorpio/Sad Angel	1971	—	2.50	5.00
❑ 233	Taurus/Can You Feel It	1972	—	2.50	5.00
❑ 237	Ride, Sally, Ride/Getting It On	1972	—	2.50	5.00
❑ 251	Capricorn's Thing/Lonely Moon Child	1973	—	2.50	5.00
❑ 511	Theme from "Enter the Dragon"/Junction Flats	1973	—	2.50	5.00
❑ 631	Getting It On '75/Chicano	1974	—	2.50	5.00

WARNER BROS.

❑ 7769	Theme from "Black Belt Jones"/Love Theme from "Black Belt Jones"	1974	—	2.50	5.00

WESTBOUND

❑ 5020	Finger Lickin' Good/Wild Child	1975	—	2.00	4.00
❑ 5028	Honky Tonk/El Tigre	1976	—	2.00	4.00
❑ 55402	Our Love Goes On Forever/Back Home	1977	—	2.00	4.00
❑ 55414	Calling Planet Earth/A Sweet Taste of Sin	1978	—	2.00	4.00

Albums

ORPHEUS

❑ D1-75617	Under the Moonlight	1989	3.00	6.00	12.00

SUSSEX

❑ SUX-7004	Evolution	1971	3.00	6.00	12.00
❑ SUX-7010	Goin' for Myself	1972	3.00	6.00	12.00
❑ SUX-7021	Electric Coffey	1972	3.00	6.00	12.00
❑ SUX-8031	Instant Coffey	1974	3.00	6.00	12.00

WESTBOUND

❑ W-212	Finger Lickin' Good	1975	2.50	5.00	10.00
❑ WD 300	Home	1977	2.50	5.00	10.00
❑ 6105	The Sweet Taste of Sin	1978	2.50	5.00	10.00

COINS, THE

45s

GEE

Number	Title (A Side/B Side)	Yr	VG	VG+	NM
❑ 10	Cheatin' Baby/Blue, Can't Get No Place with You	1954	500.00	1000.	2000.
❑ 11	Look at Me Girl/S.R. Blues	1954	500.00	1000.	2000.
❑ 1007	Look at Me Girl/Two Loves Have I	1956	150.00	300.00	600.00
—B-side by the Colonials					

MODEL

❑ 2001	Loretta/Please	1955	500.00	1000.	2000.

COLDCUT

12-Inch Singles

COLUMBIA

Number	Title (A Side/B Side)	Yr	VG	VG+	NM
❑ 44-07842	Doctorin' the House (Vocal Verse) (7" Vocal)/(Upset Remix) (Acid Shut Up Mix)	1988	3.00	6.00	12.00
—Featuring Yazz & The Plastic Population					

TOMMY BOY

❑ TB 931	People Hold On (5 versions)	1989	2.00	4.00	8.00
—Featuring Lisa Stansfield					
❑ TB 939	People Hold On (6 versions)	1989	2.00	4.00	8.00
—Featuring Lisa Stansfield					
❑ TB 940	Stop This Crazy Thing (4 versions)	1989	2.00	4.00	8.00
—Featuring Junior Reid					

45s

COLUMBIA

❑ 38-07935	Doctorin' the House/(Thief-Apella Mix)	1988	—	2.50	5.00
—Featuring Yazz & The Plastic Population					
❑ 38-07935 [PS]	Doctorin' the House/(Thief-Apella Mix)	1988	—	2.50	5.00

TOMMY BOY

❑ 22848	People Hold On (Radio Mix)/(Acapella)	1989	—	2.00	4.00
—Featuring Lisa Stansfield					
❑ 22848 [PS]	People Hold On (Radio Mix)/(Acapella)	1989	—	2.00	4.00

Albums

TOMMY BOY

❑ 25974	What's That Noise?	1989	3.00	6.00	12.00

COLE, COZY

45s

BETHLEHEM

Number	Title (A Side/B Side)	Yr	VG	VG+	NM
❑ 3067	Big Boss/Cozy and Bossa	1963	2.00	4.00	8.00

COLUMBIA

❑ 43657	Whole Lotta Shakin' Goin' On/Watch It	1966	2.00	4.00	8.00

CORAL

❑ 62339	Big Noise from Winnetka (Part 1)/Big Noise from Winnetka (Part 2)	1962	2.00	4.00	8.00
❑ 62379	Rockin' Drummer/Sing, Sing, Sing (With a Swing)	1963	2.00	4.00	8.00
—With Gary Chester					
❑ 62395	Ol' Man Moses/Christopher Columbus	1964	2.00	4.00	8.00
❑ 62417	Cozy Beat/Night Beach	1964	2.00	4.00	8.00

FELSTED

❑ 8546	Caravan Part 1/Caravan Part 2	1959	2.50	5.00	10.00

GRAND AWARD

❑ 1023	Caravan Part 1/Caravan Part 2	1959	3.00	6.00	12.00

KING

❑ 5222	Blow-Up/Flop-Down	1959	2.50	5.00	10.00
❑ 5242	Strange/D Natural Rock	1959	2.50	5.00	10.00
❑ 5254	Melody of a Dreamer/Soft	1959	2.50	5.00	10.00
❑ 5265	Boy Meets Girl/Playtime Blues	1959	2.50	5.00	10.00
—With Lee Parker					
❑ 5287	Stain Glass/D'Mitri	1959	2.50	5.00	10.00
❑ 5303	Play, Cozy, Play/Cozy's Mambo	1960	2.50	5.00	10.00
❑ 5316	Blockhead/Teen-Age Ideas	1960	2.50	5.00	10.00
❑ 5337	Drum Fever/Bag of Tricks	1960	2.50	5.00	10.00
❑ 5363	Cozy's Corner/Red Ball	1960	2.50	5.00	10.00
❑ 5390	Ha Ha Cha-Cha/The Pogo Hop	1960	2.50	5.00	10.00

LOVE

❑ 5003/4	Topsy I/Topsy II	1958	3.75	7.50	15.00
❑ 5014	Turvy I/Turvy II	1958	3.00	6.00	12.00

MERCURY

❑ 71385	St. Louis Blues/Father Cooperates	1958	3.00	6.00	12.00

MGM

❑ 11794	Hound Dog Special/Terrible Sight	1954	3.00	6.00	12.00

Albums

AUDITION

❑ 33-5943 [M]	Cozy Cole	1955	12.50	25.00	50.00

BETHLEHEM

❑ BCP-21 [M]	Jazz at the Metropole Café	1955	12.50	25.00	50.00

CHARLIE PARKER

❑ PLP-403S [S]	A Cozy Conaption of Carmen	1962	6.25	12.50	25.00
❑ PLP-403 [M]	A Cozy Conaption of Carmen	1962	5.00	10.00	20.00

COLUMBIA

❑ CL 2553 [M]	It's a Rockin' Thing	1965	3.75	7.50	15.00
❑ CS 9353 [S]	It's a Rockin' Thing	1965	5.00	10.00	20.00

CORAL

❑ CRL 57423 [M]	Drum Beat Dancing Feet	1962	3.75	7.50	15.00
❑ CRL 57457 [M]	It's a Cozy World	1964	3.75	7.50	15.00
❑ CRL 757423 [S]	Drum Beat Dancing Feet	1962	5.00	10.00	20.00
❑ CRL 757457 [S]	It's a Cozy World	1964	5.00	10.00	20.00

FELSTED

❑ 2002 [S]	Cozy's Caravan/Earl's Backroom	1958	10.00	20.00	40.00
❑ 7002 [M]	Cozy's Caravan/Earl's Backroom	1958	12.50	25.00	50.00

Number	Title (A Side/B Side)	Yr	VG	VG+	NM
GRAND AWARD					
❑ GA 33-334 [M]	After Hours	1956	10.00	20.00	40.00
KING					
❑ 673 [M]	Cozy Cole	1959	15.00	30.00	60.00
❑ KS-673 [S]	Cozy Cole	1959	37.50	75.00	150.00
LOVE					
❑ 500M [M]	Topsy	1959	25.00	50.00	100.00
❑ 500S [S]	Topsy	1959	50.00	100.00	200.00
PARIS					
❑ 122 [M]	Cozy Cole and His All-Stars	1958	12.50	25.00	50.00
PLYMOUTH					
❑ P 12-155 [M]	Cozy Cole and His All Stars	195?	7.50	15.00	30.00
SAVOY					
❑ MG-12197 [M]	Concerto for Cozy	196?	5.00	10.00	20.00
WHO'S WHO IN JAZZ					
❑ 21003	Lionel Hampton Presents Cozy Cole & Marty Napoleon	1977	2.50	5.00	10.00

COLE, COZY/JIMMY MCPARTLAND
Albums
WALDORF MUSIC HALL

Number	Title (A Side/B Side)	Yr	VG	VG+	NM
❑ MH 33-162 [10]	After Hours	195?	12.50	25.00	50.00

COLE, IKE
45s
UNITED ARTISTS

Number	Title (A Side/B Side)	Yr	VG	VG+	NM
❑ 50103	Same Old You/Wishing Doll	1966	—	—	—
Albums					
DEE GEE					
❑ 4001	Ike Cole's Tribute to His Brother Nat	1966	10.00	20.00	40.00

COLE, NAT KING
Includes material by the King Cole Trio.
45s
AMERICAN PIE

Number	Title (A Side/B Side)	Yr	VG	VG+	NM
❑ 9067	The Christmas Song/Ramblin' Rose	198?	—	2.50	5.00
—Reissue					
CAPITOL					
❑ 54-529	These Foolish Things/Cole Capers	1949	5.00	10.00	20.00
—Part of "CCF-156"					
❑ F529	These Foolish Things/Cole Capers	1950	3.75	7.50	15.00
—Part of "CCF-156"; reissue of 54-529					
❑ 54-530	Three Little Words/I'll Never Be the Same	1949	5.00	10.00	20.00
—Part of "CCF-156"					
❑ F530	Three Little Words/I'll Never Be the Same	1950	3.75	7.50	15.00
—Part of "CCF-156"; reissue of 54-530					
❑ 54-531	Blues in My Shower/How High the Moon	1949	5.00	10.00	20.00
—Part of "CCF-156"					
❑ F531	Blues in My Shower/How High the Moon	1950	3.75	7.50	15.00
—Part of "CCF-156"; reissue of 54-531					
❑ F606	Lillian/Lush Life	1949	3.75	7.50	15.00
—Add 1/3 if "O.C." (optional center) is still in the center of the record					
❑ 54-680	(It's Easy to See) The Trouble with Me Is You/Who Do You Know in Heaven	1949	5.00	10.00	20.00
❑ F889	I Almost Lost My Mind/Baby Won't You Say You Love Me	1950	3.75	7.50	15.00
—Nat King Cole records on Capitol before F889 are unconfirmed on 45 rpm, except as listed					
❑ F1010	Mona Lisa/The Greatest Inventor (Of Them All)	1950	3.75	7.50	15.00
❑ F1030	I Don't Know Why/You're the Cream in My Coffee	1950	3.75	7.50	15.00
❑ F1032	I'm in the Mood for Love/Don't Blame Me	1950	3.75	7.50	15.00
❑ F1033	(I Love You) For Sentimental Reasons/I Can't See for Lookin'	1950	3.75	7.50	15.00
❑ F1034	Little Girl/What Can I Say	1950	3.75	7.50	15.00
❑ F1035	Portrait of Jenny/Lost April	1950	3.75	7.50	15.00
❑ F1036	Exactly Like You/That's What	1950	3.75	7.50	15.00
❑ F1037	Sweet Georgia Brown/I Know That You Know	1950	3.75	7.50	15.00
❑ F1038	This Way Out/Rex Rhumba	1950	3.75	7.50	15.00
❑ F1133	Home (When Shadows Fall)/Tunnel of Love	1950	3.75	7.50	15.00
❑ F1176	Get Out and Get Under/Hey, Not Now	1950	3.75	7.50	15.00
❑ F1184	Orange Colored Sky/Jambo	1950	3.75	7.50	15.00
❑ F1203	Frosty the Snow Man/A Little Christmas Tree	1950	7.50	15.00	30.00
❑ F1270	Time Out for Tears/Get to Gettin'	1951	3.00	6.00	12.00
❑ F1365	Jet/Magic Tree	1951	3.00	6.00	12.00
❑ F1401	Always You/Destination Moon	1951	3.00	6.00	12.00
❑ F1449	Too Young/That's My Girl	1951	3.00	6.00	12.00
❑ F1468	Red Sails in the Sunset/Little Child	1951	3.00	6.00	12.00
❑ F1501	Because of Rain/Song of Delilah	1951	3.00	6.00	12.00
❑ F1565	Early American/My Brother	1951	3.00	6.00	12.00
❑ F1613	Sweet Lorraine/Kee-Mo Ky-Mo	1951	3.00	6.00	12.00
❑ F1627	Lost April/Calypso Blues	1951	3.00	6.00	12.00
❑ F1650	Embraceable You/It's Only a Paper Moon	1951	2.50	5.00	10.00
—As "The King Cole Trio"					
❑ F1663	Nature Boy/For All We Know	1951	2.50	5.00	10.00
❑ F1669	Makin' Whoopee/This Is My Night to Dream	1951	2.50	5.00	10.00
❑ F1672	Lush Life/I Miss You So	1951	2.50	5.00	10.00
❑ F1673	Mona Lisa/No Moon at All	1951	2.50	5.00	10.00
❑ F1674	Too Young/(I Love You) For Sentimental Reasons	1952	2.50	5.00	10.00
❑ F1689	Pretend/Unforgettable	1954	2.50	5.00	10.00
—Most of the Capitol 1600 series were reissues, some of material from 78s					
❑ F1747	Make Believe Land/I'll Always Remember You	1951	3.00	6.00	12.00
❑ F1808	Unforgettable/My First, My Last Love	1951	3.00	6.00	12.00
❑ F1815	I Still See Elisa/You're OK for TV	1951	3.00	6.00	12.00
❑ F1863	Walkin'/I'm Hurtin'	1951	3.00	6.00	12.00

Number	Title (A Side/B Side)	Yr	VG	VG+	NM
❑ F1893	Here's to My Lady/Miss Me	1951	3.00	6.00	12.00
❑ F1925	Wine, Women and Song/A Weaver of My Dreams	1952	3.00	6.00	12.00
❑ F1968	You Weren't There/You Will Never Grow Old	1952	2.50	5.00	10.00
❑ F1994	Easter Sunday Morning/Summer Is a Comin' On	1952	2.50	5.00	10.00
❑ SXE-2-2008 [S]	When My Sugar Walks Down the Street/Warm and Willing	196?	2.50	5.00	10.00
—"Capitol Compact 33," small hole, plays at 33 1/3 rpm					
❑ F2069	Somewhere Along the Way/What Does It Take to Make You Take Me	1952	2.50	5.00	10.00
❑ 2088	Thank You, Pretty Baby/Brazilian Love Song	1968	—	3.00	6.00
❑ F2130	Walking My Baby Back Home/Funny (Not Much)	1952	2.50	5.00	10.00
❑ F2212	Because You're Mine/I'm Never Satisfied	1952	2.50	5.00	10.00
❑ F2230	Faith Can Move Mountains/The Ruby and the Pearl	1952	2.50	5.00	10.00
❑ F2309	Strange/How (Do I Go About It)	1952	2.50	5.00	10.00
❑ F2346	Pretend/Don't Let Your Eyes Go Shopping	1953	2.50	5.00	10.00
❑ F2389	Can't I/Blue Gardenia	1953	2.50	5.00	10.00
❑ 2451	I'm Gonna Laugh You Right Out of My Life/People	1969	—	3.00	6.00
❑ F2459	I Am in Love/My Flaming Heart	1953	2.50	5.00	10.00
❑ F2498	Return to Paradise/Angel Eyes	1953	2.50	5.00	10.00
❑ F2540	A Fool Was I/If Love Is Good to Me	1953	2.50	5.00	10.00
❑ F2610	Lover Come Back to Me/That's All	1953	2.50	5.00	10.00
❑ F2616	Mrs. Santa Claus/The Little Boy That Santa Claus Forgot	1953	5.00	10.00	20.00
❑ F2687	Answer Me, My Love/Why	1953	2.50	5.00	10.00
❑ F2734	It Happens to Be Me/Alone Too Long	1954	2.50	5.00	10.00
❑ F2803	Make Her Mine/I Envy	1954	2.50	5.00	10.00
❑ F2897	Smile/It's Crazy	1954	2.50	5.00	10.00
❑ F2949	Hajji Baba (Persian Lament)/Unbelievable	1954	2.50	5.00	10.00
❑ F2955	The Christmas Song (Merry Christmas to You)/My Two Front Teeth (All I Want for Christmas)	1954	5.00	10.00	20.00
❑ F2985	Open Up the Doghouse/Long, Long Ago	1954	3.75	7.50	15.00
—With Dean Martin					
❑ F3027	Darling Je Vous Aime Beaucoup/The Sand and the Sea	1955	2.50	5.00	10.00
❑ F3095	A Blossom Fell/If I May	1955	3.75	7.50	15.00
—B-side with the Four Knights					
❑ F3136	My One Sin/Blues from Kiss Me Deadly	1955	2.50	5.00	10.00
❑ F3234	Forgive My Heart/Someone You Love	1955	2.50	5.00	10.00
❑ F3305	Take Me Back to Toyland/I'm Gonna Laugh You Right Out of My Life	1955	5.00	10.00	20.00
❑ F3328	Ask Me/Nothing Ever Changes My Love for You	1956	2.50	5.00	10.00
❑ F3390	Too Young to Go Steady/Never Let Me Go	1956	2.50	5.00	10.00
❑ F3456	That's All There Is to That/My Dream Sonata	1956	2.50	5.00	10.00
❑ F3551	Night Lights/To the Ends of the Earth	1956	2.50	5.00	10.00
❑ F3560	Mrs. Santa Claus/Take Me Back to Toyland	1956	3.75	7.50	15.00
❑ 3561	The Christmas Song (Merry Christmas to You)/The Little Boy That Santa Claus Forgot	1960	2.00	4.00	8.00
—Purple label, Capitol logo on side					
❑ 3561	The Christmas Song (Merry Christmas to You)/The Little Boy That Santa Claus Forgot	1962	—	3.00	6.00
—Orange and yellow swirl label					
❑ 3561	The Christmas Song (Merry Christmas to You)/The Little Boy That Santa Claus Forgot	1973	—	2.00	4.00
—Orange label with "Capitol" at bottom					
❑ F3561	The Christmas Song (Merry Christmas to You)/The Little Boy That Santa Claus Forgot	1956	3.75	7.50	15.00
—Original with "F" prefix, Capitol logo on top					
❑ F3619	Ballerina/You Are My First Love	1957	2.50	5.00	10.00
❑ F3702	When Rock and Roll Come to Trinidad/China Gate	1957	3.75	7.50	15.00
❑ F3737	Send for Me/My Personal Possession	1957	3.75	7.50	15.00
—B-side with the Four Knights					
❑ F3782	With You on My Mind/The Song of Raintree County	1957	2.50	5.00	10.00
❑ F3860	Angel Smile/Back in My Arms	1957	2.50	5.00	10.00
❑ F3939	Looking Back/Do I Like It	1958	2.50	5.00	10.00
❑ F4004	Come Closer to Me/Nothing in the World	1958	2.50	5.00	10.00
❑ F4056	Non Dimenticar (Don't Forget)/Bend a Little My Way	1958	2.50	5.00	10.00
❑ F4125	Madrid/Give Me Your Love	1959	2.50	5.00	10.00
❑ F4184	You Made Me Love You/I Must Be Dreaming	1959	2.50	5.00	10.00
❑ F4248	Sweet Bird of Youth/Midnight Flyer	1959	2.50	5.00	10.00
❑ F4248 [PS]	Sweet Bird of Youth/Midnight Flyer	1959	7.50	15.00	30.00
❑ 4301	The Happiest Christmas Tree/Buon Natale	1959	3.00	6.00	12.00
❑ 4301 [PS]	The Happiest Christmas Tree/Buon Natale	1959	6.25	12.50	25.00
❑ 4325	What'cha Gonna Do/Time and the River	1960	2.00	4.00	8.00
❑ 4369	Is It Better to Have Loved and Lost/That's You	1960	2.00	4.00	8.00
❑ 4393	My Love/Steady	1960	2.00	4.00	8.00
❑ 4481	If I Knew/World in My Arms	1960	2.00	4.00	8.00
❑ 4519	Illusion/When It's Summer	1961	2.00	4.00	8.00
❑ 4555	Goodnight, Little Leaguer/The First Baseball Game	1961	2.00	4.00	8.00
❑ 4555 [PS]	Goodnight, Little Leaguer/The First Baseball Game	1961	5.00	10.00	20.00
❑ 4582	Take a Fool's Advice/Make It Last	1961	2.00	4.00	8.00
❑ 4623	Let True Love Begin/Cappuccina	1961	2.00	4.00	8.00
❑ 4672	Magic Moment/Step Right Up	1961	2.00	4.00	8.00
❑ 4714	Look No Further/The Right Thing to Say	1962	2.00	4.00	8.00
❑ 4804	Ramblin' Rose/Good Times	1962	3.00	6.00	12.00
❑ 4804 [PS]	Ramblin' Rose/Good Times	1962	5.00	10.00	20.00
❑ 4870	Dear Lonely Hearts/Who's Next in Line	1962	3.00	6.00	12.00
❑ 4870 [PS]	Dear Lonely Hearts/Who's Next in Line	1962	5.00	10.00	20.00
❑ 4919	All Over the World/Nothing Goes Up (Without Coming Down)	1963	2.00	4.00	8.00

C

Number	Title (A Side/B Side)	Yr	VG	VG+	NM
❑ 4965	Those Lazy-Hazy-Crazy Days of Summer/In the Cool of Day	1963	3.00	6.00	12.00
❑ 4965 [PS]	Those Lazy-Hazy-Crazy Days of Summer/In the Cool of Day	1963	5.00	10.00	20.00
❑ 5027	That Sunday, That Summer/Mr. Wishing Well	1963	3.00	6.00	12.00
❑ 5125	My True Carrie, Love/A Rag a Bone, A Hank of Hair	1964	2.00	4.00	8.00
❑ 5155	I Don't Want to Be Hurt Anymore/People	1964	2.00	4.00	8.00
❑ 5219	Marnie/More and More of the Amore	1964	2.00	4.00	8.00
❑ 5261	L-O-V-E/I Don't Want to See Tomorrow	1964	2.00	4.00	8.00
❑ 5412	The Ballad of Cat Ballou/They Can't Make Her Cry	1965	2.00	4.00	8.00
—With Stubby Kay					
❑ 5412 [PS]	The Ballad of Cat Ballou/They Can't Make Her Cry	1965	3.75	7.50	15.00
❑ 5486	Wanderlust/You'll See	1965	2.00	4.00	8.00
❑ 5549	One Sun/Looking Back	1965	2.00	4.00	8.00
❑ 5683	Let Me Tell You, Babe/For the Want of a Kiss	1966	2.00	4.00	8.00
❑ F15509	Straighten Up and Fly Right/Nature Boy	1950	3.75	7.50	15.00
—All the Capitol 15000 series on 45s are from multi-disc box sets					
❑ F15510	You Call It Madness/The Frim Fram Sauce	1950	3.75	7.50	15.00
❑ F15511	(Get Your Kicks on) Route 66/Gee Baby Ain't I Been Good to You	1950	3.75	7.50	15.00
❑ F15552	Yes Sir That's My Baby/I Used to Love You	1950	3.75	7.50	15.00
❑ F15553	For All We Know/'Tis Autumn	1950	3.75	7.50	15.00
❑ F15554	Bop Kick/Laugh Cool Clown	1950	3.75	7.50	15.00
❑ F15564	Sweet Lorraine/It's Only a Paper Moon	1950	3.75	7.50	15.00
❑ F15565	The Man I Love/Body and Soul	1950	3.75	7.50	15.00
❑ F15566	Embraceable You/What Is This Thing Called Love	1950	3.75	7.50	15.00
❑ F15643	Jumpin' at Capitol/Love for Sale	1950	3.75	7.50	15.00
—B-side by Benny Carter Orchestra					
❑ F15728	Makin' Whoopee/Honeysuckle Rose	1951	3.00	6.00	12.00
❑ F15729	I'll String Along with You/Too Marvelous for Words	1951	3.00	6.00	12.00
❑ F15730	This Is My Night to Dream/Rhumba Azul	1951	3.00	6.00	12.00
❑ F15843	Return Trip/St. Louis Blues	1952	3.00	6.00	12.00
—B-side by Freddie Slack					
❑ F15868	Penthouse Serenade/If I Should Lose You	1952	3.00	6.00	12.00
❑ F15869	Somebody Loves Me/Down by the Old Mill Stream	1952	3.00	6.00	12.00
❑ F15870	Laura/Polka Dots and Moonbeams	1952	3.00	6.00	12.00
❑ F15922	Walkin' My Baby Back Home/Kay's Lament	1952	3.00	6.00	12.00
—B-side by Kay Starr					
❑ S7-19764	Mrs. Santa Claus/Take Me Back to Toyland	1997	—	—	3.00
❑ S7-57887	The Christmas Song/O Holy Night	1992	—	2.00	4.00
—Originals on black vinyl					
❑ S7-57887	The Christmas Song/O Holy Night	1993	—	2.00	4.00
—Second pressing on red vinyl					
❑ F90036	(All I Want for Christmas Is) My Two Front Teeth/The Christmas Song (Merry Christmas To You)	1949	5.00	10.00	20.00
—B-side is the original King Cole Trio hit version, possibly its only U.S. release on 45					
TAMPA					
❑ 134	Vom-Vim-Veedle/All for You	1957	3.00	6.00	12.00
❑ 134 [PS]	Vom-Vim-Veedle/All for You	1957	6.25	12.50	25.00
78s					
AMMOR					
❑ 108	I Like the Riff/On the Sunny Side of the Street	1942	6.25	12.50	25.00
❑ 109	Black Spider Stomp/By the River Sainte-Marie	1942	6.25	12.50	25.00
ATLAS					
❑ KC 100	F.S.T. (Fine, Sweet and Tasty)/My Lips Remember Your Kisses	1944	6.25	12.50	25.00
❑ KC 102	Got a Penny/Don't You Notice Anything New?	1944	7.50	15.00	30.00
—B-side by Don Swan and Eileen Wilson					
❑ KC 106	Got a Penny/Let's Pretend	1944	6.25	12.50	25.00
CAPITOL					
❑ 139	All for You/Vim Vom Veedle	1943	3.75	7.50	15.00
❑ 154	Straighten Up and Fly Right/I Can't See for Lookin'	1944	3.00	6.00	12.00
❑ 169	Gee, Baby, Ain't I Good to You/I Realize Now	1944	3.00	6.00	12.00
❑ 192	If You Can't Smile and Say Yes/Bring Another Drink	1945	3.00	6.00	12.00
❑ 208	I'm a Shy Guy/I Thought You Ought to Know	1945	3.00	6.00	12.00
❑ 224	Come to Baby, Do/The Frim Fram Sauce	1945	3.00	6.00	12.00
❑ 239	Sweet Georgia Brown/It Is Better to Be By Yourself	1946	3.00	6.00	12.00
❑ 256	(Get Your Kicks on) Route 66/Everyone Is Sayin' Hello Again (Why Must We Say Goodbye?)	1946	3.00	6.00	12.00
❑ 274	Oh But I Do/You Call It Madness (But I Call It Love)	1946	3.00	6.00	12.00
❑ 304	(I Love You) For Sentimental Reasons/The Best Man	1946	3.00	6.00	12.00
❑ 311	The Christmas Song (Merry Christmas to You)/In the Cool of the Evening	1946	3.00	6.00	12.00
❑ 328	That's the Beginning of the End/But She's My Buddy's Chick	1947	3.00	6.00	12.00
❑ 356	You Should Have Told Me/I Want to Thank Your Folks	1947	3.00	6.00	12.00
❑ 393	Meet Me at No Special Place (And I'll Be There at No Particular Time)/You Don't Learn That in School	1947	3.00	6.00	12.00
❑ 418	Come In Out of the Rain/Can You Look Me in the Eye	1947	3.00	6.00	12.00
❑ 437	That's What/Naughty Angeline	1947	3.00	6.00	12.00
❑ 444	I Miss You So/I Think You Get What I Mean	1947	3.00	6.00	12.00
❑ 889	I Almost Lost My Mind/Baby Won't You Say You Love Me	1950	2.00	4.00	8.00
❑ 1010	Mona Lisa/The Greatest Inventor (Of Them All)	1950	2.00	4.00	8.00
❑ 1030	I Don't Know Why/You're the Cream in My Coffee	1950	2.00	4.00	8.00

Number	Title (A Side/B Side)	Yr	VG	VG+	NM
❑ 1133	Home (When Shadows Fall)/Tunnel of Love	1950	2.00	4.00	8.00
❑ 1176	Get Out and Get Under/Hey, Not Now	1950	2.00	4.00	8.00
❑ 1184	Orange Colored Sky/Jambo	1950	2.00	4.00	8.00
❑ 1203	Frosty the Snow Man/A Little Christmas Tree	1950	3.00	6.00	12.00
❑ 1270	Time Out for Tears/Get to Gettin'	1951	2.00	4.00	8.00
❑ 1365	Jet/Magic Tree	1951	2.00	4.00	8.00
❑ 1401	Always You/Destination Moon	1951	2.00	4.00	8.00
❑ 1449	Too Young/That's My Girl	1951	2.00	4.00	8.00
❑ 1468	Red Sails in the Sunset/Little Child	1951	2.00	4.00	8.00
❑ 1501	Because of Rain/Song of Delilah	1951	2.00	4.00	8.00
❑ 1565	Early American/My Brother	1951	2.00	4.00	8.00
❑ 1747	Make Believe Land/I'll Always Remember You	1951	2.00	4.00	8.00
❑ 1808	Unforgettable/My First, My Last Love	1951	2.00	4.00	8.00
❑ 1815	I Still See Elisa/You're OK for TV	1951	2.00	4.00	8.00
❑ 1863	Walkin'/I'm Hurtin'	1951	2.00	4.00	8.00
❑ 1893	Here's to My Lady/Miss Me	1951	2.00	4.00	8.00
❑ 1925	Wine, Women and Song/A Weaver of My Dreams	1952	2.00	4.00	8.00
❑ 1968	You Weren't There/You Will Never Grow Old	1952	2.00	4.00	8.00
❑ 1994	Easter Sunday Morning/Summer Is a Comin' On	1952	2.00	4.00	8.00
❑ 2069	Somewhere Along the Way/What Does It Take to Make You Take Me	1952	2.00	4.00	8.00
❑ 2130	Walking My Baby Back Home/Funny (Not Much)	1952	2.00	4.00	8.00
❑ 2212	Because You're Mine/I'm Never Satisfied	1952	2.00	4.00	8.00
❑ 2230	Faith Can Move Mountains/The Ruby and the Pearl	1952	2.00	4.00	8.00
❑ 2309	Strange/How (Do I Go About It)	1952	2.00	4.00	8.00
❑ 2346	Pretend/Don't Let Your Eyes Go Shopping	1953	2.00	4.00	8.00
❑ 2389	Can't I/Blue Gardenia	1953	2.00	4.00	8.00
❑ 2459	I Am in Love/My Flaming Heart	1953	2.00	4.00	8.00
❑ 2498	Return to Paradise/Angel Eyes	1953	2.00	4.00	8.00
❑ 2540	A Fool Was I/If Love Is Good to Me	1953	2.00	4.00	8.00
❑ 2610	Lover Come Back to Me/That's All	1953	2.00	4.00	8.00
❑ 2616	Mrs. Santa Claus/The Little Boy That Santa Claus Forgot	1953	2.50	5.00	10.00
❑ 2687	Answer Me, My Love/Why	1953	2.00	4.00	8.00
❑ 2734	It Happens to Be Me/Alone Too Long	1954	2.00	4.00	8.00
❑ 2803	Make Her Mine/I Envy	1954	2.00	4.00	8.00
❑ 2897	Smile/It's Crazy	1954	2.00	4.00	8.00
❑ 2949	Hajji Baba (Persian Lament)/Unbelievable	1954	2.00	4.00	8.00
❑ 2955	The Christmas Song (Merry Christmas to You)/My Two Front Teeth (All I Want for Christmas)	1954	2.50	5.00	10.00
❑ 2985	Open Up the Doghouse/Long, Long Ago	1954	2.50	5.00	10.00
—With Dean Martin					
❑ 3027	Darling Je Vous Aime Beaucoup/The Sand and the Sea	1955	2.50	5.00	10.00
❑ 3095	A Blossom Fell/If I May	1955	2.50	5.00	10.00
—B-side with the Four Knights					
❑ 3136	My One Sin/Blues from Kiss Me Deadly	1955	2.50	5.00	10.00
❑ 3234	Forgive My Heart/Someone You Love	1955	2.50	5.00	10.00
❑ 3305	Take Me Back to Toyland/I'm Gonna Laugh You Right Out of My Life	1955	3.00	6.00	12.00
❑ 3328	Ask Me/Nothing Ever Changes My Love for You	1956	2.50	5.00	10.00
❑ 3390	Too Young to Go Steady/Never Let Me Go	1956	2.50	5.00	10.00
❑ 3456	That's All There Is to That/My Dream Sonata	1956	2.50	5.00	10.00
❑ 3551	Night Lights/To the Ends of the Earth	1956	2.50	5.00	10.00
❑ 10038	Jumpin' at Capitol/Love for Sale	1944	3.75	7.50	15.00
—B-side by Benny Carter					
❑ 10074	Smoke Gets in Your Eyes/(B-side unknown)	1946	3.00	6.00	12.00
❑ 10086	You're the Cream in My Coffee/(B-side unknown)	1946	3.00	6.00	12.00
❑ 10101	Makin' Whoopee/Too Marvelous for Words	1947	3.00	6.00	12.00
❑ 10102	Honeysuckle Rose/I'll String Along with You	1947	3.00	6.00	12.00
❑ 10103	Rhumba Azul/This Is My Night to Dream	1947	3.00	6.00	12.00
❑ 10189	Cole Capers/These Foolish Things	1947	3.00	6.00	12.00
❑ 10190	Three Little Words/I'll Never Be the Same	1947	3.00	6.00	12.00
❑ 10191	How High the Moon/Blues in My Shower	1947	3.00	6.00	12.00
❑ 15000	Save the Bones for Henry Jones ('Cause Henry Don't Eat No Meat)/Harmony	1947	2.50	5.00	10.00
—With Johnny Mercer					
❑ 15011	Those Things Money Can't Buy/Now He Tells Me	1947	2.50	5.00	10.00
❑ 15019	What'll I Do?/I Feel So Smoochie	1948	2.50	5.00	10.00
❑ 15026	My Baby Likes to Be-Bop/You Can't Make Money Dreamin'	1948	3.00	6.00	12.00
❑ 15036	I've Only Myself to Blame/The Geek	1948	3.00	6.00	12.00
❑ 15054	Nature Boy/Lost April	1948	2.50	5.00	10.00
❑ 15080	Put 'Em in a Box, Tie 'Em with a Ribbon (And Throw 'Em in the Deep Blue Sea)/It's the Sentimental Thing to Do	1948	2.50	5.00	10.00
❑ 15085	A Boy from Texas — A Girl from Tennessee/My Fair Lady	1948	3.00	6.00	12.00
❑ 15110	Don't Blame Me/I've Got a Way with Women	1948	3.00	6.00	12.00
❑ 15165	Little Girl/Baby, Baby All the Time	1948	3.00	6.00	12.00
❑ 15201	The Christmas Song (Merry Christmas to You)/Laguna Mood	1948	2.50	5.00	10.00
❑ 15224	Lillette/A Woman Always Understands	1948	2.50	5.00	10.00
❑ 15240	Kee-Mo-Ky-Mo (The Magic Song)/Rex Rhumba	1948	2.50	5.00	10.00
❑ 15284	Gee Baby, Ain't I Good to You/Straighten Up and Fly Right	1949	2.50	5.00	10.00
❑ 15311	I Can't See for Lookin'/(I Love You) For Sentimental Reasons	1949	2.50	5.00	10.00
❑ 15320	Flo and Joe/That's a Natural Fact	1949	3.00	6.00	12.00
❑ 15358	It Only Happens Once/No Moon at All	1949	3.00	6.00	12.00
❑ 15387	Portrait of Jenny/An Old Piano Plays the Blues	1949	3.00	6.00	12.00
❑ 15418	If You Stub Your Toe on the Moon/Don't Cry, Cry Baby	1949	3.00	6.00	12.00
❑ 20009	Sweet Lorraine/Embraceable You	1944	3.00	6.00	12.00
❑ 20010	The Man I Love/Body and Soul	1944	3.00	6.00	12.00

Number	Title (A Side/B Side)	Yr	VG	VG+	NM
❑ 20011	Prelude in C Sharp Minor/What Is This Thing Called Love	1944	3.00	6.00	12.00
❑ 20012	It's Only a Paper Moon/Easy Listening Blues	1944	3.00	6.00	12.00
❑ 20061	This Way Out/What Can I Say After I Say I'm Sorry	1946	3.00	6.00	12.00
❑ 20062	I Don't Know Why (I Just Do)/I Know That You Know	1946	3.00	6.00	12.00
❑ 20063	I'm in the Mood for Love/To a Wild Rose	1946	3.00	6.00	12.00
❑ 20064	I'm Thru with Love/Look What You've Done to Me	1946	3.00	6.00	12.00
❑ 20128	Could 'Ja/School Days	1946	3.00	6.00	12.00
—B-side by Johnny Mercer					
❑ 7-25009	Ke Mo Ki (The Magic Song)/Old Mac Donald Had a Farm	1947	3.75	7.50	15.00
❑ 7-25010	(Go to Sleep) My Sleepy Head/Nursery Rhymes (Mary Had a Little Lamb; London Bridge; Go In and Out the Window; Pop Goes the Weasel)	1947	3.75	7.50	15.00
❑ 7-25011	There's a Train Out for Dreamland/The Three Trees	1947	3.75	7.50	15.00
❑ 57-70050	My Mother Told Me/Exactly Like You	1949	3.75	7.50	15.00
DAVIS & SCHWEGLER					
❑ 108/109	There's No Anaesthetics for Love/Dixie Jamboree	1939	12.50	25.00	50.00
❑ 110/111	Ta-De-Ah/Riffin' at the Bar-B-Q	1939	12.50	25.00	50.00
❑ 112/113	Harlem Swing/I Lose Control of Myself	1939	12.50	25.00	50.00
❑ 114/115	The Land of Make Believe/That "Please Be Mineable" Feeling	1940	12.50	25.00	50.00
❑ 116/117	Dancing in the Street/You're So Different	1940	12.50	25.00	50.00
❑ 118/119	I Wouldn't Have Known It/Let's Get Happy	1940	12.50	25.00	50.00
—All Davis & Schwegler titles as "King Cole's Swingsters"					
DECCA					
❑ 8520	Sweet Lorraine/This Side Up	1941	5.00	10.00	20.00
❑ 8535	Gone with the Draft/Honeysuckle Rose	1941	5.00	10.00	20.00
❑ 8541	Early Morning Blues/Babs	1941	5.00	10.00	20.00
❑ 8556	Slow Down/Scotchin' with the Soda	1941	5.00	10.00	20.00
❑ 8571	Hit the Ramp/This Will Make You Laugh	1941	5.00	10.00	20.00
❑ 8592	Stop! The Red Light's On/I Like to Riff	1941	5.00	10.00	20.00
❑ 8604	Call the Police/Are You Fer It?	1942	5.00	10.00	20.00
❑ 8630	That Ain't Right/Hit That Jive, Jack	1942	5.00	10.00	20.00
EXCELSIOR					
❑ 00102/3	Vom, Vim, Veedle/All for You	1943	12.50	25.00	50.00
❑ SC-104/5	Pitchin' Up a Boogie/I'm Lost	1943	12.50	25.00	50.00
❑ SC-106/7	Beautiful Moons Ago/Let's Spring One	1943	12.50	25.00	50.00
PREMIER					
❑ KC 100	F.S.T. (Fine, Sweet and Tasty)/My Lips Remember Your Kisses	1944	6.25	12.50	25.00
❑ KC 103	Got a Penny/Let's Pretend	1944	7.50	15.00	30.00
SAVOY					
❑ 600	I Like to Riff/On the Sunny Side of the Street	1946	3.75	7.50	15.00
—Reissue of Ammor 108					
VARSITY					
❑ 8340	I Like to Riff/On the Sunny Side of the Street	194?	3.00	6.00	12.00
—Another reissue of Ammor 108					
7-Inch Extended Plays					
CAPITOL					
❑ EAP 1-332	(contents unknown)	195?	3.00	6.00	12.00
❑ EAP 1-332 [PS]	Penthouse Serenade, Part 1	195?	3.00	6.00	12.00
❑ EAP 2-332	(contents unknown)	195?	3.00	6.00	12.00
❑ EAP 2-332 [PS]	Penthouse Serenade, Part 2	195?	3.00	6.00	12.00
❑ EBF-332 [PS]	Penthouse Serenade	195?	3.75	7.50	15.00
—Gatefold sleeve for some copies of 1-332 and 2-332					
❑ EAP 1-357	Unforgettable/Portrait of Jennie//(I Love You) For Sentimental Reasons/Red Sails in the Sunset	195?	3.00	6.00	12.00
❑ EAP 1-357 [PS]	Unforgettable Songs by Nat King Cole, Part 1	195?	3.00	6.00	12.00
❑ EAP 2-357	What'll I Do/Lost April//Too Young/Mona Lisa	195?	3.00	6.00	12.00
❑ EAP 2-357 [PS]	Unforgettable Songs by Nat King Cole, Part 2	195?	3.00	6.00	12.00
❑ EAP 3-357	Answer Me, My Love/Hajji Baba//Pretend/Make Her Mine	195?	3.00	6.00	12.00
❑ EAP 3-357 [PS]	Unforgettable Songs by Nat King Cole, Part 3	195?	3.00	6.00	12.00
❑ EAP 1-420	*Love Is Here to Stay/A Handful of Stars/Almost Like Being in Love/Tenderly	1954	3.00	6.00	12.00
❑ EAP 1-420 [PS]	Two in Love, Part 1	1954	3.00	6.00	12.00
❑ EAP 2-420	*A Little Street Where Old Friends Meet/This Can't Be Love/Dinner for One Please, James/There Goes My Heart	1954	3.00	6.00	12.00
❑ EAP 2-420 [PS]	Two in Love, Part 2	1954	3.00	6.00	12.00
❑ EPA 1-500	*Lover Come Back/Pretend/A Fool Was I/I'm Hurtin'	1954	3.00	6.00	12.00
❑ EPA 1-500 [PS]	Songs by Nat King Cole	1954	3.00	6.00	12.00
❑ EAP 1-514	(contents unknown)	1954	3.00	6.00	12.00
❑ EAP 1-514 [PS]	Tenth Anniversary Album, Part 1	1954	3.00	6.00	12.00
❑ EAP 2-514	(contents unknown)	1954	3.00	6.00	12.00
❑ EAP 2-514 [PS]	Tenth Anniversary Album, Part 2	1954	3.00	6.00	12.00
❑ EAP 3-514	The Love Nest/But All I've Got Is Me//Lovelight/Where Were You	1954	3.00	6.00	12.00
❑ EAP 3-514 [PS]	Tenth Anniversary Album, Part 3	1954	3.00	6.00	12.00
❑ EAP 4-514	Peaches/I Can't Be Bothered//Mother Nature and Father Time/Wish I Were Somebody Else	1954	3.00	6.00	12.00
❑ EAP 4-514 [PS]	Tenth Anniversary Album, Part 4	1954	3.00	6.00	12.00
❑ EBF 1-514 [PS]	Tenth Anniversary Album, Parts 1 and 2	1954	5.00	10.00	20.00
—Gatefold sleeve for some editions of EAP 1-514 and 2-514					
❑ EBF 2-514 [PS]	Tenth Anniversary Album, Parts 3 and 4	1954	5.00	10.00	20.00
—Gatefold sleeve for some editions of EAP 3-514 and 4-514					
❑ EAP 1-633	*A Blossom Fell/Darling, Je Vous Aime Beaucoup/If I May/The Sand and the Sea	1955	3.00	6.00	12.00
❑ EAP 1-633 [PS]	Moods in Song	1955	3.00	6.00	12.00

Number	Title (A Side/B Side)	Yr	VG	VG+	NM
❑ EAP 1-782	Sometimes I'm Happy//Just You, Just Me/When I Grow Too Old to Dream	1956	2.50	5.00	10.00
❑ EAP 1-782 [PS]	After Midnight, Part 1	1956	2.50	5.00	10.00
❑ EAP 2-782	Lonely One/I Know That You Know//Sweet Lorraine	1956	2.50	5.00	10.00
❑ EAP 2-782 [PS]	After Midnight, Part 2	1956	2.50	5.00	10.00
❑ EAP 3-782	You're Looking at Me//Caravan/(Get Your Kicks on) Route 66	1956	2.50	5.00	10.00
❑ EAP 3-782 [PS]	After Midnight, Part 3	1956	2.50	5.00	10.00
❑ EAP 4-782	It's Only a Paper Moon/Don't Let It Go to Your Head//Blame It On My Youth	1956	2.50	5.00	10.00
❑ EAP 4-782 [PS]	After Midnight, Part 4	1956	2.50	5.00	10.00
❑ EBF 1-782 [PS]	After Midnight, Parts 1 & 2	1956	5.00	10.00	20.00
—Gatefold sleeve for some editions of EAP 1-782 and 2-782					
❑ EAP 1-813	Around the World/Fascination//An Affair to Remember (Our Love Affair)/There's a Gold Mine in the Sky	1957	3.00	6.00	12.00
❑ EAP 1-813 [PS]	Around the World	1957	3.00	6.00	12.00
❑ EAP 1-824	Love Is the Thing/Stay as Sweet as You Are//When I Fall in Love/Where Can I Go Without You?	1957	3.00	6.00	12.00
❑ EAP 1-824 [PS]	Love Is the Thing, Part 1	1957	3.00	6.00	12.00
❑ EAP 2-824	Maybe It's Because I Love You Too Much/It's All in the Game//Stardust/When Sunny Gets Blue	1957	3.00	6.00	12.00
❑ EAP 2-824 [PS]	Love Is the Thing, Part 2	1957	3.00	6.00	12.00
❑ EAP 3-824	(contents unknown)	1957	3.00	6.00	12.00
❑ EAP 3-824 [PS]	Love Is the Thing, Part 3	1957	3.00	6.00	12.00
❑ EAP 1-903	(contents unknown)	195?	3.00	6.00	12.00
❑ EAP 1-903 [PS]	Just One of Those Things, Part 1	195?	3.00	6.00	12.00
❑ EAP 2-903	Don't Get Around Much Anymore/The Party's Over//Once in a While/Just for the Fun of It	195?	3.00	6.00	12.00
❑ EAP 2-903 [PS]	Just One of Those Things, Part 2	195?	3.00	6.00	12.00
❑ EAP 3-903	(contents unknown)	195?	3.00	6.00	12.00
❑ EAP 3-903 [PS]	Just One of Those Things, Part 3	195?	3.00	6.00	12.00
❑ EAP 1-960	Looking Back/Send for Me//Do I Like It/Angel Smile	1958	2.50	5.00	10.00
❑ EAP 1-960 [PS]	Looking Back	1958	2.50	5.00	10.00
❑ EAP 1-993	*Overture (Introducing "Love Theme" and "Hesitating Blues")/Harlem Blues/Yellow Dog Blues/St. Louis Blues	1958	3.00	6.00	12.00
❑ EAP 1-993 [PS]	St. Louis Blues, Part 1	1958	3.00	6.00	12.00
❑ EAP 2-993	(contents unknown)	1958	3.00	6.00	12.00
❑ EAP 2-993 [PS]	St. Louis Blues, Part 2	1958	3.00	6.00	12.00
❑ EAP 3-993	(contents unknown)	1958	3.00	6.00	12.00
❑ EAP 3-993 [PS]	St. Louis Blues, Part 3	1958	3.00	6.00	12.00
❑ EAP 1-1031	*Cachito/Maria Elena/Las Mananitas/Quizas, Quizas, Quizas	1958	3.00	6.00	12.00
❑ EAP 1-1031 [PS]	Cole Espanol, Part 1	1958	3.00	6.00	12.00
❑ EAP 2-1031	(contents unknown)	1958	3.00	6.00	12.00
❑ EAP 2-1031 [PS]	Cole Espanol, Part 2	1958	3.00	6.00	12.00
❑ EAP 3-1031	(contents unknown)	1958	3.00	6.00	12.00
❑ EAP 3-1031 [PS]	Cole Espanol, Part 3	1958	3.00	6.00	12.00
❑ EAP 1-1084	Paradise/Cherchez La Femme//Impossible/Found A Million Dollar Baby (In A Five And Ten Cent Store)	195?	2.50	5.00	10.00
❑ EAP 1-1084 [PS]	The Very Thought of You, Part 1	195?	2.50	5.00	10.00
❑ EAP 2-1084	(contents unknown)	195?	2.50	5.00	10.00
❑ EAP 2-1084 [PS]	The Very Thought of You, Part 2	195?	2.50	5.00	10.00
❑ EAP-1138	(contents unknown)	195?	2.50	5.00	10.00
❑ EAP-1138 [PS]	Non Dimenticar	195?	2.50	5.00	10.00
❑ EAP 1346	(contents unknown)	195?	2.50	5.00	10.00
❑ EAP 1346 [PS]	The Happiest Christmas Tree	195?	2.50	5.00	10.00
❑ EAP-1500	(contents unknown)	196?	2.50	5.00	10.00
❑ EAP-1500 [PS]	Songs by Nat King Cole	196?	2.50	5.00	10.00
❑ EAP-1535	(contents unknown)	195?	2.50	5.00	10.00
❑ EAP-1535 [PS]	By the Beautiful Sea	195?	2.50	5.00	10.00
❑ EAP-1696	(contents unknown)	196?	2.50	5.00	10.00
❑ EAP-1696 [PS]	Love Songs by Nat King Cole	196?	2.50	5.00	10.00
❑ EAP-1709	(contents unknown)	196?	2.50	5.00	10.00
❑ EAP-1709 [PS]	Strip for Action	196?	2.50	5.00	10.00
❑ SXA-2195	Your Love/My Kind of Girl/Three Little Words//L-O-V-E/Coquette/More	1965	2.50	5.00	10.00
—33 1/3 rpm, small hole					
❑ SXA-2195 [PS]	L-O-V-E	1965	2.50	5.00	10.00
❑ EAP 1-9026	The Christmas Song/Mrs. Santa Claus//Frosty The Snowman/The Little Christmas Tree	195?	3.00	6.00	12.00
❑ EAP 1-9026 [PS]	The Christmas Song	195?	3.00	6.00	12.00
❑ EAP 1-9110	*Somewhere Along the Way/Funny (Not Much)/Walkin' My Baby Back Home/Faith Can Move Mountains	195?	3.75	7.50	15.00
❑ EAP 1-9110 [PS]	Nat King Cole's Top Pops, Part I	195?	3.75	7.50	15.00
❑ EAP 2-9110	*Because You're Mine/I'm Never Satisfied/The Ruby and the Pearl/A Weaver of Dreams	195?	3.75	7.50	15.00
❑ EAP 2-9110 [PS]	Nat King Cole's Top Pops, Part II	195?	3.75	7.50	15.00
❑ EAP 1-9120	If I Give My Heart To You/Hold My Hand//Pappa Loves Mambo/Teach Me Tonight	1954	3.00	6.00	12.00
❑ EAP 1-9120 [PS]	Nat King Cole Sings	1954	3.00	6.00	12.00
❑ EAP 1-9128	Love Is a Many-Splendored Thing/Breezin' Along with the Breeze//Autumn Leaves/You Are My Sunshine	1955	3.00	6.00	12.00
❑ EAP 1-9128 [PS]	Nat King Cole	1955	3.00	6.00	12.00
Albums					
ARCHIVE OF FOLK AND JAZZ					
❑ 290	Nature Boy	197?	2.50	5.00	10.00
CAMAY					
❑ CA-3004	Nat King Cole	196?	3.00	6.00	12.00

Number	Title (A Side/B Side)	Yr	VG	VG+	NM
CAPITOL					
❑ H 8 [10]	The King Cole Trio	1950	25.00	50.00	100.00
❑ H 29 [10]	The King Cole Trio, Volume 2	1950	25.00	50.00	100.00
❑ H 59 [10]	The King Cole Trio, Volume 3	1950	25.00	50.00	100.00
❑ H 156 [10]	Nat King Cole at the Piano	1950	25.00	50.00	100.00
❑ H 177 [10]	The King Cole Trio, Volume 4	1950	17.50	35.00	70.00
❑ H 213 [10]	Harvest of Hits	1950	17.50	35.00	70.00
❑ H 220 [10]	The Nat King Cole Trio	1950	15.00	30.00	60.00
❑ DWBB-252 [(2)]	Close-Up	1969	3.75	7.50	15.00
—Reissue of 680 and 1891					
❑ ST-310	There! I've Said It Again	1969	3.00	6.00	12.00
❑ H 332 [10]	Penthouse Serenade	1951	15.00	30.00	60.00
❑ T 332 [M]	Penthouse Serenade	1955	10.00	20.00	40.00
❑ DT 357 [R]	Unforgettable	1965	3.00	6.00	12.00
❑ H 357 [10]	Unforgettable	1952	15.00	30.00	60.00
❑ SM-357	Unforgettable	197?	2.00	4.00	8.00
—Reissue with new prefix					
❑ T 357 [M]	Unforgettable	1955	10.00	20.00	40.00
—Turquoise label					
❑ T 357 [M]	Unforgettable	1958	7.50	15.00	30.00
—Black label with colorband, "Capitol" at left					
❑ T 357 [M]	Unforgettable	1962	5.00	10.00	20.00
—Black label with colorband, "Capitol" at top					
❑ SKAO-373	Nat King Cole's Greatest	1969	3.00	6.00	12.00
❑ DT 420 [R]	Nat King Cole Sings for Two in Love	1963	3.75	7.50	15.00
❑ H 420 [10]	Nat King Cole Sings for Two in Love	1953	12.50	25.00	50.00
❑ T 420 [M]	Nat King Cole Sings for Two in Love	1955	10.00	20.00	40.00
—Turquoise label					
❑ T 420 [M]	Nat King Cole Sings for Two in Love	1958	7.50	15.00	30.00
—Black label with colorband, "Capitol" at left					
❑ T 420 [M]	Nat King Cole Sings for Two in Love	1962	5.00	10.00	20.00
—Black label with colorband, "Capitol" at top					
❑ STBB-503 [(2)]	Walkin' My Baby Back Home/A Blossom Fell	1970	3.75	7.50	15.00
❑ H 514 [10]	Tenth Anniversary Album	1954	12.50	25.00	50.00
❑ W 514 [M]	Tenth Anniversary Album	1955	10.00	20.00	40.00
❑ T 591 [M]	Vocal Classics	1955	10.00	20.00	40.00
❑ T 592 [M]	Instrumental Classics	1955	10.00	20.00	40.00
❑ DT 680 [R]	Ballads of the Day	1963	3.75	7.50	15.00
—Black label with colorband					
❑ T 680 [M]	Ballads of the Day	1956	10.00	20.00	40.00
—Turquoise label					
❑ T 680 [M]	Ballads of the Day	1958	7.50	15.00	30.00
—Black label with colorband, "Capitol" at left					
❑ T 680 [M]	Ballads of the Day	1962	5.00	10.00	20.00
—Black label with colorband, "Capitol" at top					
❑ W 689 [M]	The Piano Style of Nat King Cole	1956	10.00	20.00	40.00
—Turquoise label					
❑ W 689 [M]	The Piano Style of Nat King Cole	1958	7.50	15.00	30.00
—Black label with colorband, "Capitol" at left					
❑ W 689 [M]	The Piano Style of Nat King Cole	1962	5.00	10.00	20.00
—Black label with colorband, "Capitol" at top					
❑ W 782 [M]	After Midnight	1956	10.00	20.00	40.00
—Turquoise label					
❑ W 782 [M]	After Midnight	1958	7.50	15.00	30.00
—Black label with colorband, "Capitol" at left					
❑ W 782 [M]	After Midnight	1962	5.00	10.00	20.00
—Black label with colorband, "Capitol" at top					
❑ SM-824	Love Is the Thing	197?	2.00	4.00	8.00
—Reissue with new prefix					
❑ SW 824 [S]	Love Is the Thing	1959	7.50	15.00	30.00
—Black label with colorband, "Capitol" at left					
❑ SW 824 [S]	Love Is the Thing	1962	5.00	10.00	20.00
—Black label with colorband, "Capitol" at top					
❑ SW 824 [S]	Love Is the Thing	1969	3.00	6.00	12.00
—Lime green label					
❑ W 824 [M]	Love Is the Thing	1957	10.00	20.00	40.00
—Turquoise or gray label					
❑ W 824 [M]	Love Is the Thing	1958	7.50	15.00	30.00
—Black label with colorband, "Capitol" at left					
❑ W 824 [M]	Love Is the Thing	1962	5.00	10.00	20.00
—Black label with colorband, "Capitol" at top					
❑ DT 870 [R]	This Is Nat "King" Cole	1963	3.75	7.50	15.00
—Black label with colorband					
❑ T 870 [M]	This Is Nat "King" Cole	1957	10.00	20.00	40.00
—Turquoise or gray label					
❑ T 870 [M]	This Is Nat "King" Cole	1958	7.50	15.00	30.00
—Black label with colorband, "Capitol" at left					
❑ T 870 [M]	This Is Nat "King" Cole	1962	5.00	10.00	20.00
—Black label with colorband, "Capitol" at top					
❑ SW 903 [S]	Just One of Those Things	1959	7.50	15.00	30.00
—Black label with colorband, "Capitol" at left					
❑ SW 903 [S]	Just One of Those Things	1962	5.00	10.00	20.00
—Black label with colorband, "Capitol" at top					
❑ W 903 [M]	Just One of Those Things	1957	10.00	20.00	40.00
—Turquoise or gray label					
❑ W 903 [M]	Just One of Those Things	1958	7.50	15.00	30.00
—Black label with colorband, "Capitol" at left					
❑ W 903 [M]	Just One of Those Things	1962	5.00	10.00	20.00
—Black label with colorband, "Capitol" at top					
❑ SW 993 [S]	St. Louis Blues	1959	12.50	25.00	50.00
—Black label with colorband, "Capitol" at left					
❑ W 993 [M]	St. Louis Blues	1958	12.50	25.00	50.00
—Turquoise or gray label					
❑ W 993 [M]	St. Louis Blues	1962	10.00	20.00	40.00
—Black label with colorband, "Capitol" at left					
❑ DW 1031 [R]	Cole Espanol	196?	3.75	7.50	15.00
—Black label with colorband					
❑ SM-1031	Cole Espanol	197?	2.00	4.00	8.00
—Reissue with new prefix					
❑ W 1031 [M]	Cole Espanol	1958	7.50	15.00	30.00
—Black label with colorband, "Capitol" at left					
❑ W 1031 [M]	Cole Espanol	1962	5.00	10.00	20.00
—Black label with colorband, "Capitol" at top					
❑ SW 1084 [S]	The Very Thought of You	1959	7.50	15.00	30.00
—Black label with colorband, "Capitol" at left					
❑ SW 1084 [S]	The Very Thought of You	1962	5.00	10.00	20.00
—Black label with colorband, "Capitol" at top					
❑ W 1084 [M]	The Very Thought of You	1958	7.50	15.00	30.00
—Black label with colorband, "Capitol" at left					
❑ W 1084 [M]	The Very Thought of You	1962	5.00	10.00	20.00
—Black label with colorband, "Capitol" at top					
❑ SW 1120 [S]	Welcome to the Club	1959	10.00	20.00	40.00
—Black label with colorband, "Capitol" at left					
❑ W 1120 [M]	Welcome to the Club	1959	7.50	15.00	30.00
—Black label with colorband, "Capitol" at left					
❑ SW 1190 [S]	To Whom It May Concern	1959	10.00	20.00	40.00
—Black label with colorband, "Capitol" at left					
❑ W 1190 [M]	To Whom It May Concern	1959	7.50	15.00	30.00
—Black label with colorband, "Capitol" at left					
❑ SW 1220 [S]	A Mis Amigos	1959	10.00	20.00	40.00
—Black label with colorband, "Capitol" at left					
❑ SW 1220 [S]	A Mis Amigos	1962	6.25	12.50	25.00
—Black label with colorband, "Capitol" at top					
❑ W 1220 [M]	A Mis Amigos	1959	7.50	15.00	30.00
—Black label with colorband, "Capitol" at left					
❑ W 1220 [M]	A Mis Amigos	1962	5.00	10.00	20.00
—Black label with colorband, "Capitol" at top					
❑ SW 1249 [S]	Every Time I Feel the Spirit	1960	7.50	15.00	30.00
—Black label with colorband, "Capitol" at left					
❑ W 1249 [M]	Every Time I Feel the Spirit	1960	6.25	12.50	25.00
—Black label with colorband, "Capitol" at left					
❑ SW 1331 [S]	Tell Me About Yourself	1960	7.50	15.00	30.00
—Black label with colorband, "Capitol" at left					
❑ W 1331 [M]	Tell Me About Yourself	1960	6.25	12.50	25.00
—Black label with colorband, "Capitol" at left					
❑ SWAK 1392 [S]	Wild Is Love	1960	7.50	15.00	30.00
—Black label with colorband, "Capitol" at left					
❑ WAK 1392 [M]	Wild Is Love	1960	6.25	12.50	25.00
—Black label with colorband, "Capitol" at left					
❑ SW 1444 [S]	The Magic of Christmas	1960	5.00	10.00	20.00
❑ W 1444 [M]	The Magic of Christmas	1960	5.00	10.00	20.00
❑ SW 1574 [S]	The Touch of Your Lips	1961	6.25	12.50	25.00
—Black label with colorband, "Capitol" at left					
❑ SW 1574 [S]	The Touch of Your Lips	1962	5.00	10.00	20.00
—Black label with colorband, "Capitol" at top					
❑ W 1574 [M]	The Touch of Your Lips	1961	5.00	10.00	20.00
—Black label with colorband, "Capitol" at left					
❑ W 1574 [M]	The Touch of Your Lips	1962	3.75	7.50	15.00
—Black label with colorband, "Capitol" at top					
❑ SWCL 1613 [(3) S]	The Nat King Cole Story	1961	7.50	15.00	30.00
❑ WCL 1613 [(3) M]	The Nat King Cole Story	1961	6.25	12.50	25.00
❑ SM-1675	Nat King Cole Sings/George Shearing Plays	197?	2.00	4.00	8.00
—Reissue with new prefix					
❑ SW 1675 [S]	Nat King Cole Sings/George Shearing Plays	1962	7.50	15.00	30.00
—Black label with colorband, "Capitol" at left					
❑ SW 1675 [S]	Nat King Cole Sings/George Shearing Plays	1963	5.00	10.00	20.00
—Black label with colorband, "Capitol" at top					
❑ W 1675 [M]	Nat King Cole Sings/George Shearing Plays	1962	6.25	12.50	25.00
—Black label with colorband, "Capitol" at left					
❑ W 1675 [M]	Nat King Cole Sings/George Shearing Plays	1963	3.75	7.50	15.00
—Black label with colorband, "Capitol" at top					
❑ SW 1713 [S]	Nat King Cole Sings the Blues	1962	6.25	12.50	25.00
—Black label with colorband, "Capitol" at left					
❑ W 1713 [M]	Nat King Cole Sings the Blues	1962	5.00	10.00	20.00
—Black label with colorband, "Capitol" at left					
❑ SM-1749	More Cole Espanol	197?	2.00	4.00	8.00
—Reissue with new prefix					
❑ SW 1749 [S]	More Cole Espanol	1962	7.50	15.00	30.00
—Black label with colorband, "Capitol" at left					
❑ SW 1749 [S]	More Cole Espanol	1963	5.00	10.00	20.00
—Black label with colorband, "Capitol" at top					
❑ W 1749 [M]	More Cole Espanol	1962	6.25	12.50	25.00
—Black label with colorband, "Capitol" at left					
❑ W 1749 [M]	More Cole Espanol	1963	3.75	7.50	15.00
—Black label with colorband, "Capitol" at top					
❑ ST 1793 [S]	Ramblin' Rose	1962	5.00	10.00	20.00
❑ T 1793 [M]	Ramblin' Rose	1962	3.75	7.50	15.00
❑ ST 1838 [S]	Dear Lonely Hearts	1962	5.00	10.00	20.00
❑ T 1838 [M]	Dear Lonely Hearts	1962	3.75	7.50	15.00
❑ SW 1859 [S]	Where Did Everyone Go?	1963	5.00	10.00	20.00
❑ W 1859 [M]	Where Did Everyone Go?	1963	3.75	7.50	15.00
❑ DT 1891 [R]	Nat King Cole's Top Pops	1963	3.00	6.00	12.00
❑ T 1891 [M]	Nat King Cole's Top Pops	1963	3.75	7.50	15.00
❑ SW 1926 [S]	The Nat King Cole Story, Volume 1	1962	3.75	7.50	15.00
❑ W 1926 [M]	The Nat King Cole Story, Volume 1	1962	3.00	6.00	12.00
❑ SW 1927 [S]	The Nat King Cole Story, Volume 2	1963	3.75	7.50	15.00
❑ W 1927 [M]	The Nat King Cole Story, Volume 2	1963	3.00	6.00	12.00
❑ SW 1928 [S]	The Nat King Cole Story, Volume 3	1963	3.75	7.50	15.00
❑ W 1928 [M]	The Nat King Cole Story, Volume 3	1963	3.00	6.00	12.00
❑ SW 1929 [S]	Nat King Cole Sings the Blues, Volume 2	1963	5.00	10.00	20.00
❑ W 1929 [M]	Nat King Cole Sings the Blues, Volume 2	1963	3.75	7.50	15.00

Number	Title (A Side/B Side)	Yr	VG	VG+	NM
❑ ST 1932 [S]	Those Lazy-Hazy-Crazy Days of Summer	1963	5.00	10.00	20.00
❑ T 1932 [M]	Those Lazy-Hazy-Crazy Days of Summer	1963	3.75	7.50	15.00
❑ SM-1967 [S]	The Christmas Song	197?	2.00	4.00	8.00
—Budget-line reissue					
❑ SW 1967 [S]	The Christmas Song	1962	3.75	7.50	15.00
—Black label with colorband					
❑ SW 1967 [S]	The Christmas Song	1969	3.00	6.00	12.00
—Lime-green label					
❑ SW 1967 [S]	The Christmas Song	1971	3.00	6.00	12.00
—Red label					
❑ SW 1967 [S]	The Christmas Song	1973	2.50	5.00	10.00
—Orange label, "Capitol" at bottom					
❑ W 1967 [M]	The Christmas Song	1962	3.75	7.50	15.00
—Reissue of W 1444 with title song added and another deleted					
❑ SW 2008 [S]	Let's Face the Music	1963	5.00	10.00	20.00
❑ W 2008 [M]	Let's Face the Music	1963	3.75	7.50	15.00
❑ SM-2117	My Fair Lady	197?	2.00	4.00	8.00
—Reissue with new prefix					
❑ SW 2117 [S]	My Fair Lady	1964	5.00	10.00	20.00
—Black label with colorband					
❑ SW 2117 [S]	My Fair Lady	1969	3.00	6.00	12.00
—Lime green label					
❑ W 2117 [M]	My Fair Lady	1964	3.75	7.50	15.00
❑ ST 2118 [S]	I Don't Want to Be Hurt Anymore	1964	5.00	10.00	20.00
❑ T 2118 [M]	I Don't Want to Be Hurt Anymore	1964	3.75	7.50	15.00
❑ ST 2195 [S]	L-O-V-E	1965	5.00	10.00	20.00
❑ T 2195 [M]	L-O-V-E	1965	3.75	7.50	15.00
❑ T 2311 [M]	The Nat King Cole Trio	1965	3.00	6.00	12.00
❑ ST 2340 [S]	Songs from "Cat Ballou" and Other Motion Pictures	1965	3.75	7.50	15.00
❑ T 2340 [M]	Songs from "Cat Ballou" and Other Motion Pictures	1965	3.00	6.00	12.00
❑ DT 2348 [R]	Nature Boy	1965	3.00	6.00	12.00
❑ T 2348 [M]	Nature Boy	1965	3.75	7.50	15.00
❑ ST 2361 [S]	Looking Back	1965	3.75	7.50	15.00
❑ T 2361 [M]	Looking Back	1965	3.00	6.00	12.00
❑ MAS 2434 [M]	Nat King Cole at the Sands	1966	3.00	6.00	12.00
❑ SM-2434	Nat King Cole at the Sands	197?	2.00	4.00	8.00
—Reissue with new prefix					
❑ SMAS 2434 [S]	Nat King Cole at the Sands	1966	3.75	7.50	15.00
❑ ST 2454 [S]	Hymns and Spirituals	1966	3.75	7.50	15.00
❑ T 2454 [M]	Hymns and Spirituals	1966	3.00	6.00	12.00
❑ T 2529 [M]	The Vintage Years	1966	3.00	6.00	12.00
❑ ST 2558 [S]	The Great Songs!	1966	3.75	7.50	15.00
❑ T 2558 [M]	The Great Songs!	1966	3.00	6.00	12.00
❑ ST 2680 [S]	Sincerely, Nat King Cole	1967	3.00	6.00	12.00
❑ T 2680 [M]	Sincerely, Nat King Cole	1967	3.75	7.50	15.00
❑ ST 2759 [S]	Thank You Pretty Baby	1967	3.00	6.00	12.00
❑ T 2759 [M]	Thank You Pretty Baby	1967	3.75	7.50	15.00
❑ ST 2820 [S]	Beautiful Ballads	1967	3.00	6.00	12.00
❑ T 2820 [M]	Beautiful Ballads	1967	3.75	7.50	15.00
❑ STCL 2873 [(3) P]	The Nat King Cole Deluxe Set	1968	6.25	12.50	25.00
❑ TCL 2873 [(3) M]	The Nat King Cole Deluxe Set	1968	7.50	15.00	30.00
❑ SKAO 2944	The Best of Nat King Cole	1968	3.00	6.00	12.00
❑ H 9110 [10]	Eight Top Pops	1954	12.50	25.00	50.00
❑ M-11033 [M]	Trio Days	1972	3.75	7.50	15.00
❑ SWAK-11355	Love Is Here to Stay	1974	3.00	6.00	12.00
❑ SM-11796	After Midnight	1978	2.50	5.00	10.00
❑ SM-11804	Songs from "Cat Ballou" and Other Motion Pictures	1978	2.50	5.00	10.00
❑ SM-11882	Looking Back	1979	2.50	5.00	10.00
❑ ST-12219	16 Grandes Exitos	1982	2.50	5.00	10.00
❑ SN-16032	Ramblin' Rose	1980	2.00	4.00	8.00
❑ SN-16033	The Nat King Cole Story, Volume 1	1980	2.00	4.00	8.00
❑ SN-16034	The Nat King Cole Story, Volume 2	1980	2.00	4.00	8.00
❑ SN-16035	The Nat King Cole Story, Volume 3	1980	2.00	4.00	8.00
❑ SN-16036	The Best of Nat King Cole	1980	2.00	4.00	8.00
❑ SN-16037	Wild Is Love	1980	2.00	4.00	8.00
❑ SN-16136	A Mis Amigos	1980	2.00	4.00	8.00
❑ SN-16137	St. Louis Blues	1980	2.00	4.00	8.00
❑ SN-16162	Unforgettable	1981	2.00	4.00	8.00
❑ SN-16163	Love Is the Thing	1981	2.00	4.00	8.00
❑ DN-16164	Walkin' My Baby Back Home	1981	2.00	4.00	8.00
❑ DN-16165	A Blossom Fell	1981	2.00	4.00	8.00
❑ N-16166	Cole Espanol	1981	2.00	4.00	8.00
❑ SN-16167	More Cole Espanol	1981	2.00	4.00	8.00
❑ N-16260	The Best of the King Cole Trio — Volume 1	1982	2.00	4.00	8.00
❑ N-16281	The Best of the King Cole Trio — Volume 2	1982	2.00	4.00	8.00
❑ SQBO 90938 [(2)]	The Velvet Moods of Nat King Cole	1967	6.25	12.50	25.00
—Capitol Record Club exclusive					
❑ SQBO 91278 [(2)]	The Swingin' Moods of Nat King Cole	1967	6.25	12.50	25.00
—Capitol Record Club exclusive					
❑ SQBO-93741 [(2)]	The Man and His Music	197?	5.00	10.00	20.00
—Capitol Record Club exclusive; with booklet					
DCC COMPACT CLASSICS					
❑ LPZ-2029	Love Is the Thing	1997	30.00	60.00	120.00
—Audiophile vinyl					
❑ LPZ-2047	The Very Thought of You	1998	25.00	50.00	100.00
—Audiophile vinyl					
❑ LPZ-2061 [(2)]	The Greatest Hits	1998	30.00	60.00	120.00
—Audiophile vinyl					
DECCA					
❑ DL 8260 [M]	In the Beginning	1956	10.00	20.00	40.00
—Black label, silver print					
❑ DL 8260 [M]	In the Beginning	1960	6.25	12.50	25.00
—Black label with color bars					

Number	Title (A Side/B Side)	Yr	VG	VG+	NM
MARK 56					
❑ 739 [(2)]	Early 1940s	197?	3.75	7.50	15.00
MCA					
❑ 4020 [(2)]	From the Very Beginning	1973	3.00	6.00	12.00
MOBILE FIDELITY					
❑ 1-081	Nat King Cole Sings/George Shearing Plays	1981	10.00	20.00	40.00
—Audiophile vinyl					
MOSAIC					
❑ MR27-138 [(27)]	The Complete Capitol Recordings of the Nat King Cole Trio	199?	150.00	300.00	600.00
PAIR					
❑ PDL2-1025 [(2)]	Weaver of Dreams	1986	3.00	6.00	12.00
❑ PDL2-1026 [(2)]	Love Moods	1986	3.00	6.00	12.00
❑ PDL2-1128 [(2)]	Tenderly	1986	3.00	6.00	12.00
PICKWICK					
❑ PTP-2058 [(2)]	Nature Boy	1973	3.00	6.00	12.00
❑ SPC-3046	Love Is a Many Splendored Thing	196?	2.50	5.00	10.00
❑ SPC-3071	When You're Smiling	196?	2.50	5.00	10.00
❑ SPC-3105	Stay As Sweet As You Are	196?	2.50	5.00	10.00
❑ SPC-3154	You're My Everything	197?	2.50	5.00	10.00
❑ SPC-3249	Nature Boy	197?	2.50	5.00	10.00
SAVOY JAZZ					
❑ SJL-1205	Nat King Cole & The King Cole Trio	1989	3.00	6.00	12.00
SCORE					
❑ SLP-4019 [M]	The King Cole Trio and Lester Young	1957	20.00	40.00	80.00
TRIP					
❑ 7	The Nat "King" Cole Trio	197?	3.00	6.00	12.00
VERVE					
❑ VSP-14 [M]	Nat Cole at JATP	1966	3.75	7.50	15.00
❑ VSPS-14 [R]	Nat Cole at JATP	1966	3.00	6.00	12.00
❑ VSP-25 [M]	Nat Cole at JATP 2	1966	3.75	7.50	15.00
❑ VSPS-25 [R]	Nat Cole at JATP 2	1966	3.00	6.00	12.00

COLE, NATALIE

12-Inch Singles

Number	Title (A Side/B Side)	Yr	VG	VG+	NM
CAPITOL					
❑ SPRO-8990/1 [DJ]	I'm Catching Hell (Living Here Alone) (7:28) (stereo/mono)	1978	3.75	7.50	15.00
ELEKTRA					
❑ ED 6256 [(2) DJ]	Livin' for Love (unknown versions)	2000	3.00	6.00	12.00
❑ 67153 [(2)]	Livin' for Love (Hex HQ2 Club Mix) (Acappella) (Frankie Knuckles Classic Club Mix) (Album Version) (Hex HQ2 Instrumental) (Hex HQ2 Radio Mix) (Frankie Knuckles Classic Instrumental) (Frankie Knuckles Dubbin' 4 Love)	2000	2.50	5.00	10.00
EMI					
❑ SPRO 04265 [DJ]	Miss You Like Crazy (same on both sides?)	1989	2.50	5.00	10.00
❑ SPRO 04441/2 [DJ]	As a Matter of Fact (4 versions)	1989	2.50	5.00	10.00
❑ SPRO 04449 [DJ]	Starting Over Again (same on both sides?)	1989	3.75	7.50	15.00
❑ V-56161	Wild Women Do (7 versions)	1990	2.00	4.00	8.00
EMI MANHATTAN					
❑ V-56084	Pink Cadillac (Radio Version) (Club Vocal) (Bass It Dub)/I Wanna Be That Woman	1988	2.50	5.00	10.00
EPIC					
❑ AS 1748 [DJ]	Keep It on the Outside/I Won't Deny You	1983	2.00	4.00	8.00
❑ 49-04001	Too Much Mister/Where's Your Angel	1983	2.00	4.00	8.00
MANHATTAN					
❑ V-56053	Jump Start (Extended Remix) (Dub Version) (Radio Edit)/More Than Stars	1987	2.00	4.00	8.00
❑ SPRO-79136/7 [DJ]	Jump Start (Extended Version) (Car Mix) (Deluxe Dub Mix)	1987	3.00	6.00	12.00
❑ SPRO-79154 [DJ]	I Live for Your Love (same on both sides?)	1987	2.50	5.00	10.00
MODERN					
❑ DMD 903 [DJ]	Secrets (Extended) (LP Version)	1985	2.50	5.00	10.00
❑ 96841	Secrets (Extended) (Instrumental)	1985	2.00	4.00	8.00
❑ 96885	Dangerous (Extended Dance Mix) (Dub Mix) (Acappella)	1985	2.50	5.00	10.00

45s

Number	Title (A Side/B Side)	Yr	VG	VG+	NM
CAPITOL					
❑ 4109	This Will Be/Joey	1975	—	2.50	5.00
❑ 4193	Inseparable/How Come You Won't Stay Here	1975	—	2.00	4.00
❑ 4259	Sophisticated Lady (She's a Different Lady)/Good Morning Heartache	1976	—	2.00	4.00
❑ 4328	Mr. Melody/Not Like Mine	1976	—	2.00	4.00
❑ 4360	I've Got Love on My Mind/Unpredictable You	1976	—	2.00	4.00
❑ 4439	Party Lights/Peaceful Living	1977	—	2.00	4.00
❑ 4509	Our Love/La Costa	1977	—	2.00	4.00
❑ 4572	Annie Mae/Just Can't Stay Away	1978	—	2.00	4.00
❑ 4623	Lucy in the Sky with Diamonds/Lovers	1978	—	2.00	4.00
❑ 4690	Stand By/Who Will Carry On	1979	—	2.00	4.00
❑ 4722	Sorry/You're So Good	1979	—	2.00	4.00
❑ 4767	Your Lonely Heart/The Winner	1979	—	2.00	4.00
❑ 4869	Someone That I Used to Love/Don't Look Back	1980	—	2.00	4.00
❑ 4924	Hold On/Paradise	1980	—	2.00	4.00
❑ A-5021	You Were Right Girl/Across the Nation	1981	—	2.00	4.00
❑ A-5045	Nothin' But a Fool/The Joke Is On You	1981	—	2.00	4.00
ELEKTRA					
❑ 64816	The Christmas Song (Chestnuts Roasting on an Open Fire)/Nature Boy	1991	—	2.00	4.00
❑ 64875	Unforgettable/Cottage for Sale	1991	—	2.00	4.00
EMI					
❑ B-50185	Miss You Like Crazy/Good to Be Back	1989	—	—	3.00
❑ B-50185 [PS]	Miss You Like Crazy/Good to Be Back	1989	—	2.50	5.00

Number	Title (A Side/B Side)	Yr	VG	VG+	NM
❏ B-50213	I Do/Miss You Like Crazy	1989	—	—	3.00
❏ B-50231	As a Matter of Fact/(B-side unknown)	1989	—	2.50	5.00
EMI MANHATTAN					
❏ B-50117	Pink Cadillac/I Wanna Be That Woman	1988	—	—	3.00
❏ B-50138	When I Fall in Love/Pink Cadillac	1988	—	—	3.00
❏ B-50138 [PS]	When I Fall in Love/Pink Cadillac	1988	—	2.00	4.00
EPIC					
❏ 34-04000	Too Much Mister/Where's Your Angel	1983	—	2.00	4.00
❏ 34-04147	Keep 'Em on the Outside/I Won't Deny You	1983	—	2.00	4.00
GEFFEN					
❏ 28152	Over You/After Midnite	1987	—	—	3.00
—With Ray Parker Jr.					
MANHATTAN					
❏ B-50073	Jump Start/More Than the Stars	1987	—	—	3.00
❏ B-50073 [PS]	Jump Start/More Than the Stars	1987	—	2.00	4.00
❏ B-50094	I Live for Your Love/More Than the Stars	1987	—	—	3.00
❏ B-50094 [PS]	I Live for Your Love/More Than the Stars	1987	—	2.00	4.00
MODERN					
❏ 99589	Secrets/Nobody's Soldier	1985	—	—	3.00
❏ 99630	A Little Bit of Heaven/When I Need It Bad, You Got It Good	1985	—	—	3.00
❏ 99648	Dangerous/Love Is On the Way	1985	—	—	3.00
❏ 99648 [PS]	Dangerous/Love Is On the Way	1985	—	—	3.00
Albums					
CAPITOL					
❏ ST-11429	Inseparable	1975	2.50	5.00	10.00
❏ ST-11517	Natalie	1976	2.50	5.00	10.00
❏ SO-11600	Unpredictable	1977	2.50	5.00	10.00
❏ SW-11708	Thankful	1978	2.50	5.00	10.00
❏ SKBL-11709 [(2)]	Natalie..Live!	1978	3.00	6.00	12.00
❏ SO-11928	I Love You So	1979	2.50	5.00	10.00
❏ ST-12079	Don't Look Back	1980	2.50	5.00	10.00
❏ ST-12165	Happy Love	1981	2.50	5.00	10.00
❏ ST-12242	A Collection	1982	2.50	5.00	10.00
❏ SN-16038	Inseparable	198?	2.00	4.00	8.00
—Budget-line reissue					
❏ SN-16310	A Collection	1985	2.00	4.00	8.00
—Budget-line reissue					
ELEKTRA					
❏ 61049 [(2)]	Unforgettable	1991	5.00	10.00	20.00
EMI					
❏ E1-48902	Good to Be Back	1989	2.50	5.00	10.00
EPIC					
❏ FE 38280	I'm Ready	1983	2.50	5.00	10.00
MANHATTAN					
❏ 53051	Everlasting	1987	2.50	5.00	10.00
MOBILE FIDELITY					
❏ 1-032	Thankful	1980	5.00	10.00	20.00
—Audiophile vinyl					
MODERN					
❏ 90270	Dangerous	1985	2.50	5.00	10.00

COLE, NATALIE, AND PEABO BRYSON
Also see each artist's individual listings.

45s

Number	Title (A Side/B Side)	Yr	VG	VG+	NM
CAPITOL					
❏ 4804	Gimme Some Time/Love Will Find You	1979	—	2.00	4.00
❏ 4826	What You Won't Do for Love/Your Lonely Heart	1980	—	2.00	4.00
Albums					
CAPITOL					
❏ SOO-12025	We're the Best of Friends	1979	2.50	5.00	10.00

COLLEGIANS, THE (1)

45s

Number	Title (A Side/B Side)	Yr	VG	VG+	NM
WINLEY					
❏ 224	Zoom, Zoom, Zoom/On Your Merry Way	1958	12.50	25.00	50.00
❏ 261	Oh I Need Your Love/Tonite, Oh Tonite	1962	7.50	15.00	30.00
❏ 263	Right Around the Corner/Teenie Weenie Little Bit	1962	7.50	15.00	30.00
X-TRA					
❏ 108	Let's Go for a Ride/Heavenly Night	1958	75.00	150.00	300.00
—Small print label (title and artist about 1/8-inch high)					
❏ 108	Let's Go for a Ride/Heavenly Night	1961	15.00	30.00	60.00
—Large print label (title and artist about 1/4-inch high)					
Albums					
LOST-NITE					
❏ LLP-5 [10]	The Best of the Collegians	1981	2.50	5.00	10.00
—Red vinyl					
WINLEY					
❏ LP-6004 [M]	Sing Along with the Collegians	195?	100.00	200.00	400.00

COLLINS, ALBERT

45s

Number	Title (A Side/B Side)	Yr	VG	VG+	NM
20TH FOX					
❏ 6708	Cookin' Catfish/Taking My Time	1968	2.00	4.00	8.00
GREAT SCOTT					
❏ 007	Albert's Alley/Defrost	1963	7.50	15.00	30.00
HALLWAY					
❏ 1913	Albert's Alley/Defrost	1963	5.00	10.00	20.00
❏ 1920	Frosty/Tremble	1964	7.50	15.00	30.00
❏ 1925	Backstroke/Thaw Out	1964	5.00	10.00	20.00
IMPERIAL					
❏ 66351	Ain't Got Time/Got a Good Thing Goin'	1969	2.00	4.00	8.00
❏ 66391	Do the Sissy/Turnin' On	1969	2.00	4.00	8.00

Number	Title (A Side/B Side)	Yr	VG	VG+	NM
❏ 66412	Conversation for Collins/And Then It Started Raining	1969	2.00	4.00	8.00
KANGAROO					
❏ 103	Freeze/(B-side unknown)	1958	15.00	30.00	60.00
❏ 104	Collins Shuffle/(B-side unknown)	1958	15.00	30.00	60.00
LIBERTY					
❏ 56184	Coon 'n Collards/Do What You Want to Do	1970	2.00	4.00	8.00
TCF HALL					
❏ 104	Sno Cone (Part 1)/Sno Cone (Part 2)	1965	2.50	5.00	10.00
❏ 116	Dyin' Flu/Hot 'N' Cold	1966	2.50	5.00	10.00
❏ 127	Frost Bite/Don't Lose Your Cool	1966	2.50	5.00	10.00
Albums					
ALLIGATOR					
❏ AL-4713	Ice Pickin'	1978	2.50	5.00	10.00
❏ AL-4719	Frostbite	1980	2.50	5.00	10.00
❏ AL-4725	Frozen Alive!	1981	2.50	5.00	10.00
❏ AL-4730	Don't Lose Your Cool	1983	2.50	5.00	10.00
❏ AL-4733	Live in Japan	1984	2.50	5.00	10.00
❏ AL-4743	Showdown!	1985	2.50	5.00	10.00
—With Robert Cray and Johnny Copeland					
❏ AL-4752	Cold Snap	1986	2.50	5.00	10.00
BLUE THUMB					
❏ BTS 8	Truckin' with Albert Collins	1969	6.25	12.50	25.00
—Reissue of TCF Hall LP					
IMPERIAL					
❏ LP-12429	Love Can Be Found Anywhere	1968	7.50	15.00	30.00
❏ LP-12438	Trash Talkin'	1969	7.50	15.00	30.00
❏ LP-12449	The Compleat Albert Collins	1970	7.50	15.00	30.00
MOBILE FIDELITY					
❏ 1-217	Showdown!	1995	7.50	15.00	30.00
—With Robert Cray and Johnny Copeland; audiophile vinyl					
❏ 1-226	Cold Snap	1995	5.00	10.00	20.00
—Audiophile vinyl					
TCF HALL					
❏ 8002 [M]	The Cool Sound of Albert Collins	1965	75.00	150.00	300.00
TUMBLEWEED					
❏ TWS-103	There's Gotta Be a Change	1971	3.75	7.50	15.00

COLLINS, BOOTSY
Also see BOOTSY'S RUBBER BAND; FUNKADELIC; PARLIAMENT.

12-Inch Singles

Number	Title (A Side/B Side)	Yr	VG	VG+	NM
COLUMBIA					
❏ 44-07878	Party on Plastic (What's Bootsy Doin'?) (3 versions)/A Creative Nuisance	1988	2.50	5.00	10.00
❏ 44-08173	1st One 2 the Egg Wins (Screwin' Up) (Street Legal) (Human Race) (Street Legal Instrumental)	1988	2.50	5.00	10.00

45s

Number	Title (A Side/B Side)	Yr	VG	VG+	NM
COLUMBIA					
❏ 38-07991	Party on Plastic (What's Bootsy Doin'?)/Save What's Mine for Me	1988	—	—	3.00
❏ 38-07991 [PS]	Party on Plastic (What's Bootsy Doin'?)/Save What's Mine for Me	1988	—	—	3.00
❏ 38-08496	1st One 2 the Egg Wins (Human Race)/1st One 2 the Egg Wins (Street Legal)	1988	—	—	3.00
WARNER BROS.					
❏ 8215	Stretchin' Out (In a Rubber Band)/Physical Love	1976	—	3.00	6.00
❏ 29965	Shine-O-Myte (Rag Popping)/So Nice You Name Him Twice	1982	—	2.00	4.00
❏ 50044	Take a Lickin' and Keep On Kickin'/Shine-O-Myte (Rag Poppin')	1982	—	2.00	4.00
Albums					
COLUMBIA					
❏ FC 44107	What's Bootsy Doin'?	1988	2.50	5.00	10.00
WARNER BROS.					
❏ BSK 3667	The One Giveth, The Count Taketh Away	1982	2.50	5.00	10.00

COLLINS, LYN
Also see JAMES BROWN.

45s

Number	Title (A Side/B Side)	Yr	VG	VG+	NM
KING					
❏ 6373	Wheels of Life/Just Won't Do Right	1971	2.00	4.00	8.00
PEOPLE					
❏ 608	Think (About It)/Ain't No Sunshine	1972	2.50	5.00	10.00
❏ 615	Me and My Baby Got a Good Thing Goin'/I'll Never Let You Break My Heart Again	1972	—	3.00	6.00
❏ 618	Mama Feel Good/Fly Me to the Moon	1973	—	3.00	6.00
❏ 623	How Long Can I Keep It Up (Part 1)/How Long Can I Keep It Up (Part 2)	1973	—	3.00	6.00
❏ 626	Take Me As I Am/Make the World a Better Place	1973	—	3.00	6.00
❏ 630	We Wanted to Parrty, Parrty, Party/You Can't Beat Two People in Love	1973	—	3.00	6.00
❏ 633	Take Me Just As I Am/Don't Make Me Over	1973	—	3.00	6.00
❏ 636	Give It Up or Turnit A Loose/What the World Needs Now Is Love	1974	—	3.00	6.00
❏ 641	Wide Awake in a Dream/Rock Me Again & Again & Again & Again & Again & Again	1974	—	3.00	6.00
❏ 650	Rock Me Again & Again & Again & Again & Again/You Can't Love Me If You Don't Respect Me	1974	—	3.00	6.00
❏ 657	Baby Don't Do It/How Long Can I Keep It Up	1975	—	3.00	6.00
❏ 659	If You Don't Know Me By Now/Baby Don't Do It	1975	—	3.00	6.00
❏ 662	Mr. Big Stuff/Rock Me Again & Again & Again & Again & Again	1975	—	3.00	6.00

Number	Title (A Side/B Side)	Yr	VG	VG+	NM

Albums

PEOPLE

Number	Title (A Side/B Side)	Yr	VG	VG+	NM
❑ PE-5602	Think (About It)	1972	15.00	30.00	60.00
❑ PE-6605	Check Me Out	1975	12.50	25.00	50.00

COMMODORES

Also see LIONEL RICHIE.

12-Inch Singles

MOTOWN

Number	Title (A Side/B Side)	Yr	VG	VG+	NM
❑ M 00007D1	Brick House (6:11) (same on both sides)	1977	3.75	7.50	15.00
❑ PR-56 [DJ]	Still (5:51)/Sail On (5:35)	1979	5.00	10.00	20.00
❑ PR-70 [DJ]	Jesus Is Love (Short Version 4:26) (Long Version 6:04)	1980	5.00	10.00	20.00
❑ PR-87 [DJ]	Keep On Taking Me Higher (5:18)/Why You Wanna Try Me (4:36)	1981	3.00	6.00	12.00
❑ PR-166 [DJ]	Nightshift (Radio Edit of Club Mix 4:48) (Club Mix 7:02) (Dub Mix 7:12)	1985	3.00	6.00	12.00
❑ 4533MG	Nightshift (Edit of Club Mix 4:48) (Club Mix 7:02) (Instrumentakl Mix 7:12)	1985	2.00	4.00	8.00
❑ 4535MG	Animal Instinct (Club Mix 9:46)/Lightin' Up the Night	1985	2.00	4.00	8.00

POLYDOR

Number	Title (A Side/B Side)	Yr	VG	VG+	NM
❑ PRO 467-1 [DJ]	Goin' to the Bank (Club Mix) (Dub)	1986	3.00	6.00	12.00
❑ PRO 501-1 [DJ]	United in Love (Edit) (LP Version)	1986	2.00	4.00	8.00
❑ PRO 641-1 [DJ]	Solitaire (same on both sides)	1988	2.50	5.00	10.00
❑ PRO 684-1 [DJ]	Homeless (same on both sides)	1988	2.00	4.00	8.00
❑ 871371-1	Grrip (6 versions)	1989	2.00	4.00	8.00
❑ 885358-1	Goin' to the Bank (7:17) (4:19)	1986	2.00	4.00	8.00
❑ 885538-1	Take It from Me (4 versions)/I Wanna Rock You	1987	2.00	4.00	8.00

45s

MOTOWN

Number	Title (A Side/B Side)	Yr	VG	VG+	NM
❑ 1268	Are You Happy/There's a Song in My Heart	1973	—	3.00	6.00
❑ 1307	Machine Gun/There's a Song in My Heart	1974	—	2.50	5.00
❑ 1307 [DJ]	Machine Gun (stereo/mono)	1974	3.75	7.50	15.00
—Promo only on red vinyl					
❑ 1319	I Feel Sanctified/It Is As Good As You Make It	1974	—	2.50	5.00
❑ 1338	Slippery When Wet/The Bump	1975	—	2.50	5.00
❑ 1361	This Is Your Life/Look What You've Done to Me	1975	—	2.50	5.00
❑ 1366	Wide Open/(B-side unassigned)	1975	—	—	—
—Unreleased					
❑ 1381	Sweet Love/Better Never Than Forever	1976	—	2.00	4.00
❑ 1381 [DJ]	Sweet Love (stereo/mono)	1976	3.75	7.50	15.00
—Promo only on yellow vinyl					
❑ 1394	Come Inside/Time	1976	—	—	—
—Unreleased					
❑ 1399	High on Sunshine/Thumpin' Music	1976	—	—	—
—Unreleased					
❑ 1402	Just to Be Close to You/Thumpin' Music	1976	—	2.00	4.00
❑ 1408	Fancy Dancer/Cebu	1977	—	2.00	4.00
❑ 1418	Easy/Can't Let You Tease Me	1977	—	2.00	4.00
❑ 1425	Brick House/Captain Quickdraw	1977	—	2.00	4.00
❑ 1432	Too Hot Ta Trot/Funky Situation	1977	—	2.00	4.00
❑ 1443	Three Times a Lady/Look What You've Done to Me	1978	—	2.00	4.00
❑ 1452	Flying High/X-Rated Movie	1978	—	2.00	4.00
❑ 1457	Say Yeah/(B-side unassigned)	1978	—	—	—
—Unreleased					
❑ 1466	Sail On/Thumpin' Music	1979	—	2.00	4.00
❑ 1474	Still/Such a Woman	1979	—	2.00	4.00
❑ 1479	Wonderland/Lovin' You	1979	—	2.00	4.00
❑ 1489	Old Fashion Love/Sexy Lady	1980	—	2.00	4.00
❑ 1495	Heroes/Funky Situation	1980	—	2.00	4.00
❑ 1502	Jesus Is Love/Mighty Spirit	1980	—	3.00	6.00
❑ 1514	Lady (You Bring Me Up)/Gettin' It	1981	—	2.00	4.00
❑ 1527	Oh No/Lovin' You	1981	—	2.00	4.00
❑ 1604	Why You Wanna Try Me/X-Rated Movie	1982	—	2.00	4.00
❑ 1651	Painted Pictures/Reach High	1982	—	—	3.00
❑ 1661	Sexy Lady/Reach High	1983	—	—	3.00
❑ 1694	Only You/Cebu	1983	—	—	3.00
❑ 1719	Been Lovin' You/Turn Off the Lights	1984	—	—	3.00
❑ 1773	Nightshift/I Keep Running	1985	—	—	3.00
❑ 1773 [PS]	Nightshift/I Keep Running	1985	—	3.00	6.00
❑ 1788	Animal Instinct/Lightin' Up the Sky	1985	—	—	3.00
❑ 1802	Janet/I'm in Love	1985	—	—	3.00

MOWEST

Number	Title (A Side/B Side)	Yr	VG	VG+	NM
❑ 5009	I'm Looking for Love/At the Zoo	1972	2.00	4.00	8.00
❑ 5038	Determination/Don't You Be Worried	1973	2.00	4.00	8.00

POLYDOR

Number	Title (A Side/B Side)	Yr	VG	VG+	NM
❑ 871370-7	Grrip/Ain't Giving Up	1989	—	—	3.00
❑ 885358-7	Goin' to the Bank/Serious Love	1986	—	—	3.00
❑ 885358-7 [PS]	Goin' to the Bank/Serious Love	1986	—	—	3.00
❑ 885538-7	Take It from Me/I Wanna Rock You	1987	—	—	3.00
❑ 885538-7 [PS]	Take It from Me/I Wanna Rock You	1987	—	—	3.00
❑ 885760-7	United in Love/Talk to Me	1987	—	—	3.00
❑ 885760-7 [PS]	United in Love/Talk to Me	1987	—	—	3.00
❑ 887939-7	Solitaire/Stretchhh	1988	—	—	3.00
❑ 887939-7 [PS]	Solitaire/Stretchhh	1988	—	—	3.00

Albums

MOTOWN

Number	Title (A Side/B Side)	Yr	VG	VG+	NM
❑ PR 39 [DJ]	1978 Platinum Tour	1978	5.00	10.00	20.00
—Promo-only compilation					
❑ M5-121V1	Machine Gun	1981	2.50	5.00	10.00
—Reissue					
❑ M5-179V1	Movin' On	1981	2.00	4.00	8.00
❑ M5-222V1	Commodores	1982	2.00	4.00	8.00
❑ M5-240V1	Caught in the Act	1982	2.00	4.00	8.00
❑ M6-798	Machine Gun	1974	3.75	7.50	15.00
❑ M6-820	Caught in the Act	1975	2.50	5.00	10.00
❑ M6-848	Movin' On	1975	2.50	5.00	10.00
❑ M6-867	Hot on the Tracks	1976	2.50	5.00	10.00
❑ M7-884	Commodores	1977	2.50	5.00	10.00
❑ M9-894 [(2)]	Commodores Live!	1977	3.00	6.00	12.00
❑ M7-902	Natural High	1978	2.50	5.00	10.00
❑ M7-912	Commodores' Greatest Hits	1978	2.50	5.00	10.00
❑ M8-926	Midnight Magic	1979	2.50	5.00	10.00
❑ M8-939	Heroes	1980	2.50	5.00	10.00
❑ M8-955	In the Pocket	1981	2.50	5.00	10.00
❑ 5257 ML	Hot on the Tracks	1983	2.00	4.00	8.00
❑ 5293 ML	Natural High	1983	2.00	4.00	8.00
❑ 6028 ML	All the Great Hits	1982	2.50	5.00	10.00
❑ 6044 ML2 [(2)]	Anthology	1983	3.00	6.00	12.00
❑ 6054 ML	Commodores 13	1983	2.50	5.00	10.00
❑ 6124 ML	Nightshift	1985	2.50	5.00	10.00

POLYDOR

Number	Title (A Side/B Side)	Yr	VG	VG+	NM
❑ 831194-1	United	1986	2.50	5.00	10.00
❑ 835369-1	Rock Solid	1988	2.50	5.00	10.00

CONLEY, ARTHUR

45s

ATCO

Number	Title (A Side/B Side)	Yr	VG	VG+	NM
❑ 6463	Sweet Soul Music/Let's Go Steady	1967	2.50	5.00	10.00
❑ 6494	Shake, Rattle and Roll/You Don't Have to See Me	1967	2.00	4.00	8.00
❑ 6529	Whole Lot of Woman/Love Comes and Goes	1967	2.00	4.00	8.00
❑ 6563	Funky Street/Put Our Love Together	1968	2.00	4.00	8.00
❑ 6588	People Sure Act Funny/Burning Fire	1968	2.00	4.00	8.00
❑ 6622	Is That You Love/Aunt Dora's Love Soul Shack	1968	2.00	4.00	8.00
❑ 6640	Ob-La-Di, Ob-La-Da/Otis Sleep On	1968	2.00	4.00	8.00
❑ 6661	Speak Her Name/Run On	1969	—	3.00	6.00
❑ 6706	Star Review/Love Sure Is a Powerful Thing	1969	—	3.00	6.00
❑ 6733	Hurt/They Call the Wind Maria	1970	—	3.00	6.00
❑ 6747	God Bless/(Your Love Has Brought Me A) Mighty Long Way	1970	—	3.00	6.00
❑ 6790	Nobody's Fault But Mine/Day-O	1970	—	3.00	6.00

CAPRICORN

Number	Title (A Side/B Side)	Yr	VG	VG+	NM
❑ 0001	More Sweet Soul Music/Walking on Eggs	1972	2.50	5.00	10.00
❑ 0006	Rita/More Sweet Soul Music	1972	2.00	4.00	8.00
❑ 0047	Bless You/It's So Nice	1973	2.00	4.00	8.00
❑ 8017	I'm Living Good/I'm So Glad You're Here	1971	2.50	5.00	10.00

FAME

Number	Title (A Side/B Side)	Yr	VG	VG+	NM
❑ 1007	I Can't Stop/In the Same Old Way	1966	3.75	7.50	15.00
❑ 1009	Take Me (Just As I Am)/I'm Gonna Forget About You	1966	3.75	7.50	15.00

JOTIS

Number	Title (A Side/B Side)	Yr	VG	VG+	NM
❑ 470	I'm a Lonely Stranger/Where Lead Me	1965	5.00	10.00	20.00
❑ 472	Who's Fooling Who/There's a Place for Us	1966	5.00	10.00	20.00

PHILCO-FORD

Number	Title (A Side/B Side)	Yr	VG	VG+	NM
❑ HP-15	Sweet Soul Music/You Don't Have to See Me	1968	3.75	7.50	15.00
—4-inch plastic "Hip Pocket Record" with color sleeve					

Albums

ATCO

Number	Title (A Side/B Side)	Yr	VG	VG+	NM
❑ 33-215 [M]	Sweet Soul Music	1967	10.00	20.00	40.00
❑ SD 33-215 [S]	Sweet Soul Music	1967	7.50	15.00	30.00
❑ 33-220 [M]	Shake, Rattle & Roll	1967	10.00	20.00	40.00
❑ SD 33-220 [S]	Shake, Rattle & Roll	1967	7.50	15.00	30.00
❑ SD 33-243	Soul Directions	1968	7.50	15.00	30.00
❑ SD 33-276	More Sweet Soul	1969	7.50	15.00	30.00

CONNORS, NORMAN

12-Inch Singles

ARISTA

Number	Title (A Side/B Side)	Yr	VG	VG+	NM
❑ SP-99 [DJ]	Take It to the Limit (same on both sides?)	1980	3.75	7.50	15.00

CAPITOL

Number	Title (A Side/B Side)	Yr	VG	VG+	NM
❑ V-15376	You're My One and Only Love (5 versions)	1988	2.50	5.00	10.00

45s

ARISTA

Number	Title (A Side/B Side)	Yr	VG	VG+	NM
❑ 0343	This Is Your Life/Captain Connors	1978	—	2.00	4.00
❑ 0377	Wouldn't You Like to See/Listen	1978	—	2.00	4.00
❑ 0443	Your Love/Disco Land	1979	—	2.00	4.00
❑ 0460	Hand Me Gently/Be There In the Morning	1979	—	2.00	4.00
❑ 0548	Take It to the Limit/You Bring Me Joy	1980	—	2.00	4.00
❑ 0581	Melancholy Fire/You've Been On My Mind	1980	—	2.00	4.00
❑ 0632	She's Gone/(B-side unknown)	1981	—	2.00	4.00

BUDDAH

Number	Title (A Side/B Side)	Yr	VG	VG+	NM
❑ 499	Valentine Love/Aria	1975	—	2.50	5.00
❑ 534	We Both Need Each Other/You Are My Starship	1976	—	3.00	6.00
❑ 542	You Are My Starship/Bubbles	1976	—	2.50	5.00
❑ 554	Betcha By Golly Wow/Kwasi	1976	—	2.50	5.00
❑ 570	Once I've Been There/Romantic Journey	1977	—	2.50	5.00
❑ 580	For You Everything/Give the Drummer Some	1977	—	2.50	5.00

CAPITOL

Number	Title (A Side/B Side)	Yr	VG	VG+	NM
❑ B-44110	I Am Your Melody/Samba for Maria	1988	—	—	3.00
❑ B-44159	You're My One and Only Love/I Am Your Melody	1988	—	—	3.00

THE RIGHT STUFF

Number	Title (A Side/B Side)	Yr	VG	VG+	NM
❑ 58849	Didn't I (Blow Your Mind This Time)/River of Love	2000	—	—	3.00

Albums

ACCORD

Number	Title (A Side/B Side)	Yr	VG	VG+	NM
❑ SN-7210	Just Imagine	1982	2.00	4.00	8.00

Number	Title (A Side/B Side)	Yr	VG	VG+	NM
ARISTA					
☐ AB 4177	This Is Your Life	1978	2.50	5.00	10.00
☐ AB 4216	Invitation	1979	2.50	5.00	10.00
☐ AL 9534	Take It to the Limit	1980	2.50	5.00	10.00
☐ AL 9575	Mr. C.	1981	2.50	5.00	10.00
BUDDAH					
☐ BDS-5142	Love from the Sun	1973	3.00	6.00	12.00
☐ BDS-5611	Slewfoot	1974	3.00	6.00	12.00
☐ BDS-5643	Saturday Night Special	1975	2.50	5.00	10.00
☐ BDS-5655	You Are My Starship	1976	2.50	5.00	10.00
☐ BDS-5674	Dance of Magic	1977	2.50	5.00	10.00
—Reissue of Cobblestone 9024					
☐ BDS-5675	Dark of Light	1977	2.50	5.00	10.00
—Reissue of Cobblestone 9035					
☐ BDS-5682	Romantic Journey	1977	2.50	5.00	10.00
☐ BDS-5716	The Best of Norman Connors & Friends	1978	2.50	5.00	10.00
CAPITOL					
☐ C1-48515	Passion	1988	2.50	5.00	10.00
COBBLESTONE					
☐ 9024	Dance of Magic	1972	3.75	7.50	15.00
☐ 9035	Dark of Light	1973	3.75	7.50	15.00

CONTOURS, THE

12-Inch Singles

Number	Title (A Side/B Side)	Yr	VG	VG+	NM
MOTOWN					
☐ 4611MG	Do You Love Me (6:26) (Edited Version 2:37) (Original Version 2:53)	1988	3.75	7.50	15.00

45s

Number	Title (A Side/B Side)	Yr	VG	VG+	NM
GORDY					
☐ 7005	Do You Love Me/Move Mr. Man	1962	5.00	10.00	20.00
☐ 7012	Shake Sherry/You Better Get in Line	1963	3.75	7.50	15.00
☐ 7016	Don't Let Her Be Your Baby/It Must Be Love	1963	3.00	6.00	12.00
☐ 7019	Pa I Need a Car/You Get Ugly	1963	3.00	6.00	12.00
☐ 7029	Can You Do It/I'll Stand By You	1964	3.00	6.00	12.00
☐ 7037	Can You Jerk Like Me/That Day When She Needed Me	1964	3.00	6.00	12.00
☐ 7044	First I Look at the Purse/Searching for a Girl	1965	3.00	6.00	12.00
☐ 7052	Just a Little Misunderstanding/Determination	1966	3.00	6.00	12.00
☐ 7059	It's So Hard Being a Loser/Your Love Grows More Precious Every Day	1967	3.00	6.00	12.00
HOB					
☐ 116	I'm So Glad/Yours Is My Heart Alone	1961	30.00	60.00	120.00
MOTOWN					
☐ 1008	Whole Lotta Woman/Come On and Be Mine	1961	125.00	250.00	500.00
☐ 1012	The Stretch/Funny	1962	200.00	400.00	800.00
MOTOWN YESTERYEAR					
☐ 448	Do You Love Me/Shake Sherry	1972	—	2.00	4.00
☐ 448 [PS]	Do You Love Me/Shake Sherry	1988	—	2.50	5.00
—"Dirty Dancing" sleeve; without cut-out hole					
ROCKET					
☐ 41192	I'm a Winner/Makes Me Wanna Come Back	1980	—	2.00	4.00
TAMLA					
☐ 7012	Shake Sherry/You Better Get in Line	1963	37.50	75.00	150.00
—Tamla label used in error for a Gordy release					

Albums

Number	Title (A Side/B Side)	Yr	VG	VG+	NM
GORDY					
☐ G 901 [M]	Do You Love Me?	1962	125.00	250.00	500.00
MOTOWN					
☐ M5-188V1	Do You Love Me?	1981	2.50	5.00	10.00

COOKE, SAM

45s

Number	Title (A Side/B Side)	Yr	VG	VG+	NM
CHERIE					
☐ 4501	Darling I Need You Now/Win Your Love for Me	1971	2.00	4.00	8.00
KEEN					
☐ 8-1001	You Send Me/Love You Most of All	1960	3.75	7.50	15.00
—Gold label; early reissue series					
☐ 3-2005	Stealing Kisses/All of My Life	1958	6.25	12.50	25.00
☐ 3-2006 [M]	Win Your Love for Me/Love Song from "Houseboat" (Almost in Your Arms)	1958	6.25	12.50	25.00
☐ 5-2006 [S]	Win Your Love for Me/Love Song from "Houseboat" (Almost in Your Arms)	1959	25.00	50.00	100.00
—Blue vinyl					
☐ 3-2008	Love You Most of All/Blue Moon	1958	6.25	12.50	25.00
☐ 3-2018 [M]	Everybody Likes to Cha Cha Cha/Little Things You Do	1959	6.25	12.50	25.00
☐ 5-2018 [S]	Everybody Likes to Cha Cha Cha/Little Things You Do	1959	10.00	20.00	40.00
☐ 2022 [M]	Only Sixteen/Let's Go Steady Again	1959	6.25	12.50	25.00
☐ 5-2022 [S]	Only Sixteen/Let's Go Steady Again	1959	12.50	25.00	50.00
☐ 2101	Summertime/Summertime (Part 2)	1959	6.25	12.50	25.00
☐ 8-2105	There! I've Said It Again/One Hour Ahead of the Posse	1959	6.25	12.50	25.00
☐ 2118	Steal Away/So Glamorous	1960	5.00	10.00	20.00
☐ 2122	Mary, Mary Lou/Eee-Yi-Ee-Yi-Oh	1960	5.00	10.00	20.00
☐ 3-4002	(I Love You) For Sentimental Reasons/Desire Me	1958	6.25	12.50	25.00
—Black label					
☐ 4009	You Were Made for Me/Lonely Island	1958	6.25	12.50	25.00
☐ 3-4013	You Send Me/Summertime	195?	5.00	10.00	20.00
—Multicolor label; note slightly different number than original (34013)					
☐ 34013	You Send Me/Summertime	1957	6.25	12.50	25.00
—Black label (original)					
☐ 82111	'T'ain't Nobody's Bizness (If I Do)/No One	1960	6.25	12.50	25.00
☐ 82112	Wonderful World/Along the Navajo Trail	1960	5.00	10.00	20.00
☐ 82117	With You/I Thank God	1960	5.00	10.00	20.00
RCA					
☐ PB-14146	Bring It On Home to Me/Nothing Can Change This Love	1985	2.00	4.00	8.00
RCA VICTOR					
☐ 37-7853	That's It-I Quit-I'm Movin' On/What Do You Say	1961	15.00	30.00	60.00
—"Compact Single 33" (small hole, plays at LP speed)					
☐ 47-7701	Teenage Sonata/If You Were the Only Girl	1960	5.00	10.00	20.00
☐ 47-7730	You Understand Me/I Belong to Your Heart	1960	3.75	7.50	15.00
☐ 47-7730 [PS]	You Understand Me/I Belong to Your Heart	1960	6.25	12.50	25.00
☐ 47-7783	Chain Gang/I Fall in Love Every Day	1960	3.75	7.50	15.00
☐ 47-7783 [PS]	Chain Gang/I Fall in Love Every Day	1960	6.25	12.50	25.00
☐ 47-7816	Sad Mood/Love Me	1960	3.75	7.50	15.00
☐ 47-7853	That's It-I Quit-I'm Movin' On/What Do You Say	1961	3.75	7.50	15.00
☐ 47-7883	Cupid/Farewell, My Darling	1961	3.75	7.50	15.00
☐ 47-7883 [PS]	Cupid/Farewell, My Darling	1961	6.25	12.50	25.00
☐ 47-7927	Feel It/It's All Right	1961	3.75	7.50	15.00
☐ 47-7927 [PS]	Feel It/It's All Right	1961	6.25	12.50	25.00
☐ 47-7983	Twistin' the Night Away/One More Time	1962	3.75	7.50	15.00
☐ 47-8036	Bring It On Home to Me/Having a Party	1962	3.75	7.50	15.00
☐ 47-8088	Nothing Can Change This Love/Somebody Have Mercy	1962	3.75	7.50	15.00
☐ 47-8088 [PS]	Nothing Can Change This Love/Somebody Have Mercy	1962	6.25	12.50	25.00
☐ 47-8129	Send Me Some Lovin'/Baby, Baby, Baby	1963	3.75	7.50	15.00
☐ 47-8129 [PS]	Send Me Some Lovin'/Baby, Baby, Baby	1963	6.25	12.50	25.00
☐ 47-8164	Another Saturday Night/Love Will Find a Way	1963	3.75	7.50	15.00
☐ 47-8164 [PS]	Another Saturday Night/Love Will Find a Way	1963	6.25	12.50	25.00
☐ 47-8215	Frankie and Johnny/Cool Train	1963	3.00	6.00	12.00
☐ 47-8215 [PS]	Frankie and Johnny/Cool Train	1963	6.25	12.50	25.00
☐ 47-8247	Little Red Rooster/You Gotta Move	1963	3.00	6.00	12.00
☐ 47-8247 [PS]	Little Red Rooster/You Gotta Move	1963	6.25	12.50	25.00
☐ 47-8299	Good News/Basin Street Blues	1963	3.00	6.00	12.00
☐ 47-8299	Ain't That Good News/Basin Street Blues	1963	5.00	10.00	20.00
—Original A-side title (or a scarce reissue)					
☐ 47-8368	Good Times/Tennessee Waltz	1964	3.00	6.00	12.00
☐ 47-8426	Cousin of Mine/That's Where It's At	1964	3.00	6.00	12.00
☐ 47-8486	Shake/A Change Is Gonna Come	1964	3.00	6.00	12.00
☐ 47-8539	It's Got the Whole World Shakin'/Ease My Troublin' Mind	1965	2.50	5.00	10.00
☐ 47-8586	When a Boy Falls in Love/The Piper	1965	2.50	5.00	10.00
☐ 47-8631	Sugar Dumpling/Bridge of Tears	1965	2.50	5.00	10.00
☐ 47-8631 [PS]	Sugar Dumpling/Bridge of Tears	1965	6.25	12.50	25.00
☐ 47-8751	Feel It/That's All	1965	2.50	5.00	10.00
☐ 47-8803	Let's Go Steady Again/Trouble Blues	1966	2.50	5.00	10.00
☐ 47-8934	Meet Me at Mary's Place/If I Had a Hammer	1966	2.50	5.00	10.00
☐ SP-45-173 [DJ]	A Change Is Gonna Come (same on both sides)	1968	12.50	25.00	50.00
—Promo-only number; this appears to be a radio reissue in the wake of events going on in 1968					
☐ VP-3-2555 [S]	The Twist/Movin' & Groovin'	196?	6.25	12.50	25.00
—Small hole, plays at 33 1/3 rpm					
☐ VP-4-2555 [S]	Somebody Have Mercy/Camptown Girl	196?	6.25	12.50	25.00
—Small hole, plays at 33 1/3 rpm					
SAR					
☐ 122 [DJ]	Just for You/Made for Me	1961	25.00	50.00	100.00
—Promo only ("Audition" on label); possibly made as leverage during contract renegotiation at RCA Victor, one source claims only five (5) copies were made					
SPECIALTY					
☐ 596	Forever/Lovable	1957	7.50	15.00	30.00
—As "Dale Cook"					
☐ 619	I'll Come Running Back to You/Forever	1957	7.50	15.00	30.00
☐ 627	That's All I Need to Know/I Don't Want to Cry	1958	7.50	15.00	30.00
☐ 667	Happy in Love/I Need You Now	1959	7.50	15.00	30.00
☐ 921	Must Jesus Bear the Cross Alone/The Last Mile of the Way	1970	2.50	5.00	10.00
—With the Soul Stirrers					
☐ 928	Just Another Day/Christ Is All	1973	2.50	5.00	10.00
—With the Soul Stirrers					
☐ 930	That's Heaven to Me/Lord, Remember Me	1974	2.50	5.00	10.00
—With the Soul Stirrers					

78s

Number	Title (A Side/B Side)	Yr	VG	VG+	NM
KEEN					
☐ 4-2018	Everybody Likes to Cha Cha Cha/Little Things You Do	1959	25.00	50.00	100.00
☐ 4-4002	(I Love You) For Sentimental Reasons/Desire Me	1958	12.50	25.00	50.00
☐ 44013	You Send Me/Summertime	1957	12.50	25.00	50.00
SPECIALTY					
☐ 596	Forever/Lovable	1957	10.00	20.00	40.00
—As "Dale Cook"					
☐ 619	I'll Come Running Back to You/Forever	1957	10.00	20.00	40.00
☐ 627	That's All I Need to Know/I Don't Want to Cry	1958	12.50	25.00	50.00

7-Inch Extended Plays

Number	Title (A Side/B Side)	Yr	VG	VG+	NM
KEEN					
☐ B-2001	The Bells of Saint Mary's/Tammy//Moonlight in Vermont/So Long	1958	20.00	40.00	80.00
☐ B-2001 [PS]	Songs by Sam Cooke, Volume 1	1958	20.00	40.00	80.00
☐ B-2002	*You Send Me/The Lonesome Road/That Lucky Old Sun/Canadian Sunset	1958	20.00	40.00	80.00
☐ B-2002 [PS]	Songs by Sam Cooke, Volume 2	1958	20.00	40.00	80.00
☐ B-2003	Summertime/Danny Boy//Around the World/Ol' Man River	1958	20.00	40.00	80.00
☐ B-2003 [PS]	Songs by Sam Cooke, Volume 3	1958	20.00	40.00	80.00
☐ B-2006	*Mary, Mary Lou/The Gypsy/Oh, Look at Me Now/Someday	1958	20.00	40.00	80.00
☐ B-2006 [PS]	Encore, Volume 1	1958	20.00	40.00	80.00

Number	Title (A Side/B Side)	Yr	VG	VG+	NM
❑ B-2007	*When I Fall in Love/I Cover the Waterfront/ Running Wild/Today I Sing the Blues	1958	20.00	40.00	80.00
❑ B-2007 [PS]	Encore, Volume 2	1958	20.00	40.00	80.00
❑ B-2008	It's the Talk of the Town/Along the Navajo Trail// My Foolish Heart/Accentuate the Positive	1958	20.00	40.00	80.00
❑ B-2008 [PS]	Encore, Volume 3	1958	20.00	40.00	80.00
❑ B-2010	Love Song from Houseboat/Lonely Island//Win Your Love for Me/All of My Life	1959	20.00	40.00	80.00
❑ B-2010 [PS]	Sam Cooke Sings His Hits	1959	20.00	40.00	80.00
❑ B-2012	Let's Call the Whole Thing Off/God Bless the Child//Comes Love/Lover Girl	1959	20.00	40.00	80.00
❑ B-2012 [PS]	Tribute to the Lady, Volume 1	1959	20.00	40.00	80.00
❑ B-2013	(contents unknown)	1959	20.00	40.00	80.00
❑ B-2013 [PS]	Tribute to the Lady, Volume 2	1959	20.00	40.00	80.00
❑ B-2014	(contents unknown)	1959	20.00	40.00	80.00
❑ B-2014 [PS]	Tribute to the Lady, Volume 3	1959	20.00	40.00	80.00

RCA VICTOR

Number	Title (A Side/B Side)	Yr	VG	VG+	NM
❑ LPC-126	Chain Gang/If You Were the Only Girl//Teenage Sonata/You Understand Me	1961	5.00	10.00	20.00
❑ LPC-126 [PS]	Sam Cooke Sings	1961	5.00	10.00	20.00
❑ EPA-4375	Another Saturday Night/You Send Me//Only Sixteen/Bring It On Home to Me	1963	5.00	10.00	20.00
❑ EPA-4375 [PS]	Another Saturday Night	1963	5.00	10.00	20.00

Albums

51 WEST

Number	Title (A Side/B Side)	Yr	VG	VG+	NM
❑ Q 16032	My Foolish Heart	198?	3.00	6.00	12.00

ABKCO

Number	Title (A Side/B Side)	Yr	VG	VG+	NM
❑ 1124-1	Sam Cooke's Night Beat	1995	3.00	6.00	12.00
—Reissue					
❑ 2970-1	Sam Cooke at the Copa	1988	3.00	6.00	12.00
—Reissue					

FAMOUS

Number	Title (A Side/B Side)	Yr	VG	VG+	NM
❑ 502	Sam's Songs	1969	10.00	20.00	40.00
❑ 505	Only Sixteen	1969	10.00	20.00	40.00
❑ 508	So Wonderful	1969	10.00	20.00	40.00
❑ 509	You Send Me	1969	10.00	20.00	40.00
❑ 512	Cha-Cha-Cha	1969	10.00	20.00	40.00

KEEN

Number	Title (A Side/B Side)	Yr	VG	VG+	NM
❑ A-2001 [M]	Sam Cooke	1958	50.00	100.00	200.00
❑ A-2003 [M]	Encore	1958	50.00	100.00	200.00
❑ A-2004 [M]	Tribute to the Lady	1959	37.50	75.00	150.00
❑ AS-2004 [S]	Tribute to the Lady	1959	50.00	100.00	200.00
❑ 86101 [M]	Hit Kit	1959	62.50	125.00	250.00
❑ 86103 [M]	I Thank God	1960	100.00	200.00	400.00
❑ 86106 [M]	The Wonderful World of Sam Cooke	1960	87.50	1175.	350.00

PAIR

Number	Title (A Side/B Side)	Yr	VG	VG+	NM
❑ PDL2-1006 [(2)]	You Send Me	1986	3.75	7.50	15.00

RCA CAMDEN

Number	Title (A Side/B Side)	Yr	VG	VG+	NM
❑ ACS1-0445	You Send Me	1974	3.00	6.00	12.00
❑ CAL-2264 [M]	The One and Only Sam Cooke	1967	5.00	10.00	20.00
❑ CAS-2264 [R]	The One and Only Sam Cooke	1967	3.00	6.00	12.00
❑ CAS-2433	Sam Cooke	1970	3.00	6.00	12.00
❑ CAS-2610	The Unforgettable Sam Cooke	1972	3.00	6.00	12.00

RCA VICTOR

Number	Title (A Side/B Side)	Yr	VG	VG+	NM
❑ LPM-2221 [M]	Cooke's Tour	1960	10.00	20.00	40.00
❑ LSP-2221 [S]	Cooke's Tour	1960	12.50	25.00	50.00
❑ LPM-2236 [M]	Hits of the 50's	1960	10.00	20.00	40.00
❑ LSP-2236 [S]	Hits of the 50's	1960	12.50	25.00	50.00
❑ LPM-2293 [M]	Swing Low	1960	10.00	20.00	40.00
❑ LSP-2293 [S]	Swing Low	1960	12.50	25.00	50.00
❑ LPM-2392 [M]	My Kind of Blues	1961	10.00	20.00	40.00
❑ LSP-2392 [S]	My Kind of Blues	1961	12.50	25.00	50.00
❑ LPM-2555 [M]	Twistin' the Night Away	1962	10.00	20.00	40.00
❑ LSP-2555 [S]	Twistin' the Night Away	1962	12.50	25.00	50.00
❑ AFL1-2625	The Best of Sam Cooke	1977	3.00	6.00	12.00
—Reissue with new prefix					
❑ LPM-2625 [M]	The Best of Sam Cooke	1962	7.50	15.00	30.00
❑ LSP-2625 [R]	The Best of Sam Cooke	1962	5.00	10.00	20.00
❑ ANL1-2658	Sam Cooke at the Copa	1977	3.00	6.00	12.00
—Reissue of LSP-2970					
❑ LPM-2673 [M]	Mr. Soul	1963	7.50	15.00	30.00
❑ LSP-2673 [S]	Mr. Soul	1963	10.00	20.00	40.00
❑ LPM-2709 [M]	Night Beat	1963	7.50	15.00	30.00
❑ LSP-2709 [S]	Night Beat	1963	10.00	20.00	40.00
❑ LPM-2899 [M]	Ain't That Good News	1964	7.50	15.00	30.00
❑ LSP-2899 [S]	Ain't That Good News	1964	10.00	20.00	40.00
❑ LPM-2970 [M]	Sam Cooke at the Copa	1964	7.50	15.00	30.00
❑ LSP-2970 [S]	Sam Cooke at the Copa	1964	10.00	20.00	40.00
❑ LPM-3367 [M]	Shake	1965	6.25	12.50	25.00
❑ LSP-3367 [S]	Shake	1965	7.50	15.00	30.00
❑ LPM-3373 [M]	The Best of Sam Cooke, Volume 2	1965	6.25	12.50	25.00
❑ LSP-3373 [S]	The Best of Sam Cooke, Volume 2	1965	7.50	15.00	30.00
❑ LPM-3435 [M]	Try a Little Love	1965	6.25	12.50	25.00
❑ LSP-3435 [S]	Try a Little Love	1965	7.50	15.00	30.00
❑ LPM-3517 [M]	The Unforgettable Sam Cooke	1966	5.00	10.00	20.00
❑ LSP-3517 [S]	The Unforgettable Sam Cooke	1966	6.25	12.50	25.00
❑ AYL1-3863	The Best of Sam Cooke	1981	2.00	4.00	8.00
—Budget-line reissue					
❑ LPM-3991 [M]	The Man Who Invented Soul	1968	12.50	25.00	50.00
❑ LSP-3991 [S]	The Man Who Invented Soul	1968	6.25	12.50	25.00
❑ AFL1-5181	Live at the Harlem Square Club, 1963	1985	3.00	6.00	12.00
❑ VPS-6027 [(2)]	This Is Sam Cooke	1970	5.00	10.00	20.00
❑ CPL2-7127 [(2)]	The Man and His Music	1986	3.75	7.50	15.00

SPECIALTY

Number	Title (A Side/B Side)	Yr	VG	VG+	NM
❑ SPS-2106	Sam Cooke and the Soul Stirrers	1970	3.75	7.50	15.00
❑ SPS-2116	The Gospel Soul of Sam Cooke, Vol. 1	1970	3.75	7.50	15.00
❑ SPS-2119	Two Sides of Sam Cooke	1970	3.75	7.50	15.00
❑ SPS-2128	The Gospel Soul of Sam Cooke, Vol. 2	197?	3.75	7.50	15.00
❑ SPS-2146	That's Heaven to Me	197?	3.75	7.50	15.00

TRIP

Number	Title (A Side/B Side)	Yr	VG	VG+	NM
❑ 8030 [(2)]	The Golden Sound of Sam Cooke	1972	3.75	7.50	15.00

UPFRONT

Number	Title (A Side/B Side)	Yr	VG	VG+	NM
❑ 160	The Billie Holiday Story	1973	3.75	7.50	15.00

COOKIES, THE

45s

ATLANTIC

Number	Title (A Side/B Side)	Yr	VG	VG+	NM
❑ 1061	Precious Love/Later, Later	1955	7.50	15.00	30.00
❑ 1084	In Paradise/Passing Time	1956	7.50	15.00	30.00
❑ 1110	Down By the River/My Lover	1956	6.25	12.50	25.00
❑ 2079	Passing Time/In Paradise	1960	5.00	10.00	20.00

DIMENSION

Number	Title (A Side/B Side)	Yr	VG	VG+	NM
❑ 1002	Chains/Stranger in My Arms	1962	5.00	10.00	20.00
❑ 1008	Don't Say Nothin' Bad/Softly in the Night	1963	5.00	10.00	20.00
❑ 1008	Don't Say Nothin' Bad (About My Baby)/Softly in the Night	1963	3.75	7.50	15.00
❑ 1012	I Want a Boy for My Birthday/Will Power	1963	3.75	7.50	15.00
❑ 1020	Girls Grow Up Faster Than Boys/Only to Other People	1963	3.75	7.50	15.00
❑ 1032	I Never Dreamed/The Old Crowd	1964	3.75	7.50	15.00

JOSIE

Number	Title (A Side/B Side)	Yr	VG	VG+	NM
❑ 822	King of Hearts/Hippy-Dippy-Daddy	1957	7.50	15.00	30.00

LAMP

Number	Title (A Side/B Side)	Yr	VG	VG+	NM
❑ 8008	Don't Let Go/All Night Mambo	1954	10.00	20.00	40.00

WARNER BROS.

Number	Title (A Side/B Side)	Yr	VG	VG+	NM
❑ 7025	All My Trials/Wounded	1967	2.50	5.00	10.00
❑ 7047	Mr. Cupid (Don't You Call on Me)/Hang My Head and Cry	1967	2.50	5.00	10.00
—B-side by the Big Guys					

COOKIES, THE/LITTLE EVA/CAROLE KING

Albums

DIMENSION

Number	Title (A Side/B Side)	Yr	VG	VG+	NM
❑ DLP-6001 [M]	The Dimension Dolls, Vol. 1	1964	62.50	125.00	250.00

COOPER, LES, AND THE SOUL ROCKERS

Also see THE EMPIRES (1).

45s

ARRAWAK

Number	Title (A Side/B Side)	Yr	VG	VG+	NM
❑ 1008	I Can Do the Soul Jerk/At the World's Fair	1965	3.00	6.00	12.00

ATCO

Number	Title (A Side/B Side)	Yr	VG	VG+	NM
❑ 6644	Gonna Have a Lotta Fun/Thank God for You	1969	2.00	4.00	8.00

DIMENSION

Number	Title (A Side/B Side)	Yr	VG	VG+	NM
❑ 1023	Motor City/Swobblin'	1963	5.00	10.00	20.00

ENJOY

Number	Title (A Side/B Side)	Yr	VG	VG+	NM
❑ 2024	Owee Baby/Let's Do the Boston Monkey	1965	2.50	5.00	10.00

EVERLAST

Number	Title (A Side/B Side)	Yr	VG	VG+	NM
❑ 5016	Twistin'/Dig Yourself	1963	3.00	6.00	12.00
❑ 5019	Wiggle Wobble/Dig Yourself	1963	3.75	7.50	15.00
❑ 5023	Garbage Can/Bossa Nova Dance	1963	3.00	6.00	12.00

Albums

EVERLAST

Number	Title (A Side/B Side)	Yr	VG	VG+	NM
❑ ELP-202 [M]	Wiggle Wobble	1963	12.50	25.00	50.00

COOPERETTES, THE

45s

ABC

Number	Title (A Side/B Side)	Yr	VG	VG+	NM
❑ 11156	Peace Maker/Trouble	1968	3.00	6.00	12.00
❑ 11197	Spiral Road/Trouble	1969	3.00	6.00	12.00

BRUNSWICK

Number	Title (A Side/B Side)	Yr	VG	VG+	NM
❑ 55296	Goodbye School/Goodbye School (Part 2)	1966	3.75	7.50	15.00
❑ 55307	Don't Trust Him/Everything's Wrong	1966	3.75	7.50	15.00
❑ 55329	(Life Has) No Meaning Now/Shing-a-Ling	1967	6.25	12.50	25.00

CORDEL, PAT

45s

CLUB

Number	Title (A Side/B Side)	Yr	VG	VG+	NM
❑ 1011	Darling, Come Back/My My Tears	1956	500.00	1000.	1500.
—And the Crescents					

MICHELLE

Number	Title (A Side/B Side)	Yr	VG	VG+	NM
❑ 503	Darling, Come Back/My My Tears	1959	37.50	75.00	150.00
—And the Elegants					

VICTORY

Number	Title (A Side/B Side)	Yr	VG	VG+	NM
❑ 1001	Darling, Come Back/My My Tears	1963	20.00	40.00	80.00
—And the Elegants					

CORNELIUS BROTHERS AND SISTER ROSE

45s

PLATINUM

Number	Title (A Side/B Side)	Yr	VG	VG+	NM
❑ 105/6	Treat Her Like a Lady/Over at My Place	1970	3.00	6.00	12.00

UNITED ARTISTS

Number	Title (A Side/B Side)	Yr	VG	VG+	NM
❑ 0131	Treat Her Like a Lady/Over at My Place	1973	—	2.00	4.00
—"Silver Spotlight Series" reissue					
❑ XW208	Let Me Down Easy/Gonna Be Sweet for You	1973	—	2.50	5.00
❑ XW313	I Just Can't Stop Loving You/These Lonely Nights	1973	—	2.50	5.00
❑ XW377	Big Time Lover/Wonderful Tune	1974	—	2.50	5.00

C

Number	Title (A Side/B Side)	Yr	VG	VG+	NM
❑ XW512	Too Late to Turn Back Now/Don't Ever Be Lonely (A Poor Little Fool Like Me)	1974	—	2.00	4.00
—Reissue					
❑ XW533	Trouble Child/Got to Testify	1974	—	2.50	5.00
❑ XW534	Since I Found My Baby/I Love Music	1974	—	2.50	5.00
❑ 50721	Treat Her Like a Lady/Over at My Place	1970	—	2.50	5.00
❑ 50910	Too Late to Turn Back Now/Lift Your Love Higher	1972	—	2.50	5.00
❑ 50954	Don't Ever Be Lonely (A Poor Little Fool Like Me)/I'm So Glad to Be Loved by You	1972	—	2.50	5.00
❑ 50996	I'm Never Gonna Be Alone Anymore/Let's Stay Together	1972	—	2.50	5.00
Albums					
UNITED ARTISTS					
❑ UA-LA593-G	Greatest Hits	1976	3.00	6.00	12.00
❑ UAS-5568	Cornelius Brothers and Sister Rose	1972	3.75	7.50	15.00

CORONETS, THE
45s
CHESS

Number	Title (A Side/B Side)	Yr	VG	VG+	NM
❑ 1549	Nadine/I'm All Alone	1953	50.00	100.00	200.00
—Silver top label					
❑ 1549	Nadine/I'm All Alone	1958	3.00	6.00	12.00
—All-blue label					
❑ 1553	It Would Be Heavenly/Baby's Coming Home	1953	100.00	200.00	400.00
—Black vinyl					
❑ 1553	It Would Be Heavenly/Baby's Coming Home	1953	200.00	400.00	800.00
—Red vinyl					
GROOVE					
❑ 0114	I Love You More/Crime Doesn't Pay	1955	25.00	50.00	100.00
❑ 0116	The Bible Tells Me So/Hush	1955	37.50	75.00	150.00
STERLING					
❑ 903	Don't Deprive Me/Little Boy	1955	62.50	125.00	250.00

COSBY, BILL
45s
CAPITOL

Number	Title (A Side/B Side)	Yr	VG	VG+	NM
❑ 4258	Yes, Yes, Yes/Ben	1976	—	2.00	4.00
❑ 4299	I Luv Myself Better Than I Luv Myself/Do It To Me	1976	—	2.00	4.00
❑ 4501	Boogie on Your Face/What's in a Slang	1977	—	2.00	4.00
❑ 4523	Merry Christmas Mama (Vocal)/(Instrumental)	1977	5.00	10.00	20.00
TETRAGRAMMATON					
❑ 1539	Football/Golf	1969	—	3.00	6.00
UNI					
❑ 55184	Hikky Burr/Hikky Burr	1969	—	3.00	6.00
—A-side with the Bunions; B-side by the Bradford Band					
❑ 55223	Grover Henson Feels Forgotten/(Instrumental)	1970	—	3.00	6.00
❑ 55247	Hybish Skybish/Martin's Funeral	1970	—	2.50	5.00
—With Bad Foot Brown					
WARNER BROS.					
❑ 5499	Stand Still for My Lovin'/When I Marry	1965	2.50	5.00	10.00
❑ 7072	Little Ole Man (Uptight-Everything's Alright)/Don'cha Know	1967	2.00	4.00	8.00
❑ 7096	Hooray for the Salvation Army Band/Ursalena	1968	2.00	4.00	8.00
❑ 7126	Little Ole Man (Uptight-Everything's Alright)/Funky North Philly	1969	—	3.00	6.00
—Hall of Fame Hits (originals have green labels with "W7" logo)					
❑ 7171	Funky North Philly/Stop, Look and Listen	1968	2.00	4.00	8.00
Albums					
CAPITOL					
❑ ST-11530	Bill Cosby Is Not Himself These Days, Rat Own, Rat Own, Rat Own	1976	2.50	5.00	10.00
❑ ST-11590	My Father Confused Me…What Must I Do? What Must I Do?	1977	2.50	5.00	10.00
❑ ST-11683	Let's Boogie (Disco Bill)	1977	2.50	5.00	10.00
❑ ST-11731	Bill's Best Friend	1978	2.50	5.00	10.00
GEFFEN					
❑ GHS 24104	Those of You With or Without Children, You'll Understand	1986	2.50	5.00	10.00
MCA					
❑ 169	When I Was a Kid	197?	2.00	4.00	8.00
—Reissue of Uni 73100					
❑ 333	Fat Albert	1973	2.50	5.00	10.00
❑ 553	For Adults Only	197?	2.00	4.00	8.00
—Reissue of Uni 73112					
❑ 554	Inside the Mind of Bill Cosby	197?	2.00	4.00	8.00
—Reissue of Uni 73139					
❑ 8005 [(2)]	Bill	197?	3.00	6.00	12.00
MOTOWN					
❑ 6026 ML	Bill Cosby "Himself"	1982	2.50	5.00	10.00
TETRAGRAMMATON					
❑ T-5100 [(2)]	8:15 12:15	1969	5.00	10.00	20.00
UNI					
❑ 73066	Bill Cosby	1969	2.50	5.00	10.00
❑ 73082	"Live" Madison Square Garden Center	1970	2.50	5.00	10.00
❑ 73100	When I Was a Kid	1971	2.50	5.00	10.00
❑ 73112	For Adults Only	1971	2.50	5.00	10.00
❑ 73139	Inside the Mind of Bill Cosby	1972	2.50	5.00	10.00
WARNER BROS.					
❑ PRO 249 [DJ]	Radio Sampler Album — The Best of Bill Cosby	1969	5.00	10.00	20.00
—Promo LP with edits of 12 tracks for radio use					
❑ W 1518 [M]	Bill Cosby Is a Very Funny Fellow Right!	1964	3.75	7.50	15.00
❑ W 1567 [M]	I Started Out as a Child	1964	3.75	7.50	15.00
❑ W 1606 [M]	Why Is There Air?	1965	3.75	7.50	15.00
❑ W 1634 [M]	Wonderfulness	1966	3.75	7.50	15.00

Number	Title (A Side/B Side)	Yr	VG	VG+	NM
❑ WS 1634 [S]	Wonderfulness	1966	3.75	7.50	15.00
—Gold label					
❑ W 1691 [M]	Revenge	1967	3.75	7.50	15.00
❑ W 1709 [M]	Bill Cosby Sings/Silver Throat	1967	3.75	7.50	15.00
❑ WS 1709 [S]	Bill Cosby Sings/Silver Throat	1967	3.00	6.00	12.00
❑ W 1728 [M]	Bill Cosby Sings/Hooray for the Salvation Army Band	1968	3.75	7.50	15.00
❑ WS 1728 [S]	Bill Cosby Sings/Hooray for the Salvation Army Band	1968	3.00	6.00	12.00
❑ W 1734 [M]	To Russell, My Brother, Whom I Slept With	1968	3.75	7.50	15.00
❑ WS 1734 [S]	To Russell, My Brother, Whom I Slept With	1968	3.00	6.00	12.00
❑ WS 1757	200 M.P.H.	1968	3.00	6.00	12.00
❑ WS 1770	It's True! It's True!	1969	3.00	6.00	12.00
❑ WS 1798	The Best of Bill Cosby	1969	3.00	6.00	12.00
❑ WS 1836	More of the Best of Bill Cosby	1970	3.00	6.00	12.00

COSMIC RAYS, THE
45s
SATURN

Number	Title (A Side/B Side)	Yr	VG	VG+	NM
❑ 222	Bye Bye/Someone's in Love	1960	750.00	1500.	3000.
❑ 401	Daddy's Gonna Tell You No Lies/Dreaming	1960	500.00	1000.	2000.

COTTON, JAMES
45s
BUDDAH

Number	Title (A Side/B Side)	Yr	VG	VG+	NM
❑ 461	Boogie Thing/Fever	1975	—	2.50	5.00
❑ 468	Rocket 88/One More Mile	1975	—	2.50	5.00
LOMA					
❑ 2042	Laying in the Weeds/Complete This Order	1966	3.00	6.00	12.00
SUN					
❑ 199	My Baby/Straighten Up, Baby	1954	375.00	750.00	1500.
❑ 206	Cotton Crop Blues/Hold Me in Your Arms	1954	450.00	900.00	1800.
VERVE FORECAST					
❑ 5053	Good Time Charlie/Off the Wall	1967	2.50	5.00	10.00
❑ 5066	Feelin' Good/Don't Start Me Talkin'	1967	2.50	5.00	10.00
❑ 5107	The Coach's Better Days/(B-side unknown)	1969	2.00	4.00	8.00
78s					
SUN					
❑ 199	My Baby/Straighten Up, Baby	1954	150.00	300.00	600.00
❑ 206	Cotton Crop Blues/Hold Me in Your Arms	1954	175.00	350.00	700.00
Albums					
ALLIGATOR					
❑ AL-4737	High Compression	1984	2.50	5.00	10.00
❑ AL-4746	Live from Chicago	1986	2.50	5.00	10.00
ANTONE'S					
❑ ANT-0007	James Cotton Live	1988	3.00	6.00	12.00
BLIND PIG					
❑ BP-2587	Take Me Back	1987	2.50	5.00	10.00
BUDDAH					
❑ BDS-5620	100% Cotton	1974	3.00	6.00	12.00
❑ BDS-5650	High Energy	1975	3.00	6.00	12.00
❑ BDS-5661 [(2)]	Live & On the Move!	1976	3.75	7.50	15.00
CAPITOL					
❑ SM-814	Taking Care of Business	197?	2.50	5.00	10.00
—Reissue with new prefix					
❑ ST-814	Taking Care of Business	1971	3.75	7.50	15.00
INTERMEDIA					
❑ QS-5006	Dealing with the Devil	198?	2.50	5.00	10.00
❑ QS-5011	Two Sides of the Blues	198?	2.50	5.00	10.00
VANGUARD					
❑ VSD-79283	Cut You Loose!	1969	3.75	7.50	15.00
VERVE FORECAST					
❑ FT-3023 [M]	The James Cotton Blues Band	1967	6.25	12.50	25.00
❑ FTS-3023 [S]	The James Cotton Blues Band	1967	5.00	10.00	20.00
❑ FTS-3038	Pure Cotton	1968	5.00	10.00	20.00

COVAY, DON
Also see THE SOLDIER BOYS.
45s
ARNOLD

Number	Title (A Side/B Side)	Yr	VG	VG+	NM
❑ 1002	Pony Time/Love Boat	1961	6.25	12.50	25.00
—As "The Goodtimers"					
❑ 1002	Pony Time/Love Boat	1961	3.00	6.00	12.00
—As "Don Covay and the Goodtimers"					
ATLANTIC					
❑ 1147	Bip Bop Bip/Silver Dollar	1957	20.00	40.00	80.00
—As "Pretty Boy"					
❑ 2280	The Boomerang/Daddy Loves Baby	1965	2.50	5.00	10.00
❑ 2286	Please Do Something/A Woman's Love	1965	2.50	5.00	10.00
❑ 2301	See Saw/I Never Get Enough of Your Love	1965	2.50	5.00	10.00
❑ 2323	Sookie Sookie/Watching the Late Late Shoe	1966	2.50	5.00	10.00
❑ 2340	You Put Something On Me/Iron Out the Rough Spots	1966	2.50	5.00	10.00
❑ 2357	Somebody's Got to Love You/Temptation Was Too Strong	1966	2.50	5.00	10.00
❑ 2375	Shing-Aling '67/I Was There	1967	2.50	5.00	10.00
❑ 2407	40 Days — 40 Nights/The Usual Place	1967	2.50	5.00	10.00
❑ 2440	You've Got Me on the Critical List/Never Had No Love	1967	2.50	5.00	10.00
❑ 2481	Chain of Fools/Prove It	1968	2.50	5.00	10.00
❑ 2494	Don't Let Go/It's In the Wind	1968	2.50	5.00	10.00
❑ 2521	Gonna Send You Back to Your Mama/House on the Corner	1968	2.50	5.00	10.00

Number	Title (A Side/B Side)	Yr	VG	VG+	NM
❏ 2565	I Stole Some Love/Snake in the Grass	1968	2.50	5.00	10.00
❏ 2609	Sweet Pea/C.C. Rider Blues	1969	2.50	5.00	10.00
❏ 2666	Ice Cream Man (The Gimmie Game)/Black Woman	1969	2.50	5.00	10.00
❏ 2725	Everything I Do Goin' Be Funky/Key to the Kighway	1970	2.00	4.00	8.00
❏ 2742	Soul Stirrer/Sookie Sookie	1970	2.00	4.00	8.00

BIG

❏ 617	Switchin' in the Kitchen/Rockin' the Mule	1958	20.00	40.00	80.00

—As "Pretty Boy"

BIG TOP

❏ 3060	Hey There/I'm Coming Down with the Blues	1960	3.75	7.50	15.00

BLAZE

❏ 350	Standing in the Doorway/(B-side unknown)	1958	7.50	15.00	30.00

CAMEO

❏ 239	The Popeye Waddle/One Little Bot Had Money	1962	3.00	6.00	12.00
❏ 251	Wiggle Wobble/Do the Bug	1963	3.00	6.00	12.00

COLUMBIA

❏ 41981	Shake Wid the Snake/Every Which-a Way	1961	5.00	10.00	20.00
❏ 42058	Hand Jive Workout/See About Me	1961	5.00	10.00	20.00
❏ 42197	Now That I Need You/Teen Life Swag	1961	25.00	50.00	100.00

EPIC

❏ 9484	It's Twistin' Time/Twistin' Train	1961	3.75	7.50	15.00

—As "The Goodtimers"

JANUS

❏ 164	Sweet Thang/Standing in the Grits Line	1971	—	3.00	6.00
❏ 181	Daddy Please Don't Go Out/Shoes Under My Bed	1972	—	3.00	6.00

LANDA

❏ 704	You're Good for Me/Truth of the Lite	1965	2.50	5.00	10.00

MERCURY

❏ 71385	I Was Checkin' Out She Was Checkin' In/Money	1973	—	3.00	6.00
❏ 71430	Somebody's Been Enjoying My Home/Bad Mouthing	1973	—	3.00	6.00
❏ 71469	It's Better to Have (And Don't Need)/Leave Him (Part 1)	1974	—	3.00	6.00
❏ 73311	Overtime Man/Dungeon #3	1972	—	3.00	6.00
❏ 73648	Rumble in the Jungle/We Can't Make It No More	1975	—	3.00	6.00

NEWMAN

❏ 500	Badd Boy//(Instrumental)	1980	—	2.50	5.00

PARKWAY

❏ 894	Ain't That Silly/Turn It On	1964	3.00	6.00	12.00
❏ 910	The Froog/One Little Boy Had Money	1964	3.00	6.00	12.00

PHILADELPHIA INT'L.

❏ 3594	Right Time for Love/No Tell Motel	1976	—	2.50	5.00
❏ 3602	Travelin' in Heavy Traffic/Once You Have It	1976	—	2.50	5.00

ROSEMART

❏ 801	Mercy Mercy/Can't Stay Away	1964	3.75	7.50	15.00
❏ 802	Take This Hurt Off Me/Please Don't Let Me Know	1964	3.00	6.00	12.00

SUE

❏ 709	Betty Jean/Believe It or Not	1958	7.50	15.00	30.00

U-VON

❏ 102	Back to the Roots (Part 1)/Back to the Roots (Part 2)	1977	—	2.50	5.00

Albums

ATLANTIC

❏ 8104 [M]	Mercy	1965	10.00	20.00	40.00
❏ SD 8104 [S]	Mercy	1965	12.50	25.00	50.00
❏ 8120 [M]	See Saw	1966	10.00	20.00	40.00
❏ SD 8120 [S]	See Saw	1966	12.50	25.00	50.00
❏ SD 8237	The House of Blue Lights	1969	6.25	12.50	25.00

JANUS

❏ 3038	Different Strokes for Different Folks	1972	3.75	7.50	15.00

MERCURY

❏ SRM-1-653	Super Dude I	1973	3.00	6.00	12.00
❏ SRM-1-1020	Hot Blood	1974	3.00	6.00	12.00
❏ 835030-1	Checkin' In with Don Covay	1988	2.50	5.00	10.00

PHILADELPHIA INT'L.

❏ PZ 33958	Travelin' In Heavy Traffic	1977	2.50	5.00	10.00

COX, DEBORAH
12-Inch Singles
ARISTA

❏ ADP 2852 [DJ]	Sentimental (2 versions)	1995	—	3.00	6.00
❏ ADP 2970 [DJ]	Who Do U Love (at least 4 versions)	1996	3.00	6.00	12.00
❏ ADP 3237 [DJ]	Just Be Good to Me (Johnny's Vicious Mix) (LP Version) (Vocal Dub) (Div-a-Pella)	1996	2.00	4.00	8.00
❏ ADP 3289 [DJ]	It Could've Been You (Club Mix) (Club Mix II) (Dub Mix)/The Sound of My Tears	1996	2.00	4.00	8.00
❏ ADP 3517 [DJ]	September (LP Version) (Instrumental) (Acapella)	1998	2.00	4.00	8.00
❏ ADP 3544 [DJ]	Nobody's Supposed to Be Here (4 versions)	1998	2.50	5.00	10.00
❏ ARDP 3614 [DJ]	It's Over Now (LP Version) (Instrumental) (Acapella)	1999	2.50	5.00	10.00
❏ ARDP 3664 [DJ]	It's Over Now (Retro Future Club Mix) (Acapella) (Instrumental Dub) (Radio Mix)	1999	2.50	5.00	10.00
❏ ARDP 3673 [DJ]	It's Over Now (6 versions)	1999	2.00	4.00	8.00
❏ ARDP 3861 [DJ]	I Never Knew (3 versions)	2000	2.50	5.00	10.00
❏ 13235	Where Do We Go from Here/Just Be Good to Me (Johnny's Vicious Mix) (V-Men Vocal Dub) (Div-a-Pella)/Call Me	1996	2.00	4.00	8.00
❏ 13278	The Sound of My Tears/It Could've Been You (3 versions each?)	1996	—	3.00	6.00
❏ 13381	Things Just Ain't the Same (unknown versions)	1997	2.00	4.00	8.00
❏ 13551	Nobody's Supposed to Be Here (5 versions)	1998	—	3.50	7.00
❏ 13656 [(2)]	It's Over Now (8 versions)	1999	2.00	4.00	8.00

J

❏ 21079	Absolutely Not (Vocal 3:39) (Acapella 2:53)/(Vocal 3:39) (Instrumental 3:53)	2001	2.50	5.00	10.00
❏ 21100	Absolutely Not (unknown versions)	2001	2.00	4.00	8.00

45s
ARISTA

❏ 12950	Who Do U Love/Sentimental	1996	—	2.00	4.00

CRAWFORD, CAROLYN
45s
MERCURY

❏ 74036	Coming On Strong/Love Song for You	1978	—	2.50	5.00

—Mercury titles as "Caroline Crawford"

❏ 74054	You'll Wait/Breakdown	1979	—	2.50	5.00
❏ 76013	The Strut/I'll Be Here for You	1979	—	2.50	5.00

MOTOWN

❏ 1050	Forget About Me/Devil in His Heart	1963	10.00	20.00	40.00
❏ 1064	My Smile Is Just a Frown Turned Upside Down/I'll Come Running	1964	12.50	25.00	50.00

—Original version of A-side title

❏ 1064	My Smile Is Just a Frown (Turned Upside Down)/I'll Come Running	1964	5.00	10.00	20.00

—Revised version of A-side title

❏ 1070	My Heart/When Someone's Good to You	1964	10.00	20.00	40.00

PHILADELPHIA INT'L.

❏ 3553	Just Got to Be More Careful/Saving All the Love I Got for You	1974	—	2.50	5.00
❏ 3570	It Takes Two to Make One/No Matter How Bad Things Are, I Still Love You	1975	—	2.50	5.00
❏ 3580	Good & Plenty/If You Move, You Lose	1975	—	2.50	5.00

CRAYTON, PEE WEE
45s
ALADDIN

❏ 3112	When It Rains It Pours/Daybreak	1952	25.00	50.00	100.00
❏ 3112	When It Rains It Pours/Daybreak	1952	500.00	1000.	1500.

—Green vinyl

EDCO

❏ 1009	Ev'ry Night About This Time/(B-side unknown)	196?	6.25	12.50	25.00
❏ 1010	Money Tree/When Darkness Falls	196?	6.25	12.50	25.00

FOX

❏ 10069	Give Me One More Chance/(B-side unknown)	196?	7.50	15.00	30.00

GUYDEN

❏ 2048	I'm Still in Love with You/Time on My Hands	1961	3.75	7.50	15.00

IMPERIAL

❏ 5288	Do Unto Others/Every Dog Has a Day	1954	50.00	100.00	200.00
❏ 5297	Wine-O/Hurry Hurry	1954	125.00	250.00	500.00
❏ 5321	I Need Your Love/You Know — Yeah	1955	12.50	25.00	50.00
❏ 5338	My Idea About You/I Got News for You	1955	12.50	25.00	50.00
❏ 5345	Eyes Full of Tears/Runnin' Wild	1955	12.50	25.00	50.00
❏ 5353	Yours Truly/Be Faithful	1955	12.50	25.00	50.00

JAMIE

❏ 1190	'Tain't Nobody's Business If I Do/Little Bitty Things	1961	3.75	7.50	15.00

MODERN

❏ 892	Cool Evening/Have You Lost Your Love for Me	1951	25.00	50.00	100.00

POST

❏ 2007	Don't Go/I Must Go On	1955	10.00	20.00	40.00

RECORDED IN HOLLYWOOD

❏ 408	Pappy's Blues/Crying and Walking	1954	25.00	50.00	100.00
❏ 426	Baby Pat the Floor/I'm Your Prisoner	1954	25.00	50.00	100.00

SMASH

❏ 1774	Sabre Twist/Hillbilly Blues	1962	3.00	6.00	12.00

VEE JAY

❏ 214	A Frosty Night/The Telephone Is Ringing	1956	10.00	20.00	40.00
❏ 252	I Don't Care/I Found My Peace of Mind	1957	10.00	20.00	40.00
❏ 266	Fiddle Dee Dee/Is This the Price I Pay	1957	10.00	20.00	40.00

78s
4 STAR

❏ 1304	After Hours Boogie/Why Did You Go	1948	20.00	40.00	80.00

ALADDIN

❏ 3112	When It Rains It Pours/Daybreak	1952	12.50	25.00	50.00

IMPERIAL

❏ 5288	Do Unto Others/Every Dog Has a Day	1954	12.50	25.00	50.00
❏ 5297	Wine-O/Hurry Hurry	1954	20.00	40.00	80.00
❏ 5321	I Need Your Love/You Know — Yeah	1955	10.00	20.00	40.00
❏ 5338	My Idea About You/I Got News for You	1955	10.00	20.00	40.00
❏ 5345	Eyes Full of Tears/Runnin' Wild	1955	10.00	20.00	40.00
❏ 5353	Yours Truly/Be Faithful	1955	10.00	20.00	40.00

MODERN

❏ 20-624	Blues After Hours/I'm Still in Love with You	1948	10.00	20.00	40.00
❏ 20-643	Texas Hop/Central Avenue Blues	1948	10.00	20.00	40.00
❏ 20-658	Rock Island Line/Be-Bop	1949	7.50	15.00	30.00
❏ 20-675	I Love You So/When Darkness Falls	1949	7.50	15.00	30.00
❏ 20-707	Brand New Woman/Long After Hours	1949	7.50	15.00	30.00
❏ 20-719	Old Fashioned Way/Bounce Pee Wee	1949	7.50	15.00	30.00
❏ 20-732	Please Come Back/Rockin' the Blues	1949	7.50	15.00	30.00
❏ 20-742	Some Rainy Day/Huckle Boogie	1950	7.50	15.00	30.00
❏ 20-763	Louella Brown/Answer to Blues After Hours	1950	7.50	15.00	30.00
❏ 20-774	Good Little Woman/Dedicating the Blues	1950	7.50	15.00	30.00
❏ 20-796	Tired of Travelin'/Change Your Way of Lovin'	1950	7.50	15.00	30.00

Number	Title (A Side/B Side)	Yr	VG	VG+	NM
❑ 816	Thinking of You/Poppa Stoppa	1951	7.50	15.00	30.00
❑ 892	Cool Evening/Have You Lost Your Love for Me	1951	6.25	12.50	25.00
POST					
❑ 2007	Don't Go/I Must Go On	1955	7.50	15.00	30.00
RECORDED IN HOLLYWOOD					
❑ 408	Pappy's Blues/Crying and Walking	1954	15.00	30.00	60.00
❑ 426	Baby Pat the Floor/I'm Your Prisoner	1954	15.00	30.00	60.00
VEE JAY					
❑ 214	A Frosty Night/The Telephone Is Ringing	1956	7.50	15.00	30.00
❑ 252	I Don't Care/I Found My Peace of Mind	1957	10.00	20.00	40.00
❑ 266	Fiddle Dee Dee/Is This the Price I Pay	1957	10.00	20.00	40.00
Albums					
CROWN					
❑ CLP-5175 [M]	Pee Wee Crayton	1959	25.00	50.00	100.00
—*Black label*					
❑ CLP-5175 [M]	Pee Wee Crayton	196?	5.00	10.00	20.00
—*Gray label*					
VANGUARD					
❑ VSD-6566	The Things I Used to Do	1971	3.75	7.50	15.00

CREATIVE SOURCE
45s
POLYDOR					
❑ 14291	Pass the Feelin' On/Turn On to Music	1975	—	2.50	5.00
❑ 14334	I'll Find You Anywhere/Singin' Funky Music	1976	—	—	—
—*Canceled*					
SUSSEX					
❑ 501	You Can't Hide Love/Lovesville	1973	—	2.50	5.00
❑ 508	You're Too Good to Be True/Oh Love	1973	—	2.50	5.00
❑ 509	Who Is He and What Is He to You (Part 1)/Who Is He and What Is He to You (Part 2)	1974	—	2.50	5.00
❑ 622	Keep On Movin'/I Just Can't See Myself Without You	1974	—	2.50	5.00
❑ 632	Migration/I Just Can't See Myself Without You	1974	—	2.50	5.00

CRESTS, THE
45s
COED					
❑ 501	Pretty Little Angel/I Thank the Moon	1958	37.50	75.00	150.00
—*"Coed" in red print*					
❑ 501	Pretty Little Angel/I Thank the Moon	1958	10.00	20.00	40.00
—*"Coed" in red and black print*					
❑ 506	16 Candles/Beside You	1958	7.50	15.00	30.00
❑ 509	Six Nights a Week/I Do	1959	6.25	12.50	25.00
❑ 511	Flower of Love/Molly Mae	1959	6.25	12.50	25.00
❑ 515	The Angels Listened In/I Thank the Moon	1959	7.50	15.00	30.00
❑ 521	A Year Ago Tonight/Paper Clown	1959	6.25	12.50	25.00
❑ 525	Step by Step/Gee (But I'd Give the World)	1960	6.25	12.50	25.00
❑ 531	Trouble in Paradise/Always You	1960	6.25	12.50	25.00
❑ 535	Journey of Love/If My Heart Could Write a Letter	1960	5.00	10.00	20.00
❑ 537	Isn't It Amazing/Molly Mae	1960	5.00	10.00	20.00
❑ 543	I Remember (In the Still of the Night)/Good Golly Miss Molly	1961	6.25	12.50	25.00
❑ 561	Little Miracles/Baby I Gotta Know	1962	7.50	15.00	30.00
CORAL					
❑ 62403	You Blew Out the Candles/A Love to Last a Lifetime	1964	7.50	15.00	30.00
HARVEY					
❑ 5002	Sixteen Candles/My Juanita	1981	2.50	5.00	10.00
—*Red vinyl*					
JOYCE					
❑ 103	My Juanita/Sweetest One	1957	75.00	150.00	300.00
—*Label name: "JoYce"*					
❑ 103	My Juanita/Sweetest One	1959	12.50	25.00	50.00
—*Label name: "Joyce"*					
❑ 105	No One to Love/Wish She Was Mine	1957	75.00	150.00	300.00
KING TUT					
❑ 172	Earth Angel/Tweedlee Dee	197?	2.00	4.00	8.00
LANA					
❑ 101	16 Candles/Beside You	196?	2.00	4.00	8.00
—*Oldies reissue*					
❑ 102	Trouble in Paradise/I Thank the Moon	196?	2.00	4.00	8.00
—*Oldies reissue*					
❑ 103	Step by Step/Gee (But I'd Give the World)	196?	2.00	4.00	8.00
—*Oldies reissue*					
MUSICTONE					
❑ 1106	My Juanita/Sweetest One	1961	5.00	10.00	20.00
SCEPTER					
❑ 12112	I'm Stepping Out of the Picture/Afraid of Love	1965	3.75	7.50	15.00
SELMA					
❑ 311	Guilty/Number One with Me	1962	18.75	37.50	75.00
—*A-side has spoken intro*					
❑ 311	Guilty/Number One with Me	1962	6.25	12.50	25.00
—*A-side does not have spoken intro*					
❑ 4000	Did I Remember/Tears Will Fall	1963	7.50	15.00	30.00
TIMES SQUARE					
❑ 2	No One to Love/Wish She Was Mine	1962	5.00	10.00	20.00
—*Red vinyl*					
❑ 6	Baby/I Love You So	1964	3.75	7.50	15.00
❑ 97	Baby/I Love You So	1964	3.00	6.00	12.00
TRANS ATLAS					
❑ 696	The Actor/Three Tears in a Bucket	1962	7.50	15.00	30.00

Number	Title (A Side/B Side)	Yr	VG	VG+	NM
78s					
COED					
❑ 501	Pretty Little Angel/I Thank the Moon	1958	125.00	250.00	500.00
❑ 506	16 Candles/Beside You	1958	100.00	200.00	400.00
—*Later Crests 78s are rumored to exist in U.S. pressings; any would fetch in the hundreds for a NM copy*					
JOYCE					
❑ 103	My Juanita/Sweetest One	1957	30.00	60.00	120.00
❑ 105	No One to Love/Wish She Was Mine	1957	30.00	60.00	120.00
7-Inch Extended Plays					
COED					
❑ EPC-101	16 Candles/Six Nights a Week//The Angels Listened In/Flower of Love	1960	100.00	200.00	400.00
❑ EPC-101 [PS]	The Angels Listened In	1960	100.00	200.00	400.00
Albums					
COED					
❑ LPC-901 [M]	The Crests Sing All Biggies	1960	100.00	200.00	400.00
—*Yellow label, black print*					
❑ LPC-901 [M]	The Crests Sing All Biggies	1960	50.00	100.00	200.00
—*Red label*					
❑ LPC-904 [M]	The Best of the Crests/16 Fabulous Hits	1961	100.00	200.00	400.00
—*Label simply calls this "16 Fabulous Hits"*					
COLLECTABLES					
❑ COL-5009	Greatest Hits	1982	3.00	6.00	12.00
POST					
❑ 3000	The Crests Sing	196?	10.00	20.00	40.00
RHINO					
❑ R1-70948	The Best of the Crests	1989	3.00	6.00	12.00

CRICKETS, THE (2)
Black vocal group featuring Dean Barlow.
45s
DAVIS					
❑ 459	I'm Going to Live My Life Alone/Man from the Moon	1958	15.00	30.00	60.00
JAY DEE					
❑ 777	Dreams and Wishes/When I Met You	1953	50.00	100.00	200.00
❑ 781	Fine As Wine/I'm Not the Same One You Love	1953	50.00	100.00	200.00
❑ 785	Changing Partners/Your Love	1954	37.50	75.00	150.00
❑ 786	Just You/My Little Baby's Shoes	1954	37.50	75.00	150.00
❑ 789	Are You Looking for a Sweetheart/Never Give Up Hope	1954	37.50	75.00	150.00
❑ 795	I'm Going to Live My Life Alone/Man from the Moon	1954	37.50	75.00	150.00
MGM					
❑ 11428	You're Mine/Milk and Gin	1953	62.50	125.00	250.00
❑ 11507	I'll Cry No More/For You I Have Eyes	1953	50.00	100.00	200.00
Albums					
RELIC					
❑ LP-5040	The Crickets Featuring Dean Barlow	1987	2.50	5.00	10.00

CROPPER, STEVE
Also see BOOKER T. AND THE MG's; MAR-KEYS.
45s
MCA					
❑ 51078	Playin' My Thang/Why Do You Say You Love Me	1981	—	2.00	4.00
❑ 51115	Sandy Beaches/Fly	1981	—	2.00	4.00
❑ 52103	Night After Night/634-5789	1982	—	2.00	4.00
Albums					
MCA					
❑ 5171	Playin' My Thang	1980	2.50	5.00	10.00
❑ 5340	Night After Night	1982	2.50	5.00	10.00
VOLT					
❑ VOS-6006	With a Little Help from My Friends	1970	3.75	7.50	15.00

CROWN HEIGHTS AFFAIR
12-Inch Singles
DE-LITE					
❑ MK 79 [DJ]	Dance Lady Dance (6:25)/The Rock Is Hot (7:14)	1979	5.00	10.00	20.00
❑ MK 142 [DJ]	Sure Shot (6:20) (same on both sides)	1980	5.00	10.00	20.00
❑ PRO 225-1 [DJ]	Let Me Ride on the Wave of Your Love (5:44) (same on both sides)	1982	5.00	10.00	20.00
❑ DDS 582	Do It the French Way/Sexy Ways	1977	10.00	20.00	40.00
❑ DDS 588	Dancin' (6:13)/Love Me (6:01)	1977	10.00	20.00	40.00
SBK					
❑ V-19703	I'll Do Anything (Radio Edit 3:54) (Nineties Club Mix 6:53) (Red Zone Mix 6:04) (Marsha Mix 9:14)	1989	2.50	5.00	10.00
45s					
DE-LITE					
❑ 803	You Gave Me Love/Tell Me You Love Me	1980	—	2.00	4.00
❑ 805	Sure Shot/I See the Light	1980	—	2.00	4.00
❑ 821	Somebody Tell Me What to Do/You Gave Me Love	1982	—	2.00	4.00
❑ 823	Let Me Ride on the Wave of Your Love/Wine and Dine You	1982	—	2.00	4.00
❑ 908	Say a Prayer for Two/Galaxy of Love	1978	—	2.00	4.00
❑ 911	I Love You/Dream World	1978	—	2.00	4.00
❑ 912	Dance Lady Dance/Come Fly with Me	1979	—	2.00	4.00
❑ 915	Empty Soul of Mine/Rock Is Hot	1979	—	2.00	4.00
❑ 1570	Dreaming a Dream/Dreaming a Dream (Part 2)	1975	—	2.00	4.00
❑ 1575	Every Beat of My Heart/Every Beat of My Heart (Disco Version)	1975	—	2.00	4.00
❑ 1581	Foxy Lady/Picture Show	1976	—	2.00	4.00

Number	Title (A Side/B Side)	Yr	VG	VG+	NM
❏ 1588	Dancin'/Love Me	1976	—	2.00	4.00
❏ 1592	Do It the French Way/Sexy Ways	1977	—	2.00	4.00
❏ 1592 [PS]	Do It the French Way/Sexy Ways	1977	—	3.00	6.00
RCA VICTOR					
❏ APBO-0023	Super Rod (Part 1)/Super Rod (Part 2)	1973	—	2.50	5.00
❏ APBO-0243	Leave the Kids Alone/Rip-Off	1974	—	2.50	5.00
❏ PB-10018	Special Kind of Woman/Streaking	1974	—	2.50	5.00

CROWNS, THE (1)
45s
CHORDETTE

Number	Title (A Side/B Side)	Yr	VG	VG+	NM
❏ 1001	Party Time/Amazon Basin Pop	1962	5.00	10.00	20.00

CROWNS, THE (2)
45s
OLD TOWN

❏ 1171	Possibility/Watch Out	1964	10.00	20.00	40.00
—Old light blue Old Town label					
❏ 1171	Possibility/Watch Out	1964	3.75	7.50	15.00
—Black label with moon					

CROWNS, THE (3)
45s
R&B

❏ 6901	Kiss and Make Up/I'll Forget About You	1958	20.00	40.00	80.00

CROWNS, THE (4)
45s
VEE JAY

❏ 546	Better Luck Next Time/You Make Me Blue	1963	3.75	7.50	15.00

CROWS, THE
45s
RAMA

❏ 3	Seven Lonely Days/No Help Wanted	1953	125.00	250.00	500.00
❏ 5	Gee/I Love You So	1953	17.50	35.00	70.00
—Blue label, black vinyl					
❏ 5	Gee/I Love You So	1953	100.00	200.00	400.00
—Blue label, red vinyl					
❏ 5	Gee/I Love You So	1955	7.50	15.00	30.00
—Red label, black vinyl					
❏ 10	Heartbreaker/Call a Doctor	1953	100.00	200.00	400.00
—Black vinyl					
❏ 10	Heartbreaker/Call a Doctor	1953	200.00	400.00	800.00
—Red vinyl					
❏ 10	Heartbreaker/Call a Doctor	1953	150.00	300.00	600.00
—Black vinyl, label says "The Jewels"					
❏ 10	Heartbreaker/Call a Doctor	1953	150.00	300.00	600.00
—Black vinyl, label says "The Jewels" on one side, "The Crows" on the other					
❏ 10	Heartbreaker/Call a Doctor	1953	400.00	800.00	1200.
—Red vinyl; label says "The Jewels"					
❏ 29	Baby/Untrue	1954	50.00	100.00	200.00
❏ 30	Miss You/I Really, Really Love You So	1954	100.00	200.00	400.00
—Black vinyl					
❏ 30	Miss You/I Really, Really Love You So	1954	250.00	500.00	1000.
—Red vinyl					
❏ 50	Baby Doll/Sweet Sue (It's You)	1954	100.00	200.00	400.00
TICO					
❏ 1082	Mambo Shevitz/Mambo #5	1955	50.00	100.00	200.00
—B-side by Melino and Orchestra; black vinyl					
❏ 1082	Mambo Shevitz/Mambo #5	1955	75.00	150.00	300.00
—B-side by Melino and Orchestra; red vinyl					

CROWS, THE / THE HARPTONES
Albums
ROULETTE

❏ RE-114 [(2)]	Echoes of a Rock Era: The Groups	1973	5.00	10.00	20.00

CRUDUP, ARTHUR
45s
ACE

❏ 503	I Wonder/My Baby Boogies All the Time	1955	50.00	100.00	200.00
FIRE					
❏ 1501	Rock Me Mama/Mean Ole Frisco	1962	3.75	7.50	15.00
❏ 1502	Katie Mae/Dig Myself a Hole	1962	3.75	7.50	15.00
GROOVE					
❏ 0011	I Love My Baby/Fall on Your Knees and Pray	1954	10.00	20.00	40.00
❏ 0026	She's Got No Hair/If You Ever Been to Georgia	1954	10.00	20.00	40.00
RCA VICTOR					
❏ 22-0109	My Baby Left Me/Anytime Is the Right Time	1951	20.00	40.00	80.00
❏ 47-4367	Love Me Mama/Where Did You Stay Last Night	1951	25.00	50.00	100.00
❏ 47-4572	Goin' Back to Georgia/Mr. So and So	1952	20.00	40.00	80.00
❏ 47-4753	Worried 'Bout You Baby/Late in the Evening	1952	20.00	40.00	80.00
❏ 47-4933	Second Man Blues/Do It If You Want	1952	20.00	40.00	80.00
❏ 47-5070	Lookin' for My Baby/Pearly Lee	1952	20.00	40.00	80.00
❏ 47-5167	Keep On Drinkin'/Nelvina	1953	20.00	40.00	80.00
❏ 47-5563	War Is Over/My Wife and Woman	1953	20.00	40.00	80.00
❏ 50-0000	That's All Right/Crudup's After Hours	1949	100.00	200.00	400.00
—Gray label, orange vinyl; the first R&B 45 rpm record!					
❏ 50-0001	Boy Friend Blues/Katie May	1949	25.00	50.00	100.00
—Gray label, orange vinyl					
❏ 50-0013	Shout Sister Shout/Crudup's Vicksburg Blues	1949	25.00	50.00	100.00
—Gray label, orange vinyl					

Number	Title (A Side/B Side)	Yr	VG	VG+	NM
❏ 50-0032	Hoodoo Lady Blues/Tired of Worry	1949	25.00	50.00	100.00
—Gray label, orange vinyl					
❏ 50-0046	Come Back Baby/Mercy Blues	1949	25.00	50.00	100.00
—Gray label, orange vinyl					
❏ 50-0074	Dust My Broom/You Know That I Love You	1950	25.00	50.00	100.00
—Gray label, orange vinyl					
❏ 50-0092	Mean Old Santa Fe/Oo Wee Baby	1950	25.00	50.00	100.00
—Gray label, orange vinyl					
❏ 50-0100	Lonesome World to Me/Hand Me Down My Walking Cane	1950	25.00	50.00	100.00
—Gray label, orange vinyl					
❏ 50-0105	She's Just Like Caldonia/(B-side unknown)	1951	25.00	50.00	100.00
—Gray label, orange vinyl					
❏ 50-0109	My Baby Left Me/Anytime Is the Right Time	1951	37.50	75.00	150.00
—Gray label, orange vinyl					
❏ 50-0117	Nobody Wants Me/Star Bootlegger	1951	25.00	50.00	100.00
—Gray label, black vinyl					
❏ 50-0126	Roberta Blues/Behind Closed Doors	1951	25.00	50.00	100.00
—Gray label, black vinyl					
❏ 50-0141	I'm Gonna Dig Myself a Hole/Too Much Competition	1951	25.00	50.00	100.00
—Gray label, black vinyl					

78s
ACE

❏ 503	I Wonder/My Baby Boogies All the Time	1955	50.00	100.00	200.00
BLUEBIRD					
❏ B-8858	If I Get Lucky/Death Valley Blues	1941	15.00	30.00	60.00
❏ B-8890	Kind Lover Blues/Black Pony Blues	1942	15.00	30.00	60.00
❏ B-9019	Raised to My Hand/Give Me a 32-20	1942	10.00	20.00	40.00
❏ 34-0704	Mean Old Frisco Blues/Gonna Follow My Baby	194?	10.00	20.00	40.00
❏ 34-0717	My Mamma Don't Allow Me/Standing at My Window	194?	10.00	20.00	40.00
❏ 34-0725	Rock Me Mamma/Who's Been Foolin' You	1945	7.50	15.00	30.00
❏ 34-0736	Keep Your Arms Around Me/Cool Disposition	1945	7.50	15.00	30.00
❏ 34-0746	She's Gone/(B-side unknown)	1946	7.50	15.00	30.00
CHAMPION					
❏ 503	I Wonder/My Baby Boogies All the Time	1953	100.00	200.00	400.00
—As "Arthur 'Blues' Crump"					
GROOVE					
❏ 0011	I Love My Baby/Fall on Your Knees and Pray	1954	7.50	15.00	30.00
❏ 0026	She's Got No Hair/If You Ever Been to Georgia	1954	7.50	15.00	30.00
RCA VICTOR					
❏ 20-1949	So Glad You're Mine/Ethel Mae	1946	5.00	10.00	20.00
❏ 20-2105	I Want Your Lovin'/(B-side unknown)	1946	5.00	10.00	20.00
❏ 20-2205	That's All Right/Crudup's After Hours	1947	37.50	75.00	150.00
❏ 20-2387	That's Your Red Wagon/I Don't Know It	1947	5.00	10.00	20.00
❏ 20-2509	My Mamma Don't Allow Me/Standing at My Window	1947	5.00	10.00	20.00
—Reissue of Bluebird 34-0717					
❏ 20-2565	Train Fare Blues/No More Lovers	1947	5.00	10.00	20.00
❏ 20-2757	Dirt Road Blues/Cry Your Blues Away	1948	5.00	10.00	20.00
❏ 20-2989	Boy Friend Blues/Katie May	1948	5.00	10.00	20.00
❏ 20-3140	Just Like a Spider//(B-side unknown)	1948	5.00	10.00	20.00
❏ 20-3261	Chicago Blues/(B-side unknown)	1949	5.00	10.00	20.00
❏ 20-4367	Love Me Mama/Where Did You Stay Last Night	1951	5.00	10.00	20.00
❏ 20-4572	Goin' Back to Georgia/Mr. So and So	1952	5.00	10.00	20.00
❏ 20-4753	Worried 'Bout You Baby/Late in the Evening	1952	5.00	10.00	20.00
❏ 20-4933	Second Man Blues/Do It If You Want	1952	5.00	10.00	20.00
❏ 20-5070	Lookin' for My Baby/Pearly Lee	1952	5.00	10.00	20.00
❏ 20-5167	Keep On Drinkin'/Nelvina	1953	5.00	10.00	20.00
❏ 20-5563	War Is Over/My Wife and Woman	1953	5.00	10.00	20.00
❏ 22-0007	Gonna Be Some Changes Made/Someday	1949	6.25	12.50	25.00
❏ 22-0029	Shout Sister Shout/Crudup's Vicksburg Blues	1949	6.25	12.50	25.00
❏ 22-0048	Hoodoo Lady Blues/Tired of Worry	1949	6.25	12.50	25.00
❏ 22-0061	Come Back Baby/Mercy Blues	1949	6.25	12.50	25.00
❏ 22-0074	Dust My Broom/You Know That I Love You	1950	6.25	12.50	25.00
❏ 22-0092	Mean Old Santa Fe/Oo Wee Baby	1950	6.25	12.50	25.00
❏ 22-0100	Lonesome World to Me/Hand Me Down My Walking Cane	1950	6.25	12.50	25.00
❏ 22-0105	She's Just Like Caldonia/(B-side unknown)	1951	6.25	12.50	25.00
❏ 22-0117	Nobody Wants Me/Star Bootlegger	1951	6.25	12.50	25.00
❏ 22-0126	Roberta Blues/Behind Closed Doors	1951	6.25	12.50	25.00
❏ 22-0141	I'm Gonna Dig Myself a Hole/Too Much Competition	1951	6.25	12.50	25.00

Albums
COLLECTABLES

❏ COL-5130	Mean Ol' Frisco	1988	2.50	5.00	10.00
DELMARK					
❏ DS-614	Look on Yonder's Wall	1969	10.00	20.00	40.00
❏ DS-621	Crudup's Mood	1969	10.00	20.00	40.00
FIRE					
❏ 103 [M]	Mean Ol' Frisco	1960	300.00	600.00	900.00
RCA VICTOR					
❏ LVP-573	Father of Rock and Roll	1971	5.00	10.00	20.00
TRIP					
❏ 7501	Mean Ol' Frisco	1975	3.75	7.50	15.00

Number	Title (A Side/B Side)	Yr	VG	VG+	NM

CRUMP, ARTHUR "BLUES"
See ARTHUR CRUDUP.

CRUSADERS, THE (1)
Jazz and soul group. Originally recorded as "The Jazz Crusaders"; Pacific Jazz and World Pacific releases were under that name. Also see STIX HOOPER.

12-Inch Singles
MCA

Number	Title (A Side/B Side)	Yr	VG	VG+	NM
❏ L33-1190 [DJ]	Dead End/Night Ladies	1984	2.50	5.00	10.00
❏ L33-1748 [DJ]	This Old World's Too Funky for Me/Standing Tall	1981	3.75	7.50	15.00
—A-side with Joe Cocker					
❏ L33-1833 [DJ]	Street Life (6:02) (same on both sides)	1979	5.00	10.00	20.00
❏ 13991	New Moves (Remixed Version 5:35) (Dub Version 6:26) (Single Mix 3:45)	1984	2.00	4.00	8.00

45s
ABC BLUE THUMB

Number	Title (A Side/B Side)	Yr	VG	VG+	NM
❏ 261	Stomp and Buck Dance/A Ballad for Joe (Louis)	1975	—	2.50	5.00
❏ 267	Creole/I Feel the Love	1975	—	2.50	5.00
❏ 269	Keep That Same Old Feeling/'Til the Sun Shines	1976	—	2.50	5.00
❏ 270	And Then There Was the Blues/Feeling Funky	1976	—	2.50	5.00
❏ 272	Feel It/The Way We Was	1977	—	2.50	5.00
❏ 273	Free as the Wind/The Way We Was	1977	—	2.50	5.00
❏ 278	Bayou Bottoms/Covert Action	1978	—	2.50	5.00

BLUE THUMB

Number	Title (A Side/B Side)	Yr	VG	VG+	NM
❏ 208	Put It Where You Want It/Mosadi	1972	—	2.50	5.00
❏ 217	So Far Away/That's How I Feel	1972	—	2.50	5.00
❏ 225	Don't Let It Get You Down/Journey from Within	1973	—	2.50	5.00
❏ 232	Take It or Leave It/That's How I Feel	1973	—	2.50	5.00
❏ 245	Lay It On the Line/Let's Boogie	1974	—	2.50	5.00
❏ 249	Scratch/Way Back Home	1974	—	2.50	5.00

CHISA

Number	Title (A Side/B Side)	Yr	VG	VG+	NM
❏ 8010	Way Back Home/Jackson	1970	—	3.00	6.00
—As "Jazz Crusaders"					
❏ 8013	Pass the Plate/Greasy Spoon	1971	—	3.00	6.00

MCA

Number	Title (A Side/B Side)	Yr	VG	VG+	NM
❏ 41054	Street Life/Hustler	1979	—	2.00	4.00
❏ 41295	Sweet Gentle Love/Soul Shadows	1980	—	2.00	4.00
❏ 51029	Last Call/Honky Tonk Struttin'	1980	—	2.00	4.00
❏ 51177	I'm So Glad I'm Standing Here Today/Standing Tall	1981	—	2.00	4.00
—A-side with Joe Cocker					
❏ 51222	This Old World's Too Funky for Me/Standing Tall	1981	—	2.00	4.00
—A-side with Joe Cocker					
❏ 52098	Street Life/Overture	1982	—	2.00	4.00
—With B.B. King and the London Symphony Orchestra					
❏ 52365	New Move/Mr. Cool	1984	—	2.00	4.00
❏ 52398	Dream Street/Dead End	1984	—	2.00	4.00
❏ 52454	Gotta Lotta Shakalada/Zalal 'E Mini	1984	—	2.00	4.00
❏ 52966	The Way It Goes/Good Times	1986	—	2.00	4.00
❏ 53330	A.C. (Alternating Currents)/Mulholland Nights	1988	—	—	3.00

MOWEST

Number	Title (A Side/B Side)	Yr	VG	VG+	NM
❏ 5028	Spanish Harlem/Papa Hooper's Barrelhouse Groove	1972	—	3.00	6.00

PACIFIC JAZZ

Number	Title (A Side/B Side)	Yr	VG	VG+	NM
❏ 340	Sinnin' Sam/Tonight	1962	3.00	6.00	12.00
❏ 342	Young Rabbits/(B-side unknown)	1962	3.00	6.00	12.00
❏ 371	No Name Samba/Tough Talk	1963	2.50	5.00	10.00
❏ 88125	Uptight (Everything's Alright)/Scratch	1966	2.00	4.00	8.00
❏ 88144	Eleanor Rigby/Ooga Boogaloo	1968	—	3.00	6.00
❏ 88146	Hey Jude/Love and Peace	1969	—	3.00	6.00
❏ 88153	Get Back/Willie and Laura Mae Jones	1969	—	3.00	6.00

WORLD PACIFIC

Number	Title (A Side/B Side)	Yr	VG	VG+	NM
❏ 388	Boopie/Turkish Black	1963	2.50	5.00	10.00
—As "Jazz Crusaders"					
❏ 401	Heat Wave/On Broadway	1964	2.50	5.00	10.00
❏ 412	I Remember Tomorrow/Long John	1964	2.50	5.00	10.00
❏ 77800	The Thing/Tough Talk	1965	2.00	4.00	8.00
❏ 77806	Aqua Dulce/Soul Bourgeoise	1966	2.00	4.00	8.00

Albums
ABC BLUE THUMB

Number	Title (A Side/B Side)	Yr	VG	VG+	NM
❏ SPMK-42 [DJ]	Crusaders In-Store Sampler Album	1978	5.00	10.00	20.00
—Promo-only issue					
❏ BT-6001 [(2)]	Crusaders 1	1975	3.00	6.00	12.00
❏ BT-6010	Scratch	1975	2.50	5.00	10.00
—Reissue					
❏ 6022	Chain Reaction	1975	2.50	5.00	10.00
❏ 6024	Those Southern Knights	1976	2.50	5.00	10.00
❏ 6027 [(2)]	The Best of the Crusaders	1976	3.00	6.00	12.00
❏ 6029	Free As the Wind	1977	2.50	5.00	10.00
❏ BA-6030	Images	1978	2.50	5.00	10.00
❏ BTSY-9002 [(2)]	Southern Comfort	1974	3.00	6.00	12.00

APPLAUSE

Number	Title (A Side/B Side)	Yr	VG	VG+	NM
❏ APBL-2313	Powerhouse	197?	3.00	6.00	12.00
—Reissue of Pacific Jazz 20136					

BLUE NOTE

Number	Title (A Side/B Side)	Yr	VG	VG+	NM
❏ BN-LA170-G [(2)]	Tough Talk	1974	3.00	6.00	12.00
❏ BN-LA530-H2 [(2)]	Young Rabbits	1977	3.00	6.00	12.00
❏ LWB-530 [(2)]	Young Rabbits	1981	2.50	5.00	10.00
—Reissue of BN-LA530-H2					
❏ LT-1046	Live Sides	1980	2.50	5.00	10.00

BLUE THUMB

Number	Title (A Side/B Side)	Yr	VG	VG+	NM
❏ BT-6001 [(2)]	Crusaders 1	1972	3.75	7.50	15.00
❏ BT-6007	Unsung Heroes	1973	3.00	6.00	12.00
❏ BT-6010	Scratch	1974	3.00	6.00	12.00

Number	Title (A Side/B Side)	Yr	VG	VG+	NM
❏ BT-7000 [(2)]	The 2nd Crusade	1973	3.75	7.50	15.00

CHISA

Number	Title (A Side/B Side)	Yr	VG	VG+	NM
❏ 804	Old Socks, New Shoes…New Socks, Old Shoes	1970	3.00	6.00	12.00
—As "Jazz Crusaders"					
❏ 807	Pass the Plate	1971	3.00	6.00	12.00

CRUSADERS

Number	Title (A Side/B Side)	Yr	VG	VG+	NM
❏ 16000	Street Life	1982	6.25	12.50	25.00
—Audiophile vinyl					
❏ 16002	Ongaku-Kai: Live in Japan	1982	6.25	12.50	25.00
—Audiophile vinyl					

LIBERTY

Number	Title (A Side/B Side)	Yr	VG	VG+	NM
❏ LST-11005	Give Peace a Chance	1970	3.75	7.50	15.00
—As "Jazz Crusaders"					

MCA

Number	Title (A Side/B Side)	Yr	VG	VG+	NM
❏ 3094	Street Life	1979	2.50	5.00	10.00
❏ 5124	Rhapsody and Blues	1980	2.50	5.00	10.00
❏ 5254	Standing Tall	1981	2.50	5.00	10.00
❏ 5429	Ghetto Blaster	1984	2.50	5.00	10.00
❏ 5781	The Good and Bad Times	1987	2.50	5.00	10.00
❏ 6006 [(2)]	The Best of the Crusaders	1980	2.50	5.00	10.00
—Reissue of Blue Thumb 6027					
❏ 6014 [(2)]	Crusaders 1	198?	2.50	5.00	10.00
—Reissue of Blue Thumb 6001					
❏ 6015 [(2)]	2nd Crusade	198?	2.50	5.00	10.00
—Reissue of Blue Thumb 7000					
❏ 6016 [(2)]	Southern Comfort	198?	2.50	5.00	10.00
—Reissue of Blue Thumb 9002					
❏ 8017 [(2)]	Royal Jam	1982	3.00	6.00	12.00
❏ 37072	Scratch	198?	2.00	4.00	8.00
—Reissue of Blue Thumb 6010					
❏ 37073	Free As the Wind	198?	2.00	4.00	8.00
—Reissue of Blue Thumb 6029					
❏ 37074	Images	198?	2.00	4.00	8.00
—Reissue of Blue Thumb 6030					
❏ 37146	Chain Reaction	198?	2.00	4.00	8.00
—Reissue of Blue Thumb 6022					
❏ 37147	Those Southern Knights	198?	2.00	4.00	8.00
—Reissue of Blue Thumb 6024					
❏ 37174	Rhapsody and Blues	198?	2.00	4.00	8.00
—Reissue of 5124					
❏ 37240	Standing Tall	1985	2.00	4.00	8.00
—Reissue of 5254					
❏ 42087	The Vocal Album	1988	2.50	5.00	10.00
❏ 42168	Life in the Modern World	1988	2.50	5.00	10.00

MOBILE FIDELITY

Number	Title (A Side/B Side)	Yr	VG	VG+	NM
❏ 1-010	Chain Reaction	1979	5.00	10.00	20.00
—Audiophile vinyl					

MOTOWN

Number	Title (A Side/B Side)	Yr	VG	VG+	NM
❏ M5-195V1	The Crusaders At Their Best	1981	2.50	5.00	10.00
❏ M 796	The Crusaders At Their Best	1973	3.00	6.00	12.00

MOWEST

Number	Title (A Side/B Side)	Yr	VG	VG+	NM
❏ 118	Hollywood	1972	3.00	6.00	12.00

PACIFIC JAZZ

Number	Title (A Side/B Side)	Yr	VG	VG+	NM
❏ PJ-27 [M]	Freedom Sound	1961	6.25	12.50	25.00
❏ ST-27 [S]	Freedom Sound	1961	7.50	15.00	30.00
❏ PJ-43 [M]	Lookin' Ahead	1962	6.25	12.50	25.00
❏ ST-43 [S]	Lookin' Ahead	1962	7.50	15.00	30.00
—Black vinyl					
❏ ST-43 [S]	Lookin' Ahead	1962	15.00	30.00	60.00
—Yellow vinyl					
❏ PJ-57 [M]	The Jazz Crusaders at the Lighthouse	1962	6.25	12.50	25.00
❏ ST-57 [S]	The Jazz Crusaders at the Lighthouse	1962	7.50	15.00	30.00
❏ PJ-68 [M]	Tough Talk	1963	6.25	12.50	25.00
❏ ST-68 [S]	Tough Talk	1963	7.50	15.00	30.00
❏ PJ-76 [M]	Heat Wave	1963	6.25	12.50	25.00
❏ ST-76 [S]	Heat Wave	1963	7.50	15.00	30.00
❏ PJ-83 [M]	Stretchin' Out	1964	6.25	12.50	25.00
❏ ST-83 [S]	Stretchin' Out	1964	7.50	15.00	30.00
❏ PJ-87 [M]	The Thing	1964	6.25	12.50	25.00
❏ ST-87 [S]	The Thing	1964	7.50	15.00	30.00
❏ PJ-10092 [M]	Chili Con Soul	1965	5.00	10.00	20.00
❏ PJ-10098 [M]	Live at the Lighthouse '66	1966	5.00	10.00	20.00
❏ PJ-10106 [M]	Talk That Talk	1966	5.00	10.00	20.00
❏ PJ-10115 [M]	The Festival Album	1967	6.25	12.50	25.00
❏ PJ-10124	Uh Huh	1967	6.25	12.50	25.00
❏ ST-20092 [S]	Chili Con Soul	1965	6.25	12.50	25.00
❏ ST-20098 [S]	Live at the Lighthouse '66	1966	6.25	12.50	25.00
❏ ST-20106 [S]	Talk That Talk	1966	6.25	12.50	25.00
❏ ST-20115 [S]	The Festival Album	1967	5.00	10.00	20.00
❏ ST-20124	Uh Huh	1967	5.00	10.00	20.00
❏ ST-20131	Lighthouse '68	1968	5.00	10.00	20.00
❏ ST-20136	Powerhouse	1968	5.00	10.00	20.00
❏ ST-20165	The Jazz Crusaders at the Lighthouse '69	1969	5.00	10.00	20.00
❏ ST-20175	The Best of the Jazz Crusaders	1969	5.00	10.00	20.00
❏ T-90598 [M]	Chili Con Soul	1965	6.25	12.50	25.00
—Capitol Record Club edition					

PAUSA

Number	Title (A Side/B Side)	Yr	VG	VG+	NM
❏ 9005	The Best of the Jazz Crusaders	1979	2.50	5.00	10.00
—As "Jazz Crusaders"					

WORLD PACIFIC JAZZ

Number	Title (A Side/B Side)	Yr	VG	VG+	NM
❏ ST-20098 [S]	Live at the Lighthouse '66	1970	3.75	7.50	15.00
—Reissue with "Liberty/UA" on label					

C

Number	Title (A Side/B Side)	Yr	VG	VG+	NM

CRUSADERS, THE (U)
45s
CAMEO
| ❏ 285 | Boogie Woogie/At the Club | 1963 | 3.00 | 6.00 | 12.00 |

DKR
| ❏ (no #) | Seminole/Busted Surfboard | 1962 | 10.00 | 20.00 | 40.00 |

DOOTO
| ❏ 472 | Swinging Week-End/I Found Someone | 1963 | 3.75 | 7.50 | 15.00 |

TOWER
| ❏ 286 | The Little Drummer Boy/Battle Hymn of the Republic | 1966 | 2.50 | 5.00 | 10.00 |
| ❏ 328 | Make a Joyful Noise/Praise We the Lord | 1967 | 2.50 | 5.00 | 10.00 |

CRYSTAL, RONETTE AND CHIFFON
45s
GEFFEN
| ❏ 7-28393 | Little Shop of Horrors/Grow for Me | 1987 | 2.00 | 4.00 | 8.00 |

—B-side by Rick Moranis

CRYSTALS, THE (1)
45s
GUSTO
| ❏ 2090 | Da Doo Ron Ron/Then He Kissed Me | 1979 | — | 2.00 | 4.00 |

—Re-recordings

MICHELLE
| ❏ 4113 | Ring-a-Ting-a-Ling/Should I Keep On Waiting | 1967 | 2.50 | 5.00 | 10.00 |

PAVILLION
| ❏ 03333 | Rudolph the Red-Nosed Reindeer/I Saw Mommy Kissing Santa Claus | 1982 | — | 2.50 | 5.00 |

—B-side by The Ronettes

PHILLES
❏ 100	There's No Other (Like My Baby)/Oh Yeah, Maybe Baby	1961	10.00	20.00	40.00
❏ 102	Uptown/What a Nice Way to Turn Seventeen	1962	10.00	20.00	40.00
❏ 105	He Hit Me (And It Felt like a Kiss)/No One Ever Tells You	1962	25.00	50.00	100.00
❏ 106	He's a Rebel/I Love You Eddie	1962	15.00	30.00	60.00

—Orange label
| ❏ 106 | He's a Rebel/I Love You Eddie | 1962 | 10.00 | 20.00 | 40.00 |

—Light blue label
| ❏ 106 | He's a Rebel/I Love You Eddie | 1964 | 6.25 | 12.50 | 25.00 |

—Yellow and red label
| ❏ 109 | He's Sure the Boy I Love/Walkin' Along (La-La-La) | 1962 | 7.50 | 15.00 | 30.00 |
| ❏ 111 | (Let's Dance) The Screw — Part 1/(Let's Dance) The Screw — Part 2 | 1963 | 3000. | 4500. | 6000. |

—Light blue label; no "D.J. Only Not for Sale" on label; "Audio Matrix" stamped in dead wax (counterfeits do not have this)
| ❏ 111 [DJ] | (Let's Dance) The Screw — Part 1/(Let's Dance) The Screw — Part 2 | 1963 | 2000. | 3000. | 4000. |

—White label; copies exist with the title as "Let's Dance The Screw" (no parentheses) also, with the same value as above
| ❏ 112 | Da Doo Ron Ron (When He Walked Me Home)/Git' It | 1963 | 7.50 | 15.00 | 30.00 |
| ❏ 115 | Then He Kissed Me/Brother Julius | 1963 | 10.00 | 20.00 | 40.00 |

—Light blue label
| ❏ 115 | Then He Kissed Me/Brother Julius | 1963 | 6.25 | 12.50 | 25.00 |

—Yellow and red label
❏ 119X	Little Boy/Harry (From West Virginia) and Milt	1964	5.00	10.00	20.00
❏ 119	Little Boy/Harry (From West Virginia) and Milt	1964	6.25	12.50	25.00
❏ 122	All Grown Up/Irving (Jaggered Sixteenths)	1964	6.25	12.50	25.00

—Possible Rolling Stones involvement on instrumental B-side; "Jaggered" refers to Mick

PHILLES/COLLECTABLES
| ❏ 3200 | He's a Rebel/He Hit Me (And It Felt like a Kiss) | 1985 | — | 3.00 | 6.00 |

—Red vinyl; part of box set "Phil Spector Wall of Sound Series Vol. 2"
| ❏ 3200 | He's a Rebel/He Hit Me (And It Felt like a Kiss) | 1986 | — | 2.50 | 5.00 |

—Black vinyl
| ❏ 3201 | Then He Kissed Me/Puddin' and Tain | 1985 | — | 3.00 | 6.00 |

—Red vinyl; part of box set "Phil Spector Wall of Sound Series Vol. 2"; B-side by the Alley Cats
| ❏ 3201 | Then He Kissed Me/Puddin' and Tain | 1986 | — | 2.50 | 5.00 |

—Black vinyl
| ❏ 3202 | Uptown/He's Sure the Boy I Love | 1985 | — | 3.00 | 6.00 |

—Red vinyl; part of box set "Phil Spector Wall of Sound Series Vol. 2"
| ❏ 3202 | Uptown/He's Sure the Boy I Love | 1986 | — | 2.50 | 5.00 |

—Black vinyl
| ❏ 3204 | There's No Other (Like My Baby)/Not Too Young to Get Married | 1985 | — | 3.00 | 6.00 |

—Gold vinyl; part of box set "Phil Spector Wall of Sound Series Vol. 1"; B-side by Bob B. Soxx and the Blue Jeans
| ❏ 3204 | There's No Other (Like My Baby)/Not Too Young to Get Married | 1986 | — | 2.50 | 5.00 |

—Black vinyl; B-side by Bob B. Soxx and the Blue Jeans
| ❏ 3206 | Da Doo Ron Ron/All Grown Up | 1985 | — | 3.00 | 6.00 |

—Gold vinyl; part of box set "Phil Spector Wall of Sound Series Vol. 1"
| ❏ 3206 | Da Doo Ron Ron/All Grown Up | 1986 | — | 2.50 | 5.00 |

—Black vinyl

UNITED ARTISTS
| ❏ 927 | You Can't Tie a Good Girl Down/My Place | 1965 | 3.75 | 7.50 | 15.00 |
| ❏ 994 | I Got a Man/Are You Trying to Get Rid of Me, Baby | 1966 | 3.75 | 7.50 | 15.00 |

Albums
PHILLES
❏ PHLP-4000 [M]	Twist Uptown	1962	150.00	300.00	600.00
❏ PHLP-4001 [M]	He's a Rebel	1963	150.00	300.00	600.00
❏ PHLP-4003 [M]	The Crystals Sing the Greatest Hits, Vol. 1	1963	150.00	300.00	600.00
❏ DT-90722 [R]	Twist Uptown	1965	300.00	600.00	1200.

—Capitol Record Club edition
| ❏ T-90722 [M] | Twist Uptown | 1965 | 150.00 | 300.00 | 600.00 |

—Capitol Record Club edition

CRYSTALS, THE (2)
45s
ALADDIN
| ❏ 3355 | I Love My Baby/I Do Believe | 1957 | 15.00 | 30.00 | 60.00 |

CRYSTALS, THE (3)
45s
BRENT
| ❏ 7011 | Malaguena/Gypsy Ribbon | 1960 | 3.75 | 7.50 | 15.00 |

CUB
| ❏ 9064 | Oh My You/Watching You | 1960 | 3.75 | 7.50 | 15.00 |

INDIGO
| ❏ 114 | Dreams and Wishes/Mr. Brush | 1961 | 5.00 | 10.00 | 20.00 |

METRO
| ❏ 20026 | Better Come Back to Me/That's Where I Belong | 1960 | 3.75 | 7.50 | 15.00 |

REGALIA
| ❏ 17 | Pony in Dixie/Espresso | 1961 | 3.75 | 7.50 | 15.00 |

CRYSTALS, THE (4)
45s
DELUXE
❏ 6013	Four Women/My Dear	1953	500.00	1000.	2000.
❏ 6037	Have Faith in Me/My Love	1954	500.00	1000.	2000.
❏ 6077	God Only Knows/My Girl	1955	50.00	100.00	200.00

LUNA
| ❏ 100 | Squeeze Me Baby/Come to Me, Darling | 1954 | 100.00 | 200.00 | 400.00 |
| ❏ 5001 | Squeeze Me Baby/Come to Me, Darling | 1954 | 50.00 | 100.00 | 200.00 |

ROCKIN'
| ❏ 518 | My Girl/Don't You Go | 1953 | 62.50 | 125.00 | 250.00 |

CRYSTALS, THE (5)
45s
FELSTED
| ❏ 8566 | Mary Ellen/Blind Date | 1959 | 5.00 | 10.00 | 20.00 |

MERCURY
| ❏ 71381 | Vampire/Tropical Illusion | 1958 | 3.75 | 7.50 | 15.00 |

SPECIALTY
| ❏ 657 | In the Deep/Love You So | 1959 | 3.75 | 7.50 | 15.00 |

CUFF LINKS, THE (2)
Black vocal group.
45s
DOOTO
❏ 409	Guided Missiles/My Heart	1957	20.00	40.00	80.00
❏ 413	How You Lied/The Winner	1957	10.00	20.00	40.00
❏ 414	Twinkle/One Day Blues	1957	10.00	20.00	40.00
❏ 422	It's Too Late Now/Saxophone Rag	1957	12.50	25.00	50.00
❏ 474	Changing My Love/I Don't Want Nobody	1963	6.25	12.50	25.00

DOOTONE
| ❏ 409 | Guided Missiles/My Heart | 1956 | 50.00 | 100.00 | 200.00 |

CYMANDE
45s
JANUS
❏ 203	The Message/Zion I	1972	—	2.50	5.00
❏ 215	Bra/Ras Tafarian Folk Song	1973	—	2.50	5.00
❏ 225	Anthracite/Fug	1973	—	2.50	5.00

Albums
JANUS
| ❏ 3044 | Cymande | 1972 | 2.50 | 5.00 | 10.00 |
| ❏ 3054 | Second Time Round | 1973 | 2.50 | 5.00 | 10.00 |

CYMONE, ANDRE
12-Inch Singles
COLUMBIA
❏ 44-03059	Livin' in the New Wave (same on both sides)	1982	2.00	4.00	8.00
❏ 44-04065	Make Me Wanna Dance (Vocal 4:49) (Instrumental 4:49)	1983	2.50	5.00	10.00
❏ 44-04958	Survivin' in the 80's (2 versions)	1984	2.00	4.00	8.00
❏ 44-05249	The Dance Electric (2 versions)/Red Light	1985	2.00	4.00	8.00
❏ 44-05315	Lipstick Lover (Radio Version) (Club Version)	1985	2.50	5.00	10.00
❏ 44-05335	Satisfaction (Extended Dance Remix 5:54) (Dub Mix) (Edited Version)	1986	2.00	4.00	8.00

45s
COLUMBIA
❏ 18-03037	Livin' in the New Wave/Nite Club	1982	—	2.00	4.00
❏ 38-03301	Kelly's Eyes/Baby Don't Go	1982	—	2.00	4.00
❏ 38-04066	Make Me Wanna Dance/(Instrumental)	1983	—	2.00	4.00
❏ 38-04066 [PS]	Make Me Wanna Dance/(Instrumental)	1983	—	2.00	4.00
❏ 38-04316	Survivin' in the 80's/What Are We Doing Here	1984	—	2.00	4.00
❏ 38-05435	The Dance Electric/Red Light	1985	—	2.00	4.00
❏ 38-05435 [PS]	The Dance Electric/Red Light	1985	—	2.00	4.00
❏ 38-05710	Lipstick Lover/(Instrumental)	1985	—	2.00	4.00
❏ 38-05743	Fallin' Fallin'/Lipstick Lover	1986	—	2.50	5.00
❏ 38-05787	Satisfaction/Vacation	1986	—	2.00	4.00

Albums
COLUMBIA
❏ FC 38123	Livin' in the New Wave	1982	2.50	5.00	10.00
❏ FC 38902	Survivin' in the 80's	1983	2.50	5.00	10.00
❏ FC 40037	A.C.	1985	2.50	5.00	10.00

Here is the Coasters' first Atco EP, which collects both sides of a couple early singles. As with most R&B-related EPs, this is worth far more than those two singles.

Cozy Cole, more of a jazz drummer than an R&B cat, nonetheless had the huge 1958 hit "Topsy II" on both the R&B and pop charts. This was his sole LP for the King label.

Best known for "Do You Love Me," the Contours had charted hits as late as 1967. The album with their big hit, though, is their most sought-after on the original Gordy label.

Before hitting it big with "16 Candles," the Crests issued two singles on the Joyce label. This is the second of the two, "No One to Love." Notice the large "Y" in the "Joyce" insignia at the top of the label.

Arthur "Big Boy" Crudup is best known as the originator of "That's All Right," the song that was Elvis Presley's first released recording for Sun. Much later, in 1960, this rare album was issued on the Fire label.

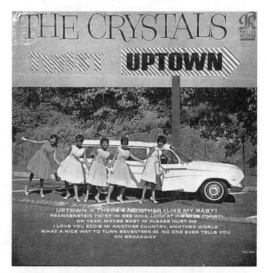

Another rare Philles album is *Twist Uptown,* the first collection by the Crystals. In fact, it was the first album released on the label, in 1962.

D

D'ANGELO

12-Inch Singles

VIRGIN

Number	Title (A Side/B Side)	Yr	VG	VG+	NM
❑ 38678	Left & Right (Radio Edit) (Explicit Edit) (Instrumental)//Untitled (How Does It Feel)/Left & Right (Album Version) (A Cappella)	1999	3.00	6.00	12.00

45s

EMI

Number	Title (A Side/B Side)	Yr	VG	VG+	NM
❑ S7-19019	Lady/(Remix with Az)	1996	—	2.00	4.00
❑ S7-19170	Me and Those Dreamin' Eyes of Mine/Brown Sugar	1996	—	2.00	4.00

VIRGIN

Number	Title (A Side/B Side)	Yr	VG	VG+	NM
❑ 58836	Untitled (How Does It Feel)/Left & Right (Feat. Method Man and Redman)	2000	—	—	3.00
❑ 58864	Send It On/The Line	2000	—	—	3.00

Albums

VIRGIN

Number	Title (A Side/B Side)	Yr	VG	VG+	NM
❑ SPRO 14969 [DJ]	Voodoo DJ Soul Essentials	2000	5.00	10.00	20.00

—Six-song promo-only sampler

Number	Title (A Side/B Side)	Yr	VG	VG+	NM
❑ 48499 [(2)]	Voodoo	2000	3.75	7.50	15.00

D'ARBY, TERENCE TRENT

12-Inch Singles

COLUMBIA

Number	Title (A Side/B Side)	Yr	VG	VG+	NM
❑ CAS 01070 [DJ]	Under My Thumb (Live) (same on both sides)	198?	5.00	10.00	20.00

—May only exist as a test pressing

Number	Title (A Side/B Side)	Yr	VG	VG+	NM
❑ CAS 1141 [DJ]	Sign Your Name (12" Remix)/(LP Version)	1988	2.00	4.00	8.00
❑ CAS 01181 [DJ]	Sign Your Name (Lee Perry Remix) (same on both sides?)	1987	3.00	6.00	12.00

—Advance pressing, no label name on label

Number	Title (A Side/B Side)	Yr	VG	VG+	NM
❑ CAS 1337 [DJ]	Dance Little Sister/If You All Get to Heaven	1988	2.00	4.00	8.00
❑ CAS 2855 [DJ]	If You Let Me Stay (Shep Pettibone Mix) (Dub) (Voice Version) (Radio Edit)	1987	2.00	4.00	8.00
❑ CAS 02888 [DJ]	Wishing Well (LP Version)/(Cool in the Shade Mix)	1987	2.00	4.00	8.00
❑ 44-07450	If You Let Me Stay (2 versions)/Loving You Is Another Word for Lonely	1987	2.00	4.00	8.00
❑ 44-07543	Wishing Well (Cool in the Shade Mix)/(What a) Wonderful World/Elevators and Hearts	1987	2.00	4.00	8.00
❑ 44-07877	Sign Your Name (12" Extended Remix) (Lee "Scratch" Perry Remix)	1988	2.50	5.00	10.00
❑ 44-07887	Dance Little Sister (12" Remix) (7" Single Edit) (Extended Remix)	1988	2.00	4.00	8.00
❑ 44-74949	Do You Love Me Like You Say? (5 versions)	1993	2.00	4.00	8.00

45s

COLUMBIA

Number	Title (A Side/B Side)	Yr	VG	VG+	NM
❑ 38-07398	If You Let Me Stay/Loving You Is Another Word for Lonely	1987	—	—	3.00
❑ 38-07398 [PS]	If You Let Me Stay/Loving You Is Another Word for Lonely	1987	—	—	3.00
❑ 38-07675	Wishing Well/Elevators and Hearts	1988	—	—	3.00
❑ 38-07675 [PS]	Wishing Well/Elevators and Hearts	1988	—	—	3.00
❑ 38-07911	Sign Your Name/Greasy Chicken	1988	—	—	3.00
❑ 38-07911 [PS]	Sign Your Name/Greasy Chicken	1988	—	—	3.00
❑ 38-08023	Dance Little Sister (Part One)/(Part Two)	1988	—	—	3.00
❑ 38-08023 [PS]	Dance Little Sister (Part One)/(Part Two)	1988	—	—	3.00
❑ 38-73074	This Side of Love/Sad Song for Sister Sarah Serenade	1989	—	3.00	6.00

Albums

COLUMBIA

Number	Title (A Side/B Side)	Yr	VG	VG+	NM
❑ BFC 40964	Introducing the Hardline According to Terence Trent D'Arby	1987	3.00	6.00	12.00
❑ C 45351	Neither Fish Nor Flesh	1989	2.50	5.00	10.00

DALE

12-Inch Singles

PAISLEY PARK

Number	Title (A Side/B Side)	Yr	VG	VG+	NM
❑ 20818	Simon Simon (Extended)/Simon Simon (Dub)/ The Perfect Stranger	1988	2.00	4.00	8.00

45s

PAISLEY PARK

Number	Title (A Side/B Side)	Yr	VG	VG+	NM
❑ 27731	Riot in English (Edit)/(LP Version)	1988	—	—	3.00
❑ 28142	Simon Simon/The Perfect Stranger	1987	—	—	3.00
❑ 28142 [PS]	Simon Simon/The Perfect Stranger	1987	—	2.00	4.00

Albums

PAISLEY PARK

Number	Title (A Side/B Side)	Yr	VG	VG+	NM
❑ 25577	Riot in English	1988	2.50	5.00	10.00

DAMITA JO

Also see BROOK BENTON AND DAMITA JO.

45s

ABC-PARAMOUNT

Number	Title (A Side/B Side)	Yr	VG	VG+	NM
❑ 9822	How Will I Know/I'll Never Cry	1957	3.75	7.50	15.00
❑ 9849	My Heart Is Home/Disillusioned Lovers	1957	3.75	7.50	15.00
❑ 10176	How Will I Know/Disillusioned Lovers	1961	2.50	5.00	10.00

BANG BANG

Number	Title (A Side/B Side)	Yr	VG	VG+	NM
❑ 4105	Why Love a Stranger/Whoa Now Boy	196?	3.00	6.00	12.00

EPIC

Number	Title (A Side/B Side)	Yr	VG	VG+	NM
❑ 9766	Tomorrow Night/Silver Dollar	1965	2.00	4.00	8.00
❑ 9797	Gotta Travel On/Something You Got	1965	2.00	4.00	8.00
❑ 9821	Nobody Knows You When You're Down and Out/ Whispering Grass (Don't Tell the Trees)	1965	2.00	4.00	8.00
❑ 9860	Sweet Pussycat/Who Could Ask for More	1965	2.00	4.00	8.00
❑ 9887	That Special Way/Tossin' and Turnin'	1966	2.00	4.00	8.00
❑ 10061	If You Go Away/When the Fog Rolls In to San Francisco	1966	2.00	4.00	8.00
❑ 10061 [DJ]	If You Go Away (same on both sides)	1966	5.00	10.00	20.00

—Promo only on yellow vinyl

Number	Title (A Side/B Side)	Yr	VG	VG+	NM
❑ 10176	No Guilty Feelings/Yellow Days	1967	2.00	4.00	8.00
❑ 10235	Dinner For One/Please, James	1967	2.00	4.00	8.00

MERCURY

Number	Title (A Side/B Side)	Yr	VG	VG+	NM
❑ 71493	The Dance Was Over/Look at Yourself	1959	3.00	6.00	12.00
❑ 71568	What Would You Do/Widow Talk	1960	3.00	6.00	12.00
❑ 71608	Little Things Mean a Lot/I Burned Your Letter	1960	3.00	6.00	12.00
❑ 71690	I'll Save the Last Dance for You/Forgive	1960	3.75	7.50	15.00
❑ 71760	Keep Your Hands Off of Him/Hush, Somebody's Calling My Name	1961	3.00	6.00	12.00
❑ 71793	Sweet Georgia Brown/Do What You Want	1961	3.00	6.00	12.00
❑ 71840	I'll Be There/Love Laid Its Hands on Me	1962	3.75	7.50	15.00
❑ 71840 [PS]	I'll Be There/Love Laid Its Hands on Me	1962	6.25	12.50	25.00
❑ 71871	Dance with a Dolly (With a Hole in Her Stocking)/ You're Nobody 'Til Somebody Loves You	1962	3.00	6.00	12.00
❑ 71929	I Didn't Know I Was Crying/I Built My World Around a Dream	1962	3.00	6.00	12.00
❑ 71946	You're Nobody 'Til Somebody Loves You/Joey	1962	3.00	6.00	12.00
❑ 71946 [PS]	You're Nobody 'Til Somebody Loves You/Joey	1962	5.00	10.00	20.00
❑ 71984	Another Dancing Partner/Please Send Me Someone to Love	1962	3.00	6.00	12.00
❑ 72019	The Window Up Above/Tennessee Waltz	1962	3.00	6.00	12.00
❑ 72019 [PS]	The Window Up Above/Tennessee Waltz	1962	5.00	10.00	20.00
❑ 72056	Dance Him By Me/Las Vegas	1962	3.00	6.00	12.00
❑ 72056 [PS]	Dance Him By Me/Las Vegas	1962	5.00	10.00	20.00
❑ 72086	Little Things/Mr. Blues (Found a Home with Me)	1963	2.50	5.00	10.00
❑ 72086 [PS]	Little Things/Mr. Blues (Found a Home with Me)	1963	5.00	10.00	20.00
❑ 72121	Drama of Love/Hobo Flats	1963	2.50	5.00	10.00
❑ 72121 [PS]	Drama of Love/Hobo Flats	1963	6.25	12.50	25.00
❑ 72162	In the Dark/Melancholy Baby	1963	2.50	5.00	10.00

RANWOOD

Number	Title (A Side/B Side)	Yr	VG	VG+	NM
❑ 820	Loving You/Reason to Believe	1968	—	3.00	6.00
❑ 826	Grown-Up Games/Lonely Letters	1968	—	3.00	6.00
❑ 844	Brother Love's Traveling Salvation Show/I'll Save the Last Dance for You	1969	—	3.00	6.00
❑ 857	Lonely Teardrops/Ain't Misbehavin'	1969	—	3.00	6.00
❑ 869	Paint Me Loving You/Tomorrow Is the First Day of the Rest of My Life	1970	—	3.00	6.00
❑ 884	Mrs. Robinson/Two Worlds	1970	—	2.50	5.00
❑ 894	Hallelujah Baby/Two Worlds	1971	—	2.50	5.00

RCA VICTOR

Number	Title (A Side/B Side)	Yr	VG	VG+	NM
❑ 47-4685	Lonesome and Blue/I Need You	1952	3.75	7.50	15.00

—By John Greer, vocals by Damita Jo

Number	Title (A Side/B Side)	Yr	VG	VG+	NM
❑ 47-5022	I'd Do It Again/I Don't Care	1952	3.75	7.50	15.00
❑ 47-5120	Go 'Way From My Window/Let Me Share Your Name	1953	3.75	7.50	15.00
❑ 47-5253	Missing/The Widow Walk	1953	3.75	7.50	15.00
❑ 47-5328	Do Me a Favor/Don't You Care	1953	3.75	7.50	15.00
❑ 47-5570	Face to Face/Sadie Thompson's Song	1953	3.75	7.50	15.00
❑ 47-5987	Win or Lose/My Tzatskele	1955	3.75	7.50	15.00
❑ 47-6096	Feelin' Kinda Happy/Nuff of That Stuff	1955	3.75	7.50	15.00

—B-side by Steve Gibson and His Red Caps

Number	Title (A Side/B Side)	Yr	VG	VG+	NM
❑ 47-6185	In My Heart/Abracadabra	1955	3.75	7.50	15.00
❑ 47-6281	Always/Freehearted	1955	3.75	7.50	15.00

VEE JAY

Number	Title (A Side/B Side)	Yr	VG	VG+	NM
❑ 661	I'm Waiting for Ships That Never Come In/Hurt a Fool	1965	2.00	4.00	8.00

Albums

ABC-PARAMOUNT

Number	Title (A Side/B Side)	Yr	VG	VG+	NM
❑ 378 [M]	The Big Fifteen	1961	20.00	40.00	80.00
❑ S-378 [S]	The Big Fifteen	1961	25.00	50.00	100.00

EPIC

Number	Title (A Side/B Side)	Yr	VG	VG+	NM
❑ LN 24131 [M]	This Is Damita Jo	1965	3.75	7.50	15.00
❑ LN 24164 [M]	One More Time with Feeling	1965	3.75	7.50	15.00
❑ LN 24202 [M]	Midnight Session	1966	3.75	7.50	15.00
❑ LN 24244 [M]	If You Go Away	1967	5.00	10.00	20.00
❑ BN 26131 [S]	This Is Damita Jo	1965	5.00	10.00	20.00
❑ BN 26164 [S]	One More Time with Feeling	1965	5.00	10.00	20.00
❑ BN 26202 [S]	Midnight Session	1966	5.00	10.00	20.00
❑ BN 26244 [S]	If You Go Away	1967	3.75	7.50	15.00

MERCURY

Number	Title (A Side/B Side)	Yr	VG	VG+	NM
❑ MG-20642 [M]	I'll Save the Last Dance for You	1961	7.50	15.00	30.00
❑ MG-20703 [M]	Damita Jo Live at the Diplomat	1962	6.25	12.50	25.00
❑ MG-20734 [M]	Sing a Country Song	1962	6.25	12.50	25.00
❑ MG-20818 [M]	This One's for Me	1963	5.00	10.00	20.00
❑ SR-60642 [S]	I'll Save the Last Dance for You	1961	10.00	20.00	40.00
❑ SR-60703 [S]	Damita Jo Live at the Diplomat	1962	7.50	15.00	30.00
❑ SR-60734 [S]	Sing a Country Song	1962	7.50	15.00	30.00
❑ SR-60818 [S]	This One's for Me	1963	6.25	12.50	25.00

RANWOOD

Number	Title (A Side/B Side)	Yr	VG	VG+	NM
❑ RLP.8037	Miss Damita Jo	1968	3.75	7.50	15.00

RCA CAMDEN

Number	Title (A Side/B Side)	Yr	VG	VG+	NM
❑ CAL-900 [M]	Go Go with Damita Jo	196?	3.75	7.50	15.00
❑ CAS-900(e) [R]	Go Go with Damita Jo	196?	3.00	6.00	12.00

SUNSET

Number	Title (A Side/B Side)	Yr	VG	VG+	NM
❑ SUS-5198	The Irresistible Damita Jo	1968	3.00	6.00	12.00

Number	Title (A Side/B Side)	Yr	VG	VG+	NM
VEE JAY					
❏ LP-1137 [M]	Damita Jo Sings	1965	6.25	12.50	25.00
❏ LPS-1137 [S]	Damita Jo Sings	1965	12.50	25.00	50.00
WING					
❏ WC-16333	This One's for Me	196?	3.00	6.00	12.00

DANLEERS, THE
45s
AMP 3

❏ 2115	One Summer Night/Wheelin' and Dealin'	1958	50.00	100.00	200.00
—By "Dandleers"					
❏ 2115	One Summer Night/Wheelin' and Dealin'	1958	10.00	20.00	40.00
—Corrected group name on label					
EPIC					
❏ 9367	I Live Half a Block from an Angel/If You Don't Care	1960	7.50	15.00	30.00
❏ 9421	I'll Always Be in Love with You/Little Lover	1960	7.50	15.00	30.00
EVEREST					
❏ 19412	Foolish/I'm Looking Around	1961	7.50	15.00	30.00
LEMANS					
❏ 004	The Truth Hurts/Baby You've Got It	1963	2.50	5.00	10.00
❏ 008	I'm Sorry/This Thing Called Love	1963	2.50	5.00	10.00
MERCURY					
❏ 71322	One Summer Night/Wheelin' and a-Dealin'	1958	5.00	10.00	20.00
❏ 71356	I Really Love You/My Flaming Heart	1958	5.00	10.00	20.00
❏ 71401	A Picture of You/Prelude to Love	1959	5.00	10.00	20.00
❏ 71441	I Can't Sleep/Your Love	1959	5.00	10.00	20.00
SMASH					
❏ 1872	Were You There/If	1964	3.00	6.00	12.00
❏ 1895	Where Is Love/The Angels Sent You	1964	3.00	6.00	12.00

DANTE
45s
A&M

❏ 788	Speedoo/Sweet Lover	1966	2.50	5.00	10.00
DARROW					
❏ 515	How Much I Care/Baby Baby	1960	10.00	20.00	40.00
DECCA					
❏ 31178	If You Don't Know/Leave Your Tears Behind You	1960	3.75	7.50	15.00
❏ 31268	Bye Bye Baby/That's Why	1961	3.75	7.50	15.00
❏ 31319	Ring or Write or Call/Say It to Me	1961	3.75	7.50	15.00
IMPERIAL					
❏ 5798	Something Happens/Are You Just My Friend	1961	3.75	7.50	15.00
❏ 5827	Miss America/Now I've Got You	1962	3.75	7.50	15.00
❏ 5867	Magic Ring/Am I the One	1962	3.75	7.50	15.00
—Imperial titles as "Dante and His Friends"					
MADISON					
❏ 130	Alley Oop/The Right Time	1960	5.00	10.00	20.00
—As "Dante and the Evergreens"					
❏ 135	Time Machine/Dream Land	1960	3.75	7.50	15.00
❏ 143	What Are You Doing New Year's Eve/Yeah Baby	1960	3.75	7.50	15.00
—As "Dante and the Evergreens"					
❏ 154	Think Sweet Thoughts/Da Doo	1961	3.75	7.50	15.00
MERCURY					
❏ 71621	How Much I Care/Baby Baby	1960	5.00	10.00	20.00
TIDE					
❏ 003	My Lament/Aching Heart	1960	5.00	10.00	20.00

DAPPS, THE
Also see HANK BALLARD.
45s
KING

❏ 6087	It's a Gas (Part 1)/It's a Gas (Part 2)	1967	5.00	10.00	20.00
❏ 6147	Bringing Up the Guitar/Gittin' a Little Hipper	1968	5.00	10.00	20.00
❏ 6201	I'll Be Sweeter Tomorrow/A Woman, a Lover, a Friend	1968	5.00	10.00	20.00

DAVIS, ANDREA
See MINNIE RIPERTON.

DAVIS, BILLY, JR.
Also see THE FIFTH DIMENSION; MARILYN McCOO AND BILLY DAVIS, JR.
45s
ABC

❏ 12106	Three Steps from True Love/Light a Candle	1975	—	2.50	5.00

DAVIS, TYRONE
45s
ABC

❏ 11030	Bet You Win/What If a Man	1967	3.00	6.00	12.00
COLUMBIA					
❏ 02269	Just My Luck/Let's Be Closer Together	1981	—	2.00	4.00
❏ 02634	Leave Well Enough Alone/I Won't Let Go	1981	—	2.00	4.00
❏ 10388	Give It Up (Turn It Loose)/You're Too Much	1976	—	2.50	5.00
❏ 10457	Close to You/Wrong Doers	1976	—	2.50	5.00
❏ 10528	This I Swear/Givin' Myself to You	1977	—	2.50	5.00
❏ 10604	All You Got/I Got Carried Away	1977	—	2.50	5.00
❏ 10684	Get It Up (Disco)/It's You, It's You	1978	—	2.50	5.00
❏ 10773	Can't Help But Say/Bunky	1978	—	2.00	4.00
❏ 10904	In the Mood/I Can't Wait	1979	—	2.00	4.00
❏ 11035	Ain't Nothing I Can Do/The Love I Need	1979	—	2.00	4.00
❏ 11128	Be With Me/Love You Forever	1979	—	2.00	4.00
❏ 11199	Can't You Tell It's Me/I Don't Think You Heard Me	1980	—	2.00	4.00
❏ 11246	Keep On Dancin'/Heart Failure	1980	—	2.00	4.00
❏ 11344	How Sweet It Is (To Be Loved By You)/I Can't Wait	1980	—	2.00	4.00
❏ 11415	I Just Can't Keep On Going/We Don't Need No Music	1980	—	2.00	4.00
DAKAR					
❏ 602	Can I Change My Mind/A Woman Needs to Be Loved	1968	2.50	5.00	10.00
❏ 605	Is It Something You've Got/Undying Love	1969	2.00	4.00	8.00
❏ 609	All the Waiting Is Not in Vain/Need Your Lovin' Everybody	1969	2.00	4.00	8.00
❏ 611	If It's Love That You're After/When I'm Not Around	1969	2.00	4.00	8.00
❏ 615	If I Didn't Love You/You Can't Keep a Good Man Down	1969	2.00	4.00	8.00
❏ 616	Turn Back the Hands of Time/I Keep Coming Back	1970	2.00	4.00	8.00
❏ 618	I'll Be Right Here/Just Because of You	1970	—	3.00	6.00
❏ 621	Let Me Back In/Love Bones	1970	—	3.00	6.00
❏ 623	Could I Forget You/Just My Way of Loving You	1971	—	3.00	6.00
❏ 624	One-Way Ticket/We Got a Love	1971	—	3.00	6.00
❏ 626	You Keep Me Holding On/We Got a Love No One Can Deny	1971	—	3.00	6.00
❏ 1452	Can I Change My Mind/A Woman Needs to Be Loved	1968	3.00	6.00	12.00
❏ 4501	I Had It All the Time/You Wouldn't Believe	1972	—	2.50	5.00
❏ 4507	Was I Just a Fool/After All This Time	1972	—	2.50	5.00
❏ 4510	Come and Get This Ring/After All This Time	1972	—	2.50	5.00
❏ 4513	If You Had a Change in Mind/Was It Just a Feelin'	1972	—	2.50	5.00
❏ 4519	Without You in My Life/How Could I Forget You	1973	—	2.50	5.00
❏ 4523	There It Is/You Wouldn't Believe	1973	—	2.50	5.00
❏ 4526	Wrapped Up in Your Warm and Tender Love/True Love Is Hard to Find	1973	—	2.50	5.00
❏ 4529	I Wish It Was Me/You Don't Have to Beg Me to Stay	1974	—	2.50	5.00
❏ 4532	What Goes Up (Must Come Down)/There's Got to Be an Answer	1974	—	2.50	5.00
❏ 4536	Happiness Is Being with You/Where Lovers Meet	1974	—	2.50	5.00
❏ 4538	I Can't Make It Without You/You Wouldn't Believe	1974	—	2.50	5.00
❏ 4541	Homewreckers/This Time	1975	—	2.50	5.00
❏ 4545	A Woman Needs to Be Loved/Just Because of You (I Can See My Way Through)	1975	—	2.50	5.00
❏ 4550	Turning Point/Don't Let It Be Too Late	1975	—	2.50	5.00
❏ 4553	So Good (To Be Home with You)/I Can't Bump	1976	—	2.50	5.00
❏ 4558	I Can't Bump, Part 2/Saving My Love for You	1976	—	2.50	5.00
❏ 4561	Ever Lovin' Girl/Forever	1976	—	2.50	5.00
❏ 4563	Where Lovers Meet (At the Dark End of the Street)/It's All in the Game	1977	—	2.50	5.00
FUTURE					
❏ 101	Sexy Thing/Save Me	1987	—	2.50	5.00
❏ 102	I'm in Love Again/Serious Love	1987	—	2.00	4.00
❏ 103	Do You Feel It/(Instrumental)	1988	—	2.00	4.00
❏ 104	It's a Miracle/Wrong Doers	1988	—	2.00	4.00
❏ 204	Flashin' Back/Flashin' Back (LP Version)	1988	—	2.00	4.00
HIGHRISE					
❏ 2005	Are You Serious/Overdrive	1982	—	2.00	4.00
❏ 2009	A Little Bit of Loving (Goes a Long Way)/Where Did We Lose	1983	—	2.00	4.00
ICHIBAN					
❏ 139	Can I Change My Mind/Hey There Lonely Girl	1989	—	2.00	4.00
—B-side by Eddie Holman					
❏ 226	I'll Always Love You/Can I Change My Mind	1991	—	—	3.00
❏ 237	Mom's Apple Pie/Do U Still Love Me	1991	—	—	3.00
❏ 255	Something's Mighty Wrong/Let Me Love You	1992	—	—	3.00
❏ 261	Running In and Out of My Life/I've Gotta Get Over You	1992	—	—	3.00
❏ 273	Don't Make Me Choose/Ain't Gonna Get It	1992	—	—	3.00
❏ 285	It's a Miracle/Do You Feel It	1993	—	—	3.00
❏ 292	I Found Myself When I Lost You/Something About a Woman	1993	—	—	3.00
OCEAN-FRONT					
❏ 2001	I Found Myself When I Lost You/(Instrumental)	1983	—	2.00	4.00
❏ 2004	Let Me Be Your Pacifier/Turning Point	1984	—	2.00	4.00

Albums
COLUMBIA

❏ PC 34268	Love and Touch	1976	3.00	6.00	12.00
❏ PC 34654	Let's Be Closer Together	1977	3.00	6.00	12.00
❏ JC 35305	I Can't Go On This Way	1978	3.00	6.00	12.00
❏ JC 35723	In the Mood with Tyrone Davis	1979	3.00	6.00	12.00
❏ JC 36230	Can't You Tell It's Me	1979	3.00	6.00	12.00
❏ JC 36598	I Just Can't Keep On Going	1980	3.00	6.00	12.00
❏ FC 37366	Everything in Place	1981	3.00	6.00	12.00
❏ PC 37979	The Best of Tyrone Davis	1982	2.50	5.00	10.00
DAKAR					
❏ DK-9005	Can I Change My Mind	1969	7.50	15.00	30.00
❏ DK-9027	Turn Back the Hands of Time	1970	7.50	15.00	30.00
❏ DK-76901	I Had It All the Time	1972	7.50	15.00	30.00
❏ DK-76902	Tyrone Davis' Greatest Hits	1972	6.25	12.50	25.00
❏ DK-76904	Without You in My Life	1973	6.25	12.50	25.00
❏ DK-76909	It's All in the Game	1974	5.00	10.00	20.00
❏ DK-76915	Homewrecker	1975	5.00	10.00	20.00
❏ DK-76918	Turning Point	1976	5.00	10.00	20.00
EPIC					
❏ PE 38626	Tyrone Davis' Greatest Hits	1983	2.00	4.00	8.00
HIGHRISE					
❏ 103	Tyrone Davis	1982	2.50	5.00	10.00
ICHIBAN					
❏ ICH 1103	I'll Always Love You	1991	3.00	6.00	12.00

Number	Title (A Side/B Side)	Yr	VG	VG+	NM

DAWN (3)
Said to be THE FIVE DISCS in disguise.

45s

LAURIE

| ❏ 3388 | I'm Afraid They're All Talking About Me/Lovers' Melody | 1967 | 3.00 | 6.00 | 12.00 |
| ❏ 3417 | Sandy/For the Love of Money | 1968 | 3.00 | 6.00 | 12.00 |

RUST

| ❏ 5128 | Baby I Love You/Bring It On Home | 1968 | 3.00 | 6.00 | 12.00 |

DAY, BOBBY

45s

CASH

| ❏ 1031 | The Truth Hurts/Let's Live Together As One | 1956 | 25.00 | 50.00 | 100.00 |

—As "Bobby Byrd and the Birds"

CLASS

❏ 207	Come Seven/So Long Baby	1957	5.00	10.00	20.00
❏ 211	Little Bitty Pretty One/When the Swallows Come Back to Capistrano	1957	6.25	12.50	25.00
❏ 215	Beep-Beep-Beep/Darling, If I Had You	1957	5.00	10.00	20.00
❏ 225	Little Turtle Dove/Saving My Life for You	1958	5.00	10.00	20.00
❏ 229	Rock-N Robin/Over and Over	1958	7.50	15.00	30.00
❏ 241	The Bluebird, the Buzzard, and the Oriole/Alone Too Long	1959	5.00	10.00	20.00
❏ 245	That's All I Want/Say Yes	1959	3.75	7.50	15.00
❏ 252	Mr. and Mrs. Rock & Roll/Gotta New Girl	1959	3.75	7.50	15.00
❏ 255	Ain't Gonna Cry No More/Love Is a One-Time Affair	1959	3.75	7.50	15.00
❏ 257	Unchained Melody/Three Young Rebs from Georgia	1959	3.75	7.50	15.00
❏ 263	My Blue Heaven/I Don't Want To	1960	3.75	7.50	15.00
❏ 705	Don't Leave Me Hangin' on a String/When I Started Dancin'	1965	3.00	6.00	12.00

CORVET

| ❏ 1017 | Why/Gotta Girl | 1958 | 15.00 | 30.00 | 60.00 |

—As "Bobby Byrd and the Impalas"

JAMIE

| ❏ 1039 | Bippin' and Boppin' Over You/Strawberry Stomp | 1957 | 7.50 | 15.00 | 30.00 |

—As "Robert Byrd and His Birdies"

RCA VICTOR

❏ 47-8133	Another Country, Another World/Know-It-All	1963	2.50	5.00	10.00
❏ 47-8196	Buzz Buzz Buzz/Pretty Little Girl Next Door	1963	2.50	5.00	10.00
❏ 47-8230	Down on My Knees/Jole Blon, Little Darling	1963	2.50	5.00	10.00
❏ 47-8316	When I See My Baby Smile/On the Street Where You Live	1964	2.50	5.00	10.00

RENDEZVOUS

❏ 130	Teenage Philosopher/Undecided	1960	3.00	6.00	12.00
❏ 133	Rockin' Robin/Over and Over	1960	3.00	6.00	12.00
❏ 136	Gee Whiz/Over and Over	1960	3.00	6.00	12.00
❏ 146	I Need Help/Life Can Be Beautiful	1961	3.00	6.00	12.00
❏ 158	King's Highway/What Fools We Mortals Be	1961	3.00	6.00	12.00
❏ 167	Don't Worry 'Bout Me/Oop-E-Du-Pers Ball	1962	3.00	6.00	12.00
❏ 175	Undecided/Slow Pokey Joe	1962	3.00	6.00	12.00

SAGE AND SAND

| ❏ 203 | Please Don't Hurt Me/Delicious Are Your Kisses | 1955 | 10.00 | 20.00 | 40.00 |

—As "Bobby Byrd"

SPARK

| ❏ 501 | Bippin' and Boppin' Over You/Strawberry Stomp | 1957 | 12.50 | 25.00 | 50.00 |

—As "Robert Byrd and His Birdies"

SURE SHOT

| ❏ 5036 | So Lonely/Spicks and Specks | 1967 | 2.00 | 4.00 | 8.00 |

ZEPHYR

| ❏ 70-018 | If We Should Meet Again/Looby Loo | 1957 | 7.50 | 15.00 | 30.00 |

—As "Bobby Byrd"

Albums

CLASS

| ❏ LP-5002 [M] | Rockin' with Robin | 1959 | 100.00 | 200.00 | 400.00 |

COLLECTABLES

| ❏ COL-5074 | Golden Classics | 198? | 2.50 | 5.00 | 10.00 |

RENDEZVOUS

| ❏ M-1312 [M] | Rockin' with Robin | 196? | 20.00 | 40.00 | 80.00 |

RHINO

| ❏ RNDF-208 | The Best of Bobby Day | 1984 | 3.00 | 6.00 | 12.00 |

DAZZ BAND

12-Inch Singles

20TH CENTURY

| ❏ TCD-90 | Keep on Rockin' (6:41)/I Searched Around | 1979 | 2.50 | 5.00 | 10.00 |

GEFFEN

❏ PRO-A-2509 [DJ]	L.O.V.E. M.I.A. (Edit) (LP Version)	1986	2.50	5.00	10.00
❏ 20499	L.O.V.E. M.I.A. (House Mix) (Clubhouse Mix)/A Place in My Heart (Cassette Version)	1986	2.50	5.00	10.00
❏ 20547	Wild and Free (4 versions)/Last Chance for Love	1986	—	3.00	6.00

MOTOWN

| ❏ PR-78 [DJ] | Shake It Up (5:05)//You Like Me Don't You (4:59)/Little Girl Don't You Worry (3:54) | 1980 | 3.75 | 7.50 | 15.00 |

—B-side by Jermaine Jackson

| ❏ PR-104 [DJ] | Keep It Live (On the K.I.L.)/Lil' Suzy | 1982 | 2.50 | 5.00 | 10.00 |

—B-side by Ozone

| ❏ PR-112 [DJ] | On the One for Fun (Vocal 6:37) (Instrumental 6:21) | 1983 | 2.50 | 5.00 | 10.00 |
| ❏ PR-125 [DJ] | Party Right Here (Vocal 5:12) (Instrumental 4:56)/Bad Girl (4:12) | 1983 | — | 3.50 | 7.00 |

❏ PR-141 [DJ]	Swoop (I'm Yours) (8:30)/Joystick (Vocal 6:13)	1984	3.00	6.00	12.00
❏ PR-157 [DJ]	Let It All Blow (Long Version 6:45) (Instrumental 6:45)	1984	—	3.50	7.00
❏ PR-164 [DJ]	Heartbeat (7:03)/Let It All Blow (Special Disco Mix 6:41)	1984	2.50	5.00	10.00
❏ 4503 MG	Let It Whip (Vocal 6:22) (Instrumental 7:00)	1982	3.00	6.00	12.00
❏ 4520 MG	Swoop (I'm Yours) (8:30)/Joystick (Vocal 6:13)	1984	2.00	4.00	8.00
❏ 4524 MG	Let It All Blow (Long Version 6:45) (Instrumental 6:11)	1984	2.50	5.00	10.00
❏ 4543 MG	Hot Spot (Club Mix 6:50)/I've Been Waiting (4:32)	1985	—	3.00	6.00

RCA

| ❏ 6998-1-RD | Anticipation (Club Mix) (Bonus Beats) (Dub)/If It's Love | 1988 | — | 3.00 | 6.00 |
| ❏ 8677-1-RD | Single Girls (Dance Remix 6:59) (Dub Dance Version 6:59) (B-Beats 2:08)/All the Way | 1988 | — | 3.50 | 7.00 |

45s

20TH CENTURY

| ❏ 2390 | I Might As Well Forget About Loving You/Dazzberry Jam | 1978 | — | 2.00 | 4.00 |

—20th Century sides as "Kinsman Dazz"

❏ 2401	Get Down with the Feelin'/Makin' Music	1979	—	2.00	4.00
❏ 2417	Keep On Rockin'/I Searched Around	1979	—	2.00	4.00
❏ 2435	Catchin' Up on Love/I Searched Around	1979	—	2.00	4.00
❏ 2453	Dancin' Free/I Searched Around	1980	—	2.00	4.00

GEFFEN

❏ 28635	L.O.V.E. M.I.A./A Place in My Heart	1986	—	—	3.00
❏ 28658	Wild and Free/Last Chance for Love	1986	—	—	3.00
❏ 28658 [PS]	Wild and Free/Last Chance for Love	1986	—	—	3.00

MOTOWN

❏ 1500	Shake It Up/Only Love	1980	—	2.00	4.00
❏ 1507	Invitation to Love/Magnetized	1981	—	2.00	4.00
❏ 1515	Knock! Knock!/Sooner or Later	1981	—	2.00	4.00
❏ 1528	Hello Girl/Let the Music Play	1981	—	2.00	4.00
❏ 1609	Let It Whip/Everyday Love	1982	—	2.00	4.00
❏ 1622	Keep It Live (On the K.I.L.)/This Time It's Forever	1982	—	2.00	4.00
❏ 1659	On the One for Fun/Just Believe in Love	1983	—	2.00	4.00
❏ 1676	Cheek to Cheek/We Can Dance	1983	—	2.00	4.00
❏ 1680	Party Right Here/Gamble with My Love	1983	—	2.00	4.00
❏ 1701	Joystick/Don't Get Caught in the Middle	1983	—	2.00	4.00
❏ 1725	Swoop (I'm Yours)/Bad Girl	1984	—	2.00	4.00
❏ 1760	Let It All Blow/Now That I Have You	1984	—	2.00	4.00
❏ 1775	Heartbeat/Rock with Me	1985	—	2.00	4.00
❏ 1800	Hot Spot/I've Been Waiting	1985	—	2.00	4.00

RCA

❏ 7614-7-R	Anticipation/If It's Love	1988	—	—	3.00
❏ 8676-7-R	Single Girls/All the Way	1988	—	—	3.00
❏ 8793-7-R	Open Sesame/(Instrumental)	1989	—	—	3.00

Albums

20TH CENTURY

| ❏ T-594 | Kinsman Dazz | 1978 | 3.75 | 7.50 | 15.00 |

—As "Kinsman Dazz"

| ❏ T-594 | Dazz | 1979 | 3.75 | 7.50 | 15.00 |

—As "Kinsman Dazz"

GEFFEN

| ❏ GHS 24110 | Wild and Free | 1986 | 2.00 | 4.00 | 8.00 |

MOTOWN

❏ M8-946M1	Invitation to Love	1980	3.00	6.00	12.00
❏ M8-957M1	Let the Music Play	1981	2.50	5.00	10.00
❏ 5350 ML	Keep It Live	1984	2.00	4.00	8.00

—Reissue of 6004

❏ 5387 ML	Greatest Hits	1986	2.00	4.00	8.00
❏ 6004 ML	Keep It Live	1982	2.50	5.00	10.00
❏ 6031 ML	On the One	1983	2.50	5.00	10.00
❏ 6084 ML	Joystick	1983	2.50	5.00	10.00
❏ 6117 ML	Jukebox	1984	2.50	5.00	10.00
❏ 6149 ML	Hot Spot	1985	2.50	5.00	10.00

RCA

| ❏ 6928-1-R | Rock the Room | 1988 | 2.00 | 4.00 | 8.00 |

DE LA SOUL

12-Inch Singles

TOMMY BOY

❏ TB 500	Millie Pulled a Pistol on Santa (Full Mix)/Keepin' the Faith (Straight Pass) (12" UK Mix) (LP Version)/Millie Pulled a Pistol on Santa (Full Mix Instrumental)/Keepin' the Faith (No Bass Mix) (Straight Pass Instrumental) (7" UK Version)	1991	3.00	6.00	12.00
❏ TB 586	Breakadawn (Vocal Version 4:15)/Stickabush 1:15/En Focus (Vocal 3:15)/The Dawn Brings Smoke (2:11)/Hsubakcits 0:15/En Focus (Instrumental 3:15)Breakadawn (Instrumental 4:15)	1993	2.50	5.00	10.00
❏ TB 595	Ego Trippin' (Part Two) (Original Version 3:52) (LA Jay Remix 4:13) (Gumbo Funk Remix 5:46)/Lovely How I Let My Mind Float (4:02)/Ego Trippin' (Part Three) (Egoristic Mix 4:42)/Ego Trippin' (Part Two) (Original Instrumental 3:52)/Ego Trippin' (Part Three) (Egoristic Instrumental 4:40)	1994	3.00	6.00	12.00
❏ TB 606 [DJ]	Ego Trippin' (Part Two) (4 versions)/Ego Trippin' (Part Three) (2 versions)	1994	5.00	10.00	20.00

—Promo-only version with radio edits

| ❏ TB 730 | Stakes Is High (Album Version) (Instrumental) (Acappella)/The Bizness (Album Version) (Clean Version) (Instrumental) | 1996 | 2.50 | 5.00 | 10.00 |

Number	Title (A Side/B Side)	Yr	VG	VG+	NM
❏ TB 752	Itzsoweezee (Hot) (4 versions)/Stakes Is High (2 versions)	1996	2.50	5.00	10.00
❏ TB 910	Plug Tunin' (Are You Ready for This? 3:41)/ Freedom of Speak (We Got More Than Three Minutes 4:16) (We Got Three Minutes 2:52)/Plug Tunin' (Something's Wrong Here 3:10)/Strictly Dan Stuckie (0:38)	1988	5.00	10.00	20.00
❏ TB 917	Jenifa (Taught Me) (Vocal 3:27)/Skip 2 My Loop (1:09)/Potholes in My Lawn (Vocal 4:13)/They Don't Know That the Soul Don't Go For That ("Potholes" Instrumental) (3:25)/Derwin ("Jenifa" Instrumental) (3:29)	1988	5.00	10.00	20.00
❏ TB 926	Me Myself and I (Radio Mix 3:40)/Ain't Hip to Be Labeled a Hippie (Vocal 1:54)/3:38 Me Myself And I (Instrumental 3:38)/What's More (Vocal 2:10)/Me Myself and I (Oblapos Mode 3:38)/ Brainwashed Follower (Vocal 3:01)/Me Myself and I (Oblapos Instrumental 3:37)	1989	5.00	10.00	20.00
❏ TB 934	Say No Go (Say No Dope Mix 6:09) (New Keys Vocal 4:50) (Radio Mix 3:50)/The Mack Daddy on the Left (3:14)/Say No Go (New Keys Instrumental 5:03)	1989	3.75	7.50	15.00
❏ TB 943	Buddy (Native Tongue Decision 7:17) (Native Tongues Instrumental 7:15)/Ghetto Thang (Vocal 3:35) (Ghetto Ximer 3:45)/Buddy (Vocal 4:56)/Ghetto Thang (Ghetto Ximer Instrumental 3:45)	1989	3.75	7.50	15.00
❏ TB 965	Ring Ring Ring (Ha Ha Hey) (Extended Decision) (Radio Decision) (Piles and Piles of Demo Tapes Bi-Da Miles) (Conley's Decision)/ Afro Connections at a Hi 5 (In the Eyes of the Hoodlum)	1991	3.00	6.00	12.00
❏ TB 990	A Roller Skating Jam Named "Saturdays" (What Yo Life Can Truly Be) (Who's Skating) (Ladies Nite Decision) (LP Version)/(Radio Home Mix) (Dave's Home Mix) (6:00 AM Mix) (Mo Mo Dub)	1991	3.00	6.00	12.00
❏ TB 2116	Oooh (Original Version) (Instrumental)/Words and Verbs	2000	2.50	5.00	10.00
—Featuring Redman					
❏ TB 2178	All Good? (Original Mix) (Ugo + Sanz Chaka's Affair)/(Razor n' Guido Duhb Mix) (MJ Cole Vocal Mix)	2000	2.50	5.00	10.00
—Featuring Chaka Khan					
❏ TB 2339	Baby Phat (3 versions)/Watch Out (3 versions)	2001	2.50	5.00	10.00

45s
TOMMY BOY

Number	Title (A Side/B Side)	Yr	VG	VG+	NM
❏ TB 7910	Plug Tunin'/Freedom of Speak	1988	2.50	5.00	10.00
❏ TB 7917	Jenifa (Taught Me)/Potholes in My Lawn	1988	2.50	5.00	10.00

TOMMY BOY/COLLECTABLES

Number	Title (A Side/B Side)	Yr	VG	VG+	NM
❏ TB 586	Breakadawn/En Focus	1993	—	3.00	6.00

Albums
TOMMY BOY

Number	Title (A Side/B Side)	Yr	VG	VG+	NM
❏ TB 1019	3 Feet High and Rising	1989	5.00	10.00	20.00
—Original edition					
❏ TB 1019 [(2)]	3 Feet High and Rising	2001	3.75	7.50	15.00
—Reissue, expanded to a two-disc set					
❏ TB 1029	De La Soul Is Dead	1991	5.00	10.00	20.00
❏ TB 1041 [(2) DJ]	De La Soul Is Dead	1991	6.25	12.50	25.00
—Promo-only two-record set					
❏ TB 1063 [DJ]	Buhloone Mindstate	1993	6.25	12.50	25.00
—Vinyl appears to be promo only					
❏ TB 1093 [DJ]	Clear Lake Auditorium	1994	6.25	12.50	25.00
—Promo-only on clear vinyl (black vinyl editions are counterfeits)					
❏ TB 1149 [(2)]	Stakes Is High	1996	3.75	7.50	15.00
❏ TB 1175 [DJ]	Stakes Is High Sampler	1996	6.25	12.50	25.00
—Promo only; contains eight songs from the full-length edition					
❏ TB 1361 [(2)]	Art Official Intelligence: Mosaic Thump	2000	3.75	7.50	15.00
❏ TB 1362 [(2)]	AOI: Bionix	2001	3.75	7.50	15.00
❏ TB 1437 [(2)]	Art Official Intelligence: Mosaic Thump Instrumentals	2000	3.75	7.50	15.00
❏ TB 1443 [(2) DJ]	AOI: Bionix//Edited	2001	3.75	7.50	15.00
—Promo-only "clean" version					
❏ TB 1546 [(2)]	AOI: Bionix Instrumentals	2002	3.75	7.50	15.00

DEAN, DEBBIE
45s
MOTOWN

Number	Title (A Side/B Side)	Yr	VG	VG+	NM
❏ 1007	Don't Let Him Shop Around/A New Girl	1961	10.00	20.00	40.00
❏ 1014	Itty, Bitty, Pity Love/But I'm Afraid	1961	7.50	15.00	30.00
❏ 1025	Everybody's Talking About My Baby/I Cried All Night	1962	10.00	20.00	40.00
❏ 1025 [PS]	Everybody's Talking About My Baby/I Cried All Night	1962	20.00	40.00	80.00

V.I.P.

Number	Title (A Side/B Side)	Yr	VG	VG+	NM
❏ 25044	Why Am I Lovin' You/Stay My Love	1967	75.00	150.00	300.00

DEAN AND JEAN
45s
EMBER

Number	Title (A Side/B Side)	Yr	VG	VG+	NM
❏ 1048	We're Gonna Get Married/Too Young to Know	1958	3.00	6.00	12.00
❏ 1054	Turn It Off/Never Let Your Love Fade Away	1959	3.00	6.00	12.00

RUST

Number	Title (A Side/B Side)	Yr	VG	VG+	NM
❏ TR 1	Seven Day Wonder/The Man Who Will Never Grow Old	196?	3.00	6.00	12.00
❏ 5044	Come Take a Walk with Me/Dance the Roach	1962	2.50	5.00	10.00
❏ 5046	Mack the Knife/You Can't Be Happy by Yourself	1962	2.50	5.00	10.00

Number	Title (A Side/B Side)	Yr	VG	VG+	NM
❏ 5067	Tra La La La La Suzy/I Love the Summertime	1963	2.50	5.00	10.00
❏ 5075	Hey Jean, Hey Dean/Please Don't Tell Me Now	1964	3.75	7.50	15.00
❏ 5081	I Wanna Be Loved/Thread Your Needle	1964	2.50	5.00	10.00
❏ 5085	Goddess of Love/The Man Who Will Never Grow Old	1964	2.50	5.00	10.00
❏ 5089	Sticks and Stones/In My Way	1964	2.50	5.00	10.00
❏ 5100	Lovingly Yours/Goddess of Love	1965	2.50	5.00	10.00
❏ 5107	She's Too Respectable/I Love the Summertime	1965	2.50	5.00	10.00

DEBARGE
Also see BUNNY DEBARGE; EL DEBARGE.
12-Inch Singles
GORDY

Number	Title (A Side/B Side)	Yr	VG	VG+	NM
❏ PR-102 [DJ]	Stop! Don't Tease Me (6:01) (3:53)	1982	3.75	7.50	15.00
❏ 4545 GG	You Wear It Well (Club Mix 6:55) (Dub Mix 5:06)/ Baby, Won't Cha Come Quick	1985	—	3.50	7.00
—As "El DeBarge with DeBarge"					
❏ 4552 GG	The Heart Is Not So Smart (Club Mix 6:27) (Radio Edit of Club Mix 3:54) (Dub Mix 6:01)/Share My World	1985	2.00	4.00	8.00
—As "El DeBarge with DeBarge"					

MOTOWN

Number	Title (A Side/B Side)	Yr	VG	VG+	NM
❏ 4532 MG	Rhythm of the Night (Long Version 6:45)/Queen of My Heart	1985	2.00	4.00	8.00

STRIPED HORSE

Number	Title (A Side/B Side)	Yr	VG	VG+	NM
❏ SH 1204	Dance All Night (Radio) (Dance) (Club) (Dub) (Instrumental)	1987	—	3.00	6.00
❏ SH 1207	You Babe (Vocal) (Instrumental)	1987	—	3.00	6.00

45s
GORDY

Number	Title (A Side/B Side)	Yr	VG	VG+	NM
❏ 1635	Stop! Don't Tease Me/Hesitated	1982	—	2.50	5.00
❏ 1645	I Like It/Hesitated	1982	—	2.00	4.00
❏ 1660	All This Love/I'm in Love with You	1983	—	2.00	4.00
❏ 1705	Time Will Reveal/I'll Never Fall in Love Again	1983	—	2.00	4.00
❏ 1723	Love Me in a Special Way/Dance the Night Away	1984	—	2.00	4.00
❏ 1770	Rhythm of the Night/Queen of My Heart	1985	—	—	3.00
❏ 1770 [PS]	Rhythm of the Night/Queen of My Heart	1985	—	2.50	5.00
❏ 1793	Who's Holding Donna Now/Be My Lady	1985	—	—	3.00
❏ 1793 [PS]	Who's Holding Donna Now/Be My Lady	1985	—	2.50	5.00
❏ 1804	You Wear It Well/Baby, Won't Cha Come Quick	1985	—	—	3.00
—As "El DeBarge with DeBarge"					
❏ 1804 [PS]	You Wear It Well/Baby, Won't Cha Come Quick	1985	—	2.00	4.00
—As "El DeBarge with DeBarge"					
❏ 1822	The Heart Is Not So Smart/Share My World	1985	—	—	3.00
—As "El DeBarge with DeBarge"					
❏ 1822 [PS]	The Heart Is Not So Smart/Share My World	1985	—	2.00	4.00
—As "El DeBarge with DeBarge"					
❏ 7198	Dance the Night Away/(B-side unknown)	1981	—	2.50	5.00
❏ 7203	What's Your Name/You're So Gentle, So Kind	1981	—	2.50	5.00

STRIPED HORSE

Number	Title (A Side/B Side)	Yr	VG	VG+	NM
❏ 7004	Dance All Night/(Instrumental)	1987	—	2.50	5.00
❏ 7004 [PS]	Dance All Night/(Instrumental)	1987	—	3.00	6.00
❏ 7007	You Babe/(Instrumental)	1987	—	3.00	6.00

Albums
GORDY

Number	Title (A Side/B Side)	Yr	VG	VG+	NM
❏ G8-1003M1	The DeBarges	1981	3.00	6.00	12.00
❏ 6012 GL	All This Love	1982	2.00	4.00	8.00
❏ 6061 GL	In a Special Way	1983	2.00	4.00	8.00
❏ 6123 GL	Rhythm of the Night	1985	2.00	4.00	8.00

MOTOWN

Number	Title (A Side/B Side)	Yr	VG	VG+	NM
❏ 5335 ML	The DeBarges	1985	2.00	4.00	8.00
—Reissue of Gordy 1003					

STRIPED HORSE

Number	Title (A Side/B Side)	Yr	VG	VG+	NM
❏ SHL 2004	Bad Boys	1987	2.50	5.00	10.00

DEBARGE, BUNNY
Also see DEBARGE.
12-Inch Singles
GORDY

Number	Title (A Side/B Side)	Yr	VG	VG+	NM
❏ 4575 MG	Save the Best for Me (Best of Your Lovin') (12-Inch Mix 6:00) (7-Inch Version 4:01) (Dub 4:40)/ Life Begins with You	1986	5.00	10.00	20.00
—Recalled and replaced with editions on Motown					

MOTOWN

Number	Title (A Side/B Side)	Yr	VG	VG+	NM
❏ 4575 MG	Save the Best for Me (Best of Your Lovin') (12-Inch Mix 6:00) (7-Inch Version 4:01) (Dub 4:40)/ Life Begins with You	1986	—	3.00	6.00

45s
GORDY

Number	Title (A Side/B Side)	Yr	VG	VG+	NM
❏ 1869	Save the Best for Me (Best of Your Lovin')/Life Begins with You	1986	—	—	3.00
❏ 1869 [PS]	Save the Best for Me (Best of Your Lovin')/Life Begins with You	1986	—	—	3.00

Albums
GORDY

Number	Title (A Side/B Side)	Yr	VG	VG+	NM
❏ 6217 GL	In Love	1987	2.00	4.00	8.00

DEBARGE, CHICO
12-Inch Singles
KEDAR

Number	Title (A Side/B Side)	Yr	VG	VG+	NM
❏ U8P-1177 [DJ]	Iggin' Me (Radio Edit) (Clean LP Version) (Instrumental) (TV Track)	1997	2.50	5.00	10.00
❏ U8P-1190 [DJ]	Trouble Man (2 versions)/Physical Train (2 versions)/Superman (2 versions)	1997	2.00	4.00	8.00

Number	Title (A Side/B Side)	Yr	VG	VG+	NM
❑ U8P-1277 [DJ]	No Guarantee (4 versions)	1998	2.00	4.00	8.00
❑ U8P-1381 [DJ]	Virgin (Album Version) (Radio Version) (Instrumental) (Acappella)	1998	2.00	4.00	8.00
MOTOWN					
❑ PR-223 [DJ]	Rainy Night (Gold-N-Boy Mix 5:50) (Rainy Night Music 4:15) (Radio Mix 4:40)/Desperate	1988	2.50	5.00	10.00
❑ U8P-1451 [DJ]	Soopaman Lover (Street) (TV Track) (Clean) (Instrumental)	1999	2.00	4.00	8.00
❑ U8P-1566 [DJ]	Give You What You Want (Fa Sure) (LP Version 4:43) (Instrumental 4:43) (Radio Edit 3:49) (Acappella 4:34)	1999	2.50	5.00	10.00
❑ U8P-1660 [DJ]	The Game (LP Version 4:49) (Clean 3:42)/ (Instrumental 4:49) (Acappella 4:49)	1999	3.00	6.00	12.00
❑ U8P-1671 [DJ]	Listen to Your Man (LP Version) (Radio Instrumental)/(Radio Version) (LP Instrumental)	2000	2.00	4.00	8.00
❑ 4567 MG	Talk to Me (12-Inch Version 7:02)/If It Takes All Night	1986	—	3.00	6.00
❑ 4572 MG	The Girl Next Door (12-Inch Version 7:14) (7-Inch Version 4:08)//(Dub 5:45)/You're Much Too Fast	1987	—	3.00	6.00
❑ 4582 MG	I Like My Body (Extended Version) (Movie Mix) (Dub Mix)/You're Much Too Fast	1986	—	3.50	7.00
❑ 4594 MG	I've Been Watching You (Extended Version 6:10) (Dub Version 3:05) (LP Version 3:32)/If It Takes All Night	1987	2.00	4.00	8.00
❑ 4610 MG	Kiss Serious (4 versions)/Shame, Shame	1988	—	3.00	6.00
❑ 20071 [DJ]	Listen to Your Man (Radio Edit) (LP Version) (Instrumental)/(same on both sides)	2000	2.00	4.00	8.00
❑ 20218 [DJ]	Sorry (LP Version) (Radio Version) (Instrumental) (Acappella)	2000	2.50	5.00	10.00
❑ 56233	Soopaman Lover (Clean) (Instrumental) (LP Version) (TV Track)	1999	2.50	5.00	10.00
❑ 56355	Give You What You Want (Fa Sure) (unknown versions)	1999	2.00	4.00	8.00
❑ 156872	Listen to Your Man (Radio Edit) (LP Version) (Instrumental)/(same on both sides)	2000	—	3.00	6.00
❑ 158524	Playa Hater (Main) (Instrumental) (Acappella)	2000	—	3.50	7.00
45s					
MOTOWN					
❑ 1858	Talk to Me/If It Takes All Night	1986	—	—	3.00
❑ 1858 [PS]	Talk to Me/If It Takes All Night	1986	—	2.00	4.00
❑ 1875	The Girl Next Door/You're Much Too Fast	1987	—	—	3.00
❑ 1875 [PS]	The Girl Next Door/You're Much Too Fast	1987	—	2.00	4.00
❑ 1890	I Like My Body/You're Much Too Fast	1987	—	2.00	4.00
❑ 1909	I've Been Watching You/If It Takes All Night	1987	—	—	3.00
❑ 1909 [PS]	I've Been Watching You/If It Takes All Night	1987	—	—	3.00
❑ 1922	Rainy Night/Desperate	1987	—	—	3.00
❑ 1935	Kiss Serious/Shame, Shame	1988	—	—	3.00
❑ 1935 [PS]	Kiss Serious/Shame, Shame	1988	—	—	3.00
Albums					
KEDAR					
❑ 53088	Long Time No See	1997	3.00	6.00	12.00
MOTOWN					
❑ 6214 ML	Chico DeBarge	1986	2.00	4.00	8.00
❑ 6249 ML	Kiss Serious	1987	2.00	4.00	8.00

DEBARGE, EL

Also see DEBARGE.

Number	Title (A Side/B Side)	Yr	VG	VG+	NM
12-Inch Singles					
GORDY					
❑ PR-183 [DJ]	Who's Johnny ("Short Circuit" Theme) (12-Inch Version 6:24) (Instrumental 4:40)	1986	3.75	7.50	15.00
MOTOWN					
❑ MOT-4618	Real Love (Extended House Mix 9:24) (Dub Version 5:40) (LP Version 4:00) (Bonus Beats) (Radio Edit 4:30)	1989	—	3.50	7.00
❑ MOT-4641	Somebody Loves You (3 versions)	1989	2.50	5.00	10.00
❑ MOT-4670	Broken Dreams (3 versions)	1989	2.00	4.00	8.00
❑ L33-17825 [DJ]	Somebody Loves You (Edit) (LP Version) (Instrumental)	1989	2.50	5.00	10.00
REPRISE					
❑ PRO-A-6960 [DJ]	Slide//Can't Get Enough/Where Is My Love?	1994	2.00	4.00	8.00
WARNER BROS.					
❑ PRO-A-5264 [DJ]	My Heart Belongs to You (Edit) (LP Version)	1992	2.00	4.00	8.00
❑ PRO-A-5460 [DJ]	You Know What I Like (Edit) (LP Version)	1992	2.50	5.00	10.00
❑ PRO-A-5602 [DJ]	Another Chance (Edit) (LP Version)	1992	2.50	5.00	10.00
❑ 40357	My Heart Belongs to You (7 versions)/You Turn Me On	1992	2.50	5.00	10.00
45s					
GORDY					
❑ 1842	Who's Johnny ("Short Circuit" Theme)/Love in a Special Way	1986	—	—	3.00
❑ 1842 [PS]	Who's Johnny ("Short Circuit" Theme)/Love in a Special Way	1986	—	—	3.00
❑ 1857	Love Always/The Walls (Came Tumbling Down)	1986	—	—	3.00
❑ 1857 [PS]	Love Always/The Walls (Came Tumbling Down)	1986	—	—	3.00
❑ 1867	Someone/Stop! Don't Tease Me	1986	—	—	3.00
❑ 1867 [PS]	Someone/Stop! Don't Tease Me	1986	—	—	3.00
MCA					
❑ 53041	Starlight Express/(Instrumental)	1987	—	—	—
MOTOWN					
❑ 1948	Real Love/(House Mix)	1989	—	—	3.00
❑ 1948 [PS]	Real Love/(House Mix)	1989	—	—	3.00
❑ 1966	Somebody Loves You/(Instrumental)	1989	—	—	3.00
❑ 1995	Broken Dreams/(Instrumental)	1989	—	2.00	4.00
REPRISE					
❑ 7-18140	Where Is My Love?/Starlight, Moonlight, Candlelight	1994	—	—	3.00
❑ 7-18155	Can't Get Enough/You to Turn Me On	1994	—	—	3.00
Albums					
GORDY					
❑ 6181 GL	El DeBarge	1986	2.00	4.00	8.00
MOTOWN					
❑ PR-189 [DJ]	El Elaborates!	1986	6.25	12.50	25.00
—Promo-only interview and music album					
❑ MOT-6264	Gemini	1989	2.50	5.00	10.00

DEL VIKINGS, THE

Usually considered to be one group, but actually three: Two of them splintered from the original group, one featuring Kripp Johnson, the other featuring Gus Backus. For convenience's sake, all are listed together.

Number	Title (A Side/B Side)	Yr	VG	VG+	NM
45s					
ABC-PARAMOUNT					
❑ 10208	I'll Never Stop Crying/Bring Back Your Heart	1961	6.25	12.50	25.00
❑ 10248	I Hear Bells (Wedding Bells)/Don't Get Slick on Me	1961	12.50	25.00	50.00
❑ 10278	Kiss Me/Face the Music	1961	6.25	12.50	25.00
❑ 10304	Big Silence/One More River to Cross	1962	6.25	12.50	25.00
❑ 10341	Confession of Love/Kilimanjaro	1962	6.25	12.50	25.00
❑ 10385	An Angel Up in Heaven/Fishing Chant	1962	12.50	25.00	50.00
❑ 10425	Too Many Miles/Sorcerer's Apprentice	1963	6.25	12.50	25.00
ALPINE					
❑ 66	Pistol Packin' Mama/The Sun	1960	20.00	40.00	80.00
❑ 66 [PS]	Pistol Packin' Mama/The Sun	1960	25.00	50.00	100.00
BIM BAM BOOM					
❑ 111	Cold Feet/A Little Man Cried	1972	—	2.50	5.00
❑ 113	Watching the Moon/You Say You Love Me	1972	—	2.50	5.00
❑ 115	I'm Spinning/Girl Girl	1972	—	2.50	5.00
DOT					
❑ 15538	Come Go with Me/How Can I Find True Love	1957	7.50	15.00	30.00
❑ 15571	What Made Maggie Run/Little Billy Boy	1957	7.50	15.00	30.00
❑ 15592	Whispering Bells/Don't Be a Fool	1957	7.50	15.00	30.00
❑ 15636	I'm Spinning/When I Come Home	1957	7.50	15.00	30.00
—As "Kripp Johnson with the Dell-Vikings"					
❑ 16092	Come Go with Me/How Can I Find True Love	1960	5.00	10.00	20.00
❑ 16236	Come Go with Me/Whispering Bells	1961	5.00	10.00	20.00
❑ 16248	I Hear Bells (Wedding Bells)/Don't Get Slick on Me	1961	5.00	10.00	20.00
DRC					
❑ 101	Can't You See/Oh I	196?	10.00	20.00	40.00
FEE BEE					
❑ 173	Welfare Blues/Hollywood and Vine	1977	—	2.50	5.00
❑ 205	Come Go with Me/How Can I Find True Love	1957	125.00	250.00	500.00
—Orange label, bee on top					
❑ 205	Come Go with Me/How Can I Find True Love	1957	62.50	125.00	250.00
—Orange label, one side has bee, the other side doesn't					
❑ 205	Come Go with Me/How Can I Find True Love	1961	7.50	15.00	30.00
—Orange label, no bee					
❑ 205	Come Go with Me/Whispering Bells	1964	5.00	10.00	20.00
❑ 206	Down in Bermuda/Maggie	1964	20.00	40.00	80.00
❑ 210	What Made Maggie Run/Uh Uh Baby	1957	20.00	40.00	80.00
❑ 210	What Made Maggie Run/When I Come Home	1957	40.00	80.00	120.00
❑ 210	What Made Maggie Run/Down by the Stream	1964	7.50	15.00	30.00
❑ 214	Whispering Bells/Don't Be a Fool	1957	100.00	200.00	400.00
❑ 218	I'm Spinning/You Say You Love Me	1957	30.00	60.00	120.00
—Bee on label					
❑ 218	I'm Spinning/You Say You Love Me	1964	7.50	15.00	30.00
—No bee on label					
❑ 221	Willette/Woke Up This Morning	1958	25.00	50.00	100.00
❑ 221	Willette/I Want to Marry You	1958	20.00	40.00	80.00
❑ 227	Tell Me/Finger Poppin' Woman	1959	20.00	40.00	80.00
❑ 902	True Love/Baby, Let Me Know	1964	7.50	15.00	30.00
—As "The Original Dell Vikings"					
GATEWAY					
❑ 743	We Three/I've Got to Know	1964	7.50	15.00	30.00
JOJO					
❑ 108	Keep On Walkin'/My Body, Your Shadow	1976	—	2.50	5.00
LUNIVERSE					
❑ 106	Somewhere Over the Rainbow/Hey, Senorita	1957	25.00	50.00	100.00
❑ 110	Yours/Heaven and Paradise	1958	5.00	10.00	20.00
❑ 113	In the Still of the Night/The White Cliffs of Dover	1958	5.00	10.00	20.00
❑ 114	There I Go/Girl Girl	1958	5.00	10.00	20.00
—The above three Luniverse 45s are bootlegs, but they perversely do have collector's value!					
MERCURY					
❑ 71132	Cool Shake/Jitterbug Mary	1957	7.50	15.00	30.00
❑ 71180	Come Along with Me/Whatcha Gonna Lose	1957	7.50	15.00	30.00
❑ 71198	I'm Spinning/When I Come Home	1957	7.50	15.00	30.00
❑ 71241	Snowbound/Your Book of Life	1957	7.50	15.00	30.00
❑ 71266	The Voodoo Man/Can't Wait	1958	7.50	15.00	30.00
❑ 71345	You Cheated/Pretty Little Things Called Girls	1958	7.50	15.00	30.00
—Black label					
❑ 71345	You Cheated/Pretty Little Things Called Girls	1958	10.00	20.00	40.00
—Blue label					
❑ 71390	How Could You/Flat Tire	1958	7.50	15.00	30.00
SCEPTER					
❑ 12367	Come Go with Me/When You're Asleep	1973	—	2.50	5.00
SHIP					
❑ 214	Sunday Kind of Love/Over the Rainbow	197?	—	2.00	4.00

Number	Title (A Side/B Side)	Yr	VG	VG+	NM

7-Inch Extended Plays

DOT

| ☐ DEP-1058 | Come Go with Me/Don't Be a Fool//Whispering Bells/What Made Maggie Run | 1957 | 25.00 | 50.00 | 100.00 |
| ☐ DEP-1058 [PS] | Come Go with Us | 1957 | 50.00 | 100.00 | 200.00 |

MERCURY

☐ EP 1-3359	Come Along with Me/A Sunday Kind of Love//(There'll Be Blue Birds Over) The White Cliffs of Dover/Now Is the Hour	1957	25.00	50.00	100.00
☐ EP 1-3359 [PS]	They Sing — They Swing, Vol. 1	1957	37.50	75.00	150.00
☐ EP 1-3362	Heart and Soul/My Foolish Heart//Down in Bermuda/I'm Sitting on Top of the World	1957	25.00	50.00	100.00
☐ EP 1-3362 [PS]	They Sing — They Swing, Vol. 2	1957	37.50	75.00	150.00
☐ EP 1-3363	Somewhere Over the Rainbow/Is It Any Wonder//Yours/Summertime	1957	25.00	50.00	100.00
☐ EP 1-3363 [PS]	They Sing — They Swing, Vol. 3	1957	37.50	75.00	150.00

Albums

COLLECTABLES

| ☐ COL-5010 | The Best of the Dell-Vikings | 198? | 3.00 | 6.00 | 12.00 |

DOT

| ☐ DLP-3685 [M] | Come Go with Me | 1966 | 50.00 | 100.00 | 200.00 |
| ☐ DLP-25685 [R] | Come Go with Me | 1966 | 37.50 | 75.00 | 150.00 |

LUNIVERSE

| ☐ LP-1000 [M] | Come Go with the Del Vikings | 1957 | 125.00 | 250.00 | 500.00 |

—Eight tracks, cover is composed of slicks. Counterfeits have more tracks and a preprinted cover (not slicks)

MERCURY

| ☐ MG-20314 [M] | They Sing — They Swing | 1957 | 75.00 | 150.00 | 300.00 |
| ☐ MG-20353 [M] | A Swinging, Singing Record Session | 1958 | 50.00 | 100.00 | 200.00 |

DEL VIKINGS, THE / THE SONNETS

Albums

CROWN

| ☐ CLP-5368 [M] | The Del Vikings and the Sonnets | 1963 | 10.00 | 20.00 | 40.00 |

DELEGATES, THE (3)

DEE CLARK was a member.

45s

VEE JAY

| ☐ 212 | The Convention/Jay's Rock | 1956 | 15.00 | 30.00 | 60.00 |

—B-side by Big Jay McNeely

| ☐ 243 | Mother's Son/I'm Gonna Be Glad | 1957 | 15.00 | 30.00 | 60.00 |

DELFONICS, THE

Also see MAJOR HARRIS.

45s

ARISTA

| ☐ 0308 | Don't Throw It All Away/I Don't Care What People Say | 1978 | — | 2.00 | 4.00 |

CAMEO

| ☐ 472 | You've Been Untrue/I Was There | 1967 | 3.75 | 7.50 | 15.00 |

MOON SHOT

| ☐ 6703 | He Don't Really Love You/Without You | 1967 | 3.75 | 7.50 | 15.00 |

PHILLY GROOVE

☐ 150	La-La Means I Love You/Can't Get Over Losing You	1968	2.50	5.00	10.00
☐ 151	I'm Sorry/You're Gone	1968	2.50	5.00	10.00
☐ 152	Break Your Promise/Alfie	1968	2.50	5.00	10.00
☐ 154	Ready Or Not Here I Come (Can't Hide from Love)/Somebody Loves You	1968	2.50	5.00	10.00
☐ 156	Funny Feeling/My New Love	1969	2.50	5.00	10.00
☐ 157	You Got Yours and I'll Get Mine/Loving Him	1969	2.50	5.00	10.00
☐ 161	Didn't I (Blow Your Mind This Time)/Down Is Up, Up Is Down	1970	2.50	5.00	10.00
☐ 162	Trying to Make a Fool of Me/Baby I Love You	1970	2.50	5.00	10.00
☐ 163	When You Get Right Down To It/I Gave to You	1970	2.50	5.00	10.00
☐ 166	Over and Over/Hey! Love	1971	2.00	4.00	8.00
☐ 169	Walk Right Up to the Sun/Round and Round	1971	2.00	4.00	8.00
☐ 172	Tell Me This Is a Dream/I'm a Man	1972	2.00	4.00	8.00
☐ 174	Think It Over/I'm a Man	1972	2.00	4.00	8.00
☐ 176	I Don't Want to Make You Wait/Baby I Miss You	1973	2.00	4.00	8.00
☐ 177	Alfie/Start All Over Again	1973	2.00	4.00	8.00
☐ 182	I Told You So/Seventeen and In Love	1973	2.00	4.00	8.00
☐ 184	Lying to Myself/Hey Baby	1974	2.00	4.00	8.00

Albums

ARISTA

| ☐ AL 8333 | The Best of the Delfonics | 198? | 2.50 | 5.00 | 10.00 |

COLLECTABLES

| ☐ COL-5109 | Golden Classics | 198? | 2.50 | 5.00 | 10.00 |

KORY

| ☐ 1002 | The Best of the Delfonics | 1977 | 3.00 | 6.00 | 12.00 |

PHILLY GROOVE

☐ 1150	La La Means I Love You	1968	20.00	40.00	80.00
☐ 1151	The Sexy Sound of Soul	1969	20.00	40.00	80.00
☐ 1152	The Delfonics Super Hits	1969	12.50	25.00	50.00
☐ 1153	The Delfonics	1970	12.50	25.00	50.00
☐ 1154	Tell Me This Is a Dream	1972	12.50	25.00	50.00
☐ 1501	Alive & Kicking	1974	12.50	25.00	50.00

POOGIE

| ☐ 121680 | The Delfonics Return | 1981 | 3.00 | 6.00 | 12.00 |

DELL VIKINGS, THE

See THE DEL-VIKINGS.

DELLS, THE

45s

20TH CENTURY

☐ 2463	I Touched a Dream/All About the Paper	1980	—	2.00	4.00
☐ 2475	Passionate Breezes/Your Song	1980	—	2.00	4.00
☐ 2504	Happy Song/Look at Us Now	1981	—	2.00	4.00
☐ 2602	Ain't It a Shame/Stay in My Corner	1982	—	2.00	4.00

ABC

☐ 12386	Super Woman/My Life Is So Wonderful	1978	—	2.50	5.00
☐ 12422	(I Wanna) Testify/Don't Save Me	1978	—	2.50	5.00
☐ 12422	(I Wanna) Testify/Drowning for Your Love	1978	—	2.50	5.00
☐ 12440	(You Bring Out) The Best in Me/Wrapped Up Tight	1978	—	2.50	5.00

ARGO

☐ 5415	God Bless the Child/I'm Going Home	1962	3.00	6.00	12.00
☐ 5428	The (Bossa Nova) Bird/Eternally	1962	3.00	6.00	12.00
☐ 5442	Hi Diddle Dee Dum Dum (It's a Good Feelin')/If It Ain't One Thing, It's Another	1963	3.00	6.00	12.00
☐ 5456	After You/Goodbye Mary Ann	1963	3.00	6.00	12.00

CADET

☐ 5538	Thinkin' About You/The Change We Go Thru (For Love)	1966	—	3.00	6.00
☐ 5551	Over Again/Run for Cover	1967	—	3.00	6.00
☐ 5563	You Belong to Someone Else/Inspiration	1967	—	3.00	6.00
☐ 5574	O-O, I Love You/There Is	1967	—	3.00	6.00
☐ 5590	There Is/Show Me	1968	2.00	4.00	8.00
☐ 5599	Wear it On Our Face/Please Don't Change Me Now	1968	—	3.00	6.00
☐ 5612	Stay in My Corner/Love Is So Simple	1969	—	3.00	6.00
☐ 5621	Always Together/I Want My Mama	1968	—	3.00	6.00
☐ 5631	Does Anybody Know I'm Here/Make Sure (You Have Somebody to Love You)	1968	—	3.00	6.00
☐ 5636	I Can't Do Enough/Hallways of My Mind	1969	—	3.00	6.00
☐ 5641	I Can Sing a Rainbow-Love Is Blue/Hallelujah Baby	1969	—	3.00	6.00
☐ 5649	Oh What a Night/Believe Me	1969	—	3.00	6.00
☐ 5658	On the Dock of the Bay/When I'm in Your Arms	1969	—	3.00	6.00
☐ 5663	Oh What a Day/The Change We Go Thru (For Love)	1970	—	3.00	6.00
☐ 5667	Open Up My Heart/Nadine	1970	—	3.00	6.00
☐ 5672	Long Lonely Nights/A Little Understanding	1970	—	3.00	6.00
☐ 5679	The Glory of Love/A Whiter Shade of Pale	1970	—	3.00	6.00
☐ 5683	The Love We Had (Stays on My Mind)/Freedom Means	1971	—	3.00	6.00
☐ 5689	It's All Up to You/Oh, My Dear	1972	—	3.00	6.00
☐ 5691	Walk On By/This Guy's in Love with You	1972	—	3.00	6.00
☐ 5694	Just As Long As We're in Love/I'd Rather Be with You	1972	—	3.00	6.00
☐ 5696	Give Your Baby a Standing Ovation/Closer	1973	—	3.00	6.00
☐ 5698	My Pretending Days Are Over/Let's Make It Last	1973	—	3.00	6.00
☐ 5700	I Miss You/Don't Make Me a Storyteller	1973	—	3.00	6.00
☐ 5702	I Wish It Was Me You Loved/Two Together Is Better Than One	1974	—	3.00	6.00
☐ 5703	Bring Back the Love of Yesterday/Learning to Love You Was Easy (It's So Hard Trying to Get Over You)	1974	—	3.00	6.00
☐ 5703	Sweeter as the Days Go By/Learning to Love You Was Easy (It's So Hard Trying to Get Over You)	1974	—	3.00	6.00

—A-side is the same song with a new title

| ☐ 5707 | The Glory of Love/You're the Greatest | 1975 | — | 3.00 | 6.00 |
| ☐ 5711 | We Got to Get Our Thing Together/The Power of Love | 1975 | 2.00 | 4.00 | 8.00 |

CHECKER

| ☐ 794 | Darling I Know/Christine | 1954 | 400.00 | 800.00 | 1200. |

—As "The El Rays"

MCA

| ☐ 41051 | Plastic People/What I Could | 1979 | — | 2.50 | 5.00 |

MERCURY

☐ 73723	We Got to Get Our Thing Together/Reminiscing	1975	—	2.50	5.00
☐ 73759	The Power of Love/Gotta Get Home to My Baby	1976	—	2.50	5.00
☐ 73807	Slow Motion/Ain't No Black and White in Music	1976	—	2.50	5.00
☐ 73842	No Way Back/Too Late for Love	1976	—	2.50	5.00
☐ 73901	Betcha Never Been Loved (Like This Before)/Get On Down	1977	—	2.50	5.00
☐ 73909	Our Love/Could It Be	1977	—	2.50	5.00
☐ 73977	Private Property/Teaser	1977	—	2.50	5.00

PHILCO-FORD

| ☐ HP-32 | There Is/Show Me | 1968 | 5.00 | 10.00 | 20.00 |

—4-inch plastic "Hip Pocket Record" with color sleeve

PRIVATE I

☐ 04343	Don't Want Nobody/You Can't Just Walk Away	1984	—	2.00	4.00
☐ 04448	One Step Closer/Come On Back to Me	1984	—	2.00	4.00
☐ 04540	Love On/Don't Want Nobody	1984	—	2.00	4.00

SKYLARK

| ☐ 558 | I Can't Help Myself/She's Just an Angel | 198? | — | 2.00 | 4.00 |
| ☐ 581 | Someone to Call Me Darling/Now I Pray | 198? | — | 2.00 | 4.00 |

VEE JAY

| ☐ 134 | Tell the World/Blues at Three | 1955 | 2500. | 3750. | 5000. |

—Red vinyl

| ☐ 134 | Tell the World/Blues at Three | 1955 | 500.00 | 1000. | 2000. |
| ☐ 166 | Dreams of Contentment/Zing, Zing, Zing | 1955 | 50.00 | 100.00 | 200.00 |

Number	Title (A Side/B Side)	Yr	VG	VG+	NM
❏ 204	Oh What a Nite/Jo-Jo	1956	30.00	60.00	120.00
❏ 230	Movin' On/I Wanna Go Home	1956	10.00	20.00	40.00
❏ 236	Why Do You Have to Go/Dance, Dance, Dance	1957	10.00	20.00	40.00
❏ 251	A Distant Love/O-Bop She-Bop	1957	10.00	20.00	40.00
❏ 258	Pain in My Heart/Time Makes You Change	1957	10.00	20.00	40.00
❏ 274	The Springer/What You Say Baby	1958	7.50	15.00	30.00
❏ 292	I'm Calling/Jeepers Creepers	1958	7.50	15.00	30.00
❏ 300	Wedding Day/My Best Girl	1958	25.00	50.00	100.00
❏ 324	Dry Your Eyes/Baby Open Up Your Heart	1959	10.00	20.00	40.00
❏ 338	Oh What a Nite/I Wanna Go Home	1960	5.00	10.00	20.00
❏ 376	Hold On to What You've Got/Swingin' Teens	1961	5.00	10.00	20.00
❏ 595	Shy Girl/What Do We Prove	1964	3.00	6.00	12.00
❏ 615	Wait Till Tomorrow/Oh What a Good Night	1964	3.00	6.00	12.00
❏ 674	Stay in My Corner/It's Not Unusual	1965	3.00	6.00	12.00
❏ 712	Poor Little Boy/Hey Sugar (Don't Get Serious)	1966	3.00	6.00	12.00

VETERAN

❏ 7-101	Thought of You Just a Little Too Much/(B-side unknown)	1989	—	2.50	5.00

Albums
20TH CENTURY

❏ T-618	I Touched a Dream	1980	3.00	6.00	12.00
❏ T-633	Whatever Turns You On	1981	3.00	6.00	12.00

ABC

❏ AA-1100	New Beginnings	1978	3.00	6.00	12.00
❏ AA-1113	Face to Face	1978	3.00	6.00	12.00

BUDDAH

❏ BDS-5053	The Dells	1969	3.75	7.50	15.00

CADET

❏ LPS-804	There Is	1968	12.50	25.00	50.00
❏ LPS-822	The Dells Musical Menu/Always Together	1969	12.50	25.00	50.00
❏ LPS-824	The Dells Greatest Hits	1969	12.50	25.00	50.00
❏ LPS-829	Love Is Blue	1969	12.50	25.00	50.00
❏ LPS-837	Like It Is, Like It Was	1970	12.50	25.00	50.00
❏ 50004	Freedom Means	1971	6.25	12.50	25.00
❏ 50017	The Dells Sing Dionne Warwicke's Greatest Hits	1972	6.25	12.50	25.00
❏ 50021	Sweet As Funk Can Be	1972	6.25	12.50	25.00
❏ 50037	Give Your Baby a Standing Ovation	1973	6.25	12.50	25.00
❏ 50046	The Dells	1973	6.25	12.50	25.00
❏ 60030	The Mighty Mighty Dells	1974	6.25	12.50	25.00
❏ 60036	The Dells' Greatest Hits, Vol. 2	1975	5.00	10.00	20.00

CHESS

❏ CH-9103	The Dells	198?	2.50	5.00	10.00
—Reissue					
❏ CH-9288	There Is	1989	2.50	5.00	10.00
—Reissue of Cadet 804					

LOST-NITE

❏ LLP-21 [10]	The Dells	1981	3.75	7.50	15.00
—Red vinyl, generic red cover					

MERCURY

❏ SRM-1-1059	We Got to Get Our Thing Together	1975	3.75	7.50	15.00
❏ SRM-1-1084	No Way Back	1976	3.75	7.50	15.00
❏ SRM-1-1145	They Said It Couldn't Be Done	1977	3.75	7.50	15.00
❏ SRM-1-3711	Love Connection	1977	3.75	7.50	15.00

PRIVATE I

❏ BFZ 39309	One Step Closer	1984	2.50	5.00	10.00

SOLID SMOKE

❏ 8029	Breezy Ballads and Tender Tunes: The Best of the Early Years (1955-65)	1984	2.50	5.00	10.00

UPFRONT

❏ UPF-105	Stay In My Corner	1968	3.75	7.50	15.00

URGENT

❏ URG-4108	The Second Time	1991	3.00	6.00	12.00

VEE JAY

❏ LP 1010 [M]	Oh What a Nite	1959	200.00	400.00	800.00
—Maroon label					
❏ LP 1010 [M]	Oh What a Nite	1961	75.00	150.00	300.00
—Black label with colorband					
❏ VJLP-1010	Oh What a Nite	198?	2.50	5.00	10.00
—Late-80s reissue on reactivated Vee Jay label. "Trade Mark Reg." on label.					
❏ LP 1141 [M]	It's Not Unusual	1965	25.00	50.00	100.00
❏ LPS 1141 [S]	It's Not Unusual	1965	37.50	75.00	150.00

VJ INTERNATIONAL

❏ 7305	The Dells In Concert	197?	3.00	6.00	12.00

ZOO

❏ 11023	I Salute You	1992	3.75	7.50	15.00

DELLS, THE, AND THE DRAMATICS
Also see each artist's individual listings.
45s
CADET

❏ 5710	Love Is Missing from Our Lives/I'm in Love	1975	—	3.00	6.00

Albums
CADET

❏ 60027	The Dells Vs. the Dramatics	1974	6.25	12.50	25.00

DELTA JOHN
See JOHN LEE HOOKER.

DESTINY'S CHILD
12-Inch Singles
COLUMBIA

❏ CAS 12584/5 [(2) DJ]	Say My Name (11 versions)	1999	3.75	7.50	15.00
❏ CAS 40443 [DJ]	Bills, Bills, Bills (Vocal 4:15) (Instrumental 4:03) (Acappella 4:00)/(same on both sides)	1999	2.00	4.00	8.00
❏ CAS 41117 [DJ]	With Me (5 versions)	1998	2.00	4.00	8.00
❏ CAS 42631 [DJ]	Bills, Bills, Bills (Remix Featuring Sporty Thievz 3:57) (LP Version 4:16) (Remix Featuring Sporty Thievz Instrumental 3:55) (Remix Featuring Sporty Thievz Acapella 4:00)	1999	2.00	4.00	8.00
❏ CAS 48875 [DJ]	Jumpin' Jumpin' (Album Version) (Instrumental) (A Cappella)/Bug a Boo (Refugee Camp Remix) (Refugee Camp Remix Instrumental) (Refugee Camp Remix A Cappella)	2000	2.00	4.00	8.00
❏ 44-78687	No, No, No (Part 2 Featuring Wyclef Jean) (Part 1) (Part 2 Without Rap)/(Part 2 A Cappella Featuring Wyclef Jean) (Part 2 Instrumental) (Part 1 Instrumental)	1997	2.00	4.00	8.00
❏ 44-79176	Bills, Bills, Bills (LP Version) (Digital Black-N-Groove Club Mix) (Acappella) (Maurice's Xclusive Livegig Mix) (Maurice's Xclusive Dub Mix)	1999	—	3.00	6.00
❏ 44-79346	Say My Name (unknown versions)	2000	2.00	4.00	8.00
❏ 44X-79446 [(2)]	Jumpin' Jumpin' (12 versions)	2000	2.00	4.00	8.00
❏ 44-79493	Independent Women Part 1 (Maurice's Independent Man Remix) (LP Version) (Instrumental) (Victor Calderone Club Mix) (Victor Calderone Drum Dub Mix)	2000	—	3.00	6.00
❏ 44-79566	Survivor (Calderone Club Mix 9:26) (Calderone Drum Dub Mix 6:45) (CB200 Club Anthem Mix 6:20) (Remix Extended Version Featuring Da Brat 4:24) (Azza'z Soul Remix 4:30)	2001	—	3.00	6.00
❏ 44-79622	Bootylicious (Richard Vission's V-Quest) (Richard Vission's DJ Dub)/(Big Boyz Remix) (Big Boyz Remix Instrumental) (Album Version) (Album Instrumental)	2001	—	3.00	6.00
❏ 44X-79672 [(2)]	Emotion (10 versions)	2001	2.00	4.00	8.00

EASTWEST

❏ ED 6113 [DJ]	Get On the Bus (LP Version) (same on both sides)	1998	2.00	4.00	8.00

45s
COLUMBIA

❏ 38 079582	Survivor/Survivor (Featuring Da Brat)	2001	—	2.00	4.00

Albums
COLUMBIA

❏ DES-01 [DJ]	This Is the Remix Sampler	2002	3.75	7.50	15.00
—Five-song sampler					
❏ CAS 56652 [DJ]	Holiday Sampler	2001	3.75	7.50	15.00
—Contains 8 tracks -- 3 versions of "Emotion," 3 versions of "8 Days of Christmas" and 2 versions of "Sexy Daddy"					
❏ C2 61063 [(2)]	Survivor	2001	3.75	7.50	15.00
❏ C2 69870 [(2)]	The Writing's on the Wall	1999	3.75	7.50	15.00
❏ C2 86431 [(2)]	This Is the Remix	2002	3.75	7.50	15.00

DETROIT EMERALDS
45s
RIC TIC

❏ 135	Show Time/(Instrumental)	1968	3.00	6.00	12.00
❏ 138	Shades Down/Ode to Billie Joe	1968	3.00	6.00	12.00
❏ 141	Take Me the Way I Am/I'll Keep On Coming Back	1968	3.00	6.00	12.00

WESTBOUND

❏ 147	Holding On/Things Are Looking Up	1969	2.00	4.00	8.00
❏ 156	If I Lose Your Love/I Bet You Get the One	1969	2.00	4.00	8.00
❏ 161	I Can't See Myself Doing Without You/Just Now and Then	1970	2.00	4.00	8.00
❏ 172	Do Me Right/Just Now and Then	1970	2.00	4.00	8.00
❏ 181	Wear This Ring (With Love)/Bet You Got the One Who Loves You	1971	—	3.00	6.00
❏ 192	You Want It, You Got It/Till You Decide to Come Home	1971	—	3.00	6.00
❏ 203	Baby Let Me Take You (In My Arms)/I'll Never Sail the Sea Again	1972	—	3.00	6.00
❏ 209	Feel the Need in Me/There's a Love for Me Somewhere	1972	—	3.00	6.00
❏ 213	You're Gettin' a Little Too Smart/Heaven Couldn't Be Like This	1973	—	3.00	6.00
❏ 220	Lee/Whatcha Gonna Wear Tomorrow	1973	—	3.00	6.00
❏ 226	I'm Qualified/Set It Out	1974	—	3.00	6.00
❏ 5005	Yes I Know I'm in Love/Rosetta Stone	1974	—	3.00	6.00
❏ 55401	Feel the Need/Love Has Come to Me	1977	—	2.50	5.00
❏ 55404	Set It Out (Part 1)/Set It Out (Part 2)	1977	—	2.50	5.00
❏ 55410	Turn On Lady/Just Don't Know About This Girl of Mine	1977	—	2.50	5.00

Albums
WESTBOUND

❏ 302	Feel the Need	1977	3.75	7.50	15.00
❏ 2006	Do Me Right	1971	10.00	20.00	40.00
❏ 2013	You Want It, You Got It	1972	10.00	20.00	40.00
❏ 2018	I'm in Love with You	1973	10.00	20.00	40.00
❏ 6101	Let's Get Together	1978	3.75	7.50	15.00

DEUCES OF RHYTHM AND THE TEMPO TOPPERS, THE
Also see LITTLE RICHARD.
45s
PEACOCK

❏ 1616	Ain't That Good News/A Fool at the Wheel	1953	20.00	40.00	80.00
❏ 1628	Always/Rice, Red Beans and Turnip Greens	1954	20.00	40.00	80.00

Number	Title (A Side/B Side)	Yr	VG	VG+	NM

DEVAUGHN, WILLIAM
45s
ROXBURY

Number	Title (A Side/B Side)	Yr	VG	VG+	NM
❏ BRBO-0236	Be Thankful for What You Got-Pt. 1/Be Thankful for What You Got-Pt. 2	1974	—	2.50	5.00
❏ 2001	Blood Is Thicker Than Water/Blood Is Thicker Than Water (Part 2)	1974	—	2.50	5.00
❏ 2005	Give the Little Man a Great Big Hand/Something Being Done	1974	—	2.50	5.00
❏ 2018	Kiss and Make Up/(B-side unknown)	1975	—	2.50	5.00

TEC

❏ 767	Figures Can't Calculate/(B-side unknown)	1980	—	2.00	4.00

Albums
ROXBURY

❏ RLX-100	Be Thankful For What You Got	1974	3.00	6.00	12.00

DIABLOS, THE (1)
See NOLAN STRONG AND THE DIABLOS.

DIAMONDS, THE (2)
Black vocal group.
45s
ATLANTIC

❏ 981	A Beggar for Your Kisses/Call, Baby, Call	1952	375.00	750.00	1500.
❏ 1003	I'll Live Again/Two Loves Have I	1953	150.00	300.00	600.00
❏ 1017	Romance in the Dark/Cherry	1954	150.00	300.00	600.00

DIBANGO, MANU
12-Inch Singles
CELLULOID

❏ CEL 171	Abele Dance/Abele Dance Dub	1984	2.00	4.00	8.00
❏ CEL 182	Makossa Rock (2 versions)/Gammatron	1985	2.00	4.00	8.00

ISLAND

❏ 8680 [DJ]	Big Blow/Aloko Party	1976	2.00	4.00	8.00

45s
ATLANTIC

❏ 2971	Soul Makossa/Lily	1973	—	2.50	5.00
❏ 2983	Dangwa/Obaso	1973	—	2.50	5.00
❏ 3000	Weya/Moni	1974	—	2.00	4.00
❏ 3263	Super Kimba/Wasa N'Doto	1975	—	2.00	4.00

WARNER BROS.

❏ 8680	Aloko Party/Big Blow	1978	—	2.00	4.00

Albums
ATLANTIC

❏ SD 7267	Soul Makossa	1973	2.50	5.00	10.00
❏ SD 7276	Makossa Man	1974	2.50	5.00	10.00

ISLAND

❏ ILPS 9526	Afrovision	1976	3.00	6.00	12.00

DIDDLEY, BO
45s
CHECKER

❏ 814	Bo Diddley/I'm a Man	1955	12.50	25.00	50.00
❏ 819	Diddley Daddy/She's Fine, She's Mine	1955	15.00	30.00	60.00

—A-side backing vocals: The Moonglows

❏ 827	Pretty Thing/Bring It to Jerome	1955	12.50	25.00	50.00
❏ 832	Diddy Wah Diddy/I Am Looking for a Woman	1956	12.50	25.00	50.00
❏ 842	Who Do You Love?/In Bad	1956	15.00	30.00	60.00
❏ 842	Who Do You Love?/I'm Bad	1956	10.00	20.00	40.00

—Note altered B-side title

❏ 850	Cops and Robbers/Down Home Special	1956	10.00	20.00	40.00
❏ 860	Hey! Bo Diddley/Mona	1957	12.50	25.00	50.00

—Originals of Checker 816-860 have "Checker" over a checkerboard on top of label

❏ 878	Say! Boss Man/Before You Accuse Me	1957	6.25	12.50	25.00
❏ 896	Dearest Darling/Hush Your Mouth	1958	6.25	12.50	25.00
❏ 907	Bo Meets the Monster/Willie and Lillie	1958	7.50	15.00	30.00
❏ 914	I'm Sorry/Oh Yeah	1959	6.25	12.50	25.00
❏ 924	Crackin' Up/The Great Grandfather	1959	6.25	12.50	25.00
❏ 931	Say Man/Clock Strikes Twelve	1959	7.50	15.00	30.00
❏ 931 [PS]	Say Man/Clock Strikes Twelve	1959	100.00	200.00	400.00
❏ 936	Say Man, Back Again/She's Alright	1959	6.25	12.50	25.00
❏ 942	Road Runner/My Story	1960	5.00	10.00	20.00
❏ 951	Walkin' and Talkin'/Crawdad	1960	5.00	10.00	20.00
❏ 965	Gun Slinger/Signifying	1960	5.00	10.00	20.00
❏ 976	No Guilty/Aztec	1961	5.00	10.00	20.00
❏ 985	Pills/Call Me	1961	7.50	15.00	30.00
❏ 997	Bo Diddley/I'm a Man	1961	5.00	10.00	20.00
❏ 1019	You Can't Judge a Book By Its Cover/I Can Tell	1962	6.25	12.50	25.00
❏ 1045	Surfers' Love Call/Greatest Lover in the World	1963	5.00	10.00	20.00
❏ 1058	Memphis/Monkey Diddle	1963	5.00	10.00	20.00
❏ 1083	Jo Ann/Mama, Keep Your Big Mouth Shut	1964	5.00	10.00	20.00
❏ 1089	Bo's Beat/Chuck's Beat	1964	5.00	10.00	20.00

—B-side by Chuck Berry

❏ 1098	Hey, Good Lookin'/You Ain't Bad	1965	3.75	7.50	15.00
❏ 1123	500% More Man/Let the Kids Dance	1965	3.75	7.50	15.00
❏ 1142	We're Gonna Get Married/Do the Frog	1966	3.75	7.50	15.00
❏ 1158	Ooh Baby/Back to School	1966	3.75	7.50	15.00
❏ 1168	Bo-Ga-Loo Before You Go/Wrecking My Love Life	1967	3.75	7.50	15.00
❏ 1200	Another Sugardaddy/I'm High Again	1968	3.75	7.50	15.00
❏ 1213	Bo Diddley 1969/Soul Train	1969	3.00	6.00	12.00
❏ 1238	The Shape I'm In/Pollution	1970	3.00	6.00	12.00

CHESS

❏ 2117	I Love You More Than You'll Ever Know/I Said Shut Up Woman	1971	2.50	5.00	10.00
❏ 2129	Bo Diddley-Itis/Infatuation	1972	2.50	5.00	10.00
❏ 2134	Bo-Jam/Husband-in-Law	1972	2.50	5.00	10.00
❏ 2142	I Don't Want No Lyin' Woman/Make a Hit Record	1973	2.50	5.00	10.00

PHILCO-FORD

❏ HP-33	I'm a Man/Song of Bo Diddley	1968	7.50	15.00	30.00

—4-inch plastic "Hip Pocket Record" with color sleeve
RCA VICTOR

❏ PB-10618	Not Fade Away/Drag On	1976	2.50	5.00	10.00

7-Inch Extended Plays
CHESS

❏ 5125	Bo Diddley/I'm a Man//Willie and Lillie/Bo Meets the Monster	1958	30.00	60.00	120.00
❏ 5125 [PS]	Bo Diddley	1958	45.00	90.00	180.00

Albums
ACCORD

❏ SN-7182	Toronto Rock and Roll Revival, Vol. 5	1982	5.00	10.00	20.00

CHECKER

❏ LP 1431 [M]	Bo Diddley	1958	37.50	75.00	150.00
❏ LP 1436 [M]	Go Bo Diddley	1959	37.50	75.00	150.00
❏ LP 2974 [M]	Have Guitar, Will Travel	1960	37.50	75.00	150.00
❏ LP 2976 [M]	Spotlight on Bo Diddley	1960	37.50	75.00	150.00
❏ LP 2977 [M]	Bo Diddley Is a Gunslinger	1961	37.50	75.00	150.00
❏ LP 2980 [M]	Bo Diddley Is a Lover	1961	37.50	75.00	150.00
❏ LP 2982 [M]	Bo Diddley's a Twister	1962	25.00	50.00	100.00
❏ LP 2982 [M]	Road Runner	1967	20.00	40.00	80.00

—Reissue of "Bo Diddley's a Twister"

❏ LP 2984 [M]	Bo Diddley	1962	25.00	50.00	100.00
❏ LP 2985 [M]	Bo Diddley and Company	1963	40.00	80.00	120.00
❏ LP 2987 [M]	Surfin' with Bo Diddley	1964	40.00	80.00	120.00
❏ LPS 2987 [R]	Surfin' with Bo Diddley	1964	7.50	15.00	30.00
❏ LP 2988 [M]	Bo Diddley's Beach Party	1963	25.00	50.00	100.00
❏ LP 2989 [M]	16 All Time Greatest Hits	1964	12.50	25.00	50.00
❏ LPS 2989 [R]	16 All Time Greatest Hits	1964	7.50	15.00	30.00
❏ LP 2992 [M]	Hey! Good Lookin'	1965	15.00	30.00	60.00
❏ LPS 2992 [R]	Hey! Good Lookin'	1965	7.50	15.00	30.00
❏ LP 2996 [M]	500% More Man	1965	15.00	30.00	60.00
❏ LPS 2996 [R]	500% More Man	1965	7.50	15.00	30.00
❏ LP 3001 [M]	The Originator	1966	7.50	15.00	30.00
❏ LPS 3001 [S]	The Originator	1966	10.00	20.00	40.00
❏ LP 3006 [M]	Go Bo Diddley	1967	12.50	25.00	50.00

—Reissue of 1436

❏ LPS 3006 [R]	Go Bo Diddley	1967	10.00	20.00	40.00
❏ LP 3007 [M]	Boss Man	1967	20.00	40.00	80.00

—Reissue of Chess 1431

❏ LPS 3007 [R]	Boss Man	1967	12.50	25.00	50.00
❏ LPS 3013	The Black Gladiator	1968	7.50	15.00	30.00

CHESS

❏ LP 1431 [M]	Bo Diddley	1958	50.00	100.00	200.00
❏ CH-9106	His Greatest Sides, Vol. 1	1984	2.50	5.00	10.00
❏ CH-9187	Have Guitar, Will Travel	1985	2.50	5.00	10.00

—Reissue of Checker 2974

❏ CH-9194	Bo Diddley	1986	2.50	5.00	10.00

—Reissue of 1431

❏ CH-9196	Go Bo Diddley	1986	2.50	5.00	10.00

—Reissue of Checker 1436

❏ CH-9264	Spotlight on Bo Diddley	1987	2.50	5.00	10.00

—Reissue of Checker 2976

❏ CH-9285	Bo Diddley Is a Gunslinger	1989	2.50	5.00	10.00

—Reissue of Checker 2977

❏ CH-9296	The London Bo Diddley Sessions	1989	2.50	5.00	10.00

—Reissue of 50029

❏ CH3-19502 [(3)]	The Chess Box	1990	10.00	20.00	40.00
❏ CH 50001	Another Dimension	1971	10.00	20.00	40.00
❏ CH 50016	Where It All Began	1972	10.00	20.00	40.00
❏ CH 50029	The London Bo Diddley Sessions	1973	6.25	12.50	25.00
❏ CH 50047	Big Bad Bo	1974	6.25	12.50	25.00
❏ 2CH 60005 [(2)]	Got My Own Bag of Tricks	1972	6.25	12.50	25.00

RCA VICTOR

❏ APL1-1229	The 20th Anniversary of Rock and Roll	1976	5.00	10.00	20.00

DIDDLEY, BO/CHUCK BERRY
Also see each artist's individual listings.
Albums
CHECKER

❏ LP 2991 [M]	Two Great Guitars	1964	15.00	30.00	60.00
❏ LPS 2991 [R]	Two Great Guitars	1964	10.00	20.00	40.00

CHESS

❏ CH-9170	Two Great Guitars	1985	2.50	5.00	10.00

—Reissue of Checker 2991

DIDDLEY, BO/MUDDY WATERS/HOWLIN' WOLF
Also see each artist's individual listings.
Albums
CHECKER

❏ LP 3010 [M]	Super, Super Blues Band	1968	12.50	25.00	50.00
❏ LPS 3010 [S]	Super, Super Blues Band	1968	10.00	20.00	40.00

CHESS

❏ CH-9169	Super, Super Blues Band	1985	2.50	5.00	10.00

—Reissue of Checker 3010

Number	Title (A Side/B Side)	Yr	VG	VG+	NM

DIDDLEY, BO/MUDDY WATERS/LITTLE WALTER
Also see each artist's individual listings.
Albums
CHECKER

❑ LP 3008 [M]	Super Blues Band	1968	12.50	25.00	50.00
❑ LPS 3008 [S]	Super Blues Band	1968	10.00	20.00	40.00

CHESS

❑ CH-9168	Super Blues Band	1985	2.50	5.00	10.00

—Reissue of Checker 3008

DIGABLE PLANETS
12-Inch Singles
PENDULUM

❑ 5657 [DJ]	Nickel Bags (4 versions)/Appointment at the Fat Clinic (2 versions)	1993	2.00	4.00	8.00
❑ 19945 [DJ]	9th Wonder (Slicker This Year) (4 versions)	1994	2.00	4.00	8.00
❑ 66285	Nickel Bags (4 versions)/Appointment at the Fat Clinic (2 versions)	1993	—	3.00	6.00
❑ 66318	Where I'm From (6 versions)	1993	2.00	4.00	8.00

45s
ELEKTRA

❑ 64674	Rebirth of Slick (Cool Like Dat)/Where I'm From	1993	—	—	3.00

PENDULUM

❑ S7-18482	Dial 7/Graffiti	1995	—	—	3.00

Albums
PENDULUM

❑ E1-30654	Blowout Comb	1994	3.00	6.00	12.00
❑ 61414	Reachin' (A New Refutation of Time and Space)	1993	3.00	6.00	12.00

DIGITAL UNDERGROUND
12-Inch Singles
CRITIQUE

❑ 15571	Oregano Flow (Radio) (Hot Sauce Mix) (Instrumental)	1996	2.50	5.00	10.00

JAKE

❑ INT8P-6424 [DJ]	Wind Me Up (Single Version) (LP Version) (Instrumental) (Acappella)	1998	2.00	4.00	8.00
❑ INT8P-6486 [DJ]	Mission (Clean Version)/Odd Couple (Clean Version)	1998	3.75	7.50	15.00

—A-side featuring Big Punisher, Shock G, Styles and Whateva; B-side featuring Humpty Hump and Biz Markie
TOMMY BOY

❑ TB 513	No Nose Job (Club) (Beatstrumental) (Radio) (Fat Bass International)	1991	2.50	5.00	10.00
❑ TB 587	The Return of the Crazy One (5 versions)/Carry the Way	1993	2.50	5.00	10.00
❑ TB 590 [DJ]	The Return of the Crazy One (Party Flava Mix) (Radio Flava Mix)	1993	2.50	5.00	10.00
❑ TB 612	Wussup Wit the Luv (3 versions)/Doo Woo You (3 versions)	1994	2.50	5.00	10.00
❑ TB 615	Wussup Wit the Luv (3 versions)/Doo Woo You (3 versions)	1994	3.00	6.00	12.00
❑ TB 932	Doowutchyalike (4 versions)/Hip Hop Doll (2 versions)	1989	3.00	6.00	12.00
❑ TB 944	The Humpty Dance (Mini Hump Radio Mix 4:40) (Bonus Hump Mix 6:28) (Humpstrumental 3:16)	1989	2.50	5.00	10.00
❑ TB 955	Doowutchyalike (Remix) (2 versions)/Packet Man (3 versions)	1990	3.00	6.00	12.00
❑ TB 993	Kiss You Back (Smack on the Cheek Mix) (LP Mix)/(Full French Kiss Mix) (Smackapella Mix)	1991	3.00	6.00	12.00

45s
TOMMY BOY/COLLECTABLES

❑ TB 944	The Humpty Dance (same on both sides)	1992	—	2.50	5.00

Albums
CRITIQUE

❑ 15452	Future Rhythm	1996	3.00	6.00	12.00

JAKE

❑ INT2-92061 [(2)]	Who Got the Gravy?	1998	3.75	7.50	15.00

TOMMY BOY

❑ TB 964 [EP]	This Is an E.P. Release	1991	3.75	7.50	15.00
❑ TB 1026	Sex Packets	1990	3.00	6.00	12.00
❑ TB 1045	Sons of the P.	1991	3.00	6.00	12.00
❑ TB 1470 [(2)]	No Nose Job: The Legend of Digital Underground	2001	3.75	7.50	15.00

DILLARD, VARETTA
45s
CUB

❑ 9073	Teaser/I Know I'm Good for You	1960	3.00	6.00	12.00
❑ 9083	Little Bitty Tear/Mercy Mr. Percy	1961	3.00	6.00	12.00
❑ 9091	You Better Come Home/I Don't Know What It Is, But I Like It	1961	3.00	6.00	12.00

GROOVE

❑ 0139	Darling, Listen to the Words of This Song/Mama Don't Want (What Poppa Don't Want)	1956	10.00	20.00	40.00
❑ 0152	Gonna Tell My Daddy/Cherry Blossom	1956	6.25	12.50	25.00
❑ 0159	Got You On My Mind/Skinny Jimmy	1956	6.25	12.50	25.00
❑ 0167	I Miss You Jimmy/If You Want to Be My Baby	1956	6.25	12.50	25.00
❑ 0177	One More Time/I Can't Help Myself	1956	6.25	12.50	25.00

RCA VICTOR

❑ 47-6869	Pray for Me Mother/Leave a Happy Fool Alone	1957	5.00	10.00	20.00
❑ 47-6936	Time Was/I Got a Lot of Love	1957	5.00	10.00	20.00
❑ 47-7057	Undecided/That's Why I Cry	1957	5.00	10.00	20.00
❑ 47-7144	Star of Fortune/The Blues of Love	1958	5.00	10.00	20.00
❑ 47-7285	What'll I Do/Just Multiply	1958	5.00	10.00	20.00

SAVOY

❑ 822	Love and Wine/Please Come Back to Me	1951	12.50	25.00	50.00
❑ 839	Hurry Up/Please Tell Me Why	1952	10.00	20.00	40.00
❑ 847	Easy, Easy Baby/A Letter in Blue	1952	10.00	20.00	40.00
❑ 851	I'm Yours/Here in My Heart	1952	10.00	20.00	40.00
❑ 871	I Cried and Cried/Double Crossing Daddy	1952	10.00	20.00	40.00
❑ 884	Three Lies/Getting Ready for My Daddy	1953	10.00	20.00	40.00
❑ 897	Mercy, Mr. Percy/No Kinda Good No How	1953	10.00	20.00	40.00
❑ 1118	I Ain't Gonna Tell/(That's the Way) My Mind Is Working	1953	7.50	15.00	30.00
❑ 1137	Send Me Some Money/Love	1954	7.50	15.00	30.00
❑ 1153	Johnny Has Gone/So Many Ways	1955	7.50	15.00	30.00
❑ 1160	You're the Answer to My Prayer/Promise Mr. Thomas	1955	7.50	15.00	30.00
❑ 1166	I'll Never Forget You/I Can't Stop Now	1955	7.50	15.00	30.00

TRIUMPH

❑ 608	Good Gravy Baby/Scorched	1959	3.75	7.50	15.00

Albums
SAVOY JAZZ

❑ SJL-1203	Mercy, Mr. Percy, Volume 1	1989	3.00	6.00	12.00

DIONNE AND FRIENDS
Also see GLADYS KNIGHT; DIONNE WARWICK; STEVIE WONDER.
45s
ARISTA

❑ 9422	That's What Friends Are For/Two Ships Passing in the Night	1985	—	—	3.00
❑ 9422 [PS]	That's What Friends Are For/Two Ships Passing in the Night	1985	—	—	3.00

DISCO-TEX AND THE SEX-O-LETTES
45s
CHELSEA

❑ 3004	Get Dancin' (Part I)/Get Dancin' (Part II)	1974	—	2.00	4.00
❑ 3015	I Wanna Dance Wit'choo (Part I)/I Wanna Dance Wit'choo (Part II)	1975	—	2.00	4.00
❑ 3026	Jam Band/Jam Band Reprise	1975	—	2.00	4.00
❑ 3040	Hot Lava/Hot Lava 2	1976	—	2.00	4.00
❑ 3045	Dancin' Kid (Part I)/Dancin' Kid (Part II)	1976	—	2.00	4.00
❑ 3054	Strollin'/We're Havin' a Party (It's Gonna Be Alright)	1976	—	2.00	4.00
❑ 3070	Wooly Bully/On Broadway	1977	—	2.00	4.00

Albums
CHELSEA

❑ CHL 505	Disco-Tex and His Sex-O-Lettes	1975	2.50	5.00	10.00
❑ CHL 516	Manhattan Millionaire	1976	2.50	5.00	10.00
❑ CHL 555	A Piece of the Rock	1977	2.50	5.00	10.00

DIXIE CUPS, THE
45s
ABC

❑ 10855	Love Ain't So Bad (After All)/Daddy Said No	1966	3.00	6.00	12.00

ABC-PARAMOUNT

❑ 10692	That's Where It's At/Two-Way-Poc-A-Way	1965	3.00	6.00	12.00
❑ 10715	I'm Not the Kind of Girl (To Marry)/What Goes Up Must Go Down	1965	3.00	6.00	12.00
❑ 10755	A-B-C Song/That's What the Kids Said	1965	3.00	6.00	12.00

ANTILLES

❑ 707	Iko Iko/Hey Hey (Indian's Coming)	1987	—	2.00	4.00

—B-side by The Wild Tchoupitoulas

❑ 707 [PS]	Iko Iko/Hey Hey (Indian's Coming)	1987	—	2.00	4.00

RED BIRD

❑ 10-001	Chapel of Love/Ain't That Nice	1964	7.50	15.00	30.00
❑ 10-006	People Say/Girls Can Tell	1964	5.00	10.00	20.00
❑ 10-012	You Should Have Seen the Way He Looked at Me/No True Love	1964	5.00	10.00	20.00
❑ 10-017	Little Bell/Another Boy Like Me	1964	5.00	10.00	20.00
❑ 10-024	Iko Iko/Gee, Baby, Gee	1965	5.00	10.00	20.00
❑ 10-024	Iko Iko/I'm Gonna Get You Yet	1965	5.00	10.00	20.00
❑ 10-032	Gee, the Moon Is Shining Bright/I'm Gonna Get You Yet	1965	5.00	10.00	20.00

Albums
ABC-PARAMOUNT

❑ 525 [M]	Riding High	1965	15.00	30.00	60.00
❑ S-525 [S]	Riding High	1965	20.00	40.00	80.00

RED BIRD

❑ RB 20-100 [M]	Chapel of Love	1964	15.00	30.00	60.00
❑ RBS 20-100 [S]	Chapel of Love	1964	20.00	40.00	80.00
❑ RB 20-103 [M]	Iko Iko	1965	37.50	75.00	150.00

DIXIEBELLES, THE
45s
SOUND STAGE 7

❑ 2507	(Down at) Papa Joe's/Rock, Rock, Rock	1963	2.50	5.00	10.00
❑ 2517	Southtown U.S.A./Why Don't You Set Me Free	1964	2.50	5.00	10.00
❑ 2521	New York Town/The Beale Street Dog	1964	2.50	5.00	10.00

Albums
SOUND STAGE 7

❑ SSM-5000 [M]	Down at Papa Joe's	1963	10.00	20.00	40.00
❑ SSS-15000 [R]	Down at Papa Joe's	1963	7.50	15.00	30.00

Number	Title (A Side/B Side)	Yr	VG	VG+	NM

DIXON, FLOYD
45s
ALADDIN

❑ 3101	Do I Love You/Time and Place	1951	50.00	100.00	200.00
—Earlier Floyd Dixon 45s on Aladdin may exist					
❑ 3111	Too Much Jelly Roll/Baby, Let's Go to the Woods	1952	50.00	100.00	200.00
❑ 3121	Blues for Cuba/Bad Neighborhood	1952	50.00	100.00	200.00
❑ 3135	Wine, Wine, Wine/Call Operator 210	1952	50.00	100.00	200.00
❑ 3144	Red Cherries/The River	1952	75.00	150.00	300.00
—Black vinyl					
❑ 3144	Red Cherries/The River	1952	175.00	350.00	700.00
—Red vinyl					
❑ 3151	Tired, Broke and Busted/Come Back Baby	1952	37.50	75.00	150.00
❑ 3166	You Played Me for a Fool/Broken Hearted Traveler	1953	37.50	75.00	150.00
❑ 3196	Lovin'/Married Woman	1953	37.50	75.00	150.00
❑ 3230	You Need Me Now/A Long Time Ago	1954	25.00	50.00	100.00

CASH

❑ 1057	Oh Baby/Never Can Tell	1957	12.50	25.00	50.00

CAT

❑ 106	Moonshine/Roll Baby Roll	1954	15.00	30.00	60.00
❑ 114	Hey Bartender/It Is True	1955	15.00	30.00	60.00

CHATTAHOOCHIE

❑ 652	Tell Me, Tell Me/There Goes My Heart	1964	2.50	5.00	10.00

CHECKER

❑ 857	Alarm Clock Blues/I'm Ashamed of Myself	1957	7.50	15.00	30.00

DODGE

❑ 807	Opportunity Blues/Daisy	1961	3.75	7.50	15.00

EBB

❑ 105	What Is Life Without a Home/Oh-Ee Little Girl	1957	7.50	15.00	30.00

IMPERIAL

❑ 5849	Tired, Broke and Busted/Call Operator 210	1962	3.00	6.00	12.00

KENT

❑ 311	Change Your Mind/Dance the Thing	1958	5.00	10.00	20.00

SPECIALTY

❑ 468	Hard Living Alone/Please Don't Go	1953	20.00	40.00	80.00
—Black vinyl					
❑ 468	Hard Living Alone/Please Don't Go	1953	50.00	100.00	200.00
—Red vinyl					
❑ 477	Hole in the Wall/Old Memories	1953	20.00	40.00	80.00
❑ 486	Ooh-Eee Ooh-Eee/Nose Job	1954	20.00	40.00	80.00

SWINGIN'

❑ 626	Tight Skirts/Wake Up and Live	1960	5.00	10.00	20.00

DR. BUZZARD'S ORIGINAL SAVANNAH BAND
45s
COLLECTABLES

❑ 4560	Cherchez La Femme/I'll Play the Fool	198?	—	—	3.00
—Reissue					

ELEKTRA

❑ 46607	Didn't I Love You Girl/The Seven Year Itch	1980	—	2.00	4.00

RCA

❑ PB-10762	I'll Play the Fool/Sunshower	1976	—	2.00	4.00
❑ PB-10827	Whispering/Cherchez La Femme/Se Si Bon//Sunshower	1976	—	2.00	4.00
❑ PB-10923	You've Got Something/Lemon in the Honey	1977	—	2.00	4.00
❑ PB-11239	Mister Love//Transistor Madness/Future D.J.	1978	—	2.00	4.00
❑ GB-11325	Whispering/Cherchez La Femme/Se Si Bon//I'll Play the Fool	1978	—	—	3.00
—Gold Standard Series reissue					

Albums
ELEKTRA

❑ 6E-218	James Monroe H.S. Presents Dr. Buzzard's Original Savannah Band Goes to Washington	1979	2.50	5.00	10.00

PASSPORT

❑ 6013	Calling All Beatniks	1986	2.50	5.00	10.00

RCA VICTOR

❑ APL1-1504	Dr. Buzzard's Original Savannah Band	1976	3.75	7.50	15.00
—Original copies have tan labels					
❑ APL1-1504	Dr. Buzzard's Original Savannah Band	1976	2.50	5.00	10.00
—Reissue on black label with "Nipper" logo					
❑ AFL1-2402	Dr. Buzzard's Original Savannah Band Meets King Pennet	1978	3.00	6.00	12.00
❑ AYL1-3767	Dr. Buzzard's Original Savannah Band	1980	2.00	4.00	8.00
—Reissue					

DR. DRE
12-Inch Singles
AFTERMATH

❑ INT8P-6766 [DJ]	Forgot About Dre (unknown versions)	2000	3.75	7.50	15.00
❑ 497333	The Next Episode (unknown versions)	2000	3.00	6.00	12.00

DEATH ROW/INTERSCOPE

❑ 53829	Dre Day/Puffin' on Blunts/One Eight Seven	1993	3.75	7.50	15.00

Albums
AFTERMATH

❑ 490486 [(2)]	2001	1999	3.75	7.50	15.00
❑ 490571 [(2)]	2001: Instrumentals	2000	5.00	10.00	20.00

DEATH ROW

❑ P1-50611	The Chronic	1993	3.75	7.50	15.00

DR. FEELGOOD AND THE INTERNS
Also see PIANO RED.
45s
COLUMBIA

❑ 43372	Doctor of Love/Let the House Rock On	1965	2.00	4.00	8.00
❑ 43615	Where Did You Go/Don't Tell Me No Dirty	1966	2.00	4.00	8.00

OKEH

❑ 7144	Mr. Moonlight/Dr. Feel-Good	1962	3.00	6.00	12.00
❑ 7153	Bald Headed Lena/What's Up Doc	1962	3.00	6.00	12.00
❑ 7156	The Right String But the Wrong Yo-Yo/What's Up Doc	1962	3.00	6.00	12.00
❑ 7161	Let's Have a Good Time Tonight/The Same Old Things Keep Happening	1962	3.00	6.00	12.00
❑ 7167	My Gal Jo/Bald Headed Lena	1963	3.00	6.00	12.00
❑ 7185	The Doctor's Boogie/Blang Dong	1963	3.00	6.00	12.00

Albums
OKEH

❑ OKM 12101 [M]	Dr. Feelgood and the Interns	1962	25.00	50.00	100.00
❑ OKS 14101 [S]	Dr. Feelgood and the Interns	1962	50.00	100.00	200.00

DR. JOHN
Also see HUEY "PIANO" SMITH.
45s
ACE

❑ 611	Good Times/Sahara	1961	6.25	12.50	25.00
—As "Mac Rebennack"					

ATCO

❑ 6607	I Walk on Gilded Splinters (Part 1)/I Walk on Gilded Splinters (Part 2)	1968	3.00	6.00	12.00
❑ 6635	Jump Sturdy/Mama Roox	1968	3.00	6.00	12.00
❑ 6697	Patriotic Flag Waver (Long)/Patriotic Flag Waver (Short)	1969	2.00	4.00	8.00
❑ 6755	Wash, Mama, Wash/Loup Gardo	1970	3.00	6.00	12.00
❑ 6882	Iko Iko/The Huey Smith Medley	1972	2.50	5.00	10.00
❑ 6898	Wang Dang Doodle/Big Chief	1972	—	3.00	6.00
❑ 6900	Let the Good Times Roll/Stack-A-Lee	1972	—	3.00	6.00
❑ 6914	Right Place Wrong Time/I Been Hoodood	1973	—	3.00	6.00
❑ 6937	Such a Night/Cold, Cold, Cold	1973	—	3.00	6.00
❑ 6957	(Everybody Wanna Get Rich) Rite Away/Mos'Scocious	1974	—	3.00	6.00
❑ 6971	Let's Make a Better World/Me Minus You Equals Loneliness	1974	—	3.00	6.00

A.F.O.

❑ 309	The Point/One Naughty Flat	1962	6.25	12.50	25.00
—As "Mac Rebennack"					

HORIZON

❑ 117	Wild Honey/Dance the Night Away with You	1979	—	2.00	4.00
❑ 125	Keep That Music Simple/I Thought I Heard New Orleans	1979	—	2.00	4.00

RCA

❑ PB-11285	Take Me Higher/Sweet Rider	1978	—	2.00	4.00

REX

❑ 1008	Storm Warning/Foolish Little Girl	1959	12.50	25.00	50.00
—As "Mac Rebennack"					

SCEPTER

❑ 12393	One Night Late/She's Just a Square	1974	—	2.50	5.00

WARNER BROS.

❑ 22976	Makin' Whoopee!/More Than You Know	1989	—	—	3.00
❑ 22976 [PS]	Makin' Whoopee!/More Than You Know	1989	—	—	3.00
❑ 49703	The Sailor and the Mermaid/One Good Turn	1981	—	2.00	4.00
—A-side with Libby Titus; B-side by Al Jarreau					

DOCTOR ROSS
45s
HI-Q

❑ 5027	Cannonball/Numbers Blues	1963	5.00	10.00	20.00
❑ 5033	Call the Doctor/New York Breakdown	1963	5.00	10.00	20.00

SUN

❑ 193	Chicago Breakdown/Come Back Baby	1954	200.00	400.00	600.00
❑ 212	The Boogie Disease/Juke Box Boogie	1954	500.00	1000.	2000.

Albums
FORTUNE

❑ F-3011 [M]	Doctor Ross, The Harmonica Boss	1962	12.50	25.00	50.00
❑ FS-3011 [S]	Doctor Ross, The Harmonica Boss	1962	25.00	50.00	100.00

TESTAMENT

❑ 2206 [M]	Doctor Ross	196?	5.00	10.00	20.00

DODDS, NELLA
45s
WAND

❑ 167	Come See About Me/You Don't Love Me Anymore	1964	3.75	7.50	15.00
❑ 171	Finders Keepers Losers Weepers/A Girl's Life	1964	3.00	6.00	12.00
❑ 178	Your Love Back/P's and Q's	1965	3.00	6.00	12.00
❑ 187	Come Back Baby/Dream Boy	1965	3.00	6.00	12.00
❑ 1111	Gee Whiz/Maybe Baby	1966	3.75	7.50	15.00
❑ 1136	Honey Boy/I Just Gotta Have You	1966	20.00	40.00	80.00

DOGGETT, BILL
Also see EARL BOSTIC.
45s
ABC-PARAMOUNT

❑ 10611	Mudcat/The Kicker	1965	—	3.00	6.00

Number	Title (A Side/B Side)	Yr	VG	VG+	NM
CHUMLEY					
❑ 90001	Blue Point of View/Funky Feet	1974	—	2.00	4.00
COLUMBIA					
❑ 42384	Buster/Ladies Choice	1962	2.50	5.00	10.00
❑ 42531	Oops/Choo Choo	1962	2.50	5.00	10.00
❑ 42689	Soda Pop/Ham Fat	1963	2.50	5.00	10.00
❑ 42792	The Worm/Hot Fudge	1963	2.50	5.00	10.00
CORAL					
❑ 61739	A Pretty Girl Is Like a Melody/If I Should Lose You	1956	3.00	6.00	12.00
KING					
❑ S-7 1611 [S]	Mr. Ballard/The Eagle Speaks	196?	6.25	12.50	25.00
—33 1/3 rpm jukebox single, small hole					
❑ 4548	Please Don't Ever Let Me Go/Glo' Glug	1952	5.00	10.00	20.00
❑ 4702	It's a Dream/The Song Is Ended	1954	5.00	10.00	20.00
❑ 4711	There's No You/Easy	1954	5.00	10.00	20.00
❑ 4720	Sweet Lorraine/Tailor Made	1954	5.00	10.00	20.00
❑ 4732	Sweet Slumber/High Heels	1954	5.00	10.00	20.00
❑ 4738	The Nearness of You/Honey	1954	5.00	10.00	20.00
❑ 4742	The Christmas Song/Winter Wonderland	1954	5.00	10.00	20.00
❑ 4759	Tara's Theme/Gumbo	1955	3.75	7.50	15.00
❑ 4769	My Reverie/King Bee	1955	3.75	7.50	15.00
❑ 4784	Wild Oats/I'll Be Around	1955	3.75	7.50	15.00
❑ 4795	Oof/Street Scene	1955	3.75	7.50	15.00
❑ 4808	Quaker City/True Blue	1955	3.75	7.50	15.00
❑ 4825	You Don't Know What Love Is/Shove Off	1955	3.75	7.50	15.00
❑ 4838	Honey Boy/Misty Moon	1955	3.75	7.50	15.00
❑ 4888	In a Sentimental Mood/Who's Who	1956	3.75	7.50	15.00
❑ 4917	Squashy/We Found Love	1956	3.75	7.50	15.00
❑ 4936	What a Difference a Day Makes/Stella by Starlight	1956	3.75	7.50	15.00
❑ 4950	Honky Tonk (Part 1)/Honky Tonk (Part 2)	1956	5.00	10.00	20.00
❑ 5000	Slow Walk/Hand in Hand	1956	3.75	7.50	15.00
❑ 5001	Honky Tonk (Vocal)/Peacock Alley	1956	3.75	7.50	15.00
—Vocal by Tommy Brown					
❑ 5020	Ram-Bunk-Shush/Blue Largo	1957	3.00	6.00	12.00
❑ 5044	Chloe/Number Three	1957	3.00	6.00	12.00
❑ 5058	Ding Dong/Cling to Me	1957	3.00	6.00	12.00
❑ 5070	Hammer Head/Shindig	1957	3.00	6.00	12.00
❑ 5080	Hot Ginger/Soft	1957	3.00	6.00	12.00
❑ 5096	Hippy Dippy/Flying Home	1957	3.00	6.00	12.00
❑ 5101	Leaps and Bounds (Part 1)/Leaps and Bounds (Part 2)	1958	3.00	6.00	12.00
❑ 5125	Boo Da Ba/Pimento	1958	3.00	6.00	12.00
❑ 5130	How Could You/Blues for Handy	1958	3.00	6.00	12.00
❑ 5138	Tanya/Blip Bop	1958	3.00	6.00	12.00
❑ 5149	Birdie/Hold It	1958	3.00	6.00	12.00
❑ 5159	Rainbow Riot (Part 1)/Rainbow Riot (Part 2)	1958	3.00	6.00	12.00
❑ 5176	Monster Party/Scott's Bluff	1959	3.00	6.00	12.00
❑ 5204	The Madison/Ocean Liner	1959	3.00	6.00	12.00
❑ 5227	After Hours/Big City Drag	1959	3.00	6.00	12.00
❑ 5256	Yucky Dock (Part 1)/Yucky Dock (Part 2)	1959	3.00	6.00	12.00
❑ 5281	The Goofy Organ/Zee	1959	3.00	6.00	12.00
❑ 5310	Smokie Part 2/Evening Dreams	1960	2.50	5.00	10.00
❑ 5319	Back Woods/Raw Turkey	1960	2.50	5.00	10.00
❑ 5339	Big Boy/Smoochie	1960	2.50	5.00	10.00
❑ 5364	Buttered Popcorn/The Slush	1960	2.50	5.00	10.00
❑ 5387	A Lover's Dream/Trav'lin' Light	1960	2.50	5.00	10.00
❑ 5419	Slidin'/Afternoon Jump	1960	2.50	5.00	10.00
❑ 5444	Honky Tonk (Part 2)/Floyd's Guitar Blues	1961	2.50	5.00	10.00
❑ 5482	Bugle Nose/The Doodle	1961	2.50	5.00	10.00
❑ 5561	High and Wide/In the Wee Hours	1961	2.50	5.00	10.00
❑ 5599	The Doodle Twist/Gene's Dream	1962	2.00	4.00	8.00
❑ 5642	George Washington Twist/Eleven O'Clock Twist	1962	2.00	4.00	8.00
❑ 5665	Teardrops/Moon Dust	1962	2.00	4.00	8.00
❑ 5684	Hometown Shout/For All We Know	1962	2.00	4.00	8.00
❑ 5718	Honky Tonk Bossa Nova (Part 2)/Ocean Liner Bossa Nova	1963	2.00	4.00	8.00
❑ 5740	Down Home Bossa Nova/Si Si Nova	1963	2.00	4.00	8.00
❑ 5788	The Fog/Groovy Movie	1963	2.00	4.00	8.00
❑ 5873	The Rail/Hey Big Boy, Hey Hey	1964	2.00	4.00	8.00
❑ 5878	Night Train (Part 1)/Night Train (Part 2)	1964	2.00	4.00	8.00
❑ 5948	Crackers/That's Enough, Lock 'Em Up	1964	2.00	4.00	8.00
❑ 5957	Snuff Box/Blood Pressure	1964	2.00	4.00	8.00
❑ 6019	Teardrops/Slidin'	1966	—	3.00	6.00
❑ 6217	Take Your Shot/Mad	1969	—	2.50	5.00
❑ 6225	Twenty-Five Miles/For Once in My Life	1969	—	2.50	5.00
❑ 6239	Honky Tonk Popcorn/Honky Tonk	1969	—	2.50	5.00
❑ 6312	The Nearness of You/Moon Dust	1970	—	2.00	4.00
❑ 6350	High Heels/Soft	1971	—	2.00	4.00
❑ 6356	In a Sentimental Mood/Eventide	1971	—	2.00	4.00
ROULETTE					
❑ 4732	Sapphire/Ko-Ko	1967	—	3.00	6.00
❑ 4749	Lovin' Mood/The Funky Wrestler	1967	—	3.00	6.00
SUE					
❑ 10-002	Fat Back/Si Si Cisco	1968	—	2.50	5.00
WARNER BROS.					
❑ 5181	Jack Rabbit/Let's Do the Hully Gully Twist	1960	3.00	6.00	12.00
❑ 5209	Let's Do the Continental/Pony Walk	1961	3.00	6.00	12.00
❑ 5223	You Can't Sit Down (Part 1)/You Can't Sit Down (Part 2)	1961	3.00	6.00	12.00
7-Inch Extended Plays					
KING					
❑ EP-259	*Early Bird/Percy Speaks/Ready Mix/Moon Dust	1954	6.25	12.50	25.00
❑ EP-259 [PS]	Bill Doggett	1954	6.25	12.50	25.00

Number	Title (A Side/B Side)	Yr	VG	VG+	NM
❑ EP-325	*The Song Is Ended/Eventide/And the Angels Sing/Tailor Made	1955	6.25	12.50	25.00
❑ EP-325 [PS]	Bill Doggett, Vol. 2	1955	6.25	12.50	25.00
❑ EP-334	*Honey/It's a Dream/High Heels/Real Gone Mambo	1955	6.25	12.50	25.00
❑ EP-334 [PS]	Bill Doggett, His Organ and Combo, Vol. 4	1955	6.25	12.50	25.00
❑ EP-346	White Christmas/Silent Ninght//Jingle Bells/I Saw Mommy Kissing Santa Claus	195?	6.25	12.50	25.00
—The label of the copy we examined has the listed typo on the song "Silent Night"					
❑ EP-346 [PS]	All-Time Christmas Favorites	195?	6.25	12.50	25.00
—The label of the copy we examined has the listed typo on the song "Silent Night"					
❑ EP-352	*Sweet Slumber/The Nearness of You/Gumbo/Tara's Theme	1955	6.25	12.50	25.00
❑ EP-352 [PS]	Bill Doggett, His Organ and Combo, Vol. 5	1955	6.25	12.50	25.00
❑ EP-382	*I'll Be Around/Street Scene/You Don't Know What Love Is/Misty Moon	1956	6.25	12.50	25.00
❑ EP-382 [PS]	Doggett Dreams	1956	6.25	12.50	25.00
❑ EP-388	*Quaker City/Oof!/Wild Oats/Shove Off	1956	6.25	12.50	25.00
❑ EP-388 [PS]	Doggett Jumps	1956	6.25	12.50	25.00
❑ EP-390	Honky Tonk (Part 1)/Honky Tonk (Part 2)//Squashy/Who's Who	1956	7.50	15.00	30.00
❑ EP-390 [PS]	Honky Tonk	1956	7.50	15.00	30.00
❑ EP-391	*Leaps and Bounds/On the Sunny Side of the Street/True Blue	1956	5.00	10.00	20.00
❑ EP-391 [PS]	Bill Doggett, Vol. 1	1956	5.00	10.00	20.00
❑ EP-392	*Honky Tonk Number Three/When Your Lover Has Gone/Big Boy/Nothin' Yet	1956	5.00	10.00	20.00
❑ EP-392 [PS]	Bill Doggett, Vol. 2	1956	5.00	10.00	20.00
❑ EP-393	*Slow Walk/Afternoon Jump/Peacock Alley/Honey Boy	1956	5.00	10.00	20.00
❑ EP-393 [PS]	Bill Doggett, Vol. 3	1956	5.00	10.00	20.00
❑ EP-394	*I Hadn't Anyone Till You/Yesterdays/A Cottage for Sale/As You Desire Me	1957	5.00	10.00	20.00
❑ EP-394 [PS]	As You Desire Me, Vol. 1	1957	5.00	10.00	20.00
❑ EP-395	*Alone/As Time Goes By/Dedicated to You/Sweet and Lovely	1957	5.00	10.00	20.00
❑ EP-395 [PS]	As You Desire Me, Vol. 2	1957	5.00	10.00	20.00
❑ EP-396	*Dream/Don't Blame Me/This Love of Mine/Fools Rush In	1957	5.00	10.00	20.00
❑ EP-396 [PS]	As You Desire Me, Vol. 3	1957	5.00	10.00	20.00
❑ EP-399	*Caravan/Solitude/I'm Just a Lucky So and So/Prelude to a Kiss	1958	3.75	7.50	15.00
❑ EP-399 [PS]	A Salute to Ellington, Vol. 1	1958	3.75	7.50	15.00
❑ EP-400	*I Let a Song Go Out of My Heart/Don't Get Around Much Anymore/I Got It Bad and That Ain't Good	1958	3.75	7.50	15.00
❑ EP-400 [PS]	A Salute to Ellington, Vol. 2	1958	3.75	7.50	15.00
❑ EP-401	*C Jam Blues/Sophisticated Lady/Perdido/Satin Doll	1958	3.75	7.50	15.00
❑ EP-401 [PS]	A Salute to Ellington, Vol. 3	1958	3.75	7.50	15.00
❑ EP-402	*Sweet Lorraine/Diane/Dinah/Cherry	1958	3.75	7.50	15.00
❑ EP-402 [PS]	Dame Dreaming, Vol. 1	1958	3.75	7.50	15.00
❑ EP-403	*Ramona/Cynthia/Tangerine/Nancy	1958	3.75	7.50	15.00
❑ EP-403 [PS]	Dame Dreaming, Vol. 2	1958	3.75	7.50	15.00
❑ EP-404	*Marcheta/Laura/Jeannine/Estrellita	1958	3.75	7.50	15.00
❑ EP-404 [PS]	Dame Dreaming, Vol. 3	1958	3.75	7.50	15.00
❑ EP-407	*Ram-Bunk-Shus/Cling to Me/Ding Dong/Chloe	1958	3.75	7.50	15.00
❑ EP-407 [PS]	Hot Doggett	1958	3.75	7.50	15.00
❑ EP-408	*Soft/Hammer Head/Shindig/Hot Ginger	1958	3.75	7.50	15.00
❑ EP-408 [PS]	Soft	1958	3.75	7.50	15.00
Albums					
ABC-PARAMOUNT					
❑ 507 [M]	Wow!	1965	5.00	10.00	20.00
❑ S-507 [S]	Wow!	1965	6.25	12.50	25.00
AFTER HOURS					
❑ AFT-4112	The Right Choice	1991	3.75	7.50	15.00
COLUMBIA					
❑ CL 1814 [M]	Oops!	1962	5.00	10.00	20.00
❑ CL 1942 [M]	Prelude to the Blues	1963	5.00	10.00	20.00
❑ CL 2082 [M]	Fingertips	1963	5.00	10.00	20.00
❑ CS 8614 [S]	Oops!	1962	6.25	12.50	25.00
❑ CS 8742 [S]	Prelude to the Blues	1963	6.25	12.50	25.00
❑ CS 8882 [S]	Fingertips	1963	6.25	12.50	25.00
KING					
❑ 295-82 [10]	Bill Doggett — His Organ and Combo	1955	37.50	75.00	150.00
❑ 295-83 [10]	Bill Doggett — His Organ and Combo, Volume 2	1955	37.50	75.00	150.00
❑ 295-89 [10]	All-Time Christmas Favorites	1955	50.00	100.00	200.00
❑ 295-102 [10]	Sentimentally Yours	1956	37.50	75.00	150.00
❑ 395-502 [M]	Moondust	1957	15.00	30.00	60.00
❑ 395-514 [M]	Hot Doggett	1957	15.00	30.00	60.00
❑ 395-523 [M]	As You Desire	1957	15.00	30.00	60.00
❑ KLP-523 [M]	As You Desire	1987	2.50	5.00	10.00
—Reissue with "Highland Records" on label					
❑ 395-531 [M]	Everybody Dance to the Honky Tonk	1958	15.00	30.00	60.00
❑ 395-532 [M]	Dame Dreaming	1958	15.00	30.00	60.00
❑ KLP-532 [M]	Dame Dreaming	1987	2.50	5.00	10.00
❑ 395-533 [M]	A Salute to Ellington	1958	15.00	30.00	60.00
❑ 395-557 [M]	The Doggett Beat for Dancing Feet	1958	15.00	30.00	60.00
❑ KLP-557 [M]	The Doggett Beat for Dancing Feet	1987	2.50	5.00	10.00
—Reissue with "Highland Records" on label					
❑ 395-563 [M]	Candle Glow	1958	15.00	30.00	60.00
❑ 395-582 [M]	Swingin' Easy	1959	15.00	30.00	60.00
❑ 395-585 [M]	Dance Awhile	1959	15.00	30.00	60.00

Number	Title (A Side/B Side)	Yr	VG	VG+	NM
❑ KLP-585 [M]	Dance Awhile	1987	2.50	5.00	10.00
—Reissue with "Highland Records" on label					
❑ 395-600 [M]	A Bill Doggett Christmas	1959	10.00	20.00	40.00
❑ 395-609 [M]	Hold It	1959	15.00	30.00	60.00
❑ 633 [M]	High and Wide	1959	12.50	25.00	50.00
❑ 641 [M]	Big City Dance Party	1959	12.50	25.00	50.00
❑ 667 [M]	Bill Doggett On Tour	1959	12.50	25.00	50.00
❑ 706 [M]	For Reminiscent Lovers, Romantic Songs	1960	12.50	25.00	50.00
❑ 723 [M]	Back Again with More	1960	12.50	25.00	50.00
❑ 759 [M]	Bonanza of 24 Songs	1960	12.50	25.00	50.00
❑ 778 [M]	The Many Moods of Bill Doggett	1960	12.50	25.00	50.00
❑ KLP-778 [M]	The Many Moods of Bill Doggett	1987	2.50	5.00	10.00
—Reissue with "Highland Records" on label					
❑ 830 [M]	American Songs in the Bossa Nova Style	1963	10.00	20.00	40.00
❑ 868 [M]	Impressions	1964	10.00	20.00	40.00
❑ 908 [M]	The Best of Bill Doggett	1964	10.00	20.00	40.00
❑ 959 [M]	Bonanza of 24 Hit Songs	1966	7.50	15.00	30.00
❑ KS-1078	Honky Tonk Popcorn	1969	12.50	25.00	50.00
❑ KS-1097	The Nearness of You	1970	6.25	12.50	25.00
❑ KS-1101	Ram-Bunk-Shush	1970	6.25	12.50	25.00
❑ KS-1104	Sentimental Journey	1970	6.25	12.50	25.00
❑ KS-1108	Soft	1970	6.25	12.50	25.00
❑ K-5009	14 Original Greatest Hits	1977	2.50	5.00	10.00
POWER PAK					
❑ 269	Hold It!	197?	2.50	5.00	10.00
ROULETTE					
❑ R 25330 [M]	Honky Tonk A La Mod	1966	5.00	10.00	20.00
❑ SR 25330 [S]	Honky Tonk A La Mod	1966	6.25	12.50	25.00
STARDAY					
❑ 3023	16 Bandstand Favorites	197?	2.50	5.00	10.00
WARNER BROS.					
❑ W 1404 [M]	3,046 People Danced 'Til 4 AM	1960	5.00	10.00	20.00
❑ WS 1404 [S]	3,046 People Danced 'Til 4 AM	1960	6.25	12.50	25.00
❑ W 1421 [M]	The Band with the Beat	1961	5.00	10.00	20.00
❑ WS 1421 [S]	The Band with the Beat	1961	6.25	12.50	25.00
❑ W 1452 [M]	Bill Doggett Swings	1962	5.00	10.00	20.00
❑ WS 1452 [S]	Bill Doggett Swings	1962	6.25	12.50	25.00
WHO'S WHO IN JAZZ					
❑ 21002	Lionel Hampton Presents Bill Doggett	1977	3.00	6.00	12.00

DOMINO, FATS

45s

Number	Title (A Side/B Side)	Yr	VG	VG+	NM
ABC					
❑ 10902	I Don't Want to Set the World on Fire/I'm Living Right	1967	2.50	5.00	10.00
ABC-PARAMOUNT					
❑ 10444	There Goes (My Heart Again)/Can't Go On Without You	1963	2.50	5.00	10.00
❑ 10475	When I'm Walking (Let Me Walk)/I've Got a Right to Cry	1963	2.50	5.00	10.00
❑ 10484	Red Sails in the Sunset/Song for Rosemary	1963	3.00	6.00	12.00
❑ 10512	Who Cares/Just a Lonely Man	1963	2.50	5.00	10.00
❑ 10531	Lazy Lady/I Don't Want to Set the World on Fire	1964	2.50	5.00	10.00
❑ 10545	If You Don't Know What Love Is/Something You Got, Baby	1964	2.50	5.00	10.00
❑ 10567	Mary, Oh Mary/Packin' Up	1964	2.50	5.00	10.00
❑ 10584	Sally Was a Good Old Girl/For You	1964	2.50	5.00	10.00
❑ 10596	Heartbreak Hill/Kansas City	1964	2.50	5.00	10.00
❑ 10631	Why Don't You Do Right/Wigs	1965	2.50	5.00	10.00
❑ 10644	Let Me Call You Sweetheart/Goodnight Sweetheart	1965	2.50	5.00	10.00
BROADMOOR					
❑ 104	The Lady in Black/Work My Way Up Steady	1967	3.75	7.50	15.00
❑ 105	Big Mouth/Wait 'Til It Happens to You	1968	5.00	10.00	20.00
IMPERIAL					
❑ 45-5058	The Fat Man/Detroit City Blues	1950	500.00	1000.	2000.
—Blue-label "script" logo; pressed in 1952 or so; counterfeits exist					
❑ 45-5099	Korea Blues/Every Night About This Time	1950	200.00	400.00	800.00
—Blue-label "script" logo; pressed in 1952 or so					
❑ 45-5167	You Know I Miss You/I'll Be Gone	1952	125.00	250.00	500.00
—Fats Domino records on Imperial before 5167 are unconfirmed on 45 rpm, except those listed above.					
❑ 45-5180	Goin' Home/Reeling and Rocking	1952	75.00	150.00	300.00
❑ 45-5197	Poor Poor Me/Trust in Me	1952	50.00	100.00	200.00
❑ 45-5209	How Long/Dreaming	1952	20.00	40.00	80.00
—Black vinyl					
❑ 45-5209	How Long/Dreaming	1952	75.00	150.00	300.00
—Red vinyl					
❑ 45-5220	Nobody Loves Me/Cheatin'	1953	20.00	40.00	80.00
—Black vinyl					
❑ 45-5220	Nobody Loves Me/Cheatin'	1953	75.00	150.00	300.00
—Red vinyl					
❑ 45-5231	Going to the River/Mardi Gras in New Orleans	1953	25.00	50.00	100.00
—Black vinyl					
❑ 45-5231	Going to the River/Mardi Gras in New Orleans	1953	125.00	250.00	500.00
—Red vinyl					
❑ 45-5240	Please Don't Leave Me/The Girl I Love	1953	15.00	30.00	60.00
—Black vinyl					
❑ 45-5240	Please Don't Leave Me/The Girl I Love	1953	75.00	150.00	300.00
—Red vinyl					
❑ 45-5251	You Said You Loved Me/Rose Mary	1953	15.00	30.00	60.00
❑ X5262	Something's Wrong/Don't Leave Me This Way	1954	12.50	25.00	50.00
—Black vinyl					
❑ X5262	Something's Wrong/Don't Leave Me This Way	1954	62.50	125.00	250.00
—Red vinyl					

Number	Title (A Side/B Side)	Yr	VG	VG+	NM
❑ X5272	Little School Girl/You Done Me Wrong	1954	15.00	30.00	60.00
❑ X5283	Baby, Please/Where Did You Stay	1954	15.00	30.00	60.00
❑ X5301	You Can Pack Your Suitcase/I Lived My Life	1954	10.00	20.00	40.00
❑ X5313	Love Me/Don't You Hear Me Calling You	1954	10.00	20.00	40.00
❑ X5323	I Know/Thinking of You	1955	12.50	25.00	50.00
—Black vinyl					
❑ X5323	I Know/Thinking of You	1955	125.00	250.00	500.00
—Red vinyl					
❑ X5340	Don't You Know/Helping Hand	1955	10.00	20.00	40.00
❑ X5348	Ain't It a Shame/La La	1955	10.00	20.00	40.00
❑ X5357	All By Myself/Troubles of My Own	1955	20.00	40.00	80.00
—Red label, script logo					
❑ X5357	All By Myself/Troubles of My Own	1955	6.25	12.50	25.00
—Red or maroon label, block logo					
❑ X5369	Poor Me/I Can't Go On	1955	6.25	12.50	25.00
❑ X5375	Bo Weevil/Don't Blame It on Me	1956	6.25	12.50	25.00
❑ X5386	I'm in Love Again/My Blue Heaven	1956	6.25	12.50	25.00
❑ X5396	When My Dreamboat Comes Home/So-Long	1956	6.25	12.50	25.00
❑ X5407	Blueberry Hill/Honey Chile	1956	6.25	12.50	25.00
—Black vinyl, red label					
❑ X5407	Blueberry Hill/Honey Chile	1956	37.50	75.00	150.00
—Red vinyl					
❑ X5407	Blueberry Hill/Honey Chile	1957	3.75	7.50	15.00
—Black vinyl, black label					
❑ X5417	Blue Monday/What's the Reason I'm Not Pleasing You	1957	6.25	12.50	25.00
❑ X5428	I'm Walkin'/I'm in the Mood for Love	1957	6.25	12.50	25.00
—Maroon or red label					
❑ X5428 [PS]	I'm Walkin'/I'm in the Mood for Love	1957	12.50	25.00	50.00
❑ X5442	Valley of Tears/It's You I Love	1957	6.25	12.50	25.00
❑ X5454	When I See You/What Will I Tell My Heart	1957	6.25	12.50	25.00
❑ X5467	Wait and See/I Still Love You	1957	6.25	12.50	25.00
❑ X5477	The Big Beat/I Want You to Know	1957	6.25	12.50	25.00
❑ X5477 [PS]	The Big Beat/I Want You to Know	1957	15.00	30.00	60.00
❑ X5492	Yes, My Darling/Don't You Know I Love You	1958	6.25	12.50	25.00
—Black vinyl					
❑ X5492	Yes, My Darling/Don't You Know I Love You	1958	37.50	75.00	150.00
—Red vinyl					
❑ X5515	Sick and Tired/No, No	1958	6.25	12.50	25.00
❑ X5526	Little Mary/The Prisoner's Song	1958	6.25	12.50	25.00
❑ X5537	Young School Girl/It Must Be Love	1958	6.25	12.50	25.00
❑ X5553	Whole Lotta Loving/Coquette	1958	7.50	15.00	30.00
—Red label					
❑ X5553	Whole Lotta Loving/Coquette	1958	6.25	12.50	25.00
—Black label					
❑ X5553	Whole Lotta Loving/Coquette	1958	37.50	75.00	150.00
—Red vinyl (translucent)					
❑ 5569	Telling Lies/When the Saints Go Marching In	1959	3.75	7.50	15.00
❑ 5585	I'm Ready/Margie	1959	3.75	7.50	15.00
❑ 5606	I Want to Walk You Home/I'm Gonna Be a Wheel Some Day	1959	5.00	10.00	20.00
❑ 5606 [PS]	I Want to Walk You Home/I'm Gonna Be a Wheel Some Day	1959	—	—	—
—Rumored to exist, but without conclusive evidence, we will delete this from future editions					
❑ 5629	Be My Guest/I've Been Around	1959	3.75	7.50	15.00
❑ 5629 [PS]	Be My Guest/I've Been Around	1959	12.50	25.00	50.00
❑ 5645	Country Boy/If You Need Me	1960	3.75	7.50	15.00
❑ 5660	Tell Me That You Love Me/Before I Grow Too Old	1960	3.75	7.50	15.00
❑ 5675	Walking to New Orleans/Don't Come Knockin'	1960	5.00	10.00	20.00
❑ 5687	Three Nights a Week/Put Your Arms Around Me Honey	1960	3.75	7.50	15.00
❑ 5704	My Girl Josephine/Natural Born Lover	1960	5.00	10.00	20.00
❑ 5723	What a Price/Ain't That Just Like a Woman	1961	3.75	7.50	15.00
❑ 5734	Shu Rah/Fell in Love on Monday	1961	3.75	7.50	15.00
❑ 5753	It Keeps Rainin'/I Just Cry	1961	3.75	7.50	15.00
❑ 5764	Let the Four Winds Blow/Good Hearted Man	1961	3.75	7.50	15.00
❑ 5779	What a Party/Rockin' Bicycle	1961	3.75	7.50	15.00
❑ 5796	Jambalaya (On the Bayou)/I Hear You Knocking	1961	3.75	7.50	15.00
❑ 5816	You Win Again/Ida Jane	1962	3.75	7.50	15.00
❑ 5833	My Real Name/My Heart Is Bleeding	1962	3.75	7.50	15.00
❑ 5863	Nothing New (Same Old Thing)/Dance with Mr. Domino	1962	3.75	7.50	15.00
❑ 5875	Did You Ever See a Dream Walking/Stop the Clock	1962	3.75	7.50	15.00
❑ 5895	Won't You Come On Back/Hands Across the Table	1962	3.75	7.50	15.00
❑ 5895	Won't You Come On Back/Your Cheatin' Heart	1962	3.75	7.50	15.00
❑ 5909	Hum Diddy Doo/Those Eyes	1963	3.75	7.50	15.00
❑ 5937	You Always Hurt the One You Love/Trouble Blues	1963	3.75	7.50	15.00
❑ 5959	Isle of Capri/True Confession	1963	3.75	7.50	15.00
❑ 5980	One Night/I Can't Go On This Way	1963	3.75	7.50	15.00
❑ 5999	Your Cheatin' Heart/Goin' Home	1963	3.75	7.50	15.00
❑ 66005	I Can't Give You Anything But Love/Goin' Home	1963	3.00	6.00	12.00
❑ 66016	When I Was Young/Your Cheatin' Heart	1964	3.00	6.00	12.00
MERCURY					
❑ 72463	I Left My Heart in San Francisco/I Done Got Over You	1965	2.50	5.00	10.00
❑ 72485	It's Never Too Late/What's That You Got	1965	2.50	5.00	10.00
❑ 72485 [PS]	It's Never Too Late/What's That You Got	1965	5.00	10.00	20.00
REPRISE					
❑ 0696	One for the Highway/Honest Papas Love Their Mamas Better	1968	3.75	7.50	15.00
❑ 0763	Lady Madonna/One for the Highway	1968	3.75	7.50	15.00
❑ 0775	Lovely Rita/Wait Till It Happens to You	1968	3.75	7.50	15.00
❑ 0810	Everybody's Got Someting to Hide (Except Me and My Monkey)/So Swell When You're Well	1969	3.75	7.50	15.00

Number	Title (A Side/B Side)	Yr	VG	VG+	NM
❑ 0891	Have You Seen My Baby?/Make Me Belong to You	1970	3.75	7.50	15.00
❑ 0944	New Orleans Ain't the Same/Sweet Patootie	1970	3.75	7.50	15.00

THE RIGHT STUFF

Number	Title (A Side/B Side)	Yr	VG	VG+	NM
❑ S7-18216	Christmas Is a Special Day/Please Come Home for Christmas (Christmas Once Again)	1994	—	2.00	4.00
—Red vinyl					
❑ S7-19768	Frosty the Snowman/Every Heart Is Home at Christmas	1997	—	2.50	5.00
—B-side by the Five Keys on Aladdin					

TOOT TOOT

Number	Title (A Side/B Side)	Yr	VG	VG+	NM
❑ 001	My Toot Toot/My Toot Toot (Rock)	1985	—	2.50	5.00
—With Doug Kershaw					
❑ 002	Don't Mess with My Popeye's/My Toot Toot	1985	—	2.50	5.00
—With Doug Kershaw					

UNITED ARTISTS

Number	Title (A Side/B Side)	Yr	VG	VG+	NM
❑ 0001	Ain't That a Shame/Goin' Home	1973	—	2.00	4.00
❑ 0002	Blue Monday/I'm Gonna Be a Wheel Someday	1973	—	2.00	4.00
❑ 0003	I'm in Love Again/Whole Lotta Lovin'	1973	—	2.00	4.00
❑ 0004	Blueberry Hill/Bo Weevil	1973	—	2.00	4.00
❑ 0005	I'm Walkin'/One Night	1973	—	2.00	4.00
❑ 0006	I Hear You Knockin'/My Blue Heaven	1973	—	2.00	4.00
❑ 0007	Walkin' to New Orleans/Country Boy	1973	—	2.00	4.00
❑ 0008	I Want to Walk You Home/It's You I Love	1973	—	2.00	4.00
❑ 0009	I'm Ready/Wait and See	1973	—	2.00	4.00
❑ 0010	My Girl Josephine/When My Dreamboat Comes Home	1973	—	2.00	4.00
❑ 0011	Three Nights a Week/Let the Four Winds Blow	1973	—	2.00	4.00
—0001 through 0011 are "Silver Spotlight Series" reissues					
❑ XW 514	The Fat Man/Valley of Tears	1974	—	2.50	5.00
—Reissue					

WARNER BROS.

Number	Title (A Side/B Side)	Yr	VG	VG+	NM
❑ 49610	Whiskey Heaven/Beers to You	1980	—	2.00	4.00
—B-side by Texas Opera Company					

78s

IMPERIAL

Number	Title (A Side/B Side)	Yr	VG	VG+	NM
❑ 5058	The Fat Man/Detroit City Blues	1950	50.00	100.00	200.00
❑ 5065	Boogie Woogie Baby/Little Bee	1950	10.00	20.00	40.00
❑ 5077	She's My Baby/Hide Away Blues	1950	10.00	20.00	40.00
❑ 5085	Brand New Baby/Hey La Bass Boogie	1950	10.00	20.00	40.00
❑ 5099	Korea Blues/Every Night About This Time	1950	10.00	20.00	40.00
❑ 5114	What's the Matter Baby/Tired of Crying	1951	10.00	20.00	40.00
❑ 5123	Don't You Lie to Me/Sometimes I Wonder	1951	10.00	20.00	40.00
❑ 5138	No No Baby/Right From Wrong	1951	10.00	20.00	40.00
❑ 5145	Careless Love/Rocking Chair	1951	10.00	20.00	40.00
❑ 5167	You Know I Miss You/I'll Be Gone	1952	10.00	20.00	40.00
❑ 5180	Goin' Home/Reeling and Rocking	1952	10.00	20.00	40.00
❑ 5197	Poor Poor Me/Trust in Me	1952	10.00	20.00	40.00
❑ 5209	How Long/Dreaming	1952	10.00	20.00	40.00
❑ 5220	Nobody Loves Me/Cheatin'	1953	7.50	15.00	30.00
❑ 5231	Going to the River/Mardi Gras in New Orleans	1953	7.50	15.00	30.00
❑ 5240	Please Don't Leave Me/The Girl I Love	1953	7.50	15.00	30.00
❑ 5251	You Said You Loved Me/Rose Mary	1953	7.50	15.00	30.00
❑ 5262	Something's Wrong/Don't Leave Me This Way	1954	6.25	12.50	25.00
❑ 5272	Little School Girl/You Done Me Wrong	1954	6.25	12.50	25.00
❑ 5283	Baby, Please/Where Did You Stay	1954	6.25	12.50	25.00
❑ 5301	You Can Pack Your Suitcase/I Lived My Life	1954	6.25	12.50	25.00
❑ 5313	Love Me/Don't You Hear Me Calling You	1954	6.25	12.50	25.00
❑ 5323	I Know/Thinking of You	1955	6.25	12.50	25.00
❑ 5340	Don't You Know/Helping Hand	1955	6.25	12.50	25.00
❑ 5348	Ain't It a Shame/La La	1955	10.00	20.00	40.00
❑ 5357	All By Myself/Troubles of My Own	1955	6.25	12.50	25.00
❑ 5369	Poor Me/I Can't Go On	1955	6.25	12.50	25.00
❑ 5375	Bo Weevil/Don't Blame It on Me	1956	6.25	12.50	25.00
❑ 5386	I'm in Love Again/My Blue Heaven	1956	7.50	15.00	30.00
❑ 5396	When My Dreamboat Comes Home/So-Long	1956	7.50	15.00	30.00
❑ 5407	Blueberry Hill/Honey Chile	1956	7.50	15.00	30.00
❑ 5417	Blue Monday/What's the Reason I'm Not Pleasing You	1957	7.50	15.00	30.00
❑ 5428	I'm Walkin'/I'm in the Mood for Love	1957	7.50	15.00	30.00
❑ 5442	Valley of Tears/It's You I Love	1957	7.50	15.00	30.00
❑ 5454	When I See You/What Will I Tell My Heart	1957	7.50	15.00	30.00
❑ 5467	Wait and See/I Still Love You	1957	7.50	15.00	30.00
❑ 5477	The Big Beat/I Want You to Know	1957	7.50	15.00	30.00
❑ 5492	Yes, My Darling/Don't You Know I Love You	1958	7.50	15.00	30.00
❑ 5515	Sick and Tired/No, No	1958	7.50	15.00	30.00
❑ 5526	Little Mary/The Prisoner's Song	1958	7.50	15.00	30.00
❑ 5537	Young School Girl/It Must Be Love	1958	10.00	20.00	40.00
❑ 5553	Whole Lotta Loving/Coquette	1958	12.50	25.00	50.00

7-Inch Extended Plays

IMPERIAL

Number	Title (A Side/B Side)	Yr	VG	VG+	NM
❑ IMP 127	Going to the River/Every Night About This Time//Going Home/Please Don't Leave Me	1955	37.50	75.00	150.00
—"Script" label					
❑ IMP 127	Going to the River/Every Night About This Time//Going Home/Please Don't Leave Me	1955	25.00	50.00	100.00
—Maroon label, block-letter logo					
❑ IMP 127	Going to the River/Every Night About This Time//Going Home/Please Don't Leave Me	1958	6.25	12.50	25.00
—Black label					
❑ IMP 127 [PS]	Fats Domino	1955	12.50	25.00	50.00
❑ IMP 138	Domino Stomp/The Girl I Love//Don't You Know/The Fat Man	1956	25.00	50.00	100.00
—Maroon label, block-letter logo					
❑ IMP 138	Domino Stomp/The Girl I Love//Don't You Know/The Fat Man	1958	6.25	12.50	25.00
—Black label					
❑ IMP 138 [PS]	Rock and Rollin' with Fats Domino	1956	12.50	25.00	50.00
❑ IMP 139	Rosemary/All By Myself//Tired of Crying/You Said You Loved Me	1956	25.00	50.00	100.00
—Maroon label, block-letter logo					
❑ IMP 139	Rosemary/All By Myself//Tired of Crying/You Said You Loved Me	1958	6.25	12.50	25.00
—Black label					
❑ IMP 139 [PS]	Rock and Rollin' with Fats Domino	1956	12.50	25.00	50.00
❑ IMP 140	Ain't It a Shame/Poor Me//Bo Weevil/Don't Blame It on Me	1956	25.00	50.00	100.00
—Maroon label, block-letter logo					
❑ IMP 140	Ain't It a Shame/Poor Me//Bo Weevil/Don't Blame It on Me	1958	6.25	12.50	25.00
—Black label					
❑ IMP 140 [PS]	Rock and Rollin' with Fats Domino	1956	12.50	25.00	50.00
❑ IMP 141	My Blue Heaven/Swanee River Hop//Second Line Jump/Goodbye	1956	25.00	50.00	100.00
—Maroon label, block-letter logo					
❑ IMP 141	My Blue Heaven/Swanee River Hop//Second Line Jump/Goodbye	1958	6.25	12.50	25.00
—Black label					
❑ IMP 141 [PS]	Rock and Rollin'	1956	12.50	25.00	50.00
❑ IMP 142	Careless Love/I Love Her//I'm in Love Again/When My Dreamboat Comes Home	1956	25.00	50.00	100.00
—Maroon label, block-letter logo					
❑ IMP 142	Careless Love/I Love Her//I'm in Love Again/When My Dreamboat Comes Home	1958	6.25	12.50	25.00
—Black label					
❑ IMP 142 [PS]	Rock and Rollin'	1956	12.50	25.00	50.00
❑ IMP 143	Are Your Going My Way/If You Need Me//My Heart Is In Your Hands/Fats Frenzy	1956	25.00	50.00	100.00
—Maroon label, block-letter logo					
❑ IMP 143	Are Your Going My Way/If You Need Me//My Heart Is In Your Hands/Fats Frenzy	1958	6.25	12.50	25.00
—Black label					
❑ IMP 143 [PS]	Rock and Rollin'	1956	12.50	25.00	50.00
❑ IMP 144	Blueberry Hill/Honey Chile//Troubles of My Own/You Done Me Wrong	1956	25.00	50.00	100.00
—Maroon label, block-letter logo					
❑ IMP 144	Blueberry Hill/Honey Chile//Troubles of My Own/You Done Me Wrong	1958	6.25	12.50	25.00
—Black label					
❑ IMP 144 [PS]	This Is Fats Domino	1956	12.50	25.00	50.00
❑ IMP 145	What's the Reason I'm Not Pleasing You/Blue Monday//Reeling and Rocking/The Fat Man's Hop	1956	25.00	50.00	100.00
—Maroon label, block-letter logo					
❑ IMP 145	What's the Reason I'm Not Pleasing You/Blue Monday//Reeling and Rocking/The Fat Man's Hop	1958	6.25	12.50	25.00
—Black label					
❑ IMP 145 [PS]	This Is Fats Domino	1956	12.50	25.00	50.00
❑ IMP 146	So Long/La La//Poor, Poor Me/Trust in Me	1956	25.00	50.00	100.00
—Maroon label, block-letter logo					
❑ IMP 146	So Long/La La//Poor, Poor Me/Trust in Me	1958	6.25	12.50	25.00
—Black label					
❑ IMP 146 [PS]	This Is Fats Domino	1956	12.50	25.00	50.00
❑ IMP 147	The Rooster Song/My Happiness//As Time Goes By/Hey La Bas	1956	25.00	50.00	100.00
—Maroon label, block-letter logo					
❑ IMP 147	The Rooster Song/My Happiness//As Time Goes By/Hey La Bas	1958	6.25	12.50	25.00
—Black label					
❑ IMP 147 [PS]	Here Comes Fats	1956	12.50	25.00	50.00
❑ IMP 148	Detroit City Blues/Hide Away Blues//She's My Baby/New Baby	1957	25.00	50.00	100.00
—Maroon label, block-letter logo					
❑ IMP 148	Detroit City Blues/Hide Away Blues//She's My Baby/New Baby	1958	6.25	12.50	25.00
—Black label					
❑ IMP 148 [PS]	Here Stands Fats Domino	1957	12.50	25.00	50.00
❑ IMP 149	Little Bee/Every Night About This Time//I'm Walkin'/Cheatin'	1957	25.00	50.00	100.00
—Maroon label, block-letter logo					
❑ IMP 149	Little Bee/Every Night About This Time//I'm Walkin'/Cheatin'	1958	6.25	12.50	25.00
—Black label					
❑ IMP 149 [PS]	Here Stands Fats Domino	1957	12.50	25.00	50.00
❑ IMP 150	I'm in the Mood for Love/You Can Pack Your Suitcase//Hey! Fat Man/I'll Be Gone	1957	25.00	50.00	100.00
—Maroon label, block-letter logo					
❑ IMP 150	I'm in the Mood for Love/You Can Pack Your Suitcase//Hey! Fat Man/I'll Be Gone	1958	6.25	12.50	25.00
—Black label					
❑ IMP 150 [PS]	Here Stands Fats Domino	1957	12.50	25.00	50.00
❑ IMP 151	Love Me/Don't You Hear Me Calling You//It's You I Love/Valley of Tears	1957	25.00	50.00	100.00
—Maroon label, block-letter logo					
❑ IMP 151	Love Me/Don't You Hear Me Calling You//It's You I Love/Valley of Tears	1958	6.25	12.50	25.00
—Black label					
❑ IMP 151 [PS]	Cookin' with Fats	1957	12.50	25.00	50.00

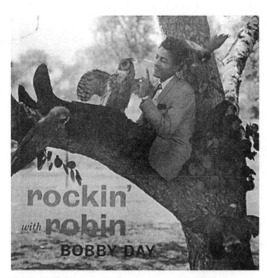

Bobby Day, who recorded under several other pseudonyms and also was with the Hollywood Flames, had his biggest hit with "Rock-In Robin" in 1958. This is the album that resulted.

The only album ever issued on Buchanan and Goodman's Luniverse label had nothing to do with break-in records – it was this highly sought-after album by the Del Vikings.

Before there was a white group of the same name, a black group called The Diamonds recorded for Atlantic. This is one side of their third and last single for the label, issued in 1954.

Bo Diddley's only EP for Chess came out in 1958. This same photo was used for the ultra-rare "Say Man" picture sleeve.

Rock and Rollin' with Fats Domino, an early EP, contains one track from 1951, two from 1953 and one from 1955. The oldest song, "Tired of Crying," was previously only issued on a 78.

Fats Domino's third album, *This Is Fats Domino,* made the pop LP charts in early 1957.

Number	Title (A Side/B Side)	Yr	VG	VG+	NM
❑ IMP 152	Thinking of You/You Know I Miss You//Where Did You Stay/Baby Please	1957	25.00	50.00	100.00
—Maroon label, block-letter logo					
❑ IMP 152	Thinking of You/You Know I Miss You//Where Did You Stay/Baby Please	1958	6.25	12.50	25.00
—Black label					
❑ IMP 152 [PS]	Rockin' with Fats	1957	12.50	25.00	50.00

Albums

ABC

Number	Title (A Side/B Side)	Yr	VG	VG+	NM
❑ S-455 [S]	Here Comes... Fats Domino	1967	3.75	7.50	15.00
❑ S-479 [S]	Fats on Fire	1967	3.75	7.50	15.00
❑ S-510 [S]	Get Away with Fats Domino	1967	3.75	7.50	15.00

ABC-PARAMOUNT

Number	Title (A Side/B Side)	Yr	VG	VG+	NM
❑ 455 [M]	Here Comes... Fats Domino	1963	5.00	10.00	20.00
❑ S-455 [S]	Here Comes... Fats Domino	1963	6.25	12.50	25.00
❑ 479 [M]	Fats on Fire	1964	5.00	10.00	20.00
❑ S-479 [S]	Fats on Fire	1964	6.25	12.50	25.00
❑ 510 [M]	Get Away with Fats Domino	1965	5.00	10.00	20.00
❑ S-510 [S]	Get Away with Fats Domino	1965	6.25	12.50	25.00
❑ ST-90167 [S]	Get Away with Fats Domino	1965	7.50	15.00	30.00
—Capitol Record Club edition					
❑ T-90167 [M]	Get Away with Fats Domino	1965	6.25	12.50	25.00
—Capitol Record Club edition					

ARCHIVE OF FOLK AND JAZZ

Number	Title (A Side/B Side)	Yr	VG	VG+	NM
❑ 280	Fats Domino	1974	2.50	5.00	10.00
❑ 330	Fats Domino, Vol. II	1975	2.50	5.00	10.00

ATLANTIC

Number	Title (A Side/B Side)	Yr	VG	VG+	NM
❑ 81751	Live in Montreux	1987	3.00	6.00	12.00

COLUMBIA

Number	Title (A Side/B Side)	Yr	VG	VG+	NM
❑ C 35996	When I'm Walking	1979	2.50	5.00	10.00
—Reissue of Harmony LP					
❑ PC 35996	When I'm Walking	1986	2.00	4.00	8.00
—Budget-line reissue					

COLUMBIA SPECIAL PRODUCTS

Number	Title (A Side/B Side)	Yr	VG	VG+	NM
❑ P2 13197 [(2)]	The Legendary Music Man	1976	3.75	7.50	15.00
—Candelite Music TV offer					

GRAND AWARD

Number	Title (A Side/B Side)	Yr	VG	VG+	NM
❑ 267 [M]	Fats Domino	196?	5.00	10.00	20.00
❑ S-267 [R]	Fats Domino	196?	2.50	5.00	10.00

HARLEM HIT PARADE

Number	Title (A Side/B Side)	Yr	VG	VG+	NM
❑ 5005	Fats' Hits	197?	2.50	5.00	10.00

HARMONY

Number	Title (A Side/B Side)	Yr	VG	VG+	NM
❑ HS 11343	When I'm Walking	1969	3.00	6.00	12.00

IMPERIAL

Number	Title (A Side/B Side)	Yr	VG	VG+	NM
❑ LP-9004 [M]	Rock and Rollin' with Fats Domino	1956	37.50	75.00	150.00
—Maroon label					
❑ LP-9004 [M]	Rock and Rollin' with Fats Domino	1958	20.00	40.00	80.00
—Black label with stars on top					
❑ LP-9004 [M]	Rock and Rollin' with Fats Domino	1964	6.25	12.50	25.00
—Black and pink label					
❑ LP-9004 [M]	Rock and Rollin' with Fats Domino	1967	5.00	10.00	20.00
—Black and green label					
❑ LP-9009 [M]	Fats Domino Rock and Rollin'	1956	37.50	75.00	150.00
—Maroon label					
❑ LP-9009 [M]	Fats Domino Rock and Rollin'	1958	20.00	40.00	80.00
—Black label with stars on top					
❑ LP-9009 [M]	Fats Domino Rock and Rollin'	1964	6.25	12.50	25.00
—Black and pink label					
❑ LP-9009 [M]	Fats Domino Rock and Rollin'	1967	5.00	10.00	20.00
—Black and green label					
❑ LP-9028 [M]	This Is Fats Domino!	1957	37.50	75.00	150.00
—Maroon label					
❑ LP-9028 [M]	This Is Fats Domino!	1958	20.00	40.00	80.00
—Black label with stars on top					
❑ LP-9028 [M]	This Is Fats Domino!	1964	6.25	12.50	25.00
—Black and pink label					
❑ LP-9028 [M]	This Is Fats Domino!	1967	5.00	10.00	20.00
—Black and green label					
❑ LP-9038 [M]	Here Stands Fats Domino	1957	37.50	75.00	150.00
—Maroon label					
❑ LP-9038 [M]	Here Stands Fats Domino	1958	20.00	40.00	80.00
—Black label with stars on top					
❑ LP-9038 [M]	Here Stands Fats Domino	1964	6.25	12.50	25.00
—Black and pink label					
❑ LP-9038 [M]	Here Stands Fats Domino	1967	5.00	10.00	20.00
—Black and green label					
❑ LP-9040 [M]	This Is Fats	1957	37.50	75.00	150.00
—Maroon label					
❑ LP-9040 [M]	This Is Fats	1958	20.00	40.00	80.00
—Black label with stars on top					
❑ LP-9040 [M]	This Is Fats	1964	6.25	12.50	25.00
—Black and pink label					
❑ LP-9040 [M]	This Is Fats	1967	5.00	10.00	20.00
—Black and green label					
❑ LP-9055 [M]	The Fabulous Mr. D.	1958	25.00	50.00	100.00
—Black label with stars on top					
❑ LP-9055 [M]	The Fabulous Mr. D.	1964	7.50	15.00	30.00
—Black and pink label					
❑ LP-9055 [M]	The Fabulous Mr. D.	1967	5.00	10.00	20.00
—Black and green label					
❑ LP-9062 [M]	Fats Domino Swings	1959	25.00	50.00	100.00
—Black label with stars on top					
❑ LP-9062 [M]	Fats Domino Swings	1964	7.50	15.00	30.00
—Black and pink label					
❑ LP-9062 [M]	Fats Domino Swings	1967	5.00	10.00	20.00
—Black and green label					
❑ LP-9065 [M]	Let's Play Fats Domino	1959	25.00	50.00	100.00
—Black label with stars on top					
❑ LP-9065 [M]	Let's Play Fats Domino	1964	7.50	15.00	30.00
—Black and pink label					
❑ LP-9065 [M]	Let's Play Fats Domino	1967	5.00	10.00	20.00
—Black and green label					
❑ LP-9103 [M]	Million Record Hits	1960	25.00	50.00	100.00
—Black label with stars on top					
❑ LP-9103 [M]	Million Record Hits	1964	7.50	15.00	30.00
—Black and pink label					
❑ LP-9103 [M]	Million Record Hits	1967	5.00	10.00	20.00
—Black and green label					
❑ LP-9127 [M]	A Lot of Dominos	1960	25.00	50.00	100.00
—Black label with stars on top					
❑ LP-9127 [M]	A Lot of Dominos	1964	7.50	15.00	30.00
—Black and pink label					
❑ LP-9127 [M]	A Lot of Dominos	1967	5.00	10.00	20.00
—Black and green label					
❑ LP-9138 [M]	I Miss You So	1961	25.00	50.00	100.00
—Black label with stars on top					
❑ LP-9138 [M]	I Miss You So	1964	7.50	15.00	30.00
—Black and pink label					
❑ LP-9138 [M]	I Miss You So	1967	5.00	10.00	20.00
—Black and green label					
❑ LP-9153 [M]	Let the Four Winds Blow	1961	25.00	50.00	100.00
—Black label with stars on top					
❑ LP-9153 [M]	Let the Four Winds Blow	1964	7.50	15.00	30.00
—Black and pink label					
❑ LP-9153 [M]	Let the Four Winds Blow	1967	5.00	10.00	20.00
—Black and green label					
❑ LP-9164 [M]	What a Party	1962	15.00	30.00	60.00
—Black label with stars on top					
❑ LP-9164 [M]	What a Party	1964	7.50	15.00	30.00
—Black and pink label					
❑ LP-9164 [M]	What a Party	1967	5.00	10.00	20.00
—Black and green label					
❑ LP-9170 [M]	Twistin' the Stomp	1962	15.00	30.00	60.00
—Black label with stars on top					
❑ LP-9170 [M]	Twistin' the Stomp	1964	7.50	15.00	30.00
—Black and pink label					
❑ LP-9170 [M]	Twistin' the Stomp	1967	5.00	10.00	20.00
—Black and green label					
❑ LP-9195 [M]	Million Sellers by Fats	1962	12.50	25.00	50.00
—Black label with stars on top					
❑ LP-9195 [M]	Million Sellers by Fats	1964	7.50	15.00	30.00
—Black and pink label					
❑ LP-9195 [M]	Million Sellers by Fats	1967	5.00	10.00	20.00
—Black and green label					
❑ LP-9208 [M]	Just Domino	1962	12.50	25.00	50.00
—Black label with stars on top					
❑ LP-9208 [M]	Just Domino	1964	7.50	15.00	30.00
—Black and pink label					
❑ LP-9208 [M]	Just Domino	1967	5.00	10.00	20.00
—Black and green label					
❑ LP-9227 [M]	Walking to New Orleans	1963	12.50	25.00	50.00
—Black label with stars on top					
❑ LP-9227 [M]	Walking to New Orleans	1964	7.50	15.00	30.00
—Black and pink label					
❑ LP-9227 [M]	Walking to New Orleans	1967	5.00	10.00	20.00
—Black and green label					
❑ LP-9239 [M]	Let's Dance with Domino	1963	12.50	25.00	50.00
—Black label with stars on top					
❑ LP-9239 [M]	Let's Dance with Domino	1964	7.50	15.00	30.00
—Black and pink label					
❑ LP-9239 [M]	Let's Dance with Domino	1967	5.00	10.00	20.00
—Black and green label					
❑ LP-9248 [M]	Here He Comes Again	1963	12.50	25.00	50.00
—Black label with stars on top					
❑ LP-9248 [M]	Here He Comes Again	1964	7.50	15.00	30.00
—Black and pink label					
❑ LP-9248 [M]	Here He Comes Again	1967	5.00	10.00	20.00
—Black and green label					
❑ LP-12066 [S]	A Lot of Dominos	1961	37.50	75.00	150.00
—Black label with silver top					
❑ LP-12066 [S]	A Lot of Dominos	1964	10.00	20.00	40.00
—Black and pink label					
❑ LP-12066 [S]	A Lot of Dominos	1967	6.25	12.50	25.00
—Black and green label					
❑ LP-12073 [S]	Let the Four Winds Blow	1961	37.50	75.00	150.00
—Black label with silver top					
❑ LP-12073 [S]	Let the Four Winds Blow	1964	10.00	20.00	40.00
—Black and pink label					
❑ LP-12073 [S]	Let the Four Winds Blow	1967	6.25	12.50	25.00
—Black and green label					
❑ LP-12091 [R]	Fats Domino Swings	1964	5.00	10.00	20.00
—Black and pink label					
❑ LP-12091 [R]	Fats Domino Swings	1967	3.75	7.50	15.00
—Black and green label					
❑ LP-12103 [R]	Million Record Hits	1964	5.00	10.00	20.00
—Black and pink label					
❑ LP-12103 [R]	Million Record Hits	1967	3.75	7.50	15.00
—Black and green label					
❑ LP-12195 [R]	Million Sellers by Fats	1964	5.00	10.00	20.00
—Black and pink label					

Number	Title (A Side/B Side)	Yr	VG	VG+	NM
❑ LP-12195 [R] Million Sellers by Fats		1967	3.75	7.50	15.00
—Black and green label					
❑ LP-12227 [R] Walking to New Orleans		1964	5.00	10.00	20.00
—Black and pink label					
❑ LP-12227 [R] Walking to New Orleans		1967	3.75	7.50	15.00
—Black and green label					
❑ LP-12248 [R] Here He Comes Again		1964	5.00	10.00	20.00
—Black and pink label					
❑ LP-12248 [R] Here He Comes Again		1967	3.75	7.50	15.00
—Black and green label					
❑ LP-12387 [R] Rock and Rollin' with Fats Domino		1968	3.00	6.00	12.00
—Rechanneled reissue of 9004					
❑ LP-12388 [R] Fats Domino Rock and Rollin'		1968	3.00	6.00	12.00
—Rechanneled reissue of 9009					
❑ LP-12389 [R] This Is Fats Domino!		1968	3.00	6.00	12.00
—Rechanneled reissue of 9028					
❑ LP-12390 [R] Here Stands Fats Domino		1968	3.00	6.00	12.00
—Rechanneled reissue of 9038					
❑ LP-12391 [R] This Is Fats		1968	3.00	6.00	12.00
—Rechanneled reissue of 9040					
❑ LP-12394 [R] The Fabulous Mr. D.		1968	3.00	6.00	12.00
—Rechanneled reissue of 9055					
❑ LP-12395 [R] Let's Play Fats Domino		1968	3.00	6.00	12.00
—Rechanneled reissue of 9065					
❑ LP-12398 [R] I Miss You So		1968	3.00	6.00	12.00
—Rechanneled reissue of 9138					
LIBERTY					
❑ LWB-122 [(2)] Cookin' with Fats (Superpak)		1981	3.00	6.00	12.00
—Budget-line reissue of UA 122					
❑ LM-1027 Million Sellers by Fats		1981	2.00	4.00	8.00
—Budget-line reissue of UA 1027					
❑ LWB-9958 [(2)] Legendary Masters		1981	2.50	5.00	10.00
—Budget-line reissue of UA 9958					
❑ LN-10135 Let's Play Fats Domino		1981	2.00	4.00	8.00
—Budget-line reissue					
❑ LN-10136 The Fabulous Mr. D.		1981	2.00	4.00	8.00
—Budget-line reissue					
MCA/SILVER EAGLE					
❑ 6170 Greatest Hits		198?	2.50	5.00	10.00
MERCURY					
❑ MG-21039 [M] Fats Domino '65		1965	6.25	12.50	25.00
❑ 21065/61065 Southland U.S.A,		1966	—	—	—
—Canceled					
❑ SR-61039 [S] Fats Domino '65		1965	10.00	20.00	40.00
PICKWICK					
❑ SPC-3111 Blueberry Hill		197?	2.50	5.00	10.00
❑ SPC-3165 When My Dreamboat Comes Home		197?	2.50	5.00	10.00
❑ SPC-3295 My Blue Heaven		1971	2.50	5.00	10.00
QUICKSILVER					
❑ QS-1016 Live Hits		198?	2.50	5.00	10.00
REPRISE					
❑ RS 6304 Fats Is Back		1968	7.50	15.00	30.00
❑ RS 6439 Fats		1970	125.00	250.00	500.00
—Officially unreleased, test pressings and coverless stock copies are known to exist					
SEARS					
❑ SPS-473 Blueberry Hill!		1970	6.25	12.50	25.00
SUNSET					
❑ SUM-1103 [M] Fats Domino		1966	3.00	6.00	12.00
❑ SUM-1158 [M] Stompin' Fats Domino		1967	3.00	6.00	12.00
❑ SUS-5103 [R] Fats Domino		1966	3.00	6.00	12.00
❑ SUS-5158 [R] Stompin' Fats Domino		1967	3.00	6.00	12.00
❑ SUS-5200 [P] Trouble in Mind		1968	5.00	10.00	20.00
❑ SUS-5299 [R] Ain't That a Shame		1970	3.00	6.00	12.00
UNITED ARTISTS					
❑ UAMG-104 [DJ] The Fats Domino Sound		1973	10.00	20.00	40.00
—Promo compilation of 30 excerpts of Fats hits					
❑ UA-LA122-F2 [(2)] Cookin' with Fats (Superpak)		1974	7.50	15.00	30.00
❑ UA-LA122-F2 [(2) DJ] Cookin' with Fats (Superpak)		1974	75.00	150.00	300.00
—Promo with one black vinyl record and one colored vinyl record					
❑ UA-LA233-G The Very Best of Fats Domino		1974	3.00	6.00	12.00
❑ LM-1027 Million Sellers by Fats		1980	2.50	5.00	10.00
❑ UAS-9958 [(2)] Legendary Masters		1972	3.75	7.50	15.00

DOMINOES, THE
See BILLY WARD AND THE DOMINOES.

DON AND DEWEY
45s

Number	Title (A Side/B Side)	Yr	VG	VG+	NM
FIDELITY					
❑ 3017 Jump Awhile/H.B. Boogie		1960	3.75	7.50	15.00
❑ 3018 Kill Me/Little Sally Walker		1960	3.75	7.50	15.00
RUSH					
❑ 1003 Don't Ever Leave Me (Don't Make Me Cry)/Heart Attack		196?	5.00	10.00	20.00
SHADE					
❑ 100 Miss Sue/My Heart Is Aching		195?	37.50	75.00	150.00
SPECIALTY					
❑ 599 Jungle Hop/A Little Love		1957	6.25	12.50	25.00
❑ 610 Leavin' It All Up to You/Jelly Bean		1957	7.50	15.00	30.00
❑ 617 Just a Little Lovin'/When the Sun Has Begun to Shine		1957	6.25	12.50	25.00
❑ 631 Justine/Bim Bam		1958	6.25	12.50	25.00
❑ 639 The Letter/Koko Joe		1958	6.25	12.50	25.00
❑ 659 Farmer John/Big Boy Pete		1959	6.25	12.50	25.00
❑ 691 Annie Lee/Get Your Hat		196?	3.00	6.00	12.00

Albums
SPECIALTY

Number	Title (A Side/B Side)	Yr	VG	VG+	NM
❑ SPS-2131 They're Rockin' 'Til Midnight, Rollin' Til Dawn		1970	7.50	15.00	30.00
—Original labels are black and gold					

DON AND JUAN
45s

Number	Title (A Side/B Side)	Yr	VG	VG+	NM
BIG TOP					
❑ 3079 What's Your Name/Chicken Necks		1961	6.25	12.50	25.00
❑ 3106 Two Fools Are We/Pot Luck		1962	5.00	10.00	20.00
❑ 3121 Magic Wand/What I Really Meant to Say		1962	10.00	20.00	40.00
❑ 3145 True Love Never Runs Smooth/Is It All Right If I Love You		1963	12.50	25.00	50.00
LANA					
❑ 150 What's Your Name/Chicken Necks		196?	—	3.00	6.00
—Early reissue					
MALA					
❑ 469 Lonely Man/Could This Be Love		1963	3.00	6.00	12.00
❑ 479 Pledging My Love/Molinda		1964	3.00	6.00	12.00
❑ 484 Sincerely/Maryana Cherie		1964	3.00	6.00	12.00
❑ 494 I Can't Help Myself/All That's Missing Is You		1964	3.00	6.00	12.00
❑ 509 The Heartbreaking Truth/Thank Goodness		1,965	7.50	15.00	30.00
TWIRL					
❑ 2021 Because I Love You/Are You Putting Me on the Shelf		1966	7.50	15.00	30.00

DONAYS, THE
45s

Number	Title (A Side/B Side)	Yr	VG	VG+	NM
BRENT					
❑ 7033 Devil in His Heart/Bad Boy		1962	10.00	20.00	40.00
—The Beatles re-made the A-side as "Devil in Her Heart"					

DOOTONES, THE
45s

Number	Title (A Side/B Side)	Yr	VG	VG+	NM
DOOTONE					
❑ 366 Teller of Fortune/Ay Si Si		1955	50.00	100.00	200.00
❑ 470 Strange Love Affair/The Day You Said Goodbye		1962	7.50	15.00	30.00
❑ 471 Sailor Boy/Down the Road		1962	7.50	15.00	30.00

DORMAN, HAROLD
45s

Number	Title (A Side/B Side)	Yr	VG	VG+	NM
RITA					
❑ 1003 Mountain of Love/To Be with You		1960	6.25	12.50	25.00
❑ 1008 I'll Come Running/River of Tears		1960	5.00	10.00	20.00
❑ 1012 Moved to Kansas City/Take a Chance on Me		1960	5.00	10.00	20.00
SANTO					
❑ 9005 In an Instant/There on Yonder Hill		1962	3.75	7.50	15.00
❑ 9051 Ain't Gonna Change/What Comes Next		1962	3.75	7.50	15.00
SUN					
❑ 362 I'll Stick By You/There They Go		1961	5.00	10.00	20.00
❑ 370 Just One Step/Uncle Jonah's Place		1961	5.00	10.00	20.00
❑ 377 Wait 'Til Saturday Night/In the Beginning		1962	5.00	10.00	20.00

DORSEY, LEE
45s

Number	Title (A Side/B Side)	Yr	VG	VG+	NM
ABC					
❑ 12326 Night People/Can I Be the One		1978	—	2.00	4.00
❑ 12361 God Must Have Blessed America/Say It Again		1978	—	2.00	4.00
ABC-PARAMOUNT					
❑ 10192 Lottie Mo/Lover of Love		1961	3.75	7.50	15.00
ACE					
❑ 640 Lonely Evening/Rock		1961	3.75	7.50	15.00
AMY					
❑ 927 Ride Your Pony/The Kitty Cat Song		1965	2.00	4.00	8.00
❑ 939 Can You Hear Me/Work, Work, Work		1965	2.00	4.00	8.00
❑ 945 Get Out of My Life, Woman/So Long		1965	2.00	4.00	8.00
❑ 952 Confusion/The Neighbors' Daughter		1966	2.00	4.00	8.00
❑ 958 Working in the Coal Mine/Mexico		1966	2.50	5.00	10.00
❑ 965 Holy Cow/Operation Heartache		1966	2.00	4.00	8.00
❑ 974 Gotta Find a Job/Rain, Rain, Rain, Go Away		1967	—	3.00	6.00
❑ 987 My Old Car/Why Wait Until Tomorrow		1967	—	3.00	6.00
❑ 994 Can't Get Away/Vista Vista		1967	—	3.00	6.00
❑ 998 Go-Go Girl/I Can Hear You Callin'		1967	—	3.00	6.00
❑ 11010 I Can't Get Away/Cynthia		1968	—	3.00	6.00
❑ 11020 Wonder Woman/A Little Dab A Do Ya		1968	—	3.00	6.00
❑ 11031 Four Corners (Part 1)/Four Corners (Part 2)		1968	—	3.00	6.00
❑ 11048 I'm Gonna Sit Right Down/Little Ba-By		1968	—	3.00	6.00
❑ 11052 What Now My Love/A Lover Was Born		1969	—	3.00	6.00
❑ 11055 Everything I Do Gonna be Funky (From Now On)/There Should Be a Book		1969	—	3.00	6.00
❑ 11057 Give It Up/Candy Man		1969	—	3.00	6.00
BELL					
❑ 908 I Can Hear You Callin'/What You Want		1970	—	2.50	5.00
CONSTELLATION					
❑ 115 Organ Grinder's Swing/I Gotta Find a New Love		1964	5.00	10.00	20.00
❑ 135 You're Breaking Me Up/Messed Around and Fell in Love		1964	5.00	10.00	20.00
FURY					
❑ 1053 Ya Ya/Give Me You		1961	3.75	7.50	15.00
❑ 1056 Do-Re-Mi/People Gonna' Talk		1961	3.00	6.00	12.00
❑ 1061 Eenie Meenie Miny Moe/Behind the 8-Ball		1962	3.00	6.00	12.00
❑ 1066 You Are My Sunshine/Give Me Your Love		1962	3.00	6.00	12.00
❑ 1074 Hoodlum Joe/When I Met My Baby		1963	3.00	6.00	12.00

Number	Title (A Side/B Side)	Yr	VG	VG+	NM
POLYDOR					
❑ 14038	Yes We Can — Part 1/O Me O, My O	1970	—	2.50	5.00
❑ 14055	Sneakin' Sally Through the Alley/Tears, Tears and More Tears	1971	—	2.50	5.00
❑ 14106	Freedom for the Stallion/If She Won't (Find Someone Who Will)	1971	—	2.50	5.00
❑ 14147	When Can I Come Home/Gator Tail	1972	—	2.50	5.00
❑ 14181	On Your Way Down/Freedom for the Stallion	1973	—	2.50	5.00
REX					
❑ 1005	Rock/Lonely Evening	1959	6.25	12.50	25.00
SANSU					
❑ 474	Love Lots of Lovin'/Take Care of Our Love	1967	3.00	6.00	12.00
—With Betty Harris					
SMASH					
❑ 1842	Hello Good Looking/Someday	1963	2.50	5.00	10.00
SPRING					
❑ 114	Occapella/Tears, Tears and More Tears	1971	—	2.50	5.00
VALIANT					
❑ 1001	Lottie Mo/Lover of Love	1958	10.00	20.00	40.00
Albums					
AMY					
❑ 8010-S [S]	Ride Your Pony	1966	10.00	20.00	40.00
❑ 8010 [M]	Ride Your Pony	1966	7.50	15.00	30.00
❑ 8011-S [S]	The New Lee Dorsey/Working in the Coal Mine-Holy Cow	1966	7.50	15.00	30.00
❑ 8011 [M]	The New Lee Dorsey/Working in the Coal Mine-Holy Cow	1966	6.25	12.50	25.00
ARISTA					
❑ AL 8387	Holy Cow! The Best of Lee Dorsey	1985	2.50	5.00	10.00
FURY					
❑ 1002 [M]	Ya Ya	1962	75.00	150.00	300.00
POLYDOR					
❑ 24-4024	Yes We Can	1970	3.00	6.00	12.00
SPHERE SOUND					
❑ SR-7003 [M]	Ya Ya	196?	25.00	50.00	100.00
—Reissue of Fury 1002					
❑ SSR-7003 [R]	Ya Ya	196?	12.50	25.00	50.00
—Rechanneled reissue of Fury 1002					

DOUGLAS, CARL
45s

Number	Title (A Side/B Side)	Yr	VG	VG+	NM
20TH CENTURY					
❑ 2140	Kung Fu Fighting/Gamblin' Man	1974	—	2.00	4.00
❑ 2168	Dance the Kung Fu/Changing Times	1975	—	2.00	4.00
❑ 2179	Blue Eyed Soul (Part 1)/Blue Eyed Soul (Part 2)	1975	—	2.00	4.00
❑ 2192	Witchfinder General/Never Had This Dream Before	1975	—	2.00	4.00
OKEH					
❑ 7268	Crazy Feeling/Keep It to Myself	1966	3.00	6.00	12.00
❑ 7287	Let the Birds Sing/Something for Nothing	1967	3.00	6.00	12.00
Albums					
20TH CENTURY					
❑ T-464	Kung Fu Fighting and Other Great Love Songs	1974	3.00	6.00	12.00

DOUGLAS, CAROL
12-Inch Singles

Number	Title (A Side/B Side)	Yr	VG	VG+	NM
MIDSONG INT'L.					
❑ L33-1975 [DJ]	Night Fever (6:20) (same on both sides)	1978	2.50	5.00	10.00
❑ 13905	Night Fever/Let You Come Into My Life	1978	3.00	6.00	12.00
45s					
20TH CENTURY					
❑ 2484	Slip Into Something Comfortable/My Simple Heart	1981	—	—	3.00
MIDLAND INT'L.					
❑ MB-10113	Doctor's Orders/Baby, Don't Let This Good Love Die	1974	—	2.00	4.00
❑ MB-10229	Hurricane Is Coming Tonight/I Fell in Love with You	1975	—	2.00	4.00
❑ MB-10304	Will We Make It Tonight/Take Me (Make Me Lose Control)	1975	—	2.00	4.00
❑ MB-10372	Headline News/Boy, YouKnow Just What I'm After	1975	—	2.00	4.00
❑ MB-10753	Midnight Love Affair/Midnight Love Affair (Long Version)	1976	—	2.00	4.00
❑ MB-10870	Dancing Queen/In the Morning	1976	—	2.00	4.00
❑ MB-10979	We Do It/Lie to Me	1977	—	2.00	4.00
MIDSONG INT'L.					
❑ 1008	I Got the Answer/We're Gonna Make It	1979	—	2.00	4.00
❑ 40860	Night Fever/Let You Come Into My Life	1978	—	2.00	4.00
—A-side appeared in the movie Saturday Night Fever, but not on the soundtrack LP					
❑ 40912	So You Win Again/Let You Come Into My Life	1978	—	2.00	4.00
❑ 40945	Let's Get Down to Doin' It Tonight/Burnin'	1978	—	2.00	4.00
RCA VICTOR					
❑ GB-10479	Doctor's Orders/Baby, Don't Let This Good Love Die	1975	—	—	3.00
—Gold Standard Series					
Albums					
MIDLAND INT'L.					
❑ BKL1-0931	The Carol Douglas Album	1975	2.50	5.00	10.00
❑ BKL1-1798	Midnight Love Affair	1976	2.50	5.00	10.00
❑ BKL1-2222	Full Bloom	1977	2.50	5.00	10.00
MIDSONG INT'L.					
❑ 3048	Burnin'	1978	2.50	5.00	10.00
❑ W 36852	The Best of Carol Douglas	1980	2.50	5.00	10.00

DOVELLS, THE
Also see LEN BARRY.
45s

Number	Title (A Side/B Side)	Yr	VG	VG+	NM
ABKCO					
❑ 4011	Bristol Stomp/You Can't Sit Down	1972	—	2.00	4.00
❑ 4029	Baby Workout/Hully Gully Baby	1973	2.50	5.00	10.00
❑ 4032	Bristol Twistin' Annie/Betty in Bermudas	1973	—	2.00	4.00
EVENT					
❑ 216	Dancing in the Street/Back on the Road Again	1974	—	2.50	5.00
❑ 3310	Roll Over Beethoven/Something About You Boy	1970	—	2.50	5.00
JAMIE					
❑ 1369	Our Winter Love/Blue	1969	2.50	5.00	10.00
MGM					
❑ 13628	There's a Girl/Love Is Everywhere	1966	2.50	5.00	10.00
❑ 14568	Don't Vote for Luke McCabe/Mary's Magic Show	1973	—	2.50	5.00
PARAMOUNT					
❑ 0134	L-O-V-E Love/We're All In This Together	1971	—	2.50	5.00
PARKWAY					
❑ 819	No, No, No/Letters of Love	1961	5.00	10.00	20.00
❑ 827	Bristol Stomp/Out in the Cold Again	1961	7.50	15.00	30.00
❑ 827	Bristol Stomp/Letters of Love	1961	3.75	7.50	15.00
❑ 833	Do the New Continental/Mope-Itty Mope Stomp	1962	3.75	7.50	15.00
❑ 833 [PS]	Do the New Continental/Mope-Itty Mope Stomp	1962	7.50	15.00	30.00
❑ 838	Bristol Twistin' Annie/The Actor	1962	3.75	7.50	15.00
❑ 838 [PS]	Bristol Twistin' Annie/The Actor	1962	7.50	15.00	30.00
❑ 845	Hully Gully Baby/Your Last Chance	1962	3.75	7.50	15.00
❑ 845 [PS]	Hully Gully Baby/Your Last Chance	1962	7.50	15.00	30.00
❑ 855	The Jitterbug/Kissin' in the Kitchen	1962	3.75	7.50	15.00
❑ 855 [PS]	The Jitterbug/Kissin' in the Kitchen	1962	7.50	15.00	30.00
❑ 861	Save Me Baby/You Can't Run Away from Yourself	1963	5.00	10.00	20.00
❑ 861 [PS]	Save Me Baby/You Can't Run Away from Yourself	1963	7.50	15.00	30.00
❑ 867	You Can't Sit Down/Stompin' Everywhere	1963	3.00	6.00	12.00
❑ 867	You Can't Sit Down/Wildwood Days	1963	3.75	7.50	15.00
❑ 867 [PS]	You Can't Sit Down/Stompin' Everywhere	1963	10.00	20.00	40.00
❑ 867 [PS]	You Can't Sit Down/Wildwood Days	1963	10.00	20.00	40.00
❑ 882	Betty in Bermudas/Dance the Froog	1963	3.00	6.00	12.00
❑ 882 [PS]	Betty in Bermudas/Dance the Froog	1963	7.50	15.00	30.00
❑ 889	Stop Monkeyin' Aroun'/No, No, No	1963	3.00	6.00	12.00
❑ 889 [PS]	Stop Monkeyin' Aroun'/No, No, No	1963	7.50	15.00	30.00
❑ 901	Be My Girl/Dragster on the Prowl	1964	5.00	10.00	20.00
❑ 911	One Potato/Happy Birthday Just the Same	1964	3.75	7.50	15.00
❑ 925	Watusi with Lucy/What in the World's Come Over You	1964	3.00	6.00	12.00
❑ 925 [PS]	Watusi with Lucy/What in the World's Come Over You	1964	7.50	15.00	30.00
SWAN					
❑ 4231	Happy/(Hey, Hey, Hey) Alright	1965	5.00	10.00	20.00
VERVE					
❑ 10701	Far Away/Sometimes	1973	—	2.50	5.00
Albums					
CAMEO					
❑ C-1082 [M]	Len Barry Sings with the Dovells	1965	7.50	15.00	30.00
❑ SC-1082 [S]	Len Barry Sings with the Dovells	1965	12.50	25.00	50.00
PARKWAY					
❑ P 7006 [M]	The Bristol Stomp	1961	20.00	40.00	80.00
—Light orange label					
❑ P 7006 [M]	The Bristol Stomp	1962	12.50	25.00	50.00
—Dark orange and yellow label					
❑ P 7010 [M]	All the Hits of the Teen Groups	1962	12.50	25.00	50.00
❑ P 7021 [M]	For Your Hully Gully Party	1962	12.50	25.00	50.00
❑ P 7025 [M]	You Can't Sit Down	1963	12.50	25.00	50.00
WYNCOTE					
❑ SW 9052 [R]	Discotheque	1965	3.75	7.50	15.00
❑ W 9052 [M]	Discotheque	1965	5.00	10.00	20.00
❑ SW 9114 [R]	The Dovells' Biggest Hits	1965	3.75	7.50	15.00
❑ W 9114 [M]	The Dovells' Biggest Hits	1965	5.00	10.00	20.00

DOWNBEATS, THE (1)
45s

Number	Title (A Side/B Side)	Yr	VG	VG+	NM
GEE					
❑ 1019	My Girl/China Girl	1956	200.00	400.00	800.00
—Red label					
❑ 1019	My Girl/China Girl	1958	7.50	15.00	30.00
—Gray label					
PEACOCK					
❑ 1689	You're So Fine/Someday She'll Come Along	1958	6.25	12.50	25.00

DOZIER, GENE, AND THE BROTHERHOOD
45s

Number	Title (A Side/B Side)	Yr	VG	VG+	NM
MINIT					
❑ 32026	House of Funk/One for Bess	1967	2.50	5.00	10.00
❑ 32031	I Wanna Testify/Mustang Sally	1967	2.50	5.00	10.00
❑ 32041	Funky Broadway/Soul Stroll	1968	2.50	5.00	10.00
Albums					
MINIT					
❑ 24010 [S]	Blues Power	1967	6.25	12.50	25.00
❑ 40010 [M]	Blues Power	1967	6.25	12.50	25.00

DOZIER, LAMONT

Also see HOLLAND-DOZIER; THE VOICE MASTERS.

12-Inch Singles
WARNER BROS.

Number	Title (A Side/B Side)	Yr	VG	VG+	NM
❑ 8802	Boogie Business/True Love Is Bittersweet	1979	2.50	5.00	10.00

45s
ABC

Number	Title (A Side/B Side)	Yr	VG	VG+	NM
❑ 11407	Trying to Hold On to My Woman/We Don't Want Nobody to Come Between Us	1973	—	2.00	4.00

—Also see "Holland-Dozier"

❑ 11438	Fish Ain't Bitin'/Breaking Out All Over	1974	—	2.00	4.00
❑ 12012	Fish Ain't Bitin'/Breaking Out All Over	1974	—	2.00	4.00
❑ 12044	Let Me Start Tonite/I Wanna Be with You	1974	—	2.00	4.00
❑ 12076	All Cried Out/Rose	1975	—	2.00	4.00
❑ 12234	Out Here on My Own/Take Off Your Make-Up	1976	—	2.00	4.00

ANNA

❑ 1125	Let's Talk It Over/Benny the Skinny Man	1960	6.25	12.50	25.00

—As "Lamont Anthony"

❑ 1125	Let's Talk It Over/Popeye	1960	62.50	125.00	250.00

—As "Lamont Anthony"

CHECKMATE

❑ 1001	Just to Be Loved/I Didn't Know	1961	62.50	125.00	250.00

—As "Lamont Anthony"

COLUMBIA

❑ 02035	Cool Me Out/Starting Over (We've Made the Necessary Changes)	1981	—	2.00	4.00
❑ 02238	Too Little Too Long/Chained (To Your Love)	1981	—	2.00	4.00

MEL-O-DY

❑ 102	Dearest One/Fortune Teller Please Tell Me	1962	25.00	50.00	100.00

M&M

❑ 502	Shout About It/(Instrumental)	1982	—	2.50	5.00

WARNER BROS.

❑ 8432	Sight for Sore Eyes/Tear Down the Walls	1977	—	2.00	4.00
❑ 8792	Boogie Business/True Love Is Bittersweet	1979	—	2.00	4.00

Albums
ABC

❑ D-804	Out Here on My Own	1973	2.50	5.00	10.00
❑ D-839	Black Bach	1974	2.50	5.00	10.00

INVICTUS

❑ KZ 33134	Love and Beauty	1974	3.00	6.00	12.00

WARNER BROS.

❑ BS 2929	Right There	1976	2.50	5.00	10.00
❑ BS 3039	Peddlin'	1977	2.50	5.00	10.00
❑ BSK 3282	Bittersweet	1979	2.50	5.00	10.00

DRAMATICS, THE

Probably all the same group. Also see THE DELLS AND THE DRAMATICS.

45s
ABC

Number	Title (A Side/B Side)	Yr	VG	VG+	NM
❑ 12090	Mr. and Mrs. Jones/I Cried All the Way Home	1975	—	2.50	5.00
❑ 12125	(I'm Going By) The Stars in Your Eyes/Trying to Get Over You	1975	—	2.50	5.00
❑ 12150	You're Fooling You/I'll Make It So Good	1975	—	2.50	5.00
❑ 12180	Treat Me Like a Man/I Was the Life of the Party	1976	—	2.50	5.00
❑ 12220	Finger Fever/Say the Word	1976	—	2.50	5.00
❑ 12235	Be My Girl/The Nicest Man Alive	1976	—	2.50	5.00
❑ 12258	I Can't Get Over You/Sundown Is Coming (Hold Back the Night)	1977	—	2.50	5.00
❑ 12299	Shake It Well/That Heaven Kind of Feeling	1977	—	2.50	5.00
❑ 12331	Ocean of Thoughts and Dreams/Come Inside	1978	—	2.50	5.00
❑ 12372	Stop Your Weeping/California Sunrise	1978	—	2.50	5.00
❑ 12400	Do What You Want to Do/Jane	1978	—	2.50	5.00
❑ 12429	Why Do You Wanna Do Me Wrong/Yo' Love (Can Only Bring Me Happiness)	1978	—	2.50	5.00
❑ 12460	I Just Wanna Dance with You/I've Got a Schoolboy Crush on You	1979	—	2.50	5.00

CADET

❑ 5704	Door to Your Heart/Choosing Up on You	1974	—	3.00	6.00
❑ 5706	Don't Make Me No Promises/Tune Up	1974	—	3.00	6.00
❑ 5710	Love Is Missing from Our Lives/I'm in Love	1975	—	3.00	6.00

—With the Dells

CAPITOL

❑ B-5103	Live It Up/She's My Kind of Girl	1982	—	2.00	4.00
❑ B-5140	Treat Me Right/Night Life	1982	—	2.00	4.00

CRACKERJACK

❑ 4015	Toy Soldier/Hello Summer	1968	15.00	30.00	60.00

FANTASY

❑ 966	Luv's Calling/Dream Lady	1985	—	—	3.00
❑ 967	One Love Ago/Dream Lady	1986	—	—	3.00

MAINSTREAM

❑ 5571	No Rebate on Love/Feel It	1976	—	2.50	5.00

MCA

❑ 12460	I Just Wanna Dance with You/I've Got a Schoolboy Crush on You	1979	—	2.00	4.00
❑ 41017	I Just Wanta Dance With You/I've Got a Schoolboy Crush on You	1979	—	2.00	4.00
❑ 41056	That's My Favorite Song/Bottom Line Woman	1979	—	2.00	4.00
❑ 41178	Welcome Back Home/Marriage on Paper Only	1980	—	2.00	4.00
❑ 41241	Be With the One You Love/If You Feel Like You Wanna Dance, Dance	1980	—	2.00	4.00
❑ 51004	Share Your Love with Me/Get It	1980	—	2.00	4.00
❑ 51041	(We Need More) Lovin' Time/You're the Best Thing in My Life	1980	—	2.00	4.00

SPORT

Number	Title (A Side/B Side)	Yr	VG	VG+	NM
❑ 101	All Because of You/If You Haven't Got Love	1967	15.00	30.00	60.00

VOLT

❑ 302	Bridge Over Troubled Water//(B-side unknown)	1989	—	2.00	4.00
❑ 4029	Since I've Been in Love/Your Love Was Strange	1969	2.00	4.00	8.00
❑ 4058	Whatcha See Is Whatcha Get/Thankful for Your Love	1971	2.00	4.00	8.00
❑ 4071	Get Up and Get Down/Fall in Love, Lady Love	1971	2.00	4.00	8.00
❑ 4075	In the Rain/Good Soul Music	1972	2.00	4.00	8.00
❑ 4082	Toast to the Fool/Your Love Was Strange	1972	2.00	4.00	8.00
❑ 4090	Hey You! Get Off My Mountain/The Devil Is Dope	1973	2.00	4.00	8.00
❑ 4099	Fell for You/Now You Got Me Loving You	1973	2.00	4.00	8.00
❑ 4105	And I Panicked/Beware of the Man	1974	2.00	4.00	8.00
❑ 4108	I Made Myself Lonely/Highway to Heaven	1974	2.00	4.00	8.00

WINGATE

❑ 18	Somewhere/Bingo!	1966	12.50	25.00	50.00

—As "The Dynamics"

❑ 22	Baby I Need You/Inky Dinky Wang Dang Doo	1966	12.50	25.00	50.00

—As "The Dynamics"

Albums
ABC

❑ D-867	The Dramatic Jackpot	1975	3.75	7.50	15.00
❑ D-916	Drama V	1975	3.75	7.50	15.00
❑ D-955	Joy Ride	1976	3.75	7.50	15.00
❑ AB-1010	Shake It Well	1977	3.75	7.50	15.00
❑ AA-1072	Do What You Wanna Do	1978	3.75	7.50	15.00
❑ AA-1125	Anytime, Anyplace	1979	3.75	7.50	15.00

CAPITOL

❑ ST-12205	New Dimension	1982	2.50	5.00	10.00

FANTASY

❑ 9642	Somewhere in Time: A Dramatic Reunion	1986	3.00	6.00	12.00

MCA

❑ 761	Dramatic Way	198?	2.00	4.00	8.00

—Reissue of 5149

❑ 762	10 1/2	198?	2.00	4.00	8.00

—Reissue of 3196

❑ AA-1125	Anytime, Anyplace	1979	3.00	6.00	12.00

—Reissue of ABC 1125

❑ 3196	10 1/2	1980	2.50	5.00	10.00
❑ 5149	Dramatic Way	1981	2.50	5.00	10.00

STAX

❑ STX-4111	Whatcha See Is Whatcha Get	1978	3.00	6.00	12.00

—Reissue of Volt 6018

❑ STX-4131	A Dramatic Experience	1979	3.00	6.00	12.00

—Reissue of Volt 6019

❑ MPS-8523	Dramatically Yours	198?	2.00	4.00	8.00

—Reissue of Volt 9501

❑ MPS-8526	The Best of the Dramatics	198?	2.50	5.00	10.00
❑ MPS-8545	The Dramatics Live	1988	2.50	5.00	10.00

VOLT

❑ V-3402	Positive State of Mind	1989	2.50	5.00	10.00
❑ V-3407	Stone Cold	1990	2.50	5.00	10.00
❑ VOS-6018	Whatcha See Is Whatcha Get	1972	6.25	12.50	25.00
❑ VOS-6019	A Dramatic Experience	1973	6.25	12.50	25.00
❑ VOS-9501	Dramatically Yours	1974	6.25	12.50	25.00

DREAMS, THE

45s
SAVOY

Number	Title (A Side/B Side)	Yr	VG	VG+	NM
❑ 1130	Darlene/A Letter to My Girl	1954	50.00	100.00	200.00
❑ 1140	Under the Willow/I'm Losing My Mind	1954	30.00	60.00	120.00

—A copy on gold vinyl with a blue Savoy label has shown up; its authenticity is unknown

❑ 1157	I'll Be Faithful/My Little Honeybun	1955	25.00	50.00	100.00

DRIFTERS, THE

Several different groups with a common heritage, thus we list them together. Also see BEN E. KING; RUDY LEWIS; CLYDE McPHATTER; BILL PINKNEY.

45s
ATLANTIC

Number	Title (A Side/B Side)	Yr	VG	VG+	NM
❑ 1006	Money Honey/The Way I Feel	1953	20.00	40.00	80.00
❑ 1019	Such a Night/Lucille	1954	17.50	35.00	70.00
❑ 1029	Honey Love/Warm Your Heart	1954	12.50	25.00	50.00
❑ 1043	Bip Bam/Someday You'll Want to Me to Want You	1954	10.00	20.00	40.00
❑ 1048	White Christmas/The Bells of St. Mary's	1954	15.00	30.00	60.00

—Yellow label, no spinner (original)

❑ 1048	White Christmas/The Bells of St. Mary's	1956	6.25	12.50	25.00

—Red label, no "fan" logo at lower left

❑ 1048	White Christmas/The Bells of St. Mary's	1962	2.00	4.00	8.00

—Red label with "fan" logo at lower left

❑ 1048	White Christmas/The Bells of St. Mary's	197?	—	2.50	5.00

—Glossy yellow label with "fan" logo

❑ 1048 [DJ]	White Christmas/The Bells of St. Mary's	196?	6.25	12.50	25.00

—White/red label promo, no "fan" logo, with holly leaves encircling "45 R.P.M."

❑ 1055	What'Cha Gonna Do/Gone	1955	12.50	25.00	50.00
❑ 1078	Adorable/Steamboat	1955	10.00	20.00	40.00
❑ 1089	Ruby Baby/Your Promise to Be Mine	1956	7.50	15.00	30.00
❑ 1101	Soldier of Fortune/I Got to Get Myself a Woman	1956	7.50	15.00	30.00
❑ 1123	Fools Fall in Love/It Was a Tear	1957	7.50	15.00	30.00
❑ 1141	Hypnotized/Drifting Away from You	1957	7.50	15.00	30.00
❑ 1161	I Know/Yodee Yakee	1957	7.50	15.00	30.00
❑ 1187	Drip Drop/Moonlight Bay	1958	7.50	15.00	30.00

—Last record by the "old" Drifters. The below Atlantic 45s are by a completely different group, although personnel changes resulted in at least one "old" Drifter (Johnny Moore) spending time with the "new" Drifters.

DRIVERS, THE

Number	Title (A Side/B Side)	Yr	VG	VG+	NM
❑ 2025	There Goes My Baby/Oh My Love	1959	6.25	12.50	25.00
❑ 2040	Dance with Me/(If You Cry) True Love, True Love	1959	5.00	10.00	20.00
❑ 2050	This Magic Moment/Baltimore	1960	5.00	10.00	20.00
❑ 2062	Lonely Winds/Hey Senorita	1960	5.00	10.00	20.00
❑ 2071	Save the Last Dance for Me/Nobody But Me	1960	5.00	10.00	20.00
❑ 2087	I Count the Tears/Suddenly There's a Valley	1960	3.75	7.50	15.00
❑ 2096	Some Kind of Wonderful/Honey Bee	1961	3.75	7.50	15.00
❑ 2105	Please Stay/No Sweet Lovin'	1961	3.75	7.50	15.00
❑ 2117	Sweets for My Sweet/Loneliness or Happiness	1961	3.75	7.50	15.00
❑ 2127	Room Full of Tears/Somebody New Dancin' with You	1961	3.75	7.50	15.00
❑ 2134	When My Little Girl Is Smiling/Mexican Divorce	1962	3.75	7.50	15.00
❑ 2143	Stranger on the Shore/What to Do	1962	3.75	7.50	15.00
❑ 2151	Sometimes I Wonder/Jackpot	1962	3.75	7.50	15.00
❑ 2162	Up On the Roof/Another Night with the Boys	1962	5.00	10.00	20.00
❑ 2182	On Broadway/Let the Music Play	1963	3.75	7.50	15.00
❑ 2191	Rat Race/If You Don't Come Back	1963	3.75	7.50	15.00
❑ 2201	I'll Take You Home/I Feel Good All Over	1963	3.75	7.50	15.00
❑ 2216	Vaya Con Dios/In the Land of Make Believe	1964	3.75	7.50	15.00
❑ 2225	One Way Love/Didn't It	1964	3.75	7.50	15.00
❑ 2237	Under the Boardwalk/I Don't Want to Go On Without You	1964	3.75	7.50	15.00
❑ 2253	I've Got Sand in My Shoes/He's Just a Playboy	1964	3.00	6.00	12.00
❑ 2260	Saturday Night at the Movies/Spanish Lace	1964	3.00	6.00	12.00
❑ 2260 [PS]	Saturday Night at the Movies/Spanish Lace	1964	10.00	20.00	40.00
❑ 2261	The Christmas Song/I Remember Christmas	1964	3.00	6.00	12.00
❑ 2261 [PS]	The Christmas Song/I Remember Christmas	1964	7.50	15.00	30.00
❑ 2268	At the Club/Answer the Phone	1965	2.50	5.00	10.00
❑ 2285	Come On Over to My Place/Chains of Love	1965	2.50	5.00	10.00
❑ 2292	Follow Me/The Outside World	1965	2.50	5.00	10.00
❑ 2298	I'll Take You Where the Music's Playing/Far from the Maddening Crowd	1965	2.50	5.00	10.00
❑ 2310	Nylon Stockings/We Gotta Sing	1965	2.50	5.00	10.00
❑ 2325	Memories Are Made of This/My Islands in the Sun	1966	2.00	4.00	8.00
❑ 2336	Up in the Streets of Harlem/You Can't Love Them All	1966	2.00	4.00	8.00
❑ 2366	Aretha/Baby What I Mean	1966	2.00	4.00	8.00
❑ 2426	Up Jumped the Devil/Ain't It the Truth	1967	2.00	4.00	8.00
❑ 2471	I Need You Now/Still Burning in My Heart	1968	2.00	4.00	8.00
❑ 2624	Your Best Friend/Steal Away	1969	2.00	4.00	8.00
❑ 2746	You Got to Pay Your Dues/Black Silk	1970	2.50	5.00	10.00
❑ 2786	A Rose By Any Other Name/Be My Lady	1971	2.50	5.00	10.00
❑ 89189	Ruby Baby/Fever	1987	—	2.00	4.00

—B-side by Little Willie John

| ❑ 89189 [PS] | Ruby Baby/Fever | 1987 | — | 2.00 | 4.00 |

—From the movie "Big Town"

BELL

❑ 45320	You've Got Your Troubles/I'm Feelin' Sad	1973	—	2.50	5.00
❑ 45387	The Songs We Used to Sing/Like Sister and Brother	1973	—	2.50	5.00
❑ 45600	Kissin' in the Back Row of the Movies/I'm Feelin' Sad	1974	—	2.50	5.00

CROWN

| ❑ 108 | The World Is Changing/Sacroiliac Swing | 1954 | 50.00 | 100.00 | 200.00 |

EMI-CAPITOL MUSIC

| ❑ S7-19351 | Christmas Time Is Here/I'll Be Home for Christmas | 1996 | — | — | 3.00 |

—As "The Drifters Featuring Rick Sheppard"

MUSICOR

| ❑ 1498 | Midsummer Night in Harlem/Lonely Drifter, Don't Cry | 1974 | — | 2.50 | 5.00 |

—As "Charlie Thomas and the Drifters"

S&J

| ❑ 800826 | (More Than a Number in My) Little Red Book/I Count the Tears | 196? | 2.50 | 5.00 | 10.00 |

—As "Bill Pinkney and the Original Drifters"

78s
ATLANTIC

❑ 1006	Money Honey/The Way I Feel	1953	12.50	25.00	50.00
❑ 1019	Such a Night/Lucille	1954	12.50	25.00	50.00
❑ 1029	Honey Love/Warm Your Heart	1954	7.50	15.00	30.00
❑ 1043	Bip Bam/Someday You'll Want to Want You	1954	7.50	15.00	30.00
❑ 1048	White Christmas/The Bells of St. Mary's	1954	7.50	15.00	30.00
❑ 1055	What'Cha Gonna Do/Gone	1955	7.50	15.00	30.00
❑ 1078	Adorable/Steamboat	1955	7.50	15.00	30.00
❑ 1089	Ruby Baby/Your Promise to Be Mine	1956	7.50	15.00	30.00
❑ 1101	Soldier of Fortune/I Got to Get Myself a Woman	1956	7.50	15.00	30.00
❑ 1123	Fools Fall in Love/It Was a Tear	1957	10.00	20.00	40.00
❑ 1141	Hypnotized/Drifting Away from You	1957	10.00	20.00	40.00
❑ 1161	I Know/Yodee Yakee	1957	10.00	20.00	40.00
❑ 1187	Drip Drop/Moonlight Bay	1958	12.50	25.00	50.00

—Last record by the "old" Drifters. The below Atlantic 78s are by a completely different group.

| ❑ 2025 | There Goes My Baby/Oh My Love | 1959 | 100.00 | 200.00 | 400.00 |

—Later Drifters 78s are rumored to exist in U.S. pressings; any would fetch in the hundreds for a NM copy

7-Inch Extended Plays
ATLANTIC

❑ 534	(contents unknown)	1954	50.00	100.00	200.00
❑ 534 [PS]	Clyde McPhatter and the Drifters	1954	75.00	150.00	300.00
❑ 592	Fools Fall in Love/Adorable//Steamboat/Ruby Baby	1957	25.00	50.00	100.00
❑ 592 [PS]	The Drifters	1957	50.00	100.00	200.00

Albums
ARISTA

| ❑ AB 4140 | Every Night Is Saturday Night | 1976 | 3.00 | 6.00 | 12.00 |

ATCO

Number	Title (A Side/B Side)	Yr	VG	VG+	NM
❑ SD 33-375 [R]	Their Greatest Recordings — The Early Years	1971	3.00	6.00	12.00

ATLANTIC

| ❑ 8003 [M] | Clyde McPhatter and the Drifters | 1956 | 125.00 | 250.00 | 500.00 |

—Black label

| ❑ 8003 [M] | Clyde McPhatter and the Drifters | 1959 | 15.00 | 30.00 | 60.00 |

—Red and purple label, white "fan" logo at right

| ❑ 8003 [M] | Clyde McPhatter and the Drifters | 1963 | 10.00 | 20.00 | 40.00 |

—Red and purple label, black "fan" logo at right

| ❑ 8022 [M] | Rockin' and Driftin' | 1958 | 150.00 | 300.00 | 600.00 |

—Black label

| ❑ 8022 [M] | Rockin' and Driftin' | 1958 | 125.00 | 250.00 | 500.00 |

—White "bullseye" label

| ❑ 8022 [M] | Rockin' and Driftin' | 1959 | 15.00 | 30.00 | 60.00 |

—Red and purple label, white "fan" logo at right

| ❑ 8022 [M] | Rockin' and Driftin' | 1963 | 10.00 | 20.00 | 40.00 |

—Red and purple label, black "fan" logo at right

| ❑ 8041 [M] | The Drifters' Greatest Hits | 1960 | 150.00 | 300.00 | 600.00 |

—Black label

| ❑ 8041 [M] | The Drifters' Greatest Hits | 1960 | 25.00 | 50.00 | 100.00 |

—Red and purple label, white "fan" logo at right

| ❑ 8041 [M] | The Drifters' Greatest Hits | 1963 | 12.50 | 25.00 | 50.00 |

—Red and purple label, black "fan" logo at right

| ❑ 8059 [M] | Save the Last Dance for Me | 1962 | 30.00 | 60.00 | 120.00 |

—Red and purple label, white "fan" logo at right

| ❑ 8059 [M] | Save the Last Dance for Me | 1963 | 15.00 | 30.00 | 60.00 |

—Red and purple label, black "fan" logo at right

| ❑ SD 8059 [S] | Save the Last Dance for Me | 1962 | 50.00 | 100.00 | 200.00 |

—Green and blue label, white "fan" logo at right

| ❑ SD 8059 [S] | Save the Last Dance for Me | 1963 | 25.00 | 50.00 | 100.00 |

—Green and blue label, black "fan" logo at right

| ❑ SD 8059 [S] | Save the Last Dance for Me | 1969 | 6.25 | 12.50 | 25.00 |

—Red and green label, white horizontal stripe through center hole

| ❑ 8073 [M] | Up on the Roof — The Best of the Drifters | 1963 | 25.00 | 50.00 | 100.00 |

—Red and purple label, black "fan" logo at right

| ❑ SD 8073 [S] | Up on the Roof — The Best of the Drifters | 1963 | 37.50 | 75.00 | 150.00 |

—Green and blue label, black "fan" logo at right

| ❑ 8093 [M] | Our Biggest Hits | 1964 | 15.00 | 30.00 | 60.00 |

—Red and purple label, white "fan" logo at right

| ❑ SD 8093 [S] | Our Biggest Hits | 1964 | 20.00 | 40.00 | 80.00 |

—Mostly red label, black "fan" logo

| ❑ 8099 [M] | Under the Boardwalk | 1964 | 20.00 | 40.00 | 80.00 |

—Black and white photo of group on cover

| ❑ 8099 [M] | Under the Boardwalk | 1964 | 12.50 | 25.00 | 50.00 |

—Color photo of group on cover

| ❑ SD 8099 [S] | Under the Boardwalk | 1964 | 30.00 | 60.00 | 120.00 |

—Black and white photo of group on cover

| ❑ SD 8099 [S] | Under the Boardwalk | 1964 | 15.00 | 30.00 | 60.00 |

—Color photo of group on cover

❑ 8103 [M]	The Good Life with the Drifters	1965	10.00	20.00	40.00
❑ SD 8103 [S]	The Good Life with the Drifters	1965	12.50	25.00	50.00
❑ 8113 [M]	I'll Take You Where the Music's Playing	1965	10.00	20.00	40.00
❑ SD 8113 [S]	I'll Take You Where the Music's Playing	1965	12.50	25.00	50.00
❑ 8153 [M]	The Drifters' Golden Hits	1968	7.50	15.00	30.00
❑ SD 8153 [P]	The Drifters' Golden Hits	1968	7.50	15.00	30.00

—Green and blue label

| ❑ SD 8153 [P] | The Drifters' Golden Hits | 1969 | 3.75 | 7.50 | 15.00 |

—Red and green label

| ❑ 81927 [(2)] | Let the Boogie-Woogie Roll: Greatest Hits 1953-1958 | 1989 | 3.75 | 7.50 | 15.00 |
| ❑ 81931 [(2)] | All-Time Greatest Hits and More: 1959-1965 | 1989 | 3.75 | 7.50 | 15.00 |

CLARION

| ❑ 608 [M] | The Drifters | 1964 | 5.00 | 10.00 | 20.00 |
| ❑ SD 608 [P] | The Drifters | 1964 | 7.50 | 15.00 | 30.00 |

GUSTO

| ❑ 0063 | Greatest Hits — The Drifters | 1980 | 2.50 | 5.00 | 10.00 |

TRIP

| ❑ TOP-16-6 | 16 Greatest Hits — The Drifters | 1976 | 2.50 | 5.00 | 10.00 |

DRIVERS, THE

45s
COMET

Number	Title (A Side/B Side)	Yr	VG	VG+	NM
❑ 2142	High Gear/Low Gear	1961	6.25	12.50	25.00

DELUXE

❑ 6094	Women/Smooth, Slow and Easy	1956	25.00	50.00	100.00
❑ 6104	My Lonely Prayer/Midnight Hours	1957	50.00	100.00	200.00
❑ 6117	Dangerous Lips/Oh Miss Nellie	1957	20.00	40.00	80.00

KING

| ❑ 5645 | Mr. Astronaut/Dry Bones Twist | 1962 | 3.00 | 6.00 | 12.00 |

LIN

| ❑ 1002 | A Man's Glory/Teeter Totter | 1954 | 100.00 | 200.00 | 400.00 |

RCA VICTOR

| ❑ 47-7023 | Blue Moon/I Get Weak | 1957 | 15.00 | 30.00 | 60.00 |

DRU HILL

12-Inch Singles
DEF SOUL

| ❑ DEF-340-1 [DJ] | You Are Everything (Radio Edit Featuring Ja Rule) (Explicit Featuring Ja Rule) (Instrumental)/(Radio Edit) (Album Version) (Instrumental) | 1999 | 2.00 | 4.00 | 8.00 |
| ❑ 562021-1 | You Are Everything (Remix Radio Version) (Remix Explicit Version) (Remix Instrumental Version)/(Original Album Version Radio) (LP Version) (Original Version Instrumental) | 1999 | — | 3.00 | 6.00 |

Number	Title (A Side/B Side)	Yr	VG	VG+	NM
ISLAND BLACK MUSIC					
❑ PR12-7235 [DJ]Tell Me (LP Version) (Acappella) (Instrumental) (Executive Mix)		1996	2.50	5.00	10.00
❑ PR12-7366 [DJ]Tell Me (Bounce Remix) (Bounce Remix Featuring Big Dex) (Bounce Remix Instrumental) (Student Remix) (Student Instrumental) (Student Acappella)		1996	2.50	5.00	10.00
❑ PR12-7485	Never Make a Promise (4 versions)	1997	2.50	5.00	10.00
❑ 572425-1	How Deep Is Your Love (unknown versions)	1998	2.00	4.00	8.00
LAFACE					
❑ LFDP-4294 [DJ]We're Not Making Love No More (Album Version) (Album Instrumental)/(same on both sides)		1997	2.00	4.00	8.00
45s					
ISLAND BLACK MUSIC					
❑ 572210-7	5 Steps/In My Bed	1998	—	2.00	4.00
❑ 572482-7	These Are the Times/You Are Everything	1998	—	—	3.00
Albums					
ISLAND BLACK MUSIC					
❑ PRLP-7317 [(2) DJ]97 — The Year of the Dru		1997	3.75	7.50	15.00
—Promo-only edition of their debut album, "Dru Hill"					
DUBS, THE					
45s					
ABC-PARAMOUNT					
❑ 10056	No One/Early in the Evening	1959	6.25	12.50	25.00
❑ 10100	Don't Laugh at Me/You Never Belong to Me	1960	12.50	25.00	50.00
❑ 10150	For the First Time/Ain't That So	1960	6.25	12.50	25.00
❑ 10198	If I Only Had Magic/Joogie Boogie	1961	7.50	15.00	30.00
❑ 10269	Lullaby/Down, Down, Down I Go	1961	7.50	15.00	30.00
CLIFTON					
❑ 2	Where Do We Go from Here/I Only Have Eyes for You	1973	—	3.00	6.00
END					
❑ 1108	Now That We Broke Up/This to Me Is Love	1962	12.50	25.00	50.00
GONE					
❑ 5002	Don't Ask Me (To Be Lonely)/Darling	1957	25.00	50.00	100.00
—Black label, "shadow" logo					
❑ 5002	Don't Ask Me (To Be Lonely)/Darling	1957	15.00	30.00	60.00
—Black label, clown-face logo					
❑ 5002	Don't Ask Me (To Be Lonely)/Darling	1957	6.25	12.50	25.00
—Multi-color label					
❑ 5011	Could This Be Magic/Such Lovin'	1957	12.50	25.00	50.00
—Black label					
❑ 5011	Could This Be Magic/Such Lovin'	1957	6.25	12.50	25.00
—Multi-color label					
❑ 5020	Beside My Love/Gonna Make a Change	1957	15.00	30.00	60.00
❑ 5034	Song in My Heart/Be Sure (My Love)	1958	15.00	30.00	60.00
❑ 5046	Chapel of Dreams/Is There a Love for Me	1958	15.00	30.00	60.00
❑ 5069	Chapel of Dreams/Is There a Love for Me	1959	12.50	25.00	50.00
❑ 5138	You're Free to Go/Is There a Love for Me	1962	12.50	25.00	50.00
JOHNSON					
❑ 097	Connie/Home Under My Hat	1973	—	3.00	6.00
❑ 098	Somebody Goofed/I Won't Have You Breaking My Heart	1973	—	3.00	6.00
❑ 102	Don't Ask Me (To Be Lonely)/Darling	1957	500.00	1000.	1500.
JOSIE					
❑ 911	Wisdom of a Fool/This I Swear	1963	5.00	10.00	20.00
LANA					
❑ 115	Could This Be Magic/Blue Velvet	1964	2.00	4.00	8.00
—A-side is an alternate take of the hit version					
❑ 116	Don't Ask Me (To Be Lonely)/Your Very First Love	1964	2.00	4.00	8.00
—A-side is an alternate take of the hit version					
MARK-X					
❑ 8008	Be Sure My Love/Song in My Heart	1960	5.00	10.00	20.00
VICKIE					
❑ 229	I'm Downtown/Lost in the Wilderness	1971	2.50	5.00	10.00
—As "Richard Blandon and the Dubs"					
WILSHIRE					
❑ 201	Just You/Your Very First Love	1963	10.00	20.00	40.00
Albums					
CANDELITE					
❑ 1003	You've Got to Be Good to Make It in New York City	197?	3.00	6.00	12.00
❑ 1004	The Best of the Dubs	197?	3.00	6.00	12.00
DUBS, THE / THE SHELLS					
Also see each artist's individual listings.					
Albums					
JOSIE					
❑ JM-4001 [M]	The Dubs Meet the Shells	1962	75.00	150.00	300.00
❑ JSS-4001 [S]	The Dubs Meet the Shells	1962	150.00	300.00	600.00
DUKAYS, THE					
Also see GENE CHANDLER.					
45s					
NAT					
❑ 4001	The Big Lie/The Girl's a Devil	1961	5.00	10.00	20.00
❑ 4002	Nite Owl/Festival of Love	1961	5.00	10.00	20.00
VEE JAY					
❑ 430	Nite Owl/Festival of Love	1962	3.75	7.50	15.00
❑ 442	I'm Gonna Love You So/Please Help	1962	3.75	7.50	15.00
❑ 460	I Feel Good All Over/I Never Knew	1962	3.75	7.50	15.00
❑ 491	Combination/Every Step	1963	3.75	7.50	15.00

D

Number	Title (A Side/B Side)	Yr	VG	VG+	NM
DUKE, GEORGE					
Also see STANLEY CLARKE AND GEORGE DUKE.					
12-Inch Singles					
ELEKTRA					
❑ ED 5162 [DJ]	Broken Glass (4 versions)	1986	2.00	4.00	8.00
EPIC					
❑ AE 595 [DJ]	Straight from the Heart/Pluck	1979	2.50	5.00	10.00
—Red vinyl					
❑ 05052	Celebrate (Extended)/(Instrumental)	1983	2.00	4.00	8.00
WARNER BROS.					
❑ PRO-A-6463 [DJ]6 O'Clock (4 versions)		1993	2.00	4.00	8.00
45s					
ELEKTRA					
❑ 69296	Love Ballad/560SL	1989	—	—	3.00
❑ 69315	Guilty/(Instrumental)	1989	—	—	3.00
❑ 69504	Good Friend/African Violet	1986	—	—	3.00
❑ 69504 [PS]	Good Friend/African Violet	1986	—	—	3.00
❑ 69524	Broken Glass/Island Girl	1986	—	—	3.00
❑ 69649	Thief in the Night/La La	1985	—	—	3.00
EPIC					
❑ 02701	Shine On/Positive Energy	1982	—	2.00	4.00
❑ 02932	Ride On Love/Let Your Love Shine	1982	—	2.00	4.00
❑ 03760	Reach Out (Part 1)/Reach Out (Part 2)	1983	—	2.00	4.00
❑ 50463	Reach For It/Just for You	1977	—	2.00	4.00
❑ 50531	Dukey Stick (Part One)/Dukey Stick(Part Two)	1978	—	2.00	4.00
❑ 50593	Movin' On/The Way I Feel	1978	—	2.00	4.00
❑ 50660	Say That You Will/I Am for Real (May the Funk Be With You)	1979	—	2.00	4.00
❑ 50719	Straight from the Heart/Pluck	1979	—	2.00	4.00
❑ 50792	I Want You for Myself/Party Down	1979	—	2.00	4.00
❑ 50853	Every Little Step I Take/Games	1980	—	2.00	4.00
Albums					
ELEKTRA					
❑ 60398	Thief in the Night	1985	2.50	5.00	10.00
❑ 60778	Night After Night	1989	2.50	5.00	10.00
EPIC					
❑ PE 34469	From Me to You	1977	2.50	5.00	10.00
—Originals have no bar code					
❑ PE 34469	From Me to You	198?	2.00	4.00	8.00
—Budget-line reissue with bar code					
❑ JE 34883	Reach For It	1977	2.50	5.00	10.00
❑ PE 34883	Reach For It	198?	2.00	4.00	8.00
—Budget-line reissue					
❑ JE 35366	Don't Let Go	1978	2.50	5.00	10.00
❑ PE 35366	Don't Let Go	198?	2.00	4.00	8.00
—Budget-line reissue					
❑ JE 35701	Follow the Rainbow	1979	2.50	5.00	10.00
❑ JE 36263	Master of the Game	1979	2.50	5.00	10.00
❑ PE 36263	Master of the Game	198?	2.00	4.00	8.00
—Budget-line reissue					
❑ FE 36483	A Brazilian Love Affair	1980	2.50	5.00	10.00
❑ FE 37532	Dream On	1982	2.50	5.00	10.00
❑ FE 38208	1976 Solo Album	1983	2.50	5.00	10.00
❑ FE 39262	Rendezvous	1984	2.50	5.00	10.00
MPS/BASF					
❑ 22018	Faces in Reflection	1974	3.00	6.00	12.00
❑ 22835	Liberated Fantasies	1976	2.50	5.00	10.00
❑ 25355	Feel	1974	2.50	5.00	10.00
❑ 25613	The Aura Will Prevail	1975	2.50	5.00	10.00
❑ 25671	I Love the Blues, She Heard My Cry	1975	2.50	5.00	10.00
PACIFIC JAZZ					
❑ PJ-LA891-H	George Duke	1978	2.50	5.00	10.00
❑ LN-10127	Save the Country	198?	2.00	4.00	8.00
PAUSA					
❑ 7042	The Aura Will Prevail	198?	2.00	4.00	8.00
—Reissue of MPS/BASF 25613					
❑ 7070	I Love the Blues	1980	2.00	4.00	8.00
PICKWICK					
❑ SPC-3588	Save the Country	1978	2.00	4.00	8.00
VERVE/MPS					
❑ 821665-1	Feel	1984	2.00	4.00	8.00
—Reissue of MPS/BASF 25355					
❑ 821837-1	The Aura Will Prevail	1984	2.00	4.00	8.00
—Reissue of Pausa 7042					
DUKE OF EARL, THE					
See GENE CHANDLER.					
DUKES, THE					
Possibly more than one group.					
45s					
FLIP					
❑ 343	Looking for You/Groceries Sir	1959	7.50	15.00	30.00
❑ 345	I Love You/Leap Year Cha Cha	1959	10.00	20.00	40.00
IMPERIAL					
❑ 5401	Teardrop Eyes/Shimmies and Shakes	1956	62.50	125.00	250.00
❑ 5415	Wini Brown/Cotton Pickin' Hands	1956	30.00	60.00	120.00
SPECIALTY					
❑ 543	Ooh Bop She Bop/Oh-Kay	1954	18.75	37.50	75.00

Number	Title (A Side/B Side)	Yr	VG	VG+	NM

DUPONTS, THE

Little Anthony's group before joining the Imperials. They are NOT the same group as the Imperials.

45s
ROULETTE

Number	Title (A Side/B Side)	Yr	VG	VG+	NM
❑ 4060	Half Past Nothing/A Screamin' Ball (At Dracula Hall)	1958	6.25	12.50	25.00

ROYAL ROOST

❑ 627	Somebody/Prove It Tonight	1957	12.50	25.00	50.00

SAVOY

❑ 1552	Must Be Falling in Love/You	1958	6.25	12.50	25.00

—As "Little Anthony Guardine and the Duponts"
WINLEY

❑ 212	Must Be Falling in Love/You	1957	20.00	40.00	80.00

DUPREE, CHAMPION JACK

45s
ATLANTIC

❑ 2032	Frankie and Johnny/Strollin'	1959	3.00	6.00	12.00

—As "Champion Jack"

❑ 2095	My Mother-in-Law/Evil Woman	1961	2.50	5.00	10.00

EVERLAST

❑ 5025	Shake Baby Shake/Walking Down the Highway	1963	2.50	5.00	10.00
❑ 5032	Highway Blues/Shake Baby Shake	1964	2.00	4.00	8.00

FEDERAL

❑ 12408	Two Below Zero/Sharp Harp	1961	3.00	6.00	12.00

GROOVE

❑ 0171	Lonely Road Blues/When I Get Married	1956	10.00	20.00	40.00

—With Mr. Bear
KING

❑ 4695	Hard Feeling/Walking Upside Your Head	1954	7.50	15.00	30.00
❑ 4706	Camille/Rub a Little Boogie	1954	7.50	15.00	30.00
❑ 4779	Blues for Everybody/Two Below Zero	1955	7.50	15.00	30.00
❑ 4797	Let the Doorbell Ring/Harelip Blues	1955	7.50	15.00	30.00
❑ 4812	Walking the Blues/Daybreak Rock	1955	7.50	15.00	30.00

—B-side by Mr. Bear and the Bearcats

❑ 4827	That's My Pa/Stumbling Block	1955	7.50	15.00	30.00
❑ 4859	Silent Partner/She Cooks Me Cabbage	1955	7.50	15.00	30.00
❑ 4876	Me and My Mule/Failing Health Blues	1956	7.50	15.00	30.00
❑ 4906	So Sorry, So Sorry/Overhead	1956	7.50	15.00	30.00
❑ 4938	Big Leg Woman/Mail Order Woman	1956	7.50	15.00	30.00
❑ 6299	Blues for Everybody/Tongue-Tied Blues	1970	—	3.00	6.00

RED ROBIN

❑ 109	Stumblin' Block Blues/Number Nine Blues	1952	100.00	200.00	400.00
❑ 112	Shake Baby Shake/Highway Blues	1952	50.00	100.00	200.00
❑ 130	Drunk Again/Shim Sham Shimmy	1954	50.00	100.00	200.00

VIK

❑ 0260	Just Like a Woman/Dirty Woman	1957	10.00	20.00	40.00
❑ 0279	Old Time Rock and Roll/Rocky Mountain	1957	10.00	20.00	40.00
❑ 0304	Shake Baby Shake/Lollipop Baby	1957	10.00	20.00	40.00

Albums
ARCHIVE OF FOLK AND JAZZ

❑ 217	Champion Jack Dupree	197?	2.50	5.00	10.00

ATLANTIC

❑ 8019 [M]	Blues from the Gutter	1959	37.50	75.00	150.00

—Black label

❑ 8019 [M]	Blues from the Gutter	1960	12.50	25.00	50.00

—White "fan" logo at right of label

❑ 8019 [M]	Blues from the Gutter	1963	5.00	10.00	20.00

—Black "fan" logo at right of label

❑ SD 8019 [S]	Blues from the Gutter	1959	50.00	100.00	200.00

—Green label

❑ SD 8019 [S]	Blues from the Gutter	1960	15.00	30.00	60.00

—Green and blue label, white "fan" logo at right of label

❑ SD 8019 [S]	Blues from the Gutter	1963	6.25	12.50	25.00

—Green and blue label, black "fan" logo at right of label

❑ 8045 [M]	Natural and Soulful Blues	1961	12.50	25.00	50.00

—White "fan" logo at right of label

❑ 8045 [M]	Natural and Soulful Blues	1963	5.00	10.00	20.00

—Black "fan" logo at right of label

❑ SD 8045 [S]	Natural and Soulful Blues	1961	15.00	30.00	60.00

—Green and blue label, white "fan" logo at right of label

❑ SD 8045 [S]	Natural and Soulful Blues	1963	6.25	12.50	25.00

—Green and blue label, black "fan" logo at right of label

❑ 8056 [M]	Champion of the Blues	1961	12.50	25.00	50.00

—White "fan" logo at right of label

❑ 8056 [M]	Champion of the Blues	1963	5.00	10.00	20.00

—Black "fan" logo at right of label

❑ SD 8056 [R]	Champion of the Blues	196?	3.75	7.50	15.00
❑ SD 8255	Blues from the Gutter	1970	3.75	7.50	15.00

BLUE HORIZON

❑ 7702	When You Feel the Feeling	1969	6.25	12.50	25.00

BULLSEYE

❑ BB-9502	Back Home In New Orleans	1990	3.00	6.00	12.00

CONTINENTAL

❑ CLP-16002 [M]	Low Down Blues	1961	62.50	125.00	250.00

FOLKWAYS

❑ FS-3825 [M]	Women Blues of Champion Jack Dupree	1961	6.25	12.50	25.00

GNP CRESCENDO

❑ GNPS-10001	Tricks	1974	3.00	6.00	12.00
❑ GNPS-10005	Happy to Be Free	1974	3.00	6.00	12.00
❑ GNPS-10013	Legacy of Blues 3	197?	3.00	6.00	12.00

JAZZ MAN

❑ BLZ-5501	Champion Jack Dupree	1982	2.50	5.00	10.00

KING

❑ 735 [M]	Champion Jack Dupree Sings the Blues	1961	75.00	150.00	300.00
❑ KS-1084	Walking the Blues	1970	3.75	7.50	15.00

LONDON

❑ PS 553	From New Orleans to Chicago	1969	5.00	10.00	20.00

OKEH

❑ OKM 12103 [M]	Cabbage Greens	1963	7.50	15.00	30.00

STORYVILLE

❑ 4010	Best of the Blues	1982	2.50	5.00	10.00
❑ 4040	I'm Growing Older Every Day	198?	2.50	5.00	10.00

DUPREE, CHAMPION JACK, AND MICKEY BAKER

Also see each artist's individual listings.
Albums
SIRE

❑ SES-97010	In Heavy Blues	1969	7.50	15.00	30.00

DUPREE, CHAMPION JACK, AND JIMMY RUSHING

Albums
AUDIO LAB

❑ AL-1512 [M]	Two Shades of Blue	1958	50.00	100.00	200.00

DUPREES, THE

45s
COED

❑ 569	You Belong to Me/Take Me As I Am	1962	5.00	10.00	20.00
❑ 571	My Own True Love/Ginny	1962	5.00	10.00	20.00
❑ 574	I'd Rather Be Here in Your Arms/I Wish I Could Believe You	1963	3.75	7.50	15.00
❑ 576	Gone with the Wind/Let's Make Love Again	1963	3.75	7.50	15.00
❑ 580	I Gotta Tell Her Now/Take Me As I Am	1963	3.75	7.50	15.00
❑ 584	Why Don't You Believe Me/The Things I Love	1963	7.50	15.00	30.00
❑ 584	Why Don't You Believe Me/My Dearest One	1963	3.75	7.50	15.00
❑ 585	Have You Heard/Love Eyes	1963	3.75	7.50	15.00
❑ 587	(It's No) Sin/The Sand and the Sea	1964	3.75	7.50	15.00
❑ 591	Please Let Her Know/Where Are You	1964	3.75	7.50	15.00
❑ 593	Unbelievable/So Many Have Told Me	1964	3.75	7.50	15.00
❑ 595	So Little Time/It Isn't Fair	1964	3.75	7.50	15.00
❑ 596	I'm Yours/Wishing Ring	1964	3.75	7.50	15.00

COLOSSUS

❑ 110	Check Yourself/The Sky's the Limit	1970	—	3.00	6.00

—As "The Italian Asphalt and Pavement Company" or "The I.A.P. Co." for short

❑ 110 [PS]	Check Yourself/The Sky's the Limit	1970	—	3.00	6.00

—As "The Italian Asphalt and Pavement Company" or "The I.A.P. Co." for short
COLUMBIA

❑ 43336	Around the Corner/They Said It Couldn't Be Done	1965	3.00	6.00	12.00
❑ 43464	Norma Jean/She Waits for Him	1965	3.00	6.00	12.00
❑ 43577	The Exodus Song/Let Them Talk	1966	3.00	6.00	12.00
❑ 43802	It's Not Time Now/Don't Want to Have to Do It	1966	2.50	5.00	10.00
❑ 44078	Be My Love/I Understand	1967	2.50	5.00	10.00

HERITAGE

❑ 804	My Special Angel/Ring of Love	1968	2.50	5.00	10.00
❑ 805	Goodnight My Love/Ring of Love	1968	2.50	5.00	10.00
❑ 805 [PS]	Goodnight My Love/Ring of Love	1968	5.00	10.00	20.00
❑ 808	My Love, My Love/The Sky's the Limit	1968	2.50	5.00	10.00
❑ 808 [PS]	My Love, My Love/The Sky's the Limit	1968	5.00	10.00	20.00
❑ 811	Two Different Worlds/Hope	1969	2.50	5.00	10.00
❑ 811 [PS]	Two Different Worlds/Hope	1969	5.00	10.00	20.00
❑ 826	Have You Heard/My Love, My Love	1970	2.50	5.00	10.00

RCA VICTOR

❑ PB-10407	The Sky's the Limit/Delicious	1975	2.50	5.00	10.00

Albums
COED

❑ LPC-905 [M]	You Belong to Me	1962	75.00	150.00	300.00
❑ LPC-906 [M]	Have You Heard	1963	50.00	100.00	200.00

COLLECTABLES

❑ COL-5008	The Best of the Duprees	198?	3.00	6.00	12.00

COLOSSUS

❑ 5000	Duprees Gold	1970	7.50	15.00	30.00

—As "The Italian Asphalt & Pavement Co."
HERITAGE

❑ HT-35002 [M]	Total Recall	1968	20.00	40.00	80.00

—Mono is promo only; in stereo cover with "DJ Monaural" sticker on front

❑ HTS-35002 [S]	Total Recall	1968	7.50	15.00	30.00

POST

❑ 1000	The Duprees Sing	196?	7.50	15.00	30.00

DUPRI, JERMAINE

Also see JD & MARIAH.
12-Inch Singles
SO SO DEF

❑ CAS 3573 [DJ]	The Party Continues (Main Mix) (Instrumental) (Acappella)/We Just Wanna Party with You (Remix) (Instrumental)	1998	2.00	4.00	8.00

—As "JD & Da Brat"

❑ 44-78786	The Party Continues (unknown versions)	1998	—	3.50	7.00

—As "JD & Da Brat"

❑ 44-78864	Money Ain't a Thang (unknown versions)	1998	2.00	4.00	8.00

—As "JD Featuring Jay-Z"

❑ 44-79417	I've Got to Have It (2 versions)/That's What I'm Looking For (2 versions)	2000	2.00	4.00	8.00
❑ 44-79590	Ballin' Out of Control (4 versions)/Hate Blood (3 versions)	2001	—	3.50	7.00

A 1960s release by Don and Dewey is "Don't Ever Leave Me," on the Rush label.

One of Lee Dorsey's biggest hits, a Top 10 smash on both the R&B and pop charts, was "Working in the Coal Mine" in 1966.

Before he recorded as Lamont Dozier, he made a record in the early 1960s under the name "Lamont Anthony." Today this one-off single for Check Mate is highly collectible.

The Drifters' *Save the Last Dance for Me,* featuring the #1 title song, was actually in print long enough to come out on the 1969-76 era red and green label with the wide white stripe through the center hole.

Jubilee Records put together this LP of tracks by two vocal groups onto one record. As with many of this type of album, the originals are quite collectible.

As with most green-label Atlantic stereo originals, *Blues from the Gutter* by Champion Jack Dupree is quite sought-after in that initial edition.

Number	Title (A Side/B Side)	Yr	VG	VG+	NM

WARNER BROS.

| ❏ PRO-A-100534 | [DJ]Lay It Down (LP Version) (Radio Version) (Instrumental) (Acappella) | 2001 | 2.00 | 4.00 | 8.00 |

—*Featuring R.O.C. and Lil' Mo*

45s

HOLLYWOOD

| ❏ ED 11085 | [DJ]It's Nothing (Clean Version) (Album Version) (Instrumental)/Rapid Fire (Album Version) (Instrumental) | 1999 | 3.75 | 7.50 | 15.00 |

—*With Da Brat featuring R.O.C.*

SO SO DEF

| ❏ 38-79079 | Going Home with Me (Clean Version)/Jazzy H*** (Clean Version) | 1998 | — | — | 3.00 |

—*A-side features Keith Sweat and R.O.C.*

Albums

SO SO DEF

| ❏ C2 69087 [(2)] | Jermaine Dupri Presents Life in 1472 — The Original Soundtrack | 1998 | 3.00 | 6.00 | 12.00 |
| ❏ C2 85830 [(2)] | Instructions | 2001 | 3.75 | 7.50 | 15.00 |

DYKE AND THE BLAZERS

45s

ORIGINAL SOUND

❏ 64	Funky Broadway — Part 1/Funky Broadway — Part 2	1966	2.50	5.00	10.00
❏ 69	So Sharp/Don't Bug Me	1967	2.00	4.00	8.00
❏ 79	Funky Walk Part 1 — East/Funky Walk Part 2 — West	1967	2.00	4.00	8.00
❏ 83	Funky Bull — Part 1/Funky Bull — Part 2	1968	2.00	4.00	8.00
❏ 86	We Got More Soul/Shotgun Slim	1969	2.00	4.00	8.00
❏ 89	Let a Woman Be a Woman — Let a Man Be a Man/Uhh	1969	2.00	4.00	8.00
❏ 90	You Are My Sunshine/City Dump	1969	2.00	4.00	8.00
❏ 91	Uhh/My Sister's and My Brother's Day Is Coming	1970	2.00	4.00	8.00
❏ 96	Runaway People/I'm So All Alone	1970	2.00	4.00	8.00

Albums

ORIGINAL SOUND

❏ LP 8876 [M]	The Funky Broadway	1967	12.50	25.00	50.00
❏ LPS 8876 [S]	The Funky Broadway	1967	18.75	37.50	75.00
❏ LPS 8877	Dyke's Greatest Hits	1968	18.75	37.50	75.00

DYNAMIC SUPERIORS

45s

MOTOWN

❏ 1324	Shoe Shoe Shine/Release Me	1974	—	3.00	6.00
❏ 1342	Leave It Alone/One-Nighter	1975	—	3.00	6.00
❏ 1357	Romeo/I Got Away	1975	—	—	—

—*Canceled?*

❏ 1359	Nobody's Gonna Change Me/I Got Away	1975	—	3.00	6.00
❏ 1365	Deception/One Nighter	1975	—	3.00	6.00
❏ 1413	Can't Stay Away (From the One I Love)/Supersensuosensation (Try Some Love)	1977	—	3.00	6.00
❏ 1419	Nowhere to Run, Pt. 1/Nowhere to Run, Pt. 2	1977	—	3.00	6.00
❏ 1428	You're What I Need/Here Comes That Feeling	1977	—	3.00	6.00

Albums

MOTOWN

❏ M6-822	Dynamic Superiors	1974	3.00	6.00	12.00
❏ M6-841	Pure Pleasure	1975	3.00	6.00	12.00
❏ M6-875	You Name It	1976	3.00	6.00	12.00
❏ M6-879	Give and Take	1977	3.00	6.00	12.00

DYSON, RONNIE

45s

COLUMBIA

❏ 10071	Captain of Your Soul/Life and Breath	1974	—	2.50	5.00
❏ 10211	Lady in Red/Cup (Runneth Over)	1975	—	2.50	5.00
❏ 10356	The More You Do It (The More I Like It Done to Me)/You and Me	1976	—	2.50	5.00
❏ 10441	(I Like Being) Close to You/Lovin' Feelin'	1976	—	2.50	5.00
❏ 10599	Don't Be Afraid/I Just Want to Be There	1977	—	2.50	5.00
❏ 10667	Ain't Nothing Wrong/Just As You Are	1978	—	2.50	5.00
❏ 10716	Sara Smile/No Way	1978	—	2.00	4.00
❏ 45110	(If You Let Me Make Love to You Then) Why Can't I Touch You?	1970	—	2.50	5.00
❏ 45240	I Don't Wanna Cry/She's Gone	1970	—	2.50	5.00
❏ 45387	When You Get Right Down To It…/Sleeping Sun	1971	—	2.50	5.00
❏ 45599	Jesus Is Just Alright/Love Is Slipping Away	1972	—	3.00	6.00
❏ 45776	One Man Band (Plays All Alone)/I Think I'll Tell Her	1973	—	2.50	5.00
❏ 45776 [PS]	One Man Band (Plays All Alone)/I Think I'll Tell Her	1973	2.00	4.00	8.00
❏ 45867	Just Don't Want to Be Lonely/Point of No Return	1973	—	2.50	5.00
❏ 45974	Wednesday in Your Garden/I Think I'll Tell Her	1973	—	3.00	6.00
❏ 46021	We Can Make It Last Forever/Just a Little Love from Me	1974	—	2.50	5.00

COTILLION

❏ 47005	Heart to Heart/Bring It On Home	1982	—	—	3.00
❏ 99811	You Better Be Fierce/(B-side unknown)	1983	—	2.00	4.00
❏ 99841	All Over Your Face/Don't Need You Now	1983	—	—	3.00

RCA VICTOR

| ❏ 74-0128 | Aquarius/Hair | 1969 | 2.50 | 5.00 | 10.00 |

—*By "Ronald Dyson & Co."*

| ❏ GB-10658 | Aquarius/Hair | 1976 | — | 2.50 | 5.00 |

—*"Gold Standard Series" reissue*

Number	Title (A Side/B Side)	Yr	VG	VG+	NM

Albums

COLUMBIA

❏ C 30223	(If You Let Me Make Love to You Then) Why Can't I Touch You?	1970	3.00	6.00	12.00
❏ KC 31305	Back Home	1972	3.00	6.00	12.00
❏ KC 32211	One Man Band	1973	3.00	6.00	12.00
❏ PC 34350	The More You Do	1976	2.50	5.00	10.00
❏ PC 34866	Love in All Flavors	1977	2.50	5.00	10.00

COTILLION

| ❏ 90119 | Brand New Day | 1982 | 2.50 | 5.00 | 10.00 |

Number	Title (A Side/B Side)	Yr	VG	VG+	NM

E

EAGER, BRENDA LEE
45s
MERCURY
❏ 73292	I'm a Lonely Woman/In My World	1972	—	3.00	6.00
❏ 73450	Let Me Be/When I'm With You	1974	—	2.50	5.00
❏ 73607	Ah, Sweet Mystery of Life/There Ain't No Way	1974	—	2.50	5.00
❏ 73627	You Gave Me Everything/When I'm With You	1974	—	2.50	5.00

PLAYBOY
❏ 6047	Good Old Fashioned Lovin'/I'll Get By	1975	—	2.50	5.00

PRIVATE I
❏ 04621	Watch My Body Talk/(Instrumental)	1984	—	2.00	4.00

EARLS, THE (1)
All of the below are by the same group or closely related.
45s
ABC
❏ 11109	It's Been a Long Time Coming/My Lonely, Lonely Room	1968	3.75	7.50	15.00

BARRY
❏ 1021	I Believe/Don't Forget	1963	10.00	20.00	40.00

CLIFTON
❏ 39	Lookin' for My Baby/Cross My Heart	1974	—	2.50	5.00
❏ 43	Lost Love/My Heart's Desire	1974	—	2.50	5.00
❏ 47	Dreams Come True/My Heart's Desire	1974	—	2.50	5.00

COLUMBIA
❏ 3-10225	Goin' Uptown/Mrs. Woman	1975	2.00	4.00	8.00

GONE
❏ 5117	I'll Never Cry/My Heart's Desire	1961	15.00	30.00	60.00

HARVEY
❏ 100	A Sunday Kind of Love/Teenage Dreams	1975	2.00	4.00	8.00

MR. G
❏ 801	If I Could Do It Over Again/Papa	1967	3.75	7.50	15.00

OLD TOWN
❏ 1130	Remember Then/Let's Waddle	1963	12.50	25.00	50.00
—Blue label					
❏ 1130	Remember Then/Let's Waddle	1963	6.25	12.50	25.00
—Mostly black label with moon					
❏ 1133	Never/I Keep a-Telling You	1963	10.00	20.00	40.00
—Blue label					
❏ 1133	Never/I Keep a-Telling You	1963	5.00	10.00	20.00
—Mostly black label with moon					
❏ 1141	Eyes/Look My Way	1963	5.00	10.00	20.00
❏ 1145	Cry, Cry, Cry/Kissin'	1963	5.00	10.00	20.00
❏ 1149	I Believe/Don't Forget	1963	10.00	20.00	40.00
—Blue label					
❏ 1149	I Believe/Don't Forget	1963	5.00	10.00	20.00
—Mostly black label with moon					
❏ 1169	Oh What a Time/Ask Anybody	1964	7.50	15.00	30.00
❏ 1181 [DJ]	Remember Me Baby/Amor	1965	12.50	25.00	50.00
—Assigned 1181 in error, as another record had been released with the number					
❏ 1182	Remember Me Baby/Amor	1965	5.00	10.00	20.00
—Error was corrected on stock copies					

POWER MARTIN
❏ 1005	Stormy Weather/Could This Be Magic	1975	—	2.50	5.00
—B-side by the Pretenders					

ROME
❏ 101	Life Is But a Dream/It's You	1961	30.00	60.00	120.00
❏ 101	Life Is But a Dream/Without You	1961	10.00	20.00	40.00
❏ 102	Lookin' for My Baby/Cross My Heart	1961	10.00	20.00	40.00
❏ 111	Stormy Weather/Could This Be Magic	1976	—	2.50	5.00
—B-side by the Pretenders					
❏ 112/3	Little Boy and Girl/Lost Love	1976	—	2.00	4.00
❏ 114/5	All Through Our Teens/Whoever You Are	1976	2.00	4.00	8.00
—Black vinyl					
❏ 114/5	All Through Our Teens/Whoever You Are	1976	3.00	6.00	12.00
—Colored vinyl					

WOODBURY
❏ 101	Tonight (Could Be the Night)/Meditation	1977	2.00	4.00	8.00

Albums
CHANCE
❏ 1001	The Earls Today	1983	3.00	6.00	12.00

OLD TOWN
❏ LP-104 [M]	Remember Me Baby	1963	125.00	250.00	500.00
—Counterfeit identification: Counterfeits have more than 1-inch trailoffs or as little as 1/2 inch trailoffs; legitimate copies have 5/8- to 3/4-inch trailoff					

WOODBURY
❏ 104	Remember Me Baby	1976	3.75	7.50	15.00

EARLS, THE (2)
45s
GEM
❏ 221	Believe Me My Love/Spinnin'	1954	100.00	200.00	400.00
❏ 227	My Marie/Out of This World	197?	2.00	4.00	8.00
—There are differences of opinion on this record. Some claim that it was released in 1954 not long after Gem 221; others claim that it's a 1970s reproduction on a number that Gem never used. As no 78s are known to exist of this title, we lean toward the latter, but would appreciate positive evidence one way or the other.					

EARTH, WIND, AND FIRE
Also see PHILIP BAILEY; WADE FLEMONS; MAURICE WHITE.
12-Inch Singles
ARC
❏ AS 853 [DJ]	Let Me Talk (Remix)/(Instrumental)	1980	2.50	5.00	10.00
❏ AS 924 [DJ]	And Love Goes On (Single Version)/(LP Version)	1980	2.50	5.00	10.00

COLUMBIA
❏ AS 1648 [DJ]	Side by Side/Something Special	1983	2.00	4.00	8.00
❏ AS 1842 [DJ]	Moonwalk/We're Living in Our Own Time	1983	2.00	4.00	8.00
❏ 44-04008	Spread Your Love/Freedom of Choice	1983	—	3.00	6.00
❏ 44-04211	Magnetic (Extended Dance Remix)/(Instrumental)	1983	—	3.00	6.00
❏ 44-04211	Magnetic (Extended Dance Remix)/(Album Version)	1983	—	3.00	6.00
❏ 44-07475	System of Survival (4 versions)	1987	—	3.00	6.00
❏ 44-07562	Evil Roy (4 versions)	1987	—	3.00	6.00
❏ 44-08140	Turn On (The Beat Box) (4 versions)	1988	—	3.00	6.00
❏ 23-10512	Saturday Nite/On Your Face	1977	3.75	7.50	15.00
❏ 23-10786	Got to Get You Into My Life/I'll Write a Song for You	1978	2.50	5.00	10.00
❏ 73157	Heritage (Extended)/Heritage (Edit)	1990	—	3.00	6.00
❏ 73193	For the Love of You (6 versions)	1990	2.00	4.00	8.00

45s
ARC
❏ 02536	Let's Groove/(Instrumental)	1981	—	2.00	4.00
❏ 02688	Wanna Be with You/Kalimba Tree	1982	—	2.00	4.00
❏ 10854	September/Love's Holiday	1978	—	2.50	5.00
❏ 11033	After the Love Has Gone/Rock That!	1979	—	2.50	5.00
❏ 11093	In the Stone/You and I	1979	—	2.00	4.00
❏ 11165	Star/You and I	1979	—	2.00	4.00
❏ 11366	Let Me Talk/(Instrumental)	1980	—	2.00	4.00
❏ 11366 [PS]	Let Me Talk/(Instrumental)	1980	—	2.50	5.00
❏ 11407	You/Share Your Love	1980	—	2.00	4.00
❏ 11434	And Love Goes On/Win or Lose	1981	—	2.00	4.00

COLUMBIA
❏ 13-03136	Let's Groove/Sing a Song	1982	—	—	3.00
—Reissue					
❏ 38-03375	Fall in Love with Me/(Instrumental)	1982	—	2.00	4.00
❏ 38-03375 [PS]	Fall in Love with Me/(Instrumental)	1982	—	2.00	4.00
❏ CNR-03566	Fall in Love with Me	1983	—	3.00	6.00
—One-sided budget release					
❏ 38-03814	Side by Side/Something Special	1983	—	2.00	4.00
❏ 38-04002	Spread Your Love/Freedom of Choice	1983	—	2.00	4.00
❏ 38-04210	Magnetic/Speed of Love	1983	—	2.00	4.00
❏ 38-04210 [PS]	Magnetic/Speed of Love	1983	—	2.00	4.00
❏ 38-04329	Touch/Sweet Sassy Lady	1984	—	2.00	4.00
❏ 38-04329 [PS]	Touch/Sweet Sassy Lady	1984	—	2.00	4.00
❏ 38-04427	Moonwalk/We're Living in Our Own Time	1984	—	2.00	4.00
❏ 38-07608	System of Survival/Writing on the Wall	1987	—	—	3.00
❏ 38-07608 [PS]	System of Survival/Writing on the Wall	1987	—	—	3.00
❏ 38-07678	You and I/Musical Interlude: New Horizons	1988	—	—	3.00
❏ 38-07687	Evil Roy/(Instrumental)	1988	—	—	3.00
❏ 38-07695	Thinking of You/Money Tight	1988	—	—	3.00
❏ 38-07695 [PS]	Thinking of You/Money Tight	1988	—	—	3.00
❏ 38-08107	Turn On (The Beat Box)/(Instrumental)	1988	—	—	3.00
❏ 3-10026	Devotion/Fair But So Uncool	1974	—	3.00	6.00
❏ 3-10056	Hot Dawgit/R.L. Tambura	1974	—	2.50	5.00
—With Ramsey Lewis					
❏ 3-10090	Shining Star/Yearnin', Learnin'	1975	—	2.50	5.00
❏ 3-10090 [PS]	Shining Star/Yearnin', Learnin'	1975	2.50	5.00	10.00
❏ 3-10103	Sun Goddess/Jungle Strut	1975	—	2.50	5.00
—With Ramsey Lewis					
❏ 3-10172	That's the Way of the World/Africano	1975	—	2.50	5.00
❏ 3-10251	Singasong/(Instrumental)	1975	—	3.00	6.00
—Original pressings have title as one word					
❏ 3-10251	Sing a Song/(Instrumental)	1975	—	2.50	5.00
—Later pressings have title as three words					
❏ 3-10309	Can't Hide Love/Gratitude	1976	—	2.50	5.00
❏ 3-10373	Getaway/(Instrumental)	1976	—	2.50	5.00
❏ 3-10373 [PS]	Getaway/(Instrumental)	1976	2.50	5.00	10.00
❏ 3-10439	Saturday Nite/Departure	1976	—	2.50	5.00
❏ 3-10492	On Your Face/Biyo	1977	—	2.50	5.00
❏ 3-10625	Serpentine Fire/(Instrumental)	1977	—	2.50	5.00
❏ 3-10688	Fantasy/Runnin'	1978	—	2.50	5.00
❏ 3-10796	Got to Get You Into My Life/I'll Write a Song for You	1978	—	2.50	5.00
❏ 4-45747	Power/M-O-M	1972	—	3.00	6.00
❏ 4-45800	Tims Is On Your Side/Where Have All the Flowers Gone	1973	—	3.00	6.00
❏ 4-45888	Evil/Clover	1973	—	2.50	5.00
❏ 4-45888 [PS]	Evil/Clover	1973	2.50	5.00	10.00
❏ 4-45953	Keep Your Head to the Sky/Build Your Nest	1973	—	2.50	5.00
❏ 4-46007	Mighty Mighty/Drum Song	1974	—	2.50	5.00
❏ 4-46007 [PS]	Mighty Mighty/Drum Song	1974	2.50	5.00	10.00
❏ 4-46070	Kalimba Story/Tee Nine Chee Bit	1974	—	2.50	5.00
❏ 73205	Heritage/Gotta Find Out	1990	—	2.50	5.00

WARNER BROS.
❏ 7480	Fan the Fire/This World Today	1971	—	3.00	6.00
❏ 7492	Love Is Life/This World Today	1971	—	3.00	6.00
❏ 7549	I Think About Lovin' You/C'mon Children	1972	—	3.00	6.00

Albums
ARC
❏ FC 35647	The Best of Earth, Wind & Fire, Vol. 1	1978	2.50	5.00	10.00
❏ FC 35730	I Am	1979	2.50	5.00	10.00
❏ PC 35730	I Am	1984	2.00	4.00	8.00
—Budget-line reissue					

Number	Title (A Side/B Side)	Yr	VG	VG+	NM
❑ KC2 36795 [(2)]Faces		1980	3.00	6.00	12.00
❑ PC 37548	Raise!	1984	2.00	4.00	8.00
—Budget-line reissue					
❑ TC 37548	Raise!	1981	2.50	5.00	10.00
❑ HC 45647	The Best of Earth, Wind & Fire, Vol. 1	1981	7.50	15.00	30.00
—Half-speed mastered edition					
❑ HC 45730	I Am	1981	7.50	15.00	30.00
—Half-speed mastered edition					
❑ HC 47548	Raise!	1982	7.50	15.00	30.00
—Half-speed mastered edition					
COLUMBIA					
❑ KC 31702	Last Days and Time	1972	3.75	7.50	15.00
❑ PC 31702	Last Days and Time	197?	2.00	4.00	8.00
—Reissue					
❑ CQ 32194 [Q]	Head to the Sky	1973	5.00	10.00	20.00
❑ KC 32194	Head to the Sky	1973	3.00	6.00	12.00
❑ PC 32194	Head to the Sky	197?	2.00	4.00	8.00
—Reissue					
❑ CQ 32712 [Q]	Open Our Eyes	1974	5.00	10.00	20.00
❑ KC 32712	Open Our Eyes	1974	3.00	6.00	12.00
❑ PC 32712	Open Our Eyes	197?	2.00	4.00	8.00
—Reissue					
❑ PC 33280	That's the Way of the World	1975	3.00	6.00	12.00
—No bar code					
❑ PC 33280	That's the Way of the World	198?	2.00	4.00	8.00
—Budget-line reissue with bar code					
❑ PG 33694 [(2)]Gratitude		1975	3.75	7.50	15.00
—No bar code					
❑ PG 33694 [(2)]Gratitude		198?	2.50	5.00	10.00
—Budget-line reissue with bar code					
❑ PC 34241	Spirit	1976	3.00	6.00	12.00
—No bar code					
❑ PC 34241	Spirit	198?	2.00	4.00	8.00
—Budget-line reissue with bar code					
❑ PCQ 34241 [Q]Spirit		1976	6.25	12.50	25.00
❑ JC 34905	All 'N All	1977	3.00	6.00	12.00
❑ PC 34905	All 'N All	198?	2.00	4.00	8.00
—Budget-line reissue					
❑ PC 38367	Powerlight	1984	2.00	4.00	8.00
—Budget-line reissue					
❑ TC 38367	Powerlight	1983	2.50	5.00	10.00
❑ QC 38980	Electric Universe	1983	2.50	5.00	10.00
❑ FC 40596	Touch the World	1987	2.50	5.00	10.00
❑ OC 45013	The Best of Earth, Wind & Fire, Vol. II	1988	2.50	5.00	10.00
❑ C 45268	Heritage	1990	3.75	7.50	15.00
❑ HC 48367	Powerlight	1983	10.00	20.00	40.00
—Half-speed mastered edition					
MOBILE FIDELITY					
❑ 1-159	That's the Way of the World	198?	7.50	15.00	30.00
—Audiophile vinyl					
PAIR					
❑ PDL2-1064 [(2)]Beat It to Life		1986	3.00	6.00	12.00
WARNER BROS.					
❑ WS 1905	Earth, Wind, and Fire	1971	5.00	10.00	20.00
—Green label					
❑ WS 1958	The Need of Love	1971	5.00	10.00	20.00
—Green label					
❑ 2WS 2798 [(2)]Another Time		1974	5.00	10.00	20.00
—"Burbank" palm trees labels					

EARTH, WIND, AND FIRE WITH THE EMOTIONS

Also see each artist's individual listings.

12-Inch Singles

ARC					
❑ 10950	Boogie Wonderland/(Instrumental)	1979	2.00	4.00	8.00
45s					
ARC					
❑ 10956	Boogie Wonderland/(Instrumental)	1979	—	2.50	5.00

EBONAIRES, THE

45s

ALADDIN					
❑ 3211	3 O'Clock in the Morning/Baby, You're the One	1953	125.00	250.00	500.00
❑ 3212	You're Nobody 'Til Somebody Loves You/Lawd, Lawd, Lawd	1954	125.00	250.00	500.00
COLONIAL					
❑ 117	We're in Love/Thinkin' and Thinkin'	1959	30.00	60.00	120.00
HOLLYWOOD					
❑ 1046	Love For Christmas/Jingle Bell Hop	1955	100.00	200.00	400.00
❑ 1062	Let's Kiss and Say Hello Again/Jivarama Hop	1956	100.00	200.00	400.00
LENA					
❑ 101	Love Call/Somewhere in My Heart	1959	50.00	100.00	200.00
MONEY					
❑ 220	The Very Best Luck in the World/Hey Baby Stop	1956	20.00	40.00	80.00

EBONYS, THE

45s

BUDDAH					
❑ 537	Makin' Love Ain't No Fun (Without the One You Love) Part 1/Part 2	1976	—	3.00	6.00
PHILADELPHIA INT'L.					
❑ 3503	You're the Reason Why/Sexy Ways	1971	2.00	4.00	8.00
❑ 3510	Determination/Do It	1971	2.00	4.00	8.00
❑ 3513 [DJ]	(Christmas Ain't Christmas, New Year's Ain't New Year's) Without The One You Love (mono/stereo)	1971	2.00	4.00	8.00
❑ 3514	Do You Like the Way I Love/I'm So Glad I'm Me	1972	2.00	4.00	8.00
❑ 3529	It's Forever/Sexy Ways	1973	—	3.50	7.00
❑ 3541	I Believe/Nation Time	1974	—	3.50	7.00
❑ 3548	Life in the Country/Hook Up and Get Down	1974	—	3.50	7.00
SOUL CLOCK					
❑ 108	Don't Knock Me/Can't Get Enough	1969	3.75	7.50	15.00
Albums					
BUDDAH					
❑ BDS 5679	Sing About Life	1976	10.00	20.00	40.00
PHILADELPHIA INT'L.					
❑ KZ 32419	The Ebonys	1973	3.00	6.00	12.00

ECHELONS, THE

45s

BAB					
❑ 129	A Christmas Long Ago (Jingle Jingle)/Mystery	19??	3.75	7.50	15.00
COLLECTABLES					
❑ 3997	A Christmas Long Ago (Jingle Jingle)/Have Yourself A Merry Little Christmas	199?	—	—	3.00
—B-side by Johnny Maestro and the Brooklyn Bridge					

ECHOES, THE (1)

45s

SEG-WAY					
❑ 103	Baby Blue/Boomerang	1961	6.25	12.50	25.00
❑ 106	Sad Eyes (Don't You Cry)/It's Raining	1961	6.25	12.50	25.00
❑ 1002	Angel of My Heart/Gee Oh Gee	1962	10.00	20.00	40.00
SMASH					
❑ 1766	Bluebirds Over the Mountain/A Chicken Ain't Nothin' But a Bird	1962	3.75	7.50	15.00
❑ 1807	Keep an Eye on Her/A Million Miles from Nowhere	1963	3.75	7.50	15.00
❑ 1850	Annabelle Lee/If Love Is	1963	3.75	7.50	15.00
SRG					
❑ 101	Baby Blue/Boomerang	1960	50.00	100.00	200.00

ECKSTINE, BILLY

Also see SARAH VAUGHAN.

45s

A&M					
❑ 1858	The Best Thing/Love Theme from "The Getaway"	1976	—	2.00	4.00
❑ 1858 [PS]	The Best Thing/Love Theme from "The Getaway"	1976	—	3.00	6.00
ENTERPRISE					
❑ 9009	Stormy/When You Look in the Mirror	1970	—	3.00	6.00
❑ 9025	I Wanna Be Your Baby/The Name of My Sorrow	1970	—	3.00	6.00
❑ 9046	When Something Is Wrong with My Baby/Today Was Tomorrow Yesterday	1972	—	3.00	6.00
❑ 9076	I Didn't Mean to Love You/I Wanna Be Your Man	1973	—	2.50	5.00
❑ 9093	If She Walked Into My Life/Remembering	1974	—	2.50	5.00
MERCURY					
❑ 71161	All of My Life/Poor Little Heart	1957	2.50	5.00	10.00
❑ 71217	Boulevard of Broken Dreams/If I Can Help Somebody	1957	2.50	5.00	10.00
❑ 71250	Gigi/Trust in Me	1957	2.50	5.00	10.00
❑ 71325	Vertigo/In the Rain	1958	2.50	5.00	10.00
❑ 71372	Prisoner of Love/Funny	1958	2.50	5.00	10.00
❑ 71861	Theme from Exodus/It Isn't Fair	1961	2.00	4.00	8.00
❑ 71907	Jeannie/Alright, Okay, You Win	1961	2.00	4.00	8.00
❑ 71967	Guilty/I Want to Talk About You	1962	2.00	4.00	8.00
❑ 72022	What Kind of Fool Am I/Till There Was You	1962	2.00	4.00	8.00
❑ 72050	You've Changed/The Beauty of True Love	1962	2.00	4.00	8.00
❑ 72128	Everything I Have Is Yours/Darling, Why Did You	1963	2.00	4.00	8.00
❑ 72264	People/Sweet Georgia Brown	1963	2.00	4.00	8.00
❑ 72302	Wanted/What Are You Afraid Of	1964	2.00	4.00	8.00
MGM					
❑ K10525	O Come, All Ye Faithful/O, Holy Night	1949	3.75	7.50	15.00
❑ K10623	My Foolish Heart/Sure Thing	1950	5.00	10.00	20.00
❑ K10643	Free/Baby Won't You Say You Love Me	1950	5.00	10.00	20.00
❑ K10684	My Destiny/Roses	1950	5.00	10.00	20.00
❑ K10690	You're All I Need/Dedicated to You	1950	5.00	10.00	20.00
❑ K10716	I Wanna Be Loved/Stardust	1950	5.00	10.00	20.00
❑ K10778	The Show Must Go On/You've Got Me Cryin' Again	1950	5.00	10.00	20.00
❑ K10796	Blue Christmas/The Lonely Shepherd	1950	5.00	10.00	20.00
❑ K10799	Be My Love/Only a Moment Ago	1950	5.00	10.00	20.00
❑ K10825	I'll Know/I've Never Been in Love Before	1951	3.75	7.50	15.00
❑ K10856	I'm So Crazy for Love/Guess I'll Have to Dream	1951	3.75	7.50	15.00
❑ K10896	If/When You Return	1951	3.75	7.50	15.00
❑ K10903	I Apologize/Bring Back the Thrill	1951	3.75	7.50	15.00
❑ K10916	I Left My Hat/Here Come the Blues	1951	3.75	7.50	15.00
❑ K10944	I'm Yours to Command/What Will I Tell My Heart	1951	3.75	7.50	15.00
❑ K10982	I'm a Fool/Lose Me	1951	3.75	7.50	15.00
❑ K10996	Pandora/Wonder Why	1951	3.75	7.50	15.00
❑ K11028	Enchanted Land/I've Got My Mind on You	1951	3.75	7.50	15.00
❑ K11073	Once/Out in the Cold	1951	3.75	7.50	15.00
❑ K11101	Taking a Chance/You're Driving Me Crazy	1951	3.75	7.50	15.00
❑ K11111	Jalousie/Strange Interlude	1951	3.75	7.50	15.00
❑ K11125	Take Me Back/Weaver of Dreams	1952	3.75	7.50	15.00
❑ K11144	Every Day/I Love You	1952	3.75	7.50	15.00
❑ K11177	Carnival/Room with a View	1952	3.75	7.50	15.00
❑ K11217	If They Ask Me/Hold Me Close to You	1952	3.75	7.50	15.00
❑ K11225	Kiss of Fire/Never Like This	1952	3.75	7.50	15.00

Number	Title (A Side/B Side)	Yr	VG	VG+	NM
❑ K11291	Have a Good Time/Strange Sensation	1952	3.75	7.50	15.00
❑ K11301	Early Autumn/Because You're Mine	1952	3.75	7.50	15.00
❑ K11351	Be Fair/Come to the Mardi Gras	1952	3.75	7.50	15.00
❑ K11396	Until Eternity/Everything Depends on You	1953	3.75	7.50	15.00
❑ K11439	A Fool in Love/Until Today	1953	3.75	7.50	15.00
❑ K11511	Send My Baby Back to Me/Laugh to Keep From Crying	1953	3.75	7.50	15.00
❑ K11550	It Can't Be Wrong/I Can Read Between the Lines	1953	3.75	7.50	15.00
❑ K11573	St. Louis Blues (Part 1)/St. Louis Blues (Part 2)	1953	3.75	7.50	15.00
❑ K11587	I'm Saving Dreams/Fortune Telling Cards	1953	3.75	7.50	15.00
❑ K11623	What Are You Doing New Year's Eve/Christmas Eve	1953	5.00	10.00	20.00
❑ K11655	Rendezvous/I'm In a Mood	1954	3.75	7.50	15.00
❑ K11694	Don't Get Around Much Anymore/Lost in Loveliness	1954	3.75	7.50	15.00
❑ K11712	No One But You/Seabreeze	1954	3.75	7.50	15.00
❑ K11744	Beloved/Temporarily Blue	1954	3.75	7.50	15.00
❑ K11803	Olay, Olay/You Leave Me Breathless	1954	3.75	7.50	15.00
❑ K11845	Mood Indigo/Do Nothing 'Till You Hear from Me	1954	3.75	7.50	15.00
❑ K11855	Love Me/One Sweet Kiss	1954	3.75	7.50	15.00
❑ K11915	What More Is There to Say/Touching Shoulders	1955	3.00	6.00	12.00
❑ K11948	Give Me Another Chance/More Than You'll Ever Know	1955	3.00	6.00	12.00
❑ K11984	Love Me or Leave Me/Only You	1955	3.00	6.00	12.00
❑ K11998	Careless Lips/A Man Doesn't Know	1955	3.00	6.00	12.00
❑ K12055	September Song/Pass the Word Around	1955	3.00	6.00	12.00
❑ K12105	La De Do De Do (The Honey Bug Song)/Farewell to Romance	1955	3.00	6.00	12.00
❑ K12160	You'll Get Yours/Lonely Avenue	1955	3.00	6.00	12.00
❑ K12180	Good-Bye/The Show Must Go On	1956	3.00	6.00	12.00
❑ K12237	Out of My Mind/My Fickle Heart	1956	3.00	6.00	12.00

MOTOWN

Number	Title (A Side/B Side)	Yr	VG	VG+	NM
❑ 1077	Had You Been Around/Down to Earth	1965	3.00	6.00	12.00
❑ 1091	Wish You Were Here/Slender Thread	1966	3.00	6.00	12.00
❑ 1100	A Warmer World/And There You Were	1966	3.00	6.00	12.00
❑ 1105	I Wonder Why (Nobody Loves Me)/I've Been Blessed	1967	3.00	6.00	12.00
❑ 1120	Is Anyone Here Going My Way/Thank You Love	1968	2.50	5.00	10.00
❑ 1131	For Love of Ivy/A Woman	1968	2.50	5.00	10.00
❑ 1143	My Cup Runneth Over/Ask the Lonely	1969	2.50	5.00	10.00

RCA VICTOR

Number	Title (A Side/B Side)	Yr	VG	VG+	NM
❑ 47-6436	The Bitter with the Sweet/Grapevine	1956	3.00	6.00	12.00
❑ 47-6488	My Heart Says No/Joey, Joey, Joey	1956	3.00	6.00	12.00
❑ 47-6524	Tennessee Rock 'n' Roll/Condemned for Life	1956	5.00	10.00	20.00
❑ 47-6691	The Chosen Few/Just Call Me Crazy	1956	3.00	6.00	12.00
❑ 47-6827	Blue Illusion/Oh My Pretty Pretty	1957	3.00	6.00	12.00

ROULETTE

Number	Title (A Side/B Side)	Yr	VG	VG+	NM
❑ 4199	Anything You Wanna Do/Like Wow	1959	3.00	6.00	12.00
❑ 4239	I Love You/I Apologize	1960	3.00	6.00	12.00

78s

DELUXE

Number	Title (A Side/B Side)	Yr	VG	VG+	NM
❑ 2000	I Stay in the Mood for You/Good Jelly Blues	1944	3.75	7.50	15.00
❑ 2001	If That's the Way You Feel/Blowing the Blues Away	1944	3.75	7.50	15.00
❑ 2002	The Real Thing Happened to Me/Opus X	1944	3.75	7.50	15.00
❑ 2003	I Want to Talk About You/I'll Wait and Pray	1945	3.75	7.50	15.00

MGM

Number	Title (A Side/B Side)	Yr	VG	VG+	NM
❑ 10043	This Is an Inside Story/Just an Old Love of Mine	1947	3.00	6.00	12.00
❑ 10069	On the Boulevard of Memories/The Wildest Gal in Town	1947	3.00	6.00	12.00
❑ 10097	Fool That I Am/Three Loves Have I	1947	3.00	6.00	12.00
❑ 10123	True/I'll Never Make the Same Mistake Again	1948	3.00	6.00	12.00
❑ 10154	I'm Out to Forget Tonight/Intrigue	1948	3.00	6.00	12.00
❑ 10208	Mr. B's Blues/I'm Falling for You	1948	3.00	6.00	12.00
❑ 10259	Everything I Have Is Yours/I'll Be Faithful	1948	3.00	6.00	12.00
❑ 10311	Fools Rush In/Blue Moon	1948	2.50	5.00	10.00
❑ 10340	Bewildered/No Orchids for My Lady	1949	2.50	5.00	10.00
❑ 10368	Caravan/A Senorita's Bouquet	1949	2.50	5.00	10.00
❑ 10383	Somehow/What's My Name	1949	2.50	5.00	10.00
❑ 10422	Night After Night/A New Shade of Blue	1949	2.50	5.00	10.00
❑ 10458	Crying/Temptation	1949	2.50	5.00	10.00
❑ 10472	Just One Way to Say I Love You/Goodbye	1949	2.50	5.00	10.00
❑ 10501	Body and Soul/If Love Is Trouble	1949	2.50	5.00	10.00
❑ 10525	O Come, All Ye Faithful/O, Holy Night	1949	2.50	5.00	10.00
❑ 10562	Fool's Paradise/You're Wonderful	1949	2.50	5.00	10.00
❑ 10602	Sitting by the Window/Lost in a Dream	1950	2.50	5.00	10.00
❑ 10605	Someone to Watch Over Me/Nobody Knows the Trouble I've Seen	1950	2.50	5.00	10.00
❑ 10606	My Old Flame/I Don't Want to Cry Alone	1950	2.50	5.00	10.00
❑ 10607	Over the Rainbow/You Go to My Head	1950	2.50	5.00	10.00
❑ 10623	My Foolish Heart/Sure Thing	1950	2.00	4.00	8.00
❑ 10643	Free/Baby Won't You Say You Love Me	1950	2.00	4.00	8.00
❑ 10684	My Destiny/Roses	1950	2.00	4.00	8.00
❑ 10690	You're All I Need/Dedicated to You	1950	2.00	4.00	8.00
❑ 10716	I Wanna Be Loved/Stardust	1950	2.00	4.00	8.00
❑ 10778	The Show Must Go On/You've Got Me Cryin' Again	1950	2.00	4.00	8.00
❑ 10796	Blue Christmas/The Lonely Shepherd	1950	2.00	4.00	8.00
❑ 10799	Be My Love/Only a Moment Ago	1950	2.00	4.00	8.00
❑ 10825	I'll Know/I've Never Been in Love Before	1951	2.00	4.00	8.00
❑ 10856	I'm So Crazy for Love/Guess I'll Have to Dream	1951	2.00	4.00	8.00
❑ 10896	If/When You Return	1951	2.00	4.00	8.00
❑ 10903	I Apologize/Bring Back the Thrill	1951	2.00	4.00	8.00
❑ 10916	I Left My Hat/Here Come the Blues	1951	2.00	4.00	8.00
❑ 10944	I'm Yours to Command/What Will I Tell My Heart	1951	2.00	4.00	8.00
❑ 10982	I'm a Fool/Lose Me	1951	2.00	4.00	8.00
❑ 10996	Pandora/Wonder Why	1951	2.00	4.00	8.00
❑ 11028	Enchanted Land/I've Got My Mind on You	1951	2.00	4.00	8.00
❑ 11073	Once/Out in the Cold	1951	2.00	4.00	8.00
❑ 11101	Taking a Chance/You're Driving Me Crazy	1951	2.00	4.00	8.00
❑ 11111	Jalousie/Strange Interlude	1951	2.00	4.00	8.00
❑ 11125	Take Me Back/Weaver of Dreams	1952	2.00	4.00	8.00
❑ 11144	Every Day/I Love You	1952	2.00	4.00	8.00
❑ 11177	Carnival/Room with a View	1952	2.00	4.00	8.00
❑ 11217	If They Ask Me/Hold Me Close to You	1952	2.00	4.00	8.00
❑ 11225	Kiss of Fire/Never Like This	1952	2.00	4.00	8.00
❑ 11291	Have a Good Time/Strange Sensation	1952	2.00	4.00	8.00
❑ 11301	Early Autumn/Because You're Mine	1952	2.00	4.00	8.00
❑ 11351	Be Fair/Come to the Mardi Gras	1952	2.00	4.00	8.00
❑ 11396	Until Eternity/Everything Depends on You	1953	2.00	4.00	8.00
❑ 11439	A Fool in Love/Until Today	1953	2.00	4.00	8.00
❑ 11511	Send My Baby Back to Me/Laugh to Keep From Crying	1953	2.00	4.00	8.00
❑ 11550	It Can't Be Wrong/I Can Read Between the Lines	1953	2.00	4.00	8.00
❑ 11573	St. Louis Blues (Part 1)/St. Louis Blues (Part 2)	1953	2.00	4.00	8.00
❑ 11587	I'm Saving Dreams/Fortune Telling Cards	1953	2.00	4.00	8.00
❑ 11623	What Are You Doing New Year's Eve/Christmas Eve	1953	2.50	5.00	10.00
❑ 11655	Rendezvous/I'm In a Mood	1954	2.00	4.00	8.00
❑ 11694	Don't Get Around Much Anymore/Lost in Loveliness	1954	2.00	4.00	8.00
❑ 11712	No One But You/Seabreeze	1954	2.00	4.00	8.00
❑ 11744	Beloved/Temporarily Blue	1954	2.00	4.00	8.00
❑ 11803	Olay, Olay/You Leave Me Breathless	1954	2.00	4.00	8.00
❑ 11845	Mood Indigo/Do Nothing 'Till You Hear from Me	1954	2.00	4.00	8.00
❑ 11855	Love Me/One Sweet Kiss	1954	2.00	4.00	8.00
❑ 11915	What More Is There to Say/Touching Shoulders	1955	2.50	5.00	10.00
❑ 11948	Give Me Another Chance/More Than You'll Ever Know	1955	2.50	5.00	10.00
❑ 11984	Love Me or Leave Me/Only You	1955	2.50	5.00	10.00
❑ 11998	Careless Lips/A Man Doesn't Know	1955	2.50	5.00	10.00
❑ 12055	September Song/Pass the Word Around	1955	2.50	5.00	10.00
❑ 12105	La De Do De Do (The Honey Bug Song)/Farewell to Romance	1955	2.50	5.00	10.00
❑ 12160	You'll Get Yours/Lonely Avenue	1955	2.50	5.00	10.00
❑ 12180	Good-Bye/The Show Must Go On	1956	2.50	5.00	10.00
❑ 12237	Out of My Mind/My Fickle Heart	1956	2.50	5.00	10.00

NATIONAL

Number	Title (A Side/B Side)	Yr	VG	VG+	NM
❑ 9014	A Cottage for Sale/I Love the Rhythm in a Riff	1945	3.75	7.50	15.00
❑ 9015	Lonesome Lover Blues/Last Night (And Now Tonight Again)	1945	3.75	7.50	15.00
❑ 9016	I'm in the Mood for Love/Long Long Journey	1946	3.75	7.50	15.00
❑ 9017	Prisoner of Love/All I Sing Is Blues	1946	3.75	7.50	15.00
❑ 9018	Blue/Second Balcony Jump	1946	3.75	7.50	15.00
❑ 9019	You Call It Madness But I Call It Love/Tell Me Pretty Baby	1946	3.75	7.50	15.00
❑ 9020	It Ain't Like That/I've Got to Pass Your House	1946	3.75	7.50	15.00
❑ 9021	Jelly Jelly/My Deep Blue Dream	1946	3.75	7.50	15.00
❑ 9023	All the Things You Are/Don't Take Your Love from Me	1947	3.00	6.00	12.00
❑ 9030	Time on My Hands/I Love the Loveliness	1947	3.00	6.00	12.00
❑ 9037	Gloomy Sunday/In the Still of the Night	1947	3.00	6.00	12.00
❑ 9041	All of Me/She's Got the Blues for Sale	1948	3.00	6.00	12.00
❑ 9049	Sophisticated Lady/The Jitney Man	1948	3.00	6.00	12.00
❑ 9052	You're My Everything/Cool Breeze	1948	3.00	6.00	12.00
❑ 9060	My Silent Love/In a Sentimental Mood	1948	3.00	6.00	12.00
❑ 9061	Without a Song/Say It Isn't So	1948	3.00	6.00	12.00
❑ 9076	I Only Have Eyes for You/The Blues	1949	3.00	6.00	12.00
❑ 9086	In My Solitude/I Do, Do You?	1949	3.00	6.00	12.00
❑ 9096	What's New/There Are Such Things	1949	3.00	6.00	12.00
❑ 9115	I Surrender Dear/Our Love	1950	3.00	6.00	12.00
❑ 9125	Love Is the Thing/Oo Bop Sh'Bam	1950	3.00	6.00	12.00
❑ 9132	Cool Breeze/Serenade in Blue	1950	3.00	6.00	12.00

RCA VICTOR

Number	Title (A Side/B Side)	Yr	VG	VG+	NM
❑ 20-6436	The Bitter with the Sweet/Grapevine	1956	3.00	6.00	12.00
❑ 20-6488	My Heart Says No/Joey, Joey, Joey	1956	3.00	6.00	12.00
❑ 20-6524	Tennessee Rock 'n' Roll/Condemned for Life	1956	5.00	10.00	20.00
❑ 20-6691	The Chosen Few/Just Call Me Crazy	1956	3.00	6.00	12.00
❑ 20-6827	Blue Illusion/Oh My Pretty Pretty	1957	3.00	6.00	12.00

7-Inch Extended Plays

EMARCY

Number	Title (A Side/B Side)	Yr	VG	VG+	NM
❑ 16041	(contents unknown)	195?	5.00	10.00	20.00
❑ 16041 [PS]	Billy's Blues	195?	5.00	10.00	20.00

MGM

Number	Title (A Side/B Side)	Yr	VG	VG+	NM
❑ X1011	(contents unknown)	195?	5.00	10.00	20.00
❑ X1011 [PS]	My Foolish Heart	195?	5.00	10.00	20.00
❑ X1015	(contents unknown)	195?	3.75	7.50	15.00
❑ X1015 [PS]	I Apologize	195?	3.75	7.50	15.00
❑ X1041	(contents unknown)	195?	5.00	10.00	20.00
❑ X1041 [PS]	Songs by Billy Eckstine	195?	5.00	10.00	20.00
❑ X1052	Tenderly/If You Could See Me Now//Laura/One for My Baby (And One More for the Road)	1953	3.75	7.50	15.00
❑ X1052 [PS]	Billy Eckstine Sings "Tenderly"	1953	3.75	7.50	15.00
❑ X-1053	(contents unknown)	195?	3.75	7.50	15.00
❑ X-1053 [PS]	Smoke Gets In Your Eyes	195?	3.75	7.50	15.00
❑ X1078	(contents unknown)	195?	3.75	7.50	15.00
❑ X1078 [PS]	St. Louis Blues	195?	3.75	7.50	15.00
❑ X-1084	(contents unknown)	195?	3.75	7.50	15.00
❑ X-1084 [PS]	A Fool in Love	195?	3.75	7.50	15.00
❑ X-1099	(contents unknown)	195?	3.75	7.50	15.00

Number	Title (A Side/B Side)	Yr	VG	VG+	NM
❑ X-1099 [PS]	Love Songs, Vol. 1	195?	3.75	7.50	15.00
❑ X-1100	(contents unknown)	195?	3.75	7.50	15.00
❑ X-1100 [PS]	Love Songs, Vol. 2	195?	3.75	7.50	15.00
❑ X-1103	(contents unknown)	195?	3.75	7.50	15.00
❑ X-1103 [PS]	Billy Eckstine Favorites, Vol. 1	195?	3.75	7.50	15.00
❑ X-1104	*Bewildered/My Foolish Heart/Everything I Have Is Yours/Fool That I Am	195?	3.75	7.50	15.00
❑ X-1104 [PS]	Billy Eckstine Favorites, Vol. 2	195?	3.75	7.50	15.00
❑ X-1110	(contents unknown)	1955	3.75	7.50	15.00
❑ X-1110 [PS]	I Let a Song Go Out of My Heart, Vol. 1	1955	3.75	7.50	15.00
❑ X-1111	(contents unknown)	1955	3.75	7.50	15.00
❑ X-1111 [PS]	I Let a Song Go Out of My Heart, Vol. 2	1955	3.75	7.50	15.00
❑ X-1152	(contents unknown)	195?	3.00	6.00	12.00
❑ X-1152 [PS]	Early Autumn	195?	3.00	6.00	12.00
Albums					
AUDIO LAB					
❑ AL-1549 [M]	Mr. B	1960	30.00	60.00	120.00
DELUXE					
❑ FA-2010 [M]	Billy Eckstine and His Orchestra	195?	20.00	40.00	80.00
EMARCY					
❑ MG-26025 [10]	Blues for Sale	1954	30.00	60.00	120.00
❑ MG-26027 [10]	The Love Songs of Mr. B	1954	30.00	60.00	120.00
❑ MG-36010 [M]	I Surrender, Dear	1955	20.00	40.00	80.00
❑ MG-36029 [M]	Blues for Sale	1955	20.00	40.00	80.00
❑ MG-36030 [M]	The Love Songs of Mr. B	1955	20.00	40.00	80.00
❑ MG-36129 [M]	Billy Eckstine's Imagination	1958	15.00	30.00	60.00
ENTERPRISE					
❑ ENS-1013	Stormy	1971	3.75	7.50	15.00
❑ ENS-1017	Feel the Warm	1971	3.75	7.50	15.00
❑ ENS-5004	Senior Soul	1972	3.75	7.50	15.00
FORUM					
❑ F-9027 [M]	Once More with Feeling	196?	3.75	7.50	15.00
❑ SF-9027 [S]	Once More with Feeling	196?	3.75	7.50	15.00
KING					
❑ 295-12 [10]	The Great Mr. B	1953	75.00	150.00	300.00
LION					
❑ L-70057 [M]	The Best of Billy Eckstine	1958	6.25	12.50	25.00
MERCURY					
❑ MG-20333 [M]	Billy's Best	1958	10.00	20.00	40.00
❑ MG-20637 [M]	Broadway, Bongos and Mr. B	1961	6.25	12.50	25.00
❑ MG-20674 [M]	Billy Eckstine and Quincy Jones at Basin St. East	1962	6.25	12.50	25.00
❑ MG-20736 [M]	Don't Worry 'Bout Me	1962	6.25	12.50	25.00
❑ MG-20796 [M]	The Golden Hits of Billy Eckstine	1963	3.75	7.50	15.00
❑ SR-60086 [S]	Billy's Best	1958	12.50	25.00	50.00
❑ SR-60637 [S]	Broadway, Bongos and Mr. B	1961	7.50	15.00	30.00
❑ SR-60674 [S]	Billy Eckstine and Quincy Jones at Basin St. East	1962	7.50	15.00	30.00
❑ SR-60736 [S]	Don't Worry 'Bout Me	1962	7.50	15.00	30.00
❑ SR-60796 [S]	The Golden Hits of Billy Eckstine	1963	5.00	10.00	20.00
METRO					
❑ M-537 [M]	Everything I Have Is Yours	1965	3.75	7.50	15.00
❑ MS-537 [R]	Everything I Have Is Yours	1965	3.00	6.00	12.00
MGM					
❑ E-153 [10]	Billy Eckstine Sings Rodgers & Hammerstein	1952	37.50	75.00	150.00
❑ E-219 [10]	Tenderly	1953	37.50	75.00	150.00
❑ E-257 [10]	I Let a Song Go Out of My Heart	1954	37.50	75.00	150.00
❑ E-523 [10]	Songs by Billy Eckstine	1951	40.00	80.00	160.00
❑ E-548 [10]	Favorites	1951	40.00	80.00	160.00
❑ E-3176 [M]	Mr. B with a Beat	1955	12.50	25.00	50.00
❑ E-3209 [M]	Rendezvous	1955	12.50	25.00	50.00
❑ E-3275 [M]	That Old Feeling	1956	12.50	25.00	50.00
MOTOWN					
❑ M 632 [M]	Prime of My Life	1965	5.00	10.00	20.00
❑ MS 632 [S]	Prime of My Life	1965	6.25	12.50	25.00
❑ M 646 [M]	My Way	1966	5.00	10.00	20.00
❑ MS 646 [S]	My Way	1966	6.25	12.50	25.00
❑ MS 677	For Love of Ivy	1969	6.25	12.50	25.00
NATIONAL					
❑ NLP-2001 [10]	Billy Eckstine Sings	1949	50.00	100.00	200.00
REGENT					
❑ MG-6052 [M]	Prisoner of Love	1957	12.50	25.00	50.00
❑ MG-6053 [M]	The Duke, the Blues and Me	1957	12.50	25.00	50.00
❑ MG-6054 [M]	My Deep Blue Dream	1957	12.50	25.00	50.00
❑ MG-6058 [M]	You Call It Madness	1957	12.50	25.00	50.00
ROULETTE					
❑ R-25052 [M]	No Cover, No Minimum	1961	6.25	12.50	25.00
❑ SR-25052 [S]	No Cover, No Minimum	1961	7.50	15.00	30.00
❑ R-25104 [M]	Once More with Feeling	1962	6.25	12.50	25.00
❑ SR-25104 [S]	Once More with Feeling	1962	7.50	15.00	30.00
SAVOY					
❑ 1127	Billy Eckstine Sings	1979	3.00	6.00	12.00
❑ SJL-2214 [(2)]	Mr. B and the Band/The Savoy Sessions	1976	3.75	7.50	15.00
TRIP					
❑ 5567	The Modern Sound of Mr. B	197?	2.50	5.00	10.00
VERVE					
❑ 819442-1 [(2)]	Everything I Have Is Yours: The MGM Years	1986	3.75	7.50	15.00
XANADU					
❑ 207	I Want to Talk About You	1987	2.50	5.00	10.00

ECKSTINE, BILLY, AND SARAH VAUGHAN
See SARAH VAUGHAN AND BILLY ECKSTINE.

Number	Title (A Side/B Side)	Yr	VG	VG+	NM
EDSELS, THE					
45s					
CAPITOL					
❑ 4588	Bone Shaker Joe/My Jealous One	1961	5.00	10.00	20.00
❑ 4675	If Your Pillow Could Talk/Shake Shake Sherry	1961	5.00	10.00	20.00
❑ 4836	Shaddy Daddy Dip Dip/Don't You Feel	1962	5.00	10.00	20.00
DOT					
❑ 16311	My Whispering Heart/Could It Be	1962	6.25	12.50	25.00
DUB					
❑ 2843	Lama Rama Ding Dong/Bells	1958	17.50	35.00	70.00
—Originals have the wrong title and the same recording as on Twin 700					
❑ 2843	Rama Lama Ding Dong/Bells	1958	12.50	25.00	50.00
—Repress with corrected title and the same recording as on Twin 700					
❑ 2843	Rama Lama Ding Dong/Bells	197?	—	2.50	5.00
—Reproduction with an alternate take of the A-side; this has confused many who believe that the original Dub and Twin records are different.					
EMBER					
❑ 1078	Three Precious Words/Let's Go	1961	6.25	12.50	25.00
MUSICTONE					
❑ 1144	Rama Lama Ding Dong/Bells	1961	3.00	6.00	12.00
ROULETTE					
❑ 4151	Do You Love Me/Rink-a-Dink-a-Doo	1959	6.25	12.50	25.00
TAMMY					
❑ 1010	What Brought Us Together/Don't Know What to Do	1960	12.50	25.00	50.00
❑ 1014	Three Precious Words/Let's Go	1960	12.50	25.00	50.00
❑ 1023	The Girl I Love/Got to FInd Out About Love	1961	10.00	20.00	40.00
❑ 1027	Count the Tears/Twenty-Four Hours	1961	10.00	20.00	40.00
TWIN					
❑ 700	Rama Lama Ding Dong/Bells	1961	6.25	12.50	25.00
EDWARDS, TOMMY					
45s					
MGM					
❑ 10884	Once There Lived a Fool/A Friend of Johnny's	1951	5.00	10.00	20.00
❑ 10921	Gypsy Heart/Operetta	1951	5.00	10.00	20.00
❑ 10973	I'll Never Know Why/A Beggar in Love	1951	5.00	10.00	20.00
❑ 10989	The Morning Side of the Mountain/For Instance	1951	6.25	12.50	25.00
❑ 11035	It's All in the Game/All Over Again	1951	6.25	12.50	25.00
❑ 11077	Solitaire/My Concerto	1951	5.00	10.00	20.00
❑ 11097	Christmas Is for Children/Kris Kringle	1951	5.00	10.00	20.00
❑ 11134	Please Mr. Sun/I May Live with You	1952	6.25	12.50	25.00
❑ 11170	Forgive Me/The Bridge	1952	5.00	10.00	20.00
❑ 11209	My Girl/Piano, Bass and Drums	1952	5.00	10.00	20.00
❑ 11268	Easy to Say/The Greatest Sinner of Them All	1952	5.00	10.00	20.00
❑ 11326	You Win Again/Sinner and Saint	1952	5.00	10.00	20.00
❑ 11395	(Now and Then, There's) A Fool Such As I/I Can't Love Another	1953	5.00	10.00	20.00
❑ 11465	Au Revoir/I Lived When I Met You	1953	5.00	10.00	20.00
❑ 11485	Take These Chains from My Heart/Paging Mr. Jackson	1953	5.00	10.00	20.00
❑ 11541	Lover's Waltz/Baby, Baby, Baby	1953	5.00	10.00	20.00
❑ 11582	So Little Time/Blue Bird	1953	5.00	10.00	20.00
❑ 11604	That's All/Secret Love	1953	5.00	10.00	20.00
❑ 11624	Every Day Is Christmas/It's Christmas Once Again	1953	5.00	10.00	20.00
❑ 11668	There Was a Time/Wall of Ice	1954	5.00	10.00	20.00
❑ 11718	The Joker (In the Card Game of Life)/Within My Heart	1954	5.00	10.00	20.00
❑ 11763	Linger in My Arms/If You Would Love Me Again	1954	5.00	10.00	20.00
❑ 11821	You Walk By/I Have That Kind of Heart	1954	5.00	10.00	20.00
❑ 11932	Serenade to a Fool/It Could Have Been Me	1955	5.00	10.00	20.00
❑ 11993	Welcome to My Heart/Spring Never Came Around This Year	1955	5.00	10.00	20.00
❑ 12054	Teardrop on a Rose/To Those Who Wait	1955	5.00	10.00	20.00
❑ 12095	Baby, Let Me Take You Dreaming/My Sweetheart	1955	5.00	10.00	20.00
❑ 12248	Love Is a Child/There Must Be a Way to Your Heart	1956	5.00	10.00	20.00
❑ 12342	The Day That I Lost You/My Ship	1956	5.00	10.00	20.00
❑ 12514	We're Not Children Anymore/Any Place, Any Time	1957	5.00	10.00	20.00
❑ 12688	It's All in the Game/Please Love Me Forever	1958	3.75	7.50	15.00
❑ 12722	Love Is All We Need/Mr. Music Man	1958	3.75	7.50	15.00
❑ 12757 [M]	Please Mr. Sun/The Morning Side of the Mountain	1959	3.75	7.50	15.00
❑ 12794	My Melancholy Baby/It's Only the Good Times	1959	3.75	7.50	15.00
❑ 12814	I've Been There/I Looked at Heaven	1959	3.75	7.50	15.00
❑ 12837	Honestly and Truly/(New In) The Ways of Love	1959	3.75	7.50	15.00
❑ 12871	Don't Fence Me In/I'm Building Castles Again	1960	3.00	6.00	12.00
❑ 12890	I Really Don't Want to Know/Unloved	1960	3.00	6.00	12.00
❑ 12890 [PS]	I Really Don't Want to Know/Unloved	1960	7.50	15.00	30.00
❑ 12916	It's Not the End of Everything/Blue Heartaches	1960	3.00	6.00	12.00
❑ 12959	Suzie Wong/As You Desire Me	1960	3.00	6.00	12.00
❑ 12981	Vaya Con Dios/One and Twenty	1961	3.00	6.00	12.00
❑ 13002	The Golden Chain/That's the Way with Love	1961	3.00	6.00	12.00
❑ 13032	I'm So Lonesome I Could Cry/My Heart Would Know	1961	3.00	6.00	12.00
❑ 13057	I'll Cry You Out of My Heart/Tables Are Turning	1962	3.00	6.00	12.00
❑ 13100	Please Don't Tell Me/Tonight I Won't Be There	1962	3.00	6.00	12.00
❑ 13128	May I/Sometimes You Win, Sometimes You Lose	1963	2.50	5.00	10.00
❑ 13172	Country Boy/Love Is Best of All	1963	2.50	5.00	10.00
❑ 13317	Take These Chains from My Heart/You WIn Again	1965	2.50	5.00	10.00
❑ SK 50112 [S]	Please Mr. Sun/The Morning Side of the Mountain	1959	6.25	12.50	25.00

Number	Title (A Side/B Side)	Yr	VG	VG+	NM
MUSICOR					
❏ 1046	Left-Over Dreams/9 Chances Out of 10	1964	2.50	5.00	10.00
❏ 1159	I Must Be Doing Something Wrong/I Cried, I Cried	1966	2.50	5.00	10.00
7-Inch Extended Plays					
MGM					
❏ X-1003	*It's All in the Game/Solitaire/Forgive Me/You Win Again	1952	10.00	20.00	40.00
❏ X-1003 [PS]	It's All in the Game	1952	10.00	20.00	40.00
❏ X-1614	*It's All in the Game/My Sugar, My Sweet/I'll Always Be with You/That's All	1958	5.00	10.00	20.00
❏ X-1614 [PS]	It's All in the Game, Vol. 1	1958	5.00	10.00	20.00
❏ X1618 [S]	(contents unknown)	1958	5.00	10.00	20.00
❏ X1618 [PS]	It's All in the Game, Vol. 2	1958	5.00	10.00	20.00
❏ X1619	Please Love Me Forever/Love Is a Sacred Thing//Now and Then There's a Fool Such as I/Love Is All We Need	1958	5.00	10.00	20.00
❏ X1619 [PS]	It's All in the Game, Vol. 3	1958	5.00	10.00	20.00
❏ SX-1666 [PS]	For Young Lovers, Vol. 1	1959	6.25	12.50	25.00
❏ SX-1666 [S]	(contents unknown)	1959	6.25	12.50	25.00
❏ X-1666 [M]	(contents unknown)	1959	5.00	10.00	20.00
❏ X-1666 [PS]	For Young Lovers, Vol. 1	1959	5.00	10.00	20.00
❏ SX-1667 [PS]	For Young Lovers, Vol. 2	1959	6.25	12.50	25.00
❏ SX-1667 [S]	(contents unknown)	1959	6.25	12.50	25.00
❏ X-1667 [M]	(contents unknown)	1959	5.00	10.00	20.00
❏ X-1667 [PS]	For Young Lovers, Vol. 2	1959	5.00	10.00	20.00
❏ SX-1668 [PS]	For Young Lovers, Vol. 3	1959	6.25	12.50	25.00
❏ SX-1668 [S]	Once There Lived a Fool/Up in a Cloud//It's Only the Good Times/Welcome Me	1959	6.25	12.50	25.00
❏ X-1668 [M]	(contents unknown)	1959	5.00	10.00	20.00
❏ X-1668 [PS]	For Young Lovers, Vol. 3	1959	5.00	10.00	20.00
Albums					
LION					
❏ L-70120 [M]	Tommy Edwards	1959	7.50	15.00	30.00
METRO					
❏ M-511 [M]	Tommy Edwards	1965	3.00	6.00	12.00
❏ MS-511 [S]	Tommy Edwards	1965	3.75	7.50	15.00
MGM					
❏ E-3732 [M]	It's All in the Game	1958	7.50	15.00	30.00
—Yellow label					
❏ E-3732 [M]	It's All in the Game	1960	5.00	10.00	20.00
—Black label					
❏ SE-3732 [S]	It's All in the Game	1959	10.00	20.00	40.00
—Yellow label					
❏ SE-3732 [S]	It's All in the Game	1960	6.25	12.50	25.00
—Black label					
❏ E-3760 [M]	For Young Lovers	1959	7.50	15.00	30.00
—Yellow label					
❏ E-3760 [M]	For Young Lovers	1960	5.00	10.00	20.00
—Black label					
❏ SE-3760 [S]	For Young Lovers	1959	10.00	20.00	40.00
—Yellow label					
❏ SE-3760 [S]	For Young Lovers	1960	6.25	12.50	25.00
—Black label					
❏ E-3805 [M]	You Started Me Dreaming	1960	5.00	10.00	20.00
❏ SE-3805 [S]	You Started Me Dreaming	1960	6.25	12.50	25.00
❏ E-3822 [M]	Step Out Singing	1960	5.00	10.00	20.00
❏ SE-3822 [S]	Step Out Singing	1960	6.25	12.50	25.00
❏ E-3838 [M]	Tommy Edwards in Hawaii	1960	5.00	10.00	20.00
❏ SE-3838 [S]	Tommy Edwards in Hawaii	1960	6.25	12.50	25.00
❏ E-3884 [M]	Tommy Edwards' Greatest Hits	1961	5.00	10.00	20.00
❏ SE-3884 [S]	Tommy Edwards' Greatest Hits	1961	6.25	12.50	25.00
❏ E-3959 [M]	Golden Coutnry Hits	1961	5.00	10.00	20.00
❏ SE-3959 [S]	Golden Coutnry Hits	1961	6.25	12.50	25.00
❏ E-4020 [M]	Stardust	1962	5.00	10.00	20.00
❏ SE-4020 [S]	Stardust	1962	6.25	12.50	25.00
❏ E-4060 [M]	Soft Strings and Two Guitars	1962	5.00	10.00	20.00
❏ SE-4060 [S]	Soft Strings and Two Guitars	1962	6.25	12.50	25.00
❏ E-4141 [M]	The Very Best of Tommy Edwards	1963	3.75	7.50	15.00
❏ SE-4141 [S]	The Very Best of Tommy Edwards	1963	5.00	10.00	20.00
REGENT					
❏ MG-6096 [M]	Tommy Edwards Sings	1958	15.00	30.00	60.00

8TH DAY, THE
Probably all the same group.

45s

Number	Title (A Side/B Side)	Yr	VG	VG+	NM
A&M					
❏ 2539	Call Me Up/I've Got My Heart in the Right Place	1983	—	2.00	4.00
❏ 2595 [DJ]	In the Valley (same on both sides)	1983	—	2.00	4.00
CADET					
❏ 5660	Hear the Grass Grow/Bring Your Love Back	1969	2.50	5.00	10.00
CRIB					
❏ 101	Let's Share the Miracle/It's Christmas Day	19??	—	2.00	4.00
INVICTUS					
❏ 9087	She's Not Just Another Woman/I Can't Fool Myself	1971	—	2.50	5.00
❏ 9098	You've Got to Crawl (Before You Walk)/It's Instrumental to Be Free	1971	—	2.50	5.00
❏ 9107	If I Could See the Light/If I Could See the Light (Part 2)	1971	—	2.50	5.00
❏ 9117	Eeny-Meeny-Miny-Mo (Three's a Crowd)/Rocks in My Head	1972	—	2.50	5.00
❏ 9124	Good Book/I Gotta Get Home	1972	—	2.50	5.00

Number	Title (A Side/B Side)	Yr	VG	VG+	NM
KAPP					
❏ 862	Hey Boy (The Girl's in Love with You)/Million Lights	1967	2.00	4.00	8.00
❏ 894	Raining Sunshine/That Good Old Fashioned Way	1968	2.00	4.00	8.00
❏ 916	Glory/Building with a Steeple	1968	2.00	4.00	8.00
Albums					
A&M					
❏ SP-4942	The 8th Day	1983	2.50	5.00	10.00
INVICTUS					
❏ ST-7306	The 8th Day	1971	3.00	6.00	12.00
❏ ST-9809	I Gotta Get Home	1973	3.00	6.00	12.00
KAPP					
❏ KS 3554	On the Eighth Day	1968	3.75	7.50	15.00

EL DORADOS
45s

Number	Title (A Side/B Side)	Yr	VG	VG+	NM
PAULA					
❏ 347	Looking In from the Outside/Since You Came Into My Life	1971	2.50	5.00	10.00
❏ 369	Loose Booty (Part 1)/Loose Booty (Part 2)	1971	2.50	5.00	10.00
TORRID					
❏ 100	In Over My Head/You Make My Heart Sing	1970	3.75	7.50	15.00
VEE JAY					
❏ 115	Baby I Need You/My Loving Baby	1954	100.00	200.00	400.00
—Red vinyl					
❏ 115	Baby I Need You/My Loving Baby	1954	20.00	40.00	80.00
❏ 118	Annie's Answer/Living with Vivian	1954	75.00	150.00	300.00
—Red vinyl					
❏ 118	Annie's Answer/Living with Vivian	1954	20.00	40.00	80.00
❏ 127	One More Chance/Little Miss Love	1954	50.00	100.00	200.00
❏ 147	At My Front Door/What's Buggin' You Baby	1955	17.50	35.00	70.00
❏ 165	I'll Be Forever Lovin' You/I Began to Realize	1955	15.00	30.00	60.00
❏ 180	Now That You've Gone/Rock 'N' Roll's for Me	1956	12.50	25.00	50.00
❏ 197	Fallen Tear/Chop Ling Soon	1956	12.50	25.00	50.00
❏ 211	Bim Bam Boom/There in the Night	1956	20.00	40.00	80.00
❏ 250	Tears on My Pillow/A Rose for My Darling	1957	7.50	15.00	30.00
❏ 263	Three Reasons Why/Boom Diddle Boom	1958	37.50	75.00	150.00
❏ 302	Oh What a Girl/The Lights Are Low	1958	37.50	75.00	150.00
Albums					
LOST-NITE					
❏ LLP-20 [10]	The El Dorados	1981	3.00	6.00	12.00
—Red vinyl					
SOLID SMOKE					
❏ 8025	Low Mileage/High Octane	1984	2.50	5.00	10.00
VEE JAY					
❏ LP-1001 [M]	Crazy Little Mama	1959	200.00	400.00	800.00
—Maroon label, thick silver band					
❏ LP-1001 [M]	Crazy Little Mama	1960	100.00	200.00	400.00
—Maroon label, thin silver band					
❏ LP-1001 [M]	Crazy Little Mama	1962	62.50	125.00	250.00
—Black label with colorband					
❏ VJLP-1001 [M]	Crazy Little Mama	198?	2.50	5.00	10.00
—Authorized reissue					

EL RAYS, THE
See THE DELLS.

ELBERT, DONNIE
45s

Number	Title (A Side/B Side)	Yr	VG	VG+	NM
ALL PLATINUM					
❏ 2330	Where Did Our Love Go/That's If You Love Me	1971	—	3.00	6.00
❏ 2333	Sweet Baby/Can't Get Over Losing You	1971	—	3.00	6.00
❏ 2336	If I Can't Have You/Can't Get Over Losing You	1972	—	3.00	6.00
❏ 2337	Little Piece of Leather/Sweet Baby	1972	—	3.00	6.00
❏ 2338	That's If You Love Me/Can't Get Over Losing You	1972	—	3.00	6.00
❏ 2346	This Feeling of Losing You/Can't Stand These Lonely Nights	1973	—	3.00	6.00
❏ 2351	Love Is Strange/(Instrumental)	1973	—	3.00	6.00
❏ 2367	What Do You Do/Will You Love Me Tomorrow	1974	—	2.50	5.00
❏ 2374	You Should Be Dancing/What Do You Do	1974	—	2.50	5.00
ATCO					
❏ 6550	Too Far Gone/In Between the Heartaches	1968	2.00	4.00	8.00
AVCO					
❏ 4587	I Can't Help Myself/Love Is Here and Now You're Gone	1972	—	3.00	6.00
❏ 4598	Ooh, Baby Baby/Tell Her for Me	1972	—	3.00	6.00
CUB					
❏ 9125	Don't Cry My Love/Love Stew	1963	3.00	6.00	12.00
DELUXE					
❏ 6125	What Can I Do/Hear My Plea	1957	5.00	10.00	20.00
❏ 6143	Believe It or Not/Tell Me So	1957	5.00	10.00	20.00
❏ 6148	Leona/Have I Sinned	1957	5.00	10.00	20.00
❏ 6156	Wild Child/Let's Do the Stroll	1958	5.00	10.00	20.00
❏ 6161	My Confession of Love/Peek-a-Boo	1958	5.00	10.00	20.00
❏ 6168	I Want to Be Near You/Come On Sugar	1958	5.00	10.00	20.00
❏ 6175	Just a Little Bit of Lovin'/When You're Near Me	1958	5.00	10.00	20.00
DERAM					
❏ 7526	Without You/Baby Please Come Home	1969	2.00	4.00	8.00
PARKWAY					
❏ 844	Set My Heart at Ease/Baby Cares	1962	3.75	7.50	15.00
RARE BULLET					
❏ 101	Can't Get Over Losing You/Got to Get Myself Together	1970	—	3.00	6.00

E

Number	Title (A Side/B Side)	Yr	VG	VG+	NM

VEE JAY
❏ 336	Hey Baby/Will You Ever Be Mine	1960	3.75	7.50	15.00
❏ 353	Baby Let Me Love You Tonight/Half as Old	1960	3.75	7.50	15.00
❏ 370	I've Loved You Baby/I Beg of You	1960	3.75	7.50	15.00

Albums
ALL PLATINUM
| ❏ 3007 | Where Did Our Love Go | 1971 | 6.25 | 12.50 | 25.00 |
| ❏ 3019 | Dancin' the Night Away | 1977 | 6.25 | 12.50 | 25.00 |

DELUXE
| ❏ 12003 | Have I Sinned | 1971 | 6.25 | 12.50 | 25.00 |

KING
| ❏ 629 [M] | The Sensational Donnie Elbert Sings | 1959 | 100.00 | 200.00 | 400.00 |

SUGAR HILL
| ❏ 256 | From the Git Go | 1981 | 3.00 | 6.00 | 12.00 |

TRIP
| ❏ 9514 | Donnie Elbert Sings | 197? | 3.75 | 7.50 | 15.00 |
| ❏ 9524 | Stop in the Name of Love | 197? | 3.75 | 7.50 | 15.00 |

ELECTRIC INDIAN, THE
Group evolved into MFSB.
45s
MARMADUKE
| ❏ 4001 | Keem-O-Sabe/Broad Street | 1969 | 5.00 | 10.00 | 20.00 |

UNITED ARTISTS
❏ 0128	Keem-O-Sabe/Stick Shift	1973	—	2.00	4.00
—"Silver Spotlight Series" reissue; B-side by The Duals					
❏ 50563	Keem-O-Sabe/Broad Street	1969	—	3.00	6.00
❏ 50613	Geronimo/Land of 1,000 Dances	1969	—	2.50	5.00
❏ 50647	Rain Dance/Storm Warning	1970	—	2.50	5.00
❏ 50701	Apotchee/Chicago Hawk	1970	—	2.50	5.00
❏ 50744	Geronimo/My Cherie Amour	1971	—	2.50	5.00

Albums
UNITED ARTISTS
| ❏ UAS 6728 | Keem-O-Sabe | 1969 | 3.75 | 7.50 | 15.00 |

ELEGANTS, THE
Also see PAT CORDEL.
45s
ABC-PARAMOUNT
| ❏ 10219 | I've Seen Everything/Tiny Cloud | 1961 | 10.00 | 20.00 | 40.00 |

APT
❏ 25005	Little Star/Getting Dizzy	1958	12.50	25.00	50.00
—All-black label					
❏ 25005	Little Star/Getting Dizzy	1958	10.00	20.00	40.00
—Black label with rainbow					
❏ 25017	Goodnight/Please Believe Me	1958	7.50	15.00	30.00
❏ 25029	Pay Day/True Love Affair	1959	7.50	15.00	30.00

BANGAR
| ❏ 613 | Minor Chaos/Lost Souls | 1964 | 7.50 | 15.00 | 30.00 |

BIM BAM BOOM
❏ 121	It's Just a Matter of Time/Lonesome Weekends	1974	—	3.00	6.00
—Colored vinyl					
❏ 121	It's Just a Matter of Time/Lonesome Weekends	1974	—	2.00	4.00
—Black vinyl					

CRYSTAL BALL
| ❏ 139 | Maybe/Woo Woo Train | 197? | — | 2.50 | 5.00 |

HULL
| ❏ 732 | Little Boy Blue/Get Well Soon | 1960 | 25.00 | 50.00 | 100.00 |

LAURIE
❏ 3283	A Letter from Viet Nam/Barbara Beware	1965	7.50	15.00	30.00
❏ 3298	Wake Up/Bring Back Wendy	1965	12.50	25.00	50.00
❏ 3324	Belinda/Lazy Love	1965	6.25	12.50	25.00
—As "Vito and the Elegants"					

PHOTO
| ❏ 2662 | Dressin' Up/A Dream Can Come True | 1963 | 12.50 | 25.00 | 50.00 |
| ❏ 2662 [PS] | Dressin' Up/A Dream Can Come True | 1963 | 37.50 | 75.00 | 150.00 |

UNITED ARTISTS
| ❏ 230 | Speak Low/Let My Prayers Be With You | 1960 | 10.00 | 20.00 | 40.00 |
| ❏ 295 | Happiness/Spiritual | 1961 | 12.50 | 25.00 | 50.00 |

78s
APT
| ❏ 25005 | Little Star/Getting Dizzy | 1958 | 125.00 | 250.00 | 500.00 |

Albums
MURRAY HILL
| ❏ 210 | Little Star | 1986 | 2.50 | 5.00 | 10.00 |

ELGINS, THE (1)
Detroit R&B group.
45s
LUMMTONE
| ❏ 113 | Your Lovely Ways/Finding a Sweetheart | 1963 | 6.25 | 12.50 | 25.00 |

TAMLA
❏ 54056	Request of a Fool/Your Baby's Back	1962	75.00	150.00	300.00
—As "The Downbeats"; with "Tamla" circling globe at top of label					
❏ 54056	Request of a Fool/Your Baby's Back	1962	7.50	15.00	30.00
—As "The Downbeats"; with "Tamla" in globe at top of label					

V.I.P.
❏ 25029	Darling Baby/Put Yourself in My Place	1965	50.00	100.00	200.00
—First pressings credited "The Downbeats"					
❏ 25029	Darling Baby/Put Yourself in My Place	1965	5.00	10.00	20.00
❏ 25037	Heaven Must Have Sent You/Stay in My Lonely Arms	1965	5.00	10.00	20.00
❏ 25043	It's Been a Long, Long Time/I Understand My Man	1966	5.00	10.00	20.00

| ❏ 25065 | Heaven Must Have Sent You/Stay in My Lonely Arms | 1970 | 2.50 | 5.00 | 10.00 |

Albums
V.I.P.
| ❏ 400 [M] | Darling Baby | 1966 | 17.50 | 35.00 | 70.00 |
| ❏ S-400 [S] | Darling Baby | 1966 | 25.00 | 50.00 | 100.00 |

ELLIS, SHIRLEY
45s
COLUMBIA
❏ 43829	Truly, Truly, Truly/Birds, Bees, Cupids and Bows	1966	2.00	4.00	8.00
❏ 44021	Soul Time/Waitin'	1967	2.00	4.00	8.00
❏ 44137	Sugar Let's Shing-a-Ling/How Lonely Is Lonely	1967	2.00	4.00	8.00

CONGRESS
❏ 202	The Nitty Gritty/Give Me a List	1963	3.75	7.50	15.00
❏ 208	(That's) What the Nitty Gritty Is/Get Out	1964	2.50	5.00	10.00
❏ 210	Shy One/Takin' Care of Business	1964	2.50	5.00	10.00
❏ 221	Such a Night/Bring It On Home to Me	1964	2.50	5.00	10.00
❏ 230	The Name Game/Whisper to the Wind	1964	3.00	6.00	12.00
❏ 230 [PS]	The Name Game/Whisper to the Wind	1964	5.00	10.00	20.00
❏ 234	The Clapping Song (Clap Pat Clap Slap)/This Is Beautiful	1965	2.50	5.00	10.00
❏ 234 [PS]	The Clapping Song (Clap Pat Clap Slap)/This Is Beautiful	1965	5.00	10.00	20.00
❏ 238	The Puzzle Song (A Puzzle in Song)/I See It, I Like It, I Want It	1965	2.50	5.00	10.00
❏ 246	I Never Will Forget/I Told You So	1965	2.50	5.00	10.00
❏ 251	One Sour Note/You Better Be Good, World	1965	2.50	5.00	10.00
❏ 260	Ever See a Diver Kiss His Wife While the Bubbles Bounce About Above the Water/Stardust	1965	2.50	5.00	10.00

Albums
COLUMBIA
| ❏ CL 2679 [M] | Sugar, Let's Shing-a-Ling | 1967 | 5.00 | 10.00 | 20.00 |
| ❏ CS 9479 [S] | Sugar, Let's Shing-a-Ling | 1967 | 6.25 | 12.50 | 25.00 |

CONGRESS
❏ CGL-3002 [M]	Shirley Ellis In Action	1964	6.25	12.50	25.00
❏ CGS-3002 [S]	Shirley Ellis In Action	1964	7.50	15.00	30.00
❏ CGL-3003 [M]	The Name Game	1965	6.25	12.50	25.00
❏ CGS-3003 [S]	The Name Game	1965	7.50	15.00	30.00

EMBERS, THE
Several different groups.
45s
ATLANTIC
| ❏ 2627 | Where Did I Go Wrong/You Got What You Want | 1969 | 2.50 | 5.00 | 10.00 |

BELL
| ❏ 664 | It Ain't No Big Thing/It Ain't Necessary | 1967 | 5.00 | 10.00 | 20.00 |

COLUMBIA
| ❏ 40287 | Sweet Lips/There'll Be No One Else But You | 1954 | 10.00 | 20.00 | 40.00 |

DOT
| ❏ 16101 | Wait for Me/Couldn't Wait Any Longer | 1960 | 3.75 | 7.50 | 15.00 |
| ❏ 16162 | Please Mr. Sun/My Dearest Darling | 1960 | 3.75 | 7.50 | 15.00 |

EMBER
| ❏ 101 | Sound of Love/Paradise Hill | 1953 | 200.00 | 400.00 | 800.00 |

EMPRESS
❏ 101	Solitaire/I'm Feeling All Right Again	1961	7.50	15.00	30.00
❏ 104	I Won't Cry Anymore/I Was Too Careful	1961	7.50	15.00	30.00
❏ 107	Abigail/I Was Too Careful	1962	7.50	15.00	30.00
❏ 108	What a Surprise/I Was Too Careful	1962	10.00	20.00	40.00

HERALD
❏ 410	Sound of Love/Paradise Hill	1953	50.00	100.00	200.00
—Black label					
❏ 410	Sound of Love/Paradise Hill	1953	20.00	40.00	80.00
—Yellow label					
❏ 410	Sound of Love/Paradise Hill	1953	37.50	75.00	150.00
—Red vinyl					

JCP
| ❏ 1008 | In My Lonely Room/Good Good Lovin' | 1964 | 15.00 | 30.00 | 60.00 |

LIBERTY
| ❏ 55944 | Evelyn/And Now I'm Blue | 1967 | 2.50 | 5.00 | 10.00 |

MGM
| ❏ 14167 | Watch Out Girl/Far Away Places | 1970 | 7.50 | 15.00 | 30.00 |

WYNNE
| ❏ 101 | Peter Gunn Cha Cha/Chinny Chin Cha Cha | 1958 | 3.75 | 7.50 | 15.00 |

EMOTIONS, THE (1)
Female R&B vocal group. Also see EARTH, WIND AND FIRE WITH THE EMOTIONS.
45s
ARC
❏ 18-02239	Turn It Out/When You Gonna Wake Up	1981	—	2.00	4.00
❏ 18-02535	Now That I Know/Here You Come Again	1981	—	2.00	4.00
❏ 11134	What's the Name of Your Love?/Layed Back	1979	—	2.50	5.00
❏ 11205	Where Is Your Love?/Layed Back	1980	—	2.50	5.00

COLUMBIA
❏ 3-10347	Flowers/I Don't Wanna Lose Your Love	1976	—	2.50	5.00
❏ 3-10544	Best of My Love/A Feeling Is	1977	—	2.50	5.00
❏ 3-10622	Don't Ask My Neighbors/Love's What's Happenin'	1977	—	2.50	5.00
❏ 3-10791	Smile/Changes	1978	—	2.50	5.00
❏ 3-10828	Whole Lotta Shakin'/Time Is Passing By	1978	—	2.50	5.00
❏ 3-10874	Walking the Line/Ain't No Doubt About It	1978	—	2.50	5.00

MOTOWN
| ❏ 1784 | I Can't Wait to Make You Mine/I'm Gonna Miss Your Love | 1985 | — | 2.00 | 4.00 |

Number	Title (A Side/B Side)	Yr	VG	VG+	NM
❑ 1792	If I Only Knew Then (What I Know Now)/Eternally	1985	—	2.00	4.00

RED LABEL

Number	Title (A Side/B Side)	Yr	VG	VG+	NM
❑ 001-1	You're the One/I Can Do Anything	1984	—	2.50	5.00
❑ 001-2	You're the Best/(B-side unknown)	1984	—	2.50	5.00
❑ 001-3	Are You Through with My Heart/(B-side unknown)	1984	—	2.50	5.00

STAX

Number	Title (A Side/B Side)	Yr	VG	VG+	NM
❑ 1056	What Do The Lonely Do At Christmas?/Santa Claus Wants Some Lovin'	197?	—	3.00	6.00

—B-side by Albert King; reissue

Number	Title (A Side/B Side)	Yr	VG	VG+	NM
❑ 3200	Shouting Out Love/Baby, I'm Through	1977	—	2.50	5.00
❑ 3205	Baby, I'm Through/Any Way You Look at It	1978	—	2.50	5.00
❑ 3215	What Do the Lonely Do at Christmas/(Instrumental)	1978	—	2.50	5.00

TWIN STACKS

Number	Title (A Side/B Side)	Yr	VG	VG+	NM
❑ 126	Somebody New/Brushfire	1968	2.50	5.00	10.00
❑ 130	I Love You But I'll Leave You/Brushfire	1968	2.50	5.00	10.00

VOLT

Number	Title (A Side/B Side)	Yr	VG	VG+	NM
❑ 4010	So I Can Love You/Got to Be the Man	1969	2.00	4.00	8.00
❑ 4021	The Best Part of a Love Affair/I Like It	1969	2.00	4.00	8.00
❑ 4031	Stealing Love/When Tomorrow Comes	1970	2.00	4.00	8.00
❑ 4045	Heart Association/The Touch of Your Lips	1970	2.00	4.00	8.00
❑ 4053	Black Christmas/(Instrumental)	1970	2.50	5.00	10.00
❑ 4054	You Make Me Want to Love You/What You See Is What You Get	1971	—	3.50	7.00
❑ 4062	If You Think It/Love Ain't Easy One-Sided	1971	—	3.50	7.00
❑ 4066	Show Me How/Boss Love Maker	1971	—	3.50	7.00
❑ 4077	My Honey and Me/Blind Alley	1972	—	3.50	7.00
❑ 4083	I Could Never Be Happy/I've Fallen in Love	1972	—	3.50	7.00
❑ 4088	From Toys to Boys/I Call This Loving You	1972	—	3.50	7.00
❑ 4095	Runnin' Back (And Forth)/I Wanna Come Back	1973	—	3.50	7.00
❑ 4100	Peace Be Still/Runnin' Back (And Forth)	1973	—	3.50	7.00
❑ 4104	What Do the Lonely Do at Christmas/(Instrumental)	1973	2.00	4.00	8.00
❑ 4106	Put a Little Love Away/I Call This Loving You	1974	—	3.50	7.00
❑ 4110	Baby I'm Through/I Wanna Come Back	1974	—	3.50	7.00
❑ 4113	Any Way You Look At It/There Are More Questions Than Answers	1974	—	3.50	7.00

Albums

ARC

Number	Title (A Side/B Side)	Yr	VG	VG+	NM
❑ JC 36149	Come Into Our World	1979	2.50	5.00	10.00
❑ FC 37456	New Affair	1981	2.50	5.00	10.00

COLUMBIA

Number	Title (A Side/B Side)	Yr	VG	VG+	NM
❑ PC 34163	Flowers	1976	2.50	5.00	10.00

—No bar code on cover

Number	Title (A Side/B Side)	Yr	VG	VG+	NM
❑ PC 34163	Flowers	198?	2.00	4.00	8.00

—With bar code on cover

Number	Title (A Side/B Side)	Yr	VG	VG+	NM
❑ PC 34762	Rejoice	1977	2.50	5.00	10.00

—No bar code on cover

Number	Title (A Side/B Side)	Yr	VG	VG+	NM
❑ PC 34762	Rejoice	198?	2.00	4.00	8.00

—With bar code on cover

Number	Title (A Side/B Side)	Yr	VG	VG+	NM
❑ JC 35385	Sunbeam	1978	2.50	5.00	10.00

MOTOWN

Number	Title (A Side/B Side)	Yr	VG	VG+	NM
❑ 6136 ML	If I Only Knew	1985	2.00	4.00	8.00

RED LABEL

Number	Title (A Side/B Side)	Yr	VG	VG+	NM
❑ 001	Sincerely	1984	2.50	5.00	10.00

STAX

Number	Title (A Side/B Side)	Yr	VG	VG+	NM
❑ STX-4100	Sunshine	1977	2.50	5.00	10.00
❑ STX-4110	So I Can Love You	1978	2.50	5.00	10.00

—Reissue of Volt 6008

Number	Title (A Side/B Side)	Yr	VG	VG+	NM
❑ STX-4112	Untouched	1978	2.50	5.00	10.00

—Reissue of Volt 6015

Number	Title (A Side/B Side)	Yr	VG	VG+	NM
❑ STX-4121	Chronicle	1979	2.50	5.00	10.00

VOLT

Number	Title (A Side/B Side)	Yr	VG	VG+	NM
❑ VOS-6008	So I Can Love You	1971	6.25	12.50	25.00
❑ VOS-6015	Untouched	1972	6.25	12.50	25.00

EMPIRES, THE (1)

LES COOPER was a member of this group.

45s

AMP 3

Number	Title (A Side/B Side)	Yr	VG	VG+	NM
❑ 132	If I'm a Fool/Zippety Zip	1957	25.00	50.00	100.00

HARLEM

Number	Title (A Side/B Side)	Yr	VG	VG+	NM
❑ 2325	Corn Whiskey/My Baby, My Baby	1954	100.00	200.00	400.00
❑ 2333	Magic Mirror/Make Me or Break Me	1955	100.00	200.00	400.00

WHIRLIN' DISC

Number	Title (A Side/B Side)	Yr	VG	VG+	NM
❑ 104	Linda/Whispering Heart	1957	17.50	35.00	70.00

WING

Number	Title (A Side/B Side)	Yr	VG	VG+	NM
❑ 90023	I Want to Know/Shirley	1955	12.50	25.00	50.00
❑ 90050	By the Riverside/Tell Me Pretty Baby	1956	10.00	20.00	40.00
❑ 90080	Don't Touch My Gal/My First Discovery	1956	10.00	20.00	40.00

EN VOGUE

12-Inch Singles

ATLANTIC

Number	Title (A Side/B Side)	Yr	VG	VG+	NM
❑ DMD 1452 [DJ]	Hold On (Radio Version with Intro 5:08) (Edit 4:15) (Edit with Intro 4:58) (Extended Version 5:18)	1990	3.75	7.50	15.00
❑ DMD 1502 [DJ]	Lies (8 versions?)	1990	3.75	7.50	15.00
❑ DMD 1561 [DJ]	You Don't Have to Worry (5 versions)	1990	3.00	6.00	12.00
❑ 86168	Lies (Avant Garde Remix Extended Version) (LP Version) (Funky Remix Extended Version) (Kwame's Boneage Remix)	1990	3.00	6.00	12.00

EASTWEST

Number	Title (A Side/B Side)	Yr	VG	VG+	NM
❑ DMD 1748 [DJ]	Time Goes On/Strange//You Don't Have to Worry/Lies/Hold On	1992	5.00	10.00	20.00
❑ DMD 1832 [DJ]	My Lovin' (You're Never Gonna Get It) (4 versions)	1992	3.00	6.00	12.00
❑ DMD 1900 [DJ]	Free Your Mind (4 versions)	1992	3.75	7.50	15.00
❑ DMD 1977 [DJ]	Love Don't Love You (4 versions)	1993	3.00	6.00	12.00
❑ DMD 2032 [DJ]	Runaway Love (Extended Version) (Hype Mix) (F Mob Instrumental Mix) (EP Version) (Edit)	1993	3.00	6.00	12.00
❑ DMD 2047 [DJ]	What Is Love (Extended Club Remix) (CD Version) (Mentalinstrum Instrumental) (B-Mental Beats)	1993	3.75	7.50	15.00
❑ DMD 2064 [DJ]	Desire (Dancehall Remix 3:57) (same on both sides)	1993	2.50	5.00	10.00
❑ ED 5877 [DJ]	Don't Let Go (Love) (Soundtrack Version) (Radio Edit) (Instrumental)/Hold On	1996	3.75	7.50	15.00
❑ ED 6033 [DJ]	Whatever (Album Version) (Radio Edit) (Instrumental) (TV Track)	1997	3.00	6.00	12.00
❑ ED 6038 [DJ]	Whatever (6 versions)	1997	2.50	5.00	10.00
❑ ED 6042 [DJ]	Whatever (Mucho Soul Mix) (Shelter Dub) (Tuff Jam's Unda Vybe Mix) (Tuff Jam's 2 in 1 Instrumental)	1997	3.00	6.00	12.00
❑ ED 6204 [DJ]	The Riddle (Album Version) (Radio Edit) (Red Zone Remix) (Red Zone Remix Instrumental) (Extended Club Remix) (Club Remix Instrumental) (Album Version Instrumental) (Album Version Acappella)	2000	3.75	7.50	15.00
❑ ED 6227 [DJ]	The Riddle (The Ultimate Riddle Edit) (The Ultimate Riddle) (Stargate Radio Remix) (Stargate Club Remix)	2000	3.75	7.50	15.00
❑ 63987	Don't Let Go (Love) (3 versions)/Hold On	1996	3.00	6.00	12.00
❑ 96059	Love Don't Love You (Remix #1) (Remix #2) (LP Version) (Remix Dub)/Yesterday	1993	3.75	7.50	15.00
❑ 96128	Free Your Mind (Theo's Rec & Wreck Mix) (Tommy's Spoiled Brat Mix) (James Club Remix) (LP Version)	1992	3.00	6.00	12.00

45s

ATLANTIC

Number	Title (A Side/B Side)	Yr	VG	VG+	NM
❑ 87812	You Don't Have to Worry/Luv Lines	1990	—	2.50	5.00
❑ 87893	Lies/(LP Version)	1990	—	2.00	4.00
❑ 87984	Hold On/Luv Lines	1990	—	2.00	4.00

EASTWEST

Number	Title (A Side/B Side)	Yr	VG	VG+	NM
❑ 64231	Don't Let Go (Love)/Hold On	1996	—	2.50	5.00
❑ 98487	Free Your Mind/Just Can't Stay Away	1992	—	2.50	5.00
❑ 98560	Giving Him Something He Can Feel/My Love (You're Never Gonna Get It) (Remix)	1992	—	2.50	5.00
❑ 98586	My Lovin' (You're Never Gonna Get It)/(Instrumental)	1992	—	2.50	5.00

Albums

ATLANTIC

Number	Title (A Side/B Side)	Yr	VG	VG+	NM
❑ 82084	Born to Sing	1990	3.75	7.50	15.00

ENCHANTERS, THE (2)

Also see GARNET MIMMS AND THE ENCHANTERS.

45s

LOMA

Number	Title (A Side/B Side)	Yr	VG	VG+	NM
❑ 2012	I Want to Be Loved/I Paid for the Party	1965	2.50	5.00	10.00
❑ 2035	You Were Meant to Be My Baby/God Bless the Girl, and Me	1966	2.50	5.00	10.00
❑ 2054	We Got Love/I've Lost All Communications	1966	2.50	5.00	10.00

WARNER BROS.

Number	Title (A Side/B Side)	Yr	VG	VG+	NM
❑ 5460	I Wanna Thank You/I'm a Good Man	1964	3.75	7.50	15.00

ENCHANTMENTS, THE

45s

FARO

Number	Title (A Side/B Side)	Yr	VG	VG+	NM
❑ 620	I'm in Love with Your Daughter/(B-side unknown)	1964	25.00	50.00	100.00

GONE

Number	Title (A Side/B Side)	Yr	VG	VG+	NM
❑ 5130	(I Love You) Sherry/Come On Home	1962	7.50	15.00	30.00

RITZ

Number	Title (A Side/B Side)	Yr	VG	VG+	NM
❑ 17003	I Love You Baby/Pains in My Heart	1963	25.00	50.00	100.00

ENCORES, THE

More than one group.

45s

BOW

Number	Title (A Side/B Side)	Yr	VG	VG+	NM
❑ 302	Barbara/Thank You	1958	25.00	50.00	100.00

CHECKER

Number	Title (A Side/B Side)	Yr	VG	VG+	NM
❑ 760	When I Look at You/Young Girls, Young Girls	1952	2000.	3000.	4000.

HOLLYWOOD

Number	Title (A Side/B Side)	Yr	VG	VG+	NM
❑ 1034	Time Is Moving On/Ha-Chi-Bi-Ri-Bi-Ri	1955	20.00	40.00	80.00

LOOK

Number	Title (A Side/B Side)	Yr	VG	VG+	NM
❑ 105	Time Is Moving On/Ha-Chi-Bi-Ri-Bi-Ri	1955	100.00	200.00	400.00

MGM

Number	Title (A Side/B Side)	Yr	VG	VG+	NM
❑ 11947	Chloe/Wa Va Ga Dot	1955	3.00	6.00	12.00

EQUALS, THE

Also see EDDY GRANT.

45s

BANG

Number	Title (A Side/B Side)	Yr	VG	VG+	NM
❑ 582	Ain't Got Nothing to Give You/Black Skin, Blue Eyed Boys	1971	2.50	5.00	10.00

E

Number	Title (A Side/B Side)	Yr	VG	VG+	NM

PRESIDENT

Number	Title (A Side/B Side)	Yr	VG	VG+	NM
❏ 103	Fire/I Won't Be There	1967	3.00	6.00	12.00
❏ 105	My Life Ain't Easy/You Got Too Many Boyfriends	1967	3.00	6.00	12.00
❏ 108	Giddy Up a Ding-Dong/I Get So Excited	1968	3.00	6.00	12.00
❏ 109	Lovely Rita/Softly, Softly	1968	3.00	6.00	12.00
❏ 110	Honey Gun/Michael and the Slipper Tree	1968	3.00	6.00	12.00
❏ 111	I Can't Let You Go/Viva Bobby Joe	1969	3.00	6.00	12.00

RCA VICTOR

❏ 47-9186	Baby Come Back/Hold Me Closer	1967	3.75	7.50	15.00
❏ 47-9583	Baby Come Back/Hold Me Closer	1968	2.50	5.00	10.00

SHOUT

❏ 247	Ain't Got Nothing to Give You/Black Skin, Blue Eyed Boys	1970	3.00	6.00	12.00

Albums
LAURIE

❏ LLP-2045 [M]	Unequalled	1967	6.25	12.50	25.00
❏ SLP-2045 [S]	Unequalled	1967	7.50	15.00	30.00

PRESIDENT

❏ PTL-1015	Equal Sensation	1968	6.25	12.50	25.00
❏ PTL-1020	The Sensational Equals	1968	6.25	12.50	25.00
❏ PTL-1025	Equals Supreme	1968	6.25	12.50	25.00
❏ PTL-1030	Strikeback	1969	6.25	12.50	25.00

RCA VICTOR

❏ LSP-4078	Baby Come Back	1968	6.25	12.50	25.00

ESQUIRES, THE (1)
Milwaukee-based R&B group.
45s
BUNKY

❏ 7750	Get On Up/Listen to Me	1967	2.50	5.00	10.00
❏ 7752	And Get Away/Everybody's Laughin'	1967	2.50	5.00	10.00
❏ 7753	You Say/State Fair	1968	2.50	5.00	10.00
❏ 7755	Why Can't I Stop/The Feeling's Gone	1968	2.50	5.00	10.00
❏ 7756	How Could It Be/I Know I Can	1968	2.50	5.00	10.00

CAPITOL

❏ 2650	Reach Out/Listen to Me	1969	2.00	4.00	8.00

CIGAR MAN

❏ 79880	The Show Ain't Over/What Good Is Music?	1980	—	3.00	6.00

JU-PAR

❏ 104	Get On Up '76/Feeling's Gone (Also Known As Disco Dancing)	1976	—	3.00	6.00

LAMARR

❏ 1001	Girls in the City/Ain't Gonna Give It Up	1971	2.00	4.00	8.00

SCEPTER

❏ 12232	You've Got the Power/No Doubt About It	1968	—	—	—
—Unreleased? (Possibly reassigned to Wand?)					

WAND

❏ 1193	You've Got the Power/No Doubt About It	1968	2.00	4.00	8.00
❏ 1195	I Don't Know/Part Angel	1969	2.00	4.00	8.00
❏ 11201	Whip It On Me/It Was Yesterday	1969	2.00	4.00	8.00

Albums
BUNKY

❏ 300	Get On Up and Get Away	1968	8.75	17.50	35.00

ESSEX, THE
Also see ANITA HUMES.
45s
BANG

❏ 537	The Eagle/Moonlight, Music, and You	1966	2.00	4.00	8.00

ROULETTE

❏ 4494	Easier Said Than Done/Are You Going My Way	1963	3.75	7.50	15.00
❏ 4515	A Walkin' Miracle/What I Don't Know Won't Hurt Me	1963	3.75	7.50	15.00
❏ 4530	She's Got Everything/Out of Sight, Out of Mind	1964	2.50	5.00	10.00
❏ 4542	What Did I Do/Curfew Lover	1964	2.50	5.00	10.00

Albums
ROULETTE

❏ R-25234 [M]	Easier Said Than Done	1963	10.00	20.00	40.00
❏ SR-25234 [S]	Easier Said Than Done	1963	12.50	25.00	50.00
❏ R-25235 [M]	A Walkin' Miracle	1963	10.00	20.00	40.00
❏ SR-25235 [S]	A Walkin' Miracle	1963	12.50	25.00	50.00
❏ R-25246 [M]	Young and Lively	1964	10.00	20.00	40.00
❏ SR-25246 [S]	Young and Lively	1964	12.50	25.00	50.00

ETERNALS, THE (1)
45s
HOLLYWOOD

❏ 68	Rockin' in the Jungle/Rock and Roll Cha Cha	1959	15.00	30.00	60.00
—White label					
❏ 68	Rockin' in the Jungle/Rock and Roll Cha Cha	1959	10.00	20.00	40.00
—Blue label					
❏ 68	Rockin' in the Jungle/Rock and Roll Cha Cha	1959	5.00	10.00	20.00
—Yellow label					
❏ 70	Babalu's Wedding Day/My Girl	1959	12.50	25.00	50.00
—Red label					
❏ 70	Babalu's Wedding Day/My Girl	1959	6.25	12.50	25.00
—Blue label					

WARWICK

❏ 611	Blind Date/Today	1961	5.00	10.00	20.00

ETTA AND HARVEY
Also see HARVEY; ETTA JAMES.

45s
CHESS

Number	Title (A Side/B Side)	Yr	VG	VG+	NM
❏ 1760	If I Can't Have You/My Heart Cries	1960	6.25	12.50	25.00
❏ 1771	Spoonful/It's a Crying Shame	1960	6.25	12.50	25.00

EVERETT, BETTY
45s
ABC

❏ 10829	In Your Arms/Nothing I Wouldn't Do	1966	2.00	4.00	8.00
❏ 10861	Bye, Bye Baby/Your Love Is Important to Me	1966	2.00	4.00	8.00
❏ 10919	Love Comes Tumbling Down/People Around Me	1967	2.00	4.00	8.00
❏ 10978	I Can't Say/My Baby Loving My Best Friend	1967	2.00	4.00	8.00

CJ

❏ 611	Why Did You Have to Go/Please Come Back	1961	5.00	10.00	20.00
—As "Bettie Everett & Daylighters"					
❏ 619	Your Lovin' Arms/Happy I Long to Be	1961	5.00	10.00	20.00
❏ 674	Days Gone By/Her New Love	1964	3.75	7.50	15.00

COBRA

❏ 5019	My Love/My Life Depends on You	1957	7.50	15.00	30.00
❏ 5024	Ain't Gonna Cry/Killer Diller	1958	6.25	12.50	25.00
❏ 5031	Weep No More/Tell Me Darling	1959	6.25	12.50	25.00

FANTASY

❏ 652	I Got to Tell Somebody/Why Are You Leaving Me	1970	—	2.50	5.00
❏ 658	Ain't Nothing Gonna Change Me/What Is It?	1971	—	2.50	5.00
❏ 667	I'm a Woman/Prove It	1971	—	2.50	5.00
❏ 687	Black Girl/Innocent Bystanders	1972	—	2.50	5.00
❏ 687	Black Girl/What Is It?	1972	—	2.50	5.00
❏ 696	Danger/Just a Matter of Time Till You're Gone	1973	—	2.50	5.00
❏ 714	Sweet Dan/Who Will Your Next Fool Be	1973	—	2.50	5.00
❏ 725	Try It, You'll Like It/Wondering	1974	—	2.50	5.00
❏ 738	Happy Endings/Keep It Up	1974	—	2.50	5.00

ONE-DERFUL

❏ 4806	I've Got a Claim on You/Your Love Is Important to Me	1962	3.75	7.50	15.00
❏ 4823	I'll Be There/Please Love Me	1964	3.00	6.00	12.00

UNI

❏ 55100	Take Me/There'll Come a Time	1968	—	3.00	6.00
❏ 55122	I Can't Say No to You/Better Tomorrow Than Today	1969	—	3.00	6.00
❏ 55141	1900 Yesterday/Maybe	1969	—	3.00	6.00
❏ 55174	Just a Man's Way/Been a Long Time	1969	—	3.00	6.00
❏ 55189	Sugar/Just Another Winter	1969	—	3.00	6.00
❏ 55219	Unlucky Girl/Better Tomorrow Than Today	1970	—	3.00	6.00

UNITED ARTISTS

❏ XW1200	True Love (You Took My Heart)/You Can Do It	1978	—	2.00	4.00

VEE JAY

❏ 513	By My Side/Prince of Players	1963	3.75	7.50	15.00
❏ 566	You're No Good/Chained to Your Love	1963	5.00	10.00	20.00
❏ 585	The Shoop Shoop Song (It's In His Kiss)/Hands Off	1964	5.00	10.00	20.00
❏ 599	I Can't Hear You/Can I Get to Know You	1964	3.75	7.50	15.00
❏ 610	It Hurts to Be in Love/Until You Were Gone	1964	3.75	7.50	15.00
❏ 628	Getting Mighty Crowded/Chained to a Memory	1964	3.75	7.50	15.00
❏ 683	The Real Thing/Gonna Be Ready	1965	3.75	7.50	15.00
❏ 699	I Don't Hurt Anymore/Too Hot to Hold	1965	3.75	7.50	15.00
❏ 716	Trouble Over the Weekend/My Shoe Won't Fly	1966	3.75	7.50	15.00

Albums
FANTASY

❏ 9447	Love Rhymes	1974	3.00	6.00	12.00
❏ 9480	Happy Endings	1975	3.00	6.00	12.00

SUNSET

❏ SUS-5220	I Need You So	1968	3.75	7.50	15.00

UNI

❏ 73048	There'll Come a Time	1969	6.25	12.50	25.00

VEE JAY

❏ LP 1077 [M]	You're No Good	1964	10.00	20.00	40.00
❏ LP 1077 [M]	It's In His Kiss	1964	7.50	15.00	30.00
❏ SR 1077 [S]	You're No Good	1964	17.50	35.00	70.00
❏ SR 1077 [S]	It's In His Kiss	1964	12.50	25.00	50.00
❏ LP 1122 [M]	The Very Best of Betty Everett	1965	10.00	20.00	40.00
❏ VJLP 1122	The Very Best of Betty Everett	198?	2.50	5.00	10.00
—Authorized reissue					
❏ VJS 1122 [S]	The Very Best of Betty Everett	1965	12.50	25.00	50.00

EVERETT, BETTY, AND JERRY BUTLER
Also see each artist's individual listings.
45s
VEE JAY

❏ 613	Let It Be Me/Ain't That Loving You Baby	1964	3.00	6.00	12.00
❏ 633	Smile/Love Is Strange	1964	3.00	6.00	12.00
❏ 676	Since I Don't Have You/Just Be True	1965	3.00	6.00	12.00
❏ 691	Fever/The Way You Do the Things You Do	1965	3.00	6.00	12.00

Albums
BUDDAH

❏ BDS-7505	Together	1969	3.75	7.50	15.00
❏ BDS-7505	Together	1969	3.75	7.50	15.00

TRADITION

❏ 2073	Starring Betty Everett with Jerry Butler	197?	3.00	6.00	12.00

VEE JAY

❏ LP-1099 [M]	Delicious Together	1964	5.00	10.00	20.00
❏ LP 1099 [M]	Delicious Together	1964	5.00	10.00	20.00
❏ VJLP-1099	Delicious Together	198?	2.50	5.00	10.00
—Reissue of original 1099; has softer vinyl					

Number	Title (A Side/B Side)	Yr	VG	VG+	NM
❑ VJLP 1099	Delicious Together	198?	3.00	6.00	12.00
—Authorized reissue					
❑ VJS-1099 [S]	Delicious Together	1964	6.25	12.50	25.00
❑ VJS 1099 [S]	Delicious Together	1964	6.25	12.50	25.00

EXCITERS, THE
45s
BANG

Number	Title (A Side/B Side)	Yr	VG	VG+	NM
❑ 515	A Little Bit of Soap/I'm Gonna Get Him Someday	1966	3.00	6.00	12.00
❑ 518	You Better Come Home/Weddings Make Me Cry	1966	7.50	15.00	30.00
FARGO					
❑ 1400	Alone Again, Naturally/(B-side unknown)	1972	2.00	4.00	8.00
RCA VICTOR					
❑ 47-9633	Take One Step (I'll Take Two)/If You Want My Love	1968	7.50	15.00	30.00
❑ 47-9723	You Don't Know What You're Missing ('Til It's Gone!)/Blowing Up My Mind	1969	7.50	15.00	30.00
❑ 48-1035	You Don't Know What You're Missing ('Til It's Gone!)/Blowing Up My Mind	1972	3.75	7.50	15.00
ROULETTE					
❑ 4591	I Want You to Be My Boy/Tonight, Tonight	1965	3.00	6.00	12.00
❑ 4591 [PS]	I Want You to Be My Boy/Tonight, Tonight	1965	12.50	25.00	50.00
❑ 4594	Are You Satisfied/Just Not Ready	1965	3.00	6.00	12.00
❑ 4614	My Father/Run Mascara	1965	3.00	6.00	12.00
❑ 4632	I Knew You Would/There They Go	1965	3.00	6.00	12.00
SHOUT					
❑ 205	Number One/You Got Love	1966	2.50	5.00	10.00
❑ 214	Soulmotion/You Know It Ain't Right	1967	2.50	5.00	10.00
TODAY					
❑ 1002	Learning How to Fly/Life, Love and Peace	1970	2.00	4.00	8.00
UNITED ARTISTS					
❑ 0029	Tell Him/Do Wah Diddy	1973	—	2.00	4.00
—"Silver Spotlight Series" reissue					
❑ 544	Tell Him/Hard Way to Go	1963	3.75	7.50	15.00
❑ 572	Drama of Love/He's Got the Power	1963	3.00	6.00	12.00
❑ 604	Get Him/It's So Exciting	1963	3.00	6.00	12.00
❑ 662	Do-Wah-Diddy/If Love Came Your Way	1963	3.00	6.00	12.00
❑ 721	Having My Fun/We Were Lovers (When the Party Began)	1964	3.00	6.00	12.00
❑ 830	Having My Fun/We Were Lovers (When the Party Began)	1965	2.50	5.00	10.00

Albums
RCA VICTOR

Number	Title (A Side/B Side)	Yr	VG	VG+	NM
❑ LSP-4211	Caviar and Chitlins	1969	7.50	15.00	30.00
ROULETTE					
❑ R 25326 [M]	The Exciters	1966	7.50	15.00	30.00
❑ SR 25326 [S]	The Exciters	1966	10.00	20.00	40.00
TODAY					
❑ 1001	Black Beauty	1971	5.00	10.00	20.00
UNITED ARTISTS					
❑ UAL-3264 [M]	Tell Him	1963	17.50	35.00	70.00
❑ UAS-6264 [S]	Tell Him	1963	37.50	75.00	150.00

F

FABULAIRES, THE
45s
EASTWEST

Number	Title (A Side/B Side)	Yr	VG	VG+	NM
❑ 103	While Walking/No No	1957	75.00	150.00	300.00
MAIN LINE					
❑ 103	While Walking/No No	1958	50.00	100.00	200.00

FABULONS, THE (1)
45s
EMBER

Number	Title (A Side/B Side)	Yr	VG	VG+	NM
❑ 1069	Smoke From Your Cigarette/Give Me Back My Ring	1960	12.50	25.00	50.00
—White label					
❑ 1069	Smoke From Your Cigarette/Give Me Back My Ring	1960	6.25	12.50	25.00
—Black label					

FABULOUS FIVE, THE
45s
KING

Number	Title (A Side/B Side)	Yr	VG	VG+	NM
❑ 5220	Janie Made a Monster/Gettin' Old	1959	3.75	7.50	15.00

FAIR, YVONNE
45s
DADE

Number	Title (A Side/B Side)	Yr	VG	VG+	NM
❑ 1851	Straighten Up/Say Yeah Yeah	1963	3.00	6.00	12.00
❑ 5006	Straighten Up/Say Yeah Yeah	1963	5.00	10.00	20.00
KING					
❑ 5594	I Found You/If I Knew	1962	3.75	7.50	15.00
—With the James Brown Band					
❑ 5654	Tell Me Why/Say So Long	1962	3.75	7.50	15.00
—With James Brown					
❑ 5687	It Hurts to Be in Love/You Can Make It If You Try	1962	3.75	7.50	15.00
—With James Brown					
❑ 6017	Tell Me Why/You Can Make It If You Try	1966	2.00	4.00	8.00
MOTOWN					
❑ 1306	Funky Music Sho Nuff Turns Me On/Let Your Hair Down	1974	—	2.50	5.00
❑ 1323	Walk Out the Door If You Wanna/It Should Have Been Me	1974	—	2.50	5.00
❑ 1323 [PS]	Walk Out the Door If You Wanna/It Should Have Been Me	1974	2.00	4.00	8.00
❑ 1344	You Can't Judge a Book By Its Cover/It's Bad for Me to See You	1975	—	2.50	5.00
❑ 1354	Love Ain't No Toy/It's Bad for Me to See You	1975	—	2.50	5.00
❑ 1384	It Should Have Been Me/Tell Me Something Good	1976	—	2.50	5.00
SMASH					
❑ 2030	Just As Sure (As You Play, You Must Pay)/Baby, Baby, Baby	1966	2.50	5.00	10.00
SOUL					
❑ 35075	Stay a Little Longer/We Should Never Be Lonely My Love	1970	—	3.00	6.00

FAITH HOPE & CHARITY
45s
20TH CENTURY

Number	Title (A Side/B Side)	Yr	VG	VG+	NM
❑ 2370	Don't Pity Me/Find What You Need	1978	—	2.00	4.00
❑ 2391	How Can I Help But Love You/Keep Me Baby	1978	—	2.00	4.00
MAXWELL					
❑ 805	So Much Love/Let's Try It Over	1970	—	3.00	6.00
❑ 808	Baby Don't Take Your Love/Make Love to Me	1970	—	3.00	6.00
RCA					
❑ PB-10749	You're My Peace of Mind/Rescue Me	1976	—	2.50	5.00
❑ PB-10865	Life Goes On/You've Gotta Tell Her	1976	—	2.50	5.00
RCA VICTOR					
❑ PB-10343	To Each His Own/Find a Way	1975	—	2.50	5.00
❑ PB-10542	Don't Go Looking for Love/Disco Dan	1976	—	2.50	5.00
SUSSEX					
❑ 216	Come Back and Finish What You Started/I Worship the Very Ground You Walk On	1971	—	2.50	5.00
❑ 224	No Trespassing/Ghosts Keep Haunting Me	1971	—	2.50	5.00
❑ 231	We Can Change the World/God Bless the World	1972	—	2.50	5.00
❑ 243	I Was There/Who Could Love You More Than I	1972	—	2.50	5.00
❑ 252	Who Made You Go/Heavy Love	1973	—	2.50	5.00

Albums
RCA VICTOR

Number	Title (A Side/B Side)	Yr	VG	VG+	NM
❑ APL1-1100	Faith, Hope & Charity	1975	3.00	6.00	12.00
❑ APL1-1827	Life Goes	1976	3.00	6.00	12.00
SUSSEX					
❑ SXSB-7019	Heavy Love	1972	3.75	7.50	15.00

FALCONS, THE (1)
Detroit R&B group. Also see EDDIE FLOYD; WILSON PICKETT.
45s
ANNA

Number	Title (A Side/B Side)	Yr	VG	VG+	NM
❑ 1110	Just for Your Love/This Heart of Mine	1959	25.00	50.00	100.00
ATLANTIC					
❑ 2153	Darling/Lah-Tee-Lah-Tah	1962	5.00	10.00	20.00
❑ 2179	Let's Kiss and Make Up/Take This Love I've Got	1963	5.00	10.00	20.00

Number	Title (A Side/B Side)	Yr	VG	VG+	NM
❏ 2207	Oh Baby/Fine, Fine, Fine	1963	5.00	10.00	20.00
BIG WHEEL					
❏ 321	I Must Love You/Love, Love, Love	1966	5.00	10.00	20.00
❏ 323/4	I Can't Help It/Standing on Guard	1966	5.00	10.00	20.00
❏ 1967	Standing On Guard/I Can't Help It	1966	5.00	10.00	20.00
❏ 1972	Good Good Feeling/You Like You Never Been Loved	1966	5.00	10.00	20.00
CHESS					
❏ 1743	Just for Your Love/This Heart of Mine	1959	6.25	12.50	25.00
FALCON					
❏ 1006	Now That It's Over/My Only Love	1957	50.00	100.00	200.00
FLICK					
❏ 001	You're So Fine/Goddess of Angels	1959	100.00	200.00	400.00
❏ 008	You Must Know I Love You/That's What I Aim to Do	1960	30.00	60.00	120.00
KUDO					
❏ 661	This Heart of Mine/Romanita	1958	100.00	200.00	400.00
LUPINE					
❏ 103	I Found a Love/Swim	1962	12.50	25.00	50.00
❏ 124	Lonely Nights/Has It Happened to You	1962	25.00	50.00	100.00
❏ 1003	I Found a Love/Swim	1962	12.50	25.00	50.00
❏ 1024	Lonely Nights/Has It Happened to You	1962	10.00	20.00	40.00
UNART					
❏ 2013-S [S]	You're So Fine/Goddess of Angels	1959	25.00	50.00	100.00
—Though labeled as stereo, this seems to be rechanneled					
❏ 2013 [M]	You're So Fine/Goddess of Angels	1959	7.50	15.00	30.00
❏ 2022	You're Mine/Country Shack	1959	6.25	12.50	25.00
UNITED ARTISTS					
❏ 0108	You're So Fine/Showtime	1973	—	2.00	4.00
—"Silver Spotlight Series" reissue					
❏ 229	The Teacher/Waiting for You	1960	5.00	10.00	20.00
❏ 255	I Plus Love Plus You/Wonderful Love	1960	5.00	10.00	20.00
❏ 289	Pow! You're in Love/Workin' Man's Song	1961	5.00	10.00	20.00
❏ 420	You're So Fine/Goddess of Angels	1962	5.00	10.00	20.00
❏ 1624	You're So Fine/Goddess of Angels	196?	2.00	4.00	8.00
—"Silver Spotlight Series" issue					
7-Inch Extended Plays					
UNITED ARTISTS					
❏ 10010	*The Teacher/Waiting for You/You're So Fine/Goddess of Angels	1960	75.00	150.00	300.00
❏ 10010 [PS]	The Falcons	1960	75.00	150.00	300.00
Albums					
RELIC					
❏ 8005	You're So Fine (The Falcons' Story Part One: 1956-1959)	1987	3.00	6.00	12.00
❏ 8006	I Found a Love (The Falcons' Story Part Two: 1960-1964)	1987	3.00	6.00	12.00

FALCONS, THE (2)
45s
CASH

Number	Title (A Side/B Side)	Yr	VG	VG+	NM
❏ 1002	Tell Me Why/I Miss You Darling	1955	125.00	250.00	500.00
FLIP					
❏ 301	Stay Mine/Du-Bi-A-Do	1954	50.00	100.00	200.00
❏ 302	You Are the Only One/Mambo Baby Tonight	1954	50.00	100.00	200.00

FAME GANG, THE
Albums
FAME

Number	Title (A Side/B Side)	Yr	VG	VG+	NM
❏ SKAO-4200	Solid Gold from Muscle Shoals	1969	6.25	12.50	25.00

FANTASTIC FOUR, THE
45s
EASTBOUND

Number	Title (A Side/B Side)	Yr	VG	VG+	NM
❏ 609	I Had the Whole World to Choose From/If You Need Me	1973	—	3.00	6.00
❏ 620	I'm Falling in Love (I Feel Good All Over)/I Believe in Miracles	1974	—	3.00	6.00
RIC-TIC					
❏ 113	Can't Stop Looking for My Baby/Can't Stop Looking for My Baby (Part 2)	1966	50.00	100.00	200.00
❏ 119	Girl Have Pity/Live Up to What She Thinks	1967	3.75	7.50	15.00
❏ 121	Can't Stop Looking for My Baby/Just the Lonely	1967	25.00	50.00	100.00
❏ 122	The Whole World Is a Stage/Ain't Love Wonderful	1967	3.75	7.50	15.00
❏ 128	You Gave Me Something (And Everything's Alright)/I Don't Wanna Live Without You	1967	3.75	7.50	15.00
❏ 130	To Share Your Love/As Long As I Live (I Live for You)	1967	3.75	7.50	15.00
❏ 134	Goddess of Love/As Long As the Feeling Is There	1968	3.75	7.50	15.00
❏ 136	Love Is a Many-Splendored Thing/Goddess of Love	1968	3.75	7.50	15.00
❏ 137	No Love Like Your Love/A Man in Love	1968	3.75	7.50	15.00
❏ 139	I've Got to Have You/Win or Lose	1968	3.75	7.50	15.00
❏ 144	I Love You Madly/(Instrumental)	1968	5.00	10.00	20.00
SOUL					
❏ 35052	I Love You Madly/(Instrumental)	1968	3.00	6.00	12.00
❏ 35058	I Feel Like I'm Falling in Love/Pin Point It Out	1969	3.75	7.50	15.00
❏ 35065	Just Another Lonely Night/I Don't Care Why You Want Me	1969	3.75	7.50	15.00
❏ 35072	On the Brighter Side of a Blue World/I'm Gonna Hurry On	1970	3.00	6.00	12.00
WESTBOUND					
❏ 5009	Alvin Stone (The Birth & Death of a Gangster)/I Believe in Miracles, I Believe in You	1975	—	2.50	5.00

Number	Title (A Side/B Side)	Yr	VG	VG+	NM
❏ 5017	Have a Little Mercy/County Line	1975	—	2.50	5.00
❏ 5030	Don't Risk Your Happiness On Foolish Things/They Took the Show on the Road	1976	—	2.50	5.00
❏ 5032	Hideaway/They Took the Show on the Road	1976	—	2.50	5.00
❏ 55403	I Got to Have Your Love/Ain't I Been Good to You	1977	—	2.50	5.00
❏ 55408	Mixed Up Moods and Attitudes/Disco Fool Blues	1978	—	2.50	5.00
❏ 55417	Sexy Lady/If This Is Love	1979	—	2.50	5.00
❏ 55419	B.Y.O.F. (Bring Your Own Funk)/If This Is Love	1979	—	2.50	5.00
Albums					
SOUL					
❏ SS-717	The Best of the Fantastic Four	1969	10.00	20.00	40.00
❏ SS-722	How Sweet He Is	1970	—	—	—
—Canceled					
WESTBOUND					
❏ 201	Alvin Stone (The Birth and Death of a Gangster)	1975	3.75	7.50	15.00
❏ 226	Night People	1976	3.75	7.50	15.00
❏ SD 306	Got to Have Your Love	1977	3.75	7.50	15.00
❏ SD 6108	BYOF (Bring Your Own Funk)	1978	3.75	7.50	15.00

FANTASTIC JOHNNY C, THE
45s
KAMA SUTRA

Number	Title (A Side/B Side)	Yr	VG	VG+	NM
❏ 511	Let's Do It Together/Peace Treaty	1970	—	2.50	5.00
❏ 515	Good Love/You Got Your Hooks in Me	1970	—	2.50	5.00
PHILCO-FORD					
❏ HP-39	Boogaloo Down Broadway/Got What You Need	1969	5.00	10.00	20.00
—4-inch plastic "Hip Pocket Record" with color sleeve					
PHIL.-LA OF SOUL					
❏ 305	Boogaloo Down Broadway/Look What Love Can Make You Do	1967	2.00	4.00	8.00
❏ 309	Got What You Need/New Love	1968	—	3.00	6.00
❏ 315	Hitch It to the Horse/Cool Broadway	1968	—	3.00	6.00
❏ 320	Baby I Need You/Some Kind of Wonderful	1968	—	3.00	6.00
❏ 327	Is There Anything Better Than Making Love/New Love	1969	—	3.00	6.00
❏ 361	Don't Depend on Me/Waitin' for the Rain	1973	—	2.00	4.00
❏ 363	Just Say the Word/I'm a Man	1973	—	2.00	4.00
Albums					
PHIL-LA OF SOUL					
❏ 4000	Boogaloo Down Broadway	1968	20.00	40.00	80.00

FASCINATORS, THE (1)
45s
BIM BAM BOOM

Number	Title (A Side/B Side)	Yr	VG	VG+	NM
❏ 110	Oh, Rose Marie/Forgive Me, My Darling	1974	2.50	5.00	10.00
CAPITOL					
❏ F-4053	Chapel Bells/I Wonder Who	1958	37.50	75.00	150.00
❏ F-4137	Come to Paradise/Who Do You Think You Are	1959	50.00	100.00	200.00
❏ F-4247	Oh Rose Marie/Fried Chicken and Macaroni	1959	50.00	100.00	200.00
❏ 4544	Chapel Bells/I Wonder Who	1961	20.00	40.00	80.00

FASCINATORS, THE (2)
45s
BLUE LAKE

Number	Title (A Side/B Side)	Yr	VG	VG+	NM
❏ 112	Can't Stop/Don't Give My Love Away	1953	500.00	1000.	2000.

FASCINATORS, THE (3)
45s
BURN

Number	Title (A Side/B Side)	Yr	VG	VG+	NM
❏ 845	I'll Be Gone/Can't You See I'm Lonely	1965	5.00	10.00	20.00

FASCINATORS, THE (4)
45s
DOOTO

Number	Title (A Side/B Side)	Yr	VG	VG+	NM
❏ 441	Teardrop Eyes/Shivers and Shakes	1958	15.00	30.00	60.00

FASCINATORS, THE (5)
45s
YOUR COPY

Number	Title (A Side/B Side)	Yr	VG	VG+	NM
❏ 1135	The Bells of My Heart/Sweet Baby	1954	250.00	500.00	1000.
—Black vinyl					
❏ 1135	The Bells of My Heart/Sweet Baby	1954	500.00	1000.	2000.
—Red vinyl					
❏ 1136	My Beauty, My Own/Don't Give It Away	1954	250.00	500.00	1000.

FASHIONS, THE (3)
45s
PHIL-L.A. OF SOUL

Number	Title (A Side/B Side)	Yr	VG	VG+	NM
❏ 354	I Don't Mind Doin' It/What Goes Up (Must Come Down)	1972	—	3.00	6.00

FATBACK
Includes records as "Fatback Band."
12-Inch Singles
COTILLION

Number	Title (A Side/B Side)	Yr	VG	VG+	NM
❏ PR 763 [DJ]	You've Got That Magic (6:43)/You've Got That Magic (3:55)	1984	2.00	4.00	8.00
SPRING					
❏ PRO 184 [DJ]	On the Floor (same on both sides)	1982	2.00	4.00	8.00
❏ 402	King Tim III (Personality Jock)/You're My Candy Sweet	1979	2.50	5.00	10.00
❏ 409	The Girl Is Fine (So Fine)/(B-side unknown)	1983	2.00	4.00	8.00
❏ 414	Spread Love/(B-side unknown)	1984	—	3.00	6.00

Number	Title (A Side/B Side)	Yr	VG	VG+	NM

45s
COTILLION
□ 99642	Lover Undercover/(B-side unknown)	1985	—	—	3.00
□ 99665	Girls on My Mind/Osiris (There's a Party Goin' On)	1985	—	—	3.00
□ 99730	You've Got That Magic/(B-side unknown)	1984	—	—	3.00
□ 99749	Call Out My Name/I Love You So	1984	—	—	3.00

EVENT
□ 217	Keep On Steppin'/Breakin' Up Is Hard to Do	1974	—	2.50	5.00
□ 219	Wicki-Wacky/Can't Fight the Flame	1974	—	2.50	5.00
□ 224	(Hey I) Feel Real Good (Part 1)/(Hey I) Feel Real Good (Part 2)	1975	—	2.50	5.00
□ 226	Yum Yum (Gimme Some)/Let the Drums Speak	1975	—	2.50	5.00
□ 227	(Are You Ready) Do the Bus Stop/Gotta Learn to Dance	1975	—	2.50	5.00
□ 229	Spanish Hustle/Put Your Love (In My Tender Care)	1976	—	2.50	5.00

PERCEPTION
□ 520	Soul March/To Be with You	1973	—	2.50	5.00
□ 526	Street Dance/Goin' to See My Baby	1973	—	2.50	5.00
□ 540	Nija (Nija) Walk (Street Walk)/Soul Man	1973	—	2.50	5.00

SPRING
□ 165	Party Time/Groovy Kind of Day	1976	—	2.50	5.00
□ 168	The Booty/If That's the Way You Want It	1976	—	2.50	5.00
□ 171	Double Dutch/Spank the Baby	1977	—	2.50	5.00
□ 174	NYCNY USA (Nik-Ne-Yoo-Sa)/Soulfinger	1977	—	2.50	5.00
□ 177	Master Booty/Zodiac Man	1977	—	2.50	5.00
□ 180	Mile High/Midnight Freak	1978	—	2.50	5.00
□ 181	I Like Girls/Get Out on the Dance Floor	1978	—	2.50	5.00
□ 188	Boogie Freak/I'm Fired Up	1978	—	2.50	5.00
□ 191	Freak the Freak the Funk (Rock)/Wild Dreams	1979	—	2.50	5.00
□ 195	(Do the) Boogie Woogie/Hesitation	1979	—	2.50	5.00
□ 199	King Tim III (Personality Jock)/You're My Candy Sweet	1979	—	3.00	6.00
□ 3005	Love in Perfect Harmony/Disco Bass	1979	—	2.00	4.00
□ 3008	Gotta Get My Hands on Some (Money)/Street Band	1980	—	2.00	4.00
□ 3012	Backstrokin'/Love Spell	1980	—	2.00	4.00
□ 3015	Let's Do It Again/Come and Get the Love	1980	—	2.00	4.00
□ 3016	Angel/Concrete Jungle	1981	—	2.00	4.00
□ 3018	Take It Any Way You Want It/Lady Groove	1981	—	2.00	4.00
□ 3020	Kool Whip/Keep Your Fingers Out of the Jam	1981	—	2.00	4.00
□ 3022	Rockin' to the Beat/Wanna Dance	1981	—	2.00	4.00
□ 3023	Na Na Hey Hey Kiss Her Goodbye/I'm So in Love	1982	—	2.00	4.00
□ 3025	On the Floor/Chillin' Out	1982	—	2.00	4.00
□ 3026	She's My Shining Star/UFO (Unidentified Funk Object)	1982	—	2.00	4.00
□ 3030	The Girl Is Fine (So Fine)/(B-side unknown)	1983	—	2.00	4.00
□ 3032	Is This the Future/Double Love Affair	1983	—	2.00	4.00
□ 3033	Up Against the Wall/With Love	1983	—	2.00	4.00
□ 3037	I Wanna Be Your Lover/(B-side unknown)	1984	—	2.00	4.00

Albums
COTILLION
| □ 90168 | Phoenix | 1984 | 2.00 | 4.00 | 8.00 |
| □ 90253 | So Delicious | 1985 | 2.00 | 4.00 | 8.00 |

EVENT
| □ 6902 | Keep On Steppin' | 1974 | 3.75 | 7.50 | 15.00 |

—As "The Fatback Band"

| □ 6904 | Yum Yum | 1975 | 3.75 | 7.50 | 15.00 |

—As "The Fatback Band"

| □ 6905 | Raising Hell | 1976 | 3.75 | 7.50 | 15.00 |

—As "The Fatback Band"

SPRING
| □ 6711 | Night Fever | 1976 | 3.00 | 6.00 | 12.00 |

—As "The Fatback Band"

| □ 6714 | NYCNYUSA | 1977 | 3.00 | 6.00 | 12.00 |

—As "The Fatback Band"

| □ 6717 | Man with a Plan | 1978 | 3.00 | 6.00 | 12.00 |

—As "The Fatback Band"

□ 6718	Fired Up 'N' Kickin'	1978	2.50	5.00	10.00
□ 6721	Bright Lites, Big City	1979	2.50	5.00	10.00
□ 6723	Fatback XII	1979	2.50	5.00	10.00
□ 6726	Hot Box	1980	2.50	5.00	10.00
□ 6729	14 Karat	1980	2.50	5.00	10.00
□ 6731	Tasty Jam	1981	2.50	5.00	10.00
□ 6734	Gigolo	1981	2.50	5.00	10.00
□ 6736	On the Floor	1982	2.50	5.00	10.00

FATBACK BAND, THE
See FATBACK.

FEATHERS, THE (1)
45s
ALADDIN
| □ 3267 | Johnny Darling/Shake 'Em Up | 1954 | 50.00 | 100.00 | 200.00 |
| □ 3277 | I Need a Girl/Standing Right There | 1955 | 50.00 | 100.00 | 200.00 |

HOLLYWOOD
| □ 1051 | Dear One/Lonesome Tonight | 1956 | 1000. | 2000. | 3000. |

SHOW TIME
□ 1104	Nona/Johnny Darling	1954	75.00	150.00	300.00
□ 1105	Why Don't You Write Me/Busy as a Bee	1954	50.00	100.00	200.00
□ 1105	Why Don't You Write Me/Where Did Caledonia Go	1954	37.50	75.00	150.00
□ 1106	Love Only You/Crashing the Party	1955	50.00	100.00	200.00

FEDERALS, THE (2)
45s
DELUXE
| □ 6112 | Come Go with Me/Cold Cash | 1957 | 20.00 | 40.00 | 80.00 |

FURY
| □ 1005 | While Our Hearts Are Young/You're the One I Love | 1957 | 25.00 | 50.00 | 100.00 |
| □ 1009 | Dear Lorraine/She's My Girl | 1958 | 25.00 | 50.00 | 100.00 |

FIESTAS, THE
45s
CHIMNEYVILLE
| □ 10216 | Tina, the Disco Queen/I'm No Better Than You | 1977 | 3.00 | 6.00 | 12.00 |
| □ 10221 | Is That Long Enough for You/I'm Gonna Make Myself | 1977 | 3.00 | 6.00 | 12.00 |

COTILLION
| □ 44117 | So Fine/Broken Heart | 1971 | 6.25 | 12.50 | 25.00 |

OLD TOWN
| □ 1062 | So Fine/Last Night I Dreamed | 1958 | 12.50 | 25.00 | 50.00 |

—Versions pressed by Columbia have a piano intro not available elsewhere. Look for "ZTSP" on label

| □ 1062 | So Fine/Last Night I Dreamed | 1958 | 7.50 | 15.00 | 30.00 |

—Standard version; no "ZTSP" on label

□ 1067	Grandma Gave a Party/I'm Your Slave	1959	6.25	12.50	25.00
□ 1069	Our Anniversary/I'm Your Slave	1959	6.25	12.50	25.00
□ 1074	Good News/That Was Me	1959	6.25	12.50	25.00
□ 1080	Dollar Bill/It Don't Make Sense	1960	6.25	12.50	25.00
□ 1090	So Nice/You Could Be My Girlfriend	1960	6.25	12.50	25.00
□ 1104	Look at That Girl/Mr. Dillon, Mr. Dillon	1961	6.25	12.50	25.00
□ 1111	Hobo's Prayer/She's Mine	1961	10.00	20.00	40.00
□ 1122	Broken Heart/Railroad Song	1962	5.00	10.00	20.00
□ 1127	I Feel Good All Over/Look at That Girl	1962	5.00	10.00	20.00
□ 1134	The Gypsy Said/Mama Put the Law Down	1963	5.00	10.00	20.00
□ 1140	The Party's Over/Try It One More Time	1963	5.00	10.00	20.00
□ 1148	Foolish Dreamer/Rock-a-By Baby	1963	5.00	10.00	20.00
□ 1166	All That's Good/Rock-a-By Baby	1964	5.00	10.00	20.00
□ 1178	Think Smart/Anna	1965	20.00	40.00	80.00
□ 1187	Love Is Strange/Love Is Good to Me	1965	3.75	7.50	15.00
□ 1189	Ain't She Sweet/I Gotta Have Your Lovin'	1965	3.75	7.50	15.00

RESPECT
| □ 2509 | I Can't Shake Your Love (Can't Shake You Loose)/A Sometimes Storm | 1972 | 2.00 | 4.00 | 8.00 |

STRAND
| □ 25046 | Come On Everybody/Julia | 1961 | 10.00 | 20.00 | 40.00 |

VIGOR
| □ 712 | So Fine/Darling You've Changed | 1974 | 2.00 | 4.00 | 8.00 |

FIFTH DIMENSION, THE
Also see BILLY DAVIS JR.; MARILYN McCOO.
45s
ABC
□ 12136	Magic in My Life/Lean On Me Always	1975	—	2.00	4.00
□ 12168	Walk Your Feet in the Sunshine/Speaking with My Heart	1976	—	2.00	4.00
□ 12181	Love Hangover/Will You Be There	1976	—	2.00	4.00

ARISTA
| □ 0101 | No Love in the Room/I Don't Know How to Look for Love | 1975 | — | 2.00 | 4.00 |

BELL
□ 860	Medley: A Change Is Gonna Come & People Gotta Be Free/The Declaration	1970	—	2.50	5.00
□ 880	Puppet Man/A Love Like Ours	1970	—	2.50	5.00
□ 895	Save the Country/Dimension 5	1970	—	2.50	5.00
□ 913	On the Beach (In the Summertime)/This Is Your Life	1970	—	2.50	5.00
□ 940	One Less Bell to Answer/Feelin' Alright?	1970	—	2.50	5.00
□ 965	Love's Lines, Angles and Rhymes/The Singer	1971	—	2.50	5.00
□ 999	Light Sings/Viva Tirado	1971	—	2.50	5.00
□ 45134	Never My Love/A Love Like Ours	1971	—	2.50	5.00
□ 45170	Together Let's Find Love/I Just Wanta Be Your Friend	1972	—	2.50	5.00
□ 45195	(Last Night) I Didn't Get to Sleep at All/The River Witch	1972	—	2.50	5.00
□ 45261	If I Could Reach You/Tomorrow Belongs to the Children	1972	—	2.50	5.00
□ 45310	Living Together, Growing Together/What Do I Need to Be Me	1973	—	2.00	4.00
□ 45338	Everything's Been Changed/There Never Was a Day	1973	—	2.00	4.00
□ 45380	Ashes to Ashes/The Singer	1973	—	2.00	4.00
□ 45425	Flashback/Diggin' for a Livin'	1973	—	2.00	4.00
□ 45612	Harlem/My Song	1974	—	2.00	4.00

MOTOWN
| □ 1437 | You Are the Reason (I Feel Like Dancing)/Slipping Into Something New | 1978 | — | 2.00 | 4.00 |
| □ 1453 | Everybody's Got to Give It Up/You're My Star | 1978 | — | 2.00 | 4.00 |

SOUL CITY
□ 752	I'll Be Loving You Forever/Train, Keep On Moving	1966	15.00	30.00	60.00
□ 753	Go Where You Wanna Go/Too Poor to Die	1967	2.00	4.00	8.00
□ 753 [PS]	Go Where You Wanna Go/Too Poor to Die	1967	5.00	10.00	20.00
□ 755	Another Day, Another Heartache/Rosecrans Blvd.	1967	2.50	5.00	10.00
□ 755 [PS]	Another Day, Another Heartache/Rosecrans Blvd.	1967	5.00	10.00	20.00
□ 756	Up-Up and Away/Which Way to Nowhere	1967	2.00	4.00	8.00

F

Number	Title (A Side/B Side)	Yr	VG	VG+	NM
❑ 760	Paper Cup/Poor Side of Town	1967	2.00	4.00	8.00
❑ 762	Carpet Man/Magic Garden	1968	2.00	4.00	8.00
❑ 766	Stoned Soul Picnic/The Sailboat Song	1968	2.00	4.00	8.00
❑ 766 [PS]	Stoned Soul Picnic/The Sailboat Song	1968	3.75	7.50	15.00
❑ 768	Sweet Blindness/Bobby's Blues	1968	2.00	4.00	8.00
❑ 768 [PS]	Sweet Blindness/Bobby's Blues	1968	3.75	7.50	15.00
❑ 770	California Soul/It'll Never Be the Same	1968	2.00	4.00	8.00
❑ 772	Aquarius/Let the Sunshine In (The Flesh Failures)//Don'tcha Hear Me Callin' To Ya	1969	2.00	4.00	8.00
❑ 772 [DJ]	Aquarius/Let the Sunshine In (The Flesh Failures) (same on both sides?)	1969	3.75	7.50	15.00

—Promo only on yellow vinyl

Number	Title (A Side/B Side)	Yr	VG	VG+	NM
❑ 772 [PS]	Aquarius/Let the Sunshine In (The Flesh Failures)//Don'tcha Hear Me Callin' To Ya	1969	3.75	7.50	15.00
❑ 776	Workin' on a Groovy Thing/Broken Wing Bird	1969	2.00	4.00	8.00
❑ 779	Wedding Bell Blues/Lovin' Stew	1969	2.00	4.00	8.00
❑ 780	Blowing Away/Skinny Man	1970	—	3.00	6.00
❑ 781	The Girls' Song/It'll Never Be the Same Again	1970	—	3.00	6.00

SUTRA

Number	Title	Yr	VG	VG+	NM
❑ 122	Surrender/Fantasy	1983	—	2.00	4.00

Albums

ABC

Number	Title	Yr	VG	VG+	NM
❑ D-897	Earthbound	1975	2.50	5.00	10.00

ARISTA

Number	Title	Yr	VG	VG+	NM
❑ ABM-1106	Greatest Hits on Earth	1975	2.00	4.00	8.00

—Reissue of Bell 1106

❑ AL 8335	Greatest Hits on Earth	198?	2.00	4.00	8.00

—Reissue of Arista 1106

BELL

Number	Title	Yr	VG	VG+	NM
❑ 1106	Greatest Hits on Earth	1972	2.50	5.00	10.00
❑ 1116	Living Together, Growing Together	1973	2.50	5.00	10.00
❑ 1315	Soul and Inspiration	1974	2.50	5.00	10.00
❑ 6045	Portrait	1970	3.00	6.00	12.00
❑ 6060	Love's Lines, Angles and Rhymes	1971	3.00	6.00	12.00
❑ 6065	Reflections	1971	2.50	5.00	10.00
❑ 6073	Individually & Collectively	1972	2.50	5.00	10.00
❑ 9000 [(2)]	The 5th Dimension/Live!!	1971	3.00	6.00	12.00

MOTOWN

Number	Title	Yr	VG	VG+	NM
❑ M7-896	Star	1978	2.50	5.00	10.00

PAIR

Number	Title	Yr	VG	VG+	NM
❑ PDL2-1108 [(2)]	The Glory Days	1986	3.00	6.00	12.00

RHINO

Number	Title	Yr	VG	VG+	NM
❑ RNDA-71104 [(2)]	The 5th Dimension Anthology	1986	3.00	6.00	12.00

SOUL CITY

Number	Title	Yr	VG	VG+	NM
❑ SCS-33900	The 5th Dimension/Greatest Hits	1970	3.00	6.00	12.00
❑ SCS-33901	The July 5th Album	1970	3.00	6.00	12.00
❑ SCM-91000 [M]	Up, Up and Away	1967	5.00	10.00	20.00
❑ SCM-91001 [M]	The Magic Garden	1967	5.00	10.00	20.00
❑ SCS-92000 [S]	Up, Up and Away	1967	3.75	7.50	15.00
❑ SCS-92001 [S]	The Magic Garden	1967	3.75	7.50	15.00
❑ SCS-92002	Stoned Soul Picnic	1968	3.75	7.50	15.00
❑ SCS-92005	The Age of Aquarius	1969	3.75	7.50	15.00

FINNEGAN, LARRY
45s

CORAL

Number	Title (A Side/B Side)	Yr	VG	VG+	NM
❑ 62313	I'll Be Back, Jack/There Ain't Nothin' in This World	1962	2.50	5.00	10.00

OLD TOWN

❑ 1113	Dear One/Candy Lips	1961	3.00	6.00	12.00
❑ 1120	Pretty Susie Sunshine/It's Walkin' Talkin' Time	1962	2.50	5.00	10.00
❑ 1136	A Kiss and a Dozen Roses/Pick Up the Pieces	1963	2.50	5.00	10.00

RIC

❑ 146	The Other Ringo (A Tribute to Ringo Starr)/When My Love Passes By	1964	3.75	7.50	15.00

FIREFLIES, THE
45s

CANADIAN AMERICAN

Number	Title (A Side/B Side)	Yr	VG	VG+	NM
❑ 117	Marianne/Give All Your Love to Me	1960	5.00	10.00	20.00

RIBBON

❑ 6901	You Were Mine/Stella Got a Fella	1959	6.25	12.50	25.00

—With "Ribbon" encased in a ribbon on label

❑ 6901	You Were Mine/Stella Got a Fella	1959	7.50	15.00	30.00

—With "Ribbon" standing alone on label

❑ 6904	I Can't Say Goodbye/What Did I Do Wrong	1959	5.00	10.00	20.00
❑ 6906	My Girl/Because of My Pride	1960	5.00	10.00	20.00

TAURUS

❑ 355	One O'Clock Twist/You Were Mine for Awhile	1962	5.00	10.00	20.00
❑ 366	Good Friends/My Prayer for You	1964	5.00	10.00	20.00
❑ 376	Runaround/Could You Mean More	1965	5.00	10.00	20.00
❑ 380	Tonight/A Time for Us	1965	5.00	10.00	20.00

Albums

TAURUS

❑ 1002 [M]	You Were Mine	196?	25.00	50.00	100.00
❑ S-1002 [S]	You Were Mine	196?	75.00	150.00	300.00

FIRST CHOICE
45s

GOLD MIND

Number	Title (A Side/B Side)	Yr	VG	VG+	NM
❑ 4004	Doctor Love/I Love You More Than Before	1977	—	2.50	5.00
❑ 4009	Love Having You Around/Indian Giver	1977	—	2.50	5.00
❑ 4017	Hold Your Horses/Now I've Thrown It All Away	1979	—	2.50	5.00
❑ 4019	Double Cross/Game of Love	1979	—	2.50	5.00
❑ 4022	Love Thang/Great Expectations	1980	—	2.50	5.00
❑ 4023	Breakaway/House for Sale	1980	—	2.50	5.00

PHILLY GROOVE

Number	Title (A Side/B Side)	Yr	VG	VG+	NM
❑ 175	Armed and Extremely Dangerous/Gonna Keep On Lovin' Him	1973	—	2.50	5.00
❑ 179	Smarty Pants/One Step Away	1973	—	2.50	5.00
❑ 183	Newsy Neighbors/This Little Woman	1974	—	2.50	5.00
❑ 200	The Player — Part 1/The Player — Part 2	1974	—	2.50	5.00
❑ 202	Guilty/Wake Up to Me	1974	—	2.50	5.00
❑ 204	Love Freeze/A Boy Named Junior	1975	—	2.50	5.00

SCEPTER

❑ 12347	One Step Away/This Is the House	1972	—	3.00	6.00

WARNER BROS.

❑ 8214	Gotta Get Away (From You Baby)/Yes, Maybe Not	1976	—	2.50	5.00
❑ 8251	Let Him Go/First Choice Theme	1976	—	2.50	5.00

Albums

GOLD MIND

❑ 7501	Delusions	1977	3.00	6.00	12.00
❑ 9502	Hold Your Horses	1979	3.00	6.00	12.00
❑ 9505	Breakaway	1980	3.00	6.00	12.00

PHILLY GROOVE

❑ 1400	Armed and Extremely Dangerous	1973	3.75	7.50	15.00
❑ 1502	The Player	1974	3.75	7.50	15.00

WARNER BROS.

❑ BS 2934	Let Us Entertain You	1976	3.75	7.50	15.00

FIRST CLASS (2)
U.S. R&B group.

45s

ALL PLATINUM

Number	Title (A Side/B Side)	Yr	VG	VG+	NM
❑ 2365	Me and My Gemini/Me and My Gemini (Part 2)	1976	—	2.50	5.00
❑ 2368	This Is It/Filled with Desire	1977	—	2.50	5.00
❑ 2372	Coming Back to You/This Is It	1977	—	2.50	5.00

EBONY SOUNDS

❑ 187	The Beginning of My End/(B-side unknown)	1975	—	2.50	5.00

TODAY

❑ 1528	What About Me/Outside Your World	1974	—	2.50	5.00

FISHBONE
12-Inch Singles

COLUMBIA

Number	Title (A Side/B Side)	Yr	VG	VG+	NM
❑ AS 2076 [DJ]	? (Modern Industry) (Dance Mix) (Original Version)	1985	2.00	4.00	8.00
❑ CAS 3082 [DJ]	Sunless Saturday/Fishy Swa Ska/Understand Me	1991	2.00	4.00	8.00
❑ 44-05223	? (Modern Industry) (3 versions)	1984	2.00	4.00	8.00
❑ CAS 5252 [DJ]	Swim (3 versions)	1993	3.00	6.00	12.00
❑ 44-05326	Party at Ground Zero (Vapor Mix 7:02) (Visual Mix 4:50)/Skankin' to the Beat	1985	2.50	5.00	10.00
❑ 44-05984	When Problems Arise (The Mix Is Risen) (Album Mix) (Problematic Mix)	1986	2.50	5.00	10.00
❑ 44-08172	Freddie's Dead (12" Mix) (Urban Mix) (Single Mix) (Zeoniquz Mix) (Zeoniquz Mix Instrumental)	1988	2.00	4.00	8.00

45s

COLUMBIA

❑ 38-04922	? (Modern Industry)/V.T.T.L.O.T.S.D.G.F.	1985	—	2.00	4.00
❑ 38-08500	Freddie's Dead/Question of Life	1988	—	2.00	4.00

WTG

❑ 31-68936	Skankin' to the Beat/In Your Eyes	1989	—	2.00	4.00

—B-side by Peter Gabriel

Albums

COLUMBIA

❑ CAS 1416 [DJ]	Interchords	198?	6.25	12.50	25.00

—Promo-only music and interviews

❑ CAS 2235 [EP]	New and Improved Bonin'	1990	3.00	6.00	12.00

—Promo-only five-song sampler

❑ B6C 40032 [EP]	Fishbone	1985	3.00	6.00	12.00
❑ BFC 40333	In Your Face	1986	3.00	6.00	12.00
❑ FC 40891	Truth and Soul	1988	3.00	6.00	12.00
❑ 4C 44097 [EP]	It's a Wonderful Life (Gonna Have a Good Time)	1987	2.50	5.00	10.00
❑ C 46142 [(2)]	The Reality of My Surroundings	1991	3.75	7.50	15.00

FISHBONE AND CURTIS MAYFIELD
Also see each artist's individual listings.

12-Inch Singles

ARISTA

Number	Title (A Side/B Side)	Yr	VG	VG+	NM
❑ 9812	He's a Flyguy (3 versions)	1988	—	3.00	6.00

45s

ARISTA

❑ 9806	He's a Flyguy/(Instrumental)	1989	—	—	2.00
❑ 9806 [PS]	He's a Flyguy/(Instrumental)	1989	—	—	3.00

FIVE BOROUGHS, THE
45s

CLASSIC ARTISTS

❑ 135	Like a Kid at Christmas/Only at Christmas	1990	—	2.50	5.00

FIVE BUDDS, THE
45s

RAMA

Number	Title (A Side/B Side)	Yr	VG	VG+	NM
❑ 1	I Was Such a Fool (To Fall in Love with You)/Midnight	1953	125.00	250.00	500.00
❑ 2	I Guess It's All Over Now/I Want Her Back	1953	125.00	250.00	500.00

Several years after their two R&B hits, Vee Jay combined recordings by the El Dorados with others by the Magnificents and created this album, which was one of the earliest to come out on the Chicago label.

Among the vocalists who passed through the Falcons were Eddie Floyd and Wilson Pickett. Floyd was one of the members on this EP, which was based around the hit song "You're So Fine."

The Fantastic Johnny C, whose real name was John Corley, had by far his biggest hit in late 1967 with "Boogaloo Down Broadway." This album came out shortly thereafter.

One of many sought-after vocal group records is this 1956 waxing on States by the Five Chances.

The Five Dollars had five singles on the Detroit-based Fortune label, one of which was picked up by Fraternity for wider distribution. "So Strange" was the second of the five.

Chicago's Five Echoes recorded for the Sabre label before going to Vee Jay in the mid-1950s. One side of their first single was "Lonely Mood."

Number	Title (A Side/B Side)	Yr	VG	VG+	NM

FIVE CHANCES, THE
45s
ATOMIC

Number	Title (A Side/B Side)	Yr	VG	VG+	NM
❏ 2494	Make Love to Me/California	1977	3.00	6.00	12.00

BLUE LAKE

| ❏ 115 | All I Want/Shake-a-Link | 1955 | 200.00 | 400.00 | 800.00 |

CHANCE

| ❏ 1157 | I May Be Small/Nagasaki | 1954 | 250.00 | 500.00 | 1000. |

FEDERAL

| ❏ 12303 | My Days Are Blue/Tell Me Why | 1957 | 125.00 | 250.00 | 500.00 |

P.S.

| ❏ 1510 | Is This Love/Need Your Love | 1960 | 75.00 | 150.00 | 300.00 |

STATES

| ❏ 156 | Gloria/Sugar Lips | 1956 | 200.00 | 400.00 | 800.00 |

—*Black vinyl*

| ❏ 156 | Gloria/Sugar Lips | 1956 | 300.00 | 600.00 | 1200. |

—*Red vinyl*

FIVE CROWNS, THE
Probably more than one group.
45s
CARAVAN

| ❏ 15609 | I Can't Pretend/Popcorn Willie | 1955 | 12.50 | 25.00 | 50.00 |

DE'BESTH

| ❏ 1121/2 | A Surprise from Outer Space/Memories of Yesterday | 1959 | 100.00 | 200.00 | 400.00 |
| ❏ 1123 | I Want You/Hillum Boy | 1959 | 100.00 | 200.00 | 400.00 |

GEE

| ❏ 1001 | Do You Remember/God Bless You | 1956 | 50.00 | 100.00 | 200.00 |

OLD TOWN

| ❏ 790 | Good Luck Darling/You Could Be My Love | 1952 | 125.00 | 250.00 | 500.00 |

—*Black vinyl*

| ❏ 790 | Good Luck Darling/You Could Be My Love | 1952 | 750.00 | 1500. | 3000. |

—*Red vinyl*

| ❏ 792 | Lullaby of the Bells/Later, Later Baby | 1952 | — | — | — |

—*Unconfirmed on 45 rpm*
RAINBOW

| ❏ 179 | A Star/You're My Inspiration | 1952 | 75.00 | 150.00 | 300.00 |

—*Black vinyl*

| ❏ 179 | A Star/You're My Inspiration | 1952 | 200.00 | 400.00 | 800.00 |

—*Red vinyl*

| ❏ 184 | Who Can Be True/$19.50 Due | 1952 | — | — | — |

—*Unconfirmed on 45 rpm*

| ❏ 202 | Keep It a Secret/Why Don't You Believe Me | 1953 | 1000. | 2000. | 4000. |

—*Red vinyl*

| ❏ 202 | Keep It a Secret/Why Don't You Believe Me | 1953 | 250.00 | 500.00 | 1000. |

—*Black vinyl*

| ❏ 206 | Alone Again/Don't Have to Hunt No More | 1953 | — | — | — |

—*Unconfirmed on 45 rpm*

| ❏ 281 | I Was Wrong/Hug Me Baby | 1954 | 125.00 | 250.00 | 500.00 |
| ❏ 335 | You Came to Me/Ooh Wee Baby | 1956 | 50.00 | 100.00 | 200.00 |

—*Reissued by "The Duvals"*
RIVIERA

| ❏ 990 | You Came to Me/Ooh Wee Baby | 1955 | 1000. | 2000. | 4000. |

TRANS WORLD

| ❏ 717 | I Can't Pretend/Popcorn Willie | 1956 | 20.00 | 40.00 | 80.00 |

FIVE DAPPS, THE
See THE DAPPS.

FIVE DELIGHTS, THE
45s
ABEL

| ❏ 228 | The Thought of Losing You/That Love Affair | 1959 | 75.00 | 150.00 | 300.00 |

NEWPORT

| ❏ 7002 | There'll Be No Goodbye/Okey Dokey Mama | 1958 | 37.50 | 75.00 | 150.00 |

UNART

| ❏ 2003 | There'll Be No Goodbye/Okey Dokey Mama | 1958 | 7.50 | 15.00 | 30.00 |

FIVE DISCS, THE
Evidently these are all the same group or closely related. Also see DAWN (3).
45s
CALO

| ❏ 202 | Adios/My Baby Loves Me | 1961 | 37.50 | 75.00 | 150.00 |

—*Green label*

| ❏ 202 | Adios/My Baby Loves Me | 1962 | 25.00 | 50.00 | 100.00 |

—*White label*
CHEER

| ❏ 1000 | Never Let You Go/That Was the Time | 1962 | 25.00 | 50.00 | 100.00 |

—*Black label*

| ❏ 1000 | Never Let You Go/That Was the Time | 1962 | 12.50 | 25.00 | 50.00 |

—*Red label*

| ❏ 1000 [DJ] | Never Let You Go/That Was the Time | 1962 | 75.00 | 150.00 | 300.00 |

—*White label, promo only*
CRYSTAL BALL

❏ 114	Mirror Mirror/Most of All I Wonder Why	1978	2.50	5.00	10.00
❏ 120	Unchained Melody/The Shrine of St. Cecelia	1978	2.50	5.00	10.00
❏ 136	Playing a Game of Love/Bells	1979	2.00	4.00	8.00
❏ 141	This Love of Ours/To the Fair	1979	2.00	4.00	8.00

DWAIN

| ❏ 803 | My Chinese Girl/Roses | 1959 | 50.00 | 100.00 | 200.00 |

—*As "Mario and the Five Discs"*

| ❏ 803 | My Chinese Girl/Roses | 1959 | 37.50 | 75.00 | 150.00 |
| ❏ 6072 | My Chinese Girl/Roses | 1959 | 500.00 | 1000. | 2000. |

EMGE

| ❏ 1004 | I Remember/The World Is a Beautiful Place | 1958 | 100.00 | 200.00 | 400.00 |

LAURIE

| ❏ 3601 | Rock and Roll Revival/Gypsy Women | 1973 | 3.75 | 7.50 | 15.00 |

MELLO MOOD

| ❏ 1002 | My Chinese Girl/Roses | 1964 | 3.75 | 7.50 | 15.00 |

PYRAMID

| ❏ 166 | Let's Fall in Love/That Was the Time | 197? | — | 3.00 | 6.00 |

RUST

| ❏ 5027 | I Remember/The World Is a Beautiful Place | 1961 | 6.25 | 12.50 | 25.00 |

VIK

| ❏ 0327 | I Remember/The World Is a Beautiful Place | 1958 | 20.00 | 40.00 | 80.00 |

YALE

| ❏ 240 | When Love Comes Knocking/Go-Go | 1961 | 100.00 | 200.00 | 400.00 |
| ❏ 243/4 | Come On Baby/I Don't Know What to Do | 1961 | 100.00 | 200.00 | 400.00 |

Albums
CRYSTAL BALL

| ❏ 119 | Unchained | 1978 | 3.75 | 7.50 | 15.00 |

MAGIC CARPET

| ❏ 1002 | The Five Discs Sing Again | 1991 | 5.00 | 10.00 | 20.00 |

—*Dark blue cover*

FIVE DOLLARS, THE
45s
FORTUNE

❏ 821	Harmony of Love/Doctor Baby	1955	25.00	50.00	100.00
❏ 826	So Strange/You Know I Can't Refuse	1956	25.00	50.00	100.00
❏ 830	I Will Wait/Hard Working Mama	1956	25.00	50.00	100.00
❏ 833	You Fool/How Do You Do the Bacon Fat	1957	20.00	40.00	80.00
❏ 854	That's the Way It Goes/My Baby-O	1960	12.50	25.00	50.00

FRATERNITY

| ❏ 821 | Harmony of Love/Doctor Baby | 1958 | 10.00 | 20.00 | 40.00 |

FIVE ECHOES, THE
45s
SABRE

| ❏ 102 | Baby Come Back to Me/Lonely Mood | 1953 | 150.00 | 300.00 | 600.00 |

—*Black vinyl*

| ❏ 102 | Baby Come Back to Me/Lonely Mood | 1953 | 750.00 | 1125. | 1500. |

—*Red vinyl*

| ❏ 105 | So Lonesome/Broke | 1954 | 150.00 | 300.00 | 600.00 |

—*Black vinyl*

| ❏ 105 | So Lonesome/Broke | 1954 | 750.00 | 1125. | 1500. |

—*Red vinyl*
VEE JAY

❏ 129	I Really Do/Tell Me Baby	1954	75.00	150.00	300.00
❏ 156	Fool's Prayer/Tastee Freeze	1955	250.00	500.00	1000.
❏ 190	Soldier Boy/Pledging to You	1956	50.00	100.00	200.00

FIVE EMBERS, THE
45s
GEM

| ❏ 224 | Please Come Home/(B-side unknown) | 1954 | 200.00 | 400.00 | 800.00 |

FIVE EMERALDS, THE
45s
S.R.C.

| ❏ 106 | I'll Beg/Let Me Take You Out Tonight | 1953 | 250.00 | 500.00 | 1000. |

—*Label uses numeral "5" in group name, and "S.R.C." has periods in it*

| ❏ 106 | I'll Beg/Let Me Take You Out Tonight | 1953 | 250.00 | 500.00 | 1000. |

—*Label spells out "Five" in group name, and "S-R-C" has hyphens in it*

| ❏ 107 | Darling/Pleasure Me | 1954 | 300.00 | 600.00 | 1200. |

FIVE JETS, THE
45s
DELUXE

❏ 6018	I Am in Love/Not a Hand to Shake	1953	37.50	75.00	150.00
❏ 6053	I'm Stuck/I Want a Woman	1954	37.50	75.00	150.00
❏ 6058	Tell Me You're Mine/Give In	1954	50.00	100.00	200.00
❏ 6064	Crazy Chicken/Everybody Do the Chicken	1954	15.00	30.00	60.00
❏ 6071	Down Slow/Please Love Me Baby	1955	20.00	60.00	120.00

KING

| ❏ 6058 | Tell Me You're Mine/Give In | 1966 | 5.00 | 10.00 | 20.00 |

FIVE KEYS, THE
45s
ALADDIN

| ❏ 3085 | With a Broken Heart/Too Late | 1951 | — | — | — |

—*Unconfirmed on 45 rpm*

❏ 3099	The Glory of Love/Hucklebuck with Jimmy	1951	250.00	500.00	1000.
❏ 3113	It's Christmas Time/Old Mac Donald	1951	250.00	500.00	1000.
❏ 3118	Yes Sir That's My Baby/Old Mac Donald	1952	250.00	500.00	1000.
❏ 3119	Darling/Goin' Downtown	1952	250.00	500.00	1000.
❏ 3127	Red Sails in the Sunset/Be Anything, But Be Mine	1952	3000.	4500.	6000.
❏ 3131	How Long/Mistakes	1952	300.00	600.00	1200.
❏ 3136	Hold Me/I Hadn't Anyone Till You	1952	200.00	400.00	800.00
❏ 3158	I Cried for You/Serve Another Round	1953	225.00	450.00	900.00
❏ 3167	Can't Keep From Crying/Come Go My Bail, Louise	1953	200.00	400.00	800.00
❏ 3175	There Ought to Be a Law/Mama (Your Daughter Told a Lie on Me)	1953	200.00	400.00	800.00

Number	Title (A Side/B Side)	Yr	VG	VG+	NM
❑ 3182	I'll Always Be in Love with You/Rocking and Crying Blues	1953	200.00	400.00	800.00
❑ 3190	These Foolish Things/Lonesome Old Story	1953	1000.	2000.	4000.
❑ 3204	Teardrops in Your Eyes/I'm So High	1953	200.00	400.00	800.00
❑ 3214	My Saddest Hour/Oh! Babe!	1953	200.00	400.00	800.00
❑ 3228	Someday Sweetheart/Love My Loving	1954	200.00	400.00	800.00
❑ 3245	Deep in My Heart/How Do You Expect Me to Get It	1954	200.00	400.00	800.00
❑ 3263	My Love/Why, Oh Why	1954	75.00	150.00	300.00
❑ 3312	Story of Love/Serve Another Round	1956	75.00	150.00	300.00
❑ S7-19768	Every Heart Is Home at Christmas/Frosty the Snowman	1997	—	2.50	5.00

—B-side by Fats Domino on The Right Stuff

BANGAR
| ❑ 661 | Run-Around/I Tell My Heart | 1965 | 3.75 | 7.50 | 15.00 |

CAPITOL
❑ F-2945	Ling, Ting, Tong/I'm Alone	1954	10.00	20.00	40.00
❑ F-3032	Close Your Eyes/Doggone It, You Did It	1955	10.00	20.00	40.00
❑ F-3127	The Verdict/Me Make Um Pow Wow	1955	10.00	20.00	40.00
❑ F-3185	Don't You Know I Love You/I Wish I'd Never Learned to Read	1955	10.00	20.00	40.00
❑ F-3267	'Cause You're My Lover/Gee Whittakers	1955	10.00	20.00	40.00
❑ F-3318	You Broke the Rules of Love/What Goes On	1956	10.00	20.00	40.00
❑ F-3392	She's the Most/I Dreamt I Dwelt in Heaven	1956	10.00	20.00	40.00

—Regular large hole
| ❑ F-3392 | She's the Most/I Dreamt I Dwelt in Heaven | 1956 | 17.50 | 35.00 | 70.00 |

—Small hole
❑ F-3455	My Pigeon's Gone/Peace and Love	1956	10.00	20.00	40.00
❑ F-3502	Out of Sight, Out of Mind/That's Right	1956	7.50	15.00	30.00
❑ F-3597	Wisdom of a Fool/Now Don't That Prove I Love You	1956	7.50	15.00	30.00
❑ F-3660	Tiger Lily/Let There Be You	1957	6.25	12.50	25.00
❑ F-3710	Four Walls/It's a Groove	1957	6.25	12.50	25.00
❑ F-3738	This I Promise You/The Blues Don't Care	1957	6.25	12.50	25.00
❑ F-3786	Boom Boom/Face of An Angel	1957	6.25	12.50	25.00
❑ F-3830	Do Anything/It's a Cryin' Shame	1957	6.25	12.50	25.00
❑ F-3861	From Me to You/Whippety Whirl	1957	6.25	12.50	25.00
❑ F-3948	You're for Me/With All My Love	1958	6.25	12.50	25.00
❑ F-4009	Emily Please/Handy Andy	1958	6.25	12.50	25.00
❑ F-4092	One Great Love/Really-O, Truly-O	1958	6.25	12.50	25.00
❑ 4828	Out of Sight, Out of Mind/From the Bottom of My Heart	1962	5.00	10.00	20.00

CLASSIC ARTISTS
| ❑ 115 | I Want You For Christmas/Express Yourself Back Home | 1989 | — | 2.50 | 5.00 |

—As "Rudy West and the Five Keys"

GROOVE
| ❑ 0031 | I'll Follow You/Lawdy Miss Mary | 1954 | 2000. | 3000. | 4000. |

—There is some debate about whether this record actually exists on 45.

INFERNO
| ❑ 4500 | Hey Girl/No Matter | 1967 | 5.00 | 10.00 | 20.00 |

KING
❑ 5251	I Took Your Love for a Toy/Ziggus	1959	7.50	15.00	30.00
❑ 5273	Dancing Senorita/Dream On	1959	5.00	10.00	20.00
❑ 5302	How Can I Forget You/I Burned Your Letter	1960	5.00	10.00	20.00
❑ 5330	Gonna Be Too Late/Rosetta	1960	5.00	10.00	20.00
❑ 5358	I Didn't Know/No, Says My Heart	1960	5.00	10.00	20.00
❑ 5398	Bimbo/Valley of Love	1960	5.00	10.00	20.00
❑ 5446	You Broke the Only Heart/That's What You're Doing to Me	1961	5.00	10.00	20.00
❑ 5496	Do Something for Me/Stop Your Crying	1961	5.00	10.00	20.00
❑ 5877	I'll Never Stop Loving You/I Can't Escape from You	1964	3.00	6.00	12.00

LIBERTY
| ❑ 1394 | It's Christmas Time/It's Christmas | 1980 | 2.00 | 4.00 | 8.00 |

—B-side by Marvin and Johnny

OWL
| ❑ 321 | A Dreamer/Your Teeth and Your Tongue | 1973 | 2.00 | 4.00 | 8.00 |

SEG-WAY
| ❑ 1008 | Out of Sight, Out of Mind/You're the One | 1962 | 3.75 | 7.50 | 15.00 |

UNITED ARTISTS
| ❑ 0150 | The Glory of Love/My Saddest Hour | 1973 | — | 2.00 | 4.00 |

—"Silver Spotlight Series" reissue

7-Inch Extended Plays

CAPITOL
❑ EAP 572	(contents unknown)	1955	25.00	50.00	100.00
❑ EAP 572 [PS]	The Five Keys	1955	25.00	50.00	100.00
❑ EAP 1-828	(contents unknown)	1957	25.00	50.00	100.00
❑ EAP 1-828 [PS]	The Five Keys On Stage! Volume 1	1957	37.50	75.00	150.00

—On cover, the far left singer has his thumb sticking out (inadvertently?) in a phallic way
| ❑ EAP 1-828 [PS] | The Five Keys On Stage! Volume 1 | 1957 | 25.00 | 50.00 | 100.00 |

—On cover, the far left singer's "offending" thumb is airbrushed out
| ❑ EAP 2-828 | (contents unknown) | 1957 | 25.00 | 50.00 | 100.00 |
| ❑ EAP 2-828 [PS] | The Five Keys On Stage! Volume 2 | 1957 | 37.50 | 75.00 | 150.00 |

—On cover, the far left singer has his thumb sticking out (inadvertently?) in a phallic way
| ❑ EAP 2-828 [PS] | The Five Keys On Stage! Volume 2 | 1957 | 25.00 | 50.00 | 100.00 |

—On cover, the far left singer's "offending" thumb is airbrushed out
| ❑ EAP 3-828 | C'est La Vie/Dream//Let There Be You/All I Need Is You | 1957 | 25.00 | 50.00 | 100.00 |
| ❑ EAP 3-828 [PS] | The Five Keys On Stage! Volume 3 | 1957 | 37.50 | 75.00 | 150.00 |

—On cover, the far left singer has his thumb sticking out (inadvertently?) in a phallic way
| ❑ EAP 3-828 [PS] | The Five Keys On Stage! Volume 3 | 1957 | 25.00 | 50.00 | 100.00 |

—On cover, the far left singer's "offending" thumb is airbrushed out

Number	Title (A Side/B Side)	Yr	VG	VG+	NM
Albums					

ALADDIN
| ❑ LP-806 [M] | The Best of the Five Keys | 1956 | 1000. | 1500. | 2000. |

—Copies of Aladdin 806 entitled "On the Town" are bootlegs.

CAPITOL
| ❑ T 828 [M] | The Five Keys On Stage! | 1957 | 75.00 | 150.00 | 300.00 |

—On cover, the far left singer has his thumb sticking out (inadvertently?) in a phallic way
| ❑ T 828 [M] | The Five Keys On Stage! | 1957 | 125.00 | 250.00 | 500.00 |

—On cover, the far left singer's "offending" thumb is airbrushed out
| ❑ M-1769 | The Fantastic Five Keys | 1977 | 5.00 | 10.00 | 20.00 |

—Reissue with new prefix
| ❑ T 1769 [M] | The Fantastic Five Keys | 1962 | 75.00 | 150.00 | 300.00 |

HARLEM HIT PARADE
| ❑ 5004 | The Five Keys | 1972 | 3.75 | 7.50 | 15.00 |

KING
❑ 688 [M]	The Five Keys	1960	200.00	400.00	800.00
❑ 692 [M]	Rhythm and Blues Hits, Past and Present	1960	150.00	300.00	600.00
❑ 5013	14 Hits	1978	3.00	6.00	12.00

SCORE
| ❑ LP-4003 [M] | The Five Keys on the Town | 1957 | 200.00 | 400.00 | 800.00 |

—Reissue of Aladdin 806.

FIVE KIDS, THE
45s
MAXWELL
| ❑ 101 | Carolyn/Oh Baby | 1955 | 1000. | 2000. | 3000. |

FIVE LYRICS, THE
45s
MUSIC CITY
| ❑ 799 | I'm Traveling Light/My Honeysweet Pea | 1956 | 375.00 | 750.00 | 1500. |

FIVE NOTES, THE
45s
CHESS
| ❑ 1614 | Show Me the Way/Park Your Lover | 1955 | 37.50 | 75.00 | 150.00 |

JEN D
| ❑ 4185 | You Are So Beautiful/Broken Hearted Baby | 1955 | 125.00 | 250.00 | 500.00 |

JOSIE
| ❑ 784 | You Are So Beautiful/Broken Hearted Baby | 1955 | 20.00 | 40.00 | 80.00 |

FIVE PLAYBOYS, THE
45s
DOT
| ❑ 15605 | When We Were Young/Pages of My Scrapbook | 1957 | 6.25 | 12.50 | 25.00 |

FEE BEE
| ❑ 213 | When We Were Young/Pages of My Scrapbook | 1958 | 12.50 | 25.00 | 50.00 |
| ❑ 232 | Angel Mine/She's My Baby | 1959 | 25.00 | 50.00 | 100.00 |

MERCURY
| ❑ 71269 | Time Will Allow/Why Be a Fool | 1958 | 6.25 | 12.50 | 25.00 |

PETITE
| ❑ 504 | She's My Baby/Mr. Echo | 1959 | 10.00 | 20.00 | 40.00 |

FIVE ROVERS, THE
45s
MUSIC CITY
| ❑ 798 | Down to the Sea/Change Your Mind | 1956 | 30.00 | 60.00 | 120.00 |

FIVE ROYALES, THE
Also includes "The Five Royals" and "The '5' Royales."
45s
ABC-PARAMOUNT
| ❑ 10348 | Catch That Teardrop/Goof Ball | 1962 | 2.50 | 5.00 | 10.00 |
| ❑ 10368 | What's In Your Heart/I Want It Like That | 1962 | 2.50 | 5.00 | 10.00 |

APOLLO
| ❑ 441 | Courage to Love/You Know I Know | 1952 | 25.00 | 50.00 | 100.00 |

—Black vinyl
| ❑ 441 | Courage to Love/You Know I Know | 1952 | 100.00 | 200.00 | 400.00 |

—Red vinyl
| ❑ 443 | Baby Don't Do It/Take All of Me | 1952 | 25.00 | 50.00 | 100.00 |

—Black vinyl
| ❑ 443 | Baby Don't Do It/Take All of Me | 1952 | 100.00 | 200.00 | 400.00 |

—Red vinyl
❑ 446	Help Me, Somebody/Crazy, Crazy, Crazy	1953	25.00	50.00	100.00
❑ 448	Too Much Lovin' (Much Too Much)/Laundromat Blues	1953	30.00	60.00	120.00
❑ 449	I Want to Thank You/All Righty	1953	20.00	40.00	80.00
❑ 452	I Do/Good Things	1954	20.00	40.00	80.00
❑ 454	Cry Some More/I Like It Like That	1954	20.00	40.00	80.00
❑ 458	What's That/Let Me Come Back Home	1954	17.50	35.00	70.00
❑ 467	With All Your Heart/6 O'Clock in the Morning	1955	17.50	35.00	70.00

HOME OF THE BLUES
❑ 112	Please, Please, Please/I Got to Know	1960	3.75	7.50	15.00
❑ 218	If You Don't Need Me/I'm Gonna Tell Them	1961	3.75	7.50	15.00
❑ 232	Take Me With You Baby/Not Going to Cry	1961	3.75	7.50	15.00
❑ 234	Nuch in Need/They Don't Know	1962	3.75	7.50	15.00
❑ 243	Catch That Teardrop/Goof Ball	1962	3.75	7.50	15.00

KING
❑ 4740	I'm Gonna Run It Down/Behave Yourself	1954	20.00	40.00	80.00
❑ 4744	Monkey Hips and Rice/Devil with the Rest	1954	20.00	40.00	80.00
❑ 4762	School Girl/One Mistake	1955	20.00	40.00	80.00
❑ 4770	Every Dog Has His Day/You Didn't Learn It at Home	1955	20.00	40.00	80.00

Number	Title (A Side/B Side)	Yr	VG	VG+	NM
❑ 4785	How I Wonder/Mohawk Squaw	1955	20.00	40.00	80.00
❑ 4806	I Need Your Lovin'/When I Get Like This	1955	12.50	25.00	50.00
❑ 4819	Women About to Make Me Go Crazy/Do Unto You	1955	12.50	25.00	50.00
❑ 4830	I Ain't Gettin' Caught/Someone Made You for Me	1955	12.50	25.00	50.00
❑ 4869	When You Walked Through the Door/Right Around the Corner	1956	12.50	25.00	50.00
❑ 4901	I Could Love You/My Wants for Love	1956	12.50	25.00	50.00
❑ 4952	Get Something Out of It/Come On and Save Me	1956	12.50	25.00	50.00
❑ 4973	Just As I Am/Mine Forevermore	1956	12.50	25.00	50.00
❑ 5032	Tears of Joy/Thirty Second Lover	1957	10.00	20.00	40.00
❑ 5053	Think/I'd Better Make a Move	1957	10.00	20.00	40.00
❑ 5082	Messin' Up/Say It	1957	10.00	20.00	40.00
❑ 5098	Dedicated to the One I Love/Don't Be Ashamed	1958	10.00	20.00	40.00
❑ 5131	Do the Cha Cha Cherry/The Feeling Is Real	1958	6.25	12.50	25.00
❑ 5141	Tell the Truth/Double or Nothing	1958	6.25	12.50	25.00
❑ 5153	The Slummer the Slum/Don't Let It Be in Vain	1958	6.25	12.50	25.00
❑ 5162	Your Only Love/The Real Thing	1958	6.25	12.50	25.00
❑ 5191	Miracle of Love/I Know It's Hard, But It's Fair	1959	6.25	12.50	25.00
❑ 5237	Tell Me You Care/Wonder Where Your Love Has Gone	1959	6.25	12.50	25.00
❑ 5266	My Sugar Sugar/It Hurts Inside	1959	6.25	12.50	25.00
❑ 5329	Don't Give No More Than You Can Take/I'm with You	1960	6.25	12.50	25.00
❑ 5357	Why/Within My Heart	1960	6.25	12.50	25.00
❑ 5453	Dedicated to the One I Love/Miracle of Love	1961	3.75	7.50	15.00
❑ 5756	Dedicated to the One I Love/Tears of Joy	1963	3.75	7.50	15.00
❑ 5892	I Wonder Where Your Love Has Gone/I Need Your Lovin' Baby	1964	3.75	7.50	15.00
—The Five Royals					
SMASH					
❑ 1936	Baby Don't Do It/I Like It Like That	1964	2.50	5.00	10.00
❑ 1963	Never Turn Your Back/Faith	1965	2.50	5.00	10.00
TODD					
❑ 1086	I'm Standing in the Shadows/Doin' Everything	1963	2.50	5.00	10.00
❑ 1088	Baby Don't Do It/There's Somebody Over There	1963	2.50	5.00	10.00
VEE JAY					
❑ 412	Much in Need/They Don't Know	1961	3.75	7.50	15.00
❑ 431	Help Me Somebody/Talk About My Woman	1962	3.75	7.50	15.00
Albums					
APOLLO					
❑ LP-488 [M]	The Rockin' 5 Royales	1956	2000.	3000.	4000.
—Purple label					
❑ LP-488 [M]	The Rockin' 5 Royales	1956	1000.	1500.	2000.
—Green label					
❑ LP-488 [M]	The Rockin' 5 Royales	1956	250.00	500.00	1000.
—Yellow label					
KING					
❑ 580 [M]	Dedicated to You	1957	125.00	250.00	500.00
❑ 616 [M]	The 5 Royales Sing for You	1959	100.00	200.00	400.00
❑ 678 [M]	The Five Royales	1960	62.50	125.00	250.00
❑ 955 [M]	24 All Time Hits	1966	25.00	50.00	100.00
❑ 5014	17 Hits	197?	3.00	6.00	12.00

FIVE SATINS, THE

Also see FRED PARRIS; THE WILDWOODS.

45s

Number	Title (A Side/B Side)	Yr	VG	VG+	NM
BUDDAH					
❑ 477	Everybody Stand and Clap Your Hands/Hey There Pretty Lady	1975	—	2.50	5.00
—As "Black Satin"					
CANDELITE					
❑ 411	She's Gone (With the Wind)/Somewhere a Voice Is Calling	1974	—	3.00	6.00
CHANCELLOR					
❑ 1110	The Masquerade Is Over/Raining in My Heart	1962	5.00	10.00	20.00
❑ 1121	Do You Remember/Downtown	1962	5.00	10.00	20.00
CUB					
❑ 9071	Your Memory/I Didn't Know	1960	6.25	12.50	25.00
❑ 9077	These Foolish Things/A Beggar with a Dream	1960	6.25	12.50	25.00
❑ 9090	Golden Earrings/Can I Come Over Tonight	1961	6.25	12.50	25.00
ELEKTRA					
❑ 47411	Memories of Days Gone By Medley/Loving You (Would Be the Sweetest Thing)	1982	5.00	10.00	20.00
—As "Fred Parris and the Five Satins"					
❑ 69888	Didn't I (Blow Your Mind)/Loving You (Would Be the Sweetest Thing)	1982	—	2.50	5.00
❑ 69938	Breaking Up/Loving You (Would Be the Sweetest Thing)	1982	—	2.50	5.00
❑ 69984	I'll Be Seeing You/Loving You (Would Be the Sweetest Thing)	1982	—	2.50	5.00
EMBER					
❑ 1005	In the Still of the Nite/The Jones Girl	1956	50.00	100.00	200.00
—Red label; has "6106A" in the trail-off vinyl					
❑ 1005	In the Still of the Nite/The Jones Girl	1956	12.50	25.00	50.00
—Red label; has "E-2105-45" in the trail-off vinyl					
❑ 1005	In the Still of the Nite/The Jones Girl	1956	7.50	15.00	30.00
—Red label; has "E-1005" in the trail-off vinyl					
❑ 1005	I'll Remember (In the Still of the Nite)/The Jones Girl	1956	7.50	15.00	30.00
—Red label					
❑ 1005	I'll Remember (In the Still of the Nite)/The Jones Girl	1959	12.50	25.00	50.00
—Multi-color "logs" label; reads "Special Demand Release"					

Number	Title (A Side/B Side)	Yr	VG	VG+	NM
❑ 1005	I'll Remember (In the Still of the Nite)/The Jones Girl	1959	7.50	15.00	30.00
—Multi-color "logs" label; no "Special Demand Release"					
❑ 1005	In the Still of the Nite/The Jones Girl	1959	10.00	20.00	40.00
—Multi-color "logs" label with original A-side title					
❑ 1005	In the Still of the Night "I'll Remember"/The Jones Girl	1961	7.50	15.00	30.00
—Black label, white logo and red flames at left; A-side title revised yet again					
❑ 1008	Weeping Willow/Wonderful Girl	1956	10.00	20.00	40.00
❑ 1014	Our Love Is Forever/Oh Happy Day	1957	10.00	20.00	40.00
❑ 1019	To the Aisle/Wish I Had My Baby	1957	10.00	20.00	40.00
—Red label					
❑ 1019	To the Aisle/Wish I Had My Baby	1960	7.50	15.00	30.00
—Multi-color "logs" label					
❑ 1019	To the Aisle/Wish I Had My Baby	1961	5.00	10.00	20.00
—Black label					
❑ 1025	Our Anniversary/Pretty Baby	1957	10.00	20.00	40.00
—Red label					
❑ 1025	Our Anniversary/Pretty Baby	1957	5.00	10.00	20.00
—Black label					
❑ 1028	A Million to One/Love with No Love in Return	1957	10.00	20.00	40.00
❑ 1038	A Night to Remember/Senorita Lolita	1958	7.50	15.00	30.00
—As "Fred Parris and the Satins"					
❑ 1056	Shadows/Toni My Love	1959	7.50	15.00	30.00
❑ 1061	I'll Be Seeing You/A Night Like This	1960	7.50	15.00	30.00
❑ 1066	Candlelight/The Time	1960	6.25	12.50	25.00
❑ 1070	Wishing Ring/Tell Me Dear	1961	6.25	12.50	25.00
FIRST					
❑ 104	When Your Love Comes Along/Skippity Doo	1959	10.00	20.00	40.00
—Orange label					
❑ 104	When Your Love Comes Along/Skippity Doo	1959	6.25	12.50	25.00
—Green label					
GLENVILLE MUSIC					
❑ 106	(I'll Remember) In the Still of the Night/The Jones Girl	196?	2.00	4.00	8.00
—Reissue					
KIRSHNER					
❑ 4251	Very Precious Oldies/You Are Love	1974	2.50	5.00	10.00
❑ 4252	Two Different Worlds/Love Is Such a Beautiful Thing	1974	2.50	5.00	10.00
KLIK					
❑ 1020	I Love You So/Story to You	1973	2.50	5.00	10.00
MAMA SADIE					
❑ 1001	In the Still of the Night "67"/Heck No (Instrumental)	1967	3.00	6.00	12.00
MUSICTONE					
❑ 1108	To the Aisle/Just to Be Near You	1961	6.25	12.50	25.00
NIGHTRAIN					
❑ 901	All Mine/The Voice	1970	2.50	5.00	10.00
RCA					
❑ 6989-7-R	In the Still of the Night/Yes	1988	—	—	3.00
—B-side by Merry Clayton					
RCA VICTOR					
❑ 74-0478	Summer in New York/Dark at the Top of My Heart	1971	2.50	5.00	10.00
ROULETTE					
❑ 4563	Ain't Gonna Cry/You Can Count on Me	1964	2.50	5.00	10.00
SAMMY					
❑ 103	No One Knows/Musical Chairs	196?	7.50	15.00	30.00
SIGNATURE					
❑ 001	Everybody's Got a Home But Me/Heartache	1990	—	2.50	5.00
STANDORD					
❑ 100	All Mine/Rose Mary	1956	175.00	350.00	700.00
—Red label					
❑ 100	All Mine/Rose Mary	1962	50.00	100.00	200.00
—Maroon label					
❑ 200	In the Still of the Nite/The Jones Girl	1956	300.00	600.00	900.00
❑ 200	In the Still of the Nite/The Jones Girl	1956	1000.	1500.	2000.
—With "Produced by Martin Kuegell" credit					
TIME MACHINE					
❑ 570	Wonder Why/No One Knows	1962	2.00	4.00	8.00
❑ 571	The Masquerade Is Over/Lonely Hearts	1962	2.00	4.00	8.00
TIMES SQUARE					
❑ 4	All Mine/Rose Mary	1962	5.00	10.00	20.00
—Blue vinyl					
❑ 21	Paradise on Earth/Monkey Business	1963	5.00	10.00	20.00
❑ 94	Paradise on Earth/Monkey Business	1964	3.75	7.50	15.00
UNITED ARTISTS					
❑ 368	On a Lover's Island/Till the End	1961	6.25	12.50	25.00
WARNER BROS.					
❑ 5367	Remember Me/Kangaroo	1963	3.00	6.00	12.00
X-BAT					
❑ 1000	When the Swallows Come Back to Capistrano/Dance Girl Dance	1995	—	2.50	5.00
—Red vinyl					
❑ 1000 [PS]	When the Swallows Come Back to Capistrano/Dance Girl Dance	1995	—	2.50	5.00
7-Inch Extended Plays					
EMBER					
❑ EEP-100	I'll Remember/The Jones Girl//Wonderful Girl/Pretty Baby	1957	50.00	100.00	200.00
❑ EEP-100 [PS]	The Five Satins Sing (Vol. 1)	1957	50.00	100.00	200.00
❑ EEP-101	To the Aisle/Sugar//Our Love Is Forever/Weeping Willow	1957	50.00	100.00	200.00

Number	Title (A Side/B Side)	Yr	VG	VG+	NM
EEP-101 [PS]	The Five Satins Sing (Vol. 2)	1957	50.00	100.00	200.00
EEP-102	Our Anniversary/I'll Get Along//Wish I Had My Baby/Moonlight and I	1957	50.00	100.00	200.00
EEP-102 [PS]	The Five Satins Sing (Vol. 3)	1957	50.00	100.00	200.00

Albums

BUDDAH

BDS-5654	Black Satin	1976	3.75	7.50	15.00

—As "Black Satin"

CELEBRITY SHOWCASE

JB-7671	The Best of the Five Satins	1970	5.00	10.00	20.00

COLLECTABLES

COL-5017	The Five Satins Sing Their Greatest Hits	198?	2.50	5.00	10.00

EMBER

ELP-100 [M]	The Five Satins Sing	1957	1000.	1500.	2000.

—Red label; group pictured on front cover; blue vinyl

ELP-100 [M]	The Five Satins Sing	1957	150.00	300.00	600.00

—Red label; group pictured on front cover; black vinyl

ELP-100 [M]	The Five Satins Sing	1959	75.00	150.00	300.00

—Mostly white "logs" label; group pictured on front cover

ELP-100 [M]	The Five Satins Sing	1959	50.00	100.00	200.00

—Mostly white "logs" label; no picture on cover

ELP-100 [M]	The Five Satins Sing	1961	25.00	50.00	100.00

—Black label; no picture on cover

ELP-401 [M]	The Five Satins Encore	1960	50.00	100.00	200.00

—Mostly white "logs" label

ELP-401 [M]	The Five Satins Encore	1961	25.00	50.00	100.00

—Black label

LOST-NITE

LLP-8 [10]	The Five Satins	1981	2.50	5.00	10.00

—Red vinyl

LLP-9 [10]	The Five Satins	1981	2.50	5.00	10.00

—Red vinyl

MOUNT VERNON

108	The Five Satins Sing	196?	7.50	15.00	30.00

RELIC

5008	The Five Satins' Greatest Hits (1956-1959), Volume 1	198?	2.50	5.00	10.00
5013	The Five Satins' Greatest Hits (1956-1959), Volume 2	198?	2.50	5.00	10.00
5024	The Five Satins' Greatest Hits (1956-1959), Volume 3	198?	2.50	5.00	10.00

FIVE SCALDERS, THE

45s

DRUMMOND

3000	If Only You Were Mine/There Will Come a Time	1956	250.00	500.00	1000.
3001	Girl Friend/Willow Blues	1956	500.00	1000.	1500.

—Blue label

3001	Girl Friend/Willow Blues	1956	250.00	500.00	1000.

—Maroon label

SUGAR HILL

3000	If Only You Were Mine/There Will Come a Time	1956	500.00	1000.	2000.

FIVE SHARKS, THE

45s

AMBER

852	The Lion Sleeps Tonight/Land of 1000 Dances	1966	2.50	5.00	10.00

OLD TIMER

604	Gloria/Flames	1964	5.00	10.00	20.00
605	Stand By Me/I'll Never Let You Go	1964	5.00	10.00	20.00

—Gold vinyl

605	Stand By Me/I'll Never Let You Go	1964	4.00	8.00	16.00

—Blue vinyl

611	Gloria/Flames	1965	5.00	10.00	20.00

—Red vinyl

611	Gloria/Flames	1965	3.75	7.50	15.00

—Black vinyl

RELIC

525	Stormy Weather (2:45)/If You Love Me	1965	2.50	5.00	10.00

SIAMESE

404	Gloria/Flames	1965	3.00	6.00	12.00

TIMES SQUARE

35	Stormy Weather (3:45)/If You Love Me	1964	15.00	30.00	60.00

—Blue vinyl

35	Stormy Weather (3:45)/If You Love Me	1964	10.00	20.00	40.00

—Black vinyl

35	Stormy Weather (2:45)/If You Love Me	1964	7.50	15.00	30.00

FIVE SHARPS, THE (1)

45s

BIM BAM BOOM

103	Stormy Weather/Sleepy Cowboy	1972	2.00	4.00	8.00

—Reissue mastered off the cracked Jubilee 78 (see below); the original master has long since disappeared

JUBILEE

5104	Stormy Weather/Sleepy Cowboy	1952	—	—	—

—Unknown on 45 RPM (3 known copies, one of which is cracked, exist on 78); all known 45s are counterfeits. Known counterfeits do not match the proper typeface of the era for the label, and the blue labels are too bright compared to authentic Jubilee 45s of the early 1950s. If a legitimate 45 would be confirmed, it could sell for more than any record ever made!

78s

JUBILEE

5104	Stormy Weather/Sleepy Cowboy	1952	5000.	7500.	10000.

FIVE SHARPS, THE (2)

A completely different group than (1), they were assembled by Jubilee to record a new version of "Stormy Weather" in the midst of the hubbub about the first Five Sharps version. (For the full story, see The Complete Book of Doo-Wop by Gribin and Schiff, Krause Publications, 2000.)

45s

JUBILEE

5478	Stormy Weather/Mammy Jammy	1964	3.00	6.00	12.00

FIVE STAIRSTEPS, THE

Includes records by "Five Stairsteps and Cubie" and "Stairsteps."

45s

BUDDAH

20	Something's Missing/Tell Me Who	1967	2.00	4.00	8.00

—As "Five Stairsteps and Cubie"

20 [PS]	Something's Missing/Tell Me Who	1967	3.75	7.50	15.00
26	A Million to One/You Make Me So Mad	1968	2.00	4.00	8.00

—As "Five Stairsteps and Cubie"

26 [PS]	A Million to One/You Make Me So Mad	1968	3.75	7.50	15.00
35	The Shadow of Your Love/Bad News	1968	2.00	4.00	8.00
165	Dear Prudence/O-o-h Child	1970	2.00	4.00	8.00
165	O-o-h Child/Who Do You Belong To	1970	—	3.00	6.00
188	Because I Love You/America Standing	1970	—	2.50	5.00
213	Didn't It Look So Easy/Peace Is Gonna Come	1971	—	2.50	5.00

—Starting with the above, as "Stairsteps"

222	Snow/Look Out	1971	—	2.50	5.00
277	I Love You—Stop/I Feel a Song (In My Heart Again)	1972	—	2.50	5.00
291	Hush Child/The Easy Way	1972	—	2.50	5.00
320	Every Single Way/Two Weeks' Notice	1972	—	2.50	5.00

CURTOM

1931	Don't Change Your Love/New Dance Craze	1968	—	3.00	6.00

—Curtom releases as "Five Stairsteps and Cubie"

1933	I Made a Mistake/Stay Close to Me	1968	—	3.00	6.00
1936	Baby Make Me Feel So Good/Little Young Lover	1969	—	3.00	6.00
1944	Madame Mary/Little Boy Blue	1969	—	3.00	6.00
1945	We Must Be in Love/Little Young Lover	1969	—	3.00	6.00

DARK HORSE

10005	From Us to You/Time	1975	—	2.50	5.00
10005 [PS]	From Us to You/Time	1975	—	3.00	6.00
10009	Tell Me Why/Salaam	1976	—	2.50	5.00

WINDY "C"

601	You Waited Too Long/Don't Waste Your Time	1966	2.50	5.00	10.00
602	World of Fantasy/Playgirl's Love	1966	2.50	5.00	10.00
603	Come Back/You Don't Love Me	1966	2.50	5.00	10.00
604	Danger, She's a Stranger/Behind Curtains	1967	2.50	5.00	10.00
605	Ain't Gonna Rest (Till I Get You)/You Can't See	1967	2.50	5.00	10.00
607	Oooh, Baby Baby/The Girl I Love	1967	2.50	5.00	10.00
608	The Touch of You/Change of Face	1967	2.50	5.00	10.00

Albums

BUDDAH

BDS-5008	Our Family Portrait	1967	5.00	10.00	20.00
BDS-5061	Stairsteps	1970	3.75	7.50	15.00

—As "Stairsteps"

BDS-5068	Step by Step by Step	1970	3.75	7.50	15.00

—As "Stairsteps"

COLLECTABLES

COL-5023	Greatest Hits	1985	2.50	5.00	10.00

CURTOM

8002	Love's Happening	1969	5.00	10.00	20.00

WINDY C

6000 [M]	The Five Stairsteps	1967	6.25	12.50	25.00
S-6000 [S]	The Five Stairsteps	1967	6.25	12.50	25.00

FIVE STARS, THE (1)

45s

ABC-PARAMOUNT

9911	Pickin' on the Wrong Chicken/Dreaming	1958	6.25	12.50	25.00

HUNT

318	Pickin' on the Wrong Chicken/Dreaming	1959	5.00	10.00	20.00

NOTE

10011	Pickin' on the Wrong Chicken/Dreaming	1958	7.50	15.00	30.00
10016	My Paradise/Friction	1958	10.00	20.00	40.00
10031	Am I Wasting My Time/Gamblin' Man	1959	7.50	15.00	30.00

FIVE SWANS, THE

45s

MUSIC CITY

795	Little Girl of My Dreams/Little Tipa Tins	1956	75.00	150.00	300.00

FIVE THRILLS, THE

45s

PARROT

796	My Baby's Gone/Feel So Good	1954	200.00	400.00	800.00
800	Gloria/Wee Wee Baby	1954	1000.	1500.	2000.

—Black vinyl

800	Gloria/Wee Wee Baby	1954	2000.	3000.	4000.

—Red vinyl

78s

PARROT

796	My Baby's Gone/Feel So Good	1954	62.50	125.00	250.00
800	Gloria/Wee Wee Baby	1954	125.00	250.00	500.00

F

Number	Title (A Side/B Side)	Yr	VG	VG+	NM

FIVE TINOS, THE
45s
SUN

Number	Title (A Side/B Side)	Yr	VG	VG+	NM
❏ 222	Sitting By My Window/Don't Do That	1955	300.00	600.00	1200.

78s
SUN

| ❏ 222 | Sitting By My Window/Don't Do That | 1955 | 150.00 | 300.00 | 600.00 |

FIVE TRUMPETS, THE
45s
GOTHAM

❏ 681	Stand By Me/Jesus Is Here Today	1951	15.00	30.00	60.00
❏ 693	My Chains Fell Off/The Lord Knows What I Need	1952	15.00	30.00	60.00
❏ 696	No Not One/A Hand I Can See	1952	15.00	30.00	60.00

RCA VICTOR

❏ 50-0014	Oh Lord/Don't Let Nobody Turn You Around	1949	17.50	35.00	70.00
—Orange vinyl					
❏ 50-0034	Swing Low Sweet Chariot/Sign of the Judgment	1949	17.50	35.00	70.00
—Orange vinyl					
❏ 50-0080	When the Saints Go Marching In/Preach My Word	1950	17.50	35.00	70.00
—Orange vinyl					

SAVOY

| ❏ 4060 | Amazing Grace/Lord I Want to Be a Christian | 1955 | 6.25 | 12.50 | 25.00 |
| ❏ 4072 | I've Got Jesus/I Shall Not Be Moved | 1956 | 6.25 | 12.50 | 25.00 |

FIVE WILLOWS, THE
45s
ALLEN

❏ 1000	My Dear, Dearest Darling/Rock, Little Francis	1953	75.00	150.00	300.00
❏ 1002	Delores/All Night Long	1953	150.00	300.00	600.00
❏ 1003	The White Cliffs of Dover/With These Hands	1953	175.00	350.00	700.00

HERALD

| ❏ 433 | Baby Come a Little Closer/Lay Your Head on My Shoulder | 1954 | 75.00 | 150.00 | 300.00 |
| ❏ 442 | Look Me in the Eyes/So Help Me | 1954 | 100.00 | 200.00 | 400.00 |

LOST-NITE

❏ 174	My Dear, Dearest Darling/Rock, Little Francis	196?	—	3.00	6.00
❏ 183	Delores/All Night Long	196?	—	3.00	6.00
❏ 187	The White Cliffs of Dover/With These Hands	196?	—	3.00	6.00
—Lost-Nite records are reissues					
❏ 192	Love Bells/Please Baby	196?	—	3.00	6.00

PEE DEE

| ❏ 290 | Love Bells/Please, Baby | 1953 | 375.00 | 750.00 | 1500. |

78s
ALLEN

❏ 1000	My Dear, Dearest Darling/Rock, Little Francis	1953	25.00	50.00	100.00
❏ 1002	Delores/All Night Long	1953	30.00	60.00	120.00
❏ 1003	The White Cliffs of Dover/With These Hands	1953	50.00	100.00	200.00

HERALD

| ❏ 433 | Baby Come a Little Closer/Lay Your Head on My Shoulder | 1954 | 20.00 | 40.00 | 80.00 |
| ❏ 442 | Look Me in the Eyes/So Help Me | 1954 | 20.00 | 40.00 | 80.00 |

PEE DEE

| ❏ 290 | Love Bells/Please, Baby | 1953 | 300.00 | 600.00 | 1200. |

FIVE WINGS, THE
45s
KING

❏ 4778	Johnny Has Gone/Johnny's Still Singing	1955	50.00	100.00	200.00
❏ 4781	Teardrops Are Falling/Rock-A-Locka	1955	100.00	200.00	400.00
—Later released on King 5199 as The Checkers.					

78s
KING

| ❏ 4778 | Johnny Has Gone/Johnny's Still Singing | 1955 | 25.00 | 50.00 | 100.00 |
| ❏ 4781 | Teardrops Are Falling/Rock-A-Locka | 1955 | 25.00 | 50.00 | 100.00 |

FLACK, ROBERTA
45s
ANGEL

| ❏ S7-19773 | The Christmas Song (Chestnuts Roasting on an Open Fire)/25th of Last December | 1997 | — | 2.00 | 4.00 |

ATLANTIC

❏ 2665	Compared to What/That's No Way to Say Goodbye	1969	2.00	4.00	8.00
❏ 2730	How Many Broken Wings/Baby Baby	1970	—	3.00	6.00
—With Les McCann					
❏ 2758	Reverend Lee/Business Goes On As Usual	1970	—	3.00	6.00
❏ 2785	Let It Be Me/Do What Cha Gotta Do	1971	—	3.00	6.00
❏ 2851	Will You Still Love Me Tomorrow/Go Up Moses	1972	—	2.50	5.00
❏ 2864	The First Time Ever I Saw Your Face/Trade Winds	1972	—	2.50	5.00
❏ 2940	Killing Me Softly with His Song/Just Like a Woman	1973	—	2.50	5.00
❏ 2982	Jesse/No Tears	1973	—	2.50	5.00
❏ 3025	Feel Like Makin' Love/When You Smile	1974	—	2.50	5.00
❏ 3203	Feel Like Makin' Love/When You Smile	1974	—	2.00	4.00
❏ 3271	Feelin' That Glow/Some Gospel According to Matthew	1975	—	2.00	4.00
❏ 3441	The 25th of Last December/Move In with Me	1977	—	2.00	4.00
❏ 3483	If Ever I See You Again/I'd Like to Be a Baby to You	1978	—	2.00	4.00
❏ 3521	When It's Over/Come Share My Love	1978	—	2.00	4.00

Number	Title (A Side/B Side)	Yr	VG	VG+	NM
❏ 3560	You Are Everything/Knowing That We're Made for Each Other	1979	—	2.00	4.00
❏ 3627	You Are My Heaven/I'll Love You Forever and Ever	1979	—	2.00	4.00
❏ 3753	Don't Make Me Wait Too Long/Only Heaven Can Wait (For Love)	1980	—	2.00	4.00
❏ 4005	Making Love/Jesse	1982	—	2.00	4.00
❏ 4005 [PS]	Making Love/Jesse	1982	—	3.00	6.00
❏ 4068	I'm the One/'Til the Morning Comes	1982	—	2.00	4.00
❏ 87607	Set the Night to Music/Natural Thing	1991	—	2.00	4.00
—A-side: With Maxi Priest					
❏ 88898	Shock to My System/You Know What It's Like	1989	—	—	3.00
❏ 88941	Uh-Uh Ooh-Ooh Look Out (Here It Comes)/You Know What It's Like	1989	—	—	3.00
❏ 88941 [PS]	Uh-Uh Ooh-Ooh Look Out (Here It Comes)/You Know What It's Like	1989	—	—	3.00
❏ 88996	Oasis/You Know What It's Like	1988	—	—	3.00
❏ 88996 [PS]	Oasis/You Know What It's Like	1988	—	—	3.00
❏ 89295	We Shall Overcome/We Shall Overcome	1987	—	—	3.00
❏ 89440	Let Me Be a Light to Shine/We Shall Overcome	1986	—	—	3.00
—With Howard Hewett					
❏ 89931	Our Love Will Stop the World/Only Heaven Can Wait (For Love)	1982	—	2.00	4.00
—A-side: With Eric Mercury					
❏ 89932	In the Name of Love/Happiness	1982	—	2.00	4.00

COLUMBIA

| ❏ 44050 | Si, Si, Senor/This Year | 1967 | 2.50 | 5.00 | 10.00 |
| ❏ 44448 | Cold, Cold Winter/If You Ever Leave Me Now | 1968 | 2.50 | 5.00 | 10.00 |

MCA

| ❏ 51126 | You Stopped Loving Me/Qual E Maundrinio | 1981 | — | 2.00 | 4.00 |
| ❏ 51173 | Lovin' You/Hittin' Me Where It Hurts | 1981 | — | 2.00 | 4.00 |

VIVA

| ❏ 29401 | This Side of Forever/Robbery Suspects | 1983 | — | 2.00 | 4.00 |
| —B-side by The Enforcers | | | | | |

7-Inch Extended Plays
ATLANTIC

❏ SD 7-7271	I'm the Girl/Conversation Love//River/When You Smile	1973	2.00	4.00	8.00
—Jukebox issue; small hole, plays at 33 1/3 rpm					
❏ SD 7-7271 [PS]	Killing Me Softly	1973	2.00	4.00	8.00

Albums
ATLANTIC

❏ SD 1569	Chapter Two	1970	2.50	5.00	10.00
❏ SD 1594	Quiet Fire	1971	2.50	5.00	10.00
❏ SD 7271	Killing Me Softly	1973	2.50	5.00	10.00
❏ SD 8230	First Take	1969	2.50	5.00	10.00
❏ SD 16013	Roberta Flack Featuring Donny Hathaway	1980	2.50	5.00	10.00
—Only two tracks feature Mr. Hathaway					
❏ SD 18131	Feel Like Makin' Love	1974	2.50	5.00	10.00
❏ SD 19149	Blue Lights in the Basement	1977	2.50	5.00	10.00
❏ SD 19154	Killing Me Softly	1978	2.00	4.00	8.00
—Reissue of 7271					
❏ SD 19186	Roberta Flack	1978	2.50	5.00	10.00
❏ SD 19317	The Best of Roberta Flack	1981	2.50	5.00	10.00
❏ SD 19354	I'm the One	1982	2.50	5.00	10.00
❏ 81916	Oasis	1988	2.50	5.00	10.00

MCA

| ❏ 5141 | Bustin' Loose | 1981 | 2.50 | 5.00 | 10.00 |

FLACK, ROBERTA, AND PEABO BRYSON
See PEABO BRYSON AND ROBERTA FLACK.

FLACK, ROBERTA, AND DONNY HATHAWAY
Also see each artist's individual listings.
45s
ATLANTIC

❏ 2808	You've Got a Friend/Gone Away	1971	—	2.50	5.00
❏ 2837	You've Lost That Lovin' Feeling/Be Real Black for Me	1971	—	2.50	5.00
❏ 2879	Where Is the Love/Mood	1972	—	2.50	5.00
❏ 3463	The Closer I Get to You/Love Is the Healing	1978	—	2.00	4.00
—B-side by Flack alone					
❏ 3661	Back Together Again/God Don't Like Ugly	1980	—	2.00	4.00

Albums
ATLANTIC

| ❏ SD 7216 | Roberta Flack and Donny Hathaway | 1972 | 2.50 | 5.00 | 10.00 |

FLAIRS, THE (1)
Also see CORNEL GUNTER; SHIRLEY GUNTER.
45s
ABC-PARAMOUNT

| ❏ 9740 | Aladdin's Lamp/Steppin' Out | 1956 | 10.00 | 20.00 | 40.00 |

FLAIR

❏ 1012	I Had a Love/She Wants to Rock	1953	100.00	200.00	400.00
❏ 1019	Tell Me You Love Me/You Should Care for Me	1953	100.00	200.00	400.00
❏ 1028	Love Me Girl/Gettin' High	1954	100.00	200.00	400.00
❏ 1041	Baby Wants/You Were Untrue	1954	100.00	200.00	400.00
❏ 1044	This Is the Night for Love/Let's Make with Some Love	1954	100.00	200.00	400.00
❏ 1051	Love Me, Love Me, Love Me/My Heart's Crying for You	1954	100.00	200.00	400.00
—As "The Chimes"					
❏ 1056	I'll Never Let You Go/Hold Me, Thrill Me, Chill Me	1955	100.00	200.00	400.00
❏ 1067	She Loves to Dance/My Darling, My Sweet	1955	100.00	200.00	400.00

Number	Title (A Side/B Side)	Yr	VG	VG+	NM
Albums					
CROWN					
❏ CLP-5356 [M]	The Flairs	1963	20.00	40.00	80.00

FLAMES, THE
More than one group. Also see THE HOLLYWOOD FLAMES.
45s
7-11

Number	Title (A Side/B Side)	Yr	VG	VG+	NM
❏ 2106	Keep On Smiling/Baby, Baby, Baby	1953	150.00	300.00	600.00
❏ 2107	Together/Baby, Pretty Baby	1953	125.00	250.00	500.00
BERTRAM					
❏ 203	I'll Never Let You Go/Crazy	1958	6.25	12.50	25.00
DOT					
❏ 15813	The Scramble (Part 1)/The Scramble (Part 2)	1958	3.75	7.50	15.00
FARGO					
❏ 1018	Making Time/Letti Lu	1961	5.00	10.00	20.00
HARLEM					
❏ 114	So Long My Darling/I'm Going to Try to Live My Life All Over	1960	1500.	2250.	3000.
—As "The Fabulous Flames"					
❏ 114	So Long My Darling/I'm Going to Try to Live My Life All Over	1960	200.00	400.00	800.00
—As "The Flames"					
SPIN					
❏ 101	Cryin' for My Baby/Starnge Land Blues	1952	125.00	250.00	500.00

FLAMING EMBER, THE
45s
FORTUNE

Number	Title (A Side/B Side)	Yr	VG	VG+	NM
❏ 869	Gone, Gone, Gone/You Can Count on Me	1965	15.00	30.00	60.00
HOT WAX					
❏ 6902	Mind, Body and Soul/Filet de Soul	1969	—	3.00	6.00
❏ 6907	Shades of Green/Don't You Wanna Wanna	1969	—	3.00	6.00
❏ 7003	Westbound #9/Why Don't You Stay	1970	—	3.00	6.00
❏ 7006	I'm Not My Brothers Keeper/Deserted Village	1970	—	3.00	6.00
❏ 7010	Stop the World and Let Me Off/Robot in a Robot's World	1970		3.00	6.00
❏ 7103	Sunshine/1200 Miles	1971	—	3.00	6.00
❏ 7109	If It's Good to You (Part 1)/If It's Good to You (Part 2)	1971		3.00	6.00
RIC-TIC					
❏ 129	Let's Have a Love-In (Vocal)/Let's Have a Love-In (Instrumental)	1967	5.00	10.00	20.00
—B-side credited to Wingate's Love-In Strings					
❏ 131	She's a Real Live Wire/Let's Have a Love-In (Instrumental)	1967	5.00	10.00	20.00
—B-side credited to Wingate's Love-In Strings					
❏ 132	Hey Mama/Let's Have a Love-In	1967	5.00	10.00	20.00
❏ 140	Bless You (My Love) (Instrumental)/Bless You (My Love) (Vocal)	1968	3.75	7.50	15.00
—B-side by Al Kent					
❏ 143	Children (Vocal)/Children (Instrumental)	1968	3.75	7.50	15.00
❏ 145	Tell It Like It Is/Just Like Children	1968	3.75	7.50	15.00
Albums					
HOT WAX					
❏ HA-702	Westbound #9	1970	3.75	7.50	15.00
❏ HA-705	Sunshine	1971	3.75	7.50	15.00

FLAMINGOS, THE
45s
CHANCE

Number	Title (A Side/B Side)	Yr	VG	VG+	NM
❏ 1133	If I Can't Have You/Someday, Somehow	1953	200.00	400.00	800.00
—Black vinyl					
❏ 1133	If I Can't Have You/Someday, Somehow	1953	1000.	1500.	2000.
—Red vinyl					
❏ 1140	That's My Desire/Hurry Home Baby	1953	150.00	300.00	600.00
—Black vinyl					
❏ 1140	That's My Desire/Hurry Home Baby	1953	375.00	750.00	1500.
—Red vinyl					
❏ 1145	Golden Teardrops/Carried Away	1953	250.00	500.00	1000.
—Black vinyl					
❏ 1145	Golden Teardrops/Carried Away	1953	750.00	1500.	3000.
—Red vinyl					
❏ 1149	Plan for Love/You Ain't Ready	1953	500.00	1000.	2000.
—Yellow and black label					
❏ 1149	Plan for Love/You Ain't Ready	1953	200.00	400.00	800.00
—Blue and silver label					
❏ 1154	Cross Over the Bridge/Listen to My Plea	1954	250.00	500.00	1000.
❏ 1162	Jump Children/Blues in the Letter	1954	150.00	300.00	600.00
CHECKER					
❏ 815	That's My Baby (Chick-a-Boom)/When	1955	20.00	40.00	80.00
❏ 821	I Want to Love You/Please Come Back Home	1955	20.00	40.00	80.00
❏ 830	I'll Be Home/Need Your Love	1956	20.00	40.00	80.00
❏ 837	A Kiss from Your Lips/Get With It	1956	20.00	40.00	80.00
❏ 846	The Vow/Shilly Dilly	1956	20.00	40.00	80.00
❏ 853	Just for a Kick/Would I Be Crying	1957	20.00	40.00	80.00
—Originals of above Checker singles are maroon with a checkerboard at top of label					
❏ 915	Whispering Stars/Dream of a Lifetime	1959	12.50	25.00	50.00
❏ 1084	Lover Come Back to Me/Your Little Guy	1964	3.75	7.50	15.00
❏ 1091	Goodnight Sweetheart/Does It Really Matter	1964	3.75	7.50	15.00
DECCA					
❏ 30335	The Ladder of Love/Let's Make Up	1957	7.50	15.00	30.00
❏ 30454	Helpless/My Faith in You	1957	7.50	15.00	30.00

Number	Title (A Side/B Side)	Yr	VG	VG+	NM
❏ 30687	Rock and Roll March/Where Mary Go	1958	7.50	15.00	30.00
❏ 30880	Kiss-A Me/Ever Since I Met Lucy	1959	7.50	15.00	30.00
❏ 30948	Jerri-Lee/Hey Now	1959	7.50	15.00	30.00
END					
❏ 1035	Please Wait for Me/That Love Is You	1958	15.00	30.00	60.00
❏ 1035	Lovers Never Say Goodbye/That Love Is You	1958	10.00	20.00	40.00
—A-sides of End 1035 are the same song, the titles were changed					
❏ 1040	I Shed a Tear at Your Wedding/But Not for Me	1959	7.50	15.00	30.00
❏ 1044	At the Prom/Love Walked In	1959	10.00	20.00	40.00
❏ 1046 [M]	I Only Have Eyes for You/Goodnight Sweetheart	1959	7.50	15.00	30.00
❏ 1046 [M]	I Only Have Eyes for You/At the Prom	1959	6.25	12.50	25.00
❏ 1046 [M]	I Only Have Eyes for You/Love Walked In	1959	6.25	12.50	25.00
❏ 1046 [S]	I Only Have Eyes for You/At the Prom	1959	12.50	25.00	50.00
—This B-side has been confirmed for the stereo version; others are not yet known					
❏ 1055 [M]	Yours/Love Walked In	1959	6.25	12.50	25.00
❏ 1055 [S]	Yours/Love Walked In	1959	12.50	25.00	50.00
❏ 1062	I Was Such a Fool/Heavenly Angel	1959	6.25	12.50	25.00
❏ 1065	Mio Amore/You, Me and the Sea	1960	6.25	12.50	25.00
❏ 1068	Nobody Loves Me Like You/Besame Mucho	1960	7.50	15.00	30.00
❏ 1068	Nobody Loves Me Like You/You, Me and the Sea	1960	6.25	12.50	25.00
❏ 1070	Besame Mucho/You, Me and the Sea	1960	6.25	12.50	25.00
❏ 1073	Mio Amore/At Night	1960	5.00	10.00	20.00
❏ 1079	Beside You/When I Fall in Love	1960	5.00	10.00	20.00
❏ 1081	Your Other Love/Lovers Gotta Cry	1960	5.00	10.00	20.00
❏ 1085	Thatr's Why I Love You/Ko Ko Mo	1961	5.00	10.00	20.00
❏ 1092	Time Was/Dream Girl	1961	5.00	10.00	20.00
❏ 1099	My Memories of You/I Want to Love You	1961	5.00	10.00	20.00
❏ 1111	It Must Be Love/I'm No Fool Anymore	1962	5.00	10.00	20.00
❏ 1116	For All We Know/Near You	1962	5.00	10.00	20.00
❏ 1121	I Know Better/Flame of Love	1963	5.00	10.00	20.00
❏ 1124	(Talk About) True Love/Come to My Party	1963	5.00	10.00	20.00
JULMAR					
❏ 506	Dealin' All the Way/Dealin' (Groovin' with Feelin')	1969	2.50	5.00	10.00
MERCURY					
❏ 72455	Temptation/Call Her on the Phone	1965	—	—	—
—Cancelled					
PARROT					
❏ 808	Dream of a Lifetime/On My Merry Way	1954	200.00	400.00	800.00
—Black vinyl					
❏ 808	Dream of a Lifetime/On My Merry Way	1954	400.00	800.00	1600.
—Red vinyl					
❏ 811	I Really Don't Want to Know/Get With It	1955	4000.	6000.	8000.
—Red vinyl					
❏ 811	I Really Don't Want to Know/Get With It	1955	2500.	2750.	5000.
—Black vinyl					
❏ 812	I'm Yours/Ko Ko Mo	1955	200.00	400.00	800.00
—Black vinyl					
❏ 812	I'm Yours/Ko Ko Mo	1955	400.00	800.00	1600.
—Red vinyl					
PHILIPS					
❏ 40308	Temptation/Call Her on the Phone	1965	3.75	7.50	15.00
❏ 40347	The Boogaloo Party/The Nearness of You	1965	3.75	7.50	15.00
❏ 40378	Brooklyn Boogaloo/Since My Baby Put Me Down	1966	3.75	7.50	15.00
❏ 40413	Itty Bitty Baby/She Shook My World	1966	3.75	7.50	15.00
❏ 40452	Koo Koo/It Keeps the Doctor Away	1967	3.75	7.50	15.00
❏ 40496	Oh Mary Don't You Worry/Do It, Do It	1967	3.75	7.50	15.00
POLYDOR					
❏ 14019	Buffalo Soldier (Long)/Buffalo Soldier (Short)	1970	2.50	5.00	10.00
❏ 14044	Straighten It Up (Get It Together)/Lover Come Back to Me	1970	2.50	5.00	10.00
RONZE					
❏ 111	Welcome Home/Gotta Have All Your Lovin'	1971	—	2.50	5.00
❏ 115	Someone to Watch Over Me/Heavy Hips	1972	—	2.50	5.00
❏ 116	Love Keeps the Doctor Away (Long)/Love Keeps the Doctor Away (Short)	1972		2.50	5.00
ROULETTE					
❏ 4524	Ol' Man River (Part 1)/Ol' Man River (Part 2)	1963	5.00	10.00	20.00
SKYLARK					
❏ 541	If I Could Love You/I Found a New Baby	197?		2.50	5.00
TIMES SQUARE					
❏ 102	A Lovely Way to Spend an Evening/Walking My Baby Back Home	1964	3.75	7.50	15.00
VEE JAY					
❏ 384	Golden Teardrops/Carried Away	1961	6.25	12.50	25.00
WORLDS					
❏ 103	Think About Me/(Instrumental)	1974	—	2.50	5.00
78s					
CHANCE					
❏ 1133	If I Can't Have You/Someday, Somehow	1953	75.00	150.00	300.00
❏ 1140	That's My Desire/Hurry Home Baby	1953	25.00	50.00	100.00
❏ 1145	Golden Teardrops/Carried Away	1953	75.00	150.00	300.00
❏ 1149	Plan for Love/You Ain't Ready	1953	62.50	125.00	250.00
❏ 1154	Cross Over the Bridge/Listen to My Plea	1954	62.50	125.00	250.00
❏ 1162	Jump Children/Blues in the Letter	1954	100.00	200.00	400.00
CHECKER					
❏ 815	That's My Baby (Chick-a-Boom)/When	1955	10.00	20.00	40.00
❏ 821	I Want to Love You/Please Come Back Home	1955	10.00	20.00	40.00
❏ 830	I'll Be Home/Need Your Love	1956	12.50	25.00	50.00
❏ 837	A Kiss from Your Lips/Get With It	1956	12.50	25.00	50.00
❏ 846	The Vow/Shilly Dilly	1956	12.50	25.00	50.00
❏ 853	Just for a Kick/Would I Be Crying	1957	15.00	30.00	60.00
END					
❏ 1035	Lovers Never Say Goodbye/That Love Is You	1958	200.00	400.00	800.00
❏ 1046	I Only Have Eyes for You/Goodnight Sweetheart	1959	175.00	350.00	700.00

F

Number	Title (A Side/B Side)	Yr	VG	VG+	NM
❏ 1046	I Only Have Eyes for You/At the Prom	1959	175.00	350.00	700.00

PARROT

Number	Title (A Side/B Side)	Yr	VG	VG+	NM
❏ 808	Dream of a Lifetime/On My Merry Way	1954	50.00	100.00	200.00
❏ 811	I Really Don't Want to Know/Get With It	1955	150.00	300.00	600.00
❏ 812	I'm Yours/Ko Ko Mo	1955	50.00	100.00	200.00

7-Inch Extended Plays
END

Number	Title (A Side/B Side)	Yr	VG	VG+	NM
❏ 205	Goodnight Sweetheart/Music Maestro Please//I Only Have Eyes for You/I'm in the Mood for Love	1959	50.00	100.00	200.00
❏ 205 [PS]	The Flamingos	1959	50.00	100.00	200.00

Albums
CHECKER

Number	Title (A Side/B Side)	Yr	VG	VG+	NM
❏ LP-1433 [M]	The Flamingos	1959	100.00	200.00	400.00
—Black label					
❏ LP-1433 [M]	The Flamingos	196?	37.50	75.00	150.00
—Blue label					
❏ LPS-3005 [R]	The Flamingos	1966	6.25	12.50	25.00
—Rechanneled reissue of 1433					

CONSTELLATION

Number	Title (A Side/B Side)	Yr	VG	VG+	NM
❏ CS-3 [M]	Collectors Showcase: The Flamingos	1964	25.00	50.00	100.00
—With hot pink lettering on cover					
❏ CS-3 [M]	Collectors Showcase: The Flamingos	1964	12.50	25.00	50.00
—With more restrained pink lettering on cover					

END

Number	Title (A Side/B Side)	Yr	VG	VG+	NM
❏ LP-304 [M]	Flamingo Serenade	1959	50.00	100.00	200.00
—Gray label with dog					
❏ LP-304 [M]	Flamingo Serenade	1959	100.00	200.00	400.00
—Black label with shadow print logo					
❏ LPS-304 [S]	Flamingo Serenade	1959	125.00	250.00	500.00
—Cover says "Stereo"					
❏ LPS-304 [S]	Flamingo Serenade	196?	50.00	100.00	200.00
—Cover says "Rechanneled Stereo" (only one track is)					
❏ LP-307 [M]	Flamingo Favorites	1960	25.00	50.00	100.00
❏ LPS-307 [R]	Flamingo Favorites	1960	17.50	35.00	70.00
❏ LP-308 [M]	Requestfully Yours	1960	25.00	50.00	100.00
❏ LPS-308 [R]	Requestfully Yours	1960	17.50	35.00	70.00
❏ LP-316 [M]	The Sound of the Flamingos	1962	25.00	50.00	100.00
❏ LPS-316 [R]	The Sound of the Flamingos	1962	17.50	35.00	70.00
❏ LPS-316 [S]	The Sound of the Flamingos	1962	50.00	100.00	200.00
—"Stereo" at upper right corner of front cover					

LOST-NITE

Number	Title (A Side/B Side)	Yr	VG	VG+	NM
❏ LLP-7 [10]	The Flamingos	1981	2.50	5.00	10.00
—Red vinyl					

PHILIPS

Number	Title (A Side/B Side)	Yr	VG	VG+	NM
❏ PHM 200206 [M]	Their Hits — Then and Now	1966	6.25	12.50	25.00
❏ PHS 600206 [S]	Their Hits — Then and Now	1966	7.50	15.00	30.00

RONZE

Number	Title (A Side/B Side)	Yr	VG	VG+	NM
❏ RLP-1001	The Flamingos Today	1972	3.75	7.50	15.00

SOLID SMOKE

Number	Title (A Side/B Side)	Yr	VG	VG+	NM
❏ 8018	Golden Teardrops	198?	2.50	5.00	10.00

FLAMINGOS, THE, AND THE MOONGLOWS
Albums
VEE JAY

Number	Title (A Side/B Side)	Yr	VG	VG+	NM
❏ LP-1052 [M]	The Flamingos Meet the Moonglows on the Dusty Road of Hits	1962	37.50	75.00	150.00
❏ VJLP-1052 [M]	The Flamingos Meet the Moonglows on the Dusty Road of Hits	198?	3.00	6.00	12.00
—Authorized reissue					

FLEMONS, WADE
Also see EARTH, WIND AND FIRE.
45s
VEE JAY

Number	Title (A Side/B Side)	Yr	VG	VG+	NM
❏ 295	Here I Stand/My Baby Likes to Rock	1958	7.50	15.00	30.00
❏ 309	Hold Me Close/You'll Remain Forever	1959	7.50	15.00	30.00
❏ 321	Slow Motion/Wailing by the River	1959	7.50	15.00	30.00
❏ 335	Goodnite, It's Time To Go/What's Happening	1959	7.50	15.00	30.00
❏ 344	Easy Lovin'/Woops Now	1960	7.50	15.00	30.00
❏ 368	Ain't That Lovin' You Baby/I'll Come Runnin'	1960	5.00	10.00	20.00
❏ 377	At the Party/Devil in Your Soul	1961	5.00	10.00	20.00
❏ 389	Please Send Me Someone to Love/Keep On Loving Me	1961	5.00	10.00	20.00
❏ 427	Half a Love/Welcome Stranger	1962	5.00	10.00	20.00
❏ 471	Ain't These Tears/I Hope, I Think, I Wish	1962	5.00	10.00	20.00
❏ 533	That Time of the Year/I Came Running	1963	3.75	7.50	15.00
❏ 578	When It Rains, It Pours/Watch Over Her	1964	3.75	7.50	15.00
—The Four Seasons sing backup on this record					
❏ 614	I Knew You When/That Other Place	1964	3.75	7.50	15.00
❏ 668	Where Did You Go Last Night/Empty Balcony	1965	3.00	6.00	12.00

Albums
VEE JAY

Number	Title (A Side/B Side)	Yr	VG	VG+	NM
❏ LP-1011 [M]	Wade Flemons	1959	37.50	75.00	150.00
—Maroon label					
❏ LP-1011 [M]	Wade Flemons	196?	20.00	40.00	80.00
—Black label					

FLOATERS, THE
45s
ABC

Number	Title (A Side/B Side)	Yr	VG	VG+	NM
❏ 12237	I Am So Glad I Took My Time/Take One Step at a Time	1976	—	2.00	4.00
❏ 12284	Float On/Everything Happens for a Reason	1977	—	2.00	4.00
❏ 12284 [PS]	Float On/Everything Happens for a Reason	1977	—	3.00	6.00
❏ 12314	You Don't Have to Say You Love Me/Take One Step at a Time	1977	—	2.00	4.00
❏ 12364	I Just Want to Be with You/Whatever Your Sign	1978	—	2.00	4.00
❏ 12399	Let's Try Love/The Time Is Now	1978	—	2.00	4.00

Albums
ABC

Number	Title (A Side/B Side)	Yr	VG	VG+	NM
❏ AB-1030	Floaters	1977	2.50	5.00	10.00
❏ AA-1047	Magic	1978	2.50	5.00	10.00

MCA

Number	Title (A Side/B Side)	Yr	VG	VG+	NM
❏ 3093	Into the Future	1979	2.50	5.00	10.00

FLOYD, EDDIE
Also see THE FALCONS.
45s
ATLANTIC

Number	Title (A Side/B Side)	Yr	VG	VG+	NM
❏ 2275	Hush Hush/Drive On	1965	3.00	6.00	12.00

LUPINE

Number	Title (A Side/B Side)	Yr	VG	VG+	NM
❏ 115	Set My Soul on Fire/Will I Be the One	1963	3.75	7.50	15.00

MALACO

Number	Title (A Side/B Side)	Yr	VG	VG+	NM
❏ 1032	Somebody Touch Me/Never Too Old	1976	—	2.50	5.00
❏ 1035	Chi-Town Hustler/In Paradise	1976	—	2.50	5.00
❏ 1039	Special Christmas Day/Mother, My Dear Mother	1976	—	2.50	5.00
❏ 1040	We Should Really Be in Love/I'll Never Be Loved	1977	—	2.50	5.00
—With Dorothy Moore					
❏ 1043	You're Gonna Walk Out on Me/Prove It to Me	1977	—	2.50	5.00

MERCURY

Number	Title (A Side/B Side)	Yr	VG	VG+	NM
❏ 73964	If You Really Love Me/It's Me	1977	—	2.00	4.00
❏ 74003	Disco Summer/Do It in the Water	1978	—	2.00	4.00

SAFICE

Number	Title (A Side/B Side)	Yr	VG	VG+	NM
❏ 336	Can This Be Christmas/I'll Be Home For Christmas	1964	3.00	6.00	12.00

STAX

Number	Title (A Side/B Side)	Yr	VG	VG+	NM
❏ 0002	I've Never Found a Girl (To Love Me Like You Do)/I'm Just the Kind of Fool	1968	—	3.00	6.00
❏ 0012	Bring It On Home to Me/The Sweet Things You Do	1968	—	3.00	6.00
❏ 0025	I've Got to Have Your Love/Girl I Love You	1969	—	3.00	6.00
❏ 0036	Don't Tell Your Mama (Where You've Been)/Consider Me	1969	—	3.00	6.00
❏ 0041	Never Never Let You Go/Ain't That Good	1969	—	3.00	6.00
—With Mavis Staples					
❏ 0051	Why Is the Wine Sweeter (On the Other Side)/People Get It Together	1969	—	3.00	6.00
❏ 0060	California Girl/The Woodman	1970	—	3.00	6.00
❏ 0072	My Girl/Laurie	1970	—	3.00	6.00
❏ 0077	The Best Years of My Life/My Little Girl	1970	—	3.00	6.00
❏ 0087	Oh How It Rained/When My Baby Said Goodbye	1971	—	3.00	6.00
❏ 0095	Blood Is Thicker Than Water/Have You Heard the Word	1971	—	3.00	6.00
❏ 0109	Yum Yum Yum (I Want Some)/Tears of Joy	1971	—	3.00	6.00
❏ 0134	You're Good Enough (To Be My Baby)/Spend All You Have on Love	1972	—	3.00	6.00
❏ 0158	Knock on Wood/Lay Your Loving on Me	1973	—	3.00	6.00
❏ 0171	Baby Lay Your Head Down (Gently on My Bed)/Check Me Out	1973	—	3.00	6.00
❏ 187	Things Get Better/Good Love, Bad Love	1966	3.00	6.00	12.00
❏ 0188	I Wanna Do Things for You/We've Been Through Too Much Together	1973	—	3.00	6.00
❏ 194	Knock on Wood/Got to Make a Comeback	1966	3.75	7.50	15.00
❏ 208	Raise Your Hand/I've Just Been Feeling Bad	1967	2.50	5.00	10.00
❏ 0209	Guess Who/Something to Write Home About	1974	—	3.00	6.00
❏ 0216	Soul Street/Highway Man	1974	—	3.00	6.00
❏ 219	Don't Rock the Boat/This House	1967	2.50	5.00	10.00
❏ 223	Love Is a Doggone Good Thing/Hey Now	1967	2.50	5.00	10.00
❏ 0232	Stealing Love/I Got a Reason to Smile	1974	—	3.00	6.00
❏ 233	On a Saturday Night/Under My Nose	1967	2.50	5.00	10.00
❏ 0239	Talk to the Man/I Got a Reason to Smile	1975	—	3.00	6.00
❏ 246	Holding On with Both Hands/Big Bird	1968	2.50	5.00	10.00
❏ 0251	I'm So Glad I Met You/I'm So Grateful	1975	—	3.00	6.00

Albums
MALACO

Number	Title (A Side/B Side)	Yr	VG	VG+	NM
❏ 6352	Experience	1977	3.00	6.00	12.00

STAX

Number	Title (A Side/B Side)	Yr	VG	VG+	NM
❏ 714 [M]	Knock on Wood	1967	17.50	35.00	70.00
❏ ST 714 [S]	Knock on Wood	1967	17.50	35.00	70.00
❏ STS-2002	I've Never Found a Girl	1968	7.50	15.00	30.00
❏ STS-2011	Rare Stamps	1969	6.25	12.50	25.00
❏ STS-2017	You've Got to Have Eddie	1969	6.25	12.50	25.00
❏ STS-2029	California Girl	1970	6.25	12.50	25.00
❏ STS-2041	Down to Earth	1971	6.25	12.50	25.00
❏ STS-3016	Baby Lay Your Head Down	1973	6.25	12.50	25.00
❏ STX-4122	Chronicle	1979	3.00	6.00	12.00
❏ STS-5512	Soul Street	1974	6.25	12.50	25.00
❏ MPS-8527	Soul Street	198?	2.50	5.00	10.00

FOR REAL
12-Inch Singles
A&M

Number	Title (A Side/B Side)	Yr	VG	VG+	NM
❏ 31458 0537 1	You Don't Wanna Miss (Massive Club Jam) (Massive Instrumental) (Down Tempo House Mix) (Silkadelic Mix) (Indasoul Mix)	1994	2.50	5.00	10.00

ROWDY

Number	Title (A Side/B Side)	Yr	VG	VG+	NM
❏ RDP 5079 [DJ]	Like I Do (Main Mix 4:08) (Acappella 3:40) (Instrumental 4:05)	1996	2.00	4.00	8.00

Number	Title (A Side/B Side)	Yr	VG	VG+	NM
❏ RDP 5086 [DJ]	Like I Do (4 versions)/Free	1996	—	3.50	7.00
❏ 35079	Like I Do (4 versions)/Free	1996	2.00	4.00	8.00

45s
ROWDY

❏ 35079	Like I Do/(Instrumental)	1996	—	—	3.00
❏ 35079 [PS]	Like I Do/(Instrumental)	1996	—	—	3.00
❏ 35097	The Saddest Song I Ever Heard/Like I Do	1997	—	—	3.00

FORD, DEE DEE
Also see DON GARDNER AND DEE DEE FORD.
45s
ABC-PARAMOUNT

❏ 10503	Just Like a Fool (I Keep Hopin')/Shoo-Fly Pie	1963	3.00	6.00	12.00

BRIAR

❏ 142	Good Morning Blues/I Just Can't Believe	1962	3.00	6.00	12.00

TODD

❏ 1049	Good Morning Blues/I Just Can't Believe	1959	3.75	7.50	15.00

FORD, FRANKIE
45s
ABC

❏ 11431	All Alone Am I/Blue Monday	1974	—	2.50	5.00

ACE

❏ 549	The Last One to Cry/Cheatin' Woman	1958	6.25	12.50	25.00
❏ 554	Sea Cruise/Roberta	1959	7.50	15.00	30.00
❏ 566	Alimony/Can't Tell My Heart (What to Do)	1959	6.25	12.50	25.00
❏ 580	Time After Time/Want to Be Your Man	1960	6.25	12.50	25.00
❏ 592	Chinatown/What's Goin' On	1960	6.25	12.50	25.00
❏ 592 [PS]	Chinatown/What's Goin' On	1960	12.50	25.00	50.00
❏ 8009	Ocean Full of Tears/Hour of Need	1963	3.75	7.50	15.00

BRIARMEADE

❏ 7600	I've Found Someone of My Own/Battle Hymn of the Republic	1976	—	2.50	5.00
❏ 7701	Desperado/Mardi Gras in New Orleans	1977	—	2.50	5.00
❏ 7901	Halfway to Paradise/I'm Proud of What I Am	1979	—	2.50	5.00

CINNAMON

❏ 752	When I Stop Dreamin'/I'm Proud of What I Am	1972	—	2.50	5.00
❏ 767	Talk to a Carpenter/When I Stop Dreamin'	1973	—	2.50	5.00

CONSTELLATION

❏ 101	Chinatown/Ocean Full of Tears	1963	3.75	7.50	15.00

DOUBLOON

❏ 101	Half a Crown/I Can't Face Tomorrow	1967	2.50	5.00	10.00

IMPERIAL

❏ 5686	You Talk Too Much/If You've Got Troubles	1960	3.75	7.50	15.00
❏ 5706	My Southern Belle/The Groom	1960	3.75	7.50	15.00
❏ 5735	Seventenn/Doghouse	1961	3.75	7.50	15.00
❏ 5749	Saturday Night Fish Fry/Love Don't Love Nobody	1961	3.75	7.50	15.00
❏ 5776	Let 'Em Talk/What Happened to You	1961	3.75	7.50	15.00
❏ 5819	They Said It Couldn't Be Done/A Man Only Does	1962	3.75	7.50	15.00

PAULA

❏ 351	Peace of Mind/I'm Proud of What I Am	1971	2.00	4.00	8.00

SYC

❏ 1227	Growing Pains/Ups and Downs	1982	—	2.00	4.00
❏ 1228	My Prayer/Gospel Ship	1983	—	2.00	4.00

7-Inch Extended Plays
ACE

❏ 105	(contents unknown)	1959	37.50	75.00	150.00
❏ 105 [PS]	The Best of Frankie Ford	1959	37.50	75.00	150.00

Albums
ACE

❏ LP 1005 [M]	Let's Take a Sea Cruise	1959	75.00	150.00	300.00

BRIARMEADE

❏ BR-5002	Frankie Ford	1976	3.00	6.00	12.00

FORMATIONS, THE
45s
BANK

❏ 1007	At the Top of the Stairs/Magic Melody	1968	7.50	15.00	30.00

MGM

❏ 13899	At the Top of the Stairs/Magic Melody	1968	2.50	5.00	10.00
❏ 13963	Love's Not Only for the Heart/Lonely Voice of Love	1968	5.00	10.00	20.00
❏ 14009	Don't Get Close/There's No Room	1968	3.00	6.00	12.00

FOUR AIMS, THE
See FOUR TOPS.

FOUR BARS, THE
45s
JOSIE

❏ 762	Grief by Day, Grief by Night/Hey Baby	1954	75.00	150.00	300.00
❏ 768	If I Give My Heart to You/Stop It! Quit It!	1954	75.00	150.00	300.00
❏ 783	Let Me Live/Why Do You Treat Me This Way	1955	150.00	300.00	600.00

REPUBLIC

❏ 7101	Memories of You/When Did You Leave Heaven	1954	150.00	300.00	600.00

FOUR BELLS, THE
45s
GEM

❏ 207	Please Tell It to Me/Long Way to Go	1953	200.00	400.00	800.00
❏ 220	Only a Miracle/My Tree	1954	200.00	400.00	800.00

FOUR BROTHERS AND A COUSIN
45s
JAGUAR

❏ 3003	Trust in Me/Whistle Stop Blues	1954	100.00	200.00	400.00
❏ 3005	Whispeing Wind/Can It Be	1954	125.00	250.00	500.00

FOUR BUDDIES, THE (1)
Vocal group from Baltimore.
45s
SAVOY

❏ 769	I Will Wait/Just to See You Smile Again	1951	100.00	200.00	400.00
❏ 769	I Will Wait/Just to See You Smile Again	1951	125.00	250.00	500.00
—As "The Four Buds"					
❏ 779	Don't Leave Me Now/Sweet Slumber	1951	100.00	200.00	400.00
❏ 789	My Summer's Gone/Why at a Time Like This	1951	75.00	150.00	300.00
❏ 817	Heart and Soul/Sin	1951	75.00	150.00	300.00
❏ 823	Window Eyes/Simply Say Goodbye	1951	75.00	150.00	300.00
❏ 845	You're Part of Me/Story Blues	1952	75.00	150.00	300.00
❏ 866	What's the Matter with Me/Sweet Tooth for My Baby	1952	75.00	150.00	300.00
❏ 888	My Mother's Eyes/Ooh Ow	1953	75.00	150.00	300.00
❏ 891	I'd Climb the Highest Mountain/I Wanna Know	1953	75.00	150.00	300.00
—B-side by Dolly Cooper					

FOUR CHEERS, THE
45s
END

❏ 1034	Fatal Charms of Love/Periwinkle Blue	1958	50.00	100.00	200.00

FOUR DEUCES, THE
45s
EVEREST

❏ 19311	Polly/Yella Shoes	1959	7.50	15.00	30.00

MUSIC CITY

❏ 790	W-P-L-J/Here Lies My Love	1955	37.50	75.00	150.00
—Maroon label					
❏ 790	W-P-L-J/Here Lies My Love	1955	10.00	20.00	40.00
—Black label					
❏ 796	Down It Went/Goose Is Gone	1955	15.00	30.00	60.00

FOUR DUKES, THE (1)
45s
DUKE

❏ 116	Crying in the Chapel/I Done Done It	1953	200.00	400.00	800.00

FOUR DUKES, THE (2)
45s
IMPERIAL

❏ 5653	Baby Won't You Please Come Home/John Henry	1960	7.50	15.00	30.00

FOUR ESQUIRES, THE
45s
CADENCE

❏ 1260	Three Things/The Sphinx Won't Tell	1955	5.00	10.00	20.00
❏ 1277	Adorable/Thunderbolt	1955	5.00	10.00	20.00

LONDON

❏ 1652	Look Homeward Angel/Santo Domingo	1956	6.25	12.50	25.00

PARIS

❏ 501	Song of April/Everyone's Sweet on My Sugar	1957	5.00	10.00	20.00
❏ 505	The Chopstick Rock/Never Look for Love	1957	5.00	10.00	20.00
❏ 509	Love Me Forever/I Ain't Been Right Since You Left	1957	5.00	10.00	20.00
❏ 512	Always and Forever/I Walk Down the Street	1958	5.00	10.00	20.00
❏ 515	All Around the Clock/The Big Dance	1958	5.00	10.00	20.00
❏ 520	Hideaway/Repeat After Me	1958	5.00	10.00	20.00
—With Rosemary June					
❏ 526	Follow Me/The Land of You and Me	1958	5.00	10.00	20.00
❏ 531	Lucky Old Sun/Non E Cosi	1959	5.00	10.00	20.00
❏ 535	Act Your Age/So Ends the Night	1959	5.00	10.00	20.00
❏ 539	Wonderful One/Wouldn't It Be Wonderful	1959	5.00	10.00	20.00
❏ 544	Make Them Mine/Peg O' My Heart	1960	5.00	10.00	20.00
❏ 549	Sweet Sixteen She'll Never Be/The Chopstick Rock	1960	5.00	10.00	20.00

PILGRIM

❏ 717	Follow Me/Summer Vacation	1956	6.25	12.50	25.00

TERRACE

❏ 7502	Can't Help Falling in Love/Merry-Go-Round of Love	1961	3.75	7.50	15.00
❏ 7516	The James Bond Theme (Double-O-Seven)/Summer Vacation	1963	6.25	12.50	25.00
—Betcha didn't know this had lyrics...					

FOUR EXCEPTIONS, THE
45s
PARKWAY

❏ 986	You Got the Power/A Sad Goodbye	1966	12.50	25.00	50.00

FOUR GRADUATES, THE
45s
CRYSTAL BALL

❏ 116	May I Have This Dance/Caught in a Lie	1978	—	2.00	4.00
❏ 119	Your Initials/Every Year About This Time	1978	—	2.00	4.00

F

Number	Title (A Side/B Side)	Yr	VG	VG+	NM
RUST					
❏ 5062	Picture of An Angel/A Lovely Way to Spend An Evening	1963	25.00	50.00	100.00
❏ 5084	Candy Queen/A Girl in Love	1964	45.00	90.00	180.00

FOUR HAVEN KNIGHTS, THE
45s

Number	Title (A Side/B Side)	Yr	VG	VG+	NM
ANGLETONE					
❏ 1066	In My Lonely Room/I'm Just a Dreamer	1958	12.50	25.00	50.00
❏ 1092	Just to Be in Love/Why Go On Pretending	1958	12.50	25.00	50.00
ATLAS					
❏ 1066	In My Lonely Room/I'm Just a Dreamer	1957	37.50	75.00	150.00
❏ 1092	Just to Be in Love/Why Go On Pretending	1957	37.50	75.00	150.00
JOSIE					
❏ 824	In My Lonely Room/I'm Just a Dreamer	1957	7.50	15.00	30.00

FOUR HOLIDAYS, THE
45s

Number	Title (A Side/B Side)	Yr	VG	VG+	NM
UNITED ARTISTS					
❏ 163	Who Can Say/Nobody Loves You Like-a Me	1959	7.50	15.00	30.00
VERVE					
❏ 10204	I Don't Wanna Go to School/Love Ya' Baby	1960	3.75	7.50	15.00

FOUR HUES, THE
45s

Number	Title (A Side/B Side)	Yr	VG	VG+	NM
CORAL					
❏ 61617	Ivory Tower/Sister Jenny	1956	7.50	15.00	30.00
CROWN					
❏ 159	Rock-a-Bye/Take Me Out of Your Heart	1955	10.00	20.00	40.00

FOUR IMPERIALS, THE
45s

Number	Title (A Side/B Side)	Yr	VG	VG+	NM
CHANT					
❏ 10067	My Girl/Teen Age Fool	1958	12.50	25.00	50.00
DIAL					
❏ 101	Valley of Tears/Time Out	1959	37.50	75.00	150.00
DOT					
❏ 15737	Lazy Bonnie/Let's Make a Scene	1958	6.25	12.50	25.00
FOX					
❏ 102	Give Me One More Chance/Look Up and Live	1958	20.00	40.00	80.00
LORELEI					
❏ 4444	Lazy Bonnie/Let's Make a Scene	1958	25.00	50.00	100.00
TWIRL					
❏ 2005	Santa's Got a Coupe de Ville/Seven Lonely Days	1960	6.25	12.50	25.00

FOUR JACKS, THE
45s

Number	Title (A Side/B Side)	Yr	VG	VG+	NM
FEDERAL					
❏ 12075	You Met a Fool/Goodbye Baby	1952	200.00	400.00	800.00
❏ 12087	The Last of the Good Rockin' Men/I'll Be Home Again	1952	125.00	250.00	500.00
MGM					
❏ 11179	You're in Love with Someone Else/Darling, Lonesome for You	1952	5.00	10.00	20.00

FOUR JEWELS, THE
45s

Number	Title (A Side/B Side)	Yr	VG	VG+	NM
CHECKER					
❏ 1039	Dapper Dan/Loaded with Goodies	1963	5.00	10.00	20.00
❏ 1069	Time for Love/That's What They Put Erasers on Pencils For	1964	5.00	10.00	20.00
START					
❏ 638	Loaded with Goodies/Fire	1963	10.00	20.00	40.00
❏ 638	Johnny Jealousy/Someone Special	1963	7.50	15.00	30.00
❏ 641	All That's Good/I Love Me Some You	1963	7.50	15.00	30.00
TEC					
❏ 3007	Baby It's You/She's Wrong for You Baby	1964	6.25	12.50	25.00

FOUR PENNIES, THE (1)
See THE CHIFFONS.

FOUR STUDENTS, THE
45s

Number	Title (A Side/B Side)	Yr	VG	VG+	NM
GROOVE					
❏ 0110	So Near and Yet So Far/Hot Rotten Soda Pop	1955	12.50	25.00	50.00

FOUR TOPS, THE
Also see DELORES CARROLL AND THE FOUR TOPS; LEVI STUBBS.
12-Inch Singles

Number	Title (A Side/B Side)	Yr	VG	VG+	NM
ARISTA					
❏ AD1-9705	Indestructible (4 versions)/Are You With Me	1988	2.00	4.00	8.00
CASABLANCA					
❏ NBD 20239	Let Me Set You Free (4:24) (same on both sides)	1981	2.50	5.00	10.00
RELIANT					
❏ REG 3691	I'm Here Again (2 versions)	1983	2.00	4.00	8.00

45s

Number	Title (A Side/B Side)	Yr	VG	VG+	NM
ABC					
❏ 12096	Seven Lonely Nights/I Can't Hold Out Much Longer	1975	—	2.00	4.00
❏ 12123	We All Gotta Stick Together/(It Would Almost) Drive Me Out of My Mind	1975	—	2.00	4.00

Number	Title (A Side/B Side)	Yr	VG	VG+	NM
❏ 12155	I'm Glad You Walked Into My Life/Mama, You're All Right with Me	1975	—	2.00	4.00
❏ 12214	Catfish/Look at My Baby	1976	—	2.00	4.00
❏ 12223	Look at My Baby/Catfish	1976	—	2.00	4.00
❏ 12236	Feel Free/I Know You Like It	1976	—	2.00	4.00
❏ 12267	Strung Out for Your Love/You Can't Hold Back on Love	1977	—	2.00	4.00
❏ 12315	Runnin' From Your Love/The Show Must Go On	1977	—	2.00	4.00
❏ 12427	Inside a Brokenhearted Man/H.E.L.P.	1978	—	2.00	4.00
❏ 12457	Just in Time/This House	1978	—	2.00	4.00
ABC DUNHILL					
❏ 4330	Keeper of the Castle/Jubilee with Soul	1972	—	2.50	5.00
❏ 4334	Guardian De Tu Castle/Jubilee with Soul	1972	—	2.50	5.00
❏ 4339	Ain't No Woman (Like the One I've Got)/The Good Lord Knows	1973	—	2.50	5.00
❏ 4354	Are You Man Enough/Peace of Mind	1973	—	2.50	5.00
❏ 4366	Sweet Understanding Love/Main Street People	1973	—	2.50	5.00
❏ 4377	I Just Can't Get You Out of My Mind/Am I My Brother's Keeper?	1973	—	2.50	5.00
❏ 4386	One Chain Don't Make No Prison/Light of Your Love	1974	—	2.50	5.00
❏ 15005	Midnight Flower/All My Love	1974	—	2.50	5.00
ARISTA					
❏ 9706	Indestructible/Are You With Me	1988	—	—	3.00
❏ 9706 [PS]	Indestructible/Are You With Me	1988	—	—	3.00
❏ 9766	If Ever a Love There Was/Indestructible	1988	—	—	3.00
—A-side with Aretha Franklin					
❏ 9766 [PS]	If Ever a Love There Was/Indestructible	1988	—	—	3.00
❏ 9801	Change of Heart/Loco in Acapulco	1989	—	—	3.00
CASABLANCA					
❏ 2338	When She Was My Girl/Something to Remember	1981	—	2.00	4.00
❏ 2344	Let Me Set You Free/From a Distance	1981	—	2.00	4.00
❏ 2345	Tonight I'm Gonna Love You All Over/I'll Never Leave Again	1981	—	2.00	4.00
❏ 2353	Sad Hearts/I Believe in You and Me	1982	—	2.00	4.00
CHESS					
❏ 1623	Could It Be You?/Kiss Me, Baby	1956	50.00	100.00	200.00
COLUMBIA					
❏ 41755	Ain't That Love/Lonely Summer	1960	15.00	30.00	60.00
❏ 43356	Ain't That Love/Lonely Summer	1965	6.25	12.50	25.00
GRADY					
❏ 012	If Only I Had Known/(B-side unknown)	1956	150.00	300.00	600.00
—As "The Four Aims"					
MOTOWN					
❏ 1062	Baby I Need Your Loving/Call On Me	1964	3.75	7.50	15.00
❏ 1069	Without the One You Love (Life's Not Worth While)/Love Has Gone	1964	3.00	6.00	12.00
❏ 1073	Ask the Lonely/Where Did You Go	1965	3.75	7.50	15.00
❏ 1073 [PS]	Ask the Lonely/Where Did You Go	1965	20.00	40.00	80.00
❏ 1076	I Can't Help Myself/Sad Souvenirs	1965	3.75	7.50	15.00
❏ 1081	It's the Same Old Song/Your Love Is Amazing	1965	3.75	7.50	15.00
❏ 1084	Something About You/Darling, I Hum Our Song	1965	3.75	7.50	15.00
❏ 1090	Shake Me, Wake Me (When It's Over)/Just As Long As You Need Me	1966	3.75	7.50	15.00
❏ 1096	Loving You Is Sweeter Than Ever/I Like Everything About You	1966	3.75	7.50	15.00
❏ 1098	Reach Out I'll Be There/Until You Love Someone	1966	3.75	7.50	15.00
❏ 1098 [PS]	Reach Out I'll Be There/Until You Love Someone	1966	20.00	40.00	80.00
❏ 1102	Standing in the Shadows of Love/Since You've Been Gone	1966	3.75	7.50	15.00
❏ 1104	Bernadette/I Got a Feeling	1967	3.00	6.00	12.00
❏ 1110	7-Rooms of Gloom/I'll Turn to Stone	1967	3.00	6.00	12.00
❏ 1113	You Keep Running Away/If You Don't Want My Love	1967	3.00	6.00	12.00
❏ 1119	Walk Away Renee/Your Love Is Wonderful	1968	3.00	6.00	12.00
❏ 1124	If I Were a Carpenter/Wonderful Baby	1968	3.00	6.00	12.00
❏ 1127	Yesterday's Dreams/For Once in My Life	1968	2.00	4.00	8.00
❏ 1132	I'm in a Different World/Remember When	1968	2.00	4.00	8.00
❏ 1147	What Is a Man/Don't Bring Back Memories	1969	2.00	4.00	8.00
❏ 1159	Don't Let Him Take Your Love from Me/The Key	1969	2.00	4.00	8.00
❏ 1164	It's All in the Game/Love (Is the Answer)	1970	2.00	4.00	8.00
❏ 1164 [PS]	It's All in the Game/Love (Is the Answer)	1970	5.00	10.00	20.00
❏ 1170	Still Water (Love)/Still Water (Peace)	1970	—	3.00	6.00
❏ 1175	Just Seven Numbers (Can Straighten Out My Life)/I Wish I Were Your Mirror	1971	—	3.00	6.00
❏ 1175 [PS]	Just Seven Numbers (Can Straighten Out My Life)/I Wish I Were Your Mirror	1971	5.00	10.00	20.00
❏ 1185	In These Changing Times/Right Before My Eyes	1971	—	3.00	6.00
❏ 1189	MacArthur Park (Part 2)/MacArthur Park (Part 1)	1971	—	3.00	6.00
❏ 1196	A Simple Game/L.A. My Town	1972	—	3.00	6.00
❏ 1198	I Can't Quit Your Love/Happy (Is a Bumpy Road)	1972	—	3.00	6.00
❏ 1210	(It's the Way) Nature Planned It/I'll Never Change	1972	—	3.00	6.00
❏ 1254	Hey Man-We Gotta Get You a Woman/How Can I Forget You	1973	—	—	—
—Unreleased					
❏ 1706	I Just Can't Walk Away/Hang	1983	—	—	3.00
❏ 1718	Make Yourself Right at Home/Sing a Song of Yesterday	1984	—	—	3.00
❏ 1790	Sexy Ways/Body and Soul	1985	—	—	3.00
❏ 1811	Don't Tell Me That It's Over/I'm Ready for Love	1985	—	—	3.00
❏ 1854	Hot Nights/Again	1986	—	—	3.00
RELIANT					
❏ 1691	I'm Here Again/(Instrumental)	1983	—	2.00	4.00
RIVERSIDE					
❏ 4534	Pennies from Heaven/Where Are You?	1962	18.75	37.50	75.00

Number	Title (A Side/B Side)	Yr	VG	VG+	NM
RSO					
❑ 1069	Back to School Again/Rock-a-Hula Luau	1982	—	—	3.00
❑ 1069 [PS]	Back to School Again/Rock-a-Hula Luau	1982	—	—	3.00

—B-side: by The Cast (from the movie Grease 2)

Number	Title (A Side/B Side)	Yr	VG	VG+	NM
TOPPS/MOTOWN					
❑ 5	I Can't Help Myself	1967	18.75	37.50	75.00
❑ 9	Baby I Need Your Loving	1967	18.75	37.50	75.00

—These are cardboard discs

Albums

Number	Title (A Side/B Side)	Yr	VG	VG+	NM
ABC					
❑ D-862	Night Lights Harmony	1975	3.00	6.00	12.00
❑ D-968	Catfish	1976	3.00	6.00	12.00
❑ D-1014	The Show Must Go On	1977	3.00	6.00	12.00
❑ AA-1092	At the Top	1978	3.00	6.00	12.00
ABC DUNHILL					
❑ DSX-50129	Keeper of the Castle	1972	3.00	6.00	12.00
❑ DSX-50144	Main Street People	1973	3.00	6.00	12.00
❑ DSX-50166	Meeting of the Minds	1974	3.00	6.00	12.00
❑ DSX-50188	Live & In Concert	1974	3.00	6.00	12.00
ARISTA					
❑ AL-8492	Indestructible	1988	2.00	4.00	8.00
CASABLANCA					
❑ NBLP 7258	Tonight!	1981	2.50	5.00	10.00
❑ NBLP 7266	One More Mountain	1982	2.50	5.00	10.00
COMMAND					
❑ CQD-40011 [Q]	Keeper of the Castle	1974	5.00	10.00	20.00
❑ CQD-40012 [Q]	Main Street People	1974	5.00	10.00	20.00
MCA					
❑ 27019	Greatest Hits	198?	2.50	5.00	10.00
MOTOWN					
❑ M5-114V1	Superstar Series, Vol. 14	1981	2.50	5.00	10.00
❑ M5-122V1	Four Tops	1981	2.00	4.00	8.00
—Reissue of 622					
❑ M5-149V1	Four Tops Reach Out	1981	2.00	4.00	8.00
—Reissue of 660					
❑ M5-209V1	The Four Tops' Greatest Hits	1981	2.00	4.00	8.00
—Reissue of 662					
❑ 622 [M]	Four Tops	1964	7.50	15.00	30.00
❑ MS-622 [S]	Four Tops	1964	10.00	20.00	40.00
❑ 634 [M]	Four Tops Second Album	1965	6.25	12.50	25.00
❑ MS-634 [S]	Four Tops Second Album	1965	7.50	15.00	30.00
❑ 647 [M]	4 Tops On Top	1966	6.25	12.50	25.00
❑ MS-647 [S]	4 Tops On Top	1966	7.50	15.00	30.00
❑ 654 [M]	Four Tops Live!	1966	6.25	12.50	25.00
❑ MS-654 [S]	Four Tops Live!	1966	7.50	15.00	30.00
❑ 657 [M]	4 Tops on Broadway	1967	6.25	12.50	25.00
❑ MS-657 [S]	4 Tops on Broadway	1967	7.50	15.00	30.00
❑ 660 [M]	Four Tops Reach Out	1967	7.50	15.00	30.00
❑ MS-660 [S]	Four Tops Reach Out	1967	6.25	12.50	25.00
❑ 662 [M]	The Four Tops Greatest Hits	1967	7.50	15.00	30.00
❑ MS-662 [S]	The Four Tops Greatest Hits	1967	5.00	10.00	20.00
❑ 669 [M]	Yesterday's Dreams	1968	7.50	15.00	30.00
❑ MS-669 [S]	Yesterday's Dreams	1968	5.00	10.00	20.00
❑ MS-675	Four Tops Now!	1969	5.00	10.00	20.00
❑ MS-695	Soul Spin	1969	5.00	10.00	20.00
❑ MS-704	Still Waters Run Deep	1970	5.00	10.00	20.00
❑ MS-721	Changing Times	1970	5.00	10.00	20.00
❑ M-740L	Four Tops Greatest Hits, Vol. 2	1971	5.00	10.00	20.00
❑ M-748L	Nature Planned It	1972	5.00	10.00	20.00
❑ M-764D [(2)]	The Best of the 4 Tops	1973	3.75	7.50	15.00
❑ M9-809A3 [(3)]	Anthology	1974	5.00	10.00	20.00
❑ 5224 ML	Still Waters Run Deep	1982	2.00	4.00	8.00
—Reissue of 704					
❑ 5258 ML	Four Tops Live!	1983	2.00	4.00	8.00
—Reissue of 654					
❑ 6066 ML	Back Where I Belong	1983	2.50	5.00	10.00
❑ 6130 ML	Magic	1985	2.50	5.00	10.00
WORKSHOP JAZZ					
❑ 217 [M]	Breakin' Through	1962	—	—	—

—This album is pictured on some early Motown inner sleeves, but is not known to exist

FOUR TUNES, THE

45s

Number	Title (A Side/B Side)	Yr	VG	VG+	NM
JUBILEE					
❑ 5128	Marie/I Gambled with Love	1953	10.00	20.00	40.00
❑ 5132	I Understand Just How You Feel/Sugar Lump	1953	7.50	15.00	30.00
❑ 5135	My Wild Irish Rose/Do-Do-Do It Again	1954	7.50	15.00	30.00
❑ 5152	Lonesome/The Greatest Feeling in the World	1954	7.50	15.00	30.00
❑ 5165	Don't Cry Darling/L'Amour Toujours, L'Amour	1954	7.50	15.00	30.00
❑ 5174	I Sold My Heart to the Junkman/Let Me Go Lover	1954	7.50	15.00	30.00
❑ 5174	I Sold My Heart to the Junkman/Good News	1954	7.50	15.00	30.00
❑ 5183	I Hope/I Close My Eyes	1955	6.25	12.50	25.00
❑ 5200	Tired of Waitin'/Time Out for Texas	1955	6.25	12.50	25.00
❑ 5212	Brooklyn Bridge/Three Little Chickens	1955	6.25	12.50	25.00
❑ 5218	You Are My Love/At the Steamboat River Ball	1955	6.25	12.50	25.00
❑ 5232	Rock and Roll Call/Our Love	1956	5.00	10.00	20.00
❑ 5239	I Gotta Go/Hold Me Closer	1956	5.00	10.00	20.00
❑ 5245	Far Away Places/Dancing with Tears in My Eyes	1956	5.00	10.00	20.00
❑ 5255	The Ballad of James Dean/Japanese Farewell	1956	5.00	10.00	20.00
❑ 5276	Cool Water/A Little on the Lonely Side	1957	5.00	10.00	20.00
❑ 6000	I Understand/Marie	196?	2.50	5.00	10.00
KAY-RON					
❑ 1000	I Want to Be Loved/Savannah Sings the Blues	1953	10.00	20.00	40.00
❑ 1005	I Understand/Just in Case You Change Your Mind	1953	10.00	20.00	40.00

Number	Title (A Side/B Side)	Yr	VG	VG+	NM
RCA VICTOR					
❑ 47-3881	Say When/Do I Worry?	1950	12.50	25.00	50.00
❑ 47-3967	How Can You Say That I Don't Care/Cool Water	1950	10.00	20.00	40.00
❑ 47-4102	Wishing You Were Here Tonight/The Last Roundup	1951	10.00	20.00	40.00
❑ 47-4198	Cool Water/Carry Me Back to the Lone Prairie	1951	10.00	20.00	40.00
❑ 47-4241	The Prisoner's Song/I Married An Angel	1951	7.50	15.00	30.00
❑ 47-4305	My Buddy/Early in the Morning	1951	7.50	15.00	30.00
❑ 47-4427	Tell Me Why/I'll See You in My Dreams	1951	10.00	20.00	40.00
❑ 47-4489	Greatest Song I Ever Heard/Come What May	1952	6.25	12.50	25.00
❑ 47-4663	I Wonder/Can I Say Any More?	1952	6.25	12.50	25.00
❑ 47-4828	They Don't Understand/Why Did You Do This	1952	6.25	12.50	25.00
❑ 47-4968	I Don't Want to Set the World On Fire/Let's Give Love Another Chance	1952	10.00	20.00	40.00
❑ 47-5532	Don't Get Around Much Anymore/Water Boy	1953	7.50	15.00	30.00
❑ 50-0008	You're Heartless/Careless Love	1949	50.00	100.00	200.00
—Gray label, orange vinyl					
❑ 50-0016	My Last Affair/I'm the Guy	1949	50.00	100.00	200.00
—Gray label, orange vinyl					
❑ 50-0042	I'm Just a Fool in Love/The Lonesome Road	1949	50.00	100.00	200.00
—Gray label, orange vinyl					
❑ 50-0072	There Goes My Heart/Am I Blue	1950	37.50	75.00	150.00
—Gray label, orange vinyl					
❑ 50-0085	Old Fashioned Love/Kentucky Babe	1950	37.50	75.00	150.00
—Gray label, orange vinyl					
❑ 50-0131	May That Day Never Come/Carry Me Back to the Lone Prairie	1951	37.50	75.00	150.00
—Gray label, orange vinyl					

7-Inch Extended Plays

Number	Title (A Side/B Side)	Yr	VG	VG+	NM
RCA VICTOR					
❑ EPA-586	(contents unknown)	1954	10.00	20.00	40.00
❑ EPA-586 [PS]	The Four Tunes	1954	10.00	20.00	40.00

Albums

Number	Title (A Side/B Side)	Yr	VG	VG+	NM
JUBILEE					
❑ LP-1039 [M]	12 x 4	1957	62.50	125.00	250.00

FOX, NORMAN, AND THE ROB ROYS

45s

Number	Title (A Side/B Side)	Yr	VG	VG+	NM
BACK BEAT					
❑ 499	Lover Doll/Little Star	197?	—	2.00	4.00
—Bootleg					
❑ 501	Tell Me Why/Audry	1957	20.00	40.00	80.00
—White label					
❑ 501	Tell Me Why/Audry	1957	10.00	20.00	40.00
—Red label					
❑ 508	Dance Girl Dance/My Dearest One	1958	20.00	40.00	80.00
CAPITOL					
❑ 4128	Dream Girl/Pizza Pie	1959	175.00	350.00	700.00
HAMMER					
❑ 544	Dream Girl/Pizza Pie	1958	7.50	15.00	30.00

FOXX, INEZ (AND CHARLIE)

45s

Number	Title (A Side/B Side)	Yr	VG	VG+	NM
DYNAMO					
❑ 102	Baby Take It All/Tightrope	1967	2.00	4.00	8.00
❑ 104	I Stand Accused/Guilty	1967	2.00	4.00	8.00
❑ 109	You Are the Man/Hard to Get	1967	2.00	4.00	8.00
❑ 112	(1-2-3-4-5-6-7) Count the Days/A Stranger I Don't Know	1967	2.00	4.00	8.00
❑ 117	Undecided/I Ain't Goin' for That	1968	2.00	4.00	8.00
❑ 119	Vaya Con Dios/Fellows in Vietnam	1968	2.00	4.00	8.00
❑ 126	Come On In/Baby Drop a Dime	1968	2.00	4.00	8.00
❑ 127	Baby Give It to Me/You Fixed My Heartache	1968	2.00	4.00	8.00
❑ 134	We Got a Chance to Be Free/Speed Ticket	1969	2.00	4.00	8.00
❑ 138	North Carolina (South Carolina)/I Got It	1970	2.00	4.00	8.00
❑ 144	You Shouldn't Have Set My Soul on Fire/Live for Today	1970	2.00	4.00	8.00
MUSICOR					
❑ 1201	No Stranger to Love/Come By Here	1966	2.50	5.00	10.00
SYMBOL					
❑ 20-001	Hurt by Love/Confusion	1964	3.00	6.00	12.00
❑ 201	La De Da, I Love You/Yankee Doodle Dandy	1964	3.00	6.00	12.00
❑ 204	Don't Do It No More/I Fancy You	1964	3.00	6.00	12.00
❑ 206	I Feel Alright/My Mama Told Me	1965	3.00	6.00	12.00
❑ 208	I've Come to One Conclusion/Down by the Seashore	1965	3.00	6.00	12.00
❑ 213	Hummingbird/If I Need Anyone	1966	3.00	6.00	12.00
❑ 919	Mockingbird/Jaybirds	1963	6.25	12.50	25.00
❑ 922	Broken Hearted Fool/He's the One You Love	1963	3.75	7.50	15.00
❑ 924	Hi Diddle Diddle/Talk with Me	1963	3.75	7.50	15.00
❑ 926	Ask Me/I See You My Love	1963	3.75	7.50	15.00
UNITED ARTISTS					
❑ XW516	Mockingbird/I Know (You Don't Love Me No More)	1974	—	2.00	4.00
—Reissue; B-side by Barbara George					
VOLT					
❑ 4087	Watch the Dog/You Hurt Me for the Last Time	1972	—	3.00	6.00
❑ 4093	One Woman's Man/The Time	1973	—	3.00	6.00
❑ 4096	Crossing Over That Bridge/You're Saving Me for a Rainy Day	1973	—	3.00	6.00
❑ 4101	I Had a Talk with My Man/The Lady, The Doctor and the Prescription	1973	—	3.00	6.00
❑ 4107	Circuit's Overloaded/There's a Hand That's Reading Out	1974	—	3.00	6.00

F

Number	Title (A Side/B Side)	Yr	VG	VG+	NM

Albums

DYNAMO

Number	Title (A Side/B Side)	Yr	VG	VG+	NM
❏ DM-7000 [M]	Come By Here	1967	7.50	15.00	30.00
❏ DM-7002 [M]	Inez and Charlie Foxx's Greatest Hits	1967	7.50	15.00	30.00
❏ DS-8000 [S]	Come By Here	1967	10.00	20.00	40.00
❏ DS-8002 [S]	Inez and Charlie Foxx's Greatest Hits	1967	10.00	20.00	40.00
❏ DS-8003	Swingin' Mockin' Band	1968	7.50	15.00	30.00

SUE

| ❏ LP-1027 [M] | Mockingbird | 1966 | 25.00 | 50.00 | 100.00 |

SYMBOL

| ❏ SYM-4400 [M] | Mockingbird | 1963 | 37.50 | 75.00 | 150.00 |

VOLT

| ❏ 6022 | Inez Foxx at Memphis | 1973 | 3.75 | 7.50 | 15.00 |

FRANKLIN, ARETHA

12-Inch Singles

ARISTA

Number	Title (A Side/B Side)	Yr	VG	VG+	NM
❏ SP-103 [DJ]	What a Fool Believes (Long Version) (Short Version)	1980	3.00	6.00	12.00
❏ SP-138 [DJ]	Jump To It (6:40) (3:58)/Just My Daydream	1982	2.50	5.00	10.00
❏ SP-147 [DJ]	Love Me Right (Dance Version) (Short Version)	1982	3.75	7.50	15.00
❏ CP 718	Jump to It (Extended Version 6:40) (Single Version 3:58)/Just My Daydream	1982	5.00	10.00	20.00
❏ 2240	Everyday People (People Remix) (Bonus Beats)/ (Everyday Remix) (People Dub)	1991	2.50	5.00	10.00
❏ ADP 2651 [(3) DJ]	A Deeper Love (9 versions)	1994	5.00	10.00	20.00
❏ ADP 2703 [DJ]	Jump To It (CJ's Masta Mix) (Gorda Dub) (Original Extended Version)	1994	3.75	7.50	15.00
❏ ADP 3455 [DJ]	A Rose Is Still a Rose (Without Intro) (With Intro)	1998	2.50	5.00	10.00
❏ ADP 3484 [(2) DJ]	A Rose Is Still a Rose (Hex Hector Club Mix 8:55) (Album Version 4:29)/(Johnny Vicious Dub 9:28) (Love to Infinity Kick Mix 7:11)//(Johnny Vicious Club Mix 10:44) (HEx Hector Drums 3:50)/(Love to Infinity Club Mix) (Love to Infinity Rhythm Radio Mix) (Album Version Instrumental)	1998	3.75	7.50	15.00
—Promo version of 13484					
❏ ADP 3486 [DJ]	A Rose Is Still a Rose (Yogi's Bystorm Remix) (Yogi's Bystorm Remix Instrumental) (Yogi's Bystorm Remix Acappella) (Desert Eagle Remix) (Desert Eagle Remix Instrumental) (Original Radio Edit)	1998	5.00	10.00	20.00
❏ ADP 3493 [DJ]	Here We Go Again (LP Version) (Instrumental) (Acappella)	1998	2.50	5.00	10.00
❏ ADP 3513 [(2) DJ]	Here We Go Again (Morales Classic Mix) (Razor-N-Guido Mix) (Morales Rascal Dub) (Razor-N-Guido Key Line) (Morales Def Zone Dub) (Mixologist Bass Mix) (Morales Bass Dub) (Album Version)	1998	6.25	12.50	25.00
❏ ADP 3514 [DJ]	Here We Go Again (Bump Mix) (Mixologist Bass Rap) (Acappella) (Bass Mix) (Instrumental)	1998	3.75	7.50	15.00
❏ AD1-9043	Get It Right (Long Version 6:22)/(Instrumental 6:31)	1983	2.50	5.00	10.00
❏ AD1-9355	Freeway of Love (Rock Mix)/(Radio Mix) (Extended Remix)	1985	2.00	4.00	8.00
❏ AD1-9411	Who's Zoomin' Who (Dance Mix) (Dub Mix)/ (Radio Mix) (Acappella Mix)	1985	2.00	4.00	8.00
❏ AD1-9454	Another Night (Dance Mix) (Dub)/(Radio Mix) (7" Edit)	1985	2.00	4.00	8.00
❏ AD1-9473	Ain't Nobody Ever Loved You (Remix 6:22) (Dub 6:59) (Single Edit 4:16) (Percapella)	1986	2.00	4.00	8.00
❏ AD1-9529	Jumpin' Jack Flash (LP Mix) (Street Mix)/(Street Mix Radio Edit) (Master Dub Mix) (Beat Dub)	1986	2.50	5.00	10.00
❏ AD1-9547	Jimmy Lee (Extended Remix 7:16) (Single Version 5:47) (Dub Mix 6:14)/Aretha Megamix	1986	2.00	4.00	8.00
❏ AD1-9560	I Knew You Were Waiting (For Me) (Edited Remix) (Percapella)/(LP Version) (Extended Remix)	1987	2.00	4.00	8.00
—With George Michael					
❏ AD1-9575	Rock-a-Lott (Street Mix) (Single Version) (Street Mix Radio Edit) (Dub Mix) (Acappella)	1987	2.00	4.00	8.00
❏ ADP 9682 [DJ]	Oh Happy Day/The Lord's Prayer//I've Been in the Storm Too Long/Packing Up, Getting Ready to Go	1988	3.75	7.50	15.00
❏ AD1-9851	It Isn't, It Wasn't, It Ain't Never Gonna Be (Extended Radio) (House Radio Mix)/(Hip Hop Radio) (New Jack Swing Dub)/Think '89	1989	2.00	4.00	8.00
—With Whitney Houston					
❏ ADP 9877 [DJ]	It Isn't, It Wasn't, It Ain't Never Gonna Be (Extended Radio Mix 6:12) (Dub Mix 6:20)/(After Hours Club Mix 7:35) (1989 Vogue Dub Mix 5:36)	1989	3.75	7.50	15.00
—With Whitney Houston					
❏ AD1-9885	Gimme Your Love (Single Edit) (Extended Remix)/Think '89	1989	2.00	4.00	8.00
—With James Brown					
❏ ADP 9906 [DJ]	Gimme Your Love (Single Edit) (Extended Remix)/Interview	1989	3.75	7.50	15.00
—With James Brown					
❏ 12702	Willing to Forgive/Jump to It (2 versions)	1994	2.50	5.00	10.00
❏ 13484 [(2)]	A Rose Is Still a Rose (Hex Hector Club Mix 8:55) (Album Version 4:29)/(Johnny Vicious Dub 9:28) (Love to Infinity Kick Mix 7:11)//(Johnny Vicious Club Mix 10:44) (HEx Hector Drums 3:50)/(Love to Infinity Club Mix) (Love to Infinity Rhythm Radio Mix) (Album Version Instrumental)	1998	3.00	6.00	12.00

Number	Title (A Side/B Side)	Yr	VG	VG+	NM
❏ 13503	Here We Go Again (Morales Classic Mix 9:25) (Album Version 3:30) (Razor-N-Guide Key Line 1:31) (Razor-N-Guido Mix 9:41) (Mixologist Bass Mix 3:26)	1999	2.50	5.00	10.00

45s

ARISTA

❏ 0569	United Together/Take Me With You	1980	—	2.00	4.00
❏ 0591	What a Fool Believes/Love Me Forever	1980	—	2.00	4.00
❏ 0600	Come to Me/School Days	1981	—	2.00	4.00
❏ 0624	Love All the Hurt Away/Whole Lotta Me	1981	—	2.00	4.00
—Aretha Franklin and George Benson					
❏ 0646	It's My Turn/Kind of Man	1981	—	2.00	4.00
❏ 0665	Livin' in the Streets/There's a Star for Everyone	1982	—	2.00	4.00
❏ 0699	Jump To It/Just My Daydream	1982	—	2.00	4.00
❏ 1023	Love Me Right/(It's Just) Your Love	1982	—	2.00	4.00
❏ 1043	This Is for Real/I Just Want to Make It Up to You	1983	—	2.00	4.00
❏ 2239	Everyday People/You Can't Take me for Granted	1991	—	2.50	5.00
❏ 9034	Get It Right/Giving In	1983	—	2.00	4.00
❏ 9095	Every Girl (Wants My Guy)/I Got Your Love	1983	—	2.00	4.00
❏ 9354	Freeway of Love/Until You Say You Love Me	1985	—	—	3.00
❏ 9354 [DJ]	Freeway of Love (Short) (Long)	1985	5.00	10.00	20.00
—Promo only on pink vinyl					
❏ 9354 [PS]	Freeway of Love/Until You Say You Love Me	1985	—	—	3.00
❏ 9410	Who's Zoomin' Who/Sweet Bitter Love	1985	—	—	3.00
❏ 9410 [PS]	Who's Zoomin' Who/Sweet Bitter Love	1985	—	—	3.00
❏ 9453	Another Night/Kind of Man	1986	—	—	3.00
❏ 9474	Ain't Nobody Ever Loved You/Push	1986	—	—	3.00
—B-side with Peter Wolf					
❏ 9528	Jumpin' Jack Flash/Integrity	1986	—	2.50	5.00
—Original stock pressings on clear vinyl					
❏ 9528	Jumpin' Jack Flash/Integrity	1986	—	—	3.00
—Second pressing on black vinyl					
❏ 9528 [DJ]	Jumpin' Jack Flash (Long Version) (Short Version)	1986	2.50	5.00	10.00
—Promo on clear vinyl					
❏ 9528 [PS]	Jumpin' Jack Flash/Integrity	1986	—	2.50	5.00
—Picture sleeve with clear vinyl pressing lists catalog number as ALC-9528					
❏ 9528 [PS]	Jumpin' Jack Flash/Integrity	1986	—	—	3.00
—Picture sleeve with black vinyl pressing lists catalog number as AL-9528					
❏ 9541	Jumpin' Jack Flash/(Street Mix Radio Edit)	1986	—	2.00	4.00
❏ 9541 [PS]	Jumpin' Jack Flash/(Street Mix Radio Edit)	1986	—	2.50	5.00
❏ 9546	Jimmy Lee/If You Need My Love Tonight	1986	—	2.00	4.00
❏ 9546 [DJ]	Jimmy Lee (Short Version 4:10)/(Long Version 5:47)	1986	—	2.00	4.00
❏ 9546 [PS]	Jimmy Lee/If You Need My Love Tonight	1986	—	2.00	4.00
—B-side by Larry Graham					
❏ 9557	Jimmy Lee/An Angel Cries	1986	—	—	3.00
❏ 9557 [PS]	Jimmy Lee/An Angel Cries	1986	—	—	3.00
❏ 9559	I Knew You Were Waiting (For Me)/(Instrumental)	1987	—	—	3.00
—With George Michael					
❏ 9559 [PS]	I Knew You Were Waiting (For Me)/(Instrumental)	1987	—	—	3.00
—With George Michael					
❏ 9574	Rock-A-Lott/Look to the Rainbow	1987	—	—	3.00
❏ 9574 [PS]	Rock-A-Lott/Look to the Rainbow	1987	—	—	3.00
❏ 9623	If You Need My Love Tonight/He'll Come Along	1987	—	—	3.00
—A-side with Larry Graham					
❏ 9672	Oh Happy Day/The Lord's Prayer	1988	—	2.50	5.00
❏ 9809	Through the Storm/Come to Me	1989	—	—	3.00
—A-side with Elton John					
❏ 9809 [PS]	Through the Storm/Come to Me	1989	—	—	3.00
❏ 9850	It Isn't, It Wasn't, It Ain't Never Gonna Be/If Ever a Love There Was	1989	—	—	3.00
—A-side with Whitney Houston; B-side with the Four Tops					
❏ 9850 [PS]	It Isn't, It Wasn't, It Ain't Never Gonna Be/If Ever a Love There Was	1989	—	—	3.00
—A-side with Whitney Houston; B-side with the Four Tops					
❏ 9884	Gimme Your Love/Think	1989	—	—	3.00
—With James Brown					
❏ 9884 [PS]	Gimme Your Love/Think	1989	—	—	3.00
—With James Brown					

ATLANTIC

❏ 2386	I Never Loved a Man (The Way I Love You)/Do Right Woman, Do Right Man	1967	2.50	5.00	10.00
❏ 2403	Respect/Dr. Feelgood	1967	2.50	5.00	10.00
❏ 2427	Baby I Love You/Going Down Now	1967	2.50	5.00	10.00
❏ 2441	(You Make Me Feel Like) A Natural Woman/Baby, Baby, Baby	1967	2.50	5.00	10.00
❏ 2464	Chain of Fools/Prove It	1967	2.50	5.00	10.00
❏ 2486	(Sweet Sweet Baby) Since You've Been Gone/ Ain't No Way	1968	2.50	5.00	10.00
❏ 2518	Think/You Send Me	1968	2.50	5.00	10.00
❏ 2546	I Say a Little Prayer/The House That Jack Built	1968	2.50	5.00	10.00
❏ 2574	See Saw/My Song	1968	2.00	4.00	8.00
❏ 2603	The Weight/Tracks of My Tears	1969	2.00	4.00	8.00
❏ 2619	I Can't See Myself Leaving You/Gentle On My Mind	1969	2.00	4.00	8.00
❏ 2650	Share Your Love with Me/Pledging My Love-The Clock	1969	2.00	4.00	8.00
❏ 2683	Eleanor Rigby/It Ain't Fair	1969	2.00	4.00	8.00
❏ 2706	Call Me/Son of a Preacher Man	1970	2.00	4.00	8.00
❏ 2731	Spirit in the Dark/The Thrill Is Gone	1970	2.00	4.00	8.00
❏ 2751	Don't Play That Song/Let It Be	1970	2.00	4.00	8.00
❏ 2772	Border Song (Holy Moses)/You and Me	1970	2.00	4.00	8.00
❏ 2787	You're All I Need to Get By/Pullin'	1971	—	3.00	6.00
❏ 2796	Bridge Over Troubled Water/Brand New Me	1971	—	3.00	6.00

The most sought-after 45 by the Five Keys is the blue-label Aladdin edition of "Red Sails in the Sunset." Near-mint copies rarely, if ever, appear; if one does, it could sell for as much as $6,000.

The Five Satins, of "In the Still of the Nite" and "To the Aisle" fame, released an album called *The 5 Satins Sing* on Ember. The label also issued it as three separate EPs, of which this is Volume 3.

One number after Elvis Presley's "Mystery Train" came the Five Tinos' "Sitting by My Window" on Sun 222. And like the Elvis records before it, near-mint copies of this one can fetch over $1,000.

Any 45 on the Chicago-based Chance label is hard to find. If it's by the Flamingos, one of the greatest of all the R&B vocal groups, that makes it even more difficult to find. Here's "That's My Desire," from 1953.

The original edition of the 1955 song "W-P-L-J" by the 4 Deuces was on a maroon Music City label. A later pressing, when it became popular in New York during the early-1960s doo-wop revival, was on a black label.

Among other classics, *Aretha Now*, released in 1968, contains Aretha Franklin's classic recordings of "Think," "See Saw" and "I Say a Little Prayer."

Number	Title (A Side/B Side)	Yr	VG	VG+	NM
❑ 2817	Spanish Harlem/Lean On Me	1971	—	3.00	6.00
❑ 2838	Rock Steady/Oh Me Oh My (I'm a Fool for You Baby)	1971	—	3.00	6.00
❑ 2866	Day Dreaming/I've Been Loving You Too Long	1972	—	3.00	6.00
❑ 2883	All the King's Horses/April Fools	1972	—	3.00	6.00
❑ 2901	Wholy Holy/Give Yourself to Jesus	1972	—	3.00	6.00
❑ 2941	Master of Eyes (The Deepness of Your Eyes)/ Moody's Mood for You	1973	—	3.00	6.00
❑ 2969	Angel/Hey Hey Now (Sister from Texas)	1973	—	3.00	6.00
❑ 2995	Until You Come Back to Me (That's What I'm Gonna Do)/If You Don't Think	1973	—	3.00	6.00
❑ 2999	I'm in Love/Oh Baby	1974	—	3.00	6.00
❑ 3200	Ain't Nothing Like the Real Thing/Eight Days a Week	1974	—	3.00	6.00
❑ 3224	Without Love/Don't Go Breaking My Heart	1974	—	3.00	6.00
❑ 3249	With Everything I Feel in Me/Sing It Again, Say It Again	1975	—	3.00	6.00
❑ 3289	Mr. D.J. (5 for the D.J.)/As Long As You Are There	1975	—	3.00	6.00
❑ 3311	You/Without You	1975	—	3.00	6.00
❑ 3326	Something He Can Feel/Loving You, Baby	1976	—	3.00	6.00
❑ 3358	Jump/Hooked on Your Love	1976	—	3.00	6.00
❑ 3373	Look Into Your Heart/Rock with Me	1977	—	3.00	6.00
❑ 3393	Break It To Me Gently/Meadows of Springtime	1977	—	3.00	6.00
❑ 3418	When I Think About You/Touch Me Up	1978	—	3.00	6.00
❑ 3468	Almighty Fire (Woman of the Future)/I'm Your Speed	1978	—	3.00	6.00
❑ 3495	More Than Just a Joy/This You Can Believe	1979	—	3.00	6.00
❑ 3605	Ladies Only/What If I Should Ever Need You	1979	—	2.50	5.00
❑ 3632	Half a Love/Only Star	1979	—	2.50	5.00
CHECKER					
❑ 861	Never Grow Old/You Grow Closer	1957	5.00	10.00	20.00
❑ 941	Precious Lord, Part 1/Precious Lord, Part 2	1960	3.75	7.50	15.00
COLUMBIA					
❑ S7 31202 [S]	Won't Be Long/Love Is the Only Thing	1961	3.00	6.00	12.00
❑ S7 31203 [S]	Sweet Lover/All Night Long	1961	3.00	6.00	12.00
❑ S7 31204 [S]	Who Needs You?/Right Now	1961	3.00	6.00	12.00
❑ S7 31205 [S]	Maybe I'm a Fool/It Ain't Necessarily So	1961	3.00	6.00	12.00
❑ S7 31206 [S]	(Blue) By Myself/Today I Sing the Blues	1961	3.00	6.00	12.00
—The above five are "Stereo Seven" 33 1/3 rpm jukebox singles from set "JS 7-38" entitled "Aretha (with the Ray Bryant Combo)"					
❑ 41793	Today I Sing the Blues/Love Is the Only Thing	1960	3.00	6.00	12.00
❑ 41923	Won't Be Long/Right Now	1961	3.00	6.00	12.00
❑ 41965	Are You Sure/Maybe I'm a Fool	1961	3.00	6.00	12.00
❑ 42157	Rock-A-Bye Your Baby with a Dixie Melody/ Operation Heartbreak	1961	3.00	6.00	12.00
❑ 42266	I Surrender, Dear/Rough Lover	1962	2.50	5.00	10.00
❑ 42266 [PS]	I Surrender, Dear/Rough Lover	1962	7.50	15.00	30.00
❑ 42456	Don't Cry, Baby/Without the One You Love	1962	2.50	5.00	10.00
❑ 42456 [PS]	Don't Cry, Baby/Without the One You Love	1962	7.50	15.00	30.00
❑ 42520	Try a Little Tenderness/Just for a Thrill	1962	2.50	5.00	10.00
❑ 42520 [PS]	Try a Little Tenderness/Just for a Thrill	1962	6.25	12.50	25.00
❑ 42625	Trouble in Mind/God Bless the Child	1962	2.50	5.00	10.00
❑ 42796	Here's Where I Came In/Say It Isn't So	1963	2.50	5.00	10.00
❑ 42796 [PS]	Here's Where I Came In/Say It Isn't So	1963	7.50	15.00	30.00
❑ 42874	Skylark/You've Got Her	1963	2.50	5.00	10.00
❑ 42933	Johnny/Kissin' by the Mistletoe	1963	2.50	5.00	10.00
❑ 43009	Soulville/Evil Gal Blues	1964	2.50	5.00	10.00
❑ 43113	Runnin' Out of Fools/It's Just a Matter of Time	1964	2.50	5.00	10.00
❑ 43177	Winter Wonderland/The Christmas Song (Chestnuts Roasting on an Open Fire)	1964	2.50	5.00	10.00
❑ 43203	Can't You Just See Me/Little Miss Raggedy Ann	1965	2.50	5.00	10.00
❑ 43241	One Step Ahead/I Can't Wait Until I See My Baby's Face	1965	2.50	5.00	10.00
❑ 43333	(No, No) I'm Losing You/Sweet Bitter Love	1965	2.50	5.00	10.00
❑ 43442	You Made Me Love You/There Is No Greater Love	1966	2.50	5.00	10.00
❑ 43515	Hands Off/Tighten Up Your Tie, Button Up Your Jacket	1966	2.50	5.00	10.00
❑ 43637	Until You Were Gone/Swanee	1966	2.50	5.00	10.00
❑ 43827	Cry Like a Baby/Swanee	1966	2.50	5.00	10.00
❑ 44181	Until You Were Gone/Lee Cross	1967	2.50	5.00	10.00
❑ 44270	Take a Look/Follow Your Heart	1967	2.50	5.00	10.00
❑ 44381	Mockingbird/A Mother's Love	1967	2.00	4.00	8.00
❑ 44441	Soulville/If Ever I Would Leave You	1968	2.00	4.00	8.00
❑ 44851	Friendly Persuasion/Jim	1969	2.00	4.00	8.00
❑ 44951	Today I Sing the Blues/People	1969	2.00	4.00	8.00
JVB					
❑ 47	Never Grow Old/You Grow Closer	1957	7.50	15.00	30.00
❑ 75	Precious Lord, Part 1/Precious Lord, Part 2	1959	7.50	15.00	30.00
PHILCO-FORD					
❑ HP-24	Respect/Soul Serenade	1968	6.25	12.50	25.00
—4-inch plastic "Hip Pocket Record" with color sleeve					

7-Inch Extended Plays

Number	Title (A Side/B Side)	Yr	VG	VG+	NM
ATLANTIC					
❑ A 1025 [DJ]	Precious Lord, Take My Hand/You've Got a Friend/Precious Memories//Wholy❑ Holy/ Mary, Don't You Weep	1972	3.75	7.50	15.00
—Mono; white label promo sampler					
❑ A 1025 [PS]	Amazing Grace	1972	5.00	10.00	20.00
❑ SD 7-7265	Somewhere/Moody's Mood//Hey Now Hey/So Swell When You're Well	1973	2.50	5.00	10.00
—Jukebox issue; small hole, plays at 33 1/3 rpm					
❑ SD 7-7265 [PS]	Hey Now Hey	1973	2.50	5.00	10.00
❑ SD 7-8207	Satisfaction/Baby, I Love You/Groovin'//Soul Serenade/Dr. Feelgood	196?	3.75	7.50	15.00
—Jukebox issue; small hole, plays at 33 1/3 rpm					
❑ SD 7-8207 [PS]	Aretha in Paris	196?	3.75	7.50	15.00
❑ SD 7-8248	Let It Be/The Weight/Eleanor Rigby//This Girl's in Love with You/Share Your Love with Me	1970	3.00	6.00	12.00
—Jukebox issue; small hole, plays at 33 1/3 rpm					
❑ SD 7-8248 [PS]	This Girl's in Love with You	1970	3.00	6.00	12.00

Albums

Number	Title	Yr	VG	VG+	NM
ARISTA					
❑ AL8-8019	Get It Right	1983	2.50	5.00	10.00
❑ AL8-8286	Who's Zoomin' Who	1985	2.50	5.00	10.00
❑ AL-8344	Jump To It	1985	2.00	4.00	8.00
—Budget-line reissue					
❑ AL-8368	Love All the Hurt Away	1985	2.00	4.00	8.00
—Budget-line reissue					
❑ AL-8442	Aretha	1986	2.50	5.00	10.00
—Different album than 9538					
❑ A2L-8497 [(2)]	One Lord, One Faith, One Baptism	1987	5.00	10.00	20.00
❑ AL-8572	Through the Storm	1989	2.50	5.00	10.00
❑ AL-9538	Aretha	1980	2.50	5.00	10.00
❑ AL-9552	Love All the Hurt Away	1981	2.50	5.00	10.00
❑ AL-9602	Jump To It	1982	2.50	5.00	10.00
ATLANTIC					
❑ SD 2-906 [(2)]	Amazing Grace	1972	5.00	10.00	20.00
❑ SD 7205	Aretha Live at Fillmore West	1971	3.75	7.50	15.00
❑ SD 7213	Yoing, Gifted & Black	1972	3.75	7.50	15.00
❑ SD 7265	Hey Now Hey (The Other Side of the Sky)	1973	3.00	6.00	12.00
❑ SD 7292	Let Me in Your Life	1974	3.00	6.00	12.00
❑ 8139 [M]	I Never Loved a Man the Way I Love You	1967	6.25	12.50	25.00
❑ SD 8139	I Never Loved a Man the Way I Love You	1969	3.00	6.00	12.00
—Green and red label					
❑ SD 8139 [S]	I Never Loved a Man the Way I Love You	1967	5.00	10.00	20.00
—Green and blue label					
❑ 8150 [M]	Aretha Arrives	1967	6.25	12.50	25.00
❑ SD 8150	Aretha Arrives	1969	3.00	6.00	12.00
—Green and red label					
❑ SD 8150 [S]	Aretha Arrives	1967	5.00	10.00	20.00
—Green and blue label					
❑ 8176 [M]	Aretha: Lady Soul	1968	7.50	15.00	30.00
❑ SD 8176	Aretha: Lady Soul	1969	3.00	6.00	12.00
—Green and red label					
❑ SD 8176 [S]	Aretha: Lady Soul	1968	5.00	10.00	20.00
—Green and blue label					
❑ SD 8186	Aretha Now	1968	5.00	10.00	20.00
—Green and blue label					
❑ SD 8186	Aretha Now	1969	3.00	6.00	12.00
—Green and red label					
❑ SD 8207	Aretha in Paris	1968	3.75	7.50	15.00
❑ 8212 [M]	Aretha Franklin: Soul '69	1969	12.50	25.00	50.00
—White label promo; no stock copies in mono					
❑ SD 8212	Aretha Franklin: Soul '69	1969	3.75	7.50	15.00
❑ SD 8227	Aretha's Gold	1969	3.75	7.50	15.00
❑ SD 8248	This Girl's in Love with You	1970	3.75	7.50	15.00
❑ SD 8265	Spirit in the Dark	1970	3.75	7.50	15.00
❑ SD 8295	Aretha's Greatest Hits	1971	3.75	7.50	15.00
❑ QD 8305 [Q]	The Best of Aretha Franklin	1974	5.00	10.00	20.00
❑ SD 18116	With Everything I Feel in Me	1974	3.00	6.00	12.00
❑ SD 18151	You	1975	3.00	6.00	12.00
❑ SD 18176	Sparkle	1976	3.00	6.00	12.00
❑ SD 18204	Ten Years of Gold	1976	3.00	6.00	12.00
❑ SD 19102	Sweet Passion	1977	3.00	6.00	12.00
❑ SD 19161	Almighty Fire	1978	3.00	6.00	12.00
❑ SD 19248	La Diva	1979	3.00	6.00	12.00
❑ 81230	Aretha's Jazz	1984	2.50	5.00	10.00
❑ 81280	The Best of Aretha Franklin	1985	2.50	5.00	10.00
❑ 81668 [(2)]	30 Greatest Hits	1986	3.75	7.50	15.00
❑ STAO-95151	Hey Now Hey (The Other Side of the Sky)	1973	3.75	7.50	15.00
—Capitol Record Club edition					
CHECKER					
❑ 10009 [M]	Songs of Faith	1965	125.00	250.00	500.00
—Original issue of this album; cover has Aretha sitting at a piano					
❑ 10009 [M]	Gospel Soul	1967	5.00	10.00	20.00
—Reissue with new title and cover					
COLUMBIA					
❑ GP 4 [(2)]	Two All-Time Great Albums in One Great Package	196?	6.25	12.50	25.00
—Contains CS 9081 and CS 9429					
❑ CL 1612 [M]	Aretha	1961	12.50	25.00	50.00
—Red and black label with six "eye" logos					
❑ CL 1612 [M]	Aretha	1963	5.00	10.00	20.00
—"Guaranteed High Fidelity" on label					
❑ CL 1612 [M]	Aretha	1965	3.75	7.50	15.00
—"360 Sound Mono" on label					
❑ CL 1761 [M]	The Electrifying Aretha Franklin	1962	10.00	20.00	40.00
—Red and black label with six "eye" logos					
❑ CL 1761 [M]	The Electrifying Aretha Franklin	1963	5.00	10.00	20.00
—"Guaranteed High Fidelity" on label					
❑ CL 1761 [M]	The Electrifying Aretha Franklin	1965	3.75	7.50	15.00
—"360 Sound Mono" on label					
❑ CL 1876 [M]	The Tender, The Moving, The Swinging Aretha Franklin	1962	10.00	20.00	40.00
—Red and black label with six "eye" logos					
❑ CL 1876 [M]	The Tender, The Moving, The Swinging Aretha Franklin	1963	5.00	10.00	20.00
—"Guaranteed High Fidelity" on label					

Number	Title (A Side/B Side)	Yr	VG	VG+	NM
❑ CL 1876 [M]	The Tender, The Moving, The Swinging Aretha Franklin	1965	3.75	7.50	15.00
—"360 Sound Mono" on label					
❑ CL 2079 [M]	Laughing on the Outside	1963	5.00	10.00	20.00
—"Guaranteed High Fidelity" on label					
❑ CL 2079 [M]	Laughing on the Outside	1965	3.75	7.50	15.00
—"360 Sound Mono" on label					
❑ CL 2163 [M]	Unforgettable	1964	5.00	10.00	20.00
—"Guaranteed High Fidelity" on label					
❑ CL 2163 [M]	Unforgettable	1965	3.75	7.50	15.00
—"360 Sound Mono" on label					
❑ CL 2281 [M]	Runnin' Out of Fools	1964	5.00	10.00	20.00
—"Guaranteed High Fidelity" on label					
❑ CL 2281 [M]	Runnin' Out of Fools	1965	3.75	7.50	15.00
—"360 Sound Mono" on label					
❑ CL 2351 [M]	Yeah!!!	1965	5.00	10.00	20.00
—"Guaranteed High Fidelity" on label					
❑ CL 2351 [M]	Yeah!!!	1966	3.75	7.50	15.00
—"360 Sound Mono" on label					
❑ CL 2521 [M]	Soul Sister	1966	5.00	10.00	20.00
❑ CL 2629 [M]	Take It Like You Give It	1967	6.25	12.50	25.00
❑ CL 2673 [M]	Aretha Franklin's Greatest Hits	1967	6.25	12.50	25.00
❑ CL 2754 [M]	Take a Look	1967	7.50	15.00	30.00
❑ CS 8412 [S]	Aretha	1961	20.00	40.00	80.00
—Red and black label with six "eye" logos					
❑ CS 8412 [S]	Aretha	1963	6.25	12.50	25.00
—"360 Sound Stereo" on label					
❑ CS 8561 [S]	The Electrifying Aretha Franklin	1962	12.50	25.00	50.00
—Red and black label with six "eye" logos					
❑ CS 8561 [S]	The Electrifying Aretha Franklin	1963	6.25	12.50	25.00
—"360 Sound Stereo" on label					
❑ CS 8676 [S]	The Tender, The Moving, The Swinging Aretha Franklin	1962	12.50	25.00	50.00
—Red and black label with six "eye" logos					
❑ CS 8676 [S]	The Tender, The Moving, The Swinging Aretha Franklin	1963	6.25	12.50	25.00
—"360 Sound Stereo" on label					
❑ CS 8879 [S]	Laughing on the Outside	1963	6.25	12.50	25.00
—"360 Sound Stereo" on label					
❑ CS 8963 [S]	Unforgettable	1964	6.25	12.50	25.00
—"360 Sound Stereo" on label					
❑ CS 9081 [S]	Runnin' Out of Fools	1964	6.25	12.50	25.00
—"360 Sound Stereo" on label					
❑ CS 9151 [S]	Yeah!!!	1965	6.25	12.50	25.00
—"360 Sound Stereo" on label					
❑ CS 9321 [S]	Soul Sister	1966	6.25	12.50	25.00
—"360 Sound Stereo" on label					
❑ CS 9429 [S]	Take It Like You Give It	1967	5.00	10.00	20.00
—"360 Sound Stereo" on label					
❑ CS 9473 [S]	Aretha Franklin's Greatest Hits	1967	5.00	10.00	20.00
—"360 Sound Stereo" on label					
❑ CS 9554 [S]	Take a Look	1967	5.00	10.00	20.00
—"360 Sound Stereo" on label					
❑ CS 9601	Aretha Franklin's Greatest Hits, Volume 2	1968	5.00	10.00	20.00
—"360 Sound Stereo" on label					
❑ CS 9776	Soft and Beautiful	1969	5.00	10.00	20.00
—"360 Sound Stereo" on label					
❑ CS 9956	Today I Sing the Blues	1970	3.75	7.50	15.00
—"360 Sound Stereo" on label					
❑ KG 31355 [(2)]	In the Beginning/The World of Aretha Franklin 1960-1967	1972	5.00	10.00	20.00
❑ KC 31953	The First 12 Sides	1973	3.00	6.00	12.00
❑ C2 37377 [(2)]	The Legendary Queen of Soul	1981	3.00	6.00	12.00
❑ PC 38042	Sweet Bitter Love	1982	2.50	5.00	10.00
❑ FC 40105	Aretha Franklin Sings the Blues	1985	2.50	5.00	10.00
❑ FC 40708	Aretha After Hours	1987	2.50	5.00	10.00
COLUMBIA SPECIAL PRODUCTS					
❑ C 10589	Take a Look	1971	3.00	6.00	12.00
HARMONY					
❑ HS 11349	Once in a Lifetime	1969	3.00	6.00	12.00
❑ HS 11418	Two Sides of Love	1970	3.00	6.00	12.00
❑ KH 30606	Greatest Hits 1960-1965	1971	3.00	6.00	12.00
❑ KH 30606	Greatest Hits 1960-1966	1972	3.00	6.00	12.00

FRANKLIN, CAROLYN
45s
RCA VICTOR

Number	Title (A Side/B Side)	Yr	VG	VG+	NM
❑ 47-9734	The Boxer/I Don't Want to Lose You	1969	—	3.00	6.00
❑ 74-0188	Reality/It's True I'm Gonna Miss You	1969	—	3.00	6.00
❑ 74-0289	Ain't That Groovy/All I Want Is to Be Your Woman	1969	—	3.00	6.00
❑ 74-0314	Everybody's Talkin'/Chain Reaction	1970	—	2.50	5.00
❑ 74-0373	You Really Didn't Mean It/All I Want Is to Be Your Woman	1970	—	2.50	5.00
❑ 74-0783	As Long As You're There/I Want to Be With You	1972	—	2.50	5.00
❑ APBO-0022	You Are Everything/If You Want Me	1973	—	2.50	5.00
❑ PB-10688	I Can't Help My Feeling So Blue/If You Want Me	1976	—	2.00	4.00

Albums
RCA VICTOR

Number	Title (A Side/B Side)	Yr	VG	VG+	NM
❑ LSP-4160	Baby Dynamite	1969	5.00	10.00	20.00
❑ LSP-4317	Chain Reaction	1970	5.00	10.00	20.00
❑ LSP-4411	I'd Rather Be Lonely	1973	5.00	10.00	20.00

FRANKLIN, ERMA
45s
BRUNSWICK

Number	Title (A Side/B Side)	Yr	VG	VG+	NM
❑ 55403	Change My Thoughts from You/Gotta Find Me a Lover	1969	2.00	4.00	8.00
❑ 55415	Saving My Love/You've Been Cancelled	1969	2.00	4.00	8.00
❑ 55424	I Just Don't Need You (At All)/It Could've Been Me	1969	2.00	4.00	8.00
❑ 55430	Whispers (Gettin' Louder)/(I Get the) Sweetest Feeling	1970	2.00	4.00	8.00
EPIC					
❑ 9488	Hello Again/It's Over	1962	5.00	10.00	20.00
❑ 9511	Each Night I Cry/Time After Time	1962	5.00	10.00	20.00
❑ 9516	Dear Mama/Never Again	1962	5.00	10.00	20.00
❑ 9559	Don't Wait Too Long/Time After Time	1962	5.00	10.00	20.00
❑ 9594	Have You Ever Had the Blues/I Don't Want No Mama's Boy	1963	3.75	7.50	15.00
❑ 9610	Abracadabra/Love Is Blind	1963	3.75	7.50	15.00
SHOUT					
❑ 218	Big Boss Man/Didn't Catch the Dog's Bone	1967	2.50	5.00	10.00
❑ 221	Piece of My Heart/Baby What You Want Me to Do	1967	3.00	6.00	12.00
❑ 230	Open Up Your Soul/I'm Just Not Ready for Love	1967	2.50	5.00	10.00
❑ 234	Right to Cry/I'm Just Not Ready for Love	1968	2.50	5.00	10.00

Albums
BRUNSWICK

Number	Title (A Side/B Side)	Yr	VG	VG+	NM
❑ BL 754147	Soul Sister	1969	5.00	10.00	20.00
EPIC					
❑ BN 619 [S]	Her Name Is Erma	1962	10.00	20.00	40.00
❑ LN 3824 [M]	Her Name Is Erma	1962	7.50	15.00	30.00

FREE MOVEMENT, THE
45s
COLUMBIA

Number	Title (A Side/B Side)	Yr	VG	VG+	NM
❑ 45512	The Harder I Try (The Bluer I Get)/Comin' Home	1972	—	2.50	5.00
❑ 45567	Could You Believe in a Dream/Love the One You're With	1972	—	2.50	5.00
❑ 45778	Every Step of the Way/I Can't Move No Mountains	1973	—	2.50	5.00
DECCA					
❑ 32818	I've Found Someone of My Own/I Can't Convince My Heart	1971	—	3.00	6.00

Albums
COLUMBIA

Number	Title (A Side/B Side)	Yr	VG	VG+	NM
❑ KC 31136	I've Found Someone of My Own	1972	3.75	7.50	15.00

FRIENDS OF DISTINCTION, THE
45s
RCA VICTOR

Number	Title (A Side/B Side)	Yr	VG	VG+	NM
❑ 74-0107	Grazing in the Grass/I Really Hope You Do	1969	—	3.00	6.00
❑ 74-0204	Going in Circles/Let Yourself Go	1969	—	3.00	6.00
❑ 74-0319	Love Or Let Me Be Lonely/This Generation	1970	—	3.00	6.00
❑ 74-0385	Time Waits for No One/Mother Nature	1970	—	2.50	5.00
❑ 74-0416	Check It Out/I Need You	1971	—	2.50	5.00
❑ 74-0516	It Don't Matter to Me/Down I Go	1971	—	2.50	5.00
❑ 74-0562	Let Me Be/Long Time Comin' My Way	1971	—	2.50	5.00
❑ 74-0679	Love Is the Way of Life/Jenny Wants to Know	1972	—	2.50	5.00
❑ 74-0787	Now Is the Time/Thumb Tripping	1972	—	2.50	5.00
❑ 74-0888	Ain't No Woman (Like the One I've Got)/Easy Evil	1973	—	2.50	5.00
❑ 74-0956	Check It Out/Love Can Make It Easier	1973	—	2.50	5.00
❑ PB-10197	Honey Baby Theme Part 1/Honey Baby Theme Part 2	1975	—	2.00	4.00
❑ PB-10220	Love Shack Part 1/Love Shack Part 2	1975	—	2.00	4.00

Albums
RCA VICTOR

Number	Title (A Side/B Side)	Yr	VG	VG+	NM
❑ APD1-0276	Greatest Hits	1973	5.00	10.00	20.00
❑ LSP-4149	Grazin'	1969	3.75	7.50	15.00
❑ LSP-4212	Highly Distinct	1969	3.75	7.50	15.00
❑ LSP-4313	Real Friends	1970	3.75	7.50	15.00
❑ LSP-4408	Whatever	1970	3.75	7.50	15.00
❑ LSP-4492	Friends & People	1971	3.75	7.50	15.00
❑ LSP-4819	Greatest Hits	1972	3.00	6.00	12.00
❑ LSP-4829	Love Can Make It Easier	1973	3.00	6.00	12.00

FULLER, JOHNNY
45s
ALADDIN

Number	Title (A Side/B Side)	Yr	VG	VG+	NM
❑ 3278	Johnny Ace's Last Letter/Fools Paradise	1955	20.00	40.00	80.00
❑ 3286	Cruel, Cruel World/My Heart Beats for You	1955	15.00	30.00	60.00
ART TONE					
❑ 828	No More/The Power	1962	5.00	10.00	20.00
CHECKER					
❑ 899	You Got Me Whistling/All Night Long	1958	6.25	12.50	25.00
FLAIR					
❑ 1054	Buddy/Hard Times	1955	37.50	75.00	150.00
HOLLYWOOD					
❑ 1043	Train Train Blues/Bad Luck Overtook Me	1955	20.00	40.00	80.00
❑ 1057	Mean Old World/How Long	1956	20.00	40.00	80.00
❑ 1063	Comin' Round the Corner/Roughest Place in Town	1956	20.00	40.00	80.00
❑ 1077	My Mama Told Me/Too Late to Change My Mind	1956	20.00	40.00	80.00
❑ 1084	Sunny Road/I Can't Succeed	1957	20.00	40.00	80.00
IMPERIAL					
❑ 5580	Heavenly Love/Whispering Wind	1959	5.00	10.00	20.00
❑ 5697	Miss You/Stop, Look and Listen	1960	5.00	10.00	20.00

F

Number	Title (A Side/B Side)	Yr	VG	VG+	NM

IRMA

Number	Title (A Side/B Side)	Yr	VG	VG+	NM
❏ 106	Weeping and Mourning/Strange Land	1958	20.00	40.00	80.00
❏ 110	First Stage of the Blues/No More, No More	1958	20.00	40.00	80.00
❏ 112	You Got Me Whistling/All Night Long	1958	15.00	30.00	60.00

MONEY

❏ 206	I Walk All Night/These Young Girls	1955	15.00	30.00	60.00

SPECIALTY

❏ 655	Haunted House/The Mighty Hand	1959	5.00	10.00	20.00
❏ 671	Swingin' at the Creek/Many Rivers, Mighty Seas	1959	5.00	10.00	20.00

FULSON, LOWELL

Also recorded as "Lowell Folsom" and "Lowell Fulsom," both included below.

45s

ALADDIN

Number	Title (A Side/B Side)	Yr	VG	VG+	NM
❏ 3088	Double Trouble/Good Woman Blues	1951	37.50	75.00	150.00
❏ 3104	Night and Day/Stormin' and Rainin'	1951	25.00	50.00	100.00
—Black vinyl					
❏ 3104	Night and Day/Stormin' and Rainin'	1951	250.00	500.00	1000.
—Green vinyl					
❏ 3217	Don't Leave Me Baby/Check with the Boys	1954	20.00	40.00	80.00
❏ 3233	Blues Never Fail/You've Gotta Reap	1954	20.00	40.00	80.00

CASH

❏ 1051	Love Society Blues/Blue Shadows	1957	10.00	20.00	40.00

CHECKER

❏ 804	Reconsider Baby/I Believe I'll Give It Up	1954	10.00	20.00	40.00
❏ 812	Loving You (Is All I Crave)/Check Yourself	1955	10.00	20.00	40.00
❏ 820	Lonely Hours/Do Me Right	1955	7.50	15.00	30.00
❏ 829	Trouble, Trouble/I Still Love You Baby	1955	7.50	15.00	30.00
❏ 841	It's Your Fault, Baby/Tollin' Bells	1956	7.50	15.00	30.00
❏ 854	Blues Rhumba/Please Don't Go	1957	6.25	12.50	25.00
❏ 865	Don't Drive Me, Baby/You're Gonna Miss Me	1957	6.25	12.50	25.00
❏ 882	I Want to Make Love to You/Rock This Morning	1958	6.25	12.50	25.00
❏ 937	It Took a Long Time/That's Alright	1960	5.00	10.00	20.00
❏ 952	Comin' Home/Have You Changed Your Mind	1960	5.00	10.00	20.00
❏ 959	I'm Glad You Reconsidered/Blue Shadows	1960	5.00	10.00	20.00
❏ 972	I Want to Know (Part 1)/I Want to Know (Part 2)	1961	3.75	7.50	15.00
❏ 992	So Many Tears/Hung Down Head	1961	3.75	7.50	15.00
❏ 1027	Shed No Tears/Can She	1962	3.75	7.50	15.00
❏ 1046	Trouble with the Blues/Love Grows Cold	1963	3.75	7.50	15.00

GRANITE

❏ 533	Do You Love Me/A Step at a Time	1975	—	2.50	5.00
❏ 538	The Old Blues Singer/Monday Morning Blues	1976	—	2.50	5.00

HOLLYWOOD

❏ 567-242	The Original Lonesome Christmas Part 1/The Original Lonesome Christmas Part 2	196?	2.50	5.00	10.00
❏ 1022	The Original Lonesome Christmas Part 1/The Original Lonesome Christmas Part 2	1955	5.00	10.00	20.00
❏ 1029	Everyday I Have the Blues/Guitar Shuffle	1955	12.50	25.00	50.00
❏ 1103	Everyday I Have the Blues/Guitar Shuffle	1962	3.75	7.50	15.00

JEWEL

❏ 801	Letter Home/Lady in the Rain	1969	2.00	4.00	8.00
❏ 802	Why Don't We Do It in the Road/Too Soon	1969	2.50	5.00	10.00
❏ 805	How Do You Want Your Man/Sleeper	1969	2.00	4.00	8.00
❏ 808	Don't Leave Me/Thug	1970	2.00	4.00	8.00
❏ 811	Do You Feel It/Don't Destroy Me	1970	2.00	4.00	8.00
❏ 813	Lonesome Christmas (Part 1)/Lonesome Christmas (Part 2)	1970	—	3.00	6.00
❏ 818	My Baby/Bluesway	1971	—	3.00	6.00
❏ 820	Teach Me/Man of Motion	1971	—	3.00	6.00
❏ 827	Change of Heart/Every Second a Fool Is Born	1972	—	3.00	6.00
❏ 832	Look at You Baby/Fed Up	1972	—	3.00	6.00

KENT

❏ 395	Every Time It Rains/My Heart Belongs to You	1964	3.00	6.00	12.00
❏ 395	Every Time It Rains/Just One More Time	1964	3.00	6.00	12.00
❏ 401	Key to My Heart/Too Many Drivers	1964	3.00	6.00	12.00
❏ 410	Strange Feeling/What's Gonna Be	1965	3.00	6.00	12.00
❏ 422	No More (Part 1)/No More (Part 2)	1965	3.00	6.00	12.00
❏ 431	Black Nights/Little Angel	1965	2.50	5.00	10.00
❏ 440	Sittin' Here Thinkin'/Shattered Dreams	1966	2.50	5.00	10.00
❏ 443	Blues Around Midnight/Talkin' Woman	1966	2.50	5.00	10.00
❏ 448	Change Your Ways/My Aching Back	1966	2.50	5.00	10.00
❏ 452	The Trouble I'm In/Ask at Any Door in Town	1966	2.50	5.00	10.00
❏ 456	Tramp/Pico	1966	2.50	5.00	10.00
❏ 463	Make a Little Love/I'm Sinking	1967	2.50	5.00	10.00
❏ 463 [PS]	Make a Little Love/I'm Sinking	1967	5.00	10.00	20.00
❏ 466	Everyday I Have the Blues/No Hard Feelings	1967	2.50	5.00	10.00
❏ 471	I Cried/The Thing	1967	2.50	5.00	10.00
❏ 474	I'm a Drifter/Hobo Meetin'	1967	2.50	5.00	10.00
❏ 477	I Wanna Spend Christmas with You Part 1/I Wanna Spend Christmas with You Part 2	1967	3.00	6.00	12.00
❏ 479	Tomorrow/Push Me	1968	2.50	5.00	10.00
❏ 486	The Letter/Let's Go Get Stoned	1968	2.50	5.00	10.00
❏ 489	Blues Pain/Mellow Together	1968	2.50	5.00	10.00
❏ 497	Sweetest Thing/What the Heck	1968	2.50	5.00	10.00
❏ 505	Lovin' Touch/Price for Love	1969	2.50	5.00	10.00
❏ 4535	Let's Go Get Stoned/Funky Broadway	1970	2.00	4.00	8.00

MOVIN'

❏ 128	Stop and Think/Baby	1964	3.00	6.00	12.00

PARROT

❏ 787	I've Been Mistreated/Juke Box Shuffle	1953	25.00	50.00	100.00
—Black vinyl					
❏ 787	I've Been Mistreated/Juke Box Shuffle	1953	50.00	100.00	200.00
—Red vinyl					

SWING TIME

Number	Title (A Side/B Side)	Yr	VG	VG+	NM
❏ 242	Lonesome Christmas (Part 1)/Lonesome Christmas (Part 2)	1951	15.00	30.00	60.00
—78 released in 1950; 45 released in 1951					
❏ 243	I'm a Night Owl (Part 1)/I'm a Night Owl (Part 2)	1951	25.00	50.00	100.00
❏ 272	Why Can't You Cry for Me/Blues with a Feeling	1951	—	—	—
—Unreleased on 45 rpm?					
❏ 289	Let's Live Right/Best Wishes	1952	12.50	25.00	50.00
❏ 290	Three O'Clock in the Morning Blues/I'm Wild About You Baby	1952	—	—	—
—Unreleased on 45 rpm?					
❏ 295	Guitar Shuffle/Mean Old Lonesome Song	1952	12.50	25.00	50.00
❏ 308	Black Widow Spider/Midnight Showers of Rain	1953	12.50	25.00	50.00
❏ 315	Raggedy Daddy Blues/Goodbye	1953	12.50	25.00	50.00
❏ 320	Ride Until the Sun Goes Down/Good Party Shuffle	1953	12.50	25.00	50.00
❏ 325	Upstairs/Let Me Ride Your Automobile	1953	12.50	25.00	50.00
❏ 330	The Blues Come Rollin' In/I Love My Baby	1954	12.50	25.00	50.00
❏ 335	Cash Box Boogie/My Daily Prayer	1954	12.50	25.00	50.00
❏ 338	I've Been Mistreated/Juke Box Shuffle	1954	12.50	25.00	50.00

78s

ALADDIN

❏ 3088	Double Trouble/Good Woman Blues	1951	6.25	12.50	25.00
❏ 3104	Night and Day/Stormin' and Rainin'	1951	6.25	12.50	25.00
❏ 3217	Don't Leave Me Baby/Check with the Boys	1954	6.25	12.50	25.00
❏ 3233	Blues Never Fail/You've Gotta Reap	1954	6.25	12.50	25.00

BIG TOWN

❏ 1068	Crying Blues/You're Gonna Miss Me When I'm Gone	1946	12.50	25.00	50.00
❏ 1070	Miss Katie Lee Blues/(B-side unknown)	1946	12.50	25.00	50.00
❏ 1071	Ramblin' Blues/Fulson's Blues	194?	12.50	25.00	50.00
❏ 1072	San Francisco Blues/Bad Luck and Trouble	194?	12.50	25.00	50.00
❏ 1074	Trouble Blues/Going to See My Baby	194?	12.50	25.00	50.00
❏ 1077	Black Widow Spider Blues/Don't Be So Evil	194?	12.50	25.00	50.00

CHECKER

❏ 804	Reconsider Baby/I Believe I'll Give It Up	1954	7.50	15.00	30.00
❏ 812	Loving You (Is All I Crave)/Check Yourself	1955	7.50	15.00	30.00
❏ 820	Lonely Hours/Do Me Right	1955	7.50	15.00	30.00
❏ 829	Trouble, Trouble/I Still Love You Baby	1955	7.50	15.00	30.00
❏ 841	It's Your Fault, Baby/Tollin' Bells	1956	7.50	15.00	30.00
❏ 854	Blues Rhumba/Please Don't Go	1957	7.50	15.00	30.00
❏ 865	Don't Drive Me, Baby/You're Gonna Miss Me	1957	7.50	15.00	30.00
❏ 882	I Want to Make Love to You/Rock This Morning	1958	10.00	20.00	40.00

COLONIAL

❏ 122	I'm Prison Bound/Goodbye, Goodbye	1949	7.50	15.00	30.00

DOWN BEAT

❏ 110	Crying Blues/You're Gonna Miss Me When I'm Gone	194?	7.50	15.00	30.00
—Reissue of Big Town 1068					
❏ 111	Miss Katie Lee Blues/Rambling Blues	194?	7.50	15.00	30.00
—Reissue of Big Town material					
❏ 112	Fulson's Blues/San Francisco Blues	194?	7.50	15.00	30.00
—Reissue of Big Town material					
❏ 113	Mean Woman Blues/Fulson Boogie	194?	7.50	15.00	30.00
—Reissue of earlier material					
❏ 114	Trouble Blues/Going to See My Baby	194?	7.50	15.00	30.00
—Reissue of Big Town 1074					
❏ 115	Black Widow Spider Blues/Don't Be So Evil	194?	7.50	15.00	30.00
—Reissue of Big Town 1077					
❏ 116	Tryin' to Find My Baby/Highway 99	194?	7.50	15.00	30.00
—Reissue of one side of Trilon 192 and one side of Trilon 193					
❏ 117	Thinkin' Blues/Down Beat Shuffle	194?	7.50	15.00	30.00
—Reissue of one side of Trilon 186 and one side of Trilon 187					
❏ 118	Midnight Showers of Rain/So Long, So Long	194?	7.50	15.00	30.00
❏ 119	Wee Hours in the Morning/My Gal at Eight	194?	7.50	15.00	30.00
❏ 120	Bad Luck Blues/I'm Going Away	194?	7.50	15.00	30.00
❏ 121	Blues Got Me Down/Black Cat Blues	194?	7.50	15.00	30.00
❏ 122	Just a Poor Boy/My Baby	194?	7.50	15.00	30.00
❏ 132	Blues and Women/Sweet Jenny Lee	1948	7.50	15.00	30.00
❏ 133	Don't You Hear Me Calling You/Television Blues	1948	7.50	15.00	30.00
❏ 134	Demon Woman/Tears at Sunrise	1948	7.50	15.00	30.00
❏ 135	Blues and Misery/Jam That Boogie	1948	7.50	15.00	30.00
—As "Tulsa Red"					
❏ 136	Black Snake Blues/My Heart Belongs to You	1948	7.50	15.00	30.00
❏ 167	Three O'Clock in the Morning/I'm Wild About You Baby	1949	7.50	15.00	30.00

DOWN TOWN

❏ 2002	Three O'Clock Blues/I'm Wild About You	1948	7.50	15.00	30.00
❏ 2021	I'm Prison Bound/My Baby Left Me	1948	7.50	15.00	30.00

GILT EDGE

❏ 5041	Miss Katie Lee Blues/Street Walking Woman	1951	10.00	20.00	40.00
❏ 5043	Mercury Boogie/Total Eclipse	1951	10.00	20.00	40.00
❏ 5050	Cryin' Won't Make Me Stay/Bad Luck and Trouble	1951	10.00	20.00	40.00

PARROT

❏ 787	I've Been Mistreated/Juke Box Shuffle	1953	12.50	25.00	50.00

RPM

❏ 305	Doin' Time Blues/Some Old Lonesome Day	1950	10.00	20.00	40.00

SCOTTY'S RADIO

❏ 101	Scotty's Blues/(B-side unknown)	1946	12.50	25.00	50.00

SWING TIME

❏ 196	Everyday I Have the Blues/Rocking After Midnight	1949	6.25	12.50	25.00
❏ 197	Cold Hearted Woman/Mama Bring Your Clothes Back Home	1949	6.25	12.50	25.00

Number	Title (A Side/B Side)	Yr	VG	VG+	NM
❏ 201	Western Union Blues/Lazy Woman Blues	1949	6.25	12.50	25.00
❏ 202	River Blues — Part 1/Part 2	1949	6.25	12.50	25.00
❏ 203	Jimmie's Blues/Ain't Nobody's Business	1949	6.25	12.50	25.00
❏ 219	I Walked All Night/Between Midnight and Day	1950	6.25	12.50	25.00
❏ 220	The Blues Is Killing Me/Did You Ever Feel Lucky	1950	6.25	12.50	25.00
❏ 226	Blue Shadows/Low Society Blues	1950	7.50	15.00	30.00
❏ 227	Back Home Blues/Baby Won't You Jump with Me	1950	6.25	12.50	25.00
❏ 230	Come Back Baby/Country Boy	1950	6.25	12.50	25.00
❏ 231	Rainy Day/Miss Lillie Brown	1950	6.25	12.50	25.00
❏ 237	Old Time Shuffle Blues/Sinner's Prayer	1950	6.25	12.50	25.00
—With Lloyd Glenn					
❏ 242	Lonesome Christmas (Part 1)/Lonesome Christmas (Part 2)	1950	6.25	12.50	25.00
❏ 243	I'm a Night Owl (Part 1)/I'm a Night Owl (Part 2)	1951	6.25	12.50	25.00
❏ 272	Why Can't You Cry for Me/Blues with a Feeling	1951	6.25	12.50	25.00
❏ 289	Let's Live Right/Best Wishes	1952	6.25	12.50	25.00
❏ 290	Three O'Clock in the Morning Blues/I'm Wild About You Baby	1952	6.25	12.50	25.00
❏ 295	Guitar Shuffle/Mean Old Lonesome Song	1952	6.25	12.50	25.00
❏ 308	Black Widow Spider/Midnight Showers of Rain	1953	6.25	12.50	25.00
❏ 315	Raggedy Daddy Blues/Goodbye	1953	6.25	12.50	25.00
❏ 320	Ride Until the Sun Goes Down/Good Party Shuffle	1953	6.25	12.50	25.00
❏ 325	Upstairs/Let Me Ride Your Automobile	1953	6.25	12.50	25.00
❏ 330	The Blues Come Rollin' In/I Love My Baby	1954	6.25	12.50	25.00
❏ 335	Cash Box Boogie/My Daily Prayer	1954	6.25	12.50	25.00
❏ 338	I've Been Mistreated/Juke Box Shuffle	1954	6.25	12.50	25.00
TRILON					
❏ 185	Jelly Jelly/Mean Woman Blues	1947	12.50	25.00	50.00
❏ 186	Thinkin' Blues/9:30 Blues	1947	12.50	25.00	50.00
❏ 187	Down Beat Shuffle/Fulson Boogie	1947	12.50	25.00	50.00
❏ 192	Tryin' to Find My Baby/Let's Throw a Boogie	1948	12.50	25.00	50.00
❏ 193	Highway 99/Whiskey Boogie	1948	12.50	25.00	50.00
Albums					
ARHOOLIE					
❏ R-2003	Early Recordings	1962	7.50	15.00	30.00
BIG TOWN					
❏ 1008	Lovemaker	1978	3.00	6.00	12.00
CHESS					
❏ 408	Hung Down Head	197?	3.75	7.50	15.00
GRANITE					
❏ 1006	Ol' Blues Singer	1976	3.75	7.50	15.00
JEWEL					
❏ LPS-5003	In a Heavy Bag	1970	3.75	7.50	15.00
❏ LPS-5009	I've Got the Blues	1973	3.75	7.50	15.00
KENT					
❏ KST-516 [S]	Lowell Fulsom	1965	10.00	20.00	40.00
❏ KST-520 [S]	Tramp	1967	10.00	20.00	40.00
❏ KST-531	Lowell Fulsom Now	1969	7.50	15.00	30.00
❏ KLP-5016 [M]	Lowell Fulsom	1965	7.50	15.00	30.00
❏ KLP-5020 [M]	Tramp	1967	7.50	15.00	30.00
ROUNDER					
❏ 2088	It's a Good Day	198?	3.00	6.00	12.00

FUNK INC.
45s

Number	Title (A Side/B Side)	Yr	VG	VG+	NM
PRESTIGE					
❏ 752	Whipper (Part 1)/Whipper (Part 2)	1972	—	3.00	6.00
❏ 754	The Thrill Is Gone/Bowlegs	1973	—	3.00	6.00
❏ 759	Dirty Red (Part 1)/Dirty Red (Part 2)	197?	—	3.00	6.00
❏ 762	Goodbye, So Long/Just Don't Mean a Thing	197?	—	3.00	6.00
Albums					
PRESTIGE					
❏ 10031	Funk Inc.	1971	3.75	7.50	15.00
❏ 10043	Chicken Lickin'	1972	3.75	7.50	15.00
❏ 10059	Hangin' Out	1973	3.75	7.50	15.00
❏ 10071	Superfunk	1973	3.75	7.50	15.00
❏ 10087	Priced to Sell	1974	3.75	7.50	15.00

FUNKADELIC
Also see GEORGE CLINTON; FUNKADELIC (2); PARLIAMENT; THE PARLIAMENTS.
45s

Number	Title (A Side/B Side)	Yr	VG	VG+	NM
MCA					
❏ 53654	By Way of the Drum/(Instrumental)	1989	—	—	3.00
WARNER BROS.					
❏ 8618	One Nation Under a Groove (Part 1)/One Nation Under a Groove (Part 2)	1978	—	2.50	5.00
❏ 8618 [PS]	One Nation Under a Groove (Part 1)/One Nation Under a Groove (Part 2)	1978	—	2.50	5.00
❏ 8735	Cholly (Funk Getting Ready to Roll)/Into You	1979	—	2.50	5.00
❏ 49040	(Not Just) Knee Deep — Part 1/(Not Just) Knee Deep — Part 2	1979	—	2.50	5.00
❏ 49117	Uncle Jam (Part 1)/Uncle Jam (Part 2)	1979	—	2.50	5.00
❏ 49667	The Electric Spanking of War Babies/The Electric Spanking of War Babies (Part 2)	1981	—	2.00	4.00
❏ 49667 [PS]	The Electric Spanking of War Babies/The Electric Spanking of War Babies (Part 2)	1981	—	2.50	5.00
❏ 49807	Shockwaves/Bullino's Bounce	1981	—	2.00	4.00
WESTBOUND					
❏ 148	Music for My Mother/(Instrumental)	1969	2.50	5.00	10.00
❏ 150	I'll Bet You/Open Your Eyes	1969	2.50	5.00	10.00
❏ 158	I Got a Thing, You Got a Thing, Everybody's Got a Thing/Fish, Chips and Sweat	1970	2.50	5.00	10.00

Number	Title (A Side/B Side)	Yr	VG	VG+	NM
❏ 167	I Wanna Know If It's Good to You?/I Wanna Know If It's Good to You? (Part 2)	1970	2.50	5.00	10.00
❏ 175	You and Your Folks, Me and My Folks/Funky Dollar Bill	1971	2.50	5.00	10.00
❏ 185	Can You Get to That?/Back in Our Minds	1971	2.50	5.00	10.00
❏ 197	I Miss My Baby/Baby I Owe You Something Good	1972	2.50	5.00	10.00
—As "U.S. Music with Funkadelic"					
❏ 198	Hit It and Quit It/A Whole Lot of B.S.	1972	2.50	5.00	10.00
❏ 205	A Joyful Process/Loose Booty	1972	2.50	5.00	10.00
❏ 218	Cosmic Slop/If You Don't Like the Effects, Don't Produce the Cause	1973	2.50	5.00	10.00
❏ 224	Standing on the Verge of Getting It On/Jimmy's Got a Little Bit of Bitch in Him	1974	2.50	5.00	10.00
❏ 5000	Red Hot Momma/Vital Juices	1975	2.00	4.00	8.00
❏ 5014	Better the Pound/Stuffs and Things	1975	2.00	4.00	8.00
❏ 5026	Let's Take It to the Stage/Bilogical Speculation	1976	2.00	4.00	8.00
❏ 5029	Undisco Kidd/How Do Yeau View You	1976	2.00	4.00	8.00
Albums					
SCARFACE/PRIORITY					
❏ 53872	One Nation Under a Groove	1993	3.75	7.50	15.00
—Limited-edition reissue of Warner Bros. 3209					
❏ 53873	Hardcore Jollies	1993	3.75	7.50	15.00
—Limited-edition reissue of Warner Bros. 2973					
❏ 53874	The Electric Spanking of War Babies	1993	3.75	7.50	15.00
—Limited-edition reissue of Warner Bros. 3482					
❏ 53875	Uncle Jam Wants You	1993	3.75	7.50	15.00
—Limited-edition reissue of Warner Bros. 3371					
WARNER BROS.					
❏ BS 2973	Hardcore Jollies	1976	6.25	12.50	25.00
❏ BS 3209	One Nation Under a Groove	1978	6.25	12.50	25.00
—Includes bonus 7-inch single with small hole (deduct 20% if missing)					
❏ BSK 3371	Uncle Jam Wants You	1979	6.25	12.50	25.00
❏ BSK 3482	The Electric Spanking of War Babies	1981	6.25	12.50	25.00
WESTBOUND					
❏ 208	Standing on the Verge of Getting It On	1975	6.25	12.50	25.00
—Reissue of Westbound 1001					
❏ 215	Let's Take It to the Stage	1975	12.50	25.00	50.00
❏ 215	Let's Take It to the Stage	1992	3.75	7.50	15.00
—Reissue with bar code					
❏ 216	Funkadelic	1975	7.50	15.00	30.00
—Reissue of Westbound 2000					
❏ 217	Free Your Mind…And Your Ass Will Follow	1975	6.25	12.50	25.00
—Reissue of Westbound 2001					
❏ 218	Maggot Brain	1975	6.25	12.50	25.00
—Reissue of Westbound 2007					
❏ 221 [(2)]	America Eats Its Young	1976	6.25	12.50	25.00
—Reissue of Westbound 2020					
❏ 223	Cosmic Slop	1976	6.25	12.50	25.00
—Reissue of Westbound 2022					
❏ 227	Tales of Kidd Funkadelic	1976	12.50	25.00	50.00
❏ 227	Tales of Kidd Funkadelic	1992	3.75	7.50	15.00
—Reissue with bar code					
❏ 303	Best of the Early Years	197?	10.00	20.00	40.00
❏ 1001	Standing on the Verge of Getting It On	1974	12.50	25.00	50.00
❏ 1001	Standing on the Verge of Getting It On	1991	3.75	7.50	15.00
—Reissue with bar code					
❏ 1004	Funkadelic's Greatest Hits	1975	12.50	25.00	50.00
❏ 2000	Funkadelic	1970	12.50	25.00	50.00
❏ 2000	Funkadelic	1990	3.75	7.50	15.00
—Reissue with bar code					
❏ 2001	Free Your Mind...And Your Ass Will Follow	1970	12.50	25.00	50.00
❏ 2001	Free Your Mind...And Your Ass Will Follow	1990	3.75	7.50	15.00
—Reissue with bar code					
❏ 2007	Maggot Brain	1971	12.50	25.00	50.00
❏ 2007	Maggot Brain	1990	3.75	7.50	15.00
—Reissue with bar code					
❏ 2020 [(2)]	America Eats Its Young	1972	15.00	30.00	60.00
❏ 2020 [(2)]	America Eats Its Young	1991	5.00	10.00	20.00
—Reissue with bar code					
❏ 2022	Cosmic Slop	1973	12.50	25.00	50.00
❏ 2022	Cosmic Slop	1991	3.75	7.50	15.00
—Reissue with bar code					

FUNKADELIC (2)
Splinter group from the original band, listed separately because GEORGE CLINTON is not involved.
45s

Number	Title (A Side/B Side)	Yr	VG	VG+	NM
LAX					
❏ 70055	Connections and Disconnections/The Witch	1981	—	2.00	4.00
Albums					
LAX					
❏ FW 37087	Connections and Disconnections	1981	2.50	5.00	10.00

FURIOUS FIVE, THE
See GRANDMASTER FLASH; GRANDMASTER MELLE MEL.

F

Number	Title (A Side/B Side)	Yr	VG	VG+	NM

G

G-CLEFS, THE
45s
LOMA

Number	Title (A Side/B Side)	Yr	VG	VG+	NM
❏ 2034	Party '66/Little Lonely Boy	1966	2.50	5.00	10.00
❏ 2048	I Can't Stand It/Whirlwind	1966	2.50	5.00	10.00

PARIS

❏ 502	Symbol of Love/Love Her in the Mornin'	1957	7.50	15.00	30.00
❏ 506	Zing Zang Zoo/Is This the Way	1957	6.25	12.50	25.00

PILGRIM

❏ 715	Ka-Ding-Dong/Darla My Darlin'	1956	7.50	15.00	30.00
—Purple label					
❏ 715	Ka-Ding-Dong/Darla My Darlin'	1956	5.00	10.00	20.00
—Red label					
❏ 720	'Cause You're Mine/Please Write While I'm Away	1956	7.50	15.00	30.00

REGINA

❏ 1314	To the Winner Goes the Prize/I Believe in All I Feel	1964	3.75	7.50	15.00
❏ 1319	Angel Listen to Me/Nobody But Betty	1964	5.00	10.00	20.00

TERRACE

❏ 7500	I Understand (Just How You Feel)/Little Girl I Love You	1961	5.00	10.00	20.00
❏ 7503	Girl Has to Know/Lad (There Never Was a Dog Like You)	1962	5.00	10.00	20.00
❏ 7507	Make Up Your Mind/They'll Call Me Away	1962	5.00	10.00	20.00
❏ 7510	A Lover's Prayer/Sitting in the Moonlight	1962	6.25	12.50	25.00
❏ 7514	All My Trials/Big Train	1963	6.25	12.50	25.00

VEEP

❏ 1218	I Have/On the Other Side of Town	1965	3.75	7.50	15.00
❏ 1226	This Time/On the Other Side of Town	1965	3.75	7.50	15.00

GALES, THE
45s
DEBRA

❏ 1002	Tommy/Around the Clock with You	1963	10.00	20.00	40.00

JVB

❏ 34	His Eyes Keep Me in Trouble/Don't Let the Sun Catch You Cryin'	1955	1000.	2000.	3000.
❏ 35	Darling Patricia/All Is Well, All Is Well	1955	125.00	250.00	500.00

J.O.B.

❏ 3001	Darling Patricia/All Is Well, All Is Well	1956	50.00	100.00	200.00

MEL-O

❏ 111	Guiding Angel/Boy Come Home	1958	62.50	125.00	250.00
❏ 113	Josephine/If I Could Forget	1958	62.50	125.00	250.00

WINN

❏ 916	I Love You/Squeeze Me	1960	125.00	250.00	500.00

GAMBLE, DEE DEE SHARP
See DEE DEE SHARP.

GAMBLE, KENNY
45s
ARCTIC

❏ 107	Down by the Seashore (Part 1)/Down by the Seashore (Part 2)	1965	50.00	100.00	200.00
❏ 114	Ain't It Baby (Part 1)/Ain't It Baby (Part 2)	1965	50.00	100.00	200.00
❏ 123	The Joke's on You/Don't Stop Loving Me	1966	50.00	100.00	200.00

COLUMBIA

❏ 43132	Our Love/You Don't Know What You Got Until You Lose It	1964	7.50	15.00	30.00

EPIC

❏ 9636	Standing in the Shadows/No Mail on Monday	1963	7.50	15.00	30.00

GANG STARR
12-Inch Singles
CHRYSALIS

❏ Y-58111	Mass Appeal (Radio Version) (Street Version) (Masstrumental)	1994	2.50	5.00	10.00

Albums
CHRYSALIS

❏ F1-21798	Step In the Arena	1991	3.75	7.50	15.00
❏ F1-21910	Daily Operation	1992	3.75	7.50	15.00
❏ F1-28435	Hard to Earn	1994	3.75	7.50	15.00

VIRGIN

❏ 45585 [(3)]	Moment of Truth	1998	3.75	7.50	15.00
❏ 47279 [(4)]	Full Clip — A Decade of Gang Starr	1999	5.00	10.00	20.00

WILD PITCH

❏ 2001	No More Mr. Nice Guy	1989	3.75	7.50	15.00
❏ E1-98709	No More Mr. Nice Guy	1992	3.00	6.00	12.00

GANT, CECIL
45s
DECCA

❏ 9-30320	I Wonder/Cecil's Boogie	1957	7.50	15.00	30.00
❏ 9-48167	Goodnight Irene/My House Fell Down	1950	12.50	25.00	50.00
—As "Gunter Lee Carr"					
❏ 9-48170	We're Gonna Rock/Yesterday	1950	12.50	25.00	50.00
—As "Gunter Lee Carr"					
❏ 9-48171	Someday You'll Be Sorry (Part 1)/Someday You'll Be Sorry (Part 2)	1950	10.00	20.00	40.00
❏ 9-48185	It's Christmas Time Again/Hello Santa Claus	1950	10.00	20.00	40.00

Number	Title (A Side/B Side)	Yr	VG	VG+	NM
❏ 9-48191	Train Time Blues No. 2/It Ain't Gonna Be Like That	1951	10.00	20.00	40.00
❏ 9-48200	Shot Gun Boogie/Rock Little Baby	1951	12.50	25.00	50.00
❏ 9-48212	Don't You Worry/My Little Baby	1951	10.00	20.00	40.00
❏ 9-48231	Owl Stew/Playin' Myself the Blues	1951	10.00	20.00	40.00
❏ 9-48249	God Bless My Daddy/The Grass Is Gettin' Greener	1951	10.00	20.00	40.00

DOT

❏ 1112	All By Myself/It Hurts Me Too	1952	10.00	20.00	40.00
—Earlier singles on Dot may not exist on 45s					
❏ 1121	Sloppy Joes/Train Time Blues	1952	10.00	20.00	40.00

GILT EDGE

❏ 5090	I Wonder/Cecil's Boogie	1955	10.00	20.00	40.00
—Reissue of 78 first released in 1944					

78s
4 STAR

❏ 1176	Special Delivery/Jump Jack Jump	1948	6.25	12.50	25.00
❏ 1205	Boogie Blues/Wake Up, Cecil, Wake Up	1948	6.25	12.50	25.00
❏ 1215	That's the Stuff You Gotta Watch/The New Cecil Boogie	1948	6.25	12.50	25.00
❏ 1221	Killer Diller Boogie/Hit That Jive, Jack	1949	6.25	12.50	25.00
❏ 1243	Soft and Mellow/Am I to Blame	1949	6.25	12.50	25.00
❏ 1284	I'm Travelin' Alone/God Bless My Daddy	1949	6.25	12.50	25.00
❏ 1339	Fare Thee Well My Baby/I'll Remember You	1949	6.25	12.50	25.00
❏ 1377	Long Distance/Vibology	1949	6.25	12.50	25.00
❏ 1452	Coming Round the Mountain/Don't Leave Me	1950	5.00	10.00	20.00
—B-side by Ivory Joe Hunter					
❏ 1482	I've Heard That Jive Before/You're Going to Cry	1950	5.00	10.00	20.00
❏ 1526	My Baby's Changed/Can't Get Youy Off My Mind	1950	5.00	10.00	20.00
❏ 1561	Rock the Boogie/I'll Go On Loving You	1951	5.00	10.00	20.00
❏ 1584	Time Will Tell/Where I Belong	1951	5.00	10.00	20.00
❏ 1606	I'm Losing You/Peace and Love	1952	5.00	10.00	20.00

BRONZE

❏ 117	I Wonder/Cecil's Boogie	1944	10.00	20.00	40.00
—"I Wonder" is a different recording than any on Gilt Edge					

BULLET

❏ 250	Loose as a Goose/Nashville Jumps	194?	6.25	12.50	25.00
❏ 255	Sloppy Joe's/Train Time Blues	194?	6.25	12.50	25.00
❏ 256	Boogie Woogie Baby/If It's True	194?	6.25	12.50	25.00
❏ 257	I'm All Alone Now/Anna Mae	194?	6.25	12.50	25.00
❏ 258	It's the Girl/Ninth Street Jive	194?	6.25	12.50	25.00
❏ 264	Every Minute of Every Hour/Boozie Boogie	194?	6.25	12.50	25.00
❏ 265	Go to Sleep Little Baby/My, My, My	194?	6.25	12.50	25.00
❏ 272	I Believe I'll Go Back Home/I Wonder	1948	6.25	12.50	25.00
❏ 280	Another Day, Another Dollar/Three Little Girls	1948	6.25	12.50	25.00
❏ 289	I'm a Good Man But a Poor Man/Cecil's Jam Session	1949	6.25	12.50	25.00
❏ 299	I Ain't Gonna Cry Anymore/Screwey Boogie	1949	6.25	12.50	25.00
❏ 300	I Hate to Say Goodbye/My Little Baby	1949	6.25	12.50	25.00
❏ 313	I'm Singing the Blues Today/Rose Room	1949	6.25	12.50	25.00
❏ 320	What's the Matter/You Can't Do Me Right (And Do Me Wrong)	1949	6.25	12.50	25.00

DECCA

❏ 30320	I Wonder/Cecil's Boogie	1957	7.50	15.00	30.00
❏ 48167	Goodnight Irene/My House Fell Down	1950	5.00	10.00	20.00
—As "Gunter Lee Carr"					
❏ 48170	We're Gonna Rock/Yesterday	1950	5.00	10.00	20.00
—As "Gunter Lee Carr"					
❏ 48171	Someday You'll Be Sorry (Part 1)/Someday You'll Be Sorry (Part 2)	1950	3.75	7.50	15.00
❏ 48185	It's Christmas Time Again/Hello Santa Claus	1950	3.75	7.50	15.00
❏ 48191	Train Time Blues No. 2/It Ain't Gonna Be Like That	1951	3.75	7.50	15.00
❏ 48200	Shot Gun Boogie/Rock Little Baby	1951	5.00	10.00	20.00
❏ 48212	Don't You Worry/My Little Baby	1951	3.75	7.50	15.00
❏ 48231	Owl Stew/Playin' Myself the Blues	1951	3.75	7.50	15.00
❏ 48249	God Bless My Daddy/The Grass Is Gettin' Greener	1951	3.75	7.50	15.00

DOT

❏ 1016	Crying to Myself/Nobody Loves You	1950	6.25	12.50	25.00
❏ 1030	Waiting for My Train/Cindy Lou	1951	6.25	12.50	25.00
❏ 1053	Alma/I'm Still in Love with You	1951	6.25	12.50	25.00
❏ 1069	Raining Blues/Goodbye Baby	1951	6.25	12.50	25.00
❏ 1112	All By Myself/It Hurts Me Too	1952	5.00	10.00	20.00
❏ 1121	Sloppy Joes/Train Time Blues	1952	5.00	10.00	20.00

GILT EDGE

❏ 500	I Wonder/Cecil's Boogie	1944	62.50	125.00	250.00
—Red picture disc with different photo on each side					
❏ 501	I Wonder/Cecil's Boogie	1944	6.25	12.50	25.00
—Four different recordings of "I Wonder" appear on different pressings of 500 and 501; no difference in value					
❏ 502	Wake Up Cecil, Wake Up/Boogie Blues	1944	6.25	12.50	25.00
❏ 503	Put Another Chair at the Table/New Boogie	1945	6.25	12.50	25.00
❏ 504	I'll Remember You (If You'll Remember Me)/Cecil's Mop Mop	1945	6.25	12.50	25.00
❏ 505	The Grass Is Getting Greener/Killer Diller Boogie	1945	6.25	12.50	25.00
❏ 506	I'm Tired/Are You Ready	1945	6.25	12.50	25.00
❏ 508	Cecil Knows Better/You're Going to Cry	1945	6.25	12.50	25.00
❏ 510	Fit as a Fiddle/(B-side unknown)	1946	6.25	12.50	25.00
❏ 511	In a Little Spanish Town/(B-side unknown)	1946	6.25	12.50	25.00
❏ 512	Rhumba Boogie Woogie/(B-side unknown)	1947	6.25	12.50	25.00
❏ 513	Way Down/Nothing Bothers Me	1947	6.25	12.50	25.00
❏ 514	I Got a Gal/(B-side unknown)	1947	6.25	12.50	25.00
❏ 515	That's the Stuff You Got to Watch/Make Believe Girl	1947	6.25	12.50	25.00
❏ 516	I Feel It/Jam Jam Blues	1947	6.25	12.50	25.00
❏ 517	Solitude/Lightning Blues	194?	6.25	12.50	25.00
❏ 518	It's a Great Life/(B-side unknown)	194?	6.25	12.50	25.00

Number	Title (A Side/B Side)	Yr	VG	VG+	NM
IMPERIAL					
❑ 5066	When You Left My Baby/You'll Be Sorry	1950	7.50	15.00	30.00
❑ 5112	Come Home/Blues by Cecil	1951	7.50	15.00	30.00
KING					
❑ 4231	Hogan's Alley/Why	1948	7.50	15.00	30.00
SWING TIME					
❑ 209	Deal Yourself Another Hand/All Because of You	1949	7.50	15.00	30.00
❑ 302	You're Going to Cry/Baby I'm Losing You	1952	6.25	12.50	25.00
Albums					
KING					
❑ 671 [M]	Cecil Gant	1960	20.00	40.00	80.00
RED MILL					
❑ (no #) [M]	Cecil Gant	1956	125.00	250.00	500.00
—Red vinyl					
SOUND					
❑ 601 [M]	The Incomparable Cecil Gant	1958	25.00	50.00	100.00

GAP BAND, THE
12-Inch Singles

Number	Title (A Side/B Side)	Yr	VG	VG+	NM
ARISTA					
❑ AD1-9777	I'm Gonna Git Ya Sucka (Extended Version 6:13) (Sugar Shack Version 6:00)/(Single Version 3:34) (Extended Edit 3:58) (Tripped Out Dub Version 6:00)	1988	—	3.50	7.00
CAPITOL					
❑ V-15493	All of My Love (Extended Mix) (Instrumental) (Just Coolin' Mix) (Radio Mix) (Percussapella) (Bonus Beats)	1989	—	3.50	7.00
❑ V-15534	Addicted to Your Love (Extended Mix) (Instrumental) (Silly Stoopid Crazy Over You Mix)/(I'll Groove 4 U Remix) (I'll Groove 4 U Rap) (I'll Groove 4 U Instrumental)	1990	2.00	4.00	8.00
MERCURY					
❑ MK 86 [DJ]	Baby Baba Boogie (7:32)/Shake	1979	3.00	6.00	12.00
❑ MK 124 [DJ]	Steppin' (Out) (same on both sides)	1979	2.00	4.00	8.00
❑ MK 138 [DJ]	Party Lights (2 versions)	1980	3.00	6.00	12.00
❑ MK 175 [DJ]	Yearning for Your Love/Humpin'	1980	2.00	4.00	8.00
❑ MDS 4006	Shake/Baby Baba Boogie	1979	2.50	5.00	10.00
❑ 884662-1	You Dropped a Bomb on Me/Party Train	1986	3.00	6.00	12.00
—Reissue in conjunction with 'The 12" Collection' LP					
PASSPORT					
❑ PB-4005	Not Guilty/Knucklehead Funkin'/Listen to the Music	1983	2.00	4.00	8.00
RAGING BULL					
❑ RB 5023	Got It Goin' On (Extended BATT Edit) (Radio Edit)	1995	2.00	4.00	8.00
❑ RB 8013	First Lover (4 versions)	1995	2.00	4.00	8.00
TOTAL EXPERIENCE					
❑ TK 214 [DJ]	You Dropped a Bomb on Me (Long Version 13:05) (LP Version 5:12)	1982	3.00	6.00	12.00
❑ TED-701	Early in the Morning (Short Version 6:30) (Long Version 7:33)	1982	2.00	4.00	8.00
❑ TED-702	You Dropped a Bomb on Me (13:05)/Humpin' (5:06)	1982	3.75	7.50	15.00
❑ TED-704	Outstanding (unknown versions)	1982	2.00	4.00	8.00
❑ TED-706	Party Train (5:55) (6:10)	1982	2.50	5.00	10.00
❑ TED-707	I'm Ready (If You're Ready) (5:51)/Shake a Leg	1983	—	3.50	7.00
❑ TED 1003	Straight from the Heart (Cardiac Mix) (Radio Mix) (Pump the Heart Dub Mix) (Thump Thump Instrumental)	1988	—	3.00	6.00
❑ TED 1005	All the Way Yours (unknown versions)	1988	—	3.00	6.00
❑ TED1-2606	Beep a Freak (Short Version, To Be LP Mix 5:10) (Dance Mix 7:47) (Instrumental)	1984	2.00	4.00	8.00
❑ TED1-2615	Disrespect (Extended LP Version with Breakdown) (LP Version) (Club Mix)	1985	2.00	4.00	8.00
❑ TED1-2624	Desire (Special Remix) (LP Version) (Dub Version)	1985	2.00	4.00	8.00
❑ TED1-2632	Going in Circles (4:31)/I Believe (4:28)	1985	—	3.50	7.00
❑ TED1-2636	Automatic Brain (Main Radio and Club Mix Vocal 7:40) (Acapella 5:10) (Dub Version 5:55) (Rap Version)	1986	2.00	4.00	8.00
❑ 2701-1-TD	Big Fun (Radio Mix) (Serious Dub Mix) (Acapella Mix) (Mega Mix) (Bandolero Mix)	1986	—	3.50	7.00
❑ 2705-1-TD	Zibble, Zibble (Get the Money) (aka: Get Loose, Get Funky) (Album Mix 5:27) (Radio Short Mix 4:04) (Dub-Zibble Money Mix 5:37)	1986	2.00	4.00	8.00
45s					
ARISTA					
❑ 9788	I'm Gonna Git Ya Sucka/Clean Up Your Act	1988	—	—	3.00
—B-side by Jermaine Jackson					
❑ 9788 [PS]	I'm Gonna Git Ya Sucka/Clean Up Your Act	1988	—	—	3.00
A&M					
❑ 1788	Hard Time Charlie/This Place Called Heaven	1976	—	2.50	5.00
CAPITOL					
❑ B-44418	All of My Love (7" Version)/(Radio Mix)	1989	—	2.00	4.00
❑ 7PRO-79045 [DJ]	We Can Make It Alright (same on both sides)	1990	—	3.00	6.00
—Vinyl is promo only					
COLLECTABLES					
❑ 4391	Early in the Morning/Open Your Mind (Wide)	199?	—	—	3.00
❑ 4478	Steppin' (Out)/Shake	199?	—	—	3.00
MEGA					
❑ 4005	Not Guilty/(B-side unknown)	1984	—	2.50	5.00
MERCURY					
❑ DJ-568 [DJ]	The Boys Are Back in Town (stereo/mono?)	1980	2.00	4.00	8.00
❑ 74053	Shake/Got to Get Away	1979	—	2.00	4.00

Number	Title (A Side/B Side)	Yr	VG	VG+	NM
❑ 74080	Open Up Your Mind (Wide)/I Can Sing	1979	—	2.00	4.00
❑ 76021	Steppin' (Out)/You Are My High	1979	—	2.00	4.00
❑ 76037	I Don't Believe You Want to Get Up and Dance (Oops, Up Side Your Head)/Who Do You Call	1980	—	2.00	4.00
❑ 76062	Party Lights/The Boys Are Back in Town	1980	—	2.00	4.00
❑ 76091	Burn Rubber (Why You Wanna Hurt Me)/Nothin' Comes to a Sleeper	1980	—	2.00	4.00
❑ 76101	Yearning for Your Love/When I Look in Your Eyes	1981	—	2.00	4.00
❑ 76114	Humpin'/No Hiding Place	1981	—	2.00	4.00
❑ 811357-7	Burn Rubber/Yearning for Your Love	1983	—	—	3.00
—Reissue					
❑ 884662-7	You Dropped a Bomb on Me/Party Train	1986	—	2.50	5.00
—Reissue in conjunction with 'The 12" Collection' LP					
RCA					
❑ 5035-7-R	Sweeter Than Candy (Penitentiary III)/ (Instrumental)	1986	—	2.00	4.00
SHELTER					
❑ 40228	Backbone/Loving You Is Everything	1974	—	3.00	6.00
❑ 40295	I-Yike-It/Tommy's Groove	1974	—	3.00	6.00
TATTOO					
❑ TB-10884	Out of the Blue (Can You Feel It)/Silly Grin	1977	—	2.50	5.00
❑ TB-10990	Little Bit of Love/Knucklehead Sunckin'	1977	—	2.50	5.00
TOTAL EXPERIENCE					
❑ 101	Straight from the Heart/(Dub Mix)	1988	—	—	3.00
❑ 101 [PS]	Straight from the Heart/(Dub Mix)	1988	—	2.00	4.00
❑ 2405	Beep a Freak/(Dub Version)	1984	—	—	3.00
❑ 2405 [PS]	Beep a Freak/(Dub Version)	1984	—	2.00	4.00
❑ 2412	I Found My Baby/(Instrumental)	1985	—	—	3.00
❑ 2418	Disrespect/(Instrumental)	1985	—	—	3.00
❑ 2427	Desire/(Album Version)	1985	—	—	3.00
❑ 2428	Automatic Brain/(Instrumental)	1986	—	2.00	4.00
❑ 2435	The Christmas Song (Chestnuts Roasting on an Open Fire)/Joy to the World	1985	—	2.50	5.00
—B-side by Oliver Scott					
❑ 2436	Going in Circles/I Believe	1986	—	—	3.00
❑ 2436 [DJ]	Going in Circles (Remix 3:59)/(Remix Instrumental with Harmonica 5:15)	1986	—	3.00	6.00
❑ 2440	Automatic Brain/(With Rap)	1986	—	—	3.00
❑ 2700	Big Fun/(Ooh Ah Dub)	1986	—	—	3.00
❑ 2703	Zibble, Zibble (Get the Money) (aka: Get Loose, Get Funky)/(Instrumental)	1987	—	—	3.00
❑ 8201	Early in the Morning/I'm in Love	1982	—	2.00	4.00
❑ 8201 [PS]	Early in the Morning/I'm in Love	1982	—	2.50	5.00
❑ 8203	You Dropped a Bomb on Me/Lonely Like Me	1982	—	2.00	4.00
❑ 8205	Outstanding/The Blues Are Back in Town	1982	—	2.00	4.00
❑ 8209	Party Train/The Special Party Train Dance Mix	1983	—	2.00	4.00
❑ 8210	Jam the Motha' (Party Mix)/(Munchkin People)	1983	—	2.00	4.00
❑ 8211	I'm Ready (If You're Ready)/Shake a Leg	1984	—	2.00	4.00
Albums					
CAPITOL					
❑ C1-90799	Round Trip	1989	2.50	5.00	10.00
MERCURY					
❑ SRM-1-3758	The Gap Band	1979	2.50	5.00	10.00
❑ SRM-1-3804	The Gap Band II	1979	2.50	5.00	10.00
❑ SRM-1-4003	The Gap Band III	1980	2.50	5.00	10.00
❑ 822788-1	The Gap Band III	198?	2.00	4.00	8.00
—Reissue					
❑ 826808-1	The 12" Collection	1986	2.00	4.00	8.00
PASSPORT					
❑ PB-6026	Strike a Groove	1983	2.50	5.00	10.00
SHELTER					
❑ 2111	Magicians' Holiday	1974	3.75	7.50	15.00
TATTOO					
❑ BJL1-2168	The Gap Band	1977	3.75	7.50	15.00
TOTAL EXPERIENCE					
❑ 2700-1-T	Gap Band 8	1986	2.00	4.00	8.00
❑ 2710-1-T	Straight from the Heart	1987	2.00	4.00	8.00
❑ TE-1-3001	Gap Band IV	1982	2.00	4.00	8.00
❑ TE-1-3004	Gap Band V — Jammin'	1983	2.00	4.00	8.00
❑ TEL8-5705	Gap Band VI	1984	2.00	4.00	8.00
❑ TEL8-5714	Gap Band VII	1986	2.00	4.00	8.00
❑ 812186-1	Gap Band V — Jammin'	198?	—	3.00	6.00
—Reissue					
❑ 822794-1	Gap Band IV	198?	—	3.00	6.00
—Reissue					
❑ 824343-1	Gap Gold/Best of the Gap Band	1985	2.00	4.00	8.00

GARDENIAS, THE (1)
45s

Number	Title (A Side/B Side)	Yr	VG	VG+	NM
FEDERAL					
❑ 12284	Flaming Love/My Baby's Tops	1956	30.00	60.00	120.00

GARDNER, DON
Also see DON GARDNER AND DEE DEE FORD.
45s

Number	Title (A Side/B Side)	Yr	VG	VG+	NM
BRUCE					
❑ 105	How Do You Speak to an Angel/Sonotone Bounce	1954	15.00	30.00	60.00
❑ 108	I'll Walk Alone/Going Down Mary	1954	12.50	25.00	50.00
❑ 127	It's a Sin to Tell a Lie/I Hear a Rhapsody	1955	12.50	25.00	50.00
CAMEO					
❑ 102	Love Only Brings Happiness/Sneakin' In	1957	10.00	20.00	40.00
DELUXE					
❑ 6133	This Nearly Was Mine/A Dagger in My Chest	1957	6.25	12.50	25.00

G

Number	Title (A Side/B Side)	Yr	VG	VG+	NM
❏ 6155	There! I've Said It Again/I Don't Want to Go Home	1958	6.25	12.50	25.00
JUBILEE					
❏ 5482	I Really Love You Baby/Talking About You	1964	2.50	5.00	10.00
❏ 5484	The Bitter with the Sweet/I Don't Know What I'm Gonna Do	1964	2.50	5.00	10.00
❏ 5493	Little Girl Blue/I'm In Such Misery	1964	2.50	5.00	10.00
JUNIOR					
❏ 393	High School Baby/Crying All Alone	1957	10.00	20.00	40.00
❏ 394	Dark Alley/Up the Street	1957	7.50	15.00	30.00
KAISER					
❏ 399	Ask Anything/Humility	1958	6.25	12.50	25.00
❏ 402	At Last/The Hump	1959	6.25	12.50	25.00
MR. G					
❏ 824	Your Love Is Driving Me Crazy/There Ain't Gonna Be No Loving	1969	2.00	4.00	8.00
SEDGRICK					
❏ 3001	Cheatin' Kind/(B-side unknown)	196?	2000.	3000.	4000.
VERVE					
❏ 10582	You Babe/I'm a Practical Guy	1967	3.00	6.00	12.00

GARDNER, DON, AND DEE DEE FORD
Also see each artist's individual listings.
45s

Number	Title (A Side/B Side)	Yr	VG	VG+	NM
FIRE					
❏ 508	I Need Your Loving/Tell Me	1962	5.00	10.00	20.00
—Red label					
❏ 508	I Need Your Loving/Tell Me	1962	3.75	7.50	15.00
—Multicolor label					
❏ 513	Don't You Worry/I'm Coming Home to Stay	1962	3.75	7.50	15.00
❏ 517	Lead Me On/TCB (Taking Care of Business)	1962	3.75	7.50	15.00
KC					
❏ 196	Glory of Love/'Deed I Do	1963	3.00	6.00	12.00
LUDIX					
❏ 104	You Upset My Soul/Son My Son	1963	3.00	6.00	12.00
Albums					
COLLECTABLES					
❏ COL-5155	Golden Classics: Need Your Lovin'	198?	3.00	6.00	12.00
FIRE					
❏ LP-105 [M]	Need Your Lovin'	1962	100.00	200.00	400.00
SUE					
❏ LP-1044 [M]	Don Gardner and Dee Dee Ford In Sweden	1965	30.00	60.00	120.00

GAYE, MARVIN
Also see THE MARQUEES (5); DIANA ROSS AND MARVIN GAYE.
12-Inch Singles

Number	Title (A Side/B Side)	Yr	VG	VG+	NM
COLUMBIA					
❏ AS 1566 [DJ]	Sexual Healing (Long Version 5:10) (Short Version 3:52)	1982	15.00	30.00	60.00
❏ CAS 2124 [DJ]	Masochistic Beauty (Vocal 4:39) (Instrumental 4:39)	1985	2.00	4.00	8.00
❏ 44-03934	Joy (2 versions?)	1983	2.00	4.00	8.00
❏ 44-05188	Sanctified Lady/(Instrumental)	1985	2.00	4.00	8.00
❏ 44H-69170	Sexual Healing/The Groove	1989	2.00	4.00	8.00
—"Mixed Masters" reissue; B-side by Rodney Franklin					
MOTOWN					
❏ M 00014D1	A Funky Space Reincarnation (8:15) (Instrumental 8:19)	1978	5.00	10.00	20.00
❏ PR-129 [DJ]	I Heard It Through the Grapevine (5:03)//The Tracks of My Tears/I Second That Emotion	1983	2.50	5.00	10.00
—B-side by Smokey Robinson and the Miracles; promo-only item issued in conjunction with the movie "The Big Chill"					
REPRISE					
❏ PRO-A-8343 [DJ]	Piece of Clay (Edit) (LP Version)	1996	2.50	5.00	10.00
TAMLA					
❏ PR-16 [DJ]	I Want You (Vocal 4:33) (Instrumental 4:36)/Love Hangover (7:49)	1976	50.00	100.00	200.00
—B-side by Diana Ross on Motown label					
❏ PR-46 [DJ]	A Funky Space Reincarnation (8:15) (same on both sides)	1979	7.50	15.00	30.00
❏ PR-178 [DJ]	The World Is Rated X (12-Inch Version 6:28)//(Single Version 3:58)/Dark Side of the World/Lonely Lover/I'm Going Home	1986	3.75	7.50	15.00

45s

Number	Title (A Side/B Side)	Yr	VG	VG+	NM
COLUMBIA					
❏ 38-03302	Sexual Healing/(Instrumental)	1982	—	2.00	4.00
❏ CNR-03344	Sexual Healing/(B-side blank)	1982	—	3.00	6.00
—One-sided budget release					
❏ 13-03585	Sexual Healing/(Instrumental)	1983	—	—	3.00
—Reissue					
❏ 38-03589	'Til Tomorrow/Rockin' After Midnight	1983	—	2.00	4.00
❏ 38-03860	Joy/(Instrumental)	1983			
—Canceled? (Replaced by 38-03935?)					
❏ 38-03870	Star Spangled Banner/Turn On Some Music	1983	—	—	—
—Canceled?					
❏ 38-03935	Joy/Turn On Some Music	1983	—	2.00	4.00
❏ 38-04861	Sanctified Lady/(Instrumental)	1985	—	2.00	4.00
❏ 38-05442	It's Madness/Ain't It Funny (How Things Turn Around)	1985	—	2.00	4.00
❏ 38-05791	Just Like/More	1986	—	2.00	4.00
DETROIT FREE PRESS					
❏ (no #) [DJ]	The Teen Beat Song/Loraine Alterman Interviews Marvin Gaye	1966	37.50	75.00	150.00

Number	Title (A Side/B Side)	Yr	VG	VG+	NM
TAMLA					
❏ (no #) [DJ]	Masquerade (Is Over)/Witchcraft	1962	150.00	300.00	600.00
—As "Marvin Gay"; label states "Single Not Available extracted from Album (TM-221)"					
❏ S4KM 0741/2 [DJ]	This Is the Life/My Way	1965	12.50	25.00	50.00
❏ 1836	The World Is Rated X/No Greater Love	1986	—	2.50	5.00
❏ 1836 [PS]	The World Is Rated X/No Greater Love	1986	—	2.50	5.00
❏ 54041	Let Your Conscience Be Your Guide/Never Let You Go	1961	100.00	200.00	400.00
❏ 54055	Sandman/I'm Yours, You're Mine	1962	15.00	30.00	60.00
❏ 54062	Masquerade (Is Over)/Witchcraft	1962	—	—	—
—Unreleased					
❏ 54063	Soldier's Plea/Taking My Time	1962	10.00	20.00	40.00
—With label credit "Marvin Gaye Love Tones"					
❏ 54063	Soldier's Plea/Taking My Time	1962	12.50	25.00	50.00
—With label credit "Marvin Gaye"					
❏ 54068	Stubborn Kind of Fellow/It Hurts Me Too	1962	7.50	15.00	30.00
❏ 54075	Hitch Hike/Hello There Angel	1963	5.00	10.00	20.00
❏ 54079	Pride and Joy/One of These Days	1963	5.00	10.00	20.00
❏ 54087	Can I Get a Witness/I'm Crazy 'Bout My Baby	1963	5.00	10.00	20.00
❏ 54093	You're a Wonderful One/When I'm Alone I Cry	1964	3.75	7.50	15.00
❏ 54095	Try It Baby/If My Heart Could Sing	1964	3.75	7.50	15.00
❏ 54095 [PS]	Try It Baby/If My Heart Could Sing	1964	15.00	30.00	60.00
❏ 54101	Baby Don't You Do It/Walk on the Wild Side	1964	3.75	7.50	15.00
❏ 54101 [PS]	Baby Don't You Do It/Walk on the Wild Side	1964	15.00	30.00	60.00
❏ 54107	How Sweet It Is To Be Loved By You/Forever	1964	3.75	7.50	15.00
❏ 54112	I'll Be Doggone/You've Been a Long Time Coming	1965	3.75	7.50	15.00
❏ 54117	Pretty Little Baby/Now That You've Won Me	1965	3.75	7.50	15.00
❏ 54122	Ain't That Peculiar/She's Got to Be Real	1965	3.75	7.50	15.00
❏ 54129	One More Heartache/When I Had Your Love	1966	3.00	6.00	12.00
❏ 54132	Take This Heart of Mine/Need Your Lovin' (Want You Back)	1966	3.00	6.00	12.00
❏ 54138	Little Darling, I Need You/Hey Diddle Diddle	1966	3.00	6.00	12.00
❏ 54153	Your Unchanging Love/I'll Take Care of You	1967	2.50	5.00	10.00
❏ 54160	You/Change What You Can	1967	2.50	5.00	10.00
❏ 54170	Chained/At Last I Found a Love	1968	2.50	5.00	10.00
❏ 54176	I Heard It Through the Grapevine/You're What's Happening (In the World Today)	1968	2.50	5.00	10.00
❏ 54181	Too Busy Thinking About My Baby/Wherever I Lay My Hat (That's My Home)	1969	2.00	4.00	8.00
❏ 54185	That's the Way Love Is/Gonna Keep On Tryin' Till I Win Your Love	1969	2.00	4.00	8.00
❏ 54190	Gonna Give Her All the Love I've Got/How Can I Forget You	1970	2.00	4.00	8.00
❏ 54195	The End of Our Road/Me and My Lonely Room	1970	2.00	4.00	8.00
❏ 54201	What's Going On/God Is Love	1971	—	3.00	6.00
❏ 54207	Mercy Mercy Me (The Ecology)/Sad Tomorrows	1971	—	3.00	6.00
❏ 54209	Inner City Blues (Make Me Wanna Holler)/Wholly Holy	1971	—	3.00	6.00
❏ 54221	You're the Man (Part 1)/You're the Man (Part 2)	1972	—	3.00	6.00
❏ 54228	Trouble Man/Don't Mess With Mister "T"	1972	—	3.00	6.00
❏ 54229	Christmas in the City/I Want to Come Home for Christmas	1972	—	—	—
—Canceled					
❏ 54234	Let's Get It On/I Wish It Would Rain	1973	—	2.00	4.00
❏ 54241	Come Get to This/Distant Lover	1973	—	2.00	4.00
❏ 54244	You Sure Love to Ball/Just to Keep You Satisfied	1974	—	2.00	4.00
❏ 54253	Distant Lover/Trouble Man	1974	—	2.00	4.00
❏ 54264	I Want You/I Want You (Instrumental)	1975	—	2.00	4.00
❏ 54273	After the Dance/Feel All My Love Inside	1976	—	2.00	4.00
❏ 54280	Got to Give It Up — Pt. 1/Got to Give It Up — Pt. 2	1977	—	2.00	4.00
❏ 54280 [PS]	Got to Give It Up — Pt. 1/Got to Give It Up — Pt. 2	1977	2.50	5.00	10.00
❏ 54298	Funky Space Reincarnation — Pt. 1/Funky Space Reincarnation — Pt. 2	1979	—	2.00	4.00
❏ 54300	Time to Get It Together/Anger	1979	2.50	5.00	10.00
—Only released in Canada					
❏ 54305	Ego Tripping Out/(Instrumental)	1979	—	2.00	4.00
❏ 54322	Funk Me/Praise	1981	—	2.00	4.00
❏ 54326	Heavy Love Affair/Far Cry	1981	—	2.00	4.00
TOPPS/MOTOWN					
❏ 6	How Sweet It Is	1967	18.75	37.50	75.00
—Cardboard record					
Albums					
COLUMBIA					
❏ FC 38197	Midnight Love	1982	2.50	5.00	10.00
❏ PC 38197	Midnight Love	1986	2.00	4.00	8.00
—Budget-line reissue					
❏ FC 39916	Dream of a Lifetime	1985	2.50	5.00	10.00
❏ 9C9 40133 [PD]	Dream of a Lifetime	1985	5.00	10.00	20.00
❏ FC 40208	Romantically Yours	1986	2.50	5.00	10.00
❏ HC 48197	Midnight Love	1984	10.00	20.00	40.00
—Half-speed mastered edition					
MOTOWN					
❏ M5-115V1	Motown Superstar Series, Vol. 15	1981	2.50	5.00	10.00
❏ M5-125V1	M.P.G.	1981	2.50	5.00	10.00
—Reissue of Tamla 292					
❏ M5-181V1	Marvin Gaye Live!	1981	2.50	5.00	10.00
—Reissue of Tamla 333					
❏ M5-191V1	Marvin Gaye's Greatest Hits	1981	2.50	5.00	10.00
—Reissue of Tamla 348					
❏ M5-192V1	Let's Get It On	1981	2.50	5.00	10.00
❏ M5-216V1	A Tribute to the Great Nat King Cole	1981	2.50	5.00	10.00
—Reissue of Tamla 261					

Number	Title (A Side/B Side)	Yr	VG	VG+	NM
❏ M5-218V1	That Stubborn Kinda' Fellow	1981	2.50	5.00	10.00
—Reissue of Tamla 239					
❏ M9-791A3 [(3)]	Anthology	1974	5.00	10.00	20.00
❏ 37463 1296-1 [DJ]	The Master 1961-1984	1995	5.00	10.00	20.00
—Vinyl is promo only; 8-song sampler from box set					
❏ 5259 ML [(2)]	Marvin Gaye Live at the London Palladium	1983	3.00	6.00	12.00
—Reissue of Tamla 352					
❏ 5306 ML	Super Hits	198?	2.50	5.00	10.00
❏ 5339 ML	What's Going On	198?	2.50	5.00	10.00
—Reissue of Tamla 322					
❏ 6058 ML	Every Great Motown Hit of Marvin Gaye	1983	2.50	5.00	10.00
❏ 6255 ML [(2)]	A Musical Testament 1964-1984	1988	3.00	6.00	12.00
NATURAL RESOURCES					
❏ NR 4007T1	The Soulful Moods of Marvin Gaye	1978	3.00	6.00	12.00
—Reissue of Tamla 221					
TAMLA					
❏ T 221 [M]	The Soulful Moods of Marvin Gaye	1961	250.00	500.00	1000.
❏ T 239 [M]	That Stubborn Kinda' Fella	1963	150.00	300.00	600.00
❏ T 242 [M]	Recorded Live — Marvin Gaye on Stage	1963	75.00	150.00	300.00
❏ T 251 [M]	When I'm Alone I Cry	1964	62.50	125.00	250.00
❏ T 252 [M]	Marvin Gaye/Greatest Hits	1964	7.50	15.00	30.00
❏ TS 252 [S]	Marvin Gaye/Greatest Hits	1964	10.00	20.00	40.00
❏ T 258 [M]	How Sweet It Is to Be Loved by You	1965	10.00	20.00	40.00
❏ TS 258 [S]	How Sweet It Is to Be Loved by You	1965	12.50	25.00	50.00
❏ T 259 [M]	Hello Broadway, This Is Marvin	1965	10.00	20.00	40.00
❏ TS 259 [S]	Hello Broadway, This Is Marvin	1965	12.50	25.00	50.00
❏ T 261 [M]	A Tribute to the Great Nat King Cole	1965	10.00	20.00	40.00
❏ TS 261 [S]	A Tribute to the Great Nat King Cole	1965	12.50	25.00	50.00
❏ T 266 [M]	Moods of Marvin Gaye	1966	10.00	20.00	40.00
❏ TS 266 [S]	Moods of Marvin Gaye	1966	12.50	25.00	50.00
❏ T 278 [M]	Marvin Gaye/Greatest Hits, Vol. 2	1967	6.25	12.50	25.00
❏ TS 278 [S]	Marvin Gaye/Greatest Hits, Vol. 2	1967	5.00	10.00	20.00
❏ T 285 [M]	In the Groove	1968	12.50	25.00	50.00
❏ TS 285 [M]	In the Groove	1968	6.25	12.50	25.00
❏ TS 285 [S]	I Heard It Through the Grapevine	1969	5.00	10.00	20.00
—Retitled version of "In the Groove"					
❏ TS 292	M.P.G.	1969	5.00	10.00	20.00
❏ TS 293	Marvin Gaye and His Girls	1969	5.00	10.00	20.00
—Includes duets with Tammi Terrell, Mary Wells, Kim Weston					
❏ TS 299	That's the Way Love Is	1969	5.00	10.00	20.00
❏ TS 300	Marvin Gaye Super Hits	1970	5.00	10.00	20.00
❏ T5-310	What's Going On	1971	3.75	7.50	15.00
❏ T5-322	Trouble Man	1972	3.75	7.50	15.00
❏ T6-329	Let's Get It On	1973	3.75	7.50	15.00
❏ T6-333	Marvin Gaye Live!	1974	3.75	7.50	15.00
❏ T6-342	I Want You	1976	3.75	7.50	15.00
❏ T6-348	Marvin Gaye's Greatest Hits	1976	3.75	7.50	15.00
❏ T7-352 [(2)]	Marvin Gaye Live at the London Palladium	1977	3.75	7.50	15.00
❏ T13-364 [(2)]	Here, My Dear	1978	3.75	7.50	15.00
❏ T8-374	In Our Lifetime	1981	2.50	5.00	10.00
❏ 6172 TL	Motown Remembers Marvin Gaye	1986	2.50	5.00	10.00

GAYE, MARVIN, AND TAMMI TERRELL
Also see each artist's individual listings.
45s
TAMLA

Number	Title (A Side/B Side)	Yr	VG	VG+	NM
❏ 54149	Ain't No Mountain High Enough/Give a Little Love	1967	2.00	4.00	8.00
❏ 54156	Your Precious Love/Hold Me Oh My Darling	1967	2.00	4.00	8.00
❏ 54161	If I Could Build My Whole World Around You/If This World Were Mine	1967	2.00	4.00	8.00
❏ 54163	Ain't Nothing Like the Real Thing/Little Ole Boy, Little Ole Girl	1968	2.00	4.00	8.00
❏ 54169	You're All I Need to Get By/Two Can Have a Party	1968	2.00	4.00	8.00
❏ 54173	You Ain't Livin' Till You're Lovin'/Keep On Lovin' Me Honey	1968	—	3.00	6.00
❏ 54179	Good Lovin' Ain't Easy to Come By/Satisfied Feelin'	1969	—	3.00	6.00
❏ 54179 [PS]	Good Lovin' Ain't Easy to Come By/Satisfied Feelin'	1969	5.00	10.00	20.00
❏ 54187	What You Gave Me/How You Gonna Keep It	1969	—	3.00	6.00
❏ 54192	The Onion Song/California Soul	1970	—	3.00	6.00
Albums					
MOTOWN					
❏ M5-102V1	Motown Superstar Series, Vol. 2	1981	2.50	5.00	10.00
❏ M5-142V1	You're All I Need	1981	2.50	5.00	10.00
—Reissue of Tamla 284					
❏ M5-200V1	United	1981	2.50	5.00	10.00
—Reissue of Tamla 277					
TAMLA					
❏ T 277 [M]	United	1967	7.50	15.00	30.00
❏ TS 277 [S]	United	1967	6.25	12.50	25.00
❏ T 284 [M]	You're All I Need	1968	12.50	25.00	50.00
❏ TS 284 [S]	You're All I Need	1968	5.00	10.00	20.00
❏ TS 294	Easy	1969	5.00	10.00	20.00
❏ TS 302	Marvin Gaye & Tammi Terrell/Greatest Hits	1970	5.00	10.00	20.00

GAYE, MARVIN, AND MARY WELLS
Also see each artist's individual listings.
45s
MOTOWN

Number	Title (A Side/B Side)	Yr	VG	VG+	NM
❏ 1057	Once Upon a Time/What's the Matter with You Baby	1964	3.75	7.50	15.00
❏ 1057 [PS]	Once Upon a Time/What's the Matter with You Baby	1964	15.00	30.00	60.00

Albums
MOTOWN

Number	Title (A Side/B Side)	Yr	VG	VG+	NM
❏ M 613 [M]	Together	1964	12.50	25.00	50.00
❏ 5260 ML	Together	1982	2.50	5.00	10.00

GAYE, MARVIN, AND KIM WESTON
Also see each artist's individual listings.
45s
TAMLA

Number	Title (A Side/B Side)	Yr	VG	VG+	NM
❏ 54104	What Good Am I Without You/I Want You 'Round	1964	3.75	7.50	15.00
❏ 54141	It Takes Two/It's Got to Be a Miracle	1966	3.00	6.00	12.00
Albums					
TAMLA					
❏ T/TS 260	Side by Side	1965	—	—	—
—Canceled					
❏ T 270 [M]	Take Two	1966	7.50	15.00	30.00
❏ TS 270 [S]	Take Two	1966	10.00	20.00	40.00

GAYNOR, GLORIA
12-Inch Singles
ATLANTIC

Number	Title (A Side/B Side)	Yr	VG	VG+	NM
❏ 369	Tease Me (2 versions)	1982	—	3.00	6.00
❏ 633	America/Runaround Love	1982	—	3.00	6.00
MCA					
❏ L33-1847 [DJ]	Love Is a Heartbeat Away (2 versions)	1979	2.50	5.00	10.00
POLYDOR					
❏ PRO 107 [DJ]	Most of All/As Time Goes By	1977	2.50	5.00	10.00
❏ PRO 111 [DJ]	Let Me Know (I Have a Right) (2 versions)	1979	2.00	4.00	8.00
❏ PD-D-504 [DJ]	Substitute (same on both sides)	1978	2.00	4.00	8.00
❏ PD-D-507 [DJ]	Anybody Wanna Party (same on both sides)	1978	2.00	4.00	8.00
❏ PD-D-517 [DJ]	Let's Mend What's Been Broken (same on both sides)	1981	2.00	4.00	8.00
SILVER BLUE					
❏ 220	I Am What I Am (From La Cage Aux Folles)/(Dub Mix)	198?	2.00	4.00	8.00
❏ 05018	Bullseye/Chain of Whispers	1984	—	3.00	6.00
45s					
ATLANTIC					
❏ 89824 [DJ]	America (same on both sides)	1983	—	2.00	4.00
—May be promo only					
❏ 89887	Stop in the Name of Love/For You, My Love	1982	—	2.00	4.00
❏ 89947	Tease Me/Mack Side	1982	—	2.00	4.00
COLUMBIA					
❏ 45909	Honey Bee/All It Took, Boy, Was Losing You	1973	—	3.00	6.00
MGM					
❏ 14706	Honey Bee/Come Tonight	1974	—	2.50	5.00
❏ 14748	Never Can Say Goodbye/We Can Just Make It	1974	—	2.00	4.00
❏ 14790	Reach Out, I'll Be There/Searchin'	1975	—	2.00	4.00
❏ 14808	Walk On By/Real Good People	1975	—	2.00	4.00
❏ 14823	(If You Want It) Do It Yourself/I'm Still Yours	1975	—	2.00	4.00
❏ 14838	How High the Moon/My Man's Gone	1975	—	2.00	4.00
POLYDOR					
❏ 2021	Let Me Know (I Have a Right)/One Plus One	1979	—	2.00	4.00
❏ 2056	Midnight Rocker/Can't Fight This Feelin'	1980	—	2.00	4.00
❏ 2089	The Luckiest Girl in the World/Ain't No Bigger Fool	1980	—	2.00	4.00
❏ 2173	Let's Mend What's Been Broken/I Love You Because	1981	—	2.00	4.00
❏ 2179	I Kinda Like Me/Fingers in the Rain	1981	—	2.00	4.00
❏ 14342	Do It Right/Touch of Lightning	1976	—	2.00	4.00
❏ 14357	Let's Make a Deal/Let's Make Love	1976	—	2.00	4.00
❏ 14391	Most of All/So Much Love	1977	—	2.00	4.00
❏ 14443	After the Lovin'/You're All I Need to Get By	1977	—	2.00	4.00
❏ 14472	This Love Affair/For the First Time in My Life	1978	—	2.00	4.00
❏ 14508	I Will Survive/Substitute	1978	—	2.00	4.00
❏ 14558	Anybody Wanna Party?/Please Be There	1979	—	2.00	4.00
SILVER BLUE					
❏ 720	I Am What I Am/More Than Enough	1983	—	2.50	5.00
❏ 04294	I Am What I Am/More Than Enough	1983	—	2.00	4.00
❏ 04422	Strive/I've Been Watching You	1984	—	2.00	4.00
Albums					
ATLANTIC					
❏ 80033	Gloria Gaynor	1982	2.50	5.00	10.00
MGM					
❏ M3G-4982	Never Can Say Goodbye	1975	2.50	5.00	10.00
❏ M3G-4997	Experience Gloria Gaynor	1975	2.50	5.00	10.00
POLYDOR					
❏ PD-1-6063	I've Got You	1976	2.50	5.00	10.00
❏ PD-1-6095	Glorious	1977	2.50	5.00	10.00
❏ PD-1-6139	Gloria Gaynor's Park Avenue Sound	1978	2.50	5.00	10.00
❏ PD-1-6184	Love Tracks	1978	2.50	5.00	10.00
❏ PD-1-6231	I Have a Right	1979	2.50	5.00	10.00
❏ PD-1-6274	Stories	1980	2.50	5.00	10.00

GAYTEN, PAUL
Also see THE TUNE WEAVERS.
45s
ANNA

Number	Title (A Side/B Side)	Yr	VG	VG+	NM
❏ 1106	The Hunch/Hot Cross Buns	1959	5.00	10.00	20.00
❏ 1112	Beatnick Beat/Scratch Back	1960	5.00	10.00	20.00
ARGO					
❏ 5257	The Music Goes Round and Round/Be My Baby	1956	6.25	12.50	25.00
❏ 5263	Driving Home Part 1/Driving Home Part 2	1957	6.25	12.50	25.00
❏ 5267	Old Buttermilk Sky/The Sweeper	1957	6.25	12.50	25.00

G

Number	Title (A Side/B Side)	Yr	VG	VG+	NM
❏ 5277	Nervous Boogie/Flatfoot Sam	1957	6.25	12.50	25.00

—*B-side by Oscar Wiles*

❏ 5300	Windy/Tickle Toe	1958	6.25	12.50	25.00

CHECKER

❏ 801	I'm Tired/Get It	1954	6.25	12.50	25.00
❏ 836	You Better Believe It/Mother Roux	1956	6.25	12.50	25.00

OKEH

❏ 6847	Lonesome for My Baby/All Alone and Lovely	1952	7.50	15.00	30.00
❏ 6870	Give Me Liberty or Give Me Death/Happy Days	1952	7.50	15.00	30.00
❏ 6908	True (You Don't Love Me)/They All Ask for You	1952	7.50	15.00	30.00
❏ 6934	Yes You Do, Yes You Do/Don't Worry Me	1953	7.50	15.00	30.00
❏ 6972	Time Is a-Passin'/Ain't Nothin' Happenin'	1953	7.50	15.00	30.00
❏ 6982	Cow Cow Blues/Ooh-Boo	1953	7.50	15.00	30.00
❏ 7003	Hurry Home/Sugar Baby	1953	7.50	15.00	30.00
❏ 7019	Mule Face/It's Over	1954	7.50	15.00	30.00
❏ 7068	True (You Don't Love Me)/Cow Cow Blues	1956	6.25	12.50	25.00

GEMS, THE (1)
45s
CHESS

Number	Title (A Side/B Side)	Yr	VG	VG+	NM
❏ 1863	One More Year/Let Your Hair Down	1963	3.00	6.00	12.00
❏ 1875	If It's the Last Thing I Do/A Girl's Impression	1963	3.00	6.00	12.00
❏ 1882	A Love of Mine/That's Why They Put Erasers On	1964	3.00	6.00	12.00
❏ 1908	I Can't Help Myself/Can't You Take a Hint	1964	3.00	6.00	12.00
❏ 1917	Love For Christmas/All Of It	1964	3.00	6.00	12.00
❏ 1930	He Makes Me Feel So Good/Happy New Love	1965	2.50	5.00	10.00
❏ 2104	Girls Can Do It/Ain't That Loving You	1971	—	3.00	6.00

GEMS, THE (2)
45s
DREXEL

Number	Title (A Side/B Side)	Yr	VG	VG+	NM
❏ 901	Deed I Do/Talk About the Weather	1954	100.00	200.00	400.00

—*Black vinyl*

❏ 901	Deed I Do/Talk About the Weather	1954	625.00	1250.	2500.

—*Red vinyl*

❏ 903	I Thought You'd Care/Kitty from New York City	1954	75.00	150.00	300.00

—*Black vinyl*

❏ 903	I Thought You'd Care/Kitty from New York City	1954	150.00	300.00	600.00

—*Red vinyl*

❏ 904	You're Tired of Love/Ol' Man River	1954	75.00	150.00	300.00

—*Black vinyl*

❏ 904	You're Tired of Love/Ol' Man River	1954	150.00	300.00	600.00

—*Red vinyl*

❏ 909	One Woman Man/The Darkest Night	1955	100.00	200.00	400.00
❏ 915	Till the Day I Die/Monkey Face Baby	1956	100.00	200.00	400.00

GENE AND EUNICE
45s
ALADDIN

Number	Title (A Side/B Side)	Yr	VG	VG+	NM
❏ 3276	Ko Ko Mo (I Need You So)/You and Me	1954	6.25	12.50	25.00
❏ 3282	This Is My Story/Move It Over Baby	1954	6.25	12.50	25.00
❏ 3292	Flim Flam/Can We Forget It	1954	6.25	12.50	25.00
❏ 3305	I Gotta Go Home/Have You Changed Your Mind	1954	6.25	12.50	25.00
❏ 3315	Hootchy Kootchy/I'll Never Believe in You	1955	5.00	10.00	20.00
❏ 3321	Let's Get Together/I'm So in Love with You	1955	5.00	10.00	20.00
❏ 3351	Bom Bom Lulu/Hi Diddle Diddle	1956	5.00	10.00	20.00
❏ 3374	The Vow/Strange World	1957	5.00	10.00	20.00
❏ 3376	Doodle Doodle Doo/Don't Treat Me This Way	1957	5.00	10.00	20.00
❏ 3414	I Mean Love/The Angels Gave You to Me	1958	5.00	10.00	20.00

CASE

❏ 1001	Poco-Loco/Go-On Kokomo	1959	7.50	15.00	30.00
❏ 1002	Ah! Ah!/You Think I'm Not Thinking	1959	7.50	15.00	30.00
❏ 1005	Without Love/(B-side unknown)	1959	6.25	12.50	25.00
❏ 1007	Sugar Babe/Let's Play the Game	1960	6.25	12.50	25.00

COMBO

❏ 64	Ko Ko Mo (I Need You So)/You and Me	1954	7.50	15.00	30.00

LILLY

❏ 512	Everlovin' Baby/Got a Right to Know	1962	3.75	7.50	15.00

UNITED ARTISTS

❏ 0151	Ko Ko Mo (I Need You So)/This Is My Story	1973	—	2.00	4.00

—*"Silver Spotlight Series" reissue*

GENTLE SOUL
45s
EPIC

Number	Title (A Side/B Side)	Yr	VG	VG+	NM
❏ 10448	Reelin'/2:30 Train	1969	3.00	6.00	12.00

GEORGE, BARBARA
45s
A.F.O.

Number	Title (A Side/B Side)	Yr	VG	VG+	NM
❏ 302	I Know (You Don't Love Me No More)/Love	1961	3.00	6.00	12.00

—*Orange and black label*

❏ 302	I Know (You Don't Love Me No More)/Love	1961	3.75	7.50	15.00

—*All-orange label*

❏ 304	You Talk About Love/Whip-O-Will	1962	2.50	5.00	10.00

SUE

❏ 763	If You Think/If When You've Done the Best You Can	1962	2.00	4.00	8.00
❏ 766	Send for Me (If You Need Some Lovin')/Bless You	1962	2.00	4.00	8.00
❏ 773	Recipe (For Perfect Fools)/Try Again	1962	2.00	4.00	8.00
❏ 796	Something's Definitely Wrong/I Need Something Different	1963	2.50	5.00	10.00

UNITED ARTISTS

Number	Title (A Side/B Side)	Yr	VG	VG+	NM
❏ XW516	I Know (You Don't Love Me No More)/Mockingbird	1974	—	2.00	4.00

—*Reissue; B-side by Charles and Inez Foxx*

Albums
A.F.O.

❏ LP 5001 [M]	I Know (You Don't Love Me No More)	1962	62.50	125.00	250.00

GEORGE AND GREER
45s
GOLDWAX

Number	Title (A Side/B Side)	Yr	VG	VG+	NM
❏ 313	You Don't Know It, But You Had Me/Good Times	1966	10.00	20.00	40.00
❏ 313	You Don't Know It, But You Had Me/Good Times	1966	7.50	15.00	30.00

—*Reissue as "George Jackson and Dan Greer"*

GILL, JOHNNY
Also see STACY LATTISAW AND JOHNNY GILL; NEW EDITION.
12-Inch Singles
COTILLION

Number	Title (A Side/B Side)	Yr	VG	VG+	NM
❏ DMD 644 [DJ]	Super Love (Special Version 4:54) (Short Version 3:59)	1983	2.50	5.00	10.00
❏ DMD 839 [DJ]	Can't Wait Til Tomorrow (Vocal)/(Dub Version) (Vocal Edited Version of Remix)	1985	3.75	7.50	15.00

GIANT

❏ PRO-A-4912 [DJ]	I'm Still Waiting (Master Mix) (Instrumental)	1991	2.50	5.00	10.00

MOTOWN

❏ L33-1088 [DJ]	Wrap My Body Tight (7" Radio Edit) (12" Remake Version) (Funk Radio)/(Soul Mix) (House Mix) (LP Version)	1991	3.00	6.00	12.00
❏ 37463 1095 1	The Floor (Instrumental) (Pop Edit) (LP Version) (Flyte Tyme Edit) (Video Edit)	1993	2.50	5.00	10.00
❏ 37463 1110 1	The Floor (L.R. Extended Mix) (L.R. Edit) (Underground Dub)/(Smoove Extended Mix) (Raw Mix) (LP Version)	1993	2.50	5.00	10.00
❏ 37463 1119 1	I Got You (LP Version 4:14) (Radio Mix 3:56) (Crazy Disco 4:40)/(Chill Mix 4:26) (Main Mix 4:40) (Dance Mix 3:55)	1993	2.50	5.00	10.00
❏ 37463 1132 1	Long Way from Home (LP Edit) (LP Edit with Early Fade)/(LP Version) (Instrumental Version)	1993	2.50	5.00	10.00
❏ 37463 1152 1	Quiet Time to Play (Live Version) (Live Edit - LP Version)/(Full Live Version) (Instrumental)	1993	3.00	6.00	12.00
❏ 37463 1162 1	Tell Me How U Want It (Radio Edit) (LP Version) (Instrumental)	1994	3.00	6.00	12.00
❏ L33-1363 [DJ]	Giving My All to You (same on both sides)	1991	2.50	5.00	10.00
❏ 37463 2017 1	It's Your Body (Radio Edit) (LP Version) (Instrumental) (Acappella)	1996	2.50	5.00	10.00

—*"Featuring Roger Troutman"*

❏ 37463 2028 1	Love in an Elevator (Radio Edit) (LP Version) (Alternative Mix) (Instrumental) (Acappella)	1997	2.50	5.00	10.00
❏ 37463 2030 1	Love in an Elevator (Radio Edit) (LP Version) (Instrumental) (A Cappella)/So Gentle (Radio Edit) (LP Version) (Instrumental) (A Cappella)	1997	2.50	5.00	10.00
❏ 37463 2094 1	Maybe (Radio Edit) (LP Version)/Having Illusions (Radio Version)	1997	2.50	5.00	10.00
❏ MOT-4657	Rub You the Right Way (2 versions)	1990	2.50	5.00	10.00
❏ MOT-4727	Fairweather Friend (unknown versions)	1990	2.50	5.00	10.00
❏ MOT12-4756	Wrap My Body Tight (5 versions)	1991	3.00	6.00	12.00
❏ 37483 4834 1	The Floor (Smoove Extended Mix) (L.R. Extended Mix) (Jazz Mix)	1993	2.50	5.00	10.00
❏ 37463 4842 1	I Got You (LP Version 4:14) (Radio Mix 3:56) (Crazy Disco 4:40)/(Chill Mix 4:26) (Main Mix 4:40) (Dance Mix 3:55)	1993	2.50	5.00	10.00
❏ L33-17921 [DJ]	Rub You the Right Way (LP Version) (Edit Version)	1990	3.00	6.00	12.00
❏ L33-18396 [DJ]	Fairweather Friend (same on both sides)	1990	2.50	5.00	10.00

45s
COTILLION

❏ 99646	Can't Wait Till Tomorrow/One Small Light	1985	—	2.00	4.00
❏ 99671	Half Crazy/Chemistry	1985	—	2.00	4.00
❏ 99671 [PS]	Half Crazy/Chemistry	1985	—	2.00	4.00
❏ 99840	When Something Is Wrong with My Baby/Half Steppin'	1983	—	2.00	4.00
❏ 99859	Super Love/I'm Sorry	1983	—	2.00	4.00

MOTOWN

❏ 919	My, My, My (same on both sides)	1990	—	2.00	4.00
❏ 1982	Rub You the Right Way/Rub You the Right Way (LP Version)	1989	—	2.50	5.00
❏ 37463 2202 7	The Floor/Album Snippets	1993	—	—	3.00

Albums
COTILLION

❏ 90103	Johnny Gill	1983	2.50	5.00	10.00
❏ 90250	Chemistry	1985	2.50	5.00	10.00

MOTOWN

❏ 6283	Johnny Gill	1990	3.00	6.00	12.00

GLADIOLAS, THE
Evolved into MAURICE WILLIAMS AND THE ZODIACS.
45s
EXCELLO

Number	Title (A Side/B Side)	Yr	VG	VG+	NM
❏ 2101	Little Darlin'/Sweetheart, Please Don't Go	1957	18.75	37.50	75.00
❏ 2110	Run, Run, Little Joe/Comin' Home to You	1957	12.50	25.00	50.00
❏ 2120	Hey Little Girl/I Wanta Know	1957	12.50	25.00	50.00
❏ 2136	Shoop Shoop/Say You'll Be Mine	1958	12.50	25.00	50.00

Number	Title (A Side/B Side)	Yr	VG	VG+	NM

GLENN, LLOYD
45s
ALADDIN

Number	Title (A Side/B Side)	Yr	VG	VG+	NM
❑ 3268	Nite Flite/Still Waters	1954	6.25	12.50	25.00
❑ 3288	Footloose/Glen's Glide	1955	6.25	12.50	25.00
❑ 3307	Sunrise/Tiddly Winks	1955	6.25	12.50	25.00
❑ 3327	Southbound Special/Blue Ivories	1956	5.00	10.00	20.00
❑ 3346	After Hours (Part 1)/After Hours (Part 2)	1956	5.00	10.00	20.00
❑ 3353	Chica-Boo/Old Time Shuffle	1957	5.00	10.00	20.00
❑ 3378	The Vamp/Ballroom Shuffle	1957	5.00	10.00	20.00
❑ 3400	Hyde Park/Love for Sale	1957	5.00	10.00	20.00
❑ 3407	Cute-Tee/Black Fantasy	1958	5.00	10.00	20.00
❑ 3446	Petite Fleur/Honky Tonk Train	1959	3.75	7.50	15.00
❑ 3459	Long Gone (Part 1)/Long Gone (Part 2)	1959	3.75	7.50	15.00

HOLLYWOOD

Number	Title (A Side/B Side)	Yr	VG	VG+	NM
❑ 1021	Merry Christmas Baby/Sleigh Ride	1954	5.00	10.00	20.00
—B-side by Charles Brown; red label					
❑ 1021	Merry Christmas Baby/Sleigh Ride	196?	2.00	4.00	8.00
—B-side by Charles Brown; color label					
❑ 1021	Merry Christmas Baby/Sleigh Ride	197?	—	2.50	5.00
—B-side by Charles Brown; black label					
❑ 1028	Chica-Boo/Old Time Shuffle	1954	6.25	12.50	25.00
❑ 1033	Sleigh Ride/China Doll	1954	6.25	12.50	25.00

IMPERIAL

Number	Title (A Side/B Side)	Yr	VG	VG+	NM
❑ 5839	Twistville/Young Date	1962	3.00	6.00	12.00

SWING TIME

Number	Title (A Side/B Side)	Yr	VG	VG+	NM
❑ 254	Chica-Boo/Jungle Town Jubilee	1951	7.50	15.00	30.00
❑ 271	Sleigh Ride/Savage Boy	1951	7.50	15.00	30.00
❑ 277	Day Break Stomp/Jungle Twilight	1952	7.50	15.00	30.00
❑ 278	Cute-Tee/Rhumba	1952	7.50	15.00	30.00
❑ 292	After Hours/Yancey Special	1952	7.50	15.00	30.00
❑ 293	Honky Tonk Train/Pine Top Boogie Woogie	1952	7.50	15.00	30.00
❑ 296	Angora/Cuba Doll	1952	7.50	15.00	30.00
❑ 311	Boogie Woogie on St. Louis Blues/Ugh	1953	7.50	15.00	30.00
❑ 324	Night Time/It Moves Me	1953	7.50	15.00	30.00
❑ 336	Not the Girl for Me/Black Fantasy	1954	7.50	15.00	30.00

Albums
ALADDIN

Number	Title (A Side/B Side)	Yr	VG	VG+	NM
❑ LP-808 [M]	Chica-Boo	1956	1000.	1500.	2000.
—Red vinyl					
❑ LP-808 [M]	Chica-Boo	1956	250.00	500.00	1000.
—Black vinyl					

BLACK & BLUE

Number	Title (A Side/B Side)	Yr	VG	VG+	NM
❑ 33077	Old Time Shuffle	1977	3.00	6.00	12.00

IMPERIAL

Number	Title (A Side/B Side)	Yr	VG	VG+	NM
❑ LP-9174 [M]	Chica-Boo	1962	37.50	75.00	150.00
❑ LP-9175 [M]	After Hours	1962	37.50	75.00	150.00
❑ LP-12174 [S]	Chica-Boo	1962	50.00	100.00	200.00
❑ LP-12175 [S]	After Hours	1962	50.00	100.00	200.00

SCORE

Number	Title (A Side/B Side)	Yr	VG	VG+	NM
❑ SLP-4006 [M]	Lloyd Glenn	1957	250.00	500.00	1000.
❑ SLP-4020 [M]	After Hours	1958	250.00	500.00	1000.

SWING TIME

Number	Title (A Side/B Side)	Yr	VG	VG+	NM
❑ 1901 [10]	Lloyd Glenn	1954	1500.	2250.	3000.

GLOBETROTTERS, THE
45s
BUDDAH

Number	Title (A Side/B Side)	Yr	VG	VG+	NM
❑ 309	Don't Rock the Boat/Hatfield Small	1972	2.50	5.00	10.00

KIRSHNER

Number	Title (A Side/B Side)	Yr	VG	VG+	NM
❑ 63-5006	Cheer Me Up/Gravy	1970	3.00	6.00	12.00
❑ 63-5006 [PS]	Cheer Me Up/Gravy	1970	3.75	7.50	15.00
❑ 63-5008	Rainy Day Bells/Meadowlark	1970	3.75	7.50	15.00
❑ 63-5012	Duke of Earl/Everybody's Got Hot Pants	1971	3.00	6.00	12.00
❑ 63-5016	Everybody Needs Love/ESP	1971	3.00	6.00	12.00

Albums
KIRSHNER

Number	Title (A Side/B Side)	Yr	VG	VG+	NM
❑ KES-108	The Globetrotters	1970	5.00	10.00	20.00

GOLDENRODS, THE
45s
VEE JAY

Number	Title (A Side/B Side)	Yr	VG	VG+	NM
❑ 307	Wish I Was Back in School/Color Cartoons	1959	62.50	125.00	250.00

GORDON, ROSCOE
45s
ABC-PARAMOUNT

Number	Title (A Side/B Side)	Yr	VG	VG+	NM
❑ 10351	A Girl to Love/As You Walk Away	1962	3.00	6.00	12.00
❑ 10407	A Little Bit of Magic/I Want Revenge	1963	3.00	6.00	12.00
❑ 10501	I Don't Stand a Chance/That's What You Did	1963	3.00	6.00	12.00
—As "Barbara & Roscoe Gordon"					

CALLA

Number	Title (A Side/B Side)	Yr	VG	VG+	NM
❑ 145	Just a Little Bit/I Really Love You	1968	2.00	4.00	8.00

CHESS

Number	Title (A Side/B Side)	Yr	VG	VG+	NM
❑ 1487	Booted/I Love You Till the Day I Die	1951	375.00	750.00	1500.

DUKE

Number	Title (A Side/B Side)	Yr	VG	VG+	NM
❑ 101	Tell Daddy/Hey Fat Girl	1952	25.00	50.00	100.00
❑ 106	T-Model Boogie/New Orleans Woman	1953	12.50	25.00	50.00
❑ 109	Too Many Women/Wise to You, Baby	1953	12.50	25.00	50.00
❑ 114	Ain't No Use/Roscoe's Mambo	1953	12.50	25.00	50.00
❑ 129	Three Can't Love/You Figure It Out	1954	12.50	25.00	50.00
❑ 165	Keep On Doggin'/Bad Dream	1957	7.50	15.00	30.00

Number	Title (A Side/B Side)	Yr	VG	VG+	NM
❑ 173	I've Loved and Lost/Tummer Tee	1957	7.50	15.00	30.00
❑ 320	Dilly Bop/You'll Never Know	1960	3.75	7.50	15.00

FLIP

Number	Title (A Side/B Side)	Yr	VG	VG+	NM
❑ 227	Weeping Blues/Just Love Me, Baby	1956	75.00	150.00	300.00
❑ 237	The Chicken (Dance with You)/Love for You Baby	1956	12.50	25.00	50.00

OLD TOWN

Number	Title (A Side/B Side)	Yr	VG	VG+	NM
❑ 1167	Gotta Keep Rollin'/Just a Little at a Time	1964	2.50	5.00	10.00
❑ 1175	It Ain't Right/Could This Be Love	1965	2.50	5.00	10.00
—As "Roscoe and Barbara"					

RPM

Number	Title (A Side/B Side)	Yr	VG	VG+	NM
❑ 324	Saddled the Cow/Ouch, Pretty Baby	1951	100.00	200.00	400.00
❑ 336	Dime a Dozen/A New Remedy for Love	1951	62.50	125.00	250.00
❑ 344	Booted/Cold, Cold Winter	1952	50.00	100.00	200.00
❑ 350	No More Doggin'/Maria	1952	50.00	100.00	200.00
❑ 358	New Orleans Woman/I Remember Your Kisses	1952	25.00	50.00	100.00
❑ 365	What You Got on Your Mind/Two Kinds of Women	1952	25.00	50.00	100.00
❑ 369	Trying/Dream Baby	1952	15.00	30.00	60.00
❑ 373	Lucille/Blues for My Baby	1953	15.00	30.00	60.00
❑ 379	I'm in Love/Just In from Texas	1953	15.00	30.00	60.00
❑ 384	We're All Loaded/Tomorrow May Be Too Late	1953	15.00	30.00	60.00

SUN

Number	Title (A Side/B Side)	Yr	VG	VG+	NM
❑ 227	Weeping Blues/Just Love Me, Baby	1956	125.00	250.00	500.00
❑ 237	The Chicken (Dance with You)/Love for You Baby	1956	50.00	100.00	200.00
❑ 257	Shoobie Oobie/Cheese and Crackers	1956	12.50	25.00	50.00
❑ 305	Sally Jo/Torro	1958	6.25	12.50	25.00

VEE JAY

Number	Title (A Side/B Side)	Yr	VG	VG+	NM
❑ 316	A Fool in Love/No More Doggin'	1959	3.75	7.50	15.00
❑ 332	Just a Little Bit/Goin' Home	1959	3.75	7.50	15.00
❑ 348	Surely I Love You/What You Do to Me	1960	3.75	7.50	15.00
❑ 385	What I Wouldn't Do/Let 'Em Try	1961	3.00	6.00	12.00

GOSPEL HILITES, THE
45s
CHECKER

Number	Title (A Side/B Side)	Yr	VG	VG+	NM
❑ 1251	Joy And A Christmas Way/One More Time	197?	—	2.50	5.00

GOSPEL STARS, THE
45s
TAMLA

Number	Title (A Side/B Side)	Yr	VG	VG+	NM
❑ 54037	He Lifted Me/Behold the Saints of God	1961	37.50	75.00	150.00
—Horizontal lines logo					
❑ 54037	He Lifted Me/Behold the Saints of God	1961	15.00	30.00	60.00
—Globe logo					

Albums
TAMLA

Number	Title (A Side/B Side)	Yr	VG	VG+	NM
❑ TM-222 [M]	The Great Gospel Stars	1961	1000.	2000.	3000.

GRAHAM, LARRY
Also see GRAHAM CENTRAL STATION; SLY AND THE FAMILY STONE.
12-Inch Singles
WARNER BROS.

Number	Title (A Side/B Side)	Yr	VG	VG+	NM
❑ PRO-A-1027 [DJ]	Don't Stop When You're Hot (edit)/(LP version)	1982	2.00	4.00	8.00
❑ PRO-A-1046 [DJ]	Sooner or Later/(Instrumental)	1982	2.00	4.00	8.00
❑ PRO-A-2065 [DJ]	I'm Sick and Tired (same on both sides)	1983	2.00	4.00	8.00

45s
WARNER BROS.

Number	Title (A Side/B Side)	Yr	VG	VG+	NM
❑ 29003	What We All Need Is More Love/Tearing Out My Heart	1985	—	—	3.00
❑ 29529	I'm Sick and Tired/I'd Rather Be Loving You	1983	—	2.00	4.00
❑ 29620	I Never Forgot Your Eyes/Movin' Inside Your Love	1983	—	2.00	4.00
❑ 29884	Let Me Come Into Your Life/What You Are Inside	1982	—	2.00	4.00
❑ 29956	Sooner or Later/I Feel Good	1982	—	2.00	4.00
❑ 29956 [PS]	Sooner or Later/I Feel Good	1982	—	2.50	5.00
❑ 49221	One in a Million You/The Entertainer	1980	—	2.00	4.00
❑ 49221 [PS]	One in a Million You/The Entertainer	1980	—	2.50	5.00
❑ 49581	When We Get Married/Tonight	1980	—	2.00	4.00
❑ 49744	Just Be My Lady/Feels Like Love	1981	—	2.00	4.00
❑ 49833	Guess Who/Sweetheart	1981	—	2.00	4.00
❑ 50068	Don't Stop When You're Hot/I Love Loving You	1982	—	2.00	4.00
❑ 50068 [PS]	Don't Stop When You're Hot/I Love Loving You	1982	—	2.50	5.00

Albums
WARNER BROS.

Number	Title (A Side/B Side)	Yr	VG	VG+	NM
❑ BSK 3447	One in a Million You	1980	2.00	4.00	8.00
❑ BSK 3554	Just Be My Lady	1981	2.00	4.00	8.00
❑ BSK 3668	Sooner or Later	1982	2.00	4.00	8.00
❑ 23878	Victory	1983	2.00	4.00	8.00
❑ 25307	Fired Up	1985	2.00	4.00	8.00

GRAHAM CENTRAL STATION
Also see LARRY GRAHAM.
12-Inch Singles
WARNER BROS.

Number	Title (A Side/B Side)	Yr	VG	VG+	NM
❑ PRO-A-639 [DJ]	Entrow (2 versions)	1976	3.75	7.50	15.00
❑ PRO-A-673 [DJ]	Now Do U Wanta Dance (same on both sides)	1977	3.75	7.50	15.00

45s
WARNER BROS.

Number	Title (A Side/B Side)	Yr	VG	VG+	NM
❑ 7782	Can You Handle It/Ghetto	1974	—	2.50	5.00
❑ 8025	Release Yourself/'Tis Your Kind of Music	1974	—	2.50	5.00
❑ 8061	Feel the Need/We Be's Gettin' Down	1974	—	2.50	5.00
❑ 8105	Your Love/I Believe in You	1975	—	2.00	4.00
❑ 8148	It's Alright/Luckiest People	1975	—	2.00	4.00

G

Number	Title (A Side/B Side)	Yr	VG	VG+	NM
❑ 8175	The Jam/The Jam (Disco Version)	1975	—	2.00	4.00
❑ 8205	Love/Why	1976	—	2.00	4.00
❑ 8235	Entrow — Part 1/Entrow — Part 2	1976	—	2.00	4.00
❑ 8288	Do Yah/I Got a Reason	1976	—	2.00	4.00
❑ 8378	Now Do-U-Wanta Dance/(B-side unknown)	1977	—	2.00	4.00
❑ 8417	Stomped Beat-Up and Whooped/Ole Smokey	1977	—	2.00	4.00
❑ 8464	Crazy Chicken/Saving My Love for You	1977	—	2.00	4.00
❑ 8602	My Radio Sure Sounds Good to Me/Turn It Out	1978	—	2.00	4.00
❑ 8665	Is It Love?/Are You Happy?	1978	—	2.00	4.00
❑ 8816	(You're a) Foxy Lady/Tonight	1979	—	2.00	4.00
❑ 49011	Star Walk/Boogie Baby	1979	—	2.00	4.00
❑ 49067	Sneaky Freak/Boogie Baby	1979	—	2.00	4.00

Albums
WARNER BROS.

Number	Title (A Side/B Side)	Yr	VG	VG+	NM
❑ BS 2763	Graham Central Station	1974	2.50	5.00	10.00
❑ BS4 2763 [Q]	Graham Central Station	1974	3.75	7.50	15.00
❑ BS 2814	Release Yourself	1974	2.50	5.00	10.00
❑ BS 2876	Ain't No 'Bout-a-Doubt It	1975	2.50	5.00	10.00
❑ BS4 2876 [Q]	Ain't No 'Bout-a-Doubt It	1975	3.75	7.50	15.00
❑ BS 2937	Mirror	1976	2.50	5.00	10.00
❑ BS 3041	Now Do U Wanta Dance	1977	2.50	5.00	10.00
❑ BSK 3175	My Radio Sure Sounds Good to Me	1978	2.50	5.00	10.00

—As "Larry Graham and Graham Central Station"

| ❑ BSK 3322 | Star Walk | 1979 | 2.50 | 5.00 | 10.00 |

—As "Larry Graham and Graham Central Station"

GRANDMASTER FLASH
12-Inch Singles
ELEKTRA

Number	Title (A Side/B Side)	Yr	VG	VG+	NM
❑ ED 5024 [DJ]	Sign of the Times (6:05) (Instrumental 5:59) (Edit of LP Version)/Larry's Dance Theme	1985	3.75	7.50	15.00
❑ ED 5052 [DJ]	Girls Love the Way He Spins (unknown versions)	1985	2.50	5.00	10.00
❑ ED 5079 [DJ]	Alternate Groove (LP Version 5:20) (Vocal Edit 3:56) (Instrumental 5:27)	1985	5.00	10.00	20.00
❑ ED 5134 [DJ]	Style (Peter Gunn Theme) (Extended Remixed Version) (Edit of LP Version) (Instrumental Version)	1986	3.75	7.50	15.00
❑ ED 5154 [DJ]	Behind Closed Doors (Extended Remix Version 5:28) (LP Version 3:38)	1986	3.75	7.50	15.00
❑ ED 5205 [DJ]	U Know What Time It Is (2 versions)	1987	3.00	6.00	12.00
❑ ED 5233 [DJ]	All Wrapped Up (Vocal Extended Mix) (Instrumental)/Kid Named Flash	1987	3.75	7.50	15.00
❑ ED 5279 [DJ]	Gold (6 versions)	1988	5.00	10.00	20.00
❑ ED 5301 [DJ]	Fly Girl (6 versions)	1988	3.00	6.00	12.00
❑ ED 5319 [DJ]	Magic Carpet Ride (Chep-O-Matic Mix) (LP Version) (Instrumental)	1988	3.00	6.00	12.00
❑ 66749	Magic Carpet Ride (unknown versions)/On the Strength	1988	3.00	6.00	12.00
❑ 66777	Gold (Extended Version) (Acapella Dub Version) (Edit of LP Version) (Acapella Version) (Instrumental)	1988	3.75	7.50	15.00
❑ 66801	All Wrapped Up (Extended 5:08) (Instrumental)/Kid Named Flash	1987	5.00	10.00	20.00
❑ 66825	U Know What Time It Is (Extended Scratch Mix) (Instrumental)/Bus Dis (Woo)	1987	2.00	4.00	8.00
❑ 66842	Behind Closed Doors (Extended Remix Version 5:28) (LP Version 3:38)/Lies	1986	3.75	7.50	15.00
❑ 66857	Style (Peter Gunn Theme) (Extended Remixed Version) (Edit of LP Version) (Instrumental Version)	1986	2.50	5.00	10.00
❑ 66908	Girls Love the Way He Spins/Larry's Dance Theme (2 versions)	1985	3.75	7.50	15.00
❑ 66922	Sign of the Times (Vocal) (Instrumental)	1985	3.00	6.00	12.00

ENJOY

| ❑ 6001 | Superappin' (12:03)/Superappin' Theme (12:01) | 1979 | 75.00 | 150.00 | 300.00 |

SUGAR HILL

| ❑ SH 457 | New York, New York (Vocal) (Instrumental) | 1983 | 3.00 | 6.00 | 12.00 |
| ❑ SH 465 | White Lines (Don't Don't Do It) (4 versions) | 1983 | 5.00 | 10.00 | 20.00 |

—As "Grandmaster and Melle Mel"

| ❑ SH 549 | Freedom (Vocal 8:13) (Instrumental 8:13) | 1980 | 5.00 | 10.00 | 20.00 |

—A wide range of prices has been noted on this record

❑ SH 555	The Birthday Party (2 versions)	1981	3.75	7.50	15.00
❑ SH 557	The Adventures of Grandmaster Flash on the Wheels of Steel/The Party Mix	1981	10.00	20.00	40.00
❑ SH 558	Showdown (Vocal 5:52) (Instrumental 5:52)	1981	10.00	20.00	40.00

—As "The Furious Five Meets the Sugarhill Gang"

❑ SH 569	It's Nasty (Genius of Love) (7:49) (8:15)	1982	3.75	7.50	15.00
❑ SH 574	Flash to the Beat (Part 1 and 2)	1982	5.00	10.00	20.00
❑ SH 584	The Message (Vocal 7:11) (Instrumental)	1982	3.75	7.50	15.00
❑ SH 590	Scorpio (unknown versions)	1982	5.00	10.00	20.00
❑ SH 32504	Freedom/New York, New York	1985	3.00	6.00	12.00

—"Old Gold" reissue

| ❑ 32505 | The Message/The Birthday Party | 1985 | 3.00 | 6.00 | 12.00 |

—"Old Gold" reissue

| ❑ 32508 | White Lines (Don't Don't Do It)/Scorpio | 1985 | 2.50 | 5.00 | 10.00 |

—"Old Gold" reissue

45s
ELEKTRA

Number	Title (A Side/B Side)	Yr	VG	VG+	NM
❑ 69380	Magic Carpet Ride/On the Strength	1988	—	3.00	6.00
❑ 69400	Fly Girl/Gold In Effect	1988	—	3.00	6.00
❑ 69416	Gold/Back in the Old Days of Hip-Hop	1988	—	2.50	5.00
❑ 69459	All Wrapped Up/Kid Named Flash	1987	—	—	3.00
❑ 69490	U Know What Time It Is/Bus Dis (Woo)	1987	—	3.00	6.00
❑ 69530	Behind Closed Doors/Lies	1986	—	2.50	5.00
❑ 69552	Style (Peter Gunn Theme)/(Instrumental)	1986	—	3.00	6.00
❑ 69617	Alternate Groove/Who's That Lady?	1985	—	2.50	5.00
❑ 69643	Girls Love the Way He Spins/Larry's Dance Theme	1985	—	3.00	6.00
❑ 69677	Sign of the Times/Larry's Dance Theme	1984	—	3.00	6.00

SUGAR HILL

❑ 756	Freedom/(Instrumental)	1980	3.75	7.50	15.00
❑ 759	The Birthday Party/(Instrumental)	1981	3.75	7.50	15.00
❑ 775	It's Nasty (Genius of Love)/(Instrumental)	1982	3.75	7.50	15.00

Albums
ELEKTRA

❑ 60389	They Said It Couldn't Be Done	1985	3.00	6.00	12.00
❑ 60723	Ba-Dop-Boom-Bang	1987	2.50	5.00	10.00
❑ 60769	On the Strength	1988	3.00	6.00	12.00

SUGAR HILL

| ❑ SH 268 | The Message | 1982 | 5.00 | 10.00 | 20.00 |

—Note: This album has been reissued to look like the original

| ❑ SH 9121 | Greatest Messages | 1984 | 5.00 | 10.00 | 20.00 |

GRANDMASTER MELLE MEL
12-Inch Singles
NEW DAY

Number	Title (A Side/B Side)	Yr	VG	VG+	NM
❑ BA 529	White Lines '89 Part II (Don't Do It Version) (Short Version) (Instrumental)	1989	2.50	5.00	10.00

POSSE

| ❑ 1234 | What's the Matter with Your World (3 versions) | 1989 | — | 3.00 | 6.00 |

SUGAR HILL

| ❑ SH 594 | Message II (Survival) (Vocal) (Instrumental) | 1982 | 3.75 | 7.50 | 15.00 |

—As "Melle Mel and Duke Bootee"

| ❑ SH 32009 | White Lines (Don't Don't Do It)/Melle Mel's Groove | 1984 | 3.00 | 6.00 | 12.00 |

—Reissue of 465 (by "Grandmaster & Melle Mel") with new B-side

❑ SH 32016	Jesse (Vocal 6:02) (Instrumental 6:02)	1984	3.75	7.50	15.00
❑ SH 32019	Beat Street/Internationally Known Parts 1 & 2	1984	3.00	6.00	12.00
❑ SH 32025	We Don't Work for Free (Vocal) (Instrumental)	1984	3.75	7.50	15.00
❑ SH 32033	Step Off (6:52) (4:32)	1984	3.75	7.50	15.00

—As "The Furious Five featuring Cowboy, Melle Mel and Scorpio"

❑ SH 32038	Pump Me Up (unknown versions)	1985	3.75	7.50	15.00
❑ SH 32039	The Mega-Melle Mix/World War III	1985	5.00	10.00	20.00
❑ SH 32044	King of the Streets (3 versions)	1985	3.75	7.50	15.00
❑ SH 32058	Vice (5:00)/World War III	1985	3.00	6.00	12.00

45s
ATLANTIC

| ❑ 89659 | Beat Street Breakdown - Part I/Part II | 1984 | — | 2.00 | 4.00 |
| ❑ 89659 [PS] | Beat Street Breakdown/Beat Street Breakdown | 1984 | — | 2.00 | 4.00 |

MCA

| ❑ 52740 | Vice/Chase | 1985 | — | 2.00 | 4.00 |
| ❑ 52740 [PS] | Vice/Chase | 1985 | — | 2.00 | 4.00 |

SUGAR HILL

| ❑ 92011 | We Don't Work for Free/(Instrumental) | 1984 | 2.50 | 5.00 | 10.00 |

Albums
NEW DAY

| ❑ ND 222 | Piano | 1989 | 2.50 | 5.00 | 10.00 |

SUGAR HILL

| ❑ SH 9205 | Grandmaster Melle Mel and the Furious Five | 1984 | 3.75 | 7.50 | 15.00 |

GRANT, EDDY
Also see THE EQUALS.
45s
CAPITOL

Number	Title (A Side/B Side)	Yr	VG	VG+	NM
❑ B-44212	Gimme Hope Jo'Anna/Don't Talk to Strangers	1988	—	—	3.00

EPIC

❑ 50766	Walking on Sunshine/Sunshine Jam	1979	—	2.00	4.00
❑ 50834	Living on the Front Line/Front Line Symphony	1980	—	2.00	4.00
❑ 50878	My Turn to Love You/Use It or Lose It	1980	—	2.00	4.00
❑ 50929	Everybody Dance/Feel the Rhythm (Of You and I)	1980	—	2.00	4.00

PORTRAIT

❑ 37-03793	Electric Avenue/Time Warp	1983	—	2.00	4.00
❑ 04039	I Don't Wanna Dance/I Don't Wanna Dance (Acapella)	1983	—	2.00	4.00
❑ 04433	Romancing the Stone/My Turn to Love You	1984	—	—	3.00
❑ 04433 [PS]	Romancing the Stone/My Turn to Love You	1984	—	2.00	4.00
❑ 04620	Boys in the Street/Time to Let Go	1984	—	—	3.00
❑ 06238	Dance Party/Rock You Good	1986	—	—	3.00

Albums
PORTRAIT

| ❑ B6R 38554 | Killer on the Rampage | 1983 | 2.50 | 5.00 | 10.00 |

—Original prefix

| ❑ FR 38554 | Killer on the Rampage | 1983 | 2.00 | 4.00 | 8.00 |

—Reissue prefix after LP became popular

| ❑ FR 39261 | Going for Broke | 1984 | 2.50 | 5.00 | 10.00 |
| ❑ BFR 40284 | Born Tuff | 1986 | 2.50 | 5.00 | 10.00 |

GRAY, DOBIE
12-Inch Singles
INFINITY

Number	Title (A Side/B Side)	Yr	VG	VG+	NM
❑ INF-16001	You Can Do It/Thank You for Tonight	1979	3.00	6.00	12.00

45s
ANTHEM

| ❑ 200 | Guess Who?/Bits and Pieces | 1972 | — | 2.50 | 5.00 |

ARISTA

| ❑ 1047 | One Can Fake It/(B-side unknown) | 1983 | — | 2.00 | 4.00 |

CAPITOL

| ❑ 2241 | We the People/Funny and Groovy | 1968 | 2.50 | 5.00 | 10.00 |

Number	Title (A Side/B Side)	Yr	VG	VG+	NM
❑ B-5562	Gonna Be a Long Night/That's One to Grown On	1986	—	—	3.00
❑ B-5596	The Dark Side of Life/A Night in the Life of a Country Boy	1986	—	—	3.00
❑ B-5647	From Where I Stand/So Far So Good	1986	—	—	3.00
❑ 5853	River Deep, Mountain High/Tennessee Waltz	1967	3.75	7.50	15.00
❑ B-44087	Take It Real Easy/You Must Have Been Reading My Heart	1987	—	—	3.00
❑ B-44126	Love Letters/Steady As She Goes	1988	—	—	3.00
CAPRICORN					
❑ 0249	If Love Must Go/Lover's Sweat	1975	—	2.00	4.00
❑ 0259	Find 'Em, Fool 'Em and Forget 'Em/Mellow Man	1976	—	2.00	4.00
❑ 0267	Let Go/Mellow Man	1976	—	2.00	4.00
CHARGER					
❑ 105	The "In" Crowd/Be a Man	1964	3.00	6.00	12.00
❑ 107	See You at the "Go-Go"/Walk with Love	1965	2.50	5.00	10.00
❑ 109	In Hollywood/Mr. Engineer	1965	2.50	5.00	10.00
❑ 113	Monkey Jerk/My Baby	1965	2.50	5.00	10.00
❑ 115	No Room to Cry/Out on the Floor	1966	2.50	5.00	10.00
CORDAK					
❑ 1602	Look at Me/Walkin' and Whistlin'	1962	3.75	7.50	15.00
DECCA					
❑ 33057	Drift Away/City Stars	1973	—	2.50	5.00
INFINITY					
❑ 50003	You Can Do It/Sharing the Night Together	1978	—	2.00	4.00
❑ 50010	Who's Lovin' You/Thank You for Tonight	1979	—	2.00	4.00
❑ 50020	Spending Time, Making Love, and Going Crazy/Let This Man Take Hold of Your Life	1979	—	2.00	4.00
❑ 50043	The In Crowd/Let This Man Take Hold of Your Life	1979	—	2.00	4.00
MCA					
❑ 40100	Loving Arms/Now That I'm Without You	1973	—	2.00	4.00
❑ 40153	Good Old Song/Reachin' for the Feelin'	1973	—	2.00	4.00
❑ 40188	Rose/Lovin' the Easy Way	1974	—	2.00	4.00
❑ 40201	There's a Honky Tonk Angel (Who'll Take Me Back In)/Lovin' the Easy Way	1974	—	2.00	4.00
❑ 40268	Watch Out for Lucy/Turning On You	1974	—	2.00	4.00
❑ 40315	The Music's Real/Roll On Sweet Mississippi	1974	—	2.00	4.00
ROBOX					
❑ RRS-117	Decorate the Night (same on both sides)	1979	—	2.50	5.00
WHITE WHALE					
❑ 300	Rose Garden/Where's the Girl Gone	1969	2.50	5.00	10.00
❑ 330	What a Way to Go/Do You Really Have a Heart	1969	50.00	100.00	200.00
❑ 342	Honey, You Can't Take It Back	1970	15.00	30.00	60.00
Albums					
CAPITOL					
❑ ST-12489	From Where I Stand	1986	2.50	5.00	10.00
CAPRICORN					
❑ CP 0163	New Ray of Sunshine	1976	2.50	5.00	10.00
CHARGER					
❑ CHR-M-2002 [M]	Dobie Gray Sings for "In" Crowders That Go "Go Go"	1965	10.00	20.00	40.00
❑ CHR-S-2002 [S]	Dobie Gray Sings for "In" Crowders That Go "Go Go"	1965	30.00	60.00	120.00
DECCA					
❑ DL 75397	Drift Away	1973	3.00	6.00	12.00
INFINITY					
❑ INF-9001	Midnight Diamond	1979	2.50	5.00	10.00
MCA					
❑ 371	Loving Arms	1973	2.50	5.00	10.00
❑ 449	Hey Dixie	1974	2.50	5.00	10.00
❑ 515	Drift Away	1974	2.50	5.00	10.00
—Reissue of Decca 75397					
ROBOX					
❑ RBX 8102	Welcome Home	1981	2.50	5.00	10.00
STRIPE					
❑ LPM 2001 [M]	Look — Dobie Gray	1963	25.00	50.00	100.00

GRAY, MACY

Number	Title (A Side/B Side)	Yr	VG	VG+	NM
12-Inch Singles					
EPIC					
❑ EAS 16903 [DJ]	Hey Young World II (LP Version) (Remix) (Instrumental) (Acappella)	2001	2.50	5.00	10.00
❑ EAS 32751 [DJ]	Sexual Revolution (4 versions)	2002	2.50	5.00	10.00
❑ E2S 41945 [(2) DJ]	Do Something (7 versions?)	1999	5.00	10.00	20.00
❑ EAS 41978 [DJ]	Do Something (Album Mix) (Black Apple Mix) (Black Apple Instrumental) (Acapella)/Caligula (Album Mix)	1999	3.75	7.50	15.00
❑ EAS 46531 [DJ]	I've Committed Murder (Clean Radio Mix) (Main Street Mix) (Acappella Street Mix) (Instrumental Mix)	2001	3.75	7.50	15.00
❑ 49-79195	Do Something (unknown versions)	1999	2.00	4.00	8.00
❑ 49-79241	Do Something (3 versions)	1999	2.00	4.00	8.00
❑ 49-79537	Still (unknown versions)	2000	2.00	4.00	8.00
45s					
EPIC					
❑ 34-79421	I Try (same on both sides)	2000	—	—	2.00
—Custom gray label					
❑ 34-79421 [PS]	I Try (same on both sides)	2000	—	—	2.00
❑ 34-79643	Sweet Baby (featuring Erykah Badu) (same on both sides)	2001	—	—	2.00
—Custom label					
❑ 34-79643 [PS]	Sweet Baby (featuring Erykah Badu) (same on both sides)	2001	—	—	2.00
Albums					
EPIC					
❑ E 69490	On How Life Is	1999	3.00	6.00	12.00
❑ E 85200	The Id	2001	3.00	6.00	12.00

GREAVES, R.B.

Number	Title (A Side/B Side)	Yr	VG	VG+	NM
45s					
20TH CENTURY					
❑ 2147	Rock and Roll/I'm Married, You're Married	1974	—	2.00	4.00
❑ 2203	Let's Try It Again/My Place or Yours	1975	—	2.00	4.00
ATCO					
❑ 6714	Take a Letter Maria/Big Bad City	1969	2.00	4.00	8.00
❑ 6726	Always Something There to Remind Me/Oh, When I Was a Boy	1969	—	3.00	6.00
❑ 6745	Fire and Rain/The Ballad of Leroy	1970	—	3.00	6.00
❑ 6778	Oh When I Was a Boy/Georgia Took Her Back	1970	—	3.00	6.00
❑ 6789	Whiter Shade of Pale/Show Me the Way to Go	1970	—	3.00	6.00
❑ 6839	Paperback Writer/Over You Now	1971	—	2.50	5.00
BAREBACK					
❑ 523	Margie, Who's Watching the Baby/(B-side unknown)	1977	—	3.00	6.00
MGM					
❑ 14483	Margie, Who's Watching the Baby/Area Code 213	1973	—	2.50	5.00
❑ 14567	All I Want to Do/Long Live the King	1973	—	2.50	5.00
MIDSONG INT'L.					
❑ 72006	Let Me Be the One Tonight/Please Mister Mailman	1980	—	2.00	4.00
SUNFLOWER					
❑ 128	Margie, Who's Watching the Baby/Area Code 213	1972	—	3.00	6.00
Albums					
ATCO					
❑ SD 33-311	R.B. Greaves	1969	5.00	10.00	20.00
INTERMEDIA					
❑ QS-5032	Rock and Roll	198?	2.50	5.00	10.00

GREEN, AL

Number	Title (A Side/B Side)	Yr	VG	VG+	NM
12-Inch Singles					
A&M					
❑ 12311	As Long As We're Together (4 versions)	1989	—	3.00	6.00
❑ 12323	The Message Is Love (6 versions)	1989	—	3.00	6.00
HI					
❑ 78510	I Feel Good (7:30)/I Feel Good (3:17)	1978	3.75	7.50	15.00
45s					
A&M					
❑ 1427	As Long As We're Together/Blessed	1989	—	—	3.00
❑ 2786	Going Away/Building Up	1985	—	2.00	4.00
❑ 2807	True Love/He Is the Light	1986	—	2.00	4.00
❑ 2919	Everything's Gonna Be Alright/So Real to Me	1987	—	—	3.00
❑ 2952	You Know and I Know/True Love	1987	—	—	3.00
❑ 2962	Soul Survivor/Jesus Will Fix It	1987	—	—	3.00
BELL					
❑ 45258	Guilty/Let Me Help You	1972	—	2.50	5.00
❑ 45305	Hot Wire/Don't Leave Me	1973	—	2.50	5.00
CAPITOL					
❑ S7-18869	Tired of Being Alone/Walk On By	1995	—	—	3.00
—B-side by Isaac Hayes					
HI					
❑ 2159	I Want to Hold Your Hand/What Am I Gonna Do with Myself	1969	2.00	4.00	8.00
❑ 2164	One Woman/Tomorrow's Dream	1969	2.00	4.00	8.00
❑ 2172	You Say It/Gotta Find a New World	1969	—	3.00	6.00
❑ 2177	Right Now, Right Now/All Because I'm a Foolish One	1970	—	3.00	6.00
❑ 2182	I Can't Get Next to You/Ride Sally Ride	1970	—	3.00	6.00
❑ 2188	Driving Wheel/True Love	1971	—	3.00	6.00
❑ 2194	Tired of Being Alone/Get Back Baby	1971	—	2.50	5.00
❑ 2202	Let's Stay Together/Tomorrow's Dream	1971	—	2.50	5.00
❑ 2211	Look What You Done for Me/La La for You	1972	—	2.50	5.00
❑ 2216	I'm Still in Love with You/Old Time Lovin'	1972	—	2.50	5.00
❑ 2227	You Ought to Be with Me/What Is This Feeling	1972	—	2.50	5.00
❑ 2235	Call Me (Come Back Home)/What a Wonderful Thing Love Is	1973	—	2.50	5.00
❑ 2247	Here I Am (Come and Take Me)/I'm Glad You're Mine	1973	—	2.50	5.00
❑ 2257	Livin' for You/It Ain't No Fun to Me	1973	—	2.50	5.00
❑ 2262	Let's Get Married/So Good to Be Here	1974	—	2.50	5.00
❑ 2274	Sha-La-La (Make Me Happy)/School Days	1974	—	2.50	5.00
❑ 2282	L-O-V-E (Love)/I Wish You Were Here	1975	—	2.50	5.00
❑ 2288	Oh Me, Oh My (Dreams in My Arms)/Strong As Death (Sweet As Love)	1975	—	2.50	5.00
❑ 2300	Full of Fire/Could I Be the One	1975	—	2.50	5.00
❑ 2306	Let It Shine/There's No Way	1976	—	2.50	5.00
❑ 2319	Keep Me Cryin'/There Is Love	1976	—	2.50	5.00
❑ 2322	I Tried to Tell Myself/Something	1977	—	2.50	5.00
❑ 2324	Love and Happiness/Glory Glory	1977	—	2.50	5.00
❑ 77505	Belle/Chariots of Fire	1977	—	2.00	4.00
❑ 77505 [PS]	Belle/Chariots of Fire	1977	—	3.00	6.00
❑ 77680	White Christmas/Winter Wonderland	2001	—	2.50	5.00
—Clear vinyl					
❑ 78511	I Feel Good/Feels Like Summer	1978	—	2.00	4.00
❑ 78522	Wait Here/To Sir with Love	1978	—	2.00	4.00
❑ 78522 [PS]	Wait Here/To Sir with Love	1978	—	3.00	6.00

Number	Title (A Side/B Side)	Yr	VG	VG+	NM
HOT LINE JOURNAL					
❏ 15000	Back Up Train/Don't Leave Me	1967	6.25	12.50	25.00
❏ 15001	Don't Hurt Me No More/Get Yourself Together	1967	7.50	15.00	30.00
❏ 15002	I'll Be Good to You/Lover's Hideaway	1967	7.50	15.00	30.00
THE RIGHT STUFF					
❏ S7-17524	Let's Stay Together/I'm Still in Love with You	1993	—	—	3.00
❏ S7-18217	I'll Be Home for Christmas/It Feels Like Christmas	1994	—	2.50	5.00
7-Inch Extended Plays					
HI					
❏ SBG 81	How Can You Mend a Broken Heart/So You're Leaving//I've Never Found a Girl/What Is This Feeling/It Ain't No Fun to Me	1972	2.50	5.00	10.00
—Jukebox issue; small hole, plays at 33 1/3 rpm					
❏ SBG 81 [PS]	Let's Stay Together	1972	2.50	5.00	10.00
❏ SBG 87	Funny How Time Slips Away/Love Is Like the Morning Sun//Have You Been Making Out O.K./Stand Up	1973	2.50	5.00	10.00
—Jukebox issue; small hole, plays at 33 1/3 rpm					
❏ SBG 87 [PS]	Call Me	1973	2.50	5.00	10.00
Albums					
A&M					
❏ SP-5150	Soul Survivor	1987	2.50	5.00	10.00
❏ SP-5228	I Get Joy	1989	2.50	5.00	10.00
BELL					
❏ 6076	Al Green	1972	5.00	10.00	20.00
—Reissue of Hot Line LP					
DCC COMPACT CLASSICS					
❏ LPZ-2058	Greatest Hits	1998	7.50	15.00	30.00
—Audiophile vinyl					
HI					
❏ 6004	The Belle Album	1977	3.00	6.00	12.00
❏ 6009	Truth 'N' Time	1978	3.00	6.00	12.00
❏ 8000	Tired of Being Alone	1977	3.00	6.00	12.00
❏ 8001	Al Green Gets Next to You	1977	3.00	6.00	12.00
❏ 8007	Let's Stay Together	1977	3.00	6.00	12.00
❏ SHL-32055	Green Is Blues	1969	3.75	7.50	15.00
❏ SHL-32062	Al Green Gets Next to You	1971	3.75	7.50	15.00
❏ SHL-32070	Let's Stay Together	1972	3.75	7.50	15.00
❏ SHL-32074	I'm Still in Love with You	1972	3.75	7.50	15.00
❏ SHL-32077	Call Me	1973	3.75	7.50	15.00
❏ SHL-32082	Livin' for You	1973	3.75	7.50	15.00
❏ SHL-32087	Al Green Explores Your Mind	1974	3.75	7.50	15.00
❏ SHL-32089	Al Green/Greatest Hits	1975	3.75	7.50	15.00
❏ SHL-32092	Al Green Is Love	1975	3.75	7.50	15.00
❏ SHL-32097	Full of Fire	1976	3.75	7.50	15.00
❏ SHL-32103	Have a Good Time	1976	3.75	7.50	15.00
❏ SHL-32105	Al Green's Greatest Hits, Volume II	1977	3.75	7.50	15.00
HOT LINE					
❏ 1500 [M]	Back Up Train	1967	12.50	25.00	50.00
—As "Al Greene"					
❏ S-1500 [S]	Back Up Train	1967	20.00	40.00	80.00
—As "Al Greene"					
KORY					
❏ 1005	Al Green	1977	2.50	5.00	10.00
—Reissue of Bell LP					
MCA					
❏ 42308	Love Ritual	1988	2.50	5.00	10.00
MOTOWN					
❏ 5283 ML	Al Green/Greatest Hits	198?	2.50	5.00	10.00
—Reissue of Hi 32089					
❏ 5284 ML	I'm Still in Love with You	198?	2.50	5.00	10.00
—Reissue of Hi 32074					
❏ 5290 ML	Let's Stay Together	198?	2.50	5.00	10.00
—Reissue of Hi 32070					
❏ 5291 ML	Al Green's Greatest Hits, Volume II	198?	2.50	5.00	10.00
—Reissue of Hi 32105					
❏ 5317 ML	Truth N' Time	198?	2.50	5.00	10.00
MYRRH					
❏ MSB-6661	The Lord Will Make a Way	1980	2.50	5.00	10.00
❏ MSB-6671	Higher Plane	1981	2.50	5.00	10.00
❏ MSB-6702	Precious Lord	1981	2.50	5.00	10.00
❏ MSB-6747	I'll Rise Again	1982	2.50	5.00	10.00
❏ MSB-6774	Al Green and the Full Gospel Tabernacle Choir	1984	2.50	5.00	10.00
❏ WR-8113	The Lord Will Make a Way	1985	2.00	4.00	8.00
—Reissue with new number and A&M logo					
❏ WR-8114	Higher Plane	1985	2.00	4.00	8.00
—Reissue with new number and A&M logo					
❏ WR-8115	Precious Lord	1985	2.00	4.00	8.00
—Reissue with new number and A&M logo					
❏ WR-8116	I'll Rise Again	1985	2.00	4.00	8.00
—Reissue with new number and A&M logo					
❏ WR-8117	White Christmas	1985	2.50	5.00	10.00
—Reissue with new number and A&M logo					
❏ WR-8118	Trust in God	1985	2.00	4.00	8.00
—Reissue with new number and A&M logo					
❏ WR-8209	Al Green and the Full Gospel Tabernacle Choir	1986	2.00	4.00	8.00
—Reissue with new number and A&M logo					
❏ 7-01-678006-6	White Christmas	1984	3.00	6.00	12.00
❏ 7-01-678306-?	Trust in God	1984	2.50	5.00	10.00
THE RIGHT STUFF					
❏ T1-27121	Let's Stay Together	1995	3.75	7.50	15.00
—Green vinyl reissue					
❏ T1-27627	I'm Still in Love with You	1995	3.75	7.50	15.00
—Green vinyl reissue					

Number	Title (A Side/B Side)	Yr	VG	VG+	NM
WORD					
❏ E 77000	One in a Million	1991	3.00	6.00	12.00

GREEN, GARLAND

45s

Number	Title (A Side/B Side)	Yr	VG	VG+	NM
CASINO					
❏ 056	I.O.U./It's a Backdoor World	1976	—	2.50	5.00
COTILLION					
❏ 44098	Plain and Simple Girl/Hey Cloud	1971	—	3.00	6.00
OCEAN-FRONT					
❏ 2000	Tryin' to Hold On/(B-side unknown)	1983	—	2.00	4.00
RCA					
❏ PB-10889	Don't Let Love Walk Out on Us/Ask Me for What You Want	1977	—	3.00	6.00
❏ PB-11023	Shake Your Shaker/Lovin' You Baby	1977	—	2.50	5.00
❏ PB-11126	Let's Celebrate/Let Me Be Your Pacifier	1977	—	2.50	5.00
REVUE					
❏ 11001	Girl I Love You/It Rained Forty Days and Nights	1967	3.75	7.50	15.00
❏ 11020	Mr. Misery/You Played on a Prayer	196?	3.00	6.00	12.00
❏ 11030	Love Now, Pay Later/Ain't That Good Enough	196?	3.00	6.00	12.00
SPRING					
❏ 142	He Didn't Know (He Kept On Talkin')/Please Come Home	1973	—	2.50	5.00
❏ 146	Sweet Loving Woman/Sending My Best Friend	1974	—	2.50	5.00
❏ 151	Let the Good Times Roll/You and I Go Good Together	1974	—	2.50	5.00
❏ 158	Bumpin' and Stompin'/Nothing Can Take You from Me	1975	—	2.50	5.00
❏ 160	Just Loving You/Nothing Can Take You from Me	1975	—	2.50	5.00
UNI					
❏ 55143	Jealous Kind of Fella/I Can't Believe You Quit Me	1969	2.00	4.00	8.00
❏ 55188	Don't Think That I Am a Violent Guy/All She Said (Was Goodbye to Me)	1969	2.00	4.00	8.00
❏ 55213	Angel Baby/You Played On a Player	1970	2.00	4.00	8.00
Albums					
RCA VICTOR					
❏ APL1-2351	Love Is What We Came Here For	1977	3.00	6.00	12.00
UNI					
❏ 73073	Jealous Kind of Fellow	1969	5.00	10.00	20.00

GREEN, VERNON, AND THE MEDALLIONS
See THE MEDALLIONS.

GREER, BIG JOHN

45s

Number	Title (A Side/B Side)	Yr	VG	VG+	NM
GROOVE					
❏ 0002	Bottle It Up and Go/You'll Never Be Mine	1954	10.00	20.00	40.00
❏ 0016	When the Roses Bloom in Lover's Lane/Too Long	1954	10.00	20.00	40.00
❏ 0038	We Wanna See Santa Do the Mambo/Wait Till After Christmas	1954	10.00	20.00	40.00
❏ 0108	Soon, Soon, Soon/I'm Glad for Your Sake	1955	10.00	20.00	40.00
❏ 0119	Come Back Maybellene/Night Crawlin'	1955	12.50	25.00	50.00
❏ 0131	A Man and a Woman/Blam	1955	15.00	30.00	60.00
—With the Four Students					
KING					
❏ 4878	Record Hop/Keep On Loving Me	1956	5.00	10.00	20.00
❏ 4941	Let Me Come Home/Come Back, Uncle John	1956	5.00	10.00	20.00
❏ 5006	Midnight Ramble/Sweet Slumber	1957	5.00	10.00	20.00
❏ 5057	Duck Walk/I Still Love You So	1957	5.00	10.00	20.00
RCA VICTOR					
❏ 47-4293	Have Another Drink/I'm Savin' All My Lovin'	1951	10.00	20.00	40.00
❏ 47-4348	Got You on My Mind/Woman Is a Five-Letter Word	1951	10.00	20.00	40.00
❏ 47-4484	Strong Red Whiskey/If You Let Me	1952	10.00	20.00	40.00
❏ 47-5037	I'm the Fat Man/Since You Went Away from Me	1952	10.00	20.00	40.00
❏ 47-5170	I'll Never Let You Go/You Played on My Piano	1953	10.00	20.00	40.00
❏ 47-5259	Ride Pretty Baby/Don't Worry 'Bout Me	1953	10.00	20.00	40.00
❏ 47-5531	Drinkin' Fool/Gettin' Mighty Lonesome for You	1953	10.00	20.00	40.00
❏ 50-0007	Drinkin' Wine Spo-Dee-O-Dee/Long Tall Gal	1949	17.50	35.00	70.00
—Orange vinyl					
❏ 50-0029	If I Told You Once/I Found a Dream	1949	17.50	35.00	70.00
—Orange vinyl					
❏ 50-0051	Rockin' Jenny Jones/I've Just Found Love	1950	17.50	35.00	70.00
—Orange vinyl					
❏ 50-0076	I'll Never Do That Again/A Fool Hasn't Got a Chance	1950	15.00	30.00	60.00
—Orange vinyl					
❏ 50-0096	Cheatin'/It's Better to Have Been Taken for Granted	1950	15.00	30.00	60.00
—Orange vinyl					
❏ 50-0104	Red Juice/Big John's a-Blowin'	1950	15.00	30.00	60.00
—Orange vinyl					
❏ 50-0108	Once There Lived a Fool/I Want Ya, I Need Ya	1951	12.50	25.00	50.00
❏ 50-0113	Why Did You Go/Our Wedding Time	1951	12.50	25.00	50.00
❏ 50-0125	Clambake Boogie/When You Love	1951	12.50	25.00	50.00
❏ 50-0137	Big Rock/How Can You Forget?	1951	12.50	25.00	50.00

GREGORY, DICK

45s

Number	Title (A Side/B Side)	Yr	VG	VG+	NM
B-SHARP					
❏ 272	Did You Need to Know/(B-side unknown)	1966	75.00	150.00	300.00
—Probably a different performer than the comedian/activist					
VEE JAY					
❏ 469	They Won't Hire Me/Benefit	1962	3.00	6.00	12.00

He was billed as "Pvt. Cecil Gant" and was known as "The G.I. Sing-Sation" when his first record, "I Wonder," was a #1 R&B hit in 1944. It was so popular that the B-side, "Cecil Boogie," also made the top 5. His record company, Gilt-Edge, released the two songs on this collectible flexible picture disc in addition to a regular 78.

Marvin Gaye's debut album, *The Soulful Moods of Marvin Gaye,* is his most collectible LP today.

Gaye's first 45, "Let Your Conscience Be Your Guide," failed to make the national charts, and is considered quite rare today.

Barbara George's only hit single, "I Know (You Don't Want Me No More)," spent a month atop the R&B charts. That led to this rather scarce LP.

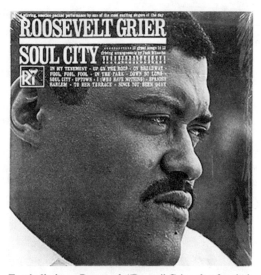

One of the most valuable R&B albums is this Lloyd Glenn collection issued by the Swing Time label in 1954. It appears to be the only LP the label issued before it disappeared.

Football player Roosevelt "Rosey" Grier also fancied himself a singer. He made many singles for many different labels over a period of well over a decade. But this was his only full-length LP of secular music.

Number	Title (A Side/B Side)	Yr	VG	VG+	NM

Albums
COLPIX

❏ CP 417 [M]	In Living Black and White	1961	6.25	12.50	25.00
❏ CP 420 [M]	East and West	1961	6.25	12.50	25.00
❏ CP 480 [M]	We All Have Problems	1964	6.25	12.50	25.00

GATEWAY

| ❏ GLP 9007 [M] | My Brother's Keeper | 1963 | 10.00 | 20.00 | 40.00 |

POPPY

❏ PP-LA176-G2 [(2)]Caught in the Act		1973	3.75	7.50	15.00
❏ PYS 40008	Dick Gregory On...	1970	3.75	7.50	15.00
❏ PYS 40011	Dick Gregory at the Village Gate	1972	3.75	7.50	15.00
❏ PYS 60001 [(2)]The Light Side: The Dark Side		1969	5.00	10.00	20.00
❏ PYS 60004 [(2)]Frankenstein		1970	3.75	7.50	15.00
❏ PYS 60005 [(2)]Dick Gregory at Kent State		1971	3.75	7.50	15.00

TOMATO

| ❏ 9001 [(3)] | The Best of Dick Gregory | 1978 | 5.00 | 10.00 | 20.00 |

VEE JAY

❏ LP 1093 [M]	Running for President	1964	6.25	12.50	25.00
❏ LP 4001 [M]	Dick Gregory Talks Turkey	1962	6.25	12.50	25.00
❏ LP 4005 [M]	Two Sides of Dick Gregory	1963	6.25	12.50	25.00

GRIER, ROOSEVELT
Most of his 1970s records, and scattered earlier ones, were as "Rosey Grier."

45s
20TH CENTURY

| ❏ 2212 | Take the Time to Love Somebody/Your Love Is Right Up My Alley | 1975 | 2.00 | 4.00 | 8.00 |

A

| ❏ 105 | Sincerely/Why Don't You Do Me Right | 1959 | 6.25 | 12.50 | 25.00 |
| ❏ 110 | Moonlight in Vermont/Smoky Morning | 1960 | 6.25 | 12.50 | 25.00 |

ABC

| ❏ 11275 | Rat Race/I Don't Want Nobody (To Lead Me On) | 1970 | — | 3.00 | 6.00 |

AGP

| ❏ 109 | Bad News/Ring Around the World | 1969 | 2.00 | 4.00 | 8.00 |

AMY

❏ 11004	Who's Got the Ball (Y'All)/Halftime	1967	3.00	6.00	12.00
❏ 11015	High Society Woman/C'mon Cupid	1968	3.00	6.00	12.00
❏ 11029	Hard to Forget/People Make the World	1968	3.00	6.00	12.00

A&M

| ❏ 1457 | Beautiful People/I'll Be Back Tomorrow | 1973 | — | 2.50 | 5.00 |
| ❏ 1500 | If You Hit a Good Lick, Lay On It/You're the Violin | 1974 | — | 2.50 | 5.00 |

BATTLE

| ❏ 45911 | Why/Lover Set Me Free | 1963 | 6.25 | 12.50 | 25.00 |

BELL

| ❏ 45459 | It's All Right to Cry/(B-side unknown) | 1974 | 2.00 | 4.00 | 8.00 |

D-TOWN

| ❏ 1058 | Pizza Pie Man/Welcome to the Club | 1965 | 10.00 | 20.00 | 40.00 |

LIBERTY

| ❏ 55413 | Struttin' 'n Twistin'/Let the Cool Wind Blow | 1962 | 3.75 | 7.50 | 15.00 |
| ❏ 55453 | The Mail Must Go Thru/Your Has Been | 1962 | 3.75 | 7.50 | 15.00 |

MGM

| ❏ 13698 | Slow Drag/Yesterday | 1967 | 3.00 | 6.00 | 12.00 |
| ❏ 13840 | Spanish Harlem/I'm Living Good | 1967 | 3.00 | 6.00 | 12.00 |

RIC

| ❏ 102 | Fool, Fool, Fool/Since You've Been Gone | 1964 | 5.00 | 10.00 | 20.00 |
| ❏ 112 | Down So Long/In My Tenement | 1964 | 5.00 | 10.00 | 20.00 |

SPINDLE TOP

| ❏ 102 | I'm Going Home/Jinny | 1961 | 5.00 | 10.00 | 20.00 |

UNITED ARTISTS

| ❏ 50893 | Bring Back the Time/Oh How I Miss You Baby | 1972 | — | 3.00 | 6.00 |

YOUNGSTOWN

| ❏ 609 | Deputy Dog/(B-side unknown) | 1966 | 7.50 | 15.00 | 30.00 |

Albums
RIC

| ❏ M-1008 [M] | Soul City | 1964 | 5.00 | 10.00 | 20.00 |
| ❏ S-1008 [S] | Soul City | 1964 | 6.25 | 12.50 | 25.00 |

WORD

| ❏ WR-8342 | Committed | 1986 | 3.00 | 6.00 | 12.00 |

GUITAR SLIM
45s
ATCO

❏ 6072	Oh Yeah/Down Through the Years	1956	10.00	20.00	40.00
❏ 6097	It Hurts to Love Someone/If I Should Lose You	1957	7.50	15.00	30.00
❏ 6108	I Won't Mind at All/Hello, How Ya' Been, Goodbye	1958	7.50	15.00	30.00
❏ 6120	If I Had My Life to Live Over/When There's No Way Out	1958	7.50	15.00	30.00

IMPERIAL

| ❏ 5278 | Woman Troubles/Cryin' in the Mornin' | 1954 | 15.00 | 30.00 | 60.00 |
| ❏ 5310 | New Arrival/Standing at the Station | 1954 | 15.00 | 30.00 | 60.00 |

SPECIALTY

❏ 482	The Things That I Used to Do/Well, I Done Get Over It	1954	12.50	25.00	50.00
❏ 490	Story of My Life/A Letter to My Girl Friend	1954	10.00	20.00	40.00
❏ 527	Later for You Baby/Troubles Don't Last	1954	6.25	12.50	25.00
❏ 536	Sufferin' Mind/Twenty-Five Lies	1955	6.25	12.50	25.00
❏ 542	Stand By Me/Our Only Child	1955	6.25	12.50	25.00
❏ 551	You're Gonna Miss Me/I Got Sumpin' for You	1955	6.25	12.50	25.00
❏ 557	Think It Over/Quicksand	1955	6.25	12.50	25.00
❏ 569	Sumthin' to Remember Me By/You Give Me Nothin' But the Blues	1956	6.25	12.50	25.00

Albums
ATLANTIC

| ❏ 81760 | The Atco Sessions | 1987 | 2.50 | 5.00 | 10.00 |

SPECIALTY

| ❏ SP-2130 | Things That I Used to Do | 1969 | 5.00 | 10.00 | 20.00 |

GUNTER, ARTHUR
45s
EXCELLO

❏ 2047	Baby Let's Play House/Blues After Hours	1954	30.00	60.00	120.00
❏ 2053	She's Mine, All Mine/You Are Doin' Me Wrong	1955	15.00	30.00	60.00
❏ 2058	Honey Babe/No Happy Home	1955	15.00	30.00	60.00
❏ 2073	Baby You Better Listen/Trouble with My Baby	1955	7.50	15.00	30.00
❏ 2084	Hear My Plea Baby/Love Has Got Me	1956	7.50	15.00	30.00
❏ 2125	Baby Can't You See/You're Always on My Mind	1958	6.25	12.50	25.00
❏ 2137	Ludella/We're Gonna Shake	1959	6.25	12.50	25.00
❏ 2147	Crazy Me/Don't Leave Me Now	1959	6.25	12.50	25.00
❏ 2164	No Naggin' No Draggin'/I Want Her Back	1959	6.25	12.50	25.00
❏ 2191	Little Blue Jeans/Mind Your Own Business Babe	1960	5.00	10.00	20.00
❏ 2201	My Heart's Always Lonesome/I'm Fallin', Love's Got Me	1961	5.00	10.00	20.00

Albums
EXCELLO

| ❏ LPS-8017 | Black and Blues | 1971 | 6.25 | 12.50 | 25.00 |

GUNTER, CORNEL
45s
ABC-PARAMOUNT

| ❏ 9698 | She Loves to Rock/In Self Defense | 1956 | 10.00 | 20.00 | 40.00 |

—As "Cornel Gunter and the Flairs"
CHALLENGE

| ❏ 59281 | If I Had the Key to Your Heart/Wishful | 1965 | 2.50 | 5.00 | 10.00 |

DOT

| ❏ 15654 | You Send Me/Call Me a Fool | 1957 | 5.00 | 10.00 | 20.00 |

EAGLE

| ❏ 301 | Baby Come Home/I Want You Madly | 1957 | 7.50 | 15.00 | 30.00 |

LIBERTY

| ❏ 55096 | If We Should Meet Again/Neighborhood Dance | 1957 | 5.00 | 10.00 | 20.00 |

LOMA

❏ 701	True Love/Peek, Peek-a-Boo	1955	25.00	50.00	100.00
❏ 703	You Broke My Heart/(Pretty Baby) I'm Used to You Now	1956	37.50	75.00	150.00
❏ 704	Keep Me Alive/Muchacha, Muchacha	1956	20.00	40.00	80.00
❏ 705	I'm Sad/One Thing	1956	25.00	50.00	100.00

—The Loma singles credit "The Ermines," and may or may not mention Gunter.
WARNER BROS.

| ❏ 5266 | Lieft Me Up Angel/Hope of Sand | 1962 | 3.00 | 6.00 | 12.00 |
| ❏ 5292 | It Ain't No Use/In a Dream of Love | 1962 | 3.00 | 6.00 | 12.00 |

GUNTER, SHIRLEY
45s
FLAIR

❏ 1020	Send Him Back/Since I Fell for You	1953	10.00	20.00	40.00
❏ 1027	Found Some Good Lovin'/Strange Romance	1954	7.50	15.00	30.00
❏ 1050	Oop Shoop/It's You	1955	7.50	15.00	30.00
❏ 1060	You're Mine/Why	1955	7.50	15.00	30.00
❏ 1065	What Difference Does It Make/Baby I Love You So	1955	7.50	15.00	30.00
❏ 1070	That's the Way I Like It/Gimme, Gimme, Gimme	1955	7.50	15.00	30.00
❏ 1076	How Can I Tell You/Ipsy Gypsy Ooh	1955	15.00	30.00	60.00

—With the Flairs
MODERN

| ❏ 979 | Please Tell Me/Come On | 1956 | 6.25 | 12.50 | 25.00 |
| ❏ 1001 | Fortune in Love/Just Got Rid of a Heartache | 1956 | 6.25 | 12.50 | 25.00 |

—With the Flairs

| ❏ 1011 | I'm So Sorry/I've Been Searching | 1956 | 6.25 | 12.50 | 25.00 |

TANGERINE

| ❏ 949 | Stuck Up/You Let My Love Grow Cold | 1965 | 2.50 | 5.00 | 10.00 |

TENDER

| ❏ 503 | Believe Me/Crazy Little Baby | 1958 | 10.00 | 20.00 | 40.00 |

GURU
Albums
CHRYSALIS

| ❏ F1-21998 | Jazzmatazz Vol. 1 | 1993 | 5.00 | 10.00 | 20.00 |
| ❏ F1-34290 [(2)] | Jazzmatazz Vol. 2: The New Reality | 1995 | 3.75 | 7.50 | 15.00 |

VIRGIN

| ❏ 50188 [(2)] | Jazzmatazz Vol. 3: Streetsoul | 2000 | 3.75 | 7.50 | 15.00 |

GUY, BUDDY
45s
ARTISTIC

| ❏ 1501 | Sit and Cry/Try to Quit You Baby | 1958 | 10.00 | 20.00 | 40.00 |
| ❏ 1503 | You Sure Can't Do/This Is the End | 1958 | 10.00 | 20.00 | 40.00 |

CHESS

❏ 1753	I Got My Eyes on You/The First Time I Met the Blues	1960	7.50	15.00	30.00
❏ 1759	Stop Around/Broken Hearted Blues	1960	6.25	12.50	25.00
❏ 1784	Let Me Love You Baby/Ten Years Ago	1961	6.25	12.50	25.00
❏ 1812	Stone Crazy/Skippin'	1962	6.25	12.50	25.00
❏ 1838	When My Left Eye Jumps/My Treasure Untold	1962	6.25	12.50	25.00
❏ 1878	No Lie/Hard But It's Fair	1963	5.00	10.00	20.00
❏ 1899	My Time After a While/I Dig Your Wig	1964	5.00	10.00	20.00

Number	Title (A Side/B Side)	Yr	VG	VG+	NM
❏ 1936	Leave My Girl Alone/Crazy Music	1965	5.00	10.00	20.00
❏ 1974	My Mother/Mother-in-Law Blues	1966	5.00	10.00	20.00
❏ 2022	Gonna Keep It to Myself/Suffer	1967	3.75	7.50	15.00
❏ 2067	She Suits Me to a Tee/Buddy's Groove	1969	3.75	7.50	15.00

VANGUARD

❏ 35060	Sweet Little Angel/Mary Had a Little Lamb	1968	3.00	6.00	12.00

78s
ARTISTIC

❏ 1501	Sit and Cry/Try to Quit You Baby	1958	37.50	75.00	150.00

Albums
BLUE THUMB

❏ BTS 20	Buddy and the Juniors	1970	6.25	12.50	25.00

CHESS

❏ LP-409	I Was Walking Through the Woods	1970	5.00	10.00	20.00
❏ LP-1527 [M]	I Left My Blues in San Francisco	1968	7.50	15.00	30.00
❏ CH-9115	Buddy Guy	1984	2.00	4.00	8.00

MCA

❏ 11165	I Was Walking Through the Woods	1995	6.25	12.50	25.00

—"Heavy Vinyl" audiophile reissue

VANGUARD

❏ VSD-79272	A Man and the Blues	1968	6.25	12.50	25.00
❏ VSD-79290	This Is Buddy Guy	1969	6.25	12.50	25.00
❏ VSD-79323	Hold That Plane!	1972	5.00	10.00	20.00

GUYTONES, THE
45s
DELUXE

Number	Title (A Side/B Side)	Yr	VG	VG+	NM
❏ 6144	You Won't Let Me Go/Ooh Bop Sha Boo (Give All Your Love to Me)	1957	20.00	40.00	80.00
❏ 6152	She's Mine/Not Wanted	1957	20.00	40.00	80.00
❏ 6159	Hunky Dory/This Is Love	1958	20.00	40.00	80.00
❏ 6163	Baby, I Don't Care/Young Dreamer	1958	15.00	30.00	60.00
❏ 6169	Tell Me (How Was I to Know)/Your Heart's Bigger Than Mine	1958	15.00	30.00	60.00

H

HALL, DARYL
Also see DARYL HALL AND JOHN OATES; THE TEMPTONES.
12-Inch Singles
RCA

Number	Title (A Side/B Side)	Yr	VG	VG+	NM
❏ 5714-1-RD	Dreamtime (Extended)/(Dub)	1986	2.00	4.00	8.00
❏ 5745-1-RD	Foolish Pride/Let It Out	1986	2.00	4.00	8.00
❏ 5748-1-RD	Foolish Pride (Extended Version) (Edit Remix) (Dub)/What's Gonna Happen to Us	1986	2.00	4.00	8.00
❏ PD-14386 [DJ]	Dreamtime (same on both sides)	1986	2.00	4.00	8.00

45s
AMY

❏ 11049	The Princess and the Soldier (Part 1)/The Princess and the Soldier (Part 2)	1969	—	3.00	6.00

EPIC

❏ 34-77139	I'm in a Philly Mood/Money Changes Everything	1993	—	—	3.00
❏ 34-77258	Stop Lovin' Me, Stop Lovin' You/(Churban Remix)	1993	—	—	3.00

PARALLAX

❏ 404	A Lonely Girl/(B-side unknown)	196?	7.50	15.00	30.00

RCA

❏ 5038-7-R	Foolish Pride/What's Gonna Happen to Us	1986	—	—	3.00
❏ 5038-7-R [PS]	Foolish Pride/What's Gonna Happen to Us	1986	—	—	3.00
❏ 5105-7-R	Someone Like You (The Guitar Solo)/Someone Like You (The Sax Solo)	1987	—	—	3.00
❏ 5105-7-R [PS]	Someone Like You (The Guitar Solo)/Someone Like You (The Sax Solo)	1987	—	—	3.00
❏ PB-12001	Something in 4/4 Time/Sacred Songs	1980	—	2.00	4.00
❏ PB-12001 [PS]	Something in 4/4 Time/Sacred Songs	1980	—	2.50	5.00
❏ PB-14387	Dreamtime/Let It Out	1986	—	—	3.00
❏ PB-14387 [PS]	Dreamtime/Let It Out	1986	—	—	3.00

Albums
RCA VICTOR

❏ AFL1-3573	Sacred Songs	1980	2.50	5.00	10.00
❏ AJL1-7196	Three Hearts in the Happy Ending Machine	1986	2.00	4.00	8.00

HALL, DARYL, AND JOHN OATES
Also see DARYL HALL.
12-Inch Singles
ARISTA

Number	Title (A Side/B Side)	Yr	VG	VG+	NM
❏ AD1-9685	Everything Your Heart Desires (If You Want the World Mix 7:53) (54th Street Remix 9:12) (No Words Can Help Dub Mix 5:57) (7th Avenue Remix 4:26)/Realove	1988	2.50	5.00	10.00
❏ AD1-9728	Missed Opportunity (Unlimited Mix 6:58) (Smooth Mix 8:57) (Radio Mix 4:39)/Soul Love	1988	2.00	4.00	8.00
❏ AD1-9768	Downtown Life (5 versions)	1989	2.00	4.00	8.00
❏ ADP-9779 [DJ]	Talking All Night (Extended Remix 6:08) (Dub Mix) (A Cappella) (LP Version) (Radio Remix)	1989	3.75	7.50	15.00

PUSH

❏ 90405-1 [(2) DJ]	Hold On to Yourself (Tommy Musto's Club Mix 5:54) (Rachid Wehbi's Extended Mix 6:07) (Tribal Path Mix 4:37) (Naughty G's Rubber Mix 6:10) (Tommy Musto's Dub Mix 5:21) (Tommy Musto's Club Instrumental 5:57) (Tribal Path Hip-Hop Mix 4:39) (Tommy Musto's Radio Mix 4:18)	1998	10.00	20.00	40.00

RCA

❏ JT-11022 [DJ]	Back Together Again/Kerry	1977	5.00	10.00	20.00

—B-side by Stephen Dees

❏ JD-11302 [DJ]	Do What You Want, Be What You Are (Long Version) (Short Version)	1977	5.00	10.00	20.00
❏ JD-11431 [DJ]	I Don't Wanna Lose You/August Day	1977	5.00	10.00	20.00
❏ JD-11770 [DJ]	Running from Paradise (6:29)/Portable Radio	1979	3.75	7.50	15.00
❏ JD-12053 [DJ]	How Does It Feel to Be Back (same on both sides)	1980	5.00	10.00	20.00
❏ PD-12297	Private Eyes/Tell Me What You Want	1981	3.00	6.00	12.00
❏ PD-12358	I Can't Go for That (No Can Do)/Unguarded Minute	1981	3.00	6.00	12.00
❏ PD-13080	Did It in a Minute/Head Above Water	1982	3.00	6.00	12.00
❏ PD-13253	Your Imagination (Extended Remix 5:41)/Sara Smile (3:07)	1982	3.00	6.00	12.00
❏ JD-13403 [DJ]	Maneater (Special Extended Club Mix)/I Can't Go for That (Club Mix)	1982	3.75	7.50	15.00
❏ PD-13428	One on One (Club Mix 5:30)/I Can't Go for That (Long)	1983	3.00	6.00	12.00
❏ PD-13508	Family Man (Extended Dance Remix)/Maneater	1983	2.50	5.00	10.00
❏ JD-13659 [DJ]	Say It Isn't So/Wait for Me (Live)	1983	3.00	6.00	12.00
❏ PW-13679	Say It Isn't So (Special Extended Dance Mix 6:49)//(Dub Version 4:47)/Kiss on My List	1983	2.50	5.00	10.00
❏ JM-13705 [DJ]	Jingle Bell Rock from Daryl/Jingle Bell Rock from John	1983	7.50	15.00	30.00

—Promo-only picture disc in plastic sleeve

❏ PD-13715	Adult Education (Special Club Mix 6:04)/Maneater	1984	2.00	4.00	8.00
❏ JD-13736 [DJ]	Adult Education (Special Extended Mix Long) (Special Extended Mix Short)	1984	3.00	6.00	12.00
❏ PW-13917	Out of Touch (Extended Remix 7:37)//(Dub Version 7:24)/Cold, Dark and Yesterday	1984	2.50	5.00	10.00
❏ JR-13927 [DJ]	Out of Touch (4:24) (same on both sides)	1984	3.00	6.00	12.00
❏ PW-13971	Method of Modern Love (7:50)//(Dub)/Bank On Your Love	1984	2.50	5.00	10.00
❏ JD-13972 [DJ]	Method of Modern Love (5:27)/Bank On Your Love	1984	3.00	6.00	12.00

Number	Title (A Side/B Side)	Yr	VG	VG+	NM
❑ JD-13983 [DJ]	Jingle Bell Rock from Daryl/Jingle Bell Rock from John	1984	3.00	6.00	12.00
—Promo-only reissue, not a picture disc					
❑ PW-14036	Some Things Are Better Left Unsaid (Special New Mix 5:24)//All American Girl/Some Things Are Better Left Unsaid (Instrumental 5:25)	1985	2.00	4.00	8.00
❑ JD-14038 [DJ]	Some Things Are Better Left Unsaid (Special New Mix 5:24) (same on both sides)	1985	3.00	6.00	12.00
❑ PW-14099	Possession Obsession//Dance on Your Knees/Everytime You Go Away	1985	2.00	4.00	8.00
❑ JR-14100 [DJ]	Possession Obsession (Special New Mix) (same on both sides)	1985	2.50	5.00	10.00
❑ PW-14179	A Nite at the Apollo Live! The Way You Do the Things You Do-My Girl//Everytime You Go Away/Adult Education	1985	2.00	4.00	8.00
❑ JR-14180 [DJ]	A Nite at the Apollo Live! The Way You Do the Things You Do-My Girl (same on both sides)	1985	2.50	5.00	10.00
❑ PD-14250	Jingle Bell Rock from Daryl/Jingle Bell Rock from John//Everytime You Go Away/When Something Is Wrong with My Baby	1985	—	—	—
—Canceled					

45s

ARISTA

Number	Title (A Side/B Side)	Yr	VG	VG+	NM
❑ 2085	So Close/So Close (Unplugged)	1990	—	—	3.00
❑ 2157	Don't Hold Back Your Love/Change of Season	1990	—	—	3.00
❑ 9684	Everything Your Heart Desires/Real Love	1988	—	—	3.00
❑ 9684 [PS]	Everything Your Heart Desires/Real Love	1988	—	—	3.00
❑ 9727	Missed Opportunity/Soul Love	1988	—	—	3.00
❑ 9727 [PS]	Missed Opportunity/Soul Love	1988	—	—	3.00
❑ 9753	Downtown Life (LP Version)/Downtown Life (Urban Mix)	1988	—	—	3.00
❑ 9753 [PS]	Downtown Life (LP Version)/Downtown Life (Urban Mix)	1988	—	—	3.00

ATLANTIC

Number	Title (A Side/B Side)	Yr	VG	VG+	NM
❑ 2922	Goodnight & Good Morning/All Our Love	1972	2.50	5.00	10.00
—As "Whole Oats"					
❑ 2939	Lilly (Are You Happy)/I'm Sorry	1973	2.00	4.00	8.00
❑ 2993	She's Gone/I'm Just a Kid (Don't Make Me Feel Like a Man)	1973	2.00	4.00	8.00
❑ 3026	Lady Rain/When the Morning Comes	1974	—	2.50	5.00
❑ 3239	Can't Stop the Music/70's Scenario	1975	—	2.50	5.00
❑ 3332	She's Gone/I'm Just a Kid (Don't Make Me Feel Like a Man)	1976	—	2.00	4.00
❑ 3332 [DJ]	She's Gone (Long Version)/She's Gone	1976	—	3.00	6.00
❑ 3397	It's Uncanny/Lilly (Are You Happy)	1977	—	2.00	4.00

CHELSEA

Number	Title (A Side/B Side)	Yr	VG	VG+	NM
❑ 3063	If That's What Makes You Happy/The Reason Why	1977	—	2.50	5.00
—B-side by "Daryl Hall and Gulliver"					
❑ 3065	Red River Blues/(B-side unknown)	1977	—	2.50	5.00
❑ 3069	Perkiomen/The Provider	1977	—	2.50	5.00

RCA

Number	Title (A Side/B Side)	Yr	VG	VG+	NM
❑ PB-10808	Do What You Want, Be What You Are/You'll Never Learn	1976	—	2.00	4.00
❑ PB-10860	Rich Girl/London Luck, & Love	1976	—	2.00	4.00
❑ PB-10860 [PS]	Rich Girl/London Luck, & Love	1976	2.00	4.00	8.00
❑ GB-10942	Sara Smile/Do What You Want, Be What You Are	1977	—	—	3.00
—Gold Standard Series					
❑ PB-10970	Back Together Again/Room to Breathe	1977	—	2.00	4.00
❑ PB-11132	Why Do Lovers (Break Each Other's Heart?)/A Girl Who Used to Be	1977	—	2.00	4.00
❑ PB-11181	Don't Change/The Emptiness	1977	—	2.00	4.00
❑ GB-11324	Rich Girl/Back Together Again	1978	—	—	3.00
—Gold Standard Series					
❑ PB-11371	It's a Laugh/Serious Music	1978	—	2.00	4.00
❑ PB-11424	I Don't Wanna Lose You/August Day	1978	—	2.00	4.00
❑ PB-11747	Wait for Me/No Brain No Pain	1979	—	2.00	4.00
❑ PB-11920	All You Want Is Heaven/Who Said the World Was Fair	1980	—	2.00	4.00
❑ GB-11970	It's a Laugh/I Don't Wanna Lose You	1980	—	—	3.00
—Gold Standard Series					
❑ PB-12048	How Does It Feel to Be Back/United State	1980	—	2.00	4.00
❑ PB-12103	You've Lost That Lovin' Feeling/Diddy Doo Wap (I Hear the Voices)	1980	—	2.00	4.00
❑ PB-12142	Kiss on My List/Africa	1981	—	2.00	4.00
❑ PB-12217	You Make My Dreams/Gotta Lotta Love	1981	—	2.00	4.00
❑ PB-12296	Private Eyes/Tell Me What You Want	1981	—	2.00	4.00
❑ GB-12318	Kiss on My List/You've Lost That Lovin' Feeling	1981	—	—	3.00
—Gold Standard Series					
❑ PB-12357	I Can't Go for That (No Can Do)/Unguarded Minute	1981	—	2.00	4.00
❑ JB-12361 [DJ]	I Can't Go for That (No Can Do)/(Club Mix)	1981	2.50	5.00	10.00
—Promo only					
❑ PB-13065	Did It in a Minute/Head Above Water	1982	—	2.00	4.00
❑ PB-13252	Your Imagination/Sara Smile	1982	—	2.00	4.00
❑ PB-13354	Maneater/Delayed Reaction	1982	—	—	3.00
❑ PB-13354 [PS]	Maneater/Delayed Reaction	1982	—	2.00	4.00
❑ PB-13421	One on One/Art of Heartbreak	1983	—	—	3.00
❑ PB-13421 [PS]	One on One/Art of Heartbreak	1983	—	2.00	4.00
❑ GB-13480	Private Eyes/I Can't Go for That (No Can Do)	1983	—	—	3.00
—Gold Standard Series					
❑ GB-13481	You Make My Dreams/Did It in a Minute	1983	—	—	3.00
—Gold Standard Series					
❑ PB-13507	Family Man/Open All Night	1983	—	—	3.00
❑ PB-13654	Say It Isn't So/Kiss on My List	1983	—	—	3.00
❑ PB-13654 [PS]	Say It Isn't So/Kiss on My List	1983	—	2.00	4.00
❑ PB-13714	Adult Education/Maneater	1984	—	—	3.00
❑ PB-13714 [PS]	Adult Education/Maneater	1984	—	2.00	4.00
❑ GB-13796	Maneater/One on One	1984	—	—	3.00
—Gold Standard Series					
❑ GB-13797	Family Man/Say It Isn't So	1984	—	—	3.00
—Gold Standard Series					
❑ PB-13916	Out of Touch/Cold, Dark, and Yesterday	1984	—	—	3.00
❑ PB-13916 [PS]	Out of Touch/Cold, Dark, and Yesterday	1984	—	—	3.00
❑ PB-13970	Method of Modern Love (Remix Edit)/Method of Modern Love	1984	—	—	3.00
❑ PB-13970 [PS]	Method of Modern Love (Remix Edit)/Method of Modern Love	1984	—	—	3.00
❑ PB-14035	Some Things Are Better Left Unsaid/All American Girl	1985	—	—	3.00
❑ PB-14035 [PS]	Some Things Are Better Left Unsaid/All American Girl	1985	—	—	3.00
❑ GB-14064	Out of Touch/Adult Education	1985	—	—	3.00
—Gold Standard Series					
❑ PB-14098	Possession Obsession/Dance on Your Knees	1985	—	—	3.00
❑ PB-14098 [PS]	Possession Obsession/Dance on Your Knees	1985	—	—	3.00
❑ PB-14178	A Nite at the Apollo Live! The Way You Do the Things You Do-My Girl/Everytime You Go Away	1985	—	—	3.00
—A-side: With David Ruffin and Eddie Kendrick (sic)					
❑ PB-14178 [PS]	A Nite at the Apollo Live! The Way You Do the Things You Do-My Girl/Everytime You Go Away	1985	—	—	3.00
—A-side: With David Ruffin and Eddie Kendrick (sic)					
❑ JR-14259 [DJ]	Jingle Bell Rock from Daryl/Jingle Bell Rock from John	1985	2.50	5.00	10.00
—Promo only on red vinyl					
❑ JR-14259 [DJ]	Jingle Bell Rock from Daryl/Jingle Bell Rock from John	1985	2.50	5.00	10.00
—Promo only on green vinyl					
❑ JR-14259 [PS]	Jingle Bell Rock from Daryl/Jingle Bell Rock from John	1985	2.50	5.00	10.00
❑ GB-14340	Method of Modern Love/Possession Obsession	1986	—	—	3.00
—Gold Standard Series					
❑ GB-14341	Some Things Are Better Left Unsaid/A Nite at the Apollo Live! The Way You Do the Things You Do-My Girl	1986	—	—	3.00
—Gold Standard Series					

RCA VICTOR

Number	Title (A Side/B Side)	Yr	VG	VG+	NM
❑ PB-10373	Camellia/Ennui on the Mountain	1975	—	2.50	5.00
❑ PB-10436	Nothing at All/Alone Too Long	1975	—	2.50	5.00
❑ PB-10530	Sara Smile/Soldering	1975	—	2.50	5.00

SIRE

Number	Title (A Side/B Side)	Yr	VG	VG+	NM
❑ 22967	Love Train/"Earth Girls Are Easy" Theme	1989	—	—	3.00
❑ 22967 [PS]	Love Train/"Earth Girls Are Easy" Theme	1989	—	—	3.00

Albums

ALLEGIANCE

Number	Title	Yr	VG	VG+	NM
❑ AV-5014	Nucleus	198?	2.00	4.00	8.00

ARISTA

Number	Title	Yr	VG	VG+	NM
❑ AL-8539	Ooh Yeah!	1988	2.50	5.00	10.00
❑ AL-8614	Change of Season	1989	3.00	6.00	12.00

ATLANTIC

Number	Title	Yr	VG	VG+	NM
❑ SD 7242	Whole Oats	1972	3.00	6.00	12.00
❑ SD 7269	Abandoned Luncheonette	1973	3.00	6.00	12.00
❑ SD 18109	War Babies	1974	3.00	6.00	12.00
❑ SD 18213	No Goodbyes	1977	2.50	5.00	10.00
❑ SD 19139	Abandoned Luncheonette	1977	2.00	4.00	8.00

CHELSEA

Number	Title	Yr	VG	VG+	NM
❑ CHL-547	Past Times Behind	1976	3.00	6.00	12.00

INTERMEDIA

Number	Title	Yr	VG	VG+	NM
❑ QS-5040	The Early Years	198?	2.00	4.00	8.00

JEM

Number	Title	Yr	VG	VG+	NM
❑ 55002	Early Years	198?	2.00	4.00	8.00

MOBILE FIDELITY

Number	Title	Yr	VG	VG+	NM
❑ 1-069	Abandoned Luncheonette	1982	5.00	10.00	20.00
—Audiophile vinyl					

RCA VICTOR

Number	Title	Yr	VG	VG+	NM
❑ APL1-1144	Daryl Hall & John Oates	1976	2.50	5.00	10.00
❑ APL1-1467	Bigger Than Both of Us	1976	2.50	5.00	10.00
❑ AFL1-2300	Beauty on a Back Street	1977	2.50	5.00	10.00
❑ AFL1-2802	Livetime!	1978	2.50	5.00	10.00
❑ AFL1-2804	Along the Red Ledge	1978	2.50	5.00	10.00
❑ AFL1-2804	Along the Red Ledge	1978	3.75	7.50	15.00
—Red vinyl					
❑ ANL1-3463	Daryl Hall & John Oates	1979	2.00	4.00	8.00
❑ AFL1-3494	X-Static	1979	2.50	5.00	10.00
❑ DJL1-3512 [DJ]	Post Static	1979	5.00	10.00	20.00
—Promo-only one-sided 4-song sampler					
❑ AQL1-3646	Voices	1980	3.00	6.00	12.00
—No "RE" of any type on back cover: Embossed lettering and sound waves, Hall's head almost touches the word "Voices" on front					
❑ AQL1-3646	Voices	1980	3.00	6.00	12.00
—"RE" on back cover: Variation unknown					
❑ AQL1-3646	Voices	1980	2.50	5.00	10.00
—"RE 2" on back cover: Cover not embossed; Hall's head 3 inches-plus below "Voices" on front cover					
❑ AQL1-3646	Voices	1980	3.00	6.00	12.00
—"RE 3" on back cover: Cover lettering in black					
❑ AQL1-3646	Voices	1980	2.00	4.00	8.00
—"RE 4" on back cover: Color photo of Hall and Oates on each side					
❑ AQL1-3646	Voices	1981	2.00	4.00	8.00
—"RE 5" on back cover: Variation unknown					

Number	Title (A Side/B Side)	Yr	VG	VG+	NM
❑ AQL1-3646	Voices	1981	2.00	4.00	8.00

—"RE 6" on back cover: Bar code on upper left back cover

Number	Title (A Side/B Side)	Yr	VG	VG+	NM
❑ DJL1-3832	RCA Radio Special Interview Series	1980	3.75	7.50	15.00
❑ AYL1-3836	Daryl Hall & John Oates	1980	2.00	4.00	8.00
❑ AYL1-3866	Bigger Than Both of Us	1980	2.00	4.00	8.00
❑ AFL1-4028	Private Eyes	1981	2.50	5.00	10.00
❑ DJL1-4179	Special Radio Series	1981	3.75	7.50	15.00
❑ AYL1-4230	Beauty on a Back Street	1981	2.00	4.00	8.00
❑ AYL1-4231	Along the Red Ledge	1981	2.00	4.00	8.00
❑ AYL1-4303	X-Static	1982	2.00	4.00	8.00
❑ AFL1-4383	H2O	1982	2.50	5.00	10.00
❑ AYL1-4722	Livetime!	1983	2.00	4.00	8.00
❑ CPL1-4858	Rock 'n Soul Part 1	1983	3.00	6.00	12.00

—Original cover: back cover says "Plus Two New Songs (Recorded September 1983)" WITHOUT mentioning what the songs are

Number	Title (A Side/B Side)	Yr	VG	VG+	NM
❑ CPL1-4858	Rock 'n Soul Part 1	1983	2.50	5.00	10.00

—"RE" on lower left back: back cover says "Plus Two New Songs (Recorded September 1983)," then mentions "Say It Isn't So" and "Adult Education"

Number	Title (A Side/B Side)	Yr	VG	VG+	NM
❑ CPL1-4858	Rock 'n Soul Part 1	1983	2.00	4.00	8.00

—"RE 2" on lower left back: Variation unknown

Number	Title (A Side/B Side)	Yr	VG	VG+	NM
❑ AFL1-5309	Big Bam Boom	1984	3.00	6.00	12.00
❑ AJL1-5336	Big Bam Boom	1984	2.50	5.00	10.00
❑ AFL1-7035	Live at the Apollo	1985	2.50	5.00	10.00

HALL, ROY (1)

Rockabilly and country singer-pianist; wrote "Whole Lot of Shakin' Goin' On." Not to be confused with the pre-World War II country singer of the same name.

45s

DECCA

Number	Title (A Side/B Side)	Yr	VG	VG+	NM
❑ 29697	Whole Lotta Shakin' Goin' On/All By Myself	1955	20.00	40.00	80.00
❑ 29786	See You Later, Alligator/Don't Stop Now	1956	12.50	25.00	50.00
❑ 29880	Blue Suede Shoes/Luscious	1956	12.50	25.00	50.00
❑ 30060	Three Alley Cats/Diggin' the Boogie	1956	12.50	25.00	50.00

FORTUNE

Number	Title (A Side/B Side)	Yr	VG	VG+	NM
❑ 170	Going Down the Road/Jealous Love	1952	10.00	20.00	40.00

—B-side by the Davis Sisters

Number	Title (A Side/B Side)	Yr	VG	VG+	NM
❑ 521	Corrine, Corrina/Don't Ask Me No Questions	1956	12.50	25.00	50.00

HI-Q

Number	Title (A Side/B Side)	Yr	VG	VG+	NM
❑ 5045	Three Alley Cats/Bedspring Motel	196?	15.00	30.00	60.00
❑ 5050	Go Go Little Queenie/Everybody Dig That Boogie	196?	15.00	30.00	60.00

HAMILTON, ROY

45s

AGP

Number	Title (A Side/B Side)	Yr	VG	VG+	NM
❑ 113	The Dark End of the Street/100 Years	1969	2.00	4.00	8.00
❑ 116	Angelica/Hang Ups	1969	2.00	4.00	8.00
❑ 125	It's Only Make Believe/100 Years	1969	2.00	4.00	8.00

CAPITOL

Number	Title (A Side/B Side)	Yr	VG	VG+	NM
❑ 2057	Let This World Be Free/Wait Until Dark	1967	2.00	4.00	8.00

EPIC

Number	Title (A Side/B Side)	Yr	VG	VG+	NM
❑ 9015	You'll Never Walk Alone/I'm Gonna Sit Right Down and Cry	1954	6.25	12.50	25.00
❑ 9047	So Let There Be Love/If You Loved Me	1954	6.25	12.50	25.00
❑ 9068	Ebb Tide/Beware	1954	6.25	12.50	25.00
❑ 9086	Hurt/Star of Love	1954	6.25	12.50	25.00
❑ 9092	I Believe/If You Are But a Dream	1955	5.00	10.00	20.00
❑ 9102	Unchained Melody/From Here to Eternity	1955	6.25	12.50	25.00
❑ 9111	Forgive This Fool/You Wanted to Change Me	1955	5.00	10.00	20.00
❑ 9118	A Little Voice/All This Is Mine	1955	5.00	10.00	20.00
❑ 9125	Without a Song/Cuban Love Song	1955	5.00	10.00	20.00
❑ 9132	Everybody's Got a Home/Take Me with You	1955	5.00	10.00	20.00
❑ 9147	There Goes My Heart/Walk Along with Kings	1956	5.00	10.00	20.00
❑ 9160	Somebody, Somewhere/Since I Fell for You	1956	5.00	10.00	20.00
❑ 9180	I Took My Grief to Him/Chained	1956	5.00	10.00	20.00
❑ 9203	The Simple Prayer/A Mother's Love	1957	5.00	10.00	20.00
❑ 9212	My Faith, My Hope, My Love/So Long	1957	5.00	10.00	20.00
❑ 9224	The Aisle/That Old Feeling	1957	5.00	10.00	20.00
❑ 9232	(All of a Sudden) My Heart Sings/I'm Gonna Lock You in My Heart	1957	5.00	10.00	20.00
❑ 9257	Don't Let Go/The Night to Love	1957	5.00	10.00	20.00
❑ 9268	Crazy Feelin'/In a Dream	1958	3.75	7.50	15.00
❑ 9274	Lips/Jungle Fever	1958	3.75	7.50	15.00
❑ 9282	Wait for Me/Everything	1958	3.75	7.50	15.00
❑ 9294	Pledging My Love/My One and Only Love	1958	3.75	7.50	15.00
❑ 9301	It's Never Too Late/Somewhere Along the Way	1959	3.75	7.50	15.00
❑ 9307	I Need Your Lovin'/Blue Prelude	1959	3.75	7.50	15.00
❑ 9323	Time Marches On/Take It Easy, Joe	1959	3.75	7.50	15.00
❑ 9342	Great Romance/On My Way Back Home	1959	3.75	7.50	15.00
❑ 9354	The Ten Commandments/Nobody Knows the Trouble I've Seen	1959	5.00	10.00	20.00
❑ 9354	The Ten Commandments/Dowm by the Riverside	1959	3.75	7.50	15.00
❑ 9372	Down by the Riverside/Nobody Knows the Trouble I've Seen	1960	3.75	7.50	15.00
❑ 9373	I Let a Song Go Out of My Heart/I Get the Blues When It Rains	1960	3.75	7.50	15.00
❑ 9374	My Story/Please Send Me Someone to Love	1960	3.75	7.50	15.00
❑ 9375	Something's Gotta Give/Cheek to Cheek	1960	—	—	—

—Unreleased?

Number	Title (A Side/B Side)	Yr	VG	VG+	NM
❑ 9376	Sing You Sinners/Blow, Gabriel, Blow	1960	3.75	7.50	15.00
❑ 9386	Having Myself a Ball/Slowly	1960	3.75	7.50	15.00

—B-side by Bobby Sykes

Number	Title (A Side/B Side)	Yr	VG	VG+	NM
❑ 9388	Never Let Me Go/I Get the Blues When It Rains	1960	—	—	—

—Unreleased?

Number	Title (A Side/B Side)	Yr	VG	VG+	NM
❑ 9390	The Clock/I Get the Blues When It Rains	1960	3.75	7.50	15.00
❑ 9398	A Lover's Prayer/Never Let Me Go	1960	3.75	7.50	15.00
❑ 9407	Lonely Hands/Your Love	1960	3.75	7.50	15.00
❑ 9434	You Can Have Her/Abide With Me	1961	3.75	7.50	15.00
❑ 9434 [PS]	You Can Have Her/Abide With Me	1961	7.50	15.00	30.00
❑ 9443	You're Gonna Need Magic/To the One I Love	1961	3.75	7.50	15.00
❑ 9443 [PS]	You're Gonna Need Magic/To the One I Love	1961	7.50	15.00	30.00
❑ 9449	No Substitute for Love/Please Louise	1961	3.75	7.50	15.00
❑ 9449 [PS]	No Substitute for Love/Please Louise	1961	7.50	15.00	30.00
❑ 9460	Excerpts from "You Can Have Her"	1961	3.75	7.50	15.00
❑ 9461	Excerpts from "You Can Have Her"	1961	3.75	7.50	15.00
❑ 9462	Excerpts from "You Can Have Her"	1961	3.75	7.50	15.00
❑ 9463	Excerpts from "You Can Have Her"	1961	3.75	7.50	15.00
❑ 9464	Excerpts from "You Can Have Her"	1961	3.75	7.50	15.00
❑ 9466	There We Were/If	1961	3.00	6.00	12.00
❑ 9492	Don't Come Cryin' to Me/If Only I Had Known	1962	3.00	6.00	12.00
❑ 9520	Climb Ev'ry Mountain/I'll Come Running Back to You	1962	3.00	6.00	12.00
❑ 9538	I Am/Earthquake	1962	3.00	6.00	12.00
❑ 10559	You'll Never Walk Alone/The Golden Boy	1969	2.00	4.00	8.00

MGM

Number	Title (A Side/B Side)	Yr	VG	VG+	NM
❑ 13138	Let Go/You Still Love Him	1963	2.50	5.00	10.00
❑ 13157	Midnight Town-Daybreak City/Intermezzo	1963	2.50	5.00	10.00
❑ 13175	Theme from "The V.I.P.'s" (The Willow)/The Sinner	1963	2.50	5.00	10.00
❑ 13217	The Panic Is On/There She Is	1964	6.25	12.50	25.00
❑ 13247	Answer Me, My Love/Unchained Melody	1964	2.50	5.00	10.00
❑ 13291	You Can Count on Me/She Makes Me Wanna Dance	1964	6.25	12.50	25.00
❑ 13315	Sweet Violets/A Thousand Years Ago	1965	2.50	5.00	10.00

RCA VICTOR

Number	Title (A Side/B Side)	Yr	VG	VG+	NM
❑ 47-8641	Heartache/Ain't It the Truth	1965	2.50	5.00	10.00
❑ 47-8705	And I Love Her/Tore Up Over You	1965	2.50	5.00	10.00
❑ 47-8813	The Impossible Dream/She's Got a Heart	1966	2.50	5.00	10.00
❑ 47-8960	Walk Hand in Hand/Crackin' Up Over You	1966	6.25	12.50	25.00
❑ 47-9061	I Taught Her Everything She Knows/Lament	1967	2.50	5.00	10.00
❑ 47-9171	So High My Love/You Shook Me Up	1967	12.50	25.00	50.00
❑ 48-1034	Walk Hand in Hand/Crackin' Up Over You	1972	2.50	5.00	10.00

7-Inch Extended Plays

EPIC

Number	Title (A Side/B Side)	Yr	VG	VG+	NM
❑ EG-7065	You'll Never Walk Alone/I'm Gonna Sit Right Down and Cry (Over You)//If I Loved You/So Let There Be Love	195?	5.00	10.00	20.00
❑ EG-7065 [PS]	You'll Never Walk Alone	195?	5.00	10.00	20.00
❑ EG-7079	Ebb Tide/Beware//If You Are But a Dream/From Here to Eternity	195?	5.00	10.00	20.00
❑ EG-7079 [PS]	Ebb Tide	195?	5.00	10.00	20.00
❑ EG-7080	(contents unknown)	195?	5.00	10.00	20.00
❑ EG-7080 [PS]	Faith, Hope and Hamilton	195?	5.00	10.00	20.00
❑ EG-7133	(contents unknown)	195?	5.00	10.00	20.00
❑ EG-7133 [PS]	Roy Hamilton	195?	5.00	10.00	20.00
❑ EG-7158	(contents unknown)	195?	3.75	7.50	15.00
❑ EG-7158 [PS]	Roy Hamilton	195?	3.75	7.50	15.00
❑ EG-7159	(contents unknown)	195?	3.75	7.50	15.00
❑ EG-7159 [PS]	Roy Hamilton	195?	3.75	7.50	15.00
❑ EG-7200	(contents unknown)	1958	3.75	7.50	15.00
❑ EG-7200 [PS]	Don't Let Go	1958	3.75	7.50	15.00
❑ EG-7205	(contents unknown)	1958	3.75	7.50	15.00
❑ EG-7205 [PS]	Lips	1958	3.75	7.50	15.00
❑ EG-7210	(contents unknown)	195?	3.75	7.50	15.00
❑ EG-7210 [PS]	With All My Love	195?	3.75	7.50	15.00
❑ EG-7214	(contents unknown)	195?	3.75	7.50	15.00
❑ EG-7214 [PS]	You Belong to My Heart	195?	3.75	7.50	15.00

Albums

EPIC

Number	Title (A Side/B Side)	Yr	VG	VG+	NM
❑ BN 518 [S]	With All My Love	1958	10.00	20.00	40.00
❑ BN 525 [S]	Why Fight The Feeling?	1959	7.50	15.00	30.00
❑ BN 530 [S]	Come Out Swingin'	1959	7.50	15.00	30.00
❑ BN 535 [S]	Have Blues, Must Travel	1959	7.50	15.00	30.00
❑ BN 551 [S]	Spirituals	1960	7.50	15.00	30.00
❑ BN 578 [S]	Soft 'n Warm	1960	7.50	15.00	30.00
❑ BN 595 [S]	You Can Have Her	1961	10.00	20.00	40.00
❑ BN 610 [S]	Only You	1961	7.50	15.00	30.00
❑ BN 632 [R]	You'll Never Walk Alone	1962	5.00	10.00	20.00
❑ LN 1023 [10]	You'll Never Walk Alone	1954	50.00	100.00	200.00
❑ LN 1103 [10]	The Voice of Roy Hamilton	1954	50.00	100.00	200.00
❑ LN 3176 [M]	Roy Hamilton	1955	15.00	30.00	60.00
❑ LN 3294 [M]	You'll Never Walk Alone	1956	17.50	35.00	70.00
❑ LN 3364 [M]	Golden Boy	1957	12.50	25.00	50.00
❑ LN 3519 [M]	With All My Love	1958	7.50	15.00	30.00
❑ LN 3545 [M]	Why Fight The Feeling?	1959	6.25	12.50	25.00
❑ LN 3561 [M]	Come Out Swingin'	1959	6.25	12.50	25.00
❑ LN 3580 [M]	Have Blues, Must Travel	1959	6.25	12.50	25.00
❑ LN 3628 [M]	Roy Hamilton At His Best	1960	10.00	20.00	40.00
❑ LN 3654 [M]	Spirituals	1960	6.25	12.50	25.00
❑ LN 3717 [M]	Soft 'n Warm	1960	6.25	12.50	25.00
❑ LN 3775 [M]	You Can Have Her	1961	7.50	15.00	30.00
❑ LN 3807 [M]	Only You	1961	6.25	12.50	25.00
❑ LN 24000 [M]	Mr. Rock and Soul	1962	6.25	12.50	25.00
❑ LN 24009 [M]	Roy Hamilton's Greatest Hits	1962	5.00	10.00	20.00
❑ LN 24316 [M]	Roy Hamilton's Greatest Hits, Vol. 2	1967	5.00	10.00	20.00
❑ BN 26000 [S]	Mr. Rock and Soul	1962	7.50	15.00	30.00
❑ BN 26009 [S]	Roy Hamilton's Greatest Hits	1962	6.25	12.50	25.00
❑ BN 26316 [S]	Roy Hamilton's Greatest Hits, Vol. 2	1967	6.25	12.50	25.00

MGM

Number	Title (A Side/B Side)	Yr	VG	VG+	NM
❑ E-4139 [M]	Warm and Soul	1963	3.75	7.50	15.00
❑ SE-4139 [S]	Warm and Soul	1963	5.00	10.00	20.00

Number	Title (A Side/B Side)	Yr	VG	VG+	NM
❑ E-4233 [M]	Sentimental, Lonely & Blue	1964	3.75	7.50	15.00
❑ SE-4233 [S]	Sentimental, Lonely & Blue	1964	5.00	10.00	20.00

RCA VICTOR

Number	Title (A Side/B Side)	Yr	VG	VG+	NM
❑ LPM-3552 [M]	The Impossible Dream	1966	3.75	7.50	15.00
❑ LSP-3552 [S]	The Impossible Dream	1966	5.00	10.00	20.00

HAMMER, MC

12-Inch Singles

BUSTIN'

Number	Title (A Side/B Side)	Yr	VG	VG+	NM
❑ BR 003	Cold Go MC Hammer (Vocal) (Instrumental)	1987	3.75	7.50	15.00
❑ 1987-2	Thrill Is Gone (Vocal 4:41) (Instrumental 4:41)	1987	3.00	6.00	12.00
❑ 1987-3	Let's Get It Started (Vocal 6:00) (Instrumental)	1987	3.75	7.50	15.00

CAPITOL

Number	Title (A Side/B Side)	Yr	VG	VG+	NM
❑ V-15411	Let's Get It Started (Extended) (Radio Edit) (Instrumental)	1988	2.00	4.00	8.00
❑ V-15428	Pump It Up (The I Rose Mix) (Dope Mix) (Radio Edit) (Instrumental)	1988	2.00	4.00	8.00
❑ V-15437	Turn This Mutha Out (2 versions)/Ring 'Em (2 versions)	1989	2.00	4.00	8.00
❑ V-15460	(Hammer Hammer) They Put Me in the Mix (2 versions)/Cold Go MC Hammer (2 versions)	1989	2.00	4.00	8.00
❑ V-15540	Help the Children (Vocal) (Instrumental)	1990	2.00	4.00	8.00
❑ V-15542	Dancin' Machine (Vocal) (Instrumental) (Club Mix)	1990	—	3.00	6.00
❑ V-15571	U Can't Touch This (LP Version) (Video Mix) (Instrumental)/Dancin' Machine (Funk Mix) (Funky Club Mix)	1991	2.50	5.00	10.00
❑ V-15585	Here Comes the Hammer (4 versions)	1991	2.00	4.00	8.00
❑ V-15586	Have You Seen Her (LP Version) (Instrumental)	1990	2.00	4.00	8.00
❑ V-15617	Pray (LP Version) (Instrumental)	1990	2.00	4.00	8.00
❑ V-15791	2 Legit 2 Quit (Legit Remix) (Get Bucked Mix)/ Addams Groove (Instrumental)	1991	2.00	4.00	8.00
❑ V-15792	This Is the Way We Roll (4 versions)	1992	2.00	4.00	8.00
❑ V-15801	Addams Groove (2 versions)	1991	2.00	4.00	8.00
❑ V-15830	Do Not Pass Me By (3 versions)	1992	—	3.00	6.00
❑ SPRO-79312/26 [DJ]	This Is the Way We Roll (5 versions)	1991	2.00	4.00	8.00
❑ SPRO-79313/25 [DJ]	Good to Go (5 versions)	1991	2.50	5.00	10.00
❑ SPRO-79314 [DJ]	2 Legit 2 Quit (Mega Mix 7:12) (Mega Mix Edit 5:10)	1991	2.50	5.00	10.00
❑ SPRO-79315/24 [DJ]	Till You Drop (3 versions)	1991	2.00	4.00	8.00
❑ SPRO-79463/4 [DJ]	Pray (Slam the Hammer Mix) (Slam the Hammer Piano Dub) (Jam the Hammer Mix) (Hit 'Um Hard Mix) (Nail 'Um Down Chant)	1990	2.50	5.00	10.00
❑ SPRO-79485/6 [DJ]	Gaining Momentum (Edit) (Momentum Jam) (Hip Hop Mix)	1992	2.50	5.00	10.00

GIANT

Number	Title (A Side/B Side)	Yr	VG	VG+	NM
❑ PRO-A-6858 [DJ]	Don't Stop (same on both sides?)	1994	2.00	4.00	8.00
❑ PRO-A-7544 [DJ]	Sultry Funk (12:34)/Bustin' Loose (12:35)	1995	3.00	6.00	12.00
❑ PRO-A-7551 [DJ]	Anything Goes on the Dance Floor (14:07)/ Keep On/I Need That Number	1995	2.00	4.00	8.00
❑ 41260	Pumps & a Bump (2 versions)/It's All Good (2 versions)	1994	2.00	4.00	8.00
❑ 41473	Don't Stop (4 versions)	1994	2.00	4.00	8.00

45s

BUSTIN'

Number	Title (A Side/B Side)	Yr	VG	VG+	NM
❑ 1987-7	Let's Get It Started/(Instrumental)	1987	5.00	10.00	20.00

CAPITOL

Number	Title (A Side/B Side)	Yr	VG	VG+	NM
❑ B-44229	Let's Get It Started/(Instrumental)	1988	—	—	3.00
❑ B-44266	Pump It Up/(Instrumental)	1988	—	—	3.00
❑ B-44290	Turn This Mutha Out/Ring 'Em	1989	—	—	3.00
❑ B-44353	(Hammer Hammer) They Put Me in the Mix/Cold Go M.C. Hammer	1989	—	—	—
—Unreleased?					
❑ B-44497	Help the Children/(Instrumental)	1989	—	—	3.00
❑ NR-44794	Addams Groove/(Instrumental)	1991	—	2.00	4.00
❑ S7-57700	2 Legit to Quit (Long)/2 Legit to Quit (Short)	1992	—	2.00	4.00
❑ S7-57730	Do Not Pass Me By/Gaining Momentum	1992	—	2.00	4.00
❑ S7-57740	Good to Go/Count It Off	1992	—	2.00	4.00
❑ 7PRO-79072 [DJ]	U Can't Touch This (same on both sides)	1990	3.75	7.50	15.00
❑ 7PRO-79150 [DJ]	Have You Seen Her (same on both sides)	1990	2.50	5.00	10.00
❑ SPRO-79175 [DJ]	2 Legit 2 Quit (2 versions)	1991	2.00	4.00	8.00
❑ 7PRO-79284/95 [DJ]	Pray (Radio Edit)/Pray (LP Version)	1990	2.50	5.00	10.00
❑ 7PRO-79667 [DJ]	(Hammer Hammer) They Put Me in the Mix (same on both sides)	1989	—	3.00	6.00
❑ 7PRO-79893 [DJ]	Dancin' Machine (same on both sides)	1990	—	3.00	6.00

COLLECTABLES

Number	Title (A Side/B Side)	Yr	VG	VG+	NM
❑ 6324	U Can't Touch This/Pray	199?	—	2.00	4.00
❑ 6325	2 Legit 2 Quit/Addams Groove	199?	—	—	3.00
❑ 6326	Have You Seen Her/Here Comes the Hammer	199?	—	—	3.00

GIANT

Number	Title (A Side/B Side)	Yr	VG	VG+	NM
❑ 18218	Pumps & a Bump (Radio Edit)/Pumps & a Bump (Album Version)	1994	—	—	3.00
❑ 18271	It's All Good/(Instrumental)	1994	—	—	3.00

Albums

BUSTIN'

Number	Title (A Side/B Side)	Yr	VG	VG+	NM
❑ BR-LP-001	Feel My Power	1987	6.25	12.50	25.00

CAPITOL

Number	Title (A Side/B Side)	Yr	VG	VG+	NM
❑ SPRO-79080 [EP]	A Bit Legit	1991	2.00	4.00	8.00
—Promo-only three-track sampler					
❑ C1-90924	Let's Get It Started	1988	2.50	5.00	10.00
❑ C1-92857	Please Hammer Don't Hurt 'Em	1990	3.75	7.50	15.00
❑ C1-98151 [(2)]	Too Legit to Quit	1991	3.75	7.50	15.00

GIANT

Number	Title (A Side/B Side)	Yr	VG	VG+	NM
❑ PRO-A-6798 [(2) DJ]	The Funky Headhunter	1994	3.75	7.50	15.00
—Vinyl version is promo only					

HANCOCK, HERBIE

12-Inch Singles

COLUMBIA

Number	Title (A Side/B Side)	Yr	VG	VG+	NM
❑ AS 751 [DJ]	Go For It (6:58)/Go For It (7:32)	1980	2.00	4.00	8.00
❑ AS 814 [DJ]	Saturday Night/Making Love	1980	2.00	4.00	8.00
❑ AS 1251 [DJ]	Everybody's Broke (3:53)/Everybody's Broke (7:05)	1981	2.00	4.00	8.00
❑ AS 1262 [DJ]	Magic Number/Everybody's Broke	1981	2.00	4.00	8.00
❑ AS 1333 [DJ]	Magic Number (Remix)/Magic Number (Edit)	1981	2.00	4.00	8.00
❑ AS 1413 [DJ]	Lite Me Up (long)/Lite Me Up (short)	1982	2.00	4.00	8.00
❑ AS 1504 [DJ]	Gettin' to the Good Part/The Fun Tracks	1982	2.00	4.00	8.00
❑ 03978	Rockit (2 versions)	1983	2.50	5.00	10.00
❑ 04200	Autodrive/Chameleon	1983	—	3.00	6.00
❑ 04637	Metal Beat (extended)/Metal Beat (edit)	1984	—	3.00	6.00
❑ 04960	Mega-Mix (same on both sides)	1984	2.00	4.00	8.00
❑ 05027	Hardrock (long)/Hardrock (short)	1984	—	3.00	6.00
❑ 07804	Vibe Alive (extended) (edit) (bonus beats)	1988	—	3.00	6.00
❑ 07896	Beat Wise (4 versions)	1988	—	3.00	6.00
❑ 10906	Ready or Not (6:43)/You Bet Your Love (8:12)	1979	2.00	4.00	8.00
❑ 11019	Tell Everybody (7:48)/Honey from the Jar (5:36)	1979	2.00	4.00	8.00
❑ 11310	Stars in Your Eyes/Go For It	1980	2.00	4.00	8.00

45s

BLUE NOTE

Number	Title (A Side/B Side)	Yr	VG	VG+	NM
❑ 1862	Watermelon Man/Three Bags Full	1962	2.00	4.00	8.00
❑ 1863	Driftin'/Alone Am I	1962	2.00	4.00	8.00
❑ 1887	Blind Man (Part 1)/Blind Man (Part 2)	196?	2.00	4.00	8.00

COLUMBIA

Number	Title (A Side/B Side)	Yr	VG	VG+	NM
❑ 02404	Everybody's Broke/Help Yourself	1981	—	2.00	4.00
❑ 02615	Magic Number/Help Yourself	1981	—	2.00	4.00
❑ 02824	Lite Me Up/Satisfied with Love	1982	—	2.00	4.00
❑ 03004	Gettin' to the Good Part/The Fun Tracks	1982	—	2.00	4.00
❑ 03318	Paradise/The Fun Tracks	1982	—	2.00	4.00
❑ 04054	Rockit (2 versions)	1983	—	2.50	5.00
❑ 04054	Rockit (2 versions)	1984	—	2.00	4.00
—Gold-label "Instant Classic" early reissue					
❑ 04268	Autodrive/Chameleon	1983	—	2.00	4.00
❑ 04473	Mega-Mix/TFS	1984	—	2.00	4.00
❑ 04565	Hardrock (2 versions)	1984	—	2.00	4.00
❑ 04565 [PS]	Hardrock (2 versions)	1984	—	2.00	4.00
❑ 04633	Metal Beat/Karabali	1984	—	2.00	4.00
❑ 07718	Vibe Alive/P. Bop	1988	—	—	3.00
❑ 07718 [PS]	Vibe Alive/P. Bop	1988	—	—	3.00
❑ 07987	Beat Wise/Chemical Residue	1988	—	—	3.00
❑ 10050	Palm Grease/Butterfly	1974	—	2.50	5.00
❑ 10094	Spank-a-Lee/Actual Proof	1975	—	2.50	5.00
❑ 10239	Suntouch/Hang Up Your Hang-Ups	1975	—	2.50	5.00
❑ 10408	Doin' It/People Music	1976	—	2.50	5.00
❑ 10563	Maiden Voyage/Spider	1977	—	2.50	5.00
❑ 10781	I Thought It Was You/No Means Yes	1978	—	2.50	5.00
❑ 10835	Sunlight/Come Running to Me	1978	—	2.50	5.00
❑ 10894	Knee Deep/You Get Your Love`	1979	—	2.50	5.00
❑ 10936	Ready Or Not/Trust Me	1979	—	2.50	5.00
❑ 11021	Tell Everybody/Honey from the Jar	1979	—	2.50	5.00
❑ 11122	Doin' It/Honey from the Jar	1979	—	2.00	4.00
❑ 11227	Go For It/Trust Me	1980	—	—	—
—Canceled?					
❑ 11236	Stars in Your Eyes/Go For It	1980	—	2.00	4.00
❑ 11323	Making Love/It All Comes Around	1980	—	2.00	4.00
❑ 46002	Chameleon/Vein Melter	1974	—	2.50	5.00
❑ 46073	Watermelon Man/Sly	1974	—	2.50	5.00

WARNER BROS.

Number	Title (A Side/B Side)	Yr	VG	VG+	NM
❑ 7358	Fat Mama/Wiggle-Waggle	1969	—	3.00	6.00
❑ 7598	Water Torture/Crossings	1972	—	3.00	6.00

Albums

BLUE NOTE

Number	Title (A Side/B Side)	Yr	VG	VG+	NM
❑ BN-LA152-F	Succotash	1974	3.00	6.00	12.00
❑ BN-LA399-H2 [(2)]	Herbie Hancock	1975	3.75	7.50	15.00
❑ BLP-4109 [M]	Takin' Off	1962	12.50	25.00	50.00
❑ BLP-4126 [M]	My Point of View	1963	8.75	17.50	35.00
❑ BLP-4147 [M]	Inventions and Dimensions	1963	8.75	17.50	35.00
❑ BLP-4175 [M]	Empyrean Isles	1964	8.75	17.50	35.00
❑ BLP-4195 [M]	Maiden Voyage	1965	8.75	17.50	35.00
❑ B1-46339	Maiden Voyage	1997	5.00	10.00	20.00
—Audiophile reissue					
❑ BST-84109	Takin' Off	1987	2.50	5.00	10.00
—"The Finest in Jazz Since 1939" reissue					
❑ BST-84109 [S]	Takin' Off	1962	10.00	20.00	40.00
—With New York, USA address on label					
❑ BST-84109 [S]	Takin' Off	1967	3.75	7.50	15.00
—With "A Division of Liberty Records" on label					
❑ BST-84126	My Point of View	1987	2.50	5.00	10.00
—"The Finest in Jazz Since 1939" reissue					
❑ BST-84126 [S]	My Point of View	1963	8.75	17.50	35.00
—With New York, USA address on label					
❑ BST-84126 [S]	My Point of View	1967	3.75	7.50	15.00
—With "A Division of Liberty Records" on label					
❑ BST-84147	Inventions and Dimensions	1987	2.50	5.00	10.00
—"The Finest in Jazz Since 1939" reissue					
❑ BST-84147 [S]	Inventions and Dimensions	1963	8.75	17.50	35.00
—With New York, USA address on label					
❑ BST-84147 [S]	Inventions and Dimensions	1967	3.75	7.50	15.00
—With "A Division of Liberty Records" on label					
❑ BST-84175	Empyrean Isles	1985	2.50	5.00	10.00
—"The Finest in Jazz Since 1939" reissue					

Number	Title (A Side/B Side)	Yr	VG	VG+	NM
❑ BST-84175 [S]Empyrean Isles		1964	8.75	17.50	35.00
—With New York, USA address on label					
❑ BST-84175 [S]Empyrean Isles		1967	3.75	7.50	15.00
—With "A Division of Liberty Records" on label					
❑ BST-84195 [S]Maiden Voyage		1965	8.75	17.50	35.00
—With New York, USA address on label					
❑ BST-84195 [S]Maiden Voyage		1967	3.75	7.50	15.00
—With "A Division of Liberty Records" on label					
❑ BST-84195 [S]Maiden Voyage		1985	2.50	5.00	10.00
—"The Finest in Jazz Since 1939" reissue					
❑ BST-84279	Speak Like a Child	1968	3.75	7.50	15.00
❑ BST-84279	Speak Like a Child	1986	2.50	5.00	10.00
—"The Finest in Jazz Since 1939" reissue					
❑ BST-84321	The Prisoner	1969	3.75	7.50	15.00
❑ BST-84321	The Prisoner	1987	2.50	5.00	10.00
—"The Finest in Jazz Since 1939" reissue					
❑ BST-84407	The Best of Herbie Hancock	1971	3.75	7.50	15.00
❑ B1-91142	The Best of Herbie Hancock	1988	2.50	5.00	10.00
COLUMBIA					
❑ KC 32212	Sextant	1973	3.00	6.00	12.00
❑ PC 32212	Sextant	198?	2.00	4.00	8.00
—Budget-line reissue					
❑ CQ 32371 [Q] Head Hunters		1973	6.25	12.50	25.00
❑ KC 32371	Head Hunters	1973	3.00	6.00	12.00
❑ PC 32371	Head Hunters	197?	2.00	4.00	8.00
—Reissue (with or without bar code)					
❑ PC 32965	Thrust	1974	3.00	6.00	12.00
—No bar code on cover					
❑ PC 32965	Thrust	198?	2.00	4.00	8.00
—Budget-line reissue with bar code					
❑ PCQ 32965 [Q]Thrust		1974	6.25	12.50	25.00
❑ PC 33812	Man-Child	1975	3.00	6.00	12.00
—No bar code on cover					
❑ PC 33812	Man-Child	198?	2.00	4.00	8.00
—Budget-line reissue with bar code					
❑ PC 34280	Secrets	1976	3.00	6.00	12.00
—No bar code on cover					
❑ PC 34280	Secrets	198?	2.00	4.00	8.00
—Budget-line reissue with bar code					
❑ PCQ 34280 [Q]Secrets		1976	6.25	12.50	25.00
❑ PG 34688 [(2)]V.S.O.P.		1977	3.75	7.50	15.00
❑ JC 34907	Sunlight	1978	3.00	6.00	12.00
❑ C2 34976 [(2)] V.S.O.P. Quintet		1978	3.75	7.50	15.00
❑ JC 35764	Feets Don't Fail Me Now	1979	3.00	6.00	12.00
❑ PC 35764	Feets Don't Fail Me Now	198?	2.00	4.00	8.00
—Budget-line reissue					
❑ JC 36309	The Best of Herbie Hancock	1979	3.00	6.00	12.00
❑ JC 36415	Monster	1980	2.50	5.00	10.00
❑ PC 36415	Monster	198?	2.00	4.00	8.00
—Budget-line reissue					
❑ JC 36578	Mr. Hands	1980	2.50	5.00	10.00
❑ PC 36578	Mr. Hands	198?	2.00	4.00	8.00
—Budget-line reissue					
❑ FC 37387	Magic Windows	1981	2.50	5.00	10.00
❑ PC 37387	Magic Windows	198?	2.00	4.00	8.00
—Budget-line reissue					
❑ FC 37928	Lite Me Up	1982	2.50	5.00	10.00
❑ PC 37928	Lite Me Up	198?	2.00	4.00	8.00
—Budget-line reissue					
❑ FC 38814	Future Shock	1983	2.50	5.00	10.00
❑ FC 39478	Sound-System	1984	2.50	5.00	10.00
❑ PC 39478	Sound-System	1985	2.00	4.00	8.00
—Budget-line reissue					
❑ FC 39870	Village Life	1985	2.50	5.00	10.00
❑ 8C8 39913 [EP]Hardrock		1984	3.00	6.00	12.00
—Picture disc					
❑ FC 40025	Perfect Machine	1988	2.50	5.00	10.00
❑ SC 40464	'Round Midnight	1986	2.50	5.00	10.00
MGM					
❑ E-4447 [M]	Blow-Up	1967	8.75	17.50	35.00
❑ SE-4447 [S]	Blow-Up	1967	10.00	20.00	40.00
—Also includes one track by the Yardbirds					
PAUSA					
❑ 9002	Succotash	198?	2.50	5.00	10.00
TRIP					
❑ UPF-194	Traces	197?	3.00	6.00	12.00
WARNER BROS.					
❑ WS 1834	Fat Albert Rotunda	1970	3.75	7.50	15.00
❑ WS 1898	Mwandishi	1971	3.75	7.50	15.00
❑ BS 2617	Crossings	1972	3.75	7.50	15.00
❑ 2WS 2807 [(2)]Treasure Chest		1974	3.75	7.50	15.00

HARMONY GRITS, THE

Members of the original DRIFTERS formed this group after their firing.

45s

Number	Title (A Side/B Side)	Yr	VG	VG+	NM
END					
❑ 1051	Am I to Be the One/I Could Have Told You	1959	6.25	12.50	25.00
❑ 1063	Gee/I Could Have Told You	1959	6.25	12.50	25.00
❑ 1063	Gee/Santa Claus Is Coming to Town	1959	10.00	20.00	40.00

HARPO, SLIM

45s

Number	Title (A Side/B Side)	Yr	VG	VG+	NM
EXCELLO					
❑ 2113	I'm a King Bee/I Got Love If You Want It	1957	15.00	30.00	60.00
❑ 2138	Wonderin' and Worryin'/Strange Love	1958	7.50	15.00	30.00

Number	Title (A Side/B Side)	Yr	VG	VG+	NM
❑ 2162	One More Day/You'll Be Sorry One Day	1959	7.50	15.00	30.00
❑ 2171	Buzz Me Babe/Late Last Night	1960	7.50	15.00	30.00
❑ 2184	Blues Hangover/What a Dream	1960	7.50	15.00	30.00
❑ 2194	Rainin' in My Heart/Don't Start Cryin' Now	1961	5.00	10.00	20.00
❑ 2239	Buzzin'/I Love the Life I'm Livin'	1963	3.75	7.50	15.00
❑ 2246	Little Queen Bee (Got a Brand New King)/I Need Money (Keep Your Alibis)	1964	3.00	6.00	12.00
❑ 2253	Still Rainin' in My Heart/We're Two of a Kind	1964	3.00	6.00	12.00
❑ 2261	Sittin' Here Wondering/What's Goin' On Baby	1964	3.00	6.00	12.00
❑ 2265	Please Don't Turn Me Down/Harpo's Blues	1965	3.00	6.00	12.00
❑ 2273	Baby Scratch My Back/I'm Gonna Miss You (LIke the Devil)	1965	3.00	6.00	12.00
❑ 2276	Goin' Away Blues/Just a Lonely Stranger	1966	2.50	5.00	10.00
❑ 2278	Midnight Blues/Shake Your Hips	1966	2.50	5.00	10.00
❑ 2282	I'm Your Bread-Maker, Baby/Loving You (The Way I Do)	1966	2.50	5.00	10.00
❑ 2285	Tip On In (Part 1)/Tip On In (Part 2)	1967	2.50	5.00	10.00
❑ 2289	I'm Gonna Keep What I've Got/I've Got to Be with You Tonight	1967	2.50	5.00	10.00
❑ 2294	Te-Ni-Lee-Ni-Nu/Mailbox Bues	1968	2.50	5.00	10.00
❑ 2301	Mohair Sam/I Just Can't Leave You	1969	2.00	4.00	8.00
❑ 2305	Just for You/That's Why I Love You	1969	2.00	4.00	8.00
❑ 2306	Folsom Prison Blues/Mututal Friend	1969	2.00	4.00	8.00
❑ 2309	I've Got My Finger on Your Trigger/The Price Is Too High	1969	2.00	4.00	8.00
❑ 2316	Rainin' in My Heart/Jody Man	1970	2.00	4.00	8.00

78s

Number	Title (A Side/B Side)	Yr	VG	VG+	NM
EXCELLO					
❑ 2113	I'm a King Bee/I Got Love If You Want It	1957	10.00	20.00	40.00

Albums

Number	Title (A Side/B Side)	Yr	VG	VG+	NM
EXCELLO					
❑ LP-8003 [M]	Raining in My Heart	1961	62.50	125.00	250.00
—Orange and blue label					
❑ LPS-8003 [M]	Raining in My Heart	196?	25.00	50.00	100.00
—All-blue label					
❑ LP-8005 [M]	Baby Scratch My Back	1966	50.00	100.00	200.00
—Orange and blue label					
❑ LPS-8005 [M]	Baby Scratch My Back	196?	25.00	50.00	100.00
—All-blue label					
❑ LPS-8008 [M]	Tip On In	1968	12.50	25.00	50.00
❑ LPS-8010 [M]	The Best of Slim Harpo	1969	12.50	25.00	50.00
❑ LPS-8013 [M]	Slim Harpo Knew the Blues	1970	12.50	25.00	50.00
RHINO					
❑ RNLP-106	The Best of Slim Harpo	198?	3.75	7.50	15.00
❑ R1-70169	Scratch My Back: The Best of Slim Harpo	1989	3.00	6.00	12.00

HARPS, THE

See THE CAMELOTS.

HARPTONES, THE

45s

Number	Title (A Side/B Side)	Yr	VG	VG+	NM
AMBIENT SOUND					
❑ 02807	Love Needs a Heart/It's You	1982	—	3.00	6.00
ANDREA					
❑ 100	What Is Your Decision/Gimme Some	1956	10.00	20.00	40.00
BRUCE					
❑ 101	A Sunday Kind of Love/I'll Never Tell	1953	1000.	2000.	3000.
—"Bruce" in script lettering					
❑ 101	A Sunday Kind of Love/I'll Never Tell	1953	20.00	40.00	80.00
—"Bruce" in block lettering					
❑ 102	My Memories of You/It Was Just for Laughs	1954	50.00	100.00	200.00
❑ 102	My Memories of You/The Laughs on You	1954	30.00	60.00	120.00
—Same B-side with different title (and missing the apostrophe)					
❑ 104	I Depended on You/Mambo Boogie	1954	20.00	40.00	80.00
❑ 109	Forever Mine/Why Should I Love You	1954	20.00	40.00	80.00
❑ 113	Since I Fell for You/Oobidee-Oobidee-Oo	1954	20.00	40.00	80.00
❑ 123	High Flying Baby/Loving a Girl Like You	1955	15.00	30.00	60.00
❑ 128	I Almost Lost My Mind/Oh Wee Baby	1955	15.00	30.00	60.00
COED					
❑ 540	Answer Me My Love/Rain Down Kisses	1960	5.00	10.00	20.00
COMPANION					
❑ 102	All in Your Mind/The Last Dance	1961	7.50	15.00	30.00
❑ 103	What Will I Tell My Heart/Foolish Me	1961	20.00	40.00	80.00
CUB					
❑ 9097	Devil in Velvet/Your Love Is a Good Love	1961	5.00	10.00	20.00
GEE					
❑ 1045	Cry Like I Cried/So Good, So Fine, You're Mine	1957	15.00	30.00	60.00
—Red label					
KT					
❑ 201	Sunset/I Gotta Have Your Love	1963	12.50	25.00	50.00
PARADISE					
❑ 101	Life Is But a Dream/You Know You're Doing Me Wrong	1954	37.50	75.00	150.00
—Maroon label					
❑ 101	Life Is But a Dream/You Know You're Doing Me Wrong	1954	15.00	30.00	60.00
—Purple label					
❑ 103	My Success/I've Got a Notion	1955	75.00	150.00	300.00
❑ 105	It All Depends on You/Guitar Shuffle	1955	37.50	75.00	150.00
—Maroon label					
❑ 105	It All Depends on You/Guitar Shuffle	1955	15.00	30.00	60.00
—Purple label					
RAMA					
❑ 203	Three Wishes/That's the Way It Goes	1956	20.00	40.00	80.00

Number	Title (A Side/B Side)	Yr	VG	VG+	NM
❏ 214	The Masquerade Is Over/On Sunday Afternoon	1956	20.00	40.00	80.00
❏ 221	The Shrine of St. Cecelia/Oo Wee Baby	1957	20.00	40.00	80.00
RAVEN					
❏ 8001	A Sunday Kind of Love/Mambo Boogie	1962	3.75	7.50	15.00
TIP TOP					
❏ 401	My Memories of You/High Flyin' Baby	1956	10.00	20.00	40.00
WARWICK					
❏ 500	I Remember/Laughing on the Outside	1959	6.25	12.50	25.00
❏ 512	Love Me Completely/Hep Teenager	1959	6.25	12.50	25.00
❏ 551	No Greater Miracle/What Kind of a Fool	1960	6.25	12.50	25.00
7-Inch Extended Plays					
BRUCE					
❏ BEP 201	A Sunday Kind of Love/Ou Wee Baby//Forever Mine/I Almost Lost My Mind	1954	2500.	3750.	5000.
❏ BEP 201 [PS]	The Sensational Harptones	1954	2500.	3750.	5000.
Albums					
AMBIENT SOUND					
❏ FZ 37718	Love Needs	1982	3.00	6.00	12.00
HARLEM HIT PARADE					
❏ 5006	The Harptones	197?	3.75	7.50	15.00
RELIC					
❏ LP-5001	The Greatest Hits of the Harptones, Vol. 1	197?	3.00	6.00	12.00
❏ LP-5003	The Greatest Hits of the Harptones, Vol. 2	197?	3.00	6.00	12.00

HARRIS, MAJOR
Also see THE DELFONICS.

12-Inch Singles

Number	Title (A Side/B Side)	Yr	VG	VG+	NM
POP ART					
❏ 1401	All My Life/(B-side unknown)	1983	—	3.00	6.00
45s					
ATLANTIC					
❏ 3217	Each Morning I Wake Up/Just a Thing I Do	1974	—	2.50	5.00
❏ 3248	Love Won't Let Me Wait/After Loving You	1975	—	2.00	4.00
❏ 3299 [DJ]	Loving You Is Mellow (mono/stereo)	1975	—	2.50	5.00
—May be promo-only					
❏ 3303	I Got Over Love/Loving You Is Mellow	1975	—	2.00	4.00
❏ 3321	Jealousy/Tynisa (What's Your Hurry)	1976	—	2.00	4.00
❏ 3336	It's Got to Be Magic/Just a Thing That I Do	1976	—	2.00	4.00
OKEH					
❏ 7314	Just Love Me/Loving You More	1968	7.50	15.00	30.00
❏ 7327	Like a Rolling Stone/Call Me Tomorrow	1969	15.00	30.00	60.00
WMOT					
❏ 02091	Here We Are/Living's Easy Now	1981	—	2.00	4.00
❏ 4002	Laid Back Love/This Is What You Mean to Me	1976	—	2.00	4.00
Albums					
ATLANTIC					
❏ SD 18119	My Way	1974	3.75	7.50	15.00
❏ SD 18160	Jealousy	1976	3.75	7.50	15.00
RCA VICTOR					
❏ APL1-2803	How Do You Take Your Love	1978	3.00	6.00	12.00
WMOT					
❏ 627	Mellow Major	1977	3.00	6.00	12.00
❏ PW 37067	The Best of Major Harris, Now and Then	1981	2.50	5.00	10.00

HARRIS, PEPPERMINT
45s

Number	Title (A Side/B Side)	Yr	VG	VG+	NM
ALADDIN					
❏ 3097	I Got Loaded/It's You, Yes It's You	1951	25.00	50.00	100.00
—Black vinyl					
❏ 3097	I Got Loaded/It's You, Yes It's You	1951	62.50	125.00	250.00
—Green vinyl					
❏ 3107	Have Another Drink and Talk to Me/Middle of Winter	1951	20.00	40.00	80.00
❏ 3108	Let the Back Door Hit You/P.H. Blues	1951	20.00	40.00	80.00
❏ 3130	Right Back On It/Maggie's Boogie	1952	20.00	40.00	80.00
❏ 3141	I Cry for My Baby/There's a Dead Cat on the Line	1952	20.00	40.00	80.00
❏ 3154	I Sure Do Miss My Baby/Hey Little Schoolgirl	1952	20.00	40.00	80.00
❏ 3177	Wasted Love/Goodbye Blues	1953	20.00	40.00	80.00
❏ 3183	Don't Leave Me Alone/Wet Rat	1953	20.00	40.00	80.00
❏ 3206	I Never Get Enough of You/Three Sheets in the Wind	1953	20.00	40.00	80.00
CASH					
❏ 1003	Cadillac Funeral/Treat Me Like I Treat You	1954	37.50	75.00	150.00
COMBO					
❏ 114	Love at First Sight/I Don't Care	1956	15.00	30.00	60.00
DART					
❏ 103	You Get Me Wondering/Messing Around with the Blues	1959	6.25	12.50	25.00
DUKE					
❏ 319	Ain't No Business/Angel Child	1960	6.25	12.50	25.00
JEWEL					
❏ 742	Marking Time/Bad, Mad Woman	1965	2.50	5.00	10.00
❏ 747	Ma Ma/Anything You Can Do	1965	2.50	5.00	10.00
❏ 762	Raining in My Heart/My Time After Awhile	1966	2.50	5.00	10.00
❏ 772	Anytime Is the Right Time/Wait Until It Happens to You	1966	2.50	5.00	10.00
❏ 789	Bad Bad Whiskey/Lonesome As Can Be	1967	2.50	5.00	10.00
❏ 795	24 Hours/Little Girl	1968	2.50	5.00	10.00
MODERN					
❏ 936	Bye Bye, Fare Thee Well/Black Cat Bone	1951	25.00	50.00	100.00
SITTIN' IN WITH					
❏ 543	Raining in My Heart/My Blues Have Rolled Away	1950	37.50	75.00	150.00
—Other Peppermint Harris 45s on this label may exist.					

Number	Title (A Side/B Side)	Yr	VG	VG+	NM
"X"					
❏ 0142	Need Your Lovin'/Just Me and You	1955	25.00	50.00	100.00
Albums					
TIME					
❏ 5 [M]	Peppermint Harris	1962	50.00	100.00	200.00

HARRIS, THURSTON
45s

Number	Title (A Side/B Side)	Yr	VG	VG+	NM
ALADDIN					
❏ 3398	Little Bitty Pretty One/I Hope You Won't Hold It Against Me	1957	10.00	20.00	40.00
❏ 3399	Do What You Did/I'm Asking Forgiveness	1957	7.50	15.00	30.00
❏ 3415	Be Baby Leba/I'm Out to Getcha	1958	7.50	15.00	30.00
❏ 3428	Only One Love Is Blessed/Smokey Joe's	1958	7.50	15.00	30.00
❏ 3430	Over and Over/You're Gonna Miss Me	1958	5.00	10.00	20.00
❏ 3435	Over Someone Else's Shoulder/Tears from My Heart	1958	5.00	10.00	20.00
❏ 3440	Purple Stew/I Heard a Rhapsody	1958	5.00	10.00	20.00
❏ 3447	From the Bottom of My Heart/You Don't Know How Much I Love You	1959	5.00	10.00	20.00
❏ 3448	Don't You Know/From the Bottom of My Heart	1959	5.00	10.00	20.00
❏ 3450	Hey Little Girl/My Love Will Last	1959	5.00	10.00	20.00
❏ 3452	Runk Bunk/Bless Your Heart	1959	5.00	10.00	20.00
❏ 3456	Slip Slop/Paradise Hill	1959	5.00	10.00	20.00
❏ 3462	Moonlight Cocktail/Recess in Heaven	1960	5.00	10.00	20.00
❏ 3468	One Scotch, One Bourbon, One Beer/Send Me Some Loving	1960	5.00	10.00	20.00
CUB					
❏ 9108	I'd Like to Start Over Again/Mr. Satan	1962	3.00	6.00	12.00
DOT					
❏ 16415	Quiet As It's Kept/Goddess of Angels	1963	2.50	5.00	10.00
❏ 16427	Poop-A-Loop/She's the One	1963	2.50	5.00	10.00
IMPERIAL					
❏ 5928	Got You on My Mind/Tears from My Heart	1963	2.50	5.00	10.00
❏ 5971	You're Gonna Need Me/I'm Asking Forgiveness	1963	2.50	5.00	10.00
REPRISE					
❏ 0255	Dance On Little Girl/Dancing Silhouettes	1964	2.50	5.00	10.00
UNITED ARTISTS					
❏ 0152	Little Bitty Pretty One/Over and Over	1973	—	2.00	4.00
—"Silver Spotlight Series" reissue					

HARRIS, WYNONIE
45s

Number	Title (A Side/B Side)	Yr	VG	VG+	NM
ATCO					
❏ 6081	Destination Love/Tell a Whale of a Tale	1956	7.50	15.00	30.00
KING					
❏ 4210	Good Rockin' Tonight/Good Morning Mister Blues	1952	37.50	75.00	150.00
—78 originally released in 1948; the only known Wynonie Harris 45 on King before 4461					
❏ 4461	Bloodshot Eyes/Confessin' the Blues	1951	30.00	60.00	120.00
❏ 4468	I'll Never Give Up/Man Have I Got Troubles	1951	30.00	60.00	120.00
❏ 4485	Lovin' Machine/Luscious Woman	1951	30.00	60.00	120.00
—Black vinyl					
❏ 4485	Lovin' Machine/Luscious Woman	1951	100.00	200.00	400.00
—Blue vinyl					
❏ 4507	My Playful Baby's Gone/Here Comes the Night	1952	25.00	50.00	100.00
❏ 4526	Keep On Churnin'/Married Women Stay Married	1952	25.00	50.00	100.00
❏ 4555	Do it Again Please/Night Train	1952	25.00	50.00	100.00
❏ 4565	Drinking Blues/Adam Come and Get Your Rib	1952	25.00	50.00	100.00
❏ 4592	Greyhound/Rot Gut	1953	25.00	50.00	100.00
❏ 4593	Bad News Baby (There'll Be Rockin' Tonight)/Bring It Back	1953	25.00	50.00	100.00
❏ 4620	Mama Your Daughter Done Lied on Me/Wasn't That Good	1953	25.00	50.00	100.00
❏ 4635	Song of the Bayou/The Deacon Doesn't Like It	1953	25.00	50.00	100.00
❏ 4662	Tremblin'/Rot Gut	1953	20.00	40.00	80.00
❏ 4668	Please Louise/Nearer My Love to Thee	1953	20.00	40.00	80.00
❏ 4685	Down Boy Down/Quiet Whiskey	1954	20.00	40.00	80.00
❏ 4716	Shake That Thing/Keep A-Talking	1954	20.00	40.00	80.00
❏ 4724	I Get a Thrill/Don't Take My Whiskey Away from Me	1954	20.00	40.00	80.00
❏ 4763	All She Wants to Do Is Mambo/Christina	1955	15.00	30.00	60.00
❏ 4774	Good Mambo Tonight/Git to Gittin' Baby	1955	15.00	30.00	60.00
❏ 4789	Fishtail Blues/Mr. Dollar	1955	15.00	30.00	60.00
❏ 4814	Drinkin' Sherry Wine/Get With the Guts	1955	12.50	25.00	50.00
❏ 4826	Wine, Wine, Sweet Wine/Man's Best Friend	1955	12.50	25.00	50.00
❏ 4839	Shot Gun Wedding/I Don't Know Where to Go	1955	12.50	25.00	50.00
❏ 4852	Good Morning Judge/Bloodshot Eyes	1955	12.50	25.00	50.00
❏ 5050	Big Ole Country Fool/That's Me Right Now	1957	7.50	15.00	30.00
❏ 5073	There's No Substitute for Love/A Tale of Woe	1957	7.50	15.00	30.00
❏ 5416	Good Rockin' Tonight/Bloodshot Eyes	1960	3.75	7.50	15.00
❏ 6011	Big Old Country Fool/Bloodshot Eyes	1965	2.50	5.00	10.00
❏ 6304	Good Rockin' Tonight/Good Morning Judge	1970	—	3.00	6.00
ROULETTE					
❏ 4291	Bloodshot Eyes/Sweet Lucy Brown	1960	3.00	6.00	12.00
78s					
ALADDIN					
❏ 171	Mr. Blues Jumped the Rabbit/Whiskey and Jelly Roll Blues	194?	7.50	15.00	30.00
❏ 172	Rugged Road/Come Back Baby	194?	7.50	15.00	30.00
APOLLO					
❏ 360	Young Man's Blues/Straighten Him Out	1945	7.50	15.00	30.00
❏ 361	That's the Stuff You Gotta Watch/Baby Love	1945	7.50	15.00	30.00

Number	Title (A Side/B Side)	Yr	VG	VG+	NM
❑ 362	Wynonie's Blues/Somebody Changed the Lock on My Door	1945	7.50	15.00	30.00
❑ 363	Here Come the Blues/She's Gone with the Wind	1945	7.50	15.00	30.00
❑ 372	Playful Baby/Poppa Treetop	1946	7.50	15.00	30.00
❑ 378	Everybody's Boogie/Time to Change Your Town	1946	7.50	15.00	30.00
❑ 381	Young and Wild/(B-side unknown)	1947	7.50	15.00	30.00
❑ 387	Rebecca's Blues/I Gotta Lyin' Woman	1947	7.50	15.00	30.00
BULLET					
❑ 251	Dig This Boogie/Lightning Struck the Poor House	194?	15.00	30.00	60.00
❑ 252	Drinkin' by Myself/My Baby's Barrel House	194?	15.00	30.00	60.00
HAMP-TONE					
❑ 1001	Good Morning Corrine/(B-side unknown)	194?	10.00	20.00	40.00
KING					
❑ 4202	Wynonie's Boogie/Rose Get Your Clothes	1948	12.50	25.00	50.00
❑ 4210	Good Rockin' Tonight/Good Morning Mister Blues	1948	12.50	25.00	50.00
❑ 4217	Love Is Like Rain/Your Money Don't Mean a Thing	1948	10.00	20.00	40.00
❑ 4226	Lollipop Mama/Blow Your Brains Out	1948	10.00	20.00	40.00
❑ 4252	Bite Again, Bite Again/Blowin' to California	1948	10.00	20.00	40.00
❑ 4276	Grandma Plays the Numbers/I Feel That Old Age Coming On	1949	10.00	20.00	40.00
❑ 4292	Drinkin' Wine Spo-Dee-O-Dee/She Just Won't Sell No More	1949	10.00	20.00	40.00
❑ 4304	All She Wants to Do Is Rock/I Want My Fanny Brown	1949	10.00	20.00	40.00
❑ 4330	Sittin' On It All the Time/Baby Shame on You	1949	10.00	20.00	40.00
❑ 4342	I Like My Baby's Pudding/I Can't Take It No More	1950	10.00	20.00	40.00
❑ 4378	Good Morning Judge/Stormy Night Blues	1950	10.00	20.00	40.00
❑ 4389	Be Mine My Love/Rock Mr. Blues	1950	10.00	20.00	40.00
❑ 4402	I Want to Love You Baby/Mr. Blues Is Coming to Town	1950	10.00	20.00	40.00
❑ 4415	Put It Back/Triplin' Woman	1950	10.00	20.00	40.00
❑ 4418	Oh Babe!/Silent George	1950	10.00	20.00	40.00
—With Lucky Millinder and His Orchestra					
❑ 4419	Teardrops from My Eyes/Please Open Your Heart	1950	10.00	20.00	40.00
—With Lucky Millinder and His Orchestra					
❑ 4445	I Believe I'll Fall in Love/A Love Untrue	1951	10.00	20.00	40.00
❑ 4448	Just Like Two Drops of Water/Tremblin'	1951	10.00	20.00	40.00
❑ 4461	Bloodshot Eyes/Confessin' the Blues	1951	12.50	25.00	50.00
❑ 4468	I'll Never Give Up/Man Have I Got Troubles	1951	7.50	15.00	30.00
❑ 4485	Lovin' Machine/Luscious Woman	1951	7.50	15.00	30.00
❑ 4507	My Playful Baby's Gone/Here Comes the Night	1952	7.50	15.00	30.00
❑ 4526	Keep On Churnin'/Married Women Stay Married	1952	7.50	15.00	30.00
❑ 4555	Do it Again Please/Night Train	1952	7.50	15.00	30.00
❑ 4565	Drinking Blues/Adam Come and Get Your Rib	1952	7.50	15.00	30.00
❑ 4592	Greyhound/Rot Gut	1953	7.50	15.00	30.00
❑ 4593	Bad News Baby (There'll Be Rockin' Tonight)/Bring It Back	1953	7.50	15.00	30.00
❑ 4620	Mama Your Daughter Done Lied on Me/Wasn't That Good	1953	7.50	15.00	30.00
❑ 4635	Song of the Bayou/The Deacon Doesn't Like It	1953	7.50	15.00	30.00
❑ 4662	Tremblin'/Rot Gut	1953	7.50	15.00	30.00
❑ 4668	Please Louise/Nearer My Love to Thee	1953	7.50	15.00	30.00
❑ 4685	Down Boy Down/Quiet Whiskey	1953	7.50	15.00	30.00
❑ 4716	Shake That Thing/Keep A-Talking	1954	7.50	15.00	30.00
❑ 4724	I Get a Thrill/Don't Take My Whiskey Away from Me	1954	7.50	15.00	30.00
❑ 4763	All She Wants to Do Is Mambo/Christina	1955	7.50	15.00	30.00
❑ 4774	Good Mambo Tonight/Git to Gittin' Baby	1955	7.50	15.00	30.00
❑ 4789	Fishtail Blues/Mr. Dollar	1955	7.50	15.00	30.00
❑ 4814	Drinkin' Sherry Wine/Get With the Guts	1955	7.50	15.00	30.00
❑ 4826	Wine, Wine, Sweet Wine/Man's Best Friend	1955	7.50	15.00	30.00
❑ 4839	Shot Gun Wedding/I Don't Know Where to Go	1955	7.50	15.00	30.00
❑ 4852	Good Morning Judge/Bloodshot Eyes	1955	7.50	15.00	30.00
❑ 5050	Big Ole Country Fool/That's Me Right Now	1957	7.50	15.00	30.00
❑ 5073	There's No Substitute for Love/A Tale of Woe	1957	7.50	15.00	30.00
PHILO					
❑ 103	Around the Clock Part 1/Part 2	1945	7.50	15.00	30.00
❑ 104	Cock-a-Doodle-Doo/Yonder Goes My Baby	1945	7.50	15.00	30.00
7-Inch Extended Plays					
KING					
❑ EP-260	*Good Rockin' Tonight/Bloodshot Eyes/All She Wants to Do Is Rock/Good Morning Judge	1954	125.00	250.00	500.00
❑ EP-260 [PS]	Wynonie Harris	1954	125.00	250.00	500.00
Albums					
KING					
❑ KS-1086	Good Rockin' Blues	1970	6.25	12.50	25.00

HARRISON, WILBERT

Number	Title (A Side/B Side)	Yr	VG	VG+	NM
45s					
BELL					
❑ 869	C.C. Rider/Since I Fell for You	1970	—	3.00	6.00
BRUNSWICK					
❑ 55511	Lovin' Operator/Love You	1974	—	3.00	6.00
❑ 55519	I'm Going to the River/I Need Some (Honey Honey)	1975	—	3.00	6.00
CHART					
❑ 626	Cool Water/Calypso Man	1956	6.25	12.50	25.00
CONSTELLATION					
❑ 122	New York World's Fair/Mama, Mama, Mama	1964	2.50	5.00	10.00
DELUXE					
❑ 6002	This Woman of Mine/The Letter	1953	15.00	30.00	60.00
❑ 6031	Nobody Knows My Trouble/Gin and Coconut Milk	1954	15.00	30.00	60.00
FURY					
❑ 1023	Kansas City/Listen, My Darling	1959	7.50	15.00	30.00
❑ 1027	Cheating Baby/Don't Wreck My Life	1959	3.75	7.50	15.00
❑ 1028	Goodbye Kansas City/1960	1960	3.75	7.50	15.00
❑ 1031	C.C. Rider/Why Did You Leave	1960	3.75	7.50	15.00
❑ 1037	Since I Fell for You/Little School Girl	1960	3.75	7.50	15.00
❑ 1041	The Horse/Da-De-Ya-Da (I'd Do Anything for You)	1961	3.75	7.50	15.00
❑ 1047	Happy in Love/Calypso Dance	1961	3.75	7.50	15.00
❑ 1055	Drafted/My Heart Is Yours	1961	3.75	7.50	15.00
❑ 1059	Let's Stick Together/Kansas City Twist	1962	3.75	7.50	15.00
❑ 1063	Let's Stick Together/My Heart Is Yours	1962	3.00	6.00	12.00
GLADES					
❑ 603	Gonna Tell You a Story/Letter Edged in Black	1959	3.00	6.00	12.00
PORT					
❑ 3003	Baby Move On/You're Still My Baby	1965	2.00	4.00	8.00
❑ 3009	Don't Take It So Hard/Sugar Lump	1965	2.00	4.00	8.00
ROCKIN'					
❑ 526	This Woman of Mine/The Letter	1952	25.00	50.00	100.00
ROULETTE					
❑ 4752	No One's Love But Yours/Mini-Parade	1967	2.00	4.00	8.00
SAVOY					
❑ 1138	Don't Drop It/The Ways of a Woman	1954	10.00	20.00	40.00
❑ 1149	Women and Whiskey/Da-De-Ya-Da (I'd Do Anything for You)	1955	7.50	15.00	30.00
❑ 1164	Florida Special/Darling, Listen to This Song	1955	7.50	15.00	30.00
❑ 1198	Confessin' My Dream/The Way I Feel	1956	7.50	15.00	30.00
❑ 1517	My Love Is True/I Know My Baby Loves Me	1957	6.25	12.50	25.00
❑ 1531	Baby Don't You Know/My Love for You Lingers On	1958	5.00	10.00	20.00
❑ 1571	Don't Drop It/Baby Don't You Know	1959	3.75	7.50	15.00
SEA HORN					
❑ 502	Say It Again/Near to You	1963	2.00	4.00	8.00
SSS INTERNATIONAL					
❑ 830	My Heart Is Yours/Pretty Little Woman	1971	—	3.00	6.00
❑ 830 [DJ]	My Heart Is Yours (mono/stereo)	1971	2.50	5.00	10.00
—Promo only on blue vinyl					
SUE					
❑ 11	Let's Work Together (Part 1)/Let's Work Together (Part 2)	1969	—	3.00	6.00
WET SOUL					
❑ 4	My Heart Is Yours/Pretty Little Woman	1970	2.00	4.00	8.00
Albums					
BUDDAH					
❑ BDS-5002	Wilbert Harrison	1971	7.50	15.00	30.00
CHELSEA					
❑ CH 523	Wilbert Harrison	1977	5.00	10.00	20.00
JUGGERNAUT					
❑ ST-8803	Shoot You Full of Love	1971	12.50	25.00	50.00
SAVOY JAZZ					
❑ SJL-1182	Listen to My Song	1987	3.00	6.00	12.00
SPHERE SOUND					
❑ SSR-7000 [M]	Kansas City	1965	62.50	125.00	250.00
❑ SSSR-7000 [R]	Kansas City	1965	50.00	100.00	200.00
SUE					
❑ SSLP-8801	Let's Work Together	1970	12.50	25.00	50.00
WET SOUL					
❑ 1001	Anything You Want	197?	12.50	25.00	50.00

HARVEY

Also see ETTA AND HARVEY; THE MOONGLOWS.

Number	Title (A Side/B Side)	Yr	VG	VG+	NM
45s					
CHESS					
❑ 1713	I Want Somebody/Da Da Goo Goo	1959	10.00	20.00	40.00
❑ 1725	Twelve Months of the Year/Don't Be Afraid of Love	1959	10.00	20.00	40.00
❑ 1749	Blue Skies/Ooh, Ouch, Stop!	1960	6.25	12.50	25.00
❑ 1760	If I Can't Have You/My Heart Cries	1960	6.25	12.50	25.00
—As "Etta and Harvey" (Etta is Etta James)					
❑ 1771	Spoonful/It's a Crying Shame	1960	6.25	12.50	25.00
—As "Etta and Harvey" (Etta is Etta James)					
❑ 1781	The First Time/Mama	1961	6.25	12.50	25.00
—As "Harvey Fuqua"					
HARVEY					
❑ 121	What Can You Do Now/Will I Do	1962	10.00	20.00	40.00
—As "Harvey and Ann"					
TRI-PHI					
❑ 1017	She Loves Me So/Any Way You Wanta	1962	10.00	20.00	40.00
❑ 1024	Memories of You/Come On and Answer Me	1963	15.00	30.00	60.00

HATFIELD, BOBBY

Also see THE RIGHTEOUS BROTHERS.

Number	Title (A Side/B Side)	Yr	VG	VG+	NM
45s					
MOONGLOW					
❑ 220	I Need a Girl/Hot Tamale	1963	6.25	12.50	25.00
VERVE					
❑ 10598	Hang-Ups/Soul Cafe	1968	2.00	4.00	8.00
❑ 10621	Brothers/What's the Matter Baby	1968	2.00	4.00	8.00
❑ 10634	Only You/The Wonder of You	1969	2.00	4.00	8.00
❑ 10639	My Prayer/I Wish I Didn't Love You So	1969	2.00	4.00	8.00
❑ 10641	Answer Me My Love/I Only Have Eyes for You	1969	2.00	4.00	8.00
WARNER BROS.					
❑ 7566	Rock 'N Roll Woman/Oo Wee Baby, I Love You	1972	—	2.50	5.00

Number	Title (A Side/B Side)	Yr	VG	VG+	NM
❑ 7649	Stay with Me/Rock 'N Roll Woman	1972	—	2.50	5.00
Albums					
MGM					
❑ SE-4727	Messin' in Muscle Shoals	1971	3.00	6.00	12.00

HATHAWAY, DONNY
Also see ROBERTA FLACK.
45s
ATCO

Number	Title (A Side/B Side)	Yr	VG	VG+	NM
❑ 6719	The Ghetto (Part 1)/The Ghetto (Part 2)	1969	—	3.00	6.00
❑ 6759	Thank You Master/Je Vous Aime	1970	—	2.50	5.00
❑ 6768	Tryin' Times/Voices Inside	1970	—	2.50	5.00
❑ 6799	This Christmas/Be There	1970	2.00	4.00	8.00
❑ 6817	Take a Love Song/Magnificent Sanctuary Band	1971	—	2.50	5.00
❑ 6828	A Song for You/Put Your Hand in the Hand	1971	—	2.50	5.00
❑ 6880	Little Ghetto Boy/We're Still Friends	1972	—	2.50	5.00
❑ 6884	Giving Up/Jealous Love	1972	—	2.50	5.00
❑ 6899	Bossa Nova/Come Back Charleston Blue	1972	—	2.50	5.00
—With Margie Joseph					
❑ 6903	I Love You More Than You'll Ever Know/Lord Help Me	1972	—	2.50	5.00
❑ 6928	Love, Love, Love/Someday We'll All Be Free	1973	—	2.50	5.00
❑ 6951	Come Little Children/The Slums	1973	—	2.50	5.00
❑ 7066	This Christmas/Be There	1975	—	2.50	5.00
❑ 7092	You Were Meant for Me/Valdez in the Country	1978	—	2.00	4.00
❑ 7320	This Christmas/Be There	1980	—	2.00	4.00
❑ 99956	This Christmas/Be There	1982	—	2.00	4.00
CURTOM					
❑ 1935	I Thank You Baby/What's This I See	1969	2.00	4.00	8.00
—By "June and Donnie"					
❑ 1971	I Thank You/Just Another Reason	1972	—	2.50	5.00
—By "June Conquest and Donnie Hathaway"; same A-side as 1935 but with revised title					
7-Inch Extended Plays					
ATCO					
❑ SD 7-7029	I Know It's You/Flying Easy//The Slums/Valdez in the Country	1973	2.00	4.00	8.00
—Jukebox issue; small hole, plays at 33 1/3 rpm					
❑ SD 7-7029 [PS]	Extension of a Man	1973	2.00	4.00	8.00
Albums					
ATCO					
❑ SD 38-107	The Best of Donny Hathaway	1978	2.50	5.00	10.00
❑ SD 33-332	Everything Is Everything	1970	3.00	6.00	12.00
❑ SD 33-360	Donny Hathaway	1971	3.00	6.00	12.00
❑ SD 33-386	Donny Hathaway Live	1972	3.00	6.00	12.00
❑ QD 7029 [Q]	Extension of a Man	1974	4.50	9.00	18.00
❑ SD 7029	Extension of a Man	1973	2.50	5.00	10.00
ATLANTIC					
❑ SD 19278	In Performance	1980	2.50	5.00	10.00

HAWKINS, DALE
45s
ABC-PARAMOUNT

Number	Title (A Side/B Side)	Yr	VG	VG+	NM
❑ 10668	I'll Fly High/La La Song	1965	2.50	5.00	10.00
ABNAK					
❑ 110	The Flag/And I Believed You	1965	3.00	6.00	12.00
ATLANTIC					
❑ 2126	Stay at Home, Lulu/I Can't Erase You	1961	5.00	10.00	20.00
❑ 2150	What a Feeling/Women, That's What's Happening	1962	5.00	10.00	20.00
BELL					
❑ 807	Back Street/Little Rain Cloud	1969	2.00	4.00	8.00
❑ 827	Heavy on My Mind/Joe	1969	2.00	4.00	8.00
CHECKER					
❑ 843	See You Soon, Baboon/Four Letter Word	1956	7.50	15.00	30.00
❑ 863	Susie-Q/Don't Treat Me This Way	1957	12.50	25.00	50.00
❑ 876	Baby, Baby/Mrs. Merguitory's Daughter	1957	7.50	15.00	30.00
❑ 892	Little Pig/Tornado	1958	6.25	12.50	25.00
❑ 900	La-Do-Dada/Cross Ties	1958	6.25	12.50	25.00
❑ 906	My Babe/A House, a Car, and a Wedding Ring	1958	6.25	12.50	25.00
❑ 913	Someday, One Day/Take My Heart	1959	6.25	12.50	25.00
❑ 916	Class Cutter (Yeah Yeah)/Lonely Nights	1959	6.25	12.50	25.00
❑ 923	Ain't That Lovin' You Baby/My Dream	1959	6.25	12.50	25.00
❑ 929	Our Turn/Lifeguard Man	1959	6.25	12.50	25.00
❑ 934	Liza Jane/Back to School Blues	1959	6.25	12.50	25.00
❑ 940	Hot Dog/Don't Break Your Promise to Me	1960	5.00	10.00	20.00
❑ 944	Poor Little Rhode Island/Every Little Girl	1960	5.00	10.00	20.00
❑ 944 [PS]	Poor Little Rhode Island/Every Little Girl	1960	75.00	150.00	300.00
❑ 962	Linda/Who	1960	5.00	10.00	20.00
❑ 970	Grandma's House/I Want to Love You	1961	5.00	10.00	20.00
LINCOLN					
❑ 002	Johnny B. Goode/Baby We Had It	196?	2.00	4.00	8.00
PAULA					
❑ 424	First Cut is the Deepest/Nothing Left to Do But Say Goodbye	1977	—	2.50	5.00
TILT					
❑ 781	Money Honey/The Same Old Way	1962	5.00	10.00	20.00
❑ 783	Forbidden Love/Wish I Hadn't Called Home	1962	5.00	10.00	20.00
❑ 785	Hawk Blows, Band Plays (Part 1)/Hawk Blows, Band Plays (Part 2)	1962	5.00	10.00	20.00
ZONK					
❑ 1002	Gotta Dance/Peaches	1973	—	2.50	5.00
Albums					
BELL					
❑ 6036	L.A., Memphis and Tyler, Texas	1969	10.00	20.00	40.00

Number	Title (A Side/B Side)	Yr	VG	VG+	NM
CHESS					
❑ ACRR-706	Dale Hawkins	1976	3.75	7.50	15.00
❑ LP-1429 [M]	Oh! Susie-Q	1958	500.00	1000.	1500.
ROULETTE					
❑ R 25175 [M]	Let's All Twist at the Miami Beach Peppermint Lounge	1962	50.00	100.00	200.00
❑ SR 25175 [S]	Let's All Twist at the Miami Beach Peppermint Lounge	1962	75.00	150.00	300.00

HAWKINS, EDWIN
45s
BUDDAH

Number	Title (A Side/B Side)	Yr	VG	VG+	NM
❑ 145	Blowin' in the Wind/Pray for Peace	1970	—	2.50	5.00
❑ 155	I Believe/He's a Friend of Mine	1970	—	2.50	5.00
❑ 200	Try the Real Thing/Praise Him	1971	—	2.50	5.00
❑ 251	Children Get Together/There's a Place for Me	1971	—	2.50	5.00
❑ 271	Give Me a Star/Jesus	1971	—	2.50	5.00
❑ 324	Jesu, Joy of Man's Desiring/(B-side unknown)	1972	—	2.50	5.00
❑ 360	Jubilation/Do My Thing	1973	—	2.50	5.00
PAVILION					
❑ 20001	Oh Happy Day/Jesus, Lover of My Soul	1969	—	3.00	6.00
❑ 20002	Ain't It Like Him/Lord Don't Move That Mountain	1969	—	3.00	6.00
Albums					
ACCORD					
❑ SN-7120	The Genius of Edwin Hawkins	1981	2.50	5.00	10.00
BIRTHRIGHT					
❑ 4020	The Comforter	197?	3.00	6.00	12.00
❑ LS 5904	The Edwin Hawkins Christmas Album	1985	3.75	7.50	15.00
❑ WR-8119	Edwin Hawkins Live	198?	2.50	5.00	10.00
❑ ST-70200	The Edwin Hawkins Christmas Album	1987	2.00	4.00	8.00
—Reissue					
❑ ST-70201	Have Mercy	1987	2.00	4.00	8.00
❑ ST-70202	Angels Will Be Singing	1987	2.00	4.00	8.00
❑ D1-70208	Live with the Oakland Symphony, Vol. 1	1988	2.00	4.00	8.00
—Reissue of Myrrh 6691					
❑ D1-70210	Live with the Oakland Symphony, Vol. 2	1988	2.00	4.00	8.00
—Reissue of Myrrh 6700					
❑ ST-70300	Give Us Peace	1987	2.00	4.00	8.00
❑ D1-70315	The Name	1988	2.50	5.00	10.00
BUDDAH					
❑ BDS-5054	Peace Is Blowin' in the Wind	1969	3.75	7.50	15.00
❑ BDS-5064	More Happy Days	1970	3.75	7.50	15.00
❑ BDS-5070	Oh Happy Day	1970	3.00	6.00	12.00
—Reissue of Pavilion LP					
❑ BDS-5086	Children (Get Together)	1971	3.75	7.50	15.00
❑ BDS-5101	I'd Like to Teach the World to Sing	1972	3.75	7.50	15.00
LECTION					
❑ 501	Imagine Heaven	1982	2.50	5.00	10.00
❑ 810639-1	The Edwin Hawkins Mass Choir	198?	2.50	5.00	10.00
MYRRH					
❑ 6691	Live with the Oakland Symphony, Vol. 1	198?	2.50	5.00	10.00
❑ 6700	Live with the Oakland Symphony, Vol. 2	198?	2.50	5.00	10.00
PAVILION					
❑ BPS-10001	Let Us Go Into the House of the Lord	1969	3.75	7.50	15.00
SAVOY					
❑ 7077 [(2)]	The Best of the Edwin Hawkins Singers	198?	3.00	6.00	12.00

HAWKINS, SCREAMIN' JAY
45s
APOLLO

Number	Title (A Side/B Side)	Yr	VG	VG+	NM
❑ 506	Please Try to Understand/Not Anymore	1957	6.25	12.50	25.00
❑ 528	Baptize Me in Wine/Not Anymore	1958	6.25	12.50	25.00
CHANCELLOR					
❑ 1117	Ashes/Nitty Gritty	1962	3.75	7.50	15.00
DECCA					
❑ 32019	All Night/I'm Not Made of Clay	1966	3.75	7.50	15.00
❑ 32100	I Put a Spell on You/You're an Exception to the Rule	1967	10.00	20.00	40.00
ENRICA					
❑ 1010	I Hear Voices/I Just Don't Care	1962	6.25	12.50	25.00
GRAND					
❑ 135	Take Me Back/I Is	1957	6.25	12.50	25.00
MERCURY					
❑ 70549	This Is All/She Put the Whammee on Me	1955	20.00	40.00	80.00
OKEH					
❑ 7072	I Put a Spell on You/Little Demon	1956	12.50	25.00	50.00
❑ 7084	You Made Me Love You/Darling, Please Forgive Me	1957	7.50	15.00	30.00
❑ 7087	Person to Person/Frenzy	1957	7.50	15.00	30.00
❑ 7101	Alligator Wine/There's Something Wrong with You	1958	7.50	15.00	30.00
PHILIPS					
❑ 40606	Stone Crazy/I'm Lonely	1969	—	3.00	6.00
❑ 40636	Too Many Teardrops/Makaka Ways	1969	—	3.00	6.00
❑ 40645	Constipation Blues/Do You Really Love Me	1969	—	3.00	6.00
❑ 40668	Moanin'/Do You Really Love Me	1970	—	3.00	6.00
❑ 40674	Our Love Is Not for Three/Take Me Back	1970	—	3.00	6.00
PROVIDENCE					
❑ 411	My Kind of Love/Po' Folks	1965	3.00	6.00	12.00
QUEEN BEE					
❑ 1314	Monkberry Moon Delight/Sweet Ginny	1973	—	3.00	6.00
RCA VICTOR					
❑ PB-10127	You Put the Spell on Me/Voodoo	1974	—	2.50	5.00

Number	Title (A Side/B Side)	Yr	VG	VG+	NM
ROULETTE					
❑ 4579	The Whammy/Strange	1964	3.00	6.00	12.00
TIMELY					
❑ 1004	Baptize Me in Wine/Not Anymore	1954	20.00	40.00	80.00
❑ 1005	I Found My Way to Wine/Please Try to Understand	1954	20.00	40.00	80.00
WING					
❑ 90005	Well, I Tried/You're All of Life to Me	1955	10.00	20.00	40.00
❑ 90055	Even Though/Talk About Me	1956	7.50	15.00	30.00
Albums					
EPIC					
❑ LN 3448 [M]	At Home with Screamin' Jay Hawkins	1958	300.00	600.00	1200.
❑ LN 3457 [M]	I Put a Spell on You	1958	125.00	250.00	500.00
❑ BN 26457 [R]	I Put a Spell on You	1969	15.00	30.00	60.00
PHILIPS					
❑ PHS 600319	What That Is	1969	10.00	20.00	40.00
❑ PHS 600336	Screamin' Jay Hawkins	1970	10.00	20.00	40.00
SOUNDS OF HAWAII					
❑ 5015	A Night at Forbidden City	196?	12.50	25.00	50.00

HAWKS, THE (1)
45s

Number	Title (A Side/B Side)	Yr	VG	VG+	NM
IMPERIAL					
❑ 5266	Joe the Grinder/Candy Girl	1954	62.50	125.00	250.00
❑ 5281	She's All Right/Good News	1954	50.00	100.00	200.00
❑ 5292	It Ain't That Way/I-Yi	1954	25.00	50.00	100.00
❑ 5306	Nobody But You/Give It Up	1954	25.00	50.00	100.00
❑ 5317	All Women Are the Same/That's What You Are	1954	25.00	50.00	100.00
❑ 5332	It's Too Late Now/I Can't See for Lookin'	1955	25.00	50.00	100.00
MODERN					
❑ 990	It's All Over/Ever Since You Been Gone	1956	62.50	125.00	250.00
POST					
❑ 2004	These Blues/Why Oh Why	1955	75.00	150.00	300.00

HAYES, ISAAC
45s

Number	Title (A Side/B Side)	Yr	VG	VG+	NM
ABC/HBS					
❑ 12118	Chocolate Chip/(Instrumental)	1975	—	2.00	4.00
❑ 12138	Come Live with Me/Body Language	1975	—	2.00	4.00
❑ 12171	Disco Connection/St. Thomas Square	1976	—	2.00	4.00
—By the "Isaac Hayes Movement"					
❑ 12176	Rock Me Easy Baby (Pt. 1)/Rock Me Easy Baby (Pt. 2)	1976	—	2.00	4.00
❑ 12206	Juicy Fruit (Disco Freak) (Pt. 1)/Juicy Fruit (Disco Freak) (Pt. 2)	1976	—	2.00	4.00
BRUNSWICK					
❑ 55258	Sweet Temptation/Laura	1964	2.50	5.00	10.00
CAPITOL					
❑ S7-18869	Walk On By/Tired of Being Alone	1995	—	—	3.00
—B-side by Al Green					
COLUMBIA					
❑ 06363	Ike's Rap/Hey Girl (Edited)	1986	—	—	3.00
❑ 06363 [PS]	Ike's Rap/Hey Girl (Edited)	1986	—	2.00	4.00
❑ 06655	Thing for You/Thank God for Love	1987	—	—	3.00
❑ 07104	If You Want My Lovin' (Do Me Right)/(Instrumental)	1987	—	—	3.00
❑ 07978	Showdown/(Instrumental)	1988	—	—	3.00
❑ 08116	Let Me Be Your Everything/Curious	1988	—	—	3.00
ENTERPRISE					
❑ 002	Precious Precious/Going to Chicago Blues	1969	2.00	4.00	8.00
❑ 9003	By the Time I Get to Phoenix/Walk On By	1969	—	3.00	6.00
❑ 9006	The Mistletoe and Me/Winter Snow	1969	—	3.00	6.00
❑ 9017	I Stand Accused/I Just Don't Know What to Do with Myself	1970	—	2.50	5.00
❑ 9028	The Look of Love/Ike's Mood	1970	—	2.50	5.00
❑ 9031	Never Can Say Goodbye/I Can't Help It If I'm Still in Love with You	1971	—	2.50	5.00
❑ 9038	Theme from Shaft/Cafe Regio's	1971	—	2.50	5.00
❑ 9042	Do Your Thing/Ellie's Love Theme	1972	—	2.50	5.00
❑ 9045	Let's Stay Together/Soulville	1972	—	2.50	5.00
❑ 9049	Ain't That Loving You (For More Reasons Than One)/Baby I'm-a Want You	1972	—	2.50	5.00
—With David Porter					
❑ 9058	Theme from The Men/Type Thang	1972	—	2.50	5.00
❑ 9065	(If Loving You Is Wrong) I Don't Want to Be Right/Rolling Down a Mountainside	1973	—	2.50	5.00
❑ 9085	Joy (Part 1)/Joy (Part 2)	1973	—	2.50	5.00
❑ 9095	Wonderful/Someone Made You for Me	1974	—	2.50	5.00
❑ 9104	Title Theme/Hung Up on My Baby	1974	—	2.50	5.00
POLYDOR					
❑ 2011	Don't Let Go/You Can't Hold Your Woman	1979	—	2.00	4.00
❑ 2068	A Few More Kisses to Go/What Does It Take	1980	—	2.00	4.00
❑ 2090	I Ain't Never/Love Has Been Good to Us	1980	—	2.00	4.00
❑ 2102	It's All in the Game/Wherever You Are	1980	—	2.00	4.00
❑ 2182	I'm So Proud/I'm Gonna Make You Love Me	1981	—	2.00	4.00
❑ 2192	Fugitive/Lifetime Thing	1981	—	2.00	4.00
❑ 14446	Out of the Ghetto/It's Heaven to Me	1977	—	2.00	4.00
❑ 14464	Moonlight Lovin' (Menage a Trois)/It's Heaven to Me	1978	—	2.00	4.00
❑ 14521	Zeke the Freak/If We Ever Needed Peace	1978	—	2.00	4.00
❑ 14534	Just the Way You Are (Part 1)/Just the Way You Are (Part 2)	1979	—	2.00	4.00

Number	Title (A Side/B Side)	Yr	VG	VG+	NM
STAX					
❑ 3209	Feel Like Makin' Love (Part 1)/Feel Like Makin' Love (Part 2)	1978	—	2.50	5.00
VIRGIN					
❑ S7-18950	Fragile/Thanks to the Fool	1995	—	2.00	4.00
❑ 38759	Only If You Were Here/Oh Come All Ye Faithful	2000	—	2.00	4.00
—B-side by Ideal					
Albums					
ABC/HBS					
❑ D-874	Chocolate Chip	1975	3.75	7.50	15.00
❑ D-923	Disco Connection	1975	3.00	6.00	12.00
❑ D-925	Groove-a-Thon	1976	3.00	6.00	12.00
❑ D-953	Juicy Fruit (Disco Freak)	1976	3.00	6.00	12.00
ATLANTIC					
❑ SD 1599	In the Beginning	1972	3.75	7.50	15.00
—Reissue of Enterprise 100					
COLUMBIA					
❑ FC 40316	U-Turn	1986	2.50	5.00	10.00
❑ FC 40941	Love Attack	1988	2.50	5.00	10.00
ENTERPRISE					
❑ E-100 [M]	Presenting Isaac Hayes	1968	10.00	20.00	40.00
❑ ES-100 [S]	Presenting Isaac Hayes	1968	7.50	15.00	30.00
❑ ENS-1001	Hot Buttered Soul	1969	5.00	10.00	20.00
❑ ENS-1010	The Isaac Hayes Movement	1970	5.00	10.00	20.00
❑ ENS-1014	To Be Continued	1970	5.00	10.00	20.00
❑ ENS-5002 [(2)]	Shaft	1971	5.00	10.00	20.00
❑ ENS-5003 [(2)]	Black Moses	1971	5.00	10.00	20.00
❑ ENS-5005 [(2)]	Live at the Sahara Tahoe	1973	3.75	7.50	15.00
❑ ENS-5007	Joy	1973	3.00	6.00	12.00
❑ ENS-7504	Tough Guys	1974	3.00	6.00	12.00
❑ ENS-7507 [(2)]	Truck Turner	1974	3.75	7.50	15.00
❑ ENS-7510	The Best of Isaac Hayes	1975	3.00	6.00	12.00
POINTBLANK					
❑ SPRO-12787 [DJ]	Funky Junky	1995	3.75	7.50	15.00
—Vinyl is promo only					
POLYDOR					
❑ PD-1-6120	New Horizon	1977	2.50	5.00	10.00
❑ PD-1-6164	For the Sake of Love	1978	2.50	5.00	10.00
❑ PD-1-6224	Don't Let Go	1979	2.50	5.00	10.00
❑ PD-1-6269	And Once Again	1980	2.50	5.00	10.00
STAX					
❑ STX-4102	Hotbed	197?	2.50	5.00	10.00
❑ STX-4114	Hot Buttered Soul	1978	2.50	5.00	10.00
—Reissue of Enterprise 1001					
❑ STX-4129	The Isaac Hayes Movement	197?	2.50	5.00	10.00
—Reissue of Enterprise 1010					
❑ STX-4133	To Be Continued	197?	2.50	5.00	10.00
—Reissue of Enterprise 1014					
❑ MPS-8509	Excerpts from Black Moses	1981	2.50	5.00	10.00
❑ MPS-8515	His Greatest Hit Singles	1982	2.50	5.00	10.00
❑ MPS-8530	Joy	1984	2.50	5.00	10.00
—Reissue of Enterprise 5007					
❑ STX-88002 [(2)]	Shaft	1979	3.00	6.00	12.00
—Reissue of Enterprise 5002					
❑ STX-88003 [(2)]	Enterprise: His Greatest Hits	1980	3.00	6.00	12.00
❑ STX-88004 [(2)]	Live at the Sahara Tahoe	198?	3.00	6.00	12.00
—Reissue of Enterprise 5005					

HAYES, ISAAC, AND DIONNE WARWICK
Also see each artist's individual listings.
45s

Number	Title (A Side/B Side)	Yr	VG	VG+	NM
ABC/HBS					
❑ 12253	By the Time I Get to Phoenix—I Say a Little Prayer/That's the Way I Like It—Cry Down	1977	—	2.00	4.00
Albums					
ABC/HBS					
❑ D-996 [(2)]	A Man and a Woman	1977	3.75	7.50	15.00
MCA					
❑ 10012 [(2)]	A Man and a Woman	198?	3.00	6.00	12.00
—Reissue of ABC/HBS 996					

HAYES, LINDA
45s

Number	Title (A Side/B Side)	Yr	VG	VG+	NM
ANTLER					
❑ 4000	I Had a Dream/You Ain't Movin' Me	1956	7.50	15.00	30.00
DECCA					
❑ 29644	Our Love's Forever Blessed/You're the Only One for Me	1955	7.50	15.00	30.00
HOLLYWOOD					
❑ 1003	Take Me Back/Yours for the Asking	1953	12.50	25.00	50.00
❑ 1009	No Next Time/Don't Do Nothin' Baby	1954	10.00	20.00	40.00
❑ 1016	Play It Right/Your Back's Out	1954	10.00	20.00	40.00
❑ 1019	Non-Cooperation/Grrr! Mambo	1954	10.00	20.00	40.00
❑ 1027	Change of Heart/Darling Angel	1954	10.00	20.00	40.00
❑ 1031	Johnny Ace's Last Letter/Why Johnny Why	1955	12.50	25.00	50.00
—With Johnny Moore					
❑ 1032	Our Love's Forever Blessed/You're the Only One for Me	1955	15.00	30.00	60.00
KING					
❑ 4752	My Name Ain't Annie/Let's Babalu	1954	18.75	37.50	75.00
❑ 4773	Please Have Mercy/Oochi Poochi	1955	12.50	25.00	50.00

Number	Title (A Side/B Side)	Yr	VG	VG+	NM

RECORDED IN HOLLYWOOD

Number	Title (A Side/B Side)	Yr	VG	VG+	NM
❏ 244	Yes! I Know (What You're Putting Down)/Sister Ann	1953	12.50	25.00	50.00
❏ 246	Big City (Part 1)/Big City (Part 2)	1953	12.50	25.00	50.00

HAYWOOD, LEON
12-Inch Singles
CASABLANCA

Number	Title (A Side/B Side)	Yr	VG	VG+	NM
❏ 812164-1	I'm Out to Catch (LP version)/(Dub Version)	1983	—	3.00	6.00

MCA

| ❏ 13911 | Disco Fever/Party | 1978 | 3.00 | 6.00 | 12.00 |

45s
20TH CENTURY

Number	Title (A Side/B Side)	Yr	VG	VG+	NM
❏ 2003	One Way Ticket to Loveland/There Ain't Enough Love Around	1972	—	3.00	6.00
❏ 2022	La La Song/Sweet Loving Fair	1973	—	3.00	6.00
❏ 2065	Keep It in the Family/Long As There's You (I Got Love)	1974	—	2.50	5.00
❏ 2103	Sugar Lump/That Sweet Woman of Mine	1974	—	2.50	5.00
❏ 2146	Believe Half of What You See (And None of What You Hear)/The Day I Laid Eyes on You	1974	—	2.50	5.00
❏ 2191	Come an' Get Yourself Some/B.M.F. Beautiful	1975	—	3.00	6.00
❏ 2191	Come an' Get Yourself Some/Who You Been Givin' It Up To	1975	—	2.50	5.00
❏ 2228	I Want'a Do Something Freaky to You/I Know What Love Is	1975	—	2.50	5.00
❏ 2264	Just Your Fool/Consider the Source	1975	—	2.50	5.00
❏ 2285	Strokin' (Part 1)/Strokin' (Part 2)	1976	—	2.50	5.00
❏ 2443	Don't Push It Don't Force It/Who You Been Givin' It Up To	1980	—	2.00	4.00
❏ 2454	If You're Lookin' for a Night of Fun (Look Past Me, I'm Not the One)/That's What Time It Is	1980	—	2.00	4.00
❏ 2469	Daydream/Love Is What We Came Here For	1980	—	2.00	4.00

ATLANTIC

| ❏ 2799 | You and Your Moody Ways/You Know What | 1971 | — | 3.00 | 6.00 |
| ❏ 2858 | Clean Up Your Own Back Yard/String Bean | 1972 | — | 3.00 | 6.00 |

CAPITOL

| ❏ 2584 | Just Your Fool/Consider the Source | 1969 | 3.75 | 7.50 | 15.00 |
| ❏ 2752 | I Wanna Thank You/I Was Sent to Love You | 1970 | 3.75 | 7.50 | 15.00 |

CASABLANCA

| ❏ 812164-7 | I'm Out to Catch/Keep It in the Family | 1983 | — | — | 3.00 |

—With Karen Roberts

| ❏ 814217-7 | T.V. Mama/Steppin' Out | 1983 | — | — | 3.00 |

COLUMBIA

| ❏ 10413 | The Streets Will Love You to Death - Part 1/The Streets Will Love You to Death - Part 2 | 1976 | — | 2.00 | 4.00 |
| ❏ 10477 | Dream Dream/Let Me Make It Good | 1977 | — | 2.00 | 4.00 |

DECCA

❏ 32164	It's Got to Be Mellow/Cornbread & Buttermilk	1967	2.00	4.00	8.00
❏ 32230	Mellow Moonlight/Tennessee Waltz	1967	2.00	4.00	8.00
❏ 32310	Mercy, Mercy, Mercy/It's the Last Time	1968	2.00	4.00	8.00
❏ 32348	I Want to Talk About My Baby/You Don't Have to See Me Cry	1968	2.00	4.00	8.00
❏ 32414	Blues Get Off My Shoulder/Everyday Will Be Like a Holiday	1968	2.00	4.00	8.00

FANTASY

| ❏ 581 | The Truth About Money/Would I | 1964 | 6.25 | 12.50 | 25.00 |

FAT FISH

| ❏ 8005 | Soul Cargo/Spice of the Blues | 1966 | 7.50 | 15.00 | 30.00 |

IMPERIAL

| ❏ 66123 | She's With Her Other Love/Pain in My Heart | 1965 | 3.75 | 7.50 | 15.00 |

—As "Leon Hayward"

| ❏ 66149 | Soul-On/1-2-3 | 1965 | 3.00 | 6.00 | 12.00 |

MCA

❏ 40793	Super Sexy/Life Goes On	1977	—	2.00	4.00
❏ 40849	Double My Pleasure/It's Gonna Be Alright	1978	—	2.00	4.00
❏ 40889	Fine and Healthy Thing/She's Built, She's Stacked	1978	—	2.00	4.00
❏ 40941	Party/Life Goes On	1978	—	2.00	4.00
❏ 40989	Disco Fever/Self Respect	1979	—	2.00	4.00
❏ 41035	Energy/You Bring Out the Freak in Me	1979	—	2.00	4.00

MODERN

| ❏ 99708 | Tenderoni/(Instrumental) | 1984 | — | — | 3.00 |

Albums
20TH CENTURY

❏ T-411	Back to Stay	1973	3.00	6.00	12.00
❏ T-440	Keep It in the Family	1974	3.00	6.00	12.00
❏ T-476	Come and Get Yourself Some	1975	2.50	5.00	10.00
❏ T-613	Naturally	1980	2.50	5.00	10.00

COLUMBIA

| ❏ PC 34363 | Intimate | 1976 | 2.50 | 5.00 | 10.00 |

DECCA

| ❏ DL 74949 | It's Got to Be Mellow | 1969 | 5.00 | 10.00 | 20.00 |

GALAXY

| ❏ 8206 | Mellow, Mellow | 196? | 5.00 | 10.00 | 20.00 |

MCA

| ❏ 2322 | Double My Pleasure | 1978 | 2.50 | 5.00 | 10.00 |
| ❏ 3090 | Energy | 1979 | 2.50 | 5.00 | 10.00 |

HEAD, ROY
45s
ABC

Number	Title (A Side/B Side)	Yr	VG	VG+	NM
❏ 12346	How You See 'Em, Now You Don't/Smooth Whiskey	1978	—	2.00	4.00
❏ 12383	Tonight's the Night/A Lady in My Room	1978	—	2.00	4.00
❏ 12418	Dixie/Love Survived	1978	—	2.00	4.00
❏ 12462	Kiss You and Make It Better/You Do It	1979	—	2.00	4.00

ABC DOT

❏ 17608	Lady Luck and Mother Nature/The Door I Used to Close	1976	—	2.00	4.00
❏ 17629	Ain't It Funny (How Times Haven't Changed)/A Bridge for Crawling Back	1976	—	2.00	4.00
❏ 17650	One Night/Deep Elem Blues	1976	—	2.00	4.00
❏ 17669	Just Because/Angel with a Broken Wing	1976	—	2.00	4.00
❏ 17706	Julianne/Velvet Strings	1977	—	2.00	4.00
❏ 17722	Come to Me/Georgia on My Mind	1977	—	2.00	4.00

ABC DUNHILL

| ❏ 4240 | I'm Not a Fool Anymore/Mama Mama | 1970 | — | 3.00 | 6.00 |

ATLANTIC AMERICA

| ❏ 99529 | There's Something on Your Mind/Everything A Man Can Do (And I Love You) | 1986 | — | — | 3.00 |

AVION

| ❏ 105 | Where Did He Go Right/(B-side unknown) | 1983 | — | 3.50 | 7.00 |

BACK BEAT

❏ 543	Teenage Letter/Pain	1965	3.00	6.00	12.00
❏ 546	Treat Her Right/So Long, My Love	1965	4.00	8.00	16.00
❏ 555	Apple of My Eye/I Pass the Day	1965	3.00	6.00	12.00
❏ 560	My Babe/Pain	1966	3.00	6.00	12.00
❏ 563	Driving Wheel/Wigglin' and Gigglin'	1966	3.00	6.00	12.00
❏ 571	Don't Cry No More/To Make a Big Man Cry	1966	3.00	6.00	12.00
❏ 576	You're (Almost) Tough/Tush Hog	1966	3.00	6.00	12.00
❏ 582	Nobody But Me/A Good Man Is Hard to Find	1967	2.50	5.00	10.00

CHURCHILL

| ❏ 7778 | After Texas/California Day | 1981 | — | 2.50 | 5.00 |

ELEKTRA

❏ 46549	In Our Room/Things I Never Could Have Left Behind	1979	—	2.00	4.00
❏ 46582	The Fire of Two Old Flames/Under Suspicion	1980	—	2.00	4.00
❏ 46653	Long Drop/Gonna Save It for My Baby	1980	—	2.00	4.00
❏ 47029	Drinking Them Long Necks/Baby's Found Another Way to Love Me	1980	—	2.00	4.00
❏ 47081	I've Never Gone to Bed With an Ugly Woman/All Night Long Is Gone	1981	—	2.00	4.00

MEGA

| ❏ 1219 | Baby's Not Home/Do What You Can Do | 1974 | — | 2.50 | 5.00 |

MERCURY

❏ 72750	Got Down on Saturday (Sunday in the Rain)/The Grass Was Green	1967	2.00	4.00	8.00
❏ 72799	Broadway Walk/Turn Out the Lights	1968	2.00	4.00	8.00
❏ 72848	Ain't Goin' Down Right/Lovin' Man on Your Hands	1968	2.00	4.00	8.00
❏ 72922	I Miss You Baby/I Want Some Action	1969	2.00	4.00	8.00

NSD

❏ 129	Play Another Gettin' Drunk and Take Somebody Home Song/Your Next One and Only	1982	—	2.50	5.00
❏ 146	The Trouble with Hearts/Naughty Smile	1982	—	2.50	5.00
❏ 156	Your Mama Don't Dance/Party Time	1982	—	2.50	5.00

SCEPTER

❏ 12116	Just a Little Bit/Treat Me Right	1965	2.50	5.00	10.00
❏ 12117	Won't Be Blue/One More Time	1965	2.50	5.00	10.00
❏ 12124	Get Back — Part 1/Get Back — Part 2	1965	2.50	5.00	10.00
❏ 12138	Convicted/One More Time	1966	2.50	5.00	10.00

SHANNON

❏ 829	The Most Wanted Woman in Town/Gingerbread Man	1975	—	2.50	5.00
❏ 833	Help Yourself to Me/To Make a Big Man Cry	1975	—	2.50	5.00
❏ 838	I'll Take It/The One That Got Away	1975	—	2.50	5.00

TEXAS CRUDE

| ❏ 614 | Break Out the Good Stuff/She Needs Time | 1985 | 2.00 | 4.00 | 8.00 |

TMI

❏ 75-0103	Rock and Roll Mood/You Got the Power	1972	—	2.50	5.00
❏ 75-0106	Why Don't We Go Somewhere and Love/Smell-A-Woman	1972	—	2.50	5.00
❏ BTBO-0111	Small Town Girl/Chug All Night	1973	—	2.50	5.00
❏ 75-0113	Carol/Clyde O'Riley	1973	—	2.50	5.00
❏ 9000	Puff of Smoke/Lord Take a Bow	1971	—	3.00	6.00
❏ 9010	Bit By Bit/Wait Till I Arrive	1972	—	3.00	6.00

TNT

| ❏ 194 | Don't Be Blue/One More Time | 1965 | 3.75 | 7.50 | 15.00 |

Albums
ABC

| ❏ AB-1054 | Tonight's the Night | 1978 | 2.50 | 5.00 | 10.00 |

ABC DOT

| ❏ DO-2051 | Head First | 1976 | 3.00 | 6.00 | 12.00 |
| ❏ DO-2066 | A Head of His Time | 1977 | 3.00 | 6.00 | 12.00 |

ABC DUNHILL

| ❏ DS-50080 | Same People | 1970 | 5.00 | 10.00 | 20.00 |

ELEKTRA

| ❏ 6E-234 | In Our Room | 1979 | 2.50 | 5.00 | 10.00 |
| ❏ 6E-298 | The Many Sides of Roy Head | 1980 | 2.50 | 5.00 | 10.00 |

MCA

| ❏ 796 | Tonight's the Night | 1980 | 2.00 | 4.00 | 8.00 |

—Reissue of ABC album

Number	Title (A Side/B Side)	Yr	VG	VG+	NM
SCEPTER					
❑ S-532 [M]	Treat Me Right	1965	7.50	15.00	30.00
❑ SS-532 [S]	Treat Me Right	1965	10.00	20.00	40.00
TMI					
❑ 1000	Dismal Prisoner	1972	3.75	7.50	15.00
TNT					
❑ 101 [M]	Roy Head and the Traits	1965	37.50	75.00	150.00
—Counterfeit alert: Authentics do NOT contain the hit "Treat Her Right."					

HEARTBEATS, THE
Also see SHEP AND THE LIMELITES.
45s

Number	Title (A Side/B Side)	Yr	VG	VG+	NM
GEE					
❑ 1043	When I Found You/Hands Off My Baby	1957	12.50	25.00	50.00
❑ 1047	500 Miles to Go/After New Year's Eve	1958	10.00	20.00	40.00
—Red label					
❑ 1047	500 Miles to Go/After New Year's Eve	1958	5.00	10.00	20.00
—Gray label					
❑ 1061	People Are Talking/Your Way	1960	5.00	10.00	20.00
❑ 1062	Darling How Long/Hurry Home Baby	1960	5.00	10.00	20.00
GUYDEN					
❑ 2011	One Million Years/Let's Get Married	1959	10.00	20.00	40.00
—Yellow label					
❑ 2011	One Million Years/Let's Get Married	1959	7.50	15.00	30.00
—Purple label					
HULL					
❑ 711	Crazy for You/Rockin-N-Rollin-N-Rhythm-N-Blues-N	1955	75.00	150.00	300.00
—Pink label, "Sheppard-Miller" as A-side composers					
❑ 711	Crazy for You/Rockin-N-Rollin-N-Rhythm-N-Blues-N	1955	50.00	100.00	200.00
—Pink label, "Miller" as A-side composer					
❑ 711	Crazy for You/Rockin-N-Rollin-N-Rhythm-N-Blues-N	1955	25.00	50.00	100.00
—Black label					
❑ 711 [DJ]	Crazy for You/Rockin-N-Rollin-N-Rhythm-N-Blues-N	1955	150.00	300.00	600.00
—White label					
❑ 713	Darling How Long/Hurry Home Baby	1956	50.00	100.00	200.00
❑ 716	People Are Talking/Your Way	1956	50.00	100.00	200.00
❑ 720	A Thousand Miles Away/Oh Baby Don't	1957	62.50	125.00	250.00
—Black label					
❑ 720	A Thousand Miles Away/Oh Baby Don't	1957	20.00	450.00	80.00
—Red label					
JUBILEE					
❑ 5202	Finally/Boil and Bubble	1955	7.50	15.00	30.00
NETWORK					
❑ 71200	Tormented/After Everybody's Gone	1955	75.00	150.00	300.00
—Cream label, black vinyl					
❑ 71200	Tormented/After Everybody's Gone	195?	30.00	60.00	120.00
—Yellow label, black vinyl					
❑ 71200	Tormented/After Everybody's Gone	195?	6.25	12.50	25.00
—Red vinyl The Network release as "The Heart Beats Quintet"					
RAMA					
❑ 216	A Thousand Miles Away/Oh Baby Don't	1956	20.00	40.00	80.00
❑ 222	Wedding Bells/I Won't Be the Fool Anymore	1957	25.00	50.00	100.00
❑ 231	I Want to Know/Everybody's Somebody's Fool	1957	25.00	50.00	100.00
ROULETTE					
❑ 4054	I Found a Job/Down on My Knees	1958	7.50	15.00	30.00
❑ 4091	One Day Next Year/Sometimes I Wonder	1958	7.50	15.00	30.00
❑ 4194	Crazy for You/Down on My Knees	1959	7.50	15.00	30.00
Albums					
EMUS					
❑ ES-12033	A Thousand Miles Away	1979	6.25	12.50	25.00
ROULETTE					
❑ R 25107 [M]	A Thousand Miles Away	1960	100.00	200.00	400.00

HEARTBEATS, THE /SHEP AND THE LIMELITES
Also see each artist's individual listings.
Albums

Number	Title (A Side/B Side)	Yr	VG	VG+	NM
ROULETTE					
❑ RE-115 [(2)]	Echoes of a Rock Era: The Groups	1972	3.75	7.50	15.00

HEARTBREAKERS, THE
Several different groups.
45s

Number	Title (A Side/B Side)	Yr	VG	VG+	NM
ATCO					
❑ 6258	The Willow Wept/You Had Time	1963	5.00	10.00	20.00
BRENT					
❑ 7037	I'm Leaving It All Up to You/Corrido Mash	1962	7.50	15.00	30.00
DONNA					
❑ 1381	Everytime I See You/Cradle Rock	1963	30.00	60.00	120.00
—Frank Zappa plays guitar on this record					
LINDA					
❑ 114	Please Answer/She Is My Baby	1964	3.75	7.50	15.00
MARKAY					
❑ 106	Since You've Been Gone/John Law	1962	20.00	40.00	80.00
MGM					
❑ 13129	It's Hard Being a Girl/Special Occasions	1963	3.75	7.50	15.00
RCA VICTOR					
❑ 47-4327	Heartbreaker/Wanda	1951	150.00	300.00	600.00
❑ 47-4508	You're So Necessary to Me/I'm Only Following My Heart	1952	150.00	300.00	600.00
❑ 47-4662	Why Don't I/Rockin' Daddy-O	1952	125.00	250.00	500.00
❑ 47-4849	There Is Time/It's OK With Me	1952	125.00	250.00	500.00
SWAN					
❑ 4242	Baby Baby/I Told You So	1966	3.75	7.50	15.00
VIK					
❑ 0261	Without a Cause/One, Two, I Love You	1957	37.50	75.00	150.00
❑ 0299	My Love/Love You Till the Day I Die	1957	62.50	125.00	250.00

HEARTS, THE
45s

Number	Title (A Side/B Side)	Yr	VG	VG+	NM
BATON					
❑ 208	Lonely Nights/Oo-Wee	1955	12.50	25.00	50.00
❑ 211	All My Love Belongs to You/Talk About Him Girlie	1955	12.50	25.00	50.00
❑ 215	Gone, Gone, Gone/Until the Real Thing Comes Along	1955	12.50	25.00	50.00
❑ 222	Disappointed Bride/Going Home to Stay	1956	7.50	15.00	30.00
❑ 228	He Drives Me Crazy/I Had a Guy	1956	6.25	12.50	25.00
J&S					
❑ 425/6	My Love Has Gone/You or Me Have Got to Go	1959	12.50	25.00	50.00
❑ 995	A Thousand Years from Today/I Feel So Good	1960	10.00	20.00	40.00
❑ 1180/1	You Weren't Home/I Couldn't Let You See Me Crying	1961	12.50	25.00	50.00
❑ 1626/7	I Want Your Love Tonight/Like Later Baby	1958	12.50	25.00	50.00
❑ 1657	Dancing in a Dream World/You Needn't Tell, I Know	1957	15.00	30.00	60.00
❑ 1660	So Long, Baby/You Say You Love Me	1957	15.00	30.00	60.00
❑ 4571/2	Goodbye Baby/There Is No Love at All	1959	10.00	20.00	40.00
❑ 10002/3	If I Had Known/There Are So Many Ways	1958	12.50	25.00	50.00
TUFF					
❑ 370	Dear Abby/(Instrumental)	1963	3.75	7.50	15.00

HEARTS OF STONE
45s

Number	Title (A Side/B Side)	Yr	VG	VG+	NM
V.I.P.					
❑ 25058	It's a Lonesome Road/Yesterday's Love Is Over	1970	2.50	5.00	10.00
❑ 25064	If I Could Give You the World/You Gotta Sacrifice	1970	2.50	5.00	10.00

HEATWAVE
12-Inch Singles

Number	Title (A Side/B Side)	Yr	VG	VG+	NM
EPIC					
❑ AS 868 [DJ]	Gangsters of the Groove (same on both sides)	1980	3.75	7.50	15.00
❑ 49-02184	Posin' Til Closin' (4:59)/Turn Around (4:58)	1981	5.00	10.00	20.00
❑ 49-02936	Lettin' It Loose (6:30)/(B-side unknown)	1982	3.00	6.00	12.00
❑ 49H-06896	Boogie Nights/The Groove Line	198?	3.00	6.00	12.00
—"Mixed Masters" reissue					
❑ 28-50371	Boogie Nights/Too Hot to Handle	1977	5.00	10.00	20.00
❑ 28-50541	The Groove Line (7:28)/Always and Forever (6:14)	1978	5.00	10.00	20.00
❑ 28-50597	Mind Blowing Decisions/Ain't No Half Steppin'	1978	3.75	7.50	15.00
❑ 28-50724	Eyeballin' (Extended Disco Mix 6:35)/(B-side unknown)	1979	3.75	7.50	15.00
❑ 48-50956	Gangsters of the Groove/Find Someone Like You	1980	3.75	7.50	15.00
45s					
EPIC					
❑ 19-02446	Posin' 'Til Closin'/Turn Around	1981	—	2.00	4.00
❑ 38-02904	Lettin' It Loose/Mind What You Find	1982	—	2.00	4.00
❑ 38-03198	Look After Love/The Big Guns	1982	—	2.00	4.00
❑ 8-50370	Boogie Nights/All You Do Is Dial	1977	—	2.50	5.00
❑ 8-50490	Always and Forever/Super Soul Sister	1977	—	2.50	5.00
❑ 8-50524	The Groove Line/Happiness Togetherness	1978	—	2.00	4.00
❑ 8-50586	Mind Blowing Decisions/Beat Your Booty	1978	—	2.00	4.00
❑ 8-50699	Eyeballin'/Birthday	1979	—	2.00	4.00
❑ 19-50736	One Night Tan/Disco	1979	—	2.00	4.00
❑ 19-50945	Gangsters of the Groove/Find Someone Like You	1980	—	2.00	4.00
❑ 19-51005	Where Did I Go Wrong/Dreamin' Your	1981	—	2.00	4.00
EPIC MEMORY LANE					
❑ 15-2377	Boogie Nights/Always and Forever	1979	—	2.00	4.00
Albums					
EPIC					
❑ PE 34761	Too Hot to Handle	1977	2.50	5.00	10.00
—Originals have orange labels					
❑ JE 35260	Central Heating	1978	2.50	5.00	10.00
—Originals have orange labels					
❑ FE 35970	Hot Property	1979	2.50	5.00	10.00
❑ FE 36873	Candles	1980	2.50	5.00	10.00
❑ FE 38065	Current	1982	2.50	5.00	10.00
❑ FE 39279	Greatest Hits	1984	2.50	5.00	10.00
❑ PE 39279	Greatest Hits	198?	2.00	4.00	8.00
—Budget-line reissue					

HEBB, BOBBY
45s

Number	Title (A Side/B Side)	Yr	VG	VG+	NM
BOOM					
❑ 60017	Betty Jo from Ohio/Sam Hall Jr.	1966	2.00	4.00	8.00
CADET					
❑ 5690	I Was a Boy When You Needed a Man/Woman in the Window	1972	—	2.50	5.00
LAURIE					
❑ 3632	True, I Love You/Proud Soul Heritage	1975	—	2.50	5.00
❑ 3638	Sunny '76/Sunny Disco	1976	—	2.50	5.00
PHILIPS					
❑ 40365	Sunny/Bread	1966	2.50	5.00	10.00
❑ 40400	A Satisfied Mind/Love, Love, Love	1966	2.00	4.00	8.00
❑ 40400 [PS]	A Satisfied Mind/Love, Love, Love	1966	3.00	6.00	12.00

Number	Title (A Side/B Side)	Yr	VG	VG+	NM
❑ 40421	Love Me/Crazy Baby	1966	2.00	4.00	8.00
❑ 40431	My Pretty Sunshine/Ooh La La	1967	2.00	4.00	8.00
❑ 40448	I Love Everything About You/Some Kind of Magic	1967	2.00	4.00	8.00
❑ 40482	Everything Is Coming Up Roses/Bound by Love	1967	2.00	4.00	8.00
❑ 40551	Dreamy/You Want to Change Me	1968	2.00	4.00	8.00
RICH					
❑ 1006	Cherry/Feel So Good	1960	3.75	7.50	15.00
❑ 1740	Just a Little Bit More/Walk Me On Alone	1962	3.75	7.50	15.00
SCEPTER					
❑ 12166	I Love Mary (Part 1)/I Love Mary (Part 2)	1966	2.00	4.00	8.00
Albums					
EPIC					
❑ BN 26523	Love Games	1970	3.00	6.00	12.00
PHILIPS					
❑ PHM 200212 [M]	Sunny	1966	6.25	12.50	25.00
—With "200-212" in trail-off; this record is mono					
❑ PHM 200212 [S]	Sunny	1966	6.25	12.50	25.00
—With "2/600-212" in trail-off; this record plays stereo, though labeled mono					
❑ PHS 600212 [S]	Sunny	1966	7.50	15.00	30.00

HENDRIX, JIMI

The albums list includes many posthumous "cash-in" records of early material.

Number	Title (A Side/B Side)	Yr	VG	VG+	NM
12-Inch Singles					
CAPITOL					
❑ SPRO 11284 [DJ]	Star Spangled Banner (same on both sides)	199?	25.00	50.00	100.00
—Promo only, blue vinyl with eight star-shaped holes in outer part of record					
45s					
AUDIO FIDELITY					
❑ 167	No Such Animal (Part 1)/No Such Animal (Part 2)	1970	3.75	7.50	15.00
❑ 167 [PS]	No Such Animal (Part 1)/No Such Animal (Part 2)	1970	10.00	20.00	40.00
EXPERIENCE HENDRIX					
❑ RTH-1007	The Jimi Hendrix Classic Singles Collection	1998	15.00	30.00	60.00
—Boxed set of 10 45s, each with picture sleeves and white sleeve, with booklet					
❑ 5651-7	Little Drummer Boy-Auld Lang Syne/Three Little Bears	1999	3.75	7.50	15.00
—Red vinyl, small hole					
❑ 5651-7	Little Drummer Boy-Auld Lang Syne/Three Little Bears	2001	—	2.50	5.00
—Green vinyl, small hole; reissue					
❑ 5651-7 [PS]	Little Drummer Boy-Auld Lang Syne/Three Little Bears	1999	—	2.50	5.00
—The same sleeve appears on both pressings of the single					
❑ 13487 [DJ]	Star Spangled Banner/Purple Haze	1999	3.75	7.50	15.00
—Promo-only picture disc					
MCA					
❑ 55336 [DJ]	Dolly Dagger/Night Bird Flying	1997	2.50	5.00	10.00
—Promo only on purple vinyl					
❑ 55336 [PS]	Dolly Dagger/Night Bird Flying	1997	2.50	5.00	10.00
❑ 55454 [DJ]	Can You Please Crawl Out Your Window?/ Burning of the Midnight Lamp	1998	—	2.00	5.00
—Promo only on orange vinyl					
❑ 55454 [PS]	Can You Please Crawl Out Your Window?/ Burning of the Midnight Lamp	1998	—	2.00	5.00
—Cardboard sleeve					
REPRISE					
❑ 0572	Hey Joe/51st Anniversary	1967	25.00	50.00	100.00
❑ 0572 [PS]	Hey Joe/51st Anniversary	1967	250.00	500.00	1000.
❑ PRO 595 [DJ]	Medley: The Little Drummer Boy-Silent Night/ Auld Lang Syne	1974	37.50	75.00	150.00
❑ PRO 595 [PS]	...And a Happy New Year	1974	20.00	40.00	80.00
❑ 0597	Purple Haze/The Wind Cries Mary	1967	6.25	12.50	25.00
❑ 0641	Foxey Lady/Hey Joe	1967	6.25	12.50	25.00
❑ 0665	Up from the Skies/One Rainy Wish	1968	7.50	15.00	30.00
❑ 0728	Purple Haze/Foxey Lady	1968	3.75	7.50	15.00
—"Back to Back Hits" series -- originals have both "r:" and "W7" logos					
❑ 0742	All Along the Watchtower/Crosstown Traffic	1971	—	3.00	6.00
—"Back to Back Hits" series					
❑ 0767	All Along the Watchtower/Burning of the Midnight Lamp	1968	7.50	15.00	30.00
❑ 0792	Crosstown Traffic/Gypsy Eyes	1968	7.50	15.00	30.00
❑ 0853	If 6 Was 9/Stone Free	1969	10.00	20.00	40.00
❑ 0905	Stepping Stone/Izabella	1970	25.00	50.00	100.00
❑ 1000	Freedom/Angel	1971	3.75	7.50	15.00
❑ 1044	Dolly Dagger/Star Spangled Banner	1971	3.75	7.50	15.00
❑ 1082	Johnny B. Goode/Lover Man	1972	3.75	7.50	15.00
❑ 1118	The Wind Cries Mary/Little Wing	1972	3.75	7.50	15.00
❑ EP 2239	Gloria (B-side blank)	1979	—	2.50	5.00
❑ EP 2239 [PS]	Gloria (B-side blank)	1979	—	2.50	5.00
—Above was a bonus record in "The Essential Jimi Hendrix, Volume 2"					
❑ 29845	Fire/Little Wing	1982	—	3.00	6.00
TRIP					
❑ 3002	Hot Trigger/Suspicious	1972	—	2.50	5.00
Albums					
ACCORD					
❑ SN-7101	Kaleidoscope	1981	2.50	5.00	10.00
❑ SN-7112	Before London	1981	2.50	5.00	10.00
❑ SN-7139	Cosmic Feeling	1981	2.50	5.00	10.00
CAPITOL					
❑ STAO-472	Band of Gypsys	1970	5.00	10.00	20.00
❑ SWBB-659 [(2)]	Get That Feeling/Flashing	1971	6.25	12.50	25.00
❑ ST 2856 [S]	Get That Feeling	1967	10.00	20.00	40.00
❑ T 2856 [M]	Get That Feeling	1967	20.00	40.00	80.00
❑ ST 2894 [S]	Flashing	1968	10.00	20.00	40.00
❑ T 2894 [M]	Flashing	1968	25.00	50.00	100.00
❑ SJ-12416	Band of Gypsys 2	1986	2.50	5.00	10.00
—Side 2 lists, and plays, three songs					
❑ SJ-12416	Band of Gypsys 2	1986	37.50	75.00	150.00
—Side 2 lists three songs, but plays four completely different songs. Four bands are visible on the record.					
❑ MLP-15022 [EP]	Johnny B. Goode	1986	2.00	4.00	8.00
❑ SN-16319	Band of Gypsys	1985	2.50	5.00	10.00
—Budget-line reissue					
❑ C1-96414	Band of Gypsys	1995	3.75	7.50	15.00
—Numbered reissue					
EXPERIENCE HENDRIX/CAPITOL					
❑ ST-472	Band of Gypsys	1997	6.25	12.50	25.00
—Limited edition on "heavy vinyl" with booklet; distributed by Classic Records					
EXPERIENCE HENDRIX/MCA					
❑ 11599 [(2)]	First Rays of the New Rising Sun	1997	12.50	25.00	50.00
—Limited edition on "heavy vinyl" with booklet					
❑ 11600 [(2)]	Electric Ladyland	1997	10.00	20.00	40.00
—Limited edition on "heavy vinyl" with booklet					
❑ 11601	Axis: Bold As Love	1997	12.50	25.00	50.00
—Limited edition on "heavy vinyl" with booklet					
❑ 11602 [(2)]	Are You Experienced?	1997	12.50	25.00	50.00
—Limited edition on "heavy vinyl" with booklet					
❑ 11607	Band of Gypsys	1997	6.25	12.50	25.00
—Limited edition on "heavy vinyl" with booklet; pressed in U.S. for export to Europe					
❑ 11608	Are You Experienced?	1997	10.00	20.00	40.00
—Limited edition on "heavy vinyl" with booklet; pressed in U.S. for export to Europe; has different cover than US version					
❑ 11671 [(2)]	Experience Hendrix: The Best of Jimi Hendrix	1998	6.25	12.50	25.00
—Despite lower number, was released after South Saturn Delta					
❑ 11684 [(2)]	South Saturn Delta	1997	6.25	12.50	25.00
—Numbered, limited edition on "heavy vinyl"					
❑ 11742 [(3)]	BBC Sessions	1998	7.50	15.00	30.00
❑ 11931 [(3)]	Live at the Fillmore East	1999	7.50	15.00	30.00
❑ 11987 [(3)]	Live at Woodstock	1999	7.50	15.00	30.00
❑ 112316 [(8)]	The Jimi Hendrix Experience	2000	17.50	35.00	70.00
—Limited edition of 5,000 in purple felt box					
❑ 112984	Smash Hits	2002	3.75	7.50	15.00
—Limited edition on "heavy vinyl"					
NUTMEG					
❑ 1001	High, Live 'N' Dirty	1978	6.25	12.50	25.00
—Red vinyl					
❑ 1001	High, Live 'N' Dirty	1978	6.25	12.50	25.00
—Black vinyl					
❑ 1002	Cosmic Turnaround	1981	3.00	6.00	12.00
PICKWICK					
❑ SPC-3528	Jimi	197?	2.50	5.00	10.00
REPRISE					
❑ MS 2025	Smash Hits	1969	10.00	20.00	40.00
—With "W7" and "r:" logos on two-tone orange label					
❑ MS 2025	Smash Hits Bonus Poster	1969	10.00	20.00	40.00
❑ MS 2025	Smash Hits	1970	3.00	6.00	12.00
—With only "r:" logo on all-orange (tan) label					
❑ MS 2025	Smash Hits	198?	2.00	4.00	8.00
—Red and black label or gold and light blue label					
❑ MS 2029	Historic Performances As Recorded at the Monterey International Pop Festival	1970	5.00	10.00	20.00
—Side 1: Jimi Hendrix; Side 2: Otis Redding					
❑ MS 2034	The Cry of Love	1971	125.00	250.00	500.00
—With "W7" and "r:" logos on two-tone orange label					
❑ MS 2034	The Cry of Love	1971	3.75	7.50	15.00
❑ MS 2040	Rainbow Bridge	1971	5.00	10.00	20.00
❑ MS 2049	Hendrix in the West	1972	5.00	10.00	20.00
❑ MS 2103	War Heroes	1972	5.00	10.00	20.00
❑ MS 2204	Crash Landing	1975	3.75	7.50	15.00
❑ MS 2229	Midnight Lightning	1975	3.75	7.50	15.00
❑ 2RS 2245 [(2)]	The Essential Jimi Hendrix	1978	5.00	10.00	20.00
❑ MSK 2276	Smash Hits	1977	2.50	5.00	10.00
—Reissue					
❑ HS 2293	The Essential Jimi Hendrix Volume Two	1979	3.75	7.50	15.00
—Add 100% if bonus single of "Gloria" with picture sleeve is enclosed					
❑ HS 2299	Nine to the Universe	1980	2.50	5.00	10.00
❑ R 6261 [M]	Are You Experienced?	1967	50.00	100.00	200.00
❑ RS 6261 [S]	Are You Experienced?	1967	12.50	25.00	50.00
—Pink, gold and green label					
❑ RS 6261 [S]	Are You Experienced?	1968	6.25	12.50	25.00
—With "W7" and "r:" logos on two-tone orange label					
❑ RS 6261 [S]	Are You Experienced?	1970	3.00	6.00	12.00
—With only "r:" logo on all-orange (tan) label					
❑ RS 6261 [S]	Are You Experienced?	198?	2.00	4.00	8.00
—Red and black label or gold and light blue label					
❑ R 6281 [M]	Axis: Bold As Love	1968	625.00	1250.	2500.
❑ RS 6281 [S]	Axis: Bold As Love	1968	20.00	40.00	80.00
—Pink, gold and green label					
❑ RS 6281 [S]	Axis: Bold As Love	1968	6.25	12.50	25.00
—With "W7" and "r:" logos on two-tone orange label					
❑ RS 6281 [S]	Axis: Bold As Love	1970	3.00	6.00	12.00
—With only "r:" logo on all-orange (tan) label					
❑ RS 6281 [S]	Axis: Bold As Love	198?	2.00	4.00	8.00
—Red and black label or gold and light blue label					
❑ 2R 6307 [(2) M]	Electric Ladyland	1968	2000.	3000.	4000.
—Mono is promo only					
❑ 2RS 6307 [(2) S]	Electric Ladyland	1968	25.00	50.00	100.00
—With "W7" and "r:" logos on two-tone orange label					
❑ 2RS 6307 [(2) S]	Electric Ladyland	1970	3.75	7.50	15.00
—With only "r:" logo on all-orange (tan) label					

Number	Title (A Side/B Side)	Yr	VG	VG+	NM
❏ 2RS 6307 [(2) S]Electric Ladyland		198?	3.00	6.00	12.00
—Red and black label or gold and light blue label					
❏ 2RS 6481 [(2)]Soundtrack Recordings from the Film Jimi					
	Hendrix	1973	6.25	12.50	25.00
❏ 22306 [(2)]	The Jimi Hendrix Concerts	1982	3.00	6.00	12.00
❏ 25119	Kiss the Sky	1984	2.50	5.00	10.00
❏ 25358	Jimi Plays Monterey	1986	2.50	5.00	10.00
❏ SKAO-91441	Axis: Bold As Love	1968	10.00	20.00	40.00
—Capitol Record Club edition; two-tone orange label with "W7" and "r:" at top					
❏ STBO-91568 [(2)]Electric Ladyland		1968	37.50	75.00	150.00
—Capitol Record Club edition					
❏ SMAS-93467	The Cry of Love	1971	15.00	30.00	60.00
—Capitol Record Club edition					
❏ SMAS-93972	Rainbow Bridge	1971	12.50	25.00	50.00
—Capitol Record Club edition					
RHINO					
❏ RNDF-254 [PD]The Jimi Hendrix Interview		1982	6.25	12.50	25.00
RYKO ANALOGUE					
❏ RALP-0038 [(2)]Live at Winterland		1988	3.75	7.50	15.00
❏ RALP-0078 [(2)]Radio One		1988	3.75	7.50	15.00
—Clear vinyl					
TRACK					
❏ 612003 [M]	Axis: Bold As Love	2000	6.25	12.50	25.00
—Classic Records issue of the original U.K. mono mix, on a reproduction of the original British label					
TRIP					
❏ 3509 [(2)]	Superpak	197?	3.75	7.50	15.00
❏ TLP-9500	Rare Hendrix	1972	3.75	7.50	15.00
❏ TLP-9501	Roots of Hendrix	1972	3.00	6.00	12.00
❏ TLP-9512	Moods	1973	3.00	6.00	12.00
❏ TLP-9523	The Genius of Jimi Hendrix	1973	3.00	6.00	12.00
UNITED ARTISTS					
❏ UA-LA505-E	The Very Best of Jimi Hendrix	1975	3.00	6.00	12.00
WARNER BROS.					
❏ HS 2299	Nine to the Universe	1980	3.00	6.00	12.00
—Reprise cover, Warner Bros. tan "pinstripe" label; possibly Columbia House edition?					

HENDRIX, JIMI, AND LITTLE RICHARD
Also see each artist's individual listings.
45s
ALA

Number	Title (A Side/B Side)	Yr	VG	VG+	NM
❏ 1175	Goodnight Irene/Why Don't You Love Me	1972	2.00	4.00	8.00

Albums
ARCHIVE OF FOLK AND JAZZ

Number	Title (A Side/B Side)	Yr	VG	VG+	NM
❏ 296	Roots of Rock	1974	3.00	6.00	12.00
PICKWICK					
❏ SPC-3347	Jimi Hendrix and Little Richard Together	1973	3.00	6.00	12.00

HENDRIX, JIMI, AND LONNIE YOUNGBLOOD
Albums
MAPLE

Number	Title (A Side/B Side)	Yr	VG	VG+	NM
❏ 6004	Two Great Experiences Together	1971	12.50	25.00	50.00

HENRY, CLARENCE
45s
ARGO

Number	Title (A Side/B Side)	Yr	VG	VG+	NM
❏ 5259	Ain't Got No Home/Troubles, Troubles	1956	5.00	10.00	20.00
❏ 5266	I'm a Country Boy/Lonely Tramp	1957	4.00	8.00	16.00
❏ 5273	I Found a Home/It Won't Be Long	1957	4.00	8.00	16.00
❏ 5305	I'm in Love/Baby Baby Please	1958	4.00	8.00	16.00
❏ 5378	I Don't Know Why/Just My Baby and Me	1960	5.00	10.00	20.00
❏ 5378	But I Do/Just My Baby and Me	1960	4.00	8.00	16.00
—A-side: Same song, new title					
❏ 5388	You Always Hurt the One You Love/Little Suzy	1961	4.00	8.00	16.00
❏ 5395	Lonely Street/Why Can't You	1961	3.75	7.50	15.00
❏ 5401	On Bended Knees/Standing in the Need of Love	1961	3.75	7.50	15.00
❏ 5408	A Little Too Much/I Wish I Could Stay the Same	1962	3.00	6.00	12.00
❏ 5414	Dream Myself a Sweetheart/Lost Without You	1962	3.00	6.00	12.00
❏ 5426	Jealous Kind/Come On and Dance	1962	3.00	6.00	12.00
❏ 5448	If I Didn't Care/It Takes Two to Tango	1963	3.00	6.00	12.00
❏ 5480	Looking Back/Long Lost and Worried	1964	2.50	5.00	10.00
CADET					
❏ 5259	Ain't Got No Home/Troubles, Troubles	1966	2.00	4.00	8.00
DIAL					
❏ 4057	This Time/Hummin' a Heartache	1967	—	3.00	6.00
❏ 4072	Shake Your Money Maker/That's When I				
	Guessed	1968	—	3.00	6.00
PARROT					
❏ 45004	Have You Ever Been Lonely/Little Green Frog	1964	2.50	5.00	10.00
❏ 45009	I Told My Pillow/Can't Hide My Tear	1964	2.50	5.00	10.00
❏ 45015	I Might As Well/Tore Up Over You	1965	2.50	5.00	10.00

Albums
ARGO

Number	Title (A Side/B Side)	Yr	VG	VG+	NM
❏ LP-4009 [M]	You Always Hurt the One You Love	1961	75.00	125.00	250.00
CADET					
❏ LP-4009 [M]	You Always Hurt the One You Love	1966	12.50	25.00	50.00
—Includes copies of Cadet LP in Argo sleeves					
ROULETTE					
❏ SR 42039	Alive and Well and Living in New Orleans	1969	6.25	12.50	25.00

HI-LITES, THE (1)
For records on Daran, see THE CHI-LITES.

HIBBLER, AL
45s
ALADDIN

Number	Title (A Side/B Side)	Yr	VG	VG+	NM
❏ 3328	Don't Take Your Love from Me/I Got It So Bad and That Ain't Good	1956	3.75	7.50	15.00
ATLANTIC					
❏ 911	Danny Boy/Song of the Wanderer	1950	—	—	—
—Unconfirmed on 45 rpm					
❏ 925	The Blues Come Falling Down/Old Folks	1951	12.50	25.00	50.00
❏ 932	Travelin' Light/If I Knew You Were There	1951	12.50	25.00	50.00
❏ 945	Now I Lay Me Down to Dream/This Is Always	1951	12.50	25.00	50.00
❏ 1071	Danny Boy/Now I Lay Me Down	1955	7.50	15.00	30.00
BRUNSWICK					
❏ 55027	Star Dust/Stormy Weather	1957	3.75	7.50	15.00
CLEF					
❏ 89095	I'm Getting Sentimental Over You/As Time Goes By	1954	3.75	7.50	15.00
DECCA					
❏ 29441	Unchained Melody/Daybreak	1955	5.00	10.00	20.00
❏ 29543	I Can't Put My Arms Around a Memory/They Say You're Laughing at Me	1955	3.75	7.50	15.00
❏ 29660	He/Breeze (Blow My Baby Back to Me)	1955	5.00	10.00	20.00
❏ 29789	11th Hour Melody/Let's Try Again	1956	3.75	7.50	15.00
❏ 29950	Away All Boats/Never Turn Back	1956	3.75	7.50	15.00
❏ 29982	After the Lights Go Down Low/I Was Telling Her About You	1956	3.75	7.50	15.00
❏ 30100	Nightfall/I'm Free	1956	3.75	7.50	15.00
❏ 30127	White Christmas/Silent Night	1956	3.75	7.50	15.00
❏ 30176	Trees/The Town Crier	1957	3.00	6.00	12.00
❏ 30268	Sweet Slumber/Because of You	1957	3.00	6.00	12.00
❏ 30337	Around the Corner from the Blues/I Complain	1957	3.00	6.00	12.00
❏ 30397	When Will I Forget You/Be Fair	1957	3.00	6.00	12.00
❏ 30483	The Crying Wind/A Wish	1957	3.00	6.00	12.00
❏ 30547	My Heart Tells Me/I'm Glad I'm Not Young Anymore	1958	3.00	6.00	12.00
❏ 30622	Honeysuckle Rose/Ain't Nothin' Wrong with That Baby	1958	3.00	6.00	12.00
❏ 30684	Softly, My Love/Your Hands	1958	3.00	6.00	12.00
❏ 30752	Love Land/Love Me Long, Hold Me Close	1958	3.00	6.00	12.00
❏ 30817	Warm Heart-Cold Feet/Mine All Mine	1959	3.00	6.00	12.00
❏ 30870	He Is Always There/What 'Tis, What 'Tis, 'Tis Spring	1959	3.00	6.00	12.00
❏ 30946	It Won't Be Easy/Lonesome and Cold	1959	3.00	6.00	12.00
MERCURY					
❏ 89011	Please/Believe It Love	1952	3.75	7.50	15.00
REPRISE					
❏ 20035	Look Away/Tall the Sky	1961	2.50	5.00	10.00
❏ 20077	Walk Away/I've Convinced Everyone But You	1962	2.50	5.00	10.00
TOP RANK					
❏ 2089	Strawberry Hill/Stranger	1960	2.50	5.00	10.00

7-Inch Extended Plays
DECCA

Number	Title (A Side/B Side)	Yr	VG	VG+	NM
❏ ED 2410	*After the Lights Go Down Low/September in the Rain/You'll Never Know/Where Are You?	195?	5.00	10.00	20.00
❏ ED 2410 [PS]	Starring Al Hibbler, Part 1	195?	5.00	10.00	20.00
❏ ED 2447	I Hadn't Anyone Till You/I'll Get Along Somehow/ /It's Been a Long, Long Time/The Town Crier	195?	5.00	10.00	20.00
❏ ED 2447 [PS]	Here's Hibbler! Part 3	195?	5.00	10.00	20.00

Albums
ARGO

Number	Title (A Side/B Side)	Yr	VG	VG+	NM
❏ LP-601 [M]	Melodies by Al Hibbler	1956	10.00	20.00	40.00
—Reissue of Marterry LP					
ATLANTIC					
❏ 1251 [M]	After the Lights Go Down Low	1957	12.50	25.00	50.00
—Black label					
❏ 1251 [M]	After the Lights Go Down Low	1961	6.25	12.50	25.00
—Mostly red label, white fan logo					
❏ 1251 [M]	After the Lights Go Down Low	1963	5.00	10.00	20.00
—Mostly red label, black fan logo					
BRUNSWICK					
❏ BL 54036 [M]	Al Hibbler with the Ellingtonians	1957	12.50	25.00	50.00
DECCA					
❏ DL 8328 [M]	Starring Al Hibbler	1956	7.50	15.00	30.00
❏ DL 8420 [M]	Here's Hibbler	1957	7.50	15.00	30.00
❏ DL 8697 [M]	Torchy and Blue	1958	7.50	15.00	30.00
❏ DL 8757 [M]	Hits by Hibbler	1958	7.50	15.00	30.00
❏ DL 8862 [M]	Al Hibbler Remembers the Big Songs of the Big Bands	1959	7.50	15.00	30.00
❏ DL 78862 [S]	Al Hibbler Remembers the Big Songs of the Big Bands	1959	10.00	20.00	40.00
DISCOVERY					
❏ 842	It's Monday Every Day	198?	3.00	6.00	12.00
—Reissue of Reprise LP					
LMI					
❏ 10001 [M]	Early One Morning	1964	7.50	15.00	30.00
MARTERRY					
❏ LP-601 [M]	Melodies by Al Hibbler	1956	20.00	40.00	80.00
MCA					
❏ 4098 [(2)]	The Best of Al Hibbler	197?	3.75	7.50	15.00
NORGRAN					
❏ MGN-4 [10]	Al Hibbler Favorites	1954	37.50	75.00	150.00
❏ MGN-15 [10]	Al Hibbler Sings Duke Ellington	1954	37.50	75.00	150.00

Number	Title (A Side/B Side)	Yr	VG	VG+	NM
OPEN SKY					
❑ OSR-3126	For Sentimental Reasons	1986	3.00	6.00	12.00
REPRISE					
❑ R-2005 [M]	It's Monday Every Day	1961	7.50	15.00	30.00
❑ R9-2005 [S]	It's Monday Every Day	1961	10.00	20.00	40.00
SCORE					
❑ SLP-4013 [M]	I Surrender, Dear	1957	25.00	50.00	100.00
VERVE					
❑ MGV-4000 [M]	Al Hibbler Sings Love Songs	1956	15.00	30.00	60.00
❑ V-4000 [M]	Al Hibbler Sings Love Songs	1961	5.00	10.00	20.00

HIDE-A-WAYS, THE
45s

Number	Title (A Side/B Side)	Yr	VG	VG+	NM
LOST-NITE					
❑ 119	Can't Help Loving That Girl of Mine/I'm Coming Home	196?	—	2.50	5.00
—Reissue label					
MGM					
❑ 55004	Cherie/Me Make Em Powwow	1955	125.00	250.00	500.00
RONNI					
❑ 1000	Can't Help Lovin' That Girl of Mine/I'm Coming Home	1954	2000.	4000.	6000.

HIGH INERGY
45s

Number	Title (A Side/B Side)	Yr	VG	VG+	NM
GORDY					
❑ 1613	First Impressions/Wrong Man, Right Touch	1982	—	2.00	4.00
❑ 1632	Beware/Wrong Man, Right Touch	1982	—	2.00	4.00
❑ 1641	Could This Be Love/Journey to Love	1982	—	2.00	4.00
❑ 1656	So Right/Don't Let Up on the Groove	1982	—	2.00	4.00
❑ 1662	He's a Pretender/Don't Let Up on the Groove	1983	—	2.00	4.00
❑ 1688	Back in My Arms Again/So Right	1983	—	2.00	4.00
❑ 7155	You Can't Turn Me Off (In the Middle of Turning Me On)/Let Me Get Close to You	1977	—	2.50	5.00
❑ 7157	Love Is All You Need/Some Kind of Magic	1978	—	2.50	5.00
❑ 7160	We Are the Future/High School	1978	—	2.50	5.00
❑ 7161	Beware/Lovin' Fever	1978	—	2.50	5.00
❑ 7166	Peaceland/Shoulda Gone Dancin'	1979	—	2.50	5.00
❑ 7172	Midnight Music Man/Come and Get It	1979	—	2.50	5.00
❑ 7174	Skate to the Rhythm/Midnight Music Man	1979	—	2.50	5.00
❑ 7178	I Love Makin' Love (To the Music)/Somebody Somewhere	1980	—	2.50	5.00
❑ 7187	Make Me Yours/I Love Makin' Love (To the Music)	1980	—	2.50	5.00
❑ 7192	Hold On to My Love/If I Love You Tonight	1980	—	2.50	5.00
❑ 7201	I Just Wanna Dance with You/Take My Life	1981	—	2.50	5.00
❑ 7207	I Just Can't Help Myself/Goin' Through the Motions	1981	—	2.50	5.00
❑ 7211	Don't Park Your Loving/Now That There's You	1981	—	2.50	5.00
Albums					
GORDY					
❑ G6-978S1	Turnin' On	1977	3.00	6.00	12.00
❑ G7-982R1	Steppin' Out	1978	3.00	6.00	12.00
❑ G7-989R1	Frenzy	1979	3.00	6.00	12.00
❑ G8-996M1	Hold On	1980	3.00	6.00	12.00
❑ G8-1005M1	High Inergy	1981	3.00	6.00	12.00
❑ 6006GL	So Right	1982	2.50	5.00	10.00
❑ 6041GL	Groove Patrol	1983	2.50	5.00	10.00

HILL, BUNKER
45s

Number	Title (A Side/B Side)	Yr	VG	VG+	NM
MALA					
❑ 451	Hide and Go Seek (Part 1)/Hide and Go Seek (Part 2)	1962	5.00	10.00	20.00
❑ 457	Red Ridin' Hood and the Wolf/Nobody Knows	1962	5.00	10.00	20.00
❑ 464	The Girl Can't Dance/You Can't Make Me Doubt My Baby	1963	6.25	12.50	25.00

HILL, LAURYN
12-Inch Singles

Number	Title (A Side/B Side)	Yr	VG	VG+	NM
RUFFHOUSE					
❑ 44 79207	Everything Is Everything (LP Version)/Ex-Factor (A Simple Mix)/Everything Is Everything (Radio Edit)/Ex-Factor (A Simple Breakdown) (A Simple Acapella)/Everything Is Everything (Instrumental)	1999	2.50	5.00	10.00
45s					
RUFFHOUSE					
❑ 38 78868	Doo Wop (That Thing)/Lost Ones (Remix)	1998	—	—	2.00
❑ 38 78868 [PS]	Doo Wop (That Thing)/Lost Ones (Remix)	1998	—	—	2.00
❑ 38 79077	Ex-Factor/When It Hurts So Bad	1999	—	—	3.00
❑ 38 79206	Everything Is Everything/Ex-Factor	1999	—	—	3.00
Albums					
RUFFHOUSE					
❑ C2 69035 [(2)]	The Miseducation of Lauryn Hill	1998	3.75	7.50	15.00

HILL, Z.Z.
45s

Number	Title (A Side/B Side)	Yr	VG	VG+	NM
ATLANTIC					
❑ 2659	It's a Hang-Up Baby/(Home Just Ain't Home at) Suppertime	1969	2.00	4.00	8.00
COLUMBIA					
❑ 10552	Love Is So Good When You're Stealing It/Need You By My Side	1977	—	2.50	5.00

Number	Title (A Side/B Side)	Yr	VG	VG+	NM
❑ 10680	This Time They Told the Truth/Near But Yet So Far	1978	—	2.50	5.00
❑ 10748	Universal Love/That's All That's Left	1978	—	2.50	5.00
HILL					
❑ 222	Don't Make Me Pay for His Mistakes/(B-side unknown)	1971	—	3.00	6.00
KENT					
❑ 404	I Could Do It All Over/You Don't Love Me	1964	2.50	5.00	10.00
❑ 416	I Need Someone (To Love Me)/Have Mercy Someone	1965	2.50	5.00	10.00
❑ 427	Hey Little Girl/Oh Darlin'	1965	2.50	5.00	10.00
❑ 432	That's It/What's More	1965	2.50	5.00	10.00
❑ 439	Everybody Has to Cry/Happiness Is All I Need	1965	2.50	5.00	10.00
❑ 444	No More Doggin'/The Kind of Love I Want	1966	2.50	5.00	10.00
❑ 449	I Found Love/Set Your Sights Higher	1966	2.50	5.00	10.00
❑ 453	You Can't Hide a Heartache/Gimme Gimme	1966	2.50	5.00	10.00
❑ 460	Oh Darling/Greatest Love	1967	2.50	5.00	10.00
❑ 464	Baby I'm Sorry/Where She At	1967	2.50	5.00	10.00
❑ 469	You Just Cheat and Lie/Everybody Needs Somebody	1967	2.50	5.00	10.00
❑ 478	What Am I Living For/You're Gonna Need My Lovin'	1967	2.50	5.00	10.00
❑ 481	Steal Away/Nothing Can Change the Love I Have for You	1967	2.50	5.00	10.00
❑ 494	You Got What I Need/Have Mercy Someone	1968	2.50	5.00	10.00
❑ 502	Don't Make Promises (You Can't Keep)/Set Your Sights Higher	1968	2.50	5.00	10.00
❑ 4547	I Need Someone (To Love Me)/Oh Darling	1971	2.00	4.00	8.00
❑ 4550	You Don't Love Me/Have Mercy Someone	1971	2.00	4.00	8.00
❑ 4560	If I Could Do It All Over/You Won't Hurt No More	1971	2.00	4.00	8.00
❑ 4577	Nothing Can Change This Love/Eveyrbody Has to Cry	1972	2.00	4.00	8.00
MALACO					
❑ 2069	Please Don't Make Me (Do Something Bad to You)/Blue Monday	1981	—	2.00	4.00
❑ 2074	Separate Ways/Chained to Your Love	1981	—	2.00	4.00
❑ 2076	Bump and Grind/Somethin' Goin' On	1981	—	2.00	4.00
❑ 2079	Cheating in the Next Room/Right Arm for Your Love	1982	—	2.00	4.00
❑ 2082	When It Rains It Pours/When Can We Do This Again	1982	—	2.00	4.00
❑ 2085	What Am I Gonna Tell Her/Get You Some Business	1982	—	2.00	4.00
❑ 2090	Open House at My House/Who You Been Givin' It To	1983	—	2.00	4.00
❑ 2094	Get a Little, Give a Little/Blind Side	1983	—	2.00	4.00
❑ 2097	Steal Away/Three Into Two Won't Go	1984	—	2.00	4.00
❑ 2103	Someone Else Is Steppin' In/Shade Tree Mechanic	1984	—	2.00	4.00
❑ 2109	I'm Gonna Stop You from Givin' Me the Blues/Personally	1984	—	2.00	4.00
❑ 2141	Down Home Blues/Please Don't Let Our Good Thing End	1988	—	2.00	4.00
MANKIND					
❑ 12003	Faithful and True/I Think I'd Do It	1971	2.00	4.00	8.00
❑ 12007	The Chokin' Kind/Hold Back	1971	2.00	4.00	8.00
❑ 12012	Second Chance/It Ain't No Use	1972	—	3.50	7.00
❑ 12015	It Ain't No Use/Ha Ha	1972	—	3.50	7.00
❑ 12017	The Chokin' Kind/A Man Needs a Woman	197?	—	3.50	7.00
M.H.					
❑ 200	You Were Wrong/(B-side unknown)	1964	2.50	5.00	10.00
UNITED ARTISTS					
❑ XW225	Ain't Nothing You Can Do/Love in the Street	1973	—	3.00	6.00
❑ XW307	I Don't Need Half a Love/Friendship Only Goes So Far	1973	—	3.00	6.00
❑ XW365	Let Them Talk/Red Rooster	1973	—	3.00	6.00
❑ XW412	Am I Groovin' You/Bad Mouth and Gossip	1974	—	3.00	6.00
❑ XW536	I Keep On Lovin' You/Whatever's Thrilling You Is Killing Me	1974	—	3.00	6.00
❑ XW631	I Created a Monster/Steppin' in the Shoes of a Fool	1975	—	3.00	6.00
❑ 50977	Your Love Makes Me Feel Good/I've Got to Get You Back	1972	—	3.50	7.00
Albums					
COLUMBIA					
❑ JC 35030	Let's Make a Deal	1978	3.00	6.00	12.00
❑ JC 36125	The Mark of Z.Z.	1979	3.00	6.00	12.00
KENT					
❑ KST-528	A Whole Lot of Soul	1969	3.75	7.50	15.00
❑ KST-560	Dues Paid in Full	1971	3.75	7.50	15.00
MALACO					
❑ 7411	The Rhyhtm & The Blues	1983	2.50	5.00	10.00
❑ 7415	I'm a Blues Man	1984	2.50	5.00	10.00
MANKIND					
❑ 201	The Brand New Z.Z. Hill	1971	3.75	7.50	15.00
UNITED ARTISTS					
❑ UA-LA417-G	Keep On Lovin' You	1975	3.00	6.00	12.00
❑ UAS 5589	The Best Thing That's Ever Happened to Me	1972	3.00	6.00	12.00

HINTON, JOE
45s

Number	Title (A Side/B Side)	Yr	VG	VG+	NM
ARVEE					
❑ 5028	My Love Is Real/I Won't Be Your Fool	1961	3.00	6.00	12.00
—Arvee titles as "Little Joe Hinton"					

Louisiana bluesman Slim Harpo had his first R&B hit in 1961 with "Rainin' in My Heart." His label, Excello, followed that with his first LP, which is hard to find.

Dale Hawkins is known for the hit "Susie-Q," which made the top 10 on the R&B charts – a feat it didn't come close to accomplishing on the pop charts. This is the rare album that came out in that song's wake.

Screamin' Jay Hawkins had his first album release in 1958, two years after his "I Put a Spell on You" failed to make either the pop or R&B charts nationally.

Leon Haywood, who had 21 R&B hits in his career, didn't become a regular presence on the charts until the mid-1970s. Before that, he recorded for several different labels, including the obscure Fat Fish label.

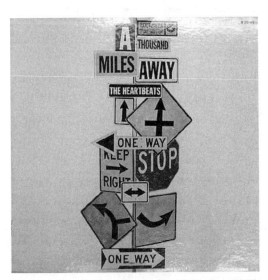

The Heartbeats had their major hit, "A Thousand Miles Away," in 1956. This album wasn't compiled and released until 1960. As a result, the LP didn't sell.

Before he became one-third of the Holland-Dozier-Holland songwriting team, Eddie Holland was a solo singer for Motown. His one big hit, "Jamie," is included on this scarce album.

Number	Title (A Side/B Side)	Yr	VG	VG+	NM
❑ 5029	Your Kind of Love/Let's Start a Romance	1961	3.00	6.00	12.00
BACK BEAT					
❑ 519	I Know/Ladder of Prayer	1958	3.75	7.50	15.00
❑ 526	Pretty Little Mama/Will You	1959	3.75	7.50	15.00
❑ 526 [PS]	Pretty Little Mama/Will You	1959	7.50	15.00	30.00
❑ 532	If You Love Me/A Thousand Cups of Happiness	1960	3.75	7.50	15.00
❑ 535	The Girls in My Life/Come On Baby	1961	3.75	7.50	15.00
❑ 537	You Know It Ain't Right/Lovre Sick Blues	1963	3.00	6.00	12.00
❑ 539	Better to Give Than Receive/There Is No In Between	1963	3.00	6.00	12.00
❑ 540	There Oughta Be a Law/You're My Girl	1964	3.00	6.00	12.00
❑ 541	Funny/You Gotta Have Love	1964	3.75	7.50	15.00
❑ 545	I Want a Little Girl/True Love	1965	3.00	6.00	12.00
❑ 547	Darling Come and Talk to Me/Everything	1965	3.00	6.00	12.00
❑ 550	Pledging My Love/Just a Kid Named Joe	1965	3.00	6.00	12.00
❑ 565	I'm Waiting/How Long Can I Last	1966	2.50	5.00	10.00
❑ 574	If I Had Only Known/Lots of Love	1966	2.50	5.00	10.00
❑ 581	Close to MyHeart/You've Been Good to Me	1967	2.50	5.00	10.00
❑ 589	I'm Satisfied/Be Ever Wonderful	1968	2.50	5.00	10.00
❑ 594	Got You on My Mind/Please	1968	2.50	5.00	10.00
SOUL					
❑ 35080	Let's Save the Children/You Are Blue	1971	6.25	12.50	25.00
Albums					
BACK BEAT					
❑ B-60 [M]	Funny (How Time Slips Away)	1965	12.50	25.00	50.00
❑ BS-60 [S]	Funny (How Time Slips Away)	1965	17.50	35.00	70.00
DUKE					
❑ DLPS-91	Duke-Peacock Remembers Joe Hinton	1969	5.00	10.00	20.00

HOGG, SMOKEY
45s

Number	Title (A Side/B Side)	Yr	VG	VG+	NM
COMBO					
❑ 11	Where Have You Been/Believe I'll Change My Towns	1952	50.00	100.00	200.00
—Also had releases on Combo 4 and 9, but these are unknown on 45					
EBB					
❑ 127	Good Morning Baby/Sure 'Nuff	1958	6.25	12.50	25.00
FEDERAL					
❑ 12109	Keep a-Walkin'/Do It No More	1953	25.00	50.00	100.00
❑ 12117	Your Little Wagon/Penny Pinching Mama	1953	25.00	50.00	100.00
❑ 12127	Gone, Gone, Gone/I Ain't Got Over It Yet	1953	25.00	50.00	100.00
IMPERIAL					
❑ 5269	When I've Been Drinkin'/Tear Me Down	1954	25.00	50.00	100.00
❑ 5290	My Baby's Gone/Train Whistle	1954	25.00	50.00	100.00
METEOR					
❑ 5021	I Declare/Dark Clouds	1955	25.00	50.00	100.00
SPECIALTY					
❑ 753	I Want My Baby for Christmas/I Want My Baby for Christmas	197?	2.50	5.00	10.00
—B-side by Jimmy Liggins					
Albums					
CROWN					
❑ CLP-5226 [M]	Smokey Hogg Sings the Blues	1962	12.50	25.00	50.00
TIME					
❑ 6 [M]	Smokey Hogg	1962	20.00	40.00	80.00
UNITED					
❑ US-7745	Smokey Hogg	1970	3.00	6.00	12.00

HOLIDAYS, THE (1)
Detroit-based R&B group.
45s

Number	Title (A Side/B Side)	Yr	VG	VG+	NM
GOLDEN WORLD					
❑ 36	Makin' Up Time/I'll Love You Forever	1966	6.25	12.50	25.00
❑ 47	No Greater Love/Watch Out Girl	1966	6.25	12.50	25.00
GROOVE CITY					
❑ 206	Easy Living/I've Lost You	196?	25.00	50.00	100.00
—As "The New Holidays"					
REVILOT					
❑ 205	Love's Creeping Up on Me/Never Alone	1967	7.50	15.00	30.00
❑ 210	I Know She Cares/I Keep Holding On	1967	7.50	15.00	30.00
❑ 226	I'll Keep Coming Back/All That Is Required of You	1968	6.25	12.50	25.00

HOLLAND, BRIAN
45s

Number	Title (A Side/B Side)	Yr	VG	VG+	NM
INVICTUS					
❑ 1265	I'm So Glad (Part 1)/I'm So Glad (Part 2)	1974	—	2.50	5.00
❑ 1272	Super Woman/Let's Get Together	1974	—	2.50	5.00
KUDO					
❑ 667	(Where's the Joy?) In Nature Boy/Shock	1958	150.00	300.00	600.00
—First name as "Briant"					

HOLLAND, EDDIE
Also see HOLLAND-DOZIER.
45s

Number	Title (A Side/B Side)	Yr	VG	VG+	NM
MERCURY					
❑ 71290	You/Little Miss Ruby	1958	25.00	50.00	100.00
MOTOWN					
❑ 1021	Jamie/Take a Chance on Me	1961	6.25	12.50	25.00
❑ 1026	You Deserve What You Got/Last Night I Had a Vision	1962	6.25	12.50	25.00
❑ 1030	If Cleopatra Took a Chance/What About Me	1962	6.25	12.50	25.00
❑ 1030 [PS]	If Cleopatra Took a Chance/What About Me	1962	25.00	50.00	100.00
❑ 1031	If It's Love (It's All Right)/It's Not Too Late	1962	6.25	12.50	25.00
❑ 1036	Darling I Hum Our Song/Just a Few Memories	1963	6.25	12.50	25.00
❑ 1043	Brenda/Baby Shake	1963	6.25	12.50	25.00
❑ 1049	I'm On the Outside Looking In/I Couldn't Cry If I Wanted To	1963	37.50	75.00	150.00
❑ 1052	Leaving Here/Brenda	1964	3.75	7.50	15.00
❑ 1058	Just Ain't Enough Love/Last Night I Had a Vision	1964	3.75	7.50	15.00
❑ 1063	Candy to Me/If You Don't Want My Love	1964	3.75	7.50	15.00
TAMLA					
❑ 102	Merry-Go-Round/It Moves Me	1959	62.50	125.00	250.00
UNITED ARTISTS					
❑ 172	Merry-Go-Round/It Moves Me	1959	7.50	15.00	30.00
❑ 191	Because I Love Her/Everybody's Going	1959	7.50	15.00	30.00
❑ 207	Magic Mirror/Will You Love Me	1960	7.50	15.00	30.00
❑ 280	The Last Laugh/Why Do You Want to Let Me Go	1960	7.50	15.00	30.00
Albums					
MOTOWN					
❑ 604 [M]	Eddie Holland	1963	100.00	200.00	400.00

HOLLAND-DOZIER
Also see LAMONT DOZIER; EDDIE HOLLAND.
45s

Number	Title (A Side/B Side)	Yr	VG	VG+	NM
INVICTUS					
❑ 1253	Slipping Away/Can't Get Enough	1973	—	2.50	5.00
❑ 1254	If You Don't Wanta Be in My Life/New Breed Kinda Woman	1973	—	2.50	5.00
❑ 1258	You Took Me from a World Outside/I'm Gonna Hijack Ya, Kidnap Ya, Take What I Want	1973	—	2.50	5.00
❑ 9110	Don't Leave Me (Part 1)/Don't Leave Me (Part 2)	1972	—	2.50	5.00
❑ 9125	Why Can't We Be Lovers/Don't Leave Me	1972	—	2.50	5.00
❑ 9133	Don't Leave Me Starvin' for Your Love (Part 1)/Don't Leave Me Starvin' for Your Love (Part 2)	1972	—	2.50	5.00
MOTOWN					
❑ 1045	What Goes Up Must Come Down/Come On Home	1963	6.25	12.50	25.00

HOLLOWAY, BRENDA
45s

Number	Title (A Side/B Side)	Yr	VG	VG+	NM
DONNA					
❑ 1358	Echo/Hey Fool	1962	10.00	20.00	40.00
❑ 1366	Game of Love/Echo-Echo-Echo	1962	12.50	25.00	50.00
❑ 1370	I'll Give My Life/More Echo	1962	12.50	25.00	50.00
TAMLA					
❑ 54094	Every Little Bit Hurts/Land of 1,000 Boys	1964	3.00	6.00	12.00
❑ 54099	I'll Always Love You/Sad Song	1964	3.75	7.50	15.00
❑ 54111	When I'm Gone/I've Been Good to You	1965	3.75	7.50	15.00
❑ 54111 [PS]	When I'm Gone/I've Been Good to You	1965	25.00	50.00	100.00
❑ 54115	Operator/I'll Be Available	1965	3.75	7.50	15.00
❑ 54121	You Can Cry on My Shoulder/How Many Times Did You Mean It	1965	5.00	10.00	20.00
❑ 54125	Sad Song/Together 'Til the End of Time	1965	5.00	10.00	20.00
❑ 54137	Hurt a Little Every Day/Where Were You	1966	7.50	15.00	30.00
❑ 54144	'Til Johnny Comes/Where Were You	1967	50.00	100.00	200.00
❑ 54148	Just Look What You've Done/Starting the Hurt All Over Again	1967	6.25	12.50	25.00
❑ 54155	You've Made Me So Very Happy/I've Got to Find It	1967	5.00	10.00	20.00
❑ 206312 [DJ]	Play It Cool, Stay in School	1966	150.00	300.00	600.00
—Promo for Women's Ad Club of Detroit					
Albums					
MOTOWN					
❑ 5242 ML	Every Little Bit Hurts	1982	3.00	6.00	12.00
TAMLA					
❑ T 257 [M]	Every Little Bit Hurts	1964	50.00	100.00	200.00
❑ TS 257 [R]	Every Little Bit Hurts	1964	37.50	75.00	150.00

HOLLOWAY, LOLEATTA
12-Inch Singles

Number	Title (A Side/B Side)	Yr	VG	VG+	NM
GOLD MIND					
❑ 402	Catch Me on the Rebound (10:51)/(7:22)	1978	3.75	7.50	15.00
❑ 4006	Hit and Run/It's Getting Stronger	1977	5.00	10.00	20.00
SELECT					
❑ 5585	Strong Enough (5 versions)	1991	2.00	4.00	8.00
STREETWISE					
❑ 2230	Crash Goes Love/Sweet Thing	1984	2.50	5.00	10.00
45s					
AWARE					
❑ 033	Our Love/Mother of Shame	1973	—	3.00	6.00
❑ 039	H-E-L-P Me My Love/(B-side unknown)	1974	—	3.00	6.00
❑ 047	Cry to Me/So Can I	1974	—	3.00	6.00
❑ 050	The Show Must Go On/I Know Where You're Coming From	1975	—	3.00	6.00
❑ 054	Casanova/Only a Fool	1975	—	3.00	6.00
GALAXY					
❑ 780	Rainbow '71/Bring It On Up	1971	2.00	4.00	8.00
GOLD MIND					
❑ 4000	Dreamin'/Worn Out Broken Heart	1976	—	3.00	6.00
❑ 4001	Hit and Run/Is It Just a Man's Way	1977	—	3.00	6.00
❑ 4007	It's Getting Stronger/How Heartaches Are Made	1977	—	3.00	6.00
❑ 4012	Only You/Good Good Feeling	1978	—	3.00	6.00
—A-side with Bunny Sigler					
❑ 4016	Catch Me on the Rebound/Mama Don't, Papa Won't	1978	—	3.00	6.00
❑ 4021	That's What You Said/There'll Come a Time	1979	—	3.00	6.00
❑ 4024	Love Sensation/Short End of the Stick	1980	2.50	5.00	10.00

Number	Title (A Side/B Side)	Yr	VG	VG+	NM
❏ 4025	I've Been Loving You Too Long/Two Became a Crowd	1980	—	3.00	6.00
SALSOUL					
❏ 2045	Run Away/Run Away (Part 2)	1977	—	3.00	6.00
—With the Salsoul Orchestra					
❏ 7034	Seconds/Columbia: The Space Shuttle	1981	—	3.00	6.00
—With the Salsoul Orchestra					
STREETWISE					
❏ 1130	Crash Goes Love/Sweet Thing	1984	—	3.00	6.00
Albums					
GOLD MIND					
❏ 7500	Loleatta	1977	5.00	10.00	20.00
❏ A-9501	Queen of the Night	1978	5.00	10.00	20.00
❏ GA-9506	Love Sensation	1979	5.00	10.00	20.00

HOLLOWAY, PATRICE
45s

Number	Title (A Side/B Side)	Yr	VG	VG+	NM
CAPITOL					
❏ 5680	Stolen Hours/Lucky My Boy	1966	20.00	40.00	80.00
❏ 5778	Love and Desire/Ecstasy	1967	15.00	30.00	60.00
❏ 5985	Stay with Your Own Kind/That's All You Got to Do	1967	12.50	25.00	50.00
TASTE					
❏ 125	Do the Del Viking (Pt. 1)/Do the Del Viking (Pt. 2)	1963	7.50	15.00	30.00

HOLLYWOOD FLAMES, THE
Also see BOBBY DAY.
45s

Number	Title (A Side/B Side)	Yr	VG	VG+	NM
ATCO					
❏ 6155	Every Day, Every Way/If I Thought I Needed You	1959	3.75	7.50	15.00
❏ 6164	Ball and Chain/I Found a Boy	1960	3.75	7.50	15.00
❏ 6171	Devil or Angel/Do You Ever Think of Me	1960	3.75	7.50	15.00
❏ 6180	Money Honey/My Heart's On Fire	1960	3.75	7.50	15.00
CHESS					
❏ 1787	Gee/Yes They Do	1961	3.00	6.00	12.00
DECCA					
❏ 29285	Peggy/Ooh La La	1954	18.75	37.50	75.00
❏ 48331	Let's Talk It Over/I Know	1955	18.75	37.50	75.00
EBB					
❏ 119	Buzz-Buzz-Buzz/Crazy	1957	7.50	15.00	30.00
❏ 131	Give Me Back My Heart/A Little Bird	1958	6.25	12.50	25.00
❏ 144	Frankenstein's Den/Strollin' on the Beach	1958	6.25	12.50	25.00
❏ 146	Chains of Love/Let's Talk It Over	1958	6.25	12.50	25.00
❏ 149	A Star Fell/I'll Get By	1958	6.25	12.50	25.00
❏ 153	I'll Be Seeing You/Just for You	1959	7.50	15.00	30.00
❏ 158	So Good/There Is Something on Your Mind	1959	6.25	12.50	25.00
❏ 162	Now That You're Gone/Hawaiian Dream	1959	6.25	12.50	25.00
❏ 163	Much Too Much/In the Dark	1959	6.25	12.50	25.00
LUCKY					
❏ 001	One Night with a Fool/Ride, Helen, Ride	1954	150.00	300.00	600.00
❏ 006	Peggy/Ooh-La-La	1954	150.00	300.00	600.00
❏ 009	Let's Talk It Over/I Know	1954	100.00	200.00	400.00
MONA-LEE					
❏ 135	Buzz-Buzz-Buzz/Crazy	1958	6.25	12.50	25.00
MONEY					
❏ 202	Fare Thee Well/I'm Leaving	1954	100.00	200.00	400.00
SWING TIME					
❏ 345	Let's Talk It Over/I Know	1953	125.00	250.00	500.00
❏ 346	Go and Get Some More/Another Soldier Gone	1953	125.00	250.00	500.00
—B-side by the Question Marks					
SYMBOL					
❏ 211	Dance Senorita/Annie Don't Love Me Anymore	1965	3.00	6.00	12.00
❏ 215	I'm Coming Home/I'm Gonna Stand By You	1966	3.00	6.00	12.00
VEE JAY					
❏ 515	Drop Me a Line/Letter to My Love	1963	3.75	7.50	15.00

HOLMAN, EDDIE
45s

Number	Title (A Side/B Side)	Yr	VG	VG+	NM
ABC					
❏ 11149	I Love You/I Surrender	1968	2.50	5.00	10.00
❏ 11240	Hey There Lonely Girl/It's All in the Game	1969	—	3.00	6.00
❏ 11261	Don't Stop Now/Since I Don't Have You	1970	—	3.00	6.00
❏ 11265	I'll Be There/Cause You're Mine Little Girl	1970	—	3.00	6.00
❏ 11276	Cathy Called/I Need Somebody	1970	—	3.00	6.00
❏ 11292	Love Story/Four Walls	1971	—	3.00	6.00
ASCOT					
❏ 2142	Go Get Your Own/Laughing at Me	1963	3.75	7.50	15.00
BELL					
❏ 712	I'm Not Gonna Give Up/I'll Cry 1,000 Tears	1968	5.00	10.00	20.00
GSF					
❏ 6873	My Mind Keeps Telling Me (That I Really Love You, Girl)/Stranded in a Dream	1972	—	3.00	6.00
❏ 6885	Young Girl/I'll Call You Joy	1972	—	3.00	6.00
PARKWAY					
❏ 106	Am I a Loser/You Know That I Will	1966	5.00	10.00	20.00
❏ 133	Somewhere Waits a Lonely Girl/Stay Mine for Heaven's Sake	1967	5.00	10.00	20.00
❏ 157	Why Do Fools Fall in Love/Never Let Me Go	1967	5.00	10.00	20.00
❏ 960	This Can't Be True/A Free Country	1965	5.00	10.00	20.00
❏ 981	Don't Stop Now/Eddie's My Name	1966	5.00	10.00	20.00
❏ 994	Return to Me/Stay Mine for Heaven's Sake	1966	5.00	10.00	20.00
SALSOUL					
❏ 2026	This Will Be a Night to Remember/Time Will Tell	1977	—	2.50	5.00

Number	Title (A Side/B Side)	Yr	VG	VG+	NM
❏ 2043	You Make My Life Complete/Somehow You Make Me Feel	1977	—	2.50	5.00
SILVER BLUE					
❏ 807	You're My Lady (Right Or Wrong)/(Instrumental)	1974	—	2.50	5.00
❏ 815	Just Say I Love Her/Darling Take Me Back	1974	—	2.50	5.00
UNITED ARTISTS					
❏ 609	Go Get Your Own/Laughing at Me	1963	—	—	—
—Unreleased					
Albums					
ABC					
❏ S-701	I Love You	1970	7.50	15.00	30.00
SALSOUL					
❏ 5511	A Night to Remember	1977	2.50	5.00	10.00

HOLMES, CECIL'S, SOULFUL SOUNDS
45s

Number	Title (A Side/B Side)	Yr	VG	VG+	NM
BUDDAH					
❏ 354	Superfly/Soulful Sounds	1973	—	2.50	5.00
❏ 391	Kung Fu/Soulful Love	1973	—	2.50	5.00
Albums					
BUDDAH					
❏ BDS-5129	The Black Motion Picture Experience	1973	3.00	6.00	12.00
❏ BDS-5139	Music for Soulful Lovers	1973	3.00	6.00	12.00

HONEY CONE, THE
45s

Number	Title (A Side/B Side)	Yr	VG	VG+	NM
HOT WAX					
❏ 6901	While You're Out Looking for Sugar?/The Feeling's Gone	1969	—	3.00	6.00
❏ 6903	Girls It Ain't Easy/The Feeling's Gone	1969	—	3.00	6.00
❏ 7001	Take Me With You/Take My Love	1970	—	3.00	6.00
❏ 7005	When Will It End/Take Me With You	1970	—	3.00	6.00
❏ 7011	Want Ads/We Belong Together	1970	—	3.00	6.00
—Mostly white label					
❏ 7011	Want Ads/We Belong Together	1970	—	2.50	5.00
—Mostly orange label					
❏ 7106	Stick-Up/V.I.P.	1971	—	3.00	6.00
❏ 7110	One Monkey Don't Stop No Show Part I/One Monkey Don't Stop No Show Part II	1971	—	3.00	6.00
❏ 7113	The Day I Found Myself/When Will It End	1971	—	3.00	6.00
❏ 7205	Sittin' on a Time Bomb (Waitin' for the Hurt to Come)/It's Better to Have Loved and Lost	1972	—	3.00	6.00
❏ 7208	Innocent Till Proven Guilty/Don't Send Me an Invitation	1972	—	3.00	6.00
❏ 7212	Ace in the Hole/Ooo Baby Baby	1972	—	3.00	6.00
❏ 7301	If I Can't Fly/Woman Can't Live by Bread Alone	1973	—	3.00	6.00
❏ 9255	The Truth Will Come Out/Somebody Is Always Messing Up a Good Thing	1974	—	3.00	6.00
Albums					
HOT WAX					
❏ HA-701	Take Me With You	1970	3.00	6.00	12.00
❏ HA-706	Sweet Replies	1971	3.00	6.00	12.00
❏ HA-707	Soulful Tapestry	1971	3.00	6.00	12.00
❏ HA-713	Love, Peace & Soul	1972	3.00	6.00	12.00

HONEYCONES, THE
45s

Number	Title (A Side/B Side)	Yr	VG	VG+	NM
EMBER					
❏ 1033	Betty Moretti/Cool It Baby	1958	5.00	10.00	20.00
❏ 1036	Op/Vision of You	1958	6.25	12.50	25.00
❏ 1042	Gee Whiz/Rockin' in the Knees	1958	5.00	10.00	20.00
❏ 1049	Tell Me Baby/Your Face	1959	5.00	10.00	20.00

HOOKER, EARL
45s

Number	Title (A Side/B Side)	Yr	VG	VG+	NM
AGE					
❏ 29106	Blue Guitar/Swear to Tell the Truth	1962	10.00	20.00	40.00
❏ 29111	These Cotton Picking Blues/How Long Can This Go On	1962	10.00	20.00	40.00
❏ 29114	That Man/Win the Dance	1963	10.00	20.00	40.00
ARGO					
❏ 5265	Guitar Rhumba/Frog Hop	1957	10.00	20.00	40.00
ARHOOLIE					
❏ 521	Wah Wah Blues/(B-side unknown)	1970	5.00	10.00	20.00
BEA & BABY					
❏ 106	Dynamite/Trying to Make a Living	1960	6.25	12.50	25.00
BLUE THUMB					
❏ 103	Boogie, Don't Blot/Funky Blues	1969	3.75	7.50	15.00
CHECKER					
❏ 1025	Tanya/Put Your Shoes On, Willie	1962	6.25	12.50	25.00
CHIEF					
❏ 7021	Messing with the Kid/Universal Rock	1960	6.25	12.50	25.00
—With Junior Wells					
❏ 7031	Rockin' the Kid/Rockin' Wild	1961	6.25	12.50	25.00
❏ 7039	Messing with the Kid/(B-side unknown)	1961	6.25	12.50	25.00
❏ 7106	Blues in D Natural/(B-side unknown)	1960	6.25	12.50	25.00
CJ					
❏ 613	Do the Chicken/Yea Yea	1961	7.50	15.00	30.00
❏ 643	Wild Moments/Chicken	1965	3.75	7.50	15.00
CUCA					
❏ 1194	Bertha/Walkin' the Floor	1964	12.50	25.00	50.00
❏ 1445	Dust My Broom/You Took All My Love	1969	5.00	10.00	20.00

H

Number	Title (A Side/B Side)	Yr	VG	VG+	NM
KING					
❏ 45-4600	Race Track/Blue Guitar Blues	1953	75.00	150.00	300.00
MEL					
❏ 1005	Messing with the Kid/(B-side unknown)	1964	6.25	12.50	25.00
MEL-LON					
❏ 1000	Want You to Rock/(B-side unknown)	1964	6.25	12.50	25.00
❏ 1001	The Leading Brand/(B-side unknown)	1964	6.25	12.50	25.00
ROCKIN'					
❏ 513	Sweet Angel/On the Hook	1952	100.00	200.00	400.00
78s					
KING					
❏ 4600	Race Track/Blue Guitar Blues	1953	25.00	50.00	100.00
ROCKIN'					
❏ 513	Sweet Angel/On the Hook	1952	30.00	60.00	120.00
Albums					
ARHOOLIE					
❏ LP 1044	2 Bugs and a Roach	1968	6.25	12.50	25.00
❏ LP 1051	Hooker and Steve	1969	6.25	12.50	25.00
❏ LP 1066	His First and Last Recordings	1970	6.25	12.50	25.00
BLUE THUMB					
❏ BTS 12	Sweet Black Angel	1969	7.50	15.00	30.00
BLUES ON BLUES					
❏ 10002	The Last of the Great Earl Hooker	197?	5.00	10.00	20.00
BLUESWAY					
❏ BLS-6032	Don't Have to Worry	1969	6.25	12.50	25.00
❏ BLS-6038	If You Miss Him	1970	6.25	12.50	25.00
❏ BLS-6072	Do You Remember the Great Earl Hooker	1973	3.75	7.50	15.00
CUCA					
❏ 3400 [M]	The Genius of Earl Hooker	1965	62.50	125.00	250.00

HOOKER, JOHN LEE
45s

Number	Title (A Side/B Side)	Yr	VG	VG+	NM
ABC					
❏ 11298	Doin' the Shout/Kick Hit 4 Hit Kix U	1971	—	3.00	6.00
❏ 11320	Never Get Out of These Blues Alive/Boogie with the Hook	1972	—	3.00	6.00
BATTLE					
❏ 45901	No More Doggin'/I Need Some Money	1962	2.50	5.00	10.00
BLUESWAY					
❏ 61010	Motor City Is Burning/Want Ad Blues	1967	2.00	4.00	8.00
❏ 61014	Mr. Lucky/Cry Before I Go	1968	—	3.00	6.00
❏ 61017	Back Biters and Syndicators/Think Twice Before You Go	1968	—	3.00	6.00
❏ 61023	I Don't Wanna Go to Vietnam/Simply the Truth	1969	—	3.00	6.00
CHANCE					
❏ 1108	Miss Lorraine/Talkin' Boogie	1951	750.00	1500.00	3000.
—As "John Lee Booker"					
❏ 1110	Graveyard Blues/I Love to Boogie	1952	750.00	1500.00	3000.
—As "John Lee Booker"					
❏ 1122	609 Boogie/Road Trouble	1952	500.00	1000.	2000.
—As "John L. Booker"					
CHART					
❏ 609	Going South/Wobbling Baby	1955	12.50	25.00	50.00
❏ 614	Blue Monday/My Baby Put Me Down	1955	12.50	25.00	50.00
CHESS					
❏ 1505	High Priced Woman/Union Station Blues	1952	300.00	600.00	1200.
❏ 1513	Sugar Mama/Walkin' the Boogie	1952	250.00	500.00	1000.
❏ 1562	It's My Own Fault/Women and Money	1954	62.50	125.00	250.00
❏ 1965	Let's Go Out Tonight/In the Mood	1966	2.50	5.00	10.00
DELUXE					
❏ 6004	Blue Monday/Lovin' Guitar Man	1953	125.00	250.00	500.00
—As "John Lee Booker"					
❏ 6009	I Came to See You Baby/I'm a Boogie Man	1953	200.00	400.00	800.00
—As "Johnny Lee"					
❏ 6032	Stuttering Blues/Pouring Down Rain	1954	100.00	200.00	400.00
—As "John Lee Booker"					
❏ 6046	My Baby Don't Love Me/Real, Real Gone	1954	100.00	200.00	400.00
—As "John Lee Booker"					
ELMOR					
❏ 303	Blues for Christmas/Big Fine Woman	1959	5.00	10.00	20.00
FEDERAL					
❏ 12377	Late Last Night/Don't You Remember Me	1960	3.75	7.50	15.00
FORTUNE					
❏ 846	609 Boogie/Curl My Baby's Hair	1959	5.00	10.00	20.00
❏ 853	Cry Baby/Love You Baby	1960	5.00	10.00	20.00
❏ 855	Crazy About That Walk/We're All God's Chillun	1960	5.00	10.00	20.00
GALAXY					
❏ 716	I Lost My Job/You Gotta Shake It Up and Go	1963	2.50	5.00	10.00
HI-Q					
❏ 5018X	609 Blues/Blues for Christmas	1961	5.00	10.00	20.00
❏ 5018	Blues for Christmas/Big Fine Woman	1960	5.00	10.00	20.00
IMPULSE					
❏ 242	Honey/Bottle Up and Go	1966	2.50	5.00	10.00
JEWEL					
❏ 824	I Feel Good (Part 1)/I Feel Good (Part 2)	1971	—	2.50	5.00
❏ 852	Stand By (Part 1)/Stand By (Part 2)	1977	—	2.00	4.00
JVB					
❏ 30	Boogie Rambler/No More Doggin'	1953	375.00	750.00	1500.
KENT					
❏ 332	Boogie Chillen/I'm in the Mood	1960	5.00	10.00	20.00

Number	Title (A Side/B Side)	Yr	VG	VG+	NM
KING					
❏ 45-4504	Moaning Blues/Stomp Boogie	1952	250.00	500.00	1000.
—As "John Lee Cooker"					
❏ 6298	Don't Go Baby/Moanin' and Stompin' Blues	1970	—	3.00	6.00
LAUREN					
❏ 361	Ballad to Abraham Lincoln (He Got Assassinated)/Mojo Hand (Louisiana Voodoo)	1961	5.00	10.00	20.00
❏ 362	I Lost My Job/You Gotta Shake It Up and Go	1961	5.00	10.00	20.00
MODERN					
❏ 45x835	How Can You Do It/I'm in the Mood	1951	100.00	200.00	400.00
❏ 45x847	Anybody Seen My Baby? (Johnny Says Come Back)/Turn Over a New Leaf	1951	75.00	150.00	300.00
❏ 45x852	Ground Hog Blues/Louise	1951	30.00	60.00	120.00
❏ 45x862	Cold Chills All Over Me/Rock Me, Mama	1952	20.00	40.00	80.00
❏ 45x876	It Hurts Me So/I Got Eyes for You	1952	20.00	40.00	80.00
—With Little Eddie Kirkland					
❏ 45x886	Key to the Highway/Bluebird Blues	1952	20.00	40.00	80.00
❏ 45x893	New Boogie Chillen/I Tried	1952	20.00	40.00	80.00
❏ 45x897	It's Been a Long Time Baby/Rock House Boogie	1952	20.00	40.00	80.00
❏ 45x901	Ride Till I Die/It's Stormin' and Rainin'	1953	15.00	30.00	60.00
❏ 45x908	Please Take Me Back/Love Money Can't Buy	1953	15.00	30.00	60.00
❏ 45x916	Too Much Boogie/Need Somebody	1953	15.00	30.00	60.00
❏ 45x923	Gotta Boogie/Down Child	1953	15.00	30.00	60.00
❏ 45x931	Jump Me/I Wonder Little Darling	1954	15.00	30.00	60.00
❏ 45x935	I Tried Hard/Let's Talk It Over	1954	12.50	25.00	50.00
❏ 45x942	Cool Little Car/Bad Boy	1954	12.50	25.00	50.00
❏ 45x948	Half a Stranger/Shake, Holler and Run	1954	12.50	25.00	50.00
❏ 45x958	Taxi Driver/You Receive Me	1955	12.50	25.00	50.00
❏ 45x966	Hug and Squeeze/The Syndicator	1955	12.50	25.00	50.00
❏ 45x978	Looking for a Woman/I'm Ready	1955	15.00	30.00	60.00
POINTBLANK					
❏ S7-19518	Dimples/Don't Look Back	1997	—	2.00	4.00
❏ 38664	Burnin' Hell/Boogie at Russian Hill	1999	—	—	3.00
RIVERSIDE					
❏ 438	I Need Some Money/No More Diggin'	1960	6.25	12.50	25.00
ROCKIN'					
❏ 524	Blue Monday/Lovin' Guitar Man	1953	250.00	500.00	1000.
—As "John Lee Booker"					
❏ 525	Stuttering Blues/Pouring Down Rain	1953	250.00	500.00	1000.
—As "John Lee Booker"					
SPECIALTY					
❏ 528	Everybody's Blues/I'm Mad	1954	10.00	20.00	40.00
STAX					
❏ 0053	Slow and Easy/Grinder Man	1969	—	3.00	6.00
VEE JAY					
❏ 164	Mambo Chillen/Time Is Marching	1955	7.50	15.00	30.00
❏ 188	Every Night/Trouble Blues	1956	7.50	15.00	30.00
❏ 205	Dimples/Baby Lee	1956	7.50	15.00	30.00
❏ 233	The Road Is So Rough/I'm So Worried Baby	1957	6.25	12.50	25.00
❏ 245	I'm So Excited/I See You When You're Weak	1957	6.25	12.50	25.00
❏ 255	Little Wheel/Rosie Mae	1957	6.25	12.50	25.00
❏ 265	You Can Lead Me, Baby/Unfriendly Baby	1958	6.25	12.50	25.00
❏ 293	I Love You Honey/You've Taken My Woman	1958	6.25	12.50	25.00
❏ 308	Maudie/I'm In the Mood	1959	6.25	12.50	25.00
❏ 319	Tennessee Blues/Boogie Chillun	1959	6.25	12.50	25.00
❏ 331	Hobo Blues/Crawlin' King Snake	1959	6.25	12.50	25.00
❏ 349	No Shoes/Solid Sender	1960	6.25	12.50	25.00
❏ 366	Dusty Road/Tupelo	1960	6.25	12.50	25.00
❏ 379	I'm Mad Again/I'm Going Upstairs	1961	6.25	12.50	25.00
❏ 397	Want Ad Blues/Take Me As I Am	1961	6.25	12.50	25.00
❏ 438	Boom Boom/Drug Store Woman	1962	6.25	12.50	25.00
❏ 453	She's Mine/A New Leaf	1962	6.25	12.50	25.00
❏ 493	Take a Look at Yourself/I Love Her	1963	12.50	25.00	50.00
❏ 493	Take a Look at Yourself/Frisco Blues	1963	5.00	10.00	20.00
❏ 538	I'm Leaving/Birmingham Blues	1963	3.75	7.50	15.00
❏ 575	Send Me Your Pillow/Don't Look Back	1964	3.75	7.50	15.00
❏ 670	Big Legs, Tight Skirt/Your Baby Ain't Sweet Like Mine	1965	3.00	6.00	12.00
❏ 708	It Serves Me Right/Flowers on the Hour	1966	2.50	5.00	10.00
78s					
ACORN					
❏ 308	Do the Boogie/Morning Blues	1949	25.00	50.00	100.00
—As "The Boogie Man"					
CHANCE					
❏ 1108	Miss Lorraine/Talkin' Boogie	1951	125.00	250.00	500.00
—As "John Lee Booker"					
❏ 1110	Graveyard Blues/I Love to Boogie	1952	125.00	250.00	500.00
—As "John Lee Booker"					
❏ 1122	609 Boogie/Road Trouble	1952	125.00	250.00	500.00
—As "John L. Booker"					
CHART					
❏ 609	Going South/Wobbling Baby	1955	12.50	25.00	50.00
❏ 614	Blue Monday/My Baby Put Me Down	1955	12.50	25.00	50.00
CHESS					
❏ 1462	Mad Man Blues/Boogie Now	1951	50.00	100.00	200.00
—As "John Lee Booker"					
❏ 1467	Ramblin' By Myself/Leave My Wife Alone	1951	37.50	75.00	150.00
❏ 1482	Ground Hog Blues/Louise	1951	37.50	75.00	150.00
❏ 1505	High Priced Woman/Union Station Blues	1952	37.50	75.00	150.00
❏ 1513	Sugar Mama/Walkin' the Boogie	1952	37.50	75.00	150.00
❏ 1562	It's My Own Fault/Women and Money	1954	17.50	35.00	70.00
DANCELAND					
❏ 403	Wayne County Ramblin' Blues/Grievin' Blues	1949	100.00	200.00	400.00
—As "Little Pork Chops"					

Number	Title (A Side/B Side)	Yr	VG	VG+	NM
DELUXE					
❏ 6004	Blue Monday/Lovin' Guitar Man	1953	37.50	75.00	150.00
—As "John Lee Booker"					
❏ 6009	I Came to See You Baby/I'm a Boogie Man	1953	75.00	150.00	300.00
—As "Johnny Lee"					
❏ 6032	Stuttering Blues/Pouring Down Rain	1954	50.00	100.00	200.00
—As "John Lee Booker"					
❏ 6046	My Baby Don't Love Me/Real, Real Gone	1954	50.00	100.00	200.00
—As "John Lee Booker"					
GONE					
❏ 60/61	Mad Man Blues/Boogie Now	1951	1000.	1500.	2000.
—As "John Lee Booker"					
GOTHAM					
❏ 506	Wandering Blues/House Rent Boogie	1950	50.00	100.00	200.00
—As "Johnny Williams"; reissue of Staff 710					
❏ 509	Questionnaire Blues/Real Gone Guy	1952	25.00	50.00	100.00
—As "Johnny Williams"					
❏ 513	Little Boy Blue/My Daddy Was a Jockey	1952	37.50	75.00	150.00
—As "Johnny Williams"					
❏ 515	Mean Old Train/Catfish	1952	25.00	50.00	100.00
—As "John Lee"					
JVB					
❏ 30	Boogie Rambler/No More Doggin'	1953	150.00	300.00	600.00
KING					
❏ 4283	Black Man Blues/Stomp Boogie	1949	37.50	75.00	150.00
—As "Texas Slim"					
❏ 4315	The Numbers/Devil's Jump	1959	37.50	75.00	150.00
—As "Texas Slim"					
❏ 4323	Nightmare Blues/I'm Gonna Kill That Woman	1949	37.50	75.00	150.00
—As "Texas Slim"					
❏ 4329	Heart Trouble Blues/Slim's Stomp	1950	37.50	75.00	150.00
—As "Texas Slim"					
❏ 4334	Wandering Blues/Don't Go Baby	1950	37.50	75.00	150.00
—As "Texas Slim"					
❏ 4366	Don't You Remember Me/Late Last Night	1950	37.50	75.00	150.00
—As "Texas Slim"					
❏ 4377	Moaning Blues/Thinking Blues	1950	50.00	100.00	200.00
—As "Texas Slim"					
❏ 4504	Moaning Blues/Stomp Boogie	1952	30.00	60.00	120.00
—As "John Lee Cooker"					
MODERN					
❏ 20-627	Sally May/Boogie Chillen	1948	75.00	150.00	300.00
❏ 20-663	Hobo Blues/Hoogie Boogie	1949	37.50	75.00	150.00
❏ 20-688	Whistlin' and Moanin' Blues/Weepin' Willow Boogie	1949	30.00	60.00	120.00
❏ 20-714	Crawling King Snake/Drifting from Door to Door	1949	30.00	60.00	120.00
❏ 20-730	Howlin' Wolf/Playin' the Races	1950	25.00	50.00	100.00
❏ 20-746	Wednesday Evening/No Friend Around	1950	25.00	50.00	100.00
❏ 20-767	Give Me Your Phone Number/Roll 'n Roll	1950	25.00	50.00	100.00
❏ 20-790	Let Your Daddy Ride/One More Time	1950	25.00	50.00	100.00
❏ 814	Queen Bee/John L's Rent House Boogie	1951	20.00	40.00	80.00
❏ 829	Women in My Life/Tease Me Baby	1951	20.00	40.00	80.00
❏ 835	How Can You Do It/I'm in the Mood	1951	20.00	40.00	80.00
❏ 847	Anybody Seen My Baby? (Johnny Says Come Back)/Turn Over a New Leaf	1951	20.00	40.00	80.00
❏ 852	Ground Hog Blues/Louise	1951	15.00	30.00	60.00
—Reissue of Chess 1482					
❏ 862	Cold Chills All Over Me/Rock Me, Mama	1952	12.50	25.00	50.00
❏ 876	It Hurts Me So/I Got Eyes for You	1952	12.50	25.00	50.00
—With Little Eddie Kirkland					
❏ 886	Key to the Highway/Bluebird Blues	1952	12.50	25.00	50.00
❏ 893	New Boogie Chillen/I Tried	1952	12.50	25.00	50.00
❏ 897	It's Been a Long Time Baby/Rock House Boogie	1952	12.50	25.00	50.00
❏ 901	Ride Till I Die/It's Stormin' and Rainin'	1953	10.00	20.00	40.00
❏ 908	Please Take Me Back/Love Money Can't Buy	1953	10.00	20.00	40.00
❏ 916	Too Much Boogie/Need Somebody	1953	10.00	20.00	40.00
❏ 923	Gotta Boogie/Down Child	1953	10.00	20.00	40.00
❏ 931	Jump Me/I Wonder Little Darling	1954	10.00	20.00	40.00
❏ 935	I Tried Hard/Let's Talk It Over	1954	10.00	20.00	40.00
❏ 942	Cool Little Car/Bad Boy	1954	10.00	20.00	40.00
❏ 948	Half a Stranger/Shake, Holler and Run	1954	10.00	20.00	40.00
❏ 958	Taxi Driver/You Receive Me	1955	10.00	20.00	40.00
❏ 966	Hug and Squeeze/The Syndicator	1955	12.50	25.00	50.00
❏ 978	Looking for a Woman/I'm Ready	1955	10.00	20.00	40.00
PRIZE					
❏ 704	Miss Rosie Mae/Highway Blues	1949	150.00	300.00	600.00
—As "Johnny Williams"					
REGAL					
❏ 3295	Boogie Chillen No. 2/Miss Eloise	1950	25.00	50.00	100.00
❏ 3304	Notoriety Woman/Never Satisfied	1950	25.00	50.00	100.00
REGENT					
❏ 1001	Goin' Mad Blues/Helpless Blues	1949	25.00	50.00	100.00
—As "Delta John"					
ROCKIN'					
❏ 524	Blue Monday/Lovin' Guitar Man	1953	62.50	125.00	250.00
—As "John Lee Booker"					
❏ 525	Stuttering Blues/Pouring Down Rain	1953	62.50	125.00	250.00
—As "John Lee Booker"					
SAVOY					
❏ 5558	Low Down Midnite Boogie/Landing Blues	1949	25.00	50.00	100.00
—As "Birmingham Sam and His Magic Guitar"					
SENSATION					
❏ 21	Burnin' Hell/Miss Sadie Mae	1949	25.00	50.00	100.00
❏ 26	Huckle Up Baby/Canal Street Blues	1949	25.00	50.00	100.00
❏ 30	Let Your Daddy Ride/Goin' on Highway 51	1950	25.00	50.00	100.00
❏ 33	My Baby's Got Somethin'/Decoration Day Blues	1950	25.00	50.00	100.00
❏ 34	Boogie Chillen No. 2/Miss Eloise	1950	30.00	60.00	120.00
SPECIALTY					
❏ 528	Everybody's Blues/I'm Mad	1954	7.50	15.00	30.00
STAFF					
❏ 710	Wandering Blues/House Rent Boogie	1950	100.00	200.00	400.00
—As "Johnny Williams"					
❏ 718	Prison Bound/Bumble Bee Blues	1952	100.00	200.00	400.00
—As "Johnny Williams"					
SWING TIME					
❏ 266	Prison Bound/Bumble Bee Blues	1952	37.50	75.00	150.00
—As "Johnny Williams"; reissue of Staff 718					
VEE JAY					
❏ 164	Mambo Chillen/Time Is Marching	1955	7.50	15.00	30.00
❏ 188	Every Night/Trouble Blues	1956	7.50	15.00	30.00
❏ 205	Dimples/Baby Lee	1956	7.50	15.00	30.00
❏ 233	The Road Is So Rough/I'm So Worried Baby	1957	7.50	15.00	30.00
❏ 245	I'm So Excited/I See You When You're Weak	1957	7.50	15.00	30.00
❏ 255	Little Wheel/Rosie Mae	1957	7.50	15.00	30.00
❏ 265	You Can Lead Me, Baby/Unfriendly Baby	1958	10.00	20.00	40.00
❏ 293	I Love You Honey/You've Taken My Woman	1958	12.50	25.00	50.00
Albums					
ABC					
❏ S-720 [(2)]	Endless Boogie	1971	5.00	10.00	20.00
❏ X-736	Never Get Out of These Blues Alive	1972	5.00	10.00	20.00
❏ XQ-736 [Q]	Never Get Out of These Blues Alive	1974	6.25	12.50	25.00
❏ X-761	Live at Soledad Prison	1972	5.00	10.00	20.00
❏ XQ-761 [Q]	Live at Soledad Prison	1974	6.25	12.50	25.00
❏ X-768	Born in Mississippi, Raised Up in Tennessee	1973	5.00	10.00	20.00
❏ XQ-768 [Q]	Born in Mississippi, Raised Up in Tennessee	1974	6.25	12.50	25.00
❏ X-838	Free Beer and Chicken	1974	3.75	7.50	15.00
❏ XQ-838 [Q]	Free Beer and Chicken	1974	6.25	12.50	25.00
ARCHIVE OF FOLK AND JAZZ					
❏ 222	John Lee Hooker	1968	3.00	6.00	12.00
❏ 347	Hooked On Blues	1980	3.00	6.00	12.00
ATCO					
❏ 33-151 [M]	Don't Turn Me From Your Door	1963	25.00	50.00	100.00
❏ SD 33-151 [R]	Don't Turn Me From Your Door	1967	12.50	25.00	50.00
ATLANTIC					
❏ SD 7228	Detroit Special	1972	5.00	10.00	20.00
BATTLE					
❏ BLP-6113 [M]	John Lee Hooker	196?	37.50	75.00	150.00
❏ BLP-6114 [M]	How Long Blues	196?	37.50	75.00	150.00
BLUESWAY					
❏ BL-6002 [M]	Live at Café A-Go-Go	1967	6.25	12.50	25.00
❏ BLS-6002 [S]	Live at Café A-Go-Go	1967	5.00	10.00	20.00
❏ BL-6012 [M]	Urban Blues	1967	6.25	12.50	25.00
❏ BLS-6012 [S]	Urban Blues	1967	5.00	10.00	20.00
❏ BLS-6023	Simply the Truth	1968	5.00	10.00	20.00
❏ BLS-6038	If You Miss 'Em	1969	5.00	10.00	20.00
❏ BLQ-6052 [Q]	Live at Kabuki-Wuki	1974	6.25	12.50	25.00
❏ BLS-6052	Live at Kabuki-Wuki	1973	3.75	7.50	15.00
BUDDAH					
❏ BDS-4002	The Very Best of John Lee Hooker	1970	3.75	7.50	15.00
❏ BDS-7506	Big Band Blues	1970	3.75	7.50	15.00
CHAMELEON					
❏ D1-74794	The Hook	1989	2.50	5.00	10.00
❏ D1-74808	The Healer	1989	2.50	5.00	10.00
CHESS					
❏ LP-1438 [M]	House of the Blues	1960	75.00	150.00	300.00
—Black label					
❏ LP-1438 [M]	House of the Blues	1966	12.50	25.00	50.00
—Blue and white label					
❏ LP-1454 [M]	John Lee Hooker Plays and Sings the Blues	1961	75.00	150.00	300.00
—Black label					
❏ LP-1454 [M]	John Lee Hooker Plays and Sings the Blues	1966	12.50	25.00	50.00
—Blue and white label					
❏ LP-1508 [M]	Real Folk Blues	1966	12.50	25.00	50.00
❏ LPS-1508 [R]	Real Folk Blues	1966	7.50	15.00	30.00
❏ CH-9199	John Lee Hooker Plays and Sings the Blues	1986	2.00	4.00	8.00
—Reissue					
❏ CH-9258	House of the Blues	1987	2.00	4.00	8.00
❏ CH-9271	The Real Folk Blues	1988	2.00	4.00	8.00
❏ 60011 [(2)]	Mad Man Blues	1973	5.00	10.00	20.00
❏ CH2-92507 [(2)]	Mad Man Blues	198?	3.00	6.00	12.00
COLLECTABLES					
❏ COL-5151	Golden Classics	198?	3.00	6.00	12.00
CROWN					
❏ CLP-5157 [M]	The Blues	1960	25.00	50.00	100.00
—Black label with silver "Crown"					
❏ CLP-5157 [M]	The Blues	1962	7.50	15.00	30.00
—Gray label					
❏ CLP-5157 [M]	The Blues	196?	3.00	6.00	12.00
—Black label with multi-color "Crown"					
❏ CLP-5232 [M]	John Lee Hooker Sings the Blues	1962	25.00	50.00	100.00
—Black label with silver "Crown"					
❏ CLP-5232 [M]	John Lee Hooker Sings the Blues	1962	7.50	15.00	30.00
—Gray label					
❏ CLP-5232 [M]	John Lee Hooker Sings the Blues	196?	3.00	6.00	12.00
—Black label with multi-color "Crown"					
❏ CLP-5295 [M]	Folk Blues	1962	7.50	15.00	30.00
—Gray label					

H

Number	Title (A Side/B Side)	Yr	VG	VG+	NM
❑ CLP-5295 [M] Folk Blues		1962	3.00	6.00	12.00
—Black label with multi-color "Crown"					
❑ CLP-5353 [M] The Great John Lee Hooker		1963	7.50	15.00	30.00
—Gray label					
❑ CLP-5353 [M] The Great John Lee Hooker		1963	3.00	6.00	12.00
—Black label with multi-color "Crown"					
EXODUS					
❑ 325 [M]	Is He the World's Greatest Blues Singer?	1966	6.25	12.50	25.00
FANTASY					
❑ 24706 [(2)]	Boogie Chillun	1972	3.75	7.50	15.00
❑ 24722 [(2)]	Black Snake	197?	3.75	7.50	15.00
GALAXY					
❑ 8201 [M]	I'm John Lee Hooker	1962	62.50	125.00	250.00
❑ 8205 [M]	Live at Sugar Hill	196?	62.50	125.00	250.00
GNP CRESCENDO					
❑ GNPS-10007 [(2)]The Best of John Lee Hooker		1974	3.75	7.50	15.00
GREENE BOTTLE					
❑ 3130 [(2)]	Johnny Lee	1972	3.75	7.50	15.00
IMPULSE!					
❑ A-9103 [M]	It Serves You Right to Suffer	1966	7.50	15.00	30.00
❑ AS-9103 [S]	It Serves You Right to Suffer	1966	10.00	20.00	40.00
JEWEL					
❑ 5005	I Feel Good	1971	3.75	7.50	15.00
KING					
❑ 727 [M]	John Lee Hooker Sings the Blues	1960	125.00	250.00	500.00
❑ KLP-727	John Lee Hooker Sings the Blues	1988	2.00	4.00	8.00
—Reissue of earlier 727					
❑ KS-1085	Moanin' and Stompin' Blues	1970	6.25	12.50	25.00
LABOR					
❑ 4	Alone	1982	2.50	5.00	10.00
MUSE					
❑ 5205	Sittin' Here Thinkin'	1980	3.00	6.00	12.00
PAUSA					
❑ PR-7197	Jealous	1986	2.50	5.00	10.00
RIVERSIDE					
❑ RLP 12-321 [M]That's My Story		1960	25.00	50.00	100.00
❑ RLP 12-838 [M]The Country Blues of John Lee Hooker		1959	25.00	50.00	100.00
SPECIALTY					
❑ SPS-2125	Alone	1970	7.50	15.00	30.00
❑ SPS-2127	Going Down Highway 51	1970	7.50	15.00	30.00
STAX					
❑ STS-2013	That's Where It's At	1970	3.75	7.50	15.00
❑ STX-4134	That's Where It's At	1979	2.50	5.00	10.00
—Reissue of 2013					
TOMATO					
❑ 7009 [(2)]	The Cream	1978	3.75	7.50	15.00
TRADITION					
❑ 2089	Real Blues	1970	3.75	7.50	15.00
UNITED ARTISTS					
❑ UA-LA127-J [(3)]John Lee Hooker's Detroit		1974	6.25	12.50	25.00
❑ UAS-5512	Coast to Coast Blues Band	1971	3.75	7.50	15.00
VEE JAY					
❑ LP-1007 [M]	I'm John Lee Hooker	1959	75.00	150.00	300.00
—Maroon label					
❑ LP-1007 [M]	I'm John Lee Hooker	1960	20.00	40.00	80.00
—Black label with colorband					
❑ VJLP-1007	I'm John Lee Hooker	1986	2.00	4.00	8.00
—Reissue of original on flimsier vinyl					
❑ LP-1023 [M]	Travelin'	1960	20.00	40.00	80.00
❑ LP-1033 [M]	The Folk Lore of John Lee Hooker	1961	12.50	25.00	50.00
❑ SR-1033 [S]	The Folk Lore of John Lee Hooker	1961	20.00	40.00	80.00
❑ LP-1043 [M]	Burnin'	1962	12.50	25.00	50.00
❑ SR-1043 [S]	Burnin'	1962	37.50	75.00	150.00
❑ LP-1049 [M]	The Best of John Lee Hooker	1962	12.50	25.00	50.00
❑ SR-1049 [P]	The Best of John Lee Hooker	1962	20.00	40.00	80.00
❑ VJLP-1049	The Best of John Lee Hooker	1986	2.00	4.00	8.00
—Reissue of original on flimsier vinyl					
❑ LP-1058 [M]	The Big Soul of John Lee Hooker	1963	12.50	25.00	50.00
❑ SR-1058 [S]	The Big Soul of John Lee Hooker	1963	37.50	75.00	150.00
❑ VJLP-1058	The Big Soul of John Lee Hooker	1986	2.00	4.00	8.00
—Reissue of original on flimsier vinyl					
❑ LP-1066 [M]	John Lee Hooker On Campus	1963	12.50	25.00	50.00
❑ SR-1066 [S]	John Lee Hooker On Campus	1963	37.50	75.00	150.00
❑ LP-1078 [M]	John Lee Hooker at Newport	1964	12.50	25.00	50.00
❑ SR-1078 [S]	John Lee Hooker at Newport	1964	37.50	751.00	150.00
❑ VJLP-1078	John Lee Hooker at Newport	1986	2.00	4.00	8.00
—Reissue of original on flimsier vinyl					
❑ DY-7301	John Lee Hooker In Person	198?	2.00	4.00	8.00
❑ LP-8502 [M]	Is He the World's Greatest Blues Singer?	1965	10.00	20.00	40.00
—This is the title on the cover; the label calls it "Is He Really the World's Greatest Blues Singer?"					
❑ VJLP-8502	Is He the World's Greatest Blues Singer?	1986	2.00	4.00	8.00
—Reissue of original on flimsier vinyl; this is the title on the cover; the label calls it "Is He Really the World's Greatest Blues Singer?"					
VERVE FOLKWAYS					
❑ FT-3003 [M]	John Lee Hooker and Seven Nights	1965	6.25	12.50	25.00
❑ FTS-3003 [S]	John Lee Hooker and Seven Nights	1965	10.00	20.00	40.00
WAND					
❑ WDS-689	On the Waterfront	1972	3.75	7.50	15.00

Number	Title (A Side/B Side)	Yr	VG	VG+	NM
HOOKER, JOHN LEE, AND CANNED HEAT					
Also see each artist's individual listings.					
45s					
UNITED ARTISTS					
❑ 50779	Whiskey and Wimmen/Let's Make It	1971	—	2.50	5.00
Albums					
LIBERTY					
❑ 35002	Hooker 'n' Heat	1971	5.00	10.00	20.00
RHINO					
❑ RNLP-801	Recorded Live at the Fox Venice Theatre	1985	3.00	6.00	12.00
❑ RNDA-71105 Infinite Boogie		1987	3.00	6.00	12.00
HOOKER, ZAKIYA					
45s					
POINTBLANK					
❑ S7-19519	Stones in My Passway/Baby You Busted	1997	—	2.00	4.00
HOOPER, STIX					
Also see THE CRUSADERS.					
12-Inch Singles					
MCA					
❑ L33-1858 [DJ] Brazos River Breakdown (6:35) (same on both sides)		1979	3.00	6.00	12.00
45s					
MCA					
❑ 41165	Brazos River Breakdown/Rum or Tequila?	1979	—	2.00	4.00
❑ 41218	Cordon Bleu/Passion	1980	—	2.00	4.00
❑ 52141	Gimme Some Space/I Touched a Dream	1982	—	2.00	4.00
Albums					
ARTFUL BALANCE					
❑ ABI-7214	Lay It on the Line	198?	3.00	6.00	12.00
MCA					
❑ 3180	The World Within	1980	2.50	5.00	10.00
❑ 5374	Touch the Feeling	1982	2.50	5.00	10.00
HOPE, LYNN					
45s					
ALADDIN					
❑ 3095	Blue Moon/Blow, Lynn, Blow	1951	10.00	20.00	40.00
❑ 3103	Too Young/Free and Easy	1951	10.00	20.00	40.00
❑ 3109	She's Funny That Way/Eleven Till Two	1951	10.00	20.00	40.00
❑ 3134	Driftin'/Sentimental Journey	1952	7.50	15.00	30.00
❑ 3155	Move It/Don't Worry 'Bout Me	1952	7.50	15.00	30.00
❑ 3165	September Song/Blues for Anna Bocoa	1953	6.25	12.50	25.00
❑ 3178	Broken Heart/Morocco	1953	6.25	12.50	25.00
❑ 3185	Jet/Tenderly	1953	6.25	12.50	25.00
❑ 3208	Swing Train/Rose Room	1953	6.25	12.50	25.00
❑ 3229	Brazil/C. Jam Blues	1954	6.25	12.50	25.00
❑ 3297	All of Me/Summertime	1955	6.25	12.50	25.00
❑ 3322	Cherry/Blues in F	1956	6.25	12.50	25.00
KING					
❑ 5336	Tenderly/Full Moon	1960	3.00	6.00	12.00
❑ 5352	Body and Soul/Sands of Sahara	1960	3.00	6.00	12.00
❑ 5378	A Ghost of a Chance/Little Landslide	1960	3.00	6.00	12.00
❑ 5431	Shockin'/Blue and Sentimental	1960	3.00	6.00	12.00
HOPKINS, LIGHTNIN'					
45s					
ACE					
❑ 516	Bad Boogie/Wonder What Is Wrong with Me	1956	10.00	20.00	40.00
ALADDIN					
❑ 3063	Shotgun Blues/Rolling Blues	1950	175.00	350.00	700.00
❑ 3077	Moonrise Blues/Honey, Honey Blues	1951	50.00	100.00	200.00
❑ 3096	Miss Me Blues/Abilene	1951	50.00	100.00	200.00
❑ 3117	You Are Not Going to Worry About My Life Anymore/Daddy Will Be Home Someday	1951	50.00	100.00	200.00
❑ 3262	So Long/My California	1954	25.00	50.00	100.00
ARHOOLIE					
❑ 508	My Woman/Lousiana Blues	1965	3.00	6.00	12.00
❑ 513	Come On Baby/Money Taker	1965	3.00	6.00	12.00
BLUESVILLE					
❑ 813	So Sorry to Leave You/Got to Move Your Baby	1960	5.00	10.00	20.00
❑ 814	Death Bells/Sail On	1961	5.00	10.00	20.00
❑ 817	Back to New Orleans/Hard to Love a Woman	1961	5.00	10.00	20.00
❑ 820	Happy Blues for John Glenn (Part 1)/Happy Blues for John Glenn (Part 2)	1962	5.00	10.00	20.00
❑ 821	Last Night Blues/Walkin' Blues	1962	5.00	10.00	20.00
❑ 822	Sinner's Prayer/Angel Child	1962	5.00	10.00	20.00
❑ 823	The Business You're Doing/Wake Up Old Lady	1963	5.00	10.00	20.00
❑ 824	Going Away/Better Stop Her	1963	5.00	10.00	20.00
❑ 825	Katie Mae/My Babe	1963	5.00	10.00	20.00
CHART					
❑ 636	Walkin' the Streets/Mussy Haired Woman	1957	7.50	15.00	30.00
DART					
❑ 123	Grievance Blues/Unsuccessful Blues	1959	5.00	10.00	20.00
❑ 152	Mary Lou/Wait to Go Home	1960	5.00	10.00	20.00
DECCA					
❑ 9-28841	The War Is Over/Policy Game	1953	20.00	40.00	80.00
❑ 9-48306	Merry Christmas/Happy New Year	1953	20.00	40.00	80.00
❑ 9-48312	Highway Blues/Cemetery Blues	1954	20.00	40.00	80.00
❑ 9-48321	I'm Wild About You Baby/Bad Things on My Mind	1954	25.00	50.00	100.00
FIRE					
❑ 1034	Mojo Hand/Glory Be	1961	5.00	10.00	20.00

Number	Title (A Side/B Side)	Yr	VG	VG+	NM
HARLEM					
❏ 2321	Contrary Mary/I'm Begging You	1954	50.00	100.00	200.00
❏ 2324	Mad Man's Boogie/Nobody Cares for Me	1954	50.00	100.00	200.00
❏ 2331	Fast Life/The Jackstropper	1955	50.00	100.00	200.00
❏ 2336	Good Old Woman/Untrue	1955	50.00	100.00	200.00
HERALD					
❏ 425	Lightnin's Boogie/Don't Think 'Cause You're Pretty	1954	7.50	15.00	30.00
❏ 428	Lightnin's Special/Life Is Used to Live	1954	7.50	15.00	30.00
❏ 436	Movin' On Out Boogie/Sick Feelin' Blues	1954	7.50	15.00	30.00
❏ 443	Nothin' But the Blues/Early Morning Boogie	1954	7.50	15.00	30.00
❏ 449	Evil Hearted Woman/They Wonder Who I Am	1955	7.50	15.00	30.00
❏ 456	My Baby's Gone/Don't Need No Job	1955	6.25	12.50	25.00
❏ 465	I Had a Gal Named Sal/Blues for My Cookie	1955	6.25	12.50	25.00
❏ 471	Hopkins Sky Hop/Lonesome in Your Home	1956	6.25	12.50	25.00
❏ 476	Grandma's Boogie/I Love You Baby	1956	6.25	12.50	25.00
❏ 483	Finally Met My Baby/That's Alright Baby	1956	6.25	12.50	25.00
❏ 490	Shine On Moon/Sitting and Thinking	1956	6.25	12.50	25.00
❏ 490	Shine On Moon/Sitting and Thinking	1956	6.25	12.50	25.00
❏ 497	Remember Me/Please Don't Go Baby	1957	6.25	12.50	25.00
❏ 504	Boogie Woogie Dance/The Blues Is a Mighty Bad Feeling	1957	5.00	10.00	20.00
❏ 520	Little Kewpie Doll/Lightnin' Don't Feel Well	1958	5.00	10.00	20.00
❏ 531	Hear Me Talkin'/Lightnin's Stomp	1958	5.00	10.00	20.00
❏ 542	Let's Move/I'm Achin'	1959	5.00	10.00	20.00
❏ 547	Flash Lightnin'/Gonna Change My Ways	1960	5.00	10.00	20.00
IMPERIAL					
❏ 5834	Feel So Bad/Shotgun	1962	3.75	7.50	15.00
❏ 5852	Picture on the Wall/Lightnin's Boogie	1962	3.75	7.50	15.00
IVORY					
❏ 91272	Got Me a Lousiana Woman/War Is Starting Again	196?	3.75	7.50	15.00
JAX					
❏ 315	No Good Woman/Been a Bad Man	1953	75.00	150.00	300.00
—Red vinyl					
❏ 318	Automobile/Organ Blues	1953	75.00	150.00	300.00
—Red vinyl					
❏ 321	Contrary Mary/I'm Begging You	1953	75.00	150.00	300.00
—Red vinyl					
❏ 635	Coffee Blues/New Short Haired Woman	1954	62.50	125.00	250.00
—Reissue of Sittin' In With 635					
❏ 642	You Caused My Heart to Weep/Tap Dance Boogie	1954	62.50	125.00	250.00
—Reissue of Sittin' In With 642					
❏ 649	New Worried Life Blues/One Kind of Favor	1954	62.50	125.00	250.00
—Reissue of Sittin' In With 649; this may be its first issue on 45 rpm					
❏ 660	Mad Blues/I've Been a Bad Man	1954	125.00	250.00	250.00
—Reissue of Sittin' In With 660					
❏ 661	Gone Again/Down to the River	1954	62.50	125.00	250.00
—Reissue of Sittin' In With 661					
JEWEL					
❏ 788	Back Door Friends/Fishing Clothes	1968	—	3.00	6.00
❏ 796	Wig Wearin' Woman/Move On Out, Part 2	1968	—	3.00	6.00
❏ 803	Lovin' Arms/Ride in Your New Auto	1969	—	3.00	6.00
❏ 807	Play with Your Poodle/Breakfast Time	1970	—	3.00	6.00
❏ 809	I'm Comin' Home/You're Too Fast	1970	—	3.00	6.00
❏ 816	My Charlie (Part 1)/My Charlie (Part 2)	1970	—	3.00	6.00
❏ 819	Rock Me Mama/Love Me This Morning	1971	—	3.00	6.00
❏ 825	Uncle Sam the Hip Hit Record Man/Found My Baby Crying	1971	—	3.00	6.00
LIGHTNING					
❏ 104	Unsuccessful Blues/Grieving Blues	1955	125.00	250.00	500.00
MERCURY					
❏ 8252x45	Everybody's Down on Me/You Do Too	1952	30.00	60.00	120.00
❏ 8274x45	Sad News from Korea/Let Me Fly Your Kite	1952	25.00	50.00	100.00
❏ 8274	Sad News from Korea/Let Me Fly Your Kite	1952	6.25	12.50	25.00
❏ 8293x45	Gone with the Wind/She's Almost Dead	1952	25.00	50.00	100.00
❏ 70081x45	Ain't It a Shame/Crazy About My Baby	1953	25.00	50.00	100.00
❏ 70191x45	My Mama Told Me/What's the Matter Now	1953	25.00	50.00	100.00
PRESTIGE					
❏ 326	I Like to Boogie/Let's Go Sit on the Lawn	1964	2.50	5.00	10.00
❏ 343	Mojo Hand/Automobile Blues	1964	2.50	5.00	10.00
❏ 374	T Model Blues/You Cook Alright	1965	2.50	5.00	10.00
❏ 391	Sinner's Prayer/Got to Move Your Baby	1965	2.50	5.00	10.00
❏ 405	I'm Gonna Build Me a Heaven (Part 1)/I'm Gonna Build Me a Heaven (Part 2)	1966	2.50	5.00	10.00
❏ 452	Mama Blues/Pneumonia Blues	1968	2.00	4.00	8.00
RPM					
❏ 45x337	Beggin' You to Stay/Bad Luck and Trouble	1951	150.00	300.00	600.00
❏ 45x346	Lonesome Dog Blues/Jake Head	1952	200.00	400.00	800.00
❏ 45x351	Don't Keep My Baby Long/Last Affair	1952	100.00	200.00	400.00
❏ 45x359	Needed Time/One Kind Favor	1952	100.00	200.00	400.00
❏ 45x378	Another Fool in Town/Candy Kitchen	1953	75.00	150.00	300.00
❏ 45x388	Black Cat/Mistreated Blues	1953	75.00	150.00	300.00
❏ 45x398	Santa Fe Blues/Some Day Baby	1954	50.00	100.00	200.00
SHAD					
❏ 5011	Hello Central/Mad As I Can Be	1959	3.75	7.50	15.00
SITTIN' IN WITH					
❏ 621	Give Me Central 209/New York Boogie	1951	125.00	250.00	500.00
❏ 621	Hello Central/New York Boogie	1952	100.00	200.00	400.00
❏ 635	Coffee Blues/New Short Haired Woman	1952	125.00	250.00	500.00
❏ 642	You Caused My Heart to Weep/Tap Dance Boogie	1952	125.00	250.00	500.00
❏ 644	Jail House Blues/"T" Model Blues	1952	125.00	250.00	500.00
❏ 647	Bald Headed Woman/Dirty House	1952	125.00	250.00	500.00
❏ 649	New Worried Life Blues/One Kind of Favor	1952	—	—	—
—Unreleased on 45 rpm?					

Number	Title (A Side/B Side)	Yr	VG	VG+	NM
❏ 652	Papa Bones Boogie/Everything Happens to Me	1953	125.00	250.00	500.00
❏ 658	Freight Train Blues (When I Started Hoboing)/Broken Hearted Blues	1953	125.00	250.00	500.00
❏ 660	Mad Blues/I've Been a Bad Man	1953	125.00	250.00	500.00
❏ 661	Gone Again/Down to the River	1953	125.00	250.00	500.00
SPHERE SOUND					
❏ 710	Santa/Black Mare Trot	196?	2.50	5.00	10.00
TNT					
❏ 8002	Lightnin' Jump/Late in the Evening	1954	175.00	350.00	700.00
❏ 8003	Moanin' Blues/Leavin' Blues	1954	175.00	350.00	700.00
VAULT					
❏ 965	Easy on Your Heels/No Education	1970	—	3.00	6.00
78s					
ACE					
❏ 516	Bad Boogie/Wonder What Is Wrong with Me	1956	10.00	20.00	40.00
ALADDIN					
❏ 165	West Coast Blues/Can't You Do Me Like You Used to Do	1947	12.50	25.00	50.00
—As "Lightnin' Hopkins and Thunder Smith"					
❏ 167	Katie Mae Blues/That Mean Old Twister	1947	12.50	25.00	50.00
❏ 168	I Feel So Bad/Rocky Mountain Blues	1947	12.50	25.00	50.00
❏ 204	Fast Mail Rambler/Thinkin' and Worryin'	1947	12.50	25.00	50.00
❏ 209	Down Now Baby/Play with Your Poodle	1947	12.50	25.00	50.00
❏ 3005	Big Mama Jump/Short Haired Woman	1948	12.50	25.00	50.00
❏ 3015	Sugar Mama/Picture on the Wall	1948	12.50	25.00	50.00
❏ 3028	Nightmare Blues/Woman, Woman	1949	10.00	20.00	40.00
❏ 3035	Morning Blues/I Have to Let You Go	1950	10.00	20.00	40.00
❏ 3052	Baby Child/Changing Weather Blues	1950	10.00	20.00	40.00
❏ 3063	Shotgun Blues/Rolling Blues	1950	17.50	35.00	70.00
❏ 3077	Moonrise Blues/Honey, Honey Blues	1951	7.50	15.00	30.00
❏ 3096	Miss Me Blues/Abilene	1951	7.50	15.00	30.00
❏ 3117	You Are Not Going to Worry About My Life Anymore/Daddy Will Be Home Someday	1951	7.50	15.00	30.00
❏ 3262	So Long/My California	1954	7.50	15.00	30.00
CHART					
❏ 636	Walkin' the Streets/Mussy Haired Woman	1957	10.00	20.00	40.00
DECCA					
❏ 28841	The War Is Over/Policy Game	1953	12.50	25.00	50.00
❏ 48306	Merry Christmas/Happy New Year	1953	15.00	30.00	60.00
❏ 48312	Highway Blues/Cemetery Blues	1954	15.00	30.00	60.00
❏ 48321	I'm Wild About You Baby/Bad Things on My Mind	1954	20.00	40.00	80.00
GOLD STAR					
❏ 613	Ida Mae/Shining Moon	194?	20.00	40.00	80.00
❏ 616	Mercy/What Can It Be	194?	20.00	40.00	80.00
❏ 624	Appetite Blues/Lonesome Home	194?	20.00	40.00	80.00
❏ 634	Lightning Blues/Walking Blues	194?	15.00	30.00	60.00
❏ 637	No Mail Blues/Ain't It a Shame	194?	15.00	30.00	60.00
❏ 640	Tim Moore's Farm/You Don't Know	1948	15.00	30.00	60.00
❏ 641	Treat Me Kind/(B-side unknown)	1949	20.00	40.00	80.00
❏ 646	Baby Please Don't Go/Death Bells	1949	20.00	40.00	80.00
❏ 652	Mad with You/Airplane Blues	1949	20.00	40.00	80.00
❏ 656	Unsuccessful Blues/(B-side unknown)	1949	15.00	30.00	60.00
❏ 662	"T" Model Blues/Jailhouse Blues	1949	17.50	35.00	70.00
❏ 664	Unkind Blues/(B-side unknown)	1949	15.00	30.00	60.00
❏ 665	European Blues/(B-side unknown)	1949	15.00	30.00	60.00
❏ 666	Automobile Blues/Zolongo	1949	25.00	50.00	100.00
❏ 669	Old Woman Blues/Untrue Blues	1950	12.50	25.00	50.00
❏ 671	Henny Penny Blues/(B-side unknown)	1950	37.50	75.00	150.00
❏ 673	Grievance Blues/(B-side unknown)	1950	20.00	40.00	80.00
❏ 3131	Big Mama Jump/Short Haired Woman	1947	25.00	50.00	100.00
HARLEM					
❏ 2321	Contrary Mary/I'm Begging You	1954	10.00	20.00	40.00
❏ 2324	Mad Man's Boogie/Nobody Cares for Me	1954	10.00	20.00	40.00
❏ 2331	Fast Life/The Jackstropper	1955	12.50	25.00	50.00
❏ 2336	Good Old Woman/Untrue	1955	12.50	25.00	50.00
HERALD					
❏ 425	Lightnin's Boogie/Don't Think 'Cause You're Pretty	1954	5.00	10.00	20.00
❏ 428	Lightnin's Special/Life Is Used to Live	1954	5.00	10.00	20.00
❏ 436	Movin' On Out Boogie/Sick Feelin' Blues	1954	5.00	10.00	20.00
❏ 443	Nothin' But the Blues/Early Morning Boogie	1954	5.00	10.00	20.00
❏ 449	Evil Hearted Woman/They Wonder Who I Am	1955	6.25	12.50	25.00
❏ 456	My Baby's Gone/Don't Need No Job	1955	6.25	12.50	25.00
❏ 465	I Had a Gal Named Sal/Blues for My Cookie	1955	6.25	12.50	25.00
❏ 471	Hopkins Sky Hop/Lonesome in Your Home	1956	6.25	12.50	25.00
❏ 476	Grandma's Boogie/I Love You Baby	1956	6.25	12.50	25.00
❏ 483	Finally Met My Baby/That's Alright Baby	1956	6.25	12.50	25.00
❏ 497	Remember Me/Please Don't Go Baby	1957	7.50	15.00	30.00
❏ 504	Boogie Woogie Dance/The Blues Is a Mighty Bad Feeling	1957	7.50	15.00	30.00
❏ 520	Little Kewpie Doll/Lightnin' Don't Feel Well	1958	10.00	20.00	40.00
❏ 531	Hear Me Talkin'/Lightnin's Stomp	1958	12.50	25.00	50.00
JAX					
❏ 315	No Good Woman/Been a Bad Man	1953	10.00	20.00	40.00
❏ 318	Automobile/Organ Blues	1953	10.00	20.00	40.00
❏ 321	Contrary Mary/I'm Begging You	1953	10.00	20.00	40.00
❏ 635	Coffee Blues/New Short Haired Woman	1954	7.50	15.00	30.00
—Reissue of Sittin' In With 635					
❏ 642	You Caused My Heart to Weep/Tap Dance Boogie	1954	7.50	15.00	30.00
—Reissue of Sittin' In With 642					
❏ 649	New Worried Life Blues/One Kind of Favor	1954	7.50	15.00	30.00
—Reissue of Sittin' In With 649					

Number	Title (A Side/B Side)	Yr	VG	VG+	NM
❑ 660	Mad Blues/I've Been a Bad Man	1954	7.50	15.00	30.00
—Reissue of Sittin' In With 660					
❑ 661	Gone Again/Down to the River	1954	7.50	15.00	30.00
—Reissue of Sittin' In With 661					
LIGHTNING					
❑ 104	Unsuccessful Blues/Grieving Blues	1955	62.50	125.00	250.00
MERCURY					
❑ 8252	Everybody's Down on Me/You Do Too	1952	7.50	15.00	30.00
❑ 8293	Gone with the Wind/She's Almost Dead	1952	6.25	12.50	25.00
❑ 70081	Ain't It a Shame/Crazy About My Baby	1953	6.25	12.50	25.00
❑ 70191	My Mama Told Me/What's the Matter Now	1953	6.25	12.50	25.00
MODERN					
❑ 20-529	Big Mama Jump/Short Haired Woman	1947	12.50	25.00	50.00
❑ 20-543	Ida Mae/Shining Moon	194?	10.00	20.00	40.00
❑ 20-552	Mercy/What Can It Be	194?	10.00	20.00	40.00
❑ 20-568	Appetite Blues/Lonesome Home	194?	10.00	20.00	40.00
❑ 20-594	Lightning Blues/Walking Blues	194?	7.50	15.00	30.00
❑ 20-621	No Mail Blues/Ain't It a Shame	1948	7.50	15.00	30.00
❑ 20-673	Tim Moore's Farm/You Don't Know	1948	7.50	15.00	30.00
RPM					
❑ 337	Beggin' You to Stay/Bad Luck and Trouble	1951	10.00	20.00	40.00
❑ 346	Lonesome Dog Blues/Jake Head	1952	25.00	50.00	100.00
❑ 351	Don't Keep My Baby Long/Last Affair	1952	12.50	25.00	50.00
❑ 359	Needed Time/One Kind Favor	1952	10.00	20.00	40.00
❑ 378	Another Fool in Town/Candy Kitchen	1953	10.00	20.00	40.00
❑ 388	Black Cat/Mistreated Blues	1953	10.00	20.00	40.00
❑ 398	Santa Fe Blues/Some Day Baby	1954	10.00	20.00	40.00
SCORE					
❑ 4002	Whiskey Head Woman/Lightnin's Blues	1949	12.50	25.00	50.00
SITTIN' IN WITH					
❑ 621	Give Me Central 209/New York Boogie	1951	30.00	60.00	120.00
❑ 621	Hello Central/New York Boogie	1952	25.00	50.00	100.00
❑ 635	Coffee Blues/New Short Haired Woman	1952	25.00	50.00	100.00
❑ 642	You Caused My Heart to Weep/Tap Dance Boogie	1952	25.00	50.00	100.00
❑ 644	Jail House Blues/"T" Model Blues	1952	25.00	50.00	100.00
❑ 647	Bald Headed Woman/Dirty House	1952	25.00	50.00	100.00
❑ 649	New Worried Life Blues/One Kind of Favor	1952	37.50	75.00	150.00
❑ 652	Papa Bones Boogie/Everything Happens to Me	1953	25.00	50.00	100.00
❑ 658	Freight Train Blues (When I Started Hoboing)/ Broken Hearted Blues	1953	25.00	50.00	100.00
❑ 660	Mad Blues/I've Been a Bad Man	1953	25.00	50.00	100.00
❑ 661	Gone Again/Down to the River	1953	25.00	50.00	100.00
TNT					
❑ 8002	Lightnin' Jump/Late in the Evening	1954	100.00	200.00	400.00
❑ 8003	Moanin' Blues/Leavin' Blues	1954	100.00	200.00	400.00
Albums					
ANALOGUE PRODUCTIONS					
❑ AAPB-014	Goin' Away	199?	10.00	20.00	40.00
—Audiophile reissue					
ARCHIVE OF FOLK AND JAZZ					
❑ 241	Lightnin' Hopkins	1969	3.75	7.50	15.00
❑ 313	Lightnin' Hopkins, Vol. 2	197?	3.75	7.50	15.00
❑ 342	Autobiography in Blues	1979	3.00	6.00	12.00
ARHOOLIE					
❑ 1011	Lightnin' Hopkins and His Guitar	196?	5.00	10.00	20.00
❑ 1022	Lightnin' Hopkins, His Brother and Barbara Dane	196?	5.00	10.00	20.00
❑ 1030	Blues Festival	196?	3.75	7.50	15.00
❑ 1034	Texas Blues Man	1968	3.75	7.50	15.00
❑ 1063	Lightnin' Hopkins in Berkeley	1969	3.75	7.50	15.00
❑ 1087	Poor Lightnin'	1970	3.75	7.50	15.00
❑ 2007	Early Recordings	197?	3.75	7.50	15.00
❑ 2010	Early Recordings Volume 2	197?	3.75	7.50	15.00
BARNABY					
❑ Z 30247	Lightnin' Hopkins in New York	1970	3.75	7.50	15.00
BLUES CLASSICS					
❑ 30	Historic Recordings 1952-1953	1986	3.00	6.00	12.00
BLUESVILLE					
❑ BVLP-1019 [M]	Lightnin'	1961	25.00	50.00	100.00
—Blue label, silver print					
❑ BVLP-1019 [M]	Lightnin'	1964	7.50	15.00	30.00
—Blue label, trident logo on right					
❑ BVLP-1029 [M]	Last Night Blues	1961	25.00	50.00	100.00
—Blue label, silver print					
❑ BVLP-1045 [M]	Blues in My Bottle	1962	25.00	50.00	100.00
—Blue label, silver print					
❑ BVLP-1045 [M]	Blues in My Bottle	1964	7.50	15.00	30.00
—Blue label, trident logo on right					
❑ BVLP-1057 [M]	Walkin' This Street	1962	25.00	50.00	100.00
—Blue label, silver print					
❑ BVLP-1057 [M]	Walkin' This Street	1964	7.50	15.00	30.00
—Blue label, trident logo on right					
❑ BVLP-1061 [M]	Lightnin' & Co.	1963	25.00	50.00	100.00
—Blue label, silver print					
❑ BVLP-1061 [M]	Lightnin' & Co.	1964	7.50	15.00	30.00
—Blue label, trident logo on right					
❑ BVLP-1070 [M]	Smokes Like Lightnin'	1963	25.00	50.00	100.00
—Blue label, silver print					
❑ BVLP-1070 [M]	Smokes Like Lightnin'	1964	7.50	15.00	30.00
—Blue label, trident logo on right					
❑ BVLP-1073 [M]	Goin' Away	1963	25.00	50.00	100.00
—Blue label, silver print					
❑ BVLP-1073 [M]	Goin' Away	1964	7.50	15.00	30.00
—Blue label, trident logo on right					

Number	Title (A Side/B Side)	Yr	VG	VG+	NM
❑ BVLP-1081 [M]	Gotta Move Your Baby	1964	7.50	15.00	30.00
—Blue label, trident logo on right					
❑ BVLP-1084 [M]	Lightnin' Hopkins' Greatest Hits	1964	10.00	20.00	40.00
❑ BVLP-1086 [M]	Down Home Blues	1964	6.25	12.50	25.00
BLUESWAY					
❑ S-6039	If You Miss 'Im	1969	5.00	10.00	20.00
BULLDOG					
❑ 1010	The Texas Bluesman	1965	3.75	7.50	15.00
CANDID					
❑ CM-8010 [M]	Lightnin' in New York	1961	30.00	60.00	120.00
❑ CS-9010 [S]	Lightnin' in New York	1961	37.50	75.00	150.00
COLLECTABLES					
❑ COL-5111	Golden Classics — Mojo Hand	198?	2.50	5.00	10.00
❑ COL-5121	The Herald Recordings/1954	198?	2.50	5.00	10.00
❑ COL-5143	Golden Classics, Part 1: Drinkin' the Blues	198?	2.50	5.00	10.00
❑ COL-5144	Golden Classics, Part 2: Prison Blues	198?	2.50	5.00	10.00
❑ COL-5145	Golden Classics, Part 3: Mama and Papa Hopkins	198?	2.50	5.00	10.00
❑ COL-5146	Golden Classics, Part 4: Nothin' But the Blues	198?	2.50	5.00	10.00
❑ COL-5203	The Lost Texas Tapes, Vol. 1	198?	2.50	5.00	10.00
❑ COL-5204	The Lost Texas Tapes, Vol. 2	198?	2.50	5.00	10.00
❑ COL-5205	The Lost Texas Tapes, Vol. 3	198?	2.50	5.00	10.00
❑ COL-5206	The Lost Texas Tapes, Vol. 4	198?	2.50	5.00	10.00
❑ COL-5207	The Lost Texas Tapes, Vol. 5	198?	2.50	5.00	10.00
CROWN					
❑ CLP-5224 [M]	Lightnin' Hopkins Sings the Blues	1962	25.00	50.00	100.00
—Black label, silver "Crown"					
❑ CLP-5224 [M]	Lightnin' Hopkins Sings the Blues	1962	12.50	25.00	50.00
—Gray label					
❑ CLP-5224 [M]	Lightnin' Hopkins Sings the Blues	196?	6.25	12.50	25.00
—Black label, multi-color logo					
DART					
❑ D-8000 [M]	Lightning Strikes Again	1960	100.00	200.00	400.00
❑ D-8000 [M]	Blues Underground	196?	50.00	100.00	200.00
—Retitled version of above					
DCC COMPACT CLASSICS					
❑ LPZ-2007	Blues Hoot	1996	7.50	15.00	30.00
—Audiophile vinyl					
FANTASY					
❑ OBC-506	Blues in My Bottle	198?	3.00	6.00	12.00
❑ OBC-522	Goin' Away	1988	3.00	6.00	12.00
❑ OBC-532	Lightnin'	1990	3.00	6.00	12.00
❑ 24702 [(2)]	Double Blues	1972	5.00	10.00	20.00
❑ 24725 [(2)]	How Many More Years	1981	3.75	7.50	15.00
FIRE					
❑ FLP 104 [M]	Mojo Hand	1960	375.00	750.00	1500.
FOLKLORE					
❑ FRLP-14021 [M]	Hootin' the Blues	1964	15.00	30.00	60.00
❑ FRST-14021 [S]	Hootin' the Blues	1964	17.50	35.00	70.00
FOLKWAYS					
❑ FS-3822 [M]	Lightnin' Hopkins	1962	10.00	20.00	40.00
❑ 31011	Roots	196?	3.75	7.50	15.00
GNP CRESCENDO					
❑ 10022	Legacy of the Blues, Volume 12	1978	3.00	6.00	12.00
GUEST STAR					
❑ G-1459 [M]	"Live" at the Bird Lounge, Houston, Texas	1964	7.50	15.00	30.00
❑ GS-1459 [R]	"Live" at the Bird Lounge, Houston, Texas	1964	5.00	10.00	20.00
HERALD					
❑ LP 1012 [M]	Lightnin' and the Blues	1959	750.00	1125.	1500.
—Black label					
❑ LP 1012 [M]	Lightnin' and the Blues	1959	200.00	400.00	800.00
—Yellow label					
❑ LP 1012 [M]	Lightnin' and the Blues	196?	125.00	250.00	500.00
—Multi-color label					
IMPERIAL					
❑ LP-9180 [M]	Lightnin' Hopkins On Stage	1962	75.00	150.00	300.00
❑ LP-9186 [M]	Lightnin' Hopkins Sings the Blues	1962	75.00	150.00	300.00
❑ LP-9211 [M]	Lightnin' Hopkins and the Blues	1963	50.00	100.00	200.00
❑ LP-12211 [R]	Lightnin' Hopkins and the Blues	1963	25.00	50.00	100.00
INTERNATIONAL ARTISTS					
❑ IA-6	Free Form Patterns	1968	50.00	100.00	200.00
—With photo on cover					
❑ IA-6	Free Form Patterns	1968	12.50	25.00	50.00
—With psychedelic art on cover					
JAZZ MAN					
❑ BLZ-5502	Lightnin' in New York	1982	2.50	5.00	10.00
JEWEL					
❑ 5000	Blue Lightnin'	1967	3.75	7.50	15.00
❑ 5001	Talkin' Some Sense	1968	3.75	7.50	15.00
❑ 5015	Great Electric Show and Dance	1970	3.75	7.50	15.00
KING					
❑ KS-1085	Moanin' Blues	1969	3.75	7.50	15.00
MAINSTREAM					
❑ 311	The Blues	1971	3.75	7.50	15.00
❑ 326	Dirty Blues	197?	3.75	7.50	15.00
❑ 405	Low Down Dirty Blues	1974	3.75	7.50	15.00
❑ S-6040 [S]	Blues	196?	7.50	15.00	30.00
❑ 56040 [M]	Blues	196?	6.25	12.50	25.00
MOUNT VERNON					
❑ 104 [M]	Nothin' But the Blues	196?	6.25	12.50	25.00
OLYMPIC GOLD MEDAL					
❑ 7110	Blues Giant	1974	3.00	6.00	12.00

Number	Title (A Side/B Side)	Yr	VG	VG+	NM
POPPY					
❏ 60002 [(2)]	Lightnin'!	1969	6.25	12.50	25.00
PRESTIGE					
❏ PRLPT-7370 [(2) M]	My Life with the Blues	1965	15.00	30.00	60.00
❏ PRST-7370 [(2) S]	My Life with the Blues	1965	17.50	35.00	70.00
❏ PRLP-7377 [M]	Soul Blues	1966	12.50	25.00	50.00
❏ PRST-7377 [S]	Soul Blues	1966	15.00	30.00	60.00
❏ PRST-7592	Lightnin' Hopkins' Greatest Hits	1969	3.75	7.50	15.00
❏ PRST-7714	The Best of Lightnin' Hopkins & His Texas Blues Band	1969	3.75	7.50	15.00
❏ PRST-7806	Hootin' the Blues	1969	3.75	7.50	15.00
❏ PRST-7811	The Blues of Lightnin' Hopkins	1969	3.75	7.50	15.00
❏ PRST-7831	Gotta Move Your Baby	1970	3.75	7.50	15.00
RHINO					
❏ RNLP 103	Los Angeles Blues	1982	2.50	5.00	10.00
SCORE					
❏ SLP-4022 [M]	Lightnin' Hopkins Strums the Blues	1958	300.00	600.00	1200.
SMITHSONIAN FOLKWAYS					
❏ SF-40019	Lightnin' Hopkins	1990	3.00	6.00	12.00
SPHERE SOUND					
❏ SSR-7001 [M]	Lightnin' Hopkins	1964	100.00	200.00	400.00
❏ SSSR-7001 [R]	Lightnin' Hopkins	1964	75.00	150.00	300.00
TIME					
❏ 1 [M]	Blues/Folk	1960	30.00	60.00	120.00
❏ 2 [M]	Blues/Folk Volume 2	1960	30.00	60.00	120.00
❏ ST-70004 [S]	Last of the Great Blues Singers	1962	30.00	60.00	120.00
❏ T-70004 [M]	Last of the Great Blues Singers	1962	30.00	60.00	120.00
TOMATO					
❏ 7004 [(2)]	Lightnin'!	1977	3.75	7.50	15.00
TRADITION					
❏ TLP-1035 [M]	Country Blues	1960	7.50	15.00	30.00
❏ TLP-1040 [M]	Autobiography in Blues	1961	7.50	15.00	30.00
❏ TLP-2056 [M]	The Best of Lightnin' Hopkins	1967	5.00	10.00	20.00
❏ TLP-2103 [M]	Lightnin' Strikes	1972	3.75	7.50	15.00
TRIP					
❏ TLP-8015	Lightnin' Hopkins	1971	3.00	6.00	12.00
UNITED					
❏ US-7713	Lightnin' Hopkins Sings the Blues	196?	3.75	7.50	15.00
❏ US-7744	Original Folk Blues	196?	3.75	7.50	15.00
❏ US-7785	A Legend in His Time	196?	3.75	7.50	15.00
UNITED ARTISTS					
❏ UAS-5512	Coast to Coast Blues Band	197?	3.75	7.50	15.00
UP FRONT					
❏ 158	Lightnin' Blues	1973	3.00	6.00	12.00
VAULT					
❏ 129	California Mudslide	1969	6.25	12.50	25.00
VEE JAY					
❏ LP 1044 [M]	Lightnin' Strikes	1962	12.50	25.00	50.00
VERVE					
❏ V-8453 [M]	Fast Life Woman	1962	10.00	20.00	40.00
VERVE FOLKWAYS					
❏ FV-9000 [M]	The Roots of Lightnin' Hopkins	1965	6.25	12.50	25.00
❏ FVS-9000 [S]	The Roots of Lightnin' Hopkins	1965	7.50	15.00	30.00
❏ FV-9022 [M]	Lightnin' Strikes	1965	6.25	12.50	25.00
❏ FVS-9022 [S]	Lightnin' Strikes	1965	7.50	15.00	30.00
VERVE FORECAST					
❏ FT-3013 [M]	Something Blue	1967	5.00	10.00	20.00
❏ FTS-3013 [S]	Something Blue	1967	6.25	12.50	25.00
❏ FTS-3031	Lightnin' Strikes	1968	5.00	10.00	20.00
WORLD PACIFIC					
❏ ST-1817 [S]	First Meetin'	1963	20.00	40.00	80.00
—Red vinyl					
❏ ST-1817 [S]	First Meetin'	1963	10.00	20.00	40.00
—Black vinyl					
❏ WP-1817 [M]	First Meetin'	1963	7.50	15.00	30.00

HORNETS, THE
More than one group.
45s

Number	Title (A Side/B Side)	Yr	VG	VG+	NM
COLUMBIA					
❏ 42999	Fruit Cake/Seven Days to Tahiti	1964	15.00	30.00	60.00
EMERALD					
❏ 501	Runt/Breakfast in Bed	196?	7.50	15.00	30.00
FLASH					
❏ 125	Crying Over You/Tango Moon	1957	62.50	125.00	250.00
LIBERTY					
❏ 55688	Motorcycle U.S.A./On the Track	1964	7.50	15.00	30.00
REV					
❏ 3515	Slow Dance/Strollin'	1958	6.25	12.50	25.00
STATES					
❏ 127	I Can't Believe/Lonesome Baby	1953	4000.	6000.	8000.
—Black vinyl					
❏ 127	I Can't Believe/Lonesome Baby	1953	7500.	10000.	15000.
—Red vinyl					
V.I.P.					
❏ 25004	She's My Baby/Give Me a Kiss	1964	15.00	30.00	60.00

HORTON, BILLIE JEAN
45s

Number	Title (A Side/B Side)	Yr	VG	VG+	NM
20TH FOX					
❏ 238	I'd Give the World (To Have You Back Again)/Angel Eyes	1961	3.75	7.50	15.00

Number	Title (A Side/B Side)	Yr	VG	VG+	NM
❏ 266	Ocean of Tears/Don't Take His Love	1961	3.75	7.50	15.00
❏ 291	Devoted to You/Octopus	1961	3.75	7.50	15.00
ABC-PARAMOUNT					
❏ 10332	Tell Him I Can't See Him Anymore/I'd Rather You Didn't Love Me	1962	3.75	7.50	15.00
ATLANTIC					
❏ 2249	I Know I'll Never See Him Again/Johnny Come Lately	1964	3.75	7.50	15.00

HOT CHOCOLATE
45s

Number	Title (A Side/B Side)	Yr	VG	VG+	NM
APPLE					
❏ 1812	Give Peace a Chance/Living Without Tomorrow	1969	2.50	5.00	10.00
—As "Hot Chocolate Band"					
BELL					
❏ 45390	Rumors/(B-side unknown)	1973	—	2.50	5.00
❏ 45466	Emma/(B-side unknown)	1974	—	3.50	7.00
BIG TREE					
❏ 16031	Emma/A Love Like Yours	1975	—	2.50	5.00
❏ 16038	Disco Queen/Makin' Music	1975	—	2.50	5.00
❏ 16047	You Sexy Thing/Amazing Skin Song	1975	—	2.50	5.00
❏ 16060	Don't Stop It Now/Beautiful Lady	1976	—	2.50	5.00
❏ 16078	Heaven Is in the Back Seat of My Cadillac/(B-side unknown)	1976	—	2.50	5.00
❏ 16096	So You Win Again/Part of Being with You	1977	—	2.50	5.00
❏ 16101	Man to Man/(B-side unknown)	1977	—	2.50	5.00
EMI-CAPITOL					
❏ S7-19894	You Sexy Thing/So You Win Again	1998	—	—	3.00
EMI AMERICA					
❏ 8143	Are You Getting Enough Happiness/One Night's Not Enough	1982	—	2.00	4.00
❏ 8157	Bed Games/It Started with a Kiss	1983	—	2.00	4.00
INFINITY					
❏ 50002	Every 1's a Winner/Power of Love	1978	—	2.00	4.00
❏ 50016	Going Through the Motions/Don't Turn It Off	1979	—	2.00	4.00
❏ 50033	I Just Love What You're Doing/Congas Man	1979	—	2.00	4.00
❏ 50048	Mindless Boogie/Dance (Get Down To It)	1979	—	2.00	4.00
RAK					
❏ 4503	You Could Have Been a Lady/Everybody's Laughing	1972	—	3.00	6.00
❏ 4506	I Believe in Love/Caveman Billy	1972	—	3.00	6.00
❏ 4508	Mary Anne/Ruth	1972	—	3.00	6.00
❏ 4513	Brother Louie/I Want to Be Free	1973	—	3.00	6.00
Albums					
BIG TREE					
❏ BT 76002	10 Greatest Hits	1977	2.50	5.00	10.00
❏ BT 89503	Cicero Park	1975	2.50	5.00	10.00
❏ BT 89512	Hot Chocolate	1975	2.50	5.00	10.00
❏ BT 89519	Man to Man	1976	2.50	5.00	10.00
EMI AMERICA					
❏ ST-17077	Mystery	1982	2.50	5.00	10.00
INFINITY					
❏ INF-9002	Every 1's a Winner	1978	2.50	5.00	10.00
❏ INF-9010	Going Through the Motions	1979	2.50	5.00	10.00

HOUSE OF PAIN
12-Inch Singles

Number	Title (A Side/B Side)	Yr	VG	VG+	NM
TOMMY BOY					
❏ TB 526	Jump Around (unknown versions)	1992	3.75	7.50	15.00
❏ TB 543	Shamrocks and Shenanigans (LP Version) (Muggs Main Mix) (Instrumental)///(Butch Vig Mix) (Salaam Main Pass)/Put Your Head Out (LP Version)	1992	3.00	6.00	12.00
❏ TB 556	Who's the Man? (Vocal) (Instrumental)/Put On Your Shit Kickers (2 versions)	1993	2.50	5.00	10.00
❏ TB 622	On Point (Radio Mix) (Lethal Dose Radio Remix) (Da Beatminerz UK Radio Remix) (Groove Merchantz Radio Remix)/Word Is Bond	1994	3.75	7.50	15.00
❏ TB 623	On Point (Album Version) (Lethal Dose Remix) (Da Beatminerz UK Remix) (A Cappella)/Word Is Bond (Album Version Featuring Diamond D)/On Point (Groove Merchantz Remix)	1994	3.00	6.00	12.00
❏ TB 740	Pass the Jinn (LP Version) (Radio Edit) (Instrumental)/Heart Full of Sorrow (LP Version) (Radio Edit) (Instrumental)	1996	3.75	7.50	15.00
❏ TB 741	Pass the Jinn (Album Version) (Instrumental)/Heart Full of Sorrow (Album Version) (Instrumental)	1996	3.00	6.00	12.00
❏ TB 744	Fed Up (Album Version) (Instrumental)/Heart Full of Sorrow (Album Version) (Instrumental)	1996	3.75	7.50	15.00
❏ TB 758	Fed Up (Remix 4:14) (Remix Instrumental 4:13)	1996	3.75	7.50	15.00
UPTOWN					
❏ UPT8P-2606 [DJ]	Who's the Man? (same on both sides)	1993	2.50	5.00	10.00
45s					
SUB POP					
❏ SP 188	Shamrocks and Shenanigans (In the Dirt Mix)/(Buds & Brew Mix)	1992	2.50	5.00	10.00
—On "lucky green vinyl"					
❏ SP 188 [PS]	Shamrocks and Shenanigans (In the Dirt Mix)/(Buds & Brew Mix)	1992	2.50	5.00	10.00
TOMMY BOY/COLLECTABLES					
❏ TB 526	Jump Around (same on both sides)	1992	2.00	4.00	8.00
—With no "Collectables" logo on label					

Number	Title (A Side/B Side)	Yr	VG	VG+	NM
❏ TB 526	Jump Around (same on both sides)	1993	—	2.50	5.00
—With "Collectables" logo on label					
❏ TB 543	Shamrocks and Shenanigans (Boom Shalock Lock Boom) (LP Version)/(Butch Vig Mix)	1992	—	2.50	5.00
❏ TB 556	Who's the Man?/Kick Some	1993	—	2.50	5.00
Albums					
TOMMY BOY					
❏ TB 1056	House of Pain	1992	3.00	6.00	12.00
❏ TB 1161	Truth Crushed to Earth Shall Rise Again	1996	3.75	7.50	15.00

HOUSTON, CISSY
12-Inch Singles
PRIVATE STOCK

Number	Title (A Side/B Side)	Yr	VG	VG+	NM
❏ PS 5108	Think It Over (6:00)/An Umbrella Song	1978	2.50	5.00	10.00

45s
COLUMBIA

Number	Title (A Side/B Side)	Yr	VG	VG+	NM
❏ 11058	Warning-Danger (This Love Affair May Be Hazardous to You)/An Umbrella Song	1979	—	2.00	4.00
❏ 11208	Break It To Me Gently/Gonna Take the Easy Way Out	1980	—	2.00	4.00
COMMONWEALTH UNITED					
❏ 3010	I'll Be There/Me — I Believe	1970	—	3.00	6.00
CONGRESS					
❏ 268	Bring Him Back/World of Broken Hearts	1966	15.00	30.00	60.00
—As "Susie Houston"					
JANUS					
❏ 131	I Just Don't Know What to Do with Myself/Empty Place	1970	—	3.00	6.00
❏ 145	Be My Baby/I'll Be There	1971	—	3.00	6.00
❏ 159	Hang On to a Dream/Darling Take Me Back	1971	—	3.00	6.00
❏ 177	I Love You/Making Love	1971	—	3.00	6.00
❏ 190	Didn't We/It's Not Easy	1972	—	3.00	6.00
❏ 206	Midnight Train to Georgia/Will You Still Love Me Tomorrow	1972	—	3.00	6.00
❏ 230	I'm So Glad I Can Love Again/One Time You Say You Love Me	1973	—	3.00	6.00
❏ 255	I Believe/Nothing Can Stop Me	1975	—	3.00	6.00
KAPP					
❏ 814	Don't Come Running to Me/One Broken Heart for Sale	1967	7.50	15.00	30.00
—As "Sissie Houston"					
PRIVATE STOCK					
❏ 45137	Love Is Something That Leads You/If I Ever Lose This Heaven	1977	—	2.50	5.00
❏ 45137	Love Is Something That Leads You/It Never Really Ended	1977	—	2.50	5.00
❏ 45153	Tomorrow/Love Is Holding On	1977	—	2.50	5.00
❏ 45171	Things to Do/It Never Really Ended	1977	—	2.50	5.00
❏ 45204	Think It Over/The Umbrella Song	1978	—	2.50	5.00
Albums					
COLUMBIA					
❏ JC 36112	Warning Danger	1979	2.50	5.00	10.00
❏ JC 36193	Step Aside for a Lady	1980	2.50	5.00	10.00
COMMONWEALTH UNITED					
❏ 6008	Cissy Houston	1970	—	—	—
—Canceled?					
JANUS					
❏ 3001	Cissy Houston	1970	3.75	7.50	15.00
PRIVATE STOCK					
❏ PS 2031	Cissy Houston	1977	3.00	6.00	12.00
❏ PS 7015	Think It Over	1978	3.00	6.00	12.00

HOUSTON, THELMA
12-Inch Singles
CENTURY 2000

Number	Title (A Side/B Side)	Yr	VG	VG+	NM
❏ 1001	Hold On (4 versions)/Athens Grooves/Olympus Thunder	1990	—	3.00	6.00
MCA					
❏ L33-1253 [DJ]	I'd Rather Spend the Bad Times with You (3 versions)	1984	2.00	4.00	8.00
❏ L33-1795 [DJ]	Working Girl (3:45)/(5:00)	1983	2.00	4.00	8.00
❏ 13963	Working Girl/Running in Circles	1983	—	3.00	6.00
❏ 23520	You Used to Hold Me So Tight (12" Version)/(Dub) (LP)	1984	—	3.00	6.00
❏ 23552	Fantasy and Heartbreak (Dance Version)/(LP Version)	1985	—	3.00	6.00
MOTOWN					
❏ 00053	Ride to the Rainbow/Love Machine	1979	2.00	4.00	8.00
RCA VICTOR					
❏ PD-12293	96 Tears/There's No Runnin' Away from Love	1981	—	3.50	7.00
REPRISE					
❏ PRO-A-4475 [DJ]	High (4 versions)	1990	2.00	4.00	8.00
❏ PRO-A-4487 [DJ]	Out of My Hands (Remix) (same on both sides)	1990	2.00	4.00	8.00
❏ 21765	High (5 versions)	1990	—	3.00	6.00
❏ 21769	Our of My Hands (5 versions)	1990	—	3.00	6.00
❏ 40080	Throw You Down (4 version)/What He Has (2 versions)	1990	—	3.00	6.00

45s
ABC DUNHILL

Number	Title (A Side/B Side)	Yr	VG	VG+	NM
❏ 11 [DJ]	Everybody Gets to Go to the Moon (same on both sides)	1969	3.75	7.50	15.00
—Special Apollo 11 promotional item					

Number	Title (A Side/B Side)	Yr	VG	VG+	NM
❏ 11 [PS]	Everybody Gets to Go to the Moon (same on both sides)	1969	5.00	10.00	20.00
—Special Apollo 11 promotional item					
❏ 4197	Sunshower/If This Was the Last Song	1969	2.50	5.00	10.00
❏ 4212	Jumpin' Jack Flash/This Is Your Life	1969	2.50	5.00	10.00
❏ 4222	Save the Country/I Just Can't Stay Away	1970	2.00	4.00	8.00
❏ 4260	The Good Earth/Ride, Louie, Ride	1970	2.00	4.00	8.00
CAPITOL					
❏ 5767	Baby Mine/Woman Behind Her Man	1966	12.50	25.00	50.00
❏ 5882	Don't Cry, My Soldier Boy/Let's Try to Make It	1967	12.50	25.00	50.00
MCA					
❏ 52196	Working Girl/Running in Circles	1983	—	—	3.00
❏ 52239	Make It Last/Just Like All the Rest	1983	—	—	3.00
❏ 52489	(I Guess) It Must Be Love/Running in Circles	1984	—	—	3.00
❏ 52491	Love Is a Dangerous Game/You Used to Hold Me So Tight	1984	—	—	3.00
❏ 52574	Keep It Light/My Lucille	1985	—	—	3.00
—B-side by B.B. King					
❏ 52582	What a Woman Feels Inside/Fantasy and Heartbreak	1985	—	—	3.00
MOTOWN					
❏ 1245	I'm Just a Part of Yesterday/Piano Man	1973	—	2.50	5.00
❏ 1260	Do You Know Where You're Going/Together	1973	—	2.50	5.00
❏ 1316	You've Been Doing Wrong for So Long/Pick Up the Week	1974	—	2.50	5.00
❏ 1385	The Bingo Long Song/Razzle Dazzle	1976	—	2.50	5.00
—B-side by William Goldstein					
❏ 1385 [PS]	The Bingo Long Song/Razzle Dazzle	1976	—	3.00	6.00
—B-side by William Goldstein					
MOWEST					
❏ 5008	I Want to Go Back There Again/Pick Up the Week	1972	—	3.00	6.00
❏ 5013	Me and Bobby McGee/No One's Gonna Be a Fool Forever	1972	—	3.00	6.00
❏ 5023	Piano Man/Me and Bobby McGee	1972	—	3.00	6.00
❏ 5027	What If/There Is a Fool	1972	—	3.00	6.00
❏ 5046	If It's the Last Thing I Do/And I Never Did	1973	—	—	—
—Unreleased					
❏ 5050	I'm Just a Part of Yesterday/Piano Man	1973	—	3.00	6.00
RCA					
❏ PB-11913	Suspicious Minds/Gone	1980	—	2.50	5.00
❏ PB-12215	If You Feel It/Hollywood	1981	—	2.00	4.00
❏ PB-12285	96 Tears/There's No Runnin' Away from Love	1981	—	2.00	4.00
TAMLA					
❏ 54275	One Out of Every Six (Censored)/Pick of the Week	1976	2.50	5.00	10.00
❏ 54278	Don't Leave Me This Way (Short Version)/Today Will Soon Be Yesterday	1977	—	2.00	4.00
❏ 54278 [DJ]	Don't Leave Me This Way (Long Version)/Don't Leave Me This Way (Short Version)	1977	—	3.00	6.00
❏ 54283	If It's the Last Thing I Do/If You Won't Let Me Walk on the Water	1977	—	2.00	4.00
❏ 54287	I'm Here Again/Sharin' Something Perfect	1977	—	2.00	4.00
❏ 54292	I Can't Go On Living Without Your Love/Any Way You Like It	1978	—	2.00	4.00
❏ 54295	I'm Not Strong Enough to Love You/Triplin'	1978	—	2.00	4.00
❏ 54297	Saturday Night, Sunday Morning/Come to Me	1979	—	2.00	4.00
Albums					
ABC DUNHILL					
❏ DS-50054	Sun Shower	1969	6.25	12.50	25.00
MCA					
❏ 5395	Thelma Houston	1983	2.50	5.00	10.00
❏ 5527	Qualifying Heat	1984	2.50	5.00	10.00
MOTOWN					
❏ M5-120V1	Superstar Series, Vol. 20	1981	2.50	5.00	10.00
❏ M5-127V1	Sunshower	1981	2.00	4.00	8.00
❏ M5-226V1	Any Way You Like It	1982	2.50	5.00	10.00
MOWEST					
❏ MW-102	Thelma Houston	1972	5.00	10.00	20.00
RCA VICTOR					
❏ AFL1-3500	Breakwater Cat	1980	2.50	5.00	10.00
❏ AFL1-3842	Never Gonna Be Another One	1981	2.50	5.00	10.00
REPRISE					
❏ 26234	Throw You Down	1990	3.75	7.50	15.00
SHEFFIELD LABS					
❏ 2	I've Got the Music in Me	1975	10.00	20.00	40.00
SHEFFIELD TREASURY					
❏ ST-200	I've Got the Music in Me	1983	5.00	10.00	20.00
—Reissue of Sheffield Labs 2					
TAMLA					
❏ T6-345R1	Any Way You Like It	1976	3.00	6.00	12.00
❏ T7-358R1	The Devil in Me	1977	2.50	5.00	10.00
❏ T7-361R1	Ready to Roll	1978	2.50	5.00	10.00

HOUSTON, THELMA, AND JERRY BUTLER
Also see each artist's individual listings.
45s
MOTOWN

Number	Title (A Side/B Side)	Yr	VG	VG+	NM
❏ 1422	It's a Lifetime Thing/Kiss Me Now	1977	—	2.50	5.00
Albums					
MOTOWN					
❏ M6-887	Thelma and Jerry	1977	2.50	5.00	10.00
❏ M7-903	Two to One	1978	2.50	5.00	10.00

Number	Title (A Side/B Side)	Yr	VG	VG+	NM

HOUSTON, WHITNEY
Also see ARETHA FRANKLIN; TEDDY PENDERGRASS.

12-Inch Singles
ARISTA

Number	Title (A Side/B Side)	Yr	VG	VG+	NM
❑ AD-2120	I'm Your Baby Tonight (Extended Remix)/I'm Knocking/Feels So Good	1990	3.00	6.00	12.00
❑ ADP 2123 [DJ]	I'm Your Baby Tonight (4 versions)	1990	3.75	7.50	15.00
❑ ADP 2370 [DJ]	I Belong to You (U.K. Mix 8:55) (U.K. Dub 8:45)/(69th St. Mix 9:27) (69th St. Dub 4:16)	1991	3.00	6.00	12.00
❑ ADP 2530 [DJ]	I'm Every Woman (2 versions)	1993	2.50	5.00	10.00
❑ ADP 2650 [DJ]	Queen of the Night (5 versions)	1993	2.50	5.00	10.00
❑ ADP 3214 [DJ]	Why Does It Hurt So Bad (LP Version) (Live Version)/I Wanna Dance with Somebody (Who Loves Me) Remix 1996 (Junior's Happy Hand Bag Mix) (Junior's X Beat Dub)	1996	3.75	7.50	15.00
❑ ADP 3287 [DJ]	Somebody Bigger Than You and I (4 versions)	1996	2.50	5.00	10.00
❑ ADP 3299 [(2) DJ]	Step by Step (7 versions)	1997	6.25	12.50	25.00
❑ ADP 3337 [DJ]	Step by Step (Tony Moran Diva x Diva Mix) (Junior Tribal x Tribal Beats) (Junior Deep Dub)	1997	3.75	7.50	15.00
❑ ADP 3578 [DJ]	It's Not Right But It's Okay (Vocal) (Instrumental) (Acappella)	1999	2.50	5.00	10.00
❑ ADP 3600 [DJ]	It's Not Right But It's Okay — Thunderpuss 2000 Remixes (Dub) (Beats) (Club) (Radio)	1999	3.00	6.00	12.00
❑ ADP 3612 [DJ]	It's Not Right But It's Okay (Johnny Vicious Momentous Mix 13:03) (Johnny Vicious Dub 8:31) (Johnny Vicious Radio Mix 4:11)	1999	3.00	6.00	12.00
❑ ADP 3618 [DJ]	Heartbreak Hotel (Hex Hector Club Mix) (Hex Hector NYC Rough Mix) (Hex Hector Radio Mix)	1998	3.00	6.00	12.00
❑ ADP 3641 [DJ]	It's Not Right But It's Okay (Album Version) (Album Version Instrumental) (Album Version Acapella) (Smooth Mix) (Smooth Instrumental) (Smooth Acapella)	1999	3.75	7.50	15.00
❑ ADP 3688 [DJ]	It's Not Right But It's Okay (KCC's Release the Love Groove Mix Bootleg 7:05) (Club 69 Future Mix 8;02) (Club 69 Future Dub 7:49)	1999	2.50	5.00	10.00
❑ ARDP 3715 [(2) DJ]	My Love Is Your Love (Thunderpuss Club) (Thunderpuss Radio) (Jonathan Peters Vocal) (Thunderpuss Severe Dub) (Acapella) (Jonathan Peters Tight Mix) (Jonathan Peters Mixshow)	1999	3.75	7.50	15.00
❑ ARDP 3727 [DJ]	My Love Is Your Love (Wyclef Remix Featuring Dyme 4:22) (LP Version 4:18) (Salaam Remix 5:33) (Wyclef Remix Instrumental 4:23) (LP Version Instrumental 4:24) (Salaam Remix Instrumental 5:36)	1999	2.50	5.00	10.00
❑ ARDP 3793 [(2) DJ]	I Learned from the Best (6 versions)	1999	5.00	10.00	20.00
❑ ARDP 3796 [DJ]	I Learned from the Best — HQ2 Mixes (Vocal 10:25) (Dub 8:25)	1999	2.50	5.00	10.00
❑ ARDP 3845 [DJ]	Fine (3 versions)	2000	2.50	5.00	10.00
❑ ARDP 3872 [(2) DJ]	Same Script, Different Cast (Joe Smooth Slang Club Mix 5:49) (Jonathan Peters Vocal Club Mix 9:35) (Jonathan Peters Goes There Dub 11:07) (Victor Romeo Slang Vocal Mix 6:19)	2000	3.75	7.50	15.00
❑ ARDP 3873 [DJ]	Same Script, Different Cast (Friburn & Urik Uncover Your Ears Mix 10:49) (Mel Hammond Beautiful Slang Dub 6:41) (Jonathan Peters Radio Edit 4:21)	2000	3.00	6.00	12.00
❑ AD1-9413	Thinking About You (Extended Dance Mix 7:19) (Dub Version 8:04) (Single Version 4:03)	1985	3.75	7.50	15.00
❑ AD1-9449	How Will I Know (Dance Remix) (Instrumental) (LP Version)	1985	2.00	4.00	8.00
❑ AD1-9599	I Wanna Dance with Somebody (Who Loves Me) (12" Remix) (Single Version)/(12" Remix Radio Edit) (Dub Mix) (Acappella Mix)	1987	2.00	4.00	8.00
❑ AD1-9632	Didn't We Almost Have It All/For the Love of You (2 versions)/Shock Me	1987	2.00	4.00	8.00
❑ AD1-9641	So Emotional (6 versions)	1987	2.50	5.00	10.00
❑ AD1-9721	Love Will Save the Day (Extended Version) (Acappella Version) (Single Version)/Dub Will Save the Day	1988	2.00	4.00	8.00
❑ 12260	My Name Is Not Susan (Extended Mix 5:56) (Dub Mix 4:28) (Extended U.K. Mix 6:16) (Alternate U.K. Mix 7:40)	1991	2.50	5.00	10.00
❑ 12520 [(2)]	I'm Every Woman (Every Woman's House Club Mix) (Every Woman's Beat)/(Clivilles & Cole House Mix I)//(Clivilles & Cole House Mix II)/(The C&C Dub) (A Cappella Mix)	1992	3.75	7.50	15.00
❑ 12916	Exhale (Shoop Shoop)/Dancing on the Smooth Edge/Moment of Truth/Do You Hear What I Hear/It Isn't, It Wasn't, It Ain't Never Gonna Be	1995	2.00	4.00	8.00
—Last track with Aretha Franklin					
❑ 12977	Count on Me/One Moment in Time/Jesus Loves Me/I Know Him So Well/Hold Up the Light	1996	3.00	6.00	12.00
—First track with CeCe Winans; last track by BeBe and CeCe Winans					
❑ 13214	Why Does It Hurt So Bad (LP Version) (Live Version)/I Wanna Dance with Somebody (Who Loves Me) Remix 1996 (Junior's Happy Hand Bag Mix) (Junior's X Beat Dub)	1996	2.50	5.00	10.00
❑ 13313 [(2)]	Step by Step (8 versions)	1997	3.75	7.50	15.00
❑ 13613 [(3)]	Heartbreak Hotel (3 versions)/It's Not Right But It's Okay (5 versions)	1998	3.75	7.50	15.00
❑ 13680	It's Not Right But It's Okay (3 versions)	1999	2.00	4.00	8.00
❑ 13823 [(2)]	I Learned from the Best (HQ2 Club Mix)/(Junior Vasquez USA Millennium Mix)//(HQ2 Dub)/(Junior Vasquez Disco Club Mix)	1999	2.50	5.00	10.00
❑ 13860	Same Script, Different Cast (unknown versions)	2000	2.50	5.00	10.00

45s
ARISTA

Number	Title (A Side/B Side)	Yr	VG	VG+	NM
❑ 2108	I'm Your Baby Tonight/I'm Knockin'	1990	—	—	3.00
❑ 2156	All the Man That I Need/Dancin' on the Smooth Edge	1990	—	—	3.00
❑ 2207	The Star Spangled Banner/America the Beautiful	1991	—	—	3.00
❑ 2222	Miracle/After We Make Love	1991	—	—	3.00
❑ 9274	You Give Good Love/Greatest Love of All	1984	—	—	3.00
❑ 9274 [PS]	You Give Good Love/Greatest Love of All	1984	—	—	3.00
❑ 9381	Saving All My Love for You/All at Once	1984	—	—	3.00
❑ 9381 [PS]	Saving All My Love for You/All at Once	1984	—	—	3.00
❑ 9412	Thinking About You/Someone for Me	1984	—	2.00	4.00
❑ 9412 [PS]	Thinking About You/Someone for Me	1984	—	2.00	4.00
❑ 9434	How Will I Know/Someone for Me	1984	—	—	3.00
❑ 9434 [PS]	How Will I Know/Someone for Me	1984	—	—	3.00
❑ 9466	Greatest Love of All/Thinking About You	1985	—	—	3.00
❑ 9466 [PS]	Greatest Love of All/Thinking About You	1985	—	—	3.00
❑ 9598	I Wanna Dance with Somebody (Who Loves Me)/Moment of Truth	1987	—	—	3.00
❑ 9598 [PS]	I Wanna Dance with Somebody (Who Loves Me)/Moment of Truth	1987	—	—	3.00
❑ 9616	Didn't We Almost Have It All/Shock Me	1987	—	—	3.00
❑ 9616 [PS]	Didn't We Almost Have It All/Shock Me	1987	—	—	3.00
❑ 9642	So Emotional/For the Love of You	1987	—	—	3.00
❑ 9642 [PS]	So Emotional/For the Love of You	1987	—	—	3.00
❑ 9674	Where Do Broken Hearts Go/Where Are You	1988	—	—	3.00
❑ 9674 [PS]	Where Do Broken Hearts Go/Where Are You	1988	—	—	3.00
❑ 9690	Just the Lonely Talking Again/If You Say My Eyes Are Beautiful	1988	—	2.50	5.00
—B-side with Jermaine Jackson					
❑ 9720	Love Will Save the Day/How Will I Know	1988	—	—	3.00
❑ 9720 [PS]	Love Will Save the Day/How Will I Know	1988	—	—	3.00
❑ 9743	One Moment in Time/Love Is a Contact Sport	1988	—	—	3.00
❑ 9743 [PS]	One Moment in Time/Love Is a Contact Sport	1988	—	—	3.00
❑ 12259	My Name Is Not Susan/(U.K. Mix)	1991	—	—	3.00
❑ 12369	I Belong to You/(International Mix)	1991	—	—	3.00
❑ 12490	I Will Always Love You/Jesus Loves Me	1992	—	—	3.00
❑ 12519	I'm Every Woman/Who Do You Love	1993	—	—	3.00
❑ 12527	I Have Nothing/Where Are You	1993	—	—	3.00
❑ 12570	Run to You/After We Make Love	1993	—	—	3.00
❑ 12885	Exhale (Shoop Shoop)/Dancin' on the Smooth Edge	1995	—	—	3.00
❑ 12976	Count on Me/One Moment in Time	1996	—	—	3.00
—A-side: Whitney Houston & Cece Winans					
❑ 13213	Why Does It Hurt So Bad/(Live Version)	1996	—	—	3.00
❑ 13293	I Believe in You and Me/Step By Step	1996	—	—	3.00
❑ 13312	Step by Step/(Teddy Riley Remix)	1997	—	—	3.00

Albums
ARISTA

Number	Title (A Side/B Side)	Yr	VG	VG+	NM
❑ AL 8212	Whitney Houston	1985	2.00	4.00	8.00
❑ AL 8405	Whitney	1987	2.00	4.00	8.00
❑ 14652 [(4)]	The Unreleased Mixes	2000	5.00	10.00	20.00
—Box set of 12-inch single remixes					
❑ AL 18616	I'm Your Baby Tonight	1990	2.50	5.00	10.00
❑ 19037 [(2)]	My Love Is Your Love	1998	3.00	6.00	12.00

HOWLIN' WOLF
45s
CADET CONCEPT

Number	Title (A Side/B Side)	Yr	VG	VG+	NM
❑ 7013	Evil/Tail Dragger	1969	2.00	4.00	8.00

CHESS

Number	Title (A Side/B Side)	Yr	VG	VG+	NM
❑ 1528	Oh! Red/My Last Affair	1952	175.00	350.00	700.00
—Note: Howlin' Wolf releases on Chess before 1528 are unknown on 45 rpm					
❑ 1557	All Night Boogie/I Love My Baby	1953	75.00	150.00	300.00
❑ 1566	No Place to Go/Rockin' Daddy	1954	25.00	50.00	100.00
❑ 1575	How Long/Evil Is Going On	1954	25.00	50.00	100.00
❑ 1584	I'll Be Around/Forty Four	1955	12.50	25.00	50.00
❑ 1593	Who Will Be Next/I Have a Little Girl	1955	10.00	20.00	40.00
❑ 1607	Come to Me Baby/Don't Mess with My Baby	1955	10.00	20.00	40.00
❑ 1618	Smoke Stack Lightning/You Can't Be Beat	1956	10.00	20.00	40.00
❑ 1632	I Asked for Water/So Glad	1956	10.00	20.00	40.00
❑ 1648	Goin' Back Home/My Life	1957	10.00	20.00	40.00
❑ 1668	Somebody in My Home/Nature	1957	10.00	20.00	40.00
❑ 1679	Sittin' On Top of the World/Poor Boy	1958	10.00	20.00	40.00
❑ 1695	Moaning for My Baby/I Didn't Know	1958	10.00	20.00	40.00
❑ 1712	I'm Leaving You/Change My Way	1959	10.00	20.00	40.00
❑ 1726	Howlin' Blues/I Better Go Now	1959	10.00	20.00	40.00
❑ 1735	Mr. Airplane Man/I've Been Abused	1959	10.00	20.00	40.00
❑ 1744	The Natchez Burning/You Gonna Wreck My Life	1959	10.00	20.00	40.00
❑ 1762	Spoonful/Howlin' for My Baby	1960	7.50	15.00	30.00
❑ 1777	Wang Dang Doodle/Back Door Man	1961	7.50	15.00	30.00
❑ 1793	Little Baby/Down in the Bottom	1961	7.50	15.00	30.00
❑ 1804	The Red Rooster/Shake for Me	1961	6.25	12.50	25.00
❑ 1813	You'll Be Mine/Goin' Down Slow	1962	6.25	12.50	25.00
❑ 1823	Just Like I Treat You/I Ain't Superstitious	1962	6.25	12.50	25.00
❑ 1844	Do the Do/Mama's Baby	1962	6.25	12.50	25.00
❑ 1870	300 Pounds of Joy/Built for Comfort	1963	5.00	10.00	20.00
❑ 1890	Tail Dragger/Hidden Charms	1964	5.00	10.00	20.00
❑ 1911	Love Me Darlin'/My Country Sugar Mama	1964	5.00	10.00	20.00
❑ 1923	Killin' Floor/Louise	1965	5.00	10.00	20.00
❑ 1928	Tell Me What I've Done/Ooh Baby	1965	3.75	7.50	15.00
❑ 1945	I Walked from Dallas/Don't Laugh at Me	1965	3.75	7.50	15.00
❑ 1968	New Crawlin' King Snake/Wild Ramblin'	1966	3.75	7.50	15.00
❑ 2009	I Had a Dream/Pop It to Me	1967	3.75	7.50	15.00
❑ 2081	Mary Sue/Hard Luck	1970	2.00	4.00	8.00

Number	Title (A Side/B Side)	Yr	VG	VG+	NM
❏ 2108	I Smell a Rat/Just As Long	1971	2.00	4.00	8.00
❏ 2118	Do the Do/Red Rooster	1971	2.00	4.00	8.00
❏ 2145	Back Door Wolf/Coon on the Moon	1973	2.00	4.00	8.00
RPM					
❏ 340	Passing By Blues/Crying at Daybreak	1952	1000.	2000.	3000.

—*Note: Howlin' Wolf releases on RPM before 340 are unknown on 45 rpm*

❏ 347	My Baby Stole Off/I Want Your Picture	1952	800.00	1600.	2400.
78s					
CHESS					
❏ 1479	Moanin' at Midnight/How Many More Years	1951	50.00	100.00	200.00
❏ 1497	Howlin' Wolf Boogie/The Wolf Is At Your Door	1952	45.00	90.00	180.00
❏ 1510	Mr. Highway Man/Getting Old and Gray	1952	37.50	75.00	150.00
❏ 1515	Saddle My Pony/Worried All the Time	1952	37.50	75.00	150.00
❏ 1528	Oh! Red/My Last Affair	1952	25.00	50.00	100.00
❏ 1557	All Night Boogie/I Love My Baby	1953	25.00	50.00	100.00
❏ 1566	No Place to Go/Rockin' Daddy	1954	15.00	30.00	60.00
❏ 1575	How Long/Evil Is Going On	1954	12.50	25.00	50.00
❏ 1584	I'll Be Around/Forty Four	1955	10.00	20.00	40.00
❏ 1593	Who Will Be Next/I Have a Little Girl	1955	10.00	20.00	40.00
❏ 1607	Come to Me Baby/Don't Mess with My Baby	1955	10.00	20.00	40.00
❏ 1618	Smoke Stack Lightning/You Can't Be Beat	1956	15.00	30.00	60.00
❏ 1632	I Asked for Water/So Glad	1956	10.00	20.00	40.00
❏ 1648	Goin' Back Home/My Life	1957	10.00	20.00	40.00
❏ 1668	Somebody in My Home/Nature	1957	10.00	20.00	40.00
❏ 1679	Sittin' On Top of the World/Poor Boy	1958	12.50	25.00	50.00
RPM					
❏ 333	Moanin' at Midnight/Riding in the Moonlight	1951	62.50	125.00	250.00
❏ 340	Passing By Blues/Crying at Daybreak	1952	50.00	100.00	200.00
❏ 347	My Baby Stole Off/I Want Your Picture	1952	50.00	100.00	200.00
Albums					
CADET					
❏ LPS-319	This Is Howlin' Wolf's New Album	1969	6.25	12.50	25.00
CHESS					
❏ 201 [(2)]	Howlin' Wolf	1976	3.75	7.50	15.00
❏ LP-1434 [M]	Moanin' in the Moonlight	1958	150.00	300.00	600.00
❏ LP-1469 [M]	Howlin' Wolf	1962	150.00	300.00	600.00
❏ LP-1502 [M]	The Real Folk Blues	1966	12.50	25.00	50.00
❏ LP-1512 [M]	More Real Folk Blues	1966	12.50	25.00	50.00
❏ LP-1540	Evil	1969	6.25	12.50	25.00
❏ CH-9107	His Greatest Sides, Vol. 1	1985	2.50	5.00	10.00
❏ CH-9182	Chicago — 26 Golden Years	1985	2.50	5.00	10.00
❏ CH-9195	Moanin' in the Moonlight	1986	2.00	4.00	8.00

—*Reissue of 1434*

❏ CH-9273	The Real Folk Blues	1988	2.50	5.00	10.00

—*Reissue of 1502*

❏ CH-9279	More Real Folk Blues	1988	2.50	5.00	10.00

—*Reissue of 1512*

❏ CH-9297	The London Howlin' Wolf Sessions	1989	2.50	5.00	10.00

—*Reissue of 60008*

❏ CH5-9332 [(5)]	The Chess Box	1991	10.00	20.00	40.00
❏ CH-50002	Message to the Young	1971	5.00	10.00	20.00
❏ CH-50015	Live and Cookin'	1972	5.00	10.00	20.00
❏ CH-50045	Back Door Wolf	1974	5.00	10.00	20.00
❏ CH-60008	The London Howlin' Wolf Sessions	1971	5.00	10.00	20.00
❏ CH-60016 [(2)]	Howlin' Wolk, AKA Chester Burnett	1972	6.25	12.50	25.00
❏ CH-93001	Change My Way	198?	2.50	5.00	10.00
CROWN					
❏ CLP-5240 [M]	Howlin' Wolf Sings the Blues	1962	6.25	12.50	25.00
CUSTOM					
❏ CM-2055 [M]	Big City Blues	196?	10.00	20.00	40.00
❏ CS-2055 [R]	Big City Blues	196?	5.00	10.00	20.00
KENT					
❏ KLP-526 [M]	Original Folk Blues	1967	3.75	7.50	15.00
❏ KST-526 [R]	Original Folk Blues	1967	3.00	6.00	12.00
❏ KST-527	Howlin' Wolf's 20 Greatest R&B Hits	1968	3.00	6.00	12.00
❏ KST-535	Underground Blues	1968	3.00	6.00	12.00
ROUNDER					
❏ SS-28	Cadillac Daddy: Memphis Recordings, 1952	1989	3.00	6.00	12.00

HUDSON, POOKIE
Lead singer with THE SPANIELS.
45s

Number	Title (A Side/B Side)	Yr	VG	VG+	NM
DOUBLE L					
❏ 711	Jealous Heart/I Know, I Know	1963	5.00	10.00	20.00
❏ 720	I Love You For Sentimental Reasons/Miracles	1963	5.00	10.00	20.00
JAMIE					
❏ 1319	This Gets To Me/All the Places I've Been	1966	15.00	30.00	60.00
PARKWAY					
❏ 839	John Brown/Turn Out the Lights	1962	5.00	10.00	20.00

HUES CORPORATION, THE
45s

Number	Title (A Side/B Side)	Yr	VG	VG+	NM
LIBERTY					
❏ 56204	Goodfootin'/We're Keepin' Our Business Together	1970	—	3.00	6.00

—*As "The Hughes Corporation"*

RCA VICTOR					
❏ 74-0813	There He Is Again/Main Chance	1972	—	2.50	5.00
❏ 74-0900	Freedom for the Stallion/Off My Cloud	1973	—	2.50	5.00
❏ APBO-0139	Go to the Poet/Miracle Maker	1973	—	2.50	5.00
❏ APBO-0232	Rock the Boat/All Goin' Down Together	1974	—	2.50	5.00
❏ PB-10066	Rockin' Soul/Go to the Poet	1974	—	2.50	5.00
❏ PB-10200	Love Corporation/He's My Home	1975	—	2.50	5.00

Number	Title (A Side/B Side)	Yr	VG	VG+	NM
❏ PB-10311	One Good Night Together/When You Look Down the Road	1975	—	2.50	5.00
❏ PB-10390	You Showed Me What Love Is/When You Look Down the Road	1975	—	2.50	5.00
❏ GB-10480	Rockin' Soul/Go to the Poet	1975	—	—	3.00

—*Gold Standard Series*

❏ GB-10481	Rock the Boat/All Goin' Down Together	1975	—	—	3.00

—*Gold Standard Series*

WARNER BROS.					
❏ 8400	I Caught Your Act/Natural Find	1977	—	2.00	4.00
❏ 8559	Give Me Everything/Needed	1978	—	2.00	4.00
❏ 8638	Love Dance/With All My Love and Affection	1978	—	2.00	4.00
Albums					
RCA VICTOR					
❏ APL1-0323	Freedom for the Stallion	1973	2.50	5.00	10.00
❏ APL1-0755	Rockin' Soul	1974	2.50	5.00	10.00
❏ APL1-0938	Love Corporation	1975	2.50	5.00	10.00
❏ ANL1-2147	Rock the Boat	1976	2.00	4.00	8.00
❏ APL1-2408	The Best of the Hues Corporation	1977	2.50	5.00	10.00
WARNER BROS.					
❏ BS 3043	I Caught Your Act	1977	2.50	5.00	10.00
❏ BSK 3196	Your Place or Mine	1978	2.50	5.00	10.00

HUGHES, FRED
45s

Number	Title (A Side/B Side)	Yr	VG	VG+	NM
BRUNSWICK					
❏ 55419	Baby Boy/Who You Really Are	1969	2.00	4.00	8.00
❏ 55439	Oo Wee Baby, I Love You/I Understand	1970	2.00	4.00	8.00
❏ 55446	Don't Let This Happen to Me/In My Time of Need	1971	2.00	4.00	8.00
CADET					
❏ 5616	Baby Don't Go/Love Is Ending	1968	2.50	5.00	10.00
VEE JAY					
❏ 684	Oo Wee Baby, I Love You/Love Me Baby	1965	3.75	7.50	15.00
❏ 703	You Can't Take It Away/My Heart Cries On	1965	3.75	7.50	15.00
❏ 718	Don't Let Me Down/My Heart Cries On	1965	3.75	7.50	15.00
Albums					
BRUNSWICK					
❏ BL 754147	Baby Boy	1970	3.75	7.50	15.00

HUGHES, JIMMY
45s

Number	Title (A Side/B Side)	Yr	VG	VG+	NM
ATLANTIC					
❏ 2454	Uncle Sam/It Ain't What You've Got	1967	2.00	4.00	8.00
FAME					
❏ 1000	Midnight Affair/When It Comes to Dancing	1965	2.50	5.00	10.00
❏ 1003	Neighbor, Neighbor/It's a Good Thing	1966	2.00	4.00	8.00
❏ 1006	I Worship the Ground You Walk On/A Shot of Rhythm and Blues	1966	2.00	4.00	8.00
❏ 1011	Why Not Tonight/I'm a Man of Action	1967	2.00	4.00	8.00
❏ 1014	Don't Lose Your Good Thing/You Can't Believe Everything That You Hear	1967	2.00	4.00	8.00
❏ 1015	Hi-Heel Sneakers/Time Will Bring You Back	1967	2.00	4.00	8.00
❏ 6401	Steal Away/Lollipops, Lace and Lipstick	1964	5.00	10.00	20.00

—*Black label*

❏ 6401	Steal Away/Lollipops, Lace and Lipstick	1964	3.00	6.00	12.00

—*Red label*

❏ 6403	Try Me/Lovely Ladies	1964	2.50	5.00	10.00
❏ 6404	I Want Justice/I'm Getting Better	1964	2.50	5.00	10.00
❏ 6407	Goodbye My Lover, Goodbye/It Was Nice	1965	2.50	5.00	10.00
❏ 6410	You Really Know How to Hurt a Guy/The Loving Physician	1965	2.50	5.00	10.00
GUYDEN					
❏ 2075	I'm Qualified/My Loving Time	1962	5.00	10.00	20.00
JAMIE					
❏ 1280	I'm Qualified/My Loving Time	1964	3.75	7.50	15.00
VOLT					
❏ 4002	I Like Everything About You/What Side of the Door	1968	2.00	4.00	8.00
❏ 4008	Let 'Em Down Baby/The Sweet Things You Do	1969	2.00	4.00	8.00
❏ 4017	Chains of Love/I'm Not Ashamed to Beg or Plead	1969	2.00	4.00	8.00
❏ 4024	I'm So Glad/Lay It on the Line	1969	2.00	4.00	8.00
Albums					
ATCO					
❏ 33-209 [M]	Why Not Tonight	1967	5.00	10.00	20.00
❏ SD 33-209 [S]	Why Not Tonight	1967	5.00	10.00	20.00
VEE JAY					
❏ VJ-1102 [M]	Steal Away	1965	6.25	12.50	25.00
❏ VJS-1102 [R]	Steal Away	1965	6.25	12.50	25.00
VOLT					
❏ VOS-6003	Something Special	1969	5.00	10.00	20.00

HUMES, ANITA
45s

Number	Title (A Side/B Side)	Yr	VG	VG+	NM
ROULETTE					
❏ 4564	Don't Fight It Baby/When Somethin's Hard to Get	1964	3.75	7.50	15.00
❏ 4575	I'm Making It Over/Just for the Boy	1964	3.75	7.50	15.00
❏ 4750	Are You Going My Way/Everybody's Got You	1967	2.50	5.00	10.00

HUMPHREY, BOBBI
12-Inch Singles

Number	Title (A Side/B Side)	Yr	VG	VG+	NM
EPIC					
❏ 50537	Home-Made Jam/Sunset Burgundy	1978	2.50	5.00	10.00
❏ 50746	Love When I'm In Your Arms/Sweet and Low	1979	2.50	5.00	10.00

Number	Title (A Side/B Side)	Yr	VG	VG+	NM
WARNER BROS.					
❑ 21716	Let's Get Started (2 versions)/Rainbows	1990	—	3.00	6.00
45s					
BLUE NOTE					
❑ XW395	Chicago, Damn/Just a Love Child	1974	—	2.50	5.00
❑ XW455	Harlem River Drive/Black and Blues	1974	—	2.50	5.00
❑ XW592	Fun House/San Francisco Lights	1975	—	2.50	5.00
❑ XW785	Uno Esta/Sweeter Than Sugar	1976	—	2.50	5.00
❑ 1971	Spanish Harlem/Sad Bag	1971	2.00	4.00	8.00
❑ 1974	Ain't No Sunchine/Sad Bag	1972	2.00	4.00	8.00
❑ 1980	Is This All/Lonely Town, Lonely Street	1972	2.00	4.00	8.00
EPIC					
❑ 50448	Dancin' to Keep From Cryin'/Theme I	1977	—	2.50	5.00
❑ 50529	Home-Made Jam/Sunset Burgundy	1978	—	2.50	5.00
❑ 50745	Love When I'm In Your Arms/Sweet and Low	1979	—	2.50	5.00
Albums					
BLUE NOTE					
❑ BN-LA142-G	Blacks and Blues	1974	2.50	5.00	10.00
❑ BN-LA344-G	Satin Doll	1974	2.50	5.00	10.00
❑ BN-LA550-G	Fancy Dancer	1975	2.50	5.00	10.00
❑ BN-LA699-G	The Best of Bobbi Humphrey	1976	2.50	5.00	10.00
❑ BST-84379	Flute-In	1971	3.00	6.00	12.00
❑ BST-84421	Dig This	1972	3.00	6.00	12.00
EPIC					
❑ PE 34704	Tailor Made	1977	2.50	5.00	10.00
❑ JE 35338	Freestyle	1978	2.50	5.00	10.00
❑ JE 35607	The Good Life	1979	2.50	5.00	10.00
❑ JE 36368	The Best of Bobbi Humphrey	1980	2.50	5.00	10.00

HUNTER, IVORY JOE

Number	Title (A Side/B Side)	Yr	VG	VG+	NM
45s					
4 STAR					
❑ 1634	Foolish Pride/Did You Mean It	1953	10.00	20.00	40.00
ATLANTIC					
❑ 1049	It May Sound Silly/I Got to Learn to Do the Mambo	1954	6.25	12.50	25.00
❑ 1066	I Want Somebody/Heven Came Down to Earth	1955	6.25	12.50	25.00
❑ 1086	A Tear Fell/I Need You By My Side	1956	6.25	12.50	25.00
❑ 1095	You Mean Everything to Me/That's Why I Dream	1956	6.25	12.50	25.00
❑ 1111	Since I Met You Baby/You Can't Stop This Rocking and Rolling	1956	7.50	15.00	30.00
❑ 1128	Empty Arms/Love's a Hurting Game	1957	5.00	10.00	20.00
❑ 1151	She's Gone/Everytime I Hear That Song	1957	5.00	10.00	20.00
❑ 1164	All About the Blues/If Only You Were Here with Me	1957	5.00	10.00	20.00
❑ 1173	You're On My Mind/Baby, Baby, Count on Me	1958	5.00	10.00	20.00
❑ 1183	I'm So Glad I Found You/Shooty Booty	1958	5.00	10.00	20.00
❑ 1191	You Flip Me Baby/Yes, I Want You	1958	5.00	10.00	20.00
❑ 2020	I Just Want to Love You/Now I Don't Worry No More	1959	3.75	7.50	15.00
CAPITOL					
❑ 4587	I'm Hooked/Because I Love You	1961	3.00	6.00	12.00
❑ 4648	May the Best Man Win/You Better Believe It Baby	1961	3.00	6.00	12.00
❑ 4688	The Life I Live/A Great Big Heart Full of Love	1962	3.00	6.00	12.00
DOT					
❑ 15880	City Lights/Stolen Moments	1958	3.75	7.50	15.00
❑ 15930	Old Fashioned Love/Cottage for Sale	1959	3.75	7.50	15.00
❑ 15957	I Love You So Much/Welcome Home Baby	1959	3.75	7.50	15.00
❑ 15986	My Search Was Ended/Did You Mean It	1959	3.75	7.50	15.00
EPIC					
❑ 10725	Heartbreak and Misery/We All Like That Groovy Feeling	1971	—	3.00	6.00
❑ 10725	Heartbreak and Misery/I'm Coming Down with the Blues	1971	—	3.00	6.00
GOLDISC					
❑ 3010	It's Love, It's Love, It's Love/You Satisfy Me Baby	1960	3.75	7.50	15.00
GOLDWAX					
❑ 307	Every Little Bit Helped Me/I Can Make You Happy	1966	5.00	10.00	20.00
KING					
❑ 4424	False Friend Blues/Send Me Pretty Mama	1951	10.00	20.00	40.00
—Ivory Joe Hunter records on King before 4422 are unconfirmed on 45 rpm					
❑ 4443	She's Gone Blues/Stop Rockin' That Train	1951	10.00	20.00	40.00
❑ 4455	Old Gal and New Gal Blues/Woo Wee Blues	1951	10.00	20.00	40.00
❑ 5166	Jealous Heart/I Like It	1958	3.75	7.50	15.00
❑ 5271	Guess Who/Don't Fall in Love with Me	1959	—	—	—
—Unreleased					
❑ 5280	Guess Who/Don't Fall in Love with Me	1959	3.75	7.50	15.00
MGM					
❑ 8011	I Almost Lost My Mind/If I Give You My Love	1949	12.50	25.00	50.00
—Original 45 issue of this record					
❑ K10578	I Almost Lost My Mind/If I Give You My Love	1949	10.00	20.00	40.00
❑ K10618	S.P. Blues/Why Fool Yourself	1950	7.50	15.00	30.00
❑ K10663	I Need You So/Leave Her Alone	1950	7.50	15.00	30.00
❑ K10733	Let Me Dream/Gimme a Pound of Round Ground	1950	7.50	15.00	30.00
❑ K10761	Old Man's Boogie/Living a Lie	1950	7.50	15.00	30.00
❑ K10818	It's A Sin/Don't You Believe Me	1950	7.50	15.00	30.00
❑ K10899	I Found My Baby/I Ain't Got No Gal	1951	7.50	15.00	30.00
❑ K10951	I Can't Get You Off My Mind/I Can't Resist You	1951	7.50	15.00	30.00
❑ K10995	You Lied/When I Lost You	1951	7.50	15.00	30.00
❑ K11052	I'm Yours/Wrong Woman Blues	1951	7.50	15.00	30.00
❑ K11132	Blue Moon/U Name It	1952	7.50	15.00	30.00
❑ K11165	Laugh/Where Shall I Go	1952	7.50	15.00	30.00
❑ K11195	I'm Sorry for You My Friend/I Will Be	1952	7.50	15.00	30.00
❑ K11263	I Get That Lonesome Feeling/I Thought I Had Loved	1952	7.50	15.00	30.00
❑ K11325	Big Bounce/Tell Her for Me	1952	7.50	15.00	30.00
❑ K11378	Rockin' Chair Boogie/Music Before Dawn	1952	7.50	15.00	30.00
❑ K11459	I Had a Girl/If You See My Baby	1953	7.50	15.00	30.00
❑ K11549	I'm Afraid/Don't Make Me Cry	1953	7.50	15.00	30.00
❑ K11599	I Must Be Talking to Myself/My Best Wishes	1953	7.50	15.00	30.00
❑ K11702	I Have a Secret/I Feel So Good	1954	6.25	12.50	25.00
❑ K11818	Do You Miss Me/Whose Arms Are You Missing	1954	6.25	12.50	25.00
PARAMOUNT					
❑ 0253	He'll Never Love You/San Antonio Rose	1973	—	3.00	6.00
SMASH					
❑ 1825	My Arms Are Waiting/Congratulations	1963	3.00	6.00	12.00
❑ 1860	There's No Forgetting You/My Lover's Prayer	1963	3.00	6.00	12.00
SOUND STAGE 7					
❑ 2623	Ivory Tower/I'll Give You All Night to Stop	1968	2.00	4.00	8.00
❑ 2635	Until the Day I Die/I Built a Wall Around Me	1969	2.00	4.00	8.00
❑ 2643	Straighten Up Baby/Baby Me Baby	1969	2.00	4.00	8.00
STAX					
❑ 155	This Kind of Woman/Can't Explain Why It Happened	1964	3.00	6.00	12.00
TEARDROP					
❑ 3058	I've Asked You for the Last Time/Heart	196?	2.50	5.00	10.00
VEE JAY					
❑ 452	Somebody's Stealing My Love/You Only Want Me When You Need Me	1962	3.00	6.00	12.00
VEEP					
❑ 1258	What's the Matter Baby/Don't You Believe Me	1967	2.00	4.00	8.00
❑ 1270	Did She Ask About Me/From the First Time We Met	1967	2.00	4.00	8.00
78s					
4 STAR					
❑ 1254	Pretty Mama Blues/Are You Hep	1949	6.25	12.50	25.00
❑ 1283	Blues at Midnight/I Love My Man	1949	6.25	12.50	25.00
❑ 1376	Please Come Back Home Baby/Seventh Street Boogie	1949	6.25	12.50	25.00
❑ 1452	Don't Leave Me/Coming Round the Mountain	1950	5.00	10.00	20.00
—B-side by Cecil Gant					
❑ 1481	She's a Killer/Empty Room Blues	1950	6.25	12.50	25.00
❑ 1535	Jumpin' at the Dew Drop Inn/We're Gonna Boogie	1950	6.25	12.50	25.00
❑ 1551	Big Wig/Grieving Blues	1951	6.25	12.50	25.00
❑ 1585	Boogie in the Rain/I Shouldn't Love You	1952	6.25	12.50	25.00
❑ 1634	Foolish Pride/Did You Mean It	1953	5.00	10.00	20.00
ATLANTIC					
❑ 1049	It May Sound Silly/I Got to Learn to Do the Mambo	1954	6.25	12.50	25.00
❑ 1066	I Want Somebody/Heven Came Down to Earth	1955	6.25	12.50	25.00
❑ 1086	A Tear Fell/I Need You By My Side	1956	7.50	15.00	30.00
❑ 1095	You Mean Everything to Me/That's Why I Dream	1956	7.50	15.00	30.00
❑ 1111	Since I Met You Baby/You Can't Stop This Rocking and Rolling	1956	10.00	20.00	40.00
❑ 1128	Empty Arms/Love's a Hurting Game	1957	7.50	15.00	30.00
❑ 1151	She's Gone/Everytime I Hear That Song	1957	7.50	15.00	30.00
❑ 1164	All About the Blues/If Only You Were Here with Me	1957	7.50	15.00	30.00
❑ 1173	You're On My Mind/Baby, Baby, Count on Me	1958	10.00	20.00	40.00
❑ 1183	I'm So Glad I Found You/Shooty Booty	1958	10.00	20.00	40.00
❑ 1191	You Flip Me Baby/Yes, I Want You	1958	12.50	25.00	50.00
EXCLUSIVE					
❑ 209	Blues at Sunrise/You Taught Me to Love	1945	6.25	12.50	25.00
—With Johnny Moore's 3 Blazes					
KING					
❑ 4183	San Francisco Blues/Don't Be No Fool, Fool	1947	6.25	12.50	25.00
❑ 4208	I Was Only Playing/Come On, Let Your Hair Down	1947	6.25	12.50	25.00
❑ 4220	Don't Fall in Love with Me/Siesta with Sonny	1948	5.00	10.00	20.00
❑ 4232	What Did You Do to Me/The Code Song	1948	5.00	10.00	20.00
❑ 4255	I Like It/No Money, No Luck Blues	1948	5.00	10.00	20.00
❑ 4275	Don't Know/In Time	1949	5.00	10.00	20.00
❑ 4291	Waiting in Vain/That's the Gal for Me	1949	5.00	10.00	20.00
❑ 4306	Guess Who/Landlord Blues	1949	5.00	10.00	20.00
❑ 4314	Jealous Heart/All States Boogie	1949	5.00	10.00	20.00
❑ 4326	I Quit My Pretty Mama/It's You, Just You	1949	5.00	10.00	20.00
❑ 4347	I Got Your Water On/Please Don't Cry Anymore	1950	5.00	10.00	20.00
❑ 4374	Time Alone Will Tell/Sometimes I Wonder	1950	5.00	10.00	20.00
❑ 4382	Changing Blues/I Have No Reason to Complain	1950	5.00	10.00	20.00
❑ 4405	Lying Woman Blues/Too Late	1950	5.00	10.00	20.00
❑ 4424	False Friend Blues/Send Me Pretty Mama	1951	3.75	7.50	15.00
❑ 4443	She's Gone Blues/Stop Rockin' That Train	1951	3.75	7.50	15.00
❑ 4455	Old Gal and New Gal Blues/Woo Wee Blues	1951	3.75	7.50	15.00
MGM					
❑ 10578	I Almost Lost My Mind/If I Give You My Love	1949	5.00	10.00	20.00
❑ 10618	S.P. Blues/Why Fool Yourself	1950	3.75	7.50	15.00
❑ 10663	I Need You So/Leave Her Alone	1950	3.75	7.50	15.00
❑ 10733	Let Me Dream/Gimme a Pound of Round Ground	1950	3.75	7.50	15.00
❑ 10761	Old Man's Boogie/Living a Lie	1950	3.75	7.50	15.00
❑ 10818	It's A Sin/Don't You Believe Me	1950	3.75	7.50	15.00
❑ 10899	I Found My Baby/I Ain't Got No Gal	1951	3.75	7.50	15.00
❑ 10951	I Can't Get You Off My Mind/I Can't Resist You	1951	3.75	7.50	15.00
❑ 10995	You Lied/When I Lost You	1951	3.75	7.50	15.00
❑ 11052	I'm Yours/Wrong Woman Blues	1951	3.75	7.50	15.00
❑ 11132	Blue Moon/U Name It	1952	3.75	7.50	15.00
❑ 11165	Laugh/Where Shall I Go	1952	3.75	7.50	15.00
❑ 11195	I'm Sorry for You My Friend/I Will Be	1952	3.75	7.50	15.00
❑ 11263	I Get That Lonesome Feeling/I Thought I Had Loved	1952	3.75	7.50	15.00
❑ 11325	Big Bounce/Tell Her for Me	1952	3.75	7.50	15.00
❑ 11378	Rockin' Chair Boogie/Music Before Dawn	1952	7.50	15.00	30.00

Number	Title (A Side/B Side)	Yr	VG	VG+	NM
❑ 11459	I Had a Girl/If You See My Baby	1953	3.75	7.50	15.00
❑ 11549	I'm Afraid/Don't Make Me Cry	1953	3.75	7.50	15.00
❑ 11599	I Must Be Talking to Myself/My Best Wishes	1953	3.75	7.50	15.00
❑ 11702	I Have a Secret/I Feel So Good	1954	3.75	7.50	15.00
❑ 11818	Do You Miss Me/Whose Arms Are You Missing	1954	3.75	7.50	15.00

PACIFIC

❑ 601	Seventh Street Boogie/Reconversion Blues	194?	7.50	15.00	30.00
❑ 602	Boogin' in the Basement/Don't Leave Me	194?	7.50	15.00	30.00
❑ 609	Tavern Swing/Bad Luck Blues	194?	7.50	15.00	30.00
❑ 612	Ivory Joe's Boogie/Gazing	194?	7.50	15.00	30.00
❑ 619	What Happened?/Right, Nine and Ten	194?	7.50	15.00	30.00
❑ 621	We're Gonna Boogie/Heavy Hearted Blues	194?	7.50	15.00	30.00
❑ 622	Why Did You Lie?/I'm Sorry	194?	7.50	15.00	30.00
❑ 623	Are You Hep?/I Love My Man	194?	7.50	15.00	30.00
❑ 630	Blues at Midnight/High Cost, Low Pay Blues	194?	7.50	15.00	30.00
❑ 632	Jammin' Down in Town/Mean Woman Blues	194?	7.50	15.00	30.00
❑ 634	You're Always Looking for More/Grieving Blues	194?	7.50	15.00	30.00
❑ 637	Pretty Mama Blues/I Don't Want No Cheese No More	1948	7.50	15.00	30.00

7-Inch Extended Plays
ATLANTIC

❑ EP 589	*Since I Met You Baby/I Got to Learn to Do the Mambo/It May Sound Silly/A Tear Fell	1958	12.50	25.00	50.00
❑ EP 589 [PS]	Ivory Joe Hunter (Since I Met You Baby)	1958	12.50	25.00	50.00
❑ EP 608	*Empty Arms/Love's a Hurting Game/She's Gone/Everytime I Hear That Song	1958	15.00	30.00	60.00
❑ EP 608 [PS]	Rock with Ivory Joe Hunter	1958	15.00	30.00	60.00

KING

❑ 265	(contents unknown)	1954	20.00	40.00	80.00
❑ 265 [PS]	Ivory Joe Hunter	1954	20.00	40.00	80.00

MGM

❑ X-1376	(contents unknown)	1957	12.50	25.00	50.00
❑ X-1376 [PS]	I Get That Lonesome Feeling, Volume 1	1957	12.50	25.00	50.00
❑ X-1377	I Get That Lonesome Feeling/I Found a New Baby//I Need You So/If You See My Baby	1957	12.50	25.00	50.00
❑ X-1377 [PS]	I Get That Lonesome Feeling, Volume 2	1957	12.50	25.00	50.00
❑ X-1378	(contents unknown)	1957	12.50	25.00	50.00
❑ X-1378 [PS]	I Get That Lonesome Feeling, Volume 3	1957	12.50	25.00	50.00

Albums
ARCHIVE OF FOLK AND JAZZ

❑ 289	Ivory Joe Hunter	1974	3.00	6.00	12.00

ATLANTIC

❑ 8008 [M]	Ivory Joe Hunter	1957	50.00	100.00	200.00
—Black label					
❑ 8008 [M]	Ivory Joe Hunter	1960	25.00	50.00	100.00
—Purple and red label					
❑ 8015 [M]	The Old and the New	1958	50.00	100.00	200.00
—Black label					
❑ 8015 [M]	The Old and the New	1960	25.00	50.00	100.00
—Purple and red label					

DOT

❑ DLP-3569 [M]	This Is Ivory Joe Hunter	1964	10.00	20.00	40.00
❑ DLP-25569 [S]	This Is Ivory Joe Hunter	1964	12.50	25.00	50.00

EPIC

❑ E 30348	The Return of Ivory Joe Hunter	1971	5.00	10.00	20.00

GOLDISC

❑ 403 [M]	The Fabulous Ivory Joe Hunter	1961	15.00	30.00	60.00

HOME COOKING

❑ 112	I'm Coming Down with the Blues	1989	3.00	6.00	12.00

KING

❑ 605 [M]	16 of His Greatest Hits	1958	100.00	200.00	400.00

LION

❑ L-70068 [M]	I Need You So	1959	15.00	30.00	60.00

MGM

❑ E-3488 [M]	I Get That Lonesome Feeling	1957	75.00	150.00	300.00

PARAMOUNT

❑ PAS-6080	I've Always Been Country	1974	3.00	6.00	12.00

POLYDOR

❑ 830897-1	Since I Met You Baby	1987	3.00	6.00	12.00

SMASH

❑ MGS-27037 [M]	Ivory Joe Hunter's Golden Hits	1963	10.00	20.00	40.00
❑ SRS-67037 [S]	Ivory Joe Hunter's Golden Hits	1963	12.50	25.00	50.00

SOUND

❑ M-603 [M]	Ivory Joe Hunter	1959	37.50	75.00	150.00

STRAND

❑ SL-1123 [M]	The Artistry of Ivory Joe Hunter	196?	10.00	20.00	40.00
❑ SLS-1123 [S]	The Artistry of Ivory Joe Hunter	196?	12.50	25.00	50.00

HUNTER, TY
45s
ANNA

❑ 1114	Everything About You/Orphan Boy	1960	6.25	12.50	25.00
❑ 1123	Every Time/I'm Free	1960	7.50	15.00	30.00

CHECK MATE

❑ 1002	Memories/The Envy of Every Man	1961	6.25	12.50	25.00
❑ 1015	Gladness to Sadness/Lonely Baby	1961	6.25	12.50	25.00

CHESS

❑ 1857	Darling, My Babe/In Time	1963	5.00	10.00	20.00
❑ 1881	Am I Losing You/Love Walked Right Out on Me	1964	3.75	7.50	15.00
❑ 1893	Bad Loser/Something Like a Storm	1964	3.75	7.50	15.00

INVICTUS

❑ 9120	Hey There Lonely Girl/I Don't See Me in Your Eyes Anymore	1972	3.75	7.50	15.00

HUTCH, WILLIE
45s
DUNHILL

❑ 4012	The Duck/Love Runs Out	1965	15.00	30.00	60.00

MAVERICK

❑ 1003	Use What You Got (Part 1)/Use What You Got (Part 2)	1968	3.75	7.50	15.00

MODERN

❑ 1021	I Can't Get Enough/Your Love Has Made Me a Man	1966	10.00	20.00	40.00

MOTOWN

❑ 1222	Brother's Gonna Work It Out/I Choose You	1973	—	2.50	5.00
❑ 1252	Slick/Mother's Theme	1973	—	2.50	5.00
❑ 1252 [PS]	Slick/Mother's Theme	1973	—	3.00	6.00
❑ 1282	Sunshine Lady/I Just Wanted to Make Her Happy	1973	—	2.50	5.00
❑ 1287	If You Ain't Got No Money (You Can't Get No Honey) Pt. 1/Pt. 2	1974	—	2.50	5.00
❑ 1292	Theme of Foxy Brown/Give Me Some of That Good Old Love	1974	—	2.50	5.00
❑ 1331	I'm Gonna Stay/Woman You Touched Me	1975	—	2.50	5.00
❑ 1339	Get Ready for the Get Down/Don't Let Nobody Tell You How to Do Your Thing	1975	—	2.50	5.00
❑ 1360	Love Power/Talk to Me	1975	—	2.00	4.00
❑ 1371	Party Down/Just Another Day	1976	—	2.00	4.00
❑ 1406	Let Me Be the One, Baby/She's Just Doing Her Thing	1976	—	2.00	4.00
❑ 1411	Shake It, Shake It/I Feel Like We Can Make It	1976	—	2.00	4.00
❑ 1416	We Gonna Have a House Party/Never Had It So Good	1977	—	2.00	4.00
❑ 1424	We Gonna Party Tonight/Precious Pearl	1977	—	2.00	4.00
❑ 1433	What You Gonna Do After the Party/I Feel Like We Can Make It	1977	—	2.00	4.00
❑ 1637	In and Out/Girl	1982	—	2.00	4.00
❑ 1797	Keep On Jammin'/The Glow	1985	—	2.00	4.00

RCA VICTOR

❑ 74-0189	Ain't Gonna Stop/Do What You Wanna Do	1969	2.50	5.00	10.00
❑ 74-0294	When a Boy Falls in Love (Part 1)/When a Boy Falls in Love (Part 2)	1969	2.50	5.00	10.00
❑ 74-0327	Magic of Love/Walking on My Love	1970	2.50	5.00	10.00

WHITFIELD

❑ 8615	All American Funkathon/And All Hell Broke Loose	1978	—	2.00	4.00
❑ 8689	Paradise/Hip Shakin' Sexy Lady	1978	—	2.00	4.00
❑ 49015	Deep in Your Love/Everybody Needs Money	1979	—	2.00	4.00
❑ 49102	Down Here on Disco Street/Kelly Green	1979	—	2.00	4.00

Albums
MOTOWN

❑ M 766	The Mack	1973	3.00	6.00	12.00
❑ M 784	Fully Exposed	1973	3.00	6.00	12.00
❑ M6-811	Foxy Brown	1974	3.00	6.00	12.00
❑ M6-815	Mark of the Beast	1974	3.00	6.00	12.00
❑ M6-838	Ode to My Lady	1975	3.00	6.00	12.00
❑ M6-854	Concert in Blues	1976	3.00	6.00	12.00
❑ M6-871	Color Her...	1977	3.00	6.00	12.00
❑ M6-874	Havin' a House Party	1977	3.00	6.00	12.00
❑ 5281 ML	The Mack	1983	2.00	4.00	8.00
—Reissue of 766					

RCA VICTOR

❑ LSP-4213	Soul Portrait: Willie Hutch	1969	3.75	7.50	15.00

WHITFIELD

❑ BSK 3226	In Tune	1978	2.50	5.00	10.00
❑ BSK 3352	Midnight Dancer	1979	2.50	5.00	10.00

HUTTO, J.B.
45s
CHANCE

❑ 1155	Now She's Gone/Combination Boogie	1954	250.00	500.00	1000.
❑ 1160	Lovin' You/Pet Cream Man	1954	1000.	2000.	4000.
—The above two may be listed on the label as "J.B. and the Hawks"					
❑ 1165	Dim Lights/Things Are So Slow	1955	750.00	1500.	3000.

78s
CHANCE

❑ 1155	Now She's Gone/Combination Boogie	1954	62.50	125.00	250.00
❑ 1160	Lovin' You/Pet Cream Man	1954	250.00	500.00	1000.
—The above two may be listed on the label as "J.B. and the Hawks"					
❑ 1165	Dim Lights/Things Are So Slow	1955	100.00	200.00	400.00

HYMAN, PHYLLIS
12-Inch Singles
ARISTA

❑ SP-42	Kiss You All Over/So Strange	1979	3.75	7.50	15.00
❑ SP-114	Tonight You and Me (3:44) (5:25)	1981	3.75	7.50	15.00
❑ SP-155	Riding the Tiger (Dance Version) (Instrumental Version)	1983	3.75	7.50	15.00
❑ AD1-9041	Riding the Tiger (Dance Version) (Instrumental)	1983	3.00	6.00	12.00

PHILADELPHIA INT'L.

❑ SPRO-9753/4 [DJ]	Old Friend (Long) (Short)/Screaming at the Moon (Long)	1986	3.00	6.00	12.00
❑ SPRO-9910 [DJ]	Living All Alone (6:03) (3:16)/What You Won't Do for Love	1986	2.50	5.00	10.00
❑ V-56032	Old Friend (Long) (Short)/Screaming at the Moon (Long) (Short)	1986	2.50	5.00	10.00
❑ SPRO-79019/20 [DJ]	Ain't You Had Enough Love (Extended Version 6:32) (Instrumental 5:28) (Percussapella Version 5:38) (Short Version 4:15)	1987	3.75	7.50	15.00

Number	Title (A Side/B Side)	Yr	VG	VG+	NM
ZOO					
ZP 17021	Don't Wanna Change the World (Extended Rap Version) (Rap Version) (No Rap Version)	1991	2.50	5.00	10.00

45s

ARISTA

Number	Title (A Side/B Side)	Yr	VG	VG+	NM
0380	Somewhere in My Lifetime/Gonna Make Changes	1978	—	2.00	4.00
0412	Kiss You All Over/So Strange	1979	—	2.00	4.00
0463	You Know How to Love Me/Give a Little More	1979	—	2.00	4.00
0495	Under Your Spell/Complete Me	1980	—	2.00	4.00
0606	Can't We Fall in Love Again/The Sunshine in My Life	1981	—	2.00	4.00

—A-side with Michael Henderson

0637	Tonight You and Me/The Sunshine in My Life	1981	—	2.00	4.00
0656	You Sure Look Good to Me/Just Another Face in the Crowd	1982	—	2.00	4.00
1061	Riding the Tiger//(Instrumental)	1983	—	2.50	5.00

—Reassigned to 9023

| 9023 | Riding the Tiger//(Instrumental) | 1983 | — | 2.00 | 4.00 |
| 9071 | Why Did You Turn Me On/Let Somebody Love You | 1983 | — | 2.00 | 4.00 |

BUDDAH

| 567 | Loving You — Losing You/Children of the World | 1977 | — | 2.50 | 5.00 |
| 577 | No One Can Love You More/Deliver the Love | 1977 | — | 2.50 | 5.00 |

DESERT MOON

| 6402 | Baby (I'm Gonna Love You)/Do Me | 1976 | — | 3.00 | 6.00 |

PHILADELPHIA INT'L.

B-50031	Old Friend/Screamin' at the Moon	1986	—	2.00	4.00
B-50031 [PS]	Old Friend/Screamin' at the Moon	1986	—	2.00	4.00
B-50059	Living All Alone/What You Won't Do for Love	1986	—	2.00	4.00
B-50059 [PS]	Living All Alone/What You Won't Do for Love	1986	—	2.00	4.00
B-50070	Ain't You Had Enough Love/First Time Together	1987	—	2.00	4.00
B-50095	You Just Don't Know/Slow Dancin'	1987	—	2.00	4.00

PRIVATE STOCK

| 45,034 | Leavin' the Good Life Behind/(B-side unknown) | 1975 | 2.50 | 5.00 | 10.00 |

Albums

ARISTA

AB 4202	Somewhere in My Lifetime	1979	3.00	6.00	12.00
AL8-8021	Goddess of Love	1983	3.00	6.00	12.00
AL 9509	You Know How to Love Me	1979	3.00	6.00	12.00
AL 9544	Can't We Fall in Love Again	1981	3.00	6.00	12.00

BUDDAH

| BDS-5681 | Phyllis Hyman | 1977 | 3.75 | 7.50 | 15.00 |

PHILADELPHIA INT'L.

| ST-53029 | Living All Alone | 1986 | 2.00 | 4.00 | 8.00 |

I

ICE-T
Also see BODY COUNT.

12-Inch Singles

ATOMIC POP

Number	Title (A Side/B Side)	Yr	VG	VG+	NM
APPRO-5003	Exodus (Clean Version Featuring Top Gunz) (Instrumental) (A Cappella - Clean)/Always Wanted Ta Be a Ho (Clean Featuring Ice's Ho) (Instrumental)/Fuck It (LP Version Featuring Elsadiq and Powerlord Jel) (Instrumental)	1999	5.00	10.00	20.00

ELECTROBEAT

| EB 002 | Killers (Vocal Mix 4:30) (Instrumental Dub 4:37)/Body Rock (Vocal Mix 6:04) (Bonus Beats 2:55) | 198? | 7.50 | 15.00 | 30.00 |

GIANT

| PRO-A-4643 [DJ] | New Jack Hustler (3 versions) | 1991 | 3.00 | 6.00 | 12.00 |
| 21845 | New Jack Hustler (4 versions) | 1991 | 2.50 | 5.00 | 10.00 |

RHINO

| 393 | Ice-A Mix (7:00)/Ice-O-Tek (5:00) | 1993 | 2.00 | 4.00 | 8.00 |

RHYME SYNDICATE

7023	That's How I'm Livin' (4 versions)/99 Problems (2 versions)	1993	—	3.00	6.00
SPRO-30046 [DJ]	I Must Stand (Clean) (Instrumental)//Where It Goes Down (Clean)/Where the Shit Goes Down (LP Version)	1996	2.50	5.00	10.00
SPRO-50897 [DJ]	Where It Goes Down (Radio)/Where the Shit Goes Down (LP Version)//Pimp Anthem	1996	3.00	6.00	12.00
53210	I Must Stand (2 versions)/Where the Shit Goes Down (2 versions)	1996	2.50	5.00	10.00
53821	Gotta Lotta Love (3 versions)	199?	—	3.50	7.00

—Reissue of Sire 40737

SIRE

PRO-A-3686 [DJ]	Lethal Weapon (Radio Version) (same on both sides?)	1989	2.00	4.00	8.00
PRO-A-5143 [DJ]	Mind Over Matter (4 versions)/Ricochet (3 versions)	1991	2.00	4.00	8.00
PRO-A-5367 [DJ]	Mind Over Matter (4 versions)	1991	2.00	4.00	8.00
20711	Make It Funky (3 versions)/Sex (2 versions)	1987	2.50	5.00	10.00
20805	Somebody Gotta Do It (Pimpin' Ain't Easy) (12" Mix) (Dub)/Our Most Requested Record (Short Version) (Long Version)	1987	3.75	7.50	15.00
20936	Colors (5 versions)/Squeeze the Trigger	1993	2.00	4.00	8.00
21026	I'm Your Pusher (3 versions)/Girls L.G.B.N.A.F. (3 versions)	1988	2.00	4.00	8.00
21149	High Rollers/The Hunted Child (3 versions)/Power (Remix) (Instrumental)	1989	2.00	4.00	8.00
21325	Lethal Weapon (2 versions)/This One's for Me/Heartbeat	1989	2.00	4.00	8.00
21426	You Played Yourself (3 versions)/Freedom of Speech	1990	2.50	5.00	10.00
21445	What Ya Wanna Do (Edit) (LP Version) (Instrumental)/The Girl Tried to Kill Me (Radio Remix)	1990	2.50	5.00	10.00
21704	Dick Tracy (4 versions)	1990	2.00	4.00	8.00
40104	Original Gangster (3 versions)/Bitches 2 (2 versions)	1991	2.00	4.00	8.00
40131	Lifestyles of the Rich and Infamous (3 versions)/The Tower (2 versions)	1991	—	3.00	6.00
40210	Ricochet (2 versions)/Mind Over Matter (Remix)	1991	2.50	5.00	10.00
40737	Gotta Lotta Love (3 versions)	1992	2.50	5.00	10.00

TECHNOHOP

| 10 | Ya Don't Quit (3 versions) | 1986 | 3.00 | 6.00 | 12.00 |
| 13 | Dog'n the Wax (3 versions)/6 in the Morning | 1986 | 3.75 | 7.50 | 15.00 |

45s

SIRE

PRO-S-2751 [DJ]	Make It Funky (same on both sides)	1987	—	3.00	6.00
19994	You Played Yourself/Freedom of Speech	1990	—	3.00	6.00
22810	Lethal Weapon/Heartbeat	1989	—	2.00	4.00
27574	High Rollers/The Hunted Child	1989	—	2.00	4.00
27768	I'm Your Pusher/Girls L.G.B.N.A.F.	1988	—	2.00	4.00
27768 [PS]	I'm Your Pusher/Girls L.G.B.N.A.F.	1988	—	2.00	4.00
27902	Colors/Squeeze the Trigger	1988	—	2.50	5.00
27902 [PS]	Colors/Squeeze the Trigger	1988	—	2.50	5.00
28126	Somebody Gotta Do It/Our Most Requested Record	1988	—	2.50	5.00

Albums

ATOMIC POP

| AP 0011 [(2)] | Greatest Hits: The Evidence | 2000 | 5.00 | 10.00 | 20.00 |

RHYME SYNDICATE

| 53858 | Home Invasion | 1993 | 2.50 | 5.00 | 10.00 |

SIRE

| PRO-A-4959 [(2) DJ] | O.G. Original Gangster | 1991 | 6.25 | 12.50 | 25.00 |

—Promo-only radio-ready version of album otherwise unavailable on U.S. vinyl

25602	Rhyme Pays	1987	2.50	5.00	10.00
25765	Power	1988	3.00	6.00	12.00
26028	The Iceberg/Freedom of Speech...Just Watch What You Say	1989	3.00	6.00	12.00

ICE CUBE

12-Inch Singles

BEST SIDE

| SPRO 81094 [DJ] | Ghetto Vet (Radio Edit) (Instrumental) | 1998 | 3.75 | 7.50 | 15.00 |
| SPRO 81141 [DJ] | Pushin' Weight (3 versions) | 1998 | 3.75 | 7.50 | 15.00 |

Number	Title (A Side/B Side)	Yr	VG	VG+	NM

CAPITOL
| ❏ 53575 | Bop Gun (One Nation)/Flash Light | 2000 | 3.75 | 7.50 | 15.00 |

—A-side featuring George Clinton; B-side by Parliament; red vinyl

JIVE
| ❏ 42398 | The World Is Mine (Clean Version) (LP Version) (Instrumental) | 1997 | 2.50 | 5.00 | 10.00 |

PRIORITY
❏ SPRO 6636 [DJ]	True to the Game (Clean Edit)/Givin' Up the Nappy Dug Out	1992	3.00	6.00	12.00
❏ SPRO 6651 [DJ]	It Was a Good Day (2 versions)/We Had to Tear This Dirty Mutha Up (2 versions)	1993	3.75	7.50	15.00
❏ SPRO 7038 [DJ]	Really Doe (Clean) (Dirty) (Instrumental)/My Skin Is My Sin (Dirty) (Instrumental)	1993	3.00	6.00	12.00
❏ 7046	You Know How We Do It/(Instrumental)	1994	2.00	4.00	8.00
❏ 7294	Endangered Species/Dead Homiez	1990	3.75	7.50	15.00
❏ 50795	Bop Gun (One Nation)/Bop Gun (One Nation) (Edit)/Down for Whatever	1994	2.50	5.00	10.00
❏ 50828	What Can I Do? (3 versions)	1994	2.50	5.00	10.00
❏ SPRO 50829 [DJ]	What Can I Do? (Eastside Remix) (Westside Remix)	1994	5.00	10.00	20.00

—Promo only; 1,000 numbered copies were issued
| ❏ 53155 | Bop Gun (One Nation) (unknown versions)/Down for Whatever | 1994 | — | 3.50 | 7.00 |

—Featuring George Clinton on "Bop Gun (One Nation)"
❏ 53813	Wicked (Radio) (Instrumental) (LP Version)/U Ain't Gonna Take My Life	1992	3.75	7.50	15.00
❏ 53817	It Was a Good Day (unknown versions)	1993	3.75	7.50	15.00
❏ 53830	Check Yo Self (2 versions)/It Was a Good Day/24 with a L	1993	3.00	6.00	12.00
❏ 53843	Really Doe (Vocal) (Instrumental)/My Skin Is My Sin	1993	2.50	5.00	10.00
❏ SPRO 81362 [DJ]	Supreme Hustle (3 versions)/Waitin' Ta Hate (3 versions)	1999	3.75	7.50	15.00
❏ SPRO 81611 [DJ]	$100 Bill, Y'All (4 versions)	2001	2.50	5.00	10.00
❏ SPRO 81613 [DJ]	In the Late Night Hour (Clean) (Instrumental) (Explicit) (Acappella)	2002	2.00	4.00	8.00

Albums
BEST SIDE
| ❏ 50015 [(2)] | War & Peace Vol. 2 (The Peace Disc) | 2000 | 3.75 | 7.50 | 15.00 |
| ❏ 50700 [(2)] | War & Peace Vol. 1 (The War Disc) | 1998 | 3.75 | 7.50 | 15.00 |
PRIORITY
❏ 7230 [EP]	Kill at Will	1990	3.00	6.00	12.00
❏ 29091 [(2)]	Greatest Hits	2001	3.75	7.50	15.00
❏ P1-53876	Lethal Injection	1993	3.75	7.50	15.00
❏ P1-53921	Bootlegs & B-Sides	1994	3.75	7.50	15.00
❏ 57120	AmeriKKKa's Most Wanted	1990	3.75	7.50	15.00
❏ 57155	Death Certificate	1991	3.75	7.50	15.00
❏ 57185	The Predator	1992	3.75	7.50	15.00

IKETTES, THE
Also see THE MIRETTES.
45s
ATCO
❏ 6212	I'm Blue (The Gong-Gong Song)/Find My Baby	1961	5.00	10.00	20.00
❏ 6223	Troubles on My Mind/Come On and Truck	1962	3.75	7.50	15.00
❏ 6232	Zizzy Zee Zum Zum/Heavenly Love	1962	3.75	7.50	15.00
❏ 6243	I Do Love You/I Had a Dream the Other Night	1962	3.75	7.50	15.00
MODERN
❏ 1005	Peaches 'N' Cream/The Biggest Players	1965	2.50	5.00	10.00
❏ 1008	(He's Gonna Be) Fine, Fine, Fine/How Come	1965	2.50	5.00	10.00
❏ 1011	I'm So Thankful/Don't Feel Sorry for Me	1965	2.00	4.00	8.00
❏ 1015	Sally Go Round the Roses/Lonely for You	1965	2.00	4.00	8.00
❏ 1024	Da Doo Ron Ron/Not That I Recall	1966	2.00	4.00	8.00
PHI-DAN
| ❏ 5009 | Down Down/What'cha Gonna Do | 1966 | 2.50 | 5.00 | 10.00 |
POMPEII
| ❏ 66683 | Beauty Is Just Skin Deep/Make Them Wait | 1968 | — | 3.00 | 6.00 |
UNITED ARTISTS
| ❏ 50866 | If You Take a Close Look/Got What It Takes | 1971 | — | 2.50 | 5.00 |
| ❏ 51103 | I'm Just Not Ready for Love/Two Timin' Double Dealin' | 1973 | — | 2.50 | 5.00 |

IMPALAS, THE
45s
20TH FOX
| ❏ 428 | Last Night I Saw a Girl/There Is Nothin' Like a Dame | 1963 | 3.00 | 6.00 | 12.00 |
BUNKY
| ❏ 7760 | Whay Should He Do/I Still Love You | 1969 | 2.00 | 4.00 | 8.00 |
| ❏ 7762 | Whip it On Me/I Still Love You | 1969 | 2.00 | 4.00 | 8.00 |
CAPITOL
| ❏ 2709 | Speed Up/Soul | 1969 | 2.00 | 4.00 | 8.00 |
CHECKER
| ❏ 999 | For the Love of Mike/I Need You So Much | 1961 | 3.00 | 6.00 | 12.00 |
CUB
| ❏ 9022 | Sorry (I Ran All the Way Home)/Fool, Fool, Fool | 1959 | 5.00 | 10.00 | 20.00 |
| ❏ 9022 | I Ran All the Way Home/Fool, Fool, Fool | 1959 | 15.00 | 30.00 | 60.00 |

—Original A-side title
❏ 9033	Oh What a Fool/Sandy Went Away	1959	5.00	10.00	20.00
❏ 9053	Peggy Darling/Bye Everybody	1959	5.00	10.00	20.00
❏ 9066	All Alone/When My Heart Does All the Talking	1960	5.00	10.00	20.00

—As "Speedo and the Impalas"
HAMILTON
| ❏ 50026 | I Was a Fool/First Date | 1960 | 5.00 | 10.00 | 20.00 |

Number	Title (A Side/B Side)	Yr	VG	VG+	NM

RED BOY
| ❏ 113 | When You Dance/I Can't See Me Without You | 1966 | 6.25 | 12.50 | 25.00 |
RITE-ON
| ❏ 101 | I Can't See Me Without You/Old Man Mose | 196? | 5.00 | 10.00 | 20.00 |
STEADY
| ❏ 044 | When You Dance/I Can't See Me Without You | 1967 | 5.00 | 10.00 | 20.00 |
SUNDOWN
| ❏ 115 | The Lonely One/Lost Boogie | 1959 | 3.75 | 7.50 | 15.00 |
7-Inch Extended Plays
CUB
| ❏ 5000 | (contents unknown) | 1959 | 100.00 | 200.00 | 400.00 |
| ❏ 5000 [PS] | Sorry (I Ran All the Way Home) | 1959 | 100.00 | 200.00 | 400.00 |

IMPERIALS, THE (1)
See LITTLE ANTHONY AND THE IMPERIALS.

IMPERIALS, THE (2)
45s
BUZZY
| ❏ 1 | My Darling/You Should Have Told Me | 1962 | 5.00 | 10.00 | 20.00 |

—Red vinyl
SAVOY
| ❏ 1104 | My Darling/You Should Have Told Me | 1954 | 50.00 | 100.00 | 200.00 |

IMPERIALS, THE (3)
45s
NEWTIME
| ❏ 503 | A Short Prayer/Where Will You Be | 1962 | 3.75 | 7.50 | 15.00 |
| ❏ 505 | The Letter/Go and Get Your Heart Broken | 1962 | 3.75 | 7.50 | 15.00 |

IMPERIALS, THE (4)
45s
OMNI
| ❏ 5501 | Who's Gonna Love Me/Better Take Time to Love | 1978 | — | 2.50 | 5.00 |

IMPERIALS MINUS TWO, THE
45s
IMPERIAL
| ❏ 5787 | A Swingin' Dream/In Any Language | 1961 | 5.00 | 10.00 | 20.00 |

IMPRESSIONS, THE
Also see JERRY BUTLER; CURTIS MAYFIELD.
45s
20TH FOX
| ❏ 172 | All Through the Night/Meanwhile, Back in My Heart | 1959 | 10.00 | 20.00 | 40.00 |
ABC
❏ 10831	Can't Satisfy/This Must End	1966	2.00	4.00	8.00
❏ 10869	Love's a-Comin'/Wade in the Water	1966	2.00	4.00	8.00
❏ 10900	You Always Hurt Me/Little Girl	1967	2.00	4.00	8.00
❏ 10932	It's Hard to Believe/You've Got Me Runnin'	1967	2.00	4.00	8.00
❏ 10964	I Can't Stay Away from You/You Ought to Be in Heaven	1967	2.00	4.00	8.00
❏ 11022	We're a Winner/It's All Over	1967	2.00	4.00	8.00
❏ 11071	We're Rolling On (Part 1)/We're Rolling On (Part 2)	1968	2.00	4.00	8.00
❏ 11103	I Loved and I Lost/Up, Up and Away	1968	2.00	4.00	8.00
❏ 11135	Don't Cry My Love/Sometimes I Wonder	1968	2.00	4.00	8.00
❏ 11188	East of Java/Just Before Sunrise	1969	2.00	4.00	8.00
ABC-PARAMOUNT
❏ 10241	Gypsy Woman/As Long As You Love Me	1961	3.75	7.50	15.00
❏ 10289	Grow Closer Together/Can't You See	1962	3.75	7.50	15.00
❏ 10328	Little Young Lover/Never Let Me Go	1962	3.75	7.50	15.00
❏ 10357	You've Come Home/Minstrel and Queen	1962	3.75	7.50	15.00
❏ 10386	I'm the One Who Loves You/I Need Your Love	1962	3.75	7.50	15.00
❏ 10431	Sad, Sad Girl and Boy/Twist and Limbo	1963	3.75	7.50	15.00
❏ 10487	It's All Right/You'll Want Me Back	1963	3.75	7.50	15.00
❏ 10511	Talking About My Baby/Never Too Much Love	1963	3.75	7.50	15.00
❏ 10537	Girl You Don't Know Me/A Woman Who Loves Me	1964	3.75	7.50	15.00
❏ 10544	I'm So Proud/I Made a Mistake	1964	3.75	7.50	15.00
❏ 10554	Keep On Pushing/I Love You (Yeah)	1964	3.75	7.50	15.00
❏ 10581	You Must Believe Me/See the Real Me	1964	3.75	7.50	15.00
❏ 10602	Amen/Long, Long Winter	1964	3.75	7.50	15.00
❏ 10622	People Get Ready/I've Been Trying	1965	3.75	7.50	15.00
❏ 10647	Woman's Got Soul/Get Up and Move	1965	3.00	6.00	12.00
❏ 10670	Meeting Over Yonder/I've Found That I've Lost	1965	3.00	6.00	12.00
❏ 10710	I Need You/Never Could You Be	1965	3.00	6.00	12.00
❏ 10725	Just One Kiss from You/Twilight Time	1965	3.00	6.00	12.00
❏ 10750	You've Been Cheatin'/Man, Oh Man	1965	3.00	6.00	12.00
❏ 10761	Since I Lost the One I Love/Falling in Love with You	1966	2.50	5.00	10.00
❏ 10789	Too Slow/No One Else	1966	2.50	5.00	10.00
ABNER
| ❏ 1013 | For Your Precious Love/Sweet Was the Wine | 1958 | 10.00 | 20.00 | 40.00 |

—As "Jerry Butler and the Impressions"
❏ 1017	Come Back My Love/Love Me	1958	7.50	15.00	30.00
❏ 1023	The Gift of Love/At the County Fair	1959	7.50	15.00	30.00
❏ 1025	Lonely One/Senorita I Love You	1959	7.50	15.00	30.00
❏ 1034	Say That You Love Me/A New Love	1960	7.50	15.00	30.00
BANDERA
| ❏ 2504 | Listen/Shorty's Got to Go | 1959 | 12.50 | 25.00 | 50.00 |
CHI-SOUND
| ❏ 2418 | Sorry/All I Wanna Do Is Make Love to You | 1979 | — | 2.50 | 5.00 |

Number	Title (A Side/B Side)	Yr	VG	VG+	NM
❑ 2438	Maybe I'm Mistaken/All I Wanna Do Is Make Love to You	1980	—	2.50	5.00
❑ 2491	For Your Precious Love/You're Mine	1981	—	2.50	5.00
❑ 2499	Love, Love, Love/Fan the Fire	1981	—	2.50	5.00

COTILLION

Number	Title (A Side/B Side)	Yr	VG	VG+	NM
❑ 44210	This Time/I'm a Fool for Love	1976	—	2.50	5.00
❑ 44211	Silent Night/I Saw Mommy Kissing Santa Claus	1976	—	3.00	6.00
❑ 44214	You'll Never Find/Stardust	1977	—	2.50	5.00
❑ 44222	Can't Get Along/You're So Right for Me	1977	—	2.50	5.00

CURTOM

Number	Title (A Side/B Side)	Yr	VG	VG+	NM
❑ SP-3 [DJ]	Merry Christmas Happy New Year	197?	3.00	6.00	12.00
❑ 0103	Sooner or Later/Miracle Woman	1975	—	2.50	5.00
❑ 0106	Same Thing It Took/I'm So Glad	1975	—	2.50	5.00
❑ 0110	Loving Power/First Impressions	1975	—	2.50	5.00
❑ 0116	Sunshine/I Wish I'd Stayed in Bed	1976	—	2.50	5.00
❑ 1932	Fool for You/I'm Loving Nothing	1968	—	3.00	6.00
❑ 1932 [PS]	Fool for You/I'm Loving Nothing	1968	3.75	7.50	15.00
❑ 1934	This Is My Country/My Woman's Love	1968	—	3.00	6.00
❑ 1937	My Deceiving Heart/You Want Somebody Else	1969	—	3.00	6.00
❑ 1940	Seven Years/The Girl I Find	1969	—	3.00	6.00
❑ 1943	Choice of Colors/Mighty Mighty Spade and Whitey	1969	—	3.00	6.00
❑ 1946	Say You Love Me/You'll Be Always Mine	1969	—	3.00	6.00
❑ 1948	Wherever She Leadeth Me/Amen (1970)	1970	—	3.00	6.00
❑ 1951	Check Out Your Mind/Can't You See	1970	—	3.00	6.00
❑ 1954	(Baby) Turn On to Me/Soulful Love	1970	—	3.00	6.00
❑ 1957	Ain't Got Time/I'm So Proud	1971	—	3.00	6.00
❑ 1959	Love Me/Do You Wanna Win	1971	—	3.00	6.00
❑ 1966	Inner City Blues/We Must Be in Love	1971	—	3.00	6.00
❑ 1970	This Loves for Real/Times Have Changed	1972	—	3.00	6.00
❑ 1973	I Need to Belong to Someone/Love Me	1972	—	3.00	6.00
❑ 1982	Preacher Man/Times Have Changed	1973	—	3.00	6.00
❑ 1985	Thin Line/I'm Loving You	1973	—	3.00	6.00
❑ 1994	If It's In You to Do Wrong/Times Have Changed	1973	—	3.00	6.00
❑ 1997	Finally Got Myself Together (I'm a Changed Man)/I'll Always Be Here	1974	—	3.00	6.00
❑ 2003	Something's Mighty, Mighty Wrong/Three the Hard Way	1974	—	3.00	6.00

FALCON

Number	Title (A Side/B Side)	Yr	VG	VG+	NM
❑ 1013	For Your Precious Love/Sweet Was the Wine	1958	15.00	30.00	60.00

—As "Jerry Butler and the Impressions"

MCA

Number	Title (A Side/B Side)	Yr	VG	VG+	NM
❑ 52995	Can't Wait 'Til Tomorrow/Love Workin' On Me	1987	—	—	3.00

PORT

Number	Title (A Side/B Side)	Yr	VG	VG+	NM
❑ 70031	Listen/Shorty's Got to Go	1962	3.75	7.50	15.00

SWIRL

Number	Title (A Side/B Side)	Yr	VG	VG+	NM
❑ 107	I Need Your Love/Don't Leave Me	1962	5.00	10.00	20.00

VEE JAY

Number	Title (A Side/B Side)	Yr	VG	VG+	NM
❑ 280	For Your Precious Love/Sweet Was the Wine	1958	4000.	6000.	8000.

—As "Jerry Butler and the Impressions"

Number	Title (A Side/B Side)	Yr	VG	VG+	NM
❑ 424	Say That You Love Me/Senorita I Love You	1962	5.00	10.00	20.00
❑ 574	The Gift of Love/At the County Fair	1963	3.75	7.50	15.00
❑ 621	Say That You Love Me/Senorita I Love You	1964	3.75	7.50	15.00

INCREDIBLE BONGO BAND, THE

45s

MGM

Number	Title (A Side/B Side)	Yr	VG	VG+	NM
❑ 14588	Bongo Rock/Bongolia	1973	—	3.00	6.00
❑ 14635	Let There Be Drums/Dueling Bongos	1973	2.00	4.00	8.00

PRIDE

Number	Title (A Side/B Side)	Yr	VG	VG+	NM
❑ 1015	Bongo Rock/Bongolia	1972	3.00	6.00	12.00
❑ 7601	Kirburi/When the Bed Breaks Down, I'll Meet You in the Spring	1974	2.50	5.00	10.00

Albums

PRIDE

Number	Title (A Side/B Side)	Yr	VG	VG+	NM
❑ 0028	Bongo Rock	1973	20.00	40.00	80.00

—Note: This album has been reissued to look like the original

Number	Title (A Side/B Side)	Yr	VG	VG+	NM
❑ 6010	The Return of the Incredible Bongo Band	1974	5.00	10.00	20.00

INDEPENDENTS, THE

45s

WAND

Number	Title (A Side/B Side)	Yr	VG	VG+	NM
❑ 11245	Just As Long As You Need Me, Part 1/Part 2	1972	—	3.00	6.00
❑ 11249	I Just Want to Be There/Can't Understand It	1972	—	3.00	6.00
❑ 11252	Leaving Me/I Love You Yes I Do	1973	—	3.00	6.00
❑ 11258	Baby I've Been Missing You/Couldn't Hear Nobody Say	1973	—	3.00	6.00
❑ 11263	It's All Over/Sara Lee	1973	—	3.00	6.00
❑ 11267	The First Time We Met/Show Me How	1973	—	3.00	6.00
❑ 11273	Arise and Shine (Let's Get It On)/I Found Love	1974	—	3.00	6.00
❑ 11279	Let This Be a Lesson to You/No Wind, No Rain	1974	—	3.00	6.00

INDIA.ARIE

12-Inch Singles

MOTOWN

Number	Title (A Side/B Side)	Yr	VG	VG+	NM
❑ 20340	Video (Main) (Instrumental) (Acappella)	2001	2.00	4.00	8.00
❑ 20414	Brown Skin (Radio Edit) (LP Version) (Instrumental) (Acappella)	2001	2.00	4.00	8.00
❑ 20565	Simple (Main) (Instrumental) (Acappella)	2001	2.00	4.00	8.00
❑ 20617	Strength, Courage and Wisdom (4 versions)	2001	2.00	4.00	8.00

Albums

MOTOWN

Number	Title (A Side/B Side)	Yr	VG	VG+	NM
❑ 440 013770-1	[(2)]Acoustic Soul	2001	3.75	7.50	15.00

INGRAM, LUTHER

45s

DECCA

Number	Title (A Side/B Side)	Yr	VG	VG+	NM
❑ 31794	Ain't That Nice/You Never Miss Your Water	1965	3.00	6.00	12.00

HIB

Number	Title (A Side/B Side)	Yr	VG	VG+	NM
❑ 698	If It's All the Same To You Babe/Exus Trek	1967	20.00	40.00	80.00

KOKO

Number	Title (A Side/B Side)	Yr	VG	VG+	NM
❑ 101	I Can't Stop/You Got to Give Love to Get Love	1968	2.50	5.00	10.00
❑ 103	Missing You/Since You Don't Want Me	1968	2.50	5.00	10.00
❑ 721	Ain't Good for Nothing/These Are the Things	1976	—	3.00	6.00
❑ 724	Let's Steal Away to the Hideaway/I've Got Your Love in My Life	1977	—	3.00	6.00
❑ 725	I Like the Feeling/Gonna Be the Next Time	1977	—	3.00	6.00
❑ 728	Do You Love Somebody/How I Miss My Baby	1977	—	3.00	6.00
❑ 731	Get to Me/Trying to Find My Love	1978	—	3.00	6.00
❑ 2101	You Can Depend on Me/Looking for a New Love	1969	2.00	4.00	8.00
❑ 2102	Pity for the Lonely/Looking for a New Love	1969	2.00	4.00	8.00
❑ 2103	Puttin' Game Down/Since You Don't Want Me	1969	2.00	4.00	8.00
❑ 2104	My Honey and Me/I Can't Stop	1969	2.00	4.00	8.00
❑ 2105	Ain't That Loving You (For More Reasons Than One)/Home Don't Seem Like Home	1970	2.00	4.00	8.00
❑ 2106	To the Other Man/I'll Just Call You Honey	1970	2.00	4.00	8.00
❑ 2107	Be Good to Me Baby/Since You Don't Want Me	1971	2.00	4.00	8.00
❑ 2108	I'll Love You Until the End/Ghetto Train	1971	2.00	4.00	8.00
❑ 2110	You Were Made for Me/Missing You	1972	2.00	4.00	8.00
❑ 2111	(If Loving You Is Wrong) I Don't Want to Be Right/Puttin' Game Down	1972	2.00	4.00	8.00
❑ 2113	I'll Be Your Shelter (In Time of Storm)/I Can't Stop	1972	2.00	4.00	8.00
❑ 2115	Always/Help Me Love	1973	2.00	4.00	8.00
❑ 2116	Love Ain't Gonna Run Me Away/To the Other Man	1973	2.00	4.00	8.00

PROFILE

Number	Title (A Side/B Side)	Yr	VG	VG+	NM
❑ 5125	Baby Don't Go Too Far/How Sweet It Would Be	1986	—	—	3.00
❑ 5132	Don't Turn Around/(B-side unknown)	1987	—	—	3.00
❑ 5143	Gotta Serve Somebody/All in the Name of Love	1987	—	—	3.00

SMASH

Number	Title (A Side/B Side)	Yr	VG	VG+	NM
❑ 2019	(I Spy) For the F.B.I./Foxey Devil	1966	5.00	10.00	20.00

Albums

KOKO

Number	Title (A Side/B Side)	Yr	VG	VG+	NM
❑ KOS-2201	I've Been Here All the Time	1971	3.75	7.50	15.00
❑ KOS-2202	If Loving You Is Wrong I Don't Want to Be Right	1972	3.75	7.50	15.00

INK SPOTS

45s

DECCA

Number	Title (A Side/B Side)	Yr	VG	VG+	NM
❑ 9-5 [PS]	Ink Spots, Volume 2	1950	3.75	7.50	15.00

—Box for 25238, 25239 and 25240

Number	Title (A Side/B Side)	Yr	VG	VG+	NM
❑ 23615	To Each His Own/I Never Had a Dream Come True	1960	2.00	4.00	8.00

—Black label, color bars at right

Number	Title (A Side/B Side)	Yr	VG	VG+	NM
❑ 9-23615	To Each His Own/I Never Had a Dream Come True	1950	6.25	12.50	25.00

—Black label, lines on either side of "Decca"; reissue of 78 from 1946

Number	Title (A Side/B Side)	Yr	VG	VG+	NM
❑ 9-23615	To Each His Own/I Never Had a Dream Come True	1955	3.00	6.00	12.00

—Black label, star under "Decca"

Number	Title (A Side/B Side)	Yr	VG	VG+	NM
❑ 23632	If I Didn't Care/Whispering Grass (Don't Tell the Trees)	1961	2.50	5.00	10.00

—Black label, color bars at right

Number	Title (A Side/B Side)	Yr	VG	VG+	NM
❑ 9-23632	If I Didn't Care/Whispering Grass (Don't Tell the Trees)	1950	6.25	12.50	25.00

—Black label, lines on either side of "Decca"

Number	Title (A Side/B Side)	Yr	VG	VG+	NM
❑ 9-23632	If I Didn't Care/Whispering Grass (Don't Tell the Trees)	1955	3.00	6.00	12.00

—Black label, star under "Decca"

Number	Title (A Side/B Side)	Yr	VG	VG+	NM
❑ 9-25238	I'll Get By (As Long As I Have You)/Just for a Thrill	1950	5.00	10.00	20.00

—Side 1 and 6 of "Album No. 9-5"

Number	Title (A Side/B Side)	Yr	VG	VG+	NM
❑ 9-25239	I'd Climb the Highest Mountain/I'm Gettin' Sentimental Over You	1950	5.00	10.00	20.00

—From "Album No. 9-5"

Number	Title (A Side/B Side)	Yr	VG	VG+	NM
❑ 9-25240	Coquette/When the Swallows Come Back to Capistrano	1950	5.00	10.00	20.00

—From "Album No. 9-5"

Number	Title (A Side/B Side)	Yr	VG	VG+	NM
❑ 25505	It's a Sin to Tell a Lie/That's When Your Heartaches Begin	1961	2.50	5.00	10.00
❑ 25533	All My Life/You Were Only Fooling	1961	3.00	6.00	12.00
❑ 9-27102	Sometime/I Was Dancing with Someone	1950	6.25	12.50	25.00
❑ 9-27214	The Way It Used to Be/Right About Now	1950	6.25	12.50	25.00
❑ 9-27256	Our Lady of Fatima/Stranger in the City	1950	6.25	12.50	25.00
❑ 9-27259	Dream Awhile/Time Out for Tears	1950	6.25	12.50	25.00
❑ 9-27391	If/A Friend of Johnny's	1951	5.00	10.00	20.00
❑ 9-27464	Tell Me You Love Me/Castles in the Sand	1951	5.00	10.00	20.00
❑ 9-27493	Do Something for Me/A Fool Grows Wise	1951	5.00	10.00	20.00
❑ 9-27632	More of the Same Sweet You/What Can You Do	1951	5.00	10.00	20.00
❑ 9-27742	I Don't Stand a Ghost of a Chance/I'm Lucky I Have You	1951	5.00	10.00	20.00
❑ 9-27996	Honest and Truly/All My Life	1952	5.00	10.00	20.00
❑ 9-29750	Memories of You/It's Funny to Everyone But Me	1955	5.00	10.00	20.00
❑ 9-29991	My Prayer/Bewildered	1956	5.00	10.00	20.00
❑ 9-30058	The Best Things in Life Are Free/I Don't Stand a Ghost of a Chance	1956	3.75	7.50	15.00

GRAND AWARD

Number	Title (A Side/B Side)	Yr	VG	VG+	NM
❑ 1001	Rock and Roll Rag/Do I Worry	1956	5.00	10.00	20.00

KING

Number	Title (A Side/B Side)	Yr	VG	VG+	NM
❑ 1297	Ebb Tide/If You Should Say Goodbye	1953	15.00	30.00	60.00

Number	Title (A Side/B Side)	Yr	VG	VG+	NM
❑ 1304	Changing Partners/Stranger in Paradise	1954	17.50	35.00	70.00
❑ 1336	Melody of Love/Am I Too Late	1954	17.50	35.00	70.00
❑ 1378	Yesterdays/Planting Rice	1954	15.00	30.00	60.00
❑ 1425	When You Come to the End of the Day/Someone's Rocking My Dreamboat	1955	12.50	25.00	50.00
❑ 1429	Melody of Love/There Is Something Missing	1955	10.00	20.00	40.00
❑ 1512	Don't Laugh at Me/Keep It Movin'	1955	10.00	20.00	40.00
❑ 4670	Here in My Lonely Room/A Fool in Love	1953	37.50	75.00	150.00
❑ 4857	Command Me/I'll Walk a Country Mile	1955	10.00	20.00	40.00

SWIFT

Number	Title (A Side/B Side)	Yr	VG	VG+	NM
❑ 1001	If I Didn't Care//Into Each Life Some Rain Must Fall/We Three	195?	3.75	7.50	15.00

VERVE

Number	Title (A Side/B Side)	Yr	VG	VG+	NM
❑ 10198	Secret Love/A Little Bird Told Me	1960	3.00	6.00	12.00

78s

BLUEBIRD

Number	Title (A Side/B Side)	Yr	VG	VG+	NM
❑ B-6530	Your Feet's Too Big/Swingin' on the Strings	1936	7.50	15.00	30.00
—Reissue of Victor 24851					

DECCA

Number	Title (A Side/B Side)	Yr	VG	VG+	NM
❑ 817	Your Feet's Too Big/'T Ain't Nobody's Biz-ness If I Do	1936	5.00	10.00	20.00
❑ 883	Christopher Columbus/Old Joe's Hittin' the Jug	1936	5.00	10.00	20.00
❑ 1036	Keep Away from My Doorstep/Stompin' at the Savoy	1936	5.00	10.00	20.00
❑ 1154	Alabama Barbeque/With Plenty of Money and You	1937	5.00	10.00	20.00
❑ 1236	Whoa Babe/Swing High, Swing Low	1937	5.00	10.00	20.00
❑ 1251	Let's Call the Whole Thing Off/Slap That Bass	1937	5.00	10.00	20.00
❑ 1731	Don't Let Old Age Creep Up on You/Yes Suh!	1938	3.75	7.50	15.00
❑ 1789	Oh! Red/That Cat Is High	1938	3.75	7.50	15.00
❑ 1870	When the Sun Goes Down/I Wish You the Best of Everything	1938	3.75	7.50	15.00
❑ 2044	Pork Chops 'n Gravy/Brown Gal	1938	3.75	7.50	15.00
❑ 2286	If I Didn't Care/Knock Kneed Sal (On the Morner's Bench)	1939	3.00	6.00	12.00
❑ 2507	It's Funny to Everyone But Me/Just for a Thrill	1939	3.00	6.00	12.00
❑ 2707	Address Unknown/You Bring Me Down	1939	3.00	6.00	12.00
❑ 2790	My Prayer/Give Her My Love	1939	3.00	6.00	12.00
❑ 2841	Bless You/I Don't Want Sympathy, I Want Love	1939	3.00	6.00	12.00
❑ 2966	Memories of You/I'm Through	1940	3.00	6.00	12.00
❑ 3077	I'm Getting Sentimental Over You/Coquette	1940	3.00	6.00	12.00
❑ 3195	When the Swallows Come Back to Capistrano/What Can I Do	1940	3.00	6.00	12.00
❑ 3258	Whispering Grass (Don't Tell the Trees)/Maybe	1940	3.00	6.00	12.00
❑ 3288	Stop Pretending/You're Breaking My Heart All Over Again	1940	3.00	6.00	12.00
❑ 3346	I'll Never Smile Again (Until I Smile at You)/I Could Make You Care	1940	3.00	6.00	12.00
❑ 3379	We Three (My Echo, My Shadow and Me)/My Greatest Mistake	1940	3.00	6.00	12.00
❑ 3432	Java Jive/Do I Worry?	1940	3.00	6.00	12.00
❑ 3468	Puttin' and Takin'/I'm Only Human	1940	3.00	6.00	12.00
❑ 3626	Please Take a Letter, Miss Brown/Ring, Telephone, Ring	1941	3.00	6.00	12.00
❑ 3656	We'll Meet Again/You're Looking for Romance (And I'm Looking for Love)	1941	3.00	6.00	12.00
❑ 3720	That's When Your Heartaches Begin/What Good Would It Do?	1941	3.00	6.00	12.00
❑ 3806	I'm Still Without a Sweetheart (Cause I'm Still in Love with You)/So Sorry	1941	3.00	6.00	12.00
❑ 3872	Why Didn't You Tell Me/Driftwood	1941	—	—	—
—Canceled					
❑ 3958	Until the Real Thing Comes Along/Keep Cool, Fool	1941	3.00	6.00	12.00
❑ 3987	I Don't Want to Set the World on Fire/Hey, Doc	1941	3.00	6.00	12.00
❑ 4045	Someone's Rocking My Dream Boat/Nothin'	1941	3.00	6.00	12.00
❑ 4112	It's a Sin to Tell a Lie/Is It a Sin (My Loving You)	1942	3.00	6.00	12.00
❑ 4194	Shout, Brother, Shout/It Isn't a Dream Anymore	1942	3.00	6.00	12.00
❑ 4303	Don't Leave Now/Foo-Gee	1942	3.00	6.00	12.00
❑ 18383	Don't Tell a Lie About Me Dear (And I Won't Tell the Truth About You)/Who Wouldn't Love You	1942	2.50	5.00	10.00
❑ 18461	Ev'ry Night About This Time/I'm Not the Same Old Me	1942	2.50	5.00	10.00
❑ 18466	Just as Though You Were Here/This Is Worth Fighting For	1942	2.50	5.00	10.00
❑ 18503	Don't Get Around Much Anymore/Street of Dreams	1942	2.50	5.00	10.00
❑ 18528	If I Cared a Little Bit Less (And You Cared a Little Bit More)/Mine, All Mine, My My	1942	2.50	5.00	10.00
❑ 18542	I Can't Stand Losing You/I'll Never Make the Same Mistake Again	1943	2.50	5.00	10.00
❑ 18579	I'll Get By (As Long As I Have You)/Someday I'll Meet You Again	1944	2.50	5.00	10.00
❑ 18583	A Lovely Way to Spend an Evening/Don't Believe Everything You Dream	1944	2.50	5.00	10.00
❑ 18587	Cow-Cow Boogie (Cuma-Ti-Yi-Yi-Ay)/When My Sugar Walks Down the Street	1944	2.50	5.00	10.00
—As "Ink Spots and Ella Fitzgerald"					
❑ 18657	I Hope to Die If I Told a Lie/Maybe It's All for the Best	1945	2.50	5.00	10.00
❑ 18711	Thoughtless/I'd Climb the Highest Mountain	1945	2.50	5.00	10.00
❑ 18755	The Sweetest Dream/I'm Gonna Turn Off the Teardrops	1946	2.50	5.00	10.00
❑ 18817	The Gypsy/Everyone Is Saying Hello Again (Why Must We Say Goodbye?)	1946	2.50	5.00	10.00
❑ 18864	Prisoner of Love/I Cover the Waterfront	1946	2.50	5.00	10.00
❑ 23356	Into Each Life Some Rain Must Fall/I'm Making Believe	1944	2.50	5.00	10.00
—As "Ink Spots and Ella Fitzgerald"					
❑ 23399	I'm Beginning to See the Light/That's the Way It Is	1945	2.50	5.00	10.00
—As "Ink Spots and Ella Fitzgerald"					
❑ 23615	To Each His Own/I Never Had a Dream Come True	1946	2.50	5.00	10.00
❑ 23632	If I Didn't Care/Whispering Grass (Don't Tell the Trees)	1946	2.50	5.00	10.00
—Reissue of A-sides of 2286 and 3258					
❑ 23634	Maybe/We Three (My Echo, My Shadow and Me)	1946	2.50	5.00	10.00
—Reissue of B-side of 3258 and A-side of 3379					
❑ 23635	I'll Never Smile Again (Until I Smile at You)/Until the Real Thing Comes Along	1946	2.50	5.00	10.00
—Reissue of A-sides of 3346 and 3958					
❑ 23695	I Get the Blues When It Rains/Either It's Love or It Isn't	1946	2.50	5.00	10.00
❑ 23757	Address Unknown/Bless You	1946	2.50	5.00	10.00
—Reissue of A-sides of 2707 and 2841					
❑ 23809	That's Where I Came In/You Can't See the Sun When You're Crying	1947	2.50	5.00	10.00
❑ 23851	I Want to Thank Your Folks/I Wasn't Meant for Love	1947	2.50	5.00	10.00
❑ 23900	Ask Anyone Who Knows/Can You Look Me in the Eyes (And Say We're Through)	1947	2.50	5.00	10.00
❑ 23936	The Gypsy/Everyone Is Saying Hello Again (Why Must We Say Goodbye?)	1947	2.00	4.00	8.00
—Reissue of 18817					
❑ 24111	Information Please/Do You Feel That Way Too?	1947	2.50	5.00	10.00
❑ 24140	Always/White Christmas	1947	2.50	5.00	10.00
❑ 24173	Just for Me/Just Plain Love	1947	2.50	5.00	10.00
❑ 24192	Home Is Where the Heart Is/Sincerely Yours	1947	2.50	5.00	10.00
❑ 24261	When You Come to the End of the Day/I'll Lose a Friend Tomorrow	1947	2.50	5.00	10.00
❑ 24286	It's All Over But the Crying/I'll Make Up for Everything	1948	2.50	5.00	10.00
❑ 24327	The Best Things in Life Are Free/I Woke Up with a Teardrop in My Eye	1948	2.50	5.00	10.00
❑ 24461	Just for Now/Where Flamingoes Fly	1948	2.50	5.00	10.00
❑ 24496	Aladdin's Lamp/My Baby Didn't Even Say Goodbye	1948	2.50	5.00	10.00
❑ 24507	You Were Only Fooling (While I Was Falling in Love)/Say Something Sweet to Your Sweetheart	1948	2.50	5.00	10.00
❑ 24517	Am I Asking Too Much/Recess in Heaven	1948	2.50	5.00	10.00
❑ 24566	No Orchids for My Lady/Bewildered	1949	2.50	5.00	10.00
❑ 24585	As You Desire Me/It Only Happens Once	1949	2.50	5.00	10.00
❑ 24611	A Kiss and a Rose/A Knock on the Door	1949	2.50	5.00	10.00
❑ 24672	If You Had to Hurt Someone/To Remind Me of You	1949	2.50	5.00	10.00
❑ 24693	You're Breaking My Heart/Who Do You Know in Heaven (That Made You the Angel You Are?)	1949	2.50	5.00	10.00
❑ 24741	Echoes/Land of Love	1949	2.50	5.00	10.00
❑ 24887	With My Eyes Wide Open I'm Dreaming/Lost in a Dream	1950	2.50	5.00	10.00
❑ 24933	My Reward/You Left Me Everything But You	1950	2.50	5.00	10.00
❑ 25047	Cow-Cow Boogie (Cuma-Ti-Yi-Yi-Ay)/That's the Way It Is	1947	2.00	4.00	8.00
—As "Ink Spots and Ella Fitzgerald"; reissue of A-side of 18587 and B-side of 23399					
❑ 25237	We'll Meet Again/My Greatest Mistake	1947	2.00	4.00	8.00
—Reissue of A-side of 3656 and B-side of 3379					
❑ 25238	I'll Get By (As Long As I Have You)/Just for a Thrill	1947	2.00	4.00	8.00
—Reissue of A-side of 18579 and B-side of 2507					
❑ 25239	I'd Climb the Highest Mountain/I'm Gettin' Sentimental Over You	1947	2.00	4.00	8.00
—Reissue of B-side of 18711 and A-side of 3077					
❑ 25240	Coquette/When the Swallows Come Back to Capistrano	1947	2.00	4.00	8.00
—Reissue of B-side of 3077 and A-side of 3195					
❑ 25344	I'm Beginning to See the Light/I'm Gonna Turn Off the Teardrops	1948	2.00	4.00	8.00
—A-side by "Ink Spots and Ella Fitzgerald"; reissue of A-side of 23399 and B-side of 18755					
❑ 25378	Ring, Telephone, Ring/Don't Leave Now	1948	2.00	4.00	8.00
—Reissue of B-side of 3626 and A-side of 4303					
❑ 25431	I Don't Want to Set the World on Fire/Someone's Rocking My Dream Boat	1948	2.00	4.00	8.00
—Reissue of A-sides of 3987 and 4045					
❑ 27102	Sometime/I Was Dancing with Someone	1950	2.50	5.00	10.00
❑ 27214	The Way It Used to Be/Right About Now	1950	2.50	5.00	10.00
❑ 27256	Our Lady of Fatima/Stranger in the City	1950	2.50	5.00	10.00
❑ 27259	Dream Awhile/Time Out for Tears	1950	2.50	5.00	10.00
❑ 27391	If/A Friend of Johnny's	1951	2.50	5.00	10.00
❑ 27464	Tell Me You Love Me/Castles in the Sand	1951	2.50	5.00	10.00
❑ 27493	Do Something for Me/A Fool Grows Wise	1951	2.50	5.00	10.00
❑ 27632	More of the Same Sweet You/What Can You Do	1951	2.50	5.00	10.00
❑ 27742	I Don't Stand a Ghost of a Chance/I'm Lucky I Have You	1951	2.50	5.00	10.00
❑ 27996	Honest and Truly/All My Life	1952	2.50	5.00	10.00
❑ 29750	Memories of You/It's Funny to Everyone But Me	1955	3.00	6.00	12.00
❑ 29991	My Prayer/Bewildered	1956	3.75	7.50	15.00
❑ 30058	The Best Things in Life Are Free/I Don't Stand a Ghost of a Chance	1956	3.75	7.50	15.00

KING

Number	Title (A Side/B Side)	Yr	VG	VG+	NM
❑ 1297	Ebb Tide/If You Should Say Goodbye	1953	7.50	15.00	30.00
❑ 1304	Changing Partners/Stranger in Paradise	1954	7.50	15.00	30.00
❑ 1336	Melody of Love/Am I Too Late	1954	7.50	15.00	30.00

Number	Title (A Side/B Side)	Yr	VG	VG+	NM
❏ 1378	Yesterdays/Planting Rice	1954	7.50	15.00	30.00
❏ 1425	When You Come to the End of the Day/ Someone's Rocking My Dreamboat	1955	7.50	15.00	30.00
❏ 1429	Melody of Love/There Is Something Missing	1955	7.50	15.00	30.00
❏ 1512	Don't Laugh at Me/Keep It Movin'	1955	7.50	15.00	30.00
❏ 4670	Here in My Lonely Room/A Fool in Love	1953	10.00	20.00	40.00
❏ 4670 [DJ]	Here in My Lonely Room/A Fool in Love	1953	20.00	40.00	80.00
—White label with biography of group on label					
❏ 4857	Command Me/I'll Walk a Country Mile	1955	7.50	15.00	30.00
VICTOR					
❏ 24851	Swingin' on the Strings/Your Feet's Too Big	1935	25.00	50.00	100.00
❏ 24876	Don't 'Low No Swingin' in Here/Swing Gate, Swing	1935	25.00	50.00	100.00

7-Inch Extended Plays
DECCA

Number	Title (A Side/B Side)	Yr	VG	VG+	NM
❏ ED 2008	The Gypsy/To Each His Own//Bless You/With My Eyes Wide Open, I'm Dreaming	195?	6.25	12.50	25.00
❏ ED 2008 [PS]	The Ink Spots, Vol. 1	195?	6.25	12.50	25.00
❏ ED 2047	*It's Funny to Everyone But Me/It's a Sin to Tell a Lie/Don't Get Around Much Anymore/My Prayer	195?	6.25	12.50	25.00
❏ ED 2047 [PS]	The Ink Spots, Volume 2	195?	6.25	12.50	25.00
KING					
❏ EP-376	*Melody of Love/Ebb Tide/Stranger in Paradise/ Yesterdays	195?	7.50	15.00	30.00
❏ EP-376 [PS]	Great Songs of Our Times	195?	7.50	15.00	30.00

Albums
ARCHIVE OF FOLK AND JAZZ

Number	Title (A Side/B Side)	Yr	VG	VG+	NM
❏ 350	The Ink Spots in London	197?	2.50	5.00	10.00
COLORTONE					
❏ 4901 [M]	The Ink Spots	1958	15.00	30.00	60.00
❏ 4947 [M]	The Ink Spots, Vol. 2	1959	15.00	30.00	60.00
CROWN					
❏ CST-144 [S]	The Ink Spots' Greatest Hits	1959	6.25	12.50	25.00
—Black vinyl					
❏ CST-144 [S]	The Ink Spots' Greatest Hits	1959	12.50	25.00	50.00
—Red vinyl					
❏ CST-175 [S]	The Ink Spots	1961	6.25	12.50	25.00
—Black vinyl					
❏ CST-175 [S]	The Ink Spots	1961	12.50	25.00	50.00
—Red vinyl					
❏ CST-217 [S]	The Sensational Ink Spots	1962	6.25	12.50	25.00
—Black vinyl					
❏ CST-217 [S]	The Sensational Ink Spots	1962	12.50	25.00	50.00
—Red vinyl					
❏ CLP-5112 [M]	The Ink Spots' Greatest Hits	1959	5.00	10.00	20.00
❏ CLP-5142 [M]	The Ink Spots	1961	5.00	10.00	20.00
❏ CLP-5187 [M]	The Sensational Ink Spots	1962	5.00	10.00	20.00
❏ CLP 5221 [M]	More Ink Spots	196?	3.75	7.50	15.00
DECCA					
❏ DXB 182 [(2) M]	The Best of the Ink Spots	1965	7.50	15.00	30.00
❏ DL 4297 [M]	Our Golden Favorites	1962	6.25	12.50	25.00
❏ DL 5056 [10]	The Ink Spots	1950	12.50	25.00	50.00
❏ DL 5071 [10]	The Ink Spots, Vol. 2	1950	12.50	25.00	50.00
❏ DL 5333 [10]	Precious Memories	1951	12.50	25.00	50.00
❏ DL 5541 [10]	Street of Dreams	1954	12.50	25.00	50.00
❏ DXSB 7182 [(2) P]	The Best of the Ink Spots	1965	5.00	10.00	20.00
❏ DL 8154 [M]	The Best of the Ink Spots	1955	10.00	20.00	40.00
—Black label, silver print					
❏ DL 8232 [M]	Time Our for Tears	1956	10.00	20.00	40.00
—Black label, silver print					
❏ DL 8768 [M]	Torch Time	1958	10.00	20.00	40.00
—Black label, silver print					
❏ DL 74297 [S]	Our Golden Favorites	1962	5.00	10.00	20.00
GRAND AWARD					
❏ GA 232 SD [S]	The Ink Spots' Greatest, Volume 3	1959	10.00	20.00	40.00
❏ GA 33-328 [M]	The Ink Spots' Greatest, Volume 1	1958	6.25	12.50	25.00
❏ GA 33-354 [M]	The Ink Spots' Greatest, Volume 2	1958	6.25	12.50	25.00
❏ GA 33-396 [M]	The Ink Spots' Greatest, Volume 3	1959	6.25	12.50	25.00
KING					
❏ 535 [M]	Something Old, Something New	1956	100.00	200.00	400.00
❏ 642 [M]	Songs That Will Live Forever	1959	75.00	150.00	300.00
—Reissue of 535					
❏ 5001	18 Hits by the Ink Spots	197?	2.50	5.00	10.00
MCA					
❏ 4005 [(2)]	The Best of the Ink Spots	197?	3.00	6.00	12.00
OPEN SKY					
❏ 3125	Just Like Old Times	198?	2.50	5.00	10.00
PAULA					
❏ 2212	The Ink Spots Sing Country	1972	2.50	5.00	10.00
TOPS					
❏ L-1561 [M]	The Ink Spots	1957	10.00	20.00	40.00
❏ L-1668 [M]	The Ink Spots, Vol. 2	1959	10.00	20.00	40.00
VERVE					
❏ MGV-2124 [M]	The Ink Spots' Favorites	1959	6.25	12.50	25.00
❏ MGVS-6096 [S]	The Ink Spots' Favorites	1959	10.00	20.00	40.00
VOCALION					
❏ VL 3606 [M]	Sincerely Yours	196?	3.00	6.00	12.00
❏ VL 3725 [M]	Lost in a Dream	1965	3.00	6.00	12.00
❏ VL 73606 [R]	Sincerely Yours	196?	2.50	5.00	10.00
❏ VL 73725 [R]	Lost in a Dream	1965	2.50	5.00	10.00
WALDORF MUSIC HALL					
❏ MH 33-144 [10]	Songs of the South Seas	195?	20.00	40.00	80.00
❏ MH 33-152 [10]	The Ink Spots Quartet	195?	20.00	40.00	80.00

INTRIGUES, THE
45s
TOOT

Number	Title (A Side/B Side)	Yr	VG	VG+	NM
❏ 609	Soul Brother (Part 1)/Soul Brother (Part 2)	1968	2.50	5.00	10.00
YEW					
❏ 1001	In a Moment/Scotchman Rock	1969	3.00	6.00	12.00
❏ 1002	I'm Gonna Love You/I Gotta Find Out for Myself	1969	2.50	5.00	10.00
❏ 1007	Just a Little Bit More/Let's Dance	1970	2.50	5.00	10.00
❏ 1010	Tuck a Little Love Away/I Know There's Love	1970	2.50	5.00	10.00
❏ 1012	The Language of Love/I Got Love	1971	2.50	5.00	10.00
❏ 1013	Mojo Hannah/To Make a World	1971	2.50	5.00	10.00
Albums					
YEW					
❏ YS-777	In a Moment	1970	7.50	15.00	30.00

INTRUDERS, THE (1)
Early Philly Soul group.
45s
GAMBLE

Number	Title (A Side/B Side)	Yr	VG	VG+	NM
❏ 201	(We'll Be) United/Up and Down the Ladder	1966	2.50	5.00	10.00
❏ 203	Devil with an Angel's Smile/A Book for the Broken Hearted	1966	2.50	5.00	10.00
❏ 203 [PS]	Devil with an Angel's Smile/A Book for the Broken Hearted	1966	3.75	7.50	15.00
❏ 204	It Must Be Love/Check Yourself	1966	2.50	5.00	10.00
❏ 205	Together/Up and Down the Ladder	1967	2.50	5.00	10.00
❏ 209	Baby I'm Lonely/A Love That's Real	1967	2.50	5.00	10.00
❏ 214	Cowboys to Girls/Turn the Hands of Time	1968	2.50	5.00	10.00
❏ 217	(Love Is Like a) Baseball Game/Friends No More	1968	2.50	5.00	10.00
❏ 221	Slow Drag/So Glad I'm Yours	1968	2.50	5.00	10.00
❏ 223	Give Her a Transplant/Girls, Girls, Girls	1969	2.50	5.00	10.00
❏ 225	Me Tarzan You Jane/Favorite Candidate	1969	2.50	5.00	10.00
❏ 231	Lollipop (I Like You)/Don't Give It Away	1969	2.50	5.00	10.00
❏ 235	Sad Girl/Let's Go Downtown	1969	2.50	5.00	10.00
❏ 240	Old Love/Every Day Is a Holiday	1969	2.50	5.00	10.00
❏ 2501	(Win, Place or Show) She's a Winner/Memories Are Here to Stay	1972	2.00	4.00	8.00
❏ 2506	I'll Always Love My Mama (Part 1)/I'll Always Love My Mama (Part 2)	1973	2.00	4.00	8.00
❏ 2508	I Wanna Know Your Name/Hang On In There	1973	2.00	4.00	8.00
❏ 4001	Tender (Was the Love We Knew)/By the Time I Get to Phoenix	1970	2.00	4.00	8.00
❏ 4004	When We Get Married/Doctor Doctor	1970	2.00	4.00	8.00
❏ 4007	This Is My Love Song/Let Me in Your Mind	1970	2.00	4.00	8.00
❏ 4009	I'm Girl Scoutin'/Wonder What Kind of Bag She's In	1971	2.00	4.00	8.00
❏ 4014	Pray for Me/Best Days of My Life	1971	2.00	4.00	8.00
❏ 4016	I Bet He Don't Love You (Like I Love You)/Do You Remember Yesterday	1971	2.00	4.00	8.00
❏ 4019	(Win, Place or Show) She's a Winner/Memories Are Here to Stay	1972	2.50	5.00	10.00
GOWEN					
❏ 1401	I'm Sold on You/Come Home Soon	1961	10.00	20.00	40.00
PHILADELPHIA INT'L.					
❏ 3624	I'll Always Love My Mama (Part 1)/I'll Always Love My Mama (Part 2)	1977	—	2.50	5.00
❏ 3689	I'll Always Love My Mama/Save the Children	1979	—	2.50	5.00
TSOP					
❏ 4758	A Nice Girl Like You/To Be Happy Is the Real Thing	1974	—	3.00	6.00
❏ 4766	Rainy Days and Mondays/Be on Time	1975	—	3.00	6.00
❏ 4771	Plain Old Fashioned Girl/Energy of Love	1975	—	3.00	6.00

ISLEY BROTHERS, THE
12-Inch Singles
T-NECK

Number	Title (A Side/B Side)	Yr	VG	VG+	NM
❏ AS 947 [DJ]	Hurry Up and Wait (3:54) (4:09)	1981	2.00	4.00	8.00
❏ 2267	Livin' in the Life/Go for Your Guns	1977	3.75	7.50	15.00
❏ 2276	Tell Me When You Need It Again/Take Me to the Next Phase	1977	3.75	7.50	15.00
❏ 2283	I Wanna Be with You (6:20)/Rockin' with Fire (5:57)	1978	3.00	6.00	12.00
❏ 2289	It's a Disco Night (Rock Don't Stop)/Ain't Givin' Up on Love	1979	3.00	6.00	12.00
❏ 03282	It's Alright with Me (Vocal) (Instrumental)	1982	2.50	5.00	10.00
❏ 04148	I Need Your Body/(Instrumental)	1983	2.00	4.00	8.00
WARNER BROS.					
❏ PRO-A-2378 [DJ]	Colder Are My Night (Edit Version) (LP Version)	1985	2.00	4.00	8.00
❏ PRO-A-4511 [DJ]	Spend the Night (Edit)/Colder Are My Nights (Edit)/Smooth Sailin' Tonight (Edit)	1989	2.00	4.00	8.00
❏ PRO-A-5417 [DJ]	Sensitive Lover (4 versions)	1992	2.00	4.00	8.00
❏ 20827	I Wish (Vocal) (Instrumental)	1987	2.00	4.00	8.00
❏ 21415	You'll Never Walk Alone (4 versions)/One of a Kind	1989	2.00	4.00	8.00

45s
ATLANTIC

Number	Title (A Side/B Side)	Yr	VG	VG+	NM
❏ 2092	Jeepers Creepers/Teach Me How to Shimmy	1961	3.75	7.50	15.00
❏ 2100	Shine On Harvest Moon/Standing on the Dance Floor	1961	3.75	7.50	15.00
❏ 2110	Your Old Lady/Write to Me	1961	3.75	7.50	15.00
❏ 2122	A Fool for You/Just One More Time	1961	3.75	7.50	15.00
❏ 2263	Looking for a Love/The Last Girl	1964	2.50	5.00	10.00
❏ 2277	Simon Says/Wild As a Tiger	1965	2.50	5.00	10.00

Number	Title (A Side/B Side)	Yr	VG	VG+	NM
❑ 2303	Move Over and Let Me Dance/Have You Ever Been Disappointed	1965	3.75	7.50	15.00
CINDY					
❑ 3009	Don't Be Jealous/This Is the End	1958	37.50	75.00	150.00
—"Cindy" in shadow print					
❑ 3009	Don't Be Jealous/This Is the End	1958	18.75	37.50	75.00
—"Cindy" in regular print					
GONE					
❑ 5022	I Wanna Know/Everybody's Gonna Rock and Roll	1958	20.00	40.00	80.00
❑ 5048	My Love/The Drag	1958	20.00	40.00	80.00
MARK-X					
❑ 7003	The Drag/Rockin' MacDonald	1957	25.00	50.00	100.00
❑ 8000	The Drag/Rockin' MacDonald	1959	7.50	15.00	30.00
PHILCO-FORD					
❑ HP-41	Twist and Shout/Rubberleg Twist	1969	6.25	12.50	25.00
—4-inch plastic "Hip Pocket Record" with color sleeve					
RCA					
❑ 447-0589	Shout (Part 1)/Shout (Part 2)	1976	—	2.00	4.00
—Gold Standard Series; black label, dog near top					
RCA VICTOR					
❑ 47-7537	I'm Gonna Knock on Your Door/Turn to Me	1959	6.25	12.50	25.00
❑ 47-7588	Shout (Part 1)/Shout (Part 2)	1959	7.50	15.00	30.00
❑ 47-7657	Respectable/Without a Song	1959	6.25	12.50	25.00
❑ 47-7718	He's Got the Whole World in His Hands/How Deep Is the Ocean	1960	6.25	12.50	25.00
❑ 47-7746	Gypsy Love Song/Open Up Your Heart	1960	6.25	12.50	25.00
❑ 47-7787	Say You Love Me Too/Tell Me Who	1960	6.25	12.50	25.00
❑ 61-7588 [S]	Shout (Part 1)/Shout (Part 2)	1959	15.00	30.00	60.00
—"Living Stereo" (large hole, plays at 45 rpm)					
❑ 447-0589	Shout (Part 1)/Shout (Part 2)	1962	3.00	6.00	12.00
—Gold Standard Series; black label, dog on top (this charted with this number in 1962)					
❑ 447-0589	Shout (Part 1)/Shout (Part 2)	1965	2.00	4.00	8.00
—Gold Standard Series; black label, dog on side					
❑ 447-0589	Shout (Part 1)/Shout (Part 2)	1969	—	2.50	5.00
—Gold Standard Series; red label					
T-NECK					
❑ 501	Testify (Part 1)/Testify (Part 2)	1964	3.75	7.50	15.00
❑ 901	It's Your Thing/Don't Give It Away	1969	—	3.00	6.00
❑ 902	I Turned You On/I Know Who You Been Socking It To	1969	—	3.00	6.00
❑ 906	Black Berries — Pt. 1/Black Berries — Pt. 2	1969	—	3.00	6.00
❑ 908	Was It Good to You/I Got to Get Myself Together	1969	—	3.00	6.00
❑ 912	Bless Your Heart/Give the Women What They Want	1969	—	3.00	6.00
❑ 914	Keep On Doin'/Save Me	1970	—	3.00	6.00
❑ 919	If He Can, You Can/Holdin' On	1970	—	3.00	6.00
❑ 921	Girls Will Be Girls, Boys Will Be Boys/Get Down Off of the Train	1970	—	3.00	6.00
❑ 924	Get Into Something/Get Into Something (Part 2)	1970	—	3.00	6.00
❑ 927	Freedom/I Need You So	1970	—	3.00	6.00
❑ 929	Warpath/I Got to Find Me One	1971	—	3.00	6.00
❑ 930	Love the One You're With/He's Got Your Love	1971	—	3.00	6.00
❑ 932	Spill the Wine/Take Inventory	1971	—	3.00	6.00
❑ 933	Lay Lady Lay/Vacuum Cleaner	1971	—	3.00	6.00
❑ 934	Lay-Away/Feel Like the World	1972	—	3.00	6.00
❑ 935	Pop That Thang/I Got to Find Me One	1972	—	3.00	6.00
❑ 936	Work to Do/Beautiful	1972	—	3.00	6.00
❑ 937	It's Too Late/Nothing to Do But Today	1973	—	3.00	6.00
❑ 02033	Hurry Up and Wait/(Instrumental)	1981	—	2.50	5.00
❑ 02151	Don't Say Goodnight (It's Time for Love) (Parts 1 & 2)	1981	—	2.00	4.00
—Reissue					
❑ 02179	I Once Had Your Love (And I Can't Let Go)/(Instrumental)	1981	—	2.50	5.00
❑ 2251	That Lady (Part 1)/That Lady (Part 2)	1973	—	2.50	5.00
❑ 2252	What It Comes Down To/Highways of My Life	1973	—	2.50	5.00
❑ 2253	Summer Breeze (Part 1)/Summer Breeze (Part 2)	1974	—	2.50	5.00
❑ 2254	Live It Up (Part 1)/Live It Up (Part 2)	1974	—	2.50	5.00
❑ 2255	Midnight Sky (Part 1)/Midnight Sky (Part 2)	1974	—	2.50	5.00
❑ 2256	Fight the Power Part 1/Fight the Power Part 2	1975	—	2.50	5.00
❑ 2259	For the Love of You (Part 1&2)/You Walk Your Way	1975	—	2.50	5.00
❑ 2260	Who Loves You Better-Part 1/Who Loves You Better-Part 2	1976	—	2.50	5.00
❑ 2261	Harvest for the World/Harvest for the World (Part 2)	1976	—	2.50	5.00
❑ 2262	The Pride (Part 1)/The Pride (Part 2)	1977	—	2.50	5.00
❑ 2264	Livin' in the Life/Go for Your Guns	1977	—	2.50	5.00
❑ 2270	Voyage to Atlantis/Do You Wanna Stay Down	1977	—	2.50	5.00
❑ 02270	Voyage to Atlantis/Do You Wanna Stay Down	1981	—	2.00	4.00
—Reissue					
❑ 2272	Take Me to the Next Phase (Part 1)/Take Me to the Next Phase (Part 2)	1978	—	2.50	5.00
❑ 2277	Groove with You/Footsteps in the Dark	1978	—	2.50	5.00
❑ 2278	Showdown (Part 1)/Showdown (Part 2)	1978	—	2.50	5.00
❑ 2279	I Wanna Be with You (Part 1)/I Wanna Be with You (Part 2)	1979	—	2.50	5.00
❑ 2284	Winner Takes All/Fun and Games	1979	—	2.50	5.00
❑ 2287	It's a Disco Night (Rock Don't Stop)/Ain't Givin' Up on Love	1979	—	2.50	5.00
❑ 2290	Don't Say Goodnight (It's Time for Love) (Part 1)/Don't Say Goodnight (It's Time for Love) (Part 2)	1980	—	2.50	5.00
❑ 2291	Here We Go Again (Part 1)/Here We Go Again (Part 2)	1980	—	2.50	5.00
❑ 2292	Say You Will (Part 1)/Say You Will (Part 2)	1980	—	2.50	5.00

Number	Title (A Side/B Side)	Yr	VG	VG+	NM
❑ 2293	Who Said?/(Can't You See) What You've Done to Me	1980	—	2.50	5.00
❑ 02293	Who Said?/(Can't You See) What You Do to Me	1981	—	2.00	4.00
—Reissue					
❑ 02531	Inside You (Part 1)/Inside You (Part 2)	1981	—	2.50	5.00
❑ 02705	Party Night/Welcome Into My Night	1982	—	2.50	5.00
❑ 02985	The Real Deal/(Instrumental)	1982	—	2.50	5.00
❑ 03281	It's Alright with Me/(Instrumental)	1982	—	2.50	5.00
❑ 03797	Between the Sheets/(Instrumental)	1983	—	2.50	5.00
❑ 03994	Choosey Lover/(Instrumental)	1983	—	2.50	5.00
❑ 04320	Let's Make Love Tonight/(Instrumental)	1984	—	2.50	5.00
TAMLA					
❑ 54128	This Old Heart of Mine (Is Weak for You)/There's No Love Left	1966	3.75	7.50	15.00
❑ 54133	Take Some Time Out for Love/Who Could Ever Doubt My Love	1966	3.00	6.00	12.00
❑ 54135	I Guess I'll Always Love You/I Hear a Symphony	1966	3.00	6.00	12.00
❑ 54146	Got to Have You Back/Just Ain't Enough Love	1967	3.00	6.00	12.00
❑ 54154	One Too Many Heartaches/That's the Way Love Is	1967	3.00	6.00	12.00
❑ 54164	Take Me in Your Arms (Rock Me a Little While)/Why When Love Is Gone	1968	3.00	6.00	12.00
❑ 54175	Behind a Painted Smile/All Because I Love You	1968	3.00	6.00	12.00
❑ 54182	Take Some Time Out for Love/Just Ain't Enough Love	1969	3.00	6.00	12.00
TEENAGE					
❑ 1004	Angels Cried/The Cow Jumped Over the Moon	1957	200.00	400.00	800.00
UNITED ARTISTS					
❑ 605	She's Gone/Tango	1963	5.00	10.00	20.00
❑ 638	Surf and Shout/Whatcha Gonna Do	1963	5.00	10.00	20.00
❑ 659	Please, Please, Please/You'll Never Leave Him	1963	5.00	10.00	20.00
❑ 714	Who's That Lady/My Little Girl	1964	5.00	10.00	20.00
❑ 798	Love Is a Wonderful Thing/Open Up Her Eyes	1964	—	—	—
—Unreleased					
❑ 923	Love Is a Wonderful Thing/Open Up Her Eyes	1965	—	—	—
—Unreleased					
VEEP					
❑ 1230	Love Is a Wonderful Thing/Open Up Her Eyes	1966	2.50	5.00	10.00
V.I.P.					
❑ 25020	I Hear a Symphony/Who Could Ever Doubt My Love	1965	200.00	400.00	800.00
WAND					
❑ 118	Right Now/The Snake	1962	3.75	7.50	15.00
❑ 124	Twist and Shout/Spanish Twist	1962	5.00	10.00	20.00
❑ 127	Twistin' with Linda/You Better Come Home	1962	3.00	6.00	12.00
❑ 131	Nobody But Me/I'm Laughing to Keep from Crying	1963	3.00	6.00	12.00
❑ 137	I Say Love/Hold On Baby	1963	3.00	6.00	12.00
WARNER BROS.					
❑ 22748	One of a Kind/You'll Never Walk Alone	1989	—	—	3.00
❑ 22900	Spend the Night (Ce Soir)/(Instrumental)	1989	—	—	3.00
❑ 22900 [PS]	Spend the Night (Ce Soir)/(Instrumental)	1989	—	—	3.00
❑ 27954	It Takes a Good Woman/(Instrumental)	1988	—	2.00	4.00
❑ 28129	I Wish/(Instrumental)	1988	—	2.00	4.00
❑ 28129 [PS]	I Wish/(Instrumental)	1988	—	2.00	4.00
❑ 28241	Come My Way/(Instrumental)	1987	—	2.00	4.00
❑ 28385	Smooth Sailin' Tonight/(Instrumental)	1987	—	2.00	4.00
❑ 28385 [PS]	Smooth Sailin' Tonight/(Instrumental)	1987	—	2.00	4.00
❑ 28764	May I?/(Instrumental)	1986	—	2.00	4.00
❑ 28860	Colder Are My Nights/(Instrumental)	1985	—	2.00	4.00
Albums					
BUDDAH					
❑ BDS-5652 [(2)]	The Best of the Isley Brothers	1976	3.75	7.50	15.00
COLLECTABLES					
❑ COL-5103	Shout!	198?	2.50	5.00	10.00
ISLAND					
❑ 7243 [(2) DJ]	Mission to Please	1996	5.00	10.00	20.00
—Promo-only vinyl in generic cover					
MOTOWN					
❑ M5-106V1	Motown Superstar Series, Volume 6	1981	2.00	4.00	8.00
❑ M5-128V1	This Old Heart of Mine	1981	2.00	4.00	8.00
—Reissue of Tamla 269					
❑ M5-143V1	Doin' Their Thing (Best of the Isley Brothers)	1981	2.00	4.00	8.00
—Reissue of Tamla 287					
PICKWICK					
❑ SPC-3331	Soul Shout!	197?	2.50	5.00	10.00
RCA CAMDEN					
❑ ACL1-0126	Rock On Brother	1973	3.00	6.00	12.00
❑ ACL1-0861	Rock Around the Clock	1975	3.00	6.00	12.00
RCA VICTOR					
❑ LPM-2156 [M]	Shout!	1959	30.00	60.00	120.00
—"Long Play" label					
❑ LSP-2156 [S]	Shout!	1959	50.00	100.00	200.00
—"Living Stereo" label					
SCEPTER					
❑ SC-552 [M]	Take Some Time Out for the Isley Brothers	1966	7.50	15.00	30.00
❑ SCS-552 [S]	Take Some Time Out for the Isley Brothers	1966	10.00	20.00	40.00
SUNSET					
❑ SUS-5257	The Isley Brothers Do Their Thing	1969	3.75	7.50	15.00
T-NECK					
❑ ASZ 137 [DJ]	Everything You Always Wanted to Hear by the Isley Brothers But Were Afraid to Ask For	1976	5.00	10.00	20.00
—Promo-only compilation					
❑ TNS-3001	It's Our Thing	1969	5.00	10.00	20.00
❑ TNS-3002	The Brothers: Isley	1969	5.00	10.00	20.00

Brenda Holloway was a rarity in early Motown days in that she wasn't from the Detroit area; she actually hailed from California. This is her only LP.

"Shotgun Blues," a #1 R&B hit in 1950, was the first Lightnin' Hopkins single to be issued on 45 rpm. Original pressings are quite rare.

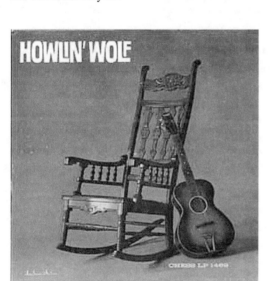

The second Howlin' Wolf LP on the Chess label was simply titled *Howlin' Wolf* and featured only a rocking chair and a guitar on the cover.

After Ivory Joe Hunter had a career revival on Atlantic, his prior label, MGM, began to re-release some of his older material. This EP is one of three that comprised the contents of the LP *I Get That Lonesome Feeling*.

The Impalas were one-hit wonders on the pop and R&B charts with "Sorry (I Ran All the Way Home)." The resulting album is tough enough to find, but it's even tougher in stereo.

How many other album covers so perfectly reflect the excitement of the songs within as this one for the Isley Brothers' *Shout*?

Number	Title (A Side/B Side)	Yr	VG	VG+	NM
❏ TNS-3006	Get Into Something	1970	3.75	7.50	15.00
❏ TNS-3007	In the Beginning (With Jimi Hendrix)	1970	5.00	10.00	20.00
❏ TNS-3008	Givin' It Back	1971	3.75	7.50	15.00
❏ TNS-3009	Brother, Brother, Brother	1972	3.75	7.50	15.00
❏ TNS-3010 [(2)]	The Isleys Live	1973	5.00	10.00	20.00
❏ TNS-3011	Isleys' Greatest Hits	1973	3.75	7.50	15.00
❏ KZ 32453	3 + 3	1973	3.00	6.00	12.00
❏ PZ 32453	3 + 3	197?	2.00	4.00	8.00
—Reissue with new prefix					
❏ ZQ 32453 [Q]	3 + 3	1974	5.00	10.00	20.00
❏ PZ 33070	Live It Up	1974	3.00	6.00	12.00
—No bar code on cover					
❏ PZQ 33070 [Q]	Live It Up	1974	5.00	10.00	20.00
❏ PZ 33536	The Heat Is On	1975	3.00	6.00	12.00
—No bar code on cover					
❏ PZ 33536	The Heat Is On	198?	2.00	4.00	8.00
—Budget-line reissue with bar code					
❏ PZ 33809	Harvest for the World	1976	3.00	6.00	12.00
—No bar code on cover					
❏ PZQ 33809 [Q]	Harvest for the World	1976	5.00	10.00	20.00
❏ PZ 34432	Go for Your Guns	1977	3.00	6.00	12.00
—No bar code on cover					
❏ PZ 34432	Go for Your Guns	198?	2.00	4.00	8.00
—Budget-line reissue with bar code					
❏ PZQ 34432 [Q]	Go for Your Guns	1977	5.00	10.00	20.00
❏ PZ 34452	Forever Gold	1977	2.50	5.00	10.00
❏ JZ 34930	Showdown	1978	2.50	5.00	10.00
❏ PZ 34930	Showdown	198?	2.00	4.00	8.00
—Budget-line reissue					
❏ KZ2 35650 [(2)]	Timeless	1978	3.00	6.00	12.00
❏ PZ2 36077 [(2)]	Winner Takes All	1979	3.00	6.00	12.00
❏ FZ 36305	Go All the Way	1980	2.50	5.00	10.00
❏ PZ 36305	Go All the Way	198?	2.00	4.00	8.00
—Budget-line reissue					
❏ FZ 37080	Grand Slam	1981	2.50	5.00	10.00
❏ PZ 37080	Grand Slam	198?	2.00	4.00	8.00
—Budget-line reissue					
❏ FZ 37533	Inside You	1981	2.50	5.00	10.00
❏ FZ 38047	The Real Deal	1982	2.50	5.00	10.00
❏ FZ 38674	Between the Sheets	1983	2.50	5.00	10.00
❏ PZ 38674	Between the Sheets	1985	2.00	4.00	8.00
—Budget-line reissue					
❏ FZ 39240	Greatest Hits, Vol. 1	1984	2.50	5.00	10.00
❏ PZ 39240	Greatest Hits, Vol. 1	1985	2.00	4.00	8.00
—Budget-line reissue					
TAMLA					
❏ T-269 [M]	This Old Heart of Mine	1966	6.25	12.50	25.00
❏ TS-269 [S]	This Old Heart of Mine	1966	7.50	15.00	30.00
❏ T-275 [M]	Soul on the Rocks	1967	6.25	12.50	25.00
❏ TS-275 [S]	Soul on the Rocks	1967	7.50	15.00	30.00
❏ TS-287	Doin' Their Thing (Best of the Isley Brothers)	1969	5.00	10.00	20.00
UNITED ARTISTS					
❏ UA-LA500-E	The Very Best of the Isley Brothers	1975	2.50	5.00	10.00
❏ UAL-3313 [M]	The Famous Isley Brothers	1963	12.50	25.00	50.00
❏ UAS-6313 [S]	The Famous Isley Brothers	1963	15.00	30.00	60.00
WAND					
❏ WD-653 [M]	Twist & Shout	1962	20.00	40.00	80.00
❏ WDS-653 [S]	Twist & Shout	1962	25.00	50.00	100.00
WARNER BROS.					
❏ 25347	Masterpiece	1985	2.50	5.00	10.00
❏ 25586	Smooth Sailin'	1987	2.50	5.00	10.00
❏ 25940	Spend the Night	1989	2.50	5.00	10.00

ISLEY JASPER ISLEY
12-Inch Singles
CBS ASSOCIATED

Number	Title (A Side/B Side)	Yr	VG	VG+	NM
❏ 4Z9-05158	Kiss and Tell (Vocal) (Instrumental)	1984	2.00	4.00	8.00
❏ 4Z9-05285	Caravan of Love/I Can't Get Over Losin' You	1985	2.00	4.00	8.00
❏ 4Z9-05329	Insatiable Woman (6:10)/Break This Chain (4:30)	1985	2.00	4.00	8.00
❏ 4Z9-06802	8th Wonder of the World (Octagon Club Mix) (Power Guitar Mix)/(Wonderdub) (Congapella)	1987	—	3.50	7.00
MAGIC SOUNDS					
❏ 4Z9-05109	Look the Other Way (5:06) (Instrumental)	1984	2.50	5.00	10.00

45s
CBS ASSOCIATED

Number	Title (A Side/B Side)	Yr	VG	VG+	NM
❏ ZS4-04741	Kiss and Tell/(Instrumental)	1985	—	2.00	4.00
❏ ZS4-04916	Serve You Right/Love Is Gonna Last Forever	1985	—	2.00	4.00
❏ ZS4-05611	Caravan of Love/I Can't Get Over Losin' You	1985	—	2.00	4.00
❏ ZS4-05760	Insatiable Woman/Break the Chain	1986	—	2.00	4.00
❏ ZS4-06111	If You Believe in Love/Sex Drive	1986	—	2.00	4.00
❏ ZS4-07018	8th Wonder of the World/Broadway's Closer to Sunset Blvd.	1987	—	2.00	4.00
❏ ZS4-07254	Givin' You Back the Love/I Can Hardly Wait	1987	—	2.00	4.00
❏ 08445	Caravan of Love/Insatiable Woman	1988	—	—	3.00
—Reissue					
MAGIC SOUNDS					
❏ ZS4-04642	Look the Other Way/(Instrumental)	1984	—	2.50	5.00

Albums
CBS ASSOCIATED

Number	Title (A Side/B Side)	Yr	VG	VG+	NM
❏ FZ 39873	Broadway's Closer to Sunset Blvd.	1984	2.50	5.00	10.00
❏ BFZ 40118	Caravan of Love	1985	2.00	4.00	8.00
❏ FZ 40409	Different Drummer	1987	2.00	4.00	8.00

Number	Title (A Side/B Side)	Yr	VG	VG+	NM

J

J.B.'S, THE
See FRED WESLEY.

J.B. AND THE HAWKS
See J.B. HUTTO.

JACKS, THE
Also see THE CADETS.
45s
KENT

Number	Title (A Side/B Side)	Yr	VG	VG+	NM
❏ 344	Why Don't You Write Me/This Empty Heart	1960	3.75	7.50	15.00
RPM					
❏ 428	Why Don't You Write Me/Smack Dab in the Middle	1955	50.00	100.00	200.00
❏ 428	Why Don't You Write Me/My Darling	1955	15.00	30.00	60.00
❏ 433	I'm Confessin'/Since My Baby's Been Gone	1955	15.00	30.00	60.00
❏ 444	This Empty Heart/My Clumsy Heart	1955	12.50	25.00	50.00
❏ 454	So Wrong/How Soon	1956	12.50	25.00	50.00
❏ 458	Sugar Baby/Why Did I Fall in Love	1956	15.00	30.00	60.00
❏ 467	Let's Make Up/Dream a Little Longer	1956	15.00	30.00	60.00

Albums
CROWN

Number	Title (A Side/B Side)	Yr	VG	VG+	NM
❏ CST-372 [R]	Jumpin' with the Jacks	1962	12.50	25.00	50.00
❏ CLP-5021 [M]	Jumpin' with the Jacks	1960	50.00	100.00	200.00
❏ CLP-5372 [M]	Jumpin' with the Jacks	1962	25.00	50.00	100.00
RELIC					
❏ 5023	The Jacks' Greatest Hits	198?	2.50	5.00	10.00
RPM					
❏ LRP-3006 [M]	Jumpin' with the Jacks	1956	1000.	1500.	2000
UNITED					
❏ US-7797	Rock 'n' Roll Hits of the 50's	197?	3.75	7.50	15.00

JACKSON, BULL MOOSE
45s
BOGUS

Number	Title (A Side/B Side)	Yr	VG	VG+	NM
❏ 12-042684	Get Off the Table, Mable (The Two Dollars Is For the Beer)/I've Got a Gal Who Lives Up on a Hill	1984	—	2.50	5.00
❏ 12-042684 [PS]	Get Off the Table, Mable (The Two Dollars Is For the Beer)/I've Got a Gal Who Lives Up on a Hill	1984	—	2.50	5.00
ENCINO					
❏ 1005	Understanding/(B-side unknown)	1957	15.00	30.00	60.00
KING					
❏ 4181	I Love You Yes I Do/Sneaky Pete	1951	15.00	30.00	60.00
—78 originally released in 1947					
❏ 4189	I Want a Bowlegged Woman/All My Love Belongs to You	1951	20.00	40.00	80.00
—78 originally released in 1948 -- 5191 and 5198 are the only legitimate 45s known before 4451					
❏ 4451	Trust in Me/Wonder When My Baby's Coming Home	1951	15.00	30.00	60.00
❏ 4462	Unless/End This Misery	1951	15.00	30.00	60.00
❏ 4472	Cherokee Boogie/I'm Lucky I Have You	1951	15.00	30.00	60.00
❏ 4493	I'll Be Home for Christmas/I Never Loved Anyone But You	1951	15.00	30.00	60.00
❏ 4524	Nosey Joe/Sad	1952	20.00	40.00	80.00
❏ 4535	(Let Me Love You) All Night Long/Bootsie	1952	15.00	30.00	60.00
❏ 4551	Bearcat Blues/There Is No Greater Love	1952	15.00	30.00	60.00
❏ 4580	Big Ten Inch Record/I Needed You	1952	50.00	100.00	200.00
❏ 4634	Meet Me with Your Black Dress On/Try to Forget Him	1953	10.00	20.00	40.00
❏ 4655	If You'll Let Me/Hodge Podge	1953	10.00	20.00	40.00
❏ 4775	If You Ain't Lovin'/I Wanna Hug Ya, Kiss Ya	1955	6.25	12.50	25.00
❏ 4802	I'm Glad for Your Sake/Must You Keep On Pretending	1955	6.25	12.50	25.00
SEVEN ARTS					
❏ 705	I Love You Yes I Do/Aw Shucks Baby	1961	5.00	10.00	20.00
WARWICK					
❏ 575	I Found My Love/More of the Same	1960	5.00	10.00	20.00

78s
KING

Number	Title (A Side/B Side)	Yr	VG	VG+	NM
❏ 4165	Goin' Back to Cleveland, Ohio/Charlie White, Short Man	1947	7.50	15.00	30.00
❏ 4181	I Love You Yes I Do/Sneaky Pete	1947	7.50	15.00	30.00
❏ 4189	I Want a Bowlegged Woman/All My Love Belongs to You	1948	7.50	15.00	30.00
❏ 4213	Three Boxes/All My Love Belongs to You	1948	7.50	15.00	30.00
❏ 4230	I Can't Go On Without You/Fare Thee Well, Deacon Jones	1948	7.50	15.00	30.00
❏ 4244	Cleveland, Ohio Blues/I Know Who Threw the Whiskey (In the Well)	1948	7.50	15.00	30.00
❏ 4250	Love Me Tonight/We Can Talk Some Trash	1948	7.50	15.00	30.00
❏ 4280	Don't Ask Me Why/Oh John	1949	7.50	15.00	30.00
❏ 4288	Little Girl Don't Cry/Moosey	1949	7.50	15.00	30.00
❏ 4305	Gone Back to Me/Houston Texas Gal	1949	7.50	15.00	30.00
❏ 4322	Why Don't You Haul Off and Love Me/Is That All I Mean to You	1949	7.50	15.00	30.00
❏ 4335	Must You Go/Not Until You Come My Way	1950	7.50	15.00	30.00
❏ 4352	A Fool in Love/Let Your Conscience Be Your Guide	1950	7.50	15.00	30.00
❏ 4373	Sometimes I Wonder/Time Alone Will Tell	1950	7.50	15.00	30.00
❏ 4412	Big Fat Mamas Are In Style Again/My Beloved	1950	7.50	15.00	30.00
❏ 4422	Have You No Mercy/Without Your Love	1950	7.50	15.00	30.00

Number	Title (A Side/B Side)	Yr	VG	VG+	NM
❑ 4433	My Little Baby/Forget and Forgive	1951	7.50	15.00	30.00
❑ 4451	Trust in Me/Wonder When My Baby's Coming Home	1951	6.25	12.50	25.00
❑ 4462	Unless/End This Misery	1951	6.25	12.50	25.00
❑ 4472	Cherokee Boogie/I'm Lucky I Have You	1951	6.25	12.50	25.00
❑ 4493	I'll Be Home for Christmas/I Never Loved Anyone But You	1951	6.25	12.50	25.00
❑ 4524	Nosey Joe/Sad	1952	7.50	15.00	30.00
❑ 4535	(Let Me Love You) All Night Long/Bootsie	1952	6.25	12.50	25.00
❑ 4551	Bearcat Blues/There Is No Greater Love	1952	6.25	12.50	25.00
❑ 4580	Big Ten Inch Record/I Needed You	1952	20.00	40.00	80.00
❑ 4634	Meet Me with Your Black Dress On/Try to Forget Him	1953	6.25	12.50	25.00
❑ 4655	If You'll Let Me/Hodge Podge	1953	6.25	12.50	25.00
❑ 4775	If You Ain't Lovin'/I Wanna Hug Ya, Kiss Ya	1955	6.25	12.50	25.00
❑ 4802	I'm Glad for Your Sake/Must You Keep On Pretending	1955	6.25	12.50	25.00
QUEEN					
❑ 4100	The Honey Dripper/Hold Me Joe	1945	10.00	20.00	40.00
❑ 4102	We Ain't Got Nothin' But the Blues/B.M. Jackson Blues	1946	10.00	20.00	40.00
❑ 4107	Jammin', Jumpin'/Oo Oo E-Bob-a-Lee-Bob	1946	10.00	20.00	40.00
❑ 4112	Buffalo Shuffle/Shorty's Got to Go	1946	10.00	20.00	40.00
❑ 4116	I Know Who Threw the Whiskey (In the Well)/Bad Man Jackson, That's Me	1946	10.00	20.00	40.00
7-Inch Extended Plays					
KING					
❑ EP-211	*I Love You, Yes I Do/I Want a Bowlegged Woman/All My Love Belongs to You/Little Girl Don't Cry	1953	37.50	75.00	150.00
❑ EP-211 [PS]	Bull Moose Jackson Sings His All Time Hits	1953	37.50	75.00	150.00
Albums					
AUDIO LAB					
❑ AL-1524 [M]	Bull Moose Jackson	1959	150.00	300.00	600.00
BOGUS					
❑ 6-0214851	Moosemania!	1985	2.50	5.00	10.00

JACKSON, CHUCK

Number	Title (A Side/B Side)	Yr	VG	VG+	NM
45s					
ABC					
❑ 11368	I Only Get This Feeling/Slowly But Surely	1973	—	3.00	6.00
❑ 11398	I Can't Break Away/Just a Little Tear	1973	—	3.00	6.00
❑ 11423	If Only You Believe/Maybe This Will Be the Morning	1974	—	3.00	6.00
❑ 12024	Take Off Your Make-Up/Talk a Little Less	1974	—	3.00	6.00
ALL PLATINUM					
❑ 2357	Love Lights/(Instrumental)	1975	—	2.50	5.00
❑ 2360	I'm Needing You, Wanting You/We Can't Hide It Anymore	1975	—	2.50	5.00
❑ 2363	If You Were My Woman (Part 1)/If You Were My Woman (Part 2)	1976	—	2.50	5.00
❑ 2370	One of Those Yesterdays/Love Lights	1976	—	2.50	5.00
❑ 2373	I Fell Asleep/One of Those Yesterdays	1976	—	2.50	5.00
AMY					
❑ 849	Come On and Love Me/Ooh Baby	1962	3.75	7.50	15.00
❑ 868	I'm Yours/Hula Lula	1962	3.75	7.50	15.00
ATCO					
❑ 6197	Never Let Me Go/Baby I Want to Marry You	1961	3.00	6.00	12.00
BELTONE					
❑ 1005	Mr. Price/Hula Lula	1961	5.00	10.00	20.00
CLOCK					
❑ 1015	Come On and Love Me/Ooh Baby	1959	6.25	12.50	25.00
—Clock sides as "Charles Jackson"					
❑ 1022	Hula Hula/I'm Yours	1960	6.25	12.50	25.00
❑ 1027	This Is It/Mr. Pride	1960	6.25	12.50	25.00
DAKAR					
❑ 4512	I Forgot to Tell You/The Man and the Woman	1972	—	3.00	6.00
DOT					
❑ 15673	Woke Up This Morning/Wilette	1957	7.50	15.00	30.00
—With Kripp Johnson					
EMI AMERICA					
❑ 8042	I Wanna Give You Some Love/Waiting in Vain	1980	—	2.00	4.00
❑ 8056	After You/Let's Get Together	1980	—	2.00	4.00
MOTOWN					
❑ 1118	(Don't Let the Boy Overpower) The Man in You/Girls, Girls, Girls	1968	2.50	5.00	10.00
❑ 1144	Are You Lonely for Me Baby/Your Wonderful Love	1969	2.50	5.00	10.00
❑ 1152	Honey Come Back/What Am I Gonna Do Without You	1969	2.50	5.00	10.00
❑ 1160	The Day My World Stood Still/Baby, I'll Get It	1970	125.00	250.00	500.00
SUGARHILL					
❑ 764	Sometimes When We Touch/(B-side unknown)	1981	—	2.00	4.00
VIBRATION					
❑ 569	We Can't Hide It Anymore/I'm Needing You, Wanting You	1977	—	2.50	5.00
—With Sylvia					
V.I.P.					
❑ 25052	The Day My World Stood Still/Baby, I'll Get It	1970	2.50	5.00	10.00
❑ 25056	Let Somebody Love Me/Two Feet from Happiness	1970	2.50	5.00	10.00
❑ 25059	Is There Anything Love Can't Do/Pet Names	1971	2.50	5.00	10.00
❑ 25067	Who You Gonna Run To/Forgive My Jealousy	1971	100.00	200.00	400.00
WAND					
❑ 106	I Don't Want to Cry/Just Once	1961	3.00	6.00	12.00
❑ 108	(It Never Happens) In Real Life/The Same Old Story	1961	3.00	6.00	12.00
❑ 110	I Wake Up Crying/Everybody Needs Love	1961	3.00	6.00	12.00
❑ 115	The Breaking Point/My Willow Tree	1961	3.00	6.00	12.00
❑ 119	What'cha Gonna Say Tomorrow/Angel of Angels	1962	3.00	6.00	12.00
❑ 122	Any Day Now (My Wild Beautiful Bird)/The Prophet	1962	3.75	7.50	15.00
❑ 126	I Keep Forgetting/Who's Gonna Pick Up the Pieces	1962	2.50	5.00	10.00
❑ 128	Gettin' Ready for the Heartbreak/In Between Tears	1962	2.50	5.00	10.00
❑ 132	Tell Him I'm Not Home/Lonely Am I	1963	2.50	5.00	10.00
❑ 132 [PS]	Tell Him I'm Not Home/Lonely Am I	1963	6.25	12.50	25.00
❑ 138	I Will Never Turn My Back on You/Tears of Joy	1963	2.50	5.00	10.00
❑ 141	Any Other Way/Big New York	1963	2.50	5.00	10.00
❑ 149	Hand It Over/Look Over Your Shoulder	1964	2.00	4.00	8.00
❑ 154	Beg Me/This Broken Heart	1964	2.00	4.00	8.00
❑ 161	Somebody New/Stand By Me	1964	2.00	4.00	8.00
❑ 169	Since I Don't Have You/Hand It Over	1964	2.00	4.00	8.00
❑ 179	I Need You/Soul Brother Twist	1965	2.00	4.00	8.00
❑ 188	If I Didn't Love You/Just a Little Bit of Your Soul	1965	2.00	4.00	8.00
❑ 1105	Good Things Come to Those Who Wait/Yah	1965	2.00	4.00	8.00
❑ 1119	All in My Mind/And That's Saying a Lot	1966	2.00	4.00	8.00
❑ 1129	These Chains of Love/Theme to the Blues	1966	2.00	4.00	8.00
❑ 1142	I've Got to Be Strong/Where Did She Stay	1967	2.00	4.00	8.00
❑ 1151	Every Man Needs a Down Home Girl/Need You There	1967	2.00	4.00	8.00
❑ 1159	Hound Dog/Love Me Tender	1967	2.00	4.00	8.00
❑ 1166	Shame on Me/Candy	1967	2.00	4.00	8.00
❑ 1178	My Child's Child/Theme to the Blues	1968	2.00	4.00	8.00
Albums					
ABC					
❑ X-798	Through All Times	1973	3.75	7.50	15.00
ALL PLATINUM					
❑ 3014	Needing You, Wanting You	1976	3.75	7.50	15.00
COLLECTABLES					
❑ COL-5115	Golden Classics	198?	2.50	5.00	10.00
EMI AMERICA					
❑ SW-17031	I Wanna Give You Some Love	1980	2.50	5.00	10.00
GUEST STAR					
❑ GS-1912 [M]	Chuck Jackson	196?	5.00	10.00	20.00
❑ GSS-1912 [R]	Chuck Jackson	196?	3.00	6.00	12.00
MOTOWN					
❑ M-667 [M]	Chuck Jackson Arrives!	1967	10.00	20.00	40.00
❑ MS-667 [S]	Chuck Jackson Arrives!	1967	6.25	12.50	25.00
❑ MS-687	Goin' Back to Chuck Jackson	1969	6.25	12.50	25.00
SCEPTER					
❑ 5100	A Tribute to Burt Bacharach	1972	3.75	7.50	15.00
SPIN-O-RAMA					
❑ 123 [M]	Starring Chuck Jackson	196?	5.00	10.00	20.00
❑ S-123 [R]	Starring Chuck Jackson	196?	3.00	6.00	12.00
STRAND					
❑ SL-1125 [M]	The Great Chuck Jackson	196?	6.25	12.50	25.00
❑ SLS-1125 [S]	The Great Chuck Jackson	196?	7.50	15.00	30.00
UNITED ARTISTS					
❑ UA-LA499-E	The Very Best of Chuck Jackson	1974	2.50	5.00	10.00
V.I.P.					
❑ 403	Teardrops Keep Fallin' on My Heart	1970	10.00	20.00	40.00
WAND					
❑ LP-650 [M]	I Don't Want to Cry	1961	10.00	20.00	40.00
❑ LP-654 [M]	Any Day Now	1962	10.00	20.00	40.00
❑ WD-655 [M]	Encore	1963	10.00	20.00	40.00
❑ WD-658 [M]	Chuck Jackson On Tour	1964	10.00	20.00	40.00
❑ WDM-667 [M]	Mr. Everything	1965	7.50	15.00	30.00
❑ WDS-667 [S]	Mr. Everything	1965	10.00	20.00	40.00
❑ WD-673 [M]	A Tribute to Rhythm and Blues	1966	7.50	15.00	30.00
❑ WDS-673 [S]	A Tribute to Rhythm and Blues	1966	10.00	20.00	40.00
❑ WD-676 [M]	A Tribute to Rhythm and Blues, Volume 2	1966	7.50	15.00	30.00
❑ WDS-676 [S]	A Tribute to Rhythm and Blues, Volume 2	1966	10.00	20.00	40.00
❑ WD-680 [M]	Dedicated to the King!!	1966	10.00	20.00	40.00
❑ WDS-680 [S]	Dedicated to the King!!	1966	12.50	25.00	50.00
❑ WD-683 [M]	Chuck Jackson's Greatest Hits	1967	5.00	10.00	20.00
❑ WDS-683 [S]	Chuck Jackson's Greatest Hits	1967	6.25	12.50	25.00

JACKSON, CHUCK, AND MAXINE BROWN

Also see each artist's individual listings.

Number	Title (A Side/B Side)	Yr	VG	VG+	NM
45s					
WAND					
❑ 181	Something You Got/Baby Take Me	1965	2.00	4.00	8.00
❑ 191	Don't Go/Can't Let You Out of My Sight	1965	2.00	4.00	8.00
❑ 198	I Need You So/Cause We're in Love	1965	2.00	4.00	8.00
❑ 1109	Plerase Don't Hurt Me/I'm Satisfied	1966	2.00	4.00	8.00
❑ 1148	Hold On I'm Comin'/Never Had It So Good	1967	2.00	4.00	8.00
❑ 1155	Daddy's Home/Don't Go	1967	2.00	4.00	8.00
❑ 1162	See See Rider/Tennessee Waltz	1967	2.00	4.00	8.00
Albums					
WAND					
❑ WD-669 [M]	Say Something	1965	7.50	15.00	30.00
❑ WDS-669 [S]	Say Something	1965	10.00	20.00	40.00
❑ WD-678 [M]	Hold On, We're Coming	1966	7.50	15.00	30.00
❑ WDS-678 [S]	Hold On, We're Coming	1966	10.00	20.00	40.00

Number	Title (A Side/B Side)	Yr	VG	VG+	NM

JACKSON, CHUCK, AND TAMMI TERRELL
Also see each artist's individual listings.
Albums
WAND
❑ WD-682 [M]	The Early Show	1967	7.50	15.00	30.00
❑ WDS-682 [S]	The Early Show	1967	7.50	15.00	30.00

JACKSON, DEON
45s
ATLANTIC
❑ 2213	Hush Little Baby/You Said You Loved Me	1963	2.50	5.00	10.00
❑ 2252	Come Back Home/Nursery Rhymes	1964	2.50	5.00	10.00
CARLA
❑ 1900	I Can't Go On/I Need a Love Like Yours	1968	2.00	4.00	8.00
❑ 1903	You'll Wake Up Wiser Baby/You Gotta Love	1968	2.00	4.00	8.00
❑ 2526	Love Makes the World Go Round/You Said You Loved Me	1966	2.50	5.00	10.00
❑ 2527	Love Takes a Long Time Growing/Hush Little Baby	1966	2.00	4.00	8.00
❑ 2530	I Can't Do Without You/That's What You Do to Me	1966	2.00	4.00	8.00
❑ 2533	When Your Love Has Gone/Hard to Get Thing Called Love	1967	2.00	4.00	8.00
❑ 2537	Ooh Baby/All on a Sunny Day	1967	2.00	4.00	8.00
SHOUT
❑ 254	I'll Always Love You/Life Can Be That Way	1969	6.25	12.50	25.00
Albums
ATCO
❑ 33-188 [M]	Love Makes the World Go Round	1966	7.50	15.00	30.00
❑ SD 33-188 [S]	Love Makes the World Go Round	1966	10.00	20.00	40.00
COLLECTABLES
❑ COL-5106	Golden Classics	198?	2.50	5.00	10.00

JACKSON, FREDDIE
12-Inch Singles
CAPITOL
❑ V-8640	Rock Me Tonight (For Old Times' Sake) (3 versions)	1985	2.00	4.00	8.00
❑ V-8650	You Are My Lady (LP Version)/I Wanna Say I Love You (Special Theme Version)	1985	2.00	4.00	8.00
❑ SPRO-9410 [DJ]	Good Morning Heartache (unknown versions)	1985	3.00	6.00	12.00
❑ SPRO-9639 [DJ]	Love Is Just a Touch Away (2 versions)	1986	2.00	4.00	8.00
❑ V-15213	He'll Never Love You (Like I Do) (Original) (Maserati Mix)/I Wanna Say I Love You	1985	—	3.50	7.00
❑ V-15254	Tasty Love (2 versions)/I Wanna Say I Love You	1986	—	3.50	7.00
❑ V-15269	Have You Ever Loved Somebody (LP Version) (7" Version) (Instrumental)	1986	—	3.00	6.00
❑ V-15279	I Don't Want to Lose Your Love (Extended 4:28) (Edit 3:59)/Love Is Just a Touch Away (Midnight Mix)	1987	—	3.00	6.00
❑ V-15317	Jam Tonight (Serious Jam Remix)/Have You Ever Loved Somebody	1987	—	3.00	6.00
❑ V-15336	Look Around (LP Version) (Edit)/I Can't Let You Go (Extended) (Dub)	1987	2.00	4.00	8.00
❑ V-15383	Nice 'n' Slow (3 versions)/You Are My Love	1988	2.00	4.00	8.00
❑ V-15398	Hey Lover (Original) (Edit)/Look Around (Edit)	1988	2.00	4.00	8.00
❑ V-15432	You and I Got a Thang (The All Night Thang) (The Main Thang) (The Whole Thang)/ It's Gonna Take a Long Long Time	1988	2.00	4.00	8.00
❑ V-15461	Crazy (For Me) (Asylum Mix) (Wacky Dub) (Stir Crazy Mix) (Club Radio Edit) (Done Properly Mix) (Done Properly Dub)	1989	2.00	4.00	8.00
❑ V-15645	Love Me Down (Radio Edit) (LP Version) (Instrumental)/All Over You (LP Version)	1990	2.00	4.00	8.00
❑ V-15668	Do Me Again (Remix Version) (Instrumental) (Radio Edit) (Let Freddie Do You Mix)	1991	2.00	4.00	8.00
❑ V-15697	Main Course (4 versions)	1991	—	3.50	7.00
❑ SPRO-79081 [DJ]	Jam Tonight (Serious Jam Remix) (Serious Edit)	1987	2.00	4.00	8.00
❑ SPRO-79372 [DJ]	I Could Use a Little Love (Right Now) (unknown versions)	1992	2.00	4.00	8.00
❑ SPRO-79525/42 [DJ]	Can I Touch You (Rega Funk Extended Mix) (Flavored Funk Mix) (Big Beat Remix) (Let 'Em Sag Remix)	1992	2.00	4.00	8.00
ORPHEUS
❑ V-72278	All Over You (LP Version)/(Instrumental Version)	1990	—	3.00	6.00
RCA
❑ RDAB-62703	Make Love Easy (Radio Version) (LP Version) (Paradise Mix) (Paradise Dub)	1993	2.00	4.00	8.00
❑ RDAB-62753	Make Love Easy (You Sure Love To Version) (You Sure Love to Ball Mix) (Smooth Mix)	1993	2.00	4.00	8.00
❑ 62791	Was It Something (E-Smoove's Raw Mix) (E-Smoove's Sleazy House Mox) (Boss' Phat Extended Mix)/(Something I Said Mix) (Main Mix)	1994	2.50	5.00	10.00
45s
CAPITOL
❑ B-5459	Rock Me Tonight (For Old Times' Sake)/(Groove Version)	1985	—	—	3.00
❑ B-5459 [PS]	Rock Me Tonight (For Old Times' Sake)/(Groove Version)	1985	—	2.50	5.00
❑ B-5495	You Are My Lady/I Wanna Say I Love You	1985	—	—	3.00
❑ B-5495 [PS]	You Are My Lady/I Wanna Say I Love You	1985	—	—	3.00
❑ B-5535	He'll Never Love You (Like I Do)/I Wanna Say I Love You	1985	—	—	3.00

Number	Title (A Side/B Side)	Yr	VG	VG+	NM
❑ B-5535 [PS]	He'll Never Love You (Like I Do)/I Wanna Say I Love You	1985	—	—	3.00
❑ B-5565	Love Is Just a Touch Away/(Sonata)	1986	—	—	3.00
❑ B-5565 [PS]	Love Is Just a Touch Away/(Sonata)	1986	—	—	3.00
❑ B-5616	Tasty Love/I Wanna Say I Love You	1986	—	—	3.00
❑ B-5616 [PS]	Tasty Love/I Wanna Say I Love You	1986	—	—	3.00
❑ B-5661	Have You Ever Loved Somebody/Tasty Love	1986	—	—	3.00
❑ B-5661 [PS]	Have You Ever Loved Somebody/Tasty Love	1986	—	—	3.00
❑ B-5680	I Don't Want to Lose Your Love/Love Is a Touch Away	1987	—	—	3.00
❑ B-5680 [PS]	I Don't Want to Lose Your Love/Love Is a Touch Away	1987	—	—	3.00
❑ B-44037	Jam Tonight/Have You Ever Loved Somebody	1987	—	—	3.00
❑ B-44075	Look Around/I Can't Let You Go	1987	—	—	3.00
❑ B-44171	Nice 'n' Slow/You Are My Love	1988	—	—	3.00
❑ B-44171 [PS]	Nice 'n' Slow/You Are My Love	1988	—	—	3.00
❑ B-44208	Hey Lover/Look Around	1988	—	—	3.00
❑ B-44208 [PS]	Hey Lover/Look Around	1988	—	—	3.00
❑ B-44283	You and I Got a Thang/It's Gonna Take a Long, Long Time	1989	—	—	3.00
❑ B-44283 [PS]	You and I Got a Thang/It's Gonna Take a Long, Long Time	1989	—	—	3.00
❑ B-44354	Crazy (For Me)/(Radio Edit)	1989	—	—	3.00
EMI
❑ S7-19350	Christmas Forever/Lovin' Little Christmas	1996			3.00
—B-side on Charisma by Danny Tate
ORPHEUS
❑ B-72277	All Over You/(Instrumental)	1990	—	2.00	4.00
RCA
❑ 64230	The Christmas Song/O Holy Night	1994	—	—	3.00
❑ 64231	One Wish/This Christmas	1994	—	—	3.00
Albums
CAPITOL
❑ ST-12404	Rock Me Tonight	1985	2.00	4.00	8.00
❑ ST-12495	Just Like the First Time	1986	2.00	4.00	8.00
❑ C1-48987	Don't Let Love Slip Away	1988	2.00	4.00	8.00
❑ C1-92217	Do Me Again	1990	3.00	6.00	12.00

JACKSON, GEORGE
45s
ATLANTIC
❑ 1024	Uh Huh/I'm Sorry	1954	12.50	25.00	50.00
CAMEO
❑ 460	When I Stop Lovin' You/That Lonely Night	1967	3.00	6.00	12.00
CHESS
❑ 2167	Things Are Gettin' Better/Mackin' on You	1975	—	3.00	6.00
DOT
❑ 16724	Blinkety Blink/There Goes My Pride	1965	3.00	6.00	12.00
FAME
❑ 1457	Find 'Em, Fool 'Em, and Forget 'Em/My Desires Are Getting the Best of Me	1969	2.00	4.00	8.00
❑ 1468	That's How Much You Mean to Me/I'm Gonna Hold On	1970	2.00	4.00	8.00
HI
❑ 2130	I'm Gonna Wait/So Good to Me	1967	3.00	6.00	12.00
❑ 2212	Aretha, Sing One for Me/I'm Gonna Wait	1972	2.00	4.00	8.00
❑ 2236	Let Them Know You Care/Patricia	1973	2.00	4.00	8.00
MERCURY
❑ 72736	Kiss Me/Tossin' and Turnin'	1967	2.50	5.00	10.00
❑ 72782	I Don't Have the Time to Love You/Don't Use Me	1968	2.50	5.00	10.00
MGM
❑ 14680	We've Only Just Begun/You Can't Run Away from Love	1973	—	3.00	6.00
❑ 14732	Willie Lump Lump/How Can I Get Next to You	1974	—	3.00	6.00
❑ 14767	Soul Train/Smoking and Drinking	1974	—	3.00	6.00
RPM
❑ 441	Hold Me Up/Heaven on Earth	1955	6.25	12.50	25.00
VERVE
❑ 10658	Love Highjacker/I Found What I Wanted	1970	6.25	12.50	25.00

JACKSON, GEORGE, AND DAN GREER
See GEORGE AND GREER.

JACKSON, J.J.
45s
CALLA
❑ 119	But It's Alright/Boogaloo Baby	1966	3.00	6.00	12.00
❑ 125	I Dig Girls/That Ain't Right	1966	2.50	5.00	10.00
❑ 130	Til Love Goes Out of Style/Seems Like I've Been Here Before	1967	2.50	5.00	10.00
❑ 133	Four Walls (Three Windows and Two Doors)/ Here We Go Again	1967	2.50	5.00	10.00
CONGRESS
❑ 6008	Fat, Black and Together/That Woman Loving	1969	2.00	4.00	8.00
EVEREST
❑ 2012	False Face/Ring Telephone	1963	3.00	6.00	12.00
LOMA
❑ 2082	Try Me/Sho Nuff (Gotta Good Thing Goin')	1967	2.00	4.00	8.00
❑ 2090	Down But Not Out/Why Does It Take So Long	1968	2.00	4.00	8.00
❑ 2096	Come See Me (I'm Your Man)/I Don't Want to Live My Life Alone	1968	2.00	4.00	8.00
❑ 2102	Too Late/You Do It Cause You Wanna	1968	2.00	4.00	8.00
❑ 2104	That Ain't Right/Courage Ain't Strength	1968	2.00	4.00	8.00

Number	Title (A Side/B Side)	Yr	VG	VG+	NM
MAGNA GLIDE					
❏ 5N-325	Let Me Try Again/(B-side unknown)	1975	—	3.00	6.00
PERCEPTION					
❏ 7	Nobody's Gonna Help You/Help Me Get to My Grits	1970	2.00	4.00	8.00
WARNER BROS.					
❏ 7130	But It's Alright/Four Walls (Three Windows and Two Doors)	1970	—	3.00	6.00
—"Back to Back Hits" series					
❏ 7278	But It's Alright/Ain't Too Proud to Beg	1969	2.00	4.00	8.00
❏ 7321	Four Walls (Three Windows and Two Doors)/That Ain't Right	1969	2.00	4.00	8.00
Albums					
CALLA					
❏ C-1101 [M]	But It's Alright/I Dig Girls	1967	5.00	10.00	20.00
❏ CS-1101 [S]	But It's Alright/I Dig Girls	1967	6.25	12.50	25.00
CONGRESS					
❏ CS-7000	The Greatest Little Soul Band in the World	1968	6.25	12.50	25.00
PERCEPTION					
❏ 3	J.J. Jackson's Dilemma	1970	3.75	7.50	15.00
WARNER BROS.					
❏ WS 1797	The Great J.J. Jackson	1969	5.00	10.00	20.00

JACKSON, JACKIE
Also see THE JACKSONS.

12-Inch Singles
POLYDOR

Number	Title (A Side/B Side)	Yr	VG	VG+	NM
❏ 871549-1	Stay (4 versions)/Who's Loving You Now	1989	2.00	4.00	8.00
❏ 889035-1	Cruzin' (12" Remix) (7" Remix) (7" Edit) (House Mix) (House Dub)	1989	2.00	4.00	8.00
45s					
POLYDOR					
❏ 871548-7	Stay/Who's Loving You Now	1989	—	—	3.00
❏ 871548-7 [PS]	Stay/Who's Loving You Now	1989	—	—	3.00
❏ 889034-7	Cruzin/(another mix)	1989	—	—	3.00
❏ 889034-7 [PS]	Cruzin/(another mix)	1989	—	—	3.00
Albums					
MOTOWN					
❏ M 785V1	Jackie Jackson	1973	3.75	7.50	15.00
POLYDOR					
❏ 837766-1	Be the One	1989	2.50	5.00	10.00

JACKSON, JANET
Also see LUTHER VANDROSS.

12-Inch Singles
A&M

Number	Title (A Side/B Side)	Yr	VG	VG+	NM
❏ AMPRO 00038	[(2) DJ]Runaway (LP Version 3:35) (Junior's Factory Mix 9:06) (Junior's Tribal Dub 4:40) (Junior's Factory Dub 6:57) (Junior's Chant Mix 9:20)/When I Think of You (Classic Club Mix) (Extended Morales House Mix '95 7:41) (Crazy Love Mix 8:44) (Incredible Boss Dub 7:10) (Jazzy Mix 10:19) (Heller & Farley Project Mix 10:41)/Runaway (Junior's Unplugged Mix 3:30)	1995	6.25	12.50	25.00
❏ 31458 1225 1	Runaway (LP Version) (Junior's Factory Mix) (Junior's Factory Dub)//When I Think of You (Extended Morales House Mix '95) (Crazy Love Mix)/Runaway (Junior's Unplugged Mix)	1995	2.50	5.00	10.00
❏ 75021 2345 1	Come Back to Me (7" I'm Beggin' You Mix) (I'm Beggin' You Mix) (Instrumental)/The Skin Game Part 1/The Skin Game Part 2 (Instrumental)	1990	2.50	5.00	10.00
—May also exist as A&M SP-12345, but this has not been confirmed					
❏ 75021 2346 1	Love Will Never Do (Without You) (6 versions)	1990	2.50	5.00	10.00
—May also exist as A&M SP-12346, but this has not been confirmed					
❏ 75021 2348 1	Black Cat (Funky 12") (Funky 7") (Video Mix Short Solo)/(3 Snaps Up 12") (3 Snaps Up 7") (3 Snaps Up Dub)	1990	3.00	6.00	12.00
❏ 75021 7447 1	[(2) DJ]Love Will Never Do (Without You) (9 versions)	1990	6.25	12.50	25.00
❏ 75021 7523 1	[(2) DJ]State of the World (United Nations 12" Mix) (State of the House 12" Mix) (World Dance Mix) (Third World 7" Mix) (United Nations Dub) (Make a Change Dub) (Third World Dub)/State of the World Suite (Medley of State of the House 12"-Make a Change Dub-World Dance Mix 14:09)	1991	10.00	20.00	40.00
❏ SP-12059	Say You Do (Special Remixed Version)/You'll Never Find (A Love Like Mine)	1983	3.75	7.50	15.00
❏ SP-12105	Don't Stand Another Chance (Special Remixed Version 6:52) (Dub Version 6:52)	1984	3.75	7.50	15.00
❏ SP-12115	Fast Girls (Specially Remixed Version 6:59)/French Blue (6:22)	1984	3.75	7.50	15.00
❏ SP-12167	What Have You Done for Me Lately (Extended Mix) (Dub Version) (A Cappella Version)	1986	2.00	4.00	8.00
❏ SP-12178	Nasty (Extended Version 6:00) (Instrumental 4:00) (A Cappella 2:55)	1986	2.00	4.00	8.00
❏ SP-12193	When I Think of You (Dance Remix) (Instrumental) (Extra Beats) (Dub A Cappella)	1986	2.00	4.00	8.00
❏ SP-12196	Nasty (Cool Summer Mix Part 1) (Cool Summer Mix Part 2)	1986	2.00	4.00	8.00
❏ SP-12209	Control (Extended Version) (Dub Version) (A Cappella Version)	1986	2.00	4.00	8.00
❏ SP-12218	Control (Video Remix) (Dub Version) (A Cappella)	1986	3.00	6.00	12.00
❏ SP-12230	The Pleasure Principle (4 versions)	1987	2.00	4.00	8.00
❏ SP-12315	Miss You Much (Mama Mix 7:22) (Sing It Yourself Mix 4:19) (Oh I Like That Mix 4:56)/You Need Me	1989	2.50	5.00	10.00
❏ SP-12335	Rhythm Nation (12" United Mix 6:35) (United Dub 6:09) (7" Edit 4:28) (12" House Nation Mix 8:06) (House Nation Groove 6:42) (7" Instrumental 4:44)	1989	2.50	5.00	10.00
❏ SP-12351	Alright (12" R&B Mix) (7" R&B Mix) (Acappella)/(12" House Mix) (Hip House Mix) (House Dub)	1990	2.50	5.00	10.00
❏ SP-12352	Escapade (Shep's Good Time Mix) (The Get Away Dub) (LP Version)/(Shep's Housecapade Mix) (Housecapade Dub) (I Can't Take No More Dub)	1990	3.00	6.00	12.00
❏ SP-17207 [DJ]	Young Love (Edit 3:39) (LP Version 4:56)	1982	3.75	7.50	15.00
❏ SP-17217 [DJ]	Come Give Your Love to Me (Edit) (LP Version)	1983	3.75	7.50	15.00
❏ SP-17925 [DJ]	Miss You Much (Slammin' R&B Mix) (Slammin' Dub) (Acapella) (Shep's House Mix) (Shep's House Dub) (The Bass You Much Mix)	1989	5.00	10.00	20.00
❏ SP-18021 [DJ]	Alright (4 versions)	1990	3.00	6.00	12.00
DEF JAM/DEF SOUL					
❏ 562828-1	Doesn't Really Matter (6 versions)	2000	2.00	4.00	8.00
VIRGIN					
❏ SPRO-12696 [DJ]	You Want This (4 versions)	1994	2.50	5.00	10.00
❏ SPRO-12732 [DJ]	Got 'Til It's Gone (5 versions)	1997	3.75	7.50	15.00
❏ SPRO-12767 [(2) DJ]	Got 'Til It's Gone (9 versions)	1997	7.50	15.00	30.00
—Limited promo edition of 3,000 on clear vinyl					
❏ SPRO-12768 [(2) DJ]	Got 'Til It's Gone (9 versions)	1997	5.00	10.00	20.00
—Promo version on black vinyl					
❏ SPRO-12791 [(2) DJ]	Together Again (Jimmy Jam Extended Deep Club Mix) (Jimmy Jam Deep Remix) (Tony Moran's 12" Club Mix) (Tony Humphries FBI Dub) (Tony Humphries Club Mix) (DJ Premier Just Tha Bass) (Tony Moran Radio) (LP Version)	1997	6.25	12.50	25.00
❏ SPRO-13108 [(2) DJ]	I Get Lonely (Janet vs. Jason Club Remix) (The Jason Nevins Radio Remix)/(Jason's Special Sauce Dub) (LP Version)//(TNT Remix) (Bonus Beat Remix)/(Jam & Lewis Feel My Bass Mix) (Jam & Lewis Feel My Bass Mix #2)	1998	5.00	10.00	20.00
❏ SPRO-13165 [(2) DJ]	Go Deep (Masters at Work Spiritual Flute Mix) (Masters at Work Bonus Beats) (Roni Size Remix) (Masters at Work Vocal Deep Disco Dub) (Jam & Lewis Radio Extended LP Mix) (Masters at Work Downtempo Mix) (Masters at Work Thunder Mix) (Masters at Work Radio Edit)	1998	6.25	12.50	25.00
❏ SPRO-13172 [DJ]	Go Deep (Timbaland-Missy Remix) (Missy Edit) (Teddy Riley Nation Remix) (TR Funk Mix)	1998	3.75	7.50	15.00
❏ SPRO-16130 [DJ]	All for You (Radio Edit 4:24) (same on both sides)	2001	2.50	5.00	10.00
❏ SPRO-16153 [DJ]	All for You (LP Version) (Instrumental)	2001	3.00	6.00	12.00
❏ SPRO-16155 [(2) DJ]	All for You (8 versions)	2001	6.25	12.50	25.00
❏ SPRO-16157 [DJ]	All for You (DJ Quik Remix) (Rock Mix) (Top Heavy Remix) (DJ Quik Remix Instrumental) (Instrumental Rock Mix) (Top Heavy Remix Instrumental)	2001	3.75	7.50	15.00
❏ SPRO-16404 [(2) DJ]	Someone to Call My Lover (8 versions)	2001	6.25	12.50	25.00
❏ Y-38422	Because of Love (5 versions)	1994	2.50	5.00	10.00
❏ Y-38435	Any Time, Any Place (2 versions?)/Throb (2 versions?)	1994	2.50	5.00	10.00
❏ Y-38455	You Want This (3 versions)/New Agenda/70's Love Groove	1994	2.00	4.00	8.00
❏ Y-38623	Together Again (3 versions)/Got 'Til It's Gone	1997	—	3.00	6.00
❏ 97522	All for You (Thunderpuss Club Mix) (Album Version)/(DJ Quik Remix) (Top Heavy Remix) (Rock Mix)	2001	—	3.00	6.00
45s					
A&M					
❏ 31458 1194 7	Runaway/When I Think of You (Morales House Mix 95)	1995	—	—	3.00
❏ 31458 1194 7 [PS]	Runaway/When I Think of You (Morales House Mix 95)	1995	—	—	3.00
❏ 1445	Miss You Much/You Need Me	1989	—	3.00	6.00
❏ 1455	Rhythm Nation/(Instrumental)	1989	—	2.00	4.00
❏ 1475	Come Back to Me/Vuelva A Mi	1990	—	3.00	6.00
—First pressing: Blue label, no bar code					
❏ 75021 1475 7	Come Back to Me/Vuelva A Mi	1990	—	2.00	4.00
—Second pressing: Blue label, longer number with bar code					
❏ 75021 1477 7	Black Cat (Video Mix Short Solo)/(Guitar Mix Featuring Vernon Reid)	1990	—	2.00	4.00
—All copies have red labels					
❏ 1479	Alright (7" R&B Mix)/(7" Remix)	1990	—	2.50	5.00
—First pressing: Blue label, no bar code					
❏ 75021 1479 7	Alright (7" R&B Mix)/(7" Remix)	1990	—	—	3.00
—Second pressing: Blue label, longer number with bar code					
❏ 1490	Escapade/(Instrumental)	1990	—	2.00	4.00
—As this was issued before 1475, 1477, and 1479, it was issued before the "75021" numerical prefix was added to A&M 45s					
❏ 75021 1538 7	Love Will Never Do (Without You)/Work It Out	1990	—	2.00	4.00
❏ 2440	Young Love/The Magic Is Working	1982	—	2.50	5.00
❏ 2440 [PS]	Young Love/The Magic Is Working	1982	—	2.50	5.00
❏ 2522	Come Give Your Love to Me/Forever Yours	1983	—	2.50	5.00
❏ 2522 [PS]	Come Give Your Love to Me/Forever Yours	1983	—	2.50	5.00
❏ 2537	Say You Do/Don't Mess Up a Good Thing	1983	—	—	—
—Canceled?					
❏ 2545	Say You Do/You'll Never Find (A Love Like Mine)	1983	—	2.50	5.00
❏ 2660	Don't Stand Another Chance/Rock 'N' Roll	1984	—	2.50	5.00
❏ 2660 [PS]	Don't Stand Another Chance/Rock 'N' Roll	1984	—	2.50	5.00
❏ 2682	Dream Street/Love and My Best Friend	1984	—	3.00	6.00

J

Number	Title (A Side/B Side)	Yr	VG	VG+	NM
❑ 2693	Fast Girls/Love and My Best Friend	1984	—	2.50	5.00
❑ 2812	What Have You Done for Me Lately/He Doesn't Know I'm Alive	1986	—	—	3.00
❑ 2812 [PS]	What Have You Done for Me Lately/He Doesn't Know I'm Alive	1986	—	—	3.00
❑ 2830	Nasty/You'll Never Find (A Love Like Mine)	1986	—	—	3.00
❑ 2830 [PS]	Nasty/You'll Never Find (A Love Like Mine)	1986	—	2.50	5.00
❑ 2855	When I Think of You/Pretty Boy	1986	—	—	3.00
❑ 2855 [PS]	When I Think of You/Pretty Boy	1986	—	—	3.00
❑ 2877	Control/Fast Girls	1986	—	—	3.00
❑ 2877 [PS]	Control/Fast Girls	1986	—	—	3.00
❑ 2906	Let's Wait Awhile/Pretty Boy	1987	—	—	3.00
❑ 2906 [PS]	Let's Wait Awhile/Pretty Boy	1987	—	—	3.00
❑ 2927	The Pleasure Principle/Fast Girls	1987	—	—	3.00
❑ 2927 [PS]	The Pleasure Principle/Fast Girls	1987	—	—	3.00

DEF JAM/DEF SOUL

Number	Title (A Side/B Side)	Yr	VG	VG+	NM
❑ 562913-7	Doesn't Really Matter (same on both sides)	2000	—	2.00	4.00

VIRGIN

Number	Title (A Side/B Side)	Yr	VG	VG+	NM
❑ S7-17332	That's the Way Love Goes/(Instrumental)	1993	—	3.00	6.00
—Original pressing on red vinyl					
❑ S7-17332	That's the Way Love Goes/(Instrumental)	1993	—	2.00	4.00
—Reissue on black vinyl					
❑ S7-17446	If/One More Chance	1993	—	2.00	4.00
❑ S7-17582	Again/(Piano Vocal)	1993	—	3.00	6.00
—Yellow vinyl					
❑ S7-17582	Again/(Piano Vocal)	1993	—	2.00	4.00
—Black vinyl					
❑ S7-17807	Because of Love/Funky Big Band	1994	—	2.00	4.00
❑ S7-18095	Any Time, Any Place (R. Kelly Mix)/Throb	1994	—	2.00	4.00
❑ S7-18307	You Want This/New Agenda	1995	—	—	3.00
❑ NR-38623	Together Again/Got 'Til It's Gone	1997	—	—	2.00
❑ NR-38623 [PS]	Together Again/Got 'Til It's Gone	1997	—	—	2.00
❑ NR-38631	I Get Lonely (TNT Remix Edit)/(Jam & Lewis Feel My Bass Mix - Radio Edit)	1998	—	—	3.00
❑ NR-38631 [PS]	I Get Lonely (TNT Remix Edit)/(Jam & Lewis Feel My Bass Mix - Radio Edit)	1998	—	—	3.00
❑ 38800	All for You/Someone to Call My Lover	2001	—	2.00	4.00

Albums

A&M

Number	Title	Yr	VG	VG+	NM
❑ 31454 0399 1 [(2)]	Design of a Decade 1986/1996	1995	3.75	7.50	15.00
❑ SP-3905	Control	1986	2.00	4.00	8.00
—Second issue; most have a black label					
❑ SP-3920	Janet Jackson's Rhythm Nation 1814	1989	3.75	7.50	15.00
❑ SP-6-4907	Janet Jackson	1982	3.00	6.00	12.00
❑ SP-4962	Dream Street	1984	3.00	6.00	12.00
❑ SP-5106	Control	1986	2.50	5.00	10.00
—Original issue; silver label with fading A&M logo					

VIRGIN

Number	Title	Yr	VG	VG+	NM
❑ 10144 [(2)]	All for You	2001	3.75	7.50	15.00

JACKSON, JERMAINE

Also see THE JACKSONS.

12-Inch Singles

ARISTA

Number	Title (A Side/B Side)	Yr	VG	VG+	NM
❑ ADP 9189 [DJ]	Tell Me I'm Not Dreamin' (Too Good to Be True)/Do What You Do/Escape from the Planet	1984	3.00	6.00	12.00
❑ AD1-9222	Dynamite/(Instrumental)/Tell Me I'm Not Dreaming (Instrumental)	1984	2.00	4.00	8.00
❑ AD1-9317	When the Rain Begins to Fall/Come to Me	1985	2.00	4.00	8.00
—A-side with Pia Zadora					
❑ AD1-9357	(Closest Thing to) Perfect/(Instrumental)	1985	2.00	4.00	8.00
❑ AD1-9445	I Think It's Love (4 versions)	1986	2.00	4.00	8.00
❑ AD1-9501	Do You Remember Me (6 versions)	1986	2.00	4.00	8.00
❑ ADP 9876 [DJ]	Don't Take It Personal (same on both sides)	1989	2.00	4.00	8.00
❑ AD1-9878	Don't Take It Personal (3 versions)	1989	2.00	4.00	8.00
❑ AD1-9934	Two Ships (In the Night) (4 versions)	1990	2.00	4.00	8.00

LAFACE

Number	Title (A Side/B Side)	Yr	VG	VG+	NM
❑ 24004	You Said, You Said (5 versions)	1991	2.00	4.00	8.00
❑ 24012	Word to the Badd!! (5 versions)	1991	3.00	6.00	12.00
❑ 24017	I Dream, I Dream (5 versions)	1992	2.50	5.00	10.00

MOTOWN

Number	Title (A Side/B Side)	Yr	VG	VG+	NM
❑ M 00001D1	Let's Be Young Tonight (5:07)/Down to Love Town (5:55)	1976	5.00	10.00	20.00
—B-side by the Originals on Soul					
❑ PR-66 [DJ]	Let's Get Serious (Short Version 3:33) (Long Version 7:55)	1980	5.00	10.00	20.00
❑ PR-73 [DJ]	Burnin' Hot (7:44)/Feelin' Free (6:32)	1980	6.25	12.50	25.00
—No label name on label					
❑ PR-101 [DJ]	Let Me Tickle Your Fancy (Vocal) (Instrumental)/Hard to Get (Vocal) (Instrumental)	1982	3.75	7.50	15.00
—No label name on label; B-side by Rick James					
❑ PR-108 [DJ]	Very Special Part (6:32)/(Instrumental)	1982	3.00	6.00	12.00

45s

ARISTA

Number	Title (A Side/B Side)	Yr	VG	VG+	NM
❑ 2029	I'd Like to Get to Know You/Spare the Rod, Love the Child	1990	—	—	3.00
❑ 9190	Dynamite/Tell Me I'm Not Dreaming (Too Good to Be True) (Instrumental)	1984	—	—	3.00
❑ 9190 [DJ]	Dynamite (same on both sides)	1984	2.00	4.00	8.00
—Promo only on red vinyl					
❑ 9190 [PS]	Dynamite/Tell Me I'm Not Dreaming (Too Good to Be True) (Instrumental)	1984	—	—	3.00
❑ 9275	Take Good Care of My Heart/Tell Me I'm Not Dreaming (Too Good to Be True) (Instrumental)	1984	—	2.50	5.00
—A-side with Whitney Houston					
❑ 9279	Do What You Do/Tell Me I'm Not Dreaming (Too Good to Be True)	1984	—	—	3.00
❑ 9356	(Closest Thing to) Perfect/(Instrumental)	1985	—	—	3.00
❑ 9356 [PS]	(Closest Thing to) Perfect/(Instrumental)	1985	—	—	3.00
❑ 9444	I Think It's Love/Voices in the Dark	1985	—	—	3.00
❑ 9444 [PS]	I Think It's Love/Voices in the Dark	1985	—	—	3.00
❑ 9495	Words Into Action/Our Love Story	1986	—	—	3.00
❑ 9495 [PS]	Words Into Action/Our Love Story	1986	—	—	3.00
❑ 9502	Do You Remember Me/Whatcha' Doin'	1986	—	—	3.00
❑ 9502 [PS]	Do You Remember Me/Whatcha' Doin'	1986	—	—	3.00
❑ 9788	Clean Up Your Act/I'm Gonna Git Ya Sucka	1988	—	—	3.00
—B-side by the Gap Band					
❑ 9788 [PS]	Clean Up Your Act/I'm Gonna Git Ya Sucka	1988	—	—	3.00
❑ 9875	Don't Take It Personal/Clean Up Your Act	1989	—	—	3.00
❑ 9875 [PS]	Don't Take It Personal/Clean Up Your Act	1989	—	—	3.00
❑ 9933	Two Ships (In the Night)/Next to You	1990	—	—	3.00
❑ 9933 [PS]	Two Ships (In the Night)/Next to You	1990	—	—	3.00

LAFACE

Number	Title (A Side/B Side)	Yr	VG	VG+	NM
❑ 24003	You Said, You Said/(Instrumental)	1991	—	2.00	4.00

MOTOWN

Number	Title (A Side/B Side)	Yr	VG	VG+	NM
❑ 1201	That's How Love Goes/I Lost My Love in the Big City	1972	—	2.50	5.00
❑ 1216	Daddy's Home/Take Me in Your Arms (Rock Me for a Little While)	1972	—	2.50	5.00
❑ 1244	You're in Good Hands/Does Your Mama Know About Me	1973	—	2.50	5.00
❑ 1386	She's the Ideal Girl/I'm So Glad You Chose Me	1976	—	—	—
—Unreleased					
❑ 1401	Let's Be Young Tonight/Boss Odyssey	1976	—	2.50	5.00
❑ 1409	You Need to Be Loved/My Touch of Madness	1977	—	2.50	5.00
❑ 1441	Castles of Sand/I Love Every Little Thing About You	1978	—	2.50	5.00
❑ 1469	Let's Get Serious/Je Vous Aime Beaucoups	1980	—	2.00	4.00
❑ 1490	You're Supposed to Keep Your Love for Me/Let It Ride	1980	—	2.00	4.00
❑ 1499	Little Girl Don't You Worry/We Can Put It Back Together	1980	—	2.00	4.00
❑ 1503	You Like Me Don't You/(Instrumental)	1981	—	2.00	4.00
❑ 1525	I'm Just Too Shy/All Because of You	1981	—	2.00	4.00
❑ 1600	Paradise in Your Eyes/I'm My Brother's Keeper	1982	—	2.00	4.00
❑ 1628	Let Me Tickle Your Fancy/Maybe Next Time	1982	—	2.00	4.00
—Devo is the backing group					
❑ 1649	Very Special Part/You're Givin' Me the Runaround	1982	—	2.00	4.00

Albums

ARISTA

Number	Title	Yr	VG	VG+	NM
❑ AL8-8203	Jermaine Jackson	1984	2.50	5.00	10.00
❑ AL8-8277	Precious Moments	1986	2.50	5.00	10.00
❑ AL-8421	Jermaine Jackson	1986	2.00	4.00	8.00
—Budget-line reissue					
❑ AL-8493	Don't Take It Personal	1989	2.50	5.00	10.00

MOTOWN

Number	Title	Yr	VG	VG+	NM
❑ M5-117V1	Motown Superstar Series, Vol. 17	1981	2.50	5.00	10.00
❑ M-752L	Jermaine	1972	2.50	5.00	10.00
❑ M-775L	Come Into My Life	1973	2.50	5.00	10.00
❑ M6-842S1	My Name Is Jermaine	1976	2.50	5.00	10.00
❑ M6-888S1	Feel the Fire	1977	2.50	5.00	10.00
❑ M7-898R1	Frontiers	1978	2.50	5.00	10.00
❑ M7-928R1	Let's Get Serious	1980	2.50	5.00	10.00
❑ M8-948M1	Jermaine	1980	2.50	5.00	10.00
❑ M8-952M1	I Like Your Style	1981	2.50	5.00	10.00
❑ 6017 ML	Let Me Tickle Your Fancy	1982	2.50	5.00	10.00

JACKSON, LA TOYA

45s

LARC

Number	Title (A Side/B Side)	Yr	VG	VG+	NM
❑ 81025	Bet'cha Gonna Need My Lovin'/(Instrumental)	1983	—	2.00	4.00

POLYDOR

Number	Title (A Side/B Side)	Yr	VG	VG+	NM
❑ 2117	Night Time Lover/Who Is She	1980	—	2.00	4.00
❑ 2137	If You Feel the Funk/Lonely Is She	1980	—	2.00	4.00
❑ 2177	Stay the Night/Camp Kuchi Kalai	1981	—	2.00	4.00
❑ 2188	I Don't Want You to Go/Love Song	1981	—	2.00	4.00

PRIVATE I

Number	Title (A Side/B Side)	Yr	VG	VG+	NM
❑ 04439	Heart Don't Lie/Without You	1984	—	2.00	4.00
❑ 04439 [PS]	Heart Don't Lie/Without You	1984	—	2.00	4.00
❑ 04572	Hot Potato/Think Twice	1984	—	2.00	4.00
❑ 05783	He's a Pretender/How Do I Tell Them	1986	—	2.00	4.00
❑ 05783 [PS]	He's a Pretender/How Do I Tell Them	1986	—	2.00	4.00
❑ 06040	Love Talk/Imagination	1986	—	2.00	4.00

RCA

Number	Title (A Side/B Side)	Yr	VG	VG+	NM
❑ 8689-7-R	You're Gonna Get Rocked/Does It Really Matter	1988	—	—	3.00
❑ 8689-7-R [PS]	You're Gonna Get Rocked/Does It Really Matter	1988	—	—	3.00
❑ 8873-7-R	Such a Wicked Love/Does It Really Matter	1989	—	—	3.00

JACKSON, LIL' SON

45s

IMPERIAL

Number	Title (A Side/B Side)	Yr	VG	VG+	NM
❑ 5204	Journey Back Home/Rockin' and Rollin' #2	1952	25.00	50.00	100.00
—Note: Lil' Son Jackson records on Imperial before 5204 are unconfirmed on 45 rpm					
❑ 5218	Black and Brown/Sad Letter Blues	1953	25.00	50.00	100.00
❑ 5229	Lonely Blues/Freight Train Blues	1953	25.00	50.00	100.00
❑ 5237	Spending Money Blues/All Alone	1953	25.00	50.00	100.00
❑ 5248	Movin' to the Country/Confession	1953	25.00	50.00	100.00
❑ 5259	Dirty Work/Little Girl	1953	25.00	50.00	100.00

Number	Title (A Side/B Side)	Yr	VG	VG+	NM
❑ 5267	Thrill Me, Baby/Doctor, Doctor	1954	20.00	40.00	80.00
❑ 5276	Big Rat/Piggly Wiggly	1954	20.00	40.00	80.00
❑ 5286	Trouble Don't Last Always/Blues by the Hour	1954	20.00	40.00	80.00
❑ 5300	Get High Everybody/Let Me Down Easy	1954	20.00	40.00	80.00
❑ 5312	How Long/Good Ole Wagon	1954	20.00	40.00	80.00
❑ 5319	My Younger Days/I Wish to Go Home	1954	20.00	40.00	80.00
❑ 5339	Sugar Mama/Messin' Up	1955	20.00	40.00	80.00
❑ 5703	Rockin' and Rollin'/Peace Breaking People	1960	3.75	7.50	15.00
❑ 5851	Everybody's Blues/Travelin' Woman	1962	3.75	7.50	15.00
❑ 5963	Prison Bound/Rolling Mill	1963	3.00	6.00	12.00
POST					
❑ 2014	No Money/Lonely Blues	1955	10.00	20.00	40.00
Albums					
ARHOOLIE					
❑ 1004 [M]	Lil' Son Jackson	1960	6.25	12.50	25.00
IMPERIAL					
❑ LP-9142 [M]	Rockin' and Rollin'	1961	100.00	200.00	400.00

JACKSON, MAHALIA

45s

Number	Title (A Side/B Side)	Yr	VG	VG+	NM
APOLLO					
❑ 235	Silent Night, Holy Night/Go Tell It On The Mountain	1951	5.00	10.00	20.00
—Note: Earlier Mahalia Jackson 45s on Apollo may exist					
❑ 240	Get Away Jordan/I Gave Up Everything	1951	5.00	10.00	20.00
❑ 245	Bless This House/The Lord's Prayer	1951	5.00	10.00	20.00
❑ 246	His Eyes Are On the Sparrow/It Is No Secret (What God Can Do)	1951	5.00	10.00	20.00
❑ 248	How I Got Over/Just As I Am	1951	5.00	10.00	20.00
❑ 258	He's the One/I'm Getting Nearer My Home	1952	5.00	10.00	20.00
❑ 262	In the Upper Room (Part 1)/In the Upper Room (Part 2)	1952	5.00	10.00	20.00
❑ 269	He Said He Would/God Spoke to Me	1953	5.00	10.00	20.00
❑ 273	I'm Going Down the River/Do You Know Him	1953	5.00	10.00	20.00
❑ 278	I Wonder If I Will Ever Rest/Coming to Jesus	1953	5.00	10.00	20.00
❑ 282	Hands of God/It's Real	1954	5.00	10.00	20.00
❑ 286	I'm On My Way/My Story	1954	5.00	10.00	20.00
❑ 289	Walking to Jerusalem/What Then	1954	5.00	10.00	20.00
❑ 291	I Walked Into the Garden/I'm Going to Tell God	1955	5.00	10.00	20.00
❑ 298	Nobody Knows/Run All the Way	1955	5.00	10.00	20.00
❑ 304	He's My Light/If You Just Keep Still	1956	4.50	9.00	18.00
❑ 311	His Eyes Are On the Sparrow/I Can Put My Trust in Jesus	1956	4.50	9.00	18.00
❑ 313	Didn't It Rain/Nobody Knows	1956	4.50	9.00	18.00
❑ 314	I'm On My Way/My Story	1956	4.50	9.00	18.00
❑ 539	Silent Night/The Lord's Prayer	1959	3.75	7.50	15.00
❑ 750	Silent Night/The Lord's Prayer	1962	3.00	6.00	12.00
❑ 750 [PS]	Silent Night/The Lord's Prayer	1962	5.00	10.00	20.00
COLUMBIA					
❑ 40411	A Rusty Old Halo/The Treasure of Love	1955	3.75	7.50	15.00
❑ 40412	Walk Over God's Heaven/Jesus Met the Woman	1955	3.75	7.50	15.00
❑ 40473	You'll Never Walk Alone/One God	1955	3.75	7.50	15.00
❑ 40529	His Hands/I See God	1955	3.75	7.50	15.00
❑ 40554	The Bible Tells Me So/Satisfied Mind	1955	3.75	7.50	15.00
❑ 40610	The Lord Is a Busy Man/You're Not Living in Vain	1955	3.75	7.50	15.00
❑ 40712	Round the Rainbow/An Evening Star	1956	3.75	7.50	15.00
❑ 40721	I Ask the Lord/I'm Going to Live	1956	3.75	7.50	15.00
❑ 40753	The Lord's Prayer/Precious Lord	1956	3.75	7.50	15.00
❑ 40777	Silent Night, Holy Night/Mary's Little Boy Chile	1956	3.75	7.50	15.00
❑ 40854	God Is So Good/I Complained	1957	3.75	7.50	15.00
❑ 41000	Trouble/He's a Light Unto My Pathway	1957	3.75	7.50	15.00
❑ 41055	Sweet Little Jesus Boy/A Star Stood Still	1957	3.00	6.00	12.00
❑ 41150	He's Got the Whole World In His Hands/Didn't It Rain	1958	3.00	6.00	12.00
❑ 41258	For My Good Fortune/Have You Any Rivers	1958	3.00	6.00	12.00
❑ 41322	Elijah Rock/Hold Me	1959	3.00	6.00	12.00
❑ 41382	Tell the World About This/Trouble of the World	1959	3.00	6.00	12.00
❑ 41779	My Country 'Tis of Thee (America)/Onward, Christian Soldiers	1960	3.00	6.00	12.00
❑ 42633	Joy To The World!/Go Tell It On The Mountain	1962	2.50	5.00	10.00
❑ 42910	We Shall Overcome/Let's Pray Together	1963	2.50	5.00	10.00
❑ 42946	In the Summer of His Years/Song for My Brother	1964	2.50	5.00	10.00
❑ 43474	Sunrise, Sunset/Like the Breeze Blows	1965	2.50	5.00	10.00
❑ 44529	Take My Hand, Precious Lord/We Shall Overcome	1968	2.00	4.00	8.00
❑ 45068	Abraham, Martin and John/Day Is Done	1970	—	3.00	6.00
❑ JZSP 137705/6 [DJ]	Happy Birthday To You, Our Lord/Silver Bells	1968	—	2.50	5.00
GRAND AWARD					
❑ 1025	Dig a Little Deeper/I'm On My Way	1959	3.75	7.50	15.00
KENWOOD					
❑ 300	In the Upper Room (Part 1)/In the Upper Room (Part 2)	1964	2.00	4.00	8.00
❑ 301	His Eyes Are On the Sparrow/Walking to Jerusalem	196?	2.00	4.00	8.00
❑ 302	How I Got Over/Didn't It Rain	196?	2.00	4.00	8.00
❑ 303	Go Tell It On the Mountain/Bless This House	196?	2.00	4.00	8.00
❑ 304	Move On Up a Little Higher (Part 1)/Move On Up a Little Higher (Part 2)	196?	2.00	4.00	8.00
❑ 305	These Are They/Get Away Jordan	196?	2.00	4.00	8.00
❑ 750	Silent Night/The Lord's Prayer	1964	2.50	5.00	10.00
NASHBORO					
❑ 750 [DJ]	Silent Night/The Lord's Prayer	197?	—	2.00	4.00
—Reissue of Kenwood 750					
U.S.A.					
❑ 109	The Holy Bible (Part 1)/The Holy Bible (Part 2)	196?	2.50	5.00	10.00

7-Inch Extended Plays

Number	Title (A Side/B Side)	Yr	VG	VG+	NM
COLUMBIA					
❑ B-2072	*Trouble in My Way/Down by the Riverside/Joshua Fit the Battle of Jericho/You'll Never Walk Alone	195?	5.00	10.00	20.00
❑ B-2072 [PS]	You'll Never Walk Alone	195?	5.00	10.00	20.00

Albums

Number	Title (A Side/B Side)	Yr	VG	VG+	NM
APOLLO					
❑ 201/202 [M]	Spirituals	1954	7.50	15.00	30.00
❑ 482 [M]	No Matter How You Pray	1959	6.25	12.50	25.00
❑ 499 [M]	Mahalia Jackson	1962	6.25	12.50	25.00
❑ 1001/2 [M]	Command Performance	1961	6.25	12.50	25.00
COLUMBIA					
❑ CL 644 [M]	Mahalia Jackson	1955	10.00	20.00	40.00
❑ CL 702 [M]	Sweet Little Jesus Boy	1955	10.00	20.00	40.00
❑ CL 899 [M]	Bless This House	1956	7.50	15.00	30.00
❑ CL 1244 [M]	Newport 1958	1959	5.00	10.00	20.00
❑ CL 1343 [M]	That Great Gettin' Up Morning	1959	5.00	10.00	20.00
❑ CL 1428 [M]	Come On Children, Let's Sing	1960	5.00	10.00	20.00
❑ CL 1473 [M]	The Power and the Glory	1960	5.00	10.00	20.00
❑ CL 1549 [M]	I Believe	1960	3.75	7.50	15.00
❑ CL 1643 [M]	Every Time I Feel the Spirit	1961	3.75	7.50	15.00
❑ CL 1726 [M]	Recorded in Europe During Her Latest Concert Tour	1962	3.75	7.50	15.00
❑ CL 1824 [M]	Great Songs of Love and Faith	1962	3.75	7.50	15.00
❑ CL 1903 [M]	Silent Night	1962	3.75	7.50	15.00
❑ CL 1936 [M]	Make a Joyful Noise Unto the Lord	1962	3.75	7.50	15.00
❑ CL 2004 [M]	Mahalia Jackson's Greatest Hits	1963	3.00	6.00	12.00
❑ CL 2130 [M]	Let's Pray Together	1964	3.00	6.00	12.00
❑ CL 2452 [M]	Mahalia Sings	1966	3.00	6.00	12.00
❑ CL 2546 [M]	Garden of Prayer	1967	3.75	7.50	15.00
❑ CL 2552 [10]	You'll Never Walk Alone	1955	12.50	25.00	50.00
❑ CL 2605 [M]	My Faith	1967	3.75	7.50	15.00
❑ CL 2690 [M]	Mahalia Jackson In Concert, Easter Sunday 1967	1967	3.75	7.50	15.00
❑ CS 8071 [S]	Newport 1958	1959	7.50	15.00	30.00
❑ CS 8153 [S]	That Great Gettin' Up Morning	1959	6.25	12.50	25.00
❑ CS 8225 [S]	Come On Children, Let's Sing	1960	6.25	12.50	25.00
❑ CS 8264 [S]	The Power and the Glory	1960	6.25	12.50	25.00
❑ CS 8349 [S]	I Believe	1960	5.00	10.00	20.00
❑ CS 8443 [S]	Every Time I Feel the Spirit	1961	5.00	10.00	20.00
❑ CS 8526 [S]	Recorded in Europe During Her Latest Concert Tour	1962	5.00	10.00	20.00
❑ CS 8624 [S]	Great Songs of Love and Faith	1962	5.00	10.00	20.00
❑ CS 8703 [S]	Silent Night	1962	5.00	10.00	20.00
❑ CS 8736 [S]	Make a Joyful Noise Unto the Lord	1962	5.00	10.00	20.00
❑ CS 8759 [R]	Mahalia Jackson	1963	3.00	6.00	12.00
❑ CS 8761 [R]	Bless This House	1963	3.00	6.00	12.00
❑ PC 8761	Bless This House	198?	2.00	4.00	8.00
—Budget-line reissue					
❑ CS 8804 [S]	Mahalia Jackson's Greatest Hits	1963	3.75	7.50	15.00
❑ CS 8930 [S]	Let's Pray Together	1964	3.75	7.50	15.00
❑ CS 9252 [S]	Mahalia Sings	1966	3.75	7.50	15.00
❑ CS 9346 [S]	Garden of Prayer	1967	3.00	6.00	12.00
❑ CS 9405 [S]	My Faith	1967	3.00	6.00	12.00
❑ CS 9490 [S]	Mahalia Jackson In Concert, Easter Sunday 1967	1967	3.00	6.00	12.00
❑ CS 9659	A Mighty Fortress	1968	3.00	6.00	12.00
❑ CS 9686	The Best-Loved Hymns of Dr. Martin Luther King Jr.	1968	3.75	7.50	15.00
❑ PC 9686	The Best-Loved Hymns of Dr. Martin Luther King Jr.	198?	2.00	4.00	8.00
—Budget-line reissue					
❑ CS 9727	Christmas with Mahalia	1968	3.00	6.00	12.00
❑ CS 9813	Right Out of the Church	1969	3.00	6.00	12.00
❑ CS 9950	What the World Needs Now	1970	3.00	6.00	12.00
❑ CG 30744 [(2)]	America's Favorite Hymns	1971	3.75	7.50	15.00
❑ KG 31379 [(2)]	The Great Mahalia Jackson	1972	3.75	7.50	15.00
❑ KC 34073	How I Got Over	1976	2.50	5.00	10.00
❑ PC 37710	Mahalia Jackson's Greatest Hits	198?	2.00	4.00	8.00
❑ 3C 38304	Silent Night	1982	2.00	4.00	8.00
—Reissue					
COLUMBIA SPECIAL PRODUCTS					
❑ P2 13200 [(2)]	(HRB Music Proudly Presents) The Best of Mahalia Jackson: Hymns, Spirituals & Songs of Inspiration	1976	3.75	7.50	15.00
FOLKWAYS					
❑ 31101	I Sing Because I'm Happy, Volume 1	198?	2.50	5.00	10.00
❑ 31102	I Sing Because I'm Happy, Volume 2	198?	2.50	5.00	10.00
GRAND AWARD					
❑ GA 265 SD	I Believe	1966	3.75	7.50	15.00
—Reissue of 326					
❑ GA 33-326 [M]	Mahalia Jackson	1955	7.50	15.00	30.00
❑ GA 33-390 [M]	Mahalia Jackson	195?	7.50	15.00	30.00
HARMONY					
❑ HS 11279	You'll Never Walk Alone	196?	2.50	5.00	10.00
❑ HS 11372	Abide With Me	1970	2.50	5.00	10.00
❑ H 30019	Sunrise, Sunset	1970	2.50	5.00	10.00
❑ KH 31111	Lord Don't Let Me Fall	1972	2.50	5.00	10.00
KENWOOD					
❑ 474	In the Upper Room	196?	3.75	7.50	15.00
❑ 479	Just As I Am	196?	3.75	7.50	15.00
❑ 482	No Matter How You Pray	196?	3.75	7.50	15.00
❑ 486	Mahalia	196?	3.75	7.50	15.00

Number	Title (A Side/B Side)	Yr	VG	VG+	NM
❏ 489	Mahalia Jackson With the Greatest Spiritual Singers	196?	3.75	7.50	15.00
❏ 500	The Best of Mahalia Jackson	196?	3.75	7.50	15.00
❏ 501	I Lift My Voice	196?	3.75	7.50	15.00
❏ 502	Sing Out	196?	3.75	7.50	15.00
❏ 1001/2 [(2)]	Command Performance	196?	5.00	10.00	20.00

PICKWICK

❏ SPC-3510	I Believe	197?	2.50	5.00	10.00

PRIORITY

❏ PU 37710	Mahalia Jackson's Greatest Hits	1981	2.50	5.00	10.00

JACKSON, MARLON
Also see THE JACKSONS.

12-Inch Singles
CAPITOL

❏ V-15323	Don't Go (unknown versions)	1987	2.00	4.00	8.00
❏ V-15346	Baby Tonight (4 versions)	1987	2.50	5.00	10.00

45s
CAPITOL

❏ B-5675	(Let Your Love Find) The Chosen One/Sardo and the Child	1987	—	2.00	4.00
❏ B-44047	Don't Go/(Instrumental)	1987	—	—	3.00
❏ B-44047 [PS]	Don't Go/(Instrumental)	1987	—	—	3.00
❏ B-44092	Baby Tonight (Radio Edit)/Baby Tonight (Video Version)	1987	—	—	3.00
❏ B-44092 [PS]	Baby Tonight (Radio Edit)/Baby Tonight (Video Version)	1987	—	—	3.00
❏ B-44122	Lovely Eyes/(Instrumental)	1988	—	—	3.00

Albums
CAPITOL

❏ CLT-46942	Baby Tonight	1987	2.50	5.00	10.00

JACKSON, MICHAEL
Also see THE JACKSONS; MICHAEL JACKSON AND PAUL McCARTNEY.

12-Inch Singles
CBS INTERNATIONAL

❏ EPSL-69007	Todo Mi Amor Eres Tu/I Just Can't Stop Loving You	1988	20.00	40.00	80.00

—Spanish version of "I Just Can't Stop Loving You," pressed in U.S. for Hispanic markets in the U.S. and elsewhere

EPIC

❏ AS 654 [DJ]	Don't Stop 'Til You Get Enough (5:45) (same on both sides?)	1979	6.25	12.50	25.00
❏ AS 687 [DJ]	Rock with You (3:39) (same on both sides)	1979	6.25	12.50	25.00
❏ EAS 0781 [DJ]	Blood on the Dance Floor — The Dubs (T&G Pool of Blood Dub) (Refugee Camp Dub) (Fire Island Dub) (A Cappella)	1997	5.00	10.00	20.00
❏ AS 1624 [DJ]	Beat It (same on both sides)	1983	5.00	10.00	20.00
❏ 49-03557	Billie Jean (Extended Version 6:20) (Instrumental 6:20)	1983	6.25	12.50	25.00
❏ 49-03915	Wanna Be Startin' Somethin' (6:30)/(Instrumental)	1983	3.00	6.00	12.00
❏ EAS 4363 [DJ]	Black or White (Club Mix) (Dub Mix) (Underground House Mix) (House Radio Mix with Guitars) (Tribal Beats)	1991	5.00	10.00	20.00
❏ EAS 4454 [DJ]	Remember the Time (unknown versions)	1992	5.00	10.00	20.00
❏ E2S 4467 [(2) DJ]	In the Closet (11 versions)	1991	7.50	15.00	30.00
❏ E2S 4533 [(2) DJ]	In the Closet (11 versions)	1991	7.50	15.00	30.00
❏ E2S 4580 [(2) DJ]	Jam (13 versions)	1991	7.50	15.00	30.00
❏ E2S 4582 [(2) DJ]	Jam (Atlanta Techno Dub 5:11) (Roger's Slam Jam Mix 4:51) (Silky Dub 4:22) (Acapella Mix 4:31) (More Than Enuff Dub 5:56) (Maurice's Jammin' Dub Mix 7:18) (Roger's Club Dub 6:14) (Roger's Club Mix 6:20) (More Than Enuff Mix 5:56) (E-Smoove's Jazzy Jam 6:44) (Atlanta Techno Mix 6:06) (Roger's Underground Mix 6:02) (Silky 12" 6:20)	1991	7.50	15.00	30.00
❏ EAS 4656 [DJ]	Jam (Roger's Jeep Mix) (Teddy's 12" Mix) (Percapella) (Teddy's Jam) (Roger's Jeep Dub) (MJ's Raw Mix)	1992	5.00	10.00	20.00
❏ E2S 4686 [(2) DJ]	Who Is It (11 versions)	1993	7.50	15.00	30.00
❏ 49-04961	Thriller/(Instrumental)	1983	2.50	5.00	10.00
❏ 49-06911	Don't Stop 'Til You Get Enough/Wanna Be Startin' Somethin'	1987	3.00	6.00	12.00

—"Mixed Masters" series

❏ E2S 7125 [(2) DJ]	Scream (12 versions)	1995	7.50	15.00	30.00
❏ E2S 7127 [(2) DJ]	Scream (unknown versions)	1995	7.50	15.00	30.00
❏ AED 7192 [DJ]	The Megamixes (10:33) (4:58) (MJ Urban Megamix)/Scream (Jam & Lewis Remix) (Jam & Lewis Instrumental)	1995	7.50	15.00	30.00
❏ AED 7298 [DJ]	You Are Not Alone (Franctified Club Mix) (Album Version) (Knuckluv Dub Version) (Classic Club Mix)	1995	5.00	10.00	20.00
❏ 49-07462	Bad (Dance Extended Mix) (7" Single Version) (Dance Remix Radio Edit) (Dub Version) (Acappella)	1987	2.50	5.00	10.00
❏ 49-07487	The Way You Make Me Feel (Dance Extended Mix) (Dance Remix Radio Edit) (Dub Version) (A Cappella)	1987	2.50	5.00	10.00
❏ 49-07510	Man in the Mirror (Single Mix) (Album Mix1)	1988	2.50	5.00	10.00
❏ 49-07583	Dirty Diana/(Instrumental)	1988	2.50	5.00	10.00
❏ E2S 7603 [DJ]	This Time Around (DM Mad Club) (DM Radio) (Maurice's Club) (Georgie's House 'n Around Mix) (Timeland Dub) (Neverland Dub) (Don's Control This Dub) (UBQ's Opera Vibe) (DM Bang Da Drums Mix)	1995	25.00	50.00	100.00

Number	Title (A Side/B Side)	Yr	VG	VG+	NM
❏ EAS 7605 [DJ]	Earth Song (Hani's Around the World Experience) (Hani's Club Experience) (Hani's Extended Radio Experience)	1995	7.50	15.00	30.00
❏ EAS 7606 [DJ]	This Time Around (unknown versions)	1995	12.50	25.00	50.00
❏ EAS 7607 [DJ]	This Time Around (4 versions)	1995	12.50	25.00	50.00
❏ E2S 7770 [(2) DJ]	They Don't Care About Us (10 versions)	1996	7.50	15.00	30.00
❏ 49-07855	Another Part of Me (Extended Dance Mix) (Radio Edit) (Dub Mix) (Acappella)	1988	2.00	4.00	8.00
❏ 49-07895	Smooth Criminal (Extended Dance Mix) (Extended Dance Mix Radio Edit) (Annie Mix) (Dub Mix) (A Cappella)	1988	2.50	5.00	10.00
❏ EAS 8337 [DJ]	Stranger in Moscow (Tee's In-House Club Mix) (Basement Boys 12" Club Mix) (Hani's Num Club Mix) (Charlie Roane's Full R&B Mix)	1996	3.75	7.50	15.00
❏ EAS 8338 [DJ]	Stranger in Moscow (Tee's Freeze Mix) (Tee's Mission Mix) (Tee'sq Cappella) (Bonus Beats) (Hani's Extended Chili Hop Mix) (Basement Boys Danger Dub)	1996	3.75	7.50	15.00
❏ EAS 9961 [DJ]	Blood on the Dance Floor (TM's Switchblade Mix) (Refugee Camp Mix) (Fire Island Vocal Mix) (TM's O-Positive Dub)	1997	3.00	6.00	12.00
❏ 28-50658	You Can't Win (Part 1 7:14)/(Part 2 2:58)	1978	6.25	12.50	25.00
❏ EAS 54863 [DJ]	Butterflies (same on both sides)	2001	3.75	7.50	15.00
❏ EAS 54911 [DJ]	You Rock My World (Track Masters Remix with Jay-Z) (same on both sides)	2001	5.00	10.00	20.00
❏ EAS 56719 [DJ]	Butterflies (Master Mix Featuring Eve) (Michael A Cappella) (Eve A Cappella) (Instrumental)	2002	5.00	10.00	20.00
❏ 49-74099	Black or White (The Clivilles & Cole House/Club Mix) (The Clivilles and Core House/Dub Mix) (House with Guitar Radio Mix) (Single Version) (Instrumental) (Tribal Beats)	1991	2.50	5.00	10.00
❏ 49-74201	Remember the Time (4 versions)/Black or White (The Underground Club Mix)`	1991	2.50	5.00	10.00
❏ 49-74267	In the Closet (Club Mix) (The Underground Mix) (Touch Me Dub) (KI's 12" Mix)	1992	2.50	5.00	10.00
❏ 49-74304	In the Closet (The Mission 9:20) (Freestyle Mix 6:20)/(The Mix of Life 7:38) (The Underground Dub 6:24)	1992	3.00	6.00	12.00
❏ 49-74334	Jam (Roger's Club Mix) (Atlanta Techno Mix) (Teddy's Jam) (Roger's Jeep Mix) (E-Smoove's Jazzy Jam)/Don't Stop 'Til You Get Enough (Roger's Underground Solution Mix)	1992	2.50	5.00	10.00
❏ 49-74420	Who Is It (4 versions)/Beat It (Moby's Sub Mix)	1993	2.50	5.00	10.00
❏ 49-78001	Scream (5 versions)/Childhood	1995	2.50	5.00	10.00
❏ 49-78003	You Are Not Alone (Franctified Club Mix) (Album Version)/MJ Megaremix (10:33)/Scream Louder (Flyte Tyme Remix)	1995	2.50	5.00	10.00
❏ 49-78008	Blood on the Dance Floor (2 versions?)/Dangerous (Roger's Dangerous Mix)	1997	2.00	4.00	8.00
❏ 49-78013	Stranger in Moscow (Hani's Num Club Mix) (TNT Danger Dub) (Basement Boys 12" Club Mix)/Blood on the Dance Floor	1997	2.50	5.00	10.00
❏ 49X-78212 [(2)]	They Don't Care About Us (7 versions)/Earth Song/Rock with You (Club Mix)/This Time Around	1996	3.75	7.50	15.00
❏ 49-78581	Beat It/Working Day and Night	1997	3.00	6.00	12.00

—"Mixed Masters" series

❏ 49-78582	Billie Jean/Off the Wall	1997	2.50	5.00	10.00

—"Mixed Masters" series

MOTOWN

❏ PR-153 [DJ]	Farewell My Summer Love (4:21)/Call on Me (3:38)//The Jackson 5 Motown Medley (6:49)	1984	3.00	6.00	12.00

45s
EPIC

❏ 15-02156	Rock with You/Off the Wall	1981	—	—	3.00

—"Memory Lane" reissue

❏ 15-02157	She's Out of My Life/Lovely One	1981	—	—	3.00

—"Memory Lane" reissue; B-side by The Jacksons

❏ 34-03509	Billie Jean/Can't Get Outta the Rain	1983	—	2.00	4.00
❏ ENR-03575	Billie Jean/(B-side blank)	1983	3.75	7.50	15.00

—One-sided budget release

❏ 34-03759	Beat It/Get On the Floor	1983	—	2.00	4.00
❏ 34-03914	Wanna Be Startin' Somethin'/(Instrumental)	1983	—	2.00	4.00
❏ 34-03914 [PS]	Wanna Be Startin' Somethin'/(Instrumental)	1983	—	2.50	5.00
❏ 34-04026	Human Nature/Baby Be Mine	1983	—	2.00	4.00
❏ 34-04026 [PS]	Human Nature/Baby Be Mine	1983	—	2.50	5.00
❏ 34-04026 [PS]	Human Nature	1983	2.50	5.00	10.00

—"Demonstration -- Not for Sale" on sleeve

❏ 34-04165	P.Y.T. (Pretty Young Thing)/Working Day and Night	1983	—	2.00	4.00
❏ 34-04165 [PS]	P.Y.T. (Pretty Young Thing)/Working Day and Night	1983	—	2.50	5.00
❏ 34-04364	Thriller/Can't Get Outta the Rain	1984	—	2.00	4.00
❏ 34-07253	I Just Can't Stop Loving You/Baby Be Mine	1987	—	—	3.00
❏ 34-07253 [PS]	I Just Can't Stop Loving You/Baby Be Mine	1987	—	—	3.00
❏ 34-07418	Bad/I Can't Help It	1987	—	—	3.00
❏ 34-07418 [PS]	Bad/I Can't Help It	1987	—	—	3.00
❏ 34-07645	The Way You Make Me Feel/(Instrumental)	1987	—	—	3.00
❏ 34-07645 [PS]	The Way You Make Me Feel/(Instrumental)	1987	—	—	3.00
❏ 34-07668	Man in the Mirror/(Instrumental)	1988	—	—	3.00
❏ 34-07668 [PS]	Man in the Mirror/(Instrumental)	1988	—	—	3.00
❏ 34-07739	Dirty Diana/(Instrumental)	1988	—	—	3.00
❏ 34-07739 [PS]	Dirty Diana/(Instrumental)	1988	—	—	3.00
❏ 34-07962	Another Part of Me/(Instrumental)	1988	—	—	3.00
❏ 34-07962 [PS]	Another Part of Me/(Instrumental)	1988	—	—	3.00
❏ 34-08044	Smooth Criminal/(Instrumental)	1988	—	—	3.00

Number	Title (A Side/B Side)	Yr	VG	VG+	NM
❑ 34-08044 [PS]	Smooth Criminal/(Instrumental)	1988	—	—	3.00
❑ 8-50654	You Can't Win (Part 1)/You Can't Win (Part 2)	1979	—	3.00	6.00
❑ 9-50742	Don't Stop 'Til You Get Enough/I Can't Help It	1979	—	2.00	4.00
❑ 9-50797	Rock with You/Working Day and Night	1979	—	2.00	4.00
❑ 9-50838	Off the Wall/Get On the Floor	1980	—	2.00	4.00
❑ 9-50871	She's Out of My Life/Get On the Floor	1980	—	2.00	4.00
❑ 34-74100	Black or White/(Instrumental)	1991	—	—	3.00
❑ 34-74200	Remember the Time/Black or White (The Underground Club Mix)	1992	—	—	3.00
❑ 34-74266	In the Closet (7" Edit)/(The Mission Radio Edit)	1992	—	—	3.00
❑ 34-74333	Jam/Rock with You (Masters At Work Remix)	1992	—	—	3.00
❑ 34-74406	Who Is It/Wanna Be Startin' Somethin'	1992	—	—	3.00
❑ 34-74708	Heal the World/She Drives Me Wild	1992	—	—	3.00
❑ 34-77060	Will You Be There/(Instrumental)	1993	—	—	3.00
❑ 34-77312	Gone Too Soon/(Instrumental)	1993	—	—	3.00
❑ 34-78000	Scream/Childhood	1995	—	—	3.00

—A-side: With Janet Jackson

❑ 34-78002	You Are Not Alone/Scream Louder	1995	—	—	3.00
❑ 38-78007	Blood on the Dance Floor/Dangerous (Roger's Dangerous Edit)	1997	—	—	3.00
❑ 34-78012	Stranger in Moscow (Radio Edit)/(Tee's Radio Mix)	1997	—	—	3.00
❑ 34-78264	They Don't Care About Us/Rock with You (Frankie Knuckles Mix)	1996	—	—	3.00
❑ 34 79656	You Rock My World (same on both sides)	2001	—	—	2.00
❑ 34 79656 [PS]	You Rock My World (same on both sides)	2001	—	—	2.00
❑ 34 79660	Cry (same on both sides)	2001	—	—	3.00

MCA

❑ S45-1786 [DJ]	Someone in the Dark (same on both sides)	1982	12.50	25.00	50.00
❑ S45-1786 [PS]	Someone in the Dark (same on both sides)	1982	12.50	25.00	50.00
❑ 40947	Ease On Down the Road/Poppy Girls	1978	—	2.50	5.00

—With Diana Ross

❑ 40947 [PS]	Ease On Down the Road/Poppy Girls	1978	—	2.50	5.00

MOTOWN

❑ 1191	Got to Be There/Maria (You Were the Only One)	1971	—	2.50	5.00
❑ 1197	Rockin' Robin/Love Is Here and Now You're Gone	1972	—	2.50	5.00
❑ 1202	I Wanna Be Where You Are/We Got a Good Thing Going	1972	—	2.50	5.00
❑ 1202 [PS]	I Wanna Be Where You Are/We Got a Good Thing Going	1972	2.50	5.00	10.00
❑ 1207	Ben/You Can Cry on My Shoulder	1972	—	2.50	5.00
❑ 1218	With a Child's Heart/Morning Glow	1973	—	2.50	5.00
❑ 1270	Doggin' Around/Up Again	1974	—	—	—

—Unreleased

❑ 1341	We're Almost There/Take Me Back	1975	—	2.50	5.00
❑ 1349	Just a Little Bit of You/Dear Michael	1975	—	2.50	5.00
❑ 1512	One Day in Your Life/Take Me Back	1981	—	2.00	4.00
❑ 1739	Farewell My Summer Love/Call On Me	1984	—	2.00	4.00
❑ 1739 [PS]	Farewell My Summer Love/Call On Me	1984	—	2.50	5.00
❑ 1757	Girl You're So Together/Touch the One You Love	1984	—	2.00	4.00
❑ 1914	Twenty-Five Miles/Up on the House Top	1987	2.00	4.00	8.00
❑ 1914 [PS]	Twenty-Five Miles/Up on the House Top	1987	2.00	4.00	8.00

Albums

EPIC

❑ FE 35745	Off the Wall	1979	2.00	4.00	8.00
❑ QE 38112	Thriller	1982	2.00	4.00	8.00
❑ 8E8 38867 [PD]	Thriller	1983	5.00	10.00	20.00
❑ OE 40600	Bad	1987	2.00	4.00	8.00
❑ 9E9 44043 [PD]	Bad	1987	3.00	6.00	12.00
❑ E2 45400 [(2)]	Dangerous	1991	3.75	7.50	15.00
❑ HE 47545	Off the Wall	1982	10.00	20.00	40.00

—Half-speed mastered edition

❑ HE 48112	Thriller	1982	10.00	20.00	40.00

—Half-speed mastered edition

❑ E3 59000 [(3)]	HIStory: Past, Present and Future — Book I	1995	5.00	10.00	20.00

—Box set with 12x12 booklet

❑ E2 68000 [(2)]	Blood on the Dance Floor: HIStory in the Mix	1997	3.75	7.50	15.00
❑ E2 69400 [(2)]	Invincible	2001	3.75	7.50	15.00

MOTOWN

❑ M5-107V1	Motown Superstar Series, Vol. 7	1981	2.00	4.00	8.00
❑ M5-130V1	Got to Be There	1981	2.50	5.00	10.00

—Reissue of Motown 747

❑ M5-153V1	Ben	1981	2.50	5.00	10.00

—Reissue of Motown 755

❑ M5-194V1	The Best of Michael Jackson	1981	2.50	5.00	10.00

—Reissue of Motown 851

❑ M 747	Got to Be There	1972	3.75	7.50	15.00
❑ M 755	Ben	1972	3.75	7.50	15.00

—With only Michael Jackson on front cover

❑ M 755	Ben	1972	15.00	30.00	60.00

—With Michael Jackson on top half of cover, rats on the bottom half

❑ M 767	Music and Me	1973	3.75	7.50	15.00
❑ M6-825S	Forever, Michael	1975	3.00	6.00	12.00
❑ M6-851S	The Best of Michael Jackson	1975	3.00	6.00	12.00
❑ M8-956M1	One Day in Your Life	1981	2.50	5.00	10.00
❑ 6099 ML	Michael Jackson and The Jackson 5 — 14 Greatest Hits	1984	2.50	5.00	10.00

—Picture disc packaged with one glove

❑ 6101 ML	Farewell My Summer Love 1984	1984	2.50	5.00	10.00

JACKSON, MICHAEL, AND PAUL MCCARTNEY

12-Inch Singles

COLUMBIA

❑ AS 1758 [DJ]	Say Say Say (same on both sides)	1983	3.00	6.00	12.00

—As "Paul McCartney and Michael Jackson"

Number	Title (A Side/B Side)	Yr	VG	VG+	NM
❑ 44-04169	Say, Say, Say//(Instrumental)/Ode to a Koala Bear	1983	2.50	5.00	10.00

—As "Paul McCartney and Michael Jackson"

45s

COLUMBIA

❑ 38-04168	Say, Say, Say/Ode to a Koala Bear	1983	—	2.00	4.00

—As "Paul McCartney and Michael Jackson"; B-side by Paul McCartney

❑ 38-04168 [PS]	Say, Say, Say/Ode to a Koala Bear	1983	—	2.00	4.00

EPIC

❑ 34-03288	The Girl Is Mine/Can't Get Outta the Rain	1982	—	2.50	5.00

—B-side by Michael Jackson

❑ 34-03288 [PS]	The Girl Is Mine/Can't Get Outta the Rain	1982	—	2.50	5.00
❑ ENR-03372	The Girl Is Mine/(B-side blank)	1982	3.00	6.00	12.00

—One-sided budget release

JACKSON, MILLIE

12-Inch Singles

JIVE

❑ 1015	Hot! Wild! Unrestricted! Crazy Love (4 versions)	1986	—	3.00	6.00
❑ 1022	Love Is a Dangerous Game/(Instrumental)	1986	—	3.00	6.00
❑ 1057	It's a Thang (4 versions)	1987	—	3.00	6.00
❑ 1109	Something You Can Feel (3 versions)	1988	—	3.00	6.00
❑ 1194	You Knocked the Love (Right Out of My Heart) (3 versions)/Let Me Show You	1989	—	3.00	6.00
❑ 1247	Will You Love Me Tomorrow (same on both sides)	1989	—	3.00	6.00

SPRING

❑ 028 [DJ]	All the Way Lover/You Created a Monster	1977	2.50	5.00	10.00
❑ 099	We Got to Hit It Off (same on both sides)	1979	2.50	5.00	10.00
❑ 195	Mess on Your Hands-Finger Rap (censored & uncensored)	1982	3.00	6.00	12.00

45s

JIVE

❑ 1007-7-J	Hot! Wild! Unrestricted! Crazy Love (long & short version)	1986	—	—	3.00
❑ 1007-7-J [PS]	Hot! Wild! Unrestricted! Crazy Love (long & short version)	1986	—	—	3.00
❑ 1009-7-J	Love Is a Dangerous Game/(Instrumental)	1986	—	—	3.00
❑ 1009-7-J [PS]	Love Is a Dangerous Game/(Instrumental)	1986	—	—	3.00
❑ 1040-7-J	An Imitation of Love/Mind Over Matter	1987	—	—	3.00
❑ 1040-7-J [PS]	An Imitation of Love/Mind Over Matter	1987	—	—	3.00
❑ 1056-7-J	It's a Thang/(Instrumental)	1987	—	—	3.00
❑ 1108-7-J	The Tide Is Turning/Cover Me (Wall to Wall)	1988	—	—	3.00
❑ 1111-7-J	Something You Can Feel/(Instrumental)	1988	—	—	3.00
❑ 1111-7-J [PS]	Something You Can Feel/(Instrumental)	1988	—	—	3.00
❑ 1246-7-J	Will You Love Me Tomorrow/Muffle That Fart	1989	—	2.00	4.00

MGM

❑ 14050	Little Bit of Something/My Heart Took a Licking	1969	2.00	4.00	8.00

SPRING

❑ 119	A Child of God (It's Hard to Believe)/You're the Joy of My Life	1971	—	2.50	5.00
❑ 123	Ask Me What You Want/I Just Can't Stand It	1972	—	2.50	5.00
❑ 127	My Man, a Sweet Man/I Gotta Get Away	1972	—	2.50	5.00
❑ 131	I Miss You Baby/I Ain't Giving Up	1972	—	2.50	5.00
❑ 134	Breakaway/Strange Things	1973	—	2.50	5.00
❑ 139	Hurts So Good/Love Doctor	1973	—	2.50	5.00
❑ 144	I Got to Try It One Time/Get Your Love Right	1974	—	2.50	5.00
❑ 147	How Do You Feel the Morning After/In the Wash	1974	—	2.50	5.00
❑ 155	The Rap/If Loving You Is Wrong I Don't Want to Be Right	1974	—	2.50	5.00
❑ 157	I'm Through Trying to Prove My Love to You/All I Want Is a Fighting Chance	1975	—	2.50	5.00
❑ 161	Leftovers/Loving Arms	1975	—	2.50	5.00
❑ 164	Bad Risk/There You Are	1976	—	2.50	5.00
❑ 167	Feel Like Making Love/I'm in Love Again	1976	—	2.50	5.00
❑ 170	I Can't Say Goodbye/Help Me Finish My Song	1977	—	2.50	5.00
❑ 173	A Love of Your Own/Live My Love for You	1977	—	2.50	5.00
❑ 175	If You're Not Back in Love by Monday/A Taste of Outside Love	1977	—	2.50	5.00
❑ 179	All the Way Lover/Cheatin' Is	1978	—	2.50	5.00
❑ 185	Sweet Music Man/Go Out and Get Some	1978	—	2.50	5.00
❑ 189	Keep the Home Fire Burnin'/Logs and Thangs	1978	—	2.50	5.00
❑ 192	Never Change Lovers in the Middle of the Night/Seeing You Again	1979	—	2.50	5.00
❑ 197	A Moment's Pleasure/Once You've Had It	1979	—	2.50	5.00
❑ 3002	We Got to Hit It Off/What Went Wrong Last Night	1979	—	2.00	4.00
❑ 3007	Didn't I Blow Your Mind/Be a Sweetheart	1980	—	2.00	4.00
❑ 3011	Despair/Wish That I Could Have Hurt That Way Again	1980	—	2.00	4.00
❑ 3013	This Is It (Part 1)/This Is It (Part 2)	1980	—	2.00	4.00
❑ 3017	I Had to Say It/It's Going to Take Some Time This Time	1981	—	2.00	4.00
❑ 3019	I Can't Stop Loving You/Loving You	1981	—	2.00	4.00
❑ 3021	Anybody That Don't Like Millie Jackson/Rose Colored Glasses	1981	—	2.50	5.00
❑ 3024	Passion/Lovers and Girlfriends	1982	—	2.00	4.00
❑ 3028	Special Occasion/Blues Don't Get Tired of Me	1982	—	2.00	4.00
❑ 3034	I Feel Like Walking in the Rain/(B-side unknown)	1983	—	2.00	4.00
❑ 3036	E.S.P./(B-side unknown)	1984	—	2.00	4.00
❑ 3040	Sister in the System/(B-side unknown)	1984	—	2.00	4.00

Albums

JIVE

❑ 1016-1-J	An Imitation of Love	1986	2.00	4.00	8.00
❑ 1103-1-J	The Tide Is Turning	1988	2.00	4.00	8.00
❑ 1186-1-J	Back to the Shit	1989	2.50	5.00	10.00
❑ 1447-1-J	Young Man, Older Woman	1991	3.00	6.00	12.00

Number	Title (A Side/B Side)	Yr	VG	VG+	NM
SPRING					
❑ SPR-5703	Millie Jackson	1972	3.00	6.00	12.00
❑ SPR-5706	It Hurts So Good	1973	3.00	6.00	12.00
❑ SPR-6701	Millie	1974	2.50	5.00	10.00
❑ SPR-6703	Caught Up	1974	2.50	5.00	10.00
❑ SPR-6708	Still Caught Up	1975	2.50	5.00	10.00
❑ SP-6712	Lovingly Yours	1976	2.50	5.00	10.00
❑ SP-6715	Feelin' Bitchy	1977	2.50	5.00	10.00
❑ SP-1-6719	Get It Out'cha System	1978	2.50	5.00	10.00
❑ SP-1-6722	A Moment's Pleasure	1979	2.50	5.00	10.00
❑ SP-2-6725 [(2)]	Live & Uncensored	1979	3.00	6.00	12.00
❑ SP-1-6727	For Men Only	1980	2.50	5.00	10.00
❑ SP-1-6730	I Had to Say It	1981	2.50	5.00	10.00
❑ SP-1-6735	Live and Outrageous (Rated XXX)	1982	2.50	5.00	10.00
❑ SP-1-6737	Hard Times	1983	2.50	5.00	10.00

JACKSON, MILLIE, AND ISAAC HAYES
Also see each artist's individual listings.
45s

Number	Title (A Side/B Side)	Yr	VG	VG+	NM
POLYDOR					
❑ 2036	Do You Wanna Make Love/I Changed My Mind	1979	—	2.00	4.00
❑ 2063	You Never Cross My Mind/Feels Like the First Time	1980	—	2.00	4.00
Albums					
POLYDOR					
❑ PD-1-6229	Royal Rappin's	1979	2.50	5.00	10.00

JACKSON, NISHA
45s

Number	Title (A Side/B Side)	Yr	VG	VG+	NM
CAPITOL					
❑ B-44064	Alive and Well/Going Down Slow	1987	—	—	3.00

JACKSON, RANDY
12-Inch Singles

Number	Title (A Side/B Side)	Yr	VG	VG+	NM
A&M					
❑ SP-12322	Perpetrators (7" Version) (Extended Version) (Gut Bucket Version) (Drum and Vocal Version) (Instrumental)	1989	2.50	5.00	10.00
—As "Randy and the Gypsys"					
❑ SP-12324	Love You Honey (6 versions)	1990	2.00	4.00	8.00
—As "Randy and the Gypsys"					
45s					
A&M					
❑ 1449	Perpetrators/(Instrumental)	1989	—	2.00	4.00
—As "Randy and the Gypsys"					
❑ 1472	Love You Honey/(Dub)	1990	—	2.00	4.00
—As "Randy and the Gypsys"					
EPIC					
❑ 8-50576	How Can I Be Sure/Love Song for Kids	1978	—	3.00	6.00
Albums					
A&M					
❑ SP-5191	Randy and the Gypsys	1989	3.00	6.00	12.00
—As "Randy and the Gypsys"					

JACKSON, REBBIE
45s

Number	Title (A Side/B Side)	Yr	VG	VG+	NM
COLUMBIA					
❑ 04547	Centipede/(Instrumental)	1984	—	2.00	4.00
❑ 04547 [PS]	Centipede/(Instrumental)	1984	—	2.50	5.00
❑ 04765	A Fork in the Road/Eternal Love	1985	—	—	3.00
❑ 04874	Play Me (I'm a Jukebox)/(Instrumental)	1985	—	—	3.00
❑ 06197	Reaction/(Instrumental)	1986	—	—	3.00
❑ 06563	You Send the Rain Away/If You Don't Call, You Don't Care	1987	—	—	3.00
—With Robin Zander (of Cheap Trick)					
❑ 07685	Plaything/Distant Conversation	1988	—	—	3.00
❑ 07685 [PS]	Plaything/Distant Conversation	1988	—	—	3.00
❑ 07799	R U Tuff Enuff/(Instrumental)	1988	—	—	3.00
—Rap by Melle Mel					
❑ 07799 [PS]	R U Tuff Enuff/(Instrumental)	1988	—	—	3.00
—Rap by Melle Mel					
❑ 08424	Centipede/(Instrumental)	1988	—	—	3.00
—Reissue					
Albums					
COLUMBIA					
❑ BFC 39238	Centipede	1984	2.50	5.00	10.00

JACKSON, RUDY
45s

Number	Title (A Side/B Side)	Yr	VG	VG+	NM
IMPERIAL					
❑ 5425	Teasing Me/Give Me Your Hand	1957	10.00	20.00	40.00
❑ 5945	Go On Lover, Go On/Who Do You Think You Are	1963	3.00	6.00	12.00
R & B					
❑ 1310	I'm Crying/Enfold Me	1955	20.00	40.00	80.00

JACKSON, WALTER
45s

Number	Title (A Side/B Side)	Yr	VG	VG+	NM
BRUNSWICK					
❑ 55502	It Doesn't Take Much/Let Me Come Back	1973	—	3.00	6.00
CHI-SOUND					
❑ XW908	Feelings/Words (Are Impossible)	1976	—	2.50	5.00
❑ XW964	Baby, I Love Your Way/What Would You Do	1977	—	2.50	5.00
❑ XW1044	It's All Over/Gonna Find Me an Angel	1977	—	2.50	5.00
❑ XW1140	If I Had My Way/We Could Fly	1978	—	2.50	5.00
❑ XW1216	Manhattan Skyline/I Won't Remember Ever Loving You	1978	—	2.50	5.00
❑ 2426	Magic Man/Golden Rays	1979	—	2.00	4.00
COLUMBIA					
❑ 02037	Tell Me Where It Hurts/When I See You	1981	—	2.00	4.00
❑ 02294	What If I Walked Out on You/Come to Me	1981	—	2.00	4.00
❑ 42528	This World of Mine/I Don't Want to Suffer	1962	6.25	12.50	25.00
❑ 42659	Starting Tomorrow/Then, Only Then	1963	5.00	10.00	20.00
❑ 42823	Opportunity/It Will Be the Last Time	1963	5.00	10.00	20.00
COTILLION					
❑ 44053	Anyway That You Want Me/Life Has Its Ups and Downs	1969	2.00	4.00	8.00
EPIC					
❑ 10408	Ad Lib/No Butterflies	1968	2.00	4.00	8.00
KELLI-ARTS					
❑ 1006	If I Had a Chance/(B-side unknown)	1982	—	2.50	5.00
OKEH					
❑ 7189	That's What Mama Say/What Would You Do	1964	3.00	6.00	12.00
❑ 7204	It's All Over/Lee Cross	1964	2.50	5.00	10.00
❑ 7215	Suddenly I'm All Alone/Special Love	1965	2.50	5.00	10.00
❑ 7219	Welcome Home/Blowin' in the Wind	1965	2.50	5.00	10.00
❑ 7229	I'll Keep On Trying/Where Have All the Flowers Gone	1965	2.50	5.00	10.00
❑ 7236	Funny (Not Much)/One Heart Lonely	1965	2.50	5.00	10.00
❑ 7247	It's an Uphill Climb to the Bottom/Tear for Tear	1966	2.00	4.00	8.00
❑ 7247 [PS]	It's an Uphill Climb to the Bottom/Tear for Tear	1966	5.00	10.00	20.00
❑ 7256	After You There Can Be Nothing/My Funny Valentine	1966	2.00	4.00	8.00
❑ 7260	A Corner in the Sun/Not You	1966	2.00	4.00	8.00
❑ 7272	Speak Her Name/They Don't Give Medals (To Yesterday's Heroes)	1967	2.00	4.00	8.00
❑ 7272 [PS]	Speak Her Name/They Don't Give Medals (To Yesterday's Heroes)	1967	5.00	10.00	20.00
❑ 7285	Deep in the Heart of Harlem/My One Chance to Make It	1967	2.00	4.00	8.00
❑ 7285 [PS]	Deep in the Heart of Harlem/My One Chance to Make It	1967	5.00	10.00	20.00
❑ 7295	Cold, Cold Winter/My Ship Is Comin' In	1967	2.00	4.00	8.00
❑ 7305	Everything/Road to Ruin	1968	2.00	4.00	8.00
U.S.A.					
❑ 104	Fool for You/Walls That Separate	196?	3.00	6.00	12.00
Albums					
CHI-SOUND					
❑ CS-LA656-G	Feeling Good	1976	3.00	6.00	12.00
❑ CS-LA733-G	I Want to Come Back As A Song	1977	3.00	6.00	12.00
❑ CS-LA844-G	Good to See You	1978	3.00	6.00	12.00
COLUMBIA					
❑ FC 37132	Tell Me Where It Hurts	1981	2.50	5.00	10.00
EPIC					
❑ E 34657	Greatest Hits	1977	2.50	5.00	10.00
❑ PE 40434	Greatest Hits	1987	2.00	4.00	8.00
OKEH					
❑ OKM 12107 [M]	It's All Over	1965	6.25	12.50	25.00
❑ OKM 12108 [M]	Welcome Home	1966	6.25	12.50	25.00
❑ OKM 12120 [M]	Speak Her Name	1967	6.25	12.50	25.00
❑ OKS 14107 [S]	It's All Over	1965	7.50	15.00	30.00
❑ OKS 14108 [S]	Welcome Home	1966	7.50	15.00	30.00
❑ OKS 14120 [S]	Speak Her Name	1967	7.50	15.00	30.00
❑ OKS 14128	Walter Jackson's Greatest Hits	1969	3.75	7.50	15.00

JACKSON FIVE, THE
See THE JACKSONS.

JACKSONS, THE
Includes records as "The Jackson Five." Also see JACKIE JACKSON; JERMAINE JACKSON; MARLON JACKSON; RANDY JACKSON; MICHAEL JACKSON.
12-Inch Singles

Number	Title (A Side/B Side)	Yr	VG	VG+	NM
EPIC					
❑ ASD 523 [DJ]	Blame It on the Boogie (Extended Disco Mix 7:00) (same on both sides)	1978	17.50	35.00	70.00
❑ AS 551 [DJ]	Shake Your Body (Down to the Ground) (7:58)/Things I Do for You	1978	7.50	15.00	30.00
❑ AS 858 [DJ]	Lovely One (same on both sides?)	1980	3.75	7.50	15.00
❑ AS 894 [DJ]	Heartbreak Hotel (same on both sides)	1980	3.75	7.50	15.00
❑ AS 936 [DJ]	Can You Feel It (same on both sides)	1981	5.00	10.00	20.00
❑ AS 1244 [DJ]	Walk Right Now/(Instrumental)	1981	2.50	5.00	10.00
❑ AS 1351 [DJ]	Heartbreak Hotel/She's Out of My Life/Jacksons Medley	1982	5.00	10.00	20.00
❑ AS 1387 [DJ]	Working Day and Night/Things I Do for You	1982	3.75	7.50	15.00
❑ EAS 1724 [DJ]	2300 Jackson Street (Short Version 4:12) (LP Version 5:06)	1989	3.00	6.00	12.00
❑ AS 1910 [DJ]	Torture/(Instrumental)	1984	3.00	6.00	12.00
❑ AS 1954 [DJ]	Body/(Instrumental)	1984	3.00	6.00	12.00
❑ 49-02403	Walk Right Now (Vocal 7:35) (Instrumental 6:55)	1981	3.75	7.50	15.00
❑ 49-05022	State of Shock (Dance Mix)/(Instrumental)	1984	2.50	5.00	10.00
—A-side vocal shared by Mick Jagger					
❑ 49-05075	Torture (Dance Mix)/(Instrumental)	1984	2.50	5.00	10.00
❑ 49H-07548	Lovely One/Can You Feel It	198?	2.50	5.00	10.00
—"Mixed Masters" reissue					
❑ 49H-08142	Blame It on the Boogie/Heartbreak Hotel	1988	2.50	5.00	10.00
—"Mixed Masters" reissue					
❑ 28-50721	Shake Your Body (Down to the Ground) (European Version 7:59)/That's What You Get (For Being Polite) (4:56)	1978	5.00	10.00	20.00
❑ 49-68233	Nothin' (That Compares 2 U) (5 versions)	1989	2.00	4.00	8.00

Number	Title (A Side/B Side)	Yr	VG	VG+	NM
❑ 49-78583	Enjoy Yourself/Blame It on the Boogie/Walk Right Now	1997	2.50	5.00	10.00
—"Mixed Masters" reissue					
❑ 49-78584	Shake Your Body (Down to the Ground)/Can You Feel It	1997	2.50	5.00	10.00
—"Mixed Masters" reissue					
MCA					
❑ 23729	Time Out for the Burglar (Extended Version 7:52) (Radio Edit 5:37) (Bonus Beats 7:44) (Instrumental 7:52)	1987	2.50	5.00	10.00
MOTOWN					
❑ 37463 1066 1 [DJ]	Who's Lovin' You (Live LP Version 5:40) (Live Radio Edit 4:02) (Original Version 3:42)	1992	3.75	7.50	15.00
❑ 37463 3004 1	I Want You Back '98 (6 versions)	1998	5.00	10.00	20.00

45s

Number	Title (A Side/B Side)	Yr	VG	VG+	NM
DYNAMO					
❑ 146	You Don't Have to Be Over Twenty-One to Fall in Love/Some Girls Want Me for Their Love	1971	10.00	20.00	40.00
EPIC					
❑ 19-01032	Can You Feel It/Everybody	1981	—	2.00	4.00
❑ 19-02132	Walk Right Now/Your Ways	1981	—	2.00	4.00
❑ 15-02157	Lovely One/She's Out of My Life	1981	—	—	3.00
—Reissue; B-side by Michael Jackson					
❑ 14-02720	The Things I Do for You/Working Day and Night	1982	—	2.00	4.00
❑ 34-04503	State of Shock/Your Ways	1984	—	2.00	4.00
—A-side with Mick Jagger					
❑ 34-04503 [PS]	State of Shock/Your Ways	1984	—	2.00	4.00
❑ 34-04575	Torture/(Instrumental)	1984	—	2.00	4.00
❑ 34-04575 [PS]	Torture/(Instrumental)	1984	—	2.00	4.00
❑ 34-04673	Body/(Instrumental)	1984	—	2.00	4.00
❑ 34-04673 [PS]	Body/(Instrumental)	1984	—	2.00	4.00
❑ 8-50595	Blame It on the Boogie/Do What You Wanna	1978	—	2.00	4.00
❑ 8-50656	Shake Your Body (Down to the Ground)/That's What You Get (For Being Polite)	1979	—	2.50	5.00
—Original issue has orange label					
❑ 8-50656	Shake Your Body (Down to the Ground)/That's What You Get (For Being Polite)	1979	—	2.00	4.00
—Second issue has dark blue label					
❑ 9-50938	Lovely One/Bless His Soul	1980	—	2.00	4.00
❑ 19-50959	Heartbreak Hotel/The Things I Do for You	1980	—	2.00	4.00
❑ 34-68688	Nothin' (That Compares 2 U)/Alright with Me	1989	—	—	3.00
❑ 34-69022	2300 Jackson Street/When I Look at You	1989	—	—	3.00
EPIC/PHILADELPHIA INT'L.					
❑ 8-50289	Enjoy Yourself/Style of Life	1976	—	2.50	5.00
❑ 8-50350	Show You the Way to Go/Blues Away	1977	—	2.50	5.00
❑ 8-50454	Goin' Places/Do What You Wanna	1977	—	2.50	5.00
❑ 8-50496	Find Me a Girl/Different Kind of Lady	1977	—	2.50	5.00
MCA					
❑ 53032	Time Out for the Burglar/News at Eleven	1987	—	—	3.00
—B-side by the Distants					
❑ 53032 [PS]	Time Out for the Burglar/News at Eleven	1987	—	—	3.00
MOTOWN					
❑ 1157	I Want You Back/Who's Lovin' You	1969	2.00	4.00	8.00
❑ 1163	ABC/The Young Folks	1970	2.00	4.00	8.00
❑ 1166	The Love You Save/I Found That Girl	1970	2.00	4.00	8.00
❑ 1166 [DJ]	I Found That Girl (same on both sides)	1970	5.00	10.00	20.00
—Red vinyl					
❑ 1166 [DJ]	The Love You Save	1970	7.50	15.00	30.00
—Blank back promo					
❑ 1171	I'll Be There/One More Chance	1970	2.00	4.00	8.00
❑ 1174	Santa Claus Is Coming to Town/Christmas Won't Be the Same This Year	1970	3.00	6.00	12.00
❑ 1177	Mama's Pearl/Darling Dear	1971	—	3.00	6.00
❑ 1177 [PS]	Mama's Pearl/Darling Dear	1971	3.75	7.50	15.00
❑ 1179	Never Can Say Goodbye/She's Good	1971	—	3.00	6.00
❑ 1186	Maybe Tomorrow/I Will Find a Way	1971	—	3.00	6.00
❑ 1194	Sugar Daddy/I'm So Happy	1971	—	3.00	6.00
❑ 1199	Little Bitty Pretty One/If I Had to Move a Mountain	1972	—	3.00	6.00
❑ 1205	Looking Through the Windows/Love Song	1972	—	3.00	6.00
❑ 1214	Corner of the Sky/To Know	1972	—	3.00	6.00
❑ 1224	Hallelujah Day/You Made Me What I Am	1973	—	3.00	6.00
❑ 1230	Boogie Man/Don't Let Your Baby Catch You	1973	—	—	—
—Unreleased					
❑ 1277	Get It Together/Touch	1973	—	3.00	6.00
❑ 1286	Dancing Machine/It's Too Late to Change the Time	1974	—	3.00	6.00
❑ 1308	Whatever You Got, I Want/I Can't Quit Your Love	1974	—	3.00	6.00
❑ 1310	I Am Love (Parts 1 & 2)/I Am Love (Part 2)	1975	—	3.00	6.00
❑ 1310	I Am Love (Part 1)/I Am Love (Part 2)	1975	2.00	4.00	8.00
❑ 1356	Forever Came Today/All I Do Is Think of You	1975	—	3.00	6.00
❑ 1365	Body Language/Call of the Wild	1975	—	—	—
—Unreleased					
❑ 2193	Who's Lovin' You/In the Still of the Night (I'll Remember)	1992	—	2.00	4.00
—B-side by Boyz II Men					
STEELTOWN					
❑ 681	Big Boy/You've Changed	1968	25.00	50.00	100.00
❑ 684	You Don't Have to Be Over Twenty-One to Fall in Love/Some Girls Want Me for Their Love	1968	25.00	50.00	100.00
❑ 689	Let Me Carry Your School Books/I Never Had a Girl	1969	20.00	40.00	80.00
—By "The Ripples and Waves plus Michael"					

7-Inch Extended Plays

Number	Title (A Side/B Side)	Yr	VG	VG+	NM
MOTOWN					
❑ M 60718	Ready or Not Here I Come/Goin' Back to Indiana/ Darling Dear//Oh How Happy/Reach In/Can I See You in the Morning	1970	3.75	7.50	15.00
—Jukebox issue; small hole, plays at 33 1/3 rpm					
❑ M 60718 [PS]	Third Album	1970	3.75	7.50	15.00
—Part of "Little LP" series (LLP #132)					

Albums

Number	Title (A Side/B Side)	Yr	VG	VG+	NM
EPIC					
❑ PE 34229	The Jacksons	1976	2.50	5.00	10.00
—Orange label					
❑ PE 34229	The Jacksons	198?	—	3.00	6.00
—Budget-line reissue with bar code and dark blue label					
❑ JE 34835	Goin' Places	1977	2.50	5.00	10.00
—Orange label					
❑ PE 34835	Goin' Places	198?	—	3.00	6.00
—Budget-line reissue					
❑ JE 35552	Destiny	1978	2.50	5.00	10.00
—Orange label					
❑ JE 35552	Destiny	1979	2.00	4.00	8.00
—Dark blue label					
❑ FE 36424	Triumph	1980	2.00	4.00	8.00
❑ KE2 37545 [(2)]	Jacksons Live	1981	3.00	6.00	12.00
❑ QE 38946	Victory	1984	2.00	4.00	8.00
❑ 8E8 39576 [PD]	Victory	1984	3.75	7.50	15.00
❑ OE 40911	2300 Jackson Street	1989	2.00	4.00	8.00
❑ HE 46424	Triumph	1982	15.00	30.00	60.00
—Half-speed mastered edition					
MOTOWN					
❑ M5-112V1	Motown Superstar Series, Vol. 12	1981	2.50	5.00	10.00
❑ M5-129V1	Diana Ross Presents the Jackson Five	1981	2.00	4.00	8.00
❑ M5-152V1	ABC	1981	2.00	4.00	8.00
❑ M5-157V1	Third Album	1981	2.00	4.00	8.00
❑ M5-201V1	Jackson 5 Greatest Hits	1981	2.00	4.00	8.00
❑ MS 700	Diana Ross Presents the Jackson 5	1969	6.25	12.50	25.00
❑ MS 709	ABC	1970	6.25	12.50	25.00
❑ MS 713	Christmas Album	1970	6.25	12.50	25.00
❑ MS 718	Third Album	1970	3.75	7.50	15.00
❑ M-735	Maybe Tomorrow	1971	3.75	7.50	15.00
❑ M-741	Jackson 5 Greatest Hits	1971	3.75	7.50	15.00
❑ M-742	Goin' Back to Indiana	1971	3.75	7.50	15.00
❑ M-750	Lookin' Through the Windows	1972	3.75	7.50	15.00
❑ M-761	Skywriter	1973	3.00	6.00	12.00
❑ M6-780	Dancing Machine	1974	3.00	6.00	12.00
❑ M6-783	Get It Together	1973	3.00	6.00	12.00
❑ M6-829	Moving Violation	1975	3.00	6.00	12.00
❑ M6-865	Joyful Jukebox Music	1976	3.00	6.00	12.00
❑ M7-868 [(3)]	Anthology	1976	5.00	10.00	20.00
❑ 37463 1294-1 [DJ]	Soulsation!	1995	5.00	10.00	20.00
—Vinyl is promo only; 4-song sampler from box set					
❑ 5228 ML	Maybe Tomorrow	1982	2.00	4.00	8.00
❑ 5250 ML	Christmas Album	1982	2.00	4.00	8.00
—Reissue of Motown 713					

JADES, THE

Many different groups.

45s

Number	Title (A Side/B Side)	Yr	VG	VG+	NM
ADONA					
❑ 1445	Hey Senorita/(B-side unknown)	1962	7.50	15.00	30.00
CAPITOL					
❑ 2281	Ain't It Funny What Love Can Do/Baby I Need Your Love	1968	—	3.00	6.00
CHRISTY					
❑ 110	Oh Why/Big Beach Party	1959	125.00	250.00	500.00
❑ 111	Tell Me Pretty Baby/Applesauce	1959	62.50	125.00	250.00
❑ 113	Don't Be a Fool/Friday Night with My Baby	1959	125.00	250.00	500.00
❑ 114	Look for a Lie/Blue Memories	1959	375.00	750.00	1500.
DORE					
❑ 687	Hold Back the Dawn/When They Ask About You	1963	5.00	10.00	20.00
DOT					
❑ 15822	I'm Pretending/Beverly	1958	20.00	40.00	80.00
GAITY					
❑ 2-23-64	Surfin' Crow/Blue Black Hair	1964	45.00	90.00	180.00
IMPERIAL					
❑ 66383	Wheel of Fortune/Gotta Find Somebody to Love	1969	—	3.00	6.00
❑ 66425	L-O-V-E I Love You/Don't Give What's Mine Away	1969	—	3.00	6.00
LIBERTY					
❑ 56192	All's Quiet on West 23rd/Love of a Woman	1970	—	2.50	5.00
MGM					
❑ 13399	There's a Kinder Way to Say Goodbye/You're So Right for Me	1965	3.00	6.00	12.00
NAU VOO					
❑ 807	Walking All Alone/Hey Little Girl	1959	37.50	75.00	150.00
OXBORO					
❑ 2002	Surfin' Crow/Blue Black Hair	1964	30.00	60.00	120.00
❑ 2005	Little Marlene/Shake Baby Shake	1965	30.00	60.00	120.00
PORT					
❑ 70042	He's My Guy/There Will Come a Day	1964	6.25	12.50	25.00
TIME					
❑ 1002	Leave Her For Me/So Blue	1957	50.00	100.00	200.00

—Lou Reed is alleged to have been in this group, but he would have been 15 at the time.

Number	Title (A Side/B Side)	Yr	VG	VG+	NM
UNI					
❑ 55019	The Glide/Flower Power	1967	2.00	4.00	8.00
❑ 55032 [DJ]	Privilege (same on both sides)	1967	2.00	4.00	8.00
VERVE					
❑ 10385	For Just Another Day/I'm By Your Side (Baby)	1966	3.00	6.00	12.00

JAGUARS, THE (1)

45s

Number	Title (A Side/B Side)	Yr	VG	VG+	NM
AARDELL					
❑ 0003	Rock It Davy, Rock It/I Wanted You	1955	12.50	25.00	50.00
❑ 0006	Be My Sweetie/Why Don't You Believe Me	1956	12.50	25.00	50.00
❑ 0011	The Way You Look Tonight/Moonlight and You	1956	62.50	125.00	250.00
—Black vinyl					
❑ 0011	The Way You Look Tonight/Moonlight and You	1956	150.00	300.00	600.00
—Red vinyl					
BARONET					
❑ 1	The Way You Look Tonight/Baby, Baby, Baby	1962	6.25	12.50	25.00
CLASSIC ARTISTS					
❑ 117	Happy Holiday/More Than Enough for Me	1989	—	3.00	6.00
—B-side by Johnny Staton and the Feathers					
❑ 136	Merry Christmas, Darling/Lost and Found	1990	—	3.00	6.00
ORIGINAL SOUND					
❑ 6	Thinking of You/Look Into My Eyes	1959	20.00	40.00	80.00
❑ 20	Thinking of You/Look Into My Eyes	1962	10.00	20.00	40.00
❑ 59	The Way You Look Tonight/Baby, Baby, Baby	1966	5.00	10.00	20.00
R-DELL					
❑ 11	The Way You Look Tonight/Baby, Baby, Baby	1956	12.50	25.00	50.00
❑ 16	I Love You Baby/Baby, Baby, Baby	1957	30.00	60.00	120.00
❑ 45	Rock It Davy, Rock It/I Wanted You	1958	10.00	20.00	40.00
❑ 107	Rock It Davy, Rock It/The Big Bear	1958	10.00	20.00	40.00
❑ 117	Girl of My Dreams/Don't Go Home	1960	15.00	30.00	60.00

JAMES, ELMORE

Some of the below were as "Elmo James."

45s

Number	Title (A Side/B Side)	Yr	VG	VG+	NM
ACE					
❑ 508	I Believe My Time Ain't Long/I Wish I Was a Catfish	1955	62.50	125.00	250.00
CHECKER					
❑ 777	Country Boogie/She Just Won't Do Right	1953	250.00	500.00	1000.
CHESS					
❑ 1756	I Can't Hold Out/The Sun Is Shining	1960	3.75	7.50	15.00
CHIEF					
❑ 7001	The Twelve Year Old Boy/Coming Home	1957	20.00	40.00	80.00
❑ 7004	It Hurts Me Too/Elmore's Contribution to Jazz	1957	20.00	40.00	80.00
❑ 7006	Cry for Me Baby/Take Me Where You Go	1957	15.00	30.00	60.00
❑ 7020	Knocking at Your Door/Calling All Blues	1960	10.00	20.00	40.00
ENJOY					
❑ 2015	It Hurts Me Too/Bleeding Heart	1965	5.00	10.00	20.00
❑ 2015	It Hurts Me Too/Pickin' the Blues	1965	3.75	7.50	15.00
❑ 2020	Mean Mistreatin' Mama/Bleeding	1965	3.75	7.50	15.00
❑ 2027	Dust My Broom/Everyday I Have the Blues	1965	3.75	7.50	15.00
FIRE					
❑ 504	Shake Your Moneymaker/Look on Yonder Wall	1962	10.00	20.00	40.00
❑ 1011	Make My Dreams Come True/Bobby's Rock	1960	7.50	15.00	30.00
❑ 1016	The Sky Is Crying/Held My Baby Last Night	1960	10.00	20.00	40.00
❑ 1024	I'm Worried/Rollin' and Tumblin'	1960	5.00	10.00	20.00
❑ 1031	Fine Little Mama/Done Somebody Wrong	1961	5.00	10.00	20.00
❑ 1503	Stranger Blues/Anna Lee	1963	3.75	7.50	15.00
❑ 2020	It Hurts Me Too/Pickin' the Blues	196?	3.75	7.50	15.00
—Red vinyl					
FLAIR					
❑ 1011	Early in the Morning/Hawaiian Boogie	1953	125.00	250.00	500.00
❑ 1014	Can't Stop Lovin'/Make a Little Love	1953	50.00	100.00	200.00
❑ 1022	Strange Kinda Feeling/Please Find My Baby	1953	50.00	100.00	200.00
❑ 1031	Make My Dreams Come True/Hand in Hand	1954	75.00	150.00	300.00
❑ 1039	Sho'nuff, I Do/1839 Blues	1954	75.00	150.00	300.00
❑ 1048	Dark and Dreary/Rock My Baby Right	1954	75.00	150.00	300.00
❑ 1057	Standing at the Cross Roads/Sunny Land	1955	62.50	125.00	250.00
❑ 1062	Late Hours at Midnight/The Way You Treat Me	1955	37.50	75.00	150.00
❑ 1069	Happy Home/No Love in My Heart	1955	37.50	75.00	150.00
❑ 1074	Dust My Blues/I Was a Fool	1955	62.50	125.00	250.00
❑ 1079	Blues Before Sunrise/Goodbye Baby	1955	50.00	100.00	200.00
JEWEL					
❑ 764	Dust My Broom/Gotta Find My Baby	1966	2.50	5.00	10.00
❑ 783	Catfish Blues/Make a Little Love	1967	2.50	5.00	10.00
KENT					
❑ 331	Dust My Blues/Happy Home	1960	3.00	6.00	12.00
❑ 394	Dust My Blues/Happy Home	1964	2.50	5.00	10.00
❑ 465	Sunnyland/Goodbye Baby	1967	2.00	4.00	8.00
❑ 508	I Believe/1839 Blues	1969	—	3.00	6.00
M-PAC					
❑ 7231	Cry for Me/Take Me Where You Go	1966	2.50	5.00	10.00
MEL					
❑ 7011	Cry for Me Baby/(B-side unknown)	197?	—	3.00	6.00
METEOR					
❑ 5000	I Believe/I Held My Baby Last Night	1953	200.00	400.00	800.00
❑ 5003	Baby What's Wrong/Sinful Woman	1953	125.00	250.00	500.00
❑ 5016	Saxony Boogie/Dumb Woman Blues	1954	75.00	150.00	300.00
❑ 5024	San Symphonic Boogie/Flaming Blues	1955	62.50	125.00	250.00
MODERN					
❑ 983	Wild About You/Long Tall Woman	1956	75.00	150.00	300.00

Number	Title (A Side/B Side)	Yr	VG	VG+	NM
VEE JAY					
❑ 249	Coming Home/The 12-Year-Old Boy	1957	6.25	12.50	25.00
❑ 259	It Hurts Me Too/Elmore's Contribution to Jazz	1957	6.25	12.50	25.00
❑ 269	Cry for Me Baby/Take Me Where You Go	1958	6.25	12.50	25.00
Albums					
BELL					
❑ 6037	Elmore James	1969	6.25	12.50	25.00
CHESS					
❑ LP-1537	Whose Muddy Shoes	1969	6.25	12.50	25.00
COLLECTABLES					
❑ COL-5112	Golden Classics	198?	3.00	6.00	12.00
❑ COL-5184	The Complete Fire and Enjoy Sessions, Part 1	198?	2.50	5.00	10.00
❑ COL-5185	The Complete Fire and Enjoy Sessions, Part 2	198?	2.50	5.00	10.00
❑ COL-5186	The Complete Fire and Enjoy Sessions, Part 3	198?	2.50	5.00	10.00
❑ COL-5187	The Complete Fire and Enjoy Sessions, Part 4	198?	2.50	5.00	10.00
CROWN					
❑ CLP-5168 [M]	Blues After Hours	1961	62.50	125.00	250.00
—Black label, silver "Crown"					
❑ CLP-5168 [M]	Blues After Hours	1962	12.50	25.00	50.00
—Gray label					
INTERMEDIA					
❑ QS-5034	Red Hot Blues	198?	2.50	5.00	10.00
KENT					
❑ KST-522 [R]	Original Folk Blues	1964	6.25	12.50	25.00
❑ KLP-5022 [M]	Original Folk Blues	1964	10.00	20.00	40.00
❑ KLP-9001	Anthology of the Blues Legend	196?	6.25	12.50	25.00
❑ KLP-9010	The Resurrection of Elmore James	196?	6.25	12.50	25.00
SPHERE SOUND					
❑ SR-7002 [M]	The Sky Is Crying	1965	45.00	90.00	180.00
❑ SSR-7002 [R]	The Sky Is Crying	1965	30.00	60.00	120.00
❑ SR-7008 [M]	I Need You	1966	37.50	75.00	150.00
❑ SSR-7008 [R]	I Need You	1966	30.00	60.00	120.00
UP FRONT					
❑ UP-122	The Great Elmore James	1970	3.00	6.00	12.00

JAMES, ETTA

45s

Number	Title (A Side/B Side)	Yr	VG	VG+	NM
ARGO					
❑ 5359	All I Could Do Was Cry/Girl of My Dreams	1960	3.00	6.00	12.00
❑ 5368	My Dearest Darling/Tough Mary	1960	3.00	6.00	12.00
❑ 5380	At Last/I Just Want to Make Love to You	1961	3.75	7.50	15.00
❑ 5385	Trust in Me/Anything to Say You're Mine	1961	2.50	5.00	10.00
❑ 5390	Dream/Fool That I Am	1961	2.50	5.00	10.00
❑ 5393	Sunday Kind of Love/Don't Cry, Baby	1961	2.50	5.00	10.00
❑ 5402	It's Too Soon to Know/Seven Day Fool	1961	2.50	5.00	10.00
❑ 5409	Something's Got a Hold on Me/Waiting for Charlie to Come Home	1962	2.50	5.00	10.00
❑ 5418	Stop the Wedding/Street of Tears	1962	2.50	5.00	10.00
❑ 5424	Next Door to the Blues/Fools Rush In	1962	2.50	5.00	10.00
❑ 5430	How Do You Speak to An Angel/Would It Make Any Difference to You	1962	2.50	5.00	10.00
❑ 5437	Pushover/I Can't Hold It In Anymore	1963	2.50	5.00	10.00
❑ 5445	Be Honest with Me/Pay Back	1963	2.50	5.00	10.00
❑ 5452	Two Sides (To Every Story)/I Worry Bout You	1963	2.50	5.00	10.00
❑ 5459	Baby What You Want Me to Do/What I Say	1964	2.50	5.00	10.00
❑ 5465	Look Who's Blue/Loving You More Every Day	1964	2.50	5.00	10.00
❑ 5477	Breaking Point/That Man Belongs Back Here with Me	1964	2.50	5.00	10.00
❑ 5485	Mellow Fellow/Bobby Is His Name	1964	2.50	5.00	10.00
CADET					
❑ 5519	Somewhere Down the Line/Do I Make Myself Clear	1966	2.00	4.00	8.00
—With Sugar Pie DeSanto					
❑ 5526	Only Time Will Tell/I'm Sorry for You	1966	2.00	4.00	8.00
❑ 5539	In the Basement — Part 1/In the Basement — Part 2	1966	2.00	4.00	8.00
—With Sugar Pie DeSanto					
❑ 5552	I Prefer You/I'm So Glad	1966	2.00	4.00	8.00
❑ 5564	Don't Take Me for Your Fool/It Must Be Your Love	1967	2.00	4.00	8.00
❑ 5568	Happiness/842-3089 (Call My Name)	1967	2.00	4.00	8.00
❑ 5578	Tell Mama/I'd Rather Go Blind	1967	2.00	4.00	8.00
❑ 5594	Security/I'm Gonna Take What He's Got	1968	2.00	4.00	8.00
❑ 5606	I Got You Babe/I Worship the Ground You Walk On	1968	2.00	4.00	8.00
❑ 5620	Fire/You Got It	1968	2.00	4.00	8.00
❑ 5630	Almost Persuaded/Steal Away	1968	2.00	4.00	8.00
❑ 5655	Miss Pitiful/Bobby Is His Name	1969	2.00	4.00	8.00
❑ 5664	Tighten Up Your Own Thing/What Fools We Mortals Be	1970	2.00	4.00	8.00
❑ 5671	The Sound of Love/When I Stop Dreaming	1970	2.00	4.00	8.00
❑ 5676	Losers Weepers — Part I/Weepers	1970	2.00	4.00	8.00
CAPITOL					
❑ B-44333	Avenue D/My Head Is a City	1989	—	2.00	4.00
—With David A. Stewart					
CHESS					
❑ 2100	The Love of My Man/Nothing from Nothing Leaves Nothing	1971	—	3.00	6.00
❑ 2112	I Think It's You/Take Out Some Insurance	1971	—	3.00	6.00
❑ 2125	I Found a Love/Nothing from Nothing Leaves Nothing	1972	—	3.00	6.00
❑ 2144	All the Way Down/Lay Back Daddy	1973	—	3.00	6.00
❑ 2148	Leave Your Hat On/Only a Fool	1974	—	3.00	6.00
❑ 2153	Out on the Street Again/Feeling Uneasy	1974	—	3.00	6.00

Number	Title (A Side/B Side)	Yr	VG	VG+	NM
❏ 2171	Lovin' Arms/Take Out Some Insurance	1975	—	3.00	6.00
❏ 31001	Jump Into Love/(B-side unknown)	1976	—	2.50	5.00
EPIC					
❏ 68593	Baby What You Want Me to Do/Max's Theme (Instrumental)	1989	—	2.00	4.00
KENT					
❏ 304	Baby, Baby, Every Night/Sunshine of Love	1958	7.50	15.00	30.00
❏ 345	Roll with Me Henry/Good Rockin' Daddy	1960	6.25	12.50	25.00
❏ 352	How Big a Fool/Good Rockin' Daddy	1961	6.25	12.50	25.00
❏ 370	Do Something Crazy/Good Rockin' Daddy	1962	6.25	12.50	25.00
MODERN					
❏ 947	The Wallflower (Roll With Me Henry)/Hold Me, Squeeze Me	1955	10.00	20.00	40.00
❏ 947	The Wallflower (Dance With Me Henry)/Hold Me, Squeeze Me	1955	6.25	12.50	25.00
❏ 957	Hey Henry (Doin' Fine, Henry)/Be Mine	1955	6.25	12.50	25.00
❏ 962	Good Rockin' Daddy/Crazy Feeling	1955	7.50	15.00	30.00
❏ 972	That's All/W-O-M-A-N	1955	6.25	12.50	25.00
❏ 984	I'm a Fool/Number One (My One and Only)	1956	6.25	12.50	25.00
❏ 988	Shortnin' Bread Rock/Tears of Joy	1956	6.25	12.50	25.00
❏ 998	Fools We Mortals Be/Tough Lover	1956	7.50	15.00	30.00
❏ 1007	Good Lookin'/Then I'll Care	1957	6.25	12.50	25.00
❏ 1016	The Pick-Up/Market Place	1957	6.25	12.50	25.00
❏ 1022	By the Light of the Silvery Moon/Come What May	1957	6.25	12.50	25.00
PHILCO-FORD					
❏ HP-31	Tell Mama/Security	1968	5.00	10.00	20.00
—4-inch plastic "Hip Pocket Record" with color sleeve					
T-ELECTRIC					
❏ 41264	It Takes Love to Keep a Woman/Mean Mother	1980	—	2.50	5.00
WARNER BROS.					
❏ 8545	Piece of My Heart/Lovesick Blues	1978	—	2.50	5.00
❏ 8611	Sugar on the Floor/Lovesick Blues	1978	—	2.50	5.00
Albums					
ARGO					
❏ LP-4003 [M]	At Last!	1961	10.00	20.00	40.00
❏ LPS-4003 [S]	At Last!	1961	15.00	30.00	60.00
❏ LP-4011 [M]	The Second Time Around	1961	7.50	15.00	30.00
❏ LPS-4011 [S]	The Second Time Around	1961	10.00	20.00	40.00
❏ LP-4013 [M]	Etta James	1962	7.50	15.00	30.00
❏ LPS-4013 [P]	Etta James	1962	10.00	20.00	40.00
—Two duets with Harvey Fuqua are rechanneled					
❏ LP-4018 [M]	Etta James Sings for Lovers	1962	7.50	15.00	30.00
❏ LPS-4018 [S]	Etta James Sings for Lovers	1962	10.00	20.00	40.00
❏ LP-4025 [M]	Etta James Top Ten	1963	7.50	15.00	30.00
❏ LPS-4025 [S]	Etta James Top Ten	1963	10.00	20.00	40.00
❏ LP-4032 [M]	Etta James Rocks the House	1964	25.00	50.00	100.00
❏ LPS-4032 [S]	Etta James Rocks the House	1964	37.50	75.00	150.00
❏ LP-4040 [M]	The Queen of Soul	1965	7.50	15.00	30.00
❏ LPS-4040 [S]	The Queen of Soul	1965	10.00	20.00	40.00
CADET					
❏ LP-802 [M]	Tell Mama	1968	6.25	12.50	25.00
❏ LPS-802 [S]	Tell Mama	1968	5.00	10.00	20.00
❏ LPS-832	Etta James Sings Funk	1969	5.00	10.00	20.00
❏ LPS-847	Losers Weepers	1970	3.75	7.50	15.00
❏ LP-4003 [M]	At Last!	1966	3.00	6.00	12.00
❏ LPS-4003 [S]	At Last!	1966	3.75	7.50	15.00
❏ LP-4011 [M]	The Second Time Around	1966	3.00	6.00	12.00
❏ LPS-4011 [S]	The Second Time Around	1966	3.75	7.50	15.00
❏ LP-4013 [M]	Etta James	1966	3.00	6.00	12.00
❏ LPS-4013 [S]	Etta James	1966	3.75	7.50	15.00
❏ LP-4018 [M]	Etta James Sings for Lovers	1966	3.00	6.00	12.00
❏ LPS-4018 [S]	Etta James Sings for Lovers	1966	3.75	7.50	15.00
❏ LP-4025 [M]	Etta James Top Ten	1966	3.00	6.00	12.00
❏ LPS-4025 [S]	Etta James Top Ten	1966	3.75	7.50	15.00
❏ LP-4040 [M]	The Queen of Soul	1966	3.00	6.00	12.00
❏ LPS-4040 [S]	The Queen of Soul	1966	3.75	7.50	15.00
❏ LP-4055 [M]	Call My Name	1967	3.75	7.50	15.00
❏ LPS-4055 [S]	Call My Name	1967	5.00	10.00	20.00
CHESS					
❏ CH2-6028 [(2)]	The Sweetest Peaches	1989	3.00	6.00	12.00
❏ CH-9110	Her Greatest Sides, Vol. 1	1984	2.50	5.00	10.00
❏ CH-9184	Etta James Rocks the House	1986	2.00	4.00	8.00
—Reissue					
❏ CH-9266	At Last!	1987	2.00	4.00	8.00
—Reissue					
❏ CH-9269	Tell Mama	1987	2.00	4.00	8.00
—Reissue					
❏ CH-9287	The Second Time Around	1989	2.00	4.00	8.00
—Reissue					
❏ ACH-19003	Etta Is Betta Than Evvah!	1976	3.75	7.50	15.00
❏ CH-50042	Etta James	1973	3.75	7.50	15.00
❏ 2CH-60004 [(2)]	Peaches	1971	5.00	10.00	20.00
❏ CH-60029	Come a Little Closer	1974	3.75	7.50	15.00
❏ CH-91509	Come a Little Closer	198?	2.00	4.00	8.00
—Reissue					
CROWN					
❏ CST-360 [R]	Etta James	1963	5.00	10.00	20.00
—With Etta smiling on cover					
❏ CST-360 [R]	Etta James	1963	5.00	10.00	20.00
—With Etta somber on cover					
❏ CLP-5209 [M]	Miss Etta James	1961	25.00	50.00	100.00
—First edition, with framed picture on cover					
❏ CLP-5209 [M]	Miss Etta James	1962	15.00	30.00	60.00
—Second edition, all-white cover with "Miss Etta James"					

Number	Title (A Side/B Side)	Yr	VG	VG+	NM
❏ CLP-5234 [M]	The Best of Etta James	1962	15.00	30.00	60.00
—Black label					
❏ CLP-5234 [M]	The Best of Etta James	1963	7.50	15.00	30.00
—Gray label					
❏ CLP-5250 [M]	Twist with Etta James	1962	15.00	30.00	60.00
—Black label					
❏ CLP-5250 [M]	Twist with Etta James	1963	7.50	15.00	30.00
—Gray label					
❏ CLP-5360 [M]	Etta James	1963	7.50	15.00	30.00
—With Etta smiling on cover					
❏ CLP-5360 [M]	Etta James	1963	7.50	15.00	30.00
—With Etta somber on cover					
INTERMEDIA					
❏ QS-5014	Etta, Red Hot 'N' Live!	198?	2.50	5.00	10.00
ISLAND					
❏ 91018	Seven Year Itch	1988	2.50	5.00	10.00
❏ 842926-1	Sticking to My Guns	1990	3.00	6.00	12.00
KENT					
❏ KST-500 [R]	Miss Etta James	1964	20.00	40.00	80.00
—Red vinyl					
❏ KST-500 [R]	Miss Etta James	1964	6.25	12.50	25.00
—Black vinyl					
❏ KLP-5000 [M]	Miss Etta James	1964	7.50	15.00	30.00
UNITED					
❏ US 7712	Etta James Sings	197?	2.50	5.00	10.00
WARNER BROS.					
❏ BSK 3156	Deep in the Night	1978	3.00	6.00	12.00

JAMES, RICK
12-Inch Singles

Number	Title (A Side/B Side)	Yr	VG	VG+	NM
GORDY					
❏ PR 72 [DJ]	Big Time (6:27)/Upside Down (4:05)	1980	12.50	25.00	50.00
—No label name on label; B-side by Diana Ross					
❏ PR-101 [DJ]	Hard to Get (Vocal) (Instrumental)/Let Me Tickle Your Fancy (Vocal) (Instrumental)	1982	3.75	7.50	15.00
—No label name on label; B-side by Jermaine Jackson					
MOTOWN					
❏ 00012	High on Your Love Suite (7:20)/You and I (8:04)	1978	3.00	6.00	12.00
❏ PR-60 [DJ]	Love Gun (10:03) (3:45)	1979	3.00	6.00	12.00
❏ PR-81 [DJ]	Give It To Me Baby (3 versions)	1981	3.00	6.00	12.00
❏ 144	17 (6:40 vocal) (5:38 instrumental)	1984	—	3.00	6.00
❏ 981 [DJ]	You and I (8:04) (same on both sides)	1978	2.50	5.00	10.00
❏ 4511	Cold Blooded/(Instrumental)	1983	—	3.00	6.00
❏ 4528	Can't Stop/Oh What a Night	1985	—	3.00	6.00
❏ 4561	Sweet and Sexy Thing (3 versions)	1986	—	3.00	6.00
❏ 4565	Forever and a Day/(Instrumental)	1986	—	3.00	6.00
REPRISE					
❏ PRO-A-3376 [DJ]	Sexual Love Affair (Club) (Remix Edit) (LP)	1988	2.00	4.00	8.00
❏ 20941	Loosey's Rap (5 versions)	1988	—	3.00	6.00
❏ 21035	This Magic Moment (3 versions)	1988	—	3.00	6.00
❏ 21036	Sexual Luv Affair (4 versions)/In the Girls Room	1988	—	3.00	6.00
45s					
A&M					
❏ 1615	Funkin' Around/My Mama	1974	6.25	12.50	25.00
GORDY					
❏ 1619	Dance Wit' Me — Part 1/Dance Wit' Me — Part 2	1982	—	2.00	4.00
❏ 1619 [PS]	Dance Wit' Me — Part 1/Dance Wit' Me — Part 2	1982	—	2.50	5.00
❏ 1634	Hard to Get/My Love	1982	—	2.00	4.00
❏ 1646	She Blew My Mind (69 Times)/(B-side unknown)	1982	—	2.00	4.00
❏ 1658	Teardrops/Throwdown	1983	—	2.00	4.00
❏ 1687	Cold Blooded/(Instrumental)	1983	—	2.00	4.00
❏ 1703	U Bring the Freak Out/He Talks	1983	—	2.00	4.00
❏ 1714	Ebony Eyes/1,2,3	1983	—	2.50	5.00
—As "Rick James and Friend"					
❏ 1714	Ebony Eyes/1,2,3	1983	—	2.00	4.00
—As "Rick James and Smokey Robinson"					
❏ 1730	17/(Instrumental)	1984	—	2.00	4.00
❏ 1763	You Turn Me On/Fire and Desire	1984	—	2.00	4.00
❏ 1776	Can't Stop/Oh What a Night	1985	—	2.00	4.00
❏ 1776 [PS]	Can't Stop/Oh What a Night	1985	—	2.50	5.00
❏ 1796	Glow/(Instrumental)	1985	—	2.00	4.00
❏ 1806	Spend the Night with Me/(Instrumental)	1985	—	2.00	4.00
❏ 1844	Sweet and Sexy Thing/(Instrumental)	1986	—	—	3.00
❏ 1844 [PS]	Sweet and Sexy Thing/(Instrumental)	1986	2.00	4.00	8.00
—Sleeve may be promo only					
❏ 1862	Forever and a Day/(Instrumental)	1986	—	—	3.00
❏ 7156	You & I/Hollywood	1978	—	2.50	5.00
❏ 7162	Mary Jane/Dream Maker	1978	—	2.50	5.00
❏ 7164	High on Your Love Suite/Stone City Band High	1979	—	2.50	5.00
❏ 7164 [PS]	High on Your Love Suite/Stone City Band High	1979	—	3.00	6.00
❏ 7167	Bustin' Out/Sexy Lady	1979	—	2.50	5.00
❏ 7171	Fool on the Street/Jefferson Hall	1979	—	2.50	5.00
❏ 7176	Love Gun/Stormy Love	1979	—	2.50	5.00
❏ 7177	Come Into My Life (Part 1)/Come Into My Life (Part 2)	1980	—	2.50	5.00
❏ 7185	Big Time/Island Lady	1980	—	2.50	5.00
❏ 7191	Gettin' it On (In the Summertime)/Summer Love	1980	—	2.50	5.00
❏ 7197	Give It to Me Baby/Don't Give Up on Love	1981	—	2.00	4.00
❏ 7205	Super Freak (Part 1)/Super Freak (Part 2)	1981	—	2.00	4.00
❏ 7215	Ghetto Life/Below the Funk (Pass the J)	1981	—	2.00	4.00
REPRISE					
❏ 27764	Sexual Love Affair/In the Girls' Room	1988	—	—	3.00
❏ 27828	Wonderful/(Instrumental)	1988	—	—	3.00
❏ 27828 [PS]	Wonderful/(Instrumental)	1988	—	—	3.00

J

Number	Title (A Side/B Side)	Yr	VG	VG+	NM
❑ 27885	Loosey's Rap/(Instrumental)	1988	—	—	3.00
—With Roxanne Shante					
❑ 27885 [PS]	Loosey's Rap/(Instrumental)	1988	—	—	3.00
WARNER BROS.					
❑ 27763	This Magic Moment-Dance with Me/ (Instrumental)	1989	—	—	3.00
❑ 27763 [PS]	This Magic Moment-Dance with Me/ (Instrumental)	1989	—	—	3.00

Albums
GORDY

Number	Title (A Side/B Side)	Yr	VG	VG+	NM
❑ G7-981	Come Get It!	1978	2.50	5.00	10.00
❑ G7-984	Bustin' Out of L. Seven	1979	2.50	5.00	10.00
❑ G8-990	Fire It Up	1979	2.50	5.00	10.00
❑ G8-995	Garden of Love	1980	2.50	5.00	10.00
❑ G8-1002	Street Songs	1981	2.00	4.00	8.00
❑ 6005 GL	Throwin' Down	1982	2.00	4.00	8.00
❑ 6043 GL	Cold Blooded	1983	2.00	4.00	8.00
❑ 6095 GL	Reflections	1984	2.00	4.00	8.00
❑ 6135 GL	Glow	1985	2.00	4.00	8.00

MOTOWN

Number	Title (A Side/B Side)	Yr	VG	VG+	NM
❑ 5263 ML	Come Get It!	198?	2.00	4.00	8.00
❑ 5382 ML	Greatest Hits	1986	2.00	4.00	8.00
❑ MOT-5405	Street Songs	1987	—	3.00	6.00

REPRISE

Number	Title (A Side/B Side)	Yr	VG	VG+	NM
❑ 25659	Wonderful	1988	2.50	5.00	10.00

JARMELS, THE
45s
LAURIE

Number	Title (A Side/B Side)	Yr	VG	VG+	NM
❑ 3085	Little Lonely One/She Loves to Dance	1961	3.75	7.50	15.00
❑ 3098	A Little Bit of Soap/The Way You Look Tonight	1961	5.00	10.00	20.00
❑ 3116	I'll Follow You/Gee Oh Gosh	1962	3.75	7.50	15.00
❑ 3124	Red Sails in the Sunset/Loneliness	1962	3.75	7.50	15.00
❑ 3142	Little Bug/One By One	1962	3.75	7.50	15.00
❑ 3174	Come On Girl/Keep Your Mind on Me	1963	3.75	7.50	15.00

Albums
COLLECTABLES

Number	Title (A Side/B Side)	Yr	VG	VG+	NM
❑ COL-5044	Golden Classics	198?	2.50	5.00	10.00

JARREAU, AL
12-Inch Singles
POLYDOR

Number	Title (A Side/B Side)	Yr	VG	VG+	NM
❑ 883513-1	Day by Day (Full Version)//Don't Push Me/Day by Day	1985	3.75	7.50	15.00
—With Shakatak					
REPRISE					
❑ PRO-A-3368 [DJ]So Good (Extended Version) (same on both sides)		1988	3.00	6.00	12.00
❑ PRO-A-5322 [DJ]Heaven and Earth (Edit) (LP Version)		1992	2.00	4.00	8.00
❑ PRO-A-5486 [DJ]It's Not Hard to Love You (Edit 3:50) (LP Version 6:11)		1992	2.00	4.00	8.00
❑ PRO-A-5676 [DJ]Superfine Love (same on both sides?)		1993	2.50	5.00	10.00
❑ 40531	Blue Angel (E-Smoove's Groovy Remix) E-Smoove's Groovy Remix Instrumental) (E-Smoove's Groovy Remix Edit) (Album Edit)/ (Ralphie's Quench Mix) (Urban Remix) (Jamie's Underground Dub)	1992	2.00	4.00	8.00
WARNER BROS.					
❑ PRO-A-933 [DJ]One Good Turn/Alonzo/Love Is Real/(If I Could) Change Your Mind		1980	3.00	6.00	12.00
❑ PRO-A-2269 [DJ]Raging Waters (LP Version) (Edit)		1985	2.50	5.00	10.00
❑ PRO-A-2530 [DJ]L Is for Lover (Remix) (LP Version)		1986	2.00	4.00	8.00
❑ PRO-A-2568 [DJ]L Is for Lover (Extended Mix) (LP Version)		1986	3.75	7.50	15.00
❑ PRO-A-2615 [DJ]Tell Me What I Gotta Do (Long Version) (Short Version) (Dub) (Instrumental)		1986	2.00	4.00	8.00
❑ 20301	Raging Waters (Dance) (Instrumental)/Fallin'	1985	2.00	4.00	8.00

45s
MCA

Number	Title (A Side/B Side)	Yr	VG	VG+	NM
❑ 53124	Moonlighting (Theme)/(Dub Version)	1987	—	—	3.00
❑ 53124 [PS]	Moonlighting (Theme)/(Dub Version)	1987	—	—	3.00
POLYDOR					
❑ 883513-7	Day by Day/Don't Push Me	1985	—	2.00	4.00
—With Shakatak					
RAYNARD					
❑ 1022	I'm Not Afraid/Ska-Bobbi	196?	37.50	75.00	150.00
❑ 1024	Shake Up/Boom Boom	196?	37.50	75.00	150.00
REPRISE					
❑ 1374	Rainbow in Your Eyes/Hold on Me	1976	—	2.50	5.00
❑ 22929	All of My Love/Killer Love	1989	—	—	3.00
❑ 27550	All or Nothing at All/Heart's Horizon	1989	—	—	3.00
❑ 27664	So Good/Pleasure Over Pain	1988	—	—	3.00
❑ 27664 [PS]	So Good/Pleasure Over Pain	1988	—	—	3.00
SESAME STREET					
❑ 49703	One Good Turn/The Sailor and the Mermaid	1981	—	2.00	4.00
—B-side by Dr. John with Libby Titus					
WARNER BROS.					
❑ PRA [DJ]	The Christmas Song//Al's Greeting/The Christmas Song	1983	—	2.50	5.00
❑ PRA [PS]	The Christmas Song//Al's Greeting/The Christmas Song	1983	—	3.00	6.00
—Promo sleeve has blank green back					
❑ 8443	Take Five/Loving You	1977	—	2.00	4.00
❑ 8481	We Got By/So Long Girl	1977	—	2.00	4.00
❑ 8677	Thinkin' About It Too/Fly	1978	—	2.00	4.00

Number	Title (A Side/B Side)	Yr	VG	VG+	NM
❑ 8751	She's Leaving Home/All	1979	—	2.00	4.00
❑ 28400	Give a Little More Lovin'/Says	1987	—	—	3.00
❑ 28538	Tell Me What I Gotta Do/Across the Midnight Sky	1986	—	—	3.00
❑ 28686	L Is for Lover/No Ordinary Romance	1986	—	—	3.00
❑ 28686 [PS]	L Is for Lover/No Ordinary Romance	1986	—	—	3.00
❑ 28925	Pretend/Black and Blues	1985	—	—	3.00
❑ 29091	Raging Waters/Fallin'	1985	—	—	3.00
❑ 29262	After All/I Keep Callin'	1984	—	—	3.00
❑ 29262 [PS]	After All/I Keep Callin'	1984	—	—	3.00
❑ 29446	The Christmas Song/Our Love	1983	—	2.00	4.00
❑ 29446 [PS]	The Christmas Song/Our Love	1983	—	2.50	5.00
❑ 29501	Trouble in Paradise/Step by Step	1983	—	—	3.00
❑ 29501 [PS]	Trouble in Paradise/Step by Step	1983	—	—	3.00
❑ 29624	Boogie Down/Our Love	1983	—	—	3.00
❑ 29720	Mornin'/Not Like This	1983	—	—	3.00
❑ 29720 [PS]	Mornin'/Not Like This	1983	—	2.50	5.00
❑ 29893	Your Precious Love/Monmouth College Fight Song	1982	—	—	3.00
—A-side with Randy Crawford					
❑ 49234	Never Givin' Up/Distracted	1980	—	2.00	4.00
❑ 49538	Gimme What You Got/Spain	1980	—	2.00	4.00
❑ 49588	Distracted/Alonzo	1980	—	2.00	4.00
❑ 49746	We're In This Love Together/Alonzo	1981	—	2.00	4.00
❑ 49842	Breakin' Away/(Round, Round, Round) Blue Ronda A La Turk	1981	—	2.00	4.00
❑ 50032	Teach Me Tonight/Easy	1982	—	2.00	4.00

Albums
BAINBRIDGE

Number	Title (A Side/B Side)	Yr	VG	VG+	NM
❑ BT-6237	Al Jarreau 1965	1982	2.00	4.00	8.00

MOBILE FIDELITY

Number	Title (A Side/B Side)	Yr	VG	VG+	NM
❑ 1-019	All Fly Home	1980	5.00	10.00	20.00
—Audiophile vinyl					

REPRISE

Number	Title (A Side/B Side)	Yr	VG	VG+	NM
❑ MS 2224	We Got By	1975	2.50	5.00	10.00
❑ MS 2248	Glow	1976	2.50	5.00	10.00
❑ 25778	Heart's Horizon	1988	2.50	5.00	10.00

WARNER BROS.

Number	Title (A Side/B Side)	Yr	VG	VG+	NM
❑ 2WS 3052 [(2)]Look to the Rainbow/Live in Europe		1977	3.00	6.00	12.00
❑ BSK 3229	All Fly Home	1978	2.50	5.00	10.00
❑ BSK 3434	This Time	1980	2.00	4.00	8.00
❑ BSK 3576	Breakin' Away	1981	2.00	4.00	8.00
❑ 23801	Jarreau	1983	2.00	4.00	8.00
❑ 25106	High Crime	1984	2.00	4.00	8.00
❑ 25331	Al Jarreau in London	1985	2.00	4.00	8.00
❑ 25477	L Is for Lover	1986	2.00	4.00	8.00

JAY AND THE TECHNIQUES
45s
EVENT

Number	Title (A Side/B Side)	Yr	VG	VG+	NM
❑ 222	I Feel Love Coming On/World of Mine	1975	—	2.50	5.00
❑ 228	Number Onederful/Don't Forget to Ask	1975	—	2.50	5.00
GORDY					
❑ 7123	I'll Be Here/Robot Man	1973	—	3.00	6.00
PHILCO-FORD					
❑ HP-22	Apples Peaches Pumpkin Pie/Loving for Money	1968	3.75	7.50	15.00
—4-inch plastic "Hip Pocket Record" with color sleeve					
SMASH					
❑ 2086	Apples, Peaches, Pumpkin Pie/Stronger Than Dirt	1967	2.00	4.00	8.00
❑ 2124	Keep the Ball Rollin'/Here We Go Again	1967	2.00	4.00	8.00
❑ 2124 [PS]	Keep the Ball Rollin'/Here We Go Again	1967	3.00	6.00	12.00
❑ 2142	Strawberry Shortcake/Still (In Love with You)	1967	2.00	4.00	8.00
❑ 2142 [PS]	Strawberry Shortcake/Still (In Love with You)	1967	3.00	6.00	12.00
❑ 2154	Baby Make Your Own Sweet Music/Help Yourself to All My Lovin'	1968	2.00	4.00	8.00
❑ 2154 [PS]	Baby Make Your Own Sweet Music/Help Yourself to All My Lovin'	1968	3.00	6.00	12.00
❑ 2171	The Singles Game/Baby How Easy Your Heart Forgets Me	1968	2.00	4.00	8.00
❑ 2171 [PS]	The Singles Game/Baby How Easy Your Heart Forgets Me	1968	3.00	6.00	12.00
❑ 2185	Hey Diddle Diddle/If I Should Lose You	1968	2.00	4.00	8.00
❑ 2217	Change Your Mind/Are You Ready for This	1969	2.00	4.00	8.00
❑ 2237	Dancin' Mood/If I Should Lose You	1969	2.00	4.00	8.00

Albums
SMASH

Number	Title (A Side/B Side)	Yr	VG	VG+	NM
❑ MGS-27095 [M]Apples, Peaches, Pumpkin Pie		1967	7.50	15.00	30.00
❑ SRS-67095 [S]Apples, Peaches, Pumpkin Pie		1967	7.50	15.00	30.00
—First cover with "live" photo of the band					
❑ SRS-67095 [S]Apples, Peaches, Pumpkin Pie		1968	5.00	10.00	20.00
—Second cover with "posed" photo of the band					
❑ SRS-67102	Love Lost and Found	1968	7.50	15.00	30.00

JAYHAWKS, THE
Also see THE MARATHONS; THE VIBRATIONS.
45s
ALADDIN

Number	Title (A Side/B Side)	Yr	VG	VG+	NM
❑ 3393	Everyone Should Know/The Creature	1957	20.00	40.00	80.00
ARGYLE					
❑ 1005	Lonely Highway/La Macerena	1961	6.25	12.50	25.00
EASTMAN					
❑ 792	Start the Fire/I Wish the World Owed Me a Living	1958	37.50	75.00	150.00
❑ 798	New Love/Betty Brown	1958	37.50	75.00	150.00

Number	Title (A Side/B Side)	Yr	VG	VG+	NM
FLASH					
❑ 105	Counting Teardrops/The Devil's Cousin	1955	50.00	100.00	200.00
❑ 109	Starnded in the Jungle/My Only Darling	1956	12.50	25.00	50.00
❑ 111	Love Train/Don't Mind Dyin'	1956	7.50	15.00	30.00

JAYNETTS, THE
45s
J&S

Number	Title (A Side/B Side)	Yr	VG	VG+	NM
❑ 1177	Out Behind the Daisies/Is It My Imagination	196?	2.00	4.00	8.00
❑ 1468/9	Chicken, Chicken, Crance or Crow/Winky Dinky	196?	2.00	4.00	8.00
❑ 1473	Peepin' In and Out the Window/Extra, Extra, Read All About It	196?	2.00	4.00	8.00
❑ 1477	Who Stole the Cookie/That's My Boy	196?	2.50	5.00	10.00
❑ 1686	Looking for Wonderland, My Lover/Make It an Extra	1965	2.00	4.00	8.00
❑ 1765/6	I Wanted to Be Free/Where Are You Tonight	196?	2.50	5.00	10.00
❑ 4418/9	Vangie Don't You Cry/My Guy Is As Sweet As Can Be	196?	2.00	4.00	8.00
TUFF					
❑ 369	Sally, Go 'Round the Roses/(Instrumental)	1963	3.75	7.50	15.00
❑ 371	Keep an Eye on Her/(Instrumental)	1963	2.50	5.00	10.00
❑ 374	Snowman, Snowman, Sweet Potato Nose/(Instrumental)	1963	3.75	7.50	15.00
❑ 377	No Love at All/Tonight You Belong to Me	1964	3.00	6.00	12.00

JAZZ CRUSADERS, THE
See THE CRUSADERS.

JAZZY JEFF AND FRESH PRINCE
Includes records as "DJ Jazzy Jeff and the Fresh Prince" and "DJ Jazzy Jeff." Also see WILL SMITH.
12-Inch Singles
JIVE

Number	Title (A Side/B Side)	Yr	VG	VG+	NM
❑ 1030	The Magnificent Jazzy Jeff/(Instrumental)/Megadope Mix	1987	2.50	5.00	10.00
❑ 1040	A Touch of Jazz (3 mixes)	1987	2.50	5.00	10.00
❑ 1092-1	Parents Just Don't Understand (4 mixes)	1988	2.00	4.00	8.00
❑ 1125-1	A Nightmare on My Street (4 mixes)	1988	2.00	4.00	8.00
❑ 1146-1	Girls Ain't Nothin' But Trouble (3 mixes)/Brand New Funk (4 mixes)	1988	—	3.00	6.00
❑ 1313-1	The Groove (6 mixes)	1989	—	3.00	6.00
❑ 1442-1	Summertime (6 mixes)	1991	—	3.00	6.00
❑ 9330	King Heroin (Don't Mess with Heroin) (3 mixes)	1985	—	3.00	6.00
—Label credit: "DJ Jazzy Jeff"					
❑ 9378	Mix So I Can Go Crazy (2 versions)/Rock It (2 versions)	1985	2.00	4.00	8.00
—Label credit: "DJ Jazzy Jeff"					
❑ 9427	Fire (2 mixes)/We Just Want to Have Fun (Gangster Boogie Dub Mix)	1985	2.00	4.00	8.00
—Label credit: "DJ Jazzy Jeff"					
❑ 42050	You Saw My Blinker/You Saw My Blinker (Edit)	1992	—	3.50	7.00
❑ 42182	I'm Looking for the One (5 versions)	1993	2.00	4.00	8.00
❑ 42202	I Wanna Rock (7 versions)	1994	—	3.50	7.00
POW WOW					
❑ 430	Real Hip Hop My Man (4 versions)	1988	2.00	4.00	8.00
—Label credit: "Jazzy Jeff"					
WORD UP					
❑ WD-001	Girls Ain't Nothing But Trouble (4 versions)	1985	3.00	6.00	12.00
❑ WD-002	Guys Ain't Nothing But Trouble (same on both sides)	1985	3.75	7.50	15.00
❑ WD-003	Just One of Those Days (same on both sides)	1985	3.75	7.50	15.00

45s
JIVE

Number	Title (A Side/B Side)	Yr	VG	VG+	NM
❑ 1029-7	The Magnificent Jazzy Jeff/(Instrumental)	1987	—	2.00	4.00
❑ 1042-7	A Touch of Jazz/(Instrumental)	1987	—	2.00	4.00
❑ 1099-7	Parents Just Don't Understand/(Instrumental)	1988	—	—	3.00
❑ 1099-7 [PS]	Parents Just Don't Understand/(Instrumental)	1988	—	—	3.00
❑ 1124-7	A Nightmare on My Street/(Instrumental)	1988	—	—	3.00
❑ 1124-7 [PS]	A Nightmare on My Street/(Instrumental)	1988	—	—	3.00
❑ 1147-7	Girls Ain't Nothin' But Trouble/Brand New Funk	1988	—	—	3.00
❑ 1147-7 [PS]	Girls Ain't Nothin' But Trouble/Brand New Funk	1988	—	—	3.00
❑ 1282-7	I Think I Can Beat Mike Tyson/(Instrumental)	1989	—	—	3.00
❑ 1282-7 [PS]	I Think I Can Beat Mike Tyson/(Instrumental)	1989	—	—	3.00
❑ 9329	King Heroin (Don't Mess with Heroin)/(instrumental)	1985	—	2.00	4.00
—Label credit: "DJ Jazzy Jeff"					
❑ 9377	Mix So I Can Go Crazy	1985	—	2.00	4.00
—Label credit: "DJ Jazzy Jeff"					
❑ 9428	Fire/We Just Want to Have Fun	1985	—	2.00	4.00
—Label credit: "DJ Jazzy Jeff"					

Albums
JIVE

Number	Title (A Side/B Side)	Yr	VG	VG+	NM
❑ 1026-1-J	Rock the House	1986	2.50	5.00	10.00
—Reissued in 1989 with same catalog number and one new track					
❑ 1091-1-J [(2)]	He's the D.J., I'm the Rapper	1988	3.00	6.00	12.00
—Without "Nightmare on My Street" disclaimer on cover					
❑ 1091-1-J RE [(2)]	He's the D.J., I'm the Rapper	1988	4.00	8.00	16.00
—With "Nightmare on My Street" disclaimer on cover (much scarcer than original)					
❑ 1188-1-J	And in This Corner...	1989	2.50	5.00	10.00
❑ 1392-1-J	Homebase	1991	3.00	6.00	12.00
❑ JL6-8399	On Fire	1985	3.00	6.00	12.00
❑ 41489-1	Code Red	1993	3.00	6.00	12.00
—LP in generic black cover with center hole and sticker					
RAPSTER					
❑ RR 008 EP [EP]	The Magnificent EP	2002	—	3.00	6.00
—By "DJ Jazzy Jeff"					
❑ RR 008 LP [(2)]	The Magnificent	2002	3.75	7.50	15.00
—By "DJ Jazzy Jeff"; full-length version with different cover than EP					
WORD UP					
❑ WDLP-0001	Rock the House	1985	6.25	12.50	25.00

JD & MARIAH
Also see MARIAH CAREY; JERMAINE DUPRI.
12-Inch Singles
SO SO DEF

Number	Title (A Side/B Side)	Yr	VG	VG+	NM
❑ CAS 41331 [DJ]	Sweetheart (Clean Version) (Instrumental) (A Cappella)/Money Ain't a Thang (Extended LP Remix) (Extended LP Instrumental)	1998	5.00	10.00	20.00
—B-side by JD Featuring Jay-Z					

45s
SO SO DEF

Number	Title (A Side/B Side)	Yr	VG	VG+	NM
❑ 38-79027	Sweetheart/(w/o rap)	1998	—	—	3.00
❑ 38-79027 [PS]	Sweetheart/(w/o rap)	1998	—	—	3.00

JELLY BEANS, THE
45s
ESKEE

Number	Title (A Side/B Side)	Yr	VG	VG+	NM
❑ 001	I'm Hip to You/You Don't Mean No Good to Me	1965	3.75	7.50	15.00
RED BIRD					
❑ 10-003	I Wanna Love Him So Bad/So Long	1964	5.00	10.00	20.00
❑ 10-011	The Kind of Boy You Can't Forget/Baby Be Mine	1964	5.00	10.00	20.00

JESSE AND MARVIN
45s
SPECIALTY

Number	Title (A Side/B Side)	Yr	VG	VG+	NM
❑ 447	Dream Girl/Daddy Loves Baby	1952	50.00	100.00	200.00
—Red vinyl					
❑ 447	Dream Girl/Daddy Loves Baby	1952	18.75	37.50	75.00
—Black vinyl					

JESTERS, THE
Also see THE PARAGONS/THE JESTERS.
45s
AMY

Number	Title (A Side/B Side)	Yr	VG	VG+	NM
❑ 859	Alexander Graham Bell/Buffalo	1962	2.00	4.00	8.00
CYCLONE					
❑ 5011	I Laughed/Now That You're Gone	1958	12.50	25.00	50.00
FEATURE					
❑ 101	Panther Pounce/Tiger Tail	1964	12.50	25.00	50.00
SIDEWALK					
❑ 910	Leave Me Alone/Don't Try to Crawl Back	1967	2.50	5.00	10.00
❑ 916	Hands of Time/If You Love Her, Tell Her So	1967	2.50	5.00	10.00
SUN					
❑ 400	Cadillac Man/My Babe	1966	7.50	15.00	30.00
ULTIMA					
❑ 705	Drag Like Boogie/A-Rab	1964	7.50	15.00	30.00
WINLEY					
❑ 218	So Strange/Love No One But You	1957	12.50	25.00	50.00
❑ 221	I'm Falling in Love/Please Let Me Love You	1957	12.50	25.00	50.00
❑ 225	The Plea/Oh Baby	1958	10.00	20.00	40.00
❑ 242	The Wind/Sally Green	1959	10.00	20.00	40.00
❑ 248	That's How It Goes/Tutti Frutti	1961	12.50	25.00	50.00
—Red vinyl					
❑ 248	That's How It Goes/Tutti Frutti	1961	7.50	15.00	30.00
—Black vinyl					
❑ 252	Come Let Me Show You/Uncle Henry's Basement	1961	7.50	15.00	30.00

Albums
COLLECTABLES

Number	Title (A Side/B Side)	Yr	VG	VG+	NM
❑ COL-5036	The Best of the Jesters	198?	2.50	5.00	10.00

JEWELS, THE (1)
Female vocal group.
45s
DIMENSION

Number	Title (A Side/B Side)	Yr	VG	VG+	NM
❑ 1034	Opportunity/Gotta Find a Way	1964	5.00	10.00	20.00
❑ 1048	Smokey Joe/But I Do	1965	3.75	7.50	15.00

JEWELS, THE (2)
Male vocal group, did the original version of the hit "Hearts of Stone."
45s
ANTLER

Number	Title (A Side/B Side)	Yr	VG	VG+	NM
❑ 1102	The Wind/Pearlie Mae	1959	10.00	20.00	40.00
IMPERIAL					
❑ 5351	Angel in My Life/Hearts Can Be Broken	1955	25.00	50.00	100.00
❑ 5362	Natural, Natural Ditty/Please Return	1955	25.00	50.00	100.00
❑ 5377	How/Rickety Rock	1956	25.00	50.00	100.00
❑ 5387	My Baby/Goin', Goin', Goin'	1956	25.00	50.00	100.00
ORIGINAL SOUND					
❑ 38	Hearts of Stone/Oh Yes I Know	1964	5.00	10.00	20.00
RPM					
❑ 474	She's a Flirt/Be-Bomp Baby	1956	17.50	35.00	70.00
R&B					
❑ 1301	Hearts of Stone/Runnin'	1954	50.00	100.00	200.00
❑ 1303	Oh Yes I Know/A Fool in Paradise	1954	75.00	150.00	300.00

J

Number	Title (A Side/B Side)	Yr	VG	VG+	NM

JEWELS, THE (3)
45s
DYNAMITE

Number	Title (A Side/B Side)	Yr	VG	VG+	NM
❏ 2000	Papa Left Mama Holdin' the Bag/This Is My Story	1966	3.75	7.50	15.00

FEDERAL

❏ 12541	My Song/This Is My Story	1966	5.00	10.00	20.00

KING

❏ 6068	Smokie Joe's/Lookie Lookie	1967	3.00	6.00	12.00

JIVE BOMBERS, THE
45s
SAVOY

❏ 1508	Bad Boy/When Your Hair Has Turned to Silver	1957	6.25	12.50	25.00
❏ 1513	If I Had a Talking Picture of You/The Blues Don't Mean a Thing	1957	5.00	10.00	20.00
❏ 1515	You Took My Love/Cherry	1957	5.00	10.00	20.00
❏ 1535	Just Around the Corner/Is This the End	1958	5.00	10.00	20.00
❏ 1560	Star Dust/You Give Your Love to Me	1959	5.00	10.00	20.00

Albums
SAVOY JAZZ

❏ SJL-1150	Bad Boy	1986	2.50	5.00	10.00

JIVE FIVE, THE
45s
AMBIENT SOUND

❏ 02742	Magic Maker, Music Maker/Oh Baby	1982	—	2.50	5.00
❏ 03053	Hey Sam/Don't Believe Him Donna	1982	—	2.50	5.00

AVCO

❏ 4568	Come Down in Time/Love Is Pain	1971	—	3.00	6.00
❏ 4589	Follow the Lamb/Let the Feeling Belong	1972	—	3.00	6.00
❏ 4589	Follow the Lamb/Lay Lady Lay	1972	—	3.00	6.00

BELTONE

❏ 1006	My True Story/When I Was Single	1961	7.50	15.00	30.00
❏ 1014	Never, Never/People from Another World	1961	5.00	10.00	20.00
❏ 2019	Hully Gully Calling Time/No, Not Again	1962	5.00	10.00	20.00
❏ 2024	What Time Is It?/Beggin' You Please	1962	5.00	10.00	20.00
❏ 2029	These Golden Rings/Do You Hear Wedding Bells	1962	5.00	10.00	20.00
❏ 2030	Lily Marlene/Johnny Never Knew	1963	5.00	10.00	20.00
❏ 2034	She's My Girl/Rain	1963	5.00	10.00	20.00

BRUT

❏ 814	All I Ever Do Is Dream About You/Super Woman (Part 2)	1973	—	3.00	6.00

DECCA

❏ 32671	(If You Let Me Make Love to You) Why Can't I Touch You/You Showed Me the Light of Love	1970	2.00	4.00	8.00
❏ 32736	I Want You to Be My Baby/Give Me Just a Chance	1970	2.00	4.00	8.00

LANA

❏ 105	My True Story/When I Was Single	196?	2.00	4.00	8.00

—Early reissue

MUSICOR

❏ 1250	Crying Like a Baby/You'll Fall in Love	1967	3.00	6.00	12.00
❏ 1270	No More Tears/You'll Fall in Love	1967	3.00	6.00	12.00
❏ 1305	Sugar (Don't Take Away My Candy)/Blues in the Ghetto	1968	3.00	6.00	12.00

SKETCH

❏ 219	United/Prove Every Word You Say	1964	3.75	7.50	15.00

UNITED ARTISTS

❏ 0100	I'm a Happy Man/It Will Stand	1973	—	2.50	5.00

—"Silver Spotlight Series" reissue; B-side by The Showmen

❏ 807	United/Prove Every Word You Say	1965	5.00	10.00	20.00
❏ 853	I'm a Happy Man/Kiss Kiss Kiss	1965	5.00	10.00	20.00
❏ 936	Please Baby Please/A Bench in the Park	1965	5.00	10.00	20.00
❏ 50004	Goin' Wild/Main Street	1966	3.75	7.50	15.00
❏ 50033	In My Neighborhood/Then Came Heartbreak	1966	3.75	7.50	15.00
❏ 50069	You're a Puzzle/Ha Ha	1966	3.75	7.50	15.00
❏ 50107	You/You Promised Me Great Things	1966	3.75	7.50	15.00

Albums
AMBIENT SOUND

❏ FZ 37717	Here We Are	1982	3.75	7.50	15.00

AMBIENT SOUND/ROUNDER

❏ ASR-801	Way Back	1985	3.00	6.00	12.00

COLLECTABLES

❏ COL-5022	Greatest Hits	198?	2.50	5.00	10.00

RELIC

❏ 5020	The Jive Five's Greatest Hits (1961-1963)	198?	2.50	5.00	10.00

UNITED ARTISTS

❏ UAL-3455 [M]	The Jive Five	1965	12.50	25.00	50.00
❏ UAS-6455 [S]	The Jive Five	1965	18.75	37.50	75.00

JIVERS, THE
45s
ALADDIN

❏ 3329	Cherie/Little Mama	1956	40.00	80.00	160.00
❏ 3347	Ray Pearl/Dear Little One	1956	30.00	60.00	120.00

JOHN, LITTLE WILLIE
45s
ATLANTIC

❏ 89189	Fever/Ruby Baby	1987	—	—	3.00

—B-side by the Drifters

❏ 89189 [PS]	Fever/Ruby Baby	1987	—	—	3.00

—From the movie "Big Town"

KING

Number	Title (A Side/B Side)	Yr	VG	VG+	NM
❏ 4818	All Around the World/Don't Leave Me Dear	1955	6.25	12.50	25.00
❏ 4841	Need Your Love So Bad/Home at Last	1955	6.25	12.50	25.00
❏ 4893	Are You Ever Coming Back/I'm Stickin' with You Baby	1956	6.25	12.50	25.00
❏ 4935	Fever/Letter from My Darling	1956	7.50	15.00	30.00
❏ 4960	Do Something for Me/My Nerves	1956	6.25	12.50	25.00
❏ 4989	I've Been Around/Suffering with the Blues	1956	6.25	12.50	25.00
❏ 5003	Will the Sun Shine Tomorrow/A Little Bit of Loving	1956	6.25	12.50	25.00
❏ 5023	Love, Life and Money/You Got to Get Up Early in the Morning	1957	6.25	12.50	25.00
❏ 5045	I've Got to Go Cry/Look What You've Done to Me	1957	6.25	12.50	25.00
❏ 5066	Young Girl/If I Thought You Needed Me	1957	6.25	12.50	25.00
❏ 5083	Uh Uh Baby/Summer Date	1957	6.25	12.50	25.00
❏ 5091	Person to Person/Until You Do	1957	6.25	12.50	25.00
❏ 5108	Talk to Me, Talk to Me/Spasms	1958	6.25	12.50	25.00
❏ 5142	Let's Rock While the Rockin' Good/You're a Sweetheart	1958	6.25	12.50	25.00
❏ 5147	Tell It Like It Is/Don't Be Ashamed to Call My Name	1958	6.25	12.50	25.00
❏ 5154	All My Love Belongs to You/Why Don't You Haul Off and Love Me	1958	6.25	12.50	25.00
❏ 5170	No Regrets/I'll Carry Your Love Wherever I Go	1959	5.00	10.00	20.00
❏ 5179	Made for Me/Do More in Life	1959	5.00	10.00	20.00
❏ 5219	Leave My Kitten Alone/Let Nobody Love You	1959	5.00	10.00	20.00
❏ 5274	Let Them Talk/Right There	1959	5.00	10.00	20.00
❏ 5318	Loving Care/My Love Is	1960	5.00	10.00	20.00
❏ 5342	I'm Shakin'/Cottage for Sale	1960	5.00	10.00	20.00
❏ 5356	Heartbreak (It's Hurtin' Me)/Do You Love Me	1960	5.00	10.00	20.00
❏ 5394	Sleep/There's a Difference	1960	5.00	10.00	20.00
❏ 5428/30 [DJ]	Walk Slow/The Hoochi Coochi Coo	1960	6.25	12.50	25.00
—White label; B-side by Hank Ballard and the Midnighters					
❏ 5428	Walk Slow/You Hurt Me	1960	3.75	7.50	15.00
❏ 5452	Leave My Kitten Alone/I'll Never Go Back on My Word	1961	3.75	7.50	15.00
❏ 5458	I'm Sorry/The Very Thought of You	1961	3.75	7.50	15.00
❏ 5503	(I've Got) Spring Fever/Flamingo	1961	3.75	7.50	15.00
❏ 5516	Take My Love (I Want to Give It All to You)/Now You Know	1961	3.75	7.50	15.00
❏ 5539	Need Your Love So Bad/Drive Me Home	1961	3.75	7.50	15.00
❏ 5577	There Is Someone in This World for Me/Autumn Leaves	1961	3.75	7.50	15.00
❏ 5591	Fever/Bo-Da-Ley Dino-Ley	1962	3.75	7.50	15.00
❏ 5602	The Masquerade Is Over/Katanga	1962	3.75	7.50	15.00
❏ 5628	Until Again My Love/Mister Glenn	1962	3.75	7.50	15.00
❏ 5641	Every Beat of My Heart/I Wish I Could Cry	1962	3.75	7.50	15.00
❏ 5667	She Thinks I Still Care/Come Back to Me	1962	3.75	7.50	15.00
❏ 5681	Doll Face/Big Blue Diamonds	1962	3.75	7.50	15.00
❏ 5694	Without a Friend/Half a Love	1962	3.75	7.50	15.00
❏ 5717	Don't Play with Love/Heaven All Around Me	1963	3.00	6.00	12.00
❏ 5744	My Baby's in Love with Another Guy/Come On Sugar	1963	3.00	6.00	12.00
❏ 5799	Let Them Talk/Talk to Me	1963	3.00	6.00	12.00
❏ 5818	So Lovely/Inside Information	1963	3.00	6.00	12.00
❏ 5823	Person to Person/I'm Shakin'	1963	3.00	6.00	12.00
❏ 5850	Bill Bailey/My Love Will Never Change	1964	3.00	6.00	12.00
❏ 5870	Rock Love/It Only Hurts for a Little While	1964	3.00	6.00	12.00
❏ 5886	All Around the World/All My Love Belongs to You	1964	3.00	6.00	12.00
❏ 5949	Do Something for Me/Don't You Know I'm in Love	1964	3.00	6.00	12.00
❏ 6003	Talk to Me/Take My Love	1965	2.50	5.00	10.00
❏ 6170	Fever/Let Them Talk	1968	2.50	5.00	10.00
❏ 6302	All Around the World/Need Your Love So Bad	1970	2.00	4.00	8.00

7-Inch Extended Plays
KING

❏ EP-423	*Talk to Me, Talk to Me/You're a Sweetheart/ Fever/Tell It Like It Is	1958	62.50	125.00	250.00
❏ EP-423 [PS]	Talk to Me	1958	62.50	125.00	250.00

Albums
BLUESWAY

❏ BLS-6069	Free at Last	1973	6.25	12.50	25.00

KING

❏ 564 [M]	Fever	1957	150.00	300.00	600.00
—White cover with "Fever" in large colorful letters					
❏ 395-564 [M]	Fever	1956	250.00	500.00	1000.
—"Nurse with thermometer" cover					
❏ 596 [M]	Talk to Me	1958	75.00	150.00	300.00
❏ 603 [M]	Mister Little Willie John	1958	62.50	125.00	250.00
❏ 691 [M]	Little Willie John In Action	1960	62.50	125.00	250.00
❏ 739 [M]	Sure Things	1961	37.50	75.00	150.00
❏ 767 [M]	The Sweet, the Hot, the Teenage Beat	1961	37.50	75.00	150.00
❏ 802 [M]	Come On and Join Little Willie John	1962	30.00	60.00	120.00
❏ 895 [M]	These Are My Favorite Songs	1964	25.00	50.00	100.00
❏ 949 [M]	Little Willie Sings All Originals	1966	25.00	50.00	100.00
❏ KS-949 [S]	Little Willie Sings All Originals	1966	37.50	75.00	150.00

JOHN, MABLE
45s
MOTOWN

❏ 54031	Who Wouldn't Love a Man Like That/You Made a Fool Out of Me	1960	125.00	250.00	500.00

—Mispress with wrong label; may have been promo only

STAX

❏ 0016	Running Out/Shouldn't I Love Him	1968	5.00	10.00	20.00
❏ 192	Your Good Thing (Is About to End)/It's Catching	1966	5.00	10.00	20.00

Queen was an early subsidiary of the Cincinnati-based label King. Bull Moose Jackson had a hit on the label – "I Know Who Threw the Whiskey (In the Well)" in 1946 – before it was swallowed by its parent. This 78 precedes that hit.

J.J. Jackson of "But It's Alright" fame was still looking for that elusive next hit in 1975, when he issued this obscure 45 on the Magna Glide label.

"You Are Not Alone" by Michael Jackson was the first single ever to debut at #1 on the *Billboard* Hot 100, in 1995. This is the picture cover from its 12-inch single release.

Elmore James' "I Believe," a Top 10 R&B hit in 1953, was his first 45-rpm single, and the value of this record reflects its rarity.

Long before he had hit records, Al Jarreau recorded two singles for the Milwaukee-based Raynard label. This is the first of them, released in 1964!

The Jewels made the original recording of "Hearts of Stone," which was an R&B chart hit in a cover by the Charms. That record is scarce enough, but the Jewels' follow-up single is even harder to find.

Number	Title (A Side/B Side)	Yr	VG	VG+	NM
❑ 205	If You Give Up What You Got/You're Taking Up Another Man's Place	1967	5.00	10.00	20.00
❑ 215	Same Time, Same Place/Bigger and Better	1967	5.00	10.00	20.00
❑ 225	I'm a Big Girl Now/Wait You Dog	1967	5.00	10.00	20.00
❑ 234	Don't Hit Me No More/Left Over Love	1967	5.00	10.00	20.00
❑ 249	Don't Get Caught/Able Mable	1968	5.00	10.00	20.00

TAMLA

Number	Title (A Side/B Side)	Yr	VG	VG+	NM
❑ 54031	Who Wouldn't Love a Man Like That/You Made a Fool Out of Me	1960	37.50	75.00	150.00
❑ 54040	No Love/Looking for a Love	1961	30.00	60.00	120.00
—Version with long intro					
❑ 54040	No Love/Looking for a Love	1961	25.00	50.00	100.00
—Version with no intro					
❑ 54050	Take Me/Action Speaks Louder Than Words	1962	20.00	40.00	80.00
❑ 54081	Who Wouldn't Love a Man Like That/Say You'll Never Let Me Go	1963	30.00	60.00	120.00

JOHN AND ERNEST
45s
RAINY WEDNESDAY

Number	Title (A Side/B Side)	Yr	VG	VG+	NM
❑ 201	Super Fly Meets Shaft/Problems	1973	—	2.50	5.00
❑ 201	Super Fly Meets Shaft/Part Two	1973	—	2.50	5.00
❑ 203	Soul President Number One/Crossover	1973	—	2.50	5.00

JOHNNIE AND JOE
45s
ABC-PARAMOUNT

Number	Title (A Side/B Side)	Yr	VG	VG+	NM
❑ 10079	I Adore You/I Want You Here Beside Me	1960	3.75	7.50	15.00
❑ 10117	Your Love/Why Do You Hurt Me So	1960	3.75	7.50	15.00

AMBIENT SOUND

❑ 03410	Kingdom of Love/Tossin' Turnin' (Yearnin' Burnin' For Your Love)	1982	—	2.50	5.00

CHESS

❑ 1641	I'll Be Spinning/Feel Alright	1956	5.00	10.00	20.00
❑ 1654	Over the Mountain; Across the Sea/My Baby's Gone, On, On	1957	6.25	12.50	25.00
—Originals with blue and silver "chess pieces" label					
❑ 1654	Over the Mountain; Across the Sea/My Baby's Gone, On, On	1958	3.00	6.00	12.00
—Reissues on blue labels with vertical "CHESS"					
❑ 1654	Over the Mountain; Across the Sea/My Baby's Gone, On, On	1963	2.50	5.00	10.00
—Reissues on other labels (multicolor, black)					
❑ 1677	I Was So Lonely/If You Tell You're Mine	1957	5.00	10.00	20.00
❑ 1693	Why Oh Why/Why Did She Go	1958	5.00	10.00	20.00
❑ 1706	My Baby's Gone/Darling	1958	5.00	10.00	20.00
❑ 1769	Across the Sea/You Said It, And Don't Forget It	1960	3.75	7.50	15.00

GONE

❑ 5024	Who Do You Love/Trust in Me	1958	7.50	15.00	30.00

J&S

❑ 1008	Over the Mountain (Part 2)/Won't You Come Back to Me	1959	6.25	12.50	25.00
❑ 1603	I Was So Lonely/If You Tell Me You're Mine	1957	6.25	12.50	25.00
❑ 1605/6	Who Do You Love/Trust in Me	1958	6.25	12.50	25.00
❑ 1630/1	Warm, Soft and Lovely/False Love Has Got to Go	1958	6.25	12.50	25.00
❑ 1654	Over the Mountain; Across the Sea/My Baby's Gone, On, On	1957	37.50	75.00	150.00
—With horizontal lines on label					
❑ 1654	Over the Mountain; Across the Sea/My Baby's Gone, On, On	1962	5.00	10.00	20.00
—Without horizontal lines on label					
❑ 1659	It Was There/There Goes My Heart	1957	6.25	12.50	25.00
❑ 1701	Where Did She Go/Red Sails in the Sunset	1959	6.25	12.50	25.00
❑ 4420	The Devil Said No, Gone With You Bad Self/You Can Always Count on Me	196?	3.75	7.50	15.00
❑ 8719	Tell Me/Sincere Love	196?	3.75	7.50	15.00
❑ 42832	You're the Loveliest Song/Let Your Mind Do the Walking	196?	3.75	7.50	15.00
❑ 87187	False Love Has Got to Go/Jamaica — Our Thing	196?	3.75	7.50	15.00

TUFF

❑ 379	Here We Go Baby/That's the Way You Go	1964	3.00	6.00	12.00

JOHNSON, BUBBER
45s
KING

Number	Title (A Side/B Side)	Yr	VG	VG+	NM
❑ 4793	Drop Me a Line/Ding Dang Doo	1955	5.00	10.00	20.00
❑ 4822	Come Home/There'll Be No One	1955	5.00	10.00	20.00
❑ 4855	It's Christmas Time/Let's Make Everyday a Christmas Day	1955	5.00	10.00	20.00
❑ 4872	Wonderful Things Happen/Keep a Light in the Window	1956	5.00	10.00	20.00
❑ 4924	My One Desire/I Lost Track of Everything	1956	5.00	10.00	20.00
❑ 4939	My Lonely Heart/Have a Little Faith in Me	1956	5.00	10.00	20.00
❑ 4988	Confidential/Let's Take a Walk	1956	5.00	10.00	20.00
❑ 5014	Butterfly/Too Many Hearts	1957	5.00	10.00	20.00
❑ 5034	Little Girls Don't Cry/The Search	1957	5.00	10.00	20.00
❑ 5068	Crazy Afternoon/So Much Tonight	1957	5.00	10.00	20.00
❑ 5089	Muddy Water/The Whisperers	1957	5.00	10.00	20.00
❑ 5117	Dedicated to the One I Love/Prince of Players	1958	3.75	7.50	15.00
❑ 5132	Finger Tips/I'm Confessin'	1958	3.75	7.50	15.00
❑ 5143	I Surrender Dear/Everybody's With You When You're Winning	1958	3.75	7.50	15.00
❑ 5148	I Can't See Why/As Long As I Live	1958	3.75	7.50	15.00
❑ 5174	One Good Reason/Time Was	1959	3.75	7.50	15.00
❑ 5193	House of Love/Until Sunrise	1959	3.75	7.50	15.00
❑ 5232	I Do (Love You)/Come On	1959	3.75	7.50	15.00
❑ 5267	Tell Me Who/I Know My Way	1959	3.75	7.50	15.00
❑ 5298	Those Who Dream/Atlanta	1959	3.75	7.50	15.00

MERCURY

❑ 8285	I've Got an Invitation/Forget It If You Can	1952	15.00	30.00	60.00

Albums
KING

❑ 569 [M]	Come Home	1957	50.00	100.00	200.00
❑ 624 [M]	Bubber Johnson Sings Sweet Love Songs	1959	37.50	75.00	150.00

JOHNSON, LONNIE
45s
BLUESVILLE

Number	Title (A Side/B Side)	Yr	VG	VG+	NM
❑ 806	Don't Ever Love/You Don't Move Me	196?	3.00	6.00	12.00
❑ 812	I'll Get Along Somehow/Memories of You	196?	3.00	6.00	12.00

FEDERAL

❑ 12376	Friendless Blues/What a Real Woman	1960	3.75	7.50	15.00

KING

❑ 4201	Tomorrow Night/What a Woman	1951	15.00	30.00	60.00
—78 released in 1948					
❑ 4459	Take Me I'm Yours/Why Should I Cry	1951	10.00	20.00	40.00
❑ 4473	It Was All in Vain/You Only Want Me When You're Lonely	1951	10.00	20.00	40.00
❑ 4492	Happy New Year, Darling/Christmas Blues	1951	12.50	25.00	50.00
—B-side by Gatemouth Moore					
❑ 4503	Seven Long Days/Darlin'	1951	10.00	20.00	40.00
❑ 4510	My Mother's Eyes/My Crazy Self	1951	10.00	20.00	40.00
❑ 4553	I'm Guilty/Can't Sleep Anymore	1952	10.00	20.00	40.00
❑ 4572	You Can't Buy Love/Just Another Day	1952	10.00	20.00	40.00
❑ 4758	Tomorrow Night/Pleasing You	1954	10.00	20.00	40.00
❑ 5293	Tomorrow Night/Pleasing You	1959	3.75	7.50	15.00
❑ 5907	Love Me Tonight/Brenda	1964	2.50	5.00	10.00
❑ 6303	Tomorrow Night/Blues Stay Away from Me	1970	—	3.00	6.00

PRESTIGE

❑ 310	Mr. Jelly Roll Baker/I'll Get Along Somehow	1964	2.50	5.00	10.00

RAMA

❑ 9	My Woman Is Gone/Don't Make Me Cry Baby	1953	15.00	30.00	60.00
—Black vinyl					
❑ 9	My Woman Is Gone/Don't Make Me Cry Baby	1953	37.50	75.00	150.00
—Red vinyl					
❑ 14	Stick With It Baby/Will You Remember	1953	15.00	30.00	60.00
❑ 19	It's Been So Long/Vaya Con Dios	1953	15.00	30.00	60.00
❑ 20	This Love of Mine/I Love a Dream	1953	15.00	30.00	60.00

78s
BLUEBIRD

❑ B-8322	Nothing But a Rat/She's My Mary	1940	10.00	20.00	40.00
❑ B-8338	Four-O-Three Blues/The Loveless Blues	1940	10.00	20.00	40.00
❑ B-8363	Why Women Go Wrong/She's Only a Woman	1940	10.00	20.00	40.00
❑ B-8387	Trust Your Husband/Jersey Belle Blues	1940	10.00	20.00	40.00
❑ B-8530	Get Yourself Together/Don't Be No Fool	1940	7.50	15.00	30.00
❑ B-8564	I'm Just Dumb/Be Careful	1940	7.50	15.00	30.00
❑ B-8684	She Ain't Right/Somebody's Got to Go	1941	7.50	15.00	30.00
❑ B-8748	Lazy Woman Blues/In Love Again	1941	7.50	15.00	30.00
❑ B-8779	Chicago Blues/I Did All I Could	1941	7.50	15.00	30.00
❑ B-8804	That's Love Blues/Crowing Rooster Blues	1941	7.50	15.00	30.00
❑ B-8980	From 20 to 44/The Last Call	1942	7.50	15.00	30.00
❑ B-9006	When You Feel Low Down/He's a Jelly Roll Baker	1942	7.50	15.00	30.00
❑ B-9022	Heart of Iron/The Devil's Woman	1942	7.50	15.00	30.00
❑ 34-0708	Rambler's Blues/(B-side unknown)	194?	6.25	12.50	25.00
❑ 34-0714	Lonesome Road/(B-side unknown)	194?	6.25	12.50	25.00
❑ 34-0732	Some Day Baby/Watch Shorty	194?	6.25	12.50	25.00
❑ 34-0742	My Love Is Down/(B-side unknown)	194?	6.25	12.50	25.00

COLUMBIA

❑ 14622-D	Jelly Killed Old Sam/The Faults of All Men and Women	1932	50.00	100.00	200.00
—As "Jimmy Jordan"					
❑ 14647-D	Cat You Been Messin' Aroun'/She's Dangerous with That Thing	1932	50.00	100.00	200.00
—As "Jimmy Jordan"					
❑ 14655-D	Winnie the Wailer/There Is No Justice	1932	50.00	100.00	200.00
—As "Jimmy Jordan"					
❑ 14667-D	Home Wrecker Blues/Hell Is a Name for All Sinners	1932	37.50	75.00	150.00
❑ 14674-D	Unselfish Love/My Love Doesn't Belong to You	1932	37.50	75.00	150.00

DECCA

❑ 7388	Hard Times Ain't Gone Nowhere/Something Fishy Blues	1937	10.00	20.00	40.00
❑ 7397	Flood Water Blues/I'm Nuts Over You	1938	10.00	20.00	40.00
❑ 7427	Swing Out Rhythm/It Ain't What You Usta Be	1938	10.00	20.00	40.00
❑ 7445	Man Killing Broad/Got the Blues for the West End	1938	10.00	20.00	40.00
❑ 7461	New Falling Rain Blues/Southbound Backwater Blues	1938	10.00	20.00	40.00
❑ 7487	Friendless and Blue/Devil's Got the Blues	1938	10.00	20.00	40.00
❑ 7509	I Ain't Gonna Be Your Fool/Mr. Johnson Swing	1938	10.00	20.00	40.00
❑ 7537	Blue Ghost Blues/Laplegged Drunk Again	1939	10.00	20.00	40.00
❑ 48078	It Ain't What You Usta Be/I'm Nuts Over You	1948	5.00	10.00	20.00

DISC

❑ 5060	Tell Me Why/I'm in Love with Love	1946	6.25	12.50	25.00
❑ 5061	My Lost Love/(B-side unknown)	1946	6.25	12.50	25.00
❑ 5062	Keep What You Got/(B-side unknown)	1946	6.25	12.50	25.00
❑ 5063	Rocks in My Bed/(B-side unknown)	194?	6.25	12.50	25.00
❑ 5064	Drifting Along Blues/(B-side unknown)	194?	6.25	12.50	25.00
❑ 5065	Blues in My Soul/(B-side unknown)	1947	6.25	12.50	25.00

HARMONY

Number	Title (A Side/B Side)	Yr	VG	VG+	NM
❑ 1087	It Feels So Good/Furniture Man Blues	1949	3.75	7.50	15.00

—Reissue of 1928 recordings; B-side by Victoria Spivey

KING

Number	Title (A Side/B Side)	Yr	VG	VG+	NM
❑ 4201	Tomorrow Night/What a Woman	1948	5.00	10.00	20.00
❑ 4212	I Am So Glad/Working Man's Blues	1948	5.00	10.00	20.00
❑ 4225	I Want My Baby/In Love Again	1948	5.00	10.00	20.00
❑ 4245	Pleasing You (As Long As I Live)/Feel So Lonesome	1948	5.00	10.00	20.00
❑ 4251	Happy New Year Darling/Backwater Blues	1948	5.00	10.00	20.00
❑ 4261	Bewildered/I Know It's Love	1949	5.00	10.00	20.00
❑ 4263	So Tired/Tell Me Little Woman	1949	5.00	10.00	20.00
❑ 4278	You're Mine You/My My Baby	1949	5.00	10.00	20.00
❑ 4297	I Found a Dream/You Take Romance	1949	5.00	10.00	20.00
❑ 4317	She's So Sweet/Don't Play Bad with My Love	1949	5.00	10.00	20.00
❑ 4336	Confused/Blues Stay Away from Me	1950	5.00	10.00	20.00
❑ 4346	I'm So Afraid/Troubles Ain't Nothin' But the Blues	1950	5.00	10.00	20.00
❑ 4388	Drunk Again/Jelly Roll Baker	1950	5.00	10.00	20.00
❑ 4411	Nothin' Clickin' Chicken/I'm So Crazy for Love	1950	5.00	10.00	20.00
❑ 4423	Little Rockin' Chair/When I'm Gone Will It Still Be Me	1951	5.00	10.00	20.00
❑ 4432	Nobody's Lovin' Me/Nothing But Trouble	1951	5.00	10.00	20.00
❑ 4450	Falling Rain Blues/Good Night Darling	1951	5.00	10.00	20.00
❑ 4459	Take Me I'm Yours/Why Should I Cry	1951	3.75	7.50	15.00
❑ 4473	It Was All in Vain/You Only Want Me When You're Lonely	1951	3.75	7.50	15.00
❑ 4492	Happy New Year, Darling/Christmas Blues	1951	5.00	10.00	20.00

—B-side by Gatemouth Moore

Number	Title (A Side/B Side)	Yr	VG	VG+	NM
❑ 4503	Seven Long Days/Darlin'	1951	3.75	7.50	15.00
❑ 4510	My Mother's Eyes/My Crazy Self	1951	3.75	7.50	15.00
❑ 4553	I'm Guilty/Can't Sleep Anymore	1952	3.75	7.50	15.00
❑ 4572	You Can't Buy Love/Just Another Day	1952	3.75	7.50	15.00
❑ 4758	Tomorrow Night/Pleasing You	1954	3.75	7.50	15.00

MONTGOMERY WARD

Number	Title (A Side/B Side)	Yr	VG	VG+	NM
❑ M-8790	Nothing But a Rat/She's My Mary	1940	10.00	20.00	40.00
❑ M-8791	Four-O-Three Blues/The Loveless Blues	1940	10.00	20.00	40.00
❑ M-8792	Why Women Go Wrong/She's Only a Woman	1940	10.00	20.00	40.00
❑ M-8793	Trust Your Husband/Jersey Belle Blues	1940	10.00	20.00	40.00

OKEH

Number	Title (A Side/B Side)	Yr	VG	VG+	NM
❑ 8253	Mr. Johnson's Blues/Falling Rain Blues	1926	50.00	100.00	200.00
❑ 8282	Love Story Blues/Very Lonesome Blues	1926	37.50	75.00	150.00
❑ 8291	Bed of Sand/Sun to Sun Blues	1926	37.50	75.00	150.00
❑ 8309	Lonesome Jail Blues/When I Was Lovin' Changed My Mind Blues	1926	37.50	75.00	150.00
❑ 8340	Baby You Don't Know My Mind/A Good Happy Home	1926	37.50	75.00	150.00
❑ 8358	Good Old Wagon/A Woman Changed My Life	1926	30.00	60.00	120.00
❑ 8376	Baby Please Tell Me/There's No Use of Lovin'	1926	30.00	60.00	120.00
❑ 8391	Oh! Doctor, The Blues/I'm Gonna Dodge the Blues	1926	30.00	60.00	120.00
❑ 8411	Lonnie's Got the Blues/I Have No Sweet Woman Now	1926	30.00	60.00	120.00
❑ 8417	Five O'Clock Blues/Johnson's Trio Stomp	1927	30.00	60.00	120.00
❑ 8435	Ball and Chain Blues/Sweet Woman See for Yourself	1927	30.00	60.00	120.00
❑ 8451	You Don't See Into the Blues Like Me/You Drove a Good Man Away	1927	30.00	60.00	120.00
❑ 8466	South Bound Water/Back Water Blues	1927	30.00	60.00	120.00
❑ 8484	Treat 'Em Right/Baby Will You Please Come Home	1927	30.00	60.00	120.00
❑ 8497	Roaming Rambler Blues/Mean Old Bedbug Blues	1927	30.00	60.00	120.00
❑ 8505	Lonesome Ghost Blues/Fickle Mama Blues	1927	30.00	60.00	120.00
❑ 8512	St. Louis Cyclone Blues/Sweet Woman You Can't Go Wrong	1927	30.00	60.00	120.00
❑ 8524	Biting Fleas Blues/Tin Can Alley Blues	1928	30.00	60.00	120.00
❑ 8537	Kansas City Blues/Kansas City Blues No. 2	1928	30.00	60.00	120.00
❑ 8557	Life Saver Blues/Blue Ghost Blues	1928	30.00	60.00	120.00
❑ 8558	Playing with the Strings/Stompin' 'Em Along Slow	1928	37.50	75.00	150.00
❑ 8574	Crowing Rooster Blues/Away Down in the Alley Blues	1928	30.00	60.00	120.00
❑ 8576	Blues in G/Burying Ground Blues	1928	37.50	75.00	150.00
❑ 8586	Sweet Potato Blues/Bed Bug Blues No. 2	1928	30.00	60.00	120.00
❑ 8601	Wrong Woman Blues/A Broken Heart That Never Smiles	1928	30.00	60.00	120.00
❑ 8618	Broken Levee Blues/Stay Out of Walnut Street Alley	1928	30.00	60.00	120.00
❑ 8635	Careless Love/When You Fall for Someone That's Not Your Own	1929	30.00	60.00	120.00
❑ 8637	Two Tone Stomp/Have to Change Keys to Play These Blues	1929	30.00	60.00	120.00
❑ 8664	It Feels So Good/It Feels So Good No. 2	1929	15.00	30.00	60.00
❑ 8677	I'm So Tired of Living Alone/Low Land Moan	1929	30.00	60.00	120.00
❑ 8691	Death Is On Your Track/I Just Want a Little Some of That	1929	30.00	60.00	120.00
❑ 8695	Bull Frog Moan/Handful of Riffs	1929	37.50	75.00	150.00
❑ 8697	It Feels So Good No. 3/It Feels So Good No. 4	1929	20.00	40.00	80.00
❑ 8709	Mr. Johnson's Blues No. 2/New Falling Rain Blues	1929	30.00	60.00	120.00
❑ 8711	Blue Guitars/Guitar Blues	1929	30.00	60.00	120.00
❑ 8722	From Now On Make Your Whoopee at Home/You Can't Give a Woman Everything She Needs	1929	30.00	60.00	120.00
❑ 8743	Deep Minor Rhythm/Hot Fingers	1929	37.50	75.00	150.00
❑ 8744	Toothache Blues/Toothache Blues No. 2	1929	30.00	60.00	120.00

—With Victoria Spivey

Number	Title (A Side/B Side)	Yr	VG	VG+	NM
❑ 8754	Baby Please Don't Leave Home No More/Sundown Blues	1930	37.50	75.00	150.00
❑ 8762	Wipe It Off/The Monkey and the Baboon	1930	50.00	100.00	200.00
❑ 8768	She's Making Whoopee in Hell Tonight/Death Valley Is Just Halfway to My Home	1930	37.50	75.00	150.00
❑ 8775	The Dirty Dozen/She Don't Know Who She Wants	1930	37.50	75.00	150.00
❑ 8786	Headed for Southland/I Got the Best Jelly Roll in Town	1930	37.50	75.00	150.00
❑ 8796	Don't Drive Me from Your Door/I Got the Best Jelly Roll in Town No. 2	1930	37.50	75.00	150.00
❑ 8802	The Bull Frog and the Toad/The Monkey and the Baboon No. 2	1930	37.50	75.00	150.00
❑ 8812	Keep It to Yourself/Once or Twice	1930	50.00	100.00	200.00
❑ 8818	Midnight Call Blues/Blue Room Blues	1930	37.50	75.00	150.00
❑ 8822	Deep Sea Blues/Long Black Train	1930	37.50	75.00	150.00
❑ 8831	No More Troubles Now/Sam You Can't Do That to Me	1931	37.50	75.00	150.00
❑ 8846	Let All Married Women Alone/Got the Blues for Murder Only	1931	37.50	75.00	150.00
❑ 8875	Just a Roaming Man/The Blues Is Only a Ghost	1931	37.50	75.00	150.00
❑ 8886	I Just Can't Stand These Blues/Another Woman Booked Out and Bound to Go	1931	37.50	75.00	150.00
❑ 8898	Beautiful But Dumb/From a Wash Woman On Up	1931	37.50	75.00	150.00
❑ 8909	I Have to Do My Time/The Southland Is All Right with Me	1931	37.50	75.00	150.00
❑ 8916	The Best Jockey in Town/Not the Chump I Used to Be	1931	37.50	75.00	150.00
❑ 8926	Sleepy Water Blues/Uncle Ned Don't Use Your Head	1932	37.50	75.00	150.00
❑ 8937	Sam You're Just a Rat/Men Get Wise to Yourself	1932	37.50	75.00	150.00
❑ 8946	I'm Nuts About That Gal/Racketeer's Blues	1933	50.00	100.00	200.00
❑ 40695	Nile of Genago/To Do This, You Gotta Know How	1926	37.50	75.00	150.00

PARADISE

Number	Title (A Side/B Side)	Yr	VG	VG+	NM
❑ 110	Tomorrow Night/(B-side unknown)	1952	10.00	20.00	40.00
❑ 123	Lonesome Day Blues/(B-side unknown)	1952	10.00	20.00	40.00

RAMA

Number	Title (A Side/B Side)	Yr	VG	VG+	NM
❑ 9	My Woman Is Gone/Don't Make Me Cry Baby	1953	6.25	12.50	25.00
❑ 14	Stick With It Baby/Will You Remember	1953	6.25	12.50	25.00
❑ 19	It's Been So Long/Vaya Con Dios	1953	6.25	12.50	25.00
❑ 20	This Love of Mine/I Love a Dream	1953	6.25	12.50	25.00

SCORE

Number	Title (A Side/B Side)	Yr	VG	VG+	NM
❑ 4005	How Could You/Love Is the Answer	1949	7.50	15.00	30.00

Albums

BLUESVILLE

Number	Title	Yr	VG	VG+	NM
❑ BVLP-1007 [M]	Blues by Lonnie	1960	50.00	100.00	200.00

—Blue label, silver print

Number	Title	Yr	VG	VG+	NM
❑ BVLP-1007 [M]	Blues by Lonnie	1964	15.00	30.00	60.00

—Blue label with trident logo at right

Number	Title	Yr	VG	VG+	NM
❑ BVLP-1011 [M]	Blues and Ballads	1960	50.00	100.00	200.00

—Blue label, silver print

Number	Title	Yr	VG	VG+	NM
❑ BVLP-1011 [M]	Blues and Ballads	1964	15.00	30.00	60.00

—Blue label with trident logo at right

Number	Title	Yr	VG	VG+	NM
❑ BVLP-1024 [M]	Losing Game	1961	50.00	100.00	200.00

—Blue label, silver print

Number	Title	Yr	VG	VG+	NM
❑ BVLP-1024 [M]	Losing Game	1964	15.00	30.00	60.00

—Blue label with trident logo at right

Number	Title	Yr	VG	VG+	NM
❑ BVLP-1062 [M]	Another Night to Cry	1963	50.00	100.00	200.00

—Blue label, silver print

Number	Title	Yr	VG	VG+	NM
❑ BVLP-1062 [M]	Another Night to Cry	1964	15.00	30.00	60.00

—Blue label with trident logo at right

COLUMBIA

Number	Title	Yr	VG	VG+	NM
❑ C 46221	Steppin' On the Blues	1990	5.00	10.00	20.00

FANTASY

Number	Title	Yr	VG	VG+	NM
❑ OBC-502	Blues by Lonnie	198?	3.00	6.00	12.00
❑ OBC-531	Blues and Ballads	1990	3.00	6.00	12.00

KING

Number	Title	Yr	VG	VG+	NM
❑ 395-520 [M]	Lonesome Road	1958	750.00	1375.	2000.
❑ 958 [M]	Lonnie Johnson 24 Twelve-Bar Blues	1966	15.00	30.00	60.00
❑ KS-958 [R]	Lonnie Johnson 24 Twelve-Bar Blues	1966	15.00	30.00	60.00
❑ KS-1083	Tomorrow Night	1970	6.25	12.50	25.00

PRESTIGE

Number	Title	Yr	VG	VG+	NM
❑ PRST-7724	The Blues of Lonnie Johnson	1970	5.00	10.00	20.00

JOHNSON, LONNIE, AND VICTORIA SPIVEY

Albums

BLUESVILLE

Number	Title	Yr	VG	VG+	NM
❑ BVLP-1044 [M]	Idle Hours	1962	37.50	75.00	150.00

—Blue label, silver print

Number	Title	Yr	VG	VG+	NM
❑ BVLP-1044 [M]	Idle Hours	1964	12.50	25.00	50.00

—Blue label with trident logo at right

Number	Title	Yr	VG	VG+	NM
❑ BVLP-1054 [M]	Woman Blues	1962	37.50	75.00	150.00

—Blue label, silver print

Number	Title	Yr	VG	VG+	NM
❑ BVLP-1054 [M]	Woman Blues	1964	12.50	25.00	50.00

—Blue label with trident logo at right

FANTASY

Number	Title	Yr	VG	VG+	NM
❑ OBC-518	Idle Hours	198?	3.00	6.00	12.00

JOHNSON, MARV

45s

GORDY

Number	Title (A Side/B Side)	Yr	VG	VG+	NM
❑ 7042	Why Do You Want to Let Me Go/I'm Not a Plaything	1965	3.75	7.50	15.00
❑ 7051	Just the Way You Are/Miss You Baby	1966	3.75	7.50	15.00
❑ 7077	I'll Pick a Rose for My Rose/You Got the Love I Love	1968	3.75	7.50	15.00

Number	Title (A Side/B Side)	Yr	VG	VG+	NM

KUDO

Number	Title (A Side/B Side)	Yr	VG	VG+	NM
❏ 663	My Baby-O/Once Upon a Time	1958	150.00	300.00	600.00

TAMLA

❏ 101	Come to Me/Whisper	1959	75.00	150.00	300.00

—No address on label

❏ 101	Come to Me/Whisper	1959	62.50	125.00	250.00

—With Gladstone St., Detroit, address on label

UNITED ARTISTS

❏ 0030	You've Got What It Takes/I Love the Way You Love	1973	—	2.50	5.00

—"Silver Spotlight Series" reissue

❏ 0031	Move Two Mountains/Come to Me	1973	—	2.50	5.00

—"Silver Spotlight Series" reissue

❏ 160	Come to Me/Whisper	1959	6.25	12.50	25.00
❏ 175	River of Tears/I'm Coming Home	1959	5.00	10.00	20.00
❏ 185	You Got What It Takes/Don't Leave Me	1959	5.00	10.00	20.00
❏ 208	I Love the Way You Love/Let Me Love You	1960	5.00	10.00	20.00
❏ 226	Ain't Gonna Be That Way/All the Love I've Got	1960	5.00	10.00	20.00
❏ 241	(You've Got to) Move Two Mountains/I Need You	1960	3.75	7.50	15.00
❏ 273	Happy Days/Baby, Baby	1960	3.75	7.50	15.00
❏ 294	Merry-Go-Round/Tell Me That You Love Me	1961	3.75	7.50	15.00
❏ 322	How Can We Tell Him/I've Got a Notion	1961	5.00	10.00	20.00
❏ 359	Show Me/Oh Mary	1961	5.00	10.00	20.00
❏ 386	Easier Said Than Done/Johnny One Stop	1961	5.00	10.00	20.00
❏ 423	Magic Mirror/With All That's In Me	1962	5.00	10.00	20.00
❏ 454	He Gave Me You/That's How Bad	1962	5.00	10.00	20.00
❏ 483	Let Yourself Go/That's Where I Lost My Baby	1962	5.00	10.00	20.00
❏ 556	Keep Tellin' Yourself/Everyone Who's Been in Love with You	1963	5.00	10.00	20.00
❏ 590	He's Got the Whole World In His Hands/Another Tear Falls	1963	5.00	10.00	20.00
❏ 617	Come On and Stop/Not Available	1963	5.00	10.00	20.00
❏ 643	Congratulations, You've Hurt Me Again/Crying on My Pillow	1963	5.00	10.00	20.00
❏ 691	Unbreakable Love/A Man Who Don't Believe in Love	1964	6.25	12.50	25.00

7-Inch Extended Plays

UNITED ARTISTS

❏ 10,007	I Love the Way You Love/Let Me Love You//You Got What It Takes/Don't Leave Me	1960	25.00	50.00	100.00
❏ 10,007 [PS]	Marv Johnson	1960	25.00	50.00	100.00
❏ 10,009	(contents unknown)	1960	25.00	50.00	100.00
❏ 10,009 [PS]	Marv Johnson	1960	25.00	50.00	100.00

Albums

UNITED ARTISTS

❏ UAL 3081 [M]	Marvelous Marv Johnson	1960	37.50	75.00	150.00
❏ UAL 3118 [M]	More Marv Johnson	1961	37.50	75.00	150.00
❏ UAL 3187 [M]	I Believe	1962	37.50	75.00	150.00
❏ UAS 6081 [S]	Marvelous Marv Johnson	1960	50.00	100.00	200.00
❏ UAS 6118 [S]	More Marv Johnson	1961	50.00	100.00	200.00
❏ UAS 6187 [S]	I Believe	1962	50.00	100.00	200.00

JONES, JIMMY

Also see THE PRETENDERS (2).

45s

ABC-PARAMOUNT

❏ 10094	Blue and Lonely/Daddy Needs Baby	1960	37.50	75.00	150.00

—As "Jimmy Jones and the Pretenders"

ARROW

❏ 717	Heaven in Your Eyes/The Whistlin' Man	1957	45.00	90.00	180.00

—As "Jimmy Jones and the Jones Boys"

BELL

❏ 682	Personal Property/39-21-40	1967	2.00	4.00	8.00
❏ 689	True Love Ways/Snap My Fingers	1967	2.00	4.00	8.00

CAPITOL

❏ 3849	If I Knew Then (What I Know Now)/Everything's Gonna Be All Right	1974	—	2.50	5.00

CONCHILLO

❏ 1	Ain't Nothing Wrong Makin' Love the First Night/Time and Changes	1976	—	3.00	6.00

CUB

❏ 9049	Handy Man/The Search Is Over	1959	6.25	12.50	25.00
❏ 9067	Good Timin'/My Precious Angel	1960	6.25	12.50	25.00
❏ 9072	That's When I Cried/I Just Go for You	1960	5.00	10.00	20.00
❏ 9072 [PS]	That's When I Cried/I Just Go for You	1960	12.50	25.00	50.00
❏ 9076	Itchin'/Ee-I-Ee-I-Oh	1960	5.00	10.00	20.00
❏ 9082	Ready for Love/For You	1960	5.00	10.00	20.00
❏ 9085	I Told You So/You Got It	1961	3.75	7.50	15.00
❏ 9093	Dear One/I Say Love	1961	3.75	7.50	15.00
❏ 9102	Mr. Music Man/Holler Hey	1961	3.75	7.50	15.00
❏ 9110	You're Much Too Young/Nights of Mexico	1962	3.75	7.50	15.00

EPIC

❏ 9339	Whenever You Need Me/You for Me to Love	1959	30.00	60.00	120.00

PARKWAY

❏ 988	Don't You Just Know It/Dynamite	1966	2.50	5.00	10.00

RAMA

❏ 210	Lover/Plain Old Love	1956	30.00	60.00	120.00

—As "Jimmy Jones and the Pretenders"

ROULETTE

❏ 4232	Lover/Plain Old Love	1960	7.50	15.00	30.00

—As "Jimmy 'Handyman' Jones"

VEE JAY

❏ 505	No Insurance (For a Broken Heart)/Mr. Fix-It	1963	3.75	7.50	15.00

Number	Title (A Side/B Side)	Yr	VG	VG+	NM

Albums

JEN JILLUS

❏ 1001	The Handy Man's Back in Town	1977	3.00	6.00	12.00

MGM

❏ E-3847 [M]	Good Timin'	1960	30.00	60.00	120.00
❏ SE-3847 [S]	Good Timin'	1960	40.00	80.00	160.00

JONES, JOE

45s

CAPITOL

❏ F2951	Adam Bit the Apple/Will Call	1954	10.00	20.00	40.00

HERALD

❏ 488	You Done Me Wrong/When Your Hair Has Turned to Silver	1956	10.00	20.00	40.00

RIC

❏ 972	You Talk Too Much/I Love You Still	1960	6.25	12.50	25.00

ROULETTE

❏ 4304	You Talk Too Much/I Love You Still	1960	3.75	7.50	15.00
❏ 4316	One Big Mouth/Here's What You Gotta Do	1960	3.00	6.00	12.00
❏ 4344	California Sun/Please Don't Talk About Me When I'm Gone	1961	3.00	6.00	12.00
❏ 4377	The Big Mule/I've Got a Uh Uh Wife	1961	3.00	6.00	12.00

Albums

ROULETTE

❏ R 25143 [M]	You Talk Too Much	1961	37.50	75.00	150.00
❏ SR 25143 [R]	You Talk Too Much	1961	25.00	50.00	100.00

JONES, ORAN "JUICE"

12-Inch Singles

COLUMBIA

❏ 44-73120	Pipe Dreams (3 versions)/To Be Immortal	1989	2.50	5.00	10.00
❏ 44-73172	Shaniqua (3 versions)/Dollar and a Dream (3 versions)/To Be Immortal	1990	2.00	4.00	8.00

DEF JAM

❏ 44-05930	The Rain/Your Song	1986	3.00	6.00	12.00
❏ 44-05968	Curiosity (2 versions)/Here I Go Again	1986	2.50	5.00	10.00
❏ 44-06730	Here I Go Again/1.2.1	1986	2.50	5.00	10.00
❏ 44-06960	Cold Spendin' My $ Money/(Instrumental)	1987	2.50	5.00	10.00

45s

COLUMBIA

❏ 38-73023	Pipe Dreams/To Be Immortal	1989	—	2.00	4.00

DEF JAM

❏ 38-06209	The Rain/Your Song	1986	—	2.00	4.00
❏ 38-06389	Curiosity/Here I Go Again	1986	—	—	3.00
❏ 38-06687	Here I Go Again/1.2.1	1987	—	—	3.00
❏ 38-07391	Cold Spendin' My Money/(Instrumental)	1987	—	—	3.00
❏ 38-07656	I Just Can't Say Goodbye/Not on the Outside	1987	—	—	3.00
❏ 68736	The Rain/Your Song	1989	—	—	3.00

—Reissue

Albums

COLUMBIA

❏ FC 45321	To Be Immortal	1989	2.50	5.00	10.00

DEF JAM

❏ BFC 40367	Juice	1986	3.00	6.00	12.00
❏ FC 40955	G.T.O. Gangsters Takin' Over	1987	3.75	7.50	15.00

JONES, QUINCY

45s

ABC

❏ 11086	For Love of Ivy/The Pussyfoot	1968	2.00	4.00	8.00

A&M

❏ 1115	Oh Happy Day/Love and Peace	1969	—	3.00	6.00
❏ 1139	Oh Happy Day/Love and Peace	1969	—	2.50	5.00
❏ 1163	Killer Joe/Maybe Tomorrow	1970	—	2.50	5.00
❏ 1184	Bridge Over Troubled Water (Part 1)/Bridge Over Troubled Water (Part 2)	1970	—	2.50	5.00
❏ 1316	What's Going On (Part 1)/What's Going On (Part 2)	1971	—	2.50	5.00
❏ 1323	Ironside/Cast Your Fate to the Wind	1972	—	2.50	5.00
❏ 1404	Love Theme from "The Getaway" (Part 1)/Love Theme from "The Getaway" (Part 2)	1973	—	2.00	4.00
❏ 1455	Sanford & Son Theme/Summer in the City	1973	—	2.00	4.00
❏ 1606	If I Ever Lose This Heaven/Along Came Betty	1974	—	2.00	4.00
❏ 1606 [PS]	If I Ever Lose This Heaven/Along Came Betty	1974	—	3.00	6.00
❏ 1638	Soul Saga/Boogie Joe, The Grinder	1974	—	2.00	4.00
❏ 1663	Body Heat/One Track Mind	1975	—	2.00	4.00
❏ 1743	Is It Love That We're Missing/Cry Baby	1975	—	2.00	4.00
❏ 1743 [PS]	Is It Love That We're Missing/Cry Baby	1975	—	3.00	6.00
❏ 1791	Mellow Madness/Paranoid	1976	—	2.00	4.00
❏ 1878	Midnight Soul Patrol/Brown Soft Shoe	1976	—	2.00	4.00
❏ 1909	"Roots" Medley/Many Rains Ago (Oluwu)	1977	—	2.00	4.00
❏ 1909 [PS]	"Roots" Medley/Many Rains Ago (Oluwu)	1977	—	3.00	6.00
❏ 1923	What Shall I Do (Hush, Hush, Somebody's Calling My Name)/Oh, Lord, Come By Here	1977	—	2.00	4.00
❏ 2043	Stuff Like That/There's a Train Leavin'	1978	—	2.00	4.00
❏ 2043 [PS]	Stuff Like That/There's a Train Leavin'	1978	—	3.00	6.00
❏ 2080	Love, I Never Had It So Good/I Heard That	1978	—	2.00	4.00
❏ 2309	Ai No Corrida/Lenta Letina	1981	—	2.00	4.00
❏ 2334	Razzamatazz/Velas	1981	—	2.00	4.00

—Featuring Patti Austin

❏ 2357	Just Once/The Dude	1981	—	2.00	4.00

—Featuring James Ingram

Number	Title (A Side/B Side)	Yr	VG	VG+	NM
❏ 2387	One Hundred Ways/Velas	1981	—	2.00	4.00
—Featuring James Ingram					
❏ 2417	There's a Train Leavin'/Something Special	1981	—	2.00	4.00
—Featuring Patti Austin					
BELL					
❏ 832	I'm a Believer/The Time for Love Is Anytime	1969	—	3.00	6.00
❏ 833	Cactus Flower Theme/The Time for Love Is Anytime	1969	—	3.00	6.00
❏ 838	Bob & Carol & Ted & Alice/Giggle Grass	1969	—	3.00	6.00
COLGEMS					
❏ 66-1016	Hangin' Paper/Lonely Bottles	1968	2.00	4.00	8.00
IMPULSE					
❏ 206	Quintessence/For Lena and Lennie	1962	3.00	6.00	12.00
MERCURY					
❏ 71425	The Syncopated Clock/Tuxedo Junction	1959	3.00	6.00	12.00
❏ 71460	Choo Choo Ch-Boogie/Marchin' the Blues	1959	3.00	6.00	12.00
❏ 71489	Moanin'/The Preacher	1959	3.00	6.00	12.00
❏ 71546	Birth of a Band/Change of Pace	1959	3.00	6.00	12.00
❏ 71665	Love Is Here to Stay/Moonglow	1960	3.00	6.00	12.00
❏ 71737	G-Man Train/Pleasingly Plump	1960	3.00	6.00	12.00
❏ 71825	Mack the Knife/Hot Saki	1961	3.00	6.00	12.00
❏ 71940	St. Louis Blues/Twistin' Chicken	1962	3.00	6.00	12.00
❏ 72012	A Taste of Honey/Shagnasty	1962	3.00	6.00	12.00
❏ 72105	Boogie Bossa Nova/Morning of the Carnival	1963	2.50	5.00	10.00
❏ 72160	Jive Samba/Comin' Home Baby	1963	2.50	5.00	10.00
❏ 72289	Baby Elephant Walk/Mr. Lucky	1964	2.50	5.00	10.00
❏ 72306	Theme from "Golden Boy"/Sea Weed	1964	2.50	5.00	10.00
❏ 72348	A Hard Day's Night/Soul Serenade	1964	2.50	5.00	10.00
❏ 72423	Non-Stop to Brazil/Gentle Rain	1965	2.50	5.00	10.00
❏ 72436	The Pawnbroker/Harlem Drive	1965	2.50	5.00	10.00
❏ 72460	Mirage/Pack It Up	1965	2.50	5.00	10.00
❏ 72496	(I Can't Get No) Satisfaction/What's New Pussycat	1965	2.50	5.00	10.00
❏ 72533	Baby Cakes/Mohair Sam	1966	2.50	5.00	10.00
QWEST					
❏ 17528	Stomp (Frankie Knuckles Mix)/Stomp (Mousse T.'s Radio Mix)	1996	—	—	3.00
❏ 17673	Slow Jams (New Edit)/Slow Jams (Remix)	1996	—	—	3.00
—Featuring Babyface and Tamia with Portrait and Barry White					
❏ 19881	Tomorrow (A Better You, A Better Me)/ (Instrumental)	1990	—	—	3.00
—Featuring Tevin Campbell					
❏ 19992	The Secret Garden (Sweet Seduction Suite)/ (Instrumental)	1990	—	—	3.00
—With Al B. Sure!, James Ingram, El DeBarge and Barry White					
❏ 19992 [PS]	The Secret Garden (Sweet Seduction Suite)/ (Instrumental)	1990	—	—	3.00
❏ 22697	I'll Be Good to You/(Instrumental)	1990	—	—	3.00
—With Ray Charles and Chaka Khan					
❏ 22697 [PS]	I'll Be Good to You/(Instrumental)	1990	—	—	3.00
RCA VICTOR					
❏ 74-0221	Ole Turkey Buzzard/Soul Full of Gold	1969	—	3.00	6.00
REPRISE					
❏ 1072	Passin' the Buck/Money Runner	1972	—	2.50	5.00
UNI					
❏ 55142	The Lost Man/Main Squeeze	1969	—	3.00	6.00
UNITED ARTISTS					
❏ 50706	Call Me Mister Tibbs/Soul Flower	1970	—	2.50	5.00
Albums					
ABC					
❏ D-782 [(2)]	Mode	1973	3.00	6.00	12.00
ABC-PARAMOUNT					
❏ 149 [M]	This Is How I Feel About Jazz	1956	25.00	50.00	100.00
❏ 186 [M]	Go West, Man!	1957	25.00	50.00	100.00
ABC IMPULSE!					
❏ AS-11 [S]	The Quintessence	1968	3.75	7.50	15.00
❏ IA-9342 [(2)]	Quintessential Charts	1978	3.00	6.00	12.00
A&M					
❏ SP-3023	Walking in Space	1969	3.00	6.00	12.00
❏ SP-3030	Gula Matari	1970	3.00	6.00	12.00
❏ SP-3037	Smackwater Jack	1971	3.00	6.00	12.00
❏ SP-3041	You've Got It Bad Girl	1973	3.00	6.00	12.00
❏ SP-3191	Body Heat	1982	2.00	4.00	8.00
—Budget-line reissue					
❏ SP-3200	The Best	1982	2.00	4.00	8.00
❏ SP-3248	The Dude	198?	2.00	4.00	8.00
—Budget-line reissue					
❏ SP-3249	Sounds…And Stuff Like That!	198?	2.00	4.00	8.00
—Budget-line reissue					
❏ SP-3278	The Best, Vol. 2	1985	2.00	4.00	8.00
❏ SP-3617	Body Heat	1974	2.50	5.00	10.00
❏ SP-3705 [(2)]	I Heard That!!	1976	3.00	6.00	12.00
❏ SP-3721	The Dude	1981	2.50	5.00	10.00
❏ SP-4526	Mellow Madness	1975	2.50	5.00	10.00
❏ SP-4626	Roots	1977	2.50	5.00	10.00
❏ SP-4685	Sounds…And Stuff Like That!	1978	2.50	5.00	10.00
❏ SP-6507 [(2)]	I Heard That!!	198?	2.50	5.00	10.00
—Budget-line reissue					
❏ QU-53041 [Q]	You've Got It Bad Girl	1974	5.00	10.00	20.00
❏ QU-53617 [Q]	Body Heat	1974	5.00	10.00	20.00
❏ QU-54526 [Q]	Mellow Madness	1975	5.00	10.00	20.00
CHESS					
❏ CH-91562	The Music of Quincy Jones	198?	2.50	5.00	10.00

Number	Title (A Side/B Side)	Yr	VG	VG+	NM
COLGEMS					
❏ COM-107 [M]	In Cold Blood	1967	5.00	10.00	20.00
❏ COS-107 [S]	In Cold Blood	1967	6.25	12.50	25.00
EMARCY					
❏ MG-36083 [M]	Jazz Abroad	1956	25.00	50.00	100.00
❏ 818177-1 [(2)]	The Birth of a Band	1984	3.00	6.00	12.00
GRP/IMPULSE!					
❏ 222	The Quintessence	199?	3.75	7.50	15.00
—Reissue on audiophile vinyl					
IMPULSE!					
❏ A-11 [M]	The Quintessence	1962	7.50	15.00	30.00
❏ AS-11 [S]	The Quintessence	1962	10.00	20.00	40.00
LIBERTY					
❏ LOM-16004 [M]	Enter Laughing	1967	6.25	12.50	25.00
❏ LOS-17004 [S]	Enter Laughing	1967	7.50	15.00	30.00
MCA					
❏ 4145 [(2)]	Quintessential Charts	198?	2.50	5.00	10.00
—Reissue of ABC Impulse 9342					
❏ 5578	The Slugger's Wife	1985	3.00	6.00	12.00
MCA/IMPULSE!					
❏ 5728	The Quintessence	1986	2.00	4.00	8.00
MERCURY					
❏ SRM-2-623 [(2)]	Ndeda	1972	3.75	7.50	15.00
❏ PPS-2014 [M]	Around the World	1961	7.50	15.00	30.00
❏ PPS-6014 [S]	Around the World	1961	10.00	20.00	40.00
❏ MG-20444 [M]	Birth of a Band	1959	12.50	25.00	50.00
❏ MG-20561 [M]	The Great, Wide World of Quincy Jones	1960	12.50	25.00	50.00
❏ MG-20612 [M]	I Dig Dancers	1960	10.00	20.00	40.00
❏ MG-20653 [M]	Quincy Jones at Newport '61	1961	7.50	15.00	30.00
❏ MG-20751 [M]	Big Band Bossa Nova	1962	7.50	15.00	30.00
❏ MG-20799 [M]	Quincy Jones Plays Hip Hits	1963	7.50	15.00	30.00
❏ MG-20863 [M]	Quincy Jones Explores the Music of Henry Mancini	1964	5.00	10.00	20.00
❏ MG-20938 [M]	Golden Boy	1964	5.00	10.00	20.00
❏ MG-21011 [M]	The Pawnbroker	1964	5.00	10.00	20.00
❏ MG-21025 [M]	Mirage	1965	5.00	10.00	20.00
❏ MG-21050 [M]	Quincy Jones Plays for Pussycats	1965	5.00	10.00	20.00
❏ MG-21063 [M]	Quincy's Got a Brand New Bag	1965	5.00	10.00	20.00
❏ MG-21070 [M]	Slender Thread	1966	5.00	10.00	20.00
❏ SR-60129 [S]	Birth of a Band	1959	15.00	30.00	60.00
❏ SR-60221 [S]	The Great, Wide World of Quincy Jones	1960	15.00	30.00	60.00
❏ SR-60612 [S]	I Dig Dancers	1960	12.50	25.00	50.00
❏ SR-60653 [S]	Quincy Jones at Newport '61	1961	10.00	20.00	40.00
❏ SR-60751 [S]	Big Band Bossa Nova	1962	10.00	20.00	40.00
❏ SR-60799 [S]	Quincy Jones Plays Hip Hits	1963	10.00	20.00	40.00
❏ SR-60863 [S]	Quincy Jones Explores the Music of Henry Mancini	1964	6.25	12.50	25.00
❏ SR-60938 [S]	Golden Boy	1964	6.25	12.50	25.00
❏ SR-61011 [S]	The Pawnbroker	1964	6.25	12.50	25.00
❏ SR-61025 [S]	Mirage	1965	6.25	12.50	25.00
❏ SR-61050 [S]	Quincy Jones Plays for Pussycats	1965	6.25	12.50	25.00
❏ SR-61063 [S]	Quincy's Got a Brand New Bag	1965	6.25	12.50	25.00
❏ SR-61070 [S]	Slender Thread	1966	6.25	12.50	25.00
MOBILE FIDELITY					
❏ 1-078	You've Got It Bad Girl	1981	6.25	12.50	25.00
—Audiophile vinyl					
NAUTILUS					
❏ NR-52	The Dude	198?	10.00	20.00	40.00
—Audiophile vinyl					
PRESTIGE					
❏ PRLP-172 [10]	Quincy Jones with the Swedish-American All Stars	1953	50.00	100.00	200.00
QWEST					
❏ 25356 [(2)]	The Color Purple	1985	5.00	10.00	20.00
—Boxed set on purple vinyl					
❏ 25389 [(2)]	The Color Purple	1985	3.75	7.50	15.00
—Gatefold package on purple vinyl					
❏ 26020	Back on the Block	1989	3.00	6.00	12.00
TRIP					
❏ 5514	The Great Wide World of Quincy Jones	1974	2.00	4.00	8.00
❏ 5554	Live at Newport '61	197?	2.00	4.00	8.00
UNITED ARTISTS					
❏ UAS-5214	They Call Me Mister Tibbs	1970	6.25	12.50	25.00
WING					
❏ SRW-16398	Around the World	1969	3.00	6.00	12.00

JORDAN, JIMMY
See LONNIE JOHNSON.

JORDAN, LOUIS
45s

Number	Title (A Side/B Side)	Yr	VG	VG+	NM
ALADDIN					
❏ 45-3223	Whiskey, Do Your Stuff/Dad Gum Yo' Hide Boy	1954	7.50	15.00	30.00
❏ 45-3227	Ooh Wee!/I'll Die Happy	1954	7.50	15.00	30.00
❏ 45-3243	Hurry Home/A Dollar Down	1954	10.00	20.00	40.00
❏ 45-3246	Messy Bessie/I Seen Watcha Done	1954	7.50	15.00	30.00
❏ 45-3249	Louis' Blues/If I Had Any Sense I'd Go Back Home	1954	7.50	15.00	30.00
❏ 45-3264	Put Some Money in the Pot Boy/Yeah, Yeah, Baby	1954	7.50	15.00	30.00
❏ 45-3270	Fat Back and Corn Liquor/The Dripper	1955	7.50	15.00	30.00
❏ 45-3280	Gal, You Need a Whippin'/Time Is a-Passin'	1955	7.50	15.00	30.00
❏ 45-3295	It's Hard to Be Good Without You/Gotta Go	1955	7.50	15.00	30.00
DECCA					
❏ 9-27058	Onion/Psych-Loco	1950	7.50	15.00	30.00

J

Number	Title (A Side/B Side)	Yr	VG	VG+	NM
❑ 9-27114	Blue Light Boogie — Part 1/Part 2	1950	6.25	12.50	25.00
❑ 9-27129	Show Me How/I Want a Roof Over My Head	1950	6.25	12.50	25.00
❑ 9-27203	Tamburitza Boogie/Trouble Then Satisfaction	1950	6.25	12.50	25.00
❑ 9-27212	You Rascal You/Life Is So Peculiar	1950	6.25	12.50	25.00
❑ 9-27324	Lemonade/(You Dyed Your Hair) Chartreuse	1950	6.25	12.50	25.00
❑ 9-27428	Teardrops from My Eyes/It's a Great, Great Pleasure	1951	6.25	12.50	25.00
❑ 9-27547	Weak Minded Blues/Is My Pop In There?	1951	6.25	12.50	25.00
❑ 9-27620	I Can't Give You Anything But Love, Baby/You Will Always Have a Friend	1951	6.25	12.50	25.00
❑ 9-27648	If You're So Smart, How Come You Ain't Rich?/ How Blue Can You Get	1951	6.25	12.50	25.00
❑ 9-27694	Three Handed Woman/Please Don't Leave Me	1951	6.25	12.50	25.00
❑ 9-27784	Cock-a-Doodle-Doo/Trust in Me	1951	6.25	12.50	25.00
❑ 9-27806	May Every Day Be Christmas/Bone Dry	1951	6.25	12.50	25.00
❑ 9-27898	Lay Somethin' on the Bar/No Sale	1951	6.25	12.50	25.00
❑ 9-27969	Louisville Lodge Meeting/Work Baby Work	1952	5.00	10.00	20.00
❑ 9-28088	Never Trust a Woman/Slow Down	1952	5.00	10.00	20.00
❑ 9-28211	Azure-Te (Paris Blues)/Junco Partner	1952	5.00	10.00	20.00
❑ 9-28225	Jordan for President/Oil Well, Texas	1952	5.00	10.00	20.00
❑ 9-28335	All of Me/There Goes My Heart	1952	5.00	10.00	20.00
❑ 9-28444	You're Much Too Fat/Friendship	1952	5.00	10.00	20.00
❑ 9-28543	A Man's Best Friend Is a Bed/You Didn't Want Me Baby	1953	5.00	10.00	20.00
❑ 9-28664	It's Better to Wait for Love/Just Like a Butterfly	1953	5.00	10.00	20.00
❑ 9-28756	House Party/Hog Wash	1953	5.00	10.00	20.00
❑ 9-28820	Time Marches On/There Must Be a Way	1953	5.00	10.00	20.00
❑ 9-28883	You Know It Too/I Want You to Be My Baby	1953	5.00	10.00	20.00
❑ 9-28983	Fat Sam from Birmingham/The Soona Baby	1954	3.75	7.50	15.00
❑ 9-29018	Lollypop/Nobody Knows You When You're Down and Out	1954	3.75	7.50	15.00
❑ 9-29166	Only Yesterday/I Didn't Know What Time It Was	1954	3.75	7.50	15.00
❑ 9-29263	Wake Up Jacob/If It's True	1954	3.75	7.50	15.00
❑ 9-29424	Perdido/Locked Up	1955	3.75	7.50	15.00
❑ 9-29860	I Gotta Move/Everything That's Made of Wood	1956	3.75	7.50	15.00
❑ 9-30223	Run Joe/Time Marches On	1957	3.00	6.00	12.00
MERCURY					
❑ 70993x45	Cat Scratchin'/Big Bess	1956	3.75	7.50	15.00
❑ 71023x45	Ain't Nobody Here But Us Chickens/Choo Choo Ch'Boogie	1956	3.75	7.50	15.00
❑ 71052x45	Morning Light/Rock Dock	1957	5.00	10.00	20.00
❑ 71106x45	Fire/Ella Mae	1957	3.75	7.50	15.00
❑ 71206x45	Peace of Mind/I Never Had a Chance	1957	3.75	7.50	15.00
❑ 71319x45	Sweet Hunk of Junk/Wish I Could Make Some Money	1958	3.75	7.50	15.00
PZAZZ					
❑ 015	Santa Claus, Santa Claus/Sakatumi	1968	2.00	4.00	8.00
TANGERINE					
❑ 924	Texarkana Twist/You're My Mule	1962	2.50	5.00	10.00
❑ 926	Workin' Man/The Meeting	1962	2.50	5.00	10.00
❑ 930	Hardhead/You Never Know When a Cheating Woman Changes Her Mind	196?	2.50	5.00	10.00
❑ 933	Point of No Return/Don't Send Me No Flowers	196?	2.50	5.00	10.00
❑ 937	What'd I Say/Old Age	196?	2.50	5.00	10.00
❑ 942	Time Is Running Out/Troubadour	196?	2.50	5.00	10.00
❑ 947	Ain't Nobody Here But Us Chickens/Saturday Nite Fish Fry	196?	2.00	4.00	8.00
❑ 958	Comin' Down/65 Bars	196?	2.00	4.00	8.00
VIK					
❑ 4X-0192	Rock 'n' Roll Call/Baby, You're Just Too Much	1956	3.75	7.50	15.00
WARWICK					
❑ 583	Bills/Fifty Cents	1960	3.00	6.00	12.00
❑ 621	I See a Million People/I'm Going Home	1961	3.00	6.00	12.00
"X"					
❑ 4X-0116	Whatever Lola Wants/It's Been Said	1955	3.75	7.50	15.00
❑ 4X-0148	Bananas/Baby Let's Do It	1955	3.75	7.50	15.00
78s					
ALADDIN					
❑ 3223	Whiskey, Do Your Stuff/Dad Gum Yo' Hide Boy	1954	3.75	7.50	15.00
❑ 3227	Ooh Wee!/I'll Die Happy	1954	3.75	7.50	15.00
❑ 3243	Hurry Home/A Dollar Down	1954	5.00	10.00	20.00
❑ 3246	Messy Bessie/I Seen Watcha Done	1954	3.75	7.50	15.00
❑ 3249	Louis' Blues/If I Had Any Sense I'd Go Back Home	1954	3.75	7.50	15.00
❑ 3264	Put Some Money in the Pot Boy/Yeah, Yeah, Baby	1954	3.75	7.50	15.00
❑ 3270	Fat Back and Corn Liquor/The Dripper	1955	5.00	10.00	20.00
❑ 3279	Gal, You Need a Whippin'/Time Is a-Passin'	1955	5.00	10.00	20.00
❑ 3295	It's Hard to Be Good Without You/Gotta Go	1955	5.00	10.00	20.00
DECCA					
❑ 7556	Barnacle Bill the Sailor/Honey in the Bee Ball	1939	6.25	12.50	25.00
❑ 7590	Flat Face/Doug the Jitterbug	1939	6.25	12.50	25.00
❑ 7609	At the Swing Cats' Ball/Keep a-Knockin'	1939	6.25	12.50	25.00
❑ 7623	Sam Jones Done Snagged His Britches/Swingin' in the Cocoanut Trees	1939	6.25	12.50	25.00
❑ 7675	Honeysuckle Rose/But I'll Be Back	1940	5.00	10.00	20.00
❑ 7693	You Ain't Nowhere/Fore Day Blues	1940	5.00	10.00	20.00
❑ 7705	You Run Your Mouth and I'll Run My Business/ Hard Lovin' Blues	1940	5.00	10.00	20.00
❑ 7719	You're My Meat/Jake, What a Snake	1940	5.00	10.00	20.00
❑ 7723	June Tenth Jamboree/I'm Alabama Bound	1940	5.00	10.00	20.00
❑ 7729	You Got to Go When the Wagon Comes/After School Swing Session	1940	5.00	10.00	20.00
❑ 7745	Lovie Joe/Somebody Done Hoodooed the Hoodoo Man	1940	5.00	10.00	20.00

Number	Title (A Side/B Side)	Yr	VG	VG+	NM
❑ 7777	Never Let Your Left Hand Know/Penthouse in the Basement	1940	5.00	10.00	20.00
❑ 8500	Do You Call That a Buddy?/Pompton Turnpike	1940	5.00	10.00	20.00
❑ 8501	A Chicken Ain't Nothin' But a Bird/I Know You	1940	5.00	10.00	20.00
❑ 8525	Pinetop's Boogie Woogie/T-Bone Blues	1941	5.00	10.00	20.00
❑ 8537	The Two Little Squirrels/Pan-Pan	1941	5.00	10.00	20.00
❑ 8560	Brotherly Love/Saxa-Woogie	1941	5.00	10.00	20.00
❑ 8581	St. Vitus' Dance/The Boogie-Woogie Came to Town	1941	5.00	10.00	20.00
❑ 8593	Knock Me a Kiss/I'm Gonna Move to the Outskirts of Town	1942	5.00	10.00	20.00
❑ 8605	The Green Grass Grows All Around/How 'Bout That?	1942	5.00	10.00	20.00
❑ 8627	Small Town Boy/Mama Mama Blues	1942	5.00	10.00	20.00
❑ 8638	I'm Gonna Leave You on the Outskirts of Town/ It's a Low Down Dirty Shame	1942	5.00	10.00	20.00
❑ 8645	What's the Use of Getting Sober (When You Gonna Get Drunk Again)/The Chicks I Pick Are Slender and Tender and Tall	1942	5.00	10.00	20.00
❑ 8653	Five Guys Named Moe/That'll Just 'Bout Knock Me Out	1943	5.00	10.00	20.00
❑ 8654	Ration Blues/Deacon Jones	1943	5.00	10.00	20.00
❑ 8659	Is You Is or Is You Ain't (Ma' Baby)/G.I. Jive	1944	5.00	10.00	20.00
❑ 8668	Mop! Mop!/You Can't Get That No More	1945	3.75	7.50	15.00
❑ 8670	Caldonia/Somebody Done Changed the Lock on My Door	1945	6.25	12.50	25.00
❑ 18734	Buzz Me/Don't Worry 'Bout That Mule	1945	3.75	7.50	15.00
❑ 18762	Salt Pork, West Virginia/Reconversion Blues	1946	3.75	7.50	15.00
❑ 18818	Beware/Don't Let the Sun Catch You Cryin'	1946	3.75	7.50	15.00
❑ 23546	Stone Cold Dead in the Market/Petootie Pie	1946	3.75	7.50	15.00
❑ 23610	Choo Choo Ch' Boogie/That Chick's Too Young to Fry	1946	5.00	10.00	20.00
❑ 23628	Knock Me a Kiss/I'm Gonna Move to the Outskirts of Town	1946	3.00	6.00	12.00
❑ 23629	What's the Use of Getting Sober (When You Gonna Get Drunk Again)/The Chicks I Pick Are Slender and Tender and Tall	1946	3.00	6.00	12.00
❑ 23630	Is You Is or Is You Ain't (Ma' Baby)/Five Guys Named Moe	1946	3.00	6.00	12.00
❑ 23631	It's a Low Down Dirty Shame/Mama Mama Blues	1946	3.00	6.00	12.00
❑ 23669	Ain't That Just Like a Woman (They'll Do It Every Time)/If It's Love You Want Baby, That's Me	1946	3.75	7.50	15.00
❑ 23741	Ain't Nobody Here But Us Chickens/Let the Good Times Roll	1946	5.00	10.00	20.00
❑ 23810	Texas and Pacific/I Like 'Em Fat Like That	1947	3.75	7.50	15.00
❑ 23841	Open the Door, Richard!/It's So Easy	1947	3.75	7.50	15.00
❑ 23901	Jack, You're Dead/I Know What You're Puttin' Down	1947	3.75	7.50	15.00
❑ 23931	Beware/Don't Let the Sun Catch You Cryin'	1947	3.00	6.00	12.00
❑ 23932	Caldonia/Somebody Done Changed the Lock on My Door	1947	3.00	6.00	12.00
❑ 24104	Boogie Woogie Blue Plate/Sure Had a Wonderful Time	1947	3.75	7.50	15.00
❑ 24155	Early in the Mornin'/Look Out	1947	3.75	7.50	15.00
❑ 24300	Barnyard Boogie/How Long Must I Wait for You	1948	3.75	7.50	15.00
❑ 24381	Reet, Petite and Gone/Inflation Blues	1948	3.75	7.50	15.00
❑ 24448	Run Joe/All for the Love of Lil	1948	3.75	7.50	15.00
❑ 24483	Don't Burn the Candle at Both Ends/We Can't Agree	1948	3.75	7.50	15.00
❑ 24502	Daddy-O/You're on the Right Track Baby (But You're Goin' the Wrong Way)	1948	3.75	7.50	15.00
❑ 24527	Pettin' and Pokin'/Why'd You Do It Baby	1949	3.75	7.50	15.00
❑ 24571	Roamin' Blues/Have You Got the Gumption	1949	3.75	7.50	15.00
❑ 24587	You Broke Your Promise/Safe, Sane and Single	1949	3.75	7.50	15.00
❑ 24633	Cole Slaw (Sorghum Switch)/Every Man to His Own Profession	1949	3.75	7.50	15.00
❑ 24643	You Run Your House, I'll Run My Business/A Chicken Ain't Nothin' But a Bird	1949	3.75	7.50	15.00
❑ 24673	Beans and Corn Bread/Chicky-Mo Craney Cow	1949	3.75	7.50	15.00
❑ 24725	Saturday Night Fish Fry (Part I)/(Part II)	1949	10.00	20.00	40.00
❑ 24815	School Days/I Know What I've Got	1949	3.75	7.50	15.00
❑ 24877	Push Ka Pee Shee Pie/Hungry Man	1950	3.75	7.50	15.00
❑ 24981	Baby's Gonna Go Bye Bye/Heed My Warning	1950	3.75	7.50	15.00
❑ 25394	Pinetop's Boogie Woogie/Saxa-Woogie	1948	3.00	6.00	12.00
❑ 25473	Honeysuckle Rose/T-Bone Blues	1949	3.00	6.00	12.00
❑ 27058	Onion/Psych-Loco	1950	2.50	5.00	10.00
❑ 27114	Blue Light Boogie — Part 1/Part 2	1950	2.50	5.00	10.00
❑ 27129	Show Me How/I Want a Roof Over My Head	1950	2.50	5.00	10.00
❑ 27203	Tamburitza Boogie/Trouble Then Satisfaction	1950	2.50	5.00	10.00
❑ 27212	You Rascal You/Life Is So Peculiar	1950	2.50	5.00	10.00
❑ 27324	Lemonade/(You Dyed Your Hair) Chartreuse	1950	2.50	5.00	10.00
❑ 27428	Teardrops from My Eyes/It's a Great, Great Pleasure	1951	2.50	5.00	10.00
❑ 27547	Weak Minded Blues/Is My Pop In There?	1951	2.50	5.00	10.00
❑ 27620	I Can't Give You Anything But Love, Baby/You Will Always Have a Friend	1951	2.50	5.00	10.00
❑ 27648	If You're So Smart, How Come You Ain't Rich?/ How Blue Can You Get	1951	2.50	5.00	10.00
❑ 27694	Three Handed Woman/Please Don't Leave Me	1951	2.50	5.00	10.00
❑ 27784	Cock-a-Doodle-Doo/Trust in Me	1951	2.50	5.00	10.00
❑ 27806	May Every Day Be Christmas/Bone Dry	1951	2.50	5.00	10.00
❑ 27898	Lay Somethin' on the Bar/No Sale	1951	2.50	5.00	10.00
❑ 27969	Louisville Lodge Meeting/Work Baby Work	1952	2.50	5.00	10.00
❑ 28088	Never Trust a Woman/Slow Down	1952	2.50	5.00	10.00
❑ 28211 [PS]	Azure-Te (Paris Blues)/Junco Partner	1952	2.50	5.00	10.00
❑ 28225	Jordan for President/Oil Well, Texas	1952	2.50	5.00	10.00

The original cover of Little Willie John's *Fever* LP shows a picture of a nurse with a thermometer. This was eventually changed to a cover with no such photo on it.

Mable John, Little Willie John's sister, had a Top 10 R&B hit for Stax in 1966. Before that, she recorded for Tamla without success. This was one of those flop 45s.

Though he began recording in 1926, Lonnie Johnson didn't finally taste mainstream success until "Tomorrow Night" in 1948. King, the label for which he had his big hit, began releasing LPs of his material in the 1950s; this is one of them.

Marv Johnson's third and final album for United Artists was this collection of sacred songs. It is quite difficult to find, especially in stereo.

Jimmy Jones' MGM album contains both of his big hits, "Handy Man" and the title song, "Good Timin'."

Louis Jordan's records spent 113 weeks atop the *Billboard* R&B singles charts, a record by far. This album, released in 1957 on the Score label, is his most valuable.

Number	Title (A Side/B Side)	Yr	VG	VG+	NM
❏ 28335	All of Me/There Goes My Heart	1952	2.50	5.00	10.00
❏ 28444	You're Much Too Fat/Friendship	1952	2.50	5.00	10.00
❏ 28543	A Man's Best Friend Is a Bed/You Didn't Want Me Baby	1953	2.50	5.00	10.00
❏ 28664	It's Better to Wait for Love/Just Like a Butterfly	1953	2.50	5.00	10.00
❏ 28756	House Party/Hog Wash	1953	2.50	5.00	10.00
❏ 28820	Time Marches On/There Must Be a Way	1953	2.50	5.00	10.00
❏ 28883	You Know It Too/I Want You to Be My Baby	1953	2.50	5.00	10.00
❏ 28983	Fat Sam from Birmingham/The Soona Baby	1954	2.50	5.00	10.00
❏ 29018	Lollypop/Nobody Knows You When You're Down and Out	1954	2.50	5.00	10.00
❏ 29166	Only Yesterday/I Didn't Know What Time It Was	1954	2.50	5.00	10.00
❏ 29263	Wake Up Jacob/If It's True	1954	2.50	5.00	10.00
❏ 29424	Perdido/Locked Up	1955	2.50	5.00	10.00
❏ 29860	I Gotta Move/Everything That's Made of Wood	1956	3.00	6.00	12.00
❏ 30223	Run Joe/Time Marches On	1957	3.75	7.50	15.00

Albums

CIRCLE

Number	Title (A Side/B Side)	Yr	VG	VG+	NM
❏ 53	Louis Jordan and the Tympany Five: 1944-45	198?	2.50	5.00	10.00
❏ 97	More Louis Jordan and His Tympany Five	198?	2.50	5.00	10.00

CLASSIC JAZZ

Number	Title (A Side/B Side)	Yr	VG	VG+	NM
❏ 148	I Believe in Music	198?	3.00	6.00	12.00

DECCA

Number	Title (A Side/B Side)	Yr	VG	VG+	NM
❏ DL 5035 [M]	Greatest Hits	1968	7.50	15.00	30.00
❏ DL 8551 [M]	Let the Good Times Roll	1958	25.00	50.00	100.00
—Black label, silver print					
❏ DL 75035 [R]	Greatest Hits	1968	3.75	7.50	15.00

MCA

Number	Title (A Side/B Side)	Yr	VG	VG+	NM
❏ 274	Greatest Hits	197?	2.50	5.00	10.00
❏ 1337	Greatest Hits, Vol. 2	198?	2.50	5.00	10.00
❏ 4079 [(2)]	The Best of Louis Jordan	197?	3.00	6.00	12.00

MERCURY

Number	Title (A Side/B Side)	Yr	VG	VG+	NM
❏ MG-20242 [M]	Somebody Up There Digs Me	1957	30.00	60.00	120.00
❏ MG-20331 [M]	Man, We're Wailin'	1958	30.00	60.00	120.00

SCORE

Number	Title (A Side/B Side)	Yr	VG	VG+	NM
❏ SLP-4007 [M]	Go Blow Your Horn	1957	50.00	100.00	200.00

TANGERINE

Number	Title (A Side/B Side)	Yr	VG	VG+	NM
❏ 1503 [M]	Hallelujah	1964	5.00	10.00	20.00
❏ S-1503 [S]	Hallelujah	1964	6.25	12.50	25.00

WING

Number	Title (A Side/B Side)	Yr	VG	VG+	NM
❏ MGW-12126 [M]	Somebody Up There Digs Me	1962	6.25	12.50	25.00

JOSEPH, MARGIE

12-Inch Singles

H.C.R.C.

Number	Title (A Side/B Side)	Yr	VG	VG+	NM
❏ 03338	Knockout (Part 1)/Knockout (Part 2)	1982	2.00	4.00	8.00

45s

ATLANTIC

Number	Title (A Side/B Side)	Yr	VG	VG+	NM
❏ 2907	Born to Wander/Let's Go Somewhere and Love	1972	—	2.50	5.00
❏ 2933	Touch Your Woman/I'm So Glad I'm Your Woman	1973	—	2.50	5.00
❏ 2954	Let's Stay Together/I'd Rather Go Blind	1973	—	2.50	5.00
❏ 2988	Come Lay Some Lovin' on Me/Ridin' High	1973	—	2.50	5.00
❏ 3032	My Love/Sweet Surrender	1974	—	2.50	5.00
❏ 3220	Words (Are Impossible)/I Still Love You	1974	—	2.50	5.00
❏ 3269	I Can't Move No Mountains/Just As Soon As the Feeling's Over	1975	—	2.50	5.00
❏ 3290	Stay Still/Just As Soon As the Feeling's Over	1975	—	2.50	5.00
❏ 3445	Come On Back to Me Lover/He Came Into My Life	1978	—	2.00	4.00
❏ 3509	I Feel His Love Getting Stronger/How Will I Know	1978	—	2.00	4.00
❏ 3525	I Don't Want to Get Over You/Love Takes Tears	1978	—	2.00	4.00

COTILLION

Number	Title (A Side/B Side)	Yr	VG	VG+	NM
❏ 44201	Hear the Words, Feel the Feeling/I Get Carried Away	1976	—	2.00	4.00
❏ 44207	Don't Turn the Lights Off/All Cried Out	1976	—	2.00	4.00
❏ 99737	Big Strong Man/(B-side unknown)	1984	—	2.00	4.00
❏ 99771	Ready for the Night/(B-side unknown)	1984	—	2.00	4.00

H.C.R.C.

Number	Title (A Side/B Side)	Yr	VG	VG+	NM
❏ 03337	Knockout (Part 1)/Knockout (Part 2)	1982	—	2.00	4.00

VOLT

Number	Title (A Side/B Side)	Yr	VG	VG+	NM
❏ 4012	One More Chance/Never Can You Be	1969	2.00	4.00	8.00
❏ 4023	What You Gonna Do/Nobody	1969	2.00	4.00	8.00
❏ 4037	Your Sweet Lovin'/What's Wrong Baby	1970	—	3.00	6.00
❏ 4046	Punish Me/A Sweeter Tomorrow	1970	—	3.00	6.00
❏ 4056	Stop! In the Name of Love/Make Me Believe You'll Stay	1971	—	3.00	6.00
❏ 4061	The Other Woman Got My Man and Gone/I'll Always Love You	1971	—	3.00	6.00

Albums

ATLANTIC

Number	Title (A Side/B Side)	Yr	VG	VG+	NM
❏ SD 7248	Margie Joseph	1973	3.00	6.00	12.00
❏ SD 7277	Sweet Surrender	1974	3.00	6.00	12.00
❏ SD 18126	Margie	1975	3.00	6.00	12.00
❏ SD 19182	Feeling My Way	1978	2.50	5.00	10.00

COTILLION

Number	Title (A Side/B Side)	Yr	VG	VG+	NM
❏ SD 9906	Hear the Words, Feel the Feeling	1976	3.00	6.00	12.00

H.C.R.C.

Number	Title (A Side/B Side)	Yr	VG	VG+	NM
❏ 20009	Knockout	1983	2.50	5.00	10.00

VOLT

Number	Title (A Side/B Side)	Yr	VG	VG+	NM
❏ VOS-6012	Margie Joseph Makes a New Impression	1971	7.50	15.00	30.00
❏ VOS-6016	Phase II	1971	7.50	15.00	30.00

JOSEPH, MARGIE, AND BLUE MAGIC
Also see each artist's individual listings.

45s

ATCO/WMOT

Number	Title (A Side/B Side)	Yr	VG	VG+	NM
❏ 7030	What's Come Over Me/You and Me (Got a Good Thing Goin')	1975	—	2.50	5.00

JOSIE AND THE PUSSYCATS
Also see PATRICE HOLLOWAY.

45s

CAPITOL

Number	Title (A Side/B Side)	Yr	VG	VG+	NM
❏ CP 58-1	Letter to Mama/Inside, Outside, Upside Down	1970	5.00	10.00	20.00
❏ CP 58-1 [PS]	Letter to Mama/Inside, Outside, Upside Down	1970	7.50	15.00	30.00
❏ CP 59-2	With Every Beat of My Heart/Josie	1970	5.00	10.00	20.00
❏ CP 59-2 [PS]	With Every Beat of My Heart/Josie	1970	7.50	15.00	30.00
❏ CP 60-3	Voodoo/If That Isn't Love	1970	5.00	10.00	20.00
❏ CP 60-3 [PS]	Voodoo/If That Isn't Love	1970	7.50	15.00	30.00
❏ CP 61-4	I Wanna Make You Happy/It's Gotta Be Him	1970	5.00	10.00	20.00
❏ CP 61-4 [PS]	I Wanna Make You Happy/It's Gotta Be Him	1970	7.50	15.00	30.00
❏ 2967	Every Beat of My Heart/It's All Right with Me	1970	5.00	10.00	20.00
—Same song as CP 59, but a slightly different title and a mono mix					
❏ 3045	Stop, Look and Listen/You've Come a Long Way, Baby	1971	5.00	10.00	20.00

JOYTONES, THE

45s

RAMA

Number	Title (A Side/B Side)	Yr	VG	VG+	NM
❏ 191	All My Love Belongs to You/You Just Won't Treat Me Right	1956	37.50	75.00	150.00
❏ 202	Gee What a Boy/Is This Really the End	1956	75.00	150.00	300.00
❏ 215	My Foolish Heart/Jimbo Jango	1956	125.00	250.00	500.00

JULIAN, DON, AND THE MEADOWLARKS
Also see THE LARKS.

45s

CLASSIC ARTISTS

Number	Title (A Side/B Side)	Yr	VG	VG+	NM
❏ 101	Quickie Wedding/Our Love	1988	—	2.00	4.00
❏ 105	White Christmas/Marry Christmas, Baby	1988	—	3.00	6.00

DOOTO

Number	Title (A Side/B Side)	Yr	VG	VG+	NM
❏ 424	Blue Moon/Big Mama Wants to Rock	1957	12.50	25.00	50.00

DOOTONE

Number	Title (A Side/B Side)	Yr	VG	VG+	NM
❏ 359	Heaven and Paradise/Embarrassing Moments	1955	75.00	150.00	300.00
❏ 367	Always and Always/I Got Tore Up	1955	18.75	37.50	75.00
—Red label					
❏ 367	Always and Always/I Got Tore Up	1955	12.50	25.00	50.00
—Maroon label					
❏ 372	This Must Be Paradise/Mine All Mine	1955	15.00	30.00	60.00
❏ 394	Please Love a Fool/Oop Boopy Oop	1956	12.50	25.00	50.00
❏ 405	I Am a Believer/Boogie Woogie Teenager	1956	20.00	40.00	80.00

DYNAMITE

Number	Title (A Side/B Side)	Yr	VG	VG+	NM
❏ 1112	Heaven Only Knows/Popeye	1962	7.50	15.00	30.00

ORIGINAL SOUND

Number	Title (A Side/B Side)	Yr	VG	VG+	NM
❏ 3	Please Say You Want Me/Doin' the Cha Cha Cha	1959	10.00	20.00	40.00
❏ 12	There's a Girl/Blue Moon	1960	7.50	15.00	30.00

RPM

Number	Title (A Side/B Side)	Yr	VG	VG+	NM
❏ 399	Love Only You/Real Pretty Mama	1954	75.00	150.00	300.00
—As "The Meadow Larks"					
❏ 406	LSMFT Blues (Lord Find My Sweet Theresa)/Pass the Gin	1954	750.00	1500.	3000
—As "The Meadow Larks"					

7-Inch Extended Plays

DOOTO

Number	Title (A Side/B Side)	Yr	VG	VG+	NM
❏ 203	(contents unknown)	1958	50.00	100.00	200.00
❏ 203 [PS]	Don Julian and the Meadowlarks	1958	50.00	100.00	200.00
—Reissue of Dootone 203					

DOOTONE

Number	Title (A Side/B Side)	Yr	VG	VG+	NM
❏ 203	(contents unknown)	1956	100.00	200.00	400.00
❏ 203 [PS]	Don Julian and the Meadowlarks	1956	100.00	200.00	400.00

Number	Title (A Side/B Side)	Yr	VG	VG+	NM

K

K.C. AND THE SUNSHINE BAND
Includes K.C. as a solo performer.
12-Inch Singles
EPIC

Number	Title (A Side/B Side)	Yr	VG	VG+	NM
❏ 03187	(You Said) You'd Gimme Some More (7:33)/ (Instrumental)	1982	2.00	4.00	8.00

SUNSHINE SOUND

❏ 207	Do You Wanna Go Party (7:27) (10:00)	1979	2.00	4.00	8.00

45s
CASABLANCA

❏ 2227	Yes I'm Ready/With Your Love	1979	—	2.00	4.00
—As "Teri DeSario with K.C."					
❏ 2278	Dancin' in the Streets/Moonlight Madness	1980	—	2.00	4.00
—As "Teri DeSario with K.C."					
❏ 812991-7	Yes I'm Ready/Dancin' in the Streets	1983	—	2.00	4.00
—As "Teri DeSario with K.C."; reissue					

EPIC

❏ 03286	When You Dance to the Music/(You Said) You'd Gimme Some More	1982	—	2.00	4.00
❏ 03356	On the Line/Don't Run	1983	—	2.00	4.00
—B-side features Teri DeSario					

MECA

❏ 1001	Give It Up/(Instrumental)	1983	—	2.00	4.00
—K.C. solo					

SUNSHINE SOUND

❏ 02545	Love Me/Don't Say No	1981	—	2.00	4.00
❏ 02652	It Happens Every Night/Stand Up	1981	—	2.00	4.00

T.K.

❏ 1001	Blow Your Whistle/I'm Going to Do Something Good to You	1973		2.50	5.00
—As "K.C. and the Sunshine Junkanoo Band"					
❏ 1003	Sound Your Funky Horn/Why Don't We Get Together	1974	—	2.50	5.00
❏ 1005	Queen of Clubs/Do It Good	1974	—	2.50	5.00
❏ 1008	I'm a Pushover/You Don't Know	1974	—	2.50	5.00
❏ 1009	Get Down Tonight/You Don't Know	1975	—	2.00	4.00
❏ 1010	Shotgun Shuffle/Hey J	1975	—	2.00	4.00
—As "The Sunshine Band"					
❏ 1015	That's the Way (I Like It)/What Makes You Happy	1975	—	2.00	4.00
❏ 1018	Rock Your Baby/S.O.S.	1976	—	2.00	4.00
—As "The Sunshine Band"					
❏ 1019	(Shake, Shake, Shake) Shake Your Booty/ Boogie Shoes	1976	—	2.00	4.00
❏ 1020	I Like to Do It/Come On In	1976	—	2.00	4.00
❏ 1022	I'm Your Boogie Man/Wrap Your Arms Around Me	1977	—	2.00	4.00
❏ 1023	Keep It Comin' Love/Baby I Love You	1977	—	2.00	4.00
❏ 1023 [PS]	Keep It Comin' Love/Baby I Love You	1977	—	2.50	5.00
❏ 1025	Boogie Shoes/I Get Lifted	1978	—	2.00	4.00
❏ 1025 [PS]	Boogie Shoes/I Get Lifted	1978	—	3.00	6.00
❏ 1026	Black Water Gold (Part 1)/Black Water Gold (Part 2)	1978	—	2.00	4.00
—As "The Sunshine Band"					
❏ 1028	It's the Same Old Song/Let's Go Party	1978	—	2.00	4.00
❏ 1028 [PS]	It's the Same Old Song/Let's Go Party	1978	—	2.00	4.00
❏ 1030	Do You Feel All Right/I Will Love You Tomorrow	1978	—	2.00	4.00
❏ 1030 [PS]	Do You Feel All Right/I Will Love You Tomorrow	1978	—	2.00	4.00
❏ 1031	Who Do Ya Love/Sho-Nuff	1978	—	2.00	4.00
❏ 1031 [PS]	Who Do Ya Love/Sho-Nuff	1978	—	2.00	4.00
❏ 1033	Do You Wanna Go Party/Come to My Island	1979	—	2.00	4.00
❏ 1035	Please Don't Go/I Betcha Didn't Know That	1979	—	2.00	4.00
❏ 1036	Let's Go Rock and Roll/I've Got the Feeling	1980	—	2.00	4.00
❏ 1037	Que Pasa?/Por Favor No Te Vayas	1980	—	2.00	4.00
❏ 1038	Make Me a Star/Do Me	1980	—	2.00	4.00
—K.C. solo					
❏ 1044	Space Cadet/Do Me	1981	—	2.00	4.00
—K.C. solo					
❏ 1048	Redlight/I Don't Wanna Make Love	1982	—	2.00	4.00
—K.C. solo					

Albums
EPIC

❏ FE 37490	The Painter	1981	2.50	5.00	10.00
❏ PE 37490	The Painter	1982	2.00	4.00	8.00
—Budget-line reissue					
❏ FE 38073	All in a Night's Work	1982	2.50	5.00	10.00
❏ PE 38073	All in a Night's Work	1984	2.00	4.00	8.00
—Budget-line reissue					

MECA

❏ 8301	KC Ten	1984	2.50	5.00	10.00

SUNSHINE SOUND

❏ 614	Space Cadet/Solo Flight	1981	2.50	5.00	10.00

T.K.

❏ 500	Do It Good	1974	3.00	6.00	12.00
❏ 603	K.C. and the Sunshine Band	1975	2.50	5.00	10.00
❏ 604	The Sound of Sunshine	1975	2.50	5.00	10.00
—By "The Sunshine Band" (all instrumental)					
❏ 605	Part 3	1976	2.50	5.00	10.00
❏ 607	Who Do Ya (Love)	1978	2.50	5.00	10.00
❏ 611	Do You Wanna Go Party	1979	2.50	5.00	10.00
❏ 612	Greatest Hits	1980	2.50	5.00	10.00

K.C. AND THE SUNSHINE BAND AND KOOL & THE GANG FEATURING JT TAYLOR
45s
EMI-CAPITOL

❏ S7-19725	Casper, the Friendly Ghost/Delicious	1997	—	—	3.00
—B-side by Shampoo					

K-DOE, ERNIE
45s
DUKE

❏ 378	My Mother-in-Law (Is In My Hair Again)/Looking Into the Future	1964	2.00	4.00	8.00
❏ 387	Little Bit of Everything/Someone	1965	2.00	4.00	8.00
❏ 400	Please Don't Stop/Boomerang	1966	2.00	4.00	8.00
❏ 404	Little Marie/Somebody Told Me	1966	2.00	4.00	8.00
❏ 411	Later for Tomorrow/Dancin' Man	1966	2.00	4.00	8.00
❏ 420	Love Me Like I Wanna/Don't Kill My Groove	1967	2.00	4.00	8.00
❏ 423	(It Will Have to Do) Until the Real Thing Comes Along/Little Marie	1967	2.00	4.00	8.00
❏ 437	Gotta Pack My Bag/How Sweet You Are	1968	2.00	4.00	8.00
❏ 450	I'm Sorry/Trying to Make You Love Me	1969	2.00	4.00	8.00
❏ 456	I'll Make Everything Be Alright/Wishing in Vain	1969	2.00	4.00	8.00

EMBER

❏ 1050	My Love for You/Tuff-Enuff	1959	6.25	12.50	25.00
❏ 1075	My Love for You/Shirley's Tuff	1961	3.75	7.50	15.00

INSTANT

❏ 3260	Baby, SInce I Met You/Sufferin' So	1963	2.50	5.00	10.00
❏ 3264	Reaping What I Sow/Talking Out of My Head	1964	2.50	5.00	10.00

ISLAND

❏ 031	Let Me Love You/So Good	1975	—	3.00	6.00

JANUS

❏ 167	Here Come the Girls/Long Way Home	1971	—	3.00	6.00

MINIT

❏ 604	Make You Love Me/There's a Will, There's a Way	1959	7.50	15.00	30.00
❏ 614	'Tain't It the Truth/Hello My Lover	1960	5.00	10.00	20.00
❏ 623	Mother-in-Law/Wanted, $10,000 Reward	1961	6.25	12.50	25.00
—Side 1 is at the correct speed. Trail-off number is "SO-738-2"					
❏ 623	Mother-in-Law/Wanted, $10,000 Reward	1961	50.00	100.00	200.00
—Side 1 was accidentally mis-mastered at 33 1/3 rpm. Trail-off number is "45-SO-738"					
❏ 627	Te-Ta-Te-Ta-Ta/Real Man	1961	3.75	7.50	15.00
❏ 634	A Certain Girl/I Cried My Last Tear	1961	3.75	7.50	15.00
❏ 641	Popeye Joe/Come On Home	1962	3.75	7.50	15.00
❏ 645	Hey Hey/Love You the Best	1962	3.75	7.50	15.00
❏ 651	Beating Like a Tom-Tom/I Got to Find Somebody	1962	3.75	7.50	15.00
❏ 656	Loving You/Get Out of My House	1962	3.75	7.50	15.00
❏ 661	Easier Said Than Done/Be Sweet	1963	3.75	7.50	15.00
❏ 665	I'm the Boss/Pennies Worth o' Happiness	1963	3.75	7.50	15.00
❏ 32042	Real Man/Te Ta Te Ta Ta	1968	2.50	5.00	10.00

SANSU

❏ 1006	Stoop Down/(B-side unknown)	197?	5.00	10.00	20.00
❏ 1016	Hotcha Mama/She Gave It All to Me	197?	5.00	10.00	20.00

SPECIALTY

❏ 563	Eternity/Do Baby Do	1955	10.00	20.00	40.00
—As "Ernest Kador"					

UNITED ARTISTS

❏ 0110	Mother-in-Law/A Wonderful Dream	1973	—	2.50	5.00
—"Silver Spotlight Series" reissue; B-side by the Majors					

Albums
JANUS

❏ JLS-3030	Ernie K-Doe	1971	6.25	12.50	25.00

MINIT

❏ LP-0002 [M]	Mother-in-Law	1961	50.00	100.00	200.00
—Orange label					
❏ LP-24002 [R]	Mother-in-Law	196?	37.50	75.00	150.00
—Black label, not issued until after Imperial bought Minit					

KAY-GEES, THE
45s
DELITE

❏ 903	Kilowatt/Kilowatt Invasion	1978	—	2.00	4.00
❏ 906	Cheek to Cheek/Tango Hustle	1978	—	2.00	4.00
❏ 913	Heavenly Love/Burn Me Up	1979	—	2.00	4.00

GANG

❏ 321	You've Got to Keep On Bumpin' (Pt 1)/You've Got to Keep On Bumpin' (Pt 2)	1974	—	2.50	5.00
❏ 1322	Master Plan/(B-side unknown)	1974	—	2.50	5.00
❏ 1323	Get Down/My Favorite Song	1975	—	2.50	5.00
❏ 1325	Hustle Wit Every Muscle (Theme from "Party" TV Show)/(Instrumental)	1975	—	2.50	5.00
❏ 1326	Waiting at the Bus Stop (Part 1)/Waiting at the Bus Stop (Part 2)	1976	—	2.50	5.00

Albums
DE-LITE

❏ 9505	Kilowatt	1978	2.50	5.00	10.00
❏ 9510	Burn Me Up	1979	2.50	5.00	10.00

GANG

❏ 101	Keep On Bumpin' & Masterplan	1975	2.50	5.00	10.00
❏ 102	Find a Friend	1975	2.50	5.00	10.00

KELLY, R.

12-Inch Singles

JIVE

Number	Title (A Side/B Side)	Yr	VG	VG+	NM
❑ 42030	Honey Love (Nobody's Home Mix) (Midnight Mix) (Sensuous Mix) (Radio Fade)	1992	3.75	7.50	15.00
❑ 42185	Sex Me (Parts 1 and 2) (4 versions)/Born Into the 90's (Remix)	1993	3.00	6.00	12.00
❑ 42206	Bump N' Grind (4 versions)/Definition of a Hotti	1994	3.75	7.50	15.00
❑ 42343	You Remind Me of Something (Vocal) (Instrumental)	1995	2.50	5.00	10.00
❑ 42427	I Believe I Can Fly (LP Version) (Radio Edit) (Instrumental)/Hump Bounce/Religious Love/I Can't Sleep Baby (If I) (Remix Radio-Video Version)	1996	2.00	4.00	8.00
❑ 42484	Gotham City (LP Version) (Acapella/Music) (Instrumental)/(Remix) (Remix Radio) (Remix Instrumental)	1997	2.50	5.00	10.00
❑ 42540	Half on a Baby (Radio Version) (Instrumental) (Extended Video Version)	1998	2.00	4.00	8.00
❑ 42566	Half on a Baby (3 versions)	1998	2.00	4.00	8.00
❑ 42600	Did You Ever Think (Vocal) (Instrumental) (Edit) (Acappella)	1998	2.50	5.00	10.00
❑ 42604	Did You Ever Think (Remix) (Remix Instrumental) (LP Version) (LP Instrumental)/Home Alone	1999	2.00	4.00	8.00
❑ 42640	If I Could Turn Back the Hands of Time (unknown versions)	1999	2.00	4.00	8.00
❑ 42740	I Wish (unknown versions)	2000	2.00	4.00	8.00
❑ 42755	I Wish (To the Homies That We Lost) (Clean) (Uncensored) (Radio Edit) (LP Version)	2000	2.00	4.00	8.00
❑ 42877	Fiesta (Remix Featuring Jay-Z Clean) (Remix Featuring Jay-Z Street) (Remix Featuring Jay-Z Instrumental) (Clean LP Version) (Street LP Version) (Instrumental LP Version)	2001	2.00	4.00	8.00
❑ 42946	Feelin' On Yo Booty (6 versions)	2001	2.00	4.00	8.00

45s

JIVE

Number	Title (A Side/B Side)	Yr	VG	VG+	NM
❑ 42373	Down Low (Nobody Has to Know)/I Can't Sleep Baby (If I)	1996	—	—	3.00
❑ 42422	I Believe I Can Fly/Religious Love	1996	—	—	3.00
❑ 42473	Gotham City (LP Version)/Gotham City (Acapella/Music)	1997	—	—	3.00
❑ 42623	If I Could Turn Back the Hands of Time/Dancing with a Rich Man	1999	—	—	3.00
❑ 42744	I Wish (Cleanest Edit) (same on both sides)	2000	—	—	3.00

Albums

JIVE

Number	Title (A Side/B Side)	Yr	VG	VG+	NM
❑ 41579 [(2)]	R. Kelly	1995	3.75	7.50	15.00
❑ 41625 [(3)]	R.	1998	5.00	10.00	20.00
❑ 41748 [(2)]	TP-2.com	2000	3.75	7.50	15.00

KELLY, R., AND CELINE DION

45s

JIVE

Number	Title (A Side/B Side)	Yr	VG	VG+	NM
❑ 42557	I'm Your Angel (same on both sides)	1998	—	—	3.00

KENDRICK, NAT, AND THE SWANS

James Brown's backing band, later known as the J.B.'s. Also see FRED WESLEY.

45s

DADE

Number	Title (A Side/B Side)	Yr	VG	VG+	NM
❑ 1804	(Do the) Mashed Potatoes (Part 1)/(Do the) Mashed Potatoes (Part 2)	1959	3.75	7.50	15.00
❑ 1808	Dish Rag (Part 1)/Dish Rag (Part 2)	1960	3.75	7.50	15.00
❑ 1812	Hot Chili/Slow Down	1960	3.75	7.50	15.00
❑ 5003	Wobble Wobble (Part 1)/Wobble Wobble (Part 2)	1961	3.75	7.50	15.00
❑ 5004	(Do the) Mashed Potatoes (Part 1)/(Do the) Mashed Potatoes (Part 2)	1961	3.00	6.00	12.00

KENDRICKS, EDDIE

Also see DARYL HALL AND JOHN OATES; DAVID RUFFIN AND EDDIE KENDRICK; THE TEMPTATIONS.

12-Inch Singles

Number	Title (A Side/B Side)	Yr	VG	VG+	NM
ARISTA					
❑ SP-15 [DJ]	Ain't No Smoke Without Fire (5:58)/Whip (5:05)	1978	3.00	6.00	12.00
CORNER STONE					
❑ 3001	Surprise Attack (3 versions)	1984	2.00	4.00	8.00

45s

Number	Title (A Side/B Side)	Yr	VG	VG+	NM
ARISTA					
❑ 0325	Ain't No Smoke Without Fire/Love, Love, Love	1978	—	2.00	4.00
❑ 0346	The Best of Strangers Now/Don't Underestimate the Power of Love	1978	—	2.00	4.00
❑ 0466	I Just Want to Be the One in Your Life/I Can't Let You Walk Away	1979	—	2.00	4.00
❑ 0500	Your Love Has Been So Good/I Never Used to Dance	1980	—	2.00	4.00
ATLANTIC					
❑ 3796	Looking for Love/Need Your Lovin'	1981	—	2.00	4.00
❑ 3874 [DJ]	I Don't Need Nobody Else (same on both sides)	1981	—	2.50	5.00
—May be promo only					
CORNER STONE					
❑ 1001	Surprise Attack/(B-side unknown)	1984	—	2.00	4.00
TAMLA					
❑ 54203	It's So Hard for Me to Say Good-Bye/This Used to Be the Home of Johnnie Mae	1971	—	2.50	5.00
❑ 54210	Can I/I Did It All for You	1971	—	2.50	5.00
❑ 54218	Eddie's Love/Let Me Run Into Your Lonely Heart	1972	—	2.50	5.00
❑ 54222	If You Let Me/Just Memories	1972	—	2.50	5.00
❑ 54230	Girl You Need a Change of Mind (Part 1)/Girl You Need a Change of Mind (Part 2)	1973	—	2.50	5.00
❑ 54236	Darling Come Back Home/Loving You the Second Time Around	1973	—	2.50	5.00
❑ 54238	Keep On Truckin' (Part 1)/Keep On Truckin' (Part 2)	1973	—	2.50	5.00
❑ 54243	Boogie Down/Can't Help What I Am	1974	—	2.50	5.00
❑ 54247	Son of Sagittarius/Trust Your Heart	1974	—	2.50	5.00
❑ 54249	Tell Her Love Has Felt the Need/Loving You the Second Time Around	1974	—	2.50	5.00
❑ 54255	One Tear/The Thin Man	1974	—	2.50	5.00
❑ 54257	Shoeshine Boy/Hooked on Your Love	1975	—	2.50	5.00
❑ 54260	Get the Cream Off the Top/Honey Brown	1975	—	2.50	5.00
❑ 54263	Happy/Deep and Quiet Love	1975	—	2.50	5.00
❑ 54266	He's a Friend/All of My Life	1976	—	2.50	5.00
❑ 54266 [DJ]	He's a Friend (stereo/mono)	1976	3.75	7.50	15.00
—Promo only on red vinyl					
❑ 54270	Get It While It's Hot/Never Gonna Leave You	1976	—	2.50	5.00
❑ 54277	Goin' Up in Smoke/Thanks for the Memories	1976	—	2.50	5.00
❑ 54285	Date with the Rain/Born Again	1977	—	2.50	5.00
❑ 54289	Baby/I Want to Live (My Life with You)	1977	—	—	—
—Unreleased					
❑ 54290	Baby/Intimate Friends	1977	—	2.50	5.00

Albums

Number	Title (A Side/B Side)	Yr	VG	VG+	NM
ARISTA					
❑ AB 4170	Vintage '78	1978	2.50	5.00	10.00
❑ AB 4250	Something More	1979	2.50	5.00	10.00
ATLANTIC					
❑ SD 19294	Love Keys	1981	2.50	5.00	10.00
MOTOWN					
❑ M5-151V1	Eddie Kendricks	1981	2.00	4.00	8.00
—Reissue of Tamla 327					
❑ M5-196V1	He's a Friend	1981	2.00	4.00	8.00
—Reissue of Tamla 343					
TAMLA					
❑ T-309	All By Myself	1971	2.50	5.00	10.00
❑ T 315L	People...Hold On	1972	2.50	5.00	10.00
❑ T 327L	Eddie Kendricks	1973	2.50	5.00	10.00
❑ T 330V1	Boogie Down!	1974	2.50	5.00	10.00
❑ T6-335	For You	1974	2.50	5.00	10.00
❑ T6-338	The Hit Man	1975	2.50	5.00	10.00
❑ T6-343	He's a Friend	1976	2.50	5.00	10.00
❑ T6-346	Goin' Up in Smoke	1976	2.50	5.00	10.00
❑ T7-354	Eddie Kendricks at His Best	1977	2.50	5.00	10.00
❑ T8-356	Slick	1978	2.50	5.00	10.00

KENNER, CHRIS

45s

Number	Title (A Side/B Side)	Yr	VG	VG+	NM
BATON					
❑ 220	Grandma's House/Don't Let Her Pin That Charge	1956	10.00	20.00	40.00
IMPERIAL					
❑ 5448	Sick and Tired/Nothing Will Keep Me from You	1957	6.25	12.50	25.00
❑ 5488	Will You Be Mine/I Have News for You	1958	6.25	12.50	25.00
❑ 5767	Sick and Tired/Nothing Will Keep Me from You	1961	3.00	6.00	12.00
INSTANT					
❑ 3229	I Like It Like That, Part 1/I Like It Like That, Part 2	1961	3.75	7.50	15.00
❑ 3234	A Very True Story/Packin' Up	1961	3.00	6.00	12.00
❑ 3237	Something You Got/Come See About Me	1961	3.00	6.00	12.00
❑ 3244	How Far/Time	1962	3.00	6.00	12.00
❑ 3247	Let Me Show You How (To Twist)/Johnny Little	1962	3.00	6.00	12.00
❑ 3252	Land of 1000 Dances/That's My Girl	1962	3.00	6.00	12.00
❑ 3257	Come Back and See/Go Thru Life	1963	3.00	6.00	12.00
❑ 3263	What's Wrong with Life/Never Reach Perfection	1963	3.00	6.00	12.00
❑ 3265	She Can Dance/Anybody Here See My Baby	1964	3.00	6.00	12.00
❑ 3277	I'm Lonely, Take Me/Cinderella	1966	2.50	5.00	10.00
❑ 3280	All Night Rambler, Part 1/All Night Rambler, Part 2	1966	2.50	5.00	10.00
❑ 3283	Shoo Rah/Stretch My Hands to You	1967	2.50	5.00	10.00
❑ 3286	Fumigate Funky Broadway/Wind the Clock	1967	2.50	5.00	10.00
❑ 3290	Memories of a King (Let Freedom Ring), Part 1/Memories of a King (Let Freedom Ring), Part 2	1968	3.00	6.00	12.00
❑ 3293	Mini-Skirts and Soul/Sad Mistake	1968	2.50	5.00	10.00
PRIGAN					
❑ 2002	Don't Make No Noise/Right Kind of Girl	196?	5.00	10.00	20.00
RON					
❑ 335	Rocket to the Moon/Life's Just a Struggle	1961	3.00	6.00	12.00
UPTOWN					
❑ 708	Life of My Baby/They Took My Money	1965	2.50	5.00	10.00
❑ 716	I'm the Greatest/Get On This Train	1965	2.50	5.00	10.00
VALIANT					
❑ 3229	I Like It Like That, Part 1/I Like It Like That, Part 2	1960	10.00	20.00	40.00

Albums

Number	Title (A Side/B Side)	Yr	VG	VG+	NM
ATLANTIC					
❑ 8117 [M]	Land of 1,000 Dances	1965	20.00	40.00	80.00
COLLECTABLES					
❑ COL-5116	Golden Classics: I Like It Like That	198?	3.00	6.00	12.00

KENT, AL

45s

BARITONE

Number	Title (A Side/B Side)	Yr	VG	VG+	NM
❑ 942	Hold Me/Tell Me Why	1960	37.50	75.00	150.00

Number	Title (A Side/B Side)	Yr	VG	VG+	NM

CHECKER
| ❑ 881 | Dat's Why (I Love You So)/Am I the Man | 1958 | 15.00 | 30.00 | 60.00 |

RIC-TIC
❑ 123	The Way You Been Acting Lately/(Instrumental)	1967	5.00	10.00	20.00
❑ 127	You've Got to Pay the Price/Where Do I Go from Here	1967	5.00	10.00	20.00
❑ 133	Finders Keepers/Ooh! Pretty Lady	1967	5.00	10.00	20.00
❑ 140	Bless You (My Love)/(Instrumental)	1968	3.75	7.50	15.00

WINGATE
| ❑ 004 | You Know I Love You/Country Boy | 1965 | 6.25 | 12.50 | 25.00 |

WIZARD
| ❑ 100 | Hold Me/You Know Me | 1959 | 25.00 | 50.00 | 100.00 |

KEYNOTES, THE
Possibly all the same group.
45s
APOLLO
❑ 478	Suddenly/Zenda	1955	37.50	75.00	150.00
❑ 484	I Don't Know/A Star	1955	20.00	40.00	80.00
❑ 493	Really Wish You Were Here/Bye Bye Baby	1956	30.00	60.00	120.00
❑ 498	Now I Know/Zup Zup	1956	25.00	50.00	100.00
❑ 503	In the Evening/O Yeah Hm-m-m	1956	20.00	40.00	80.00
❑ 513	One Little Kiss/Now I Know	1957	20.00	40.00	80.00

DOT
| ❑ 15225 | Who/They Say | 1954 | 7.50 | 15.00 | 30.00 |

INDEX
| ❑ 101 | Open the Door (To Your Heart)/Dum-De, Dum-Dum | 1958 | 25.00 | 50.00 | 100.00 |

POP
| ❑ 111 | Carelessly/Congratulations Baby | 1957 | 20.00 | 40.00 | 80.00 |

TOP RANK
| ❑ 2005 | With These Rings/We're Not Getting Along | 1959 | 3.75 | 7.50 | 15.00 |

KEYS, ALICIA
12-Inch Singles
J
❑ 21041	Girlfriend (Club Mix 3:30) (Instrumental Version 3:30) (Acappella Mix 3:30)/Fallin' (Mix 3:16)	2001	3.00	6.00	12.00
❑ J1PV-21073	Fallin' (Remix Featuring Busta Rhymes and Rampage) (Instrumental) (Without Rap) (Radio Version)	2001	2.50	5.00	10.00
❑ J1PV-21112	A Woman's Worth (Vocal Mix 4:10) (Instrumental 4:10)/(same on both sides)	2001	2.50	5.00	10.00
❑ 21144	A Woman's Worth (Club Mix 4:28) (Radio Mix 4:28) (Instrumental Mix 5:02) (Acappella Mix 4:25)	2002	2.00	4.00	8.00
❑ J1PV-21144	A Woman's Worth (Club Mix 4:28) (Radio Mix 4:28) (Instrumental Mix 5:02) (Acappella Mix 4:25)	2002	2.50	5.00	10.00
❑ J1PV-21184 [(2)]	Butterflyz (4 versions)	2002	3.00	6.00	12.00
45s
J
| ❑ 21101 | Fallin'/Fallin' Remix | 2001 | — | — | 3.00 |

KEYSTONERS, THE
45s
EPIC
| ❑ 9187 | The Magic Kiss/After I Propose | 1956 | 15.00 | 30.00 | 60.00 |

G&M
| ❑ 102 | The Magic Kiss/I'd Write About the Blues | 1956 | 75.00 | 150.00 | 300.00 |

OKEH
| ❑ 7210 | The Magic Kiss/After I Propose | 1964 | 5.00 | 10.00 | 20.00 |

RIFF
| ❑ 202 | Sleep and Dream/T.V. Gal | 1961 | 50.00 | 100.00 | 200.00 |

KEYTONES, THE
45s
CHELSEA
| ❑ 101 | I Don't Care/La-Do-Da Da | 1962 | 7.50 | 15.00 | 30.00 |
| ❑ 1013 | Sweet Chariot/One, Two, Three | 1963 | 3.75 | 7.50 | 15.00 |

OLD TOWN
| ❑ 1041 | Wonders of the World/A Fool in Love | 1957 | 75.00 | 150.00 | 300.00 |
| ❑ 1041 | Seven Wonders of the World/A Fool in Love | 1957 | 25.00 | 50.00 | 100.00 |

KHAN, CHAKA
Also see RUFUS.
12-Inch Singles
FOX
| ❑ 62974 [DJ] | Miles Blowin' (Vinyl Republic Dub) (Disco 9000 Mix) (Afro Cube Mix) | 1994 | 3.75 | 7.50 | 15.00 |

MCA
| ❑ MCA8P-3494 [DJ] | Love Me Still (LP Version) (Instrumental)/(same on both sides) | 1995 | 2.50 | 5.00 | 10.00 |
| ❑ 23604 | Own the Night (3 versions) | 1985 | — | 3.00 | 6.00 |

REPRISE
❑ PRO-A-8454 [DJ]	Never Miss the Water (Album Version) (Radio Edit) (Stylus Remix) (Stylus Street Mix) (A Cappella)	1996	3.00	6.00	12.00
❑ PRO-A-8638 [DJ]	Never Miss the Water (Deeper Mix) (Lewis and Rich Remix) (Deeper Dub) (Addis-Polvere Remix)	1996	2.50	5.00	10.00
❑ 43787	Never Miss the Water (unknown versions)	1996	2.50	5.00	10.00

WARNER BROS.
❑ PRO-A-787 [DJ]	Life Is a Dance/Some Love	1979	3.75	7.50	15.00
❑ PRO-A-883 [DJ]	Papillon (aka Hot Butterfly)/Too Much Love	1980	5.00	10.00	20.00
❑ PRO-A-909 [DJ]	Get Ready, Get Set (Stereo) (Mono)	1980	2.50	5.00	10.00
❑ PRO-A-3316 [DJ]	It's My Party (Edit) (LP Version)	1988	—	3.00	6.00
❑ PRO-A-3451 [DJ]	Baby Me (3 CK's and a Baby Mix) (Big Baby Mix Radio Edit) (Instrumental Mix) (Midget Mix)	1989	2.50	5.00	10.00
❑ PRO-A-3481 [DJ]	Baby Me (Babysitting Mix) (same on both sides)	1988	—	3.00	6.00
❑ PRO-A-3571 [DJ]	Soul Talkin' (Edit) (Serious Soul Edit)	1988	2.50	5.00	10.00
❑ PRO-A-5783 [DJ]	I Want (unknown versions)	1992	2.00	4.00	8.00
❑ 20249	I Feel for You (Remix 7:12)/Chinatown (LP Version 4:33)	1984	—	3.00	6.00
❑ 20296	This Is My Night (6:11)/Caught in the Act	1984	—	3.00	6.00
❑ 20367	(Krush Groove) Can't Stop the Street (Vocal) (Instrumental)	1985	—	3.00	6.00
❑ 20487	Love of a Lifetime (Extended)/Coltrane Dreams (Long)	1986	—	3.00	6.00
❑ 20561	Tight Fit (Extended Version)/Who's It Gonna Be	1986	—	3.00	6.00
❑ 21097	It's My Party (New Party Mix 8:40) (Club Instrumental 5:05) (LP Version 5:10) (Club Edit 5:10) (Dance Dub 5:18)/Where Are You Tonite	1988	—	3.00	6.00
❑ 21179	Baby Me/Everybody Needs Some Love	1989	—	3.50	7.00
❑ 21250	Soul Talkin' (Soul Mix) (Soul Edit)/I'm Every Woman (Remix) (Remix Edit)/Ain't Nobody	1988	2.00	4.00	8.00
❑ 29721	Tearin' It Up (Long Version Remix 7:21) (Instrumental Version 8:07)	1983	3.00	6.00	12.00

45s
ARISTA
| ❑ 12957 | My Funny Valentine/Not Gon' Cry | 1996 | — | — | 3.00 |
—B-side by Mary J. Blige

ATLANTIC
| ❑ 89449 | The Other Side of the World/(Instrumental) | 1986 | — | — | 3.00 |

MCA
| ❑ 52730 | Own the Night/(Instrumental) | 1985 | — | — | 3.00 |
| ❑ 52730 [PS] | Own the Night/(Instrumental) | 1985 | — | — | 3.00 |

REPRISE
| ❑ 17503 | Never Miss the Water/Papillon (AKA Hot Butterfly) | 1996 | — | — | 3.00 |
—A-side with Me'Shell NdegeOcello

WARNER BROS.
| ❑ 8683 | I'm Every Woman/Woman in a Man's World | 1978 | — | 2.50 | 5.00 |
—Tan label
| ❑ 8683 | I'm Every Woman/Woman in a Man's World | 1978 | 2.00 | 4.00 | 8.00 |
—"Burbank" palm trees label
❑ 8683 [PS]	I'm Every Woman/Woman in a Man's World	1978	—	2.50	5.00
❑ 8740	Life Is a Dance/Some Love	1979	—	2.00	4.00
❑ 22913	Soul Talkin'/I'm Every Woman	1989	—	—	3.00
❑ 27541	Baby Me/Everybody Needs Some Love	1989	—	—	3.00
❑ 27678	It's My Party/Where Are You Tonite	1988	—	—	3.00
❑ 27678 [PS]	It's My Party/Where Are You Tonite	1988	—	—	3.00
❑ 28459	Earth to Mickey/My Destiny	1987	—	—	3.00
❑ 28576	Tight Fit/Who's It Gonna Be	1986	—	—	3.00
❑ 28576 [PS]	Tight Fit/Who's It Gonna Be	1986	—	—	3.00
❑ 28671	Love of a Lifetime/Coltrane Dreams	1986	—	—	3.00
❑ 28671 [PS]	Love of a Lifetime/Coltrane Dreams	1986	—	—	3.00
❑ 28923	(Krush Groove) Can't Stop the Street/ (Instrumental)	1985	—	—	3.00
❑ 28923 [PS]	(Krush Groove) Can't Stop the Street/ (Instrumental)	1985	—	—	3.00
❑ 29025	Through the Fire/La Flamme	1985	—	—	3.00
❑ 29097	This Is My Night/Caught in the Act	1985	—	—	3.00
❑ 29097 [PS]	This Is My Night/Caught in the Act	1985	—	—	3.00
❑ 29195	I Feel for You/Chinatown	1984	—	2.00	4.00
❑ 29195 [PS]	I Feel for You/Chinatown	1984	—	2.00	4.00
❑ 29745	Tearin' It Up/So Not to Worry	1983	—	2.00	4.00
❑ 29881	Got to Be There/Pass It On, A Sure Thing	1982	—	2.00	4.00
❑ 49216	Clouds/What You Did	1980	—	2.00	4.00
❑ 49256	Papillon (AKA Hot Butterfly)/Too Much Love	1980	—	2.00	4.00
❑ 49571	Get Ready, Get Set/So Naughty	1980	—	2.00	4.00
❑ 49692	What Cha' Gonna Do for Me/Lover's Touch	1981	—	2.00	4.00
❑ 49759	We Can Work It Out/Only Once	1981	—	2.00	4.00
❑ 49804	Any Old Sunday/Heed the Warning	1981	—	2.00	4.00
❑ 49847	And the Melody Still Lingers On/I Know You, I Live You	1981	—	2.00	4.00

Albums
REPRISE
| ❑ PRO-A-8478 [DJ] | Epiphany: The Best of Chaka Khan Sampler | 1996 | 3.75 | 7.50 | 15.00 |
—Promo-only six-song sampler

WARNER BROS.
❑ BSK 3245	Chaka	1978	2.50	5.00	10.00
❑ BSK 3385	Naughty	1980	2.50	5.00	10.00
❑ HS 3526	What Cha' Gonna Do for Me	1981	2.50	5.00	10.00
❑ 23729	Chaka Khan	1982	2.50	5.00	10.00
❑ 25162	I Feel for You	1984	2.50	5.00	10.00
❑ 25425	Destiny	1986	2.50	5.00	10.00
❑ 25707	C.K.	1988	2.50	5.00	10.00
❑ 25946 [(2)]	Life Is a Dance: The Remix Project	1989	3.75	7.50	15.00

KING, ALBERT
45s
ATLANTIC
| ❑ 2604 | The Hunter/As the Years Go Passing By | 1969 | 2.00 | 4.00 | 8.00 |

BOBBIN
| ❑ 114 | Why Are You So Mean to Me/Ooh-Ee Baby | 1959 | 6.25 | 12.50 | 25.00 |
| ❑ 119 | Need You By My Side/The Time Has Come | 1960 | 6.25 | 12.50 | 25.00 |

Number	Title (A Side/B Side)	Yr	VG	VG+	NM
❏ 126	Blues at Sunrise/Let's Have a Natural Ball	1960	6.25	12.50	25.00
❏ 129	I Walked All Night Long/I've Made Nights By Myself	1961	6.25	12.50	25.00
❏ 130	Travelin' to California/Dyna-Flow	1961	6.25	12.50	25.00
❏ 131	Don't Thow Your Love on Me So Strong/This Morning	1961	6.25	12.50	25.00
❏ 135	I Get Evil/What Can I Do to Change Your Mind	1962	6.25	12.50	25.00
❏ 141	I'll Do Anything for You/Got to Be Some Changes Made	1963	6.25	12.50	25.00
❏ 143	Old Blue Ribbon/I've Made Nights By Myself	1963	6.25	12.50	25.00
KING					
❏ 5575	Don't Throw Your Love on Me So Strong/This Morning	1961	3.00	6.00	12.00
❏ 5588	Travelin' to California/Dyna-Flow	1961	3.00	6.00	12.00
❏ 5751	This Funny Feeling/Had You Told It Like It Was	1963	3.00	6.00	12.00
❏ 6265	Travelin' to California/Don't Throw Your Love on Me So Strong	1969	2.00	4.00	8.00
PARROT					
❏ 798	Bad Luck Blues/Be On Your Merry Way	1954	400.00	800.00	1200.
STAX					
❏ 0020	Night Stomp/Blues Power	1968	2.00	4.00	8.00
❏ 0034	Drowning on Dry Land (Vocal)/(Instrumental)	1969	2.00	4.00	8.00
❏ 0058	Wrapped Up in Love Again/Cockroach	1969	2.00	4.00	8.00
❏ 0069	Can't You See What You're Doing to Me/Cold Sweat	1970	2.00	4.00	8.00
❏ 0101	Everybody Wants to Go to Heaven/Lovejoy, Ill.	1971	—	3.50	7.00
❏ 0121	Angel of Mercy/Funky London	1972	—	3.50	7.00
❏ 0135	I'll Play the Blues for You (Part 1)/I'll Play the Blues for You (Part 2)	1972	—	3.50	7.00
❏ 0147	Breaking Up Somebody's Home/Little Brother	1972	—	3.50	7.00
❏ 0166	The High Cost of Loving/Playing on Me	1973	—	3.50	7.00
❏ 0189	That's What the Blues Is All About/I Wanna Get Funky	1973	—	3.50	7.00
❏ 190	Laundromat Blues/Overall Junction	1966	2.50	5.00	10.00
❏ 197	Funk-Shun/Pretty Woman (Can't Make You Love Me)	1966	2.50	5.00	10.00
❏ 201	Crosscut Saw/Down Don't Bother Me	1966	2.50	5.00	10.00
❏ 217	Born Under a Bad Sign/Personal Manager	1967	2.50	5.00	10.00
❏ 0217	I Can Hear Nothing But the Blues/Flat Tire	1974	—	3.50	7.00
❏ 0228	Crosscut Saw/Don't Burn Down the Bridge	1974	—	3.50	7.00
❏ 0234	Santa Claus Wants Some Lovin'/Don't Burn Down the Bridges	1974	—	3.50	7.00
❏ 241	Cold Feet/Drive a Hard Bargain	1967	2.50	5.00	10.00
❏ 252	(I Love) Lucy/You're Gonna Need Me	1968	2.50	5.00	10.00
❏ 1056	Santa Claus Wants Some Lovin'/What Do The Lonely Do At Christmas?	197?	—	3.00	6.00
—B-side by Emotions; reissue					
❏ 1073	Christmas Comes Once A Year/I'll Be Your Santa Claus	197?	—	2.50	5.00
—B-side by Rufus Thomas; reissue					
❏ 3203	The Pinch Paid Off (Part 1)/The Pinch Paid Off (Part 2)	1978	—	2.50	5.00
❏ 3225	Santa Claus Wants Some Lovin'/Don't Burn Down the Bridges	1979	—	3.00	6.00
TOMATO					
❏ 10001	Call My Job/Love Shack	1978	—	2.50	5.00
❏ 10002	Chump Change/Good Time Charlie	1978	—	2.50	5.00
❏ 10009	The Very Thought of You/I Get Evil	1979	—	2.50	5.00
❏ 10012	Born Under a Bad Sign/I've Got the Blues	1979	—	2.50	5.00
UTOPIA					
❏ PB-10544	Cadillac Assembly Line/Nobody Wants a Loser	1976	—	2.50	5.00
❏ PB-10682	Sensation, Communication Together/Gonna Make It Somehow	1976	—	2.50	5.00
❏ PB-10770	Guitar Man/Rub My Back	1976	—	2.50	5.00
❏ PB-10879	Ain't Nothing You Can Do/I Don't Care What My Baby Do	1977	—	2.50	5.00
Albums					
ATLANTIC					
❏ SD 8213	King of the Blues Guitar	1969	6.25	12.50	25.00
FANTASY					
❏ 9627	San Francisco '83	1983	2.50	5.00	10.00
❏ 9633	I'm in a Phone Booth, Baby	1984	2.50	5.00	10.00
KING					
❏ 852 [M]	Big Blues	1963	125.00	250.00	500.00
❏ KS-1060	Travelin' to California	1969	6.25	12.50	25.00
MODERN BLUES					
❏ MBLP-723	Let's Have a Natural Ball	198?	2.50	5.00	10.00
STAX					
❏ ST-723 [M]	Born Under a Bad Sign	1967	20.00	40.00	80.00
❏ STS-723 [S]	Born Under a Bad Sign	1967	30.00	60.00	120.00
❏ STS-2003	Live Wire/Blues Power	1968	12.50	25.00	50.00
❏ STS-2010	Years Gone By	1969	6.25	12.50	25.00
❏ STS-2015	King Does the King's Thing	1969	6.25	12.50	25.00
❏ STS-2040	Lovejoy	1971	5.00	10.00	20.00
❏ STS-3009	I'll Play the Blues for You	1972	5.00	10.00	20.00
❏ STX-4101	The Pinch	1977	3.00	6.00	12.00
❏ STX-4128	Live Wire/Blues Power	1979	2.50	5.00	10.00
—Reissue of 2003					
❏ STX-4132	Montreux Festival	1980	2.50	5.00	10.00
—Retitled reissue of 5520					
❏ STS-5505	I Wanna Get Funky	1974	3.75	7.50	15.00
❏ STS-5520	Montreux Festival	1975	3.75	7.50	15.00
❏ MPS-8504	Blues for Elvis	1981	2.50	5.00	10.00
—Retitled reissue of 2015					

Number	Title (A Side/B Side)	Yr	VG	VG+	NM
❏ MPS-8513	I'll Play the Blues for You	1981	2.50	5.00	10.00
—Reissue of 3309					
❏ MPS-8517	Lovejoy	1981	2.50	5.00	10.00
—Reissue of 2040					
❏ MPS-8522	Years Gone By	1982	2.50	5.00	10.00
—Reissue of 2010					
❏ MPS-8534	The Lost Session	1986	2.50	5.00	10.00
❏ MPS-8536	I Wanna Get Funky	1987	2.50	5.00	10.00
—Reissue of 5505					
❏ MPS-8546	Blues at Sunrise	1988	2.50	5.00	10.00
❏ MPS-8556	Wednesday Night in San Francisco	1990	2.50	5.00	10.00
❏ MPS-8557	Tuesday Night in San Francisco	1990	2.50	5.00	10.00
SUNDAZED					
❏ LP 5031	Born Under a Bad Sign	1999	3.75	7.50	15.00
—Reissue on 180-gram vinyl					
TOMATO					
❏ TOM-6002	King Albert	1978	3.00	6.00	12.00
❏ TOM-7022	New Orleans Heat	1979	3.00	6.00	12.00
UTOPIA					
❏ BUL1-1387	Truckload of Lovin'	1976	3.00	6.00	12.00
❏ BUL1-1731	Albert	1976	3.00	6.00	12.00
❏ CUL2-2205 [(2)]	Albert Live	1977	3.75	7.50	15.00

KING, ALBERT/STEVE CROPPER/POP STAPLES

45s

STAX

Number	Title (A Side/B Side)	Yr	VG	VG+	NM
❏ 0047	Tupelo (Part 1)/Tupelo (Part 2)	1969	2.00	4.00	8.00
❏ 0048	Water/Opus de Soul	1969	2.00	4.00	8.00

Albums

STAX

Number	Title	Yr	VG	VG+	NM
❏ STS-2020	Jammed Together	1969	6.25	12.50	25.00
❏ MPS-8544	Jammed Together	1988	2.50	5.00	10.00
—Reissue					

KING, ALBERT/LITTLE MILTON

Albums

STAX

Number	Title	Yr	VG	VG+	NM
❏ STX-4123	Chronicle	1979	3.00	6.00	12.00
—One side devoted to each artist					

KING, ALBERT/OTIS RUSH

Albums

CHESS

Number	Title	Yr	VG	VG+	NM
❏ LPS 1538	Door to Door	1969	6.25	12.50	25.00
❏ CH-9322	Door to Door	1990	2.50	5.00	10.00
—Reissue					

KING, B.B.

Also see BOBBY BLAND AND B.B. KING.

12-Inch Singles

MCA

Number	Title (A Side/B Side)	Yr	VG	VG+	NM
❏ L33-1284 [DJ]	My Lucille (Extended)/Into the Night	1985	2.00	4.00	8.00
❏ 2118 [DJ]	The Blues Come Over Me (6 versions)	1991	—	3.00	6.00
❏ L33-17810 [DJ]	Lay Another Log on the Fire/Go On	1989	—	3.00	6.00
❏ 23831	Habit to Me (LP Version) (TV Mix)	1988	—	3.00	6.00

45s

ABC

Number	Title (A Side/B Side)	Yr	VG	VG+	NM
❏ 10856	Don't Answer the Door (Part 1)/Don't Answer the Door (Part 2)	1966	3.75	7.50	15.00
❏ 10889	Waitin' on You/Night Life	1966	3.75	7.50	15.00
❏ 11268	Hummingbird/Ask Me No Questions	1970	2.00	4.00	8.00
❏ 11280	Chains and Things/King's Special	1970	2.00	4.00	8.00
❏ 11290	Ask Me No Questions/Nobody Loves Me But My Mother	1971	2.00	4.00	8.00
❏ 11302	Help the Poor/Lucille's Granny	1971	2.00	4.00	8.00
❏ 11310	Ghetto Woman/Seven Minutes	1971	2.00	4.00	8.00
❏ 11316	Ain't Nobody Home/Alexi's Boogie	1971	2.00	4.00	8.00
❏ 11319	Sweet Sixteen/I've Been Blue Too Long	1972	—	3.00	6.00
❏ 11321	I Got Some Help I Don't Need/Lucille's Granny	1972	—	3.00	6.00
❏ 11330	Guess Who/Better Lovin' Man	1972	—	3.00	6.00
❏ 11339	Summer in the City/Five Long Years	1972	—	3.00	6.00
❏ 11373	To Know You Is to Love You/I Can't Leave	1973	—	3.00	6.00
❏ 11406	I Like to Live the Love/Love	1973	—	3.00	6.00
❏ 11433	Who Are You/On to Me	1974	—	3.00	6.00
❏ 12029	Philadelphia/Up at 5 A.M.	1974	—	3.00	6.00
❏ 12053	Friends/My Song	1974	—	3.00	6.00
❏ 12158	When I'm Wrong/Have Faith	1976	—	3.00	6.00
❏ 12247	Slow and Easy/I Wonder Why	1977	—	3.00	6.00
❏ 12380	Never Make a Move Too Soon/Let Me Make You Cry a Little Longer	1978	—	3.00	6.00
❏ 12412	I Just Can't Leave Your Love Alone/Midnight Believer	1978	—	3.00	6.00
ABC-PARAMOUNT					
❏ 10316	I'm Gonna Sit In Till You Give In/You Ask Me	1962	3.75	7.50	15.00
❏ 10334	Blues at Midnight/My Baby's Coming Home	1962	3.75	7.50	15.00
❏ 10361	Chains of Love/Sneakin' Around	1962	3.75	7.50	15.00
❏ 10367	Tomorrow Night/Mother's Love	1962	3.75	7.50	15.00
❏ 10390	Guess Who/By Myself	1962	3.75	7.50	15.00
❏ 10455	On My Word of Honor/Young Dreamers	1963	3.75	7.50	15.00
❏ 10486	How Do I Love You/Slowly Losing My Mind	1963	3.75	7.50	15.00
❏ 10527	How Blue Can You Get/Please Accept My Love	1964	3.75	7.50	15.00
❏ 10552	Help the Poor/I Wouldn't Have It Any Other Way	1964	3.75	7.50	15.00
❏ 10576	Whole Lotta Lovin'/The Hurt	1964	3.75	7.50	15.00
❏ 10597	Never Trust a Woman/Worryin' Blues	1964	3.75	7.50	15.00

Number	Title (A Side/B Side)	Yr	VG	VG+	NM
❑ 10616	Please Send Me Someone to Love/The Worst Thing in My Life	1965	3.75	7.50	15.00
❑ 10634	Everyday I Have the Blues/It's My Own Fault	1965	3.75	7.50	15.00
❑ 10675	Tired of Your Jive/Night Owl	1965	3.75	7.50	15.00
❑ 10724	All Over Again/The Things You Put Me Through	1965	3.75	7.50	15.00
❑ 10754	Goin' to Chicago Blues/I'd Rather Drink Muddy Water	1965	3.75	7.50	15.00
❑ 10766	Tormented/You're Still a Square	1966	3.75	7.50	15.00
BLUESWAY					
❑ 61004	Think It Over/I Don't Want You Cutting Off Your Hair	1967	2.50	5.00	10.00
❑ 61007	Worried Dream/That's Wrong, Little Mama	1967	2.50	5.00	10.00
❑ 61011	Raining in My Heart/Heartbreaker	1967	2.50	5.00	10.00
❑ 61012	Sweet Sixteen (Part 1)/Sweet Sixteen (Part 2)	1968	2.50	5.00	10.00
❑ 61015	Paying the Cost to Be the Boss/Having My Say	1968	2.50	5.00	10.00
❑ 61018	I'm Gonna Do What They Do to Me/Losing Faith in You	1968	2.50	5.00	10.00
❑ 61019	You Put It On Me/B.B. Jones	1968	2.50	5.00	10.00
❑ 61021	Dance with Me/Please Send Me Someone to Love	1968	2.50	5.00	10.00
❑ 61022	Don't Waste My Time/Get Myself Somebody	1969	2.50	5.00	10.00
❑ 61024	Why I Sing the Blues/Friends	1969	2.50	5.00	10.00
❑ 61026	Get Off My Back Woman/I Want You So Bad	1969	2.50	5.00	10.00
❑ 61029	Just a Little Love/My Mood	1969	2.50	5.00	10.00
❑ 61032	The Thrill Is Gone/You're Mean	1969	3.00	6.00	12.00
❑ 61032 [PS]	The Thrill Is Gone/You're Mean	1969	5.00	10.00	20.00
❑ 61035	So Excited/Confessin' the Blues	1970	2.00	4.00	8.00
KENT					
❑ 301	You Know I Go for You/Why Do Everything Happen to Me	1958	5.00	10.00	20.00
❑ 307	Days of Old/Don't Look Now, But You Got the Blues	1958	5.00	10.00	20.00
❑ 315	Please Accept My Love/You've Been an Angel	1958	6.25	12.50	25.00
—With the Vocal Chords					
❑ 317	Worry Worry/I Am	1959	5.00	10.00	20.00
❑ 319	The Fool/Come By Here	1959	5.00	10.00	20.00
❑ 325	A Lonely Lover's Plea/Woman in Love	1959	5.00	10.00	20.00
❑ 327	Everyday I Have the Blues/Time to Say Goodbye	1959	5.00	10.00	20.00
❑ 329	Sugar Mama/Mean Old Friend	1959	5.00	10.00	20.00
❑ 330	Sweet Sixteen, Pt. 1/Sweet Sixteen, Pt. 2	1960	5.00	10.00	20.00
❑ 333	Got a Right to Love My Baby/My Own Fault	1960	3.75	7.50	15.00
❑ 336	Please Love Me/Crying Won't Help You	1960	3.75	7.50	15.00
❑ 337	Blind Love/You Upset Me Baby	1960	3.75	7.50	15.00
❑ 338	Ten Long Years/Everyday I Have the Blues	1960	3.75	7.50	15.00
❑ 339	Did You Ever Love a Woman/Three O'Clock Blues	1960	3.75	7.50	15.00
❑ 340	Sweet Little Angel/You Done Lost Your Good Thing Now	1960	3.75	7.50	15.00
❑ 346	Partin' Time/Good Man Gone Bad	1960	3.75	7.50	15.00
❑ 350	Waking Dr. Bill/You Done Lost Your Good Thing Now	1960	3.75	7.50	15.00
❑ 351	Things Are Not the Same/Fishin' After Me	1961	3.75	7.50	15.00
❑ 353	Bad Luck Soul/Get Out of Here	1961	3.75	7.50	15.00
❑ 358	Hold That Train/Understand	1961	3.75	7.50	15.00
❑ 360	Peace of Mind/Someday	1961	3.75	7.50	15.00
❑ 362	You're Breaking My Heart/Bad Case of Love	1961	3.75	7.50	15.00
❑ 365	My Sometime Baby/Lonely	1962	3.00	6.00	12.00
❑ 372	Gonna Miss You Around Here/Hully Gully Twist	1962	3.00	6.00	12.00
❑ 373	3 O'Clock Stomp/Mashed Potato Twist	1962	3.00	6.00	12.00
❑ 381	Tell Me Baby/Mashing the Popeye	1962	3.00	6.00	12.00
❑ 383	Going Down Slow/When My Heart Beats Like a Hammer	1962	3.00	6.00	12.00
❑ 386	Your Letter/Blues for Me	1962	3.00	6.00	12.00
❑ 387	Christmas Celebration/Easy Listening	1962	3.00	6.00	12.00
❑ 388	Whole Lot of Loving/Down Now	1963	3.00	5.00	10.00
❑ 389	Trouble in Mind/Long Nights	1963	3.00	5.00	10.00
❑ 390	My Reward/The Road I Travel	1963	3.00	5.00	10.00
❑ 391	The Letter/You Never Know	1963	3.00	5.00	10.00
❑ 392	Army of the Lord/Precious Lord	1964	3.00	7.50	15.00
❑ 393	Rock Me Baby/I Can't Lose	1964	3.00	5.00	10.00
❑ 396	Let Me Love You/You're Gonna Miss Me	1964	3.00	5.00	10.00
❑ 403	Beautician Blues/I Can Hear My Name	1964	3.00	5.00	10.00
❑ 412	Christmas Celebration/Easy Listening	1964	3.00	6.00	12.00
❑ 415	Got 'Em Bad/The Worst Thing in My Life	1965	3.00	6.00	12.00
❑ 421	Please Love Me/Baby Look at You	1965	3.00	6.00	12.00
❑ 426	Blue Shadows/And Like That	1965	3.00	6.00	12.00
❑ 429	Just a Dream/Why Do Everything Happen to Me	1965	3.00	6.00	12.00
❑ 435	Mercy, Mercy, Mercy/Broken Promise	1965	3.00	6.00	12.00
❑ 441	Eyesight to the Blind/Just Like a Woman	1966	3.00	6.00	12.00
❑ 445	Five Long Years/Love, Honor and Obey	1966	3.00	6.00	12.00
❑ 447	Ain't Nobody's Business/I Wonder Why	1966	3.00	6.00	12.00
❑ 450	I Stay in the Mood/Early Every Morning	1966	3.00	6.00	12.00
❑ 458	It's a Mean World/Blues Stay Away	1966	2.00	4.00	8.00
❑ 462	The Jungle/Long Gone Baby	1967	2.00	4.00	8.00
❑ 467	Treat Me Right/Who Can Your Good Man Be	1967	2.00	4.00	8.00
❑ 470	Bad Breaks/Growing Old	1967	2.00	4.00	8.00
❑ 475	Sweet Thing/Soul Beat	1967	2.00	4.00	8.00
❑ 484	Worry, Worry, Worry/Why Do Everything Happen to Me	1968	—	3.00	6.00
❑ 492	The Woman I Love/Blues for Me	1968	—	3.00	6.00
❑ 499	Slow Burn/3 O'Clock Blues	1968	—	3.00	6.00
❑ 510	Your Fool/Shoutin' the Blues	1969	—	3.00	6.00
❑ 4513	I'm Cracking Up Over You/Powerhouse	1969	2.50	5.00	10.00
❑ 4515	Dreams/House Rocker	1970	2.50	5.00	10.00
❑ 4526	Worried Life/Walkin' Dr. Bill	1970	2.50	5.00	10.00
❑ 4542	That Evil Child/Tell Me Baby	1971	2.00	4.00	8.00
❑ 4549	I'll Survive/Long Nights	1971	2.00	4.00	8.00
❑ 4562	Precious Lord/Swing Low, Sweet Chariot	1972	2.00	4.00	8.00
❑ 4566	Don't Get Around Much Anymore/Poontanging	1972	2.00	4.00	8.00
❑ 4572	Recession Blues/Walkin' Dr. Bill	1972	2.00	4.00	8.00
MCA					
❑ 41062	Happy Birthday Blues/Better Not Look Down	1979	—	2.00	4.00
❑ 51101	There Must Be a Better World Somewhere/You're Going with Me	1981	—	2.00	4.00
❑ 52057	Since I Met You Baby/One of Those Nights	1982	—	—	3.00
❑ 52098	Street Life/Overture	1982	—	—	3.00
—With the Crusaders and the London Symphony Orchestra					
❑ 52125	Love Me Tender/The World I Never Made	1982	—	—	3.00
❑ 52218	Sell My Monkey/Inflation Blues	1983	—	—	3.00
❑ 52530	Into the Night/Century City Chase of J.B. in Teheran	1985	—	—	3.00
❑ 52530 [PS]	Into the Night/Century City Chase of J.B. in Teheran	1985	—	—	3.00
❑ 52574	My Lucille/Keep It Light	1985	—	—	3.00
—B-side by Thelma Houston					
❑ 52675	Big Boss Man/My Guitar Sings the Blues	1985	—	—	3.00
❑ 52751	Memory Lane/Six Silver Strings	1985	—	—	3.00
❑ 53269	(You've Become a) Habit to Me/(You've Become a) Habit to Me (Long)	1988	—	—	3.00
❑ 53644	Lay Another Log on the Fire/Go On	1989	—	—	3.00
❑ 54339	The Blues Come Over Me (Wild & Bluesy Club Mix Edit)/The Blues Come Over Me (Integrity Mix)	1992	—	2.00	4.00
POINTBLANK					
❑ 58820	Christmas Celebration/White Christmas	1999	—	—	3.00
—B-side by Hadda Brooks					
RPM					
❑ 339	3 O'Clock Blues/That Ain't the Way to Do It	1951	225.00	450.00	900.00
—B.B. King singles on RPM before 339 are unconfirmed on 45 rpm					
❑ 348	Fine Lookin' Woman/She Don't Move Me No More	1952	75.00	150.00	300.00
❑ 355	Shake It Up and Go/My Own Fault, Darling	1952	37.50	75.00	150.00
❑ 360	Gotta Find My Baby/Someday Somewhere	1952	25.00	50.00	100.00
❑ 363	You Know I Love You/You Didn't Want Me	1952	20.00	40.00	80.00
❑ 374	Story from My Heart and Soul/Boogie Woogie Woman	1952	37.50	75.00	150.00
❑ 380	Woke Up This Morning (My Baby She Was Gone)/Don't Have to Cry	1953	25.00	50.00	100.00
❑ 386	Please Love Me/Highway Bound	1953	37.50	75.00	150.00
❑ 391	Please Hurry Home/Neighborhood Affair	1953	20.00	40.00	80.00
❑ 395	Why Did You Leave Me/Blind Love	1953	20.00	40.00	80.00
❑ 403	Praying to the Lord/Please Help Me	1954	7.50	15.00	30.00
❑ 408	Love Me Baby/The Woman I Love	1954	7.50	15.00	30.00
❑ 411	Everything I Do Is Wrong/Don't You Want a Man Like Me	1954	7.50	15.00	30.00
❑ 412	When My Heart Beats Like a Hammer/Bye Bye Baby	1954	7.50	15.00	30.00
❑ 416	You Upset Me Baby/Whole Lotta' Love	1954	7.50	15.00	30.00
❑ 421	Every Day I Have the Blues/Sneakin' Around	1955	7.50	15.00	30.00
❑ 425	Lonely and Blue/Jump with You Baby	1955	7.50	15.00	30.00
❑ 430	I'm in Love/Shut Your Mouth	1955	7.50	15.00	30.00
❑ 435	Talkin' the Blues/Boogie Rock	1955	7.50	15.00	30.00
❑ 437	Ten Long Years/What Can I Do	1955	7.50	15.00	30.00
❑ 450	I'm Cracking Up Over You/Ruby Lee	1956	6.25	12.50	25.00
❑ 451	Crying Won't Help You/Sixteen Tons	1956	6.25	12.50	25.00
❑ 451	Crying Won't Help You/Can't We Talk It Over	1956	6.25	12.50	25.00
❑ 457	Did You Ever Love a Woman/Let's Do the Boogie	1956	6.25	12.50	25.00
❑ 459	Dark Is the Night (Part 1)/Dark Is the Night (Part 2)	1956	6.25	12.50	25.00
❑ 468	Bad Luck/Sweet Little Angel	1956	6.25	12.50	25.00
❑ 479	On My Word of Honor/Bim Bam	1956	6.25	12.50	25.00
❑ 486	You Don't Know/Early in the Morning	1957	6.25	12.50	25.00
❑ 490	How Do I Love You/You Can't Fool My Heart	1957	6.25	12.50	25.00
❑ 492	Troubles, Troubles, Troubles/I Want to Get Married	1957	6.25	12.50	25.00
❑ 494	Quit My Baby/Be Careful with a Fool	1957	6.25	12.50	25.00
❑ 498	I Wonder/I Need You So Bad	1957	6.25	12.50	25.00
❑ 501	The Key to My Kingdom/My Heart Belongs to Only You	1957	6.25	12.50	25.00
78s					
BULLET					
❑ 309	Miss Martha King/When Your Baby Packs Up and Goes	1949	250.00	500.00	1000.
❑ 315	Got the Blues/Take a Swing with Me	1949	175.00	350.00	700.00
RPM					
❑ 304	Mistreated Woman/B.B. Boogie	1950	37.50	75.00	150.00
❑ 311	Other Night Blues/Walkin' and Cryin'	1950	30.00	60.00	120.00
❑ 318	My Baby's Gone/Don't You Want a Man Like Me	1951	30.00	60.00	120.00
❑ 323	She's Dynamite/B.B. Blues	1951	30.00	60.00	120.00
❑ 330	She's a Mean Woman/Hard Working Woman	1951	30.00	60.00	120.00
❑ 339	3 O'Clock Blues/That Ain't the Way to Do It	1951	30.00	60.00	120.00
❑ 348	Fine Lookin' Woman/She Don't Move Me No More	1952	15.00	30.00	60.00
❑ 355	Shake It Up and Go/My Own Fault, Darling	1952	12.50	25.00	50.00
❑ 360	Gotta Find My Baby/Someday Somewhere	1952	12.50	25.00	50.00
❑ 363	You Know I Love You/You Didn't Want Me	1952	10.00	20.00	40.00
❑ 374	Story from My Heart and Soul/Boogie Woogie Woman	1952	20.00	40.00	80.00
❑ 380	Woke Up This Morning (My Baby She Was Gone)/Don't Have to Cry	1953	12.50	25.00	50.00
❑ 386	Please Love Me/Highway Bound	1953	12.50	25.00	50.00

Number	Title (A Side/B Side)	Yr	VG	VG+	NM
❏ 391	Please Hurry Home/Neighborhood Affair	1953	10.00	20.00	40.00
❏ 395	Why Did You Leave Me/Blind Love	1953	10.00	20.00	40.00
❏ 403	Praying to the Lord/Please Help Me	1954	7.50	15.00	30.00
❏ 408	Love Me Baby/The Woman I Love	1954	7.50	15.00	30.00
❏ 411	Everything I Do Is Wrong/Don't You Want a Man Like Me	1954	7.50	15.00	30.00
❏ 412	When My Heart Beats Like a Hammer/Bye Bye Baby	1954	7.50	15.00	30.00
❏ 416	You Upset Me Baby/Whole Lotta' Love	1954	7.50	15.00	30.00
❏ 421	Every Day I Have the Blues/Sneakin' Around	1955	7.50	15.00	30.00
❏ 425	Lonely and Blue/Jump with You Baby	1955	7.50	15.00	30.00
❏ 430	I'm in Love/Shut Your Mouth	1955	7.50	15.00	30.00
❏ 435	Talkin' the Blues/Boogie Rock	1955	7.50	15.00	30.00
❏ 437	Ten Long Years/What Can I Do	1955	7.50	15.00	30.00
❏ 450	I'm Cracking Up Over You/Ruby Lee	1956	7.50	15.00	30.00
❏ 451	Crying Won't Help You/Sixteen Tons	1956	7.50	15.00	30.00
❏ 451	Crying Won't Help You/Can't We Talk It Over	1956	7.50	15.00	30.00
❏ 457	Did You Ever Love a Woman/Let's Do the Boogie	1956	7.50	15.00	30.00
❏ 459	Dark Is the Night (Part 1)/Dark Is the Night (Part 2)	1956	7.50	15.00	30.00
❏ 468	Bad Luck/Sweet Little Angel	1956	7.50	15.00	30.00
❏ 479	On My Word of Honor/Bim Bam	1956	7.50	15.00	30.00
❏ 486	You Don't Know/Early in the Morning	1957	10.00	20.00	40.00
❏ 490	How Do I Love You/You Can't Fool My Heart	1957	10.00	20.00	40.00
❏ 492	Troubles, Troubles, Troubles/I Want to Get Married	1957	10.00	20.00	40.00
❏ 494	Quit My Baby/Be Careful with a Fool	1957	10.00	20.00	40.00
❏ 498	I Wonder/I Need You So Bad	1957	10.00	20.00	40.00
❏ 501	The Key to My Kingdom/My Heart Belongs to Only You	1957	10.00	20.00	40.00

Albums

ABC

Number	Title (A Side/B Side)	Yr	VG	VG+	NM
❏ D-704	Blues Is King	1970	3.00	6.00	12.00
—Reissue of BluesWay 6001					
❏ D-709	Blues on Top of Blues	1970	3.00	6.00	12.00
—Reissue of BluesWay 6011					
❏ D-712	Lucille	1970	3.00	6.00	12.00
—Reissue of BluesWay 6016					
❏ D-713	Indianola Mississippi Seeds	1970	3.00	6.00	12.00
❏ D-723	Live in Cook County Jail	1971	3.00	6.00	12.00
❏ D-724	Live at the Regal	1971	3.00	6.00	12.00
—Reissue of ABC-Paramount 509					
❏ D-730	B.B. King in London	1971	3.00	6.00	12.00
❏ D-743	L.A. Midnight	1972	3.00	6.00	12.00
❏ X-759	Guess Who	1972	3.00	6.00	12.00
❏ X-767	The Best of B.B. King	1973	3.00	6.00	12.00
❏ X-794	To Know You Is to Love You	1973	3.00	6.00	12.00
❏ D-813	His Best/The Electric B.B. King	1974	3.00	6.00	12.00
—Reissue of BluesWay 6022					
❏ D-819	Live and Well	1974	3.00	6.00	12.00
—Reissue of BluesWay 6031					
❏ D-825	Friends	1974	3.00	6.00	12.00
❏ D-868	Completely Well	1975	3.00	6.00	12.00
—Reissue of BluesWay 6037					
❏ D-878	Back in the Alley	1975	3.00	6.00	12.00
—Reissue of BluesWay 6050					
❏ D-898	Lucille Talks Back	1975	3.00	6.00	12.00
❏ AB-977	King Size	1977	3.00	6.00	12.00
❏ AA-1061	Midnight Believer	1978	3.00	6.00	12.00

ABC-PARAMOUNT

Number	Title (A Side/B Side)	Yr	VG	VG+	NM
❏ 456 [M]	Mr. Blues	1963	7.50	15.00	30.00
❏ S-456 [S]	Mr. Blues	1963	10.00	20.00	40.00
❏ 509 [M]	Live at the Regal	1965	10.00	20.00	40.00
❏ S-509 [S]	Live at the Regal	1965	12.50	25.00	50.00
❏ 528 [M]	Confessin' the Blues	1965	7.50	15.00	30.00
❏ S-528 [S]	Confessin' the Blues	1965	10.00	20.00	40.00

BLUESWAY

Number	Title (A Side/B Side)	Yr	VG	VG+	NM
❏ BL-6001 [M]	Blues Is King	1967	10.00	20.00	40.00
❏ BLS-6001 [S]	Blues Is King	1967	6.25	12.50	25.00
❏ BLS-6011	Blues on Top of Blues	1968	6.25	12.50	25.00
❏ BLS-6016	Lucille	1968	6.25	12.50	25.00
❏ BLS-6022	His Best/The Electric B.B. King	1969	5.00	10.00	20.00
❏ BLS-6031	Live and Well	1969	5.00	10.00	20.00
❏ BLS-6037	Completely Well	1969	5.00	10.00	20.00
❏ BLS-6050	Back in the Alley	1970	5.00	10.00	20.00

CROWN

Number	Title (A Side/B Side)	Yr	VG	VG+	NM
❏ CST-147 [R]	B.B. King Wails	1960	3.00	6.00	12.00
—Black vinyl					
❏ CST-147 [R]	B.B. King Wails	1960	25.00	50.00	100.00
—Red vinyl					
❏ CST-152 [R]	B.B. King Sings Spirituals	1960	3.00	6.00	12.00
—Black vinyl					
❏ CST-152 [R]	B.B. King Sings Spirituals	1960	25.00	50.00	100.00
—Red vinyl					
❏ CST-195 [S]	King of the Blues	1961	5.00	10.00	20.00
—Black vinyl; this album is in true stereo, contrary to prior reports					
❏ CST-195 [S]	King of the Blues	1961	30.00	60.00	120.00
—Red vinyl; this album is in true stereo, contrary to prior reports					
❏ CST-309 [R]	Blues in My Heart	1963	3.00	6.00	12.00
❏ CST-359 [P]	B.B. King	1963	3.00	6.00	12.00
—Half of the album is in stereo, half is rechanneled					
❏ CLP-5020 [M]	Singin' the Blues	1957	25.00	50.00	100.00
—Black label, silver "Crown"					
❏ CLP-5020 [M]	Singin' the Blues	1963	5.00	10.00	20.00
—Gray label, black "Crown"					

Number	Title (A Side/B Side)	Yr	VG	VG+	NM
❏ CLP-5020 [M]	Singin' the Blues	196?	3.00	6.00	12.00
—Black label, multi-color "Crown"					
❏ CLP-5063 [M]	The Blues	1958	20.00	40.00	80.00
—Black label, silver "Crown"					
❏ CLP-5063 [M]	The Blues	1963	5.00	10.00	20.00
—Gray label, black "Crown"					
❏ CLP-5063 [M]	The Blues	196?	3.00	6.00	12.00
—Black label, multi-color "Crown"					
❏ CLP-5115 [M]	B.B. King Wails	1959	20.00	40.00	80.00
—Black label, silver "Crown"					
❏ CLP-5115 [M]	B.B. King Wails	1963	5.00	10.00	20.00
—Gray label, black "Crown"					
❏ CLP-5115 [M]	B.B. King Wails	196?	3.00	6.00	12.00
—Black label, multi-color "Crown"					
❏ CLP-5119 [M]	B.B. King Sings Spirituals	1960	15.00	30.00	60.00
—Gray label, black "Crown"					
❏ CLP-5119 [M]	B.B. King Sings Spirituals	196?	3.00	6.00	12.00
—Black label, multi-color "Crown"					
❏ CLP-5143 [M]	The Great B.B. King	1961	15.00	30.00	60.00
—Gray label, black "Crown"					
❏ CLP-5143 [M]	The Great B.B. King	196?	3.00	6.00	12.00
—Black label, multi-color "Crown"					
❏ CLP-5167 [M]	King of the Blues	1961	15.00	30.00	60.00
—Gray label, black "Crown"					
❏ CLP-5167 [M]	King of the Blues	196?	3.00	6.00	12.00
—Black label, multi-color "Crown"					
❏ CLP-5188 [M]	My Kind of Blues	1961	15.00	30.00	60.00
—Gray label, black "Crown"					
❏ CLP-5188 [M]	My Kind of Blues	196?	3.00	6.00	12.00
—Black label, multi-color "Crown"					
❏ CLP-5230 [M]	More B.B. King	1962	15.00	30.00	60.00
—Gray label, black "Crown"					
❏ CLP-5230 [M]	More B.B. King	196?	3.00	6.00	12.00
—Black label, multi-color "Crown"					
❏ CLP-5248 [M]	Twist with B.B. King	1962	15.00	30.00	60.00
—Gray label, black "Crown"					
❏ CLP-5248 [M]	Twist with B.B. King	196?	3.00	6.00	12.00
—Black label, multi-color "Crown"					
❏ CLP-5286 [M]	Easy Listening Blues	1962	15.00	30.00	60.00
—Gray label, black "Crown"					
❏ CLP-5286 [M]	Easy Listening Blues	196?	3.00	6.00	12.00
—Black label, multi-color "Crown"					
❏ CLP-5309 [M]	Blues in My Heart	1963	10.00	20.00	40.00
—Gray label, black "Crown"					
❏ CLP-5309 [M]	Blues in My Heart	196?	3.00	6.00	12.00
—Black label, multi-color "Crown"					
❏ CLP-5359 [M]	B.B. King	1963	10.00	20.00	40.00
—Gray label, black "Crown"					
❏ CLP-5359 [M]	B.B. King	196?	3.00	6.00	12.00
—Black label, multi-color "Crown"					

CRUSADERS

Number	Title (A Side/B Side)	Yr	VG	VG+	NM
❏ 16013	Live in London	1982	6.25	12.50	25.00
—Part of MCA's "Audiophile Series"					

CUSTOM

Number	Title (A Side/B Side)	Yr	VG	VG+	NM
❏ CM-2046 [M]	Blues for Me	196?	3.00	6.00	12.00
❏ CM-2049 [M]	I Love You So	196?	3.00	6.00	12.00
❏ CM-2052 [M]	The Soul of B.B. King	196?	3.00	6.00	12.00

DIRECT DISK

Number	Title (A Side/B Side)	Yr	VG	VG+	NM
❏ SD-16616	Midnight Believer	1980	12.50	25.00	50.00
—Audiophile vinyl					

GALAXY

Number	Title (A Side/B Side)	Yr	VG	VG+	NM
❏ 202 [M]	16 Greatest Hits	1963	15.00	30.00	60.00
❏ 8202 [S]	16 Greatest Hits	1963	20.00	40.00	80.00

GRP

Number	Title (A Side/B Side)	Yr	VG	VG+	NM
❏ GR-9637	Live at the Apollo	1991	3.75	7.50	15.00

KENT

Number	Title (A Side/B Side)	Yr	VG	VG+	NM
❏ KST-512 [R]	Rock Me Baby	1964	3.75	7.50	15.00
❏ KST-513 [R]	Let Me Love You	1965	3.75	7.50	15.00
❏ KST-515 [R]	B.B. King Live on Stage	1965	3.75	7.50	15.00
❏ KST-516 [R]	The Soul of B.B. King	1966	3.75	7.50	15.00
❏ KST-517 [R]	Pure Soul	1966	3.75	7.50	15.00
❏ KST-521 [R]	The Jungle	1967	3.75	7.50	15.00
❏ KST-529 [R]	Boss of the Blues	1968	3.75	7.50	15.00
❏ KST-533 [(2)]	From the Beginning	1969	5.00	10.00	20.00
❏ KST-535	Underground Blues	1969	3.75	7.50	15.00
❏ KST-539	The Incredible Soul of B.B. King	1970	3.75	7.50	15.00
❏ KST-548	Turn On to B.B. King	1970	3.75	7.50	15.00
❏ KST-552	Greatest Hits, Volume 1	1971	3.75	7.50	15.00
❏ KST-561	Better Than Ever	1971	3.75	7.50	15.00
❏ KST-563	Doing My Thing, Lord	1971	3.75	7.50	15.00
❏ KST-565	B.B. King Live	1972	3.75	7.50	15.00
❏ KST-568	The Original Sweet Sixteen	1972	3.75	7.50	15.00
❏ KLP-5012 [M]	Rock Me Baby	1964	5.00	10.00	20.00
❏ KLP-5013 [M]	Let Me Love You	1965	5.00	10.00	20.00
❏ KLP-5015 [M]	B.B. King Live on Stage	1965	5.00	10.00	20.00
❏ KLP-5016 [M]	The Soul of B.B. King	1966	5.00	10.00	20.00
❏ KLP-5017 [M]	Pure Soul	1966	5.00	10.00	20.00
❏ KLP-5021 [M]	The Jungle	1967	5.00	10.00	20.00
❏ KLP-5029 [M]	Boss of the Blues	1968	5.00	10.00	20.00

MCA

Number	Title (A Side/B Side)	Yr	VG	VG+	NM
❏ 3151	Take It Home	1979	2.50	5.00	10.00
❏ 5162	There Must Be a Better World Somewhere	1981	2.50	5.00	10.00
❏ 5307	Love Me Tender	1982	2.50	5.00	10.00
❏ 5413	Blues 'N' Jazz	1983	2.50	5.00	10.00
❏ 5616	Six Silver Strings	1985	2.50	5.00	10.00

Number	Title (A Side/B Side)	Yr	VG	VG+	NM
6455	Live at San Quentin	1990	3.00	6.00	12.00
2-8016 [(2)]	"Now Appearing" at Ole Miss	1980	3.00	6.00	12.00
27005	Live in Cook County Jail	1980	2.00	4.00	8.00
—Reissue of ABC 723					
27006	Live at the Regal	1980	2.00	4.00	8.00
—Reissue of ABC 724					
27007	His Best/The Electric B.B. King	1980	2.00	4.00	8.00
—Reissue of ABC 813					
27008	Live and Well	1980	2.00	4.00	8.00
—Reissue of ABC 819					
27009	Completely Well	1980	2.00	4.00	8.00
—Reissue of ABC 868					
27010	Back in the Alley	1980	2.00	4.00	8.00
—Reissue of ABC 878					
27011	Midnight Believer	1980	2.00	4.00	8.00
—Reissue of ABC 1061					
27028	Take It Home	1981	2.00	4.00	8.00
—Reissue of MCA 3151					
27034	There Must Be a Better World Somewhere	1983	2.00	4.00	8.00
—Reissue of MCA 5162					
27074	The Best of B.B. King	1984	2.00	4.00	8.00
—Reissue of ABC 767					
42183	The King of the Blues: 1989	1989	2.50	5.00	10.00
MOBILE FIDELITY					
1-235	Lucille	1995	6.25	12.50	25.00
—Audiophile vinyl					
PICKWICK					
SPC-3593	Live at the Regal	197?	2.00	4.00	8.00
SPC-3654	Live in Cook County Jail	197?	2.00	4.00	8.00
STAX					
ORS-4508	16 Original Big Hits	198?	2.00	4.00	8.00
UNITED					
US-7703	Heart Full of Blues	197?	2.00	4.00	8.00
US-7705	Easy Listening Blues	197?	2.00	4.00	8.00
—Reissue of Crown 5286					
US-7708	Blues for Me	197?	2.00	4.00	8.00
—Reissue of Custom 2046					
US-7711	I Love You So	197?	2.00	4.00	8.00
—Reissue of Custom 2049					
US-7714	The Soul of B.B. King	197?	2.00	4.00	8.00
—Reissue of Custom 2052					
US-7721	Swing Low	197?	2.00	4.00	8.00
US-7724	My Kind of Blues	197?	2.00	4.00	8.00
—Reissue of Crown 5188					
US-7726	Singin' the Blues	197?	2.00	4.00	8.00
—Reissue of Crown 5020					
US-7728	The Great B.B. King	197?	2.00	4.00	8.00
—Reissue of Crown 5143					
US-7732	The Blues	197?	2.00	4.00	8.00
—Reissue of Crown 5063					
US-7733	Rock Me, Baby	197?	2.00	4.00	8.00
—Reissue of Kent 5012					
US-7734	Let Me Love You	197?	2.00	4.00	8.00
—Reissue of Kent 513					
US-7736	B.B. King Live on Stage	197?	2.00	4.00	8.00
—Reissue of Kent 515					
US-7742	The Jungle	197?	2.00	4.00	8.00
—Reissue of Kent 521					
US-7750	Boss of the Blues	197?	2.00	4.00	8.00
—Reissue of Kent 529					
US-7756	The Incredible Soul of B.B. King	197?	2.00	4.00	8.00
—Reissue of Kent 539					
US-7763	Turn On with B.B. King	197?	2.00	4.00	8.00
—Reissue of Kent 548					
US-7766	Greatest Hits, Volume 1	197?	2.00	4.00	8.00
—Reissue of Kent 552					
US-7773	The Original Sweet Sixteen	197?	2.00	4.00	8.00
—Reissue of Kent 568					
US-7788	9 x 9	197?	2.00	4.00	8.00

KING, B.B./ERIC CLAPTON
45s
REPRISE

Number	Title (A Side/B Side)	Yr	VG	VG+	NM
7-16831	Riding with the King/Key to the Highway	2000	—	—	3.00
7-16832	Worried Life Blues/Days of Old	2000	—	—	3.00
7-16833	Marry You/Three O'Clock Blues (Edit)	2000	—	—	3.00
7-16834	When My Heart Beats Like a Hammer (Edit)/I Wanna Be	2000	—	—	3.00
7-16835	Help the Poor/Hold On I'm Coming	2000	—	—	3.00
7-16836	Come Rain or Come Shine/Ten Long Years	2000	—	—	3.00

KING, BEN E.
Also see AVERAGE WHITE BAND; THE DRIFTERS.
45s
ATCO

Number	Title (A Side/B Side)	Yr	VG	VG+	NM
6166	Show Me the Way/Brace Yourself	1960	4.00	8.00	16.00
6185	Spanish Harlem/First Taste of Love	1960	5.00	10.00	20.00
6194	Stand By Me/On the Horizon	1961	5.00	10.00	20.00
6203	Amor/Souvenir of Mexico	1961	4.00	8.00	16.00
6207	Young Boy Blues/Here Comes the Night	1961	4.00	8.00	16.00
6215	Ecstasy/Yes	1962	4.00	8.00	16.00
6222	Don't Play That Song (You Lied)/Hermit of Misty Mountain	1962	4.00	8.00	16.00
6231	Too Bad/My Heart Cries for You	1962	3.00	6.00	12.00

Number	Title (A Side/B Side)	Yr	VG	VG+	NM
6237	I'm Standing By/Walking in the Footsteps of a Fool	1962	3.00	6.00	12.00
6246	Tell Daddy/Auf Weidersehn, My Dear	1962	3.00	6.00	12.00
6256	How Can I Forget/Gloria Gloria	1963	3.00	6.00	12.00
6267	I (Who Have Nothing)/The Beginning of Time	1963	3.00	6.00	12.00
6275	I Could Have Danced All Night/Gypsy	1963	3.00	6.00	12.00
6284	What Now My Love/Groovin'	1964	2.50	5.00	10.00
6288	That's When It Hurts/Around the Corner	1964	2.50	5.00	10.00
6303	What Can a Man Do/Si, Senor	1964	2.50	5.00	10.00
6315	It's All Over/Let the Water Run Down	1964	2.50	5.00	10.00
6328	Seven Letters/River of Tears	1964	2.50	5.00	10.00
6343	The Record (Baby I Love You)/The Way You Shake It	1965	2.50	5.00	10.00
6357	She's Gone Again/Not Now (I'll Tell You When)	1965	2.50	5.00	10.00
6371	Cry No More/There's No Place to Hide	1965	2.50	5.00	10.00
6390	Goodnight My Love/I Can't Break the News to Myself	1965	2.50	5.00	10.00
6413	So Much Love/Don't Drive Me Away	1966	2.00	4.00	8.00
6431	Get in a Hurry/I Swear by Stars Above	1966	2.00	4.00	8.00
6454	They Don't Give Medals to Yesterday's Heroes/What Is Soul	1966	2.00	4.00	8.00
6472	A Man Without a Dream/Tears, Tears, Tears	1967	2.00	4.00	8.00
6493	Katherine/Teeny Weeny Little Bit	1967	2.00	4.00	8.00
6527	Don't Take Your Sweet Love Away/She Knows What to Do for Me	1967	2.50	5.00	10.00
6557	We Got a Thing Goin' On/What 'Cha Gonna Do About It	1968	2.00	4.00	8.00
—With Dee Dee Sharp					
6571	Don't Take Your Love from Me/Forgive This Soul	1968	2.00	4.00	8.00
6596	Where's the Girl/It's Amazing	1968	2.00	4.00	8.00
6637	It Ain't Fair/Till I Can't Take It Anymore	1968	2.00	4.00	8.00
6666	Hey Little One/When You Love Someone	1969	2.50	5.00	10.00
ATLANTIC					
3241	Supernatural Thing — Part 1/Supernatural Thing — Part 2	1975	—	2.50	5.00
3274	Do It in the Name of Love/Imagination	1975	—	2.50	5.00
3308	We Got Love/I Had a Love	1975	—	2.50	5.00
3337	I Betch'a You Didn't Know/Smooth Sailing	1976	—	2.50	5.00
3359	One More Time/Somebody's Knocking	1976	—	2.50	5.00
3402	Get It Up/Keepin' It To Myself	1977	—	2.50	5.00
—With the Average White Band					
3427	A Star in the Ghetto/What Is Soul?	1977	—	2.50	5.00
—With the Average White Band					
3444	Fool for You Anyway/The Message	1977	—	2.50	5.00
—With the Average White Band					
3494	I See the Light/Tippin'	1978	—	2.50	5.00
3535	Fly Away to My Wonderland/Spoiled	1978	—	2.50	5.00
3635	Music Trance/And This Is Love	1979	—	2.00	4.00
3808	Street Tough/Why Is the Question	1981	—	2.00	4.00
3839	You Made the Difference in My Life/Souvenirs of Love	1981	—	2.00	4.00
89234	Spanish Harlem/First Taste of Love	1987	—	—	3.00
89361	Stand By Me/Yakety Yak	1986	—	—	3.00
—B-side by the Coasters					
89361 [DJ]	Stand By Me Medley (same on both sides)	1986	2.00	4.00	8.00
—Contains excerpts from all 10 songs on the "Stand By Me" soundtrack album. It is listed here because it uses the same number as the stock release of "Stand By Me."					
89361 [PS]	Stand By Me/Yakety Yak	1986	—	—	3.00
89361 [PS]	Stand By Me Medley	1986	2.00	4.00	8.00
—Promo-only sleeve accompanying above medley. Stock and promo sleeves are identical in front but different on back.					
ICHIBAN					
254	You've Got All of Me/It's All Right	1992	—	—	3.00
257	You Still Move Me/I'm Gonna Be Somebody	1992	—	—	3.00
MANDALA					
2512	Take Me to the Pilot/I Guess It's Goodbye	1972	—	2.50	5.00
2513	Into the Mystic/White Moon	1972	—	2.50	5.00
2518	Spread Myself Around/Travellin' Woman	1973	—	2.50	5.00
MANHATTAN					
50078	Save the Last Dance for Me/Wheel of Love	1987	—	—	3.00
50078 [PS]	Save the Last Dance for Me/Wheel of Love	1987	—	—	3.00
MAXWELL					
800	I Can't Take It Like a Man/(B-side unknown)	1969	2.00	4.00	8.00
THE RIGHT STUFF					
S7-19728	4th of July, Asbury Park (Sandy)/Janey, Don't You Lose Heart	1997	—	—	3.00
—B-side by Mrs. Fun/Tina & The B-Side Movement					

Albums
ATCO

Number	Title (A Side/B Side)	Yr	VG	VG+	NM
33-133 [M]	Spanish Harlem	1961	25.00	50.00	100.00
—Yellow label with harp					
33-133 [M]	Spanish Harlem	1962	10.00	20.00	40.00
—Gold and gray label					
SD 33-133 [S]	Spanish Harlem	1961	37.50	75.00	150.00
—Yellow label with harp					
SD 33-133 [S]	Spanish Harlem	1962	12.50	25.00	50.00
—Purple and brown label					
33-137 [M]	Ben E. King Sings for Soulful Lovers	1962	10.00	20.00	40.00
SD 33-137 [S]	Ben E. King Sings for Soulful Lovers	1962	15.00	30.00	60.00
33-142 [M]	Don't Play That Song	1962	10.00	20.00	40.00
SD 33-142 [S]	Don't Play That Song	1962	15.00	30.00	60.00
33-165 [M]	Ben E. King's Greatest Hits	1964	7.50	15.00	30.00
SD 33-165 [S]	Ben E. King's Greatest Hits	1964	10.00	20.00	40.00
—Purple and brown label					

K

Number	Title (A Side/B Side)	Yr	VG	VG+	NM
❑ SD 33-165 [S]	Ben E. King's Greatest Hits	1969	3.00	6.00	12.00
—Yellow label					
❑ SD 33-165 [S]	Ben E. King's Greatest Hits	197?	2.00	4.00	8.00
—Any other color label					
❑ 33-174 [M]	Seven Letters	1965	10.00	20.00	40.00
❑ SD 33-174 [S]	Seven Letters	1965	12.50	25.00	50.00
ATLANTIC					
❑ SD 18132	Supernatural	1975	3.00	6.00	12.00
❑ SD 18169	I Have a Love	1976	3.00	6.00	12.00
❑ SD 18191	Rhapsody	1976	3.00	6.00	12.00
❑ SD 19200	Let Me Live in Your Life	1978	3.00	6.00	12.00
❑ SD 19269	Music Trance	1980	2.50	5.00	10.00
❑ SD 19300	Street Tough	1981	2.50	5.00	10.00
❑ 81716	Stand By Me: The Best of Ben E. King	1987	2.00	4.00	8.00
—Includes seven Ben E. King tracks and three by the Drifters					
CLARION					
❑ 606 [M]	Young Boy Blues	1966	6.25	12.50	25.00
❑ SD 606 [S]	Young Boy Blues	1966	7.50	15.00	30.00
MANDALA					
❑ MLP 3007	The Beginning of It All for Ben E. King	1972	5.00	10.00	20.00
❑ MLP-3008 [DJ]	Audio Biography	1972	7.50	15.00	30.00
—Promo-only interview by Richard Robinson					
MAXWELL					
❑ ML-88001	Rough Edges	1969	5.00	10.00	20.00

KING, EARL

45s

Number	Title (A Side/B Side)	Yr	VG	VG+	NM
ACE					
❑ 509	Those Lonely, Lonely Nights/Baby You Can Get Your Gun	1955	15.00	30.00	60.00
❑ 514	My Love Is Strong/Little Girl	1956	12.50	25.00	50.00
❑ 517	It Must Have Been Love/I'll Take You Back Home	1956	12.50	25.00	50.00
❑ 520	Is Everything Alright/Mother Told Me Not to Go	1956	12.50	25.00	50.00
❑ 529	Those Lonely, Lonely Feelings/You Can Fly High	1957	12.50	25.00	50.00
❑ 543	I'll Never Get Tired/Well'o, Well'o, Well'o Baby	1958	12.50	25.00	50.00
❑ 564	Weary Silent Night/Everybody's Carried Away	1959	10.00	20.00	40.00
❑ 598	Don't You Know You're Wrong/Buddy It's Time to Go	1960	10.00	20.00	40.00
IMPERIAL					
❑ 5713	Come On — Part 1/Come On — Part 2	1960	6.25	12.50	25.00
❑ 5730	Love Me Now/The Things That I Used to Do	1961	6.25	12.50	25.00
❑ 5750	Come Along with Me/You're More to Me Than Gold	1961	6.25	12.50	25.00
❑ 5774	You Better Know/Mama and Papa	1961	6.25	12.50	25.00
❑ 5811	Trick Bag/Always a First Time	1962	6.25	12.50	25.00
❑ 5858	We Are Just Friends/You're More to Me That Gold	1962	6.25	12.50	25.00
❑ 5891	Come Along with Me/Case of Love	1962	6.25	12.50	25.00
REX					
❑ 1015	I Can't Help Myself/Darling Honey, Angel Child	1961	5.00	10.00	20.00
SPECIALTY					
❑ 495	A Mother's Love/I'm Your Best Bet Baby	1954	15.00	30.00	60.00
❑ 531	No One But Me/Eating and Sleeping	1954	15.00	30.00	60.00
❑ 558	Funny Face/Sittin' and Wonderin'	1955	15.00	30.00	60.00

KING, EVELYN "CHAMPAGNE"

12-Inch Singles

Number	Title (A Side/B Side)	Yr	VG	VG+	NM
EMI					
❑ V-56146	Day to Day (Dance Mix 8:01) (Dub Mix 7:18) (Bonus Beats) (Acappella) (7" Edit 4:01)	1989	—	3.50	7.00
❑ V-56155	Day to Day (12" Blazin' Remix) (7" Blazin' Edit) (Dub Mix) (Blazin' Instrumental)	1989	2.50	5.00	10.00
❑ V-56181	Do Right (12-Inch House [Yeah That's Right Mix]) (Do the Right Thing Mix) (Dub Mix) (7-Inch Do the Right Thing Mix) (7-Inch House Mix)	1990	2.50	5.00	10.00
EMI MANHATTAN					
❑ SPRO-04068 [DJ]	Flirt (Loose Booty Mix 7:05) (Sin-Strumental Mix 6:11) (Booty to Booty Dub Mix 7:57)	1988	2.50	5.00	10.00
—As "Evelyn King"					
❑ V-56075	Flirt (Pump It Up Mix) (Flirt to Flirt Dub)	1988	—	3.50	7.00
—As "Evelyn King"					
❑ V-56101	Hold On to What You've Got (Extended UK Mix 8:28) (Grip Your Hips Mix 6:34) (Extended LP Mix 8:32) (Get a Grip Mix 6:34) (Radio Mix 5:49) (Set It Off Dub)	1988	—	3.50	7.00
PRIVATE I					
❑ 4Z9-05283	Give It Up (Killer Dance Mix) (Dub Mix)	1985	2.00	4.00	8.00
RCA					
❑ PD-11213	Shame/Nobody Knows	1978	2.50	5.00	10.00
❑ PD-11415	I Don't Know If It's Right (8:15)/We're Going to a Party	1978	3.75	7.50	15.00
❑ PD-11587	Music Box (7:27)/It's OK	1979	3.00	6.00	12.00
❑ PD-12090	Let's Get Funky Tonight (6:28)/Just a Little Bit of Love	1980	3.00	6.00	12.00
❑ PD-12244	I'm in Love/The Other Side of Love	1981	2.50	5.00	10.00
—As "Evelyn King"					
❑ PD-13018	Spirit of the Dancer/I Can't Take It	1981	2.00	4.00	8.00
—As "Evelyn King"					
❑ PD-13274	Love Come Down/(Instrumental)	1982	3.00	6.00	12.00
—As "Evelyn King"					
❑ PD-13396	Betcha She Don't Love You (Vocal) (Instrumental)	1982	2.00	4.00	8.00
—As "Evelyn King"					
❑ PD-13462	Get Loose/Spirit of the Dancer	1983	2.50	5.00	10.00
—As "Evelyn King"					
❑ PD-13683	Action/Let's Get Crazy	1983	2.00	4.00	8.0
❑ JD-13749 [DJ]	Shake Down (6:20) (6:46)	1984	2.50	5.00	10.0
❑ PW-13765	Shake Down (Original Version) (Dub Version)/Tell Me Something Good	1984	2.00	4.00	8.0
❑ PW-13826	Teenager (12-Inch Remix 5:20) (Instrumental Mix 5:15) (Dub Version 5:01)	1984	2.00	4.00	8.0
❑ PW-13915	Just for the Night (4:45) (TV Track 4:45)/So in Love	1984	2.50	5.00	10.0
❑ PW-13981	Out of Control (Remix Version 5:50) (Instrumental) (Vocal Dub Version 6:35)/Show Me (Don't Tell Me)	1984	2.50	5.00	10.0
❑ PW-14202	Your Personal Touch (Dance Version) (LP Version)/Talking in My Sleep	1985	2.00	4.00	8.0
❑ PW-14309	High Horse (Remixed Version 6:10) (Dub Version 6:00) (LP Mix 4:26)/Take a Chance	1986	2.00	4.00	8.0
❑ PW-14374	Slow Down (Remix) (LP Version) (Dub A) (Dub B)	1986	2.00	4.00	8.0
❑ 62350	Shame '92 (2 versions)/Shame '77 (2 versions)	1992	2.50	5.00	10.0

45s

Number	Title (A Side/B Side)	Yr	VG	VG+	NM
EMI MANHATTAN					
❑ B-50101	Flirt/(Instrumental)	1988	—	—	3.0
—As "Evelyn King"					
❑ B-50101 [PS]	Flirt/(Instrumental)	1988	—	2.00	4.0
—As "Evelyn King"					
❑ B-50142	Hold On to What You've Got/(Set It Off Dub)	1988	—	—	3.0
❑ 50164	Kisses Don't Lie/(Instrumental)	1988	—	—	3.0
PRIVATE I					
❑ ZS4-05627	Give It Up/Armies of the Night	1985	—	2.00	4.0
—B-side by Sparks					
RCA					
❑ PB-11025	Dancin', Dancin', Dancin'/Till I Come Off the Road	1977	2.50	5.00	10.0
❑ PB-11122	Shame/Dancin', Dancin', Dancin'	1977	—	2.50	5.0
❑ PB-11386	I Don't Know If It's Right/We're Going to a Party	1978	—	2.00	4.0
❑ PB-11386 [PS]	I Don't Know If It's Right/We're Going to a Party	1978	—	2.50	5.0
❑ PB-11586	Music Box/It's Okay	1979	—	2.00	4.0
❑ PB-11680	Out There/Make Up Your Mind	1979	—	2.00	4.0
❑ PD-11681	Out There/Make Up Your Mind	1979	3.00	6.00	12.0
❑ GB-11969	Shame/I Don't Know If It's Right	1980	—	—	3.0
—Gold Standard Series					
❑ PB-12075	Let's Get Funky Tonight/Just a Little Bit of Love	1980	—	2.00	4.0
❑ PB-12156	I Need Your Love/Bedroom Eyes	1981	—	2.00	4.0
❑ PB-12243	I'm in Love/The Other Side of Love	1981	—	2.00	4.0
—As "Evelyn King"					
❑ PB-12243 [PS]	I'm in Love/The Other Side of Love	1981	—	2.50	5.0
—As "Evelyn King"					
❑ PB-12322	Don't Hide Our Love/The Best Is Yet to Come	1981	—	2.00	4.0
—As "Evelyn King"					
❑ PB-13017	Spirit of the Dancer/I Can't Take It	1981	—	2.00	4.0
—As "Evelyn King"					
❑ PB-13273	Love Come Down/(Instrumental)	1982	—	2.00	4.0
—As "Evelyn King"					
❑ PB-13380	Betcha She Don't Love You/Get Up Off Your Love	1982	—	2.00	4.0
—As "Evelyn King"					
❑ JB-13398 [DJ]	Betcha She Don't Love You (Long)/(Short)	1982	2.00	4.00	8.0
—As "Evelyn King"; promo-only number					
❑ PB-13461	Get Loose/Spirit of the Dancer	1983	—	2.00	4.0
—As "Evelyn King"					
❑ GB-13493	Love Come Down/I'm in Love	1983	—	—	3.0
—As "Evelyn King"; Gold Standard Series					
❑ PB-13682	Action/Let's Get Crazy	1983	—	2.00	4.0
❑ PB-13748	Shake Down/Tell Me Something Good	1984	—	2.00	4.0
❑ PB-13825	Teenager/Don't It Feel Good	1984	—	2.00	4.0
❑ PB-13914	Just for the Night/So In Love	1984	—	2.00	4.0
❑ PB-13914 [PS]	Just for the Night/So In Love	1984	—	2.50	5.0
❑ PB-13980	Out of Control/Show Me (Don't Tell Me)	1984	—	—	3.0
❑ PB-13980 [PS]	Out of Control/Show Me (Don't Tell Me)	1984	—	2.00	4.0
❑ PB-14048	Till Midnight/I'm So Romantic	1985	—	—	3.0
❑ PW-14049	Till Midnight (Remixed Version) (Dub Version) (Instrumental) (Acappella)	1985	2.00	4.00	8.0
❑ PB-14201	Your Personal Touch/Talking in My Sleep	1985	—	—	3.0
❑ PB-14201 [PS]	Your Personal Touch/Talking in My Sleep	1985	—	—	3.0
❑ PB-14308	High Horse/Take a Chance	1986	—	—	3.0
❑ PB-14373	Slow Down/Better Deal	1986	—	—	3.0

Albums

Number	Title (A Side/B Side)	Yr	VG	VG+	NM
EMI					
❑ E1-92049	The Girl Next Door	1989	3.00	6.00	12.0
EMI MANHATTAN					
❑ E1-46968	Flirt	1988	2.00	4.00	8.0
RCA VICTOR					
❑ APL1-2466	Smooth Talk	1978	2.50	5.00	10.0
❑ AFL1-3033	Music Box	1979	2.50	5.00	10.0
❑ AFL1-3543	Call on Me	1980	2.50	5.00	10.0
❑ AFL1-3962	I'm in Love	1981	2.50	5.00	10.0
—As "Evelyn King"					
❑ AFL1-4337	Get Loose	1982	2.00	4.00	8.0
—As "Evelyn King"					
❑ AFL1-4725	Face to Face	1983	2.00	4.00	8.0
❑ AFL1-5308	So Romantic	1984	2.00	4.00	8.0
❑ AFL1-7015	A Long Time Coming (A Change Is Gonna Come)	1985	2.50	5.00	10.0

KING, FREDDIE

45s

Number	Title (A Side/B Side)	Yr	VG	VG+	NM
COTILLION					
❑ 44015	Funky/Play It Cool	1968	2.00	4.00	8.0
❑ 44058	I Wonder Why/Yonder Wall	1970	2.00	4.00	8.0

Number	Title (A Side/B Side)	Yr	VG	VG+	NM
EL-BEE					
❏ 157	Country Boy/That's What You Think	1956	100.00	200.00	400.00
FEDERAL					
❏ 12384	Have You Ever Loved a Woman/You've Got to Love Her with a Feeling	1960	10.00	20.00	40.00
❏ 12401	Hideaway/I Love the Woman	1961	7.50	15.00	30.00
❏ 12415	Lonesome Whistle Blues/It's Too Bad Things Are Going So Tough	1961	7.50	15.00	30.00
❏ 12428	San-Ho-Zay/See See Baby	1961	7.50	15.00	30.00
❏ 12432	I'm Tore Down/Sen-Say-Shun	1961	7.50	15.00	30.00
❏ 12439	Christmas Tears/I Hear Jingle Bells	1961	7.50	15.00	30.00
❏ 12443	If You Believe in What You Do/Heads Up	1961	5.00	10.00	20.00
❏ 12450	Takin' Care of Business/The Stumble	1962	5.00	10.00	20.00
❏ 12456	Side Tracked/Sittin' on the Boat Dock	1962	5.00	10.00	20.00
❏ 12462	What About Love/Texas Oil	1962	5.00	10.00	20.00
❏ 12470	Come On/Just Pickin'	1962	5.00	10.00	20.00
❏ 12475	In the Open/I'm On My Way to Atlanta	1962	5.00	10.00	20.00
❏ 12482	The Bossa Nova Watusi Twist/Look Ma, I'm Crying	1963	3.75	7.50	15.00
❏ 12491	(I'd Love To) Make Love to You/One Hundred Years	1963	3.75	7.50	15.00
❏ 12499	(The Welfare) Turns Its Back on You/You're Barkin' Up the Wrong Tree	1963	3.75	7.50	15.00
❏ 12509	Surf Monkey/Monkey Donkey	1963	5.00	10.00	20.00
❏ 12515	Meet Me at the Station/Ting-a-Ling	1964	3.75	7.50	15.00
❏ 12518	Driving Sideways/Someday After Awhile (You'll Be Gone)	1964	3.00	6.00	12.00
❏ 12521	She Put the Whammy on Me/High Rise	1964	3.00	6.00	12.00
❏ 12529	Now I've Got a Woman/Onion Rings	1964	3.00	6.00	12.00
❏ 12532	Some Other Day, Some Other Time/Manhole	1965	3.00	6.00	12.00
❏ 12535	If You Have It/I Love You More Every Day	1965	3.00	6.00	12.00
❏ 12537	Full Time Love/She's the One	1965	3.00	6.00	12.00
KING					
❏ 6057	Use What You've Got/Double Eyed Whammy	1966	3.00	6.00	12.00
❏ 6080	You've Got Me Licked/The Girl from Kookamunga	1967	3.00	6.00	12.00
❏ 6264	Have You Ever Loved a Woman/Hideaway	1969	2.00	4.00	8.00
RSO					
❏ 505	My Credit Didn't Go Through/Texas Flyer	1975	—	2.50	5.00
❏ 516	Boogie Bump/It's Your Love	1975	—	2.50	5.00
SHELTER					
❏ 7303	Going Down/Toke Down	1971	—	3.00	6.00
❏ 7320	Me and My Guitar/Downtown in Lodi	1972	—	3.00	6.00
❏ 7333	Woman Across the River/Help Me Through the Day	1973	—	3.00	6.00
❏ 40410	Going Down/Me and My Guitar	1975	—	2.50	5.00
Albums					
COTILLION					
❏ SD 9004	Freddie King Is a Blues Master	1969	6.25	12.50	25.00
❏ SD 9016	My Feeling for the Blues	1970	6.25	12.50	25.00
KING					
❏ 762 [M]	Freddie King Sings the Blues	1961	62.50	125.00	250.00
❏ 773 [M]	Let's Hide Away and Dance Away	1961	62.50	125.00	250.00
❏ 821 [M]	Bossa Nova and Blues	1962	37.50	75.00	150.00
❏ 856 [M]	Freddie King Goes Surfin'	1963	20.00	40.00	80.00
❏ KS-856 [S]	Freddie King Goes Surfin'	1963	30.00	60.00	120.00
❏ 928 [M]	A Bonanza of Instrumentals	1965	12.50	25.00	50.00
❏ KS-928 [S]	A Bonanza of Instrumentals	1965	15.00	30.00	60.00
❏ 964 [M]	24 Vocals and Instrumentals	1966	6.25	12.50	25.00
❏ KS-1059	Hide Away	1969	3.75	7.50	15.00
MCA					
❏ 690	The Best of Freddie King	1979	2.00	4.00	8.00
—Reissue of Shelter 52021					
MODERN BLUES					
❏ MB2LP-721 [(2)]Just Pickin'		198?	3.75	7.50	15.00
❏ MBLP-722	Freddie King Sings	198?	2.50	5.00	10.00
RSO					
❏ RS-1-3025	Freddie King 1934-1976	1977	3.00	6.00	12.00
❏ SD 4803	Burglar	1974	3.00	6.00	12.00
❏ SD 4811	Larger Than Life	1975	3.00	6.00	12.00
SHELTER					
❏ 2140	The Best of Freddie King	1975	3.75	7.50	15.00
—Original with MCA distribution					
❏ SW-8905	Getting Ready	1971	3.75	7.50	15.00
❏ SW-8913	Texas Cannonball	1972	3.75	7.50	15.00
❏ SW-8919	Woman Across the River	1973	3.75	7.50	15.00
❏ SRL 52021	The Best of Freddie King	1977	3.00	6.00	12.00
—Second edition with ABC distribution					
STARDAY/GUSTO					
❏ 5012	17 Original Hits	1977	2.50	5.00	10.00
❏ 5033	Hide Away	1978	2.50	5.00	10.00

KING, FREDDIE/LULA REED/BOBBY THOMPSON
Albums

Number	Title (A Side/B Side)	Yr	VG	VG+	NM
KING					
❏ 777 [M]	Boy-Girl-Boy	1962	62.50	125.00	250.00

KING, REV. MARTIN LUTHER
45s

Number	Title (A Side/B Side)	Yr	VG	VG+	NM
GORDY					
❏ 7023	I Have a Dream/We Shall Overcome	1963	7.50	15.00	30.00
❏ 7023	I Have a Dream/We Shall Overcome	1968	2.00	4.00	8.00
—B-side by Liz Lands; "Gordy" on side of label					

Number	Title (A Side/B Side)	Yr	VG	VG+	NM
MERCURY					
❏ 72814	I Have a Dream/I've Been to the Mountain Top-Eulogy	1968	2.00	4.00	8.00
Albums					
20TH CENTURY					
❏ TCF-3110 [M]	Freedom March on Washington	1963	7.50	15.00	30.00
❏ S-3201	The Rev. Dr. Martin Luther King, Jr.	1968	5.00	10.00	20.00
BUDDAH					
❏ BDS-2002	Man of Love	1968	5.00	10.00	20.00
CREED					
❏ 3201 [M]	I Have a Dream	1968	5.00	10.00	20.00
DOOTO					
❏ DTL-831 [M]	Martin Luther King at Zion Hill	1962	7.50	15.00	30.00
❏ DTL-841	The American Dream	1968	5.00	10.00	20.00
GORDY					
❏ G-906 [M]	The Great March to Freedom	1963	10.00	20.00	40.00
—"Gordy" in script at top of label					
❏ G-906 [M]	The Great March to Freedom	1968	3.75	7.50	15.00
—Later pressings					
❏ G-908 [M]	The Great March on Washington	1963	10.00	20.00	40.00
—"Gordy" in script at top of label					
❏ G-908 [M]	The Great March on Washington	1968	3.75	7.50	15.00
—Later pressings					
❏ G-929	...Free at Last	1968	7.50	15.00	30.00
—Original with gatefold cover					
MERCURY					
❏ SR-61170	In Search of Freedom	1968	5.00	10.00	20.00
MR. MAESTRO					
❏ 1000 [M]	The March on Washington	1963	7.50	15.00	30.00
SUNSET					
❏ 21033	The Struggle for Freedom	1968	3.75	7.50	15.00
UNART					
❏ S 21033	In the Struggle for Freedom and Human Dignity	1968	5.00	10.00	20.00

KING CURTIS
45s

Number	Title (A Side/B Side)	Yr	VG	VG+	NM
ABC-PARAMOUNT					
❏ 10133	Beatnick Hoedown/King Neptune's Guitar	1960	3.75	7.50	15.00
ALCOR					
❏ 1016	Jay Walk/The Lone Prairie	1961	5.00	10.00	20.00
APOLLO					
❏ 507	King's Rock/Dynamite at Midnight	1957	7.50	15.00	30.00
ATCO					
❏ 6114	The Birth of the Blues/Just Smoochin'	1958	5.00	10.00	20.00
❏ 6124	You Made Me Love You/Ific	1958	5.00	10.00	20.00
❏ 6135	Castle Rock/Chili	1959	5.00	10.00	20.00
❏ 6143	Honey Dripper (Part 1)/Honey Dripper (Part 2)	1959	5.00	10.00	20.00
❏ 6152	Heavenly Blues/Restless Guitar	1959	5.00	10.00	20.00
❏ 6387	Spanish Harlem/The Boss	1965	2.50	5.00	10.00
❏ 6406	On Broadway/Quicksand	1966	2.00	4.00	8.00
❏ 6419	Make the World Go Away/You've Lost That Lovin' Feeling	1966	2.00	4.00	8.00
❏ 6429	Dancing in the Streets/He'll Have to Go	1966	2.00	4.00	8.00
❏ 6447	Pots and Pans (Part 1)/Pots and Pans (Part 2)	1966	2.00	4.00	8.00
❏ 6457	Something on Your Mind/Soul Theme	1966	2.00	4.00	8.00
❏ 6476	Jump Back/When Something Is Wrong with My Baby	1967	2.00	4.00	8.00
❏ 6496	You Don't Miss Your Water/Green Onions	1967	2.00	4.00	8.00
❏ 6511	Memphis Soul Stew/Blue Nocturne	1967	2.00	4.00	8.00
❏ 6516	Ode to Billie Joe/In the Pocket	1967	2.00	4.00	8.00
—As "The Kingpins"					
❏ 6534	For What It's Worth/Cook Out	1968	2.00	4.00	8.00
❏ 6547	I Never Loved a Man (The Way I Love You)/I Was Made to Love Her	1968	2.00	4.00	8.00
❏ 6562	(Sittin' On) The Dock of the Bay/This Is Soul	1968	2.00	4.00	8.00
❏ 6582	(Theme from) Valley of the Dolls/Eighth Wonder	1968	2.00	4.00	8.00
❏ 6598	I Heard It Through the Grapevine/Whiter Shade of Pale	1968	2.00	4.00	8.00
❏ 6613	Harper Valley P.T.A./Makin' Hey	1968	2.00	4.00	8.00
❏ 6630	The Christmas Song/What Are You Doing New Year's Eve?	1968	3.00	6.00	12.00
❏ 6664	Games People Play/Foot Pattin' (Part 2)	1969	2.00	4.00	8.00
❏ 6680	Instant Groove/Sweet Inspiration	1969	2.00	4.00	8.00
❏ 6695	Little Green Apples/La Jeanne	1969	2.00	4.00	8.00
❏ 6711	C.C. Rider/Rocky Roll	1969	2.00	4.00	8.00
❏ 6720	Pop Corn Willie/Patty Cake	1969	2.00	4.00	8.00
❏ 6738	Soulin'/Teasin'	1970	—	3.00	6.00
❏ 6762	Get Ready/Bridge Over Troubled Water	1970	—	3.00	6.00
❏ 6779	Whole Lotta Love/Floatin'	1970	—	3.00	6.00
❏ 6785	Changes (Part 1)/Changes (Part 2)	1970	—	3.00	6.00
❏ 6834	Changes (Part 1)/Changes (Part 2)	1971	—	3.00	6.00
❏ 6908	Ridin' Thumb (Part 1)/Ridin' Thumb (Part 2)	1972	—	3.00	6.00
CAPITOL					
❏ 4788	Beach Party/Turn 'Em On	1962	2.50	5.00	10.00
❏ 4841	Beautiful Brown Eyes/Your Cheatin' Heart	1962	2.50	5.00	10.00
❏ 4891	Strollin' Home/Mess Around	1962	2.50	5.00	10.00
❏ 4998	Do the Monkey/Feel All Right	1963	2.50	5.00	10.00
❏ 5061	Theme from "Lilies of the Field" (Part 1)/Theme from "Lilies of the Field" (Part 2)	1963	2.50	5.00	10.00
❏ 5109	Soul Serenade/More Soul	1964	2.50	5.00	10.00
❏ 5212	Summer Dream/Melancholy Serenade	1964	2.50	5.00	10.00
❏ 5270	Stranger on the Shore/Hide Away	1964	2.50	5.00	10.00
❏ 5324	Sister Sadie/Tanya	1964	2.50	5.00	10.00
❏ 5377	Bill Bailey/Soul Twine	1965	2.50	5.00	10.00

Number	Title (A Side/B Side)	Yr	VG	VG+	NM
❏ 5490	The Prance/Slow Drag	1965	2.50	5.00	10.00
DELUXE					
❏ 6142	The Stranger/Steel Guitar Rag	1957	6.25	12.50	25.00
❏ 6157	Wicky Wacky (Part 1)/Wicky Wacky (Part 2)	1958	6.25	12.50	25.00
ENJOY					
❏ 1000	Soul Twist/Twisting Time	1962	3.75	7.50	15.00
❏ 1001	Twisting with the King/Wobble Twist	1962	3.75	7.50	15.00
EVEREST					
❏ 19406	Jay Walk/The Lone Prairie	1961	3.75	7.50	15.00
EVERLAST					
❏ 5030	Soul Twist/Twisting Time	1965	2.50	5.00	10.00
GEM					
❏ 208	Tenor in the Sky/No More Crying on My Pillow	1954	10.00	20.00	40.00
GROOVE					
❏ 1060	Movin' On/Rockabye Baby	1956	6.25	12.50	25.00
KING					
❏ 5647	King Curtis Stomp/Steel Guitar Rag	1962	3.00	6.00	12.00
MONARCH					
❏ 702	Wine Head/I've Got News for You Baby	1953	15.00	30.00	60.00
NEW JAZZ					
❏ 45-510	Soul Meeting/All the Way	1961	3.75	7.50	15.00
SEG-WAY					
❏ 1006	Hot Rod/Bonaparte's Retreat	1962	3.75	7.50	15.00
SKY ROCKET					
❏ 106	Madisonville (Part 1)/Madisonville (Part 2)	1960	5.00	10.00	20.00
TRU SOUND					
❏ 401	Trouble in Mind/But That's Alright	1961	3.75	7.50	15.00
❏ 406	Twistin' and Jivin'/I Have to Worry	1961	3.75	7.50	15.00
❏ 412	So Rare/Hucklebuck Twist	1961	3.75	7.50	15.00
❏ 415	Free for All/When the Saints Go Marching In	1962	3.75	7.50	15.00
❏ 422	Low Down/I'll Wait for You	1962	3.75	7.50	15.00
Albums					
ATCO					
❏ 33-113 [M]	Have Tenor Sax, Will Blow	1959	10.00	20.00	40.00
❏ SD 33-113 [S]	Have Tenor Sax, Will Blow	1959	15.00	30.00	60.00
❏ 33-189 [M]	That Lovin' Feeling	1966	5.00	10.00	20.00
❏ SD 33-189 [S]	That Lovin' Feeling	1966	6.25	12.50	25.00
❏ 33-198 [M]	Live at Small's Paradise	1966	5.00	10.00	20.00
❏ SD 33-198 [S]	Live at Small's Paradise	1966	6.25	12.50	25.00
❏ 33-211 [M]	The Great Memphis Hits	1967	5.00	10.00	20.00
❏ SD 33-211 [S]	The Great Memphis Hits	1967	6.25	12.50	25.00
❏ 33-231 [M]	King Size Soul	1967	6.25	12.50	25.00
❏ SD 33-231 [S]	King Size Soul	1967	5.00	10.00	20.00
❏ 33-247 [M]	Sweet Soul	1968	7.50	15.00	30.00
❏ SD 33-247 [S]	Sweet Soul	1968	5.00	10.00	20.00
❏ SD 33-266	The Best of King Curtis	1968	5.00	10.00	20.00
❏ SD 33-293	Instant Groove	1969	5.00	10.00	20.00
❏ SD 33-338	Get Ready	1970	5.00	10.00	20.00
❏ SD 33-359	Live at Fillmore West	1971	5.00	10.00	20.00
❏ SD 33-385	Everybody's Talkin'	1972	5.00	10.00	20.00
ATLANTIC					
❏ SD 1637	Blues Montreux	1973	3.00	6.00	12.00
CAPITOL					
❏ ST 1756 [S]	Country Soul	1963	10.00	20.00	40.00
❏ T 1756 [M]	Country Soul	1963	7.50	15.00	30.00
❏ ST 2095 [S]	Soul Serenade	1964	7.50	15.00	30.00
❏ T 2095 [M]	Soul Serenade	1964	6.25	12.50	25.00
❏ ST 2341 [S]	King Curtis Plays the Hits Made Famous by Sam Cooke	1965	7.50	15.00	30.00
❏ T 2341 [M]	King Curtis Plays the Hits Made Famous by Sam Cooke	1965	6.25	12.50	25.00
❏ ST 2858 [S]	The Best of King Curtis	1968	6.25	12.50	25.00
❏ T 2858 [M]	The Best of King Curtis	1968	12.50	25.00	50.00
—Red and white "Starline" label; may be promo only					
❏ SM-11798	Soul Serenade	1978	2.50	5.00	10.00
—Reissue					
❏ SM-11963	The Best of King Curtis	1979	2.50	5.00	10.00
—Reissue					
CLARION					
❏ 615 [M]	The Great "K" Curtis	1966	5.00	10.00	20.00
❏ SD 615 [S]	The Great "K" Curtis	1966	6.25	12.50	25.00
COLLECTABLES					
❏ COL-5119	Soul Twist	198?	2.50	5.00	10.00
❏ COL-5156	Golden Classics: Enjoy…The Best of King Curtis	198?	2.50	5.00	10.00
ENJOY					
❏ ENLP-2001 [M]	Soul Twist	1962	12.50	25.00	50.00
EVEREST					
❏ SDBR-1121 [S]	Azure	1961	18.75	37.50	75.00
❏ LPBR-5121 [M]	Azure	1961	12.50	25.00	50.00
FANTASY					
❏ OJC-198	The New Scene of King Curtis	1985	2.50	5.00	10.00
—Reissue of New Jazz 8237					
❏ OBC-512	Trouble in Mind	1988	2.50	5.00	10.00
—Reissue of Tru-Sound 15001					
NEW JAZZ					
❏ NJLP-8237 [M]	The New Scene of King Curtis	1960	15.00	30.00	60.00
—Purple label					
❏ NJLP-8237 [M]	The New Scene of King Curtis	1965	7.50	15.00	30.00
—Blue label with trident logo on right					
PRESTIGE					
❏ PRLP-7222 [M]	Soul Meeting	1962	12.50	25.00	50.00
❏ PRST-7222 [S]	Soul Meeting	1962	18.75	37.50	75.00

Number	Title (A Side/B Side)	Yr	VG	VG+	NM
❏ PRST-7709	The Best of King Curtis	1969	3.75	7.50	15.00
❏ PRST-7775	The Best of King Curtis — One More Time	1970	3.75	7.50	15.00
❏ PRST-7789	King Soul	1970	3.75	7.50	15.00
❏ PRST-7833	Soul Meeting	1971	3.75	7.50	15.00
—Reissue of 7222					
❏ 24033 [(2)]	Jazz Groove	198?	3.75	7.50	15.00
RCA CAMDEN					
❏ CAS-2242	Sax in Motion	1968	3.75	7.50	15.00
RCA VICTOR					
❏ LPM-2492 [M]	Arthur Murray's Music for Dancing: The Twist!	1962	6.25	12.50	25.00
❏ LSP-2492 [S]	Arthur Murray's Music for Dancing: The Twist!	1962	7.50	15.00	30.00
TRU-SOUND					
❏ TS-15001 [M]	Trouble in Mind	1961	12.50	25.00	50.00
❏ TS-15008 [M]	It's Party Time	1962	12.50	25.00	50.00
❏ TS-15009 [M]	Doin' the Dixie Twist	1962	12.50	25.00	50.00

KING FLOYD
45s
CHIMNEYVILLE

Number	Title (A Side/B Side)	Yr	VG	VG+	NM
❏ 435	Groove Me/What Our Love Needs	1970	—	3.00	6.00
❏ 437	Baby Let Me Kiss You/Please Don't Leave Me Lonely	1971	—	2.50	5.00
❏ 437 [PS]	Baby Let Me Kiss You/Please Don't Leave Me Lonely	1971	2.00	4.00	8.00
❏ 439	Got to Have Your Lovin'/Let Us Be	1971	—	2.50	5.00
❏ 442	It's Wonderful/Let Me See You Do That Thing	1971	—	2.50	5.00
❏ 443	Woman Don't Go Astray/Everybody Needs Somebody	1972	—	2.50	5.00
❏ 446	Think About It/Here It Is	1973	—	2.50	5.00
❏ 1779	So Much Confusion/So Much Confusion (Part 2)	1973	—	2.50	5.00
❏ 10202	I Feel Like Dynamite/Handle with Care	1974	—	2.50	5.00
❏ 10205	Don't Cry No More/I'm Missing You	1974	—	2.50	5.00
❏ 10206	Can't Give It Up/I'm Gonna Fall in Love with You	1975	—	2.50	5.00
❏ 10207	We Can Love/Making Love	1975	—	2.50	5.00
—With Dorothy Moore					
❏ 10209	Hey Baby/I Really Love You	1976	—	2.50	5.00
❏ 10212	Body English/I Really Love You	1976	—	2.50	5.00
❏ 10218	Stop, Look and Listen/Trouble	1977	—	2.50	5.00
❏ 10222	So True/Doing That No More	197?	—	2.50	5.00
❏ 10224	I Wanna Slow Dance Wit 'Cha/Stop, Look and Listen	197?	—	2.50	5.00
DIAL					
❏ 1027	Can You Dig It/Learning to Forget You	1974	—	3.00	6.00
ORIGINAL SOUND					
❏ 52	Why Did She Leave Me/Walkin' and Thinkin'	1964	3.75	7.50	15.00
PULSAR					
❏ 2401	Times Have Changed/Groov-a-Ling	1969	2.50	5.00	10.00
—With the Three Queens					
❏ 2406	Together We Can Do It/You Got the Love I Need	1969	2.50	5.00	10.00
UPTOWN					
❏ 719	Love Makes the World Go Round/Walkin' and Thinkin'	1965	3.00	6.00	12.00
❏ 733	Come On Home (Where You Belong)/I Don't Care (No More)	1966	3.00	6.00	12.00
V.I.P.					
❏ 25061	Heartaches/Together We Can Do Anything	1970	5.00	10.00	20.00
Albums					
CHIMNEYVILLE					
❏ SD 9047	King Floyd	1971	3.75	7.50	15.00
PULSAR					
❏ 10602	A Man in Love	1969	5.00	10.00	20.00
V.I.P.					
❏ 407	The Heart of the Matter	1970	10.00	20.00	40.00

KING PINS, THE (1)
45s
FEDERAL

Number	Title (A Side/B Side)	Yr	VG	VG+	NM
❏ 12480	Believe in Me/Don't Wait Pretty Baby	1963	5.00	10.00	20.00
❏ 12484	It Won't Be This Way (Always)/How Long Will It Last	1963	5.00	10.00	20.00
❏ 12505	The Monkey One More Time/With the Other Guy	1963	3.75	7.50	15.00
❏ 12512	Hop Scotch/Wonderful One	1964	3.75	7.50	15.00
❏ 12517	Two Hearts/I Won't Have It	1964	3.75	7.50	15.00
❏ 12519	I Got the Monkey Off My Back/You're Using Me	1964	3.75	7.50	15.00

KINSMAN DAZZ
See DAZZ BAND.

KITTENS, THE
Probably more than one group.
45s
ABC

Number	Title (A Side/B Side)	Yr	VG	VG+	NM
❏ 10835	The Masquerade Is Over/It's Gotta Be Love	1966	2.50	5.00	10.00
ABC-PARAMOUNT					
❏ 10619	Shindig/I Got to Know Him	1965	3.00	6.00	12.00
❏ 10730	Lookie Lookie/We Find Him Guilty	1965	3.00	6.00	12.00
❏ 10783	Is It Our Baby/Undecided You	1966	3.00	6.00	12.00
ALPINE					
❏ 64	Dark, Dark Sunglasses/Itsy Bitsy Teeny Weeny Yellow Polka Dot Bikini	1960	7.50	15.00	30.00
❏ 67	A Letter on His Sweater/Broken Dreams	1960	7.50	15.00	30.00
CHESS					
❏ 2027	Hey Operator/Ain't No More Room	1967	2.00	4.00	8.00
❏ 2055	How Long Can I Go On/I've Got to Get Over You	1968	2.00	4.00	8.00

Number	Title (A Side/B Side)	Yr	VG	VG+	NM
CHESTNUT					
❑ 203	Count Every Star/I'm Worried	1963	12.50	25.00	50.00
DON-EL					
❑ 122	Walter/Lite Bulb	1963	3.75	7.50	15.00
❑ 205	I Need Your Love Tonight/Johnny's Place	1963	3.75	7.50	15.00
MURBO					
❑ 1015	Joey Has a New Love/Lonely Summer	1967	2.50	5.00	10.00
UNART					
❑ 2010	It's All Over Now/Letter to Donna	1959	12.50	25.00	50.00

KNIGHT, FREDERICK

45s

1-2-3

Number	Title (A Side/B Side)	Yr	VG	VG+	NM
❑ 1724	Have a Little Mercy/Sauerkraut	1970	3.75	7.50	15.00
JUANA					
❑ 1948	Let Me Ring Your Bell Again/When It Ain't Right	1980	—	2.50	5.00
❑ 3402	I'm Falling in Love Again/Done Got Over Lover	1976	—	2.50	5.00
❑ 3404	Sugar/I'm Falling in Love	1976	—	2.50	5.00
❑ 3408	High Society//(Instrumental)	1976	—	2.50	5.00
❑ 3411	Staying Power/Wrapped in Your Love	1977	—	2.50	5.00
❑ 3415	Sit Down on Your Love/Staying Power	1977	—	2.50	5.00
❑ 3418	You and Me/When It Ain't Right with My Baby	1978	—	2.50	5.00
❑ 3420	My Music Makes Me Feel Good/When It Ain't Right with My Baby	1978	—	2.50	5.00
❑ 3423	You Can't Deny Me/If You Love Your Baby	1979	—	2.50	5.00
❑ 3700	The Old Songs/Bundle of Love	1981	—	2.50	5.00
❑ 3702	You're the Best Thing in My Life/(B-side unknown)	1981	—	2.50	5.00
STAX					
❑ 0117	I've Been Lonely for So Long/Lean on Me	1972	2.00	4.00	8.00
❑ 0139	Trouble/A Friend	1972	—	3.50	7.00
❑ 0167	Take Me On Home Witcha/This Is My Song of Love to You	1973	—	3.50	7.00
❑ 0201	I Let My Chance Go By/Suzy	1974	—	3.50	7.00
TRUTH					
❑ 3202	Passing Through/Sometimes Storm	1974	—	3.00	6.00
❑ 3216	I Betcha Didn't Know That/Let's Make a Deal	1974	—	3.00	6.00
❑ 3228	I Wanna Play with You/I Miss You	1975	—	3.00	6.00
Albums					
STAX					
❑ STS-3011	I've Been Lonely So Long	1973	5.00	10.00	20.00

KNIGHT, GLADYS, AND THE PIPS

Includes Gladys Knight solo and the Pips without Gladys. Also see DIONNE AND FRIENDS.

12-Inch Singles

BUDDAH

Number	Title (A Side/B Side)	Yr	VG	VG+	NM
❑ DSC 115	Love Is Always On Your Mind/(Instrumental)	1977	3.00	6.00	12.00
❑ DSC 126	It's a Better Than Good Time/(Instrumental)	1978	3.00	6.00	12.00
COLUMBIA					
❑ AS 803 [DJ]	Taste of Bitter Love/Bourgie, Bourgie	1980	3.00	6.00	12.00
❑ AS 1307 [DJ]	I Will Fight (4:10)/God Is (3:48)	1981	2.50	5.00	10.00
❑ AS 1643 [DJ]	Save the Overtime (For Me) (5:07) (same on both sides)	1983	3.00	6.00	12.00
❑ CAS 2052 [DJ]	Keep Givin' Me Love (same on both sides)	1985	2.00	4.00	8.00
❑ 44-03969	Save the Overtime (For Me)/(Instrumental)	1983	2.00	4.00	8.00
❑ 44-04965	When You're Far Away//(Instrumental)	1983	—	3.00	6.00
❑ 44-05161	My Time (2 versions)	1984	2.50	5.00	10.00
❑ 23-10996	You Bring Out the Best in Me (8:20)/You Loved Away the Pain	1979	3.75	7.50	15.00
MCA					
❑ L33-1456 [DJ]	Men (5 versions)	1990	2.00	4.00	8.00
❑ L33-1621 [DJ]	Where Would I Be (Vocal) (Instrumental) (Suite)	1991	2.00	4.00	8.00
❑ L33-1653 [DJ]	Meet Me in the Middle (LP Version) (Instrumental) (7" Version) (Suite)	1991	3.75	7.50	15.00
❑ L33-1694 [DJ]	Superwoman (LP Mix 6:19) (Radio Edit 5:37) (Instrumental Mix 6:15) (Single Version 4:29)	1991	2.00	4.00	8.00
❑ L33-2080 [DJ]	Meet Me in the Middle (6 versions)	1991	2.00	4.00	8.00
❑ MCA8P-3311 [DJ]	This Time (Spike Club Mix 8:48) (Spike Beats Mix) (Radio Mix) (Spike Next Dub 9:35)	1994	2.00	4.00	8.00
❑ L33-17429 [DJ]	Lovin' On Next to Nothin' (Extended) (Radio Edit) (Instrumental) (Percussapella)	1987	2.00	4.00	8.00
❑ L33-17431 [DJ]	Love Overboard (4 versions)	1987	2.00	4.00	8.00
❑ L33-17444 [DJ]	Love Overboard (6:10) (5:44)	1987	2.00	4.00	8.00
❑ L33-17546 [DJ]	Lovin' on Next to Nothin' (5 versions)	1988	2.50	5.00	10.00
❑ L33-17561 [DJ]	It's Gonna Take All Our Love (same on both sides)	1988	2.00	4.00	8.00
❑ 23713	Send It To Me (Extended Version 7:34)/When You Love Somebody (It's Christmas Everyday) (6:12)	1986	3.00	6.00	12.00
❑ 23803	Love Overboard (Extended Version 6:00)/(Instrumental)	1987	—	3.00	6.00
❑ 23804	Lovin' On Next to Nothin' (Extended Version) (Instrumental)	1987	—	3.00	6.00
❑ 23871	It's Gonna Take All Our Love/(Instrumental)	1988	2.00	4.00	8.00
❑ 25371 [DJ]	If I Were Your Woman II (LP Version) (Instrumental) (Acappella)/(same on both sides)	2001	3.00	6.00	12.00
❑ 54130	Men (Extended Club Version 7:13) (Instrumental)	1990	—	3.00	6.00

45s

BRUNSWICK

Number	Title (A Side/B Side)	Yr	VG	VG+	NM
❑ 55048	Whistle My Love/Ching Ching	1958	30.00	60.00	120.00
BUDDAH					
❑ 363	Where Peaceful Waters Flow/Perfect Love	1973	—	2.50	5.00
❑ 363 [PS]	Where Peaceful Waters Flow/Perfect Love	1973	2.00	4.00	8.00
❑ 383	Midnight Train to Georgia/(Instrumental)	1973	—	3.00	6.00

Number	Title (A Side/B Side)	Yr	VG	VG+	NM
❑ 383	Midnight Train to Georgia/Window Raising Granny	1973	—	2.50	5.00
❑ 393	I've Got to Use My Imagination/I Can See Clearly Now	1973	—	2.50	5.00
❑ 403	Best Thing That Ever Happened to Me/Once in a Lifetime	1974	—	2.50	5.00
❑ 423	On and On/The Makings of You	1974	—	2.50	5.00
❑ 423 [PS]	On and On/The Makings of You	1974	2.00	4.00	8.00
❑ 433	I Feel a Song (In My Heart)/Don't Burn Down the Bridge	1974	—	2.50	5.00
❑ 453	Love Finds It's Own Way/Better You Go Your Way	1975	—	2.50	5.00
❑ 463	The Way We Were-Try to Remember/The Need to Be	1975	—	2.50	5.00
❑ 487	Money/Street Brothers	1975	—	2.50	5.00
❑ 513	Part Time Love/Where Did I Put His Memory	1975	—	2.50	5.00
❑ 523	Make Yours a Happy Home/The Going Up and the Coming Down	1976	—	2.50	5.00
❑ 544	So Sad the Song/(Instrumental)	1976	—	2.50	5.00
❑ 569	Baby Don't Change Your Mind/I Love to Feel That Feelin'	1977	—	2.50	5.00
❑ 584	Sorry Doesn't Always Make It Right/You Put a New Life in My Body	1977	—	2.50	5.00
❑ 592	The One and Only/Pipe Dreams	1978	—	2.50	5.00
❑ 598	It's a Better Than Good Time/Everybody's Got to Find a Way	1978	—	2.50	5.00
❑ 601	I'm Coming Home Again/Love Gives You the Power	1978	—	2.50	5.00
❑ 605	Sail Away/I'm Still Caught Up with You	1979	—	2.50	5.00
❑ 1974 [DJ]	Do You Hear What I Hear/Silent Night	1974	—	3.00	6.00
❑ 1974 [PS]	Do You Hear What I Hear/Silent Night	1974	—	3.00	6.00
CASABLANCA					
❑ 912	If I Could Bring Back Yesterday/Since I Found Love	1978	—	2.00	4.00
—As "The Pips"					
❑ 949	Baby I'm Your Fool/Lights of the City	1978	—	2.00	4.00
—As "The Pips"					
COLUMBIA					
❑ 11-02113	Forever Yesterday (For the Children)/(Instrumental)	1981	—	2.00	4.00
❑ 11-02113 [PS]	Forever Yesterday (For the Children)/(Instrumental)	1981	—	2.50	5.00
❑ 18-02413	If That'll Make You Happy/Love Was Made for Two	1981	—	2.00	4.00
❑ 18-02549	I Will Fight/God Is	1981	—	2.00	4.00
❑ 18-02706	Friend of Mine/Reach High	1982	—	2.00	4.00
❑ 38-03418	That Special Time of Year/Santa Claus Is Comin' to Town	1982	—	2.50	5.00
❑ 38-03761	Save the Overtime (For Me)/Ain't No Greater Love	1983	—	2.00	4.00
❑ 38-04033	You're Number 1 in My Book/Oh La De Dah	1983	—	2.00	4.00
❑ 38-04219	Hero (The Wind Beneath My Wings)/Seconds	1983	—	2.50	5.00
❑ 38-04333	Here's That Sunny Day/Oh La De Da	1984	—	2.00	4.00
❑ 38-04369	When You're Far Away/Seconds	1984	—	2.00	4.00
❑ 38-04761	My Time/(Instrumental)	1985	—	2.00	4.00
❑ 38-04761 [PS]	My Time/(Instrumental)	1985	—	2.50	5.00
❑ 38-04873	Keep Givin' Me Love/Do You Wanna Have Some Fun	1985	—	2.00	4.00
❑ 38-05679	Till I See You Again/Strivin'	1985	—	2.00	4.00
❑ 3-10922	Am I Too Late/It's the Same Old Song	1979	—	2.00	4.00
❑ 3-10997	You Bring Out the Best in Me/You Loved Away the Pain	1979	—	2.00	4.00
❑ 3-11088	The Best Thing We Can Do Is Say Goodbye/You Don't Have to Say I Love You	1979	—	2.00	4.00
❑ 1-11239	Landlord/We Need Hearts	1980	—	2.00	4.00
❑ 1-11330	Taste of Bitter Love/Add It Up	1980	—	2.00	4.00
❑ 1-11375	Bourgie', Bourgie'/Get the Love	1980	—	2.00	4.00
❑ 11-11409	When a Child Is Born/The Lord's Prayer	1980	—	2.50	5.00
—With Johnny Mathis					
ENJOY					
❑ 2012	What Shall I Do/Love Call	1964	3.75	7.50	15.00
EVERLAST					
❑ 5025	Happiness/I Had a Dream Last Night	1963	6.25	12.50	25.00
—As "The Pips"					
FURY					
❑ 1050	Every Beat of My Heart/Room in Your Heart	1961	6.25	12.50	25.00
—Re-recordings of the same songs on Huntom and Vee Jay					
❑ 1052	Guess Who/Stop Running Around	1961	3.75	7.50	15.00
❑ 1054	Letter Full of Tears/You Broke Your Promise	1961	3.75	7.50	15.00
❑ 1064	Operator/I'll Trust in You	1962	3.75	7.50	15.00
❑ 1067	Darling/Linda	1962	5.00	10.00	20.00
—As "The Pips"					
❑ 1073	Come See About Me/I Want That Kind of Love	1963	7.50	15.00	30.00
HUNTOM					
❑ 2510	Every Beat of My Heart/Room in Your Heart	1961	125.00	250.00	500.00
—As "The Pips"					
MAXX					
❑ 326	Giving Up/Maybe, Maybe Baby	1964	3.75	7.50	15.00
❑ 329	Lovers Always Forget/Another Love	1964	3.75	7.50	15.00
❑ 331	Either Way I Lose/Go Away, Stay Away	1964	3.75	7.50	15.00
❑ 334	Who Knows/Stop and Get a Hold of Myself	1965	3.75	7.50	15.00
❑ 335	Tell Her You're Mine/If I Should Ever Be in Love	1965	3.75	7.50	15.00
MCA					
❑ 53002	Send It to Me/When You Love Somebody (It's Christmas Every Day)	1987	—	—	3.00

Number	Title (A Side/B Side)	Yr	VG	VG+	NM
❏ 53002 [PS]	Send It to Me/When You Love Somebody (It's Christmas Every Day)	1987	—	—	3.00
❏ 53210	Love Overboard/(Instrumental)	1987	—	—	3.00
❏ 53210 [PS]	Love Overboard/(Instrumental)	1987	—	—	3.00
❏ 53211	Lovin' on Next to Nothin'/(Instrumental)	1988	—	—	3.00
❏ 53211 [PS]	Lovin' on Next to Nothin'/(Instrumental)	1988	—	—	3.00
❏ 53351	It's Gonna Take All Our Love/(Instrumental)	1988	—	—	3.00
❏ 53657	Licence to Kill/You	1989	—	—	3.00
❏ 53676	Licence to Kill/Pam	1989	—	—	3.00

—B-side by National Philharmonic Orchestra

❏ 54117	Men/(Instrumental)	1991	—	—	3.00

SCOTTI BROS.

❏ ZS4-06267	Loving on Borrowed Time (Love Theme from Cobra)/Angel of the City	1986	—	—	3.00

—A-side: Gladys Knight and Bill Medley; B-side: Robert Tepper

SOUL

❏ 35023	Just Walk in My Shoes/Stepping Closer to Your Heart	1966	2.00	4.00	8.00
❏ 35033	Take Me in Your Arms and Love Me/Do You Love Me Just a Little More?	1967	2.00	4.00	8.00
❏ 35034	Everybody Needs Love/Since I've Lost You	1967	2.00	4.00	8.00
❏ 35039	I Heard It Through the Grapevine/It's Time to Go Now	1967	2.50	5.00	10.00
❏ 35042	The End of Our Road/Don't Let Her Take Your Love from Me	1968	2.00	4.00	8.00
❏ 35045	It Should Have Been Me/You Don't Love Me No More	1968	2.00	4.00	8.00
❏ 35047	I Wish It Would Rain/It's Summer	1968	2.00	4.00	8.00
❏ 35057	Didn't You Know (You'd Have to Cry Sometime)/Keep an Eye	1969	2.00	4.00	8.00
❏ 35063	The Nitty Gritty/Got Myself a Good Man	1969	2.00	4.00	8.00
❏ 35068	Friendship Train/Cloud Nine	1969	2.00	4.00	8.00
❏ 35071	You Need Love Like I Do (Don't You)/You're My Everything	1970	2.00	4.00	8.00
❏ 35078	If I Were Your Woman/The Tracks of My Tears	1970	—	3.50	7.00
❏ 35083	I Don't Want to Do Wrong/Is There a Place In His Heart for Me	1971	—	3.00	6.00
❏ 35091	Make Me the Woman You Come Home To/If You're Gonna Leave (Just Leave)	1972	—	3.00	6.00
❏ 35094	Help Me Make It Through the Night/If You're Gonna Leave (Just Leave)	1972	—	3.00	6.00
❏ 35098	Neither One of Us (Wants to Be the First to Say Goodbye)/Can't Give It Up No More	1972	—	3.00	6.00
❏ 35105	Daddy Could Swear I Declare/For Once in My Life	1973	—	3.00	6.00
❏ 35107	All I Need Is Time/The Only Time You Love Me (Is When You're Losing Me)	1973	—	3.00	6.00
❏ 35111	Betwen Her Goodbye and My Hello/This Child Needs Its Father	1974	—	3.00	6.00

TRIP

❏ 3004	It Hurt Me So Bad/What Will Become of Me	1973	—	3.00	6.00
❏ 3004 [PS]	It Hurt Me So Bad/What Will Become of Me	1973	3.00	6.00	12.00

VEE JAY

❏ 386	Every Beat of My Heart/Room in Your Heart	1961	5.00	10.00	20.00

—By "The Pips"

❏ 386	Every Beat of My Heart/Ain'tcha Got Some Room (In Your Heart for Me)	1961	5.00	10.00	20.00

—By "The Pips"; same B-side, different title

❏ 545	A Love Like Mine/Queen of Tears	1963	5.00	10.00	20.00

Albums

ACCORD

❏ SN-7103	Every Beat of My Heart	1981	2.50	5.00	10.00
❏ SN-7105	Letter Full of Tears	1981	2.50	5.00	10.00
❏ SN-7131	I Feel a Song	1981	2.50	5.00	10.00
❏ SN-7188	It's Showtime	1982	2.50	5.00	10.00

ALLEGIANCE

❏ AV-5002	Glad to Be...	198?	2.50	5.00	10.00

BELL

❏ 1323	In the Beginning	1975	3.00	6.00	12.00
❏ 6013	Tastiest Hits	1968	5.00	10.00	20.00

BUDDAH

❏ BDS-5141	Imagination	1973	3.00	6.00	12.00
❏ BDS-5602	Claudine	1974	7.50	15.00	30.00
❏ BDS-5612	I Feel a Song	1974	3.00	6.00	12.00
❏ BDS-5639	2nd Anniversary	1975	3.00	6.00	12.00
❏ BDS-5653	The Best of Gladys Knight & The Pips	1976	3.00	6.00	12.00
❏ BDS-5676	Pipe Dreams	1976	3.00	6.00	12.00
❏ BDS-5689	Still Together	1977	3.00	6.00	12.00
❏ BDS-5701	The One and Only	1978	3.00	6.00	12.00
❏ BDS-5714	Miss Gladys Knight	1978	3.00	6.00	12.00

CASABLANCA

❏ NBLP 7081	At Last…The Pips	1977	2.50	5.00	10.00

—As "The Pips"

❏ NBLP 7113	Callin'	1978	2.50	5.00	10.00

—As "The Pips"

COLLECTABLES

❏ COL-5154	Golden Classics: Letter Full of Tears	198?	2.50	5.00	10.00

COLUMBIA

❏ JC 35704	Gladys Knight	1979	2.50	5.00	10.00
❏ PC 35704	Gladys Knight	198?	2.00	4.00	8.00

—Budget-line reissue

❏ JC 36387	About Love	1980	2.50	5.00	10.00
❏ PC 36387	About Love	198?	2.00	4.00	8.00

—Budget-line reissue

❏ FC 37086	Touch	1981	2.50	5.00	10.00

Number	Title (A Side/B Side)	Yr	VG	VG+	NM
❏ PC 37086	Touch	198?	2.00	4.00	8.00

—Budget-line reissue

❏ FC 38114	That Special Time of Year	1982	2.50	5.00	10.00
❏ PC 38114	That Special Time of Year	1983	2.00	4.00	8.00

—Same as above with new prefix

❏ FC 38205	Visions	1983	2.50	5.00	10.00
❏ PC 38205	Visions	198?	2.00	4.00	8.00

—Budget-line reissue

❏ FC 39423	Life	1985	2.50	5.00	10.00
❏ PC 39423	Life	198?	2.00	4.00	8.00

—Budget-line reissue

❏ FC 40376	Greatest Hits	1986	2.50	5.00	10.00
❏ FC 40878	The Best of Gladys Knight and the Pips/The Columbia Years	1988	2.50	5.00	10.00

FURY

❏ 1003 [M]	Letter Full of Tears	1962	125.00	250.00	500.00

LOST-NITE

❏ LLP-17 [10]	The Best of Gladys Knight and the Pips	1981	3.00	6.00	12.00

—Red vinyl

MAXX

❏ 3000 [M]	Gladys Knight and the Pips	1964	37.50	75.00	150.00

MCA

❏ 10329	Good Woman	1991	3.75	7.50	15.00
❏ 42004	All Our Love	1987	2.50	5.00	10.00

MOTOWN

❏ M5-113V	Motown Superstar Series, Vol. 13	1981	2.50	5.00	10.00
❏ M5-126V1	Everybody Needs Love	1981	3.00	6.00	12.00

—Reissue of Soul 706

❏ M5-148V1	Nitty Gritty	1981	3.00	6.00	12.00

—Reissue of Soul 713

❏ M5-193V1	Neither One of Us	1981	3.00	6.00	12.00

—Reissue of Soul 737

❏ M 792S2 [(2)]	Anthology	1974	3.75	7.50	15.00
❏ MOT 5303	All the Great Hits of Gladys Knight and the Pips	198?	2.00	4.00	8.00

NATURAL RESOURCES

❏ NR 4004T1	Silk N' Soul	1978	2.50	5.00	10.00

—Reissue of Soul 711

PAIR

❏ PDL2-1198	The Best of Gladys Knight and the Pips	1987	3.00	6.00	12.00

PICKWICK

❏ SPC-3349	Every Beat of My Heart	197?	2.50	5.00	10.00

SOUL

❏ S 706 [M]	Everybody Needs Love	1967	5.00	10.00	20.00
❏ SS 706 [S]	Everybody Needs Love	1967	6.25	12.50	25.00
❏ S 707 [M]	Feelin' Bluesy	1968	10.00	20.00	40.00

—Mono copies are white label promo only; cover has "Monaural Record DJ Copy" sticker

❏ SS 707 [S]	Feelin' Bluesy	1968	6.25	12.50	25.00
❏ SS 711	Silk N' Soul	1968	6.25	12.50	25.00
❏ SS 713	Nitty Gritty	1969	6.25	12.50	25.00
❏ SS 723	Gladys Knight and the Pips Greatest Hits	1970	3.75	7.50	15.00
❏ SS 730	All in a Knight's Work	1970	3.75	7.50	15.00
❏ SS 731	If I Were Your Woman	1971	3.75	7.50	15.00
❏ S 736L	Standing Ovation	1971	3.75	7.50	15.00
❏ S 737L	Neither One of Us	1973	3.75	7.50	15.00
❏ S 739L	All I Need Is Time	1973	3.75	7.50	15.00
❏ S 741	Knight Time	1974	3.00	6.00	12.00
❏ S 744	A Little Knight Music	1975	3.00	6.00	12.00

SPHERE SOUND

❏ SR-7006 [M]	Gladys Knight and the Pips	196?	50.00	100.00	200.00
❏ SSR-7006 [R]	Gladys Knight and the Pips	196?	30.00	60.00	120.00

SPRINGBOARD

❏ SPB-4035	Early Hits	1972	2.50	5.00	10.00
❏ SPB-4050	How Do You Say Goodbye	1973	2.50	5.00	10.00

TRIP

❏ TLP-9509	It Hurt Me So Bad	1973	2.50	5.00	10.00

UNITED ARTISTS

❏ UA-LA503-E	The Very Best of Gladys Knight and the Pips	1975	3.00	6.00	12.00

UPFRONT

❏ UPF 130	Gladys Knight and the Pips	197?	2.50	5.00	10.00
❏ UPF 185	Gladys Knight and the Pips	197?	2.50	5.00	10.00

VEE JAY

❏ D1-74796	Every Beat of My Heart: The Greatest Hits of the Early Years	1989	3.75	7.50	15.00

KNIGHT, JEAN

45s

CHELSEA

❏ 3020	Don't Ask for 24 Hours/Hold Back the Night	1975	—	2.50	5.00
❏ 3035	Jesse James Is an Outlaw/Hold Back the Night	1975	—	2.50	5.00

COTILLION

❏ 46020	You Got the Papers (But I Got the Man)/Anything You Can Do (I Can Do As Well)	1981	—	2.00	4.00
❏ 46027	Keep It Comin'/One on One	1981	—	2.00	4.00
❏ 47002	You Show Me Yours, I'll Show You Mine/(B-side unknown)	1982	—	2.00	4.00

—All of the above with Premium

DIAL

❏ 1026	Dirt/Jesse Joe	1974	—	2.50	5.00

ICHIBAN

❏ 97-422	Bill/Bus Stop	1997	—	—	3.00

JETSTREAM

❏ 706	Doggin' Around/The Man That Left Me	1965	2.50	5.00	10.00

Number	Title (A Side/B Side)	Yr	VG	VG+	NM
MIRAGE					
❏ 99606	Let the Good Times Roll/Magic	1985	—	—	3.00
❏ 99643	My Toot Toot/My Heart Is Willing (And My Body Is Too)	1985	—	—	3.00
❏ 99643 [PS]	My Toot Toot/My Heart Is Willing (And My Body Is Too)	1985	—	—	3.00
STAX					
❏ 0088	Mr. Big Stuff/Why I Keep Living These Memories	1971	—	3.00	6.00
❏ 0105	You Think You're Hot Stuff/Don't Talk About Jody	1971	—	2.50	5.00
❏ 0116	Carry On/Call Me Your Fool	1972	—	2.50	5.00
❏ 0136	Helping Man/Pick Up the Pieces	1972	—	2.50	5.00
❏ 0150	Do Me/Save the Last Kiss for Me	1972	—	2.50	5.00
TRIBE					
❏ 8304	Lonesome Tonight/Love	1964	3.00	6.00	12.00
❏ 8306	T'Ain't It the Truth/I'm So Glad for Your Sake	1965	3.00	6.00	12.00
❏ 8313	Anyone Can Love Him/A Tear	1966	3.00	6.00	12.00
Albums					
COTILLION					
❏ SD 5230	Jean Knight and Premium	1981	3.75	7.50	15.00
MIRAGE					
❏ 90282	My Toot Toot	1985	2.50	5.00	10.00
STAX					
❏ STS-2045	Mr. Big Stuff	1971	10.00	20.00	40.00
❏ MPS-8554	Mr. Big Stuff	198?	2.50	5.00	10.00

KNOCKOUTS, THE (1)

Number	Title (A Side/B Side)	Yr	VG	VG+	NM
45s					
SCEPTER					
❏ 1269	Got My Mojo Workin'/Every Day of the Week	1964	3.00	6.00	12.00
SHAD					
❏ 5013	Darling Lorraine/Riot in Room 3C	1959	12.50	25.00	50.00
—With long ending on A-side					
❏ 5013	Darling Lorraine/Riot in Room 3C	1959	6.25	12.50	25.00
—With short ending on A-side					
❏ 5018	Please Be Mine/Rich Boy, Poor Boy	1960	6.25	12.50	25.00
TRIBUTE					
❏ 199	Got My Mojo Working (Part 1)/Got My Mojo Working (Part 2)	1964	3.75	7.50	15.00
❏ 201	Tweet-Tweet/What's On Your Mind	1964	4.00	8.00	16.00

KOOL AND THE GANG

Also see K.C. AND THE SUNSHINE BAND.

Number	Title (A Side/B Side)	Yr	VG	VG+	NM
12-Inch Singles					
DE-LITE					
❏ MK 179-1 [DJ]	Take My Heart (same on both sides)	1983	—	3.00	6.00
❏ MK 208-1 [DJ]	Big Fun (same on both sides)	1982	3.75	7.50	15.00
❏ PRO 245-1 [DJ]	Home Is Where the Heart Is (same on both sides)	1983	2.00	4.00	8.00
❏ PRO 261-1 [DJ]	Tonight (Dance Mix) (same on both sides)	1983	2.00	4.00	8.00
❏ PRO 274-1 [DJ]	Tonight (AOR Mix) (same on both sides)	1984	2.50	5.00	10.00
❏ PRO 278-1 [DJ]	Straight Ahead (same on both sides)	1983	—	3.00	6.00
❏ DDS 503 [DJ]	Celebremos (5:25)/Morning Star	1981	7.50	15.00	30.00
❏ DDS 507	Tonight/Celebration	1984	3.00	6.00	12.00
❏ 880623-1	Fresh (Remix) (Dance Mix)	1985	2.00	4.00	8.00
❏ 880947-1	Cherish (Remix 5:40)/Fresh-Misled (Remix 6:10)	1985	2.00	4.00	8.00
❏ 884199-1	Emergency (Remix) (Dub Mix) (Special Mix)/You Are the One	1985	3.00	6.00	12.00
MERCURY					
❏ PRO 478-1 [DJ]	Stone Love (Club Mix) (House Mix)/Dance Champion	1986	2.00	4.00	8.00
❏ PRO 739-1 [DJ]	Raindrops (3 versions)	1989	2.00	4.00	8.00
❏ 870513-1	Rags to Riches (5 versions)	1988	2.00	4.00	8.00
❏ 870572-1	Rags to Riches (4 versions)	1988	2.00	4.00	8.00
❏ 874403-1	Raindrops (3 versions)/Amor, Amore	1989	2.00	4.00	8.00
❏ 888074-1	Victory (12" Version) (7" Version)/Bad Woman	1986	2.00	4.00	8.00
❏ 888292-1	Stone Love (Club Version) (House Mix)/Dance Champion	1986	2.00	4.00	8.00
❏ 888712-1	Holiday (12" Club Remix 5:48) (Dub Version 5:45) (7" Version 3:35) (Jam Mix 5:20)	1988	2.00	4.00	8.00
45s					
DE-LITE					
❏ 519	Kool and the Gang/Raw Hamburger	1969	—	3.00	6.00
❏ 523	The Gangs Back Again/Kools Back Again	1969	—	3.00	6.00
❏ 525	Kool It (Here Comes the Fuzz)/Can't Stop	1970	—	3.00	6.00
❏ 529	Let the Music Take Your Mind/Chocolate Buttermilk	1970	—	3.00	6.00
❏ 534	Funky Man/1,2,3,4,5,6,7,8	1970	—	3.00	6.00
❏ 538	Who's Gonna Take the Weight (Part One)/Who's Gonna Take the Weight (Part Two)	1970	—	3.00	6.00
❏ 540	I Want to Take You Higher/Pneumonia	1971	—	3.00	6.00
❏ 543	The Penguin/Lucky for Me	1971	—	3.00	6.00
❏ 544	N.T. (Part One)/N.T. (Part Two)	1971	—	3.00	6.00
❏ 546	Love the Life You Live, Part I/Love the Life You Live, Part II	1972	—	3.00	6.00
❏ 547	You've Lost That Lovin' Feeling/Ike's Mood	1972	—	3.00	6.00
❏ 550	Music Is the Messenger, Part I/Music Is the Messenger, Part II	1972	—	3.00	6.00
❏ 552	Good Times/The Frog	1972	—	3.00	6.00
❏ 553	Funky Granny/Blowing with the Wind	1973	—	3.00	6.00
❏ 555	Country Junkie/I Remember John W. Coltrane	1973	—	3.00	6.00
❏ 557	Funky Stuff/More Funky Stuff	1973	—	3.00	6.00
❏ 559	Jungle Boogie/North, East, South, West	1973	—	2.50	5.00
❏ 561	Hollywood Swinging/Dujii	1974	—	2.50	5.00

Number	Title (A Side/B Side)	Yr	VG	VG+	NM
❏ 801	Ladies Night/If You Feel Like Dancin'	1979	—	2.00	4.00
❏ 802	Too Hot/Tonight's the Night	1979	—	2.00	4.00
❏ 804	Hangin' Out/Got You Into My Life	1980	—	2.00	4.00
❏ 807	Celebration/Morning Star	1980	—	2.00	4.00
❏ 810	Take It to the Top/Love Affair	1981	—	2.00	4.00
❏ 813	Jones Vs. Jones/Night People	1981	—	2.00	4.00
❏ 815	Take My Heart/Just Friends	1981	—	2.50	5.00
—First pressings have no subtitle					
❏ 815	Take My Heart (You Can Have It If You Want It)/Just Friends	1981	—	2.00	4.00
❏ 816	Steppin' Out/Love Festival	1982	—	2.00	4.00
❏ 818	Get Down On It/Steppin' Out	1982	—	2.00	4.00
❏ 822	Big Fun/No Show	1982	—	2.00	4.00
❏ 824	Let's Go Dancin' (Ooh, La, La, La)/Be My Lady	1982	—	2.00	4.00
❏ 825	Street Kids/As One	1983	—	2.00	4.00
❏ 829	Joanna/A Place for Us	1983	—	—	3.00
❏ 830	Tonight/Home Is Where the Heart Is	1984	—	—	3.00
❏ 831	Straight Ahead/September Love	1984	—	—	3.00
❏ 901	Slick Superchick/Life's a Song	1978	—	2.50	5.00
❏ 905	A Place in Space/The Force	1978	—	2.50	5.00
❏ 909	I Like Music/It's All You Need	1978	—	2.50	5.00
❏ 910	Everybody's Dancin'/Stay Awhile	1978	—	2.50	5.00
❏ 1562	Higher Plane/Wild Is Love	1974	—	2.50	5.00
❏ 1563	Rhyme Tyme People/Father, Father	1974	—	2.50	5.00
❏ 1567	Spirit of the Boogie/Summer Madness	1975	—	2.50	5.00
❏ 1573	Caribbean Festival/Caribbean Festival (Disco Version)	1975	—	2.50	5.00
❏ 1577	Winter Sadness/Father, Father	1975	—	2.50	5.00
❏ 1579	Love and Understanding (Come Together)/Sunshine and Love	1976	—	2.50	5.00
❏ 1583	Universal Sound/Ancestral Ceremony	1976	—	2.50	5.00
❏ 1586	Open Sesame — Part 1/Open Sesame — Part 2	1976	—	2.50	5.00
❏ 1590	Super Band/Sunshine	1977	—	2.50	5.00
❏ 880431-7	Misled/Rollin'	1984	—	—	3.00
❏ 880623-7	Fresh/In the Heart	1985	—	—	3.00
❏ 880623-7 [PS]	Fresh/In the Heart	1985	—	2.00	4.00
❏ 880869-7	Cherish/(Instrumental)	1985	—	—	3.00
❏ 880869-7 [PS]	Cherish/(Instrumental)	1985	—	2.00	4.00
❏ 884199-7	Emergency/You Are the One	1985	—	—	3.00
MERCURY					
❏ PRO 621-7 [DJ]	Rags to Riches (Lightnin' Licks Remix) (same on both sides)	1988	—	3.00	6.00
❏ PRO 621-7 [PS]	Rags to Riches (Lightnin' Licks Remix) (same on both sides)	1988	—	3.00	6.00
❏ 870513-7	Rags to Riches/Rags to Riches (Remix)	1988	—	—	3.00
❏ 870513-7 [PS]	Rags to Riches/Rags to Riches (Remix)	1988	—	—	3.00
❏ 872038-7	Strong/Funky Stuff	1988	—	—	3.00
❏ 874402-7	Raindrops/Amor Amore	1989	—	—	3.00
❏ 876072-7	Never Give Up/Amor Amore	1989	—	—	3.00
❏ 888074-7	Victory/Bad Woman	1986	—	—	3.00
❏ 888074-7 [PS]	Victory/Bad Woman	1986	—	—	3.00
❏ 888292-7	Stone Love/Dance Champion	1987	—	—	3.00
❏ 888292-7 [PS]	Stone Love/Dance Champion	1987	—	—	3.00
❏ 888712-7	Holiday/(Jam Mix)	1987	—	—	3.00
❏ 888712-7 [PS]	Holiday/(Jam Mix)	1987	—	—	3.00
❏ 888867-7	In a Special Way/God's Country	1987	—	—	3.00
❏ 888867-7 [PS]	In a Special Way/God's Country	1987	—	—	3.00
Albums					
DE-LITE					
❏ MK-48 [DJ]	History of Kool and the Gang	1979	3.75	7.50	15.00
❏ 2003	Kool and the Gang	1969	6.25	12.50	25.00
❏ 2008	Live at the Sex Machine	1971	3.00	6.00	12.00
❏ 2009	The Best of Kool and the Gang	1971	3.00	6.00	12.00
❏ 2010	Live at PJ's	1971	3.00	6.00	12.00
❏ 2011	Music Is the Message	1972	3.00	6.00	12.00
❏ 2012	Good Times	1973	3.00	6.00	12.00
❏ 2013	Wild and Peaceful	1973	2.50	5.00	10.00
❏ 2014	Light of Worlds	1974	2.50	5.00	10.00
❏ 2015	Kool & The Gang Greatest Hits!	1975	2.50	5.00	10.00
❏ 2016	Spirit of the Boogie	1975	2.50	5.00	10.00
❏ 2018	Love and Understanding	1976	2.50	5.00	10.00
❏ 2023	Open Sesame	1976	2.50	5.00	10.00
❏ 4001	Kool Jazz	1973	2.50	5.00	10.00
❏ 8502	Something Special	1981	2.50	5.00	10.00
❏ 8505	As One	1982	2.50	5.00	10.00
❏ 8508	In the Heart	1983	2.50	5.00	10.00
❏ 9501	The Force	1978	2.50	5.00	10.00
❏ 9507	Kool & The Gang Spin Their Top Ten Hits	1978	2.50	5.00	10.00
❏ 9509	Everybody's Dancin'	1979	2.50	5.00	10.00
❏ 9513	Ladies Night	1979	2.50	5.00	10.00
❏ 9518	Celebrate!	1980	2.50	5.00	10.00
❏ 814351-1	In the Heart	1984	2.00	4.00	8.00
—Reissue					
❏ 822534-1	Something Special	1984	2.00	4.00	8.00
—Reissue					
❏ 822535-1	As One	1984	2.00	4.00	8.00
—Reissue					
❏ 822536-1	Kool & The Gang Spin Their Top Ten Hits	1984	2.00	4.00	8.00
—Reissue					
❏ 822537-1	Ladies Night	1984	2.00	4.00	8.00
—Reissue					
❏ 822538-1	Celebrate!	1984	2.00	4.00	8.00
—Reissue					
❏ 822943-1	Emergency	1984	2.00	4.00	8.00

Number	Title (A Side/B Side)	Yr	VG	VG+	NM

MERCURY
❑ 830398-1	Forever	1986	2.00	4.00	8.00
❑ 834780-1	Everything's Kool & the Gang: Greatest Hits & More	1988	2.00	4.00	8.00
❑ 838233-1	Sweat	1989	2.00	4.00	8.00

KOOL GENTS
DEE CLARK was a member of this group.
45s
VEE JAY
| ❑ 173 | This Is the Night/Do Ya Do | 1956 | 50.00 | 100.00 | 200.00 |
| ❑ 207 | You Know/I Can't Help Myself | 1956 | 50.00 | 100.00 | 200.00 |

KRUSH GROOVE ALL-STARS
Also see KURTIS BLOW; RUN-D.M.C.
12-Inch Singles
WARNER BROS.
| ❑ PRO-A-2391 [DJ]Krush Groovin' (2 versions) | | 1985 | 3.75 | 7.50 | 15.00 |
45s
WARNER BROS.
| ❑ 28843 | Krush Groove/Kold Krush | 1985 | — | 2.50 | 5.00 |

L

L.L. COOL J
12-Inch Singles
DEF JAM
Number	Title (A Side/B Side)	Yr	VG	VG+	NM
❑ DJ-001	I Need a Beat (Vocal) (Zootie Mix) (Instrumental)	1984	6.25	12.50	25.00
❑ DJ-005	I Want You (Vocal) (Instrumental)/Dangerous (Vocal) (Instrumental) (Burnt Mix)	1985	6.25	12.50	25.00
❑ CAS 1733 [DJ]Big Ole Butt (Edit) (LP Version)		1989	3.00	6.00	12.00
❑ CAS 5010 [DJ]Now I'm Comin'/(Instrumental)		1993	2.00	4.00	8.00
❑ CAS 5193 [DJ]Pink Cookies in a Plastic Bag Getting Crushed by Buildings/Funkadelic Relic		1992	2.00	4.00	8.00
❑ 44-05291	I Can Give You More (Vocal)/(Instrumental)/I Can't Live Without My Radio	1985	3.75	7.50	15.00
❑ 44-05349	Rock the Bells (Original Version 7:11) (Radio Version 4:00)	1985	3.75	7.50	15.00
❑ 44-05907	You'll Rock (Remix)/I Need a Beat	1986	3.75	7.50	15.00
❑ 44-06799	I'm Bad (4:40)/Get Down	1987	3.75	7.50	15.00
❑ 44-07476	Go Cut Creator Go/Kanday	1987	3.00	6.00	12.00
❑ 44-07563	Going Back to Cali/Jack the Ripper	1987	3.75	7.50	15.00
❑ 44-68792	I'm That Type of Guy/It Gets No Rougher	1989	3.00	6.00	12.00
❑ 44-68864	Big Ole Butt (12" Remix) (LP Version)/One Shot at Love	1989	3.75	7.50	15.00
❑ 44-73147	Jingling Baby (Remixed and Still Jingling) (LP Version)/Illegal Search (Keep On Searchin' Mix) (Pre-Trial Hearing Mix)	1990	3.00	6.00	12.00
❑ 44-73458	The Boomin' System (3 versions)	1990	3.00	6.00	12.00
❑ 44-73610	Around the Way Girl (LP Version) (Untouchables Remix) (New Bass Mix) (Instrumental) (Jazzy Mix)	1990	3.00	6.00	12.00
❑ 44-73703	Mama Said Knock You Out (Original Recipe - Long) (Original Recipe - Short) (For Steering Pleasure) (Bonus Beats) (Hot Mix - Short) (Hot Mix - Long) (7 A.M. Mix)	1991	3.00	6.00	12.00
❑ 44-73821	6 Minutes of Pleasure (Hey Girl Remix) (LP Version) (Remix Instrumental)/Eat 'Em Up L Chill (Chill Remix) (LP Version) (Remix Instrumental)	1991	3.00	6.00	12.00
❑ 44-74810	How I'm Comin' (LP Version) (Instrumental)/Buckin' Em Down (LP Version) (Instrumental)	1993	2.50	5.00	10.00
❑ 44-74983	Pink Cookies in a Plastic Bag Getting Crushed by Buildings (LP Version) (Instrumental) (Remix) (Remix Instrumental)/Back Seat (Of My Jeep)	1993	2.50	5.00	10.00
❑ 44-77097	Stand By Your Man (LP Version) (New Jack Street Mix) (New Jack Street Mix Instrumental) (Hip Hop Mix 2) (Hip Hop Mix 1)/Soul Survivor (LP Version) (A Cappella)	1993	3.00	6.00	12.00
❑ 562279-1	Say What/First Degree/Violators	1999	2.50	5.00	10.00
❑ 562827-1	Imagine That (6 versions?)	2000	2.00	4.00	8.00
❑ 568081-1	Phenomenon (3 versions)/Hot Hot Hot (3 versions)	1997	2.50	5.00	10.00
❑ 572645-1	Take It Off (3 versions)/Back Where I Belong (3 versions)	2000	2.50	5.00	10.00
❑ 572665-1	You and Me (3 versions)/Fuhgidabowdit (2 versions)	2000	2.50	5.00	10.00
—With Kelly Price					
❑ 577495-1	Hey Lover (Radio Edit) (Instrumental) (LP Version) (Acappella)	1995	2.50	5.00	10.00
GEFFEN					
❑ PRO-A-1063 [DJ]Ain't Nobody/Pimp'n Ain't EZ		1996	3.00	6.00	12.00
❑ 22195	Ain't Nobody (Vocal) (Instrumental)	1996	3.00	6.00	12.00
❑ 22229	Ain't Nobody/Pimp'n Ain't EZ	1996	3.00	6.00	12.00
MOTOWN					
❑ L33-18371 [DJ]To Da Break of Dawn (4 versions)		1990	2.50	5.00	10.00
UPTOWN					
❑ L33-1696 [DJ] Strictly Business (Radio) (Instrumental) (Extended Club) (Acapella)		1991	2.50	5.00	10.00
❑ 54246	Strictly Business (Radio Version) (Instrumental) (Extended Club Mix) (Acapella)	1991	2.00	4.00	8.00
WARNER BROS.					
❑ PRO-A-9897 [DJ]Deepest Bluest (Shark's Fin) (Radio) (Instrumental) (Acapella)		1999	2.00	4.00	8.00
❑ PRO-A-9956 [DJ]Say What/Smokeman//Burn Baby Burn/I Found Another Man		1999	3.75	7.50	15.00
WARNER SUNSET					
❑ DMD 2545 [DJ]Shut 'Em Down (Radio Mix) (Video Mix) (Clean Acapella) (LP Version) (Instrumental) (Acapella)		2000	2.00	4.00	8.00
❑ 84652	Shut 'Em Down (unknown versions)	2000	2.50	5.00	10.00
45s					
DEF JAM					
❑ CS7 1604 [DJ]I'm That Type of Guy (Radio Edit) (same on both sides)		1989	—	3.00	6.00
❑ 38-05665	I Can't Live Without My Radio/I Can Give You More	1985	—	—	3.00
❑ 38-05840	Rock the Bells/El Shabazz	1986	—	2.00	4.00
❑ 38-06061	You'll Rock/I Need a Beat	1986	—	2.00	4.00
❑ 38-07120	I'm Bad/Get Down	1987	—	2.00	4.00
❑ 38-07350	I Need Love/My Rhyme Ain't Done	1987	—	—	3.00
❑ 38-07620	Go Cut Creator Go/Kanday	1987	—	—	3.00
❑ 38-07620 [PS] Go Cut Creator Go/Kanday	1987	—	2.50	5.00
❑ 38-07679	Going Back to Cali/Jack the Ripper	1988	—	—	3.00
❑ 38-07679 [PS] Going Back to Cali/Jack the Ripper	1988	—	2.00	4.00
❑ 13-08380	I Can't Live Without My Radio/Rock the Bells	1988	—	—	3.00
—Reissue					

Number	Title (A Side/B Side)	Yr	VG	VG+	NM
❏ 13-08381	I Need Love/I'm Bad	1988	—	—	3.00
—Reissue
❏ 38-68902	I'm That Type of Guy/It Gets No Rougher	1989	—	—	3.00
❏ 38-69056	Big Ole Butt/One Shot at Love	1989	—	2.00	4.00
❏ 38-73609	Around the Way Girl/Mama Said Knock You Out	1991	—	2.00	4.00
❏ 576120-7	Doin It (On the Air)/Hey Lover (Radio Edit)	1996	—	2.00	4.00
❏ 577494-7	Hey Lover (Radio Edit) (same on both sides)	1995	—	—	3.00
—Featuring Boyz II Men
MOTOWN
❏ 921	To Da Break of Dawn/(Instrumental)	1990	—	2.50	5.00
Albums
DEF JAM
❏ FC 40239	Radio	1985	3.00	6.00	12.00
❏ FC 40793	Bigger and Deffer	1987	3.00	6.00	12.00
❏ OC 45173	Walking with a Panther	1989	3.75	7.50	15.00
❏ C 46888	Mama Said Knock You Out	1990	3.75	7.50	15.00
❏ C2 53325 [(2)]	14 Shots to the Dome	1993	3.75	7.50	15.00
❏ 523845-1	Mr. Smith	1995	3.00	6.00	12.00
❏ 524125-1 [(2)]	All World	1996	3.75	7.50	15.00
❏ 539186-1 [(2)]	Phenomenon	1997	3.75	7.50	15.00
❏ 546819-1 [(2)]	G.O.A.T. Featuring James T. Smith the Greatest of All Time	2000	3.75	7.50	15.00

L.T.D.
Also see JEFFREY OSBORNE.
45s
A&M

Number	Title (A Side/B Side)	Yr	VG	VG+	NM
❏ 1514	Elegant Love/Success	1974	—	2.50	5.00
❏ 1537	What Goes Around/To the Bone	1974	—	2.50	5.00
❏ 1665	Don't Lose Your Cool/Thank You Mother	1975	—	2.50	5.00
❏ 1681	Trying to Find a Way/I Told You I'd Be Back	1975	—	2.50	5.00
❏ 1731	Rated X/Ain't No Way	1975	—	2.50	5.00
❏ 1847	Love Ballad/Let the Music Keep Playing	1976	—	2.50	5.00
❏ 1847 [PS]	Love Ballad/Let the Music Keep Playing	1976	—	3.00	6.00
❏ 1897	Love to the World/Get Your It Together	1976	—	2.50	5.00
❏ 1974	(Every Time I Turn Around) Back in Love Again/Material Things	1977	—	2.50	5.00
❏ 1974 [PS]	(Every Time I Turn Around) Back in Love Again/Material Things	1977	2.00	4.00	8.00
❏ 2005	Never Get Enough of Your Love/Make Someone Smile Today	1978	—	2.50	5.00
❏ 2005 [PS]	Never Get Enough of Your Love/Make Someone Smile Today	1978	—	3.00	6.00
❏ 2057	Holding On (When Love Is Gone)/Together Forever	1978	—	2.50	5.00
❏ 2095	We Both Deserve Each Other's Love/It's Time to Be Real	1978	—	2.50	5.00
❏ 2142	Dance "N" Sing "N"/Give It All	1979	—	2.50	5.00
❏ 2142 [PS]	Dance "N" Sing "N"/Give It All	1979	—	3.00	6.00
❏ 2176	Share My Love/Sometimes	1979	—	2.50	5.00
❏ 2192	Stranger/Sometimes	1979	—	2.50	5.00
❏ 2250	Where Did We Go Wrong/Stand Up L.T.D.	1980	—	2.50	5.00
❏ 2283	Shine On/Love Is What You Need	1980	—	2.50	5.00
❏ 2346	Shine On (Spanish Version)/Where Did We Go Wrong	1981	—	2.50	5.00
❏ 2382	Kickin' Back/Now	1981	—	2.50	5.00
❏ 2395	April Love/Stay on the One	1982	—	2.50	5.00
❏ 2414	Cuttin' It Up/Love Magic	1982	—	2.00	4.00
MONTAGE
❏ 908	For You/Party with You (All Night)	1983	—	2.00	4.00
Albums
A&M
❏ SP-3119	L.T.D.	198?	2.00	4.00	8.00
—Budget-line reissue
❏ SP-3146	Love to the World	198?	2.00	4.00	8.00
—Budget-line reissue
❏ SP-3148	Something to Love	198?	2.00	4.00	8.00
—Budget-line reissue
❏ SP-3602	L.T.D.	1974	3.00	6.00	12.00
❏ SP-3660	Gittin' Down	1975	3.00	6.00	12.00
❏ SP-4589	Love to the World	1976	2.50	5.00	10.00
❏ SP-4646	Something to Love	1977	2.50	5.00	10.00
❏ SP-4705	Togetherness	1978	2.50	5.00	10.00
❏ SP-4771	Devotion	1979	2.50	5.00	10.00
❏ SP-4819	Shine On	1980	2.50	5.00	10.00
❏ SP-4881	Love Magic	1981	2.50	5.00	10.00

LABELLE
Also see PATTI LaBELLE; PATTI LaBELLE AND THE BLUE BELLES.
45s
EPIC

Number	Title (A Side/B Side)	Yr	VG	VG+	NM
❏ 50048	Lady Marmalade/Space Children	1974	—	3.00	6.00
❏ 50097	Night Bird/What Can I Do for You	1975	—	3.00	6.00
❏ 50140	Messin' My Mind/Take the Night Off	1975	—	3.00	6.00
❏ 50168	Slow Burn/Far As We Felt Like Going	1975	—	3.00	6.00
❏ 50262	Get You Somebody New/Who's Watching the Watcher	1976	—	3.00	6.00
❏ 50315	Isn't It a Shame/Gypsy Moths	1976	—	3.00	6.00
RCA VICTOR
❏ 74-0965	Open Up Your Heart/Going Up a Holiday	1973	2.00	4.00	8.00
❏ APBO-0157	Mr. Sunshine Man/Sunshine	1973	2.00	4.00	8.00
WARNER BROS.
❏ 7512	Morning Much Better/Shades of Difference	1971	2.00	4.00	8.00
❏ 7579	Moonshadow/If I Can't Have You	1972	2.00	4.00	8.00
❏ 7624	Touch Me All Over/Ain't It Sad It's All Over	1972	2.00	4.00	8.00

Albums
EPIC

Number	Title (A Side/B Side)	Yr	VG	VG+	NM
❏ KE 33075	Nightbirds	1974	3.00	6.00	12.00
❏ PE 33075	Nightbirds	197?	2.00	4.00	8.00
—Reissue with new prefix
❏ PE 33579	Phoenix	1975	2.50	5.00	10.00
❏ PEQ 33579 [Q]	Phoenix	1975	3.75	7.50	15.00
❏ PE 34189	Chameleon	1976	2.50	5.00	10.00
—Original with no bar code and orange label
❏ PE 34189	Chameleon	198?	2.00	4.00	8.00
—Reissue with bar code and dark blue label
RCA VICTOR
❏ APL1-0205	Pressure Cookin'	1973	3.00	6.00	12.00
❏ AYL1-4176	Pressure Cookin'	1982	2.00	4.00	8.00
—"Best Buy Series" reissue
WARNER BROS.
❏ WS 1943	LaBelle	1971	3.75	7.50	15.00
❏ BS 2618	Moonshadow	1972	3.75	7.50	15.00

LABELLE, PATTI
Also see LaBELLE; PATTI LaBELLE AND THE BLUE BELLES.
12-Inch Singles
EPIC

Number	Title (A Side/B Side)	Yr	VG	VG+	NM
❏ 50664	Music Is My Way of Life (2 versions)	1979	3.00	6.00	12.00
MCA
❏ 1131 [DJ]	'Twas Love/Reason for the Season	1990	2.00	4.00	8.00
❏ 2074 [DJ]	Somebody Loves You Baby (4 versions)	1991	2.00	4.00	8.00
❏ 2433 [DJ]	All Right Now (6 versions)	1992	2.00	4.00	8.00
❏ 3140 [DJ]	All This Love (3 versions)	1994	2.00	4.00	8.00
❏ 3160 [DJ]	All This Love (4 versions)	1994	2.00	4.00	8.00
❏ L33-17339 [DJ]	Just the Facts (same on both sides)	1987	2.00	4.00	8.00
❏ L33-18014 [DJ]	Yo Mister (same on both sides)	1989	2.00	4.00	8.00
❏ L33-18108 [DJ]	I Can't Complain/(Instrumental)	1989	2.00	4.00	8.00
❏ 23534	New Attitude (Extended Mix)/Axel F (Extended Mix)	1985	2.50	5.00	10.00
—B-side by Harold Faltermeyer
❏ 23567	Stir It Up (3 versions)	1985	2.50	5.00	10.00
❏ 23607	On My Own/Stir It Up	1986	—	3.00	6.00
—A-side with Michael McDonald
❏ 23649	Something Special (5 versions)	1986	2.00	4.00	8.00
❏ 23651	Oh, People (Extended)/(Instrumental)	1986	2.00	4.00	8.00
❏ 23773	Just the Facts (4 versions)	1987	2.50	5.00	10.00
❏ 23984	Yo Mister (3 versions)	1989	2.00	4.00	8.00
❏ 54541	All Right Now (Extended) (Remix) (Dub)	1992	2.00	4.00	8.00
❏ 54851	The Right Kinda Lover (Fusion Extended Remix) (Def Jam Remix) (Club Remix)	1994	2.50	5.00	10.00
❏ 54933	All This Love (Hip Hop Mix) (Patti's Buttah Mix)/Our World	1994	2.00	4.00	8.00
❏ 55113	Turn It Out (4 mixes)	1995	2.00	4.00	8.00
PHILADELPHIA INT'L.
❏ 04176	If Only You Knew/I'll Never, Never Give Up	1983	2.50	5.00	10.00
❏ 05296	Shy (Remix)/Shy (Dub Mix)	1985	2.00	4.00	8.00

45s
ARISTA

Number	Title (A Side/B Side)	Yr	VG	VG+	NM
❏ 12929	My Love, Sweet Love/Sittin' Up in My Room	1996	—	—	3.00
—B-side by Brandy
BEVERLY GLEN
❏ 2012	Love Has Finally Come at Last/American Dream	1984	—	2.00	4.00
—With Bobby Womack
❏ 2018	It Takes a Lot of Strength to Say Goodbye/Who's Foolin' Who	1984	—	2.00	4.00
—With Bobby Womack
ELEKTRA
❏ 69887	The Best Is Yet to Come/Bye Bye Love	1982	—	2.00	4.00
—With Grover Washington Jr.
EPIC
❏ 50445	Joy to Have Your Love/Do I Stand a Chance	1977	—	3.00	6.00
❏ 50487	You Are My Friend/I Think About You	1977	—	3.00	6.00
❏ 50510	Since I Don't Have You/Dan Swit Me	1978	—	3.00	6.00
❏ 50550	Teach Me Tonight/Quiet Time	1978	—	3.00	6.00
❏ 50583	Little Girls/You Make It So Hard	1978	—	3.00	6.00
❏ 50659	It's Alright with Me/Music Is My Way of Life	1979	—	2.50	5.00
❏ 50718	Music Is My Way of Life/My Best Was Good Enough	1979	—	2.50	5.00
❏ 50763	Love Is Just a Touch Away/Love and Learn	1979	—	2.50	5.00
❏ 50852	Come and Dance with Me/Release	1980	—	2.50	5.00
❏ 50872	I Don't Go Shopping/Come and Dance with Me	1980	—	2.50	5.00
❏ 50910	Ain't That Enough/Don't Make Your Angel Cry	1980	—	2.50	5.00
MCA
❏ 52517	New Attitude/Shoot Out	1984	—	2.00	4.00
—B-side by Harold Faltermeyer
❏ 52517 [PS]	New Attitude/Shoot Out	1984	—	2.00	4.00
❏ 52610	Stir It Up/The Discovery	1985	—	2.00	4.00
—B-side by Harold Faltermeyer
❏ 52610 [PS]	Stir It Up/The Discovery	1985	—	2.00	4.00
❏ 52770	On My Own/Stir It Up	1986	—	—	3.00
—A-side with Michael McDonald
❏ 52770 [PS]	On My Own/Stir It Up	1986	—	2.00	4.00
❏ 52876	Something Special (Is Gonna Happen Tonight)/(Instrumental)	1986	—	—	3.00
❏ 52877	Oh, People/Love Attack	1986	—	—	3.00
❏ 52877 [PS]	Oh, People/Love Attack	1986	—	2.00	4.00
❏ 52945	Kiss Away the Pain/(Instrumental)	1986	—	—	3.00

Number	Title (A Side/B Side)	Yr	VG	VG+	NM
❑ 53064	The Last Unbroken Heart/Miami Vice: New York Theme	1987	—	—	3.00
—A-side with Bill Champlin; B-side by Harold Faltermeyer					
❑ 53064 [PS]	The Last Unbroken Heart/Miami Vice: New York Theme	1987	—	—	3.00
❑ 53100	Just the Facts/(Instrumental)	1987	—	—	3.00
❑ 53358	If You Asked Me To/(Instrumental)	1988	—	—	3.00
❑ 53728	Yo Mister/I Can Fly	1989	—	—	3.00
❑ 53774	I Can't Complain/I Can Fly	1989	—	—	3.00
❑ 54481	When You Love Somebody (I'm Saving My Love for You)/Temptation	1992	—	—	3.00
❑ 54513	All Right Now/All Right Now (Remix Dub)	1992	—	—	3.00
❑ 54673	The Right Kinda Lover/(Instrumental)	1993	—	—	3.00
PHILADELPHIA INT'L.					
❑ 02309	Rocking Pneumonia and the Boogie Woogie Flu/Over the Rainbow	1981	—	2.00	4.00
❑ 02655	The Spirit's In It/The Family	1981	—	2.00	4.00
❑ 04248	If Only You Knew/I'll Never, Never Give Up	1983	—	2.00	4.00
❑ 04399	I'm in Love Again/Love, Need and Want It	1984	—	2.00	4.00
❑ 05436	I Can't Forget You/Living Doubt	1985	—	2.00	4.00
❑ 05755	If You Don't Know Me By Now/(Instrumental)	1986	—	2.00	4.00
❑ 05877	Look to the Rainbow/What Can I Do for You	1986	—	2.00	4.00
Albums					
EPIC					
❑ PE 34847	Patti LaBelle	1977	2.50	5.00	10.00
—Original with no bar code and orange label					
❑ PE 34847	Patti LaBelle	1986	2.00	4.00	8.00
—Reissue with bar code and dark blue label					
❑ JE 35335	Tasty	1978	2.50	5.00	10.00
❑ JE 35772	It's Alright with Me	1979	2.50	5.00	10.00
❑ JE 36381	Released	1980	2.50	5.00	10.00
❑ FE 36997	Best of Patti LaBelle	1981	2.50	5.00	10.00
❑ PE 36997	Best of Patti LaBelle	198?	2.00	4.00	8.00
—Budget-line reissue					
MCA					
❑ 5737	Winner in You	1986	2.50	5.00	10.00
❑ 6292	Be Yourself	1989	2.50	5.00	10.00
❑ 10439	Burnin'	1991	3.00	6.00	12.00
PHILADELPHIA INT'L.					
❑ FZ 37380	The Spirit's In It	1981	2.50	5.00	10.00
❑ PZ 37380	The Spirit's In It	198?	2.00	4.00	8.00
—Budget-line reissue					
❑ FZ 38539	I'm in Love Again	1983	2.50	5.00	10.00
❑ FZ 40020	Patti	1985	2.50	5.00	10.00

LABELLE, PATTI, AND THE BLUE BELLES

Also see THE BLUE BELLES; LaBELLE.

Number	Title (A Side/B Side)	Yr	VG	VG+	NM
45s					
ATLANTIC					
❑ 2311	All or Nothing/You Forgot How to Love	1965	3.00	6.00	12.00
❑ 2318	A Groovy Kind of Love/Over the Rainbow	1966	2.50	5.00	10.00
❑ 2333	Ebb Tide/Patti's Prayer	1966	2.50	5.00	10.00
❑ 2347	I'm Still Waiting/Family Man	1966	2.50	5.00	10.00
❑ 2373	Take Me for a Little While/I Don't Want to Go On Without You	1967	2.50	5.00	10.00
❑ 2390	(There's) Always Something There to Remind Me/Tender Words	1967	2.50	5.00	10.00
❑ 2408	Unchained Melody/Dreamer	1967	2.50	5.00	10.00
❑ 2446	Oh My Love/I Need Your Love	1967	2.50	5.00	10.00
❑ 2548	He's My Man/Wonderful	1968	2.50	5.00	10.00
❑ 2610	Dance to the Rhythm of Love/He's Gone	1969	2.50	5.00	10.00
❑ 2629	Loving Blues/Pride's No Match for Love	1969	2.50	5.00	10.00
❑ 2712	Suffer/Trustin' in You	1970	2.50	5.00	10.00
KING					
❑ 5777	Down the Aisle (Wedding Song)/C'est La Vie	1963	3.75	7.50	15.00
NEWTIME					
❑ 510	Love Me Just a Little/The Joke's On You	1962	5.00	10.00	20.00
NEWTOWN					
❑ 5000	I Sold My Heart to the Junkman/Itty Bitty Twist	1962	5.00	10.00	20.00
—Credited to "The Blue-Belles" but actually recorded by The Starlets					
❑ 5006	I Found a New Love/Pitter Patter	1962	5.00	10.00	20.00
—Most of the Newtown sides credit "The Blue-Belles"					
❑ 5007	Tear After Tear/Go On, This Is Goodbye	1962	5.00	10.00	20.00
❑ 5009	Cool Water/When Johnny Comes Marching Home	1962	5.00	10.00	20.00
❑ 5019	Academy Award/Decatur Street	1963	5.00	10.00	20.00
❑ 5777	Down the Aisle (Wedding Song)/C'est La Vie	1963	3.75	7.50	15.00
NICETOWN					
❑ 5020	You'll Never Walk Alone/Where Are You	1963	3.75	7.50	15.00
PARKWAY					
❑ 896	You'll Never Walk Alone/Decatur Street	1964	3.00	6.00	12.00
❑ 896 [PS]	You'll Never Walk Alone/Decatur Street	1964	20.00	40.00	80.00
❑ 913	One Phone Call/You Will Fill My Eyes No More	1964	3.00	6.00	12.00
❑ 935	Danny Boy/I Believe	1964	3.00	6.00	12.00
PEAK					
❑ 7042	I've Got to Let Him Know/I Sold My Heart to the Junkman	1962	6.25	12.50	25.00
—Credited to "The Blue-Belles" but actually recorded by The Starlets					
❑ 7042 [PS]	I've Got to Let Him Know/I Sold My Heart to the Junkman	1962	20.00	40.00	80.00
Albums					
ATLANTIC					
❑ 8119 [M]	Over the Rainbow	1966	7.50	15.00	30.00
❑ SD 8119 [S]	Over the Rainbow	1966	10.00	20.00	40.00
❑ 8147 [M]	Dreamer	1967	7.50	15.00	30.00
❑ SD 8147 [S]	Dreamer	1967	10.00	20.00	40.00
MISTLETOE					
❑ MLP-1204	Merry Christmas from LaBelle	1976	5.00	10.00	20.00
NEWTOWN					
❑ 631 [M]	Sweethearts of the Apollo	1963	100.00	200.00	400.00
❑ 632 [M]	Sleigh Bells, Jingle Bells and Blue Bells	1963	75.00	150.00	300.00
PARKWAY					
❑ P-7043 [M]	The Bluebelles On Stage	1965	37.50	75.00	150.00
—With bonus single					
❑ P-7043 [M]	The Bluebelles On Stage	1965	30.00	60.00	120.00
—Without bonus single					
TRIP					
❑ 3508	Patti LaBelle and the Bluebelles	197?	2.50	5.00	10.00
❑ 8000	Patti LaBelle and the Bluebelles' Greatest Hits	1971	2.50	5.00	10.00
❑ 9525	Early Hits	197?	2.50	5.00	10.00
UNITED ARTISTS					
❑ UA-LA504-E	The Very Best of Patti LaBelle and the Bluebelles	1975	2.50	5.00	10.00

LAMPLIGHTERS, THE

Number	Title (A Side/B Side)	Yr	VG	VG+	NM
45s					
FEDERAL					
❑ 12149	Part of Me/Turn Me Loose	1953	75.00	150.00	300.00
❑ 12152	Give Me/Be-Bop Wino	1953	37.50	75.00	150.00
❑ 12166	Smootchie/I Can't Stand It	1954	37.50	75.00	150.00
❑ 12176	Tell Me You Came/I Used to Cry Mercy, Mercy	1954	37.50	75.00	150.00
❑ 12182	Salty Dog/Ride, Jockey, Ride	1954	37.50	75.00	150.00
❑ 12192	Five Minutes Longer/You Hear	1954	37.50	75.00	150.00
❑ 12197	Yum! Yum!/Goody Good Times	1954	37.50	75.00	150.00
❑ 12206	I Wanna Know/Believe in Me	1955	37.50	75.00	150.00
❑ 12212	Roll On/Love, Rock and Thrill	1955	37.50	75.00	150.00
❑ 12242	Don't Make It So Good/Hug a Little, Kiss a Little	1955	37.50	75.00	150.00
❑ 12255	You Were Sent Down from Heaven/Bo-Peep	1956	25.00	50.00	100.00
❑ 12261	It Ain't Right/Everything's All Right	1956	25.00	50.00	100.00
KING					
❑ 5890	Be-Bop Wino/Thunderbird	1964	3.75	7.50	15.00
—B-side by Dossie Terry					

LANCE, MAJOR

Number	Title (A Side/B Side)	Yr	VG	VG+	NM
45s					
COLUMBIA					
❑ 10488	Come On, Have Yourself a Good Time/Come What May	1977	—	2.50	5.00
CURTOM					
❑ 1953	Stay Away from Me (I Love You Too Much)/Gypsy Woman	1970	—	3.00	6.00
❑ 1956	Must Be Love Coming Down/Little Young Lover	1970	—	3.00	6.00
DAKAR					
❑ 608	Follow the Leader/Since You've Been Gone	1969	2.00	4.00	8.00
❑ 612	Shadows of a Memory/Sweeter As the Days Go By	1969	2.00	4.00	8.00
KAT FAMILY					
❑ 03024	I Wanna Go Home/(Instrumental)	1982	—	2.00	4.00
❑ 04185	Are You Leaving Me/I Wanna Go Home	1983	—	2.00	4.00
MERCURY					
❑ 71582	I've Got a Girl/Phyllis	1960	7.50	15.00	30.00
OKEH					
❑ 7175	The Monkey Time/Mama Didn't Know	1963	3.75	7.50	15.00
❑ 7181	Hey Little Girl/Crying in the Rain	1963	3.00	6.00	12.00
❑ 7187	Um, Um, Um, Um, Um, Um/Sweet Music	1964	3.75	7.50	15.00
❑ 7187 [PS]	Um, Um, Um, Um, Um, Um/Sweet Music	1964	7.50	15.00	30.00
❑ 7191	The Matador/Gonna Get Married	1964	2.50	5.00	10.00
❑ 7197	It Ain't No Use/Girls	1964	2.50	5.00	10.00
❑ 7200	Think Nothing About It/It's Alright	1964	12.50	25.00	50.00
❑ 7203	Rhythm/Please Don't Say No More	1964	2.50	5.00	10.00
❑ 7203 [PS]	Rhythm/Please Don't Say No More	1964	3.75	7.50	15.00
❑ 7209	Sometimes I Wonder/I'm So Lost	1965	2.50	5.00	10.00
❑ 7216	Come See/You Belong to Me My Love	1965	2.50	5.00	10.00
❑ 7216 [PS]	Come See/You Belong to Me My Love	1965	3.75	7.50	15.00
❑ 7223	Ain't It a Shame/Gotta Get Away	1965	2.50	5.00	10.00
❑ 7226	Too Hot to Hold/Dark and Lovely	1965	2.50	5.00	10.00
❑ 7233	Everybody Loves a Good Time/I Just Can't Help It	1965	3.75	7.50	15.00
❑ 7250	Little Young Lover/Investigate	1966	3.75	7.50	15.00
❑ 7250 [PS]	Little Young Lover/Investigate	1966	5.00	10.00	20.00
❑ 7255	It's the Beat/You'll Want Me Back	1966	2.50	5.00	10.00
❑ 7266	Ain't No Soul (In These Shoes)/I	1966	3.75	7.50	15.00
❑ 7284	You Don't Want Me No More/Wait Till I Get You in Your Arms	1967	12.50	25.00	50.00
❑ 7298	Without a Doubt/Forever	1967	2.50	5.00	10.00
OSIRIS					
❑ 001	You're Everything I Need/(Instrumental)	1975	—	2.50	5.00
PLAYBOY					
❑ 6017	Um, Um, Um, Um, Um, Um/Last of the Red Hot Lovers	1974	—	2.50	5.00
❑ 6020	Sweeter/Wild and Free	1975	—	2.50	5.00
SOUL					
❑ 35123	I Never Thought I'd Be Losing You/Chicago Disco	1977	—	2.50	5.00
VOLT					
❑ 4079	I Wanna Make Up/That's the Story of My Life	1972	—	3.00	6.00
❑ 4085	Ain't No Sweat/Since I Lost My Baby's Love	1972	—	3.00	6.00
Albums					
KAT FAMILY					
❑ FZ 38898	The Major's Back	1983	3.00	6.00	12.00

Chris Kenner, of "I Like It Like That" fame, recorded at least this one single for the Prigan label, which was partially owned by Lloyd Price.

This was Ben E. King's first solo album. The title song actually was a bigger hit on the pop charts than R&B.

Freddy (or Freddie) King had his first hit with the instrumental "Hide Away" in 1961. This sought-after all-instrumental album followed.

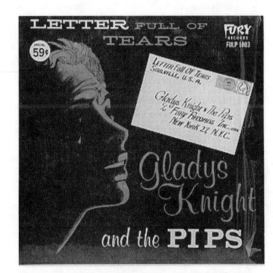

The rarest Gladys Knight and the Pips LP is *Letter Full of Tears*, released in 1962 on the Fury label in the wake of the title song's hit status.

After Jeffrey and Billy Osborne left L.T.D. in the early 1980s, the group had a few more hits before disappearing. Their last hit, "For You" in 1983, was on the small Montage label.

Sweethearts of the Apollo was the first full-length LP by Patti LaBelle and the Blue-Belles, on the Newtown label in 1963.

Number	Title (A Side/B Side)	Yr	VG	VG+	NM

OKEH

❏ OKM-12105 [M]	The Monkey Time	1963	10.00	20.00	40.00
❏ OKM-12106 [M]	Um, Um, Um, Um, Um, Um	1964	10.00	20.00	40.00
❏ OKM-12110 [M]	Major's Greatest Hits	1965	7.50	15.00	30.00
❏ OKS-14105 [S]	The Monkey Time	1963	12.50	25.00	50.00
❏ OKS-14106 [S]	Um, Um, Um, Um, Um, Um	1964	12.50	25.00	50.00
❏ OKS-14110 [S]	Major's Greatest Hits	1965	10.00	20.00	40.00

SOUL

❏ S7-751	Now Arriving	1978	3.00	6.00	12.00

LANDS, LIZ
45s
GORDY

❏ 7023	We Shall Overcome/I Have a Dream	1963	6.25	12.50	25.00

—*B-side by Rev. Martin Luther King*

❏ 7026	May What He Lived For Live/He's Got the Whole World in His Hands	1963	7.50	15.00	30.00
❏ 7030	Midnight Journey/Keep Me	1964	12.50	25.00	50.00

—*The Temptations sing backup*

ONE-DERFUL

❏ 4847	One Man's Poison/Don't Shut Me Out	1967	3.75	7.50	15.00

T&L

❏ 201	Silent Night (Part 1)/Silent Night (Part 2)	19??	2.00	4.00	8.00

LANE, MICKEY LEE
45s
MALA

❏ 12032	Tutti Frutti/With Your Love	1968	2.00	4.00	8.00

SWAN

❏ 4183	Shaggy Dog/Oo-Oo	1964	3.00	6.00	12.00
❏ 4199	The Zoo/(They're All in the) Senior Class	1965	2.50	5.00	10.00
❏ 4210	Little Girl (I Was Wrong)/When You're in Love	1965	2.50	5.00	10.00
❏ 4222	Hey Sah-Lo-Ney/Of Yesterday	1965	2.50	5.00	10.00
❏ 4252	The Only Thing to Do/She Don't Want To	1966	2.50	5.00	10.00

LARKS, THE (1)
Also see DON JULIAN AND THE MEADOWLARKS.
45s
MONEY

❏ 106	The Jerk/Forget Me	1964	5.00	10.00	20.00
❏ 109	Mickey's East Coast Jerk/Soul Jerk	1965	3.00	6.00	12.00
❏ 110	The Slauson Shuffle/Soul Jerk	1965	3.00	6.00	12.00
❏ 112	The Roman/Heavenly Father	1965	3.00	6.00	12.00
❏ 115	Can You Do the Duck/Sad Sad Boy	1965	3.00	6.00	12.00
❏ 119	Lost My Love Yesterday/The Answer Came Too Late	1966	3.00	6.00	12.00
❏ 122	Philly Dog/Heaven Only Knows	1966	3.00	6.00	12.00
❏ 127	The Skate/Come Back Baby	1967	3.00	6.00	12.00
❏ 601	I Love You/I Want You Back	1973	—	3.00	6.00
❏ 604	My Favorite Beer Joint/(Instrumental)	1973	—	3.00	6.00
❏ 607	Shorty the Pimp (Part 1)/Shorty the Pimp (Part 2)	1974	—	3.00	6.00

—*Money 604 and 607 as "Don Julian and the Larks"*

Albums
COLLECTABLES

❏ COL-5176	Golden Classics: The Jerk	198?	2.50	5.00	10.00

MONEY

❏ LP-1102 [M]	The Jerk	1965	10.00	20.00	40.00
❏ ST-1102 [S]	The Jerk	1965	12.50	25.00	50.00
❏ LP-1107 [M]	Soul Kaleidoscope	1966	10.00	20.00	40.00
❏ ST-1107 [S]	Soul Kaleidoscope	1966	12.50	25.00	50.00
❏ LP-1110 [M]	Superslick	1967	10.00	20.00	40.00
❏ ST-1110 [S]	Superslick	1967	12.50	25.00	50.00

LARKS, THE (2)
45s
SHERYL

❏ 334	It's Unbelievable/I Can't Believe It	1961	7.50	15.00	30.00
❏ 338	There Is a Girl/Let's Drink a Toast	1961	6.25	12.50	25.00

LARKS, THE (3)
45s
APOLLO

❏ 429	Little Side Car/Hey Little Girl	1951	1000.	2000.	4000.
❏ 430	Ooh, It Feels So Good/I Don't Believe in Tomorrow	1951	1000.	2000.	4000.
❏ 435	My Lost Love/How Long Must I Wait for You	1952	250.00	500.00	1000.
❏ 437	Darlin'/Lucy Brown	1952	250.00	500.00	1000.
❏ 475	No Mama No/Honey from the Bee	1955	100.00	200.00	400.00
❏ 1180	Hopefully Yours/When I Leave These Prison Walls	1951	1000.	2000.	4000.
❏ 1184	My Reverie/Let's Say a Prayer	1951	500.00	1000.	2000.

—*Black vinyl*

❏ 1184	My Reverie/Let's Say a Prayer	1951	4000.	6000.	8000.

—*Red vinyl*

❏ 1189	Shadrack/Honey in the Rock	1952	500.00	1000.	2000.
❏ 1190	Stolen Love/In My Lonely Room	1952	625.00	1250.	2500.

—*Black vinyl*

❏ 1190	Stolen Love/In My Lonely Room	1952	2500.	3750.	5000.

—*Red vinyl*

❏ 1194	I Live True to You/Hold Me	1952	250.00	500.00	1000.

LLOYDS

❏ 108	Margie/Rockin' in the Rockin' Room	1954	200.00	400.00	800.00
❏ 110	Tippin' In/If It's a Crime	1954	200.00	400.00	800.00
❏ 112	No Other Girl/The World Is Waiting for the Sunrise	1954	200.00	400.00	800.00
❏ 114	Forget It/I Live True to You	1954	150.00	300.00	600.00

78s
APOLLO

❏ 427	Eyesight to the Blind/I Ain't Fattenin' Frogs for Snakes	1951	50.00	100.00	200.00
❏ 429	Little Side Car/Hey Little Girl	1951	50.00	100.00	200.00
❏ 430	Ooh, It Feels So Good/I Don't Believe in Tomorrow	1951	50.00	100.00	200.00
❏ 435	My Lost Love/How Long Must I Wait for You	1952	50.00	100.00	200.00
❏ 437	Darlin'/Lucy Brown	1952	37.50	75.00	150.00
❏ 475	No Mama No/Honey from the Bee	1955	37.50	75.00	150.00
❏ 1180	Hopefully Yours/When I Leave These Prison Walls	1951	62.50	125.00	250.00
❏ 1184	My Reverie/Let's Say a Prayer	1951	100.00	200.00	400.00
❏ 1189	Shadrack/Honey in the Rock	1952	87.50	175.00	350.00
❏ 1190	Stolen Love/In My Lonely Room	1952	100.00	200.00	400.00
❏ 1194	I Live True to You/Hold Me	1952	62.50	125.00	250.00

LLOYDS

❏ 108	Margie/Rockin' in the Rockin' Room	1954	50.00	100.00	200.00
❏ 110	Tippin' In/If It's a Crime	1954	50.00	100.00	200.00
❏ 112	No Other Girl/The World Is Waiting for the Sunrise	1954	50.00	100.00	200.00
❏ 114	Forget It/I Live True to You	1954	50.00	100.00	200.00

LARKS, THE (U)
It's doubtful that any of these are groups (1) or (3). Some could be by group (2).
45s
CROSS FIRE

❏ 74-49/50	Fabulous Cars and Diamond Rings/Life Is Sweeter Now	1961	5.00	10.00	20.00

GUYDEN

❏ 2098	I Want Her to Love Me/(Instrumental)	1963	3.00	6.00	12.00
❏ 2103	Fabulous Cars and Diamond Rings/Life Is Sweeter Now	1964	3.00	6.00	12.00

JETT

❏ 3001	Love You So/Love Me True	1965	15.00	30.00	60.00

NASCO

❏ 028	I Love You/I Want You Back	1972	2.00	4.00	8.00

STACY

❏ 969	Food Sticks/Scavenger	1963	3.00	6.00	12.00

VIOLET

❏ 1051	I Want Her to Love Me/(Instrumental)	1962	5.00	10.00	20.00

LARKTONES, THE
45s
ABC-PARAMOUNT

❏ 9909	The Letter/Rockin' Swingin' Man	1958	7.50	15.00	30.00

RIKI

❏ 140	Why Are You Tearing Us Apart/Nosy Neighbor	1960	15.00	30.00	60.00

LASALLE, DENISE
45s
ABC

❏ 12225	Hellfire Loving/I Get What I Want	1976	—	2.50	5.00
❏ 12238	Freedom to Express Yourself/Second Breath	1977	—	2.00	4.00
❏ 12312	Love Me Right/Fool Me Good	1977	—	2.00	4.00
❏ 12353	One Life to Live/Before You Take It to the Streets	1978	—	2.00	4.00
❏ 12419	Workin' Overtime/No Matter What They Say	1978	—	2.00	4.00
❏ 12443	P.A.R.T.Y. (Where It Is)/Under the Influence	1979	—	2.00	4.00

CHESS

❏ 2005	A Love Reputation/One Little Thing	1967	2.50	5.00	10.00
❏ 2044	Private Property/I've Been Waiting	1968	2.50	5.00	10.00
❏ 2058	Count Down (And Fly Me to the Moon)/A Promise Is a Promise	1968	2.50	5.00	10.00

MALACO

❏ 2089	Lady in the Street/I Was Not the Best Woman	198?	—	2.00	4.00
❏ 2092	Lay Me Down/I Was Telling Him About You	198?	—	2.00	4.00
❏ 2095	Down Home Blues/Down Home Blues (X-Rated)	198?	—	2.00	4.00
❏ 2098	Right Place, Right Time/He's Not Available	1984	—	2.00	4.00

—*With Latimore*

❏ 2105	Treat Your Man Like a Baby/Come to Bed	1985	—	2.00	4.00
❏ 2112	My Tu-Tu/Give Me Yo' Strongest Whiskey	1985	—	2.00	4.00
❏ 2124	Santa Claus Got the Blues/Love Is a Five Letter Word	1985	—	2.50	5.00
❏ 2131	What's Going On in My House/He's That Way Sometime	1986	—	2.00	4.00
❏ 2138	Hold What You Got/Footsteps of a Fool	1986	—	2.00	4.00
❏ 2152	Bring It On Home to Me/Write This One Off (As Actors)	1987	—	2.00	4.00
❏ 2156	Caught in Your Mess/I Forgot to Remember	1987	—	2.00	4.00
❏ 2167	Drop That Zero/Chain Letter	1988	—	2.00	4.00

MCA

❏ 41222	I'm So Hot/Miracle, You and Me	1980	—	2.00	4.00
❏ 51046	I'm Trippin' on You/I'll Get You Some Help	1981	—	2.00	4.00
❏ 51098	Sharing Your Love/I'll Get You Some Help	1981	—	2.00	4.00

TARPEN

❏ 6603	A Love Reputation/One Little Thing	1967	6.25	12.50	25.00

WESTBOUND

❏ 162	Heartbreaker of the Year/Hung Up, Strung Out	1971	2.00	4.00	8.00
❏ 182	Trapped by a Thing Called Love/Keep It Coming	1971	—	3.00	6.00
❏ 201	Now Run and Tell That/The Deeper I Go	1972	—	3.00	6.00
❏ 206	Man Sized Job/I'm Over You	1972	—	3.00	6.00

Number	Title (A Side/B Side)	Yr	VG	VG+	NM
215	What It Takes to Get a Good Woman (That's What It's Gonna Take to Keep Her)/Making a Good Thing Better	1973	—	3.00	6.00
219	Your Man and Your Best Friend/What Am I Doing Wrong	1973	—	3.00	6.00
221	Don't Nobody Live Here (By the Name of Fool)/ Goody Goody Getter	1973	—	3.00	6.00
223	Get Up Off My Mind/The Best Thing I Ever Had	1974	—	3.00	6.00
229	Trying to Forget/We've Got Love	1974	—	3.00	6.00
5004	My Brand on You/Anytime Is the Right Time	1975	—	2.50	5.00
5008	Here I Am Again/Hung Up, Strung Out	1975	—	2.50	5.00
5019	Married, But Not to Each Other/Who's the Fool	1976	—	2.50	5.00
Albums					
ABC					
D-966	Second Breath	1976	3.00	6.00	12.00
D-1027	The Bitch Is Bad	1977	3.00	6.00	12.00
AA-1087	Under the Influence	1978	3.00	6.00	12.00
MALACO					
7412	A Lady in the Street	198?	2.50	5.00	10.00
7417	Right Place, Right Time	1984	2.50	5.00	10.00
7422	Love Talkin'	198?	2.50	5.00	10.00
7434	Rain and Fire	198?	2.50	5.00	10.00
7441	It's Lying Time Again	198?	2.50	5.00	10.00
7447	Hittin' Where It Hurts	198?	2.50	5.00	10.00
7454	Still Trapped	198?	2.50	5.00	10.00
7464	Love Me Right	198?	2.50	5.00	10.00
MCA					
759	Unwrapped	198?	2.00	4.00	8.00
—Reissue of 3089					
760	I'm So Hot	198?	2.00	4.00	8.00
—Reissue of 3239					
3089	Unwrapped	1979	2.50	5.00	10.00
3239	I'm So Hot	1980	2.50	5.00	10.00
WESTBOUND					
209	Here I Am Again	1975	3.00	6.00	12.00
2012	Trapped by a Thing Called Love	1972	3.75	7.50	15.00
2016	On the Loose	1973	3.75	7.50	15.00

LAST POETS, THE
45s

Number	Title (A Side/B Side)	Yr	VG	VG+	NM
BLUE THUMB					
216	Tribute to Orabi/Bird's Word	1972	3.00	6.00	12.00
DOUGLAS					
ADS 8	O.D./Black Thighs	1971	3.75	7.50	15.00
ADS 8 [PS]	O.D./Black Thighs	1971	7.50	15.00	30.00
ZS7 6500	True Blues/Black Is	1971	3.00	6.00	12.00
Albums					
BLUE THUMB					
BT-39	Chastisement	1972	7.50	15.00	30.00
BT-52	At Last	1973	7.50	15.00	30.00
CASABLANCA					
NBLP 7051	Delights of the Garden	1977	6.25	12.50	25.00
CELLULOID					
6101	The Last Poets	198?	2.50	5.00	10.00
6105	This Is Madness	198?	2.50	5.00	10.00
6108	Oh My People	198?	2.50	5.00	10.00
6136	Delights of the Garden	198?	2.50	5.00	10.00
COLLECTABLES					
COL-6500	Right On!	198?	2.50	5.00	10.00
DOUGLAS					
3	The Last Poets	1970	12.50	25.00	50.00
Z 30583	This Is Madness	1971	12.50	25.00	50.00
Z 30811	The Last Poets	1971	10.00	20.00	40.00
JUGGERNAUT					
8802	Right On!	1971	12.50	25.00	50.00
—As "The Original Last Poets"					

LATIMORE
12-Inch Singles

Number	Title (A Side/B Side)	Yr	VG	VG+	NM
T.K. DISCO					
400	Goodbye Heartache/We Got to Hit It Off	1979	3.75	7.50	15.00
45s					
ATLANTIC					
2639	I Pity the Fool/I'm Just an Ordinary Man	1969	2.00	4.00	8.00
DADE					
2013	Girl, I Got News for You/Ain't Gonna Cry No More	1967	2.50	5.00	10.00
2014	There She Is/It Was So Nice While It Lasted	1967	2.50	5.00	10.00
2015	It's Just a Matter of Time/Let's Move and Groove Together	1967	2.50	5.00	10.00
2017	The Power and the Glory/Love Don't Love Me	1968	2.50	5.00	10.00
2020	Have a Little Faith/I'm a Believer	1968	2.50	5.00	10.00
2022	I Pity the Fool/I'm Just an Ordinary Man	1968	2.50	5.00	10.00
2026	I'll Be Good to You/Life's Little Ups and Downs	1969	2.50	5.00	10.00
GLADES					
1714	Jolie/There's No End	1973	2.00	4.00	8.00
1716	Stormy Monday/There's No End	1973	—	3.00	6.00
1720	If You Were My Woman/Put Pride Aside	1974	—	3.00	6.00
1722	Let's Straighten It Out/Ain't Nobody Gonna Make Me Change My Mind	1974	—	3.00	6.00
1726	Keep the Home Fires Burnin'/That's How It Is	1975	—	3.00	6.00
1729	There's a Red-Neck in the Soul Band/Just One Step	1975	—	3.00	6.00
1733	Qualified Man/She Don't Lose Her Groove	1976	—	3.00	6.00
1739	Somethin' 'Bout 'Cha/Sweet Vibrations	1976	—	3.00	6.00
1742	I Get Lifted/All the Way Lover	1977	—	3.00	6.00
1744	Let Me Live the Life I Love/It Ain't Where You Been	1977	—	3.00	6.00
1750	Dig a Little Deeper/Let Me Go	1978	—	3.00	6.00
1752	Long Distance Love/Out to Get 'Cha	1979	—	3.00	6.00
1755	Goodbye Heartache/We Got to Hit It Off	1979	—	3.00	6.00
1756	Discoed to Death/Just One Step	1979	—	3.00	6.00
1761	Take Me to the Mountaintop/Joy	1980	—	3.00	6.00
MALACO					
2083	Let the Doorknob Hit'cha/Do That To Me One More Time	1982	—	2.00	4.00
2084	Ain't Nothing You Can Do/Bad Risk	198?	—	2.00	4.00
2093	I'll Do Anything for You/Hell Fire Lovin'	198?	—	2.00	4.00
2098	Right Place, Right Time/He's Not Available	1984	—	2.00	4.00
—With Denise LaSalle					
2099	One Shirt, Soulless Shoes/You	1984	—	2.00	4.00
2119	Good Time Man/You Crowed in My Bed	198?	—	2.00	4.00
2130	Sunshine Lady/There's No Limit to My Love	1986	—	2.00	4.00
Albums					
GLADES					
6502	Latimore	1973	3.00	6.00	12.00
6503	More, More, More	1974	3.00	6.00	12.00
7505	Latimore 3	1975	3.00	6.00	12.00
7509	It Ain't Where You Been	1976	2.50	5.00	10.00
7515	Dig a Little Deeper	1978	2.50	5.00	10.00
MALACO					
7409	Singing in the Key of Love	198?	2.50	5.00	10.00
7414	I'll Do Anything for You	198?	2.50	5.00	10.00
7423	Good Time Man	198?	2.50	5.00	10.00
7436	Every Way But Wrong	198?	2.50	5.00	10.00
7443	Slow Down	198?	2.50	5.00	10.00
7456	The Only Way Is Up	198?	2.50	5.00	10.00
7468	Catchin' Up	1993	3.00	6.00	12.00

LATTISAW, STACY
12-Inch Singles

Number	Title (A Side/B Side)	Yr	VG	VG+	NM
COTILLION					
DSKO 168 [DJ]	When You're Young and In Love (9:20)/Rock with Me (6:33)	1979	3.00	6.00	12.00
295 [DJ]	Feel My Love Tonight (4:12) (same on both sides)	1981	2.00	4.00	8.00
MOTOWN					
PR-190 [DJ]	Nail It to the Wall (12" Version 6:10) (12" Instrumental 4:46) (Edit of 12" Vocal 3:54)	1986	2.00	4.00	8.00
PR-197 [DJ]	Jump Into My Life (Dance Mix 7:11) (7" Version 4:17)/(Dub 6:15) (Acapella Mix 4:26)	1987	—	3.50	7.00
PR 231 [DJ]	Let Me Take You Down (same on both sides)	1988	2.00	4.00	8.00
4563 MG	Nail It to the Wall (12" Version 6:10) (12" Instrumental 4:46) (Edit of 12" Vocal 3:54)	1986	—	3.50	7.00
4574 MG	Jump Into My Life (Dance Mix 7:11) (7" Version 4:17)//(Dub 6:15)/Long Shot	1987	—	3.00	6.00
MOT-4615	Call Me (3 versions)	1988	—	3.00	6.00
MOT-4653	What You Need (Extended) (Instrumental)	1989	—	3.00	6.00
L33-17914 [DJ]	What You Need (Extended) (Edit) (Instrumental)	1989	—	3.00	6.00
L33-18083 [DJ]	Dance for You (Radio Edit) (Extended) (Dub)	1989	—	3.00	6.00
L33-18094 [DJ]	What You Need (12" Remix) (Dub) (Radio Edit) (Club)	1989	2.50	5.00	10.00
L33-18197 [DJ]	I Don't Have the Heart (Radio Edit) (LP Version) (Instrumental)	1990	2.00	4.00	8.00
45s					
ATLANTIC OLDIES SERIES					
OS 13226	Let Me Be Your Angel/Dynamite	198?	—	—	3.00
COTILLION					
44250	When You're Young and In Love/Three Wishes	1979	—	3.00	6.00
44250 [PS]	When You're Young and In Love/Three Wishes	1979	—	3.00	6.00
45015	Dynamite!/Dreaming	1980	—	2.50	5.00
46001	Let Me Be Your Angel/You Don't Love Me Anymore	1980	—	2.50	5.00
46015	Love On a Two-Way Street/Baby I Love You	1981	—	2.50	5.00
46024	It Was So Easy/Screaming Off the Top	1981	—	2.50	5.00
46026	Feel My Love Tonight/Young Girl	1981	—	2.50	5.00
47011	Don't Throw It All Away/Down for You	1982	—	2.50	5.00
99614	He's Just Not You/Coming Alive	1985	—	2.00	4.00
99635	I'm Not the Same Girl/Toughen Up	1985	—	2.00	4.00
99635 [PS]	I'm Not the Same Girl/Toughen Up	1985	—	2.00	4.00
99819	Million Dollar Babe/The Ways of Love	1983	—	2.50	5.00
99855	Miracles/Black Pumps and Pink Lipstick	1983	—	2.50	5.00
99943	Hey There Lonely Boy/Tonight I'm Gonna Make You Mine	1982	—	2.50	5.00
99968	Attack of the Name Game/I Could Love You So Divine	1982	—	2.50	5.00
MOTOWN					
1859	Nail It to the Wall/(Instrumental)	1986	—	—	3.00
1859 [PS]	Nail It to the Wall/(Instrumental)	1986	—	2.00	4.00
1874	Jump Into My Life/Long Shot	1987	—	—	3.00
1891	Take Me All the Way/Little Bit of Heaven	1987	—	—	3.00
1912	Every Drop of Your Love/Long Shot	1987	—	—	3.00
1912 [PS]	Every Drop of Your Love/Long Shot	1987	—	2.00	4.00
1934	Let Me Take You Down/The Hard Way	1988	—	—	3.00
1945	Call Me/Call Me (With Rap)	1988	—	—	3.00
1945 [PS]	Call Me/Call Me (With Rap)	1988	—	2.00	4.00
1978	What You Need/(Instrumental)	1989	—	—	3.00

L

Number	Title (A Side/B Side)	Yr	VG	VG+	NM
Albums					
COTILLION					
❑ SD 5214	Young and In Love	1979	3.00	6.00	12.00
❑ SD 5219	Let Me Be Your Angel	1980	2.50	5.00	10.00
❑ SD 16049	With You	1981	2.50	5.00	10.00
❑ 90002	Sneakin' Out	1982	2.50	5.00	10.00
❑ 90106	Sixteen	1983	2.50	5.00	10.00
❑ 90280	I'm Not the Same Girl	1985	2.50	5.00	10.00
MOTOWN					
❑ 6212ML	Take Me All the Way	1986	2.00	4.00	8.00
❑ 6247ML	Personal Attention	1988	2.00	4.00	8.00

LATTISAW, STACY, AND JOHNNY GILL

Also see each artist's individual listings.

Number	Title (A Side/B Side)	Yr	VG	VG+	NM
12-Inch Singles					
COTILLION					
❑ 749 [DJ]	Block Party (5:25) (same on both sides)	1984	2.00	4.00	8.00
MOTOWN					
❑ MOT-4701	Where Do We Go from Here (Extended) (Radio Version) (Instrumental)	1989	—	3.00	6.00
45s					
COTILLION					
❑ 99725	Block Party/Come Out of the Shadows	1984	—	2.00	4.00
❑ 99750	Baby It's You/50-50 Love	1984	—	2.00	4.00
❑ 99785	Perfect Combination/Heartbreak Look	1984	—	2.00	4.00
MOTOWN					
❑ 2026	Where Do We Go from Here/(Instrumental)	1989	—	2.50	5.00
Albums					
COTILLION					
❑ 90136	Perfect Combination	1984	2.50	5.00	10.00

LAVETTE, BETTY

Number	Title (A Side/B Side)	Yr	VG	VG+	NM
45s					
ATCO					
❑ 6891	Heart of Gold/You'll Wake Up Wisely	1972	—	3.00	6.00
❑ 6913	Your Turn to Cry/Soul Tambourine	1973	—	3.00	6.00
ATLANTIC					
❑ 2160	My Man — He's a Lovin' Man/Shut Your Mouth	1962	3.00	6.00	12.00
—As "Betty LaVett"					
❑ 2198	You'll Never Change/Here I Am	1963	3.00	6.00	12.00
—As "Betty LaVett"					
CALLA					
❑ 102	Let Me Down Easy/What I Don't Know (Won't Hurt Me)	1965	2.50	5.00	10.00
❑ 104	I Feel Good (All Over)/Only Your Love Can Save Me	1965	2.50	5.00	10.00
❑ 106	Stand Up Like a Man/I'm Just a Fool for You	1965	2.50	5.00	10.00
KAREN					
❑ 1540	Love Makes the World Go Round/Almost	1968	2.00	4.00	8.00
❑ 1544	Get Away/What Condition My Condition Is In	1968	2.00	4.00	8.00
❑ 1545	With a Little Help from My Friends/Hey Love	1969	2.00	4.00	8.00
❑ 1548	Ticket to the Moon/Let Me Down Easy	1969	2.00	4.00	8.00
LUPINE					
❑ 123	Witch Craft in the Air/You Killed the Love	1964	10.00	20.00	40.00
—As "Betty LaVett"					
❑ 1021	Witch Craft in the Air/You Killed the Love	1964	6.25	12.50	25.00
—As "Betty LaVett"					
MOTOWN					
❑ 1532	Right in the Middle (Of Falling in Love)/You Seen One, You Seen 'Em All	1981	—	2.50	5.00
—As "Bettye LaVette"					
❑ 1614	Either Way, We Lose/I Can't Stop	1982	—	2.50	5.00
—As "Bettye LaVette"					
SILVER FOX					
❑ 17	He Made a Woman Out of Me/Nearer to You	1969	—	3.00	6.00
❑ 21	Do Your Duty/Love's Made a Fool Out of Me	1970	—	3.00	6.00
❑ 24	Games People Play/My Train's Comin' In	1970	—	3.00	6.00
SSS INTERNATIONAL					
❑ 839	Take Another Piece of My Heart/At the Mercy of a Man	1971	—	3.00	6.00
WEST END					
❑ 1213	Doin' the Best That I Can/(Instrumental)	1983	—	2.50	5.00
—As "Bettye LaVette"					

LAWS, HUBERT

Number	Title (A Side/B Side)	Yr	VG	VG+	NM
45s					
ATLANTIC					
❑ 5046	Miss Thing/Blue Eyed Peas and Rice	1965	2.00	4.00	8.00
COLUMBIA					
❑ 02694	Goodbye for Now (Theme from "Reds")/(Instrumental)	1982	—	2.00	4.00
❑ 10736	False Faces/The Baron	1978	—	2.00	4.00
❑ 10811	It Happens Every Day/Love Gets Better	1978	—	2.00	4.00
❑ 11022	Land of Passion/Heartbeats	1979	—	2.00	4.00
❑ 11368	Wildfire/Family	1980	—	2.00	4.00
CTI					
❑ 3	Fire and Rain/Theme from Love Story	1971	—	2.50	5.00
❑ 13	Amazing Grace (Part 1)/Amazing Grace (Part 2)	1973	—	2.50	5.00
❑ 21	Mean Lene/Come All Ye Disconsolate	1974	—	2.50	5.00
❑ 27	The Chicago Theme (Love Loop)/I Had a Dream	1975	—	2.50	5.00
❑ 501	La Jean/Let It Be	197?	—	2.00	4.00
❑ 505	Feelin' Alright/Let It Be	197?	—	2.00	4.00
Albums					
ATLANTIC					
❑ 1432 [M]	The Laws of Jazz	1965	3.00	6.00	12.00
❑ SD 1432 [S]	The Laws of Jazz	1965	3.75	7.50	15.00
❑ 1452 [M]	Flute By-Laws	1966	3.00	6.00	12.00
❑ SD 1452 [S]	Flute By-Laws	1966	3.75	7.50	15.00
❑ SD 1509	Laws Cause	1970	3.00	6.00	12.00
❑ SD 1624	Wild Flower	1973	2.50	5.00	10.00
❑ SD 8813	The Laws of Jazz	198?	2.00	4.00	8.00
—Reissue of 1432					
CBS					
❑ M 39858	Blanchard: New Earth Symphony; Telemann: Suite in A; Amazing Grace	1985	3.00	6.00	12.00
COLUMBIA					
❑ PC 34330	Romeo and Juliet	1976	3.00	6.00	12.00
❑ JC 35022	Say It with Silence	1978	2.50	5.00	10.00
❑ JC 35708	Land of Passion	1979	2.50	5.00	10.00
❑ FC 36365	The Best of Hubert Laws	198?	2.50	5.00	10.00
❑ JC 36396	Family	1980	2.50	5.00	10.00
❑ FC 38850	Make It Last	1983	2.50	5.00	10.00
CTI					
❑ CTX-3 + 3 [(2)]	In the Beginning	1974	3.75	7.50	15.00
❑ 1002	Crying Song	1970	5.00	10.00	20.00
❑ 6000	Crying Song	1970	3.00	6.00	12.00
—Reissue of 1002					
❑ 6006	Afro-Classic	1971	3.00	6.00	12.00
❑ 6012	Rite of Spring	1972	3.00	6.00	12.00
❑ 6022	Morning Star	1972	3.00	6.00	12.00
❑ 6025	Carnegie Hall	1973	3.00	6.00	12.00
❑ 6058	The Chicago Theme	1975	3.00	6.00	12.00
❑ 6065	Then There Was Light, Vol. 1	1976	3.00	6.00	12.00
❑ 6066	Then There Was Light, Vol. 2	1976	3.00	6.00	12.00
❑ 7075	San Francisco	1976	3.00	6.00	12.00
❑ 8015	The Chicago Theme	198?	2.00	4.00	8.00
—Reissue of 6058					
❑ 8019	Afro-Classic	198?	2.00	4.00	8.00
—Reissue of 6006					
❑ 8020	Rite of Spring	198?	2.00	4.00	8.00
—Reissue of 6012					

LAWS, RONNIE

Number	Title (A Side/B Side)	Yr	VG	VG+	NM
45s					
BLUE NOTE					
❑ XW738	Always There/Tidal Wave	1975	—	2.50	5.00
❑ XW848	Carmen/All the Time	1976	—	2.50	5.00
❑ XW1007	Just Love/Nuthin' But Nuthin'	1977	—	2.50	5.00
❑ XW1036	Friends and Strangers/Goodtime Ride	1977	—	2.50	5.00
CAPITOL					
❑ B-5241	In the Groove/Summer Fool	1983	—	—	3.00
❑ B-5241 [PS]	In the Groove/Summer Fool	1983	—	2.00	4.00
❑ B-5274	Mr. Nice Guy/Off and On Again	1983	—	—	3.00
❑ B-5421	City Girl/Rolling	1984	—	—	3.00
❑ B-5465	(You Are) Paradise/Stay Awake	1985	—	—	3.00
COLUMBIA					
❑ 06240	Come to Me/Take a Chance	1986	—	—	3.00
❑ 06574	Mirror Town/Midnight Side	1986	—	—	3.00
❑ 07629	Rhythm of Romance/Nite Life	1987	—	—	3.00
❑ 07787	Smoke House/All Day Rhythm	1988	—	—	3.00
LIBERTY					
❑ 1424	Stay Awake/Summer Fool	1981	—	2.00	4.00
❑ 1442	There's a Way/Just As You Are	1981	—	2.00	4.00
❑ 1459	Heavy On Easy/Just As You Are	1982	—	2.00	4.00
UNITED ARTISTS					
❑ 1264	Love Is Here/Grace	1978	—	2.00	4.00
❑ 1278	All for You/These Days	1979	—	2.00	4.00
❑ 1334	Every Generation/Every Generation (Part 2)	1980	—	2.00	4.00
❑ 1334 [PS]	Every Generation/Every Generation (Part 2)	1980	—	2.50	5.00
❑ 1354	Love's Victory/It's One	1980	—	2.00	4.00
❑ 1376	Young Child/(B-side unknown)	1980	—	2.00	4.00
Albums					
BLUE NOTE					
❑ BN-LA452-G	Pressure Sensitive	1975	3.00	6.00	12.00
❑ BN-LA628-G	Fever	1976	3.00	6.00	12.00
❑ BN-LA730-H	Friends and Strangers	1977	2.50	5.00	10.00
CAPITOL					
❑ ST-12261	Mr. Nice Guy	1983	2.50	5.00	10.00
❑ ST-12375	Classic Masters	1984	2.50	5.00	10.00
COLUMBIA					
❑ BFC 40089	Mirror Town	1986	2.50	5.00	10.00
❑ FC 40902	All Day Rhythm	1987	2.50	5.00	10.00
LIBERTY					
❑ LO-628	Fever	198?	2.00	4.00	8.00
—Reissue of Blue Note 628					
❑ LW-730	Friends and Strangers	198?	2.00	4.00	8.00
—Reissue of Blue Note 730					
❑ LO-881	Flame	198?	2.00	4.00	8.00
—Reissue of United Artists 881					
❑ LT-1001	Every Generation	1981	2.00	4.00	8.00
—Reissue of United Artists 1001					
❑ LN-10164	Pressure Sensitive	198?	2.00	4.00	8.00
—Reissue of Blue Note 452					
❑ LN-10232	Flame	198?	2.00	4.00	8.00
—Budget-line reissue					

Number	Title (A Side/B Side)	Yr	VG	VG+	NM
❏ LN-10255	Fever	198?	2.00	4.00	8.00
—Budget-line reissue					
❏ LN-10307	Solid Ground	1986	2.00	4.00	8.00
—Budget-line reissue					
❏ LO-51087	Solid Ground	1981	2.50	5.00	10.00
UNITED ARTISTS					
❏ UA-LA881-H	Flame	1978	2.50	5.00	10.00
❏ LT-1001	Every Generation	1980	2.50	5.00	10.00

LEE, BRENDA (2)

Her real name is Brenda Lee Jones. She is no relation to the more famous pop and country singer Brenda Lee (Brenda Mae Tarpley).

45s

Number	Title (A Side/B Side)	Yr	VG	VG+	NM
APOLLO					
❏ 490	I Ain't Gonna Give Nobody None/I'll Never Get Rich Again	1956	7.50	15.00	30.00

LEE, CURTIS

45s

Number	Title (A Side/B Side)	Yr	VG	VG+	NM
DUNES					
❏ 801	California GH-903/Then I'll Know	1960	5.00	10.00	20.00
❏ 2001	Special Love/"D" in Love	1960	5.00	10.00	20.00
❏ 2003	Pledge of Love/Then I'll Know	1961	5.00	10.00	20.00
❏ 2003 [PS]	Pledge of Love/Then I'll Know	1961	6.25	12.50	25.00
❏ 2007	Pretty Little Angel Eyes/Gee, How I Wish You Were Here	1961	6.25	12.50	25.00
❏ 2008	Under the Moon of Love/Beverly Jean	1961	6.25	12.50	25.00
—2007 and 2008 were Phil Spector productions					
❏ 2012	Just Another Fool/A Night at Daddy Gee's	1962	5.00	10.00	20.00
❏ 2015	Does He Mean That Much to You/The Wobble	1962	5.00	10.00	20.00
❏ 2020	Lonely Weekends/Better Him Than Me	1963	5.00	10.00	20.00
❏ 2021	Pickin' Up the Pieces of My Heart/Mr. Mistaker	1963	5.00	10.00	20.00
HOT					
❏ 7	I Never Knew What Love Could Do/Gotta Have You	1960	18.75	37.50	75.00
MIRA					
❏ 240	Sweet Baby/Is She In Your Town	1967	5.00	10.00	20.00
ROJAC					
❏ 114	Get In My Bag/Everybody's Going Wild	1967	3.00	6.00	12.00
SABRA					
❏ 517	Let's Take a Ride/I'm Asking Forgiveness	1960	6.25	12.50	25.00
WARRIOR					
❏ 1555	With All My Heart/Pure Love	1959	7.50	15.00	30.00

LEE, JACKIE (1)

Male R&B singer whose biggest hit was "The Duck."

45s

Number	Title (A Side/B Side)	Yr	VG	VG+	NM
ABC					
❏ 11146	One for the Road/Darkest Days	1968	5.00	10.00	20.00
CAPITOL					
❏ 3145	25 Miles to Louisiana/Pershing Square	1971	—	3.00	6.00
KEYMEN					
❏ 109	Glory of Love/Bring It Home	1968	2.50	5.00	10.00
❏ 114	African Boo-Ga-Loo/Bring It Home	1968	2.50	5.00	10.00
MIRWOOD					
❏ 5502	The Duck/Let Your Conscience Be Your Guide	1965	3.00	6.00	12.00
❏ 5509	Your P-E-R-S-O-N-A-L-I-T-Y/Try My Method	1966	2.50	5.00	10.00
❏ 5510	The Shotgun and the Duck/Do the Temptation Walk	1966	2.50	5.00	10.00
❏ 5519	You're Everything/Would You Believe	1966	2.50	5.00	10.00
❏ 5527	Don't Be Ashamed/Oh, My Darlin'	1966	2.50	5.00	10.00
❏ 5528	Baby I'm Satisfied/Whether It's Right or Wrong	1966	2.50	5.00	10.00
—With Dolores Hall					
UNI					
❏ 55206	The Chicken/I Love You	1970	2.00	4.00	8.00
❏ 55259	Your Sweetness Is My Weakness/You Were Searching for a Love	1970	2.00	4.00	8.00
Albums					
MIRWOOD					
❏ MW-7000 [M]	The Duck	1966	5.00	10.00	20.00
❏ SW-7000 [S]	The Duck	1966	6.25	12.50	25.00

LEE, JOHN

See JOHN LEE HOOKER.

LEE, JULIA

45s

Number	Title (A Side/B Side)	Yr	VG	VG+	NM
CAPITOL					
❏ F838	Ain't It a Crime/Don't Save It Too Long	1950	10.00	20.00	40.00
—Note: Julia Lee singles before 838 are unknown on 45 rpm					
❏ F956	Do You Want It/Decent Woman Blues	1950	10.00	20.00	40.00
❏ F1009	There Goes My Heart/Nobody Knows You When You're Down and Out	1950	10.00	20.00	40.00
❏ F1111	My Man Stands Out/Don't Come Too Soon	1950	12.50	25.00	50.00
❏ F1252	It Won't Be Long/Bleeding Hearted Blues	1950	10.00	20.00	40.00
❏ F1376	Lotus Blossom/Pipe Dreams	1951	7.50	15.00	30.00
❏ F1432	Ugly Papa/I Know It's Wrong	1951	7.50	15.00	30.00
❏ F1589	Mama Don't Allow It/The Breeze	1951	7.50	15.00	30.00
❏ F1798	Scream in the Night/If You Hadn't Gone Away	1951	7.50	15.00	30.00
❏ F1896	Charmaine/Out in the Cold Again	1951	7.50	15.00	30.00
❏ F2203	Last Call for Alcohol/Goin' to Chicago Blues	1952	12.50	25.00	50.00
78s					
CAPITOL					
❏ 308	Gotta Gimme Whatcha Got/Lies	1946	5.00	10.00	20.00
❏ 320	When a Woman Loves a Man/Julia's Blues	1946	5.00	10.00	20.00

Number	Title (A Side/B Side)	Yr	VG	VG+	NM
❏ 340	Oh Marie/On My Way Out	1947	5.00	10.00	20.00
❏ 379	I'll Get Along Somehow/Young Girl Blues	1947	5.00	10.00	20.00
❏ 838	Ain't It a Crime/Don't Save It Too Long	1950	3.75	7.50	15.00
❏ 956	Do You Want It/Decent Woman Blues	1950	3.75	7.50	15.00
❏ 1009	There Goes My Heart/Nobody Knows You When You're Down and Out	1950	3.75	7.50	15.00
❏ 1111	My Man Stands Out/Don't Come Too Soon	1950	5.00	10.00	20.00
❏ 1252	It Won't Be Long/Bleeding Hearted Blues	1950	3.75	7.50	15.00
❏ 1376	Lotus Blossom/Pipe Dreams	1951	3.75	7.50	15.00
❏ 1432	Ugly Papa/I Know It's Wrong	1951	3.75	7.50	15.00
❏ 1589	Mama Don't Allow It/The Breeze	1951	3.75	7.50	15.00
❏ 1798	Scream in the Night/If You Hadn't Gone Away	1951	3.75	7.50	15.00
❏ 1896	Charmaine/Out in the Cold Again	1951	3.75	7.50	15.00
❏ 2203	Last Call for Alcohol/Goin' to Chicago Blues	1952	5.00	10.00	20.00
❏ 15060	That's What I Like/Crazy World	1948	5.00	10.00	20.00
❏ 15106	All I Ever Do Is Worry/Wise Guys (You're a Wise Guy)	1948	5.00	10.00	20.00
❏ 15144	Tell Me, Daddy/Until the Real Thing Comes Along	1948	5.00	10.00	20.00
❏ 15203	Christmas Spirits/Charmaine	1948	5.00	10.00	20.00
❏ 15300	Cold-Hearted Daddy/Living Back Street for You	1949	5.00	10.00	20.00
❏ 15367	I Didn't Like It the First Time (The Spinach Song)/Sit Down and Drink It Over	1949	5.00	10.00	20.00
❏ 40008	Since I've Been with You/A Porter's Love Song (Opportunity Knocks But Once)	1947	5.00	10.00	20.00
❏ 40028	Snatch and Grab It/I Was Wrong	1947	10.00	20.00	40.00
❏ 40056	Doubtful Blues/My Sin	1948	5.00	10.00	20.00
❏ 40082	King Size Papa/When You're Smiling (The Whole World Smiles with You)	1948	10.00	20.00	40.00
❏ 70006	Take It or Leave It/The Glory of Love	1949	6.25	12.50	25.00
❏ 70015	Tonight's the Night/After Hours Waltz	1949	6.25	12.50	25.00
❏ 70031	You Ain't Got It No More/Oh Chuck It in a Bucket	1949	6.25	12.50	25.00
❏ 70051	Dragging My Heart Around/Blues for Someone	1949	6.25	12.50	25.00
MERCURY					
❏ 8005	If It's Good/Show Me Missouri Blues	1946	7.50	15.00	30.00
❏ 8013	Lotus Blossom/Dream Lucky Blues	1946	7.50	15.00	30.00
Albums					
CAPITOL					
❏ H 228 [10]	Party Time	1950	30.00	60.00	120.00
❏ T 228 [M]	Party Time	195?	20.00	40.00	80.00

LEE, LAURA

12-Inch Singles

Number	Title (A Side/B Side)	Yr	VG	VG+	NM
FANTASY					
❏ D-133	Sat-Is-Fac-Tion (6:20)/Your Song	1979	3.00	6.00	12.00
45s					
ARIOLA AMERICA					
❏ 7652	Love's Got Me Tired (But I Ain't Tired of Love)/You're Barking Up the Wrong Tree	1976	—	2.50	5.00
CHESS					
❏ 1989	Stop Giving Your Man Away/You Need Me	1967	3.00	6.00	12.00
❏ 2013	Dirty Man/It's Mighty Hard	1967	2.50	5.00	10.00
❏ 2030	Wanted: Lover, No Experience Necessary/Up Tight, Good Man	1967	2.50	5.00	10.00
❏ 2041	As Long As I Got You/A Man with Some Backbone	1968	2.50	5.00	10.00
❏ 2052	Need to Belong/He Will Break Your Heart	1968	2.50	5.00	10.00
❏ 2062	Hang It Up/It's How You Make It Good	1968	2.50	5.00	10.00
❏ 2068	Mama's Got a Good Thing/Love More Than Pride	1969	2.50	5.00	10.00
COTILLION					
❏ 44054	What a Man/Separation Line	1970	2.00	4.00	8.00
❏ 44073	Together/But You Know I Love You	1970	2.00	4.00	8.00
FANTASY					
❏ 865	Sat-Is-Fac-Tion/Your Song	1979	—	2.50	5.00
HOT WAX					
❏ 7007	Wedlock Is a Padlock/Her Picture Matches Mine	1970	2.00	4.00	8.00
❏ 7105	Women's Love Rights/Her Picture Matches Mine	1971	2.00	4.00	8.00
❏ 7111	Love and Liberty/I Don't Want Nothing Old But Money	1971	2.00	4.00	8.00
❏ 7201	Since I Fell for You/I Don't Want Nothing Old But Money	1972	—	3.50	7.00
❏ 7204	Rip Off/Two Lovely Pillows	1972	—	3.50	7.00
❏ 7207	If You Can Beat Me Rockin' (You Can Have My Chair)/If I'm Good Enough to Love	1972	—	3.50	7.00
❏ 7210	Crumbs Off the Table/You've Got to Save Me	1972	—	3.50	7.00
❏ 7302	(If You Want to Try Love Again) Remember Me/If I'm Good Enough to Love	1973	—	3.50	7.00
❏ 7305	I'll Catch You When You Fall/I Can't Hold On Much Longer	1973	—	3.50	7.00
INVICTUS					
❏ 1264	I Need It Just As Bad As You/If I'm Good Enough to Love	1974	—	3.00	6.00
❏ 1273	Don't Leave Me Starving for Your Love/Remember Me	1974	—	3.00	6.00
RIC-TIC					
❏ 111	To Win Your Heart/So Will I	1966	3.75	7.50	15.00
Albums					
CHESS					
❏ CH-50031	Love More Than Pride	1972	5.00	10.00	20.00
HOT WAX					
❏ HA-708	Women's Love Rights	1971	3.75	7.50	15.00
❏ HA-714	Laura Lee	1972	3.75	7.50	15.00
❏ HA-715	The Best of Laura Lee	1973	3.75	7.50	15.00
INVICTUS					
❏ KZ 33133	Laura Lee	1974	2.50	5.00	10.00

L

Number	Title (A Side/B Side)	Yr	VG	VG+	NM
LEE AND THE LEOPARDS					
45s					
FORTUNE					
❑ 867	What About Me/Don't Press Your Luck	1964	12.50	25.00	50.00
GORDY					
❑ 7002	Come Into My Palace/Trying to Make It	1962	15.00	30.00	60.00
LAURIE					
❑ 3197	Come Into My Palace/Trying to Make It	1963	6.25	12.50	25.00
LENOIR, J.B.					
45s					
CHECKER					
❑ 844	Let Me Die with the One I Love/If I Give My Love to You	1956	10.00	20.00	40.00
❑ 856	Don't Touch My Head/I've Been Down So Long	1957	10.00	20.00	40.00
❑ 874	What About Your Daughter/Five Years	1957	7.50	15.00	30.00
❑ 901	Daddy Talk to Your Son/She Don't Know	1958	7.50	15.00	30.00
J.O.B.					
❑ 1012	The Mojo/How Can I Leave	1952	50.00	100.00	200.00
❑ 1102	Play a Little While/Louise	1952	30.00	60.00	120.00
PARROT					
❑ 802	Eisenhower Blues/I'm in Korea	1954	100.00	200.00	400.00
❑ 802	Tax Paying Blues/I'm in Korea	1954	250.00	500.00	1000.
—A-side is similar, though not identical, to "Eisenhower Blues"					
❑ 802	Tax Paying Blues/I'm in Korea	1954	500.00	1000.	2000.
—Red vinyl					
❑ 809	Mama Talk to Your Daughter/Man, Watch Your Woman	1955	20.00	40.00	80.00
❑ 814	Mama Your Daughter Is Going to Miss Me/What Have I Done	1955	25.00	50.00	100.00
❑ 821	Fine Girls/I Lost My Baby	1955	37.50	75.00	150.00
SHAD					
❑ 5012	Back Door/Louella	1959	5.00	10.00	20.00
U.S.A.					
❑ 744	I Feel So Good/Sing Um the Way I Feel	1963	5.00	10.00	20.00
VEE JAY					
❑ 352	Do What I Say/Oh Baby	1960	3.00	6.00	12.00
—As "J.B. Lenore"					
Albums					
CHESS					
❑ LP-410	Natural Man	1970	10.00	20.00	40.00
❑ CH-9323	Natural Man	1990	3.00	6.00	12.00
POLYDOR					
❑ 24-4011	J.B. Lenoir	1970	3.75	7.50	15.00
LEVERT					
Also see GERALD LEVERT.					
12-Inch Singles					
ATCO					
❑ DMD 1225 [DJ]	Addicted to You (12" Club Remix) (Dub Version) (Accapella Bonus Beat) (Dance Remix)	1988	—	3.00	6.00
❑ PR 2411 [DJ]	Addicted to You (same on both sides?)	1988	—	3.50	7.00
❑ 96624	Addicted to You (Club Version) (Dub) (Acappella)	1988	2.00	4.00	8.00
ATLANTIC					
❑ DMD 1009 [DJ]	Fascination (4 versions)	1987	—	3.50	7.00
❑ DMD 1073 [DJ]	Casanova (5 versions)	1987	2.00	4.00	8.00
❑ DMD 1103 [DJ]	My Forever Love (same on both sides?)	1987	—	3.50	7.00
❑ DMD 1144 [DJ]	Sweet Sensation (Vocal Remix 6:00) (Vocal Radio 4:34) (Vocal Edit 3:50) (Instrumental Dub 4:35)	1988	—	3.00	6.00
❑ DMD 1259 [DJ]	Pull Over (5 versions)	1988	—	3.50	7.00
❑ DMD 1286 [DJ]	Just Coolin' (Extended Hip Hop Mix) (Hip Hop Dub Mix) (Original Version Re-Edit)	1989	2.00	4.00	8.00
❑ DMD 1322 [DJ]	Gotta Get the Money (Radio Mix) (Edited Version) (Alternate Remix)/(Extended Remix Version) (Dub I) (Dub II)	1989	—	3.50	7.00
❑ DMD 1547 [DJ]	Rope a Dope Style (10 versions)	1990	3.75	7.50	15.00
❑ DMD 2403 [DJ]	True Dat (Remix Extended Version) (Album Version Extended) (Remix Instrumental)/(Hip Hop Remix Extended) (Hip Hop Instrumental)	1997	2.00	4.00	8.00
❑ PR 2535 [DJ]	Pull Over (Straight Radio Version) (Edit) (Radio Remix) (Extended Club Mix) (Percappella Version) (Bonus Beats)	1988	2.00	4.00	8.00
❑ PR 2587 [DJ]	Just Coolin' (3 versions)	1989	2.00	4.00	8.00
❑ PR 3069 [DJ]	Feel Real (same on both sides?)	1988	2.50	5.00	10.00
❑ PR 3991 [DJ]	Give a Little Love (same on both sides?)	1991	2.00	4.00	8.00
❑ 85431	True Dat (5 versions)	1997	—	3.50	7.00
❑ 85771	Good Ol' Days (5 versions)	1993	2.50	5.00	10.00
❑ 86129	Rope a Dope Style (4 versions)	1990	2.00	4.00	8.00
❑ 86313	Smilin' (3 versions)	1989	2.50	5.00	10.00
❑ 86422	Gotta Get the Money (4 versions)	1989	—	3.50	7.00
❑ 86459	Just Coolin' (Extended Hip Hop Version) (Hip Hop Dub) (Original Version)	1989	—	3.00	6.00
❑ 86480	Pull Over (Extended Version) (Dub)	1988	—	3.00	6.00
❑ 86663	Casanova (Extended Mix)/Throwdown	1987	—	3.00	6.00
❑ 86673	Casanova (Extended Mix)/(Dance Mix) (Dub Mix) (A Cappella)	1987	—	3.50	7.00
❑ 86780	(Pop, Pop, Pop, Pop) Goes My Mind/Looking for Love	1986	—	3.50	7.00
TEMPRE					
❑ 1835	I'm Still (2 versions)/I Want Too	1985	2.50	5.00	10.00
45s					
ATCO					
❑ 99292	Addicted to You/(Vocal Remix)	1988	—	—	3.00
❑ 99292 [PS]	Addicted to You/(Vocal Remix)	1988	—	—	3.00

Number	Title (A Side/B Side)	Yr	VG	VG+	NM
ATLANTIC					
❑ 87366	ABC-123 (Radio Edit)/(LP Version)	1993	—	2.00	4.00
❑ 87379	Good Ol' Days (Single Edit)/(Remix)	1993	—	2.00	4.00
❑ 88842	Smilin' (With Rap)/(Without Rap)	1989	—	—	3.00
❑ 88910	Gotta Get the Money/Join In the Fun	1989	—	—	3.00
❑ 88959	Just Coolin'/(Hip Hop Version)	1989	—	—	3.00
❑ 88959 [PS]	Just Coolin'/(Hip Hop Version)	1989	—	—	3.00
❑ 88987	Pull Over/(Instrumental)	1988	—	—	3.00
❑ 88987 [PS]	Pull Over/(Instrumental)	1988	—	—	3.00
❑ 89124	Sweet Sensation/Love the Way U Love Me	1988	—	—	3.00
❑ 89124 [PS]	Sweet Sensation/Love the Way U Love Me	1988	—	—	3.00
❑ 89182	My Forever Love/Kiss and Make Up	1987	—	—	3.00
❑ 89182 [PS]	My Forever Love/Kiss and Make Up	1987	—	—	3.00
❑ 89217	Casanova/Throwdown	1987	—	—	3.00
❑ 89217 [PS]	Casanova/Throwdown	1987	—	—	3.00
❑ 89311	Fascination/Pose	1987	—	—	3.00
❑ 89350	Let's Go Out Tonight/Grip	1986	—	—	3.00
❑ 89350 [PS]	Let's Go Out Tonight/Grip	1986	—	2.00	4.00
❑ 89389	(Pop, Pop, Pop, Pop) Goes My Mind/Looking for Love	1986	—	—	3.00
❑ 89389 [PS]	(Pop, Pop, Pop, Pop) Goes My Mind/Looking for Love	1986	—	2.00	4.00
ATLANTIC OLDIES SERIES					
❑ 84955	Casanova/(Pop, Pop, Pop, Pop) Goes My Mind	199?	—	—	3.00
TEMPRE					
❑ 5505	I'm Still/I Want Too	1985	—	3.00	6.00
Albums					
ATLANTIC					
❑ 81669	Bloodline	1986	2.00	4.00	8.00
❑ 81773	The Big Throwdown	1987	2.00	4.00	8.00
❑ 81926	Just Coolin'	1988	2.00	4.00	8.00
❑ 82164	Rope a Dope Style	1990	3.00	6.00	12.00
❑ 82462	For Real Tho'	1993	3.75	7.50	15.00
TEMPRE					
❑ TL 1234	I Get Hot	1985	3.75	7.50	15.00
LEVERT, GERALD					
Also see LEVERT.					
12-Inch Singles					
EASTWEST					
❑ DMD 1722 [DJ]	Private Line (5 versions)	1991	2.00	4.00	8.00
❑ ED 5806 [DJ]	Already Missing You (2 versions)/Where Ever You Are	1995	2.00	4.00	8.00
—With Eddie Levert, Sr.					
❑ ED 6007 [DJ]	Wind Beneath My Wings (LP Version) (Radio Edit)	1998	—	3.50	7.00
❑ ED 6110 [DJ]	Thinkin' Bout It (Blaq Rain Radio Remix) (Blaq Rain Radio Remix Edit) (Blaq Rain Remix)/ (same on both sides)	1998	2.00	4.00	8.00
❑ ED 6112 [DJ]	Thinkin' Bout It (Blaq Rain Remix) (Mucho Remix) (LP Version)/(Blaze 12" Dance Remix) (Blaze Dance Remix Dub) (Acappella)	1998	3.00	6.00	12.00
❑ ED 6120 [DJ]	Taking Everything (Soap Opera Remix Extended Version) (Soap Opera Remix Edit)/(Soap Opera Remix Instrumental) (Soap Opera Remix Acappella)	1998	3.00	6.00	12.00
❑ ED 6122 [DJ]	Taking Everything (Millennium 2000 Extended Dance Remix) (Millennium 2000 Instrumental) (Acappella)/(Timmy Regisford's Club Edit) (Timmy's Instrumental)	1998	2.00	4.00	8.00
❑ ED 6191 [DJ]	Nothin' to Somethin' (Millennium 2000 Mix Amended Version) (Millennium 2000 Mix)/ (Millennium 2000 Dub Amended Version)	1999	3.00	6.00	12.00
❑ ED 6222 [DJ]	Baby U Are (LP Version) (Radio Edit)/ (Instrumental) (Acappella)	2000	3.00	6.00	12.00
❑ 63809	Thinkin' Bout It (Blaq Rain Remix) (Mucho Remix) (Album Version)/(Blaze 12" Dance Remix) (Blaze Dance Remix Dub) (Acappella)	1998	3.00	6.00	12.00
❑ 96280	Private Line (4 versions)	1991	—	3.00	6.00
45s					
EASTWEST					
❑ 98577	School Me/Baby Hold On to Me	1992	—	2.00	4.00
LEWIS, BARBARA					
45s					
ATLANTIC					
❑ 2141	My Heart Went Do Dat Da/The Longest Night of the Year	1962	3.00	6.00	12.00
❑ 2159	My Mama Told Me/Gonna Love You Till the Day I Die	1962	3.00	6.00	12.00
❑ 2184	Hello Stranger/Think a Little Sugar	1963	5.00	10.00	20.00
❑ 2200	Straighten Up Your Heart/If You Love Her	1963	3.00	6.00	12.00
❑ 2214	Puppy Love/Snap Your Fingers	1963	3.00	6.00	12.00
❑ 2227	Someday We're Gonna Love Again/Spend a Little Time	1964	2.50	5.00	10.00
❑ 2255	Come Home/Pushin' a Good Thing Too Far	1964	2.50	5.00	10.00
❑ 2283	Baby, I'm Yours/I Say Love	1965	3.75	7.50	15.00
❑ 2300	Make Me Your Baby/Love to Be Loved	1965	3.75	7.50	15.00
❑ 2316	Don't Forget About Me/It's Magic	1965	2.50	5.00	10.00
❑ 2346	Make Me Belong to You/Girls Need Loving Care	1966	2.00	4.00	8.00
❑ 2361	I Remember the Feeling/Baby What You Want Me to Do	1966	2.00	4.00	8.00
❑ 2400	Love Makes the World Go Round/I'll Make Him Love Me	1967	2.00	4.00	8.00
❑ 2413	Fool, Fool, Fool/Only All the Time	1967	2.00	4.00	8.00

Number	Title (A Side/B Side)	Yr	VG	VG+	NM
❏ 2482	Thankful for What I Got/Sho Nuff	1968	2.00	4.00	8.00
❏ 2514	On Bended Knees/I'll Keep Believing	1968	2.00	4.00	8.00
❏ 2550	I'm All You've Got/You're a Dream Maker	1968	2.00	4.00	8.00

ENTERPRISE

Number	Title (A Side/B Side)	Yr	VG	VG+	NM
❏ 9012	You Made Me a Woman/Just the Way You Are Today	1970	—	3.00	6.00
❏ 9027	Ask the Lonely/Why Did It Take You So Long	1970	—	3.00	6.00
❏ 9029	Anyway/That's the Way I Like It	1970	—	3.00	6.00

KAREN

❏ 313	My Heart Went Do Dat Da/The Longest Night of the Year	1961	7.50	15.00	30.00

REPRISE

❏ 1146	Rock and Roll Lullaby/I'm So Thankful	1972	—	2.50	5.00

7-Inch Extended Plays

ATLANTIC

❏ LSD 8110 [DJ]	Baby I'm Yours/Hy Heart Went Do Da Dat/Puppy Love//Hello Stranger/Someday We're Gonna Love Again/Snap Your Fingers	196?	3.75	7.50	15.00

—Jukebox mini-LP, small hole, plays at 33 1/3 rpm

❏ LSD 8110 [PS]	Baby I'm Yours	196?	3.75	7.50	15.00

Albums

ATLANTIC

❏ 8086 [M]	Hello Stranger	1963	10.00	20.00	40.00
❏ SD 8086 [S]	Hello Stranger	1963	12.50	25.00	50.00
❏ 8090 [M]	Snap Your Fingers	1964	10.00	20.00	40.00
❏ SD 8090 [S]	Snap Your Fingers	1964	12.50	25.00	50.00
❏ 8110 [M]	Baby, I'm Yours	1965	10.00	20.00	40.00
❏ SD 8110 [S]	Baby, I'm Yours	1965	12.50	25.00	50.00
❏ 8118 [M]	It's Magic	1966	7.50	15.00	30.00
❏ SD 8118 [S]	It's Magic	1966	10.00	20.00	40.00
❏ SD 8173	Workin' on a Groovy Thing	1968	6.25	12.50	25.00
❏ SD 8286	The Best of Barbara Lewis	1971	5.00	10.00	20.00

COLLECTABLES

❏ COL-5104	Golden Classics	198?	2.50	5.00	10.00

ENTERPRISE

❏ ENS-1006	The Many Grooves of Barbara Lewis	1970	6.25	12.50	25.00

LEWIS, BOBBY (1)

R&B singer; not to be confused with the country singer of the same name, who recorded for Ace of Hearts, Capricorn, GRT, HME, RPA and United Artists.

45s

ABC-PARAMOUNT

❏ 10565	That's Right/Fannie Lewis	1964	3.00	6.00	12.00
❏ 10592	Jealous Love/Stark Raving Wild	1964	3.00	6.00	12.00

BELTONE

❏ 1002	Tossin' and Turnin'/Oh Yes I Love You	1961	6.25	12.50	25.00
❏ 1012	One Track Mind/Are You Ready	1961	6.25	12.50	25.00
❏ 1015	What a Walk/Cry No More	1961	3.75	7.50	15.00
❏ 1016	Yes, Oh Yes, It Did/Mamie in the Afternoon	1962	3.75	7.50	15.00
❏ 2018	A Man's Gotta Be a Man/Day by Day I Need Your Love	1962	3.75	7.50	15.00
❏ 2023	I'm Tossin' and Turnin' Again/Nothin' But the Blues	1962	3.75	7.50	15.00
❏ 2026	Lonely Teardrops/Boom-a-Chick-Chick	1962	3.75	7.50	15.00
❏ 2035	Nothin' But the Blues/Intermission	1963	3.75	7.50	15.00

LOST-NITE

❏ 146	Tossin' An' Turnin'/Oh Yes I Love You	196?	—	3.00	6.00

—Reissue; note slightly different spelling of A-side

MERCURY

❏ 71245	Mumbles Blues/Oh Baby	1957	6.25	12.50	25.00

PHILIPS

❏ 40519	Soul Seekin'/Give Me Your Yesterdays	1968	5.00	10.00	20.00

ROULETTE

❏ 4182	You Better Stop/Fire of Love	1959	3.75	7.50	15.00
❏ 4382	Solid as a Rock/Oh Mr. Somebody	1961	3.75	7.50	15.00

SPOTLIGHT

❏ 394	Mumbles Blues/Oh Baby	1957	7.50	15.00	30.00
❏ 397	Solid as a Rock/You Even Forgot My Name	1957	7.50	15.00	30.00

Albums

BELTONE

❏ 4000 [M]	Tossin' and Turnin'	1961	50.00	100.00	200.00

LEWIS, CLARENCE

45s

FURY

❏ 1032	Cupid's Little Helper/Half a Heart	1960	3.75	7.50	15.00

RED ROBIN

❏ 136	Lost Everything/Your Heart Must Be Made of Stone	1955	20.00	40.00	80.00

LEWIS, RAMSEY

12-Inch Singles

COLUMBIA

❏ 05311	This Ain't No Fantasy (Extended with Male)/ (Extended with Female)	1985	—	3.00	6.00
❏ 06850	7-11 (Club Mix) (Booster Mix)	1987	—	3.00	6.00
❏ 10937	Aquarius-Let the Sunshine In/Just Can't Give You Up	1979	3.00	6.00	12.00

45s

ARGO

❏ 108-S [S]	Scarlet Ribbons/Here 'Tis	1960	5.00	10.00	20.00
❏ 110-S [S]	Solo Para Ti/These Foolish Things	1960	5.00	10.00	20.00
❏ 5303	Black Eyed Peas/Carmen	1958	3.00	6.00	12.00
❏ 5322	Tracy Blues/Delilah	1958	3.00	6.00	12.00

Number	Title (A Side/B Side)	Yr	VG	VG+	NM
❏ 5344	C.C. Rider/Consider the Source	1959	3.00	6.00	12.00
❏ 5351	Ol' Devil Moon/Please Send Me Someone to Love	1959	3.00	6.00	12.00
❏ 5352	The Chant/Here 'Tis	1959	3.00	6.00	12.00
❏ 5362	Little Liza Jane/Put Your Little Foot Right Out	1960	3.00	6.00	12.00
❏ 5377	Santa Claus Is Coming to Town/Winter Wonderland	1960	3.00	6.00	12.00
❏ 5387	Blues for the Night Owl/Hello, Cello	1961	2.50	5.00	10.00
❏ 5398	Never on Sunday/The Ripper	1961	2.50	5.00	10.00
❏ 5407	Sound of Christmas/Merry Christmas Baby	1961	3.00	6.00	12.00
❏ 5411	I Got Plenty of Nothin'/Thanks for the Memory	1962	2.50	5.00	10.00
❏ 5413	Blue Spring/Spring Fever	1962	2.50	5.00	10.00
❏ 5423	Blueberry Hill/Memphis in June	1962	2.50	5.00	10.00
❏ 5431	Maha de Carnaval/Tangleweed 'Round My Heart	1963	2.00	4.00	8.00
❏ 5438	Look-a Here/Andaluza	1963	2.00	4.00	8.00
❏ 5454	Lonely Avenue/Come On Baby	1963	2.00	4.00	8.00
❏ 5467	Dance Mystique/For the Love of a Princess	1964	2.00	4.00	8.00
❏ 5474	Why Don't You Do It Right/Travel On	1964	2.00	4.00	8.00
❏ 5481	Something You Got/My Babe	1964	2.00	4.00	8.00
❏ 5488	Jingle Bells/Egg Nog	1964	2.50	5.00	10.00
❏ 5496	Let It Be Me/It Had Better Be Tonight	1965	2.00	4.00	8.00
❏ 5506	The "In" Crowd/Since I Fell for You	1965	2.50	5.00	10.00

CADET

❏ 5377	Santa Claus Is Coming To Town/Winter Wonderland	1966	2.00	4.00	8.00

—Reissue of Argo 5377

❏ 5423	Blueberry Hill/Memphis in June	1966	—	3.00	6.00
❏ 5431	Maha de Carnaval/Tangleweed 'Round My Heart	1966	—	3.00	6.00
❏ 5481	Something You Got/My Babe	1966	—	3.00	6.00
❏ 5496	Let It Be Me/It Had Better Be Tonight	1966	—	3.00	6.00
❏ 5506	The "In" Crowd/Since I Fell for You	1966	—	3.00	6.00
❏ 5522	Hang On Sloopy/Movin' Easy	1965	2.00	4.00	8.00
❏ 5525	A Hard Day's Night/All My Love Belongs to You	1966	2.00	4.00	8.00
❏ 5531	Hi Heel Sneakers — Pt. 1/Hi Heel Sneakers — Pt. 2	1966	2.00	4.00	8.00
❏ 5541	Wade in the Water/Ain't That Peculiar	1966	2.00	4.00	8.00
❏ 5547	Up Tight/Money in the Pocket	1966	2.00	4.00	8.00
❏ 5553	Rudolph the Red-Nosed Reindeer/Day Tripper	1966	2.00	4.00	8.00
❏ 5556	One, Two, Three/Down by the Riverside	1967	2.00	4.00	8.00
❏ 5562	Function at the Junction/Hey, Mrs. Jones	1967	2.00	4.00	8.00
❏ 5565	Saturday Night After the Movies/China Gate	1967	2.00	4.00	8.00
❏ 5573	Dancing in the Street/Girls Talk	1967	2.00	4.00	8.00
❏ 5583	Soul Man/Struttin' Lightly	1967	2.00	4.00	8.00
❏ 5593	The Look of Love/Bear Mash	1968	—	3.00	6.00
❏ 5596	Jade Easy/Party Time	1968	—	3.00	6.00
❏ 5609	Since You've Been Gone/Les Fleurs	1968	—	3.00	6.00
❏ 5629	Mary's Boy Child/Have Yourself a Merry Little Christmas	1968	—	3.00	6.00
❏ 5640	Julia/Do What You Wanna	1969	—	3.00	6.00
❏ 5645	If You've Got It, Flaunt It/Wanderin' Rose	1969	—	3.00	6.00
❏ 5662	Mary's Boy Child/My Cherie Amour	1969	—	3.00	6.00
❏ 5668	Everybody's Talkin'/Love I Feel for You	1970	—	3.00	6.00
❏ 5674	Them Changes/Unsilent Minority	1970	—	3.00	6.00
❏ 5678	Do Whatever Sets You Free/Close Your Eyes and Remember	1970	—	3.00	6.00
❏ 5681	Candida/Love Me Now	1971	—	3.00	6.00
❏ 5684	He Ain't Heavy, He's My Brother/Up in Yonder	1971	—	3.00	6.00
❏ 5695	Summertime/Look-a There	1973	—	3.00	6.00

COLUMBIA

❏ 02043	So Much More/Romance Me	1981	—	2.00	4.00
❏ 02572	Lakeshore Cowboy/Michelle	1981	—	2.00	4.00
❏ 02704	You Never Know/Lynn	1982	—	2.00	4.00
❏ 03274	Up Where We Belong/Chance Encounter	1982	—	2.00	4.00
❏ 04524	The Two of Us/Song Without Words (Remembering)	1984	—	2.00	4.00
❏ 04655	Quiet Storm/Ram	1984	—	2.00	4.00
❏ 05640	This Ain't No Fantasy/The Quest	1985	—	—	3.00
❏ 05819	Ram Jam/Slow Dancin'	1986	—	—	3.00
❏ 07220	7-11/My Love Will Lead You Home	1987	—	—	3.00
❏ 10056	Hot Dawgit/R.L. Tambura	1974	—	2.50	5.00

—A-side with Earth, Wind and Fire

❏ 10103	Sun Goddess/Jungle Strut	1975	—	2.50	5.00

—A-side with Earth, Wind and Fire

❏ 10235	What's the Name of This Funk (Spider Man)/Juacklyn	1975	—	2.50	5.00
❏ 10293	Don't It Feel Good/Fish Bite	1976	—	2.50	5.00
❏ 10382	Brazilica/Salongo	1976	—	2.50	5.00
❏ 10571	Spring High/The Messenger	1977	—	2.50	5.00
❏ 10643	Skippin'/Camino El Bueno	1977	—	2.50	5.00
❏ 10698	Tequila Mockingbird/My Angel's Smile	1978	—	2.50	5.00
❏ 10827	All the Way Live/Toccata	1978	—	2.50	5.00
❏ 10932	Aquarius-Let the Sunshine In/Just Can't Give You Up	1979	—	2.50	5.00
❏ 11042	Wearin' It Out/Spanoletta	1979	—	2.50	5.00
❏ 45634	Slipping Into Darkness/Collage	1972	—	2.50	5.00
❏ 45707	Upendo Mi Pamoja/Eternal Peace	1972	—	2.50	5.00
❏ 45766	Kufanya Mapenzi (Making Love)/What It Is	1973	—	2.50	5.00
❏ 45847	Dreams/Hang On Sloopy	1973	—	2.50	5.00
❏ 45973	Hi-Heel Sneakers/Wade in the Water	1973	—	2.50	5.00
❏ 46037	Summer Breeze/Everywhere Calypso	1974	—	2.50	5.00

7-Inch Extended Plays

ARGO

❏ EP-1084	Sleigh Ride/Christmas Blues//Sound of Christmas/The Christmas Song	1961	2.50	5.00	10.00
❏ EP-1084 [PS]	Sound of Christmas	1961	3.00	6.00	12.00

Number	Title (A Side/B Side)	Yr	VG	VG+	NM
Albums					
ARGO					
❏ LP-611 [M]	Gentleman of Swing	1958	12.50	25.00	50.00
❏ LPS-611 [S]	Gentleman of Swing	1959	15.00	30.00	60.00
❏ LP-627 [M]	Gentleman of Jazz	1958	12.50	25.00	50.00
❏ LPS-627 [S]	Gentleman of Jazz	1959	15.00	30.00	60.00
❏ LP-642 [M]	The Ramsey Lewis Trio with Lee Winchester	1959	10.00	20.00	40.00
❏ LPS-642 [S]	The Ramsey Lewis Trio with Lee Winchester	1959	12.50	25.00	50.00
❏ LP-645 [M]	An Hour with the Ramsey Lewis Trio	1959	10.00	20.00	40.00
❏ LPS-645 [S]	An Hour with the Ramsey Lewis Trio	1959	12.50	25.00	50.00
❏ LP-665 [M]	Stretching Out	1960	10.00	20.00	40.00
❏ LPS-665 [S]	Stretching Out	1960	12.50	25.00	50.00
❏ LP-671 [M]	The Ramsey Lewis Trio in Chicago	1961	10.00	20.00	40.00
❏ LPS-671 [S]	The Ramsey Lewis Trio in Chicago	1961	12.50	25.00	50.00
❏ LP-680 [M]	More Music from the Soil	1961	10.00	20.00	40.00
❏ LPS-680 [S]	More Music from the Soil	1961	12.50	25.00	50.00
❏ LP-687 [M]	Sound of Christmas	1961	10.00	20.00	40.00
❏ LPS-687 [S]	Sound of Christmas	1961	12.50	25.00	50.00
❏ LP-693 [M]	The Sound of Spring	1962	6.25	12.50	25.00
❏ LPS-693 [S]	The Sound of Spring	1962	7.50	15.00	30.00
❏ LP-701 [M]	Country Meets the Blues	1962	6.25	12.50	25.00
❏ LPS-701 [S]	Country Meets the Blues	1962	7.50	15.00	30.00
❏ LP-705 [M]	Bossa Nova	1962	6.25	12.50	25.00
❏ LPS-705 [S]	Bossa Nova	1962	7.50	15.00	30.00
❏ LP-715 [M]	Pot Luck	1963	6.25	12.50	25.00
❏ LPS-715 [S]	Pot Luck	1963	7.50	15.00	30.00
❏ LP-723 [M]	Barefoot Sunday Blues	1963	6.25	12.50	25.00
❏ LPS-723 [S]	Barefoot Sunday Blues	1963	7.50	15.00	30.00
❏ LP-732 [M]	Bach to the Blues	1964	6.25	12.50	25.00
❏ LPS-732 [S]	Bach to the Blues	1964	7.50	15.00	30.00
❏ LP-741 [M]	The Ramsey Lewis Trio at the Bohemian Caverns	1964	6.25	12.50	25.00
❏ LPS-741 [S]	The Ramsey Lewis Trio at the Bohemian Caverns	1964	7.50	15.00	30.00
❏ LP-745 [M]	More Sounds of Christmas	1964	6.25	12.50	25.00
❏ LPS-745 [S]	More Sounds of Christmas	1964	7.50	15.00	30.00
❏ LP-755 [M]	Choice! The Best of the Ramsey Lewis Trio	1965	7.50	15.00	30.00
❏ LPS-755 [S]	Choice! The Best of the Ramsey Lewis Trio	1965	10.00	20.00	40.00
❏ LP-757 [M]	The In Crowd	1965	6.25	12.50	25.00
❏ LPS-757 [S]	The In Crowd	1965	7.50	15.00	30.00
CADET					
❏ LP-611 [M]	Gentleman of Swing	1966	3.00	6.00	12.00
❏ LPS-611 [S]	Gentleman of Swing	1966	3.75	7.50	15.00
❏ LP-627 [M]	Gentleman of Jazz	1966	3.00	6.00	12.00
❏ LPS-627 [S]	Gentleman of Jazz	1966	3.75	7.50	15.00
❏ LP-645 [M]	An Hour with the Ramsey Lewis Trio	1966	3.00	6.00	12.00
❏ LPS-645 [S]	An Hour with the Ramsey Lewis Trio	1966	3.75	7.50	15.00
❏ LP-665 [M]	Stretching Out	1966	3.00	6.00	12.00
❏ LPS-665 [S]	Stretching Out	1966	3.75	7.50	15.00
❏ LP-671 [M]	The Ramsey Lewis Trio in Chicago	1966	3.00	6.00	12.00
❏ LPS-671 [S]	The Ramsey Lewis Trio in Chicago	1966	3.75	7.50	15.00
❏ LP-680 [M]	More Music from the Soil	1966	3.00	6.00	12.00
❏ LPS-680 [S]	More Music from the Soil	1966	3.75	7.50	15.00
❏ LPS-680 [S]	More Music from the Soil	197?	3.00	6.00	12.00
—Reissue with "A Division of All Platinum Record Group" on label					
❏ LP-687X [M]	Sound of Christmas	1966	5.00	10.00	20.00
—Reissue of Argo 687					
❏ LPS-687X [S]	Sound of Christmas	1966	5.00	10.00	20.00
—Reissue of Argo 687-S					
❏ LP-693 [M]	The Sound of Spring	1966	3.00	6.00	12.00
❏ LPS-693 [S]	The Sound of Spring	1966	3.75	7.50	15.00
❏ LP-701 [M]	Country Meets the Blues	1966	3.00	6.00	12.00
❏ LPS-701 [S]	Country Meets the Blues	1966	3.75	7.50	15.00
❏ LP-705 [M]	Bossa Nova	1966	3.00	6.00	12.00
❏ LPS-705 [S]	Bossa Nova	1966	3.75	7.50	15.00
❏ LP-715 [M]	Pot Luck	1966	3.00	6.00	12.00
❏ LPS-715 [S]	Pot Luck	1966	3.75	7.50	15.00
❏ LP-723 [M]	Barefoot Sunday Blues	1966	3.00	6.00	12.00
❏ LPS-723 [S]	Barefoot Sunday Blues	1966	3.75	7.50	15.00
❏ LP-732 [M]	Bach to the Blues	1966	3.00	6.00	12.00
❏ LPS-732 [S]	Bach to the Blues	1966	3.75	7.50	15.00
❏ LP-741 [M]	The Ramsey Lewis Trio at the Bohemian Caverns	1966	3.00	6.00	12.00
❏ LPS-741 [S]	The Ramsey Lewis Trio at the Bohemian Caverns	1966	3.75	7.50	15.00
❏ LP-745 [M]	More Sounds of Christmas	1966	3.75	7.50	15.00
❏ LPS-745 [S]	More Sounds of Christmas	1966	5.00	10.00	20.00
❏ LP-750 [M]	You Better Believe It	1966	3.00	6.00	12.00
❏ LPS-750 [S]	You Better Believe It	1966	3.75	7.50	15.00
❏ LP-755 [M]	Choice! The Best of the Ramsey Lewis Trio	1965	3.75	7.50	15.00
❏ LPS-755 [S]	Choice! The Best of the Ramsey Lewis Trio	1965	5.00	10.00	20.00
❏ LP-757 [M]	The In Crowd	1965	3.00	6.00	12.00
❏ LPS-757 [S]	The In Crowd	1965	3.75	7.50	15.00
❏ LP-761 [M]	Hang On Ramsey!	1966	3.75	7.50	15.00
❏ LPS-761 [S]	Hang On Ramsey!	1966	5.00	10.00	20.00
❏ LP-771 [M]	Swingin'	1966	3.75	7.50	15.00
❏ LPS-771 [S]	Swingin'	1966	5.00	10.00	20.00
❏ LP-774 [M]	Wade in the Water	1966	3.75	7.50	15.00
❏ LPS-774 [S]	Wade in the Water	1966	5.00	10.00	20.00
❏ LP-782 [M]	The Movie Album	1967	5.00	10.00	20.00
❏ LPS-782 [S]	The Movie Album	1967	3.75	7.50	15.00
❏ LP-790 [M]	Goin' Latin	1967	5.00	10.00	20.00
❏ LPS-790 [S]	Goin' Latin	1967	3.75	7.50	15.00
❏ LP-794 [M]	Dancing in the Street	1967	5.00	10.00	20.00
❏ LPS-794 [S]	Dancing in the Street	1967	3.75	7.50	15.00
❏ LPS-799	Up Pops Ramsey Lewis	1968	3.75	7.50	15.00
❏ LPS-811	Maiden Voyage	1968	3.75	7.50	15.00
❏ LPS-821	Mother Nature's Son	1969	3.75	7.50	15.00
❏ LPS-827	Another Voyage	1969	3.75	7.50	15.00
❏ LPS-836	Ramsey Lewis, The Piano Player	1970	3.75	7.50	15.00
❏ LPS-839	The Best of Ramsey Lewis	1970	3.75	7.50	15.00
❏ LPS-844	Them Changes	1970	3.75	7.50	15.00
❏ 50020	Groover	1973	3.00	6.00	12.00
❏ 50058 [(2)]	Solid Ivory	1974	3.75	7.50	15.00
❏ 60001	Back to the Roots	1971	3.00	6.00	12.00
❏ 60018 [(2)]	Inside Ramsey Lewis	1972	3.75	7.50	15.00
CBS					
❏ FM 42661	A Classic Encounter	1988	2.50	5.00	10.00
CHESS					
❏ 9001 [(2)]	Solid Ivory	197?	3.00	6.00	12.00
—Reissue of Cadet 50058					
❏ CH 9716	Sound of Christmas	1984	2.50	5.00	10.00
—Reissue of Argo 687-S					
COLUMBIA					
❏ CQ 31096 [Q]	Upendo Ni Pamoja	1972	4.50	9.00	18.00
❏ KC 31096	Upendo Ni Pamoja	1972	3.00	6.00	12.00
❏ KC 32030	Funky Serenity	1973	3.00	6.00	12.00
❏ KC 32490	Ramsey Lewis' Newly Recorded All-Time, Non-Stop Golden Hits	1973	3.00	6.00	12.00
❏ PC 32490	Ramsey Lewis' Newly Recorded All-Time, Non-Stop Golden Hits	197?	2.00	4.00	8.00
—Reissue with new prefix					
❏ KC 32897	Solar Wind	1974	3.00	6.00	12.00
❏ KC 33194	Sun Goddess	1974	2.50	5.00	10.00
❏ PC 33194	Sun Goddess	197?	2.00	4.00	8.00
—Reissue with new prefix					
❏ CG 33663 [(2)]	Upendo Ni Pamoja/Funky Serenity	1975	3.00	6.00	12.00
❏ PC 33800	Don't It Feel Good	1975	2.50	5.00	10.00
—Originals have no bar code					
❏ PC 33800	Don't It Feel Good	198?	2.00	4.00	8.00
—Budget-line reissue with bar code					
❏ PC 34173	Salongo	1976	2.50	5.00	10.00
—Originals have no bar code					
❏ PC 34173	Salongo	198?	2.00	4.00	8.00
—Budget-line reissue with bar code					
❏ PC 34696	Love Notes	1977	2.50	5.00	10.00
❏ JC 35018	Tequila Mockingbird	1977	2.50	5.00	10.00
❏ JC 35483	Legacy	1978	2.50	5.00	10.00
❏ PC 35483	Legacy	198?	2.00	4.00	8.00
—Budget-line reissue					
❏ JC 35815	Ramsey	1979	2.50	5.00	10.00
❏ FC 36364	The Best of Ramsey Lewis	1980	2.50	5.00	10.00
❏ JC 36423	Routes	1980	2.50	5.00	10.00
❏ PC 36423	Routes	198?	2.00	4.00	8.00
—Budget-line reissue					
❏ FC 37153	Three Piece Suite	1981	2.50	5.00	10.00
❏ FC 37687	Live at the Savoy	1982	2.50	5.00	10.00
❏ PC 37687	Live at the Savoy	198?	2.00	4.00	8.00
—Budget-line reissue					
❏ FC 38294	Chance Encounter	1983	2.50	5.00	10.00
❏ FC 38787	Les Fleurs	1983	2.50	5.00	10.00
❏ FC 39158	Reunion	1983	2.50	5.00	10.00
❏ FC 40108	Fantasy	1985	2.50	5.00	10.00
❏ FC 40677	Keys to the City	1987	2.50	5.00	10.00
❏ HC 43194	Sun Goddess	1982	12.50	25.00	50.00
—Half-speed mastered edition					
❏ FC 44190	Urban Renewal	1989	3.75	7.50	15.00
❏ HC 47687	Live at the Savoy	1982	20.00	40.00	80.00
—Half-speed mastered edition					
COLUMBIA JAZZ ODYSSEY					
❏ PC 37019	Blues for the Night Owl	1981	2.50	5.00	10.00
EMARCY					
❏ MG-36150 [M]	Down to Earth	1958	10.00	20.00	40.00
❏ SR-80029 [S]	Down to Earth	1958	12.50	25.00	50.00
MERCURY					
❏ MG-20536 [M]	Down to Earth	1965	5.00	10.00	20.00
❏ SR-60536 [S]	Down to Earth	1965	6.25	12.50	25.00

LEWIS, RAMSEY, AND JEAN DUSHON

Albums

ARGO

Number	Title (A Side/B Side)	Yr	VG	VG+	NM
❏ 750S [S]	You Better Believe Me	1965	7.50	15.00	30.00
❏ 750 [M]	You Better Believe Me	1965	6.25	12.50	25.00

LEWIS, RAMSEY, AND NANCY WILSON

Also see each artist's individual listings.

Albums

COLUMBIA

Number	Title (A Side/B Side)	Yr	VG	VG+	NM
❏ FC 39326	The Two of Us	1984	2.50	5.00	10.00

LEWIS, RUDY

Also see THE DRIFTERS.

45s

ATLANTIC

Number	Title (A Side/B Side)	Yr	VG	VG+	NM
❏ 2193	I've Loved You So Long/Baby I Dig Love	1963	3.00	6.00	12.00
RCA VICTOR					
❏ 47-7792	Moonbeam/Beer, Beer and More Beer	1960	5.00	10.00	20.00
—With the Sputnicks					

LEWIS, SMILEY

45s

DOT

Number	Title (A Side/B Side)	Yr	VG	VG+	NM
❏ 16674	I Wonder/Lookin' for My Woman	1964	2.50	5.00	10.00

Number	Title (A Side/B Side)	Yr	VG	VG+	NM

IMPERIAL

| 5194 | The Bells Are Ringing/Lillie Mae | 1952 | 30.00 | 60.00 | 120.00 |

Note: Smiley Lewis records on Imperial before 5194 are unconfirmed on 45 rpm

5208	Gumbo Blues/It's So Peaceful	1952	25.00	50.00	100.00
5224	Gypsy Blues/You're Not the One	1953	25.00	50.00	100.00
5234	Play Girl/Big Mamou	1953	20.00	40.00	80.00
5234	Play Girl/Big Mamou	1953	62.50	125.00	250.00

Red vinyl

5241	Caldonia's Party/Oh Baby	1953	20.00	40.00	80.00
5252	Little Fernandez/It's Music	1953	20.00	40.00	80.00
5268	Down the Road/Blue Monday	1954	20.00	40.00	80.00
5279	I Love You for Sentimental Reasons/The Rocks	1954	20.00	40.00	80.00
5296	Can't Stop Loving You/That Certain Door	1954	20.00	40.00	80.00
5316	Too Many Drivers/Ooh La La	1954	20.00	40.00	80.00
5325	Jailbird/Farewell	1955	20.00	40.00	80.00
5349	Real Gone Lover/Nobody Knows	1955	20.00	40.00	80.00
5356	I Hear You Knocking/Bumpity Bump	1955	20.00	40.00	80.00
5372	Queen of Hearts/Come On	1956	20.00	40.00	80.00
5380	One Night/Ain't Gonna Do It	1956	20.00	40.00	80.00
5389	She's Got Me (Hook, Line and Sinker)/Please Listen to Me	1956	20.00	40.00	80.00
5404	Down Yonder We Go Ballin'/Someday You'll Want Me	1956	20.00	40.00	80.00
5418	Shame, Shame, Shame/No No	1957	15.00	30.00	60.00
5431	You Are My Sunshine/Sweeter Words Have Never Been Spoken	1957	10.00	20.00	40.00
5450	Go On Fool/Goin' to Jump and Shout	1957	7.50	15.00	30.00
5470	Rootin' and Tootin'/I Can't Believe	1957	7.50	15.00	30.00
5478	Bad Luck Blues/School Days Are Back Again	1957	7.50	15.00	30.00
5531	Lil' Liza Jane/My Love Is Gone	1958	6.25	12.50	25.00
5662	Oh Red!/I Want to Be with Her	1960	3.75	7.50	15.00
5676	Last Night/Ain't Goin' There No More	1960	3.75	7.50	15.00
5719	Stormy Monday Blues/Tell Me Who	1961	3.75	7.50	15.00
5820	Gumbo Blues/Tee Nah Nah	1962	3.75	7.50	15.00

KNIGHT

| 2007 | Baby Please/I Shall Not Be Moved | 1959 | 3.75 | 7.50 | 15.00 |
| 2011 | Lost Weekend/By the Water | 1959 | 3.75 | 7.50 | 15.00 |

LOMA

| 2024 | Bells Are Ringing/Walkin' the Girl | 1965 | 2.50 | 5.00 | 10.00 |

OKEH

| 7146 | I'm Coming Down with the Blues/Tune-Up | 1962 | 3.00 | 6.00 | 12.00 |

LIGHTFOOT, PAPA

45s

ALADDIN

| 3171 | After a While (Blue Lights)/P.L.'s Blues | 1953 | 50.00 | 100.00 | 200.00 |
| 3304 | Blue Lights/Jumpin' with Jarvis | 1955 | 37.50 | 75.00 | 150.00 |

IMPERIAL

| 5289 | Wine, Women, Whiskey/Mean Old Train | 1954 | 37.50 | 75.00 | 150.00 |

SAVOY

| 1161 | Mean Old Train/Wild Fire | 1955 | 7.50 | 15.00 | 30.00 |

Albums

SAULT

| 130 | Natchez Trace | 1969 | 3.75 | 7.50 | 15.00 |

—As "Papa George Lightfoot"

LIGHTNIN' SLIM

45s

ACE

| 505 | Bad Feeling Blues/Lightning Slim Boogie | 1955 | 37.50 | 75.00 | 150.00 |

EXCELLO

2066	I Can't Be Successful/Lightnin' Blues	1955	10.00	20.00	40.00
2075	Sugar Plum/Just Made Twenty One	1956	7.50	15.00	30.00
2080	Goin' Home/Wonderin' and Goin'	1956	7.50	15.00	30.00
2096	Have Your Way/Bad Luck and Trouble	1956	7.50	15.00	30.00
2106	Mean Old Lonesome Train/I'm Grown	1957	7.50	15.00	30.00
2116	I'm a Rollin' Stone/Love Me Mama	1957	7.50	15.00	30.00
2131	Hoo-Doo Blues/It's Mighty Crazy	1958	7.50	15.00	30.00
2142	My Starter Won't Work/Long Leanie Mama	1958	7.50	15.00	30.00
2150	Feelin' Awful Blues/I'm Leavin' You Baby	1959	7.50	15.00	30.00
2160	Sweet Little Woman/Lightnin's Troubles	1959	7.50	15.00	30.00
2169	Rooster Blues/G.I. Slim	1959	7.50	15.00	30.00
2179	My Little Angel Child/Too Close Blues	1960	6.25	12.50	25.00
2186	Cool Down Baby/Nothin' But the Devil	1960	6.25	12.50	25.00
2195	Somebody Knockin'/I Just Don't Know	1961	6.25	12.50	25.00
2203	Hello Mary Lee/I'm Tired Waitin' Baby	1961	6.25	12.50	25.00
2215	Mind Your Own Business/You're Old Enough to Understand	1962	6.25	12.50	25.00
2224	Winter Time Blues/I'm Warnin' You Baby	1962	6.25	12.50	25.00
2228	If You Ever Need Me/I'm Evil	1963	6.25	12.50	25.00
2234	Loving Around the Clock/You Know You're So Fine	1963	6.25	12.50	25.00
2240	Blues at Night/Don't Mistreat Me Baby	1963	6.25	12.50	25.00
2245	You Give Me the Blues/Strangest Feelin'	1964	6.25	12.50	25.00
2252	Greyhound Blues/She's My Crazy Little Baby	1964	6.25	12.50	25.00
2258	Baby Please Come Back/You Move Me Baby	1964	6.25	12.50	25.00
2262	Have Mercy on Me Baby/I've Been a Fool for You Darlin'	1965	6.25	12.50	25.00
2267	Bad Luck Blues/Can't Live This Life No More	1965	6.25	12.50	25.00
2269	Don't Start Me Talkin'/Darlin' You're the One	1965	5.00	10.00	20.00
2272	I Hate to See You Leave/Love Is Just a Gamble	1965	5.00	10.00	20.00
2320	My Babe/Good Morning Heartaches	1971	2.50	5.00	10.00

FEATURE

3006	Rock Me, Mama/Bad Luck	1954	75.00	150.00	300.00
3008	I Can't Live Happy/New Orleans Bound	1954	15.00	30.00	60.00
3012	Bugger Bugger Boy/Ethel Mae	1954	15.00	30.00	60.00

Number	Title (A Side/B Side)	Yr	VG	VG+	NM

Albums

EXCELLO

| ❏ LP 8000 [M] | Rooster Blues | 1960 | 200.00 | 400.00 | 800.00 |
| ❏ LPS 8000 [M] | Rooster Blues | 196? | 12.50 | 25.00 | 50.00 |

—Thogh labeled "Electronic Stereo," this record is mono

| ❏ LP 8004 [M] | Lightnin' Slim's Bell Ringer | 1965 | 75.00 | 150.00 | 300.00 |
| ❏ LPS 8004 [M] | Lightnin' Slim's Bell Ringer | 196? | 12.50 | 25.00 | 50.00 |

—Thogh labeled "Electronic Stereo," this record is mono

| ❏ LPS 8018 | High and Low Down | 1971 | 3.75 | 7.50 | 15.00 |
| ❏ LPS 8023 | London Gumbo | 1972 | 3.75 | 7.50 | 15.00 |

INTERMEDIA

| ❏ QS-5062 | That's All Right | 198? | 2.50 | 5.00 | 10.00 |

LIL BOW WOW

12-Inch Singles

SO SO DEF

❏ CAS 56658 [DJ]	Thank You (LP Version) (Radio Edit) (Instrumental)/(TV Track) (A Cappella)	2001	2.50	5.00	10.00
❏ 44-79476	Bounce with Me (Album Version) (Radio Remix Featuring Lil' Mo and R.O.C.) (Extended Remix) (Instrumental) (Radio Instrumental) (Acappella)	2000	—	3.50	7.00
❏ 44-79487	Bow Wow (That's My Name)/This Playboy (6 versions)	2000	2.00	4.00	8.00
❏ 44-79612	Ghetto Girls (LP Version) (Instrumental) (Acapella)/Puppy Love (Remarqable Remix) (Instrumental) (Acappella)	2001	—	3.00	6.00

45s

SO SO DEF

| ❏ 38-79556 | Bow Wow (That's My Name)/Puppy Love | 2001 | — | — | 3.00 |

—B-side featuring Jagged Edge

Albums

SO SO DEF

| ❏ C2 69981 [(2)] | Beware of Dog | 2000 | 3.75 | 7.50 | 15.00 |

LIL' JOHNNY

12-Inch Singles

WARNER BROS.

| ❏ PRO-A-100609 [DJ] | I Got You (unknown versions) | 2001 | — | 3.00 | 6.00 |

45s

WARNER BROS.

| ❏ 7-16744 | I Got You/Wheel of Fortune | 2001 | — | — | 3.00 |

LIL' KIM

12-Inch Singles

UNDEAS/BIG BEAT

❏ DMD 2419 [DJ]	Not Tonight (4 versions)/Drugs	1997	2.00	4.00	8.00
❏ 95574	Not Tonight (Remix) (Remix Instrumental)/Drugs (Album Version)//Crush on You (Remix) (Remix Instrumental)/Drugs (Instrumental)	1997	2.50	5.00	10.00
❏ 95631	No Time (Album Version) (Instrumental) (Single Version) (A Cappella)	1996	2.50	5.00	10.00

UNDEAS/QUEEN BEE

❏ DMD 2514 [DJ]	Suck My D!#k (LP Version) (Instrumental) (Acappella)	2000	2.50	5.00	10.00
❏ DMD 2562 [DJ]	No Matter What They Say (Radio Edit) (Instrumental) (LP Version) (Acappella)	2000	3.00	6.00	12.00
❏ 84703	No Matter What They Say (Radio Edit) (Instrumental) (Album Version) (Acappella)	2000	2.00	4.00	8.00
❏ 85032	How Many Licks (Clean Album Version) (Instrumental) (Dirty Album Version) (Acappella)	2000	2.00	4.00	8.00
❏ PR 300272 [DJ]	The Notorious K.I.M. (Clean) (Instrumental) (Acappella) (LP Version)	2000	5.00	10.00	20.00
❏ PR 300359 [DJ]	How Many Licks (Clean Album Version) (Instrumental) (Dirty Album Version) (Acappella)	2000	2.00	4.00	8.00

45s

UNDEAS/QUEEN BEE

| ❏ 7-84770 | No Matter What They Say/Single Black Female | 2000 | — | — | 3.00 |

Albums

UNDEAS

| ❏ 92733 [(2)] | Hard Core | 1996 | 5.00 | 10.00 | 20.00 |
| ❏ 92840 [(2)] | The Notorious K.I.M. | 2000 | 3.75 | 7.50 | 15.00 |

LIL' ROMEO

12-Inch Singles

SME/PRIORITY

❏ 50208	My Baby (unknown versions)	2001	—	3.00	6.00
❏ SPRO 81504 [DJ]	My Baby (4 versions)	2001	—	3.50	7.00
❏ SPRO 81549 [DJ]	The Girlies (Radio Version) (TV Mix) (Instrumental Version) (A Cappella Version)/My Baby (International Mix) (House Mix)	2001	2.50	5.00	10.00

45s

SME/PRIORITY

| ❏ 79849 | My Baby/The Girlies | 2001 | — | 2.00 | 4.00 |

Albums

SME/PRIORITY

| ❏ 50198 | Lil' Romeo | 2001 | 3.75 | 7.50 | 15.00 |

LIPPS, INC.

45s

CASABLANCA

❏ 1006	Rock It/(Instrumental)	1979	—	2.00	4.00
❏ 2233	Funkytown/All Night Dancing	1980	—	2.50	5.00
❏ 2281	Rock It/Power	1980	—	2.00	4.00

L

Number	Title (A Side/B Side)	Yr	VG	VG+	NM
❑ 2303	How Long/There They Are	1980	—	2.00	4.00
❑ 2326	The Gossip Song/Jazzy	1981	—	2.00	4.00
❑ 2342	Hold Me Down/Always Lookin'	1981	—	2.00	4.00
❑ 2348	Designer Music/Background Singer	1981	—	2.00	4.00

Albums

CASABLANCA

Number	Title (A Side/B Side)	Yr	VG	VG+	NM
❑ NBLP 7197	Mouth to Mouth	1980	2.50	5.00	10.00
❑ NBLP 7242	Pucker Up	1980	2.50	5.00	10.00
❑ NBLP 7262	Designer Music	1981	2.50	5.00	10.00
❑ 811022-1	Four	1983	2.50	5.00	10.00

LIPSTIQUE

Albums

TOM N JERRY

Number	Title (A Side/B Side)	Yr	VG	VG+	NM
❑ TJ-4701	At the Discotheque	1978	5.00	10.00	20.00

LITTLE ANTHONY AND THE IMPERIALS

45s

Number	Title (A Side/B Side)	Yr	VG	VG+	NM
APOLLO					
❑ 521	The Fires Burn No More/Lift Up Your Hands	1957	15.00	30.00	60.00
—As "The Chesters"					
AVCO					
❑ 4635	I'm Falling in Love with You/What Good Am I Without You	1974	—	2.50	5.00
❑ 4645	I Don't Have to Worry/Loneliest House on the Block	1974	—	2.50	5.00
❑ 4651	Hold On (Just a Little Bit Longer)/I've Got to Let You Go (Part 1)	1975	—	2.50	5.00
❑ 4655	I'll Be Loving You Sooner or Later/Young Girl	1975	—	2.50	5.00
DCP					
❑ 1104	I'm On the Outside (Looking In)/Please Go	1964	2.50	5.00	10.00
❑ 1119	Goin' Out of My Head/Make It Easy on Yourself	1964	2.50	5.00	10.00
❑ 1128	Hurt So Bad/Reputation	1965	2.50	5.00	10.00
❑ 1128 [PS]	Hurt So Bad/Reputation	1965	10.00	20.00	40.00
❑ 1136	Take Me Back/Our Song	1965	2.00	4.00	8.00
❑ 1149	I Miss You So/Get Out of My Life	1965	2.00	4.00	8.00
❑ 1154	Hurt/Never Again	1966	2.00	4.00	8.00
END					
❑ 1027	Tears on My Pillow/Two People in the World	1958	10.00	20.00	40.00
—As "The Imperials"					
❑ 1027	Tears on My Pillow/Two People in the World	1958	6.25	12.50	25.00
—As "Little Anthony and the Imperials"					
❑ 1036	So Much/Oh Yeah	1958	6.25	12.50	25.00
❑ 1038	The Diary/Cha Cha Henry	1959	6.25	12.50	25.00
❑ 1039	When You Wish Upon a Star/Wishful Thinking	1959	6.25	12.50	25.00
❑ 1047	A Prayer and a Juke Box/River Path	1959	6.25	12.50	25.00
❑ 1053	So Near and Yet So Far/I'm Alright	1959	6.25	12.50	25.00
❑ 1060	Shimmy, Shimmy, Ko-Ko Bop/I'm Still in Love with You	1959	7.50	15.00	30.00
❑ 1067	My Empty Room/Bayou, Bayou, Baby	1960	3.75	7.50	15.00
❑ 1074	I'm Taking a Vacation from Love/Only Sympathy	1960	3.75	7.50	15.00
❑ 1080	Limbo (Part 1)/Limbo (Part 2)	1960	3.75	7.50	15.00
❑ 1083	Formula of Love/Dream	1961	3.75	7.50	15.00
❑ 1086	Please Say You Want Me/So Near Yet So Far	1961	3.75	7.50	15.00
❑ 1091	Traveling Stranger/Say Yea	1961	3.75	7.50	15.00
❑ 1104	Dream/A Lovely Way to Spend an Evening	1961	3.75	7.50	15.00
JANUS					
❑ 160	Father, Father/Each One, Teach One	1971	—	3.00	6.00
❑ 166	Madeline/Universe	1971	—	3.00	6.00
❑ 178	(Where Do I Begin) Love Story/There's an Island	1972	—	3.00	6.00
LIBERTY					
❑ 55119	The Glory of Love/C'mon Tiger (Gimme a Growl)	1958	7.50	15.00	30.00
—As "The Imperials"					
MCA					
❑ 41258	Daylight/Your Love	1980	—	2.00	4.00
—Little Anthony solo					
NEWTIME					
❑ 503	A Short Prayer/Where Will You Be	196?	3.00	6.00	12.00
—As "Anthony and the Imperials"					
PCM					
❑ 202	This Time We're Winning/Your Love	1983	—	2.00	4.00
PURE GOLD					
❑ 101	Nothing from Nothing/Running with the Wrong Crowd	1976	—	2.50	5.00
ROULETTE					
❑ 4379	That Lil' Ole Lovemaker Me/It Just Ain't Fair	1961	3.00	6.00	12.00
—Little Anthony solo					
❑ 4477	Lonesome Romeo/I've Got a Lot to Offer Darling	1963	3.00	6.00	12.00
—Little Anthony solo					
UNITED ARTISTS					
❑ 0117	Goin' Out of My Head/I'm On the Outside (Looking In)	1973	—	2.00	4.00
—"Silver Spotlight Series" reissue					
❑ 0118	Hurt So Bad/Take Me Back	1973	—	2.00	4.00
—"Silver Spotlight Series" reissue					
❑ 50552	Out of Sight, Out of Mind/Summer's Comin'	1969	—	3.00	6.00
❑ 50598	The Ten Commandments of Love/Let the Sunshine In	1969	—	3.00	6.00
❑ 50625	It'll Never Be the Same Again/Don't Get Close	1970	—	3.00	6.00
❑ 50677	World of Darkness/The Change	1970	—	3.00	6.00
❑ 50720	Help Me Find a Way (To Say I Love You)/If I Love You	1970	—	3.00	6.00
VEEP					
❑ 1228	Better Use Your Head/The Wonder of It All	1966	2.00	4.00	8.00
❑ 1228 [PS]	Better Use Your Head/The Wonder of It All	1966	10.00	20.00	40.00
❑ 1233	You Better Take It Easy Baby/Gonna Fix You Good (Every Time You're Bad)	1966	2.00	4.00	8.00
❑ 1239	Tears on My Pillow/Who's Sorry Now	1966	—	3.00	6.00
❑ 1240	I'm On the Outside (Looking In)/Please Go	1966	—	3.00	6.00
❑ 1241	Goin' Out of My Head/Shing-a-Ling	1966	—	3.00	6.00
❑ 1242	Hurt So Bad/Reputation	1966	—	3.00	6.00
❑ 1243	Take Me Back/Our Song	1966	—	3.00	6.00
❑ 1244	I Miss You So/Get Out of My Life	1966	—	3.00	6.00
❑ 1245	Hurt/Never Again	1966	—	3.00	6.00
❑ 1248	It's Not the Same/Down on Love	1966	2.00	4.00	8.00
❑ 1255	Don't Tie Me Down/Where There's a Will There's a Way	1967	2.00	4.00	8.00
❑ 1262	Hold On to Someone/Lost in Love	1967	2.00	4.00	8.00
❑ 1269	You Only Live Twice/Hungry Heart	1967	2.00	4.00	8.00
❑ 1275	Beautiful People/If I Remember to Forget	1967	2.00	4.00	8.00
❑ 1278	I'm Hypnotized/Hungry Heart	1968	2.00	4.00	8.00
❑ 1283	What Greater Love/In the Back of My Heart	1968	2.00	4.00	8.00
❑ 1285	Yesterday Has Gone/My Love Is a Rainbow	1968	2.00	4.00	8.00
❑ 1293	The Flesh Failures (Let the Sunshine In)/Gentle Rain	1969	2.00	4.00	8.00
❑ 1303	Anthem (Revelation)/Goodbye Good Times	1969	2.00	4.00	8.00

7-Inch Extended Plays

Number	Title (A Side/B Side)	Yr	VG	VG+	NM
END					
❑ 203	(contents unknown)	1959	50.00	100.00	200.00
❑ 203 [PS]	Little Anthony and the Imperials	1959	75.00	150.00	300.00
❑ 204	(contents unknown)	1959	50.00	100.00	200.00
❑ 204 [PS]	We Are Little Anthony and the Imperials	1959	75.00	150.00	300.00

Albums

Number	Title (A Side/B Side)	Yr	VG	VG+	NM
ACCORD					
❑ SN-7216	Tears on My Pillow	1983	2.50	5.00	10.00
AVCO					
❑ AV-11012	On a New Street	1973	5.00	10.00	20.00
DCP					
❑ DCL-3801 [M]	I'm On the Outside Looking In	1964	6.25	12.50	25.00
❑ DCL-3808 [M]	Goin' Out of My Head	1965	6.25	12.50	25.00
❑ DCL-3809 [M]	The Best of Little Anthony and the Imperials	1965	5.00	10.00	20.00
❑ DCS-6801 [S]	I'm On the Outside Looking In	1964	7.50	15.00	30.00
❑ DCS-6808 [S]	Goin' Out of My Head	1965	7.50	15.00	30.00
❑ DCS-6809 [S]	The Best of Little Anthony and the Imperials	1965	6.25	12.50	25.00
END					
❑ LP 303 [M]	We Are The Imperials Featuring Little Anthony	1959	62.50	125.00	250.00
❑ LP 311 [M]	Shades of the 40's	1960	50.00	100.00	200.00
FORUM					
❑ F-9107 [M]	Little Anthony and the Imperials' Greatest Hits	196?	3.75	7.50	15.00
❑ FS-9107 [R]	Little Anthony and the Imperials' Greatest Hits	196?	3.00	6.00	12.00
LIBERTY					
❑ LM-1017	Out of Sight, Out of Mind	1981	2.00	4.00	8.00
—Reissue of United Artists 1017					
❑ LN-10133	The Best of Little Anthony and the Imperials	1981	2.00	4.00	8.00
—Budget-line reissue					
PICKWICK					
❑ SPC-3029	The Hits of Little Anthony and the Imperials	196?	3.00	6.00	12.00
RHINO					
❑ R1-70919	The Best of Little Anthony and the Imperials	1989	3.00	6.00	12.00
ROULETTE					
❑ R-25294 [M]	Little Anthony and the Imperials' Greatest Hits	1965	6.25	12.50	25.00
❑ SR-25294 [R]	Little Anthony and the Imperials' Greatest Hits	1965	5.00	10.00	20.00
❑ SR-42007	Forever Yours	1968	3.75	7.50	15.00
SONGBIRD					
❑ 3245	Daylight	1980	2.50	5.00	10.00
SUNSET					
❑ SUS-5287	Little Anthony and the Imperials	1970	3.75	7.50	15.00
UNITED ARTISTS					
❑ UA-LA026-G [(2)]	Legendary Masters Series	1972	6.25	12.50	25.00
❑ UA-LA255-G	The Very Best of Little Anthony and the Imperials	1974	2.50	5.00	10.00
❑ LM-1017	Out of Sight, Out of Mind	1980	2.50	5.00	10.00
—Reissue of United Artists 6720					
❑ UAS 6720	Out of Sight, Out of Mind	1969	5.00	10.00	20.00
VEEP					
❑ VP 13510 [M]	I'm On the Outside Looking In	1966	3.75	7.50	15.00
❑ VP 13511 [M]	Goin' Out of My Head	1966	3.75	7.50	15.00
❑ VP 13512 [M]	The Best of Little Anthony and the Imperials	1966	3.75	7.50	15.00
❑ VP 13513 [M]	Payin' Our Dues	1966	3.75	7.50	15.00
❑ VP 13514 [M]	Reflections	1967	3.75	7.50	15.00
❑ VP 13516 [M]	Movie Grabbers	1967	3.75	7.50	15.00
❑ VPS 16510 [S]	I'm On the Outside Looking In	1966	5.00	10.00	20.00
❑ VPS 16511 [S]	Goin' Out of My Head	1966	5.00	10.00	20.00
❑ VPS 16512 [S]	The Best of Little Anthony and the Imperials	1966	5.00	10.00	20.00
❑ VPS 16513 [S]	Payin' Our Dues	1966	5.00	10.00	20.00
❑ VPS 16514 [S]	Reflections	1967	5.00	10.00	20.00
❑ VPS 16516 [S]	Movie Grabbers	1967	5.00	10.00	20.00
❑ VPS 16519	The Best of Little Anthony, Volume 2	1968	3.75	7.50	15.00

LITTLE BUBBER

45s

IMPERIAL

Number	Title (A Side/B Side)	Yr	VG	VG+	NM
❑ 5225	High Class Woman/Come Back Baby	1953	20.00	40.00	80.00
❑ 5238	Runnin' Around/Never Trust a Woman	1953	20.00	40.00	80.00

LITTLE CAESAR AND THE CONSULS

45s

MALA

Number	Title (A Side/B Side)	Yr	VG	VG+	NM
❑ 512	(My Girl) Sloopy/Poison Ivy	1965	3.75	7.50	15.00
❑ 518	You've Really Got a Hold on Me/It's So Easy	1965	3.00	6.00	12.00
❑ 523	Hey Girl/You Laugh Too Much	1966	3.00	6.00	12.00

Number	Title (A Side/B Side)	Yr	VG	VG+	NM

LITTLE CAESAR AND THE EMPIRE
45s
PARKWAY
| ❏ 152 | Everybody Dance Now/(Instrumental) | 1967 | 6.25 | 12.50 | 25.00 |

LITTLE CAESAR AND THE ROMANS
45s
DEL-FI
❏ 4158	Those Oldies But Goodies (Remind Me of You)/ She Don't Wanna Dance	1961	7.50	15.00	30.00
❏ 4164	Hully Gully Again/Frankie and Johnny	1961	6.25	12.50	25.00
❏ 4166	Memories of Those Oldies But Goodies/Fever	1961	15.00	30.00	60.00
❏ 4170	Ten Commandments of Love/C.C. Rider	1961	12.50	25.00	50.00
❏ 4176	Popeye One More Time/Yoyo Yo Yoyo	1962	6.25	12.50	25.00
	SCEPTER				
❏ 12237	Baby Love/When Will I Get Over You	1969	2.00	4.00	8.00

—As "Caesar and the Romans"

| ❏ 12264 | Jailhouse Rock/Leavin' My Past Behind | 1969 | 2.00 | 4.00 | 8.00 |

—As "Caesar and the Romans"

Albums
DEL-FI
| ❏ DFLP-1218 [M] | Memories of Those Oldies But Goodies | 1961 | 75.00 | 150.00 | 300.00 |

LITTLE ESTHER
See LITTLE ESTHER PHILLIPS.

LITTLE EVA
45s
AMY
❏ 943	Stand By Me/That's My Man	1965	2.00	4.00	8.00
	BELL				
❏ 45264	The Loco-Motion/Will You Love Me Tomorrow	1972	—	2.50	5.00
	DIMENSION				
❏ 1000	The Loco-Motion/He Is the Boy	1962	5.00	10.00	20.00
❏ 1003	Keep Your Hands Off/Where Do I Go	1962	3.75	7.50	15.00

—Some copies have this shortened title

| ❏ 1003 | Keep Your Hands Off My Baby/Where Do I Go | 1962 | 3.00 | 6.00 | 12.00 |

—Most copies have longer, and correct, title

❏ 1006	Let's Turkey Trot/Down Home	1963	3.00	6.00	12.00
❏ 1011	Old Smokey Locomotion/Just a Little Girl	1963	3.00	6.00	12.00
❏ 1013	The Trouble with Boys/What I Gotta Do	1963	3.00	6.00	12.00
❏ 1019	Let's Start the Party Again/Please Hurt Me	1963	3.00	6.00	12.00
❏ 1021	The Christmas Song/I Wish You a Merry Christmas	1963	3.75	7.50	15.00

—With Big Dee Irwin

| ❏ 1021 [PS] | The Christmas Song/I Wish You a Merry Christmas | 1963 | 10.00 | 20.00 | 40.00 |

—With Big Dee Irwin

❏ 1035	Makin' with the Magilla/Run to Her	1964	2.50	5.00	10.00
❏ 1035	Makin' with the Magilla/Conga	1964	2.50	5.00	10.00
❏ 1035 [PS]	Makin' with the Magilla/Run to Her	1964	10.00	20.00	40.00
❏ 1042	Wake Up John/Takin' Back What I Said	1964	2.50	5.00	10.00
	SPRING				
❏ 101	Mama Said/Something About You Boy	1970	—	3.00	6.00
❏ 107	Night After Night/Something About You Boy	1970	—	3.00	6.00
	VERVE				
❏ 10459	Bend It/Just One Word Isn't Enough	1966	2.00	4.00	8.00
❏ 10529	Everything Is Beautiful About You Boy/Take a Step in My Direction	1967	2.00	4.00	8.00

Albums
DIMENSION
| ❏ DLP-6000 [M] | LLLLLoco-Motion | 1962 | 37.50 | 75.00 | 150.00 |

—Without "Keep Your Hands Off My Baby"

| ❏ DLP-6000 [M] | LLLLLoco-Motion | 1962 | 50.00 | 100.00 | 200.00 |

—With "Keep Your Hands Off My Baby"

| ❏ DLPS-6000 [R] | LLLLLoco-Motion | 1962 | 37.50 | 75.00 | 150.00 |

—Without "Keep Your Hands Off My Baby"

| ❏ DLPS-6000 [R] | LLLLLoco-Motion | 1962 | 50.00 | 100.00 | 200.00 |

—With "Keep Your Hands Off My Baby"

LITTLE IVA AND HER BAND
45s
MIRACLE
| ❏ 2 | When I Needed You/Continental Strut | 1960 | 500.00 | 1000. | 1500. |

LITTLE JOE
45s
BRUNSWICK
| ❏ 55369 | Holiday/Fool on the Hill | 1968 | 2.00 | 4.00 | 8.00 |

Albums
BRUNSWICK
| ❏ BL 754135 | Little Joe (Sure Can Sing) | 1968 | 5.00 | 10.00 | 20.00 |

LITTLE JOE AND THE THRILLERS
45s
ENJOY
❏ 2011	Peanuts and Popcorn/Chicken Little Boo Boo	1964	2.50	5.00	10.00
	EPIC				
❏ 9293	Mine/It's Too Bad We Had to Say Goodbye	1958	3.75	7.50	15.00
❏ 9431	Run Little Girl/Public Opinion	1961	3.00	6.00	12.00
	MGM				
❏ 14129	Somehow, Someway/Days 'Til Morning	1970	—	2.50	5.00
❏ 14230	People Show/Baby I Could Be So Good at Lovin' You	1971	—	2.50	5.00
❏ 14290	Don't Take the Rain Away/The Children	1971	—	2.50	5.00
❏ 14361	Shelly Made Me Smile/Words and Music	1972	—	2.50	5.00
❏ 14466	Baby I Could Be So Good at Lovin' You/Cherry Pink and Apple Blossom White	1972	—	2.50	5.00
❏ 14662	Folks Who Live on the Hill/Baby I Could Be So Good at Lovin' You	1973	—	2.50	5.00
	OKEH				
❏ 7075	Let's Do the Slop/This I Know	1956	3.75	7.50	15.00
❏ 7088	Peanuts/Lilly Lou	1957	5.00	10.00	20.00
❏ 7094	Lonesome/The Echoes Keep Calling Me	1957	3.75	7.50	15.00
❏ 7099	Don't Leave Me Alone/What's Happened to Your Halo	1958	3.75	7.50	15.00
❏ 7107	Mine/It's Too Bad We Had to Say Goodbye	1958	3.75	7.50	15.00
❏ 7116	Cherry (Part 1)/Cherry (Part 2)	1959	3.00	6.00	12.00
❏ 7121	I'm Tryin'/Strange Dreams	1959	3.00	6.00	12.00
❏ 7127	Give Me All Your Love/I'll Never Let You Go	1959	3.00	6.00	12.00
❏ 7134	Ev'ry Now and Then/Goodnight, Little Girl	1960	3.00	6.00	12.00
❏ 7136	Stay/Please Don't Go	1960	3.00	6.00	12.00
❏ 7140	Run Little Girl/Public Opinion	1961	3.00	6.00	12.00
	REPRISE				
❏ 20142	Peanuts/No, No, I Can't Stop	1963	2.50	5.00	10.00

7-Inch Extended Plays
EPIC
| ❏ EG-7198 | (contents unknown) | 1958 | 25.00 | 50.00 | 100.00 |
| ❏ EG-7198 [PS] | Little Joe and the Thrillers | 1958 | 25.00 | 50.00 | 100.00 |

LITTLE JOEY AND THE FLIPS
45s
JOY
| ❏ 262 | Bongo Stomp/Lost Love | 1962 | 3.75 | 7.50 | 15.00 |
| ❏ 268 | Bongo Gully/It Was Like Heaven | 1962 | 3.00 | 6.00 | 12.00 |

LITTLE MILTON
45s
BOBBIN
❏ 101	I'm a Lonely Man/That Will Never Do	1958	6.25	12.50	25.00
❏ 103	Long Distance Operator/I Found Me a New Love	1959	6.25	12.50	25.00
❏ 112	Strange Dreams/I'm Tryin'	1959	6.25	12.50	25.00
❏ 117	Hold Me Tight/Same Old Blues	1959	6.25	12.50	25.00
❏ 120	Dead Love/My Baby Pleases Me	1960	6.25	12.50	25.00
❏ 125	Let It Be Known/Hey Girl	1960	6.25	12.50	25.00
❏ 128	I'm in Love/Cross My Heart	1961	6.25	12.50	25.00
	CHECKER				
❏ 977	Saving My Love for You/Lonely No More	1961	3.75	7.50	15.00
❏ 994	So Mean to Me/I Need Somebody	1961	3.75	7.50	15.00
❏ 1012	Satisfied/Someone to Love	1962	3.75	7.50	15.00
❏ 1020	I Wonder Why/Losing Hand	1962	3.75	7.50	15.00
❏ 1048	She Put a Spell on Me/Never Too Old	1963	3.75	7.50	15.00
❏ 1063	Meddlin'/One of These Old Days	1963	3.75	7.50	15.00
❏ 1078	Sacrifice/What Kind of Love Is This	1964	3.75	7.50	15.00
❏ 1096	Blind Man/Blues in the Night	1964	3.75	7.50	15.00
❏ 1105	We're Gonna Make It/Can't Hold Back the Tears	1965	3.75	7.50	15.00
❏ 1113	Who's Cheating Who?/Ain't No Big Deal on You	1965	3.75	7.50	15.00
❏ 1118	Help Me Help You/Without My Sweet Baby	1965	3.75	7.50	15.00
❏ 1128	My Baby's Something Else/Your People	1965	3.75	7.50	15.00
❏ 1132	Sometimes/We Got the Winning Hand	1965	3.75	7.50	15.00
❏ 1138	I'm Mighty Grateful/When Does Heartache End	1966	3.75	7.50	15.00
❏ 1149	Man Loves Two/Believe in Me	1966	3.75	7.50	15.00
❏ 1162	Feel So Bad/You Colored My Blues Right	1966	5.00	10.00	20.00
❏ 1172	I'll Never Turn My Back on You/Don't Leave Her	1967	3.00	6.00	12.00
❏ 1178	I'm Shorty/Sitting Home Alone	1967	3.00	6.00	12.00
❏ 1186	A Whole Lot of Fun Before the Weekend Is Done/ Real True Love	1967	3.00	6.00	12.00
❏ 1189	More and More/Cost of Living	1967	3.00	6.00	12.00
❏ 1194	I Know What I Want/You Mean Everything to Me	1968	3.00	6.00	12.00
❏ 1203	At the Dark End of the Street/I (Who Have Nothing)	1968	3.00	6.00	12.00
❏ 1208	Let Me Down Easy/Lonely Drifter	1968	3.00	6.00	12.00
❏ 1212	Grits Ain't Groceries (All Around the World)/I Can't Quit You Baby	1969	3.00	6.00	12.00
❏ 1217	Just a Little Bit/Spring	1969	3.00	6.00	12.00
❏ 1221	Poor Man/So Blue	1969	3.00	6.00	12.00
❏ 1225	Let's Get Together/I'll Always Love You	1969	3.00	6.00	12.00
❏ 1226	If Walls Could Talk/Loving You	1969	3.00	6.00	12.00
❏ 1227	Baby I Love You/Don't Talk Back	1970	3.00	6.00	12.00
❏ 1231	Somebody's Changin' My Sweet Baby's Mind/I'm Tired	1970	3.00	6.00	12.00

—As "Little Milton Campbell"

❏ 1236	Many Rivers to Cross/Mother's Love	1970	3.00	6.00	12.00
❏ 1239	I Play Dirty/Nothing Beats a Failure	1971	2.00	4.00	8.00
	GLADES				
❏ 1734	Friend of Mine/(Instrumental)	1976	—	2.50	5.00
❏ 1738	Baby It Ain't No Way/Bring It On Back	1976	—	2.50	5.00
❏ 1741	Just One Step/(Instrumental)	1977	—	2.50	5.00
❏ 1743	Loving You (Is the Best Thing to Happen to Me)/ 9:59 A.M.	1977	—	2.50	5.00
❏ 1747	Me for You, You for Me/My Thing Is You	1977	—	2.50	5.00
	MALACO				
❏ 2104	The Blues Is All Right/Come Back Kind of Loving	1985	—	2.00	4.00
❏ 2108	Misty Blue/Catch You on the Way Down	1985	—	2.00	4.00
❏ 2123	Lonesome Christmas/Come To Me	1985	—	2.00	4.00
❏ 2127	I Will Survive/4:59 A.M.	1986	—	2.00	4.00
❏ 2134	Real Good Woman/Annie Mae's Café	198?	—	2.00	4.00
❏ 2147	His Old Lady and My Old Lady/(B-side unknown)	198?	—	2.00	4.00
❏ 2162	Bad Dream/The Woman I Love	198?	—	2.00	4.00

L

Number	Title (A Side/B Side)	Yr	VG	VG+	NM

MCA

Number	Title (A Side/B Side)	Yr	VG	VG+	NM
❑ 52184	Age Ain't Nothin' But a Number/(Instrumental)	1983	—	2.00	4.00
❑ 52254	Living on the Dark Side of Love/Why Are You So Hard to Please	1983	—	2.00	4.00

METEOR

| ❑ 5040 | Love at First Sight/Let's Boogie Baby | 1957 | 50.00 | 100.00 | 200.00 |
| ❑ 5045 | Let My Baby Be/Oh My Little Baby | 1957 | 200.00 | 400.00 | 800.00 |

STAX

❑ 0100	If That Ain't a Reason (For Your Woman to Leave You)/Mr. Mailman	1971	—	3.00	6.00
❑ 0111	That's What Love Will Make You Do/I'm Livin' Off the Love You Give	1972	—	3.00	6.00
❑ 0124	Walking the Back Streets and Crying/Before the Honeymoon	1972	—	3.00	6.00
❑ 0141	I'm Gonna Cry a River/What It Is	1972	—	3.00	6.00
❑ 0148	Lovin' Stick/Rainy Day	1972	—	3.00	6.00
❑ 0174	What It Is/Who Can Handle Me Is You	1973	—	3.00	6.00
❑ 0191	Tin Pan Alley/Sweet Woman of Mine	1974	—	3.00	6.00
❑ 0210	Behind Closed Doors/Bet You I Win	1974	—	3.00	6.00
❑ 0229	Let Me Back In/Let Your Loss Be Your Lesson	1974	—	3.00	6.00
❑ 0238	If You Talk in Your Sleep/Sweet Woman of Mine	1975	—	3.00	6.00
❑ 0252	How Could You Do It to Me/Packed Up and Took My Mind	1975	—	3.00	6.00

SUN

❑ 194	Beggin' My Baby/Somebody Told Me	1954	75.00	150.00	300.00
❑ 200	If You Love Me/Alone and Blue	1954	150.00	300.00	600.00
❑ 220	Looking for My Baby/Lonesome for My Baby	1955	200.00	400.00	800.00

Albums

CHECKER

| ❑ LP-2995 [M] | We're Gonna Make It | 1965 | 25.00 | 50.00 | 100.00 |
| —Black label |
| ❑ LP-2995 [M] | We're Gonna Make It | 1966 | 17.50 | 35.00 | 70.00 |
| —Blue label with red and black checkers |
| ❑ LP-2995 [M] | We're Gonna Make It | 196? | 6.25 | 12.50 | 25.00 |
| —Blue, fading to white, label |
❑ LP-3002 [M]	Little Milton Sings Big Blues	1966	12.50	25.00	50.00
❑ LP-3011	Grits Ain't Groceries	1969	6.25	12.50	25.00
❑ LP-3012	If Walls Could Talk	1970	6.25	12.50	25.00

CHESS

| ❑ 204 [(2)] | Little Milton | 1976 | 3.75 | 7.50 | 15.00 |
| ❑ CH-9252 | We're Gonna Make It | 1986 | 2.50 | 5.00 | 10.00 |
| —Reissue of Checker 2995 |
| ❑ CH-9265 | Little Milton Sings Big Blues | 1987 | 2.50 | 5.00 | 10.00 |
| —Reissue of Checker 3002 |
| ❑ CH-9289 | If Walls Could Talk | 1989 | 2.50 | 5.00 | 10.00 |
| —Reissue of Checker 3012 |
| ❑ CH-50013 | Little Milton's Greatest Hits | 1972 | 3.75 | 7.50 | 15.00 |

GLADES

| ❑ 7508 | Friend of Mine | 1976 | 3.00 | 6.00 | 12.00 |
| ❑ 7511 | Me for You, You for Me | 1977 | 3.00 | 6.00 | 12.00 |

MALACO

❑ 7419	Playin' for Keeps	198?	3.00	6.00	12.00
❑ 7427	I Will Survive	198?	3.00	6.00	12.00
❑ 7435	Annie Mae's Café	198?	3.00	6.00	12.00
❑ 7445	Movin' to the Country	198?	3.00	6.00	12.00
❑ 7448	Back to Back	198?	3.00	6.00	12.00
❑ 7453	Too Much Pain	198?	3.00	6.00	12.00

MCA

| ❑ 5414 | Age Ain't Nothin' But a Number | 1983 | 2.50 | 5.00 | 10.00 |

ROUNDER

| ❑ SS-35 | The Sun Masters | 198? | 3.00 | 6.00 | 12.00 |

STAX

| ❑ STS-3012 | Waiting for Little Milton | 1973 | 5.00 | 10.00 | 20.00 |
| ❑ 4117 | Waiting for Little Milton | 1978 | 3.00 | 6.00 | 12.00 |
| —Reissue of 3012 |
❑ 5514	Blues 'n' Soul	1974	5.00	10.00	20.00
❑ MPS-8514	Walking the Back Streets	1981	2.50	5.00	10.00
❑ MPS-8518	Blues 'n' Soul	1981	2.50	5.00	10.00
—Reissue of 5514
❑ MPS-8529	Grits Ain't Groceries	198?	2.50	5.00	10.00
—Despite the title, this is NOT a reissue of Checker 3011, but a later live recording
❑ MPS-8550	What It Is	198?	2.50	5.00	10.00

LITTLE MISS CORNSHUCKS

45s

CHESS

| ❑ 1785 | No Teasing Around/It Do Me No Good | 1961 | 3.75 | 7.50 | 15.00 |

Albums

CHESS

| ❑ LP-1453 [M] | The Loneliest Gal in Town | 1961 | 50.00 | 100.00 | 200.00 |

LITTLE OTIS

45s

TAMLA

| ❑ 54058 | I Out-Duked the Duke/Baby I Need You | 1962 | 7.50 | 15.00 | 30.00 |

LITTLE PORK CHOPS

See JOHN LEE HOOKER.

LITTLE RICHARD

Also see THE DEUCES OF RHYTHM AND THE TEMPO TOPPERS; JIMI HENDRIX.

12-Inch Singles

MCA

| ❑ L33-17101 [DJ] | Great Gosh A' Mighty! (same on both sides) | 1986 | 2.00 | 4.00 | 8.00 |

SPECIALTY

Number	Title (A Side/B Side)	Yr	VG	VG+	NM
❑ SPS 4000	Lucille/Heebie-Jeebies Love	198?	2.00	4.00	8.00

WTG

| ❑ 08169 | Twins (5 versions) | 1988 | — | 3.00 | 6.00 |
| —With Philip Bailey |

45s

ATLANTIC

| ❑ 2181 | Crying in the Chapel/Hole in the Wall | 1963 | 3.00 | 6.00 | 12.00 |
| ❑ 2192 | It Is No Secret (What God Can Do)/Travelin' Shoes | 1963 | 3.00 | 6.00 | 12.00 |

BELL

| ❑ 45385 | Good Golly Miss Molly/Good Golly Miss Molly (Part 2) | 1973 | — | 2.50 | 5.00 |

BRUNSWICK

❑ 55362	She's Together/Try Some of Mine	1968	2.00	4.00	8.00
❑ 55377	Stingy Jenny/Baby Don't You Tear My Clothes	1968	2.00	4.00	8.00
❑ 55386	Soul Train/Can I Count on You	1968	2.00	4.00	8.00

CORAL

| ❑ 62366 | Milky White Way/Need Him | 1963 | 2.50 | 5.00 | 10.00 |

CRITIQUE

| ❑ 99392 | Happy Endings/California Girls | 1987 | — | 2.00 | 4.00 |
| —A-side with the Beach Boys; B-side is The Beach Boys without Little Richard |

ELEKTRA

| ❑ 69370 | Tutti Frutti/Rave On | 1988 | — | — | 3.00 |
| —B-side by John Cougar Mellencamp |
| ❑ 69384 | Tutti Frutti/Powerful Stuff | 1988 | — | — | 3.00 |
| —B-side by the Fabulous Thunderbirds |
| ❑ 69385 | Tutti Frutti/Kokomo | 1988 | — | — | 3.00 |
| —B-side by the Beach Boys |

END

| ❑ 1057 | Troubles of the World/Save Me Lord | 1959 | 3.75 | 7.50 | 15.00 |
| ❑ 1058 | Milky White Way/I've Just Come From the Fountain | 1959 | 3.75 | 7.50 | 15.00 |

GREEN MOUNTAIN

| ❑ 413 | In the Middle of the Night/Where Will I Find a Place to Sleep This Evening | 1973 | — | 2.50 | 5.00 |

KENT

| ❑ 4567 | Mississippi/In the Name | 1972 | — | — | — |
| —Unreleased |
| ❑ 4568 | Don't You Know I/In the Name | 1972 | — | 2.50 | 5.00 |

MAINSTREAM

| ❑ 5572 | Try to Help Your Brother/Funk Proof | 1975 | — | 2.50 | 5.00 |

MANTICORE

| ❑ 7007 | Call My Name/Steal Miss Liza (Miss Liza Jane) | 1975 | — | 2.00 | 4.00 |

MCA

| ❑ 52780 | Great Gosh A-Mighty! (It's a Matter of Time)/The Ride | 1986 | — | — | 3.00 |
| —B-side by Charlie Midnight |
| ❑ 52780 [PS] | Great Gosh A-Mighty! (It's a Matter of Time)/The Ride | 1986 | — | — | 3.00 |

MERCURY

❑ 71884	He's Not Just a Soldier/Joy, Joy, Joy	1962	3.75	7.50	15.00
❑ 71911	Do You Care/Ride On King Jesus	1962	3.75	7.50	15.00
❑ 71965	Why Don't You Change Your Ways/He Got What He Wanted	1962	3.75	7.50	15.00

MODERN

❑ 1018	Holy Mackeral/Baby, Don't You Want a Man Like Me	1966	3.00	6.00	12.00
❑ 1018 [PS]	Holy Mackeral/Baby, Don't You Want a Man Like Me	1966	5.00	10.00	20.00
❑ 1019	Do You Feel It (Part 1)/Do You Feel It (Part 2)	1966	3.00	6.00	12.00
❑ 1022	Directly from My Heart to You/I'm Back	1966	3.00	6.00	12.00
❑ 1030	Slippin' and Slidin'/Bring It Back Home to Me	1967	3.00	6.00	12.00
❑ 1043	Baby What You Want Me to Do (Part 1)/Baby What You Want Me to Do (Part 2)	1967	3.00	6.00	12.00

OKEH

❑ 7251	Poor Dog (Who Can't Wag His Own Tail)/Well	1966	3.75	7.50	15.00
❑ 7251 [PS]	Poor Dog (Who Can't Wag His Own Tail)/Well	1966	6.25	12.50	25.00
❑ 7262	I Need Love/Commandments of Love	1966	3.00	6.00	12.00
❑ 7271	Hurry Sundown/I Don't Want to Discuss It	1967	3.00	6.00	12.00
❑ 7278	Don't Deceive Me (Please Don't Go)/Never Gonna Let You Go	1967	3.00	6.00	12.00
❑ 7286	Money/Little Bit of Something	1967	3.00	6.00	12.00
❑ 7325	Lucille/Whole Lotta Shakin' Goin' On	1969	2.50	5.00	10.00

PEACOCK

| ❑ 1658 | Little Richard's Boogie/Directly from My Heart to You | 1956 | 37.50 | 75.00 | 150.00 |
| ❑ 1673 | Maybe I'm Right/I Love My Baby | 1957 | 20.00 | 40.00 | 80.00 |

RCA VICTOR

❑ 47-4392	Taxi Blues/Every Hour	1951	225.00	450.00	900.00
❑ 47-4582	Get Rich Quick/Thinkin' 'Bout My Mother	1952	200.00	400.00	800.00
❑ 47-4772	Why Did You Leave Me?/Ain't Nothin' Happenin'	1952	200.00	400.00	800.00
❑ 47-5025	Please Have Mercy on Me/I Brought It All on Myself	1952	150.00	300.00	600.00

REPRISE

❑ 0907	Freedom Blues/Dew Drop Inn	1970	2.50	5.00	10.00
❑ 0942	Greenwood Mississippi/I Saw Her Standing There	1970	2.50	5.00	10.00
❑ 1005	Shake a Hand (If You Can)/Somebody Saw You	1971	2.00	4.00	8.00
❑ 1043	Green Power/Dancing in the Street	1971	2.00	4.00	8.00
❑ 1062	Money Is/Money Runner	1972	2.00	4.00	8.00
—B-side by Quincy Jones
❑ 1130	Mockingbird Sally/Nuki Suki	1972	2.00	4.00	8.00

Number	Title (A Side/B Side)	Yr	VG	VG+	NM
SPECIALTY					
❏ 561	Tutti-Frutti/I'm Just a Lonely Guy	1955	12.50	25.00	50.00
❏ 572	Long Tall Sally/Slippin' and Slidin' (Peepin' and Hidin')	1956	10.00	20.00	40.00
❏ 579	Rip It Up/Ready Teddy	1956	10.00	20.00	40.00
❏ 584	Heebie-Jeebies/She's Got it	1956	10.00	20.00	40.00
❏ 591	The Girl Can't Help It/All Around the World	1956	10.00	20.00	40.00
❏ 598	Lucille/Send Me Some Lovin'	1957	10.00	20.00	40.00
❏ 606	Jenny, Jenny/Miss Ann	1957	10.00	20.00	40.00
❏ 606 [PS]	Jenny, Jenny/Miss Ann	1957	15.00	30.00	60.00
❏ 611	Keep a Knockin/Can't Believe You Wanna Leave	1957	7.50	15.00	30.00
❏ 611 [PS]	Keep a Knockin/Can't Believe You Wanna Leave	1957	15.00	30.00	60.00
❏ 624	Good Golly, Miss Molly/Hey-Hey-Hey-Hey!	1958	7.50	15.00	30.00
❏ 624 [PS]	Good Golly, Miss Molly/Hey-Hey-Hey-Hey!	1958	12.50	25.00	50.00
❏ 633/624	Ooh! My Soul/True, Fine Mama	1958	20.00	40.00	80.00

—*Some copies have the B-side misnumbered; all other information is correct, including the master number*

Number	Title (A Side/B Side)	Yr	VG	VG+	NM
❏ 633	Ooh! My Soul/True, Fine Mama	1958	6.25	12.50	25.00
❏ 633 [PS]	Ooh! My Soul/True, Fine Mama	1958	12.50	25.00	50.00
❏ 645	Baby Face/I'll Never Let You Go	1958	6.25	12.50	25.00
❏ 652	She Knows How to Rock/Early One Morning	1958	6.25	12.50	25.00
❏ 660	By the Light of the Silvery Moon/Wonderin'	1959	6.25	12.50	25.00
❏ 664	Kansas City/Lonesome and Blue	1959	6.25	12.50	25.00
❏ 670	Shake a Hand/All Night Long	1959	6.25	12.50	25.00
❏ 680	Whole Lotta Shakin' Goin' On/Maybe I'm Right	1959	6.25	12.50	25.00
❏ 681	I Got It/Baby	1960	6.25	12.50	25.00
❏ 686	The Most I Can Offer/Directly from My Heart	1964	3.75	7.50	15.00
❏ 692	Bama Lama Bama Loo/Annie Is Back	1964	3.75	7.50	15.00
❏ 697	Keep a Knockin/Bama Lama Bama Loo	1964	3.75	7.50	15.00
❏ 699	Poor Boy Paul/Wonderin'	1964	3.75	7.50	15.00
❏ 734	Chicken Little Baby/Oh Why	1974	—	3.00	6.00
VEE JAY					
❏ 612	Whole Lotta Shakin' Goin' On/Goodnight Irene	1964	2.50	5.00	10.00
❏ 625	Blueberry Hill/Cherry Red	1964	2.50	5.00	10.00
❏ 652	It Ain't Whatcha Do/Cross Over	1965	2.50	5.00	10.00
❏ 665	Without Love/Dance What You Wanna	1965	2.50	5.00	10.00
❏ 698	I Don't Know What You've Got But It's Got Me — Part I/I Don't Know What You've Got But It's Got Me — Part II	1965	2.50	5.00	10.00
WARNER BROS.					
❏ 28491	Big House Reunion/Somebody's Comin'	1987	—	2.00	4.00
WTG					
❏ 08492	Twins (Long)/Twins (Short)	1988	—	2.00	4.00

—*With Philip Bailey*

78s

Number	Title (A Side/B Side)	Yr	VG	VG+	NM
PEACOCK					
❏ 1658	Little Richard's Boogie/Directly from My Heart to You	1956	20.00	40.00	80.00
❏ 1673	Maybe I'm Right/I Love My Baby	1957	12.50	25.00	50.00
RCA VICTOR					
❏ 20-4392	Taxi Blues/Every Hour	1951	75.00	150.00	300.00
❏ 20-4582	Get Rich Quick/Thinkin' 'Bout My Mother	1952	62.50	125.00	250.00
❏ 20-4772	Why Did You Leave Me?/Ain't Nothin' Happenin'	1952	62.50	125.00	250.00
❏ 20-5025	Please Have Mercy on Me/I Brought It All on Myself	1952	62.50	125.00	250.00
SPECIALTY					
❏ 561	Tutti-Frutti/I'm Just a Lonely Guy	1955	10.00	20.00	40.00
❏ 572	Long Tall Sally/Slippin' and Slidin' (Peepin' and Hidin')	1956	10.00	20.00	40.00
❏ 579	Rip It Up/Ready Teddy	1956	10.00	20.00	40.00
❏ 584	Heebie-Jeebies/She's Got it	1956	10.00	20.00	40.00
❏ 591	The Girl Can't Help It/All Around the World	1956	10.00	20.00	40.00
❏ 598	Lucille/Send Me Some Lovin'	1957	10.00	20.00	40.00
❏ 606	Jenny, Jenny/Miss Ann	1957	10.00	20.00	40.00
❏ 611	Keep a Knockin'/Can't Believe You Wanna Leave	1957	10.00	20.00	40.00
❏ 624	Good Golly, Miss Molly/Hey-Hey-Hey-Hey!	1958	10.00	20.00	40.00
❏ 633	Ooh! My Soul/True, Fine Mama	1958	10.00	20.00	40.00

7-Inch Extended Plays

Number	Title (A Side/B Side)	Yr	VG	VG+	NM
RCA CAMDEN					
❏ CAE-416	Ain't Nothin' Happenin'/Why Did You Leave Me//Every Hour/I Brought It All on Myself	1955	37.50	75.00	150.00
❏ CAE-416 [PS]	Little Richard	1955	37.50	75.00	150.00
❏ CAE-446	Taxi Blues/Please Have Mercy on Me//Get Rich Quick/Thinkin' 'Bout My Mother	1956	25.00	50.00	100.00
❏ CAE-446 [PS]	Little Richard Rocks	1956	25.00	50.00	100.00
SPECIALTY					
❏ SEP-400	Long Tall Sally/Miss Ann//She's Got It/Can't Believe You Wanna Leave	1957	25.00	50.00	100.00
❏ SEP-400 [PS]	Here's Little Richard	1957	25.00	50.00	100.00
❏ SEP-401	Slippin' and Slidin'/Oh Why//Ready Teddy/Baby	1957	25.00	50.00	100.00
❏ SEP-401 [PS]	Here's Little Richard	1957	25.00	50.00	100.00
❏ SEP-402	Tutti-Frutti/True, Fine Mama//Rip It Up/Jenny, Jenny	1957	25.00	50.00	100.00
❏ SEP-402 [PS]	Here's Little Richard	1957	25.00	50.00	100.00
❏ SEP-403	Keep a Knockin'/By the Light of the Silvery Moon//Lucille/Hey-Hey-Hey-Hey	1958	20.00	40.00	80.00
❏ SEP-403 [PS]	Little Richard	1958	20.00	40.00	80.00
❏ SEP-404	Ooh! My Soul/All Around the World//Good Golly, Miss Molly/Babyface	1958	20.00	40.00	80.00
❏ SEP-404 [PS]	Little Richard	1958	20.00	40.00	80.00
❏ SEP-405	(contents unknown)	1958	20.00	40.00	80.00
❏ SEP-405 [PS]	Little Richard	1958	20.00	40.00	80.00

Number	Title (A Side/B Side)	Yr	VG	VG+	NM
Albums					
20TH FOX					
❏ FXG-5010 [M] Little Richard Sings Gospel		1959	25.00	50.00	100.00
❏ SGM-5010 [S] Little Richard Sings Gospel		1959	37.50	75.00	150.00
ACCORD					
❏ SN-7123	Tutti Frutti	1981	2.50	5.00	10.00
AUDIO ENCORES					
❏ 1002	Little Richard	1980	6.25	12.50	25.00
BUDDAH					
❏ BDS-7501	Little Richard	1969	7.50	15.00	30.00
CORAL					
❏ CRL 57446 [M] Coming Home		1963	10.00	20.00	40.00
❏ CRL 757446 [S] Coming Home		1963	12.50	25.00	50.00
CROWN					
❏ CLP-5362 [M] Little Richard Sings Freedom Songs		1963	5.00	10.00	20.00
CUSTOM					
❏ 2061 [M]	Little Richard Sings Spirituals	196?	3.00	6.00	12.00
EPIC					
❏ EG 30428 [(2)] Cast a Long Shadow		1971	5.00	10.00	20.00
❏ PE 40389	Little Richard's Greatest Hits	1986	2.50	5.00	10.00
❏ PE 40390	The Explosive Little Richard	1986	2.50	5.00	10.00
EXACT					
❏ 206	The Best of Little Richard	1980	2.50	5.00	10.00
GNP CRESCENDO					
❏ GNP-9033	The Big Hits	1974	3.00	6.00	12.00
GRT					
❏ 2103	The Original Little Richard	1977	2.50	5.00	10.00
GUEST STAR					
❏ GS-1429 [M] Little Richard with Sister Rosetta Tharpe		196?	3.00	6.00	12.00
❏ GSS-1429 [R] Little Richard with Sister Rosetta Tharpe		196?	3.00	6.00	12.00
KAMA SUTRA					
❏ KSBS-2023	Little Richard	1970	6.25	12.50	25.00
MERCURY					
❏ MG-20656 [M] It's Real		1961	12.50	25.00	50.00
❏ SR-60656 [S] It's Real		1961	15.00	30.00	60.00
MODERN					
❏ 100 [M]	His Greatest Hits/Recorded Live	1966	5.00	10.00	20.00
❏ 103 [M]	The Explosive Little Richard	1966	5.00	10.00	20.00
❏ 1000 [S]	His Greatest Hits/Recorded Live	1966	6.25	12.50	25.00
❏ 1003 [S]	The Explosive Little Richard	1966	6.25	12.50	25.00
OKEH					
❏ OKM 12117 [M] The Explosive Little Richard		1967	6.25	12.50	25.00
❏ OKM 12121 [M] Little Richard's Greatest Hits		1967	6.25	12.50	25.00
❏ OKS 14117 [S] The Explosive Little Richard		1967	5.00	10.00	20.00
❏ OKS 14121 [S] Little Richard's Greatest Hits		1967	5.00	10.00	20.00
PICKWICK					
❏ SPC-3258	King of the Gospel Singers	197?	2.50	5.00	10.00
RCA CAMDEN					
❏ CAL-420 [M]	Little Richard	1956	50.00	100.00	200.00
❏ CAS-2430(e)	Every Hour with Little Richard	1970	3.00	6.00	12.00
REPRISE					
❏ MS 2107	The Second Coming	1973	5.00	10.00	20.00
❏ RS 6406	The Rill Thing	1971	5.00	10.00	20.00
❏ RS 6462	King of Rock and Roll	1972	5.00	10.00	20.00
RHINO					
❏ R1-70236	Shut Up! A Collection of Rare Tracks, 1951-1964	1988	3.00	6.00	12.00
SCEPTER					
❏ CTN-18020	The Best of Little Richard	1972	3.00	6.00	12.00
SPECIALTY					
❏ 100 [M]	Here's Little Richard	1957	175.00	350.00	700.00
❏ SP-2100 [M]	Here's Little Richard	1957	50.00	100.00	200.00
—*Thick vinyl*					
❏ SP-2103 [M]	Little Richard	1958	37.50	75.00	150.00
—*Front cover photo occupies the entire cover*					
❏ SP-2103 [M]	Little Richard	196?	25.00	50.00	100.00
—*Front cover photo partially obscured by a black triangle at uper right; thick vinyl*					
❏ SP-2103 [M]	Little Richard	197?	5.00	10.00	20.00
—*Reissue with thinner vinyl*					
❏ SP-2104 [M]	The Fabulous Little Richard	1958	37.50	75.00	150.00
—*Thick vinyl*					
❏ SP-2104 [M]	The Fabulous Little Richard	197?	5.00	10.00	20.00
—*Reissue with thinner vinyl*					
❏ SP-2111	Little Richard — His Biggest Hits	1963	12.50	25.00	50.00
—*Thick vinyl*					
❏ SP-2111 [M]	Little Richard — His Biggest Hits	197?	5.00	10.00	20.00
—*Reissue with thinner vinyl*					
❏ SP-2113	Little Richard's Grooviest 17 Original Hits	1968	6.25	12.50	25.00
—*Thick vinyl*					
❏ SP-2136	Well Alright!	1970	5.00	10.00	20.00
❏ SP-8508 [(5)]	The Specialty Sessions	1989	10.00	20.00	40.00
SPIN-O-RAMA					
❏ 119 [M]	Clap Your Hands	196?	3.00	6.00	12.00
TRIP					
❏ 8013 [(2)]	Greatest Hits	1972	3.00	6.00	12.00
UNITED					
❏ US-7775	His Greatest Hits/Recorded Live	197?	2.50	5.00	10.00
❏ US-7777	The Wild and Frantic Little Richard	197?	2.50	5.00	10.00
UNITED ARTISTS					
❏ UA-LA497-E	The Very Best of Little Richard	1975	2.50	5.00	10.00
UPFRONT					
❏ UPF-123	The Best of Little Richard	197?	2.50	5.00	10.00
❏ UPF-197	Little Richard Sings Gospel	197?	2.50	5.00	10.00

L

Number	Title (A Side/B Side)	Yr	VG	VG+	NM
VEE JAY					
❑ LP-1107 [M]	Little Richard Is Back!	1964	12.50	25.00	50.00
❑ LPS-1107 [S]	Little Richard Is Back!	1964	17.50	35.00	70.00
❑ VJLP-1107	Little Richard's Back	198?	2.50	5.00	10.00
—Reissue with thin vinyl					
❑ LP-1124 [M]	Little Richard's Greatest Hits	1965	6.25	12.50	25.00
❑ LPS-1124 [S]	Little Richard's Greatest Hits	1965	10.00	20.00	40.00
❑ VJLP-1124	Little Richard's Greatest Hits	198?	2.50	5.00	10.00
—Reissue with thin vinyl					
❑ DY-7304	Talkin' 'Bout Soul	198?	3.00	6.00	12.00
VEE JAY/CHAMELEON					
❑ D1-74797	Rip It Up	1989	3.00	6.00	12.00
WING					
❑ MGW-12288 [M]	King of the Gospel Singers	1964	3.75	7.50	15.00
❑ SRW-16288 [S]	King of the Gospel Singers	1964	5.00	10.00	20.00

LITTLE WALTER

Number	Title (A Side/B Side)	Yr	VG	VG+	NM
45s					
CHANCE					
❑ 1116	That's All Right/Just Keep Loving Her	1952	1000.	2000.	3000.
—As "Little Walter J."					
CHECKER					
❑ 758	Juke/Can't Hold On Much Longer	1952	50.00	100.00	200.00
❑ 764	Mean Old World/Sad Hours	1952	30.00	60.00	120.00
❑ 767	Don't Have to Hunt No More/Tonight with a Fool	1953	20.00	40.00	80.00
❑ 770	Off the Wall/Tell Me Mama	1953	20.00	40.00	80.00
—Black vinyl					
❑ 770	Off the Wall/Tell Me Mama	1953	750.00	1500.	3000.
—Red vinyl					
❑ 780	Blues with a Feeling/Quarter to Twelve	1953	25.00	50.00	100.00
❑ 786	Lights Out/You're So Fine	1953	12.50	25.00	50.00
❑ 793	Oh Baby/Rocker	1954	10.00	20.00	40.00
❑ 799	You'd Better Watch Yourself/Blue Light	1954	10.00	20.00	40.00
—Black vinyl					
❑ 799	You'd Better Watch Yourself/Blue Light	1954	25.00	50.00	100.00
—Red vinyl					
❑ 805	Last Night/Mellow Down Easy	1954	15.00	30.00	60.00
❑ 811	My Babe/Thunder Bird	1955	10.00	20.00	40.00
❑ 817	Roller Coaster/I Got to Go	1955	10.00	20.00	40.00
❑ 825	Too Late/I Hate to See You Go	1955	10.00	20.00	40.00
❑ 833	Who/It Ain't Right	1956	10.00	20.00	40.00
❑ 838	Flying Saucer/One More Chance with You	1956	10.00	20.00	40.00
❑ 845	Teenage Beat/What a Feeling	1956	10.00	20.00	40.00
❑ 852	It's Too Late Brother/Take Me Back	1957	10.00	20.00	40.00
❑ 859	Everybody Needs Somebody/Nobody But You	1957	10.00	20.00	40.00
❑ 867	Boom, Boom — Out Goes the Light/Temperature	1957	10.00	20.00	40.00
❑ 890	The Toddle/Confessin' the Blues	1958	7.50	15.00	30.00
❑ 904	Key to the Highway/Rock Bottom	1958	7.50	15.00	30.00
❑ 919	My Baby's Sweeter/Crazy Mixed-Up World	1959	6.25	12.50	25.00
❑ 930	Everything's Gonna Be All Right/Back Track	1959	6.25	12.50	25.00
❑ 938	Break It Up/Me and Piney Brown	1960	5.00	10.00	20.00
❑ 945	Ah'w Baby/I Had My Fun	1960	5.00	10.00	20.00
❑ 955	My Babe/Blue Midnight	1960	5.00	10.00	20.00
❑ 968	I Don't Play/As Long As I Have You	1961	5.00	10.00	20.00
❑ 986	Crazy Legs/Crazy for My Baby	1961	5.00	10.00	20.00
❑ 1013	Just You Fool/I Got to Find My Baby	1962	3.75	7.50	15.00
❑ 1043	Up the Line/Southern Feeling	1963	3.75	7.50	15.00
❑ 1071	Diggin' My Potatoes/Snake Dancer	1964	3.75	7.50	15.00
❑ 1081	Dead Presidents/I'm a Business Man	1964	3.75	7.50	15.00
❑ 1117	Mean Ole Frisco/Blue and Lonesome	1965	3.75	7.50	15.00
78s					
CHANCE					
❑ 1116	That's All Right/Just Keep Loving Her	1952	125.00	250.00	500.00
—As "Little Walter J."					
CHECKER					
❑ 758	Juke/Can't Hold On Much Longer	1952	30.00	60.00	120.00
❑ 764	Mean Old World/Sad Hours	1952	12.50	25.00	50.00
❑ 767	Don't Have to Hunt No More/Tonight with a Fool	1953	12.50	25.00	50.00
❑ 770	Off the Wall/Tell Me Mama	1953	12.50	25.00	50.00
❑ 780	Blues with a Feeling/Quarter to Twelve	1953	12.50	25.00	50.00
❑ 786	Lights Out/You're So Fine	1953	10.00	20.00	40.00
❑ 793	Oh Baby/Rocker	1954	10.00	20.00	40.00
❑ 799	You'd Better Watch Yourself/Blue Light	1954	10.00	20.00	40.00
❑ 805	Last Night/Mellow Down Easy	1954	10.00	20.00	40.00
❑ 811	My Babe/Thunder Bird	1955	10.00	20.00	40.00
❑ 817	Roller Coaster/I Got to Go	1955	10.00	20.00	40.00
❑ 825	Too Late/I Hate to See You Go	1955	10.00	20.00	40.00
❑ 833	Who/It Ain't Right	1956	12.50	25.00	50.00
❑ 838	Flying Saucer/One More Chance with You	1956	12.50	25.00	50.00
❑ 845	Teenage Beat/What a Feeling	1956	12.50	25.00	50.00
❑ 852	It's Too Late Brother/Take Me Back	1957	12.50	25.00	50.00
❑ 859	Everybody Needs Somebody/Nobody But You	1957	12.50	25.00	50.00
❑ 867	Boom, Boom — Out Goes the Light/Temperature	1957	12.50	25.00	50.00
❑ 890	The Toddle/Confessin' the Blues	1958	15.00	30.00	60.00
❑ 904	Key to the Highway/Rock Bottom	1958	25.00	50.00	100.00
ORA NELLE					
❑ 711	Ora-Nelle Blues/I Just Keep Loving Her	1947	200.00	400.00	800.00
—Credited to "Little Walter J.--Harmonica; Othum Brown---Guitar"					
REGAL					
❑ 3296	Muscadine Blues/Bad Acting Woman	1950	2000.	3500.	5000.
Albums					
CHECKER					
❑ LP-1428 [M]	The Best of Little Walter	1957	125.00	250.00	500.00
—Black or maroon label					
❑ LP-3004 [M]	The Best of Little Walter	1967	12.50	25.00	50.00
—Reissue of 1428					
CHESS					
❑ 2ACMB-202 [(2)]	Little Walter	1976	5.00	10.00	20.00
—Reissue of 60014					
❑ CHV-416 [M]	Confessin' the Blues	1974	3.00	6.00	12.00
❑ LP-1535 [M]	Hate to See You Go	1969	6.25	12.50	25.00
❑ 2CH-60014 [(2)]	Boss Blues Harmonica	1972	5.00	10.00	20.00

LITTLEFIELD, LITTLE WILLIE

Number	Title (A Side/B Side)	Yr	VG	VG+	NM
45s					
BULLSEYE					
❑ 1005	Ruby-Ruby/Easy Go	1958	7.50	15.00	30.00
FEDERAL					
❑ 12101	Sticking on You Baby/Blood Is Redder Than Wine	1952	25.00	50.00	100.00
❑ 12110	K.C. Loving/Pleading at Midnight	1953	25.00	50.00	100.00
❑ 12137	The Midnight Hour Was Shining/My Best Wishes and Regards	1953	25.00	50.00	100.00
❑ 12148	Miss K.C.'s Fine/Rock-a-Bye Baby	1953	25.00	50.00	100.00
❑ 12163	Please Don't Go-o-o-o-oh/Don't Take My Heart Little Girl	1954	20.00	40.00	80.00
❑ 12174	Goofy Dust Blues/Falling Tears	1954	20.00	40.00	80.00
❑ 12221	Jim Wilson's Boogie/Sitting on the Curbstone	1955	15.00	30.00	60.00
❑ 12351	Kansas City/Midnight Hour Was Shining	1959	7.50	15.00	30.00
RHYTHM					
❑ 107	Baby Shame/Mistreated	1956	37.50	75.00	150.00
❑ 108	Ruby-Ruby/Easy Go	1956	37.50	75.00	150.00
❑ 115	I Need a Pay Day/I Want a Little Girl	195?	25.00	50.00	100.00
❑ 124	Theresa/The Day the Rains Came	195?	20.00	40.00	80.00
❑ 130	I Wanna Love You/Goodbye Baby	195?	20.00	40.00	80.00

LOLLIPOPS, THE (1)

Number	Title (A Side/B Side)	Yr	VG	VG+	NM
45s					
ATCO					
❑ 6787	Nothing's Gonna Stop Our Love/I Believe in Love	1970	—	3.00	6.00
GORDY					
❑ 7089	Cheating Is Telling On You/Need Your Love	1969	200.00	400.00	800.00
IMPACT					
❑ 1021	Lovin' Good Feelin'/Step Aside Baby	1967	7.50	15.00	30.00
V.I.P.					
❑ 25051	Cheating Is Telling On You/Need Your Love	1968	6.25	12.50	25.00

LONG, SHORTY (1)

Number	Title (A Side/B Side)	Yr	VG	VG+	NM
45s					
SOUL					
❑ 35001	Devil with the Blue Dress/Wind It Up	1964	6.25	12.50	25.00
❑ 35005	It's a Crying Shame/Out to Get You	1964	6.25	12.50	25.00
❑ 35021	Function at the Junction/Call On Me	1966	3.75	7.50	15.00
❑ 35031	Chantilly Lace/Your Love Is Amazing	1966	3.75	7.50	15.00
❑ 35040	Night Fo' Last/(Instrumental)	1968	2.50	5.00	10.00
❑ 35044	Here Comes the Judge/Sing What You Wanna	1968	2.50	5.00	10.00
❑ 35054	I Had a Dream/Ain't No Justice	1969	2.50	5.00	10.00
❑ 35064	A Whiter Shade of Pale/When You Are Available	1969	2.50	5.00	10.00
TRI-PHI					
❑ 1006	I'll Be There/Bad Willie	1962	12.50	25.00	50.00
❑ 1015	Too Smart/I'll Be There	1962	17.50	35.00	70.00
❑ 1021	What's the Matter/Going Away	1963	15.00	30.00	60.00
Albums					
SOUL					
❑ SS-709	Here Comes the Judge	1968	5.00	10.00	20.00
❑ SS-719	The Prime of Shorty Long	1969	3.75	7.50	15.00

LOVE, DARLENE

Also see THE BLOSSOMS; THE CRYSTALS.

Number	Title (A Side/B Side)	Yr	VG	VG+	NM
45s					
ARISTA					
❑ 74621 124767	All Alone on Christmas/(Instrumental)	1992	—	2.50	5.00
❑ 74621 124767 [PS]	All Alone on Christmas/(Instrumental)	1992	—	2.50	5.00
—45 and sleeve released only in Europe					
COLUMBIA					
❑ 07984	He's Sure the Man I Love/Everybody Needs	1988	—	2.50	5.00
ELEKTRA					
❑ 69647	River Deep, Mountain High/Leader of the Pack	1985	—	2.00	4.00
—B-side by Leader of the Pack					
❑ 69647 [PS]	River Deep, Mountain High/Leader of the Pack	1985	—	2.00	4.00
PASSPORT					
❑ 7926	Christmas (Baby Please Come Home)/Playing for Keeps	1983	3.00	6.00	12.00
PHILLES					
❑ 111	(Today I Met) The Boy I'm Gonna Marry/My Heart Beat a Little Bit Faster	1963	7.50	15.00	30.00
❑ 111	(Today I Met) The Boy I'm Gonna Marry/Playing for Keeps	1963	5.00	10.00	20.00
❑ 114	Wait 'Til My Bobby Gets Home/Take It From Me	1963	5.00	10.00	20.00
❑ 117	A Fine Fine Boy/Nino & Sonny (Big Trouble)	1963	5.00	10.00	20.00
❑ 119	Christmas (Baby Please Come Home)/Harry and Milt Meet Hal B.	1963	10.00	20.00	40.00
❑ 123	Stumble and Fall/(He's a) Quiet Guy	1964	200.00	400.00	800.00
—Yellow and red label stock copy; has been verified to exist					
❑ 123	Stumble and Fall/(He's a) Quiet Guy	1964	75.00	150.00	300.00
—Yellow and red label, "D.J. Copy Not for Sale" on label					

Composed by the second Sonny Boy Williamson, "Eyesight to the Blind" was a top-5 R&B hit by the East Coast group The Larks in 1951.

Barbara Lewis' second album, *Snap Your Fingers*, features mostly remakes of slightly older soul hits.

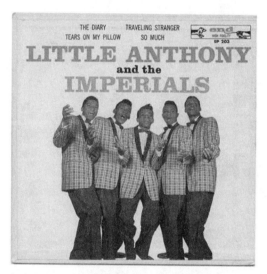

As is true with most R&B-oriented EPs of the 1950s, this one by Little Anthony and the Imperials on End is very hard to find, especially with its cover intact.

Little Eva's only album, based around the hit "The Loco-Motion," mostly consisted of covers of current hits. A later edition added the song "Keep Your Hands Off My Baby."

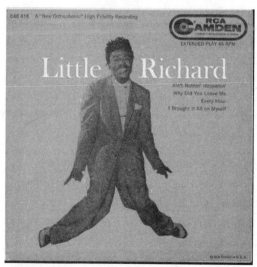

When he became popular on Specialty, RCA compiled some of Little Richard's early-1950s recordings into EPs in hopes of getting some reflected sales. This is one of them.

Blues singer Little Walter was only 17 when his made "Ora-Nelle Blues," his debut single, which came out in 1947

Number	Title (A Side/B Side)	Yr	VG	VG+	NM
❏ 123 [DJ]	Stumble and Fall/(He's a) Quiet Guy	1964	37.50	75.00	150.00
—White label promo					
❏ 125X	Christmas (Baby Please Come Home)/Winter Wonderland	1965	6.25	12.50	25.00
❏ 125	Christmas (Baby Please Come Home)/X-Mas Blues	1964	100.00	200.00	400.00
REPRISE					
❏ 0534	Too Late to Say You're Sorry/If	1966	2.50	5.00	10.00
WARNER/SPECTOR					
❏ 0401	Christmas (Baby Please Come Home)/Winter Wonderland	1974	2.50	5.00	10.00
❏ 0410	Lord, If You're a Woman/Stumble and Fall	1975	2.50	5.00	10.00
Albums					
COLUMBIA					
❏ FC 40605	Paint Another Picture	1988	3.00	6.00	12.00

LOVE, HOT SHOT
45s
SUN

Number	Title (A Side/B Side)	Yr	VG	VG+	NM
❏ 196	Wolf Call Boogie/Harmonica Jam	1954	1000.	2000.	4000.

78s
SUN

Number	Title (A Side/B Side)	Yr	VG	VG+	NM
❏ 196	Wolf Call Boogie/Harmonica Jam	1954	125.00	250.00	500.00

LOVE CHILDS AFRO CUBAN BLUES BAND
12-Inch Singles
MIDSONG INT'L.

Number	Title (A Side/B Side)	Yr	VG	VG+	NM
❏ MD-10983	Oye Como Va (9:56)/Medley: Spanish Harlem-Dancin' to Spandisco	1977	3.00	6.00	12.00

45s
ROULETTE

Number	Title (A Side/B Side)	Yr	VG	VG+	NM
❏ 7172	Life and Death in G & A/Bang Bang	1975	—	2.50	5.00
❏ 7180	Black Skin Blue Eyed Boys/Ask Me	1975	—	2.50	5.00

Albums
MIDSONG INT'L.

Number	Title (A Side/B Side)	Yr	VG	VG+	NM
❏ BKL1-2292	Spandisco	1977	2.50	5.00	10.00

ROULETTE

Number	Title (A Side/B Side)	Yr	VG	VG+	NM
❏ 3016	Out Among 'Em	1975	2.50	5.00	10.00

LOVE NOTES, THE (1)
45s
HOLIDAY

Number	Title (A Side/B Side)	Yr	VG	VG+	NM
❏ 2605	United/Tonight	1957	15.00	30.00	60.00
—Glossy label					
❏ 2605	United/Tonight	1957	5.00	10.00	20.00
—Flat (matte) label					
❏ 2607	If I Could Make You Mine/Don't Go	1957	10.00	20.00	40.00

LOVE NOTES, THE (2)
45s
IMPERIAL

Number	Title (A Side/B Side)	Yr	VG	VG+	NM
❏ 5254	Surrender Your Heart/Get On My Train	1953	300.00	600.00	1200.
RAINBOW					
❏ 266	I'm Sorry/Sweet Lulu	1954	75.00	150.00	300.00
RIVIERA					
❏ 970	I'm Sorry/Sweet Lulu	1954	200.00	400.00	800.00
❏ 975	Since I Fell for You/Don't Be No Fool	1954	250.00	500.00	1000.
—Authentic copies have a lavender (light purple) label, counterfeits have a pink label					

LOVE NOTES, THE (3)
45s
WILSHIRE

Number	Title (A Side/B Side)	Yr	VG	VG+	NM
❏ 200	Nancy/Our Songs of Love	1963	10.00	20.00	40.00
❏ 203	Gloria/The Mathematics of Love	1963	25.00	50.00	100.00

LOVE, PEACE AND HAPPINESS
Also see THE NEW BIRTH; THE NITE-LITERS.
45s
RCA VICTOR

Number	Title (A Side/B Side)	Yr	VG	VG+	NM
❏ 74-0402	Don't Blame the Young Folks for the Drug Society/You've Got to Be the One for Me	1970	—	3.00	6.00
❏ 74-0468	Message to the Establishment/Love Is Far Stronger Than We	1971	—	2.50	5.00
❏ 74-0584	Strip Me Naked/Unborn Child	1971	—	2.50	5.00
❏ 74-0740	I Don't Want to Do Wrong/Lonely Room	1972	—	2.50	5.00

Albums
RCA VICTOR

Number	Title (A Side/B Side)	Yr	VG	VG+	NM
❏ LSP-4535	Love Is Stronger	1971	3.00	6.00	12.00
❏ LSP-4721	Here 'Tis	1972	3.00	6.00	12.00

LOVE UNLIMITED
12-Inch Singles
UNLIMITED GOLD

Number	Title (A Side/B Side)	Yr	VG	VG+	NM
❏ 1410	High Steppin', Hip Dressin' Fella (You Got It Together)/(Instrumental)	1979	3.00	6.00	12.00

45s
20TH CENTURY

Number	Title (A Side/B Side)	Yr	VG	VG+	NM
❏ 2025	Oh Love, Well We Finally Made It/Yes, We Finally Made It	1973	—	2.50	5.00
❏ 2062	It May Be Winter Outside (But In My Heart It's Spring)/It's Winter Again	1973	—	2.50	5.00
❏ 2082	Under the Influence of Love/(Instrumental)	1974	—	2.50	5.00

Number	Title (A Side/B Side)	Yr	VG	VG+	NM
❏ 2110	People of Tomorrow Are the Children of Today/So Nice to Hear	1974	—	2.50	5.00
❏ 2141	I Belong to You/And Only You	1974	—	2.50	5.00
❏ 2183	Share a Little Love in Your Heart/I Love You So, Never Gonna Let You Go	1975	—	2.50	5.00
MCA					
❏ 40009	Fragile/I'll Be Yours Forever	1973	—	3.00	6.00
UNI					
❏ 55319	Walkin' in the Rain with the One I Love/I Should Have Known	1972	—	3.00	6.00
❏ 55342	Is It Really True Boy — Is It Really Me?/Another Chance	1972	—	3.00	6.00
❏ 55349	Are You Really Sure/Another Chance	1972	—	3.00	6.00
UNLIMITED GOLD					
❏ 1409	High Steppin', Hip Dressin' Fella (You Got It Together)/(Instrumental)	1979	—	2.50	5.00
❏ 1412	I'm So Glad That I'm a Woman/Gotta Be Where You Are	1980	—	2.50	5.00
❏ 1417	If You Want Me, Say It/When I'm In Your Arms, Everything's Okay	1980	—	2.50	5.00
❏ 7001	I Did It for Love/(Instrumental)	1977	—	2.50	5.00

Albums
20TH CENTURY

Number	Title (A Side/B Side)	Yr	VG	VG+	NM
❏ T-414	Under the Influence of…	1973	2.50	5.00	10.00
❏ T-443	In Heat	1974	2.50	5.00	10.00
MCA					
❏ 181	Love Unlimited	1973	3.00	6.00	12.00
—Reissue of Uni 73131					
❏ 316	Under the Influence of…	1973	—	—	—
—Canceled; issued on 20th Century 414					
UNI					
❏ 73131	Love Unlimited	1972	3.75	7.50	15.00
UNLIMITED GOLD					
❏ 101	He's All I Got	1977	2.50	5.00	10.00
❏ JZ 36130	Love Is Back	1979	2.50	5.00	10.00

LOVE UNLIMITED ORCHESTRA
12-Inch Singles
20TH CENTURY

Number	Title (A Side/B Side)	Yr	VG	VG+	NM
❏ TCD-61	Theme from King Kong/Blues Concerto	1976	3.75	7.50	15.00
❏ TCD-66	Don't You Know How Much I Love You/Hey Look at Me, I'm in Love	1978	3.75	7.50	15.00
UNLIMITED GOLD					
❏ 1406	Jamaican Girl/I'm in the Mood	1979	3.00	6.00	12.00
❏ 1414	Young America/Freeway Flyer	1980	3.00	6.00	12.00
❏ 02135	Lift Your Voice and Say (United We Can Live in Peace Today)/My Fantasies	1981	2.50	5.00	10.00
❏ 02479	Welcome Aboard/Strange	1981	2.50	5.00	10.00
❏ 02636	Night Life in the City/Wind	1981	2.50	5.00	10.00
❏ 03882	My Laboratory Is Ready for You/Goodbye Concerto	1983	2.50	5.00	10.00

45s
20TH CENTURY

Number	Title (A Side/B Side)	Yr	VG	VG+	NM
❏ 2069	Love's Theme/Sweet Moments	1973	—	2.50	5.00
❏ 2090	Rhapsody in White/Barry's Theme	1974	—	2.50	5.00
❏ 2107	Theme from "Together Brothers"/Find the Man Brothers	1974	—	2.50	5.00
❏ 2145	Baby Blues/What a Groove	1974	—	2.50	5.00
❏ 2162	Satin Soul/Just Living It Up	1975	—	2.50	5.00
❏ 2197	Forever in Love/Only You Can Make Me Blue	1975	—	2.50	5.00
❏ 2281	Midnight Groove/It's Only What I Feel	1976	—	2.50	5.00
❏ 2301	My Sweet Summer Suite/Just Living It Up	1976	—	2.50	5.00
❏ 2325	Theme from King Kong (Pt. 1)/Theme from King Kong (Pt. 2)	1977	—	2.50	5.00
❏ 2348	Brazilian Love Song/My Sweet Summer Suite	1977	—	2.50	5.00
❏ 2364	Whisper Softly/Hey Look at Me, I'm in Love	1978	—	2.50	5.00
❏ 2367	Don't You Know How Much I Love You/Hey Look at Me, I'm in Love	1978	—	2.50	5.00
❏ 2399	Theme from "Superman"/Theme from "Shaft"	1978	—	2.50	5.00
UNLIMITED GOLD					
❏ 1405	Jamaican Girl/I'm in the Mood	1979	—	2.50	5.00
❏ 1413	Young America/Freeway Flyer	1980	—	2.50	5.00
❏ 1421	I Wanna Boogie and Woogie with You/I'm in the Mood	1980	—	2.50	5.00
❏ 1423	Vieni Qua Bella Mi/Bayou	1980	—	2.50	5.00
❏ 02134	Lift Your Voice and Say (United We Can Live in Peace Today)/My Fantasies	1981	—	2.00	4.00
❏ 02478	Welcome Aboard/Strange	1981	—	2.00	4.00
❏ 02635	Night Life in the City/Wind	1981	—	2.00	4.00
❏ 03881	My Laboratory Is Ready for You/Goodbye Concerto	1983	—	2.00	4.00

Albums
20TH CENTURY

Number	Title (A Side/B Side)	Yr	VG	VG+	NM
❏ T-101	Together Brothers	1974	3.00	6.00	12.00
❏ T-433	Rhapsody in White	1974	2.50	5.00	10.00
❏ T-458	White Gold	1974	2.50	5.00	10.00
❏ T-480	Music Maestro Please	1975	2.50	5.00	10.00
❏ T-517	My Sweet Summer Suite	1976	2.50	5.00	10.00
❏ T-554	My Musical Bouquet	1978	2.50	5.00	10.00
❏ T-582	Movie Themes	1978	2.50	5.00	10.00
UNLIMITED GOLD					
❏ FZ 37425	Welcome Aboard	1981	2.50	5.00	10.00
❏ FZ 38366	Rise	1983	2.50	5.00	10.00

LOVERS, THE (1)

Husband-and-wife R&B duo.

45s

Number	Title (A Side/B Side)	Yr	VG	VG+	NM
ALADDIN					
❑ 3419	Tell Me/Love Bug Bit Me	1958	10.00	20.00	40.00
IMPERIAL					
❑ 5845	Darling It's Wonderful/I Want to Be Loved	1962	5.00	10.00	20.00
❑ 5960	Tell Me/Let's Elope	1963	5.00	10.00	20.00
❑ 66055	Darling It's Wonderful/I Want to Be Loved	1964	3.75	7.50	15.00
LAMP					
❑ 2005	Darling It's Wonderful/Gotta Whole Lot of Livin' to Do	1957	12.50	25.00	50.00
❑ 2013	I Wanna Be Loved/Let's Elope	1957	12.50	25.00	50.00
❑ 2018	Tell Me/Love Bug Bit Me	1958	12.50	25.00	50.00
POST					
❑ 10007	Darling It's Wonderful/Gotta Whole Lot of Livin' to Do	1963	3.75	7.50	15.00

LUKE

Also see THE 2 LIVE CREW.

12-Inch Singles

Number	Title (A Side/B Side)	Yr	VG	VG+	NM
LUKE					
❑ 215	I Wanna Rock (5 versions)	1992	2.50	5.00	10.00
❑ 216	Breakdown (Nasty Mix) (Rave Mix) (Radio Mix)/Ain't That a Bitch	1992	2.00	4.00	8.00
❑ 217	Breakdown (Radio Mix) (Rave Mix) (DJ Laz Boomin Bass Mix) (Nasty Mix) (Radio Rave Mix)/Wake Up America Part I & II/Ain't That a Bitch	1992	2.00	4.00	8.00
❑ 233	You & Me (3 versions)/Head, Head and More Head (3 versions)	1993	3.00	6.00	12.00
❑ 458	You & Me (3 versions)/Head, Head and More Head (3 versions)	1993	3.75	7.50	15.00
❑ 466	Cowards in Compton (6 versions)/Once a Punk, Always a Punk (Dirty Version)	1993	2.50	5.00	10.00
❑ 468	Work It Out (9 versions)	1993	2.50	5.00	10.00
❑ 474	Hop (9 versions)/Take It Off	1993	2.00	4.00	8.00
❑ 487	Where Them Ho's At (4 versions)/Where Them Girls At (3 versions)/Megamix	1994	2.00	4.00	8.00
❑ DMD 1780 [DJ]	I Wanna Rock (4 versions)	1992	2.00	4.00	8.00
❑ PR12-7838 [DJ]	Raise the Roof (8 versions)	1998	2.50	5.00	10.00
❑ 572251-1	Raise the Roof (unknown versions)	1998	2.00	4.00	8.00
LUTHER CAMPBELL					
❑ 167001	Bounce to Da Beat (5 versions)	1996	—	3.00	6.00

Albums

Number	Title (A Side/B Side)	Yr	VG	VG+	NM
LIL' JOE					
❑ 260 [(2)]	Luke's Booty Calls & Chants	2000	3.75	7.50	15.00
LUKE					
❑ 200 [(2)]	In the Nude	1993	3.00	6.00	12.00
❑ 201 [(2)]	In the Nude (Edited)	1993	3.75	7.50	15.00
❑ 6996 [(2)]	Freak for Life 6996	1994	3.75	7.50	15.00
—Vinyl may be promo only					
❑ 7694 [(2) DJ]	Changin' the Game	1997	3.75	7.50	15.00
—Vinyl is promo only					
❑ 91830 [(2)]	I Got Shit on My Mind	1992	3.75	7.50	15.00
❑ 91842 [(2)]	I Got Sumthin' on My Mind	1992	3.75	7.50	15.00
—Clean version of 91830					
LUTHER CAMPBELL					
❑ 161000-1 [(2)]	Uncle Luke	1996	3.00	6.00	12.00

LUTCHER, JOE

78s

Number	Title (A Side/B Side)	Yr	VG	VG+	NM
CAPITOL					
❑ 15109	How Fine Can You Be?/Mo-Jo Stomp	1948	3.75	7.50	15.00
❑ 15170	Bagdad Bebop/Toodle-Oo	1948	3.75	7.50	15.00
❑ 15297	Joe-Joe Jump/Walk Into My Heart	1948	3.75	7.50	15.00
❑ 15361	Lucky Lindy Boogie/Sauterne Special	1949	3.75	7.50	15.00
❑ 40052	Strato-Cruiser/Sunday Blues	1947	3.75	7.50	15.00
❑ 40071	Shuffle Boogie/Bebop Blues	1948	3.75	7.50	15.00
❑ 40101	No Name Boogie/Hit the Block	1948	3.75	7.50	15.00
MODERN					
❑ 20-661	Rockola/Pasadena Rumboogie	1949	5.00	10.00	20.00
❑ 20-672	Mardi Gras/Ojai	1949	5.00	10.00	20.00
❑ 20-708	Foothill Drive/Joe's Lament	1950	5.00	10.00	20.00
❑ 20-736	Rag Mop/Beige Boom	1950	5.00	10.00	20.00
SPECIALTY					
❑ 303	The Rockin' Boogie/Blues for Sale	1948	5.00	10.00	20.00
—Reissue of Specialty 512					
❑ 304	The Traffic Song/Society Boogie	1948	5.00	10.00	20.00
❑ 512	The Rockin' Boogie/Blues for Sale	1947	6.25	12.50	25.00

LUTCHER, NELLIE

45s

Number	Title (A Side/B Side)	Yr	VG	VG+	NM
CAPITOL					
❑ F798	Little Sally Walker/Only You	1950	7.50	15.00	30.00
—Capitol 45s in the 15000, 40000 and 70000 series are unknown					
❑ F847	For You My Love/Can I Come In for a Second	1950	6.25	12.50	25.00
—With Nat King Cole					
❑ F878	I'll Never Get Tired/That's a Plenty	1950	7.50	15.00	30.00
❑ F1026	Kinda Blue and Low/Lovable	1950	7.50	15.00	30.00
❑ F1217	To Be Forgotten/That'll Just About Knock Me Out	1950	7.50	15.00	30.00
❑ F1420	Pa's Not Home/I Really Couldn't Love You	1951	6.25	12.50	25.00
❑ F1604	Fine Brown Frame/Hurry On Down	1951	6.25	12.50	25.00
—Reissue of early tracks making their first appearance on 45					
❑ F1728	Humoresque/The Song Is Ended	1951	6.25	12.50	25.00
❑ F1789	Birth of the Blues/I Want to Be Near You	1951	6.25	12.50	25.00
❑ F1829	Mean to Me/Let the Worry Bird Worry You	1951	6.25	12.50	25.00
❑ F1978	The Heart of a Clown/What a Difference a Day Made	1952	6.25	12.50	25.00
❑ F2038	That's How It Goes/Keepin' Out of Mischief Now	1952	6.25	12.50	25.00
DECCA					
❑ 9-29464	Please Come Back/It's Been Said	1955	3.75	7.50	15.00
EPIC					
❑ 5-9005	Whee, Baby/Blues for Bill Bailey	1953	5.00	10.00	20.00
LIBERTY					
❑ F-55018	Blue Skies/You Made Me Love You	1956	3.75	7.50	15.00
❑ F-55027	All of a Sudden/Have You Ever Been Lonely	1956	3.75	7.50	15.00
OKEH					
❑ 5-6935	Muchly, Verily/How Many More	1953	7.50	15.00	30.00

78s

Number	Title (A Side/B Side)	Yr	VG	VG+	NM
CAPITOL					
❑ 798	Little Sally Walker/Only You	1950	3.00	6.00	12.00
❑ 847	For You My Love/Can I Come In for a Second	1950	3.00	6.00	12.00
—With Nat King Cole					
❑ 878	I'll Never Get Tired/That's a Plenty	1950	3.00	6.00	12.00
❑ 1026	Kinda Blue and Low/Lovable	1950	3.00	6.00	12.00
❑ 1217	To Be Forgotten/That'll Just About Knock Me Out	1950	3.00	6.00	12.00
❑ 1420	Pa's Not Home/I Really Couldn't Love You	1951	3.00	6.00	12.00
❑ 1728	Humoresque/The Song Is Ended	1951	3.00	6.00	12.00
❑ 1789	Birth of the Blues/I Want to Be Near You	1951	3.00	6.00	12.00
❑ 1829	Mean to Me/Let the Worry Bird Worry You	1951	3.00	6.00	12.00
❑ 1978	The Heart of a Clown/What a Difference a Day Made	1952	3.00	6.00	12.00
❑ 2038	That's How It Goes/Keepin' Out of Mischief Now	1952	3.00	6.00	12.00
❑ 15032	Fine Brown Frame/Let Me Love You Tonight	1948	5.00	10.00	20.00
❑ 15064	Come and Get It, Honey/He Sends Me	1948	3.75	7.50	15.00
❑ 15112	Imagine You Having Eyes for Me/I Thought About You	1948	3.75	7.50	15.00
❑ 15148	Cool Water/Lake Charles Boogie	1948	3.75	7.50	15.00
❑ 15180	Alexander's Ragtime Band/My Little Boy	1948	3.75	7.50	15.00
❑ 15279	Wish I Was in Walla Walla/A Maid's Prayer	1948	3.75	7.50	15.00
❑ 15352	Say a Little Prayer for Me/My New Papa Got to Love Everything	1949	3.75	7.50	15.00
❑ 40002	Hurry On Down/That Lady's in Love with You	1947	3.75	7.50	15.00
❑ 40017	He's a Real Gone Guy/Let Me Love You Tonight	1947	3.75	7.50	15.00
❑ 40042	You Better Watch Yourself, Bub/My Mother's Eyes	1947	3.75	7.50	15.00
❑ 40063	The Song Is Ended (But the Melody Lingers On)/Do You or Don't You Love Me?	1948	3.75	7.50	15.00
❑ 70001	A Chicken Ain't Nothin' But a Bird/Ditto from Me to You	1949	5.00	10.00	20.00
❑ 70009	Kiss Me Sweet/Baby Please Stop and Think About Me	1949	5.00	10.00	20.00
❑ 70026	Fine and Mellow/Princess Poo-Loo-Ly	1949	5.00	10.00	20.00
❑ 70044	Glad Rag Doll/Lutcher's Leap	1949	5.00	10.00	20.00
DECCA					
❑ 29464	Please Come Back/It's Been Said	1955	3.75	7.50	15.00
EPIC					
❑ 9005	Whee, Baby/Blues for Bill Bailey	1953	3.00	6.00	12.00
LIBERTY					
❑ 55018	Blue Skies/You Made Me Love You	1956	5.00	10.00	20.00
❑ 55027	All of a Sudden/Have You Ever Been Lonely	1956	5.00	10.00	20.00
OKEH					
❑ 6935	Muchly, Verily/How Many More	1953	3.75	7.50	15.00

Albums

Number	Title (A Side/B Side)	Yr	VG	VG+	NM
CAPITOL					
❑ H 232 [10]	Real Gone	1950	15.00	30.00	60.00
❑ T 232 [M]	Real Gone	1955	10.00	20.00	40.00
EPIC					
❑ LN 1108 [10]	Whee! Nellie	1955	12.50	25.00	50.00
LIBERTY					
❑ LRP-3014 [M]	Our New Nellie	1956	10.00	20.00	40.00

LYMON, FRANKIE

Also see FRANKIE LYMON AND THE TEENAGERS.

45s

Number	Title (A Side/B Side)	Yr	VG	VG+	NM
BIG KAT					
❑ 7008	I Want You to Be My Girl/Portable on My Shoulder	1968	2.50	5.00	10.00
❑ 7008 [PS]	I Want You to Be My Girl/Portable on My Shoulder	1968	3.00	6.00	12.00
COLUMBIA					
❑ 43094	Somewhere/Sweet and Lovely	1964	12.50	25.00	50.00
GEE					
❑ 1039	Goody Goody/Creation of Love	1957	6.25	12.50	25.00
❑ 1052	I'm Not Too Young to Dream/Goody Good Girl	1959	6.25	12.50	25.00
ROULETTE					
❑ 4026	So Goes My Love/My Girl	1957	6.25	12.50	25.00
❑ 4035	It's Christmas Once Again/Little Girl	1957	6.25	12.50	25.00
❑ 4044	Footsteps/Thumb Thumb	1958	5.00	10.00	20.00
❑ 4068	Mama Don't Allow It/Portable on My Shoulder	1958	5.00	10.00	20.00
❑ 4093	Melinda/The Only Way to Love	1958	5.00	10.00	20.00
❑ 4128	No Matter What You've Done/Up Jumped a Rabbit	1959	5.00	10.00	20.00
❑ 4150	Before I Fall Asleep/What a Little Moonlight Can Do	1959	5.00	10.00	20.00
❑ 4257	Little Bitty Pretty One/Creation of Love	1960	5.00	10.00	20.00
❑ 4283	Buzz, Buzz, Buzz/Waitin' in School	1960	5.00	10.00	20.00
❑ 4310	Jailhouse Rock/Silhouettes	1961	5.00	10.00	20.00
❑ 4348	Change Partners/So Young	1961	5.00	10.00	20.00

Number	Title (A Side/B Side)	Yr	VG	VG+	NM
❑ 4391	I Put the Bomp/So Young	1962	5.00	10.00	20.00
TCF					
❑ 11	Teacher Teacher/To Each His Own	1964	3.75	7.50	15.00
7-Inch Extended Plays					
ROULETTE					
❑ EPR-1-304	Let's Fall in Love/My Baby Just Cares for Me// Goody Goody/Somebody Loves Me	1958	50.00	100.00	200.00
❑ EPR-1-304 [PS]	Frankie Lymon at the London Palladium	1958	50.00	100.00	200.00

LYMON, FRANKIE, AND THE TEENAGERS
Also see FRANKIE LYMON; THE TEENAGERS.

45s

Number	Title (A Side/B Side)	Yr	VG	VG+	NM
GEE					
❑ 1002	Why Do Fools Fall in Love/Please Be Mine	1956	20.00	40.00	80.00
—Red and gold label					
❑ 1002	Why Do Fools Fall in Love/Please Be Mine	1956	12.50	25.00	50.00
—Red and black label; vocal duet on B-side					
❑ 1002	Why Do Fools Fall in Love/Please Be Mine	1956	7.50	15.00	30.00
—Red and black label; vocal solo on B-side. All of the above credit "The Teenagers featuring Frankie Lymon"					
❑ 1002	Why Do Fools Fall in Love/My Girl	1958	6.25	12.50	25.00
—White label, "Gee Records" at top; note different B-side					
❑ 1002	Why Do Fools Fall in Love/Please Be Mine	1959	3.75	7.50	15.00
—Gray label, "Gee Records" at bottom; label credit is "The Teenagers featuring Frankie Lymon"					
❑ 1012	I Want You to Be My Girl/I'm Not a Know-It-All	1956	12.50	25.00	50.00
—As "The Teenagers featuring Frankie Lymon"					
❑ 1012	I Want You to Be My Girl/I'm Not a Know-It-All	1956	7.50	15.00	30.00
—As "Frankie Lymon and the Teenagers"					
❑ 1018	I Promise to Remember/Who Can Explain	1956	7.50	15.00	30.00
❑ 1022	The ABC's of Love/Share	1956	7.50	15.00	30.00
❑ 1026	I'm Not a Juvenile Delinquent/Baby Baby	1957	7.50	15.00	30.00
❑ 1032	Teenage Love/Paper Castles	1957	7.50	15.00	30.00
❑ 1035	Am I Fooling Myself Again/Love Is a Clown	197?	—	—	—
—Evidently a 1970s bootleg to fill in a gap in the Gee Records discography					
❑ 1036	Miracle of Love/Out in the Cold Again	1957	7.50	15.00	30.00
❑ 1039	Goody Goody/Creation of Love	1957	10.00	20.00	40.00
—Actually a Frankie Lymon solo recording; the first pressing credited the entire group					

7-Inch Extended Plays

Number	Title (A Side/B Side)	Yr	VG	VG+	NM
GEE					
❑ GEP-601	Teenage Love/Why Do Fools Fall in Love//I Want You to Be My Girl/Love Is a Clown	1956	37.50	75.00	150.00
❑ GEP-601 [PS]	The Teenagers Go Rock'n	1956	50.00	100.00	200.00
❑ GEP-602	Paper Castles/Share//Am I Fooling Myself Again/ I'm Not a Know-It-All	1957	50.00	100.00	200.00
❑ GEP-602 [PS]	The Teenagers Go Romantic	1957	50.00	100.00	200.00

Albums

Number	Title (A Side/B Side)	Yr	VG	VG+	NM
ACCORD					
❑ SN-7203	Why Do Fools Fall in Love	1982	2.50	5.00	10.00
GEE					
❑ GLP-701 [M]	The Teenagers Featuring Frankie Lymon	1956	125.00	250.00	500.00
—Red label					
❑ GLP-701 [M]	The Teenagers Featuring Frankie Lymon	1961	37.50	75.00	150.00
—Gray label					
❑ GLP-701 [M]	The Teenagers Featuring Frankie Lymon	197?	3.00	6.00	12.00
—White label on thinner vinyl					
MURRAY HILL					
❑ 148 [(5)]	Frankie Lymon and the Teenagers	198?	17.50	35.00	70.00
RHINO					
❑ R1-70918	The Best of Frankie Lymon and the Teenagers	1989	3.00	6.00	12.00

LYMON, LEWIS, AND THE TEENCHORDS
45s

Number	Title (A Side/B Side)	Yr	VG	VG+	NM
END					
❑ 1003	Too Young/Your Last Chance	1957	25.00	50.00	100.00
❑ 1007	I Found Out Why/Tell Me Love	1958	20.00	40.00	80.00
❑ 1113	Too Young/Your Last Chance	1962	5.00	10.00	20.00
FURY					
❑ 1000	I'm So Happy (Tra-La-La-La-La-La)/Lydia	1957	50.00	100.00	200.00
—Maroon label					
❑ 1000	I'm So Happy (Tra-La-La-La-La-La)/Lydia	1958	10.00	20.00	40.00
—Yellow label					
❑ 1003	Honey, Honey (You Don't Know)/Please Tell the Angels	1957	20.00	40.00	80.00
❑ 1006	I'm Not Too Young to Fall in Love/Falling in Love	1957	20.00	40.00	80.00
JUANITA					
❑ 101	Dance Girl/Them There Eyes	1958	12.50	25.00	50.00

Albums

Number	Title (A Side/B Side)	Yr	VG	VG+	NM
COLLECTABLES					
❑ COL-5049	Lewis Lymon and the Teenchords Meet the Kodaks	198?	2.50	5.00	10.00
LOST-NITE					
❑ LLP-13 [10]	Lewis Lymon and the Teenchords	1981	2.50	5.00	10.00
—Red vinyl					

LYNN, BARBARA
45s

Number	Title (A Side/B Side)	Yr	VG	VG+	NM
ATLANTIC					
❑ 2450	This Is the Thanks I Get/Ring, Telephone, Ring	1967	2.00	4.00	8.00
❑ 2513	Why Can't You Love Me/You're Losing Me	1968	2.00	4.00	8.00
❑ 2553	Love Ain't Never Hurt Nobody/You're Gonna See a Lot More	1968	2.00	4.00	8.00
❑ 2585	People Like Me/He Ain't Gonna Do Right	1968	2.00	4.00	8.00
❑ 2812	(Until Then) I'll Suffer/Take Your Love and Run	1971	—	3.00	6.00
❑ 2853	Nice and Easy/I'm a One Woman Man	1972	—	3.00	6.00

Number	Title (A Side/B Side)	Yr	VG	VG+	NM
❑ 2880	(Daddy Hotstuff) You're Too Hot to Hold/You Better Quit It	1972	—	3.00	6.00
❑ 2931	You Make Me So Hot/It Ain't No Good to Be Too Good	1973	—	3.00	6.00
JAMIE					
❑ 1220	You'll Lose a Good Thing/Lonely Heartache	1962	5.00	10.00	20.00
❑ 1233	Second Fiddle Girl/Letter to Mommy and Daddy	1962	3.00	6.00	12.00
❑ 1240	You're Gonna Need Me/I'm Sorry I Met You	1962	3.00	6.00	12.00
❑ 1244	Don't Be Cruel/You Can't Be Satisfied	1963	3.00	6.00	12.00
❑ 1251	To Love or Not to Love/Promises	1963	3.00	6.00	12.00
❑ 1260	(I Cried at) Laura's Wedding/You Better Stop	1963	3.00	6.00	12.00
❑ 1265	Everybody Loves Somebody/Dedicate the Blues to Me	1963	3.00	6.00	12.00
❑ 1269	Money/Jealous Love	1964	3.00	6.00	12.00
❑ 1277	Oh! Baby (We Got a Good Thing Goin')/Unfair	1964	3.00	6.00	12.00
❑ 1286	Don't Spread It Around/Let Her Knock Herself Out	1964	3.00	6.00	12.00
❑ 1292	It's Better to Have It/People Gonna Talk	1964	3.00	6.00	12.00
❑ 1295	(Don't Pretend) Just Lay It on the Line/Careless Hands	1965	2.00	4.00	8.00
—With Lee Maye					
❑ 1297	Keep On Pushing Your Luck/I've Taken All I'm Gonna Take	1965	2.00	4.00	8.00
❑ 1301	Can't Buy Me Love/That's What Friends Are For	1965	2.00	4.00	8.00
❑ 1304	All I Need Is Your Love/You're Gonna Be Sorry	1965	2.00	4.00	8.00
TRIBE					
❑ 8316	Running Back/I'm a Good Woman	1966	2.00	4.00	8.00
❑ 8319	You Left the Water Running/Until I'm Free	1966	2.00	4.00	8.00
❑ 8322	Watch the One That Brings Bad News/AUB A-Go-Go	1967	2.00	4.00	8.00
❑ 8324	I Don't Want a Playboy/New Kind of Love	1967	2.00	4.00	8.00

Albums

Number	Title (A Side/B Side)	Yr	VG	VG+	NM
ATLANTIC					
❑ 8171 [M]	Here Is Barbara Lynn	1968	12.50	25.00	50.00
❑ SD 8171 [S]	Here Is Barbara Lynn	1968	10.00	20.00	40.00
JAMIE					
❑ JLP-3023 [M]	You'll Lose a Good Thing	1962	12.50	25.00	50.00
❑ JLPS-3023 [R]	You'll Lose a Good Thing	1962	12.50	25.00	50.00
❑ JLP-3026 [M]	Sister of Soul	1964	—	—	—
—Canceled					
❑ JLPS-3026 [S]	Sister of Soul	1964	—	—	—
—Canceled					

LYNN, CHERYL
12-Inch Singles

Number	Title (A Side/B Side)	Yr	VG	VG+	NM
COLUMBIA					
❑ AS 1743 [DJ]	Preppie (Vocal) (Instrumental)	1983	2.00	4.00	8.00
❑ AS 1843 [DJ]	This Time/Change the Channel	1984	3.00	6.00	12.00
❑ 43-02103	Shake It Up Tonight/Baby	1981	3.00	6.00	12.00
❑ 44-02914	Instant Love (5:10)/I Just Wanna Be Your Fantasy	1982	2.50	5.00	10.00
❑ 44-04257	Encore (8:18)/Free (7:25)	1983	2.50	5.00	10.00
❑ 44-05220	Fidelity/High Fidelity (Dub Mix)	1985	2.50	5.00	10.00
❑ 23-10869	Got to Be Real (5:10)/Star Love (7:23)	1978	3.75	7.50	15.00
❑ 43-11261	Keep It Hot (5:26)/In Love (3:48)	1980	5.00	10.00	20.00
MANHATTAN					
❑ SPRO-9952/3 [DJ]	New Dress (Extended Version) (Dub) (LP Version)	1987	2.00	4.00	8.00
❑ V-56040	New Dress (Extended Version) (Instrumental)/ Everyday	1987	—	3.50	7.00
❑ V-56054	If You Were Mine (Dance Mix) (Radio Mix) (Instrumental)	1987	2.00	4.00	8.00
VIRGIN					
❑ DMD 1375 [DJ]	Every Time I Try to Say Goodbye (12") (Radio Edit) (Club Mix) (Instrumental)	1989	2.00	4.00	8.00
❑ DMD 1419 [DJ]	Whatever It Takes (2 versions)	1989	2.50	5.00	10.00
❑ DMD 1471 [DJ]	Upset! (12" Mix) (Nervy Mix) (Instrumental)	1990	2.00	4.00	8.00
❑ 96488	Upset! (12" Mix) (Nervy Mix) (Instrumental)	1990	2.00	4.00	8.00
❑ 96534	Every Time I Try to Say Goodbye (12" Version) (Radio Edit) (Club Mix) (Instrumental)	1989	2.00	4.00	8.00

45s

Number	Title (A Side/B Side)	Yr	VG	VG+	NM
COLUMBIA					
❑ 11-02102	Shake It Up Tonight/Baby	1981	—	2.00	4.00
❑ 18-02511	In the Night/If You'll Be True to Me	1981	—	2.00	4.00
❑ 18-02648	Show You How/What's On Your Mind	1981	—	2.50	5.00
❑ 18-02905	Instant Love/I Just Wanna Be Your Fantasy	1982	—	2.00	4.00
❑ 18-03204	If This World Were Mine/I Just Wanna Be Your Fantasy	1982	—	2.00	4.00
—A-side with Luther Vandross					
❑ 38-03475	Look Before You Leap/Day After Day	1982	—	2.00	4.00
❑ 38-04153	Preppie/Free	1983	—	2.00	4.00
❑ 38-04256	Encore/Free	1983	—	2.00	4.00
❑ 38-04429	This Time/Change the Channel	1984	—	2.00	4.00
❑ 38-04932	Fidelity/Free	1985	—	—	3.00
❑ 38-05605	Fade to Black/Loafin'	1985	—	—	3.00
❑ 3-10808	Got to Be Real (3:42)/Come In From the Rain	1978	—	3.00	6.00
—Original copies contain an edited version of the A-side					
❑ 3-10808	Got to Be Real (5:10)/Come In From the Rain	1978	—	2.50	5.00
—Reissue copies contain full-length version of A-side					
❑ 3-10907	Star Love/You're the One	1979	—	2.50	5.00
❑ 1-11174	I've Got Faith in You/Chances	1979	—	2.50	5.00
❑ 1-11234	In Love/Love Bomb	1980	—	2.50	5.00
❑ 13-33386	Got to Be Real/Star Love	198?	—	2.00	4.00
—Originals have red "Hall of Fame" labels					
MANHATTAN					
❑ B-50056	New Dress/Everyday	1987	—	—	3.00
❑ B-50056 [PS]	New Dress/Everyday	1987	—	—	3.00

Number	Title (A Side/B Side)	Yr	VG	VG+	NM
❏ B-50074	If You Were Mine/(Instrumental)	1987	—	—	3.00
❏ B-50074 [PS]	If You Were Mine/(Instrumental)	1987	—	—	3.00
❏ B-50099	Start Over/(B-side unknown)	1987	—	2.50	5.00

PRIVATE I

❏ ZS4-04736	At Last You're Mine/Look What You've Done to Me	1985	—	—	3.00

—B-side by Marc Tanner

❏ ZS4-04736 [PS]	At Last You're Mine/Look What You've Done to Me	1985	—	2.00	4.00

—B-side by Marc Tanner

❏ ZS4-04736 [PS]	At Last You're Mine	1985	—	3.00	6.00

—"Demonstration -- Not for Sale" on sleeve; no B-side listed

VIRGIN

❏ 99142	Whatever It Takes/(Instrumental)	1989	—	2.00	4.00
❏ 99180	Every Time I Try to Say Goodbye/(Instrumental)	1989	—	2.00	4.00
❏ 99180 [PS]	Every Time I Try to Say Goodbye/(Instrumental)	1989	—	2.00	4.00

Albums

COLUMBIA

❏ JC 35486	Cheryl Lynn	1978	2.50	5.00	10.00

—Original issue

❏ JC 35486 [DJ]	Cheryl Lynn	1978	3.75	7.50	15.00

—White-label promo only (not a designate promo)

❏ PC 35486	Cheryl Lynn	198?	2.00	4.00	8.00

—Budget-line reissue; orange label with six "Columbia"s around outer edge

❏ PC 35486	Cheryl Lynn	2001	2.50	5.00	10.00

—Reissue on 180-gram vinyl from original LP master; red label with single white "Columbia" at top

❏ JC 36145	In Love	1979	2.50	5.00	10.00
❏ FC 37034	In the Night	1981	2.50	5.00	10.00
❏ FC 38057	Instant Love	1982	2.50	5.00	10.00
❏ FC 38961	Preppie	1983	2.50	5.00	10.00
❏ FC 40024	It's Gonna Be Right	1985	2.50	5.00	10.00

MANHATTAN

❏ ST-53035	Start Over	1987	2.00	4.00	8.00

VIRGIN

❏ 91254	Whatever It Takes	1989	3.00	6.00	12.00

M

M/A/R/R/S
12-Inch Singles
4TH & B'WAY

Number	Title (A Side/B Side)	Yr	VG	VG+	NM
❏ 452	Pump Up the Volume (4 versions)/Anitina	1987	2.00	4.00	8.00

45s
4TH & B'WAY

❏ 7452	Pump Up the Volume (Radio Edit)/Anitina	1987	—	2.00	4.00

—No mention of "Bright Lights Big City" on label

❏ 7452	Pump Up the Volume (From Bright Lights Big City)/Anitina	1987	—	—	3.00
❏ 7452 [PS]	Pump Up the Volume (From Bright Lights Big City)/Anitina	1987	—	—	3.00

—Both versions have same picture sleeve

COLLECTABLES

❏ 2610	Pump Up the Volume/(instrumental)	199?	—	—	3.00

—Reissue

M.C. HAMMER
See HAMMER, MC.

MADONNA
12-Inch Singles
MAVERICK

❏ PRO-A-5665 [DJ]	Erotica (LP Version) (Radio Edit)	1992	3.75	7.50	15.00
❏ PRO-A-5860	[(2) DJ]Erotica (Kenlou B-Boy Mix 6:23) (Kenlou B-Boy Instrumental 5:54) (Madonna's In My Jeep Mix 5:46) (Jeep Beats 5:48) (Underground Tribal Beats 3:30) (Underground Club Mix 4:53) (Masters At Work Dub 4:51) (Bass Hit Dub 4:47) (WØ 12" 6:07) (WØ Dub 4:53) (House Instrumental 4:49)	1992	12.50	25.00	50.00

—Promo-only two-record set

❏ PRO-A-5928	[(2) DJ]Deeper and Deeper (Shep's Deep Makeover Mix 9:07) (Shep's Deep Bass Dub 5:00) (Shep's Deeper Dub 6:08) (Shep's Classic 12" 7:26) (Shep's Fierce Deeper Dub 5:59) (Shep's Deep Beats 2:57) (David's Klub Mix 7:39) (David's Love Dub 5:37) (David's Deeper Dub 5:22) (David's Classic 12" 7:02) (Momo's Fantasy 2:55) (Shep's Deepstrumental 5:31)	1992	10.00	20.00	40.00

—Promo-only two-record set

❏ PRO-A-6074	[(2) DJ]Fever (Murk Boys Miami Mix 7:10) (Oscar G.'s Dope Dub 4:55) (Murk Boys Deep South Mix 6:28) (Back To The Dub 2 4:52) (12" Instrumental 4:56) (Extended 12" 6:05) (T's Extended Dub A 2:56) (T's Extended Dub B 5:03) (Hot Sweat 12" 7:55) (Shep's Remedy Dub 4:29) (Peggy's Nightclub Mix 4:55) (Bugged Out Bonzai Dub 4:48)	1993	25.00	50.00	100.00

—Promo-only two-record set on red vinyl

❏ PRO-A-7323-A	[DJ]Take a Bow (InDaSoul Mix 4:57) (Album Edit 4:31) (Silky Soul Mix 4:10) (InDaSoul Instrumental 4:57) (Silky Soul Instrumental 4:10) (Album Instrumental, 5:20)	1994	5.00	10.00	20.00
❏ PRO-A-7600-A	[DJ]Bedtime Story Chapter II (Lush Vocal Mix 6:47) (Luscious Dub Mix 7:38) (Percapella Mix 6:31) (Unconscious In The Jungle Mix 6:26)	1995	50.00	100.00	200.00
❏ PRO-A-7719-A	[DJ]Human Nature (Runway Club Mix 8:18) (I'm Not Your Bitch Mix 8:10) (Runway Club Mix Radio Edit 3:58) (Bottom Heavy Dub 8:08) (Howie Tee Remix 4:47) (Howie Tee Clean Remix Radio Edit 4:07)	1995	6.25	12.50	25.00

—"Advance Only" on label and on regular black vinyl

❏ PRO-A-7719	[DJ]Human Nature (Runway Club Mix 8:18) (I'm Not Your Bitch Mix 8:10) (Runway Club Mix Radio Edit 3:58) (Bottom Heavy Dub 8:08) (Howie Tee Remix 4:47) (Howie Tee Clean Remix Radio Edit 4:07)	1995	10.00	20.00	40.00

—Brown vinyl (when held to a light)

❏ PRO-A-7758	[DJ]Human Nature (Human Club Mix 9:00) (Love Is The Nature Mix 6:40)	1995	6.25	12.50	25.00
❏ PRO-A-8244	[DJ]Love Don't Live Here Anymore (Ext. Journey 8:03) (Hot Mix Edit 6:44) (Hot Mix Radio Edit 4:50) (Edge Factor Dub 8:31) (Early Morning Dub 10:04)	1996	12.50	25.00	50.00

—White label

❏ PRO-A-8244	[DJ]Love Don't Live Here Anymore (Ext. Journey 8:03) (Hot Mix Edit 6:44) (Hot Mix Radio Edit 4:50) (Edge Factor Dub 8:31) (Early Morning Dub 10:04)	1996	12.50	25.00	50.00

—Red label

❏ PRO-A-9254	[DJ]Frozen (William Orbit Widescreen Mix 6:34) (William Orbit Drumapella 5:15) (Victor Calderone Drumapella 5:09)	1998	12.50	25.00	50.00
❏ PRO-A-9327	[(2) DJ]Ray of Light (Album Version 5:21) (Sasha's Ultra Violet Mix 10:45) (Victor Calderone Club Mix 9:29) (William Orbit Liquid Mix 8:05)	1998	15.00	30.00	60.00
❏ PRO-A-9333-A	[(2) DJ]Ray of Light (Album Version 5:21) (Sasha's Ultra Violet Mix 10:45) (Victor Calderone Club Mix 9:29) (William Orbit Liquid Mix 8:05)	1998	12.50	25.00	50.00

—"Advance Only" promo with less detailed labels than 9327

Number	Title (A Side/B Side)	Yr	VG	VG+	NM
❑ PRO-A-9359 [DJ]Ray of Light: New Mixes (Sasha Twilo Mix 10:58) (Sasha Strip Down Mix 5:00) (William Orbit Ultra Violet Mix 6:59) (Victor Calderone Drum Mix 5:26)	1998	15.00	30.00	60.00
❑ PRO-A-9499 [DJ]The Power of Good-Bye (Fabien's Good God Mix 8:25) (Slater's Filtered Mix 6:05) (Slater's Super Luper Mix 8:45) (Dallas Austin Low End Mix 4:33)	1998	10.00	20.00	40.00
❑ PRO-A-9630-A [(2) DJ]Nothing Really Matters (Club 69 Vocal Club Mix 7:39) (Club 69 Radio Mix 3:45) (Club 69 Mix-Show Mix 5:40) (Club 69 Future Mix 8:33) (Club 69 Phunk Mix 8:00) (Album Version 4:27) (Club 69 Future Dub 5:48) (Kruder & Dorfmeister Remix 11:10)	1999	12.50	25.00	50.00
❑ PRO-A-9647-A [(2) DJ]Nothing Really Matters (Club 69 Vocal Club Mix 7:39) (Club 69 Radio Mix 3:45) (Club 69 Future Mix 8:33) (Club 69 Mix-Show Mix 5:40) (Club 69 Phunk Mix 8:00) (Vikram Radio Mix 7:42) (Club 69 Future Dub 5:48) (Kruder & Dorfmeister Remix 11:10)	1999	12.50	25.00	50.00
❑ PRO-A-9665-A [DJ]Nothing Really Matters (Vikram Cybercut 13:44) (Kruder & Dorfmeister Remix 11:10)	1999	10.00	20.00	40.00
❑ PRO-A-9700-A [DJ]Nothing Really Matters (Club 69 Speed Mix 10:35) (Club 69 Speed Dub 10:25)	1999	10.00	20.00	40.00
❑ PRO-A-9838-A [DJ]Beautiful Stranger (Calderone Club Mix 10:13) (Calderone Radio Mix 4:04) (New Club Edit 5:12) (Album Version 4:21)	1999	10.00	20.00	40.00
—"Advance Only" version, white label					
❑ PRO-A-9838 [DJ]Beautiful Stranger (Calderone Club Mix 10:13) (Calderone Radio Mix 4:04) (New Club Edit 5:12) (Album Version 4:21)	1999	7.50	15.00	30.00
—Red label					
❑ PRO-A-9922-A [DJ]Beautiful Stranger (Calderone Club Mix 10:12) (Album Version 4:21) (Calderone Radio Mix 4:04) (Calderone Dub Mix 6:22)	1999	7.50	15.00	30.00
❑ 40585	Erotica (Kenlou B-Boy Mix 6:25) (Jeep Beats 5:51) (Madonna's In My Jeep Mix 5:50) (WØ 12" 6:09) (Underground Club Mix 4:54) (Bass Hit Dub 4:48)	1992	2.00	4.00	8.00
❑ 40722	Deeper and Deeper (Shep's Classic 12" 7:26) (Shep's Deep Makeover Mix 9:07) (Shep's Deep Beats 2:57) (David's Klub Mix 7:39) (David's Deeper Dub 5:22) (Shep's Deeper Dub 6:08)	1992	2.00	4.00	8.00
❑ 40793	Bad Girl (Extended Mix, 6:29/Fever (Extended 12" Mix 6:08) (Shep's Remedy Dub 4:29) (Murk Boys Miami Mix 7:10) (Murk Boys Deep South Mix 6:28) (Oscar G.'s Dope Dub 4:55)	1993	2.00	4.00	8.00
❑ 40988	Rain (Radio Remix, 4:33) (LP Version 5:30)/Up Down Suite (Dub Version 12:17)/Waiting (Remix 4:40)	1993	2.00	4.00	8.00
❑ 41355	I'll Remember (Guerilla Beach Mix 6:17) (Album Version 4:22) (Guerilla Groove Mix 6:07) (Orbit Alternative Remix 4:30)	1994	2.00	4.00	8.00
❑ 41355 [DJ]	I'll Remember (Guerilla Beach Mix 6:17) (Album Version 4:22) (Guerilla Groove Mix 6:07) (Orbit Alternative Remix 4:30)	1994	3.75	7.50	15.00
—Same as stock copy, except labels say "Advance Copy - Promotion Only"					
❑ 41772	Secret (Junior's Sound Factory Mix 10:16) (Junior's Sound Factory Dub 7:57) (Junior's Luscious Club Mix 6:19) (Junior's Luscious Club Dub 6:20) (Allstar Mix 5:11)	1994	2.00	4.00	8.00
❑ 41772 [DJ]	Secret (Junior's Sound Factory Mix 10:16) (Junior's Sound Factory Dub 7:57) (Junior's Luscious Club Mix 6:19) (Junior's Luscious Club Dub 6:20) (Allstar Mix 5:11)	1994	2.00	4.00	8.00
—Same as stock copy, except labels say "Advance Copy - Promotion Only"					
❑ 41880	Human Nature (Runway Club Mix 8:18) (I'm Not Your Bitch Mix 8:10) (Runway Club Mix Radio Edit 3:58) (Bottom Heavy Dub 7:55) (Howie Tee Remix 4:47) (Howie Tee Clean Remix 4:46) (Radio Version 4:30) (Love Is The Nature Mix 6:40)	1995	2.00	4.00	8.00
❑ 41887	Take a Bow (InDaSoul Mix 4:57) (Album Edit 4:31) (Silky Soul Mix 4:10) (InDaSoul Instrumental 4:57) (Album Instrumental 5:20)	1994	—	3.00	6.00
❑ 41895	Bedtime Story (Junior's Sound Factory Mix 9:15) (Junior's Sound Factory Dub 8:14) (Orbital Mix 7:42) (Junior's Wet Dream Mix 8:33) (Junior's Wet Dream Dub 7:30)	1995	—	3.00	6.00
❑ 42372 [(2)]	What It Feels Like for a Girl (Paul Oakenfold Perfecto Mix 7:18) (Richard Vission Velvet Masta Mix 8:08)/(Above & Beyond 12" Club Mix 7:27) (Richard Vission Velvet Masta Edit 3:39)//(Calderone & Quayle Dark Side Mix 6:42) (Tracy Young Cool Out Radio Mix 4:45)/(Above & Beyond Club Radio Edit 3:45) (Tracy Young Club Mix 8:54)	2001	2.00	4.00	8.00
❑ 43649	You'll See (Album Version 4:39) (Instrumental 4:44) (Spanish Version 4:21)/Live To Tell (Live from the "Who's That Girl" Tour 8:14)	1995	2.50	5.00	10.00
❑ 43993	Frozen (Album Version 6:12) (Stereo MC's Remix 5:45) (Extended Club Mix 11:17) (Meltdown Mix 8:09)	1998	2.00	4.00	8.00
❑ 44523 [(2)]	Ray of Light (Sasha Untra Violet Mix 10:45) (Sasha Strip Down Mix 5:00)/(Victor Calderone Club Mix 9:29) (William Orbit Liquid Mix 8:06)//				
❑ 44613 [(2)]	(Sasha Twilo Mix 10:58) (Victor Calderone Drum Mix 5:26)/(William Orbit Ultra Violet Mix 6:59) (Album Version 5:21)	1998	3.00	6.00	12.00
❑ 44613 [(2)]	Nothing Really Matters (Club 69 Vocal Club Mix 7:51) (Album Version 4:27)/(Club 69 Future Mix 8:19) (Club 69 Radio Mix 3:45)//(Club 69 Phunk Mix) (Vikram Radio Remix)/(Club 69 Future Dub 5:48) (Kruder & Dorfmeister Remix 11:10)	1999	6.25	12.50	25.00
—Original edition, quickly recalled, has records labeled "Record One" and "Record Two," but both play the Record Two mixes. Holding the two records (Side 1 or especially Side 2 of each) next to each other will reveal a nearly identical groove. The dead wax of the copy we've examined has "0-44613-A-SR1" on Record 1 Side 1; "0-44613-B-SR1" on Record 1 Side 2; "PRO-A-9647-C/0-44613-C" on Record 2 Side 1; and "PRO-A-9630-D SR1" on Record 2 Side 2.					
❑ 44613 [(2)]	Nothing Really Matters (Club 69 Vocal Club Mix 7:51) (Album Version 4:27)/(Club 69 Future Mix 8:19) (Club 69 Radio Mix 3:45)//(Club 69 Phunk Mix) (Vikram Radio Remix)/(Club 69 Future Dub 5:48) (Kruder & Dorfmeister Remix 11:10)	1999	2.50	5.00	10.00
—Correct edition, with two different records inside					
❑ 44909 [(2)]	Music (HQ2 Club Mix 8:46) (Groove Armada 12" Mix 5:30) (Calderone Anthem 11:55) (Album Version 3:44) (Deep Dish Dot Com Mix 11:21) (The Young Collective Club Remix 13:16)	2000	2.00	4.00	8.00
❑ 44910 [(2)]	Don't Tell Me (Timo Maas Mix 6:56) (Tracy Young Club Mix 11:00) (Vission Remix 7:52) (Thunderpuss 2001 Hands in the Air Anthem 10:20) (Victor Calderone Sensory Mix 6:48) (Vission Radio Mix 3:48) (Thunderpuss 2001 Hands in the Air Radio 4:26)	2001	2.00	4.00	8.00
❑ PRO-A-100018 [DJ]American Pie (Victor Calderone Vocal Dub Mix 6:15) (Victor Calderone Filter Dub Mix 6:00)/ (Richard "Humpty" Vission Visits Madonna 5:45) (Richard "Humpty" Vission Radio Mix 4:26)	2000	5.00	10.00	20.00
❑ PRO-A-100115 [DJ]American Pie (Victor Calderone Vocal Club Mix 9:06) (Victor Calderone Extended Vocal Club Mix 10:30)	2000	6.25	12.50	25.00
❑ PRO-A-100303 [DJ]Music (Album Version 3:44) (same on both sides)	2000	3.00	6.00	12.00
—In generic black sleeve with "Remixes to Come" sticker					
❑ PRO-A-100304 [(2) DJ]Music (Calderone Anthem Mix 11:55) (The Young Collective Club Remix 13:16) (Groove Armada's Flagship Dub 9:29) (Victor Calderone Radio Edit 4:25) (Groove Armada's 12" Revival 5:30) (Groove Armada's 7" Edit 3:38) (Groove Armada's Bonus Beats 4:50)	2000	6.25	12.50	25.00
—In generic black sleeve with "More Mixes to Come" sticker					
❑ PRO-A-100305 [DJ]Music (HQ2 Club Mix 8:50) (HQ2 Radio Mix 4:04)/(Deep Dish Dot Com Remix 11:21) (Deep Dish Dot Com Radio Edit 4:15)	2000	3.75	7.50	15.00
—With custom labels and picture cover					
❑ PRO-A-100512 [DJ]Don't Tell Me (Thunderpuss Club Mix 7:50) (Richard Humpty Vission Remix 7:51)/(Tracy Young Club Mix 11:00) (Thunderpuss Radio Mix 3:40)	2000	3.75	7.50	15.00
❑ PRO-A-100514-A [DJ]Don't Tell Me (Timo Maas Mix) (Victor Calderone Sensory Mix) (Thunderpuss 2001 Hands in the Air Anthem)	2001	3.75	7.50	15.00
❑ PRO-A-100620-A [(2) DJ]What It Feels Like for a Girl (Paul Oakenfold Perfecto Mix 7:18) (Richard Vission Velvet Masta Mix 8:08) (Saturday Night Mix 5:22) (Above & Beyond 12" Club Mix 7:27) (Richard Vission Velvet Masta Edit 3:39) (Calderone & Quayle Dark Side Mix 6:42) (Above & Beyond Club Radio Edit 3:45) (Tracy Young Club Mix 8:54) (Tracy Young Cool Out Radio Mix 4:45)	2001	7.50	15.00	30.00
—"Advance Only" on label					
❑ PRO-A-100620 [(2) DJ]What It Feels Like for a Girl (Paul Oakenfold Perfecto Mix 7:18) (Richard Vission Velvet Masta Mix 8:08) (Saturday Night Mix 5:22) (Above & Beyond 12" Club Mix 7:27) (Richard Vission Velvet Masta Edit 3:39) (Calderone & Quayle Dark Side Mix 6:42) (Above & Beyond Club Radio Edit 3:45) (Tracy Young Club Mix 8:54) (Tracy Young Cool Out Radio Mix 4:45)	2001	7.50	15.00	30.00
❑ PRO-A-100771-A [DJ]Impressive Instant (Peter Rauhofer's Universal Club Mix 9:40) (Peter Rauhofer's Drowned World Dub 8:40)	2001	3.75	7.50	15.00
❑ PRO-A-100790-A [DJ]GHV2 Johnny Rocks & Mac Quayle Megamix (8:17)/GHV2 Tracy Young's Shake & Stir Club Mix (11:53)	2001	3.75	7.50	15.00
❑ PRO-A-100797-A [DJ]GHV2 Tracy Young's Shake & Stir Club Mix (11:53) (same on both sides)	2001	3.75	7.50	15.00
❑ PRO-A-100820-A [DJ]GHV2 Johnny Rocks & Mac Quayle Dub (9:02)/GHV2 Johnny Rocks & Mac Quayle Club Mix (8:18)	2002	5.00	10.00	20.00
SIRE					
❑ PRO-A-2069 [DJ]Lucky Star (5:30)/Holiday (6:08)	1983	7.50	15.00	30.00
❑ PRO-A-2120 [DJ]Borderline (New Mix 6:54) (Instrumental 5:41)	1984	10.00	20.00	40.00
❑ PRO-A-2172 [DJ]Like a Virgin (3:35) (same on both sides)	1984	5.00	10.00	20.00
❑ PRO-A-2223 [DJ]Like a Virgin (Extended Remix 6:07) (same on both sides)	1984	7.50	15.00	30.00
❑ PRO-A-2257 [DJ]Material Girl (3:56) (same on both sides)	1985	6.25	12.50	25.00
❑ PRO-A-2292 [DJ]Angel (3:40) (Extended Dance Mix 6:15)	1985	3.00	6.00	12.00
❑ PRO-A-2353 [DJ]Dress You Up (12" Formal Mix 6:15) (same on both sides)	1985	3.75	7.50	15.00

Number	Title (A Side/B Side)	Yr	VG	VG+	NM
❑ PRO-A-2470	[DJ]Live to Tell (Edit 4:37) (LP Version 5:49)	1986	10.00	20.00	40.00
❑ PRO-A-2517	[DJ]Papa Don't Preach (LP Version 4:27) (Edit 3:47)	1986	6.25	12.50	25.00
❑ PRO-A-2905	[DJ]Where's the Party (Extended Remix 7:31) (Dub 6:22)/Spotlight (Extended Remix 6:24) (Dub 4:49)	1987	12.50	25.00	50.00
❑ PRO-A-2906	[DJ]Into the Groove (New Remix 8:31) (Dub 6:22)/ Everybody (New Remix 7:06)	1987	12.50	25.00	50.00
❑ PRO-A-2907	[DJ]Holiday (New Remix 6:59) (Dub 6:57)/Over and Over (Extended Remix 7:11) (Dub 6:43)	1987	15.00	30.00	60.00
❑ PRO-A-3472	[DJ]Like a Prayer (12" Dance Mix 7:50) (Instrumental Dub 6:11) (Bass Dub 5:48) (12" Club Version 6:35) (Dub Beats 4:40) (7" Remix/ Edit 5:41)	1989	5.00	10.00	20.00
❑ PRO-A-3791	[DJ]Keep It Together (12" Remix 7:50) (Dub 7:00) (12" Mix 6:48) (Bonus Beats 3:56)	1990	3.00	6.00	12.00
❑ PRO-A-4582	[DJ]Justify My Love (Album Version 4:58) (same on both sides)	1990	3.00	6.00	12.00
❑ PRO-A-4613	[DJ]Justify My Love (Orbit Edit 4:30) (Hip Hop Mix 6:30) (Orbit 12" Mix 7:16) (The Beast Within Mix 6:10)	1990	5.00	10.00	20.00
❑ PRO-A-4710	[(2) DJ]Rescue Me (Titanic Vocal, 8:15) (Lifeboat Vocal 5:20) (Lifeboat Dub 6:02) (Houseboat Vocal 6:56) (Houseboat Dub 5:23) (Demanding Dub 5:20) (S.O.S. Mix 6:23) (Disaster Dub 3:20)	1990	10.00	20.00	40.00
—Promo-only two-record set					
❑ 20212	Borderline (New Mix 6:54)/Lucky Star (New Mix 7:13)	1984	2.50	5.00	10.00
❑ 20239	Like a Virgin (Extended Dance Remix 6:07)/Stay (4:04)	1984	—	3.00	6.00
❑ 20304	Material Girl (Extended Dance Remix 6:06)/ Pretender (4:28)	1985	2.00	4.00	8.00
❑ 20335	Angel (Extended Dance Remix 6:15)/Into the Groove (4:40)	1985	2.00	4.00	8.00
❑ 20369	Dress You Up (12" Formal Mix 6:15) (Casual Instrumental Mix 4:36)/Shoo-Be-Doo (5:14)	1985	2.00	4.00	8.00
❑ 20461	Live to Tell (LP Version 5:49) (Edit 4:37) (Instrumental 5:49)	1986	2.00	4.00	8.00
❑ 20492	Papa Don't Preach (Extended Remix 5:43)/ Pretender (4:28)	1986	—	3.00	6.00
❑ 20533	True Blue (Color Mix 6:37) (Instrumental 6:56)/ Ain't No Big Deal (4:12)/True Blue (Remix Edit 4:22)	1986	2.00	4.00	8.00
❑ 20597	Open Your Heart (Extended 10:35) (Dub 6:40)/ White Heat (4:25)	1986	2.00	4.00	8.00
❑ 20633	La Isla Bonita (Extended Remix 5:20) (Extended Instrumental 5:14)	1987	—	3.00	6.00
❑ 20692	Who's That Girl (Extended Version 6:28) (Dub Version, 5:05)/White Heat (4:25)	1987	2.00	4.00	8.00
❑ 20762	Causing a Commotion (Silver Screen Mix 6:33) (Dub 7:04) (Movie House Mix 9:40)/Jimmy Jimmy (3:54)	1987	2.50	5.00	10.00
❑ 21170	Like a Prayer (12" Dance Mix, 7:50) (12" Extended Remix 7:21) (Churchapella 6:14)//(12" Club Version 6:35) (7" Remix Edit 5:41)/Act of Contrition (2:18)	1989	2.50	5.00	10.00
❑ 21225	Express Yourself (Non-Stop Express Mix 7:54) (Stop & Go Dubs 10:40)//(Local Mix 6:20)/The Look Of Love (4:03)	1989	—	3.00	6.00
❑ 21427	Keep It Together (12" Remix 7:44) (Dub 7:00) (12" Extended Mix 7:20) (12" Mix 6:48) (Bonus Beats 3:56) (Instrumental 5:52)	1990	—	3.00	6.00
❑ 21513	Vogue (12" Version 8:19) (Bette Davis Dub 7:24) (Strike-A-Pose Dub 7:37)	1990	—	3.00	6.00
❑ 21577	Hanky Panky (Bare Bottom 12" Mix 6:34) (Bare Bones Single Mix 3:50)/More (4:58)	1990	—	3.00	6.00
❑ 21813	Rescue Me (Titanic Vocal 8:15) (Lifeboat Vocal 5:20) (Houseboat Vocal 6:56) (S.O.S. Mix 6:23)	1991	2.00	4.00	8.00
❑ 21820	Justify My Love (Orbit 12" Mix 7:16) (Hip Hop Mix 6:30) (The Beast Within Mix 6:10)/Express Yourself (1990 Remix) (Long Version 9:30)	1990	2.00	4.00	8.00
❑ 29715	Burning Up (5:56)/Physical Attraction (6:35)	1983	2.50	5.00	10.00
❑ 29899	Everybody (5:56) (Dub 9:23)	1982	2.50	5.00	10.00
WARNER BROS.					
❑ PRO-A-8544-A	[DJ]Don't Cry for Me Argentina (Miami Mix Alternate Ending 7:59) (Miami Mix Spanglish Mix 6:57) (Miami Mix Edit 4:29)/(Miami Dub Mix 6:23) (Miami Mix Instrumental Version 6:55) (Miami Spanglish Mix Edit 4:28)	1997	6.25	12.50	25.00
—"Advance Only" on label					
❑ PRO-A-8544	[DJ]Don't Cry for Me Argentina (Miami Mix Alternate Ending 7:59) (Miami Mix Spanglish Mix 6:57) (Miami Mix Edit 4:29)/(Miami Dub Mix 6:23) (Miami Mix Instrumental Version 6:55) (Miami Spanglish Mix Edit 4:28)	1997	5.00	10.00	20.00
❑ PRO-A-8984-A	[DJ]Buenos Aires (Te Amo 12" Extended Vocal Version 7:53) (Te Amo Radio Version 4:09) (Te Amo Instrumental 7:52) (Te Amo Single Edit 5:23)	1997	10.00	20.00	40.00
—"Advance Only" on label					
❑ PRO-A-8984	[DJ]Buenos Aires (Te Amo 12" Extended Vocal Version 7:53) (Te Amo Radio Version 4:09) (Te Amo Instrumental 7:52) (Te Amo Single Edit 5:23)	1997	10.00	20.00	40.00

Number	Title (A Side/B Side)	Yr	VG	VG+	NM
❑ 43809	Don't Cry for Me Argentina (Miami Mix Alternate Ending 7:59) (Miami Spanglish Mix 6:57) (Miami Mix Edit 4:29)/(Miami Dub Mix 6:23) (Miami Mix Instrumental Version 6:55) (Miami Spanglish Mix Edit 4:28)	1997	2.00	4.00	8.00
WEA					
❑ 43993	[DJ] Frozen (Album Version) (Stereo MC's Remix) (Extended Club Mix) (Meltdown Mix)	1998	100.00	200.00	400.00
—Rare test pressing with handwritten labels; fewer than 10 copies known to exist					
45s					
GEFFEN					
❑ GGEF 0540	Gambler/Crazy for You	198?	—	—	3.00
—"Back to Back Hits" series; first issue of A-side on U.S. 45					
❑ 29051	Crazy for You/No More Words	1985	—	—	3.00
—B-side by Berlin					
❑ 29051 [PS]	Crazy for You/No More Words	1985	—	—	3.00
MAVERICK					
❑ 16711	Deeper and Deeper/Secret	2001	—	—	3.00
❑ 16712	Erotica/Bedtime Story	2001	—	—	3.00
❑ 16713	Frozen/Take a Bow	2001	—	—	3.00
—Both sides are edits; the original 45s had full-length versions					
❑ 16714	The Power of Good-Bye/Human Nature	2001	—	—	3.00
❑ 16715	Ray of Light/Beautiful Stranger	2001	—	—	3.00
❑ 16716	Don't Tell Me/What It Feels Like for a Girl	2001	—	—	3.00
❑ 16717	Music//Drowned World/Substitute for Love	2001	—	—	3.00
❑ 16825	Don't Tell Me (Album Version)/(Thunderpuss' 2001 Hands in the Air Radio)	2001	—	2.00	4.00
❑ 16826	Music/Cyberraga	2000	—	2.00	4.00
❑ 17102	Nothing Really Matters/To Have and Not to Hold	1999	—	2.00	4.00
❑ 17160	The Power of Good-Bye/Mer Girl	1998	—	—	3.00
❑ 17206	Ray of Light/Has to Be	1998	—	—	3.00
❑ 17244	Frozen/Shanti-Ashtangi	1998	—	—	3.00
❑ 17714	Love Don't Live Here Anymore (Soulpower Radio Remix)/(Album Remix)	1996	—	—	3.00
❑ 17719	You'll See/Live to Tell (Live Edit)	1995	—	—	3.00
❑ 17882	Human Nature/Sanctuary	1995	—	—	3.00
❑ 17924	Bedtime Story/Survival	1995	—	—	3.00
❑ 18000	Take a Bow/(InDaSoul Mix)	1994	—	—	3.00
❑ 18035	Secret/(Instrumental)	1994	—	—	3.00
❑ 18247	I'll Remember/Secret Garden	1994	—	—	3.00
❑ 18505	Rain/Waiting	1993	—	—	3.00
❑ 18639	Deeper and Deeper/(Instrumental)	1992	—	—	3.00
❑ 18650	Bad Girl/Fever	1993	—	—	3.00
❑ 18782	Erotica/(Instrumental)	1992	—	—	3.00
SIRE					
❑ GSRE 0494	Borderline/Holiday	198?	—	—	3.00
—"Back to Back Hits" reissue					
❑ GSRE 0506	Live a Virgin/Lucky Star	198?	—	—	3.00
—"Back to Back Hits" reissue					
❑ GSRE 0507	Material Girl/Angel	198?	—	—	3.00
—"Back to Back Hits" reissue					
❑ GSRE 0539	Into the Groove/Dress You Up	198?	—	—	3.00
—"Back to Back Hits" series; first issue of A-side on U.S. 45					
❑ PRO-S-2023	[DJ]Physical Attraction (same on both sides)	1983	12.50	25.00	50.00
❑ 18822	This Used to Be My Playground/(Long Version)	1992	—	—	3.00
❑ 19485	Justify My Love/Express Yourself 1990	1990	—	—	3.00
❑ 19490	Rescue Me/(Alternate Single Mix)	1990	—	—	3.00
❑ 19789	Hanky Panky/More	1990	—	—	3.00
❑ 19863	Vogue (Single Version)/Vogue (Bette Davis Dub)	1990	—	—	3.00
❑ 19986	Keep It Together/(Instrumental)	1990	—	—	3.00
❑ 19986 [PS]	Keep It Together/(Instrumental)	1990	20.00	40.00	80.00
❑ 21860	Express Yourself/Cherish	199?	—	—	3.00
—"Back to Back Hits" reissue					
❑ 21861	Like a Prayer/Oh Father	199?	—	—	3.00
—"Back to Back Hits" reissue					
❑ 21940	Who's That Girl/Causing a Commotion	198?	—	—	3.00
—"Back to Back Hits" reissue					
❑ 21941	La Isla Bonita/Open Your Heart	198?	—	—	3.00
—"Back to Back Hits" reissue					
❑ 21985	Live to Tell/True Blue	198?	—	—	3.00
—"Back to Back Hits" reissue					
❑ 21986	Papa Don't Preach/Everybody	198?	—	—	3.00
—"Back to Back Hits" reissue					
❑ 22723	Oh Father/Pray for Spanish Eyes	1989	—	—	3.00
❑ 22723 [PS]	Oh Father/Pray for Spanish Eyes	1989	—	—	—
—The purported sleeve appears to be a fake. Current opinion is that there is NO genuine U.S. picture sleeve.					
❑ 22883	Cherish/Supernatural	1989	—	—	3.00
❑ 22883 [PS]	Cherish/Supernatural	1989	—	—	3.00
❑ 22948	Express Yourself/The Look of Love	1989	—	—	3.00
❑ 22948 [PS]	Express Yourself/The Look of Love	1989	—	—	3.00
❑ 27539	Like a Prayer/Act of Contrition	1989	—	—	3.00
❑ 27539 [DJ]	Like a Prayer (7" Remix Edit)/(7" Version with Fade)	1989	2.50	5.00	10.00
❑ 27539 [PS]	Like a Prayer/Act of Contrition	1989	—	—	3.00
❑ 28224	Causing a Commotion/Jimmy, Jimmy	1987	—	—	3.00
❑ 28224 [PS]	Causing a Commotion/Jimmy, Jimmy	1987	—	—	3.00
❑ 28341	Who's That Girl?/White Heat	1987	—	—	3.00
❑ 28341 [PS]	Who's That Girl?/White Heat	1987	—	—	3.00
❑ 28425	La Isla Bonita/(Instrumental)	1987	—	—	3.00
❑ 28425 [PS]	La Isla Bonita/(Instrumental)	1987	—	—	3.00
❑ 28508	Open Your Heart/White Heat	1986	—	—	3.00
❑ 28508 [PS]	Open Your Heart/White Heat	1986	—	—	3.00
❑ 28591	True Blue/Ain't No Big Deal	1986	—	2.50	5.00
—Blue vinyl					

Number	Title (A Side/B Side)	Yr	VG	VG+	NM
❑ 28591	True Blue/Ain't No Big Deal	1986	—	—	3.00
❑ 28591 [PS]	True Blue/Ain't No Big Deal	1986	—	2.50	5.00
—"Limited edition blue vinyl pressing" on sleeve					
❑ 28591 [PS]	True Blue/Ain't No Big Deal	1986	—	—	3.00
—No mention of limited edition on sleeve					
❑ 28660	Papa Don't Preach/Pretender	1986	—	—	3.00
❑ 28660 [PS]	Papa Don't Preach/Pretender	1986	—	—	3.00
❑ 28717	Live to Tell/(Instrumental)	1986	—	—	3.00
❑ 28717 [PS]	Live to Tell/(Instrumental)	1986	—	—	3.00
❑ 28919	Dress You Up/Shoo-Be-Doo	1985	—	—	3.00
❑ 28919 [PS]	Dress You Up/Shoo-Be-Doo	1985	12.50	25.00	50.00
❑ 29008	Angel/(12" Remix Edit)	1985	—	—	3.00
❑ 29008 [PS]	Angel/(12" Remix Edit)	1985	—	—	3.00
❑ 29083	Material Girl/Pretender	1985	—	—	3.00
❑ 29083 [PS]	Material Girl/Pretender	1985	—	—	3.00
❑ 29177	Lucky Star/I Know It	1984	—	2.00	4.00
❑ 29210	Like a Virgin/Stay	1984	—	—	3.00
❑ 29210 [PS]	Like a Virgin/Stay	1984	—	—	3.00
❑ 29354	Borderline/Think of Me	1984	—	2.00	4.00
❑ 29354 [PS]	Borderline/Think of Me	1984	20.00	40.00	80.00
—Fold-out poster sleeve					
❑ 29478	Holiday/(Instrumental)	1983	—	2.00	4.00
❑ 29478	Holiday/I Know It	1983	—	2.00	4.00
❑ 29841	Everybody/(Instrumental)	1982	5.00	10.00	20.00
—Deduct 50% for promo copy					
WARNER BROS.					
❑ 17495	You Must Love Me/Rainbow High	1996	—	2.00	4.00
Albums					
MAVERICK					
❑ PRO-A-5904 [(2) DJ]	Erotica	1992	15.00	30.00	60.00
—Vinyl is promo only					
❑ PRO-A-7311 [(2) DJ]	Bedtime Stories	1994	20.00	40.00	80.00
—Promo only on pink vinyl					
❑ PRO-A-9378 [(2) DJ]	Ray of Light	1998	12.50	25.00	50.00
—Vinyl is promo only; generic cover with sticker					
❑ PRO-A-100500-A [(2) DJ]	Music	2000	7.50	15.00	30.00
—Vinyl is promo only; generic white die-cut sleeve					
❑ PRO-A-100871 [(3) DJ]	GHV2 Remixed — The Best of 1991-2001	2001	10.00	20.00	40.00
—Promo-only remixes of 12 songs from the "GHV2" CD; comes in generic black jacket with hole in center					
SIRE					
❑ PRO-A-2892	You Can Dance	1987	7.50	15.00	30.00
—Promo-only; contains single edits of the seven songs on the stock editions					
❑ 23867	Madonna	1983	5.00	10.00	20.00
—First pressing with 4:48 version of "Burning Up"; this version has only been found on copies with a gold promo stamp on the cover					
❑ 23867	Madonna	1983	2.50	5.00	10.00
—Second pressing with 3:49 version of "Burning Up"					
❑ W1-23867	Madonna	1984	3.75	7.50	15.00
—Columbia House edition					
❑ 25157	Like a Virgin	1984	15.00	30.00	60.00
—White vinyl with silver colored spine					
❑ 25157	Like a Virgin	1984	12.50	25.00	50.00
—White vinyl with cream colored spine					
❑ 25157	Like a Virgin	1984	2.50	5.00	10.00
❑ W1-25157	Like a Virgin	1985	3.75	7.50	15.00
—Columbia House edition					
❑ 25442	True Blue	1986	3.00	6.00	12.00
—With poster					
❑ 25442	True Blue	1986	2.00	4.00	8.00
—Without poster					
❑ W1-25442	True Blue	1986	3.75	7.50	15.00
—Columbia House edition; issued with poster					
❑ 25535	You Can Dance	1987	3.00	6.00	12.00
—With gold obi "Madonna and Dancing"					
❑ 25535	You Can Dance	1987	2.00	4.00	8.00
—Without gold obi					
❑ W1-25535	You Can Dance	1987	3.75	7.50	15.00
—Columbia House edition; not issued with obi					
❑ 25844	Like a Prayer	1989	2.50	5.00	10.00
❑ W1-25844	Like a Prayer	1989	3.75	7.50	15.00
—Columbia House edition					
❑ 26209	I'm Breathless	1990	2.50	5.00	10.00
❑ W1-26209	I'm Breathless	1990	3.75	7.50	15.00
—Columbia House edition					
❑ 26440 [(2)]	The Immaculate Collection	1990	3.75	7.50	15.00
❑ W1-26440 [(2)]	The Immaculate Collection	1990	5.00	10.00	20.00
—Columbia House edition					
❑ R 100572	I'm Breathless	1990	3.75	7.50	15.00
—BMG Direct Marketing edition					
❑ R 101029	Like a Prayer	1989	3.75	7.50	15.00
—BMG Direct Marketing edition					
❑ R 134536	You Can Dance	1987	3.75	7.50	15.00
—RCA Music Service edition; not issued with obi					
❑ R 143811	True Blue	1986	3.75	7.50	15.00
—RCA Music Service edition; issued with poster					
❑ R 161153	Like a Virgin	1985	3.75	7.50	15.00
—RCA Music Service edition					
❑ R 164288	Madonna	1984	3.75	7.50	15.00
—RCA Music Service edition					
❑ R 254164 [(2)]	The Immaculate Collection	1990	5.00	10.00	20.00
—BMG Direct Marketing edition					

MAESTRO, JOHNNY

Number	Title (A Side/B Side)	Yr	VG	VG+	NM
45s					
APT					
❑ 25075	Phone Booth on the Highway/She's All Mine Alone	1965	12.50	25.00	50.00
BUDDAH					
❑ 201	The Rains Came/Never Knew THis Kind of Hurt Before	1971	2.50	5.00	10.00
❑ 236	Yours Until Tomorrow/Man in a Band	1971	2.50	5.00	10.00
❑ 289 [DJ]	Snow (mono/stereo)	1971	2.50	5.00	10.00
—May be promo only					
CAMEO					
❑ 256	Over the Weekend/I'll Be There	1963	7.50	15.00	30.00
❑ 305	Lean on Me/(It's Harder to) Make Up My Mind	1964	5.00	10.00	20.00
COED					
❑ 527	Say It Isn't So/The Great Physician	1960	6.25	12.50	25.00
—As "Johnny Masters"					
❑ 545	Model Girl/We've Got to Tell Them	1961	6.25	12.50	25.00
—As "Johnny Mastro"					
❑ 549	What a Surprise/Warning Voice	1961	6.25	12.50	25.00
❑ 552	Mr. Happiness/Test of Love	1961	6.25	12.50	25.00
❑ 557	I.O.U./The Way You Look Tonight	1961	7.50	15.00	30.00
❑ 562	Besame Baby/It Must Be Love	1962	25.00	50.00	100.00
PARKWAY					
❑ 118	My Times/Is It You	1966	5.00	10.00	20.00
❑ 987	Heartburn/Try Me	1966	3.75	7.50	15.00
❑ 987 [DJ]	Heartburn	1966	15.00	30.00	60.00
—One-sided white label promo					
❑ 999	I Care About You/Come See Me (I'm Your Man)	1966	3.75	7.50	15.00
UNITED ARTISTS					
❑ 474	Before I Loved Her/Fifty Million Heartbeats	1962	10.00	20.00	40.00
Albums					
BUDDAH					
❑ BDS-5091	The Johnny Maestro Story	1971	10.00	20.00	40.00
—With inserts; deduct 40% if missing					

MAGNIFICENTS, THE

Number	Title (A Side/B Side)	Yr	VG	VG+	NM
45s					
CHECKER					
❑ 1016	The Dribble Twist/Do You Mind	1962	3.75	7.50	15.00
KANSOMA					
❑ 03	The Dribble Twist/Do You Mind	1962	7.50	15.00	30.00
VEE JAY					
❑ 183	Up On the Mountain/Why Did She Go	1956	18.75	37.50	75.00
❑ 208	Hiccup/Caddy Bo	1956	25.00	50.00	100.00
❑ 235	Off the Mountain/Lost Lovers	1957	18.75	37.50	75.00
❑ 281	Don't Leave Me/Ozeta	1958	25.00	50.00	100.00
❑ 367	Up On the Mountain/Let's Do the Cha Cha	1960	5.00	10.00	20.00

MAIN INGREDIENT, THE

Number	Title (A Side/B Side)	Yr	VG	VG+	NM
12-Inch Singles					
RCA					
❑ PD-13046	Party People/Save Me	1981	3.00	6.00	12.00
45s					
MERCURY					
❑ 73831	Magic Touch/Very White	1976	—	2.50	5.00
—As "Tony Sylvester and the New Ingredient"					
❑ 73871	Puzuzu/Soca	1977	—	2.50	5.00
—As "Tony Sylvester and the New Ingredient"					
POLYDOR					
❑ 889910-7	I Just Wanna Love You/When We Need It Bad	1989	—	—	3.00
RCA					
❑ PB-12060	Think Positive/Spoiled	1980	—	2.00	4.00
—RCA 1980s titles as "Cuba Gooding and the Main Ingredient"					
❑ PB-12107	What Can a Miracle Do/Makes No Diff'rence to Me	1980	—	2.00	4.00
❑ PB-12320	Evening of Love/(Instrumental)	1981	—	—	—
—Unreleased					
❑ PB-12340	I Only Have Eyes for You/Only	1981	—	2.00	4.00
❑ PB-13045	Party People/Save Me	1982	—	2.00	4.00
RCA VICTOR					
❑ 47-9748	I Was Born to Lose You/Psychedelic Ride	1969	—	3.00	6.00
❑ 74-0252	Get Back/Brotherly Love	1969	—	3.00	6.00
❑ 74-0313	The Girl I Left Behind/Can't Stand Your Love	1970	—	2.50	5.00
❑ 74-0340	You've Been My Inspiration/Life Won't Be the Same (Without You)	1970	—	2.50	5.00
❑ 74-0385	Need Your Love/I'm Better Off Without You	1970	—	2.50	5.00
❑ 74-0401	I'm So Proud/Brother Love	1970	—	2.50	5.00
❑ 74-0456	Spinning Around (I Must Be Falling in Love)/Magic Shoes	1971	—	2.50	5.00
❑ 74-0517	Black Seeds Keep On Growing/Baby Change Your Mind	1971	—	2.50	5.00
❑ 74-0603	I'm Leaving This Time/Another Day Has Come	1971	—	2.50	5.00
❑ 74-0731	Everybody Plays the Fool/Who Can I Turn To	1972	—	3.00	6.00
❑ 74-0856	You've Got to Take It (If You Want It)/Travelling	1973	—	2.50	5.00
❑ 74-0939	You Can Call Me Rover/I'm Better Off Without You	1973	—	2.50	5.00
❑ APBO-0046	Girl Blue/Movin' On	1973	—	2.50	5.00
❑ AMBO-0124	Everybody Plays the Fool/I'm So Proud	1973	—	2.00	4.00
—Gold Standard Series					
❑ APBO-0205	Just Don't Want to Be Lonely/Goodbye My Love	1974	—	2.50	5.00
❑ APBO-0305	Happiness Is Just Around the Bend/Why Can't We All Unite	1974	—	2.50	5.00
❑ PB-10095	California My Way/Looks Like Rain	1974	—	2.50	5.00

Number	Title (A Side/B Side)	Yr	VG	VG+	NM
❑ PB-10224	Rolling Down a Mountainside/Family Man	1975	—	2.50	5.00
❑ PB-10334	The Good Old Days/I Want to Make You Glad	1975	—	2.50	5.00
❑ PB-10431	Shame on the World/Lillian	1975	—	2.50	5.00
❑ GB-10482	Why Can't We All Unite/Happiness Is Just Around the Corner	1975	—	2.00	4.00

—Gold Standard Series

| ❑ GB-10483 | Just Don't Want to Be Lonely/Goodbye My Love | 1975 | — | 2.00 | 4.00 |

—Gold Standard Series

ZAKIA

| ❑ 015 | Do Me Right/(B-side unknown) | 1986 | — | 2.00 | 4.00 |

Albums
COLLECTABLES

| ❑ COL-5101 | Golden Classics | 198? | 2.50 | 5.00 | 10.00 |

POLYDOR

| ❑ 841249-1 | I Just Wanna Love You | 1989 | 3.00 | 6.00 | 12.00 |

RCA VICTOR

❑ APL1-0314	Greatest Hits	1974	3.00	6.00	12.00
❑ APL1-0335	Euphrates River	1974	3.00	6.00	12.00
❑ APL1-0644	Rolling Down a Mountainside	1975	3.00	6.00	12.00
❑ APL1-1003	Shame On the World	1975	3.00	6.00	12.00
❑ APL1-1558	Music Maximus	1977	3.00	6.00	12.00
❑ APL1-1858	Super Hits	1977	3.00	6.00	12.00
❑ ANL1-2667	Rolling Down a Mountainside	1978	2.50	5.00	10.00

—Reissue of APL1-0644

❑ AFL1-3641	Ready for Love	1980	2.50	5.00	10.00
❑ AFL1-3963	I Only Have Eyes for You	1981	2.50	5.00	10.00
❑ LSP-4253	The Main Ingredient L.T.D.	1970	3.00	6.00	12.00
❑ LSP-4412	Tasteful Soul	1971	3.00	6.00	12.00
❑ LSP-4483	Black Seeds	1971	3.00	6.00	12.00
❑ LSP-4677	Bitter Sweet	1972	3.00	6.00	12.00
❑ LSP-4834	Afrodisiac	1973	3.00	6.00	12.00

MAJESTICS, THE (1)
45s
CHESS

| ❑ 1802 | Oasis (Part 1)/Oasis (Part 2) | 1961 | 5.00 | 10.00 | 20.00 |

V.I.P.

| ❑ 25028 [DJ] | Say You/All for Someone | 1965 | 250.00 | 500.00 | 1000. |

—Promo only; stock copies credited "The Monitors"

MAJESTICS, THE (2)
45s
CHEX

❑ 1000	Give Me a Cigarette/Shoppin' and Hoppin'	1962	25.00	50.00	100.00
❑ 1000	Give Me a Cigarette/So I Can Forget	1962	10.00	20.00	40.00
❑ 1004	Unhappy and Blue/Treat Me Like You Want	1962	12.50	25.00	50.00
❑ 1006	Lonely Heart/Gwendolyn	1962	7.50	15.00	30.00
❑ 1009	Baby/Teach Me How to Limbo	1963	6.25	12.50	25.00

MAJESTICS, THE (3)
45s
20TH FOX

| ❑ 171 | The Lone Stranger/Sweet One | 1959 | 6.25 | 12.50 | 25.00 |

CONTOUR

| ❑ 501 | Teen Age Gossip/Hard Times | 1960 | 20.00 | 40.00 | 80.00 |

FARO

| ❑ 592 | TV Cowboys/So You Want to Rock | 1959 | 6.25 | 12.50 | 25.00 |

FOXIE

| ❑ 7004 | The Lone Stranger/Sweet One | 1960 | 5.00 | 10.00 | 20.00 |

NRC

| ❑ 502 | Please Don't Say No/Divided Heart | 1958 | 62.50 | 125.00 | 250.00 |

SIOUX

| ❑ 91459 | The Lone Stranger/Sweet One | 1959 | 12.50 | 25.00 | 50.00 |

MAJESTICS, THE (4)
45s
DUNES

| ❑ 2014 | The Boss Walk (Part 1)/The Boss Walk (Part 2) | 1962 | 10.00 | 20.00 | 40.00 |

SAM

❑ 112	Jaguar/Blue Feeling	1962	12.50	25.00	50.00
❑ 117	Riptide/Big Noise from Makaba	1962	12.50	25.00	50.00
❑ 123	XL-3/My Little Baby	1963	12.50	25.00	50.00

MAJESTICS, THE (5)
45s
JORDAN

| ❑ 1057 | Angel of Love/Searching for a New Love | 1961 | 75.00 | 150.00 | 300.00 |

—Yellow vinyl

| ❑ 1057 | Angel of Love/Searching for a New Love | 1961 | 12.50 | 25.00 | 50.00 |

—Black vinyl
LINDA

| ❑ 111 | Strange World/Everything Is Gonna Be All Right | 1963 | 15.00 | 30.00 | 60.00 |
| ❑ 121 | Girl of My Dreams/It Hurts Me | 1963 | 25.00 | 50.00 | 100.00 |

NU-TONE

| ❑ 123 | Angel of Love/Searching for a New Love | 1961 | 17.50 | 35.00 | 70.00 |

PIXIE

| ❑ 6901 | Angel of Love/Searching for a New Love | 1961 | 7.50 | 15.00 | 30.00 |

MAJESTICS, THE (6)
Sam Moore of SAM AND DAVE was in this group.
45s
MARLIN

| ❑ 802 | Nitey Nite/Cave Man Rock | 1956 | 250.00 | 500.00 | 1000. |

MAJESTICS, THE (7)
45s
MGM

| ❑ 13488 | Love Has Forgotten Me/Smile Through My Tears | 1966 | 3.00 | 6.00 | 12.00 |

MAJOR LANCE
See listing under LANCE, MAJOR.

MAJORS, THE (1)
45s
IMPERIAL

❑ 5855	A Wonderful Dream/Time Will Tell	1962	5.00	10.00	20.00
❑ 5879	She's a Troublemaker/A Little Bit Now, A Little Bit Later	1962	3.75	7.50	15.00
❑ 5914	What in the World/Anything You Can Do	1963	3.00	6.00	12.00
❑ 5936	Tra La La/What Have You Been Doin'	1963	3.00	6.00	12.00
❑ 5968	One Happy Ending/Get Up Now	1963	3.00	6.00	12.00
❑ 5991	Which Way Did She Go/Your Life Begins (Sweet 16)	1963	3.00	6.00	12.00
❑ 66009	I'll Be There/Ooh Wee Baby	1963	3.00	6.00	12.00

UNITED ARTISTS

| ❑ 0110 | A Wonderful Dream/Mother-in-Law | 1973 | — | 2.50 | 5.00 |

—"Silver Spotlight Series" reissue; B-side by Ernie K-Doe
Albums
IMPERIAL

| ❑ LP-9222 [M] | Meet the Majors | 1963 | 37.50 | 75.00 | 150.00 |
| ❑ LP-12222 [S] | Meet the Majors | 1963 | 75.00 | 150.00 | 300.00 |

MAJORS, THE (2)
45s
DERBY

| ❑ 763 | At Last/You Ran Away from My Heart | 1951 | 200.00 | 400.00 | 800.00 |
| ❑ 779 | Laughing on the Outside/Come On Up to My Room | 1951 | 150.00 | 300.00 | 600.00 |

MAJORS, THE (3)
45s
FELSTED

❑ 8501	Blue Sunset/Rockin' the Boogie	1958	7.50	15.00	30.00
❑ 8576	Come Go with Me/Les Qua	1959	6.25	12.50	25.00
❑ 8707	Come Go with Me/Les Qua	1964	3.75	7.50	15.00

MAJORS, THE (4)
45s
ORIGINAL

| ❑ 1003 | Big Eyes/Go 'Way | 1954 | 100.00 | 200.00 | 400.00 |

MALCOLM X
Black Muslim leader whose speeches were often sampled on early hip-hop records.
12-Inch Singles
TOMMY BOY

| ❑ TB 840 | No Sell Out (Vocal 5:44) (Instrumental 7:09) | 1983 | 3.00 | 6.00 | 12.00 |

45s
TOMMY BOY

| ❑ 840 | No Sell Out/(Instrumental) | 1983 | — | 2.50 | 5.00 |

Albums
DOUGLAS

❑ SD 795 [M]	Malcolm X Talks to Young People	1968	7.50	15.00	30.00
❑ SD 797	His Wit and Wisdom	196?	7.50	15.00	30.00
❑ Z 30743 [M]	By Any Means Necessary	1971	7.50	15.00	30.00

PAUL WINLEY

| ❑ 135 | The Ballot or the Bullet | 197? | 5.00 | 10.00 | 20.00 |

RCA

| ❑ 66132 | Words from the Frontlines: Excerpts from the Great Speeches of Malcolm X | 1992 | 5.00 | 10.00 | 20.00 |

UPFRONT

| ❑ UPF-152 | Malcolm X Speaks to the People in Harlem | 197? | 3.75 | 7.50 | 15.00 |

WARNER BROS.

❑ BS 2619	Malcolm X	1972	6.25	12.50	25.00
❑ PRO-A-5943 [DJ]	Malcolm X Speaks	1992	5.00	10.00	20.00
❑ PRO-A-5957 [DJ]	Music and Dialog from the Historic 1992 Documentary Film Malcolm X	1992	5.00	10.00	20.00

MALLETT, SAUNDRA, AND THE VANDELLAS
Also see MARTHA AND THE VANDELLAS.
45s
TAMLA

| ❑ 54067 | Camel Walk/It's Gonna Be Hard Times | 1962 | 250.00 | 500.00 | 1000. |

MANDRILL
45s
ARISTA

❑ 0274	Funky Monkey/Gilley Hines	1977	—	2.00	4.00
❑ 0304	Can You Get It/Holiday	1978	—	2.00	4.00
❑ 0326	Happy Beat/Holiday	1978	—	2.00	4.00
❑ 0375	Too Late/Holiday	1978	—	2.00	4.00
❑ 0490	My Kind of Girl/Lo Siento Mucho	1980	—	2.00	4.00
❑ 0507	Getting in the Mood/(B-side unknown)	1980	—	2.00	4.00
❑ 0529	Dance of Love/When You Shake	1980	—	2.00	4.00

MONTAGE

| ❑ 1222 | Put Your Money Where the Funk Is/(B-side unknown) | 1982 | — | 2.00 | 4.00 |
| ❑ 1224 | Soar Like an Eagle/Starry-Eyed | 1982 | — | 2.00 | 4.00 |

M

Number	Title (A Side/B Side)	Yr	VG	VG+	NM

POLYDOR

Number	Title (A Side/B Side)	Yr	VG	VG+	NM
❏ 14070	Mandrill/Warning Blues	1971	—	2.50	5.00
❏ 14085	Rollin' On/Symphonic Revolution	1971	—	2.50	5.00
❏ 14127	Kofijahm/I Refuse to Smile	1972	—	2.50	5.00
❏ 14142	Cohelo/Git It All	1972	—	2.50	5.00
❏ 14156	Children of the Sun/Ace Is High	1972	—	2.50	5.00
❏ 14163	Fencewalk/Hagalo	1973	—	2.50	5.00
❏ 14187	Hang Loose/Polk Street Carnival	1973	—	2.50	5.00
❏ 14200	Mango Meat/Afrikus Retrospectus	1973	—	2.50	5.00
❏ 14214	Love Song/Two Sisters of Mystery	1974	—	2.50	5.00
❏ 14235	Positive Thing/Positive Thing Plus	1974	—	2.50	5.00
❏ 14257	Road to Love/Armadillo	1974	—	2.50	5.00

UNITED ARTISTS

Number	Title (A Side/B Side)	Yr	VG	VG+	NM
❏ XW673	Tee Vee/Silk	1975	—	2.00	4.00
❏ XW778	Disco-Lypso/Solid	1976	—	2.00	4.00

Albums

ARISTA

Number	Title	Yr	VG	VG+	NM
❏ AL 4144	We Are One	1977	2.50	5.00	10.00
❏ AL 4195	New Worlds	1978	2.50	5.00	10.00
❏ AL 9527	Getting In the Mood	1980	2.50	5.00	10.00

LIBERTY

Number	Title	Yr	VG	VG+	NM
❏ LN-10196	Rebirth	1983	2.00	4.00	8.00

MONTAGE

Number	Title	Yr	VG	VG+	NM
❏ ST-72008	Energize	1982	3.00	6.00	12.00

POLYDOR

Number	Title	Yr	VG	VG+	NM
❏ 24-4060	Mandrill	1971	3.00	6.00	12.00
❏ PD-5025	Mandrill Is	1972	3.00	6.00	12.00
❏ PD-5043	Composite Truth	1973	3.00	6.00	12.00
❏ PD-5059	Just Outside of Town	1973	3.00	6.00	12.00
❏ PD-1-6047	The Best of Mandrill	1975	3.00	6.00	12.00
❏ PD-2-9002	[(2)]Mandrilland	1976	3.75	7.50	15.00

UNITED ARTISTS

Number	Title	Yr	VG	VG+	NM
❏ UA-LA408-G	Solid	1975	3.00	6.00	12.00
❏ UA-LA577-G	Beast from the East	1976	3.00	6.00	12.00

MANHATTANS, THE (1)

Well-known male R&B vocal group.

12-Inch Singles

COLUMBIA

Number	Title (A Side/B Side)	Yr	VG	VG+	NM
❏ AS 1316 [DJ]	Let Your Love Come Down (same on both sides)	1981	2.50	5.00	10.00
❏ 03940	Crazy (5:00) (Instrumental)	1983	2.00	4.00	8.00
❏ 05973	Maybe Tomorrow/Where Did We Go Wrong	1986	2.00	4.00	8.00

45s

CARNIVAL

Number	Title (A Side/B Side)	Yr	VG	VG+	NM
❏ 504	I've Got Everything But You/For the Very First Time	1964	5.00	10.00	20.00
❏ 506	There Goes a Fool/Call Somebody Please	1964	10.00	20.00	40.00
❏ 507	I Wanna Be (Your Everything)/What's It Gonna Be	1965	3.75	7.50	15.00
❏ 509	Searchin' for My Baby/I'm the One That Love Forgot	1965	3.75	7.50	15.00
❏ 512	Follow Your Heart/The Boston Money	1965	3.75	7.50	15.00
❏ 514	Baby I Need You/Teach Me the Philly Dog	1966	3.75	7.50	15.00
❏ 517	Can I/That New Girl	1966	3.75	7.50	15.00
❏ 522	I Betcha (Couldn't Love Me)/Sweet Little Girl	1966	3.75	7.50	15.00
❏ 524	It's That Time of the Year/Alone on New Year's Eve	1966	5.00	10.00	20.00
❏ 526	All I Need Is Your Love/Our Love Will Never Die	1967	3.75	7.50	15.00
❏ 529	When We're Made As One/Baby I'm Sorry	1967	3.75	7.50	15.00
❏ 533	I Call It Love/Manhattan Stomp	1967	3.75	7.50	15.00
❏ 542	I Don't Wanna Go/Love Is Breaking Out	1968	3.75	7.50	15.00
❏ 545	Til You Come Back to Me/Call Somebody Please	1968	3.75	7.50	15.00

COLUMBIA

Number	Title (A Side/B Side)	Yr	VG	VG+	NM
❏ 02164	Shining Star/Summertime in the City	1981	—	—	3.00
—Reissue					
❏ 02191	Just One Moment Away/When I Leave Tomorrow	1981	—	2.00	4.00
❏ 02548	Let Your Love Come Down/I Gotta Thank You	1981	—	2.00	4.00
❏ 02666	Money, Money/I Wanta Thank You	1982	—	2.00	4.00
❏ 03939	Crazy/Gonna Find You	1983	—	2.00	4.00
❏ 04110	Forever By Your Side/Locked Up in Your Love	1983	—	2.00	4.00
❏ 04754	You Send Me/You're Gonna Love Being Loved By Me	1985	—	2.00	4.00
❏ 04754 [PS]	You Send Me/You're Gonna Love Being Loved By Me	1985	—	2.00	4.00
❏ 04930	Don't Say No/Dreamin'	1985	—	2.00	4.00
❏ 06376	Where Did We Go Wrong/Maybe Tomorrow	1986	—	2.00	4.00
—With Regina Belle					
❏ 07010	Mr. D.J./All I Need	1987	—	2.00	4.00
❏ 10045	Don't Take Your Love/The Day the Robins Sang to Me	1974	—	2.50	5.00
❏ 10140	Hurt/Nursery Rhymes	1975	—	2.50	5.00
❏ 10310	Kiss and Say Goodbye/Wonderful World of Love	1976	—	2.50	5.00
❏ 10430	I Kinda Miss You/Gypsy Man	1976	—	2.50	5.00
❏ 10495	It Feels So Good to Be Loved By You/On the Street (Where I Live)	1977	—	2.50	5.00
❏ 10586	We Never Danced to a Love Song/Let's Start It All Over Again	1977	—	2.50	5.00
❏ 10674	Am I Losing You/Movin'	1978	—	2.50	5.00
❏ 10766	Everybody Has a Dream/Happiness	1978	—	2.50	5.00
❏ 10921	Here Comes the Hurt Again/Don't Say Goodbye	1979	—	2.50	5.00
❏ 11024	The Way We Were-Memories/New York City	1979	—	2.50	5.00
❏ 11222	Shining Star/I'll Never Run Away from Love Again	1980	—	2.00	4.00
❏ 11321	Girl of My Dreams/The Closer You Are	1980	—	2.00	4.00

Number	Title (A Side/B Side)	Yr	VG	VG+	NM
❏ 11398	I'll Never Find Another (Another Just Like You)/Rendezvous	1980	—	2.00	4.00
❏ 45838	There's No Me Without You/I'm Not a Run-Around	1973	—	3.00	6.00
❏ 45927	You'd Better Believe It/Soul Train	1973	—	3.00	6.00
❏ 45971	Wish That You Were Mine/It's So Hard Loving You	1973	—	3.00	6.00
❏ 46081	Summertime in the City/The Other Side of Me	1974	—	3.00	6.00
❏ 60511	Do You Really Mean Goodbye/Rendezvous	1981	—	2.00	4.00

DELUXE

Number	Title (A Side/B Side)	Yr	VG	VG+	NM
❏ 109	The Picture Became Quite Clear/Oh Lord, How I Wish I Could Sleep	1969	2.50	5.00	10.00
❏ 115	It's Gonna Take a Lot to Bring Me Back/Give Him Up	1970	2.50	5.00	10.00
❏ 122	If My Heart Could Speak/Loneliness	1970	2.50	5.00	10.00
❏ 129	From Atlanta to Goodbye/Fantastic Journey	1970	2.50	5.00	10.00
❏ 132	Let Them Talk/Straight to My Heart	1970	2.50	5.00	10.00
❏ 136	Do You Ever/I Can't Stand for You to Leave Me	1971	2.50	5.00	10.00
❏ 137	A Million to One/Cry If You Wanna Cry	1971	2.50	5.00	10.00
❏ 139	One Life to Live/It's the Only One	1972	2.50	5.00	10.00
❏ 144	Back Up/Fever	1972	2.50	5.00	10.00
❏ 146	Rainbow Week/Loneliness	1973	2.50	5.00	10.00
❏ 152	Do You Ever/If My Heart Could Speak	1973	2.50	5.00	10.00

STARFIRE

Number	Title (A Side/B Side)	Yr	VG	VG+	NM
❏ 121	Alone on New Year's Eve/It's That Time of the Year	1979	—	2.50	5.00

VALLEY VUE

Number	Title (A Side/B Side)	Yr	VG	VG+	NM
❏ 75723	Sweet Talk/(B-side unknown)	1989	—	3.00	6.00
❏ 75749	Why You Wanna Love Me Like That/(B-side unknown)	1989	—	3.00	6.00

Albums

CARNIVAL

Number	Title	Yr	VG	VG+	NM
❏ CMLP-201	[M]Dedicated to You	1966	62.50	125.00	250.00
❏ CSLP-201	[S] Dedicated to You	1966	125.00	250.00	500.00
❏ CMLP-202	[M]For You and Yours	1967	37.50	75.00	150.00
❏ CSLP-202	[S] For You and Yours	1967	75.00	150.00	300.00

COLLECTABLES

Number	Title	Yr	VG	VG+	NM
❏ COL-5135	Dedicated to You: Golden Carnival Classics, Part One	198?	2.50	5.00	10.00
❏ COL-5136	For You and Yours: Golden Carnival Classics, Part Two	198?	2.50	5.00	10.00

COLUMBIA

Number	Title	Yr	VG	VG+	NM
❏ KC 32444	There's No Me Without You	1973	3.75	7.50	15.00
❏ PC 32444	There's No Me Without You	198?	2.00	4.00	8.00
—Budget-line reissue					
❏ KC 33064	That's How Much I Love You	1975	3.75	7.50	15.00
❏ PC 33820	The Manhattans	1976	3.00	6.00	12.00
—No bar code on back cover					
❏ PC 33820	The Manhattans	198?	2.00	4.00	8.00
—With bar code on back cover					
❏ PC 34450	It Feels So Good	1977	3.00	6.00	12.00
—No bar code on back cover					
❏ PC 34450	It Feels So Good	198?	2.00	4.00	8.00
—With bar code on back cover					
❏ PCQ 34450	[Q]It Feels So Good	1977	5.00	10.00	20.00
❏ JC 35252	There's No Good in Goodbye	1978	3.00	6.00	12.00
❏ JC 35693	Love Talk	1979	3.00	6.00	12.00
❏ PC 35693	After Midnight	198?	2.00	4.00	8.00
—Budget-line reissue					
❏ JC 36411	After Midnight	1980	3.00	6.00	12.00
❏ JC 36861	Manhattans Greatest Hits	1980	3.00	6.00	12.00
❏ FC 37156	Black Tie	1981	2.50	5.00	10.00
❏ PC 37156	Black Tie	198?	2.00	4.00	8.00
—Budget-line reissue					
❏ FC 38600	Forever By Your Side	1983	2.50	5.00	10.00
❏ FC 39277	Too Hot to Stop It	1985	2.50	5.00	10.00

DELUXE

Number	Title	Yr	VG	VG+	NM
❏ 12000	With These Hands	1971	6.25	12.50	25.00
❏ 12004	A Million to One	1972	6.25	12.50	25.00

SOLID SMOKE

Number	Title	Yr	VG	VG+	NM
❏ 8007	Follow Your Heart	1981	2.50	5.00	10.00

VALLEY VUE

Number	Title	Yr	VG	VG+	NM
❏ D1-72946	Sweet Talk	1989	3.00	6.00	12.00

MANHATTANS, THE (2)

45s

COLPIX

Number	Title (A Side/B Side)	Yr	VG	VG+	NM
❏ 115	Big Wheel Express/Powder Blue	1959	7.50	15.00	30.00

MANHATTANS, THE (U)

Some of these are likely group (1); others could be group (2); others are probably neither.

45s

AVANTI

Number	Title (A Side/B Side)	Yr	VG	VG+	NM
❏ 1401	What Should I Do/Later for You	1963	6.25	12.50	25.00

BIG MACK

Number	Title (A Side/B Side)	Yr	VG	VG+	NM
❏ 3911	Why Should I Cry/The Feeling Is Mutual	196?	50.00	100.00	200.00

CAPITOL

Number	Title (A Side/B Side)	Yr	VG	VG+	NM
❏ 4591	Molly Brown Medley/I Ain't Down Yet	1961	5.00	10.00	20.00
❏ 4730	La La La/Sing All the Day	1962	5.00	10.00	20.00

ENJOY

Number	Title (A Side/B Side)	Yr	VG	VG+	NM
❏ 2008	Come On Back/Long Time No See	1964	5.00	10.00	20.00
—As "Ronnie and the Manhattans"					

GOLDEN WORLD

Number	Title (A Side/B Side)	Yr	VG	VG+	NM
❏ 14	Just a Little Loving/Beautiful Brown Eyes	1964	7.50	15.00	30.00

Number	Title (A Side/B Side)	Yr	VG	VG+	NM
KING					
❏ 5228	Ebb Tide (Part 1)/Ebb Tide (Part 2)	1959	3.75	7.50	15.00
❏ 5259	Sugar Tooth/Like Saying Something	1959	3.75	7.50	15.00
PINEY					
❏ 107	Live It Up/Go Baby Go	1962	15.00	30.00	60.00
❏ 108	Crazy Love/The Hawk and the Crow	1962	12.50	25.00	50.00
WARNER					
❏ 1015	How Do I Say I'm Sorry/Love Is Where You Find It	1958	30.00	60.00	120.00

MANN, HERBIE
12-Inch Singles
ATLANTIC

Number	Title (A Side/B Side)	Yr	VG	VG+	NM
❏ DSKO 172 [DJ]	Jisco Dazz/Body Oil	1979	2.50	5.00	10.00
❏ DK 4708	Superman/Etagui	1978	2.50	5.00	10.00

45s
ATLANTIC

Number	Title (A Side/B Side)	Yr	VG	VG+	NM
❏ 2262	Theme from Malamondo/Fiddler on the Roof	1964	2.50	5.00	10.00
❏ 2363	Is Paris Burning?/Happy Brass	1966	2.00	4.00	8.00
❏ 2379	The Honeydripper/The Puppet	1967	—	3.00	6.00
❏ 2392	Day Tripper/A Good Thing (Is Hard to Come By)	1967	2.00	4.00	8.00
—With Tamiko Jones					
❏ 2393	Uskudar/Turkish Coffee	1967	—	3.00	6.00
❏ 2399	The Beat Goes On/Free for All	1967	—	3.00	6.00
❏ 2444	To Sir with Love/Hold Back (Just a Little Longer)	1967	—	3.00	6.00
❏ 2451	Cottage for Sale/Live for Life	1967	—	3.00	6.00
—With Carmen McRae					
❏ 2498	By the Time I Get to Phoenix/Sports Car	1968	—	3.00	6.00
❏ 2621	Memphis Underground/New Orleans	1969	—	3.00	6.00
❏ 2661	Battle Hymn of the Republic/Hold On, I'm Comin'	1969	—	3.00	6.00
❏ 2671	It's a Funky Thing — Right On (Part 1)/It's a Funky Thing — Right On (Part 2)	1969	—	3.00	6.00
❏ 2882	Respect Yourself/Mississippi Gambler	1972	—	2.50	5.00
❏ 2960	Do It Again/Turtle Baby	1973	—	2.50	5.00
❏ 3009	Now I've Found a Lady/Spin Ball	1974	—	2.50	5.00
❏ 3037	Anata/Sound of Wood Wind	1974	—	2.50	5.00
❏ 3219	My Girl/Rivers of Babylon	1974	—	2.50	5.00
❏ 3246	Hijack/Orient Express	1975	—	2.00	4.00
❏ 3282	Waterbed/Body Oil	1975	—	2.00	4.00
❏ 3313	Stars and Stripes Forever (Part 1)/Stars and Stripes Forever (Part 2)	1976	—	2.50	5.00
❏ 3343	Cajun Moon/So Git It While You Can	1976	—	2.00	4.00
❏ 3390	Birdwalk/Aria	1977	—	2.00	4.00
❏ 3536	The Closer I Get to You/Watermelon Man	1978	—	2.00	4.00
❏ 3547	Superman/Etagui	1978	—	2.00	4.00
❏ 3547 [PS]	Superman/Etagui	1978	—	3.00	6.00
❏ 3575	Jisco Dazz/Time Is a Thief	1979	—	2.00	4.00
❏ 5009	Uhuru/High Life	1960	3.00	6.00	12.00
❏ 5010	Walkin'/(B-side unknown)	1961	3.00	6.00	12.00
❏ 5015	This Little Girl of Mine/Why Don't You Do Right	1961	3.00	6.00	12.00
❏ 5019	Carnival/La La La	1962	3.00	6.00	12.00
❏ 5020	Sumemrtime/Comin' Home Baby	1962	3.00	6.00	12.00
❏ 5023	Right Now/Boroquino	1962	3.00	6.00	12.00
❏ 5026	Blues Walk Bossa Nova/It Must Be Love Bossa Nova	1962	3.00	6.00	12.00
❏ 5031	Bag's Groove/New York Is a Jungle Festival	1963	2.50	5.00	10.00
❏ 5032	The Girl from Ipanema/Soft Winds	1964	2.50	5.00	10.00
❏ 5036	Love in Peace/One Note Samba	1964	2.50	5.00	10.00
❏ 5037	Harlem Nocturne/Not Now — Not Later	1964	2.50	5.00	10.00
❏ 5038	Down By the Riverside/Insensatez	1964	2.50	5.00	10.00
❏ 5044	Soul Guajira/Hushi Mushi	1965	2.00	4.00	8.00
❏ 5048	The Joker/Feeling Good	1965	2.00	4.00	8.00
❏ 5064	Today/Arrastao	1966	2.00	4.00	8.00
❏ 5065	Our Man Flint/Yesterday	1966	2.00	4.00	8.00
❏ 5070	Theme from This Is My Beloved/Scratch	1966	2.00	4.00	8.00
❏ 5074	Philly Dog/Frere Jacques	1966	2.00	4.00	8.00
❏ 89880	Theme from "Tootsie"/(B-side unknown)	1983	—	2.00	4.00
A&M					
❏ 896	Unchain My Heart/Glory of Love	1968	2.00	4.00	8.00
❏ 923	Upa, Neguinho/The Letter	1968	2.50	5.00	10.00
BETHLEHEM					
❏ 3040	Chicken Little/My Little Suede Shoes	1962	2.50	5.00	10.00
❏ 11036	Love Is a Simple Thing/Jasmine	1959	3.00	6.00	12.00
❏ 11037	Surrey with the Fringe on Top/Sorimao	1959	3.00	6.00	12.00
❏ 11038	Cuban Love Song/Scuffles	1959	3.00	6.00	12.00
PRESTIGE					
❏ 113	Let's March (Part 1)/Let's March (Part 2)	1957	5.00	10.00	20.00
❏ 318	Cherry Point/Early Morning Blues	1964	2.50	5.00	10.00
❏ 416	Tutti Flutee (Part 1)/Tutti Flutee (Part 2)	1966	2.00	4.00	8.00

Albums
ATLANTIC

Number	Title (A Side/B Side)	Yr	VG	VG+	NM
❏ SD 2-300 [(2)]	The Evolution of Mann	1972	3.75	7.50	15.00
❏ 1343 [M]	The Common Ground	1960	3.75	7.50	15.00
❏ SD 1343 [S]	The Common Ground	1960	5.00	10.00	20.00
❏ 1371 [M]	The Family of Mann	1961	3.75	7.50	15.00
❏ SD 1371 [S]	The Family of Mann	1961	5.00	10.00	20.00
❏ 1380 [M]	Herbie Mann at the Village Gate	1962	3.75	7.50	15.00
❏ SD 1380 [S]	Herbie Mann at the Village Gate	1962	5.00	10.00	20.00
❏ 1384 [M]	Right Now	1962	3.75	7.50	15.00
❏ SD 1384 [S]	Right Now	1962	5.00	10.00	20.00
❏ 1397 [M]	Do the Bossa Nova with Herbie Mann	1962	3.75	7.50	15.00
❏ SD 1397 [S]	Do the Bossa Nova with Herbie Mann	1962	5.00	10.00	20.00
❏ 1407 [M]	Herbie Mann Returns to the Village Gate	1963	3.75	7.50	15.00
❏ SD 1407 [S]	Herbie Mann Returns to the Village Gate	1963	5.00	10.00	20.00
❏ 1413 [M]	Herbie Mann Live at Newport	1963	3.75	7.50	15.00

Number	Title (A Side/B Side)	Yr	VG	VG+	NM
❏ SD 1413 [S]	Herbie Mann Live at Newport	1963	5.00	10.00	20.00
❏ 1422 [M]	Latin Fever	1964	3.75	7.50	15.00
❏ SD 1422 [S]	Latin Fever	1964	5.00	10.00	20.00
❏ 1426 [M]	Nirvana	1964	3.75	7.50	15.00
❏ SD 1426 [S]	Nirvana	1964	5.00	10.00	20.00
❏ 1433 [M]	My Kinda Groove	1965	3.75	7.50	15.00
❏ SD 1433 [S]	My Kinda Groove	1965	5.00	10.00	20.00
❏ 1437 [M]	The Roar of the Greasepaint, The Smell of the Crowd	1965	3.75	7.50	15.00
❏ SD 1437 [S]	The Roar of the Greasepaint, The Smell of the Crowd	1965	5.00	10.00	20.00
❏ 1445 [M]	Standing Ovation at Newport	1965	3.75	7.50	15.00
❏ SD 1445 [S]	Standing Ovation at Newport	1965	5.00	10.00	20.00
❏ 1454 [M]	Herbie Mann Today	1966	3.75	7.50	15.00
❏ SD 1454 [S]	Herbie Mann Today	1966	5.00	10.00	20.00
❏ 1462 [M]	Monday Night at the Village Gate	1966	3.75	7.50	15.00
❏ SD 1462 [S]	Monday Night at the Village Gate	1966	5.00	10.00	20.00
❏ 1464 [M]	Our Mann Flute	1966	3.75	7.50	15.00
❏ SD 1464 [S]	Our Mann Flute	1966	5.00	10.00	20.00
❏ 1471 [M]	New Mann at Newport	1967	5.00	10.00	20.00
❏ SD 1471 [S]	New Mann at Newport	1967	3.75	7.50	15.00
❏ 1475 [M]	Impressions of the Middle East	1967	5.00	10.00	20.00
❏ SD 1475 [S]	Impressions of the Middle East	1967	3.75	7.50	15.00
❏ 1483 [M]	The Beat Goes On	1967	5.00	10.00	20.00
❏ SD 1483 [S]	The Beat Goes On	1967	3.75	7.50	15.00
❏ 1490 [M]	The Herbie Mann String Album	1968	6.25	12.50	25.00
❏ SD 1490 [S]	The Herbie Mann String Album	1968	3.75	7.50	15.00
❏ SD 1497	Wailing Dervishes	1968	3.75	7.50	15.00
❏ SD 1507	Windows Open	1969	3.00	6.00	12.00
❏ 1513 [M]	The Inspiration I Feel	1969	7.50	15.00	30.00
—Mono is promo only					
❏ SD 1513 [S]	The Inspiration I Feel	1969	3.75	7.50	15.00
❏ SD 1522	Memphis Underground	1969	3.00	6.00	12.00
❏ SD 1536	Live at the Whisky A-Go-Go	1969	3.00	6.00	12.00
❏ SD 1540	Concerto Grosso in D Blues	1969	3.00	6.00	12.00
❏ SD 1544	The Best of Herbie Mann	1970	3.00	6.00	12.00
❏ SD 1610	Mississippi Gambler	1972	3.00	6.00	12.00
❏ QD 1632 [Q]	Hold On, I'm Comin'	1973	5.00	10.00	20.00
❏ SD 1632	Hold On, I'm Comin'	1973	3.00	6.00	12.00
❏ SD 1642	Turtle Bay	1973	3.00	6.00	12.00
❏ SD 1648	London Underground	1974	3.00	6.00	12.00
❏ SD 1655	Reggae	1974	3.00	6.00	12.00
❏ SD 1658	First Light	1974	3.00	6.00	12.00
❏ SD 1670	Discotheque	1975	3.00	6.00	12.00
❏ SD 1676	Waterbed	1975	3.00	6.00	12.00
❏ SD 1682	Surprises	1976	3.00	6.00	12.00
❏ 8141 [M]	Mann and a Woman	1967	5.00	10.00	20.00
❏ SD 8141 [S]	Mann and a Woman	1967	3.75	7.50	15.00
❏ SD 16046	Mellow	1981	2.50	5.00	10.00
❏ SD 18209	Bird in a Silver Cage	1977	2.50	5.00	10.00
❏ SD 19112	Herbie Mann & Fire Island	1977	2.50	5.00	10.00
❏ SD 19169	Brazil — Once Again	1978	2.50	5.00	10.00
❏ SD 19221	Super Mann	1979	2.50	5.00	10.00
❏ SD 19252	Yellow Fever	1980	2.50	5.00	10.00
❏ 80077	Astral Island	1983	2.50	5.00	10.00
❏ 81285	See Through Spirits	1986	2.50	5.00	10.00
❏ 90141	Nirvana	1984	2.50	5.00	10.00
A&M					
❏ 2003 [M]	Glory of Love	1967	5.00	10.00	20.00
❏ SP-3003	Glory of Love	198?	3.75	7.50	15.00
—Audiophile reissue (labeled as such)					
❏ SP-3003 [S]	Glory of Love	1967	3.00	6.00	12.00
❏ SP-3008	Trust in Me/Soul Flutes	1969	3.00	6.00	12.00
BETHLEHEM					
❏ BCP-24 [M]	Flamingo, My Goodness — Four Flutes, Vol. 2	1955	12.50	25.00	50.00
❏ BCP-40 [M]	The Herbie Mann-Sam Most Quintet	1956	12.50	25.00	50.00
❏ BCP-58 [M]	Herbie Mann Plays	1956	12.50	25.00	50.00
❏ BCP-63 [M]	Love and the Weather	1956	12.50	25.00	50.00
❏ BCP-1018 [10]	East Coast Jazz 4	1954	25.00	50.00	100.00
❏ BCP-6020 [M]	The Mann with the Most	1960	10.00	20.00	40.00
❏ BCP-6067 [M]	The Epitome of Jazz	1963	7.50	15.00	30.00
COLUMBIA					
❏ CS 1068	Big Boss	1970	3.00	6.00	12.00
❏ CL 2388 [M]	Latin Mann	1965	3.75	7.50	15.00
❏ CS 9188 [S]	Latin Mann	1965	5.00	10.00	20.00
COLUMBIA SPECIAL PRODUCTS					
❏ JCS 9188	Latin Mann	197?	3.00	6.00	12.00
—Part of "Jazz Greats" Collectors' Series					
EMBRYO					
❏ 520	Stone Flute	1970	3.00	6.00	12.00
❏ 526	Muscle Shoals Nitty Gritty	1970	3.00	6.00	12.00
❏ 531	Memphis Two-Step	1971	3.00	6.00	12.00
❏ 532	Push Push	1971	3.00	6.00	12.00
EPIC					
❏ LN 3395 [M]	Salute to the Flute	1957	15.00	30.00	60.00
❏ LN 3499 [M]	Herbie Mann with the Ilcken Trio	1958	15.00	30.00	60.00
FINNADAR					
❏ 9014	Gagaku and Beyond	197?	2.50	5.00	10.00
JAZZLAND					
❏ JLP-5 [M]	Herbie Mann Quintet	1960	7.50	15.00	30.00
—Reissue of Riverside 245					
MILESTONE					
❏ 47010	Let Me Tell You	1973	3.00	6.00	12.00

Number	Title (A Side/B Side)	Yr	VG	VG+	NM

NEW JAZZ

Number	Title (A Side/B Side)	Yr	VG	VG+	NM
❑ NJLP-8211 [M]	Just Walkin'	1958	12.50	25.00	50.00
—Purple label					
❑ NJLP-8211 [M]	Just Walkin'	1964	6.25	12.50	25.00
—Blue label with trident logo					

PRESTIGE

❑ PRLP-7101 [M]	Flute Souffle	1957	20.00	40.00	80.00
❑ PRLP-7124 [M]	Flute Flight	1957	20.00	40.00	80.00
❑ PRLP-7136 [M]	Mann in the Morning	1958	20.00	40.00	80.00
❑ PRLP-7432 [M]	The Best of Herbie Mann	1965	3.75	7.50	15.00
❑ PRST-7432 [R]	The Best of Herbie Mann	1965	3.00	6.00	12.00
❑ PRST-7659	Herbie Mann in Sweden	1969	3.00	6.00	12.00

RIVERSIDE

❑ RLP 12-234 [M]	Sultry Serenade	1957	15.00	30.00	60.00
—Blue on white label					
❑ RLP 12-234 [M]	Sultry Serenade	1958	10.00	20.00	40.00
—Blue label with reel and microphone logo					
❑ RLP 12-245 [M]	Great Ideas of Western Mann	1957	10.00	20.00	40.00
❑ S-3029	Moody Mann	1969	3.00	6.00	12.00
❑ 6084	Great Ideas of Western Mann	197?	2.50	5.00	10.00

SAVOY

❑ MG-12102 [M]	Flute Suite	1957	12.50	25.00	50.00
❑ MG-12107 [M]	Mann Alone	1957	12.50	25.00	50.00
❑ MG-12108 [M]	Yardbird Suite	1957	12.50	25.00	50.00

SAVOY JAZZ

❑ SJL-1102	Be Bop Synthesis	197?	2.50	5.00	10.00

SOLID STATE

❑ SS-18020	Jazz Impressions of Brazil	1968	3.00	6.00	12.00
❑ SS-18023	St. Thomas	1968	3.00	6.00	12.00

SURREY

❑ S-1015 [M]	Big Band	1965	3.75	7.50	15.00
❑ SS-1015 [S]	Big Band	1965	5.00	10.00	20.00

TRIP

❑ 5031	Super Mann	1974	2.50	5.00	10.00

UNITED ARTISTS

❑ UAL-4042 [M]	African Suite	1959	7.50	15.00	30.00
❑ UAS-5042 [S]	African Suite	1959	10.00	20.00	40.00
❑ UAS-5638	Brazil Blues	1972	3.00	6.00	12.00
❑ UAJ-14009 [M]	Brasil, Bossa Nova and Blue	1962	7.50	15.00	30.00
❑ UAJ-14022 [M]	St. Thomas	1962	7.50	15.00	30.00
❑ UAJS-15009 [S]	Brasil, Bossa Nova and Blue	1962	10.00	20.00	40.00
❑ UAJS-15022 [S]	St. Thomas	1962	10.00	20.00	40.00

VERVE

❑ VSP-8 [M]	Bongo, Conga and Flute	1966	3.75	7.50	15.00
❑ VSPS-8 [R]	Bongo, Conga and Flute	1966	3.00	6.00	12.00
❑ VSP-19 [M]	Big Band Mann	1966	3.75	7.50	15.00
❑ VSPS-19 [R]	Big Band Mann	1966	3.00	6.00	12.00
❑ MGVS-6074 [S]	Flautista! — Herbie Mann Plays Afro-Cuban Jazz	1960	7.50	15.00	30.00
❑ MGV-8247 [M]	The Magic Flute of Herbie Mann	1958	10.00	20.00	40.00
❑ V-8247 [M]	The Magic Flute of Herbie Mann	1961	5.00	10.00	20.00
❑ MGV-8336 [M]	Flautista! — Herbie Mann Plays Afro-Cuban Jazz	1959	10.00	20.00	40.00
❑ V-8336 [M]	Flautista! — Herbie Mann Plays Afro-Cuban Jazz	1961	5.00	10.00	20.00
❑ V6-8336 [S]	Flautista! — Herbie Mann Plays Afro-Cuban Jazz	1961	3.75	7.50	15.00
❑ MGV-8392 [M]	Flute, Brass, Vibes and Percussion	1960	7.50	15.00	30.00
❑ V-8392 [M]	Flute, Brass, Vibes and Percussion	1961	5.00	10.00	20.00
❑ V-8527 [M]	The Sound of Mann	1963	5.00	10.00	20.00
❑ V6-8527 [S]	The Sound of Mann	1963	3.75	7.50	15.00
❑ V6-8821 [(2)]	Et Tu Flute	1973	3.75	7.50	15.00

MANN, REV. COLUMBUS

45s

CYE

❑ 1001	Soon Very Soon (He's Coming Back)/(B-side unknown)	196?	10.00	20.00	40.00

TAMLA

❑ 54047	Jesus Loves/They Shall Be Mine	1961	12.50	25.00	50.00

Albums

TAMLA

❑ T-227 [M]	They Shall Be Mine	1962	2000.	3000.	4000.

WINGATE

❑ 701 [M]	He Satisfies Me	196?	300.00	600.00	900.00

MAR-KEYS

45s

SATELLITE

❑ 107	Last Night/Night Before	1960	7.50	15.00	30.00

STAX

❑ 112	Morning After/Diana	1961	3.00	6.00	12.00
❑ 114	About Noon/Sack-O-Woe	1961	3.00	6.00	12.00
❑ 115	Foxy/One Degree North	1961	3.00	6.00	12.00
❑ 121	Pop-Eye Stroll/Po-Dunk	1962	3.00	6.00	12.00
❑ 124	What's Happening/You Got It	1962	3.00	6.00	12.00
❑ 129	Sailor Man Waltz/Sack-O-Woe	1963	3.00	6.00	12.00
❑ 133	The Dribble/Bo Time	1963	3.00	6.00	12.00
❑ 156	Beach Bash/Bush Bash	1964	2.50	5.00	10.00
❑ 166	The Shovel/Banana Juice	1965	2.50	5.00	10.00
❑ 181	Grab This Thing (Part 1)/Grab This Thing (Part 2)	1965	2.50	5.00	10.00
❑ 185	Philly Dog/Honey Pot	1966	2.50	5.00	10.00

Albums

ATLANTIC

❑ 8055 [M]	Last Night	1961	25.00	50.00	100.00
—White "fan" logo on right					
❑ 8055 [M]	Last Night	1962	12.50	25.00	50.00
—Black "fan" logo on right					
❑ SD 8055 [R]	Last Night	1966	10.00	20.00	40.00
❑ 8062 [M]	Do the Pop-Eye with the Mar-Keys	1962	12.50	25.00	50.00
❑ SD 8062 [R]	Do the Pop-Eye with the Mar-Keys	1966	10.00	20.00	40.00

STAX

❑ ST-707 [M]	The Great Memphis Sound	1966	12.50	25.00	50.00
❑ STS-707 [R]	The Great Memphis Sound	1966	10.00	20.00	40.00
❑ STS-2025	Damifiknew	1969	5.00	10.00	20.00
❑ STS-2036	Memphis Experience	1971	5.00	10.00	20.00

MAR-KEYS/BOOKER T. AND THE MG'S

Also see each artist's individual listings.

Albums

STAX

❑ ST-720 [M]	Back to Back	1967	5.00	10.00	20.00
❑ STS-720 [S]	Back to Back	1967	6.25	12.50	25.00

MAR-VELS, THE

45s

ANGIE

❑ 1005	Go On and Have Yourself a Ball/How Do I Keep the Girls Away	1963	5.00	10.00	20.00

BUTANE

❑ 778	Go On and Have Yourself a Ball/How Do I Keep the Girls Away	1963	3.75	7.50	15.00

IN

❑ 102	Surfing at Makeha/Endless Nights	1964	12.50	25.00	50.00

LOVE

❑ 5011/2	Cherry Lips/Could Be You	1958	7.50	15.00	30.00

TAMMY

❑ 1016	Somewhere in Life/Voo Doo Hurt	1961	75.00	150.00	300.00
❑ 1019	My Guardian Angel/Marble Stomp	1961	75.00	150.00	300.00

MARATHONS, THE (1)

Two different groups posing as one. After the success of "Peanut Butter" on Arvee, the label hired another group to be The Marathons after losing a legal battle to keep the "real" group, which was really THE VIBRATIONS in disguise. And the Vibrations had formerly been THE JAYHAWKS. Confused yet?

45s

ARGO

❑ 5389	Peanut Butter/Down in New Orleans	1961	3.75	7.50	15.00
—As "Vibrations Named By Others As MARATHONS"					

ARVEE

❑ 5027	Peanut Butter/Talkin' Trash	1961	5.00	10.00	20.00
❑ 5038	Tight Sweater/C. Percy Mercy of Scotland	1961	3.00	6.00	12.00
❑ 5048	Chicken Spaceman/You Bug Me Baby	1962	3.00	6.00	12.00

CHESS

❑ 1790	Peanut Butter/Down in New Orleans	1961	4.00	8.00	16.00

PLAZA

❑ 507	Mashed Potatoes One More Time/Little Pancho	1962	3.00	6.00	12.00

Albums

ARVEE

❑ A-428 [M]	Peanut Butter	1961	45.00	90.00	180.00

MARATHONS, THE (2)

Completely unrelated to groups (1).

45s

SABRINA

❑ 334	Don't Know Why/The Stranger	1959	30.00	60.00	120.00

MARAUDERS, THE

More than one group.

45s

ALMO

❑ 221	Like You/Slippin' and Slidin'	1965	3.75	7.50	15.00

HAWK

❑ 4002	Sand Flea/Stomp Watch	1962	12.50	25.00	50.00

LAURIE

❑ 3356	Out of Sight, Out of Mind/Jug Band Music	1966	5.00	10.00	20.00

LEE

❑ 9449	Nightmare/Lovin'	1965	7.50	15.00	30.00

SKYVIEW

❑ 001	Since I Met You/I Don't Know How	1966	5.00	10.00	20.00
❑ 001 [PS]	Since I Met You/I Don't Know How	1966	12.50	25.00	50.00

MARCELS, THE

45s

888

❑ 101	How Deep Is the Ocean/Lonely Boy	1964	3.75	7.50	15.00

ALL EARS

❑ 810085	Blue Moon/Clap Your Hands (When I Clap My Hands)	1981	—	3.00	6.00

BARON

❑ 109	Betty Lou/Take Me Back	197?	2.00	4.00	8.00

CHARTBOUND

❑ 009	Letter Full of Tears/Tell Me	197?	2.00	4.00	8.00

COLPIX

❑ 186	Blue Moon/Goodbye to Love	1961	7.50	15.00	30.00
❑ 186 [PS]	Blue Moon/Goodbye to Love	1961	15.00	30.00	60.00
❑ 196	Summertime/Teeter-Totter Love	1961	6.25	12.50	25.00
❑ 606	You Are My Sunshine/Find Another Fool	1961	6.25	12.50	25.00
❑ 612	Heartaches/My Love for You	1961	6.25	12.50	25.00

Number	Title (A Side/B Side)	Yr	VG	VG+	NM
❏ 612 [PS]	Heartaches/My Love for You	1961	25.00	50.00	100.00
❏ 617	Merry Twist-Mas/Don't Cry for Me This Christmas	1961	6.25	12.50	25.00
❏ 617 [PS]	Merry Twist-Mas/Don't Cry for Me This Christmas	1961	30.00	60.00	120.00
❏ 624	My Melancholy Baby/Really Need Your Love	1962	5.00	10.00	20.00
❏ 629	Footprints in the Sand/Twistin' Fever	1962	12.50	25.00	50.00
❏ 640	Flowerpot/Hold On	1962	7.50	15.00	30.00
❏ 651	Loved Her the Whole Week Through/Friendly Loans	1962	6.25	12.50	25.00
❏ 665	Alright, Okay, You Win/Lollipop Baby	1962	6.25	12.50	25.00
❏ 683	That Old Black Magic/Don't Turn Your Back on Me	1963	6.25	12.50	25.00
❏ 687	Give Me Back Your Love/I Wanna Be the Leader	1963	7.50	15.00	30.00
❏ 694	One Last Kiss/Teeter-Totter Love	1963	25.00	50.00	100.00
❏ 694	One Last Kiss/You Got to Be Sincere	1963	50.00	100.00	200.00

KYRA
❏ 100	Comes Love/Your Red Wagon	1964	25.00	50.00	100.00
—Red vinyl					
❏ 100	Comes Love/Your Red Wagon	1964	12.50	25.00	50.00

MONOGRAM
❏ 112	I'll Be Forever Loving You/A Fallen Tear	1974	3.00	6.00	12.00
❏ 113	Sweet Was the Wine/Over the Rainbow	1974	3.00	6.00	12.00
❏ 115	Two People in the World/Most of All	1974	3.00	6.00	12.00

OWL
❏ 324	(You Gave Me) Peace of Mind/Crazy Bells	197?	2.00	4.00	8.00

QUEEN BEE
❏ 47001	In the Still of the Night/High on a Hill	1973	3.75	7.50	15.00

ROCKY
❏ 13711	(You Gave Me) Peace of Mind/That Lucky Old Sun	1975	2.00	4.00	8.00
—As "The Fabulous Marcels"					

ST. CLAIR
❏ 13711	(You Gave Me) Peace of Mind/That Lucky Old Sun	1975	2.50	5.00	10.00
—As "The Fabulous Marcels"					

Albums

COLPIX
❏ CP-416 [M]	Blue Moon	1961	87.50	175.00	350.00
—Gold label					
❏ CP-416 [M]	Blue Moon	1963	30.00	60.00	120.00
—Blue label					

MARCHAN, BOBBY
45s

ACE
❏ 523	Chickee Wah-Wah/Don't Take Your Love from Me	1956	10.00	20.00	40.00
❏ 532	I'll Never Let You Go/I Can't Stop Loving You	1957	7.50	15.00	30.00
❏ 557	Rockin' Behind the Iron Curtain/You Can't Stop Her	1959	7.50	15.00	30.00
❏ 3004	Push the Button/My Day Is Coming	1974	—	2.50	5.00
❏ 3008	God Bless Our Love/My Day Is Coming	1975	—	2.50	5.00
❏ 3016	Baby Get Your Yo-Yo/What Can I Do	1975	—	2.50	5.00

ALADDIN
❏ 3189	Just a Little Walk/Have Mercy	1953	15.00	30.00	60.00

BOBBY ROBINSON
❏ (# unknown)	There's Something on Your Mind/(B-side unknown)	1973	—	3.00	6.00

CAMEO
❏ 405	There's Something About My Baby/Everything a Poor Man Needs	1966	2.50	5.00	10.00
❏ 429	Shake Your Tambourine/Just Be Yourself	1966	2.50	5.00	10.00
❏ 453	Meet Me in Church/Hooked	1967	2.00	4.00	8.00
❏ 469	You Better Hold On/Help Yourself	1967	2.00	4.00	8.00
❏ 489	Rockin' Pneumonia/Someone to Take Your Place	1967	2.00	4.00	8.00

DIAL
❏ 1152	Bump Your Bootie/Ain't Nothing Wrong with Whitey	1975	—	2.50	5.00
❏ 3022	I Gotta Sit Down and Cry/I Got a Thing Going	1964	2.50	5.00	10.00
❏ 4002	Get Down to It/Half a Mind	1964	2.50	5.00	10.00
❏ 4007	Hello Happiness/Funny Style	1965	2.50	5.00	10.00
❏ 4020	I Feel It Coming/Gimme Your Love	1965	2.50	5.00	10.00
❏ 4065	I Just Want What Belongs to Me/Sad Sack	1967	2.00	4.00	8.00

FIRE
❏ 510	Yes It's Written All Over Your Face/Look at My Heart	1962	3.75	7.50	15.00
❏ 1014	Snoopin' and Accusin'/This Is the Life	1959	3.75	7.50	15.00
❏ 1022	There's Something On Your Mind (Part 1)/There's Something On Your Mind (Part 2)	1960	6.25	12.50	25.00
❏ 1027	Booty Green/It Hurts Me to My Heart	1960	3.75	7.50	15.00
❏ 1028	You're Still My Baby (Part 1)/You're Still My Baby (Part 2)	1960	3.75	7.50	15.00
❏ 1035	All in My Mind/I Miss You So	1961	3.75	7.50	15.00
❏ 1037	What You Don't Know Don't Hurt You/I Need Someone (I Need You)	1961	3.75	7.50	15.00

GALE
❏ 4M-101	Chickee Wah Wah/Give a Helping Hand	1957	6.25	12.50	25.00

GAMBLE
❏ 216	(Ain't No Reason) For Girls to Be Lonely Part 1/Part 2	1968	2.00	4.00	8.00

MERCURY
❏ 73908	I Wanna Bump with the Big Fat Woman/Disco Rabbit	1977	—	2.50	5.00

Number	Title (A Side/B Side)	Yr	VG	VG+	NM

VOLT
❏ 108	What Can I Do (Part 1)/What Can I Do (Part 2)	1963	3.00	6.00	12.00

Albums

COLLECTABLES
❏ COL-5113	Golden Classics	198?	2.50	5.00	10.00

SPHERE SOUND
❏ SSR-7004 [M]	There's Something on Your Mind	1964	75.00	150.00	300.00

MARESCA, ERNIE
45s

LAURIE
❏ 3345	The Good Life/A Bum Can't Cry	1966	2.50	5.00	10.00
❏ 3371	My Son/My Shadow and Me	1967	2.50	5.00	10.00
❏ 3447	What Is a Marine/The Night My Papa Died	1968	2.00	4.00	8.00
❏ 3496	Blind Date/People Get Jealous	1969	2.00	4.00	8.00
❏ 3519	The Spirit of Woodstock/Web of Love	1969	2.00	4.00	8.00
❏ 3671	The Night My Poppa Died/Please Don't Play Me a Seven	1978	—	3.00	6.00
❏ 3698	You're the Only Girl for Me/Medley	1980	—	3.00	6.00
—B-side by the Belmonts					

PROVIDENCE
❏ 417	Rockin' Blvd. St./Am I Better Off Than Them	1965	12.50	25.00	50.00

RUST
❏ 5076	The Beetle Dance/Theme from Lilly, Lilly	1964	3.75	7.50	15.00

SEVILLE
❏ 107	Lonesome Blues/I Don't Know Why	1960	3.75	7.50	15.00
❏ 45-117	Shout! Shout! (Knock Yourself Out)/Crying Like a Baby	1962	6.25	12.50	25.00
❏ 5N-117	Shout! Shout! (Knock Yourself Out)/Crying Like a Baby	197?	—	3.00	6.00
—Reissue on all-black label; note different prefix					
❏ 119	Down on the Beach/Mary Jane	1962	3.75	7.50	15.00
❏ 119 [PS]	Down on the Beach/Mary Jane	1962	5.00	10.00	20.00
❏ 122	Something to Shout About/How Many Times	1962	3.75	7.50	15.00
❏ 125	Love Express/Lorelei	1963	12.50	25.00	50.00
❏ 129	The Rovin' Kind/Please Be Fair	1963	3.75	7.50	15.00
❏ 138	I Can't Dance/It's Their World	1965	3.75	7.50	15.00

MARKHAM, PIGMEAT
45s

CHESS
❏ 1828	Hold That Ladder (Part 1)/Hold That Ladder (Part 2)	1962	2.50	5.00	10.00
❏ 1891	Open the Door, Richard (Part 1)/Open the Door, Richard (Part 2)	1964	2.00	4.00	8.00
❏ 2049	Here Comes the Judge/The Trial	1968	—	3.50	7.00
❏ 2059	Sock It To 'Em Judge/The Hip Judge	1968	—	3.00	6.00
❏ 2087	Pig's Popcorn/Who's Got the Number	1969	—	3.00	6.00

Albums

CHESS
❏ LP-1451 [M]	The Trial	1961	6.25	12.50	25.00
❏ LP-1462 [M]	Pigmeat Markham At the Party	1962	6.25	12.50	25.00
❏ LP-1467 [M]	Anything Goes	1962	6.25	12.50	25.00
❏ LP-1475 [M]	The World's Greatest Clown	1963	6.25	12.50	25.00
❏ LP-1484 [M]	Open the Door, Richard	1964	6.25	12.50	25.00
❏ LP-1493 [M]	Mr. Funny Man	1965	6.25	12.50	25.00
❏ LP-1500 [M]	This'll Kill Ya	1965	6.25	12.50	25.00
❏ LP-1505 [M]	If You Can't Be Good, Be Careful	1966	3.75	7.50	15.00
❏ LPS-1505 [S]	If You Can't Be Good, Be Careful	1966	5.00	10.00	20.00
❏ LP-1515 [M]	Mr. Vaudeville	1967	3.75	7.50	15.00
❏ LPS-1515 [S]	Mr. Vaudeville	1967	5.00	10.00	20.00
❏ LP-1517 [M]	Save Your Soul, Baby	1967	5.00	10.00	20.00
❏ LPS-1517 [S]	Save Your Soul, Baby	1967	5.00	10.00	20.00
❏ LP-1521 [M]	Backstage	1968	5.00	10.00	20.00
❏ LPS-1521 [S]	Backstage	1968	5.00	10.00	20.00
❏ LPS-1525	Here Comes the Judge	1968	5.00	10.00	20.00
❏ LPS-1526	Tune Me In	1968	3.75	7.50	15.00
❏ LPS-1529	Hustlers	1969	3.75	7.50	15.00
❏ LPS-1534	Bag	1970	3.75	7.50	15.00
❏ CH-9166	Here Comes the Judge	1985	2.50	5.00	10.00
—Reissue of 1525					

JEWEL
❏ 5007	Crap-Shootin' Rev	1972	3.00	6.00	12.00
❏ 5012	Will the Real Pigmeat Markham Please Sit Down	1973	3.00	6.00	12.00

MARKIE, BIZ
12-Inch Singles

COLD CHILLIN'
❏ PRO-A-3087 [DJ]	Vapors/Biz Is Goin' Off	1988	3.75	7.50	15.00
❏ CDC 3507	Vapors/Bad by Myself	1997	2.00	4.00	8.00
—Reissue of earlier tracks					
❏ CDC 3510	Let Me Turn You On/Spring Again	1997	2.00	4.00	8.00
—Reissue of earlier tracks					
❏ CDC 3512	Something for the Radio/The Mudd Foot	1997	2.00	4.00	8.00
—Reissue of earlier tracks					
❏ CDC 3513	Just Rhymin' with Biz/Let Go My Eggo	1997	2.00	4.00	8.00
—Reissue of earlier tracks					
❏ CDC 3526	Nobody Beats the Biz (unknown versions)	1997	2.00	4.00	8.00
—Reissue of earlier tracks					
❏ CDC 3534	Pickin' Boogers/Doo Doo	199?	2.00	4.00	8.00
—Reissue of earlier tracks					
❏ PRO-A-4925 [DJ]	What Comes Around Goes Around (3 versions)	1991	3.75	7.50	15.00
❏ PRO-A-6106 [DJ]	Let Me Turn You On (Edit) (LP Version)	1993	3.75	7.50	15.00

Number	Title (A Side/B Side)	Yr	VG	VG+	NM
❑ PRO-A-6415 [DJ]	Young Girl Bluez (LP Version) (Instrumental)	1993	3.00	6.00	12.00
❑ 21342	Just a Friend/(Instrumental)	1989	3.75	7.50	15.00
❑ 40264	T.S.R. (2 versions)/Busy Doin' Nuthin' (2 versions)	1991	3.75	7.50	15.00
❑ 41032	Young Girl Bluez (2 versions)/I'm the Biz Markie (2 versions)/Family Tree	1993	3.75	7.50	15.00

PRISM

Number	Title (A Side/B Side)	Yr	VG	VG+	NM
❑ (# unknown)	Make the Music with Your Mouth (Vocal) (Instrumental)/The Biz Dance (Vocal) (Instrumental)/They're Coming to Take Me Away	1986	7.50	15.00	30.00

45s

COLD CHILLIN'

Number	Title (A Side/B Side)	Yr	VG	VG+	NM
❑ 22784	Just a Friend/(Instrumental)	1989	—	2.00	4.00
❑ 22784 [PS]	Just a Friend/(Instrumental)	1989	2.00	4.00	8.00
❑ 27784	This Is Something for the Radio/(Dub Dash Apella)	1989	—	2.50	5.00
❑ 27890	Vapors/The Do Do	1988	—	2.50	5.00

PRISM

Number	Title (A Side/B Side)	Yr	VG	VG+	NM
❑ 2008	Make the Music with Your Mouth/(B-side unknown)	1986	2.50	5.00	10.00

Albums

COLD CHILLIN'

Number	Title (A Side/B Side)	Yr	VG	VG+	NM
❑ CDC 5003 [(2)]	Biz's Baddest Beats	1995	3.75	7.50	15.00
❑ PRO-A-5179 [DJ]	I Need a Haircut	1991	10.00	20.00	40.00

—Promo-only issue on vinyl; includes "Alone Again," which sampled the Gilbert O'Sullivan hit without authorization and resulted in the entire album's withdrawal from sale

❑ CDC 9000	I Need a Haircut	1995	3.00	6.00	12.00

—Reissue with banned track, "Alone Again," deleted

❑ CDC 9001	Goin' Off	1995	3.00	6.00	12.00

—Reissue of 25675

❑ CDC 9009	The Biz Never Sleeps	1995	3.00	6.00	12.00

—Reissue of 26003

❑ 25675	Goin' Off	1988	3.75	7.50	15.00
❑ 26003	The Biz Never Sleeps	1989	3.75	7.50	15.00
❑ 45261	All Samples Cleared!	1993	3.75	7.50	15.00

LANDSPEED

Number	Title (A Side/B Side)	Yr	VG	VG+	NM
❑ LSR 8802 [(3)]	Best of Cold Chillin'	2000	5.00	10.00	20.00

MARLEY, BOB, AND THE WAILERS

12-Inch Singles

COTILLION

Number	Title (A Side/B Side)	Yr	VG	VG+	NM
❑ PR 291 [DJ]	Reggae on Broadway (6:00) (3:15)	1981	3.00	6.00	12.00
❑ PR 414 [DJ]	Chances Are (same on both sides)	1981	3.75	7.50	15.00

ISLAND

❑ DMD 628 [DJ]	Buffalo Soldier/Buffalo Dub	1983	2.50	5.00	10.00
❑ DMD 668 [DJ]	Mix Up, Mix Up (LP Version) (Edit Version)	1983	2.50	5.00	10.00

TUFF GONG

❑ 864693-1	Iron Zion Lion (4 versions)/Could You Be Loved	1992	3.00	6.00	12.00

45s

BLACK HEART

❑ 8042	African Herbsman/Stand Alone	1974	3.00	6.00	12.00

CLOCK TOWER

❑ 505	Duppy Conqueror/Duppy Version	1971	6.25	12.50	25.00

COTILLION

❑ 46023	Reggae on Broadway/Gonna Get You	1981	—	2.50	5.00
❑ 46029	Chances Are/(B-side unknown)	1981	—	2.50	5.00

G&C

❑ C&G-5000	Trench Town Rock/Version	197?	5.00	10.00	20.00

ISLAND

❑ 005	I Shot the Sheriff/Put It On	1974	—	3.00	6.00
❑ 027	Lively Up Yourself/So Jah Seh	1975	—	3.00	6.00
❑ 037	No Woman, No Cry/Kinky Reggae	1975	—	3.00	6.00
❑ 060	Roots, Rock, Reggae/Cry to Me	1976	—	3.00	6.00
❑ 072	Who the Cap Fit/(B-side unknown)	1976	—	3.00	6.00
❑ 089	Exodus/(Instrumental)	1977	—	3.00	6.00
❑ 092	Waiting in Vain/Roots	1977	—	3.00	6.00
❑ 099	Is This Love/Crisis	1978	—	3.00	6.00
❑ PR 670 [DJ]	Stir It Up (same on both sides)	1984	2.50	5.00	10.00
❑ 1211	Rock It Baby/Stop That Train	1972	2.00	4.00	8.00
❑ 1215	Concrete Jungle/No More Trouble	1973	2.00	4.00	8.00
❑ 1218	Get Up, Stand Up/Slave Driver	1973	2.00	4.00	8.00
❑ 49080	Wake Up and Live/Wake Up and Live (Dub)	1979	—	3.00	6.00
❑ 49156	Kaya/One Drop	1980	—	3.00	6.00
❑ 49547	Ride Natty Ride/Could You Be Loved	1980	—	3.00	6.00
❑ 49636	Redemption Song/Coming In from the Cold	1980	—	3.00	6.00
❑ 49755	Jamming/No Woman, No Cry	1981	—	3.00	6.00
❑ 99740	Blackman Redemption/Is This Love	1984	—	2.00	4.00
❑ 99837	Mix Up, Mix Up/French Town	1983	—	2.00	4.00
❑ 99882	Buffalo Soldier/Buffalo Dub	1983	—	2.00	4.00
❑ 99882 [PS]	Buffalo Soldier/Buffalo Dub	1983	—	3.00	6.00
❑ 562356-7	Kinky Reggae (Raga Mix)/Kinky Reggae (Kinky Mix)	1999	—	2.00	4.00

JAD

❑ 211	Bend Down Low/Mellow Mood	1968	25.00	50.00	100.00

—As "Bob, Rita and Peter"

SHELTER

❑ 7309	Doppy Conquer/Justice	1971	3.00	6.00	12.00

—B-side by the Upsetters

TRANQUILITY

❑ T0024	It Hurts to Be Alone/(B-side unknown)	1965	50.00	100.00	200.00

—As "The Wailers"

TUFF GONG

Number	Title (A Side/B Side)	Yr	VG	VG+	NM
❑ TG-5002	Ammunition/Kingston 12 Shuffle	197?	5.00	10.00	20.00

—B-side by U-Roy

❑ TG-5004	Lick Samba/Version	197?	5.00	10.00	20.00
❑ TG-5005	Lively Up Yourself/Guava Jelly	197?	5.00	10.00	20.00
❑ TG-5007	Craven Choke Puppy/Version	197?	5.00	10.00	20.00
❑ TG-5009	Steppin' (Walking) Razor/The Letter	197?	5.00	10.00	20.00
❑ TG-5014	Midnight Ravers/Version	197?	5.00	10.00	20.00

UPSETTER

❑ (# unknown)	More Axe/The Axe Man	1971	6.25	12.50	25.00
❑ 007	Cross the Nation/Version	1970	5.00	10.00	20.00

—B-side by the Upsetters

❑ 007	Cross the Nation/All in One (Medley)	1970	5.00	10.00	20.00
❑ 009	Small Axe/Version	1970	5.00	10.00	20.00

—B-side by the Upsetters

❑ 9001	Secondhand/Secondhand Part 2	1971	5.00	10.00	20.00

Albums

ACCORD

❑ SN-7211	Jamaican Storm	1982	2.50	5.00	10.00

CALLA

❑ CAS-1240 [(2)]	The Birth of a Legend	1976	3.75	7.50	15.00
❑ ZX 34759	The Birth of a Legend	1977	2.50	5.00	10.00

—Reissue of Record 1 of Calla 1240

❑ ZX 34760	Early Music	1977	2.50	5.00	10.00

—Reissue of Record 2 of Calla 1240

COLUMBIA

❑ PZ 34759	The Birth of a Legend	198?	2.00	4.00	8.00

—Budget-line reissue of Calla 34759

❑ PZ 34760	Early Music	198?	2.00	4.00	8.00

—Budget-line reissue of Calla 34760

COTILLION

❑ SD 5228	Chances Are	1981	2.50	5.00	10.00

ISLAND

❑ ISLD 11 [(2)]	Babylon by Bus	1978	3.75	7.50	15.00

—Island distribution

❑ ISLD 11 [(2)]	Babylon by Bus	1979	3.00	6.00	12.00

—Warner Bros. distribution

❑ ILPS 9241	Catch a Fire	1975	3.75	7.50	15.00

—Reissue with standard cover; Island distribution

❑ ILPS 9241	Catch a Fire	1978	3.00	6.00	12.00

—Reissue; Warner Bros. distribution

❑ ILPS 9256	Burnin'	1974	3.75	7.50	15.00

—Island distribution

❑ ILPS 9256	Burnin'	1978	3.00	6.00	12.00

—Warner Bros. distribution

❑ ILPS 9281	Natty Dread	1974	3.75	7.50	15.00

—Island distribution

❑ ILPS 9281	Natty Dread	1978	3.00	6.00	12.00

—Warner Bros. distribution

❑ SW-9329	Catch a Fire	1973	12.50	25.00	50.00

—"Cigarette lighter" cover with flip-open top; Capitol distribution

❑ SMAS-9338	Burnin'	1973	5.00	10.00	20.00

—Capitol distribution

❑ ILPS 9376	Live!	1975	3.00	6.00	12.00

—Island distribution

❑ ILPS 9376	Live!	1978	2.50	5.00	10.00

—Warner Bros. distribution

❑ ILPS 9383	Rastaman Vibration	1976	3.00	6.00	12.00

—Island distribution

❑ ILPS 9383	Rastaman Vibration	1978	2.50	5.00	10.00

—Warner Bros. distribution

❑ ILPS 9383 [DJ]	Rastaman Vibration	1976	25.00	50.00	100.00

—Promotional package with burlap box and press kit

❑ ILPS 9498	Exodus	1977	3.00	6.00	12.00

—Island distribution (all have multicolor labels)

❑ ILPS 9498	Exodus	1978	2.50	5.00	10.00

—Warner Bros. distribution

❑ ILPS 9517	Kaya	1978	3.00	6.00	12.00

—Island distribution

❑ ILPS 9517	Kaya	1979	2.50	5.00	10.00

—Warner Bros. distribution

❑ ILPS 9542	Survival	1979	3.00	6.00	12.00
❑ ILPS 9596	Uprising	1980	3.00	6.00	12.00
❑ 90029 [(2)]	Babylon by Bus	1983	3.00	6.00	12.00
❑ 90030	Catch a Fire	1983	2.00	4.00	8.00
❑ 90031	Burnin'	1983	2.00	4.00	8.00
❑ 90032	Live!	1983	2.00	4.00	8.00
❑ 90033	Rastaman Vibration	1983	2.00	4.00	8.00
❑ 90034	Exodus	1983	2.00	4.00	8.00
❑ 90035	Kaya	1983	2.00	4.00	8.00
❑ 90036	Uprising	1983	2.00	4.00	8.00
❑ 90037	Natty Dread	1983	2.00	4.00	8.00

—90029-90037 are reissues with Atco distribution

❑ 90085	Confrontation	1983	2.50	5.00	10.00
❑ 90169	Legend	1984	2.50	5.00	10.00
❑ 90520	Rebel Music	1986	2.50	5.00	10.00
❑ 524419-1	Dreams of Freedom	1997	3.00	6.00	12.00
❑ 546404-1	Chant Down Babylon	1999	3.00	6.00	12.00

MOBILE FIDELITY

❑ 1-221	Exodus	1995	6.25	12.50	25.00

—Audiophile vinyl

❑ 1-236	Catch a Fire	1995	6.25	12.50	25.00

—Audiophile vinyl

TUFF GONG

❑ 524103-1	Natural Mystic	1995	3.75	7.50	15.00

Number	Title (A Side/B Side)	Yr	VG	VG+	NM
❑ 846197-1 [(2)]	Babylon by Bus	1990	3.75	7.50	15.00
❑ 846200-1	Burnin'	1990	3.00	6.00	12.00
❑ 846201-1	Catch a Fire	1990	3.00	6.00	12.00
❑ 846202-1	Survival	1990	3.00	6.00	12.00
❑ 846203-1	Live!	1990	3.00	6.00	12.00
❑ 846204-1	Natty Dread	1990	3.00	6.00	12.00
❑ 846205-1	Rastaman Vibration	1990	3.00	6.00	12.00
❑ 846206-1	Rebel Music	1990	3.00	6.00	12.00
❑ 846207-1	Confrontation	1990	3.00	6.00	12.00
❑ 846208-1	Exodus	1990	3.00	6.00	12.00
❑ 846209-1	Kaya	1990	3.00	6.00	12.00
❑ 846210-1	Legend	1990	3.00	6.00	12.00
❑ 846211-1	Uprising	1990	3.00	6.00	12.00
❑ 848243-1	Talkin' Blues	1991	3.00	6.00	12.00

MARQUEES, THE (5)

MARVIN GAYE was in this group.

45s

OKEH

Number	Title (A Side/B Side)	Yr	VG	VG+	NM
❑ 7096	Hey Little School Girl/Wyatt Earp	1957	30.00	60.00	120.00

MARTHA AND THE VANDELLAS

Also see SAUNDRA MALLETT AND THE VANDELLAS; MARTHA REEVES; THE VELLS.

45s

A&M

Number	Title (A Side/B Side)	Yr	VG	VG+	NM
❑ 3022	Nowhere to Run/I Got You (I Feel Good)	1988	—	2.00	4.00

—B-side by James Brown

Number	Title (A Side/B Side)	Yr	VG	VG+	NM
❑ 3022 [PS]	Nowhere to Run/I Got You (I Feel Good)	1988	—	2.00	4.00

—"Good Morning Vietnam" sleeve

GORDY

Number	Title (A Side/B Side)	Yr	VG	VG+	NM
❑ 7011	I'll Have to Let Him Go/My Baby Won't Come Back	1962	6.25	12.50	25.00
❑ 7014	Come and Get These Memories/Jealous Love	1963	7.50	15.00	30.00
❑ 7022	Heat Wave/A Love Like Yours	1963	5.00	10.00	20.00
❑ 7025	Quicksand/Darling, I Hum Our Song	1963	3.75	7.50	15.00
❑ 7027	Live Wire/Old Love	1964	3.75	7.50	15.00
❑ 7031	In My Lonely Room/A Tear for the Girl	1964	3.75	7.50	15.00
❑ 7033	Dancing in the Street/There He Is (At My Door)	1964	3.75	7.50	15.00
❑ 7033 [PS]	Dancing in the Street/There He Is (At My Door)	1964	30.00	60.00	120.00
❑ 7036	Wild One/Dancing Slow	1964	3.00	6.00	12.00
❑ 7039	Nowhere to Run/Motoring	1965	3.00	6.00	12.00
❑ 7045	You've Been in Love Too Long/Love (Makes You Do Foolish Things)	1965	3.00	6.00	12.00
❑ 7048	My Baby Loves Me/Never Leave Your Baby's Side	1965	3.00	6.00	12.00
❑ 7053	What Am I Gonna Do Without Your Love/Go Ahead and Laugh	1966	3.00	6.00	12.00
❑ 7056	I'm Ready for Love/He Doesn't Love Her Anymore	1966	3.75	7.50	15.00

—"Gordy" logo at top

Number	Title (A Side/B Side)	Yr	VG	VG+	NM
❑ 7056	I'm Ready for Love/He Doesn't Love Her Anymore	1966	3.00	6.00	12.00

—"Gordy" logo at left

Number	Title (A Side/B Side)	Yr	VG	VG+	NM
❑ 7058	Jimmy Mack/Third Finger, Left Hand	1967	2.50	5.00	10.00
❑ 7062	Love Bug Leave My Heart Alone/One Way Out	1967	2.50	5.00	10.00
❑ 7067	Honey Chile/Show Me the Way	1967	2.50	5.00	10.00

—Starting here, as "Martha Reeves and the Vandellas"

Number	Title (A Side/B Side)	Yr	VG	VG+	NM
❑ 7070	I Promise to Wait My Love/Forget Me Not	1968	2.50	5.00	10.00
❑ 7075	I Can't Dance to That Music You're Playin'/I Tried	1968	2.50	5.00	10.00
❑ 7080	Sweet Darlin'/Without You	1968	2.50	5.00	10.00
❑ 7085	(We've Got) Honey Love/I'm In Love (And I Know It)	1969	2.00	4.00	8.00
❑ 7094	Taking My Love (And Leaving Me)/Heartless	1969	2.00	4.00	8.00
❑ 7098	I Should Be Pround/Love, Guess Who	1970	2.00	4.00	8.00
❑ 7103	I Gotta Let You Go/You're the Loser Now	1970	2.00	4.00	8.00
❑ 7110	Bless You/Hope I Don't Get My Heart Broke	1971	2.00	4.00	8.00
❑ 7113	In and Out of My Life/Your Love Makes It All Worthwhile	1972	2.00	4.00	8.00
❑ 7118	Tear It On Down/I Want You Back	1972	2.00	4.00	8.00
❑ 7127	Baby Don't Leave Me/I Won't Be the Fool I've Been Again	1973	2.00	4.00	8.00

TOPPS/MOTOWN

Number	Title (A Side/B Side)	Yr	VG	VG+	NM
❑ 7	Dancing in the Street	1967	18.75	37.50	75.00

—Cardboard record

Number	Title (A Side/B Side)	Yr	VG	VG+	NM
❑ 14	Love Is Like a Heat Wave	1967	18.75	37.50	75.00

—Cardboard record

Albums

GORDY

Number	Title (A Side/B Side)	Yr	VG	VG+	NM
❑ G-902 [M]	Come and Get These Memories	1963	100.00	200.00	400.00
❑ GS-902 [S]	Come and Get These Memories	1963	200.00	400.00	800.00
❑ G-907 [M]	Heat Wave	1963	37.50	75.00	150.00
❑ GS-907 [R]	Heat Wave	1963	37.50	75.00	150.00

—"Stereo" banner pre-printed on cover

Number	Title (A Side/B Side)	Yr	VG	VG+	NM
❑ GS-907 [S]	Heat Wave	1963	100.00	200.00	400.00

—Mono cover with "Stereo" sticker

Number	Title (A Side/B Side)	Yr	VG	VG+	NM
❑ G-915 [M]	Dance Party	1965	10.00	20.00	40.00
❑ GS-915 [S]	Dance Party	1965	15.00	30.00	60.00
❑ G-917 [M]	Greatest Hits	1966	6.25	12.50	25.00
❑ GS-917 [S]	Greatest Hits	1966	7.50	15.00	30.00
❑ G-920 [M]	Watchout!	1966	6.25	12.50	25.00
❑ GS-920 [S]	Watchout!	1966	7.50	15.00	30.00
❑ G-925 [M]	Martha and the Vandellas Live!	1967	7.50	15.00	30.00
❑ GS-925 [S]	Martha and the Vandellas Live!	1967	6.25	12.50	25.00
❑ G-926 [M]	Ridin' High	1968	10.00	20.00	40.00

—Mono is promo only

Number	Title (A Side/B Side)	Yr	VG	VG+	NM
❑ GS-926 [S]	Ridin' High	1968	5.00	10.00	20.00
❑ GS-944	Sugar 'N Spice	1969	5.00	10.00	20.00
❑ GS-952	Natural Resources	1970	5.00	10.00	20.00
❑ GS-958	Black Magic	1972	5.00	10.00	20.00

MOTOWN

Number	Title (A Side/B Side)	Yr	VG	VG+	NM
❑ M5-111V1	Motown Superstar Series, Vol. 11	1981	2.50	5.00	10.00
❑ M5-145V1	Heat Wave	1981	2.50	5.00	10.00

—Reissue of Gordy 907

Number	Title (A Side/B Side)	Yr	VG	VG+	NM
❑ M5-204V1	Greatest Hits	1981	2.50	5.00	10.00

—Reissue of Gordy 917

Number	Title (A Side/B Side)	Yr	VG	VG+	NM
❑ M7-778 [(2)]	Anthology	1974	3.75	7.50	15.00

MARVELETTES, THE

45s

A&M

Number	Title (A Side/B Side)	Yr	VG	VG+	NM
❑ 1201	Danger Heartbreak Dead Ahead/Baby Please Don't Go	1988	—	2.00	4.00

—B-side by Them

Number	Title (A Side/B Side)	Yr	VG	VG+	NM
❑ 1201 [PS]	Danger Heartbreak Dead Ahead/Baby Please Don't Go	1988	—	2.00	4.00

—"Good Morning Vietnam" sleeve

GORDY

Number	Title (A Side/B Side)	Yr	VG	VG+	NM
❑ 7024	Too Hurt to Cry, Too Much in Love to Say Goodbye/Come On Home	1963	20.00	40.00	80.00

—As "The Darnells"

TAMLA

Number	Title (A Side/B Side)	Yr	VG	VG+	NM
❑ 54046	Please Mr. Postman/So Long Baby	1961	6.25	12.50	25.00
❑ 54046 [PS]	Please Mr. Postman/So Long Baby	1961	30.00	60.00	120.00
❑ 54054	Twistin' Postman/I Want a Guy	1962	5.00	10.00	20.00
❑ 54054 [PS]	Twistin' Postman/I Want a Guy	1962	25.00	50.00	100.00
❑ 54060	Playboy/All the Love I've Got	1962	5.00	10.00	20.00
❑ 54065	Beechwood 4-5789/Someday, Someway	1962	5.00	10.00	20.00
❑ 54072	Strange I Know/Too Strong to Be Strung Along	1962	3.75	7.50	15.00
❑ 54077	Forever/Locking Up My Heart	1963	3.75	7.50	15.00
❑ 54082	Tie a String Around My Finger/My Daddy Knows Best	1963	5.00	10.00	20.00
❑ 54088	As Long As I Know He's Mine/Little Girl Blue	1963	3.00	6.00	12.00
❑ 54091	He's a Good Guy (Yes He Is)/Goddess of Love	1964	3.00	6.00	12.00
❑ 54091 [DJ]	Yes He Is	1964	18.75	37.50	75.00

—One-sided promo with different title than stock copy

Number	Title (A Side/B Side)	Yr	VG	VG+	NM
❑ 54097	You're My Remedy/A Little Bit of Sympathy, A Little Bit of Love	1964	2.50	5.00	10.00
❑ 54097 [PS]	You're My Remedy/A Little Bit of Sympathy, A Little Bit of Love	1964	15.00	30.00	60.00
❑ 54105	Two Many Fish in the Sea/A Need for Love	1964	10.00	20.00	40.00

—Some copies feature the above incorrect A-side title

Number	Title (A Side/B Side)	Yr	VG	VG+	NM
❑ 54105	Too Many Fish in the Sea/A Need for Love	1964	2.50	5.00	10.00
❑ 54116	I'll Keep Holding On/No Time for Tears	1965	2.50	5.00	10.00
❑ 54120	Danger, Heartbreak Dead Ahead/Your Cheating Ways	1965	2.50	5.00	10.00
❑ 54126	Don't Mess with Bill/Anything You Wanna Do	1965	2.50	5.00	10.00
❑ 54131	You're the One/Paper Boy	1966	2.50	5.00	10.00
❑ 54143	The Hunter Gets Captured by the Game/I Think I Can Change You	1967	2.50	5.00	10.00
❑ 54150	When You're Young and In Love/The Day You Take One, You Have to Take the Other	1967	2.50	5.00	10.00
❑ 54158	My Baby Must Be a Magician/I Need Someone	1967	2.50	5.00	10.00
❑ 54166	Here I Am Baby/Keep Off, No Trespassing	1968	2.50	5.00	10.00
❑ 54171	Destination: Anywhere/What's So Easy for Two Is So Hard for One	1968	2.50	5.00	10.00
❑ 54177	I'm Gonna Hold On Long As I Can/Don't Make Hurting Me a Habit	1968	2.50	5.00	10.00
❑ 54186	That's How Heartaches Are Made/Rainy Mourning	1969	2.50	5.00	10.00
❑ 54198	Marionette/After All	1970	2.00	4.00	8.00
❑ 54213	A Breath Taking Guy/You're the One for Me Baby	1972	2.00	4.00	8.00

TOPPS/MOTOWN

Number	Title (A Side/B Side)	Yr	VG	VG+	NM
❑ 12	Please Mr. Postman	1967	18.75	37.50	75.00

—Cardboard record

7-Inch Extended Plays

TAMLA

Number	Title (A Side/B Side)	Yr	VG	VG+	NM
❑ 60274	The Hunter Gets Captured by the Game/When You're Young and In Love/I Know Better//He Was Really Sayin' Somethin'/The Day You Take One/Keep Off, No Trespassing	196?	10.00	20.00	40.00

—Jukebox issue; small hole, plays at 33 1/3 rpm

Number	Title (A Side/B Side)	Yr	VG	VG+	NM
❑ 60274 [PS]	The Marvelettes	196?	10.00	20.00	40.00

Albums

MOTOWN

Number	Title (A Side/B Side)	Yr	VG	VG+	NM
❑ M5-180V1	Greatest Hits	1981	2.50	5.00	10.00

—Reissue of Tamla 253

Number	Title (A Side/B Side)	Yr	VG	VG+	NM
❑ M7-827 [(2)]	Anthology	1975	3.75	7.50	15.00
❑ 5266 ML	Please Mr. Postman	1982	2.50	5.00	10.00

—Reissue of Tamla 228

TAMLA

Number	Title (A Side/B Side)	Yr	VG	VG+	NM
❑ T-228 [M]	Please Mr. Postman	1961	150.00	300.00	600.00

—White label

Number	Title (A Side/B Side)	Yr	VG	VG+	NM
❑ T-228 [M]	Please Mr. Postman	1963	75.00	150.00	300.00

—Yellow label with globes logo

Number	Title (A Side/B Side)	Yr	VG	VG+	NM
❑ T-229 [M]	Smash Hits of 62'	1962	600.00	900.00	1200.

—Title as listed on front cover; large black "M" with song titles in circles

Number	Title (A Side/B Side)	Yr	VG	VG+	NM
❑ T-229 [M]	The Marveletts Sing	1962	125.00	250.00	500.00

—Title as listed on front cover (misspelled); all-black cover with white circles

Number	Title (A Side/B Side)	Yr	VG	VG+	NM
❑ T-229 [M]	The Marveletts Sing	1963	62.50	125.00	250.00

—Yellow label with side-by-side globes logo

Number	Title (A Side/B Side)	Yr	VG	VG+	NM
❑ T-231 [M]	Playboy	1962	125.00	250.00	500.00

—Yellow label with overlapping record and globe logo

MARVELLOS, THE (1)

Number	Title (A Side/B Side)	Yr	VG	VG+	NM
❑ T-231 [M]	Playboy	1962	150.00	300.00	600.00
—White label					
❑ T-231 [M]	Playboy	1963	62.50	125.00	250.00
—Yellow label with side-by-side globes logo					
❑ T-237 [M]	The Marvelous Marvelettes	1963	37.50	75.00	150.00
❑ T-243 [M]	Recorded Live On Stage	1963	20.00	40.00	80.00
❑ T-253 [M]	Greatest Hits	1966	7.50	15.00	30.00
—Yellow cover					
❑ T-253 [M]	Greatest Hits	1967	6.25	12.50	25.00
—Green cover					
❑ TS-253 [S]	Greatest Hits	1966	10.00	20.00	40.00
—Yellow cover					
❑ TS-253 [S]	Greatest Hits	1967	5.00	10.00	20.00
—Green cover					
❑ T-274 [M]	The Marveletttes	1967	7.50	15.00	30.00
❑ TS-274 [S]	The Marveletttes	1967	5.00	10.00	20.00
❑ T-286 [M]	Sophisticated Soul	1968	10.00	20.00	40.00
❑ TS-286 [S]	Sophisticated Soul	1968	5.00	10.00	20.00
❑ TS-288	In Full Bloom	1969	3.75	7.50	15.00
❑ TS-305	Return of the Marvelettes	1970	3.75	7.50	15.00

MARVELLOS, THE (1)

45s

CHA CHA

Number	Title (A Side/B Side)	Yr	VG	VG+	NM
❑ 756	Come Back My Love/Boyee Yoing	1963	7.50	15.00	30.00

STEPHENY

❑ 1818	Come Back My Love/Boyee Yoing	1958	50.00	100.00	200.00

MARVELLOS, THE (2)

45s

EXODUS

❑ 6214	Salty Sam/She Told Me Lies	1962	50.00	100.00	200.00
❑ 6216	I Ask of You/Hip Enough	1962	30.00	60.00	120.00

REPRISE

❑ 20088	Salty Sam/She Told Me Lies	1962	7.50	15.00	30.00

MARVELLOS, THE (3)

45s

LOMA

❑ 2045	Something's Burning/We Go Together	1966	3.00	6.00	12.00
❑ 2061	You're Such a Sweet Thing/Why Do You Want to Hurt the One You Love	1966	3.00	6.00	12.00

MODERN

❑ 1054	Down in the City/In the Sunshine	1967	2.50	5.00	10.00

WARNER BROS.

❑ 7011	Don't Play with My Heart/Let Me Keep You Satisfied	1967	2.50	5.00	10.00
❑ 7054	Piece of Silk/Yes I Do	1967	2.50	5.00	10.00

MARVELLOS, THE (U)

Could be group (1); it's doubtful that these could be either of the other two.

45s

MARVELLO

❑ 5005	Red Hot Momma/I Need a Girl	1955	75.00	150.00	300.00

THERON

❑ 117	You're the Dream/Calypso Mama	1957	100.00	200.00	400.00

MARVELOWS, THE

45s

ABC

❑ 10820	Fade Away/You've Been Going to Sally	1966	2.50	5.00	10.00
❑ 11011	In the Morning/Talkin' 'Bout Ya, Baby	1967	2.00	4.00	8.00
—As "The Mighty Marvelows"					
❑ 11073	I'm So Confused/I'm Without a Girl	1968	2.00	4.00	8.00
—As "The Mighty Marvelows"					
❑ 11139	Hey, Hey Girl/Wait, Be Cool	1968	2.00	4.00	8.00
—As "The Mighty Marvelows"					
❑ 11189	You're Breaking My Heart/This Town's Too Much	1969	2.00	4.00	8.00
—As "The Mighty Marvelows"					

ABC-PARAMOUNT

❑ 10613	A Friend/Hey, Hey Baby	1965	2.50	5.00	10.00
❑ 10629	I Do/My Heart	1965	3.75	7.50	15.00
❑ 10708	Shim Sham/Your Little Sister	1965	2.50	5.00	10.00
❑ 10756	Do It/I've Got My Eyes on You	1965	2.50	5.00	10.00

Albums

ABC

❑ S-643	The Mighty Marvelows	1968	7.50	15.00	30.00

MARVELS, THE (1)

Early version of THE DUBS.

45s

ABC-PARAMOUNT

❑ 9771	I Won't Have You Breaking My Heart/Jump Rock and Roll	1956	150.00	300.00	600.00

MARVELS, THE (2)

45s

LAURIE

❑ 3106	I Shed So Many Tears/So Young, So Sweet	1958	17.50	35.00	70.00
—Also released as "The Marvells"					

MARVELS, THE (3)

45s

MUN-RAB

Number	Title (A Side/B Side)	Yr	VG	VG+	NM
❑ 1008	Just Another Fool/You Crack Me Up	1959	375.00	750.00	1500.

MARVELS, THE (U)

May be group (2).

45s

WINN

❑ 1916	For Sentimental Reasons/Come Back	1961	50.00	100.00	200.00

MARVIN AND JOHNNY

45s

ALADDIN

❑ 3371	Yak Yak/Pretty Eyes	1957	7.50	15.00	30.00
❑ 3408	You're in My Heart/Smack Smack	1958	7.50	15.00	30.00
❑ 3439	It's Christmas/The Valley of Love	1958	7.50	15.00	30.00

FELSTED

❑ 8681	Hot Biscuits and Gravy/Tired of Being Alone	1963	3.00	6.00	12.00

JAMIE

❑ 1188	Once Upon a Time/Tick Tock	1961	3.00	6.00	12.00

LIBERTY

❑ 1394	It's Christmas/It's Christmas Time	1980	—	2.50	5.00
—B-side by the Five Keys					

MODERN

❑ 933	Tick Tock/Cherry Pie	1954	18.75	37.50	75.00
❑ 941	Sugar/Kiss Me	1954	12.50	25.00	50.00
❑ 946	Little Honey/Honey Girl	1955	12.50	25.00	50.00
❑ 949	Ko Ko Mo/Sometimes I Wonder	1955	10.00	20.00	40.00
❑ 952	I Love You, Yes I Do/Baby Won't You Marry Me	1955	10.00	20.00	40.00
❑ 959	Butler Ball/Sugar Mama	1955	10.00	20.00	40.00
❑ 968	Will You Love Me/Sweet Dreams	1956	7.50	15.00	30.00
❑ 974	Ain't That Right/Let Me Know	1956	7.50	15.00	30.00

SPECIALTY

❑ 479	Baby Doll/I'm Not a Fool	1953	15.00	30.00	60.00
❑ 479	Baby Doll/I'm Not a Fool	1953	25.00	50.00	100.00
—Red vinyl					
❑ 488	Jo Jo/How Long Has She Been Gone	1954	15.00	30.00	60.00
❑ 498	School of Love/Boy Loves Girl	1954	15.00	30.00	60.00
❑ 530	Day In — Day Out/Flip	1954	15.00	30.00	60.00
❑ 554	Ding Dong Baby/Mamo Mamo	1955	12.50	25.00	50.00

SWINGIN'

❑ 641	I'm Tired of Being Alone/Baby You Don't Know	1962	3.00	6.00	12.00
❑ 645	Pretty One/Second Helping of Cherry Pie	1963	3.00	6.00	12.00

Albums

CROWN

❑ CST-381 [R]	Marvin and Johnny	1963	3.00	6.00	12.00
❑ CLP-5381 [M]	Marvin and Johnny	1963	12.50	25.00	50.00

MARYLANDERS, THE

45s

JUBILEE

❑ 5079	I'm a Sentimental Fool/Sittin' By the River	1952	100.00	200.00	400.00
❑ 5091	Make Me Thrill Again/Please Love Me	1952	100.00	200.00	400.00
❑ 5114	Fried Chicken/Good Old 99	1953	100.00	200.00	400.00
—Red vinyl					
❑ 5114	Fried Chicken/Good Old 99	1953	75.00	150.00	300.00

MASON, BARBARA

12-Inch Singles

WEST END

❑ 22164	Another Man (4 versions)	1983	—	3.00	6.00

WMOT

❑ 02237	Let Me Give You Love/(Instrumental)	1981	2.00	4.00	8.00

45s

ARCTIC

❑ 102	Girls Have Feelings Too/Come to Me	1964	3.00	6.00	12.00
❑ 105	Yes I'm Ready/Keep Him	1965	5.00	10.00	20.00
❑ 108	Sad, Sad Girl/Come to Me	1965	3.00	6.00	12.00
❑ 112	You Got What It Takes/If You Don't (Love Me, Tell Me So)	1965	3.00	6.00	12.00
❑ 116	Don't Ever Want to Lose Your Love/Is It Me	1965	3.00	6.00	12.00
❑ 120	I Need Love/Bobby Is My Baby	1966	2.50	5.00	10.00
❑ 126	Hello Baby/Poor Girl I'm in Trouble	1966	2.50	5.00	10.00
❑ 134	You Can Depend on Me/Game of Love	1967	2.00	4.00	8.00
❑ 137	Oh, How It Hurts/Ain't Got Nobody	1967	2.00	4.00	8.00
❑ 140	Dedicated to the One I Love/Half a Love	1968	2.00	4.00	8.00
❑ 142	Half a Love/(I Can Feel Your Love) Slipping Away	1968	2.00	4.00	8.00
❑ 146	Don't Ever Go Away/I'm No Good for You	1968	2.00	4.00	8.00
❑ 148	Take It Easy/You Never Loved Me	1969	2.00	4.00	8.00
❑ 154	You Better Stop It/Happy Girl	1969	2.00	4.00	8.00

BUDDAH

❑ 249	The Pow Pow Song (Sorry Sorry Baby)/Your Old Flame	1971	—	3.00	6.00
❑ 296	Bed and Board/Yes It's You	1972	—	2.50	5.00
❑ 319	Woman and Man/Who Will You Hurt Next	1972	—	2.50	5.00
❑ 331	Give Me Your Love/You Can Be with the One You Don't Love	1972	—	2.50	5.00
❑ 355	Yes I'm Ready/Who Will You Hurt Next	1973	—	2.50	5.00
❑ 375	Child of Tomorrow/Out of This World	1973	—	2.50	5.00
❑ 395	Caught in the Middle/Give Him Up	1973	—	2.50	5.00
❑ 405	World War III/I Miss You Gordon	1974	—	2.50	5.00
❑ 424	Our Day Will Come/Half Sister, Half Brother	1974	—	2.50	5.00

Number	Title (A Side/B Side)	Yr	VG	VG+	NM
❑ 441	From His Woman to You/When You Wake Up in Georgia	1974	—	2.50	5.00
❑ 459	Shackin' Up/One Man Between Us	1975	—	2.50	5.00
❑ 481	Make It Last/We Got Each Other	1975	—	2.50	5.00
—With the Futures					
❑ 481 [PS]	Make It Last/We Got Each Other	1975	2.00	4.00	8.00
CRUSADER					
❑ 111	Dedicated to You/Trouble Child	1965	2.50	5.00	10.00
NATIONAL GENERAL					
❑ 005	Raindrops Keep Fallin' on My Head/If You Knew Him Like I Do	1970	—	3.00	6.00
PRELUDE					
❑ 71103	I Am Your Woman, She Is Your Wife/Take Me Tonight	1978	—	2.50	5.00
❑ 71111	Darling Come Back Home Soon/It Was You Boy	1978	—	2.50	5.00
WEST END					
❑ 1264	Another Man (Vocal) (Short)/Another Man (Instrumental)	1984	—	2.00	4.00
WMOT					
❑ 02506	She's Got the Papers (But I've Got the Man)/(Instrumental)	1981	—	2.00	4.00
❑ 5352	I'll Never Love the Same Way Twice/(B-side unknown)	1980	—	2.00	4.00
❑ 70077	On and Off/You're All Inside of Me	1981	—	2.00	4.00
Albums					
ARCTIC					
❑ ALP-1000 [M]	Yes, I'm Ready	1965	7.50	15.00	30.00
❑ ALPS-1000 [P]	Yes, I'm Ready	1965	12.50	25.00	50.00
❑ ALPS-1004	Oh, How It Hurts	1968	7.50	15.00	30.00
BUDDAH					
❑ BDS-5117	Give Me Your Love	1972	3.00	6.00	12.00
❑ BDS-5140	Lady Love	1973	3.00	6.00	12.00
❑ BDS-5610	Transition	1974	3.00	6.00	12.00
❑ BDS-5628	Love's the Thing	1975	3.00	6.00	12.00
NATIONAL GENERAL					
❑ 2001	If You Knew Him Like I Do	1970	7.50	15.00	30.00

MASON, BARBARA, AND BUNNY SIGLER

Also see each artist's individual listings.

Number	Title (A Side/B Side)	Yr	VG	VG+	NM
Albums					
CURTOM					
❑ CU 5014	Locked in This Position	1977	2.50	5.00	10.00

MATHIS, JOHNNY/DENIECE WILLIAMS

Also see DENIECE WILLIAMS.

Number	Title (A Side/B Side)	Yr	VG	VG+	NM
45s					
COLUMBIA					
❑ 38-04379	Love Won't Let Me Wait/Lead Me to Your Love	1984	—	—	3.00
❑ 3-10693	Too Much, Too Little, Too Late/Emotion	1978	—	2.50	5.00
❑ 3-10693	Too Much, Too Little, Too Late/I Wrote a Symphony on My Guitar	1978	2.50	5.00	10.00
—B-side by Johnny Mathis solo					
❑ 3-10772	You're All I Need to Get By/You're a Special Part of My Life	1978	—	2.50	5.00
❑ 3-10772 [PS]	You're All I Need to Get By	1978	2.50	5.00	10.00
—Sleeve is promo only					
❑ 3-10826	That's What Friends Are For/I Just Can't Get Over You	1978	—	2.50	5.00
❑ 33360	Too Much, Too Little, Too Late/You're All I Need to Get By	198?	—	2.00	4.00
—Red label					
❑ 33360	Too Much, Too Little, Too Late/You're All I Need to Get By	198?	—	—	3.00
—Gray label					
Albums					
COLUMBIA					
❑ JC 35435	That's What Friends Are For	1978	2.50	5.00	10.00
❑ PC 35435	That's What Friends Are For	198?	2.00	4.00	8.00
—Budget-line reissue					

MAXIM TRIO, THE

Also see RAY CHARLES.

Number	Title (A Side/B Side)	Yr	VG	VG+	NM
78s					
DOWN BEAT					
❑ 171	Confession Blues/I Love You, I Love You	1949	15.00	30.00	60.00
❑ 178	Blues Before Sunrise/How Long Blues	1949	15.00	30.00	60.00
❑ 179	A Sentimental Blues/You'll Never Miss the Water	1949	15.00	30.00	60.00
SWING TIME					
❑ 211	Alone in the City/Can Anyone Ask for Any More	1949	12.50	25.00	50.00
❑ 212	Here I Am/Rockin' Chair Blues	1949	12.50	25.00	50.00
❑ 213	The Honey Bee/If I Gave You My Love	1949	12.50	25.00	50.00

MAYE, LEE

Also recorded as "Arthur Lee Maye."

Number	Title (A Side/B Side)	Yr	VG	VG+	NM
45s					
ABC					
❑ 11028	If You Leave Me/The Greatest Love I've Ever Known	1967	2.00	4.00	8.00
BUDDAH					
❑ 141	He'll Have to Go/Jus' Lookin'	1969	—	3.00	6.00
CASH					
❑ 1063	Will You Be Mine/Honey Honey	1958	37.50	75.00	150.00
❑ 1065	All I Want Is Someone to Love/Pounding	1958	30.00	60.00	120.00
DIG					
❑ 124	This Is the Night for Love/(B-side unknown)	1956	62.50	125.00	250.00
❑ 133	A Fool's Prayer/(B-side unknown)	1957	37.50	75.00	150.00
FLIP					
❑ 330	Hey Pretty Baby/'Cause You're Mine Alone	1958	20.00	40.00	80.00
—As "Arthur Lee Maye"					
IMPERIAL					
❑ 5790	Will You Be Mine/Honey Honey	1961	5.00	10.00	20.00
JAMIE					
❑ 1272	Who Made You What You Are/Loving Fool	1964	2.50	5.00	10.00
❑ 1276	How's the World Treating You/Loving Fool	1964	2.50	5.00	10.00
❑ 1284	Only a Dream/The Breaks of Life	1964	2.50	5.00	10.00
❑ 1287	Even a Nobody/Who Made You What You Are	1964	2.50	5.00	10.00
❑ 1295	(Don't Pretend) Just Lay It on the Line/Careless Hands	1965	2.00	4.00	8.00
—With Barbara Lynn					
LENOX					
❑ 5566	Half Way (Out of Love with You)/I Can't Please You	1963	3.00	6.00	12.00
MODERN					
❑ 944	Set My Heart Free/I Wanna Love	1954	150.00	300.00	600.00
—As "Arthur Lee Maye and the Crowns"					
RPM					
❑ 424	Truly/Oochie Pachie	1955	50.00	100.00	200.00
—As "Arthur Lee Maye and the Crowns"					
❑ 429	Loop De Loop/Love Me Always	1955	30.00	60.00	120.00
—As "Arthur Lee Maye"					
❑ 438	Do the Bop/Please Don't Leave Me	1955	37.50	75.00	150.00
—As "Arthur Lee Maye and the Crowns"					
SPECIALTY					
❑ 573	Gloria/Oo-Rooba-Lee	1956	15.00	30.00	60.00
—As "Arthur Lee Maye and the Crowns"					
TOWER					
❑ 243	When My Heart Hurts No More/At the Party	1966	2.00	4.00	8.00

MAYER, NATHANIEL

Number	Title (A Side/B Side)	Yr	VG	VG+	NM
45s					
FORTUNE					
❑ 449	Village of Love/I Want a Woman	1962	6.25	12.50	25.00
❑ 487	Hurting Love/Leave Me Alone	1962	7.50	15.00	30.00
—Fortune 449 and 487 were part of the United Artists numbering system					
❑ 542	My Last Dance with You/My Little Darling	1962	5.00	10.00	20.00
❑ 545	Village of Love/I Want a Woman	1962	5.00	10.00	20.00
❑ 547	Hurting Love/Leave Me Alone	1962	5.00	10.00	20.00
❑ 550	Mr. Santa Claus/(B-side unknown)	1962	7.50	15.00	30.00
❑ 550	Work It Out/Well, I've Got News	1962	3.75	7.50	15.00
❑ 554	I Had a Dream/I'm Not Gonna Cry	1963	3.75	7.50	15.00
❑ 557	Going Back to the Village of Love/My Last Dance with You	1963	3.75	7.50	15.00
❑ 562	The Place I Know/Don't Come Back	196?	3.75	7.50	15.00
❑ 563	Village of Love/I Want a Woman	196?	3.00	6.00	12.00
❑ 567	From Now On/I Want Love and Affection	196?	3.00	6.00	12.00
Albums					
FORTUNE					
❑ 8014 [M]	Goin' Back to the Village of Love	1964	75.00	150.00	300.00
—Light blue label					
❑ 8014 [M]	Goin' Back to the Village of Love	196?	37.50	75.00	150.00
—Purple label					
❑ 8014 [M]	Goin' Back to the Village of Love	196?	15.00	30.00	60.00
—Yellow label					
❑ 8014 [M]	Goin' Back to the Village of Love	197?	3.75	7.50	15.00
—Bluish purple label, with much more flexible vinyl than earlier pressings					

MAYFIELD, CURTIS

Also see FISHBONE; THE IMPRESSIONS.

Number	Title (A Side/B Side)	Yr	VG	VG+	NM
12-Inch Singles					
CAPITOL					
❑ V-15602	Superfly 1990 (6 versions)	1990	2.00	4.00	8.00
—With Ice-T					
CURTOM					
❑ 12-PO-22 [DJ]	I Mo Git U Sucka/He's a Fly Guy	198?	2.50	5.00	10.00
❑ 12-PO-52 [DJ]	Got to Be Real/On and On	198?	2.50	5.00	10.00
RSO/CURTOM					
❑ 1016 [DJ]	Tell Me, Tell Me (7:16)//Heartbeat/Over the Hump	1979	2.50	5.00	10.00
45s					
BOARDWALK					
❑ NB7-11-122	She Don't Let Nobody (But Me)/You Get All My Love	1981	—	2.00	4.00
❑ NB7-11-132	Toot An'Toot An'Toot/Come Free Your People	1981	—	2.00	4.00
❑ NB7-11-155	Hey Baby (Give It All to Me)/Summer Hot	1982	—	2.00	4.00
❑ NB7-11-169	Dirty Laundry/Nobody But You	1982	—	2.00	4.00
COLUMBIA					
❑ 10147	Stash That Butt, Sucker/Zanzibar	1975	—	2.50	5.00
CRC					
❑ 001	Baby It's You/(B-side unknown)	1985	—	3.00	6.00
CURTOM					
❑ 0105	So in Love/Hard Times	1975	—	2.50	5.00
❑ 0118	Only You Babe/Love to the People	1976	—	2.50	5.00
❑ 0122	Party Night/P.S. I Love You	1976	—	2.50	5.00
❑ 0125	Show Me Love/Just Want to Be with You	1977	—	2.50	5.00
❑ 0131	Do Do Wap Is Strong in Here/Need Someone to Love	1977	—	2.50	5.00
❑ 0135	You Are, You Are/Get a Little Bit (Give, Get, Take and Have)	1978	—	2.50	5.00

Number	Title (A Side/B Side)	Yr	VG	VG+	NM
❑ 0135 [PS]	You Are, You Are/Get a Little Bit (Give, Get, Take and Have)	1978	—	3.00	6.00
❑ 0141	Do It All Night/Party Party	1978	—	2.50	5.00
❑ 0142	In Love, In Love, In Love/Keeps Me Loving You	1978	—	2.50	5.00
❑ 1955	(Don't Worry) If There's a Hell Below We're All Going to Go/The Makings of You	1970	—	3.00	6.00
❑ 1960	Beautiful Brother of Mine/Give It Up	1971	—	3.00	6.00
❑ 1963	Mighty Mighty (Spade and Whitey)/(B-side unknown)	1971	—	3.00	6.00
❑ 1966	Get Down/We're a Winner	1971	—	3.00	6.00
❑ 1968	We Got to Have Peace/We're a Winner	1972	—	3.00	6.00
❑ 1968 [PS]	We Got to Have Peace/We're a Winner	1972	2.00	4.00	8.00
❑ 1972	Beautiful Brother of Mine/Love to Keep You In My Mind	1972	—	3.00	6.00
❑ 1974	Move On Up/Underground	1972	—	3.00	6.00
❑ 1975	Freddie's Dead (Theme from "Superfly")/Underground	1972	—	3.00	6.00
❑ 1978	Superfly/Underground	1972	—	3.00	6.00
❑ 1978 [PS]	Superfly/Underground	1972	2.00	4.00	8.00
❑ 1987	Future Shock/The Other Side of Town	1973	—	3.00	6.00
❑ 1991	If I Were Only a Child Again/Think	1973	—	3.00	6.00
❑ 1993	Can't Say Nothin'/Future Song	1973	—	3.00	6.00
❑ 1999	Kung Fu/Right On for the Darkness	1974	—	3.00	6.00
❑ 1999 [PS]	Kung Fu/Right On for the Darkness	1974	2.00	4.00	8.00
❑ 2005	Sweet Exorcist/Suffer	1974	—	3.00	6.00
❑ 2006	Mother's Son/Love Me	1974	—	3.00	6.00
RSO/CURTOM					
❑ 919	This Year/(Instrumental)	1979	—	2.50	5.00
❑ 941	You're So Good to Me/Between You, Babe, and Me	1979	—	2.50	5.00
—With Linda Clifford					
❑ 1029	Love's Sweet Sensation/(Instrumental)	1980	—	2.50	5.00
—With Linda Clifford					
❑ 1036	Love Me, Love Me Now/It's Alright	1980	—	2.50	5.00
❑ 1046	Tripping Out/Never Stop Loving	1980	—	2.50	5.00
Albums					
BOARDWALK					
❑ NB1-33239	Love Is the Place	1981	2.50	5.00	10.00
❑ NB1-33256	Honesty	1982	2.50	5.00	10.00
CRC					
❑ 2001	We Come in Peace with a Message of Love	1985	3.00	6.00	12.00
CURTOM					
❑ CUR-2003	There's No Place Like America Today	198?	2.00	4.00	8.00
—Reissue of 5001					
❑ CUR-2005	Something to Believe In	198?	2.00	4.00	8.00
—Reissue of RSO 3077					
❑ CUR-2008	Take It to the Street	198?	2.50	5.00	10.00
❑ CUR-2901 [(2)]	Live in Europe	198?	3.00	6.00	12.00
❑ CUR-2902 [(2)]	Greatest Hits of All Time (Classic Collection)	198?	3.00	6.00	12.00
❑ CU 5001	There's No Place Like America Today	1975	3.00	6.00	12.00
❑ CU 5007	Give, Get, Take and Have	1976	3.00	6.00	12.00
❑ CU 5013	Never Say You Can't Survive	1977	3.00	6.00	12.00
❑ CUK 5022	Do It All Night	1978	3.00	6.00	12.00
❑ CRS-8005	Curtis	1970	3.75	7.50	15.00
❑ CRS-8008 [(2)]	Curtis/Live!	1971	5.00	10.00	20.00
❑ CRS-8009	Roots	1971	3.75	7.50	15.00
❑ CRS-8014	Superfly	1972	5.00	10.00	20.00
❑ CRS-8015	Back to the World	1973	3.75	7.50	15.00
❑ CRS-8018	Curtis in Chicago	1973	3.75	7.50	15.00
❑ CRS-8601	Sweet Exorcist	1974	3.00	6.00	12.00
❑ CRS-8604	Got to Find a Way	1974	3.00	6.00	12.00
RSO					
❑ RS-1-3053	Heartbeat	1979	2.50	5.00	10.00
❑ RS-1-3077	Something to Believe In	1980	2.50	5.00	10.00

MAYFIELD, PERCY

Number	Title (A Side/B Side)	Yr	VG	VG+	NM
45s					
ATLANTIC					
❑ 3207	I Don't Want to Be President/Nothin' Stays the Same Forever	1974	—	2.50	5.00
BRUNSWICK					
❑ 55390	Walking on a Tightrope/P.M. Blues	1968	2.00	4.00	8.00
CHESS					
❑ 1599	Double Dealing/Are You Out There	1955	15.00	30.00	60.00
IMPERIAL					
❑ 5577	One Love/My Reward	1959	3.75	7.50	15.00
❑ 5620	My Heart Is a Prisoner/My Memories	1959	3.75	7.50	15.00
KING					
❑ 4480	Two Years of Torture/Half Awake	1951	15.00	30.00	60.00
RCA VICTOR					
❑ 74-0307	To Live the Past/Lying Woman (Not Trustworthy)	1970	—	3.00	6.00
❑ 74-0348	A Highway Is Like a Woman/You Wear Your Hair Too Long	1970	—	3.00	6.00
❑ 74-0379	Daddy Wants You to Come Home/Weakness Is a Thing Called Man	1970	—	3.00	6.00
❑ 74-0462	The Flirt/California Blues	1971	—	3.00	6.00
SPECIALTY					
❑ 375	Please Send Me Someone to Love/Strange Things Happening	1950	20.00	40.00	80.00
❑ 390	Lost Love/Life Is Suicide	1951	15.00	30.00	60.00
❑ 400	What a Fool I Was/Nightless Lover	1951	15.00	30.00	60.00
❑ 408	Prayin' For Your Return/My Blues	1951	15.00	30.00	60.00
❑ 416	Cry Baby/Hopeless	1952	10.00	20.00	40.00
❑ 425	The Big Question/The Hurt Is On	1952	10.00	20.00	40.00
❑ 432	Louisiana/Two Hearts Are Greater Than One	1952	10.00	20.00	40.00
❑ 439	Lonesome Highway/My Heart	1952	10.00	20.00	40.00
❑ 460	Lost Mind/Lonely One	1953	10.00	20.00	40.00
—Black vinyl					
❑ 460	Lost Mind/Lonely One	1953	20.00	40.00	80.00
—Colored vinyl					
❑ 473	The Bachelor Blues/How Deep Is the Well	1953	10.00	20.00	40.00
—Black vinyl					
❑ 473	The Bachelor Blues/How Deep Is the Well	1953	20.00	40.00	80.00
—Colored vinyl					
❑ 485	I Need Love So Bad/Loose Lips	1954	10.00	20.00	40.00
❑ 499	You Don't Exist No More/Sugar Mama, Peach Papa	1954	10.00	20.00	40.00
❑ 537	My Heart Is Cryin'/You Were Lyin' to Me	1954	10.00	20.00	40.00
❑ 544	Baby You're Rich/The Voice Within	1955	7.50	15.00	30.00
❑ 607	Diggin' the Moonglow/Please Believe Me	1956	7.50	15.00	30.00
❑ 690	When Did You Leave Heaven/What Must I Do	1960	5.00	10.00	20.00
❑ 723	Lost Mind/River's Invitation	1973	—	3.00	6.00
TANGERINE					
❑ 923	Never No More/I Reached for a Tear	1962	3.00	6.00	12.00
❑ 927	Never Say Now/Life Is Suicide	1963	2.50	5.00	10.00
❑ 931	River's Invitation/Baby Please	1963	2.50	5.00	10.00
❑ 934	The Hunt Is On/Cookin' in Style	1963	2.50	5.00	10.00
❑ 935	You Don't Exist No More/Memory Pain	1964	2.50	5.00	10.00
❑ 941	Stranger in My Own Home Town/Maybe It's Because of Love	1964	2.50	5.00	10.00
❑ 950	Fading Love/Stand By	1965	2.00	4.00	8.00
❑ 957	Give Me Time to Explain/My Jug and I	1965	2.00	4.00	8.00
❑ 966	It's Time to Make a Change/We Both Must Cry	1966	2.00	4.00	8.00
❑ 973	My Love/My Bottle Is My Companion	1966	2.00	4.00	8.00
❑ 977	As Long As You're Mine/Ha Ha in the Daytime	1967	2.00	4.00	8.00
❑ 979	Don't Start Lyin' to Me/Pretty Eyed Baby	1967	2.00	4.00	8.00
Albums					
BRUNSWICK					
❑ BL 754145	Walking on a Tightrope	1968	5.00	10.00	20.00
INTERMEDIA					
❑ QS-5010	Please Send Me Someone to Love	198?	2.50	5.00	10.00
RCA VICTOR					
❑ LSP-4269	Percy Mayfield Sings Percy Mayfield	1970	3.75	7.50	15.00
❑ LSP-4444	Weakness Is a Thing Called Man	1970	3.75	7.50	15.00
❑ LSP-4558	Blues And Then Some	1971	3.75	7.50	15.00
SPECIALTY					
❑ SPS-2126	The Best of Percy Mayfield	1970	5.00	10.00	20.00
❑ SP-7001	Poet of the Blues	1990	3.75	7.50	15.00
TANGERINE					
❑ TRC-1505 [M]	My Jug and I	1966	5.00	10.00	20.00
❑ TRCS-1505 [S]	My Jug and I	1966	6.25	12.50	25.00
❑ TRC-1510 [M]	Bought Blues	1967	5.00	10.00	20.00
❑ TRCS-1510 [S]	Bought Blues	1967	6.25	12.50	25.00

MAYS, WILLIE

Number	Title (A Side/B Side)	Yr	VG	VG+	NM
45s					
DUKE					
❑ 350	My Sad Heart/If You Love Me	1962	2.50	5.00	10.00
❑ 418	My Sad Heart/If You Love Me	1967	2.00	4.00	8.00
EPIC					
❑ 9066	Say Hey (The Willie Mays Song)/Out of the Bushes	1954	6.25	12.50	25.00
—With the Treniers					

MCCARTNEY, PAUL, AND STEVIE WONDER

Also see STEVIE WONDER.

Number	Title (A Side/B Side)	Yr	VG	VG+	NM
12-Inch Singles					
COLUMBIA					
❑ 44-02878	Ebony and Ivory//Rainclouds/Ebony and Ivory (Solo)	1982	3.00	6.00	12.00
—B-side by McCartney solo					
45s					
COLUMBIA					
❑ 18-02860	Ebony and Ivory/Rainclouds	1982	—	2.00	4.00
—B-side by McCartney solo					
❑ 18-02860 [PS]	Ebony and Ivory/Rainclouds	1982	—	2.00	4.00

MCCOO, MARILYN

Also see THE FIFTH DIMENSION; MARILYN McCOO AND BILLY DAVIS, JR.

Number	Title (A Side/B Side)	Yr	VG	VG+	NM
45s					
RCA					
❑ PB-13677	Heart Stop Beating in Time/Understand Your Man	1983	—	2.00	4.00
❑ PB-13761	I Believe in You and Me/Just Like You	1984	—	2.00	4.00

MCCOO, MARILYN, AND BILLY DAVIS, JR.

Also see each artist's individual listings; THE FIFTH DIMENSION.

Number	Title (A Side/B Side)	Yr	VG	VG+	NM
45s					
ABC					
❑ 12170	I Hope We Get to Love in Time/There's Got to Be a Happy Ending	1976	—	2.00	4.00
❑ 12208	You Don't Have to Be a Star (To Be in My Show)/We've Got to Get It On Again	1976	—	2.00	4.00
❑ 12262	Your Love/My Love for You (Will Always Be the Same)	1977	—	2.00	4.00
❑ 12298	Look What You've Done to My Heart/In My Lifetime	1977	—	2.00	4.00
❑ 12316	Wonderful/Hard Road Down	1977	—	2.00	4.00

Number	Title (A Side/B Side)	Yr	VG	VG+	NM
❑ 12324	My Reason to Be Is You/Two of Us	1978	—	2.00	4.00
COLUMBIA					
❑ 10806	Shine On Silver Moon/I Got the Words, You Got the Music	1978	—	2.00	4.00

MCCOY, VAN
12-Inch Singles
H&L

❑ 2002	Rhythms of the World (10:12)//Soul Cha Cha/That's the Joint	1976	5.00	10.00	20.00

45s
AVCO

❑ 4639	Love Is the Answer/Killing Me Softly	1974	—	2.50	5.00
❑ 4648	Boogie Down/Rainy Night in Georgia	1975	—	2.50	5.00
❑ 4653	The Hustle/Hey Girl, Come and Get It	1975	—	2.00	4.00
❑ 4660	Change with the Times/Goodnight Baby	1975	—	2.00	4.00
COLUMBIA					
❑ 43415	Keep Loving Me/Butterfly	1965	3.00	6.00	12.00
❑ 43495	Starlight Starbright/This Is the Way We Fall in Love	1965	2.00	4.00	8.00
❑ 43694	I Will Wait for You/The House That Love Built	1966	2.00	4.00	8.00
EPIC					
❑ 10470	I Started a Joke/Toney's Theme	1969	—	3.50	7.00
H&L					
❑ 4667	Night Walk/Love Child	1976	—	2.00	4.00
❑ 4670	Party/The Disco Kid	1976	—	2.00	4.00
❑ 4677	The Shuffle/That's the Joint	1976	—	2.00	4.00
❑ 4682	Soul Cha Cha/Oriental Boogie	1977	—	2.00	4.00
LIBERTY					
❑ 55457	Follow Your Heart/Lonely	1962	3.00	6.00	12.00
MCA					
❑ 40885	My Favorite Fantasy/You're So Right for Me	1978	—	2.00	4.00
❑ 40938	Trying to Make the Best of It/Two Points	1978	—	2.00	4.00
❑ 40984	Lonely Dancer/Decisions	1979	—	2.00	4.00
ROCK'N					
❑ 101	Mr. D.J./Never Trust a Friend	1961	12.50	25.00	50.00

Albums
AVCO

❑ AV-69002	Love Is the Answer	1974	2.50	5.00	10.00
❑ AV-69006	Disco Baby	1975	2.50	5.00	10.00
❑ AV-69009	The Disco Kid	1975	2.50	5.00	10.00
BUDDAH					
❑ BDS-5103	Soul Improvisations	1971	3.75	7.50	15.00
❑ BDS-5648	From Disco to Love	1975	2.50	5.00	10.00
—Retitled reissue of 5103					
COLUMBIA					
❑ CL 2497 [M]	Night Time Is the Lonely Time	1966	5.00	10.00	20.00
❑ CS 9297 [S]	Night Time Is the Lonely Time	1966	6.25	12.50	25.00
H&L					
❑ HL-69002	Love Is the Answer	1976	2.00	4.00	8.00
—Reissue of Avco 69002					
❑ HL-69006	Disco Baby	1976	2.00	4.00	8.00
—Reissue of Avco 69006					
❑ HL-69009	The Disco Kid	1976	2.00	4.00	8.00
—Reissue of Avco 69009					
❑ HL-69012	The Real McCoy	1976	2.50	5.00	10.00
❑ HL-69014	Rhythms of the World	1976	2.50	5.00	10.00
❑ HL-69016	The Hustle and Best of Van McCoy	1976	2.50	5.00	10.00
❑ HL-69022	Van McCoy and His Magnificent Movie Machine	1977	2.50	5.00	10.00
MCA					
❑ 3036	My Favorite Fantasy	1978	2.50	5.00	10.00
❑ 3054	A Woman Called Moses	1978	2.50	5.00	10.00
❑ 3071	Lovely Dancer	1979	2.50	5.00	10.00

MCCRACKLIN, JIMMY
45s
ART-TONE

❑ 825	Just Got to Know/The Drag	1961	3.00	6.00	12.00
❑ 826	Christmas Time (Part 1)/Christmas Time (Part 2)	1961	3.00	6.00	12.00
❑ 827	Shame, Shame, Shame/I'm the One	1962	3.00	6.00	12.00
❑ 831	That's No Big Thing/Susie and Pat	1962	3.00	6.00	12.00
CHECKER					
❑ 885	The Walk/I'm to Blame	1958	6.25	12.50	25.00
❑ 893	Everybody Rock/Get Tough	1958	3.75	7.50	15.00
CHESS					
❑ 1809	I Know/Later On	1961	2.50	5.00	10.00
❑ 1826	One Track Love/Trottin'	1962	2.50	5.00	10.00
HI					
❑ 2023	Things I Meant to Say/Here Today and Gone Tomorrow	1960	3.00	6.00	12.00
HOLLYWOOD					
❑ 1054	It's All Right/Fare You Well	1955	12.50	25.00	50.00
IMPERIAL					
❑ 5892	Bitter Pill/Head Over Flip	1962	2.50	5.00	10.00
❑ 5906	I Don't Care/Just Got to Know	1963	2.50	5.00	10.00
❑ 5911	Advice/No No	1963	2.50	5.00	10.00
❑ 5926	The Bitter and the Sweet/Just Pretending	1963	2.50	5.00	10.00
❑ 5955	That's the Way (It Goes)/I'll See It Through	1963	2.50	5.00	10.00
❑ 5977	Every Night/The Slightest Idea	1963	2.50	5.00	10.00
❑ 5982	Sooner or Later/Looking for a Woman	1963	2.50	5.00	10.00
❑ 66010	I Did Wrong/Someone	1964	2.00	4.00	8.00
❑ 66035	Just Like It Is/Let's Do It All	1964	2.00	4.00	8.00
❑ 66067	Believe in Me/Set Six	1964	2.00	4.00	8.00

Number	Title (A Side/B Side)	Yr	VG	VG+	NM
❑ 66094	Every Night, Every Day/Can't Raise Me	1965	2.00	4.00	8.00
❑ 66116	Arkansas (Part 1)/Arkansas (Part 2)	1965	2.00	4.00	8.00
❑ 66129	Think/Steppin' Up in Class	1965	2.00	4.00	8.00
❑ 66147	My Answer/Beulah	1966	2.00	4.00	8.00
❑ 66168	Come On Home (Back Where You Belong)/Something That Belongs to Me	1966	2.00	4.00	8.00
❑ 66180	Just Let Me Cry/These Boots Are Made for Walkin'	1966	2.00	4.00	8.00
❑ 66207	It's Got to Be Love/Sorry	1966	2.00	4.00	8.00
IRMA					
❑ 102	You're the One/I Wanna Make Love to You	1956	7.50	15.00	30.00
❑ 103	Take a Chance/Fare Well	1956	7.50	15.00	30.00
❑ 107	I'm the One/Savoy's Jump	1957	7.50	15.00	30.00
❑ 109	Beer Tavern Girl/Love for You	1957	7.50	15.00	30.00
KENT					
❑ 369	I've Got Eyes for You/I'm Gonna Tell Your Mother	1962	2.50	5.00	10.00
LIBERTY					
❑ 56198	Believe Me/I Never Thought	1970	—	2.50	5.00
MERCURY					
❑ 71412	The Wobble/With Your Love	1959	3.75	7.50	15.00
❑ 71516	Let's Do It (The Chicken Scratch)/Georgia Slop	1959	3.75	7.50	15.00
❑ 71613	Doomed Lover/By Myself	1960	3.00	6.00	12.00
❑ 71666	You Rascal You/No One to Love Me	1960	3.00	6.00	12.00
❑ 71747	What's That (Part 1)/The Bridge	1961	3.00	6.00	12.00
❑ 71766	No One to Love Me/(B-side unknown)	1961	3.00	6.00	12.00
MINIT					
❑ 32018	Let the Door Hit You/This Thing	1967	—	3.00	6.00
❑ 32022	Dog (Part 1)/Dog (Part 2)	1967	—	3.00	6.00
❑ 32033	Get Together/How You Like Your Love	1967	—	3.00	6.00
❑ 32044	Pretty Little Sweet Thing/A & I	1968	—	3.00	6.00
❑ 32052	Love, Love, Love/Married Life	1968	—	3.00	6.00
❑ 32064	Drown in My Own Tears/What's Going On	1969	—	3.00	6.00
❑ 32086	I Had to Get With It/You Ain't Nothin' But a Devil	1969	—	3.00	6.00
❑ 32092	Stick to My Mind/I Just Live by the Rules	1970	—	3.00	6.00
MODERN					
❑ 926	Blues Blasters' Boogie/The Panic's On	1954	10.00	20.00	40.00
❑ 934	Darlin' Share Your Love/Give My Heart a Break	1954	10.00	20.00	40.00
❑ 951	Please Forgive Me Baby/Couldn't Be a Dream	1954	10.00	20.00	40.00
❑ 967	Gonna Tell Your Mother/That Ain't Right	1955	10.00	20.00	40.00
PEACOCK					
❑ 1605	My Days Are Limited/She's Gone	1952	15.00	30.00	60.00
❑ 1615	She Felt Too Good/Share and Share Alike	1953	15.00	30.00	60.00
❑ 1634	I Cried/The End	1953	15.00	30.00	60.00
❑ 1639	The Cheater/My Story	1954	15.00	30.00	60.00
❑ 1683	I Need Your Loving/The Swinging Thing	1958	6.25	12.50	25.00

Albums
CHESS

❑ LP-1464 [M]	Jimmy McCracklin Sings	1961	30.00	60.00	120.00
CROWN					
❑ CLP-5244 [M]	Twist with Jimmy McCracklin	1962	12.50	25.00	50.00
—Black label, silver "Crown"					
❑ CLP-5244 [M]	Twist with Jimmy McCracklin	1962	6.25	12.50	25.00
—Gray label					
❑ CLP-5244 [M]	Twist with Jimmy McCracklin	196?	3.75	7.50	15.00
—Black label, multi-color "Crown"					
EVEJIM					
❑ EJR-4013	Same Lovin'	198?	3.00	6.00	12.00
IMPERIAL					
❑ LP-9219 [M]	I Just Gotta Know	1964	6.25	12.50	25.00
❑ LP-9285 [M]	Every Night, Every Day	1965	6.25	12.50	25.00
❑ LP-9297 [M]	Think	1965	6.25	12.50	25.00
❑ LP-9306 [M]	My Answer	1966	6.25	12.50	25.00
❑ LP-9316 [M]	The New Soul of Jimmy McCracklin	1966	6.25	12.50	25.00
❑ LP-12219 [S]	I Just Gotta Know	1964	7.50	15.00	30.00
❑ LP-12285 [S]	Every Night, Every Day	1965	7.50	15.00	30.00
❑ LP-12297 [S]	Think	1965	7.50	15.00	30.00
❑ LP-12306 [S]	My Answer	1966	7.50	15.00	30.00
❑ LP-12316 [S]	The New Soul of Jimmy McCracklin	1966	7.50	15.00	30.00
MINIT					
❑ LP-4009 [M]	The Best of Jimmy McCracklin	1967	7.50	15.00	30.00
❑ LP-24009 [S]	The Best of Jimmy McCracklin	1967	6.25	12.50	25.00
❑ LP-24011	Let's Get Together	1968	6.25	12.50	25.00
❑ LP-24017	Stinger Man	1969	6.25	12.50	25.00
STAX					
❑ STS-2047	Yesterday Is Gone	1972	5.00	10.00	20.00
❑ MPS-8506	High on the Blues	1980	2.50	5.00	10.00

MCCRAE, GEORGE
12-Inch Singles
GOLD MOUNTAIN

❑ 81205	Own the Night/Own the Night (Dub)	1984	2.00	4.00	8.00
T.K. DISCO					
❑ 22	Love in Motion (5:00)/Givin' Back the Feeling (5:31)	1977	3.00	6.00	12.00
❑ 62	Kiss Me (The Way I Like It) (3:42) (5:47)	1977	3.00	6.00	12.00
❑ 91	Let's Dance (6:10)/Hey Sexy Dancer	1978	3.00	6.00	12.00

45s
SOUL CITY

❑ XW456	Taking It All Off/Please Help Me Find My Baby	1974	—	3.00	6.00
T.K.					
❑ 1004	Rock Your Baby (Part 1)/Rock Your Baby (Part 2)	1974	—	2.50	5.00
❑ 1006	I Get Lifted/I Can't Leave You Alone	1974	—	2.50	5.00
❑ 1011	Look At You/I Need Someone Like You	1975	—	2.50	5.00

Number	Title (A Side/B Side)	Yr	VG	VG+	NM
❏ 1014	I Ain't Lyin'/You Don't Know	1975	—	2.50	5.00
❏ 1016	Honey I/Sing a Happy Song	1975	—	2.50	5.00
❏ 1021	I'm Gonna Stay with My Baby Tonight/Love in Motion	1977	—	2.50	5.00
❏ 1024	Kiss Me (The Way I Like It) Part 1/Kiss Me (The Way I Like It) Part 2	1977	—	2.50	5.00
❏ 1029	Let's Dance (People All Over the World)/Let George Do It	1978	—	2.50	5.00
❏ 1032	I Want You Around Me/Are You Looking for Love	1979	—	2.50	5.00
❏ 1034	Don't You Feel My Love/You Got Me Going Crazy	1979	—	2.50	5.00

UNITED ARTISTS

❏ 50811	Taking It All Off/Please Help Me Find My Baby	1971	2.50	5.00	10.00

Albums

GOLD MOUNTAIN

❏ GM 80008	Own the Night	1984	2.50	5.00	10.00

T.K.

❏ 501	Rock Your Baby	1974	2.50	5.00	10.00
❏ 602	George McCrae	1975	2.50	5.00	10.00
❏ 606	Diamond Touch	1977	2.50	5.00	10.00

MCCRAE, GEORGE AND GWEN
Also see each artist's individual listings.

45s

CAT

❏ 2002	Winners Together or Losers Apart/Homesick Lovesick	1976	—	2.50	5.00
❏ 2004	I'll Do the Rockin'/Mechanical Body	1976	—	2.50	5.00

Albums

CAT

❏ 2606	Together	1976	2.50	5.00	10.00

MCCRAE, GWEN
12-Inch Singles

ATLANTIC

❏ PR 387 [DJ]	Keep the Fire Burning (same on both sides)	1982	—	3.00	6.00

BLACK JACK

❏ 0021	Do You Know What I Mean (Long Version) (Short Version) (Dub)	1984	2.00	4.00	8.00

45s

ATLANTIC

❏ 3853	Funky Sensation/Have a Good Time	1981	—	2.00	4.00
❏ 3881	Poison/(B-side unknown)	1981	—	2.00	4.00
❏ 89910	Keep the Fire Burning/Hang On	1982	—	2.00	4.00
❏ 89961	I Need to Be with You/(B-side unknown)	1982	—	2.00	4.00

CAT

❏ 1987	He Keeps Something Groovy Goin' On/Your Love Is Worse Than a Cold Love	1973	—	2.50	5.00
❏ 1989	For Your Love/Your Love	1973	—	2.50	5.00
❏ 1992	It's Worth the Hurt/90% of Me Is You	1974	—	2.50	5.00
❏ 1994	Move Me Baby/He Don't Ever Lose His Groove	1974	—	2.50	5.00
❏ 1996	Rockin' Chair/It Keeps On Raining	1975	—	2.50	5.00
❏ 1999	Love Insurance/He Keeps Something Groovy Goin' On	1975	—	2.50	5.00
❏ 2000	Cradle of Love/Easy Rock	1976	—	2.50	5.00
❏ 2005	Damn Right It's Good/Love Without Sex	1976	—	2.50	5.00
❏ 2011	Starting All Over Again/At Bedtime	1977	—	2.50	5.00
❏ 2014	The Melody of Life/The Joy	197?	—	2.50	5.00
❏ 2015	Maybe I'll Find Somebody New/All This Love That I'm Givin'	197?	—	2.50	5.00

COLUMBIA

❏ 45214	Lead Me On/Lay It On Me	1970	—	2.50	5.00
❏ 45320	Been So Long/Lay It On Me	1971	—	2.50	5.00
❏ 45448	Ain't Nothing You Can Do/Goin' Down the Road Feelin' Bad	1971	—	2.50	5.00
❏ 45578	You Were Always on My Mind/He's Not You	1972	—	2.50	5.00
❏ 45684	I'm Losing the Feeling/Leave the Driving to Us	1972	—	2.50	5.00

Albums

ATLANTIC

❏ 80014	On My Way	1982	2.50	5.00	10.00

CAT

❏ 2603	Gwen McCrae	1974	2.50	5.00	10.00
❏ 2605	Rockin' Chair	1975	2.50	5.00	10.00
❏ 2608	Something So Right	1976	2.50	5.00	10.00

MCDANIELS, GENE
45s

ATLANTIC

❏ 2805	The Lord Is Back/Tell Me Mr. President	1971	—	3.00	6.00

—As "Eugene McDaniels"

COLUMBIA

❏ 43800	Something Blue/Cause I Love You So	1966	2.50	5.00	10.00
❏ 44010	Touch of Your Lips/Sweet Lover No More	1967	2.50	5.00	10.00

LIBERTY

❏ 55231	In Times Like These/Once Before	1959	3.75	7.50	15.00
❏ 55265	The Green Door/Facts of Life	1960	3.75	7.50	15.00
❏ 55308	A Hundred Pounds of Clay/Take a Chance on Love	1961	4.00	8.00	16.00
❏ 55344	A Tear/She's Come Back	1961	3.75	7.50	15.00
❏ 55371	Tower of Strength/The Secret	1961	4.00	8.00	16.00
❏ 55405	Chip Chip/Another Tear Falls	1962	3.75	7.50	15.00
❏ 55444	Funny/Chapel of Tears	1962	3.75	7.50	15.00
❏ 55480	Point of No Return/Warmer Than a Whisper	1962	3.75	7.50	15.00
❏ 55510	Spanish Lace/Somebody's Waiting	1962	3.75	7.50	15.00

Number	Title (A Side/B Side)	Yr	VG	VG+	NM
❏ 55541	The Puzzle/Cry Baby Cry	1963	3.00	6.00	12.00
❏ 55597	It's a Lonely Town/False Friends	1963	3.00	6.00	12.00
❏ 55637	Old Country/Anyone Else	1963	3.00	6.00	12.00
❏ 55723	Make Me a Present of You/In Times Like These	1964	3.00	6.00	12.00
❏ 55752	Emily/Forgotten Man	1964	3.00	6.00	12.00
❏ 55805	A Miracle/Walk with a Winner	1965	2.50	5.00	10.00
❏ 55834	Hang On/Will It Last Forever	1965	2.50	5.00	10.00

MGM

❏ 14613	Ol' Heartbreak Top Ten/River	1973	—	2.50	5.00

ODE

❏ 66107	Lady Fair/Natural Juices	1975	—	2.00	4.00

UNITED ARTISTS

❏ 0053	A Hundred Pounds of Clay/Tower of Strength	1973	—	2.00	4.00

—"Silver Spotlight Series" reissue

❏ 0054	Chip Chip/Point of No Return	1973	—	2.00	4.00

—"Silver Spotlight Series" reissue

MCDONALD, MICHAEL
Also see THE REGENTS (5).

12-Inch Singles

MCA

❏ 23641	Sweet Freedom (4 versions)	1986	2.00	4.00	8.00

REPRISE

❏ PRO-A-4395 [DJ]	All We Got (4 versions)	1990	2.50	5.00	10.00
❏ PRO-A-4398 [DJ]	Tear It Up (same on both sides)	1990	2.00	4.00	8.00
❏ PRO-A-6538 [DJ]	Hey Girl (Edit) (LP Version) (Radio Remix)	1993	2.00	4.00	8.00
❏ 21734	All We Got (5 versions)/Show Me	1990	2.00	4.00	8.00

WARNER BROS.

❏ PRO-A-2325 [DJ]	No Lookin' Back (same on both sides)	1985	2.00	4.00	8.00

45s

BELL

❏ 45182	Dear Me/I Think I Love You Again	1972	2.00	4.00	8.00

—All Bell records as "Mike McDonald"

❏ 45219	Good Old Time Love Song/When I'm Home	1972	2.00	4.00	8.00
❏ 45259 [DJ]	Drivin' Wheel/(B-side unknown)	1972	2.00	4.00	8.00

—Stock copy may not exist

❏ 45308 [DJ]	Where Do I Go from Here/(B-side unknown)	1973	2.00	4.00	8.00

—Stock copy may not exist

MCA

❏ 52857	Sweet Freedom/The Freedom Eights	1986	—	—	3.00
❏ 52857 [PS]	Sweet Freedom/The Freedom Eights	1986	—	—	3.00

QWEST

❏ 29394	Yah Mo B There/Come in Da Machine	1983	—	2.00	4.00

—A-side with James Ingram; B-side: James Ingram solo

RCA VICTOR

❏ 74-0405	God Knows/If You Won't, I Will	1970	3.75	7.50	15.00

—As "Mike McDonald"

REPRISE

❏ 18469	I Stand for You/East of Eden	1993	—	—	3.00

WARNER BROS.

❏ 28596	Our Love (Theme from "No Mercy")/Don't Let Me Down	1986	—	—	3.00
❏ 28847	Lost in the Parade/By Heart	1985	—	2.00	4.00
❏ 28960	No Lookin' Back/Don't Let Me Down	1985	—	—	3.00
❏ 28960 [PS]	No Lookin' Back/Don't Let Me Down	1985	—	—	3.00
❏ 29743	Believe in It/Playin' by the Rules	1983	—	2.00	4.00
❏ 29862	I Gotta Try/Believe in It	1982	—	2.00	4.00
❏ 29862 [PS]	I Gotta Try/Believe in It	1982	—	2.00	4.00
❏ 29933	I Keep Forgettin'/Losin' End	1982	—	2.50	5.00

—First pressing has no subtitle on A-side

❏ 29933	I Keep Forgettin' (Every Time You're Near)/Losin' End	1982	—	2.00	4.00

—Second pressing has subtitle on A-side

❏ 29933 [PS]	I Keep Forgettin'/Losin' End	1982	—	2.50	5.00

—First pressing has no subtitle on A-side

❏ 29933 [PS]	I Keep Forgettin' (Every Time You're Near)/Losin' End	1982	—	2.00	4.00

—Second pressing has subtitle on A-side

Albums

MOBILE FIDELITY

❏ 1-149	If That's What It Takes	1985	5.00	10.00	20.00

—Audiophile vinyl

REPRISE

❏ 25979	Take It to Heart	1990	3.00	6.00	12.00

WARNER BROS.

❏ 23703	If That's What It Takes	1982	2.50	5.00	10.00
❏ 25291	No Lookin' Back	1985	2.50	5.00	10.00

MCFADDEN AND WHITEHEAD
45s

CAPITOL

❏ B-5176	One More Time/Best of Me	1982	—	2.00	4.00
❏ B-5206	Are You Lonely/Riding the Creat	1983	—	2.00	4.00

PHILADELPHIA INT'L.

❏ 3681	Ain't No Stoppin' Us Now/I Got the Love	1979	—	2.00	4.00
❏ 3725	I've Been Pushed Aside/(B-side unknown)	1979	—	2.00	4.00

TSOP

❏ 4788	I Heard It in a Love Song/Always Room for One More	1980	—	2.00	4.00
❏ 4792	Ain't No Stoppin' Us Now (The Philadelphia Phillies Version) (same on both sides)	1980	—	2.50	5.00
❏ 4796	That Lets Me Know I'm in Love/I Know What I'm Gonna Do	1980	—	2.00	4.00

Number	Title (A Side/B Side)	Yr	VG	VG+	NM
❏ 4799	Ain't No Stoppin' Us Now (The Phiadelphia Eagles Version)/same (The Philadelphia Phillies Version)	1980	—	2.50	5.00

Albums
PHILADELPHIA INT'L.

❏ JZ 35800	McFadden and Whitehead	1979	3.00	6.00	12.00

TSOP

❏ JZ 36773	I Heard It in a Love Song	1980	3.00	6.00	12.00

MCGHEE, BROWNIE
Also see SONNY TERRY AND BROWNIE McGHEE.

45s
DOT

❏ 1184	Cheatin' and Lyin'/Need Someone to Love	1954	62.50	125.00	250.00

HARLEM

❏ 2323	Worrying Over You/Christina	1954	15.00	30.00	60.00
❏ 2329	My Confession (I Want to Thank You)/Bluebird, Bluebird	1954	15.00	30.00	60.00

JAX

❏ 302	Smiling and Crying Blues/A Letter to Lightnin' Hopkins	1951	30.00	60.00	120.00
❏ 304	I Feel So Good/Key to the Highway	1952	30.00	60.00	120.00
❏ 307	Meet You in the Morning/Brownie's Blues	1952	30.00	60.00	120.00
❏ 310	Guitar Strangers Blues/Dissatisfied Woman	1952	30.00	60.00	120.00
❏ 312	I'm 10,000 Years Old/Cherry Red	1952	30.00	60.00	120.00
❏ 322	New Bad Blood Blues/Pawnshop Blues	1953	30.00	60.00	120.00

RED ROBIN

❏ 111	Don't Dog Your Woman/Daisy	1953	62.50	125.00	250.00

SAVOY

❏ 835	Diamond Ring/So Much Trouble	1952	7.50	15.00	30.00
❏ 872	Tell Me Baby/Bad Nerves	1952	7.50	15.00	30.00
❏ 899	Sweet Baby Blues/4 O'Clock in the Morning	1953	7.50	15.00	30.00
❏ 1177	I'd Love to Love You/Anna Mae	1955	5.00	10.00	20.00
❏ 1185	When It's Love Time/My Fault	1956	5.00	10.00	20.00
❏ 1564	Living with the Blues/Be My Friend	1959	3.75	7.50	15.00

Albums
BLUESVILLE

❏ BVLP-1042 [M]	Brownie's Blues	1962	20.00	40.00	80.00
—Blue label, silver print					
❏ BVLP-1042 [M]	Brownie's Blues	1964	6.25	12.50	25.00
—Blue label, trident logo at right					

FANTASY

❏ OBC-505	Brownie's Blues	198?	3.00	6.00	12.00

FOLKWAYS

❏ FP-30 [10]	Brownie McGhee Blues	1951	30.00	60.00	120.00
❏ FA-2030 [10]	Brownie McGhee Blues	1951	25.00	50.00	100.00
❏ 2421/2 [(2)]	Traditional Blues Vol. 1 and 2	197?	3.75	7.50	15.00
❏ 3557	Brownie McGhee Sings the Blues	197?	3.00	6.00	12.00

SAVOY JAZZ

❏ SJL-1204	Jumpin' the Blues	1989	3.00	6.00	12.00

MCGHEE, BROWNIE, AND SONNY TERRY
See SONNY TERRY AND BROWNIE McGHEE.

MCGHEE, STICK

45s
ATLANTIC

❏ 873	Drinkin' Wine Spo-Dee-O-Dee/Blues Mixture (I'd Rather Drink Muddy Water)	1971	5.00	10.00	20.00
—Yellow label, "fan" logo at lower left; first issue of this number on 45					
❏ 955	Wee Wee Hours (Part 1)/Wee Wee Hours (Part 2)	1952	25.00	50.00	100.00
—Note: Stick McGhee records on Atlantic before 955 are unconfirmed on 45 rpm					
❏ 991	New Found Love/Meet You in the Morning	1953	20.00	40.00	80.00

HERALD

❏ 553	Money Fever/Sleep-In Job	1960	3.75	7.50	15.00

KING

❏ 4610	Little Things We Used to Do/Head Happy with Wine	1953	25.00	50.00	100.00
❏ 4628	Whiskey, Women and Loaded Dice/Blues in My Heart and Tears in My Eyes	1953	25.00	50.00	100.00
❏ 4672	Jungle Juice/Dealing from the Bottom	1953	25.00	50.00	100.00
❏ 4700	I'm Doin' All This Time/Wiggle Waggin' Woo	1954	25.00	50.00	100.00
❏ 4783	Double Crossin' Liquor/Six to Eight	1955	30.00	60.00	120.00
❏ 4800	Get Your Mind Out the Gutter/Sad, Bad, Glad	1955	25.00	50.00	100.00

LONDON

❏ 978	You Gotta Have Something on the Ball//(B-side unknown)	1951	62.50	125.00	250.00

SAVOY

❏ 1148	Things Have Changed/Help Me Baby	1955	7.50	15.00	30.00

78s
ATLANTIC

❏ 873	Drinkin' Wine Spo-Dee-O-Dee/Blues Mixture (I'd Rather Drink Muddy Water)	1949	25.00	50.00	100.00
❏ 898	Drank Up All the Wine Last Night/Southern Menu	1950	15.00	30.00	60.00
❏ 909	My Baby's Comin' Back/Venus Blues	1950	15.00	30.00	60.00
❏ 912	Let's Do It/She's Gone	1950	15.00	30.00	60.00
❏ 926	Tennessee Waltz Blues/Housewarmin' Boogie	1951	15.00	30.00	60.00
❏ 937	One Monkey Don't Stop the Show/Blue Barrel House	1951	15.00	30.00	60.00
❏ 955	Wee Wee Hours (Part 1)/Wee Wee Hours (Part 2)	1952	10.00	20.00	40.00
❏ 991	New Found Love/Meet You in the Morning	1953	10.00	20.00	40.00

DECCA

❏ 48104	Drinkin' Wine Spo-Dee-O-Dee/Baby Baby Blues	1949	10.00	20.00	40.00

ESSEX

❏ 709	My Little Rose/(B-side unknown)	195?	7.50	15.00	30.00

HARLEM

❏ 1018	Drinkin' Wine Spo-Dee-O-Dee/(B-side unknown)	1947	75.00	150.00	300.00

KING

❏ 4610	Little Things We Used to Do/Head Happy with Wine	1953	7.50	15.00	30.00
❏ 4628	Whiskey, Women and Loaded Dice/Blues in My Heart and Tears in My Eyes	1953	7.50	15.00	30.00
❏ 4672	Jungle Juice/Dealing from the Bottom	1953	7.50	15.00	30.00
❏ 4700	I'm Doin' All This Time/Wiggle Waggin' Woo	1954	7.50	15.00	30.00
❏ 4783	Double Crossin' Liquor/Six to Eight	1955	10.00	20.00	40.00
❏ 4800	Get Your Mind Out the Gutter/Sad, Bad, Glad	1955	10.00	20.00	40.00

LONDON

❏ 978	You Gotta Have Something on the Ball//(B-side unknown)	1951	17.50	35.00	70.00

SAVOY

❏ 1148	Things Have Changed/Help Me Baby	1955	6.25	12.50	25.00

MCGHEE, STICK, AND JOHN LEE HOOKER
Also see each artist's individual listings.

Albums
AUDIO LAB

❏ AL-1520 [M]	Highway of Blues	1959	87.50	175.00	350.00

MCGRIFF, JIMMY

12-Inch Singles
T.K. DISCO

❏ 79	Sky Hawk/Tailgunner	1976	3.00	6.00	12.00

45s
BLUE NOTE

❏ 1968	Black Pearl/Groove Alley	1971	—	2.50	5.00

CAPITOL

❏ 2875	Sugar Sugar/Fat Cakes	1970	—	2.50	5.00
❏ 3019	The Bird/Plain Brown Bag	1971	—	2.50	5.00

GROOVE MERCHANT

❏ 1003	Groove Grease/Mr. Lucky	1972	—	2.50	5.00
❏ 1006	Theme from Shaft/Let's Stay Together	1972	—	2.50	5.00
❏ 1014	Everyday I Have the Blues/It's You I Adore	1973	—	2.50	5.00
❏ 1025	If You're Ready (Come Go with Me)/(B-side unknown)	1974	—	2.50	5.00
❏ 1029	Main Squeeze/The Sermon	1975	—	2.50	5.00
❏ 1033	Stump Juice/The Worm Turns	1976	—	2.50	5.00

JELL

❏ 503	Soul Song Of Christmas (Silent Nite)/Chip! Chip!	1965	2.00	4.00	8.00

MILESTONE

❏ 313	I'm Walkin'/(B-side unknown)	1984	—	2.00	4.00

SOLID STATE

❏ 2501	I Cover the Waterfront/Slow But Sure	1966	2.00	4.00	8.00
❏ 2502	Cherry/The Comeback	1966	2.00	4.00	8.00
❏ 2510	I Can't Give You Anything But Love, Baby/(I Can't Get No) Satisfaction	1967	2.00	4.00	8.00
❏ 2515	Tennessee Waltz/Swingin' Shepherd Blues	1967	2.00	4.00	8.00
❏ 2516	Days of Wine and Roses/You Are My Sunshine	1967	2.00	4.00	8.00
❏ 2520	I've Got a Woman/Kiko	1968	—	3.00	6.00
❏ 2522	Honey/Since You've Been Gone	1968	—	3.00	6.00
❏ 2524	The Worm/Keep Loose	1968	—	3.00	6.00
❏ 2528	Step One/South Wes	1969	—	3.00	6.00
❏ 2531	Charlotte/Trying to Come By	1969	—	3.00	6.00
❏ 2534	Back on the Street/Chris Cross	1970	—	3.00	6.00

SUE

❏ 105	Hello Betty/Close Your Eyes	1964	2.00	4.00	8.00
❏ 110	All Day Long/When You're Smiling	1964	2.00	4.00	8.00
❏ 112	Topkapi/Theme from "The Man with the Golden Arm"	1964	2.00	4.00	8.00
❏ 120	Sho 'Nuff/Bilbo	1965	2.00	4.00	8.00
❏ 123	Discotheque U.S.A./People	1965	2.00	4.00	8.00
❏ 128	Turn Blue/Bump De Bump	1965	2.00	4.00	8.00
❏ 770	I've Got a Woman (Part 1)/I've Got a Woman (Part 2)	1962	2.50	5.00	10.00
❏ 777	All About My Girl/M.G. Blues	1963	2.00	4.00	8.00
❏ 786	The Last Minute (Part 1)/The Last Minute (Part 2)	1963	2.00	4.00	8.00
❏ 791	One of Mine/Broadway	1963	2.00	4.00	8.00
❏ 802	Lonely Avenue (Part 1)/Lonely Avenue (Part 2)	1963	2.00	4.00	8.00
❏ 804	Christmas with McGriff Part 1/Part 2	1963	3.00	6.00	12.00
❏ 804	Winter with McGriff Pt. 1/Winter with McGriff Pt. 2	1963	2.50	5.00	10.00
❏ 10001	Kiko/Jumpin' at the Woodside	1964	2.00	4.00	8.00

UNITED ARTISTS

❏ 50826	Pretty Baby/I Need Love So Bad	1971	—	2.50	5.00
—With Junior Parker					

7-Inch Extended Plays
SOLID STATE

❏ SSLP 9-18002	I Cover the Waterfront/Hallelujah//See See Rider/Boston Bust Out	196?	3.00	6.00	12.00
—Jukebox issue; small hole, plays at 33 1/3 rpm					
❏ SSLP 9-18002 [PS]	A Bag Full of Soul	196?	3.00	6.00	12.00

Albums
BLUE NOTE

❏ BST-84350	Electric Funk	1970	3.75	7.50	15.00
❏ BST-84364	Something to Listen To	1971	3.75	7.50	15.00
❏ BST-84374	Black Pearl	1971	3.75	7.50	15.00

CAPITOL

❏ ST-569	Dudes Doin' Business	1970	3.75	7.50	15.00
❏ ST-616	Soul Sugar	1970	3.75	7.50	15.00

Number	Title (A Side/B Side)	Yr	VG	VG+	NM
COLLECTABLES					
❏ COL-5147	Blues for Mr. Jimmy	198?	2.50	5.00	10.00
GROOVE MERCHANT					
❏ 503	Groove Grease	1972	3.75	7.50	15.00
❏ 506	Let's Stay Together	1972	3.75	7.50	15.00
❏ 509	Fly Dude	1973	3.75	7.50	15.00
❏ 520	Come Together	1973	3.00	6.00	12.00
❏ 529	If You're Ready Come Go with Me	1974	3.00	6.00	12.00
❏ 534	Main Squeeze	1975	3.00	6.00	12.00
❏ 2203	Black and Blues	1971	3.75	7.50	15.00
❏ 2205	Good Things Don't Happen Every Day	1971	3.75	7.50	15.00
❏ 3300 [(2)]	Giants of the Organ In Concert	1974	3.75	7.50	15.00
❏ 3309	Stump Juice	1976	3.00	6.00	12.00
❏ 3311	Mean Machine	1976	3.00	6.00	12.00
❏ 4403 [(2)]	Flyin' Time	197?	3.75	7.50	15.00
JAM					
❏ 002	City Lights	1982	3.00	6.00	12.00
❏ 005	Movin' Upside the Blues	1983	3.00	6.00	12.00
LRC					
❏ 9316	Tailgunner	1977	3.75	7.50	15.00
❏ 9320	Outside Looking In	1978	3.75	7.50	15.00
MILESTONE					
❏ M-9116	Countdown	1984	2.50	5.00	10.00
❏ M-9126	Skywalk	1985	2.50	5.00	10.00
❏ M-9135	State of the Art	1986	2.50	5.00	10.00
❏ M-9148	The Starting Five	1987	2.50	5.00	10.00
❏ M-9163	Blue to the 'Bone	1988	2.50	5.00	10.00
QUINTESSENCE					
❏ 25061	Soul	1978	3.00	6.00	12.00
SOLID STATE					
❏ SM-17001 [M]	The Big Band of Jimmy McGriff	1966	3.75	7.50	15.00
❏ SM-17002 [M]	A Bag Full of Soul	1966	3.75	7.50	15.00
❏ SM-17006 [M]	Cherry	1967	5.00	10.00	20.00
❏ SS-18001 [S]	The Big Band of Jimmy McGriff	1966	5.00	10.00	20.00
❏ SS-18002 [S]	A Bag Full of Soul	1966	5.00	10.00	20.00
❏ SS-18006 [S]	Cherry	1967	5.00	10.00	20.00
❏ SS-18017	A Bag Full of Blues	1968	5.00	10.00	20.00
❏ SS-18030	I've Got a New Woman	1968	5.00	10.00	20.00
❏ SS-18036	Honey	1968	5.00	10.00	20.00
❏ SS-18045	The Worm	1968	5.00	10.00	20.00
❏ SS-18053	Step I	1969	5.00	10.00	20.00
❏ SS-18060	A Thing to Come By	1969	5.00	10.00	20.00
❏ SS-18063	The Way You Look Tonight	1970	5.00	10.00	20.00
SUE					
❏ LP-1012 [M]	I've Got a Woman	1962	7.50	15.00	30.00
❏ STLP-1012 [S]	I've Got a Woman	1962	10.00	20.00	40.00
❏ LP-1013 [M]	One of Mine	1963	7.50	15.00	30.00
❏ STLP-1013 [S]	One of Mine	1963	10.00	20.00	40.00
❏ LP-1017 [M]	Jimmy McGriff at the Apollo	1963	7.50	15.00	30.00
❏ STLP-1017 [S]	Jimmy McGriff at the Apollo	1963	10.00	20.00	40.00
❏ LP-1018 [M]	Christmas with McGriff	1963	7.50	15.00	30.00
❏ STLP-1018 [S]	Christmas with McGriff	1963	10.00	20.00	40.00
❏ LP-1020 [M]	Jimmy McGriff at the Organ	1963	7.50	15.00	30.00
❏ STLP-1020 [S]	Jimmy McGriff at the Organ	1963	10.00	20.00	40.00
❏ LP-1033 [M]	Topkapi	1964	7.50	15.00	30.00
❏ STLP-1033 [S]	Topkapi	1964	10.00	20.00	40.00
❏ LP-1039 [M]	Blues for Mister Jimmy	1965	7.50	15.00	30.00
❏ STLP-1039 [S]	Blues for Mister Jimmy	1965	10.00	20.00	40.00
❏ LP-1043 [M]	Toast to Greatest Hits	1966	5.00	10.00	20.00
❏ STLP-1043 [S]	Toast to Greatest Hits	1966	6.25	12.50	25.00
SUNSET					
❏ SUS-5264	The Great Jimmy McGriff	1969	2.50	5.00	10.00
UNITED ARTISTS					
❏ UAS-5597	Jimmy McGriff and Junior Parker	1972	3.75	7.50	15.00
VEEP					
❏ VP-13515 [M]	Live Where the Action Is	1966	5.00	10.00	20.00
❏ VP-13522 [M]	Greatest Organ Hits	1967	6.25	12.50	25.00
❏ VPS-16515 [S]	Live Where the Action Is	1966	6.25	12.50	25.00
❏ VPS-16522 [S]	Greatest Organ Hits	1967	5.00	10.00	20.00

MCKNIGHT, BRIAN
12-Inch Singles

Number	Title (A Side/B Side)	Yr	VG	VG+	NM
MERCURY					
❏ PRO 1083-1 [DJ]	One Last Cry (unknown versions)	1993	2.50	5.00	10.00
❏ 574761-1	You Should Be Mine (Don't Waste Your Time) (4 versions)	1997	2.50	5.00	10.00
❏ 852227-1	On the Down Low (Remix With Rap Featuring Paid & Live) (Remix TV Track) (Remix Featuring Power of Three) (Remix Without Rap) (Jeep Mix Featuring Paid & Live) (LP Version)	1995	2.00	4.00	8.00
❏ 864493-1	Goodbye My Love (unknown versions)	1992	2.00	4.00	8.00
MOTOWN					
❏ U8P-1646 [(2) DJ]	Back at One (Groove Brothers Club Mix) (Johnny Viscious Dub Mix)/(Johnny Viscious Club Mix)//(same versions on Record 2?)	1999	5.00	10.00	20.00
❏ 37463 3072 1 [DJ]	The Only One for Me (Victor Franco Extended Mix 5:25) (LP Version 5:13) (Bornola Extended Mix 6:57) (Bornola Acapella 4:21)	1998	2.50	5.00	10.00
❏ MOTR 20025 [DJ]	Stay or Let It Go (Album Version) (Instrumental)/(JMH Dub) (A Cappella)	2000	2.00	4.00	8.00
❏ MOTR 20237 [DJ]	6,8,12 (Jonathan Peters Sound Factory Vocal 10:19) (Jonathan Peters Sound Factory Acapella 6:00) (C&C Club Mix 8:20) (C&C Pop Radio 4:03)	2000	—	3.50	7.00
❏ MOTR 20554 [DJ]	Love of My Life (Radio) (Main) (Instrumental) (Acappella)	2001	2.00	4.00	8.00
❏ 012-156248-1	Stay or Let It Go (LP Version) (Instrumental)/ (JMH Dub) (A Cappella)	2000	—	3.50	7.00
❏ 012-156501-1	Back at One (unknown versions)	1999	2.00	4.00	8.00
❏ 012-158125-1	6,8,12 (Jonathan Peters Sound Factory Club Mix 6:55) (Jonathan Peters Sound Club Instrumental 6:55)/Back at One (Groove Brothers Club Mix 6:45) (Groove Brothers Club Instrumental 6:45)	2000	—	3.50	7.00

45s

Number	Title (A Side/B Side)	Yr	VG	VG+	NM
COLLECTABLES					
❏ 4938	One Last Cry/The Way Love Goes	1994	—	—	3.00
MOTOWN					
❏ 012-156402-7	Back at One/Anytime	1999	—	—	3.00
❏ 422-860768-7	Anytime/The Only One for Me	1998	—	—	3.00

MCLOLLIE, OSCAR
45s

Number	Title (A Side/B Side)	Yr	VG	VG+	NM
CLASS					
❏ 206	Here I Am/Say	1957	3.75	7.50	15.00
❏ 228	Hey Girl — Hey Boy/Let Me Know Let Me Know	1958	3.75	7.50	15.00
—With Jeanette Baker					
❏ 238	Let's Get Together/Rock-a-Cha	1958	3.75	7.50	15.00
—With Jeanette Baker					
❏ 243	Convicted/My Heart Speaks	1959	3.75	7.50	15.00
❏ 265	The Honey Jump/Call It Love	1960	3.75	7.50	15.00
❏ 503	Rain/Casino	1956	5.00	10.00	20.00
MERCURY					
❏ 70964	Blue Velvet/The Penalty	1956	6.25	12.50	25.00
MODERN					
❏ 902	The Honey Jump (Part 1)/The Honey Jump (Part 2)	1952	15.00	30.00	60.00
❏ 915	Be Cool My Heart/All the Oil in Texas	1952	12.50	25.00	50.00
❏ 920	Falling in Love with You/Lolly Pop	1953	12.50	25.00	50.00
❏ 938	Hot Banana/Wiggle Toe	1954	10.00	20.00	40.00
❏ 943	God Gave Us Christmas/Dig That Crazy Santa Claus	1954	10.00	20.00	40.00
❏ 950	Pretty Girl/Hey Lolly Lolly	1955	10.00	20.00	40.00
❏ 955	Pagliacci (With a Broken Heart)/Eternal Love	1955	10.00	20.00	40.00
❏ 970	Roll, Hot Rod, Roll/Convicted	1955	10.00	20.00	40.00
❏ 976	God Gave Us Christmas/(B-side unknown)	1955	7.50	15.00	30.00
WING					
❏ 90083	God's Green Earth/Got Your Love in My Heart	1956	6.25	12.50	25.00

Albums

Number	Title (A Side/B Side)	Yr	VG	VG+	NM
CROWN					
❏ CLP-5016 [M]	Oscar McLollie and His Honey Jumpers	1956	100.00	200.00	400.00
—Opinions differ as to whether this LP actually exists. Value is probably conservative.					

MCNAIR, BARBARA
45s

Number	Title (A Side/B Side)	Yr	VG	VG+	NM
AUDIO FIDELITY					
❏ 153	Love Has a Way/(B-side unknown)	1969	2.50	5.00	10.00
❏ 162	After St. Francis/I Can Tell	1969	2.50	5.00	10.00
CORAL					
❏ 61923	Till There Was You/Bobby	1958	6.25	12.50	25.00
❏ 61972	He's Got the Whole World in His Hands/Flipped Over You	1958	7.50	15.00	30.00
❏ 61996	Indiscreet/Waltz Me Around	1958	6.25	12.50	25.00
❏ 62020	Too Late This Spring/See If I Care	1958	6.25	12.50	25.00
❏ 62071	Goin' Steady with the Moon/I Feel a Feeling	1959	6.25	12.50	25.00
❏ 62116	Lover's Prayer/Old Devil Moon	1959	6.25	12.50	25.00
KC					
❏ 109	Cross Over the Bridge/Gloryland	1962	12.50	25.00	50.00
❏ 112	A Little Bird Told Me/Nobody Rings My Bell	1963	10.00	20.00	40.00
MOTOWN					
❏ 1087	Touch of Time/You're Gonna Love My Baby	1965	6.25	12.50	25.00
❏ 1099	What a Day/Everything Is Good About You	1966	6.25	12.50	25.00
❏ 1106	Here I Am Baby/My World Is Empty Without You	1966	6.25	12.50	25.00
❏ 1112	Steal Away Tonight/For Once in My Life	1967	125.00	250.00	500.00
❏ 1123	Where Would I Be Without You/For Once in My Life	1968	6.25	12.50	25.00
❏ 1133	You Could Never Love Him/Fancy Passes	1968	6.25	12.50	25.00
SIGNATURE					
❏ 12024	He's a King/Murray, What's Your Hurry	1960	5.00	10.00	20.00
❏ 12033	All About Love/You Done Me Wrong	1960	5.00	10.00	20.00
❏ 12049	Kansas City/Love Talk	1960	5.00	10.00	20.00
WARNER BROS.					
❏ 5633	Wanted Me/It Was Never Like This	1965	7.50	15.00	30.00

Albums

Number	Title (A Side/B Side)	Yr	VG	VG+	NM
AUDIO FIDELITY					
❏ AFSD-6222	More Today Than Yesterday	1969	5.00	10.00	20.00
MOTOWN					
❏ 644 [M]	Here I Am	1966	12.50	25.00	50.00
❏ S-644 [S]	Here I Am	1966	15.00	30.00	60.00
❏ S-680	The Real Barbara McNair	1969	7.50	15.00	30.00
SIGNATURE					
❏ SM 1042 [M]	Love Talk	1960	10.00	20.00	40.00
❏ SS 1042 [S]	Love Talk	1960	12.50	25.00	50.00
WARNER BROS.					
❏ W 1541 [M]	I Enjoy Being a Girl	1964	6.25	12.50	25.00
❏ WS 1541 [S]	I Enjoy Being a Girl	1964	7.50	15.00	30.00
❏ W 1570 [M]	The Livin' End	1964	6.25	12.50	25.00
❏ WS 1570 [S]	The Livin' End	1964	7.50	15.00	30.00

Fifties R&B

1. Wynonie Harris had the biggest hit version of "Good Rockin' Tonight," in 1948. That is one of the four songs that King compiled onto this extremely rare EP in the 1950s.

2. One of the rarest of all Sun 45s is "Wolf Call Boogie" by Hot Shot Love.

3. Pretty early in their hit-making career, the Dominos became Billy Ward and the Dominoes. This early 10-inch LP was the first long-playing collection of their hits.

4. The first LP of Ray Charles material to appear was this Atlantic collection, *Rock and Roll,* in 1957.

5. Howlin' Wolf's first album, *Moanin' in the Moonlight*, came out in 1958. Before that, all his material had been on various 45s and 78s.

6. *I'm John Lee Hooker,* a compilation of material he recorded for Vee Jay, was his first full-length LP, in 1959.

The Golden Motown Era

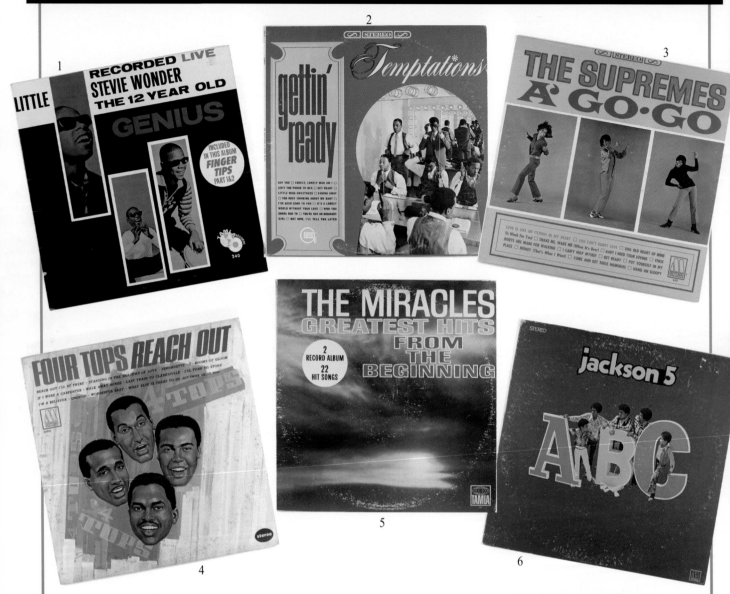

1. At the time (1963), Little Stevie Wonder seemed to be more a novelty act than anything else. But he did have Motown's first chart-topping album – and many more in years to come.

2. *Gettin' Ready,* which includes "Get Ready" and "Ain't Too Proud to Beg," was the third of 10 consecutive Temptations albums to hit #1 on the R&B charts.

3. *The Supremes A' Go-Go*, which includes "You Can't Hurry Love," became their first pop #1 album in 1966.

4. The Four Tops' 1967 album *Reach Out* includes six hit singles – a rarity for 1960s albums that weren't "greatest hits" releases.

5. Released in early 1965, *The Miracles Greatest Hits from the Beginning* is a two-record set with 22 singles – and it actually predates their big 1965 hits, "The Tracks of My Tears" and "Ooo Baby Baby."

6. The Jackson Five began recording for Motown in late 1969 and were an instant success for the label. Their second album, *ABC,* spent three months at #1 on the R&B charts.

Sixties Soul

1. James Brown's *Live at the Apollo,* issued in 1963, is one of the great live albums of any era in any genre of music.

2. *The Impressions Keep On Pushing,* released in 1964, made the top 10 of both the pop and R&B album charts.

3. *Lady Soul*, Aretha Franklin's third album for Atlantic, couldn't have been more accurately named. It contains four of her 1967-68 hits including "Chain of Fools," "Since You've Been Gone" and "A Natural Woman."

4. Few albums in R&B history have been so aptly named as the late-1966 *Complete & Unbelievable … The Otis Redding Dictionary of Soul.* Among others, it contains "Fa-Fa-Fa-Fa-Fa (Sad Song)" and his version of "Try a Little Tenderness."

5. Sly & the Family Stone had their first hit in 1968 with "Dance to the Music." This is the album that resulted; it didn't really sell that well at first, but it picked up a year later.

6. Solomon Burke's only album for the Bell label, *Proud Mary* in 1969, moved John Fogerty so much that he ended up writing the back cover liner notes.

Sounds of the Seventies

1. War began as a backing band for Eric Burdon, but once the band went "solo," it made its more essential music. *The World Is a Ghetto*, issued in late 1972, hit #1 on the pop LP charts.

2. Al Green, along with producer Willie Mitchell, came up with a distinctive soul sound that was a constant presence on the charts from 1971-75. *I'm Still in Love with You* was the third album in that run, issued late in 1972.

3. After years in the business, Barry White finally found his musical niche by singing sultry, seductive odes to love in a deep voice. His 1974 album *Can't Get Enough* was one of six to top the R&B LP charts, and the only one to do the same on the pop charts.

4. The O'Jays had been recording, with relatively limited success, throughout the 1960s. Only when they joined the Philadelphia International label did they break through. The 1975 LP *Family Reunion* contains the hits "I Love Music" and "Livin' for the Weekend."

5. The Isley Brothers had been around since the late 1950s, but their peak of popularity was in the 1970s. *Harvest for the World,* issued in 1976, was the third of five straight #1 R&B LPs of new material for the group.

6. The Brothers Johnson, formerly members of Billy Preston's band, had much success on their own. One of their three #1 R&B hits was "Strawberry Letter 23" from 1977.

Motown: The 70s and Beyond

1. The first Marvin Gaye album over which he had complete artistic control, 1971's *What's Going On*, remains a landmark LP that continues to speak to new generations of R&B fans.

2. Stevie Wonder recorded a series of albums in the 1970s that were both artistic and commercial successes. *Talking Book*, issued in 1972, featured "Superstition" and "You Are the Sunshine of My Life."

3. After leaving the Supremes, Diana Ross had a couple quick hit singles, then went off to film *Lady Sings the Blues* before doing *Touch Me in the Morning* in 1973.

4. The Commodores were one of Motown's biggest acts of the 1970s and early 1980s. *In the Pocket*, from 1981, was their last album before Lionel Richie went solo.

5. In the mid-1980s, family act DeBarge spent a lot of time near the top of the charts. One of their biggest hits was "Rhythm of the Night" in 1985; this is its picture sleeve.

6. Boyz II Men won praise both for their groove and for their vocal talents. Their first hit single was 1991's "Motownphilly."

Funk and Disco

1. The multi-racial K.C. and the Sunshine Band, led by Harry Wayne Casey, raced up both the R&B and pop charts with its horn-based disco. Here's the picture sleeve from 1977's "Keep It Comin' Love."

2. L.T.D.'s biggest hit on both the R&B and pop charts was "(Every Time I Turn Around) Back in Love Again," in late 1977 and early 1978. This is its picture sleeve.

3. "Flash Light" by Parliament, from 1978, was the funk band's first #1 R&B single, and one of their two biggest pop hits.

4. *I Am,* the first Earth, Wind and Fire album after their 1978 greatest-hits collection, contained five R&B hits by itself, including "After the Love Is Gone," which was renamed "After the Love Has Gone" for single release.

5. For the most part, Donna Summer was somewhat more successful on the pop charts than on the R&B charts. One album that was an across-the-board smash was 1979's *Bad Girls.*

6. Kool and the Gang had most of their 1970s success with funk, but became even more popular in the 1980s by toning down and polishing their sound. Four big hits came from 1984's *Emergency.*

The 1980s

1. Grandmaster Flash and the Furious Five issued one of the most influential rap records of all time, "The Message," in 1982. It also appears on this LP of the same name.

2. In 1982, the Gap Band, which had been recording since the mid-1970s, had their most successful album, *Gap Band IV.* It contained two #1 R&B hits and one #2 R&B hit.

3. It wasn't his biggest R&B hit, but Prince's album *1999,* issued in 1982, broke him into the mainstream in 1983.

4. Other than perhaps "Rapper's Delight," no rap record had a greater effect on its long-term popularity than Run-D.M.C.'s 1986 crossover hit, "Walk This Way."

5. Janet Jackson escaped the shadow of her older brothers in 1986 with her huge hit album *Control.*

6. Keith Sweat had one of the biggest hits of the so-called "new jack swing" style with his "I Want Her."

1. TLC's 1995 single "Waterfalls," the trio's biggest pop hit, not only was issued on 45, but also came with this picture sleeve.

2. 2Pac's last album before he was gunned down, *All Eyez on Me*, was issued in 1996 on vinyl as a four-record set.

3. Macy Gray didn't have her first hit single – "I Try" – until more than half a year after its album, *On How Life Is,* first made the charts in 1999.

4. Destiny's Child, led by the multitalented Beyoncé Knowles, has gone through several permutations in its short history, but remains popular.

5. Alicia Keys' chart-topping single from 2001, "Fallin'," was issued on this 45 rpm single.

6. Mary J. Blige, who has been a hitmaker since 1992, had her 2001 album *No More Drama* released two different times with two different covers. This is the first edition.

Number	Title (A Side/B Side)	Yr	VG	VG+	NM

MCNEELY, BIG JAY
45s
ALADDIN
❏ 3242	Real Crazy Cool/Let's Split	1954	7.50	15.00	30.00

BAYOU
| ❏ 014 | Hometown Jamboree/Teenage Hop | 1953 | 20.00 | 40.00 | 80.00 |
| ❏ 018 | Catastrophe/Calamity | 1953 | 20.00 | 40.00 | 80.00 |

FEDERAL
❏ 12102	The Goof/Big Jay Shuffle	1952	10.00	20.00	40.00
❏ 12111	Just Crazy/Penthouse Serenade	1952	10.00	20.00	40.00
❏ 12141	Nervous Man, Nervous/Rock Candy	1953	10.00	20.00	40.00
❏ 12151	3-D/Texas Turkey	1953	10.00	20.00	40.00
❏ 12168	Mule Walk/Ice Water	1954	10.00	20.00	40.00
❏ 12179	Hot Cinders/Whipped Cream	1954	10.00	20.00	40.00
❏ 12186	Let's Work/Hard Tack	1954	10.00	20.00	40.00
❏ 12191	Beachcomber/Strip Tease Swing	1954	10.00	20.00	40.00

IMPERIAL
| ❏ 5219 | Deacon's Express/Jet Fury | 1953 | 12.50 | 25.00 | 50.00 |

—Note: Earlier Big Jay McNeely releases on Imperial are unknown on 45 rpm

SAVOY
| ❏ 798 | The Deacon's Hop/Thirty Five Thirty | 1951 | 15.00 | 30.00 | 60.00 |
| ❏ 1143 | Deacon Hop/The Hucklebuck | 1955 | 7.50 | 15.00 | 30.00 |

—With Paul Williams

SWINGIN'
❏ 614	There Is Something on Your Mind/Back...Shack...Track	1959	6.25	12.50	25.00
❏ 618	I Got the Message/Psycho Serenade	1959	3.75	7.50	15.00
❏ 622	Minnie/My Darling Dear	1960	3.75	7.50	15.00
❏ 627	I Love You, Oh Darling/Oh, What a Fool	1960	3.75	7.50	15.00
❏ 629	After Midnight/Before Midnight	1961	3.75	7.50	15.00
❏ 637	Without a Love/The Squat	1962	3.75	7.50	15.00

VEE JAY
| ❏ 142 | Big Jay's Hop/Three Blind Mice | 1955 | 10.00 | 20.00 | 40.00 |
| ❏ 212 | Jay's Rock/The Convention | 1956 | 15.00 | 30.00 | 60.00 |

—B-side by the Delegates

WARNER BROS.
| ❏ 5401 | You Don't Have to Go/Big Jay's Count | 1963 | 3.00 | 6.00 | 12.00 |

78s
ALADDIN
| ❏ 3050 | Jay's Frantic/Deacon's Blowout | 1950 | 7.50 | 15.00 | 30.00 |
| ❏ 3242 | Real Crazy Cool/Let's Split | 1954 | 5.00 | 10.00 | 20.00 |

BAYOU
| ❏ 014 | Hometown Jamboree/Teenage Hop | 1953 | 10.00 | 20.00 | 40.00 |
| ❏ 018 | Catastrophe/Calamity | 1953 | 10.00 | 20.00 | 40.00 |

EXCLUSIVE
| ❏ 122x | K & H Boogie/Junie Flip | 194? | 7.50 | 15.00 | 30.00 |

FEDERAL
❏ 12102	The Goof/Big Jay Shuffle	1952	5.00	10.00	20.00
❏ 12111	Just Crazy/Penthouse Serenade	1952	5.00	10.00	20.00
❏ 12141	Nervous Man, Nervous/Rock Candy	1953	5.00	10.00	20.00
❏ 12151	3-D/Texas Turkey	1953	5.00	10.00	20.00
❏ 12168	Mule Walk/Ice Water	1954	5.00	10.00	20.00
❏ 12179	Hot Cinders/Whipped Cream	1954	5.00	10.00	20.00
❏ 12186	Let's Work/Hard Tack	1954	5.00	10.00	20.00
❏ 12191	Beachcomber/Strip Tease Swing	1954	5.00	10.00	20.00

IMPERIAL
❏ 5115	All That Wine Is Gone/Don't Cry Baby	1951	6.25	12.50	25.00
❏ 5130	Sad Story/Insect Ball	1951	6.25	12.50	25.00
❏ 5164	Let's Do It/I'll Never Love Again	1952	6.25	12.50	25.00
❏ 5169	The Deacon Blows for Ray/Tall Brown Woman	1952	6.25	12.50	25.00
❏ 5170	The Deacon Rides Again/Blow, Blow, Blow	1952	6.25	12.50	25.00
❏ 5176	Jay Walk/Night Ride	1952	6.25	12.50	25.00
❏ 5186	True Love/That Old Mule	1952	6.25	12.50	25.00
❏ 5219	Deacon's Express/Jet Fury	1953	5.00	10.00	20.00

SAVOY
❏ 682	Wild Wig/Benson's Groove	1948	7.50	15.00	30.00
❏ 685	The Deacon's Hop/Artie's Jump	1949	10.00	20.00	40.00
❏ 1143	Deacon Hop/The Hucklebuck	1955	6.25	12.50	25.00

—With Paul Williams

VEE JAY
| ❏ 142 | Big Jay's Hop/Three Blind Mice | 1955 | 7.50 | 15.00 | 30.00 |
| ❏ 212 | Jay's Rock/The Convention | 1956 | 10.00 | 20.00 | 40.00 |

—B-side by the Delegates

7-Inch Extended Plays
FEDERAL
❏ EP-246	Big Jake Shuffle/3-D//Nervous Man Nervous/The Goof	1953	75.00	150.00	300.00
❏ EP-246 [PS]	Go! Go! Go! With Big Jay McNeely	1953	75.00	150.00	300.00
❏ EP-301	*Mule Milk/Hot Cinders/Ice Water/Whipped Cream	1954	50.00	100.00	200.00
❏ EP-301 [PS]	Big Jay McNeely, Volume 2	1954	50.00	100.00	200.00
❏ EP-332	(contents unknown)	1954	50.00	100.00	200.00
❏ EP-332 [PS]	Wild Man of the Saxophone	1954	50.00	100.00	200.00
❏ EP-373	(contents unknown)	1955	25.00	50.00	100.00
❏ EP-373 [PS]	Just Crazy	1955	25.00	50.00	100.00

Albums
COLLECTABLES
| ❏ COL-5133 | Golden Classics | 198? | 2.50 | 5.00 | 10.00 |

FEDERAL
| ❏ 295-96 [10] | Big Jay McNeely | 1954 | 750.00 | 1500. | 3000. |
| ❏ 395-530 [M] | Big Jay McNeely in 3-D | 1956 | 200.00 | 400.00 | 800.00 |

KING
| ❏ 650 [M] | Big Jay McNeely in 3-D | 1959 | 125.00 | 250.00 | 500.00 |

SAVOY
❏ MG-15045 [10]	A Rhythm and Blues Concert	1955	1000.	1500.	2000.

WARNER BROS.
| ❏ W 1533 [M] | Big Jay McNeely | 1963 | 20.00 | 40.00 | 80.00 |
| ❏ WS 1533 [S] | Big Jay McNeely | 1963 | 25.00 | 50.00 | 100.00 |

MCPHATTER, CLYDE
Also see THE DRIFTERS.
45s
AMY
❏ 941	Everybody's Somebody's Fool/I Belong to You	1965	3.75	7.50	15.00
❏ 950	Little Bit of Sunshine/Everybody Loves a Good Time	1966	3.00	6.00	12.00
❏ 968	A Shot of Rhythm and Blues/I'm Not Going to Work Today	1966	3.00	6.00	12.00
❏ 975	Sweet and Innocent/Lavender Lace	1967	3.00	6.00	12.00
❏ 993	I Dreamt I Died/Lonely People Can't Afford to Cry	1967	3.00	6.00	12.00

ATLANTIC
| ❏ 1070 | Everybody's Laughing/Hot Ziggity | 1955 | 7.50 | 15.00 | 30.00 |
| ❏ 1077 | Love Has Joined Us Together/I Gotta Have You | 1955 | 7.50 | 15.00 | 30.00 |

—With Ruth Brown
❏ 1081	Seven Days/I'm Not Worthy	1956	7.50	15.00	30.00
❏ 1092	Treasure of Love/When You're Sincere	1956	10.00	20.00	40.00
❏ 1106	Thirty Days/I'm Lonely Tonight	1956	7.50	15.00	30.00
❏ 1117	Without Love (There Is Nothing)/I Make Believe	1956	7.50	15.00	30.00
❏ 1133	No Matter What/Just to Hold My Hand	1957	6.25	12.50	25.00
❏ 1149	Long Lonely Nights/Heartaches	1957	6.25	12.50	25.00
❏ 1158	You'll Be There/Rock and Cry	1957	6.25	12.50	25.00
❏ 1170	That's Enough for Me/No Love Like Her Love	1958	6.25	12.50	25.00
❏ 1185	Come What May/Let Me Know	1958	6.25	12.50	25.00
❏ 1199	A Lover's Question/I Can't Stand Up Long	1958	6.25	12.50	25.00
❏ 2018	Lovey Dovey/My Island of Dreams	1959	5.00	10.00	20.00
❏ 2028	Since You've Been Gone/Try, Try Baby	1959	5.00	10.00	20.00

—B-side actually the "old" Drifters (uncredited)
| ❏ 2038 | You Went Back on Your Word/There You Go | 1959 | 5.00 | 10.00 | 20.00 |

—B-side actually the "old" Drifters (uncredited)
| ❏ 2049 | Just Give Me a Ring/Don't Dog Me | 1960 | 5.00 | 10.00 | 20.00 |

—B-side actually the "old" Drifters (uncredited)
| ❏ 2060 | Deep Sea Ball/Let the Boogie-Woogie Roll | 1960 | 5.00 | 10.00 | 20.00 |

—B-side actually the "old" Drifters (uncredited)
| ❏ 2082 | If I Didn't Love You Like I Do/Go! Yes Go! | 1960 | 5.00 | 10.00 | 20.00 |

—B-side actually the "old" Drifters (uncredited)

DECCA
| ❏ 32719 | Book of Memories/I'll Belong to You | 1970 | 2.00 | 4.00 | 8.00 |
| ❏ 32753 | Why Can't We Get Together/Mixed-Up Cup | 1970 | 2.00 | 4.00 | 8.00 |

DERAM
| ❏ 85032 | Thank You Love/Only a Fool | 1968 | 2.50 | 5.00 | 10.00 |
| ❏ 85039 | Baby You've Got It/Baby I Could Be So Good at Loving You | 1969 | 2.50 | 5.00 | 10.00 |

MERCURY
❏ 71660	Ta Ta/I Ain't Givin' Up Nothin'	1960	3.75	7.50	15.00
❏ 71692	I Just Want to Love You/You're for Me	1960	3.75	7.50	15.00
❏ 71692 [PS]	I Just Want to Love You/You're for Me	1960	7.50	15.00	30.00
❏ 71740	One More Chance/Before I Fall in Love Again	1960	3.75	7.50	15.00
❏ 71740 [PS]	One More Chance/Before I Fall in Love Again	1960	7.50	15.00	30.00
❏ 71783	Tomorrow Is a-Comin'/I'll Love You Till the Cows Come Home	1961	3.75	7.50	15.00
❏ 71783 [PS]	Tomorrow Is a-Comin'/I'll Love You Till the Cows Come Home	1961	7.50	15.00	30.00
❏ 71809	A Whole Heap o'Love/You're Movin' Me	1961	3.75	7.50	15.00
❏ 71809 [PS]	A Whole Heap o'Love/You're Movin' Me	1961	7.50	15.00	30.00
❏ 71841	I Never Knew/Happiness	1961	3.75	7.50	15.00
❏ 71841 [PS]	I Never Knew/Happiness	1961	6.25	12.50	25.00
❏ 71868	Same Time, Same Place/Your Second Choice	1961	3.75	7.50	15.00
❏ 71868 [PS]	Same Time, Same Place/Your Second Choice	1961	7.50	15.00	30.00
❏ 71941	Lover Please/Let's Forget About the Past	1962	5.00	10.00	20.00
❏ 71941 [PS]	Lover Please/Let's Forget About the Past	1962	10.00	20.00	40.00
❏ 71987	Little Bitty Pretty One/Next to Me	1962	3.75	7.50	15.00
❏ 71987 [PS]	Little Bitty Pretty One/Next to Me	1962	10.00	20.00	40.00
❏ 72025	Maybe/I Do Believe	1962	3.75	7.50	15.00
❏ 72025 [PS]	Maybe/I Do Believe	1962	7.50	15.00	30.00
❏ 72051	The Best Man Cried/Stop	1962	3.75	7.50	15.00
❏ 72051 [PS]	The Best Man Cried/Stop	1962	7.50	15.00	30.00
❏ 72166	So Close to Being in Love/From One to One	1963	3.75	7.50	15.00
❏ 72166 [PS]	So Close to Being in Love/From One to One	1963	7.50	15.00	30.00
❏ 72220	Deep in the Heart of Harlem/Happy Good Times	1963	3.75	7.50	15.00
❏ 72220 [PS]	Deep in the Heart of Harlem/Happy Good Times	1963	7.50	15.00	30.00
❏ 72253	Second Window, Second Floor/In My Tenement	1964	3.75	7.50	15.00
❏ 72317	Lucille/Baby, Baby	1964	3.75	7.50	15.00
❏ 72407	Crying Won't Help You Now/I Found My Love	1965	3.75	7.50	15.00
❏ 72407 [PS]	Crying Won't Help You Now/I Found My Love	1965	7.50	15.00	30.00

MGM
❏ 12780	I Told Myself a Lie/The Masquerade Is Over	1959	5.00	10.00	20.00
❏ 12816	Twice As Nice/Where Did I Make My Mistake	1959	5.00	10.00	20.00
❏ 12843 [M]	Let's Try Again/Bless You	1959	5.00	10.00	20.00
❏ 12877	Think Me a Kiss/When the Right Time Comes Along	1960	5.00	10.00	20.00
❏ 12949	One Right After Another/This Is Not Goodbye	1960	5.00	10.00	20.00
❏ 12988	The Glory of Love/Take a Step	1961	5.00	10.00	20.00
❏ SK-50134 [S]	Let's Try Again/Bless You	1959	10.00	20.00	40.00

78s
ATLANTIC
| ❏ 1070 | Everybody's Laughing/Hot Ziggity | 1955 | 7.50 | 15.00 | 30.00 |

M

Number	Title (A Side/B Side)	Yr	VG	VG+	NM
❏ 1077	Love Has Joined Us Together/I Gotta Have You	1955	7.50	15.00	30.00
—With Ruth Brown					
❏ 1081	Seven Days/I'm Not Worthy	1956	10.00	20.00	40.00
❏ 1092	Treasure of Love/When You're Sincere	1956	12.50	25.00	50.00
❏ 1106	Thirty Days/I'm Lonely Tonight	1956	10.00	20.00	40.00
❏ 1117	Without Love (There Is Nothing)/I Make Believe	1956	10.00	20.00	40.00
❏ 1133	No Matter What/Just to Hold My Hand	1957	10.00	20.00	40.00
❏ 1149	Long Lonely Nights/Heartaches	1957	10.00	20.00	40.00
❏ 1158	You'll Be There/Rock and Cry	1957	10.00	20.00	40.00
❏ 1170	That's Enough for Me/No Love Like Her Love	1958	12.50	25.00	50.00
❏ 1185	Come What May/Let Me Know	1958	12.50	25.00	50.00
❏ 1199	A Lover's Question/I Can't Stand Up Long	1958	25.00	50.00	100.00

7-Inch Extended Plays
ATLANTIC

Number	Title (A Side/B Side)	Yr	VG	VG+	NM
❏ EP 584	*Without Love (There Is Nothing)/Thirty Days/I Make Believe/Treasure of Love	1958	62.50	125.00	250.00
❏ EP 584 [PS]	Clyde McPhatter	1958	62.50	125.00	250.00
❏ EP 605	*Honey Love/What'cha Gonna Do/Seven Days/Long Lonely Nights	1958	62.50	125.00	250.00
❏ EP 605 [PS]	Rock with Clyde McPhatter	1958	62.50	125.00	250.00
❏ EP 618	A Lover's Question/I Can't Stand Up Alone//Lovey Dovey/My Island of Dreams	1959	62.50	125.00	250.00
❏ EP 618 [PS]	Clyde McPhatter	1959	62.50	125.00	250.00

Albums
ALLEGIANCE

Number	Title (A Side/B Side)	Yr	VG	VG+	NM
❏ AV-5029	The Pretty One	198?	2.50	5.00	10.00

ATLANTIC

Number	Title (A Side/B Side)	Yr	VG	VG+	NM
❏ 8024 [M]	Love Ballads	1958	125.00	250.00	500.00
—Black label					
❏ 8024 [M]	Love Ballads	1960	50.00	100.00	200.00
—Brown and purple label					
❏ 8024 [M]	Love Ballads	1960	100.00	200.00	400.00
—White "bullseye" label					
❏ 8031 [M]	Clyde	1959	125.00	250.00	500.00
—Black label					
❏ 8031 [M]	Clyde	1960	100.00	200.00	400.00
—White "bullseye" label					
❏ 8031 [M]	Clyde	1960	50.00	100.00	200.00
—Brown and purple label					
❏ 8077 [M]	The Best of Clyde McPhatter	1963	50.00	100.00	200.00

DECCA

Number	Title (A Side/B Side)	Yr	VG	VG+	NM
❏ DL 75231	Welcome Home	1970	6.25	12.50	25.00

MERCURY

Number	Title (A Side/B Side)	Yr	VG	VG+	NM
❏ MG-20597 [M]	Ta Ta	1960	12.50	25.00	50.00
❏ MG-20655 [M]	Golden Blues Hits	1961	12.50	25.00	50.00
❏ MG-20711 [M]	Lover Please	1962	12.50	25.00	50.00
❏ MG-20750 [M]	Rhythm and Soul	1962	12.50	25.00	50.00
❏ MG-20783 [M]	Clyde McPhatter's Greatest Hits	1963	7.50	15.00	30.00
❏ MG-20902 [M]	Songs of the Big City	1964	7.50	15.00	30.00
❏ MG-20915 [M]	Live at the Apollo	1964	7.50	15.00	30.00
❏ SR-60262 [S]	Ta Ta	1960	17.50	35.00	70.00
❏ SR-60655 [S]	Golden Blues Hits	1961	17.50	35.00	70.00
❏ SR-60711 [S]	Lover Please	1962	17.50	35.00	70.00
❏ SR-60750 [S]	Rhythm and Soul	1962	17.50	35.00	70.00
❏ SR-60783 [S]	Clyde McPhatter's Greatest Hits	1963	10.00	20.00	40.00
❏ SR-60902 [S]	Songs of the Big City	1964	10.00	20.00	40.00
❏ SR-60915 [S]	Live at the Apollo	1964	10.00	20.00	40.00

MGM

Number	Title (A Side/B Side)	Yr	VG	VG+	NM
❏ E-3775 [M]	Let's Start Over Again	1959	37.50	75.00	150.00
❏ SE-3775 [S]	Let's Start Over Again	1959	50.00	100.00	200.00
❏ E-3866 [M]	Clyde McPhatter's Greatest Hits	1960	17.50	35.00	70.00
❏ SE-3866 [S]	Clyde McPhatter's Greatest Hits	1960	20.00	40.00	80.00

WING

Number	Title (A Side/B Side)	Yr	VG	VG+	NM
❏ MGW-12224 [M]	May I Sing for You?	1962	6.25	12.50	25.00
❏ SRW-16224 [S]	May I Sing for You?	1962	7.50	15.00	30.00

MCTELL, BLIND WILLIE
Albums
BLUESVILLE

Number	Title (A Side/B Side)	Yr	VG	VG+	NM
❏ BVLP-1040 [M]	Last Session	1962	30.00	60.00	120.00
—Blue label, silver print					
❏ BVLP-1040 [M]	Last Session	1964	7.50	15.00	30.00
—Blue label, trident logo at right					

MELODEON

Number	Title (A Side/B Side)	Yr	VG	VG+	NM
❏ 7323 [M]	1940	1956	37.50	75.00	150.00

MEADOWLARKS, THE
See DON JULIAN AND THE MEADOWLARKS.

MEDALLIONS, THE (1)
45s
DOOTO

Number	Title (A Side/B Side)	Yr	VG	VG+	NM
❏ 419	For Better or For Worse/I Wonder, Wonder, Wonder	1957	7.50	15.00	30.00
—As "Vernon Green and the Medallions"					
❏ 425	A Lover's Prayer/Unseen	1957	7.50	15.00	30.00
—As "Vernon Green and the Medallions"					
❏ 446	Magic Mountain/59 Volvo	1959	6.25	12.50	25.00
—As "Vernon Green and the Medallions"					
❏ 454	Behind the Door/Rocket Ship	1959	6.25	12.50	25.00
—As "Vernon Green and the Medallions"					

DOOTONE

Number	Title (A Side/B Side)	Yr	VG	VG+	NM
❏ 347	The Letter/Buick 59	1955	50.00	100.00	200.00
—Red label					
❏ 347	The Letter/Buick 59	1955	15.00	30.00	60.00
—Black label					
❏ 357	The Telegram/Coupe de Ville Baby	1955	15.00	30.00	60.00
—Maroon label					
❏ 357	The Telegram/Coupe de Ville Baby	1955	37.50	75.00	150.00
—Blue label					
❏ 364	Edna/Speeding	1955	15.00	30.00	60.00
❏ 373	My Pretty Baby/I'll Never Love Again	1955	15.00	30.00	60.00
—As "Johnny Twovoice and the Medallions"					
❏ 379	Dear Darling/Don't Shoot Baby	1955	17.50	35.00	70.00
❏ 393	I Want a Love/Dance and Swing	1956	12.50	25.00	50.00
❏ 400	Shedding Tears for You/Push Button Automobile	1956	15.00	30.00	60.00
—As "Vernon Green and the Medallions"					
❏ 407	My Mary Lou/Did You Have Fun	1956	15.00	30.00	60.00
—As "Vernon Green and the Medallions"					
❏ 479	Can You Talk/You Don't Know	1964	3.75	7.50	15.00

MINIT

Number	Title (A Side/B Side)	Yr	VG	VG+	NM
❏ 32034	Look at Me, Look at Me/Am I Ever Gonna See My Baby	1968	5.00	10.00	20.00
—As "Vernon Green and the Medallions"					

PAN WORLD

Number	Title (A Side/B Side)	Yr	VG	VG+	NM
❏ 71	Dear Ann/Shimmy Shimmy Shake	1962	12.50	25.00	50.00
—As "Vernon Green and the Medallions"					

7-Inch Extended Plays
DOOTONE

Number	Title (A Side/B Side)	Yr	VG	VG+	NM
❏ 202	(contents unknown)	1958	25.00	50.00	100.00
❏ 202 [PS]	Rhythm and Blues	1958	37.50	75.00	150.00

MEDLEY, BILL
Also see THE RIGHTEOUS BROTHERS.
45s
A&M

Number	Title (A Side/B Side)	Yr	VG	VG+	NM
❏ 1285	A Song for You/We've Only Just Begun	1971	—	2.50	5.00
❏ 1309	You've Lost That Lovin' Feeling/We've Only Just Begun	1971	—	2.50	5.00
❏ 1311	A Song for You/We've Only Just Begun	1971	—	2.00	4.00
❏ 1336	Help Me Make It Through the Night/Hung on You	1972	—	2.00	4.00
❏ 1350	Freedom for the Stallion/Damn Good Friend	1972	—	2.00	4.00
❏ 1371	A Simple Man/Missing You Too Long	1972	—	2.00	4.00
❏ 1434	Put a Little Love Away/It's Not Easy	1973	—	2.00	4.00

CURB

Number	Title (A Side/B Side)	Yr	VG	VG+	NM
❏ 10542	Most of All You/I'm Gonna Be Strong	1989	—	—	3.00
❏ 76890	Don't Let Go/Bridge Over Troubled Water	1990	—	—	3.00

ELEKTRA

Number	Title (A Side/B Side)	Yr	VG	VG+	NM
❏ 69281	Rude Awakening/Leave Love Behind	1989	—	—	3.00
—B-side by Jonathan Elias					

LIBERTY

Number	Title (A Side/B Side)	Yr	VG	VG+	NM
❏ 1402	Don't Know Much/Woman	1981	—	2.00	4.00
❏ 1412	Stay the Night/Grandma and Grandpa	1981	—	2.00	4.00

MCA

Number	Title (A Side/B Side)	Yr	VG	VG+	NM
❏ 53443	Brown Eyed Woman/You've Lost That Lovin' Feelin'	1988	—	—	3.00

MGM

Number	Title (A Side/B Side)	Yr	VG	VG+	NM
❏ 13931	I Can't Make It Alone/One Day Girl	1968	2.00	4.00	8.00
❏ 13959	Brown Eyed Woman/Let the Good Times Roll	1968	2.00	4.00	8.00
❏ 14000	Peace Brother Peace/Winter Won't Come This Year	1968	2.00	4.00	8.00
❏ 14025	Something's So Wrong/This Is a Love Song	1969	2.00	4.00	8.00
❏ 14081	Reaching Back/Someone Is Standing Outside	1969	2.00	4.00	8.00
❏ 14099	Evie/Let Me Love Again	1969	2.00	4.00	8.00
❏ 14119	Hold On, I'm Comin'/Makin' My Way	1970	—	3.00	6.00
❏ 14145	Nobody Knows/Something's So Wrong	1970	—	3.00	6.00
❏ 14179	Gone/What Have You Got to Lose	1970	—	3.00	6.00
❏ 14202	Wasn't It Easy/Gone	1970	—	3.00	6.00

PARAMOUNT

Number	Title (A Side/B Side)	Yr	VG	VG+	NM
❏ 0089	Swing Low, Sweet Chariot/(B-side unknown)	1971	—	3.00	6.00

PLANET

Number	Title (A Side/B Side)	Yr	VG	VG+	NM
❏ YB-13317	Right Here and Now/The Best of My Life	1982	—	2.00	4.00
❏ YB-13425	I'm No Angel/I Need You in My Life	1983	—	—	3.00
❏ YB-13474	For You/I Need You in My Life	1983	—	—	3.00

RCA

Number	Title (A Side/B Side)	Yr	VG	VG+	NM
❏ 5224-7-RX	(I've Had) The Time of My Life/Love Is Strange	1987	—	—	3.00
—A-side: With Jennifer Warnes; B-side by Mickey and Sylvia					
❏ 5224-7-RX [PS]	(I've Had) The Time of My Life/Love Is Strange	1987	—	2.00	4.00
—A-side: With Jennifer Warnes; B-side by Mickey and Sylvia					
❏ PB-13692	I've Got Dreams to Remember/Till Your Memory's Gone	1983	—	—	3.00
❏ PB-13753	I Still Do/I've Got Dreams to Remember	1984	—	—	3.00
❏ PB-13851	Turn It Loose/I've Always Got the Heart to Sing the Blues	1984	—	—	3.00
❏ PB-13962	She Keeps Me in One Piece/Old Friend	1984	—	—	—
—Unreleased					
❏ PB-14021	Is There Anything I Can Do/Old Friend	1985	—	—	3.00
❏ PB-14081	Women in Love/Stand Up	1985	—	—	3.00

REPRISE

Number	Title (A Side/B Side)	Yr	VG	VG+	NM
❏ 0413	I Surrender to Your Touch/Leavin' Town	1965	3.75	7.50	15.00

SCOTTI BROTHERS

Number	Title (A Side/B Side)	Yr	VG	VG+	NM
❏ ZS4-07938	He Ain't Heavy, He's My Brother/The Bridge	1988	—	—	3.00
—B-side by Georgio Moroder					

UNITED ARTISTS

Number	Title (A Side/B Side)	Yr	VG	VG+	NM
❏ XW1256	Lay a Little Lovin' On Me/Wasn't That You Last Night	1978	—	2.00	4.00
❏ XW1270	Statue of a Fool/Wasn't That You Last Night	1978	—	2.00	4.00
❏ 1349	Hello Rock & Roll/Still a Fool	1980	—	2.00	4.00

The Manhattans are best known for their 1970s and early 1980s hits on Columbia. Long before that, they made some strong recordings for Carnival. Two albums came out, both of which are quite rare. This is the first.

Here is the picture sleeve for "Heartaches," the Marcels' second and final R&B hit in 1961.

Another of the rare early Motown albums is the Marvelettes' *Please Mr. Postman*, issued in 1961. The white-label stock version is especially desirable.

Big "J" in 3-D by Big Jay McNeely was issued twice, first on Federal, then on King. This is the King edition, and even this one is hard to find.

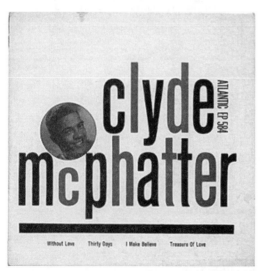

The first Atlantic EP of Clyde McPhatter tunes put several of his earliest solo hits together in one four-song package.

The Mello-Kings' hit was "Tonite Tonite." This is their EP, which is much more difficult to find than the single.

Number	Title (A Side/B Side)	Yr	VG	VG+	NM
VERVE					
❏ 10569	That Lucky Old Sun/My Darling Clementine	1967	2.50	5.00	10.00
Albums					
A&M					
❏ SP-3505	A Song for You	1971	3.00	6.00	12.00
❏ SP-3517	Smile	1972	3.00	6.00	12.00
LIBERTY					
❏ LT-1097	Sweet Thunder	1981	2.00	4.00	8.00
—Reissue of United Artists 1097					
MGM					
❏ SE-4583	Bill Medley 100%	1968	5.00	10.00	20.00
❏ SE-4603	Soft and Soulful	1969	5.00	10.00	20.00
❏ SE-4640	Someone Is Standing Outside	1969	5.00	10.00	20.00
❏ SE-4702	Nobody Knows	1970	3.75	7.50	15.00
❏ SE-4741	Gone	1970	3.75	7.50	15.00
RCA VICTOR					
❏ BXL1-4434	Right Here and Now	1982	2.50	5.00	10.00
❏ CPL1-5352	Still Hung Up on You	1984	2.50	5.00	10.00
❏ MHL1-8519 [EP]	I Still Do	1985	2.00	4.00	8.00
UNITED ARTISTS					
❏ UA-LA929-H	Lay a Little Lovin' on Me	1978	2.50	5.00	10.00
❏ LT-1097	Sweet Thunder	1980	2.50	5.00	10.00

MEGATRONS, THE
45s

Number	Title (A Side/B Side)	Yr	VG	VG+	NM
ACOUSTICON					
❏ 101	Velvet Waters/The Merry Piper	1959	3.75	7.50	15.00
AUDICON					
❏ 101	Velvet Waters/The Merry Piper	1959	3.00	6.00	12.00
❏ 104	Whispering Winds/Tootie Flutie	1960	2.50	5.00	10.00
❏ 107	Dance of the Silhouettes/Ranchero	1960	2.50	5.00	10.00
❏ 110	Julienne/By the Waters of the Minnetonka	1960	2.50	5.00	10.00
LAURIE					
❏ 3291	Velvet Waters/The Merry Piper	1965	2.00	4.00	8.00
❏ 3310	A Love That Will Last Forever/The Detroit Sound	1965	2.00	4.00	8.00

MEL AND TIM
45s

Number	Title (A Side/B Side)	Yr	VG	VG+	NM
BAMBOO					
❏ 106	I've Got Puredee/(Instrumental)	1969	—	3.00	6.00
❏ 107	Backfield in Motion/Do It Right Baby	1969	2.00	4.00	8.00
—White label, not a promo					
❏ 107	Backfield in Motion/Do It Right Baby	1969	—	3.00	6.00
—Multicolor label					
❏ 109	Good Guys Only Win in the Movies/I Found That I Was Wrong	1970	—	3.00	6.00
❏ 112	Feeling Bad/I've Got Puredee	1970	—	3.00	6.00
❏ 114	Mail Call Time/Forget It, I've Got It	1970	—	3.00	6.00
❏ 116	We've Got a Groove to Move On/Never on Time	1970	—	3.00	6.00
❏ 118	I'm the One/Put An Extra Plus to Your Love	1971	—	3.00	6.00
STAX					
❏ 0127	Starting All Over Again/It Hurts to Want It So Bad	1972	—	2.50	5.00
❏ 0154	I May Not Be What You Want/Too Much Wheelin' and Dealin'	1973	—	2.50	5.00
❏ 0160	Heaven Knows/Don't Mess with My Money, My Honey, Oh My Woman	1973	—	2.50	5.00
❏ 0202	Those Little Things That Count/The Same Folks	1974	—	2.50	5.00
❏ 0224	Forever and a Day/That's the Way I Want to Live My Life	1974	—	2.50	5.00
Albums					
BAMBOO					
❏ BMS-8001	Good Guys Only Win in the Movies	1970	6.25	12.50	25.00
STAX					
❏ STS-3007	Starting All Over Again	1972	5.00	10.00	20.00
❏ STS-5501	Mel and Tim	1974	5.00	10.00	20.00

MEL-O-DOTS, THE
45s

Number	Title (A Side/B Side)	Yr	VG	VG+	NM
APOLLO					
❏ 1192	One More Time/Just How Long	1952	750.00	1500.	3000.

MELLO-HARPS, THE
45s

Number	Title (A Side/B Side)	Yr	VG	VG+	NM
CASINO					
❏ 104	Gumma Gumma/No Good	1959	15.00	30.00	60.00
DO-RE-MI					
❏ 203	Love Is a Vow/Valerie	1956	4000.	6000.	8000.
TIN PAN ALLEY					
❏ 145/6	I Love Only You/Ain't Got the Money	1955	100.00	200.00	400.00
❏ 157/8	What Good Are My Dreams/Gone	1956	150.00	300.00	600.00
❏ 159	I Couldn't Believe/My Bleeding Heart	1956	150.00	300.00	600.00

MELLO-KINGS, THE
45s

Number	Title (A Side/B Side)	Yr	VG	VG+	NM
HERALD					
❏ 502	Tonite Tonite/Do Baby Do	1957	125.00	250.00	500.00
—First pressing credits "The Mellotones"					
❏ 502	Tonite Tonite/Do Baby Do	1957	12.50	25.00	50.00
—Label corrected to "The Mello-Kings"; script print inside flag					
❏ 502	Tonite Tonite/Do Baby Do	1961	6.50	12.50	25.00
—Reissue; block print inside flag					
❏ 507	Chapel on the Hill/Sassafras	1957	7.50	15.00	30.00

Number	Title (A Side/B Side)	Yr	VG	VG+	NM
❏ 511	Baby Tell Me Why Why Why/The Only Girl I'll Ever Know	1958	7.50	15.00	30.00
❏ 518	Valerie/She's Real Cool	1958	7.50	15.00	30.00
❏ 536	Chip Chip/Running to You	1959	7.50	15.00	30.00
—Both sides play as labeled					
❏ 536	Chip Chip/Running to You	1959	37.50	75.00	150.00
—Mispressing; plays "Rockin' at the Bandstand"/"Down in Cuba" by the Royal Holidays					
❏ 548	Our Love Is Beautiful/Dear Mr. Jock	1960	6.25	12.50	25.00
❏ 554	Kid Stuff/I Promise	1960	6.25	12.50	25.00
❏ 561	Penny/Till There Were None	1961	6.25	12.50	25.00
❏ 567	Love at First Sight/She's Real Cool	1961	6.25	12.50	25.00
LESCAY					
❏ 3009	Walk Softly/But You Lied	1962	7.50	15.00	30.00
7-Inch Extended Plays					
HERALD					
❏ HEP-451	Tonite, Tonite/She's Real Cool/The Only Girl/Do Baby Do	1957	75.00	150.00	300.00
❏ HEP-451 [PS]	The Fabulous Mello-Kings	1957	100.00	200.00	400.00
Albums					
COLLECTABLES					
❏ COL-5020	Greatest Hits	198?	2.50	5.00	10.00
HERALD					
❏ H-1013 [M]	Tonight-Tonight	1960	125.00	250.00	500.00
—Yellow label					
❏ H-1013 [M]	Tonight-Tonight	196?	62.50	125.00	250.00
—Multi-color label					
RELIC					
❏ LP-5035	Greatest Hits	198?	3.00	6.00	12.00

MELLO-MOODS, THE
45s

Number	Title (A Side/B Side)	Yr	VG	VG+	NM
GAMBLE					
❏ 2512	Stop Taking My Love for Granted/Inspirational Pleasure	1972	2.50	5.00	10.00
HAMILTON					
❏ 143	I'm Lost/I Woke Up This Morning	1953	25.00	50.00	100.00
PRESTIGE					
❏ 799	Call on Me/I Tried and Tried and Tried	1953	175.00	350.00	700.00
❏ 856	I'm Lost/I Woke Up This Morning	1953	175.00	350.00	700.00
ROBIN					
❏ 104	I Couldn't Sleep a Wink Last Night/And You Just Can't Go Through Life Alone	1952	750.00	1500.	3000.
❏ 105	Where Are You (Now That I Need You)/How Could You	1952	1250.	2500.	5000.
78s					
ROBIN					
❏ 104	I Couldn't Sleep a Wink Last Night/And You Just Can't Go Through Life Alone	1952	125.00	250.00	500.00
❏ 105	Where Are You (Now That I Need You)/How Could You	1952	75.00	150.00	300.00

MELLO-TONES, THE
More than one group.
45s

Number	Title (A Side/B Side)	Yr	VG	VG+	NM
COLUMBIA					
❏ 1-904	When the Rain Gates Unfold/What Are They Doing in Heaven	1950	100.00	200.00	400.00
—Microgroove 33 1/3 rpm 7-inch record, small hole					
❏ 6-904	When the Rain Gates Unfold/What Are They Doing in Heaven	1950	100.00	200.00	400.00
—Originally released on Columbia's short-lived special numbering system for 7-inch records					
❏ 39051	When The Rain Gates Unfold/What Are They Doing in Heaven	1950	75.00	150.00	300.00
❏ 39215	Looking for a City/Flysing Saucers	1951	75.00	150.00	300.00
DECCA					
❏ 48318	Winos on Parade/Man Loves Woman	1954	100.00	200.00	400.00
❏ 48319	I'm Just Another One in Love with You/I'm Gonna Get	1954	100.00	200.00	400.00
FASCINATION					
❏ 1001	Rosie Lee/I'll Never Fall in Love Again	1957	37.50	75.00	150.00
GEE					
❏ 1037	Rosie Lee/I'll Never Fall in Love Again	1957	10.00	20.00	40.00
❏ 1040	Ca-Sandra/Rattle Shake Roll	1957	10.00	20.00	40.00
OKEH					
❏ 6828	Rough and Rocky Road/Cool by the River Banks	1951	75.00	150.00	300.00

MELLOW DROPS, THE
45s

Number	Title (A Side/B Side)	Yr	VG	VG+	NM
IMPERIAL					
❏ 5324	When I Grow Too Old to Dream/The Crazy Song	1955	50.00	100.00	200.00

MELLOW MOODS, THE
45s

Number	Title (A Side/B Side)	Yr	VG	VG+	NM
RONNIE					
❏ 202	The Christmas Song/Love Me	19??	2.50	5.00	10.00
—B-side by the Rainbows					

MELLOWLARKS, THE
45s

Number	Title (A Side/B Side)	Yr	VG	VG+	NM
ARGO					
❏ 5285	Sing a Silly Sing Song/Farewell to You, My Nancy	1958	6.25	12.50	25.00

Number	Title (A Side/B Side)	Yr	VG	VG+	NM

MELLOWS, THE
45s
CANDLELIGHT

❏ 1011	Moon of Silver/You're Gone	1956	37.50	75.00	150.00
❏ 1012	Farewell Farewell/No More Loneliness	1956	37.50	75.00	150.00

CELESTE

❏ 3002	Lucky Guy/My Darling	1956	30.00	60.00	120.00
❏ 3004	I'm Yours/Sweet Lorraine	1956	150.00	300.00	600.00

JAY DEE

❏ 793	How Sentimental Can I Be/Nothin' to Do	1954	50.00	100.00	200.00
❏ 797	Smoke from Your Cigarette/Pretty Baby	1954	62.50	125.00	250.00
❏ 801	I Was a Fool to Let You Go/I Still Care	1955	50.00	100.00	200.00
❏ 807	Yesterday's Memories/Loveable Lilly	1955	37.50	75.00	150.00

MELO GENTS, THE
45s
WARNER BROS.

❏ 5056	Baby Be Mine/Get Off My Back	1959	12.50	25.00	50.00

MELODEARS, THE
45s
GONE

❏ 5033	Summer Romance/Charock	1958	3.75	7.50	15.00
❏ 5040	It's Love Because/They Don't Say	1958	3.75	7.50	15.00

MELODEERS, THE
45s
STUDIO

❏ 9908	Rudolph the Red-Nosed Reindeer/Wishing Is for Fools	1959	5.00	10.00	20.00

MELODY MAKERS, THE
45s
HOLLIS

❏ 1001	Carolina Moon/Let's Make Love Worthwhile	1957	25.00	50.00	100.00
❏ 1002	The Nearnes of You/Gotta Go	1957	37.50	75.00	150.00

MELVIN, HAROLD, AND THE BLUE NOTES
Also see THE BLUE NOTES (1); TEDDY PENDERGRASS.
12-Inch Singles
PHILLY WORLD

❏ PR 751 [DJ]	Today's Your Lucky Day (6:20) (7:07)	1984	2.00	4.00	8.00

SOURCE

❏ 13950	Prayin' (5:56)/Your Love Is Takin' Me on a Journey (5:55)	1979	3.00	6.00	12.00

45s
ABC

❏ 12240	Reaching for the World/Stay Together	1976	—	2.50	5.00
❏ 12268	After You Love Me, Why Do You Leave Me/Big Singing Star	1977	—	2.50	5.00
—With Sharon Paige					
❏ 12327	Baby, You Got My Nose Open/Try to Live a Day	1978	—	2.50	5.00
❏ 12368	Power of Love/Now Is the Time	1978	—	2.50	5.00

ARCTIC

❏ 135	Go Away/What Can a Man Do	1967	2.50	5.00	10.00

LANDA

❏ 703	Get Out (And Let Me Cry)/You May Not Love Me	1964	4.00	8.00	16.00
—As "The Blue Notes"					

MCA

❏ 41291	Tonight's the Night/If You're Looking for Someone to Love	1980	—	2.00	4.00
—With Sharon Paige					
❏ 51190	Hang On In There/If You Love Me, Really Love Me	1982	—	2.00	4.00

PHILADELPHIA INT'L.

❏ 3516	I Miss You (Part I)/I Miss You (Part II)	1972	—	2.50	5.00
❏ 3520	If You Don't Know Me By Now/Let Me Into Your World	1972	—	2.50	5.00
❏ 3525	Yesterday I Had the Blues/Ebony Woman	1973	—	2.50	5.00
❏ 3525 [PS]	Yesterday I Had the Blues/Ebony Woman	1973	—	3.00	6.00
❏ 3533	The Love I Lost (Part 1)/The Love I Lost (Part 2)	1973	—	2.50	5.00
❏ 3543	Satisfaction Guaranteed (Or Take Your Love Back)/I'm Weak for You	1974	—	2.50	5.00
❏ 3552	Where Are All My Friends/Let It Be You	1974	—	2.50	5.00
❏ 3562	Bad Luck (Part 1)/Bad Luck (Part 2)	1975	—	2.50	5.00
❏ 3569	Hope That We Can Be Together Soon/Be for Real	1975	—	2.50	5.00
—With Sharon Paige					
❏ 3579	Wake Up Everybody (Part 1)/Wake Up Everybody (Part 2)	1975			5.00
❏ 3588	Tell the World How I Feel About 'Cha Baby/You Know How to Make Me Feel So Good	1976	—	2.50	5.00

PHILLY WORLD

❏ 99709	I Really Love You/I Can't Let Go	1984	—	2.00	4.00
❏ 99735	Today's Your Lucky Day (Long)/Today's Your Lucky Day (Short)	1984	—	2.00	4.00
❏ 99761	Don't Give Me Up/(Instrumental)	1984	—	2.00	4.00

SOURCE

❏ 41156	Prayin' (Part 1)/Prayin' (Part 2)	1979	—	2.00	4.00
❏ 41157	Tonight's the Night/Your Love Is Taking Me on a Journey	1979	—	2.00	4.00
❏ 41231	I Should Be Your Lover (Part 1)/I Should Be Your Lover (Part 2)	1980	—	2.00	4.00

Albums
ABC

❏ AB-969	Reaching for the World	1977	2.50	5.00	10.00
❏ AB-1041	Now Is the Time	1978	2.50	5.00	10.00

MCA

❏ 5261	All Things Happen in Time	1981	2.50	5.00	10.00

PHILADELPHIA INT'L.

❏ KZ 31648	Harold Melvin and the Blue Notes	1972	3.00	6.00	12.00
❏ KZ 32407	Black & Blue	1973	3.00	6.00	12.00
❏ ZQ 32407 [Q]	Black & Blue	1973	5.00	10.00	20.00
❏ PZ 33148	To Be True	1975	3.00	6.00	12.00
❏ PZ 33808	Wake Up Everybody	1975	3.00	6.00	12.00
❏ PZQ 33808 [Q]	Wake Up Everybody	1975	5.00	10.00	20.00
❏ PZ 34232	Collector's Item — All Their Greatest Hits!	1976	3.00	6.00	12.00

PHILLY WORLD

❏ 90187	Talk It Up (Tell Everybody)	1985	2.50	5.00	10.00

SOURCE

❏ 3197	The Blue Album	1980	2.50	5.00	10.00

MEMORIES, THE
45s
WAY-LIN

❏ 101	Love Bells/I Promise	1959	100.00	200.00	400.00

MEMPHIS MINNIE
45s
CHECKER

❏ 771	Broken Heart/Me and My Chauffeur	1953	1000.	2000.	3000.

J.O.B.

❏ 1101	Kissing in the Dark/World of Trouble	1952	250.00	500.00	1000.

78s
BANNER

❏ 32525	Bumble Bee/Bumble Bee No. 2	1932	50.00	100.00	200.00
❏ 32556	I'm Talking About You/I'm Talking About You No. 2	1932	50.00	100.00	200.00
❏ 32796	Fishin' Blues/Where Is My Good Man	1933	50.00	100.00	200.00
❏ 32797	Kind Treatment Blues/Outdoor Blues	1933	50.00	100.00	200.00

BLUEBIRD

❏ B-6141	Keep On Going/I'm Waiting on You	1935	50.00	100.00	200.00
—As "Texas Tessie"					
❏ B-6187	When the Sun Goes Down/Atlanta Town	1936	50.00	100.00	200.00
—B-side by Collins Chasey					
❏ B-6199	Doctor, Doctor Blues/Selling My Pork Chops	1936	37.50	75.00	150.00
❏ B-6202	Hustlin' Woman Blues/Got the Blues About My Baby	1936	62.50	125.00	250.00
❏ B-6429	You Wrecked My Happy Home/You Got the Right Key	1936	50.00	100.00	200.00
—As "Texas Tessie"; B-side by Trixie Butler					

CHECKER

❏ 771	Broken Heart/Me and My Chauffeur	1953	100.00	200.00	400.00

COLUMBIA

❏ 20054	Fish Man Blues/Lean Meat Won't Fry	1948	3.75	7.50	15.00
—Reissue of 37579					
❏ 36895	True Love/Please Set a Date	1946	5.00	10.00	20.00
❏ 37295	Mean Mistreater Blues/I'm So Glad	1947	5.00	10.00	20.00
❏ 37455	When You Love Me/Love Comes and Goes	1947	5.00	10.00	20.00
—Reissue of Okeh 6733					
❏ 37462	I'm Not a Bad Girl/It Was You Baby	1947	5.00	10.00	20.00
—Reissue of Okeh 6624					
❏ 37579	Fish Man Blues/Lean Meat Won't Fry	1947	5.00	10.00	20.00
❏ 37689	Boy Friend Blues/Nothin' in Ramblin'	1947	5.00	10.00	20.00
—Reissue of Okeh 05670					
❏ 37690	It's Hard to Please My Man/Lonesome Shark Blues	1947	5.00	10.00	20.00
—Reissue of Okeh 05728					
❏ 37977	Hold Me Blues/Killer Diller Blues	1948	5.00	10.00	20.00
❏ 38099	Three Times Seven Blues/Shout the Boogie	1948	5.00	10.00	20.00

CONQUEROR

❏ 9025	I'm a Gamblin' Woman/Caught Me Wrong Again	1938	10.00	20.00	40.00
❏ 9026	Walking and Crying Blues/New Caught Me Wrong Again	1938	10.00	20.00	40.00
❏ 9162	I'd Rather See Him Dead/Long As I Can See You Smile	1938	10.00	20.00	40.00
❏ 9198	Good Soppin'/Black Widow Stinger	1939	10.00	20.00	40.00
❏ 9275	Low Down Man Blues/Bad Outside Friends	1939	10.00	20.00	40.00
❏ 9282	Keep Your Big Mouth Closed/Call the Fire Wagon	1939	10.00	20.00	40.00
❏ 9372	Boy Friend Blues/It's Hard to Please My Man	1940	10.00	20.00	40.00
❏ 9763	Fingerprint Blues/Ma Rainey	1940	10.00	20.00	40.00
❏ 9764	Nothin' in Ramblin'/Lonesome Shark Blues	1940	10.00	20.00	40.00
❏ 9933	Me and My Chauffeur Blues/In My Girlish Days	1941	10.00	20.00	40.00
❏ 9934	My Gauge Is Going Up/Can't Afford to Lose My Man	1941	10.00	20.00	40.00
❏ 9935	I Got to Make a Change Blues/Pigmeat on the Line	1941	10.00	20.00	40.00
❏ 9936	This Is Your Last Chance/Down by the Riverside	1941	10.00	20.00	40.00

DECCA

❏ 7019	Chickasaw Train Blues/Banana Man Blues	1934	75.00	150.00	300.00
❏ 7037	Keep It to Yourself/Moaning the Blues	1934	75.00	150.00	300.00
❏ 7048	Dirty Mother for You/You Can't Give It Away	1935	75.00	150.00	300.00
❏ 7084	Sylvester and His Mule Blues/When You're Asleep	1935	62.50	125.00	250.00
❏ 7102	Reachin' Pete/Down in New Orleans	1935	62.50	125.00	250.00
❏ 7125	Jockey Man Blues/Weary Woman's Blues	1935	50.00	100.00	200.00
❏ 7146	Squat It/(B-side unknown)	1935	50.00	100.00	200.00

M

Number	Title (A Side/B Side)	Yr	VG	VG+	NM
J.O.B.					
❏ 1101	Kissing in the Dark/World of Trouble	1952	75.00	150.00	300.00
MELOTONE					
❏ M 12729	Fishin' Blues/Outdoor Blues	1933	50.00	100.00	200.00
❏ M 12730	Where Is My Good Man/Kind Treatment Blues	1933	50.00	100.00	200.00
OKEH					
❏ 05670	Boy Friend Blues/Nothin' in Ramblin'	1940	25.00	50.00	100.00
❏ 05728	It's Hard to Please My Man/Lonesome Shark Blues	1940	15.00	30.00	60.00
❏ 05811	Fingerprint Blues/Ma Rainey	1940	15.00	30.00	60.00
❏ 06288	Me and My Chauffeur Blues/Can't Afford to Lose My Man	1941	20.00	40.00	80.00
❏ 06410	In My Girlish Days/My Gauge Is Going Up	1941	15.00	30.00	60.00
❏ 06505	This Is Your Last Chance/Pigmeat on the Line	1941	15.00	30.00	60.00
❏ 6624	I'm Not a Bad Girl/It Was You Baby	1942	12.50	25.00	50.00
❏ 6707	Looking the World Over/Black Rat Swing	1942	12.50	25.00	50.00
—B-side by Little Son Joe					
❏ 6733	When You Love Me/Love Comes and Goes	1945	10.00	20.00	40.00
❏ 8948	My Butcher Man/Too Late	1934	75.00	150.00	300.00
ORIOLE					
❏ 8157	Bumble Bee/Bumble Bee No. 2	1932	50.00	100.00	200.00
❏ 8165	I'm Talking About You/I'm Talking About You No. 2	1932	50.00	100.00	200.00
REGAL					
❏ 3259	Why Did I Make You Cry/Kidman Blues	1950	17.50	35.00	70.00
VOCALION					
❏ 1476	Bumble Bee/I'm Talking About You	1930	75.00	150.00	300.00
❏ 1512	I'm Gonna Bake My Biscuits/Mister Tango Blues	1930	100.00	200.00	400.00
❏ 1550	What's the Matter with the Mill?/North Memphis Blues	1930	100.00	200.00	400.00
❏ 1556	Bumble Bee No. 2/I'm Talkin' 'Bout You No. 2	1930	62.50	125.00	250.00
❏ 1588	Frankie Jean/Memphis Minnie Blues	1931	100.00	200.00	400.00
❏ 1601	Garage Fire Blues/Grandpa and Grandma Blues	1931	125.00	250.00	500.00
❏ 1603	Good Girl Blues/Georgia Skin Blues	1931	75.00	150.00	300.00
❏ 1618	New Bumble Bee/New Dirty Dozen	1931	100.00	200.00	400.00
❏ 1631	Plymouth Rock Blues/I Called You This Morning	1931	100.00	200.00	400.00
—B-side by Kansas Joe (McCoy)					
❏ 1638	You Dirty Mistreater/Dirt Dauber Blues	1931	100.00	200.00	400.00
❏ 1653	Tricks Ain't Walkin' No More/Somebody's Got to Help You	1931	100.00	200.00	400.00
❏ 1658	Soo Cow Soo/After a While Blues	1931	100.00	200.00	400.00
❏ 1665	Lay My Money Down/Hard Down Lie	1932	100.00	200.00	400.00
❏ 1673	Don't Bother It/Today Today Blues	1932	100.00	200.00	400.00
❏ 1678	Crazy Cryin' Blues/I Don't Want That Junk Outa You	1932	100.00	200.00	400.00
❏ 1682	Minnie Minnie Bumble Bee/If You Want Me to Love You	1932	100.00	200.00	400.00
—A-side with Tampa Red; b-side by Georgia Tom & Kansas Joe					
❏ 1688	Socket Blues/You Stole My Cake	1932	125.00	250.00	500.00
—B-side by Kansas Joe (McCoy)					
❏ 1698	Where Is My Good Man/Outdoor Blues	1932	62.50	125.00	250.00
❏ 1711	Fishin' Blues/Kind Treatment Blues	1932	62.50	125.00	250.00
❏ 1718	Jailhouse Trouble Blues/You Know You Done Me Wrong	1932	100.00	200.00	400.00
—B-side by Kansas Joe (McCoy)					
❏ 02711	Drunken Barrel House Blues/Stinging Snake Blues	1934	75.00	150.00	300.00
❏ 03046	Joe Louis Strut/He's In the Ring	1935	25.00	50.00	100.00
❏ 03144	Biting Bug Blues/You Ain't Done Nothin' to Me	1936	25.00	50.00	100.00
❏ 03187	Ain't Nobody Home But Me/Minnie's Lonesome Song	1936	25.00	50.00	100.00
❏ 03222	Ice Man (Come On Up)/Hoodoo Lady	1936	37.50	75.00	150.00
❏ 03258	I'm a Gamblin' Woman/Caught Me Wrong Again	1936	25.00	50.00	100.00
❏ 03285	If You See My Rooster (Please Run Him Home)/My Strange Man	1936	25.00	50.00	100.00
❏ 03398	Dragging My Heart Around/Out in the Cold	1937	20.00	40.00	80.00
❏ 03436	I Don't Want You No More/Good Morning	1937	20.00	40.00	80.00
❏ 03474	It's Hard to Be Mistreated/Man, You Won't Give Me No Money	1937	20.00	40.00	80.00
❏ 03541	Ball and Chain Blues/I'm a Bad Luck Woman	1937	20.00	40.00	80.00
❏ 03581	Black Cat Blues/Haunted House	1937	20.00	40.00	80.00
❏ 03612	Down in the Alley/Look What You Got	1937	20.00	40.00	80.00
❏ 03651	Keep On Sailing/Hot Stuff	1937	20.00	40.00	80.00
❏ 03697	You Can't Rule Me/No Need You Doggin' Me	1937	20.00	40.00	80.00
❏ 03768	Living the Best I Can/Wants Cake When I'm Hungry	1938	15.00	30.00	60.00
❏ 03894	My Baby Don't Want Me No More/Moonshine	1938	15.00	30.00	60.00
❏ 03966	Walking and Crying Blues/New Caught Me Wrong Again	1938	15.00	30.00	60.00
❏ 04250	I've Been Treated Wrong/Has Anybody Seen My Man?	1938	15.00	30.00	60.00
❏ 04295	Good Biscuits/Keep On Eating	1938	15.00	30.00	60.00
❏ 04356	Keep On Walking/I Hate to See the Sun Go Down	1938	15.00	30.00	60.00
❏ 04506	I'd Rather See Him Dead/Long As I Can See You Smile	1938	15.00	30.00	60.00
❏ 04694	Good Soppin'/Black Widow Stinger	1939	15.00	30.00	60.00
❏ 04797	Low Down Man Blues/Bad Outside Friends	1939	15.00	30.00	60.00
❏ 04858	Keep Your Big Mouth Closed/Call the Fire Wagon	1939	15.00	30.00	60.00
❏ 04898	Don't Lead My Baby Wrong/Worried Baby Blues	1939	15.00	30.00	60.00
❏ 05004	Poor and Wanderin' Woman Blues/Key to the World	1939	15.00	30.00	60.00
—B-side by Little Son Joe					

Number	Title (A Side/B Side)	Yr	VG	VG+	NM
MEMPHIS SLIM					
45s					
JOSIE					
❏ 973	Come Again/Little Lonely Girl	1967	2.50	5.00	10.00
KING					
❏ 6301	Messin' Around with the Blues/Mistake in Life	1970	2.00	4.00	8.00
MERCURY					
❏ 8251x45	Train Time/Blue Evening	1951	12.50	25.00	50.00
❏ 8266x45	No Mail Blues/Gonna Need My Help Some Day	1952	12.50	25.00	50.00
❏ 8281x45	The Question/Never Let Me Love	1952	12.50	25.00	50.00
❏ 70063x45	The Train Is Coming/Drivin' Me Mad	1953	10.00	20.00	40.00
MONEY					
❏ 212	My Country Gal/Treat Me Like I Treat You	1955	10.00	20.00	40.00
PEACOCK					
❏ 1602	Sitting and Thinking/Living Like a King	1952	12.50	25.00	50.00
STRAND					
❏ 25041	Four Walls/Lonesome	1961	6.25	12.50	25.00
UNITED					
❏ 138	Back Alley/Living the Life I Love	1952	15.00	30.00	60.00
❏ 156	The Come Back/Five O'Clock Blues	1953	15.00	30.00	60.00
—Black vinyl					
❏ 156	The Come Back/Five O'Clock Blues	1953	37.50	75.00	150.00
—Red vinyl					
❏ 166	Call Before You Go Home/This Is My Lucky Day	1953	15.00	30.00	60.00
—Black vinyl					
❏ 166	Call Before You Go Home/This Is My Lucky Day	1953	37.50	75.00	150.00
—Red vinyl					
❏ 176	Wish Me Well/Sassy Mae	1954	15.00	30.00	60.00
—Black vinyl					
❏ 176	Wish Me Well/Sassy Mae	1954	37.50	75.00	150.00
—Red vinyl					
❏ 182	I Love My Baby/Four Years of Torment	1954	12.50	25.00	50.00
❏ 186	Memphis Slim U.S.A./Blues All Around My Head	1954	12.50	25.00	50.00
❏ 189	She's Alright/Two of a Kind	1955	12.50	25.00	50.00
❏ 201	Go to Find My Baby/Blue and Lonesome	1956	10.00	20.00	40.00
VEE JAY					
❏ 271	Stroll On Little Girl/Guitar Cha Cha Cha	1958	5.00	10.00	20.00
❏ 294	This Time I'm Through/What's the Matter	1958	5.00	10.00	20.00
❏ 330	Steppin' Out/My Gal Keeps Me Crying	1959	5.00	10.00	20.00
❏ 343	The Come Back/Slim's Blues	1960	3.75	7.50	15.00
WARNER BROS.					
❏ 7500	Chicago Seven/Boogie Woogie 1-9-7-0	1971	2.00	4.00	8.00
78s					
BLUEBIRD					
❏ B-8584	Grinder Man Blues/Beer Drinking Woman	1940	20.00	40.00	80.00
❏ B-8615	Empty Room Blues/You Didn't Mean Me No Good	1941	17.50	35.00	70.00
❏ B-8645	Shelby County Blues/I See My Great Mistake	1941	17.50	35.00	70.00
❏ B-8749	Jasper's Gal/Two of a Kind	1941	17.50	35.00	70.00
❏ B-8784	Me, Myself and I/Maybe I'll Lend You a Dime	1941	17.50	35.00	70.00
❏ B-8834	Whiskey Store Blues/You Got to Help Me Some	1941	17.50	35.00	70.00
❏ B-8903	Old Taylor/I Believe I'll Settle Down	1942	17.50	35.00	70.00
❏ B-8945	Whiskey and Gin Blues/You Gonna Worry Too?	1942	17.50	35.00	70.00
❏ B-8974	This Life I'm Living/Caught the Old Coon at Last	1942	17.50	35.00	70.00
❏ B-9028	Don't Think You're Smart/Lend Me Your Love	1942	17.50	35.00	70.00
CHESS					
❏ 1491	Walking Alone/Rockin' the Pad	1952	15.00	30.00	60.00
FEDERAL					
❏ 12007	Life Is Like That/Nobody Loves Me	1951	10.00	20.00	40.00
—Reissue of sides issued on Miracle 111 and 145, respectively					
❏ 12015	Motherless Child/Pacemaker Boogie	1951	10.00	20.00	40.00
—Reissue of Miracle 110					
❏ 12021	Messin' Around/Midnight Jump	1951	10.00	20.00	40.00
—Reissue of Miracle 125					
❏ 12033	Lend Me Your Love/Darling I Miss You So	1951	10.00	20.00	40.00
—Reissue of sides issued on Miracle 103 and 102, respectively					
HY-TONE					
❏ 10	Grinder Man Blues/Mistake in Life	1946	12.50	25.00	50.00
—Reissue of Melody Lane Record Shop 10					
❏ 17	Slim's Boogie/Little Mary	1946	12.50	25.00	50.00
❏ 18	Don't Ration (My Love)/(Now I) Got the Blues	1946	12.50	25.00	50.00
❏ 19	A Letter Home/Cheatin' Around	1946	12.50	25.00	50.00
KING					
❏ 4284	Cheatin' Around/Now I Got the Blues	1949	10.00	20.00	40.00
❏ 4312	A Letter Home/Slim's Boogie	1949	10.00	20.00	40.00
❏ 4324	Little Mary/Mistake in Life	1949	10.00	20.00	40.00
❏ 4327	Grinder Man Blues/Don't Ration Love	1950	10.00	20.00	40.00
MASTER					
❏ 1010	Believe I'll Settle Down/Country Girl	1949	10.00	20.00	40.00
❏ 1020	Restless Nights/If You Live That Life	1950	10.00	20.00	40.00
❏ 1030	Love at First Sight/Jumping Bean	1950	10.00	20.00	40.00
MELODY LANE RECORD SHOP					
❏ 10	Grinder Man Blues/Mistake in Life	1946	15.00	30.00	60.00
MERCURY					
❏ 8251	Train Time/Blue Evening	1951	5.00	10.00	20.00
❏ 8266	No Mail Blues/Gonna Need My Help Some Day	1952	5.00	10.00	20.00
❏ 8281	The Question/Never Let Me Love	1952	5.00	10.00	20.00
❏ 70063	The Train Is Coming/Drivin' Me Mad	1953	5.00	10.00	20.00
MIRACLE					
❏ 102	Kilroy Has Been Here/Darling I Miss You So	1947	12.50	25.00	50.00
❏ 103	Rockin' the House/Lend Me Your Love	1947	12.50	25.00	50.00
❏ 110	Motherless Child/Pacemaker Boogie	1947	12.50	25.00	50.00
❏ 111	Harlem Bound/Life Is Like That	1947	12.50	25.00	50.00
❏ 125	Messin' Around/Midnight Jump	1948	12.50	25.00	50.00

Number	Title (A Side/B Side)	Yr	VG	VG+	NM
❏ 132	Frisco Bay/Timsy's Whimsey	1948	12.50	25.00	50.00
❏ 136	Blue and Lonesome/Help Me Some	1949	12.50	25.00	50.00
❏ 145	Angel Child/Nobody Loves Me	1949	12.50	25.00	50.00
❏ 153	You and I/Throw This Poor Dog a Bone	1949	12.50	25.00	50.00
MONEY					
❏ 212	My Country Gal/Treat Me Like I Treat You	1955	7.50	15.00	30.00
OLD SWING-MASTER					
❏ 1010	Believe I'll Settle Down/Country Girl	1949	12.50	25.00	50.00
PEACOCK					
❏ 1517	Mean Little Woman/The Girl I Love	1949	10.00	20.00	40.00
❏ 1602	Sitting and Thinking/Living Like a King	1952	6.25	12.50	25.00
PREMIUM					
❏ 850	Flock Rocker/I Guess I'm a Fool	1950	10.00	20.00	40.00
❏ 860	Slim's Blues/Havin' Fun	1950	10.00	20.00	40.00
❏ 867	Mother Earth/Really Got the Blues	1950	10.00	20.00	40.00
❏ 873	Trouble, Trouble/My Baby Left Me	1951	10.00	20.00	40.00
❏ 878	'Fore Day/Feelin' Low	1951	10.00	20.00	40.00
UNITED					
❏ 138	Back Alley/Living the Life I Love	1952	6.25	12.50	25.00
❏ 156	The Come Back/Five O'Clock Blues	1953	6.25	12.50	25.00
❏ 166	Call Before You Go Home/This Is My Lucky Day	1953	6.25	12.50	25.00
❏ 176	Wish Me Well/Sassy Mae	1954	7.50	15.00	30.00
❏ 182	I Love My Baby/Four Years of Torment	1954	7.50	15.00	30.00
❏ 186	Memphis Slim U.S.A./Blues All Around My Head	1954	7.50	15.00	30.00
❏ 189	She's Alright/Two of a Kind	1955	7.50	15.00	30.00
❏ 201	Go to Find My Baby/Blue and Lonesome	1956	10.00	20.00	40.00
Albums					
BATTLE					
❏ BM-6118 [M]	Alone with My Friends	1963	12.50	25.00	50.00
❏ BM-6122 [M]	Baby Please Come Home	1963	12.50	25.00	50.00
BLUESVILLE					
❏ BVLP-1018 [M]	Just Blues	1961	30.00	60.00	120.00
—*Blue label, silver print*					
❏ BVLP-1018 [M]	Just Blues	1964	7.50	15.00	30.00
—*Blue label, trident logo at right*					
❏ BVLP-1031 [M]	No Strain	1961	30.00	60.00	120.00
—*Blue label, silver print*					
❏ BVLP-1031 [M]	No Strain	1964	7.50	15.00	30.00
—*Blue label, trident logo at right*					
❏ BVLP-1053 [M]	All Kinds of Blues	1962	25.00	50.00	100.00
—*Blue label, silver print*					
❏ BVLP-1053 [M]	All Kinds of Blues	1964	7.50	15.00	30.00
—*Blue label, trident logo at right*					
❏ BVLP-1075 [M]	Steady Rollin' Blues	1963	25.00	50.00	100.00
—*Blue label, silver print*					
❏ BVLP-1075 [M]	Steady Rollin' Blues	1964	7.50	15.00	30.00
—*Blue label, trident logo at right*					
BUDDAH					
❏ BDS-7505	Mother Earth	1969	5.00	10.00	20.00
CANDID					
❏ CM-8023 [M]	Slim's Tribute to Big Bill Broonzy	1961	15.00	30.00	60.00
❏ CM-8024 [M]	Memphis Slim U.S.A.	1962	15.00	30.00	60.00
❏ CS-9023 [S]	Slim's Tribute to Big Bill Broonzy	1961	20.00	40.00	80.00
❏ CS-9024 [S]	Memphis Slim U.S.A.	1962	20.00	40.00	80.00
CHESS					
❏ LP-1455 [M]	Memphis Slim	1961	37.50	75.00	150.00
—*Black label*					
❏ LP-1510 [M]	The Real Folk Blues	1966	20.00	40.00	80.00
DISC					
❏ D-105 [M]	If the Rabbit Had a Gun	1964	10.00	20.00	40.00
FOLKWAYS					
❏ FG-3524 [M]	The Real Boogie Woogie	1959	25.00	50.00	100.00
❏ FG-3535 [M]	Memphis Slim…And the Real Honky Tonk	1960	25.00	50.00	100.00
❏ FG-3536 [M]	Chicago Blues	1961	25.00	50.00	100.00
JUBILEE					
❏ JGM-8003 [M]	Legend of the Blues	1967	6.25	12.50	25.00
❏ JGS-8003 [S]	Legend of the Blues	1967	6.25	12.50	25.00
KING					
❏ 885 [M]	Memphis Slim Sings Folk Blues	1964	12.50	25.00	50.00
SCEPTER					
❏ SM-535 [M]	Self Portrait	1966	5.00	10.00	20.00
❏ SMS-535 [S]	Self Portrait	1966	6.25	12.50	25.00
SPIN-O-RAMA					
❏ 149 [M]	Lonesome Blues	196?	5.00	10.00	20.00
STRAND					
❏ SL-1046 [M]	The World's Foremost Blues Singer	1962	10.00	20.00	40.00
❏ SLS-1046 [S]	The World's Foremost Blues Singer	1962	12.50	25.00	50.00
UNITED ARTISTS					
❏ UAL-3137 [M]	Broken Soul Blues	1961	15.00	30.00	60.00
❏ UAS-6137 [S]	Broken Soul Blues	1961	20.00	40.00	80.00
VEE JAY					
❏ LP-1012 [M]	Memphis Slim at the Gate of the Horn	1959	50.00	100.00	200.00
—*Maroon label*					
❏ LP-1012 [M]	Memphis Slim at the Gate of the Horn	1961	30.00	60.00	120.00
—*Black rainbow label, oval logo*					

MEMPHIS WILLIE B
Albums
BLUESVILLE

Number	Title (A Side/B Side)	Yr	VG	VG+	NM
❏ BVLP-1034 [M]	Introducing Memphis Willie B	1961	25.00	50.00	100.00
—*Blue label, silver print*					
❏ BVLP-1034 [M]	Introducing Memphis Willie B	1964	7.50	15.00	30.00
—*Blue label, trident logo at right*					

Number	Title (A Side/B Side)	Yr	VG	VG+	NM
❏ BVLP-1048 [M]	Hard Working Man Blues	1962	25.00	50.00	100.00
—*Blue label, silver print*					
❏ BVLP-1048 [M]	Hard Working Man Blues	1964	7.50	15.00	30.00
—*Blue label, trident logo at right*					

METERS, THE
Also see AARON NEVILLE.
45s
JOSIE

Number	Title (A Side/B Side)	Yr	VG	VG+	NM
❏ 1001	Sophisticated Cissy/Sehorn's Farm	1968	2.50	5.00	10.00
❏ 1005	Cissy Strut/Here Comes the Meter Man	1969	2.50	5.00	10.00
❏ 1008	Ease Back/Ann	1969	2.50	5.00	10.00
❏ 1013	Dry Spell/Look-Ka Py Py	1969	2.50	5.00	10.00
❏ 1015	Look-Ka Py Py/This Is My Last Affair	1970	2.50	5.00	10.00
❏ 1018	Chicken Strut/Hey! Last Minute	1970	2.50	5.00	10.00
❏ 1021	Hand Clapping Song/Joog	1970	2.50	5.00	10.00
❏ 1024	A Message from the Meters/Zony Mash	1970	2.50	5.00	10.00
❏ 1026	Stretch Your Rubber Band/Groovy Lady	1971	2.50	5.00	10.00
❏ 1029	(The World Is a Bit Under the Weather) Doodle-Oop/I Need More Time	1971	2.50	5.00	10.00
❏ 1031	Good Old Funky Music/Sassy Lady	1971	2.50	5.00	10.00
REPRISE					
❏ 1086	Do the Dirt/Smiling	1972	2.00	4.00	8.00
❏ 1106	Cabbage Alley/The Flower Song	1972	2.00	4.00	8.00
❏ 1135	Chug Chug Chug-A-Lug (Part 1)/Chug Chug Chug-A-Lug (Part 2)	1972	2.00	4.00	8.00
❏ 1307	Hey Pocky A-Way/Africa	1974	—	3.00	6.00
❏ 1314	People Say/Loving You Is On My Mind	1974	—	3.00	6.00
❏ 1338	Running Fast/They All Ask'd for You	1975	—	3.00	6.00
❏ 1357	Disco Is the Thing Today/Mister Moon	1976	—	3.00	6.00
❏ 1372	Trick Bag/Find Yourself	1976	—	3.00	6.00
WARNER BROS.					
❏ 8434	Be My Lady/No More Okey Doke	1977		2.50	5.00
Albums					
JOSIE					
❏ JOS-4010	The Meters	1969	17.50	35.00	70.00
❏ JOS-4011	Look-Ka Py Py	1970	17.50	35.00	70.00
❏ JOS-4012	Struttin'	1970	17.50	35.00	70.00
REPRISE					
❏ MS 2076	Cabbage Alley	1972	17.50	35.00	70.00
❏ MS 2200	Rejuvenation	1974	12.50	25.00	50.00
❏ MS 2228	Fire on the Bayou	1975	12.50	25.00	50.00
❏ MS 2252	Trick Bag	1976	12.50	25.00	50.00
ROUNDER					
❏ 2103	Look-Ka Py Py	1990	5.00	10.00	20.00
—*Reissue of Josie 4011*					
❏ 2104	Good Old Funky Music	1990	5.00	10.00	20.00
SUNDAZED					
❏ LP 5081	Kickback	2001	3.00	6.00	12.00
VIRGO					
❏ 12002	The Best of the Meters	1972	12.50	25.00	50.00
WARNER BROS.					
❏ BS 3042	New Directions	1977	12.50	25.00	50.00

MFSB
45s
PHILADELPHIA INT'L.

Number	Title (A Side/B Side)	Yr	VG	VG+	NM
❏ 3528	Family Affair/Layin' Low	1973	—	2.50	5.00
❏ 3540	TSOP (The Sound of Philadelphia)/Something for Nothing	1974	—	2.50	5.00
❏ 3547	Love Is the Message/My One and Only Love	1974	—	2.50	5.00
❏ 3567	Sexy/Human Machine	1975	—	2.50	5.00
❏ 3576	T.L.C. (Tender Lovin' Care)/Love Has No Time or Place	1975	—	2.50	5.00
❏ 3578	The Zip/My Mood	1975	—	2.50	5.00
❏ 3583	Smile Happy/When Your Love Is Gone	1976	—	2.50	5.00
❏ 3589	Philadelphia Freedom/South Philly	1976	—	2.50	5.00
❏ 3600	Summertime And I'm Feelin' Mellow/Hot Summer Nights	1976	—	2.50	5.00
❏ 3607	We Got the Time/(B-side unknown)	1976	—	2.50	5.00
❏ 3626	I'm On Your Side/Picnic in the Park	1977	—	2.50	5.00
❏ 3641	K-Jee/My Mood	1978	—	2.50	5.00
❏ 3650	Use Ta Be My Guy/Redwood Beach	1978	—	2.50	5.00
❏ 3663	Let's Party Down/To Be in Love	1978	—	2.50	5.00
❏ 3668	Dance with Me Tonight/Is It Something I Said	1979	—	2.50	5.00
TSOP					
❏ 02022	Mysteries of the World/Thank You Miss Scott	1981	—	2.00	4.00
❏ 4797	Manhattan Skyline/Metamorphosis	1980	—	2.00	4.00
Albums					
PHILADELPHIA INT'L.					
❏ KZ 32046	MFSB	1973	2.50	5.00	10.00
❏ KZ 32707	Love Is the Message	1974	2.50	5.00	10.00
❏ ZQ 32707 [Q]	Love Is the Message	1974	4.50	9.00	18.00
❏ PZ 33158	Universal Love	1975	2.50	5.00	10.00
❏ PZ 33845	Philadelphia Freedom	1975	2.50	5.00	10.00
❏ PZQ 33845 [Q]	Philadelphia Freedom	1975	4.50	9.00	18.00
❏ PZ 34238	Summertime	1976	2.50	5.00	10.00
❏ PZ 34658	The End of Phase One	1977	2.50	5.00	10.00
❏ JZ 35516	The Gamble-Huff Orchestra	1978	2.50	5.00	10.00
TSOP					
❏ JZ 36405	Mysteries of the World	1980	2.50	5.00	10.00

Number	Title (A Side/B Side)	Yr	VG	VG+	NM

MICKEY AND SYLVIA
Also see MICKEY BAKER; SYLVIA (1).
45s
ALL PLATINUM

Number	Title (A Side/B Side)	Yr	VG	VG+	NM
❏ 2307	Lovedrops/Because You Do It to Me	1969	—	3.00	6.00
❏ 2310	Anytime/Souling with Mickey and Sylvia	1969	—	3.00	6.00

CAT

❏ 102	Fine Love/Speedy Life	1954	10.00	20.00	40.00

—As "Little" Sylvia Vanderpool and Mickey Baker
GROOVE

❏ 0164	No Good Lover/Walkin' in the Rain	1956	7.50	15.00	30.00
❏ 0175	Love Is Strange/I'm Going Home	1956	7.50	15.00	30.00

KING

❏ 5737	Baby, Let's Dance/Oh Yea, Ah Ah	1963	3.00	6.00	12.00
❏ 6006	Love Is Strange/Darling	1965	2.50	5.00	10.00

RAINBOW

❏ 316	I'm So Glad/Se De Boom Run Dun	1955	7.50	15.00	30.00
❏ 318	Forever and a Day/Ride, Sally, Ride	1955	7.50	15.00	30.00

RCA

❏ 5224-7-RX	Love Is Strange/(I've Had) The Time of My Life	1987	—	—	3.00

—B-side by Bill Medley and Jennifer Warnes
RCA VICTOR

❏ 37-7877	Love Is the Only Thing/Love Lesson	1961	12.50	25.00	50.00

—"Compact Single 33" (small hole, plays at LP speed)

❏ 47-7403	To the Valley/Oh Yeah! Uh-Huh	1958	5.00	10.00	20.00
❏ 47-7774 [M]	Sweeter As the Days Go By/Mommy Out De Light	1960	3.75	7.50	15.00
❏ 47-7811 [M]	What Would I Do/This Is My Story	1960	5.00	10.00	20.00
❏ 47-7877	Love Is the Only Thing/Love Lesson	1961	3.75	7.50	15.00
❏ 47-8517	Let's Shake Some More/Gypsy	1965	3.00	6.00	12.00
❏ 47-8582	Fallin' in Love/From the Beginning of Time	1965	3.00	6.00	12.00
❏ 61-7774 [S]	Sweeter As the Days Go By/Mommy Out De Light	1960	10.00	20.00	40.00

—"Living Stereo" (large hole, plays at 45 rpm)

❏ 61-7811 [S]	What Would I Do/This Is My Story	1960	10.00	20.00	40.00

—"Living Stereo" (large hole, plays at 45 rpm)

❏ APAO-0080	Love Is Strange/Dearest	1973	—	3.00	6.00

STANG

❏ 5004	Rocky Raccoon/Souling with Mickey and Sylvia	1969	2.00	4.00	8.00
❏ 5047	Baby You're So Fine/Anytime You Want To	1973	—	3.00	6.00

VIK

❏ 0252	Love Is Strange/I'm Going Home	1957	7.50	15.00	30.00
❏ 0267	There Oughta Be a Law/Dearest	1957	6.25	12.50	25.00
❏ 0280	Two Shadows on Your Window/Love Will Make You Fail in School	1957	6.25	12.50	25.00
❏ 0290	Love Is a Treasure/Let's Have a Picnic	1957	6.25	12.50	25.00
❏ 0297	There'll Be No Backin' Out/Where Is My Honey	1957	6.25	12.50	25.00
❏ 0324	Rock and Stroll Room/Bewildered	1958	5.00	10.00	20.00
❏ 0334	It's You I Love/True, True Love	1958	5.00	10.00	20.00

WILLOW

❏ 23000	Baby, You're So Fine/Lovedrops	1961	3.75	7.50	15.00
❏ 23002	Darling (I Miss You So)/I'm Guilty	1961	3.75	7.50	15.00
❏ 23004	Since I Fell for You/He Gave Me Everything	1962	3.75	7.50	15.00
❏ 23006	Love Is Strange/Walking in the Rain	1962	3.75	7.50	15.00

7-Inch Extended Plays
GROOVE

❏ EGA-18	Love Is Strange/I'm Going Home//Walkin' in the Rain/No Good Lover	1957	37.50	75.00	150.00
❏ EGA-18 [PS]	Love Is Strange	1957	37.50	75.00	150.00

VIK

❏ 262	*There Oughta Be a Law/I'm So Glad/Dearest/Se De Boom Run Dun	1957	20.00	40.00	80.00
❏ 262 [PS]	Love Is Strange	1957	20.00	40.00	80.00

Albums
RCA CAMDEN

❏ CAL-863 [M]	Love Is Strange	1965	12.50	25.00	50.00
❏ CAS-863(e) [R]	Love Is Strange	1965	7.50	15.00	30.00

RCA VICTOR

❏ APM1-0327	Do It Again	1973	3.00	6.00	12.00

VIK

❏ LX-1102 [M]	New Sounds	1957	100.00	200.00	400.00

MIDDLETON, TONY
Also see THE WILLOWS.
45s
ABC-PARAMOUNT

❏ 10695	You Spoiled My Reputation/If I Could Write a Song	1965	7.50	15.00	30.00

ALFA

❏ 113	My Home Town/Please Take Me	1962	3.00	6.00	12.00

ALTO

❏ 2001	Untouchable/I Need You	1960	3.00	6.00	12.00

A&M

❏ 1084	Angela/Keep On Dancing	1969	5.00	10.00	20.00
❏ 1124	Harlem Lady/Sound of Goodbye	1969	3.75	7.50	15.00

BIG TOP

❏ 3037	Unchained Melody/Sweet Baby of Mine	1960	7.50	15.00	30.00

ELDORADO

❏ 508	First Taste of Love/Only My Heart	1957	7.50	15.00	30.00

GONE

❏ 5015	Let's Fall in Love/Say Yeah	1957	15.00	30.00	60.00

MALA

❏ 544	Out of This World/My Baby Likes to Boogaloo	1966	6.25	12.50	25.00

MGM

❏ 13493	Don't Ever Leave Me/To the Ends of the Earth	1966	10.00	20.00	40.00

MR. G

❏ 811	Let Me Down Easy (Part 1)/Let Me Down Easy (Part 2)	1968	3.00	6.00	12.00
❏ 815	Good Morning World/(B-side unknown)	1968	3.00	6.00	12.00

PHILIPS

❏ 40151	I Need You Tonight/Send Me Away	1963	3.00	6.00	12.00
❏ 40184	Too Hot to Handle/I Just Couldn't Help Myself	1964	3.00	6.00	12.00

ROULETTE

❏ 4345	Is It This or Is It That/I'm Gonna Try Love One More Time	1961	6.25	12.50	25.00

ROYAL FLUSH

❏ 102	Lady Fingers/A Garden in the Ghetto	1976	—	3.00	6.00

SAXONY

❏ 104	I'm On My Way/(B-side unknown)	1958	12.50	25.00	50.00

SCEPTER

❏ 12290	Border Song (Holy Moses)/Silliest People	1970	2.50	5.00	10.00

TOY

❏ 3803	Rock and Roll Lullaby/Sittin' in the Sunshine	1972	2.00	4.00	8.00

TRIUMPH

❏ 600	Count Your Blessings (See What Love Has Done)/I Just Want Somebody	1959	6.25	12.50	25.00
❏ 605	The Universe/Blackjack	1959	6.25	12.50	25.00

UNITED ARTISTS

❏ 410	Drifting/Memories Are Made of This	1962	3.75	7.50	15.00

MIDNIGHT STAR
45s
SOLAR

Number	Title (A Side/B Side)	Yr	VG	VG+	NM
❏ YB-11903	Make It Last/Follow the Path	1980	—	2.00	4.00
❏ YB-12035	Two in Love/You're the Star	1980	—	2.00	4.00
❏ YB-12221	I've Been Watching You/Searching for Love	1981	—	2.50	5.00
❏ B-44284	Snake in the Grass/Snake in the Grass (TV Mix)	1988	—	—	3.00
❏ 47933	I've Been Watching You/Searching for Love	1981	—	2.00	4.00
❏ 47947	Hold Out/I Won't Let You Be Lonely	1981	—	2.00	4.00
❏ 47948	Tuff/I Got What You Need	1981	—	2.00	4.00
❏ 48003	Can't Give You Up/Hold Out	1982	—	2.00	4.00
❏ 48012	Hot Spot/I Won't Let You Be Lonely	1982	—	2.00	4.00
❏ 68961	Love Song/(Instrumental)	1989	—	—	3.00
❏ 69472	Stay Here by My Side/Searching for Love	1987	—	—	3.00
❏ 69501	Engine No. 9/Searching for Love	1986	—	—	3.00
❏ 69525	Midas Touch/Searching for Love	1986	—	—	3.00
❏ 69547	Headlines/Headlines (Dub)	1986	—	—	3.00
❏ 69547 [PS]	Headlines/Headlines (Dub)	1986	—	2.00	4.00
❏ 69638	Body Snatchers/Curious	1985	—	—	3.00
❏ 69659	Scientific Love/Make Time (To Fall in Love)	1985	—	—	3.00
❏ 69684	Operator/Playmates	1984	—	—	3.00
❏ 69704	Night Rider/Slow Jam	1984	—	2.00	4.00
❏ 69753	No Parking (On the Dance Floor)/Feels So Good	1984	—	2.00	4.00
❏ 69790	Wet My Whistle/You Can't Stop Me	1983	—	2.00	4.00
❏ 69828	Freak-A-Zoid/Move Me	1983	—	2.00	4.00
❏ 69932	Victory/Love Is Alive	1982	—	2.00	4.00
❏ 70011	Freak-A-Zoid/Curious	1988	—	—	3.00
❏ 70027	Don't Rock the Boat/(B-side unknown)	1988	—	—	3.00
❏ 74002	90 Days (Same as Cash)/(Instrumental)	1989	—	—	3.00
❏ 74520	Luv-U-Up (Radio Edit)/(Instrumental)	1990	—	—	3.00

Albums
SOLAR

❏ BXL1-3491	The Beginning	1980	5.00	10.00	20.00
❏ 60145	Victory	1982	3.00	6.00	12.00
❏ 60241	No Parking on the Dance Floor	1983	2.50	5.00	10.00
❏ 60384	Planetary Invasion	1984	2.50	5.00	10.00
❏ 60454	Headlines	1986	2.50	5.00	10.00
❏ D1-72564	Midnight Star	1988	2.50	5.00	10.00

MIDNIGHTERS, THE
Also see HANK BALLARD AND THE MIDNIGHTERS; THE ROYALS (1).
45s
FEDERAL

❏ 12169	Work With Me Annie/Until I Die	1954	25.00	50.00	100.00

—Silver top label; as "The Midnighters (Formerly Known As the Royals)"

❏ 12169	Work With Me Annie/Until I Die	1954	10.00	20.00	40.00

—All-green label; as "The Midnighters (Formerly Known As the Royals)"

❏ 12177	Give It Up/That Woman	1954	20.00	40.00	80.00

—As "The Midnighters Formerly the Royals"

❏ 12185	Sexy Ways/Don't Say Your Last Goodbye	1954	20.00	40.00	80.00

—As "The Midnighters Formerly the Royals"

❏ 12195	Annie Had a Baby/She's the One	1954	15.00	30.00	60.00
❏ 12200	Annie's Aunt Fanny/Crazy Loving	1954	15.00	30.00	60.00
❏ 12202	Tell Them/Stingy Little Thing	1954	15.00	30.00	60.00
❏ 12205	She's the One/Moonrise	1955	15.00	30.00	60.00
❏ 12210	Ashamed of Myself/Ring-a-Ling-Ling	1955	15.00	30.00	60.00
❏ 12220	Why Are We Apart/Switchie, Witchie, Titchie	1955	15.00	30.00	60.00
❏ 12224	Henry's Got Flat Feet (Can't Dance No More)/Whatsoever You Do	1955	15.00	30.00	60.00
❏ 12227	It's Love Baby (24 Hours a Day)/Looka Here	1955	15.00	30.00	60.00
❏ 12230	Give It Up/That Woman	1955	15.00	30.00	60.00
❏ 12240	Rock and Roll Wedding/That House on the Hill	1955	15.00	30.00	60.00
❏ 12243	Don't Change Your Pretty Ways/We'll Never Meet Again	1955	15.00	30.00	60.00
❏ 12251	Partners for Life/Sweet Mama, Do Right	1956	15.00	30.00	60.00
❏ 12260	Rock Granny Roll/Open Up the Back Door	1956	15.00	30.00	60.00
❏ 12270	Tore Up Over You/Early One Morning	1956	12.50	25.00	50.00

Number	Title (A Side/B Side)	Yr	VG	VG+	NM
❑ 12285	I'll Be Home Some Day/Come On and Get It	1957	12.50	25.00	50.00
❑ 12288	Let Me Hold Your Hand/Oh Bah Baby	1957	12.50	25.00	50.00
❑ 12293	E Basta Cosi/In the Doorway Crying	1957	12.50	25.00	50.00
❑ 12299	Oh, So Happy/Is Your Love for Real	1957	10.00	20.00	40.00
❑ 12305	Let 'Em Roll/What Made You Change Your Mind	1957	10.00	20.00	40.00
❑ 12317	Stay By My Side/Daddy's Little Baby	1958	10.00	20.00	40.00
❑ 12339	Baby Please/Ow-Wow-Oo-Wee	1958	10.00	20.00	40.00

7-Inch Extended Plays

FEDERAL

Number	Title (A Side/B Side)	Yr	VG	VG+	NM
❑ 333	Work with Me Annie/Moonrise//Sexy Ways/Get It	1955	75.00	150.00	300.00
—Green label, silver top					
❑ 333	Work with Me Annie/Moonrise//Sexy Ways/Get It	1955	37.50	75.00	150.00
—All-green label					
❑ 333 [PS]	The Midnighters Sing Their Greatest Hits	1955	50.00	100.00	200.00
—Pink cover					
❑ 333 [PS]	The Midnighters Sing Their Greatest Hits	1955	50.00	100.00	200.00
—Purple cover					

Albums

FEDERAL

Number	Title (A Side/B Side)	Yr	VG	VG+	NM
❑ 295-90 [10]	Their Greatest Hits	1954	4000.	6000.	8000.
❑ 541 [M]	Their Greatest Hits	1955	375.00	750.00	1500.
—Red cover					
❑ 541 [M]	Their Greatest Hits	1955	250.00	500.00	1000.
—Yellow cover					
❑ 581 [M]	The Midnighters, Volume 2	1955	300.00	600.00	1200.

KING

Number	Title (A Side/B Side)	Yr	VG	VG+	NM
❑ 541 [M]	Their Greatest Jukebox Hits	1958	100.00	200.00	400.00
—Crownless black label, "King" is two inches wide on label					
❑ 541 [M]	Their Greatest Jukebox Hits	196?	75.00	150.00	300.00
—Crownless black label, "King" is three inches wide on label. Above two have a girl on the cover.					
❑ 541 [M]	Their Greatest Jukebox Hits	196?	50.00	100.00	200.00
—Reissue with Hank Ballard on cover					
❑ 581 [M]	The Midnighters, Volume 2	1958	75.00	150.00	300.00
—Crownless black label, "King" is two inches wide on label					
❑ 581 [M]	The Midnighters, Volume 2	196?	50.00	100.00	200.00
—Crownless black label, "King" is three inches wide on label					

MIGHTY CLOUDS OF JOY

12-Inch Singles

EPIC

Number	Title (A Side/B Side)	Yr	VG	VG+	NM
❑ 50693	Joy in These Changing Times/(Instrumental)	1979	3.00	6.00	12.00

45s

ABC

Number	Title (A Side/B Side)	Yr	VG	VG+	NM
❑ 12164	Mighty High/Touch My Soul	1976	—	2.00	4.00
❑ 12196	You Are So Beautiful/Everything Is All	1976	—	2.00	4.00
❑ 12241	There's Love in the World (Tell the Lonely People)/(B-side unknown)	1976	—	2.00	4.00
❑ 12281	God Is Not Dead/Music Is My Way of Life	1977	—	2.00	4.00
❑ 12322	Look on the Bright Side/(B-side unknown)	1978	—	2.00	4.00

ABC DUNHILL

Number	Title (A Side/B Side)	Yr	VG	VG+	NM
❑ 15012	Time/(B-side unknown)	1974	—	2.50	5.00
❑ 15025	Mighty Cloud of Joy/Everything Is Going Up	1974	—	2.50	5.00

EPIC

Number	Title (A Side/B Side)	Yr	VG	VG+	NM
❑ 50690	Joy in These Changing Times/We're Gonna Have a Good Time	1979	—	2.00	4.00
❑ 50691	I've Been in the Storm Too Long/We're Blessed	1979	—	2.00	4.00
❑ 50788	I Get a Blessing Every Day/Rainy Day Friend	1979	—	2.00	4.00
❑ 50875	What a Difference You've Made in My Life/We're Blessed	1980	—	2.00	4.00

MYRRH

Number	Title (A Side/B Side)	Yr	VG	VG+	NM
❑ 241	Glow Love/(B-side unknown)	1982	—	2.00	4.00

PEACOCK

Number	Title (A Side/B Side)	Yr	VG	VG+	NM
❑ 1823	Jesus Lead Us Safely/Ain't Got Long Here	1961	3.00	6.00	12.00
❑ 1839	I'll Be Alright/My Religion	1961	3.00	6.00	12.00
❑ 1857	Time Has Changed/I Love Jesus	1962	2.50	5.00	10.00
❑ 1869	Family Circle/None But the Righteous	1962	2.50	5.00	10.00
❑ 1895	Glory Hallelujah/Lord Hold My Hand	1962	2.50	5.00	10.00
❑ 1896	Nearer to Thee/You'll Never Know	1962	2.50	5.00	10.00
❑ 3025	I'll Go (Part 1)/I'll Go (Part 2)	1964	2.50	5.00	10.00
❑ 3050	A Friend in Jesus/Two Wings	1965	2.50	5.00	10.00
❑ 3064	He's Able/Swing Low	1965	2.50	5.00	10.00
❑ 3077	See How They Done My Lord/Look for Me in Heaven	1966	2.50	5.00	10.00
❑ 3080	Nobody Can Turn Me Around/Touch Me Lord	1966	2.50	5.00	10.00
❑ 3099	I'm Glad About It/Let Jesus Lead You	1966	2.50	5.00	10.00
❑ 3132	Somewhere Around God's Throne/The Holy Ghost	1967	2.00	4.00	8.00
❑ 3144	Pray for Me/Call Him Up	1968	2.00	4.00	8.00
❑ 3167	How Far Have I Strayed/Just to Behold His Face	1969	2.00	4.00	8.00
❑ 3175	In This World Alone/Why Do Men Treat the Lord	1970	2.00	4.00	8.00
❑ 3189	Heavy Load/I'll Be Alright Someday	1972	—	3.00	6.00

Albums

ABC

Number	Title (A Side/B Side)	Yr	VG	VG+	NM
❑ D-899	Kickin'	1975	2.50	5.00	10.00
❑ D-986	The Truth Is the Power	1976	2.50	5.00	10.00
❑ D-1038	Live and Direct	1977	2.50	5.00	10.00

ABC DUNHILL

Number	Title (A Side/B Side)	Yr	VG	VG+	NM
❑ DSX-50177	It's Time	1974	2.50	5.00	10.00

HOB

Number	Title (A Side/B Side)	Yr	VG	VG+	NM
❑ 288	"Live" Zion Songs	196?	3.75	7.50	15.00

KING

Number	Title (A Side/B Side)	Yr	VG	VG+	NM
❑ SG3-1107	Out Talking to Yourself	1970	3.75	7.50	15.00

MCA

Number	Title (A Side/B Side)	Yr	VG	VG+	NM
❑ 1091 [(2)]	The Very Best of Mighty Clouds of Joy	198?	2.50	5.00	10.00
❑ 28008	Family Circle	198?	2.00	4.00	8.00
—Reissue of Peacock 114					
❑ 28012	The Bright Side	198?	2.00	4.00	8.00
—Reissue of Peacock 121					
❑ 28017	Mighty Clouds of Joy At the Music Hall	198?	2.00	4.00	8.00
—Reissue of Peacock 134					
❑ 28019	The Best of Mighty Clouds of Joy	198?	2.00	4.00	8.00
—Reissue of Peacock 136					
❑ 28025	The Untouchables	198?	2.00	4.00	8.00
—Reissue of Peacock 151					
❑ 28028	Songs of Rev. Julius Cheeks and the Nightingales	198?	2.00	4.00	8.00
—Reissue of Peacock 163					
❑ 28030	God Bless America	198?	2.00	4.00	8.00
—Reissue of Peacock 170					
❑ 28032	Live at the Apollo	198?	2.00	4.00	8.00
—Reissue of Peacock 173					
❑ 28040	The Best of Mighty Clouds of Joy — Volume 2	198?	2.00	4.00	8.00

MYRRH

Number	Title (A Side/B Side)	Yr	VG	VG+	NM
❑ MSB-6663	Cloudburst	1980	2.50	5.00	10.00
❑ MSB-6681	The Truth Is the Power	1981	2.50	5.00	10.00
❑ MSB-6694	Miracle Man	1982	2.50	5.00	10.00
❑ MSB-6712	Request Line	1983	2.50	5.00	10.00
❑ WR-8121	Mighty Clouds Alive	1984	2.50	5.00	10.00
❑ WR-8122	Sing and Shout	1984	2.50	5.00	10.00

PEACOCK

Number	Title (A Side/B Side)	Yr	VG	VG+	NM
❑ 114	Family Circle	196?	5.00	10.00	20.00
❑ 121	The Bright Side	196?	5.00	10.00	20.00
❑ 134	Mighty Clouds of Joy At the Music Hall	196?	5.00	10.00	20.00
❑ 136	The Best of Mighty Clouds of Joy	196?	5.00	10.00	20.00
❑ 151	The Untouchables	196?	5.00	10.00	20.00
❑ 161	Out Talking to Yourself	196?	5.00	10.00	20.00
❑ 163	Songs of Rev. Julius Cheeks and the Nightingales	196?	5.00	10.00	20.00
❑ 170	God Bless America	1971	3.75	7.50	15.00
❑ 173	Live at the Apollo	1972	3.75	7.50	15.00

PRIORITY

Number	Title (A Side/B Side)	Yr	VG	VG+	NM
❑ RV 37707	Changing Times	1982	2.50	5.00	10.00

MIGHTY FAITH INCREASERS, THE

45s

BETHLEHEM

Number	Title (A Side/B Side)	Yr	VG	VG+	NM
❑ 3072	Lord, Come See About Me/Temptation	1963	3.00	6.00	12.00

Albums

KING

Number	Title (A Side/B Side)	Yr	VG	VG+	NM
❑ 806 [M]	The Mighty Faith Increasers with Willa Dorsey	1962	37.50	75.00	150.00
❑ 814 [M]	A Festival of Spiritual Songs	1962	37.50	75.00	150.00

MIGHTY MARVELOWS, THE

See THE MARVELOWS.

MILBURN, AMOS

45s

ALADDIN

Number	Title (A Side/B Side)	Yr	VG	VG+	NM
❑ 3014	Chicken Shack Boogie/It Took a Long, Long Time	1950	50.00	100.00	200.00
—78 originally released in 1948					
❑ 3018	Bewildered/A and M Blues	1950	30.00	60.00	120.00
—78 originally released in 1948					
❑ 3068	Bad, Bad Whiskey/I'm Going to Tell My Mama	1950	125.00	250.00	500.00
—Note: Amos Milburn singles on Aladdin before 3068 are unconfirmed on 45 rpm except those listed					
❑ 3080	Let's Rock a While/Tears, Tears, Tears	1951	20.00	40.00	80.00
❑ 3090	Everybody Clap Hands/That Was Your Last Mistake	1951	20.00	40.00	80.00
❑ 3093	Ain't Nothin' Shaking/Just One More Drink	1951	20.00	40.00	80.00
❑ 3105	She's Gone Again/Boogie Woogie	1951	20.00	40.00	80.00
❑ 3124	Thinking and Drinking/Trouble in Mind	1952	20.00	40.00	80.00
❑ 3125	Flying Home/Put Something in My Hand	1952	20.00	40.00	80.00
❑ 3133	I Won't Be Your Fool Anymore/Roll Mr. Jelly	1952	20.00	40.00	80.00
❑ 3146	Button Your Lip/Everything I Do Is Wrong	1952	20.00	40.00	80.00
❑ 3150	Kiss Me Again/Greyhound	1952	20.00	40.00	80.00
❑ 3159	Rock, Rock, Rock/Boo Hoo	1953	15.00	30.00	60.00
❑ 3164	Let Me Go Home, Whiskey/Three Times a Fool	1953	15.00	30.00	60.00
❑ 3168	Long, Long Day/Please Mr. Johnson	1953	15.00	30.00	60.00
❑ 3197	One Scotch, One Bourbon, One Beer/What Can I Do	1953	25.00	50.00	100.00
❑ 3218	Good, Good Whiskey/Let's Have a Party	1954	20.00	40.00	80.00
❑ 3226	How Could You Hurt Me So/Rocky Mountain	1954	15.00	30.00	60.00
❑ 3240	Milk and Water/I'm Still a Fool for You	1954	15.00	30.00	60.00
❑ 3248	Glory of Love/Baby, Baby All the Time	1954	15.00	30.00	60.00
❑ 3253	Vicious, Vicious Vodka/I Done Done It	1954	15.00	30.00	60.00
❑ 3269	That's It/One, Two, Three Everybody	1954	15.00	30.00	60.00
❑ 3281	Why Don't You Do Right/I Love You Anyway	1955	10.00	20.00	40.00
❑ 3293	All Is Well/My Happiness Depends on You	1955	10.00	20.00	40.00
❑ 3306	House Party/I Guess I'll Go	1955	10.00	20.00	40.00
❑ 3320	French Fried Potatoes and Ketchup/I Need Someone	1956	10.00	20.00	40.00
❑ 3332	Chicken Shack Boogie/Juice, Juice, Juice	1956	10.00	20.00	40.00
❑ 3340	Girl of My Dreams/Everyday of the Week	1956	10.00	20.00	40.00
❑ 3363	Rum and Coca-Cola/Soft Pollow	1957	7.50	15.00	30.00
❑ 3370	Greyhound/Dear Angel	1957	7.50	15.00	30.00
❑ 3383	Thinking of You Baby/If I Could Be with You	1957	7.50	15.00	30.00

IMPERIAL

Number	Title (A Side/B Side)	Yr	VG	VG+	NM
❑ 5831	I'm Still a Fool for You/Rocky Mountain	1962	3.00	6.00	12.00

KING

Number	Title (A Side/B Side)	Yr	VG	VG+	NM
❑ 5405	Christmas (Comes But Once a Year)/Please Come Home for Christmas	1960	3.00	6.00	12.00
—B-side by Charles Brown					

Number	Title (A Side/B Side)	Yr	VG	VG+	NM
❏ 5464	I Wanna Go Back Home/My Little Baby	1961	3.00	6.00	12.00
—With Charles Brown					
❏ 5483	My Sweet Baby's Love/Heartaches That Make You Cry	1961	3.00	6.00	12.00
❏ 5529	Movin' Time/The Hammer	1961	3.00	6.00	12.00
❏ 6095	Whiz O Shoo Pepi/Same Old Thing	1967	2.50	5.00	10.00
MOTOWN					
❏ 1038	I'll Make It Up to You Somehow/My Baby Gave Me Another Chance	1963	7.50	15.00	30.00
❏ 1046	My Daily Prayer/(B-side unknown)	1963	7.50	15.00	30.00
UNITED ARTISTS					
❏ 0149	Chicken Shack Boogie/Revitalized	1973	—	2.00	4.00
—"Silver Spotlight Series" reissue					

78s

ALADDIN

Number	Title (A Side/B Side)	Yr	VG	VG+	NM
❏ 159	After Midnight/Amos' Blues	194?	12.50	25.00	50.00
❏ 160	My Baby's Boogin'/Darling How Long	194?	12.50	25.00	50.00
❏ 161	Down the Road a Piece/Don't Beg Me	194?	12.50	25.00	50.00
❏ 174	Operation Boogie (Blues)/Cinch Blues	194?	12.50	25.00	50.00
❏ 191	Money Hustlin' Woman/Real Gone	194?	12.50	25.00	50.00
❏ 201	My Love Is Limited/Blues at Sundown	194?	12.50	25.00	50.00
❏ 202	Sad and Blue/That's My Choice	194?	12.50	25.00	50.00
❏ 206	Train Time Blues/Bye Bye Boogie	194?	12.50	25.00	50.00
❏ 211	I Still Love You/Pool Playing Blues	194?	12.50	25.00	50.00
❏ 3014	Chicken Shack Boogie/It Took a Long, Long Time	1948	25.00	50.00	100.00
❏ 3018	Bewildered/A and M Blues	1948	15.00	30.00	60.00
❏ 3023	Hold Me Baby/Jitterbug Parade	1949	15.00	30.00	60.00
❏ 3026	In the Middle of the Night/Pot Luck Boogie	1949	15.00	30.00	60.00
❏ 3032	Roomin' House Boogie/Empty Arms Blues	1949	15.00	30.00	60.00
❏ 3037	Let's Make Christmas Merry, Baby/Bow Wow	1949	15.00	30.00	60.00
❏ 3038	Real Pretty Mama Blues/Drifting Blues	1949	15.00	30.00	60.00
❏ 3043	I'm Just a Fool in Love/How Long Has This Train Been Gone	1950	12.50	25.00	50.00
❏ 3049	Walking Blues/Johnson Rag	1950	12.50	25.00	50.00
❏ 3056	Square Dance Boogie/Anybody's Blues	1950	12.50	25.00	50.00
❏ 3058	I Love Her/Birmingham Bounce	1950	—	—	—
—Canceled					
❏ 3059	Hard Luck Blues/Ten Years of Fortune	1950	12.50	25.00	50.00
❏ 3064	Sax Shack Boogie/Remember	1950	12.50	25.00	50.00
❏ 3068	Bad, Bad Whiskey/I'm Going to Tell My Mama	1950	15.00	30.00	60.00
❏ 3068	Bad, Bad Whiskey/I'm Going to Tell My Mama	1950	150.00	300.00	600.00
—Green wax					
❏ 3080	Let's Rock a While/Tears, Tears, Tears	1951	10.00	20.00	40.00
❏ 3090	Everybody Clap Hands/That Was Your Last Mistake	1951	10.00	20.00	40.00
❏ 3093	Ain't Nothin' Shaking/Just One More Drink	1951	10.00	20.00	40.00
❏ 3105	She's Gone Again/Boogie Woogie	1951	10.00	20.00	40.00
❏ 3124	Thinking and Drinking/Trouble in Mind	1952	10.00	20.00	40.00
❏ 3125	Flying Home/Put Something in My Hand	1952	10.00	20.00	40.00
❏ 3133	I Won't Be Your Fool Anymore/Roll Mr. Jelly	1952	10.00	20.00	40.00
❏ 3146	Button Your Lip/Everything I Do Is Wrong	1952	10.00	20.00	40.00
❏ 3150	Kiss Me Again/Greyhound	1952	10.00	20.00	40.00
❏ 3159	Rock, Rock, Rock/Boo Hoo	1953	7.50	15.00	30.00
❏ 3164	Let Me Go Home, Whiskey/Three Times a Fool	1953	7.50	15.00	30.00
❏ 3168	Long, Long Day/Please Mr. Johnson	1953	7.50	15.00	30.00
❏ 3197	One Scotch, One Bourbon, One Beer/What Can I Do	1953	10.00	20.00	40.00
❏ 3218	Good, Good Whiskey/Let's Have a Party	1954	10.00	20.00	40.00
❏ 3226	How Could You Hurt Me So/Rocky Mountain	1954	7.50	15.00	30.00
❏ 3240	Milk and Water/I'm Still a Fool for You	1954	7.50	15.00	30.00
❏ 3248	Glory of Love/Baby, Baby All the Time	1954	7.50	15.00	30.00
❏ 3253	Vicious, Vicious Vodka/I Done Done It	1954	7.50	15.00	30.00
❏ 3269	That's It/One, Two, Three Everybody	1954	7.50	15.00	30.00
❏ 3281	Why Don't You Do Right/I Love You Anyway	1955	7.50	15.00	30.00
❏ 3293	All Is Well/My Happiness Depends on You	1955	7.50	15.00	30.00
❏ 3306	House Party/I Guess I'll Go	1955	7.50	15.00	30.00
❏ 3320	French Fried Potatoes and Ketchup/I Need Someone	1956	10.00	20.00	40.00
❏ 3332	Chicken Shack Boogie/Juice, Juice, Juice	1956	10.00	20.00	40.00
❏ 3340	Girl of My Dreams/Everyday of the Week	1956	10.00	20.00	40.00
❏ 3363	Rum and Coca-Cola/Soft Pollow	1957	10.00	20.00	40.00
❏ 3370	Greyhound/Dear Angel	1957	10.00	20.00	40.00
❏ 3383	Thinking of You Baby/If I Could Be with You	1957	10.00	20.00	40.00

Albums

ALADDIN

Number	Title (A Side/B Side)	Yr	VG	VG+	NM
❏ LP-704 [10]	Rockin' the Boogie	1955	200.00	4000.	8000.
—Red vinyl, blue cover					
❏ LP-704 [10]	Rockin' the Boogie	1955	1000.	2000.	4000.
—Black vinyl					
❏ LP-810 [M]	Rockin' the Boogie	1958	—	—	—
—Canceled					
IMPERIAL					
❏ LP-9176 [M]	Million Sellers	1962	125.00	250.00	500.00
MOTOWN					
❏ 608 [M]	The Return of Amos Milburn, "The" Blues Boss	1963	225.00	450.00	900.00
SCORE					
❏ LP-4012 [M]	Let's Have a Party	1957	200.00	400.00	800.00
❏ LP-4035 [M]	Amos Milburn Sings the Blues	1958	—	—	—
—Canceled					

MILBURN, AMOS/WYNONIE HARRIS/ETC.

Albums

ALADDIN

Number	Title (A Side/B Side)	Yr	VG	VG+	NM
❏ LP-703 [10]	Party After Hours	1955	2000.	4000.	8000.
—Red vinyl, blue cover					
❏ LP-703 [10]	Party After Hours	1955	1000.	2000.	4000.
—Black vinyl					

MILES, BUDDY

45s

ATLANTIC

Number	Title (A Side/B Side)	Yr	VG	VG+	NM
❏ 3852 [DJ]	Can You Hold Me (same on both sides)	1981	—	2.00	4.00
—May be promo only					
❏ 4006 [DJ]	Sunshine of Your Love (same on both sides)	1982	—	2.00	4.00
—May be promo only					
CASABLANCA					
❏ 839	Rockin' and Rollin' on the Streets of Hollywood/Livin' in the Right Space	1975	—	2.00	4.00
❏ 849	Nasty Disposition/Do It to Me	1975	—	2.00	4.00
❏ 859	Reuben "The Hurricane"/Where You Gonna Run To Lady	1976	—	2.00	4.00
COLUMBIA					
❏ 10030	Pain/We Get Love	1974	—	2.50	5.00
❏ 10089	Pull Yourself Together/I'm Just a Kiss Away	1975	—	2.50	5.00
❏ 45826	Love Affair/Life Is What You Make It	1973	—	2.50	5.00
❏ 45876	Elvira/Hear No Evil	1973	—	2.50	5.00
❏ 45969	Crazy Love/Thinking of You	1973	—	2.50	5.00
MERCURY					
❏ 72860	The Train (Part 1)/The Train (Part 2)	1968	2.00	4.00	8.00
❏ 72903	This Lady/'69 Freedom Special	1969	2.00	4.00	8.00
❏ 72945	Memphis Train/My Chant	1969	—	3.00	6.00
❏ 73008	Them Changes/Spot on the Wall	1970	—	3.00	6.00
❏ 73086	Down By the River/Hearts Delight	1970	—	3.00	6.00
❏ 73119	Dreams/Your Feeling Is Mine	1970	—	3.00	6.00
❏ 73159	We Got to Live Together (Part 1)/We Got to Live Together (Part 2)	1970	—	3.00	6.00
❏ 73170	Runaway Child/(B-side unknown)	1970	—	3.00	6.00
❏ 73205	Wholesale Love/That's the Way Life Is	1971	—	2.50	5.00
❏ 73238	Them Changes/The Way I Feel Tonight	1971	—	2.50	5.00
❏ 73261	Give Away None of My Love/Take It Off Him and Put It On Me	1972	—	2.50	5.00
❏ 73277	Life Is What You Make It (Part 1)/Life Is What You Make It (Part 2)	1972	—	2.50	5.00

Albums

ATLANTIC

Number	Title (A Side/B Side)	Yr	VG	VG+	NM
❏ SD 2-4000 [(2)]	Sneak Attack	1982	3.00	6.00	12.00
CASABLANCA					
❏ NBLP 7019	More Miles Per Gallon	1975	2.50	5.00	10.00
❏ NBLP 7024	Bicentennial Gathering of the Tribes	1976	2.50	5.00	10.00
COLUMBIA					
❏ CQ 32048 [Q]	Chapter VII	1973	5.00	10.00	20.00
❏ KC 32048	Chapter VII	1973	3.00	6.00	12.00
❏ CQ 32694 [Q]	Booger Bear	1973	5.00	10.00	20.00
❏ KC 32694	Booger Bear	1973	3.00	6.00	12.00
❏ KC 33089	All the Faces	1974	3.00	6.00	12.00
MERCURY					
❏ SRM-1-608	A Message to the People	1971	3.75	7.50	15.00
❏ SRM-2-7500 [(2)]	Buddy Miles Live	1971	3.75	7.50	15.00
❏ SR-61196	Expressway to Your Skull	1968	5.00	10.00	20.00
❏ SR-61222	Electric Church	1969	5.00	10.00	20.00
❏ SR-61280	Them Changes	1970	3.75	7.50	15.00
❏ SR-61313	We Got to Live Together	1970	3.75	7.50	15.00

MILLER, BOBBY

45s

CONSTELLATION

Number	Title (A Side/B Side)	Yr	VG	VG+	NM
❏ 103	The Big Question/I Don't Believe You	1963	5.00	10.00	20.00
❏ 111	The Big Question/Uncle Willie Time	1963	5.00	10.00	20.00
❏ 116	Whoa (She's All Mine)/Take It in Stride	1964	5.00	10.00	20.00
❏ 127	This Is My Dance/Simon Says	1964	5.00	10.00	20.00
❏ 134	I'm For the Girls/Love Take the Case	1964	7.50	15.00	30.00

MILLER SISTERS, THE

45s

ACME

Number	Title (A Side/B Side)	Yr	VG	VG+	NM
❏ 111	Let's Start Anew/The Flip Skip	1957	12.50	25.00	50.00
❏ 717	You Made Me a Promise/Crazy Billboard Song	1957	10.00	20.00	40.00
❏ 721	Let's Start Anew/The Flip Skip	1958	10.00	20.00	40.00
EMBER					
❏ 1004	Guess Who/How Am I to Know	1956	7.50	15.00	30.00
FLIP					
❏ 504	Someday You Will Pay/I Knew You Would	1955	50.00	100.00	200.00
GLODIS					
❏ 1003	Pop Your Finger/You Got to Reap What You Sow	1961	3.75	7.50	15.00
GMC					
❏ 10006	I'm Telling It Like It Is/Until You Come Home I'll Walk Alone	1967	2.50	5.00	10.00
HERALD					
❏ 455	Hippity Ha/Until You're Mine	1955	12.50	25.00	50.00
❏ 527	Hippity Ha/Until You're Mine	1958	5.00	10.00	20.00
HULL					
❏ 718	Please Don't Leave/Do You Wanna Go	1956	10.00	20.00	40.00

Number	Title (A Side/B Side)	Yr	VG	VG+	NM
❑ 736	Just Wait and See/Black Pepper	1960	6.25	12.50	25.00
—B-side by Leo Price and Band					
❑ 750	Roll Back the Rug (And Twist)/Don't You Forget	1962	6.25	12.50	25.00
❑ 752	I Cried All Night/Hully Gully Reel	1962	5.00	10.00	20.00
MILLER					
❑ 1140	Oh Lover/Remember That	1960	5.00	10.00	20.00
❑ 1141	Pony Dance/Give Me Some Old Fashioned Love	1960	5.00	10.00	20.00
❑ 1143	Please Mr. D.J./(B-side unknown)	1960	5.00	10.00	20.00
ONYX					
❑ 507	Sugar Candy/My Own	1957	12.50	25.00	50.00
RAYNA					
❑ 5001	I Miss You So/Dance Little Sister	1962	3.75	7.50	15.00
❑ 5004	Oh Why/Walk On	1962	3.75	7.50	15.00
RIVERSIDE					
❑ 4535	Dance Close/Tell Him	1962	5.00	10.00	20.00
ROULETTE					
❑ 4491	Baby Your Baby/Silly Girl	1963	3.00	6.00	12.00
STARDUST					
❑ 3001	Feel Good/Cooncha	1964	2.50	5.00	10.00
SUN					
❑ 230	There's No Right Way to Do Me Wrong/You Can Tell Me	1956	12.50	25.00	50.00
❑ 255	Finders Keepers/Ten Cats Down	1956	12.50	25.00	50.00
❑ 504	Someday You Will Pay/I Knew You Would	1955	37.50	75.00	150.00
YORKTOWN					
❑ 75	Looking Over My Life/Si Senor	1965	2.50	5.00	10.00
MILLINDER, LUCKY					
45s					
KING					
❑ 4449	Chew Tobacco Rag/Georgia Rose	1951	15.00	30.00	60.00
❑ 4453	I'm Waiting Just for You/Bongo Boogie	1951	15.00	30.00	60.00
❑ 4476	The Grape Vine/No One Else Could Be	1951	15.00	30.00	60.00
❑ 4496	The Right Kind of Love/It's Been a Long, Long Time	1951	15.00	30.00	60.00
❑ 4534	Ram-Bunk-Shush/Loaded with Love	1952	15.00	30.00	60.00
❑ 4545	When I Have You My Love/Please Be Careful	1952	25.00	50.00	100.00
❑ 4557	Lord Knows I Tried/Heavy Sugar	1952	25.00	50.00	100.00
❑ 4571	Backslider's Ball/Please Be Careful	1952	25.00	50.00	100.00
❑ 4792	It's a Sad, Sad Feeling/Ow	1955	20.00	40.00	80.00
—With the Admirals					
❑ 4803	Goody Goody Love/I'm Here, Love	1955	7.50	15.00	30.00
❑ 5240	Heavy Sugar/Honeydripper	1959	3.00	6.00	12.00
RCA VICTOR					
❑ 47-2961	Tomorrow/I Ain't Got Nothin' to Lose	1949	12.50	25.00	50.00
❑ 47-3005	Awful Natural/In the Middle of the Night	1949	12.50	25.00	50.00
❑ 47-3128	I'll Never Be Free/Journey's End	1949	12.50	25.00	50.00
❑ 50-0054	D Natural Blues/Little Girl, Don't Cry	1949	15.00	30.00	60.00
—Gray label, orange vinyl					
❑ 50-0088	Let It Be/Sweet Slumber	1950	12.50	25.00	50.00
WARWICK					
❑ 582	Big Fat Mama/Slide My Trombone	1960	3.00	6.00	12.00
78s					
DECCA					
❑ 3956	Slide, Mr. Trombone/Rock, Daniel	1941	6.25	12.50	25.00
❑ 4041	Big Fat Mama/Trouble in Mind	1941	6.25	12.50	25.00
❑ 4099	How About That Mess?/Let Me Off Uptown	1942	6.25	12.50	25.00
❑ 4146	Hey Huss/Ride, Red, Ride	1942	6.25	12.50	25.00
❑ 4261	We're Gonna Have to Slap the Dirty Little Jap/Fightin' Doug MacArthur	1942	6.25	12.50	25.00
❑ 18353	Savoy/Rock Me	1942	5.00	10.00	20.00
❑ 18386	Shout, Sister, Shout/I Want a Tall Skinny Papa	1942	5.00	10.00	20.00
❑ 18496	When the Lights Go On Again (All Over the World)/That's All	1942	5.00	10.00	20.00
❑ 18529	Apollo Jump/Are You Ready?	1943	5.00	10.00	20.00
❑ 18569	Sweet Slumber/Don't Cry Baby	1943	5.00	10.00	20.00
❑ 18569	Sweet Slumber/Don't Cry, Baby	1943	5.00	10.00	20.00
❑ 18609	Hurry, Hurry/I Can't See for Lookin'	1944	5.00	10.00	20.00
❑ 18674	Who Threw the Whiskey in the Well/Shipyard Social Function	1945	5.00	10.00	20.00
❑ 18835	There's Good Blues Tonight/Chittlin' Time	1946	5.00	10.00	20.00
❑ 18867	Shorty's Got to Go/Some Day	1946	5.00	10.00	20.00
❑ 23825	More, More, More/How Big Can You Get, Little Man?	1947	3.75	7.50	15.00
❑ 23949	You Can't Put Out a Fire/The Spider and the Fly	1947	3.75	7.50	15.00
❑ 24384	Don't Hesitate Too Long/Tonight He Sailed Again	1948	3.75	7.50	15.00
❑ 24495	Fare Thee Well, Denim Jones/Berserk Boogie	1948	3.75	7.50	15.00
❑ 48053	Big Fat Mama/Trouble in Mind	1947	5.00	10.00	20.00
❑ 48057	Shout, Sister, Shout/That's All	1947	5.00	10.00	20.00
KING					
❑ 4379	My Little Baby/Let It Roll Again	1950	6.25	12.50	25.00
❑ 4398	Clap Your Hands/Who Said Shorty Wasn't Coming Back	1950	6.25	12.50	25.00
❑ 4436	The Jumping Jack/Mr. Trumpet Man	1951	6.25	12.50	25.00
❑ 4449	Chew Tobacco Rag/Georgia Rose	1951	6.25	12.50	25.00
❑ 4453	I'm Waiting Just for You/Bongo Boogie	1951	6.25	12.50	25.00
❑ 4476	The Grape Vine/No One Else Could Be	1951	6.25	12.50	25.00
❑ 4496	The Right Kind of Love/It's Been a Long, Long Time	1951	6.25	12.50	25.00
❑ 4534	Ram-Bunk-Shush/Loaded with Love	1952	6.25	12.50	25.00
❑ 4545	When I Have You My Love/Please Be Careful	1952	6.25	12.50	25.00
❑ 4557	Lord Knows I Tried/Heavy Sugar	1952	6.25	12.50	25.00
❑ 4571	Backslider's Ball/Please Be Careful	1952	6.25	12.50	25.00

Number	Title (A Side/B Side)	Yr	VG	VG+	NM
❑ 4792	It's a Sad, Sad Feeling/Ow	1955	12.50	25.00	50.00
—With the Admirals					
❑ 4803	Goody Good Love/I'm Here, Love	1955	7.50	15.00	30.00
RCA VICTOR					
❑ 20-3351	D Natural Blues/Little Girl, Don't Cry	1949	5.00	10.00	20.00
❑ 20-3496	Tomorrow/I Ain't Got Nothin' to Lose	1949	5.00	10.00	20.00
❑ 20-3622	I'll Never Be Free/Journey's End	1949	5.00	10.00	20.00
❑ 22-0088	Let It Be/Sweet Slumber	1950	5.00	10.00	20.00
MILLS, STEPHANIE					
12-Inch Singles					
20TH CENTURY					
❑ TCD-86	Whatcha Gonna Do with My Lovin'/Put Your Body In It	1979	3.75	7.50	15.00
❑ TCD-99	You Can Get Over (9:00)/Deeper Inside Your Love	1979	3.75	7.50	15.00
❑ TCD-106	Sweet Sensation (Long Version 6:26)/Wish That You Were Mine	1980	2.50	5.00	10.00
❑ TCD-110	Sweet Sensation (6:26)/Wish That You Were Mine (4:33)	1980	3.00	6.00	12.00
❑ TCD-2460	Never Knew Love Like This Before/Still Mine	1980	2.00	4.00	8.00
❑ TCD-2501	Top of My List/Magic	1981	2.00	4.00	8.00
CASABLANCA					
❑ NBD 20244	Last Night (same on both sides)	1982	—	3.50	7.00
❑ 810337-1	You Can't Run from My Love (7:25) (4:24)	1983	3.00	6.00	12.00
❑ 814168-1	Pilot Error (Club Mix 6:20) (Album Version 5:07)	1983	2.00	4.00	8.00
❑ 880180-1	The Medicine Song (Vocal 6:30)/(Dub 5:49)	1984	—	3.50	7.00
❑ 880445-1	Edge of the Razor (Dance Mix) (Dub Mix)/Rough Trade	1984	2.00	4.00	8.00
MCA					
❑ MCA8P-2348	[DJ]All Day, All Night (3:59) (4:44)	1992	2.50	5.00	10.00
❑ MCA8P-2486	[DJ]All Day, All Night (Radio Edit 3:59) (Soulpower Radio Mix 3:48) (Stephanie N Tha House Mix 4:14)	1992	3.00	6.00	12.00
❑ MCA8P-2528	[DJ]Never Do You Wrong (Remix Radio Version 4:10) (Remix Dub 6:42) (House Club Mix 6:30)/(Dark Stupid Dub 5:35) (Club Mix #2 5:54) (Drumapella 5:39) (House Instrumental 5:05)	1993	2.00	4.00	8.00
❑ L33-17076	[DJ]Stand Back (Extended Version) (Radio Edit) (Instrumental) (Acapella) (Bonus Beats)	1985	2.50	5.00	10.00
❑ L33-17097	[DJ]I Have Learned to Respect the Power of Love (same on both sides)	1985	2.50	5.00	10.00
❑ L33-17110	[DJ]I Have Learned to Respect the Power of Love (4 versions)	1986	2.00	4.00	8.00
❑ L33-17130	[DJ]Rising Desire (same on both sides)	1986	2.00	4.00	8.00
❑ L33-18107	[DJ]Comfort of a Man (3 versions)/Love Hasn't Been Easy on Me	1990	2.50	5.00	10.00
❑ L33-18343	[DJ]Real Love (Extended Vocal Version) (LP Version) (Instrumental)	1990	2.00	4.00	8.00
❑ L33-18370	[DJ]Real Love (Remix Vocal) (Tell It Like It Is) (Radio Edit) (Instrumental) (Interlude)	1990	3.75	7.50	15.00
❑ 23564	Bit by Bit (3 versions)	1985	2.00	4.00	8.00
❑ 23598	Stand Back (Extended Version) (Radio Edit) (Instrumental)	1985	2.00	4.00	8.00
❑ 23644	Rising Desire/I Have Learned to Respect the Power of Love	1986	2.00	4.00	8.00
❑ 23674	Time of Your Life (Club) (Radio Edit) (Instrumental) (Acappella) (Bonus Beats)	1986	2.00	4.00	8.00
❑ 23740	I Feel Good All Over (unknown versions)	1987	2.50	5.00	10.00
❑ 23774	(You're Puttin') A Rush on Me (Extended Version) (Rushapella) (Bonus Beats)	1987	2.50	5.00	10.00
❑ 23805	Secret Lady (5:24) (Instrumental)	1987	—	3.50	7.00
❑ 23887	If I Were Your Woman (Vocal) (Suite)	1988	—	3.50	7.00
❑ 24036	Real Love (unknown versions)	1990	2.00	4.00	8.00
❑ 54503	All Day, All Night (Soulpower Mix) (12" Mix) (Crazy Dane Mix)	1992	2.00	4.00	8.00
❑ 54579	Never Do You Wrong (Remix Dub) (House Dub) (Dark Stupid Dub)	1983	3.00	6.00	12.00
45s					
20TH CENTURY					
❑ 2403	Whatcha Gonna Do with My Lovin'/Starlight	1979	—	2.00	4.00
❑ 2427	You Can Get Over/Better Than Ever	1979	—	2.00	4.00
❑ 2449	Sweet Sensation/Wish That You Were Mine	1980	—	2.00	4.00
❑ 2449 [PS]	Sweet Sensation/Wish That You Were Mine	1980	—	2.50	5.00
❑ 2460	Never Knew Love Like This Before/Still Mine	1980	—	2.00	4.00
❑ 2492	Two Hearts/I Just Wanna Stay	1981	—	2.00	4.00
—A-side with Teddy Pendergrass					
❑ 2506	Night Games/Magic	1981	—	2.00	4.00
ABC					
❑ 12051	You Do It to Me/Movin' in the Right Direction	1975	2.00	4.00	8.00
CASABLANCA					
❑ 2352	Last Night/Wailin'	1982	—	2.00	4.00
❑ 2354	Keep Away Girls/True Love Don't Come Easy	1982	—	2.00	4.00
❑ 810336-7	You Can't Run From My Love/'Ole Love	1983	—	2.00	4.00
❑ 814142-7	Pilot Error/His Name Is Michael	1983	—	2.00	4.00
❑ 814747-7	How Come U Don't Call Me Anymore?/Here I Am	1983	—	2.00	4.00
❑ 880180-7	The Medicine Song/(Instrumental)	1984	—	2.00	4.00
❑ 880445-7	Edge of the Razor/Rough Trade	1984	—	2.00	4.00
❑ 880662-7	Give It Half a Chance/In My Life	1985	—	2.00	4.00
COLLECTABLES					
❑ 4318	Never Knew Love Like This Before/Whatcha Gonna Do with My Lovin'	199?	—	—	3.00
❑ 4354	Sweet Sensation/The Medicine Song	199?	—	—	3.00
❑ 90182	I Feel Good All Over/Home	199?	—	—	3.00

M

MILLS BROTHERS, THE

Number	Title (A Side/B Side)	Yr	VG	VG+	NM
MCA					
❑ S45-17117 [DJ]	I Have Learned to Respect the Power of Love (same on both sides)	1986	—	2.50	5.00
❑ 52617	Bit by Bit/Exotic Skates	1985	—	—	3.00
❑ 52617 [PS]	Bit by Bit/Exotic Skates	1985	—	—	3.00
❑ 52731	Stand Back/I Have Learned to Respect the Power of Love	1985	—	2.00	4.00
❑ 52731 [PS]	Stand Back/I Have Learned to Respect the Power of Love	1985	—	2.00	4.00
❑ 52799	I Have Learned to Respect the Power of Love/ Stand Back	1986	—	—	3.00
❑ 52799 [PS]	I Have Learned to Respect the Power of Love/ Stand Back	1985	—	—	3.00
❑ 52843	Rising Desire/Under Pressure	1986	—	—	3.00
❑ 52843 [PS]	Rising Desire/Under Pressure	1986	—	—	3.00
❑ 53056	I Feel Good All Over/(Instrumental)	1987	—	—	3.00
❑ 53056 [PS]	I Feel Good All Over/(Instrumental)	1987	—	—	3.00
❑ 53151	(You're Puttin') A Rush on Me/(Instrumental)	1987	—	—	3.00
❑ 53151 [PS]	(You're Puttin') A Rush on Me/(Instrumental)	1987	—	—	3.00
❑ 53209	Secret Lady/(Instrumental)	1987	—	—	3.00
❑ 53209 [PS]	Secret Lady/(Instrumental)	1987	—	—	3.00
❑ 53275	If I Were Your Woman/(Instrumental)	1988	—	—	3.00
❑ 53624	Something in the Way (You Make Me Feel)/Love Hasn't Been Easy on Me	1989	—	—	3.00
❑ 53712	Home/Love Hasn't Been Easy on Me	1989	—	—	3.00
❑ 53769	Comfort of a Man/Love Hasn't Been Easy on Me	1990	—	2.00	4.00
❑ 54573	Never Do You Wrong (Radio Version)/(Remix Radio Version)	1993	—	2.00	4.00
❑ 79031	Real Love/(Instrumental)	1990	—	2.00	4.00
MOTOWN					
❑ 1382	This Empty Place/I See You for the First Time	1975	2.00	4.00	8.00
PARAMOUNT					
❑ 0290	I Knew It Was Love/The Passion and the Pain	1974	2.00	4.00	8.00

Albums

Number	Title (A Side/B Side)	Yr	VG	VG+	NM
20TH CENTURY					
❑ T-583	Whatcha Gonna Do ... With My Lovin'?	1979	2.50	5.00	10.00
❑ T-603	Sweet Sensation	1980	2.50	5.00	10.00
❑ T-700	Stephanie	1981	2.50	5.00	10.00
ABC					
❑ ABCD-869	Movin' in the Right Direction	1975	3.75	7.50	15.00
CASABLANCA					
❑ NBLP 7265	Tantalizingly Hot	1982	2.50	5.00	10.00
❑ 811364-1	Merciless	1983	2.50	5.00	10.00
❑ 822421-1	I've Got the Cure	1984	2.50	5.00	10.00
❑ 832519-1	In My Life: Greatest Hits	1987	2.50	5.00	10.00
MCA					
❑ 5669	Stephanie Mills	1985	2.00	4.00	8.00
❑ 5996	If I Were Your Woman	1987	2.00	4.00	8.00
❑ 6312	Home	1989	2.50	5.00	10.00
❑ 10690	Something Real	1992	3.75	7.50	15.00
MOTOWN					
❑ M5-227-V1	For the First Time	1982	2.00	4.00	8.00
—Reissue of 859					
❑ M6-859S1	For the First Time	1975	3.00	6.00	12.00
❑ 6033 ML	Love Has Lifted Me	1983	12.50	25.00	50.00

MILLS BROTHERS, THE

45s

Number	Title (A Side/B Side)	Yr	VG	VG+	NM
DECCA					
❑ 9-33 [PS]	Famous Barber Shop Ballads, Volume One	1950	3.75	7.50	15.00
—Box for 24761, 24762 and 24763					
❑ 9-11051 T	Paper Doll/Tiger Rag	195?	5.00	10.00	20.00
—"Collectors' Classics" reissue on maroon label; part of "Curtain Call," 1-707					
❑ 23930	You Always Hurt the One You Love/Till Then	1960	2.00	4.00	8.00
—Black label with color bar					
❑ 9-23930	You Always Hurt the One You Love/Till Then	1950	5.00	10.00	20.00
—Reissue of 78 from 1944; black label with lines on either side of "Decca"					
❑ 9-23930	You Always Hurt the One You Love/Till Then	1955	3.00	6.00	12.00
—Black label with star under "Decca"					
❑ 9-24694	Someday/On a Chinese Honeymoon	1950	5.00	10.00	20.00
❑ 9-24756	If I Had My Way/Sweet Genevieve	1950	5.00	10.00	20.00
❑ 9-24761	You Tell Me Your Dreams, I'll Tell Mine/ Sweet Adeline	1950	3.75	7.50	15.00
❑ 9-24762	My Gal Sal/Just a Dream of You, Dear	1950	3.75	7.50	15.00
❑ 9-24763	Meet Me Tonight in Dreamland/Can't You Hear Me Callin', Caroline	1950	3.75	7.50	15.00
—The above three comprise "Album 9-33"					
❑ 9-24872	Daddy's Little Girl/If I Live to Be a Hundred	1950	5.00	10.00	20.00
❑ 9-25046	Lazy River/Cielito Lindo	1950	5.00	10.00	20.00
❑ 25516	Across the Alley from the Alamo/Don't Be a Baby, Baby	1961	2.00	4.00	8.00
❑ 27157	Paper Doll/I'll Be Around	1960	2.00	4.00	8.00
—Black label with color bar					
❑ 9-27157	Paper Doll/I'll Be Around	1950	5.00	10.00	20.00
—Reissue of 78 from 1943; black label with lines on either side of "Decca"					
❑ 9-27157	Paper Doll/I'll Be Around	1955	3.00	6.00	12.00
—Black label with star under "Decca"					
❑ 9-27184	A Star for Everyone/I'm Afraid to Love You	1950	5.00	10.00	20.00
❑ 9-27236	Daddy's Little Boy/I Still Love You	1950	5.00	10.00	20.00
❑ 9-27253	Nevertheless (I'm in Love with You)/Thirsty for Your Kisses	1950	5.00	10.00	20.00
❑ 9-27267	Funny Feelin'/I Don't Mind Being Alone	1950	5.00	10.00	20.00
❑ 9-27400	Around the World/You Don't Have to Drop a Heart to Break It	1951	3.75	7.50	15.00

Number	Title (A Side/B Side)	Yr	VG	VG+	NM
❑ 9-27447	Please Don't Talk About Me When I'm Gone/You Know You Belong to Someone Else	1951	3.75	7.50	15.00
—With Tommy Dorsey					
❑ 9-27579	Mister and Mississippi/Wonderful, Wasn't It	1951	3.75	7.50	15.00
❑ 9-27615	Love Me/Who Knows Love	1951	3.75	7.50	15.00
❑ 9-27683	Lord Ups an' Downs/A Cottage with a Prayer	1951	5.00	10.00	20.00
❑ 9-27762	I Ran All the Way Home/Get Her Off My Hands	1951	3.75	7.50	15.00
❑ 9-27889	Be My Life's Companion/Love Lies	1951	3.75	7.50	15.00
❑ 9-28021	High and Dry/You're Not Worth My Tears	1952	3.75	7.50	15.00
❑ 9-28180	Pretty As a Picture/When You Come Back to Me	1952	3.75	7.50	15.00
❑ 9-28309	Just When We're Falling in Love/Blue and Sentimental	1952	3.75	7.50	15.00
❑ 9-28384	The Glow-Worm/After All	1952	3.75	7.50	15.00
❑ 9-28458	Lazy River/Wish Me Good Luck, Amigo	1952	3.75	7.50	15.00
❑ 9-28459	Someone Loved Someone/A Shoulder to Weep On	1952	3.75	7.50	15.00
❑ 9-28586	Twice As Much/I Want Someone to Care For	1953	3.00	6.00	12.00
❑ 9-28670	Say Si Si/I'm With You	1953	3.00	6.00	12.00
❑ 9-28736	Pretty Butterfly/Don't Let Me Dream	1953	3.00	6.00	12.00
❑ 9-28818	Who Put the Devil in Evelyn's Eyes/Beware	1953	3.00	6.00	12.00
❑ 9-28945	The Jones Boy/She Was Five and He Was Ten	1953	3.00	6.00	12.00
❑ 9-29019	I Had to Call You Up to Say I'm Sorry/You Didn't Want Me When You Had Me	1954	3.00	6.00	12.00
❑ 9-29115	A Carnival in Venice/Go In and Out the Window	1954	3.00	6.00	12.00
❑ 9-29185	How Blue/Why Do I Keep Lovin' You	1954	3.00	6.00	12.00
❑ 9-29276	You're Nobody 'Til Somebody Loves You/Every Second of Every Day	1954	3.00	6.00	12.00
❑ 9-29382	Paper Valentine/The Urge	1954	3.00	6.00	12.00
❑ 9-29496	Opus One/There You Are	1955	3.00	6.00	12.00
❑ 9-29511	Smack Dab in the Middle/Kiss Me and Kill Me with Love	1955	3.00	6.00	12.00
❑ 9-29564	Daddy's Little Girl/Daddy's Little Boy	1955	3.00	6.00	12.00
❑ 9-29686	Suddenly There's a Valley/Gum Drop	1955	3.00	6.00	12.00
❑ 9-29754	I Believe in Santa Claus/You Don't Have to Be a Santa Claus	1955	3.00	6.00	12.00
❑ 9-29781	All the Way 'Round the World/I've Changed My Mind a Thousand Times	1956	2.50	5.00	10.00
❑ 9-29853	Dream of You/In a Mellow Tone	1956	2.50	5.00	10.00
❑ 9-29897	Standing on the Corner/King Porter Stomp	1956	2.50	5.00	10.00
❑ 9-30024	Don't Get Caught (Short on Love)/That's Right	1956	2.50	5.00	10.00
❑ 9-30136	That's All I Need/Tell Me More	1956	2.50	5.00	10.00
❑ 9-30224	In De Banana Tree/Knocked-Out Nightingale	1957	2.50	5.00	10.00
❑ 9-30299	Queen of the Senior Prom/My Troubled Mind	1957	2.50	5.00	10.00
❑ 30430	Two Minute Tango/Change for a Penny	1957	2.50	5.00	10.00
❑ 30546	The Barbershop Quartet/You Only Told Me Half	1958	2.50	5.00	10.00
DOT					
❑ 15695	Get a Job/I Found a Million Dollar Baby	1958	3.75	7.50	15.00
❑ 15827	Me and My Shadow/Music, Maestro, Please	1958	2.50	5.00	10.00
❑ 15858	Yellow Bird/Baby Clementine	1958	2.00	4.00	8.00
❑ 15909	You Can't Be True Dear/Beaver	1959	2.50	5.00	10.00
❑ 15950	Lullaby in Ragtime/Te Quiero	1959	2.50	5.00	10.00
❑ 15987	You Always Hurt the One You Love/(B-side unknown)	1959	2.50	5.00	10.00
❑ 16037	Paper Doll/The Glow-Worm	1960	2.00	4.00	8.00
❑ 16049	I Miss You So/Oh Ma Ma	1960	2.00	4.00	8.00
❑ 16091	Highways Are Happy Ways/I Got You	1960	2.00	4.00	8.00
❑ 16234	Yellow Bird/Baby Clementine	1961	2.00	4.00	8.00
❑ 16258	I'll Take Care of Your Cares/Ballerina	1961	2.00	4.00	8.00
❑ 16360	I Found the Only Girl for Me/Queen of the Senior Prom	1961	2.00	4.00	8.00
❑ 16432	Tonight You Belong to Me/You Broke the Only Heart That Ever Loved You	1963	—	3.50	7.00
❑ 16451	The End of the World/Big City	1963	—	3.50	7.00
❑ 16579	Don't Blame Me/It Hurts Me More Than It Hurts You	1964	—	3.50	7.00
❑ 16703	Welcome Home/Chum Chum Chittilum Chum	1965	—	3.50	7.00
❑ 16733	Bye Bye Blackbird/Chum Chum Chittilum Chum	1965	—	3.50	7.00
❑ 16972	Smack Dab in the Middle/Honeysuckle Rose Blues Bossa Nova	1967	—	3.00	6.00
❑ 17041	Cab Driver/Fortuosity	1967	—	3.00	6.00
❑ 17096	My Shy Violet/Flower Road	1968	—	3.00	6.00
❑ 17162	The Ol' Race Track/But for Love	1968	—	3.00	6.00
❑ 17198	Dream/Jimtown Road	1968	—	3.00	6.00
❑ 17235	A Guy on the Go/What Have I Done for Her Lately	1969	—	3.00	6.00
❑ 17285	I'll Never Forgive Myself/Up to Maggie Jones	1969	—	3.00	6.00
❑ 17321	It Ain't No Big Thing/Help Yourself to Some Tomorrow	1969	—	3.00	6.00
PARAMOUNT					
❑ 0046	Smile Away Every Rainy Day/Between Winston-Salem and Nashville, Tennessee	1970	—	2.50	5.00
❑ 0095	Happy Songs of Love/I'm Sorry I Answered the Phone	1971	—	2.50	5.00
❑ 0117	L-O-V-E/Strollin'	1971	—	2.50	5.00
❑ 0147	Come Summer/Sally Sunshine	1972	—	2.50	5.00
❑ 0181	There's No Life on the Moon/A Donut and a Dream	1972	—	2.50	5.00
RANWOOD					
❑ 961	Truck Stop/He Gives Me Love	1973	—	2.00	4.00
❑ 1003	Tiger Rag/On a Chinese Honeymoon	1974	—	2.00	4.00
❑ 1020	You Are My Sunshine/Between Winston-Salem and Nashville, Tennessee	1974	—	2.00	4.00
❑ 1040	El Paso/Till Then	197?	—	2.00	4.00
❑ 1042	Daisies Never Tell/Sawdust Heart	197?	—	2.00	4.00
❑ 1054	Coney Island Washboard/Nevertheless	197?	—	2.00	4.00

Number	Title (A Side/B Side)	Yr	VG	VG+	NM
78s					
BANNER					
❑ 33210	Sleepy Head/Jungle Fever	193?	6.25	12.50	25.00
❑ 33211	St. Louis Blues/Coney Island Washboard	193?	6.25	12.50	25.00
❑ 33212	Goodbye Blues/How Am I Doing?	193?	6.25	12.50	25.00
❑ 33213	Loveless Love/I Heard	193?	6.25	12.50	25.00
❑ 33214	Rockin' Chair/Sweet Sue	193?	6.25	12.50	25.00
❑ 33215	Chinatown, My Chinatown/Bugle Call Rag	193?	6.25	12.50	25.00
❑ 33254	I Found a New Baby/Baby Won't You Please Come Home	193?	6.25	12.50	25.00
❑ 33255	Dirt Dishin' Daisy/Fiddlin' Joe	193?	6.25	12.50	25.00
BRUNSWICK					
❑ 6197	Tiger Rag/Nobody's Sweetheart	1931	7.50	15.00	30.00
❑ 6225	You Rascal You/Baby, Won't You Please Come Home	1931	7.50	15.00	30.00
❑ 6240	Dinah/Can't We Talk It Over	1931	5.00	10.00	20.00
—A-side by "Bing Crosby and Mills Brothers"; B-side by Bing Crosby solo					
❑ 6269	I Heard/How'm I Doin', Hey-Hey	1932	10.00	20.00	40.00
❑ 6276	Shine/Shadows on the Window	1932	5.00	10.00	20.00
—A-side by "Bing Crosby and Mills Brothers"; B-side by Bing Crosby solo					
❑ 6278	Good-Bye, Blues/Rockin' Chair	1932	7.50	15.00	30.00
❑ 6305	Chinatown, My Chinatown/Loveless Love	1932	6.25	12.50	25.00
❑ 6330	St. Louis Blues/Sweet Sue	1932	6.25	12.50	25.00
❑ 6357	Bugle Call Rag/The Old Man of the Mountain	1932	6.25	12.50	25.00
❑ 6377	It Don't Mean a Thing (If It Ain't Got That Swing)/ Coney Island Washboard	1932	6.25	12.50	25.00
❑ 6430	Dirt Dishin' Daisy/Git Along	1933	6.25	12.50	25.00
❑ 6485	Shine/Dinah	1933	5.00	10.00	20.00
—As "Bing Crosby and Mills Brothers"					
❑ 6490	Any Time, Any Day, Anywhere/Fiddlin' Joe	1933	6.25	12.50	25.00
❑ 6517	Doin' the New Lowdown/I Can't Give You Anything But Love	1933	10.00	20.00	40.00
—A-side credited to "Don Redman & His Orchestra"; B-side by Ethel Waters with the Duke Ellington Orchestra					
❑ 6519	Diga Diga Doo/I Can't Give You Anything But Love	1933	10.00	20.00	40.00
❑ 6525	Smoke Rings/My Honey's Loving Arms	1933	7.50	15.00	30.00
—B-side by the Dorsey Brothers Orchestra (vocal by Bing Crosby)					
❑ 6785	I Found a New Baby/Jungle Fever	1934	6.25	12.50	25.00
❑ 6894	Swing It, Sister/Money in My Pockets	1934	6.25	12.50	25.00
❑ 6913	Sleepy Head/Put On Your Old Gray Bonnet	1934	6.25	12.50	25.00
CONQUEROR					
❑ 8400	I Heard/St. Louis Blues	193?	5.00	10.00	20.00
❑ 8426	Sleepy Head/Jungle Fever	193?	5.00	10.00	20.00
DECCA					
❑ 165	Ida, Sweet as Apple Cider/My Gal Sal	1934	5.00	10.00	20.00
❑ 166	Old Fashioned Love/Miss Otis Regrets	1934	5.00	10.00	20.00
❑ 167	Rockin' Chair/Tiger Rag	1934	5.00	10.00	20.00
❑ 176	Nagasaki/Lazybones	1934	5.00	10.00	20.00
❑ 228	Some of These Days/I've Found a New Baby	1934	5.00	10.00	20.00
❑ 267	Sweeter Than Sugar/Limehouse Blues	1934	5.00	10.00	20.00
❑ 380	Sweet Georgia Brown/There Goes My Headache	1935	5.00	10.00	20.00
❑ 402	What's the Reason/Don't Be Afraid to Tell Your Mother	1935	5.00	10.00	20.00
❑ 497	Sweet Lucy Brown/Moanin' for You	1935	5.00	10.00	20.00
❑ 961	Shoe Shine Boy/Rhythm Saved the World	1936	5.00	10.00	20.00
❑ 1082	Solitude/London Rhythm	1937	5.00	10.00	20.00
❑ 1147	Swing for Sale/Pennies from Heaven	1937	5.00	10.00	20.00
❑ 1148	Dedicated to You/Big Boy Blue	1937	5.00	10.00	20.00
—With Ella Fitzgerald					
❑ 1227	The Love Bug Will Bite You/Rockin' Chair Swing	1937	5.00	10.00	20.00
❑ 1245	Daling Nelly Gray/Carry Me Back to Old Virginny	1937	3.75	7.50	15.00
—With Louis Armstrong					
❑ 1360	The Old Folks at Home/Long About Midnight	1937	3.75	7.50	15.00
—A-side with Louis Armstrong					
❑ 1490	In the Shade of the Old Apple Tree/Since We Fell Out of Love	1937	3.75	7.50	15.00
—A-side with Louis Armstrong					
❑ 1876	The Flat Foot Floogie/Caravan	1938	3.75	7.50	15.00
—A-side with Louis Armstrong					
❑ 1892	My Walking Stick/The Song Is Ended	1938	3.75	7.50	15.00
—With Louis Armstrong					
❑ 1964	Sixty Seconds Got Together/Julius Caesar	1938	3.75	7.50	15.00
❑ 2008	The Lambeth Walk/The Yam	1938	3.75	7.50	15.00
❑ 2029	Just a Kid Named Joe/Funiculi, Funicula	1938	3.75	7.50	15.00
❑ 2285	Sweet Adeline/You Tell Me Your Dream, I'll Tell You Mine	1939	3.75	7.50	15.00
❑ 2441	Goodbye Blues/Sweet Sue, Just You	1939	3.75	7.50	15.00
❑ 2599	Way Down Home/Side Kick Joe	1939	3.75	7.50	15.00
❑ 2804	Meet Me Tonight in Dreamland/Asleep in the Deep	1939	3.75	7.50	15.00
❑ 2982	Put On Your Old Gray Bonnet/It Don't Mean a Thing (If It Ain't Got That Swing)	1940	3.75	7.50	15.00
❑ 3132	Old Black Joe/Swanee River	1940	3.00	6.00	12.00
❑ 3151	W.P.A./Marie	1940	3.00	6.00	12.00
—With Louis Armstrong					
❑ 3180	Boog It/Cherry	1940	3.00	6.00	12.00
—With Louis Armstrong					
❑ 3225	Just a Dream of You, Dear/My Gal Sal	1940	3.00	6.00	12.00
❑ 3291	Marie/Sleepy Time Gal	1940	3.00	6.00	12.00
—A-side with Louis Armstrong					
❑ 3331	Moonlight Bay/On the Banks of the Wabash	1940	3.00	6.00	12.00
❑ 3381	Once Upon a Dream/When You Were Sweet Sixteen	1940	3.00	6.00	12.00
—A-side with Louis Armstrong					

Number	Title (A Side/B Side)	Yr	VG	VG+	NM
❑ 3455	Can't Yo Hear Me Callin' Caroline?/Love's Old Sweet Song	1940	3.00	6.00	12.00
❑ 3486	A Bird in the Hand/When You Said Goodbye	1941	3.00	6.00	12.00
❑ 3545	By the Watermelon Vine, Lindy Lou/I've Been in Love Before	1941	3.00	6.00	12.00
—A-side with Benny Carter; B-side credited to Benny Carter and His Orchestra					
❑ 3567	How Did She Look?/Did Anyone Call?	1941	3.00	6.00	12.00
❑ 3598	I Wish/Put Another Chair at the Table	1941	3.00	6.00	12.00
❑ 3688	Georgia on My Mind/Shine	1941	3.00	6.00	12.00
❑ 3705	Darling Nellie Gray/Break the News to Mother	1941	3.00	6.00	12.00
❑ 3763	Down, Down, Down/Rig-a-Jig-Jig	1941	3.00	6.00	12.00
❑ 3789	Brazilian Nuts/Cielito Lindo	1941	3.00	6.00	12.00
❑ 3901	If It's True/The Very Thought of You	1941	3.00	6.00	12.00
❑ 4070	The Bells of San Raquel/I Guess I'll Be On My Way	1941	3.00	6.00	12.00
❑ 4108	Window Washer Man/Delilah	1942	3.00	6.00	12.00
❑ 4187	Lazy River/627 Stomp	1942	3.00	6.00	12.00
❑ 4251	Dreamsville, Ohio/Beyond the Stars	1942	3.00	6.00	12.00
❑ 4348	Way Down Home/When You Were Sweet Sixteen	1942	3.00	6.00	12.00
❑ 18318	Paper Doll/I'll Be Around	1942	2.50	5.00	10.00
❑ 18473	In Old Champlain/I Met Her on Monday	1942	2.50	5.00	10.00
❑ 18599	You Always Hurt the One You Love/Till Then	1944	2.50	5.00	10.00
❑ 18663	I Wish/Put Another Chair at the Table	1945	2.50	5.00	10.00
❑ 18753	Don't Be a Baby, Baby/Never Make a Promise in Vain	1946	2.50	5.00	10.00
❑ 18834	I Don't Know Enough About You/There's No One But You	1946	2.50	5.00	10.00
❑ 23623	Sweet Adeline/You Tell Me Your Dream, I'll Tell You Mine	1946	2.00	4.00	8.00
—Reissue of 2285					
❑ 23625	Meet Me Tonight in Dreamland/Can't Yo Hear Me Callin' Caroline?	1946	2.00	4.00	8.00
—Reissue of A-sides of 2804 and 3455					
❑ 23626	Moonlight Bay/On the Banks of the Wabash	1946	2.00	4.00	8.00
—Reissue of 3331					
❑ 23627	Way Down Home/When You Were Sweet Sixteen	1946	2.00	4.00	8.00
—Reissue of 4348					
❑ 23638	I Guess I'll Get the Papers and Go Home/Too Many Irons in the Fire	1946	2.50	5.00	10.00
❑ 23713	I'm Afraid to Love You/You Broke the Only Heart That Ever Loved You	1946	2.50	5.00	10.00
❑ 23863	Across the Alley from the Alamo/Dream Dream Dream	1947	2.50	5.00	10.00
❑ 23930	You Always Hurt the One You Love/Till Then	1947	2.00	4.00	8.00
—Reissue of 18599					
❑ 23979	Oh! My Achin' Heart/What You Don't Know Won't Hurt You	1947	2.50	5.00	10.00
❑ 24180	You Never Miss the Water Till the Well Runs Dry/ After You	1947	2.50	5.00	10.00
❑ 24252	I'll Never Make the Same Mistake Again/I'm Sorry I Didn't Say I'm Sorry	1947	2.50	5.00	10.00
❑ 24329	If You Had All the World and Its Gold/Tell Me a Story	1948	2.50	5.00	10.00
❑ 24333	Manana (Is Soon Enough for Me)/I Wish I Knew the Name (Of the Girl of My Dreams)	1948	2.50	5.00	10.00
❑ 24382	S-H-I-N-E/Love Is Fun	1948	2.50	5.00	10.00
❑ 24409	Confess/Someone Cares	1948	2.50	5.00	10.00
❑ 24441	I Couldn't Call My Baby/Baby, Don't Be Mad at Me	1948	2.50	5.00	10.00
❑ 24472	I'll Never Be Without a Dream/Two Blocks Down, Turn to the Left	1948	2.50	5.00	10.00
❑ 24509	Gloria/I Want to Be the Only One	1948	2.50	5.00	10.00
❑ 24534	Down Among the Sheltering Palms/Is It True What They Say About Dixie	1948	2.50	5.00	10.00
—With Al Jolson					
❑ 24550	I Love You So Much It Hurts/I've Got My Love to Keep Me Warm	1949	2.50	5.00	10.00
❑ 24621	Words/I'm Happy Being Me	1949	2.50	5.00	10.00
❑ 24656	Gather Your Dreams/Single Saddle	1949	2.50	5.00	10.00
❑ 24679	Out of Love/Lora-Belle Lee	1949	2.50	5.00	10.00
❑ 24694	Someday/On a Chinese Honeymoon	1949	2.50	5.00	10.00
❑ 24749	Who'll Be the Next One (To Cry Over You)/I Want You to Want Me	1949	2.50	5.00	10.00
❑ 24756	If I Had My Way/Sweet Genevieve	1949	2.00	4.00	8.00
❑ 24757	'Til We Meet Again/Honey Dat I Love So Well	1949	2.00	4.00	8.00
❑ 24758	Love's Old Sweet Song/Long, Long Ago	1949	2.00	4.00	8.00
❑ 24759	On the Banks of the Wabash/Moonlight Bay	1949	2.00	4.00	8.00
❑ 24761	You Tell Me Your Dreams, I'll Tell You Mine/ Sweet Adeline	1949	2.00	4.00	8.00
❑ 24762	My Gal Sal/Just a Dream of You, Dear	1949	2.00	4.00	8.00
❑ 24763	Meet Me Tonight in Dreamland/Can't You Hear Me Callin', Caroline	1949	2.00	4.00	8.00
❑ 24764	Way Down Home/When You Were Sweet Sixteen	1949	2.00	4.00	8.00
❑ 24768	On This Christmas Eve/My Christmas Song for You	1949	2.50	5.00	10.00
❑ 24872	Daddy's Little Girl/If I Live to Be a Hundred	1950	2.50	5.00	10.00
❑ 24994	Open the Gates of Dreamland/I've Shed a Hundred Tears	1950	2.50	5.00	10.00
❑ 25046	Lazy River/Cielito Lindo	1947	2.50	5.00	10.00
—Reissue of A-side of 4187 and B-side of 3789					
❑ 25284	If It's True/The Very Thought of You	1948	2.00	4.00	8.00
—Reissue of 3901					
❑ 25361	Dedicated to You/Big Boy Blue	1949	2.00	4.00	8.00
—With Ella Fitzgerald; reissue of 1148					

Number	Title (A Side/B Side)	Yr	VG	VG+	NM
❑ 27157	Paper Doll/I'll Be Around	1950	2.00	4.00	8.00
—Reissue of 18318					
❑ 27184	A Star for Everyone/I'm Afraid to Love You	1950	2.50	5.00	10.00
❑ 27236	Daddy's Little Boy/I Still Love You	1950	2.50	5.00	10.00
❑ 27253	Nevertheless (I'm in Love with You)/Thirsty for Your Kisses	1950	2.50	5.00	10.00
❑ 27267	Funny Feelin'/I Don't Mind Being Alone	1950	2.50	5.00	10.00
❑ 27400	Around the World/You Don't Have to Drop a Heart to Break It	1951	2.50	5.00	10.00
❑ 27447	Please Don't Talk About Me When I'm Gone/You Know You Belong to Someone Else	1951	2.50	5.00	10.00
—With Tommy Dorsey					
❑ 27579	Mister and Mississippi/Wonderful, Wasn't It	1951	2.50	5.00	10.00
❑ 27615	Love Me/Who Knows Love	1951	2.50	5.00	10.00
❑ 27683	Lord Ups an' Downs/A Cottage with a Prayer	1951	2.50	5.00	10.00
❑ 27762	I Ran All the Way Home/Get Her Off My Hands	1951	2.50	5.00	10.00
❑ 27889	Be My Life's Companion/Love Lies	1951	2.50	5.00	10.00
❑ 28021	High and Dry/You're Not Worth My Tears	1952	2.50	5.00	10.00
❑ 28180	Pretty As a Picture/When You Come Back to Me	1952	2.50	5.00	10.00
❑ 28309	Just When We're Falling in Love/Blue and Sentimental	1952	2.50	5.00	10.00
❑ 28384	The Glow-Worm/After All	1952	2.50	5.00	10.00
❑ 28458	Lazy River/Wish Me Good Luck, Amigo	1952	2.50	5.00	10.00
❑ 28459	Someone Loved Someone/A Shoulder to Weep On	1952	2.50	5.00	10.00
❑ 28586	Twice As Much/I Want Someone to Care For	1953	2.50	5.00	10.00
❑ 28670	Say Si Si/I'm With You	1953	2.50	5.00	10.00
❑ 28736	Pretty Butterfly/Don't Let Me Dream	1953	2.50	5.00	10.00
❑ 28818	Who Put the Devil in Evelyn's Eyes/Beware	1953	2.50	5.00	10.00
❑ 28945	The Jones Boy/She Was Five and He Was Ten	1953	3.00	6.00	12.00
❑ 29019	I Had to Call You Up to Say I'm Sorry/You Didn't Want Me When You Had Me	1954	2.50	5.00	10.00
❑ 29115	A Carnival in Venice/Go In and Out the Window	1954	2.50	5.00	10.00
❑ 29185	How Blue/Why Do I Keep Lovin' You	1954	2.50	5.00	10.00
❑ 29276	You're Nobody 'Til Somebody Loves You/Every Second of Every Day	1954	2.50	5.00	10.00
❑ 29382	Paper Valentine/The Urge	1954	2.50	5.00	10.00
❑ 29496	Opus One/There You Are	1955	2.50	5.00	10.00
❑ 29511	Smack Dab in the Middle/Kiss Me and Kill Me with Love	1955	2.50	5.00	10.00
❑ 29564	Daddy's Little Girl/Daddy's Little Boy	1955	2.50	5.00	10.00
❑ 29686	Suddenly There's a Valley/Gum Drop	1955	2.50	5.00	10.00
❑ 29754	I Believe in Santa Claus/You Don't Have to Be a Santa Claus	1955	2.50	5.00	10.00
❑ 29781	All the Way 'Round the World/I've Changed My Mind a Thousand Times	1956	2.50	5.00	10.00
❑ 29853	Dream of You/In a Mellow Tone	1956	2.50	5.00	10.00
❑ 29897	Standing on the Corner/King Porter Stomp	1956	2.50	5.00	10.00
❑ 30024	Don't Get Caught (Short on Love)/That's Right	1956	2.50	5.00	10.00
❑ 30136	That's All I Need/Tell Me More	1956	2.50	5.00	10.00
❑ 30224	In De Banana Tree/Knocked-Out Nightingale	1957	3.00	6.00	12.00
❑ 30299	Queen of the Senior Prom/My Troubled Mind	1957	3.00	6.00	12.00
—Note: Later 78s by the Mills Brothers may exist					
HARMONY					
❑ 1001	St. Louis Blues/Any Time, Any Day, Anywhere	1949	2.50	5.00	10.00
—Reissue of A-sides of Brunswick 6330 and 6490					
❑ 1002	Put On Your Old Gray Bonnet/Smoke Rings	1949	2.50	5.00	10.00
—Reissue of A-side of Brunswick 6525 and B-side of Brunswick 6913					
MELOTONE					
❑ M 13177	Sleepy Head/Jungle Fever	193?	6.25	12.50	25.00
❑ M 13178	St. Louis Blues/Coney Island Washboard	193?	6.25	12.50	25.00
❑ M 13179	Goodbye Blues/How Am I Doing?	193?	6.25	12.50	25.00
❑ M 13180	Loveless Love/I Heard	193?	6.25	12.50	25.00
❑ M 13181	Rockin' Chair/Sweet Sue	193?	6.25	12.50	25.00
❑ M 13182	Chinatown, My Chinatown/Bugle Call Rag	193?	6.25	12.50	25.00
❑ M 13221	I Found a New Baby/Baby Won't You Please Come Home	193?	6.25	12.50	25.00
❑ M 13222	Dirt Dishin' Daisy/Fiddlin' Joe	193?	6.25	12.50	25.00
ORIOLE					
❑ 3005	Sleepy Head/Jungle Fever	193?	6.25	12.50	25.00
❑ 3006	St. Louis Blues/Coney Island Washboard	193?	6.25	12.50	25.00
❑ 3007	Goodbye Blues/How Am I Doing?	193?	6.25	12.50	25.00
❑ 3008	Loveless Love/I Heard	193?	6.25	12.50	25.00
❑ 3009	Rockin' Chair/Sweet Sue	193?	6.25	12.50	25.00
❑ 3010	Chinatown, My Chinatown/Bugle Call Rag	193?	6.25	12.50	25.00
❑ 3034	I Found a New Baby/Baby Won't You Please Come Home	193?	6.25	12.50	25.00
❑ 3035	Dirt Dishin' Daisy/Fiddlin' Joe	193?	6.25	12.50	25.00
PERFECT					
❑ 13056	Sleepy Head/Jungle Fever	193?	6.25	12.50	25.00
—Other 78s on Perfect probably exist; similar price range					
ROMEO					
❑ 2379	Sleepy Head/Jungle Fever	193?	6.25	12.50	25.00
❑ 2380	St. Louis Blues/Coney Island Washboard	193?	6.25	12.50	25.00
❑ 2381	Goodbye Blues/How Am I Doing?	193?	6.25	12.50	25.00
❑ 2382	Loveless Love/I Heard	193?	6.25	12.50	25.00
❑ 2383	Rockin' Chair/Sweet Sue	193?	6.25	12.50	25.00
❑ 2384	Chinatown, My Chinatown/Bugle Call Rag	193?	6.25	12.50	25.00
❑ 2408	I Found a New Baby/Baby Won't You Please Come Home	193?	6.25	12.50	25.00
❑ 2409	Dirt Dishin' Daisy/Fiddlin' Joe	193?	6.25	12.50	25.00
7-Inch Extended Plays					
DECCA					
❑ ED 582 [PS]	Souvenir Album	195?	3.00	6.00	12.00
—Cover for 2-EP set (91176, 91177)					
❑ ED 2010	Lazy River/I'm Afraid to Love You//Blue and Sentimental/I've Got My Love to Keep Me Warm	195?	3.75	7.50	15.00
❑ ED 2010 [PS]	The Mills Brothers, Volume 1	195?	3.75	7.50	15.00
❑ ED 2044	*Caravan/Solitude/It Don't Mean a Thing/Georgia on My Mind	195?	3.75	7.50	15.00
❑ ED 2044 [PS]	The Mills Brothers, Vol. 2	195?	3.75	7.50	15.00
❑ ED 2513	One Dozen Roses/Rose Room//Mexicali Rose/Honeysuckle Rose	195?	3.75	7.50	15.00
❑ ED 2513 [PS]	One Dozen Roses	195?	3.75	7.50	15.00
❑ ED 2573	Oh How I Miss You Tonight/You Only Told Me Half the Story//When I Lost You/Will ❑ You Remember Tomorrow	195?	3.75	7.50	15.00
❑ ED 2573 [PS]	Mills Brothers in Hi-Fi: Barbershop Ballads	195?	3.75	7.50	15.00
❑ ED 2742	Daddy's Little Girl/Daddy's Little Boy//You're Nobody 'Til Somebody Loves You/Queen of the Senior Prom	195?	3.00	6.00	12.00
❑ ED 2742 [PS]	The Mills Brothers	195?	3.00	6.00	12.00
❑ 91176	Paper Doll/I'll Be Around//You Always Hurt the One You Love/Till Then	195?	3.00	6.00	12.00
—Part of 2-EP set ED 582					
❑ 91177	Too Many Irons in the Fire/I Guess I'll Get the Papers and Go Home//You Never Miss the Water Till the Well Runs Dry/After You	195?	3.00	6.00	12.00
—Part of 2-EP set ED 582					
DOT					
❑ DLP 592	Say Si Si/Time Was/It Happened in Monterey//Perfidia/Yours/South of the Border	196?	3.00	6.00	12.00
—Jukebox issue; small hole, plays at 33 1/3 rpm					
❑ DLP 592 [PS]	Say Si Si and Other Great Latin Hits	196?	3.00	6.00	12.00
❑ DEP-1087	Glow Worm/Lazy River//Till Then/Paper Doll	195?	2.50	5.00	10.00
❑ DEP-1087 [PS]	Great Hits	195?	2.50	5.00	10.00
Albums					
ABC					
❑ 1027 [(2)]	The Best of the Mills Brothers, Volume 2	1978	3.00	6.00	12.00
❑ 4004	16 Great Performances	1975	2.50	5.00	10.00
ABC SONGBIRD					
❑ SBDP-255	Inspiration	1974	2.50	5.00	10.00
ARCHIVE OF FOLK AND JAZZ					
❑ 300	The Mills Brothers	197?	2.50	5.00	10.00
❑ 328	The Mills Brothers, Volume 2	197?	2.50	5.00	10.00
DECCA					
❑ DXB 193 [(2) M]	The Best of the Mills Brothers	1965	5.00	10.00	20.00
❑ DL 4084 [M]	Our Golden Favorites	1960	5.00	10.00	20.00
❑ DL 5050 [10]	Barber Shop Ballads	1950	12.50	25.00	50.00
❑ DL 5051 [10]	Barber Shop Ballads	1950	12.50	25.00	50.00
❑ DL 5102 [10]	Souvenir Album	1950	12.50	25.00	50.00
❑ DL 5337 [10]	Wonderful Words	1951	12.50	25.00	50.00
❑ DL 5506 [10]	Meet the Mills Brothers	1954	12.50	25.00	50.00
❑ DL 5516 [10]	Four Boys and a Guitar	1954	12.50	25.00	50.00
❑ DXSB 7193 [(2) R]	The Best of the Mills Brothers	1965	3.75	7.50	15.00
❑ DL 8148 [M]	Souvenir Album	1955	7.50	15.00	30.00
❑ DL 8209 [M]	Singin' and Swingin'	1956	7.50	15.00	30.00
❑ DL 8219 [M]	Memory Lane	1956	7.50	15.00	30.00
❑ DL 8491 [M]	One Dozen Roses	1957	7.50	15.00	30.00
❑ DL 8664 [M]	The Mills Brothers in Hi-Fi	1958	7.50	15.00	30.00
❑ DL 8827 [M]	Glow with the Mills Brothers	1958	7.50	15.00	30.00
❑ DL 8890 [M]	Barber Shop Harmony	1959	7.50	15.00	30.00
❑ DL 8892 [M]	Harmonizin' with the Mills Brothers	1959	7.50	15.00	30.00
❑ DL 74084 [R]	Our Golden Favorites	196?	3.00	6.00	12.00
❑ DL 75174 [R]	Golden Favorites, Volume 2	1970	2.50	5.00	10.00
DOT					
❑ DLP-3103 [M]	Mmmm, The Mills Brothers	1958	5.00	10.00	20.00
❑ DLP-3157 [M]	The Mills Brothers' Great Hits	1958	5.00	10.00	20.00
❑ DLP-3208 [M]	Great Barbershop Hits	1959	5.00	10.00	20.00
❑ DLP-3232 [M]	Merry Christmas	1959	5.00	10.00	20.00
❑ DLP-3237 [M]	The Mills Brothers Sing	1960	5.00	10.00	20.00
❑ DLP-3308 [M]	The Mills Brothers' Great Hits, Volume 2	1960	3.75	7.50	15.00
❑ DLP-3338 [M]	Yellow Bird	1960	3.75	7.50	15.00
❑ DLP-3363 [M]	San Antonio Rose	1961	3.75	7.50	15.00
❑ DLP-3368 [M]	Great Hawaiian Hits	1961	3.75	7.50	15.00
❑ DLP-3465 [M]	Beer Barrel Polka and Other Hits	1962	3.00	6.00	12.00
❑ DLP-3508 [M]	The End of the World	1963	3.00	6.00	12.00
❑ DLP-3565 [M]	Gems by the Mills Brothers	1964	3.00	6.00	12.00
❑ DLP-3568 [M]	Hymns We Love	1964	3.00	6.00	12.00
❑ DLP-3592 [M]	Say Si Si and Other Great Latin Hits	1964	3.00	6.00	12.00
❑ DLP-3652 [M]	Ten Years of Hits 1954-1964	1965	3.00	6.00	12.00
❑ DLP-3699 [M]	These Are the Mills Brothers	1966	3.00	6.00	12.00
❑ DLP-3744 [M]	That Country Feeling	1966	3.00	6.00	12.00
❑ DL-3766 [M]	The Mills Brothers Today	1966	3.00	6.00	12.00
❑ DLP-3783 [M]	The Mills Brothers Live	1967	3.75	7.50	15.00
❑ DLP-25103 [S]	Mmmm, The Mills Brothers	1958	7.50	15.00	30.00
❑ DLP-25157 [S]	The Mills Brothers' Great Hits	1958	7.50	15.00	30.00
—Black vinyl					
❑ DLP-25157 [S]	The Mills Brothers' Great Hits	195?	15.00	30.00	60.00
—Blue vinyl					
❑ DLP-25208 [S]	Great Barbershop Hits	1959	7.50	15.00	30.00
❑ DLP-25232 [S]	Merry Christmas	1959	7.50	15.00	30.00
—Same as above, but in stereo; with cursive "Dot" logo					
❑ DLP-25232 [S]	Merry Christmas	1968	3.00	6.00	12.00
—With "Dot"/"Paramount" logo					
❑ DLP-25237 [S]	The Mills Brothers Sing	1960	7.50	15.00	30.00
❑ DLP-25308 [S]	The Mills Brothers' Great Hits, Volume 2	1960	5.00	10.00	20.00
❑ DLP-25338 [S]	Yellow Bird	1960	5.00	10.00	20.00
❑ DLP-25363 [S]	San Antonio Rose	1961	5.00	10.00	20.00
❑ DLP-25368 [S]	Great Hawaiian Hits	1961	5.00	10.00	20.00

Number	Title (A Side/B Side)	Yr	VG	VG+	NM
❏ DLP-25465 [S]	Beer Barrel Polka and Other Hits	1962	3.75	7.50	15.00
❏ DLP-25508 [S]	The End of the World	1963	3.75	7.50	15.00
❏ DLP-25565 [S]	Gems by the Mills Brothers	1964	3.75	7.50	15.00
❏ DLP-25568 [S]	Hymns We Love	1964	3.75	7.50	15.00
❏ DLP-25592 [S]	Say Si Si and Other Great Latin Hits	1964	3.75	7.50	15.00
❏ DLP-25652 [S]	Ten Years of Hits 1954-1964	1965	3.75	7.50	15.00
❏ DLP-25699 [S]	These Are the Mills Brothers	1966	3.75	7.50	15.00
❏ DLP-25744 [S]	That Country Feeling	1966	3.75	7.50	15.00
❏ DLP-25766 [S]	The Mills Brothers Today	1966	3.75	7.50	15.00
❏ DLP-25783 [S]	The Mills Brothers Live	1967	3.75	7.50	15.00
❏ DLP-25809	Fortuosity	1968	3.75	7.50	15.00
❏ DLP-25872	My Shy Violet	1968	3.75	7.50	15.00
❏ DLP-25927	Dream	1969	3.75	7.50	15.00
❏ DLP-25960	The Mills Brothers In Motion	1970	3.75	7.50	15.00

GNP CRESCENDO

Number	Title (A Side/B Side)	Yr	VG	VG+	NM
❏ GNP-9106	Four Boys and a Guitar	197?	2.50	5.00	10.00

HAMILTON

| ❏ HL-116 [M] | The Mills Brothers Sing for You | 1964 | 3.00 | 6.00 | 12.00 |
| ❏ HS-12116 [S] | The Mills Brothers Sing for You | 1964 | 3.00 | 6.00 | 12.00 |

MARK 56

| ❏ 709 | Original Radio Broadcasts | 197? | 2.50 | 5.00 | 10.00 |

MCA

❏ 132	Golden Favorites, Volume 2	1973	2.50	5.00	10.00
❏ 188	Old Golden Favorites	1973	2.50	5.00	10.00
❏ 717	16 Great Performances	1980	2.00	4.00	8.00
❏ 4039 [(2)]	The Best of the Mills Brothers	197?	3.00	6.00	12.00
❏ 15029	Merry Christmas	198?	2.50	5.00	10.00
❏ 27083	The Mills Brothers Great Hits	1980	2.00	4.00	8.00
❏ 28116	Were You There	198?	2.00	4.00	8.00

MCA SPECIAL MARKETS

| ❏ MSM2-35067 [(2)] | Classic Mills Brothers | 198? | 2.50 | 5.00 | 10.00 |

PARAMOUNT

❏ PAS-1010	The Best of the Mills Brothers	1973	3.00	6.00	12.00
❏ PAS-1027 [(2)]	The Best of the Mills Brothers, Volume 2	1974	3.75	7.50	15.00
❏ PAS-5025	No Turnin' Back	1971	3.00	6.00	12.00
❏ PAS-6024	What a Wonderful World	1972	3.00	6.00	12.00
❏ PAS-6038	A Donut and a Dream	1973	3.00	6.00	12.00

PICKWICK

❏ SPC-1025	Merry Christmas	1979	2.50	5.00	10.00
—Reissue of Dot album with one fewer track					
❏ 2008	Songs You Remember	197?	2.50	5.00	10.00
❏ 2030	The Mills Brothers	1973	2.50	5.00	10.00
❏ SPC-3076	14 Karat Gold	196?	2.50	5.00	10.00
❏ SPC-3107	Anytime	197?	2.50	5.00	10.00
❏ SPC-3137	Dream a Little Dream	197?	2.50	5.00	10.00
❏ SPC-3158	Till We Meet Again	197?	2.50	5.00	10.00
❏ SPC-3220	Cab Driver	197?	2.50	5.00	10.00

RANWOOD

❏ 7035 [(2)]	22 Great Hits	1985	2.50	5.00	10.00
❏ 8123	Cab Driver	197?	2.50	5.00	10.00
❏ 8133	The Mills Brothers Story	197?	2.50	5.00	10.00
❏ 8139	Country's Greatest Hits	197?	2.50	5.00	10.00
❏ 8152	50th Anniversary	197?	2.50	5.00	10.00
❏ 8198	Command Performance	198?	2.00	4.00	8.00

SUNNYVALE

| ❏ 1023 | Timeless | 1978 | 2.50 | 5.00 | 10.00 |

VOCALION

❏ VL 3607 [M]	In a Mellow Tone	196?	3.00	6.00	12.00
❏ VL 73607 [R]	In a Mellow Tone	196?	2.50	5.00	10.00
❏ VL 73859 [R]	Such Sweet Singing	1969	2.50	5.00	10.00

MILTON, ROY

45s

CENCO

| ❏ 114 | I Can't Go On/Thelma Lou | 1960 | 3.75 | 7.50 | 15.00 |

DOOTONE

❏ 363	I Can't Go On/Fools Are Getting Scarcer	1955	12.50	25.00	50.00
❏ 369	You Got Me Reeling and Rocking/Nothing Left	1955	12.50	25.00	50.00
❏ 377	I Want to Go Home/I Never Would Have Made It	1955	12.50	25.00	50.00
❏ 398	Baby I'm Gone/Cry Some Baby	1956	12.50	25.00	50.00

KING

❏ 4993	You're Gonna Suffer Baby/One Zippy Zam	1956	5.00	10.00	20.00
❏ 5035	Succotash/I'm Grateful	1957	5.00	10.00	20.00
❏ 5069	Rockin' Pneumonia/Skid Row	1957	5.00	10.00	20.00
❏ 5074	Jeep's Blues/A Brand New Me	1957	5.00	10.00	20.00
❏ 5663	Jeep's Blues/R.M. Blues	1962	3.75	7.50	15.00

SPECIALTY

❏ 403	It's Later Than You Think/Numbers Blues	1951	15.00	30.00	60.00
❏ 407	T-Town Twist/I Have News for You	1951	15.00	30.00	60.00
❏ 414	Best Wishes/Short, Sweet and Snappy	1951	15.00	30.00	60.00
❏ 429	So Tired/Thelma Lou	1952	20.00	40.00	80.00
❏ 436	Flying Saucer/As Time Goes By	1952	20.00	40.00	80.00
❏ 438	Night and Day (I Miss You So)/Am I Wasting My Time	1952	20.00	40.00	80.00
❏ 446	Believe Me Baby/Blue Turning Gray All Over	1952	25.00	50.00	100.00
❏ 455	Some Day/Don't You Remember Baby	1953	12.50	25.00	50.00
❏ 464	Early in the Morning/Let Me Give You All My Love	1953	12.50	25.00	50.00
—Black vinyl					
❏ 464	Early in the Morning/Let Me Give You All My Love	1953	50.00	100.00	200.00
—Red vinyl					
❏ 480	Baby, You Don't Know	1953	12.50	25.00	50.00
—Original pressings have a white line through the black bars on either side of the center hole					
❏ 480	Baby, You Don't Know	1961	5.00	10.00	20.00
—Reissues have solid black bars on either side of the center hole					

Number	Title (A Side/B Side)	Yr	VG	VG+	NM
❏ 489	Make Me Know It/A Bird in Hand	1954	10.00	20.00	40.00
❏ 526	It's Too Late/Gonna Leave You Baby	1954	10.00	20.00	40.00
❏ 538	How Can I Live Without You?/Tell It Like It Is	1954	10.00	20.00	40.00
❏ 545	What Can I Do?/Baby, Don't Do That to Me	1955	7.50	15.00	30.00
❏ 721	R.M. Blues/Best Wishes	1969	2.00	4.00	8.00

WARWICK

| ❏ 549 | Early in the Morning/Bless Your Heart | 1960 | 5.00 | 10.00 | 20.00 |
| ❏ 662 | Red Light/So Tired | 1961 | 5.00 | 10.00 | 20.00 |

78s

DOOTONE

❏ 363	I Can't Go On/Fools Are Getting Scarcer	1955	7.50	15.00	30.00
❏ 369	You Got Me Reeling and Rocking/Nothing Left	1955	7.50	15.00	30.00
❏ 377	I Want to Go Home/I Never Would Have Made It	1955	7.50	15.00	30.00
❏ 398	Baby I'm Gone/Cry Some Baby	1956	7.50	15.00	30.00

JUKE BOX

| ❏ 503 | Milton's Boogie/Groovy Blues | 1946 | 10.00 | 20.00 | 40.00 |
| ❏ 504 | R.M. Blues/Rhythm Cocktail | 1946 | 10.00 | 20.00 | 40.00 |

KING

❏ 4993	You're Gonna Suffer Baby/One Zippy Zam	1956	6.25	12.50	25.00
❏ 5035	Succotash/I'm Grateful	1957	6.25	12.50	25.00
❏ 5069	Rockin' Pneumonia/Skid Row	1957	6.25	12.50	25.00
❏ 5074	Jeep's Blues/A Brand New Me	1957	6.25	12.50	25.00

ROY MILTON

| ❏ 103/4 | I'll Always Be in Love with You/Mr. Fine | 194? | 12.50 | 25.00 | 50.00 |

SPECIALTY

❏ 314	Everything I Do Is Wrong/Hop, Skip and Jump	1948	6.25	12.50	25.00
❏ 317	New Year's Resolution/Porter's Love Song	1948	7.50	15.00	30.00
❏ 328	The Hucklebuck/Sympathetic Blues	1949	6.25	12.50	25.00
❏ 330	Junior Jumps/There Is Something Missing	1949	6.25	12.50	25.00
❏ 341	Tain't Me/I'm Wakin' Up Baby	1949	6.25	12.50	25.00
❏ 349	Information Blues/My Sweetheart	1950	6.25	12.50	25.00
❏ 358	Where There Is No Love/Junior Jives	1950	6.25	12.50	25.00
❏ 366	Playboy Blues/Cryin' and Singin' the Blues	1950	6.25	12.50	25.00
❏ 372	Bartender's Boogie/Sad Feeling	1950	6.25	12.50	25.00
❏ 381	Oh Babe/Christmas Time Blues	1950	6.25	12.50	25.00
❏ 386	Bye Bye Baby Blues/That's the One for Me	1951	6.25	12.50	25.00
❏ 403	It's Later Than You Think/Numbers Blues	1951	6.25	12.50	25.00
❏ 407	T-Town Twist/I Have News for You	1951	6.25	12.50	25.00
❏ 414	Best Wishes/Short, Sweet and Snappy	1951	6.25	12.50	25.00
❏ 429	So Tired/Thelma Lou	1952	6.25	12.50	25.00
❏ 436	Flying Saucer/As Time Goes By	1952	6.25	12.50	25.00
❏ 438	Night and Day (I Miss You So)/Am I Wasting My Time	1952	6.25	12.50	25.00
❏ 446	Believe Me Baby/Blue Turning Gray All Over	1952	6.25	12.50	25.00
❏ 455	Some Day/Don't You Remember Baby	1953	6.25	12.50	25.00
❏ 464	Early in the Morning/Let Me Give You All My Love	1953	6.25	12.50	25.00
❏ 480	I Stood By/Baby Don't You Know	1953	6.25	12.50	25.00
❏ 489	Make Me Know It/A Bird in Hand	1954	6.25	12.50	25.00
❏ 503	Milton's Boogie/Groovy Blues	1947	6.25	12.50	25.00
—Reissue of Juke Box 503					
❏ 504	R.M. Blues/Rhythm Cocktail	1947	6.25	12.50	25.00
—Reissue of Juke Box 504					
❏ 510	True Blues/Camille's Boogie	1947	6.25	12.50	25.00
❏ 511	Red Light/It Should Never Have Been This Way	1947	6.25	12.50	25.00
❏ 513	Sunny Side of the Street/I'll Always Be in Love with You	1947	6.25	12.50	25.00
❏ 514	Blues in My Heart/Groovin' with Joe	1947	6.25	12.50	25.00
❏ 515	Mr. Fine/Rainy Day Confession Blues	1947	6.25	12.50	25.00
❏ 516	Them There Eyes/Little Boy Blue	1947	6.25	12.50	25.00
❏ 517	Pack Your Sack, Jack/When I Grow Too Old to Dream	1947	6.25	12.50	25.00
❏ 518	Thrill Me/Big Fat Mama	1947	6.25	12.50	25.00
❏ 519	What's the Use/Roy Rides	1947	6.25	12.50	25.00
❏ 522	Keep a Dollar in Your Pocket/My Blue Heaven	1948	6.25	12.50	25.00
❏ 524	Train Blues/I've Had My Moments	1948	6.25	12.50	25.00
❏ 526	It's Too Late/Gonna Leave You Baby	1954	6.25	12.50	25.00
❏ 538	How Can I Live Without You?/Tell It Like It Is	1954	6.25	12.50	25.00
❏ 545	What Can I Do?/Baby, Don't Do That to Me	1955	6.25	12.50	25.00

Albums

KENT

| ❏ KST-554 [R] | The Great Roy Milton | 196? | 7.50 | 15.00 | 30.00 |
| ❏ KLP-5054 [M] | The Great Roy Milton | 1963 | 12.50 | 25.00 | 50.00 |

MIMMS, GARNET, AND THE ENCHANTERS

Includes Garnet Mimms credited alone. Also see THE ENCHANTERS (2).

45s

ARISTA

❏ 0239	What It Is (Part 1)/What It Is (Part 2)	1977	—	2.00	4.00
❏ 0289	Johnny Porter/Tail Snatcher	1977	—	2.00	4.00
❏ 0332	Right Here in the Palm of My Hand/Tail Snatcher	1978	—	2.00	4.00

GSF

| ❏ 6874 | Another Place/Stop and Check Yourself | 1972 | — | 3.00 | 6.00 |
| ❏ 6887 | I'll Keep On Loving/Somebody, Someplace | 1972 | — | 3.00 | 6.00 |

UNITED ARTISTS

❏ 0109	Cry Baby/For Your Precious Love	1973	—	2.00	4.00
—"Silver Spotlight Series" reissue					
❏ 629	Cry Baby/Don't Change Your Heart	1963	3.75	7.50	15.00
❏ 658	Baby Don't You Weep/For Your Precious Love	1963	3.00	6.00	12.00
❏ 658 [PS]	Baby Don't You Weep/For Your Precious Love	1963	15.00	30.00	60.00
❏ 694	Tell Me Baby/Anytime You Want Me	1964	3.00	6.00	12.00
❏ 715	One Girl/A Quiet Place	1964	3.00	6.00	12.00
❏ 773	One Woman Man/Look Away	1964	3.00	6.00	12.00
❏ 796	A Little Bit of Soap/I'll Make It Up to You	1964	3.00	6.00	12.00
❏ 848	So Close/It Was Easier to Hurt Her	1965	3.00	6.00	12.00

M

Number	Title (A Side/B Side)	Yr	VG	VG+	NM
❑ 868	Welcome Home/The Adventures of Moll Flanders	1965	3.00	6.00	12.00
❑ 887	Everytime/That Goes to Show You	1965	3.00	6.00	12.00
❑ 951	Looking for You/More Than a Miracle	1965	3.00	6.00	12.00
❑ 995	Prove It to Me/I'll Take Good Care of You	1966	3.00	6.00	12.00
❑ 50058	My Baby/Keep On Smilin'	1966	—	—	—
—Unreleased					
VEEP					
❑ 1232	Thinkin'/It's Been Such a Long Time Comin'	1966	2.00	4.00	8.00
❑ 1234	My Baby/Keep On Smilin'	1966	2.00	4.00	8.00
❑ 1252	All About Love/The Truth Hurts	1967	2.00	4.00	8.00
VERVE					
❑ 10596	Stop and Think It Over/I Can Hear My Baby Crying	1968	2.00	4.00	8.00
❑ 10624	Can You Top This/We Can Find That Love	1968	2.00	4.00	8.00
❑ 10642	Take Me/Happy Landing	1969	2.00	4.00	8.00
❑ 10650	Sad Song/Get It While You Can	1970	2.00	4.00	8.00

Albums

Number	Title	Yr	VG	VG+	NM
ARISTA					
❑ AL 4153	Garnet Mimms Has It All	1978	3.00	6.00	12.00
UNITED ARTISTS					
❑ UAL 3305 [M]	Cry Baby and 11 Other Hits	1963	20.00	40.00	80.00
❑ UAL 3396 [M]	As Long As I Have You	1964	12.50	25.00	50.00
❑ UAL 3498 [M]	I'll Take Good Care of You	1966	12.50	25.00	50.00
❑ UAS 6305 [S]	Cry Baby and 11 Other Hits	1963	25.00	50.00	100.00
❑ UAS 6396 [S]	As Long As I Have You	1964	17.50	35.00	70.00
❑ UAS 6498 [S]	I'll Take Good Care of You	1966	17.50	35.00	70.00

MINORBOPS, THE

45s

Number	Title	Yr	VG	VG+	NM
LAMP					
❑ 2012	Need You Tonight/Want You for My Own	1957	62.50	125.00	250.00

MINT CONDITION

12-Inch Singles

Number	Title	Yr	VG	VG+	NM
PERSPECTIVE					
❑ PSPRO 00282 [DJ]	What Kind of Man Would I Be (4 versions)/I Want It Again (LP Version) (Instrumental)	1997	3.00	6.00	12.00
❑ PSPRO 00375 [DJ]	You Don't Have to Hurt No More (LP Version) (Radio Edit) (Instrumental) (A Cappella)/Change Your Mind (LP Version) (Instrumental) (A Cappella)	1997	3.00	6.00	12.00
❑ PSPRO 00420 [DJ]	You Don't Have to Hurt No More (M Doc's Hip Hop Remix) (M Doc's Hip Hop Remix Instrumental) (Silk's House Remix Instrumental)/(Silk's House Remix) Silk's Scat Dub)	1997	3.00	6.00	12.00
❑ PSPRO 00512 [DJ]	Let Me Be the One (LP Version) (Ummah Remix Featuring Phife) (A Cappella)/(Ummah Remix Featuring Q-Tip) (Silk's House Remix)	1997	2.50	5.00	10.00
❑ 28968 1201 1	Are You Free (12" Peppermint Mix) (12" Spearmint Mix)/(10" After Dinner Mix) (LP Version)	1991	3.00	6.00	12.00
❑ 31458 7449 1	U Send Me Swingin' (unknown versions)	1993	3.00	6.00	12.00
❑ 31458 7461 1	Someone to Love (Extended Remix) Extended Remix Without Vocal Sample) (Instrumental)/(Remix Radio Edit) (Remix Radio Edit Without Vocal Sample) (LP Version)	1994	2.50	5.00	10.00
❑ 31458 7565 1	You Don't Have to Hurt No More (4 versions)/Change Your Mind (3 versions)	1997	3.75	7.50	15.00
❑ 31458 8364 1	So Fine (For Da Nine Four Remix) (Instrumental Remix) (Stewdells's Party Remix) (Party Instrumental Remix)	1995	2.50	5.00	10.00

45s

Number	Title	Yr	VG	VG+	NM
A&M/COLLECTABLES					
❑ 31458 8744 1	U Send Me Swingin'/Someone to Love	199?	—	—	3.00
PERSPECTIVE					
❑ 31458 7564 7	You Don't Have to Hurt No More/What Kind of Man Would I Be	1997	—	—	3.00

Albums

Number	Title	Yr	VG	VG+	NM
PERSPECTIVE					
❑ 28968 1001 1	Meant to Be Mint	1991	3.75	7.50	15.00

MINT JULEPS, THE

45s

Number	Title	Yr	VG	VG+	NM
HERALD					
❑ 481	Bells of Love/Vip-a-Dip	1956	25.00	50.00	100.00
—With script logo inside flag					
❑ 481	Bells of Love/Vip-a-Dip	1956	6.25	12.50	25.00
—With block logo inside flag					

MIRACLES, THE

Includes records as "Smokey Robinson and the Miracles." Also see SMOKEY ROBINSON.

12-Inch Singles

Number	Title	Yr	VG	VG+	NM
COLUMBIA					
❑ AS 283 [DJ]	Spy for Brotherhood (6:04) (same on both sides)	1976	5.00	10.00	20.00
❑ 23-10515	Spy for Brotherhood (6:04)/Women (Make the World Go 'Round) (4:50)	1977	5.00	10.00	20.00
MOTOWN					
❑ PR-129 [DJ]	The Tracks of My Tears/I Second That Emotion//I Heard It Through the Grapevine (5:03)	1983	2.50	5.00	10.00
—As "Smokey Robinson and the Miracles"; B-side by Marvin Gaye; promo-only item issued in conjunction with the movie "The Big Chill"					

45s

Number	Title	Yr	VG	VG+	NM
CHESS					
❑ 1734	Bad Girl/I Love Your Baby	1959	15.00	30.00	60.00
—Blue label with vertical Chess logo (original)					
❑ 1734	Bad Girl/I Love Your Baby	1963	6.25	12.50	25.00
—Black label					
❑ 1734	Bad Girl/I Love Your Baby	1966	5.00	10.00	20.00
—Blue label with "Chess" at top					
❑ 1768	I Need a Change/All I Want (Is You)	1960	10.00	20.00	40.00
COLUMBIA					
❑ 3-10464	Spy for Brotherhood/The Bird Must Fly Away	1976	—	2.50	5.00
❑ 3-10517	Women (Make the World Go 'Round)/I Can Touch the Sky	1977	—	2.50	5.00
❑ 3-10706	Mean Machine/The Magic of Your Eyes (Laura's Eyes)	1978	—	2.50	5.00
END					
❑ 1016	Got a Job/My Mama Done Told Me	1958	15.00	30.00	60.00
❑ 1029	Money/I Cry	1958	12.50	25.00	50.00
—Mostly gray-white label, no mention of Roulette Records					
❑ 1029	Money/I Cry	1958	10.00	20.00	40.00
—Multicolor label with "A Division of Roulette Records Inc." on label					
❑ 1084	Money/I Cry	1961	6.25	12.50	25.00
MOTOWN					
❑ G 1/G 2	Bad Girl/I Love Your Baby	1959	1250.	1875.	2500.
❑ TLX-2207	Bad Girl/I Love Your Baby	1959	1250.	1875.	2500.
STANDARD GROOVE					
❑ 13090 [DJ]	I Care About Detroit	1968	50.00	100.00	200.00
—With Tamla globe logo on label					
❑ 13090 [DJ]	I Care About Detroit	1968	37.50	75.00	150.00
—With no Tamla logo on label					
TAMLA					
❑ EX-009 [DJ]	The Christmas Song/Christmas Everyday	1963	50.00	100.00	200.00
❑ 54028	The Feeling Is So Fine/You Can Depend On Me	1960	125.00	250.00	500.00
—With alternate take of B-side; matrix number followed by "A" in trail-off wax					
❑ 54028	The Feeling Is So Fine/You Can Depend On Me	1960	100.00	200.00	400.00
❑ 54028	Way Over There/Depend On Me	1960	15.00	30.00	60.00
—With overdubbed strings on A-side					
❑ 54028	Way Over There/Depend on Me	1960	37.50	75.00	150.00
—No strings on A-side recording					
❑ 54034	Shop Around/Who's Lovin' You	1960	45.00	90.00	180.00
—Original take, withdrawn shortly after release. In trail-off wax is "H55518A."					
❑ 54034	Shop Around/Who's Lovin' You	1960	7.50	15.00	30.00
—Hit take. In trail-off wax is "L-1." Horizontal lines label.					
❑ 54034	Shop Around/Who's Lovin' You	1960	3.00	6.00	12.00
—Hit take. In trail-off wax is "L-1." Globe label.					
❑ 54036	Ain't It Baby/The Only One I Love	1961	37.50	75.00	150.00
❑ 54044	Mighty Good Lovin'/Broken Hearted	1961	12.50	25.00	50.00
❑ 54044 [PS]	Mighty Good Lovin'/Broken Hearted	1961	37.50	75.00	150.00
❑ 54048	Everybody's Gotta Pay Some Dues/I Can't Believe	1961	12.50	25.00	50.00
❑ 54048	You Gotta Pay Some Dues/I Can't Believe	1961	25.00	50.00	100.00
—Alternate A-side title					
❑ 54048 [PS]	Everybody's Gotta Pay Some Dues/I Can't Believe	1961	50.00	100.00	200.00
❑ 54053	What's So Good About Good-By/I've Been Good to You	1962	7.50	15.00	30.00
❑ 54053 [PS]	What's So Good About Good-By/I've Been Good to You	1962	30.00	60.00	120.00
❑ 54059	I'll Try Something New/You Never Miss a Good Thing	1962	5.00	10.00	20.00
❑ 54059 [PS]	I'll Try Something New/You Never Miss a Good Thing	1962	30.00	60.00	120.00
❑ 54069	Way Over There/If Your Mother Only Knew	1962	5.00	10.00	20.00
❑ 54073	You've Really Got a Hold on Me/Happy Landing	1962	5.00	10.00	20.00
❑ 54078	A Love She Can Count On/I Can Take a Hint	1963	5.00	10.00	20.00
❑ 54083	Mickey's Monkey/Whatever Makes You Happy	1963	5.00	10.00	20.00
❑ 54089	I Gotta Dance to Keep from Crying/Such Is Love, Such Is Life	1963	3.75	7.50	15.00
❑ 54092	(You Can't Let the Boy Overpower) The Man in You/Heartbreak Road	1964	3.75	7.50	15.00
❑ 54098	I Like It Like That/You're So Fine and Sweet	1964	3.75	7.50	15.00
❑ 54098 [PS]	I Like It Like That/You're So Fine and Sweet	1964	30.00	60.00	120.00
❑ 54102	That's What Love Is Made Of/Would I Love You	1964	3.75	7.50	15.00
❑ 54109	Come On Do the Jerk/Baby Don't You Go	1964	3.75	7.50	15.00
❑ 54113	Ooo Baby Baby/All That's Good	1965	3.75	7.50	15.00
❑ 54118	The Tracks of My Tears/A Fork in the Road	1965	3.75	7.50	15.00
❑ 54123	My Girl Has Gone/Since You Won My Heart	1965	3.75	7.50	15.00
❑ 54127	Going to A-Go-Go/Choosey Beggar	1965	3.75	7.50	15.00
❑ 54127 [PS]	Going to A-Go-Go/Choosey Beggar	1965	25.00	50.00	100.00
❑ 54134	Whole Lot of Shakin' in My Heart (Since I Met You)/Oh Be My Lover	1966	2.50	5.00	10.00
❑ 54140	Come 'Round Here — I'm the One You Need/Save Me	1966	2.50	5.00	10.00
❑ 54140 [PS]	Come 'Round Here — I'm the One You Need/Save Me	1966	25.00	50.00	100.00
❑ 54145	The Love I Saw in You Was Just a Mirage/Come Spy with Me	1967	2.00	4.00	8.00
—Starting here, through Tamla 54225, as "Smokey Robinson and the Miracles"					
❑ 54152	More Love/Swept for You Baby	1967	2.00	4.00	8.00
❑ 54159	I Second That Emotion/You Must Be Love	1967	2.00	4.00	8.00
❑ 54162	If You Can Want/When the Words from Your Heart Get Caught Up in Your Throat	1968	2.00	4.00	8.00
—"Tamla" in box on label					

Number	Title (A Side/B Side)	Yr	VG	VG+	NM
❑ 54162	If You Can Want/When the Words from Your Heart Get Caught Up in Your Throat	1968	3.75	7.50	15.00

—"Tamla" in globe on label

Number	Title (A Side/B Side)	Yr	VG	VG+	NM
❑ 54167	Yester Love/Much Better Off	1968	2.00	4.00	8.00
❑ 54172	Special Occasion/Give Her Up	1968	2.00	4.00	8.00
❑ 54178	Baby, Baby Don't Cry/Your Mother's Only Daughter	1968	2.00	4.00	8.00
❑ 54183	Here I Go Again/Doggone Right	1969	2.00	4.00	8.00
❑ 54184	Abraham, Martin, and John/Much Better Off	1969	2.00	4.00	8.00
❑ 54189	Point It Out/Darling Dear	1969	2.00	4.00	8.00
❑ 54194	Who's Gonna Take the Blame/I Gotta Thing For You	1970	2.00	4.00	8.00
❑ 54199	The Tears of a Clown/Promise Me	1970	—	3.00	6.00
❑ 54205	I Don't Blame You at All/That Girl	1971	—	3.00	6.00
❑ 54206	Crazy About the La La La/Oh Baby Baby I Love You	1971	—	3.00	6.00
❑ 54211	Satisfaction/Flower Girl	1971	—	3.00	6.00
❑ 54220	We've Come Too Far to End It Now/When Sundown Comes	1972	—	3.00	6.00
❑ 54225	I Can't Stand to See You Cry/With Your Love Came	1972	—	3.00	6.00
❑ 54237	Don't Let It End (Til You Let It Begin)/Wigs and Lashes	1973	—	2.50	5.00

—Starting here, name reverts to The Miracles

Number	Title (A Side/B Side)	Yr	VG	VG+	NM
❑ 54240	Give Me Just Another Day/I Wanna Be with You	1973	—	2.50	5.00
❑ 54248	Do It Baby/I Wanna Be with You	1974	—	2.50	5.00
❑ 54256	Don't Cha Love It/Up Again	1974	—	2.50	5.00
❑ 54259	You Are Love/Gemini	1975	—	2.50	5.00
❑ 54262	Love Machine (Part 1)/Love Machine (Part 2)	1975	—	2.50	5.00
❑ 54268	Night Life/Smog	1976	—	2.50	5.00

TOPPS/MOTOWN

Number	Title (A Side/B Side)	Yr	VG	VG+	NM
❑ 11	Shop Around	1967	18.75	37.50	75.00

—Cardboard record

Albums

COLUMBIA

Number	Title (A Side/B Side)	Yr	VG	VG+	NM
❑ PC 34460	Love Crazy	1977	3.00	6.00	12.00
❑ PCQ 34460 [Q]	Love Crazy	1977	5.00	10.00	20.00
❑ JC 34910	The Miracles	1978	3.00	6.00	12.00

MOTOWN

Number	Title (A Side/B Side)	Yr	VG	VG+	NM
❑ M5-133V1	Do It Baby	1981	2.00	4.00	8.00

—Reissue of Tamla 334

Number	Title (A Side/B Side)	Yr	VG	VG+	NM
❑ M5-136V1	Away We a Go-Go	1981	2.00	4.00	8.00

—Reissue of Tamla 271

Number	Title (A Side/B Side)	Yr	VG	VG+	NM
❑ M5-156V1	The Tears of a Clown	1981	2.00	4.00	8.00

—Reissue of Tamla 276

Number	Title (A Side/B Side)	Yr	VG	VG+	NM
❑ M5-160V1	Hi, We're the Miracles	1981	2.00	4.00	8.00

—Reissue of Tamla 220

Number	Title (A Side/B Side)	Yr	VG	VG+	NM
❑ M5-210V1	Greatest Hits, Vol. 2	1981	2.00	4.00	8.00

—Reissue of Tamla 280

Number	Title (A Side/B Side)	Yr	VG	VG+	NM
❑ M5-217V1	Doin' Mickey's Monkey	1981	2.00	4.00	8.00

—Reissue of Tamla 245

Number	Title (A Side/B Side)	Yr	VG	VG+	NM
❑ M5-220V1	Recorded Live On Stage	1981	2.00	4.00	8.00

—Reissue of Tamla 241

Number	Title (A Side/B Side)	Yr	VG	VG+	NM
❑ M8-238M2 [(2)]	Greatest Hits from the Beginning	1982	3.00	6.00	12.00

—Reissue of Tamla 254

Number	Title (A Side/B Side)	Yr	VG	VG+	NM
❑ M 793R3 [(3)]	Smokey Robinson and the Miracles Anthology	1974	5.00	10.00	20.00
❑ 5253 ML	The Season for Miracles	1982	2.00	4.00	8.00

—Reissue of Tamla 307

Number	Title (A Side/B Side)	Yr	VG	VG+	NM
❑ 5254 ML	Christmas with the Miracles	1982	2.00	4.00	8.00

—Reissue of Tamla 236

TAMLA

Number	Title (A Side/B Side)	Yr	VG	VG+	NM
❑ T 220 [M]	Hi We're the Miracles	1961	150.00	300.00	600.00

—White label

Number	Title (A Side/B Side)	Yr	VG	VG+	NM
❑ T 223 [M]	Cookin' with the Miracles	1962	200.00	400.00	800.00

—White label

Number	Title (A Side/B Side)	Yr	VG	VG+	NM
❑ T 230 [M]	I'll Try Something New	1962	150.00	300.00	600.00

—White label

Number	Title (A Side/B Side)	Yr	VG	VG+	NM
❑ T 236 [M]	Christmas with the Miracles	1963	75.00	150.00	300.00

—Originals have two globes on the top of the label

Number	Title (A Side/B Side)	Yr	VG	VG+	NM
❑ T 238 [M]	The Fabulous Miracles	1963	75.00	150.00	300.00
❑ T 238 [M]	You've Really Got a Hold on Me	1963	50.00	100.00	200.00

—Retitled version of "The Fabulous Miracles"

Number	Title (A Side/B Side)	Yr	VG	VG+	NM
❑ T 241 [M]	The Miracles On Stage	1963	50.00	100.00	200.00
❑ T 245 [M]	Doin' Mickey's Monkey	1963	50.00	100.00	200.00
❑ TS 245 [S]	Doin' Mickey's Monkey	1963	75.00	150.00	300.00
❑ T 254 [(2) M]	Greatest Hits from the Beginning	1965	12.50	25.00	50.00
❑ TS 254 [(2) P]	Greatest Hits from the Beginning	1965	10.00	20.00	40.00
❑ T 267 [M]	Going to a Go-Go	1966	7.50	15.00	30.00
❑ TS 267 [S]	Going to a Go-Go	1966	10.00	20.00	40.00
❑ T 271 [M]	Away We a Go-Go	1966	6.25	12.50	25.00
❑ TS 271 [S]	Away We a Go-Go	1966	7.50	15.00	30.00
❑ T 276 [M]	Make It Happen	1967	6.25	12.50	25.00
❑ TS 276 [S]	Make It Happen	1967	7.50	15.00	30.00
❑ TS 276 [S]	The Tears of a Clown	1970	3.75	7.50	15.00

—Retitled version of "Make It Happen"

Number	Title (A Side/B Side)	Yr	VG	VG+	NM
❑ TS 280	Greatest Hits, Vol. 2	1968	6.25	12.50	25.00
❑ TS 289	Live!	1969	5.00	10.00	20.00
❑ T 290 [M]	Special Occasion	1968	12.50	25.00	50.00
❑ TS 290 [S]	Special Occasion	1968	5.00	10.00	20.00
❑ TS 295	Time Out for Smokey Robinson & the Miracles	1969	5.00	10.00	20.00
❑ TS 297	Four in Blue	1969	5.00	10.00	20.00
❑ TS 301	What Love Has…Joined Together	1970	3.75	7.50	15.00
❑ TS 306	A Pocket Full of Miracles	1970	3.75	7.50	15.00
❑ T 307	The Season for Miracles	1970	3.75	7.50	15.00
❑ TS 312	One Dozen Roses	1971	3.75	7.50	15.00

Number	Title (A Side/B Side)	Yr	VG	VG+	NM
❑ TS 318	Flying High Together	1972	3.75	7.50	15.00
❑ TS 320 [(2)]	1957-1972	1972	5.00	10.00	20.00
❑ T 325F	Renaissance	1973	3.00	6.00	12.00
❑ T6-334	Do It Baby	1974	3.00	6.00	12.00
❑ T6-336	Don't Cha Love It	1975	3.00	6.00	12.00
❑ T6-339	City of Angels	1975	3.00	6.00	12.00
❑ T6-344	The Power of Music	1976	3.00	6.00	12.00
❑ T7-357	Greatest Hits	1977	3.00	6.00	12.00

MIRACLES, THE (2)

No relation to the more famous group above.

45s

BATON

Number	Title (A Side/B Side)	Yr	VG	VG+	NM
❑ 210	A Lover's Chant/Come Home with Me	1955	37.50	75.00	150.00

CASH

Number	Title (A Side/B Side)	Yr	VG	VG+	NM
❑ 1008	You're An Angel/A Gal Named Jo	1955	50.00	100.00	200.00

MIRETTES, THE

Also see THE IKETTES.

45s

MINIT

Number	Title (A Side/B Side)	Yr	VG	VG+	NM
❑ 32045	Help Wanted/Play Fair	1968	2.50	5.00	10.00

MIRWOOD

Number	Title (A Side/B Side)	Yr	VG	VG+	NM
❑ 5514	He's Alright with Me/Your Kind Ain't No Good	1966	3.00	6.00	12.00
❑ 5531	He's Alright with Me/Now That I Found You Baby	1967	2.50	5.00	10.00

REVUE

Number	Title (A Side/B Side)	Yr	VG	VG+	NM
❑ 11004	In the Midnight Hour/To Love Somebody	1968	2.50	5.00	10.00
❑ 11017	Take Me for a Little While/Real Thing	1968	2.00	4.00	8.00
❑ 11029	First Love/I'm a Whole New Thing	1968	2.00	4.00	8.00

UNI

Number	Title (A Side/B Side)	Yr	VG	VG+	NM
❑ 55110	Stand By Your Man/If Everybody'd Help Somebody	1969	—	3.00	6.00
❑ 55126	Heart Full of Gladness/You Ain't Trying to Cross Over	1969	—	3.00	6.00
❑ 55147	Whirlpool/You Ain't Trying to Cross Over	1969	—	3.00	6.00
❑ 55161	Rap Run It On Down/Sweet Soul Sister	1969	—	3.00	6.00

—A-side: Nate Turner and the Mirettes; B-side: Venetta Fields and the Mirettes

Albums

REVUE

Number	Title (A Side/B Side)	Yr	VG	VG+	NM
❑ RS-7205	In the Midnight Hour	1968	3.75	7.50	15.00

UNI

Number	Title (A Side/B Side)	Yr	VG	VG+	NM
❑ 73062	Whirlpool	1969	3.75	7.50	15.00

MITCHELL, BILLY

45s

ATLANTIC

Number	Title (A Side/B Side)	Yr	VG	VG+	NM
❑ 933	My Love, My Desire/Pack Up All Your Bags	1951	75.00	150.00	300.00
❑ 950	If I Had Known/Verna Lee	1951	50.00	100.00	200.00
❑ 954	Let's Have a Ball Tonight/Someday You'll Be Sorry	1952	50.00	100.00	200.00
❑ 974	Ghost Train/Bald Headed Woman	1952	50.00	100.00	200.00

—With Joe Morris

CALLA

Number	Title (A Side/B Side)	Yr	VG	VG+	NM
❑ 165	Oh Happy Day/The Chokin' Kind	1969	2.00	4.00	8.00
❑ 167	Too Busy Thinking 'Bout My Baby/Crystal Blue Persuasion	1969	2.00	4.00	8.00

IMPERIAL

Number	Title (A Side/B Side)	Yr	VG	VG+	NM
❑ 5520	Satellite Be-Bop/Pickin' on the Wrong Chicken	1958	5.00	10.00	20.00

JUBILEE

Number	Title (A Side/B Side)	Yr	VG	VG+	NM
❑ 5400	Short Skirts/You Know I Do	1961	3.75	7.50	15.00

UNITED ARTISTS

Number	Title (A Side/B Side)	Yr	VG	VG+	NM
❑ 235	Call to Me (I'll Be Here)/Where	1960	3.75	7.50	15.00

WARWICK

Number	Title (A Side/B Side)	Yr	VG	VG+	NM
❑ 501	It Doesn't Matter to Me/Stop a Little While	1959	3.75	7.50	15.00

MITCHELL, BOBBY

45s

IMPERIAL

Number	Title (A Side/B Side)	Yr	VG	VG+	NM
❑ 5236	I'm Cryin'/Rack 'Em Back	1953	50.00	100.00	200.00
❑ 5250	One Friday Morning/Four-Eleven-Forty-Four	1953	50.00	100.00	200.00
❑ 5270	Baby's Gone/Sister Lucy	1954	30.00	60.00	120.00
❑ 5282	Angel Child/School Boy Blues	1954	30.00	60.00	120.00
❑ 5295	The Wedding Bells Are Ringing/Meant for Me	1954	30.00	60.00	120.00
❑ 5309	I'm a Young Man/She Couldn't Be Found	1954	30.00	60.00	120.00
❑ 5326	I Wish I Knew/Nothing Sweet As You	1955	20.00	40.00	80.00
❑ 5346	I Cried/I'm in Love	1955	15.00	30.00	60.00
❑ 5378	Try Rock and Roll/No, No, No	1956	12.50	25.00	50.00
❑ 5392	Goin' 'Round in Circles/I Try So Hard	1956	12.50	25.00	50.00
❑ 5412	You Are My Angel/I've Got My Fingers Crossed	1956	12.50	25.00	50.00
❑ 5440	You Always Hurt the One You Love/I Would Like to Know	1957	10.00	20.00	40.00
❑ 5475	I'm Gonna Be a Wheel Someday/You Better Go Home	1957	12.50	25.00	50.00
❑ 5511	I Love to Hold You/64 Hours	1958	10.00	20.00	40.00
❑ 5558	Hearts of Fire/You're Going to Be Sorry	1959	10.00	20.00	40.00
❑ 5882	My Southern Bell/When First We Met	1962	3.00	6.00	12.00
❑ 5923	I Don't Want to Be a Wheel No More/I Got to Call That Number	1963	3.00	6.00	12.00

RON

Number	Title (A Side/B Side)	Yr	VG	VG+	NM
❑ 337	Sand Me Your Picture/You're Doing Me Wrong	1961	3.00	6.00	12.00
❑ 342	Mama Don't Allow/There's Only One of You	1961	3.00	6.00	12.00

M

MITCHELL, WILLIE

45s

HI

Number	Title (A Side/B Side)	Yr	VG	VG+	NM
❑ 2044	The Crawl (Part 1)/The Crawl (Part 2)	1962	2.50	5.00	10.00
❑ 2053	Drippin'/Buddy Bear	1962	2.50	5.00	10.00
❑ 2058	Easy Now/Sunrise Serenade	1962	2.50	5.00	10.00
❑ 2066	Percolatin'/Empty Rooms	1963	2.50	5.00	10.00
❑ 2075	20-75/Secret Home	1964	2.00	4.00	8.00
❑ 2083	Percolatin'/Check Me	1964	2.00	4.00	8.00
❑ 2091	Buster Browne/Woodchopper's Ball	1965	2.00	4.00	8.00
❑ 2097	That Driving Beat/Everything Is Gonna Be Alright	1965	2.00	4.00	8.00
❑ 2103	Bad Eye/Sugar T	1966	—	3.00	6.00
❑ 2112	Mercy/Sticks and Stones	1966	—	3.00	6.00
❑ 2119	Misty/Barefootin'	1967	—	3.00	6.00
❑ 2125	Au Shucks/Slippin' and Slidin'	1967	—	3.00	6.00
❑ 2132	Lucky/Ooh Baby, You Turn Me On	1967	—	3.00	6.00
❑ 2140	Soul Serenade/Mercy, Mercy, Mercy	1968	—	3.00	6.00
❑ 2147	Prayer Meetin'/Run Daddy	1968	—	3.00	6.00
❑ 2151	Up-Hard/Beale Street Mood	1968	—	3.00	6.00
❑ 2151	Up-Hard/Red Light	1968	—	3.00	6.00
❑ 2154	30-60-90/Take Five	1969	—	3.00	6.00
❑ 2158	Young People/Kitten Korner	1969	—	3.00	6.00
❑ 2167	My Babe/Teenie's Dream	1969	—	3.00	6.00
❑ 2175	Six to Go/Robin's Nest	1970	—	2.50	5.00
❑ 2181	Wade in the Water/Tails Out	1970	—	2.50	5.00
❑ 2190	Too Sweet/Restless	1971	—	2.50	5.00
❑ 2196	Breaking Point/Roadhouse	1971	—	2.50	5.00
❑ 2237	Last Tango in Paris/Six to Go	1973	—	2.00	4.00

HOME OF THE BLUES

Number	Title (A Side/B Side)	Yr	VG	VG+	NM
❑ 111	Thirty-Five Thirty/Yvonne	1960	3.00	6.00	12.00
❑ 119	One Mint Julep/I've Got a Right	1961	3.00	6.00	12.00
❑ 123	I Like It/Willie's House Party	1961	3.00	6.00	12.00

Albums

BEARSVILLE

Number	Title (A Side/B Side)	Yr	VG	VG+	NM
❑ BRK 3520	... Listen ... Dance	1980	2.50	5.00	10.00

HI

Number	Title (A Side/B Side)	Yr	VG	VG+	NM
❑ 8002	Willie Mitchell Live	1977	2.50	5.00	10.00
❑ HL-32010 [M]	Sunrise Serenade	1963	10.00	20.00	40.00
❑ SHL-32010 [S]	Sunrise Serenade	1963	6.25	12.50	25.00
❑ HL-32021 [M]	Hold It	1964	6.25	12.50	25.00
❑ SHL-32021 [S]	Hold It	1964	7.50	15.00	30.00
❑ HL-32026 [M]	It's Dance Time	1965	6.25	12.50	25.00
❑ HL-32029 [M]	Driving Beat	1966	6.25	12.50	25.00
❑ SHL-32029 [S]	Driving Beat	1966	7.50	15.00	30.00
❑ HL-32034 [M]	The Hit Sound of Willie Mitchell	1967	7.50	15.00	30.00
❑ SHL-32034 [S]	The Hit Sound of Willie Mitchell	1967	6.25	12.50	25.00
❑ SHL-32036 [S]	It's Dance Time	1965	7.50	15.00	30.00
❑ HL-32039 [M]	Ooh Baby, You Turn Me On	1967	7.50	15.00	30.00
❑ SHL-32039 [S]	Ooh Baby, You Turn Me On	1967	6.25	12.50	25.00
❑ SHL-32042	Willie Mitchell Live	1968	6.25	12.50	25.00
❑ SHL-32045	Solid Soul	1968	6.25	12.50	25.00
❑ SHL-32048	On Top	1969	6.25	12.50	25.00
❑ SHL-32050	Soul Bag	1969	6.25	12.50	25.00
❑ SHL-32056	The Many Moods of Willie Mitchell	1970	6.25	12.50	25.00
❑ SHL-32058	Robin's Nest	1970	6.25	12.50	25.00
❑ SHL-32068/9 [(2)]	The Best of Willie Mitchell	1971	7.50	15.00	30.00

MOMENTS, THE

R&B trio. For legal reasons, their records on EMI America, EMI Manhattan, Panoramic and Polydor were issued under the name "Ray, Goodman and Brown."

45s

ALL PLATINUM

Number	Title (A Side/B Side)	Yr	VG	VG+	NM
❑ 2350	Sho Nuff Boogie (Part 1)/Sho Nuff Boogie (Part 2)	1974	—	2.50	5.00
—With Sylvia					

EMI AMERICA

Number	Title (A Side/B Side)	Yr	VG	VG+	NM
❑ 8365	Take It to the Limit/(Instrumental)	1986	—	—	3.00
❑ 8365 [PS]	Take It to the Limit/(Instrumental)	1986	—	—	3.00
❑ 8378	Celebrate Our Love/(Instrumental)	1987	—	—	3.00
❑ 8378 [PS]	Celebrate Our Love/(Instrumental)	1987	—	—	3.00
❑ 43022	Tonight (Baby)/Good Love	1987	—	—	3.00

EMI MANHATTAN

Number	Title (A Side/B Side)	Yr	VG	VG+	NM
❑ 50155	Where Did You Get That Body, (Baby)?/Where Are You Now	1988	—	—	3.00
❑ 50155 [PS]	Where Did You Get That Body, (Baby)?/Where Are You Now	1988	—	—	3.00

HOG

Number	Title (A Side/B Side)	Yr	VG	VG+	NM
❑ 1000	Baby I Want You/(B-side unknown)	196?	500.00	1000.	2000.

PANORAMIC

Number	Title (A Side/B Side)	Yr	VG	VG+	NM
❑ 201	Who's Gonna Make the First Move/Look Like Lovers	1984	—	2.00	4.00

POLYDOR

Number	Title (A Side/B Side)	Yr	VG	VG+	NM
❑ 2033	Special Lady/Deja Vu	1979	—	2.50	5.00
❑ 2077	Inside of You/Treat Her Right	1980	—	2.00	4.00
❑ 2116	My Prayer/The Way It Should Be	1980	—	2.00	4.00
❑ 2135	Happy Anniversary/You	1980	—	2.00	4.00
❑ 2159	Shoestrings/Me	1981	—	2.00	4.00
❑ 2191	How Can Love Be So Right (Yet So Wrong)/Each Time Is Like the First Time	1981	—	2.00	4.00
❑ 2203	Stay/Good Ole Days	1982	—	2.00	4.00
❑ 2208	Till the Right One Comes Along/Heaven in the Rain	1982	—	2.00	4.00
❑ 2222	Gambled on Your Love/Pool of Love	1982	—	2.00	4.00
❑ 2227	After All/Love Minus One	1982	—	2.00	4.00
❑ 810056-7	Special Lady/My Prayer	1983	—	—	3.00
—Reissue					

STANG

Number	Title (A Side/B Side)	Yr	VG	VG+	NM
❑ 5000	Not on the Outside/Understanding	1968	2.00	4.00	8.00
❑ 5003	Sunday/Everybody Loves My Baby	1969	—	3.00	6.00
❑ 5005	I Do/Pocketful of Heartbreaks	1969	—	3.00	6.00
❑ 5008	I'm So Lost/Where	1969	—	3.00	6.00
❑ 5009	Lovely Way She Loves/I've Got to Keep On Loving, Love	1969	—	3.00	6.00
❑ 5012	Love on a Two-Way Street/I Won't Do Anything	1970	2.00	4.00	8.00
❑ 5016	If I Didn't Care/You Make Me Feel Good	1970	—	3.00	6.00
❑ 5017	All I Have/The Hurt's On Me	1970	—	3.00	6.00
❑ 5020	I Can't Help It/To You with Love	1971	—	3.00	6.00
❑ 5024	That's How It Feels/That's How It Feels (Long)	1971	—	3.00	6.00
❑ 5031	Lucky Me/I Lost One Bird in the Hand (Reaching Out for Two in the Bush)	1971	—	3.00	6.00
❑ 5033	To You with Love/Key to My Happiness	1971	—	3.00	6.00
❑ 5036	Thanks a Lot/I Lost One Bird in the Hand (Reaching Out for Two in the Bush)	1972	—	3.00	6.00
❑ 5041	Just Because He Wants to Make Love (Doesn't Mean He Loves You)/So This Is Our Goodbye	1972	—	3.00	6.00
❑ 5045	My Thing/Thanks a Lot	1972	—	3.00	6.00
❑ 5048	Girl I'm Gonna Miss You/I Think So	1973	—	2.50	5.00
❑ 5050	Gotta Find a Way/Sweeter As the Days Go By	1973	—	2.50	5.00
❑ 5052	Sexy Mama/Where Can I Find Her	1973	—	3.00	6.00
❑ 5054	Sweet Sweet Lady/Next Time I See You	1974	—	2.50	5.00
❑ 5056	What's Your Name/Mama I Miss You	1974	—	2.50	5.00
❑ 5057	Girls (Part 1)/Girls (Part 2)	1974	—	2.50	5.00
—With the Whatnauts					
❑ 5060	Look at Me (I'm in Love)/You've Come a Long Way	1975	—	2.50	5.00
❑ 5064	Got to Get to Know You/I Feel So Bad	1975	—	2.50	5.00
❑ 5066	Nine Times/When the Morning Comes	1976	—	2.50	5.00
❑ 5068	With You/The Next Time I See You	1976	—	2.50	5.00
❑ 5071	We Don't Cry Out Loud/Come In Girl	1977	—	2.50	5.00
❑ 5073	I Don't Wanna Go/Oh I Could Have Loved You	1977	—	2.50	5.00
❑ 5075	I Could Have Loved You/Jack in the Box	1978	—	2.50	5.00
❑ 5076	Rain in My Backyard/Disco Man	1978	—	2.50	5.00

SUGAR HILL

Number	Title (A Side/B Side)	Yr	VG	VG+	NM
❑ 758	Baby Let's Rap Now (Part 1)/Baby Let's Rap Now (Part 2)	1980	—	2.50	5.00
❑ 769	Record Breakin' Love Affair/(B-side unknown)	1981	—	2.50	5.00

Albums

CHESS

Number	Title (A Side/B Side)	Yr	VG	VG+	NM
❑ CH2-92517 [(2)]	Greatest Hits	198?	3.00	6.00	12.00

POLYDOR

Number	Title (A Side/B Side)	Yr	VG	VG+	NM
❑ PD-1-6240	Ray, Goodman & Brown	1979	2.50	5.00	10.00
❑ PD-1-6299	Ray, Goodman & Brown II	1980	2.50	5.00	10.00
❑ PD-1-6341	Stay	1981	2.50	5.00	10.00

STANG

Number	Title (A Side/B Side)	Yr	VG	VG+	NM
❑ ST-1000	Not On the Outside, But On the Inside Strong	1969	7.50	15.00	30.00
❑ ST-1002	The Moments On Top	1970	7.50	15.00	30.00
❑ ST-1003	A Moment with the Moments	1970	7.50	15.00	30.00
❑ ST-1004	Moments Greatest Hits	1971	5.00	10.00	20.00
❑ ST-1006	The Moments Live at the New York State Womans Prison	1971	6.25	12.50	25.00
❑ ST-1009	The Other Side of the Moments	1972	6.25	12.50	25.00
❑ ST-1015	Live at the Miss Black America Pageant	1972	5.00	10.00	20.00
❑ ST-1019	The Best of the Moments	1975	3.75	7.50	15.00
❑ ST-1022	My Thing	1973	3.75	7.50	15.00
❑ ST-1023	The Sexy Moments	1974	3.75	7.50	15.00
❑ ST-1026	Look at Me	1975	3.75	7.50	15.00
❑ ST-1030	Moments With You	1976	3.75	7.50	15.00
❑ 2ST-1033 [(2)]	Greatest Hits	1977	5.00	10.00	20.00
❑ ST-1034	Sharp	1978	3.75	7.50	15.00

MONARCHS, THE (1)

45s

MONUMENT

Number	Title (A Side/B Side)	Yr	VG	VG+	NM
❑ 03484	Look Homeward, Angel/This Old Heart	1983	—	2.50	5.00

SOUND STAGE 7

Number	Title (A Side/B Side)	Yr	VG	VG+	NM
❑ 2502	This Old Heart/'Til I Hear It From You	1963	3.00	6.00	12.00
❑ 2516	Look Homeward, Angel/What Made You Change Your Mind	1964	3.00	6.00	12.00
❑ 2530	Climb Every Mountain/Take Me Home	1964	3.00	6.00	12.00

MONARCHS, THE (3)

45s

MELBA

Number	Title (A Side/B Side)	Yr	VG	VG+	NM
❑ 101	Pretty Little Girl/In My Younger Days	1956	20.00	40.00	80.00

NEIL

Number	Title (A Side/B Side)	Yr	VG	VG+	NM
❑ 101	Pretty Little Girl/In My Younger Days	1956	37.50	75.00	150.00
❑ 103	Always Be Faithful/How Are You	1956	30.00	60.00	120.00

MONDELLOS, THE

45s

RHYTHM

Number	Title (A Side/B Side)	Yr	VG	VG+	NM
❑ 102	Come Back Home/100 Years from Today	1956	50.00	100.00	200.00
—As "Alice Jean and the Mondellos"					
❑ 105	Over the Rainbow/Never Leave Me Alone	1956	37.50	75.00	150.00
—As "Yul McClay and the Mondellos"					
❑ 106	That's What I Call Love/Daylight Saving Time	1956	37.50	75.00	150.00
❑ 109	Hard to Please/Happiness Street	1957	37.50	75.00	150.00

After "Love Is Strange" was a hit on Groove, a different RCA subsidiary, Vik, put out *New Sounds,* a collection of Mickey and Sylvia tracks.

It started a wave of answer songs that lasted well over a year. Here is the 1954 hit "Work with Me Annie" by the Midnighters on the silver-top Federal 45. Very early pressings credited this single to "The Royals."

Rockin' the Boogie by Amos Milburn on an Aladdin 10-inch disc is among the most sought-after R&B albums. It's even more rare with a red vinyl record.

In 1968, the Miracles – as "Smokey Robinson and the Miracles" – recorded a special record to help boost their hometown of Detroit. "I Care About Detroit" was issued with two different label variations, of which this is slightly more common.

Before Smokey and the gang became famous, there was another group called the Miracles. "A Lover's Chant," issued on Baton in 1955, is a three-figure disc in near-mint condition.

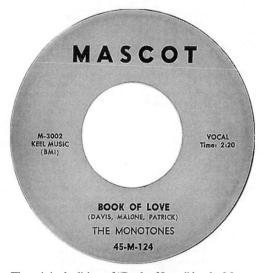

The original edition of "Book of Love" by the Monotones appeared on the Mascot label before it became a big national hit on Argo.

M

Number	Title (A Side/B Side)	Yr	VG	VG+	NM
❑ 114	My Heart/That's What I Call Love	1957	37.50	75.00	150.00
—As "Rudy Lambert and the Mondellos"					
❑ 128	That Old Feeling/Sunday Kind of Love	1957	37.50	75.00	150.00
—As "Rudy Lambert and the Mondellos"					

MONITORS, THE (1)

45s

Number	Title (A Side/B Side)	Yr	VG	VG+	NM
SOUL					
❑ 35049	Step by Step (Hand in Hand)/Time Is Passing By	1968	3.75	7.50	15.00
V.I.P.					
❑ 25028	Say You/All for Someone	1965	5.00	10.00	20.00
❑ 25032	Greetings (This Is Uncle Sam)/Number One in Your Heart	1965	5.00	10.00	20.00
❑ 25039	Since I Lost You Girl/Don't Put Off Till Tomorrow What You Can Do Today	1966	5.00	10.00	20.00
❑ 25046	Bring Back the Love/The Further You Look, The Less You See	1967	5.00	10.00	20.00
❑ 25049	Step by Step (Hand in Hand)/Time Is Passing By	1968	12.50	25.00	50.00

MONITORS, THE (2)

45s

Number	Title (A Side/B Side)	Yr	VG	VG+	NM
ALADDIN					
❑ 3309	Tonight's the Night/Candy Coated Kisses	1955	25.00	50.00	100.00

MONOTONES, THE (1)

Male vocal group from New Jersey.

45s

Number	Title (A Side/B Side)	Yr	VG	VG+	NM
ARGO					
❑ 5290	Book of Love/You Never Loved Me	1958	7.50	15.00	30.00
❑ 5301	Tom Foolery/Zombi	1958	7.50	15.00	30.00
❑ 5321	The Legend of Sleepy Hollow/Soft Shadows	1958	7.50	15.00	30.00
❑ 5339	Tell It to the Judge/Fools Will Be Fools	1959	12.50	25.00	50.00
HULL					
❑ 735	Reading the Book of Love/Dream	1960	12.50	25.00	50.00
❑ 743	Daddy's Home, But Momma's Gone/Tattle Tale	1961	12.50	25.00	50.00
MASCOT					
❑ 124	Book of Love/You Never Loved Me	1957	200.00	400.00	800.00

MONTEREYS, THE

More than one group.

45s

Number	Title (A Side/B Side)	Yr	VG	VG+	NM
ARWIN					
❑ 130	Goodbye My Love/It Hurts Me So	1961	10.00	20.00	40.00
BLAST					
❑ 219	Face in the Crowd/Step Right Up	1965	100.00	200.00	400.00
DOMINION					
❑ 1019	First Kiss/Just One More Kiss	1964	10.00	20.00	40.00
EASTWEST					
❑ 121	I'll Love You Again/The American Teens	1958	6.25	12.50	25.00
GNP CRESCENDO					
❑ 314	For Sentimental Reasons/I Still Love You	1964	6.25	12.50	25.00
IMPALA					
❑ 213	Without a Girl/So Deep	1959	30.00	60.00	120.00
MAJOR					
❑ 1009	A Crowded Room/You Said That You Loved Me	1959	17.50	35.00	70.00
PRINCE					
❑ 5060	Rita/Billy Bud	1960	3.75	7.50	15.00
ROSE					
❑ 109	You're the Girl for Me/Ape Shape	1958	25.00	50.00	100.00
SATURN					
❑ 1002	My Girl/With You	1956	10.00	20.00	40.00
TRANS AMERICAN					
❑ 1000/1	Darlin' Send Me a Letter/Late Darlin'	1960	150.00	300.00	600.00

MONTGOMERY, TAMMY

Later known as TAMMI TERRELL.

45s

Number	Title (A Side/B Side)	Yr	VG	VG+	NM
CHECKER					
❑ 1072	If I Would Marry You/This Time Tomorrow	1964	10.00	20.00	40.00
—Maroon label					
❑ 1072	If I Would Marry You/This Time Tomorrow	1964	6.25	12.50	25.00
—Mostly blue label with red and black checkers					
SCEPTER					
❑ 1224	If You See Bill/It's Mine	1961	15.00	30.00	60.00
TRY ME					
❑ 28001	I Cried/If You Don't Think	1962	7.50	15.00	30.00
—As "Tana Montgomery"					
WAND					
❑ 123	Voice of Experience/I Wancha' to Be Sure	1962	7.50	15.00	30.00

MOONGLOWS, THE

Also see HARVEY.

45s

Number	Title (A Side/B Side)	Yr	VG	VG+	NM
BIG P					
❑ 101	Sincerely '72/You've Chosen Me	1972	2.50	5.00	10.00
CHAMPAGNE					
❑ 7500	I Just Can't Tell No Lie/I've Been Your Dog (Ever Since I've Been Your Man)	1952	375.00	750.00	1500.
CHANCE					
❑ 1147	Baby Please/Whistle My Love	1953	250.00	500.00	1000.
—Black vinyl					
❑ 1147	Baby Please/Whistle My Love	1953	1500.	2250.	3000.
—Red vinyl					
❑ 1150	Just a Lonely Christmas/Hey, Santa Claus	1953	1500.	2250.	3000.
—Red vinyl (this may not exist legitimately on black vinyl)					
❑ 1152	Secret Love/Real Gone Mama	1954	375.00	750.00	1500.
—Silver and blue label					
❑ 1152	Secret Love/Real Gone Mama	1954	250.00	500.00	1000.
—Yellow and black label					
❑ 1156	I Was Wrong/Ooh Rockin' Daddy	1954	150.00	300.00	600.00
—Yellow and black label					
❑ 1156	I Was Wrong/Ooh Rockin' Daddy	1954	150.00	300.00	600.00
—Black and white label					
❑ 1161	My Gal/219 Train	1954	2500.	3750.	5000.
CHESS					
❑ 1581	Sincerely/Tempting	1954	15.00	30.00	60.00
—Blue label, silver top					
❑ 1589	Most of All/She's Gone	1955	15.00	30.00	60.00
—Blue label, silver top					
❑ 1598	Foolish Me/Slow Down	1955	15.00	30.00	60.00
—Blue label, silver top					
❑ 1605	Starlite/In Love	1955	15.00	30.00	60.00
—Blue label, silver top					
❑ 1611	In My Diary/Lover, Love Me	1955	15.00	30.00	60.00
—Blue label, silver top					
❑ 1619	We Go Together/Chickie Um Bah	1956	12.50	25.00	50.00
—Blue label, silver top					
❑ 1629	See Saw/When I'm With You	1956	12.50	25.00	50.00
—Blue label, silver top					
❑ 1646	Over and Over Again/I Knew from the Start	1957	15.00	30.00	60.00
—With slower version of A-side; "8189A" in in the run-off area					
❑ 1646	Over and Over Again/I Knew from the Start	1957	12.50	25.00	50.00
—With normal version of A-side; blue label, silver top					
❑ 1651	I'm Afraid the Masquerade Is Over/Don't Say Goodbye	1957	12.50	25.00	50.00
—Blue label, silver top					
❑ 1661	Please Send Me Someone to Love/Mr. Engineer (Bring Her Back to Me)	1957	12.50	25.00	50.00
—Blue label, silver top					
❑ 1669	The Beating of My Heart/Confess It to Your Heart	1957	12.50	25.00	50.00
—In general, for the above singles, the blue label with vertical "Chess" versions are 60% of the above values; yellow early-1960s label versions and black mid-1960s versions are 40% of above; and blue late-1960s versions, with "Chess" on top, are about 20%					
❑ 1681	Too Late/Here I Am	1958	7.50	15.00	30.00
❑ 1689	In the Middle of the Night/Soda Pop	1958	7.50	15.00	30.00
❑ 1701	This Love/Sweeter Than Words	1958	7.50	15.00	30.00
❑ 1705	Ten Commandments of Love/Mean Old Blues	1958	7.50	15.00	30.00
—As "Harvey and the Moonglows"					
❑ 1717	Love Is a River/I'll Never Stop Wanting You	1959	6.25	12.50	25.00
❑ 1738	Mama Loocie/Unemployment	1959	6.25	12.50	25.00
—As "Harvey and the Moonglows"					
❑ 1770	Beatnick/Junior	1960	6.25	12.50	25.00
❑ 1811	Blue Velvet/Penny Arcade	1962	6.25	12.50	25.00
—As "Bobby Lester and the Moonglows"					
CRIMSON					
❑ 1003	My Imagination/Gee	1964	5.00	10.00	20.00
LOST NITE					
❑ 275	Just a Lonely Christmas/Baby Please	196?	3.00	6.00	12.00
—Reissue					
MELLO					
❑ 69	Just a Lonely Christmas/Hey, Santa Claus	19??	2.00	4.00	8.00
—Reissue					
RCA VICTOR					
❑ 74-0759	Sincerely/I Was Wrong	1972	—	2.50	5.00
❑ 74-0839	When I'm With You/You've Chosen Me	1972	—	2.50	5.00
VEE JAY					
❑ 423	Secret Love/Real Gone Mama	1962	6.25	12.50	25.00

78s

Number	Title (A Side/B Side)	Yr	VG	VG+	NM
CHAMPAGNE					
❑ 7500	I Just Can't Tell No Lie/I've Been Your Dog (Ever Since I've Been Your Man)	1952	250.00	500.00	1000.
CHANCE					
❑ 1147	Baby Please/Whistle My Love	1953	75.00	150.00	300.00
❑ 1150	Just a Lonely Christmas/Hey, Santa Claus	1953	75.00	150.00	300.00
❑ 1152	Secret Love/Real Gone Mama	1954	75.00	150.00	300.00
❑ 1156	I Was Wrong/Ooh Rockin' Daddy	1954	62.50	125.00	250.00
❑ 1161	My Gal/219 Train	1954	125.00	250.00	500.00
CHESS					
❑ 1581	Sincerely/Tempting	1954	12.50	25.00	50.00
❑ 1589	Most of All/She's Gone	1955	12.50	25.00	50.00
❑ 1598	Foolish Me/Slow Down	1955	12.50	25.00	50.00
❑ 1605	Starlite/In Love	1955	12.50	25.00	50.00
❑ 1611	In My Diary/Lover, Love Me	1955	12.50	25.00	50.00
❑ 1619	We Go Together/Chickie Um Bah	1956	12.50	25.00	50.00
❑ 1629	See Saw/When I'm With You	1956	12.50	25.00	50.00
❑ 1646	Over and Over Again/I Knew from the Start	1957	12.50	25.00	50.00
❑ 1651	I'm Afraid the Masquerade Is Over/Don't Say Goodbye	1957	12.50	25.00	50.00
❑ 1661	Please Send Me Someone to Love/Mr. Engineer (Bring Her Back to Me)	1957	12.50	25.00	50.00
❑ 1669	The Beating of My Heart/Confess It to Your Heart	1957	12.50	25.00	50.00
❑ 1681	Too Late/Here I Am	1958	12.50	25.00	50.00
❑ 1689	In the Middle of the Night/Soda Pop	1958	12.50	25.00	50.00
❑ 1701	This Love/Sweeter Than Words	1958	12.50	25.00	50.00
❑ 1705	Ten Commandments of Love/Mean Old Blues	1958	15.00	30.00	60.00
—As "Harvey and the Moonglows"					

Number	Title (A Side/B Side)	Yr	VG	VG+	NM
7-Inch Extended Plays					
CHESS					
5122	(contents unknown)	1959	62.50	125.00	250.00
5122 [PS]	Look! It's the Moonglows	1959	62.50	125.00	250.00
5123	True Love/Penny Arcade//I'll Stop Waiting/ Sweeter Than Words	1959	62.50	125.00	250.00
5123 [PS]	Look! It's the Moonglows, Vol. 2	1959	62.50	125.00	250.00
Albums					
CHESS					
LP 1430 [M]	Look! It's the Moonglows	1959	125.00	250.00	500.00
LP 1471 [M]	The Best of Bobby Lester & the Moonglows	1962	75.00	150.00	300.00
—Black label					
LP 1471 [M]	The Best of Bobby Lester & the Moonglows	1966	12.50	25.00	50.00
—Blue, fading to white label					
CH-9111	Their Greatest Sides	1986	3.00	6.00	12.00
CH-9193	Look! It's the Moonglows	1987	3.00	6.00	12.00
—Reissue of 1430					
CONSTELLATION					
C-2 [M]	Collectors Showcase — The Moonglows	1964	25.00	50.00	100.00
—Light blue lettering					
C-2 [M]	Collectors Showcase — The Moonglows	1964	12.50	25.00	50.00
—Dark blue lettering					
LOST-NITE					
LP-23 [10]	The Moonglows	1981	3.00	6.00	12.00
RCA VICTOR					
LSP-4722	The Return of the Moonglows	1972	3.75	7.50	15.00

MOORE, GATEMOUTH
45s
KING

Number	Title (A Side/B Side)	Yr	VG	VG+	NM
4492	Christmas Blues/Happy New Year, Darling	1951	12.50	25.00	50.00
—B-side by Lonnie Johnson					
78s					
ARISTOCRAT					
905	The Bible's Being Fulfilled Every Day/Glory, Glory, Hallelujah	1949	7.50	15.00	30.00
CHESS					
1437	I'm Going Through/Thank You Jesus	1950	7.50	15.00	30.00
KING					
4178	I'm a Fool to Care/Highway 61 Blues	1947	7.50	15.00	30.00
4187	Gamblin' Woman/Satisfying Papa	1947	7.50	15.00	30.00
4195	Christmas Blues/Teasin' Brown	1947	7.50	15.00	30.00
4211	Hey Mr. Gatemouth/Don't You Know I Love You Baby	1948	7.50	15.00	30.00
4224	East of the Sun/Gotta Walk	1948	7.50	15.00	30.00
4256	Something I'm Gonna Be/You're My Specialty Baby	1948	7.50	15.00	30.00
4492	Christmas Blues/Happy New Year, Darling	1951	5.00	10.00	20.00
—B-side by Lonnie Johnson					
NATIONAL					
4004	Walking My Blues Away/Bum Dee Dah Ra Dee	1946	6.25	12.50	25.00
4010	Christmas Blues/Israel	1946	6.25	12.50	25.00
4015	They Can't Do This to Me/Love Doctor Blues	1947	6.25	12.50	25.00
Albums					
AUDIO FIDELITY					
AFLP-1921 [M]	Revival!	196?	15.00	30.00	60.00
AFSD-5921 [S]	Revival!	196?	20.00	40.00	80.00
BLUESWAY					
BLS 6074	After 21 Years	1973	5.00	10.00	20.00
KING					
684 [M]	Gatemouth Moore Sings Blues	1960	1250.	2500.	5000.

MOORE, JACKIE
12-Inch Singles
COLUMBIA

Number	Title (A Side/B Side)	Yr	VG	VG+	NM
10994	This Time Baby/Let's Go Somewhere and Make Love	1979	2.50	5.00	10.00
11136	How's Your Love Life Baby/(Instrumental)	1979	2.50	5.00	10.00
11293	With Your Love/Helpless	1980	2.50	5.00	10.00
DIVA					
004	This Old Heart of Mine (4 versions)	198?	2.00	4.00	8.00
SUNNYVIEW					
421	Love Is the Answer (4:23) (6:03)	1985	—	3.00	6.00
45s					
ATLANTIC					
2681	Precious Precious/Will Power	1969	—	2.50	5.00
2798	Sometimes It's Got to Rain (In Your Love Life)/ Wonderful Marvelous	1971	—	2.50	5.00
2830	Time/Cover Me	1971	—	2.50	5.00
2861	Darling Baby/Something in a Love	1972	—	2.50	5.00
2902	It Ain't Who You Know/They Tell Me of an Uncloudy Day	1972	—	2.50	5.00
2956	Sweet Charlie Babe/If	1973	—	2.50	5.00
2989	Both Ends Against the Middle/Clean Up Your Own Yard	1973	—	2.50	5.00
CATAWBA					
1010	Holding Back/(B-side unknown)	1983	—	2.00	4.00
COLUMBIA					
04599	This Time Baby/Let's Go Somewhere and Make Love	1984	—	—	3.00
10779	Personally/Ain't No Trouble Like Love Trouble	1978	—	2.00	4.00
10993	This Time Baby/Let's Go Somewhere and Make Love	1979	—	2.00	4.00

Number	Title (A Side/B Side)	Yr	VG	VG+	NM
11140	How's Your Love Life Baby/Do Ya Got What It Takes	1979	—	2.00	4.00
11288	Helpless/With Your Love	1980	—	2.00	4.00
11363	Love Won't Let Me Wait/With Your Love	1980	—	2.00	4.00
KAYVETTE					
5122	Make Me Feel Like a Woman/Singin' Funky Music Turns Me On	1975	—	2.50	5.00
5124	Puttin' It Down to You/Never Is Forever	1975	—	2.50	5.00
5125	It's Harder to Leave/(B-side unknown)	1976	—	2.50	5.00
5127	Disco Body (Shake It to the East, Shake It to the West)/Tired of Hiding	1976	—	2.50	5.00
5129	Make Me Yours/Somebody Loves You	1977	—	2.50	5.00
5139	Heart Be Still/Singin' Funky Music Turns Me On	1981	—	2.00	4.00
5140	Who's Next/Singin' Funky Music Turns Me On	1981	—	2.00	4.00
SHOUT					
232	Dear John/Here I Am	1968	2.00	4.00	8.00
239	Why Don't You Call on Me/(B-side unknown)	1968	2.00	4.00	8.00
Albums					
ATLANTIC					
SD 7285	Sweet Charlie Babe	1973	3.75	7.50	15.00
COLUMBIA					
JC 35991	On My Way	1979	2.50	5.00	10.00
JC 36455	With Your Love	1980	2.50	5.00	10.00
KAYVETTE					
801	Make Me Feel Like a Woman	1975	3.75	7.50	15.00

MOORE, MELBA
12-Inch Singles
CAPITOL

Number	Title (A Side/B Side)	Yr	VG	VG+	NM
8543	Mind Up Tonight (Extended) (Instrumental)	1982	—	3.00	6.00
8586	Love Me Right (Extended) (Instrumental)	1983	—	3.00	6.00
8627	Read My Lips/Got to Have Your Love	1985	2.00	4.00	8.00
8647	When You Love Me Like This/Winner (Instrumental Edit)	1985	—	3.00	6.00
SPRO-9335/6 [DJ]	Read My Lips (Special Mix) (Single Version)	1985	—	3.00	6.00
SPRO-9381/2 [DJ]	Read My Lips (Remix) (Extended Version)	1985	—	3.00	6.00
SPRO-9446/7 [DJ]	When You Love Me Like This (Club Mix) (Monster Groove Mix)	1985	2.00	4.00	8.00
SPRO-9500 [DJ]	I Can't Believe (It's Over) (Extended Version) (Edit Version)	1985	2.00	4.00	8.00
SPRO-9717 [DJ]	Love the One I'm With (5:44) (same on both sides)	1986	—	3.00	6.00
SPRO-9776 [DJ]	Love the One I'm With (3 versions)	1986	—	3.00	6.00
SPRO-9858/9980 [DJ]	Falling (Single Version) (LP Version)	1986	2.00	4.00	8.00
V-15236	Love the One I'm With (5:44)/Don't Go Away	1986	—	3.00	6.00
V-15256	A Little Bit More (4:54) (4:15)/When We Touch	1986	—	3.00	6.00
—With Freddie Jackson					
V-15280	It's Been So Long (2 versions)/Don't Go Away	1987	—	3.00	6.00
V-15426	Love and Kisses (3 versions)/I'm in Love	1988	—	3.00	6.00
V-15561	Do You Really Want My Love (4 versions)	1990	—	3.00	6.00
EMI AMERICA					
SPRO-9817 [DJ]	Love's Comin' At Ya (7" Version) (LP Version)	1981	2.00	4.00	8.00
EPIC					
AS 660 [DJ]	Miss Thing (same on both sides)	1979	2.00	4.00	8.00
50665	Pick Me Up, I'll Dance/(Instrumental)	1979	3.00	6.00	12.00
50771	Miss Thing/Need Love	1979	3.00	6.00	12.00
50807	Hot and Tasty/Night People	1979	3.00	6.00	12.00
45s					
BUDDAH					
452	I Am His Lady/If I Lose You	1975	—	2.50	5.00
469	Natural Part of Everything/Must Be Dues	1975	—	2.50	5.00
496	Starting to Fall/Must Be Dues	1975	—	2.50	5.00
—With Jo Ellen Cohn					
519	This Is It/Stay Awhile	1976	—	2.50	5.00
519 [PS]	This Is It/Stay Awhile	1976	2.00	4.00	8.00
535	Lean On Me/One Less Morning	1976	—	2.50	5.00
562	The Way You Make Me Feel/So Many Mountains	1977	—	2.50	5.00
568	The Long and Winding Road/Ain't No Love Lost	1977	—	2.50	5.00
572	My Sensitive, Passionate Man/The Greatest Feeling	1977	—	2.50	5.00
589	Standing Right Here/Living Free	1977	—	2.50	5.00
596	I Don't Know No One Else to Turn To/Just Another Link	1978	—	2.50	5.00
CAPITOL					
B-5180	Mind Up Tonight/(Instrumental)	1982	—	—	3.00
B-5208	Underlove/(Instrumental)	1983	—	—	3.00
B-5288	Keepin' My Lover Satisfied/(Instrumental)	1983	—	—	3.00
B-5288 [PS]	Keepin' My Lover Satisfied/(Instrumental)	1983	—	2.00	4.00
B-5308	Livin' for Your Love/Got to Have Your Love	1984	—	—	3.00
B-5308 [PS]	Livin' for Your Love/Got to Have Your Love	1984	—	2.00	4.00
B-5343	Love Me Right/Never Say Never	1984	—	—	3.00
B-5343 [PS]	Love Me Right/Never Say Never	1984	—	2.00	4.00
B-5415	(Can't Take Half) All of You/Let Me Be Yours	1984	—	—	3.00
—With Lillo Thomas					
B-5415 [PS]	(Can't Take Half) All of You/Let Me Be Yours	1984	—	2.00	4.00
B-5437	Read My Lips/Got to Have Your Love	1985	—	—	3.00
B-5437 [PS]	Read My Lips/Got to Have Your Love	1985	—	2.00	4.00
B-5484	When You Love Me Like This/Winner	1985	—	—	3.00
B-5484 [PS]	When You Love Me Like This/Winner	1985	—	2.00	4.00
B-5520	I Can't Believe It (It's Over)/King of No Heart	1985	—	—	3.00
B-5577	Love the One I'm With (A Lot of Love)/Don't Go Away	1986	—	—	3.00
—With Kashif					

Number	Title (A Side/B Side)	Yr	VG	VG+	NM
❏ B-5577 [PS]	Love the One I'm With (A Lot of Love)/Don't Go Away	1986	—	—	3.00
❏ B-5632	A Little Bit More/When We Touch	1986	—	—	3.00

—A-side with Freddie Jackson

Number	Title (A Side/B Side)	Yr	VG	VG+	NM
❏ B-5651	Falling/(B-side unknown)	1986	—	—	3.00
❏ B-5681	It's Been So Long/Don't Go Away	1987	—	—	3.00
❏ B-5681 [PS]	It's Been So Long/Don't Go Away	1987	—	—	3.00
❏ B-44012	I'm Not Gonna Let You Go/Dreams	1987	—	—	3.00
❏ B-44012 [PS]	I'm Not Gonna Let You Go/Dreams	1987	—	—	3.00
❏ B-44148	I Can't Complain/There I Go Falling in Love Again	1988	—	—	3.00

—A-side with Freddie Jackson

Number	Title (A Side/B Side)	Yr	VG	VG+	NM
❏ B-44148 [PS]	I Can't Complain/There I Go Falling in Love Again	1988	—	—	3.00
❏ B-44195	I'm in Love/Stay	1988	—	—	3.00

—With Kashif

Number	Title (A Side/B Side)	Yr	VG	VG+	NM
❏ B-44195 [PS]	I'm in Love/Stay	1988	—	—	3.00
❏ B-44265	Love and Kisses/I'm in Love	1988	—	—	3.00

EMI AMERICA

Number	Title (A Side/B Side)	Yr	VG	VG+	NM
❏ 8092	Take My Love/Just You, Just Me	1981	—	2.00	4.00
❏ 8104	Let's Stand Together/What a Woman Needs	1981	—	2.00	4.00
❏ 8114	Piece of the Rock/(Instrumental)	1982	—	2.00	4.00
❏ 8126	Love's Comin' At Ya/(Instrumental)	1982	—	2.00	4.00

EPIC

Number	Title (A Side/B Side)	Yr	VG	VG+	NM
❏ 50600	You Stepped Into My Life/There's No Other Like You	1978	—	2.00	4.00
❏ 50663	Pick Me Up, I'll Dance/Where Did You Ever Go	1979	—	2.00	4.00
❏ 50762	Miss Thing/Need Love	1979	—	2.00	4.00
❏ 50805	Hot and Tasty/Night People	1979	—	2.00	4.00
❏ 50909	Everything So Good About You/Next to You	1980	—	2.00	4.00
❏ 50954	Rest Inside My Love/Something on My Mind	1980	—	2.00	4.00

MERCURY

Number	Title (A Side/B Side)	Yr	VG	VG+	NM
❏ 72942	I Messed Up a Good Thing/I'll Do It All Over Again	1969	2.00	4.00	8.00
❏ 72989	We're Living to Give (Each Other)/(B-side unknown)	1969	2.00	4.00	8.00
❏ 73040	Time and Love/(B-side unknown)	1970	2.00	4.00	8.00
❏ 73072	I Got Love/I Love Making Love to You	1970	2.00	4.00	8.00
❏ 73134	Look What You're Doing to the Man/Patience Is Rewarded	1970	2.00	4.00	8.00
❏ 73183	If I Had a Million/Loving You Comes So Easy	1971	2.00	4.00	8.00
❏ 73217	He Ain't Heavy, He's My Brother/Take Up a Course in Happiness	1971	2.00	4.00	8.00
❏ 73289	Love Letters/I Ain't Got to Love Nobody Else	1972	2.00	4.00	8.00

MUSICOR

Number	Title (A Side/B Side)	Yr	VG	VG+	NM
❏ 1189	Does Love Believe in Me/Don't Cry, Sing Along with the Music	1966	2.50	5.00	10.00

Albums

ACCORD

Number	Title (A Side/B Side)	Yr	VG	VG+	NM
❏ SN-7129	Sweet Melba	1981	2.50	5.00	10.00

BUDDAH

Number	Title (A Side/B Side)	Yr	VG	VG+	NM
❏ BDS-5629	Peach Melba	1975	2.50	5.00	10.00
❏ BDS-5657	This Is It	1976	2.50	5.00	10.00
❏ BDS-5677	Melba	1976	2.50	5.00	10.00
❏ BDS-5695	Portrait of Melba Moore	1977	2.50	5.00	10.00
❏ BDS-5720	Dancin' with Melba	1979	2.50	5.00	10.00

CAPITOL

Number	Title (A Side/B Side)	Yr	VG	VG+	NM
❏ ST-12243	The Other Side of the Rainbow	1982	2.50	5.00	10.00
❏ ST-12305	Never Say Never	1983	2.50	5.00	10.00
❏ ST-12382	Read My Lips	1985	2.50	5.00	10.00
❏ ST-12471	A Lot of Love	1986	2.50	5.00	10.00
❏ C1-92355	Soul Exposed	1990	3.00	6.00	12.00

EMI AMERICA

Number	Title (A Side/B Side)	Yr	VG	VG+	NM
❏ ST-17060	What a Woman Needs	1981	2.50	5.00	10.00

EPIC

Number	Title (A Side/B Side)	Yr	VG	VG+	NM
❏ JE 35507	Melba	1978	2.50	5.00	10.00
❏ JE 36128	Burn	1979	2.50	5.00	10.00
❏ JE 36412	Closer	1980	2.50	5.00	10.00

MERCURY

Number	Title (A Side/B Side)	Yr	VG	VG+	NM
❏ SRM-1-622	Live!	1972	3.00	6.00	12.00
❏ SR-61255	Living to Give	1970	3.75	7.50	15.00
❏ SR-61287	I Got Love	1970	3.75	7.50	15.00
❏ SR-61321	Look What You're Doing to the Man	1971	3.75	7.50	15.00

MOORE, MELVIN
45s
KING

Number	Title (A Side/B Side)	Yr	VG	VG+	NM
❏ 4539	Possessed/Hold Me, Kiss Me, Squeeze Me	1952	25.00	50.00	100.00

MOORE, RUDY
45s
FEDERAL

Number	Title (A Side/B Side)	Yr	VG	VG+	NM
❏ 12253	My Little Angel/I'm Mad with You	1956	12.50	25.00	50.00
❏ 12259	The Buggy Ride/Ring-a-Ling-Dong	1956	12.50	25.00	50.00
❏ 12276	Step It Up and Go/Let Me Come Home	1956	25.00	50.00	100.00
❏ 12280	Bobbie Dobbie/I'll Be Home to See You Tomorrow Night	1956	12.50	25.00	50.00

MOORE, SAM
Also see SAM AND DAVE.
45s
ATLANTIC

Number	Title (A Side/B Side)	Yr	VG	VG+	NM
❏ 2762	Give You Plenty Lovin'/Tennessee Waltz	1970	—	3.00	6.00
❏ 2791	Keep On Sockin' It To Me/Stop	1971	—	3.00	6.00
❏ 2814	Shop Around/If I Should Lose Your Love	1971	—	3.00	6.00

MORGAN, DEBELAH
45s
ATLANTIC

Number	Title (A Side/B Side)	Yr	VG	VG+	NM
❏ 7-84783	Dance with Me/Dance with Me (Soul Central Mix)	2000	—	—	3.0

MORRIS, JOE
45s
ATLANTIC

Number	Title (A Side/B Side)	Yr	VG	VG+	NM
❏ 914	Any Time, Any Place, Any Where/Come Back Daddy Daddy	1950	125.00	250.00	500.0

—With Laura Tate; Atlantic's earliest number on 45; Morris' 78s on Atlantic before 914 were not issued on 45

Number	Title (A Side/B Side)	Yr	VG	VG+	NM
❏ 985	I'm Goin' to Leave You/That's What Makes My Baby Fat	1953	25.00	50.00	100.0
❏ 1160	Going, Going, Gone/Sinner Woman	1957	5.00	10.00	20.0

HERALD

Number	Title (A Side/B Side)	Yr	VG	VG+	NM
❏ 420	Travelin' Man/No, It Can't Be Done	1954	10.00	20.00	40.0

—Black vinyl

Number	Title (A Side/B Side)	Yr	VG	VG+	NM
❏ 420	Travelin' Man/No, It Can't Be Done	1954	20.00	40.00	80.0

—Red vinyl

Number	Title (A Side/B Side)	Yr	VG	VG+	NM
❏ 446	Be Careful/Way Down Yonder	1955	7.50	15.00	30.0

78s
ATLANTIC

Number	Title (A Side/B Side)	Yr	VG	VG+	NM
❏ 855	Love Groovin'/Jump with Me	1949	6.25	12.50	25.0
❏ 859	The Spider/Mad Moon	1949	6.25	12.50	25.0
❏ 866	The Applejack/Easy Riff	1949	6.25	12.50	25.0
❏ 870	Weasel Walk/Wow	1949	6.25	12.50	25.0
❏ 878	Beans and Cornbread/Bottle Top	1949	6.25	12.50	25.0
❏ 885	Boogie Woogie March/Chick-A-Boogie	1949	6.25	12.50	25.0
❏ 892	Jax Boogie/Tia-Juana	1950	6.25	12.50	25.0
❏ 914	Any Time, Any Place, Any Where/Come Back Daddy Daddy	1950	20.00	40.00	80.0

—With Laura Tate

Number	Title (A Side/B Side)	Yr	VG	VG+	NM
❏ 923	Don't Take Your Love Away from Me/Stormy Weather	1950	20.00	40.00	80.0

—With Laura Tate

Number	Title (A Side/B Side)	Yr	VG	VG+	NM
❏ 931	Yeah Yeah Yeah/Jump Everybody Jump	1951	10.00	20.00	40.0
❏ 940	Midnight Grinder/Love Fever Blues	1951	10.00	20.00	40.0
❏ 942	You're My Darling/I Hope You're Satisfied	1951	10.00	20.00	40.0

—With Laura Tate

Number	Title (A Side/B Side)	Yr	VG	VG+	NM
❏ 985	I'm Goin' to Leave You/That's What Makes My Baby Fat	1953	10.00	20.00	40.0
❏ 1160	Going, Going, Gone/Sinner Woman	1957	7.50	15.00	30.0

DECCA

Number	Title (A Side/B Side)	Yr	VG	VG+	NM
❏ 48123	Sneaking Around/Portia's Boogie	1949	6.25	12.50	25.0
❏ 48126	Broken Hearted Blues/Lowdown Baby	1950	6.25	12.50	25.0
❏ 48135	Wig Head Mama Blues/My Home Over There	1950	6.25	12.50	25.0

HERALD

Number	Title (A Side/B Side)	Yr	VG	VG+	NM
❏ 420	Travelin' Man/No, It Can't Be Done	1954	6.25	12.50	25.0
❏ 446	Be Careful/Way Down Yonder	1955	6.25	12.50	25.0

MOSES, LEE
45s
FRONT PAGE

Number	Title (A Side/B Side)	Yr	VG	VG+	NM
❏ 2301	Time and Place/I Can't Take No Chances	1970	5.00	10.00	20.0

GATES

Number	Title (A Side/B Side)	Yr	VG	VG+	NM
❏ 1502	Bad Girl/Dark End of the Street	1967	20.00	40.00	80.0

MUSICOR

Number	Title (A Side/B Side)	Yr	VG	VG+	NM
❏ 1242	Bad Girl (Part 1)/(Part 2)	1967	7.50	15.00	30.0

MURMAIDS, THE
45s
CHATTAHOOCHIE

Number	Title (A Side/B Side)	Yr	VG	VG+	NM
❏ 628	Popsicles and Icicles/Blue Dress	1963	5.00	10.00	20.0
❏ 628	Popsicles and Icicles/Huntington Flats	1963	3.75	7.50	15.0
❏ 628	Popsicles and Icicles/Bunny Stomp	1963	3.75	7.50	15.0
❏ 628	Popsicles and Icicles/Comedy and Tragedy	1963	3.75	7.50	15.0
❏ 636	Heartbreak Ahead/He's Good to Me	1964	2.50	5.00	10.0
❏ 641	Wild and Wonderful/Bull Talk	1964	2.50	5.00	10.0
❏ 668	Stuffed Animals/Little White Lies	1965	2.50	5.00	10.0
❏ 711	Little Boys/Go Away	1966	2.50	5.00	10.0

LIBERTY

Number	Title (A Side/B Side)	Yr	VG	VG+	NM
❏ 56069	Paper Sun/Song Through Perception	1968	—	—	—

—Unreleased

Number	Title (A Side/B Side)	Yr	VG	VG+	NM
❏ 56078	Paper Sun/Song Through Perception	1968	2.50	5.00	10.0

Albums
CHATTAHOOCHIE

Number	Title (A Side/B Side)	Yr	VG	VG+	NM
❏ CHLP-628 [M]	The Mermaids Resurface!	1981	7.50	15.00	30.0

MUSICAL YOUTH
12-Inch Singles
MCA

Number	Title (A Side/B Side)	Yr	VG	VG+	NM
❏ L33-1108 [DJ]	Heartbreaker (short)/Heartbreaker (long)	1983	2.50	5.00	10.0
❏ L33-1147 [DJ]	She's Trouble/Incommunicado	1983	2.50	5.00	10.0
❏ 13965	Never Gonna Give You Up/Mirror Mirror/Rub N Dub	1983	—	3.00	6.0
❏ 13986	She's Trouble (2 versions)/Sixteen	1983	2.50	5.00	10.0

45s
MCA

Number	Title (A Side/B Side)	Yr	VG	VG+	NM
❏ 52149	Pass the Dutchie/Give Love a Chance	1982	—	—	3.0
❏ 52149 [PS]	Pass the Dutchie/Give Love a Chance	1982	—	—	3.0
❏ 52203	Never Gonna Give You Up/Rub 'N' Dub	1983	—	—	3.0
❏ 52216	Heartbreaker/Rockers	1983	—	—	3.0

Number	Title (A Side/B Side)	Yr	VG	VG+	NM
❏ 52312	She's Trouble/Yard Style	1983	—	—	3.00
❏ 52312 [PS]	She's Trouble/Yard Style	1983	—	—	3.00
❏ 52364	Tell Me Why/What Cha Talking 'Bout	1984	—	—	3.00

Albums

MCA

Number	Title (A Side/B Side)	Yr	VG	VG+	NM
❏ 5389	The Youth of Today	1983	2.50	5.00	10.00
❏ 5454	Different Style	1983	2.50	5.00	10.00

MYA

12-Inch Singles

INTERSCOPE

Number	Title (A Side/B Side)	Yr	VG	VG+	NM
❏ INT8P-6303	[DJ]It's All About Me (Radio Version) (LP Version) (Instrumental) (Acappella)	1998	2.00	4.00	8.00
❏ INT8P-6377	[DJ]It's All About Me (Hula's Club Mix) (Hula's Radio Mix)/(Mijango's House Mix) (Slammin' Sam's Wild Wesside Mix)	1998	2.50	5.00	10.00
❏ INT8P-6383	[DJ]It's All About Me (New R&B Remox Clean 3:44) (New R&B Remix 3:44)/(New R&B Instrumental 3:44) (New R&B Acapella 3:44) (LP Version 4:26)	1998	2.00	4.00	8.00
❏ INT8P-6436	[DJ]Movin' On (Ralphi's Vox Club) (Ralphi's Dub)/ (Fernando's Club Mix) (Fernando's Radio Edit) (Ralphi's Dub Beats)	1998	2.00	4.00	8.00
❏ INT8P-6459	[DJ]Movin' On (University Mix Radio Edit #1 4:23) (University Mix Radio Edit #2 4:02)/(University Mix Dirty Version 5:09) (University Mix Instrumental 5:08) (University Mix Acapella 5:09)	1998	2.50	5.00	10.00
❏ INT8P-6553	[DJ]My First Night with You (Soul Solution Extended Vox) (Cibola Extended Mix)/ (Fernando G's Extended Vox) (Boris and Beck's Roxy Dub)	1999	2.50	5.00	10.00
❏ INTR-10056	[DJ]Best of Me (Main Version) (Instrumental) (Acappella)/(same on both sides)	2000	2.50	5.00	10.00
❏ INTR-10110	[DJ]Best of Me (Fernando Garibay Club Mix 5:48) (Fernando Garibay Radio Edit 3:25) (LP Version 4:12)	2000	2.50	5.00	10.00
❏ INTR-10120	[DJ]Case of the Ex (Whatcha Gonna Do) (4 versions)	2000	2.00	4.00	8.00
❏ INTR-10219	[DJ]Free (Jimmy Jam and Terry Lewis Version) (same on both sides?)	2000	2.50	5.00	10.00
❏ INTR-10234	[DJ]Free (Radio Edit) (LP Version) (Instrumental) (Acappella)	2000	2.50	5.00	10.00
❏ 95032	Movin' On (4 versions)	1998	—	3.00	6.00
❏ 497457-1	Case of the Ex (Whatcha Gonna Do) (unknown versions)	2000	2.00	4.00	8.00

RUFFNATION

Number	Title (A Side/B Side)	Yr	VG	VG+	NM
❏ PRO-A-100366	[DJ]Free (Ricco Version) (Jimmy Jam and Terry Lewis Version) (Howard and Cross Version)// (Instrumental) (A Cappella)/L.I.Z. (Clean Version)	2000	2.50	5.00	10.00

—Last track by Liz Leite

45s

INTERSCOPE/UNIVERSITY

Number	Title (A Side/B Side)	Yr	VG	VG+	NM
❏ 97088	My First Night with You/Baby It's Yours	1999	—	—	3.00

Albums

INTERSCOPE

Number	Title (A Side/B Side)	Yr	VG	VG+	NM
❏ 90166 [(2)]	Mya	1998	3.00	6.00	12.00
❏ 490640-1 [(2)]	Fear of Flying	2000	3.75	7.50	15.00

MYSTICS, THE

45s

AMBIENT SOUND

Number	Title (A Side/B Side)	Yr	VG	VG+	NM
❏ 02871	Now That Summer Is Here/Prayer to An Angel	1982	—	2.50	5.00

BLACK CAT

| ❏ 101 | Snoopy/Ooh Poo Pah Doo | 1966 | 10.00 | 20.00 | 40.00 |

CONSTELLATION

| ❏ 138 | She's Got Everything/Just a Loser | 1964 | 3.00 | 6.00 | 12.00 |

DOT

| ❏ 16862 | Now and For Always/Didn't We Have a Good Time | 1966 | 2.50 | 5.00 | 10.00 |

KING

| ❏ 5678 | Mashed Potatoes With Me/The Hoppy Hop | 1962 | 3.75 | 7.50 | 15.00 |
| ❏ 5735 | The Jumpin' Bean/Just For Your Love | 1963 | 3.75 | 7.50 | 15.00 |

LAURIE

❏ 3028 [M]	Hushabye/Adam and Eve	1959	7.50	15.00	30.00
❏ S-3028 [S]	Hushabye/Adam and Eve	1959	30.00	60.00	120.00
❏ 3038	Don't Take the Stars/So Tenderly	1959	6.25	12.50	25.00
❏ 3047	All Through the Night/To Think of You Again	1960	6.25	12.50	25.00
❏ 3058	White Cliffs of Dover/Blue Star	1960	6.25	12.50	25.00
❏ 3086	Star Crossed Lovers/Goodbye Mr. Blue	1961	6.25	12.50	25.00
❏ 3104	Sunday Kind of Love/Darling I Know How	1961	7.50	15.00	30.00

NOLTA

| ❏ 353 | The Fox/Dan | 1963 | 3.75 | 7.50 | 15.00 |

Albums

AMBIENT SOUND

| ❏ FZ 37716 | Crazy for You | 1982 | 2.50 | 5.00 | 10.00 |

COLLECTABLES

| ❏ COL-5043 | 16 Golden Classics | 198? | 2.50 | 5.00 | 10.00 |

N

N.W.A.

12-Inch Singles

PRIORITY

Number	Title (A Side/B Side)	Yr	VG	VG+	NM
❏ SPRO 81104	[DJ]Express Yourself (Radio Edit) (Instrumental) (Explicit LP)/Straight Outta Comption (Radio Edit) (Instrumental) (Explicit LP)	1998	5.00	10.00	20.00

—A-side featuring Silkk The Shocker; B-side featuring King Tee, MC Eiht and Dre

RUTHLESS

❏ MRC 1034	Panic Zone/Dope Man (2 versions)/B-Ball (2 versions)	1987	10.00	20.00	40.00
❏ 7263	Gangsta Gangsta (LP Version) (Radio Edit)// Something Like That/Quiet on Tha Set/ Something 2 Dance 2	1989	6.25	12.50	25.00
❏ 7291	100 Miles and Runnin' (unknown versions)	1990	3.00	6.00	12.00

45s

RUTHLESS

| ❏ 7206 | Express Yourself/Straight Outta Compton | 1989 | 2.50 | 5.00 | 10.00 |
| ❏ 7206 [PS] | Express Yourself/Straight Outta Compton | 1989 | 2.50 | 5.00 | 10.00 |

Albums

PRIORITY

| ❏ SPRO 30080 | [DJ]Greatest Hits/In-Store Play | 1996 | 5.00 | 10.00 | 20.00 |

—Promo-only "clean" versions for retailer use

RUTHLESS

❏ MRC 1057	N.W.A. and the Posse	1987	6.25	12.50	25.00
❏ 7224 [EP]	100 Miles and Runnin'	1990	3.75	7.50	15.00
❏ 50561 [(2)]	Greatest Hits	1996	3.75	7.50	15.00
❏ 57102	Straight Outta Compton	1989	5.00	10.00	20.00
❏ 57119	N.W.A. and the Posse	1990	3.75	7.50	15.00

—Reissue of MRC 1057

| ❏ 57126 | Efil4zaggin (Niggaz4life) | 1991 | 5.00 | 10.00 | 20.00 |

N2DEEP

12-Inch Singles

PROFILE

Number	Title (A Side/B Side)	Yr	VG	VG+	NM
❏ PRO 7383	Toss Up (Original Version) (Jaw Remix) (Radio) (Instrumental)/Do Tha Crew (LP Version) (Instrumental)	1993	2.00	4.00	8.00
❏ PRO 7395	The Weekend (Remix) (LP Version) (Instrumental)/V-Town (LP Version) (Instrumental)	1993	2.00	4.00	8.00

45s

PROFILE

| ❏ 5383 | Toss-Up/Back to the Hotel | 1993 | — | 2.00 | 4.00 |

NAJEE

12-Inch Singles

EMI

Number	Title (A Side/B Side)	Yr	VG	VG+	NM
❏ SPRO 04355	[DJ]Tokyo Blue/Gina	1990	—	3.50	7.00
❏ SPRO 4663	[DJ]Cruise Control (4 versions)	1990	3.75	7.50	15.00
❏ SPRO 4730	[DJ]My Old Friend (2 versions)	1991	2.00	4.00	8.00
❏ V-56128	Najee's Nasty Groove (2 versions)	1989	2.00	4.00	8.00

EMI AMERICA

❏ SPRO 9890	[DJ]Sweet Love (same on both sides)	1986	2.50	5.00	10.00
❏ SPRO 9977	[DJ]Feel So Good to Me (same on both sides)	1987	2.50	5.00	10.00
❏ V-19233	Feel So Good to Me (Extended Version) (Extended Instrumental Mix)	1987	2.50	5.00	10.00
❏ V-19249	Betcha Don't Know (2 versions)/We're Still Family	1987	2.50	5.00	10.00

45s

EMI

| ❏ B-50181 | Najee's Nasty Groove/Najee's Nasty Groovemix | 1989 | — | — | 3.00 |

EMI AMERICA

❏ B-8362	Sweet Love/We're Still Family	1986	—	—	3.00
❏ B-8362 [PS]	Sweet Love/We're Still Family	1986	—	—	3.00
❏ B-8381	Feel So Good to Me/(Saxless Version)	1987	—	—	3.00
❏ B-43019	Betcha Don't Know/We're Still Family	1987	—	—	3.00
❏ B-43019 [PS]	Betcha Don't Know/We're Still Family	1987	—	—	3.00
❏ B-50103	Mysterious/We're Still Family	1987	—	—	3.00

EMI MANHATTAN

| ❏ B-50136 | Personality/Feel So Good to Me | 1988 | — | — | 3.00 |
| ❏ B-51060 | So Hard to Let Go/(Instrumental) | 1988 | — | — | 3.00 |

Albums

EMI

| ❏ E1-92248 | Tokyo Blue | 1990 | 2.50 | 5.00 | 10.00 |

EMI AMERICA

| ❏ ST-17241 | Najee's Theme | 1986 | 2.50 | 5.00 | 10.00 |

EMI MANHATTAN

| ❏ E1-90096 | Day by Day | 1988 | 2.50 | 5.00 | 10.00 |

NATIVE BOYS, THE

45s

COMBO

Number	Title (A Side/B Side)	Yr	VG	VG+	NM
❏ 113	Strange Love/Cherrlyn	1956	15.00	30.00	60.00
❏ 115	Tears/When I Met You	1956	17.50	35.00	70.00
❏ 119	Laughing Love/Valley of Lovers	1956	17.50	35.00	70.00
❏ 120	Oh Let Me Dream/I've Got a Feeling	1956	15.00	30.00	60.00

MODERN

| ❏ 939 | Native Girl/It Won't Take Long | 1954 | 100.00 | 200.00 | 400.00 |

N

Number	Title (A Side/B Side)	Yr	VG	VG+	NM

NATURAL FOUR, THE
45s
ABC

Number	Title (A Side/B Side)	Yr	VG	VG+	NM
❏ 11205	Why Should We Stop Now/You Did This for Me	1969	2.00	4.00	8.00
❏ 11236	Same Thing in Mind/The Situation Needs No Explanation	1969	3.00	6.00	12.00
❏ 11253	Hurt/I Thought You Were Mine	1969	6.25	12.50	25.00
❏ 11257	Message from a Black Man/Stepping On Up	1970	3.00	6.00	12.00

CURTOM

Number	Title (A Side/B Side)	Yr	VG	VG+	NM
❏ 0101	Heaven Right Here on Earth/While We're Away	1975	—	2.50	5.00
❏ 0104	Love's So Wonderful/What's Happening Here	1975	—	2.50	5.00
❏ 0114	It's the Music/It's the Music (Disco Version)	1976	—	2.50	5.00
❏ 0119	Free/Nothing Beats a Failure (But a Try)	1976	—	2.50	5.00
❏ 1981	Things Will Be Better Tomorrow/Eddie, You Should Know Better	1973	—	2.50	5.00
❏ 1984	Try Love Again/Eddie, You Should Know Better	1973	—	2.50	5.00
❏ 1990	Can This Be Real/Try Love Again	1973	—	2.50	5.00
❏ 1995	Love That Really Counts/Love's Society	1974	—	2.50	5.00
❏ 2000	You Bring Out the Best in Me/You Can't Keep Running Away	1974	—	2.50	5.00

Albums
CURTOM

Number	Title (A Side/B Side)	Yr	VG	VG+	NM
❏ CU 5004	Heaven Right Here on Earth	1975	5.00	10.00	20.00
❏ CRT-8600	The Natural Four	1974	5.00	10.00	20.00

NATURALS, THE (1)
45s
CALLA

Number	Title (A Side/B Side)	Yr	VG	VG+	NM
❏ 181	I Can't Share You/Young Generation	1972	—	3.00	6.00

MOTOWN

Number	Title (A Side/B Side)	Yr	VG	VG+	NM
❏ 1208	Good Things/Where Was I When Love Came By	1972	—	3.00	6.00

SHOUT

Number	Title (A Side/B Side)	Yr	VG	VG+	NM
❏ 307	Color Him Father/Crystal Blue Persuasion	197?	—	3.00	6.00
❏ 310	Cold Day in Hell/(B-side unknown)	197?	—	3.00	6.00

NAUGHTY BY NATURE
12-Inch Singles
ARISTA

Number	Title (A Side/B Side)	Yr	VG	VG+	NM
❏ ADP 3598	[DJ]Dirt All By My Lonely (Radio Mix) (TV Track) (Club Mix) (Radio Mix Acapella)	1998	—	3.50	7.00
❏ ADP 3606	[DJ]Live or Die (Radio) (TV Track) (Club) (Acappella)	1999	—	3.00	6.00
❏ ADP 3675	[DJ]Jamboree (Club Version) (Instrumental) (Radio Version) (Acappella)	1999	3.75	7.50	15.00
❏ ADP 3743	[DJ]Holiday (Radio Mix) (Instrumental) (Club Mix) (Acapella)	1999	3.00	6.00	12.00
❏ 13697	Jamboree (4 versions)/On the Run (2 versions)	1999	2.50	5.00	10.00

SOUL

Number	Title (A Side/B Side)	Yr	VG	VG+	NM
❏ 2125	Uptown Anthem (3 versions)	1991	—	3.50	7.00

TOMMY BOY

Number	Title (A Side/B Side)	Yr	VG	VG+	NM
❏ TB 361	The Megamix (Extended Club Version) (Radio Edit)	1999	3.75	7.50	15.00
❏ TB 427	Mourn You 'Til I Join You (LP Version) (Instrumental)/Nothing to Lose (Naughty Live LP Version) (Instrumental)	1997	2.50	5.00	10.00
❏ TB 519	Uptown Anthem/Guard Your Grill (3 versions)	1992	2.00	4.00	8.00
❏ TB 554	Hip Hop Hooray (LP Version) (Instrumental) (Extended Mix)/The Hood Comes First (LP Version) (Instrumental)	1993	3.00	6.00	12.00
❏ TB 569	It's On (Kay Gee Remix) (Instrumental) (Beatnuts Remix) (Acappella)/Hip Hop Hooray (Pete Rock Remix)	1993	2.00	4.00	8.00
❏ TB 583	Written On Ya Kitten (QDIII Radio Edit) (Q-Funk Radio Edit) (Instrumental) (Shandi's Smooth Radio Edit)/Klickow-Klickow (Vocal) (Instrumental)	1993	3.00	6.00	12.00
❏ TB 666	Craziest (Raw Party Mix) (Raw Party Instrumental) (Clean Radio Edit) (Extended Original Mix) (Acappella)	1995	2.00	4.00	8.00
❏ TB 670	Craziest (3 versions)/Holdin' Fort (3 versions)	1995	2.50	5.00	10.00
❏ TB 682	Feel Me Flow (4 versions)/Hang Out and Hustle	1995	3.00	6.00	12.00
❏ TB 686	Feel Me Flow (4 versions)/Craziest	1995	2.50	5.00	10.00
❏ TB 703	Clap Yo Hands (Video Edit) (Kay Gee Funky Mix) (A Cappella) (Video Instrumental)/The Chain Remains (Clean Album Version) (Album Version)/Clap Yo Hands (Kay Gee Funky Mix Instrumental)	1995	3.00	6.00	12.00
❏ TB 706	Clap Yo Hands (Clean Video Edit) (Video Instrumental) (Extended Video Edit) (Kay Gee Funky Mix Radio Edit) (Kay Gee Funky Mix Instrumental) (Acappella)	1995	2.00	4.00	8.00
❏ TB 988	O.P.P. (Vocal) (Instrumental)/Wickedest Man Alive	1991	3.00	6.00	12.00
❏ TB 999	Everything's Gonna Be Alright (3 versions)/O.P.P. (Live)	1991	2.50	5.00	10.00

45s
TOMMY BOY

Number	Title (A Side/B Side)	Yr	VG	VG+	NM
❏ TB 512	O.P.P./Everything's Gonna Be Alright	1991	2.50	5.00	10.00
—Original on green and bluish label					
❏ TB 512	O.P.P./Everything's Gonna Be Alright	1991	—	2.00	4.00
—Reissue on white label, no "Collectables" on label					

TOMMY BOY/COLLECTABLES

Number	Title (A Side/B Side)	Yr	VG	VG+	NM
❏ TB 512	O.P.P./Everything's Gonna Be Alright	1992	—	—	3.00
—White label with "Collectables" on label					
❏ TB 554	Hip Hop Hooray (same on both sides)	1993	—	—	3.00

Number	Title (A Side/B Side)	Yr	VG	VG+	NM
❏ TB 670	Craziest (same on both sides)	1995	—	—	3.00
❏ TB 682	Feel Me Flow (same on both sides)	1995	—	—	3.00

Albums
ARISTA

Number	Title (A Side/B Side)	Yr	VG	VG+	NM
❏ 19047 [(2)]	Nineteen Naughty Nine — Nature's Fury	1999	5.00	10.00	20.00

TOMMY BOY

Number	Title (A Side/B Side)	Yr	VG	VG+	NM
❏ TBLP-1051	Naughty By Nature	1991	3.75	7.50	15.00
❏ TBLP-1069	19 Naughty III	1993	5.00	10.00	20.00
❏ TBLP-1111	Poverty's Paradise	1995	3.00	6.00	12.00
❏ TBLP-1310	Nature's Finest: Naughty by Nature's Greatest Hits	1999	3.75	7.50	15.00

NDEGEOCELLO, ME'SHELL
12-Inch Singles
MAVERICK

Number	Title (A Side/B Side)	Yr	VG	VG+	NM
❏ PRO-A-6485	[DJ]Dred Loc (same on both sides)	1993	2.00	4.00	8.00
❏ PRO-A-6852	[DJ]Outside Your Door (3 versions)	1993	2.00	4.00	8.00
❏ PRO-A-8216	[DJ]Leviticus: Faggot (Glee Club Vocal Mix) (Glee Club FM Edit) (The Faggot Vs. Bitch Mix) (Album Version)	1996	2.00	4.00	8.00
❏ PRO-A-8318	[DJ]Who Is He and What Is He to You (DT's Twilo Mix) (DT's Twilo Edit) (DT's N.Y.D.C. Edit) (DT's N.Y.D.C. Mix) (Alive with Pleasure Dub)	1996	3.00	6.00	12.00
❏ PRO-A-8349	[DJ]Who Is He and What Is He to You (6 versions)	1996	2.00	4.00	8.00
❏ PRO-A-8542	[DJ]Stay (6 versions)	1996	2.00	4.00	8.00
❏ PRO-A-8554 [(2) DJ]Stay (8 versions)		1997	3.75	7.50	15.00
❏ 41039	Dred Loc (5 versions)	1993	2.00	4.00	8.00
❏ 41316	If That's Your Boyfriend (He Wasn't Last Night) (Mad Sex Mix Extended) (Li'l Louis Freaky Mix) (Mad Sex Instrumental) (Existential Meditation on the Probability of You Kissing My Mind Mix) (Tiramisu Mix Extended) (The Gentrified 9 Mix) (Album Version)	1993	2.50	5.00	10.00
❏ 42453	Earth (4 versions)/Trust/Teaching	2001	—	3.00	6.00
❏ PRO-A-100798	[DJ]Pocketbook (unknown versions)	2001	3.00	6.00	12.00
❏ PRO-A-100814	[DJ]Earth (Ben Watt Lazy Dog Remix 8:42) (LP Version 5:14)	2001	3.00	6.00	12.00
❏ PRO-A-100880	[DJ]Pocketbook (Rockwilder and Missy Elliott Remix Featuring Redman and Tweet) (LP Version) (Instrumental)	2002	3.00	6.00	12.00

45s
MAVERICK

Number	Title (A Side/B Side)	Yr	VG	VG+	NM
❏ 17449	Stay/The Teaching	1997	—	—	3.00
❏ 17600	Who Is He and What Is He to You/Leviticus: Faggot	1996	—	2.00	4.00
❏ 18326	If That's Your Boyfriend (He Wasn't Last Night)/Two Lonely Hearts (On the Subway)	1993	—	—	3.00

Albums
MAVERICK

Number	Title (A Side/B Side)	Yr	VG	VG+	NM
❏ PRO-A-6622 [(2) DJ]Plantation Lullabies		1993	5.00	10.00	20.00
—Promo-only U.S. vinyl release					

NEVILLE, AARON
Also see THE METERS.
45s
A&M

Number	Title (A Side/B Side)	Yr	VG	VG+	NM
❏ 31458 0312 7	The Grand Tour/Don't Take Away My Heaven	1993	—	2.00	4.00
❏ 31458 0442 7	Please Come Home for Christmas/Louisiana Christmas Day	1993	—	2.50	5.00
❏ 31458 1112 7	For the Good Times/Crying in the Chapel	1995	—	2.00	4.00
❏ 75021 1563 7	Everybody Plays the Fool/House on a Hill	1991	—	2.00	4.00

BELL

Number	Title (A Side/B Side)	Yr	VG	VG+	NM
❏ 746	You Can Give, But You Can't Take/Where Is My Baby	1968	2.00	4.00	8.00
❏ 781	Speak to Me/You Don't Love Me Anymore	1969	2.00	4.00	8.00
❏ 834	All These Things/She's On My Mind	1969	2.00	4.00	8.00

MERCURY

Number	Title (A Side/B Side)	Yr	VG	VG+	NM
❏ 73310	Baby I'm-a Want You/Mojo Hannah	1972	—	3.00	6.00
❏ 73387	Hercules/Going Home	1973	—	3.00	6.00

MINIT

Number	Title (A Side/B Side)	Yr	VG	VG+	NM
❏ 612	Over You/Every Day	1960	3.75	7.50	15.00
—As "Arron Neville"					
❏ 618	Show Me the Way/Get Out of My Life	1960	3.00	6.00	12.00
❏ 624	Don't Cry/Reality	1961	3.00	6.00	12.00
❏ 631	Let's Live/I Found Another Love	1961	3.00	6.00	12.00
❏ 639	How Many Times/I'm Waitin' at the Station	1962	3.00	6.00	12.00
❏ 650	Humdinger/Sweet Little Mama	1962	3.00	6.00	12.00
❏ 657	Wrong Number/How Could I Help But Love You	1963	3.00	6.00	12.00

PAR-LO

Number	Title (A Side/B Side)	Yr	VG	VG+	NM
❏ 101	Tell It Like It Is/Why Worry	1966	5.00	10.00	20.00
—Black and white label					
❏ 101	Tell It Like It Is/Why Worry	1966	6.25	12.50	25.00
—Turquoise label, silver print					
❏ 101	Tell It Like It Is/Why Worry	1966	6.25	12.50	25.00
—Yellow label, red and black print					
❏ 103	She Took You for a Ride/Space Man	1967	2.00	4.00	8.00

POLYDOR

Number	Title (A Side/B Side)	Yr	VG	VG+	NM
❏ 14426	Greatest Love/Performance	1977	—	2.00	4.00

WHO DAT?

Number	Title (A Side/B Side)	Yr	VG	VG+	NM
❏ VPAG-4476/7	Who Dat? (The History of the Saints)/(Extended Version)	1987	2.00	4.00	8.00

Albums
MINIT

Number	Title (A Side/B Side)	Yr	VG	VG+	NM
❏ LP 24007 [R]	Like It 'Tis	1967	7.50	15.00	30.00

Number	Title (A Side/B Side)	Yr	VG	VG+	NM
❑ LP 40007 [M]	Like It 'Tis	1967	10.00	20.00	40.00
PAR-LO					
❑ 1 [M]	Tell It Like It Is	1967	20.00	40.00	80.00
❑ 1 [S]	Tell It Like It Is	1967	50.00	100.00	200.00

NEW BIRTH, THE

Also see LOVE, PEACE AND HAPPINESS; THE NITE-LITERS.

45s

Number	Title (A Side/B Side)	Yr	VG	VG+	NM
ARIOLA AMERICA					
❑ 7760	I Love You/Fastest Gun	1979	—	2.00	4.00
BUDDAH					
❑ 464	Granddaddy (Part 1)/Granddaddy (Part 2)	1975	—	2.00	4.00
❑ 470	Dream Merchant/Why Did It	1975	—	2.00	4.00
RCA VICTOR					
❑ 74-0400	What'll I Do/One Way Bus	1970	—	3.00	6.00
❑ 74-0520	It's Impossible/Honeybee	1971	—	2.50	5.00
❑ 74-0657	Unh Song/Two Kinds of People	1972	—	2.50	5.00
❑ 74-0774	Come Back in My Life (Part 1)/Come Back in My Life (Part 2)	1972	—	2.50	5.00
❑ 74-0912	I Can Understand It/Oh Baby, I Love the Way	1973	—	2.50	5.00
❑ APBO-0003	Until It's Time for You to Go/You Are What I'm All About	1973	—	2.50	5.00
❑ APBO-0185	It's Been a Long Time/Keep On Doin' It	1973	—	2.50	5.00
❑ APBO-0265	Wildflower/Got to Get a Knutt	1974	—	2.50	5.00
❑ PB-10017	I Wash My Hands of the Whole Damn Deal Part 1/Part 2	1974	—	2.50	5.00
❑ PB-10110	Comin' From All Sides/Patiently	1974	—	2.50	5.00
❑ PB-10242	Do It Again/Pretty Music	1975	—	2.50	5.00
WARNER BROS.					
❑ 8217	The Long and Winding Road/Hurry Hurry	1976	—	2.00	4.00
❑ 8256	Fallin' in Love — Part I/Fallin' in Love — Part II	1976	—	2.00	4.00
❑ 8292	We Are All God's Children — Part I/We Are All God's Children — Part II	1976	—	2.00	4.00
❑ 8422	Deeper/Deeper (Part 2)	1977	—	2.00	4.00
❑ 8499	The Mighty Army/Hurry Hurry	1977	—	2.00	4.00
❑ 8536	How Will I Live/Squeezing Too Much Living	1978	—	2.00	4.00

Albums

Number	Title (A Side/B Side)	Yr	VG	VG+	NM
ARIOLA AMERICA					
❑ SW-50062	Platinum City	1979	2.50	5.00	10.00
BUDDAH					
❑ BDS-5636	Blind Baby	1975	2.50	5.00	10.00
COLLECTABLES					
❑ COL-5100	Golden Classics	1988	2.50	5.00	10.00
RCA VICTOR					
❑ APD1-0285 [Q]	It's Been a Long Time	1974	5.00	10.00	20.00
❑ APL1-0285	It's Been a Long Time	1974	2.50	5.00	10.00
❑ APL1-0494	Comin' From All Ends	1974	2.50	5.00	10.00
❑ APL1-1021	The Best of the New Birth	1975	2.50	5.00	10.00
❑ ANL1-2145	Birth Day	1977	2.50	5.00	10.00
—Reissue of 4797					
❑ AFL1-4411	I'm Back	1982	2.50	5.00	10.00
❑ LSP-4450	The New Birth	1970	3.75	7.50	15.00
❑ LSP-4526	Ain't No Big Thing, But It's Growing	1971	3.75	7.50	15.00
❑ LSP-4697	Coming Together	1972	3.75	7.50	15.00
❑ LSP-4797	Birth Day	1973	3.00	6.00	12.00
WARNER BROS.					
❑ BS 2953	Love Potion	1976	2.50	5.00	10.00
❑ BSK 3071	Behold the Mighty Army	1977	2.50	5.00	10.00

NEW EDITION

12-Inch Singles

Number	Title (A Side/B Side)	Yr	VG	VG+	NM
MCA					
❑ L33-1259 [DJ]	Mr. Telephone Man (2 versions)	1984	2.50	5.00	10.00
❑ L33-1620 [DJ]	Boys to Men (Extended) (Edit) (Instrumental)	1991	—	3.50	7.00
❑ MCA8P-3776 [DJ]	Hit Me Off (4 versions)	1996	3.00	6.00	12.00
❑ MCA8P-3789 [DJ]	Hit Me Off (6 versions)	1996	2.50	5.00	10.00
❑ MCA8P-3792 [DJ]	Hit Me Off (Franktified Club Mix) (Franktified Club Mix With Rap) (Dub of Definity) (Franktified Dub Version)	1996	2.50	5.00	10.00
❑ MCA8P-3869 [DJ]	You Don't Have to Worry (6 versions)	1996	2.50	5.00	10.00
❑ MCA8P-3892 [DJ]	I'm Still in Love with You (Concrete Jungle Full Version 4:45) (Concrete Jungle Instrumental 4:44) (Concrete Jungle Drumapella 4:45)/(Unplugged Full Version 5:05) (Unplugged Instrumental 5:08) (Brooklyn Baller's Full Version 4:52) (Brooklyn Baller's Instrumental)	1996	2.50	5.00	10.00
❑ L33-17015 [DJ]	My Secret (Didja Gitit Yet?) (same on both sides)	1985	—	3.00	6.00
❑ L33-17275 [DJ]	Tears on My Pillow (same on both sides)	1987	2.00	4.00	8.00
❑ L33-17626 [DJ]	N.E. Heart Break (same on both sides)	1989	—	3.00	6.00
❑ L33-17636 [DJ]	You're Not My Kind of Girl (same on both sides)	1988	—	3.00	6.00
❑ L33-17655 [DJ]	You're Not My Kind of Girl (5 versions)	1988	2.00	4.00	8.00
❑ L33-17710 [DJ]	You're Not My Kind of Girl (Extended Version) (Radio Edit) (Instrumental) (Percussapella) (Bonus Beats)	1988	2.00	4.00	8.00
❑ L33-17773 [DJ]	Crucial (Remix) (Dub Version) (Instrumental) (Acappella) (Dance Remix)	1989	2.00	4.00	8.00
❑ 23515	Cool It Now (Extended Version) (Dub Version)	1984	2.00	4.00	8.00
❑ 23544	Kinda Girls We Like (3 versions)	1985	—	3.50	7.00
❑ 23595	Count Me Out (Extended Version)/(Instrumental) (A Cappella)	1985	2.00	4.00	8.00
❑ 23608	A Little Bit of Love (Is All It Takes) (2 versions)	1986	—	3.00	6.00
❑ 23669	Earth Angel/School	1986	—	3.00	6.00
❑ 23692	Once in a Lifetime Groove (Extended Version)/(Dub) (Acappella) (Bonus Beats)	1986	—	3.50	7.00
❑ 23782	Helplessly in Love (Vocal) (Instrumental)	1987	—	3.50	7.00
❑ 23830	If It Isn't Love (Club Mix) (Instrumental)	1988	—	3.50	7.00
❑ 23891	N.E. Heart Break (Extended) (Instrumental) (Faux Live Radio Version)	1989	—	3.00	6.00
❑ 23903	You're Not My Kind of Girl (Vocal 8:40) (Instrumental 8:40)	1988	—	3.00	6.00
❑ 23919	Can You Stand the Rain (Extended Version) (Instrumental)	1988	—	3.00	6.00
❑ 23934	Crucial (Dance Remix) (Dub) (Acappella)	1989	—	3.00	6.00
❑ 54205	Boys to Men (Extended) (Instrumental)	1991	—	3.50	7.00
❑ 55224	Hit Me Off (5 versions)	1996	—	3.00	6.00
❑ 55278	I'm Still in Love with You/You Don't Have to Worry	1996	2.00	4.00	8.00
STREETWISE					
❑ SWRL 2208	Candy Girl (6:58) (6:55)	1983	3.75	7.50	15.00

45s

Number	Title (A Side/B Side)	Yr	VG	VG+	NM
MCA					
❑ 52455	Cool It Now/(Instrumental)	1984	—	2.00	4.00
❑ 52455 [PS]	Cool It Now/(Instrumental)	1984	—	2.00	4.00
❑ 52484	Mr. Telephone Man/(Instrumental)	1984	—	2.00	4.00
❑ 52484 [PS]	Mr. Telephone Man/(Instrumental)	1984	—	2.00	4.00
❑ 52553	Lost in Love/Gold Mine	1985	—	2.00	4.00
❑ 52553 [PS]	Lost in Love/Gold Mine	1985	—	2.00	4.00
❑ 52627	My Secret (Didja Gitit Yet?)/I'm Leaving You Again	1985	—	2.00	4.00
❑ 52627 [PS]	My Secret (Didja Gitit Yet?)/I'm Leaving You Again	1985	—	2.00	4.00
❑ 52703	Count Me Out/Good Boys	1985	—	—	3.00
❑ 52703 [PS]	Count Me Out/Good Boys	1985	—	—	3.00
❑ 52745	It's Christmas (All Over the World)/All I Want for Christmas Is My Girl	1985	—	2.00	4.00
—Red vinyl stock copy					
❑ 52745 [DJ]	It's Christmas (All Over the World) (same on both sides)	1985	—	3.00	6.00
—Promo on red vinyl					
❑ 52745 [PS]	It's Christmas (All Over the World)/All I Want for Christmas Is My Girl	1985	—	2.00	4.00
❑ 52768	A Little Bit of Love (Is All It Takes)/Sneakin' Around	1986	—	—	3.00
❑ 52768 [PS]	A Little Bit of Love (Is All It Takes)/Sneakin' Around	1986	—	—	3.00
❑ 52829	With You All the Way/All for Love	1986	—	—	3.00
❑ 52829 [PS]	With You All the Way/All for Love	1986	—	—	3.00
❑ 52905	Earth Angel/With You All the Way	1986	—	—	3.00
❑ 52959	Once in a Lifetime Groove/Once in a Lifetime Groove (Acapella)	1986	—	—	3.00
❑ 52959 [PS]	Once in a Lifetime Groove/Once in a Lifetime Groove (Acapella)	1986	—	—	3.00
❑ 53019	Tears on My Pillow/Bring Back the Memories	1987	—	2.50	5.00
—Little Anthony appears on this record					
❑ 53019 [PS]	Tears on My Pillow/Bring Back the Memories	1987	—	2.50	5.00
❑ 53079	Duke of Earl/What's Your Name	1987	—	—	3.00
❑ 53164	Helplessly in Love/(Instrumental)	1987	—	—	3.00
❑ 53264	If It Isn't Love/(Instrumental)	1988	—	—	3.00
❑ 53264 [PS]	If It Isn't Love/(Instrumental)	1988	—	—	3.00
❑ 53391	N.E. Heart Break/(Instrumental)	1988	—	—	3.00
❑ 53405	You're Not My Kind of Girl/(Instrumental)	1988	—	—	3.00
❑ 53405 [PS]	You're Not My Kind of Girl/(Instrumental)	1988	—	—	3.00
❑ 53464	Can You Stand the Rain/(Instrumental)	1988	—	—	3.00
❑ 53464 [PS]	Can You Stand the Rain/(Instrumental)	1988	—	—	3.00
❑ 53500	Crucial (Dance Remix)/Crucial (Uptown Mix Instrumental)	1989	—	—	3.00
❑ 53500 [PS]	Crucial (Dance Remix)/Crucial (Uptown Mix Instrumental)	1989	—	—	3.00
STREETWISE					
❑ 1108	Candy Girl/(Instrumental)	1983	2.00	4.00	8.00
❑ 1111	Is This the End/(Instrumental)	1983	2.00	4.00	8.00
❑ 1116	Popcorn Love/Jealous Girl	1983	2.00	4.00	8.00

Albums

Number	Title (A Side/B Side)	Yr	VG	VG+	NM
MCA					
❑ 5515	New Edition	1984	2.00	4.00	8.00
❑ 5679	All for Love	1985	2.00	4.00	8.00
❑ 5912	Under the Blue Moon	1986	2.00	4.00	8.00
❑ 11480	Home Again	1996	3.75	7.50	15.00
❑ 39040 [EP]	Christmas All Over the World	1985	2.00	4.00	8.00
❑ 42207	Heart Break	1988	2.00	4.00	8.00
STREETWISE					
❑ 3301	Candy Girl	1983	3.00	6.00	12.00

NEW 2 LIVE CREW, THE

See THE 2 LIVE CREW.

NEW YORK CITY

45s

Number	Title (A Side/B Side)	Yr	VG	VG+	NM
CHELSEA					
❑ BCBO-0025	Make Me Twice the Man/Uncle James	1973	—	2.50	5.00
❑ 78-0113	I'm Doin' Fine Now/Ain't It So	1973	—	2.50	5.00
❑ BCBO-0150	Quick, Fast, In a Hurry/Set the Record Straight	1973	—	2.50	5.00
❑ 3000	Happiness Is/Darling Take Me Back	1974	—	2.50	5.00
❑ 3008	Love Is What You Make It/Do You Remember Yesterday	1974	—	2.50	5.00
❑ 3010	Got to Get You Back In My Life/Reach Out	1975	—	2.50	5.00
❑ 3031	Can't Survive Without My Sweets/Take My Hand	1975	—	2.50	5.00

Albums

Number	Title (A Side/B Side)	Yr	VG	VG+	NM
CHELSEA					
❑ BCL1-0198	I'm Doin' Fine Now	1973	3.75	7.50	15.00

N

Number	Title (A Side/B Side)	Yr	VG	VG+	NM
❑ CHL 500	Soulful Road	1974	3.75	7.50	15.00
❑ CHL 514	The Best of New York City	1977	3.00	6.00	12.00

NEW YORKERS, THE (1)
With FRED PARRIS of THE FIVE SATINS.
45s
WALL

Number	Title (A Side/B Side)	Yr	VG	VG+	NM
❑ 547	Miss Fine/Dream a Little Dream	1961	7.50	15.00	30.00
❑ 548	Tears in My Eyes/A Little Bit	1961	7.50	15.00	30.00

NEWPORTS, THE (1)
45s
CRYSTAL BALL

Number	Title (A Side/B Side)	Yr	VG	VG+	NM
❑ 129	Jingle Bells/My Juanita	1979	2.00	4.00	8.00
GUYDEN					
❑ 2067	If I Could Tonight/A Fellow Needs a Girl	1962	7.50	15.00	30.00
❑ 2116	Tears/Disillusioned Love	1964	7.50	15.00	30.00

NEWPORTS, THE (2)
45s
KENT

Number	Title (A Side/B Side)	Yr	VG	VG+	NM
❑ 380	The Wonder of Love/Dixie Women	1962	7.50	15.00	30.00

NICKY AND THE NOBLES
45s
END

Number	Title (A Side/B Side)	Yr	VG	VG+	NM
❑ 1021	Schoolhouse Rock/A Way to Tell Her	1958	12.50	25.00	50.00
❑ 1098	School Bells/School Day Crush	1961	6.25	12.50	25.00
GONE					
❑ 5039	School Bells/School Day Crush	1958	15.00	30.00	60.00
—Black label					
❑ 5039	School Bells/School Day Crush	1958	6.25	12.50	25.00
—Multicolor label					
❑ 5039	School Bells/School Days	1958	25.00	50.00	100.00
—With B-side title variation					

NIGHTINGALE, MAXINE
45s
A&M

Number	Title (A Side/B Side)	Yr	VG	VG+	NM
❑ 2335	You Touched Me/Rendezvous	1981	—	2.00	4.00
—With Brian Short					
UNITED ARTISTS					
❑ XW752	Right Back Where We Started From/Believe in What You Do	1975	—	2.50	5.00
❑ XW820	One Last Ride/Gotta Be the One	1976	—	2.00	4.00
❑ XW865	Life Has Just Begun/(I Think I Wanna) Possess You	1976	—	2.00	4.00
❑ XW944	If I Ever Lose This Heaven/Love Hit Me	1977	—	2.00	4.00
❑ XW983	Love Hit Me (Part 1)/Love Hit Me (Part 2)	1977	—	2.00	4.00
❑ XW1015	How Much Love/Will You Be My Lover	1977	—	2.00	4.00
❑ XW1159	Right Back Where We Started From/Will You Be My Lover	1978	—	—	3.00
—Reissue					
WINDSONG					
❑ CB-11530	Lead Me On/Love Me Like You Mean It	1979	—	2.00	4.00
❑ CB-11729	(Bringing Out) The Girl in Me/Hideaway	1979	—	2.00	4.00
❑ CB-11729 [PS]	(Bringing Out) The Girl in Me/Hideaway	1979	—	2.00	4.00
❑ CB-12020	Take Your Heart/Why Did You Turn Me On	1980	—	2.00	4.00
❑ CB-12117	All Night with Me/Tight Spot	1980	—	2.00	4.00

Albums
HIGHRISE

Number	Title (A Side/B Side)	Yr	VG	VG+	NM
❑ HR 101	It's a Beautiful Thing	198?	3.00	6.00	12.00
RCA VICTOR					
❑ AFL1-3528	Bittersweet	1980	2.50	5.00	10.00
UNITED ARTISTS					
❑ UA-LA626-G	Right Back Where We Started From	1976	3.00	6.00	12.00
❑ UA-LA731-G	Night Life	1977	3.00	6.00	12.00
WINDSONG					
❑ BXL1-3404	Lead Me On	1979	2.50	5.00	10.00

94 EAST
Early band led by PRINCE.
45s
HOT PINK

Number	Title (A Side/B Side)	Yr	VG	VG+	NM
❑ 3223	Just Another Sucker/(B-side unknown)	1986	—	3.00	6.00
POLYDOR					
❑ 14414	Be My Fortune Teller/I Just Wanna Be	1977	—	—	—
—Unreleased?					

Albums
HOT PINK

Number	Title (A Side/B Side)	Yr	VG	VG+	NM
❑ HLP 3223	Minneapolis Genius — 94 East	1977	10.00	20.00	40.00
—Deduct 25% for cut-outs					

98 DEGREES
12-Inch Singles
UNIVERSAL

Number	Title (A Side/B Side)	Yr	VG	VG+	NM
❑ UNIR-20322 [DJ]	Give Me Just One Night (Una Noche) (Hex Hector Club Mix) (Hex Hector Radio Edit) (Hex Hector Dub) (Hex Hector Percussion Beats)	2000	2.50	5.00	10.00
❑ 012 158418-1	Give Me Just One Night (Una Noche) (3 versions?)	2000	2.00	4.00	8.00

Number	Title (A Side/B Side)	Yr	VG	VG+	NM
45s					
MOTOWN					
❑ 860674-7	Invisible Man/(Instrumental)	1997	—	—	3.00
UNIVERSAL					
❑ 012 158224-7	Give Me Just One Night (Una Noche)/I Do (Cherish You)	2000	—	—	3.00
Albums					
MOTOWN					
❑ 314 530796 1	98 Degrees	1997	3.75	7.50	15.00

NINO AND THE EBB TIDES
45s
ACME

Number	Title (A Side/B Side)	Yr	VG	VG+	NM
❑ 720	Franny Franny/Darling I'll Love Only You	1958	75.00	150.00	300.00
MADISON					
❑ 162	Those Oldies But Goodies (Remind Me of You)/Don't Run Away	1961	10.00	20.00	40.00
❑ 166	Juke Box Saturday Night/(Someday) I'll Fall in Love	1961	7.50	15.00	30.00
MALA					
❑ 480	Automatic Reaction/Linda Lou Garrett Like 24 Karat	1964	5.00	10.00	20.00
MARCO					
❑ 105	Little Miss Blue/Someday	1961	12.50	25.00	50.00
MR. PEACOCK					
❑ 102	Wished I Was Home/Happy Guy	1961	6.25	12.50	25.00
❑ 117	Lovin' Time/Stamps, Baby, Stamps	1962	6.25	12.50	25.00
MR. PEEKE					
❑ 123	Tonight I'll Be Lonely/Nursery Rhymes	1963	6.25	12.50	25.00
RECORTE					
❑ 405	Puppy Love/You Make Me Rock 'N' Roll	1958	12.50	25.00	50.00
❑ 408	The Real Meaning of Christmas/Two Purple Shadows in the Snow	1958	75.00	150.00	300.00
❑ 409	I'm Confessin'/Tell the World I Do	1959	12.50	25.00	50.00
❑ 413	Don't Look Around/I Love Girls	1959	25.00	50.00	100.00

NITE-LITERS, THE
Also see LOVE, PEACE AND HAPPINESS; THE NEW BIRTH.
45s
RCA VICTOR

Number	Title (A Side/B Side)	Yr	VG	VG+	NM
❑ 74-0374	Con-Funk-Shun/Down and Dirty	1970	—	3.00	6.00
❑ 74-0461	K-Jee/Tanga Boo Gonk	1971	—	2.50	5.00
❑ 74-0591	Afro-Strut/(We've Got to) Pull Together	1971	—	2.50	5.00
❑ 74-0714	Cherish Every Precious Moment/I've Got Dreams to Remember	1972	—	2.50	5.00
❑ 74-0812	Funky-Doo/Do the Granny	1972	—	2.50	5.00
❑ APBO-0244	Pe-Foul/Serenade for a Jive Turkey	1974	—	2.50	5.00
Albums					
RCA VICTOR					
❑ LSP-4493	Morning, Noon & The Nite-Liters	1971	3.75	7.50	15.00
❑ LSP-4580	Instrumental Directions	1972	3.75	7.50	15.00

NITE RIDERS, THE
45s
MGM

Number	Title (A Side/B Side)	Yr	VG	VG+	NM
❑ 12487	Sippin' Coffee/Tank Town	1957	7.50	15.00	30.00
TEEN					
❑ 116	Starlight and You/I Know You're In There	1955	10.00	20.00	40.00
❑ 118	Got Me a Six-Button Benny/Don't Hang Up the Phone	1955	10.00	20.00	40.00
❑ 120	When a Man Cries/Waiting in the Schoolroom	1955	10.00	20.00	40.00

NOBLES, THE (1)
45s
ABC-PARAMOUNT

Number	Title (A Side/B Side)	Yr	VG	VG+	NM
❑ 9984	Till the End of Time/Standing Loose	1958	6.25	12.50	25.00
❑ 10012	Just for Me/To Me	1959	6.25	12.50	25.00

NOBLES, THE (2)
45s
KLIK

Number	Title (A Side/B Side)	Yr	VG	VG+	NM
❑ 305	Poor Rock and Roll/Ting-a-Ling	1958	50.00	100.00	200.00
TIMES SQUARE					
❑ 1	Poor Rock and Roll/Ting-a-Ling	1963	7.50	15.00	30.00
—Blue vinyl					
❑ 1	Poor Rock and Roll/Ting-a-Ling	1963	6.25	12.50	25.00
—Green vinyl					
❑ 12	Crime Doesn't Pay/Darkness	1963	5.00	10.00	20.00
—All copies on blue vinyl					
❑ 33	Why Be a Fool/The Search	1964	5.00	10.00	20.00

NUTMEGS, THE
45s
BABY GRAND

Number	Title (A Side/B Side)	Yr	VG	VG+	NM
❑ 800	Story Untold '72/Tell Me	1972	2.00	4.00	8.00
HERALD					
❑ 452	Story Untold/Make Me Lose My Mind	1955	17.50	35.00	70.00
❑ 459	Ship of Love/Rock Me	1955	10.00	20.00	40.00
❑ 466	Whispering Sorrows/Betty Lou	1955	12.50	25.00	50.00
❑ 475	Key to the Kingdom (Of Your Heart)/Gift O' Gabbin' Woman	1956	12.50	25.00	50.00
❑ 492	Love So True/Comin' Home	1956	10.00	20.00	40.00
❑ 538	My Sweet Dream/My Story	1959	10.00	20.00	40.00

Number	Title (A Side/B Side)	Yr	VG	VG+	NM
❑ 574	Rip Van Winkle/Crazy 'Bout You	1962	6.25	12.50	25.00
NIGHTRAIN					
❑ 905	Shifting Sands/Take Me and Make Me	1973	2.00	4.00	8.00
TEL					
❑ 1014	A Dream of Love/Someone, Somewhere (Help Me)	1960	25.00	50.00	100.00
TIMES SQUARE					
❑ 6	Let Me Tell You/Hello	1963	6.25	12.50	25.00
—Blue vinyl					
❑ 14	The Way Love Should Be/Wide Hoop Skirts	1963	5.00	10.00	20.00
❑ 19	Down to Earth/Coo Coo Cuddle Coo	1963	5.00	10.00	20.00
—B-side by the Admirations					
❑ 22	Why Must We Go to School/Ink Dries Quicker Than Tears	1963	5.00	10.00	20.00
—B-side by the Volumes					
❑ 27	Down in Mexico/My Sweet Dreams	1964	5.00	10.00	20.00
❑ 103	You're Crying/Wa-Do-Wa	1964	5.00	10.00	20.00
7-Inch Extended Plays					
HERALD					
❑ 452	*Story Untold/Betty Lou/Comin' Home/ Whispering Sorrows	1960	25.00	50.00	100.00
❑ 452 [PS]	Story Untold	1960	30.00	60.00	120.00
Albums					
COLLECTABLES					
❑ COL-5018	Greatest Hits	198?	2.50	5.00	10.00
QUICKSILVER					
❑ QS-1001	Shoo-Wop-a-Doo-Wop	198?	2.50	5.00	10.00
RELIC					
❑ LP-5002	The Nutmegs Featuring Leroy Griffin	198?	2.50	5.00	10.00
❑ LP-5011	Greatest Hits (1955-1959)	198?	2.50	5.00	10.00

NUYORICAN SOUL
12-Inch Singles
GIANT STEP/BLUE THUMB

Number	Title (A Side/B Side)	Yr	VG	VG+	NM
❑ 3093	You Can Do It (Baby) (Nuyorican Style Mix) (George's Groove) (Bar Beats)	1996	7.50	15.00	30.00
❑ 3094 [(2)]	Runaway (Original Flava 12" Mix) (Philly Beats)/ (Mongoloids in Space)//(Mousse T's Jazz Funk Experience) (Mousse T's Soul Dub)/(Ronnie's Guitar Instrumental) (India's Ambient Dream) (Don't Sample This A Cappella)	1997	7.50	15.00	30.00

45s
GIANT STEP/BLUE THUMB

Number	Title (A Side/B Side)	Yr	VG	VG+	NM
❑ 3105	Runaway (Original Radio Edit)/(Original Radio Edit w/Spanish)	1997	—	3.00	6.00
—With generic white sleeve with "Nuyorican Soul" sticker on it					

O

O'BRYAN
12-Inch Singles
CAPITOL

Number	Title (A Side/B Side)	Yr	VG	VG+	NM
❑ V-8568	Soul Train's a-Comin'/Soft Touch	1983	5.00	10.00	20.00
❑ V-8583	Lovelite/(Instrumental)	1984	2.50	5.00	10.00
❑ V-8605	Breakin' Together (Club Mix 6:22)/(Dub Version 6:22)	1984	2.50	5.00	10.00
❑ SPRO-9174 [DJ]	Breakin' Together (2 versions?)	1984	2.50	5.00	10.00
❑ SPRO-9731 [DJ]	The Gigolo (same on both sides)	1981	2.50	5.00	10.00
❑ SPRO-9889 [DJ]	I'm Freaky (2 versions?)	1983	3.75	7.50	15.00
❑ V-15250	Tenderoni (12" Version) (Dub Version) (LP Version)	1986	2.50	5.00	10.00
❑ V-15275	Driving Force (3 versions)/Surrender	1987	2.50	5.00	10.00
❑ V-15301	You Have Got to Come to Me (3 versions)	1987	3.75	7.50	15.00

45s
CAPITOL

Number	Title (A Side/B Side)	Yr	VG	VG+	NM
❑ A-5067	The Gigolo/Can't Live Without Your Love	1981	—	2.00	4.00
❑ B-5117	Still Water (Love)/Right from the Start	1982	—	2.00	4.00
❑ B-5117 [PS]	Still Water (Love)/Right from the Start	1982	—	2.50	5.00
❑ B-5203	I'm Freaky/(Instrumental)	1983	—	2.00	4.00
❑ B-5224	You and I/Together Always	1983	—	2.00	4.00
❑ B-5291	Soul Train's a-Comin'/Soft Touch	1983	—	3.00	6.00
❑ B-5329	Lovelite/(Instrumental)	1984	—	2.00	4.00
❑ B-5329 [PS]	Lovelite/(Instrumental)	1984	—	2.00	4.00
❑ B-5376	Breakin' Together/(Dub)	1984	—	2.00	4.00
❑ B-5376 [PS]	Breakin' Together/(Dub)	1984	—	2.00	4.00
❑ B-5414	Go On and Cry/You Gotta Use It	1984	—	2.00	4.00
❑ B-5617	Tenderoni/(Instrumental)	1986	—	2.00	4.00
❑ B-5673	Driving Force/Surrender	1987	—	2.00	4.00
❑ B-5673 [PS]	Driving Force/Surrender	1987	—	2.00	4.00
❑ B-44010	You Have Got to Come to Me/Dreamin' About You	1987	—	2.00	4.00

Albums
CAPITOL

Number	Title (A Side/B Side)	Yr	VG	VG+	NM
❑ ST-12192	Doin' Alright	1982	2.50	5.00	10.00
❑ ST-12256	You and I	1983	2.50	5.00	10.00
❑ ST-12332	Be My Lover	1984	2.50	5.00	10.00
❑ ST-12520	Surrender	1986	2.50	5.00	10.00

O'JAYS, THE
12-Inch Singles
EMI

Number	Title (A Side/B Side)	Yr	VG	VG+	NM
❑ SPRO-04305/24 [DJ]	Have You Had Your Love Today (2 versions)/Lovin' You	1989	2.50	5.00	10.00
❑ 4853/4 [DJ]	Merry Christmas Baby/The Christmas Song	1991	2.50	5.00	10.00
❑ V-56127	Have You Had Your Love Today (4 versions)	1989	—	3.00	6.00
❑ V-56207	Don't Let Me Down (6 versions)	1990	2.00	4.00	8.00
PHILADELPHIA INT'L.					
❑ 4Z8-3708	Sing a Happy Song (5:00)/Get On Out and Party (5:02)	1979	3.75	7.50	15.00
❑ 4Z8-3713	I Love Music (6:33)/Livin' for the Weekend (6:29)	1979	6.25	12.50	25.00
—First issue of these two dance hits on a 12-inch single					
❑ 4Z9-05000	Extraordinary Girl (5:18)/(Instrumental)	1984	2.50	5.00	10.00
❑ 4Z9-05040	Let Me Show You (How Much I Really Love You) (unknown versions)	1984	2.50	5.00	10.00
❑ V-56049	Don't Take Your Love Away (3 versions)/I Just Want Somebody to Love Me	1987	2.00	4.00	8.00
❑ SPRO-79129/30 [DJ]	Lovin' You (5:15)/Don't Let the Dream Get Away (4:16)	1987	2.50	5.00	10.00
VOLCANO					
❑ 34272	What's Stopping You (4 versions)	1997	—	3.00	6.00
❑ 37226	Pay the Bills (Main Mix) (Instrumental)/(same on both sides)	1997	2.50	5.00	10.00

45s
APOLLO

Number	Title (A Side/B Side)	Yr	VG	VG+	NM
❑ 759	Miracles/Can't Take It	1961	7.50	15.00	30.00
ASTROSCOPE					
❑ 106	Wisdom of a Child/Peace	1974	2.00	4.00	8.00
❑ 110	Peace/Don't You Know a True Love (When You See Her)	1974	2.00	4.00	8.00
BELL					
❑ 691	I'll Be Sweeter Tomorrow (Than I Was Today)/I Dig Your Act	1967	2.50	5.00	10.00
❑ 704	Look Over Your Shoulder/I'm So Glad I Found You	1968	2.50	5.00	10.00
❑ 737	The Choice/Going, Going, Gone	1968	2.50	5.00	10.00
❑ 749	I Miss You/Now That I Found You	1968	2.50	5.00	10.00
❑ 770	Don't You Know a True Love/That's All Right	1969	2.00	4.00	8.00
❑ 45378	Look Over Your Shoulder/Four for the Price of One	1973	—	2.50	5.00
EMI					
❑ S7-17491	Somebody Else Will/Decisions	1993	—	2.00	4.00
❑ S7-18914	Have Yourself a Merry Little Christmas/I Can Hardly Wait 'Til Christmas	1995		2.00	4.00
❑ B-50180	Have You Had Your Love Today/Pot Can't Call the Kettle Black	1989	—	—	3.00
❑ B-50212	Out of My Mind (Radio Mix)/(Soul 2 Mix)	1989	—	—	3.00
❑ B-50230	Serious Hold on Me/(Instrumental)	1989	—	2.00	4.00
IMPERIAL					
❑ 5942	How Does It Feel/Crack Up Laughing	1963	3.75	7.50	15.00
❑ 5976	Lonely Drifter/That's Enough	1963	2.50	5.00	10.00

O

Number	Title (A Side/B Side)	Yr	VG	VG+	NM
❏ 66007	Stand Tall/The Storm Is Over	1963	2.50	5.00	10.00
❏ 66025	I'll Never Stop Loving You/My Dearest Beloved	1964	2.50	5.00	10.00
❏ 66037	You're on Top/Lovely Dee	1964	2.50	5.00	10.00
❏ 66076	Girl Machine/Oh How You Hurt Me	1964	2.50	5.00	10.00
❏ 66102	Lipstick Traces/Think It Over, Baby	1965	2.50	5.00	10.00
❏ 66121	Whip It On Me Baby/I've Cried My Last Tear	1965	2.50	5.00	10.00
❏ 66131	You're the One (You're the Only One)/Let It All Come Out	1965	2.50	5.00	10.00
❏ 66145	I'll Never Let You Go/It Won't Hurt	1965	2.50	5.00	10.00
❏ 66162	I'll Never Forget You/Pretty Words	1966	10.00	20.00	40.00
❏ 66177	No Time for You/It's a Blowin' Wind	1966	2.50	5.00	10.00
❏ 66197	Friday Night/Stand In for Love	1966	2.50	5.00	10.00
❏ 66200	Lonely Drifter/That's Enough	1966	2.50	5.00	10.00
LITTLE STAR					
❏ 124	How Does It Feel/Crack Up Laughing	1963	6.25	12.50	25.00
❏ 125	Dream Girl/Joey St. Vincent	1963	6.25	12.50	25.00
❏ 1401	Now He's Home/Just to Be with You	1962	6.25	12.50	25.00
MINIT					
❏ 32015	Hold On/Working on Your Case	1967	2.50	5.00	10.00
NEPTUNE					
❏ 12	One Night Affair/There's Someone (Waiting Back Home)	1969	2.00	4.00	8.00
❏ 18	Branded Bad/You're the Best Thing Since Candy	1969	2.00	4.00	8.00
❏ 20	Christmas Ain't Christmas New Year's Ain't New Year's Without the One You Love/There's Someone Waiting	1969	2.50	5.00	10.00
❏ 22	Deeper (In Love with You)/I've Got the Groove	1970	2.00	4.00	8.00
❏ 31	Looky Looky (Look at Me Girl)/Let Me in Your World	1970	2.00	4.00	8.00
❏ 33	Christmas Ain't Christmas New Year's Ain't New Year's Without the One You Love/Just Can't Get Enough	1970	2.00	4.00	8.00
PHILADELPHIA INT'L.					
❏ ZS8-02096	Forever Mine/Girl, Don't Let It Get You Down	1981	—	—	3.00
—Reissue					
❏ ZS5-02834	I Just Want to Satisfy/Don't Walk Away Mad	1982	—	2.00	4.00
❏ ZS4-02982	My Favorite Person/One by One	1982	—	2.00	4.00
❏ ZS5-03009	Your Body's Here with Me (But Your Mind's on the Other Side of Town)/Out in the Real World	1982	—	2.00	4.00
❏ 3101	Hurry Up and Come Back/Identify	1979	—	2.50	5.00
❏ 3517	Back Stabbers/Sunshine	1972	—	2.50	5.00
❏ 3522	992 Arguments/Listen to the Clock on the Wall	1972	—	2.50	5.00
❏ 3524	Love Train/Who Am I	1973	—	2.50	5.00
❏ 3531	Time to Get Down/Shiftless, Shady, Jealous Kind of People	1973	—	2.50	5.00
❏ 3535	Put Your Hands Together/You Got Your Hooks in Me	1973	—	2.50	5.00
❏ 3537	Christmas Ain't Christmas New Year's Ain't New Year's Without the One You Love/Just Can't Get Enough	1973	—	3.00	6.00
❏ 3544	For the Love of Money/People Keep Tellin' Me	1974	—	2.50	5.00
❏ 3558	Sunshine (Part 1)/Sunshine (Part 2)	1974	—	2.50	5.00
❏ 3565	Give the People What They Want/What Am I Waiting For	1975	—	2.50	5.00
❏ 3573	Let Me Make Love to You/Survival	1975	—	2.50	5.00
❏ 3577	I Love Music (Part 1)/I Love Music (Part 2)	1975	—	2.50	5.00
❏ 3581	Christmas Ain't Christmas New Year's Ain't New Year's Without the One You Love/Just Can't Get Enough	1975	—	2.50	5.00
❏ 3587	Livin' for the Weekend/Stairway to Heaven	1976	—	2.50	5.00
❏ 3596	Family Reunion/Unity	1976	—	2.50	5.00
❏ 3601	Message in Our Music/She's Only a Woman	1976	—	2.50	5.00
❏ 3610	Darlin' Darlin' Baby (Sweet, Tender, Love)/A Prayer	1976	—	2.50	5.00
❏ 3631	Work On Me/Let's Spend Some Time Together	1977	—	2.50	5.00
❏ 3642	Use Ta Be My Girl/This Time Baby	1978	—	2.50	5.00
❏ 3652	Brandy/Take Me to the Stars	1978	—	2.50	5.00
❏ 3666	Cry Together/Strokety Stroke	1978	—	2.50	5.00
❏ 3707	Sing a Happy Song/One in a Million (Girl)	1979	—	2.50	5.00
❏ 3726	I Want You Here with Me/Get On Out and Party	1979	—	2.50	5.00
❏ 3727	Forever Mine/Get On Out and Party	1979	—	2.50	5.00
❏ ZS4-03892	I Can't Stand the Pain/A Letter to My Friends	1983	—	2.00	4.00
❏ ZS4-04069	Put Our Heads Together/Nice and Easy	1983	—	2.00	4.00
❏ ZS4-04437	Extraordinary Girl/I Really Need You Now	1984	—	2.00	4.00
❏ ZS4-04535	Let Me Show You (How Much I Really Love You)/Love You Direct	1984	—	2.00	4.00
❏ B-50013	Just Another Lonely Night/What Good Are These Arms of Mine	1985	—	—	3.00
❏ B-50021	What a Woman/I Love America	1985	—	—	3.00
❏ B-50067	Don't Take Your Love Away/I Just Want Somebody to Love Me	1987	—	—	3.00
❏ B-50084	Lovin' You/Don't Let the Dream Get Away	1987	—	—	3.00
❏ B-50104	Let Me Touch You/Undercover Lover	1987	—	—	3.00
❏ B-50122	I Just Want Someone to Love Me/Lovin' You	1988	—	—	3.00
SARU					
❏ 1220	Shattered Man/La De Da (Means I'm Out to Get You)	1971	—	3.00	6.00
TSOP					
❏ 3771	Christmas Ain't Christmas New Year's Ain't New Year's Without the One You Love/Just Can't Get Enough	1980	—	2.50	5.00
❏ 4790	Girl, Don't Let It Get You Down/You're the Girl of My Dreams	1980	—	2.00	4.00
❏ 4791	Once Is Not Enough/To Prove I Love You	1980	—	2.00	4.00

Number	Title (A Side/B Side)	Yr	VG	VG+	NM
❏ 70050	You Won't Fall/You'll Never Know (All There Is to Know 'Bout Love)	1981	—	2.00	4.00
Albums					
BELL					
❏ 6014	Back on Top	1968	5.00	10.00	20.00
❏ 6082	The O'Jays	1973	3.00	6.00	12.00
EMI					
❏ E1-90921	Serious	1989	2.50	5.00	10.00
❏ E1-93390	Emotionally Yours	1991	3.75	7.50	15.00
❏ E1-96420	Home for Christmas	1991	3.75	7.50	15.00
IMPERIAL					
❏ LP 9290 [M]	Comin' Through	1965	10.00	20.00	40.00
❏ LP 12290 [S]	Comin' Through	1965	12.50	25.00	50.00
KORY					
❏ 1006	The O'Jays	1977	2.50	5.00	10.00
LIBERTY					
❏ LN-10119	Greatest Hits	1980	2.00	4.00	8.00
—Budget-line reissue of Imperial material					
MINIT					
❏ LP-24008 [S]	Soul Sounds	1967	12.50	25.00	50.00
❏ LP-40008 [M]	Soul Sounds	1967	10.00	20.00	40.00
NEPTUNE					
❏ 202	The O'Jays in Philadelphia	1969	7.50	15.00	30.00
PHILADELPHIA INT'L.					
❏ ASZ 140 [DJ]	Everything You Always Wanted to Hear by the O'Jays But Were Afraid to Ask For	1975	3.75	7.50	15.00
❏ KZ 31712	Back Stabbers	1972	3.00	6.00	12.00
❏ KZ 32120	The O'Jays in Philadelphia	1973	3.00	6.00	12.00
—Reissue of Neptune LP					
❏ KZ 32408	Ship Ahoy	1973	2.50	5.00	10.00
❏ PZ 32408	Ship Ahoy	198?	2.00	4.00	8.00
—Budget-line reissue					
❏ PZQ 32408 [Q]Ship Ahoy		1974	3.75	7.50	15.00
❏ KZ 32953	The O'Jays Live in London	1974	2.50	5.00	10.00
❏ PZQ 32953 [Q]The O'Jays Live in London		1974	3.75	7.50	15.00
❏ PZ 33150	Survival	1975	2.50	5.00	10.00
❏ PZ 33807	Family Reunion	1975	2.50	5.00	10.00
—No bar code on back cover					
❏ PZ 33807	Family Reunion	198?	2.00	4.00	8.00
—Budget-line reissue with bar code					
❏ PZQ 33807 [Q]Family Reunion		1975	3.75	7.50	15.00
❏ PZ 34245	Message in the Music	1976	2.50	5.00	10.00
❏ PZ 34684	Travelin' at the Speed of Thought	1977	2.50	5.00	10.00
❏ PZG 35024 [(2)]The O'Jays: Collector's Items		1978	3.00	6.00	12.00
❏ Z2 35024 [(2)] The O'Jays: Collector's Items		198?	2.50	5.00	10.00
—Reissue					
❏ JZ 35355	So Full of Love	1978	2.50	5.00	10.00
❏ PZ 35355	So Full of Love	198?	2.00	4.00	8.00
—Budget-line reissue					
❏ FZ 36027	Identify Yourself	1979	2.50	5.00	10.00
❏ FZ 37999	My Favorite Person	1982	2.50	5.00	10.00
❏ FZ 38518	When Will I See You Again	1983	2.50	5.00	10.00
❏ PZ 38518	When Will I See You Again	1985	2.00	4.00	8.00
—Budget-line reissue					
❏ FZ 39251	Greatest Hits	1984	2.50	5.00	10.00
❏ 53015	Love Fever	1985	2.50	5.00	10.00
❏ 53036	Let Me Touch You	1987	2.50	5.00	10.00
SUNSET					
❏ SUS-5222	Full of Soul	1968	3.75	7.50	15.00
—Reissue of Imperial LP					
TSOP					
❏ FZ 36416	The Year 2000	1980	2.50	5.00	10.00
UNITED ARTISTS					
❏ UAS-5655	The O'Jays Greatest Hits	1972	3.00	6.00	12.00
VOLCANO					
❏ 31149	Love You to Tears	1997	3.75	7.50	15.00

O'KAYSIONS, THE

45s

ABC

Number	Title (A Side/B Side)	Yr	VG	VG+	NM
❏ 11094	Girl Watcher/Deal Me In	1968	2.00	4.00	8.00
❏ 11153	Love Machine/Dedicated to the One I Love	1968	—	3.00	6.00
❏ 11207	Twenty-Four Hours from Tulsa/Colors	1969	—	3.00	6.00
COTILLION					
❏ 44089	Happiness/Watch Out Girl	1970	—	2.50	5.00
❏ 44134	Life and Things/Travelin' Life	1971	—	2.50	5.00
NORTH STATE					
❏ 1001	Girl Watcher/Deal Me In	1968	25.00	50.00	100.00
❏ 1001 [PS]	Girl Watcher/Deal Me In	1968	75.00	150.00	300.00
Albums					
ABC					
❏ S-664	Girl Watcher	1968	10.00	20.00	40.00

O'NEAL, ALEXANDER

12-Inch Singles

TABU

Number	Title (A Side/B Side)	Yr	VG	VG+	NM
❏ ZAS 1363 [DJ]The Little Drummer Boy (2 versions)/Sleigh Ride (2 versions)		1988	3.00	6.00	12.00
❏ 4Z9-05140	Innocent (Extended) (Instrumental)	1985	2.00	4.00	8.00
❏ 4Z9-05361	What's Missing (Remix) (Instrumental)	1986	2.00	4.00	8.00
❏ 4Z9-05937	You Were Meant to Be My Lady (Not My Girl) (Extended Dance Remix) (Acapella) (Remix) (Party Mix)	1986	2.50	5.00	10.00

Number	Title (A Side/B Side)	Yr	VG	VG+	NM
❏ 4Z9-06788	Fake (Extended Mix) (Edited Version)/(Patty Mix) (A Cappella) (Instrumental)	1987	2.00	4.00	8.00
❏ 4Z9-07480	Criticize (Remix) (Edit) (Critical Mix) (Critical Dub)	1987	2.00	4.00	8.00
❏ 4Z9-07539	Never Knew Love Like This (4 versions)	1987	2.50	5.00	10.00

—Featuring Cherrelle

Number	Title (A Side/B Side)	Yr	VG	VG+	NM
❏ 4Z9-07812	The Lovers (Extended) (A Cappella) (Radio Edit) (Instrumental)	1988	2.00	4.00	8.00
❏ 31458 8082 1	Love Makes No Sense (5 versions)	1993	3.00	6.00	12.00
❏ 31458 8092 1	Love Makes No Sense (Brothers in Rhythm Remix 7:37) (Brothers in Rhythm Dub 6:15)	1993	2.50	5.00	10.00
❏ 31458 8154 1	In the Middle (4 versions)	1993	2.50	5.00	10.00
❏ 31458 8192 1	Aphrodisia (6 versions)	1993	2.50	5.00	10.00
❏ 45-73626	All True Man (Radio Mix) (Classic Club Mix) (Big House Mix) (Big House Instrumental Mix)	1990	2.50	5.00	10.00
❏ 45-73932	The Yoke (G.U.O.T.R.) (Radio Edit) (LP Version) (12" Remix) (Dub) (Radio Edit #2)	1991	2.50	5.00	10.00

45s
TABU

Number	Title (A Side/B Side)	Yr	VG	VG+	NM
❏ ZS4-04718	Innocent/Are You the One?	1985	—	2.00	4.00
❏ ZS4-04718 [PS]	Innocent/Are You the One?	1985	—	2.00	4.00
❏ ZS4-05418	If You Were Here Tonight/(Long Version)	1985	—	2.00	4.00
❏ ZS4-05418 [PS]	If You Were Here Tonight/(Long Version)	1985	—	2.00	4.00
❏ ZS4-05646	A Broken Heart Can Mend/Do You Wanna Like I Do	1985	—	2.00	4.00
❏ ZS4-05850	What's Missing/Are You the One?	1986	—	—	3.00
❏ ZS4-06222	You Were Meant to Be My Lady (Not My Girl)/(Acapella)	1986	—	2.00	4.00
❏ ZS4-07100	Fake/A Broken Heart Can Mend	1987	—	—	3.00
❏ ZS4-07100 [PS]	Fake/A Broken Heart Can Mend	1987	—	—	3.00
❏ ZS4-07600	Criticize/A Broken Heart Can Mend	1987	—	—	3.00
❏ ZS4-07600 [PS]	Criticize/A Broken Heart Can Mend	1987	—	—	3.00
❏ ZS4-07646	Never Knew Love Like This/What's Missing	1987	—	—	3.00

—A-side featuring Cherrelle

Number	Title (A Side/B Side)	Yr	VG	VG+	NM
❏ ZS4-07646 [PS]	Never Knew Love Like This/What's Missing	1987	—	—	3.00

—A-side featuring Cherrelle

Number	Title (A Side/B Side)	Yr	VG	VG+	NM
❏ 31458 7706-7	Love Makes No Sense (Radio Edit)/(LP Version)	1993	—	2.00	4.00
❏ ZS4-07795	The Lovers/(Instrumental)	1988	—	—	3.00
❏ ZS4-07795 [PS]	The Lovers/(Instrumental)	1988	—	—	3.00
❏ ZS4-08501	Our First Christmas/My Gift To You	1988	—	2.00	4.00
❏ ZS4-68562	(What Can I Say) To Make You Love Me/(Remix)	1989	—	—	3.00
❏ 35-73627	All True Man/(Instrumental)	1990	—	2.00	4.00
❏ 35-73810	What Is This Thing Called Love?/Sentimental	1990	—	2.00	4.00

Albums
TABU

Number	Title (A Side/B Side)	Yr	VG	VG+	NM
❏ FZ 39331	Alexander O'Neal	1985	2.00	4.00	8.00
❏ FZ 40320	Hearsay	1987	2.00	4.00	8.00
❏ OZ 44492	All Mixed Up	1989	2.50	5.00	10.00
❏ OZ 45016	My Gift to You	1988	2.50	5.00	10.00
❏ Z 45349	All True Man	1991	3.75	7.50	15.00

O'NEAL, SHAQUILLE
12-Inch Singles
JIVE

Number	Title (A Side/B Side)	Yr	VG	VG+	NM
❏ 42176	(I Know I Got) Skillz (unknown versions)	1993	3.75	7.50	15.00
❏ 42200	I'm Outstanding (unknown versions)	1994	3.00	6.00	12.00
❏ 42215	Shoot Pass Slam (6 versions)	1994	3.00	6.00	12.00
❏ 42266	Biological Didn't Bother (6 versions)	1994	3.00	6.00	12.00

T.W.ISM.

Number	Title (A Side/B Side)	Yr	VG	VG+	NM
❏ 6063 [DJ]	You Can't Stop the Reign (Remix) (Acappella) (Single) (Instrumental)	1996	3.75	7.50	15.00

—Promo only on yellow vinyl

Number	Title (A Side/B Side)	Yr	VG	VG+	NM
❏ 6152	Connected (unknown versions)	1997	2.50	5.00	10.00

Albums
JIVE

Number	Title (A Side/B Side)	Yr	VG	VG+	NM
❏ 41529	Shaq Diesel	1993	3.75	7.50	15.00

—Issued in generic cover

Number	Title (A Side/B Side)	Yr	VG	VG+	NM
❏ 41550	Shaq-Fu: Da Return	1994	3.00	6.00	12.00

T.W.ISM.

Number	Title (A Side/B Side)	Yr	VG	VG+	NM
❏ 6064 [EP]	You Can't Stop the Reign	1996	2.00	4.00	8.00

—Promo only four-track sampler

Number	Title (A Side/B Side)	Yr	VG	VG+	NM
❏ INT2-90087 [(2)]	You Can't Stop the Reign	1996	3.75	7.50	15.00

OAK CLIFF T-BONE
See T-BONE WALKER.

OAKTOWN'S 3.5.7.
12-Inch Singles
BUST IT

Number	Title (A Side/B Side)	Yr	VG	VG+	NM
❏ V-15729	Turn It Up (Edit) (Dub) (Instrumental)	1991	2.00	4.00	8.00
❏ V-15795	It's Not Your Money (Extended) (Dub) (Bonus Beats) (Radio Edit) (Instrumental) (LP Version)	1991	2.50	5.00	10.00
❏ SPRO-79194/5 [DJ]	Honey (Extended) (Dubstrumental) (LP Version)	1991	2.50	5.00	10.00
❏ SPRO-79887/8 [DJ]	Turn It Up (Club Mix) (Club Edit) (Bonus Beats) (Extended) (Radio Edit) (Club Dub Mix)	1991	2.50	5.00	10.00

CAPITOL

Number	Title (A Side/B Side)	Yr	VG	VG+	NM
❏ V-15446	Yeah! Yeah! Yeah! (3 versions)/3.5.7. Straight At Yo	1989	2.50	5.00	10.00
❏ V-15495	3.5.7. Straight At You (Vocal) (Dub)	1989	2.50	5.00	10.00
❏ V-15510	Juicy Gotcha Krazy (Vocal) (LP Version) (Instrumental)	1990	2.50	5.00	10.00
❏ V-15596	We Like It (Video Version) (Instrumental)	1990	2.50	5.00	10.00

45s
CAPITOL

Number	Title (A Side/B Side)	Yr	VG	VG+	NM
❏ 7PRO-79037/9	It's Not Your Money (Radio Edit)/(Instrumental)	1991	—	3.50	7.00

—7-inch vinyl is promo only

Number	Title (A Side/B Side)	Yr	VG	VG+	NM
❏ 7PRO-79171/242	We Like It (Video Version)/(LP Version)	1990	—	3.00	6.00

—7-inch version is promo only

Number	Title (A Side/B Side)	Yr	VG	VG+	NM
❏ 7PRO-79495	Yeah! Yeah! Yeah! (same on both sides)	1989	—	2.50	5.00
❏ 7PRO-79778/920	Juicy Gotcha Krazy (Vocal)/(Instrumental)	1989	—	3.00	6.00

—7-inch vinyl is promo only

Albums
BUST IT

Number	Title (A Side/B Side)	Yr	VG	VG+	NM
❏ C1-92996	Fully Loaded	1991	3.75	7.50	15.00

CAPITOL

Number	Title (A Side/B Side)	Yr	VG	VG+	NM
❏ C1-90926	Wild and Loose	1989	2.50	5.00	10.00

OCEAN, BILLY
12-Inch Singles
EPIC

Number	Title (A Side/B Side)	Yr	VG	VG+	NM
❏ AS 1280 [DJ]	Another Day Won't Matter (same on both sides)	1981	3.00	6.00	12.00
❏ 48-02049	Night (Feel Like Gettin' Down)/Stay the Night	1981	2.50	5.00	10.00
❏ 49-02943	Calypso Funkin' (6:25)/City Limits	1982	2.00	4.00	8.00

JIVE

Number	Title (A Side/B Side)	Yr	VG	VG+	NM
❏ 1279-1-JD	Licence to Chill (Extended) (7" Version) (Instrumental)/Pleasure	1989	2.00	4.00	8.00
❏ 1311-1-JD	I Sleep Much Better (In Someone Else's Bed) (4 versions)/Gun for Hire	1989	2.00	4.00	8.00

JIVE/ARISTA

Number	Title (A Side/B Side)	Yr	VG	VG+	NM
❏ JD1-9215	Caribbean Queen (No More Love on the Run) (Special Mix) (Instrumental) (Diamond Mix)	1984	—	3.00	6.00
❏ JD1-9280	Loverboy (3 versions)	1984	—	3.00	6.00
❏ JD1-9373	Mystery Lady (Extended Version)//African Queen (No More Love on the Run)/European Queen (No More Love on the Run)	1985	2.00	4.00	8.00
❏ JD1-9431	When the Going Get Tough, the Tough Get Going (4 versions)	1985	—	3.00	6.00
❏ JD1-9509	Love Zone (Extended) (Instrumental) (LP Version)/There'll Be Sad Songs (To Make You Cry)	1986	—	3.50	7.00
❏ JD1-9536	Love Is Forever/Suddenly	1986	2.00	4.00	8.00
❏ JD1-9679	Get Outta My Dreams, Get Into My Car (Extended Version) (Instrumental) (7" Version)/Showdown/Special Mix (Medley 9:40)	1986	—	3.50	7.00
❏ JD1-9741	Tear Down These Walls (4 versions)/Without You	1988	—	3.50	7.00

NEXT PLATEAU

Number	Title (A Side/B Side)	Yr	VG	VG+	NM
❏ NP 50054	Love Really Hurts Without You (Dance Version) (Dub Version) (7" Version)	1987	2.00	4.00	8.00

TLO

Number	Title (A Side/B Side)	Yr	VG	VG+	NM
❏ 9101	Hold On Brother (Club) (Dub) (Radio)	1986	2.50	5.00	10.00

45s
ARIOLA AMERICA

Number	Title (A Side/B Side)	Yr	VG	VG+	NM
❏ 7621	Love Really Hurts Without You/You're Running Out of Fools	1976	—	3.00	6.00
❏ 7630	L.O.D. (Love On Delivery)/Mr. Business Man	1976	—	3.00	6.00

EPIC

Number	Title (A Side/B Side)	Yr	VG	VG+	NM
❏ 19-02053	Night (Feel Like Gettin' Down)/Stay the Night	1981	—	2.00	4.00
❏ 14-02464	Are You Ready/Taking Chances	1981	—	2.00	4.00
❏ 14-02485	Another Day Won't Matter/Whatever Turns You On	1981	—	2.00	4.00
❏ 14-02942	Calypso Funkin'/City Limits	1982	—	2.00	4.00
❏ 14-03174	Inner Feelings/Tryin' to Get Through to You	1982	—	2.00	4.00
❏ 8-50810	American Hearts/My Love	1979	—	2.50	5.00

JIVE

Number	Title (A Side/B Side)	Yr	VG	VG+	NM
❏ 1283-7-J	Licence to Chill/Pleasure	1989	—	—	3.00
❏ 1283-7-J [PS]	Licence to Chill/Pleasure	1989	—	—	3.00

JIVE/ARISTA

Number	Title (A Side/B Side)	Yr	VG	VG+	NM
❏ 9199	Caribbean Queen (No More Love on the Run)/(Instrumental)	1984	—	—	3.00
❏ 9284	Loverboy/(Dub)	1984	—	—	3.00
❏ 9284 [PS]	Loverboy/(Dub)	1984	—	—	3.00
❏ 9323	Suddenly/Lucky Man	1985	—	—	3.00
❏ 9323 [PS]	Suddenly/Lucky Man	1985	—	—	3.00
❏ 9374	Mystery Lady/African Queen (No More Love on the Run)	1985	—	—	3.00
❏ 9374 [PS]	Mystery Lady/African Queen (No More Love on the Run)	1985	—	—	3.00
❏ 9432	When the Going Gets Tough, the Tough Get Going/(Instrumental)	1985	—	—	3.00
❏ 9432 [PS]	When the Going Gets Tough, the Tough Get Going/(Instrumental)	1985	—	—	3.00
❏ 9465	There'll Be Sad Songs (To Make You Cry)/If I Should Lose You	1986	—	—	3.00
❏ 9465 [PS]	There'll Be Sad Songs (To Make You Cry)/If I Should Lose You	1986	—	—	3.00
❏ 9510	Love Zone/(Instrumental)	1986	—	—	3.00
❏ 9510 [PS]	Love Zone/(Instrumental)	1986	—	—	3.00
❏ 9540	Love Is Forever/Dance Floor	1986	—	—	3.00
❏ 9540 [PS]	Love Is Forever/Dance Floor	1986	—	—	3.00
❏ 9678	Get Outta My Dreams, Get Into My Car/Showdown	1988	—	—	3.00
❏ 9678 [PS]	Get Outta My Dreams, Get Into My Car/Showdown	1988	—	—	3.00
❏ 9707	The Colour of Love/It's Never Too Late to Try	1988	—	—	3.00
❏ 9707 [PS]	The Colour of Love/It's Never Too Late to Try	1988	—	—	3.00
❏ 9740	Tear Down These Walls/Without You	1988	—	—	3.00
❏ 9740 [PS]	Tear Down These Walls/Without You	1988	—	—	3.00

Number	Title (A Side/B Side)	Yr	VG	VG+	NM

Albums

EPIC

| ❏ FE 37406 | Nights (Feel Like Gettin' Down) | 1981 | 3.75 | 7.50 | 15.00 |
| ❏ PE 37406 | Nights (Feel Like Gettin' Down) | 1985 | 2.00 | 4.00 | 8.00 |

—Budget-line reissue with new prefix

| ❏ FE 38129 | Inner Feelings | 1982 | 3.75 | 7.50 | 15.00 |
| ❏ PE 38129 | Inner Feelings | 1985 | 2.00 | 4.00 | 8.00 |

—Budget-line reissue with new prefix

JIVE

| ❏ 1271-1-J | Greatest Hits | 1989 | 2.50 | 5.00 | 10.00 |

JIVE/ARISTA

| ❏ JL8-8213 | Suddenly | 1984 | 3.75 | 7.50 | 15.00 |

—Original cover: Photo of Billy Ocean on blue background

| ❏ JL8-8213 | Suddenly | 1984 | 2.00 | 4.00 | 8.00 |

—Second cover: Drawing of Billy Ocean on white background

| ❏ JL8-8409 | Love Zone | 1986 | 2.00 | 4.00 | 8.00 |
| ❏ JL8-8495 | Tear Down These Walls | 1988 | 2.00 | 4.00 | 8.00 |

ODYSSEY
12-Inch Singles

RCA

❏ PD-11063	Native New Yorker//Easy Come, Easy Go/Hold De Mota Down	1977	5.00	10.00	20.00
❏ PD-11400	Single Again/What Time Does the Balloon Go Up/Pride	1978	2.50	5.00	10.00
❏ PD-11445	Lucky Star (4:25)/You Wouldn't Know a Real Live True Love If It Walked Right Up, Kissed You on the	1978	2.50	5.00	10.00
❏ PC-11512	Native New Yorker//Easy Come, Easy Go/Hold De Mota Down	1978	3.75	7.50	15.00
❏ PD-11963	Don't Tell Me, Tell Her (6:05)/Use It Up and Wear It Out	1980	2.00	4.00	8.00
❏ PD-12057	Hang Together (6:00)/Never Had It at All	1980	2.50	5.00	10.00
❏ PD-12241	Going Back to My Roots/Baba Awa (Roots Suite)	1981	2.50	5.00	10.00
❏ PD-13218	Inside Out/Love's Alright	1982	2.00	4.00	8.00
❏ PD-13341	Together (6:17)/Native New Yorker (5:35)	1982	2.50	5.00	10.00

45s

RCA

❏ PB-11129	Native New Yorker/Ever Lovin' Sam	1977	—	2.00	4.00
❏ PB-11245	Weekend Lover/Golden Hand	1978	—	2.00	4.00
❏ PB-11399	Single Again/What Time Does the Balloon Go Up	1978	—	2.50	5.00
❏ PB-11444	Lucky Star/You Wouldn't Know a Real Live True Love If It Walked Right Up, Kissed You on the	1978	—	2.50	5.00
❏ PB-11962	Don't Tell Me, Tell Her/Use It Up and Wear It Out	1980	—	2.00	4.00
❏ PB-12056	Hang Together/Never Had It at All	1980	—	2.50	5.00
❏ PB-12240	Going Back to My Roots/Baba Awa (Roots Suite)	1981	—	2.00	4.00
❏ PB-12348	It Will Be Alright/Baby That's All I Want	1981	—	2.50	5.00
❏ PB-13217	Inside Out/Love's Alright	1982	—	2.00	4.00
❏ PB-13340	Together/Native New Yorker	1982	—	2.50	5.00

Albums

RCA VICTOR

❏ APL1-2204	Odyssey	1977	2.50	5.00	10.00
❏ AFL1-3031	Hollywood Party Tonight	1978	2.50	5.00	10.00
❏ AFL1-3526	Hang Together	1980	2.50	5.00	10.00
❏ AFL1-3910	I Got the Melody	1981	2.50	5.00	10.00
❏ AFL1-4240	Happy Together	1982	2.50	5.00	10.00

OHIO PLAYERS, THE
Also see THE OHIO UNTOUCHABLES.

12-Inch Singles

AIR CITY

| ❏ A-402 | Sight for Sore Eyes/(Instrumental) | 1984 | — | 3.00 | 6.00 |

ARISTA

| ❏ SP-46 [DJ] | Everybody Up (9:32) (3:57) | 1979 | 3.00 | 6.00 | 12.00 |

BOARDWALK

| ❏ AS 941 [DJ] | Try a Little Tenderness/DDDDDDDance | 1981 | 3.75 | 7.50 | 15.00 |

—B-side by Rox

MERCURY

| ❏ MK-43 [DJ] | Magic Trick/Good Luck Charm | 1976 | 3.75 | 7.50 | 15.00 |

TRACK

| ❏ 58813 | Sweat (3 versions)/Rock the House | 1988 | — | 3.00 | 6.00 |

45s

AIR CITY

❏ 402	Sight for Sore Eyes/(Instrumental)	1984	—	2.00	4.00
❏ 402 [PS]	Sight for Sore Eyes/(Instrumental)	1984	—	2.00	4.00
❏ 1007	Follow Me/(B-side unknown)	1984	—	2.50	5.00

ARISTA

| ❏ 0408 | Everybody Up/Take De Funk Off, Fly | 1979 | — | 2.00 | 4.00 |
| ❏ 0440 | Don't Say Goodbye/Say It | 1979 | — | 2.00 | 4.00 |

BOARDWALK

❏ NB7-11-133	Star of the Party/I Better Take a Coffee Break	1981	—	2.00	4.00
❏ WS8-02063	Skinny/Call Me	1981	—	2.00	4.00
❏ 5708	Try a Little Tenderness/Try to Be a Man	1981	—	2.00	4.00

CAPITOL

| ❏ 2385 | Bad Bargain/Here Today and Gone Tomorrow | 1969 | 2.50 | 5.00 | 10.00 |
| ❏ 2523 | Find Someone to Love/Over the Rainbow | 1969 | 2.50 | 5.00 | 10.00 |

COMPASS

| ❏ 7015 | Tresspassin'/You Don't Mean It | 1967 | 3.00 | 6.00 | 12.00 |
| ❏ 7018 | It's a Crying Shame/I've Got to Hold On | 1968 | 3.00 | 6.00 | 12.00 |

MERCURY

❏ 73480	Jive Turkey (Part 1)/Streakin' Cheek to Cheek	1974	—	2.50	5.00
❏ 73609	Skin Tight/Heaven Must Be Like This	1974	—	2.50	5.00
❏ 73643	Fire/Together	1974	—	2.50	5.00

❏ 73675	I Want to Be Free/Smoke	1975	—	2.50	5.00
❏ 73713	Sweet Sticky Thing/Alone	1975	—	2.50	5.00
❏ 73734	Love Rollercoaster/It's All Over	1975	—	2.50	5.00
❏ 73753	Happy Holidays (Part 1)/Happy Holidays (Part 2)	1975	—	3.00	6.00
❏ 73775	Fopp/Let's Love	1976	—	2.50	5.00
❏ 73814	Who'd She Coo?/Bi-Centennial	1976	—	2.50	5.00
❏ 73860	Far East Mississippi/Only a Child Can Love	1976	—	2.50	5.00
❏ 73881	Feel the Beat (Everybody Disco)/Contradiction	1976	—	2.50	5.00
❏ 73913	Body Vibes/Don't Fight My Love	1977	—	2.50	5.00
❏ 73932	O-H-I-O/Can You Still Love Me	1977	—	2.50	5.00
❏ 73956	Merry Go Round/Angel	1977	—	2.50	5.00
❏ 73974	Good Luck Charm (Part 1)/Good Luck Charm (Part 2)	1977	—	2.50	5.00
❏ 73983	Magic Trick/Mr. Mean	1978	—	2.50	5.00
❏ 74014	Funk-O-Nots/Sleepwalkin'	1978	—	2.50	5.00
❏ 74031	Time Slips Away/Nott Enuff	1978	—	2.50	5.00

TANGERINE

| ❏ 978 | Neighbors/A Thing Called Love | 1967 | 3.00 | 6.00 | 12.00 |

TRACK

| ❏ 58812 | Let's Play (From Now On)/Show Off | 1988 | — | — | 3.00 |
| ❏ 58815 | Sweat/Rock the House | 1988 | — | — | 3.00 |

WESTBOUND

❏ 188	Pain (Part 1)/Pain (Part 2)	1971	—	3.00	6.00
❏ 204	Pleasure/I Wanna Hear from You	1972	—	3.00	6.00
❏ 208	Walt's First Trip/Varce Is Love	1972	—	3.00	6.00
❏ 214	Funky Worm/Paint Me	1973	—	3.00	6.00
❏ 216	Ecstasy/Not So Sad and Lonely	1973	—	3.00	6.00
❏ 228	Sleep Talk/Food Stamps Y'All	1974	—	3.00	6.00
❏ 5018	Rattlesnake/Gone Forever	1976	—	3.00	6.00

Albums

ACCORD

| ❏ SN-7102 | Young and Ready | 1981 | 2.00 | 4.00 | 8.00 |

ARISTA

| ❏ AB 4226 | Everybody Up | 1979 | 2.00 | 4.00 | 8.00 |

BOARDWALK

| ❏ FW 37090 | Tenderness | 1981 | 2.00 | 4.00 | 8.00 |

CAPITOL

| ❏ ST-192 | Observations in Time | 1969 | 12.50 | 25.00 | 50.00 |
| ❏ ST-11291 | The Ohio Players | 1974 | 3.00 | 6.00 | 12.00 |

—Reissue of 192

MERCURY

| ❏ SRM-1-705 | Skin Tight | 1974 | 3.00 | 6.00 | 12.00 |

—Red label

| ❏ SRM-1-705 | Skin Tight | 1974 | 2.50 | 5.00 | 10.00 |

—Chicago skyline label

❏ SRM-1-1013	Fire	1974	2.50	5.00	10.00
❏ SRM-1-1038	Honey	1975	2.50	5.00	10.00
❏ SRM-1-1088	Contradiction	1976	2.50	5.00	10.00
❏ SRM-1-1122	Ohio Players Gold	1976	2.50	5.00	10.00
❏ SRM-1-3701	Angel	1977	2.50	5.00	10.00
❏ SRM-1-3707	Mr. Mean	1977	2.50	5.00	10.00
❏ SRM-1-3730	Jass-Ay-Lay-Dee	1978	2.50	5.00	10.00
❏ 824461-1	Ohio Players Gold	198?	2.00	4.00	8.00

—Reissue of 1122

TRACK

| ❏ TRK 58810 | Back | 1988 | 2.50 | 5.00 | 10.00 |

TRIP

| ❏ 8029 | First Impression | 1972 | 3.00 | 6.00 | 12.00 |

UNITED ARTISTS

| ❏ UA-LA502-E | The Very Best of The Ohio Players | 1975 | 3.00 | 6.00 | 12.00 |

WESTBOUND

| ❏ 211 | Rattlesnake | 1975 | 3.00 | 6.00 | 12.00 |
| ❏ 219 | Pain | 1976 | 3.00 | 6.00 | 12.00 |

—Reissue of 2015

| ❏ 220 | Pleasure | 1976 | 3.00 | 6.00 | 12.00 |

—Reissue of 2017

| ❏ 222 | Ecstasy | 1976 | 3.00 | 6.00 | 12.00 |

—Reissue of 2021

❏ 304	The Best of the Early Years	1977	3.75	7.50	15.00
❏ 1003	Climax	1974	3.75	7.50	15.00
❏ 1005	Ohio Players Greatest Hits	1975	3.75	7.50	15.00
❏ 2015	Pain	1972	5.00	10.00	20.00
❏ 2017	Pleasure	1973	5.00	10.00	20.00
❏ 2021	Ecstasy	1973	5.00	10.00	20.00

OHIO UNTOUCHABLES, THE
Early version of THE OHIO PLAYERS.

45s

LUPINE

❏ 109	She's My Heart's Desire/What to Do	1962	12.50	25.00	50.00
❏ 110	Love Is Amazing/Forgive Me Darling	1962	12.50	25.00	50.00
❏ 116/7	I'm Tired/Uptown	1962	10.00	20.00	40.00
❏ 1009	She's My Heart's Desire/What to Do	1964	5.00	10.00	20.00
❏ 1010	Love Is Amazing/Forgive Me Darling	1964	5.00	10.00	20.00
❏ 1011	I'm Tired/Uptown	1964	3.75	7.50	15.00

OL' DIRTY BASTARD
12-Inch Singles

ELEKTRA

❏ ED 5766 [DJ]	Shimmy Shimmy Ya (Studo Tone Remix) (Instrumental)	1995	2.50	5.00	10.00
❏ ED 6176 [DJ]	Got Your Money (unknown versions)	1999	3.00	6.00	12.00
❏ ED 6193 [DJ]	Recognize (Amended Version) (Original Version) (Instrumental)//(same on both sides)	1999	3.00	6.00	12.00

Number	Title (A Side/B Side)	Yr	VG	VG+	NM
❑ 63718	Got Your Money (unknown versions)	1999	2.50	5.00	10.00
❑ 66128	Shimmy Shimmy Ya (5 versions?)/Baby C'mon	1995	2.00	4.00	8.00
❑ 66166	Brooklyn Zoo (Lord Digga Remix) (Lord Digga Instrumental) (LP Version) (Instrumental)/Give It To Ya Raw (LP Version) (SD50 Remix)	1995	2.00	4.00	8.00

Albums
ELEKTRA

Number	Title	Yr	VG	VG+	NM
❑ ED 5796 [(2) DJ]	Return to the 36 Chambers: The Dirty Version	1995	3.75	7.50	15.00

—Promo-only version

| ❑ ED 6187 [(2) DJ] | N***a Please | 1999 | 5.00 | 10.00 | 20.00 |

—Promo-only version

| ❑ 61659 [(2)] | Return to the 36 Chambers: The Dirty Version | 1995 | 3.75 | 7.50 | 15.00 |
| ❑ 62414 [(2)] | Nigga Please | 1999 | 3.75 | 7.50 | 15.00 |

OL' SKOOL
12-Inch Singles
UNIVERSAL

Number	Title	Yr	VG	VG+	NM
❑ 1524 [DJ]	Only One (Radio Edit) (Instrumental)//(same on both sides)	1999	2.50	5.00	10.00
❑ 56145	Set You Free (unknown versions)	1997	2.00	4.00	8.00

Albums
UNIVERSAL

| ❑ 53104 | Ol' Skool | 1998 | 3.00 | 6.00 | 12.00 |

OLLIE AND JERRY
12-Inch Singles
POLYDOR

Number	Title	Yr	VG	VG+	NM
❑ PRO 284-1 [DJ]	Breakin' ... There's No Stopping Us (Club Mix 6:51) (Instrumental 5:33)	1984	3.75	7.50	15.00
❑ 821708-1	Breakin' ... There's No Stopping Us (Club Mix) (Instrumental)	1984	3.00	6.00	12.00
❑ 881534-1	Electric Boogaloo (Dance Mix) (Instrumental)	1984	3.00	6.00	12.00

45s
POLYDOR

| ❑ 821708-7 | Breakin' ... There's No Stoppin' Us/Showdown | 1984 | — | 2.00 | 4.00 |
| ❑ 881461-7 | Electric Boogaloo/Physical Clash | 1984 | — | 2.00 | 4.00 |

OLLIE AND THE NIGHTINGALES
45s
STAX

Number	Title	Yr	VG	VG+	NM
❑ 0014	You're Leaving Me/Showered with Love	1968	—	3.00	6.00
❑ 0027	The Mellow Way You Treat Your Man/Don't Do What I Did	1969	—	3.00	6.00
❑ 0045	I've Got a Feeling/You'll Never Do Wrong	1969	—	3.00	6.00
❑ 0065	I'll Be Your Anything/Bracing Myself for the Fall	1970	—	3.00	6.00
❑ 245	I Got a Sure Thing/Girl You Have My Heart Singing	1968	2.00	4.00	8.00

OLYMPICS, THE
45s
ARVEE

Number	Title	Yr	VG	VG+	NM
❑ 562	(Baby) Hully Gully/Private Eye	1959	6.25	12.50	25.00
❑ 595	Big Boy Pete/The Slop	1960	6.25	12.50	25.00
❑ 5006	Shimmy Like Kate/Workin' Hard	1960	5.00	10.00	20.00
❑ 5020	Dance by the Light of the Moon/Dodge City	1960	5.00	10.00	20.00
❑ 5023	Little Pedro/The Bullfight	1961	5.00	10.00	20.00
❑ 5031	Stay Where You Are/Dooley	1961	10.00	20.00	40.00
❑ 5044	Mash Them 'Taters/The Stomp	1961	5.00	10.00	20.00
❑ 5051	Everybody Likes to Cha Cha Cha/The Twist	1962	3.75	7.50	15.00
❑ 5056	Baby It's Hot/The Scotch	1962	3.75	7.50	15.00
❑ 5073	What'd I Say (Part 1)/What'd I Say (Part 2)	1963	3.75	7.50	15.00
❑ 6501	Big Boy Pete '65/Stay Where You Are	1965	3.00	6.00	12.00

DEMON

❑ 1508	Western Movies/Well!	1958	7.50	15.00	30.00
❑ 1512	Dance with the Teacher/Everybody Needs Love	1958	6.25	12.50	25.00
❑ 1514	Your Love/The Chicken	1959	6.25	12.50	25.00

DUO DISC

| ❑ 104 | The Boogler (Part 1)/The Boogler (Part 2) | 1964 | 3.00 | 6.00 | 12.00 |
| ❑ 105 | Return of Big Boy Pete/Return of the Watusi | 1964 | 3.00 | 6.00 | 12.00 |

JUBILEE

| ❑ 5674 | The Cartoon Song/Things That Make Me Laugh | 1969 | 2.00 | 4.00 | 8.00 |

LOMA

❑ 2010	I'm Comin' Home/Rainin' in My Heart	1965	2.50	5.00	10.00
❑ 2013	Good Lovin'/Olympic Shuffle	1965	2.50	5.00	10.00
❑ 2017	Baby I'm Yours/No More Will I Cry	1965	2.50	5.00	10.00

MGM

| ❑ 14505 | Worm in Your Wheatgerm/The Apartment | 1973 | — | 2.50 | 5.00 |

MIRWOOD

❑ 5504	We Go Together (Pretty Baby)/Secret Agents	1966	2.00	4.00	8.00
❑ 5513	Mine Exclusively/Secret Agents	1966	2.00	4.00	8.00
❑ 5523	Baby Do the Philly Dog/Western Movies	1966	2.00	4.00	8.00
❑ 5525	The Bounce/The Duck	1966	2.00	4.00	8.00
❑ 5529	The Same Old Thing/I'll Do a Little Bit More	1967	2.00	4.00	8.00
❑ 5533	Big Boy Pete/(Baby) Hully Gully	1967	2.00	4.00	8.00

PARKWAY

| ❑ 6003 | Lookin' for a Love/Good Things | 1968 | 2.00 | 4.00 | 8.00 |

TITAN

| ❑ 1718 | The Chicken/Cool Short | 1961 | 6.25 | 12.50 | 25.00 |

TRI DISC

❑ 105	Return of Big Boy Pete/Return of the Watusi	1962	3.75	7.50	15.00
❑ 106	The Bounce/Fireworks	1963	3.75	7.50	15.00
❑ 107	Dancin' Holiday/Do the Slauson Shuffle	1963	3.75	7.50	15.00
❑ 110	Bounce Again/A New Dancin' Partner	1963	3.75	7.50	15.00
❑ 112	The Broken Hip/So Goodbye	1963	3.75	7.50	15.00

Number	Title (A Side/B Side)	Yr	VG	VG+	NM
WARNER BROS.					
❑ 7369	Girl, You're My Kind of People/Please, Please, Please	1970	—	3.00	6.00

7-Inch Extended Plays
ARVEE

| ❑ 423 | (contents unknown) | 1960 | 50.00 | 100.00 | 200.00 |
| ❑ 423 [PS] | Doin' the Hully Gully | 1960 | 50.00 | 100.00 | 200.00 |

Albums
ARVEE

❑ A-423 [M]	Doin' the Hully Gully	1960	40.00	80.00	160.00
❑ A-424 [M]	Dance by the Light of the Moon	1961	30.00	60.00	120.00
❑ A-429 [M]	Party Time	1961	30.00	60.00	120.00

EVEREST

| ❑ 4109 | The Olympics | 1981 | 2.50 | 5.00 | 10.00 |

MIRWOOD

| ❑ MS-7003 [S] | Something Old, Something New | 1966 | 12.50 | 25.00 | 50.00 |
| ❑ MW-7003 [M] | Something Old, Something New | 1966 | 10.00 | 20.00 | 40.00 |

POST

| ❑ 8000 | The Olympics Sing | 196? | 6.25 | 12.50 | 25.00 |

RHINO

| ❑ RNDF-207 | The Official Record Album of the Olympics | 1983 | 3.00 | 6.00 | 12.00 |

TRI-DISC

| ❑ 1001 [M] | Do the Bounce | 1963 | 20.00 | 40.00 | 80.00 |

ONE CAUSE ONE EFFECT
12-Inch Singles
CAPITOL

Number	Title	Yr	VG	VG+	NM
❑ V-15606	Up with Hope, Down with Dope (4 versions)	1990	2.00	4.00	8.00
❑ V-15652	Midnite Lover (2 versions)	1990	2.50	5.00	10.00
❑ V-15655	Turntable Genius (LP Version) (Radio Edit) (Extended Mix) (Instrumental)	1991	2.50	5.00	10.00

45s
CAPITOL

| ❑ 7PRO-79227/86 | Up with Hope, Down with Dope (Single Mix)/ (12" Remix) | 1990 | 2.00 | 4.00 | 8.00 |

—7-inch vinyl is promo only

100 PROOF AGED IN SOUL
45s
HOT WAX

Number	Title	Yr	VG	VG+	NM
❑ 6904	Too Many Cooks (Spoil the Soup)/Not Enough Love to Satisfy	1969	3.00	6.00	12.00

—First pressings as "Aged in Soul"

| ❑ 6904 | Too Many Cooks (Spoil the Soup)/Not Enough Love to Satisfy | 1969 | — | 3.00 | 6.00 |

—Later pressings as "100 Proof Aged in Soul"

❑ 7004	Somebody's Been Sleeping/I've Come to Save You	1970	—	3.00	6.00
❑ 7009	One Man's Leftovers (Is Another Man's Feast)/If I Could See the Light in the Window	1970	—	3.00	6.00
❑ 7104	Driveway/Love Is Sweeter	1971	—	3.00	6.00
❑ 7108	90 Day Freeze (On Her Love)/Not Enough Love to Satisfy	1971	—	3.00	6.00
❑ 7202	Everything Good Is Bad/I'd Rather Fight Than Switch	1972	—	3.00	6.00
❑ 7206	Don't Scratch/If I Could See the Light in the Window	1972	—	3.00	6.00
❑ 7211	Nothing Sweeter Than Love/Since You've Been Gone	1972	—	3.00	6.00

Albums
HOT WAX

| ❑ 704 | Somebody's Been Sleeping in My Bed | 1970 | 3.75 | 7.50 | 15.00 |
| ❑ 712 | 100 Proof Aged in Soul | 1971 | 3.75 | 7.50 | 15.00 |

112
12-Inch Singles
BAD BOY

Number	Title	Yr	VG	VG+	NM
❑ 9087 [DJ]	Cupid (Radio Mix) (Instrumental)	1997	3.75	7.50	15.00
❑ 9215 [DJ]	Anywhere (Club Mix) (Radio Mix) (Instrumental)/ (Emperor Searcy Remix Radio Mix) (Album Version) (Acappella)	1999	2.50	5.00	10.00
❑ 9231 [DJ]	Love You Like I Did (LP Version) (Instrumental) (Acapella)/The Only One (LP Version) (Instrumental) (Acapella)	1999	3.75	7.50	15.00
❑ 9342 [DJ]	It's Over Now (Radio 4:24) (Instrumental 4:24) (Radio Mix 4:24) (Acappella 4:24)	2000	3.75	7.50	15.00
❑ 9358 [DJ]	Dance with Me (4 versions)	2001	3.00	6.00	12.00
❑ 9363 [DJ]	Peaches and Cream (Radio) (Instrumental) (Club Mix)	2001	2.00	4.00	8.00
❑ 79071	Only You (Club Mix Featuring The Notorious B.I.G.) (Bad Boy Remix Featuring The Notorious B.I.G. and Mase) (Slow Remix)/(Club Mix Instrumental) (Bad Boy Remix Instrumental) (Slow Remix Instrumental)	1996	3.00	6.00	12.00
❑ 79076	Come See Me (Album Version) (Bad Boy Remix Featuring Black Rob)/Why Don't You Love Me/ Come See Me (Album Version Instrumental) (Bad Boy Remix Instrumental)	1996	3.00	6.00	12.00
❑ 79102	Cupid/Cry On!/I Can't Believe//Cupid (Instrumental)/I Can't Believe (Instrumental)	1997	3.75	7.50	15.00
❑ 79214	Anywhere (6 versions)	1999	2.50	5.00	10.00
❑ 79360	It's Over Now (unknown versions)/Peaches and Cream (unknown versions)	2000	2.00	4.00	8.00
❑ 79387	Peaches and Cream (unknown versions)	2001	—	3.00	6.00

O

Number	Title (A Side/B Side)	Yr	VG	VG+	NM
45s					
BAD BOY					
❑ 79087	Cupid/Only You	1997	—	2.00	4.00
Albums					
BAD BOY					
❑ 73021 [(2)]	Room 112	1998	3.75	7.50	15.00
❑ 73039	Part III	2000	3.00	6.00	12.00

ONE WAY
12-Inch Singles

Number	Title (A Side/B Side)	Yr	VG	VG+	NM
CAPITOL					
❑ V-15390	Driving Me Crazy (5 versions)	1988	—	3.00	6.00
—As "Al Hudson and One Way"					
❑ V-15435	Say You Will/Get Up Off It	1988	—	3.00	6.00
—As "Al Hudson and One Way"					
MCA					
❑ L33-1124 [DJ]	Shine on Me (2 versions)	1983	2.00	4.00	8.00
❑ L33-1173 [DJ]	Mr. Groove/Lady You Are	1984	2.50	5.00	10.00
❑ L33-1200 [DJ]	Smile/(Instrumental)	1984	2.00	4.00	8.00
❑ L33-1294 [DJ]	Let's Talk (9:45) (LP Version) (Dub 10:20)	1986	2.50	5.00	10.00
❑ L33-1717 [DJ]	Push/All Over Again	1981	3.00	6.00	12.00
❑ L33-1747 [DJ]	Show Me/Get Up	1981	3.75	7.50	15.00
❑ L33-1755 [DJ]	Who's Foolin' Who (3:54) (5:13)	1982	3.75	7.50	15.00
❑ L33-1764 [DJ]	Cutie Pie/Give Me One More Chance	1982	3.75	7.50	15.00
❑ L33-1853 [DJ]	Music/Now That I Found You	1980	3.75	7.50	15.00
❑ L33-1884 [DJ]	Do Your Thang (6:25)/Copy This	1980	3.75	7.50	15.00
❑ L33-1890 [DJ]	Pop It/I'm in Love with Lovin' You	1980	3.75	7.50	15.00
❑ 13972	Let's Get Together (7:49)/Didn't You Know It	1983	3.00	6.00	12.00
❑ L33-17020 [DJ]	Serving It (same on both sides)	1985	2.50	5.00	10.00
❑ L33-17042 [DJ]	More Than Friends, Less Than Lovers (5:11)/ Serving It (5:13)	1985	2.00	4.00	8.00
❑ L33-17269 [DJ]	You Better Quit (same on both sides)	1987	3.00	6.00	12.00
❑ 23659	Don't Think About It (Extended) (Radio) (Instrumental) (Bass Appella) (Bonus Beats)	1986	2.00	4.00	8.00
❑ 23714	Whammy (Extended) (Radio Edit) (Instrumental) (Hornapella) (Bonus Beats)	1987	2.00	4.00	8.00
❑ 23716	You Better Quit (4 versions)	1987	2.00	4.00	8.00
45s					
CAPITOL					
❑ B-44183	Driving Me Crazy/(Part 2)	1988	—	—	3.00
—As "Al Hudson and One Way"					
❑ B-44264	Get Up Off It/Driving Me Crazy	1988	—	—	3.00
—As "Al Hudson and One Way"					
MCA					
❑ 41170	Music/Now That I Found You	1980	—	2.00	4.00
❑ 41238	Do Your Thang/Copy This	1980	—	2.00	4.00
❑ 41298	Pop It/I'm in Love with Lovin' You	1980	—	2.00	4.00
❑ 51021	Something in the Past/You're the One	1980	—	2.00	4.00
❑ 51054	My Lady/I Didn't Mean to Break Your Heart	1981	—	2.00	4.00
❑ 51110	Push/All Over Again	1981	—	2.00	4.00
❑ 51165	Pull Fancy Dancer/Pull — Part 1//Part 2	1981	—	2.00	4.00
❑ 52004	Who's Foolin' Who/Sweet Lady	1982	—	2.00	4.00
❑ 52049	Cutie Pie/Give Me One More Chance	1982	—	2.00	4.00
❑ 52112	Runnin' Away/You	1982	—	2.00	4.00
❑ 52133	Wild Night/One of Us	1982	—	2.00	4.00
❑ 52164	Can I/Middle of Our Lives	1983	—	2.00	4.00
❑ 52228	Shine on Me/Together Forever	1983	—	2.00	4.00
❑ 52278	Let's Get Together/Didn't You Know It	1983	—	2.00	4.00
❑ 52324	Shake It Till It's Tight/So Afraid It's Over	1983	—	2.00	4.00
❑ 52348	Lady You Are/Can't Get Enough of Your Love	1984	—	2.00	4.00
❑ 52409	Mr. Groove/Dynomite	1984	—	2.00	4.00
❑ 52480	Don't Stop/Can't Get Enough of Your Love	1984	—	2.00	4.00
❑ 52552	Let's Talk/(Part 2)	1985	—	2.00	4.00
❑ 52631	Serving It/Believe in Me	1985	—	2.00	4.00
❑ 52699	More Than Friends, Less Than Lovers/ Condemned	1985	—	2.00	4.00
❑ 52893	Don't Think About It/(Part 2)	1986	—	—	3.00
❑ 52893 [PS]	Don't Think About It/(Part 2)	1986	—	—	3.00
❑ 53005	Whammy/(Instrumental)	1987	—	—	3.00
❑ 53020	You Better Quit/Oh Girl	1987	—	—	3.00
❑ 53020 [PS]	You Better Quit/Oh Girl	1987	—	—	3.00
Albums					
CAPITOL					
❑ C1-48990	New Beginning	1988	3.00	6.00	12.00
—As "Al Hudson and One Way"					
MCA					
❑ 3178	One Way Featuring Al Hudson	1979	2.50	5.00	10.00
❑ 5127	One Way Featuring Al Hudson	1980	2.50	5.00	10.00
—Not the same album as 3178					
❑ 5163	Love Is ... One Way	1981	2.50	5.00	10.00
❑ 5247	Fancy Dancer	1981	2.50	5.00	10.00
❑ 5279	Who's Foolin' Who	1982	2.50	5.00	10.00
❑ 5369	Wild Night	1982	2.50	5.00	10.00
❑ 5428	Shine on Me	1983	2.50	5.00	10.00
❑ 5470	Lady	1984	2.50	5.00	10.00
❑ 5552	Wrap Your Body	1985	2.50	5.00	10.00
❑ 5823	One Way IX	1986	2.50	5.00	10.00

ONYX
12-Inch Singles

Number	Title (A Side/B Side)	Yr	VG	VG+	NM
CHAOS					
❑ OAS 4977 [DJ]	Bacup/Throw Ya Gunz (2 versions)/Bacdafucup	1993	5.00	10.00	20.00
❑ OAS 5564 [DJ]	Da Next Niguz (4:08) (3:48)	1993	5.00	10.00	20.00

Number	Title (A Side/B Side)	Yr	VG	VG+	NM
❑ 42-74766	Throw Ya Gunz (Radio Version) (LP Version) (Instrumental)/Blac Vagina Finda	1993	2.50	5.00	10.00
❑ 42-74882	Slam (2 versions)/Da Next Niguz (2 versions)	1993	2.50	5.00	10.00
❑ 42-74982	Shiftee (Radio Version) (Shy Tixon Remix) (Spikinspan Remix) (A Cappella) (Instrumental)/ Bichasniguz	1993	2.50	5.00	10.00
DEF JAM					
❑ 568569-1	Shut 'Em Down (3 versions)/Raze It Up	1998	2.00	4.00	8.00
❑ 568983-1	React (2 versions)/Broke Willies (2 versions)/ Shut 'Em Down (2 versions)	1998	2.00	4.00	8.00
❑ 579621-1	Live!!! (2 versions)/Kill Dem All	1995	2.50	5.00	10.00
TOMMY BOY					
❑ TB 434	The Worst (4 versions)	1997	2.50	5.00	10.00
—With Wu-Tang Clan					
Albums					
DEF JAM					
❑ 230 [(2) DJ]	Shut 'Em Down	1998	5.00	10.00	20.00
—Promo-only version in generic cover					
❑ 536988-1	Shut 'Em Down	1998	3.75	7.50	15.00
JMJ/RAL					
❑ 529265-1	All We Got Iz Us	1995	3.00	6.00	12.00

OPALS, THE (1)
45s

Number	Title (A Side/B Side)	Yr	VG	VG+	NM
APOLLO					
❑ 462	My Heart's Desire/Oh But She Did	1954	50.00	100.00	200.00
—Original with flat (non-glossy) label					
❑ 462	My Heart's Desire/Oh But She Did	1958	10.00	20.00	40.00
—Reissue with glossy label					

OPALS, THE (2)
45s

Number	Title (A Side/B Side)	Yr	VG	VG+	NM
BELTONE					
❑ 2025	Love/Two-Sided Love	1962	6.25	12.50	25.00

OPALS, THE (3)
45s

Number	Title (A Side/B Side)	Yr	VG	VG+	NM
OKEH					
❑ 7188	Does It Matter/Tender Lover	1964	6.25	12.50	25.00
❑ 7202	You Can't Hurt Me No More/Rhythm	1964	6.25	12.50	25.00
❑ 7224	I'm So Afraid/Restless Lover	1965	6.25	12.50	25.00

ORCHIDS, THE (3)
45s

Number	Title (A Side/B Side)	Yr	VG	VG+	NM
KING					
❑ 4661	Oh Why/All Night Baby	1953	100.00	200.00	400.00
❑ 4663	I've Been a Fool from the Start/Beginning to Miss You	1953	100.00	200.00	400.00
PARROT					
❑ 815	Newly Wed/You're Everything to Me	1955	100.00	200.00	400.00
❑ 819	I Can't Refuse/You Said You Loved Me	1955	62.50	125.00	250.00
78s					
KING					
❑ 4661	Oh Why/All Night Baby	1953	25.00	50.00	100.00
❑ 4663	I've Been a Fool from the Start/Beginning to Miss You	1953	25.00	50.00	100.00
PARROT					
❑ 815	Newly Wed/You're Everything to Me	1955	20.00	40.00	80.00
❑ 819	I Can't Refuse/You Said You Loved Me	1955	20.00	40.00	80.00

ORIGINALS, THE (1)
12-Inch Singles

Number	Title (A Side/B Side)	Yr	VG	VG+	NM
FANTASY					
❑ D-101	Don't Put Me On/Take This Love	1978	3.75	7.50	15.00
❑ D-118	Blue Moon (8:27)/While the Cat's Away (7:34)	1979	3.00	6.00	12.00
❑ D-130	J-E-A-L-O-U-S (Means I Love You)/Jezebel (You've Got Me Under Your Spell)	1979	3.00	6.00	12.00
PHASE II					
❑ AS 917 [DJ]	Waitin' on a Letter/Mr. Postman (8:40) (Instrumental 8:56)	1981	2.50	5.00	10.00
❑ 4W8-5655	Waitin' on a Letter/Mr. Postman (8:40)//The Magic Is You (5:00)	1981	2.00	4.00	8.00
SOUL					
❑ M 00001D1	Down to Love Town (5:55)/Let's Be Young Tonight (5:07)	1976	5.00	10.00	20.00
—B-side by Jermaine Jackson on Motown					
45s					
FANTASY					
❑ 820	Take This Love/Ladies (We Need You)	1978	—	2.50	5.00
❑ 847	Blue Moon/Ladies (We Need You)	1979	—	2.50	5.00
❑ 856	J-E-A-L-O-U-S (Means I Love You)/Jezebel (You've Got Me Under Your Spell)	1979	—	2.50	5.00
MOTOWN					
❑ PR-1 [DJ]	Young Train (same on both sides?)	1973	50.00	100.00	200.00
❑ 1355	Good Lovin' Is Just a Dime Away/Nothing Can Take the Place (Of Your Love)	1975	—	3.00	6.00
❑ 1370	50 Years/Financial Affair	1975	—	3.00	6.00
❑ 1379	Everybody's Got to Do Something/(Instrumental)	1975	—	3.00	6.00
PHASE II					
❑ WS8-02061	Baby I'm for Real/Share Your Love with Me	1981	—	2.00	4.00
❑ WS8-02147	The Magic Is You/Let Me Dance	1981	—	2.00	4.00
❑ ZS5-02724	Baby I'm for Real/The Magic Is You	1982	—	2.00	4.00
—As "Hank Dixon and the Originals"					

Number	Title (A Side/B Side)	Yr	VG	VG+	NM
❏ 5653	Waitin' on a Letter/Mr. Postman//(B-side unknown)	1981	—	2.50	5.00
SOUL					
❏ 35029	Goodnight Irene/Need Your Loving (Want It Back)	1967	3.00	6.00	12.00
❏ 35056	We've Got a Way Out Love/You're the One	1969	3.00	6.00	12.00
❏ 35061	Green Grow the Lilacs/You're the One	1969	3.00	6.00	12.00
❏ 35066	Baby I'm for Real/The Moment of Truth	1969	2.00	4.00	8.00
❏ 35069	The Bells/I'll Wait for You	1970	2.00	4.00	8.00
❏ 35074	We Can Make It Baby/I Like Your Style	1970	2.00	4.00	8.00
❏ 35074	We Can Make It/I Like Your Style	1970	3.00	6.00	12.00
❏ 35079	God Bless Whoever Sent You/Desperate Young Man	1970	2.00	4.00	8.00
❏ 35085	Keep Me/A Man Without Love	1971	—	3.00	6.00
❏ 35093	I'm Someone Who Cares/Once I Have You	1972	—	3.00	6.00
❏ 35102	Be My Love/Endlessly Love	1973	—	3.00	6.00
❏ 35109	First Lady (Sweet Mother's Love)/There's a Chance When You Love, You Love	1973	—	3.00	6.00
❏ 35112	Supernatural Voodoo Woman (Part 1)/Supernatural Voodoo Woman (Part 2)	1974	—	3.00	6.00
❏ 35113	Game Called Love/Ooh You Put a Spell on Me	1974	—	3.00	6.00
❏ 35115	You're My Only World/So Near (And Yet So Far)	1974	—	3.00	6.00
❏ 35117	Touch/Ooh You Put a Spell on Me	1975	—	3.00	6.00
❏ 35119	Down to Love Town/Just to Be Closer to You	1976	—	3.00	6.00
❏ 35121 [DJ]	Call On Your Six Million Dollar Man (mono/stereo)	1977	—	3.00	6.00
Albums					
FANTASY					
❏ F-9546	Another Time, Another Place	1978	2.50	5.00	10.00
❏ F-9577	Come Away with Me	1979	2.50	5.00	10.00
MOTOWN					
❏ M5-110V	Motown Superstar Series, Vol. 10	1982	2.50	5.00	10.00
❏ M7-826	California Sunset	1975	3.75	7.50	15.00
PHASE II					
❏ JW 37075	Yesterday and Today	1981	3.00	6.00	12.00
SOUL					
❏ SS-716	Baby I'm for Real	1969	10.00	20.00	40.00
❏ SS-724	Portrait of the Originals	1970	6.25	12.50	25.00
❏ SS-729	Naturally Together	1971	6.25	12.50	25.00
❏ SS-734	Definitions	1971	5.00	10.00	20.00
❏ SS-740	The Game Called…	1973	3.75	7.50	15.00
❏ SS-743	California Sunset	1974	—	—	—
—Unreleased					
❏ S7-746	Communique	1976	3.75	7.50	15.00
❏ S7-749	Down to Love Town	1977	3.75	7.50	15.00

ORIOLES, THE
Also see SONNY TIL.
45s
ABNER

Number	Title (A Side/B Side)	Yr	VG	VG+	NM
❏ 1016	Sugar Girl/Didn't I Say	1958	15.00	30.00	60.00
CHARLIE PARKER					
❏ 211	Secret Love/The Wobble	1962	5.00	10.00	20.00
❏ 212	In the Chapel in the Moonlight/Hey! Little Woman	1962	5.00	10.00	20.00
❏ 213	Back to the Chapel Again/((It's Gonna Be a) Lonely Christmas	1962	5.00	10.00	20.00
❏ 214	What Are You Doing New Year's Eve/Don't Mess Around with My Love	1962	5.00	10.00	20.00
❏ 215	It's Too Soon to Know/I Miss You So	1963	3.75	7.50	15.00
❏ 216	Write and Tell Me Why/Don't Tell Her What Happens to Me	1963	3.75	7.50	15.00
❏ 219	I Miss You So/Hey! Little Woman	1963	3.75	7.50	15.00
HARLEM SOUND					
❏ 1001	Lonely Christmas/What Are You Doing New Year's Eve	19??	—	2.50	5.00
JUBILEE					
❏ 5000	It's Too Soon to Know/Barbara Lee	1951	1000.	2000.	4000.
❏ 5005	Tell Me So/Deacon Jones	1951	500.00	1000.	2000.
❏ 5016	So Much/Forgive and Forget	1951	500.00	1000.	2000.
❏ 5017	What Are You Doing New Year's Eve/Lonely Christmas	1951	200.00	400.00	800.00
❏ 5017 [PS]	What Are You Doing New Year's Eve/Lonely Christmas	1954	250.00	500.00	1000.
❏ 5025	At Night/Every Dog-Gone Time	1951	250.00	500.00	1000.
❏ 5040	I Cross My Fingers/Can't Seem to Laugh Anymore	1951	500.00	1000.	2000.
❏ 5045	Oh Holy Night/The Lord's Prayer	1951	150.00	300.00	600.00
—Original on blue label					
❏ 5045	Oh Holy Night/The Lord's Prayer	196?	6.25	12.50	25.00
—Reissue on black label					
❏ 5045 [PS]	Oh Holy Night/The Lord's Prayer	1954	150.00	300.00	600.00
❏ 5051	I Miss You So/You Are My First Love	1951	1000.	1500.	2000.
—Red vinyl					
❏ 5051	I Miss You So/You Are My First Love	1951	200.00	400.00	800.00
❏ 5055	Pal of Mine/Happy Go Lucky Local Blues	1951	200.00	400.00	800.00
❏ 5061	I'm Just a Fool in Love/Hold Me, Squeeze Me	1951	200.00	400.00	800.00
❏ 5065	Baby, Please Don't Go/Don't Tell Her What's Happened to Me	1951	1000.	1500.	2000.
—Red vinyl					
❏ 5065	Baby, Please Don't Go/Don't Tell Her What's Happened to Me	1951	150.00	300.00	600.00
—Black vinyl					
❏ 5071	When You're Not Around/How Blind Can You Be	1952	150.00	300.00	600.00
❏ 5074	Trust in Me/Shrimp Boats	1952	125.00	250.00	500.00
❏ 5076	Proud of You/You Never Cared for Me	1952	125.00	250.00	500.00
❏ 5082	It's All Over Because We're Through/Waiting	1952	125.00	250.00	500.00

Number	Title (A Side/B Side)	Yr	VG	VG+	NM
❏ 5084	Barfly/Getting Tired, Tired, Tired	1952	100.00	200.00	400.00
❏ 5092	Don't Cry Baby/See See Rider	1952	375.00	750.00	1500.
—Red vinyl					
❏ 5092	Don't Cry Baby/See See Rider	1952	100.00	200.00	400.00
❏ 5102	You Belong to Me/I Don't Want to Take a Chance	1952	125.00	250.00	500.00
❏ 5107	I Miss You So/Till Then	1952	375.00	750.00	1500.
—Red vinyl					
❏ 5107	I Miss You So/Till Then	1952	100.00	200.00	400.00
❏ 5107	I Miss You So/Till Then	1963	6.25	12.50	25.00
—Reissue, credited to "Sonny Til and the Orioles"					
❏ 5108	Teardrops on My Pillow/Hold Me, Thrill Me, Kiss Me	1953	375.00	750.00	1500.
—Red vinyl					
❏ 5108	Teardrops on My Pillow/Hold Me, Thrill Me, Kiss Me	1953	100.00	200.00	400.00
❏ 5115	Bad Little Girl/Dem Days	1953	100.00	200.00	400.00
❏ 5120	I Cover the Waterfront/One More Time	1953	300.00	600.00	1200.
—Red vinyl					
❏ 5120	I Cover the Waterfront/One More Time	1953	100.00	200.00	400.00
❏ 5122	Crying in the Chapel/Don't You Think I Ought to Know	1953	20.00	40.00	80.00
❏ 5127	In the Mission of St. Augustine/Write and Tell Me Why	1953	12.50	25.00	50.00
❏ 5134	There's No One But You/Rose of Calvary	1954	12.50	25.00	50.00
❏ 5137	Secret Love/Don't Go to Strangers	1954	12.50	25.00	50.00
❏ 5143	Maybe You'll Be There/Drowning Every Hope I Ever Had	1954	20.00	40.00	80.00
❏ 5154	In the Chapel in the Moonlight/Thank the Lord, Thank the Lord	1954	12.50	25.00	50.00
❏ 5161	If You Believe/Longing	1954	12.50	25.00	50.00
❏ 5172	Runaround/Count Your Blessings Instead of Sheep	1954	12.50	25.00	50.00
❏ 5177	I Love You Mostly/Fair Exchange	1955	10.00	20.00	40.00
❏ 5189	I Need You Baby/The Good Lord Will Smile	1955	10.00	20.00	40.00
❏ 5221	Please Sing My Blues Tonight/Moody Over You	1955	10.00	20.00	40.00
❏ 5231	Angel/Don't Go to Strangers	1956	15.00	30.00	60.00
❏ 5363	Tell Me So/At Night	1959	3.75	7.50	15.00
—As "Sonny Til and the Orioles"					
❏ 5384	Come On Home/The First of Summer	1960	3.75	7.50	15.00
—As "Sonny Til and the Orioles"					
❏ 6001	Crying in the Chapel/Forgive and Forget	1959	3.75	7.50	15.00
—As "Sonny Til and the Orioles"					
LANA					
❏ 109	What Are You Doing New Year's Eve/Crying in the Chapel	196?	—	3.00	6.00
VEE JAY					
❏ 196	I Just Got Lucky/Happy 'Til the Letter	1956	7.50	15.00	30.00
❏ 228	For All We Know/Never Leave Me Baby	1956	7.50	15.00	30.00
❏ 244	Sugar Girl/Didn't I Say	1957	10.00	20.00	40.00
VIRGO					
❏ 6017	What Are You Doing New Year's Eve/Crying in the Chapel	1972	—	2.00	4.00
78s					
IT'S A NATURAL					
❏ 5000	It's Too Soon to Know/Barbara Lee	1948	75.00	150.00	300.00
JUBILEE					
❏ 5000	It's Too Soon to Know/Barbara Lee	1948	37.50	75.00	150.00
❏ 5001	To Be with You/Dare to Dream	1949	62.50	125.00	250.00
❏ 5001	To Be with You/Lonely Christmas	1949	75.00	150.00	300.00
❏ 5001	Lonely Christmas/Dare To Dream	1949	75.00	150.00	300.00
❏ 5002	Please Give My Heart a Break/It Seems So Long Ago	1949	37.50	75.00	150.00
❏ 5005	Tell Me So/Deacon Jones	1949	37.50	75.00	150.00
❏ 5008	I Challenge Your Kiss/Donkey Serenade	1949	37.50	75.00	150.00
❏ 5009	A Kiss and a Rose/It's a Cold Summer	1949	37.50	75.00	150.00
❏ 5016	So Much/Forgive and Forget	1949	37.50	75.00	150.00
❏ 5017	What Are You Doing New Year's Eve/Lonely Christmas	1949	30.00	60.00	120.00
❏ 5018	Would You Still Be the One/Is My Heart Wasting Time	1950	37.50	75.00	150.00
❏ 5025	At Night/Every Dog-Gone Time	1951	37.50	75.00	150.00
❏ 5026	Moonlight/I Remember When	1950	37.50	75.00	150.00
❏ 5028	You're Gone/Everything They Said Came True	1950	37.50	75.00	150.00
❏ 5031	I'd Rather Have You Under the Moon/We're Supposed to Be Through	1950	37.50	75.00	150.00
❏ 5037	I Need You So/Goodnight Irene	1950	37.50	75.00	150.00
❏ 5040	I Cross My Fingers/Can't Seem to Laugh Anymore	1951	37.50	75.00	150.00
❏ 5045	Oh Holy Night/The Lord's Prayer	1951	37.50	75.00	150.00
❏ 5051	I Miss You So/You Are My First Love	1951	37.50	75.00	150.00
❏ 5055	Pal of Mine/Happy Go Lucky Local Blues	1951	25.00	50.00	100.00
❏ 5057	Would I Love You/When You're a Long, Long Way from Home	1951	30.00	60.00	120.00
❏ 5061	I'm Just a Fool in Love/Hold Me, Squeeze Me	1951	25.00	50.00	100.00
❏ 5065	Baby, Please Don't Go/Don't Tell Her What's Happened to Me	1951	25.00	50.00	100.00
❏ 5071	When You're Not Around/How Blind Can You Be	1952	25.00	50.00	100.00
❏ 5074	Trust in Me/Shrimp Boats	1952	25.00	50.00	100.00
❏ 5076	Proud of You/You Never Cared for Me	1952	25.00	50.00	100.00
❏ 5082	It's All Over Because We're Through/Waiting	1952	25.00	50.00	100.00
❏ 5084	Barfly/Getting Tired, Tired, Tired	1952	25.00	50.00	100.00
❏ 5092	Don't Cry Baby/See See Rider	1952	25.00	50.00	100.00
❏ 5102	You Belong to Me/I Don't Want to Take a Chance	1952	30.00	60.00	120.00
❏ 5107	I Miss You So/Till Then	1952	25.00	50.00	100.00

O

Number	Title (A Side/B Side)	Yr	VG	VG+	NM
❑ 5108	Teardrops on My Pillow/Hold Me, Thrill Me, Kiss Me	1953	25.00	50.00	100.00
❑ 5115	Bad Little Girl/Dem Days	1953	25.00	50.00	100.00
❑ 5120	I Cover the Waterfront/One More Time	1953	20.00	40.00	80.00
❑ 5122	Crying in the Chapel/Don't You Think I Ought to Know	1953	15.00	30.00	60.00
❑ 5127	In the Mission of St. Augustine/Write and Tell Me Why	1953	7.50	15.00	30.00
❑ 5134	There's No One But You/Rose of Calvary	1954	7.50	15.00	30.00
❑ 5137	Secret Love/Don't Go to Strangers	1954	7.50	15.00	30.00
❑ 5143	Maybe You'll Be There/Drowining Every Hope I Ever Had	1954	7.50	15.00	30.00
❑ 5154	In the Chapel in the Moonlight/Thank the Lord, Thank the Lord	1954	7.50	15.00	30.00
❑ 5161	If You Believe/Longing	1954	7.50	15.00	30.00
❑ 5172	Runaround/Count Your Blessings Instead of Sheep	1954	7.50	15.00	30.00
❑ 5177	I Love You Mostly/Fair Exchange	1955	7.50	15.00	30.00
❑ 5189	I Need You Baby/The Good Lord Will Smile	1955	7.50	15.00	30.00
❑ 5221	Please Sing My Blues Tonight/Moody Over You	1955	7.50	15.00	30.00
❑ 5231	Angel/Don't Go to Strangers	1956	10.00	20.00	40.00

7-Inch Extended Plays
JUBILEE

| ❑ 5000 | Too Soon to Know/Forgive and Forget//Tell Me So/At Night | 1954 | 250.00 | 500.00 | 1000. |
| ❑ 5000 [PS] | The Orioles Sing | 1954 | 250.00 | 500.00 | 1000. |

Albums
BIG A

| ❑ LP-2001 | The Orioles' Greatest All-Time Hits | 1969 | 7.50 | 15.00 | 30.00 |

CHARLIE PARKER

| ❑ PLP-816S [S] | Modern Sounds of the Orioles | 1962 | 25.00 | 50.00 | 100.00 |
| ❑ PLP-816 [M] | Modern Sounds of the Orioles | 1962 | 20.00 | 40.00 | 80.00 |

COLLECTABLES

| ❑ COL-5014 | Sonny Til and the Orioles' Greatest Hits | 198? | 3.00 | 6.00 | 12.00 |

MURRAY HILL

| ❑ M 61234 [(5)] | For Collectors Only | 1983 | 10.00 | 20.00 | 40.00 |

ORLONS, THE
45s
ABC

| ❑ 10894 | Everything/Keep Your Hands Off My Baby | 1967 | 2.50 | 5.00 | 10.00 |
| ❑ 10948 | Kissin' Time/Once Upon a Time | 1967 | 2.50 | 5.00 | 10.00 |

CALLA

| ❑ 113 | Spinnin' Top/Anyone Who Had a Heart | 1966 | 2.50 | 5.00 | 10.00 |

CAMEO

❑ 105 [DJ]	Big Girls Don't Cry/Pop Pop Pop-Pie	1962	10.00	20.00	40.00
—Yellow label, black print, promo only					
❑ 198	I'll Be True/Heart Darling Angel	1961	12.50	25.00	50.00
❑ 211	Mr. 21/Please Let It Be Me	1961	12.50	25.00	50.00
❑ 218	The Wah-Watusi/Holiday Hill	1962	5.00	10.00	20.00
❑ 231	Don't Hang Up/The Conservative	1962	5.00	10.00	20.00
❑ 231 [PS]	Don't Hang Up/The Conservative	1962	10.00	20.00	40.00
❑ 243	South Street/Them Terrible Boots	1963	5.00	10.00	20.00
❑ 243 [PS]	South Street/Them Terrible Boots	1963	10.00	20.00	40.00
❑ 257	Not Me/My Best Friend	1963	5.00	10.00	20.00
❑ 257 [PS]	Not Me/My Best Friend	1963	7.50	15.00	30.00
❑ 273	Cross Fire!/It's No Big Thing	1963	5.00	10.00	20.00
❑ 273 [PS]	Cross Fire!/It's No Big Thing	1963	7.50	15.00	30.00
❑ 287	Bon-Doo-Wah/Don't Throw Your Love Away	1963	3.75	7.50	15.00
❑ 287 [PS]	Bon-Doo-Wah/Don't Throw Your Love Away	1963	7.50	15.00	30.00
❑ 295	Shimmy Shimmy/Everything Nice	1964	3.75	7.50	15.00
❑ 295 [PS]	Shimmy Shimmy/Everything Nice	1964	6.25	12.50	25.00
❑ 319	Rules of Love/Heartbreak Hotel	1964	3.75	7.50	15.00
❑ 319 [PS]	Rules of Love/Heartbreak Hotel	1964	6.25	12.50	25.00
❑ 332	Knock! Knock! (Who's There)/Goin' Places	1964	3.75	7.50	15.00
❑ 332 [PS]	Knock! Knock! (Who's There)/Goin' Places	1964	6.25	12.50	25.00
❑ 346	I Ain't Coming Back/Envy (In My Eyes)	1965	3.00	6.00	12.00
❑ 352	Come On Down Baby/I Ain't Coming Back	1965	3.00	6.00	12.00
❑ 372	Don't You Want My Lovin'/I Can't Take It	1965	3.00	6.00	12.00
❑ 384	No Love But Your Love/Envy (In My Eyes)	1965	10.00	20.00	40.00

Albums
CAMEO

❑ C 1020 [M]	The Wah-Watusi	1962	15.00	30.00	60.00
❑ C 1033 [M]	All the Hits by the Orlons	1962	15.00	30.00	60.00
❑ C 1041 [M]	South Street	1963	15.00	30.00	60.00
❑ C 1054 [M]	Not Me	1963	12.50	25.00	50.00
❑ C 1061 [M]	The Orlons' Biggest Hits	1964	12.50	25.00	50.00
❑ C 1073 [M]	Down Memory Lane with the Orlons	1964	12.50	25.00	50.00

ORLONS, THE / THE DOVELLS
Albums
CAMEO

| ❑ C 1067 [M] | Golden Hits of the Orlons and the Dovells | 1964 | 12.50 | 25.00 | 50.00 |

OSBORNE, JEFFREY
Also see L.T.D.; DIONNE WARWICK.
12-Inch Singles
ARISTA

| ❑ 2212 | If My Brother's in Trouble (Extended Hip-Hop Mix) (R&B Single Version) (Club Mix) (Dub Mix) | 1991 | 2.50 | 5.00 | 10.00 |

A&M

❑ SP-12061	Stay with Me Tonight/Who You Talkin' To	1983	3.75	7.50	15.00
❑ SP-12080	Stay with Me Tonight (Extended) (Dub)	1983	3.00	6.00	12.00
❑ SP-12089	Plane Love/(Dub)	1983	—	3.50	7.00

Number	Title (A Side/B Side)	Yr	VG	VG+	NM
❑ SP-12111	You Can't Be Serious (unknown versions)	1984	3.75	7.50	15.00
❑ SP-12116	The Borderlines (6:52) (7:57)	1984	2.50	5.00	10.00
❑ SP-12169	You Should Be Mine (The Woo Woo Song) (2 versions?)/Who Would Have Guessed	1986	2.00	4.00	8.00
❑ SP-12190	Soweto (Remixed Version) (Dub Version)	1986	2.00	4.00	8.00
❑ SP-12199	Room with a View (6:11) (7:31)	1986	2.00	4.00	8.00
❑ SP-12280	She's on the Left (3 versions)	1988	2.00	4.00	8.00
❑ SP-12301	Stay with Me Tonight/Plane Love	1989	—	3.50	7.00
—Reissue					
❑ SP-17194 [DJ]	I Really Don't Need No Light (same on both sides)	1982	3.00	6.00	12.00
❑ SP-17218 [DJ]	New Love/Baby	1983	3.75	7.50	15.00
❑ SP-17241 [DJ]	Don't You Get So Mad (same on both sides?)	1983	3.00	6.00	12.00
❑ SP-17298 [DJ]	Don't Stop (same on both sides)	1984	2.50	5.00	10.00
❑ SP-17629 [DJ]	Can't Go Back on a Promise (same on both sides)	1988	2.00	4.00	8.00
❑ SP-17699 [DJ]	All Because of You (same on both sides)	1988	3.00	6.00	12.00

45s
ARISTA

| ❑ 2127 | Only Human/Never | 1990 | — | 2.00 | 4.00 |

A&M

❑ 1227	She's on the Left/A Second Chance	1988	—	—	3.00
❑ 1227 [PS]	She's on the Left/A Second Chance	1988	—	—	3.00
❑ 1250	Can't Go Back on a Promise/La Cuenta, Por Favor	1988	—	—	3.00
❑ 1266	All Because of You/La Cuenta, Por Favor	1989	—	—	3.00
❑ 2410	I Really Don't Need No Light/One Million Kisses	1982	—	2.00	4.00
❑ 2434	On the Wings of Love/I'm Beggin'	1982	—	2.00	4.00
❑ 2434 [PS]	On the Wings of Love/I'm Beggin'	1982	—	2.50	5.00
❑ 2530	Eenie Meenie/New Love	1983	—	2.00	4.00
❑ 2561	Don't You Get So Mad/So Much Love	1983	—	2.00	4.00
❑ 2591	Stay with Me Tonight/Baby	1983	—	2.00	4.00
❑ 2618	We're Going All the Way/Two Wrongs Don't Make a Right	1984	—	2.00	4.00
❑ 2618 [PS]	We're Going All the Way/Two Wrongs Don't Make a Right	1984	—	2.00	4.00
❑ 2687	Don't Stop/Forever Mine	1984	—	2.00	4.00
❑ 2687 [PS]	Don't Stop/Forever Mine	1984	—	2.00	4.00
❑ 2695	The Borderlines/I'll Make Believe	1984	—	2.00	4.00
❑ 2724	Let Me Know/Live for Today	1985	—	2.00	4.00
❑ 2814	You Should Be Mine (The Woo Woo Song)/Who Would Have Guessed	1986	—	—	3.00
—B-side with Portia Griffin					
❑ 2814 [PS]	You Should Be Mine (The Woo Woo Song)/Who Would Have Guessed	1986	—	—	3.00
❑ 2863	Soweto/Love's Not Ready	1986	—	—	3.00
❑ 2863 [PS]	Soweto/Love's Not Ready	1986	—	—	3.00
❑ 2866	Room with a View/The Power	1986	—	—	3.00
❑ 2866 [PS]	Room with a View/The Power	1986	—	—	3.00
❑ 2894	In Your Eyes/Come Midnight	1986	—	—	3.00

Albums
ARISTA

| ❑ AL 8620 | Only Human | 1990 | 3.75 | 7.50 | 15.00 |

A&M

❑ SP-3272	Jeffrey Osborne	198?	—	3.00	6.00
—Budget-line reissue of 4896					
❑ SP-4896	Jeffrey Osborne	1982	2.00	4.00	8.00
❑ SP-4940	Stay with Me Tonight	1983	2.00	4.00	8.00
❑ SP-5017	Don't Stop	1984	2.00	4.00	8.00
❑ SP-5103	Emotional	1986	2.00	4.00	8.00
❑ SP-5205	One Love — One Dream	1988	2.00	4.00	8.00

OTIS, JOHNNY
45s
ATLANTIC

| ❑ 2409 | Keep the Faith — Part I/Keep the Faith — Part II | 1967 | 3.00 | 6.00 | 12.00 |

CAPITOL

❑ F3799/3802	The Johnny Otis Show	1957	100.00	200.00	400.00
—Four-record set with four-pocket cover. Price is for entire set. Records alone are valued separately below.					
❑ F3799	Can't You Hear Me Callin'/My Ding-a-Ling	1957	12.50	25.00	50.00
❑ F3800	Ma, He's Makin' Eyes at Me/In the Dark	1957	12.50	25.00	50.00
❑ F3801	Stay with Me/Tell Me So	1957	12.50	25.00	50.00
❑ F3802	It's Too Soon to Know/Star of Love	1957	12.50	25.00	50.00
❑ F3852	Bye Bye Baby/Good Golly	1957	6.25	12.50	25.00
❑ F3889	Well, Well, Well/You Just Kissed Me Goodbye	1958	6.25	12.50	25.00
❑ F3966	Willie and the Hand Jive/Ring-a-Ling	1958	7.50	15.00	30.00
❑ F4060	Willie Did the Cha Cha/Crazy Country Hop	1958	6.25	12.50	25.00
❑ F4156	My Dear/You	1959	5.00	10.00	20.00
❑ F4168 [M]	Castin' My Spell/Telephone Baby	1959	5.00	10.00	20.00
❑ F4168 [S]	Castin' My Spell/Telephone Baby	1959	12.50	25.00	50.00
❑ F4226	Three Girls Named Molly (Doin' the Hully Gully)/I'll Do the Same for You	1959	5.00	10.00	20.00
❑ F4260	Let the Sun Shine in My Life/Baby, Just You	1959	5.00	10.00	20.00
❑ 4326	Mumblin' Mosie/Hey Baby, Don't You Know	1960	3.75	7.50	15.00

DIG

❑ 119	Hey! Hey! Hey! Hey!/Let the Sunshine in My Heart	1956	7.50	15.00	30.00
❑ 122	The Midnite Creeper (Part 1)/The Midnite Creeper (Part 2)	1956	7.50	15.00	30.00
❑ 132	My Eyes Are Full of Tears/Turtle Dove	1957	7.50	15.00	30.00
❑ 134	Wa Wa (Part 1)/Wa Wa (Part 2)	1957	7.50	15.00	30.00
❑ 139	Stop, Look and Love Me/The Night Is Young	1957	7.50	15.00	30.00

ELDO

❑ 106	The New Bo Diddley/The Jelly Roll	1960	3.75	7.50	15.00
❑ 152	Keep the Faith (Part 1)/Keep the Faith (Part 2)	1968	2.00	4.00	8.00
❑ 153	Long Distance/Banana Peels	1968	2.00	4.00	8.00

"Tell It Like It Is" was the #1 R&B hit the first five weeks of 1967. This rather tough-to-find LP came out shortly thereafter.

Herald Records compiled this EP of songs by the Nutmegs and issued it in 1960 or so, five years after "Story Untold" had been a hit.

Before they became one of the foremost Philly Soul groups in the 1970s, the O'Jays struggled for years. This album came out on Imperial in 1965 and didn't sell well.

The O'Kaysions were a white band from Wilson, N.C. who released the soulful "Girl Watcher" on the local North State label before it became big on ABC. Only the original label release had this picture sleeve.

"I Challenge Your Kiss" was just one of many R&B hits that the Orioles had in the late 1940s and early 1950s.

Johnny Otis and his revolving cast of band members had many R&B hits in the pre-rock years. By 1957, though, rock 'n' roll was the thing, so this collection called *Rock 'n Roll Hit Parade* came out on the Dig label. Below Otis' photo are the words "King of Rock & Roll."

Number	Title (A Side/B Side)	Yr	VG	VG+	NM

EPIC

❏ 10606	You Can Depend on Me/The Watts Breakaway	1970	—	3.00	6.00
❏ 10757	Willie and the Hand Jive/Goin' Back to L.A.	1971	—	3.00	6.00

—With Delmar Evans

HAWK SOUND

❏ 1003	Jaws/Good to the Last Drop	1975	—	2.50	5.00

KENT

❏ 506	Country Girl/Bye Bye Baby	1969	2.00	4.00	8.00
❏ 4521	Shuggie's Blues/Cool Ade	1969	2.00	4.00	8.00

KING

❏ 5581	Hand Jive One More Time/Baby I Got News for You	1961	3.75	7.50	15.00
❏ 5606	She's All Right/It Must Be Love	1962	3.75	7.50	15.00
❏ 5634	Queen of the Twist/I Know My Love Is True	1962	3.75	7.50	15.00
❏ 5690	The Hey Hey Hey Song/Early in the Morning Blues	1962	3.75	7.50	15.00
❏ 5707	Somebody Call the Station/Yes	1963	3.00	6.00	12.00
❏ 5790	Bye, Bye Baby/The Hash	1963	3.00	6.00	12.00

MERCURY

❏ 8263	Oopy Doo/Stardust	1952	12.50	25.00	50.00
❏ 8273	One-Nighter Blues/Goomp Blues	1952	12.50	25.00	50.00
❏ 8289	Call Operator 210/Baby Baby Blues	1952	12.50	25.00	50.00
❏ 8295	Gypsy Blues/The Candle's Burning Low	1952	12.50	25.00	50.00
❏ 70038	Why Don't You Believe Me/Wishing Well	1953	12.50	25.00	50.00
❏ 70050	Love Bug Boogie/Brown Skin Butterball	1953	12.50	25.00	50.00

OKEH

❏ 7332	Watts Breakaway/You Can Depend On Me	1969	—	3.00	6.00

PEACOCK

❏ 1625	Young Girl/Rock Me Baby	1953	20.00	40.00	80.00
❏ 1636	Shake It/I Won't Be Your Fool No More	1954	12.50	25.00	50.00
❏ 1648	Sittin' Here Drinkin'/You Got Me Crying	1955	12.50	25.00	50.00
❏ 1675	Butter Ball/Dandy's Boogie	1957	12.50	25.00	50.00

SAVOY

❏ 731	Double Crossing Blues/Ain't Nothin' Shakin'	1950	30.00	60.00	120.00
❏ 731	Double Crossing Blues/Back Alley Blues	1950	25.00	50.00	100.00

—B-side by the Beale Street Gang

❏ 750	Cupid Boogie/Just Can't Get Free	1950	15.00	30.00	60.00
❏ 764	Wedding Blues/Far Away Blues (Xmas Blues)	1950	15.00	30.00	60.00
❏ 766	Rockin' Blues/My Heart Tells Me	1950	15.00	30.00	60.00
❏ 777	Gee Baby/Mambo Boogie	1951	12.50	25.00	50.00
❏ 780	Doggin' Blues/Living and Loving You	1951	12.50	25.00	50.00
❏ 787	I Dream/Hangover Blues	1951	12.50	25.00	50.00
❏ 788	All Nite Long/New Love	1951	12.50	25.00	50.00
❏ 812	Warning Blues/I'll Ask My Heart	1951	12.50	25.00	50.00
❏ 815	Harlem Nocturne/Midnight in the Barrelhouse	1951	12.50	25.00	50.00
❏ 824	Get Together Blues/Chittlin' Switch	1951	12.50	25.00	50.00
❏ 855	It Ain't the Beauty/Gonna Take a Train	1952	12.50	25.00	50.00

7-Inch Extended Plays

CAPITOL

❏ EAP 1-940	Hum Ding a Ling/It's Too Soon to Know//Stay with Me/Ma (He's Makin' Eyes at Me)	1958	37.50	75.00	150.00
❏ EAP 1-940 [PS]	The Johnny Otis Show	1958	37.50	75.00	150.00

Albums

ALLIGATOR

❏ AL-4726	The New Johnny Otis Show	1982	2.50	5.00	10.00

CAPITOL

❏ T 940 [M]	The Johnny Otis Show	1958	62.50	125.00	250.00
❏ C1-92858 [(2)]	The Capitol Years	1989	3.75	7.50	15.00

DIG

❏ 104 [M]	Rock and Roll Hit Parade, Volume 1	1957	300.00	600.00	900.00

—Gold cover with thick cardboard and thick vinyl records. Counterfeits have noticeably thinner vinyl.

❏ 104 [M]	Rock and Roll Hit Parade, Volume 1	1958	150.00	300.00	600.00

—Yellow cover with thick cardboard and thick vinyl records. Counterfeits have noticeably thinner vinyl.

EPIC

❏ BN 26524	Cuttin' Up	1970	6.25	12.50	25.00
❏ EG 30473 [(2)]	The Johnny Otis Show Live at Monterey	1971	7.50	15.00	30.00

KENT

❏ KST-534	Cold Shot	1968	6.25	12.50	25.00

SAVOY

❏ SJL-2230 [(2)]	The Original Johnny Otis Show	1978	3.75	7.50	15.00
❏ SJL-2252 [(2)]	The Original Johnny Otis Show, Vol. 2	1980	3.75	7.50	15.00

OTIS, SHUGGIE

45s

EPIC

❏ 10603	Hurricane/Jennie Lee	1970	—	3.00	6.00
❏ 10798	Strawberry Letter 23/Ice Cold Daydream	1971	2.00	4.00	8.00
❏ 10978	Purple (Part 1)/Purple (Part 2)	1973	—	3.00	6.00
❏ 50054	Inspiration Information/Aht Uh Mi Hed	1975	—	3.00	6.00

LUAKA BOP

❏ 77666	Aht Uh Mi Hed/Strawberry Letter 23	2001	—	2.00	4.00

Albums

EPIC

❏ BN 26511	Here Comes Shuggie Otis	1970	3.75	7.50	15.00
❏ KE 30752	Freedom Flight	1971	3.75	7.50	15.00
❏ PE 33059	Inspiration Information	1975	3.75	7.50	15.00

OTIS AND CARLA

Also see OTIS REDDING; CARLA THOMAS.

45s

ATCO

❏ 6665	When Something Is Wrong with My Baby/Ooh Carla, Ooh Otis	1968	2.50	5.00	10.00

STAX

❏ 216	Tramp/Tell It Like It Is	1967	2.50	5.00	10.00
❏ 228	Knock on Wood/Let Me Be Good to You	1967	2.50	5.00	10.00
❏ 244	Lovey Dovey/New Year's Resolution	1968	2.50	5.00	10.00

Albums

STAX

❏ ST-716 [M]	King and Queen	1967	8.75	17.50	35.00
❏ STS-716 [S]	King and Queen	1967	12.50	25.00	50.00

SUNDAZED

❏ LP 5069 [S]	King and Queen	2001	3.00	6.00	12.00

—Reissue on 180-gram vinyl

OUTKAST

12-Inch Singles

LAFACE

❏ 4070 [DJ]	Southernplayalisticadillacmuzik (Album Version 5:18) (Instrumental)	1997	3.75	7.50	15.00
❏ 4092 [DJ]	Player's Ball (Album Version 4:22) (same on both sides)	1994	3.75	7.50	15.00
❏ 4187 [DJ]	Elevators (Me & You) (6 versions)	1996	3.75	7.50	15.00
❏ 4225 [DJ]	Jazzy Belle (LP Version) (Instrumental) (Clean Album Version) (Acappella)	1997	3.00	6.00	12.00
❏ 4227 [DJ]	Atliens (6 versions)	1996	2.50	5.00	10.00
❏ 4235 [DJ]	Jazzy Belle (6 versions)	1997	3.00	6.00	12.00
❏ 4278 [DJ]	In Due Time (4 versions)	1997	2.50	5.00	10.00
❏ 4367 [DJ]	Rosa Parks (4 versions)	1998	2.50	5.00	10.00
❏ 4466 [DJ]	B.O.B. (Radio Mix) (Instrumental)/(Club Mix) (Acappella)	2000	2.50	5.00	10.00
❏ 4511 [DJ]	Bombs Over Baghdad (unknown versions)	2000	2.00	4.00	8.00
❏ 4529 [DJ]	So Fresh, So Clean (Radio Mix) (Instrumental) (Club Mix) (Acappella)	2000	3.00	6.00	12.00
❏ 24067	Player's Ball (Extended Version) (Radio Dirty Version) (Remix Version) (Instrumental)	1994	3.75	7.50	15.00
❏ 24086	Git Up, Git Out (5 versions)	1994	2.50	5.00	10.00
❏ 24178	Elevators (Me & You) (Crazy C Trunk Rattlin' Mix) (ONP 86 Mix) (Album Acappella)/(Crazy C Trunk Rattlin' Instrumental) (ONP 86 Instrumental) (Album Version)	1996	3.75	7.50	15.00
❏ 24525	Ms. Jackson (Radio Mix) (Instrumental)/Sole Sunday (Radio Mix) (Instrumental)	2000	3.00	6.00	12.00
❏ 24537	So Fresh, So Clean (unknown versions)/Gangsta Sh*t (unknown versions)	2000	2.50	5.00	10.00

Albums

LAFACE

❏ 6153 [(3) DJ]	Aquemini	1998	5.00	10.00	20.00

—Promo-only censored version

❏ 26029 [(2)]	Atliens	1996	3.75	7.50	15.00
❏ 26053 [(2)]	Aquemini	1998	3.75	7.50	15.00
❏ 26072 [(2)]	Stankonia	2000	3.75	7.50	15.00

OZONE

12-Inch Singles

MOTOWN

❏ PR-100 [DJ]	Li'l Suzy (Vocal) (Instrumental)	1982	3.00	6.00	12.00

45s

MOTOWN

❏ 1487	Walk On/This Is Funkin' Insane	1980	—	2.00	4.00
❏ 1510	Ozonic Bee Bop/Preacher's Gone Home	1981	—	2.00	4.00
❏ 1518	Mighty Mighty/Rock and Roll (Pop and Soul)	1981	—	2.00	4.00
❏ 1521	Gigolette/(Instrumental)	1981	—	2.00	4.00
❏ 1529	Come On In/Over and Over Again	1982	—	2.00	4.00
❏ 1605	Do What Cha Wanna/Come On In	1982	—	2.00	4.00
❏ 1617	Keep On Dancin'/Your Love Stays on My Mind	1982	—	2.00	4.00
❏ 1627	Li'l Suzy/I'm Not Easy	1982	—	2.00	4.00
❏ 1668	Strut My Thang/Don't Leave Me Now	1983	—	2.00	4.00
❏ 1691	Here I Go Again/Our Hearts	1983	—	2.00	4.00

Albums

MOTOWN

❏ M8-962M1	Send It	1981	5.00	10.00	20.00
❏ 6011ML	Li'l Suzy	1982	5.00	10.00	20.00
❏ 6037ML	Glasses	1983	5.00	10.00	20.00

Number	Title (A Side/B Side)	Yr	VG	VG+	NM

P

P. FUNK ALL STARS
45s
CBS ASSOCIATED

❏ 04032	Generator Pop/Hydraulic Pump	1983	—	2.00	4.00

HUMP

❏ 1	Hydraulic Pump (Part 1)/Hydraulic Pump (Part 2)	1981	—	2.50	5.00
❏ 3	One of Those Summers/It's Too Funky in Here	1982	—	2.50	5.00

UNCLE JAM

❏ 04408	Pumpin' It Up/Pumpin' It Up (Special Mix)	1984	—	2.00	4.00

Albums
CBS ASSOCIATED

❏ FZ 39168	Urban Dancefloor Guerrilas	1983	3.75	7.50	15.00

P.M. DAWN
12-Inch Singles
GEE STREET

❏ PR12-6707-1 [DJ]	Paper Doll (2 versions?)	1992	2.00	4.00	8.00
❏ PR12-6783-1 [DJ]	Nocturnal Is in the House (Original) (Instrumental) (Acappella)/Get Off Mine (Stereo Field Dub)	1993	2.00	4.00	8.00
❏ 854477-1	Sometimes I Miss You So Much (LP Version) (Al B Intro) (Acappella) (Dallas Austin Remix) (Dallas Austin Instrumental) (Dallas Austin Beat Mix)	1996	2.00	4.00	8.00
❏ 862025-1	Looking Through Patient Eyes (Extended) (Radio) (Instrumental)	1993	2.00	4.00	8.00
❏ 862217-1	Looking Through Patient Eyes (Pete Rock Mix 2) (Album Mix) (Radio Mix)/Plastic (Radio Mix)	1993	2.50	5.00	10.00
❏ 862475-1	The Ways of the Wind (U.S. 12" Remix 6:59) (U.K. 12" Remix 6:17) (Underground Dub 6:28) (Cash Money Groove Mix 5:03)	1993	2.00	4.00	8.00
❏ 864967-1	Plastic (Extended) (Radio) (Funk U Tomorrow Mix) (Instrumental Dub)	1992	2.00	4.00	8.00
❏ 866095-1	Set Adrift on Memory Bliss (Richie's Street Groove) (Atmospheric Vocal)/A Watcher's Point of View (3 versions)	1991	2.00	4.00	8.00
❏ 866319-1	A Watcher's Point of View (3 versions)/Twisted Mellow	1991	2.00	4.00	8.00
❏ 866375-1	Paper Doll (Club Mix) (Radio Mix) (Instrumental)/For the Love of Peace	1992	2.00	4.00	8.00
❏ 866821-1	Reality Used to Be a Friend of Mine (Club Mix) (Radio Mix) (LP Version)/Comatose	1992	2.00	4.00	8.00

LAFACE

❏ 24036	I'd Die Without You (Extended Jeep Mix) (Remix Dub) (Remix Instrumental) (Extended Remix Radio Edit)	1992	2.00	4.00	8.00

REPRISE

❏ PRO-A-100442 [DJ]	Night in the City (Stereo Dub 7:58) (Stereo Dub Instrumental 7:58) (Lenny B. Radio Mix 4:34)	2000	2.00	4.00	8.00

45s
GEE STREET/ISLAND

❏ 854408-7	Downtown Venus/She Dreams Persistent Maybes	1995	—	—	3.00
❏ 854476-7	Sometimes I Miss You So Much (LP Version)/ (Dallas Austin Remix)	1995	—	—	3.00
❏ 862024-7	Looking Through Patient Eyes/The Ways of the Wind	1993	—	—	3.00

Albums
GEE STREET

❏ PRLP-6768-1 [(2) DJ]	The Bliss Album...?	1993	5.00	10.00	20.00

—Promo-only vinyl edition

❏ 524147-1 [(2)]	Jesus Wept	1995	5.00	10.00	20.00

PACIFIC GAS & ELECTRIC
45s
COLUMBIA

❏ 45009	Redneck/Bluebuster	1969	—	3.00	6.00
❏ 45158	Are You Ready?/Staggolee	1970	—	3.00	6.00

—Available with at least three different label variations, all equal in value

❏ 45221	Elvira/Father Come On Home	1970	—	2.50	5.00
❏ 45304	The Time Has Come/Death Row No. 172	1971	—	2.50	5.00
❏ 45444	One More River to Cross/Rocky Roller's Lament	1971	—	2.50	5.00
❏ 45519	Thank God for You Baby/See the Monkey Run	1971	—	2.50	5.00
❏ 45621	Heat Wave/We Did What We Could	1972	—	2.50	5.00

POWER

❏ 1701	Wade in the Water/Live Love	1969	2.50	5.00	10.00

Albums
ABC DUNHILL

❏ DSX-50157	Pacific Gas and Electric Starring Charlie Allen	1974	3.00	6.00	12.00

BRIGHT ORANGE

❏ 701	Get It On	1968	10.00	20.00	40.00

COLUMBIA

❏ CS 1017	Are You Ready	1970	3.75	7.50	15.00

—"360 Sound" label

❏ CS 1017	Are You Ready	1970	3.00	6.00	12.00

—Orange label

❏ CS 9900	Pacific Gas and Electric	1969	3.75	7.50	15.00

—"360 Sound" label

❏ CS 9900	Pacific Gas and Electric	1970	3.00	6.00	12.00

—Orange label

❏ C 30362	PG&E	1971	3.00	6.00	12.00
❏ C 32019	The Best of Pacific Gas & Electric	1972	3.00	6.00	12.00

POWER

❏ 701	Get It On	1969	6.25	12.50	25.00

PAGE, GENE
12-Inch Singles
ARISTA

❏ SP-13 [DJ]	Close Encounters of the Third Kind (6:00) (3:38)	1978	2.50	5.00	10.00

ATLANTIC

❏ DSKO 69 [DJ]	Wild Cherry (6:00) (same on both sides)	1976	3.00	6.00	12.00

45s
ARISTA

❏ 0302	Close Encounters of the Third Kind/When You Wish Upon a Star	1978	—	2.50	5.00
❏ 0322	Theme from "Star Trek"/Sho Like to Ride on a Star	1978	—	2.50	5.00
❏ 0337	Moonglow-Love Theme/Beyond the Hole in Space	1978	—	2.50	5.00
❏ 0492	Love Starts After Dark/I Wanna Dance	1980	—	2.00	4.00
❏ 0516	Put a Little Love in Your Lovin'/With You in the Night	1980	—	2.00	4.00

ATLANTIC

❏ 3247	All My Dreams Are Coming True/Cream Corner	1975	—	2.50	5.00
❏ 3322	Wild Cherry/Fantasy Woman	1976	—	2.50	5.00
❏ 3338	Into My Thing/Organ Grinder	1976	—	2.50	5.00

Albums
ARISTA

❏ AL 4174	Close Encounters	1978	2.50	5.00	10.00
❏ AL 4262	Love Starts After Dark	1980	2.50	5.00	10.00

ATLANTIC

❏ SD 18111	Hot City	1974	3.00	6.00	12.00
❏ SD 18161	Lovelock!	1975	3.00	6.00	12.00

PARADONS, THE
45s
MILESTONE

❏ 2003	Diamonds and Pearls/I Want Love	1960	12.50	25.00	50.00

—Maroon label

❏ 2003	Diamonds and Pearls/I Want Love	1960	7.50	15.00	30.00

—Red label

❏ 2003	Diamonds and Pearls/I Want Love	1960	5.00	10.00	20.00

—Green label

❏ 2005	Bells Ring/Please Tell Me	1960	7.50	15.00	30.00
❏ 2015	I Had a Dream/Never, Never	1962	10.00	20.00	40.00

TUFFEST

❏ 102	Never Again/This Is Love	1961	37.50	75.00	150.00

WARNER BROS.

❏ 5186	Take All of Me/So Fine, So Fine, So Fine	1960	5.00	10.00	20.00

PARAGONS, THE
45s
BUDDAH

❏ 478	Oh Lovin' You/Con Me	1975	—	3.00	6.00

MUSIC CLEF

❏ 3001/2	Time After Time/Baby, Take My Hand	1963	5.00	10.00	20.00

MUSICRAFT

❏ 1102	Wedding Bells/Blue Velvet	1960	6.25	12.50	25.00

TAP

❏ 500	If/Hey Baby	1961	12.50	25.00	50.00
❏ 503	In the Midst of the Night/Begin the Beguine	1961	10.00	20.00	40.00
❏ 504	These Are the Things I Love/If You Love Me	1961	10.00	20.00	40.00

TIMES SQUARE

❏ 9	So You Will Know/Don't Cry Baby	1963	5.00	10.00	20.00

WINLEY

❏ 215	Hey Little School Girl/Florence	1957	12.50	25.00	50.00
❏ 220	Let's Start All Over Again/Stick With Me Baby	1957	12.50	25.00	50.00
❏ 223	Two Hearts Are Better Than One/Give Me Love	1958	10.00	20.00	40.00
❏ 227	The Vows of Love/Twilight	1958	10.00	20.00	40.00
❏ 227	The Wows of Love/Twilight	1958	250.00	500.00	1000.

—With misspelled A-side title

❏ 228	Don't Cry Baby/So You Will Know	1958	10.00	20.00	40.00
❏ 236	Darling, I Love You/Doll Baby	1959	10.00	20.00	40.00
❏ 240	So You Will Know/Doll Baby	1959	7.50	15.00	30.00
❏ 250	Kneel and Pray/Just a Moment	1961	7.50	15.00	30.00

Albums
COLLECTABLES

❏ COL-5035	The Best of the Paragons	198?	2.50	5.00	10.00

LOST-NITE

❏ LLP-4 [10]	The Best of the Paragons	1981	2.50	5.00	10.00

—Red vinyl; in die-cut cover with sticker

PARAGONS, THE & THE HARPTONES
Also see each artist's individual listings.
Albums
MUSICTONE

❏ M-8001 [M]	The Paragons vs. the Harptones	1964	10.00	20.00	40.00

PARAGONS, THE & THE JESTERS
Also see each artist's individual listings.
Albums
JOSIE

❏ 4008 [M]	The Paragons Meet the Jesters	1962	50.00	100.00	200.00

Number	Title (A Side/B Side)	Yr	VG	VG+	NM
JUBILEE					
❏ JLP-1098 [M]	The Paragons Meet the Jesters	1959	75.00	150.00	300.00
—Blue label, black vinyl					
❏ JLP-1098 [M]	The Paragons Meet the Jesters	1959	750.00	1125.	1500.
—Multi-color splash vinyl					
❏ JLP-1098 [M]	The Paragons Meet the Jesters	196?	37.50	75.00	150.00
—Flat black label					
❏ JLP-1098 [M]	The Paragons Meet the Jesters	196?	15.00	30.00	60.00
—Black label with multi-color logo					
WINLEY					
❏ LP-6003 [M]	War! The Jesters vs. the Paragons	195?	125.00	250.00	500.00

PARAMOURS, THE
BIL MEDLEY and BOBBY HATFIELD, later THE RIGHTEOUS BROTHERS.
45s

Number	Title (A Side/B Side)	Yr	VG	VG+	NM
MOONGLOW					
❏ 214	That's All I Want Tonight/There She Goes	1962	5.00	10.00	20.00
❏ 214	That's All I Want Tonight/There She Goes	1962	10.00	20.00	40.00
—Red vinyl					
SMASH					
❏ 1701	That's the Way We Love/Prison Break	1961	5.00	10.00	20.00
❏ 1718	Cutie Cutie/Miss Social Climber	1961	5.00	10.00	20.00

PARIS SISTERS, THE
45s

Number	Title (A Side/B Side)	Yr	VG	VG+	NM
CAPITOL					
❏ 2081	Golden Days/Greener Days	1968	2.00	4.00	8.00
CAVALIER					
❏ 828	Christmas in My Home Town/Man with the Mistletoe Moustache	197?	—	3.00	6.00
DECCA					
❏ 29372	Ooh La La/Whose Arms Are You Missing	1954	6.25	12.50	25.00
❏ 29488	Baby, Honey, Baby/Huckleberry Pie	1955	6.25	12.50	25.00
❏ 29527	His and Hers/Truly Do	1955	6.25	12.50	25.00
—With Gary Crosby					
❏ 29574	The Know How/I Wanna	1955	6.25	12.50	25.00
❏ 29744	Lover Boy/Oh Yes You Do	1955	6.25	12.50	25.00
❏ 29891	I Love You Dear/Mistaken	1956	6.25	12.50	25.00
❏ 29970	Daughter! Daughter!/So Much — So Very Much	1956	6.25	12.50	25.00
❏ 30554	Don't Tell Anybody/Mind Reader	1958	5.00	10.00	20.00
GNP CRESCENDO					
❏ 410	Stand Naked Clown/Ugliest Girl in Town	1968	2.00	4.00	8.00
GREGMARK					
❏ 2	Be My Boy/I'll Be Crying Tomorrow	1961	5.00	10.00	20.00
❏ 6	I Love How You Love Me/All Through the Night	1961	6.25	12.50	25.00
❏ 10	He Knows I Love Him Too Much/Lonely Girl's Prayer	1962	5.00	10.00	20.00
❏ 12	Let Me Be the One/What Am I to Do	1962	5.00	10.00	20.00
❏ 13	Yes I Love You/Once Upon a While Ago	1962	5.00	10.00	20.00
—All the Gregmark records were Phil Spector productions					
IMPERIAL					
❏ 5465	Old Enough to Cry/Tell Me More	1957	5.00	10.00	20.00
❏ 5487	Some Day/My Original Love	1958	5.00	10.00	20.00
MERCURY					
❏ 72320	Once Upon a Time/When I Fall in Love	1964	2.50	5.00	10.00
❏ 72320 [PS]	Once Upon a Time/When I Fall in Love	1964	5.00	10.00	20.00
❏ 72468	Always Waitin'/Why Do I Take It from You	1965	2.50	5.00	10.00
❏ 72468 [PS]	Always Waitin'/Why Do I Take It from You	1965	5.00	10.00	20.00
MGM					
❏ 13236	Dream Lover/Lonely Girl	1964	3.75	7.50	15.00
❏ 13236 [PS]	Dream Lover/Lonely Girl	1964	6.25	12.50	25.00
REPRISE					
❏ 0440	Sincerely/Too Good to Be True	1965	2.50	5.00	10.00
❏ 0472	I'm Me/You	1966	2.50	5.00	10.00
❏ 0511	It's My Party/My Good Friend	1966	2.50	5.00	10.00
❏ 0548	Some of Your Lovin'/Long After Tonight Is All Over	1967	2.50	5.00	10.00

Albums

Number	Title (A Side/B Side)	Yr	VG	VG+	NM
REPRISE					
❏ R-6259 [M]	Everything Under the Sun	1967	10.00	20.00	40.00
❏ RS-6359 [S]	Everything Under the Sun	1967	15.00	30.00	60.00
SIDEWALK					
❏ DT 5906 [R]	Golden Hits of the Paris Sisters	1967	7.50	15.00	30.00
❏ T 5906 [M]	Golden Hits of the Paris Sisters	1967	12.50	25.00	50.00
UNIFILMS					
❏ 505 [M]	The Paris Sisters Sing Songs from Glass House	1966	10.00	20.00	40.00
❏ S-505 [S]	The Paris Sisters Sing Songs from Glass House	1966	12.50	25.00	50.00

PARKER, JUNIOR
Also includes records as "Little Junior Parker."
45s

Number	Title (A Side/B Side)	Yr	VG	VG+	NM
BLUE ROCK					
❏ 4064	I Got Money/Lover to Friend	1968	2.00	4.00	8.00
❏ 4067	Reconsider Baby/Lovin' Man on Your Hands	1968	2.00	4.00	8.00
❏ 4080	Ain't Gon' Be No Cuttin' Loose/I'm So Satisfied	1969	2.00	4.00	8.00
❏ 4088	Easy Lovin'/You Can't Keep a Good Woman Down	1969	2.00	4.00	8.00
CAPITOL					
❏ 2857	The Outside Man/Darling, Depend on Me	1970	—	3.00	6.00
❏ 2997	Drownin' on Dry Land/River's Invitation	1970	—	3.00	6.00
DUKE					
❏ 120	Dirty Friend Blues/Can't Understand	1954	15.00	30.00	60.00
❏ 127	Please Baby Please/Sittin', Drinkin' and Thinkin'	1954	15.00	30.00	60.00

Number	Title (A Side/B Side)	Yr	VG	VG+	NM
❏ 137	Backtracking/I Wanna Ramble	1954	17.50	35.00	70.00
❏ 147	Driving Me/There Better Not Be No Feel	1956	12.50	25.00	50.00
❏ 157	Mother-in-Law Blues/That's My Baby	1956	12.50	25.00	50.00
❏ 164	Next Time You See Her/My Dolly Bee	1957	7.50	15.00	30.00
❏ 168	That's Alright/Pretty Baby	1957	7.50	15.00	30.00
❏ 177	Peaches/Pretty Little Doll	1957	7.50	15.00	30.00
❏ 184	Wondering/Sitting and Thinking	1958	6.25	12.50	25.00
❏ 193	Barefoot Rock/What Did I Do	1958	6.25	12.50	25.00
❏ 301	Sweet Home Chicago/Sometimes	1959	5.00	10.00	20.00
❏ 306	Five Long Years/I'm Holding On	1959	5.00	10.00	20.00
❏ 309	Stranded/Blue Letter	1959	5.00	10.00	20.00
❏ 315	Dangerous Woman/Belinda Marie	1960	3.75	7.50	15.00
❏ 317	The Next Time/You're On My Mind	1960	3.75	7.50	15.00
❏ 326	I'll Learn to Love Again/That's Just Alright	1960	3.75	7.50	15.00
❏ 330	Stand By Me/I'll Forget About You	1960	3.75	7.50	15.00
❏ 335	Driving Wheel/Seven Days	1961	6.25	12.50	25.00
❏ 341	In the Dark/How Long Can This Go On	1961	3.00	6.00	12.00
❏ 345	Annie Get Your Yo-Yo/Mary Jo	1961	3.00	6.00	12.00
❏ 351	I Feel Alright Again/Sweeter As the Days Go By	1962	3.00	6.00	12.00
❏ 357	Foxy Devil/Someone Somewhere	1962	3.00	6.00	12.00
❏ 362	It's a Pity/Last Night	1963	3.00	6.00	12.00
❏ 364	If You Don't Love Me/I Can't Forget About You	1963	3.00	6.00	12.00
❏ 367	The Tables Have Turned/Yonders Wall	1963	3.00	6.00	12.00
❏ 371	Strange Things Happening/I'm Gonna Stop	1964	3.00	6.00	12.00
❏ 376	Things I Used to Do/That's Why I'm Always Crying	1964	3.00	6.00	12.00
❏ 384	I'm in Love/Jivin' Woman	1964	3.00	6.00	12.00
❏ 389	Crying for My Baby/Guess You Don't Know (The Golden Rule)	1965	3.00	6.00	12.00
❏ 394	These Kind of Blues (Part 1)/These Kind of Blues (Part 2)	1966	3.00	6.00	12.00
❏ 398	Walking the Floor Over You/Goodbye Little Girl	1966	3.00	6.00	12.00
❏ 406	Get Away Blues/Why Do You Make Me Cry	1966	3.00	6.00	12.00
❏ 413	Man or Mouse/Wait for Another Day	1966	3.00	6.00	12.00
MERCURY					
❏ 72620	Baby Please/Just Like a Fish	1966	2.50	5.00	10.00
❏ 72651	You Can Make It If You Care/Ooh Wee Baby, That's the Way You Make Me Feel	1967	2.50	5.00	10.00
❏ 72672	Country Girl/Sometimes I Wonder	1967	2.50	5.00	10.00
❏ 72699	I Can't Put My Finger On It/If I Had Your Love	1967	2.50	5.00	10.00
❏ 72733	Hurtin' Inside/What a Fool I Was	1967	2.50	5.00	10.00
❏ 72793	It Must Be Love/Your Love's All Over	1968	2.00	4.00	8.00
MINIT					
❏ 32080	Worried Life Blues/Let the Good Times Roll	1969	—	3.00	6.00
SUN					
❏ 187	Feelin' Good/Fussin' and Fightin' Blues	1953	100.00	200.00	400.00
—As "Little Junior's Blue Flames"					
❏ 192	Mystery Train/Love My Baby	1954	75.00	150.00	300.00
—As "Little Junior's Blue Flames"					

Albums

Number	Title (A Side/B Side)	Yr	VG	VG+	NM
ABC					
❏ AC-30010	The ABC Collection	1976	3.75	7.50	15.00
ABC DUKE					
❏ DLP-76	Driving Wheel	1974	3.75	7.50	15.00
❏ DLP-83	The Best of Junior Parker	1974	3.75	7.50	15.00
BLUE ROCK					
❏ SRB-64004	Honey-Drippin' Blues	1969	3.75	7.50	15.00
BLUESWAY					
❏ BLS-6066	Sometime Tomorrow	1973	3.75	7.50	15.00
CAPITOL					
❏ ST-564	Outside Man	1970	3.75	7.50	15.00
DUKE					
❏ DLP-76 [M]	Driving Wheel	1962	37.50	75.00	150.00
—With Cadillac on front cover					
❏ DLP-76 [M]	Driving Wheel	196?	25.00	50.00	100.00
—With Wagon Wheel on front cover					
❏ DLP-83 [M]	The Best of Junior Parker	1967	12.50	25.00	50.00
❏ DLPS-83 [P]	The Best of Junior Parker	1967	10.00	20.00	40.00
GROOVE MERCHANT					
❏ 513	Love Ain't Nothin'	1974	3.75	7.50	15.00
MCA					
❏ 27046	The Best of Junior Parker	1980	2.50	5.00	10.00
MERCURY					
❏ MG-21101 [M]	Like It Is	1967	7.50	15.00	30.00
❏ SR-61101 [S]	Like It Is	1967	6.25	12.50	25.00
MINIT					
❏ 24024	Blues Man	1969	6.25	12.50	25.00
UNITED ARTISTS					
❏ UAS-6823	I Tell Stories Sad and True	1971	3.75	7.50	15.00

PARKER, JUNIOR, AND BOBBY BLAND
Also see each artist's individual listings.
Albums

Number	Title (A Side/B Side)	Yr	VG	VG+	NM
ABC DUKE					
❏ DLP-72	Blues Consolidated	1974	3.75	7.50	15.00
DUKE					
❏ DLP-72 [M]	Blues Consolidated	1961	37.50	75.00	150.00

PARKER, JUNIOR, AND JIMMY MCGRIFF
Also see each artist's individual listings.
Albums

Number	Title (A Side/B Side)	Yr	VG	VG+	NM
CAPITOL					
❏ ST-569	Dudes Doin' Business	1971	3.75	7.50	15.00

Number	Title (A Side/B Side)	Yr	VG	VG+	NM
UNITED ARTISTS					
❏ UAS-6814	100 Proof Black Magic	1971	3.75	7.50	15.00

PARKER, RAY, JR.
Includes records as "Raydio" and "Ray Parker Jr. and Raydio."

45s
ARISTA

Number	Title (A Side/B Side)	Yr	VG	VG+	NM
❏ 0283	Jack and Jill/Get Down	1977	—	2.50	5.00
—As "Raydio"					
❏ 0283 [PS]	Jack and Jill/Get Down	1977	—	3.00	6.00
—As "Raydio"					
❏ 0328	Is This a Love Thing/Let's Go All the Way	1978	—	2.50	5.00
—As "Raydio"					
❏ 0353	Honey I'm Rich/Betcha You Can't Love Me Just Once	1978	—	2.50	5.00
—As "Raydio"					
❏ 0399	You Can't Change That/Rock On	1979	—	2.50	5.00
—As "Raydio"					
❏ 0441	More Than One Way to Love a Woman/Hot Stuff	1979	—	2.50	5.00
—As "Raydio"					
❏ 0494	Two Places at the Same Time/Everybody Makes Mistakes	1980	—	2.00	4.00
—As "Ray Parker Jr. and Raydio"					
❏ 0522	For Those Who Like to Groove/Can't Keep from Cryin'	1980	—	2.00	4.00
—As "Ray Parker Jr. and Raydio"					
❏ 0554	Can't Keep from Cryin'/It's Time to Party Now	1980	—	2.00	4.00
—As "Ray Parker Jr. and Raydio"					
❏ 0575	Little Bit of You/It's Time to Party Now	1980	—	2.00	4.00
—As "Ray Parker Jr. and Raydio"					
❏ 0592	A Woman Needs Love (Just Like You Do)/So Into You	1981	—	2.00	4.00
—As "Ray Parker Jr. and Raydio"					
❏ 0616	That Old Song/Old Pro	1981	—	2.00	4.00
—As "Ray Parker Jr. and Raydio"					
❏ 0616 [PS]	That Old Song/Old Pro	1981	—	2.00	4.00
—As "Ray Parker Jr. and Raydio"					
❏ 0641	It's Your Night/Old Pro	1981	—	2.00	4.00
—As "Ray Parker Jr. and Raydio"					
❏ 0669	The Other Woman/Stay the Night	1982	—	2.00	4.00
❏ 0695	Let Me Go/Stop, Look Before You Love	1982	—	2.00	4.00
❏ 1014	It's Our Own Affair/Just Havin' Fun	1982	—	2.00	4.00
❏ 1030	Bad Boy/Let's Get Off	1982	—	2.00	4.00
❏ 1035	Christmas Time Is Here/(Instrumental)	1982	—	2.50	5.00
❏ 1035 [PS]	Christmas Time Is Here/(Instrumental)	1982	—	3.00	6.00
❏ 1051	The People Next Door/Streetlove	1983	—	2.00	4.00
❏ 9048	Woman Out of Control/She Still Feels the Need	1983	—	2.00	4.00
❏ 9116	I Still Can't Get Over Losing You/She Still Feels the Need	1983	—	2.00	4.00
❏ 9198	In the Heat of the Night/N2 U2	1984	—	2.00	4.00
❏ 9212	Ghostbusters/(Instrumental)	1984	—	—	3.00
❏ 9293	Jamie/Christmas Time Is Here	1984	—	—	3.00
❏ 9352	Girls Are More Fun/I'm in Love	1985	—	—	3.00
❏ 9352 [PS]	Girls Are More Fun/I'm in Love	1985	—	—	3.00
❏ 9451	One Sided Love Affair//(B-side unknown)	1985	—	—	3.00
ATLANTIC					
❏ 89456	One Sunny Day//(B-side unknown)	1986	—	—	3.00
—With Helen Terry					
❏ 89456 [PS]	One Sunny Day//(B-side unknown)	1986	—	—	3.00
FLASHBACK					
❏ 9288	Christmas Time Is Here/(Instrumental)	1984	—	—	3.00
—Reissue					
GEFFEN					
❏ 28152	Over You/After Midnite	1987	—	—	3.00
❏ 28152 [PS]	Over You/After Midnite	1987	—	—	3.00
—With Natalie Cole					
❏ 28417	I Don't Think That Man Should Sleep Alone/After Midnight	1987	—	—	3.00
❏ 28417 [PS]	I Don't Think That Man Should Sleep Alone/After Midnight	1987	—	—	3.00

Albums
ARISTA

Number	Title (A Side/B Side)	Yr	VG	VG+	NM
❏ AB 4163	Raydio	1978	3.75	7.50	15.00
—As "Raydio"					
❏ AB 4212	Rock On	1979	3.75	7.50	15.00
—As "Raydio"					
❏ AL8-8087	Woman Out of Control	1983	2.50	5.00	10.00
❏ AL8-8266	Chartbusters	1984	2.50	5.00	10.00
❏ AL8-8280	Sex and the Single Man	1985	2.50	5.00	10.00
❏ AL 9515	Two Places at the Same Time	1980	2.50	5.00	10.00
—As "Ray Parker Jr. and Raydio"					
❏ AL 9543	A Woman Needs Love	1981	2.50	5.00	10.00
—As "Ray Parker Jr. and Raydio"					
❏ AL 9590	The Other Woman	1982	2.50	5.00	10.00
❏ AL 9612	Greatest Hits	1982	2.50	5.00	10.00
GEFFEN					
❏ GHS 24124	After Dark	1987	2.50	5.00	10.00
MCA					
❏ 10327	I Love You Like You Are	1991	3.00	6.00	12.00

PARKER, ROBERT
45s
IMPERIAL

Number	Title (A Side/B Side)	Yr	VG	VG+	NM
❏ 5842	Mash Potatoes All Night Long/Twistin' Out of Space	1962	3.00	6.00	12.00
❏ 5889	You're Lookin' Good/Little Things Mean a Lot	1962	3.00	6.00	12.00
❏ 5916	Please Forgive Me/You Got It	1963	3.00	6.00	12.00
ISLAND					
❏ 044	Give Me the Country Side of Life/It's Hard But It's Fair	1975	—	2.00	4.00
❏ 074	A Little Bit Something/Better Luck in the Summer	1976	—	2.00	4.00
NOLA					
❏ 721	Barefootin'/Let's Go Baby (Where the Action Is)	1966	5.00	10.00	20.00
❏ 724	Ring Around the Roses/She's Coming Home	1966	3.00	6.00	12.00
❏ 726	Happy Feet/The Scratch	1966	3.00	6.00	12.00
❏ 729	Tip Toe/Soul Kind of Loving	1966	3.00	6.00	12.00
❏ 730	A Letter To Santa/C.C. Rider	1966	3.00	6.00	12.00
❏ 733	Yak Yak Yak/Secret Agents	1967	3.00	6.00	12.00
❏ 735	Everybody's Hip-Hugging/Foxy Mama	1967	3.00	6.00	12.00
❏ 738	I Caught You in a Lie/Holdin' Out	1967	3.00	6.00	12.00
❏ 739	Barefootin' Boogaloo/Soul Sister	196?	3.75	7.50	15.00
RON					
❏ 327	All Nite Long (Part 1)/All Nite Long (Part 2)	1959	3.75	7.50	15.00
❏ 331	Walkin'/Across the Track	1960	3.75	7.50	15.00
SILVER FOX					
❏ 12	You Shakin' Things Up/You See Me	1969	—	3.00	6.00

Albums
NOLA

Number	Title (A Side/B Side)	Yr	VG	VG+	NM
❏ LP-1001 [M]	Barefootin'	1966	7.50	15.00	30.00

PARLET
Female offshoot of PARLIAMENT.

12-Inch Singles
CASABLANCA

Number	Title (A Side/B Side)	Yr	VG	VG+	NM
❏ NBD 20161	Ridin' High (9:40)/(B-side blank)	1979	5.00	10.00	20.00

45s
CASABLANCA

Number	Title (A Side/B Side)	Yr	VG	VG+	NM
❏ 919	Pleasure Principle/(Pt. 2)	1978	—	2.50	5.00
❏ 932	Cookie Jar/Are You Dreaming	1978	—	2.50	5.00
❏ 975	Ridin' High/(Pt. 2)	1979	—	2.50	5.00
❏ 995	Don't Ever Stop/Huff-N-Puff	1979	—	2.50	5.00
❏ 2260	Wolf Tickets/(Pt. II)	1980	—	2.50	5.00
❏ 2293	Help from My Friends/Watch Me Do My Thang	1980	—	2.50	5.00

Albums
CASABLANCA

Number	Title (A Side/B Side)	Yr	VG	VG+	NM
❏ NBLP 7094	Pleasure Principle	1978	5.00	10.00	20.00
❏ NBLP 7146	Invasion of the Booty Snatchers	1979	5.00	10.00	20.00

PARLIAMENT
Also see BOOTSY'S RUBBER BAND; THE BRIDES OF FUNKENSTEIN; GEORGE CLINTON; BOOTSY COLLINS; FUNKADELIC; FUNKADELIC (2); P. FUNK ALL STARS; PARLET; THE PARLIAMENTS.

12-Inch Singles
CASABLANCA

Number	Title (A Side/B Side)	Yr	VG	VG+	NM
❏ NBD 20113	Flash Light (10:31)/(B-side blank)	1977	10.00	20.00	40.00
❏ NBD 20208	Theme from The Black Hole/Big Bang Theory//(B-side blank)	1979	5.00	10.00	20.00
❏ 876585-1	Flash Light (10:31)/P-Funk (Wants to Get Funked Up) (7:34)	198?	2.50	5.00	10.00
—"Timepieces" reissue					

45s
CASABLANCA

Number	Title (A Side/B Side)	Yr	VG	VG+	NM
❏ 0003	The Goose (Part 1)/The Goose (Part 2)	1974	—	3.00	6.00
❏ 0013	Up for the Down Stroke/Presence of a Brain	1974	—	3.00	6.00
❏ 0104	Up for the Down Stroke/Presence of a Brain	1974	—	2.50	5.00
❏ 803	Up for the Down Stroke/Presence of a Brain	1974	—	2.50	5.00
❏ 811	Testify/I Can Move You	1974	—	2.50	5.00
❏ 831	Chocolate City/Chocolate City (Part 2)	1975	—	2.50	5.00
❏ 843	Ride On/Big Footin'	1975	—	2.50	5.00
❏ 852	P. Funk (Wants to Get Funked Up)/Night of the Tempasaurus Peoples	1976	—	2.50	5.00
❏ 856	Tear the Roof Off the Sucker (Give Up the Funk)/P-Funk	1976	—	2.50	5.00
—Blue label					
❏ 856	Tear the Roof Off the Sucker (Give Up the Funk)/P-Funk	1976	—	2.00	4.00
—Tan label					
❏ 864	Star Child (Mothership Connection)/Supergroovealistic	1976	—	2.50	5.00
❏ 871	Do That Stuff/Handcuffs	1976	—	2.50	5.00
❏ 875	Dr. Funkenstein/Children of Production	1977	—	2.50	5.00
❏ 892	Fantasy Is Reality/The Landing (Of the Mothership)	1977	—	2.50	5.00
❏ 900	Bop Gun (Endangered Species)/I've Been Watchin' You	1977	—	2.50	5.00
❏ 909	Flash Light/Swing Down, Sweet Chariot	1978	—	2.50	5.00
❏ 921	Funkentelechy/Funkentelechy (Part 2)	1978	—	2.50	5.00
❏ 950	Aqua Boogie (A Psychoalphadiscobetabioaquadoloop)/(You're a Fish and I'm a) Water Sign	1978	—	2.50	5.00
❏ 950 [PS]	Aqua Boogie (A Psychoalphadiscobetabioaquadoloop)/(You're a Fish and I'm a) Water Sign	1978	2.50	5.00	10.00
❏ 976	Rumpofsteelskin/Liquid Sunshine	1979	—	2.50	5.00
❏ 2222	Party People/Party People (Part 2)	1979	—	2.50	5.00
❏ 2235	Theme from The Black Hole/(You're a Fish and I'm a) Water Sign	1980	—	2.50	5.00
❏ 2250	The Big Bang Theory/The Big Bang Theory (Part 2)	1980	—	2.50	5.00

Number	Title (A Side/B Side)	Yr	VG	VG+	NM
❑ 2317	Agony of DeFeet/The Freeze	1980	—	2.50	5.00
❑ 2330	Crush It/Body Language	1981	—	2.50	5.00
INVICTUS					
❑ 9077	I Call My Baby Pussy Cat/Little Ole Country Boy	1970	2.50	5.00	10.00
❑ 9091	Red Hot Mama/Little Ole Country Boy	1971	2.50	5.00	10.00
❑ 9095	Breakdown/Little Ole Country Boy	1971	2.50	5.00	10.00
❑ 9123	Come In Out of the Rain/Little Ole Country Boy	1972	2.00	4.00	8.00
Albums					
CASABLANCA					
❑ NBLP 7002	Up for the Down Stroke	1974	10.00	20.00	40.00
❑ NBLP 7014	Chocolate City	1975	10.00	20.00	40.00
❑ NBLP 7022	Mothership Connection	1976	7.50	15.00	30.00
❑ NBLP 7034	The Clones of Dr. Funkenstein	1976	7.50	15.00	30.00
❑ NBLP 7053 [(2)]	Parliament Live/P. Funk Earth Tour	1977	10.00	20.00	40.00
❑ NBLP 7084	Funkentelechy vs. the Placebo Syndrome	1977	7.50	15.00	30.00
❑ NBLP 7125	Motor-Booty Affair	1978	7.50	15.00	30.00
❑ NBPIX 7125 [PD]	Motor-Booty Affair	1978	10.00	20.00	40.00
❑ NBLP 7195	Gloryhallastoopid (Or Pin the Tale on the Funky)	1979	7.50	15.00	30.00
❑ NBLP 7249	Trombipulation	1980	7.50	15.00	30.00
❑ NBLP 9003	Up for the Down Stroke	1974	12.50	25.00	50.00
—Original pressing, distributed by Warner Bros.					
❑ 822637-1	Greatest Hits	1984	3.75	7.50	15.00
❑ 824501-1	Funkentelechy vs. the Placebo Syndrome	1985	3.75	7.50	15.00
❑ 824502-1	Mothership Connection	1985	3.75	7.50	15.00
INVICTUS					
❑ ST-7302	Osmium	1970	25.00	50.00	100.00

PARLIAMENTS, THE

All of the below are probably the same group, a Detriot-based R&B group led by GEORGE CLINTON that evolved into PARLIAMENT and FUNKADELIC.

45s

Number	Title (A Side/B Side)	Yr	VG	VG+	NM
APT					
❑ 25036	Poor Willie/Party Boys	1959	10.00	20.00	40.00
ATCO					
❑ 6675	A New Day Begins/I'll Wait	1969	5.00	10.00	20.00
FLIPP					
❑ 100/1	Lonely Island/You Make Me Wanna Cry	1960	10.00	20.00	40.00
—Red label					
❑ 100/1	Lonely Island/You Make Me Wanna Cry	1960	7.50	15.00	30.00
—Yellow label					
GOLDEN WORLD					
❑ 46	Heart Trouble/That Was My Girl	1966	12.50	25.00	50.00
LEN					
❑ 101	Don't Need You Anymore/Honey, Take Me Home with You	1958	20.00	40.00	80.00
REVILOT					
❑ 207	(I Wanna) Testify/I Can Feel the Ice Melting	1967	3.75	7.50	15.00
❑ 211	All Your Goodies Are Gone (The Loser's Seat)/Don't Be Sore at Me	1967	3.75	7.50	15.00
❑ 214	Little Man/The Goose (That Laid the Golden Egg)	1968	3.75	7.50	15.00
❑ 217	Look at What I Almost Missed/What You Been Growing	1968	3.75	7.50	15.00
❑ 223	Good Old Music/Time	1968	3.75	7.50	15.00
❑ 228	A New Day Begins/I'll Wait	1968	7.50	15.00	30.00
SYMBOL					
❑ 917	You're Cute/I'll Get You Yet	1962	6.25	12.50	25.00
U.S.A.					
❑ 719	My Only Love/To Be Alone	1961	5.00	10.00	20.00

PARRIS, FRED

Not to be confused with the similarly-named Freddie Paris, a different singer. Also see THE CHAMPLAINS; THE CHEROKEES (5); THE FIVE SATINS; THE NEW YORKERS (1); THE WILDWOODS.

45s

Number	Title (A Side/B Side)	Yr	VG	VG+	NM
ATCO					
❑ 6439	Land of the Broken Hearts/Bring It Home to Daddy	1966	2.50	5.00	10.00
BIRTH					
❑ 101	Dark at the Top of My Heart/Benediction	196?	2.00	4.00	8.00
CHECKER					
❑ 1108	No Use in Crying/Walk a Little Faster	1965	2.50	5.00	10.00
GREEN SEA					
❑ 106	Blushing Bride/Giving My Love to You	1966	2.50	5.00	10.00
❑ 107	I'll Be Hangin' On/I Can Really Satisfy	1966	2.50	5.00	10.00
KLIK					
❑ 7905	The Voice/She's Gone (With the Wind)	1958	50.00	100.00	200.00
—With the Scarlets and Passionettes					
MAMA SADIE					
❑ 1001	In the Still of the Nite "67"/Heck No	1967	2.50	5.00	10.00

PARROTS, THE (1)

45s

Number	Title (A Side/B Side)	Yr	VG	VG+	NM
CHECKER					
❑ 772	Don't Leave Me/Weep, Weep, Weep	1953	125.00	250.00	500.00

PARROTS, THE (2)

45s

Number	Title (A Side/B Side)	Yr	VG	VG+	NM
MALA					
❑ 558	They All Got Carried Away/Hey, Put the Clock Back on the Wall	1967	3.00	6.00	12.00

Number	Title (A Side/B Side)	Yr	VG	VG+	NM
PASSIONS, THE (1)					
45s					
ABC-PARAMOUNT					
❑ 10436	The Bully/The Empty Seat	1963	6.25	12.50	25.00
AUDICON					
❑ 102	Just to Be with You/Oh Melancholy Me	1959	10.00	20.00	40.00
❑ 105	I Only Want You/This Is My Love	1960	7.50	15.00	30.00
—Red label					
❑ 105	I Only Want You/This Is My Love	1960	5.00	10.00	20.00
—Red, black and white label					
❑ 106	Gloria/Jungle Drums	1960	7.50	15.00	30.00
❑ 108	Beautiful Dreamer/One Look Is All It Took	1960	7.50	15.00	30.00
❑ 112	Made for Lovers/You Don't Have Me Anymore	1961	10.00	20.00	40.00
DIAMOND					
❑ 146	Sixteen Candles/The Third Floor	1963	10.00	20.00	40.00
JUBILEE					
❑ 5406	Lonely Road/One Look Is All It Took	1961	5.00	10.00	20.00
OCTAVIA					
❑ 8005	Aphrodite/I've Gotta Know	1962	200.00	400.00	800.00

Number	Title (A Side/B Side)	Yr	VG	VG+	NM
PASTELS, THE					
45s					
ARGO					
❑ 5287	Been So Long/My One and Only Dream	1958	6.25	12.50	25.00
❑ 5297	You Don't Love Me Anymore/Let's Go to the Rock 'N' Roll Ball	1958	7.50	15.00	30.00
❑ 5314	So Far Away/Don't Knock	1958	6.25	12.50	25.00
ARK					
❑ 298	Jungle Run/K-Nif	196?	12.50	25.00	50.00
JUBILEE					
❑ 5495	First Star/Tokyo Melody	1965	3.00	6.00	12.00
MASCOT					
❑ 123	Been So Long/My One and Only Dream	1957	75.00	150.00	300.00
UNITED					
❑ 196	Put Your Arms Around Me/Boom De De Boom	1957	20.00	40.00	80.00

Number	Title (A Side/B Side)	Yr	VG	VG+	NM
PAUL, BILLY					
12-Inch Singles					
PHILADELPHIA INT'L.					
❑ 3678	Bring the Family Back (5:53)/It's Critical (6:33)	1979	3.00	6.00	12.00
❑ 3706	False Faces (6:52)/(B-side unknown)	1979	3.00	6.00	12.00
45s					
GAMBLE					
❑ 232	Somewhere/Bluesette	1968	3.00	6.00	12.00
JUBILEE					
❑ 5081	That's Why I Dream/Why Am I	1952	7.50	15.00	30.00
❑ 5086	You Didn't Know/The Stars Are Mine	1952	7.50	15.00	30.00
NEPTUNE					
❑ 30	Mrs. Robinson/Let's Fall in Love All Over	1970	2.50	5.00	10.00
PHILADELPHIA INT'L.					
❑ 3120	Jesus Boy (You Only Look Like a Man)/Love Buddies	1980	—	2.50	5.00
❑ 3509	Love Buddies/Magic Carpet Ride	1971	—	3.00	6.00
❑ 3515	This Is Your Life/I Wish It Were Yesterday	1972	—	3.00	6.00
❑ 3521	Me and Mrs. Jones/Your Song	1972	—	2.50	5.00
❑ 3526	Am I Black Enough for You/I'm Gonna Make It This Time	1973	—	2.50	5.00
❑ 3538	Thanks for Saving My Life/I Was Married	1974	—	2.50	5.00
❑ 3551	Be Truthful to Me/I Wish It Was Yesterday	1974	—	2.50	5.00
❑ 3563	Billy's Back Home/I've Got So Much to Live For	1975	—	2.50	5.00
❑ 3572	When It's Your Turn to Go/July, July, July, July	1975	—	2.50	5.00
❑ 3584	Let's Make a Baby/My Head's On Straight	1976	—	2.50	5.00
❑ 3593	People Power/I Want Cha Baby	1976	—	2.50	5.00
❑ 3613	How Good Is Your Game/I Think I'll Stay Home Today	1977	—	2.50	5.00
❑ 3621	Let 'Em In/We All Got a Mission	1977	—	2.50	5.00
❑ 3630	I Trust You/Love Won't Come Easy	1977	—	2.50	5.00
❑ 3635	Only the Strong Survive/Where I Belong	1977	—	2.50	5.00
❑ 3639	Everybody's Breakin' Up/Sooner or Later	1978	—	2.50	5.00
❑ 3645	One Man's Junk/Don't Give Up on Love	1978	—	2.50	5.00
❑ 3676	Bring the Family Back/It's Critical	1979	—	2.50	5.00
❑ 3699	False Faces/I Gotta Put This Life Down	1979	—	2.50	5.00
❑ 3736	You're My Sweetness/(B-side unknown)	1979	—	2.50	5.00
Albums					
GAMBLE					
❑ SG-5002	Feeling Good at the Cadillac Club	1968	7.50	15.00	30.00
ICHIBAN					
❑ ICH-1025	Wide Open	198?	2.50	5.00	10.00
NEPTUNE					
❑ 201	Ebony Woman	1970	5.00	10.00	20.00
PHILADELPHIA INT'L.					
❑ Z 30580	Going East	1971	3.00	6.00	12.00
❑ KZ 31793	360 Degrees of Billy Paul	1972	3.00	6.00	12.00
❑ ZQ 31793 [Q]	360 Degrees of Billy Paul	1972	5.00	10.00	20.00
❑ KZ 32118	Ebony Woman	1973	3.00	6.00	12.00
—Reissue of Neptune LP					
❑ KZ 32119	Feeling Good at the Cadillac Club	1973	3.00	6.00	12.00
—Reissue of Gamble LP					
❑ KZ 32409	War of the Gods	1973	2.50	5.00	10.00
❑ ZQ 32409 [Q]	War of the Gods	1973	5.00	10.00	20.00
❑ KZ 32952	Live in Europe	1974	2.50	5.00	10.00
❑ ZQ 32952 [Q]	Live in Europe	1974	5.00	10.00	20.00
❑ PZ 33157	Got My Head On Straight	1975	2.50	5.00	10.00

Number	Title (A Side/B Side)	Yr	VG	VG+	NM
❑ PZ 33843	When Love Is New	1975	2.50	5.00	10.00
❑ PZ 34389	Let 'Em In	1976	2.50	5.00	10.00
❑ PZ 34923	Only the Strong Survive	1977	2.50	5.00	10.00
❑ JZ 35756	First Class	1979	2.50	5.00	10.00
❑ Z2 36314 [(2)]	The Best of Billy Paul	1980	3.75	7.50	15.00

TOTAL EXPERIENCE
| ❑ TEL8-5711 | Lately | 1985 | 2.50 | 5.00 | 10.00 |

PAYNE, FREDA
12-Inch Singles
CAPITOL
❑ 8509	I'll Do Anything for You (7:40)/(Instrumental)	1978	3.00	6.00	12.00
❑ SPRO-8922/3 [DJ]	Happy Days Are Here Again-Happy Music/I'll Do Anything for You	1978	3.75	7.50	15.00
❑ SPRO-9219 [DJ]	Red Hot (7:01) (same on both sides)	1979	2.50	5.00	10.00

SUTRA
| ❑ SUD 009 | In Motion (5:35)/(Instrumental) | 1982 | 3.75 | 7.50 | 15.00 |

45s
ABC
| ❑ 12079 | Shadows on the Wall/I Get Carried Away | 1975 | — | 2.50 | 5.00 |
| ❑ 12139 | Lost in Love/You | 1975 | — | 2.50 | 5.00 |

ABC-PARAMOUNT
| ❑ 10366 | Desafinado/He Who Laughs Last | 1962 | 5.00 | 10.00 | 20.00 |
| ❑ 10437 | Pretty Baby/Grin and Bear It | 1963 | 5.00 | 10.00 | 20.00 |

ABC DUNHILL
| ❑ 15018 | It's Yours to Have/Run for Life | 1974 | — | 2.50 | 5.00 |

CAPITOL
❑ 4383	I Can't Live on a Memory/I Get High (On Your Memory)	1976	—	2.50	5.00
❑ 4431	Baby, You've Got What It Takes/Bring Back the Joy	1977	—	2.50	5.00
❑ 4494	Love Magnet/Loving You Means So Much to Me	1977	—	2.50	5.00
❑ 4537	Feed Me Your Love/Stares and Whispers	1978	—	2.50	5.00
❑ 4631	Happy Days Are Here Again-Happy Music (Dance the Night Away)/Falling in Love	1978	—	2.50	5.00
❑ 4695	I'll Do Anything for You (Part 1)/I'll Do Anything for You (Part 2)	1979	—	2.50	5.00
❑ 4775	Red Hot/Longest Night	1979	—	2.50	5.00
❑ 4805	Can't Wait/Longest Night	1979	—	2.50	5.00

IMPULSE!
| ❑ 221 | It's Time/Sweet September | 1963 | 5.00 | 10.00 | 20.00 |

INVICTUS
❑ 1255	Two Wrongs Don't Make a Right/We've Gotta Find a Way Back to Love	1973	—	3.00	6.00
❑ 1257	For No Reason/Mother Misery's Favorite Child	1973	—	3.00	6.00
❑ 9073	The Unhooked Generation/Easiest Way to Fall	1969	—	3.00	6.00
❑ 9075	Band of Gold/Easiest Way to Fall	1970	—	3.00	6.00
❑ 9080	Deeper and Deeper/The Unhooked Genration	1970	—	3.00	6.00
❑ 9085	Cherish What Is Dear to You (While It Is Near to You)/They Don't Owe Me a Thing	1971	—	3.00	6.00
❑ 9085 [PS]	Cherish What Is Dear to You (While It Is Near to You)/They Don't Owe Me a Thing	1971	2.50	5.00	10.00
❑ 9092	Bring the Boys Home/I Shall Not Be Moved	1971	—	3.00	6.00
❑ 9100	You Brought the Joy/Suddenly It's Yesterday	1971	—	3.00	6.00
❑ 9109	I'm Not Getting Any Better/The Road We Didn't Take	1972	—	3.00	6.00
❑ 9128	She's in My Life/Through the Memory of My Mind	1972	—	3.00	6.00

MGM
| ❑ 13509 | You've Lost That Lovin' Feelin'/Sad Sad September | 1966 | 5.00 | 10.00 | 20.00 |

SUTRA
| ❑ 117 | In Motion/(Instrumental) | 1982 | — | 2.50 | 5.00 |

Albums
ABC
| ❑ D-901 | Out of Payne Comes Love | 1976 | 3.00 | 6.00 | 12.00 |

ABC DUNHILL
| ❑ DSX-50176 | Payne and Pleasure | 1974 | 3.75 | 7.50 | 15.00 |

ABC IMPULSE!
| ❑ AS-53 [S] | After the Lights Go Down Low…And Much More | 1968 | 3.75 | 7.50 | 15.00 |

CAPITOL
❑ ST-11700	Stares and Whispers	1977	3.00	6.00	12.00
❑ ST-11864	Supernatural	1978	3.00	6.00	12.00
❑ ST-12003	Hot	1979	3.00	6.00	12.00

IMPULSE!
| ❑ A-53 [M] | After the Lights Go Down Low…And Much More | 1964 | 7.50 | 15.00 | 30.00 |
| ❑ AS-53 [S] | After the Lights Go Down Low…And Much More | 1964 | 10.00 | 20.00 | 40.00 |

INVICTUS
❑ ST-7301	Band of Gold	1970	3.75	7.50	15.00
❑ SMAS-7307	Contact	1971	3.75	7.50	15.00
❑ ST-9804	The Best of Freda Payne	1972	3.75	7.50	15.00
❑ Z 32493	Reaching Out	1973	3.75	7.50	15.00

MGM
❑ GAS-128	Freda Payne (Golden Archive Series)	1970	3.75	7.50	15.00
❑ E-4370 [M]	How Do You Say I Don't Love You Anymore	1966	5.00	10.00	20.00
❑ SE-4370 [S]	How Do You Say I Don't Love You Anymore	1966	6.25	12.50	25.00

PEACHES AND HERB
Herb Fame with at least three different female singers who were "Peaches."
12-Inch Singles
POLYDOR
| ❑ PRO 165 [DJ] | Freeway (6:03) (same on both sides) | 1981 | 3.00 | 6.00 | 12.00 |

Number	Title (A Side/B Side)	Yr	VG	VG+	NM
45s					
COLUMBIA					
❑ 03872	Remember/Come to Me	1983	—	2.00	4.00
❑ 04081	In My World/Keep On Smiling	1983	—	2.00	4.00
❑ 45386	The Sound of Silence/The Two of Us	1971	—	2.50	5.00
❑ 45554	God Save This World/I Can't Forget the One I Love	1972	—	2.50	5.00

DATE
❑ 1523	Let's Fall in Love/We're In This Thing Together	1966	2.50	5.00	10.00
❑ 1549	Close Your Eyes/I Will Watch Over You	1967	2.50	5.00	10.00
❑ 1549 [PS]	Close Your Eyes/I Will Watch Over You	1967	3.75	7.50	15.00
❑ 1555	Cupid-Venus/Darling, How Long	1967	3.75	7.50	15.00
❑ 1563	For Your Love/I Need Your Love So Desperately	1967	2.50	5.00	10.00
❑ 1563 [PS]	For Your Love/I Need Your Love So Desperately	1967	3.75	7.50	15.00
❑ 1574	Love Is Strange/It's True I Love You	1967	2.50	5.00	10.00
❑ 1574 [PS]	Love Is Strange/It's True I Love You	1967	3.75	7.50	15.00
❑ 1586	Two Little Kids/We've Got to Love One Another	1967	2.00	4.00	8.00
❑ 1592	The Ten Commandments of Love/What a Lovely Way (To Say Goodnight)	1968	2.00	4.00	8.00
❑ 1603	United/Thank You	1968	2.00	4.00	8.00
❑ 1603 [PS]	United/Thank You	1968	3.75	7.50	15.00
❑ 1623	Let's Make a Promise/Me and You	1968	2.00	4.00	8.00
❑ 1623 [PS]	Let's Make a Promise/Me and You	1968	3.75	7.50	15.00
❑ 1633	We've Got to Love One Another/So True	1968	2.50	5.00	10.00
❑ 1637	When He Touches Me (Nothing Else Matters)/Thank You	1969	2.00	4.00	8.00
❑ 1649	Let Me Be the One/I Need Your Love So Desperately	1969	2.00	4.00	8.00
❑ 1655	Cupid/Darling, How Long	1969	2.00	4.00	8.00
❑ 1669	It's Just a Game, Love/Satisfy My Hunger	1970	2.00	4.00	8.00
❑ 1676	Soothe Me with Your Love/We're So Much in Love	1970	2.00	4.00	8.00

MCA
| ❑ 40701 | We're Still Together/Love Is Here Beside Us | 1977 | — | 2.50 | 5.00 |
| ❑ 40782 | It Will Never Be the Same Again/I'm Counting on You | 1977 | — | 2.50 | 5.00 |

MERCURY
| ❑ 73350 | Keep It Coming/I'm a-Hurtin' Inside | 1973 | — | 2.50 | 5.00 |
| ❑ 73388 | Can't It Wait/Thank Heaven for You | 1973 | — | 2.50 | 5.00 |

POLYDOR
❑ 2031	Roller-Skatin' Mate (Part 1)/Roller-Skatin' Mate (Part 2)	1979	—	2.00	4.00
❑ 2053	I Pledge My Love/(I Want Us) Back Together	1980	—	2.00	4.00
❑ 2115	Funtime (Part 1)/Funtime (Part 2)	1980	—	2.00	4.00
❑ 2140	One Child of Love/Hearsay	1980	—	2.00	4.00
❑ 2157	Surrender/Love Stealers	1981	—	2.00	4.00
❑ 2178	Freeway/Pickin' Up the Pieces	1981	—	2.00	4.00
❑ 2187	Bluer Than Blue/Go with the Flow	1981	—	2.00	4.00
❑ 14514	Shake Your Groove Thing/All Your Love (Get It Here)	1978	—	2.00	4.00
❑ 14547	Reunited/Easy as Pie	1979	—	2.00	4.00
❑ 14577	We've Got Love/Four's a Traffic Jam	1979	—	2.00	4.00

Albums
COLUMBIA
| ❑ FC 38746 | Remember | 1983 | 2.50 | 5.00 | 10.00 |

DATE
❑ TEM 3004 [M]	Let's Fall in Love	1967	5.00	10.00	20.00
❑ TEM 3005 [M]	For Your Love	1967	6.25	12.50	25.00
❑ TEM 3007 [M]	Golden Duets	1968	7.50	15.00	30.00
❑ TES 4004 [S]	Let's Fall in Love	1967	6.25	12.50	25.00
❑ TES 4005 [S]	For Your Love	1967	5.00	10.00	20.00
❑ TES 4007 [S]	Golden Duets	1968	5.00	10.00	20.00
❑ TES 4012	Peaches and Herb's Greatest Hits	1968	5.00	10.00	20.00

EPIC
❑ E 36089	Love Is Strange	1979	2.50	5.00	10.00
—Reissue of Date material					
❑ JE 36099	Peaches and Herb's Greatest Hits	1979	2.50	5.00	10.00
—Reissue of Date 4012					

MCA
| ❑ 2261 | Peaches and Herb | 1977 | 3.00 | 6.00 | 12.00 |

POLYDOR
❑ PD-1-6172	2 Hot!	1978	2.50	5.00	10.00
❑ PD-1-6239	Twice the Fire	1979	2.50	5.00	10.00
❑ PD-1-6298	Worth the Wait	1980	2.50	5.00	10.00
❑ PD-1-6332	Sayin' Something!	1981	2.50	5.00	10.00

PEEBLES, ANN
12-Inch Singles
HI
| ❑ 78519 | I Didn't Take Your Man/(B-side unknown) | 1978 | 3.00 | 6.00 | 12.00 |

45s
HI
❑ 2157	Walk Away/I Can't Let You Go	1969	—	3.00	6.00
❑ 2165	Give Me Some Credit/Solid Foundation	1969	—	3.00	6.00
❑ 2173	Generation Gap Between Us/I'll Get Along	1970	—	3.00	6.00
❑ 2178	Part Time Love/I Still Love You	1970	—	3.00	6.00
❑ 2186	I Pity the Fool/Heartaches, Heartaches	1971	—	3.00	6.00
❑ 2198	Slipped, Tripped and Fell in Love/99 Lbs.	1971	—	3.00	6.00
❑ 2205	Breaking Up Somebody's Home/Troubles, Heartaches and Sadness	1972	—	3.00	6.00
❑ 2219	Somebody's On Your Case/I've Been There Before	1972	—	3.00	6.00
❑ 2232	I'm Gonna Tear Your Playhouse Down/One Way Street	1973	—	3.00	6.00
❑ 2248	I Can't Stand the Rain/I've Been There Before	1973	—	3.00	6.00

Number	Title (A Side/B Side)	Yr	VG	VG+	NM
❑ 2265	(You Keep Me) Hangin' On/Heartaches, Heartaches	1974	—	3.00	6.00
❑ 2271	Do I Need You/Love Vibration	1974	—	3.00	6.00
❑ 2278	Until You Came Into My Life/Put Yourself in My Place	1974	—	3.00	6.00
❑ 2284	Beware/You Got to Feed the Fire	1975	—	3.00	6.00
❑ 2294	Come to Mama/I'm Leaving You	1975	—	3.00	6.00
❑ 2302	Dr. Love Power/I Still Love You	1976	—	3.00	6.00
❑ 2309	I Don't Lend My Man/I Need Somebody	1976	—	3.00	6.00
❑ 2320	Fill This World with Love/It Was Jealousy	1976	—	3.00	6.00
❑ 77502	If This Is Heaven/Sailing	1977	—	2.50	5.00
❑ 78509	Old Man with Young Ideas/A Good Day for Lovin'	1978	—	2.50	5.00
❑ 78518	I Didn't Take Your Man/Being Here with You	1978	—	2.50	5.00
❑ 79528	If You've Got the Time (I've Got the Love)/Let Your Lovelight Shine	1979	—	2.50	5.00
❑ 80533	I'd Rather Leave While I'm in Love/Heartaches	1980	—	2.50	5.00
❑ 81534	Mon Belle-Amour/(B-side unknown)	1981	—	2.50	5.00
Albums					
HI					
❑ HLP-6002	If This Is Heaven	1977	3.00	6.00	12.00
❑ HLP-6007	The Handwriting Is On the Wall	1978	3.00	6.00	12.00
❑ HLP-8005	Part Time Love	197?	3.00	6.00	12.00
—Reissue of 32059					
❑ HLP-8009	Straight from the Heart	197?	3.00	6.00	12.00
—Reissue of 32065					
❑ SHL-32059	Part Time Love	1971	5.00	10.00	20.00
❑ SHL-32065	Straight from the Heart	1972	5.00	10.00	20.00
❑ XSHL-32079	I Can't Stand the Rain	1974	5.00	10.00	20.00
❑ SHL-32091	Tellin' It	1975	5.00	10.00	20.00

PELICANS, THE
45s
IMPERIAL

Number	Title (A Side/B Side)	Yr	VG	VG+	NM
❑ 5307	Chimes/Ain't Gonna Do It	1954	250.00	500.00	1000.
PARROT					
❑ 793	White Cliffs of Dover/Aurelia	1954	750.00	1500.	3000.
—Black vinyl					
❑ 793	White Cliffs of Dover/Aurelia	1954	3000.	4500.	6000.
—Red vinyl					
78s					
IMPERIAL					
❑ 5307	Chimes/Ain't Gonna Do It	1954	125.00	250.00	500.00
PARROT					
❑ 793	White Cliffs of Dover/Aurelia	1954	375.00	750.00	1500.

PENDERGRASS, TEDDY
Also see HAROLD MELVIN AND THE BLUE NOTES.
45s
ASYLUM

Number	Title (A Side/B Side)	Yr	VG	VG+	NM
❑ 69401	Joy/Let Me Be Closer	1988	—	—	3.00
❑ 69422	2 A.M./(Instrumental)	1988	—	2.00	4.00
❑ 69538	Lert Me Be Closer/Love Emergency	1986	—	2.00	4.00
❑ 69568	Love 4/2//One of Us Feels in Love	1986	—	2.00	4.00
❑ 69595	Never Felt Like Dancin'/Love Emergency	1985	—	2.00	4.00
❑ 69628	Somewhere I Belong/Hot Love	1985	—	2.00	4.00
❑ 69628 [PS]	Somewhere I Belong/Hot Love	1985	—	2.00	4.00
❑ 69669	In My Time/Stay with Me	1985	—	2.00	4.00
❑ 69696	You're My Choice Tonight (Choose Me)/So Sad the Song	1984	—	2.00	4.00
❑ 69720	Hold Me/Love	1984	—	2.00	4.00
—With Whitney Houston					
❑ 69720 [PS]	Hold Me/Love	1984	—	2.00	4.00
ELEKTRA					
❑ 69312	The Last Time/(B-side unknown)	1989	—	—	3.00
❑ 69358	Love Is the Power/I'm Ready	1988	—	—	3.00
❑ 69358 [PS]	Love Is the Power/I'm Ready	1988	—	—	3.00
❑ 69422	2 A.M./(Instrumental)	1988	—	—	3.00
PHILADELPHIA INT'L.					
❑ 02095	Can't You Try/Love T.K.O.	1981	—	2.00	4.00
❑ 02462	I Can't Live Without Your Love/You Must Live On	1981	—	2.00	4.00
❑ 02619	You're My Latest, Greatest Inspiration/Keep On Lovin' Me	1981	—	2.00	4.00
❑ 02856	Nine Times Out of Ten/This Gift of Life	1982	—	2.00	4.00
❑ 3107	Can't We Try/Plenty Good Lovin'	1980	—	2.50	5.00
❑ 3116	Love T.K.O./I Just Called to Say	1980	—	2.50	5.00
❑ 03116	Love T.K.O./I Just Called to Say	1982	—	—	3.00
—Reissue					
❑ 03284	I Can't Win for Losing/Don't Lead Me Out Along the Road	1982	—	2.00	4.00
❑ 03325	I Can't Win for Losing	1982	—	3.00	6.00
—One-sided budget release					
❑ 3622	I Don't Love You Anymore/Somebody Told Me	1977	—	2.50	5.00
❑ 3633	The Whole Town's Laughing at Me/The More I Get, The More I Want	1977	—	2.50	5.00
❑ 3648	Close the Door/Get Up, Get Down, Get Funky, Get Loose	1978	—	2.50	5.00
❑ 3657	Only You/It Don't Hurt Now	1978	—	2.50	5.00
❑ 3669	Life Is a Song Worth Singing/Cold, Cold World	1978	—	2.50	5.00
❑ 3696	Turn Off the Lights/If You Know Like I Know	1979	—	2.50	5.00
❑ 3717	Come Go with Me/Do Me	1979	—	2.50	5.00
❑ 3733	Shout and Scream/Close the Door	1979	—	2.50	5.00
❑ 3742	It's You I Love/Where Did All the Lovin' Go	1980	—	2.50	5.00
❑ 04302	Life Is for the Living/I Want My Baby Back	1984	—	2.00	4.00
❑ 70062	Is It Still Good to You/Girl You Know	1981	—	2.00	4.00

Number	Title (A Side/B Side)	Yr	VG	VG+	NM
Albums					
ASYLUM					
❑ 60317	Love Language	1984	2.00	4.00	8.00
❑ 60447	Workin' It Back	1985	2.00	4.00	8.00
ELEKTRA					
❑ 60775	Joy	1988	2.00	4.00	8.00
PHILADELPHIA INT'L.					
❑ PZ 34390	Teddy Pendergrass	1977	2.50	5.00	10.00
—No bar code on back cover					
❑ PZ 34390	Teddy Pendergrass	198?	2.00	4.00	8.00
—With bar code on back cover					
❑ PZ 35095	Life Is a Song Worth Singing	1978	2.50	5.00	10.00
—No bar code on back cover					
❑ PZ 35095	Life Is a Song Worth Singing	198?	2.00	4.00	8.00
—With bar code on back cover					
❑ FZ 36003	Teddy	1979	2.50	5.00	10.00
❑ PZ 36003	Teddy	198?	2.00	4.00	8.00
—Budget-line reissue with new prefix					
❑ KZ2 36294 [(2)]Teddy Live! Coast to Coast		1979	3.00	6.00	12.00
❑ FZ 36745	TP	1980	2.50	5.00	10.00
❑ PZ 36745	TP	198?	2.00	4.00	8.00
—Budget-line reissue with new prefix					
❑ FZ 37491	It's Time for Love	1981	2.50	5.00	10.00
❑ PZ 37491	It's Time for Love	198?	2.00	4.00	8.00
—Budget-line reissue with new prefix					
❑ FZ 38118	This One's for You	1982	2.50	5.00	10.00
❑ PZ 38118	This One's for You	198?	2.00	4.00	8.00
—Budget-line reissue with new prefix					
❑ FZ 38646	Heaven Only Knows	1983	2.50	5.00	10.00
❑ PZ 38646	Heaven Only Knows	1985	2.00	4.00	8.00
—Budget-line reissue with new prefix					
❑ FZ 39252	Greatest Hits	1984	2.50	5.00	10.00
❑ HZ 47491	It's Time for Love	198?	10.00	20.00	40.00
—Half-speed mastered edition					

PENGUINS, THE
45s
ATLANTIC

Number	Title (A Side/B Side)	Yr	VG	VG+	NM
❑ 1132	Pledge of Love/I Knew I'd Fall in Love	1957	7.50	15.00	30.00
DOOTO					
❑ 348	Earth Angel/Hey Senorita	1959	5.00	10.00	20.00
—Reissue on altered label name and yellow label					
❑ 428	That's How Much I Need You/Be My Lovin' Baby	1957	10.00	20.00	40.00
❑ 432	Sweet Love/Let Me Make Up Your Mind	1958	7.50	15.00	30.00
❑ 435	Do Not Pretend/If You're Mine	1958	7.50	15.00	30.00
DOOTONE					
❑ 345	No There Ain't No News Today/When I Am Gone	1954	75.00	150.00	300.00
—B-side by Dootsie Williams Orchestra					
❑ 348	Earth Angel/Hey Senorita	1954	37.50	75.00	150.00
—First pressings on glossy red labels					
❑ 348	Earth Angel/Hey Senorita	1955	12.50	25.00	50.00
—Maroon label					
❑ 348	Earth Angel/Hey Senorita	1955	10.00	20.00	40.00
—Blue label					
❑ 348	Earth Angel/Hey Senorita	1955	7.50	15.00	30.00
—Black label					
❑ 353	Love Will Make Your Mind Go Wild/Ookey Ook	1954	17.50	35.00	70.00
—First pressings on glossy red label					
❑ 353	Love Will Make Your Mind Go Wild/Ookey Ook	1955	12.50	25.00	50.00
—Maroon label					
❑ 353	Love Will Make Your Mind Go Wild/Ookey Ook	1955	10.00	20.00	40.00
—Blue label					
❑ 353	Love Will Make Your Mind Go Wild/Ookey Ook	1955	7.50	15.00	30.00
—Black label					
❑ 362	Baby, Let's Make Some Love/Kiss a Fool Goodbye	1955	12.50	25.00	50.00
ELDO					
❑ 119	Universal Twist/To Keep Our Love	1962	5.00	10.00	20.00
GLENVILLE					
❑ 101	Earth Angel/Hey Senorita	197?	—	3.00	6.00
—Reissue					
MERCURY					
❑ 70610	Don't Do It/Be Mine or Be a Fool	1955	12.50	25.00	50.00
—Black vinyl					
❑ 70610	Don't Do It/Be Mine or Be a Fool	1955	50.00	100.00	200.00
—Red vinyl					
❑ 70654	Walkin' Down Broadway/It Only Happens with You	1955	12.50	25.00	50.00
❑ 70703	Promises, Promises, Promises/The Devil That I See	1955	12.50	25.00	50.00
❑ 70762	A Christmas Prayer/Jingle Jangle	1956	20.00	40.00	80.00
❑ 70799	My Troubles Are Not At an End/She's Gone, Gone	1956	12.50	25.00	50.00
—Maroon label					
❑ 70799	My Troubles Are Not At an End/She's Gone, Gone	1956	6.25	12.50	25.00
—Black label					
❑ 70943	Earth Angel/Ice	1956	10.00	20.00	40.00
—Not the same recording as the hit on Dootone					
❑ 71033	Cool Baby Cool/Will You Be Mine	1957	10.00	20.00	40.00
ORIGINAL SOUND					
❑ 27	Memories of El Monte/Be Mine	1963	25.00	50.00	100.00
—Black and red label					
❑ 27	Memories of El Monte/Be Mine	1963	12.50	25.00	50.00
—Black and silver label; A-side written by Frank Zappa					
❑ 54	Heavenly Angel/Big Bobo's Party Train	1965	6.25	12.50	25.00

Number	Title (A Side/B Side)	Yr	VG	VG+	NM
POWER					
❑ 7023	Earth Angel/Hey Senorita	195?	2.00	4.00	8.00
—Reissue from "S.P.C. Newark, N.J."					
SUN STATE					
❑ 001	Believe Me/The Pony Rock	1962	6.25	12.50	25.00
WING					
❑ 90076	Dealer of Dreams/Peace of Mind	1956	7.50	15.00	30.00
7-Inch Extended Plays					
DOOTO					
❑ 241	Butterball/Heart of a Fool//Money Talks/Lover or Fool	1959	30.00	60.00	120.00
❑ 241 [PS]	The Cool, Cool Penguins Vol. 1	1959	30.00	60.00	120.00
❑ 243	(contents unknown)	1959	30.00	60.00	120.00
❑ 243 [PS]	The Cool, Cool Penguins, Vol. 2	1959	30.00	60.00	120.00
❑ 244	(contents unknown)	1959	30.00	60.00	120.00
❑ 244 [PS]	The Cool, Cool Penguins, Vol. 3	1959	30.00	60.00	120.00
DOOTONE					
❑ 101	Earth Angel/I Ain't Gonna Cry No More//Love Will Make Your Mind Go Wild/Baby Let's Make Some Love	1955	62.50	125.00	250.00
❑ 101 [PS]	The Penguins	1955	62.50	125.00	250.00
—Issued in "Dootone" jacket rather than custom jacket					
Albums					
COLLECTABLES					
❑ COL-5045	Golden Classics	198?	2.50	5.00	10.00
DOOTO					
❑ DTL-204 [M]	The Best Vocal Groups...Rhythm and Blues	1959	50.00	100.00	200.00
—Reissue of Dootone 204; blue and yellow label					
❑ DTL-204 [M]	The Best Vocal Groups...Rhythm and Blues	196?	25.00	50.00	100.00
—Black label with gold/orange/blue ring. This is NOT a counterfeit.					
❑ DTL-242 [M]	The Cool, Cool Penguins	1959	175.00	350.00	700.00
—Red and yellow label					
❑ DTL-242 [M]	The Cool, Cool Penguins	1959	175.00	350.00	700.00
—Blue and yellow label					
❑ DTL-242 [M]	The Cool, Cool Penguins	196?	50.00	100.00	200.00
—Black label with gold/orange/blue ring. This is NOT a counterfeit.					
DOOTONE					
❑ DTL-204 [M]	The Best Vocal Groups...Rhythm and Blues	1957	375.00	750.00	1500.
—Also includes tracks by the Medallions, Don Julian and the Meadowlarks, and the Dootones. Flat maroon label.					
❑ DTL-204 [M]	The Best Vocal Groups...Rhythm and Blues	195?	125.00	250.00	500.00
—As above; glossy maroon label					

PENTAGONS, THE

Number	Title (A Side/B Side)	Yr	VG	VG+	NM
45s					
DONNA					
❑ 1337	To Be Loved (Forever)/Down at the Beach	1961	7.50	15.00	30.00
❑ 1344	I Like the Way You Look (At Me)/For a Love That Is Mine	1961	7.50	15.00	30.00
FLEET INT'L.					
❑ 100	Down at the Beach/To Be Loved (Forever)	1960	50.00	100.00	200.00
—Original record has "Down at the Beach" labeled as "100-1" and "To Be Loved (Forever)" as "100-2"					
JAMIE					
❑ 1201	I Wonder/She's Mine	1961	3.75	7.50	15.00
❑ 1210	Until Then/I'm in Love	1962	3.75	7.50	15.00

PEOPLE'S CHOICE

Number	Title (A Side/B Side)	Yr	VG	VG+	NM
45s					
CASABLANCA					
❑ 2322	My Feet Won't Move, But My Shoes Did the Boogie/You Ought to Be Dancin'	1980	—	2.00	4.00
PALMER					
❑ 5020	Easy to Be True/Savin' My Love for You	1967	62.50	125.00	250.00
PHIL-L.A. OF SOUL					
❑ 349	I Likes to Do It/Big Ladies Man	1971	—	3.00	6.00
❑ 352	Wootie-T-Woo/'Cause That's the Way I Know	1971	—	3.00	6.00
❑ 356	Magic/Oh How I Love It	1972	—	3.00	6.00
❑ 358	Let Me Do My Thing/On a Cloudy Day	1972	—	3.00	6.00
PHILADELPHIA INT'L.					
❑ 3649	Turn Me Loose/Soft and Tender	1978	—	2.00	4.00
❑ 3658	Rough-Ride/Stay with Me	1978	—	2.00	4.00
PHILIPS					
❑ 40653	Keep On Holding On/Just Look What You've Done	1969	3.00	6.00	12.00
TSOP					
❑ 4751	Love Shot/The Big Hurt	1973	—	2.50	5.00
❑ 4759	Party Is a Groovy Thing/Asking for Trouble	1974	—	2.50	5.00
❑ 4769	Do It Any Way You Wanna/The Big Hurt	1975	—	2.50	5.00
❑ 4773	Nursery Rhymes (Part 1)/Nursery Rhymes (Part 2)	1975	—	2.50	5.00
❑ 4781	Here We Go Again/Mickey D's	1976	—	2.50	5.00
❑ 4782	Movin' In All Directions/Mellow Hood	1976	—	2.50	5.00
❑ 4784	Cold Blooded & Down-Right Funky/Jam, Jam, Jam (All Night Long)	1976	—	2.50	5.00
❑ 4786	If You Gonna Do It (Put Your Mind To It) (Part I)/ If You Gonna Do It (Put Your Mind To It) (Part II)	1977	—	2.50	5.00
Albums					
PHILADELPHIA INT'L.					
❑ JZ 35363	Turn Me Loose	1978	2.50	5.00	10.00
TSOP					
❑ KZ 33154	Boogie Down U.S.A.	1975	2.50	5.00	10.00
❑ PZ 34124	We Got the Rhythm	1976	2.50	5.00	10.00

PERSONALITIES, THE

Number	Title (A Side/B Side)	Yr	VG	VG+	NM
45s					
SAFARI					
❑ 1002	Woe Woe Baby/Yours to Command	1957	50.00	100.00	200.00
—With giraffe on label					
❑ 1002	Woe Woe Baby/Yours to Command	1957	12.50	25.00	50.00
—No giraffe on label					

PERSUADERS, THE

More than one group?

Number	Title (A Side/B Side)	Yr	VG	VG+	NM
45s					
ATCO					
❑ 6822	Thin Line Between Love and Hate/Thigh Spy	1971	2.50	5.00	10.00
❑ 6919	Bad, Bold and Beautiful Girl/Please Stay	1973	—	3.50	7.00
❑ 6943	Some Guys Have All the Luck/Love Attack	1973	2.00	4.00	8.00
❑ 6956	Best Thing That Ever Happened to Me/The Way She Is	1974	—	3.50	7.00
❑ 6964	All Strung Out on You/Once in a Lifetime Thing	1974	—	3.50	7.00
❑ 7012	I've Been Through This Before/Stay with Me	1975	—	3.50	7.00
BUM BUM					
❑ 701	Miserlou/World of Wonder	196?	7.50	15.00	30.00
CALLA					
❑ 3006	I Need Love/Sure Shot	1977	—	3.00	6.00
❑ 3007	Trying to Love Two Women/Quickest Way Out	1977	—	3.00	6.00
CARLTON					
❑ 568	Arabella/Viva El Matador	1962	3.75	7.50	15.00
WIN OR LOSE					
❑ 220	Love Gonna Pack Up (And Walk Out)/You Musta Put Something In Your Love	1971	2.00	4.00	8.00
❑ 222	If This Is What You Call Love (I Don't Want No Part of It)/Thanks for Loving Me	1972	2.00	4.00	8.00
❑ 225	Peace in the Valley of Love/What Is the Definition of Love	1972	2.00	4.00	8.00
WINLEY					
❑ 235	Tears/What Could It Be	1959	37.50	75.00	150.00
Albums					
ATCO					
❑ SD 7021	The Persuaders	1973	5.00	10.00	20.00
❑ SD 7046	Best Thing That Ever Happened to Me	1974	5.00	10.00	20.00
CALLA					
❑ PZ 34802	It's All About Love	1977	3.75	7.50	15.00
COLLECTABLES					
❑ COL-5139	Thin Line Between Love and Hate (Golden Classics)	198?	2.50	5.00	10.00
WIN OR LOSE					
❑ SD 33-387	Thin Line Between Love and Hate	1972	6.25	12.50	25.00

PERSUASIONS, THE

Number	Title (A Side/B Side)	Yr	VG	VG+	NM
45s					
A&M					
❑ 1531	I Really Got It Bad for You/We're All Goin' Home	1974	—	3.00	6.00
❑ 1631	With This Ring/Somewhere to Lay My Head	1974	—	3.00	6.00
❑ 1658	I Just Want to Sing with My Friends/Somewhere to Lay My Head	1975	—	3.00	6.00
❑ 1698	One Thing on My Mind/Darlin'	1975	—	3.00	6.00
CAPITOL					
❑ 3162	Let It Be/It's You That I Need	1971	2.00	4.00	8.00
❑ 3242	Don't Know Why I Love You/Tempts Jam	1971	2.00	4.00	8.00
❑ 3317	People Get Ready/Buffalo Soldier	1972	2.00	4.00	8.00
❑ 3425	The Ten Commandments of Love/Good Times	1972	2.00	4.00	8.00
❑ 3492	Three Angels (Part 1)/Three Angels (Part 2)	1972	2.00	4.00	8.00
ELEKTRA					
❑ 45396	Papa-Oom-Mow-Mow/Women and Drinkin'	1977	—	2.50	5.00
MCA					
❑ 40080	Good Old Accapella/You Must Believe in Me	1973	—	3.00	6.00
❑ 40118	Chapel of Love/Love You Most of All	1973	—	3.00	6.00
REPRISE					
❑ 0977	Since I Fell for You/Without a Song	1970	2.00	4.00	8.00
TOWER					
❑ 146	Try Me/I'll Go Crazy	1965	2.50	5.00	10.00
❑ 197	Big Brother/Deep Down Love	1966	2.50	5.00	10.00
Albums					
A&M					
❑ SP-3635	More Than Before	1974	3.00	6.00	12.00
❑ SP-3656	I Just Want to Sing with My Friends	1974	3.00	6.00	12.00
CAPITOL					
❑ SM-791	We Came to Play	197?	2.50	5.00	10.00
—Reissue with new prefix					
❑ ST-791	We Came to Play	1971	6.25	12.50	25.00
❑ ST-872	Street Corner Symphony	1972	6.25	12.50	25.00
❑ ST-11101	Spread the Word	1972	6.25	12.50	25.00
CATAMOUNT					
❑ 905	Stardust	197?	10.00	20.00	40.00
ELEKTRA					
❑ 7E-1099	Chirpin'	1977	3.00	6.00	12.00
FLYING FISH					
❑ FF-093	Comin' At Ya	1979	3.00	6.00	12.00
MCA					
❑ 326	We Still Ain't Got No Band	1973	3.75	7.50	15.00
REPRISE					
❑ RS 6394	Acapella	1970	7.50	15.00	30.00

Number	Title (A Side/B Side)	Yr	VG	VG+	NM
ROUNDER					
❏ 3053	Good News	1981	2.50	5.00	10.00
❏ 3083	No Frills	1984	2.50	5.00	10.00

PHILLIPS, ESTHER
Includes records as "Little Esther" and "Little Esther Phillips."

12-Inch Singles
MERCURY

Number	Title (A Side/B Side)	Yr	VG	VG+	NM
❏ 90 [DJ]	Oo-Oop-Oo-Oop (Long Version)/Oo-Oop-Oo-Oop (Edit)	1979	3.00	6.00	12.00
❏ 101 [DJ]	Our Day Will Come (same on both sides)	1979	3.00	6.00	12.00
WINNING					
❏ 1002	Turn Me Out (4:39) (5:51)	1983	2.50	5.00	10.00

45s
ATLANTIC

Number	Title (A Side/B Side)	Yr	VG	VG+	NM
❏ 2223	Hello Walls/Double Crossing Blues	1964	3.75	7.50	15.00
—With Jimmy Ricks					
❏ 2229	No Headstone on My Grave/Mo Jo Hannah	1964	3.75	7.50	15.00
❏ 2251	It's Too Soon to Know/You're the Reason I'm Living	1964	3.75	7.50	15.00
❏ 2265	Half a Heart/Some Things You Never Get Used To	1964	3.75	7.50	15.00
❏ 2281	And I Love Him/Shangri-La	1965	3.00	6.00	12.00
❏ 2294	Moonglow & Theme from Picnic/Makin' Whoopee	1965	3.00	6.00	12.00
❏ 2304	Let Me Know When It's Over/I Saw Me	1965	3.00	6.00	12.00
❏ 2324	Just Say Goodbye/I Could Have Told You	1966	3.00	6.00	12.00
❏ 2335	When a Woman Loves a Man/Ups and Downs	1966	3.00	6.00	12.00
❏ 2360	Somebody Else Is Taking My Place/When Love Comes to the Human Race	1966	3.00	6.00	12.00
❏ 2370	Fever/Try Me	1966	3.00	6.00	12.00
❏ 2411	Release Me/Don't Feel Rained	1967	2.50	5.00	10.00
❏ 2417	I'm Sorry/Cheater Man	1967	2.50	5.00	10.00
❏ 2745	Brand New Day/Set Me Free	1970	—	3.00	6.00
❏ 2775	Crazy Love/All God Has Is Us	1970	—	3.00	6.00
❏ 2783	Catch Me I'm Falling/Woman Will Do Wrong	1971	—	3.00	6.00
❏ 2800	Cry Me a River Blues/I'm Getting 'Long Alright	1971	—	3.00	6.00
DECCA					
❏ 28804	If You Want Me/Talkin' All Out of My Head	1953	10.00	20.00	40.00
❏ 48305	Please Don't Send Me/Stop Crying	1953	10.00	20.00	40.00
❏ 48314	Sit Back Down/He's a No Good Man	1954	15.00	30.00	60.00
FEDERAL					
❏ 12023	I'm a Bad, Bad Girl/Don't Make a Fool Out of Me	1951	20.00	40.00	80.00
❏ 12036	Heart to Heart/Looking for a Man to Satisfy My Soul	1951	125.00	250.00	500.00
—With the Dominoes					
❏ 12042	Cryin' and Singin' the Blues/Tell Him That I Need Him	1951	20.00	40.00	80.00
❏ 12055	Ring-a-Ding-Doo/The Crying Blues	1952	17.50	35.00	70.00
❏ 12063	Summertime/The Storm	1952	17.50	35.00	70.00
❏ 12065	Better Beware/I'll Be There	1952	17.50	35.00	70.00
❏ 12078	Aged and Mellow/Bring My Lovin' Back to Me	1952	17.50	35.00	70.00
❏ 12090	Somebody New/Ramblin' Blues	1952	17.50	35.00	70.00
❏ 12100	Saturday Night Daddy/Mainliner	1952	75.00	150.00	300.00
—With Bobby Nunn					
❏ 12108	Last Laugh Blues/Flesh, Blood and Bones	1952	17.50	35.00	70.00
—With Little Willie Littlefield					
❏ 12115	Hollerin' and Screamin'/Turn the Lamp Down Low	1953	17.50	35.00	70.00
—With Little Willie Littlefield					
❏ 12122	You Took My Love Too Fast/Street Lights	1953	75.00	150.00	300.00
—With Bobby Nunn					
❏ 12126	Hound Dog/Sweet Lips	1953	17.50	35.00	70.00
❏ 12142	Cherry Wine/Love Oh Love	1953	17.50	35.00	70.00
KUDU					
❏ 904	Home Is Where the Hatred Is/Til My Back Ain't Got No Bone	1972	—	2.50	5.00
❏ 906	Baby I'm for Real/That's All Right with Me	1972	—	2.50	5.00
❏ 910	I've Never Found a Man (To Love Me Like You Do)/Cherry Red	1972	—	2.50	5.00
❏ 915	Use Me/Let Me in Your Life	1973	—	2.50	5.00
❏ 917	Justified/Too Many Roads	1973	—	2.50	5.00
❏ 921	Such a Night/Can't Trust Your Neighbor	1974	—	2.50	5.00
❏ 922	Disposable Society/(B-side unknown)	1974	—	2.50	5.00
❏ 925	What a Difference a Day Makes/Turn Around, Look at Me	1975	—	2.50	5.00
❏ 929	For All We Know/Fever	1976	—	2.50	5.00
❏ 936	Boy I Really Tied One On/Magic's in the Air	1976	—	2.50	5.00
❏ 938	Higher and Higher/All the Way Down	1976	—	2.50	5.00
LENOX					
❏ 5555	Release Me/Don't Feel Rained On	1962	7.50	15.00	30.00
❏ 5560	Am I That Easy to Forget/I Really Don't Want to Know	1963	5.00	10.00	20.00
❏ 5565	You Never Miss Your Water (Till the Well Runs Dry)/If You Want It (I've Got It)	1963	5.00	10.00	20.00
—As "Little Esther Phillips and Big Al Downing"					
❏ 5570	Why Should We Try Anymore/While It Lasted	1963	5.00	10.00	20.00
❏ 5575	Don't Let Me Go/Why Was I Born	1963	5.00	10.00	20.00
❏ 5577	A Lover's Hymn/God Bless the Child Who's Got His Own	1963	5.00	10.00	20.00
MERCURY					
❏ 73967	Love Addict/I've Never Been a Woman Before	1977	—	2.00	4.00
❏ 74030	There You Go Again (There She Goes Again)/Stormy Weather	1978	—	2.00	4.00
❏ 74060	Oo-Oop-Oo-Oop/I'll Close My Eyes	1979	—	2.00	4.00
❏ 74077	Our Day Will Come/Mr. Melody	1979	—	2.00	4.00

Number	Title (A Side/B Side)	Yr	VG	VG+	NM
ROULETTE					
❏ 7031	Too Late to Worry, Too Blue to Cry/I'm in the Mood for Love	1969	—	3.50	7.00
❏ 7049	Tonight I'll Be Staying Here with You/Sweet Dreams	1969	—	3.50	7.00
❏ 7059	Nobody But You/Too Much of a Man	1969	—	3.50	7.00
SAVOY					
❏ 1193	You Can Bet Your Life/'Tain't Whatcha Say It's Whatcha Do	1956	6.25	12.50	25.00
❏ 1516	Longing in My Heart/If It's News to Me	1957	5.00	10.00	20.00
❏ 1563	It's So Good/Do You Ever Think of Me	1959	3.75	7.50	15.00
WARWICK					
❏ 610	Gee Baby/Wild Child	1961	3.75	7.50	15.00
WINNING					
❏ 1001	Turn Me Out/(B-side unknown)	1983	—	2.50	5.00

Albums
ATLANTIC

Number	Title (A Side/B Side)	Yr	VG	VG+	NM
❏ SD 1565	Burnin'	1970	6.25	12.50	25.00
❏ SD 1680	Confessin' the Blues	1975	3.75	7.50	15.00
❏ 8102 [M]	And I Love Him	1965	12.50	25.00	50.00
—Cover has a pink Cupid on it					
❏ 8102 [M]	And I Love Him	1966	7.50	15.00	30.00
—Cover has a black photo on it					
❏ SD 8102 [S]	And I Love Him	1965	20.00	40.00	80.00
—Cover has a pink Cupid on it					
❏ SD 8102 [S]	And I Love Him	1966	10.00	20.00	40.00
—Cover has a black photo on it					
❏ 8122 [M]	Esther	1966	7.50	15.00	30.00
❏ SD 8122 [S]	Esther	1966	10.00	20.00	40.00
❏ 8130 [M]	The Country Side of Esther Phillips	1966	7.50	15.00	30.00
—Reissue of Lenox 227					
❏ SD 8130 [S]	The Country Side of Esther Phillips	1966	10.00	20.00	40.00
—Reissue of Lenox S-227					
❏ 90670	Confessin' the Blues	1987	2.50	5.00	10.00
—Reissue of 1680					
CBS ASSOCIATED					
❏ PZ 40710	What a Diff'rence a Day Makes	1987	2.00	4.00	8.00
—Reissue of Kudu 23					
❏ PZ 40935	From a Whisper to a Scream	1988	2.00	4.00	8.00
—Reissue of Kudu 05					
KING					
❏ 622 [M]	Memory Lane	1959	1000.	2000.	4000.
KUDU					
❏ 05	From a Whisper to a Scream	1972	3.00	6.00	12.00
❏ 09	Alone Again, Naturally	1972	3.00	6.00	12.00
❏ 14	Black-Eyed Blues	1973	3.00	6.00	12.00
❏ 18	Performance	1974	3.00	6.00	12.00
❏ 23	What a Diff'rence a Day Makes	1975	3.00	6.00	12.00
❏ 28	For All We Know	1976	3.00	6.00	12.00
❏ 31	Capricorn Princess	1976	3.00	6.00	12.00
LENOX					
❏ 227 [M]	Release Me	1962	25.00	50.00	100.00
❏ S-227 [S]	Release Me	1962	50.00	100.00	200.00
MERCURY					
❏ SRM-1-1187	You've Come a Long Way, Baby	1977	2.50	5.00	10.00
❏ SRM-1-3733	All About Esther Phillips	1978	2.50	5.00	10.00
❏ SRM-1-3769	Here's Esther — Are You Ready?	1979	2.50	5.00	10.00
❏ SRM-1-4005	A Good Black Is Hard to Crack	1981	2.50	5.00	10.00
MUSE					
❏ MR-5302	A Way to Say Goodbye	1986	3.00	6.00	12.00
SAVOY JAZZ					
❏ SJL-2258	The Complete Savoy Recordings	1984	2.50	5.00	10.00

PIANO RED
Also see DR. FEELGOOD AND THE INTERNS.

45s
CHECKER

Number	Title (A Side/B Side)	Yr	VG	VG+	NM
❏ 911	Get Up Mare/So Worried	1958	7.50	15.00	30.00
GROOVE					
❏ 0023	Decatur Street Blues/Big Rock Joe from Kokomo	1954	7.50	15.00	30.00
❏ 0101	Pay It No Mind/Jump, Man, Jump	1955	7.50	15.00	30.00
❏ 0118	Six O'Clock Bounce/Goodbye	1955	7.50	15.00	30.00
❏ 0126	Red's Blues/Gordy's Rock	1955	7.50	15.00	30.00
❏ 0136	Jumpin' with Daddy/She Knocks Me Out	1956	7.50	15.00	30.00
❏ 0145	I'm Nobody's Fool/That's My Desire	1956	7.50	15.00	30.00
❏ 0169	Woo-Ee/You Were Mine for Awhile	1956	7.50	15.00	30.00
JAX					
❏ 1000	This Old World/I Feel Good	1959	3.75	7.50	15.00
❏ 1006	Guitar Walk/I've Been Walkin'	1959	3.75	7.50	15.00
KING					
❏ 6330	I Want a Bowlegged Woman/Underground Atlanta	1970	—	2.50	5.00
RCA VICTOR					
❏ 47-4265	Diggin' the Boogie/Let's Have a Good Time Tonight	1951	15.00	30.00	60.00
❏ 47-4380	Hey Good Lookin'/It Makes No Difference Now	1951	15.00	30.00	60.00
❏ 47-4524	Bouncin' with Red/Count the Days I'm Gone	1952	15.00	30.00	60.00
❏ 47-4766	She Walks Right In/Sales Tax Boogie	1952	15.00	30.00	60.00
❏ 47-4957	Yoo Doopee Doo/Daybreak	1952	15.00	30.00	60.00
❏ 47-5101	I'm Gonna Rock Some More/Everybody's Boogie	1952	12.50	25.00	50.00
❏ 47-5224	She's Dynamite/I'm Gonna Tell Everybody	1953	10.00	20.00	40.00
❏ 47-5337	Decatur Street Boogie/Your Mouth's Got a Hole In It	1953	10.00	20.00	40.00
❏ 47-5544	Right and Read, Taxi, Taxi 6963	1953	10.00	20.00	40.00

Number	Title (A Side/B Side)	Yr	VG	VG+	NM
❑ 47-6856	Wild Fire/Rock Baby	1957	5.00	10.00	20.00
❑ 47-6953	Peachtree Parade/Please Don't Talk About Me	1957	5.00	10.00	20.00
❑ 47-7065	South/Coo Cha	1957	5.00	10.00	20.00
❑ 47-7217	Comin' On/One Glimpse of Heaven	1958	5.00	10.00	20.00
❑ 50-0099	Rockin' with Red/Red's Boogie	1950	37.50	75.00	150.00
—Gray label, orange vinyl					
❑ 50-0106	The Wrong Yo-Yo/My Gal Jo	1951	15.00	30.00	60.00
❑ 50-0118	Jumpin' the Boogie/Just Right Bounce	1951	15.00	30.00	60.00
❑ 50-0130	Layin' the Boogie/Baby What's Wrong	1951	15.00	30.00	60.00

7-Inch Extended Plays

Number	Title (A Side/B Side)	Yr	VG	VG+	NM
GROOVE					
❑ EGA-3	(contents unknown)	1956	25.00	50.00	100.00
❑ EGA-3 [PS]	Jump, Man, Jump	1956	25.00	50.00	100.00
❑ EGA-26	(contents unknown)	1956	15.00	30.00	60.00
❑ EGA-26 [PS]	Piano Red In Concert, Vol. 1	1956	15.00	30.00	60.00
❑ EGA-27	(contents unknown)	1956	15.00	30.00	60.00
❑ EGA-27 [PS]	Piano Red In Concert, Vol. 2	1956	15.00	30.00	60.00
❑ EGA-28	(contents unknown)	1956	15.00	30.00	60.00
❑ EGA-28 [PS]	Piano Red In Concert, Vol. 3	1956	15.00	30.00	60.00
RCA VICTOR					
❑ EPA-587	(contents unknown)	1954	25.00	50.00	100.00
❑ EPA-587 [PS]	Rockin' with Red	1954	25.00	50.00	100.00
❑ EPA-5091	(contents unknown)	1959	25.00	50.00	100.00
—Maroon label					
❑ EPA-5091	(contents unknown)	1959	12.50	25.00	50.00
—Black label					
❑ EPA-5091 [PS]	Rockin' with Red	1959	12.50	25.00	50.00

Albums

Number	Title (A Side/B Side)	Yr	VG	VG+	NM
ARHOOLIE					
❑ 1064	William Perryman (Alone with Piano)	197?	3.00	6.00	12.00
EUPHONIC					
❑ 1212	Percussive Piano	198?	2.50	5.00	10.00
GROOVE					
❑ LG-1001 [M]	Jump Man, Jump	1956	—	—	—
—The existence of this LP has not been confirmed					
❑ LG-1002 [M]	Piano Red in Concert	1956	150.00	300.00	600.00
KING					
❑ KS-1117	Happiness Is Piano Red	1970	5.00	10.00	20.00
RCA CAMDEN					
❑ ACL1-0547	Rockin' with Red	1974	3.00	6.00	12.00
SOUTHLAND					
❑ 8	Willie Perryman-Piano Red-Dr. Feelgood	1983	3.75	7.50	15.00

PICKETT, WILSON

Also see THE FALCONS.

12-Inch Singles

Number	Title (A Side/B Side)	Yr	VG	VG+	NM
MOTOWN					
❑ 217	Land of a Thousand Dances (4 versions)/Just Let Her Know	1987	2.00	4.00	8.00

45s

Number	Title (A Side/B Side)	Yr	VG	VG+	NM
ATLANTIC					
❑ 2233	I'm Gonna Cry/For Better or Worse	1964	3.75	7.50	15.00
❑ 2271	Come Home Baby/Take a Little Love	1965	3.75	7.50	15.00
❑ 2289	In the Midnight Hour/I'm Not Tired	1965	3.75	7.50	15.00
❑ 2306	Don't Fight It/It's All Over	1965	3.75	7.50	15.00
❑ 2320	634-5789 (Soulsville, U.S.A.)/That's a Man's Way	1966	3.75	7.50	15.00
❑ 2334	Ninety-Nine and a Half (Won't Do)/Danger Zone	1966	3.75	7.50	15.00
❑ 2348	Land of 1000 Dances/You're So Fine	1966	3.75	7.50	15.00
❑ 2365	Mustang Sally/Three Time Loser	1966	3.75	7.50	15.00
❑ 2381	Eveybody Needs Somebody to Love/Nothing You Can Do	1967	3.00	6.00	12.00
❑ 2394	I Found a Love — Part I/I Found a Love — Part II	1967	3.00	6.00	12.00
❑ 2412	Soul Dance Number Three/You Can't Stand Alone	1967	3.00	6.00	12.00
❑ 2430	Funky Broadway/I'm Sorry About That	1967	3.00	6.00	12.00
❑ 2448	Stag-O-Lee/I'm In Love	1967	3.00	6.00	12.00
❑ 2484	Jealous Love/I've Come a Long Way	1968	2.50	5.00	10.00
❑ 2504	She's Lookin' Good/We've Got to Have Love	1968	2.50	5.00	10.00
❑ 2528	I'm a Midnight Mover/Deborah	1968	2.50	5.00	10.00
❑ 2558	I Found a True Love/For Better or Worse	1968	2.50	5.00	10.00
❑ 2575	A Man and a Half/People Make the World (What It Is)	1968	2.50	5.00	10.00
❑ 2591	Hey Jude/Search Your Heart	1968	2.50	5.00	10.00
❑ 2611	Mini-Skirt Minnie/Back in Your Arms	1969	2.00	4.00	8.00
❑ 2631	Born to Be Wild/Toe Hold	1969	2.00	4.00	8.00
❑ 2648	Hey Joe/Night Owl	1969	2.00	4.00	8.00
❑ 2682	You Keep Me Hangin' On/Now You See Me, Now You Don't	1969	2.00	4.00	8.00
❑ 2722	Sugar, Sugar/Cole, Cooke, and Redding	1970	2.00	4.00	8.00
❑ 2753	She Said Yes/It's Still Good	1970	—	3.00	6.00
❑ 2765	Engine Number Nine/International Playboy	1970	—	3.00	6.00
❑ 2781	Don't Let the Green Grass Fool You/Ain't No Doubt About It	1971	—	3.00	6.00
❑ 2797	Don't Knock My Love (Part 1)/Don't Knock My Love (Part 2)	1971	—	3.00	6.00
❑ 2824	Call My Name, I'll Be There/Woman Let Me Down Home	1971	—	3.00	6.00
❑ 2852	Fire and Water/Pledging My Love	1971	—	3.00	6.00
❑ 2878	Funk Factory/One Step Away	1972	—	3.00	6.00
❑ 2909	Mama Told Me Not to Come/Covering the Same Old Ground	1972	—	3.00	6.00
❑ 2961	Come Right Here/International Playboy	1973	—	3.00	6.00
BIG TREE					
❑ 16121	Who Turned You On/Dance You Down	1978	—	2.50	5.00
❑ 16129	Groovin'/Time to Let the Sun Shine In	1978	—	2.50	5.00
CORREC-TONE					
❑ 501	Let Me Be Your Boy/My Heart Belongs to You	1962	15.00	30.00	60.00
CUB					
❑ 9113	Let Me Be Your Boy/My Heart Belongs to You	1962	7.50	15.00	30.00
DOUBLE L					
❑ 713	If You Need Me/Baby Call on Me	1963	5.00	10.00	20.00
❑ 717	It's Too Late/I'm Gonna Love You	1963	5.00	10.00	20.00
❑ 724	I'm Down to My Last Heartbreak/I Can't Stop	1963	3.75	7.50	15.00
EMI AMERICA					
❑ 8027	I Want You/Love of My Life	1979	—	2.50	5.00
❑ 8034	Live with Me/Granny	1980	—	2.50	5.00
❑ 8070	Ain't Gonna Give You No More/Don't Underestimate the Power of Love	1981	—	2.50	5.00
❑ 8082	Back on the Right Track/It's You	1981	—	2.50	5.00
ERVA					
❑ 318	Love Dagger/Time to Let the Sun Shine on Me	1977	—	2.50	5.00
MOTOWN					
❑ 1898	Don't Turn Away/Can't Stop Now	1987	—	2.00	4.00
❑ 1916	In the Midnight Hour/Just Let Her Know	1987	—	2.00	4.00
❑ 1938	Love Never Let Me Down/Just Let Her Know	1988	—	2.00	4.00
❑ 53407	Love Never Let Me Down/Just Let Her Know	1988	—	2.00	4.00
PHILCO-FORD					
❑ HP-11	Land of a 1000 Dances/Midnight Hour	1967	3.75	7.50	15.00
—4-inch plastic "Hip Pocket Record" with color sleeve					
RCA VICTOR					
❑ 74-0908	Mr. Magic Man/I Sho' Love You	1973	—	3.00	6.00
❑ APBO-0049	Take a Closer Look at the Woman You're With/Two Woman and a Wife	1973	—	3.00	6.00
❑ APBO-0174	Soft Soul Boogie Woogie/Take That Pollution Out of Your Throat	1973	—	3.00	6.00
❑ APBO-0309	Take Your Pleasure Where You FInd It/What Good Is a Lie	1974	—	3.00	6.00
❑ PB-10067	I Was Too Nice/Isn't That So	1974	—	3.00	6.00
VERVE					
❑ 10378	Let Me Be Your Boy/My Heart Belongs to You	1966	5.00	10.00	20.00
WICKED					
❑ 8101	The Best Part of a Man/How Will I Ever Know	1975	—	3.00	6.00
❑ 8102	Love Will Keep Us Together/It's Gonna Be Good	1976	—	3.00	6.00

7-Inch Extended Plays

Number	Title (A Side/B Side)	Yr	VG	VG+	NM
ATLANTIC					
❑ SD 8129	Something You Got/Barefootin'/Land of 1000 Dances//In the Midnight Hour/Ninety-Nine and a Half (Won't Do)/I'm Drifting	1966	3.75	7.50	15.00
—Jukebox issue; small hole, plays at 33 1/3 rpm					
❑ SD 8129 [PS]	The Exciting Wilson Pickett	1966	3.75	7.50	15.00
❑ SD 7-8250	Groovy Little Woman/Funky Way/It's Still Good//This Old Town/You Keep Me Hangin' On	1970	3.00	6.00	12.00
—Jukebox issue; small hole, plays at 33 1/3 rpm					
❑ SD 7-8250 [PS]	Right On	1970	3.00	6.00	12.00

Albums

Number	Title (A Side/B Side)	Yr	VG	VG+	NM
ATLANTIC					
❑ SD 2-501 [(2)]	Wilson Pickett's Greatest Hits	1973	5.00	10.00	20.00
❑ 8114 [M]	In the Midnight Hour	1965	10.00	20.00	40.00
❑ SD 8114 [R]	In the Midnight Hour	1965	7.50	15.00	30.00
❑ 8129 [M]	The Exciting Wilson Pickett	1966	10.00	20.00	40.00
❑ SD 8129 [R]	The Exciting Wilson Pickett	1966	7.50	15.00	30.00
❑ 8136 [M]	The Wicked Pickett	1967	10.00	20.00	40.00
❑ SD 8136 [R]	The Wicked Pickett	1967	7.50	15.00	30.00
❑ 8145 [M]	The Sound of Wilson Pickett	1967	10.00	20.00	40.00
❑ SD 8145 [P]	The Sound of Wilson Pickett	1967	10.00	20.00	40.00
❑ 8151 [M]	The Best of Wilson Pickett	1967	10.00	20.00	40.00
❑ SD 8151 [R]	The Best of Wilson Pickett	1967	5.00	10.00	20.00
❑ SD 8175	I'm in Love	1968	6.25	12.50	25.00
❑ SD 8183	The Midnight Mover	1968	6.25	12.50	25.00
❑ SD 8215	Hey Jude	1969	5.00	10.00	20.00
❑ SD 8250	Right On	1970	5.00	10.00	20.00
❑ SD 8270	Wilson Pickett in Philadelphia	1970	5.00	10.00	20.00
❑ 8290 [M]	The Best of Wilson Pickett, Vol. II	1971	6.25	12.50	25.00
—Mono copies are promo only					
❑ SD 8290 [S]	The Best of Wilson Pickett, Vol. II	1971	3.75	7.50	15.00
❑ SD 8300	Don't Knock My Love	1971	3.75	7.50	15.00
❑ 81283	The Best of Wilson Pickett	1985	2.50	5.00	10.00
BIG TREE					
❑ SD 76011	Funky Situation	1978	3.00	6.00	12.00
DOUBLE-L					
❑ DL-2300 [M]	It's Too Late	1963	12.50	25.00	50.00
❑ SDL-8300 [S]	It's Too Late	1963	17.50	35.00	70.00
EMI AMERICA					
❑ SW-17019	I Want You	1979	3.00	6.00	12.00
❑ SW-17043	Right Track	1981	3.00	6.00	12.00
MOTOWN					
❑ 6244 ML	American Soul Man	1987	2.50	5.00	10.00
RCA VICTOR					
❑ APL1-0312	Miz Lena's Boy	1973	3.75	7.50	15.00
❑ APL1-0495	Pickett in the Pocket	1974	3.75	7.50	15.00
❑ APL1-0856	Join Me and Let's Be Free	1975	3.75	7.50	15.00
❑ ANL1-2149	Join Me and Let's Be Free	1977	2.50	5.00	10.00
—Reissue					
❑ LSP-4858	Mr. Magic Man	1973	3.75	7.50	15.00
TRIP					
❑ 8010	Wickedness	1972	2.50	5.00	10.00
WAND					
❑ WD-672 [M]	Great Wilson Pickett Hits	1966	7.50	15.00	30.00
❑ WDS-672 [R]	Great Wilson Pickett Hits	1966	5.00	10.00	20.00

Number	Title (A Side/B Side)	Yr	VG	VG+	NM

WICKED

Number	Title (A Side/B Side)	Yr	VG	VG+	NM
❑ 9001	Chocolate Mountain	1976	6.25	12.50	25.00

PINKNEY, BILL
Also see THE DRIFTERS.
45s
FONTANA

❑ 1956	Don't Call Me/I Do the Jerk	1964	3.00	6.00	12.00

GAME

❑ 394	Ol' Man River/Millionaire	196?	12.50	25.00	50.00

PHILLIPS INT'L.

❑ 3524	After the Hop/Sally's Got a Sister	1958	5.00	10.00	20.00

—As "Bill Pinky"

VEEP

❑ 1264	I Found Some Lovin'/The Masquerade Is Over	1967	2.50	5.00	10.00

PIPES, THE (1)
45s
CARLTON

❑ 575	Teamwork/Soon I Will Be Done	1962	5.00	10.00	20.00

PIPES, THE (2)
45s
DOOTO

❑ 388	Be Fair/Let Me Give You Money	1958	6.25	12.50	25.00
❑ 401	You Are An Angel/I Love the Life I Live	1958	6.25	12.50	25.00

DOOTONE

❑ 388	Be Fair/Let Me Give You Money	1956	75.00	150.00	300.00
❑ 401	You Are An Angel/I Love the Life I Live	1956	75.00	150.00	300.00

PIPS, THE
See GLADYS KNIGHT AND THE PIPS.

PIRATES, THE
Early version of THE TEMPTATIONS.
45s
MEL-O-DY

❑ 105	Mind Over Matter (I'm Gonna Make You Mine)/ I'll Love You Till I Die	1962	25.00	50.00	100.00

PLANET PATROL
12-Inch Singles
TOMMY BOY

❑ TB 319	Play at Your Own Risk (Lil' John Remix Main 6.25) (Lil' John Remix Instrumental 6.20) (Lil' John Remix Radio Edit 4.03) (Original Version 7.50)	1998	2.00	4.00	8.00
❑ TB 825	Play at Your Own Risk (Vocal 7:59) (Instrumental 8:20)	1982	6.25	12.50	25.00
❑ TB 835	Cheap Thrills (Vocal) (Instrumental)	1983	3.75	7.50	15.00
❑ TB 837	I Didn't Know I Loved You (Till I Saw You Rock & Roll) (Vocal) (Instrumental)/Play at Your Own Risk	1983	5.00	10.00	20.00
❑ TB 843	It Wouldn't Have Made Any Difference/Don't Tell Me	1983	3.75	7.50	15.00
❑ TB 846	Danger Zone (Vocal) (Instrumental) (A Cappella)	1984	5.00	10.00	20.00

Albums
TOMMY BOY

❑ TBLP-1002	Planet Patrol	1983	10.00	20.00	40.00

—Originals on purple vinyl

❑ TBLP-1002	Planet Patrol	1983	3.75	7.50	15.00

—Black vinyl

PLATTERS, THE
More than one group has used this name over the years, but all are related. Also see TONY WILLIAMS.
45s
ANTLER

❑ 3000/1	I Do It All the Time/Shake What Your Mama Gave You	1982	—	3.00	6.00

AVALANCHE

❑ XW224	Sunday with You/If the World Loved	1973	2.00	4.00	8.00

—As "The Buck Ram Platters"

ENTREE

❑ 107	Won't You Be My Friend/Run While It's Dark	1965	2.00	4.00	8.00

—As "The Platters 1965"

FEDERAL

❑ 12153	Give Thanks/Hey Now	1953	100.00	200.00	400.00

—As "Tony Williams and the Platters"

❑ 12164	I'll Cry When You're Gone/I Need You All the Time	1954	250.00	500.00	1000.
❑ 12181	Roses of Picardy/Beer Barrel Polka	1954	75.00	150.00	300.00
❑ 12188	Tell the World/Love All Night	1954	50.00	100.00	200.00
❑ 12198	Voo-Vee-Ah-Bee/Shake It Up Mambo	1954	50.00	100.00	200.00
❑ 12204	Maggie Doesn't Work Here Anymore/Take Me Back, Take Me Back	1955	50.00	100.00	200.00
❑ 12244	Only You (And You Alone)/You Made Me Cry	1955	75.00	150.00	300.00
❑ 12250	Tell the World/I Need You All the Time	1956	30.00	60.00	120.00
❑ 12271	Give Thanks/I Need You All the Time	1956	20.00	40.00	80.00

MERCURY

❑ 10001 [S]	Smoke Gets In Your Eyes/No Matter What You Are	1959	12.50	25.00	50.00
❑ 10007 [S]	Remember When/Love of a Lifetime	1959	10.00	20.00	40.00
❑ 70633	Only You (And You Alone)/Bark, Battle and Ball	1955	12.50	25.00	50.00

—Earliest pressings have pink labels

Number	Title (A Side/B Side)	Yr	VG	VG+	NM
❑ 70633	Only You (And You Alone)/Bark, Battle and Ball	1955	10.00	20.00	40.00

—Black label

❑ 70753	The Great Pretender/I'm Just a Dancing Partner	1955	10.00	20.00	40.00

—Maroon label

❑ 70753	The Great Pretender/I'm Just a Dancing Partner	1955	5.00	10.00	20.00

—Black label

❑ 70819	(You've Got) The Magic Touch/Winner Take All	1956	10.00	20.00	40.00

—Maroon label

❑ 70819	(You've Got) The Magic Touch/Winner Take All	1956	5.00	10.00	20.00

—Black label

❑ 70893	My Prayer/Heaven on Earth	1956	10.00	20.00	40.00

—Maroon label

❑ 70893	My Prayer/Heaven on Earth	1956	5.00	10.00	20.00

—Black label

❑ 70948	You'll Never Never Know/It Isn't Right	1956	7.50	15.00	30.00

—Maroon label

❑ 70948	You'll Never Never Know/It Isn't Right	1956	5.00	10.00	20.00

—Black label

❑ 71011	One in a Million/On My Word of Honor	1956	7.50	15.00	30.00
❑ 71032	I'm Sorry/He's Mine	1957	7.50	15.00	30.00

—Maroon label

❑ 71032	I'm Sorry/He's Mine	1957	5.00	10.00	20.00

—Black label

❑ 71093	My Dream/I Wanna	1957	7.50	15.00	30.00

—Maroon label

❑ 71093	My Dream/I Wanna	1957	5.00	10.00	20.00

—Black label

❑ 71184	Only Because/The Mystery of You	1957	6.25	12.50	25.00
❑ 71246	Helpless/Indifferent	1957	6.25	12.50	25.00
❑ 71289	Twilight Time/Out of My Mind	1958	6.25	12.50	25.00
❑ 71320	You're Making a Mistake/My Old Flame	1958	6.25	12.50	25.00
❑ 71353	I Wish/It's Raining Outside	1958	6.25	12.50	25.00

—Black label

❑ 71353	I Wish/It's Raining Outside	1958	7.50	15.00	30.00

—Blue label

❑ 71383	Smoke Gets In Your Eyes/No Matter What You Are	1958	6.25	12.50	25.00

—Black label

❑ 71383	Smoke Gets In Your Eyes/No Matter What You Are	1958	7.50	15.00	30.00

—Blue label

❑ 71427	Enchanted/The Sound and the Fury	1959	5.00	10.00	20.00
❑ 71467 [M]	Remember When/Love of a Lifetime	1959	5.00	10.00	20.00
❑ 71502	Where/Wish It Were Me	1959	5.00	10.00	20.00
❑ 71538	My Secret/What Does It Matter	1959	5.00	10.00	20.00
❑ 71563	Harbor Lights/Sleepy Lagoon	1960	5.00	10.00	20.00
❑ 71563 [PS]	Harbor Lights/Sleepy Lagoon	1960	10.00	20.00	40.00
❑ 71624	Ebb Tide/(I'll Be With You) In Apple Blossom Time	1960	5.00	10.00	20.00
❑ 71656	Red Sails in the Sunset/Sad River	1960	5.00	10.00	20.00
❑ 71656 [PS]	Red Sails in the Sunset/Sad River	1960	7.50	15.00	30.00
❑ 71697	To Each His Own/Down the River of Golden Dreams	1960	5.00	10.00	20.00
❑ 71697 [PS]	To Each His Own/Down the River of Golden Dreams	1960	7.50	15.00	30.00
❑ 71749	If I Didn't Care/True Lover	1961	3.75	7.50	15.00
❑ 71749 [PS]	If I Didn't Care/True Lover	1961	7.50	15.00	30.00
❑ 71791	Trees/Immortal Love	1961	3.75	7.50	15.00
❑ 71791 [PS]	Trees/Immortal Love	1961	7.50	15.00	30.00
❑ 71847	I'll Never Smile Again/You Don't Say	1961	3.75	7.50	15.00
❑ 71847 [PS]	I'll Never Smile Again/You Don't Say	1961	7.50	15.00	30.00
❑ 71904	Song for the Lonely/You'll Never Know	1961	3.75	7.50	15.00
❑ 71921	It's Magic/Reaching for a Star	1962	3.75	7.50	15.00
❑ 71921 [PS]	It's Magic/Reaching for a Star	1962	7.50	15.00	30.00
❑ 71986	More Than You Know/Every Little Moment	1962	3.00	6.00	12.00
❑ 72060	Memories/Heartbreak	1962	3.00	6.00	12.00
❑ 72107	Once in a While/I'll See You in My Dreams	1963	2.50	5.00	10.00
❑ 72129	Strangers/Here Comes Heaven Again	1963	2.50	5.00	10.00
❑ 72194	Viva Ju Joy/Quando Caliente El Sol	1963	2.50	5.00	10.00
❑ 72242	Java Jive/Michael Row the Boat Ashore	1964	2.50	5.00	10.00
❑ 72305	Sincerely/P.S. I Love You	1964	2.50	5.00	10.00
❑ 72359	Love Me Tender/Little Things Mean a Lot	1964	2.50	5.00	10.00
❑ 76160	Platterama Medley/Red Sails in the Sunset	1982	—	3.00	6.00

MUSICOR

❑ 1166	I Love You 1000 Times/Don't Hear, Speak, See No Evil	1966	2.00	4.00	8.00
❑ 1195	Alone in the Light (Without You)/Devri	1966	2.00	4.00	8.00
❑ 1211	I'll Be Home/(You've Got) The Magic Touch	1966	2.00	4.00	8.00
❑ 1229	With This Ring/If I Had a Love	1967	2.50	5.00	10.00
❑ 1251	Washed Ashore (On a Lonely Island in the Sea)/ What Name Shall I Give You, My Love	1967	2.00	4.00	8.00
❑ 1251	Washed Ashore (On a Lonely Island in the Sea)/ One in a Million	1967	2.00	4.00	8.00
❑ 1262	On Top of My Mind/Shing-a-Ling-a-Loo	1967	2.00	4.00	8.00
❑ 1275	Sweet, Sweet Lovin'/Sonata	1967	2.00	4.00	8.00
❑ 1288	Love Must Go On/How Beautiful Our Love Is	1968	2.00	4.00	8.00
❑ 1302	So Many Tears/Think Before You Walk Away	1968	2.00	4.00	8.00
❑ 1322	Hard to Get a Thing Called Love/Why	1968	2.00	4.00	8.00
❑ 1341	Fear of Loving You/Sonata	1968	2.00	4.00	8.00
❑ 1443	Be My Love/Sweet Sweet Lovin'	1971	2.00	4.00	8.00

OWL

❑ 320	Sixteen Tons/Are You Sincere	1973	2.00	4.00	8.00

RAM

❑ 1002	Only You/Here Comes the Boogie Man	1977	2.00	4.00	8.00
❑ 1004/5	My Ship Is Coming In/Guilty	1977	2.00	4.00	8.00
❑ 4852	Personality/Who's Sorry Now	1978	2.00	4.00	8.00

Number	Title (A Side/B Side)	Yr	VG	VG+	NM
78s					
FEDERAL					
❑ 12153	Give Thanks/Hey Now	1953	50.00	100.00	200.00
—As "Tony Williams and the Platters"					
❑ 12164	I'll Cry When You're Gone/I Need You All the Time	1954	50.00	100.00	200.00
❑ 12181	Roses of Picardy/Beer Barrel Polka	1954	50.00	100.00	200.00
❑ 12188	Tell the World/Love All Night	1954	50.00	100.00	200.00
❑ 12198	Voo-Vee-Ah-Bee/Shake It Up Mambo	1954	50.00	100.00	200.00
❑ 12204	Maggie Doesn't Work Here Anymore/Take Me Back, Take Me Back	1955	50.00	100.00	200.00
❑ 12244	Only You (And You Alone)/You Made Me Cry	1955	75.00	150.00	300.00
❑ 12250	Tell the World/I Need You All the Time	1956	37.50	75.00	150.00
❑ 12271	Give Thanks/I Need You All the Time	1956	25.00	50.00	100.00
MERCURY					
❑ 70633	Only You (And You Alone)/Bark, Battle and Ball	1955	12.50	25.00	50.00
—Earliest pressings have pink labels					
❑ 70633	Only You (And You Alone)/Bark, Battle and Ball	1955	7.50	15.00	30.00
—Black label					
❑ 70753	The Great Pretender/I'm Just a Dancing Partner	1955	10.00	20.00	40.00
❑ 70819	(You've Got) The Magic Touch/Winner Take All	1956	10.00	20.00	40.00
❑ 70893	My Prayer/Heaven on Earth	1956	10.00	20.00	40.00
❑ 70948	You'll Never Never Know/It Isn't Right	1956	10.00	20.00	40.00
❑ 71011	One in a Million/On My Word of Honor	1956	10.00	20.00	40.00
❑ 71032	I'm Sorry/He's Mine	1957	10.00	20.00	40.00
❑ 71093	My Dream/I Wanna	1957	10.00	20.00	40.00
❑ 71184	Only Because/The Mystery of You	1957	10.00	20.00	40.00
❑ 71246	Helpless/Indifferent	1957	10.00	20.00	40.00
❑ 71289	Twilight Time/Out of My Mind	1958	25.00	50.00	100.00
7-Inch Extended Plays					
FEDERAL					
❑ EP-378	*Only You (And You Alone)/I Need You All the Time/Tell the World/Give Thanks	1956	100.00	200.00	400.00
❑ EP-378 [PS]	The Platters Sing for Only You	1956	100.00	200.00	400.00
KING					
❑ 378	(contents unknown)	1956	37.50	75.00	150.00
❑ 378 [PS]	The Platters	1956	37.50	75.00	150.00
—Reissue of Federal EP					
❑ 651	(contents unknown)	1956	40.00	80.00	160.00
—"Federal" 651 is a counterfeit; all originals are on King					
❑ 651 [PS]	The Platters	1956	40.00	80.00	160.00
MERCURY					
❑ SR 621	Summertime/People Will Say We're in Love/More Than You Know//Stormy Weather/Every Little Movement/Poor Butterfly	196?	7.50	15.00	30.00
—Jukebox issue; small hole, plays at 33 1/3 rpm					
❑ SR 621 [PS]	Encore of Broadway Golden Hits	196?	7.50	15.00	30.00
❑ EP 1-3336	My Prayer/Have Mercy//On My Word of Honor/I'm Sorry	1957	10.00	20.00	40.00
❑ EP 1-3336 [PS]	The Platters	1957	10.00	20.00	40.00
❑ EP 1-3343	Heart of Stone/I'd Climb the Highest Mountain//September in the Rain/You've Changed	1957	10.00	20.00	40.00
❑ EP 1-3343 [PS]	The Platters (Part 1)	1957	10.00	20.00	40.00
❑ EP 1-3344	I'll Get By/I'll Give You My Word//In the Still of the Night/Wagon Wheels	1957	10.00	20.00	40.00
❑ EP 1-3344 [PS]	The Platters (Part 2)	1957	10.00	20.00	40.00
❑ EP 1-3345	Take Me in Your Arms/You Can Depend on Me//Temptation/I Don't Know Why	1957	10.00	20.00	40.00
❑ EP 1-3345 [PS]	The Platters (Part 3)	1957	10.00	20.00	40.00
❑ EP 1-3353	(contents unknown)	1958	10.00	20.00	40.00
❑ EP 1-3353 [PS]	The Flying Platters (Part 1)	1958	10.00	20.00	40.00
❑ EP 1-3354	(contents unknown)	1958	10.00	20.00	40.00
❑ EP 1-3354 [PS]	The Flying Platters (Part 2)	1958	10.00	20.00	40.00
❑ EP 1-3355	Mean to Me/Oh Promise Me//Time and Tide/Don't Forget	1958	10.00	20.00	40.00
❑ EP 1-3355 [PS]	The Flying Platters	1958	10.00	20.00	40.00
❑ EP 1-3393	(contents unknown)	1958	10.00	20.00	40.00
❑ EP 1-3393 [PS]	Twilight Time	1958	10.00	20.00	40.00
Albums					
CANDELITE MUSIC					
❑ CMI 1000 [(5)]	The 50 Golden Hits of the Platters	197?	10.00	20.00	40.00
COLUMBIA SPECIAL PRODUCTS					
❑ P 11834 [S]	Christmas with the Platters	1973	3.75	7.50	15.00
—Reissue of Mercury SR-60841 with fewer tracks					
FEDERAL					
❑ 549 [M]	The Platters	1957	400.00	800.00	1600.
KING					
❑ 651 [M]	The Platters	1959	200.00	400.00	800.00
❑ KLP-651 [M]	The Platters	1987	2.50	5.00	10.00
—Reissue with "Highland Records" on label					
❑ 5002	19 Hits of the Platters	197?	3.00	6.00	12.00
MERCURY					
❑ SRM-1-4050	Platterama	1982	2.50	5.00	10.00
❑ MG-20146 [M]	The Platters	1956	25.00	50.00	100.00
❑ MG-20216 [M]	The Platters, Volume Two	1956	25.00	50.00	100.00
❑ MG-20298 [M]	The Flying Platters	1957	25.00	50.00	100.00
❑ MG-20366 [M]	The Flying Platters Around the World	1958	7.50	15.00	30.00
❑ MG-20410 [M]	Remember When?	1959	7.50	15.00	30.00
❑ MG-20472 [M]	Encore of Golden Hits	1960	7.50	15.00	30.00
❑ MG-20481 [M]	Reflections	1960	6.25	12.50	25.00
❑ MG-20589 [M]	Life Is Just a Bowl of Cherries	1960	6.25	12.50	25.00
❑ MG-20591 [M]	More Encore of Golden Hits	1960	6.25	12.50	25.00
❑ MG-20613 [M]	Encore of Broadway Golden Hits	1961	5.00	10.00	20.00
❑ MG-20669 [M]	Song for the Lonely	1962	5.00	10.00	20.00
❑ MG-20759 [M]	Moonlight Memories	1963	5.00	10.00	20.00

Number	Title (A Side/B Side)	Yr	VG	VG+	NM
❑ MG-20782 [M]	The Platters Present All-Time Movie Hits	1963	5.00	10.00	20.00
❑ MG-20808 [M]	The Platters Sing Latino	1963	5.00	10.00	20.00
❑ MG-20841 [M]	Christmas with the Platters	1963	7.50	15.00	30.00
❑ MG-20893 [M]	Encore of Golden Hits of the Groups	1964	5.00	10.00	20.00
❑ MG-20933 [M]	10th Anniversary Album	1964	5.00	10.00	20.00
❑ MG-20983 [M]	The New Soul of the Platters	1965	3.75	7.50	15.00
❑ SR-60043 [S]	The Flying Platters Around the World	1959	12.50	25.00	50.00
❑ SR-60087 [S]	Remember When?	1959	12.50	25.00	50.00
❑ SR-60160 [S]	Reflections	1960	7.50	15.00	30.00
❑ SR-60243 [P]	Encore of Golden Hits	1960	10.00	20.00	40.00
❑ SR-60245 [S]	Life Is Just a Bowl of Cherries	1960	7.50	15.00	30.00
❑ SR-60252 [S]	More Encore of Golden Hits	1960	7.50	15.00	30.00
❑ SR-60613 [S]	Encore of Broadway Golden Hits	1961	6.25	12.50	25.00
❑ SR-60669 [S]	Song for the Lonely	1962	6.25	12.50	25.00
❑ SR-60759 [S]	Moonlight Memories	1963	6.25	12.50	25.00
❑ SR-60782 [S]	The Platters Present All-Time Movie Hits	1963	6.25	12.50	25.00
❑ SR-60808 [S]	The Platters Sing Latino	1963	6.25	12.50	25.00
❑ SR-60841 [S]	Christmas with the Platters	1963	10.00	20.00	40.00
—Same as above, but in stereo					
❑ SR-60893 [S]	Encore of Golden Hits of the Groups	1964	6.25	12.50	25.00
❑ SR-60933 [S]	10th Anniversary Album	1964	6.25	12.50	25.00
❑ SR-60983 [S]	The New Soul of the Platters	1965	5.00	10.00	20.00
❑ 828246-1	More Encore of Golden Hits	198?	2.00	4.00	8.00
—Reissue					
❑ 828254-1	Encore of Golden Hits	198?	2.00	4.00	8.00
—Reissue					
MUSIC DISC					
❑ MDS-1002	Only You	1969	3.00	6.00	12.00
MUSICOR					
❑ MM-2091 [M]	I Love You 1,000 Times	1966	3.75	7.50	15.00
❑ MM-2111 [M]	The Platters Have the Magic Touch	1966	3.75	7.50	15.00
❑ MM-2125 [M]	Going Back to Detroit	1967	3.75	7.50	15.00
❑ MM-2141 [M]	New Golden Hits of the Platters	1967	5.00	10.00	20.00
❑ MS-3091 [S]	I Love You 1,000 Times	1966	5.00	10.00	20.00
❑ MS-3111 [S]	The Platters Have the Magic Touch	1966	5.00	10.00	20.00
❑ MS-3125 [S]	Going Back to Detroit	1967	3.75	7.50	15.00
❑ MS-3141 [S]	New Golden Hits of the Platters	1967	3.75	7.50	15.00
❑ MS-3156	Sweet, Sweet Lovin'	1968	3.75	7.50	15.00
❑ MS-3171	I Get the Sweetest Feeling	1968	3.75	7.50	15.00
❑ MS-3185	Singing the Great Hits Our Way	1969	3.75	7.50	15.00
❑ MS-3231	Golden Hour	1973	3.00	6.00	12.00
❑ MS-3254	The Golden Hits of the Platters	1973	3.00	6.00	12.00
PICKWICK					
❑ PTP-2083 [(2)]	Only You	1973	3.00	6.00	12.00
❑ SPC-3236	Super Hits	197?	2.50	5.00	10.00
RHINO					
❑ RNFP-71495 [(2)]	Anthology (1955-1967)	1986	3.00	6.00	12.00
SPRINGBOARD					
❑ SPB-4059	The Platters	197?	2.50	5.00	10.00
WING					
❑ MGW-12112 [M]	Encores!	1959	7.50	15.00	30.00
—With liner notes on back cover					
❑ MGW-12112 [M]	Encores!	196?	3.75	7.50	15.00
—With photos of other Wing LPs on back cover					
❑ MGW-12226 [M]	Flying Platters	1963	3.00	6.00	12.00
❑ MGW-12272 [M]	Reflections	1964	3.00	6.00	12.00
❑ MGW-12346 [M]	10th Anniversary Album	196?	3.00	6.00	12.00
❑ SRW-16112 [R]	Encores!	196?	3.00	6.00	12.00
❑ SRW-16226 [S]	Flying Platters	1963	3.00	6.00	12.00
❑ SRW-16272 [S]	Reflections	1964	3.00	6.00	12.00
❑ SRW-16346 [S]	10th Anniversary Album	196?	3.00	6.00	12.00

POETS, THE (1)

Number	Title (A Side/B Side)	Yr	VG	VG+	NM
45s					
SYMBOL					
❑ 214	She Blew a Good Thing/Out to Lunch	1966	3.75	7.50	15.00
❑ 216	So Young (And So Innocent)/A Sure Thing	1966	3.00	6.00	12.00
❑ 219	I'm Particular/I've Only Two Hearts	1966	3.00	6.00	12.00
VEEP					
❑ 1286	The Hustler/Soul Brothers Holiday	1968	5.00	10.00	20.00

POETS, THE (3)

Number	Title (A Side/B Side)	Yr	VG	VG+	NM
45s					
FLASH					
❑ 129	Vowels of Love/Dead	1958	50.00	100.00	200.00
—Black label					
❑ 129	Vowels of Love/Dead	1958	15.00	30.00	60.00
—Maroon label					

POETS, THE (4)

Number	Title (A Side/B Side)	Yr	VG	VG+	NM
45s					
IMPERIAL					
❑ 5664	Honey Chile/I'm in Love	1960	3.75	7.50	15.00

POINTER, ANITA

Also see THE POINTER SISTERS.

Number	Title (A Side/B Side)	Yr	VG	VG+	NM
12-Inch Singles					
RCA					
❑ 6625-1-RD	Overnight Success (Dance Mix) (Instrumental)	1987	—	3.50	7.00
❑ 8306-1-RDCD [(2)]	More Than a Memory (6 versions)	1988	2.50	5.00	10.00
❑ 8403-1-RD	More Than a Memory (East Coast Mix) (East Coast Dub) (Bonus Beats) (West Coast 12" Mix) (Instrumental) (Acapella)	1988	2.00	4.00	8.00

Number	Title (A Side/B Side)	Yr	VG	VG+	NM
❑ 8441-1-RD	More Than a Memory (2 versions)/Have a Little Faith in Love	1988	2.00	4.00	8.00

45s

RCA

Number	Title (A Side/B Side)	Yr	VG	VG+	NM
❑ 5291-7-R	Overnight Success/Love Me Like You Do	1987	—	—	3.00
❑ 6847-7-R	More Than a Memory/Have a Little Faith in Love	1987	—	—	3.00

Albums

RCA

Number	Title (A Side/B Side)	Yr	VG	VG+	NM
❑ 6419-1-R	Love for What It Is	1987	2.00	4.00	8.00

POINTER, BONNIE

Also see THE POINTER SISTERS.

12-Inch Singles

MOTOWN

Number	Title (A Side/B Side)	Yr	VG	VG+	NM
❑ M00020-D1	Heaven Must Have Sent You (New Version 6:59) (LP Version 5:12)	1979	2.50	5.00	10.00

PRIVATE I

Number	Title (A Side/B Side)	Yr	VG	VG+	NM
❑ 4Z9-04996	Your Touch (Club Version 6:36) (Dub Version)	1984	—	3.50	7.00
❑ 4Z9-05117	Premonition (Dance Mix) (Dub Version)	1984	—	3.50	7.00
❑ 4Z9-05166	The Beast in Me (7:27)/Tight Blue Jeans (3:43)	1985	—	3.50	7.00

45s

MOTOWN

Number	Title (A Side/B Side)	Yr	VG	VG+	NM
❑ 1451	Free Me from My Freedom-Tie Me to a Tree (Handcuff Me)/(Instrumental)	1978	—	2.00	4.00
—Black vinyl					
❑ 1451	Free Me from My Freedom-Tie Me to a Tree (Handcuff Me)/(Instrumental)	1978	2.00	4.00	8.00
—Stock copy on red vinyl					
❑ 1451 [PS]	Free Me from My Freedom-Tie Me to a Tree (Handcuff Me)/(Instrumental)	1978	—	3.00	6.00
❑ 1459	Heaven Must Have Sent You/Heaven Must Have Sent You (LP Version)	1979	—	2.00	4.00
❑ 1478	I Can't Help Myself (Sugar Pie, Honey Bunch)/I Wanna Make It (In Your World)	1979	—	2.00	4.00
❑ 1484	Deep Inside My Soul/I Love to Sing to You	1980	—	2.00	4.00

PRIVATE I

Number	Title (A Side/B Side)	Yr	VG	VG+	NM
❑ ZS4-04449	Your Touch/There's Nobody Quite Like You	1984	—	—	3.00
❑ ZS4-04658	Premonition/Tight Blue Jeans	1984	—	—	3.00
❑ ZS4-04819	The Beast in Me/There's Nobody Quite Like You	1985	—	—	3.00
❑ ZS4-04819 [PS]	The Beast in Me/There's Nobody Quite Like You	1985	—	—	3.00

Albums

MOTOWN

Number	Title (A Side/B Side)	Yr	VG	VG+	NM
❑ M7-911R1	Bonnie Pointer	1978	3.00	6.00	12.00
❑ M7-929M1	Bonnie Pointer	1979	2.50	5.00	10.00
—The above two are different albums					

PRVATE I

Number	Title (A Side/B Side)	Yr	VG	VG+	NM
❑ FZ 39406	If the Price Is Right	1984	2.00	4.00	8.00

POINTER, JUNE

Also see THE POINTER SISTERS.

12-Inch Singles

COLUMBIA

Number	Title (A Side/B Side)	Yr	VG	VG+	NM
❑ 44-68780	Tight on Time (I'll Fit U In) (12" Office Mix) (Club 7" Career Mix) (7" Remix) (Single Version [with DJ]) (12" Overtime Club Mix) (Bonus Beat) (Acappella)	1989	2.00	4.00	8.00

PLANET

Number	Title (A Side/B Side)	Yr	VG	VG+	NM
❑ YD-13521	Ready for Some Action (5:59)/Always	1983	2.00	4.00	8.00

45s

COLUMBIA

Number	Title (A Side/B Side)	Yr	VG	VG+	NM
❑ 38-68748	Tight on Time (I'll Fit U In)/Fool for Love	1989	—	—	3.00

PLANET

Number	Title (A Side/B Side)	Yr	VG	VG+	NM
❑ YB-13522	Ready for Some Action/Always	1983	—	2.00	4.00
❑ YB-13592	Don't Mess With Bill/I Understand	1983	—	2.00	4.00

Albums

COLUMBIA

Number	Title (A Side/B Side)	Yr	VG	VG+	NM
❑ FC 44315	June Pointer	1989	3.00	6.00	12.00

PLANET

Number	Title (A Side/B Side)	Yr	VG	VG+	NM
❑ BXL1-4508	Baby Sister	1983	2.50	5.00	10.00

POINTER, RUTH

Also see THE POINTER SISTERS.

45s

EPIC

Number	Title (A Side/B Side)	Yr	VG	VG+	NM
❑ 34-08115	Enemies Like You and Me/I Need You	1988	—	—	3.00
—With Billy Vera					

POINTER SISTERS, THE

Also see ANITA POINTER; BONNIE POINTER; JUNE POINTER; RUTH POINTER.

12-Inch Singles

COLUMBIA

Number	Title (A Side/B Side)	Yr	VG	VG+	NM
❑ 07883	Power of Persuasion (3 versions)	1988	—	3.00	6.00

MCA

Number	Title (A Side/B Side)	Yr	VG	VG+	NM
❑ 23769	Be There (4 versions)	1987	—	3.00	6.00

MOTOWN

Number	Title (A Side/B Side)	Yr	VG	VG+	NM
❑ 4661	Friend's Advice (Don't Take It) (3 versions)	1990	—	3.00	6.00
❑ L33-17922 [DJ]	Friend's Advice (Don't Take It) (5 versions)	1990	2.00	4.00	8.00

PLANET

Number	Title (A Side/B Side)	Yr	VG	VG+	NM
❑ 11403 [DJ]	Happiness (same on both sides)	1979	2.00	4.00	8.00
❑ 11406 [DJ]	Come and Get Your Love/Dirty Work/Echoes of Love/Hypnotized	1979	3.00	6.00	12.00
❑ 11407 [DJ]	Fire/Happiness	1979	3.00	6.00	12.00
—Red vinyl					
❑ JD-13328 [DJ]	I'm So Excited	1982	2.50	5.00	10.00
—One-sided promo					
❑ YD-13429	I'm So Excited/If You Wanna Get Back My Love	1983	2.50	5.00	10.00
❑ YD-13721	Automatic (4:48) (6:06)	1984	2.00	4.00	8.00
❑ YD-13781	Jump (For My Love) (6:24)/(Instrumental)/Heartbeat	1984	2.00	4.00	8.00
❑ JR-13858 [DJ]	I'm So Excited (same on both sides)	1984	2.50	5.00	10.00
❑ YD-13952	Neutron Dance (4:59)/Telegraph Your Love	1984	2.00	4.00	8.00
❑ YD-14042	Baby Come and Get It (7:14)/Operator	1985	2.00	4.00	8.00

RCA

Number	Title (A Side/B Side)	Yr	VG	VG+	NM
❑ 5774-1-RDAC [DJ]	Goldmine (2 versions)/Sexual Power	1986	—	3.00	6.00
❑ 6491-1-RDAC [DJ]	Mercury Rising (3 versions)	1986	—	3.00	6.00
❑ 6865-1-RD	He Turned Me Out (4 versions)	1988	—	3.00	6.00
❑ PD-14127	Dare Me (Long) (Instrumental)/I'll Be There	1985	—	3.00	6.00
❑ PD-14196	Twist My Arm (Dance Mix)/(Instrumental)/Easy Persuasion	1985	2.00	4.00	8.00
❑ PD-14225	Freedom (4:18) (6:21)	1985	—	3.00	6.00

45s

ATLANTIC

Number	Title (A Side/B Side)	Yr	VG	VG+	NM
❑ 2845	Don't Try to Take the Fifth/Tulsa County	1971	5.00	10.00	20.00
❑ 2893	Destination No More Heartaches/Send Him Back	1972	5.00	10.00	20.00

BLUE THUMB

Number	Title (A Side/B Side)	Yr	VG	VG+	NM
❑ 229	Yes We Can Can/Jada	1973	—	3.00	6.00
❑ 243	Wang Dang Doodle/Cloudburst	1973	—	3.00	6.00
❑ 248	Steam Heat/Shaky Flat Blues	1974	—	3.00	6.00
❑ 254	Fairytale/Love In Them Thar Hills	1974	2.50	5.00	10.00
—First pressing has a gray to white label and no reference to ABC					
❑ 254	Fairytale/Love In Them Thar Hills	1974	—	2.50	5.00
—Second pressing has a multicolor label with ABC logo					
❑ 262	Live Your Life Before You Die/Shaky Flat Blues	1975	—	2.50	5.00
❑ 265	How Long (Betcha' Got a Chick on the Side)/Easy Days	1975	—	2.50	5.00
❑ 268	Going Down Slowly/Sleeping Alone	1975	—	2.50	5.00
❑ 271	You Gotta Believe/Shaky Flat Blues	1976	—	2.50	5.00
❑ 275	Having a Party/Lonely Gal	1977	—	2.50	5.00
❑ 277	I Need a Man/I'll Get By Without You	1978	—	2.50	5.00

COLUMBIA

Number	Title (A Side/B Side)	Yr	VG	VG+	NM
❑ 08015	Power of Persuasion/(Instrumental)	1988	—	—	3.00
❑ 08015 [PS]	Power of Persuasion/(Instrumental)	1988	—	—	3.00

MCA

Number	Title (A Side/B Side)	Yr	VG	VG+	NM
❑ 53120	Be There/(Instrumental)	1987	—	—	3.00
❑ 53120 [PS]	Be There/(Instrumental)	1987	—	—	3.00

MOTOWN

Number	Title (A Side/B Side)	Yr	VG	VG+	NM
❑ 902	Friends' Advice (Don't Take It)/Friends' Advice (Don't Take It) (Dub)	1990	—	2.00	4.00

PLANET

Number	Title (A Side/B Side)	Yr	VG	VG+	NM
❑ YB-13254	American Music/I Want to Do It with You	1982	—	2.00	4.00
❑ YB-13327	I'm So Excited/Nothing But a Heartache (Live)	1982	—	2.00	4.00
❑ YB-13430	If You Wanna Get Back Your Lady/I'm So Excited	1983	—	2.00	4.00
❑ GB-13485	American Music/I'm So Excited	1983	—	—	3.00
—Gold Standard Series					
❑ YB-13639	I Need You/If You Wanna Get Back Your Lady	1983	—	2.00	4.00
❑ YB-13730	Automatic/Nightline	1984	—	2.00	4.00
❑ YB-13780	Jump (For My Love)/Heart Beat	1984	—	2.00	4.00
❑ GB-13795	I Need You/If You Wanna Get Back Your Lady	1984	—	—	3.00
—Gold Standard Series					
❑ YB-13857	I'm So Excited/Dance Electric	1984	—	2.00	4.00
❑ YB-13951	Neutron Dance/Telegraph Your Love	1984	—	2.00	4.00
❑ YB-14041	Baby Come and Get It/Operator	1985	—	2.00	4.00
❑ YB-14041 [PS]	Baby Come and Get It/Operator	1985	—	2.00	4.00
❑ GB-14072	Jump (For My Love)/Automatic	1985	—	—	3.00
—Gold Standard Series					
❑ GB-14076	Fire/He's So Shy	1985	—	—	3.00
—Gold Standard Series					
❑ GB-14077	Slow Hand/Should I Do It	1985	—	—	3.00
—Gold Standard Series					
❑ 45901	Fire/Love Is Like a Rolling Stone	1978	—	2.00	4.00
❑ 45901 [PS]	Fire/Love Is Like a Rolling Stone	1978	—	3.00	6.00
❑ 45902	Happiness/Too Late	1979	—	2.00	4.00
❑ 45906	Blind Faith/The Shape I'm In	1979	—	2.00	4.00
❑ 47916	He's So Shy/Movin' On	1980	—	2.00	4.00
❑ 47918	Es Tan Timido/Cosas Especiales	1980	—	3.00	6.00
❑ 47920	Could I Be Dreaming/Evil	1980	—	2.00	4.00
❑ 47925	Where Did the Time Go/Special Things	1981	—	2.00	4.00
❑ 47929	Slow Hand/Holdin' Out for Love	1981	—	2.00	4.00
❑ 47937	What a Surprise/Fall in Love Again	1981	—	2.00	4.00
❑ 47945	Sweet Lover Man/Got to Find Love	1981	—	2.00	4.00
❑ 47960	Should I Do It/We're Gonna Make It	1982	—	2.00	4.00

RCA

Number	Title (A Side/B Side)	Yr	VG	VG+	NM
❑ 5062-7-R	Goldmine/Sexual Power	1986	—	—	3.00
❑ 5062-7-R [PS]	Goldmine/Sexual Power	1986	—	—	3.00
❑ 5112-7-R	All I Know Is the Way I Feel/Translation	1987	—	—	3.00
❑ 5230-7-R	Mercury Rising/Say the Word	1987	—	—	3.00
❑ 6865-7-R	He Turned Me Out/Translation	1988	—	—	3.00
❑ 6865-7-R [PS]	He Turned Me Out/Translation	1988	—	—	3.00
❑ 8378-7-R	I'm in Love/Uh-Oh	1988	—	—	3.00
❑ PB-14126	Dare Me/I'll Be There	1985	—	—	3.00
❑ PB-14126 [PS]	Dare Me/I'll Be There	1985	—	—	3.00
❑ PB-14197	Twist My Arm/Easy Persuasion	1986	—	—	3.00
❑ PB-14197 [PS]	Twist My Arm/Easy Persuasion	1986	—	—	3.00
❑ PB-14224	Freedom/Telegraph Your Love	1985	—	—	3.00
❑ PB-14224 [PS]	Freedom/Telegraph Your Love	1985	—	—	3.00
❑ GB-14354	Neutron Dance/Baby Come and Get It	1986	—	—	3.00
—Gold Standard Series					

The Paramours were an early version of the Righteous Brothers. Bill Medley wrote the pictured record, "There She Goes."

Best known for their huge hit "Earth Angel," the Penguins recorded a lot more material, but most of it is forgotten today. Here's a sampling, one of three EP volumes of *The Cool, Cool Penguins* from 1959.

When the Platters began having hits on Mercury, King Records compiled some of their earlier recordings, including the original version of "Only You," into this now-rare LP.

This is the only LP by the Poppies, who recorded for Epic in 1966. One of the singers in the group was Dorothy Moore, who went on to solo success with "Misty Blue."

In the late 1950s and early 1960s, many record labels issued stereo 45s in addition to the mono editions they already put out. All of these are harder to find than their mono counterparts; one of these is this stereo 45 of "Personality" by Lloyd Price.

Prince's first 45-rpm single was "Soft and Wet," issued in 1978. It became a top 20 R&B hit, a fairly auspicious start. Based on its July 1978 release date, this *ought* to exist on the older Warner Bros. "Burbank" label, but we've never seen one.

P

Number	Title (A Side/B Side)	Yr	VG	VG+	NM

SBK

| ❏ S7-17637 | Don't Walk Away/Tell It to My Heart | 1993 | — | 2.00 | 4.00 |

Albums

ABC BLUE THUMB

❏ BT-6021	Steppin	1975	3.00	6.00	12.00
❏ BT-6023	Having a Party	1977	3.00	6.00	12.00
❏ BTSY-6026 [(2)]	The Best of the Pointer Sisters	1976	3.75	7.50	15.00

BLUE THUMB

❏ BTS-48	The Pointer Sisters	1973	3.00	6.00	12.00
❏ BTS-6009	That's a Plenty	1974	3.00	6.00	12.00
❏ BTS-8002 [(2)]	Live at the Opera House	1974	3.75	7.50	15.00

MCA

| ❏ 3275 | Retrospect | 1981 | 2.50 | 5.00 | 10.00 |

—Reissue of Blue Thumb material

MOTOWN

| ❏ 6287 ML | Right Rhythm | 1990 | 3.00 | 6.00 | 12.00 |

PLANET

❏ P-1	Energy	1978	2.50	5.00	10.00
❏ P-9	Special Things	1980	2.50	5.00	10.00
❏ P-18	Black and White	1981	2.50	5.00	10.00
❏ BXL1-4355	So Excited!	1982	2.50	5.00	10.00
❏ BEL1-4705A	Break Out	1984	2.00	4.00	8.00

—Reissue has "I'm So Excited" plus a remix of "Jump (For My Love)"

| ❏ BXL1-4705 | Break Out | 1983 | 2.50 | 5.00 | 10.00 |

—Original does not have "I'm So Excited"

| ❏ P-9003 | Priority | 1979 | 2.50 | 5.00 | 10.00 |
| ❏ 60203 | Pointer Sisters' Greatest Hits | 1982 | 2.50 | 5.00 | 10.00 |

RCA

| ❏ 5609-1-R | Hot Together | 1986 | 2.50 | 5.00 | 10.00 |
| ❏ 6562-1-R | Serious Slammin' | 1988 | 2.50 | 5.00 | 10.00 |

RCA VICTOR

| ❏ AYL1-5088 | Special Things | 1985 | 2.00 | 4.00 | 8.00 |

—Budget-line reissue

| ❏ AYL1-5089 | Priority | 1985 | 2.00 | 4.00 | 8.00 |

—Budget-line reissue

| ❏ AYL1-5091 | Energy | 1985 | 2.00 | 4.00 | 8.00 |

—Budget-line reissue

| ❏ AYL1-5092 | Black and White | 1985 | 2.00 | 4.00 | 8.00 |

—Budget-line reissue

| ❏ AJL1-5487 | Contact | 1985 | 2.50 | 5.00 | 10.00 |

PONI-TAILS, THE

45s

ABC-PARAMOUNT

❏ 9846	Wild Eyes and Tender Lips/It's Just My Luck to Be Fifteen	1957	5.00	10.00	20.00
❏ 9934	Born Too Late/Come On Joey Dance With Me	1958	6.25	12.50	25.00
❏ 9934 [DJ]	Born Too Late/Come On Joey Dance With Me	1958	12.50	25.00	50.00

—White label promo with artist's name spelled "Pony-Tails"

❏ 9969	Close Friends/Seven Minutes in Heaven	1958	5.00	10.00	20.00
❏ 9995	Early to Bed/Father Time	1959	5.00	10.00	20.00
❏ 10027	Moody/Ooh-Pah Polka	1959	5.00	10.00	20.00
❏ 10047	I'll Be Seeing You/I'll Keep Tryin'	1959	5.00	10.00	20.00
❏ 10077	Before We Say Goodnight/Come Be My Love	1960	5.00	10.00	20.00
❏ 10114	Who, When and Why/Oh My, You	1960	5.00	10.00	20.00

MARC

| ❏ 1001 | Can I Be Sure/Still in Your Teens | 1957 | 6.25 | 12.50 | 25.00 |

POINT

| ❏ 8 | Your Wild Heart/Que La Bozena | 1957 | 6.25 | 12.50 | 25.00 |

POPCORN BLIZZARD, THE

45s

DE-LITE

| ❏ 516 | Good Thing Going/My Suzanne | 1969 | 5.00 | 10.00 | 20.00 |
| ❏ 522 | Good Good Day/I Just Saw a Face | 1969 | 5.00 | 10.00 | 20.00 |

POPPIES, THE

Dorothy Moore of "Misty Blue" fame was in this group.

45s

EPIC

❏ 9893	I Wonder Why/Lullaby of Love	1966	2.50	5.00	10.00
❏ 10019	He's Ready/He's Got Real Love	1966	2.50	5.00	10.00
❏ 10019 [PS]	He's Ready/He's Got Real Love	1966	5.00	10.00	20.00
❏ 10059	Do It with Soul/He Means So Much to Me	1966	3.00	6.00	12.00
❏ 10086	There's a Pain in My Heart/My Love and I	1966	6.25	12.50	25.00

TUFF

| ❏ 372 | Johnny Don't Cry/(Instrumental) | 1964 | 3.75 | 7.50 | 15.00 |

Albums

EPIC

| ❏ LN 24200 [M] | Lullaby of Love | 1966 | 10.00 | 20.00 | 40.00 |
| ❏ BN 26200 [S] | Lullaby of Love | 1966 | 12.50 | 25.00 | 50.00 |

PORTER, DAVID

45s

ENTERPRISE

| ❏ 9014 | Can't See You When I Want To/One Part, Two Parts | 1970 | — | 3.00 | 6.00 |
| ❏ 9049 | Ain't That Loving You (For More Reasons Than One)/Baby I'm-a Want You | 1972 | — | 2.50 | 5.00 |

—With Isaac Hayes

| ❏ 9050 | I'm Afraid the Masquerade Is Over/Sloopy | 1972 | — | 2.50 | 5.00 |
| ❏ 9055 | Wanna Be Your Somebody/When the Chips Are Down | 1972 | — | 2.50 | 5.00 |

| ❏ 9071 | As Long As You're the One Somebody in the World/When You Have to Sneak | 1973 | — | 2.50 | 5.0 |
| ❏ 9090 | Falling Out, Falling In/I Got You and I'm Glad | 1973 | — | 2.50 | 5.0 |

STAX

| ❏ 163 | Can't See You When I Want To/Win You Over | 1965 | 5.00 | 10.00 | 20.0 |

Albums

ENTERPRISE

❏ ENS-1009	Gritty, Groovy, & Gettin' It	1970	5.00	10.00	20.0
❏ ENS-1012	David Porter…Into a Real Thing	1971	5.00	10.00	20.0
❏ ENS-1019	Victim of the Joke?	1972	5.00	10.00	20.00
❏ ENS-1026	Sweat and Love	1973	5.00	10.00	20.0

PRESIDENTS, THE (1)

45s

SUSSEX

❏ 200	For You/Gotta Keep Movin'	1970	—	3.50	7.0
❏ 207	5-10-15-20 (25-30 Years of Love)/I'm Still Dancing	1970	2.00	4.00	8.0
❏ 212	Triangle of Love (Hey Diddle Diddle)/Sweet Magic	1971	—	3.50	7.0
❏ 217	The Sweetest Thing This Side of Heaven/It's All Over Now	1971	—	3.50	7.0

Albums

SUSSEX

| ❏ SXBX-7005 | 5-10-15-20 (25-30 Years of Love) | 1970 | 6.25 | 12.50 | 25.00 |

PRESIDENTS, THE (2)

Not the same as group (1). The Sussex group's success forced this group to change its name, as reflected in the label credit on their final DeLuxe 45.

45s

DELUXE

❏ 113	Gold Walk/I Want My Baby	1969	2.00	4.00	8.0
❏ 120	Snoopy/Stinky	1969	2.00	4.00	8.0
❏ 127	Which Way/Peter Rabbit	1970	2.00	4.00	8.0
❏ 134	Lover's Psalm/Our Meeting	1971	—	3.00	6.0

—As "The President's Band"

PRESLEY, ELVIS

12-Inch Singles

RCA

| ❏ EP-0517 [DJ] | Little Sister/Rip It Up | 1983 | 25.00 | 50.00 | 100.0 |
| ❏ 60570 | A Little Less Conversation (12" Extended Remix)/(Radio Remix Edit) (Original Version) | 2002 | 3.00 | 6.00 | 12.0 |

—Credited to "Elvis vs JXL"

45s

COLLECTABLES

| ❏ COL-0103 [(23)] | Elvis #1 Hit Singles Collection | 2001 | 25.00 | 50.00 | 100.0 |

—Contains reproductions, on red vinyl, of 18 RCA singles and all five Sun singles, using facsimiles of original labels and reproductions of original picture sleeves, and all-new sleeves for those songs not issued originally with picture sleeves; with poster and all in wooden box

| ❏ COL-0134 [(23)] | Elvis Hit Singles Collection Volume 2 | 2002 | 25.00 | 50.00 | 100.0 |

—Contains reproductions, on red vinyl, of 23 RCA singles not in the first box, using facsimiles of original labels and reproductions of original picture sleeves, and all-new sleeves for those songs no. issued originally with picture sleeves; with poster and all in wooden box

| ❏ COL-4500 | Good Rockin' Tonight/I Don't Care If the Sun Don't Shine | 1986 | — | — | 3.0 |

—Black vinyl

| ❏ COL-4500 | Good Rockin' Tonight/I Don't Care If the Sun Don't Shine | 1992 | — | 2.00 | 4.00 |

—Gold vinyl

| ❏ COL-4501 | You're a Heartbreaker/Milkcow Blues Boogie | 1986 | — | — | 3.0 |

—Black vinyl

| ❏ COL-4501 | You're a Heartbreaker/Milkcow Blues Boogie | 1992 | — | 2.00 | 4.00 |

—Gold vinyl

| ❏ COL-4502 | Baby Let's Play House/I'm Left, You're Right, She's Gone | 1986 | — | — | 3.0 |

—Black vinyl

| ❏ COL-4502 | Baby Let's Play House/I'm Left, You're Right, She's Gone | 1992 | — | 2.00 | 4.00 |

—Gold vinyl

| ❏ COL-4503 | I Got a Woman/I'm Counting on You | 1986 | — | — | 3.0 |

—Black vinyl

| ❏ COL-4503 | I Got a Woman/I'm Counting on You | 1992 | — | 2.00 | 4.00 |

—Gold vinyl

| ❏ COL-4504 | I'll Never Let You Go (Little Darlin')/I'm Gonna Sit Right Down and Cry (Over You) | 1986 | — | — | 3.00 |

—Black vinyl

| ❏ COL-4504 | I'll Never Let You Go (Little Darlin')/I'm Gonna Sit Right Down and Cry (Over You) | 1992 | — | 2.00 | 4.00 |

—Gold vinyl

| ❏ COL-4505 | Tryin' to Get to You/I Love You Because | 1986 | — | — | 3.00 |

—Black vinyl

| ❏ COL-4505 | Tryin' to Get to You/I Love You Because | 1992 | — | 2.00 | 4.00 |

—Gold vinyl

| ❏ COL-4506 | Money Honey/One-Sided Love Affair | 1986 | — | — | 3.00 |

—Black vinyl

| ❏ COL-4506 | Money Honey/One-Sided Love Affair | 1992 | — | 2.00 | 4.00 |

—Gold vinyl

| ❏ COL-4507 | Too Much/Playing for Keeps | 1986 | — | — | 3.00 |

—Black vinyl

| ❏ COL-4507 | Too Much/Playing for Keeps | 1992 | — | 2.00 | 4.00 |

—Gold vinyl

| ❏ COL-4508 | A Big Hunk o'Love/My Wish Came True | 1986 | — | — | 3.0 |

—Black vinyl

Number	Title (A Side/B Side)	Yr	VG	VG+	NM
COL-4508	A Big Hunk o'Love/My Wish Came True	1992	—	2.00	4.00
Gold vinyl					
COL-4509	Stuck on You/Fame and Fortune	1986	—	—	3.00
Black vinyl					
COL-4509	Stuck on You/Fame and Fortune	1992	—	2.00	4.00
Gold vinyl					
COL-4510	I Feel So Bad/Wild in the Country	1986	—	—	3.00
Black vinyl					
COL-4510	I Feel So Bad/Wild in the Country	1992	—	2.00	4.00
Gold vinyl					
COL-4511	She's Not You/Jailhouse Rock	1986	—	—	3.00
Black vinyl					
COL-4511	She's Not You/Jailhouse Rock	1992	—	2.00	4.00
Gold vinyl					
COL-4512	One Broken Heart for Sale/Devil in Disguise	1986	—	—	3.00
Black vinyl					
COL-4512	One Broken Heart for Sale/Devil in Disguise	1992	—	2.00	4.00
Gold vinyl					
COL-4513	Bossa Nova Baby/Such a Night	1986	—	—	3.00
Black vinyl					
COL-4513	Bossa Nova Baby/Such a Night	1992	—	2.00	4.00
Gold vinyl					
COL-4514	Love Me/Flaming Star	1986	—	—	3.00
Black vinyl					
COL-4514	Love Me/Flaming Star	1992	—	2.00	4.00
Gold vinyl					
COL-4515	Follow That Dream/When My Blue Moon Turns to Gold Again	1986	—	—	3.00
Black vinyl					
COL-4515	Follow That Dream/When My Blue Moon Turns to Gold Again	1992	—	2.00	4.00
Gold vinyl					
COL-4516	Frankie and Johnny/Love Letters	1986	—	—	3.00
Black vinyl					
COL-4516	Frankie and Johnny/Love Letters	1992	—	2.00	4.00
Gold vinyl					
COL-4517	U.S. Male/Until It's Time for You to Go	1986	—	—	3.00
Black vinyl					
COL-4517	U.S. Male/Until It's Time for You to Go	1992	—	2.00	4.00
Gold vinyl					
COL-4518	Old Shep/You'll Never Walk Alone	1986	—	—	3.00
Black vinyl					
COL-4518	Old Shep/You'll Never Walk Alone	1992	—	2.00	4.00
Gold vinyl					
COL-4519	Poor Boy/An American Trilogy	1986	—	—	3.00
Black vinyl					
COL-4519	Poor Boy/An American Trilogy	1992	—	2.00	4.00
Gold vinyl					
COL-4520	How Great Thou Art/His Hand in Mine	1986	—	—	3.00
Black vinyl					
COL-4520	How Great Thou Art/His Hand in Mine	1992	—	2.00	4.00
Gold vinyl					
COL-4521	Big Boss Man/Paralyzed	1986	—	—	3.00
Black vinyl					
COL-4521	Big Boss Man/Paralyzed	1992	—	2.00	4.00
Gold vinyl					
COL-4522	Fools Fall in Love/Blue Suede Shoes	1986	—	—	3.00
Black vinyl					
COL-4522	Fools Fall in Love/Blue Suede Shoes	1992	—	2.00	4.00
Gold vinyl					
COL-4564	The Elvis Medley/Always on My Mind	1986	—	—	3.00
COL-4738	Ask Me/The Girl of My Best Friend	1997	—	—	3.00
COL-4743	Girls! Girls! Girls!/Ain't That Loving You Baby	1997	—	—	3.00
COL-4744	It's Only Love/Beyond the Reef	1997	—	—	3.00
04764	Witchcraft/Spinout	1997	—	—	3.00
80000	(Now and Then There's) A Fool Such As I/I Need Your Love Tonight	1997	—	2.00	4.00
—Gray marbled vinyl					
80001	Separate Ways/Always On My Mind	1997	—	2.00	4.00
—Gray marbled vinyl					
80002	An American Trilogy/Until It's Time for You to Go	1997	—	2.00	4.00
—Gray marbled vinyl					
80003	Crying in the Chapel/I Believe in the Man in the Sky	1997	—	2.00	4.00
—Gray marbled vinyl					
80004	Don't/I Beg of You	1997	—	2.00	4.00
—Gray marbled vinyl					
80005	Don't Cry Daddy/Rubberneckin'	1997	—	2.00	4.00
—Gray marbled vinyl					
80006	Good Luck Charm/Anything That's Part of You	1997	—	2.00	4.00
—Gray marbled vinyl					
80007	Guitar Man/Hi-Heel Sneakers	1997	—	2.00	4.00
—Gray marbled vinyl					
80008	Hard Headed Woman/Don't Ask Me Why	1997	—	2.00	4.00
—Gray marbled vinyl					
80009	Heartbreak Hotel/I Was the One	1997	—	2.00	4.00
—Gray marbled vinyl					
80010	Mystery Train/I Forgot to Remember to Forget	1997	—	2.00	4.00
—Gray marbled vinyl					
80011	One Night/I Got Stung	1997	—	2.00	4.00
—Gray marbled vinyl					
80012	I Really Don't Want to Know/There Goes My Everything	1997	—	2.00	4.00
—Gray marbled vinyl					
80013	I Want You, I Need You, I Love You/My Baby Left Me	1997	—	2.00	4.00
—Gray marbled vinyl					

Number	Title (A Side/B Side)	Yr	VG	VG+	NM
80014	If I Can Dream/Edge of Reality	1997	—	2.00	4.00
—Gray marbled vinyl					
80015	Kentucky Rain/My Little Friend	1997	—	2.00	4.00
—Gray marbled vinyl					
80016	Kiss Me Quick/Suspicion	1997	—	2.00	4.00
—Gray marbled vinyl					
80017	Kissin' Cousins/It Hurts Me	1997	—	2.00	4.00
—Gray marbled vinyl					
80018	Marie's the Name His Latest Flame/Little Sister	1997	—	2.00	4.00
—Gray marbled vinyl					
80019	(Let Me Be You) Teddy Bear/Loving You	1997	—	2.00	4.00
—Gray marbled vinyl					
80020	The Wonder of You/Mama Liked the Roses	1997	—	2.00	4.00
—Gray marbled vinyl					
80021	Memories/Charro	1997	—	2.00	4.00
—Gray marbled vinyl					
80022	My Boy/Thinking About You	1997	—	2.00	4.00
—Gray marbled vinyl					
80023	Way Down/My Way	1997	—	2.00	4.00
—Gray marbled vinyl					
80024	Patch It Up/You Don't Have to Say You Love Me	1997	—	2.00	4.00
—Gray marbled vinyl					
80025	Surrender/Lonely Man	1997	—	2.00	4.00
—Gray marbled vinyl					
80026	That's All Right/Blue Moon of Kentucky	1997	—	2.00	4.00
—Gray marbled vinyl					
80027	Wear My Ring Around Your Neck/Doncha' Think It's Time	1997	—	2.00	4.00
—Gray marbled vinyl					
80028	Puppet on a String/Wooden Heart	1997	—	2.00	4.00
—Gray marbled vinyl					
RCA					
447-0600	I Forgot to Remember to Forget/Mystery Train	1977	—	2.00	4.00
—Note: All RCA releases with a "447" prefix are from the Gold Standard Series and are black label, dog near top					
447-0601	That's All Right/Blue Moon of Kentucky	1977	—	2.00	4.00
447-0602	Good Rockin' Tonight/I Don't Care If the Sun Don't Shine	1977	—	2.00	4.00
447-0603	Milkcow Blues Boogie/You're a Heartbreaker	1977	—	2.00	4.00
447-0604	Baby Let's Play House/I'm Left, You're Right, She's Gone	1977	—	2.00	4.00
447-0605	Heartbreak Hotel/I Was the One	1977	—	2.00	4.00
447-0607	I Want You, I Need You, I Love You/My Baby Left Me	1977	—	2.00	4.00
447-0608	Hound Dog/Don't Be Cruel	1977	—	2.00	4.00
447-0609	Blue Suede Shoes/Tutti Frutti	1977	—	2.00	4.00
447-0613	Blue Moon/Just Because	1977	—	2.00	4.00
447-0614	Money Honey/One-Sided Love Affair	1977	—	2.00	4.00
447-0615	Lawdy Miss Clawdy/Shake, Rattle, and Roll	1977	—	2.00	4.00
447-0616	Love Me Tender/Anyway You Want Me (That's How I Will Be)	1977	—	2.00	4.00
447-0617	Too Much/Playing for Keeps	1977	—	2.00	4.00
447-0618	All Shook Up/That's When Your Heartaches Begin	1977	—	2.00	4.00
447-0619	Jailhouse Rock/Treat Me Nice	1977	—	2.00	4.00
447-0620	(Let Me Be Your) Teddy Bear/Loving You	1977	—	2.00	4.00
447-0621	Don't/I Beg of You	1977	—	2.00	4.00
447-0622	Wear My Ring Around Your Neck/Don'tcha Think It's Time	1977	—	2.00	4.00
447-0623	Hard Headed Woman/Don't Ask Me Why	1977	—	2.00	4.00
447-0624	One Night/I Got Stung	1977	—	2.00	4.00
447-0625	(Now and Then There's) A Fool Such As I/I Need Your Love Tonight	1977	—	2.00	4.00
447-0626	A Big Hunk o'Love/My Wish Came True	1977	—	2.00	4.00
447-0627	Stuck on You/Fame and Fortune	1977	—	2.00	4.00
447-0628	It's Now or Never/A Mess of Blues	1977	—	2.00	4.00
447-0629	Are You Lonesome To-Night?/I Gotta Know	1977	—	2.00	4.00
447-0630	Surrender/Lonely Man	1977	—	2.00	4.00
447-0631	I Feel So Bad/Wild in the Country	1977	—	2.00	4.00
447-0634	(Marie's the Name) His Latest Flame/Little Sister	1977	—	2.00	4.00
447-0635	Can't Help Falling in Love/Rock-a-Hula Baby	1977	—	2.00	4.00
447-0636	Good Luck Charm/Anything That's Part of You	1977	—	2.00	4.00
447-0637	She's Not You/Just Tell Her Jim Said Hello	1977	—	2.00	4.00
447-0638	Return to Sender/Where Do You Come From	1977	—	2.00	4.00
447-0639	Kiss Me Quick/Suspicion	1977	—	2.00	4.00
447-0640	One Broken Heart for Sale/They Remind Me Too Much of You	1977	—	2.00	4.00
447-0641	(You're the) Devil in Disguise/Please Don't Drag That String Around	1977	—	2.00	4.00
447-0642	Bossa Nova Baby/Witchcraft	1977	—	2.00	4.00
447-0643	Crying in the Chapel/I Believe in the Man in the Sky	1977	—	2.00	4.00
447-0644	Kissin' Cousins/It Hurts Me	1977	—	2.00	4.00
447-0645	Such a Night/Never Ending	1977	—	2.00	4.00
447-0646	Viva Las Vegas/What'd I Say	1977	—	2.00	4.00
447-0647	Blue Christmas/Santa Claus Is Back in Town	1977	—	2.00	4.00
447-0647 [PS]	Blue Christmas/Santa Claus Is Back in Town	1977	2.50	5.00	10.00
—Does not mention "Gold Standard Series" on sleeve					
447-0648	Do the Clam/You'll Be Gone	1977	—	2.00	4.00
447-0649	Ain't That Loving You Baby/Ask Me	1977	—	2.00	4.00
447-0650	Puppet on a String/Wooden Heart	1977	—	2.00	4.00
447-0651	Joshua Fit the Battle/Known Only to Him	1977	—	2.00	4.00
447-0653	(Such An) Easy Question/It Feels So Right	1977	—	2.00	4.00
447-0654	I'm Yours/(It's a) Long, Lonely Highway	1977	—	2.00	4.00
447-0655	Tell Me Why/Blue River	1977	—	2.00	4.00
447-0656	Frankie and Johnny/Please Don't Stop Loving Me	1977	—	2.00	4.00

P

Number	Title (A Side/B Side)	Yr	VG	VG+	NM
❑ 447-0657	Love Letters/Come What May	1977	—	2.00	4.00
❑ 447-0658	Spinout/All That I Do	1977	—	2.00	4.00
❑ 447-0659	Indescribably Blue/Fools Fall in Love	1977	—	2.00	4.00
❑ 447-0661	There's Always Me/Judy	1977	—	2.00	4.00
❑ 447-0662	Big Boss Man/You Don't Know Me	1977	—	2.00	4.00
❑ 447-0663	Guitar Man/High Heel Sneakers	1977	—	2.00	4.00
❑ 447-0664	U.S. Male/Stay Away	1977	—	2.50	5.00
❑ 447-0665	You'll Never Walk Alone/We Call on Him	1977	—	2.00	4.00
❑ 447-0666	Let Yourself Go/Your Time Hasn't Come Yet, Baby	1977	—	2.00	4.00
❑ 447-0667	A Little Less Conversation/Almost in Love	1977	—	2.00	4.00
❑ 447-0668	If I Can Dream/Edge of Reality	1977	—	2.00	4.00
❑ 447-0669	Memories/Charro	1977	—	2.00	4.00
❑ 447-0670	How Great Thou Art/His Hand in Mine	1977	—	2.00	4.00
❑ 447-0671	In the Ghetto/Any Day Now	1977	—	2.00	4.00
❑ 447-0672	Clean Up Your Own Back Yard/The Fair Is Moving On	1977	—	2.00	4.00
❑ 447-0673	Suspicious Minds/You'll Think of Me	1977	—	2.00	4.00
❑ 447-0674	Don't Cry Daddy/Rubberneckin'	1977	—	2.00	4.00
❑ 447-0675	Kentucky Rain/My Little Friend	1977	—	2.00	4.00
❑ 447-0676	The Wonder of You/Mama Liked the Roses	1977	—	2.00	4.00
❑ 447-0677	I've Lost You/The Next Step Is Love	1977	—	2.00	4.00
❑ 447-0678	You Don't Have to Say You Love Me/Patch It Up	1977	—	2.00	4.00
❑ 447-0679	I Really Don't Want to Know/There Goes My Everything	1977	—	2.00	4.00
❑ 447-0680	Where Did They Go, Lord/Rags to Riches	1977	—	2.00	4.00
❑ 447-0681	If Every Day Was Like Christmas/How Would You Like to Be	1977	—	2.00	4.00
❑ 447-0682	Life/Only Believe	1977	—	2.00	4.00
❑ 447-0683	I'm Leavin'/Heart of Rome	1977	—	2.00	4.00
❑ 447-0684	It's Only Love/The Sound of Your Cry	1977	—	2.00	4.00
❑ 447-0685	An American Trilogy/Until It's Time for You to Go	1977	—	2.00	4.00
❑ DME1-1803R	King of the Whole Wide World/King Creole	1997	3.75	7.50	15.00
—Red vinyl, marked as a promotional copy (about 3,000 pressed)					
❑ DME1-1803	King of the Whole Wide World/King Creole	1997	2.00	4.00	8.00
—Gold vinyl (about 7,000 pressed)					
❑ DME1-1803 [DJ]	King of the Whole Wide World/King Creole	1997	100.00	200.00	400.00
—Test pressings of above on green, blue, white and clear vinyl. Value is for any of them.					
❑ DME1-1803 [PS]	King of the Whole Wide World/King Creole	1997	2.00	4.00	8.00
—Same picture sleeve with either edition					
❑ 8760-7-R	Heartbreak Hotel/Heartbreak Hotel	1988	—	2.50	5.00
—B-side by David Keith					
❑ 8760-7-R [PS]	Heartbreak Hotel/Heartbreak Hotel	1988	—	3.00	6.00
—"Pink Cadillac" sleeve					
❑ 8760-7-R [PS]	Heartbreak Hotel/Heartbreak Hotel	1988	20.00	40.00	80.00
—Promo-only sleeve of RCA executive Butch Waugh dressed as Elvis					
❑ GB-10485	Take Good Care of Her/I've Got a Thing About You, Baby	1977	—	2.00	4.00
—Gold Standard Series; black label					
❑ GB-10486	Separate Ways/Always on My Mind	1977	—	2.00	4.00
—Gold Standard Series; black label					
❑ GB-10487	T-R-O-U-B-L-E/Mr. Songman	1977	—	2.00	4.00
—Gold Standard Series; black label					
❑ GB-10488	Promised Land/It's Midnight	1977	—	2.00	4.00
—Gold Standard Series; black label					
❑ GB-10489	My Boy/Thinking About You	1977	—	2.00	4.00
—Gold Standard Series; black label					
❑ PB-10601	Hurt/For the Heart	1976	25.00	50.00	100.00
—Second pressings (very rare) on the 1976-88 "dog near top" black label					
❑ JB-10857 [DJ]	Moody Blue/She Thinks I Still Care	1976	250.00	500.00	1000.
—Colored vinyl pressings exist in five different colors -- red, white, gold, blue, green. Value is for any of them.					
❑ PB-10857	Moody Blue/She Thinks I Still Care	1976	—	2.50	5.00
❑ PB-10857 [PS]	Moody Blue/She Thinks I Still Care	1976	2.50	5.00	10.00
❑ JH-10951 [DJ]	Let Me Be There (mono/stereo)	1977	50.00	100.00	200.00
—Promo only					
❑ PB-10998	Way Down/Pledging My Love	1977	—	2.50	5.00
❑ PB-10998 [PS]	Way Down/Pledging My Love	1977	2.50	5.00	10.00
❑ PB-11099	Hound Dog/Don't Be Cruel	1977	—	2.00	4.00
❑ PB-11099 [PS]	Hound Dog/Don't Be Cruel	1977	—	2.00	4.00
—From boxes "15 Golden Records, 30 Golden Hits" and "20 Golden Hits in Full Color Sleeves"					
❑ PB-11100	In the Ghetto/Any Day Now	1977	—	2.00	4.00
❑ PB-11100 [PS]	In the Ghetto/Any Day Now	1977	—	2.00	4.00
—From boxes "15 Golden Records, 30 Golden Hits" and "20 Golden Hits in Full Color Sleeves"					
❑ PB-11101	Jailhouse Rock/Treat Me Nice	1977	—	2.00	4.00
❑ PB-11101 [PS]	Jailhouse Rock/Treat Me Nice	1977	—	2.00	4.00
—From box "15 Golden Records, 30 Golden Hits"					
❑ PB-11102	Can't Help Falling in Love/Rock-a-Hula Baby	1977	—	2.00	4.00
❑ PB-11102 [PS]	Can't Help Falling in Love/Rock-a-Hula Baby	1977	—	2.00	4.00
—From boxes "15 Golden Records, 30 Golden Hits" and "20 Golden Hits in Full Color Sleeves"					
❑ PB-11103	Suspicious Minds/You'll Think of Me	1977	—	2.00	4.00
❑ PB-11103 [PS]	Suspicious Minds/You'll Think of Me	1977	—	2.00	4.00
—From box "15 Golden Records, 30 Golden Hits"					
❑ PB-11104	Are You Lonesome To-Night?/I Gotta Know	1977	—	2.00	4.00
❑ PB-11104 [PS]	Are You Lonesome To-Night?/I Gotta Know	1977	—	2.00	4.00
—From boxes "15 Golden Records, 30 Golden Hits" and "20 Golden Hits in Full Color Sleeves"					
❑ PB-11105	Heartbreak Hotel/I Was the One	1977	—	2.00	4.00
❑ PB-11105 [PS]	Heartbreak Hotel/I Was the One	1977	—	2.00	4.00
—From boxes "15 Golden Records, 30 Golden Hits" and "20 Golden Hits in Full Color Sleeves"					
❑ PB-11106	All Shook Up/That's When Your Heartaches Begin	1977	—	2.00	4.00
❑ PB-11106 [PS]	All Shook Up/That's When Your Heartaches Begin	1977	—	2.00	4.00
—From boxes "15 Golden Records, 30 Golden Hits" and "20 Golden Hits in Full Color Sleeves"					
❑ PB-11107	Blue Suede Shoes/Tutti Frutti	1977	—	2.00	4.00

Number	Title (A Side/B Side)	Yr	VG	VG+	N
❑ PB-11107 [PS]	Blue Suede Shoes/Tutti Frutti	1977	—	2.00	4
—From boxes "15 Golden Records, 30 Golden Hits" and "20 Golden Hits in Full Color Sleeves"					
❑ PB-11108	Love Me Tender/Any Way You Want Me (That's How I Will Be)	1977	—	2.00	4.
❑ PB-11108 [PS]	Love Me Tender/Any Way You Want Me (That's How I Will Be)	1977	—	2.00	4.
—From boxes "15 Golden Records, 30 Golden Hits" and "20 Golden Hits in Full Color Sleeves"					
❑ PB-11109	(Let Me Be Your) Teddy Bear/Loving You	1977	—	2.00	4.
❑ PB-11109 [PS]	(Let Me Be Your) Teddy Bear/Loving You	1977	—	2.00	4.
—From boxes "15 Golden Records, 30 Golden Hits" and "20 Golden Hits in Full Color Sleeves"					
❑ PB-11110	It's Now or Never/A Mess of Blues	1977	—	2.00	4.
❑ PB-11110 [PS]	It's Now or Never/A Mess of Blues	1977	—	2.00	4
—From box "15 Golden Records, 30 Golden Hits"					
❑ PB-11111	Return to Sender/Where Do You Come From	1977	—	2.00	4.
❑ PB-11111 [PS]	Return to Sender/Where Do You Come From	1977	—	2.00	4.
—From boxes "15 Golden Records, 30 Golden Hits" and "20 Golden Hits in Full Color Sleeves"					
❑ PB-11112	One Night/I Got Stung	1977	—	2.00	4.
❑ PB-11112 [PS]	One Night/I Got Stung	1977	—	2.00	4.
—From box "15 Golden Records, 30 Golden Hits"					
❑ PB-11113	Crying in the Chapel/I Believe in the Man in the Sky	1977	—	2.00	4.
❑ PB-11113 [PS]	Crying in the Chapel/I Believe in the Man in the Sky	1977	—	2.00	4.
—From box "15 Golden Records, 30 Golden Hits"					
❑ PB-11165	My Way/America	1977	—	2.50	5.
❑ PB-11165	My Way/America the Beautiful	1977	5.00	10.00	20.
❑ PB-11165 [PS]	My Way/America	1977	2.50	5.00	10.
❑ PB-11165 [PS]	My Way/America the Beautiful	1977	6.25	12.50	25.
❑ PB-11212	Unchained Melody/Softly, As I Leave You	1978	2.50	5.00	10.
—Erroneously states "Vocal Accompaniment by Sherrill Nielsen" on "Unchained Melody" side					
❑ PB-11212	Unchained Melody/Softly, As I Leave You	1978	—	2.50	5.
—No credit to Sherrill Nielsen on the "Unchained Melody" side					
❑ PB-11212 [PS]	Unchained Melody/Softly, As I Leave You	1978	2.50	5.00	10.
❑ PP-11301	15 Golden Records, 30 Golden Hits	1977	15.00	30.00	60.
—Includes 15 records (11099-11113) and outer box					
❑ PB-11320	(Let Me Be Your) Teddy Bear/Puppet on a String	1978	—	2.50	5.
❑ PB-11320 [PS]	(Let Me Be Your) Teddy Bear/Puppet on a String	1978	2.50	5.00	10.
❑ GB-11326	Moody Blue/For the Heart	1978	—	2.00	4.
—Gold Standard Series					
❑ PP-11340	20 Golden Hits in Full Color Sleeves	1977	20.00	40.00	80.
—Includes 10 records (11099, 11100, 11102, 11104-11109, 11111) and outer box					
❑ GB-11504	Way Down/My Way	1979	—	2.00	4.
—Gold Standard Series					
❑ PB-11533	Are You Sincere/Solitaire	1979	—	2.50	5.
❑ PB-11533 [PS]	Are You Sincere/Solitaire	1979	2.50	5.00	10.
❑ PB-11679	There's a Honky Tonk Angel (Who Will Take Me Back In)/I Got a Feelin' in My Body	1979	3.75	7.50	15.
—Has full production credits (background vocals, strings) listed in error on both sides					
❑ PB-11679	There's a Honky Tonk Angel (Who Will Take Me Back In)/I Got a Feelin' in My Body	1979	—	2.50	5.
—Has production credits removed; only producers are listed					
❑ PB-11679 [PS]	There's a Honky Tonk Angel (Who Will Take Me Back In)/I Got a Feelin' in My Body	1979	2.50	5.00	10.
❑ GB-11988	Unchained Melody/Are You Sincere	1980	—	2.00	4.
—Gold Standard Series					
❑ JH-12158 [DJ]	Guitar Man (mono/stereo)	1981	75.00	150.00	300.
—Promo only on red vinyl					
❑ PB-12158	Guitar Man/Faded Love	1981	—	2.50	5.
❑ PB-12158 [PS]	Guitar Man/Faded Love	1981	2.50	5.00	10.
❑ JB-12205 [DJ]	Lovin' Arms/You Asked Me To	1981	75.00	150.00	300.
—Promo only on green vinyl					
❑ PB-12205	Lovin' Arms/You Asked Me To	1981	—	3.00	6.
—Not issued with picture sleeve (bootlegs exist)					
❑ PB-13058	There Goes My Everything/You'll Never Walk Alone	1982	—	2.50	5.0
❑ PB-13058 [PS]	There Goes My Everything/You'll Never Walk Alone	1982	2.50	5.00	10.
❑ GB-13275	Suspicious Minds/You'll Think of Me	1982	—	2.00	4.
—Gold Standard Series					
❑ JH-13302	The Impossible Dream (The Quest)/An American Trilogy	1982	25.00	50.00	100.
❑ JH-13302 [PS]	The Impossible Dream (The Quest)/An American Trilogy	1982	25.00	50.00	100.0
—Promo only, distributed to visitors to Elvis' birthplace in Tupelo, Mississippi, in 1982.					
❑ JB-13351 [DJ]	The Elvis Medley (Long Version)/The Elvis Medley (Short Version)	1982	75.00	150.00	300.0
—Promo only on gold vinyl					
❑ PB-13351	The Elvis Medley/Always on My Mind	1982	—	2.50	5.
❑ PB-13351 [PS]	The Elvis Medley/Always on My Mind	1982	2.50	5.00	10.
❑ JB-13500 [DJ]	I Was the One/Wear My Ring Around Your Neck	1983	75.00	150.00	300.0
—Promo only on gold vinyl					
❑ PB-13500	I Was the One/Wear My Ring Around Your Neck	1983	—	2.50	5.
❑ PB-13500 [PS]	I Was the One/Wear My Ring Around Your Neck	1983	2.50	5.00	10.
❑ JB-13547 [DJ]	Little Sister/Paralyzed	1983	75.00	150.00	300.0
—Promo only on blue vinyl					
❑ PB-13547	Little Sister/Paralyzed	1983	—	2.50	5.
❑ PB-13547 [PS]	Little Sister/Paralyzed	1983	2.50	5.00	10.0
❑ JB-13875 [DJ]	Baby Let's Play House/Hound Dog	1984	50.00	100.00	200.0
—Gold vinyl, custom label					
❑ PB-13875	Baby Let's Play House/Hound Dog	1984	10.00	20.00	40.
—Gold vinyl, custom label					
❑ PB-13875 [PS]	Baby Let's Play House/Hound Dog	1984	10.00	20.00	40.0
❑ PB-13885	Blue Suede Shoes/Tutti Frutti	1984	—	2.00	4.0
—From box "Elvis' Greatest Hits, Golden Singles, Volume 1"; gold vinyl					
❑ PB-13885 [PS]	Blue Suede Shoes/Tutti Frutti	1984	—	2.00	4.0

Number	Title (A Side/B Side)	Yr	VG	VG+	NM
PB-13886	Don't Be Cruel/Hound Dog	1984	—	2.00	4.00
	—From box "Elvis' Greatest Hits, Golden Singles, Volume 1"; gold vinyl				
PB-13886 [PS]	Don't Be Cruel/Hound Dog	1984	—	2.00	4.00
PB-13887	I Want You, I Need You, I Love You/Love Me	1984	—	2.00	4.00
	—From box "Elvis' Greatest Hits, Golden Singles, Volume 1"; gold vinyl				
PB-13887 [PS]	I Want You, I Need You, I Love You/Love Me	1984	—	2.00	4.00
PB-13888	All Shook Up/(Let Me Be Your) Teddy Bear	1984	—	2.00	4.00
	—From box "Elvis' Greatest Hits, Golden Singles, Volume 1"; gold vinyl				
PB-13888 [PS]	All Shook Up/(Let Me Be Your) Teddy Bear	1984	—	2.00	4.00
PB-13889	It's Now or Never/Surrender	1984	—	2.00	4.00
	—From box "Elvis' Greatest Hits, Golden Singles, Volume 1"; gold vinyl				
PB-13889 [PS]	It's Now or Never/Surrender	1984	—	2.00	4.00
PB-13890	In the Ghetto/If I Can Dream	1984	—	2.00	4.00
	—From box "Elvis' Greatest Hits, Golden Singles, Volume 1"; gold vinyl				
PB-13890 [PS]	In the Ghetto/If I Can Dream	1984	—	2.00	4.00
PB-13891	That's All Right/Blue Moon of Kentucky	1984	—	2.00	4.00
	—From box "Elvis' Greatest Hits, Golden Singles, Volume 2"; gold vinyl				
PB-13891 [PS]	That's All Right/Blue Moon of Kentucky	1984	—	2.00	4.00
PB-13892	Heartbreak Hotel/Jailhouse Rock	1984	—	2.00	4.00
	—From box "Elvis' Greatest Hits, Golden Singles, Volume 2"; gold vinyl				
PB-13892 [PS]	Heartbreak Hotel/Jailhouse Rock	1984	—	2.00	4.00
PB-13893	Love Me Tender/Loving You	1984	—	2.00	4.00
	—From box "Elvis' Greatest Hits, Golden Singles, Volume 2"; gold vinyl				
PB-13893 [PS]	Love Me Tender/Loving You	1984	—	2.00	4.00
PB-13894	(Marie's the Name) His Latest Flame/Little Sister	1984	—	2.00	4.00
	—From box "Elvis' Greatest Hits, Golden Singles, Volume 2"; gold vinyl				
PB-13894 [PS]	(Marie's the Name) His Latest Flame/Little Sister	1984	—	2.00	4.00
PB-13895	Are You Lonesome Tonight/Can't Help Falling in Love	1984	—	2.00	4.00
	—From box "Elvis' Greatest Hits, Golden Singles, Volume 2"; gold vinyl				
PB-13895 [PS]	Are You Lonesome Tonight/Can't Help Falling in Love	1984	—	2.00	4.00
PB-13896	Suspicious Minds/Burning Love	1984	—	2.00	4.00
	—From box "Elvis' Greatest Hits, Golden Singles, Volume 2"; gold vinyl				
PB-13896 [PS]	Suspicious Minds/Burning Love	1984	—	2.00	4.00
PB-13897	Elvis' Greatest Hits, Golden Singles, Volume 1	1984	3.75	7.50	15.00
	—Box set of six 45s with sleeves (13885-13890) with box				
PB-13898	Elvis' Greatest Hits, Golden Singles, Volume 2	1984	3.75	7.50	15.00
	—Box set of six 45s with sleeves (13891-13896) with box				
PB-13929	Blue Suede Shoes/Promised Land	1984	3.75	7.50	15.00
	—Blue vinyl; incorrect label -- "Blue Suede Shoes" side says "Stereo" and "Promised Land" side says "Mono"				
PB-13929	Blue Suede Shoes/Promised Land	1984	3.00	6.00	12.00
	—Blue vinyl; correct label -- "Blue Suede Shoes" side says "Mono" and "Promised Land" side says "Stereo"				
PB-13929 [PS]	Blue Suede Shoes/Promised Land	1984	2.50	5.00	10.00
PB-14090	Always on My Mind/My Boy	1985	2.50	5.00	10.00
	—Purple vinyl				
PB-14090 [PS]	Always on My Mind/My Boy	1985	2.50	5.00	10.00
PB-14237	Merry Christmas Baby/Santa Claus Is Back in Town	1985	3.75	7.50	15.00
	—"Elvis 50th Anniversary" label				
PB-14237	Merry Christmas Baby/Santa Claus Is Back in Town	1985	—	2.50	5.00
	—Normal black RCA label				
PB-14237	Merry Christmas Baby/Santa Claus Is Back in Town	1985	3.75	7.50	15.00
	—Green vinyl				
PB-14237 [PS]	Merry Christmas Baby/Santa Claus Is Back in Town	1985	3.00	6.00	12.00
60575	A Little Less Conversation (JXL Radio Edit Remix)/(Original Version)	2002	2.00	4.00	8.00
	—Credited to "Elvis Presley: Elvis vs JXL"				
62402	Don't Be Cruel/Ain't That Lovin' You Baby (Fast Version)	1992	—	2.50	5.00
62402 [PS]	Don't Be Cruel/Ain't That Lovin' You Baby (Fast Version)	1992	—	2.50	5.00
	—Generic white sleeve with "Elvis -- The King of Rock 'n' Roll" sticker				
62403	Blue Christmas/Love Me Tender	1992	—	2.50	5.00
62403 [PS]	Blue Christmas/Love Me Tender	1992	—	2.50	5.00
	—Generic white sleeve with "Elvis -- The King of Rock 'n' Roll" sticker				
62411	Silver Bells (Unreleased Version)/Silver Bells	1993	—	2.50	5.00
62449	Heartbreak Hotel/Hound Dog	1992	—	2.50	5.00
64476	Heartbreak Hotel/I Was the One//Heartbreak Hotel (Alternate Take 5)/I Was the One (Alternate Take 2)	1996	—	—	3.00
64476 [PS]	Heartbreak Hotel/I Was the One//Heartbreak Hotel (Alternate Take 5)/I Was the One (Alternate Take 2)	1996	—	—	3.00
RCA VICTOR					
37-7850	Surrender/Lonely Man	1961	150.00	300.00	600.00
	—"Compact Single 33" (small hole, plays at LP speed)				
37-7850 [PS]	Surrender/Lonely Man	1961	250.00	500.00	1000.
	—Special picture sleeve for above record				
37-7880	I Feel So Bad/Wild in the Country	1961	250.00	500.00	1000.
	—"Compact Single 33" (small hole, plays at LP speed)				
37-7880 [PS]	I Feel So Bad/Wild in the Country	1961	300.00	600.00	1200.
	—Special picture sleeve for above record				
37-7908	(Marie's the Name) His Latest Flame/Little Sister	1961	375.00	750.00	1500.
	—"Compact Single 33" (small hole, plays at LP speed)				
37-7908 [PS]	(Marie's the Name) His Latest Flame/Little Sister	1961	1000.	1500.	2000.
	—Special picture sleeve for above record				
37-7908 [PS]	(Marie's the Name) His Latest Flame/Little Sister	1961	1125.	1688.	2250.
	—Special picture sleeve for above record; says "Stereo-Orthophonic" on sleeve in error				
37-7968	Can't Help Falling in Love/Rock-a-Hula Baby	1961	1000.	1500.	2000.
	—"Compact Single 33" (small hole, plays at LP speed)				

Number	Title (A Side/B Side)	Yr	VG	VG+	NM
37-7968 [PS]	Can't Help Falling in Love/Rock-a-Hula Baby	1961	2000.	3000.	4000.
	—Special picture sleeve for above record				
37-7992	Good Luck Charm/Anything That's Part of You	1962	1250.	1875.	2500.
	—"Compact Single 33" (small hole, plays at LP speed)				
37-7992 [PS]	Good Luck Charm/Anything That's Part of You	1962	2500.	3750.	5000.
	—Special picture sleeve for above record				
47-6357	I Forgot to Remember to Forget/Mystery Train	1955	15.00	30.00	60.00
	—No horizontal line on label				
47-6357	I Forgot to Remember to Forget/Mystery Train	1955	15.00	30.00	60.00
	—With horizontal line on label				
47-6357 [PS]	This Is His Life: Elvis Presley	1955	375.00	750.00	1500.
	—Promo-only sleeve issued with above single; no stock picture sleeve was issued. This was formerly listed under "I Want You, I Need You, I Love You," as the sleeve does not have a number. Consensus opinion now places it with "Mystery Train."				
47-6380	That's All Right/Blue Moon of Kentucky	1955	15.00	30.00	60.00
	—No horizontal line on label				
47-6380	That's All Right/Blue Moon of Kentucky	1955	15.00	30.00	60.00
	—With horizontal line on label				
47-6381	Good Rockin' Tonight/I Don't Care If the Sun Don't Shine	1955	15.00	30.00	60.00
	—With horizontal line on label				
47-6381	Good Rockin' Tonight/I Don't Care If the Sun Don't Shine	1955	15.00	30.00	60.00
	—No horizontal line on label				
47-6382	Milkcow Blues Boogie/You're a Heartbreaker	1955	15.00	30.00	60.00
	—No horizontal line on label				
47-6382	Milkcow Blues Boogie/You're a Heartbreaker	1955	15.00	30.00	60.00
	—With horizontal line on label				
47-6383	Baby Let's Play House/I'm Left, You're Right, She's Gone	1955	15.00	30.00	60.00
	—With horizontal line on label				
47-6383	Baby Let's Play House/I'm Left, You're Right, She's Gone	1955	15.00	30.00	60.00
	—No horizontal line on label				
47-6420	Heartbreak Hotel/I Was the One	1956	10.00	20.00	40.00
	—No horizontal line on label				
47-6420	Heartbreak Hotel/I Was the One	1956	10.00	20.00	40.00
	—With horizontal line on label				
47-6540	I Want You, I Need You, I Love You/My Baby Left Me	1956	10.00	20.00	40.00
	—No horizontal line on label				
47-6540	I Want You, I Need You, I Love You/My Baby Left Me	1956	10.00	20.00	40.00
	—With horizontal line on label				
47-6604	Don't Be Cruel/Hound Dog	1956	7.50	15.00	30.00
	—No horizontal line on label				
47-6604	Don't Be Cruel/Hound Dog	1956	7.50	15.00	30.00
	—With horizontal line on label				
47-6604 [PS]	Don't Be Cruel/Hound Dog	1956	50.00	100.00	200.00
	—"Don't Be Cruel" listed on top of "Hound Dog!"				
47-6604 [PS]	Don't Be Cruel/Hound Dog	1956	30.00	60.00	120.00
	—"Hound Dog!" listed on top of "Don't Be Cruel"				
47-6636	Blue Suede Shoes/Tutti Frutti	1956	20.00	40.00	80.00
	—No horizontal line on label				
47-6636	Blue Suede Shoes/Tutti Frutti	1956	20.00	40.00	80.00
	—With horizontal line on label				
47-6637	I Got a Woman/I'm Countin' On You	1956	20.00	40.00	80.00
	—With horizontal line on label				
47-6637	I Got a Woman/I'm Countin' On You	1956	20.00	40.00	80.00
	—No horizontal line on label				
47-6638	I'm Gonna Sit Right Down and Cry (Over You)/I'll Never Let You Go (Little Darlin')	1956	17.50	35.00	70.00
	—No horizontal line on label				
47-6638	I'm Gonna Sit Right Down and Cry (Over You)/I'll Never Let You Go (Little Darlin')	1956	17.50	35.00	70.00
	—With horizontal line on label				
47-6639	Tryin' to Get to You/I Love You Because	1956	17.50	35.00	70.00
	—With horizontal line on label				
47-6639	Tryin' to Get to You/I Love You Because	1956	17.50	35.00	70.00
	—No horizontal line on label				
47-6640	Blue Moon/Just Because	1956	15.00	30.00	60.00
	—No horizontal line on label				
47-6640	Blue Moon/Just Because	1956	15.00	30.00	60.00
	—With horizontal line on label				
47-6641	Money Honey/One-Sided Love Affair	1956	12.50	25.00	50.00
	—With horizontal line on label				
47-6641	Money Honey/One-Sided Love Affair	1956	12.50	25.00	50.00
	—No horizontal line on label				
47-6642	Lawdy Miss Clawdy/Shake, Rattle, and Roll	1956	10.00	20.00	40.00
	—No horizontal line on label				
47-6642	Lawdy Miss Clawdy/Shake, Rattle, and Roll	1956	50.00	100.00	200.00
	—With horizontal line on label, but with no dog				
47-6642	Lawdy Miss Clawdy/Shake, Rattle, and Roll	1956	10.00	20.00	40.00
	—With horizontal line on label, dog on label as usual				
47-6643	Love Me Tender/Anyway You Want Me (That's How I Will Be)	1956	7.50	15.00	30.00
	—No horizontal line on label				
47-6643	Love Me Tender/Anyway You Want Me (That's How I Will Be)	1956	7.50	15.00	30.00
	—With horizontal line on label				
47-6643	Love Me Tender/Anyway You Want Me (That's How I Will Be)	1956	10.00	20.00	40.00
	—No reference to the movie "Love Me Tender" on label				
47-6643 [PS]	Love Me Tender/Anyway You Want Me (That's How I Will Be)	1956	45.00	90.00	180.00
	—Black and white sleeve				

Number	Title (A Side/B Side)	Yr	VG	VG+	NM
❏ 47-6643 [PS]	Love Me Tender/Anyway You Want Me (That's How I Will Be)	1956	18.75	37.50	75.00

—*Black and green sleeve*

❏ 47-6643 [PS]	Love Me Tender/Anyway You Want Me (That's How I Will Be)	1956	10.00	20.00	40.00

—*Black and dark pink sleeve*

❏ 47-6643 [PS]	Love Me Tender/Anyway You Want Me (That's How I Will Be)	1956	7.50	15.00	30.00

—*Black and light pink sleeve*

❏ 47-6800	Too Much/Playing for Keeps	1957	7.50	15.00	30.00

—*No horizontal line on label*

❏ 47-6800	Too Much/Playing for Keeps	1957	50.00	100.00	200.00

—*With horizontal line on label, but with no dog*

❏ 47-6800	Too Much/Playing for Keeps	1957	7.50	15.00	30.00

—*With horizontal line on label, dog on label as normal*

❏ 47-6800 [PS]	Too Much/Playing for Keeps	1957	22.50	45.00	90.00
❏ 47-6870	All Shook Up/That's When Your Heartaches Begin	1957	7.50	15.00	30.00

—*No horizontal line on label*

❏ 47-6870	All Shook Up/That's When Your Heartaches Begin	1957	7.50	15.00	30.00

—*With horizontal line on label*

❏ 47-6870 [PS]	All Shook Up/That's When Your Heartaches Begin	1957	22.50	45.00	90.00
❏ 47-7000	(Let Me Be Your) Teddy Bear/Loving You	1957	10.00	20.00	40.00

—*Label says "Let Me Be Your TEDDY BEAR" (no parentheses)*

❏ 47-7000	(Let Me Be Your) Teddy Bear/Loving You	1957	7.50	15.00	30.00

—*Parentheses around "Let Me Be Your", no horizontal line on label*

❏ 47-7000	(Let Me Be Your) Teddy Bear/Loving You	1957	7.50	15.00	30.00

—*Parentheses around "Let Me Be Your", with horizontal line on label*

❏ 47-7000 [PS]	(Let Me Be Your) Teddy Bear/Loving You	1957	30.00	60.00	120.00
❏ 47-7035	Jailhouse Rock/Treat Me Nice	1957	7.50	15.00	30.00

—*No horizontal line on label*

❏ 47-7035	Jailhouse Rock/Treat Me Nice	1957	7.50	15.00	30.00

—*With horizontal line on label*

❏ 47-7035	Jailhouse Rock/Treat Me Nice	1957	5000.	7500.	10000.

—*Gold label; gold vinyl*

❏ 47-7035 [PS]	Jailhouse Rock/Treat Me Nice	1957	25.00	50.00	100.00
❏ 47-7150	Don't/I Beg of You	1958	6.25	12.50	25.00

—*No horizontal line on label*

❏ 47-7150	Don't/I Beg of You	1958	6.25	12.50	25.00

—*With horizontal line on label*

❏ 47-7150 [PS]	Don't/I Beg of You	1958	22.50	45.00	90.00
❏ 47-7240	Wear My Ring Around Your Neck/Don'tcha Think It's Time	1958	6.25	12.50	25.00
❏ 47-7240 [PS]	Wear My Ring Around Your Neck/Don'tcha Think It's Time	1958	22.50	45.00	90.00
❏ 47-7280	Hard Headed Woman/Don't Ask Me Why	1958	6.25	12.50	25.00
❏ 47-7280 [PS]	Hard Headed Woman/Don't Ask Me Why	1958	17.50	35.00	70.00
❏ 47-7410	One Night/I Got Stung	1958	6.25	12.50	25.00
❏ 47-7410 [PS]	One Night/I Got Stung	1958	17.50	35.00	70.00
❏ 47-7506	(Now and Then There's) A Fool Such As I/I Need Your Love Tonight	1959	6.25	12.50	25.00
❏ 47-7506 [PS]	(Now and Then There's) A Fool Such As I/I Need Your Love Tonight	1959	250.00	500.00	1000.

—*Sleeve promotes the "Elvis Sails" EP*

❏ 47-7506 [PS]	(Now and Then There's) A Fool Such As I/I Need Your Love Tonight	1959	15.00	30.00	60.00

—*Sleeve lists Elvis' EPs and Gold Standard singles*

❏ 47-7600	A Big Hunk o'Love/My Wish Came True	1959	6.25	12.50	25.00
❏ 47-7600 [PS]	A Big Hunk o'Love/My Wish Came True	1959	17.50	35.00	70.00
❏ 47-7740	Stuck on You/Fame and Fortune	1960	5.00	10.00	20.00
❏ 47-7740 [PS]	Stuck on You/Fame and Fortune	1960	15.00	30.00	60.00
❏ 47-7777	It's Now or Never/A Mess of Blues	1960	250.00	500.00	1000.

—*An early mispress is missing the piano part on the A-side. Has the number "L2WW-0100-3S" or "L2WW-0100-4S" in trail-off wax.*

❏ 47-7777	It's Now or Never/A Mess of Blues	1960	5.00	10.00	20.00

—*All other pressings with overdubbed piano*

❏ 47-7777 [PS]	It's Now or Never/A Mess of Blues	1960	15.00	30.00	60.00
❏ 47-7810	Are You Lonesome To-Night?/I Gotta Know	1960	5.00	10.00	20.00
❏ 47-7810 [PS]	Are You Lonesome To-Night?/I Gotta Know	1960	15.00	30.00	60.00
❏ 47-7850	Surrender/Lonely Man	1961	5.00	10.00	20.00
❏ 47-7850 [PS]	Surrender/Lonely Man	1961	15.00	30.00	60.00
❏ 47-7880	I Feel So Bad/Wild in the Country	1961	5.00	10.00	20.00
❏ 47-7880 [PS]	I Feel So Bad/Wild in the Country	1961	12.50	25.00	50.00
❏ 47-7908	(Marie's the Name) His Latest Flame/Little Sister	1961	5.00	10.00	20.00

—*All copies of this record actually read "Marie's the Name HIS LATEST FLAME" (no parentheses)*

❏ 47-7908 [PS]	(Marie's the Name) His Latest Flame/Little Sister	1961	12.50	25.00	50.00
❏ 47-7968	Can't Help Falling in Love/Rock-a-Hula Baby	1961	5.00	10.00	20.00
❏ 47-7968 [PS]	Can't Help Falling in Love/Rock-a-Hula Baby	1961	10.00	20.00	40.00
❏ 47-7992	Good Luck Charm/Anything That's Part of You	1962	5.00	10.00	20.00
❏ 47-7992 [PS]	Good Luck Charm/Anything That's Part of You	1962	10.00	20.00	40.00

—*Titles in blue and pink letters*

❏ 47-7992 [PS]	Good Luck Charm/Anything That's Part of You	1962	10.00	20.00	40.00

—*Titles in rust and lavender letters*

❏ 47-8041	She's Not You/Just Tell Her Jim Said Hello	1962	5.00	10.00	20.00
❏ 47-8041 [PS]	She's Not You/Just Tell Her Jim Said Hello	1962	10.00	20.00	40.00
❏ 47-8100	Return to Sender/Where Do You Come From	1962	5.00	10.00	20.00
❏ 47-8100 [PS]	Return to Sender/Where Do You Come From	1962	10.00	20.00	40.00
❏ 47-8134	One Broken Heart for Sale/They Remind Me Too Much of You	1963	3.00	6.00	12.00
❏ 47-8134 [PS]	One Broken Heart for Sale/They Remind Me Too Much of You	1963	7.50	15.00	30.00
❏ 47-8188	(You're the) Devil in Disguise/Please Don't Drag That String Along	1963	50.00	100.00	200.00

—*First pressing with incorrect B-side title*

❏ 47-8188	(You're the) Devil in Disguise/Please Don't Drag That String Around	1963	3.00	6.00	12.00

—*Second pressing with correct B-side title*

❏ 47-8188 [PS]	(You're the) Devil in Disguise/Please Don't Drag That String Around	1963	7.50	15.00	30.00

—*All sleeves have correct B-side title*

❏ 47-8243	Bossa Nova Baby/Witchcraft	1963	3.00	6.00	12.00
❏ 47-8243 [PS]	Bossa Nova Baby/Witchcraft	1963	7.50	15.00	30.00

—*"Coming Soon" on sleeve*

❏ 47-8243 [PS]	Bossa Nova Baby/Witchcraft	1963	7.50	15.00	30.00

—*"Ask For" on sleeve*

❏ 47-8243 [PS]	Bossa Nova Baby/Witchcraft	1963	7.50	15.00	30.00

—*No reference to another album on sleeve*

❏ 47-8307	Kissin' Cousins/It Hurts Me	1964	3.00	6.00	12.00
❏ 47-8307 [PS]	Kissin' Cousins/It Hurts Me	1964	6.25	12.50	25.00
❏ 47-8360	Viva Las Vegas/What'd I Say	1964	3.00	6.00	12.00
❏ 47-8360 [PS]	Viva Las Vegas/What'd I Say	1964	6.25	12.50	25.00

—*"Coming Soon" on sleeve*

❏ 47-8360 [PS]	Viva Las Vegas/What'd I Say	1964	12.50	25.00	50.00

—*"Ask For" on sleeve*

❏ 47-8400	Such a Night/Never Ending	1964	3.00	6.00	12.00
❏ 47-8400 [DJ]	Such a Night/Never Ending	1964	2500.	3750.	5000.

—*An inexplicably rare regular white label promo*

❏ 47-8400 [PS]	Such a Night/Never Ending	1964	6.25	12.50	25.00
❏ 47-8440	Ain't That Loving You Baby/Ask Me	1964	2.50	5.00	10.00
❏ 47-8440 [PS]	Ain't That Loving You Baby/Ask Me	1964	6.25	12.50	25.00

—*"Coming Soon" on sleeve*

❏ 47-8440 [PS]	Ain't That Loving You Baby/Ask Me	1964	6.25	12.50	25.00

—*"Ask For" on sleeve*

❏ 47-8500	Do the Clam/You'll Be Gone	1965	2.50	5.00	10.00
❏ 47-8500 [PS]	Do the Clam/You'll Be Gone	1965	6.25	12.50	25.00
❏ 47-8585	(Such An) Easy Question/It Feels So Right	1965	2.50	5.00	10.00
❏ 47-8585 [PS]	(Such An) Easy Question/It Feels So Right	1965	6.25	12.50	25.00

—*"Coming Soon" on sleeve*

❏ 47-8585 [PS]	(Such An) Easy Question/It Feels So Right	1965	6.25	12.50	25.00

—*"Ask For" on sleeve*

❏ 47-8657	I'm Yours/(It's a) Long, Lonely Highway	1965	2.50	5.00	10.00
❏ 47-8657 [PS]	I'm Yours/(It's a) Long, Lonely Highway	1965	6.25	12.50	25.00
❏ 47-8740	Tell Me Why/Blue River	1965	2.50	5.00	10.00
❏ 47-8740 [PS]	Tell Me Why/Blue River	1965	6.25	12.50	25.00
❏ 47-8780	Frankie and Johnny/Please Don't Stop Loving Me	1966	2.50	5.00	10.00
❏ 47-8780 [PS]	Frankie and Johnny/Please Don't Stop Loving Me	1966	6.25	12.50	25.00
❏ 47-8870	Love Letters/Come What May	1966	2.50	5.00	10.00
❏ 47-8870 [PS]	Love Letters/Come What May	1966	6.25	12.50	25.00

—*"Coming Soon" on sleeve*

❏ 47-8870 [PS]	Love Letters/Come What May	1966	6.25	12.50	25.00

—*"Ask For" on sleeve*

❏ 47-8941	Spinout/All That I Do	1966	2.50	5.00	10.00
❏ 47-8941 [PS]	Spinout/All That I Do	1966	6.25	12.50	25.00

—*"Watch For" on sleeve*

❏ 47-8941 [PS]	Spinout/All That I Do	1966	6.25	12.50	25.00

—*"Ask For" on sleeve*

❏ 47-8950	If Every Day Was Like Christmas/How Would You Like to Be	1966	5.00	10.00	20.00
❏ 47-8950 [PS]	If Every Day Was Like Christmas/How Would You Like to Be	1966	10.00	20.00	40.00
❏ 47-9056	Indescribably Blue/Fools Fall in Love	1966	2.50	5.00	10.00
❏ 47-9056 [PS]	Indescribably Blue/Fools Fall in Love	1966	6.25	12.50	25.00
❏ 47-9115	Long Legged Girl (With the Short Dress On)/ That's Someone You Never Forget	1967	2.50	5.00	10.00
❏ 47-9115 [PS]	Long Legged Girl (With the Short Dress On)/ That's Someone You Never Forget	1967	6.25	12.50	25.00

—*"Coming Soon" on sleeve*

❏ 47-9115 [PS]	Long Legged Girl (With the Short Dress On)/ That's Someone You Never Forget	1967	6.25	12.50	25.00

—*"Ask For" on sleeve*

❏ 47-9287	There's Always Me/Judy	1967	2.50	5.00	10.00
❏ 47-9287 [PS]	There's Always Me/Judy	1967	6.25	12.50	25.00
❏ 47-9341	Big Boss Man/You Don't Know Me	1967	2.50	5.00	10.00
❏ 47-9341 [PS]	Big Boss Man/You Don't Know Me	1967	6.25	12.50	25.00
❏ 47-9425	Guitar Man/High Heel Sneakers	1968	2.50	5.00	10.00
❏ 47-9425 [PS]	Guitar Man/High Heel Sneakers	1968	6.25	12.50	25.00

—*"Coming Soon" on sleeve*

❏ 47-9425 [PS]	Guitar Man/High Heel Sneakers	1968	6.25	12.50	25.00

—*"Ask For" on sleeve*

❏ 47-9465	U.S. Male/Stay Away	1968	2.50	5.00	10.00
❏ 47-9465 [PS]	U.S. Male/Stay Away	1968	6.25	12.50	25.00
❏ 47-9547	Let Yourself Go/Your Time Hasn't Come Yet, Baby	1968	2.50	5.00	10.00
❏ 47-9547 [PS]	Let Yourself Go/Your Time Hasn't Come Yet, Baby	1968	6.25	12.50	25.00

—*"Coming Soon" on sleeve*

❏ 47-9547 [PS]	Let Yourself Go/Your Time Hasn't Come Yet, Baby	1968	6.25	12.50	25.00

—*"Ask For" on sleeve*

❏ 47-9600	You'll Never Walk Alone/We Call on Him	1968	3.00	6.00	12.00
❏ 47-9600 [PS]	You'll Never Walk Alone/We Call on Him	1968	25.00	50.00	100.00
❏ 47-9610	A Little Less Conversation/Almost in Love	1968	2.50	5.00	10.00
❏ 47-9610 [PS]	A Little Less Conversation/Almost in Love	1968	6.25	12.50	25.00
❏ 47-9670	If I Can Dream/Edge of Reality	1968	2.00	4.00	8.00

—*First Elvis single on orange label*

❏ 47-9670 [PS]	If I Can Dream/Edge of Reality	1968	5.00	10.00	20.00

—*Mentions his NBC-TV special on sleeve*

❏ 47-9670 [PS]	If I Can Dream/Edge of Reality	1968	5.00	10.00	20.00

—*Does not mention his NBC-TV special on sleeve*

❏ 47-9731	Memories/Charro	1969	2.00	4.00	8.00

Number	Title (A Side/B Side)	Yr	VG	VG+	NM
47-9731 [PS]	Memories/Charro	1969	5.00	10.00	20.00
47-9741	In the Ghetto/Any Day Now	1969	2.00	4.00	8.00
47-9741 [PS]	In the Ghetto/Any Day Now	1969	5.00	10.00	20.00
—"Coming Soon" on sleeve					
47-9741 [PS]	In the Ghetto/Any Day Now	1969	5.00	10.00	20.00
—"Ask For" on sleeve					
47-9747	Clean Up Your Own Back Yard/The Fair Is Moving On	1969	2.00	4.00	8.00
47-9747 [PS]	Clean Up Your Own Back Yard/The Fair Is Moving On	1969	5.00	10.00	20.00
47-9764	Suspicious Minds/You'll Think of Me	1969	2.00	4.00	8.00
47-9764 [PS]	Suspicious Minds/You'll Think of Me	1969	5.00	10.00	20.00
47-9768	Don't Cry Daddy/Rubberneckin'	1969	2.00	4.00	8.00
47-9768 [PS]	Don't Cry Daddy/Rubberneckin'	1969	3.75	7.50	15.00
47-9791	Kentucky Rain/My Little Friend	1969	2.00	4.00	8.00
47-9791 [PS]	Kentucky Rain/My Little Friend	1969	3.75	7.50	15.00
47-9835	The Wonder of You/Mama Liked the Roses	1970	2.00	4.00	8.00
47-9835 [PS]	The Wonder of You/Mama Liked the Roses	1970	3.75	7.50	15.00
47-9873	I've Lost You/The Next Step Is Love	1970	—	3.00	6.00
47-9873 [PS]	I've Lost You/The Next Step Is Love	1970	3.75	7.50	15.00
47-9916	You Don't Have to Say You Love Me/Patch It Up	1970	—	3.00	6.00
47-9916 [PS]	You Don't Have to Say You Love Me/Patch It Up	1970	3.75	7.50	15.00
47-9960	I Really Don't Want to Know/There Goes My Everything	1971	—	3.00	6.00
47-9960 [PS]	I Really Don't Want to Know/There Goes My Everything	1971	3.75	7.50	15.00
—"Coming Soon" on sleeve					
47-9960 [PS]	I Really Don't Want to Know/There Goes My Everything	1971	3.75	7.50	15.00
—"Ask For" on sleeve					
47-9980	Where Did They Go, Lord/Rags to Riches	1971	—	3.00	6.00
47-9980 [PS]	Where Did They Go, Lord/Rags to Riches	1971	5.00	10.00	20.00
47-9985	Life/Only Believe	1971	—	3.00	6.00
47-9985 [PS]	Life/Only Believe	1971	7.50	15.00	30.00
47-9998	I'm Leavin'/Heart of Rome	1971	—	3.00	6.00
47-9998 [PS]	I'm Leavin'/Heart of Rome	1971	5.00	10.00	20.00
48-1017	It's Only Love/The Sound of Your Cry	1971	—	3.00	6.00
48-1017 [PS]	It's Only Love/The Sound of Your Cry	1971	3.75	7.50	15.00
61-7740 [S]	Stuck on You/Fame and Fortune	1960	100.00	200.00	400.00
—"Living Stereo" (large hole, plays at 45 rpm)					
61-7777 [S]	It's Now or Never/A Mess of Blues	1960	100.00	200.00	400.00
—"Living Stereo" (large hole, plays at 45 rpm)					
61-7810 [S]	Are You Lonesome To-Night?/I Gotta Know	1960	150.00	300.00	600.00
—"Living Stereo" (large hole, plays at 45 rpm)					
61-7850 [S]	Surrender/Lonely Man	1961	200.00	400.00	800.00
—"Living Stereo" (large hole, plays at 45 rpm)					
68-7850 [S]	Surrender/Lonely Man	1961	1000.	1500.	2000.
—"Compact Stereo 33" in "Living Stereo"					
74-0130	How Great Thou Art/His Hand in Mine	1969	6.25	12.50	25.00
74-0130 [PS]	How Great Thou Art/His Hand in Mine	1969	37.50	75.00	150.00
74-0572	Merry Christmas Baby/O Come All Ye Faithful	1971	3.75	7.50	15.00
74-0572 [PS]	Merry Christmas Baby/O Come All Ye Faithful	1971	10.00	20.00	40.00
74-0619	Until It's Time for You to Go/We Can Make the Morning	1971	—	3.00	6.00
74-0619 [PS]	Until It's Time for You to Go/We Can Make the Morning	1971	3.75	7.50	15.00
74-0651	He Touched Me/The Bosom of Abraham	1972	37.50	75.00	150.00
—"He Touched Me" actually plays at about 35 rpm in error. A-side has "AWKS-1277" stamped in trail-off wax.					
74-0651	He Touched Me/The Bosom of Abraham	1972	2.00	4.00	8.00
—"He Touched Me" plays correctly. A-side has "APKS-1277" stamped in trail-off wax.					
74-0651 [PS]	He Touched Me/The Bosom of Abraham	1972	30.00	60.00	120.00
74-0672	An American Trilogy/The First Time Ever I Saw Your Face	1972	5.00	10.00	20.00
74-0672 [PS]	An American Trilogy/The First Time Ever I Saw Your Face	1972	10.00	20.00	40.00
74-0769	Burning Love/It's a Matter of Time	1972	—	3.00	6.00
—Originals have orange labels					
74-0769	Burning Love/It's a Matter of Time	1974	37.50	75.00	150.00
—Very rare reissues have gray labels					
74-0769 [PS]	Burning Love/It's a Matter of Time	1972	3.75	7.50	15.00
74-0815	Separate Ways/Always on My Mind	1972	—	3.00	6.00
74-0815 [PS]	Separate Ways/Always on My Mind	1972	3.75	7.50	15.00
74-0910	Steamroller Blues/Fool	1973	—	3.00	6.00
74-0910 [PS]	Steamroller Blues/Fool	1973	3.75	7.50	15.00
447-0600	I Forgot to Remember to Forget/Mystery Train	1959	3.75	7.50	15.00
—Note: All RCA Victor releases with a "447" prefix are from the Gold Standard Series. Black label, dog on top					
447-0600	I Forgot to Remember to Forget/Mystery Train	1965	2.50	5.00	10.00
—Black label, dog on left					
447-0600	I Forgot to Remember to Forget/Mystery Train	1969	6.25	12.50	25.00
—Orange label					
447-0600	I Forgot to Remember to Forget/Mystery Train	1970	2.00	4.00	8.00
—Red label					
447-0601	That's All Right/Blue Moon of Kentucky	1959	3.75	7.50	15.00
—Black label, dog on top					
447-0601	That's All Right/Blue Moon of Kentucky	1965	2.50	5.00	10.00
—Black label, dog on left					
447-0601	That's All Right/Blue Moon of Kentucky	1969	2.00	4.00	8.00
—Red label; B-side artist credit is misspelled "Elvis Presely"					
447-0601 [DJ]	That's All Right/Blue Moon of Kentucky	1964	25.00	50.00	100.00
447-0601 [PS]	That's All Right/Blue Moon of Kentucky	1964	50.00	100.00	200.00
447-0602	Good Rockin' Tonight/I Don't Care If the Sun Don't Shine	1959	3.75	7.50	15.00
—Black label, dog on top					

Number	Title (A Side/B Side)	Yr	VG	VG+	NM
❑ 447-0602	Good Rockin' Tonight/I Don't Care If the Sun Don't Shine	1965	2.50	5.00	10.00
—Black label, dog on left					
❑ 447-0602	Good Rockin' Tonight/I Don't Care If the Sun Don't Shine	1970	2.00	4.00	8.00
—Red label					
❑ 447-0602 [DJ]	Good Rockin' Tonight/I Don't Care If the Sun Don't Shine	1964	25.00	50.00	100.00
❑ 447-0602 [PS]	Good Rockin' Tonight/I Don't Care If the Sun Don't Shine	1964	50.00	100.00	200.00
❑ 447-0603	Milkcow Blues Boogie/You're a Heartbreaker	1959	3.75	7.50	15.00
—Black label, dog on top					
❑ 447-0603	Milkcow Blues Boogie/You're a Heartbreaker	1965	2.50	5.00	10.00
—Black label, dog on left					
❑ 447-0603	Milkcow Blues Boogie/You're a Heartbreaker	1969	6.25	12.50	25.00
—Orange label					
❑ 447-0603	Milkcow Blues Boogie/You're a Heartbreaker	1970	2.00	4.00	8.00
—Red label					
❑ 447-0604	Baby Let's Play House/I'm Left, You're Right, She's Gone	1959	3.75	7.50	15.00
—Black label, dog on top					
❑ 447-0604	Baby Let's Play House/I'm Left, You're Right, She's Gone	1965	2.50	5.00	10.00
—Black label, dog on left					
❑ 447-0604	Baby Let's Play House/I'm Left, You're Right, She's Gone	1970	2.00	4.00	8.00
—Red label					
❑ 447-0605	Heartbreak Hotel/I Was the One	1959	3.75	7.50	15.00
—Black label, dog on top					
❑ 447-0605	Heartbreak Hotel/I Was the One	1965	2.50	5.00	10.00
—Black label, dog on left					
❑ 447-0605	Heartbreak Hotel/I Was the One	1969	6.25	12.50	25.00
—Orange label					
❑ 447-0605	Heartbreak Hotel/I Was the One	1970	2.00	4.00	8.00
—Red label					
❑ 447-0605 [DJ]	Heartbreak Hotel/I Was the One	1964	25.00	50.00	100.00
❑ 447-0605 [PS]	Heartbreak Hotel/I Was the One	1964	50.00	100.00	200.00
❑ 447-0607	I Want You, I Need You, I Love You/My Baby Left Me	1959	3.75	7.50	15.00
—Black label, dog on top					
❑ 447-0607	I Want You, I Need You, I Love You/My Baby Left Me	1965	2.50	5.00	10.00
—Black label, dog on left					
❑ 447-0607	I Want You, I Need You, I Love You/My Baby Left Me	1969	6.25	12.50	25.00
—Orange label					
❑ 447-0607	I Want You, I Need You, I Love You/My Baby Left Me	1970	2.00	4.00	8.00
—Red label					
❑ 447-0608	Hound Dog/Don't Be Cruel	1959	3.75	7.50	15.00
—Black label, dog on top					
❑ 447-0608	Hound Dog/Don't Be Cruel	1965	2.50	5.00	10.00
—Black label, dog on left					
❑ 447-0608	Hound Dog/Don't Be Cruel	1969	6.25	12.50	25.00
—Orange label					
❑ 447-0608	Hound Dog/Don't Be Cruel	1970	2.00	4.00	8.00
—Red label					
❑ 447-0608 [DJ]	Hound Dog/Don't Be Cruel	1964	25.00	50.00	100.00
❑ 447-0608 [PS]	Hound Dog/Don't Be Cruel	1964	50.00	100.00	200.00
❑ 447-0609	Blue Suede Shoes/Tutti Frutti	1959	3.75	7.50	15.00
—Black label, dog on top					
❑ 447-0609	Blue Suede Shoes/Tutti Frutti	1965	2.50	5.00	10.00
—Black label, dog on left					
❑ 447-0609	Blue Suede Shoes/Tutti Frutti	1969	6.25	12.50	25.00
—Orange label					
❑ 447-0609	Blue Suede Shoes/Tutti Frutti	1970	2.00	4.00	8.00
—Red label					
❑ 447-0610	I Got a Woman/I'm Countin' On You	1959	3.75	7.50	15.00
—Black label, dog on top					
❑ 447-0611	I'm Gonna Sit Right Down and Cry (Over You)/I'll Never Let You Go (Little Darlin')	1959	3.75	7.50	15.00
—Black label, dog on top					
❑ 447-0612	Tryin' to Get to You/I Love You Because	1959	3.75	7.50	15.00
—Black label, dog on top					
❑ 447-0613	Blue Moon/Just Because	1959	3.75	7.50	15.00
—Black label, dog on top					
❑ 447-0613	Blue Moon/Just Because	1965	2.50	5.00	10.00
—Black label, dog on left					
❑ 447-0613	Blue Moon/Just Because	1969	6.25	12.50	25.00
—Orange label					
❑ 447-0613	Blue Moon/Just Because	1970	2.00	4.00	8.00
—Red label					
❑ 447-0614	Money Honey/One-Sided Love Affair	1959	3.75	7.50	15.00
—Black label, dog on top					
❑ 447-0614	Money Honey/One-Sided Love Affair	1965	2.50	5.00	10.00
—Black label, dog on left					
❑ 447-0614	Money Honey/One-Sided Love Affair	1969	6.25	12.50	25.00
—Orange label					
❑ 447-0614	Money Honey/One-Sided Love Affair	1970	2.00	4.00	8.00
—Red label					
❑ 447-0615	Lawdy Miss Clawdy/Shake, Rattle, and Roll	1959	3.75	7.50	15.00
—Black label, dog on top					
❑ 447-0615	Lawdy Miss Clawdy/Shake, Rattle, and Roll	1965	2.50	5.00	10.00
—Black label, dog on left					
❑ 447-0615	Lawdy Miss Clawdy/Shake, Rattle, and Roll	1969	6.25	12.50	25.00
—Orange label					

Number	Title (A Side/B Side)	Yr	VG	VG+	NM
❑ 447-0615	Lawdy Miss Clawdy/Shake, Rattle, and Roll	1970	2.00	4.00	8.00
—Red label					
❑ 447-0616	Love Me Tender/Anyway You Want Me (That's How I Will Be)	1959	3.75	7.50	15.00
—Black label, dog on top					
❑ 447-0616	Love Me Tender/Anyway You Want Me (That's How I Will Be)	1965	2.50	5.00	10.00
—Black label, dog on left					
❑ 447-0616	Love Me Tender/Anyway You Want Me (That's How I Will Be)	1969	6.25	12.50	25.00
—Orange label					
❑ 447-0616	Love Me Tender/Anyway You Want Me (That's How I Will Be)	1970	2.00	4.00	8.00
—Red label					
❑ 447-0617	Too Much/Playing for Keeps	1959	3.75	7.50	15.00
—Black label, dog on top					
❑ 447-0617	Too Much/Playing for Keeps	1965	2.50	5.00	10.00
—Black label, dog on left					
❑ 447-0617	Too Much/Playing for Keeps	1969	6.25	12.50	25.00
—Orange label					
❑ 447-0617	Too Much/Playing for Keeps	1970	2.00	4.00	8.00
—Red label					
❑ 447-0618	All Shook Up/That's When Your Heartaches Begin	1959	3.75	7.50	15.00
—Black label, dog on top					
❑ 447-0618	All Shook Up/That's When Your Heartaches Begin	1965	2.50	5.00	10.00
—Black label, dog on left					
❑ 447-0618	All Shook Up/That's When Your Heartaches Begin	1969	6.25	12.50	25.00
—Orange label					
❑ 447-0618	All Shook Up/That's When Your Heartaches Begin	1970	2.00	4.00	8.00
—Red label					
❑ 447-0618 [DJ]	All Shook Up/That's When Your Heartaches Begin	1964	25.00	50.00	100.00
❑ 447-0618 [PS]	All Shook Up/That's When Your Heartaches Begin	1964	50.00	100.00	200.00
❑ 447-0619	Jailhouse Rock/Treat Me Nice	1959	3.75	7.50	15.00
—Black label, dog on top					
❑ 447-0619	Jailhouse Rock/Treat Me Nice	1965	2.50	5.00	10.00
—Black label, dog on left					
❑ 447-0619	Jailhouse Rock/Treat Me Nice	1969	6.25	12.50	25.00
—Orange label					
❑ 447-0619	Jailhouse Rock/Treat Me Nice	1970	2.00	4.00	8.00
—Red label					
❑ 447-0620	(Let Me Be Your) Teddy Bear/Loving You	1959	3.75	7.50	15.00
—Black label, dog on top					
❑ 447-0620	(Let Me Be Your) Teddy Bear/Loving You	1965	2.50	5.00	10.00
—Black label, dog on left					
❑ 447-0620	(Let Me Be Your) Teddy Bear/Loving You	1969	6.25	12.50	25.00
—Orange label					
❑ 447-0620	(Let Me Be Your) Teddy Bear/Loving You	1970	2.00	4.00	8.00
—Red label					
❑ 447-0621	Don't/I Beg of You	1961	3.00	6.00	12.00
—Black label, dog on top					
❑ 447-0621	Don't/I Beg of You	1965	2.50	5.00	10.00
—Black label, dog on left					
❑ 447-0621	Don't/I Beg of You	1969	6.25	12.50	25.00
—Orange label					
❑ 447-0621	Don't/I Beg of You	1970	2.00	4.00	8.00
—Red label					
❑ 447-0622	Wear My Ring Around Your Neck/Don'tcha Think It's Time	1961	3.00	6.00	12.00
—Black label, dog on top					
❑ 447-0622	Wear My Ring Around Your Neck/Don'tcha Think It's Time	1965	2.50	5.00	10.00
—Black label, dog on left					
❑ 447-0622	Wear My Ring Around Your Neck/Don'tcha Think It's Time	1969	6.25	12.50	25.00
—Orange label					
❑ 447-0622	Wear My Ring Around Your Neck/Don'tcha Think It's Time	1970	2.00	4.00	8.00
—Red label					
❑ 447-0623	Hard Headed Woman/Don't Ask Me Why	1961	3.75	7.50	15.00
—Black label, dog on top					
❑ 447-0623	Hard Headed Woman/Don't Ask Me Why	1965	2.50	5.00	10.00
—Black label, dog on left					
❑ 447-0623	Hard Headed Woman/Don't Ask Me Why	1969	6.25	12.50	25.00
—Orange label					
❑ 447-0623	Hard Headed Woman/Don't Ask Me Why	1970	2.00	4.00	8.00
—Red label					
❑ 447-0624	One Night/I Got Stung	1961	3.00	6.00	12.00
—Black label, dog on top					
❑ 447-0624	One Night/I Got Stung	1965	2.50	5.00	10.00
—Black label, dog on left					
❑ 447-0624	One Night/I Got Stung	1969	6.25	12.50	25.00
—Orange label					
❑ 447-0624	One Night/I Got Stung	1970	2.00	4.00	8.00
—Red label					
❑ 447-0625	(Now and Then There's) A Fool Such As I/I Need Your Love Tonight	1961	3.75	7.50	15.00
—Black label, dog on top					
❑ 447-0625	(Now and Then There's) A Fool Such As I/I Need Your Love Tonight	1965	2.50	5.00	10.00
—Black label, dog on left					
❑ 447-0625	(Now and Then There's) A Fool Such As I/I Need Your Love Tonight	1969	6.25	12.50	25.00
—Orange label					
❑ 447-0625	(Now and Then There's) A Fool Such As I/I Need Your Love Tonight	1970	2.00	4.00	8.0
—Red label					
❑ 447-0626	A Big Hunk o'Love/My Wish Came True	1962	3.75	7.50	15.0
—Black label, dog on top					
❑ 447-0626	A Big Hunk o'Love/My Wish Came True	1965	2.50	5.00	10.00
—Black label, dog on left					
❑ 447-0626	A Big Hunk o'Love/My Wish Came True	1969	6.25	12.50	25.00
—Orange label					
❑ 447-0626	A Big Hunk o'Love/My Wish Came True	1970	2.00	4.00	8.00
—Red label					
❑ 447-0627	Stuck on You/Fame and Fortune	1962	3.00	6.00	12.0
—Black label, dog on top					
❑ 447-0627	Stuck on You/Fame and Fortune	1965	2.50	5.00	10.00
—Black label, dog on left					
❑ 447-0627	Stuck on You/Fame and Fortune	1969	6.25	12.50	25.00
—Orange label					
❑ 447-0627	Stuck on You/Fame and Fortune	1970	2.00	4.00	8.00
—Red label					
❑ 447-0628	It's Now or Never/A Mess of Blues	1962	3.00	6.00	12.0
—Black label, dog on top					
❑ 447-0628	It's Now or Never/A Mess of Blues	1965	2.50	5.00	10.00
—Black label, dog on left					
❑ 447-0628	It's Now or Never/A Mess of Blues	1969	6.25	12.50	25.0
—Orange label					
❑ 447-0628	It's Now or Never/A Mess of Blues	1970	2.00	4.00	8.00
—Red label					
❑ 447-0629	Are You Lonesome To-Night?/I Gotta Know	1962	3.75	7.50	15.0
—Black label, dog on top					
❑ 447-0629	Are You Lonesome To-Night?/I Gotta Know	1965	2.50	5.00	10.00
—Black label, dog on left					
❑ 447-0629	Are You Lonesome To-Night?/I Gotta Know	1969	6.25	12.50	25.00
—Orange label					
❑ 447-0629	Are You Lonesome To-Night?/I Gotta Know	1970	2.00	4.00	8.00
—Red label					
❑ 447-0630	Surrender/Lonely Man	1962	6.25	12.50	25.0
—Black label, dog on top					
❑ 447-0630	Surrender/Lonely Man	1965	2.50	5.00	10.0
—Black label, dog on left					
❑ 447-0630	Surrender/Lonely Man	1969	6.25	12.50	25.00
—Orange label					
❑ 447-0630	Surrender/Lonely Man	1970	2.00	4.00	8.0
—Red label					
❑ 447-0631	I Feel So Bad/Wild in the Country	1962	3.00	6.00	12.0
—Black label, dog on top					
❑ 447-0631	I Feel So Bad/Wild in the Country	1965	2.50	5.00	10.0
—Black label, dog on left					
❑ 447-0631	I Feel So Bad/Wild in the Country	1970	2.00	4.00	8.00
—Red label					
❑ 447-0634	(Marie's the Name) His Latest Flame/Little Sister	1962	3.00	6.00	12.0
—Black label, dog on top					
❑ 447-0634	(Marie's the Name) His Latest Flame/Little Sister	1965	2.50	5.00	10.0
—Black label, dog on left					
❑ 447-0634	(Marie's the Name) His Latest Flame/Little Sister	1969	6.25	12.50	25.00
—Orange label					
❑ 447-0634	(Marie's the Name) His Latest Flame/Little Sister	1970	2.00	4.00	8.0
—Red label					
❑ 447-0635	Can't Help Falling in Love/Rock-a-Hula Baby	1962	3.00	6.00	12.0
—Black label, dog on top					
❑ 447-0635	Can't Help Falling in Love/Rock-a-Hula Baby	1965	2.50	5.00	10.0
—Black label, dog on left					
❑ 447-0635	Can't Help Falling in Love/Rock-a-Hula Baby	1969	6.25	12.50	25.0
—Orange label					
❑ 447-0635	Can't Help Falling in Love/Rock-a-Hula Baby	1970	2.00	4.00	8.0
—Red label					
❑ 447-0636	Good Luck Charm/Anything That's Part of You	1962	3.00	6.00	12.0
—Black label, dog on top					
❑ 447-0636	Good Luck Charm/Anything That's Part of You	1965	2.50	5.00	10.0
—Black label, dog on left					
❑ 447-0636	Good Luck Charm/Anything That's Part of You	1969	6.25	12.50	25.0
—Orange label					
❑ 447-0636	Good Luck Charm/Anything That's Part of You	1970	2.00	4.00	8.0
—Red label					
❑ 447-0637	She's Not You/Just Tell Her Jim Said Hello	1963	3.00	6.00	12.0
—Black label, dog on top					
❑ 447-0637	She's Not You/Just Tell Her Jim Said Hello	1965	2.50	5.00	10.0
—Black label, dog on left					
❑ 447-0637	She's Not You/Just Tell Her Jim Said Hello	1969	6.25	12.50	25.00
—Orange label					
❑ 447-0637	She's Not You/Just Tell Her Jim Said Hello	1970	2.00	4.00	8.0
—Red label					
❑ 447-0638	Return to Sender/Where Do You Come From	1963	3.00	6.00	12.0
—Black label, dog on top					
❑ 447-0638	Return to Sender/Where Do You Come From	1965	2.50	5.00	10.0
—Black label, dog on left					
❑ 447-0638	Return to Sender/Where Do You Come From	1969	6.25	12.50	25.00
—Orange label					
❑ 447-0638	Return to Sender/Where Do You Come From	1970	2.00	4.00	8.0
—Red label					
❑ 447-0639	Kiss Me Quick/Suspicion	1964	2.50	5.00	10.00
—Black label, dog on top					
❑ 447-0639	Kiss Me Quick/Suspicion	1969	6.25	12.50	25.00
—Orange label					

Number	Title (A Side/B Side)	Yr	VG	VG+	NM
447-0639	Kiss Me Quick/Suspicion	1970	2.00	4.00	8.00
—Red label					
447-0639 [PS]	Kiss Me Quick/Suspicion	1964	10.00	20.00	40.00
447-0640	One Broken Heart for Sale/They Remind Me Too Much of You	1964	6.25	12.50	25.00
—Black label, dog on top					
447-0640	One Broken Heart for Sale/They Remind Me Too Much of You	1965	2.50	5.00	10.00
—Black label, dog on left					
447-0640	One Broken Heart for Sale/They Remind Me Too Much of You	1969	6.25	12.50	25.00
—Orange label					
447-0640	One Broken Heart for Sale/They Remind Me Too Much of You	1970	2.00	4.00	8.00
—Red label					
447-0641	(You're the) Devil in Disguise/Please Don't Drag That String Around	1964	6.25	12.50	25.00
—Black label, dog on top					
447-0641	(You're the) Devil in Disguise/Please Don't Drag That String Around	1965	2.50	5.00	10.00
—Black label, dog on left					
447-0641	(You're the) Devil in Disguise/Please Don't Drag That String Around	1970	2.00	4.00	8.00
—Red label					
447-0642	Bossa Nova Baby/Witchcraft	1964	6.25	12.50	25.00
—Black label, dog on top					
447-0642	Bossa Nova Baby/Witchcraft	1965	2.50	5.00	10.00
—Black label, dog on left					
447-0642	Bossa Nova Baby/Witchcraft	1969	6.25	12.50	25.00
—Orange label					
447-0642	Bossa Nova Baby/Witchcraft	1970	2.00	4.00	8.00
—Red label					
447-0643	Crying in the Chapel/I Believe in the Man in the Sky	1965	2.50	5.00	10.00
—Black label, dog on left					
447-0643	Crying in the Chapel/I Believe in the Man in the Sky	1970	2.00	4.00	8.00
—Red label					
447-0643 [PS]	Crying in the Chapel/I Believe in the Man in the Sky	1965	7.50	15.00	30.00
447-0644	Kissin' Cousins/It Hurts Me	1965	2.50	5.00	10.00
—Black label, dog on left					
447-0644	Kissin' Cousins/It Hurts Me	1969	6.25	12.50	25.00
—Orange label					
447-0644	Kissin' Cousins/It Hurts Me	1970	2.00	4.00	8.00
—Red label					
447-0645	Such a Night/Never Ending	1965	10.00	20.00	40.00
—Black label, dog on top					
447-0645	Such a Night/Never Ending	1965	2.50	5.00	10.00
—Black label, dog on left					
447-0645	Such a Night/Never Ending	1969	6.25	12.50	25.00
—Orange label					
447-0645	Such a Night/Never Ending	1970	2.00	4.00	8.00
—Red label					
447-0646	Viva Las Vegas/What'd I Say	1965	6.25	12.50	25.00
—Black label, dog on top					
447-0646	Viva Las Vegas/What'd I Say	1965	2.50	5.00	10.00
—Black label, dog on left					
447-0646	Viva Las Vegas/What'd I Say	1969	6.25	12.50	25.00
—Orange label					
447-0646	Viva Las Vegas/What'd I Say	1970	2.00	4.00	8.00
—Red label					
447-0647	Blue Christmas/Santa Claus Is Back in Town	1965	3.00	6.00	12.00
—Black label, dog on side					
447-0647	Blue Christmas/Santa Claus Is Back in Town	1969	6.25	12.50	25.00
—Orange label					
447-0647	Blue Christmas/Santa Claus Is Back in Town	1970	2.00	4.00	8.00
—Red label					
447-0647 [PS]	Blue Christmas/Santa Claus Is Back in Town	1965	7.50	15.00	30.00
—Has "Gold Standard Series" on sleeve					
447-0648	Do the Clam/You'll Be Gone	1965	2.50	5.00	10.00
—Black label, dog on left					
447-0648	Do the Clam/You'll Be Gone	1970	2.50	5.00	10.00
—Red label					
447-0649	Ain't That Loving You Baby/Ask Me	1965	2.50	5.00	10.00
—Black label, dog on left					
447-0649	Ain't That Loving You Baby/Ask Me	1970	2.00	4.00	8.00
—Red label					
447-0650	Puppet on a String/Wooden Heart	1965	2.50	5.00	10.00
—Black label, dog on left					
447-0650	Puppet on a String/Wooden Heart	1970	2.00	4.00	8.00
—Red label					
447-0650 [PS]	Puppet on a String/Wooden Heart	1965	7.50	15.00	30.00
447-0651	Joshua Fit the Battle/Known Only to Him	1966	3.75	7.50	15.00
—Black label, dog on left					
447-0651	Joshua Fit the Battle/Known Only to Him	1970	2.00	4.00	8.00
—Red label					
447-0651 [PS]	Joshua Fit the Battle/Known Only to Him	1966	50.00	100.00	200.00
447-0652	Milky White Way/Swing Down Sweet Chariot	1966	3.75	7.50	15.00
—Black label, dog on left					
447-0652	Milky White Way/Swing Down Sweet Chariot	1970	2.00	4.00	8.00
—Red label					
447-0652 [PS]	Milky White Way/Swing Down Sweet Chariot	1966	50.00	100.00	200.00
447-0653	(Such An) Easy Question/It Feels So Right	1966	2.50	5.00	10.00
—Black label, dog on left					
447-0653	(Such An) Easy Question/It Feels So Right	1970	2.00	4.00	8.00
—Red label					

Number	Title (A Side/B Side)	Yr	VG	VG+	NM
447-0654	I'm Yours/(It's a) Long, Lonely Highway	1966	2.50	5.00	10.00
—Black label, dog on left					
447-0654	I'm Yours/(It's a) Long, Lonely Highway	1970	2.00	4.00	8.00
—Red label					
447-0655	Tell Me Why/Blue River	1968	2.50	5.00	10.00
—Black label, dog on left					
447-0655	Tell Me Why/Blue River	1970	2.00	4.00	8.00
—Red label					
447-0656	Frankie and Johnny/Please Don't Stop Loving Me	1968	2.50	5.00	10.00
—Black label, dog on left					
447-0656	Frankie and Johnny/Please Don't Stop Loving Me	1969	6.25	12.50	25.00
—Orange label					
447-0656	Frankie and Johnny/Please Don't Stop Loving Me	1970	2.00	4.00	8.00
—Red label					
447-0657	Love Letters/Come What May	1968	2.50	5.00	10.00
—Black label, dog on left					
447-0657	Love Letters/Come What May	1970	2.00	4.00	8.00
—Red label					
447-0658	Spinout/All That I Do	1968	2.50	5.00	10.00
—Black label, dog on left					
447-0658	Spinout/All That I Do	1970	2.00	4.00	8.00
—Red label					
447-0659	Indescribably Blue/Fools Fall in Love	1969	6.25	12.50	25.00
—Orange label					
447-0659	Indescribably Blue/Fools Fall in Love	1970	2.00	4.00	8.00
—Red label					
447-0660	Long Legged Girl (With the Short Dress On)/That's Someone You Never Forget	1970	10.00	20.00	40.00
447-0661	There's Always Me/Judy	1970	3.75	7.50	15.00
447-0662	Big Boss Man/You Don't Know Me	1970	2.50	5.00	10.00
447-0663	Guitar Man/High Heel Sneakers	1970	2.00	4.00	8.00
447-0664	U.S. Male/Stay Away	1970	2.00	4.00	8.00
447-0665	You'll Never Walk Alone/We Call on Him	1970	2.50	5.00	10.00
447-0666	Let Yourself Go/Your Time Hasn't Come Yet, Baby	1970	2.00	4.00	8.00
447-0667	A Little Less Conversation/Almost in Love	1970	2.00	4.00	8.00
447-0668	If I Can Dream/Edge of Reality	1970	2.00	4.00	8.00
447-0669	Memories/Charro	1970	2.00	4.00	8.00
447-0670	How Great Thou Art/His Hand in Mine	1970	2.50	5.00	10.00
447-0671	In the Ghetto/Any Day Now	1970	2.00	4.00	8.00
447-0672	Clean Up Your Own Back Yard/The Fair Is Moving On	1970	2.00	4.00	8.00
447-0673	Suspicious Minds/You'll Think of Me	1970	2.00	4.00	8.00
447-0674	Don't Cry Daddy/Rubberneckin'	1970	2.00	4.00	8.00
447-0675	Kentucky Rain/My Little Friend	1971	2.00	4.00	8.00
447-0676	The Wonder of You/Mama Liked the Roses	1971	2.00	4.00	8.00
447-0677	I've Lost You/The Next Step Is Love	1971	2.00	4.00	8.00
447-0678	You Don't Have to Say You Love Me/Patch It Up	1972	2.00	4.00	8.00
447-0679	I Really Don't Want to Know/There Goes My Everything	1972	2.00	4.00	8.00
447-0680	Where Did They Go, Lord/Rags to Riches	1972	2.00	4.00	8.00
447-0681	If Every Day Was Like Christmas/How Would You Like to Be	1972	2.00	4.00	8.00
447-0682	Life/Only Believe	1972	2.50	5.00	8.00
447-0683	I'm Leavin'/Heart of Rome	1972	2.00	4.00	8.00
447-0684	It's Only Love/The Sound of Your Cry	1972	2.00	4.00	8.00
447-0685	An American Trilogy/Until It's Time for You to Go	1973	2.00	4.00	8.00
447-0720	Blue Christmas/Wooden Heart	1964	3.75	7.50	15.00
447-0720 [PS]	Blue Christmas/Wooden Heart	1964	15.00	30.00	60.00
CR-15 [DJ]	Old Shep	1956	250.00	500.00	1000.
—One-sided promo					
SP-45-76 [DJ]	Don't Wear My Ring Around Your Neck	1960	200.00	400.00	800.00
SP-45-76 [PS]	Don't Wear My Ring Around Your Neck	1960	1000.	1500.	2000.
APBO-0088	Raised on Rock/For Ol' Times Sake	1973	—	3.00	6.00
APBO-0088 [PS]	Raised on Rock/For Ol' Times Sake	1973	3.75	7.50	15.00
4-834-115 [DJ]	I'll Be Back	1966	4000.	6000.	8000.
—One-sided promo with designation "For Special Academy Consideration Only"					
SP-45-118 [DJ]	King of the Whole Wide World/Home Is Where the Heart Is	1962	50.00	100.00	200.00
SP-45-118 [PS]	King of the Whole Wide World/Home Is Where the Heart Is	1962	75.00	150.00	300.00
SP-45-139 [DJ]	Roustabout/One Track Heart	1964	75.00	150.00	300.00
SP-45-162 [DJ]	How Great Thou Art/So High	1967	37.50	75.00	150.00
SP-45-162 [DJ]	How Great Thou Art/So High	1967	50.00	100.00	200.00
APBO-0196	Take Good Care of Her/I've Got a Thing About You, Baby	1973	—	3.00	6.00
APBO-0196 [PS]	Take Good Care of Her/I've Got a Thing About You, Baby	1973	3.75	7.50	15.00
APBO-0280	If You Talk in Your Sleep/Help Me	1974	3.00	6.00	12.00
—On label, the title "If You Talk in Your Sleep" is all on one line					
APBO-0280	If You Talk in Your Sleep/Help Me	1974	—	3.00	6.00
—On label, the title "If You Talk" is on one line and "In Your Sleep" is on another line					
APBO-0280 [PS]	If You Talk in Your Sleep/Help Me	1974	3.75	7.50	15.00
HO7W-0808 [DJ]	Blue Christmas (same on both sides)	1957	375.00	750.00	1500.
PB-10074	Promised Land/It's Midnight	1974	—	2.50	5.00
—Orange label (available at the same time as gray label)					
PB-10074	Promised Land/It's Midnight	1974	—	2.50	5.00
—Gray label (available at the same time as orange label)					
PB-10074	Promised Land/It's Midnight	1975	6.25	12.50	25.00
—Tan label (reissue)					
PB-10074 [PS]	Promised Land/It's Midnight	1975	2.50	5.00	10.00
GB-10156	Burning Love/Steamroller Blues	1975	2.00	4.00	8.00
—Gold Standard Series; red label					
GB-10156	Burning Love/Steamroller Blues	1977	—	2.00	4.00
—Gold Standard Series; black label					

P

Number	Title (A Side/B Side)	Yr	VG	VG+	NM
❑ GB-10157	Raised on Rock/If You Talk in Your Sleep	1975	2.00	4.00	8.00
—Gold Standard Series; red label					
❑ GB-10157	Raised on Rock/If You Talk in Your Sleep	1977	—	2.00	4.00
—Gold Standard Series; black label					
❑ PB-10191	My Boy/Thinking About You	1975	—	2.50	5.00
—Orange label					
❑ PB-10191	My Boy/Thinking About You	1975	—	2.50	5.00
—Tan label					
❑ PB-10191 [PS]	My Boy/Thinking About You	1975	2.50	5.00	10.00
❑ PB-10278	T-R-O-U-B-L-E/Mr. Songman	1975	—	2.50	5.00
—Orange label					
❑ PB-10278	T-R-O-U-B-L-E/Mr. Songman	1975	25.00	50.00	100.00
—Gray label					
❑ PB-10278	T-R-O-U-B-L-E/Mr. Songman	1975	2.50	5.00	10.00
—Tan label					
❑ PB-10278 [PS]	T-R-O-U-B-L-E/Mr. Songman	1975	2.50	5.00	10.00
❑ PB-10401	Bringing It Back/Pieces of My Life	1975	50.00	100.00	200.00
—Orange label					
❑ PB-10401	Bringing It Back/Pieces of My Life	1975	—	2.50	5.00
—Tan label					
❑ PB-10401 [PS]	Bringing It Back/Pieces of My Life	1975	2.50	5.00	10.00
❑ GB-10485	Take Good Care of Her/I've Got a Thing About You, Baby	1975	2.00	4.00	8.00
—Gold Standard Series; red label					
❑ GB-10486	Separate Ways/Always on My Mind	1975	2.00	4.00	8.00
—Gold Standard Series; red label					
❑ GB-10487	T-R-O-U-B-L-E/Mr. Songman	1975	2.00	4.00	8.00
—Gold Standard Series; red label					
❑ GB-10488	Promised Land/It's Midnight	1975	2.00	4.00	8.00
—Gold Standard Series; red label					
❑ GB-10489	My Boy/Thinking About You	1975	2.00	4.00	8.00
—Gold Standard Series; red label					
❑ PB-10601	Hurt/For the Heart	1976	—	2.50	5.00
—Originals on tan labels					
❑ PB-10601 [PS]	Hurt/For the Heart	1976	2.50	5.00	10.00
SUN					
❑ 209	That's All Right/Blue Moon of Kentucky	1954	2000.	4000.	6000.
—A mint copy of this has sold for over $17,000, but so far that is an aberration					
❑ 210	Good Rockin' Tonight/I Don't Care If the Sun Don't Shine	1954	1500.	2500.	3500.
❑ 215	Milkcow Blues Boogie/You're a Heartbreaker	1955	2000.	3500.	5000.
❑ 217	Baby Let's Play House/I'm Left, You're Right, She's Gone	1955	1000.	2000.	3000.
❑ 223	I Forgot to Remember to Forget/Mystery Train	1955	625.00	1250.	2500.
78s					
RCA VICTOR					
❑ 20-6357	I Forgot to Remember to Forget/Mystery Train	1955	37.50	75.00	150.00
❑ 20-6380	That's All Right/Blue Moon of Kentucky	1955	37.50	75.00	150.00
❑ 20-6381	Good Rockin' Tonight/I Don't Care If the Sun Don't Shine	1955	37.50	75.00	150.00
❑ 20-6382	Milkcow Blues Boogie/You're a Heartbreaker	1955	37.50	75.00	150.00
❑ 20-6383	Baby Let's Play House/I'm Left, You're Right, She's Gone	1955	37.50	75.00	150.00
❑ 20-6420	Heartbreak Hotel/I Was the One	1956	25.00	50.00	100.00
❑ 20-6540	I Want You, I Need You, I Love You/My Baby Left Me	1956	25.00	50.00	100.00
❑ 20-6604	Don't Be Cruel/Hound Dog	1956	25.00	50.00	100.00
❑ 20-6636	Blue Suede Shoes/Tutti Frutti	1956	25.00	50.00	100.00
❑ 20-6637	I Got a Woman/I'm Countin' On You	1956	25.00	50.00	100.00
❑ 20-6638	I'm Gonna Sit Right Down and Cry (Over You)/I'll Never Let You Go (Little Darlin')	1956	25.00	50.00	100.00
❑ 20-6639	Tryin' to Get to You/I Love You Because	1956	25.00	50.00	100.00
❑ 20-6640	Blue Moon/Just Because	1956	25.00	50.00	100.00
❑ 20-6641	Money Honey/One-Sided Love Affair	1956	25.00	50.00	100.00
❑ 20-6642	Lawdy Miss Clawdy/Shake, Rattle, and Roll	1956	25.00	50.00	100.00
❑ 20-6643	Love Me Tender/Anyway You Want Me (That's How I Will Be)	1956	25.00	50.00	100.00
❑ 20-6800	Too Much/Playing for Keeps	1957	25.00	50.00	100.00
❑ 20-6870	All Shook Up/That's When Your Heartaches Begin	1957	25.00	50.00	100.00
❑ 20-7000	(Let Me Be Your) Teddy Bear/Loving You	1957	25.00	50.00	100.00
❑ 20-7035	Jailhouse Rock/Treat Me Nice	1957	25.00	50.00	100.00
❑ 20-7150	Don't/I Beg of You	1958	30.00	60.00	120.00
❑ 20-7240	Wear My Ring Around Your Neck/Don'tcha Think It's Time	1958	30.00	60.00	120.00
❑ 20-7280	Hard Headed Woman/Don't Ask Me Why	1958	30.00	60.00	120.00
❑ 20-7410	One Night/I Got Stung	1958	125.00	250.00	500.00
SUN					
❑ 209	That's All Right/Blue Moon of Kentucky	1954	750.00	1500.	3000.
❑ 210	Good Rockin' Tonight/I Don't Care If the Sun Don't Shine	1954	450.00	900.00	1800.
❑ 215	Milkcow Blues Boogie/You're a Heartbreaker	1955	625.00	1250.	2500.
❑ 217	Baby Let's Play House/I'm Left, You're Right, She's Gone	1955	375.00	750.00	1500.
❑ 223	I Forgot to Remember to Forget/Mystery Train	1955	250.00	500.00	1000.
7-Inch Extended Plays					
RCA					
❑ DTF0-2006 [PS]	Aloha from Hawaii Via Satellite	1973	25.00	50.00	100.00
❑ DTF0-2006 [S]	Something/You Gave Me a Mountain/I Can't Stop Loving You//My Way/What Now My Love/I'm So Lonesome I Could Cry	1973	20.00	40.00	80.00
—Jukebox issue; small hole, plays at 33 1/3 rpm					
RCA VICTOR					
❑ SPD-22 [PS]	Elvis Presley	1956	100.00	200.00	400.00
—Bonus given to buyers of a Victrola					

Number	Title (A Side/B Side)	Yr	VG	VG+	NM
❑ SPD-22 [(2)]	Elvis Presley	1956	100.00	200.00	400.00
—Value is for both discs together					
❑ SPD-23 [PS]	Elvis Presley	1956	1000.	2000.	300
—Bonus given to buyers of a more expensive Victrola					
❑ SPD-23 [(3)]	Elvis Presley	1956	1000.	2000.	300
—Value is for all three discs together					
❑ SPA-7-37 [DJ]	Perfect for Parties	1956	15.00	30.00	60.0
—Without horizontal line on label					
❑ SPA-7-37 [DJ]	Perfect for Parties	1956	15.00	30.00	60.0
—With horizontal line on label					
❑ SPA-7-37 [PS]	Perfect for Parties	1956	15.00	30.00	60.0
❑ LPC-128	Flaming Star/Summer Kisses, Winter Tears//Are You Lonesome To-Night?/It's Now or Never	1961	10.00	20.00	40.0
—"Compact 33 Double" with small hole					
❑ LPC-128 [PS]	Elvis By Request	1961	10.00	20.00	40.0
❑ EPA-747	Blue Suede Shoes/Tutti Frutti//I Got a Woman/Just Because	1956	12.50	25.00	50.0
—Without horizontal line on label					
❑ EPA-747	Blue Suede Shoes/Tutti Frutti//I Got a Woman/Just Because	1956	12.50	25.00	50.0
—With horizontal line on label					
❑ EPA-747	Blue Suede Shoes/Tutti Frutti//I Got a Woman/Just Because	1956	50.00	100.00	200.0
—With horizontal line on label, but with no dog					
❑ EPA-747	Blue Suede Shoes/Tutti Frutti//I Got a Woman/Just Because	1956	50.00	100.00	200.0
—With incorrect label on Side 1 that lists, as song 3, "I'm Gonna Sit Right Down and Cry (Over You)" which does not appear on this record. Known copies of this version do not have horizontal line on label.					
❑ EPA-747	Blue Suede Shoes/Tutti Frutti//I Got a Woman/Just Because	1965	7.50	15.00	30.0
—Black label, dog on left					
❑ EPA-747	Blue Suede Shoes/Tutti Frutti//I Got a Woman/Just Because	1969	20.00	40.00	80.0
—Orange label					
❑ EPA-747 [PS]	Elvis Presley	1956	250.00	500.00	100
—Temporary envelope sleeve with dark blue print, "Blue Suede Shoes by Elvis Presley" in big lette					
❑ EPA-747 [PS]	Elvis Presley	1956	150.00	300.00	600.0
—Temporary envelope sleeve with black print, "Blue Suede Shoes by Elvis Presley" in big letters					
❑ EPA-747 [PS]	Elvis Presley	1956	12.50	25.00	50.0
—Five different back covers exist, all with titles on front cover; any are of equal value					
❑ EPA-747 [PS]	Elvis Presley	1965	7.50	15.00	30.0
—No titles at top of front cover					
❑ EPA-821	Heartbreak Hotel/I Was the One//Money Honey/I Forgot to Remember to Forget	1956	12.50	25.00	50.0
—Without horizontal line on label					
❑ EPA-821	Heartbreak Hotel/I Was the One//Money Honey/I Forgot to Remember to Forget	1956	12.50	25.00	50.0
—With horizontal line on label					
❑ EPA-821	Heartbreak Hotel/I Was the One//Money Honey/I Forgot to Remember to Forget	1956	50.00	100.00	200.0
—With horizontal line on label, but with no dog					
❑ EPA-821	Heartbreak Hotel/I Was the One//Money Honey/I Forgot to Remember to Forget	1965	7.50	15.00	30.0
—Black label, dog on left					
❑ EPA-821	Heartbreak Hotel/I Was the One//Money Honey/I Forgot to Remember to Forget	1969	20.00	40.00	80.0
—Orange label					
❑ EPA-821 [PS]	Heartbreak Hotel	1956	12.50	25.00	50.0
❑ EPA-830	Shake, Rattle and Roll/I Love You Because//Blue Moon/Lawdy, Miss Clawdy	1956	12.50	25.00	50.0
—Without horizontal line on label					
❑ EPA-830	Shake, Rattle and Roll/I Love You Because//Blue Moon/Lawdy, Miss Clawdy	1956	12.50	25.00	50.0
—With horizontal line on label					
❑ EPA-830	Shake, Rattle and Roll/I Love You Because//Blue Moon/Lawdy, Miss Clawdy	1956	50.00	100.00	200.0
—With horizontal line on label, but with no dog					
❑ EPA-830	Shake, Rattle and Roll/I Love You Because//Blue Moon/Lawdy, Miss Clawdy	1965	7.50	15.00	30.0
—Black label, dog on left					
❑ EPA-830	Shake, Rattle and Roll/I Love You Because//Blue Moon/Lawdy, Miss Clawdy	1969	20.00	40.00	80.0
—Orange label					
❑ EPA-830 [PS]	Elvis Presley	1956	12.50	25.00	50.0
❑ EPA-940	Don't Be Cruel/I Want You, I Need You, I Love You//Hound Dog/My Baby Left Me	1956	12.50	25.00	50.0
—Without horizontal line on label					
❑ EPA-940	Don't Be Cruel/I Want You, I Need You, I Love You//Hound Dog/My Baby Left Me	1956	12.50	25.00	50.0
—With horizontal line on label					
❑ EPA-940	Don't Be Cruel/I Want You, I Need You, I Love You//Hound Dog/My Baby Left Me	1956	50.00	100.00	200.0
—With horizontal line on label, but with no dog					
❑ EPA-940 [PS]	The Real Elvis	1956	12.50	25.00	50.0
❑ EPA-965	Anyway You Want Me (That's How I Will Be)/I'm Left, You're Right, She's Gone/I Don't Care If the Sun Don't Shine/Mystery Train	1956	10.00	20.00	40.0
—Without horizontal line on label					
❑ EPA-965	Anyway You Want Me (That's How I Will Be)/I'm Left, You're Right, She's Gone/I Don't Care If the Sun Don't Shine/Mystery Train	1956	10.00	20.00	40.0
—With horizontal line on label					
❑ EPA-965	Anyway You Want Me (That's How I Will Be)/I'm Left, You're Right, She's Gone/I Don't Care If the Sun Don't Shine/Mystery Train	1956	50.00	100.00	200.0
—With horizontal line on label, but with no dog					

Number	Title (A Side/B Side)	Yr	VG	VG+	NM
❑ EPA-965	Anyway You Want Me (That's How I Will Be)/I'm Left, You're Right, She's Gone//I Don't Care If the Sun Don't Shine/Mystery Train	1965	7.50	15.00	30.00
—Black label, dog on left					
❑ EPA-965	Anyway You Want Me (That's How I Will Be)/I'm Left, You're Right, She's Gone//I Don't Care If the Sun Don't Shine/Mystery Train	1969	20.00	40.00	80.00
—Orange label					
❑ EPA-965 [PS]	Anyway You Want Me	1956	12.50	25.00	50.00
—With song titles and catalog number on front					
❑ EPA-965 [PS]	Anyway You Want Me	196?	10.00	20.00	40.00
—Without song titles and catalog number on front					
❑ EPA-992	Rip It Up/Love Me//When My Blue Moon Turns to Gold Again/Paralyzed	1956	10.00	20.00	40.00
—Without horizontal line on label					
❑ EPA-992	Rip It Up/Love Me//When My Blue Moon Turns to Gold Again/Paralyzed	1956	10.00	20.00	40.00
—With horizontal line on label					
❑ EPA-992	Rip It Up/Love Me//When My Blue Moon Turns to Gold Again/Paralyzed	1956	50.00	100.00	200.00
—With horizontal line on label; but with no dog					
❑ EPA-992	Rip It Up/Love Me//When My Blue Moon Turns to Gold Again/Paralyzed	1965	7.50	15.00	30.00
—Black label, dog on left					
❑ EPA-992	Rip It Up/Love Me//When My Blue Moon Turns to Gold Again/Paralyzed	1969	20.00	40.00	80.00
—Orange label					
❑ EPA-992 [PS]	Elvis (Volume 1)	1956	12.50	25.00	50.00
❑ EPA-993	So Glad You're Mine/Old Shep//Ready Teddy/Anyplace Is Paradise	1956	10.00	20.00	40.00
—Without horizontal line on label					
❑ EPA-993	So Glad You're Mine/Old Shep//Ready Teddy/Anyplace Is Paradise	1956	10.00	20.00	40.00
—With horizontal line on label					
❑ EPA-993	So Glad You're Mine/Old Shep//Ready Teddy/Anyplace Is Paradise	1956	50.00	100.00	200.00
—With horizontal line on label, but with no dog					
❑ EPA-993	So Glad You're Mine/Old Shep//Ready Teddy/Anyplace Is Paradise	1965	7.50	15.00	30.00
—Black label, dog on left					
❑ EPA-993	So Glad You're Mine/Old Shep//Ready Teddy/Anyplace Is Paradise	1969	20.00	40.00	80.00
—Orange label					
❑ EPA-993 [PS]	Elvis (Volume 2)	1956	12.50	25.00	50.00
—Titles at top of front cover					
❑ EPA-993 [PS]	Elvis (Volume 2)	1965	7.50	15.00	30.00
—No titles at top of front cover					
❑ EPA-994	Long Tall Sally/First in Line//How Do You Think I Feel/How's the World Treating You	1956	12.50	25.00	50.00
—Without horizontal line on label					
❑ EPA-994	Long Tall Sally/First in Line//How Do You Think I Feel/How's the World Treating You	1956	12.50	25.00	50.00
—With horizontal line on label					
❑ EPA-994	Long Tall Sally/First in Line//How Do You Think I Feel/How's the World Treating You	1956	50.00	100.00	200.00
—With horizontal line on label, but with no dog					
❑ EPA-994	Long Tall Sally/First in Line//How Do You Think I Feel/How's the World Treating You	1965	7.50	15.00	30.00
—Black label, dog on left					
❑ EPA-994	Long Tall Sally/First in Line//How Do You Think I Feel/How's the World Treating You	1969	20.00	40.00	80.00
—Orange label					
❑ EPA-994 [PS]	Strictly Elvis (Elvis, Vol. 3)	1956	12.50	25.00	50.00
—With titles listed on front cover					
❑ EPA-994 [PS]	Strictly Elvis (Elvis, Vol. 3)	1965	7.50	15.00	30.00
—No titles listed on front cover					
❑ EPB-1254 [PS]	Elvis Presley	1956	50.00	100.00	200.00
—Three different back covers exist hyping other non-Elvis RCA Victor releases; any are of equal value					
❑ EPB-1254 [PS]	Elvis Presley	1956	37.50	75.00	150.00
—With no hype of other non-Elvis releases on back					
❑ EPB-1254 [PS]	Elvis Presley... the most talked-about new personality in the last ten years of recorded music	1956	375.00	750.00	1500.
❑ EPB-1254 [(2)]	Elvis Presley	1956	50.00	100.00	200.00
—Without horizontal line on label; eight songs on two discs; value is for both discs together					
❑ EPB-1254 [(2)]	Elvis Presley	1956	50.00	100.00	200.00
—With horizontal line on label; eight songs on two discs; value is for both discs together					
❑ EPB-1254 [(2)]	Elvis Presley	1956	375.00	750.00	1500.
—Two records have three songs on each side (12 total), as opposed to the two of the standard release					
❑ EPA-1-1515	Loving You/Party//(Let Me Be Your) Teddy Bear/True Love	1957	10.00	20.00	40.00
—Without horizontal line on label					
❑ EPA-1-1515	Loving You/Party//(Let Me Be Your) Teddy Bear/True Love	1957	10.00	20.00	40.00
—With horizontal line on label					
❑ EPA-1-1515	Loving You/Party//(Let Me Be Your) Teddy Bear/True Love	1965	7.50	15.00	30.00
—Black label, dog on left					
❑ EPA-1-1515	Loving You/Party//(Let Me Be Your) Teddy Bear/True Love	1969	20.00	40.00	80.00
—Orange label					
❑ EPA-1-1515 [PS]	Loving You, Vol. I	1957	10.00	20.00	40.00
❑ EPA-2-1515	Lonesome Cowboy/Hot Dog//Mean Woman Blues/Got a Lot of Livin' to Do	1957	10.00	20.00	40.00
—Without horizontal line on label					
❑ EPA-2-1515	Lonesome Cowboy/Hot Dog//Mean Woman Blues/Got a Lot of Livin' to Do	1957	10.00	20.00	40.00
—With horizontal line on label					
❑ EPA-2-1515	Lonesome Cowboy/Hot Dog//Mean Woman Blues/Got a Lot of Livin' to Do	1965	7.50	15.00	30.00
—Black label, dog on left					
❑ EPA-2-1515	Lonesome Cowboy/Hot Dog//Mean Woman Blues/Got a Lot of Livin' to Do	1969	20.00	40.00	80.00
—Orange label					
❑ EPA-2-1515 [PS]	Loving You, Vol. II	1957	10.00	20.00	40.00
—With song titles on top of front cover					
❑ EPA-2-1515 [PS]	Loving You, Vol. II	1965	7.50	15.00	30.00
—No song titles on top of front cover					
❑ EPA-4006	Love Me Tender/Let Me//Poor Boy/We're Gonna Move	1956	12.50	25.00	50.00
—Without horizontal line on label					
❑ EPA-4006	Love Me Tender/Let Me//Poor Boy/We're Gonna Move	1956	12.50	25.00	50.00
—With horizontal line on label					
❑ EPA-4006	Love Me Tender/Let Me//Poor Boy/We're Gonna Move	1956	50.00	100.00	200.00
—With horizontal line on label, but with no dog					
❑ EPA-4006	Love Me Tender/Let Me//Poor Boy/We're Gonna Move	1965	7.50	15.00	30.00
—Black label, dog on left					
❑ EPA-4006	Love Me Tender/Let Me//Poor Boy/We're Gonna Move	1969	20.00	40.00	80.00
—Orange label					
❑ EPA-4006 [PS]	Love Me Tender	1956	12.50	25.00	50.00
—With song titles on top of front cover					
❑ EPA-4006 [PS]	Love Me Tender	1965	7.50	15.00	30.00
—No song titles on top of front cover					
❑ EPA-4041	I Need You So/Have I Told You Lately//Blueberry Hill/Is It So Strange	1957	12.50	25.00	50.00
—Without horizontal line on label					
❑ EPA-4041	I Need You So/Have I Told You Lately//Blueberry Hill/Is It So Strange	1957	12.50	25.00	50.00
—With horizontal line on label					
❑ EPA-4041	I Need You So/Have I Told You Lately//Blueberry Hill/Is It So Strange	1957	50.00	100.00	200.00
—With horizontal line on label, but with no dog					
❑ EPA-4041	I Need You So/Have I Told You Lately//Blueberry Hill/Is It So Strange	1965	7.50	15.00	30.00
—Black label, dog on left					
❑ EPA-4041	I Need You So/Have I Told You Lately//Blueberry Hill/Is It So Strange	1969	20.00	40.00	80.00
—Orange label					
❑ EPA-4041 [PS]	Just for You (Elvis Presley)	1957	12.50	25.00	50.00
❑ EPA-4054	(There'll Be) Peace in the Valley (For Me)/It Is No Secret (What God Can Do)//I Believe/Take My Hand, Precious Lord	1957	10.00	20.00	40.00
—Without horizontal line on label					
❑ EPA-4054	(There'll Be) Peace in the Valley (For Me)/It Is No Secret (What God Can Do)//I Believe/Take My Hand, Precious Lord	1957	10.00	20.00	40.00
—With horizontal line on label					
❑ EPA-4054 [PS]	Peace in the Valley	1957	10.00	20.00	40.00
❑ EPA-4108	Santa Bring My Baby Back (To Me)/Blue Christmas//Santa Claus Is Back in Town/I'll Be Home for Christmas	1957	10.00	20.00	40.00
—Black label, dog on top					
❑ EPA-4108	Santa Bring My Baby Back (To Me)/Blue Christmas//Santa Claus Is Back in Town/I'll Be Home for Christmas	1965	7.50	15.00	30.00
—Black label, dog on left					
❑ EPA-4108	Santa Bring My Baby Back (To Me)/Blue Christmas//Santa Claus Is Back in Town/I'll Be Home for Christmas	1969	20.00	40.00	80.00
—Orange label					
❑ EPA-4108 [PS]	Elvis Sings Christmas Songs	1957	10.00	20.00	40.00
❑ EPA-4114	Jailhouse Rock/Young and Beautiful//I Want to Be Free/Don't Leave Me Now/(You're So Square) Baby I Don't Care	1957	10.00	20.00	40.00
—Black label, dog on top					
❑ EPA-4114	Jailhouse Rock/Young and Beautiful//I Want to Be Free/Don't Leave Me Now/(You're So Square) Baby I Don't Care	1965	7.50	15.00	30.00
—Black label, dog on left					
❑ EPA-4114	Jailhouse Rock/Young and Beautiful//I Want to Be Free/Don't Leave Me Now/(You're So Square) Baby I Don't Care	1969	20.00	40.00	80.00
—Orange label					
❑ EPA-4114 [PS]	Jailhouse Rock	1957	10.00	20.00	40.00
❑ EPA-4319	King Creole/New Orleans//As Long As I Have You/Lover Doll	1958	10.00	20.00	40.00
❑ EPA-4319 [PS]	King Creole	1958	12.50	25.00	50.00
—With copyright notice on front cover					
❑ EPA-4319 [PS]	King Creole	1958	10.00	20.00	40.00
—Without copyright notice on front cover					
❑ EPA-4321	Trouble/Young Dreams//Crawfish/Dixieland Rock	1958	10.00	20.00	40.00
—Black label, dog on top					
❑ EPA-4321	Trouble/Young Dreams//Crawfish/Dixieland Rock	1965	7.50	15.00	30.00
—Black label, dog on left					

P

Number	Title (A Side/B Side)	Yr	VG	VG+	NM
❑ EPA-4321	Trouble/Young Dreams//Crawfish/Dixieland Rock	1969	20.00	40.00	80.00
—Orange label					
❑ EPA-4321 [PS]King Creole, Vol. 2		1958	10.00	20.00	40.00
❑ EPA-4325	Press Interview with Elvis Presley//Elvis Presley's Newsreel Interview/Pat Hernon Interviews Elvis...	1958	20.00	40.00	80.00
❑ EPA-4325 [PS]Elvis Sails		1958	20.00	40.00	80.00
—With 1959 calendar and a hole to make it suitable for hanging					
❑ EPA-4340	White Christmas/Here Comes Santa Claus//Oh Little Town of Bethlehem/Silent Night	1958	17.50	35.00	70.00
—Black label, dog on top					
❑ EPA-4340	White Christmas/Here Comes Santa Claus//Oh Little Town of Bethlehem/Silent Night	1965	10.00	20.00	40.00
—Black label, dog on left					
❑ EPA-4340	White Christmas/Here Comes Santa Claus//Oh Little Town of Bethlehem/Silent Night	1969	10.00	40.00	80.00
—Orange label					
❑ EPA-4340 [PS]Christmas with Elvis		1958	20.00	40.00	80.00
—With copyright notice and "Printed in U.S.A." at lower right					
❑ EPA-4340 [PS]Christmas with Elvis		1965	10.00	20.00	40.00
—Without copyright notice and "Printed in U.S.A." at lower right					
❑ EPA-4368	Follow That Dream/Angel//What a Wonderful Life/I'm Not the Marrying Kind	1962	7.50	15.00	30.00
—Black label, dog on top, no playing times on label					
❑ EPA-4368	Follow That Dream/Angel//What a Wonderful Life/I'm Not the Marrying Kind	1962	10.00	20.00	40.00
—Black label, dog on top, with playing times on label					
❑ EPA-4368	Follow That Dream/Angel//What a Wonderful Life/I'm Not the Marrying Kind	1965	6.25	12.50	25.00
—Black label, dog on left					
❑ EPA-4368	Follow That Dream/Angel//What a Wonderful Life/I'm Not the Marrying Kind	1969	20.00	40.00	80.00
—Orange label					
❑ EPA-4368 [PS]Follow That Dream		1962	37.50	75.00	150.00
—Paper sleeve with "Coin Operator -- DJ Prevue" at top; print is in red					
❑ EPA-4368 [PS]Follow That Dream		1962	10.00	20.00	40.00
—Incorrect playing times on back cover; "Follow That Dream" is listed as 1:35 but is actually 1:38, and two others are wrong also					
❑ EPA-4368 [PS]Follow That Dream		1965	6.25	12.50	25.00
—Correct playing times on back cover					
❑ EPA-4371	King of the Whole Wide World/This Is Living/Riding the Rainbow//Home Is Where the Heart Is/I Got Lucky/A Whistling Tune	1962	10.00	20.00	40.00
—Black label, dog on top					
❑ EPA-4371	King of the Whole Wide World/This Is Living/Riding the Rainbow//Home Is Where the Heart Is/I Got Lucky/A Whistling Tune	1965	7.50	15.00	30.00
—Black label, dog on left					
❑ EPA-4371	King of the Whole Wide World/This Is Living/Riding the Rainbow//Home Is Where the Heart Is/I Got Lucky/A Whistling Tune	1969	20.00	40.00	80.00
—Orange label					
❑ EPA-4371 [PS]Kid Galahad		1962	10.00	20.00	40.00
❑ EPA-4382	If You Think I Don't Need You/I Need Somebody to Lean On//C'mon Everybody/Today, Tomorrow and Forever	1964	10.00	20.00	40.00
—Black label, dog on top					
❑ EPA-4382	If You Think I Don't Need You/I Need Somebody to Lean On//C'mon Everybody/Today, Tomorrow and Forever	1965	7.50	15.00	30.00
—Black label, dog on left					
❑ EPA-4382	If You Think I Don't Need You/I Need Somebody to Lean On//C'mon Everybody/Today, Tomorrow and Forever	1969	20.00	40.00	80.00
—Orange label					
❑ EPA-4382 [PS]Viva Las Vegas		1964	10.00	20.00	40.00
❑ EPA-4383	I Feel That I've Known You Forever/Slowly But Surely//Night Rider/Dirty Feeling	1965	7.50	15.00	30.00
—Black label, dog on left					
❑ EPA-4383	I Feel That I've Known You Forever/Slowly But Surely//Night Rider/Dirty Feeling	1969	20.00	40.00	80.00
—Orange label					
❑ EPA-4383 [PS]Tickle Me		1965	7.50	15.00	30.00
—"Coming Soon" on front cover					
❑ EPA-4383 [PS]Tickle Me		1965	7.50	15.00	30.00
—"Ask For" on front cover					
❑ EPA-4383 [PS]Tickle Me		1969	8.75	17.50	35.00
—No blurb for new album on front cover					
❑ EPA-4387	Easy Come, Easy Go/The Love Machine/Yoga Is As Yoga Does//You Gotta Shop/Sing You Children/I'll Take Love	1967	7.50	15.00	30.00
—All copies appear to be black label, dog on left					
❑ EPA-4387 [PS]Easy Come, Easy Go		1967	7.50	15.00	30.00
❑ EPA-5088	Hard Headed Woman/Good Rockin' Tonight//Don't/I Beg of You	1959	15.00	30.00	60.00
—Black label, dog on top					
❑ EPA-5088	Hard Headed Woman/Good Rockin' Tonight//Don't/I Beg of You	1959	100.00	200.00	400.00
—Maroon label					
❑ EPA-5088	Hard Headed Woman/Good Rockin' Tonight//Don't/I Beg of You	1965	7.50	15.00	30.00
—Black label, dog on left					
❑ EPA-5088	Hard Headed Woman/Good Rockin' Tonight//Don't/I Beg of You	1969	20.00	40.00	80.00
—Orange label					
❑ EPA-5088 [PS]A Touch of Gold		1959	15.00	30.00	60.00

Number	Title (A Side/B Side)	Yr	VG	VG+	NM
❑ EPA-5101	Wear My Ring Around Your Neck/Treat Me Nice//One Night/That's All Right	1959	15.00	30.00	60.00
—Black label, dog on top					
❑ EPA-5101	Wear My Ring Around Your Neck/Treat Me Nice//One Night/That's All Right	1959	100.00	200.00	400.00
—Maroon label					
❑ EPA-5101	Wear My Ring Around Your Neck/Treat Me Nice//One Night/That's All Right	1965	7.50	15.00	30.00
—Black label, dog on left					
❑ EPA-5101	Wear My Ring Around Your Neck/Treat Me Nice//One Night/That's All Right	1969	20.00	40.00	80.00
—Orange label					
❑ EPA-5101 [PS]A Touch of Gold, Volume II		1959	15.00	30.00	60.00
❑ EPA-5120	Don't Be Cruel/I Want You, I Need You, I Love You//Hound Dog/My Baby Left Me	1959	15.00	30.00	60.00
—Black label, dog on top					
❑ EPA-5120	Don't Be Cruel/I Want You, I Need You, I Love You//Hound Dog/My Baby Left Me	1959	150.00	300.00	600.00
—Maroon label					
❑ EPA-5120	Don't Be Cruel/I Want You, I Need You, I Love You//Hound Dog/My Baby Left Me	1965	6.25	12.50	25.00
—Black label, dog on left					
❑ EPA-5120	Don't Be Cruel/I Want You, I Need You, I Love You//Hound Dog/My Baby Left Me	1969	20.00	40.00	80.00
—Orange label					
❑ EPA-5120 [PS]The Real Elvis		1959	15.00	30.00	60.00
❑ EPA-5121	(There'll Be) Peace in the Valley (For Me)/It Is No Secret (What God Can Do)//I Believe/Take My Hand, Precious Lord	1959	7.50	15.00	30.00
—Black label, dog on top					
❑ EPA-5121	(There'll Be) Peace in the Valley (For Me)/It Is No Secret (What God Can Do)//I Believe/Take My Hand, Precious Lord	1959	100.00	200.00	400.00
—Maroon label					
❑ EPA-5121	(There'll Be) Peace in the Valley (For Me)/It Is No Secret (What God Can Do)//I Believe/Take My Hand, Precious Lord	1965	6.25	12.50	25.00
—Black label, dog on left					
❑ EPA-5121	(There'll Be) Peace in the Valley (For Me)/It Is No Secret (What God Can Do)//I Believe/Take My Hand, Precious Lord	1969	20.00	40.00	80.00
—Orange label					
❑ EPA-5121 [PS]Peace in the Valley		1959	10.00	20.00	40.00
—Three slightly different cover variations with no difference in value					
❑ EPA-5122	King Creole/New Orleans//As Long As I Have You/Lover Doll	1959	7.50	15.00	30.00
—Black label, dog on top					
❑ EPA-5122	King Creole/New Orleans//As Long As I Have You/Lover Doll	1959	1000.	1500.	2000.
—Maroon label					
❑ EPA-5122	King Creole/New Orleans//As Long As I Have You/Lover Doll	1965	6.25	12.50	25.00
—Black label, dog on left					
❑ EPA-5122	King Creole/New Orleans//As Long As I Have You/Lover Doll	1969	20.00	40.00	80.00
—Orange label					
❑ EPA-5122 [PS]King Creole		1959	10.00	20.00	40.00
—With "Gold Standard Series" on front cover					
❑ EPA-5122 [PS]King Creole		1965	7.50	15.00	30.00
—Without "Gold Standard Series" on front cover					
❑ EPA-5141	All Shook Up/Don't Ask Me Why//Too Much/Blue Moon of Kentucky	1959	17.50	35.00	70.00
—Black label, dog on top					
❑ EPA-5141	All Shook Up/Don't Ask Me Why//Too Much/Blue Moon of Kentucky	1959	100.00	200.00	400.00
—Maroon label					
❑ EPA-5141	All Shook Up/Don't Ask Me Why//Too Much/Blue Moon of Kentucky	1959	7.50	15.00	30.00
—Black label, dog on left					
❑ EPA-5141	All Shook Up/Don't Ask Me Why//Too Much/Blue Moon of Kentucky	1959	20.00	40.00	80.00
—Orange label					
❑ EPA-5141 [PS]A Touch of Gold, Volume 3		1959	17.50	35.00	70.00
❑ EPA-5157	Press Interview with Elvis Presley//Elvis Presley's Newsreel Interview/Pat Hernon Interviews Elvis...	1965	7.50	15.00	30.00
—Black label, dog on top					
❑ EPA-5157	Press Interview with Elvis Presley//Elvis Presley's Newsreel Interview/Pat Hernon Interviews Elvis...	1969	20.00	40.00	80.00
—Orange label					
❑ EPA-5157 [PS]Elvis Sails		1965	7.50	15.00	30.00
❑ G8-MW-8705 [DJ]TV Guide Presents Elvis Presley		1956	300.00	600.00	1200.
—Blue label, locked grooves (needle has to be lifted to play each of the four excerpts)					
❑ 599-9141	Blue Moon of Kentucky/Love Me Tender//Mystery Train/Milkcow Boogie Blues	1957	100.00	200.00	400.00
—This is "Side 6" and "Side 15" of various artists box set SPD-26, "Great Country/Western Hits"; notice the error in title on the second side					

Albums

BOXCAR

❑ (no #)	Having Fun with Elvis on Stage	1974	37.50	75.00	150.00
—All-talking record sold at Elvis concerts in 1974					

DCC COMPACT CLASSICS

❑ LPZ-2037 [S] Elvis Is Back!		1997	30.00	60.00	120.00
—Audiophile vinyl					
❑ LPZ-2040 [(2)]24 Karat Hits!		1997	30.00	60.00	120.00
—Audiophile vinyl					

Many of Elvis Presley's earliest recordings came from the R&B canon. His second Sun single, "Good Rockin' Tonight," was a remake of a song composed by Roy Brown and taken to #1 on the R&B charts by Wynonie Harris.

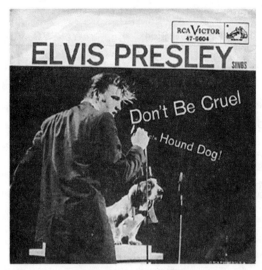

Today, it can be easy to forget that Elvis Presley was quite popular in R&B circles during his heyday. He had 34 Top 20 songs on the R&B charts, six of which hit #1. This picture sleeve represents two of those six chart-toppers, "Don't Be Cruel" and "Hound Dog."

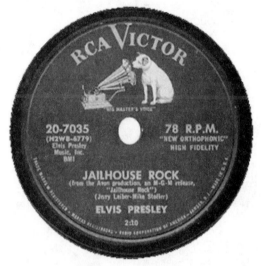

Elvis' fifth #1 single on the R&B charts was "Jailhouse Rock," the last record by anyone to hit the top of the pop, country and R&B charts. Not as often seen as the 45 is this 78-rpm edition.

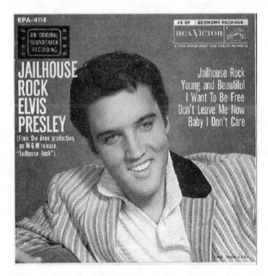

Also making the R&B charts was an additional track from the EP of songs from the movie *Jailhouse Rock,* "(You're So Square) Baby I Don't Care."

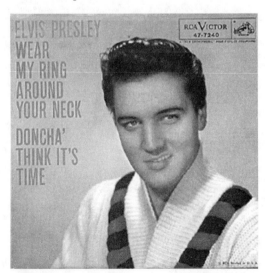

"Wear My Ring Around Your Neck" was Elvis' final #1 R&B hit. Interestingly, it didn't hit the top of either the pop or country charts.

One of the rarest Elvis artifacts is this sleeve accompanying a promo-only 45 coupling of "Don't" and "Wear My Ring Around Your Neck."

P

Number	Title (A Side/B Side)	Yr	VG	VG+	NM

FOTOPLAY
| ❑ FSP-1001 [PD] | To Elvis: Love Still Burning | 1978 | 6.25 | 12.50 | 25.00 |

—Tribute-song picture disc of Elvis; in plastic bag with 11x11 insert
| ❑ FSP-1001 [PD] | To Elvis: Love Still Burning | 1978 | 7.50 | 15.00 | 30.00 |

—In white cardboard cover with black printing
| ❑ FSP-1001 [PD] | To Elvis: Love Still Burning | 1978 | 3.75 | 7.50 | 15.00 |

—In black cardboard cover with white printing

GOLDEN EDITIONS
| ❑ KING-1 | The First Year (Elvis, Scotty and Bill) | 1979 | 3.75 | 7.50 | 15.00 |
| ❑ GEL-101 | The First Year (Elvis, Scotty and Bill) | 1979 | 5.00 | 10.00 | 20.00 |

GREAT NORTHWEST
| ❑ GV-2004 | The King Speaks (February 1961, Memphis, Tennessee) | 1977 | 2.50 | 5.00 | 10.00 |

—Label says this is on "Green Valley" while sleeve says "Great Northwest"
| ❑ GNW-4005 | The Elvis Tapes | 1977 | 3.00 | 6.00 | 12.00 |
| ❑ GNW-4006 | The King Speaks (February 1961, Memphis, Tennessee) | 1977 | 2.00 | 4.00 | 8.00 |

—Both label and sleeve say this is on "Great Northwest"

GREEN VALLEY
| ❑ GV-2001/3 [(2)] | Elvis (Speaks to You) | 1978 | 7.50 | 15.00 | 30.00 |

—Elvis interviews plus tracks by the Jordanaires
| ❑ GV-2001 | Elvis Exclusive Live Press Conference (Memphis, Tennessee, February 1961) | 1977 | 10.00 | 20.00 | 40.00 |

—Issued with two slightly different covers

GUSTO
| ❑ SD-995 | Interviews with Elvis (Canada 1957) | 1978 | 10.00 | 20.00 | 40.00 |

—Reissue of Great Northwest album

HALW
| ❑ HALW-0001 | The First Years | 1978 | 7.50 | 15.00 | 30.00 |

—With stamped, limited edition number
| ❑ HALW-0001 | The First Years | 1978 | 5.00 | 10.00 | 20.00 |

—Without limited edition number

K-TEL
| ❑ NU 9900 | Love Songs | 1981 | 5.00 | 10.00 | 20.00 |

LOUISIANA HAYRIDE
| ❑ LH-3061 | Beginning Years | 1984 | 5.00 | 10.00 | 20.00 |

—With booklet and facsimile contract

MARVENCO
| ❑ 101 | Beginning (1954-1955) | 1988 | 3.75 | 7.50 | 15.00 |

—Pink vinyl with booklet and facsimile contract

MOBILE FIDELITY
| ❑ 1-059 | From Elvis in Memphis | 1982 | 12.50 | 25.00 | 50.00 |

—Audiophile vinyl

MUSIC WORKS
| ❑ PB-3601 | The First Live Recordings | 1984 | 3.75 | 7.50 | 15.00 |
| ❑ PB-3602 | The Hillbilly Cat | 1984 | 3.75 | 7.50 | 15.00 |

OAK
| ❑ 1003 | Vintage 1955 Elvis | 1990 | 15.00 | 30.00 | 60.00 |

PAIR
❑ PDL2-1010 [(2)]	Double Dynamite	1982	5.00	10.00	20.00
❑ PDL2-1037 [(2)]	Remembering	1983	7.50	15.00	30.00
❑ PDL2-1185 [(2)]	Elvis Aron Presley Forever	1988	5.00	10.00	20.00

PICKWICK
| ❑ (no #) [(7)] | The Pickwick Pack (unofficial title) | 1978 | 15.00 | 30.00 | 60.00 |

—Seven Pickwick albums in special package and cardboard wrapper; one of the LPs is Elvis' Christmas Album
| ❑ (no #) [(7)] | The Pickwick Pack (unofficial title) | 1979 | 15.00 | 30.00 | 60.00 |

—Seven Pickwick albums in special package and cardboard wrapper; one of the LPs is Frankie and Johnny
❑ CAS-2304	Elvis Sings Flaming Star	1976	2.50	5.00	10.00
❑ CAS-2408	Let's Be Friends	1975	2.50	5.00	10.00
❑ CAL-2428 [M]	Elvis' Christmas Album	1975	3.00	6.00	12.00

—Same contents as RCA Camden LP; no Christmas trim on border
| ❑ CAL-2428 [M] | Elvis' Christmas Album | 1976 | 2.50 | 5.00 | 10.00 |

—Same as above, but with Christmas trim on cover border
❑ CAS-2440	Almost in Love	1975	2.50	5.00	10.00
❑ CAL-2472	You'll Never Walk Alone	1975	2.50	5.00	10.00
❑ CAL-2518	C'mon Everybody	1975	2.50	5.00	10.00
❑ CAS-2533	I Got Lucky	1975	2.50	5.00	10.00
❑ CAS-2567	Elvis Sings Hits from His Movies, Volume 1	1975	2.50	5.00	10.00
❑ CAS-2595	Burning Love And Hits from His Movies, Vol. 2	1975	3.00	6.00	12.00

—First cover contains a notice about the upcoming "Aloha from Hawaii" show
| ❑ CAS-2595 | Burning Love And Hits from His Movies, Vol. 2 | 1976 | 2.00 | 4.00 | 8.00 |

—Reissue deletes the "Aloha from Hawaii" notice
❑ CAS-2611	Separate Ways	1975	2.50	5.00	10.00
❑ DL2-5001 [(2)]	Double Dynamite	1975	6.25	12.50	25.00
❑ ACL-7007	Frankie and Johnny	1976	2.50	5.00	10.00
❑ ACL-7064	Mahalo from Elvis	1978	5.00	10.00	20.00

PREMORE
| ❑ PL-589 | Early Elvis (1954-1956 Live at the Louisiana Hayride) | 1989 | 7.50 | 15.00 | 30.00 |

RCA
| ❑ 2023-1-R | The Million Dollar Quartet | 1990 | 3.00 | 6.00 | 12.00 |

—With Jerry Lee Lewis, Carl Perkins, and perhaps Johnny Cash
❑ 2227-1-R	The Great Performances	1990	10.00	20.00	40.00
❑ 3114-1-R [(3)]	Collectors Gold	1991	50.00	100.00	200.00
❑ 5600-1-R	Return of the Rocker	1986	5.00	10.00	20.00
❑ 6221-1-R [(2)]	The Memphis Record	1987	7.50	15.00	30.00
❑ 6313-1-R	Elvis Talks!	1987	7.50	15.00	30.00
❑ 6382-1-R	The Number One Hits	1987	7.50	15.00	30.00
❑ 6383-1-R [(2)]	The Top Ten Hits	1987	7.50	15.00	30.00
❑ 6414-1-R [(2)]	The Complete Sun Sessions	1987	7.50	15.00	30.00
❑ 6738-1-R	Essential Elvis: The First Movies	1988	6.25	12.50	25.00
❑ 6985-1-R	The Alternate Aloha	1988	5.00	10.00	20.00
❑ 8468-1-R	Elvis in Nashville (1956-1971)	1988	10.00	20.00	40.00
❑ 9586-1-R	Elvis Gospel 1957-1971 (Known Only to Him)	1989	10.00	20.00	40.00
❑ 9589-1-R	Essential Elvis, Vol. 2 (Stereo '57)	1989	6.25	12.50	25.00
❑ 07863-67642-1	Elvis' Golden Records	1997	7.50	15.00	30.00

—Reissue for the Tower Records chain with 6 bonus tracks
| ❑ 07863-67643-1 | Elvis' Gold Records Volume 2 — 50,000,000 Elvis Fans Can't Be Wrong | 1997 | 7.50 | 15.00 | 30.00 |

—Reissue for the Tower Records chain with 10 bonus tracks
| ❑ 07863-68079-1 [(2)] | 30 #1 Hits | 2002 | 5.00 | 10.00 | 20.00 |

RCA CAMDEN
❑ CAS-2304	Elvis Sings Flaming Star	1969	7.50	15.00	30.00
❑ CAS-2408	Let's Be Friends	1970	7.50	15.00	30.00
❑ CAL-2428 [M]	Elvis' Christmas Album	1970	7.50	15.00	30.00

—Blue label, non-flexible vinyl
| ❑ CAL-2428 [M] | Elvis' Christmas Album | 1971 | 3.00 | 6.00 | 12.00 |

—Blue label, flexible vinyl
| ❑ CAS-2440 | Almost in Love | 1970 | 10.00 | 20.00 | 40.00 |

—Last song on Side 2 is "Stay Away, Joe"
| ❑ CAS-2440 | Almost in Love | 1973 | 6.25 | 12.50 | 25.00 |

—Last song on Side 2 is "Stay Away"
❑ CAL-2472	You'll Never Walk Alone	1974	7.50	15.00	30.00
❑ CALX-2472	You'll Never Walk Alone	1971	3.75	7.50	15.00
❑ CAL-2518	C'mon Everybody	1971	5.00	10.00	20.00
❑ CAL-2533	I Got Lucky	1971	6.25	12.50	25.00
❑ CAS-2567	Elvis Sings Hits from His Movies, Volume 1	1972	5.00	10.00	20.00
❑ CAS-2595	Burning Love And Hits from His Movies, Vol. 2	1972	6.25	12.50	25.00

—With star on front cover advertising a bonus photo, the presence of which doubles the value of this LP
| ❑ CAS-2595 | Burning Love And Hits from His Movies, Vol. 2 | 1972 | 2.50 | 5.00 | 10.00 |

—No star on cover, no bonus photo
| ❑ CAS-2611 | Separate Ways | 1973 | 7.50 | 15.00 | 30.00 |

RCA SPECIAL PRODUCTS
| ❑ DPL2-0056(e) [(2)] | Elvis | 1973 | 12.50 | 25.00 | 50.00 |

—Mustard labels
| ❑ DPL2-0056(e) [(2)] | Elvis | 1973 | 6.25 | 12.50 | 25.00 |

—Blue labels
| ❑ DPL2-0056(e) [(2)] | Elvis Commemorative Album | 1978 | 20.00 | 40.00 | 80.00 |

—Reissue of "Elvis" (same number) with new title and gold vinyl
| ❑ DPL2-0168 [(2)] | Elvis in Hollywood | 1976 | 15.00 | 30.00 | 60.00 |

—Blue labels; with 20-page booklet
| ❑ DML5-0263 [(5)] | The Elvis Story | 1977 | 15.00 | 30.00 | 60.00 |

—Available through Candelite Music via mail order
❑ DML1-0264	His Songs of Inspiration	1977	3.75	7.50	15.00
❑ DPL5-0347 [(5)]	Memories of Elvis (A Lasting Tribute to the King of Rock 'N' Roll)	1978	20.00	40.00	80.00
❑ DML1-0348	The Greatest Show on Earth	1978	3.75	7.50	15.00
❑ DML6-0412 [(6)]	The Legendary Recordings of Elvis Presley	1979	25.00	50.00	100.00
❑ DML1-0413	The Greatest Moments in Music	1980	3.75	7.50	15.00
❑ DML1-0437	Rock 'N Roll Forever	1981	3.75	7.50	15.00
❑ DVL1-0461	The Legendary Magic of Elvis Presley	1980	3.75	7.50	15.00
❑ DML3-0632 [(3)]	The Elvis Presley Collection	1984	20.00	40.00	80.00

—Available through Candelite Music via mail order
| ❑ DPL1-0647 | Elvis Country | 1984 | 7.50 | 15.00 | 30.00 |
| ❑ DVM1-0704 | Elvis (One Night with You) | 1984 | 15.00 | 30.00 | 60.00 |

—With poster (deduct 25% if missing)
❑ SVL3-0710 [(3)]	50 Years — 50 Hits	1985	7.50	15.00	30.00
❑ DVL2-0728 [(2)]	His Songs of Faith and Inspiration	1986	12.50	25.00	50.00
❑ SVL2-0824 [(2)]	Good Rockin' Tonight	1988	5.00	10.00	20.00
❑ CAL-2428 [M]	Elvis' Christmas Album	1986	7.50	15.00	30.00

—Reissue for The Special Music Company

RCA VICTOR
| ❑ (no #) | International Hotel, Las Vegas Nevada, Presents Elvis, 1969 | 1969 | 1250. | 1875. | 2500 |

—Gift box to guests at Elvis' July 31-Aug, 1, 1969 shows. Includes LPM-4088 and LSP-4155; press release; 1969 catalog; three photos; and thank-you note from Elvis and the Colonel. Most of the value is for the box.
| ❑ (no #) | International Hotel, Las Vegas Nevada, Presents Elvis, 1970 | 1970 | 1250. | 1875. | 2500 |

—Gift box to guests at Elvis' Jan. 28, 1970 show. Includes LSP-6020 and 47-9791; press release; 1970 catalog; photo; booklet; and dinner menu. Most of the value is for the box.
| ❑ PRS-279 | Singer Presents Elvis Singing Flaming Star and Others | 1968 | 25.00 | 50.00 | 100.00 |

—Sold only at Singer sewing machine dealers; reissued on RCA Camden 2304
| ❑ APL1-0283 | Elvis | 1973 | 12.50 | 25.00 | 50.00 |
| ❑ CPL1-0341 | A Legendary Performer, Volume 1 | 1974 | 6.25 | 12.50 | 25.00 |

—Includes booklet (deduct 40% if missing); with die-cut hole in front cover
| ❑ CPL1-0341 | A Legendary Performer, Volume 1 | 1986 | 3.75 | 7.50 | 15.00 |

—No die-cut hole in cover and no booklet
| ❑ APL1-0388 | Raised on Rock/For Ol' Times Sake | 1973 | 7.50 | 15.00 | 30.00 |

—Orange label
| ❑ APL1-0388 | Raised on Rock/For Ol' Times Sake | 1975 | 7.50 | 15.00 | 30.00 |

—Tan label
| ❑ APL1-0388 | Raised on Rock/For Ol' Times Sake | 1977 | 3.00 | 6.00 | 12.00 |

—Black label, dog near top
| ❑ SP-33-461 [DJ] | Special Palm Sunday Programming | 1967 | 175.00 | 350.00 | 700.00 |

—White label promo. Add 25% for cue sheet.
| ❑ AFL1-0475 | Good Times | 1977 | 3.00 | 6.00 | 12.00 |

—Black label, dog near top; includes copies with sticker wrapped around spine with new number
| ❑ CPL1-0475 | Good Times | 1974 | 12.50 | 25.00 | 50.00 |

—Orange label
| ❑ CPL1-0475 | Good Times | 1976 | 3.00 | 6.00 | 12.00 |

—Black label, dog near top
| ❑ SPS-33-571 [DJ] | Elvis As Recorded at Madison Square Garden | 1972 | 75.00 | 150.00 | 300.00 |

—"Radio Station Banded Special Version"; came in plain white cover with stickers
| ❑ AFL1-0606 | Elvis Recorded Live on Stage in Memphis | 1977 | 3.00 | 6.00 | 12.00 |

—Black label, dog near top; includes copies with sticker wrapped around spine with new number

Number	Title (A Side/B Side)	Yr	VG	VG+	NM
❏ APD1-0606 [Q]Elvis Recorded Live on Stage in Memphis		1974	50.00	100.00	200.00

—"RCA QuadraDisc" labels

| ❏ CPL1-0606 | Elvis Recorded Live on Stage in Memphis | 1974 | 6.25 | 12.50 | 25.00 |

—Orange label

| ❏ CPL1-0606 | Elvis Recorded Live on Stage in Memphis | 1975 | 6.25 | 12.50 | 25.00 |

—Tan label

| ❏ DJL1-0606 [DJ]Elvis Recorded Live on Stage in Memphis | | 1974 | 75.00 | 150.00 | 300.00 |

—Special banded version for radio airplay

| ❏ AFM1-0818 | Having Fun with Elvis on Stage | 1977 | 6.25 | 12.50 | 25.00 |

—Black label, dog near top

| ❏ CPM1-0818 | Having Fun with Elvis on Stage | 1974 | 7.50 | 15.00 | 30.00 |

—Commercial issue of Boxcar LP; orange label

| ❏ CPM1-0818 | Having Fun with Elvis on Stage | 1975 | 5.00 | 10.00 | 20.00 |

—Tan label

| ❏ DJM1-0835 [DJ]Elvis Presley Interview Record: An Audio Self-Portrait | | 1984 | 20.00 | 40.00 | 80.00 |

—Promotional item for "50th Anniversary" series; later issued as RCA 6313-1-R

| ❏ AFL1-0873 | Promised Land | 1977 | 3.75 | 7.50 | 15.00 |

—Black label, dog near top

| ❏ APD1-0873 [Q]Promised Land | | 1975 | 50.00 | 100.00 | 200.00 |

—"RCA QuadraDisc" label

| ❏ APD1-0873 [Q]Promised Land | | 1977 | 30.00 | 60.00 | 120.00 |

—Black label, dog near top; quadraphonic reissue

| ❏ APL1-0873 | Promised Land | 1975 | 15.00 | 30.00 | 60.00 |

—Orange label

| ❏ APL1-0873 | Promised Land | 1975 | 5.00 | 10.00 | 20.00 |

—Tan label

| ❏ ANL1-0971(e) Pure Gold | | 1975 | 3.75 | 7.50 | 15.00 |

—Orange label

| ❏ ANL1-0971(e) Pure Gold | | 1976 | 3.00 | 6.00 | 12.00 |

—Yellow label

| ❏ LOC-1035 [M] Elvis' Christmas Album | | 1957 | 125.00 | 250.00 | 500.00 |

—Gatefold cover; title printed in gold on LP spine; includes bound-in booklet but not sticker

| ❏ LOC-1035 [M] Elvis' Christmas Album | | 1957 | 125.00 | 250.00 | 500.00 |

—Gatefold cover; title printed in silver on LP spine; includes bound-in booklet but not sticker

| ❏ LOC-1035 [M] Elvis' Christmas Album | | 1957 | 7500. | 11250. | 15000. |

—Red vinyl; unique

| ❏ LOC-1035 [M] Elvis' Christmas Album Sticker | | 1957 | 37.50 | 75.00 | 150.00 |

—Gold sticker with "To_____" and "From_____" blanks

| ❏ AFL1-1039 | Elvis Today | 1977 | 3.00 | 6.00 | 12.00 |

—Black label, dog near top; includes copies with sticker wrapped around spine with new number

| ❏ APD1-1039 [Q]Elvis Today | | 1975 | 50.00 | 100.00 | 200.00 |

—"RCA QuadraDisc" labels

| ❏ APD1-1039 [Q]Elvis Today | | 1977 | 37.50 | 75.00 | 150.00 |

—Black label, dog near top; quadraphonic reissue

| ❏ APL1-1039 | Elvis Today | 1975 | 15.00 | 30.00 | 60.00 |

—Orange label

| ❏ APL1-1039 | Elvis Today | 1975 | 7.50 | 15.00 | 30.00 |

—Tan label

| ❏ AFL1-1254(e) [R]Elvis Presley | | 1977 | 3.00 | 6.00 | 12.00 |

—Black label, dog near top; includes copies with sticker wrapped around spine with new number

| ❏ LPM-1254 [M] Elvis Presley | | 1956 | 125.00 | 250.00 | 500.00 |

—Version 1: "Long Play" on label; "Elvis" in pale pink, "Presley" in pale green on cover; pale green logo box in upper right front cover

| ❏ LPM-1254 [M] Elvis Presley | | 1956 | 100.00 | 200.00 | 400.00 |

—Version 2: "Long Play" on label; "Elvis" in pale pink, "Presley" in neon green on cover; neon green logo box in upper right front cover

| ❏ LPM-1254 [M] Elvis Presley | | 1956 | 62.50 | 125.00 | 250.00 |

—Version 3: "Long Play" on label; "Elvis" in pale pink, "Presley" in neon green on cover; black logo box in upper right front cover

| ❏ LPM-1254 [M] Elvis Presley | | 1958 | 50.00 | 100.00 | 200.00 |

—Version 4: "Long Play" on label; "Elvis" in neon pink, almost red, "Presley" in neon green on cover; black logo box in upper right front cover

| ❏ LPM-1254 [M] Elvis Presley | | 1963 | 30.00 | 60.00 | 120.00 |

—"Mono" on label; cover photo is slightly left of center, otherwise same as Version 4 above

| ❏ LPM-1254 [M] Elvis Presley | | 1964 | 15.00 | 30.00 | 60.00 |

—"Monaural" on label

| ❏ LSP-1254(e) [R]Elvis Presley | | 1962 | 50.00 | 100.00 | 200.00 |

—"Stereo Electronically Reprocessed" and silver "RCA Victor" on label

| ❏ LSP-1254(e) [R]Elvis Presley | | 1965 | 10.00 | 20.00 | 40.00 |

—"Stereo Electronically Reprocessed" and white "RCA Victor" on label

| ❏ LSP-1254(e) [R]Elvis Presley | | 1968 | 7.50 | 15.00 | 30.00 |

—Orange label, non-flexible vinyl

| ❏ LSP-1254(e) [R]Elvis Presley | | 1975 | 3.75 | 7.50 | 15.00 |

—Tan label

| ❏ LSP-1254(e) [R]Elvis Presley | | 1976 | 3.00 | 6.00 | 12.00 |

—Black label, dog near top

| ❏ ANL1-1319 [S]His Hand in Mine | | 1976 | 3.75 | 7.50 | 15.00 |

—Reissue with more tightly cropped photo of Elvis on front cover

| ❏ CPL1-1349 | A Legendary Performer, Volume 2 | 1976 | 7.50 | 15.00 | 30.00 |

—Includes booklet (deduct 40% if missing); with die-cut hole in front cover

| ❏ CPL1-1349 | A Legendary Performer, Volume 2 | 1976 | 15.00 | 30.00 | 60.00 |

—Without false starts and outtakes of "Such a Night" and "Cane and a High Starched Collar," which are supposed to be there. End of matrix number may be "31."

| ❏ CPL1-1349 | A Legendary Performer, Volume 2 | 1986 | 3.75 | 7.50 | 15.00 |

—No die-cut hole in cover and no booklet

| ❏ AFL1-1382(e) [R]Elvis | | 1977 | 3.00 | 6.00 | 12.00 |

—Black label, dog near top; includes copies with sticker wrapped around spine with new number

| ❏ LPM-1382 [M] Elvis | | 1956 | 75.00 | 150.00 | 300.00 |

—Back cover has ads for other albums. At least 11 different variations of this are known, all of equal value.

| ❏ LPM-1382 [M] Elvis | | 1956 | 75.00 | 150.00 | 300.00 |

—Back cover has no ads for other albums. "Long Play" on label.

| ❏ LPM-1382 [M] Elvis | | 1956 | 200.00 | 400.00 | 800.00 |

—With alternate take of "Old Shep" on side 2. Matrix number on the "Old Shep" side ends in "15S," "17S" or "19S," but should be played for positive ID. On alternate take, Elvis sings "he grew old AND his eyes were growing dim" (no AND on standard press)

| ❏ LPM-1382 [M] Elvis | | 1956 | 100.00 | 200.00 | 400.00 |

—With tracks listed on labels as "Band 1" through "Band 6"

| ❏ LPM-1382 [M] Elvis | | 1963 | 20.00 | 40.00 | 80.00 |

—"Mono" on label

| ❏ LPM-1382 [M] Elvis | | 1965 | 15.00 | 30.00 | 60.00 |

—"Monaural" on label

| ❏ LSP-1382(e) [R]Elvis | | 1962 | 50.00 | 100.00 | 200.00 |

—"Stereo Electronically Reprocessed" and silver "RCA Victor" on label

| ❏ LSP-1382(e) [R]Elvis | | 1964 | 12.50 | 25.00 | 50.00 |

—"Stereo Electronically Reprocessed" and white "RCA Victor" on label

| ❏ LSP-1382(e) [R]Elvis | | 1968 | 7.50 | 15.00 | 30.00 |

—Orange label, non-flexible vinyl

| ❏ LSP-1382(e) [R]Elvis | | 1971 | 5.00 | 10.00 | 20.00 |

—Orange label, flexible vinyl

| ❏ LSP-1382(e) [R]Elvis | | 1975 | 3.75 | 7.50 | 15.00 |

—Tan label

| ❏ LSP-1382(e) [R]Elvis | | 1976 | 3.00 | 6.00 | 12.00 |

—Black label, dog near top

| ❏ AFL1-1506 | From Elvis Presley Boulevard, Memphis, Tennessee | 1977 | 3.00 | 6.00 | 12.00 |

—Black label, dog near top; with sticker wrapped around spine with new number (old number still on label)

| ❏ AFL1-1506 | From Elvis Presley Boulevard, Memphis, Tennessee | 1977 | 2.50 | 5.00 | 10.00 |

—Black label, dog near top; new number is on cover and label

| ❏ APL1-1506 | From Elvis Presley Boulevard, Memphis, Tennessee | 1976 | 7.50 | 15.00 | 30.00 |

—Tan label

| ❏ AFL1-1515(e) [R]Loving You | | 1977 | 3.00 | 6.00 | 12.00 |

—Black label, dog near top; includes copies with sticker wrapped around spine with new number

| ❏ LPM-1515 [M] Loving You | | 1957 | 75.00 | 150.00 | 300.00 |

—"Long Play" on label

| ❏ LPM-1515 [M] Loving You | | 1963 | 25.00 | 50.00 | 100.00 |

—"Mono" on label

| ❏ LPM-1515 [M] Loving You | | 1964 | 12.50 | 25.00 | 50.00 |

—"Monaural" on label

| ❏ LSP-1515(e) [R]Loving You | | 1962 | 37.50 | 75.00 | 150.00 |

—"Stereo Electronically Reprocessed" and silver "RCA Victor" on label

| ❏ LSP-1515(e) [R]Loving You | | 1964 | 12.50 | 25.00 | 50.00 |

—"Stereo Electronically Reprocessed" and white "RCA Victor" on label

| ❏ LSP-1515(e) [R]Loving You | | 1968 | 10.00 | 20.00 | 40.00 |

—Orange label, non-flexible vinyl

| ❏ LSP-1515(e) [R]Loving You | | 1971 | 5.00 | 10.00 | 20.00 |

—Orange label, flexible vinyl

| ❏ LSP-1515(e) [R]Loving You | | 1975 | 5.00 | 10.00 | 20.00 |

—Tan label

| ❏ LSP-1515(e) [R]Loving You | | 1976 | 3.00 | 6.00 | 12.00 |

—Black label, dog near top

| ❏ AFM1-1675 | The Sun Sessions | 1977 | 3.75 | 7.50 | 15.00 |

—Black label, dog near top; includes copies with sticker wrapped around spine with new number

| ❏ APM1-1675 | The Sun Sessions | 1976 | 5.00 | 10.00 | 20.00 |

—Tan label

| ❏ APM1-1675 | The Sun Sessions | 1976 | 3.00 | 6.00 | 12.00 |

—Black label, dog near top

| ❏ AFL1-1707(e) [R]Elvis' Golden Records | | 1977 | 3.00 | 6.00 | 12.00 |

—Black label, dog near top; includes copies with sticker wrapped around spine with new number

| ❏ AQL1-1707(e) [R]Elvis' Golden Records | | 1979 | 2.50 | 5.00 | 10.00 |

—Another reissue with new prefix

| ❏ LPM-1707 [M] Elvis' Golden Records | | 1958 | 62.50 | 125.00 | 250.00 |

—Title on cover in light blue letters; no song titles listed on front cover

| ❏ LPM-1707 [M] Elvis' Golden Records | | 1958 | 37.50 | 75.00 | 150.00 |

—Title on cover in light blue letters; no song titles listed on front cover; "RE" on back cover

| ❏ LPM-1707 [M] Elvis' Golden Records | | 1963 | 15.00 | 30.00 | 60.00 |

—"Mono" on label; title on cover in white letters; song titles added to front cover

| ❏ LPM-1707 [M] Elvis' Golden Records | | 1964 | 10.00 | 20.00 | 40.00 |

—"Monaural" on label; "RE2" on back cover

| ❏ LSP-1707(e) [R]Elvis' Golden Records | | 1962 | 50.00 | 100.00 | 200.00 |

—"Stereo Electronically Reprocessed" and silver "RCA Victor" on label

| ❏ LSP-1707(e) [R]Elvis' Golden Records | | 1964 | 12.50 | 25.00 | 50.00 |

—"Stereo Electronically Reprocessed" and white "RCA Victor" on label

| ❏ LSP-1707(e) [R]Elvis' Golden Records | | 1968 | 7.50 | 15.00 | 30.00 |

—Orange label, non-flexible vinyl

| ❏ LSP-1707(e) [R]Elvis' Golden Records | | 1971 | 5.00 | 10.00 | 20.00 |

—Orange label, flexible vinyl

| ❏ LSP-1707(e) [R]Elvis' Golden Records | | 1975 | 5.00 | 10.00 | 20.00 |

—Tan label

| ❏ LSP-1707(e) [R]Elvis' Golden Records | | 1976 | 3.00 | 6.00 | 12.00 |

—Black label, dog near top

| ❏ AFL1-1884(e) [R]King Creole | | 1977 | 3.00 | 6.00 | 12.00 |

—Black label, dog near top; includes copies with sticker wrapped around spine with new number

| ❏ LPM-1884 [M] King Creole | | 1958 | 50.00 | 100.00 | 200.00 |

—"Long Play" on label; contrary to some other sources, this was NOT issued with a bonus photo

| ❏ LPM-1884 [M] King Creole | | 1963 | 20.00 | 40.00 | 80.00 |

—"Mono" on label

| ❏ LPM-1884 [M] King Creole | | 1964 | 15.00 | 30.00 | 60.00 |

—"Monaural" on label

| ❏ LSP-1884(e) [R]King Creole | | 1962 | 37.50 | 75.00 | 150.00 |

—"Stereo Electronically Reprocessed" and silver "RCA Victor" on label

| ❏ LSP-1884(e) [R]King Creole | | 1964 | 15.00 | 30.00 | 60.00 |

—"Stereo Electronically Reprocessed" and white "RCA Victor" on label

| ❏ LSP-1884(e) [R]King Creole | | 1968 | 10.00 | 20.00 | 40.00 |

—Orange label, non-flexible vinyl

| ❏ LSP-1884(e) [R]King Creole | | 1971 | 5.00 | 10.00 | 20.00 |

—Orange label, flexible vinyl

| ❏ LSP-1884(e) [R]King Creole | | 1975 | 5.00 | 10.00 | 20.00 |

—Tan label

P

Number	Title (A Side/B Side)	Yr	VG	VG+	NM
❑ LSP-1884(e) [R]King Creole		1976	3.00	6.00	12.00

—Black label, dog near top

❑ ANL1-1936 Elvis Sings the Wonderful World of Christmas		1975	3.75	7.50	15.00

—New number; same contents as LSP-4579. Orange label.

❑ ANL1-1936 Elvis Sings the Wonderful World of Christmas		1976	3.00	6.00	12.00

—Tan label

❑ ANL1-1936 Elvis Sings the Wonderful World of Christmas		1977	2.50	5.00	10.00

—Black label, dog near top

❑ LPM-1951 [M] Elvis' Christmas Album		1958	37.50	75.00	150.00

—Same contents as LOC-1035, but with non-gatefold blue cover; "Long Play" at bottom of label

❑ LPM-1951 [M] Elvis' Christmas Album		1963	17.50	35.00	70.00

—"Mono" at bottom of label: "RE" on lower left front cover (photos on back were altered)

❑ LPM-1951 [M] Elvis' Christmas Album		1964	10.00	20.00	40.00

—"Monaural" at bottom of label; "RE" on lower left front cover

❑ LSP-1951(e) [R]Elvis' Christmas Album		1964	12.50	25.00	50.00

—Black label, dog on top; "Stereo Electronically Reprocessed" at bottom of label

❑ LSP-1951(e) [R]Elvis' Christmas Album		1968	15.00	30.00	60.00

—Orange label, non-flexible vinyl

❑ AFL1-1990(e) [R]For LP Fans Only		1977	3.00	6.00	12.00

—Black label, dog near top; includes copies with sticker wrapped around spine with new number

❑ LPM-1990 [M] For LP Fans Only		1959	62.50	125.00	250.00

—"Long Play" on label

❑ LPM-1990 [M] For LP Fans Only		1963	20.00	40.00	80.00

—"Mono" on label

❑ LPM-1990 [M] For LP Fans Only		1964	12.50	25.00	50.00

—"Monaural" on label

❑ LSP-1990(e) [R]For LP Fans Only		1965	75.00	150.00	300.00

—"Stereo Electronically Reprocessed" on label; error cover with same photo on both front and back

❑ LSP-1990(e) [R]For LP Fans Only		1965	12.50	25.00	50.00

—"Stereo Electronically Reprocessed" on label; normal cover with different front and back cover photos

❑ LSP-1990(e) [R]For LP Fans Only		1968	7.50	15.00	30.00

—Orange label, non-flexible vinyl

❑ LSP-1990(e) [R]For LP Fans Only		1975	5.00	10.00	20.00

—Tan label

❑ LSP-1990(e) [R]For LP Fans Only		1976	3.00	6.00	12.00

—Black label, dog near top

❑ AFL1-2011(e) [R]A Date with Elvis		1977	3.00	6.00	12.00

—Black label, dog near top; includes copies with sticker wrapped around spine with new number

❑ LPM-2011 [M] A Date with Elvis		1959	100.00	200.00	400.00

—"Long Play" on label; gatefold cover, no sticker on cover

❑ LPM-2011 [M] A Date with Elvis		1959	125.00	250.00	500.00

—"Long Play" on label; gatefold cover, with sticker on cover

❑ LPM-2011 [M] A Date with Elvis		1963	25.00	50.00	100.00

—"Mono" on label; no gatefold cover

❑ LPM-2011 [M] A Date with Elvis		1965	12.50	25.00	50.00

—"Monaural" on label

❑ LSP-2011(e) [R]A Date with Elvis		1965	12.50	25.00	50.00

—Black label, "Stereo Electronically Reprocessed" on label

❑ LSP-2011(e) [R]A Date with Elvis		1968	7.50	15.00	30.00

—Orange label, non-flexible vinyl

❑ LSP-2011(e) [R]A Date with Elvis		1971	5.00	10.00	20.00

—Orange label, flexible vinyl

❑ LSP-2011(e) [R]A Date with Elvis		1975	5.00	10.00	20.00

—Tan label

❑ LSP-2011(e) [R]A Date with Elvis		1977	3.00	6.00	12.00

—Black label, dog near top

❑ AFL1-2075(e) [R]Elvis' Gold Records Volume 2 — 50,000,000 Elvis Fans Can't Be Wrong		1977	3.00	6.00	12.00

—Black label, dog near top; includes copies with sticker wrapped around spine with new number

❑ LPM-2075 [M] Elvis' Gold Records Volume 2 — 50,000,000 Elvis Fans Can't Be Wrong		1960	50.00	100.00	200.00

—"Long Play" on label; "Magic Millions" on upper right front cover with RCA Victor logo

❑ LPM-2075 [M] Elvis' Gold Records Volume 2 — 50,000,000 Elvis Fans Can't Be Wrong		1963	20.00	40.00	80.00

—"Mono" on label; "RE" on lower right front cover

❑ LPM-2075 [M] Elvis' Gold Records Volume 2 — 50,000,000 Elvis Fans Can't Be Wrong		1964	12.50	25.00	50.00

—"Monaural" on label; label has words "50,000,000 Elvis Presley Fans Can't Be Wrong"

❑ LPM-2075 [M] Elvis' Gold Records Volume 2 — 50,000,000 Elvis Fans Can't Be Wrong		1964	12.50	25.00	50.00

—"Monaural" on label; label only has "Elvis' Gold Records - Vol. 2"

❑ LSP-2075(e) [R]Elvis' Gold Records Volume 2 — 50,000,000 Elvis Fans Can't Be Wrong		1962	37.50	75.00	150.00

—"Stereo Electronically Reprocessed" on label; label has words "50,000,000 Elvis Presley Fans Can't Be Wrong"

❑ LSP-2075(e) [R]Elvis' Gold Records Volume 2 — 50,000,000 Elvis Fans Can't Be Wrong		1964	12.50	25.00	50.00

—"Stereo Electronically Reprocessed" and white "RCA Victor" on label

❑ LSP-2075(e) [R]Elvis' Gold Records Volume 2 — 50,000,000 Elvis Fans Can't Be Wrong		1968	7.50	15.00	30.00

—Orange label, non-flexible vinyl

❑ LSP-2075(e) [R]Elvis' Gold Records Volume 2 — 50,000,000 Elvis Fans Can't Be Wrong		1971	5.00	10.00	20.00

—Orange label, flexible vinyl

❑ LSP-2075(e) [R]Elvis' Gold Records Volume 2 — 50,000,000 Elvis Fans Can't Be Wrong		1975	5.00	10.00	20.00

—Tan label

❑ LSP-2075(e) [R]Elvis' Gold Records Volume 2 — 50,000,000 Elvis Fans Can't Be Wrong		1976	3.00	6.00	12.00

—Black label, dog near top

❑ AFL1-2231 [S]Elvis Is Back!		1977	3.00	6.00	12.00

—Black label, dog near top; includes copies with sticker wrapped around spine with new number

❑ LPM-2231 [M] Elvis Is Back!		1960	37.50	75.00	150.00

—With sticker attached to front cover. Side 2, Song 4 is listed as "The Girl Next Door."

Number	Title (A Side/B Side)	Yr	VG	VG+	NM
❑ LPM-2231 [M] Elvis Is Back!		1960	37.50	75.00	150.00

—With sticker attached to front cover. Side 2, Song 4 is listed as "The Girl Next Door Went a-Walking."

❑ LPM-2231 [M] Elvis Is Back!		1960	50.00	100.00	200.00

—With no sticker attached to front cover. Side 2, Song 4 is listed as "The Girl Next Door."

❑ LPM-2231 [M] Elvis Is Back!		1960	50.00	100.00	200.00

—With no sticker attached to front cover. Side 2, Song 4 is listed as "The Girl Next Door Went a-Walking."

❑ LPM-2231 [M] Elvis Is Back!		1963	15.00	30.00	60.00

—"Mono" on label; song titles printed on front cover

❑ LPM-2231 [M] Elvis Is Back!		1964	15.00	30.00	60.00

—"Monaural" on label

❑ LSP-2231 [S] Elvis Is Back!		1960	75.00	150.00	300.00

—"Living Stereo" on label; with sticker attached to front cover. Side 2, Song 4 is listed as "The Girl Next Door."

❑ LSP-2231 [S] Elvis Is Back!		1960	75.00	150.00	300.00

—"Living Stereo" on label; with sticker attached to front cover. Side 2, Song 4 is listed as "The Girl Next Door Went a-Walking."

❑ LSP-2231 [S] Elvis Is Back!		1960	75.00	150.00	300.00

—"Living Stereo" on label; with no sticker attached to front cover. Side 2, Song 4 is listed as "The Girl Next Door."

❑ LSP-2231 [S] Elvis Is Back!		1960	75.00	150.00	300.00

—"Living Stereo" on label; with no sticker attached to front cover. Side 2, Song 4 is listed as "The Girl Next Door Went a-Walking."

❑ LSP-2231 [S] Elvis Is Back!		1964	15.00	30.00	60.00

—"Stereo" on label; song titles printed on front cover

❑ LSP-2231 [S] Elvis Is Back!		1968	10.00	20.00	40.00

—Orange label, non-flexible vinyl

❑ LSP-2231 [S] Elvis Is Back!		1975	5.00	10.00	20.00

—Tan label

❑ LSP-2231 [S] Elvis Is Back!		1976	3.75	7.50	15.00

—Black label, dog on top

❑ AFL1-2256 [S]G.I. Blues		1977	3.00	6.00	12.00

—Black label, dog near top; includes copies with sticker wrapped around spine with new number

❑ LPM-2256 [M] G.I. Blues		1960	125.00	250.00	500.00

—"Long Play" on label; with sticker on front cover advertising the presence of "Wooden Heart"

❑ LPM-2256 [M] G.I. Blues		1960	30.00	60.00	120.00

—"Long Play" on label; with no sticker on front cover

❑ LPM-2256 [M] G.I. Blues		1963	25.00	50.00	100.00

—"Mono" on label

❑ LPM-2256 [M] G.I. Blues		1964	12.50	25.00	50.00

—"Monaural" on label

❑ LSP-2256 [S] G.I. Blues		1960	150.00	300.00	600.00

—"Living Stereo" on label; with sticker on front cover advertising the presence of "Wooden Heart"

❑ LSP-2256 [S] G.I. Blues		1960	25.00	50.00	100.00

—"Living Stereo" on label; with no sticker on front cover

❑ LSP-2256 [S] G.I. Blues		1964	12.50	25.00	50.00

—"Stereo" on black label

❑ LSP-2256 [S] G.I. Blues		1968	10.00	20.00	40.00

—Orange label, non-flexible vinyl

❑ LSP-2256 [S] G.I. Blues		1971	5.00	10.00	20.00

—Orange label, flexible vinyl

❑ LSP-2256 [S] G.I. Blues		1975	6.25	12.50	25.00

—Tan label

❑ LSP-2256 [S] G.I. Blues		1976	3.00	6.00	12.00

—Black label, dog near top

❑ AFL1-2274 Welcome to My World		1977	3.00	6.00	12.00

—Black label, dog near top; includes copies with sticker wrapped around spine with new number

❑ APL1-2274 Welcome to My World		1977	5.00	10.00	20.00

—Black label, dog near top

❑ AQL1-2274 Welcome to My World		1979	2.50	5.00	10.00

—Black label, dog near top; includes copies with sticker wrapped around spine with new number

❑ LPM-2328 [M] His Hand in Mine		1960	30.00	60.00	120.00

—"Long Play" on label

❑ LPM-2328 [M] His Hand in Mine		1963	15.00	30.00	60.00

—"Mono" on label

❑ LPM-2328 [M] His Hand in Mine		1964	12.50	25.00	50.00

—"Monaural" on label

❑ LSP-2328 [S] His Hand in Mine		1960	50.00	100.00	200.00

—"Living Stereo" on label

❑ LSP-2328 [S] His Hand in Mine		1964	150.00	300.00	600.00

—"Stereo" and silver "RCA Victor" on black label

❑ LSP-2328 [S] His Hand in Mine		1964	25.00	50.00	100.00

—"Stereo" and white "RCA Victor" on black label

❑ LSP-2328 [S] His Hand in Mine		1968	12.50	25.00	50.00

—Orange label, non-flexible vinyl

❑ LSP-2328 [S] His Hand in Mine		1975	5.00	10.00	20.00

—Tan label

❑ LSP-2328 [S] His Hand in Mine		197?	5.00	10.00	20.00

—Orange label, flexible vinyl

❑ AHL1-2347 Greatest Hits, Volume One		1981	6.25	12.50	25.00

—With embossed cover

❑ AHL1-2347 Greatest Hits, Volume One		1983	3.75	7.50	15.00

—Without embossed cover

❑ AFL1-2370 [S]Something for Everybody		1977	3.00	6.00	12.00

—Black label, dog near top; includes copies with sticker wrapped around spine with new number

❑ LPM-2370 [M] Something for Everybody		1961	30.00	60.00	120.00

—"Long Play" on label; back cover advertises RCA Compact 33 singles and doubles

❑ LPM-2370 [M] Something for Everybody		1963	20.00	40.00	80.00

—"Mono" on label; back cover advertises "Viva Las Vegas" EP

❑ LPM-2370 [M] Something for Everybody		1964	12.50	25.00	50.00

—"Monaural" on label; back cover advertises "Viva Las Vegas" EP

❑ LSP-2370 [S] Something for Everybody		1961	50.00	100.00	200.00

—"Living Stereo" on label; back cover advertises RCA Compact 33 singles and doubles

❑ LSP-2370 [S] Something for Everybody		1963	25.00	50.00	100.00

—"Stereo" and silver "RCA Victor" on black label; back cover advertises Elvis' Christmas Album and His Hand in Mine LPs and "Viva Las Vegas" EP

Number	Title (A Side/B Side)	Yr	VG	VG+	NM
❑ LSP-2370 [S]	Something for Everybody	1964	12.50	25.00	50.00
—"Stereo" and white "RCA Victor" on black label; back cover advertises "Viva Las Vegas" EP					
❑ LSP-2370 [S]	Something for Everybody	1968	10.00	20.00	40.00
—Orange label, non-flexible vinyl; final back cover change advertises Elvis (NBC-TV Special), Elvis' Christmas Album and His Hand in Mine LPs					
❑ LSP-2370 [S]	Something for Everybody	1971	5.00	10.00	20.00
—Orange label, flexible vinyl					
❑ LSP-2370 [S]	Something for Everybody	1975	5.00	10.00	20.00
—Tan label					
❑ LSP-2370 [S]	Something for Everybody	1976	3.00	6.00	12.00
—Black label, dog near top					
❑ AFL1-2426 [S]	Blue Hawaii	1977	3.00	6.00	12.00
—Black label, dog near top; with sticker wrapped around spine with new number					
❑ LPM-2426 [M]	Blue Hawaii	1961	25.00	50.00	100.00
—"Long Play" on label; with sticker on cover advertising the presence of "Can't Help Falling in Love" and "Rock-a-Hula Baby"					
❑ LPM-2426 [M]	Blue Hawaii	1962	15.00	30.00	60.00
—"Long Play" on label; no sticker on front cover					
❑ LPM-2426 [M]	Blue Hawaii	1963	12.50	25.00	50.00
—"Mono" on label					
❑ LPM-2426 [M]	Blue Hawaii	1964	10.00	20.00	40.00
—"Monaural" on label					
❑ LSP-2426 [S]	Blue Hawaii	1961	37.50	75.00	150.00
—"Living Stereo" on label and upper right front cover; with sticker on cover advertising the presence of "Can't Help Falling in Love" and "Rock-a-Hula Baby"					
❑ LSP-2426 [S]	Blue Hawaii	1962	20.00	40.00	80.00
—"Living Stereo" on label and upper right front cover; no sticker on front cover					
❑ LSP-2426 [S]	Blue Hawaii	1964	12.50	25.00	50.00
—"Stereo" on label; "Victor Stereo" on upper right front cover					
❑ LSP-2426 [S]	Blue Hawaii	1968	10.00	20.00	40.00
—Orange label, non-flexible vinyl					
❑ LSP-2426 [S]	Blue Hawaii	1971	50.00	10.00	20.00
—Orange label, flexible vinyl					
❑ LSP-2426 [S]	Blue Hawaii	1975	50.00	10.00	20.00
—Tan label					
❑ LSP-2426 [S]	Blue Hawaii	1977	3.00	6.00	12.00
—Black label, dog near top					
❑ LSP-2426 [S]	Blue Hawaii	197?	250.00	500.00	1000.
—One-of-a-kind blue vinyl pressing with black label, dog near top					
❑ AFK1-2428	Moody Blue	1977	1500.	2250.	3000.
—Alternate cover slick (never put on an actual cover), with the words "Moody Blue" inside the large word "Elvis." See any late-1970s Elvis inner sleeve for a black and white photo of the scrapped cover.					
❑ AFL1-2428	Moody Blue	1977	2.50	5.00	10.00
—Blue vinyl					
❑ AFL1-2428	Moody Blue	1977	50.00	100.00	200.00
—Black vinyl					
❑ AFL1-2428 [DJ]	Moody Blue	1977	500.00	1000.	2000.
—Experimental colored vinyl pressings (with no cover), any color or combination except blue or black					
❑ AQL1-2428	Moody Blue	1979	6.25	12.50	25.00
—Reissue with new prefix					
❑ AFL1-2523 [S]	Pot Luck with Elvis	1977	3.00	6.00	12.00
—Black label, dog near top; includes copies with sticker wrapped around spine with new number					
❑ LPM-2523 [M]	Pot Luck with Elvis	1962	25.00	50.00	100.00
—"Long Play" on label					
❑ LPM-2523 [M]	Pot Luck with Elvis	1964	30.00	60.00	120.00
—"Monaural" on label					
❑ LSP-2523 [S]	Pot Luck with Elvis	1962	37.50	75.00	150.00
—"Living Stereo" on label					
❑ LSP-2523 [S]	Pot Luck with Elvis	1964	15.00	30.00	60.00
—"Stereo" on black label					
❑ LSP-2523 [S]	Pot Luck with Elvis	1968	10.00	20.00	40.00
—Orange label, non-flexible vinyl					
❑ LSP-2523 [S]	Pot Luck with Elvis	1975	5.00	10.00	20.00
—Tan label					
❑ LSP-2523 [S]	Pot Luck with Elvis	1976	3.00	6.00	12.00
—Black label, dog near top					
❑ APL1-2558 [S]	Harum Scarum	1977	3.00	6.00	12.00
—Black label, dog near top					
❑ APL1-2560 [S]	Spinout	1977	3.00	6.00	12.00
—Black label, dog near top					
❑ APL1-2564 [S]	Double Trouble	1977	3.00	6.00	12.00
—Black label, dog near top; includes copies with sticker wrapped around spine with new number					
❑ APL1-2565	Clambake	1977	3.00	6.00	12.00
❑ APL1-2568 [S]	It Happened at the World's Fair	1977	3.00	6.00	12.00
❑ AFL2-2587 [(2)]	Elvis in Concert	197?	250.00	500.00	1000.
—Both records on translucent blue vinyl; possibly an in-house demo at the RCA Indianapolis pressing plant					
❑ APL2-2587 [(2)]	Elvis in Concert	1977	6.25	12.50	25.00
❑ CPL2-2587 [(2)]	Elvis in Concert	1982	10.00	20.00	40.00
❑ AFL1-2621 [S]	Girls! Girls! Girls!	1977	3.00	6.00	12.00
—Black label, dog near top; includes copies with sticker wrapped around spine with new number					
❑ LPM-2621 [M]	Girls! Girls! Girls!	1962	20.00	40.00	80.00
—"Long Play" on label					
❑ LPM-2621 [M]	Girls! Girls! Girls!	1963	15.00	30.00	60.00
—"Mono" on label					
❑ LPM-2621 [M]	Girls! Girls! Girls!	1964	10.00	20.00	40.00
—"Monaural" on label					
❑ LPM/LSP-2621	Girls! Girls! Girls! Bonus 1963 Calendar	1962	37.50	75.00	150.00
—With listing of other Elvis records on back					
❑ LSP-2621 [S]	Girls! Girls! Girls!	1962	37.50	75.00	150.00
—"Living Stereo" on label					
❑ LSP-2621 [S]	Girls! Girls! Girls!	1964	15.00	30.00	60.00
—"Stereo" on black label					
❑ LSP-2621 [S]	Girls! Girls! Girls!	1968	10.00	20.00	40.00
—Orange label, non-flexible vinyl					
❑ LSP-2621 [S]	Girls! Girls! Girls!	1971	5.00	10.00	20.00
—Orange label, flexible vinyl					
❑ LSP-2621 [S]	Girls! Girls! Girls!	1975	6.25	12.50	25.00
—Tan label					
❑ LSP-2621 [S]	Girls! Girls! Girls!	1976	3.00	6.00	12.00
—Black label, dog near top					
❑ CPD2-2642 [(2) Q]	Aloha from Hawaii Via Satellite	1975	7.50	15.00	30.00
—Orange labels					
❑ CPD2-2642 [(2) Q]	Aloha from Hawaii Via Satellite	1977	20.00	40.00	80.00
—Black labels, dog near top					
❑ CPL2-2642 [(2) Q]	Aloha from Hawaii Via Satellite	1984	3.00	6.00	12.00
—New prefix; single-pocket instead of gatefold jacket					
❑ LPM-2697 [M]	It Happened at the World's Fair	1963	30.00	60.00	120.00
❑ LPM/LSP-2697	It Happened at the World's Fair Photo	1963	62.50	125.00	250.00
❑ LSP-2697 [S]	It Happened at the World's Fair	1963	50.00	100.00	200.00
—"Living Stereo" and silver "RCA Victor" on black label					
❑ LSP-2697 [S]	It Happened at the World's Fair	1964	20.00	40.00	80.00
—"Stereo" and white "RCA Victor" on black label					
❑ AFL1-2756 [S]	Fun in Acapulco	1977	3.00	6.00	12.00
—Black label, dog near top; includes copies with sticker wrapped around spine with new number					
❑ LPM-2756 [M]	Fun in Acapulco	1963	20.00	40.00	80.00
—"Mono" on label					
❑ LPM-2756 [M]	Fun in Acapulco	1964	12.50	25.00	50.00
—"Monaural" on label					
❑ LSP-2756 [S]	Fun in Acapulco	1963	25.00	50.00	100.00
—"Stereo" and silver "RCA Victor" on black label					
❑ LSP-2756 [S]	Fun in Acapulco	1964	15.00	30.00	60.00
—"Stereo" and white "RCA Victor" on black label					
❑ LSP-2756 [S]	Fun in Acapulco	1968	10.00	20.00	40.00
—Orange label, non-flexible vinyl					
❑ LSP-2756 [S]	Fun in Acapulco	1975	6.25	12.50	25.00
—Tan label					
❑ LSP-2756 [S]	Fun in Acapulco	1976	3.00	6.00	12.00
—Black label, dog near top					
❑ AFL1-2765 [S]	Elvis' Golden Records, Volume 3	1977	3.00	6.00	12.00
—Black label, dog near top; includes copies with sticker wrapped around spine with new number					
❑ LPM-2765 [M]	Elvis' Golden Records, Volume 3	1963	25.00	50.00	100.00
—"Mono" on label					
❑ LPM-2765 [M]	Elvis' Golden Records, Volume 3	1964	15.00	30.00	60.00
—"Monaural" on label					
❑ LSP-2765 [S]	Elvis' Golden Records, Volume 3	1963	37.50	75.00	150.00
—"Stereo" and silver "RCA Victor" on black label					
❑ LSP-2765 [S]	Elvis' Golden Records, Volume 3	1964	12.50	25.00	50.00
—"Stereo" and white "RCA Victor" on black label					
❑ LSP-2765 [S]	Elvis' Golden Records, Volume 3	1968	10.00	20.00	40.00
—Orange label, non-flexible vinyl					
❑ LSP-2765 [S]	Elvis' Golden Records, Volume 3	1975	5.00	10.00	20.00
—Tan label					
❑ LSP-2765 [S]	Elvis' Golden Records, Volume 3	1976	3.00	6.00	12.00
—Black label, dog near top					
❑ AFL1-2772	He Walks Beside Me	1978	6.25	12.50	25.00
—Includes 20-page photo booklet					
❑ AFL1-2894 [S]	Kissin' Cousins	1977	3.00	6.00	12.00
—Black label, dog near top; includes copies with sticker wrapped around spine with new number					
❑ LPM-2894 [M]	Kissin' Cousins	1964	20.00	40.00	80.00
—"Mono" on label; front cover has a small black and white photo of six cast members in lower right					
❑ LPM-2894 [M]	Kissin' Cousins	1964	50.00	100.00	200.00
—"Mono" on label; front cover does NOT have black and white photo in lower right					
❑ LPM-2894 [M]	Kissin' Cousins	1964	25.00	50.00	100.00
—"Monaural" on label; front cover has a small black and white photo of six cast members in lower right					
❑ LPM-2894 [M]	Kissin' Cousins	1964	50.00	100.00	200.00
—"Monaural" on label; front cover does NOT have black and white photo in lower right					
❑ LSP-2894 [S]	Kissin' Cousins	1964	30.00	60.00	120.00
—"Stereo" and silver "RCA Victor" on black label; front cover has a small black and white photo of six cast members in lower right					
❑ LSP-2894 [S]	Kissin' Cousins	1964	50.00	100.00	200.00
—"Stereo" and silver "RCA Victor" on black label; front cover does NOT have black and white photo in lower right					
❑ LSP-2894 [S]	Kissin' Cousins	1964	15.00	30.00	60.00
—"Stereo" and white "RCA Victor" on black label; all front covers have the cast photo in lower right					
❑ LSP-2894 [S]	Kissin' Cousins	1968	10.00	20.00	40.00
—Orange label, non-flexible vinyl					
❑ LSP-2894 [S]	Kissin' Cousins	1971	5.00	10.00	20.00
—Orange label, flexible vinyl					
❑ LSP-2894 [S]	Kissin' Cousins	1975	6.25	12.50	25.00
—Tan label					
❑ LSP-2894 [S]	Kissin' Cousins	1976	3.00	6.00	12.00
—Black label, dog near top					
❑ LSP-2894 [S]	Kissin' Cousins	1976	375.00	750.00	1500.
—Black label, dog near top; blue vinyl					
❑ CPL1-2901	Elvis Sings for Children and Grownups Too!	1978	5.00	10.00	20.00
—With two slits for removable greeting card on back cover (card should be with package)					
❑ CPL1-2901	Elvis Sings for Children and Grownups Too!	1978	2.50	5.00	10.00
—With greeting card graphic printed on back cover, and no slits on back cover					
❑ AFL1-2999 [S]	Roustabout	1977	3.00	6.00	12.00
—Black label, dog near top; includes copies with sticker wrapped around spine with new number					
❑ LPM-2999 [M]	Roustabout	1964	25.00	50.00	100.00
—"Mono" on label					
❑ LPM-2999 [M]	Roustabout	1965	15.00	30.00	60.00
—"Monaural" on label					
❑ LSP-2999 [S]	Roustabout	1964	150.00	300.00	600.00
—"Stereo" and silver "RCA Victor" on black label					
❑ LSP-2999 [S]	Roustabout	1964	15.00	30.00	60.00
—"Stereo" and white "RCA Victor" on black label					
❑ LSP-2999 [S]	Roustabout	1968	10.00	20.00	40.00
—Orange label, non-flexible vinyl					
❑ LSP-2999 [S]	Roustabout	1971	5.00	10.00	20.00
—Orange label, flexible vinyl					

Number	Title (A Side/B Side)	Yr	VG	VG+	NM
❑ LSP-2999 [S]	Roustabout	1975	5.00	10.00	20.00
—Tan label					
❑ LSP-2999 [S]	Roustabout	1976	3.00	6.00	12.00
—Black label, dog near top					
❑ CPL1-3078 [PD]	A Legendary Performer, Volume 3	1978	6.25	12.50	25.00
—Picture disc applied to blue vinyl LP; with booklet (deduct 40% if missing)					
❑ CPL1-3082	A Legendary Performer, Volume 3	1978	6.25	12.50	25.00
—Includes booklet (deduct 40% if missing); with die-cut hole in front cover					
❑ CPL1-3082	A Legendary Performer, Volume 3	1986	2.00	4.00	8.00
—No die-cut hole in cover and no booklet					
❑ AQL1-3279	Our Memories of Elvis	1979	5.00	10.00	20.00
❑ AFL1-3338 [S]	Girl Happy	1977	3.00	6.00	12.00
—Black label, dog near top; includes copies with sticker wrapped around spine with new number					
❑ LPM-3338 [M]	Girl Happy	1965	15.00	30.00	60.00
❑ LSP-3338 [S]	Girl Happy	1965	15.00	30.00	60.00
—"Stereo" on black label					
❑ LSP-3338 [S]	Girl Happy	1968	10.00	20.00	40.00
—Orange label, non-flexible vinyl					
❑ LSP-3338 [S]	Girl Happy	1971	5.00	10.00	20.00
—Orange label, flexible vinyl					
❑ LSP-3338 [S]	Girl Happy	1975	6.25	12.50	25.00
—Tan label					
❑ LSP-3338 [S]	Girl Happy	1976	3.00	6.00	12.00
—Black label, dog near top					
❑ AQL1-3448	Our Memories of Elvis, Volume 2	1979	5.00	10.00	20.00
❑ AFL1-3450 [P]	Elvis for Everyone	1977	3.00	6.00	12.00
—Black label, dog near top; includes copies with sticker wrapped around spine with new number					
❑ LPM-3450 [M]	Elvis for Everyone	1965	15.00	30.00	60.00
❑ LSP-3450 [P]	Elvis for Everyone	1965	15.00	30.00	60.00
—Black label, "Stereo" on label					
❑ LSP-3450 [P]	Elvis for Everyone	1968	10.00	20.00	40.00
—Orange label, non-flexible vinyl					
❑ LSP-3450 [P]	Elvis for Everyone	1971	5.00	10.00	20.00
—Orange label, flexible vinyl					
❑ LSP-3450 [P]	Elvis for Everyone	1975	5.00	10.00	20.00
—Tan label					
❑ LSP-3450 [P]	Elvis for Everyone	1976	3.00	6.00	12.00
—Black label, dog near top					
❑ DJL1-3455 [DJ]	Pure Elvis	1979	150.00	300.00	600.00
—Promo-only item for Our Memories of Elvis, Volume 2; contains original version of five songs on one side, "unsweetened" versions of same songs on the other					
❑ LPM-3468 [M]	Harum Scarum	1965	15.00	30.00	60.00
❑ LPM/LSP-3468	Harum Scarum Bonus Photo	1965	15.00	30.00	60.00
❑ LSP-3468 [S]	Harum Scarum	1965	15.00	30.00	60.00
—"Stereo" on black label					
❑ LPM-3553 [M]	Frankie and Johnny	1966	15.00	30.00	60.00
❑ LPM/LSP-3553	Frankie and Johnny Bonus Print	1966	15.00	30.00	60.00
❑ LSP-3553 [S]	Frankie and Johnny	1966	15.00	30.00	60.00
—"Stereo" on black label					
❑ AFL1-3643 [S]	Paradise, Hawaiian Style	1977	3.00	6.00	12.00
—Black label, dog near top; includes copies with sticker wrapped around spine with new number					
❑ LPM-3643 [M]	Paradise, Hawaiian Style	1966	15.00	30.00	60.00
❑ LSP-3643 [S]	Paradise, Hawaiian Style	1966	15.00	30.00	60.00
—"Stereo" on black label					
❑ LSP-3643 [S]	Paradise, Hawaiian Style	1968	10.00	20.00	40.00
—Orange label, non-flexible vinyl					
❑ LSP-3643 [S]	Paradise, Hawaiian Style	1971	5.00	10.00	20.00
—Orange label, flexible vinyl					
❑ LSP-3643 [S]	Paradise, Hawaiian Style	1975	3.75	7.50	15.00
—Tan label					
❑ LSP-3643 [S]	Paradise, Hawaiian Style	1976	3.00	6.00	12.00
—Black label, dog near top					
❑ AYL1-3683 [S]	Blue Hawaii	1980	2.50	5.00	10.00
—"Best Buy Series" reissue					
❑ AYL1-3684 [S]	Spinout	1980	2.00	4.00	8.00
—"Best Buy Series" reissue					
❑ CPL8-3699 [(8)]	Elvis Aron Presley	1980	25.00	50.00	100.00
—Box set; regular issue with booklet					
❑ CPL8-3699 [(8)]	Elvis Aron Presley	1980	62.50	125.00	250.00
—Box set; "Reviewer Series" edition (will be identified as such on the cover)					
❑ LPM-3702 [M]	Spinout	1966	15.00	30.00	60.00
❑ LPM/LSP-3702	Spinout Bonus Photo	1966	15.00	30.00	60.00
❑ LSP-3702 [S]	Spinout	1966	15.00	30.00	60.00
—"Stereo" on black label					
❑ DJL1-3729 [DJ]	Elvis Aron Presley (Excerpts)	1980	30.00	60.00	120.00
—Promo-only excerpts of songs from box set					
❑ AYL1-3732	Pure Gold	1980	2.00	4.00	8.00
—"Best Buy Series" reissue					
❑ AYL1-3733 [R]	King Creole	1980	2.00	4.00	8.00
—"Best Buy Series" reissue; includes copies with sticker wrapped around spine with new number					
❑ AYL1-3734 [S]	Harum Scarum	1980	2.00	4.00	8.00
—"Best Buy Series" reissue					
❑ AYL1-3735 [S]	G.I. Blues	1980	2.00	4.00	8.00
—"Best Buy Series" reissue					
❑ AFL1-3758 [S]	How Great Thou Art	1977	3.00	6.00	12.00
—Black label, dog near top; includes copies with sticker wrapped around spine with new number					
❑ AQL1-3758 [S]	How Great Thou Art	1979	2.50	5.00	10.00
—Reissue with new prefix					
❑ LPM-3758 [M]	How Great Thou Art	1967	15.00	30.00	60.00
—"Mono Dynagroove" on label					
❑ LSP-3758 [S]	How Great Thou Art	1967	15.00	30.00	60.00
—"Stereo Dynagroove" on black label					
❑ LSP-3758 [S]	How Great Thou Art	1968	10.00	20.00	40.00
—Orange label, non-flexible vinyl					
❑ LSP-3758 [S]	How Great Thou Art	1971	6.25	12.50	25.00
—Orange label, flexible vinyl					

Number	Title (A Side/B Side)	Yr	VG	VG+	NM
❑ LSP-3758 [S]	How Great Thou Art	1975	5.00	10.00	20.00
—Tan label					
❑ LSP-3758 [S]	How Great Thou Art	1976	3.00	6.00	12.00
—Black label, dog near top					
❑ DJL1-3781 [DJ]	Elvis Aron Presley (Selections)	1980	30.00	60.00	120.00
—Promo-only complete versions of songs from box set					
❑ LPM-3787 [M]	Double Trouble	1967	15.00	30.00	60.00
—With bonus photo announcement on cover					
❑ LPM-3787 [M]	Double Trouble	1967	20.00	40.00	80.00
—With no bonus photo announcement on cover					
❑ LPM/LSP-3787	Double Trouble Bonus Photo	1967	12.50	25.00	50.00
❑ LSP-3787 [S]	Double Trouble	1967	15.00	30.00	60.00
—With bonus photo announcement on cover					
❑ LSP-3787 [S]	Double Trouble	1967	17.50	35.00	70.00
—With no bonus photo announcement on cover; black label "Stereo"					
❑ LSP-3787 [S]	Double Trouble	1968	10.00	20.00	40.00
—Orange label, non-flexible vinyl					
❑ LSP-3787 [S]	Double Trouble	1975	5.00	10.00	20.00
—Tan label					
❑ LSP-3787 [S]	Double Trouble	1977	3.00	6.00	12.00
—Black label, dog near top					
❑ AYL1-3892	Elvis in Person at the International Hotel, Las Vegas, Nevada	1981	2.00	4.00	8.00
—"Best Buy Series" reissue					
❑ AYM1-3893	The Sun Sessions	1981	2.00	4.00	8.00
—"Best Buy Series" reissue; includes copies with sticker wrapped around spine with new number					
❑ LPM-3893 [M]	Clambake	1967	62.50	125.00	250.00
❑ LPM/LSP-3893	Clambake Bonus Photo	1967	12.50	25.00	50.00
❑ LSP-3893 [S]	Clambake	1967	15.00	30.00	60.00
❑ AYM1-3894	Elvis (NBC-TV Special)	1981	2.00	4.00	8.00
—"Best Buy Series" reissue					
❑ AAL1-3917	Guitar Man	1981	7.50	15.00	30.00
❑ AFL1-3921 [P]	Elvis' Gold Records, Volume 4	1976	3.75	7.50	15.00
—Tan label with new prefix					
❑ AFL1-3921 [P]	Elvis' Gold Records, Volume 4	1977	3.00	6.00	12.00
—Black label, dog near top; includes copies with sticker wrapped around spine with new number					
❑ LPM-3921 [M]	Elvis' Gold Records, Volume 4	1968	500.00	1000.	2000.
—"Monaural" on label					
❑ LSP-3921 [P]	Elvis' Gold Records, Volume 4	1968	12.50	25.00	50.00
—"Stereo" and white "RCA Victor" on black label					
❑ LSP-3921 [P]	Elvis' Gold Records, Volume 4	1968	10.00	20.00	40.00
—Orange label, non-flexible vinyl					
❑ LSP-3921 [P]	Elvis' Gold Records, Volume 4	1975	6.25	12.50	25.00
—Tan label					
❑ LSP-3921 [P]	Elvis' Gold Records, Volume 4	1976	3.00	6.00	12.00
—Black label, dog near top					
❑ LSP-3921 [P]	Elvis' Gold Records, Volume 4	197?	5.00	10.00	20.00
—Orange label, flexible vinyl					
❑ AYL1-3935 [S]	His Hand in Mine	1981	2.00	4.00	8.00
—"Best Buy Series" reissue; includes copies with sticker wrapped around spine with new number					
❑ AYL1-3956	Elvis Country ("I'm 10,000 Years Old")	1981	2.00	4.00	8.00
—"Best Buy Series" reissue					
❑ AFL1-3989 [S]	Speedway	1977	3.00	6.00	12.00
—Black label, dog near top; includes copies with sticker wrapped around spine with new number					
❑ LPM-3989 [M]	Speedway	1968	500.00	1000.	2000.
❑ LPM/LSP-3989	Speedway Bonus Photo	1968	12.50	25.00	50.00
❑ LSP-3989 [S]	Speedway	1968	15.00	30.00	60.00
—"Stereo" on black label					
❑ LSP-3989 [S]	Speedway	1968	10.00	20.00	40.00
—Orange label, non-flexible vinyl					
❑ LSP-3989 [S]	Speedway	1971	5.00	10.00	20.00
—Orange label, flexible vinyl					
❑ LSP-3989 [S]	Speedway	1975	5.00	10.00	20.00
—Tan label					
❑ LSP-3989 [S]	Speedway	1976	3.00	6.00	12.00
—Black label, dog near top					
❑ CPL2-4031 [(2)]	This Is Elvis	1980	3.75	7.50	15.00
❑ AFM1-4088	Elvis (NBC-TV Special)	1977	3.00	6.00	12.00
—Black label, dog near top; includes copies with sticker wrapped around spine with new number					
❑ LPM-4088	Elvis (NBC-TV Special)	1968	10.00	20.00	40.00
—Orange label, non-flexible vinyl					
❑ LPM-4088	Elvis (NBC-TV Special)	1971	7.50	15.00	30.00
—Orange label, flexible vinyl					
❑ LPM-4088	Elvis (NBC-TV Special)	1975	5.00	10.00	20.00
—Tan label					
❑ LPM-4088	Elvis (NBC-TV Special)	1976	3.75	7.50	15.00
—Black label, dog near top					
❑ AYL1-4114	That's the Way It Is	1981	2.00	4.00	8.00
—"Best Buy Series" reissue; includes copies with sticker wrapped around spine with new number					
❑ AYL1-4115 [S]	Kissin' Cousins	1981	2.00	4.00	8.00
—"Best Buy Series" reissue; includes copies with sticker wrapped around spine with new number					
❑ AYL1-4116 [S]	Something for Everybody	1981	2.00	4.00	8.00
—"Best Buy Series" reissue; includes copies with sticker wrapped around spine with new number					
❑ AFL1-4155	From Elvis in Memphis	1977	3.00	6.00	12.00
—Black label, dog near top; includes copies with sticker wrapped around spine with new number					
❑ LSP-4155	From Elvis in Memphis	1969	10.00	20.00	40.00
—Orange label, non-flexible vinyl					
❑ LSP-4155	From Elvis in Memphis Bonus Photo	1969	10.00	20.00	40.00
❑ LSP-4155	From Elvis in Memphis	1971	7.50	15.00	30.00
—Orange label, flexible vinyl					
❑ LSP-4155	From Elvis in Memphis	1975	6.25	12.50	25.00
—Tan label					
❑ LSP-4155	From Elvis in Memphis	1976	3.75	7.50	15.00
—Black label, dog near top					
❑ AYL1-4232 [P]	Elvis for Everyone	1982	2.00	4.00	8.00
—"Best Buy Series" reissue					

Number	Title (A Side/B Side)	Yr	VG	VG+	NM
❑ AFL1-4362	On Stage February, 1970	1977	3.00	6.00	12.00
—Black label, dog near top; includes copies with sticker wrapped around spine with new number					
❑ AQL1-4362	On Stage February, 1970	1983	2.00	4.00	8.00
—Reissue with some cover changes					
❑ LSP-4362	On Stage February, 1970	1970	10.00	20.00	40.00
—Orange label, non-flexible vinyl					
❑ LSP-4362	On Stage February, 1970	1971	6.25	12.50	25.00
—Orange label, flexible vinyl					
❑ LSP-4362	On Stage February, 1970	1975	6.25	12.50	25.00
—Tan label					
❑ LSP-4362	On Stage February, 1970	1976	7.50	15.00	30.00
—Black label, dog near top					
❑ CPL1-4395	Memories of Christmas	1982	3.75	7.50	15.00
—With greeting card (deduct 1/3 if missing)					
❑ AFL1-4428	Elvis in Person at the International Hotel, Las Vegas, Nevada	1977	3.00	6.00	12.00
—Black label, dog near top; includes copies with sticker wrapped around spine with new number					
❑ LSP-4428	Elvis in Person at the International Hotel, Las Vegas, Nevada	1970	12.50	25.00	50.00
—Orange label, non-flexible vinyl					
❑ LSP-4428	Elvis in Person at the International Hotel, Las Vegas, Nevada	1971	10.00	20.00	40.00
—Orange label, flexible vinyl					
❑ LSP-4428	Elvis in Person at the International Hotel, Las Vegas, Nevada	1975	6.25	12.50	25.00
—Tan label					
❑ LSP-4428	Elvis in Person at the International Hotel, Las Vegas, Nevada	1976	3.75	7.50	15.00
—Black label, dog near top					
❑ AFL1-4429	Back in Memphis	1977	3.00	6.00	12.00
—Black label, dog near top; with sticker wrapped around spine with new number					
❑ LSP-4429	Back in Memphis	1970	10.00	20.00	40.00
—Orange label, non-flexible vinyl					
❑ LSP-4429	Back in Memphis	1971	7.50	15.00	30.00
—Orange label, flexible vinyl					
❑ LSP-4429	Back in Memphis	1975	6.25	12.50	25.00
—Tan label					
❑ LSP-4429	Back in Memphis	1977	3.75	7.50	15.00
—Black label, dog near top					
❑ AFL1-4445	That's the Way It Is	1977	3.00	6.00	12.00
—Black label, dog near top; includes copies with sticker wrapped around spine with new number					
❑ LSP-4445	That's the Way It Is	1970	20.00	40.00	80.00
—Orange label, non-flexible vinyl					
❑ LSP-4445	That's the Way It Is	1971	6.25	12.50	25.00
—Orange label, flexible vinyl					
❑ LSP-4445	That's the Way It Is	1975	5.00	10.00	20.00
—Tan label					
❑ LSP-4445	That's the Way It Is	1976	3.75	7.50	15.00
—Black label, dog near top					
❑ AFL1-4460	Elvis Country ("I'm 10,000 Years Old")	1977	3.00	6.00	12.00
—Black label, dog near top; includes copies with sticker wrapped around spine with new number					
❑ LSP-4460	Elvis Country ("I'm 10,000 Years Old")	1971	10.00	20.00	40.00
—Orange label, non-flexible vinyl					
❑ LSP-4460	Elvis Country ("I'm 10,000 Years Old")	1971	6.25	12.50	25.00
—Orange label, flexible vinyl					
❑ LSP-4460	Elvis Country ("I'm 10,000 Years Old") Bonus Photo	1971	3.75	7.50	15.00
—Available in either orange-label pressing					
❑ LSP-4460	Elvis Country ("I'm 10,000 Years Old")	1975	6.25	12.50	25.00
—Tan label					
❑ LSP-4460	Elvis Country ("I'm 10,000 Years Old")	1976	3.75	7.50	15.00
—Black label, dog near top					
❑ LSP-4460	Elvis Country ("I'm 10,000 Years Old")	197?	500.00	1000.	2000.
—Green vinyl; black label, dog near top					
❑ AFL1-4530	Love Letters from Elvis	1977	3.00	6.00	12.00
—Black label, dog near top; includes copies with sticker wrapped around spine with new number					
❑ AHL1-4530	The Elvis Medley	1982	3.00	6.00	12.00
❑ LSP-4530	Love Letters from Elvis	1971	10.00	20.00	40.00
—Orange label; "Love Letters from" on one line of cover, "Elvis" on a second line					
❑ LSP-4530	Love Letters from Elvis	1971	7.50	15.00	30.00
—Orange label; "Love Letters" on one line of cover; "from" on a second line, "Elvis" on a third line					
❑ LSP-4530	Love Letters from Elvis	1975	7.50	15.00	30.00
—Tan label; "Love Letters from" on one line of cover, "Elvis" on a second line					
❑ LSP-4530	Love Letters from Elvis	1975	6.25	12.50	25.00
—Tan label; "Love Letters" on one line of cover; "from" on a second line, "Elvis" on a third line					
❑ LSP-4530	Love Letters from Elvis	1976	5.00	10.00	20.00
—Black label, dog near top					
❑ LSP-4579	Elvis Sings the Wonderful World of Christmas	1971	7.50	15.00	30.00
—Orange label. Bonus postcard is priced separately					
❑ LSP-4579	Elvis Sings the Wonderful World of Christmas Postcard	1971	5.00	10.00	20.00
❑ AFL1-4671	Elvis Now	1977	3.00	6.00	12.00
—Black label, dog near top; includes copies with sticker wrapped around spine with new number					
❑ LSP-4671	Elvis Now	1972	7.50	15.00	30.00
—Orange label					
❑ LSP-4671	Elvis Now	1975	6.25	12.50	25.00
—Tan label					
❑ LSP-4671	Elvis Now	1976	3.75	7.50	15.00
—Black label, dog near top					
❑ LSP-4671 [DJ]	Elvis Now	1972	25.00	50.00	100.00
—Orange label; with white timing sticker on front cover					
❑ AHL1-4678	I Was the One	1983	2.50	5.00	10.00
❑ AFL1-4690	He Touched Me	1977	3.00	6.00	12.00
—Black label, dog near top; includes copies with sticker wrapped around spine with new number					
❑ LSP-4690	He Touched Me	1972	10.00	20.00	40.00
—Orange label					
❑ LSP-4690	He Touched Me	1975	5.00	10.00	20.00
—Tan label					
❑ LSP-4690	He Touched Me	1976	3.75	7.50	15.00
—Black label, dog near top					
❑ LSP-4690 [DJ]	He Touched Me	1972	25.00	50.00	100.00
—Orange label; with white timing sticker on front cover					
❑ AFL1-4776	Elvis As Recorded at Madison Square Garden	1977	3.00	6.00	12.00
—Black label, dog near top; includes copies with sticker wrapped around spine with new number					
❑ AQL1-4776	Elvis As Recorded at Madison Square Garden	1980	2.00	4.00	8.00
—Another reissue with new prefix					
❑ LSP-4776	Elvis As Recorded at Madison Square Garden	1972	7.50	15.00	30.00
—Orange label					
❑ LSP-4776	Elvis As Recorded at Madison Square Garden	1975	5.00	10.00	20.00
—Tan label					
❑ LSP-4776	Elvis As Recorded at Madison Square Garden	1976	3.75	7.50	15.00
—Black label, dog near top					
❑ LSP-4776 [DJ]	Elvis As Recorded at Madison Square Garden	1972	25.00	50.00	100.00
—Orange label; with white timing sticker on front cover					
❑ CPL1-4848	A Legendary Performer, Volume 4	1983	7.50	15.00	30.00
—Includes booklet (deduct 40% if missing); with die-cut hole in front cover					
❑ CPL1-4848	A Legendary Performer, Volume 4	1986	5.00	10.00	20.00
—No die-cut hole in cover					
❑ AFL1-4941	Elvis' Gold Records, Volume 5	1984	2.50	5.00	10.00
❑ CPM6-5172 [(6)]	A Golden Celebration	1984	25.00	50.00	100.00
❑ AFM1-5182	Rocker	1984	5.00	10.00	20.00
❑ AFM1-5196 [M]	Elvis' Golden Records	1984	5.00	10.00	20.00
—50th Anniversary reissue in mono with banner					
❑ AFM1-5197 [M]	Elvis' Gold Records Volume 2 — 50,000,000 Elvis Fans Can't Be Wrong	1984	5.00	10.00	20.00
—50th Anniversary reissue in mono with banner					
❑ AFM1-5198 [M]	Elvis Presley	1984	5.00	10.00	20.00
—50th Anniversary reissue in mono with banner					
❑ AFM1-5199 [M]	Elvis	1984	5.00	10.00	20.00
—50th Anniversary reissue in mono with banner					
❑ AFL1-5353	A Valentine Gift for You	1985	5.00	10.00	20.00
—Red vinyl					
❑ AFL1-5353	A Valentine Gift for You	1985	2.50	5.00	10.00
—Black vinyl					
❑ AFL1-5418	Reconsider Baby	1985	5.00	10.00	20.00
—All copies on blue vinyl					
❑ AFL1-5430	Always on My Mind	1985	5.00	10.00	20.00
—All copies on purple vinyl					
❑ AFM1-5486 [M]	Elvis' Christmas Album	1985	5.00	10.00	20.00
—Same as LOC-1035; green vinyl with booklet					
❑ AFM1-5486 [M]	Elvis' Christmas Album	1985	3.75	7.50	15.00
—Same as LOC-1035; black vinyl with booklet					
❑ UNRM-5697/8 [DJ]	Special Christmas Programming	1967	300.00	600.00	1200.
—White label promo. Add 25% for script.					
❑ LSP-6020	From Memphis to Vegas/From Vegas to Memphis Bonus Photos	1969	12.50	25.00	50.00
—Four different photos came with LP, but no more than two per set. Value is for any two different of the four photos.					
❑ LSP-6020 [(2)]	From Memphis to Vegas/From Vegas to Memphis	1969	25.00	50.00	100.00
—Orange labels, non-flexible vinyl; with composers of "Words" correctly listed as Barry, Robin and Maurice Gibb					
❑ LSP-6020 [(2)]	From Memphis to Vegas/From Vegas to Memphis	1969	37.50	75.00	150.00
—Orange labels, non-flexible vinyl; with composers of "Words" incorrectly listed as Tommy Boyce and Bobby Hart					
❑ LSP-6020 [(2)]	From Memphis to Vegas/From Vegas to Memphis	1971	10.00	20.00	40.00
—Orange labels, flexible vinyl					
❑ LSP-6020 [(2)]	From Memphis to Vegas/From Vegas to Memphis Bonus Photos	1975	7.50	15.00	30.00
—Tan labels					
❑ LSP-6020 [(2)]	From Memphis to Vegas/From Vegas to Memphis Bonus Photos	1976	5.00	10.00	20.00
—Black label, dog near top					
❑ VPSX-6089 [(2) DJ]	Aloha from Hawaii Via Satellite	1973	500.00	1000.	2000.
—Orange or dark orange label; with white timing sticker on front cover					
❑ VPSX-6089 [(2) Q]	Aloha from Hawaii Via Satellite	1973	25.00	50.00	100.00
—Dark orange labels, "QuadraDisc" on top, "RCA" on bottom					
❑ VPSX-6089 [(2) Q]	Aloha from Hawaii Via Satellite	1973	2500.	3750.	5000.
—Stokely-Van Camp employee version with Saturn-shaped sticker on front cover with "Chicken of the Sea" and mermaid					
❑ VPSX-6089 [(2) Q]	Aloha from Hawaii Via Satellite	1973	10.00	20.00	40.00
—Lighter orange labels, "RCA" on side					
❑ LPM-6401	Worldwide 50 Gold Award Hits, Vol. 1 Photo Book	1970	10.00	20.00	40.00
—Two different books have been found in this LP box; price is for either					
❑ LPM-6401 [(4)]	Worldwide 50 Gold Award Hits, Vol. 1	1970	20.00	40.00	80.00
—Orange labels, non-flexible vinyl; with blurb for photo book on cover					
❑ LPM-6401 [(4)]	Worldwide 50 Gold Award Hits, Vol. 1	1970	20.00	40.00	80.00
—Orange labels, flexible vinyl; with blurb for photo book on cover					
❑ LPM-6401 [(4)]	Worldwide 50 Gold Award Hits, Vol. 1	1975	10.00	20.00	40.00
—Tan labels					
❑ LPM-6401 [(4)]	Worldwide 50 Gold Award Hits, Vol. 1	1977	7.50	15.00	30.00
—Black labels, dog near top					
❑ LPM-6402	The Other Sides: Worldwide 50 Gold Award Hits, Vol. 2 Poster	1971	6.25	12.50	25.00
❑ LPM-6402	The Other Sides: Worldwide 50 Gold Award Hits, Vol. 2 Swatch and Envelope	1971	6.25	12.50	25.00
❑ LPM-6402 [(4)]	The Other Sides: Worldwide 50 Gold Award Hits, Vol. 2	1971	17.50	35.00	70.00
—Orange labels, flexible vinyl; with blurb for inserts on cover					

Number	Title (A Side/B Side)	Yr	VG	VG+	NM
❑ LPM-6402 [(4)]	The Other Sides: Worldwide 50 Gold Award Hits, Vol. 2	1975	7.50	15.00	30.00
—Tan labels					
❑ LPM-6402 [(4)]	The Other Sides: Worldwide 50 Gold Award Hits, Vol. 2	1977	5.00	10.00	20.00
—Black labels, dog near top					
❑ KKL1-7065	A Canadian Tribute	1978	5.00	10.00	20.00
—Gold vinyl, embossed cover					
❑ R 213690 [(2)]	Worldwide Gold Award Hits, Parts 1 & 2	1974	30.00	60.00	120.00
—RCA Record Club version; one label is orange, the other is tan (orange label on both records is unknown)					
❑ R 213690 [(2)]	Worldwide Gold Award Hits, Parts 1 & 2	1974	10.00	20.00	40.00
—RCA Record Club version; tan labels					
❑ R 213690 [(2)]	Worldwide Gold Award Hits, Parts 1 & 2	1977	6.25	12.50	25.00
—RCA Record Club version; black labels, dog near top					
❑ R 213736 [(2) S]	Aloha from Hawaii Via Satellite	1973	17.50	35.00	70.00
—RCA Record Club edition in stereo instead of quadraphonic; orange labels					
❑ R 213736 [(2) S]	Aloha from Hawaii Via Satellite	1975	15.00	30.00	60.00
—RCA Record Club edition in stereo instead of quadraphonic; tan labels					
❑ R 213736 [(2) S]	Aloha from Hawaii Via Satellite	1977	7.50	5.00	30.00
—RCA Record Club edition in stereo instead of quadraphonic; black labels, dog near top					
❑ R 214657 [(2)]	Worldwide Gold Award Hits, Parts 3 & 4	1978	5.00	10.00	20.00
—RCA Record Club version; black labels, dog near top					
❑ R 233299(e) [(2)]	Country Classics	1980	10.00	20.00	40.00
—RCA Music Service exclusive					
❑ R 234340 [(2)]	From Elvis with Love	1978	10.00	20.00	40.00
—RCA Music Service exclusive					
❑ R 244047 [(2)]	The Legendary Concert Performances	1978	10.00	20.00	40.00
—RCA Music Service exclusive					
❑ R 244069 [(2)]	Country Memories	1978	10.00	20.00	40.00
—RCA Music Service exclusive					
READER'S DIGEST					
❑ 010/A [(7)]	His Greatest Hits	1983	15.00	30.00	60.00
—Yellow box					
❑ 010/A [(7)]	His Greatest Hits	1990	10.00	20.00	40.00
—White box					
❑ RD-10/A [(8)]	His Greatest Hits	1979	100.00	200.00	400.00
—White box					
❑ RBA-072/D	Great Hits of 1956-57	1987	5.00	10.00	20.00
❑ RD4A-181/D	Elvis Sings Inspirational Favorites	1983	5.00	10.00	20.00
❑ RB4-191/A [(7)]	The Legend Lives On	1986	15.00	30.00	60.00
❑ RDA-242/D	Elvis Sings Country Favorites	1984	15.00	30.00	60.00
SHOW-LAND					
❑ LP-2001	The First of Elvis	1979	25.00	50.00	100.00
SILHOUETTE					
❑ 10001/2 [(2)]	Personally Elvis	1979	7.50	15.00	30.00
—Interview records; no music					
SUN					
❑ 1001	The Sun Years — Interviews and Memories	1977	6.25	12.50	25.00
—With "Memphis, Tennessee" on label					
❑ 1001	The Sun Years — Interviews and Memories	1977	2.00	4.00	8.00
—With "Nashville, U.S.A." on label; white cover with brown print					
❑ 1001	The Sun Years — Interviews and Memories	1977	3.75	7.50	15.00
—With "Nashville, U.S.A." on label; dark yellow cover with brown print					
TIME-LIFE					
❑ STL-106 [(2)]	Elvis Presley: 1954-1961	1986	7.50	15.00	30.00
❑ STW-106	Country Music	1981	5.00	10.00	20.00
❑ STL-126 [(2)]	Elvis the King: 1954-1965	1989	20.00	40.00	80.00

PRESLEY, ELVIS (2)

45s

Number	Title (A Side/B Side)	Yr	VG	VG+	NM
CIN KAY					
❑ 064	Tell Me Pretty Baby (same on both sides)	1978	—	—	2.50
❑ 064 [PS]	Tell Me Pretty Baby (same on both sides)	1978	—	—	2.50
ELVIS CLASSIC					
❑ EC-5478	Tell Me Pretty Baby (same on both sides)	1978	—	—	2.50
❑ EC-5478 [PS]	Tell Me Pretty Baby (same on both sides)	1978	—	—	2.50
—The above are two different issues of a record that purported to be the "real" Elvis' first studio recording, but turned out to be an utter fake					

PRESTON, BILLY

12-Inch Singles

Number	Title (A Side/B Side)	Yr	VG	VG+	NM
MEGATONE					
❑ 124	And Dance (5:41)/Kick It (5:46)	1984	—	3.00	6.00
MOTOWN					
❑ PR-64 [DJ]	Give It Up Hot/Sock-It, Rocket	1979	3.00	6.00	12.00
❑ 4570	Since I Held You Close (3 versions)/It Don't Get Better Than This	1986	—	3.00	6.00

45s

Number	Title (A Side/B Side)	Yr	VG	VG+	NM
APPLE					
❑ 1808	That's the Way God Planned It/What About You	1969	2.00	4.00	8.00
❑ 1808	That's the Way God Planned It/What About You	1972	2.00	4.00	8.00
—With "Mono" on both sides of record and reference to LP					
❑ 1808 [PS]	That's the Way God Planned It/What About You	1969	2.50	5.00	10.00
❑ P-1808/PRO 6555 [DJ]	That's the Way God Planned It (Parts 1 & 2) (mono/stereo)	1969	15.00	30.00	60.00
❑ 1814	Everything's All Right/I Want to Thank You	1969	2.00	4.00	8.00
❑ 1817	All That I've Got (I'm Gonna Give It to You)/As I Get Older	1970	2.00	4.00	8.00
❑ 1817 [PS]	All That I've Got (I'm Gonna Give It to You)/As I Get Older	1970	3.75	7.50	15.00
❑ 1826	My Sweet Lord/Little Girl	1970	2.00	4.00	8.00
❑ 1826	My Sweet Lord/Little Girl	1970	3.00	6.00	12.00
—With star on A-side label					

Number	Title (A Side/B Side)	Yr	VG	VG+	NM
APPLE/AMERICOM					
❑ 1808P/M-433	That's the Way God Planned It (Edit)/What About You	1969	100.00	200.00	400.00
—Four-inch flexi-disc sold from vending machines					
A&M					
❑ 1320	Outa-Space/I Wrote a Simple Song	1972	—	2.50	5.00
❑ 1340	Should Have Known Better/The Bus	1972	—	2.50	5.00
❑ 1380	Slaughter/God Loves You	1972	—	2.50	5.00
❑ 1380 [PS]	Slaughter/God Loves You	1972	—	3.00	6.00
❑ 1411	Will It Go Round in Circles/Blackbird	1973	—	2.00	4.00
❑ 1463	Space Race/We're Gonna Make It	1973	—	2.00	4.00
❑ 1463 [PS]	Space Race/We're Gonna Make It	1973	—	3.00	6.00
❑ 1492	You're So Unique/How Long Has the Train Been Gone	1973	—	2.00	4.00
❑ 1536	Creature Feature/My Soul Is a Witness	1974	—	2.00	4.00
❑ 1544	Nothing from Nothing/My Soul Is a Witness	1974	—	2.00	4.00
❑ 1544 [PS]	Nothing from Nothing/My Soul Is a Witness	1974	—	3.00	6.00
❑ 1644	Struttin'/You Are So Beautiful	1974	—	2.00	4.00
❑ 1735	Fancy Lady/Song of Joy	1975	—	2.00	4.00
❑ 1735 [PS]	Fancy Lady/Song of Joy	1975	—	3.00	6.00
❑ 1768	Do It While You Can/Song of Joy	1975	—	2.00	4.00
❑ 1892	Do What You Want/I've Got the Spirit	1976	—	2.00	4.00
❑ 1925	Girl/Ecstasy	1977	—	2.00	4.00
❑ 1954	Wide Stride/When You Are Mine	1977	—	2.00	4.00
❑ 1980	A Whole New Thing/Wide Stride	1977	—	2.00	4.00
❑ 2012	I Really Miss You/Attitudes	1978	—	2.00	4.00
❑ 2071	Get Back/Space Race	1978	—	2.00	4.00
CAPITOL					
❑ 2309	Hey Brother (Part 1)/Hey Brother (Part 2)	1968	2.00	4.00	8.00
❑ 5611	The Girl's Got "It"/The Night	1966	2.00	4.00	8.00
❑ 5660	In the Midnight Hour/Advice	1966	2.00	4.00	8.00
❑ 5730	Sunny/Let the Music Play	1966	2.00	4.00	8.00
❑ 5797	Phony Friends/Can't She Tell	1966	2.00	4.00	8.00
MGM					
❑ 14001	The Split/It's Just a Love Game	1968	2.00	4.00	8.00
MOTOWN					
❑ 1470	It Will Come In Time/All I Wanted Was You	1979	—	2.00	4.00
❑ 1505	Sock-It Rocket/Hope	1981	—	2.00	4.00
❑ 1511	A Change Is Gonna Come/You	1981	—	2.00	4.00
❑ 1625	I'm Never Gonna Say Goodbye/Love You So	1982	—	2.00	4.00
VEE JAY					
❑ 646	Don't Let the Sun Catch You Cryin'/(B-side unknown)	1965	—	—	—
—Canceled?					
❑ 653	Don't Let the Sun Catch You Cryin'/Billy's Bag	1965	2.50	5.00	10.00
❑ 692	Log Cabin/Drown in My Own Tears	1965	2.50	5.00	10.00

Albums

Number	Title (A Side/B Side)	Yr	VG	VG+	NM
APPLE					
❑ ST-3359	That's the Way God Planned It	1969	12.50	25.00	50.00
—Cover has close-up of Billy Preston					
❑ ST-3359	That's the Way God Planned It	1972	5.00	10.00	20.00
—Cover has multiple images of Billy Preston					
❑ ST-3370	Encouraging Words	1970	5.00	10.00	20.00
A&M					
❑ SP-3205	The Best of Billy Preston	1982	2.50	5.00	10.00
❑ SP-3507	I Wrote a Simple Song	1971	3.00	6.00	12.00
❑ SP-3516	Music Is My Life	1972	3.00	6.00	12.00
❑ SP-3526	Everybody Likes Some Kind of Music	1973	3.00	6.00	12.00
❑ SP-3637	Live European Tour	1974	3.00	6.00	12.00
❑ SP-3645	The Kids & Me	1974	3.00	6.00	12.00
❑ SP-4532	It's My Pleasure	1975	3.00	6.00	12.00
❑ SP-4587	Billy Preston	1976	3.00	6.00	12.00
❑ SP-4657	It's a Whole New Thing	1977	3.00	6.00	12.00
BUDDAH					
❑ BDS-7502	Billy Preston	1969	3.75	7.50	15.00
CAPITOL					
❑ ST 2532 [S]	Wildest Organ in Town!	1966	10.00	20.00	40.00
❑ T 2532 [M]	Wildest Organ in Town!	1966	7.50	15.00	30.00
❑ DT 2607 [R]	Club Meetin'	1967	—	—	—
❑ T 2607 [M]	Club Meetin'	1967	—	—	—
—The above versions of Club Meetin' may not exist					
DERBY					
❑ LPM-701 [M]	16 Year Old Soul	1963	62.50	125.00	250.00
EXODUS					
❑ 304 [M]	Early Hits of 1965	1965	6.25	12.50	25.00
GNP CRESCENDO					
❑ GNPS-2071 [(2)]	Soul'd Out	1973	3.75	7.50	15.00
MCA					
❑ 28037	Gospel Soul	198?	2.00	4.00	8.00
—Reissue of Peacock LP					
MOTOWN					
❑ M7-925	Late at Night	1980	2.50	5.00	10.00
❑ M8-941	The Way I Am	1981	2.50	5.00	10.00
❑ M7-958	Billy Preston & Syreeta	1981	2.50	5.00	10.00
❑ 6020 ML	Pressin' On	1982	2.50	5.00	10.00
MYRRH					
❑ 6605	Behold	1978	2.50	5.00	10.00
❑ 6607	Universal Love	1979	2.50	5.00	10.00
PEACOCK					
❑ 179	Gospel Soul	197?	3.00	6.00	12.00
PICKWICK					
❑ SPC-3315	Organ Transplant	197?	2.50	5.00	10.00

Number	Title (A Side/B Side)	Yr	VG	VG+	NM
VEE JAY					
❑ LP-1123 [M]	The Most Exciting Organ Ever	1965	7.50	15.00	30.00
❑ LPS-1123 [S]	The Most Exciting Organ Ever	1965	12.50	25.00	50.00
❑ LP-1142 [M]	Greatest Hits	1966	7.50	15.00	30.00
❑ LPS-1142 [S]	Greatest Hits	1966	12.50	25.00	50.00

PRESTON, BILLY, AND SYREETA

Also see each artist's individual listings.

45s

Number	Title (A Side/B Side)	Yr	VG	VG+	NM
MOTOWN					
❑ 1460	With You I'm Born Again/Go For It	1979	—	2.50	5.00
❑ 1477	With You I'm Born Again/All I Wanted Was You	1979	—	2.00	4.00
❑ 1520	Searchin'/Hey You	1981	—	2.00	4.00
❑ 1522	Just for You (Put the Boogie in Your Body)/Hey You	1981	—	2.00	4.00
TAMLA					
❑ 54312	Dance For Me Children/One More Time for Love	1980	—	2.00	4.00
❑ 54319	Please Stay/Signed, Sealed, Delivered (I'm Yours)	1980	—	2.00	4.00

PRESTON, JOHNNY

45s

Number	Title (A Side/B Side)	Yr	VG	VG+	NM
ABC					
❑ 11085	I'm Only Human/There's No One Like You	1968	2.50	5.00	10.00
❑ 11187	Kick the Can/I've Just Been Wasting My Time	1969	2.50	5.00	10.00
HALLWAY					
❑ 1201	All Around the World/Just Plain Hurt	1964	3.75	7.50	15.00
❑ 1204	Willie and the Hand Jive/I've Got My Eyes on You	1964	3.75	7.50	15.00
❑ 1927	Running Bear '65/Dedicated to the One I Love	1965	3.75	7.50	15.00
IMPERIAL					
❑ 5924	This Little Bitty Tear/The Day the World Stood Still	1963	2.50	5.00	10.00
❑ 5947	I've Got My Eyes on You/I Couldn't Take It Again	1963	2.50	5.00	10.00
MERCURY					
❑ 10027 [S]	Cradle of Love/City of Tears	1960	12.50	25.00	50.00
❑ 10036 [S]	Feel So Fine/I'm Starting to Go Steady	1960	15.00	30.00	60.00
❑ 71474	Running Bear/My Heart Knows	1959	6.25	12.50	25.00
❑ 71598 [M]	Cradle of Love/City of Tears	1960	5.00	10.00	20.00
❑ 71598 [PS]	Cradle of Love/City of Tears	1960	7.50	15.00	30.00
❑ 71651 [M]	Feel So Fine/I'm Starting to Go Steady	1960	5.00	10.00	20.00
❑ 71651 [PS]	Feel So Fine/I'm Starting to Go Steady	1960	7.50	15.00	30.00
❑ 71691	Charming Billy/Up in the Air	1960	5.00	10.00	20.00
❑ 71728	New Baby for Christmas/(I Want a) Rock and Roll Guitar	1960	5.00	10.00	20.00
❑ 71761	Leave My Kitten Alone/Token of Love	1961	5.00	10.00	20.00
❑ 71761 [PS]	Leave My Kitten Alone/Token of Love	1961	7.50	15.00	30.00
❑ 71803	I Feel Good/Willy Walk	1961	5.00	10.00	20.00
❑ 71803 [PS]	I Feel Good/Willy Walk	1961	10.00	20.00	40.00
❑ 71865	Let Them Talk/She Once Belonged to Me	1961	5.00	10.00	20.00
❑ 71908	Free Me/Kissin' Tree	1961	5.00	10.00	20.00
❑ 71908 [PS]	Free Me/Kissin' Tree	1961	7.50	15.00	30.00
❑ 71951	Let's Leave It That Way/Broken Hearts Anonymous	1962	3.75	7.50	15.00
❑ 72049	Let the Big Boss Man (Pull You Through)/The Day After Forever	1962	3.75	7.50	15.00
TCF HALL					
❑ 101	Running Bear '65/Dedicated to the One I Love	1965	2.50	5.00	10.00
❑ 110	Sounds Like Trouble/You Can Make It If You Try	1965	3.75	7.50	15.00
❑ 120	I'm Askin' Forgiveness/Good Good Lovin'	1965	2.50	5.00	10.00

Albums

Number	Title (A Side/B Side)	Yr	VG	VG+	NM
MERCURY					
❑ MG-20592 [M]	Running Bear	1960	25.00	50.00	100.00
❑ MG-20609 [M]	Come Rock with Me	1960	25.00	50.00	100.00
❑ SR-60250 [S]	Running Bear	1960	37.50	75.00	150.00
—Black label					
❑ SR-60250 [S]	Running Bear	1981	3.00	6.00	12.00
—Reissue on Chicago skyline label					
❑ SR-60609 [S]	Come Rock with Me	1960	37.50	75.00	150.00
WING					
❑ MGW-12246 [M]	Running Bear	1963	5.00	10.00	20.00
❑ SRW-16246 [S]	Running Bear	1963	6.25	12.50	25.00

PRETENDERS, THE (2)

Also see JIMMY JONES.

45s

Number	Title (A Side/B Side)	Yr	VG	VG+	NM
APT					
❑ 25026	Blue and Lonely/Daddy Needs Baby	1959	125.00	250.00	500.00
CENTRAL					
❑ 2605	Blue and Lonely/Daddy Needs Baby	1958	375.00	750.00	1500.

PRETENDERS, THE (3)

45s

Number	Title (A Side/B Side)	Yr	VG	VG+	NM
BETHLEHEM					
❑ 3050	The Day You Are Mine/Ding Dong Bells	1962	50.00	100.00	200.00

PRETENDERS, THE (4)

45s

Number	Title (A Side/B Side)	Yr	VG	VG+	NM
CHATTAHOOCHIE					
❑ 685	Pepita's Theme/Tijuana Taxi	1965	5.00	10.00	20.00

PRETENDERS, THE (U)

The Rama and Whirlin' Disc records could be by group (2). None of these, or any of the above, are by the group fronted by Chrissie Hynde; they are outside the scope of this book.

45s

Number	Title (A Side/B Side)	Yr	VG	VG+	NM
POWER-MARTIN					
❑ 1001	Smile/I'm So Happy	1961	25.00	50.00	100.00
RAMA					
❑ 198	Possessive Love/I've Got to Have You Baby	1956	30.00	60.00	120.00
WHIRLIN' DISC					
❑ 106	Close Your Eyes/Part-Time Sweetheart	1957	62.50	125.00	250.00

PRETTY POISON

12-Inch Singles

Number	Title (A Side/B Side)	Yr	VG	VG+	NM
SVENGALI					
❑ SR 8403	Nightime (Dance Mix) (Dub Mix)/In the Heat of the Night	1984	2.50	5.00	10.00
❑ SR 8704	Catch Me (I'm Falling) (Dance Mix 5:31) (Instrumental 5:10) (Bonus House Beats 2:05)/ (Radio Mix 3:54) (Still Falling 7:32) (Extra Bonus Beats 2:28) (Original Mix 3:54)	1987	3.00	6.00	12.00
❑ SR 9204	Better Better Be Good to Me (6 versions)	1992	—	3.50	7.00
❑ SR 9609	Let Freedom Ring (unknown versions)	1996	—	3.50	7.00
❑ SR 9611 [(2)]	Catch Me (I'm Falling) '98 (unknown versions)	1996	3.75	7.50	15.00
TRACER					
❑ TRA 400	Better Better Be Good to Me (Extended Violet Mix) (Urban Monster Mix) (Hard Core Poison) (Fonky R&B Club Mix) (Top Hop E Rop A Pop Mix) (Winkings Techno XtaC)	1992	2.00	4.00	8.00
VIRGIN					
❑ DMD 1080 [DJ]	Catch Me (I'm Falling) (4 versions)	1987	2.00	4.00	8.00
❑ DMD 1100 [DJ]	Catch Me (I'm Falling) (Spanish Ultimix) (same on both sides)	1987	—	3.50	7.00
❑ DMD 1143 [DJ]	Nightime (Shep Pettibone Mix) (Poisonous Mix) (Dub) (Cold House Mix)	1988	2.00	4.00	8.00
❑ DMD 1190 [DJ]	Nightime (4 versions)	1988	—	3.50	7.00
❑ DMD 1204 [DJ]	When I Look Into Your Eyes (3 versions)/ Nightime (Welcome to Our House Mix)	1988	2.00	4.00	8.00
❑ 96642	When I Look Into Your Eyes (Dance Mix) (Hip Hop Mix)/Nightime (Welcome to Our House Mix)	1988	—	3.50	7.00
❑ 96710	Nightime (Shep Pettibone Mix) (Poisonous Mix) (Dub) (Cold House Mix)	1988	—	3.50	7.00
❑ 96735	Catch Me (I'm Falling) (Spanish Ultimix) (Dub Mix)	1987	2.50	5.00	10.00
❑ 96752	Catch Me (I'm Falling) (4 versions)	1987	—	3.00	6.00

45s

Number	Title (A Side/B Side)	Yr	VG	VG+	NM
POISON POPS					
❑ (no #)	Gimme Gimme (Your Autograph)/Kill You	1981	5.00	10.00	20.00
—Small center hole; original paper sleeve has handwritten phone number					
❑ (no #) [PS]	Gimme Gimme (Your Autograph)/Kill You	1981	5.00	10.00	20.00
SVENGALI					
❑ 2913	Expiration/The Realm of Existence	1981	3.75	7.50	15.00
—Plays at 33 1/3 rpm					
❑ 2913 [PS]	Expiration/The Realm of Existence	1981	3.75	7.50	15.00
—Fold-over sleeve					
VIRGIN					
❑ 99310	When I Look Into Your Eyes/(Hip Hop Mix)	1988	—	—	3.00
❑ 99350	Nightime/(Spanish Mix)	1988	—	—	3.00
❑ 99350 [PS]	Nightime/(Spanish Mix)	1988	2.50	5.00	10.00
❑ 99416	Catch Me (I'm Falling)/(Spanish Mix)	1987	—	—	3.00
❑ 99416 [PS]	Catch Me (I'm Falling)/(Spanish Mix)	1987	—	3.50	7.00
—Lips sleeve					
❑ 99416 [PS]	Catch Me (I'm Falling)/(Spanish Mix)	1987	—	2.50	5.00
—"Hiding Out" sleeve					

Albums

Number	Title (A Side/B Side)	Yr	VG	VG+	NM
SVENGALI					
❑ SRPP-1 [EP]	Laced	1984	5.00	10.00	20.00
VIRGIN					
❑ 90885	Catch Me I'm Falling	1987	2.50	5.00	10.00
❑ R 144099	Catch Me I'm Falling	1988	3.00	6.00	12.00
—BMG Direct Marketing edition					

PRICE, LLOYD

45s

Number	Title (A Side/B Side)	Yr	VG	VG+	NM
ABC					
❑ 1237	Stagger Lee/Personality	1969	—	3.00	6.00
—"Golden Treasure Chest" reissue; contains the "samitized" version of "Stagger Lee" with Mr. Lee and Billy arguing over a woman					
❑ 11016	Personality/Just Because	1967	2.00	4.00	8.00
ABC-PARAMOUNT					
❑ 9792	Just Because/Why	1957	5.00	10.00	20.00
❑ 9972 [M]	Stagger Lee/You Need Love	1958	5.00	10.00	20.00
—Most, if not all, copies contain the "raunchy" version of "Stagger Lee" with Mr. Lee and Billy playing cards					
❑ S-9972 [S]	Stagger Lee/You Need Love	1958	10.00	20.00	40.00
❑ 9997 [M]	Where Were You (On Our Wedding Day)?/Is It Really Love	1959	5.00	10.00	20.00
❑ S-9997 [S]	Where Were You (On Our Wedding Day)?/Is It Really Love	1959	10.00	20.00	40.00
❑ 10018 [M]	Personality/Have You Ever Had the Blues	1959	5.00	10.00	20.00
❑ 10018 [M]	(You've Got) Personality/Have You Ever Had the Blues	1959	5.00	10.00	20.00
—Note longer title					
❑ S-10018 [S]	Personality/Have You Ever Had the Blues	1959	12.50	25.00	50.00
❑ 10032 [M]	I'm Gonna Get Married/Three Little Pigs	1959	5.00	10.00	20.00

P

Number	Title (A Side/B Side)	Yr	VG	VG+	NM
❏ S-10032 [S]	I'm Gonna Get Married/Three Little Pigs	1959	12.50	25.00	50.00
❏ 10062	Come Into My Heart/Won't Cha Come Home	1959	3.75	7.50	15.00
❏ S-10062 [S]	Come Into My Heart/Won't Cha Come Home	1959	12.50	25.00	50.00
❏ 10075	Lady Luck/Never Let Me Go	1960	3.75	7.50	15.00
❏ 10102	No If's — No And's/For Love	1960	3.75	7.50	15.00
❏ 10123	Question/If I Look a Little Blue	1960	3.75	7.50	15.00
❏ 10139	Just Call Me (And I'll Understand)/Who Could've Told You	1960	3.75	7.50	15.00
❏ 10162	(You Better) Know What You're Doin'/That's Why Tears Come and Go	1960	3.75	7.50	15.00
❏ 10177	Boo Hoo/I Made You Cry	1961	3.75	7.50	15.00
❏ 10197	One Hundred Percent/Say I'm the One	1961	3.75	7.50	15.00
❏ 10206	String of Pearls/Chantilly Lace	1961	3.75	7.50	15.00
❏ 10221	Mary and Man-O/I Ain't Givin' Up Nothin'	1961	3.75	7.50	15.00
❏ 10229	Talk to Me/I Cover the Waterfront	1961	3.75	7.50	15.00
❏ 10288	Be a Leader/'Nother Fairy Tale	1962	3.75	7.50	15.00
❏ 10299	Twistin' the Blues/Pop Eye's Irresistable You	1962	3.75	7.50	15.00
❏ 10342	Counterfeit Friends/Your Picture	1962	3.75	7.50	15.00
❏ 10372	Under Your Spell Again/Happy Birthday Mama	1962	3.75	7.50	15.00
❏ 10412	Who's Sorry Now/Hello Bill	1963	3.75	7.50	15.00
DOUBLE-L					
❏ 714	Pistol Packin' Mama/Tennessee Waltz	1963	2.50	5.00	10.00
❏ 722	Misty/Cry On	1963	2.50	5.00	10.00
❏ 728	Merry Christmas Mama/Auld Lang Syne	1963	3.00	6.00	12.00
❏ 729	Billie Baby/Try a Little Bit of Tenderness	1964	2.50	5.00	10.00
❏ 729 [PS]	Billie Baby/Try a Little Bit of Tenderness	1964	6.25	12.50	25.00
❏ 730	I'll Be a Fool for You/You're Nobody Till Somebody Loves You	1964	2.50	5.00	10.00
❏ 736	Go On Little Girl/You're Reading Me	1965	2.50	5.00	10.00
❏ 739	Every Night/Peeping and Hiding	1966	2.50	5.00	10.00
❏ 740	Send Me Some Loving/Somewhere Along the Way	1966	2.50	5.00	10.00
GSF					
❏ 6882	Sing a Song/(B-side unknown)	1972	—	3.00	6.00
❏ 6894	Love Music/Just for Baby	1973	—	3.00	6.00
❏ 6904	Trying to Slip (Away)/They Get Down	1973	—	3.00	6.00
HURD					
❏ 82	Misty '66/Saturday Night	1966	2.00	4.00	8.00
JAD					
❏ 208	Luv, Luv, Luv/Take All	1968	2.00	4.00	8.00
❏ 212	Don't Stop Now/The Truth	1968	2.00	4.00	8.00
KRC					
❏ 301	Lonely Chair/The Chicken and the Bop	1957	12.50	25.00	50.00
❏ 303	Hello Little Girl/Georgianna	1957	6.25	12.50	25.00
❏ 305	How Many Times/To Love and Be Loved	1957	6.25	12.50	25.00
❏ 587	Just Because/Why	1957	20.00	40.00	80.00
❏ 5000	No Limit to Love/Such a Mess	195?	6.25	12.50	25.00
❏ 5002	Gonna Let You Come Back Home/Down by the River	195?	6.25	12.50	25.00
LPG					
❏ 111	What Did You Do with My Love/Love Music	1976	—	3.00	6.00
LUDIX					
❏ 4747	Feelin' Good/Cupid's Bandwagon	197?	—	3.00	6.00
MONUMENT					
❏ 856	Don't Cry/I Love You, I Just Love You	1964	2.50	5.00	10.00
❏ 865	Amen/I'd Fight the World	1964	2.50	5.00	10.00
❏ 877	Oh, Lady Luck/Woman	1965	2.50	5.00	10.00
❏ 887	If I Had My Life to Live Over/Two for Love	1965	2.50	5.00	10.00
PARAMOUNT					
❏ 0168	In the Eyes of God/The Legend of Nigger Charley	1972	—	3.00	6.00
REPRISE					
❏ 0499	I Won't Cry Anymore/The Man Who Took the Valise Off the Floor at Grand Central Station at Noon	1966	2.00	4.00	8.00
SCEPTER					
❏ 12310	Hooked on a Feeling/If You Really Love Him	1971	—	3.00	6.00
❏ 12327	Mr. and Mrs. Untrue/Natural SInner	1971	—	3.00	6.00
SPECIALTY					
❏ 428	Lawdy Miss Clawdy/Mailman Blues	1952	62.50	125.00	250.00
❏ 428	Lawdy Miss Clawdy/Mailman Blues	1952	375.00	750.00	1500.
—Red vinyl					
❏ 440	Oooh-Oooh-Oooh/Restless Heart	1952	25.00	50.00	100.00
❏ 452	Ain't It a Shame?/Tell Me Pretty Baby	1953	25.00	50.00	100.00
❏ 452	Ain't It a Shame?/Tell Me Pretty Baby	1953	50.00	100.00	200.00
—Red vinyl					
❏ 457	What's the Matter Now?/So Long	1953	25.00	50.00	100.00
❏ 457	What's the Matter Now?/So Long	1953	50.00	100.00	200.00
—Red vinyl					
❏ 463	Where You At?/Baby Don't Turn Your Back on Me	1953	25.00	50.00	100.00
❏ 463	Where You At?/Baby Don't Turn Your Back on Me	1953	50.00	100.00	200.00
—Red vinyl					
❏ 471	I Wish Your Picture Was You/Frog Legs	1953	25.00	50.00	100.00
❏ 483	Let Me Come Home, Baby/Too Late for Tears	1954	20.00	40.00	80.00
❏ 483	Let Me Come Home, Baby/Too Late for Tears	1954	50.00	100.00	200.00
—Red vinyl					
❏ 494	Walkin' the Track/Jimmie Lee	1954	20.00	40.00	80.00
❏ 535	Oo-Ee Baby/Chee-Koo Baby	1954	10.00	20.00	40.00
❏ 540	Trying to Find Someone to Love/Lord, Lord, Amen!	1955	10.00	20.00	40.00
❏ 571	Woe Ho Ho/I Yi Yi Gomen-a-Sai (I'm Sorry)	1956	10.00	20.00	40.00
❏ 578	Country Boy Rock/Rock 'N' Dance	1956	12.50	25.00	50.00
❏ 582	Forgive Me, Clawdy/I'm Glad	1956	7.50	15.00	30.00
❏ 602	Baby Please Come Home/Breaking My Heart (All Over Again)	1957	7.50	15.00	30.00

Number	Title (A Side/B Side)	Yr	VG	VG+	NM
❏ 661	Lawdy Miss Clawdy/Mailman Blues	1959	5.00	10.00	20.00
TURNTABLE					
❏ 501	I Understand/The Grass Will Sing (For You)	1969	2.00	4.00	8.00
❏ 502	I Heard It Through the Grapevine/It's Your Thing	1969	2.00	4.00	8.00
❏ 506	Bad Conditions/The Truth	1969	2.00	4.00	8.00
❏ 509	Lawdy Miss Clawdy/Little Volcano	1969	2.00	4.00	8.00
7-Inch Extended Plays					
ABC-PARAMOUNT					
❏ 277	(contents unknown)	1959	25.00	50.00	100.00
❏ 277 [PS]	The Exciting Lloyd Price	1959	25.00	50.00	100.00
❏ 315	(contents unknown)	1960	25.00	50.00	100.00
❏ 315 [PS]	Mr. Personality Sings the Blues	1960	25.00	50.00	100.00
❏ A-324	Lady Luck/Personality//Stagger Lee/I'm Gonna Get Married	1960	25.00	50.00	100.00
❏ A-324 [PS]	Mr. Personality's Big Hits	1960	25.00	50.00	100.00
Albums					
ABC					
❏ S-297	Mr. Personality	1967	3.75	7.50	15.00
—Reissue on revised label					
❏ S-324 [R]	Mr. Personality's Big 15	1968	3.75	7.50	15.00
—Reissue on revised label					
❏ X-763	16 Greatest Hits	1972	3.75	7.50	15.00
❏ AC-30006	The ABC Collection	1976	3.75	7.50	15.00
❏ DW-94842	16 Greatest Hits	1972	5.00	10.00	20.00
—Capitol Record Club edition					
ABC-PARAMOUNT					
❏ 277 [M]	The Exciting Lloyd Price	1959	10.00	20.00	40.00
❏ S-277 [S]	The Exciting Lloyd Price	1959	20.00	40.00	80.00
❏ 297 [M]	Mr. Personality	1959	10.00	20.00	40.00
❏ S-297 [S]	Mr. Personality	1959	20.00	40.00	80.00
❏ 315 [M]	Mr. Personality Sings the Blues	1960	10.00	20.00	40.00
❏ S-315 [S]	Mr. Personality Sings the Blues	1960	20.00	40.00	80.00
❏ 324 [M]	Mr. Personality's 15 Hits	1960	10.00	20.00	40.00
—Label calls this "Mr. Personality's Big Hits"					
❏ 346 [M]	The Fantastic Lloyd Price	1960	10.00	20.00	40.00
❏ S-346 [R]	The Fantastic Lloyd Price	196?	6.25	12.50	25.00
❏ 366 [M]	Lloyd Price Sings the Million Sellers	1961	10.00	20.00	40.00
❏ S-366 [S]	Lloyd Price Sings the Million Sellers	1961	12.50	25.00	50.00
❏ 382 [M]	Cookin' with Lloyd Price	1961	10.00	20.00	40.00
❏ S-382 [S]	Cookin' with Lloyd Price	1961	12.50	25.00	50.00
DOUBLE-L					
❏ DL-2301 [M]	The Lloyd Price Orchestra	1963	6.25	12.50	25.00
❏ DL-2303 [M]	Misty	1963	6.25	12.50	25.00
❏ SDL-8301 [S]	The Lloyd Price Orchestra	1963	10.00	20.00	40.00
❏ SDL-8303 [S]	Misty	1963	10.00	20.00	40.00
GRAND PRIX					
❏ 422 [M]	Mr. Rhythm and Blues	196?	3.00	6.00	12.00
❏ S-422 [R]	Mr. Rhythm and Blues	196?	2.50	5.00	10.00
GUEST STAR					
❏ G-1910 [M]	Come to Me	196?	3.00	6.00	12.00
❏ GS-1910 [R]	Come to Me	196?	2.50	5.00	10.00
JAD					
❏ 1002	Lloyd Price Now	1969	6.25	12.50	25.00
LPG					
❏ 001	Music…Music	1976	2.50	5.00	10.00
MCA					
❏ 1503	Greatest Hits	1982	2.00	4.00	8.00
MONUMENT					
❏ MLP-8032 [M]	Lloyd Swings for Sammy	1965	6.25	12.50	25.00
❏ SLP-18032 [S]	Lloyd Swings for Sammy	1965	10.00	20.00	40.00
PICKWICK					
❏ SPC-3518	Big Hits	197?	2.00	4.00	8.00
SCEPTER					
❏ CTN-18006	The Best of Lloyd Price	1972	2.50	5.00	10.00
SPECIALTY					
❏ SP-2105	Lloyd Price	198?	3.00	6.00	12.00
—1980s reissue					
❏ SP-2105 [M]	Lloyd Price	1959	45.00	90.00	180.00
TRIP					
❏ TOP 16-5	16 Greatest Hits	1976	2.50	5.00	10.00
TURNTABLE					
❏ TTS-5001	Lloyd Price Now	197?	3.75	7.50	15.00
UPFRONT					
❏ UPF-126	Misty	197?	3.00	6.00	12.00

PRIEST, MAXI
45s
VIRGIN

Number	Title (A Side/B Side)	Yr	VG	VG+	NM
❏ 38675	Mary's Got a Baby (featuring Beenie Man)/We Tomorrow's People	1999	—	—	3.0

PRIMETTES, THE
Early version of THE SUPREMES.
45s
LUPINE

Number	Title (A Side/B Side)	Yr	VG	VG+	NM
❏ 120	Tears of Sorrow/Pretty	1962	75.00	150.00	300.0

PRINCE
12-Inch Singles
ARISTA

❏ ARDP-3750 [(2) DJ]The Greatest Romance Ever Sold (Radio Edit Featuring Eve 4:32) (Jason Nevins Romance Beats 6:03)/(Neptunes Extended

Number	Title (A Side/B Side)	Yr	VG	VG+	NM
	Remix Featuring Q-Tip 5:08) (Jason Nevins Remix Edit 3:36)//(Adam & Eve Remix Featuring Eve 4:30) (Album Version 5:29)/(Jason Nevins Extended Remix 6:41) (Neptunes Remix Edit Featuring Q-Tip 3:42)	1999	5.00	10.00	20.00
❑ ARDP-3764 [DJ]	The Greatest Romance Ever Sold (Album Version 5:30) (Radio Edit 4:30)/(Adam & Eve Remix Featuring Eve 4:28) (Radio Edit Featuring Eve 4:32)	1999	3.00	6.00	12.00
❑ ARDP-3783 [DJ]	The Greatest Romance Ever Sold — Jason Nevins Mixes (4 versions)	1999	3.75	7.50	15.00
❑ 13750 [(2)]	The Greatest Romance Ever Sold (Radio Edit Featuring Eve 4:32) (Jason Nevins Romance Beats 6:03)/(Neptunes Extended Remix Featuring Q-Tip 5:08) (Jason Nevins Remix Edit 3:36)//(Adam & Eve Remix Featuring Eve 4:30) (Album Version 5:29)/(Jason Nevins Extended Remix 6:41) (Neptunes Remix Edit Featuring Q-Tip 3:42)	1999	2.50	5.00	10.00

NPG

Number	Title (A Side/B Side)	Yr	VG	VG+	NM
❑ SPRO-11672 [DJ]	Somebody's Somebody (Ultrafantasy Edit 3:45)/(Radio Edit 4:30) (Live Studio Mix 3:45)	1996	3.75	7.50	15.00
❑ SPRO-11698 [DJ]	Face Down (X-tended Rap Money Mix 4:56) (Instrumental Money Mix 3:58)//I Can't Make You Love Me (Album Version 6:38)/Face Down (A Cappella 2:21)	1997	5.00	10.00	20.00
❑ 19991 [DJ]	1999 (The New Master 7:09) (Rosario 1:19) (The Inevitable Mix 5:44) (Keep Steppin' 4:33)/(Rosie and Doug E. in a Deep House 6:23) (The New Master Single Edit 4:30) (Acapella 5:11)	1998	5.00	10.00	20.00

—Promo only on purple vinyl

NPG/BELLMARK

Number	Title (A Side/B Side)	Yr	VG	VG+	NM
❑ 72514	The Most Beautiful Girl in the World/Beautiful	1994	2.00	4.00	8.00
❑ SPRO 72516 [DJ]	The Most Beautiful Girl in the World (Staxowax 5:00) (Mustang Mix 6:22) (Brian's Mix 4:30)/(Beautiful 5:55) (Original Mix 4:39)	1994	3.75	7.50	15.00

PAISLEY PARK

Number	Title (A Side/B Side)	Yr	VG	VG+	NM
❑ PRO-A-2300 [DJ]	America (3:40) (same on both sides)	1985	3.75	7.50	15.00
❑ PRO-A-2313 [DJ]	Raspberry Beret (3:31) (same on both sides)	1985	3.75	7.50	15.00
❑ PRO-A-2331 [DJ]	Pop Life (3:43) (same on both sides)	1985	3.75	7.50	15.00
❑ PRO-A-2448 [DJ]	Kiss (Edit 3:46) (same on both sides)	1986	3.00	6.00	12.00
❑ PRO-A-2458 [DJ]	Kiss (Extended Version 7:16) (same on both sides)	1986	3.75	7.50	15.00
❑ PRO-A-2476 [DJ]	Mountains (LP Version 3:58) (Extended Version 10:03)	1986	3.75	7.50	15.00
❑ PRO-A-2687 [DJ]	Sign "O" the Times (Edit 3:44) (LP Version 4:57)	1987	2.50	5.00	10.00
❑ PRO-A-2758 [DJ]	If I Was Your Girlfriend (4:54) (same on both sides)	1987	3.00	6.00	12.00
❑ PRO-A-2770 [DJ]	I Could Never Take the Place of Your Man (Fade 3:39) (LP Version 6:31)	1987	3.75	7.50	15.00
❑ PRO-A-2771 [DJ]	U Got the Look (Long Look 6:45) (same on both sides)	1987	3.75	7.50	15.00
❑ PRO-A-2927 [DJ]	Hot Thing (Edit 3:40) (Extended Remix 8:32)	1987	5.00	10.00	20.00
❑ PRO-A-3283 [DJ]	I Wish U Heaven (LP Version 2:43) (same on both sides)	1988	3.00	6.00	12.00
❑ PRO-A-4345 [DJ]	Thieves in the Temple (Album Version 3:20) (same on both sides)	1990	2.50	5.00	10.00
❑ PRO-A-4515 [DJ]	New Power Generation (Album Version 3:15) (same on both sides)	1990	2.50	5.00	10.00
❑ PRO-A-4578 [DJ]	New Power Generation (Funky Weapon Remix 5:01) (same on both sides)	1990	3.75	7.50	15.00
❑ PRO-A-4977 [DJ]	Gett Off (Urge Mix) (Urge Dub) (Flutestramental)/(Thrust Mix) (Thrust Dub) (Rosie's Dub)	1991	3.75	7.50	15.00
❑ PRO-A-5137 [DJ]	Cream (Remixes)	1991	7.50	15.00	30.00

—Price is for Specialty test pressing; it's not known if any actual promo 12-inch singles with this number were pressed

Number	Title (A Side/B Side)	Yr	VG	VG+	NM
❑ PRO-A-5141 [DJ]	Insatiable (Edit 4:01) (Album Version 6:37)	1991	3.75	7.50	15.00
❑ PRO-A-5148 [DJ]	Diamonds and Pearls (Edit 4:20) (Album Version 4:45)	1991	3.75	7.50	15.00
❑ PRO-A-5298 [DJ]	Money Don't Matter 2 Night (Edit 4:11) (Album Version 4:48)	1992	3.75	7.50	15.00
❑ PRO-A-5301 [DJ]	Willing and Able (Edit 4:15) (Album Version 4:59)	1992	10.00	20.00	40.00
❑ PRO-A-5570 [DJ]	Sexy MF (5:25) (same on both sides)	1992	3.00	6.00	12.00
❑ PRO-A-5770 [DJ]	My Name Is Prince (Edit 4:05) (6:36)	1992	3.75	7.50	15.00
❑ PRO-A-5890 [DJ]	Damn U (Album Version 4:01) (same on both sides)	1992	3.00	6.00	12.00
❑ PRO-A-5985 [DJ]	The Morning Papers (Album Version 3:57) (same on both sides)	1993	3.00	6.00	12.00
❑ PRO-A-5993 [DJ]	Pink Cashmere (Vocal Version 3:56)/(Guitar Version 3:58) (Album Version 6:12)	1993	6.25	12.50	25.00

—With picture cover (deduct 40% if missing)

Number	Title (A Side/B Side)	Yr	VG	VG+	NM
❑ PRO-A-5994 [DJ]	Nothing Compares 2 U (Edit 4:17) (Album Version 4:58)	1993	3.00	6.00	12.00
❑ 20355	Raspberry Beret (New Mix 7:25)/She's Always in My Hair (New Mix 6:48)	1985	3.75	7.50	15.00
❑ 20357	Pop Life (Fresh Dance Mix 6:16)/Hello (Fresh Dance Mix 6:38)	1985	2.50	5.00	10.00
❑ 20389	America (21:46)/Girl (7:36)	1985	2.50	5.00	10.00
❑ 20442	Kiss (Extended Version 7:16)/Love or $ (Extended Version)	1986	3.00	6.00	12.00
❑ 20465	Mountains (Extended Version 10:03)/Alexa de Paris (Extended Version 4:54)	1986	3.00	6.00	12.00
❑ 20516	Anotherloverholenyohead (Extended Version 7:52)/Girls and Boys (LP Version 5:30)	1986	2.50	5.00	10.00
❑ 20648	Sign "O" the Times (LP Version 4:57)/La, La, La, He, He, Hee (Highly Explosive 10:32)	1987	2.50	5.00	10.00
❑ 20697	If I Was Your Girlfriend (4:54)/Shockadelica (Extended Version 6:12)	1987	2.50	5.00	10.00
❑ 20727	U Got the Look (Long Look 6:45) (Single Cut 3:58)/Housequake (Album Cut 4:38) (7 Minutes MoQuake 7:15)	1987	3.75	7.50	15.00
❑ 20728	I Could Never Take the Place of Your Man (LP Version 6:31)/Hot Thing (Edit 3:40)//(Extended Remix 8:32) (Dub Version 6:53)	1987	2.50	5.00	10.00
❑ 20930	Alphabet St. (Album Version 5:40)/Alphabet St. "This is not music, this is a trip" (7:48)	1988	2.50	5.00	10.00
❑ 21005	Glam Slam (Remix 8:52)/Escape (Free yo mind from this rat race) (6:26)	1988	2.50	5.00	10.00
❑ 21074	I Wish U Heaven (Part 1, 2 and 3)/Scarlet Pussy (6:09)	1988	2.50	5.00	10.00
❑ 21598	Thieves in the Temple (Remix 8:03) (Thieves in the House Mix 6:50) (Temple House Dub 5:06)	1990	2.00	4.00	8.00
❑ 21783	New Power Generation (Funky Weapon Remix 5:01)/T.C.'s Rap (Featuring T.C. Ellis 3:11)/ Brother with a Purpose (Featuring Tony Mosley 4:18)//Get Off (4:41)/The Lubricated Lady (2:39)/Loveleft, Loveright (5:00)	1990	2.00	4.00	8.00
❑ 40138	Gett Off (Extended Remix 8:31) (Houstyle 8:20)/ Violet the Organ Grinder (4:59)//Gett Off (Flutestramental 7:26)/Gangster Glam (6:04)/ Clockin' the Jizz (Instrumental 4:51)	1991	2.50	5.00	10.00
❑ 40197	Cream (Album Version 4:12) (N.P.G. Mix 5:47)/ Things Have Gotta Change (Tony M. Rap 3:57)/ 2 the Wire (Creamy Instrumental 3:13)/Get Some Solo (1:31)//Do Your Dance (KC's Remix 5:58)/Housebangers (4:23)/Q in Doubt (Instrumental 4:00)/Ethereal Mix (4:43)	1991	2.50	5.00	10.00
❑ 40574	7 (Album Version 5:09) (After 6 Edit 4:20) (After 6 Long Version 5:15)//(Acoustic Version 3:54) (Album Edit 4:23)/2 Whom It May Concern (4:01)	1992	2.50	5.00	10.00
❑ 40700	My Name Is Prince (12" Club Mix 8:11) (House Mix 7:18)//(Original Mix Edit 8:06) (Hard Core 12" Mix 7:55)/Sexy M.F. (12" Remix 7:34)	1992	2.50	5.00	10.00
❑ 40700 [DJ]	My Name Is Prince (12" Club Mix 8:11) (House Mix 7:18)//(Original Mix Edit 8:06) (Hard Core 12" Mix 7:55)/Sexy M.F. (12" Remix 7:34)	1992	6.25	12.50	25.00

—White label promo in generic cover

WARNER BROS.

Number	Title (A Side/B Side)	Yr	VG	VG+	NM
❑ PRO-A-741 [DJ]	Just As Long As We're Together/Soft and Wet	1978	25.00	50.00	100.00

—The only Prince 12-inch single with the "Burbank" label

Number	Title (A Side/B Side)	Yr	VG	VG+	NM
❑ PRO-A-781 [DJ]	Soft and Wet (same on both sides)	1978	20.00	40.00	80.00
❑ PRO-A-832 [DJ]	I Wanna Be Your Lover (same on both sides)	1979	20.00	40.00	80.00
❑ PRO-A-848 [DJ]	Why You Wanna Treat Me So Bad?/Bambi	1979	20.00	40.00	80.00
❑ PRO-A-870 [DJ]	Still Waiting/Why You Wanna Treat Me So Bad?//Sexy Dancer	1980	15.00	30.00	60.00
❑ PRO-A-904 [DJ]	Uptown (Edit 4:09) (Long Version 5:29)	1980	15.00	30.00	60.00
❑ PRO-A-915 [DJ]	Head/Sister/Partyup//(B-side blank)	1980	20.00	40.00	80.00
❑ PRO-A-916 [DJ]	When You Were Mine/Gotta Broken Heart Again//Uptown	1980	15.00	30.00	60.00
❑ PRO-A-929 [DJ]	Dirty Mind (same on both sides)	1980	15.00	30.00	60.00
❑ PRO-A-937 [DJ]	Gotta Stop (Messin' About)/Partyup (Edit)// Head/When U Were Mine/Uptown	1981	20.00	40.00	80.00
❑ PRO-A-938 [DJ]	Gotta Stop (Messin' About) (same on both sides)	1981	15.00	30.00	60.00
❑ PRO-A-980 [DJ]	Controversy (3:39) (Long Version 7:18)	1981	12.50	25.00	50.00
❑ PRO-A-1002 [DJ]	Let's Work (Dance Remix, Long Version 8:02)/ (7" Single Version 2:56)	1982	15.00	30.00	60.00
❑ PRO-A-1035 [DJ]	Do Me, Baby (Edit 3:57)/Private Joy (4:25)	1982	15.00	30.00	60.00
❑ PRO-A-1070 [DJ]	1999 (Album Version) (Single Version 3:35)	1982	15.00	30.00	60.00
❑ PRO-A-1082 [DJ]	Let's Pretend We're Married/D.M.S.R.// Automatic	1982	12.50	25.00	50.00
❑ PRO-A-2001 [DJ]	Little Red Corvette (LP Version 4:58) (Dance Remix 8:00)	1983	10.00	20.00	40.00
❑ PRO-A-2042 [DJ]	1999 (Single Version 3:35)//Free/Automatic	1983	12.50	25.00	50.00
❑ PRO-A-2080 [DJ]	Delirious (LP Version 3:56) (Single Edit 2:36)	1983	7.50	15.00	30.00
❑ PRO-A-2139 [DJ]	When Doves Cry (Long Version 5:52)(Short Version 3:49)	1984	6.25	12.50	25.00
❑ PRO-A-2173 [DJ]	Let's Go Crazy (Edit 3:46) (Album Version 4:40)	1984	7.50	15.00	30.00
❑ PRO-A-2182 [DJ]	Let's Go Crazy (Special Dance Mix 7:35) (Album Version 4:40)	1984	10.00	20.00	40.00
❑ PRO-A-2192 [DJ]	Purple Rain (Edit 4:02) (LP Version 8:45)	1984	10.00	20.00	40.00

—Purple vinyl

Number	Title (A Side/B Side)	Yr	VG	VG+	NM
❑ PRO-A-2233 [DJ]	I Would Die 4 U (2:57) (same on both sides)	1984	5.00	10.00	20.00
❑ PRO-A-2263 [DJ]	Take Me With U (same on both sides)	1985	7.50	15.00	30.00
❑ PRO-A-3579 [DJ]	Batdance (Edit 4:06) (LP Version 6:13)	1989	2.50	5.00	10.00
❑ PRO-A-3702 [DJ]	Batdance (The Batmix 7:15) (Radio Edit 4:09)/ (Vicki Vale Mix 5:55) (Radio Edit 4:13)	1989	3.00	6.00	12.00
❑ PRO-A-3704 [DJ]	Scandalous (LP Version 6:15) (Edit 4:12)	1989	3.75	7.50	15.00
❑ PRO-A-3705 [DJ]	Partyman (LP Version 3:11) (same on both sides)	1989	2.50	5.00	10.00
❑ PRO-A-7000 [DJ]	Letitgo (Edit 4:17) (Album Version 5:33)	1994	3.75	7.50	15.00
❑ PRO-A-7481 [DJ]	Purple Medley (Edit 3:34)/(11:03)	1995	5.00	10.00	20.00
❑ PRO-A-7594 [DJ]	I Hate U (Edit 4:27) (5:58)	1995	3.75	7.50	15.00
❑ PRO-A-7941 [DJ]	Gold (Album Version 7:23) (Radio Edit with Guitar Solo 4:22)//Rock 'N' Roll Is Alive! (and it lives in Minneapolis)/Gold (Alternate Radio Mix with Guitar Solo 4:36)	1995	5.00	10.00	20.00

—Promo only on gold vinyl

Number	Title (A Side/B Side)	Yr	VG	VG+	NM
❑ 20120	1999/Little Red Corvette	1983	6.25	12.50	25.00

Number	Title (A Side/B Side)	Yr	VG	VG+	NM
❑ 20170	Let's Pretend We're Married (7:20)/Irresistible Bitch (4:11)	1983	5.00	10.00	20.00
❑ 20228	When Doves Cry (5:54)/17 Days (3:54)	1984	2.50	5.00	10.00
❑ 20246	Let's Go Crazy (Special Dance Mix 7:35)/Erotic City (7:24)	1984	2.50	5.00	10.00
❑ 20267	Purple Rain (8:45)/God (3:59)	1984	6.25	12.50	25.00
—Purple vinyl					
❑ 20267	Purple Rain (8:45)/God (3:59)	1984	—	—	—
—Black vinyl; can someone confirm the existence of this record as a stock copy?					
❑ 20291	I Would Die 4 U (Extended Version 10:00)/ Another Lonely Christmas (6:47)	1984	3.75	7.50	15.00
—Oversized picture label with die-cut custom sleeve					
❑ 21257	Batdance (The Batmix 7:15)//(Vicki Vale Mix 5:55)/200 Balloons (5:05)	1989	2.50	5.00	10.00
❑ 21370	Partyman (The Purple Party Mix 6:02) (Partyman Music Mix 4:31)//(The Video Mix 6:20)/Feel U Up (Short Stroke 3:42)	1989	2.50	5.00	10.00
❑ 21422	The Scandalous Sex Suite (The Crime 6:24/The Passion 6:14/The Rapture 6:39)//Sex (7:02)/ When 2 R in Love (4:02)	1989	2.50	5.00	10.00
❑ 41745-A [DJ]	Letitgo (Caviar Radio Edit 4:49) (Cavi' Street Edit 5:02) (Instrumental 5:02) (On the Cool-Out Tip Radio Edit 4:34)/(Sherm Stick Edit 5:42) (-Sherm Stick Edit 5:42) (Original Radio Edit 4:15) (Original Album Version 5:33)	1994	3.00	6.00	12.00
—White promo label, "Advance Only." on label, generic white jacket					
❑ 41745	Letitgo (Caviar Radio Edit 4:49) (Cavi' Street Edit 5:02) (Instrumental 5:02) (On the Cool-Out Tip Radio Edit 4:34)/(Sherm Stick Edit 5:42) (-Sherm Stick Edit 5:42) (Original Radio Edit 4:15) (Original Album Version 5:33)	1994	2.00	4.00	8.00
❑ 41833-A [DJ]	Space (Universal Love Radio Remix 3:58) (Universal Love Remix 6:10) (Funky Stuff Remix 5:41)/(Acoustic Remix 4:41) (Funky Stuff Dub 4:48)	1994	3.00	6.00	12.00
—White label promo, "Advance Only." on label					
❑ 41833	Space (Universal Love Radio Remix 3:58) (Universal Love Remix 6:10) (Funky Stuff Remix 5:41)/(Acoustic Remix 4:41) (Funky Stuff Dub 4:48)	1994	2.00	4.00	8.00
❑ 43503	Purple Medley (11:03) (Edit 3:14)/Kirk J's B Sides Remix (7:01)	1995	2.50	5.00	10.00
❑ 43592	I Hate U (Extended Remix 6:17) (7" Edit 4:27)/ (Quiet Night Mix by Eric Leeds 3:55) (Album Version 6:07)	1995	2.00	4.00	8.00
❑ DWBS 50028	Let's Work (Dance Remix, Long Version 8:02)/ Gotta Stop (Messin' About) (2:55)	1982	15.00	30.00	60.00

(NO LABEL)

Number	Title (A Side/B Side)	Yr	VG	VG+	NM
❑ JUN 7 [DJ]	Gett Off (Approx: Damn Near 10 Min.)/(B-side blank)	1991	50.00	100.00	200.00
—1500 copies were pressed; catalog number is Prince's birthday (June 7)					
❑ L-39777 [DJ]	Sexy MF (5:25) (same on both sides)	1992	25.00	50.00	100.00
—Gold vinyl record; with custom cover, "Sexy MF" sticker, card, envelope and fan (deduct for missing items)					
❑ L-39777 [DJ]	Sexy MF (5:25) (same on both sides)	1992	10.00	20.00	40.00
—Gold vinyl record; with generic "Jacket Made in Canada" cover and none of the other goodies					

45s

PAISLEY PARK

Number	Title (A Side/B Side)	Yr	VG	VG+	NM
❑ GWB 0528	Purple Rain/Raspberry Beret	1986	—	—	3.00
—"Back to Back Hits" reissue					
❑ GWB 0529	Pop Life/America	1986	—	—	3.00
—"Back to Back Hits" reissue					
❑ PRO-S-2939 [DJ]	Hot Thing (same on both sides)	1987	3.00	6.00	12.00
❑ PRO-S-3211 [DJ]	Glam Slam (Shep Pettibone Remix 4:22)/(Edit 3:28)	1988	3.75	7.50	15.00
❑ PRO-S-3371 [DJ]	I Wish U Heaven (Radio Edit of Remix 4:25)/ (Single Edit of Remix 5:45)	1988	3.75	7.50	15.00
❑ 15990	Insatiable/Diamonds and Pearls	1993	—	—	3.00
—"Back to Back Hits" reissue					
❑ 15991	Cream/Gett Off	1993	—	—	3.00
—"Back to Back Hits" reissue					
❑ 18371	Pink Cashmere/Soft and Wet	1993	—	—	3.00
❑ 18372	Peach/Nothing Compares 2 U (Live)	1993	—	—	3.00
❑ 18583	The Morning Papers/Live 4 Love	1993	—	—	3.00
❑ 18700	Damn U/2 Whom It May Concern	1993	—	—	3.00
❑ 18707	My Name Is Prince/Sexy Mutha	1992	—	—	3.00
❑ 18817	Sexy M.F./Strollin'	1992	—	—	3.00
❑ 18824	7/(Acoustic Version)	1992	—	—	3.00
❑ 19020	Money Don't Matter 2 Night/Call the Law	1992	—	—	3.00
❑ 19083	Diamonds and Pearls/X-Cerpts	1991	—	—	3.00
❑ 19090	Insatiable/I Love U in Me	1991	—	—	3.00
❑ 19175	Cream/Horny Pony	1991	—	—	3.00
❑ 19225	Gett Off/Horny Pony	1991	—	—	3.00
❑ 19525	New Power Generation/New Power Generation (Part II)	1990	—	—	3.00
❑ 19751	Thieves in the Temple/Thieves in the Temple Part II	1990	—	—	3.00
❑ 27745	I Wish U Heaven/Scarlet Pussy	1988	—	—	3.00
❑ 27745 [DJ]	I Wish U Heaven (same on both sides)	1988	2.00	4.00	8.00
❑ 27745 [PS]	I Wish U Heaven/Scarlet Pussy	1988	—	2.50	5.00
❑ 27806	Glam Slam/Escape	1988	—	—	3.00
❑ 27806 [DJ]	Glam Slam (same on both sides)	1988	2.00	4.00	8.00
❑ 27806 [PS]	Glam Slam/Escape	1988	—	—	3.00
—Heavy plastic sleeve with title sticker					
❑ 27900	Alphabet St./Alphabet St. (Cont.)	1988	—	—	3.00
❑ 27900 [DJ]	Alphabet St./Alphabet St. (Cont.)	1988	2.00	4.00	8.00
❑ 27900 [PS]	Alphabet St./Alphabet St. (Cont.)	1988	—	—	3.00
—Heavy PVC sleeve with title sticker					
❑ 28288	I Could Never Take the Place of Your Man/Hot Thing	1987	—	—	3.00
❑ 28288 [DJ]	I Could Never Take the Place of Your Man (same on both sides)	1987	2.00	4.00	8.00
❑ 28288 [PS]	I Could Never Take the Place of Your Man/Hot Thing	1987	—	—	3.00
❑ 28289	U Got the Look/Housequake	1987	—	—	3.00
❑ 28289 [DJ]	U Got the Look (same on both sides)	1987	2.00	4.00	8.00
❑ 28289 [PS]	U Got the Look/Housequake	1987	—	—	3.00
❑ 28334	If I Was Your Girlfriend/Shockadelica	1987	—	—	3.00
❑ 28334 [DJ]	If I Was Your Girlfriend (same on both sides)	1987	2.00	4.00	8.00
❑ 28334 [PS]	If I Was Your Girlfriend/Shockadelica	1987	—	—	3.00
❑ 28399	Sign "O" the Times/La, La, La, Hee, Hee, Hee	1987	—	—	3.00
❑ 28399 [DJ]	Sign "O" the Times (same on both sides)	1987	2.00	4.00	8.00
❑ 28399 [PS]	Sign "O" the Times/La, La, La, Hee, Hee, Hee	1987	—	—	3.00
❑ 28620	Anotherloverholenyohead/Girls and Boys	1986	—	—	3.00
❑ 28620 [DJ]	Anotherloverholenyohead (same on both sides)	1986	2.00	4.00	8.00
❑ 28620 [DJ]	Girls and Boys (same on both sides)	1986	3.00	6.00	12.00
❑ 28620 [PS]	Anotherloverholenyohead/Girls and Boys	1986	—	—	3.00
❑ 28711	Mountains/Alexa de Paris	1986	—	—	3.00
❑ 28711 [DJ]	Mountains (same on both sides)	1986	2.00	4.00	8.00
❑ 28711 [PS]	Mountains/Alexa de Paris	1986	—	—	3.00
❑ 28751	Kiss/Love or $	1986	—	—	3.00
❑ 28751 [DJ]	Kiss (same on both sides)	1986	2.00	4.00	8.00
❑ 28751 [PS]	Kiss/Love or $	1986	—	—	3.00
❑ 28972	Raspberry Beret/She's Always In My Hair	1985	—	—	3.00
❑ 28972 [DJ]	Raspberry Beret (same on both sides)	1985	2.00	4.00	8.00
—Unlike stock copies, the promo does not have custom labels; the "Paisley Park" logo is at 9 o'clock, a color "WB" shield is at 3 o'clock					
❑ 28972 [PS]	Raspberry Beret/She's Always In My Hair	1985	—	—	3.00
❑ 28998	Pop Life/Hello	1985	—	—	3.00
❑ 28998 [DJ]	Pop Life (same on both sides)	1985	2.00	4.00	8.00
❑ 28998 [PS]	Pop Life/Hello	1985	—	—	3.00
❑ 28999	America/Girl	1985	—	2.00	4.00
❑ 28999 [DJ]	America (same on both sides)	1985	2.00	4.00	8.00
❑ 28999 [PS]	America/Girl	1985	—	2.00	4.00
❑ 29052	Paisley Park/She's Always In My Hair	1985	—	—	—
—Unreleased in U.S.; this pairing, with similar numbers, exists in many European countries					
❑ 29052 [PS]	Paisley Park/She's Always In My Hair	1985	125.00	250.00	500.00
—Evidently, some U.S. picture sleeves exist (not to be confused with European sleeves for this record)					

WARNER BROS.

Number	Title (A Side/B Side)	Yr	VG	VG+	NM
❑ GWB 0392	I Wanna Be Your Lover/Why You Wanna Treat Me So Bad?	1982	—	2.00	4.00
—"Back to Back Hits" reissue					
❑ GWB 0468	1999/Little Red Corvette	1984	—	—	3.00
—"Back to Back Hits" reissue					
❑ GWB 0476	Delirious/Let's Pretend We're Married	1984	—	—	3.00
—"Back to Back Hits" reissue					
❑ GWB 0516	When Doves Cry/Let's Go Crazy	1985	—	—	3.00
—"Back to Back Hits" reissue					
❑ GWB 0517	I Would Die 4 U/Take Me With U	1985	—	—	3.00
—"Back to Back Hits" reissue					
❑ 8619	Soft and Wet/So Blue	1978	7.50	15.00	30.00
—Two slightly different variations exist; one has the time of each side under the catalog number, the other has the time of each side after the titles					
❑ 8619 [DJ]	Soft and Wet (stereo/mono)	1978	3.75	7.50	15.00
❑ 8713	Just As Long As We're Together/In Love	1978	7.50	15.00	30.00
❑ 8713 [DJ]	Just As Long As We're Together (stereo/mono)	1978	3.75	7.50	15.00
❑ 17715	Gold/Rock 'N' Roll Is Alive! (and it lives in Minneapolis)	1995	—	—	3.00
❑ 17811	I Hate U (Edit)/(Quite Night Mix by Eric Leeds)	1995	—	—	3.00
❑ 17903	Purple Medley/Kirk J's B Sides Remix	1995	—	—	3.00
❑ 18012	Space (Universal Love Radio Remix)/(Album Version)	1994	—	—	3.00
❑ 18074	Letitgo/Solo	1994	—	—	3.00
❑ 20129 [PD]	Little Red Corvette/1999	1983	10.00	20.00	40.00
—7-inch picture disc with custom sticker; numbered as if a 12-inch single					
❑ 21858	I Could Never Take the Place of Your Man/ Alphabet St.	1989	—	—	3.00
—"Back to Back Hits" series					
❑ 21859	Batdance/Partyman	1989	—	—	3.00
—"Back to Back Hits" series					
❑ 21938	Sign "O" the Times/U Got the Look	1988	—	—	3.00
—"Back to Back Hits" series					
❑ 21980	Anotherloverholenyohead/Mountains	1987	—	—	3.00
—"Back to Back Hits" series					
❑ 21981	Uptown/Controversy	1987	—	—	3.00
—"Back to Back Hits" series					
❑ 21982	Kiss/Soft and Wet	1987	—	—	3.00
—"Back to Back Hits" series					
❑ 22757	The Arms of Orion/I Love U in Me	1989	—	—	3.00
❑ 22757 [PS]	The Arms of Orion/I Love U in Me	1989	—	—	3.00
—With Sheena Easton					
❑ 22814	Partyman/Feel U Up	1989	—	—	3.00
❑ 22814 [DJ]	Partyman (same on both sides)	1989	3.00	6.00	12.00
❑ 22814 [PS]	Partyman/Feel U Up	1989	—	—	3.00
❑ 22824	Scandalous/When 2 R In Love	1989	—	—	3.00
❑ 22824 [DJ]	Scandalous (same on both sides)	1989	5.00	10.00	20.00
—The last Prince promo 45 -- though "Partyman" has a lower number, it was released earlier, as opposed to the usual backwards numbering of Warner Bros. from 1982 on					
❑ 22824 [PS]	Scandalous/When 2 R In Love	1989	—	—	3.00
❑ 22924	Batdance/200 Balloons	1989	—	—	3.00
❑ 22924 [DJ]	Batdance (same on both sides)	1989	2.50	5.00	10.00

Number	Title (A Side/B Side)	Yr	VG	VG+	NM
❑ 22924 [PS]	Batdance/200 Balloons	1989	—	—	3.00
❑ 29079	Take Me With U/Baby I'm a Star	1985	—	2.00	4.00
❑ 29079 [DJ]	Take Me With U (same on both sides)	1985	2.00	4.00	8.00
❑ 29079 [PS]	Take Me With U/Baby I'm a Star	1985	—	2.00	4.00
❑ 29121	I Would Die 4 U/Another Lonely Christmas	1984	—	2.00	4.00
❑ 29121 [DJ]	I Would Die 4 U (same on both sides)	1984	2.00	4.00	8.00
❑ 29121 [PS]	I Would Die 4 U/Another Lonely Christmas	1984	—	2.00	4.00
❑ 29174	Purple Rain/God	1984	—	2.00	4.00
—Purple vinyl					
❑ 29174	Purple Rain/God	1984	—	—	—
—Black vinyl; can someone confirm the existence of this record as a stock copy?					
❑ 29174 [DJ]	Purple Rain (same on both sides)	1984	2.00	4.00	8.00
—Purple vinyl					
❑ 29174 [PS]	Purple Rain/God	1984	2.00	4.00	8.00
—Plastic semi-transparent sleeve					
❑ 29216	Let's Go Crazy/Erotic City	1984	—	2.00	4.00
❑ 29216 [DJ]	Let's Go Crazy (same on both sides)	1984	2.00	4.00	8.00
❑ 29216 [PS]	Let's Go Crazy/Erotic City	1984	2.00	4.00	8.00
❑ 29286	When Doves Cry/17 Days	1984	5.00	10.00	20.00
—Purple vinyl					
❑ 29286	When Doves Cry/17 Days	1984	—	—	3.00
—Black vinyl					
❑ 29286 [DJ]	When Doves Cry (3:49)/(5:52)	1984	2.50	5.00	10.00
—Purple vinyl promo					
❑ 29286 [DJ]	When Doves Cry (3:49)/(5:52)	1984	2.00	4.00	8.00
—Black vinyl					
❑ 29286 [PS]	When Doves Cry/17 Days	1984	—	—	3.00
❑ 29503	Delirious/Horny Toad	1983	—	3.00	6.00
—Label erroneously lists A-side time at 3:56					
❑ 29503	Delirious/Horny Toad	1983	—	—	5.00
—Label lists correct A-side time of 2:36					
❑ 29503 [DJ]	Delirious (stereo/mono)	1983	2.50	5.00	10.00
—Label on both sides lists incorrect A-side time of 3:56					
❑ 29503 [PS]	Delirious/Horny Toad	1983	12.50	25.00	50.00
—Fold-out poster sleeve					
❑ 29548	Let's Pretend We're Married/Irresistible Bitch	1983	—	2.50	5.00
❑ 29548 [DJ]	Let's Pretend We're Married (stereo/mono)	1983	2.00	4.00	8.00
❑ 29548 [PS]	Let's Pretend We're Married/Irresistible Bitch	1983	2.50	5.00	10.00
❑ 29746	Little Red Corvette/All the Critics Love U in New York	1983	—	2.50	5.00
❑ 29746 [DJ]	Little Red Corvette (Edit 3:08)/(Dance Remix 4:32)	1983	3.00	6.00	12.00
❑ 29896	1999/How Come U Don't Call Me Anymore?	1982	—	2.50	5.00
❑ 29896 [DJ]	1999 (stereo/mono)	1982	2.00	4.00	8.00
❑ 29896 [PS]	1999/How Come U Don't Call Me Anymore?	1982	2.50	5.00	10.00
❑ 29942	Do Me, Baby/Private Joy	1982	3.75	7.50	15.00
❑ 29942 [DJ]	Do Me, Baby (stereo/mono)	1982	—	3.75	7.50
❑ 49050	I Wanna Be Your Lover/My Love Is Forever	1979	2.50	5.00	10.00
❑ 49050 [DJ]	I Wanna Be Your Lover (stereo/mono)	1979	3.75	7.50	15.00
❑ 49050 [DJ]	My Love Is Forever (stereo/mono)	1979	5.00	10.00	20.00
❑ 49050 [PS]	My Love Is Forever	1979	20.00	40.00	80.00
—Promo-only sleeve; withdrawn when "I Wanna Be Your Lover" was pushed as the A-side					
❑ 49178	Why You Wanna Treat Me So Bad?/Baby	1980	7.50	15.00	30.00
❑ 49178 [DJ]	Why You Wanna Treat Me So Bad? (stereo/mono)	1980	3.75	7.50	15.00
❑ 49178 [PS]	Why You Wanna Treat Me So Bad?/Baby	1980	15.00	30.00	60.00
❑ 49226	Still Waiting/Bambi	1980	3.75	7.50	15.00
❑ 49226 [DJ]	Still Waiting (stereo/mono)	1980	2.00	4.00	8.00
❑ 49559	Uptown/Crazy You	1980	3.75	7.50	15.00
❑ 49559 [DJ]	Uptown (stereo/mono)	1980	—	3.75	7.50
❑ 49559 [PS]	Uptown/Crazy You	1980	3.75	7.50	15.00
❑ 49638	Dirty Mind/When We're Dancing Close and Slow	1980	3.75	7.50	15.00
❑ 49638 [DJ]	Dirty Mind (stereo/mono)	1980	—	3.75	7.50
❑ 49808	Controversy/When You Were Mine	1981	3.75	7.50	15.00
❑ 49808 [DJ]	Controversy (stereo/mono)	1981	2.00	4.00	8.00
❑ 50002	Let's Work/Ronnie Talk to Russia	1982	3.75	7.50	15.00
❑ 50002 [DJ]	Let's Work (stereo/mono)	1982	2.00	4.00	8.00

Albums

ARISTA

Number	Title (A Side/B Side)	Yr	VG	VG+	NM
❑ 14624 [(2)]	Rave Un2 the Joy Fantastic	1999	3.00	6.00	12.00
NPG/BELLMARK					
❑ 71003 [EP]	The Beautiful Experience	1994	5.00	10.00	20.00
NPG/REDLINE					
❑ 70004 [(2)]	The Rainbow Children	2001	6.25	12.50	25.00
PAISLEY PARK					
❑ 25286	Around the World in a Day	1985	2.50	5.00	10.00
—Original copies have a fold-over flap (deduct 25% or more if missing)					
❑ 25395	Parade	1986	2.00	4.00	8.00
❑ 25577 [(2)]	Sign "O" The Times	1987	3.75	7.50	15.00
❑ W1-25577 [(2)]	Sign "O" The Times	1987	4.50	9.00	18.00
—Columbia House edition					
❑ 25677-DJ [(2)]	The Black Album	1987	750.00	1500.	3000.
—Entire album on two 12-inch records that play at 45 RPM					
❑ 25677	The Black Album	1987	500.00	1000.	2000.
—Withdrawn prior to release, though a few copies escaped. Numerous counterfeits exist on other labels and colored vinyl.					
❑ 25720-DJ [DJ]	Lovesexy	1988	5.00	10.00	20.00
—Gold stamped and stickered cover (no UPC) with promo labels; tracks are banded					
❑ 25720	Lovesexy	1988	3.00	6.00	12.00
❑ 27493 [(2)]	Graffiti Bridge	1990	3.75	7.50	15.00
—Also includes The Time, Tevin Campbell					
❑ R 124370	Around the World in a Day	1985	3.00	6.00	12.00
—RCA Music Service edition					
❑ R 140234	Parade	1986	3.00	6.00	12.00
—RCA Music Service edition					
❑ R 154087	Lovesexy	1988	3.50	7.00	14.00
—BMG Direct Marketing edition					
❑ R 234107 [(2)]	Graffiti Bridge	1990	4.50	9.00	18.00
—Also includes The Time, Tevin Campbell; BMG Direct Marketing edition					
❑ R 261991 [(2)]	Sign "O" The Times	1987	4.50	9.00	18.00
—BMG Direct Marketing edition					
WARNER BROS.					
❑ BSK 3150	For You	1978	5.00	10.00	20.00
—First edition on Burbank "palm trees" label					
❑ BSK 3150	For You	1978	3.00	6.00	12.00
—White WB label					
❑ BSK 3366	Prince	1979	3.00	6.00	12.00
❑ BSK 3478	Dirty Mind	1980	3.00	6.00	12.00
❑ BSK 3601	Controversy	1981	3.00	6.00	12.00
❑ PRO-A-7270 [(2) DJ]	Come	1994	7.50	15.00	30.00
—Promo-only vinyl					
❑ PRO-A-7330 [DJ]	The Black Album	1994	12.50	25.00	50.00
—Promo-only vinyl					
❑ PRO-A-7835 [(2) DJ]	The Gold Experience	1995	20.00	40.00	80.00
—Promo-only gold vinyl with numbered gold foil jacket					
❑ 23720 [(2)]	1999	1982	3.75	7.50	15.00
❑ 25110	Purple Rain	1984	12.50	25.00	50.00
—Purple vinyl; comes with poster					
❑ 25110	Purple Rain	1984	2.50	5.00	10.00
—With poster					
❑ 25936	Batman (Soundtrack)	1989	2.50	5.00	10.00
❑ 45793 [DJ]	The Black Album	1994	50.00	100.00	200.00
—White vinyl; 300 copies, numbered in gold on the label (from 051 to 350)					
❑ 45793 [DJ]	The Black Album	1994	25.00	50.00	100.00
—Peach vinyl; 1,000 copies					
❑ 45793 [DJ]	The Black Album	1994	125.00	250.00	500.00
—Gray marbled vinyl; 50 copies					
❑ R 160175	Purple Rain	1984	3.00	6.00	12.00
—RCA Music Service edition; includes poster					
❑ R 160344	Batman (Soundtrack)	1989	3.00	6.00	12.00
—BMG Direct Marketing edition					
❑ R 252483 [(2)]	1999	1982	4.50	9.00	18.00
—RCA Music Service edition					

PRINCE BUSTER

45s

AMY

Number	Title (A Side/B Side)	Yr	VG	VG+	NM
❑ 906	Everybody Ska/30 Pieces of Silver	1964	3.75	7.50	15.00
ATLANTIC					
❑ 2231	Don't Make Me Cry/That Lucky Old Sun	1964	3.75	7.50	15.00
PHILIPS					
❑ 40427	Ten Commandments/Don't Make Me Cry	1967	3.00	6.00	12.00
RCA VICTOR					
❑ 47-9114	Ten Commandments from Woman to Man/Ain't That Saying a Lot	1967	3.00	6.00	12.00

Albums

RCA VICTOR

Number	Title (A Side/B Side)	Yr	VG	VG+	NM
❑ LPM-3792 [M]	Ten Commandments	1967	6.25	12.50	25.00
❑ LSP-3792 [S]	Ten Commandments	1967	7.50	15.00	30.00

PRISONAIRES, THE

45s

SUN

Number	Title (A Side/B Side)	Yr	VG	VG+	NM
❑ 186	Just Walking in the Rain/Baby Please	1953	125.00	250.00	500.00
❑ 186	Just Walking in the Rain/Baby Please	1953	2500.	3750.	5000.
—Red vinyl					
❑ 189	Softly and Tenderly/My God Is Real	1953	175.00	350.00	700.00
❑ 191	A Prisoner's Prayer/I Know	1953	125.00	250.00	500.00
❑ 207	There Is Love in You/What'll You Do Next	1954	5000.	8500.	12000.

78s

SUN

Number	Title (A Side/B Side)	Yr	VG	VG+	NM
❑ 186	Just Walking in the Rain/Baby Please	1953	25.00	50.00	100.00
❑ 189	Softly and Tenderly/My God Is Real	1953	100.00	200.00	400.00
❑ 191	A Prisoner's Prayer/I Know	1953	75.00	150.00	300.00
❑ 207	There Is Love in You/What'll You Do Next	1954	500.00	1000.	2000.

PRODUCT G&B, THE

12-Inch Singles

COLUMBIA

Number	Title (A Side/B Side)	Yr	VG	VG+	NM
❑ CAS 48771 [DJ]	Tired of Being Broke (Explicit Version with Rap) (Clean Version with Rap) (Instrumental) (Jail Rap)	2000	2.00	4.00	8.00
J					
❑ J1PV-21010	Cluck, Cluck (Main Mix) (Instrumental) (Club Mix)	2001	2.00	4.00	8.00
❑ 21044	Cluck, Cluck (unknown versions)	2001	—	3.50	7.00
❑ J1PV-21138 [(2)]	Dirty Dancin' (unknown versions)	2002	2.50	5.00	10.00

45s

J

Number	Title (A Side/B Side)	Yr	VG	VG+	NM
❑ 21049	Cluck, Cluck (Main Version)/(Instrumental)	2001	—	—	3.00
❑ 21148	Dirty Dancin'/Black Rose	2002	—	—	3.00
—A-side featuring Carlos Santana					

PROFILES, THE (1)

45s

BAMBOO

Number	Title (A Side/B Side)	Yr	VG	VG+	NM
❑ 104	Got to Be Love (Something Stupid)/You Don't Care About Me	1969	2.00	4.00	8.00
❑ 108	Be Careful/I Still Love You	1969	2.00	4.00	8.00
❑ 115	A Little Misunderstanding/Got to Be Love	1970	2.00	4.00	8.00

Number	Title (A Side/B Side)	Yr	VG	VG+	NM
DUO					
❏ 7449	If I Didn't Love You//(B-side unknown)	1968	2.50	5.00	10.00
PROFILES, THE (2)					
45s					
GAIT					
❏ 1444	Never/Right By Her Side	1962	50.00	100.00	200.00
PRYSOCK, ARTHUR					
45s					
BETHLEHEM					
❏ 3100	The Girls I Never Kissed/Funny World	1972	—	3.00	6.00
DECCA					
❏ 25684	When Day Is Done/What Will I Tell My Heart	1965	2.00	4.00	8.00
❏ 27722	Blue Velvet/Morning Side Of the Mountain	1951	3.75	7.50	15.00
❏ 27769	Sin/The Love of a Gypsy	1951	3.75	7.50	15.00
❏ 27871	A Man Ain't Supposed to Cry/I Didn't Sleep a Wink Last Night	1951	3.75	7.50	15.00
❏ 27967	Wheel of Fortune/'Til the Stars Fall in the Ocean	1952	3.75	7.50	15.00
❏ 27978	I Hear a Rhapsody/Am I to Blame	1952	3.75	7.50	15.00
❏ 28270	School of Love/Sentimental Fool	1952	3.75	7.50	15.00
❏ 28700	I'd Give Anything/This Is the Time	1953	3.75	7.50	15.00
❏ 28867	My Mood/Temptation	1953	3.75	7.50	15.00
❏ 28950	Nobody Cares/Jean	1953	3.75	7.50	15.00
❏ 29118	Baby Don't You Cry/My Last Goodbye	1954	3.75	7.50	15.00
❏ 31710	Wheel of Fortune/I Cover the Waterfront	1964	2.00	4.00	8.00
❏ 31775	Baby, Don't You Cry/I Didn't Sleep a Wink Last Night	1965	2.00	4.00	8.00
GUSTO					
❏ 9023	Today I Started Loving You Again/It Ain't No Big Thing	1979	—	3.00	6.00
KING					
❏ 6243	Soul Soliloquy/(I Wanna Go) Where the Soul Trees Grow	1969	—	3.00	6.00
❏ 6271	The 23rd Psalm/I Believe	1969	—	3.00	6.00
❏ 6276	Save Your Love for Me/If I Were Young Again	1969	—	3.00	6.00
❏ 6279	Go Ahead and Fly/How Do I Tell Her	1969	—	3.00	6.00
❏ 6307	Have a Good Time/Frisco Line	1970	—	3.00	6.00
❏ 6315	Lord, Is That Me/My Home Is Not a Home Without You	1970	—	3.00	6.00
❏ 6353	Cry/Unforgettable	1971	—	3.00	6.00
❏ 6354	It Ain't No Big Thing/Big Blue Diamonds	1971	—	3.00	6.00
❏ 6364	Precious Memories/Just a Closer Walk with Thee	1971	—	3.00	6.00
MCA					
❏ 40943	Here's to Good Friends/All I Can Do Is Cry	1978	2.00	4.00	8.00
—The song that became the "Tonight, let it be Lowenbrau" commercial					
MERCURY					
❏ 70352	Take Care of Yourself/I'll Never Let You Cry	1954	3.75	7.50	15.00
❏ 70414	This I Know/If You Don't, Somebody Will	1954	3.75	7.50	15.00
❏ 70502	Show Me How to Mambo/I'm in Heaven Tonight	1954	3.75	7.50	15.00
❏ 70599	I Have Lied/Morning, Noon and Night	1955	3.75	7.50	15.00
OLD TOWN					
❏ 100	In the Rain/Thank Heaven for You	1973	—	2.50	5.00
❏ 103	Color My World/Good Morning News	1974	—	2.50	5.00
❏ 106	Hurt So Bad/Love Makes It Right	1974	—	2.50	5.00
❏ 108	I Wantcha Baby/One Broken Heart	1975	—	2.50	5.00
❏ 1000	When Love Is New/All I Need Is You	1976	—	2.50	5.00
❏ 1001	I Wantcha Baby/One Broken Heart	1977	—	2.50	5.00
❏ 1002	You Can Do It/You Can Do It (Part 2)	1977	—	2.50	5.00
❏ 1003	Since I Fell for You/Between Hello and Goodbye	1978	—	2.50	5.00
❏ 1055	I Love You So/The Greatest Gift	1958	3.00	6.00	12.00
❏ 1060	I Just Want to Make Love to You/Keep a Light in the Window	1958	3.00	6.00	12.00
❏ 1073	I Worry About You/My Faith	1959	3.00	6.00	12.00
❏ 1079	The Very Thought of You/If Ever I Should Fall in Love	1960	2.50	5.00	10.00
❏ 1087	This Is My Love/Do You Believe	1960	2.50	5.00	10.00
❏ 1092	Good Rockin' Tonight/My Everything	1960	2.50	5.00	10.00
❏ 1101	This Time/I Wonder Where Our Love Has Gone	1961	2.50	5.00	10.00
❏ 1106	One More Time/Speak to Me	1961	2.50	5.00	10.00
❏ 1115	April in Paris/When I Fall in Love	1962	2.50	5.00	10.00
❏ 1125	Where Can I Go/Pianissimo	1962	2.50	5.00	10.00
❏ 1132	Our Love Will Last/Come and See This Old Fool	1963	2.50	5.00	10.00
❏ 1138	My Special Prayer/You Can't Come In	1963	2.50	5.00	10.00
❏ 1144	There Will Never Be Another You/Crawdad	1963	2.50	5.00	10.00
❏ 1146	Stella by Starlight/My Wish	1963	2.50	5.00	10.00
❏ 1155	Ebb Tide/Are You Ready for a Laugh	1964	2.00	4.00	8.00
❏ 1163	Close Your Eyes/My Everlasting Love	1964	2.00	4.00	8.00
❏ 1170	Fly Me to the Moon/Without the One You Love	1964	2.00	4.00	8.00
❏ 1174	Full Moon and Empty Arms/You Always Hurt the One You Love	1964	2.00	4.00	8.00
❏ 1177	Teardrops in the Rain/I'm Crossing Over	1965	2.00	4.00	8.00
❏ 1183	It's Too Late, Baby Too Late/Who Can I Turn To	1965	2.00	4.00	8.00
❏ 1185	Open Up Your Heart/Only a Fool Breaks His Own Heart	1965	2.00	4.00	8.00
❏ 1188	Again/I Got the Blues So Bad	1965	2.00	4.00	8.00
❏ 1191	My Funny Valentine/House by the Side of the Road	1966	2.00	4.00	8.00
❏ 1196	Because/Let It Be Me	1966	2.00	4.00	8.00
VERVE					
❏ 10470	You Don't Have to Say You Love Me/10,000 Kisses, 10,000 Hugs	1966	—	3.00	6.00
❏ 10515	Love Me/She's a Woman	1967	—	3.00	6.00
❏ 10544	Before You Break My Heart/Goodbye, So Long	1967	—	3.00	6.00

Number	Title (A Side/B Side)	Yr	VG	VG+	NM
❏ 10574	A Working Man's Prayer/No More in Life	1967	—	3.00	6.00
❏ 10592	Madam/No Sun Today	1968	—	3.00	6.00
❏ 10620	I Must Be Doing Something Right/Young Runaways	1968	—	3.00	6.00
❏ 10633	My Special Prayer/Pretty Girl	1969	—	3.00	6.00
Albums					
DECCA					
❏ DL 4581 [M]	Strictly Sentimental	1965	3.75	7.50	15.00
❏ DL 4628 [M]	Showcase	1965	3.75	7.50	15.00
❏ DL 74581 [S]	Strictly Sentimental	1965	5.00	10.00	20.00
❏ DL 74628 [S]	Showcase	1965	5.00	10.00	20.00
KING					
❏ KS-1064	The Country Side of Arthur Prysock	1969	3.00	6.00	12.00
❏ KS-1066	Where the Soul Trees Go	1970	3.00	6.00	12.00
❏ KS-1067	The Lord Is My Shepherd	1970	3.00	6.00	12.00
❏ KS-1088	Fly My Love	1970	3.00	6.00	12.00
❏ KS-1134	Unforgettable	1971	3.00	6.00	12.00
MCA					
❏ 3061	Here's To Good Friends	1978	2.50	5.00	10.00
MGM					
❏ GAS-134	Arthur Prysock (Golden Archive Series)	1970	3.00	6.00	12.00
❏ SE-4694	Arthur Prysock	1970	3.00	6.00	12.00
MILESTONE					
❏ M-9139	A Rockin' Good Way	1986	2.50	5.00	10.00
❏ M-9146	This Guy's in Love with You	1987	2.50	5.00	10.00
❏ M-9157	Today's Love Songs, Tomorrow's Blues	1988	2.50	5.00	10.00
OLD TOWN					
❏ 12-001	Arthur Prysock '74	1973	3.00	6.00	12.00
❏ 12-002	Love Makes It Right	1974	3.00	6.00	12.00
❏ 12-004	All My Life	1976	3.00	6.00	12.00
❏ LP-102 [M]	I Worry About You	1962	12.50	25.00	50.00
❏ LP-2004 [M]	Arthur Prysock Sings Only for You	1962	12.50	25.00	50.00
❏ LP-2005 [M]	Coast to Coast	1963	10.00	20.00	40.00
❏ LP-2006 [M]	A Portrait of Arthur Prysock	1963	10.00	20.00	40.00
❏ LP-2007 [M]	Everlasting Songs for Everlasting Lovers	1964	10.00	20.00	40.00
❏ LP-2008 [M]	Intimately Yours	1964	10.00	20.00	40.00
❏ LP-2009 [M]	A Double Header with Arthur Prysock	1965	10.00	20.00	40.00
❏ LP-2010 [M]	In a Mood	1965	10.00	20.00	40.00
❏ T-90604 [M]	A Portrait of Arthur Prysock	1965	10.00	20.00	40.00
—Capitol Record Club edition					
POLYDOR					
❏ PD-2-8901 [(2)]	Silk and Satin	1977	3.75	7.50	15.00
VERVE					
❏ V6-650 [(2)]	24 Karat Hits	1969	3.75	7.50	15.00
❏ V-5009 [M]	Art and Soul	1966	3.00	6.00	12.00
❏ V6-5009 [S]	Art and Soul	1966	3.75	7.50	15.00
❏ V-5011 [M]	The Best of Arthur Prysock	1967	3.00	6.00	12.00
❏ V6-5011 [S]	The Best of Arthur Prysock	1967	3.75	7.50	15.00
❏ V-5012 [M]	A Portrait of Arthur Prysock	1967	3.75	7.50	15.00
❏ V6-5012 [S]	A Portrait of Arthur Prysock	1967	3.75	7.50	15.00
❏ V-5014 [M]	Mister Prysock	1967	3.75	7.50	15.00
❏ V6-5014 [S]	Mister Prysock	1967	3.75	7.50	15.00
❏ V-5029 [M]	Love Me	1968	3.75	7.50	15.00
❏ V6-5029 [S]	Love Me	1968	3.00	6.00	12.00
❏ V-5038 [M]	The Best of Arthur Prysock, Volume 2	1968	5.00	10.00	20.00
—All mono copies appear to be yellow label promos					
❏ V6-5038 [S]	The Best of Arthur Prysock, Volume 2	1968	3.00	6.00	12.00
❏ V-5048 [M]	To Love or Not to Love	1968	7.50	15.00	30.00
—May be promo only					
❏ V6-5048 [S]	To Love or Not to Love	1968	3.00	6.00	12.00
❏ V6-5059	I Must Be Doing Something Right	1968	3.00	6.00	12.00
❏ V6-5070	This Is My Beloved	1969	3.00	6.00	12.00
PRYSOCK, ARTHUR/COUNT BASIE					
Albums					
VERVE					
❏ V-8646 [M]	Arthur Prysock/Count Basie	1966	3.75	7.50	15.00
❏ V6-8646 [S]	Arthur Prysock/Count Basie	1966	5.00	10.00	20.00
❏ 827011-1	Arthur Prysock/Count Basie	1985	2.00	4.00	8.00
—Reissue					
PRYSOCK, RED					
45s					
CHESS					
❏ 2042	I Heard It Through the Grapevine/Groovy Sax	1968	2.00	4.00	8.00
KING					
❏ 5595	Hand Clapping One More Time/Smokestack	1962	2.50	5.00	10.00
❏ 5644	Quick as a Flash/Old Folks	1962	2.50	5.00	10.00
❏ 5669	Harem Girl/Ride Away	1962	2.50	5.00	10.00
❏ 5704	Here We Go Again/Can't Sit Down	1963	2.50	5.00	10.00
MERCURY					
❏ 70367	Jump Red Jump/Body and Soul	1954	5.00	10.00	20.00
❏ 70419	Happy Feet/Blow Your Horn	1954	5.00	10.00	20.00
❏ 70460	Hey There/Fats' Place	1954	5.00	10.00	20.00
❏ 70540	Rock 'n' Roll/Little Jamie	1955	5.00	10.00	20.00
❏ 70602	The Zonked/Horn Blows	1955	5.00	10.00	20.00
❏ 70674	Hand Clappin'/Shoe String	1955	5.00	10.00	20.00
❏ 70698	Jumbo/Hand Clappin'	1955	5.00	10.00	20.00
❏ 70733	Finger Tips/Short Circuit	1955	5.00	10.00	20.00
❏ 70787	Zip/Red Speaks	1956	3.75	7.50	15.00
❏ 70918	Rock and Roll Party/Rock and Roll Mambo	1956	3.75	7.50	15.00
❏ 70985	Teen-Age Rock/Paquino Walk	1956	3.75	7.50	15.00
❏ 71054	Head Snappin'/Pog Wog	1957	3.75	7.50	15.00
❏ 71175	Rooster Walk/Two Point Eight	1957	3.75	7.50	15.00

Number	Title (A Side/B Side)	Yr	VG	VG+	NM
❏ 71214	What's the Word, Thunderbird/Satellite	1957	3.75	7.50	15.00
❏ 71358	Billie's Blues/Willow Weep for Me	1958	3.00	6.00	12.00
❏ 71411	Margie/Chop Suey	1959	3.00	6.00	12.00
❏ 71476	Riffin' with Red/And the Angels Sing	1959	3.00	6.00	12.00
❏ 71573	Deep Purple/Offshore	1960	3.00	6.00	12.00
❏ 71735	More Handclappin'/Twistin' 'n' Bendin'	1960	3.00	6.00	12.00
❏ 71786	Charleston Twist/Bony Maronie	1961	3.00	6.00	12.00

RED ROBIN

Number	Title (A Side/B Side)	Yr	VG	VG+	NM
❏ 107	Wiggles/Crying My Heart Out	1952	30.00	60.00	120.00
❏ 117	Hard Rock/Jump for George	1953	25.00	50.00	100.00
❏ 139	Jackpot/The Hammer	1956	20.00	40.00	80.00

Albums

MERCURY

Number	Title (A Side/B Side)	Yr	VG	VG+	NM
❏ MG-20088 [M]	Rock 'n Roll	1955	50.00	100.00	200.00
❏ MG-20211 [M]	Fruit Boots	1957	30.00	60.00	120.00
❏ MG-20307 [M]	The Beat	1957	20.00	40.00	80.00
❏ MG-20512 [M]	Swing Softly Red	1958	12.50	25.00	50.00
❏ SR-60188 [S]	Swing Softly Red	1959	20.00	40.00	80.00

WING

Number	Title (A Side/B Side)	Yr	VG	VG+	NM
❏ MGW-12007 [M]	Fruit Boots	1959	10.00	20.00	40.00
—Originals have liner notes on back cover					
❏ MGW-12007 [M]	Fruit Boots	196?	5.00	10.00	20.00
—Reissues have other LPs listed on back cover					
❏ SRW-16007 [R]	Fruit Boots	196?	3.00	6.00	12.00

PUBLIC ENEMY
12-Inch Singles
ATOMIC POP

Number	Title (A Side/B Side)	Yr	VG	VG+	NM
❏ (# unknown)	Do You Wanna Go Our Way??? (Clean) (Instrumental)/LSD//41:19 (Clean) (Street) (Instrumental)	1999	2.00	4.00	8.00
—Green vinyl					

DEF JAM

Number	Title (A Side/B Side)	Yr	VG	VG+	NM
❏ PE-2 [DJ]	Give It Up (3 versions)/Bedlam (Clean) (Instrumental)	1994	3.75	7.50	15.00
❏ PRO 1130-1 [DJ]	Give It Up (Main Version) (Instrumental)/(Dirty Drums in Memphis Mixx) (Memphis Dirty Instrumental) (Upapella)	1994	3.75	7.50	15.00
❏ CAS 1477 [DJ]	Black Steel in the Hour of Chaos (3 versions)	1989	3.75	7.50	15.00
❏ CAS 2082 [DJ]	Brothers Gonna Work It Out (4 mixes)/Anti-Nigger Machine (censored)	1990	3.00	6.00	12.00
❏ DEF 2331 [DJ]	He Got Game (Flava's Radio Edit) (Flava's Edit) (Instrumental)	1998	2.50	5.00	10.00
❏ DEF 2341 [DJ]	Resurrection (Radio Edit) (LP Version) (Instrumental)	1998	2.00	4.00	8.00
❏ 44-06719	Public Enemy #1 (Vocal) (Instrumental)/Timebomb/Son of Public Enemy (Flavor Whop Version)	1987	3.00	6.00	12.00
❏ 44-06861	You're Gonna Get Yours (Vocal) (Terminator X Dub)//Miuzi Weighs a Ton/Rebel Without a Pause (Vocal) (Instrumental)	1987	3.75	7.50	15.00
❏ 44-07491	Bring the Noise/Sophisticated	1987	3.75	7.50	15.00
❏ 4W9-07846	Don't Believe the Hype/The Rhythm, the Rebel//Prophets of Rage (2 versions)	1988	2.50	5.00	10.00
❏ 44-68216	Black Steel in the Hour of Chaos (4 versions?)	1989	3.75	7.50	15.00
❏ 44-73179	911 Is a Joke (vocal & instrumental)/Revolutionary Generation (vocal & instrumental)	1990	3.00	6.00	12.00
❏ 44-73391	Brothers Gonna Work It Out (2 mixes)/Anti-Nigger Machine/Powersex/Power to the People	1990	3.00	6.00	12.00
❏ 44-73613	Can't Do Nuttin' For Ya Man (2 versions)/Get the F___ Outta Dodge/Burn Hollywood Burn	1990	3.00	6.00	12.00
❏ 44-73869	Can't Truss It (3 mixes)/Move!	1991	3.00	6.00	12.00
❏ 44-74165	Shut 'Em Down (4 versions)/By the Time I Get to Arizona	1992	3.75	7.50	15.00
❏ 44-74254	Nighttrain (4 mixes)/More News at 11	1992	3.75	7.50	15.00
❏ 42-74487	Hazy Shade of Criminal (LP Version) (Instrumental) (Acappella)/Tie Goes to the Runner (LP Version) (Instrumental)	1992	3.00	6.00	12.00
❏ 568927-1	Resurrection (Radio Edit) (LP Version) (Instrumental)/He Got Game (Flava's Radio Edit) (Flava's Edit) (Instrumental)	1998	2.50	5.00	10.00
❏ 853317-1	Give It Up (Main Version 4:44) (Instrumental 4:44)//Live and Undrugged Pt. 2 (2:36)//Give It Up (Dirty Drums in Memphis Mixx 5:17)/Bedlam (Vocal 4:13) (Instrumental 4:13)	1994	3.00	6.00	12.00
❏ 853939-1	What Kind of Power We Got (3 versions)/Mao Tse-Tung (2 versions)/I Stand Accused (3 versions)	1995	3.00	6.00	12.00

MCA

Number	Title (A Side/B Side)	Yr	VG	VG+	NM
❏ MCA8P-2586 [DJ]	Livin' in a Zoo (4 versions)	1992	5.00	10.00	20.00

MOTOWN

Number	Title (A Side/B Side)	Yr	VG	VG+	NM
❏ 4647	Fight the Power (Extended) (Radio Edit) (Flavor Flav Meets Spike Lee Version)	1989	2.50	5.00	10.00
❏ L33-17878 [DJ]	Fight the Power (same on both sides?)	1989	2.00	4.00	8.00

PERSPECTIVE

Number	Title (A Side/B Side)	Yr	VG	VG+	NM
❏ 28968 1723 1	Get Off My Back (4 versions)	1992	3.00	6.00	12.00

45s
DEF JAM

Number	Title (A Side/B Side)	Yr	VG	VG+	NM
❏ 38-06670	Public Enemy #1/(B-side unknown)	1987	—	3.00	6.00
❏ 38-07222	You're Gonna Get Yours/Miuzi Weighs a Ton	1987	—	3.00	6.00
❏ WS4-07934	Don't Believe the Hype/Prophets of Rage	1988	—	2.00	4.00
❏ 38-08072	Night of the Living Baseheads/Cold Lampin' With Flavor	1988	—	2.50	5.00
❏ 38-08072 [PS]	Night of the Living Baseheads/Cold Lampin' With Flavor	1988	—	3.00	6.00

Number	Title (A Side/B Side)	Yr	VG	VG+	NM
❏ 38-68613	Black Steel in the Hour of Chaos/Caught, Can We Get a Witness	1989	—	2.50	5.00

MOTOWN

Number	Title (A Side/B Side)	Yr	VG	VG+	NM
❏ 1972	Fight the Power/(Flavor Flav Meets Spike Lee Version)	1989	—	2.50	5.00

Albums

ATOMIC POP

Number	Title (A Side/B Side)	Yr	VG	VG+	NM
❏ 0001 [(2)]	There's a Poison Goin' On	1999	6.25	12.50	25.00
—Red vinyl					

DEF JAM

Number	Title (A Side/B Side)	Yr	VG	VG+	NM
❏ BFC 40658	Yo! Bum Rush the Show	1987	3.00	6.00	12.00
❏ BFW 44303	It Takes a Nation of Millions to Hold Us Back	1988	3.00	6.00	12.00
❏ C 45413	Fear of a Black Planet	1990	3.00	6.00	12.00
❏ C2 47374 [(2)]	Apocalypse 91... The Enemy Strikes Black	1991	3.75	7.50	15.00
❏ C2 53014 [(2)]	Greatest Misses	1993	3.75	7.50	15.00
❏ 523362-1 [(2)]	Muse Sick-N-Hour Mess Age	1994	2.50	5.00	10.00
❏ 558130-1 [(2)]	He Got Game	1998	3.75	7.50	15.00

PURDIE, BERNARD
Albums

DATE

Number	Title (A Side/B Side)	Yr	VG	VG+	NM
❏ TEM 3006 [M]	Soul Drums	1967	5.00	10.00	20.00
❏ TES 4006 [S]	Soul Drums	1967	5.00	10.00	20.00

PRESTIGE

Number	Title (A Side/B Side)	Yr	VG	VG+	NM
❏ 10013	Purdie Good	1971	3.75	7.50	15.00
❏ 10038	Shaft	1972	5.00	10.00	20.00

PURIFY, JAMES AND BOBBY
45s
BELL

Number	Title (A Side/B Side)	Yr	VG	VG+	NM
❏ 648	I'm Your Puppet/So Many Reasons	1966	3.75	7.50	15.00
❏ 660	Wish You Didn't Have to Go/You Can't Keep a Good Man Down	1967	2.00	4.00	8.00
❏ 669	Shake a Tail Feather/Goodness Gracious	1967	3.00	6.00	12.00
❏ 680	I Take What I Want/Sixteen Tons	1967	2.00	4.00	8.00
❏ 685	Let Love Come Between Us/I Don't Want to Have to Wait	1967	2.00	4.00	8.00
❏ 700	Do Unto Me/Everybody Needs Somebody	1967	2.00	4.00	8.00
❏ 721	I Can Remember/I Was Born to Lose Out	1968	2.00	4.00	8.00
❏ 735	Help Yourself (To All of My Lovin')/Last Piece of Love	1968	2.00	4.00	8.00
❏ 751	Untie Me/We're Finally Gonna Make It	1968	2.00	4.00	8.00
❏ 774	I Don't Know What It Is You Got/Section C	1969	2.00	4.00	8.00

CASABLANCA

Number	Title (A Side/B Side)	Yr	VG	VG+	NM
❏ 812	Do Your Thing/Why Love	1974	—	2.50	5.00
❏ 827	Man Can't Be a Man Without a Woman/You and Me Together Forever	1975	—	2.50	5.00
❏ 830	All the Love I Got/(B-side unknown)	1975	—	2.50	5.00

MERCURY

Number	Title (A Side/B Side)	Yr	VG	VG+	NM
❏ 73767	I'm Your Puppet/Lay Me Down Easy	1976	—	2.50	5.00
❏ 73806	Morning Glory/Turning Back the Pages	1976	—	2.50	5.00
❏ 73884	I Ain't Got to Love Nobody Else/What's Better Than Love	1977	—	2.50	5.00
❏ 73893	Get Closer/What's Better Than Love	1977	—	2.50	5.00

PHILCO-FORD

Number	Title (A Side/B Side)	Yr	VG	VG+	NM
❏ HP-28	I'm Your Puppet/Goodnight Gracious	1968	3.75	7.50	15.00
—4-inch plastic "Hip Pocket Record" with color sleeve					

SPHERE SOUND

Number	Title (A Side/B Side)	Yr	VG	VG+	NM
❏ 77004	I'm Your Puppet/Everybody Needs Somebody	196?	2.00	4.00	8.00

Albums

BELL

Number	Title (A Side/B Side)	Yr	VG	VG+	NM
❏ 6003 [M]	James and Bobby Purify	1966	6.25	12.50	25.00
❏ S-6003 [S]	James and Bobby Purify	1966	7.50	15.00	30.00
❏ 6010 [M]	The Pure Sound of the Purifys	1967	6.25	12.50	25.00
❏ S-6010 [S]	The Pure Sound of the Purifys	1967	7.50	15.00	30.00

MERCURY

Number	Title (A Side/B Side)	Yr	VG	VG+	NM
❏ SRM-1-1134	The Purify Brothers	1977	3.00	6.00	12.00

P

Number	Title (A Side/B Side)	Yr	VG	VG+	NM

Q

Q-FEEL
12-Inch Singles
JIVE

Number	Title (A Side/B Side)	Yr	VG	VG+	NM
❏ 1221-1-JD	Dancing in Heaven (Orbital Be-Bop) (6 versions)/ At the Top (All the Way to St. Tropez)	1989	2.00	4.00	8.00

JIVE/ARISTA

Number	Title (A Side/B Side)	Yr	VG	VG+	NM
❏ VJ 12004	Dancing in Heaven (Orbital Be-Bop) (2 versions)	1983	2.50	5.00	10.00

45s
JIVE

Number	Title (A Side/B Side)	Yr	VG	VG+	NM
❏ 1220-7-J	Dancing in Heaven (Orbital Be-Bop)/At the Top (All the Way to St. Tropez)	1989	—	—	3.00
❏ 1220-7-J [PS]	Dancing in Heaven (Orbital Be-Bop)/At the Top (All the Way to St. Tropez)	1989	—	—	3.00

JIVE/ARISTA

Number	Title (A Side/B Side)	Yr	VG	VG+	NM
❏ 2001	Dancing in Heaven (Orbital Be-Bop)/At the Top (All the Way to St. Tropez)	1983	—	2.50	5.00

Albums
JIVE/ARISTA

Number	Title (A Side/B Side)	Yr	VG	VG+	NM
❏ VA 66005	Q-Feel	1983	3.00	6.00	12.00

Q-TIP
12-Inch Singles
ARISTA

Number	Title (A Side/B Side)	Yr	VG	VG+	NM
❏ 3821	Let's Ride (Radio Mix) (Club Mix) (Instrumental)/ Higher (Club Mix) (Instrumental)	2000	2.50	5.00	10.00

VIOLATOR

Number	Title (A Side/B Side)	Yr	VG	VG+	NM
❏ 562170-1	Vivrant Thing//Do What Playas Do/You Know Why	1999	2.00	4.00	8.00

Albums
ARISTA

Number	Title (A Side/B Side)	Yr	VG	VG+	NM
❏ 14619 [(2)]	Amplified	1999	3.75	7.50	15.00

QKUMBA ZOO
12-Inch Singles
ARISTA

Number	Title (A Side/B Side)	Yr	VG	VG+	NM
❏ 3252 [(2)]	The Child (Inside) (8 versions)	1996	2.50	5.00	10.00
❏ 3303	I'm Scared, You're Scared (3 versions)/Cloud Eyes	1997	2.00	4.00	8.00
❏ 3377	I'm Scared, You're Scared (4 versions)	1997	2.00	4.00	8.00

45s
ARISTA

Number	Title (A Side/B Side)	Yr	VG	VG+	NM
❏ 13259	The Child (Inside)/The Child (Inside) (Remix)	1996	—	—	3.00

Albums
ARISTA

Number	Title (A Side/B Side)	Yr	VG	VG+	NM
❏ ADP 3251 [EP]	Qkumka Zoo	1996	2.50	5.00	10.00

—Five-song promo-only sampler

QT
12-Inch Singles
ROWDY

Number	Title (A Side/B Side)	Yr	VG	VG+	NM
❏ 35094	My Baby Mama (6 versions)	1996	2.50	5.00	10.00

QUAD CITY DJ'S
12-Inch Singles
BIG BEAT

Number	Title (A Side/B Side)	Yr	VG	VG+	NM
❏ (# unknown)	C'mon N' Ride It (The Train) (unknown versions)	1996	2.00	4.00	8.00
❏ DMD 2332 [DJ]	Space Jam (4 versions)	1996	2.00	4.00	8.00
❏ DMD 2409 [DJ]	Let's Do It (5 versions?)	1997	2.50	5.00	10.00
❏ DMD 2424 [DJ]	Summer Jam (6 versions)	1997	2.50	5.00	10.00
❏ 95571	Summer Jam (unknown versions)	1997	2.00	4.00	8.00

WARNER SUNSET

Number	Title (A Side/B Side)	Yr	VG	VG+	NM
❏ 85454	Space Jam (5 versions)	1996	—	3.50	7.00

Albums
BIG BEAT

Number	Title (A Side/B Side)	Yr	VG	VG+	NM
❏ 82905 [(2)]	Get On Up and Dance	1996	2.50	5.00	10.00

QUEEN LATIFAH
12-Inch Singles
MOTOWN

Number	Title (A Side/B Side)	Yr	VG	VG+	NM
❏ 37463 1136 1	U.N.I.T.Y. (Censored Version) (LP Version) (Instrumental)	1993	3.00	6.00	12.00
❏ 37463 1149 1	U.N.I.T.Y. (7 versions)	1993	3.00	6.00	12.00
❏ 37463 1158 1	Just Another Day (8 versions)	1994	3.75	7.50	15.00
❏ 37463 1167 1	U.N.I.T.Y. (6 versions)	1994	3.00	6.00	12.00
❏ 37463 1169 1	Just Another Day (5 versions)	1994	3.00	6.00	12.00
❏ 37463 1174 1	Black Hand Side (LP Version) (Radio Version Censored)/(Instrumental) (A Cappella)	1994	3.75	7.50	15.00
❏ 37463 1196 1	Black Hand Side (Al's Remix Edit) (Jay's Lab Groove) (Al's Remix Extended)//Weekend Love (LP Version) (Instrumental)/Black Hand Side (A Cappella)	1994	3.75	7.50	15.00
❏ 37463 3006 1	Paper (Radio Without Talk) (Radio) (Instrumental) (Acappella)	1998	3.75	7.50	15.00
❏ 37463 3044 1	Bananas (Radio Version) (LP Version) (Instrumental) (Acappella)	1998	3.00	6.00	12.00

—Featuring Apache

Number	Title (A Side/B Side)	Yr	VG	VG+	NM
❏ 37463 3047 1	Bananas (4 versions)	1998	2.50	5.00	10.00

—Featuring Apache

Number	Title (A Side/B Side)	Yr	VG	VG+	NM
❏ 37463 4847 1	U.N.I.T.Y. (Big Titty Mix Uncensored) (LP Version) (Remix Instrumental)/(Beat-apella) (Bonus Beats) (Acapella)	1993	2.50	5.00	10.00
❏ 37463 4857 1	Black Hand Side (3 versions)/Weekend Love (2 versions)	1994	3.75	7.50	15.00

TOMMY BOY

Number	Title (A Side/B Side)	Yr	VG	VG+	NM
❏ TB 402	It's Alright (4 versions)	1997	2.50	5.00	10.00
❏ TB 506	Latifah's Had It Up 2 Here (4 versions)/That's the Way We Flow	1991	3.00	6.00	12.00
❏ TB 515	How Do I Love Thee (2 versions)	1993	3.00	6.00	12.00
❏ TB 524	How Do I Love Thee (6 versions)	1992	3.00	6.00	12.00
❏ TB 527	How Do I Love Thee (Extended Mix) (Deep House Mix)	1992	3.75	7.50	15.00
❏ TB 922	Dance for Me (2 versions)/Inside Out (3 versions)	1989	3.00	6.00	12.00
❏ TB 942	Ladies First (5 versions)	1989	3.00	6.00	12.00

—Featuring Monie Love

Number	Title (A Side/B Side)	Yr	VG	VG+	NM
❏ TB 948	Come Into My House (5 versions)/Latifah's Law	1990	2.50	5.00	10.00
❏ TB 991	Fly Girl (3 versions)/Nature of a Sista	1991	3.00	6.00	12.00

Albums
MOTOWN

Number	Title (A Side/B Side)	Yr	VG	VG+	NM
❏ 37463 0895 1 [DJ]	Order in the Court	1998	3.75	7.50	15.00

—Promo-only eight-song sampler from LP

Number	Title (A Side/B Side)	Yr	VG	VG+	NM
❏ 530895-1 [(2)]	Order in the Court	1998	3.75	7.50	15.00

TOMMY BOY

Number	Title (A Side/B Side)	Yr	VG	VG+	NM
❏ TB 1022	All Hail the Queen	1989	3.75	7.50	15.00
❏ TB 1035	Nature of a Sista'	1991	3.75	7.50	15.00

QUIN-TONES, THE
45s
HUNT

Number	Title (A Side/B Side)	Yr	VG	VG+	NM
❏ 321	Down the Aisle of Love/Please Dear	1958	12.50	25.00	50.00
❏ 322	There'll Be No Sorrow/What Am I to Do	1958	15.00	30.00	60.00

RED TOP

Number	Title (A Side/B Side)	Yr	VG	VG+	NM
❏ 108	Down the Aisle of Love/Please Dear	1958	30.00	60.00	120.00

—Red label

Number	Title (A Side/B Side)	Yr	VG	VG+	NM
❏ 108	Down the Aisle of Love/Please Dear	1958	10.00	20.00	40.00
❏ 116	Heavenly Father/I Watch the Stars	1959	25.00	50.00	100.00

QUINTONES, THE (1)
45s
CHESS

Number	Title (A Side/B Side)	Yr	VG	VG+	NM
❏ 1685	I Try So Hard/Ding Dong	1957	10.00	20.00	40.00

QUINTONES, THE (2)
45s
GEE

Number	Title (A Side/B Side)	Yr	VG	VG+	NM
❏ 1009	I'm Willing/Strange As It Seems	1956	250.00	500.00	1000.

QUINTONES, THE (3)
45s
PHILLIPS INT'L.

Number	Title (A Side/B Side)	Yr	VG	VG+	NM
❏ 3586	Times Sho' Gettin' Ruff/Softie	1963	5.00	10.00	20.00

QUINTONES, THE (U)
45s
PARK

Number	Title (A Side/B Side)	Yr	VG	VG+	NM
❏ 111/2	South Sea Island/More Than a Notion	1957	100.00	200.00	400.00

78s
JORDAN

Number	Title (A Side/B Side)	Yr	VG	VG+	NM
❏ 1601	The Lonely Telephone/Just a Little Loving	1956	300.00	600.00	1200.

QUOTATIONS, THE
Several different groups.
45s
ADMIRAL

Number	Title (A Side/B Side)	Yr	VG	VG+	NM
❏ 753	In the Night/Oh No, I Still Love Her	1964	5.00	10.00	20.00

DEVENUS

Number	Title (A Side/B Side)	Yr	VG	VG+	NM
❏ 107	It Can Happen to You/You Don't Have to Worry	1968	3.00	6.00	12.00

DOWNSTAIRS

Number	Title (A Side/B Side)	Yr	VG	VG+	NM
❏ 1003	Night/Why Do You Do Me Like You Do	1970	2.00	4.00	8.00

IMPERIAL

Number	Title (A Side/B Side)	Yr	VG	VG+	NM
❏ 66338	Havin' a Good Time/Can I Have Someone	1968	2.50	5.00	10.00
❏ 66368	Havin' a Good Time (With My Baby)/Can I Have Someone (For Once)	1969	2.50	5.00	10.00

LIBERTY

Number	Title (A Side/B Side)	Yr	VG	VG+	NM
❏ 55527	Listen, My Children, And You Shall Hear/Speak Softly and Carry a Big Horn	1962	6.25	12.50	25.00

VERVE

Number	Title (A Side/B Side)	Yr	VG	VG+	NM
❏ 10245	Imagination/Ala-Men-Say	1961	7.50	15.00	30.00
❏ 10252	This Love of Mine/We'll Reach Heaven Together	1962	7.50	15.00	30.00
❏ 10261	See You in September/Sumemrtime Goodbye	1962	12.50	25.00	50.00

Number	Title (A Side/B Side)	Yr	VG	VG+	NM

R

RADIANTS, THE
45s
ABC

❑ 12394	I Need a Vacation/Just Like You	1978	—	2.50	5.00

CHESS

❑ 1832	Father Knows Best/One Day I'll SHow You	1962	3.75	7.50	15.00
❑ 1849	Please Don't Leave Me/Heartbreak Society	1963	3.75	7.50	15.00
❑ 1872	I'm in Love/Shy Guy	1963	3.75	7.50	15.00
❑ 1887	Noble the Bargain Man/I Got to Dance to Keep My Baby	1964	3.75	7.50	15.00
❑ 1904	Voice Your Choice/If I Only Had You	1964	3.00	6.00	12.00
❑ 1925	It Ain't No Big Thing/I Got a Girl	1965	3.00	6.00	12.00
❑ 1939	Whole Lot of Love/Tomorrow	1965	3.00	6.00	12.00
❑ 1954	I Want to Thank You, Baby/Baby You've Got It	1966	3.00	6.00	12.00

—As "Maurice and the Radiants"

❑ 1986	(Don't It Make You) Feel Kind of Bad/Anything You Do Is Alright	1967	3.00	6.00	12.00
❑ 2021	Don't Take Your Love/The Clown Is Clever	1967	3.00	6.00	12.00
❑ 2037	Hold On/I'm Glad I'm the Loser	1968	3.00	6.00	12.00
❑ 2057	Tears of a Clown/I'm Just a Man	1968	3.00	6.00	12.00
❑ 2066	Choo Choo/Ida Mae Foster	1969	2.50	5.00	10.00
❑ 2078	Book of Love/Another Mule Is Kicking In Your Stall	1969	2.50	5.00	10.00
❑ 2083	I'm So Glad I'm the Loser/Shadow of a Doubt	1970	2.50	5.00	10.00

TWINIGHT

❑ 153	My Sunshine Girl/Don't Wanna Face the Truth	1971	2.00	4.00	8.00

RAELETTS, THE
Backing vocalists for RAY CHARLES.
45s
TANGERINE

❑ 972	One Hurt Deserves Another/One Room Paradise	1967	2.00	4.00	8.00
❑ 976	Into Something Fine/Lover's Blues	1967	2.00	4.00	8.00
❑ 984	I'm Gett'n Long Alright/All I Need Is His Love	1968	2.00	4.00	8.00
❑ 986	I Want to Thank You/It's Almost Here	1968	2.00	4.00	8.00
❑ 1006	I Want To (Do Everything for You)/Keep It to Yourself	1970	2.00	4.00	8.00
❑ 1014	Bad Water/That Goes to Show You	1970	2.00	4.00	8.00
❑ 1017	Here I Go Again/Leave My Man Alone	1971	2.00	4.00	8.00
❑ 1024	Come Get It, I Got It/Try a Little Kindness	197?	2.00	4.00	8.00
❑ 1029	You Must Be Doing Alright/You Have a Way with Me	197?	2.00	4.00	8.00
❑ 1031	Many Rivers to Cross/If You Wanna Keep Him	197?	2.00	4.00	8.00

Albums
TANGERINE

❑ TRCS-1515	Yesterday, Today, Tomorrow	1972	3.75	7.50	15.00

RAINBOWS, THE (1)
45s
ARGYLE

❑ 1012	Shirley/Stay	1962	6.25	12.50	25.00

FIRE

❑ 1012	Mary Lee/Evening	1960	5.00	10.00	20.00

PILGRIM

❑ 703	Mary Lee/Evening	1956	12.50	25.00	50.00
❑ 711	Shirley/Stay	1956	50.00	100.00	200.00

RAMA

❑ 209	Minnie/They Say	1956	150.00	300.00	600.00

RED ROBIN

❑ 134	Mary Lee/Evening	1955	150.00	300.00	600.00

—Note: Red Robin 141 is a bootleg

RANDY AND THE GYPSYS
See RANDY JACKSON.

RANDY AND THE RADIANTS
45s
SUN

❑ 395	The Mountain's High/Peek-a-Boo	1965	6.25	12.50	25.00
❑ 398	My Way of Thinking/Truth from My Eyes	1966	6.25	12.50	25.00

RANDY AND THE RAINBOWS
45s
AMBIENT SOUND

❑ 02872	Debbie/Try the Impossible	1982	—	2.50	5.00

B.T. PUPPY

❑ 535	I'll Be Seeing You/Oh to Get Away	1967	2.50	5.00	10.00

MIKE

❑ 4001	Lovely Lies/I'll Forget Her Tomorrow	1966	3.00	6.00	12.00
❑ 4004	Quarter to Three/He's a Fugitive	1966	3.00	6.00	12.00
❑ 4008	Bonnie's Part of Town/Can It Be	1966	3.00	6.00	12.00

RUST

❑ 5059	Denise/Come Back	1963	7.50	15.00	30.00

—Blue label

❑ 5059	Denise/Come Back	1963	5.00	10.00	20.00

—Mostly white label

❑ 5073	She's My Angel/Why Do Kids Grow Up	1964	3.75	7.50	15.00
❑ 5080	Happy Teenager/Dry Your Eyes	1964	3.75	7.50	15.00
❑ 5091	Little Star/Sharin'	1964	3.75	7.50	15.00
❑ 5101	Joy Ride/Little Hot Rod Suzie	1965	3.75	7.50	15.00

Albums
AMBIENT SOUND

❑ ASR-601	Remember	1985	3.00	6.00	12.00
❑ FZ 37715	C'mon, Let's Go	1982	3.00	6.00	12.00

RARE EARTH
45s
PRODIGAL

❑ 0637	Crazy Love/Is Your Teacher Cool	1977	—	2.50	5.00
❑ 0640	Warm Ride/Would You Like to Come Along	1978	—	2.50	5.00
❑ 0643	I Can Feel My Love Risin'/S.O.S. (Stop Her On Sight)	1978	—	2.50	5.00

RARE EARTH

❑ 960/961 [DJ]	What'd I Say (stereo/mono)	1972	6.25	12.50	25.00

—Blue vinyl, promo only, white label

❑ 5010	Generation (Light of the Sky)/Magic Key	1969	3.00	6.00	12.00
❑ 5012	Get Ready/Magic Key	1970	—	3.00	6.00
❑ 5017	(I Know) I'm Losing You/When Joanie Smiles	1970	—	3.00	6.00
❑ 5021	Born to Wander/Here Comes the Night	1970	—	3.00	6.00
❑ 5031	I Just Want to Celebrate/The Seed	1971	—	3.00	6.00
❑ 5031 [PS]	I Just Want to Celebrate/The Seed	1971	2.50	5.00	10.00
❑ 5038	Hey Big Brother/Under God's Light	1971	—	3.00	6.00
❑ 5043	What'd I Say/Nice to Be with You	1972	—	3.00	6.00
❑ 5048	Good Time Sally/Love Shines Down	1972	—	3.00	6.00
❑ 5052	We're Gonna Have a Good Time/Would You Like to Come Along	1973	—	3.00	6.00
❑ 5053	Ma/(Instrumental)	1973	—	3.00	6.00
❑ 5054	Hum Along and Dance/Come with Me	1973	—	3.00	6.00
❑ 5056	Big John Is My Name/Ma	1974	—	3.00	6.00
❑ 5057	Chained/Fresh from the Can	1974	—	3.00	6.00
❑ 5058	It Makes You Happy (But It Ain't Gonna Last Too Long)/Boogie with Me Children	1975	—	3.00	6.00
❑ 5059	Let Me Be Your Sunshine/Keep Me Out of the Storm	1976	—	3.00	6.00
❑ 5060	Midnight Lady/Walking Shtick	1976	—	3.00	6.00

RCA

❑ PB-13076	Howzabout Some Love/Let Me Take You Out	1982	—	—	—

—Unreleased

VERVE

❑ 10622	Stop-Where Did Our Love Go/Mother's Oats	1968	3.00	6.00	12.00

Albums
MOTOWN

❑ M5-116V1	Motown Superstar Series, Vol. 16	1981	2.50	5.00	10.00
❑ M5-202V1	Ecology	1981	2.00	4.00	8.00
❑ 5229 ML	Get Ready	1982	2.00	4.00	8.00

PRODIGAL

❑ P6-10019	Rare Earth	1977	2.50	5.00	10.00
❑ P7-10025	Band Together	1978	2.50	5.00	10.00
❑ P7-10027	Grand Slam	1979	2.50	5.00	10.00

RARE EARTH

❑ RS 507	Get Ready	1969	7.50	15.00	30.00

—Original cover has a rounded top

❑ RS 507	Get Ready	1970	3.00	6.00	12.00

—Regular square cover

❑ RS 510	Generation	1970	—	—	—

—Canceled

❑ RS 514	Ecology	1970	3.75	7.50	15.00
❑ RS 520	One World	1971	3.75	7.50	15.00
❑ R 534 [(2)]	Rare Earth in Concert	1971	3.75	7.50	15.00
❑ R 543	Willie Remembers	1972	3.00	6.00	12.00
❑ R6-546	Ma	1973	3.00	6.00	12.00
❑ R6-548	Back to Earth	1975	3.00	6.00	12.00
❑ R7-550	Midnight Lady	1976	3.00	6.00	12.00

VERVE

❑ V6-5066	Dreams/Answers	1968	12.50	25.00	50.00

RASCALS, THE
Includes "The Young Rascals."
45s
ATLANTIC

❑ 2312	I Ain't Gonna Eat Out My Heart Anymore/Slow Down	1965	3.75	7.50	15.00

—From here through Atlantic 2463, as "The Young Rascals"

❑ 2321	Good Lovin'/Mustang Sally	1966	3.75	7.50	15.00
❑ 2338	You Better Run/Love Is a Beautiful Thing	1966	2.50	5.00	10.00
❑ 2338 [PS]	You Better Run/Love Is a Beautiful Thing	1966	5.00	10.00	20.00
❑ 2353	Come On Up/What Is the Reason	1966	2.50	5.00	10.00
❑ 2377	I've Been Lonely Too Long/If You Knew	1967	2.50	5.00	10.00
❑ 2377 [PS]	I've Been Lonely Too Long/If You Knew	1967	5.00	10.00	20.00
❑ 2401	Groovin'/Sueno	1967	2.00	4.00	8.00
❑ 2401 [PS]	Groovin'/Sueno	1967	5.00	10.00	20.00
❑ 2424	A Girl Like You/It's Love	1967	2.00	4.00	8.00
❑ 2424 [PS]	A Girl Like You/It's Love	1967	5.00	10.00	20.00
❑ 2428	Groovin' (Spanish)/Groovin' (Italian)	1967	5.00	10.00	20.00
❑ 2438	How Can I Be Sure/I'm So Happy Now	1967	2.00	4.00	8.00
❑ 2463	It's Wonderful/Of Course	1967	2.00	4.00	8.00
❑ 2493	A Beautiful Morning/Rainy Day	1968	—	3.00	6.00

—First record as "The Rascals"

❑ 2493 [PS]	A Beautiful Morning/Rainy Day	1968	5.00	10.00	20.00
❑ 2537	People Got to Be Free/My World	1968	—	3.00	6.00
❑ 2537 [PS]	People Got to Be Free/My World	1968	3.00	6.00	12.00
❑ 2584	A Ray of Hope/Any Dance'll Do	1968	—	3.00	6.00
❑ 2584 [PS]	A Ray of Hope/Any Dance'll Do	1968	3.00	6.00	12.00
❑ 2599	Heaven/Baby I'm Blue	1969	—	3.00	6.00

R

Number	Title (A Side/B Side)	Yr	VG	VG+	NM
❑ 2634	See/Away Away	1969	—	3.00	6.00
❑ 2634 [PS]	See/Away Away	1969	3.00	6.00	12.00
❑ 2664	Carry Me Back/Real Thing	1969	—	3.00	6.00
❑ 2664 [PS]	Carry Me Back/Real Thing	1969	3.00	6.00	12.00
❑ 2695	Hold On/I Believe	1969	—	3.00	6.00
❑ 2695 [PS]	Hold On/I Believe	1969	3.00	6.00	12.00
❑ 2743	Glory Glory/You Don't Know	1970	—	3.00	6.00
❑ 2743 [PS]	Glory Glory/You Don't Know	1970	3.00	6.00	12.00
❑ 2773	Right On/Almost Home	1970	—	3.00	6.00
COLUMBIA					
❑ 45400	Love Me/Happy Song	1971	—	3.00	6.00
❑ 45491	Lucky Day/Love Letter	1971	—	3.00	6.00
❑ 45568	Brother Tree/Saga of New York	1972	—	3.00	6.00
❑ 45600	Echoes/Hummin' Song	1972	—	3.00	6.00
❑ 45649	Jungle Walk/Saga of New York	1972	2.50	5.00	10.00
PHILCO-FORD					
❑ HP-18	A Girl Like You/I've Been Lonely Too Long	1967	3.75	7.50	15.00
—4-inch plastic "Hip Pocket Record" with color sleeve					
7-Inch Extended Plays					
ATLANTIC					
❑ SD 7-8169	Please Love Me/It's Wonderful/I'm Gonna Love You//Easy Rollin'/Rainy Day	1968	5.00	10.00	20.00
—Jukebox issue; small hole, plays at 33 1/3 rpm					
❑ SD 7-8169 [PS]	Once Upon a Dream	1968	5.00	10.00	20.00
Albums					
ATLANTIC					
❑ ST-137 [DJ]	Freedom Suite Sampler	1969	12.50	25.00	50.00
❑ SD 2-901 [(2)]	Freedom Suite	1969	5.00	10.00	20.00
❑ 8123 [M]	The Young Rascals	1966	7.50	15.00	30.00
❑ SD 8123 [S]	The Young Rascals	1966	10.00	20.00	40.00
—Green and blue label					
❑ SD 8123 [S]	The Young Rascals	1966	12.50	25.00	50.00
—Purple and green label					
❑ SD 8123 [S]	The Young Rascals	1969	3.00	6.00	12.00
—Red and green label					
❑ 8134 [M]	Collections	1967	6.25	12.50	25.00
❑ SD 8134 [S]	Collections	1967	7.50	15.00	30.00
—Green and blue label					
❑ SD 8134 [S]	Collections	1969	3.00	6.00	12.00
—Red and green label					
❑ 8148 [M]	Groovin'	1967	6.25	12.50	25.00
❑ SD 8148 [S]	Groovin'	1967	7.50	15.00	30.00
—Green and blue label					
❑ SD 8148 [S]	Groovin'	1969	3.00	6.00	12.00
—Red and green label					
❑ 8169 [M]	Once Upon a Dream	1968	10.00	20.00	40.00
❑ SD 8169 [S]	Once Upon a Dream	1968	6.25	12.50	25.00
—Green and blue label					
❑ SD 8169 [S]	Once Upon a Dream	1969	3.00	6.00	12.00
—Red and green label					
❑ 8190 [M]	Time Peace/The Rascals' Greatest Hits	1968	12.50	25.00	50.00
—Mono is promo only					
❑ SD 8190 [S]	Time Peace/The Rascals' Greatest Hits	1968	6.25	12.50	25.00
—Green and blue label					
❑ SD 8190 [S]	Time Peace/The Rascals' Greatest Hits	1968	3.75	7.50	15.00
—Purple and gold label					
❑ SD 8190 [S]	Time Peace/The Rascals' Greatest Hits	1969	3.00	6.00	12.00
—Red and green label					
❑ SD 8246	See	1969	3.75	7.50	15.00
❑ SD 8276	Search and Nearness	1970	3.75	7.50	15.00
COLUMBIA					
❑ G 30462 [(2)]	Peaceful World	1971	3.75	7.50	15.00
❑ KC 31103	The Island of Real	1972	3.00	6.00	12.00
PAIR					
❑ PDL2-1106 [(2)]	Rock and Roll Treasures	1986	3.75	7.50	15.00
RHINO					
❑ RNLP 70237	The Young Rascals	1988	2.50	5.00	10.00
❑ RNLP 70238	Collections	1988	2.50	5.00	10.00
❑ RNLP 70239	Groovin'	1988	2.50	5.00	10.00
❑ R1-70240	Once Upon a Dream	1988	2.50	5.00	10.00
❑ R1-70241	Freedom Suite	1988	2.50	5.00	10.00
❑ R1-70242	Searching for Ecstasy: The Rest of the Rascals 1969-1972	1988	2.50	5.00	10.00
SUNDAZED					
❑ LP 5116	The Young Rascals	2002	3.00	6.00	12.00
❑ LP 5117	Collections	2002	3.00	6.00	12.00
❑ LP 5118	Groovin'	2002	3.00	6.00	12.00
❑ LP 5119	Once Upon a Dream	2002	3.00	6.00	12.00
WARNER SPECIAL PRODUCTS					
❑ SP-2502 [(2)]	24 Greatest Hits	1971	5.00	10.00	20.00
WES FARRELL					
❑ PFT-1002 [DJ]	Songs from the Rascals	197?	6.25	12.50	25.00
—Promo-only publisher's demo					

RAVENS, THE

Also see JIMMY RICKS.

Number	Title (A Side/B Side)	Yr	VG	VG+	NM
45s					
ARGO					
❑ 5255	Kneel and Pray/I Can't Believe	1956	10.00	20.00	40.00
❑ 5261	A Simple Prayer/Water Boy	1956	20.00	40.00	80.00
❑ 5276	That'll Be the Day/Dear One	1957	7.50	15.00	30.00
❑ 5284	Here Is My Heart/Lazy Mule	1957	7.50	15.00	30.00
CHECKER					
❑ 871	That'll Be the Day/Dear One	1957	5.00	10.00	20.00
COLUMBIA					
❑ 1-903	Don't Look Now/Time Takes Care of Everything	1950	375.00	750.00	1500.
—Microgroove 33 1/3 single					
❑ 6-903	Don't Look Now/Time Takes Care of Everything	1950	175.00	350.00	700.00
❑ 1-925	My Baby's Gone/I'm So Crazy for Love	1950	375.00	750.00	1500.
—Microgroove 33 1/3 single					
❑ 6-925	My Baby's Gone/I'm So Crazy for Love	1950	150.00	300.00	600.00
❑ 4-39112	You Don't Have to Drop a Heart/Midnight Blues	1950	500.00	1000.	2000.
❑ 4-39194	You're Always in My Dreams/Gotta Find My Baby	1951	500.00	1000.	2000.
❑ 4-39408	You Foolish Thing/Honey I Don't Want You	1951	500.00	1000.	2000.
JUBILEE					
❑ 45-5184	Bye Bye Baby Blues/Happy Go Lucky Baby	1955	7.50	15.00	30.00
❑ 45-5203	Green Eyes/The Bells of San Rafael	1955	7.50	15.00	30.00
—As "Jimmy Ricks and the Ravens"					
❑ 45-5217	On Chapel Hill/We'll Raise a Ruckus Tonight	1955	7.50	15.00	30.00
❑ 45-5237	I'll Always Be in Love with You/(Take Me Back To My) Boots and Saddles	1956	7.50	15.00	30.00
—As "Jimmy Ricks and the Ravens"					
MERCURY					
❑ 5764x45	There's No Use Pretending/Wagon Wheels	1951	75.00	150.00	300.00
❑ 5800x45	Begin the Beguine/Looking for My Baby	1952	62.50	125.00	250.00
❑ 5853x45	Why Did You Leave Me/Chloe	1952	62.50	125.00	250.00
❑ 8259x45	There's No Use Pretending/Wagon Wheels	1951	100.00	200.00	400.00
❑ 8291x45	Rock Me All Night Long/One Sweet Letter	1952	37.50	75.00	150.00
❑ 70060x45	I'll Be Back/Don't Mention My Name	1953	50.00	100.00	200.00
❑ 70119x45	Come a Little Bit Closer/She's Got to Go	1953	37.50	75.00	150.00
❑ 70213x45	Who'll Be the Fool/Rough Ridin'	1953	37.50	75.00	150.00
❑ 70240x45	Without a Song/Walkin' My Blues Away	1953	37.50	75.00	150.00
❑ 70307x45	September Song/Escortin' Or Courtin'	1954	37.50	75.00	150.00
❑ 70330x45	Going Home/Lonesome Road	1954	37.50	75.00	150.00
❑ 70413x45	I've Got You Under My Skin/Love Is No Dream	1954	62.50	125.00	250.00
—Pink label					
❑ 70413x45	I've Got You Under My Skin/Love Is No Dream	1954	25.00	50.00	100.00
—Black label					
❑ 70505x45	White Christmas/Silent Night	1954	50.00	100.00	200.00
—Pink label					
❑ 70505x45	White Christmas/Silent Night	1954	25.00	50.00	100.00
—Black label					
❑ 70554x45	Ol' Man River/Write Me a Letter	1955	50.00	100.00	200.00
—Pink label					
❑ 70554x45	Ol' Man River/Write Me a Letter	1955	25.00	50.00	100.00
—Black label					
NATIONAL					
❑ 9111x45	Count Every Star/I'm Gonna Paper All My Walls with Your Love	1950	1500.	2250.	3000.
—The only known Ravens single on a National 45					
OKEH					
❑ 6825	The Whiffenpoof Song/I Get All My Lovin' on a Saturday Night	1951	125.00	250.00	500.00
❑ 6843	That Old Gang of Mine/Everything But You	1951	125.00	250.00	500.00
❑ 6888	Mam'selle/Calypso Song	1952	100.00	200.00	400.00
SAVOY					
❑ 1540	White Christmas/Silent Night	1958	5.00	10.00	20.00
TOP RANK					
❑ 2003	Into the Shadows/The Rising Sun	1959	6.25	12.50	25.00
❑ 2016	Solitude/Hole in the Middle of the Moon	1959	6.25	12.50	25.00
78s					
ARGO					
❑ 5255	Kneel and Pray/I Can't Believe	1956	15.00	30.00	60.00
❑ 5261	A Simple Prayer/Water Boy	1956	25.00	50.00	100.00
❑ 5276	That'll Be the Day/Dear One	1957	15.00	30.00	60.00
❑ 5284	Here Is My Heart/Lazy Mule	1957	15.00	30.00	60.00
CHECKER					
❑ 871	That'll Be the Day/Dear One	1957	10.00	20.00	40.00
COLUMBIA					
❑ 39050	Don't Look Now/Time Takes Care of Everything	1950	37.50	75.00	150.00
❑ 39070	My Baby's Gone/I'm So Crazy for Love	1950	37.50	75.00	150.00
❑ 39112	You Don't Have to Drop a Heart/Midnight Blues	1950	50.00	100.00	200.00
❑ 39194	You're Always in My Dreams/Gotta Find My Baby	1951	50.00	100.00	200.00
❑ 39408	You Foolish Thing/Honey I Don't Want You	1951	50.00	100.00	200.00
HUB					
❑ 3030	Lullaby/Honey	1946	37.50	75.00	150.00
❑ 3032	Out of a Dream/My Sugar Is So Refined	1946	30.00	60.00	120.00
❑ 3033	Bye Bye Baby Blues/Once and For All	1946	30.00	60.00	120.00
JUBILEE					
❑ 5184	Bye Bye Baby Blues/Happy Go Lucky Baby	1955	7.50	15.00	30.00
❑ 5203	Green Eyes/The Bells of San Rafael	1955	7.50	15.00	30.00
—As "Jimmy Ricks and the Ravens"					
❑ 5217	On Chapel Hill/We'll Raise a Ruckus Tonight	1955	7.50	15.00	30.00
❑ 5237	I'll Always Be in Love with You/(Take Me Back To My) Boots and Saddles	1956	7.50	15.00	30.00
—As "Jimmy Ricks and the Ravens"					
KING					
❑ 4234	Bye Bye Baby Blues/Once and For All	1948	20.00	40.00	80.00
❑ 4260	Out of a Dream/Blues in the Clouds	1948	20.00	40.00	80.00
—B-side by the Three Clouds					
❑ 4272	Honey/Matinee Hour in New Orleans	1949	20.00	40.00	80.00
—B-side by the Three Clouds					
❑ 4293	My Sugar Is So Refined/Playing Around	1949	20.00	40.00	80.00
—B-side by the Three Clouds					
MERCURY					
❑ 5764	There's No Use Pretending/Wagon Wheels	1951	12.50	25.00	50.00
❑ 5800	Begin the Beguine/Looking for My Baby	1952	12.50	25.00	50.00
❑ 5853	Why Did You Leave Me/Chloe	1952	12.50	25.00	50.00

Number	Title (A Side/B Side)	Yr	VG	VG+	NM
❏ 8259	There's No Use Pretending/Wagon Wheels	1951	15.00	30.00	60.00
❏ 8291	Rock Me All Night Long/One Sweet Letter	1952	10.00	20.00	40.00
❏ 70060	I'll Be Back/Don't Mention My Name	1953	10.00	20.00	40.00
❏ 70119	Come a Little Bit Closer/She's Got to Go	1953	10.00	20.00	40.00
❏ 70213	Who'll Be the Fool/Rough Ridin'	1953	10.00	20.00	40.00
❏ 70240	Without a Song/Walkin' My Blues Away	1953	10.00	20.00	40.00
❏ 70307	September Song/Escortin' Or Courtin'	1954	10.00	20.00	40.00
❏ 70330	Going Home/Lonesome Road	1954	10.00	20.00	40.00
❏ 70413	I've Got You Under My Skin/Love Is No Dream	1954	7.50	15.00	30.00
❏ 70505	White Christmas/Silent Night	1954	7.50	15.00	30.00
❏ 70554	Ol' Man River/Write Me a Letter	1955	7.50	15.00	30.00

NATIONAL

Number	Title (A Side/B Side)	Yr	VG	VG+	NM
❏ 9034	For You/Marzel Means Good Luck	1947	25.00	50.00	100.00
❏ 9035	Ol' Man River/Would You Believe Me	1947	25.00	50.00	100.00
❏ 9038	Write Me a Letter/Summertime	1947	25.00	50.00	100.00
❏ 9039	Searching for Love/For You	1948	25.00	50.00	100.00
❏ 9040	Be I Bumble or Not/Fool That I Am	1948	25.00	50.00	100.00
❏ 9042	Together/There's No You	1948	25.00	50.00	100.00
❏ 9045	Send for Me If You Need Me/Until the Real Thing Comes Along	1948	25.00	50.00	100.00
❏ 9053	September Song/Once in a While	1948	25.00	50.00	100.00
❏ 9056	It's Too Soon to Know/Be On Your Merry Way	1948	25.00	50.00	100.00
❏ 9059	I Don't Know Why I Love You Like I Do/How Could I Know	1948	25.00	50.00	100.00
❏ 9062	White Christmas/Silent Night	1948	25.00	50.00	100.00
❏ 9064	Always/The Rooster	1949	25.00	50.00	100.00
❏ 9065	Deep Purple/Leave My Gal Alone	1949	25.00	50.00	100.00
❏ 9073	Ricky's Blues/The House I Live In	1949	25.00	50.00	100.00
❏ 9085	There's Nothing Like a Woman in Love/Careless Love	1949	25.00	50.00	100.00
❏ 9089	If You Didn't Mean It/Someday	1949	25.00	50.00	100.00
❏ 9098	I'm Afraid of You/Get Wise Baby	1949	25.00	50.00	100.00
❏ 9101	I Don't Have to Ride No More/I've Been a Fool	1950	25.00	50.00	100.00
❏ 9111	Count Every Star/I'm Gonna Paper All My Walls with Your Love	1950	25.00	50.00	100.00
❏ 9131	Phantom Stage Coach/I'm Gonna Take to the Road	1950	20.00	40.00	80.00
❏ 9148	Lilacs in the Rain/Time Is Marching On	1951	20.00	40.00	80.00

OKEH

Number	Title (A Side/B Side)	Yr	VG	VG+	NM
❏ 6825	The Whiffenpoof Song/I Get All My Lovin' on a Saturday Night	1951	25.00	50.00	100.00
❏ 6843	That Old Gang of Mine/Everything But You	1951	25.00	50.00	100.00
❏ 6888	Mam'selle/Calypso Song	1952	20.00	40.00	80.00

RENDITION

Number	Title (A Side/B Side)	Yr	VG	VG+	NM
❏ 5001	Write Me a Letter/Marie	1951	20.00	40.00	80.00

7-Inch Extended Plays

KING

Number	Title (A Side/B Side)	Yr	VG	VG+	NM
❏ 310	*Honey/Bye Bye Baby Blues/Out of a Dream/My Sugar Is So Refined	1954	125.00	250.00	500.00
❏ 310 [PS]	The Ravens Featuring Jimmy Ricks	1954	125.00	250.00	500.00

RENDITION

Number	Title (A Side/B Side)	Yr	VG	VG+	NM
❏ 104	(contents unknown)	195?	375.00	750.00	1500.
❏ 104 [PS]	Ol' Man River	195?	500.00	1000.	2000.

Albums

HARLEM HIT PARADE

Number	Title (A Side/B Side)	Yr	VG	VG+	NM
❏ 1007	The Ravens	1975	2.50	5.00	10.00

REGENT

Number	Title (A Side/B Side)	Yr	VG	VG+	NM
❏ MG-6062 [M]	Write Me a Letter	1957	75.00	150.00	300.00
—Green label					
❏ MG-6062 [M]	Write Me a Letter	195?	37.50	75.00	150.00
—Red label					

SAVOY JAZZ

Number	Title (A Side/B Side)	Yr	VG	VG+	NM
❏ SJL-2227 [(2)]	The Greatest Group of Them All	1978	3.00	6.00	12.00

RAWLS, LOU

12-Inch Singles

PHILADELPHIA INT'L.

Number	Title (A Side/B Side)	Yr	VG	VG+	NM
❏ 3686	Let Me Be Good to You/Lover's Holiday	1979	2.50	5.00	10.00

45s

ARISTA

Number	Title (A Side/B Side)	Yr	VG	VG+	NM
❏ 0103	Baby You Don't Know How Good You Are/Hour Glass	1975	—	3.00	6.00

BELL

Number	Title (A Side/B Side)	Yr	VG	VG+	NM
❏ 45608	She's Gone/Hour Glass	1974	—	3.00	6.00
❏ 45616	Who Can Tell Us Why?/Now You're Coming Back Michelle	1974	—	3.00	6.00

CANDIX

Number	Title (A Side/B Side)	Yr	VG	VG+	NM
❏ 305	In My Little Black Book/Just Thought You'd Like to Know	1960	5.00	10.00	20.00
❏ 312	When We Get Old/Eighty Ways	1961	5.00	10.00	20.00

CAPITOL

Number	Title (A Side/B Side)	Yr	VG	VG+	NM
❏ 2026	Little Drummer Boy/A Child with a Toy	1967	2.00	4.00	8.00
❏ 2084	Evil Woman/My Ancestors	1968	2.00	4.00	8.00
❏ 2172	Soul Serenade/You're Good for Me	1968	2.00	4.00	8.00
❏ 2252	Down Here on the Ground/I'm Satisfied (The Duffy Theme)	1968	2.00	4.00	8.00
❏ 2348	The Split/Why Can't I Speak	1968	2.00	4.00	8.00
❏ 2408	It's You/Sweet Charity	1969	2.00	4.00	8.00
❏ 2550	Your Good Thing (Is About to End)/Season of the Witch	1969	2.00	4.00	8.00
❏ 2668	I Can't Make It Alone/Make the World Go Away	1969	2.00	4.00	8.00
❏ 2734	You've Made Me So Very Happy/Let's Burn Down the Cornfield	1970	2.00	4.00	8.00

Number	Title (A Side/B Side)	Yr	VG	VG+	NM
❏ 2856	Bring It On Home/Can You Dig It-Take Me for What I Am	1970	2.00	4.00	8.00
❏ 2942	Win Your Love for Me/Coppin' a Plea	1970	2.00	4.00	8.00
❏ 4622	That Lucky Old Sun/In My Heart	1961	3.75	7.50	15.00
❏ 4669	Nine-Pound Hammer/Above My Head	1961	3.75	7.50	15.00
❏ 4695	The Wedding (The Bride)/The Biggest Lover in Town	1962	3.00	6.00	12.00
❏ 4743	Trust Me/Please Let Me Be the First to Know	1962	3.00	6.00	12.00
❏ 4761	Save Your Love for Me/Trust Me	1962	3.00	6.00	12.00
❏ 4803	Stormy Monday/Sweet Lover	1962	3.00	6.00	12.00
—With Les McCann					
❏ 5049	Tobacco Road/Blues for Four-String Guitar	1963	3.00	6.00	12.00
❏ 5160	The House Next Door/Come On In, Mr. Blues	1964	3.00	6.00	12.00
❏ 5227	Love Is Blind/I Fell in Love	1964	3.00	6.00	12.00
❏ 5424	Three O'Clock in the Morning/Nothing Really Feels the Same	1965	3.00	6.00	12.00
❏ 5505	What'll I Do/Can I Please	1965	3.00	6.00	12.00
❏ 5655	The Shadow of Your Smile/Southside Blues	1966	2.50	5.00	10.00
❏ 5709	Love Is a Hurtin' Thing/Memory Lane	1966	2.50	5.00	10.00
❏ 5790	You Can Bring Me All Your Heartaches/A Woman Who's a Woman	1966	2.50	5.00	10.00
❏ 5824	Trouble Down Here Below/The Life That I Lead	1967	2.50	5.00	10.00
❏ 5824 [PS]	Trouble Down Here Below/The Life That I Lead	1967	2.50	5.00	10.00
❏ 5869	Dead End Street/Yes It Hurts, Doesn't It	1967	2.50	5.00	10.00
❏ 5941	Show Business/When Love Goes Wrong	1967	2.50	5.00	10.00
❏ S7-18908	What Are You Doing New Year's Eve?/Have Yourself a Merry Little Christmas	1995	—	—	3.00

EPIC

Number	Title (A Side/B Side)	Yr	VG	VG+	NM
❏ 02999	Now Is the Time for Love/Will You Kiss Me One More Time	1982	—	2.00	4.00
❏ 03299	Together Again/Here Comes Garfield	1982	—	2.00	4.00
—Lou Rawls and Desiree Goyette					
❏ 03357	Let Me Show You How/Watch Your Back	1982	—	2.00	4.00
❏ 03758	Wind Beneath My Wings/Midnight Sun	1983	—	2.00	4.00
❏ 03944	Couple More Years/Upside Down	1983	—	2.00	4.00
❏ 04079	The One I Sing My Love Songs To/You Can't Take It With You	1983	—	2.00	4.00
❏ 04550	All-Time Lover/When We Were Young	1984	—	2.00	4.00
❏ 04677	Close Company/The Lady in My Life	1984	—	2.00	4.00
❏ 04773	Close Company/Forever I Do	1985	—	2.00	4.00
❏ 05714	Learn to Love Again/Ready or Not	1985	—	2.00	4.00
❏ 05831	Are You With Me/(Instrumental)	1986	—	2.00	4.00
❏ 05831 [PS]	Are You With Me/(Instrumental)	1986	—	2.00	4.00
❏ 06145	Stop Me from Starting This Feeling/Never Entered My Mind	1986	—	2.00	4.00

GAMBLE & HUFF

Number	Title (A Side/B Side)	Yr	VG	VG+	NM
❏ 310	I Wish You Belonged to Me/(B-side unknown)	1987	—	2.50	5.00

MGM

Number	Title (A Side/B Side)	Yr	VG	VG+	NM
❏ 14262	A Natural Man/You Can't Hold On	1971	—	3.00	6.00
❏ 14262	A Natural Man/Believe in Me	1971	—	3.00	6.00
❏ 14349	His Song Shall Be Sung/I'm Waiting	1972	—	3.00	6.00
❏ 14428	Politician/Walk On In	1972	—	3.00	6.00
❏ 14489	Man of Value/Learning Cup	1973	—	3.00	6.00
❏ 14527	Star Spangled Banner/Just a Closer Walk with Thee	1973	—	3.00	6.00
❏ 14574	Send for Me/Morning Comes Around	1973	—	3.00	6.00
❏ 14652	Dead End Street/Love Is a Hurtin' Thing	1973	—	3.00	6.00

PHILADELPHIA INT'L.

Number	Title (A Side/B Side)	Yr	VG	VG+	NM
❏ 3102	Ain't That Loving You (For More Reasons Than One)/(B-side unknown)	1980	—	2.50	5.00
❏ 3114	I Go Crazy/Be Anything (But Be Mine)	1980	—	2.50	5.00
❏ 3592	You'll Never Find Another Love Like Mine/Let's Fall in Love All Over Again	1976	—	2.50	5.00
❏ 3604	Groovy People/This Song Will Last Forever	1976	—	2.50	5.00
❏ 3623	See You When I Git There/Spring Again	1977	—	2.50	5.00
❏ 3634	Lady Love/Not the Staying Kind	1977	—	2.50	5.00
❏ 3643	One Life to Live/If I Coulda, Woulda, Shoulda	1978	—	2.50	5.00
❏ 3653	There Will Be Love/Unforgettable	1978	—	2.50	5.00
❏ 3672	Send In the Clowns/This Song Will Last Forever	1978	—	2.50	5.00
❏ 3684	Let Me Be Good to You/Lover's Holiday	1979	—	2.50	5.00
❏ 3738	Sit Down and Talk to Me/(B-side unknown)	1979	—	2.50	5.00
❏ 70051	Hoochie Coochie Man/You've Lost That Lovin' Feelin'	1981	—	2.50	5.00

7-Inch Extended Plays

CAPITOL

Number	Title (A Side/B Side)	Yr	VG	VG+	NM
❏ SU 1824	Black and Blue/Everyday I Have the Blues/Kansas City//Roll 'Em Pete/Strange Fruit/How Long, How Long Blues	196?	2.50	5.00	10.00
—Jukebox issue; small hole, plays at 33 1/3 rpm					
❏ SU 1824 [PS]	Black and Blue	196?	2.50	5.00	10.00
—Jukebox issue; small hole, plays at 33 1/3 rpm					

Albums

ALLEGIANCE

Number	Title (A Side/B Side)	Yr	VG	VG+	NM
❏ AV-5016	Trying As Hard As I Can	198?	2.50	5.00	10.00

BELL

Number	Title (A Side/B Side)	Yr	VG	VG+	NM
❏ 1318	She's Gone	1974	3.00	6.00	12.00

BLUE NOTE

Number	Title (A Side/B Side)	Yr	VG	VG+	NM
❏ B1-91441	Stormy Monday	1990	3.00	6.00	12.00
—Reissue of Capitol 1714					
❏ B1-91937	At Last	1989	3.00	6.00	12.00
❏ B1-93841	It's Supposed to Be Fun	1990	3.75	7.50	15.00

CAPITOL

Number	Title (A Side/B Side)	Yr	VG	VG+	NM
❏ ST-122	The Way It Was	1969	3.75	7.50	15.00
❏ ST-215	The Way It Was — The Way It Is	1969	3.75	7.50	15.00

R

Number	Title (A Side/B Side)	Yr	VG	VG+	NM
❑ ST 8-0215	The Way It Was — The Way It Is	1969	5.00	10.00	20.00
—Capitol Record Club edition					
❑ SWBB-261 [(2)]Close-Up		1969	5.00	10.00	20.00
—Reissue of 1824 and 2042 in one package					
❑ ST-325	Your Good Thing	1969	3.75	7.50	15.00
❑ ST-427	You've Made Me So Very Happy	1970	3.75	7.50	15.00
❑ ST-479	Bring It On Home	1970	3.75	7.50	15.00
❑ STBB-720 [(2)]Down Here on the Ground/I'd Rather Drink					
	Muddy Water	1971	5.00	10.00	20.00
❑ SM-1714	Stormy Monday	197?	2.50	5.00	10.00
—Reissue with new prefix					
❑ ST 1714 [S]	Stormy Monday	1962	6.25	12.50	25.00
❑ T 1714 [M]	Stormy Monday	1962	5.00	10.00	20.00
❑ ST 1824 [S]	Black and Blue	1963	6.25	12.50	25.00
❑ T 1824 [M]	Black and Blue	1963	5.00	10.00	20.00
❑ ST 2042 [S]	Tobacco Road	1964	6.25	12.50	25.00
❑ T 2042 [M]	Tobacco Road	1964	5.00	10.00	20.00
❑ ST 2273 [S]	Nobody But Lou	1965	6.25	12.50	25.00
❑ T 2273 [M]	Nobody But Lou	1965	5.00	10.00	20.00
❑ ST 2401 [S]	Lou Rawls and Strings	1965	6.25	12.50	25.00
❑ T 2401 [M]	Lou Rawls and Strings	1965	5.00	10.00	20.00
❑ SM-2459	Lou Rawls Live!	197?	2.50	5.00	10.00
—Reissue with new prefix					
❑ ST 2459 [S]	Lou Rawls Live!	1966	5.00	10.00	20.00
❑ T 2459 [M]	Lou Rawls Live!	1966	3.75	7.50	15.00
❑ SM-2566	Lou Rawls Soulin'	197?	2.50	5.00	10.00
—Reissue with new prefix					
❑ ST 2566 [S]	Lou Rawls Soulin'	1966	5.00	10.00	20.00
❑ T 2566 [M]	Lou Rawls Soulin'	1966	3.75	7.50	15.00
❑ ST 2632 [S]	Lou Rawls Carryin' On!	1966	5.00	10.00	20.00
❑ T 2632 [M]	Lou Rawls Carryin' On!	1966	3.75	7.50	15.00
❑ ST 2713 [S]	Too Much!	1967	3.75	7.50	15.00
❑ T 2713 [M]	Too Much!	1967	5.00	10.00	20.00
❑ ST 2756 [S]	That's Lou	1967	3.75	7.50	15.00
❑ T 2756 [M]	That's Lou	1967	5.00	10.00	20.00
❑ ST 2790 [S]	Merry Christmas, Ho, Ho, Ho	1967	3.00	6.00	12.00
❑ T 2790 [M]	Merry Christmas, Ho, Ho, Ho	1967	3.75	7.50	15.00
❑ ST 2864 [S]	Feelin' Good	1968	3.75	7.50	15.00
❑ T 2864 [M]	Feelin' Good	1968	7.50	15.00	30.00
❑ ST 2927	You're Good for Me	1968	3.75	7.50	15.00
❑ SKAO 2948	The Best of Lou Rawls	1968	3.75	7.50	15.00
❑ SM-2948	The Best of Lou Rawls	197?	2.50	5.00	10.00
—Reissue with new prefix					
❑ SKBB-11585 [(2)]The Best of Lou Rawls		1976	3.00	6.00	12.00
❑ SN-16096	The Best of Lou Rawls	1980	2.00	4.00	8.00
—Budget-line reissue					
❑ SN-16097	Lou Rawls Live!	1980	2.00	4.00	8.00
—Budget-line reissue					
EPIC					
❑ FE 37448	Now Is the Time	1982	2.50	5.00	10.00
❑ FE 38553	When the Night Comes	1983	2.50	5.00	10.00
❑ FE 39403	Close Company	1984	2.50	5.00	10.00
❑ FE 40210	Love All Your Blues Away	1986	2.50	5.00	10.00
MGM					
❑ SE-4771	Natural Man	1971	3.00	6.00	12.00
❑ SE-4809	Silk & Soul	1972	3.00	6.00	12.00
❑ SE-4861	A Man of Value	1973	3.00	6.00	12.00
❑ SE-4965	Live at the Century Plaza	1974	3.00	6.00	12.00
PHILADELPHIA INT'L.					
❑ PZ 33757	All Things in Time	1976	2.50	5.00	10.00
—No bar code on cover					
❑ PZ 33957	All Things in Time	198?	2.00	4.00	8.00
—With bar code on cover					
❑ PZ 34488	Unmistakably Lou	1977	2.50	5.00	10.00
❑ PZ 34488	Unmistakably Lou	1986	2.00	4.00	8.00
—Budget-line reissue					
❑ JZ 35036	When You Hear Lou, You've Heard It All	1977	2.50	5.00	10.00
❑ PZ2 35517 [(2)]Lou Rawls Live		1978	3.00	6.00	12.00
❑ JZ 36006	Let Me Be Good to You	1979	2.50	5.00	10.00
❑ PZ 36006	Let Me Be Good to You	198?	2.00	4.00	8.00
—Budget-line reissue					
❑ JZ 36304	Sit Down and Talk to Me	1979	2.50	5.00	10.00
❑ PZ 36304	Sit Down and Talk to Me	198?	2.00	4.00	8.00
—Budget-line reissue					
❑ JZ 36774	Shades of Blue	1980	2.50	5.00	10.00
❑ FZ 39285	Classics	1984	2.50	5.00	10.00
PICKWICK					
❑ SPC-3156	Come On In, Mr. Blues	1971	2.50	5.00	10.00
❑ SPC-3228	Gee Baby	1972	2.50	5.00	10.00
POLYDOR					
❑ PD-1-6086	Naturally	1976	2.50	5.00	10.00

RAY, GOODMAN AND BROWN
See THE MOMENTS.

RAY-O-VACS, THE
45s
ATCO

Number	Title (A Side/B Side)	Yr	VG	VG+	NM
❑ 6085	Party Time/Crying All Alone	1957	6.25	12.50	25.00
DECCA					
❑ 48162	Besame Mucho/You Gotta Love My Baby Too	1950	6.25	12.50	25.00
❑ 48181	A Kiss in the Dark/Got Two Arms	1950	6.25	12.50	25.00
❑ 48197	Goodnight My Love/Take Me Back to My Boots				
	and Saddle	1951	6.25	12.50	25.00

Number	Title (A Side/B Side)	Yr	VG	VG+	NM
❑ 48211	You Can Depend on Me/If You Ever Should				
	Leave Me	1951	6.25	12.50	25.00
❑ 48221	My Baby's Gone/Let's	1951	6.25	12.50	25.00
❑ 48234	What's Mine Is Mine/I Still Love You Baby	1951	6.25	12.50	25.00
❑ 48260	Charmaine/Hands Across the Table	1951	6.25	12.50	25.00
❑ 48274	When the Swallows Come Back to Capistrano/				
	She's a Real Lovin' Baby	1952	6.25	12.50	25.00
JOSIE					
❑ 763	Darling/Ridin' High	1954	7.50	15.00	30.00
❑ 781	I Still Love You/Daddy	1955	7.50	15.00	30.00
JUBILEE					
❑ 5098	What Can I Say/Start Lovin' Me	1952	7.50	15.00	30.00
❑ 5124	Outside of Paradise/You Know	1953	7.50	15.00	30.00
KAISER					
❑ 384	Crying All Alone/Party Time	1956	7.50	15.00	30.00
❑ 389	Wine-O/Hong Kong	1956	7.50	15.00	30.00
SHARP					
❑ 103	I'll Always Be in Love with You/Little Boy	1960	5.00	10.00	20.00

RAYDIO
See RAY PARKER JR.

RAYS, THE
45s
AMY

Number	Title (A Side/B Side)	Yr	VG	VG+	NM
❑ 900	Love Another Girl/Sad Saturday	1964	2.00	4.00	8.00
CAMEO					
❑ 117	Silhouettes/Daddy Cool	1957	6.25	12.50	25.00
❑ 128	Rendezvous/Triangle	1958	7.50	15.00	30.00
❑ 133	Rags to Riches/The Man Above	1958	7.50	15.00	30.00
CHESS					
❑ 1613	Tippity Top/Moo-Goo-Gai-Pan	1956	6.25	12.50	25.00
❑ 1678	How Long Must I Wait/Second Fiddle	1957	6.25	12.50	25.00
UNART					
❑ 2001	Souvenirs of Summertime/Elevator Operator	1958	10.00	20.00	40.00
XYZ					
❑ 100	My Steady Girl/No One Loves You Like I Do	1957	15.00	30.00	60.00
❑ 102	Silhouettes/Daddy Cool	1957	50.00	100.00	200.00
—Gray label					
❑ 102	Silhouettes/Daddy Cool	1957	15.00	30.00	60.00
—Blue label					
❑ 106	Souvenirs of Summertime/Elevator Operator	1958	12.50	25.00	50.00
❑ 600	Why Do You Look the Other Way/Zimbo Lula	1959	12.50	25.00	50.00
❑ 605	It's a Cryin' Shame/Mediterranean Moon	1959	10.00	20.00	40.00
❑ 607	Magic Moon/Louie Hoo Hoo	1960	10.00	20.00	40.00
—Blue label					
❑ 607	Magic Moon/Louie Hoo Hoo	1960	6.25	12.50	25.00
—Red label					
❑ 608	Old Devil Moon/Silver Starlight	1960	6.25	12.50	25.00

7-Inch Extended Plays
CHESS

Number	Title (A Side/B Side)	Yr	VG	VG+	NM
❑ 5120	(contents unknown)	1958	100.00	200.00	400.00
❑ 5120 [PS]	The Rays	1958	100.00	200.00	400.00

RECORD, EUGENE
Also see THE CHI-LITES.
12-Inch Singles
WARNER BROS.

Number	Title (A Side/B Side)	Yr	VG	VG+	NM
❑ WBSD 8774	Magnetism (7:03)//Medley: I Don't Mind/Take				
	Everything (11:45)	1979	3.00	6.00	12.00
❑ WBSD 8845	Medley: I Don't Mind/Take Everything (7:55)/				
	Magnetism (9:21)	1979	3.00	6.00	12.00
❑ DWBS 8890	Where Are You/Sweet Insanity	1979	2.50	5.00	10.00

45s
WARNER BROS.

Number	Title (A Side/B Side)	Yr	VG	VG+	NM
❑ 8322	Laying Beside You/Love Don't Live by Sex Alone	1977	—	2.50	5.00
❑ 8386	Mother of Love/Overdose of Joy	1977	—	2.50	5.00
❑ 8570	You Are the Star of My Show/Trying to Get to You	1978	—	2.50	5.00
❑ 8836	Take Everything/I Don't Mind	1979	—	2.50	5.00
❑ 49060	Where Are You/Sweet Insanity	1979	—	2.00	4.00
❑ 49126	Help Yourself to Love/Fan the Fire	1979	—	2.00	4.00

Albums
WARNER BROS.

Number	Title (A Side/B Side)	Yr	VG	VG+	NM
❑ BS 3018	Eugene Record	1977	3.75	7.50	15.00
❑ BSK 3097	Trying to Get to You	1978	3.75	7.50	15.00
❑ BSK 3284	Welcome to My Fantasy	1979	3.75	7.50	15.00

REDDING, OTIS
Also see OTIS AND CARLA; THE SHOOTERS.
45s
ATCO

Number	Title (A Side/B Side)	Yr	VG	VG+	NM
❑ 6592	Hard to Handle/Amen	1968	2.50	5.00	10.00
❑ 6612	I've Got Dreams to Remember/Nobody's Fault				
	But Mine	1968	2.50	5.00	10.00
❑ 6631	White Christmas/Merry Christmas, Baby	1968	2.50	5.00	10.00
❑ 6636	Papa's Got a Brand New Bag/Direct Me	1968	2.50	5.00	10.00
❑ 6654	A Lover's Question/You Made a Man Out of Me	1969	2.50	5.00	10.00
❑ 6677	Love Man/I Can't Turn You Loose	1969	2.50	5.00	10.00
❑ 6700	Free Me/Higher and Higher	1969	2.50	5.00	10.00
❑ 6723	Look at the Girl/That's a Good Idea	1969	2.50	5.00	10.00
❑ 6742	Demonstration/Johnny's Heartbreak	1970	2.00	4.00	8.00
❑ 6766	Giving Away None of My Love/Snatch a Little				
	Piece	1970	2.00	4.00	8.00

Number	Title (A Side/B Side)	Yr	VG	VG+	NM
❑ 6802	Try a Little Tenderness/I've Been Loving You Too Long (To Stop Now)	1971	—	3.00	6.00
❑ 6907	My Girl/Good to Me	1972	—	2.50	5.00
❑ 7069	White Christmas/Merry Christmas, Baby	1976	—	2.50	5.00
❑ 7321	White Christmas/Merry Christmas, Baby	1980	—	2.00	4.00
❑ 99955	White Christmas/Merry Christmas, Baby	1982	—	2.00	4.00

BETHLEHEM

❑ 3083	Shout Bamalama/Fat Girl	1964	5.00	10.00	20.00

CONFEDERATE

❑ 135	Shout Bamalama/Fat Girl	1962	12.50	25.00	50.00

FINER ARTS

❑ 2016	She's Alright/Tough Enuff	1961	12.50	25.00	50.00

—Originally released on Trans World by "The Shooters"

KING

❑ 6149	Shout Bamalama/Fat Girl	1968	2.50	5.00	10.00

ORBIT

❑ 135	Shout Bamalama/Fat Girl	1961	75.00	150.00	300.00

PHILCO-FORD

❑ HP-13	Shake/Fa-Fa-Fa-Fa-Fa	1967	5.00	10.00	20.00

—4-inch plastic "Hip Pocket Record" with color sleeve

STONE

❑ 209	You Left the Water Running/The Otis Jam	1976	3.00	6.00	12.00

—B-side by the Memphis Studio Band

VOLT

❑ 103	These Arms of Mine/Hey, Hey Baby	1962	5.00	10.00	20.00
❑ 109	That's What My Heart Needs/Mary's Little Lamb	1963	5.00	10.00	20.00
❑ 112	Pain in My Heart/Something Is Worrying Me	1963	5.00	10.00	20.00
❑ 116	Come to Me/Don't Leave Me This Way	1964	3.75	7.50	15.00
❑ 117	Security/I Want to Thank You	1964	3.75	7.50	15.00
❑ 121	Chained and Bound/Your One and Only Man	1964	3.75	7.50	15.00
❑ 124	Mr. Pitiful/That's How Strong My Love Is	1965	3.75	7.50	15.00
❑ 126	I've Been Loving You Too Long (To Stop Now)/ I'm Depending on You	1965	3.75	7.50	15.00
❑ 128	Respect/Ole Man Trouble	1965	3.75	7.50	15.00
❑ 130	I Can't Turn You Loose/Just One More Day	1965	3.75	7.50	15.00
❑ 132	Satisfaction/Any Ole Way	1966	3.75	7.50	15.00
❑ 136	My Lover's Prayer/Don't Mess with Cupid	1966	3.75	7.50	15.00
❑ 138	Fa-Fa-Fa-Fa-Fa (Sad Song)/Good to Me	1966	3.75	7.50	15.00
❑ 141	Try a Little Tenderness/I'm Sick Y'All	1966	3.75	7.50	15.00
❑ 146	I Love You More Than Words Can Say/Let Me Come On Home	1967	3.00	6.00	12.00
❑ 149	Shake/You Don't Miss Your Water	1967	3.00	6.00	12.00
❑ 152	Glory of Love/I'm Coming Home	1967	3.00	6.00	12.00
❑ 157	(Sittin' On) The Dock of the Bay/Sweet Lorene	1968	3.00	6.00	12.00

—Black and red label

❑ 157	(Sittin' On) The Dock of the Bay/Sweet Lorene	1968	2.50	5.00	10.00

—Multicolor (mostly brown) label

❑ 163	The Happy Song (Dum-Dum)/Open That Door	168	2.50	5.00	10.00

Albums

ATCO

❑ 33-161 [M]	Pain in My Heart	1964	62.50	125.00	250.00
❑ SD 33-161 [R]	Pain in My Heart	1968	62.50	125.00	250.00
❑ 33-252 [M]	The Immortal Otis Redding	1968	12.50	25.00	50.00

—Mono is white label promo only

❑ SD 33-252 [S]	The Immortal Otis Redding	1968	3.75	7.50	15.00
❑ SD 33-261	History of Otis Redding	1968	3.75	7.50	15.00

—Reissue of Volt 418

❑ SD 33-265	Otis Redding In Person at the Whiskey A-Go-Go	1968	3.75	7.50	15.00
❑ SD 33-284	Otis Blue/Otis Redding Sings Soul	1969	3.75	7.50	15.00

—Reissue of Volt 412

❑ SD 33-285	The Soul Album	1969	3.75	7.50	15.00

—Reissue of Volt 413

❑ SD 33-286	Otis Redding Live in Europe	1969	3.75	7.50	15.00

—Reissue of Volt 416

❑ SD 33-287	Complete & Unbelievable…The Otis Redding Dictionary of Soul	1969	3.75	7.50	15.00

—Reissue of Volt 415

❑ SD 33-288	The Dock of the Bay	1969	3.75	7.50	15.00

—Reissue of Volt 419

❑ SD 33-289	Love Man	1969	3.75	7.50	15.00
❑ SD 33-333	Tell the Truth	1970	3.75	7.50	15.00
❑ SD 2-801 [(2)]	The Best of Otis Redding	1972	5.00	10.00	20.00

ATLANTIC

❑ SD 19346	Recorded Live	198?	2.50	5.00	10.00
❑ 81282	The Best of Otis Redding	1985	2.50	5.00	10.00
❑ 81762 [(4)]	The Otis Redding Story	1987	7.50	15.00	30.00

PAIR

❑ PDL2-1062 [(2)]	The Legend of Otis Redding	1984	3.75	7.50	15.00

SUNDAZED

❑ LP 5063 [M]	Complete & Unbelievable ... The Otis Redding Dictionary of Soul	2001	3.00	6.00	12.00

—Reissue on 180-gram vinyl

❑ LP 5064 [M]	Otis Blue/Otis Redding Sings Soul	2001	3.00	6.00	12.00

—Reissue on 180-gram vinyl

VOLT

❑ 411 [M]	The Great Otis Redding Sings Soul Ballads	1965	22.50	45.00	90.00
❑ S-411 [R]	The Great Otis Redding Sings Soul Ballads	1968	27.50	55.00	110.00
❑ 412 [M]	Otis Blue/Otis Redding Sings Soul	1965	10.00	20.00	40.00
❑ S-412 [S]	Otis Blue/Otis Redding Sings Soul	1965	12.50	25.00	50.00
❑ 413 [M]	The Soul Album	1966	10.00	20.00	40.00
❑ S-413 [S]	The Soul Album	1966	12.50	25.00	50.00
❑ 415 [M]	Complete & Unbelievable…The Otis Redding Dictionary of Soul	1966	10.00	20.00	40.00
❑ S-415 [S]	Complete & Unbelievable…The Otis Redding Dictionary of Soul	1966	12.50	25.00	50.00

Number	Title (A Side/B Side)	Yr	VG	VG+	NM
❑ 416 [M]	Otis Redding Live in Europe	1967	7.50	15.00	30.00
❑ S-416 [S]	Otis Redding Live in Europe	1967	10.00	20.00	40.00
❑ 418 [M]	History of Otis Redding	1967	10.00	20.00	40.00
❑ S-418 [S]	History of Otis Redding	1967	7.50	15.00	30.00
❑ S-419	The Dock of the Bay	1968	7.50	15.00	30.00

REDDINGS, THE
12-Inch Singles
BELIEVE IN A DREAM

❑ AS 991 [DJ]	You're the Only One (5:28) (same on both sides)	1981	2.50	5.00	10.00
❑ AS 1287 [DJ]	Class (Is What You Got) (same on both sides)	1981	2.00	4.00	8.00
❑ AS 1406 [DJ]	I Know You Got Another (same on both sides)	1982	2.00	4.00	8.00
❑ AS 1788 [DJ]	Moon Rock/I'm Ready	1983	—	3.50	7.00
❑ 4Z9-03975	On the Outside Looking In (3:48)/Hand Dance (5:22)	1983	—	3.50	7.00

POLYDOR

❑ 881890-1	In My Pants (LP) (Remix 5:56)/Where Did Our Love Go	1985	2.50	5.00	10.00
❑ 883236-1	Parasite (LP) (Remix) (Dub)	1985	2.00	4.00	8.00
❑ 887395-1	So in Love with You (7" Version) (Dub Version) (Instrumental) (Bonus Beats) (12" Club Mix)	1988	—	3.50	7.00
❑ 887681-1	Call the Law (7" Remix) (The Outlaw Mix) (7" Version) (The Illegal Mix) (Dub)	1988	—	3.00	6.00

45s
BELIEVE IN A DREAM

❑ ZS6-02066	You're the Only One/Come In Out of the Rain	1981	—	2.00	4.00
❑ ZS5-02437	Class (Is What You Got)/Main Nerve	1981	—	2.00	4.00
❑ ZS5-02767	I Know You Got Another/Seriously	1982	—	2.00	4.00
❑ ZS5-02836	(Sittin' On) The Dock of the Bay/Time Won't Wait	1982	—	2.00	4.00
❑ ZS5-03161	Steamin' Hot/You Can Be a Star	1982	—	2.00	4.00
❑ ZS4-03916	On the Outside Looking In/Erotic Groove	1983	—	2.00	4.00
❑ ZS4-04067	Hand Dance/Erotic Groove	1983	—	2.00	4.00
❑ ZS4-04249	Moon Rock/I'm Ready	1983	—	2.00	4.00
❑ ZS6 5600	Remote Control/The Awakening	1980	—	2.50	5.00
❑ ZS6 5602	I Want It/It's Friday Night	1981	—	2.50	5.00

POLYDOR

❑ 881767-7	Where Did Our Love Go/Parasite	1985	—	—	3.00
❑ 887395-7	So in Love with You/(Instrumental)	1988	—	—	3.00
❑ 887395-7 [PS]	So in Love with You/(Instrumental)	1988	—	—	3.00
❑ 887681-7	Call the Law/(Remix)	1988	—	—	3.00
❑ 887681-7 [PS]	Call the Law/(Remix)	1988	—	—	3.00

Albums
BELIEVE IN A DREAM

❑ JZ 36875	Awakening	1980	2.50	5.00	10.00
❑ FZ 37175	Class	1981	2.50	5.00	10.00
❑ FZ 37974	Steamin' Hot	1982	2.50	5.00	10.00
❑ FZ 38690	Back to Basics	1983	2.50	5.00	10.00

POLYDOR

❑ 823324-1	If Looks Could Kill	1985	2.00	4.00	8.00
❑ 835292-1	The Reddings	1988	2.50	5.00	10.00

REDNOW, EIVETS
See STEVIE WONDER.

REED, JAMES
45s
BIG TOWN

❑ 117	Things Ain't What They Used to Be/You Better Hold Me	1954	37.50	75.00	150.00

FLAIR

❑ 1034	My Mama Told Me/This Is the End	1954	50.00	100.00	200.00
❑ 1042	Dr. Brown/You Better Hold Me	1954	50.00	100.00	200.00

MONEY

❑ 201	Oh People/My Love Is Real	1954	50.00	100.00	200.00

RHYTHM

❑ 1775	Tin Pan Alley/Biggest Place in Town	1954	125.00	250.00	500.00

REED, JIMMY
45s
ABC

❑ 10887	Got Nowhere to Go/Two Ways to Skin (A Cat)	1966	2.00	4.00	8.00

BLUESWAY

❑ 61003	I Wanna Know/Two Heads Are Better Than One	1967	2.00	4.00	8.00
❑ 61006	Don't Press Your Luck Woman/Feel Like I Want to Ramble	1967	2.00	4.00	8.00
❑ 61013	Buy Me a Hound Dog/Crazy About Oklahoma	1968	2.00	4.00	8.00
❑ 61020	Peepin' and Hidin'/My Baby Told Me	1968	2.00	4.00	8.00
❑ 61025	Don't Light My Fire/The Judge Should Know	1969	2.00	4.00	8.00

CANYON

❑ 38	Hard Walkin' Hannah (Part 1)/Hard Walkin' Hannah (Part 2)	196?	2.00	4.00	8.00

CHANCE

❑ 1142	High and Lonesome/Roll and Rhumba	1953	700.00	1400.	2100.

EXODUS

❑ 2005	Knockin' At Your Door/Dedication to Sonny	1966	2.50	5.00	10.00
❑ 2008	Cousin Peaches/Crazy 'Bout Oklahoma	1966	2.50	5.00	10.00

RRG

❑ 44001	Christmas Present Blues/Crying Blind	19??	2.00	4.00	8.00

VEE JAY

❑ 100	High and Lonesome/Roll and Rumba	1953	300.00	600.00	1200.

—Red vinyl

❑ 100	High and Lonesome/Roll and Rumba	1953	150.00	300.00	600.00
❑ 105	I Found My Baby/Jimmy's Boogie	1953	100.00	200.00	400.00

—Red vinyl

Number	Title (A Side/B Side)	Yr	VG	VG+	NM
❏ 105	I Found My Baby/Jimmy's Boogie	1953	50.00	100.00	200.00
❏ 119	You Don't Have to Go/Boogie in the Dark	1954	75.00	150.00	300.00
—Red vinyl					
❏ 119	You Don't Have to Go/Boogie in the Dark	1954	20.00	40.00	80.00
❏ 132	Pretty Thing/I'm Gonna Ruin You	1955	25.00	50.00	100.00
❏ 153	I Don't Go for That/She Don't Want Me No More	1955	12.50	25.00	50.00
❏ 168	Ain't That Lovin' You Baby/Baby, Don't Say That No More	1956	10.00	20.00	40.00
❏ 186	Can't Stand to See You Go/Rockin' with Reed	1956	10.00	20.00	40.00
❏ 203	I Love You Baby/My First Plea	1956	7.50	15.00	30.00
❏ 226	You've Got Me Dizzy/Honey, Don't Let Me Go	1956	7.50	15.00	30.00
❏ 237	Honey, Where You Going/Little Rain	1957	7.50	15.00	30.00
❏ 248	The Sun Is Shining/Baby, What's On Your Mind	1957	7.50	15.00	30.00
❏ 253	Honest I Do/Signals of Love	1957	7.50	15.00	30.00
❏ 270	You're Something Else/A String to My Heart	1958	7.50	15.00	30.00
❏ 275	You Got Me Crying/Go On to School	1958	7.50	15.00	30.00
❏ 287	I Know It's a Sin/Down in Virginia	1958	7.50	15.00	30.00
❏ 298	I'm Gonna Get My Baby/Odds and Ends	1958	7.50	15.00	30.00
❏ 304	I Told You Baby/Ends and Odds (Instrumental)	1958	7.50	15.00	30.00
❏ 314	Take Out Some Insurance/You Know I Love You	1959	7.50	15.00	30.00
❏ 326	I Wanna Be Loved/Going to New York	1959	7.50	15.00	30.00
❏ 333	Baby What You Want Me to Do/Caress Me, Baby	1959	7.50	15.00	30.00
❏ 347	Found Love/Where Can You Be	1960	6.25	12.50	25.00
❏ 357	Hush Hush/Going to the River, Part 2	1960	6.25	12.50	25.00
❏ 373	Laughing at the Blues/Close Together	1961	6.25	12.50	25.00
❏ 380	Big Boss Man/I'm a Love You	1961	6.25	12.50	25.00
❏ 398	Bright Lights, Big City/I'm Mr. Luck	1961	6.25	12.50	25.00
❏ 425	Aw, Shucks, Hush Your Mouth/Baby, What's Wrong	1962	5.00	10.00	20.00
❏ 449	Tell Me You Love Me/Good Lover	1962	5.00	10.00	20.00
❏ 459	I'll Change My Style/Too Much	1962	5.00	10.00	20.00
❏ 473	Let's Get Together/Oh, John	1962	5.00	10.00	20.00
❏ 509	There'll Be a Day/Shame, Shame, Shame	1963	3.75	7.50	15.00
❏ 552	Mary Mary/I'm Gonna Help You	1963	3.75	7.50	15.00
❏ 570	Outskirts of Town/St. Louis Blues	1963	3.75	7.50	15.00
❏ 584	See See Rider/Wee Wee Baby Blues	1964	3.75	7.50	15.00
❏ 593	Help Yourself/Heading for a Fall	1964	3.75	7.50	15.00
❏ 616	Oh John/Down in Mississippi	1964	3.75	7.50	15.00
❏ 622	I'm Going Upside Your Head/The Devil's Shoestring	1964	3.75	7.50	15.00
❏ 642	I Wanna Be Loved/A New Leaf	1965	3.75	7.50	15.00
❏ 702	I'm the Man Down There/Left Handed Woman	1965	3.75	7.50	15.00
❏ 709	Don't Think I'm Through/When Girls Do It	1966	3.75	7.50	15.00

Albums

ANTILLES

❏ 7007	Cold Chills	197?	3.75	7.50	15.00

ARCHIVE OF FOLK AND JAZZ

| ❏ 234 | Jimmy Reed | 197? | 3.00 | 6.00 | 12.00 |

BLUESVILLE

❏ BLS-6054	I Ain't From Chicago	1973	3.75	7.50	15.00
❏ BLS-6067	The Ultimate Jimmy Reed	1973	3.75	7.50	15.00
❏ BLS-6073 [(2)]	Jimmy Reed at Carnegie Hall	1973	5.00	10.00	20.00

BLUESWAY

❏ BL-6004 [M]	The New Jimmy Reed Album	1967	5.00	10.00	20.00
❏ BLS-6004 [S]	The New Jimmy Reed Album	1967	5.00	10.00	20.00
❏ BL-6009 [M]	Soulin'	1967	5.00	10.00	20.00
❏ BLS-6009 [S]	Soulin'	1967	5.00	10.00	20.00
❏ BLS-6015	Big Boss Man	1968	5.00	10.00	20.00
❏ BLS-6024	Down in Virginia	1969	5.00	10.00	20.00

BUDDAH

| ❏ BDS-4003 | The Very Best of Jimmy Reed | 1969 | 3.75 | 7.50 | 15.00 |
| —Reissue of Vee Jay 1039 | | | | | |

CHAMELEON

| ❏ D1-74762 | Bright Lights, Big City | 1988 | 2.50 | 5.00 | 10.00 |

GNP CRESCENDO

| ❏ GNPS-10006 [(2)] | The Best of Jimmy Reed | 1974 | 3.75 | 7.50 | 15.00 |

SUNSET

| ❏ SUS-5218 | Somethin' Else | 1968 | 3.00 | 6.00 | 12.00 |

TRADITION

| ❏ 2069 | Wailin' the Blues | 1969 | 3.00 | 6.00 | 12.00 |

TRIP

| ❏ 8012 [(2)] | History of Jimmy Reed | 1971 | 3.75 | 7.50 | 15.00 |

VEE JAY

❏ LP-1004 [M]	I'm Jimmy Reed	1958	55.00	110.00	220.00
—Maroon label					
❏ LP-1004 [M]	I'm Jimmy Reed	1961	20.00	40.00	80.00
—Black label with colorband					
❏ VJLP-1004	I'm Jimmy Reed	198?	2.50	5.00	10.00
—Reissue with glossy labels					
❏ LP-1008 [M]	Rockin' with Reed	1959	50.00	100.00	200.00
—Maroon label					
❏ LP-1008 [M]	Rockin' with Reed	1961	20.00	40.00	80.00
—Black label with colorband					
❏ VJLP-1008	Rockin' with Reed	198?	2.50	5.00	10.00
—Reissue with glossy labels					
❏ LP-1022 [M]	Found Love	1959	50.00	100.00	200.00
—Maroon label					
❏ LP-1022 [M]	Found Love	1961	20.00	40.00	80.00
—Black label with colorband					
❏ LP-1025 [M]	Now Appearing	1960	20.00	40.00	80.00
❏ VJLP-1025	Now Appearing	198?	2.50	5.00	10.00
—Reissue with glossy labels					
❏ 2LP-1035 [(2) M]	Jimmy Reed at Carnegie Hall	1961	12.50	25.00	50.00
❏ 2SR-1035 [(2) S]	Jimmy Reed at Carnegie Hall	1961	17.50	35.00	70.00

Number	Title (A Side/B Side)	Yr	VG	VG+	NM
❏ VJLP2-1035 [(2)]	Jimmy Reed at Carnegie Hall	198?	3.00	6.00	12.00
—Reissue with glossy labels					
❏ LP-1039 [M]	The Best of Jimmy Reed	1962	10.00	20.00	40.00
❏ SR-1039 [S]	The Best of Jimmy Reed	1962	15.00	30.00	60.00
❏ VJLP-1039	The Best of Jimmy Reed	198?	2.50	5.00	10.00
—Reissue with glossy labels					
❏ LP-1050 [M]	Just Jimmy Reed	1962	10.00	20.00	40.00
❏ SR-1050 [S]	Just Jimmy Reed	1962	15.00	30.00	60.00
❏ LP-1067 [M]	T'Ain't No Big Thing…But He Is Jimmy Reed	1963	10.00	20.00	40.00
❏ SR-1067 [S]	T'Ain't No Big Thing…But He Is Jimmy Reed	1963	15.00	30.00	60.00
❏ LP-1072 [M]	The Best of the Blues	1963	10.00	20.00	40.00
❏ LP-1073 [M]	The 12 String Guitar Blues	1963	10.00	20.00	40.00
❏ SR-1073 [S]	The 12 String Guitar Blues	1963	37.50	7.50	150.00
❏ LP-1080 [M]	More of the Best of Jimmy Reed	1964	10.00	20.00	40.00
❏ SR-1080 [S]	More of the Best of Jimmy Reed	1964	37.50	75.00	150.00
❏ LP-1095 [M]	Jimmy Reed at Soul City	1964	10.00	20.00	40.00
❏ VJLP-1095	Jimmy Reed at Soul City	198?	2.50	5.00	10.00
—Reissue with glossy labels					
❏ VJS-7303	Blues Is My Business	198?	2.50	5.00	10.00
❏ LP-8501 [M]	The Legend, The Man	1965	10.00	20.00	40.00
❏ VJLP-8501	The Legend, The Man	198?	2.50	5.00	10.00
—Reissue with glossy labels					
❏ VJS-8501 [S]	The Legend, The Man	1965	37.50	75.00	150.00

REED, LULA

45s

KING

❏ 4578	Let Me Be Your Love/My Story	1952	20.00	40.00	80.00
❏ 4590	Heavenly Road/My Mother's Prayer	1953	12.50	25.00	50.00
❏ 4630	I'm Losing You/My Poor Heart	1953	12.50	25.00	50.00
❏ 4649	Don't Make Me Love You/Goin' Back to Mexico	1953	12.50	25.00	50.00
❏ 4688	Your Key Don't Fit No More/Watch Dog	1953	12.50	25.00	50.00
❏ 4703	Troubles on Your Mind/Bump on a Log	1954	10.00	20.00	40.00
❏ 4714	If the Sun Isn't Shining in Your Window/Just Whisper	1954	10.00	20.00	40.00
❏ 4726	Wonderful Love/I'll Upset You Baby	1954	10.00	20.00	40.00
❏ 4737	What Could I Do But Believe in Jesus/A Quiet Time with Jesus	1954	12.50	25.00	50.00
❏ 4748	Sick and Tired/Jealous Love	1954	10.00	20.00	40.00
❏ 4767	Rock Love/I'm Gone, Yes I'm Gone	1955	6.25	12.50	25.00
❏ 4796	Without Love/Caught Me When My Love Was Down	1955	6.25	12.50	25.00
❏ 4811	I'm Giving All My Love/Why Don't You Come Home	1955	6.25	12.50	25.00
❏ 4899	Let's Call It a Day/I'll Drown in My Own Tears	1956	6.25	12.50	25.00
❏ 4969	Sample Man/Three Men	1956	6.25	12.50	25.00
❏ 4996	Every Second/Waste No More Tears	1956	6.25	12.50	25.00

Albums

KING

| ❏ 604 [M] | Blue and Moody | 1958 | 500.00 | 1000. | 2000. |

REESE, DELLA

45s

ABC

❏ 10815	Stranger on Earth/If It's the Last Thing I Do	1966	2.00	4.00	8.00
❏ 10841	It Was a Very Good Year/Solitary Woman	1966	2.00	4.00	8.00
❏ 10876	Sunny/That's Life	1966	2.00	4.00	8.00
❏ 10931	Soon/Every Other Day	1967	—	3.00	6.00
❏ 10962	I Heard You Cried Last Night/On the South Side of Chicago	1967	—	3.00	6.00
❏ 11017	Let's Make the Most of a Beautiful Thing/Sorry Baby	1967	—	3.00	6.00
❏ 11051	I Gotta Be Me/Never My Love	1968	—	3.00	6.00

ABC-PARAMOUNT

❏ 10691	After Loving You/How Do You Keep from Crying	1965	2.00	4.00	8.00
❏ 10721	And That Reminds Me/I Only Want a Buddy, Not a Sweetheart	1965	2.00	4.00	8.00
❏ 10759	'T'Ain't Nobody's Bizness If I Do/I Ain't Ready for That	1965	2.00	4.00	8.00

AVCO

| ❏ 4521 | Simple Song of Freedom/(B-side unknown) | 1970 | — | 3.50 | 7.00 |
| ❏ 4586 | If It Feels Good Do It/Good Lovin' Makes It Right | 1972 | — | 2.50 | 5.00 |

AVCO EMBASSY

❏ 4515	Games People Play/Compared to What	1969	—	3.00	6.00
❏ 4545	Billy My Love/(B-side unknown)	1970	—	3.00	6.00
❏ 4566	The Troublemaker/The Love I've Been Looking For	1971	—	3.00	6.00

CHI-SOUND

| ❏ XW978 | I'll Be Your Sunshine/Nothing But a True Love | 1977 | — | 2.00 | 4.00 |

JUBILEE

❏ 5198	In the Still of the Night/Kiss My Love Goodbye	1955	3.75	7.50	15.00
❏ 5214	Time After Time/Fine Sugar	1955	3.75	7.50	15.00
❏ 5233	I've Got My Love to Keep Me Warm/Years from Now	1956	3.75	7.50	15.00
❏ 5247	Headin' Home/Daybreak Serenade	1956	3.75	7.50	15.00
❏ 5251	My Melancholy Baby/One for My Baby	1956	3.75	7.50	15.00
❏ 5263	In the Meantime/The More I See You	1956	3.75	7.50	15.00
❏ 5278	How About You/How Can You Not Believe	1957	3.75	7.50	15.00
❏ 5292	And That Reminds Me/I Cried for You	1957	3.00	6.00	12.00
❏ 5307	I Only Want to Love You/By Love Possessed	1957	3.00	6.00	12.00
❏ 5317	How Can You Lose (What You Never Had)/If Not for You	1958	3.00	6.00	12.00
❏ 5323	I've Got a Feelin' You're Foolin'/C'mon, C'mon	1958	3.00	6.00	12.00
❏ 5332	I Wish/You Gotta Love Everybody	1958	3.00	6.00	12.00
❏ 5345	Sermonette/Dreams End at Dawn	1958	3.00	6.00	12.00

Number	Title (A Side/B Side)	Yr	VG	VG+	NM
❑ 5346	When I Grow Too Old to Dream/You're Just in Love	1958	3.00	6.00	12.00
—Della Reese and Kirk Stuart					
❑ 5369	Time Was/Once Upon a Dream	1959	3.00	6.00	12.00
❑ 5375	I Don't Want to Walk Without You/I'm Nobody's Baby	1959	3.00	6.00	12.00
❑ 5453	Sermonette/You Gotta Love Somebody	1963	2.50	5.00	10.00
RCA VICTOR					
❑ 47-7591	Don't You Know/Soldier Won't You Marry Me	1959	2.50	5.00	10.00
❑ 47-7644	Not One Minute More/You're My Love	1959	2.50	5.00	10.00
❑ 47-7683	Someday/The Lady Is a Tramp	1960	2.50	5.00	10.00
❑ 47-7706	Someday You'll Want Me to Want You/Faraway Boy	1960	2.50	5.00	10.00
❑ 47-7750	Everyday/There's No Two Ways About It	1960	2.50	5.00	10.00
❑ 47-7750 [PS]	Everyday/There's No Two Ways About It	1960	5.00	10.00	20.00
❑ 47-7784	And Now/There's Nothin' Like a Boy	1960	2.50	5.00	10.00
❑ 47-7784 [PS]	And Now/There's Nothin' Like a Boy	1960	5.00	10.00	20.00
❑ 47-7833	The Most Beautiful Words/You Mean All the World to Me	1961	2.50	5.00	10.00
❑ 47-7867	The Touch of Your Lips/Won'cha Come Home, Bill Bailey	1961	2.50	5.00	10.00
❑ 47-7884	I Possess/A Far, Far Better Thing	1961	2.50	5.00	10.00
❑ 47-7961	One/What Do You Think, Joe	1961	2.50	5.00	10.00
❑ 47-7996	Ninety-Nine and a Half Won't Do/You Don't Know How Blessed You Are	1962	2.50	5.00	10.00
❑ 47-8021	Rome Adventure/Here's That Rainy Day	1962	2.50	5.00	10.00
❑ 47-8070	I Love You So Much It Hurts/Blow Out the Sun	1962	2.50	5.00	10.00
❑ 47-8093	As Long As He Needs Me/It Makes No Difference Now	1962	2.50	5.00	10.00
❑ 47-8093 [PS]	As Long As He Needs Me/It Makes No Difference Now	1962	3.75	7.50	15.00
❑ 47-8145	Be My Love/I Behold You	1963	2.50	5.00	10.00
❑ 47-8187	More/Serenade	1963	2.50	5.00	10.00
❑ 47-8260	Angel D'Amore/Forbidden Games	1963	2.50	5.00	10.00
❑ 47-8337	The Bottom of Old Smokey/A Clock That's Got No Hands	1964	2.00	4.00	8.00
❑ 47-8394	If I Didn't Care/Wind in the Willows	1964	2.00	4.00	8.00
❑ 48-1018	Ninety-Nine and a Half Won't Do/And Now	1971	—	2.00	4.00
❑ 74-0558	You Came a Long Way from St. Louis/Nobody's Sweetheart	1971	—	2.00	4.00
7-Inch Extended Plays					
RCA VICTOR					
❑ EPA-4349	Don't You Know/Soldier, Won't You Marry Me//Not One Minute More/You're My Love	1959	3.75	7.50	15.00
❑ EPA-4349 [PS]	Don't You Know	1959	3.75	7.50	15.00
Albums					
ABC					
❑ 569 [M]	Della Reese Live	1966	3.75	7.50	15.00
❑ S-569 [S]	Della Reese Live	1966	5.00	10.00	20.00
❑ 589 [M]	One More Time	1967	5.00	10.00	20.00
❑ S-589 [S]	One More Time	1967	3.75	7.50	15.00
❑ 612 [M]	Della on Strings of Blue	1967	5.00	10.00	20.00
❑ S-612 [S]	Della on Strings of Blue	1967	3.75	7.50	15.00
❑ S-636	I Gotta Be Me...This Trip Out	1968	3.75	7.50	15.00
❑ AC-30002	The ABC Collection	1976	3.75	7.50	15.00
ABC-PARAMOUNT					
❑ ABC-524 [M]	C'mon and Hear Della Reese	1965	3.75	7.50	15.00
❑ ABCS-524 [S]	C'mon and Hear Della Reese	1965	5.00	10.00	20.00
❑ ABC-540 [M]	I Like It Like Dat!	1966	3.75	7.50	15.00
❑ ABCS-540 [S]	I Like It Like Dat!	1966	5.00	10.00	20.00
AVCO EMBASSY					
❑ 33004	Black Is Beautiful	1969	3.75	7.50	15.00
❑ 33017	Right Now	1970	3.75	7.50	15.00
JAZZ A LA CARTE					
❑ 3	One of a Kind	1978	3.75	7.50	15.00
JUBILEE					
❑ JLP-1026 [M]	Melancholy Baby	1957	7.50	15.00	30.00
❑ JGM-1071 [M]	A Date with Della Reese at Mr. Kelly's in Chicago	1963	3.75	7.50	15.00
—Black label, multi-colored spokes around "jubilee"					
❑ JGM-1071 [M]	A Date with Della Reese at Mr. Kelly's in Chicago	196?	5.00	10.00	20.00
—Black label with all-silver print					
❑ JGS-1071 [S]	A Date with Della Reese at Mr. Kelly's in Chicago	1965	3.75	7.50	15.00
—Black label, multi-colored spokes around "jubilee," yellow spoke goes nowhere near center hole; new prefix					
❑ JLP-1071 [M]	A Date with Della Reese at Mr. Kelly's in Chicago	1959	6.25	12.50	25.00
—Originals have blue labels					
❑ SDJLP-1071 [S]	A Date with Della Reese at Mr. Kelly's in Chicago	1959	7.50	15.00	30.00
—Originals have blue labels					
❑ SDJLP-1071 [S]	A Date with Della Reese at Mr. Kelly's in Chicago	1959	6.25	12.50	25.00
—Black label with all-silver print					
❑ SDJLP-1071 [S]	A Date with Della Reese at Mr. Kelly's in Chicago	1962	5.00	10.00	20.00
—Black label, multi-colored spokes around "jubilee," yellow spoke goes almost to center hole					
❑ JLP-1083 [M]	Amen	1959	6.25	12.50	25.00
❑ SDJLP-1083 [S]	Amen	1959	7.50	15.00	30.00
❑ JGM-1095 [M]	The Story of the Blues	1962	3.75	7.50	15.00
—Black label, multi-colored spokes around "jubilee," yellow spoke goes almost to center hole; new prefix					
❑ JGS-1095 [S]	The Story of the Blues	1964	3.75	7.50	15.00
—Black label, multi-colored spokes around "jubilee," yellow spoke goes nowhere near center hole					
❑ JLP-1095 [M]	The Story of the Blues	1960	6.25	12.50	25.00
—Original labels are black with all-silver print					
❑ JLP-1095 [M]	The Story of the Blues	1960	5.00	10.00	20.00
—Black label, multi-colored spokes around "jubilee," yellow spoke goes almost to center hole					
❑ SDJLP-1095 [S]	The Story of the Blues	1960	7.50	15.00	30.00
—Original labels are black with all-silver print					
❑ SDJLP-1095 [S]	The Story of the Blues	1962	6.25	12.50	25.00
—Black label, multi-colored spokes around "jubilee," yellow spoke goes almost to center hole					
❑ JLP-1109 [M]	What Do You Know About Love	1960	6.25	12.50	25.00
❑ JLP-1116 [M]	And That Reminds Me	1960	6.25	12.50	25.00
❑ JGM-5002 [M]	The Best of Della Reese	196?	3.75	7.50	15.00
❑ JGS-5002 [S]	The Best of Della Reese	196?	5.00	10.00	20.00
PICKWICK					
❑ SPC-3058	And That Reminds Me	196?	3.00	6.00	12.00
RCA VICTOR					
❑ LPM-2157 [M]	Della	1960	5.00	10.00	20.00
❑ LSP-2157 [S]	Della	1960	6.25	12.50	25.00
❑ LPM-2204 [M]	Della by Starlight	1960	5.00	10.00	20.00
❑ LSP-2204 [S]	Della by Starlight	1960	6.25	12.50	25.00
❑ LPM-2280 [M]	Della Della Cha-Cha-Cha	1961	5.00	10.00	20.00
❑ LSP-2280 [S]	Della Della Cha-Cha-Cha	1961	6.25	12.50	25.00
❑ LPM-2391 [M]	Special Delivery	1961	5.00	10.00	20.00
❑ LSP-2391 [S]	Special Delivery	1961	6.25	12.50	25.00
❑ LPM-2419 [M]	The Classic Della	1962	5.00	10.00	20.00
❑ LSP-2419 [S]	The Classic Della	1962	6.25	12.50	25.00
❑ LPM-2568 [M]	Della on Stage	1962	5.00	10.00	20.00
❑ LSP-2568 [S]	Della on Stage	1962	6.25	12.50	25.00
❑ LPM-2711 [M]	Waltz with Me	1963	5.00	10.00	20.00
❑ LSP-2711 [S]	Waltz with Me	1963	6.25	12.50	25.00
❑ LPM-2814 [M]	Moody	1963	5.00	10.00	20.00
❑ LSP-2814 [S]	Moody	1963	6.25	12.50	25.00
❑ LPM-2872 [M]	Della Reese at Basin Street East	1964	5.00	10.00	20.00
❑ LSP-2872 [S]	Della Reese at Basin Street East	1964	6.25	12.50	25.00
❑ LSP-4651	The Best of Della Reese	1972	3.00	6.00	12.00

REEVES, MARTHA

Also see MARTHA AND THE VANDELLAS.

Number	Title (A Side/B Side)	Yr	VG	VG+	NM
45s					
ARISTA					
❑ 0124	Love Blind/This Time I'll Be Sweeter	1975	—	2.50	5.00
—Also see "Martha and the Vandellas"					
❑ 0160	Now That We Found Love/Higher and Higher	1975	—	2.00	4.00
❑ 0211	The Rest of My Life/Thank You	1976	—	2.00	4.00
❑ 0228	You've Lost That Lovin' Feelin'/Now That We Found Love	1977	—	2.00	4.00
FANTASY					
❑ 825	Love Don't Come No Stronger/You're Like Sunshine	1978	—	2.00	4.00
❑ 868	Dancin' in the Streets (Skatin' in the Streets)/When You Came	1979	—	2.00	4.00
❑ 887	Really Like Your Rap/That's What I Want	1979	—	2.00	4.00
MCA					
❑ 40194	Power of Love/Stand By Me	1974	—	2.50	5.00
❑ 40274	Stand By Me/Wild Night	1974	—	2.50	5.00
❑ 40329	My Man/Facsimile	1974	—	2.50	5.00
Albums					
ARISTA					
❑ AL 4105	The Rest of My Life	1976	3.00	6.00	12.00
FANTASY					
❑ F-9549	We'll Meet Again	1978	3.00	6.00	12.00
❑ F-9591	Gotta Keep Moving	1980	3.00	6.00	12.00
MCA					
❑ 414	Martha Reeves	1974	3.00	6.00	12.00

REGALS, THE (1)

Number	Title (A Side/B Side)	Yr	VG	VG+	NM
45s					
ALADDIN					
❑ 3266	Run Pretty Baby/May the Good Lord Bless and Keep You	1954	30.00	60.00	120.00
ATLANTIC					
❑ 1062	I'm So Lonely/Got the Water Boiling	1955	15.00	30.00	60.00
MGM					
❑ 11869	There'll Always Be a Christmas/When You're Home with the Ones You Love	1954	10.00	20.00	40.00

REGALS, THE (2)

Number	Title (A Side/B Side)	Yr	VG	VG+	NM
45s					
LAST CHANCE					
❑ 109	See You in the Morning/Yes My Love	1961	2.50	5.00	10.00
LAVENDER					
❑ 1452	See You in the Morning/Yes My Love	1960	7.50	15.00	30.00
UNITED ARTISTS					
❑ 380	Icy Fingers/Tiger Tears	1961	7.50	15.00	30.00

REGENTS, THE (1)

Number	Title (A Side/B Side)	Yr	VG	VG+	NM
45s					
COUSINS					
❑ 1002	Barbara-Ann/I'm So Lonely	1961	300.00	600.00	1200.
GEE					
❑ 1065	Barbara-Ann/I'm So Lonely	1961	7.50	15.00	30.00
❑ 1071	Runaround/Laura My Darling	1961	6.25	12.50	25.00
❑ 1073	Don't Be a Fool/Liar	1961	6.25	12.50	25.00
❑ 1075	Lonesome Boy/Oh Baby	1961	6.25	12.50	25.00
Albums					
GEE					
❑ GLP-706 [M]	Barbara Ann	1961	37.50	75.00	150.00
❑ SGLP-706	Barbara Ann	197?	6.25	12.50	25.00
—Reissue by Publishers Central Bureau (clearly marked as such on cover)					
❑ SGLP-706 [S]	Barbara Ann	1961	62.50	125.00	250.00

Number	Title (A Side/B Side)	Yr	VG	VG+	NM

REGENTS, THE (2)
45s
ARGO

Number	Title (A Side/B Side)	Yr	VG	VG+	NM
❏ 5268	Isle of Trinidad/Bamboo Tree	1957	6.25	12.50	25.00

REGENTS, THE (3)
45s
BLUE CAT

❏ 110	Playmates/Me and You	1965	2.50	5.00	10.00

DOT

❏ 16970	The Russian Spy and I/Bald Headed Woman	1966	2.50	5.00	10.00

PENTHOUSE

❏ 502	Words/Worryin' Kind	1966	2.50	5.00	10.00

REGENTS, THE (4)
45s
KAYO

❏ 101	(That's What I Call) A Real Good Time/No Hard Feelings	1960	6.25	12.50	25.00

PEORIA

❏ 8	Summertime Blues/(B-side unknown)	196?	3.75	7.50	15.00

REGENTS, THE (5)
MICHAEL McDONALD, later of THE DOOBIE BROTHERS, was in this group.
45s
REPRISE

❏ 0430	She's Got Her Own Way of Lovin'/When I Die, Don't You Cry	1965	7.50	15.00	30.00

REID, CLARENCE
45s
ALSTON

❏ 3717	Baptize Me in Your Love/Whatever It Takes	1975	—	2.50	5.00
❏ 3720	Come On With It/Mr. Smith's Wife	1976	—	2.50	5.00
❏ 3723	Shake Your Butt/Caution! Love Ahead	1976	—	2.50	5.00
❏ 3733	Just Another Guy in the Band/I'm Excited	1977	—	2.50	5.00
❏ 3748	You Get Me Up/It's Hell Trying to Get to Heaven	1979	—	2.50	5.00
❏ 4572	Fools Are Not Born (They Are Made)/Part-Time Lover	1969	2.00	4.00	8.00
❏ 4574	Nobody But You Babe/Send Me Back My Money	1969	2.00	4.00	8.00
❏ 4578	I'm a Man of My Word/I'm Gonna Tear You a New Heart	1969	2.00	4.00	8.00
❏ 4582	I've Been Trying/Don't Look Too Hard	1970	—	3.00	6.00
❏ 4584	Chicken Hawk/That's How It Is	1970	—	3.00	6.00
❏ 4588	Masterpiece/Down the Road of Love	1970	—	3.00	6.00
❏ 4592	Direct Me/You Knock Me Out	1971	—	3.00	6.00
❏ 4597	You Got to Fight/Three Is a Crowd	1971	—	3.00	6.00
❏ 4598	I Get My Kicks/Gotta Take It Home to Mother	1971	—	3.00	6.00
❏ 4602	Love Every Woman You Can/Ten Tons of Dynamite	1971	—	3.00	6.00
❏ 4603	Good Old Days/Ten Tons of Dynamite	1972	—	3.00	6.00
❏ 4608	I'm Gonna Do Something Good to You/Real Woman	1972	—	3.00	6.00
❏ 4613	Ruby/Two People in Love	1972	—	3.00	6.00
❏ 4616	Till I Get My Share/With Friends Like These	1973	—	3.00	6.00
❏ 4621	Funky Party/Winter Man	1974	—	3.00	6.00

DIAL

❏ 3018	I Got My Shake/There'll Come a Day	1964	3.75	7.50	15.00
❏ 4019	I Refuse to Give Up/Somebody Will	1965	3.00	6.00	12.00
❏ 4040	Gimmie a Try/Part of Your Love	1966	3.00	6.00	12.00

PHIL-L.A. OF SOUL

❏ 301	Cadillac Annie/Tired Blood	1967	2.50	5.00	10.00

WAND

❏ 1106	Somebody Will/I Refuse to Give Up	1966	6.25	12.50	25.00
❏ 1121	I'm Your Yes Man/Your Love Is All the Help I Need	1966	10.00	20.00	40.00

Albums
ATCO

❏ SD 33-307	Dancin' with Nobody But You Babe	1969	7.50	15.00	30.00

REMUS, EUGENE
45s
MOTOWN

❏ 1001	You Never Miss a Good Thing/Hold Me Tight	1960	150.00	300.00	600.00
❏ 1001	You Never Miss a Good Thing/Gotta Have Your Lovin'	1960	125.00	250.00	500.00

REPARATA AND THE DELRONS
45s
BIG TREE

❏ 114	Just You/There's So Little Time	1971	—	2.50	5.00

KAPP

❏ 989	(That's What Sends Men to) The Bowery/I've Got an Awful Lot of Losing to Do	1969	—	3.00	6.00
❏ 2010	San Juan/We're Gonna Hold the Night	1969	—	3.00	6.00
❏ 2050	Waking in the Rain/Got Fear of Losing You	1969	—	3.00	6.00

LAURIE

❏ 3252	Your Big Mistake/Leave Us Alone	1964	7.50	15.00	30.00
—As "The Delrons"

❏ 3589	Octopus' Garden/Your Life Is Gone	1972	—	2.50	5.00
—As "Reparata"

MALA

❏ 573	I Believe/It's Waiting There for You	1967	—	3.00	6.00
❏ 589	Captain of Your Ship/Toom Toom Is a Little Boy	1968	3.00	6.00	12.00

❏ 12000	Saturday Night Didn't Happen/Panic	1968	—	3.00	6.00
❏ 12016	You Can't Change a Young Boy's Mind/Weather Forecast	1968	—	3.00	6.00
❏ 12026	Heaven Only Knows/Summer Laughter	1968	—	3.00	6.00

POLYDOR

❏ 14271	Shoes/Song for All	1975	—	2.00	4.00
—As "Reparata"

❏ 14298	Jezebee Lancer the Belly Dancer/We Need You	1975	—	—	—
—Unreleased

RCA VICTOR

❏ 47-8721	I Can Tell/Take a Look Around You	1965	2.50	5.00	10.00
❏ 47-8820	I'm Nobody's Baby Now/The Loneliest Girl in Town	1966	3.75	7.50	15.00
❏ 47-8921	Mama's Little Girl/He Don't Want Me	1966	2.50	5.00	10.00
❏ 47-9123	Boys and Girls/That Kind of Trouble That I Love	1967	2.50	5.00	10.00
❏ 47-9185	I Can Hear the Rain/Always Waitin'	1967	2.50	5.00	10.00

WORLD ARTISTS

❏ 1036	Whenever a Teenager Cries/He's My Guy	1964	3.00	6.00	12.00
❏ 1051	Tommy/Mama Don't Allow	1965	3.00	6.00	12.00
❏ 1057	He's the Greatest/A Summer Thought	1965	3.00	6.00	12.00
❏ 1062	The Boy I Love/I Found My Place	1965	3.00	6.00	12.00

Albums
AVCO EMBASSY

❏ AVE-33008	Rock and Roll Revolution	1970	6.25	12.50	25.00

WORLD ARTISTS

❏ WAM-2006 [M]	Whenever a Teenager Cries	1965	12.50	25.00	50.00
❏ WAS-3006 [S]	Whenever a Teenager Cries	1965	15.00	30.00	60.00

REVLONS, THE
More than one group.
45s
CAPITOL

❏ 4739	Dry Your Eyes/She'll Come to Me	1962	7.50	15.00	30.00

PARKWAY

❏ 107	Ya Ya/It Could Happen to You	1966	3.00	6.00	12.00

RAE COX

❏ 105	This Restless Heart/I Promise Love	1961	7.50	15.00	30.00

TIMES SQUARE

❏ 15	Ride Away/Betty	1963	6.25	12.50	25.00
—B-side by the Centuries

TOY

❏ 101	What a Love This Is/Did I Make a Mistake	1962	5.00	10.00	20.00

REYNOLDS, LAWRENCE
45s
COLUMBIA

❏ 4-45722	Love Can Be a Drag (Sometimes)/Mr. Magician	1972	—	3.50	7.00

WARNER BROS.

❏ 7322	Jesus Is a Soul Man/I Know a Good Girl (When I Hold One)	1969	2.00	4.00	8.00
❏ 7374	It Was Love/Messing with My Mind	1970	2.00	4.00	8.00
❏ 7384	Hey Mr. Preacher/Life Turned Her That Way	1970	2.00	4.00	8.00
❏ 7421	Does It Show/Doing His Thing	1970	2.00	4.00	8.00

Albums
WARNER BROS.

❏ WS 1825	Jesus Is a Soul Man	1969	5.00	10.00	20.00

RHODES, TODD
45s
KING

❏ 4469	Gin, Gin, Gin/I Shouldn't Cry But I Do	1951	25.00	50.00	100.00
❏ 4486	Good Man/Evening Breeze	1951	15.00	30.00	60.00
❏ 4509	Your Daddy's Doggin' Around/Red Boy Is Back	1952	15.00	30.00	60.00
❏ 4528	Rocket 69/Possessed	1952	12.50	25.00	50.00
❏ 4556	Snuff Dipper/Trying	1952	12.50	25.00	50.00
—B-side by La Vern Baker

❏ 4566	Pig Latin Blues/Blue Autumn	1952	12.50	25.00	50.00
❏ 4583	Hog Maw and Cabbage Slaw/Must I Cry Again	1952	12.50	25.00	50.00
—B-side by La Vern Baker

❏ 4601	Thunderbolt Boogie/Lost Child	1953	12.50	25.00	50.00
—B-side by La Vern Baker

❏ 4648	Your Mouth Got a Hole In It/Feathers	1953	10.00	20.00	40.00
❏ 4666	Let Down Blues/Beet Patch	1953	10.00	20.00	40.00
❏ 4736	Silver Sunset/Specks	1954	7.50	15.00	30.00
❏ 4755	Chicken Strut/Echoes	1954	7.50	15.00	30.00

RHYTHM ACES, THE (1)
45s
ACE

❏ 518	Rock and Roll March/Look What You've Done	1956	10.00	20.00	40.00
—B-side by Bob Douglas

VEE JAY

❏ 124	I Wonder Why/Get Lost	1954	500.00	1000.	2000.
—Red vinyl

❏ 124	I Wonder Why/Get Lost	1954	50.00	100.00	200.00
—Black vinyl

❏ 138	Whisper to Me/Olly, Olly, Oxsen Free	1955	500.00	1000.	2000.
—Red vinyl

❏ 138	Whisper to Me/Olly, Olly, Oxsen Free	1955	50.00	100.00	200.00
—Black vinyl

❏ 160	That's My Sugar/Flippety Flop	1955	30.00	60.00	120.00

Number	Title (A Side/B Side)	Yr	VG	VG+	NM
RHYTHM ACES, THE (2)					
45s					
MARK-X					
❏ 8004	Boppin' Sloppin' Baby/Crazy Jealousy	1960	7.50	15.00	30.00
RHYTHM ACES, THE (3)					
45s					
ROULETTE					
❏ 4268	Mohawk Rock/It'll Do	1960	3.75	7.50	15.00
❏ 4426	Raunchy Twist/Mockin' Bird Twist	1962	3.75	7.50	15.00
SIOUX					
❏ 82260	Allan's Rock/Go Get It	1960	7.50	15.00	30.00
❏ 102261	Yahma/What'd I Say Twist	1961	7.50	15.00	30.00
UNIVERSAL ARTISTS					
❏ 3160	Mohawk Rock/It'll Do	1960	10.00	20.00	40.00
RHYTHM HERITAGE					
45s					
ABC					
❏ 12063	Theme from "Young Frankenstein"/I Wouldn't Treat a Dog (The Way You Treated Me)	1975	—	2.50	5.00
❏ 12135	Theme from S.W.A.T./I Wouldn't Treat a Dog (The Way You Treated Me)	1975	—	2.50	5.00
—Version 1: With short version of A-side					
❏ 12135	Theme from S.W.A.T./I Wouldn't Treat a Dog (The Way You Treated Me)	1975	—	2.00	4.00
—Version 2: With long version of A-side; "RE-1" on label next to matrix number					
❏ 12177	Baretta's Theme (Keep Your Eye on the Sparrow)/My Cherie Amour	1976	—	2.00	4.00
❏ 12205	Disco-Fied/(It's Time to) Boogie Down	1976	—	2.00	4.00
❏ 12243	Gonna Fly Now (Theme from "Rocky")/Last Night on Earth	1976	—	2.00	4.00
❏ 12273	Theme from "Starsky and Hutch"/Disco Queen	1977	—	2.00	4.00
❏ 12334 [DJ]	Holdin' Out for You Love (mono/stereo)	1978	—	2.00	4.00
—May be promo only					
❏ 12378	Language of Love/Sail Away with Me	1978	—	2.00	4.00
Albums					
ABC					
❏ D-934	Disco-Fied	1976	2.50	5.00	10.00
❏ D-987	Last Night on Earth	1977	2.50	5.00	10.00
❏ AA-1037	The Sky's the Limit	1978	2.50	5.00	10.00
RHYTHMETTES, THE					
45s					
BRUNSWICK					
❏ 55012	Mind Reader/Mister Love	1957	3.75	7.50	15.00
❏ 55050	That's a-Plenty/Till My Baby Comes Home	1958	3.00	6.00	12.00
❏ 55083	Elaine/Bow Legged Woman	1958	3.00	6.00	12.00
❏ 55097	I'll Be With You in Apple Blossom Time/Page from the Future	1958	3.00	6.00	12.00
CORAL					
❏ 62186	High School Lovers/Snow Queen	1960	2.50	5.00	10.00
RCA VICTOR					
❏ 47-6089	Only You/Him	1955	5.00	10.00	20.00
❏ 47-6244	Show Me the Way/The Bridge of Love	1955	3.75	7.50	15.00
❏ 47-6349	Take My Hand, Show Me the Way/I've Got to Know	1955	3.75	7.50	15.00
❏ 47-6539	Homin' Pigeon/Boom-Boom	1956	3.75	7.50	15.00
❏ 47-6742	Winter Snow/Take a Look in the Mirror	1956	3.75	7.50	15.00
RIBBONS, THE					
45s					
MARSH					
❏ 202	Ain't Gonna Kiss Ya/My Baby Said	1963	3.75	7.50	15.00
❏ 203	After Last Night/This Is Our Melody	1963	3.00	6.00	12.00
PARKWAY					
❏ 912	Meoldie D'Amour/They Played a Sad Song	1964	3.00	6.00	12.00
RICHIE, LIONEL					
Also see COMMODORES.					
45s					
MERCURY					
❏ 852856-7	Don't Wanna Lose You (Radio Version)/Don't Wanna Lose You (Album Version)	1996	—	—	3.00
MOTOWN					
❏ 1519	Endless Love/(Instrumental)	1981	—	2.00	4.00
—With Diana Ross					
❏ 1644	Truly/Just Put Some Love in Your Heart	1982	—	2.00	4.00
❏ 1657	You Are/You Mean More to Me	1983	—	2.00	4.00
❏ 1657 [PS]	You Are/You Mean More to Me	1983	—	2.50	5.00
❏ 1677	My Love/Round and Round	1983	—	2.00	4.00
❏ 1677 [PS]	My Love/Round and Round	1983	—	2.50	5.00
❏ 1698	All Night Long (All Night)/Wandering Stranger	1983	—	2.00	4.00
❏ 1710	Running with the Night/Serves You Right	1983	—	2.00	4.00
❏ 1722	Hello/You Mean More to Me	1984	—	2.00	4.00
❏ 1746	Stuck on You/Round and Round	1984	—	2.00	4.00
❏ 1746 [PS]	Stuck on You/Round and Round	1984	—	2.00	4.00
❏ 1762	Penny Lover/Tell Me	1984	—	2.00	4.00
❏ 1762 [PS]	Penny Lover/Tell Me	1984	—	2.50	
❏ 1819	Say You, Say Me/Can't Slow Down	1985	—	—	3.00
❏ 1819 [PS]	Say You, Say Me/Can't Slow Down	1985	—	2.00	4.00
—Two different sleeves were released, each of equal value					
❏ 1843	Dancing on the Ceiling/Love Will Find a Way	1986	—	—	3.00
❏ 1843 [PS]	Dancing on the Ceiling/Love Will Find a Way	1986	—	—	3.00

Number	Title (A Side/B Side)	Yr	VG	VG+	NM
❏ 1866	Love Will Conquer All/The Only One	1986	—	—	3.00
❏ 1866 [PS]	Love Will Conquer All/The Only One	1986	—	—	3.00
❏ 1873	Ballerina Girl/Deep River Woman	1986	—	—	3.00
—B-side with Alabama					
❏ 1873 [PS]	Ballerina Girl/Deep River Woman	1986	—	2.00	4.00
❏ 1883	Se La/Serves You Right	1987	—	—	3.00
❏ 1883 [PS]	Se La/Serves You Right	1987	—	—	3.00
❏ 2160	Do It To Me (Edit)/Do It To Me (LP Version)	1992	—	2.00	4.00
Albums					
MOTOWN					
❏ 6007 ML	Lionel Richie	1982	2.00	4.00	8.00
❏ 6059ML	Can't Slow Down	1983	2.00	4.00	8.00
❏ 6158 ML	Dancing on the Ceiling	1986	2.00	4.00	8.00
❏ MOT-6338 [(2)]	Back to Front	1992	5.00	10.00	20.00
—U.S. vinyl available only through Columbia House					
RICKS, JIMMY					
Also see THE RAVENS.					
45s					
ARNOLD					
❏ 1011	Canadian Sunset/Change of Heart	1961	3.75	7.50	15.00
ATCO					
❏ 6220	Daddy Rolling Stone/Homesick	1962	5.00	10.00	20.00
ATLANTIC					
❏ 2246	Trouble in Mind/Romance in the Dark	1964	3.75	7.50	15.00
BATON					
❏ 236	I'm a Fool to Want You/Bad Man of Missouri	1957	10.00	20.00	40.00
DECCA					
❏ 30443	What Have I Done/Lazy Mule	1957	6.25	12.50	25.00
FELSTED					
❏ 8560	Secret Love/If It Didn't Hurt So Much	1959	6.25	12.50	25.00
❏ 8582	Leaning On Your Love/Here Come the Tears Again	1959	6.25	12.50	25.00
FURY					
❏ 1070	I Wonder/Let Me Down Easy	1962	5.00	10.00	20.00
JOSIE					
❏ 796	She's Fine, She's Mine/The Unbeliever	1956	10.00	20.00	40.00
JUBILEE					
❏ 5559	Lonely Man/If You Ever Loved Someone	1967	3.00	6.00	12.00
❏ 5561	Wigglin' and Gigglin'/Long, Long Arm of Love	1967	3.00	6.00	12.00
❏ 5579	Don't Go to Strangers/Lonely Man	1967	3.00	6.00	12.00
❏ 5608	It's All in the Game/Baby Don't Leave Me	1967	3.00	6.00	12.00
❏ 5619	Snap Your Fingers/Wigglin' and Gigglin'	1968	3.00	6.00	12.00
MAINSTREAM					
❏ 625	Girl of My Dreams/Glow Worm	1965	3.75	7.50	15.00
MERCURY					
❏ 8296	Love Is the Thing/Too Soon	1952	20.00	40.00	80.00
PARIS					
❏ 504	Do You Promise/The Sugar Man Song	1957	7.50	15.00	30.00
SIGNATURE					
❏ 12040	I Needed Your Love/Timber	1960	5.00	10.00	20.00
❏ 12051	The Christmas Song/Love Is the Thing	1960	5.00	10.00	20.00
Albums					
JUBILEE					
❏ JGS-8021	Tell Her You Love Her	1969	12.50	25.00	50.00
MAINSTREAM					
❏ S-6050 [S]	Vibrations	1965	15.00	30.00	60.00
❏ 56050 [M]	Vibrations	1965	12.50	25.00	50.00
SIGNATURE					
❏ SM-1032 [M]	Jimmy Ricks	1961	75.00	150.00	300.00
❏ SM-1032 [M]	Jimmy Ricks	1961	50.00	100.00	200.00
—White label promo					
RIDGLEY, TOMMY					
45s					
ATLANTIC					
❏ 1009	Ooh Lawdy My Baby/I'm Gonna Cross That River	1953	15.00	30.00	60.00
❏ 1039	Jam Up/Wish I Had Never	1954	10.00	20.00	40.00
❏ 2136	Jam Up Twist/Wish I Had Never	1962	3.75	7.50	15.00
DECCA					
❏ 48226	Anything But Love/Once in a Lifetime	1951	20.00	40.00	80.00
HERALD					
❏ 501	When I Meet My Girl/Whatcha Gonna Do	1957	5.00	10.00	20.00
❏ 508	Baby Do Liddle/Just a Memory	1957	5.00	10.00	20.00
❏ 513	Come back Baby/Woncha Gone	1958	5.00	10.00	20.00
❏ 526	Mairzy Doats and Dozy Doats/I've Heard That Story Before	1958	5.00	10.00	20.00
❏ 537	I'll Be True/Girl Across the Street	1959	5.00	10.00	20.00
❏ 540	Tina/How I Feel	1959	5.00	10.00	20.00
IMPERIAL					
❏ 5198	I Live My Life/Lavinia	1952	37.50	75.00	150.00
❏ 5203	Looped/Junie Mae	1952	37.50	75.00	150.00
❏ 5214	Monkey Man/Nobody Cares	1953	37.50	75.00	150.00
❏ 5223	Good Times/A Day Is Coming	1953	37.50	75.00	150.00
RIC					
❏ 968	Is It True/Let's Try and Talk It Over	1959	3.75	7.50	15.00
❏ 973	Do You Remember/Please Hurry Home	1960	3.75	7.50	15.00
❏ 978	Double Eye Whammy/Should I Ever Love Again	1961	3.75	7.50	15.00
❏ 982	Three Times/The Only Girl for Me	1961	3.75	7.50	15.00
❏ 984	The Girl from Kooka Monga/In the Same Old Way	1961	3.75	7.50	15.00
❏ 990	My Ordinary Girl/She's Got What It Takes	1962	3.00	6.00	12.00
❏ 993	Heavenly/I Love You Yes I Do	1963	3.00	6.00	12.00
❏ 994	Honest I Do/I've Heard That Story Before	1963	3.00	6.00	12.00

Number	Title (A Side/B Side)	Yr	VG	VG+	NM

RONN
| ❑ 36 | It's the Same Old Way/I'm Not the Same Person | 1969 | 2.50 | 5.00 | 10.00 |

WHITE CLIFFS
| ❑ 260 | Hey Little Chick/Did You Tell Him | 1967 | 2.50 | 5.00 | 10.00 |

RIGHTEOUS BROTHERS, THE
Also see BOBBY HATFIELD; BILL MEDLEY; THE PARAMOURS; PHIL SPECTOR.

45s
HAVEN
❑ 800	Hold On to What You Got/Let Me Make the Music	1976	—	2.00	4.00
❑ 7002	Rock and Roll Heaven/I Just Wanna Be Me	1974	—	2.50	5.00
❑ 7004	Give It to the People/Love Is not a Dirty Word	1974	—	2.00	4.00
❑ 7006	Dream On/Dr. Rock and Roll	1974	—	2.00	4.00
❑ 7011	High Blood Pressure/Never Say I Love You	1975	—	2.00	4.00
❑ 7014	Young Blood/Substitute	1975	—	2.00	4.00

MOONGLOW
| ❑ 215 | Little Latin Lupe Lu/I'm So Lonely | 1963 | 5.00 | 10.00 | 20.00 |
| ❑ 215 [DJ] | Little Latin Lupe Lu/I'm So Lonely | 1963 | 12.50 | 25.00 | 50.00 |
—Red vinyl promo
❑ 221	Gotta Tell You How I Feel/If You're Lying, You'll Be Crying	1963	5.00	10.00	20.00
❑ 223	My Babe/Fee-Fi-Fidily-I-Oh	1963	5.00	10.00	20.00
❑ 224	Ko Ko Joe/B-Flat Blues	1963	5.00	10.00	20.00
❑ 231	Try to Find Another Man/I Still Love You	1964	5.00	10.00	20.00
❑ 234	Bring Your Love to Me/If You're Lying, You'll Be Crying	1964	5.00	10.00	20.00
❑ 235	This Little Girl of Mine/If You're Lying, You'll Be Crying	1964	3.75	7.50	15.00
❑ 238	Bring Your Love to Me/Fannie Mae	1965	3.75	7.50	15.00
❑ 239	You Can Have Her/Love or Magic	1965	3.75	7.50	15.00
❑ 242	Justine/In That Great Gettin' Up Morning	1965	3.75	7.50	15.00
❑ 243	For Your Love/Gotta Tell You How I Feel	1965	3.75	7.50	15.00
❑ 244	Georgia on My Mind/My Tears Will Go Away	1966	3.75	7.50	15.00
❑ 245	I Need a Girl/Bring Your Love to Me	1966	3.75	7.50	15.00

PHILLES
❑ 124	You've Lost That Lovin' Feelin'/There's a Woman	1964	3.75	7.50	15.00
❑ 127	Just Once in My Life/The Blues	1965	3.75	7.50	15.00
❑ 127 [PS]	Just Once in My Life/The Blues	1965	7.50	15.00	30.00
❑ 129	Unchained Melody/Hung on You	1965	3.75	7.50	15.00
—With "Producer: Phil Spector" on the "Unchained Melody" side
| ❑ 129 | Unchained Melody/Hung on You | 1965 | 7.50 | 15.00 | 30.00 |
—With no producer credit on the "Unchained Melody" side
❑ 130	Ebb Tide/(I Love You) For Sentimental Reasons	1965	3.75	7.50	15.00
❑ 130 [PS]	Ebb Tide/(I Love You) For Sentimental Reasons	1965	7.50	15.00	30.00
❑ 132	The White Cliffs of Dover/She's Mine, All Mine	1966	5.00	10.00	20.00

VERVE
| ❑ CS8-5 | Celebrity Scene: The Righteous Brothers | 1967 | 15.00 | 30.00 | 60.00 |
—Box set of five singles (10520-10524). Price includes box, all 5 singles, jukebox title strips, bio. Records are sometimes found by themselves, so they are also listed separately.
❑ 10383	(You're My) Soul and Inspiration/B Side Blues	1966	3.75	7.50	15.00
❑ 10383 [PS]	(You're My) Soul and Inspiration/B Side Blues	1966	7.50	15.00	30.00
❑ 10403	Rat Race/Green Onions	1966	3.75	7.50	15.00
❑ 10406	He/He Will Break Your Heart	1966	2.50	5.00	10.00
❑ 10406 [PS]	He/He Will Break Your Heart	1966	5.00	10.00	20.00
❑ 10430	Go Ahead and Cry/Things Didn't Go Your Way	1966	2.50	5.00	10.00
❑ 10449	On This Side of Goodbye/A Man Without a Dream	1966	2.50	5.00	10.00
❑ 10479	Along Came Jones/Jimmy's Blues	1967	2.00	4.00	8.00
❑ 10507	Melancholy Music Man/Don't Give Up on Me	1967	2.00	4.00	8.00
❑ 10520	(You're My) Soul and Inspiration/Go Ahead and Cry	1967	2.50	5.00	10.00
❑ 10521	Hold On, I'm Coming/He Will Break Your Heart	1967	2.50	5.00	10.00
❑ 10522	Melancholy Music Man/I Believe	1967	2.50	5.00	10.00
❑ 10523	I (Who Have Nothing)/Island in the Sun	1967	2.50	5.00	10.00
❑ 10524	My Girl/Something You Got	1967	2.50	5.00	10.00
❑ 10551	Stranded in the Middle of No Place/Been So Nice	1967	2.00	4.00	8.00
❑ 10551 [PS]	Stranded in the Middle of No Place/Been So Nice	1967	3.75	7.50	15.00
❑ 10577	Here I Am/So Many Lonely Nights Ahead	1968	2.00	4.00	8.00
❑ 10637	Let the Good Times Roll/You've Lost That Lovin' Feelin'	1968	2.00	4.00	8.00
❑ 10648	And the Party Goes On/Woman, Man Needs Ya	1968	2.00	4.00	8.00
❑ 10649	Good N' Nuff/Po' Folks	1968	2.00	4.00	8.00
❑ 871882-7	Unchained Melody/Hung on You	1989	—	2.00	4.00

Albums
HAVEN
| ❑ ST-9201 | Give It to the People | 1974 | 3.75 | 7.50 | 15.00 |
| ❑ ST-9203 | Sons of Mrs. Righteous | 1975 | 3.75 | 7.50 | 15.00 |

MGM
| ❑ GAS-102 | The Righteous Brothers (Golden Archive Series) | 1970 | 3.75 | 7.50 | 15.00 |
| ❑ SE-4885 | The History of the Righteous Brothers | 1973 | 3.75 | 7.50 | 15.00 |

MOONGLOW
❑ MLP-1001 [M]	Right Now!	1963	10.00	20.00	40.00
❑ MSP-1001 [S]	Right Now!	1963	15.00	30.00	60.00
❑ MLP-1002 [M]	Some Blue-Eyed Soul	1964	10.00	20.00	40.00
❑ MSP-1002 [S]	Some Blue-Eyed Soul	1964	15.00	30.00	60.00
❑ MLP-1003 [M]	This Is New!	1965	10.00	20.00	40.00
❑ MSP-1003 [S]	This Is New!	1965	15.00	30.00	60.00
❑ MLP-1004 [M]	The Best of the Righteous Brothers	1966	6.25	12.50	25.00
❑ MSP-1004 [S]	The Best of the Righteous Brothers	1966	7.50	15.00	30.00

PHILLES
❑ PHLP-4007 [M]	You've Lost That Lovin' Feelin'	1964	6.25	12.50	25.00
❑ PHLPS-4007 [S]	You've Lost That Lovin' Feelin'	1964	10.00	20.00	40.00
❑ PHLP-4008 [M]	Just Once in My Life	1965	6.25	12.50	25.00
❑ PHLPS-4008 [S]	Just Once in My Life	1965	10.00	20.00	40.00
❑ PHLP-4009 [M]	Back to Back	1965	6.25	12.50	25.00
❑ PHLPS-4009 [S]	Back to Back	1965	10.00	20.00	40.00
❑ ST-90692 [S]	You've Lost That Lovin' Feelin'	1965	12.50	25.00	50.00
—Capitol Record Club edition
| ❑ T-90692 [M] | You've Lost That Lovin' Feelin' | 1965 | 12.50 | 25.00 | 50.00 |
—Capitol Record Club edition

RHINO
| ❑ R1-71488 [(2)] | Anthology | 1989 | 3.75 | 7.50 | 15.00 |

VERVE
❑ V-5001 [M]	Soul and Inspiration	1966	5.00	10.00	20.00
❑ V6-5001 [S]	Soul and Inspiration	1966	6.25	12.50	25.00
❑ V-5004 [M]	Go Ahead and Cry	1966	5.00	10.00	20.00
❑ V6-5004 [S]	Go Ahead and Cry	1966	6.25	12.50	25.00
❑ V-5010 [M]	Sayin' Somethin'	1967	5.00	10.00	20.00
❑ V6-5010 [S]	Sayin' Somethin'	1967	6.25	12.50	25.00
❑ V-5020 [M]	Greatest Hits	1967	6.25	12.50	25.00
❑ V6-5020 [S]	Greatest Hits	1967	5.00	10.00	20.00
❑ V-5031 [M]	Souled Out	1967	7.50	15.00	30.00
❑ V6-5031 [S]	Souled Out	1967	5.00	10.00	20.00
❑ V6-5051	Standards	1968	5.00	10.00	20.00
❑ V6-5058	One for the Road	1968	7.50	15.00	30.00
—With The Blossoms credited on the back cover
| ❑ V6-5058 | One for the Road | 1968 | 5.00 | 10.00 | 20.00 |
—Without The Blossoms credited on the back cover
❑ V6-5071	Greatest Hits, Vol. 2	1969	5.00	10.00	20.00
❑ V6-5076	Re-Birth	1970	5.00	10.00	20.00
❑ ST-91057 [S]	Sayin' Somethin'	1967	6.25	12.50	25.00
—Capitol Record Club edition
| ❑ 823662-1 | Greatest Hits | 198? | 2.50 | 5.00 | 10.00 |

RIPERTON, MINNIE
Also see ROTARY CONNECTION.

45s
CAPITOL
❑ 4706	Memory Lane/I'm a Woman	1979	—	2.00	4.00
❑ 4761	Lover and Friend/Return to Forever	1979	—	2.00	4.00
❑ 4902	Here We Go/Return to Forever	1980	—	2.00	4.00
❑ 4955	Give Me Time/Island in the Sun	1980	—	2.00	4.00

CHESS
| ❑ 1980 | Lonely Girl/You Gave Me Soul | 1966 | 2.50 | 5.00 | 10.00 |
—As "Andrea Davis"

EPIC
❑ 11139	Every Time He Comes Around/Reasons	1974	—	2.50	5.00
❑ 50020	Edge of a Dream/Seeing You This Way	1974	—	2.50	5.00
❑ 50057	Lovin' You/Edge of a Dream	1974	—	2.50	5.00
❑ 50128	Don't Let Anyone Bring You Down/Inside My Love	1975	—	2.50	5.00
❑ 50155	When It Comes Down To It/Minnie's Lament	1975	—	2.50	5.00
❑ 50166	Simple Things/Minnie's Lament	1975	—	2.50	5.00
❑ 50190	Adventures in Paradise/When It Comes Down To It	1976	—	2.50	5.00
❑ 50337	Stick Together (Part One)/Stick Together (Part Two)	1977	—	2.50	5.00
❑ 50351	Young, Willing and Able/Stick Together	1977	—	2.50	5.00
❑ 50394	Wouldn't Matter Where You Are	1977	—	2.50	5.00
❑ 50427	How Could I Love You More/Young, Willing and Able	1977	—	2.50	5.00

GRT
| ❑ 42 | Oh! By the Way/Le Fleur | 1972 | — | 3.00 | 6.00 |

Albums
ACCORD
| ❑ SN-7205 | Wistful Memories | 1981 | 2.50 | 5.00 | 10.00 |

CAPITOL
| ❑ SO-11936 | Minnie | 1979 | 2.50 | 5.00 | 10.00 |
| ❑ SN-12004 | Perfect Angel | 1979 | 2.50 | 5.00 | 10.00 |
—Reissue of Epic 32561
| ❑ SN-12005 | Adventures in Paradise | 1979 | 2.50 | 5.00 | 10.00 |
—Reissue of Epic 33454
| ❑ SN-12006 | Stay in Love | 1979 | 2.50 | 5.00 | 10.00 |
—Reissue of Epic 34191
❑ SOO-12097	Love Lives Forever	1980	2.50	5.00	10.00
❑ ST-12189	The Best of Minnie Riperton	1981	2.50	5.00	10.00
❑ SN-16145	Perfect Angel	1980	2.00	4.00	8.00
—Budget-line reissue
| ❑ SN-16146 | Adventures in Paradise | 1980 | 2.00 | 4.00 | 8.00 |
—Budget-line reissue
| ❑ SN-16147 | Stay in Love | 1980 | 2.00 | 4.00 | 8.00 |
—Budget-line reissue

EPIC
❑ KE 32561	Perfect Angel	1974	3.00	6.00	12.00
❑ PE 33454	Adventures in Paradise	1975	3.00	6.00	12.00
❑ PEQ 33454 [Q]	Adventures in Paradise	1975	5.00	10.00	20.00
❑ PE 34191	Stay in Love	1977	3.00	6.00	12.00

GRT
| ❑ 30001 | Come To My Garden | 1970 | 3.75 | 7.50 | 15.00 |

JANUS
| ❑ 7011 | Come To My Garden | 1974 | 3.00 | 6.00 | 12.00 |
—Reissue of GRT LP

RIPLEY COTTON CHOPPERS
78s
SUN
| ❑ 190 | Silver Bells/Blues Waltz | 1953 | 1000. | 2000. | 3000. |
—Unknown on 45 rpm, though nine Suns with lower numbers do exist on 45s.

Number	Title (A Side/B Side)	Yr	VG	VG+	NM

RIPPLES AND WAVES PLUS MICHAEL, THE
See THE JACKSONS.

RITCHIE FAMILY, THE
12-Inch Singles
CASABLANCA

❏ NBD 20192	Put Your Feet to the Beat (6:58)/Bad Reputation (6:01)	1979	3.75	7.50	15.00

RCA

❏ PD-13093	I'll Do My Best (For You Baby)/You've Got Me Dancin'	1982	—	3.00	6.00
❏ PD-13551	All Night All Right/Fantasy	1983	—	3.00	6.00

45s
20TH CENTURY

❏ 2218	Brazil/Hot Trip	1975	—	2.00	4.00
❏ 2252	I Want to Dance with You (Dance with Me)/Lady Champagne	1975	—	2.00	4.00

CASABLANCA

❏ 2206	Put Your Feet to the Beat/It's a Man's World	1979	—	2.00	4.00
❏ 2259	Give Me a Break/Bad Reputation	1980	—	2.00	4.00
❏ 2292	All My Love/I'll Never Be Able to Set You Free	1980	—	2.00	4.00

MARLIN

❏ 3306	The Best Disco in Town/The Best Disco in Town (Part 2)	1976	—	2.00	4.00
❏ 3309	Life Is Music/Lady Luck	1977	—	2.00	4.00
❏ 3316	Quiet Village/Voodoo	1977	—	2.00	4.00
❏ 3323	American Generation/Music Man	1978	—	2.00	4.00

RCA

❏ PB-13092	I'll Do My Best (For You Baby)/You've Got Me Dancin'	1982	—	—	3.00
❏ PB-13281	Walk with Me/Tonight I Need to Have Your Love	1982	—	—	3.00
❏ PB-13550	All Night All Right/Fantasy	1983	—	—	3.00

Albums
20TH CENTURY

❏ T-498	Brazil	1975	2.50	5.00	10.00

CASABLANCA

❏ NBLP-7166	Bad Reputation	1979	2.50	5.00	10.00
❏ NBLP-7223	Give Me a Break	1980	2.50	5.00	10.00

MARLIN

❏ 2201	Arabian Nights	1976	2.50	5.00	10.00
❏ 2203	Life Is Music	1977	2.50	5.00	10.00
❏ 2206	African Queens	1977	2.50	5.00	10.00
❏ 2215	American Generation	1978	2.50	5.00	10.00

RCA VICTOR

❏ AFL1-4324	I'll Do My Best	1982	2.50	5.00	10.00
❏ AFL1-4601	All Night, All Night	1983	2.50	5.00	10.00

RIVIERAS, THE (1)
R&B vocal group from northern New Jersey.
45s
COED

❏ 503	Count Every Star/True Love Is Hard to Find	1958	12.50	25.00	50.00
❏ 508	Moonlight Serenade/Neither Rain Nor Snow	1959	10.00	20.00	40.00
❏ 513	Our Love/True Love Is Hard to Find	1959	7.50	15.00	30.00
❏ 513	Our Love/Midnight Flyer	1959	7.50	15.00	30.00
❏ 522	Since I Made You Cry/11th Hour Melody	1959	7.50	15.00	30.00
❏ 529	Blessing of Love/Moonlight Cocktails	1960	6.25	12.50	25.00
❏ 538	My Friend/Great Big Eyes	1960	6.25	12.50	25.00
❏ 542	Easy to Remember/Stay in My Heart	1960	6.25	12.50	25.00
❏ 551	El Doraado/Refrigerator	1961	6.25	12.50	25.00
❏ 592	Moonlight Cocktails/Midnight Flyer	1964	3.75	7.50	15.00

Albums
POST

❏ 2000	The Rivieras Sing	196?	10.00	20.00	40.00

RIVILEERS, THE
45s
BATON

❏ 200	A Thousand Stars/Hey Chiquita	1953	50.00	100.00	200.00
❏ 201	Forever/Darling Farewell	1954	30.00	60.00	120.00
❏ 205	Carolyn/Eternal Love	1954	30.00	60.00	120.00
❏ 207	(I Love You) For Sentimental Reasons/I Want to See My Baby	1955	15.00	30.00	60.00
❏ 209	Little Girl/Don't Ever Leave Me	1955	15.00	30.00	60.00
❏ 241	A Thousand Stars/Who Is the Girl	1957	10.00	20.00	40.00

RIVINGTONS, THE
45s
AGC

❏ 5	I Lost the Love/Mind Your Man	1968	2.00	4.00	8.00

A.R.E. AMERICAN

❏ 100	All That Glitters/You Move Me Baby	1964	3.75	7.50	15.00

BATON MASTER

❏ 202	Teach Me Tonight/Reach Our Goal	1967	2.00	4.00	8.00

COLUMBIA

❏ 43581	A Rose Growing in the Ruins/Tend to Business	1966	3.00	6.00	12.00
❏ 43772	Yadi Yadi Yum Yum/Yadi Yadi Revisited	1966	3.00	6.00	12.00

J.D.

❏ 122	Don't Hate Your Father (Part 1)/Don't Hate Your Father (Part 2)	1976	—	2.50	5.00

LIBERTY

❏ 1484 [DJ]	Papa-Oom-Mow-Mow (same on both sides)	1982	—	3.00	6.00

—Reissue; promo only

❏ 55427	Papa-Oom-Mow-Mow/Deep Water	1962	6.25	12.50	25.00
❏ 55513	Kickapoo Joy Juice/My Reward	1962	3.75	7.50	15.00
❏ 55528	Mama-Oom-Mow-Mow/Waiting	1962	3.75	7.50	15.00
❏ 55553	The Bird's the Word/I'm Losing My Grip	1963	5.00	10.00	20.00
❏ 55585	The Shaky Bird (Part 1)/The Shaky Bird (Part 2)	1963	3.75	7.50	15.00
❏ 55610	Little Sally Walker/Cherry	1963	7.50	15.00	30.00
❏ 55671	Fairy Tales/Wee Jee Walk	1964	3.75	7.50	15.00

QUAN

❏ 1379	I Don't Want a New Baby/You're Gonna Pay	1967	2.50	5.00	10.00

RCA VICTOR

❏ 74-0301	Pop Your Corn (Part 1)/Pop Your Corn (Part 2)	1969	2.00	4.00	8.00

REPRISE

❏ 0293	I Tried/One Monkey Don't Stop No Show	1964	3.00	6.00	12.00

UNITED ARTISTS

❏ 0096	Papa-Oom-Mow-Mow/The Bird's the Word	1973	—	2.00	4.00

—"Silver Spotlight Series" reissue

VEE JAY

❏ 634	All That Glitters/You Move Me Baby	1964	3.00	6.00	12.00
❏ 649	I Love You Always/Years of Tears	1965	3.00	6.00	12.00
❏ 677	The Willy/Just Got to Be Mine	1965	3.00	6.00	12.00

WAND

❏ 11253	Papa-Oom-Mow-Mow/I Don't Want a New Baby	1973	—	2.50	5.00

Albums
LIBERTY

❏ LRP-3282 [M]	Doin' the Bird	1963	25.00	50.00	100.00
❏ LST-7282 [S]	Doin' the Bird	1963	50.00	100.00	200.00

ROBERT AND JOHNNY
45s
OLD TOWN

❏ 1021	I Believe You/Train to Paradise	1956	12.50	25.00	50.00
❏ 1029	You're Mine/Million Dollar Bills	1956	10.00	20.00	40.00
❏ 1038	Don't Do It/Baby Come Home	1957	10.00	20.00	40.00
❏ 1043	Broken Hearted Man/Indian Marriage	1957	10.00	20.00	40.00
❏ 1047	We Belong Together/In the Rain	1958	12.50	25.00	50.00
❏ 1052	I Know/Marry Me	1958	10.00	20.00	40.00
❏ 1052	I Believe in You/Marry Me	1958	10.00	20.00	40.00
❏ 1058	Eternity with You/I'm Truly, Truly Yours	1958	7.50	15.00	30.00
❏ 1065	Give Me the Key to Your Heart/Truly in Love	1959	7.50	15.00	30.00
❏ 1068	Dream Girl/Oh My Love	1959	7.50	15.00	30.00
❏ 1072	Wear This Ring/Bad Dan	1959	7.50	15.00	30.00
❏ 1078	Hear My Heartbeat/Try Me Pretty Baby	1960	6.25	12.50	25.00
❏ 1086	We Belong Together/In the Rain	1960	6.25	12.50	25.00
❏ 1100	You're Mine/Please Me Please	1961	5.00	10.00	20.00
❏ 1108	Togetherness/I Got You	1961	5.00	10.00	20.00
❏ 1117	Wear This Ring/Broken Hearted Man	1962	5.00	10.00	20.00

SUE

❏ 792	A Perfect Wife/Brown, Pretty Brown Eyes	1963	6.25	12.50	25.00

ROBINS, THE (1)
Vocal group from Los Angeles. Part of the group splintered off and became the core of THE COASTERS.
45s
ATCO

❏ 6059	Smokey Joe's Cafe/Just Like a Fool	1956	12.50	25.00	50.00

CROWN

❏ 106	I Made a Vow/Double Crossing Baby	1954	100.00	200.00	400.00
❏ 120	Key to My Heart/All I Do Is Rock	1954	75.00	150.00	300.00

KNIGHT

❏ 2001	Quarter to Twelve/Pretty Little Dolly	1958	12.50	25.00	50.00
❏ 2008	It's Never Too Late/A Little Bird Told Me	1958	20.00	40.00	80.00

RCA VICTOR

❏ 20-5271	Oh Why/All Night Baby	1953	20.00	40.00	80.00
❏ 47-5175	(Now and Then There's) A Fool Such As I/My Heart's the Biggest Fool	1953	125.00	250.00	500.00
❏ 47-5271	Oh Why/All Night Baby	1953	100.00	200.00	400.00
❏ 47-5434	How Would You Know/Let's Go to the Dance	1953	100.00	200.00	400.00
❏ 47-5486	My Baby Done Told Me/I'll Do It	1953	75.00	150.00	300.00
❏ 47-5489	Ten Days in Jail/Empty Bottles	1953	50.00	100.00	200.00
❏ 47-5564	Get It Off Your Mind/Don't Stop Now	1953	50.00	100.00	200.00

SPARK

❏ 103	Riot in Cell Block #9/Wrap It Up	1954	75.00	150.00	300.00

—Copies on yellow labels are bootlegs

❏ 107	Loop De Loop Mambo/Framed	1954	75.00	150.00	300.00

—Silver top label

❏ 107	Loop De Loop Mambo/Framed	1954	25.00	50.00	100.00

—Red label

❏ 110	If Teardrops Were Kisses/Whadaya Want	1955	75.00	150.00	300.00

—Red label

❏ 110	If Teardrops Were Kisses/Whadaya Want	1955	25.00	50.00	100.00

—Blue label

❏ 113	One Kiss/I Love Paris	1955	75.00	150.00	300.00
❏ 116	I Must Be Dreamin'/The Hatchet Man	1955	50.00	100.00	200.00

—Red label

❏ 116	I Must Be Dreamin'/The Hatchet Man	1955	12.50	25.00	50.00

—Yellow label

❏ 122	Smokey Joe's Cafe/Just Like a Fool	1955	87.50	175.00	350.00

WHIPPET

❏ 200	Cherry Lips/Out of the Picture	1956	20.00	40.00	80.00
❏ 201	Hurt Me/Merry-Go-Rock	1956	17.50	35.00	70.00
❏ 203	That Old Black Magic/Since I First Met You	1956	17.50	35.00	70.00
❏ 206	A Fool in Love/All of a Sudden My Heart Sings	1957	17.50	35.00	70.00
❏ 208	Every Night/Where's the Fire	1957	17.50	35.00	70.00
❏ 211	In My Dreams/Keep Your Mind on Me	1957	17.50	35.00	70.00

Number	Title (A Side/B Side)	Yr	VG	VG+	NM
❑ 212	Snowball/You Wanted Fun	1958	17.50	35.00	70.00
78s					
ALADDIN					
❑ 3031	Don't Like the Way You're Doing/Come Back Baby	1949	125.00	250.00	500.00
RCA VICTOR					
❑ 20-5175	(Now and Then There's) A Fool Such As I/My Heart's the Biggest Fool	1953	37.50	75.00	150.00
❑ 20-5434	How Would You Know/Let's Go to the Dance	1953	20.00	40.00	80.00
❑ 20-5486	My Baby Done Told Me/I'll Do It	1953	20.00	40.00	80.00
❑ 20-5489	Ten Days in Jail/Empty Bottles	1953	20.00	40.00	80.00
❑ 20-5564	Get It Off Your Mind/Don't Stop Now	1953	20.00	40.00	80.00
RECORDED IN HOLLYWOOD					
❑ 112	Race of Man/Bayou Baby Blues	1951	75.00	150.00	300.00
❑ 150	School Girl Blues/Early Morning Blues	1951	75.00	150.00	300.00
SAVOY					
❑ 726	If It's So Baby/If I Didn't Love You So	1950	20.00	40.00	80.00
SPARK					
❑ 103	Riot in Cell Block #9/Wrap It Up	1954	15.00	30.00	60.00
❑ 107	Loop De Loop Mambo/Framed	1954	12.50	25.00	50.00
❑ 110	If Teardrops Were Kisses/Whadaya Want	1955	12.50	25.00	50.00
❑ 113	One Kiss/I Love Paris	1955	15.00	30.00	60.00
❑ 116	I Must Be Dreamin'/The Hatchet Man	1955	12.50	25.00	50.00
❑ 122	Smokey Joe's Cafe/Just Like a Fool	1955	17.50	35.00	70.00
Albums					
GNP CRESCENDO					
❑ GNPS-9034	The Best of the Robins	1975	3.75	7.50	15.00
WHIPPET					
❑ WLP-703 [M]	Rock 'n' Roll with the Robins	1958	200.00	400.00	800.00

ROBINSON, BILL, AND THE QUAILS

Number	Title (A Side/B Side)	Yr	VG	VG+	NM
45s					
DATE					
❑ 1620	Do I Love You/Lay My Head on Your Shoulder	1969	2.50	5.00	10.00
DELUXE					
❑ 6030	Lonely Star/Quit Pushin'	1954	50.00	100.00	200.00
❑ 6047	I Know She's Gone/Baby Don't Want Me No More	1954	75.00	150.00	300.00
❑ 6057	A Little Bit of Love/Somewhere Somebody Cares	1954	50.00	100.00	200.00
❑ 6059	Why Do I Wait/Heaven Is the Place	1954	50.00	100.00	200.00
❑ 6074	Love of My Life/Oh Sugar	1955	37.50	75.00	150.00
❑ 6085	The Things She Used to Do/Pretty Huggin' Baby	1955	17.50	35.00	70.00
—As "The Quails"					

ROBINSON, FREDDY

Number	Title (A Side/B Side)	Yr	VG	VG+	NM
45s					
CHECKER					
❑ 1143	The Creeper/Go Go Girl	1966	2.50	5.00	10.00
LIBERTY					
❑ 56214	Carmalita/Stone Stallion	1970	—	3.00	6.00
LIMELIGHT					
❑ 3005	Not Like Now/Five Feet of Lovin'	1963	3.00	6.00	12.00
MERCURY					
❑ 71270	Be Mine/You and Me	1958	3.00	6.00	12.00
PACIFIC JAZZ					
❑ 88152	Before Six/The Coming Atlantis	1969	—	3.00	6.00
❑ 88155	Black Fox/The Oogue Boogum Song	1970	—	3.00	6.00
QUEEN					
❑ 24005	The Buzzard/The Hawk	196?	2.50	5.00	10.00

ROBINSON, JANICE

Number	Title (A Side/B Side)	Yr	VG	VG+	NM
45s					
WARNER BROS.					
❑ 16911	Nothing I Would Change/What Can Happen to Us	1999	—	—	3.00

ROBINSON, SMOKEY

Also see THE MIRACLES; RON AND BILL.

Number	Title (A Side/B Side)	Yr	VG	VG+	NM
12-Inch Singles					
MOTOWN					
❑ M00004D1	Vitamin U/Chalk It Up	1977	5.00	10.00	20.00
—B-side by Jerry Butler					
❑ 00027	Get Ready/(Instrumental)	1979	3.00	6.00	12.00
❑ PR-92 [DJ]	Tell Me Tomorrow/Right in the Middle (vocal) (instrumental)	1982	2.50	5.00	10.00
—B-side by Bettye Lavette					
❑ L33-17828 [DJ]	(It's the) Same Old Love (3 versions)	1990	—	3.00	6.00
❑ L33-18141 [DJ]	Everything You Touch (3 versions)/It's the Same Old Feeling	1990	—	3.00	6.00
❑ 50109	Everything You Touch (3 versions)/It's the Same Old Feeling	1990	—	3.50	7.00
TAMLA					
❑ 145 [DJ]	And I Don't Love You (7:10)/And I Don't Love You (Dub)	1984	2.00	4.00	8.00
45s					
COLUMBIA					
❑ 07727	I Know You by Heart/Could I Have Your Autograph	1988	—	—	3.00
—With Dolly Parton					
MOTOWN					
❑ 914	(It's the) Same Old Love/(Instrumental)	1990	—	2.00	4.00
❑ 1877	Just to See Her/I'm Gonna Love You Like There's No Tomorrow	1987	—	—	3.00
❑ 1877 [PS]	Just to See Her/I'm Gonna Love You Like There's No Tomorrow	1987	2.00	4.00	8.00
❑ 1897	One Heartbeat/Love Will Set You Free (Theme from Solarbabies)	1987	—	—	3.00
❑ 1897 [PS]	One Heartbeat/Love Will Set You Free (Theme from Solarbabies)	1987	—	3.00	6.00
❑ 1911	What's Too Much/I've Made Love to You a Thousand Times	1987	—	—	3.00
❑ 1911 [PS]	What's Too Much/I've Made Love to You a Thousand Times	1987	—	2.50	5.00
❑ 1925	Love Don't Give No Reason/Hanging On by a Thread	1988	—	—	3.00
❑ 1925 [PS]	Love Don't Give No Reason/Hanging On by a Thread	1988	—	2.50	5.00
SBK					
❑ 07379	Double Good Everything/Guess What I Got for You	1991	—	2.00	4.00
TAMLA					
❑ 1601	Tell Me Tomorrow (Part 1)/Tell Me Tomorrow (Part 2)	1982	—	2.00	4.00
❑ 1615	Old Fashioned Love/Destiny	1982	—	2.00	4.00
❑ 1630	Are You Still Here/Yes It's You Lady	1982	—	2.00	4.00
❑ 1655	I've Made Love to You a Thousand Times/Into Each Rain Some Life Must Fall	1983	—	2.00	4.00
❑ 1678	Touch the Sky/All My Life's a Lie	1983	—	2.00	4.00
❑ 1684	Blame It on Love/Even Tho'	1983	—	2.00	4.00
—With Barbara Mitchell					
❑ 1700	Don't Play Another Love Song/Wouldn't You Like to Know	1983	—	2.00	4.00
❑ 1735	And I Don't Love You/Dynamite	1984	—	2.00	4.00
❑ 1756	I Can't Find/Gimme What You Want	1984	—	2.00	4.00
❑ 1786	First Time on a Ferris Wheel/Train of Thought	1985	—	2.00	4.00
❑ 1828	Hold On to Your Love/Train of Thought	1985	—	2.00	4.00
❑ 1828 [PS]	Hold On to Your Love/Train of Thought	1985	—	3.00	6.00
❑ 1839	Sleepless Nights/Close Encounters of the First Kind	1986	—	2.00	4.00
❑ 1839 [PS]	Sleepless Nights/Close Encounters of the First Kind	1986	—	2.50	5.00
❑ 1855	Girl I'm Standing There/Because of You (It's the Best It's Ever Been)	1986	—	2.00	4.00
❑ 1868	Love Will Set You Free (Theme from Solarbabies) (Parts 1 & 2)	1986	—	2.00	4.00
❑ 54233	Sweet Harmony/Want to Know My Mind	1973	—	2.50	5.00
❑ 54239	Baby Come Close/A Silent Partner in a Three-Way Love Affair	1973	—	2.50	5.00
❑ 54246	It's Her Turn to Live/Just My Soul Responding	1974	—	2.50	5.00
❑ 54250	Virgin Man/Fulfill Your Need	1974	—	2.50	5.00
❑ 54251	I Am, I Am/The Family Song	1974	—	2.50	5.00
❑ 54258	Baby That's Backatcha/Just Passing Through	1975	—	2.50	5.00
❑ 54261	The Agony and the Ecstasy/Wedding Song	1975	—	2.50	5.00
❑ 54265	Quiet Storm/Asleep on My Love	1975	—	2.50	5.00
❑ 54267	Open/Coincidentally	1976	—	2.50	5.00
❑ 54269	When You Came/Coincidentally	1976	3.00	6.00	12.00
—Released only in Canada					
❑ 54272	An Old Fashioned Man/(B-side unassigned)	1976	—	—	—
—Unreleased					
❑ 54276	An Old Fashioned Man/Just Passing Through	1976	—	2.50	5.00
❑ 54279	There Will Come a Day (I'm Gonna Happen to You)/Humming Song	1977	—	2.50	5.00
❑ 54284	Vitamin U/Holly	1977	—	2.50	5.00
❑ 54288	Theme from Big Time (Part 1)/Theme from Big Time (Part 2)	1977	—	2.50	5.00
❑ 54293	Daylight and Darkness/Why You Wanna See My Bad Side	1978	—	2.50	5.00
❑ 54296	I'm Loving You Softly/Shoe Soul	1978	—	2.50	5.00
❑ 54301	Get Ready/Ever Had a Dream	1979	—	2.00	4.00
❑ 54306	Cruisin'/Ever Had a Dream	1979	—	2.00	4.00
❑ 54311	Let Me Be the Clock/Travelin' Through	1980	—	2.00	4.00
❑ 54313	Heavy on Pride/I Love the Nearness of You	1980	—	2.00	4.00
❑ 54318	I Want to Be Your Love/Wine, Women and Song	1980	—	2.00	4.00
❑ 54321	Being with You/What's In Your Life for Me	1981	—	2.00	4.00
❑ 54325	Aquicontigo/Being with You (Aquicontigo)	1981	—	2.00	4.00
❑ 54327	You Are Forever/I Hear the Children Singing	1981	—	2.00	4.00
❑ 54332	Who's Sad/Food for Thought	1981	—	2.00	4.00
Albums					
MOTOWN					
❑ M5-118V1	Motown Superstar Series, Vol. 18	1981	2.50	5.00	10.00
❑ M5-134V1	Smokey	1981	2.00	4.00	8.00
—Reissue of Tamla 328					
❑ M5-154V1	Deep in My Soul	1981	2.00	4.00	8.00
—Reissue of Tamla 350					
❑ M5-168V1	Pure Smokey	1981	2.00	4.00	8.00
—Reissue of Tamla 331					
❑ M5-197V1	A Quiet Storm	1981	2.00	4.00	8.00
—Reissue of Tamla 337					
❑ 5267ML	Where There;s Smoke	1982	2.00	4.00	8.00
—Reissue of Tamla 366					
❑ 5349ML	Being with You	1983	2.00	4.00	8.00
—Reissue of Tamla 375					
❑ MOT-6226	One Heartbeat	1987	2.50	5.00	10.00
❑ MOT-6268	Love, Smokey	1990	3.00	6.00	12.00
TAMLA					
❑ T 328	Smokey	1973	3.00	6.00	12.00
❑ T6-331	Pure Smokey	1974	3.00	6.00	12.00
❑ T6-337	A Quiet Storm	1975	3.00	6.00	12.00
❑ T6-341	Smokey's Family Robinson	1976	3.00	6.00	12.00
❑ T6-350	Deep in My Soul	1977	3.00	6.00	12.00

Number	Title (A Side/B Side)	Yr	VG	VG+	NM
❏ T7-359	Love Breeze	1978	3.00	6.00	12.00
❏ T9-363 [(2)]	Smokin'	1979	3.75	7.50	15.00
❏ T7-366	Where There's Smoke	1979	2.50	5.00	10.00
❏ T8-367	Warm Thoughts	1980	2.50	5.00	10.00
❏ T8-375	Being with You	1981	2.50	5.00	10.00
❏ 6001TL	Yes It's You Lady	1982	2.50	5.00	10.00
❏ 6030TL	Touch the Sky	1983	2.50	5.00	10.00
❏ 6064TL	Blame It on Love & All the Great Hits	1983	2.50	5.00	10.00
❏ 6098TL	Essar	1984	2.50	5.00	10.00
❏ 6156TL	Smoke Signals	1986	2.50	5.00	10.00

ROBINSON, SMOKEY, AND THE MIRACLES
See THE MIRACLES.

ROBINSON, VICKI SUE
12-Inch Singles
PRELUDE

Number	Title (A Side/B Side)	Yr	VG	VG+	NM
❏ 532	Hot Summer Night/(Version)	1981	3.00	6.00	12.00

PROFILE

❏ 7025	To Sir with Love/(Instrumental)	1983	2.00	4.00	8.00
❏ 7039	Everlasting Love/(Instrumental)	1983	2.00	4.00	8.00

RCA

❏ PD-11029	Hold Tight/Falling in Love	1977	3.75	7.50	15.00
❏ PD-11228	Trust in Me (7:03)/Don't Try to Win Me Back Again (6:06)	1978	3.00	6.00	12.00
❏ PD-11442	Nighttime Fantasy (8:15)/Feels So Good It Must Be Wrong	1979	3.00	6.00	12.00
❏ PC-11507	Turn the Beat Around/Hold Tight	1979	3.00	6.00	12.00
❏ PC-11520	Nighttime Fantasy (8:15)/Feels So Good It Must Be Wrong	1980	2.00	4.00	8.00
❏ PD-11721	What's Happening in My Life (5:42)/Movin' On	1979	3.00	6.00	12.00

45s
PRELUDE

❏ 8038	Hot Summer Nights/(Version)	1981	—	2.00	4.00

PROFILE

❏ 5025	To Sir with Love/(Instrumental)	1983	—	2.00	4.00
❏ 5039	Everlasting Love/(Instrumental)	1983	—	2.00	4.00

RCA

❏ PB-10775	Daylight/Never Gonna Let You Go	1976	—	2.00	4.00
❏ PB-10863	Should I Stay-I Won't Let You Go/When You're Loving Me	1976	—	2.00	4.00
❏ GB-10944	Turn the Beat Around/Daylight	1977	—	—	3.00
—Gold Standard Series					
❏ PB-11028	Falling in Love/Hold Tight	1977	—	2.00	4.00
❏ PB-11227	Trust in Me/Don't Try to Win Me Back Again	1978	—	2.00	4.00
❏ PB-11280	Freeway Song/Half and Half	1978	—	2.00	4.00
❏ PB-11384	Jealousy/We Found Each Other	1978	—	2.00	4.00
❏ PB-11441	Nighttime Fantasy/Feel So Good It Must Be Wrong	1978	—	2.00	4.00
❏ PB-11720	What's Happening in My Life/Movin' On	1979	—	2.00	4.00

RCA VICTOR

❏ PB-10282	Baby, Now That I've Found You/Thanks a Million	1975	—	2.00	4.00
❏ PB-10435	Never Gonna Let You Go (Part 1)/Never Gonna Let You Go (Part 2)	1975	—	2.00	4.00
❏ PB-10562	Turn the Beat Around/Lack of Respect	1976	—	2.50	5.00

Albums
RCA VICTOR

❏ APL1-1256	Never Gonna Let You Go	1976	3.00	6.00	12.00
❏ APL1-1829	Vicki Sue Robinson	1977	3.00	6.00	12.00
❏ AFL1-2294	Half and Half	1978	3.00	6.00	12.00
❏ AYL1-3949	Turn the Beat Around	1981	2.00	4.00	8.00

ROCKETEERS, THE (1)
45s
GLAD HAMP

❏ 2017	Drag Strip/Summertime	1963	10.00	20.00	40.00

ROCKETEERS, THE (2)
45s
HERALD

❏ 415	Foolish One/Gonna Feed My Baby Poison	1953	175.00	350.00	700.00
—Black vinyl					
❏ 415	Foolish One/Gonna Feed My Baby Poison	1953	500.00	1000.	2000.
—Red vinyl					

ROCKETEERS, THE (3)
45s
MODERN

❏ 999	Talk It Over Baby/Hey Rube	1956	12.50	25.00	50.00

ROCKETEERS, THE (4)
45s
M.J.C.

❏ 501	My Reckless Heart/They Turned the Party Out Down at Bessie's House	1958	500.00	1000.	2000.

ROCKETEERS, THE (U)
45s
VAL-UE

❏ 102	Rippin' and Rockin'/Downtown	1960	7.50	15.00	30.00

ROGERS, JIMMY
45s
CHESS

Number	Title (A Side/B Side)	Yr	VG	VG+	NM
❏ 1506	I Used to Love a Woman/Back Door Friend	1952	50.00	100.00	200.00
—Earlier Jimmy Rogers 45s on Chess are not known to exist					
❏ 1519	The Last Time/Out on the Road	1952	50.00	100.00	200.00
❏ 1543	Left Me with a Broken Heart/Act Like You Love Me	1953	50.00	100.00	200.00
❏ 1574	Chicago Bound/Sloppy Drunk	1954	75.00	150.00	300.00
❏ 1616	You're the One/Blues All Day Long	1956	12.50	25.00	50.00
❏ 1643	Walking By Myself/If It Ain't Me	1956	12.50	25.00	50.00
❏ 1659	One Kiss/I Can't Believe	1957	12.50	25.00	50.00
❏ 1687	What Have I Done/Trace of You	1958	10.00	20.00	40.00
❏ 1721	Rock This House/My Last Meal	1959	7.50	15.00	30.00

ROGERS, TIMMIE
45s
CADET

❏ 5685	Super Soul Brothers/It Rolls Through Everything	1971	—	2.50	5.00

CAMEO

❏ 116	Back to School Again/I've Got a Dog Who Loves Me	1957	7.50	15.00	30.00
❏ 131	Take Me to Your Leader/Fla-Ga-La-Pa	1958	6.25	12.50	25.00

CAPITOL

❏ F2406	Saturday Night/If I Were You, Baby	1953	6.25	12.50	25.00
❏ F2509	Oh Yeah/Nothin' Wrong with Nothin'	1953	6.25	12.50	25.00

EPIC

❏ 9813	If You Can't Smile and Say Yes (Please Don't Cry and Say No)/Chum Goy Tum Toy Fricasee (Soy Soy Soo)	1965	2.00	4.00	8.00
❏ 9899	Everybody Wants to Go to Heaven, But Nobody Wants to Die/Too Young to Go Steady	1966	2.00	4.00	8.00

MERCURY

❏ 70451	If I Give My Heart to You/Teedle-Dee Teedle-Dum	1954	10.00	20.00	40.00

PAR-TEE

❏ 1303	Watergate/Snake Hips	1973	—	2.50	5.00

PARKWAY

❏ 814	I Love Ya, I Love Ya, I Love Ya/Tee-Hee	1960	3.75	7.50	15.00

PHILIPS

❏ 40074	Oh Yeah/Fla-Ga-La-Pa	1962	2.50	5.00	10.00

SIGNATURE

❏ 12037	First Proposal/Underwater Cha Cha Cha	1960	3.75	7.50	15.00

Albums
PHILIPS

❏ PHM 200088 [M]	If I Were President	1963	5.00	10.00	20.00
❏ PHS 600088 [S]	If I Were President	1963	6.25	12.50	25.00

RON AND BILL
Ron White and Bill "SMOKEY" ROBINSON.
45s
ARGO

❏ 5350	It/Don't Say Bye Bye	1959	12.50	25.00	50.00

TAMLA

❏ 54025	It/Don't Say Bye Bye	1960	30.00	60.00	120.00

RONETTES, THE
Also see RONNIE SPECTOR.
45s
A&M

❏ 1040	You Came, You Saw, You Conquered/Oh, I Love You	1969	4.00	8.00	16.00

BUDDAH

❏ 384	Go Out and Get It/Lover, Lover	1973	5.00	10.00	20.00
—As "Ronnie Spector and the Ronettes"					
❏ 408	I Wish I Never Saw the Sunshine/I Wonder What He's Doing	1974	5.00	10.00	20.00

COLPIX

❏ 601	I Want a Boy/Sweet Sixteen	1961	25.00	50.00	100.00
—As "Ronnie and the Relatives"					
❏ 646	I'm Gonna Quit While I'm Ahead/I'm On the Wagon	1962	15.00	30.00	60.00

DIMENSION

❏ 1046	He Did It/Recipe for Love	1965	12.50	25.00	50.00

MAY

❏ 111	My Darling Angel/I'm Gonna Quit While I'm Ahead	1961	37.50	75.00	150.00
—As "Ronnie and the Relatives"					
❏ 114	Silhouettes/You Bet I Would	1962	12.50	25.00	50.00
❏ 138	Memory/Good Girls	1963	12.50	25.00	50.00

PAVILLION

❏ 03333	I Saw Mommy Kissing Santa Claus/Rudolph the Red-Nosed Reindeer	1982	—	2.50	5.00
—B-side by The Crystals					

PHILLES

❏ 116	Be My Baby/Tedesco and Pittman	1963	7.50	15.00	30.00
❏ 118	Baby I Love You/Miss Joan and Mr. Sam	1963	7.50	15.00	30.00
❏ 120	(The Best Part of) Breakin' Up/Big Red	1964	7.50	15.00	30.00
❏ 121	Do I Love You?/Bebe and Susu	1964	7.50	15.00	30.00
❏ 123	Walkin' in the Rain/How Does It Feel	1964	10.00	20.00	40.00
❏ 123 [PS]	Walkin' in the Rain/How Does It Feel	1964	37.50	75.00	150.00
❏ 126	Born to Be Together/Blues for Baby	1965	6.25	12.50	25.00
❏ 126 [PS]	Born to Be Together/Blues for Baby	1965	37.50	75.00	150.00
❏ 128	Is This What I Get for Loving You?/Oh, I Love You	1965	6.25	12.50	25.00
❏ 128 [PS]	Is This What I Get for Loving You?/Oh, I Love You	1965	37.50	75.00	150.00
❏ 133	I Can Hear Music/When I Saw You	1966	7.50	15.00	30.00

R

Number	Title (A Side/B Side)	Yr	VG	VG+	NM
Albums					
COLPIX					
❏ CP-486 [M]	The Ronettes Featuring Veronica	1965	50.00	100.00	200.00
—Gold label					
❏ CP-486 [M]	The Ronettes Featuring Veronica	1965	25.00	50.00	100.00
—Blue label					
❏ SCP-486 [S]	The Ronettes Featuring Veronica	1965	75.00	150.00	300.00
—Gold label					
❏ SCP-486 [S]	The Ronettes Featuring Veronica	1965	37.50	75.00	150.00
—Blue label					
PHILLES					
❏ PHLP-4006 [M]	Presenting the Fabulous Ronettes Featuring Veronica	1964	200.00	400.00	800.00
—Blue and black label					
❏ PHLP-4006 [M]	Presenting the Fabulous Ronettes Featuring Veronica	1964	100.00	200.00	400.00
—Yellow and red label					
❏ PHLP-ST-4006 [S]	Presenting the Fabulous Ronettes Featuring Veronica	1965	150.00	300.00	600.00
❏ ST-90721 [S]	Presenting the Fabulous Ronettes Featuring Veronica	1965	100.00	200.00	400.00
—Capitol Record Club edition					
❏ T-90721 [M]	Presenting the Fabulous Ronettes Featuring Veronica	1965	62.50	125.00	250.00
—Capitol Record Club edition					

RONNIE AND THE HI-LITES
45s
ABC-PARAMOUNT

Number	Title (A Side/B Side)	Yr	VG	VG+	NM
❏ 10685	High School Romance/Too Young	1965	5.00	10.00	20.00
JOY					
❏ 260	I Wish That We Were Married/Twistin' and Kissin'	1962	6.25	12.50	25.00
❏ 265	Be Kind/Send My Love (Special Delivery)	1962	5.00	10.00	20.00
RAVEN					
❏ 8000	Valerie/The Fact of the Matter	1963	5.00	10.00	20.00
WIN					
❏ 250	A Slow Dance/What the Next Day May Bring	1963	5.00	10.00	20.00
❏ 251	The Fact of the Matter/You Keep Me Guessin'	1963	5.00	10.00	20.00
❏ 252	High School Romance/Uptown-Downtown	1963	6.25	12.50	25.00

ROOMATES, THE
Also see CATHY JEAN AND THE ROOMATES.
45s
BAN

Number	Title (A Side/B Side)	Yr	VG	VG+	NM
❏ 691	A Place Called Love/Knowing You	1985	—	2.50	5.00
CAMEO					
❏ 233	Sunday Kind of Love/A Lovely Way to Spend An Evening	1962	7.50	15.00	30.00
CANADIAN AMERICAN					
❏ 166	My Heart/Just for Tonight	1964	10.00	20.00	40.00
PHILIPS					
❏ 40105	Gee/Answer Me, My Love	1963	6.25	12.50	25.00
❏ 40153	The Nearness of You/Don't Cheat on Me	1963	6.25	12.50	25.00
PROMO					
❏ 2211	I Want a Little Girl/Making Believe	196?	5.00	10.00	20.00
—Sources conflict as to date (1960 or 1964)					
VALMOR					
❏ 008	Glory of Love/Never Know	1961	5.00	10.00	20.00
❏ 010	Band of Gold/O Baby Love	1961	5.00	10.00	20.00
❏ 013	My Foolish Heart/My Kisses for Your Thoughts	1962	5.00	10.00	20.00

ROOSTERS, THE
More than one group.
45s
A&M

Number	Title (A Side/B Side)	Yr	VG	VG+	NM
❏ 746	Shake a Tail Feather/Rooster Walk	1964	3.00	6.00	12.00
EPIC					
❏ 9487	Let's Try Again/Pretty Girl	1962	3.75	7.50	15.00
FELSTED					
❏ 8642	Chicken Hop/Fun House	1962	3.75	7.50	15.00
PHILIPS					
❏ 40504	Love Machine/I'm Suspectin'	1968	2.50	5.00	10.00
❏ 40559	Good Good Lovin'/Home Down Right	1968	2.00	4.00	8.00
SHAR-DEE					
❏ 704	Chicken Hop/Fun House	1959	5.00	10.00	20.00

ROSE ROYCE
45s
ATLANTIC

Number	Title (A Side/B Side)	Yr	VG	VG+	NM
❏ 88942	Perfect Lover/You Get Right Down To It	1989	—	—	3.00
C&R					
❏ 7684	Magic Touch/(B-side unknown)	1984	—	2.50	5.00
EPIC					
❏ 02818	Best Love/Dance with Me	1982	—	2.00	4.00
❏ 02996	Fire in the Funk/Still in Love	1982	—	2.00	4.00
❏ 03319	Somehow We Made It Through the Rain/You Blew It	1982	—	2.00	4.00
MCA					
❏ 40615	Car Wash/Water	1976	—	2.50	5.00
—With Rose Royce's name prominent on label					
❏ 40615	Car Wash/Water	1976	2.00	4.00	8.00
—With "Music Composed and Produced by Norman Whitfield" and no mention of Rose Royce on either side					

Number	Title (A Side/B Side)	Yr	VG	VG+	NM
❏ 40662	I Wanna Get Next to You/Sunrise	1976	—	2.50	5.00
❏ 40721	I'm Going Down/Yo Yo	1977	—	2.50	5.00
❏ 40814	Put Your Money Where Your Mouth Is/You're On My Mind	1977	—	2.50	5.00
OMNI					
❏ 99476	Lonely Road/I Found Someone	1987	—	—	3.00
❏ 99488	Doesn't Have to Be That Way/You're My Peace of Mind	1986	—	—	3.00
WHITFIELD					
❏ 8440	Do Your Dance — Part 1/Do Your Dance — Part 2	1977	—	2.50	5.00
❏ 8491	Ooh Boy/You Can't Please Everybody	1977	—	2.50	5.00
❏ 8531	Wishing on a Star/Love, More Love	1978	—	2.50	5.00
❏ 8629	I'm in Love (And I Love the Feeling)/Get Up Off Your Fat	1978	—	2.50	5.00
❏ 8712	Love Don't Live Here Anymore/That's What's Wrong with Me	1978	—	2.50	5.00
❏ 8789	First Come, First Serve/Let Me Be the First to Know	1979	—	2.50	5.00
❏ 49049	Is It Love You're After/You Can't Run from Yourself	1979	—	2.50	5.00
❏ 49127	What You Waitin' For/Shine Your Light	1979	—	2.50	5.00
❏ 49274	Pop Your Fingers/I Wonder Where You Are Tonight	1980	—	2.50	5.00
❏ 49583	You're a Winner/Pazazz	1980	—	2.50	5.00
❏ 49624	Funkin' Around/Help Yourself	1980	—	2.50	5.00
❏ 49681	Golden Touch/Love Is In the Air	1981	—	2.50	5.00
❏ 49735	I Wanna Make It with You/Love Is in the Air	1981	—	2.50	5.00
❏ 49830	Fight It/R.R. Express	1981	—	2.50	5.00
Albums					
ATLANTIC					
❏ 81944	Perfect Lover	1989	3.75	7.50	15.00
EPIC					
❏ FE 37939	Stronger Than Ever	1982	3.75	7.50	15.00
OMNI					
❏ 90557	Fresh Cut	1986	3.00	6.00	12.00
WHITFIELD					
❏ WH 3074	Rose Royce II/In Full Bloom	1977	3.00	6.00	12.00
❏ WHK 3227	Rose Royce III/Strikes Again!	1978	3.00	6.00	12.00
❏ WHS 3387	Rose Royce IV/Rainbow Connection	1979	3.00	6.00	12.00
❏ WHK 3457	Greatest Hits	1980	2.50	5.00	10.00
❏ WHK 3512	Golden Touch	1980	3.00	6.00	12.00
❏ WHK 3620	Jump Street	1981	3.00	6.00	12.00

ROSIE AND THE ORIGINALS
45s
BRUNSWICK

Number	Title (A Side/B Side)	Yr	VG	VG+	NM
❏ 55205	Lonely Blue Nights/We'll Have a Chance	1961	6.25	12.50	25.00
—By "Rosie, formerly with the Originals"					
❏ 55212	My Darling Forever/The Time Is Near	1961	6.25	12.50	25.00
—By "Rosie, formerly with the Originals"					
ERA BACK TO BACK HITS					
❏ 038	Angel Baby/Bumble Boogie	197?	—	3.00	6.00
—B-side by B. Bumble and the Stingers					
HIGHLAND					
❏ 1011	Angel Baby/Give Me Love	1960	6.25	12.50	25.00
❏ 1032	Lonely Blue Nights/We'll Have a Chance	196?	6.25	12.50	25.00
—Actually a reissue of Brunswick 55205, but harder to find					
Albums					
BRUNSWICK					
❏ BL 54102 [M]	Lonely Blue Nights with Rosie	1961	37.50	75.00	150.00
❏ BL 754102 [S]	Lonely Blue Nights with Rosie	1961	50.00	100.00	200.00

ROSS, DIANA
Also see THE SUPREMES.
12-Inch Singles
MCA

Number	Title (A Side/B Side)	Yr	VG	VG+	NM
❏ L33-1801 [DJ]	Ease On Down the Road (6:02) (same on both sides)	1978	15.00	30.00	60.00
—With Michael Jackson					
MOTOWN					
❏ M 00010D1	Your Love Is So Good for Me (6:32)/I Can't Go On Living Without Your Love (4:32)	1978	6.25	12.50	25.00
—B-side by Thelma Houston					
❏ M 00011D1	What You Gave Me (6:06)/Free Me from My Freedom-Tie Me to a Tree (Handcuff Me) (8:25)	1978	5.00	10.00	20.00
—B-side by Bonnie Pointer					
❏ PR-16 [DJ]	Love Hangover (7:49)/I Want You (Vocal 4:33) (Instrumental 4:36)	1976	50.00	100.00	200.00
—B-side by Marvin Gaye on Tamla label					
❏ M 00026D1	The Boss (Remix 7:23)/Lovin', Livin' and Givin' (5:11)	1979	3.75	7.50	15.00
❏ PR 42 [DJ]	What You Gave Me (6:06) (same on both sides)	1978	3.75	7.50	15.00
❏ PR 54 [DJ]	It's My House/No One Gets the Prize/The Boss	1979	5.00	10.00	20.00
—No label name on label					
❏ PR 72 [DJ]	Upside Down (4:05)/Big Time (6:27)	1980	12.50	25.00	50.00
—No label name on label; B-side by Rick James					
❏ PR-75 [DJ]	I'm Coming Out (5:23)//Rock and Roll Me (3:38)/Shake It Lady (3:09)	1980	12.50	25.00	50.00
—No label name on label; first song on B-side by Mira Waters; second song on B-side by Legend					
❏ P12-1008 [DJ]	You're Gonna Love It (6 versions)	1991	2.00	4.00	8.00
❏ 37463 1011 1	Waiting in the Wings (LP Version) (Remix Edit) (Extended)	1992	5.00	10.00	20.00

Number	Title (A Side/B Side)	Yr	VG	VG+	NM
❏ P12-1014 [DJ]	You're Gonna Love It (E-Smoove's Groovy Radio Edit 4:51) (E-Smoove's Groovy Remix 6:20) (E-Smoove's Groovy Instrumental 6:20)/ (Underground Mix 7:29) (The Reel House Mix 6:59) (Mo's Flutestrumental 7:10)	1991	2.00	4.00	8.00
❏ 37463 1212 1	The Boss (EP Version) (Radio Edit) (BYC Mix)/ I'm Coming Out (EP Version (Radio Edit) (Monstrumental)	1994	5.00	10.00	20.00
❏ 37463 1322 1	Take Me Higher (6 versions)	1995	3.00	6.00	12.00
❏ 37463 1379 1	If You're Not Gonna Love Me Right (4 versions)	1996	3.00	6.00	12.00
❏ 37463 1392 1	Voice of the Heart/If You're Not Gonna Love Me Right	1996	2.50	5.00	10.00
❏ U8P-1519 [DJ]	Until We Meet Again (4 versions)	1999	3.00	6.00	12.00
❏ L33-1643 [DJ]	When You Tell Me That You Love Me (same on both sides)	1991	3.00	6.00	12.00
❏ 37463 3001 1	I Will Survive (12" Vocal Mix) (LP Version) (7" Vocal Mix) (12" Instrumental) (7" Acapella)	1997	3.75	7.50	15.00
❏ MOT-4632	Love Hangover '89 (12" Version) (Urban Remix) (Dance Mix)	1989	2.00	4.00	8.00
❏ MOT-4639	Workin' Overtime (3 versions)	1989	2.50	5.00	10.00
❏ MOT-4678	Bottom Line (3 versions)	1989	2.00	4.00	8.00
❏ 37463 4812 1	You're Gonna Love It (4 versions)	1991	—	3.00	6.00
❏ L33-17770 [DJ]	Love Hangover '89 (5 versions)	1989	2.00	4.00	8.00
❏ L33-17827 [DJ]	Workin' Overtime (6 versions)	1989	2.00	4.00	8.00
❏ L33-17909 [DJ]	Paradise (Club Mix 7:45) (Dub Mix 8:08) (7" Version 3:58)	1989	2.50	5.00	10.00
❏ L33-17963 [DJ]	This House (4:20) (5:34)	1989	2.00	4.00	8.00
❏ L33-18048 [DJ]	Bottom Line (7" Remix) (Extended Remix) (LP Version) (Instrumental)	1989	2.00	4.00	8.00
❏ 56266	Until We Meet Again (4 versions)	1999	2.00	4.00	8.00
RCA					
❏ 6416-1-RD	Dirty Looks (Remix Version 7:43) (Bonus Beats) (Instrumental Version 5:51)	1987	2.50	5.00	10.00
❏ PD-13022	Mirror, Mirror (6:06)/Sweet Nothings	1981	3.75	7.50	15.00
❏ PD-13202	Work That Body (6:32)/Two Can Make It	1982	3.00	6.00	12.00
❏ PD-13382	Muscles (6:38)/I Am Me	1982	2.50	5.00	10.00
❏ PD-13568	Pieces of Ice (7:19)/(Instrumental)	1983	2.50	5.00	10.00
❏ PD-13625	Up Front (Special Club Remix 6:56)/Love or Loneliness	1983	3.75	7.50	15.00
❏ PD-13672	Let's Go Up/Girls	1983	2.50	5.00	10.00
❏ JD-13865 [DJ]	Swept Away (Long Version 7:37)/(Shorter Version 5:20)	1984	3.75	7.50	15.00
❏ PD-13865	Swept Away (Long Version 7:37)/(Instrumental 7:14)	1984	2.50	5.00	10.00
❏ JR-14033 [DJ]	Telephone (4:08) (same on both sides)	1985	3.00	6.00	12.00
❏ JD-14183 [DJ]	Eaten Alive (Extended Version 5:51)/ (Instrumental 5:51)	1985	2.50	5.00	10.00
—White label, different prefix from stock copy					
❏ PD-14183	Eaten Alive (Extended Version 5:51)/ (Instrumental 5:51)	1985	2.50	5.00	10.00
❏ JD-14245 [DJ]	Chain Reaction (3:47) (same on both sides)	1985	2.50	5.00	10.00
❏ JR-14267 [DJ]	Chain Reaction (6:52) (same on both sides)	1985	2.00	4.00	8.00
❏ PD-14267	Chain Reaction (6:52)/More and More	1985	2.50	5.00	10.00
45s					
MCA					
❏ 40947	Ease On Down the Road/Poppy Girls	1978	—	2.50	5.00
—With Michael Jackson; B-side by Quincy Jones					
❏ 40947 [PS]	Ease On Down the Road/Poppy Girls	1978	—	2.50	5.00
—With Michael Jackson					
❏ 53448	If We Hold On Together/(Instrumental)	1988	—	—	3.00
❏ 53448 [PS]	If We Hold On Together/(Instrumental)	1988	—	—	3.00
MOTOWN					
❏ (no #) [PS]	Diana Ross TV Special 4/8/71	1971	2.00	4.00	8.00
—Special sleeve issued with some Motown (usually Diana Ross) 45s in March and April 1971					
❏ 1165	Reach Out and Touch (Somebody's Hand)/Dark Side of the World	1970	—	2.50	5.00
❏ 1165 [PS]	Reach Out and Touch (Somebody's Hand)/Dark Side of the World	1970	3.00	6.00	12.00
❏ 1169	Ain't No Mountain High Enough/Can't It Wait Until Tomorrow	1970	—	2.50	5.00
❏ 1169 [PS]	Ain't No Mountain High Enough/Can't It Wait Until Tomorrow	1970	3.00	6.00	12.00
❏ 1176	Remember Me/What About You	1971	—	2.50	5.00
❏ 1176 [PS]	Remember Me/What About You	1971	3.00	6.00	12.00
❏ 1184	Reach Out I'll Be There/Close to You	1971	—	2.50	5.00
❏ 1188	Surrender/I'm a Winner	1971	—	2.50	5.00
❏ 1192	I'm Still Waiting/A Simple Thing Like Cry	1971	—	2.50	5.00
❏ 1211	Good Morning Heartache/God Bless the Child	1972	—	2.50	5.00
❏ 1211 [PS]	Good Morning Heartache/God Bless the Child	1972	2.50	5.00	10.00
❏ 1239	Touch Me in the Morning/I Won't Last a Day Without You	1973	—	2.50	5.00
❏ 1278	Last Time I Saw Him/Save the Children	1973	—	2.50	5.00
❏ 1295	Sleepin'/You	1974	—	2.50	5.00
❏ 1335	Sorry Doesn't Always Make It Right/Together	1975	—	2.50	5.00
❏ 1335 [PS]	Sorry Doesn't Always Make It Right/Together	1975	3.00	6.00	12.00
❏ 1377	Do You Know Where You're Going To/No One's Gonna Be a Fool Forever	1975	3.00	6.00	12.00
—Possibly Canadian release only, with different A-side title					
❏ 1377	Theme from Mahogany (Do You Know Where You're Going To)/No One's Gonna Be a Fool Forever	1975	—	2.50	5.00
❏ 1377 [PS]	Theme from Mahogany (Do You Know Where You're Going To)/No One's Gonna Be a Fool Forever	1975	5.00	10.00	20.00
❏ 1387	I Thought It Took a Little Time (But Today I Fell in Love)/After You	1976	—	2.50	5.00

Number	Title (A Side/B Side)	Yr	VG	VG+	NM
❏ 1387 [PS]	I Thought It Took a Little Time (But Today I Fell in Love)/After You	1976	2.50	5.00	10.00
❏ 1392	Love Hangover/Kiss Me Now	1976	—	2.50	5.00
❏ 1398	One Love in My Lifetime/Smile	1976	—	2.50	5.00
❏ 1427	Gettin' Ready for Love/Confide in Me	1977	—	2.50	5.00
❏ 1436	Your Love Is So Good for Me/Baby It's Me	1978	—	2.50	5.00
❏ 1442	You Got It/Too Shy to Say	1978	—	2.50	5.00
❏ 1449 [DJ]	Top of the World (same on both sides)	1978	12.50	25.00	50.00
—Promo only; withdrawn before stock copies were pressed					
❏ 1450	Lovin' Livin' and Givin'/Baby It's Me	1978	—	—	—
—Unreleased					
❏ 1456	What You Gave Me/Together	1979	—	2.00	4.00
❏ 1462	The Boss/I'm in the World	1979	—	2.00	4.00
❏ 1471	It's My House/Sparkle	1979	—	2.00	4.00
❏ 1491	I'm Coming Out/Give Up	1980	—	2.00	4.00
❏ 1494	Upside Down/Friend to Friend	1980	—	2.00	4.00
❏ 1496	It's My Turn/Together	1980	—	2.00	4.00
❏ 1496 [PS]	It's My Turn/Together	1980	3.00	6.00	12.00
❏ 1508	One More Chance/After You	1981	—	2.00	4.00
❏ 1513	To Love Again/Crying My Heart Out for You	1981	—	2.00	4.00
❏ 1519	Endless Love/(Instrumental)	1981	—	2.00	4.00
—With Lionel Richie					
❏ 1531	My Old Piano/Now That You're Gone	1981	—	2.00	4.00
❏ 1626	We Can Never Light That Old Flame Again/Old Funky Rolls	1982	—	2.00	4.00
❏ 1964	Workin' Overtime/(Instrumental)	1989	—	—	3.00
❏ 1964 [PS]	Workin' Overtime/(Instrumental)	1989	—	—	3.00
❏ 1998	This House/Paradise	1989	—	—	3.00
❏ 2003	Bottom Line/(Instrumental)	1989	—	—	3.00
❏ 2139	When You Tell Me That You Love Me/You and I	1991	—	2.00	4.00
❏ S45-17886 [DJ]	Workin' Overtime (4:18) (same on both sides)	1989	2.50	5.00	10.00
RCA					
❏ 5172-7-R	Dirty Looks/So Close	1987	—	—	3.00
❏ 5172-7-R [PS]	Dirty Looks/So Close	1987	—	—	3.00
❏ 5297-7-R	Tell Me Again/I Am Me	1987	—	—	3.00
❏ 5297-7-R [PS]	Tell Me Again/I Am Me	1987	—	—	3.00
❏ PB-12349	Why Do Fools Fall in Love/Think I'm in Love	1981	—	2.00	4.00
❏ JB-13013 [DJ]	Endless Love (Long)/(Short)	1981	3.00	6.00	12.00
—Promo only					
❏ PB-13021	Mirror, Mirror/Sweet Nothings	1981	—	2.00	4.00
❏ PB-13201	Work That Body/You Can Make It	1982	—	2.00	4.00
❏ PB-13348	Muscles/I Am Me	1982	—	2.00	4.00
❏ PB-13348 [PS]	Muscles/I Am Me	1982	—	2.00	4.00
❏ PB-13424	So Close/Fool for Your Love	1983	—	2.00	4.00
❏ GB-13479	Why Do Fools Fall in Love/Mirror, Mirror	1983	—	—	3.00
—Gold Standard Series					
❏ PB-13549	Pieces of Ice/Still in Love	1983	—	2.00	4.00
❏ PB-13549 [PS]	Pieces of Ice/Still in Love	1983	—	2.00	4.00
❏ PB-13624	Up Front/Love or Loneliness	1983	—	2.00	4.00
❏ PB-13671	Let's Go Up/Girls	1983	—	2.00	4.00
❏ GB-13798	Muscles/Pieces of Ice	1984	—	—	3.00
—Gold Standard Series					
❏ PB-13864	Swept Away/Fight for It	1984	—	—	3.00
❏ PB-13864 [PS]	Swept Away/Fight for It	1984	—	—	3.00
❏ PB-13966	Missing You/We Are the Children of the World	1984	—	—	3.00
❏ PB-13966 [PS]	Missing You/We Are the Children of the World	1984	—	—	3.00
❏ PB-14032	Telephone/Fool for Your Love	1985	—	—	3.00
❏ PB-14032 [PS]	Telephone/Fool for Your Love	1985	—	—	3.00
❏ PB-14181	Eaten Alive/(Instrumental)	1985	—	—	3.00
❏ PB-14181 [PS]	Eaten Alive/(Instrumental)	1985	—	—	3.00
❏ PB-14244	Chain Reaction/More and More	1985	—	2.00	4.00
❏ PB-14244	Chain Reaction (Special New Mix)/More and More	1986	—	—	3.00
❏ PB-14244 [PS]	Chain Reaction/More and More	1985	—	—	3.00
❏ GB-14342	Missing You/Swept Away	1986	—	—	3.00
—Gold Standard Series					
7-Inch Extended Plays					
MOTOWN					
❏ M 60724	My Place/Baby It's Love/The Long and Winding Road//How About You/I'm Still Waiting/ Everything Is Everything	1970	3.00	6.00	12.00
—Jukebox issue; small hole, plays at 33 1/3 rpm					
❏ M 60724 [PS]	Everything Is Everything	1970	3.00	6.00	12.00
—Part of "Little LP" series (LLP #133)					
Albums					
MOTOWN					
❏ M5-135V1	Diana Ross	1981	2.00	4.00	8.00
—Reissue of 711					
❏ M5-155V1	Diana!	1981	2.00	4.00	8.00
—Reissue of 719					
❏ M5-163V1	Touch Me in the Morning	1981	2.00	4.00	8.00
—Reissue of 772					
❏ M5-169V1	Diana Ross Live at Caesars Palace	1981	2.00	4.00	8.00
—Reissue of 801					
❏ M5-198V1	The Boss	1981	2.00	4.00	8.00
—Reissue of 923					
❏ M5-214V1	Duets with Diana	1981	2.50	5.00	10.00
❏ MS-711	Diana Ross	1970	3.75	7.50	15.00
❏ MS-719	Diana!	1971	3.75	7.50	15.00
❏ MS-723	Surrender	1971	3.75	7.50	15.00
❏ MS-724	Everything Is Everything	1970	3.75	7.50	15.00
❏ M-758D [(2)]	Lady Sings the Blues	1972	3.75	7.50	15.00
—With booklet; all but four tracks are by Diana Ross					
❏ M-772L	Touch Me in the Morning	1973	3.75	7.50	15.00
❏ M6-801S1	Diana Ross Live at Caesars Palace	1974	3.00	6.00	12.00

R

Number	Title (A Side/B Side)	Yr	VG	VG+	NM
❏ M7-812V1	Last Time I Saw Him	1974	3.00	6.00	12.00
❏ M6-861S1	Diana Ross	1976	3.00	6.00	12.00
❏ M6-869S1	Diana Ross' Greatest Hits	1976	3.00	6.00	12.00
❏ M7-877R2 [(2)]	An Evening with Diana Ross	1977	3.75	7.50	15.00
❏ M7-890R1	Baby It's Me	1977	3.00	6.00	12.00
❏ M7-907R1	Ross	1978	3.00	6.00	12.00
❏ M8-923M1	The Boss	1979	2.50	5.00	10.00
❏ M8-936	Diana	1980	2.50	5.00	10.00
❏ M8-951M1	To Love Again	1981	2.50	5.00	10.00
❏ M13-960C2 [(2)]	All the Great Hits	1981	3.00	6.00	12.00
❏ 5294 ML	Diana Ross	1983	2.00	4.00	8.00
—Reissue of 861					
❏ 6049 ML2 [(2)]	Diana Ross Anthology	1983	3.75	7.50	15.00
❏ MOT-6274	Workin' Overtime	1989	2.50	5.00	10.00
❏ 37463-6377-1	The Remixes	1994	3.00	6.00	12.00
NAUTILUS					
❏ NR-37	Diana	1981	10.00	20.00	40.00
—Audiophile vinyl					
RCA VICTOR					
❏ AFL1-4153	Why Do Fools Fall in Love	1981	2.50	5.00	10.00
❏ AFL1-4384	Silk Electric	1982	2.50	5.00	10.00
❏ AFL1-4677	Ross	1983	2.00	4.00	8.00
❏ AFL1-5009	Swept Away	1984	2.00	4.00	8.00
❏ AYL1-5162	Why Do Fools Fall in Love	1985	—	3.00	6.00
—"Best Buy Series" reissue					
❏ AFL1-5422	Eaten Alive	1985	2.00	4.00	8.00
❏ 6388-1-R	Red Hot Rhythm and Blues	1987	2.00	4.00	8.00

ROSS, DIANA, AND MARVIN GAYE
Also see each artist's individual listings.
45s
MOTOWN

Number	Title (A Side/B Side)	Yr	VG	VG+	NM
❏ 1269	My Mistake (Was to Love You)/Include Me in Your Life	1973	—	2.50	5.00
❏ 1280	You're a Special Part of Me/I'm Falling in Love with You	1973	—	2.50	5.00
❏ 1296	Don't Knock My Love/Just Say Just Say	1974	—	2.50	5.00

Albums
MOTOWN

Number	Title (A Side/B Side)	Yr	VG	VG+	NM
❏ M5-124V1	Diana & Marvin	1981	2.00	4.00	8.00
—Reissue					
❏ M7-803	Diana & Marvin	1973	3.75	7.50	15.00

ROSS, DIANA; MARVIN GAYE; SMOKEY ROBINSON; AND STEVIE WONDER
Also see each artist's individual listings.
45s
MOTOWN

Number	Title (A Side/B Side)	Yr	VG	VG+	NM
❏ 1455	Pops, We Love You/(Instrumental)	1979	—	2.00	4.00
❏ 1455 [DJ]	Pops, We Love You (same on both sides)	1979	2.50	5.00	10.00
—Promo only on green vinyl					

ROSS, DIANA, AND THE SUPREMES
See THE SUPREMES.

ROSS, JACKIE
45s
BRUNSWICK

Number	Title (A Side/B Side)	Yr	VG	VG+	NM
❏ 55325	Keep Your Chin Up/Love Is Easy to Lose	1967	2.00	4.00	8.00
❏ 55361	Mr. Sunshine/Walk on My Side	1968	2.00	4.00	8.00
CAPITOL					
❏ 4308	I Can't Stand to See You Go/Ain't No Fun to Me	1976	—	2.00	4.00
CHESS					
❏ 1903	Selfish One/Everything But Love	1964	2.00	4.00	8.00
❏ 1913	I've Got the Skill/Change Your Ways	1964	2.00	4.00	8.00
❏ 1915	Haste Makes Waste/Wasting Time	1964	2.00	4.00	8.00
❏ 1920	Jerk and Twine/New Lover	1965	2.00	4.00	8.00
❏ 1929	You Really Know How to Hurt a Girl/Dynamite Lovin'	1965	2.00	4.00	8.00
❏ 1938	Take Me for a Little While/Honey Dear	1965	2.00	4.00	8.00
❏ 1940	We Can Do It/Honey Dear	1965	2.00	4.00	8.00
GSF					
❏ 6886	Woman Get Nothing from Love/Do I	1972	—	2.50	5.00
❏ 6895	A One Woman Man/Take the Weight Off Me	1973	—	2.50	5.00
MERCURY					
❏ 73041	Angel of the Morning/Showcase	1970	—	3.00	6.00
❏ 73185	Glory Be/I Must Give You Time	1971	—	3.00	6.00
SAR					
❏ 129	Hard Times/Hold Me	1962	3.75	7.50	15.00
—As "Jacki Ross"					
SCEPTER					
❏ 12345	The World's in a Hell of a Shape/What Would You Give	1972	—	2.50	5.00

Albums
CHESS

Number	Title (A Side/B Side)	Yr	VG	VG+	NM
❏ LP-1489 [M]	In Full Bloom	1966	7.50	15.00	30.00
❏ LPS-1489 [S]	In Full Bloom	1966	10.00	20.00	40.00

ROTARY CONNECTION
Also see MINNIE RIPERTON.
45s
CADET CONCEPT

Number	Title (A Side/B Side)	Yr	VG	VG+	NM
❏ DJ-1 [DJ]	Lady Jane/Amen	1968	3.75	7.50	15.00
❏ 7000	Like a Rollin' Stone/Turn Me On	1967	2.50	5.00	10.00

Number	Title (A Side/B Side)	Yr	VG	VG+	NM
❏ 7002	Ruby Tuesday/Soul Man	1968	2.50	5.00	10.00
❏ 7007	Paper Castle/Teach Me How to Fly	1968	2.50	5.00	10.00
❏ 7008	Aladdin/Magical World	1968	2.50	5.00	10.00
❏ 7009	Silent Night Chant/Peace At Least	1968	3.00	6.00	12.00
❏ 7014	The Weight/Respect	1969	2.50	5.00	10.00
❏ 7018	Want You to Know/Memory Band	1969	2.50	5.00	10.00
❏ 7021	Love Me Now/May Our Amens Be True	1970	2.50	5.00	10.00
❏ 7027	Stormy Monday Blues/Teach Me How to Fly	1970	2.50	5.00	10.00
❏ 7028	Hey Love/If I Sing My Song	1971	2.50	5.00	10.00
—As "New Rotary Connection"					
JANUS					
❏ 249	Living Alone/Magical World	1975	—	2.50	5.00
—As "Minnie Riperton and Rotary Connection"					

Albums
CADET

Number	Title (A Side/B Side)	Yr	VG	VG+	NM
❏ CS-50006	Hey Love	1971	5.00	10.00	20.00
CADET CONCEPT					
❏ LP-312 [M]	Rotary Connection	1968	15.00	30.00	60.00
—Mono appears to be promo only					
❏ LPS-312 [S]	Rotary Connection	1968	6.25	12.50	25.00
❏ LPS-317	Aladdin	1968	6.25	12.50	25.00
❏ LPS 318	Peace	1969	5.00	10.00	20.00
❏ LPS-322	Songs	1969	6.25	12.50	25.00
❏ LSP-328	Dinner Music	1970	6.25	12.50	25.00

ROULETTES, THE
More than one group.
45s
CHAMP

Number	Title (A Side/B Side)	Yr	VG	VG+	NM
❏ 102	I See a Star/Come On, Baby	1958	20.00	40.00	80.00
EBB					
❏ 124	The Way You Carry On/You Don't Care Anymore	1957	7.50	15.00	30.00
SCEPTER					
❏ 1204	Hasten Jason/Wouldn't It Be Goin' Steady	1959	150.00	300.00	600.00
UNITED ARTISTS					
❏ 718	Can You Go/Soon You'll Be Leaving Me	1964	2.50	5.00	10.00
❏ 990	Long Cigarette/Junk	1966	2.50	5.00	10.00

ROVERS, THE (1)
45s
CAPITOL

Number	Title (A Side/B Side)	Yr	VG	VG+	NM
❏ F3078	Why Oh-h/Ichi-Bon Tami Dachi	1955	12.50	25.00	50.00
MUSIC CITY					
❏ 750	Why Oh-h/Ichi-Bon Tami Dachi	1954	20.00	40.00	80.00
—Black vinyl					
❏ 750	Why Oh-h/Ichi-Bon Tami Dachi	1954	62.50	125.00	250.00
—Red vinyl					
❏ 780	Salute to Johnny Ace/Jadda	1955	20.00	40.00	80.00
—Black vinyl					
❏ 780	Salute to Johnny Ace/Jadda	1955	62.50	125.00	250.00
—Red vinyl					

ROY C
45s
ALAGA

Number	Title (A Side/B Side)	Yr	VG	VG+	NM
❏ 1000	In Divorce Court/I Don't Want to Worry	1970	2.50	5.00	10.00
❏ 1003	Falling in Love/I Found a Man in My Bed	1970	2.50	5.00	10.00
❏ 1005	A Merry Black Christmas/I Don't Want To Worry	1970	2.50	5.00	10.00
❏ 1006	Got to Get Enough (Of Your Sweet Love Stuff)/An Open Letter to the President	1971	2.50	5.00	10.00
❏ 1007	I Wasn't There/Those Days Are Gone	1971	2.50	5.00	10.00
❏ 1008	I'll Never Leave You Lonely/I'm Gonna Love (Somebody Else's Woman)	1972	2.50	5.00	10.00
❏ 1009	Since I Met You Baby/Lonely I Was	1972	2.50	5.00	10.00
—With Linda Caver					
❏ 1013	I Caught You in the Act/Back Into My Arms	1973	2.50	5.00	10.00
❏ 1014	Since God Made a Woman/We're On the Road to Hell	1973	2.50	5.00	10.00
BLACK HAWK					
❏ 12101	Shotgun Wedding/(B-side unknown)	1965	3.00	6.00	12.00
MERCURY					
❏ 73391	Don't Blame the Man/I'm Bustin' My Rocks	1973	—	3.00	6.00
❏ 73445	She Kept On Walkin'/Back Into My Arms	1973	—	3.00	6.00
❏ 73605	Loneliness Has Got a Hold on Me/If I Could Love You Forever	1974	—	2.50	5.00
❏ 73672	Love Me Till Tomorrow Comes/Virgin Girl	1975	—	2.50	5.00
❏ 73735	My Girl (Reggae)/The Second Time Around	1975	—	2.50	5.00
❏ 73780	Every Woman Has a Right/Don't Stop Short of Satisfaction	1976	—	2.50	5.00
❏ 73848	You Can't Judge a Man (By the Color of His Skin)/I Wanna Do It Again	1976	—	2.50	5.00
❏ 73981	From the Outside Looking In (He Used to Be My Friend)/After Loving You	1977	—	2.50	5.00
SHOUT					
❏ 206	Gone Gone/Stop What You're Doing	1966	2.50	5.00	10.00
UPTOWN					
❏ 731	Shotgun Wedding/High School Dropout	1966	2.50	5.00	10.00

Albums
MERCURY

Number	Title (A Side/B Side)	Yr	VG	VG+	NM
❏ SRM-1-678	Sex and Soul	1974	3.75	7.50	15.00
❏ SRM-1-1056	Nice	1976	3.75	7.50	15.00
❏ SRM-1-1192	More	1978	3.75	7.50	15.00

Number	Title (A Side/B Side)	Yr	VG	VG+	NM

ROYAL DRIFTERS, THE
45s
TEEN

❏ 506	S'Why Hard/Little Linda	1959	25.00	50.00	100.00
❏ 508	To Each His Own/Da Kind	1959	37.50	75.00	150.00

ROYALETTES, THE
45s
CHANCELLOR

❏ 1133	No Big Thing/Yesterday's Lovers	1963	5.00	10.00	20.00
❏ 1140	Willie the Wolf/Blue Summer	1963	3.75	7.50	15.00
MGM					
❏ 13283	He's Gone/Don't You Cry	1964	3.00	6.00	12.00
❏ 13327	Poor Boy/Watch What Happens	1965	3.00	6.00	12.00
❏ 13366	It's Gonna Take a Miracle/Out of Sight, Out of Mind	1965	3.75	7.50	15.00
❏ 13405	I Want to Meet Him/Never Again	1965	3.00	6.00	12.00
❏ 13451	You Bring Me Down/Only When You're Lonely	1966	3.00	6.00	12.00
❏ 13507	It's a Big Mistake/It's Better Not to Know	1966	3.00	6.00	12.00
❏ 13544	I Don't Want to Be the One/An Affair to Remember	1966	3.00	6.00	12.00
❏ 13588	Love Without An End/When Summer's Gone	1966	3.00	6.00	12.00
❏ 13627	My Man/Take My Love	1966	3.00	6.00	12.00
ROULETTE					
❏ 4768	River of Ters/Something Wonderful	1967	2.50	5.00	10.00
WARNER BROS.					
❏ 5439	There He Goes/Come to Me	1964	3.75	7.50	15.00

Albums
MGM

❏ E-4332 [M]	It's Gonna Take a Miracle	1965	5.00	10.00	20.00
❏ SE-3323 [S]	It's Gonna Take a Miracle	1965	6.25	12.50	25.00
❏ E-4366 [M]	The Elegant Sound of the Royalettes	1966	5.00	10.00	20.00
❏ SE-4366 [S]	The Elegant Sound of the Royalettes	1966	6.25	12.50	25.00

ROYALS, THE (1)
Later known as THE MIDNIGHTERS. Also see HANK BALLARD AND THE MIDNIGHTERS.
45s
FEDERAL

❏ 12064AA	Every Beat of My Heart/All Night Long	1952	1000.	2000.	3000.
—Blue vinyl					
❏ 12064	Every Beat of My Heart/All Night Long	1952	375.00	750.00	1500.
❏ 12077	I Know I Love You So/Starting From Tonight	1952	625.00	1250.	2500.
❏ 12088	Moonrise/Fifth Street Blues	1952	500.00	1000.	2000.
❏ 12088	Moonrise/Fifth Street Blues	1952	1000.	2000.	3000.
—Blue vinyl					
❏ 12098	A Love in My Heart/I'll Never Let You Go	1952	250.00	500.00	1000.
❏ 12113	Are You Forgetting?/What Did I Do	1952	150.00	300.00	600.00
❏ 12121	The Shrine of St. Cecelia/I Feel So Blue	1953	200.00	400.00	800.00
❏ 12133	Get It/No It Ain't	1953	50.00	100.00	200.00
❏ 12150	Hello Miss Fine/I Feel That-A-Way	1953	50.00	100.00	200.00
❏ 12160	That's It/Someone Like You	1953	62.50	125.00	250.00
❏ 12169	Work With Me Annie/Until I Die	1954	62.50	125.00	250.00
—Original pressing; for reissues, see "Midnighters, The"					
❏ 12177 [DJ]	Give It Up/That Woman	1954	75.00	150.00	300.00
—Evidently, some promos exist crediting The Royals					

ROYALS, THE (2)
Also see CHUCK WILLIS.
45s
OKEH

❏ 6832	If You Love Me/Dreams of You	1951	250.00	500.00	1000.

ROYALS, THE (3)
45s
PENGUIN

❏ 1008	Thunder Wagon/Teen Beat	1959	7.50	15.00	30.00

ROYALS, THE (4)
45s
VAGABOND

❏ 134	Surfin' Lagoon/Wild Safari	1962	12.50	25.00	50.00
❏ 444	Christmas Party/White Christmas	1963	12.50	25.00	50.00
—Black vinyl					
❏ 444	Christmas Party/White Christmas	1963	25.00	50.00	100.00
—Red vinyl					

ROYALS, THE (5)
This Royals later became The Scooters.
45s
VENUS

❏ 103	Someday We'll Meet Again/I Want You to Be My Mambo Baby	1954	100.00	200.00	400.00

RUBY AND THE ROMANTICS
45s
ABC

❏ 10911	Twilight Time/Una Bella Brazilian Melody	1967	2.50	5.00	10.00
❏ 10941	Only Heaven Knows/This Is No Laughing Matter	1967	2.50	5.00	10.00
❏ 11065	On a Clear Day You Can See Forever/More Than Yesterday, Less Than Tomorrow	1968	2.50	5.00	10.00
A&M					
❏ 1042	Hurting Each Other/Baby, I Could Be So Good at Loving You	1969	2.00	4.00	8.00

KAPP

❏ 501	Our Day Will Come/Moonlight and Music	1963	3.75	7.50	15.00
❏ 525	My Summer Love/Sweet Love and Sweet Forgiveness	1963	3.00	6.00	12.00
❏ 544	Hey There Lonely Boy/Not a Moment Too Soon	1963	3.00	6.00	12.00
❏ 544 [PS]	Hey There Lonely Boy/Not a Moment Too Soon	1963	3.75	7.50	15.00
❏ 557	Young Wings Can Fly (Higher Than You Know)/Day Dreaming	1963	3.00	6.00	12.00
❏ 557 [PS]	Young Wings Can Fly (Higher Than You Know)/Day Dreaming	1963	3.75	7.50	15.00
❏ 578	Our Everlasting Love/Much Better Off Than I've Ever Been	1964	3.00	6.00	12.00
❏ 601	Baby Come Home/Every Day's a Holiday	1964	3.00	6.00	12.00
❏ 615	When You're Young and In Love/I Cry Alone	1964	3.00	6.00	12.00
❏ 646	Does He Really Care for Me/Nevertheless (I'm in Love with You)	1965	3.00	6.00	12.00
❏ 665	We'll Meet Again/Your Baby Doesn't Love You Anymore	1965	3.00	6.00	12.00
❏ 702	Nobody But My Baby/Imagination	1965	3.00	6.00	12.00
❏ 759	We Can Make It/Remember Me	1966	2.50	5.00	10.00
❏ 773	Hey There Lonely Boy/Think	1966	2.50	5.00	10.00
❏ 839	I Know/We'll Love Again	1967	2.50	5.00	10.00

Albums
ABC

❏ S-638	More Than Yesterday	1968	5.00	10.00	20.00
KAPP					
❏ KL-1323 [M]	Our Day Will Come	1963	7.50	15.00	30.00
❏ KL-1341 [M]	Till Then	1963	6.25	12.50	25.00
❏ KL-1458 [M]	The Greatest Hits Album	1966	5.00	10.00	20.00
❏ KL-1526 [M]	Ruby and the Romantics	1967	6.25	12.50	25.00
❏ KS-3323 [S]	Our Day Will Come	1963	10.00	20.00	40.00
❏ KS-3341 [S]	Till Then	1963	7.50	15.00	30.00
❏ KS-3458 [S]	The Greatest Hits Album	1966	6.25	12.50	25.00
❏ KS-3526 [S]	Ruby and the Romantics	1967	6.25	12.50	25.00
MCA					
❏ 541	The Greatest Hits Album	197?	2.50	5.00	10.00
PICKWICK					
❏ SPC-3519	Makin' Out	197?	2.50	5.00	10.00

RUFFIN, DAVID
Also see DARYL HALL AND JOHN OATES; JIMMY AND DAVID RUFFIN; THE TEMPTATIONS; THE VOICE MASTERS.
45s
ANNA

❏ 1127	I'm in Love/One of These Days	1961	15.00	30.00	60.00
CHECK MATE					
❏ 1003	You Can Get What I Got/Action Speaks Louder Than Words	1961	15.00	30.00	60.00
❏ 1010	Mr. Bus Driver — Hurry!/Knock You Out (With Love)	1962	15.00	30.00	60.00
MOTOWN					
❏ 1140	My Whole World Ended (The Moment You Left Me)/I've Got to Find Myself a Brand New Baby	1968	—	3.00	6.00
❏ 1149	I've Lost Everything I've Ever Loved/We'll Have a Good Thing Going On	1969	—	3.00	6.00
❏ 1158	I'm So Glad I Fell for You/I Pray Every Day You Won't Regret Loving Me	1969	—	3.00	6.00
❏ 1178	Each Day Is a Lifetime/Don't Stop Loving Me	1971	—	3.00	6.00
❏ 1187	You Can Come Right Back to Me/Dinah	1971	—	3.00	6.00
❏ 1204	A Day in the Life of a Working Man/A Little More Trust	1972	—	3.00	6.00
❏ 1223	Blood Donors Needed/Go On with Your Bad Self	1973	—	3.00	6.00
❏ 1259	Common Man/I'm Just a Mortal Man	1973	—	3.00	6.00
❏ 1327	Me and Rock and Roll (Are Here to Stay)/Smiling Faces Sometimes	1974	—	3.00	6.00
❏ 1332	Take Me Clear from Here/I Just Want to Celebrate	1975	—	—	—
—Unreleased					
❏ 1336	Superstar/No Matter Where	1975	—	2.50	5.00
❏ 1376	Walk Away from Love/Love Can Be Hazardous to Your Health	1975	—	2.50	5.00
❏ 1388	Heavy Love/Love Can Be Hazardous To Your Health	1976	—	2.50	5.00
❏ 1393	Everything's Coming Up Love/No Matter Where	1976	—	2.50	5.00
❏ 1405	On and Off/Statue of a Fool	1976	—	2.50	5.00
❏ 1420	Just Let Me Hold You for a Night/Rode by the Place (Where We Used to Stay)	1977	—	2.50	5.00
❏ 1435	You're My Peace of Mind/Rose By the Place (Where We Used to Stay)	1978	—	2.50	5.00
WARNER BROS.					
❏ 49030	Sexy Dancer/Break My Heart	1979	—	2.00	4.00
❏ 49123	I Get Excited/Chain on the Brain	1979	—	2.00	4.00
❏ 49277	Slow Dance/Don't You Go Home	1980	—	2.00	4.00
❏ 49577	Still in Love with You/I Wanna Be with You	1980	—	2.00	4.00

Albums
MOTOWN

❏ M5-146V1	My Whole World Ended	1981	2.00	4.00	8.00
—Reissue					
❏ M5-211V1	At His Best	1981	2.00	4.00	8.00
—Reissue					
❏ MS-685	My Whole World Ended	1969	5.00	10.00	20.00
❏ MS-696	Feelin' Good	1969	3.75	7.50	15.00
❏ M 733	David Ruffin	1971	—	—	—
—Canceled					
❏ M-762	David Ruffin	1973	3.00	6.00	12.00
❏ M6-818	Me 'N' Rock 'N' Roll Are Here to Stay	1974	3.00	6.00	12.00

Number	Title (A Side/B Side)	Yr	VG	VG+	NM
❑ M6-849	Who I Am	1975	3.00	6.00	12.00
❑ M6-866	Everything's Coming Up Love	1976	3.00	6.00	12.00
❑ M6-885	In My Stride	1977	3.00	6.00	12.00
❑ M7-895	At His Best	1978	3.00	6.00	12.00

WARNER BROS.

Number	Title (A Side/B Side)	Yr	VG	VG+	NM
❑ BSK 3306	So Soon We Change	1979	2.50	5.00	10.00
❑ BSK 3416	Gentleman Ruffin	1980	2.50	5.00	10.00

RUFFIN, DAVID, AND EDDIE KENDRICK
Also see each artist's individual listings; DARYL HALL AND JOHN OATES; THE TEMPTATIONS.
45s
RCA

Number	Title (A Side/B Side)	Yr	VG	VG+	NM
❑ 5313-7-R	I Couldn't Believe It/Don't Know Why You're Dreamin'	1987	—	—	3.00
❑ 6925-7-R	One More for the Lonely Hearts Club/Don't Know Why You're Dreaming	1988	—	—	3.00

RUFFIN, JIMMY
45s
ATCO

Number	Title (A Side/B Side)	Yr	VG	VG+	NM
❑ 6926	Tears of Joy/Goin' Home	1973	2.00	4.00	8.00

CHESS

Number	Title (A Side/B Side)	Yr	VG	VG+	NM
❑ 2160	Tell Me What You Want/Do You Know Me	1974	—	2.50	5.00
❑ 2168	What You See (Ain't Always What You Get)/Boy from Mississippi	1975	—	2.50	5.00

EPIC

Number	Title (A Side/B Side)	Yr	VG	VG+	NM
❑ 50339	Fallin' in Love with You/Fallin' in Love with You	1977	—	2.50	5.00
❑ 50384	Fallin' in Love with You/Fallin' in Love with You	1977	—	2.50	5.00

MIRACLE

Number	Title (A Side/B Side)	Yr	VG	VG+	NM
❑ 1	Don't Feel Sorry for Me/Heart	1961	50.00	100.00	200.00

RSO

Number	Title (A Side/B Side)	Yr	VG	VG+	NM
❑ 1021	Hold On to My Love/(Instrumental)	1980	—	2.50	5.00
❑ 1042	Night of Love/Searchin'	1980	—	2.50	5.00

SOUL

Number	Title (A Side/B Side)	Yr	VG	VG+	NM
❑ 35002	Since I've Lost You/I Want Her Love	1964	10.00	20.00	40.00
❑ 35016	As Long As There Is L-O-V-E/How Can I Say I'm Sorry	1965	2.50	5.00	10.00
❑ 35022	What Becomes of the Brokenhearted/Baby I've Got It	1966	3.75	7.50	15.00
❑ 35027	I've Passed This Way Before/Tomorrow's Tears	1966	2.50	5.00	10.00
❑ 35032	Gonna Give Her All the Love I've Got/World So Wide (Nowhere to Hide from Your Heart)	1967	2.00	4.00	8.00
❑ 35035	Don't You Miss Me A Little Bit Baby/I Want Her Love	1967	2.00	4.00	8.00
❑ 35043	I'll Say Forever My Love/Everybody Needs Love	1968	2.00	4.00	8.00
❑ 35046	Don't Let Him Take Your Love from Me/Lonely, Lonely Man Am I	1968	2.00	4.00	8.00
❑ 35053	Sad and Lonesome Feeling/Gonna Keep On Trying Till I Win Your Love	1968	2.00	4.00	8.00
❑ 35060	Farewell Is a Lonely Sound/If You Will Let Me, I Know I Can	1969	2.00	4.00	8.00
❑ 35077	Maria (You Were the Only One)/Living in a World I Created For Myself	1970	2.00	4.00	8.00
❑ 35092	Our Favorite Melody/You Gave Me Love	1972	—	3.00	6.00

Albums
RSO

Number	Title (A Side/B Side)	Yr	VG	VG+	NM
❑ RS-1-3078	Sunrise	1980	2.50	5.00	10.00

SOUL

Number	Title (A Side/B Side)	Yr	VG	VG+	NM
❑ 704 [M]	Top Ten	1967	12.50	25.00	50.00
—One-color cover					
❑ 704 [M]	Top Ten	1967	6.25	12.50	25.00
—Full-color cover					
❑ S-704 [S]	Top Ten	1967	6.25	12.50	25.00
❑ S-708	Ruff'n Ready	1969	6.25	12.50	25.00
❑ SS-727	The Groove Governor	1970	5.00	10.00	20.00

RUFFIN, JIMMY AND DAVID
Also see DAVID RUFFIN; JIMMY RUFFIN.
45s
SOUL

Number	Title (A Side/B Side)	Yr	VG	VG+	NM
❑ 35076	Stand By Me/Your Love Was Worth Waiting For	1970	—	2.50	5.00
❑ 35082	When My Love Hand Comes Do Down/Steppin' On a Dream	1971	—	2.50	5.00
❑ 35086	Lo and Behold/The Things We Have to Do	1971	—	2.50	5.00

Albums
MOTOWN

Number	Title (A Side/B Side)	Yr	VG	VG+	NM
❑ M5-108V1	Motown Superstar Series, Vol. 8	1981	2.50	5.00	10.00

SOUL

Number	Title (A Side/B Side)	Yr	VG	VG+	NM
❑ SS-728	I Am My Brother's Keeper	1970	5.00	10.00	20.00

RUFUS
Includes records as "Rufus featuring Chaka Khan" and "Rufus and Chaka." Also see CHAKA KHAN.
45s
ABC

Number	Title (A Side/B Side)	Yr	VG	VG+	NM
❑ 11356	Slip 'N Slide/I Finally Found You	1973	2.00	4.00	8.00
❑ 11376	Whoever's Thrilling You (Is Killing Me)/I Finally Found You	1973	—	3.00	6.00
❑ 11394	Feel Good/Keep It Coming	1973	—	3.00	6.00
❑ 11427	Tell Me Something Good/Smokin' Room	1974	—	3.00	6.00
❑ 12010	Tell Me Something Good/Smokin' Room	1974	—	2.50	5.00
❑ 12032	You Got the Love/Rags to Rufus	1974	—	2.50	5.00
❑ 12066	Once You Get Started/Rufusized	1975	—	2.50	5.00
❑ 12099	Please Pardon Me (You Remind Me of a Friend)/Somebody's Watching You	1975	—	2.50	5.00

Number	Title (A Side/B Side)	Yr	VG	VG+	NM
❑ 12149	Sweet Thing/Circles	1975	—	2.50	5.00
❑ 12179	Dance Wit' Me/Everybody's Got an Aura	1976	—	2.50	5.00
❑ 12197	Jive Talkin'/On Time	1976	—	2.50	5.00
❑ 12239	At Midnight (My Love Will Lift You Up)/Better Days	1976	—	2.50	5.00
❑ 12269	Holywood/Earth Song	1977	—	2.50	5.00
❑ 12296	Everlasting Love/Close the Door	1977	—	2.50	5.00
❑ 12349	Stay/My Ship Will Sail	1978	—	2.50	5.00
❑ 12390	Blue Love/Turn	1978	—	2.50	5.00
❑ 12444	Keep It Together (Declaration of Love)/Red Hot Poker	1979	—	2.50	5.00

EPIC

Number	Title (A Side/B Side)	Yr	VG	VG+	NM
❑ 10691	Read All About It/Brand New Day	1971	3.00	6.00	12.00
❑ 10691 [PS]	Read All About It/Brand New Day	1971	5.00	10.00	20.00
❑ 10726	Follow the Lamb/Fire One, Fire Two, Fire Three	1971	3.00	6.00	12.00

MCA

Number	Title (A Side/B Side)	Yr	VG	VG+	NM
❑ 41025	Ain't Nobody Like You/You're to Blame	1979	—	2.00	4.00
❑ 41131	Do You Love What You Feel/Dancin' Mood	1979	—	2.00	4.00
❑ 41191	What Am I Missing/Any Love	1980	—	2.00	4.00
❑ 41230	I'm Dancing for Your Love/Walk the Rockway	1980	—	2.00	4.00
❑ 51070	Tonight We Love/Afterwards	1981	—	2.00	4.00
❑ 51125	Party 'Til You're Broke/Hold On to a Friend	1981	—	2.00	4.00
❑ 51203	Sharing the Love/We Got the Way	1981	—	2.00	4.00
❑ 52002	True Love/Better Together	1982	—	2.00	4.00

WARNER BROS.

Number	Title (A Side/B Side)	Yr	VG	VG+	NM
❑ 29406	One Million Kisses/Stay	1983	—	2.00	4.00
❑ 29555	Ain't Nobody/Sweet Thing	1983	—	2.00	4.00
❑ 29675	Blinded by the Boogie/You're Really Out of Line	1983	—	2.00	4.00
❑ 29790	Take It to the Hop/Distant Lover	1983	—	2.00	4.00

Albums
ABC

Number	Title (A Side/B Side)	Yr	VG	VG+	NM
❑ X-783	Rufus	1973	2.50	5.00	10.00
❑ X-809	Rags to Rufus	1974	2.50	5.00	10.00
❑ D-837	Rufusized	1974	2.50	5.00	10.00
❑ D-909	Rufus Featuring Chaka Khan	1975	2.50	5.00	10.00
❑ D-975	Ask Rufus	1977	2.50	5.00	10.00
❑ AA-1049	Street Player	1978	2.50	5.00	10.00
❑ AA-1049 [PD]	Street Player	1978	6.25	12.50	25.00
—Promo-only picture disc					
❑ AA-1098	Numbers	1979	2.50	5.00	10.00
❑ AA-1098 [PD]	Numbers	1979	5.00	10.00	20.00
—Promo-only picture disc					

COMMAND

Number	Title (A Side/B Side)	Yr	VG	VG+	NM
❑ CQD-40023 [Q]Rufusized		1974	5.00	10.00	20.00
❑ CQD-40024 [Q]Rags to Rufus		1974	5.00	10.00	20.00

MCA

Number	Title (A Side/B Side)	Yr	VG	VG+	NM
❑ 642	Rufus	1980	—	3.00	6.00
—Reissue of ABC 783					
❑ 5103	Masterjam	1979	2.50	5.00	10.00
❑ 5159	Party 'Til You're Broke	1981	2.50	5.00	10.00
❑ 5270	Camouflage	1982	2.50	5.00	10.00
❑ 5339	The Very Best of Rufus	1983	2.50	5.00	10.00
❑ 37034	Rags to Rufus	1980	—	3.00	6.00
—Reissue of ABC 809					
❑ 37035	Rufusized	1980	—	3.00	6.00
—Reissue of ABC 837					
❑ 37036	Rufus Featuring Chaka Khan	1980	—	3.00	6.00
—Reissue of ABC 909					
❑ 37037	Ask Rufus	1980	—	3.00	6.00
—Reissue of ABC 975					
❑ 37038	Street Player	1980	—	3.00	6.00
—Reissue of ABC 1049					
❑ 37039	Numbers	1980	—	3.00	6.00
—Reissue of ABC 1098					
❑ 37157	Masterjam	198?	—	3.00	6.00
—Reissue of 5103					

WARNER BROS.

Number	Title (A Side/B Side)	Yr	VG	VG+	NM
❑ 23679 [(2)]	Live: Stompin' at the Savoy	1983	3.00	6.00	12.00
❑ 23753	Seal in Red	1984	2.50	5.00	10.00

RUFUS AND CARLA
Also see CARLA THOMAS; RUFUS THOMAS.
45s
ATCO

Number	Title (A Side/B Side)	Yr	VG	VG+	NM
❑ 6177	Cause I Love You/Deep Down Inside	1960	6.25	12.50	25.00
—As "Carla and Rufus"					
❑ 6199	I Didn't Believe/Yeah, Yea-Ah	1961	6.25	12.50	25.00
—As "Rufus and Friend"					

SATELLITE

Number	Title (A Side/B Side)	Yr	VG	VG+	NM
❑ 102	Cause I Love You/Deep Down Inside	1960	10.00	20.00	40.00

STAX

Number	Title (A Side/B Side)	Yr	VG	VG+	NM
❑ 151	That's Really Some Good/Night Time Is the Right Time	1964	3.00	6.00	12.00
❑ 176	When You Move You Lose/We're Tight	1965	3.00	6.00	12.00
❑ 184	Birds and Bees/Never Let You Go	1966	3.00	6.00	12.00

Albums
STAX

Number	Title (A Side/B Side)	Yr	VG	VG+	NM
❑ STX-4124	Chronicle	1979	3.75	7.50	15.00

RUN-D.M.C.
12-Inch Singles
ARISTA/PROFILE

Number	Title (A Side/B Side)	Yr	VG	VG+	NM
❑ PRDP-7405 [DJ]Simmons Incorporated (Clean Mix) (Instrumental)/(Street Mix) (Acappella)		1999	3.75	7.50	15.00

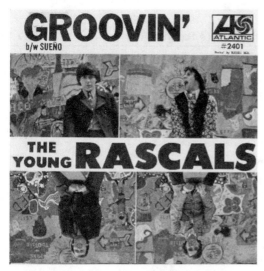

The Rascals had five singles make the R&B charts. The biggest of these, "Groovin'," got to #3. Here is its picture sleeve.

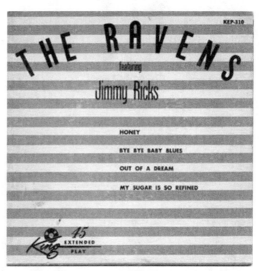

One of the hardest of all R&B EPs to find is this collection of tracks by the Ravens on the King label. All of these songs first appeared on 78s on the Hub label in 1946.

As important and influential as Otis Redding was, he only had one #1 R&B hit – the same song that hit #1 on the pop charts, "(Sittin' on) The Dock of the Bay." Here is the posthumous album that features the hit.

This compilation of tracks by the Robins on the Whippet label is rather difficult to find. It's interesting how they try to "picture" the words "rock" and "roll" on this cover.

The Ronettes' album on Philles has been sought-after for years, especially in stereo, as pictured here.

Before his days with the Temptations, David Ruffin attempted a solo career. This was the first of two obscure singles on the Check Mate label.

Number	Title (A Side/B Side)	Yr	VG	VG+	NM
❏ PRDP-7426 [DJ]	It's Over (Club) (Acappella) (Radio) (Instrumental)	2000	2.50	5.00	10.00
❏ PRDP-7431 [DJ]	Let's Stay Together (Original) (Instrumental)	2001	2.00	4.00	8.00
❏ 17421	Walk This Way (Vocal)/(Instrumental)	2000	2.00	4.00	8.00
—Reissue					
❏ 17422	Here We Go (Album Version) (Live at the Funhouse)	2000	2.50	5.00	10.00
—Reissue					
❏ 17423	My Adidas/Peter Piper	2000	2.50	5.00	10.00
—Reissue					
❏ 17424	Down with the King (Album Version) (Instrumental)	2000	2.50	5.00	10.00
—Reissue					
❏ 17425	Run's House (Vocal) (Instrumental)/Beats to the Rhyme (Vocal) (Instrumental)	2000	2.00	4.00	8.00
—Reissue					
PROFILE					
❏ ADP-3597 [DJ]	Beginning (No Further Delay) (Main Mix) (Instrumental) (Acappella)	1998	2.50	5.00	10.00
❏ PRO-7019	It's Like That/Sucker M.C.'s	1983	7.50	15.00	30.00
❏ PRO-7036	Hard Times (Vocal) (Instrumental)//Jam Master Jay (Vocal) (Instrumental)	1983	6.25	12.50	25.00
—Original					
❏ PRO-7036	Hard Times (Vocal) (Instrumental)//Jam Master Jay (Vocal) (Instrumental)	1995	3.00	6.00	12.00
—Reissue on black label					
❏ PRO-7045	Rock Box (Vocal Dub Version) (Dub Version)	1984	6.25	12.50	25.00
—Original					
❏ PRO-7045	Rock Box (Vocal Dub Version) (Dub Version)	1995	3.00	6.00	12.00
—Reissue on black label					
❏ PRO-7051	30 Days (5:45) (Instrumental 7:20)	1984	5.00	10.00	20.00
—Original on gray label					
❏ PRO-7051	30 Days (5:45) (Instrumental 7:20)	1995	3.00	6.00	12.00
—Reissue on black label					
❏ PRO-7064	King of Rock (Vocal) (Instrumental)	1985	6.25	12.50	25.00
—Original on gray label					
❏ PRO-7064	King of Rock (Vocal) (Instrumental)	1995	3.00	6.00	12.00
—Reissue on black label					
❏ PRO-7069	You Talk Too Much/(Instrumental)/Daryll & Joe (Krush Groove 3)	1985	6.25	12.50	25.00
—Original with gray label					
❏ PRO-7069	You Talk Too Much/(Instrumental)/Daryll & Joe (Krush Groove 3)	1995	3.00	6.00	12.00
—Reissue with black label					
❏ PRO-7079	Here We Go (Album Version) (Live at the Funhouse)	1985	6.25	12.50	25.00
—Original on gray label					
❏ PRO-7079	Here We Go (Album Version) (Live at the Funhouse)	1995	3.00	6.00	12.00
—Reissue on black label					
❏ PRO-7080	Jam-Master Jammin' (3 versions)	1985	6.25	12.50	25.00
❏ PRO-7088	Can You Rock It Like This/Together Forever	1985	6.25	12.50	25.00
❏ PRO-7102	My Adidas/Peter Piper	1986	6.25	12.50	25.00
—Original on gray label					
❏ PRO-7112	Walk This Way (Vocal)/(Instrumental)	1986	6.25	12.50	25.00
—With Steve Tyler and Joe Perry of Aerosmith; original with gray label and picture cover					
❏ PRO-7112	Walk This Way (Vocal)/(Instrumental)	1995	3.00	6.00	12.00
—With Steve Tyler and Joe Perry of Aerosmith; reissue with black label					
❏ PRO-7119	You Be Illin' (Remix) (Instrumental)/Hit It Run	1986	6.25	12.50	25.00
❏ PRO-7131	It's Tricky (4 versions)/Proud to Be Black	1987	5.00	10.00	20.00
—Original					
❏ PRO-7131	It's Tricky (4 versions)/Proud to Be Black	1995	2.50	5.00	10.00
—Reissue on black label					
❏ PRO-7202	Run's House (Vocal) (Instrumental)/Beats to the Rhyme (Vocal) (Instrumental)	1988	3.75	7.50	15.00
❏ PRO-7211	Mary, Mary (Vocal) (Instrumental)/Rock Box	1988	3.75	7.50	15.00
❏ PRO-7224	I'm Not Going Out Like That (2 versions)/How'd Ya Do It Dee	1988	3.00	6.00	12.00
❏ PRO-7234	Papa Crazy (2 versions)/Tougher Than Leather (2 versions)	1988	3.75	7.50	15.00
❏ PRO-7262	Pause (3 versions)/Ghostbusters	1989	3.75	7.50	15.00
❏ PRO-7315	What's It All About (3 versions)/The Ave. (3 versions)	1990	3.75	7.50	15.00
❏ PRO-7328	Faces (Album Version) (Instrumental)/Back from Hell (Remix)	1991	3.75	7.50	15.00
❏ PRO-7391	Down with the King (unknown versions)	1993	3.00	6.00	12.00
❏ PRO-7400	Ooh, Whatcha Gonna Do (Vocal) (Instrumental) (Radio)	1993	2.50	5.00	10.00
SM:)E					
❏ SM-9065	It's Tricky (Drop the Break) (Battle Beat Dub) (Jason's Battle Blaster) (Acappella Break) (Bonus Beat Break)	1997	2.00	4.00	8.00
—As "Run-D.M.C. vs. Jason Nevins"					
❏ SM-9069	It's Like That (3 versions)	1998	2.00	4.00	8.00
—As "Run-D.M.C. vs. Jason Nevins"					
45s					
MCA					
❏ 53680	Ghost Busters/(Ghost Power Instrumental)	1989	2.00	4.00	8.00
PROFILE					
❏ 5019	It's Like That/It's Like That (instrumental)	1983	—	2.50	5.00
❏ 5036	Hard Times-Jam Master Jay/Hard Times-Jam Master Jay (instrumental)	1983	—	2.50	5.00
❏ 5045	Rock Box/Rock Box (Dub Version)	1984	—	2.50	5.00
❏ 5051	30 Days/30 Days (instrumental)	1984	—	2.50	5.00
❏ 5058	Hollis Crew/Hollis Crew (instrumental)	1984	—	2.50	5.00
❏ 5064	King of Rock/King of Rock (instrumental)	1985	—	2.50	5.00

Number	Title (A Side/B Side)	Yr	VG	VG+	NM
❏ 5069	You Talk Too Much/Daryll and Joe (Krush Groove)	1985	—	2.50	5.00
❏ 5080	Jam-Master Jammin'/Jam-Master Jammin' (instrumental)	1985	—	2.50	5.00
❏ 5088	Can You Rock Like This/Together Forever	1986	—	2.50	5.00
❏ 5102	My Adidas/Peter Piper	1986	—	2.00	4.00
❏ 5102 [PS]	My Adidas/Peter Piper	1986	—	2.00	4.00
❏ 5112	Walk This Way/King of Rock	1986	—	2.00	4.00
—A-side with Steven Tyler and Joe Perry of Aerosmith					
❏ 5112 [PS]	Walk This Way/King of Rock	1986	—	2.00	4.00
❏ 5119	You Be Illin'/Hit It Run	1986	—	2.00	4.00
❏ 5119 [PS]	You Be Illin'/Hit It Run	1986	—	2.00	4.00
❏ 5131	It's Tricky/Proud to Be Black	1987	—	2.00	4.00
❏ 5131 [PS]	It's Tricky/Proud to Be Black	1987	—	2.00	4.00
❏ 5202	Run's House/Beats to the Rhyme	1988	—	2.00	4.00
❏ 5202 [PS]	Run's House/Beats to the Rhyme	1988	—	2.00	4.00
❏ 5211	Mary, Mary/Rock Box	1988	—	2.00	4.00
❏ 5211 [PS]	Mary, Mary/Rock Box	1988	—	2.00	4.00
❏ 5224	I'm Not Going Out Like That/How'd Ya Do It Dee	1988	—	2.00	4.00
❏ 5224 [PS]	I'm Not Going Out Like That/How'd Ya Do It Dee	1988	—	2.00	4.00
❏ 5235	Christmas in Hollis/Let the Jingle Bells Rock	1988	—	2.00	4.00
—B-side by Sweet Tee; red vinyl					
Albums					
ARISTA					
❏ 16400 [(2)]	Crown Royal	2001	3.75	7.50	15.00
PROFILE					
❏ PRO-1202	Run-D.M.C.	1984	3.00	6.00	12.00
❏ PRO-1205	King of Rock	1985	3.00	6.00	12.00
❏ PRO-1217	Raising Hell	1986	3.00	6.00	12.00
❏ PRO-1265	Tougher Than Leather	1988	3.00	6.00	12.00
❏ PRO-1401	Back from Hell	1990	3.00	6.00	12.00
❏ PRO-1419 [[(2)]	Together Forever: Greatest Hits 1983-1991	1991	3.75	7.50	15.00

RUNAROUNDS, THE
Probably more than one group.

45s

Number	Title (A Side/B Side)	Yr	VG	VG+	NM
CAPITOL					
❏ 5644	Perfect Woman/You're a Drag	1966	6.25	12.50	25.00
COUSINS					
❏ 1004	Mashed Potato Mary/I'm All Alone	1964	5.00	10.00	20.00
FELSTED					
❏ 8704	Send Her Back/Carrie, You're An Angel	1964	7.50	15.00	30.00
KC					
❏ 116	Unbelievable/Hurray for Love	1963	6.25	12.50	25.00
❏ 116	Unbelievable/Hurray for Love	1963	10.00	20.00	40.00
—Brown vinyl					
MGM					
❏ 13763	My Little Girl/You Lied	1967	3.75	7.50	15.00
PIO					
❏ 107	The Nearest Thing to Heaven/Lover's Lane	1961	37.50	75.00	150.00
TARHEEL					
❏ 065	Are You Looking for a Sweetheart/Let Them Talk	1963	5.00	10.00	20.00

RUSHEN, PATRICE
12-Inch Singles

Number	Title (A Side/B Side)	Yr	VG	VG+	NM
ARISTA					
❏ AD1-9563	Watch Out (Extended Remix) (Edited Remix) (Single Version) (Dub Mix)/Over the Phone	1987	—	3.00	6.00
❏ AD1-9605	Anything Can Happen (East Coast Extended Mix) (East Coast Dub) (7" Version) (West Coast Extended Mix)/All My Love	1987	—	3.00	6.00
❏ AD1-9645	Come Back to Me (Extended) (Babyfingers Instrumental) (Beat) (7" Version) (Acappella) (Dub Version)/Somewhere	1987	—	3.00	6.00
ELEKTRA					
❏ ED 4961 [DJ]	Feels So Real (Won't Let Go) (same on both sides)	1984	2.50	5.00	10.00
❏ ED 5003 [DJ]	Get Off (You Fascinate Me) (same on both sides)	1984	3.00	6.00	12.00
❏ AS 11404 [DJ]	Hang It Up (Disco Mix 7:26)/Play! (Disco Mix 8:14)	1978	3.75	7.50	15.00
❏ AS 11436 [DJ]	Haven't You Heard (stereo/mono?)	1979	5.00	10.00	20.00
❏ AS 11445 [DJ]	Let the Music Take Me/Message in the Music	1980	2.50	5.00	10.00
❏ AS 11486 [DJ]	Never Gonna Give You Up (Long Version) (Short Version)	1981	3.75	7.50	15.00
❏ AS 11555 [DJ]	Forget Me Nots (7:11)/(She Will) Take You Down to Love	1982	3.75	7.50	15.00
❏ 67959	I Was Tired of Being Alone (Glad I Got Cha) (unknown versions)	1982	2.50	5.00	10.00
❏ 67999 [DJ]	Breakout! (5:44) (stereo/mono)	1982	2.50	5.00	10.00

45s

Number	Title (A Side/B Side)	Yr	VG	VG+	NM
ARISTA					
❏ 9562	Watch Out/Over the Phone	1987	—	—	3.00
❏ 9562 [PS]	Watch Out/Over the Phone	1987	—	—	3.00
❏ 9604	Anything Can Happen/All My Love	1987	—	—	3.00
❏ 9604 [PS]	Anything Can Happen/All My Love	1987	—	—	3.00
❏ 9644	Come Back to Me/Somewhere	1987	—	—	3.00
❏ 9644 [PS]	Come Back to Me/Somewhere	1987	—	—	3.00
ELEKTRA					
❏ 45549	Hang It Up/It's Just a Natural Thing	1978	—	2.50	5.00
❏ 46024	When I Found You/Play!	1979	—	2.50	5.00
❏ 46044	Changes (In Your Life)/Music of the Earth	1979	—	2.50	5.00
❏ 46551	Haven't You Heard/Keepin' Faith in Love	1979	—	2.00	4.00
❏ 46604	Let the Music Take Me/Message in the Music	1980	—	2.00	4.00
❏ 46647	Givin' It Up Is Givin' Up/Settle for My Love	1980	—	2.00	4.00
—A-side with D.J. Rogers					

Number	Title (A Side/B Side)	Yr	VG	VG+	NM
❏ 47067	Look Up/The Dream	1980	—	2.00	4.00
❏ 47113	Never Gonna Give You Up (Part I)/(Part II)	1981	—	2.00	4.00
❏ 47143	Don't Blame Me/Time Will Tell	1981	—	2.00	4.00
❏ 47427	Forget Me Nots/(She Will) Take You Down to Love	1982	—	2.50	5.00
❏ 47427 [PS]	Forget Me Nots/(She Will) Take You Down to Love	1982	—	2.50	5.00
❏ 69586	Number 1/(B-side unknown)	1985	—	2.00	4.00
❏ 69678	Heartache Heartbreak/Gotta Find It	1984	—	2.00	4.00
❏ 69702	Get Off (You Fascinate Me)/(Instrumental)	1984	—	2.00	4.00
❏ 69742	Feels So Real (Won't Let Go)/(Instrumental)	1984	—	2.00	4.00
❏ 69930	I Was Tired of Being Alone (Glad I Got Cha)/Where There Is Love	1982	—	2.00	4.00
❏ 69992	Breakout!/Haven't You Heard	1982	—	2.00	4.00

PRESTIGE

❏ 764	Kickin' Back/What's the Story	1975	2.50	5.00	10.00
❏ 766	Let Your Heart Be Free/Sojourn	1977	2.50	5.00	10.00

Albums
ARISTA

❏ AL-8401	Watch Out!	1987	2.50	5.00	10.00

ELEKTRA

❏ 6E-160	Patrice	1978	2.50	5.00	10.00
❏ 6E-243	Pizzazz	1979	2.50	5.00	10.00
❏ 6E-302	Posh	1980	2.50	5.00	10.00
❏ 60015	Straight from the Heart	1982	2.50	5.00	10.00
❏ 60360	Patrice Rushen Now	1984	2.50	5.00	10.00
❏ 60465	Anthology of Patrice Rushen	1986	2.50	5.00	10.00

PRESTIGE

❏ 10089	Prelusion	1974	5.00	10.00	20.00
❏ 10098	Before the Dawn	1976	5.00	10.00	20.00
❏ 10101	Shout It Out	1977	3.75	7.50	15.00
❏ 10110	Let There Be Funk	1980	3.75	7.50	15.00

S

SADE
12-Inch Singles
EPIC

Number	Title (A Side/B Side)	Yr	VG	VG+	NM
❏ EAS 01121 [DJ]	Paradise (extended)/Paradise (7" Mix)	1988	2.00	4.00	8.00
❏ EAS 01499 [DJ]	Love Is Stronger Than Pride (same on both sides)	1988	2.00	4.00	8.00
❏ EAS 04876 [DJ]	No Ordinary Love (3 versions)/Paradise (Remix)	1992	3.75	7.50	15.00
❏ 77117	Cherish the Day (3 mixes)/Feel No Pain/No Ordinary Love	1993	2.00	4.00	8.00

PORTRAIT

❏ AS 2293 [DJ]	Never As Good As the First Time (2 mixes)/Keep Hangin' On	1986	2.00	4.00	8.00
❏ 05122	Hang On to Your Love (2 versions)	1984	2.00	4.00	8.00
❏ 05375	Never As Good As the First Time (extended)/Keep Hangin' On (Live Instrumental)	1986	2.00	4.00	8.00

45s
EPIC

❏ 07904	Paradise/Super Bien Total	1988	—	—	3.00
❏ 07904 [PS]	Paradise/Super Bien Total	1988	—	—	3.00
❏ 07977	Nothing Can Come Between Us/Make Some Room	1988	—	—	3.00
❏ 08465	Smooth Operator/Hang On to Your Love	1988	—	—	3.00
—Reissue					
❏ 08466	Your Love Is King/Cherry Pie	1988	—	—	3.00
—Reissue					
❏ 08467	The Sweetest Taboo/Never As Good As the First Time	1988	—	—	3.00
—Reissue					
❏ 08503	Turn My Back on You/Keep Looking	1988	—	—	3.00
❏ 68595	Love Is Stronger Than Pride/Make Some Room	1989	—	—	3.00
❏ 74734	No Ordinary Love/Paradise (Remix)	1992	—	—	3.00
❏ 74848	Kiss of Life/Room 55	1993	—	—	3.00
❏ 74903	Feel No Pain/Love Is Stronger Than Pride	1993	—	—	3.00
❏ 74980	Cherish the Day (Sade Remix Short Version)/Cherish the Day (Ronin Remix)	1993	—	—	3.00
❏ 79508	By Your Side (same on both sides)	2000	—	—	3.00

PORTRAIT

❏ 04664	Hang On to Your Love/Cherry Pie	1984	—	—	3.00
❏ 04664 [PS]	Hang On to Your Love/Cherry Pie	1984	—	—	3.00
❏ 04664 [PS]	Hang On to Your Love	1984	—	2.50	5.00
—"Demonstration -- Not for Sale" on rear					
❏ 04807	Smooth Operator/Spirit	1985	—	—	3.00
❏ 04807 [PS]	Smooth Operator/Spirit	1985	—	—	3.00
❏ 04807 [PS]	Smooth Operator	1985	—	2.50	5.00
—"Demonstration -- Not for Sale" on rear					
❏ 05408	Your Love Is King/Love Affair with Life	1985	—	—	3.00
❏ 05408 [DJ]	Your Love Is King (Short Version)/Your Love Is King (Long Version)	1985	—	2.00	4.00
❏ 05408 [PS]	Your Love Is King/Love Affair with Life	1985	—	—	3.00
❏ 05437	Your Love Is King/Love Affair with Life	1985	—	—	3.00
❏ 05437 [PS]	Your Love Is King/Love Affair with Life	1985	—	—	3.00
❏ 05713	The Sweetest Taboo/You're Not the Man	1985	—	—	3.00
❏ 05713 [PS]	The Sweetest Taboo/You're Not the Man	1985	—	—	3.00
❏ 05846	Never As Good As the First Time/Keep Hangin' On	1986	—	—	3.00
❏ 05846 [PS]	Never As Good As the First Time/Keep Hangin' On	1986	—	—	3.00
❏ 06121	Is It a Crime/Punch Drunk	1986	—	—	3.00
❏ 06121 [PS]	Is It a Crime/Punch Drunk	1986	—	—	3.00

Albums
EPIC

❏ OE 44210	Stronger Than Pride	1988	2.50	5.00	10.00
❏ E2 66686 [(2)]	The Best of Sade	1994	3.75	7.50	15.00

PORTRAIT

❏ BFR 39581	Diamond Life	1984	3.00	6.00	12.00
❏ BFR 40263	Promise	1985	2.50	5.00	10.00

SAFARIS, THE
45s
DEE JAY

❏ 203	My Image of a Girl (Is You)/C'mon Everybody	1989	—	2.00	4.00
—Red vinyl					
❏ 203 [PS]	My Image of a Girl (Is You)/C'mon Everybody	1989	—	2.00	4.00

ELDO

❏ 101	Image of a Girl/Four Steps to Love	1960	6.25	12.50	25.00
❏ 105	The Girl with the Story in Her Eyes/Summer Nights	1960	6.25	12.50	25.00
❏ 110	In the Still of the Night/Shadows	1960	7.50	15.00	30.00
❏ 113	Garden of Love/Soldier of Fortune	1961	7.50	15.00	30.00

VALIANT

❏ 6036	Kick Out/Lonely Surf Guitar	1963	7.50	15.00	30.00

ST. LOUIS JIMMY
45s
DUKE

❏ 110	Drinkin' Woman/Why Work	1953	30.00	60.00	120.00

HERALD

❏ 407	Hard Luck Boogie/Good Book Blues	1953	50.00	100.00	200.00
❏ 408	Your Evil Ways/Whiskey Drinkin' Woman	1953	50.00	100.00	200.00

S

Number	Title (A Side/B Side)	Yr	VG	VG+	NM

PARROT

Number	Title (A Side/B Side)	Yr	VG	VG+	NM
❑ 823	Going Down Slow/Murder in the First Degree	1955	50.00	100.00	200.00

SALSOUL ORCHESTRA, THE
12-Inch Singles
SALSOUL

❑ 358 [DJ]	Deck the Halls (7:29)/The Salsoul Christmas Suite (7:59)	1981	3.00	6.00	12.00

45s
SALSOUL

❑ 2002	Salsoul Hustle/Salsoul Hustle (Part 2)	1975	—	2.50	5.00
❑ 2004	Tangerine/Salsoul Hustle	1975	—	2.50	5.00
❑ 2007	You're Just the Right Size/Chicago Bus Stop (Ooh I Like It)	1976	—	2.50	5.00
❑ 2011	Nice 'n' Naasty/Nightcrawler	1976	—	2.50	5.00
❑ 2016	My Love Is Free/(B-side unknown)	1976	—	2.50	5.00
❑ 2018	Ritzy Mambo/Salsoul: 3001	1977	—	2.50	5.00
❑ 2037	Short Shorts/It's a New Day	1977	—	2.50	5.00
❑ 2038	Getaway/Magic Bird of Fire	1977	—	2.50	5.00
❑ 2052	We Wish You a Merry Christmas/Merry Christmas All	1976	—	2.50	5.00
❑ 2052 [PS]	We Wish You a Merry Christmas/Merry Christmas All	1976	—	3.00	6.00
❑ 2064	West Side Encounter — West Side Story (Medley)/Evergreen	1978	—	2.00	4.00
❑ 2072	Sgt. Pepper's Lonely Hearts Club Band/Ease On Down the Road	1978	—	2.00	4.00
❑ 2077	The Little Drummer Boy/Christmas Time	1978	—	2.50	5.00
❑ 2086	Somebody to Love/(B-side unknown)	1979	—	2.00	4.00
❑ 2093	Street Sense/Sun After the Rain	1979	—	2.00	4.00
❑ 2096	How High/Nothing Can Change This Love	1979	—	2.00	4.00
❑ 2155	Deck The Halls/The Salsoul Christmas Suite	1981	—	2.00	4.00
❑ 7026	Take Some Time Out (For Love)/(B-side unknown)	1982	—	—	3.00
❑ 7050	How I Love It So/(B-side unknown)	1983	—	—	3.00

Albums
SALSOUL

❑ CA-1001	Christmas Jollies	198?	2.00	4.00	8.00
—Reissue					
❑ CA-1004	Christmas Jollies II	198?	2.00	4.00	8.00
—Reissue					
❑ SZS 5501	The Salsoul Orchestra	1975	2.50	5.00	10.00
❑ SZS 5502	Nice 'n' Naasty	1976	2.50	5.00	10.00
❑ SZS 5507	Christmas Jollies	1976	3.00	6.00	12.00
❑ SZS 5515	Magic Journey	1977	2.50	5.00	10.00
❑ SA-8500	Up the Yellow Brick Road	1978	2.50	5.00	10.00
❑ SA-8508	Greatest Disco Hits/Music for Non-Stop Dancing	1978	2.50	5.00	10.00
❑ SA-8516	Street Sense	1979	2.50	5.00	10.00
❑ SA-8528	How High	1980	2.50	5.00	10.00
❑ SA 8547	Christmas Jollies II	1981	3.00	6.00	12.00
❑ SA-8552	Heat It Up	1982	2.50	5.00	10.00

SALT-N-PEPA
12-Inch Singles
LONDON

❑ PR12-7075-1 [DJ]	Ain't Nuthin' But a She Thing (Album Version) (Remix) (Instrumental)	1995	—	3.50	7.00

LONDON/RED ANT

❑ PR12-7678-1 [DJ]	R U Ready (5 versions)	1997	2.50	5.00	10.00
❑ 828595-1	Gitty Up (Bystorm 1 Mix) (Bystorm 2 Mix) (Album Version) (Instrumental) (Soul Solution Mix) (David Sussman Mix) (Acapella)	1998	—	3.00	6.00

MCA

❑ MCA8P-3809 [DJ]	Champagne (LP Version) (Remix) (Instrumental)	1996	—	3.50	7.00

NEXT PLATEAU

❑ NP 50043	I'll Take Your Man/(Instrumental)	1986	3.75	7.50	15.00
❑ NP 50053	Beauty and the Beat (5 versions)	1986	2.50	5.00	10.00
❑ NP 50055	My Mike Sounds Nice (Vocal) (Instrumental)/It's All Right	1987	2.00	4.00	8.00
❑ NP 50063	Tramp (3 versions)/Push It (2 versions)/Idle Chatter	1987	2.50	5.00	10.00
❑ NP 50071	I Am Down (Vocal 4:09) (Acappella) (Instrumental)/Chick on the Side (Love Bandit) (Remix) (Remix Instrumental)/Pass the Salt-N-Pepa (Medley)	1987	2.00	4.00	8.00
❑ NP 50077	Shake Your Thang (Club) (Radio) (Instrumental) (Acappella)/Spinderella's Not a Fella (Vocal) (Instrumental) (Acappella)	1988	2.50	5.00	10.00
❑ NP 50083	Get Up Everybody (Long Version) (Radio) (Instrumental) (Club Mix) (Acappella)/Twist and Shout (Vocal) (Instrumental) (Acappella)	1988	2.50	5.00	10.00
❑ NP 50101	Expression (Half-step) (No Shorts) (Acapella) (Instrumental) (Bonus Beats)/Clubhouse (Vocal) (Instrumental)	1989	2.00	4.00	8.00
❑ NP 50137	Do You Want Me (3 versions)/Gotcha (Once Again)	1990	2.00	4.00	8.00
❑ NP 50157	Let's Talk About Sex (3 versions)/Swift	1991	2.50	5.00	10.00
❑ NP 50165	You Showed Me (4 versions)	1992	2.50	5.00	10.00
❑ NP 50185	Do You Want Me '92 (4 versions)	1992	2.00	4.00	8.00
❑ 857315-1	Shoop (4 versions)/Emphatically No/AIDS P.S.A.	1993	2.00	4.00	8.00
❑ 857391-1	Whatta Man (4 versions)	1993	2.00	4.00	8.00
❑ 857715-1	None of Your Business (3 versions)/Shoop/Heaven 'N' Hell (Carron Hall Mix)	1994	2.00	4.00	8.00
❑ 869863-1	Start Me Up (4 versions)	1992	2.00	4.00	8.00

POP ART

❑ PA 1413	The Show Stoppa (Vocal) (Instrumental) (Def Mix)	1985	3.75	7.50	15.00
—As "Super Nature"					

SOUL

❑ 2127 [DJ]	He's Gamin' On Ya (3 versions)	1991	—	3.00	6.00

45s
LONDON

❑ 850346-7	Ain't Nuthin' But a She Thing (Album Version)/ (Remix)	1995	—	—	3.00
❑ 857356-7	Shoop/Whatta Man	1994	—	—	3.00

NEXT PLATEAU

❑ KF 315	Tramp/Push It	1987	2.50	5.00	10.00
❑ KF 315	Push It (Remix) (same on both sides)	1987	—	2.50	5.00
❑ KF 319	Shake Your Thang/Spinderella's Not a Fella (But a Girl D.J.)	1988	—	—	3.00
❑ KF 319 [PS]	Shake Your Thang/Spinderella's Not a Fella (But a Girl D.J.)	1988	—	—	3.00
❑ KF 321	Twist and Shout/Get Up Everybody (Get Up)	1988	—	—	3.00
❑ KF 321 [PS]	Twist and Shout/Get Up Everybody (Get Up)	1988	—	—	3.00
❑ KF 329	Expression (Half-step)/(Brixton Radio Remix)	1989	—	3.00	6.00

Albums
LONDON

❑ 828392-1	Very Necessary	1993	3.00	6.00	12.00

LONDON/RED ANT

❑ 828959-1 [(2)]	Brand New	1997	3.00	6.00	12.00

NEXT PLATEAU

❑ PL 1011	A Salt with a Deadly Pepa	1988	3.00	6.00	12.00
❑ PL 1019	Blacks' Magic	1989	3.00	6.00	12.00

SAM AND DAVE
Also see SAM MOORE.
45s
ALSTON

❑ 777	Never, Never/Lotta Lovin'	1964	5.00	10.00	20.00

ATLANTIC

❑ 2517	You Don't Know What You Mean to Me/This Is Your World	1968	—	3.00	6.00
❑ 2540	Can't You Find Another Way (Of Doing It)/Still Is the Night	1968	—	3.00	6.00
❑ 2568	Everybody Got to Believe in Somebody/If I Didn't Have a Girl Like You	1968	—	3.00	6.00
❑ 2590	Soul Sister, Brown Sugar/Come On In	1968	—	3.00	6.00
❑ 2608	Born Again/Get It	1969	—	3.00	6.00
❑ 2668	Holdin' On/Ooh Ooh Ooh	1969	—	3.00	6.00
❑ 2714	I'm Not an Indian Giver/Baby-Baby Don't Stop Now	1970	—	3.00	6.00
❑ 2728	One Part Love, Two Parts Pain/When You Steal from Me	1970	—	3.00	6.00
❑ 2733	When You Steal from Me (You're Only Hurting Yourself)/You Easily Excite Me	1970	—	3.00	6.00
❑ 2839	Don't Pull Your Love/Jody Ryder Got Killed	1971	—	3.00	6.00

CONTEMPO

❑ 7004	We Can Work It Out/Why Did You Do It	1977	—	2.50	5.00

MARLIN

❑ 6100	I Need Love/Keep a-Walkin'	1961	10.00	20.00	40.00
❑ 6104	No More Pain/My Love Belongs to You	1961	10.00	20.00	40.00

ROULETTE

❑ 4419	I Need Love/Keep a-Walkin'	1962	3.00	6.00	12.00
❑ 4445	No More Pain/My Love Belongs to You	1962	3.00	6.00	12.00
❑ 4461	She's Alright/It Feels So Nice	1962	3.00	6.00	12.00
❑ 4480	It Was So Nice While It Lasted/You Ain't No Big Thing, Baby	1963	3.00	6.00	12.00
❑ 4508	If She'll Still Have Me/Listening for My Name	1963	3.00	6.00	12.00
❑ 4533	I Found Out/I Got a Thing Going On	1963	3.00	6.00	12.00
❑ 4671	It Feels So Nice/It Was So Nice While It Lasted	1966	2.00	4.00	8.00

STAX

❑ 168	Goodnight Baby/A Place Nobody Can Find	1965	3.75	7.50	15.00
❑ 175	I Take What I Want/Sweet Home	1965	3.00	6.00	12.00
❑ 180	You Don't Know Like I Know/Blame Me (Don't Blame My Heart)	1965	3.00	6.00	12.00
❑ 189	Hold On! I'm a-Comin'/I Got Everything I Need	1966	3.75	7.50	15.00
❑ 198	Said I Wasn't Gonna Tell Nobody/If You Got the Loving	1966	2.50	5.00	10.00
❑ 204	You Got Me Hummin'/Sleep Good Tonight	1967	2.50	5.00	10.00
❑ 210	When Something Is Wrong with My Baby/Small Portion of Your Love	1967	2.50	5.00	10.00
❑ 218	Soothe Me/I Can't Stand Up for Falling Down	1967	2.50	5.00	10.00
❑ 231	Soul Man/May I Baby	1967	3.00	6.00	12.00
❑ 242	I Thank You/Wrap It Up	1968	3.00	6.00	12.00

UNITED ARTISTS

❑ XW438	A Little Bit of Good (Cures a Whole Lot of Bad)/ Blinded by Love	1974	—	3.00	6.00
❑ XW531	Under the Boardwalk/Give It What You Can	1974	—	3.00	6.00

Albums
ATLANTIC

❑ SD 8205	I Thank You	1968	6.25	12.50	25.00
❑ SD 8218	The Best of Sam and Dave	1969	5.00	10.00	20.00
❑ 81279	The Best of Sam and Dave	1985	2.50	5.00	10.00
❑ 81718	Soul Men	1987	2.50	5.00	10.00
—Reissue of Stax 725					

GUSTO

❑ 0045	Sweet and Funky Gold	197?	2.50	5.00	10.00

Number	Title (A Side/B Side)	Yr	VG	VG+	NM
ROULETTE					
❑ R-25323 [M]	Sam and Dave	1966	7.50	15.00	30.00
❑ SR-25323 [S]	Sam and Dave	1966	10.00	20.00	40.00
STAX					
❑ ST-708 [M]	Hold On, I'm Comin'	1966	10.00	20.00	40.00
❑ STS-708 [S]	Hold On, I'm Comin'	1966	12.50	25.00	50.00
❑ ST-712 [M]	Double Dynamite	1966	7.50	15.00	30.00
❑ STS-712 [S]	Double Dynamite	1966	10.00	20.00	40.00
❑ ST-725 [M]	Soul Men	1967	7.50	15.00	30.00
❑ STS-725 [S]	Soul Men	1967	10.00	20.00	40.00
UNITED ARTISTS					
❑ UA-LA524-G	Back At 'Cha!	1975	3.00	6.00	12.00

SAN REMO GOLDEN STRINGS
45s
GORDY					
❑ 7060	Festival Time/Joy Road	1967	6.25	12.50	25.00
RIC-TIC					
❑ 104	Hungry for Love/All Turned On	1965	3.00	6.00	12.00
❑ 108	I'm Satisfied/Blueberry Hill	1965	3.00	6.00	12.00
❑ 112	Festival Time/Joy Road	1966	3.00	6.00	12.00
❑ 116	International Love Theme/Quanto Si Bella	1966	3.00	6.00	12.00
Albums					
GORDY					
❑ G-923 [M]	Hungry for Love	1967	6.25	12.50	25.00
❑ GS-923 [S]	Hungry for Love	1967	7.50	15.00	30.00
❑ GS-928	Swing	1968	5.00	10.00	20.00
RIC-TIC					
❑ 901 [M]	Hungry for Love	1966	12.50	25.00	50.00
❑ S-901 [S]	Hungry for Love	1966	15.00	30.00	60.00

SAPPHIRES, THE (1)
45s
ABC-PARAMOUNT					
❑ 10559	Hearts Are Made to Be Broken/Let's Break Up for Awhile	1964	3.75	7.50	15.00
❑ 10590	Thank You for Loving Me/Our Love Is Everywhere	1964	3.75	7.50	15.00
❑ 10639	Gee I'm Sorry, Baby/Gotta Have Your Love	1965	3.75	7.50	15.00
❑ 10693	Evil One/How Could I Say Goodbye	1965	3.75	7.50	15.00
❑ 10753	You'll Never Stop Me from Loving You/Gonna Be a Big Thing	1965	3.75	7.50	15.00
❑ 10778	Our Love Is Everywhere/Slow Fizz	1966	3.75	7.50	15.00
ITZY					
❑ 8	Who Do You Love/Oh So Soon	1963	10.00	20.00	40.00
SWAN					
❑ 4143	Your True Love/Where Is Johnny Now	1963	3.75	7.50	15.00
❑ 4162	Who Do You Love/Oh So Soon	1963	3.75	7.50	15.00
❑ 4177	I Found Out Too Late/I've Got Mine, You Better Get Yours	1964	3.75	7.50	15.00
❑ 4184	Gotta Be More Than Friends/Moulin Rouge	1964	3.75	7.50	15.00
Albums					
COLLECTABLES					
❑ COL-5007	Who Do You Love	198?	2.50	5.00	10.00
SWAN					
❑ LP-513 [M]	Who Do You Love	1964	75.00	150.00	300.00

SATELLITES, THE
More than one group.
45s
ABC-PARAMOUNT					
❑ 10038	Linda Jean/Rockateen	1959	10.00	20.00	40.00
CLASS					
❑ 234	Heavenly Angel/You Ain't Sayin' Nothin'	1958	7.50	15.00	30.00
CUPID					
❑ (no #)	Linda Jean/Rockateen	1959	20.00	40.00	80.00
D-M-G					
❑ 4001	Each Night/Darktown Strutters Ball	1960	7.50	15.00	30.00
MALYNN					
❑ 231	Heavenly Angel/You Ain't Sayin' Nothin'	1958	6.25	12.50	25.00
PALACE					
❑ 102	Buzz Buzz/We Like Birdland	1960	5.00	10.00	20.00
PARROT					
❑ 313	Bodacious/El San Juan	1966	6.25	12.50	25.00
UNITED ARTISTS					
❑ 141	I Found a Girl/My Piggie's Gotta Dance	1958	10.00	20.00	40.00

SATINTONES, THE
45s
MOTOWN					
❑ 1000	Sugar Daddy/My Beloved	1960	100.00	200.00	400.00
—Without strings. Matrix number of A-side is "MNT 12345"					
❑ 1000	Sugar Daddy/My Beloved	1960	100.00	200.00	400.00
—With strings. Matrix number of A-side is "1000 G-3"					
❑ 1006	Tomorrow and Always/A Love That Can Never Be	1961	62.50	125.00	250.00
—Without strings					
❑ 1006	Angel/A Love That Can Never Be	1961	375.00	750.00	1500.
❑ 1006	Tomorrow and Always/A Love That Can Never Be	1961	62.50	125.00	250.00
—With strings					
❑ 1010	I Know How It Feels/My Kind of Love	1961	50.00	100.00	200.00
❑ 1020	Zing Went the Strings of My Heart/Faded Letter	1962	50.00	100.00	200.00
TAMLA					
❑ 54026	Motor City/Going to the Hop	1960	200.00	400.00	800.00

SCARLETS, THE (1)
45s
DOT					
❑ 16004	Stampede/Park Avenue	1959	6.25	12.50	25.00
PRINCE					
❑ 1207	Stampede/Park Avenue	1959	12.50	25.00	50.00

SCARLETS, THE (2)
45s
EVENT					
❑ 4287	Dear One/I've Lost	1958	10.00	20.00	40.00
RED ROBIN					
❑ 128	Dear One/I've Lost	1954	125.00	250.00	500.00
❑ 133	Darling, I'm Yours/Love Doll	1954	125.00	250.00	500.00
❑ 135	True Love/Cry Baby	1955	125.00	250.00	500.00
❑ 138	Kiss Me/Indian Fever	1955	150.00	300.00	600.00

SCOTT, BILLY
45s
CAMEO					
❑ 121	You're the Greatest/That's Why I Was Born	1957	6.25	12.50	25.00
❑ 143	A Million Boys/The Town of Never Worry	1958	5.00	10.00	20.00
EVEREST					
❑ 19315	Carole/Stairway to the Stars	1959	3.75	7.50	15.00
LAMON					
❑ 10114	Merry Christmas/A Night to Remember	1983	—	2.00	4.00

SCOTT, FREDDIE
Also see THE SYMPHONICS (2).
45s
COLPIX					
❑ 692	Hey Girl/The Slide	1963	3.00	6.00	12.00
❑ 709	I Got a Woman/Brand New World	1963	2.50	5.00	10.00
❑ 724	Where Does Love Go/Where Have All the Flowers Gone	1964	2.50	5.00	10.00
❑ 752	On Broadway/If I Had a Hammer	1964	2.50	5.00	10.00
COLUMBIA					
❑ 43112	Mr. Heartache/One Heartache Too Many	1964	2.50	5.00	10.00
❑ 43199	Lonely Man/I'll Try Again	1964	2.50	5.00	10.00
❑ 43316	Don't Let It End/Come Up Singing	1965	2.50	5.00	10.00
❑ 43623	One Iddy Biddy Needle/Forget Me If You Can	1966	2.50	5.00	10.00
JOY					
❑ 250	Baby, You're a Long Time Dead/Lost the Right	1961	3.00	6.00	12.00
❑ 255	I Gotta Stand Tall/When the Wind Changes	1961	3.00	6.00	12.00
❑ 280	I Gotta Stand Tall/When the Wind Changes	1963	2.50	5.00	10.00
PROBE					
❑ 481	I Shall Be Released/Girl I Love You	1970	—	3.00	6.00
P.I.P.					
❑ 8932	Deep Is the Night/The Great If	1972	—	2.50	5.00
SHOUT					
❑ 207	Are You Lonely for Me/Where Were You	1966	2.00	4.00	8.00
❑ 211	Cry to Me/No One Could Ever Love You	1967	2.00	4.00	8.00
❑ 212	Am I Grooving You/Never You Mind	1967	2.00	4.00	8.00
❑ 216	He Will Break Your Heart/I'll Be Gone	1967	2.00	4.00	8.00
❑ 220	He Ain't Give You None/Run Joy	1967	2.00	4.00	8.00
❑ 227	Just Like a Flower/Spanish Harlem	1968	2.00	4.00	8.00
❑ 233	(You) Got What I Need/Powerful Love	1968	2.50	5.00	10.00
❑ 238	Loving You Is Killing Me/Eileen	1968	2.00	4.00	8.00
❑ 245	Forever My Darling/(You) Got What I Need	1969	2.50	5.00	10.00
VANGUARD					
❑ 35137	I Guess God Wants It This Way/Please Listen	1971	—	2.50	5.00
Albums					
COLPIX					
❑ CP-461 [M]	Freddie Scott Sings and Sings and Sings	1964	15.00	30.00	60.00
—Gold label					
❑ CP-461 [M]	Freddie Scott Sings and Sings and Sings	1965	10.00	20.00	40.00
—Blue label					
❑ SCP-461 [R]	Freddie Scott Sings and Sings and Sings	1965	7.50	1.00	30.00
—Blue label					
❑ SCP-461 [S]	Freddie Scott Sings and Sings and Sings	1964	30.00	60.00	120.00
—Gold label					
COLUMBIA					
❑ CL 2258 [M]	Everything I Have Is Yours	1964	5.00	10.00	20.00
❑ CL 2660 [M]	Lonely Man	1967	5.00	10.00	20.00
❑ CS 9058 [S]	Everything I Have Is Yours	1964	6.25	12.50	25.00
❑ CS 9460 [S]	Lonely Man	1967	6.25	12.50	25.00
PROBE					
❑ CPLP-4517	I Shall Be Released	1970	6.25	12.50	25.00
SHOUT					
❑ SLP-501 [M]	Are You Lonely for Me	1967	5.00	10.00	20.00
❑ SLPS-501 [S]	Are You Lonely for Me	1967	6.25	12.50	25.00

SCOTT, FREDDIE, AND THE CHIMES
45s
ARROW					
❑ 724	Please Call/A Letter Came This Morning	1958	10.00	20.00	40.00
❑ 726	Lovin' Baby/A Faded Memory	1958	10.00	20.00	40.00

SCOTT, PEGGY, AND JO JO BENSON
45s
SSS INTERNATIONAL					
❑ 736	Lover's Holiday/Here with Me	1968	2.00	4.00	8.00

S

Number	Title (A Side/B Side)	Yr	VG	VG+	NM
❑ 748	Pickin' Wild Mountain Berries/Pure Love and Pleasure	1968	2.00	4.00	8.00
❑ 761	Soulshake/We Were Made for Each Other	1969	2.00	4.00	8.00
❑ 769	I Want to Love You Baby/We Got Our Bag	1969	2.00	4.00	8.00
❑ 781	Sugarmaker/Lover's Heaven	1969	2.00	4.00	8.00
❑ 805	Let's Spend a Day Out in the Country/Little Things That Count	1970	—	3.00	6.00

Albums
SSS INTERNATIONAL

Number	Title (A Side/B Side)	Yr	VG	VG+	NM
❑ 1	Soulshake	1968	6.25	12.50	25.00
❑ 2	Lover's Heaven	1969	6.25	12.50	25.00

SCOTT-ADAMS, PEGGY
45s
MISS BUTCH

Number	Title (A Side/B Side)	Yr	VG	VG+	NM
❑ 209	Bill/Help Yourself	1997	—	2.00	4.00
❑ 212	I'm in Love/Leave Me Alone	1997	—	2.00	4.00
❑ 222	That's How I Do It/You're Too Freaky for Me	1999	—	2.00	4.00
❑ 223	Mommy's No Dummy/You Will Always Be My Man	1999	—	2.00	4.00
❑ 229	Christmas Friends of Mine/Silent Night	1999	—	2.00	4.00

SECRETS, THE (1)
Girl group.
45s
OMEN

Number	Title (A Side/B Side)	Yr	VG	VG+	NM
❑ 15	Here I Am/I Feel a Thrill Coming On	1966	3.00	6.00	12.00

PHILIPS

Number	Title (A Side/B Side)	Yr	VG	VG+	NM
❑ 40146	The Boy Next Door/Learnin' to Forget	1963	3.75	7.50	15.00
❑ 40173	Hey Big Boy/The Other Side of Town	1964	3.00	6.00	12.00
❑ 40173 [PS]	Hey Big Boy/The Other Side of Town	1964	5.00	10.00	20.00
❑ 40196	Here He Comes Now!/Oh Donnie	1964	3.00	6.00	12.00
❑ 40222	He's the Boy/He Doesn't Want You	1964	3.00	6.00	12.00

SENSATIONS, THE
Also see YVONNE BAKER.
45s
ARGO

Number	Title (A Side/B Side)	Yr	VG	VG+	NM
❑ 5391	Music, Music, Music/A Part of Me	1961	2.50	5.00	10.00
❑ 5405	Let Me In/Oh Yes I'll Be True	1961	3.00	6.00	12.00
—Brown label					
❑ 5405	Let Me In/Oh Yes I'll Be True	1961	5.00	10.00	20.00
—Black label					
❑ 5412	That's My Desire/Eyes	1962	2.50	5.00	10.00
—By "Yvonne Baker and the Sensations"					
❑ 5420	Party Across the Hall/No Changes	1962	2.50	5.00	10.00
—By "Yvonne Baker and the Sensations"					
❑ 5446	When My Lover Comes Home/Father Dear	1963	2.50	5.00	10.00
—By "Yvonne Baker and the Sensations"					

ATCO

Number	Title (A Side/B Side)	Yr	VG	VG+	NM
❑ 6056	Yes Sir, That's My Baby/Sympathy	1955	10.00	20.00	40.00
❑ 6067	Please Mr. Disc Jockey/Ain't He Sweet	1956	10.00	20.00	40.00
❑ 6075	Cry Baby Cry/My Heart Cries for You	1956	10.00	20.00	40.00
❑ 6083	Little Wallflower/Such a Love	1957	10.00	20.00	40.00
❑ 6090	My Debut to Love/You Made Me Love You	1957	10.00	20.00	40.00
❑ 6115	Kiddy Car Love/Romance in the Dark	1958	10.00	20.00	40.00

JUNIOR

Number	Title (A Side/B Side)	Yr	VG	VG+	NM
❑ 1002	We Were Meant to Be/It's Good Enough for Me	1963	3.00	6.00	12.00
❑ 1005	You Made a Fool of Me/That's What You've Gotta Do	1963	5.00	10.00	20.00
❑ 1010	I Can't Change/Mend the Torn Pieces	1964	3.00	6.00	12.00
❑ 1021	We Were Meant to Be/It's Good Enough for Me	1964	3.00	6.00	12.00

TOLLIE

Number	Title (A Side/B Side)	Yr	VG	VG+	NM
❑ 9009	You Made a Fool of Me/That's What You've Gotta Do	1964	2.50	5.00	10.00

Albums
ARGO

Number	Title (A Side/B Side)	Yr	VG	VG+	NM
❑ LP-4022 [M]	Let Me In/Music, Music, Music	1963	125.00	250.00	500.00

SENTIMENTALS, THE
45s
CHECKER

Number	Title (A Side/B Side)	Yr	VG	VG+	NM
❑ 875	I Want to Love You/Tommie Teenager	1957	10.00	20.00	40.00

CORAL

Number	Title (A Side/B Side)	Yr	VG	VG+	NM
❑ 62100	We Three/Understanding Love	1959	6.25	12.50	25.00
❑ 62172	Deep Down in My Heart/Two Different Worlds	1960	6.25	12.50	25.00

MINT

Number	Title (A Side/B Side)	Yr	VG	VG+	NM
❑ 801	I Want to Love You/Tommie Teenager	1957	12.50	25.00	50.00
❑ 802	Sunday Kind of Love/Wedding Bells	1957	10.00	20.00	40.00
❑ 803	I'm Your Fool, Always/Rock Me, Mama	1958	10.00	20.00	40.00
❑ 805	You're Mine/Danny Boy	1958	10.00	20.00	40.00
❑ 807	Found a New Baby/I'll Miss These Things	196?	3.00	6.00	12.00
❑ 808	This Time/I Want to Love You	196?	3.00	6.00	12.00

VANITY

Number	Title (A Side/B Side)	Yr	VG	VG+	NM
❑ 589	Love Is a Gamble/If It Isn't for You	1959	6.25	12.50	25.00

SEQUINS, THE
More than one group.
45s
ASCOT

Number	Title (A Side/B Side)	Yr	VG	VG+	NM
❑ 2140	You Can't Sit Still/Mr. Leader of the Band	1963	3.75	7.50	15.00

A&M

Number	Title (A Side/B Side)	Yr	VG	VG+	NM
❑ 761	I'll Be Satisfied/Who Says You Can't Jerk to the Old Time Music	1965	3.00	6.00	12.00

CAMEO

Number	Title (A Side/B Side)	Yr	VG	VG+	NM
❑ 161	To Be Young/The Mountains	1959	5.00	10.00	20.00

GOLD STAR

Number	Title (A Side/B Side)	Yr	VG	VG+	NM
❑ 101	Hey Romeo/I've Got to Overcome	1970	—	3.00	6.00

RED ROBIN

Number	Title (A Side/B Side)	Yr	VG	VG+	NM
	Why Can't You Treat Me Right/Don't Fall in Love	1956	100.00	200.00	400.00

TERRACE

Number	Title (A Side/B Side)	Yr	VG	VG+	NM
❑ 7511	Love Me Forever/You're Dancing Now	1962	3.75	7.50	15.00
❑ 7515	Hideaway/I Ain't Gonna Cry (No More)	1963	3.75	7.50	15.00

SERENADERS, THE (1)
45s
CHOCK FULL O' HITS

Number	Title (A Side/B Side)	Yr	VG	VG+	NM
❑ 101	I Wrote a Letter/Never Let Me Go	1957	75.00	150.00	300.00
❑ 102	Dance Darling, Dance/Give Me a Girl	1957	50.00	100.00	200.00

MGM

Number	Title (A Side/B Side)	Yr	VG	VG+	NM
❑ 12623	I Wrote a Letter/Never Let Me Go	1958	25.00	50.00	100.00
❑ 12666	Dance Darling, Dance/Give Me a Girl	1958	30.00	60.00	120.00

MOTOWN

Number	Title (A Side/B Side)	Yr	VG	VG+	NM
❑ 1046	If Your Heart Says Yes/I'll Cry Tomorrow	1963	1000.	1500.	2000.

RAE COX

Number	Title (A Side/B Side)	Yr	VG	VG+	NM
❑ 101	Gotta Go to School/My Girl Flip-Flop	1959	15.00	30.00	60.00

RIVERSIDE

Number	Title (A Side/B Side)	Yr	VG	VG+	NM
❑ 4549	Adios, My Love/Two Lovers Make One Fool	1963	25.00	50.00	100.00

V.I.P.

Number	Title (A Side/B Side)	Yr	VG	VG+	NM
❑ 25002	If Your Heart Says Yes/I'll Cry Tomorrow	1964	25.00	50.00	100.00

SERENADERS, THE (2)
45s
CORAL

Number	Title (A Side/B Side)	Yr	VG	VG+	NM
❑ 60720	It's Funny/Confession Is Good for the Soul	1952	75.00	150.00	300.00
❑ 65093	Misery/But I Forgive You	1952	75.00	150.00	300.00

DELUXE

Number	Title (A Side/B Side)	Yr	VG	VG+	NM
❑ 6022	Please, Please Forgive Me/Baby	1953	125.00	250.00	500.00

JVB

Number	Title (A Side/B Side)	Yr	VG	VG+	NM
❑ 2001	Tomorrow Night/Why Don't You Do Right	1952	100.00	200.00	400.00

RED ROBIN

Number	Title (A Side/B Side)	Yr	VG	VG+	NM
❑ 115	Will She Know?/I Want to Love You Baby	1953	375.00	750.00	1500.

SWING TIME

Number	Title (A Side/B Side)	Yr	VG	VG+	NM
❑ 347	M-A-Y-B-E-L-L/Ain't Gonna Cry No More	1954	300.00	600.00	1200.

702
12-Inch Singles
BIV 10

Number	Title (A Side/B Side)	Yr	VG	VG+	NM
❑ 37463 2027 1	Get It Together (LP Version) (Radio Edit) (Instrumental) (Acappella)	1997	2.00	4.00	8.00
❑ 37643 2042 1	Get It Together (Bass Mix Extended w/Doug Lazy) (Bass Mix Instrumental)/(Lush Mix) (LP Version) (A Cappella w/Doug Lazy)	1997	2.00	4.00	8.00
❑ 37463 2054 1	No Doubt (Radio Edit) (LP Version)/ (Instrumental) (A Cappella)	1997	2.00	4.00	8.00

MOTOWN

Number	Title (A Side/B Side)	Yr	VG	VG+	NM
❑ U8P-1558 [DJ]	You Don't Know (LP Version) (Instrumental)/ (Radio Edit) (A Cappella)	1999	—	3.50	7.00
❑ MOTR-20018 [DJ]	You Don't Know (CL Remix) (Haus-a-Holics Club Mix) (Charles Bass Mix) (Charles Rub-a-Dub)	1999	2.50	5.00	10.00
❑ MOTR-20027-1 [DJ]	Gotta Leave (LP Version 5:08) (Instrumental 5:11) (Acappella 4:26)/(Remix 5:16) (Remix Instrumental 5:16)	2000	2.00	4.00	8.00
❑ 012-156722-1	Gotta Leave (LP Version 5:08) (Instrumental 5:11) (Acappella 4:26)/(Remix 5:16) (Remix Instrumental 5:16)	2000	2.00	4.00	8.00
❑ 422-860723-1	Where My Girls At? (4 versions)	1999	—	3.50	7.00

45s
BIV 10

Number	Title (A Side/B Side)	Yr	VG	VG+	NM
❑ 422-860648-7	Get It Together/Steelo	1997	—	—	3.00

SEVILLES, THE
45s
CAL-GOLD

Number	Title (A Side/B Side)	Yr	VG	VG+	NM
❑ 172	Don't You Know I Care/(B-side unknown)	1962	5.00	10.00	20.00

GALAXY

Number	Title (A Side/B Side)	Yr	VG	VG+	NM
❑ 717	Treat You Right/Hey, Hey, Hey	1963	3.75	7.50	15.00
❑ 721	Charlena/Loving You	1963	3.75	7.50	15.00
❑ 727	Creation/Baby	1964	3.75	7.50	15.00

JC

Number	Title (A Side/B Side)	Yr	VG	VG+	NM
❑ 116	Charlena/Loving You (Is My Desire)	1960	7.50	15.00	30.00
❑ 118	Louella/Salt Mine	1961	6.25	12.50	25.00
❑ 120	Fat Sally/Working Hard	1961	5.00	10.00	20.00

SH-BOOMS, THE
See THE CHORDS.

SHADES, THE
More than one group.
45s
ALADDIN

Number	Title (A Side/B Side)	Yr	VG	VG+	NM
❑ 3453	Dear Lori/One Touch of Heaven	1959	75.00	150.00	300.00

AOK

Number	Title (A Side/B Side)	Yr	VG	VG+	NM
❑ 1028	Ginger Bread Man/The Hip	1967	7.50	15.00	30.00

Number	Title (A Side/B Side)	Yr	VG	VG+	NM
BIG TOP					
❏ 3003	Sun Glasses/Undivided Attention	1958	25.00	50.00	100.00
—B-side by The Knott Sisters					

SHADES OF BLUE
45s
IMPACT

❏ 1007	Oh, How Happy/Little Orphan Boy	1966	5.00	10.00	20.00
❏ 1014	Lonely Summer/With This Ring	1966	5.00	10.00	20.00
❏ 1015	Happiness/The Night	1966	5.00	10.00	20.00
❏ 1026	All I Want Is Love/How Do You Save a Dying Love	1967	5.00	10.00	20.00
❏ 1028	Penny Arcade/Funny Kind of Love	1967	5.00	10.00	20.00
Albums					
IMPACT					
❏ IM-101 [M]	Happiness Is the Shades of Blue	1966	12.50	25.00	50.00
❏ IM-1001 [S]	Happiness Is the Shades of Blue	1966	15.00	30.00	60.00

SHAGGY
12-Inch Singles
MCA

❏ MCAR-25243	[DJ]It Wasn't Me (4 versions)	2000	2.00	4.00	8.00
❏ MCAR-25290	[DJ]It Wasn't Me (Vocal 12") (Vocal 12" Instrumental) (Punch Remix) (LP Version)	2000	—	3.50	7.00
❏ MCAR-25370	[DJ]Angel (5 versions)	2001	—	3.00	6.00
❏ MCAR-25391	[DJ]Freaky Girl (4 versions)	2001	2.00	4.00	8.00
❏ 088-155782-1	It Wasn't Me (unknown versions)	2000	—	3.50	7.00
❏ 088-155820-1	Angel (LP Version) (Dance Hall Remix) (Dance Hall Remix Instrumental)	2001	—	3.00	6.00
VIRGIN					
❏ SPRO-11019	[DJ]In the Summertime (3 versions)	1995	—	3.00	6.00
❏ SPRO-11092	[DJ]Why You Treat Me So Bad (Salaam Clean Radio) (Salaam Alternate Intro Remix) (Sting Club Mix) (Radio Mix)	1996	—	3.50	7.00
❏ SPRO-12270	[DJ]Piece of My Heart (Tee's Urban Mix) (TNT Low Down Edit) (LP Version) (Ragga Time Mix) (Duke Mix) (Ragga Instrumental)	1997	—	3.50	7.00
❏ SPRO-12722	[DJ]Piece of My Heart (Urban Remix) (Urban Remix Instrumental) (LP version featuring Marsha) (Urban Remix Acappella)	1997	—	3.50	7.00
❏ SPRO-12724	[DJ]Boombastic (LP Version) (Sting Remix)	1995	2.00	4.00	8.00
❏ SPRO-13128	[DJ]Sexy Body Girls (Tiger Version) (Lion Version) (Tiger Instrumental Version)/Big Up	1993	2.50	5.00	10.00
❏ Y-38420	Nice and Lovely (Radio Mix) (Ram Mix) (Version 12" Dub)//(Errol Moore R&B Mix) (Frankie Cutlass Hip Hop Mix)/Victoria's Secret	1993	2.00	4.00	8.00
❏ SPRO-38529	[DJ]Why You Treat Me So Bad (Club Mix) (Radio Mix) (LP Version)/Demand a Ride/The Train Is Coming (Film Version) (Urban Mix)	1996	—	3.50	7.00
❏ Y-38601	Piece of My Heart (6 versions)	1997	—	3.00	6.00
45s					
MCA					
❏ 088-155695-7	Dance and Shout/Wasn't Me	2000	—	—	3.00
❏ 088 155782-7	It Wasn't Me (Album Version)/It Wasn't Me (Vocal Club)	2000	—	—	3.00
❏ 088-155820-7	Angel (featuring Rayvon)/Chica Bonita	2001	—	2.00	4.00
VIRGIN					
❏ S7-17447	Oh Carolina/Love Me Up	1993	—	2.00	4.00
❏ S7-17599	Nice and Lovely/Victoria's Secret	1993	—	2.00	4.00
❏ S7-18586	In the Summertime/Boombastic	1995	—	2.50	5.00
❏ S7-19108	Why You Treat Me So Bad/Demand the Ride	1996	—	2.00	4.00
Albums					
MCA					
❏ 112096	Hotshot	2000	3.75	7.50	15.00
❏ 112827 [(2)]	Hotshot Ultramix	2002	3.75	7.50	15.00
VIRGIN					
❏ 44487	Midnite Lover	1997	3.00	6.00	12.00

SHALAMAR
Also see JODY WATLEY.
45s
COLUMBIA

❏ 04372	Dancing in the Sheets/(Instrumental)	1984	—	2.00	4.00
❏ 04372 [PS]	Dancing in the Sheets/(Instrumental)	1984	—	2.00	4.00
❏ 08421	Dancing in the Sheets/(Instrumental)	1988	—	—	3.00
—Reissue					
MCA					
❏ 52335	Deadline U.S.A./One More Time Around the Block Ophelia	1984	—	2.00	4.00
—B-side by Gary U.S. Bonds					
❏ 52345	Deadline U.S.A./Knock Me On My Feet	1984	—	2.00	4.00
❏ 52594	Don't Get Stopped in Beverly Hills/The Discovery	1985	—	—	3.00
—B-side by Harold Faltermeyer					
❏ 52594 [PS]	Don't Get Stopped in Beverly Hills/The Discovery	1985	—	—	3.00
SOLAR					
❏ YB-11379	Take That to the Bank/Shalamar Disco Gardens	1978	—	2.00	4.00
❏ YB-11542	Stay Close to Love/Cindy, Cindy	1979	—	2.00	4.00
❏ YB-11709	The Second Time Around/Leave It All Up to Love	1979	—	2.00	4.00
❏ YB-11709	Right in the Socket/Girl	1980	—	2.00	4.00
❏ GB-11979	Uptown Festival (Part 1)/Take That to the Bank	1980	—	—	3.00
—Gold Standard Series					
❏ YB-12049	I Owe You One/Right Time for Us	1980	—	2.00	4.00
❏ YB-12152	Full of Fire/Let's Find the Time for Love	1981	—	2.00	4.00
❏ GB-12231	The Second Time Around/Right in the Socket	1981	—	—	3.00
—Gold Standard Series					

Number	Title (A Side/B Side)	Yr	VG	VG+	NM
❏ YB-12250	This Is For the Lover in You/Some Things Never Change	1981	—	2.00	4.00
❏ YB-12329	Sweeter As the Days Go By/The Final Analysis	1981	—	2.00	4.00
❏ YB-13033	Talk to Me/Appeal	1981	—	2.00	4.00
❏ YB-13262	Attention to My Baby/Somewhere There's a Love	1982	—	—	—
—Unreleased					
❏ GB-13486	Make That Move/It's a Love Thing	1983	—	—	3.00
—Gold Standard Series; B-side by the Whispers					
❏ 48005	A Night to Remember/On Top of the World	1982	—	2.00	4.00
❏ 48013	I Can Make You Feel Good/I Just Stopped By Because I Had To	1982	—	2.00	4.00
❏ 69635	Just One of the Guys/Hard Way	1985	—	2.00	4.00
❏ 69660	My Girl Loves Me/Right Here	1985	—	2.00	4.00
❏ 69765	You Can Count on Me/The Look	1984	—	2.00	4.00
❏ 69787	Over and Over/You Won't Miss Love (Until It's Gone)	1983	—	2.00	4.00
❏ 69819	Dead Giveaway/I Don't Wanna Be the Last to Know	1983	—	2.00	4.00
❏ 69819 [PS]	Dead Giveaway/I Don't Wanna Be the Last to Know	1983	—	2.50	5.00
❏ 69958	There It Is/(B-side unknown)	1982	—	2.00	4.00
❏ 70008	Circumstantial Evidence/(Instrumental)	1987	—	—	3.00
❏ 70013	Games/(Instrumental)	1987	—	—	3.00
❏ 70021	I Want You (To Be My Playthang)/(Instrumental)	1988	—	—	3.00
SOUL TRAIN					
❏ SB-10885	Uptown Festival (Part 1)/Uptown Festival (Part 2)	1977	—	2.50	5.00
❏ SB-11045	Ooh, Baby, Baby/You Know	1977	—	2.50	5.00
Albums					
SOLAR					
❏ S-28	Friends	1982	2.50	5.00	10.00
❏ BXL1-2895	Disco Gardens	1978	3.75	7.50	15.00
❏ BXL1-3479	Big Fun	1979	3.00	6.00	12.00
❏ BZL1-3577	Three for Love	1980	2.50	5.00	10.00
❏ BXL1-3984	Go For It	1981	3.00	6.00	12.00
❏ BXL1-4262	Greatest Hits	1982	3.00	6.00	12.00
❏ 60239	The Look	1983	2.50	5.00	10.00
❏ 60385	Heart Break	1984	2.50	5.00	10.00
❏ ST-72556	Circumstantial Evidence	1987	2.50	5.00	10.00
❏ Z 75315	Wake Up	1990	3.00	6.00	12.00
SOUL TRAIN					
❏ BVL1-2289	Uptown Festival	1977	3.75	7.50	15.00

SHANGRI-LAS, THE
45s
MERCURY

❏ 72645	I'll Never Learn/Sweet Sounds of Summer	1966	5.00	10.00	20.00
❏ 72670	Footsteps on the Roof/Take the Time	1967	5.00	10.00	20.00
RED BIRD					
❏ 10-008	Remember (Walkin' in the Sand)/It's Easier to Cry	1964	6.25	12.50	25.00
❏ 10-014	Leader of the Pack/What Is Love	1964	6.25	12.50	25.00
❏ 10-018	Give Him a Great Big Kiss/Twist and Shout	1964	6.25	12.50	25.00
❏ 10-019	Maybe/Shout	1964	5.00	10.00	20.00
❏ 10-025	Out in the Streets/The Boy	1965	5.00	10.00	20.00
❏ 10-030	Give Us Your Blessings/Heaven Only Knows	1965	5.00	10.00	20.00
❏ 10-036	Right Now and Not Later/The Train from Kansas City	1965	5.00	10.00	20.00
❏ 10-043	I Can Never Go Home Anymore/Bull Dog	1965	5.00	10.00	20.00
❏ 10-043	I Can Never Go Home Anymore/Sophisticated Boom Boom	1965	7.50	15.00	30.00
❏ 10-048	Long Live Our Love/Sophisticated Boom Boom	1966	5.00	10.00	20.00
❏ 10-048	Long Live Our Love/Bull Dog	1966	5.00	10.00	20.00
❏ 10-053	He Cried/Dressed in Black	1966	5.00	10.00	20.00
❏ 10-068	Past, Present and Future/Love You More Than Yesterday	1966	5.00	10.00	20.00
❏ 10-068	Past, Present and Future/Paradise	1966	5.00	10.00	20.00
SCEPTER					
❏ 1291	Wishing Well/Hate to Say I Told You So	1964	5.00	10.00	20.00
SMASH					
❏ 1866	Simon Says/Simon Speaks	1963	10.00	20.00	40.00
SPOKANE					
❏ 4006	Wishing Well/Hate to Say I Told You So	1964	7.50	15.00	30.00
Albums					
COLLECTABLES					
❏ COL-5011	Remember…Their Greatest Hits	198?	2.50	5.00	10.00
MERCURY					
❏ MG-21099 [M]	The Shangri-Las' Golden Hits	1966	10.00	20.00	40.00
❏ SR-61099 [S]	The Shangri-Las' Golden Hits	1966	12.50	25.00	50.00
POLYDOR					
❏ 824807-1	Golden Hits of the Shangri-Las	1985	2.50	5.00	10.00
POST					
❏ 4000	The Shangri-Las Sing	196?	5.00	10.00	20.00
RED BIRD					
❏ 20101 [M]	Leader of the Pack	1965	37.50	75.00	150.00
❏ 20104 [M]	Shangri-Las '65	1965	37.50	75.00	150.00
❏ 20104 [M]	I Can Never Go Home Anymore	1966	25.00	50.00	100.00
—Retitled version with title song added and "Sophisticated Boom Boom" dropped					

SHARMEERS, THE
45s
RED TOP

❏ 109	A School Girl in Love/You're My Love	1958	37.50	75.00	150.00

S

Number	Title (A Side/B Side)	Yr	VG	VG+	NM

SHARMETTES, THE
45s
KING

❏ 5648	Answer Me/My Dream	1962	3.75	7.50	15.00
❏ 5686	I Want to Be Loved/Tell Me	1962	3.75	7.50	15.00

SHARP, DEE DEE
Includes records as "Dee Dee Sharp Gamble."
45s
ATCO

❏ 6445	Bye Bye Baby/My Best Friend's Man	1966	2.50	5.00	10.00
❏ 6502	Baby I Love You/What Am I Gonna Do	1967	2.00	4.00	8.00
❏ 6557	We Got a Thing Goin' On/What 'Cha Gonna Do About It	1968	2.00	4.00	8.00
—With Ben E. King					
❏ 6576	Woman Will Do Wrong/You're Just a Fool in Love	1968	2.00	4.00	8.00
❏ 6587	This Love Won't Run Out/Help Me Find My Glove	1968	2.00	4.00	8.00

CAMEO

❏ 212	Mashed Potato Time/Set My Heart at Ease	1962	5.00	10.00	20.00
❏ 219	Gravy (For My Mashed Potatoes)/Baby Cakes	1962	3.75	7.50	15.00
❏ 219 [PS]	Gravy (For My Mashed Potatoes)/Baby Cakes	1962	6.25	12.50	25.00
❏ 230	Ride!/The Night	1962	3.75	7.50	15.00
❏ 230 [PS]	Ride!/The Night	1962	6.25	12.50	25.00
❏ 244	Do the Bird/Lover Boy	1963	3.75	7.50	15.00
❏ 244 [PS]	Do the Bird/Lover Boy	1963	6.25	12.50	25.00
❏ 260	Rock Me in the Cradle of Love/You'll Never Be Mine	1963	3.75	7.50	15.00
❏ 260 [PS]	Rock Me in the Cradle of Love/You'll Never Be Mine	1963	6.25	12.50	25.00
❏ 274	Wild!/Why Doncha Ask Me	1963	3.75	7.50	15.00
❏ 274 [PS]	Wild!/Why Doncha Ask Me	1963	6.25	12.50	25.00
❏ 296	Where Did I Go Wrong/Willyam, Willyam	1964	3.00	6.00	12.00
❏ 296 [PS]	Where Did I Go Wrong/Willyam, Willyam	1964	5.00	10.00	20.00
❏ 329	Never Pick a Pretty Boy/He's No Ordinary Guy	1964	3.00	6.00	12.00
❏ 335	Deep Dark Secret/Good	1964	3.00	6.00	12.00
❏ 347	To Know Him Is to Love Him/There Ain't Nothin' I Wouldn't Do for You	1965	2.50	5.00	10.00
❏ 357	Let's Twine/That's What My Mama Said	1965	2.50	5.00	10.00
❏ 375	I Really Love You/Standing in the Need of Love	1965	2.50	5.00	10.00
❏ 375 [PS]	I Really Love You/Standing in the Need of Love	1965	3.75	7.50	15.00
❏ 382	It's a Funny Situation/There Ain't Nothin' I Wouldn't Do for You	1965	2.50	5.00	10.00

FAIRMOUNT

❏ 1004	(It's Wonderful) The Love I Feel for You/Willyam, Wilyam	1966	2.50	5.00	10.00

GAMBLE

❏ 219	What Kind of Lady/You're Gonna Miss Me (When I'm Gone)	1968	5.00	10.00	20.00
❏ 4005	The Bottle or Me/You're Gonna Miss Me (When I'm Gone)	1969	3.75	7.50	15.00

PHILADELPHIA INT'L.

❏ 02041	Breaking and Entering/I Love You Anyway	1981	—	2.00	4.00
❏ 3512	Conquer the World Together/We Gotta Good Thing Goin'	1971	—	3.00	6.00
—With Bunny Sigler					
❏ 3625	Flashback/Nobody Can Take Your Place	1977	—	2.50	5.00
❏ 3636	I'd Really Love to See You Tonight/What Color Is Love	1977	—	2.50	5.00
❏ 3638	I Believe in Love/Just As Long As I Know You're Mine	1978	—	2.50	5.00
❏ 3644	Tryin' to Get the Feeling Again/I Wanna Be Your Woman	1978	—	2.50	5.00
❏ 70058	I Love You Anyway/Easy Money	1981	—	2.00	4.00
—Philadelphia International records as "Dee Dee Sharp Gamble"					

TSOP

❏ 4776	Happy 'Bout the Whole Thing/Touch My Life	1976	—	2.50	5.00
❏ 4778	I'm Not in Love/Make It Till Tomorrow	1976	—	2.50	5.00

Albums
CAMEO

❏ C-1018 [M]	It's Mashed Potato Time	1962	15.00	30.00	60.00
❏ C-1022 [M]	Songs of Faith	1962	10.00	20.00	40.00
❏ SC-1022 [S]	Songs of Faith	1962	12.50	25.00	50.00
❏ C-1027 [M]	All the Hits	1962	10.00	20.00	40.00
❏ SC-1027 [S]	All the Hits	1962	12.50	25.00	50.00
❏ C-1032 [M]	All the Hits, Vol. 2	1963	10.00	20.00	40.00
❏ SC-1032 [S]	All the Hits, Vol. 2	1963	12.50	25.00	50.00
❏ C-1050 [M]	Do the Bird	1963	10.00	20.00	40.00
❏ SC-1050 [S]	Do the Bird	1963	12.50	25.00	50.00
❏ C-1062 [M]	Biggest Hits	1963	10.00	20.00	40.00
❏ C-1074 [M]	Down Memory Lane	1963	10.00	20.00	40.00
❏ C-2002 [M]	18 Golden Hits	1964	10.00	20.00	40.00
❏ SC-2002 [S]	18 Golden Hits	1964	12.50	25.00	50.00

PHILADELPHIA INT'L.

❏ PZ 33839	Happy 'Bout the Whole Thing	1976	2.50	5.00	10.00
❏ PZ 34437	What Color Is Love	1977	2.50	5.00	10.00
❏ JZ 36370	Dee Dee	1980	2.50	5.00	10.00

SHARP, DEE DEE, AND CHUBBY CHECKER
Also see each artist's individual listings.
45s
CAMEO

❏ 103 [DJ]	Do You Love Me?/One More Time	1962	10.00	20.00	40.00
—Yellow label, black print, promo only					

Albums
CAMEO

❏ C-1029 [M]	Down to Earth	1962	10.00	20.00	40.00
❏ SC-1029 [S]	Down to Earth	1962	12.50	25.00	50.00

SHARPS, THE
Possibly more than one group.
45s
ALADDIN

❏ 3401	What Will I Gain/Shufflin'	1957	12.50	25.00	50.00
❏ 3401	What Will I Gain/Shufflin'	1957	100.00	200.00	400.00
—Purple vinyl					

CHESS

❏ 1690	6 Months, 3 Weeks, 2 Days/Cha-Cho Bop	1958	7.50	15.00	30.00
—B-side by Jack McVea					

COMBO

❏ 146	All My Love/Look What You've Done to Me	1958	12.50	25.00	50.00

DOT

❏ 15806	All My Love/Look What You've Done to Me	1958	3.75	7.50	15.00

JAMIE

❏ 1040	Sweet Sweetheart/Come On	1957	10.00	20.00	40.00
❏ 1108	Have Love, Will Travel/Look at Me	1958	12.50	25.00	50.00
❏ 1114	Here's My Heart/Gig-A-Lene	1958	7.50	15.00	30.00

LAMP

❏ 2007	Our Love Is Here to Stay/Lock My Heart	1957	7.50	15.00	30.00

STAR-HI

❏ 10406	Double Clutch/If Love Is What You Want	1960	7.50	15.00	30.00

TAG

❏ 2200	6 Months, 3 Weeks, 2 Days/Cha-Cho Bop	1957	25.00	50.00	100.00
—B-side by Jack McVea					

VIK

❏ 0264	Sweet Sweetheart/Come On	1957	6.25	12.50	25.00

WIN

❏ 702	Teenage Girl/We Three	1958	12.50	25.00	50.00

SHARPTONES, THE
45s
POST

❏ 2009	Since I Fell for You/Made to Love	1955	100.00	200.00	400.00

SHEIKS, THE
More than one group. Some of these were labeled "The Shieks."
45s
AMY

❏ 807	Come On Back/Please Don't Take Away the Girl I Love	1960	50.00	100.00	200.00

CAT

❏ 116	Walk That Walk/The Kissing Song (Sweetie Lover)	1955	10.00	20.00	40.00

EF-N-DE

❏ 1000	Give Me Another Chance/Baby Don't You Cry	1955	200.00	400.00	600.00

FEDERAL

❏ 12237	So Fine/Sentimental Heart	1955	37.50	75.00	150.00

JAMIE

❏ 1147	Candlelight Cafe/The Song of Old Paree	1959	5.00	10.00	20.00

LEGRAND

❏ 1013	What I'd Do for Your Love/Why Should I Dance	1961	25.00	50.00	100.00
❏ 1016	Cocoanut Woman/Twist That Twist	1962	6.25	12.50	25.00

MGM

❏ 12876	Baghdad Rock (Part 1)/Baghdad Rock (Part 2)	1960	5.00	10.00	20.00

SHELLS, THE
45s
END

❏ 1022	Pretty Little Girl/Sippin' Soda	1958	37.50	75.00	150.00
❏ 1050	Whispering Wings/Shooma Dom Dom	1959	12.50	25.00	50.00

GONE

❏ 5103	Pretty Little Girl/Sippin' Soda	1961	6.25	12.50	25.00

JOHNSON

❏ 099	My Cherie/Explain It to Me	1972	—	3.00	6.00
❏ 104	Baby Oh Baby/Angel Eyes	1957	10.00	20.00	40.00
❏ 104	Baby Oh Baby/What's in An Angel's Eyes	1960	3.75	7.50	15.00
—Note lengthened B-side title					
❏ 106	Don't Say Goodbye/Pleading	1958	25.00	50.00	100.00
❏ 107	Explain It to Me/An Island Unknown	1961	6.25	12.50	25.00
❏ 109	Better Forget Him/Can't Take It	1961	6.25	12.50	25.00
❏ 110	In the Dim Light of the Dark/O-Mi Yum-Mi Yum-Mi	1961	6.25	12.50	25.00
❏ 112	Sweetest One/Baby Walk On In	1961	7.50	15.00	30.00
❏ 119	Deep in My Heart/((It's a) Happy Holiday	1962	7.50	15.00	30.00
❏ 120	The Drive/A Toast to Your Birthday	1962	7.50	15.00	30.00
❏ 127	On My Honor/My Royal Love	1963	12.50	25.00	50.00
❏ 332	Explain It to Me/An Island Unknown	1961	3.75	7.50	15.00

JOSIE

❏ 912	Deep in My Heart/Our Wedding Day	1963	5.00	10.00	20.00

ROULETTE

❏ 4156	The Thief/She Wasn't Meant for Me	1959	7.50	15.00	30.00

Albums
CANDELITE

❏ 1000	Accapella	197?	3.75	7.50	15.00

COLLECTABLES

❏ COL-5077	Golden Classics	198?	2.50	5.00	10.00

Number	Title (A Side/B Side)	Yr	VG	VG+	NM

SHEP AND THE LIMELITES
Also see THE HEARTBEATS; SHANE SHEPPARD.
45s
HULL

Number	Title (A Side/B Side)	Yr	VG	VG+	NM
❏ 740	Daddy's Home/This I Know	1961	10.00	20.00	40.00
—Pink label					
❏ 740	Daddy's Home/This I Know	1961	6.25	12.50	25.00
—Red label					
❏ 740	Daddy's Home/This I Know	1961	5.00	10.00	20.00
—Tan label. Note: Any colored vinyl version is a counterfeit.					
❏ 742	Ready for Your Love/You'll Be Sorry	1961	5.00	10.00	20.00
❏ 747	Three Steps from the Altar/Oh What a Feeling	1961	5.00	10.00	20.00
❏ 748	Our Anniversary/Who Told the Sandman	1962	5.00	10.00	20.00
❏ 751	What Did Daddy Do/Teach Me, Teach Me How to Twist	1962	5.00	10.00	20.00
❏ 753	Gee Baby, What About You/Everything Is Going to Be Alright	1962	5.00	10.00	20.00
❏ 756	Remember Baby/The Monkey	1963	5.00	10.00	20.00
❏ 757	Stick By Me (And I'll Stick By You)/It's All Over Now	1963	5.00	10.00	20.00
❏ 759	Steal Away (With Your Baby)/For All My Love	1963	5.00	10.00	20.00
❏ 761	Easy to Remember (When You Want to Forget)/Why, Why Won't You Believe Me	1964	5.00	10.00	20.00
❏ 767	I'm All Alone/Why Did You Fall for Me	1964	5.00	10.00	20.00
❏ 770	Party for Two/You Better Believe	1965	7.50	15.00	30.00
❏ 772	In Case I Forget/I'm a-Hurting Inside	1965	5.00	10.00	20.00

Albums
HULL

Number	Title	Yr	VG	VG+	NM
❏ 1001 [M]	Our Anniversary	1962	300.00	600.00	1200.

ROULETTE

| ❏ R-25350 [M] | Our Anniversary | 1967 | 20.00 | 40.00 | 80.00 |
| ❏ SR-25350 [R] | Our Anniversary | 1967 | 12.50 | 25.00 | 50.00 |

SHEPPARD, SHANE
Also see SHEP AND THE LIMELITES.
45s
APT

Number	Title	Yr	VG	VG+	NM
❏ 25039	Too Young to Wed/Two Loving Hearts	1960	12.50	25.00	50.00
❏ 25046	One Week from Today/I'm So Lonely (What Can I Do)	1960	10.00	20.00	40.00

SHEPPARDS, THE
More than one group?
45s
ABNER

Number	Title	Yr	VG	VG+	NM
❏ 7006	Elevator Operator/Loving You	1961	3.00	6.00	12.00

APEX

❏ 7750	Loving You/Island of Love	1959	10.00	20.00	40.00
❏ 7752	Just Like You/Feel Like Lovin'	1959	6.25	12.50	25.00
❏ 7755	It's Crazy/Meant to Be	1960	6.25	12.50	25.00
❏ 7759	Just When I Need You Most/Society Gal	1960	6.25	12.50	25.00
❏ 7760	Come Home, Come Home/Just Like You	1960	6.25	12.50	25.00
❏ 7762	Tragic/Feel Like Lovin'	1961	6.25	12.50	25.00

BUNKY

| ❏ 7764 | Island of Love/Steal Away | 1969 | — | 3.00 | 6.00 |
| ❏ 7766 | I'm Not Wanted/Your Love (Has a Hole in It) | 1969 | — | 3.00 | 6.00 |

CONSTELLATION

| ❏ 123 | Island of Love/Give a Hug to Me | 1964 | 2.50 | 5.00 | 10.00 |
| ❏ 176 | Island of Love/Give a Hug to Me | 1966 | 2.00 | 4.00 | 8.00 |

IMPACT

| ❏ 1018 | Poor Man's Thing/When Johnny Comes Marching Home | 1967 | 7.50 | 15.00 | 30.00 |

OKEH

| ❏ 7173 | Walkin'/Pretend You're Still Mine | 1963 | 2.50 | 5.00 | 10.00 |

PAM

| ❏ 1001 | Never Let Me Go/Give a Hug to Me | 1961 | 3.00 | 6.00 | 12.00 |

SHARP

| ❏ 6039 | What's the Name of the Game/Glitter in Your Eyes | 1961 | 3.00 | 6.00 | 12.00 |

UNITED

| ❏ 198 | Sherry/Mozelle | 1957 | 62.50 | 125.00 | 250.00 |

VEE JAY

| ❏ 406 | Every Now and Then/Glitter in Your Eyes | 1961 | 3.00 | 6.00 | 12.00 |
| ❏ 441 | Tragic/Come to Me | 1962 | 5.00 | 10.00 | 20.00 |

Albums
COLLECTABLES

| ❏ COL-5078 | Golden Classics | 198? | 2.50 | 5.00 | 10.00 |

CONSTELLATION

| ❏ C-4 [M] | Collectors Showcase: The Sheppards | 1964 | 20.00 | 40.00 | 80.00 |
| ❏ CS-4 [R] | Collectors Showcase: The Sheppards | 1964 | 10.00 | 20.00 | 40.00 |

SOLID SMOKE

| ❏ SS-8004 | The Sheppards | 1980 | 2.50 | 5.00 | 10.00 |
| ❏ SS-8028 | 18 Dusty Diamonds | 1984 | 2.50 | 5.00 | 10.00 |

SHIELDS, THE
45s
ATCO

Number	Title	Yr	VG	VG+	NM
❏ 7071	The Way I Feel Tonight/All Right by Me	1977	—	2.50	5.00

CONTINENTAL

| ❏ 4072 | You Told Another Lie/Barnyard Dance | 1961 | 100.00 | 200.00 | 400.00 |

DOT

❏ 136	You Cheated/Nature Boy	196?	2.50	5.00	10.00
—Reissue; black label					
❏ 15805	You Cheated/That's the Way It's Gonna Be	1958	6.25	12.50	25.00

Number	Title (A Side/B Side)	Yr	VG	VG+	NM
❏ 15856	I'm Sorry Now/Nature Boy	1958	7.50	15.00	30.00
❏ 15940	Fare Thee Well/Play the Game Fair	1959	6.25	12.50	25.00

TENDER

❏ 513	You Cheated/That's the Way It's Gonna Be	1958	37.50	75.00	150.00
—No reference to Dot Records on label					
❏ 513	You Cheated/That's the Way It's Gonna Be	1958	10.00	20.00	40.00
—With reference to Dot Records on label					
❏ 518	I'm Sorry Now/Nature Boy	1958	15.00	30.00	60.00
❏ 521	Fare Thee Well/Play the Game Fair	1959	15.00	30.00	60.00

TRANSCONTINENTAL

| ❏ 1013 | The Girl Around the Corner/Fare Thee Well, My Love | 1960 | 25.00 | 50.00 | 100.00 |

SHIRELLES, THE
45s
BELL

Number	Title	Yr	VG	VG+	NM
❏ 760	A Most Unusual Boy/Look What You've Done to My Heart	1969	2.50	5.00	10.00
❏ 787	Looking Glass/Playthings	1969	2.50	5.00	10.00
❏ 815	Never Give You Up/Go Away and Find Yourself	1969	2.50	5.00	10.00

BLUE ROCK

| ❏ 4051 | Don't Mess with Cupid/Sweet Sweet Lovin' | 1968 | 2.50 | 5.00 | 10.00 |
| ❏ 4066 | Call Me/There's a Storm Goin' Home in My Heart | 1968 | 2.50 | 5.00 | 10.00 |

DECCA

❏ 25506	I Met Him on a Sunday/My Love Is a Charm	196?	3.75	7.50	15.00
—Early reissue					
❏ 30588	I Met Him on a Sunday/I Want You to Be My Boyfriend	1958	6.25	12.50	25.00
❏ 30669	My Love Is a Charm/Slop Time	1958	10.00	20.00	40.00
❏ 30761	Stop Me/I Got the Message	1958	10.00	20.00	40.00

PHILCO-FORD

| ❏ HP-30 | Soldier Boy/My Heart Belongs to You | 1968 | 5.00 | 10.00 | 20.00 |
| —4-inch plastic "Hip Pocket Record" with color sleeve | | | | | |

RCA VICTOR

❏ 47-0902	Let's Give Each Other Love/Deep in the Night	1973	2.00	4.00	8.00
❏ 48-1019	No Sugar Tonight/Strange, I Still Love You	1971	2.50	5.00	10.00
❏ 48-1032	Brother, Brother/Sunday Dreaming	1972	2.50	5.00	10.00
❏ APBO-0192	Touch the Wind (Eres Tu)/Do What You've a Mind To	1973	2.00	4.00	8.00

SCEPTER

❏ 1203	Dedicated to the One I Love/Look A Here Baby	1958	10.00	20.00	40.00
—White label					
❏ 1203	Dedicated to the One I Love/Look A Here Baby	1958	5.00	10.00	20.00
—Red label					
❏ 1205	A Teardrop and a Lollipop/Doin' the Ronde	1959	7.50	15.00	30.00
—White label					
❏ 1205	A Teardrop and a Lollipop/Doin' the Ronde	1959	5.00	10.00	20.00
—Red label					
❏ 1207	Please Be My Boyfriend/I Saw a Tear	1960	7.50	15.00	30.00
—White label					
❏ 1207	Please Be My Boyfriend/I Saw a Tear	1960	5.00	10.00	20.00
—Red label					
❏ 1208	Tonight's the Night/The Dance Is Over	1960	7.50	15.00	30.00
—White label					
❏ 1208	Tonight's the Night/The Dance Is Over	1960	5.00	10.00	20.00
—Red label					
❏ 1208	Tonight's the Night/The Dance Is Over	1960	6.25	12.50	25.00
—Pink label					
❏ 1211	Tomorrow/Boys	1960	10.00	20.00	40.00
—Original A-side title					
❏ 1211	Will You Love Me Tomorrow/Boys	1960	7.50	15.00	30.00
—Revised A-side title					
❏ 1217	Mama Said/Blue Holiday	1961	5.00	10.00	20.00
❏ 1220	A Thing of the Past/What a Sweet Thing That Was	1961	5.00	10.00	20.00
❏ 1223	Big John/Twenty-One	1961	5.00	10.00	20.00
❏ 1227	Baby It's You/Things I Want to Hear (Pretty Words)	1961	5.00	10.00	20.00
❏ 1228	Soldier Boy/Love Is a Swingin' Thing	1962	3.75	7.50	15.00
❏ 1234	Welcome Home Baby/Mama, Here Comes the Bride	1962	3.75	7.50	15.00
❏ 1237	Stop the Music/It's Love That Really Counts	1962	3.75	7.50	15.00
❏ 1243	Everybody Loves a Lover/I Don't Think So	1962	3.75	7.50	15.00
❏ 1248	Foolish Little Girl/Not for All the Money in the World	1963	3.75	7.50	15.00
❏ 1248 [PS]	Foolish Little Girl/Not for All the Money in the World	1963	10.00	20.00	40.00
❏ 1255	Don't Say Goodnight and Mean Goodbye/I Didn't Mean to Hurt You	1963	3.00	6.00	12.00
❏ 1255 [PS]	Don't Say Goodnight and Mean Goodbye/I Didn't Mean to Hurt You	1963	10.00	20.00	40.00
❏ 1259	What Does a Girl Do?/Don't Let It Happen to You	1963	3.00	6.00	12.00
❏ 1260	It's a Mad, Mad, Mad, Mad World/31 Flavors	1963	3.00	6.00	12.00
❏ 1264	Tonight You're Gonna Fall in Love with Me/20th Century Rock and Roll	1963	3.00	6.00	12.00
❏ 1267	Sha-La-La/His Lips Get In the Way	1964	3.00	6.00	12.00
❏ 1278	Thank You Baby/Doomsday	1964	3.00	6.00	12.00
❏ 1284	Maybe Tonight/Lost Love	1964	3.00	6.00	12.00
❏ 1292	Are You Still My Baby/I Saw a Tear	1964	3.00	6.00	12.00
❏ 1296	Shh, I'm Watching the Movies/A Plus B	1964	3.00	6.00	12.00
❏ 12101	March (You'll Be Sorry)/Everybody's Goin' Mad	1965	2.50	5.00	10.00
❏ 12114	My Heart Belongs to You/Love That Man	1965	2.50	5.00	10.00
❏ 12123	(Mama) My Soldier Boy Is Coming Home/Soldier Boy	1965	2.50	5.00	10.00
❏ 12132	I Met Him on a Sunday — '66/Love That Man	1966	2.50	5.00	10.00
❏ 12150	Till My Baby Comes Home/Que Sera, Sera	1966	2.50	5.00	10.00

S

Number	Title (A Side/B Side)	Yr	VG	VG+	NM
❑ 12162	Shades of Blue/Looking Around	1966	2.50	5.00	10.00
❑ 12162	Shades of Blue/After Midnight	1966	2.50	5.00	10.00
❑ 12178	Teasin' Me/Look Away	1966	2.50	5.00	10.00
❑ 12185	Don't Go Home (My Little Baby)/Nobody Baby After You	1967	2.50	5.00	10.00
❑ 12192	Too Much of a Good Thing/Bright Shiny Colors	1967	2.50	5.00	10.00
❑ 12198	Last Minute Miracle/No Doubt About It	1967	2.50	5.00	10.00
❑ 12209	Wild and Sweet/Wait Till I Give the Signal	1968	2.50	5.00	10.00
❑ 12217	Hippie Walk (Part 1)/Hippie Walk (Part 2)	1968	2.50	5.00	10.00

TIARA

Number	Title (A Side/B Side)	Yr	VG	VG+	NM
❑ 6112	I Met Him on a Sunday/I Want You to Be My Boyfriend	1958	200.00	400.00	800.00

UNITED ARTISTS

Number	Title (A Side/B Side)	Yr	VG	VG+	NM
❑ 50648	There Goes My Baby-Be My Baby/Strange, I Still Love You	1970	2.00	4.00	8.00
❑ 50693	It's Gonna Take a Miracle/Lost	1970	2.00	4.00	8.00
❑ 50740	Take Me for a Little While/Dedicated to the One I Love	1971	2.00	4.00	8.00

Albums

RCA VICTOR

Number	Title (A Side/B Side)	Yr	VG	VG+	NM
❑ LSP-4581	Happy and In Love	1971	3.75	7.50	15.00
❑ LSP-4698	The Shirelles	1972	3.75	7.50	15.00

RHINO

Number	Title (A Side/B Side)	Yr	VG	VG+	NM
❑ RNDA-1101 [(2)]	Anthology (1959-1967)	1984	3.00	6.00	12.00

SCEPTER

Number	Title (A Side/B Side)	Yr	VG	VG+	NM
❑ S-501 [M]	Tonight's the Night	1961	50.00	100.00	200.00
—"Scepter" in scroll at top of label					
❑ SPM-501 [M]	Tonight's the Night	1962	15.00	30.00	60.00
—"Scepter Records" at left of label					
❑ SPS-501 [S]	Tonight's the Night	1965	25.00	50.00	100.00
❑ S-502 [M]	The Shirelles Sing to Trumpets and Strings	1961	50.00	100.00	200.00
—"Scepter" in scroll at top of label					
❑ SPM-502 [M]	The Shirelles Sing to Trumpets and Strings	1962	15.00	30.00	60.00
—"Scepter Records" at left of label					
❑ SPS-502 [S]	The Shirelles Sing to Trumpets and Strings	1965	25.00	50.00	100.00
❑ SPM-504 [M]	Baby It's You	1962	25.00	50.00	100.00
❑ SPS-504 [S]	Baby It's You	1965	25.00	50.00	100.00
❑ SPM-505 [M]	A Twist Party	1962	20.00	40.00	80.00
❑ SPS-505 [S]	A Twist Party	1965	25.00	50.00	100.00
❑ SPM-507 [M]	The Shirelles' Greatest Hits	1962	10.00	20.00	40.00
❑ SPS-507 [S]	The Shirelles' Greatest Hits	1965	12.50	25.00	50.00
❑ SPM-511 [M]	Foolish Little Girl	1963	12.50	25.00	50.00
❑ SPS-511 [S]	Foolish Little Girl	1965	20.00	40.00	80.00
❑ SPM-514 [M]	It's a Mad, Mad, Mad, Mad World	1963	10.00	20.00	40.00
❑ SPS-514 [S]	It's a Mad, Mad, Mad, Mad World	1963	12.50	25.00	50.00
❑ SPM-516 [M]	The Shirelles Sing the Golden Oldies	1964	10.00	20.00	40.00
❑ SPS-516 [S]	The Shirelles Sing the Golden Oldies	1964	12.50	25.00	50.00
❑ SPM-560 [M]	The Shirelles' Greatest Hits, Volume 2	1967	5.00	10.00	20.00
❑ SPS-560 [S]	The Shirelles' Greatest Hits, Volume 2	1967	6.25	12.50	25.00
❑ SPM-562 [M]	Spontaneous Combustion	1967	10.00	20.00	40.00
❑ SPS-562 [S]	Spontaneous Combustion	1967	12.50	25.00	50.00
❑ SPS-569	Eternally Soul	1968	7.50	15.00	30.00
❑ SPS-2-599 [(2)]	Remember When	1972	5.00	10.00	20.00

SPRINGBOARD

Number	Title (A Side/B Side)	Yr	VG	VG+	NM
❑ 4006	The Shirelles Sing Their Very Best	1973	2.00	4.00	8.00

UNITED ARTISTS

Number	Title (A Side/B Side)	Yr	VG	VG+	NM
❑ UA-LA340-E	The Very Best of the Shirelles	1974	2.50	5.00	10.00

SHIRLEY (AND COMPANY)

Shirley Goodman, earlier of SHIRLEY AND LEE.

45s

VIBRATION

Number	Title (A Side/B Side)	Yr	VG	VG+	NM
❑ 532	Shame, Shame, Shame/(Instrumental)	1974	—	2.50	5.00
❑ 535	Cry, Cry, Cry/(Instrumental)	1975	—	2.50	5.00
❑ 539	Disco Shirley/Keep On Rolling On	1975	—	2.50	5.00
❑ 542	I Like to Dance/Jim Doc C'ain	1976	—	2.50	5.00
❑ 579	Revelations True/(Instrumental)	1978	—	2.50	5.00

Albums

VIBRATION

Number	Title (A Side/B Side)	Yr	VG	VG+	NM
❑ 128	Shame Shame Shame	1975	2.50	5.00	10.00

SHIRLEY AND LEE

Also see SHIRLEY (AND COMPANY).

45s

ALADDIN

Number	Title (A Side/B Side)	Yr	VG	VG+	NM
❑ 3153	I'm Gone/Sweethearts	1952	25.00	50.00	100.00
❑ 3173	Baby/Shirley Come Back to Me	1953	30.00	60.00	120.00
❑ 3192	Shirley's Back/So In Love	1953	15.00	30.00	60.00
❑ 3205	Two Happy People/The Proposal	1953	12.50	25.00	50.00
❑ 3222	Why Did I/Lee Goofed	1954	12.50	25.00	50.00
❑ 3244	Confessin'/Keep On	1954	12.50	25.00	50.00
❑ 3258	Comin' Over/Takes Money	1954	12.50	25.00	50.00
❑ 3289	Feel So Good/You'd Be Thinking of Me	1955	10.00	20.00	40.00
❑ 3302	Let's Dream/I'll Do It	1955	10.00	20.00	40.00
❑ 3325	Let the Good Times Roll/Do You Mean to Hurt Me So	1956	15.00	30.00	60.00
❑ 3338	I Feel Good/Now That It's Over	1956	6.25	12.50	25.00
❑ 3362	When I Saw You/That's What I Want to Do	1957	5.00	10.00	20.00
❑ 3369	I Want to Dance/Marry Me	1957	5.00	10.00	20.00
❑ 3380	Rock All Night/Don't You Know I Love You	1957	5.00	10.00	20.00
❑ 3390	Rockin' with the Clock/The Flirt	1957	5.00	10.00	20.00
❑ 3405	Love No One But You (I Love You So)/I'll Thrill You	1958	5.00	10.00	20.00
❑ 3418	Everybody's Rocking/Don't Leave Me Here to Cry	1958	5.00	10.00	20.00
❑ 3432	Come On and Have Your Fun/All I Want to Do Is Cry	1958	5.00	10.00	20.00
❑ 3455	True Love/When Day Is Done	1959	5.00	10.00	20.00

IMPERIAL

Number	Title (A Side/B Side)	Yr	VG	VG+	NM
❑ 013	Let the Good Times Roll/Feel So Good	196?	2.50	5.00	10.00
—"The Golden Series" reissue; gold label, Imperial logo at top					
❑ 5818	Together We Stand (Divided We Fall)/The Joker	1962	2.50	5.00	10.00
❑ 5854	My Last Letter/I'm Early Enough	1962	2.50	5.00	10.00
❑ 5868	Don't Stop Now/A Little Thing	1962	2.50	5.00	10.00
❑ 5922	The Golden Rule/Hey Little Boy	1963	2.50	5.00	10.00
❑ 5970	Dancing World/I'm Gone	1963	2.50	5.00	10.00
❑ 5979	Paper Doll/The Brink of Disaster	1963	2.50	5.00	10.00
❑ 66000	Somebody Put a Jukebox in the Study Hall/Never Let Me Go	1963	2.50	5.00	10.00

UNITED ARTISTS

Number	Title (A Side/B Side)	Yr	VG	VG+	NM
❑ 0087	Let the Good Times Roll/Feel So Good	1973	—	2.00	4.00
—"Silver Spotlight Series" reissue					
❑ XW274	Let the Good Times Roll/That's What I Wanna Do	1973	—	2.50	5.00

WARWICK

Number	Title (A Side/B Side)	Yr	VG	VG+	NM
❑ 581	Let the Good Times Roll/Keep Loving Me	1960	3.00	6.00	12.00
❑ 609	Two Peas in a Pod/Your Love Makes the Difference	1961	3.00	6.00	12.00
❑ 664	Well-a, Well-a/Our Kids	1961	3.00	6.00	12.00
❑ 679	Let's Live It Up/Girl, You're Married Now	1962	3.00	6.00	12.00

Albums

ALADDIN

Number	Title (A Side/B Side)	Yr	VG	VG+	NM
❑ 807 [M]	Let the Good Times Roll	1956	375.00	750.00	1500.

IMPERIAL

Number	Title (A Side/B Side)	Yr	VG	VG+	NM
❑ LP-9179 [M]	Let the Good Times Roll	1962	75.00	150.00	300.00
—Reissue of Aladdin LP					

SCORE

Number	Title (A Side/B Side)	Yr	VG	VG+	NM
❑ SLP-4023 [M]	Let the Good Times Roll	1957	200.00	400.00	800.00
—Reissue of Aladdin LP					

WARWICK

Number	Title (A Side/B Side)	Yr	VG	VG+	NM
❑ W-2028 [M]	Let the Good Times Roll	1961	37.50	75.00	150.00
❑ W-2028ST [S]	Let the Good Times Roll	1961	75.00	150.00	300.00

SHOOTERS, THE

With OTIS REDDING.

45s

TRANS WORLD

Number	Title (A Side/B Side)	Yr	VG	VG+	NM
❑ 6908	Tuff Enuff/She's All Right	1960	25.00	50.00	100.00

SHOWMEN, THE

With General Johnson, later of CHAIRMEN OF THE BOARD.

45s

AMY

Number	Title (A Side/B Side)	Yr	VG	VG+	NM
❑ 11036	Action/What Would It Take	1968	2.00	4.00	8.00

IMPERIAL

Number	Title (A Side/B Side)	Yr	VG	VG+	NM
❑ 66033	It Will Stand/Country Fool	1964	3.00	6.00	12.00
❑ 66071	Country Fool/Somebody Help Me	1964	3.00	6.00	12.00

LIBERTY

Number	Title (A Side/B Side)	Yr	VG	VG+	NM
❑ 56166	It Will Stand/Country Fool	1970	—	3.00	6.00

MINIT

Number	Title (A Side/B Side)	Yr	VG	VG+	NM
❑ 632	It Will Stand/Country Fool	1961	7.50	15.00	30.00
—Orange label					
❑ 632	It Will Stand/Country Fool	1961	5.00	10.00	20.00
—Black label					
❑ 643	The Wrong Girl/Fate Planned It This Way	1962	12.50	25.00	50.00
❑ 647	Com'n Home/I Love You, Can't You See	1962	6.25	12.50	25.00
❑ 654	True Fine Mama/The Owl Sees You	1962	6.25	12.50	25.00
❑ 662	39-21-46/Swish Fish	1963	6.25	12.50	25.00
❑ 32007	39-21-46/Swish Fish	1966	2.50	5.00	10.00

SWAN

Number	Title (A Side/B Side)	Yr	VG	VG+	NM
❑ 4213	In Paradise/Take It Baby	1965	2.50	5.00	10.00
❑ 4219	Our Love Will Grow/You're Everything	1965	2.50	5.00	10.00
❑ 4241	Please Try and Understand/Honey House	1966	2.50	5.00	10.00

UNITED ARTISTS

Number	Title (A Side/B Side)	Yr	VG	VG+	NM
❑ 0100	It Will Stand/I'm a Happy Man	1973	—	2.50	5.00
—"Silver Spotlight Series" reissue; B-side by the Jive Five					

Albums

COLLECTABLES

Number	Title (A Side/B Side)	Yr	VG	VG+	NM
❑ COL-5162	Golden Classics	198?	2.50	5.00	10.00

SIGLER, BUNNY

12-Inch Singles

GOLD MIND

Number	Title (A Side/B Side)	Yr	VG	VG+	NM
❑ 501	Glad to Be Your Lover (8:48)/I'm Funkin' You Tonight (5:30)	1979	3.00	6.00	12.00

45s

CRAIG

Number	Title (A Side/B Side)	Yr	VG	VG+	NM
❑ 501	I Won't Cry/Come On Home	1961	7.50	15.00	30.00
—As Bunny "Mr. Emotions" Sigler					

DECCA

Number	Title (A Side/B Side)	Yr	VG	VG+	NM
❑ 31880	Everything's Gonna Be All Right/For Cryin' Out Loud	1965	6.25	12.50	25.00
❑ 31947	Will You Love Me Tomorrow/Comparatively Speaking	1966	3.00	6.00	12.00
❑ 32183	Will You Love Me Tomorrow/Let Them Talk	1967	2.50	5.00	10.00

GOLD MIND

Number	Title (A Side/B Side)	Yr	VG	VG+	NM
❑ 4008	Let Me Party with You (Part 1) (Party, Party, Party)/Let Me Party with You (Part 2) (Party, Party, Party)	1977	—	2.50	5.00

Long before their days as hitmakers on Stax, Sam and Dave recorded for the small Marlin label. "No More Pain," produced by Steve Alaimo, was the second of two that came. Both Marlin singles were released nationally on Roulette.

The Sensations are best known for their hit "Let Me In." This album on Argo, which is hard to find, tried to capitalize on it.

Our Anniversary, the album on Hull by Shep and the Limelites, is considered to be quite rare and could fetch four figures in near-mint condition.

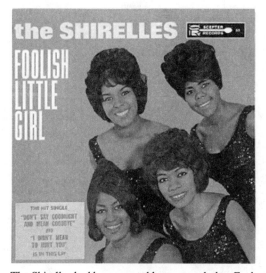

The Shirelles had been around long enough that *Foolish Little Girl* was their sixth LP.

In 1958, the Silhouettes had a #1 hit on both the pop and R&B charts with "Get a Job." About 10 years later, their only album, with both old and newer tracks, was issued on the obscure Goodway label and is hardly ever seen.

Gene Simmons, better known as "Jumpin' Gene" and no relation to the band member from Kiss, made his first 45 for the Sun label.

S

Number	Title (A Side/B Side)	Yr	VG	VG+	NM
❏ 4010	I Got What You Need/It's Time to Twist	1978	—	2.50	5.00
❏ 4012	Only You/Good Good Feeling	1978	—	3.00	6.00

—A-side with Loleatta Holloway; B-side is Holloway solo

❏ 4014	Don't Even Try (Give It Up)/I'm a Fool	1978	—	2.50	5.00
❏ 4018	By the Way You Dance (I Knew It Was You)/Glad to Be Your Lover	1979	—	2.50	5.00
❏ 4020	I'm Funking You Tonight with My Music/Glad to Be Your Lover	1979	—	2.50	5.00

NEPTUNE

❏ 14	Where Do the Lonely Go/Great Big Liar	1969	2.00	4.00	8.00
❏ 15	We're Only Human/Sure Didn't Take Long	1969	2.00	4.00	8.00

—With Cindy Scott

❏ 24	Conquer the World Together/We're Only Human	1970	2.00	4.00	8.00

—With Cindy Scott

❏ 25	Don't Stop Doing What You're Doing/Where Do the Lonely Go	1970	2.00	4.00	8.00

PARKWAY

❏ 123	Girl Don't Make Me Wait/Always in the Wrong Place (At the Wrong Time)	1966	2.50	5.00	10.00
❏ 153	Let the Good Times Roll & Feel So Good/There's No Love Left (In This Old Heart of Mine)	1967	3.00	6.00	12.00
❏ 6000	Lovey Dovey & You're So Fine/Sunny Sunday	1967	2.50	5.00	10.00
❏ 6001	Follow Your Heart/Can You Dig It	1967	2.50	5.00	10.00

PHILADELPHIA INT'L.

❏ 3505	Everybody Needs Good Lovin' (Part 1)/Everybody Needs Good Lovin' (Part 2)	1971	—	3.00	6.00
❏ 3512	Conquer the World Together/We Gotta Good Thing Goin'	1971	—	3.00	6.00

—With Dee Dee Sharp

❏ 3519	Heaven Knows I've Changed/Regina	1972	—	3.00	6.00
❏ 3523	Tossin' and Turnin'/Picture Us	1972	—	3.00	6.00
❏ 3532	Theme from "Five Fingers of Death"/Regina	1973	—	3.00	6.00
❏ 3536	That's How Long I'll Be Loving You/Heaven Knows I've Changed	1973	—	3.00	6.00
❏ 3545	Love Train (Part 1)/Love Train (Part 2)	1974	—	3.00	6.00
❏ 3554	Keep Smilin'/Somebody Free	1974	—	3.00	6.00
❏ 3560	Shake Your Booty/Your Love Is Good	1975	—	3.00	6.00
❏ 3575	Somebody Free/That's How Long I'll Be Loving You	1975	—	3.00	6.00
❏ 3582	Jingle Bells (Part 1)/Jingle Bells (Part 2)	1975	—	2.50	5.00
❏ 3597	My Music/Can't Believe That You Love Me	1976	—	3.00	6.00
❏ 3608	Somebody Loves You/Woman, Woman	1976	—	3.00	6.00

SALSOUL

❏ 2114	How Can I Tell Her (It's Over)/Since the Day I First Saw You	1980	—	2.00	4.00
❏ 2125	Super Duper Duper Superman/Kool Aid	1980	—	2.00	4.00

V-TONE

❏ 500	Family Dance/Hold On	196?	5.00	10.00	20.00

Albums

GOLD MIND

❏ 7502	Let Me Party with You	1978	3.00	6.00	12.00
❏ 9503	I've Always Wanted to Sing... Not Just Write Songs	1979	3.00	6.00	12.00

PARKWAY

❏ P-50000 [M]	Let the Good Times Roll	1967	10.00	20.00	40.00
❏ PS-50000 [S]	Let the Good Times Roll	1967	10.00	20.00	40.00

PHILADELPHIA INT'L.

❏ KZ 32589	That's How Long I'll Be Loving You	1974	3.75	7.50	15.00
❏ KZ 33249	Keep Smilin'	1974	3.75	7.50	15.00
❏ PZ 34267	My Music	1976	3.75	7.50	15.00

SALSOUL

❏ SA-8531	Let It Snow	1980	3.00	6.00	12.00

SILHOUETTES, THE
45s
ACE

❏ 552	I Sold My Heart to the Junkman/What Would You Do	1958	5.00	10.00	20.00
❏ 562	Evelyn/Never Will Part	1959	5.00	10.00	20.00

—As "Bill Horton and the Silhouettes"

EMBER

❏ 1029	Get a Job/I Am Lonely	1958	7.50	15.00	30.00

—Red label

❏ 1029	Get a Job/I Am Lonely	1958	10.00	20.00	40.00

—Orange label

❏ 1029	Get a Job/I Am Lonely	1960	5.00	10.00	20.00

—Black label

❏ 1032	Headin' for the Poorhouse/Miss Thing	1958	5.00	10.00	20.00
❏ 1037	Bing Bong/Voodoo Eyes	1958	5.00	10.00	20.00

GOODWAY

❏ 101	Not Me Baby/Gaucho Serenade	1966	50.00	100.00	200.00

—As "The New Silhouettes"

GRAND

❏ 142	Wish I Could Be There/Move On Over	1956	50.00	100.00	200.00

IMPERIAL

❏ 5899	The Push/Which Way Did She Go	1962	3.00	6.00	12.00

JUNIOR

❏ 391	Get a Job/I Am Lonely	1957	200.00	400.00	800.00

—Brown label (first press)

❏ 391	Get a Job/I Am Lonely	1957	150.00	300.00	600.00

—Blue label (second press)

❏ 396	I Sold My Heart to the Junkman/What Would You Do	1958	25.00	50.00	100.00
❏ 400	Evelyn/Never Will Part	1959	50.00	100.00	200.00
❏ 993	Your Love/Rent Man	1963	7.50	15.00	30.00

Number	Title (A Side/B Side)	Yr	VG	VG+	NM

UNITED ARTISTS

❏ 147	I Sold My Heart to the Junkman/What Would You Do	1958			

—Canceled

Albums

GOODWAY

❏ GLP-100	The Silhouettes 1958-1968/Get a Job	1968	75.00	150.00	300.00

SILVA TONES, THE
45s
ARGO

❏ 5281	Chi-Wa-Wa (That's All I Want from You)/Roses Are Blooming	1957	6.25	12.50	25.00
❏ 5281	That's All I Want from You/Roses Are Blooming	1957	7.50	15.00	30.00

MONARCH

❏ 615	That's All I Want from You/Weepin' and a-Wailin'	1957	12.50	25.00	50.00

—Yellow label

❏ 615	That's All I Want from You/Roses Are Blooming	1957	7.50	15.00	30.00

—Black label

SIMMONS, "JUMPIN'" GENE
45s
AGP

❏ 119	Back Home Again/Don't Worry About Me	1969	2.00	4.00	8.00

CHECKER

❏ 948	Bad Boy Willie/Goin' Back to Memphis	1960	3.00	6.00	12.00

DELTUNE

❏ 1201	Why Didn't I Think of That/Tennessee Party Time	1977	2.00	4.00	8.00

—As "Gene Simmons"

EPIC

❏ 10601	She's There When I Come Home/Magnolia Street	1970	—	3.00	6.00

HI

❏ 2034	Teddy Bear/Your True Love	1961	2.50	5.00	10.00
❏ 2050	Caldonia/Be Her Number One	1962	2.50	5.00	10.00
❏ 2076	Haunted House/Hey, Hey Little Girl	1964	3.75	7.50	15.00

—As "Gene Simmons"

❏ 2076	Haunted House/Hey, Hey Little Girl	1964	3.75	7.50	15.00

—As "Jumpin' Gene Simmons"

❏ 2080	The Dodo/The Jump	1964	2.50	5.00	10.00
❏ 2086	Skinnie Minnie/I'm a Ramblin' Man	1965	2.50	5.00	10.00
❏ 2092	Mattie Rae/Folsom Prison Blues	1965	2.50	5.00	10.00
❏ 2102	The Batman/Bossy Boss	1966	3.75	7.50	15.00
❏ 2113	Go On Shoes/Keep That Meat in the Pan	1966	2.50	5.00	10.00

MALA

❏ 12012	I'm Just a Loser/Lila	1968	2.50	5.00	10.00

SANDY

❏ 1027	The Waiting Game/Shenandoah Waltz	1959	5.00	10.00	20.00

—As "Morris Gene Simmons"

SUN

❏ 299	Drinkin' Wine/I Done Told You	1958	37.50	75.00	150.00

—As "Gene Simmons"

Albums

HI

❏ HL 2018 [M]	Jumpin' Gene Simmons	1964	12.50	25.00	50.00
❏ SHL 32018 [S]	Jumpin' Gene Simmons	1964	17.50	35.00	70.00

SIMON, JOE
12-Inch Singles
SPRING

❏ 025 [DJ]	One Step at a Time (5:33) (3:39)	1977	3.75	7.50	15.00
❏ 057 [DJ]	Love Vibration (same on both sides)	1978	3.00	6.00	12.00

45s
COMPLEAT

❏ 140	It Turns Me Inside Out/Morning, Noon and Night	1985	—	2.00	4.00
❏ 146	Mr. Right or Mr. Right Now/Let Me Have My Way with You	1985	—	2.00	4.00

DOT

❏ 16570	Just Like Yesterday/Only a Dream	1964	2.00	4.00	8.00

HUSH

❏ 103	It's a Miracle/Land of Love	1960	3.00	6.00	12.00
❏ 104	Call My Name/Everybody Needs Somebody	1961	3.00	6.00	12.00
❏ 106	Pledge of Love/It's All Over	1961	3.00	6.00	12.00
❏ 107	I See Your Face/Troubles	1961	3.00	6.00	12.00
❏ 108	Land of Love/I Keep Remembering	1962	3.00	6.00	12.00

POSSE

❏ 5001	Baby, When Love Is In Your Heart (It's In Your Eyes)/Are We Breaking Up	1980	—	2.50	5.00
❏ 5005	Glad You Came My Way/I Don't Wanna Make Love	1980	—	2.50	5.00
❏ 5010	Are We Breaking Up/We're Together	1981	—	2.50	5.00
❏ 5014	Fallin' in Love with You/Magnolia	1981	—	2.50	5.00
❏ 5018	You Give Life to Me/(Instrumental)	1982	—	2.50	5.00

—With Clare Bathe

❏ 5019	Go Sam/(Instrumental)	1982	—	2.50	5.00
❏ 5021	Get Down, Get Down "82"/It Be's That Way Sometime	1982	—	2.50	5.00
❏ 5038	Deeper Than Love/Step by Step	198?	—	2.50	5.00

SOUND STAGE 7

❏ 1508	Misty Blue/That's the Way I Want Our Love	1972	—	2.50	5.00
❏ 1512	Who's Julie/The Girl's Alright with Me	1973	—	2.50	5.00
❏ 1514	Someone to Lean On/I Got a Whole Lotta Lovin'	1974	—	2.50	5.00
❏ 1521	Funny How Time Slips Away/Message from Maria	1976	—	2.50	5.00

Number	Title (A Side/B Side)	Yr	VG	VG+	NM
❏ 2564	Teenager's Prayer/Long Hot Summer	1966	2.00	4.00	8.00
❏ 2569	Too Many Teardrops/What Makes a Man Feel Good	1966	2.00	4.00	8.00
❏ 2577	My Special Prayer/Travelin' Man	1966	2.00	4.00	8.00
❏ 2583	Put Your Trust in Me (Depend on Me)/Just a Dream	1967	2.00	4.00	8.00
❏ 2589	Nine Pound Steel/The Girl's Alright with Me	1967	2.00	4.00	8.00
❏ 2602	No Sad Songs/Come On and Get It	1967	2.00	4.00	8.00
❏ 2608	(You Keep Me) Hangin' On/Long Hot Summer	1968	2.00	4.00	8.00
❏ 2617	Message from Maria/I Worry About You	1968	2.00	4.00	8.00
❏ 2622	Looking Back/Standing in the Safety Zone	1968	2.00	4.00	8.00
❏ 2628	The Chokin' Kind/Come On and Get It	1969	—	3.00	6.00
❏ 2634	Baby, Don't Be Looking in My Mind/Don't Let Me Lose the Feeling	1969	—	3.00	6.00
❏ 2637	Oon-Guela (Part 1)/Oon-Guela (Part 2)	1969	2.00	4.00	8.00
❏ 2641	It's Hard to Get Along/San Francisco Is a Lonely Town	1969	—	3.00	6.00
❏ 2651	Moon Walk Part 1/Moon Walk Part 2	1969	—	3.00	6.00
❏ 2656	Farther On Down the Road/Wounded Man	1970	—	3.00	6.00
❏ 2664	Yours Love/I Got a Whole Lotta Lovin'	1970	—	3.00	6.00
❏ 2667	That's the Way I Want Our Love/When	1970	—	3.00	6.00
SPRING					
❏ 108	Your Time to Cry/I Love You More (Than Anything)	1970	—	2.50	5.00
❏ 113	Help Me Make It Through the Night/To Lay Down Beside You	1971	—	2.50	5.00
❏ 113 [PS]	Help Me Make It Through the Night/To Lay Down Beside You	1971	—	3.00	6.00
❏ 115	You're the One for Me/I Ain't Givin' Up	1971	—	2.50	5.00
❏ 118	Georgia Blues/All My Hard Times	1971	—	2.50	5.00
❏ 120	Drowning in the Sea of Love/Let Me Be the One	1971	—	2.50	5.00
❏ 124	Pool of Bad Luck/Glad to Be Your Lover	1972	—	2.50	5.00
❏ 128	Power of Love/The Mirror Don't Lie	1972	—	2.50	5.00
❏ 130	Trouble in My Home/I Found My Dad	1972	—	2.50	5.00
❏ 133	Step by Step/Talk Don't Bother Me	1973	—	2.50	5.00
❏ 138	Theme from Cleopatra Jones/Who Is That Lady	1973	—	2.50	5.00
❏ 138 [PS]	Theme from Cleopatra Jones/Who Is That Lady	1973	—	3.00	6.00
❏ 141	River/Love Never Hurt Nobody	1973	—	2.50	5.00
❏ 145	Carry Me/Do You Know What It's Like to Be Lonesome	1974	—	2.50	5.00
❏ 149	The Best Time of My Life/What We Gonna Do Now	1974	—	2.50	5.00
❏ 156	Get Down, Get Down (Get On the Floor)/In My Baby's Arms	1975	—	2.50	5.00
❏ 159	Music in My Bones/Fire Burning	1975	—	2.50	5.00
❏ 163	I Need You, You Need Me/I'll Take Care (Of You)	1975	—	2.50	5.00
❏ 166	Come Get to This/Let the Good Times Roll	1976	—	2.50	5.00
❏ 169	Easy to Love/Can't Stand the Pain	1976	—	2.50	5.00
❏ 172	You Didn't Have to Play No Games/What's Left to Do	1977	—	2.50	5.00
❏ 176	One Step at a Time/Track of Your Love	1977	—	2.50	5.00
❏ 178	For Your Love, Love, Love/I've Got a Jones on You Baby	1977	—	2.50	5.00
❏ 184	I.O.U./It Must Be Love	1978	—	2.50	5.00
❏ 190	Love Vibration/(Instrumental)	1978	—	2.50	5.00
❏ 194	Going Through These Changes/I Can't Stand a Liar	1979	—	2.50	5.00
❏ 3003	I Wanna Taste Your Love/Make Every Moment Count	1979	—	2.50	5.00
❏ 3006	Hooked on Disco Music/I Still Love You	1980	—	2.50	5.00
VEE JAY					
❏ 609	My Adorable One/Say (That My Love Is True)	1964	2.00	4.00	8.00
❏ 663	When You're Near/When I'm Gone	1965	2.00	4.00	8.00
❏ 694	Let's Do It Over/The Whoo Pee	1965	2.00	4.00	8.00
Albums					
BUDDAH					
❏ BDS-7512	Joe Simon	1969	6.25	12.50	25.00
COMPLEAT					
❏ 671015-1	Mr. Right	1985	3.00	6.00	12.00
POSSE					
❏ 10002	Glad You Came My Way	1981	3.00	6.00	12.00
❏ 10003	By Popular Demand	1982	3.00	6.00	12.00
SOUND STAGE 7					
❏ 5000 [(2)]	The World of Joe Simon	197?	3.00	6.00	12.00
—Reissue of 32536					
❏ SSM-5003 [M] Pure Soul		1967	7.50	15.00	30.00
❏ SSS-15003 [S] Pure Soul		1967	10.00	20.00	40.00
❏ SSS-15004	No Sad Songs	1968	10.00	20.00	40.00
❏ SSS-15005	Simon Sings	1968	10.00	20.00	40.00
❏ SSS-15006	The Chokin' Kind	1969	7.50	15.00	30.00
❏ SSS-15008	Joe Simon…Better Than Ever	1969	7.50	15.00	30.00
❏ SSS-15009	The Best of Joe Simon	1972	3.75	7.50	15.00
❏ KZ 31916	Greatest Hits	1972	3.00	6.00	12.00
❏ ZG 32536 [(2)]	The World of Joe Simon	1974	3.75	7.50	15.00
❏ ZG 33879 [(2)]	The Chokin' Kind/Joe Simon…Better Than Ever	1975	3.75	7.50	15.00
SPRING					
❏ SPR-4701	The Sounds of Simon	1971	6.25	12.50	25.00
❏ SPR-5702	Drowning in the Sea of Love	1972	6.25	12.50	25.00
❏ SPR-5704	The Power of Joe Simon	1973	6.25	12.50	25.00
❏ SPR-5705	Simon Country	1973	3.75	7.50	15.00
❏ SPR-6702	Mood, Heart and Soul	1974	3.75	7.50	15.00
❏ SPR-6706	Get Down	1975	3.75	7.50	15.00
❏ SPR-6710	Today	1975	3.75	7.50	15.00
❏ SPR-6713	Easy to Love	1976	3.75	7.50	15.00
❏ SPR-6716	Bad Case of Love	1977	3.75	7.50	15.00
❏ SPR-6720	Love Vibrations	1979	3.75	7.50	15.00

SIMONE, NINA

45s

Number	Title (A Side/B Side)	Yr	VG	VG+	NM
BETHLEHEM					
❏ 3031	My Baby Just Cares for Me/He Needs Me	1962	2.00	4.00	8.00
❏ 3099	I Loves You Porgy/My Baby Just Cares for Me	1970	—	2.50	5.00
❏ 11021	I Loves You, Porgy/Love Me or Leave Me	1959	3.00	6.00	12.00
❏ 11052	Little Girl Blue/He Needs Me	1960	2.50	5.00	10.00
❏ 11055	Don't Smoke in Bed/African Mailman	1960	2.50	5.00	10.00
❏ 11057	Mood Indigo/Central Park Blues	1960	2.50	5.00	10.00
❏ 11087	For All We Know/Good Bait	1960	2.50	5.00	10.00
❏ 11088	You'll Never Walk Alone/Plain Gold Ring	1960	2.50	5.00	10.00
❏ 11089	He's Got the Whole World in His Hands/Central Park Blues	1960	2.50	5.00	10.00
COLPIX					
❏ 116	Solitaire/Chilly Winds	1959	2.50	5.00	10.00
❏ 124	Children Go Where I Send Thee/Willow Weep for Me	1959	2.50	5.00	10.00
❏ 135	It Might As Well Be Spring/The Other Woman	1959	2.50	5.00	10.00
❏ 143	Summertime/Fine and Mellow	1960	2.50	5.00	10.00
❏ 151	Since My Love Has Gone/Tomorrow (We Shall Meet Once More)	1960	2.50	5.00	10.00
❏ 156	If Only for Tonight/(B-side unknown)	1960	2.50	5.00	10.00
❏ 158	Nobody Knows You When You're Down and Out/Black Is the Color of My True Love's Hair	1960	2.50	5.00	10.00
❏ 175	Trouble in Mind/Cotton-Eyed Joe	1960	2.50	5.00	10.00
❏ 197	The Work Song/Memphis in June	1961	2.50	5.00	10.00
❏ 608	You Can Have Him/Gin House Blues	1961	2.50	5.00	10.00
❏ 614	Come On Back, Jack/You've Been Gone Too Long	1961	2.50	5.00	10.00
❏ 635	In the Evening by the Moonlight/Chilly Winds Don't Blow	1962	2.00	4.00	8.00
❏ 647	I Got It Bad/I Want a Little Sugar in My Bowl	1962	2.00	4.00	8.00
❏ 703	Blackbird/Little Liza Jane	1963	2.00	4.00	8.00
CTI					
❏ 44	Baltimore/The Family	1978	—	2.50	5.00
❏ 46	Forget/Baltimore	1978	—	2.50	5.00
❏ 49	The Family/That's All I Want from You	1978	—	2.50	5.00
PHILIPS					
❏ 40194	I Loves You Porgy/Old Jim Crow	1964	2.00	4.00	8.00
❏ 40216	Mississippi Goddam/Sea Lion Woman	1964	2.00	4.00	8.00
❏ 40232	Don't Let Me Be Misunderstood/A Monster	1964	2.00	4.00	8.00
❏ 40254	I Am Blessed/How Can I	1965	2.00	4.00	8.00
❏ 40286	I Put a Spell on You/Gimme Some	1965	2.00	4.00	8.00
❏ 40337	Either Way I Lose/Break Down and Let It All Out	1965	2.00	4.00	8.00
❏ 40359	Why Keep On Breaking My Heart/I Love Your Lovin' Ways	1966	—	3.00	6.00
❏ 40376	See-Line Woman/I Love Your Lovin' Ways	1966	—	3.00	6.00
❏ 40404	What More Can I Say/Four Women	1966	—	3.00	6.00
❏ 40418	Don't Pay Them No Mind/(B-side unknown)	1966	—	3.00	6.00
RCA VICTOR					
❏ 47-9120	Do I Move You/Day and Night	1967	—	3.00	6.00
❏ 47-9286	It Be's That Way Sometime/You'll Go to Hell	1967	—	3.00	6.00
❏ 47-9375	Cherish/I Wish I Knew How It Would Feel to Be Free	1967	—	3.00	6.00
❏ 47-9447	To Love Somebody/I Can't See Nobody	1968	—	3.00	6.00
❏ 47-9532	Why (Part 1)/Why (Part 2)	1968	—	3.00	6.00
❏ 47-9602	Do What You Gotta Do/Peace of Mind	1968	—	3.00	6.00
❏ 47-9686	Ain't Got No; I Got Life/Real, Real	1968	—	3.00	6.00
❏ 47-9730	Revolution (Part 1)/Revolution (Part 2)	1969	—	3.00	6.00
❏ 47-9749	Suzanne/Turn, Turn, Turn (To Everything There Is a Season)	1969	—	3.00	6.00
❏ 74-0269	To Be Young, Gifted and Black/Save Me	1969	—	3.00	6.00
❏ 74-0311	Who Knows Where the Time Goes/The Assignment Song	1970	—	3.00	6.00
❏ 74-0467	Here Comes the Sun/New World Coming	1971	—	—	—
—Canceled					
❏ 74-0471	New World Coming/O-o-h Child	1971	—	3.00	6.00
❏ 74-0514	Here Comes the Sun/Angel of the Morning	1971	—	3.00	6.00
❏ 74-0871	My Sweet Lord-Today Is a Killer/Poppies	1973	—	3.00	6.00
Albums					
ACCORD					
❏ SN-7108	In Concert	1981	2.50	5.00	10.00
BETHLEHEM					
❏ BCP-6003	Nina Simone's Finest	197?	3.00	6.00	12.00
❏ BCP-6028 [M]	Jazz As Played in an Exclusive Side Street Club	1959	20.00	40.00	80.00
❏ BCP-6028 [M]	The Original Nina Simone	1961	7.50	15.00	30.00
—Retitled reissue					
❏ SBCP-6028 [S]	Jazz As Played in an Exclusive Side Street Club	1959	25.00	50.00	100.00
❏ SBCP-6028 [S]	The Original Nina Simone	1961	10.00	20.00	40.00
—Retitled reissue					
❏ BCP-6041 [M]	Nina Simone and Her Friends	1960	10.00	20.00	40.00
❏ SBCP-6041 [S]	Nina Simone and Her Friends	1960	12.50	25.00	50.00
—With Carmen McRae and Chris Connor					
CANYON					
❏ 7705	Gifted and Black	1971	3.75	7.50	15.00
COLPIX					
❏ CP-407 [M]	The Amazing Nina Simone	1959	6.25	12.50	25.00
❏ SCP-407 [S]	The Amazing Nina Simone	1959	7.50	15.00	30.00
❏ CP-409 [M]	Nina at Town Hall	1960	6.25	12.50	25.00
❏ SCP-409 [S]	Nina at Town Hall	1960	7.50	15.00	30.00
❏ CP-412 [M]	Nina at Newport	1960	6.25	12.50	25.00
❏ SCP-412 [S]	Nina at Newport	1960	7.50	15.00	30.00
❏ CP-419 [M]	Forbidden Fruit	1961	6.25	12.50	25.00
❏ SCP-419 [S]	Forbidden Fruit	1961	7.50	15.00	30.00
❏ CP-421 [M]	Nina Simone at the Village Gate	1961	6.25	12.50	25.00

S

Number	Title (A Side/B Side)	Yr	VG	VG+	NM
❑ SCP-421 [S]	Nina Simone at the Village Gate	1961	7.50	15.00	30.00
❑ CP-425 [M]	Nina Sings Ellington	1962	6.25	12.50	25.00
❑ SCP-425 [S]	Nina Sings Ellington	1962	7.50	15.00	30.00
❑ CP-443 [M]	Nina's Choice	1963	6.25	12.50	25.00
❑ SCP-443 [S]	Nina's Choice	1963	7.50	15.00	30.00
❑ CP-455 [M]	Nina Simone at Carnegie Hall	1963	6.25	12.50	25.00
❑ SCP-455 [S]	Nina Simone at Carnegie Hall	1963	7.50	15.00	30.00
❑ CP-465 [M]	Folksy Nina	1964	6.25	12.50	25.00
❑ SCP-465 [S]	Folksy Nina	1964	7.50	15.00	30.00
❑ CP-496 [M]	Nina with Strings	1966	6.25	12.50	25.00
❑ SCP-496 [S]	Nina with Strings	1966	7.50	15.00	30.00

CTI

Number	Title	Yr	VG	VG+	NM
❑ 7084	Baltimore	1978	3.00	6.00	12.00

PHILIPS

Number	Title	Yr	VG	VG+	NM
❑ PHM 200135 [M]	Nina Simone In Concert	1964	3.75	7.50	15.00
❑ PHM 200148 [M]	Broadway...Blues...Ballads	1964	3.75	7.50	15.00
❑ PHM 200172 [M]	I Put a Spell on You	1965	3.75	7.50	15.00
❑ PHM 200187 [M]	Pastel Blues	1965	3.75	7.50	15.00
❑ PHM 200202 [M]	Let It All Out	1966	3.75	7.50	15.00
❑ PHM 200207 [M]	Wild Is the Wind	1966	3.75	7.50	15.00
❑ PHM 200219 [M]	The High Priestess of Soul	1967	3.75	7.50	15.00
❑ PHS 600135 [S]	Nina Simone In Concert	1964	5.00	10.00	20.00
❑ PHS 600148 [S]	Broadway...Blues...Ballads	1964	5.00	10.00	20.00
❑ PHS 600172 [S]	I Put a Spell on You	1965	5.00	10.00	20.00
❑ PHS 600187 [S]	Pastel Blues	1965	5.00	10.00	20.00
❑ PHS 600202 [S]	Let It All Out	1966	5.00	10.00	20.00
❑ PHS 600207 [S]	Wild Is the Wind	1966	5.00	10.00	20.00
❑ PHS 600219 [S]	The High Priestess of Soul	1967	5.00	10.00	20.00
❑ PHS 600298	The Best of Nina Simone	1969	5.00	10.00	20.00
❑ 822846-1	The Best of Nina Simone	198?	2.50	5.00	10.00

PM

Number	Title	Yr	VG	VG+	NM
❑ 018	A Very Rare Evening	1979	3.00	6.00	12.00

QUINTESSENCE

Number	Title	Yr	VG	VG+	NM
❑ 25421	Silk and Soul	1979	2.50	5.00	10.00

RCA VICTOR

Number	Title	Yr	VG	VG+	NM
❑ AFL1-0241	It Is Finished — Nina 1974	1977	2.50	5.00	10.00
—Reissue with new prefix					
❑ APL1-0241	It Is Finished — Nina 1974	1974	3.00	6.00	12.00
❑ AFL1-1788	Poets	1977	2.50	5.00	10.00
—Reissue with new prefix					
❑ APL1-1788	Poets	1976	3.00	6.00	12.00
❑ LPM-3789 [M]	Nina Simone Sings the Blues	1967	6.25	12.50	25.00
❑ LSP-3789 [S]	Nina Simone Sings the Blues	1967	3.75	7.50	15.00
❑ LPM-3837 [M]	Silk and Soul	1967	6.25	12.50	25.00
❑ LSP-3837 [S]	Silk and Soul	1967	3.75	7.50	15.00
❑ LSP-4065	'Nuff Said	1968	3.75	7.50	15.00
❑ LSP-4102	Nina Simone and Piano	1968	3.75	7.50	15.00
❑ LSP-4152	To Love Somebody	1969	3.75	7.50	15.00
❑ LSP-4248	Black Gold	1970	3.75	7.50	15.00
❑ AFL1-4374	The Best of Nina Simone	1977	2.50	5.00	10.00
—Reissue with new prefix					
❑ LSP-4374	The Best of Nina Simone	1970	3.75	7.50	15.00
❑ AFL1-4536	Here Comes the Sun	1977	2.50	5.00	10.00
—Reissue with new prefix					
❑ LSP-4536	Here Comes the Sun	1971	3.75	7.50	15.00
❑ LSP-4757	Emergency Ward!	1972	3.75	7.50	15.00

SALSOUL

Number	Title	Yr	VG	VG+	NM
❑ SA-8546	Little Girl Blue	1982	2.50	5.00	10.00

TRIP

Number	Title	Yr	VG	VG+	NM
❑ 8020 [(2)]	Live in Europe	1973	3.00	6.00	12.00
❑ 8021 [(2)]	Black Is the Color	1973	3.00	6.00	12.00
❑ 9521	Portrait	197?	2.50	5.00	10.00

VERVE

Number	Title	Yr	VG	VG+	NM
❑ 831437-1	Let It Be Me	1987	2.50	5.00	10.00

SIMPLY RED
12-Inch Singles
EASTWEST

Number	Title (A Side/B Side)	Yr	VG	VG+	NM
❑ DMD 1738 [DJ]	Something Got Me Started (Hurley's House Remix 5:56) (Hurley's Dub 5:44) (E-Smoove's Late Nite Mix 5:00) (E-Smoove Dub 5:44)	1991	2.50	5.00	10.00
❑ ED 5841 [(2) DJ]	Remembering the First Time (6 versions)	1995	3.75	7.50	15.00
❑ ED 5888 [DJ]	Angel (Soundtrack Version) (Mousse T Soul Mix) (Smooth Soul Mix) (Club Mix) (Simply Red Mix) (Radio Remix)	1996	3.00	6.00	12.00
❑ ED 6012 [DJ]	Angel (Temple Dub 7.14) (Club Mix 6.06) (Instrumental 6.05)	1996	2.00	4.00	8.00
❑ ED 6089 [DJ]	The Air That I Breathe (3 versions)	1998	3.75	7.50	15.00
❑ ED 6111 [DJ]	Mellow My Mind (RH Factor Pop Mix) (RH Factor Radio Edit) (RH Factor Club Mix) (RH Factor Dub)	1998	2.50	5.00	10.00
❑ ED 6190 [(2) DJ]	Ain't That a Lot of Love (Phats 'n' Small Mutant Disco Mix) (Phats 'n' Small Mutant Disco Dub) (Club 39 Underground Club) (Club 39 Underground Dub) (Johnny Vicious Filter Factory Club) (Johnny Vicious Filter Factory Dub)	1999	3.75	7.50	15.00
❑ 96290	Something Got Me Started (4 versions)	1991	2.00	4.00	8.00

ELEKTRA

Number	Title	Yr	VG	VG+	NM
❑ ED 5088 [DJ]	Money$ Too Tight (To Mention) (Cutback Mix) (Dub Mix) (7" Version)	1985	2.00	4.00	8.00
❑ ED 5112 [DJ]	Come to My Aid (Survival Mix) (Heavy Dub)/ Granma's Hands	1985	2.00	4.00	8.00
❑ ED 5210 [DJ]	The Right Thing (Extended Version) (LP Version) (Edit)	1987	—	3.00	6.00
❑ ED 5227 [DJ]	Infidelity (LP Version) (Stretch Mix)	1987	—	3.00	6.00
❑ ED 5247 [DJ]	Maybe Someday ... (LP Version) (same on both sides)	1987	—	3.00	6.00
❑ ED 5268 [DJ]	Suffer (Edit of LP Version) (same on both sides)	1987	2.00	4.00	8.00
❑ ED 5358 [DJ]	It's Only Love (Valentine Mix) (Valentine Mix Edit)	1989	—	3.50	7.00
❑ ED 5378 [DJ]	If You Don't Know Me By Now (same on both sides)	1989	2.00	4.00	8.00
❑ ED 5407 [DJ]	You've Got It (same on both sides)	1989	2.00	4.00	8.00
❑ 66703	If You Don't Know Me By Now/Move On Out (Live)/Shine (Live)	1989	2.00	4.00	8.00
❑ 66807	Infidelity (Stretch Mix)/Love Fire (Massive Red Mix)/Lady Godiva's Room	1987	2.00	4.00	8.00
❑ 66816	The Right Thing/There's a Light/Every Time We Say Goodbye	1987	2.00	4.00	8.00
❑ 66872	Holding Back the Years/Drowning in My Own Tears/Picture Book	1986	2.50	5.00	10.00
❑ 66883	Money$ Too Tight (To Mention) (Cutback Mix) (Single Version) (Dub Version)	1985	2.00	4.00	8.00

45s
ELEKTRA

Number	Title	Yr	VG	VG+	NM
❑ 65939	If You Don't Know Me By Now/You've Got It	199?	—	—	3.00
—"Spun Gold" reissue					
❑ 65979	Holding Back the Years/Money$ Too Tight (To Mention)	198?	—	—	3.00
—"Spun Gold" reissue					
❑ 69269	You've Got It/She'll Have to Go	1989	—	2.00	4.00
❑ 69297	If You Don't Know Me By Now/Move On Out	1989	—	—	3.00
❑ 69297 [PS]	If You Don't Know Me By Now/Move On Out	1989	—	—	3.00
❑ 69317	It's Only Love/Turn It Up	1989	—	—	3.00
❑ 69317 [PS]	It's Only Love/Turn It Up	1989	—	—	3.00
❑ 69428	Suffer/Let Me Have It All	1987	—	—	3.00
❑ 69448	Maybe Someday.../Broken Man	1987	—	—	3.00
❑ 69448 [PS]	Maybe Someday.../Broken Man	1987	—	—	3.00
❑ 69468	Infidelity/Lady Godiva's Room	1987	—	—	3.00
❑ 69468 [PS]	Infidelity/Lady Godiva's Room	1987	—	—	3.00
❑ 69487	The Right Thing/There's a Light	1987	—	—	3.00
❑ 69487 [PS]	The Right Thing/There's a Light	1987	—	—	3.00
❑ 69528	Money$ Too Tight (To Mention)/Picture Book (Dub)	1986	—	—	3.00
❑ 69528 [PS]	Money$ Too Tight (To Mention)/Picture Book (Dub)	1986	—	—	3.00
❑ 69564	Holding Back the Years/I Won't Feel Bad	1986	—	—	3.00
❑ 69574	Come to My Aid (Remix)/Look At You Now	1986	—	2.50	5.00
❑ 69574 [PS]	Come to My Aid (Remix)/Look At You Now	1986	2.00	4.00	8.00
❑ 69607	Money$ Too Tight (To Mention)/Open Up the Red Box	1985	—	2.50	5.00
❑ 69607 [PS]	Money$ Too Tight (To Mention)/Open Up the Red Box	1985	—	2.50	5.00

Albums
ELEKTRA

Number	Title	Yr	VG	VG+	NM
❑ ED 5236 [DJ]	Simply Red Billboard Interview	1989	10.00	20.00	40.00
—Nelson George interviews Mick Hucknall and Lamont Dozier; promo-only					
❑ 60452	Picture Book	1985	2.00	4.00	8.00
❑ 60727	Men and Women	1987	2.00	4.00	8.00
❑ 60828	A New Flame	1989	2.50	5.00	10.00
❑ R 101012	A New Flame	1989	3.00	6.00	12.00
—BMG Direct Marketing edition					
❑ R 152858	Men and Women	1987	2.50	5.00	10.00
—RCA Music Service edition					
❑ R 153936	Picture Book	1985	2.50	5.00	10.00
—RCA Music Service edition					

SIMPSON, VALERIE
Also see ASHFORD AND SIMPSON.
45s
TAMLA

Number	Title	Yr	VG	VG+	NM
❑ 54204	Back to Nowhere/Can't It Wait Until Tomorrow	1971	—	2.50	5.00
❑ 54224	Silly Wasn't I/I Believe I'm Gonna Take This Ride	1972	—	2.50	5.00
❑ 54231	Genius/One More Baby Child Born	1973	—	2.50	5.00

Albums
TAMLA

Number	Title	Yr	VG	VG+	NM
❑ T 311	Valerie Simpson Exposed	1971	3.75	7.50	15.00
❑ T 317	Valerie Simpson	1972	3.75	7.50	15.00
❑ T6-351	Keep It Comin'	1977	3.00	6.00	12.00

SISTER SLEDGE
12-Inch Singles
ATLANTIC

Number	Title	Yr	VG	VG+	NM
❑ DSKO 97 [DJ]	As (same on both sides)	1977	3.75	7.50	15.00
❑ 850 [DJ]	Frankie (Club Mix) (Dub Mix)/Hold Out Poppy	1985	—	3.00	6.00
❑ 868 [DJ]	Dancing on the Jagged Edge/(Dub)	1985	—	3.00	6.00
❑ 979 [DJ]	Here to Stay (2 mixes)/Make a Wish	1986	—	3.00	6.00
—B-side by Joe Cruz					
❑ 86862	Dancing on the Jagged Edge/(Dub)	1985	—	3.00	6.00

COTILLION

Number	Title	Yr	VG	VG+	NM
❑ 229 [DJ]	Reach Your Peak (5:26) (same on both sides)	1980	2.00	4.00	8.00
❑ 277 [DJ]	He's Just a Runaway (6:05) (3:57)	1981	2.00	4.00	8.00
❑ 645 [DJ]	B.Y.O.B. (Bring Your Own Body) (6:43) (3:50)	1983	—	3.00	6.00

RHINO

Number	Title	Yr	VG	VG+	NM
❑ 76019	We Are Family (2 mixes)/Lost in Music (2 mixes)	1993	2.00	4.00	8.00

45s
ATCO

Number	Title	Yr	VG	VG+	NM
❑ 6924	The Weatherman/Have You Met My Friend	1973	—	3.00	6.00
❑ 6940	Mama Never Told Me/Neither One of Us	1973	—	3.00	6.00

Number	Title (A Side/B Side)	Yr	VG	VG+	NM
❏ 7008	Love Don't You Go Through No Changes on Me/Don't You Miss Him	1974	—	2.50	5.00
❏ 7020	Circle of Love (Caught in the Middle)/Cross My Heart	1975	—	2.50	5.00
❏ 7035	Love Ain't Easy/Love Has Found Me	1975	—	2.50	5.00

ATLANTIC

❏ 89357	Here to Stay/Make a Wish	1986	—	—	3.00

—*B-side by Joe Cruz*

❏ 89466	You're Fine/(B-side unknown)	1985	—	—	3.00
❏ 89520	You Need Me/Dancing on the Jagged Edge	1985	—	—	3.00
❏ 89547	Frankie/Hold Out Poppy	1985	—	—	3.00
❏ 89547 [PS]	Frankie/Hold Out Poppy	1985	—	2.00	4.00

COTILLION

❏ 44202	Thank You for Today/Have Love Will Travel	1976	—	2.50	5.00
❏ 44208	Cream of the Crop/Love Ain't Easy	1976	—	2.50	5.00
❏ 44220	Blockbuster Boy/Moondancer	1977	—	2.50	5.00
❏ 44226	Baby, It's the Rain/Hold Onto This Feeling	1977	—	2.50	5.00
❏ 44234	Do It to the Max/I've Seen Better Days	1978	—	2.50	5.00
❏ 44245	He's the Greatest Dancer/Somebody Loves Me	1978	—	2.00	4.00
❏ 44251	We Are Family/Easier to Love	1979	—	2.00	4.00
❏ 45001	Lost in Music/Thinking of You	1979	—	2.00	4.00
❏ 45007	Got to Love Somebody/Good Girl Now	1979	—	2.00	4.00
❏ 45013	Reach Your Peak/You Fooled Around	1980	—	2.00	4.00
❏ 45020	Let's Go on Vacation/Easy Street	1980	—	2.00	4.00
❏ 46007	All American Girls/Happy Feelings	1981	—	2.00	4.00
❏ 46012	Next Time You'll Know/If You Really Want Me	1981	—	2.00	4.00
❏ 46017	He's Just a Runaway/He's Just a Runaway (Long Version)	1981	—	2.00	4.00
❏ 47000	My Guy/Il Macquillace Lady	1982	—	2.00	4.00
❏ 47007	All the Man That I Need/Light Footin'	1982	—	2.00	4.00
❏ 99834	Gotta Get Back to Love/Lifetime Lover	1983	—	2.00	4.00
❏ 99885	B.Y.O.B. (Bring Your Own Baby)/(B-side unknown)	1983	—	2.00	4.00

Albums

ATCO

❏ SD 36-105	Circle of Love	1975	5.00	10.00	20.00

ATLANTIC

❏ 81255	When the Boys Meet the Girls	1985	2.50	5.00	10.00

COTILLION

❏ SD 5209	We Are Family	1979	2.50	5.00	10.00
❏ SD 5231	The Sisters	1982	2.50	5.00	10.00
❏ SD 9919	Together	1976	3.00	6.00	12.00
❏ SD 16012	Love Somebody Today	1980	2.50	5.00	10.00
❏ SD 16027	All American Girls	1981	2.50	5.00	10.00
❏ 90069	Bet Cha Say That to All the Girls	1983	2.50	5.00	10.00

SIX TEENS, THE

45s

FLIP

❏ 315	A Casual Look/Teenage Promise	1956	5.00	10.00	20.00
❏ 317	Send Me Flowers/Afar Into the Night	1956	3.75	7.50	15.00
❏ 320	My Special Guy/Only Jim	1956	3.75	7.50	15.00
❏ 322	Arrow of Love/Was It a Dream of Mine	1957	3.75	7.50	15.00
❏ 326	Baby You're Dynamite/My Surprise	1957	3.75	7.50	15.00
❏ 329	My Secret/Stop Playing Ping Pong	1958	3.75	7.50	15.00
❏ 333	Danny/Love's Funny That Way	1958	3.75	7.50	15.00
❏ 338	Baby-O/Oh, It's Crazy	1958	5.00	10.00	20.00
❏ 346	Why Do I Go to School/Heaven Knows I Love You	1959	6.25	12.50	25.00
❏ 350	So Happy/That Wonderful Secret of Love	1960	3.75	7.50	15.00
❏ 351	A Little Prayer/Suddenly in Love	1960	3.75	7.50	15.00

SKYLINERS, THE

45s

ATCO

❏ 6270	Since I Fell for You/I'd Die	1963	10.00	20.00	40.00

CALICO

❏ 103/4	Since I Don't Have You/One Night, One Night	1959	12.50	25.00	50.00
❏ 106	This I Swear/Tomorrow	1959	7.50	15.00	30.00
❏ 109	It Happened Today/Lonely Way	1959	7.50	15.00	30.00
❏ 114	How Much/Lorraine from Spain	1960	6.25	12.50	25.00
❏ 117	Pennies from Heaven/I'll Be Seeing You	1960	6.25	12.50	25.00
❏ 120	Believe Me/Happy Time	1960	6.25	12.50	25.00

CAMEO

❏ 215	Three Coins in the Fountain/Everyone But You	1962	10.00	20.00	40.00

CAPITOL

❏ 3979	Where Have They Gone/I Could Have Loved You So Well	1974	6.25	12.50	25.00

—*As "Jimmy Beaumont and the Skyliners"*

CLASSIC ARTISTS

❏ 123	You're My Christmas Present/Another Lonely New Year's Eve	1990	—	2.50	5.00

COLPIX

❏ 188	I'll Close My Eyes/The Door Is Still Open	1961	10.00	20.00	40.00
❏ 607	Ba'ion Rhythms/The End of a Story	196?	10.00	20.00	40.00

—*As "Jimmy Beaumont and the Skyliners"*

❏ 613	Close Your Eyes/Our Love Will Last	1961	10.00	20.00	40.00

DRIVE

❏ 6250	Our Day Is Here/The Day the Clown Died	1976	2.00	4.00	8.00

JUBILEE

❏ 5506	The Loser/Everything Is Fine	1965	3.75	7.50	15.00
❏ 5512	Who Do You Love/Get Yourself a Baby	1965	3.75	7.50	15.00
❏ 5520	I Run to You/Don't Hurt Me Baby	1965	3.75	7.50	15.00

MOTOWN

❏ 1046 [DJ]	Since I Fell for You/I'd Die	1963	1000.	1500.	2000.

—*Record never got beyond the test pressing stage (2 known copies)*

ORIGINAL SOUND

❏ 35	Since I Don't Have You/One Night, One Night	1963	3.75	7.50	15.00
❏ 36	Pennies from Heaven/I'll Be Seeing You	1963	3.75	7.50	15.00
❏ 37	This I Swear/It Happened Today	1963	3.75	7.50	15.00

TORTOISE INT'L.

❏ PB-11243	Oh How Happy/We've Got Love on Our Side	1978	2.00	4.00	8.00
❏ PB-11312	Smile On Me/Love Bug (Done Bit Me Again)	1978	2.00	4.00	8.00

VISCOUNT

❏ 104	Comes Love/Tell Me	1962	5.00	10.00	20.00

Albums

CALICO

❏ LP-3000 [M]	The Skyliners	1959	200.00	400.00	600.00

—*Yellow and blue label*

❏ LP-3000 [M]	The Skyliners	196?	50.00	100.00	200.00

—*Blue label*

KAMA SUTRA

❏ KSBS-2026	Once Upon a Time	1971	6.25	12.50	25.00

ORIGINAL SOUND

❏ OS-5010 [M]	Since I Don't Have You	1963	12.50	25.00	50.00
❏ OSS-8873 [S]	Since I Don't Have You	1963	17.50	35.00	70.00
❏ OSS-8873 [S]	Since I Don't Have You	197?	3.75	7.50	15.00

—*Reissue on thinner vinyl*

SLADES, THE

45s

DOMINO

❏ 500	You Cheated/The Waddle	1958	10.00	20.00	40.00
❏ 800	You Gambled/No Time	1959	10.00	20.00	40.00
❏ 901	Just You/It's Better to Love	1959	7.50	15.00	30.00
❏ 906	It's Your Turn/Take My Heart	1961	10.00	20.00	40.00
❏ 1000	Summertime/You Must Try	1961	7.50	15.00	30.00

LIBERTY

❏ 55118	Baby/You Mean Everything to Me	1957	12.50	25.00	50.00

—*As "The Spades," in error*

❏ 55118	Baby/You Mean Everything to Me	1957	6.25	12.50	25.00

SLEDGE, PERCY

12-Inch Singles

CAPRICORN

❏ PRO 672 [DJ]	When She's Touching Me (same on both sides)	1977	3.00	6.00	12.00

45s

ATLANTIC

❏ 2326	When a Man Loves a Woman/Love Me Like You Mean It	1966	5.00	10.00	20.00
❏ 2342	Warm and Tender Love/Sugar Puddin'	1966	2.50	5.00	10.00
❏ 2358	It Tears Me Up/Heart of a Child	1966	2.50	5.00	10.00
❏ 2383	Baby, Help Me/You Got That Something Wonderful	1967	2.50	5.00	10.00
❏ 2396	Out of Left Field/It Can't Be Stopped	1967	2.50	5.00	10.00
❏ 2414	Love Me Tender/What Am I Living For	1967	2.50	5.00	10.00
❏ 2434	Just Out of Reach (Of My Two Empty Arms)/Hard to Believe	1967	2.50	5.00	10.00
❏ 2453	Cover Me/Behind Every Great Man There Is a Woman	1967	2.50	5.00	10.00
❏ 2490	Take Time to Know Her/It's All Wrong But It's Alright	1968	3.00	6.00	12.00
❏ 2539	Sudden Stop/Between These Arms	1968	2.50	5.00	10.00
❏ 2563	You're All Around Me/Self-Preservation	1968	2.50	5.00	10.00
❏ 2594	My Special Prayer/Bless Your Little Sweet Soul	1969	2.00	4.00	8.00
❏ 2616	Any Day Now/The Angels Listened In	1969	2.50	5.00	10.00
❏ 2646	Woman of the Night/Kind Woman	1969	2.00	4.00	8.00
❏ 2679	Faithful and True/True Love Travels on a Gravel Road	1969	2.00	4.00	8.00
❏ 2719	Too Many Rivers to Cross/Push Mr. Pride Aside	1970	2.00	4.00	8.00
❏ 2754	Help Me Make It Through the Night/Thief in the Night	1970	2.00	4.00	8.00
❏ 2826	Stop the World Tonight/That's the Way I Want to Live	1971	—	3.00	6.00
❏ 2848	Rainbow Road/Standing on the Mountain	1971	—	3.00	6.00
❏ 2886	Sunday Brother/Everything You'll Ever Need	1972	—	3.00	6.00
❏ 2963	Sunshine/Unchanging Love	1973	—	3.00	6.00
❏ 89262	When a Man Loves a Woman/Cover Me	1987	—	—	3.00
❏ 89262 [PS]	When a Man Loves a Woman/Cover Me	1987	—	2.00	4.00

CAPRICORN

❏ 0209	I'll Be Your Everything/Blue Water	1974	—	2.50	5.00
❏ 0220	If This Is the Last Time/Behind Closed Doors	1975	—	2.50	5.00
❏ 0273	When a Boy Becomes a Man/When She Touches Me	1977	—	2.50	5.00

MONUMENT

❏ 03612	You Had to Be There/Hard Lovin' Woman	1983	—	2.00	4.00
❏ 03878	She's Too Pretty to Cry/Home Type Thing	1983	—	2.00	4.00

PHILCO-FORD

❏ HP-12	When a Man Loves a Woman/Baby Help Me	1967	6.25	12.50	25.00

—*4-inch plastic "Hip Pocket Record" with color sleeve*

Albums

ATLANTIC

❏ 8125 [M]	When a Man Loves a Woman	1966	12.50	25.00	50.00
❏ SD 8125 [R]	When a Man Loves a Woman	1966	7.50	15.00	30.00
❏ 8132 [M]	Warm and Tender Soul	1966	12.50	25.00	50.00
❏ SD 8132 [R]	Warm and Tender Soul	1966	7.50	15.00	30.00
❏ 8146 [M]	The Percy Sledge Way	1967	12.50	25.00	50.00

S

Number	Title (A Side/B Side)	Yr	VG	VG+	NM
❑ SD 8146 [S]	The Percy Sledge Way	1967	12.50	25.00	50.00
❑ SD 8180	Take Time to Know Her	1968	12.50	25.00	50.00
❑ SD 8210	The Best of Percy Sledge	1969	6.25	12.50	25.00

CAPRICORN

❑ CP 0147	I'll Be Your Everything	1974	3.75	7.50	15.00

MONUMENT

❑ FW 38532	Percy	1983	3.00	6.00	12.00

SLY
See SLY STEWART.

SLY AND THE FAMILY STONE
Also see LARRY GRAHAM; SLY STEWART.
45s
EPIC

Number	Title (A Side/B Side)	Yr	VG	VG+	NM
❑ 10229	Higher/Underdog	1967	2.50	5.00	10.00
❑ 10256	Dance to the Music/Let Me Hear It from You	1967	2.50	5.00	10.00
❑ 10353	Life/M'Lady	1968	2.00	4.00	8.00
❑ 10407	Everyday People/Sing a Simple Song	1968	2.50	5.00	10.00
❑ 10407 [PS]	Everyday People/Sing a Simple Song	1968	3.00	6.00	12.00
❑ 10450	Stand!/I Want to Take You Higher	1969	2.50	5.00	10.00
❑ 10450 [PS]	Stand!/I Want to Take You Higher	1969	3.00	6.00	12.00
❑ 10497	Hot Fun in the Summertime/Fun	1969	2.50	5.00	10.00
❑ 10555	Thank You Falettinme Be Mice Elf Agin/Everybody Is a Star	1969	—	3.00	6.00
❑ 10555 [PS]	Thank You Falettinme Be Mice Elf Agin/Everybody Is a Star	1969	2.50	5.00	10.00
❑ 10805	Family Affair/Luv N' Haight	1971	—	3.00	6.00
❑ 10829	Runnin' Away/Brave & Strong	1972	—	3.00	6.00
❑ 10850	Smilin'/Luv N' Haight	1972	—	3.00	6.00
❑ 11017	If You Want Me to Stay/Thankful N' Thoughtful	1973	—	3.00	6.00
❑ 11017	If You Want Me to Stay/Babies Makin' Babies	1973	—	3.00	6.00
❑ 11060	Frisky/If It Were Left Up to Me	1973	—	3.00	6.00
❑ 11140	Time for Livin'/Small Talk	1974	—	3.00	6.00
❑ 50035	Loose Booty/Can't Strain My Brain	1974	—	3.00	6.00
❑ 50119	Hot Fun in the Summertime/Fun	1975	2.00	4.00	8.00
❑ 50135	I Get High on You/That's Lovin' You	1975	—	2.50	5.00
❑ 50175	Li Lo Li/Who Do You Love	1975	—	2.50	5.00
❑ 50201	Greed/Crossword Puzzle	1976	—	2.50	5.00
❑ 50331	Family Again/Nothing Less Than Happiness	1977	—	2.50	5.00

LOADSTONE

❑ 3951	I Ain't Got Nobody/I Can't Turn You Loose	1967	5.00	10.00	20.00

WARNER BROS.

❑ 29682	High Y'All/Ha Ha He He	1983	—	2.00	4.00
❑ 49062	Sheer Energy/Remember Who You Are	1979	—	2.00	4.00
❑ 49132	Who's to Say/Same Thing	1979	—	2.00	4.00

7-Inch Extended Plays
EPIC

❑ 7-30986	You Caught Me Smilin'/Runnin' Away/Space Cowboy//Just Like a Baby/P.O.E.T.	1971	3.75	7.50	15.00
—Jukebox issue; small hole, plays at 33 1/3 rpm					
❑ 7-30986 [PS]	There's a Riot Goin' On	1971	3.75	7.50	15.00

Albums
EPIC

❑ AS 264 [DJ]	Everything You Always Wanted to Hear by Sly and the Family Stone But Were Afraid to Ask For	1976	6.25	12.50	25.00
—Promo-only compilation					
❑ LN 24324 [M]	A Whole New Thing	1967	5.00	10.00	20.00
❑ LN 24371 [M]	Dance to the Music	1968	10.00	20.00	40.00
❑ BN 26324 [S]	A Whole New Thing	1967	5.00	10.00	20.00
❑ BN 26371 [S]	Dance to the Music	1968	3.75	7.50	15.00
❑ BN 26397	Life	1968	3.75	7.50	15.00
❑ BN 26456	Stand!	1969	3.75	7.50	15.00
❑ PE 26456	Stand!	1986	2.00	4.00	8.00
—Budget-line reissue					
❑ EQ 30325 [Q]	Sly and the Family Stone's Greatest Hits	1971	25.00	50.00	100.00
—Has alternate mixes of "Hot Fun in the Summertime," "Thank You" and "Everybody Is a Star," which are not rechanneled stereo as they are on other LPs					
❑ KE 30325	Sly and the Family Stone's Greatest Hits	1970	3.00	6.00	12.00
—Yellow label, gatefold cover					
❑ PE 30325	Sly and the Family Stone's Greatest Hits	1979	2.00	4.00	8.00
—Budget-line reissue					
❑ E 30333	Life	1971	3.00	6.00	12.00
—Reissue of 26397					
❑ E 30334	Dance to the Music	1971	3.00	6.00	12.00
—Reissue of 26371					
❑ E 30335	A Whole New Thing	1971	3.00	6.00	12.00
—Reissue of 26324					
❑ KE 30986	There's a Riot Goin' On	1971	3.00	6.00	12.00
—Yellow label, gatefold cover					
❑ KE 32134	Fresh	1973	2.50	5.00	10.00
—Orange label					
❑ PE 32930	Small Talk	1974	2.50	5.00	10.00
—Orange label					
❑ PEQ 32930 [Q]	Small Talk	1974	6.25	12.50	25.00
❑ PE 33835	High on You	1975	2.50	5.00	10.00
—Orange label					
❑ PEQ 33835 [Q]	High on You	1975	6.25	12.50	25.00
❑ PE 34348	Heard Ya Missed Me, Well I'm Back	1976	2.50	5.00	10.00
—Orange label					
❑ JE 35974	Ten Years Too Soon	1979	2.50	5.00	10.00
❑ E2 37071 [(2)]	Anthology	1981	3.75	7.50	15.00

WARNER BROS.

❑ BSK 3303	Back on the Right Track	1979	2.50	5.00	10.00
❑ 23700	Ain't But the Right Way	1983	2.50	5.00	10.00

SLY FOX
12-Inch Singles
CAPITOL

Number	Title (A Side/B Side)	Yr	VG	VG+	NM
❑ 8639	Let's Go All the Way (extended)/Bonus Beats	1985	—	3.00	6.00
❑ SPRO 9643/4 [DJ]	Let's Go All the Way (3 versions)	1985	—	3.00	6.00

45s
CAPITOL

❑ 5463	Let's Go All the Way/Let's Go All the Way (Bonus Beats)	1985	—	2.50	5.00
❑ 5505	Como Tu Te Llama (What Is Your Name)/Won't Let You Go	1985	—	2.50	5.00
❑ 5552	Let's Go All the Way/Como Tu Te Llama (What Is Your Name)	1986	—	—	3.00
❑ 5581	Stay True/If Push Comes to Shove	1986	—	—	3.00
❑ 5581 [PS]	Stay True/If Push Comes to Shove	1986	—	—	3.00

Albums
CAPITOL

❑ ST-12367	Let's Go All the Way	1985	2.00	4.00	8.00
❑ ST-512367	Let's Go All the Way	1985	2.50	5.00	10.00
—Columbia House edition					

SMALL, MILLIE
45s
ATCO

Number	Title (A Side/B Side)	Yr	VG	VG+	NM
❑ 6384	Tongue Tied/Blood Shot Eyes	1965	2.50	5.00	10.00

ATLANTIC

❑ 2266	Bring It On Home to Me/I've Fallen in Love with a Snowman	1965	2.50	5.00	10.00

BRIT

❑ 7002	My Street/Mixed-Up, Lonely, Self-Centered, Spoiled Kind of Boy	1965	3.00	6.00	12.00

SMASH

❑ 1893	My Boy Lollipop/Something's Gotta Be Done	1964	3.75	7.50	15.00
❑ 1920	Sweet William/What Am I Living For	1964	3.00	6.00	12.00
❑ 1940	I Love the Way You Love/Bring It On Home to Me	1964	3.00	6.00	12.00
❑ 1946	Don't You Know/Tom Hark	1964	3.00	6.00	12.00

Albums
SMASH

❑ MGS-27055 [M]	My Boy Lollipop	1964	12.50	25.00	50.00
❑ SRS-67055 [R]	My Boy Lollipop	1964	10.00	20.00	40.00

SMITH, ARLENE
Also see THE CHANTELS.
45s
BIG TOP

Number	Title (A Side/B Side)	Yr	VG	VG+	NM
❑ 3073	Love, Love, Love/He Knows I Love Him Too Much	1961	7.50	15.00	30.00

SPECTORIOUS

❑ 150	Good Girls/Everything	196?	25.00	50.00	100.00

SMITH, HUEY "PIANO"
45s
ACE

Number	Title (A Side/B Side)	Yr	VG	VG+	NM
❑ 521	Everybody's Wailin'/Little Liza Jane	1956	6.25	12.50	25.00
❑ 530	Rockin' Pneumonia and the Boogie Woogie Flu (Part 1/Part 2)	1957	7.50	15.00	30.00
❑ 538	Free, Single and Disengaged/Just a Lonely Clown	1957	6.25	12.50	25.00
❑ 545	Don't You Just Know It/High Blood Pressure	1958	6.25	12.50	25.00
❑ 548	Havin' a Good Time/We Like Birdland	1958	6.25	12.50	25.00
❑ 553	Don't You Know Yockomo/Well, I'll Be John Brown	1958	6.25	12.50	25.00
❑ 562	Would You Believe It (I Have a Cold)/Genevieve	1959	5.00	10.00	20.00
❑ 571	Tu-Ber-Cu-Lucas and the Sinus Blues/Dearest Darling	1959	5.00	10.00	20.00
❑ 584	Beatnik Blues/For Cryin' Out Loud	1960	3.75	7.50	15.00
❑ 638	She Got Low Down/Mean, Mean, Mean	1961	3.75	7.50	15.00
❑ 639	She Got Low Down/Mean, Mean, Mean//Little Liza Jane/Rockin' Pnuemonia	1961	6.25	12.50	25.00
❑ 649	Pop-Eye/Scald Dog	1962	3.75	7.50	15.00
❑ 672	Every Once in a While/Somebody Told It	1962	3.00	6.00	12.00
❑ 8002	Talk to Me Baby/If It Ain't One Thing, It's Another	1962	3.00	6.00	12.00
❑ 8008	Let's Bring 'Em Back Again/Quiet as It's Kept	1963	3.75	7.50	15.00

CONSTELLATION

❑ 102	He's Back Again/Quiet As It's Kept	1963	2.50	5.00	10.00

COTILLION

❑ 44142	Rockin' Pneumonia and the Boogie Woogie Flu (Part 1/Part 2)	1971	—	3.00	6.00

IMPERIAL

❑ 5721	The Little Moron/Someone to Love	1961	3.00	6.00	12.00
❑ 5747	Behind the Wheel — Part 1/Behind the Wheel — Part 2	1961	3.00	6.00	12.00
❑ 5772	More Girls/Sassy Sara	1961	3.00	6.00	12.00
❑ 5789	Don't Knock It/Shag-a-Tooth	1961	3.00	6.00	12.00

INSTANT

❑ 3287	I'll Never Forget/Bury Me Dead	1967	2.00	4.00	8.00
❑ 3297	Two Way Pockaway (Part 1)/Two Way Pockaway (Part 2)	1969	2.00	4.00	8.00
❑ 3301	Epitaph of Uncle Tom/Eight Bars of Amen	1969	2.00	4.00	8.00
❑ 3303	You Got Too (Part 1)/You Got Too (Part 2)	1969	2.00	4.00	8.00
❑ 3305	Ballad of a Black Man/The Whatcha Call 'Em	1970	2.00	4.00	8.00

SAVOY

❑ 1113	You Made Me Cry/You're Down with Me	1953	25.00	50.00	100.00

Number	Title (A Side/B Side)	Yr	VG	VG+	NM
VIN					
❑ 1024	I Didn't Do It/They Kept On	1960	3.75	7.50	15.00
Albums					
ACE					
❑ LP-1004 [M]	Having a Good Time	1959	100.00	200.00	400.00
❑ LP-1015 [M]	For Dancing	1961	62.50	125.00	250.00
❑ LP-1027 [M]	'Twas the Night Before Christmas	1962	62.50	125.00	250.00
❑ LP-1027 [M]	'Twas the Night Before Christmas	198?	3.75	7.50	15.00
—Reissue with "Dr. John Band" credited on front cover and label					
❑ LP-2021	Rock 'n' Roll Revival	197?	7.50	15.00	30.00
❑ 2038	Good Old Rock & Roll	198?	3.75	7.50	15.00
GRAND PRIX					
❑ K-418 [M]	Huey "Piano" Smith	196?	5.00	10.00	20.00
❑ KS-418 [R]	Huey "Piano" Smith	196?	3.00	6.00	12.00
RHINO					
❑ RNLP-70222	Serious Clownin': The History of Huey "Piano" Smith and the Clowns	1986	3.00	6.00	12.00

SMITH, JIMMY

Number	Title (A Side/B Side)	Yr	VG	VG+	NM
45s					
BLUE NOTE					
❑ 1635	High and Mighty/You Get Cha	195?	3.00	6.00	12.00
❑ 1636	The Preacher/Midnight Sun	195?	3.00	6.00	12.00
❑ 1637	Tenderly/Joy	195?	3.00	6.00	12.00
❑ 1641	The Champ (Part 1)/The Champ (Part 2)	195?	3.00	6.00	12.00
❑ 1642	Bubbis/Bayou	195?	3.00	6.00	12.00
❑ 1643	Judo Mambo/Autumn Leaves	195?	3.00	6.00	12.00
❑ 1644	Willow Weep for Me/Fiddlin' the Minors	195?	3.00	6.00	12.00
❑ 1652	I Cover the Waterfront/I Can't Give You Anything	195?	3.00	6.00	12.00
❑ 1660	New Preacher (Part 1)/New Preacher (Part 2)	195?	3.00	6.00	12.00
❑ 1665	Where or When (Part 1)/Where or When (Part 2)	195?	3.00	6.00	12.00
❑ 1666	Love Is a Many-Splendored Thing (Part 1)/Love Is a Many-Splendored Thing (Part 2)	195?	3.00	6.00	12.00
❑ 1667	How High the Moon/Summertime	195?	3.00	6.00	12.00
❑ 1668	Plum Nellie/I'm Getting Sentimental	195?	3.00	6.00	12.00
❑ 1676	All Day Long (Part 1)/All Day Long (Part 2)	195?	3.00	6.00	12.00
❑ 1677	Funk's Oasis (Part 1)/Funk's Oasis (Part 2)	195?	3.00	6.00	12.00
❑ 1682	I Can't Get Started/Penthouse Serenade	195?	3.00	6.00	12.00
❑ 1683	East of the Sun/The Very Thought of You	195?	3.00	6.00	12.00
❑ 1685	Blue Moon (Part 1)/Blue Moon (Part 2)	195?	3.00	6.00	12.00
❑ 1686	There'll Never Be Another You/Jitterbug Waltz	195?	3.00	6.00	12.00
❑ 1703	After Hours (Part 1)/After Hours (Part 2)	195?	3.00	6.00	12.00
❑ 1704	Just Friends/Lover Man	195?	3.00	6.00	12.00
❑ 1711	The Swingin' Shepherd Blues/Cha Cha J.	195?	3.00	6.00	12.00
❑ 1727	Ain't No Use/Angel Eyes	195?	3.00	6.00	12.00
—With Bill Henderson					
❑ 1728	Ain't That Love/Willow Weep for Me	195?	3.00	6.00	12.00
—With Bill Henderson					
❑ 1765	Makin' Whoopee/What's New	196?	2.50	5.00	10.00
❑ 1766	Mack the Knife/When Johnny Comes Marching Home	196?	2.50	5.00	10.00
❑ 1767	Alfredo/I Got a Woman	196?	2.50	5.00	10.00
❑ 1768	Come On Baby/See See Rider	196?	2.50	5.00	10.00
❑ 1769	Since I Fell for You/Motorin' Along	196?	2.50	5.00	10.00
—With Kenny Burrell					
❑ 1819	Midnight Special (Part 1)/Midnight Special (Part 2)	1962	2.50	5.00	10.00
❑ 1820	Jumpin' the Blues/One O'Clock Blues	1962	2.50	5.00	10.00
❑ 1851	Ain't She Sweet/Everybody Loves My Baby	1962	2.50	5.00	10.00
❑ 1852	Honeysuckle Rose/Lulu's Back in Town	1962	2.50	5.00	10.00
❑ 1877	Back at the Chicken Shack (Part 1)/Back at the Chicken Shack (Part 2)	1963	2.50	5.00	10.00
❑ 1878	Minor Chant (Part 1)/Minor Chant (Part 2)	1963	2.50	5.00	10.00
❑ 1879	Sermon (Part 1)/Sermon (Part 2)	1963	2.50	5.00	10.00
❑ 1904	When My Dreamboat Comes Home (Part 1)/ When My Dreamboat Comes Home (Part 2)	1964	2.50	5.00	10.00
❑ 1905	Matilda, Matilda/Can Heat	1964	2.50	5.00	10.00
❑ 1906	Pork Chop (Part 1)/Pork Chop (Part 2)	1964	2.50	5.00	10.00
❑ 1909	Prayer Meetin' (Part 1)/Prayer Meetin' (Part 2)	1964	2.50	5.00	10.00
❑ 1910	Red Top (Part 1)/Red Top (Part 2)	1964	2.50	5.00	10.00
❑ 1925	I Cover the Waterfront/I Can't Give You Anything But Love	1966	2.00	4.00	8.00
❑ 1927	Bucket!/Sassy Mae	1966	2.00	4.00	8.00
MERCURY					
❑ 73895	Can't Hide Love/No Place in Space	1977	—	2.00	4.00
❑ 73972	I've Got Love on My Mind/Side Mouthin'	1977	—	2.00	4.00
PRIDE					
❑ 7602	Groovin'/Why Can't We Live Together	1974	—	2.50	5.00
VERVE					
❑ CS6-5 [(5)]	Celebrity Scene: Jimmy Smith	1967	15.00	30.00	60.00
—Box set of five singles (10502-10506). Price includes box, all 5 singles, jukebox title strips, bio. Records are sometimes found by themselves, so they are also listed separately.					
❑ 10255	Walk on the Wild Side (Part 1)/Walk on the Wild Side (Part 2)	1962	2.00	4.00	8.00
❑ 10262	Ol' Man River/Bashin'	1962	2.00	4.00	8.00
❑ 10278	Step Right Up (Part 1)/Step Right Up (Part 2)	1963	2.00	4.00	8.00
❑ 10283	Hobo Flats (Part 1)/Hobo Flats (Part 2)	1963	2.00	4.00	8.00
❑ 10298	Blueberry Hill/Walk Right In	1963	2.00	4.00	8.00
❑ 10299	Theme from "Any Number Can Win"/What'd I Say	1963	2.00	4.00	8.00
❑ 10314	Who's Afraid of Virginia Woolf?/Who's Afraid of Virginia Woolf? (Part 2)	1964	2.00	4.00	8.00
❑ 10330	The Cat/Basin Street Blues	1964	2.00	4.00	8.00
❑ 10346	Goldfinger (Part 1)/Goldfinger (Part 2)	1965	2.00	4.00	8.00
❑ 10363	The Organ Grinder's Swing/I'll Close My Eyes	1965	2.00	4.00	8.00
—With Kenny Burrell and Grady Tate					
❑ 10382	Theme from "Where the Spies Are"/Slow Theme from "Where the Spies Are"	1966	2.00	4.00	8.00
❑ 10393	Got My Mojo Working (Part 1)/Got My Mojo Working (Part 2)	1966	2.00	4.00	8.00
❑ 10424	Who Do You Love (Part 1)/Who Do You Love (Part 2)	1966	2.00	4.00	8.00
❑ 10467	Cat in a Tree (Part 1)/Cat in a Tree (Part 2)	1966	2.00	4.00	8.00
❑ 10502 [DJ]	Walk on the Wild Side (Part 1)/Walk on the Wild Side (Part 2)	1967	2.50	5.00	10.00
❑ 10503 [DJ]	The Cat/Basin Street Blues	1967	2.50	5.00	10.00
❑ 10504 [DJ]	Got My Mojo Working (Part 1)/Got My Mojo Working (Part 2)	1967	2.50	5.00	10.00
❑ 10505 [DJ]	I'm Your Hoochie Coochie Man (Part 1)/I'm Your Hoochie Coochie Man (Part 2)	1967	2.50	5.00	10.00
❑ 10506 [DJ]	Cat in a Tree (Part 1)/Cat in a Tree (Part 2)	1967	2.50	5.00	10.00
❑ 10536	Respect/Funky Broadway	1967	2.00	4.00	8.00
❑ 10583	Chain of Fools (Part 1)/Chain of Fools (Part 2)	1968	2.00	4.00	8.00
❑ 10623	Mission: Impossible/Gentle Rain	1968	2.00	4.00	8.00
❑ 10652	Groove Drops/By the Time I Get to Phoenix	1970	—	3.00	6.00
❑ 10660	One Bad Apple/Theme from "The Night Visitor"	1971	—	3.00	6.00
❑ 10668	Jimmy Smith Is a Midnight Cowboy/Recession or Depression	1971	—	3.00	6.00
❑ 10672	For Everyone Under the Sun/Sag' Shootin' His Arrow	1972	—	3.00	6.00
❑ 10695	Lolita/Straight Ahead	1972	—	3.00	6.00
❑ 10724	And I Love You So/Ritual (Funky 5/4)	1973	—	3.00	6.00
Albums					
BLUE NOTE					
❑ BN-LA400-H2 [(2)]	Jimmy Smith	1975	3.75	7.50	15.00
❑ LT-992	Confirmation	1979	2.50	5.00	10.00
❑ LT-1054	Cool Blues	1980	2.50	5.00	10.00
❑ LT-1092	On the Sunny Side	1981	2.50	5.00	10.00
❑ BLP-1512 [M]	Jimmy Smith at the Organ, Vol. 1	1956	37.50	75.00	150.00
—"Deep groove" version (deep indentation under label on both sides)					
❑ BLP-1512 [M]	Jimmy Smith at the Organ, Vol. 1	1956	25.00	50.00	100.00
—Regular edition, Lexington Ave. address on label					
❑ BLP-1512 [M]	Jimmy Smith at the Organ, Vol. 1	1963	6.25	12.50	25.00
—With New York, USA address on label					
❑ BLP-1514 [M]	Jimmy Smith at the Organ, Vol. 2	1956	37.50	75.00	150.00
—"Deep groove" version (deep indentation under label on both sides)					
❑ BLP-1514 [M]	Jimmy Smith at the Organ, Vol. 2	1956	25.00	50.00	100.00
—Regular edition, Lexington Ave. address on label					
❑ BLP-1514 [M]	Jimmy Smith at the Organ, Vol. 2	1963	6.25	12.50	25.00
—With New York, USA address on label					
❑ BLP-1525 [M]	The Incredible Jimmy Smith at the Organ, Vol. 3	1956	37.50	75.00	150.00
—"Deep groove" version (deep indentation under label on both sides)					
❑ BLP-1525 [M]	The Incredible Jimmy Smith at the Organ, Vol. 3	1956	25.00	50.00	100.00
—Regular edition, Lexington Ave. address on label					
❑ BLP-1525 [M]	The Incredible Jimmy Smith at the Organ, Vol. 3	1963	6.25	12.50	25.00
—With New York, USA address on label					
❑ BLP-1528 [M]	The Incredible Jimmy Smith at Club Baby Grand, Wilmington, Delaware, Vol. 1	1956	37.50	75.00	150.00
—"Deep groove" version (deep indentation under label on both sides)					
❑ BLP-1528 [M]	The Incredible Jimmy Smith at Club Baby Grand, Wilmington, Delaware, Vol. 1	1956	25.00	50.00	100.00
—Regular edition, Lexington Ave. address on label					
❑ BLP-1528 [M]	The Incredible Jimmy Smith at Club Baby Grand, Wilmington, Delaware, Vol. 1	1963	6.25	12.50	25.00
—With New York, USA address on label					
❑ BLP-1529 [M]	The Incredible Jimmy Smith at Club Baby Grand, Wilmington, Delaware, Vol. 2	1956	37.50	75.00	150.00
—"Deep groove" version (deep indentation under label on both sides)					
❑ BLP-1529 [M]	The Incredible Jimmy Smith at Club Baby Grand, Wilmington, Delaware, Vol. 2	1956	25.00	50.00	100.00
—Regular edition, Lexington Ave. address on label					
❑ BLP-1529 [M]	The Incredible Jimmy Smith at Club Baby Grand, Wilmington, Delaware, Vol. 2	1963	6.25	12.50	25.00
—With New York, USA address on label					
❑ BLP-1547 [M]	A Date with Jimmy Smith, Vol. 1	1957	30.00	60.00	120.00
—"Deep groove" version (deep indentation under label on both sides)					
❑ BLP-1547 [M]	A Date with Jimmy Smith, Vol. 1	1957	20.00	40.00	80.00
—Regular edition, W. 63rd St. address on label					
❑ BLP-1547 [M]	A Date with Jimmy Smith, Vol. 1	1963	6.25	12.50	25.00
—With New York, USA address on label					
❑ BLP-1548 [M]	A Date with Jimmy Smith, Vol. 2	1957	30.00	60.00	120.00
—"Deep groove" version (deep indentation under label on both sides)					
❑ BLP-1548 [M]	A Date with Jimmy Smith, Vol. 2	1957	20.00	40.00	80.00
—Regular edition, W. 63rd St. address on label					
❑ BLP-1548 [M]	A Date with Jimmy Smith, Vol. 2	1963	6.25	12.50	25.00
—With New York, USA address on label					
❑ BLP-1551 [M]	Jimmy Smith at the Organ, Vol. 1	1957	30.00	60.00	120.00
—"Deep groove" version (deep indentation under label on both sides)					
❑ BLP-1551 [M]	Jimmy Smith at the Organ, Vol. 1	1957	20.00	40.00	80.00
—Regular edition, W. 63rd St. address on label					
❑ BLP-1551 [M]	Jimmy Smith at the Organ, Vol. 1	1963	6.25	12.50	25.00
—With New York, USA address on label					
❑ BLP-1552 [M]	Jimmy Smith at the Organ, Vol. 2	1957	30.00	60.00	120.00
—"Deep groove" version (deep indentation under label on both sides)					
❑ BLP-1552 [M]	Jimmy Smith at the Organ, Vol. 2	1957	20.00	40.00	80.00
—Regular edition, W. 63rd St. address on label					
❑ BLP-1552 [M]	Jimmy Smith at the Organ, Vol. 2	1963	6.25	12.50	25.00
—With New York, USA address on label					
❑ BLP-1556 [M]	The Sounds of Jimmy Smith	1957	30.00	60.00	120.00
—"Deep groove" version (deep indentation under label on both sides)					
❑ BLP-1556 [M]	The Sounds of Jimmy Smith	1957	20.00	40.00	80.00
—Regular edition, W. 63rd St. address on label					

Number	Title (A Side/B Side)	Yr	VG	VG+	NM
❑ BLP-1556 [M]	The Sounds of Jimmy Smith	1963	6.25	12.50	25.00
—With New York, USA address on label					
❑ BLP-1563 [M]	Jimmy Smith Plays Pretty Just for You	1957	30.00	60.00	120.00
—"Deep groove" version (deep indentation under label on both sides)					
❑ BLP-1563 [M]	Jimmy Smith Plays Pretty Just for You	1957	20.00	40.00	80.00
—Regular edition, W. 63rd St. address on label					
❑ BLP-1563 [M]	Jimmy Smith Plays Pretty Just for You	1963	6.25	12.50	25.00
—With New York, USA address on label					
❑ BST-1563 [S]	Jimmy Smith Plays Pretty Just for You	1959	20.00	40.00	80.00
—"Deep groove" version (deep indentation under label on both sides)					
❑ BST-1563 [S]	Jimmy Smith Plays Pretty Just for You	1959	12.50	25.00	50.00
—Regular edition, W. 63rd St. address on label					
❑ BST-1563 [S]	Jimmy Smith Plays Pretty Just for You	1963	5.00	10.00	20.00
—With New York, USA address on label					
❑ BLP-1585 [M]	Groovin' at Small's Paradise, Vol. 1	1958	30.00	60.00	120.00
—"Deep groove" version (deep indentation under label on both sides)					
❑ BLP-1585 [M]	Groovin' at Small's Paradise, Vol. 1	1958	20.00	40.00	80.00
—Regular edition, W. 63rd St. address on label					
❑ BLP-1585 [M]	Groovin' at Small's Paradise, Vol. 1	1963	6.25	12.50	25.00
—With New York, USA address on label					
❑ BST-1585 [S]	Groovin' at Small's Paradise, Vol. 1	1959	20.00	40.00	80.00
—"Deep groove" version (deep indentation under label on both sides)					
❑ BST-1585 [S]	Groovin' at Small's Paradise, Vol. 1	1959	12.50	25.00	50.00
—Regular edition, W. 63rd St. address on label					
❑ BST-1585 [S]	Groovin' at Small's Paradise, Vol. 1	1963	5.00	10.00	20.00
—With New York, USA address on label					
❑ BLP-1586 [M]	Groovin' at Small's Paradise, Vol. 2	1958	30.00	60.00	120.00
—"Deep groove" version (deep indentation under label on both sides)					
❑ BLP-1586 [M]	Groovin' at Small's Paradise, Vol. 2	1958	20.00	40.00	80.00
—Regular edition, W. 63rd St. address on label					
❑ BLP-1586 [M]	Groovin' at Small's Paradise, Vol. 2	1963	6.25	12.50	25.00
—With New York, USA address on label					
❑ BST-1586 [S]	Groovin' at Small's Paradise, Vol. 2	1959	20.00	40.00	80.00
—"Deep groove" version (deep indentation under label on both sides)					
❑ BST-1586 [S]	Groovin' at Small's Paradise, Vol. 2	1959	12.50	25.00	50.00
—Regular edition, W. 63rd St. address on label					
❑ BST-1586 [S]	Groovin' at Small's Paradise, Vol. 2	1963	5.00	10.00	20.00
—With New York, USA address on label					
❑ BLP-4002 [M]	House Party	1959	30.00	60.00	120.00
—"Deep groove" version (deep indentation under label on both sides)					
❑ BLP-4002 [M]	House Party	1959	20.00	40.00	80.00
—Regular edition, W. 63rd St. address on label					
❑ BLP-4002 [M]	House Party	1963	6.25	12.50	25.00
—With New York, USA address on label					
❑ BST-4002 [S]	House Party	1959	20.00	40.00	80.00
—"Deep groove" version (deep indentation under label on both sides)					
❑ BST-4002 [S]	House Party	1959	12.50	25.00	50.00
—Regular edition, W. 63rd St. address on label					
❑ BST-4002 [S]	House Party	1963	5.00	10.00	20.00
—With New York, USA address on label					
❑ BLP-4011 [M]	The Sermon	1959	30.00	60.00	120.00
—"Deep groove" version (deep indentation under label on both sides)					
❑ BLP-4011 [M]	The Sermon	1959	20.00	40.00	80.00
—Regular edition, W. 63rd St. address on label					
❑ BLP-4011 [M]	The Sermon	1963	6.25	12.50	25.00
—With New York, USA address on label					
❑ BST-4011 [S]	The Sermon	1959	20.00	40.00	80.00
—"Deep groove" version (deep indentation under label on both sides)					
❑ BST-4011 [S]	The Sermon	1959	12.50	25.00	50.00
—Regular edition, W. 63rd St. address on label					
❑ BST-4011 [S]	The Sermon	1963	5.00	10.00	20.00
—With New York, USA address on label					
❑ BLP-4030 [M]	Crazy Baby	1960	30.00	60.00	120.00
—"Deep groove" version (deep indentation under label on both sides)					
❑ BLP-4030 [M]	Crazy Baby	1960	20.00	40.00	80.00
—Regular edition, W. 63rd St. address on label					
❑ BLP-4030 [M]	Crazy Baby	1963	6.25	12.50	25.00
—With New York, USA address on label					
❑ BLP-4050 [M]	Home Cookin'	1961	12.50	25.00	50.00
—With W. 63rd St. address on label					
❑ BLP-4050 [M]	Home Cookin'	1963	5.00	10.00	20.00
—With New York, USA address on label					
❑ BLP-4078 [M]	Midnight Special	1961	12.50	25.00	50.00
—With 61st St. address on label					
❑ BLP-4078 [M]	Midnight Special	1963	5.00	10.00	20.00
—With New York, USA address on label					
❑ BLP-4100 [M]	Jimmy Smith Plays Fats Waller	1962	12.50	25.00	50.00
—With 61st St. address on label					
❑ BLP-4100 [M]	Jimmy Smith Plays Fats Waller	1963	5.00	10.00	20.00
—With New York, USA address on label					
❑ BLP-4117 [M]	Back at the Chicken Shack	1963	6.25	12.50	25.00
❑ BLP-4141 [M]	Rockin' the Boat	1963	6.25	12.50	25.00
❑ BLP-4164 [M]	Prayer Meetin'	1964	6.25	12.50	25.00
❑ BLP-4200 [M]	Softly as a Summer Breeze	1965	6.25	12.50	25.00
❑ BLP-4235 [M]	Bucket!	1966	6.25	12.50	25.00
❑ BLP-4255 [M]	I'm Movin' On	1967	7.50	15.00	30.00
❑ BST-81512 [R]	Jimmy Smith at the Organ, Vol. 1	1967	3.00	6.00	12.00
❑ BST-81514 [R]	Jimmy Smith at the Organ, Vol. 2	1967	3.00	6.00	12.00
❑ BST-81525 [R]	The Incredible Jimmy Smith at the Organ, Vol. 3	1967	3.00	6.00	12.00
❑ BST-81528 [R]	The Incredible Jimmy Smith at Club Baby Grand, Wilmington, Delaware, Vol. 1	1967	3.00	6.00	12.00
❑ BST-81529 [R]	The Incredible Jimmy Smith at Club Baby Grand, Wilmington, Delaware, Vol. 2	1967	3.00	6.00	12.00
❑ BST-81547 [R]	A Date with Jimmy Smith, Vol. 1	1967	3.00	6.00	12.00
❑ BST-81548 [R]	A Date with Jimmy Smith, Vol. 2	1967	3.00	6.00	12.00
❑ BST-81551 [R]	Jimmy Smith at the Organ, Vol. 1	1967	3.00	6.00	12.00
❑ BST-81552 [R]	Jimmy Smith at the Organ, Vol. 2	1967	3.00	6.00	12.00

Number	Title (A Side/B Side)	Yr	VG	VG+	NM
❑ BST-81556 [R]	The Sounds of Jimmy Smith	1967	3.00	6.00	12.00
❑ BST-81563 [S]	Jimmy Smith Plays Pretty Just for You	1967	3.75	7.50	15.00
❑ BST-81585 [S]	Groovin' at Small's Paradise, Vol. 1	1967	3.75	7.50	15.00
❑ BST-81586 [S]	Groovin' at Small's Paradise, Vol. 1	1967	3.75	7.50	15.00
❑ BST-84002	House Party	1985	2.50	5.00	10.00
—"The Finest in Jazz Since 1939" reissue					
❑ BST-84002 [S]	House Party	1967	3.75	7.50	15.00
❑ BST-84011 [S]	The Sermon	1967	3.75	7.50	15.00
❑ B1-84030	Crazy Baby	1988	2.50	5.00	10.00
—"The Finest in Jazz Since 1939" reissue					
❑ BST-84030 [S]	Crazy Baby	1960	12.50	25.00	50.00
—With W. 63rd St. address on label					
❑ BST-84030 [S]	Crazy Baby	1963	5.00	10.00	20.00
—With New York, USA address on label					
❑ BST-84030 [S]	Crazy Baby	1967	3.75	7.50	15.00
—With "A Division of Liberty Records" on label					
❑ BST-84050 [S]	Home Cookin'	1961	12.50	25.00	50.00
—With W. 63rd St. address on label					
❑ BST-84050 [S]	Home Cookin'	1963	5.00	10.00	20.00
—With New York, USA address on label					
❑ BST-84050 [S]	Home Cookin'	1967	3.75	7.50	15.00
—With "A Division of Liberty Records" on label					
❑ B1-84078	Midnight Special	1989	2.50	5.00	10.00
—"The Finest in Jazz Since 1939" reissue					
❑ BST-84078 [S]	Midnight Special	1961	12.50	25.00	50.00
—With 61st St. address on label					
❑ BST-84078 [S]	Midnight Special	1963	5.00	10.00	20.00
—With New York, USA address on label					
❑ BST-84078 [S]	Midnight Special	1967	3.75	7.50	15.00
—With "A Division of Liberty Records" on label					
❑ BST-84100 [S]	Jimmy Smith Plays Fats Waller	1962	12.50	25.00	50.00
—With 61st St. address on label					
❑ BST-84100 [S]	Jimmy Smith Plays Fats Waller	1963	5.00	10.00	20.00
—With New York, USA address on label					
❑ BST-84100 [S]	Jimmy Smith Plays Fats Waller	1967	3.75	7.50	15.00
—With "A Division of Liberty Records" on label					
❑ BST-84117	Back at the Chicken Shack	1985	2.50	5.00	10.00
—"The Finest in Jazz Since 1939" reissue					
❑ BST-84117 [S]	Back at the Chicken Shack	1963	7.50	15.00	30.00
—With New York, USA address on label					
❑ BST-84117 [S]	Back at the Chicken Shack	1967	3.75	7.50	15.00
—With "A Division of Liberty Records" on label					
❑ BST-84141 [S]	Rockin' the Boat	1963	7.50	15.00	30.00
—With New York, USA address on label					
❑ BST-84141 [S]	Rockin' the Boat	1967	3.75	7.50	15.00
—With "A Division of Liberty Records" on label					
❑ B1-84164	Prayer Meetin'	1988	2.50	5.00	10.00
—"The Finest in Jazz Since 1939" reissue					
❑ BST-84164 [S]	Prayer Meetin'	1964	7.50	15.00	30.00
—With New York, USA address on label					
❑ BST-84164 [S]	Prayer Meetin'	1967	3.75	7.50	15.00
—With "A Division of Liberty Records" on label					
❑ BST-84200 [S]	Softly as a Summer Breeze	1965	7.50	15.00	30.00
—With New York, USA address on label					
❑ BST-84200 [S]	Softly as a Summer Breeze	1967	3.75	7.50	15.00
—With "A Division of Liberty Records" on label					
❑ BST-84235 [S]	Bucket!	1966	7.50	15.00	30.00
—With New York, USA address on label					
❑ BST-84235 [S]	Bucket!	1967	3.75	7.50	15.00
—With "A Division of Liberty Records" on label					
❑ BST-84255 [S]	I'm Movin' On	1967	5.00	10.00	20.00
❑ BST-84269	Open House	1968	5.00	10.00	20.00
❑ BST-84296	Plain Talk	1969	5.00	10.00	20.00
❑ B1-85125	Go For Whatcha Know	198?	2.50	5.00	10.00
❑ BST-89901 [(2)]	Jimmy Smith's Greatest Hits!	1969	6.25	12.50	25.00
❑ B1-91140	The Best of Jimmy Smith	1988	2.50	5.00	10.00
ELEKTRA MUSICIAN					
❑ 60175	Off the Top	1983	2.50	5.00	10.00
❑ 60301	Keep On Comin'	1984	2.50	5.00	10.00
GUEST STAR					
❑ 1344 [M]	Jimmy Smith	196?	3.00	6.00	12.00
❑ G 1914 [M]	Jimmy Smith	196?	3.00	6.00	12.00
INNER CITY					
❑ 1121	The Cat Strikes Again	1981	2.50	5.00	10.00
MERCURY					
❑ SRM-1-1127	Sit On It!	1976	2.50	5.00	10.00
❑ SRM-1-1189	It's Necessary	1977	2.50	5.00	10.00
❑ SRM-1-3716	Unfinished Business	1978	2.50	5.00	10.00
METRO					
❑ M-521 [M]	Jimmy Smith at the Village Gate	1965	3.00	6.00	12.00
❑ MS-521 [S]	Jimmy Smith at the Village Gate	1965	3.00	6.00	12.00
MGM					
❑ GAS-107	Jimmy Smith (Golden Archive Series)	1970	3.75	7.50	15.00
❑ SE-4709	The Other Side	1970	3.00	6.00	12.00
❑ SE-4751	I'm Gon' Git Myself Together	1971	3.00	6.00	12.00
MILESTONE					
❑ M-9176	Prime Time	198?	2.50	5.00	10.00
MOSAIC					
❑ MQ5-154 [(5)]	The Complete February 1957 Jimmy Smith Blue Note Sessions	199?	20.00	40.00	80.00
PICKWICK					
❑ SPC-3023	Stranger in Paradise	196?	2.50	5.00	10.00
PRIDE					
❑ 6011	Black Smith	1974	3.00	6.00	12.00

Number	Title (A Side/B Side)	Yr	VG	VG+	NM

SUNSET

Number	Title (A Side/B Side)	Yr	VG	VG+	NM
❑ SUM-1175 [M]	Jimmy Smith Plays the Standards	1967	3.75	7.50	15.00
❑ SUS-5175 [S]	Jimmy Smith Plays the Standards	1967	3.00	6.00	12.00
❑ SUS-5316	Just Friends	1971	3.00	6.00	12.00

VERVE

Number	Title (A Side/B Side)	Yr	VG	VG+	NM
❑ V6-652-2 [(2)]	24 Karat Hits	196?	3.75	7.50	15.00
❑ UMV-2073	Organ Grinder Swing	198?	2.50	5.00	10.00
—Reissue of 8628					
❑ V-8474 [M]	Bashin'	1962	5.00	10.00	20.00
❑ V6-8474 [S]	Bashin'	1962	6.25	12.50	25.00
❑ V-8544 [M]	Hobo Flats	1963	5.00	10.00	20.00
❑ V6-8544 [S]	Hobo Flats	1963	6.25	12.50	25.00
❑ V-8552 [M]	Any Number Can Win	1963	5.00	10.00	20.00
❑ V6-8552 [S]	Any Number Can Win	1963	6.25	12.50	25.00
❑ V-8583 [M]	Who's Afraid of Virginia Woolf?	1964	5.00	10.00	20.00
❑ V6-8583 [S]	Who's Afraid of Virginia Woolf?	1964	6.25	12.50	25.00
❑ V-8587 [M]	The Cat	1964	5.00	10.00	20.00
❑ V6-8587 [S]	The Cat	1964	6.25	12.50	25.00
❑ V-8604 [M]	Christmas '64	1964	5.00	10.00	20.00
❑ V6-8604 [S]	Christmas '64	1964	6.25	12.50	25.00
❑ V-8618 [M]	The Monster	1965	3.75	7.50	15.00
❑ V6-8618 [S]	The Monster	1965	5.00	10.00	20.00
❑ V-8628 [M]	Organ Grinder Swing	1965	3.75	7.50	15.00
❑ V6-8628 [S]	Organ Grinder Swing	1965	5.00	10.00	20.00
❑ V-8641 [M]	Got My Mojo Workin'	1966	3.75	7.50	15.00
❑ V6-8641 [S]	Got My Mojo Workin'	1966	5.00	10.00	20.00
❑ V-8652 [M]	Peter and the Wolf	1966	5.00	10.00	20.00
❑ V6-8652 [S]	Peter and the Wolf	1966	6.25	12.50	25.00
❑ V-8666 [M]	Christmas Cookin'	1966	5.00	10.00	20.00
❑ V6-8666 [S]	Christmas Cookin'	1966	6.25	12.50	25.00
❑ V-8667 [M]	Hoochie Coochie Man	1966	3.75	7.50	15.00
❑ V6-8667 [S]	Hoochie Coochie Man	1966	5.00	10.00	20.00
❑ V-8705 [M]	Respect	1967	5.00	10.00	20.00
❑ V6-8705 [S]	Respect	1967	3.75	7.50	15.00
❑ V-8721 [M]	The Best of Jimmy Smith	1967	5.00	10.00	20.00
❑ V6-8721 [S]	The Best of Jimmy Smith	1967	3.75	7.50	15.00
❑ V6-8745 [S]	Stay Loose	1968	3.75	7.50	15.00
❑ V6-8750	Livin' It Up!	1968	3.75	7.50	15.00
❑ V6-8770	The Boss	1969	3.75	7.50	15.00
❑ V6-8794	Groove Drops	1970	3.75	7.50	15.00
❑ V6-8800	Plain Brown Wrapper	1971	3.00	6.00	12.00
❑ V6-8806	Root Down	1972	3.00	6.00	12.00
❑ V6-8809	Bluesmith	1973	3.00	6.00	12.00
❑ V6-8814 [(2)]	History of Jimmy Smith	1973	3.75	7.50	15.00
❑ V6-8832	Portuguese Soul	1974	3.00	6.00	12.00
❑ SMAS-90643 [S]	The Monster	1965	6.25	12.50	25.00
—Capitol Record Club edition					
❑ 823308-1	Bashin'	1986	2.50	5.00	10.00
—Reissue of 8474					

SMITH, JIMMY, AND WES MONTGOMERY
Albums

VERVE

Number	Title (A Side/B Side)	Yr	VG	VG+	NM
❑ UMV-2069	Jimmy and Wes, The Dynamic Duo	198?	2.50	5.00	10.00
—Reissue of 8678					
❑ V-8678 [M]	Jimmy and Wes, The Dynamic Duo	1967	5.00	10.00	20.00
❑ V6-8678 [S]	Jimmy and Wes, The Dynamic Duo	1967	3.75	7.50	15.00
❑ V6-8766	The Further Adventures of Jimmy Smith and Wes Montgomery	1969	3.75	7.50	15.00

SMITH, O.C.
45s

BIG TOP

Number	Title (A Side/B Side)	Yr	VG	VG+	NM
❑ 3039	You Are My Sunshine/Well I'm Dancin'	1960	3.00	6.00	12.00
—As "Ocie Smith"					

CADENCE

Number	Title (A Side/B Side)	Yr	VG	VG+	NM
❑ 1304	Slow Walk/Forbidden Fruit	1956	3.75	7.50	15.00
—As "Ocie Smith"					
❑ 1312	If You Don't Love Me/Bad Man of Missouri	1957	3.75	7.50	15.00
—As "Ocie Smith"					
❑ 1329	Lighthouse/Too Many	1957	3.75	7.50	15.00
—As "Ocie Smith"					

CARIBOU

Number	Title (A Side/B Side)	Yr	VG	VG+	NM
❑ 9017	Together/Just Couldn't Help Myself	1976	—	2.50	5.00
❑ 9021	Simple Wife/Come with Me	1977	—	2.50	5.00

COLUMBIA

Number	Title (A Side/B Side)	Yr	VG	VG+	NM
❑ 10031	La La Peace Song/When Morning Comes	1974	—	2.50	5.00
❑ 43525	That's Life/I'm Your Man	1966	2.00	4.00	8.00
❑ 43809	Beyond the Next Hill/On Easy Street	1966	2.00	4.00	8.00
❑ 44151	Double Life/The Season	1967	2.00	4.00	8.00
❑ 44425	The Son of Hickory Holler's Tramp/The Best Man	1968	2.00	4.00	8.00
❑ 44555	Main Street Mission/Gas Food Lodging	1968	2.00	4.00	8.00
❑ 44616	Little Green Apples/Long Black Limousine	1968	2.00	4.00	8.00
❑ 44705	Isn't It Lonely Together/I Ain't the Worryin' Kind	1968	—	3.00	6.00
❑ 44751	Honey (I Miss You)/Keep On Keepin' On	1969	—	3.00	6.00
❑ 44859	Friend, Lover, Woman, Wife/I Taught Her Everything She Knows	1969	—	3.00	6.00
❑ 44948	Daddy's Little Man/If I Leave You Now	1969	—	3.00	6.00
❑ 44948 [PS]	Daddy's Little Man/If I Leave You Now	1969	2.00	4.00	8.00
❑ 45038	Me and You/Can't Take My Eyes Off You	1969	—	3.00	6.00
❑ 45098	Isn't Life Beautiful/Moody	1970	—	3.00	6.00
❑ 45160	Primrose Lane/Melodee	1970	—	3.00	6.00
❑ 45206	Baby I Need Your Loving/San Francisco Is a Lonely Town	1970	—	3.00	6.00
❑ 45301	Downtown U.S.A./That's What Life Is All About	1971	—	3.00	6.00

Number	Title (A Side/B Side)	Yr	VG	VG+	NM
❑ 45343	Clean Up Your Own Back Yard/I've Been There	1971	—	3.00	6.00
❑ 45435	Help Me Make It Through the Night/Diamond in the Rough	1971	—	3.00	6.00
❑ 45655	Don't Misunderstand/If You Touch Me	1972	—	3.00	6.00
❑ 45863	La La Peace Song/When Morning Comes	1973	—	3.00	6.00

FAMILY

Number	Title (A Side/B Side)	Yr	VG	VG+	NM
❑ 5000	Dreams Come True/(B-side unknown)	1980	—	2.50	5.00

MGM

Number	Title (A Side/B Side)	Yr	VG	VG+	NM
❑ 12321	Just Kiss Me/At Last My Baby's Coming Home	1956	3.75	7.50	15.00
—As "Ocie Smith"					

MOTOWN

Number	Title (A Side/B Side)	Yr	VG	VG+	NM
❑ 1623	Love Changes/Got to Know	1982	—	2.50	5.00
❑ 1636	I Betcha/That's One for Love	1982	—	2.50	5.00

RENDEZVOUS

Number	Title (A Side/B Side)	Yr	VG	VG+	NM
❑ 101	What'cha Gonna Do/(B-side unknown)	1986	—	2.00	4.00
❑ 102	You're the First, the Last, My Everything/(B-side unknown)	1986	—	2.00	4.00
❑ 103	Brenda/(B-side unknown)	1986	—	2.00	4.00

SHADY BROOK

Number	Title (A Side/B Side)	Yr	VG	VG+	NM
❑ 1045	Love to Burn/Give Me Time	1978	—	2.50	5.00
❑ 1049	Living Without Your Love/Can't Be the One to Say It's Over	1978	—	2.50	5.00
❑ 45012	Love Is Forever/(B-side unknown)	197?	—	2.50	5.00

SOUTH BAY

Number	Title (A Side/B Side)	Yr	VG	VG+	NM
❑ 1003	Love Changes/Got to Know	1982	—	3.00	6.00

7-Inch Extended Plays

COLUMBIA

Number	Title (A Side/B Side)	Yr	VG	VG+	NM
❑ 7-9680	The Son of Hickory Holler's Tramp/Little Green Apples//By the Time I Get to Phoenix/Sitting on the Dock of the Bay	1968	3.00	6.00	12.00
—Jukebox issue; small hole, plays at 33 1/3 rpm					
❑ 7-9680 [PS]	Hickory Holler Revisited	1968	3.00	6.00	12.00

Albums

CARIBOU

Number	Title (A Side/B Side)	Yr	VG	VG+	NM
❑ PZ 34471	Together	1977	2.50	5.00	10.00

COLUMBIA

Number	Title (A Side/B Side)	Yr	VG	VG+	NM
❑ CL 2714 [M]	The Dynamic O.C. Smith	1967	5.00	10.00	20.00
❑ CS 9514 [S]	The Dynamic O.C. Smith	1967	3.75	7.50	15.00
❑ CS 9680 [M]	Hickory Holler Revisited	1968	6.25	12.50	25.00
—White label promo "Special Mono Radio Station Copy" with stereo number					
❑ CS 9680 [S]	Hickory Holler Revisited	1968	3.00	6.00	12.00
❑ CS 9756	For Once in My Life	1969	3.00	6.00	12.00
❑ CS 9908	O.C. Smith at Home	1969	3.00	6.00	12.00
❑ C 30227	O.C. Smith's Greatest Hits	1970	3.00	6.00	12.00
❑ C 30664	Help Me Make It Through the Night	1971	3.00	6.00	12.00
❑ KC 33247	La La Peace Song	1974	2.50	5.00	10.00

HARMONY

Number	Title (A Side/B Side)	Yr	VG	VG+	NM
❑ KH 30317	O.C. Smith	1971	2.50	5.00	10.00

MOTOWN

Number	Title (A Side/B Side)	Yr	VG	VG+	NM
❑ 6019 ML	Love Changes	1982	2.50	5.00	10.00

SHADYBROOK

Number	Title (A Side/B Side)	Yr	VG	VG+	NM
❑ 012	Love	1978	2.50	5.00	10.00

SMITH, OCIE
See O.C. SMITH.

SMITH, WILL
Also see JAZZY JEFF AND FRESH PRINCE.

12-Inch Singles

COLUMBIA

Number	Title (A Side/B Side)	Yr	VG	VG+	NM
❑ CAS 0786 [DJ]	Men in Black (Album Version) (Track Masters Instrumental) (Track Masters Acappella)/(MIB Master Mix) (MIB Alternate Mix) (MIB Instrumental)	1997	—	3.50	7.00
❑ CAS 3128 [DJ]	Just Cruisin' (Radio Edit) (Instrumental) (Acappella) (LP Version)	1997	2.00	4.00	8.00
❑ CAS 40827 [DJ]	Wild Wild West (4 versions)	1999	—	3.00	6.00
❑ CAS 41314 [DJ]	Miami (LP Version) (Instrumental)	1998	2.50	5.00	10.00
❑ CAS 47133 [DJ]	So Fresh (LP Version) (Instrumental) (Acappella)	1999	2.50	5.00	10.00
—Featuring Biz Markie and Slick Rick					
❑ CAS 48757 [DJ]	Freakin' It (3 versions)	1999	3.00	6.00	12.00
❑ CAS 59867 [DJ]	Black Suits Comin' (Nod Ya Head) (6 versions)	2002	3.00	6.00	12.00
❑ 44-79038	Just the Two of Us (Radio Edit) (Rodney Jenkins Remix Featuring Brian McKnight) (Spanish Version Featuring DLG)/(Korean Version Featuring Turbo) (Instrumental)	1998	—	3.50	7.00
❑ 44-79287	Will 2K (Album Version) (Instrumental) (A Cappella)	1999	—	3.50	7.00
❑ 44-79341	Freakin' It (4 versions)/Pump Me Up	1999	—	3.50	7.00

INTERSCOPE

Number	Title (A Side/B Side)	Yr	VG	VG+	NM
❑ INT8P-6610 [DJ]	Wild Wild West (Album Version) (Instrumental)/(same on both sides)	1999	2.00	4.00	8.00

45s

COLUMBIA

Number	Title (A Side/B Side)	Yr	VG	VG+	NM
❑ 38-78804	Gettin' Jiggy Wit It/Men in Black	1998	—	—	2.00
❑ 38-78804 [PS]	Gettin' Jiggy Wit It/Men in Black	1998	—	—	2.00
❑ 38-79286	Will 2K/(Instrumental)	1999	—	—	3.00

Albums

COLUMBIA

Number	Title (A Side/B Side)	Yr	VG	VG+	NM
❑ C2 68683 [(2)]	Big Willie Style	1997	3.75	7.50	15.00
❑ C2 69985 [(2)]	Willennium	1999	3.75	7.50	15.00
❑ C2 86189 [(2)]	Born to Reign	2002	3.75	7.50	15.00

S

Number	Title (A Side/B Side)	Yr	VG	VG+	NM

SOF-TONES, THE
45s
CEE BEE

❏ 1062	Oh Why//(B-side unknown)	195?	4000.	6000.	8000.

SOLDIER BOYS, THE
Also see DON COVAY.
45s
SCEPTER

❏ 1230	I'm Your Soldier Boy/You Picked Me	1962	15.00	30.00	60.00

SOLITAIRES, THE
Probably more than one group.
45s
ARGO

❏ 5316	Walking Along/Please Kiss This Letter	1958	7.50	15.00	30.00
MGM					
❏ 13221	Fool That I Am/Fair Weather Lover	1964	7.50	15.00	30.00
OLD TOWN					
❏ 1000	Blue Valentine/Wonder Boy	1954	100.00	200.00	400.00
—Black vinyl					
❏ 1000	Blue Valentine/Wonder Boy	1954	375.00	750.00	1500.
—Red vinyl					
❏ 1003	Chapel of St. Clair/If I Loved You	1954	—	—	—
—Unreleased?					
❏ 1006/7	Please Remember My Heart/South of the Border	1954	175.00	350.00	700.00
—Black vinyl					
❏ 1006/7	Please Remember My Heart/South of the Border	1954	1000.	2000.	3000.
—Red vinyl					
❏ 1006/8	Please Remember My Heart/Chances I've Taken	1954	37.50	75.00	150.00
❏ 1008	Chances I've Taken/Lonely	1954	175.00	350.00	700.00
❏ 1008	Please Remember My Heart/Chances I've Taken	196?	6.25	12.50	25.00
—Blue label					
❏ 1010	I Don't Stand a Ghost of a Chance/Girl of Mine	1955	125.00	250.00	500.00
❏ 1012	My Dear/What Did She Say	1955	100.00	200.00	400.00
—Logo in Old English style					
❏ 1012	My Dear/What Did She Say	1956	18.75	37.50	75.00
—Logo in block letters					
❏ 1014	The Wedding/Don't Fall in Love	1955	25.00	50.00	100.00
❏ 1015	Magic Rose/Later for You Baby	1955	25.00	50.00	100.00
❏ 1019	The Honeymoon/Fine Little Girl	1956	25.00	50.00	100.00
❏ 1026	You've Sinned/The Angels Sang	1956	25.00	50.00	100.00
❏ 1026	You've Sinned/You're Back with Me	1956	75.00	150.00	300.00
❏ 1032	Give Me One More Chance/Nothing Like a Little Love	1956	50.00	100.00	200.00
❏ 1034	Walking Along/Please Kiss This Letter	1957	18.75	37.50	75.00
—Yellow label					
❏ 1034	Walking Along/Please Kiss This Letter	196?	6.25	12.50	25.00
—Blue label					
❏ 1044	I Really Love You So/Thrill of Love	1957	100.00	200.00	400.00
❏ 1049	Walkin' and Talkin'/No More Sorrows	1958	25.00	50.00	100.00
❏ 1059	Please Remember My Heart/Big Mary's House	1958	10.00	20.00	40.00
❏ 1066	Embraceable You/Round Goes My Heart	1959	10.00	20.00	40.00
❏ 1071	Light a Candle in the Chapel/Helpless	1959	10.00	20.00	40.00
❏ 1096	Lonesome Lover/Pretty Thing	1961	10.00	20.00	40.00
❏ 1139	The Time Is Here/Honey Babe	1963	7.50	15.00	30.00

SONICS, THE (1)
Male vocal group.
45s
AMCO

❏ 001	It's You/Preacher Man	1962	50.00	100.00	200.00
CHECKER					
❏ 922	This Broken Heart/You Made Me Cry	1959	6.25	12.50	25.00
HARVARD					
❏ 801	This Broken Heart/You Made Me Cry	1959	100.00	200.00	400.00
❏ 922	This Broken Heart/You Made Me Cry	1959	12.50	25.00	50.00
JAMIE					
❏ 1235	Sugaree/Beautiful Brown Eyes	1962	5.00	10.00	20.00
X-TRA					
❏ 107	Once in a Lifetime/It Ain't True	1958	500.00	1000.	2000.

SONNETS, THE
45s
GUYDEN

❏ 2112	I Can't Get Sentimental/Forever for You	1964	3.75	7.50	15.00
HERALD					
❏ 477	Please Won't You Call Me/Why Should We Break Up	1956	15.00	30.00	60.00

SOUL, JIMMY
45s
20TH FOX

❏ 413	Respectable/I Wish I Could Dance	1963	2.50	5.00	10.00
SPQR					
❏ 3221	My Little Room/Ella Is Yella	1964	2.50	5.00	10.00
❏ 3300	Twistin' Matilda/I Can't Hold Out Any Longer	1962	3.00	6.00	12.00
❏ 3302	When Matilda Comes Back/Some Kinda Nut	1962	3.00	6.00	12.00
❏ 3304	Guess Things Happen That Way/My Baby Loves to Bowl	1963	3.00	6.00	12.00
❏ 3305	If You Wanna Be Happy/Don't Release Me	1963	3.75	7.50	15.00
❏ 3305 [PS]	If You Wanna Be Happy/Don't Release Me	1963	7.50	15.00	30.00
❏ 3310	Treat 'Em Tough/Church Street in the Summertime	1963	3.00	6.00	12.00
❏ 3312	Go 'Way Christina/Everybody's Gone Ape	1963	3.00	6.00	12.00
❏ 3314	Change Partners/I Hate You Baby	1963	3.00	6.00	12.00
❏ 3315	My Girl-She Sure Can Cook/A Woman Is Smarter in Every Kinda Way	1964	2.50	5.00	10.00
❏ 3318	You Can't Have Your Cake/Take Me to Los Angeles	1964	2.50	5.00	10.00
❏ 3319	Twistin' Matilda/Treat 'Em Tough	1964	2.50	5.00	10.00
Albums					
SPQR					
❏ E 16001	If You Wanna Be Happy	1963	37.50	75.00	150.00

SOUL BROTHERS SIX
45s
ATLANTIC

❏ 2406	Some Kind of Wonderful/I'll Be Loving You	1967	3.75	7.50	15.00
❏ 2456	You Better Check Yourself/What Can You Do When You Ain't Got Nobody	1967	3.00	6.00	12.00
❏ 2535	Your Love Is Such a Wonderful Love/I Can't Live Without You	1968	3.00	6.00	12.00
❏ 2592	Somebody Else Is Loving My Baby/Thank You Baby for Loving Me	1969	3.00	6.00	12.00
❏ 2645	What You Got (Is So Good for Me)/Drive	1969	3.00	6.00	12.00
PHIL-L.A. OF SOUL					
❏ 355	Funky Funky Way of Making Love/Let Me Be the One	1972	—	3.00	6.00
❏ 360	You're My World/You Gotta Come a Little Closer	1973	—	3.00	6.00
❏ 365	Let Me Do What We Ain't Doin'/Lost the Will to Live	1974	—	3.00	6.00

SOUL CHILDREN, THE
45s
EPIC

❏ 50178	Finders Keepers/Midnight Sunshine	1976	—	2.50	5.00
❏ 50236	If You Move I'll Fall/Little Understanding	1976	—	2.50	5.00
❏ 50345	Where Is Your Woman Tonight?/Merry-Go-Round	1977	—	2.50	5.00
❏ 50405	There Always/You Don't Need a Ring	1977	—	2.50	5.00
STAX					
❏ 0008	Give 'Em Love/Move Over	1968	2.00	4.00	8.00
❏ 0018	I'll Understand/Doin' Our Thing	1969	2.00	4.00	8.00
❏ 0030	Tighten Up My Thang/Take Up the Slack	1969	2.00	4.00	8.00
❏ 0050	The Sweeter He Is — Part 1/The Sweeter He Is — Part 2	1969	2.00	4.00	8.00
❏ 0062	Hold On, I'm Coming/Make It Good	1970	—	3.50	7.00
❏ 0075	Give Me One Good Reason Why/Finish Me Off	1970	—	3.50	7.00
❏ 0086	Let's Make a Sweet Thing Sweeter/Finish Me Off	1971	—	3.50	7.00
❏ 0119	Hearsay/Don't Take My Sunshine	1972	—	3.50	7.00
❏ 0132	Don't Take My Kindness for Weakness/Just the One	1972	—	3.50	7.00
❏ 0152	It Ain't Always What You Do (It's Who You Let See You Do It)/All That Shines Ain't Gold	1973	—	3.50	7.00
❏ 0170	Love Is a Hurtin' Thing/Poem on the School House Door	1973	—	3.50	7.00
❏ 0182	I'll Be the Other Woman/Come Back Kind of Love	1973	—	3.00	6.00
❏ 0218	Love Makes It Right/Love Makes It Right — Part 2	1974	—	3.00	6.00
❏ 0230	What's Happening Baby/What's Happening Baby — Part 2	1974	—	3.00	6.00
❏ 3206	Can't Give Up a Good Thing/Signed, Sealed and Delivered	1978	—	2.50	5.00
❏ 3211	Summer in the Shade/Hard Living with a Woman	1978	—	2.50	5.00
❏ 3214	Who You Used to Be/Believing	1978	—	2.50	5.00
Albums					
EPIC					
❏ PE 33902	Finders Keepers	1976	3.75	7.50	15.00
❏ PE 34455	Where Is Your Woman Tonight	1977	3.75	7.50	15.00
STAX					
❏ STS-2018	Soul Children	1969	7.50	15.00	30.00
❏ STS-2043	The Best of Two Worlds	1971	7.50	15.00	30.00
❏ STS-3003	Genesis	1972	7.50	15.00	30.00
❏ STX-4105	Open Door Policy	1978	3.75	7.50	15.00
❏ STX-4120	Chronicle	1979	3.00	6.00	12.00
❏ STS-5507	Friction	1974	7.50	15.00	30.00

SOUL CLAN, THE
SOLOMON BURKE, ARTHUR CONLEY, DON COVAY, BEN E. KING and JOE TEX.
45s
ATLANTIC

❏ 2530	Soul Meeting/That's How It Feels	1968	2.50	5.00	10.00
❏ 2530 [PS]	Soul Meeting/That's How It Feels	1968	3.75	7.50	15.00

SOUL COMFORTERS, THE
45s
HOLLYWOOD

❏ 1042	White Christmas/Silent Night	1955	7.50	15.00	30.00

SOUL DUO, THE
45s
SHIPTOWN

❏ 132	Just A Sad Xmas/Can't Nobody Love Me	19??	—	3.00	6.00

SOUL GENERATION, THE

45s

EBONY SOUNDS

Number	Title (A Side/B Side)	Yr	VG	VG+	NM
❑ 175	That's the Way It's Got to Be (Body and Soul)/ Mandingo Woman	1972	2.50	5.00	10.00
❑ 176	Million Dollars/Super Fine	1973	2.50	5.00	10.00
❑ 177	A Ray of Hope/Young Bird	1973	2.50	5.00	10.00
❑ 181	I Wonder What She's Doin'/Key to Your Heart	1973	3.00	6.00	12.00
❑ 181	Praying for a Miracle/In Your Way	1974	3.75	7.50	15.00

Albums

EBONY SOUNDS

Number	Title (A Side/B Side)	Yr	VG	VG+	NM
❑ 2000	Beyond Body and Soul	1972	5.00	10.00	20.00

SOUL SISTERS, THE

45s

Number	Title (A Side/B Side)	Yr	VG	VG+	NM
GUYDEN					
❑ 2066	The Warm-Up/Because I Love You	1962	6.25	12.50	25.00
KAYO					
❑ 5101	I Can't Let Him Go/(B-side unknown)	1963	6.25	12.50	25.00
SUE					
❑ 10-005	Good Time Tonight/Foolish Dreamer	1964	3.75	7.50	15.00
❑ 107	Loop de Loop/Long Gone	1964	3.75	7.50	15.00
❑ 111	Just a Moment Ago/I Won't Be Your Fool Anymore	1964	3.75	7.50	15.00
❑ 130	Think About the Good Times/The Right Time	1965	3.75	7.50	15.00
❑ 140	Flashback/Give Me Some Satisfaction	1966	3.75	7.50	15.00
❑ 799	I Can't Stand It/Blueberry Hill	1964	3.75	7.50	15.00
VEEP					
❑ 1291	A Thousand Mountains/You Got 'Em Beat	1968	3.00	6.00	12.00

Albums

SUE

Number	Title (A Side/B Side)	Yr	VG	VG+	NM
❑ LP-1022 [M]	I Can't Stand It	1964	50.00	100.00	200.00
❑ STLP-1022 [S]	I Can't Stand It	1964	100.00	200.00	400.00

SOUL SOCIETY, THE

45s

DOT

Number	Title (A Side/B Side)	Yr	VG	VG+	NM
❑ 17136	Sidewinder/Afro-Desia	1968	2.50	5.00	10.00

Albums

DOT

Number	Title (A Side/B Side)	Yr	VG	VG+	NM
❑ DLP-25842	Satisfaction	1969	6.25	12.50	25.00

SOUL SURVIVORS

45s

Number	Title (A Side/B Side)	Yr	VG	VG+	NM
ATCO					
❑ 6627	Turn Out the Fire/Go Out Walking	1968	2.00	4.00	8.00
❑ 6650	Tell Daddy/Mama Soul	1969	2.00	4.00	8.00
❑ 6735	Still Got My Head/Tempting 'Bout to Get Me	1970	2.00	4.00	8.00
CRIMSON					
❑ 1010	Expressway to Your Heart/Hey Gyp	1967	3.00	6.00	12.00
❑ 1012	Explosion (In Your Soul)/Dathon's Theme	1967	2.50	5.00	10.00
❑ 1016	Poor Man's Dream/Impossible Mission	1968	2.50	5.00	10.00
DECCA					
❑ 32080	Devil with a Blue Dress On/Shakin' with Linda	1967	3.75	7.50	15.00
DOT					
❑ 16793	Look at Me/Can't Stand to Be in Love with You	1965	5.00	10.00	20.00
❑ 16830	Hung Up on Losin'/Snow Man	1966	3.00	6.00	12.00
PHILADELPHIA INT'L.					
❑ 3595	Happy Birthday America (Part 1)/Happy Birthday America (Part 2)	1976	—	2.50	5.00
❑ 3595 [PS]	Happy Birthday America (Part 1)/Happy Birthday America (Part 2)	1976	2.00	4.00	8.00
TSOP					
❑ 4756	City of Brotherly Love/The Best Time Was the Last Time	1974	—	3.00	6.00
❑ 4760	What It Takes/Virgin Girl	1974	—	3.00	6.00
❑ 4768	Your Love/Lover to Me	1975	—	3.00	6.00

Albums

Number	Title (A Side/B Side)	Yr	VG	VG+	NM
ATCO					
❑ SD 33-277	Take Another Look	1969	6.25	12.50	25.00
CRIMSON					
❑ CR-502 S [S]	When the Whistle Blows Anything Goes	1967	7.50	15.00	30.00
❑ CR-502 [M]	When the Whistle Blows Anything Goes	1967	12.50	25.00	50.00
TSOP					
❑ KZ 33186	The Soul Survivors	1975	3.00	6.00	12.00

SOULFUL STRINGS, THE

45s

CADET

Number	Title (A Side/B Side)	Yr	VG	VG+	NM
❑ 5559	Paint It Black/Love Is a Hurtin' Thing	1967	—	3.00	6.00
❑ 5576	Burning Spear/Within You Without You	1968	—	3.00	6.00
❑ 5607	(Sittin' On) The Dock of the Bay/The Stripper	1968	—	3.00	6.00
❑ 5617	The Who Who Song/Jericho	1968	—	3.00	6.00
❑ 5633	I Wish It Would Rain/Listen Here	1969	—	3.00	6.00
❑ 5654	A Love Song/Zabezi	1969	—	3.00	6.00

Albums

CADET

Number	Title (A Side/B Side)	Yr	VG	VG+	NM
❑ LP-776 [M]	Paint It Black	1967	3.75	7.50	15.00
❑ LPS-776 [S]	Paint It Black	1967	3.00	6.00	12.00
❑ LPS-796	Groovin' with the Soulful Strings	1967	3.00	6.00	12.00
❑ LPS-805	Another Exposure	1968	3.00	6.00	12.00
❑ LPS-814	The Magic of Christmas	1968	3.00	6.00	12.00
❑ LPS-820	In Concert/Back by Demand	1969	3.00	6.00	12.00
❑ LPS-834	String Fever	1969	3.00	6.00	12.00
❑ LPS-846	Gamble-Huff	1971	2.50	5.00	10.00
❑ 50022 [(2)]	Best of the Soulful Strings	1973	3.00	6.00	12.00

SOUVENIRS, THE

May be three different groups.

45s

Number	Title (A Side/B Side)	Yr	VG	VG+	NM
DOOTO					
❑ 412	So Long Daddy/Arlene, Sweet Little Texas Queen	1957	12.50	25.00	50.00
INFERNO					
❑ 2001	I Could Have Danced All Night/It's Too Bad	1967	12.50	25.00	50.00
REPRISE					
❑ 20065	The Worm/The Bump	1962	3.75	7.50	15.00
❑ 20066	The Real McCoy/The Watusi	1962	3.75	7.50	15.00

SPANIELS, THE

Also see POOKIE HUDSON.

45s

Number	Title (A Side/B Side)	Yr	VG	VG+	NM
BUDDAH					
❑ 153	Goodnight Sweetheart/Maybe	1969	2.00	4.00	8.00
CALLA					
❑ 172	Fairy Tales/Jealous Heart	1970	—	3.00	6.00
CANTERBURY					
❑ 101	Peace of Mind/She Sang to Me/Danny Boy	1974	—	2.50	5.00
CHANCE					
❑ 1141	Baby It's You/Bounce	1953	125.00	250.00	500.00
❑ 1141	Baby It's You/Bounce	1953	375.00	750.00	1500.
—Red vinyl					
LOST-NITE					
❑ 262	Baby It's You/Bounce	197?	—	2.00	4.00
❑ 265	The Bells Ring Out/House Cleaning	197?	—	2.00	4.00
❑ 268	Goodnite, Sweetheart, Goodnite/You Don't Move Me	197?	—	2.00	4.00
❑ 271	Do-Wah/Don'cha Go	197?	—	2.00	4.00
❑ 274	Play It Cool/Let's Make Up	197?	—	2.00	4.00
❑ 277	False Love/Do You Really	197?	—	2.00	4.00
❑ 280	You Painted Pictures/Hey, SIster Lizzie	197?	—	2.00	4.00
❑ 283	Dear Heart/Why Won't You Dance	197?	—	2.00	4.00
❑ 286	Everyone's Laughing/I.O.U.	197?	—	2.00	4.00
❑ 289	I Lost You/Crazy Baby	197?	—	2.00	4.00
❑ 292	You Gave Me Peace of Mind/Please Don't Tease	197?	—	2.00	4.00
❑ 295	You're Gonna Cry/I Like It Like That	197?	—	2.00	4.00
❑ 298	Stormy Weather/Here Is Why I Love You	197?	—	2.00	4.00
❑ 301	Tina/Great Googley Moo	197?	—	2.00	4.00
❑ 304	Since I Fell for You/Baby Come Along with Me	197?	—	2.00	4.00
❑ 307	This Is a Lovely Way to Spend an Evening/Red Sails in the Sunset	197?	—	2.00	4.00
❑ 446	I Know/Bus Fare Home	197?	—	2.00	4.00
NEPTUNE					
❑ 124	I Love You For Sentimental Reasons/Meek Man	1961	5.00	10.00	20.00
—As "Pookie Hudson and the Spaniels"					
NORTH AMERICAN					
❑ 001	Fairy Tales/Jealous Heart	1970	—	2.50	5.00
❑ 002	Stand in Line/Lonely Man	1970	—	2.50	5.00
❑ 1114	Come Back to These Arms/Money Blues	1970	—	2.50	5.00
OWL					
❑ 328	Little Goe/The Posse	1973	—	2.50	5.00
VEE JAY					
❑ 101	Baby It's You/Bounce	1953	1125.	2250.	4500.
—Red vinyl					
❑ 101	Baby It's You/Bounce	1953	200.00	400.00	800.00
—Black vinyl, maroon label					
❑ 101	Baby It's You/Bounce	1961	10.00	20.00	40.00
—Black vinyl, black label					
❑ 103	The Bells Ring Out/House Cleaning	1953	150.00	300.00	600.00
—Red vinyl					
❑ 103	The Bells Ring Out/House Cleaning	1953	75.00	150.00	300.00
❑ 107	Goodnite, Sweetheart, Goodnite/You Don't Move Me	1953	200.00	400.00	800.00
—Red vinyl; no "Trade Mark Reg" on label					
❑ 107	Goodnite, Sweetheart, Goodnite/You Don't Move Me	1953	75.00	150.00	300.00
—Black vinyl; as "Spanials"					
❑ 107	Goodnite, Sweetheart, Goodnite/You Don't Move Me	1953	50.00	100.00	200.00
—Black vinyl, correct spelling					
❑ 107	Goodnite, Sweetheart, Goodnite/You Don't Move Me	1993	2.00	4.00	8.00
—Red vinyl; "Trade Mark Reg" on label; included in Vee-Jay CD box set					
❑ 116	Play It Cool/Let's Make Up	1954	125.00	250.00	500.00
—Red vinyl					
❑ 116	Play It Cool/Let's Make Up	1954	25.00	50.00	100.00
❑ 131	Do-Wah/Don'cha Go	1955	125.00	250.00	500.00
—Red vinyl					
❑ 131	Do-Wah/Don'cha Go	1955	20.00	40.00	80.00
❑ 154	You Painted Pictures/Hey, Sister Lizzie	1955	15.00	30.00	60.00
❑ 154	You Painted Pictures/Hey, Sister Lizzie	1955	12.50	25.00	50.00
—As "Spanials"					
❑ 178	False Love/Do You Really	1956	37.50	75.00	150.00
❑ 189	Dear Heart/Why Won't You Dance	1956	37.50	75.00	150.00
❑ 202	Since I Fell for You/Baby Come Along with Me	1956	37.50	75.00	150.00
❑ 229	Please Don't Tease/You Gave Me Peace of Mind	1956	15.00	30.00	60.00

Number	Title (A Side/B Side)	Yr	VG	VG+	NM
❏ 246	Everyone's Laughing/I.O.U.	1957	15.00	30.00	60.00
❏ 257	You're Gonna Cry/I Need Your Kisses	1957	15.00	30.00	60.00
❏ 264	I Love You/Crazee Babee	1958	15.00	30.00	60.00
❏ 278	Tina/Great Googly Moo	1958	15.00	30.00	60.00
❏ 290	Stormy Weather/Here Is Why I Love You	1958	15.00	30.00	60.00
❏ 301	Baby It's You/Heart and Soul	1958	15.00	30.00	60.00
❏ 310	Trees/I Like It Like That	1959	15.00	30.00	60.00
❏ 328	These Three Words/100 Years from Today	1959	15.00	30.00	60.00
❏ 342	People Will Say We're in Love/The Bells Ring Out	1960	25.00	50.00	100.00
❏ 350	I Know/Bus Fare Home	1960	10.00	20.00	40.00

Albums
LOST-NITE

❏ LLP-19 [10]	The Spaniels	1981	3.00	6.00	12.00

—Red vinyl
VEE JAY

❏ LP-1002 [M]	Goodnite, It's Time to Go	1958	150.00	300.00	600.00

—Maroon label; group pictured on cover

❏ LP-1002 [M]	Goodnite, It's Time to Go	1961	50.00	100.00	200.00

—Black label; dogs on cover

❏ VJLP-1002 [M]	Goodnite, It's Time to Go	198?	3.00	6.00	12.00

—Legitimate reissue on flimsier vinyl than originals

❏ LP-1024 [M]	The Spaniels	1960	75.00	150.00	300.00

SPARKS OF RHYTHM, THE
45s
APOLLO

Number	Title (A Side/B Side)	Yr	VG	VG+	NM
❏ 479	Women, Women, Women/Don't Love You Anymore	1955	75.00	150.00	300.00
❏ 481	Hurry Home/Stars Are in the Sky	1955	75.00	150.00	300.00
❏ 541	Handy Man/Everybody Rock and Roll	1959	12.50	25.00	50.00

SPARROWS, THE
Probably two different groups.
45s
DAVIS

❏ 456	Love Me Tender/Come Back to Me	1957	75.00	150.00	300.00

JAY DEE

❏ 783	Tell Me Baby/Why Did You Leave Me	1953	125.00	250.00	500.00
❏ 790	I'll Be Loving You/Hey!	1954	125.00	250.00	500.00

SPECTOR, PHIL
Also see THE TEDDY BEARS; THE RIGHTEOUS BROTHERS.
45s
PAVILLION

❏ AE7 1354 [DJ]	Phil Spector's Christmas Medley (same on both sides)	1981	3.75	7.50	15.00

—Promo-only sampler from the Pavillion reissue of Phil Spector's Christmas Album
PHILLES

❏ (no #) [DJ]	Thanks for Giving Me the Right Time! (same on both sides)	1965	250.00	500.00	1000.

—Has Phil's picture on label; actually plays "Ebb Tide" by the Righteous Brothers

SPECTOR, RONNIE
Also see THE RONETTES; VERONICA.
12-Inch Singles
COLUMBIA

❏ CAS 2701 [DJ]	Who Can Sleep (same on both sides)	1987	2.00	4.00	8.00

EPIC

❏ ASF 350 [DJ]	Say Goodbye to Hollywood/Baby Please Don't Go	1977	10.00	20.00	40.00

TOM CAT

❏ JD-10380 [DJ]	You'd Be Good for Me (same on both sides)	197?	7.50	15.00	30.00

—Promo only on red vinyl
45s
ALSTON

❏ 3738	It's a Heartache/I Wanna Come Over	1978	2.00	4.00	8.00

APPLE

❏ 1832	Try Some, Buy Some/Tandoori Chicken	1971	—	3.50	7.00
❏ 1832	Try Some, Buy Some/Tandoori Chicken	1971	2.00	4.00	8.00

—With star on A-side label

❏ 1832 [PS]	Try Some, Buy Some/Tandoori Chicken	1971	2.50	5.00	10.00

COLUMBIA

❏ 07082	Who Can Sleep/When We Danced	1987	—	2.00	4.00
❏ 07082 [PS]	Who Can Sleep/When We Danced	1987	—	2.00	4.00
❏ 07300	Love on a Rooftop/Good Love Is Hard to Find	1987	—	2.00	4.00

EPIC

❏ 50374	Say Goodbye to Hollywood/Baby Please Don't Go	1977	2.50	5.00	10.00
❏ 50374 [PS]	Say Goodbye to Hollywood/Baby Please Don't Go	1977	6.25	12.50	25.00

POLISH

❏ 202	Darlin'/Tonight	1980	—	2.50	5.00

TOM CAT

❏ JB-10380 [DJ]	You'd Be Good for Me/Something Tells Me	1975	2.50	5.00	10.00

—Promo only on blue vinyl

❏ PB-10380	You'd Be Good for Me/Something Tells Me	1975	—	2.50	5.00

WARNER/SPECTOR

❏ 0409	Paradise/When I Saw You	1976	2.50	5.00	10.00

Albums
COLUMBIA

❏ C 40620	Unfinished Business	1987	2.50	5.00	10.00

POLISH

❏ PRG-808	Siren	1980	3.00	6.00	12.00

SPEECH
Also see ARRESTED DEVELOPMENT.
45s
CHRYSALIS

Number	Title (A Side/B Side)	Yr	VG	VG+	NM
❏ S7-18947	Like Marvin Gaye Said (What's Going On)/Impregnated Tidbits of Dope Hits	1995	—	—	3.00

SPEEDO AND THE IMPALAS
See THE IMPALAS.

SPELLMAN, BENNY
45s
ACE

❏ 630	That's All I Ask of You/Roll On Big Wheel	1961	5.00	10.00	20.00

ALON

❏ 9018	Tain't the Truth/No Don't Stop	1965	2.50	5.00	10.00
❏ 9024	The Word Game/I Feel Good	1965	5.00	10.00	20.00
❏ 9027	It Must Be Love/Spirit of Loneliness	1965	2.50	5.00	10.00
❏ 9031	It's for You/This Is My Love	1966	2.50	5.00	10.00

ATLANTIC

❏ 2291	The Word Game/I Feel Good	1965	2.50	5.00	10.00

MINIT

❏ 606	Life Is Too Short/Ammerette	1960	3.75	7.50	15.00
❏ 613	Darling No Matter Where/I Didn't Know	1960	3.75	7.50	15.00
❏ 644	Lipstick Traces (On a Cigarette)/Fortune Teller	1962	3.00	6.00	12.00
❏ 652	Every Now and Then/I'm in Love	1962	3.00	6.00	12.00
❏ 659	Stickin' Whicha' Baby/You Got to Get It	1963	3.00	6.00	12.00
❏ 664	Ammerette/Talk About Love	1963	3.00	6.00	12.00

SANSU

❏ 462	But If You Love Her/Sinner Girl	1967	2.00	4.00	8.00

WATCH

❏ 6336	Slow Down Baby (You Drive Too Fast)/Someday They'll Understand	1964	2.50	5.00	10.00

SPENCER, TRACIE
12-Inch Singles
CAPITOL

Number	Title (A Side/B Side)	Yr	VG	VG+	NM
❏ SPRO-15129 [DJ]	Still in My Heart (HQ2 Remix 8:54) (HQ2 Remix Instrumental 8:52)	2000	3.00	6.00	12.00
❏ V-15378	Symptoms of True Love (Symptomatic Dance Mix 6:18) (Symptomatic Edit 3:57) (Percussapella 5:23) (Mercyful Energy Mix 5:49) (Have Mercy LP Mix 5:03)	1988	2.00	4.00	8.00
❏ V-15397	Hide and Seek (2 versions)/Symptoms of True Love (U.K. Mix)	1988	2.00	4.00	8.00
❏ V-15633	Save Your Love (To the Rescue Club Mix) (Save the Drums Mix) (Groove Your Love Mix) (Hot Radio Mix)	1990	—	3.50	7.00
❏ V-15649	This House (6 versions)	1990	—	3.50	7.00
❏ V-15704	This Time Make It Funky (7" Mix) (Extended Mix) (T-Funk I) (Extended Instrumental)	1991	—	3.50	7.00
❏ 58777	It's All About You (Not About Me) (Radio Edit) (Album Version) (Instrumental)/(same on both sides)	1999	—	3.50	7.00
❏ 58807	Still in My Heart (4 versions)	2000	2.00	4.00	8.00
❏ SPRO-79171 [DJ]	Love Me (Edited Mix) (Long Mix)	1992	2.50	5.00	10.00
❏ SPRO-79373/4 [DJ]	Symptoms of True Love (Split Level Mix 5:06) (Piano Dub 5:07) (Instrumental 4:18)	1988	2.00	4.00	8.00
❏ SPRO 79442 [DJ]	Imagine (same on both sides?)	1989	—	3.50	7.00
❏ SPRO-79665/708 [DJ]	This Time Make It Funky (Extended Mix 6:35) (Radio Mix) (T-Funk II 5:38) (Funky Guitar Mix 5:36)	1991	2.00	4.00	8.00
❏ SPRO-79869 [DJ]	Tender Kisses (unknown versions)	1991	2.50	5.00	10.00

45s
CAPITOL

❏ B-44140	Symptoms of True Love/(Acappella Version)	1988	—	—	3.00
❏ B-44140 [PS]	Symptoms of True Love/(Acappella Version)	1988	—	2.00	4.00
❏ B-44198	Hide and Seek/Symptoms of True Love	1988	—	—	3.00
❏ B-44198 [PS]	Hide and Seek/Symptoms of True Love	1988	—	2.00	4.00
❏ B-44268	Imagine/Hide and Seek	1989	—	—	3.00
❏ B-44268 [PS]	Imagine/Hide and Seek	1989	—	2.00	4.00
❏ 58777	It's All About You (Not About Me)/It's On Tonight	1999	—	—	3.00
❏ 58807	Still in My Heart/If U Wanna Get Down	2000	—	2.00	4.00
❏ 7PRO-79241	Save Your Love (same on both sides)	1990	—	3.00	6.00

—Vinyl is promo only
Albums
CAPITOL

❏ C1-48186	Tracie Spencer	1988	2.00	4.00	8.00
❏ C1-92153	Make the Difference	1990	3.00	6.00	12.00

SPIDERS, THE (1)
45s
IMPERIAL

❏ 5265	I Didn't Want to Do It/You're the One	1954	25.00	50.00	100.00
❏ 5280	Tears Begin to Flow/I'll Stop Cryin'	1954	25.00	50.00	100.00
❏ 5291	I'm Searching/I'm Slippin' In	1954	62.50	125.00	250.00
❏ 5305	The Real Thing/Mm Mm Baby	1954	25.00	50.00	100.00
❏ 5318	She Keeps Me Wondering/(3 x 7) = "21"	1954	25.00	50.00	100.00
❏ 5331	That's Enough/Lost and Bewildered	1955	18.75	37.50	75.00
❏ 5344	Am I the One/Sukey, Sukey, Sukey	1955	18.75	37.50	75.00
❏ 5354	Bells in My Heart/For a Thrill	1955	25.00	50.00	100.00

—Red label

❏ 5354	Bells in My Heart/For a Thrill	1957	7.50	15.00	30.00

—Black label

Number	Title (A Side/B Side)	Yr	VG	VG+	NM
❏ 5366	Is It True/Witchcraft	1955	25.00	50.00	100.00
—Blue label					
❏ 5366	Is It True/Witchcraft	1955	10.00	20.00	40.00
—Red label					
❏ 5376	Don't Pity Me/How I Feel	1956	10.00	20.00	40.00
—Featuring Chuck Carbo					
❏ 5393	A-1 in My Heart/Dear Mary	1956	7.50	15.00	30.00
—As "The Spiders with Chuck Carbo"					
❏ 5618	I Didn't Want to Do It/You're the One	1959	7.50	15.00	30.00
❏ 5714	You're the One/Tennessee Slim	1960	7.50	15.00	30.00
❏ 5739	Witchcraft/(True) You Don't Love Me	1961	7.50	15.00	30.00

SPINNERS

Many, though not all, of these did not use the article "The" before the name. These are all by the group known as "The Detroit Spinners" in the U.K.

45s
ATLANTIC

Number	Title (A Side/B Side)	Yr	VG	VG+	NM
❏ 2904	I'll Be Around/How Could I Let You Get Away	1972	—	2.50	5.00
❏ 2927	Could It Be I'm Falling in Love/Just You and Me Baby	1972	—	2.50	5.00
❏ 2962	One of a Kind (Love Affair)/Don't Let the Green Grass Fool You	1973	—	2.50	5.00
❏ 2973	Ghetto Child/We Belong Together	1973	—	2.50	5.00
❏ 3006	Mighty Love — Pt. 1/Mighty Love — Pt. 2	1974	—	2.50	5.00
❏ 3027	I'm Coming Home/He'll Never Love You Like I Do	1974	—	2.50	5.00
❏ 3029	Then Came You/Just As Long As We Have Love	1974	—	3.00	6.00
❏ 3202	Then Came You/Just As Long As We Have Love	1974	—	2.50	5.00
—With Dionne Warwicke					
❏ 3206	Love Don't Love Nobody (Part 1)/Love Don't Love Nobody (Part 2)	1974	—	2.50	5.00
❏ 3252	Living a Little, Loving a Little/Smile, We Have Each Other	1975	—	2.50	5.00
❏ 3268	Sadie/Lazy Susan	1975	—	2.50	5.00
❏ 3284	Games People Play/I Don't Want to Lose You	1975	2.50	5.00	10.00
❏ 3284	They Just Can't Stop it (Games People Play)/I Don't Want to Lose You	1975	—	2.50	5.00
—Same A-side, altered title					
❏ 3309	Love Or Leave/You Made a Promise to Me	1975	—	2.50	5.00
❏ 3341	Wake Up Susan/If You Can't Be in Love	1976	—	2.50	5.00
❏ 3355	The Rubberband Man/Now That We're Together	1976	—	2.50	5.00
❏ 3382	You're Throwing a Good Love Away/You're All I Need in Life	1977	—	2.50	5.00
❏ 3400	Me and My Music/I'm Riding Your Shadow	1977	—	2.50	5.00
❏ 3425	Heaven on Earth (So Fine)/I'm Tired of Giving	1977	—	2.50	5.00
❏ 3462	Easy Come, Easy Go/Love Is One Step Away	1978	—	2.50	5.00
❏ 3483	If You Wanna Do a Dance/One in a Life Proposal	1978	—	2.50	5.00
❏ 3546	Are You Ready for Love/Once You Fall in Love	1978	—	2.50	5.00
❏ 3590	Don't Let the Man Get You/I Love the Music	1979	—	2.50	5.00
❏ 3619	Body Language/With My Eyes	1979	—	2.50	5.00
❏ 3637	Working My Way Back to You/Disco Ride	1979	2.00	4.00	8.00
—Original pressings mention only one song on the A-side					
❏ 3637	Working My Way Back to You/Forgive Me, Girl/Disco Ride	1979		2.00	4.00
❏ 3664	Cupid-I've Loved You for a Long Time/Pipedreams	1980	—	2.00	4.00
❏ 3757	Love Trippin'/Now That You're Mine Again	1980	—	2.00	4.00
❏ 3765	I Just Want to Fall in Love/Heavy on the Sunshine	1980	—	2.00	4.00
❏ 3798	Yesterday Once More-Nothing Remains the Same/Be My Love	1981	—	2.00	4.00
❏ 3814	Long Live Soul Music/Give Your Lady What She Wants	1981	—	2.00	4.00
❏ 3827	Winter of Our Love/The Deacon	1981	—	2.00	4.00
❏ 3848	What You Feel Is Real/Street Talk	1981	—	2.00	4.00
—With Gino Soccio					
❏ 3865	You Go Your Way (I'll Go Mine)/Got to Be Love	1981	—	2.00	4.00
❏ 3882 [DJ]	Love Connection (same on both sides)	1981	—	2.50	5.00
—May be promo only					
❏ 4007	Never Thought I'd Fall in Love/Send a Little Love	1982	—	2.00	4.00
❏ 89226	Spaceballs/Spaceballs (Dub Version)	1987	—	—	3.00
❏ 89648	(We Have Come Into) Our Time for All/All Your Love	1984	—	2.00	4.00
❏ 89689	Right or Wrong/Love Is In Season	1984	—	2.00	4.00
❏ 89862	City Full of Memories/No Other Love	1983	—	2.00	4.00
❏ 89922	Funny How Time Slips Away/I'm Calling You Now	1982	—	2.00	4.00
❏ 89962	Magic in the Moonlight/So Far Away	1982	—	2.00	4.00
MIRAGE					
❏ 99580	She Does/(B-side unknown)	1986	—	—	3.00
❏ 99604	Put Us Together Again/Show Us Your Magic	1985	—	—	3.00
MOTOWN					
❏ 1067	Sweet Thing/How Can I	1964	3.75	7.50	15.00
❏ 1078	I'll Always Love You/Tomorrow May Never Come	1965	3.75	7.50	15.00
❏ 1093	Truly Yours/Where Is That Girl	1966	3.75	7.50	15.00
❏ 1109	For All We Know/Cross My Heart	1967	3.75	7.50	15.00
❏ 1136	I Just Can't Help But Feel the Pain/Bad, Bad Weather	1968	3.75	7.50	15.00
❏ 1155	In My Diary/(She's Gonna Love Me) At Sundown	1969	375.00	750.00	1500.
❏ 1235	Together We Can Make Such Sweet Music/Bad, Bad Weather	1973	2.00	4.00	8.00
TRI-PHI					
❏ 1001	That's What Girls Are Made For/Heebie-Jeebies	1961	6.25	12.50	25.00
❏ 1004	Love (I'm So Glad I Found You)/Sudbuster	1961	6.25	12.50	25.00
❏ 1007	What Did She Use/Itching for My Baby, I Know Where to Scratch	1962	6.25	12.50	25.00
❏ 1010	She Loves Me So/Whistling About You	1962	6.25	12.50	25.00

Number	Title (A Side/B Side)	Yr	VG	VG+	NM
❏ 1013	I've Been Hurt/I Got Your Water Boiling Baby (I'm Gonna Cook Your Goose)	1962	6.25	12.50	25.00
❏ 1018	She Don't Love Me/Too Young, Too Much, Too Soon	1962	7.50	15.00	30.00
V.I.P.					
❏ 25050	In My Diary/(She's Gonna Love Me) At Sundown	1969	6.25	12.50	25.00
❏ 25054	Message from a Black Man/(She's Gonna Love Me) At Sundown	1970	3.00	6.00	12.00
❏ 25057	It's a Shame/Together We Can Make Such Sweet Music	1970	3.00	6.00	12.00
❏ 25060	We'll Have It Made/My Whole World Ended (The Moment You Left Me)	1971	3.00	6.00	12.00

7-Inch Extended Plays
ATLANTIC

Number	Title (A Side/B Side)	Yr	VG	VG+	NM
❏ SD 7-7256	One Of a Kind (Love Affair)/Just You and Me Baby/ I'll Be Around//Just Can't Get You Out of My Mind/Could It Be I'm Falling in Love	1973	3.00	6.00	12.00
—Jukebox issue; small hole, plays at 33 1/3 rpm					
❏ SD 7-7256	Spinners	1973	3.00	6.00	12.00
—Part of "Little LP" series (LLP #216)					
❏ SD 7-7296	Since I Been Gone/Love Has Gone Away//Ain't No Price on Happiness/I'm Glad You Walked Into My Life	1974	2.50	5.00	10.00
—Jukebox issue; small hole, plays at 33 1/3 rpm					
❏ SD 7-7296 [PS]	Mighty Love	1974	2.50	5.00	10.00

Albums
ATLANTIC

Number	Title (A Side/B Side)	Yr	VG	VG+	NM
❏ SD 2-910 [(2)]	Spinners Live!	1975	3.75	7.50	15.00
❏ QD 7256 [Q]	Spinners	1974	5.00	10.00	20.00
❏ SD 7256	Spinners	1973	3.00	6.00	12.00
❏ SD 7296	Mighty Love	1974	3.00	6.00	12.00
❏ SD 16032	Labor of Love	1981	2.50	5.00	10.00
❏ QD 18118 [Q]	New and Improved	1974	5.00	10.00	20.00
❏ SD 18118	New and Improved	1974	3.00	6.00	12.00
❏ SD 18141	Pick of the Litter	1975	3.00	6.00	12.00
❏ SD 18181	Happiness is Being with the Spinners	1976	3.00	6.00	12.00
❏ SD 19100	Yesterday, Today & Tomorrow	1977	3.00	6.00	12.00
❏ SD 19146	Spinners/8	1977	3.00	6.00	12.00
❏ SD 19179	The Best of the Spinners	1978	3.00	6.00	12.00
❏ SD 19219	From Here to Eternally	1979	3.00	6.00	12.00
❏ SD 19256	Dancin' and Lovin'	1980	2.50	5.00	10.00
❏ SD 19270	Love Trippin'	1980	2.50	5.00	10.00
❏ SD 19318	Can't Shake This Feelin'	1981	2.50	5.00	10.00
❏ 80020	Grand Slam	1982	2.50	5.00	10.00
MIRAGE					
❏ 90456	Lovin' Feelings	1985	2.50	5.00	10.00
MOTOWN					
❏ M5-109V1	Motown Superstar Series, Vol. 9	1982	2.00	4.00	8.00
❏ M5-132V1	The Original Spinners	1981	3.00	6.00	12.00
—Reissue of Motown 639					
❏ M5-199V1	The Best of the Spinners	1981	3.00	6.00	12.00
—Reissue of Motown 769					
❏ M 639 [M]	The Original Spinners	1967	6.25	12.50	25.00
❏ MS 639 [P]	The Original Spinners	1967	7.50	15.00	30.00
❏ M 769	The Best of the Spinners	1973	3.75	7.50	15.00
VOLT					
❏ V-3403	Down to Business	1989	3.00	6.00	12.00
V.I.P.					
❏ 405	2nd Time Around	1970	10.00	20.00	40.00

SQUIRES, THE (1)
45s
ALADDIN

Number	Title (A Side/B Side)	Yr	VG	VG+	NM
❏ 3360	Dreamy Eyes/Danglin' with My Heart	1957	25.00	50.00	100.00
KICKS					
❏ 1	Dream Come True/Lucy Lou	1954	200.00	400.00	800.00
MAMBO					
❏ 105	Sindy/Do-Be-Do-Be-Wop-Wop	1955	37.50	75.00	150.00
VITA					
❏ 105	Sindy/Do-Be-Do-Be-Wop-Wop	1960	25.00	50.00	100.00
❏ 113	Sweet Girl/Me and My Deal	1955	25.00	50.00	100.00
❏ 116	Heavenly Angel/Sweet Girl	1955	25.00	50.00	100.00

SQUIRES, THE (4)
45s
COMBO

Number	Title (A Side/B Side)	Yr	VG	VG+	NM
❏ 35	Let's Give Love a Try/Whop	1952	125.00	250.00	500.00
❏ 42	Oh Darling/My Little Girl	1953	150.00	300.00	600.00

STACEY Q
45s
ATLANTIC

Number	Title (A Side/B Side)	Yr	VG	VG+	NM
❏ 88819	Heartbeat/Incognito	1990	—	2.00	4.00
❏ 88893	Give You All My Love/Out of My Heart	1989	—	—	3.00
❏ 88991	Favorite Things/Another Chance	1988	—	—	3.00
❏ 89081	I Love You/Dance the Night	1988	—	—	3.00
❏ 89135	Don't Make a Fool of Yourself/Fly By Night	1988	—	—	3.00
❏ 89135 [PS]	Don't Make a Fool of Yourself/Fly By Night	1988	—	—	3.00
❏ 89207	Music Out of Bounds/Don't Let Me Down	1987	—	—	3.00
❏ 89267	Insecurity/He Doesn't Understand	1987	—	—	3.00
❏ 89331	We Connect/Don't Break My Heart	1986	—	—	3.00
❏ 89331 [PS]	We Connect/Don't Break My Heart	1986	—	—	3.00
❏ 89381	Two of Hearts/Dancing Nowhere	1986	—	2.00	4.00
❏ 89381 [PS]	Two of Hearts/Dancing Nowhere	1986	—	2.00	4.00

Number	Title (A Side/B Side)	Yr	VG	VG+	NM
ON THE SPOT					
❏ 110	Shy Girl (same on both sides)	1987	—	2.50	5.00
Albums					
ATLANTIC					
❏ 81676	Better Than Heaven	1986	2.50	5.00	10.00
❏ 81802	Hard Machine	1988	2.50	5.00	10.00
❏ 81962	Nights Like This	1989	2.50	5.00	10.00

STANSFIELD, LISA
12-Inch Singles
ARISTA

Number	Title (A Side/B Side)	Yr	VG	VG+	NM
❏ AD 2025	You Can't Deny It (Extended Version 7:53) (Single Version 4:21)//(Sky King Mix 8:21)/Lay Me Down (4:16)	1990	2.00	4.00	8.00
❏ AD 2038	You Can't Deny It (Extended Version - Short 5:04) (Extended Version - Long 7:53)/(Sky King Mix 8:21) (Percapella 4:14)	1990	2.50	5.00	10.00
❏ ADP 2038 [DJ]	You Can't Deny It (Extended Remix 7:39) (Dubmental 6:47)//(R&B Radio Remix 5:01) (Silky Sax Mix 7:39)	1990	3.00	6.00	12.00
❏ AD 2049	This Is the Right Time (Extended Remix 9:44) (Dub 4:42)//(Rhythm Mix 7:51) (Rhythm Dub 6:51) (Rhythm Edit 4:30)	1990	2.00	4.00	8.00
❏ ADP 3339 [DJ]	Never, Never Gonna Give You Up (Album Mix 4:40)/(Groove Mix 5:01)//(Frankie's Hard and Sexy Mix 4:13) (Frankie's Hard R&B Club Mix 6:54)	1997	2.50	5.00	10.00
❏ ADP 3410 [(2) DJ]	Never, Never Gonna Give You Up (Hani Num Club Mix 9:03) (Mark Picchiotti Dub 8:18)/ (Nikolas & Sibley Club Mix 8:36) (Frankie's Classic Morning Mix 8:46)//(Mark Picchiotti Club Mix 9:55) (Hani's Vocal Reprise 1:56) (Hani's Bonus Beats 2:03)/(Hani's Analog Bath Mix 8:30) (Nickolas & Sibley Dub 5:23)	1997	6.25	12.50	25.00
❏ ADP 3424 [DJ]	Never Gonna Fall (Junior's Return to 27th and 10th Anthem 10:23)//(Victor Calderone Remix 8:43) (Junior's Tribal Beats 6:06)	1997	2.50	5.00	10.00
❏ ADP-3458 [DJ]	I'm Leavin' (Main Club Mix 10:08) (Radio Mix 4:18) (NYC Rough Mix 10:08) (Leavin' Drums 3:07)	1998	3.00	6.00	12.00
❏ AD1-9929	All Around the World (Long Version 7:02) (American Club Remix 11:48)/Affection	1989	2.00	4.00	8.00
❏ ADP-9937 [DJ]	All Around the World (Long Version 7:02) (Single Mix) (American Club Remix 11:48) (American Club Edit)	1990	5.00	10.00	20.00
❏ 12363	Change (Ultimate Club Mix 7:54) (Misty Dub Mix 7:31)/(Driza Bone Dub Mix 6:08) (Single Mix 4:18)	1991	2.00	4.00	8.00
❏ 12399	All Woman (5:16)/Everything Will Get Better (Sax on the Beach Mix 6:35) (Ian & Andy's 12" 8:01) (Underground Club Mix 9:54)	1991	2.00	4.00	8.00
❏ 12451	A Little More Love (Album Edit 4:10) (Album Version 4:34)/Set Your Loving Free (Kenlou 12-Inch Mix 7:26) (Dubmaster Edit 4:41)	1992	2.00	4.00	8.00
GIANT					
❏ PRO-A-7109 [DJ]	Make It Right (R. Kelly Remix) (Single Mix) (R. Kelly Extended Groove Remix) (Rhetro G Mix)	1994	3.00	6.00	12.00
❏ PRO-A-7240 [DJ]	Make It Right (Kenny Dope Extended Remix 5:58) (Rhetro G' Mix 4:16) (R. Kelly Extended Groove Remix 5:19) (R. Kelly Remix No. 1 4:04)	1994	3.00	6.00	12.00

45s
ARISTA

Number	Title (A Side/B Side)	Yr	VG	VG+	NM
❏ 2024	You Can't Deny It/Lay Me Down	1990	—	—	3.00
❏ 2049	This Is the Right Time/Apple Heart	1990	—	2.00	4.00
❏ 9928	All Around the World/Affection	1989	—	2.00	4.00
❏ 9928 [PS]	All Around the World/Affection	1989	—	2.00	4.00
❏ 12328	All Around the World/This Is the Right Time	1991	—	—	3.00
—Reissue with "Collectables" logo on label					
❏ 12362	Change/It's Got to Be Real	1991	—	2.00	4.00
❏ 12398	All Woman/Everything Will Get Better	1991	—	2.00	4.00
Albums					
ARISTA					
❏ AL-8554	Affection	1990	2.50	5.00	10.00
❏ 19012 [(2)]	The #1 Remixes	1998	3.75	7.50	15.00
❏ R 134198	Affection	1990	3.00	6.00	12.00
—BMG Music Service edition					

STAPLE SINGERS, THE
Also see MAVIS STAPLES.
12-Inch Singles
PRIVATE I

Number	Title (A Side/B Side)	Yr	VG	VG+	NM
❏ 05078	Slippery People (5:30)/(Instrumental)	1984	—	2.50	5.00
❏ 05266	Are You Ready? (Extended) (Dub)	1985	—	2.50	5.00

45s
20TH CENTURY

Number	Title (A Side/B Side)	Yr	VG	VG+	NM
❏ 2508	Hold On to Your Dreams/Cold and Windy Night	1981	—	2.00	4.00
CURTOM					
❏ 0109	Let's Do It Again/After Sex	1975	—	2.00	4.00
❏ 0113	New Orleans/A Whole Lot of Love	1976	—	2.00	4.00
EPIC					
❏ 9748	Be Careful of Stones That You Throw/More Than a Hammer and Nail	1964	2.50	5.00	10.00
❏ 9776	Do Something for Yourself/Samson and Delilah	1965	2.50	5.00	10.00
❏ 9825	Freedom Highway/The Funeral	1965	2.50	5.00	10.00
❏ 9880	Why/What Are They Doing	1965	2.50	5.00	10.00

Number	Title (A Side/B Side)	Yr	VG	VG+	NM
❏ 10054	King of Kings/Step Aside	1966	2.50	5.00	10.00
❏ 10104	Pray On/It's Been a Change	1966	2.50	5.00	10.00
❏ 10158	Why (Am I Treated So Bad)/What Are They Doing (In Heaven Today)	1967	2.00	4.00	8.00
❏ 10220	For What It's Worth/Are You Sure	1967	2.00	4.00	8.00
❏ 10264	Deliver Me/He	1967	2.00	4.00	8.00
❏ 10294	Let's Get Together/Power of Love	1968	2.00	4.00	8.00
❏ 10339	Crying in the Chapel/Nothing Lasts Forever	1968	2.00	4.00	8.00
❏ 10742	For What It's Worth/Why	1971	—	3.00	6.00
PRIVATE I					
❏ 04384	H-A-T-E (Don't Live Here Anymore)/Can You Hang	1984	—	2.00	4.00
❏ 04583	Slippery People/On My Own Again	1984	—	2.00	4.00
❏ 04711	This Is Our Night/Turning Point	1984	—	2.00	4.00
❏ 05565	Are You Ready/Love Wowks in Strange Ways	1985	—	2.00	4.00
❏ 05565 [PS]	Are You Ready/Love Wowks in Strange Ways	1985	—	3.00	6.00
❏ 05727	Nobody Can Make It on Their Own/Reasons to Love	1985	—	2.00	4.00
RIVERSIDE					
❏ 4518	Gloryland/Hammer and Nails	1962	3.00	6.00	12.00
❏ 4531	Gambling Man/Use What You Got	1962	3.00	6.00	12.00
❏ 4540	There Was a Star/The Virgin Mary Had One Son	1962	3.00	6.00	12.00
❏ 4553	I Can't Help from Cryin'/Let That Liar Again	1963	3.00	6.00	12.00
❏ 4563	Cotton Fields/This Land	1963	3.00	6.00	12.00
❏ 4568	Blowing in the Wind/Wish I Had Answered	1963	3.00	6.00	12.00
SHARP					
❏ 603	This May Be the Last Time/This Same Jesus	1960	3.75	7.50	15.00
STAX					
❏ 0007	Long Walk to D.C./Stay with Us	1968	—	3.00	6.00
❏ 0019	The Ghetto/Got to Be Some Changes Made	1968	—	3.00	6.00
❏ 0031	(Sittin' On) The Dock of the Bay/Top of the Mountain	1969	—	3.00	6.00
❏ 0039	The Gardener/The Challenge	1969	—	3.00	6.00
❏ 0052	When Will We Be Paid/Tend to Your Own Business	1969	—	3.00	6.00
❏ 0066	Give a Damn/God Bless the Children	1970	—	3.00	6.00
❏ 0074	Brand New Day/God Bless the Children	1970	—	3.00	6.00
❏ 0083	Heavy Makes You Happy (Sha-Na-Boom-Boom)/Love Is Plentiful	1970	—	3.00	6.00
❏ 0084	Who Took the Merry Out of Christmas/ (Instrumental)	1970	2.00	4.00	8.00
❏ 0093	You've Got to Earn It/I'm a Lover	1971	—	2.50	5.00
❏ 0104	Respect Yourself/You're Gonna Make Me Cry	1971	—	2.50	5.00
❏ 0125	I'll Take You There/I'm Just Another Soldier	1972	—	2.50	5.00
❏ 0137	This World/Are You Sure	1972	—	2.50	5.00
❏ 0156	Oh La De Da/We the People	1973	—	2.50	5.00
❏ 0164	Be What You Are/I Like the Things About Me	1973	—	2.50	5.00
—B-side by Cal Starr					
❏ 0179	If You're Ready (Come Go with Me)/Love Comes in All Colors	1973	—	2.50	5.00
❏ 0196	Touch a Hand, Make a Friend/Tellin' Lies	1974	—	2.50	5.00
❏ 0213	What's Your Thing/Whicha Way Did It Go	1974	—	2.50	5.00
—B-side by Pops Staples					
❏ 0215	City in the Sky/That's What Friends Are For	1974	—	2.50	5.00
❏ 0227	My Main Man/Who Made the Man	1974	—	2.50	5.00
❏ 0248	Back Road Into Town/My Main Man	1975	—	2.50	5.00
UNITED					
❏ 165	It Rained Children/Won't You Sit Down	1955	100.00	200.00	400.00
VEE JAY					
❏ 169	God's Wonderful Love/If I Could Hear My Mother	1956	5.00	10.00	20.00
❏ 224	Uncloudy Day/I Know I Got Religion	1956	5.00	10.00	20.00
❏ 846	Let Me Ride/I'm Coming Home	1957	5.00	10.00	20.00
❏ 856	I Had a Dream/Help Me Jesus	1958	3.75	7.50	15.00
❏ 866	Love Is the Way/On My Way to Heaven	1959	3.75	7.50	15.00
❏ 870	I'm Leaving/Going Away	1959	3.75	7.50	15.00
❏ 881	Downward Road/So Soon	1959	3.75	7.50	15.00
❏ 893	Pray On/Too Close	1960	3.00	6.00	12.00
❏ 902	I've Been Scorned/Don't Knock	1961	3.00	6.00	12.00
❏ 912	Sit Down Servant/Swing Low	1962	3.00	6.00	12.00
❏ 930	Swing Low Sweet Chariot/I'm So Glad	1963	3.00	6.00	12.00
WARNER BROS.					
❏ 8279	Love Me, Love Me, Love Me/Pass It On	1976	—	2.00	4.00
❏ 8317	Sweeter Than the Sweet/Making Love	1977	—	2.00	4.00
❏ 8460	See a Little Further (Than My Bed)/Let's Go to the Disco	1977	—	2.00	4.00
❏ 8510	I Honestly Love You/Family Tree	1978	—	2.00	4.00
❏ 8669	Unlock Your Mind/Mystery Train	1978	—	2.00	4.00
❏ 8748	Chica Boom/Handwriting on the Wall	1979	—	2.00	4.00
❏ 49598	God Can/Unlock Your Mind	1980	—	2.00	4.00
—Warner Bros. titles as "The Staples"					
Albums					
20TH CENTURY					
❏ T-636	Hold On to Your Dream	1981	2.50	5.00	10.00
ARCHIVE OF GOSPEL MUSIC					
❏ 62	The Staple Singers	1968	3.00	6.00	12.00
❏ 72	The Staple Singers, Vol. 2	1969	3.00	6.00	12.00
BUDDAH					
❏ BDS-2009	The Best of the Staple Singers	1969	5.00	10.00	20.00
❏ BDS-7508	Will the Circle Be Unbroken	1969	5.00	10.00	20.00
CURTOM					
❏ CU 5005	Let's Do It Again	1975	3.00	6.00	12.00
EPIC					
❏ LN 24132 [M]	Amen	1965	5.00	10.00	20.00
❏ LN 24163 [M]	Freedom Highway	1965	5.00	10.00	20.00

Number	Title (A Side/B Side)	Yr	VG	VG+	NM
❏ LN 24196 [M]	Why	1966	5.00	10.00	20.00
❏ LN 24237 [M]	Pray On	1967	6.25	12.50	25.00
❏ LN 24332 [M]	For What It's Worth	1967	6.25	12.50	25.00
❏ BN 26132 [S]	Amen	1965	6.25	12.50	25.00
❏ BN 26163 [S]	Freedom Highway	1965	6.25	12.50	25.00
❏ BN 26196 [S]	Why	1966	6.25	12.50	25.00
❏ BN 26237 [S]	Pray On	1967	5.00	10.00	20.00
❏ BN 26332 [S]	For What It's Worth	1967	5.00	10.00	20.00
❏ BN 26373	What the World Needs Now Is Love	1968	5.00	10.00	20.00
❏ EG 30635 [(2)]	The Staple Singers Make You Happy	1971	5.00	10.00	20.00
FANTASY					
❏ 9423	Use What You Got	1973	3.75	7.50	15.00
❏ 9442	The 25th Day of December	1973	3.75	7.50	15.00
HARMONY					
❏ KH 31775	Tell It Like It Is	1972	3.00	6.00	12.00
MILESTONE					
❏ 47028 [(2)]	A Great Day	197?	3.75	7.50	15.00
PICKWICK					
❏ 7001	The Staple Singers	197?	2.50	5.00	10.00
PRIVATE I					
❏ FZ 39460	The Turning Point	1984	2.50	5.00	10.00
❏ BFZ 40109	The Staple Singers	1985	2.50	5.00	10.00
STAX					
❏ STS-2004	Soul Folk in Action	1968	6.25	12.50	25.00
❏ STS-2016	We'll Get Over	1969	5.00	10.00	20.00
❏ STS-2034	The Staple Swingers	1971	5.00	10.00	20.00
❏ STS-3002	Be Altitude: Respect Yourself	1972	3.75	7.50	15.00
❏ STS-3015	Be What You Are	1973	3.75	7.50	15.00
❏ STX-4116	Be Altitude: Respect Yourself	198?	2.50	5.00	10.00
—Reissue of 3002					
❏ STX-4119	Chronicle	198?	2.50	5.00	10.00
❏ STS-5515	City in the Sky	1974	3.75	7.50	15.00
❏ STS-5523	The Best of the Staple Singers	1975	3.75	7.50	15.00
❏ MPS-8511	This Time Around	198?	2.50	5.00	10.00
❏ MPS-8532	We'll Get Over	198?	2.50	5.00	10.00
—Reissue of 2016					
❏ MPS-8553	Be What You Are	1990	3.00	6.00	12.00
—Reissue of 3015					
TRIP					
❏ 7000	Uncloudy Day	197?	2.50	5.00	10.00
❏ 7014	Swing Low	197?	2.50	5.00	10.00
❏ 7019	The Best of the Staple Singers	197?	2.50	5.00	10.00
❏ 8014	The Other Side of the Staple Singers	1972	2.50	5.00	10.00
VEE JAY					
❏ LP-5000 [M]	Uncloudy Day	1959	7.50	15.00	30.00
❏ LP-5008 [M]	Will the Circle Be Unbroken	1960	7.50	15.00	30.00
❏ LP-5014 [M]	Swing Low	1961	7.50	15.00	30.00
❏ LP-5019 [M]	Best of the Staple Singers	1962	7.50	15.00	30.00
❏ LP-5030 [M]	Swing Low Sweet Chariot	1963	7.50	15.00	30.00
VEE JAY/CHAMELEON					
❏ D1-74782 [(2)]	The Best of the Staple Singers	1988	3.75	7.50	15.00
WARNER BROS.					
❏ BS 2945	Pass It On	1976	3.00	6.00	12.00
—As "The Staples"					
❏ BS 3084	Family Tree	1977	3.00	6.00	12.00
—As "The Staples"					
❏ BSK 3192	Unlock Your Mind	1978	3.00	6.00	12.00
—As "The Staples"					

STAPLES, GORDON, AND THE MOTOWN STRINGS

45s

MOTOWN

❏ 1180	Strung Out/Sounds of the Zodiac	1971	7.50	15.00	30.00
❏ 1180 [DJ]	Strung Out (same on both sides)	1971	7.50	15.00	30.00
—Red vinyl promo					

STAPLES, MAVIS

Also see THE STAPLE SINGERS.

12-Inch Singles

PAISLEY PARK

❏ PRO-A-4397 [DJ]	Melody Cool (Edit) (LP)	1990	2.00	4.00	8.00
❏ PRO-A-5991 [DJ]	The Voice (same on both sides)	1993	2.50	5.00	10.00
❏ 21287	Jaguar (4 versions)	1989	2.00	4.00	8.00
❏ 21748	Melody Cool (4 versions)/Time Waits for No One (Edit)	1990	2.00	4.00	8.00
WARNER BROS.					
❏ PRO-A-2444 [DJ]	Show Me How It Works (same on both sides)	1986	—	3.00	6.00
❏ 8837	Tonight I Feel Like Dancing/If I Can't Have You	1979	3.00	6.00	12.00

45s

CURTOM

❏ 0132	A Piece of the Action/Till Blossoms Bloom	1977	—	2.00	4.00
PAISLEY PARK					
❏ 22968	20th Century Express/All the Discomforts of Home	1989	—	—	3.00
PHONO					
❏ 1051	Love Gone Bad/(B-side unknown)	1984	—	2.50	5.00
VOLT					
❏ 4044	I Have Learned to Do Without You/Since I Fell for You	1970	—	2.50	5.00
❏ 4086	Endlessly/Don't Change Me Now	1972	—	2.50	5.00
WARNER BROS.					
❏ PRO-S-3878 [DJ]	Christmas Vacation (same on both sides)	1989	—	2.50	5.00
❏ 8838	Tonight I Feel Like Dancing/If I Can't Have You	1979	—	2.00	4.00

Number	Title (A Side/B Side)	Yr	VG	VG+	NM
❏ 28765	Show Me How It Works/Half Time	1986	—	—	3.00
❏ 49054	Oh What a Feeling/If I Can't Have You	1979	—	2.00	4.00
Albums					
CURTOM					
❏ CU 5019	A Piece of the Action	1977	3.00	6.00	12.00
PAISLEY PARK					
❏ 25798	Time Waits for No One	1989	3.00	6.00	12.00
STAX					
❏ STX-4118	Mavis Staples	198?	2.50	5.00	10.00
—Reissue of Volt 6007					
❏ MPS-8539	Only for the Lonely	1987	2.50	5.00	10.00
—Reissue of Volt 6010					
VOLT					
❏ VOS-6007	Mavis Staples	1969	5.00	10.00	20.00
❏ VOS-6010	Only for the Lonely	1970	5.00	10.00	20.00
WARNER BROS.					
❏ BSK 3319	Oh What a Feeling	1979	3.00	6.00	12.00

STARLETS, THE (1)

Later recorded as THE ANGELS (1).

45s

ASTRO

❏ 202/3	P.S. I Love You/Where Is My Love Tonight	1960	7.50	15.00	30.00
❏ 204	Romeo and Juliet/Listen for a Lonely Tambourine	1960	6.25	12.50	25.00

STARLETS, THE (2)

45s

CHESS

❏ 1997	My Baby's Real/Loving You Is Something New	1967	6.25	12.50	25.00
❏ 2038	I Wanna Be Good to You/Watered Down	1968	5.00	10.00	20.00

STARLETS, THE (3)

This is the same group that, as THE BLUE-BELLES, recorded "I Sold My Heart to the Junkman."

45s

LUTE

❏ 5909	I'm So Young/He's Got It	1960	6.25	12.50	25.00
PAM					
❏ 1003	Better Tell Him No/You Are the One	1961	5.00	10.00	20.00
❏ 1004	My Last Cry/Money Hungry	1961	5.00	10.00	20.00

STARLETTES, THE

45s

CHECKER

❏ 895	Please Ring My Phone/Jungle Love	1958	37.50	75.00	150.00

STARR, EDWIN

12-Inch Singles

20TH CENTURY

❏ TCD-62	I Just Wanna Do My Thing/Mr. Davenport and Mr. James	1977	3.75	7.50	15.00
❏ TCD-107 [DJ]	Tell a Star (same on both sides)	1980	2.50	5.00	10.00
❏ TCD-128 [DJ]	Real Live #10 (stereo/mono)	1981	2.50	5.00	10.00
A.S.K.					
❏ S-29116	Hit Me with Your Love/Over and Over	198?	2.00	4.00	8.00

45s

20TH CENTURY

❏ 2338	I Just Wanna Do My Thing/Mr. Davenport and Mr. James	1977	—	2.00	4.00
❏ 2389	I'm So Into You/Don't Waste Your Time	1978	—	2.00	4.00
❏ 2396	Contact/Don't Waste Your Time	1978	—	2.00	4.00
❏ 2408	H.A.P.P.Y. Radio/My Friend	1979	—	2.00	4.00
❏ 2420	It's Called the Rock/Patiently	1979	—	2.00	4.00
❏ 2423	It's Called the Rock/H.A.P.P.Y. Radio	1979	—	2.00	4.00
❏ 2441	It's Called the Rock/H.A.P.P.Y. Radio	1980	—	2.00	4.00
❏ 2445	Stronger Than You Think I Am/(Instrumental)	1980	—	2.00	4.00
❏ 2450	Tell-A-Star/Boop Boop Song	1980	—	2.00	4.00
❏ 2455	Get Up-Whirlpool/Better and Better	1980	—	2.00	4.00
❏ 2477	Twenty-Five Miles/Never Turn My Back on You	1980	—	2.00	4.00
❏ 2496	Real Live #10/Sweat	1981	—	2.00	4.00
GORDY					
❏ 7066	Gonna Keep On Tryin' 'Til I Win Your Love/I Want My Baby Back	1967	—	3.00	6.00
❏ 7071	I Am the Man for You Baby/My Weakness Is You	1968	—	3.00	6.00
❏ 7078	Way Over There/If My Heart Could Tell the Story	1968	—	3.00	6.00
❏ 7083	Twenty-Five Miles/Love Is the Destination	1969	—	3.00	6.00
❏ 7087	I'm Still a Struggling Man/Pretty Little Angel	1969	—	3.00	6.00
❏ 7090	Oh How Happy/Ooh Baby Baby	1969	—	3.00	6.00
—With Blinky					
❏ 7097	Time/Running Back and Forth	1970	—	3.00	6.00
❏ 7101	War/He Who Picks a Rose	1970	—	3.00	6.00
❏ 7104	Stop the War Now/Gonna Keep On Tryin' 'Til I Win Your Love	1970	—	3.00	6.00
❏ 7107	Funky Music Sho Nuff Turns Me On/Cloud Nine	1971	—	3.00	6.00
GRANITE					
❏ 522	Pain/I'll Never Forget You	1975	—	2.50	5.00
❏ 528	Stay with Me/Party	1975	—	2.50	5.00
❏ 532	Abyssinia Jones/Beginning	1975	—	2.50	5.00
MONTAGE					
❏ 1216	Tired of It/(B-side unknown)	1982	—	2.00	4.00
MOTOWN					
❏ 1276	You've Got My Soul on Fire/Love (The Lonely People's Prayer)	1973	—	2.50	5.00

Number	Title (A Side/B Side)	Yr	VG	VG+	NM
❑ 1284	Ain't It Hell Up in Harlem/Don't It Feel Good to Be Free	1973	—	2.50	5.00
❑ 1300	Big Papa/Like We Used to Do	1974	—	2.50	5.00
❑ 1326	Who's Right or Wrong/Lonely Rainy Days in San Diego	1974	—	2.50	5.00

RIC-TIC

Number	Title (A Side/B Side)	Yr	VG	VG+	NM
❑ 103	Agent Double-O-Soul/(Instrumental)	1965	3.75	7.50	15.00
❑ 107	Back Street/(Instrumental)	1965	3.75	7.50	15.00
❑ 109X [DJ]	Scott's On Swingers (S.O.S.)/I Have Faith in You	1966	12.50	25.00	50.00
❑ 109	Stop Her on Sight (S.O.S.)/I Have Faith in You	1966	3.75	7.50	15.00
❑ 114	Headline News/Harlem	1966	3.75	7.50	15.00
❑ 118	It's My Turn Now/Girls Are Getting Prettier	1967	3.75	7.50	15.00
❑ 120	You're My Mellow/My Kind of Woman	1967	15.00	30.00	60.00

SOUL

Number	Title (A Side/B Side)	Yr	VG	VG+	NM
❑ 35096	Take Me Clear from Here/Ball of Confusion	1972	—	3.00	6.00
❑ 35100	Who Is the Leader of the People/Don't Tell Me I'm Crazy	1972	—	3.00	6.00
❑ 35103	There You Go/(Instrumental)	1973	—	3.00	6.00

Albums

20TH CENTURY

Number	Title (A Side/B Side)	Yr	VG	VG+	NM
❑ T-538	Edwin Starr	1977	2.50	5.00	10.00
❑ T-559	Clean	1978	2.50	5.00	10.00
❑ T-591	Happy Radio	1979	2.50	5.00	10.00
❑ T-615	Stronger Than You	1980	2.50	5.00	10.00
❑ T-634	The Best of Edwin Starr	1981	2.50	5.00	10.00

GORDY

Number	Title (A Side/B Side)	Yr	VG	VG+	NM
❑ GS-931	Soul Master	1968	6.25	12.50	25.00
❑ GS-940	25 Miles	1969	6.25	12.50	25.00
❑ GS-945	Just We Two	1969	5.00	10.00	20.00
—With Blinky					
❑ GS-948	War & Peace	1970	5.00	10.00	20.00
❑ GS-956	Involved	1971	5.00	10.00	20.00

GRANITE

Number	Title (A Side/B Side)	Yr	VG	VG+	NM
❑ 1005	Free to Be Myself	1975	3.00	6.00	12.00

MOTOWN

Number	Title (A Side/B Side)	Yr	VG	VG+	NM
❑ M5-103V1	Superstar Series, Vol. 3	1981	2.50	5.00	10.00
❑ M5-170V1	War & Peace	1981	2.50	5.00	10.00

PICKWICK

Number	Title (A Side/B Side)	Yr	VG	VG+	NM
❑ SPC-3387	25 Miles	197?	2.50	5.00	10.00

STATON, CANDI

12-Inch Singles

LA

Number	Title (A Side/B Side)	Yr	VG	VG+	NM
❑ 8012	Without You I Cry (4:47)/(B-side unknown)	1981	2.50	5.00	10.00

SUGAR HILL

Number	Title (A Side/B Side)	Yr	VG	VG+	NM
❑ 568	Count On Me/(Instrumental)	1981	2.50	5.00	10.00
❑ 571	Suspicious Minds/Love and Be Free	1982	2.50	5.00	10.00

WARNER BROS.

Number	Title (A Side/B Side)	Yr	VG	VG+	NM
❑ PRO-A-772 [DJ]	Honest I Do Love You (6:31) (same on both sides)	1978	3.00	6.00	12.00
❑ PRO-A-827 [DJ]	Chance (5:34)/Rock (7:16)	1979	3.00	6.00	12.00
❑ PRO-A-867 [DJ]	Looking for Love (same on both sides)	1980	3.00	6.00	12.00
❑ 8820	When You Wake Up Tomorrow/Rough Times	1979	3.00	6.00	12.00

45s

FAME

Number	Title (A Side/B Side)	Yr	VG	VG+	NM
❑ XW256	Something's Burning/It's Not Love	1973	—	2.50	5.00
❑ XW328	Love Chain/I'm Gonna Hold On	1973	—	2.50	5.00
❑ 1456	I'd Rather Be an Old Man's Sweetheart (Than a Young Man's Fool)/For You	1969	—	3.00	6.00
❑ 1459	Never in Public/You Don't Love Me No More	1969	—	3.00	6.00
❑ 1460	I'm Just a Prisoner (Of Your Good Lovin')/Heart on a String	1969	—	3.00	6.00
❑ 1466	Sweet Feeling/Evidence	1970	—	3.00	6.00
❑ 1472	Stand By Your Man/How Can I Put Out the Flame (When You Keep the Fire Burning)	1970	—	3.00	6.00
❑ 1476	He Called Me Baby/What Would Become of Me	1970	—	3.00	6.00
❑ 1478	Mr. and Mrs. Untrue/Too Hurt to Cry	1971	—	3.00	6.00
❑ 91000	In the Ghetto/Sure As Sin	1972	—	2.50	5.00
❑ 91005	Lovin' You, Lovin' Me/You Don't Love Me No More	1972	—	2.50	5.00
❑ 91009	Do It in the Name of Love/The Thanks I Get for Loving You	1972	—	2.50	5.00

LA

Number	Title (A Side/B Side)	Yr	VG	VG+	NM
❑ 0080	Without You I Cry/(B-side unknown)	1981	—	2.50	5.00

SUGAR HILL

Number	Title (A Side/B Side)	Yr	VG	VG+	NM
❑ 770	Count on Me/(B-side unknown)	1981	—	2.50	5.00
❑ 776	Suspicious Minds/(B-side unknown)	1982	—	2.50	5.00
❑ 784	Hurry Sundown/Count on Me	1982	—	2.50	5.00

UNITY

Number	Title (A Side/B Side)	Yr	VG	VG+	NM
❑ 711	Now That You Have the Upper Hand/(B-side unknown)	196?	37.50	75.00	150.00

WARNER BROS.

Number	Title (A Side/B Side)	Yr	VG	VG+	NM
❑ 8038	As Long As He Takes Care of Business/Little Taste of Love	1974	—	2.00	4.00
❑ 8078	Here I Am Again/Your Opening Night	1975	—	2.00	4.00
❑ 8112	Six Nights and a Day/We Can Work It Out	1975	—	2.00	4.00
❑ 8181	Young Hearts Run Free/I Know	1976	—	2.00	4.00
❑ 8249	Run to Me/What a Feeling	1976	—	2.00	4.00
❑ 8320	A Dreamer of a Dream/When You Want Love	1977	—	2.00	4.00
❑ 8387	Nights on Broadway/You Are	1977	—	2.00	4.00
❑ 8461	Music Speaks Louder Than Words/Cotton Candi	1977	—	2.00	4.00
❑ 8477	Listen to the Music/Music Speaks Louder Than Words	1977	—	2.00	4.00
❑ 8582	Victim/So Blue	1978	—	2.00	4.00
❑ 8691	Honest I Do Love You/I'm Gonna Make Me Love You	1978	—	2.00	4.00
❑ 8821	When You Wake Up Tomorrow/Rough Times	1979	—	2.00	4.00
❑ 49061	Chance/I Live	1979	—	2.00	4.00
❑ 49240	Looking for Love/It's Real	1980	—	2.00	4.00
❑ 49240 [PS]	Looking for Love/It's Real	1980	—	3.00	6.00
❑ 49536	The Hunter Gets Captured by the Game/If You Feel the Need	1980	—	2.00	4.00

Albums

FAME

Number	Title (A Side/B Side)	Yr	VG	VG+	NM
❑ 1800	Candi Staton	1972	5.00	10.00	20.00
❑ ST-4201	I'm a Prisoner	1970	5.00	10.00	20.00
❑ ST-4202	Stand By Your Man	1971	5.00	10.00	20.00

WARNER BROS.

Number	Title (A Side/B Side)	Yr	VG	VG+	NM
❑ BS 2830	Candi	1974	3.00	6.00	12.00
❑ BS 2948	Young Hearts Run Free	1976	3.00	6.00	12.00
❑ BS 3040	Music Speaks Louder Than Words	1977	3.00	6.00	12.00
❑ BSK 3207	House of Love	1978	3.00	6.00	12.00
❑ BSK 3333	Chance	1979	3.00	6.00	12.00
❑ BSK 3428	Candi Staton	1980	3.00	6.00	12.00

STEVENSON, B.W.

45s

MCA

Number	Title (A Side/B Side)	Yr	VG	VG+	NM
❑ 41151	A Special Wish/Holding a Special Place for You	1979	—	2.00	4.00
❑ 41166	Headin' Home/Holding a Special Place for You	1980	—	2.00	4.00

PRIVATE STOCK

Number	Title (A Side/B Side)	Yr	VG	VG+	NM
❑ 45208	Holdin' On for Dear Love/I'm a Better Man for Lovin' You	1979	—	2.00	4.00

RCA VICTOR

Number	Title (A Side/B Side)	Yr	VG	VG+	NM
❑ 47-0728	Say What I Feel/Lonesome Song	1972	—	2.50	5.00
❑ 47-0778	On My Own/Highway One	1972	—	2.50	5.00
❑ 47-0840	Minuet for My Lady/Don't Go to Mexico	1972	—	2.50	5.00
❑ 47-0952	Shambala/My Feet Are So Weary	1973	—	3.00	6.00
❑ APBO-0030	My Maria/August Evening Lady	1973	—	3.00	6.00
❑ APBO-0171	River of Love/Lucky Touch	1973	—	2.50	5.00
❑ APBO-0242	Song for Katy/Look for the Light	1974	—	2.00	4.00
❑ APBO-0279	Remember Me/Roll On	1974	—	2.00	4.00
❑ PB-10012	Here We Go Again/Little Bit of Understanding	1974	—	2.00	4.00
❑ GB-10158	My Maria/Shambala	1975	—	—	3.00
—Gold Standard Series					

WARNER BROS.

Number	Title (A Side/B Side)	Yr	VG	VG+	NM
❑ 8184	Jerrry's Bar and Grill/Way Down by the Ocean	1976	—	2.00	4.00
❑ 8247	Dream Baby/Wastin' Time	1976	—	2.00	4.00
❑ 8343	Down to the Station/May You Find Yourself in Heaven	1977	—	2.00	4.00

Albums

MCA

Number	Title (A Side/B Side)	Yr	VG	VG+	NM
❑ 3215	Lifeline	1980	2.50	5.00	10.00

RCA VICTOR

Number	Title (A Side/B Side)	Yr	VG	VG+	NM
❑ APL1-0088	My Maria	1973	3.00	6.00	12.00
❑ APL1-0410	Calabasas	1974	3.00	6.00	12.00
❑ APL1-2394	The Best of B.W. Stevenson	1977	2.50	5.00	10.00
❑ LSP-4685	B.W. Stevenson	1972	3.75	7.50	15.00
❑ LSP-4794	Lead Free	1972	3.75	7.50	15.00

WARNER BROS.

Number	Title (A Side/B Side)	Yr	VG	VG+	NM
❑ BS 2901	We Be Sailin'	1976	2.50	5.00	10.00
❑ BS 3012	Lost	1977	2.50	5.00	10.00

STEWART, AMII

45s

ARIOLA AMERICA

Number	Title (A Side/B Side)	Yr	VG	VG+	NM
❑ 7736	Knock on Wood/When You Are Beautiful	1979	—	2.50	5.00
❑ 7753	Light My Fire-137 Disco Heaven/Am I Losing	1979	—	2.00	4.00
❑ 7771	Jealousy/Step Into the Love Line	1979	—	2.00	4.00

EMERGENCY

Number	Title (A Side/B Side)	Yr	VG	VG+	NM
❑ 4548	Friends/Picture	1985	—	2.00	4.00

HANDSHAKE

Number	Title (A Side/B Side)	Yr	VG	VG+	NM
❑ 02441	Why'd You Have to Be So Sexy/Where Did Our Love Go	1981	—	2.00	4.00
❑ 02591	I'm Gonna Get Your Love/Premier	1981	—	2.00	4.00
❑ 02844	Digital Love/Tonight	1982	—	2.00	4.00
❑ 5300	My Guy-My Girl/Now	1980	—	2.00	4.00
—With Johnny Bristol					

Albums

ARIOLA AMERICA

Number	Title (A Side/B Side)	Yr	VG	VG+	NM
❑ SW 50054	Knock on Wood	1979	3.00	6.00	12.00
❑ SW 50072	Paradise Bird	1979	2.50	5.00	10.00

STEWART, BILLY

45s

ARGO

Number	Title (A Side/B Side)	Yr	VG	VG+	NM
❑ 5256	Billy's Blues (Part 1)/Billy's Blues (Part 2)	1956	10.00	20.00	40.00

CHESS

Number	Title (A Side/B Side)	Yr	VG	VG+	NM
❑ 1625	Billy's Blues (Part 1)/Billy's Blues (Part 2)	1956	15.00	30.00	60.00
❑ 1820	Reap What You Sow/Fat Boy	1962	3.00	6.00	12.00
❑ 1835	True Fine Lovin'/Wedding Bells	1962	3.00	6.00	12.00
❑ 1852	Scramble/Oh What Can the Matter Be	1963	3.00	6.00	12.00
❑ 1868	Strange Feeling/Sugar and Spice	1963	3.00	6.00	12.00
❑ 1888	Count Me Out/A Fat Boy Can Cry	1964	2.50	5.00	10.00
❑ 1905	Tell It Like It Is/My Sweet Senorita	1964	2.50	5.00	10.00
❑ 1922	I Do Love You/Keep Loving	1965	2.50	5.00	10.00
❑ 1932	Sitting in the Park/Once Again	1965	2.50	5.00	10.00

Number	Title (A Side/B Side)	Yr	VG	VG+	NM
❏ 1941	How Nice It Is/No Girl	1965	2.50	5.00	10.00
❏ 1948	Because I Love You/Mountain of Love	1965	2.50	5.00	10.00
❏ 1960	Love Me/Why Am I Lonely	1966	2.50	5.00	10.00
❏ 1966	Summertime/To Love, To Love	1966	3.75	7.50	15.00
—Black label					
❏ 1966	Summertime/To Love, To Love	1966	3.00	6.00	12.00
—Blueish label					
❏ 1978	Secret Love/Look Back and Smile	1966	2.50	5.00	10.00
❏ 1991	Every Day I Have the Blues/Ol' Man River	1967	2.50	5.00	10.00
❏ 2002	Cross My Heart/Why (Do I Love You So)	1967	2.50	5.00	10.00
❏ 2053	Tell Me the Truth/What Have I Done	1968	2.50	5.00	10.00
❏ 2063	I'm in Love (Oh Yes I Am)/Crazy 'Bout You Baby	1969	2.50	5.00	10.00
❏ 2080	By the Time I Get to Phoenix/We'll Always Be Together	1969	2.50	5.00	10.00
OKEH					
❏ 7095	Baby, You're My Only Love/Billy's Heartache	1957	75.00	150.00	300.00
UNITED ARTISTS					
❏ 340	This Is a Fine Time/Young in Years	1961	3.75	7.50	15.00
Albums					
CHESS					
❏ LP-1496 [M]	I Do Love You	1965	20.00	40.00	80.00
—Red cover, black "wheel"					
❏ LP-1496 [M]	I Do Love You	196?	7.50	15.00	30.00
—Green "woman" cover					
❏ LPS-1496 [S]	I Do Love You	1965	25.00	50.00	100.00
—Red cover, black "wheel"					
❏ LPS-1496 [S]	I Do Love You	196?	10.00	20.00	40.00
—Green "woman" cover					
❏ LP-1499 [M]	Unbelievable	1966	7.50	15.00	30.00
❏ LPS-1499 [S]	Unbelievable	1966	10.00	20.00	40.00
❏ LP-1513 [M]	Billy Stewart Teaches Old Standards New Tricks	1967	7.50	15.00	30.00
❏ LPS-1513 [S]	Billy Stewart Teaches Old Standards New Tricks	1967	10.00	20.00	40.00
❏ LPS-1547	Billy Stewart Remembered	1970	6.25	12.50	25.00
❏ CH-9104	The Greatest Sides	198?	2.50	5.00	10.00
❏ CH-50059	Cross My Heart	1974	3.75	7.50	15.00

STEWART, SLY

Sylvester Stewart, later "Sly" of SLY AND THE FAMILY STONE.

12-Inch Singles

EPIC

Number	Title (A Side/B Side)	Yr	VG	VG+	NM
❏ 50794	Dance to the Music/Sing a Simple Song	1979	3.75	7.50	15.00
—As "Sly Stone"					

45s

AUTUMN

❏ 3	I Just Learned How to Swim/Scat Swim	1964	5.00	10.00	20.00
—Sylvester Stewart, later "Sly" of The Family Stone					
❏ 14	Buttermilk — Part 1/Buttermilk — Part 2	1965	5.00	10.00	20.00
—As "Sly"					
❏ 26	Temptation Walk/Temptation Walk — Part 2	1966	5.00	10.00	20.00
A&M					
❏ 2890	Eek-Ah-Bo-Static Automatic/Black Girls	1986	—	—	3.00
—B-side by Rae Dawn Chong					
❏ 2896	Love and Affection/Black Girls	1986	—	—	3.00
—A-side as "Sly Stone and Martha Davis"; B-side by Rae Dawn Chong					
EPIC					
❏ 50795	Dance to the Music/Sing a Simple Song	1979	—	2.50	5.00
—As "Sly Stone"					
G&P					
❏ 901	Help Me With My Heart/A Long Time Away	1962	62.50	125.00	250.00
—As "Sylvester Stewart"					
LUKE					
❏ 1008	A Long Time Alone/I'm Just a Fool	1961	62.50	125.00	250.00
—As "Danny Stewart"					

STRIKES, THE

45s

IMPERIAL

❏ 5433	Baby I'm Sorry/If You Can't Rock Me	1957	12.50	25.00	50.00
❏ 5446	Rockin'/I Don't Want to Cry Over You	1957	12.50	25.00	50.00
LIN					
❏ 5006	Baby I'm Sorry/If You Can't Rock Me	1957	18.75	37.50	75.00

STRONG, BARRETT

45s

ANNA

❏ 1111	Money (That's What I Want)/Oh I Apologize	1960	7.50	15.00	30.00
❏ 1116	You Know What to Do/Yes, No, Maybe You	1960	6.25	12.50	25.00
ATCO					
❏ 6225	Seven Sins/What Went Wrong	1962	10.00	20.00	40.00
CAPITOL					
❏ 4052	Is It True/Anywhere	1975	—	2.50	5.00
❏ 4120	Surrender/There's Something About You	1975	—	2.50	5.00
❏ 4223	Gonna Make It Right/The Man Up in the Sky	1976	—	2.50	5.00
EPIC					
❏ 11011	Stand Up and Cheer for the Preacher (Part 1)/Stand Up and Cheer for the Preacher (Part 2)	1973	—	2.50	5.00
PHASE II					
❏ 02048	Rock It Easy/Love Will Make It Right	1981	—	2.00	4.00
TAMLA					
❏ 54022	Let's Rock/(B-side unknown)	1960	1000.	1500.	2000.
❏ 54027	Money (That's What I Want)/Oh I Apologize	1960	30.00	60.00	120.00
—Horizontal lines label					
❏ 54027	Money (That's What I Want)/Oh I Apologize	1960	12.50	25.00	50.00
—Globe label					

Number	Title (A Side/B Side)	Yr	VG	VG+	NM
❏ 54029	You Know What to Do/Yes, No, Maybe So	1960	12.50	25.00	50.00
❏ 54033	I'm Gonna Cry/Whirl Wind	1960	12.50	25.00	50.00
❏ 54035	You Got What It Takes/Money and Me	1961	12.50	25.00	50.00
❏ 54043	Two Wrongs Don't Make a Right/Misery	1961	12.50	25.00	50.00
TOLLIE					
78s					
❏ 9023	Make Up Your Mind/I Better Run	1964	7.50	15.00	30.00
ANNA					
78s					
❏ 1111	Money (That's What I Want)/Oh I Apologize	1959	200.00	400.00	800.00
Albums					
CAPITOL					
❏ ST-11376	Stronghold	1975	3.00	6.00	12.00

STRONG, NOLAN, AND THE DIABLOS

Some of these refer only to "The Diablos," others only to "Nolan Strong."

45s

FORTUNE

❏ 509/10	Adios, My Desert Love/(I Want) An Old Fashioned Girl	1954	25.00	50.00	100.00
❏ 511	The Wind/Baby, Be Mine	1954	25.00	50.00	100.00
❏ 511	The Wind/Baby, Be Mine	196?	5.00	10.00	20.00
—Later pressing adds reference to LP on which it appears					
❏ 514	Hold Me Until Eternity/Route 16	1955	25.00	50.00	100.00
❏ 516	Daddy Rockin' Strong/Do You Remember What You Did Last Night	1955	25.00	50.00	100.00
❏ 518	The Way You Dog Me Around/Jump, Shake and Move	1955	25.00	50.00	100.00
❏ 519	You're the Only Girl, Dolores/You Are	1956	20.00	40.00	80.00
❏ 522	Teardrop from Heaven/Try Me One More Time	1956	20.00	40.00	80.00
❏ 525	Can't We Talk This Over/The Mambo of Love	1957	20.00	40.00	80.00
❏ 529	For Old Times' Sake/My Heart Will Always Belong to You	1959	10.00	20.00	40.00
❏ 531	I Am With You/Goodbye Matilda	1959	10.00	20.00	40.00
❏ 532	If I Could Be with You Tonite/I Wanna Know	1959	10.00	20.00	40.00
❏ 536	Since You're Gone/What You Gonna Do	1960	7.50	15.00	30.00
❏ 544	Blue Moon/I Don't Care	1962	5.00	10.00	20.00
❏ 546	Mind Over Matter (I'm Gonna Make You Mine)/Beside You	1962	5.00	10.00	20.00
❏ 553	I Really Love You/You're My Love	1963	5.00	10.00	20.00
❏ 556	(Yeah, Baby) It's Because of You/You're Every Beat of My Heart	1963	5.00	10.00	20.00
❏ 564	Are You Making a Fool Out of Me/You're My Happiness	1964	3.75	7.50	15.00
❏ 569	(What Did That Genie Mean When He Said) Ali-Coochie/(You're Not Good Looking But) You're Presentable	1964	3.75	7.50	15.00
❏ 574	The Way You Dog Me Around/Jump with Me	1980	3.75	7.50	15.00
PYRAMID					
❏ 159	White Christmas/Danny Boy	19??	3.75	7.50	15.00
Albums					
FORTUNE					
❏ LP-8010 [M]	Fortune of Hits	1961	55.00	110.00	220.00
—Purple label, thick vinyl					
❏ LP-8010 [M]	Fortune of Hits	196?	12.50	25.00	50.00
—Yellow label					
❏ LP-8010 [M]	Fortune of Hits	197?	3.75	7.50	15.00
—Purple label, thinner, more flexible vinyl					
❏ LP-8012 [M]	Fortune of Hits, Vol. 2	1962	55.00	110.00	220.00
—Purple label, thick vinyl					
❏ LP-8012 [M]	Fortune of Hits, Vol. 2	196?	12.50	25.00	50.00
—Yellow label					
❏ LP-8012 [M]	Fortune of Hits, Vol. 2	197?	3.75	7.50	15.00
—Purple label, thinner, more flexible vinyl					
❏ LP-8015 [M]	Mind Over Matter	1963	62.50	125.00	250.00
—Purple label, thick vinyl					
❏ LP-8015 [M]	Mind Over Matter	196?	15.00	30.00	60.00
—Yellow label					
❏ LP-8015 [M]	Mind Over Matter	197?	5.00	10.00	20.00
—Purple label, thinner, more flexible vinyl					

STUBBS, LEVI

Also see FOUR TOPS.

12-Inch Singles

GEFFEN

❏ PRO-A-2666 [DJ]	Mean Green Mother from Outer Space (Edit) (LP Version)	1986	2.50	5.00	10.00

STUDENTS, THE

45s

ARGO

❏ 5386	I'm So Young/Every Day of the Week	1961	5.00	10.00	20.00
CHECKER					
❏ 902	I'm So Young/Every Day of the Week	1958	10.00	20.00	40.00
❏ 1004	My Vow to You/That's How I Feel	1962	3.75	7.50	15.00
NOTE					
❏ 10012	I'm So Young/Every Day of the Week	1958	125.00	250.00	500.00
❏ 10019	My Vow to You/That's How I Feel	1959	100.00	200.00	400.00
RED TOP					
❏ 100	My Heart Is an Open Door/Mommy and Daddy	1958	50.00	100.00	200.00
—Blue label					
❏ 100	My Heart Is an Open Door/Mommy and Daddy	1958	10.00	20.00	40.00
—Red label					

S

Number	Title (A Side/B Side)	Yr	VG	VG+	NM

STYLERS, THE (1)
45s
GOLDEN CREST
❑ 117	You Tell Me/Blues in the Night	1957	10.00	20.00	40.00
❑ 117 [PS]	You Tell Me/Blues in the Night	1957	25.00	50.00	100.00
❑ 129	Kiss and Run Lover/Girlie, Girlie, Girlie	1957	10.00	20.00	40.00
JUBILEE
❑ 5168	Believe It or Not/The World Is Yours	1954	10.00	20.00	40.00
❑ 5188	Shoo Shoo Sha La La/I Love Ya Like Crazy	1955	10.00	20.00	40.00
❑ 5246	Lost John/Huffin' and Puffin'	1956	10.00	20.00	40.00
❑ 5253	Confession of a Sinner/Gonna Tell 'Em	1956	10.00	20.00	40.00
❑ 5279	Breaker of Hearts/Miracle in Milan	1957	7.50	15.00	30.00

STYLES, THE (1)
45s
JOSIE
| ❑ 920 | I Love You for Sentimental Reasons/School Bells to Chapel Bells | 1964 | 15.00 | 30.00 | 60.00 |
SERENE
| ❑ 1501 | Scarlet Angel/Gotta Go, Go, Go | 1961 | 37.50 | 75.00 | 150.00 |

STYLES, THE (2)
45s
MODERN
| ❑ 1048 | I Know You Know That I Know/Baby You're Alive | 1967 | 3.00 | 6.00 | 12.00 |
SWAN
| ❑ 4258 | I Do Love You/Hush Little Girl | 1966 | 3.00 | 6.00 | 12.00 |

STYLISTICS, THE
12-Inch Singles
H&L
| ❑ 2008 | The Lion Sleeps Tonight (5:29)/Fly! (6:09) | 1977 | 3.75 | 7.50 | 15.00 |
STREETWISE
❑ 2236	Give a Little Love/Give a Little Love (Sing Along Version)	1984	2.00	4.00	8.00
❑ 2237	Some Things Never Change/Row Your Love	1985	2.00	4.00	8.00
❑ 2238	Special/(B-side unknown)	1985	2.00	4.00	8.00
❑ 2241	Let's Go Rockin' (Tonight)/(B-side unknown)	1986	2.00	4.00	8.00
45s
AMHERST
| ❑ 301 | Because I Love You Girl/My Love, Come Live With Me | 1985 | — | 2.00 | 4.00 |
AVCO
❑ 4581	You Are Everything/Country Living	1971	—	2.50	5.00
❑ 4591	Betcha by Golly, Wow/Ebony Eyes	1972	—	2.50	5.00
❑ 4595	People Make the World Go Round/Point of No Return	1972	—	2.50	5.00
❑ 4603	I'm Stone in Love with You/Make It Last	1972	—	2.50	5.00
❑ 4611	Break Up to Make Up/You and Me	1973	—	2.50	5.00
❑ 4618	You'll Never Get to Heaven (If You Break My Heart)/If You Don't Watch Out	1973	—	2.50	5.00
❑ 4625	Rockin' Roll Baby/Pieces	1973	—	2.50	5.00
❑ 4634	You Make Me Feel Brand New/Only for the Children	1974	—	2.50	5.00
❑ 4640	Let's Put It All Together/I Take It Out on You	1974	—	2.50	5.00
❑ 4647	Heavy Fallin' Out/Go Now	1974	—	2.50	5.00
❑ 4649	Star on a TV Show/Hey Girl, Come and Get It	1975	—	2.50	5.00
❑ 4652	Thank You Baby/Sing, Baby, Sing	1975	—	2.50	5.00
❑ 4656	Can't Give You Anything (But My Love)/I'd Rather Be Hurt by You	1975	—	2.50	5.00
❑ 4661	Funky Weekend/If You Are There	1975	—	2.50	5.00
❑ 4664	You Are Beautiful/Michael and Me	1976	—	2.50	5.00
❑ 4664 [PS]	You Are Beautiful/Michael and Me	1976	2.50	5.00	10.00
AVCO EMBASSY
| ❑ 4555 | You're a Big Girl Now/Let the Junkie Beat the Pusher | 1970 | — | 3.00 | 6.00 |
| ❑ 4572 | Stop, Look, Listen (To Your Heart)/If I Love You | 1971 | — | 3.00 | 6.00 |
H&L
❑ 4669	Can't Help Falling in Love/Jenny	1976	—	2.00	4.00
❑ 4674	Because I Love You, Girl/You Are	1976	—	2.00	4.00
❑ 4676	Only You/What Goes Around Comes Around	1976	—	2.00	4.00
❑ 4678	I Got a Letter/Satin Doll	1977	—	2.00	4.00
❑ 4681	Shame and Scandal in the Family/That Don't Shake Me	1977	—	2.00	4.00
❑ 4686	I'm Coming Home/I Run to You	1977	—	2.00	4.00
❑ 4695	Fool of the Year/Good Thing Goin'	1978	—	2.00	4.00
MERCURY
❑ 74005	First Impressions/Your Love's Too Good to Be Forgotten	1978	—	2.00	4.00
❑ 74022	I Can't Stop Livin'/You're the Best Thing in My Life	1978	—	2.00	4.00
❑ 74042	Love at First Sight/Broken Wing	1979	—	2.00	4.00
❑ 74057	Don't Know Where I'm Going/You Make Me Feel So Doggone Good	1979	—	2.00	4.00
PHILADELPHIA INT'L.
| ❑ 02901 | Callin' You/Don't Come Telling Me Lies | 1982 | — | 2.00 | 4.00 |
| ❑ 03085 | Lighten Up/We Should Be Lovers | 1982 | — | 2.00 | 4.00 |
SEBRING
| ❑ 8370 | You're a Big Girl Now/Let the Junkie Beat the Pusher | 1970 | 7.50 | 15.00 | 30.00 |
STREETWISE
❑ 1136	Give a Little Love/Give a Little Love (Sing Along Version)	1984	—	2.00	4.00
❑ 1137	Some Things Never Change/Row Your Love	1985	—	2.00	4.00
❑ 1138	Special/(B-side unknown)	1985	—	2.00	4.00
TSOP
❑ 02195	What's Your Name/Almost There	1981	—	2.00	4.00
❑ 02588	Mine All Mine/Closer Than Close	1981	—	2.00	4.00
❑ 02702	Habit/I've Got This Feeling	1982	—	2.00	4.00
❑ 4789	Hurry Up This Way Again/It Started Out	1980	—	2.00	4.00
❑ 4798	And I'll See You No More/Driving Me Wild	1980	—	2.00	4.00
Albums
AMHERST
❑ AMH-743	The Best of the Stylistics	1986	2.50	5.00	10.00
❑ AMH-744	All-Time Classics	1986	2.50	5.00	10.00
❑ AMH-745	The Best of the Stylistics, Vol. 2	1986	2.50	5.00	10.00
❑ AMH-746	Greatest Love Hits	1986	2.50	5.00	10.00
AVCO
❑ 11006	Round 2: The Stylistics	1972	5.00	10.00	20.00
❑ 11010	Rockin' Roll Baby	1973	5.00	10.00	20.00
❑ AV-33023	The Stylistics	1971	5.00	10.00	20.00
❑ AV-69001	Let's Put It All Together	1974	3.75	7.50	15.00
❑ AV-69004	Heavy	1974	3.75	7.50	15.00
❑ AV-69005	The Best of the Stylistics	1975	3.75	7.50	15.00
❑ 69008	Thank You Baby	1975	3.75	7.50	15.00
❑ 69010	You Are Beautiful	1975	3.75	7.50	15.00
H&L
| ❑ 69013 | Fabulous | 1976 | 3.00 | 6.00 | 12.00 |
| ❑ 69032 | Wonder Woman | 1978 | 3.00 | 6.00 | 12.00 |
MERCURY
| ❑ SRM-1-3727 | In Fashion | 1978 | 3.00 | 6.00 | 12.00 |
| ❑ SRM-1-3753 | Love Spell | 1979 | 3.00 | 6.00 | 12.00 |
PHILADELPHIA INT'L.
| ❑ FZ 37955 | 1982 | 1982 | 2.50 | 5.00 | 10.00 |
TSOP
| ❑ JZ 36470 | Hurry Up This Way Again | 1980 | 2.50 | 5.00 | 10.00 |
| ❑ FZ 37458 | Closer Than Close | 1981 | 2.50 | 5.00 | 10.00 |

STYLISTS, THE
45s
V.I.P.
| ❑ 25066 | What Is Love/Where Did the Children Go | 1970 | 6.25 | 12.50 | 25.00 |

SUGAR HILL GANG
12-Inch Singles
DIAMOND HEAD
| ❑ (no #) | Boyz from Da Hill (2 versions)/Here We Go (3 versions) | 1994 | 2.00 | 4.00 | 8.00 |
SUGAR HILL
❑ SH 459	Kick It Live from 9 to 5/(Instrumental)	1983	3.00	6.00	12.00
❑ SH 468	Girls (unknown versions)	1983	5.00	10.00	20.00
❑ SH 524	Rapper's Delight (Hip Hop Remix 4:00) (7:00)/Hot Hot Summer Day	1987	3.00	6.00	12.00
❑ SH 542	Rapper's Delight (Long 15:00) (Short 6:30)	1979	7.50	15.00	30.00
❑ SH 545	Rapper's Reprise (Jam-Jam)/Sugar Hill Groove	1980	5.00	10.00	20.00
❑ SH 547	Hot Hot Summer Day (6:58)/(Instrumental)	1980	5.00	10.00	20.00
❑ SH 553	8th Wonder/Sugar Hill Groove	1980	6.25	12.50	25.00
❑ SH 567	Apache/(instrumental)	1981	6.25	12.50	25.00
❑ SH 578	Funk Box/(Instrumental)	1982	5.00	10.00	20.00
❑ SH 581	The Lover in You/(Instrumental)	1982	5.00	10.00	20.00
❑ SH 597	The Word Is Out/(Instrumental)	1983	3.75	7.50	15.00
❑ SH 32021	Livin' in the Fast Lane/(Instrumental)	1984	3.75	7.50	15.00
❑ SH 32030	Troy/Girls	1985	3.75	7.50	15.00
❑ SH 32037	Work, Work the Body/(Instrumental)	1985	5.00	10.00	20.00
❑ SH 32051	The Down Beat/(Instrumental)	1985	3.75	7.50	15.00
45s
SUGAR HILL
❑ 752 [DJ]	Rapper's Delight (4:55)/(6:30)	1979	6.25	12.50	25.00
❑ 755	Here I Am/Rapper's Delight	1980	3.75	7.50	15.00
❑ 774	Apache/Rapper's Delight	1981	2.50	5.00	10.00
❑ 92016	The Down Beat/(B-side unknown)	1984	2.50	5.00	10.00
Albums
SUGAR HILL
❑ SH 245	Sugar Hill Gang	1980	5.00	10.00	20.00
❑ SH 249	8th Wonder	1981	3.75	7.50	15.00
❑ SH 9206	Livin' in the Fast Lane	1984	3.00	6.00	12.00

SUMMER, DONNA
12-Inch Singles
ATLANTIC
❑ DMD 1333 [DJ]	This Time I Know It's for Real (Extended Remix 7:21) (Instrumental 3:34)/If It Makes You Feel Good	1989	3.75	7.50	15.00
❑ DMD 1382 [DJ]	Love's About to Change My Heart (PWL 12" Mix) (PWL 7" Mix) (Clivilles & Cole 12" Mix) (Dub 2) (Clivilles & Cole 7" Mix)	1989	2.50	5.00	10.00
❑ DMD 1431 [DJ]	Breakaway (Extended Mix 6:08) (Power Radio Mix 4:02)/I Don't Wanna Get Hurt (12" Mix)	1989	3.75	7.50	15.00
❑ DMD 1709 [DJ]	When Love Cries (Vocal Club Dub) (Radio Mix) (Club Mix) (Instrumental)	1991	2.50	5.00	10.00
❑ DMD 1758 [DJ]	Work That Magic (4:34) (6:20) (5:00)/Let There Be Peace	1991	3.00	6.00	12.00
❑ DMD 2574 [(2) DJ]	The Power of One (Johnathan Peters Club Mix) (Johnathan Peters Radio Mix) (Tommy Musto Vocal Mix) (Musto Beats) (Gel Dub) (JP Sound Factory Dub) (Sound Factory Club Mix) (Drum-a-Pella)	2000	7.50	15.00	30.00
❑ 85021	The Power of One (4 versions)	2000	3.00	6.00	12.00

Number	Title (A Side/B Side)	Yr	VG	VG+	NM
❑ 85961	When Love Cries (4 versions)	1991	2.00	4.00	8.00
❑ 86255	Breakaway (Extended Mix) (Power Radio Mix)/I Don't Wanna Get Hurt (12" Mix)	1989	2.50	5.00	10.00
❑ 86309	Love's About to Change My Heart (5 versions)	1989	2.50	5.00	10.00
❑ 86415	This Time I Know It's for Real (Extended) (Instrumental) (LP Version)	1989	2.50	5.00	10.00
CASABLANCA					
❑ NBD 100	Winter Melody/Spring Affair	1977	3.75	7.50	15.00
❑ PRO 1148 [DJ]	Love to Love You Baby (16:49)/Flash Light (10:43)	1994	5.00	10.00	20.00
—B-side by Parliament; promo-only reissue					
❑ NBLP 7041	Love to Love You Baby (16:50)/Try Me, I Know We Can Make It (17:55)	1976	5.00	10.00	20.00
—One song on each side, yet it has an LP catalog number					
❑ NBD 20104	I Feel Love (8:15)/Theme from "The Deep" (Down, Deep Inside) (6:06)//(B-side blank)	1977	5.00	10.00	20.00
❑ NBD 20112 [DJ]	Rumour Has It/I Love You//(B-side blank)	1978	3.75	7.50	15.00
❑ NBD 20148 [DJ]	Mac Arthur Park Suite (17:33)/(B-side blank)	1978	3.75	7.50	15.00
❑ NBD 20159 [DJ]	Hot Stuff (Long Version)/(B-side blank)	1979	3.00	6.00	12.00
❑ NBD 20167	Hot Stuff/Bad Girls//(B-side blank)	1979	3.75	7.50	15.00
❑ NBD 20193 [DJ]	Dim All the Lights (7:10)/(B-side blank)	1979	6.25	12.50	25.00
❑ NBD 20199	No More Tears (Enough Is Enough) (11:40)/(B-side blank)	1979	2.50	5.00	10.00
—With Barbra Streisand					
❑ NBD 20226 [DJ]	Walk Away (Disco Mix 7:15)/(B-side blank)	1979	3.75	7.50	15.00
❑ 856357-1	Melody of Love (Classic Club Mix) (Boss Mix) (Epris Mix) (Mijango's Powertools Trip #1)	1994	2.50	5.00	10.00
EPIC					
❑ EAS 42153 [DJ]	I Will Go with You (Con Te Partiro) (Club 69 Future Mix) (Rosabel Dark Dub) (Rosabel Main Vox 12") (Hex Hector Extended Vocal Mix)	1999	2.50	5.00	10.00
❑ EAS 42547 [DJ]	I Will Go with You (Con Te Partiro) (Club 69 Underground Anthem) (Welcome Summertime Fun Extended Mix) (Warren Rigg Summer Dub) (Club 69 Underground Dub)	1999	3.00	6.00	12.00
❑ EAS 42676 [DJ]	I Will Go with You (Con Te Partiro) (Skill Masters Remix 5:08) (Messy Boys Jazz Dub 6:37) (Welcome Downtempo Extended Remix 4:46) (Trouser Enthusiasts Twisted Kiss Mix 10:18) (Johnny Newman Drifting Mix 5:59)	1999	3.75	7.50	15.00
❑ EAS 42892 [DJ]	Love Is the Healer (Thunderpuss 2000 Club Mix 8:58) (Eric Kupper's I Feel Healed 7" Mix) (JP's Sound Factory Mix 9:27) (Thunderpuss 2000 Radio Mix 3:19)	1999	3.00	6.00	12.00
❑ EAS 46473 [DJ]	Love Is the Healer (4 versions)	1999	3.75	7.50	15.00
❑ 49-79202	I Will Go with You (Con Te Partiro) (4 versions)	1999	2.50	5.00	10.00
❑ 49-79226	I Will Go with You (Con Te Partiro) (Club 69 Underground Anthem) (Rosabel Dark Dub) (Warren Rigg Summer Dub) (Club 69 Trippy Dub)	1999	2.00	4.00	8.00
GEFFEN					
❑ PRO-A-910 [DJ]	The Wanderer (stereo/mono)	1980	3.75	7.50	15.00
❑ PRO-A-925 [DJ]	Cold Love/Looking Up/Who Do You Think You're Foolin'	1980	2.50	5.00	10.00
❑ PRO-A-1041 [DJ]	Love Is In Control (Edit) (LP)	1982	2.50	5.00	10.00
❑ PRO-A-2180 [DJ]	There Goes My Baby (same on both sides)	1984	2.50	5.00	10.00
❑ PRO-A-2802 [DJ]	Dinner with Gershwin (7:43) (same on both sides)	1987	2.50	5.00	10.00
❑ PRO-A-3036 [DJ]	All Systems Go (Dance Mix)/Fascination	1987	2.50	5.00	10.00
❑ 20273	Supernatural Love (Extended Dance Remix 6:12)/Face the Music (4:14)	1984	2.00	4.00	8.00
❑ 20635	Dinner with Gershwin (Extended) (Instrumental)	1987	2.00	4.00	8.00
❑ 29938	Love Is In Control (Dance Remix 7:03)/(Instrumental)	1982	2.00	4.00	8.00
INTERHIT					
❑ 10164	Carry On (Outta Control Mix) (Hot Tracks Mix) (Slammin' Cox Mix) (Hysteria Mix)	1997	2.50	5.00	10.00
—With Giorgio Moroder					
MERCURY					
❑ PRO 226-1 [DJ]	Unconditional Love (Club Mix 5:20)/(Instrumental 4:40)	1983	3.00	6.00	12.00
❑ 812370-1	She Works Hard for the Money (Special Long Version) (Instrumental)	1983	2.50	5.00	10.00
❑ 814592-1	Unconditional Love (Remix)/She Works Hard for the Money (Remix)	1983	2.50	5.00	10.00
UNIVERSAL					
❑ U8P-1130 [DJ]	Whenever There Is Love (Club Mix) (Club Dub) (Riff Dub) (Tribal Beats) (Instrumental) (7" Mix)	1998	10.00	20.00	40.00

45s

Number	Title (A Side/B Side)	Yr	VG	VG+	NM
ATLANTIC					
❑ 88792	Breakaway/Thinkin' Bout My Baby	1989	—	2.00	4.00
❑ 88840	Love's About to Change My Heart (PWL 7" Mix)/(Clivilles & Cole 7" Mix)	1989	—	—	3.00
❑ 88899	This Time I Know It's for Real/If It Makes You Feel Good	1989	—	—	3.00
❑ 88899 [PS]	This Time I Know It's for Real/If It Makes You Feel Good	1989	—	2.00	4.00
CASABLANCA					
❑ 872	Spring Affair/Come with Me	1976	—	2.50	5.00
❑ 874	Winter Melody/Spring Affair	1977	—	2.50	5.00
❑ 884	Can't We Just Sit Down (And Talk It Over)/I Feel Love	1977	—	3.00	6.00
—Original copies have "Can't We Just Sit Down" labeled as "Side A"					
❑ 884	I Feel Love/Can't We Just Sit Down (And Talk It Over)	1977	—	2.50	5.00
—Second pressings have "I Feel Love" listed as "Side A"					
❑ 884 [DJ]	Can't We Just Sit Down (And Talk It Over) (stereo/mono)	1977	2.50	5.00	10.00
❑ 884 [DJ]	I Feel Love (stereo/mono)	1977	2.00	4.00	8.00
—Both sides are shorter than the version on the stock 45					
❑ 907	I Love You/Once Upon a Time	1977	—	2.50	5.00
❑ 916	Rumour Has It/Once Upon a Time	1978	—	2.50	5.00
❑ 926	Last Dance/With Your Love	1978	—	2.00	4.00
❑ 939	Mac Arthur Park/Once Upon a Time	1978	—	2.00	4.00
❑ 959	Heaven Knows/Only One Love	1979	—	2.00	4.00
—A-side with Brooklyn Dreams					
❑ 978	Hot Stuff/Journey to the Center of Your Heart	1979	—	2.00	4.00
❑ 988	Bad Girls/On My Honor	1979	—	2.00	4.00
❑ 2201	Dim All the Lights/There Will Always Be a You	1979	—	2.00	4.00
❑ 2236	On the Radio/There Will Always Be a You	1980	—	2.00	4.00
❑ 2273	Our Love/Sunset People	1980	—	2.50	5.00
❑ 2300	Walk Away/Could It Be Magic	1980	—	2.00	4.00
❑ 858366-7	Melody of Love/The Christmas Song	1994	—	—	3.00
❑ 858366-7 [PS]	Melody of Love/The Christmas Song	1994	—	—	3.00
EPIC					
❑ 38-79201	I Will Go with You (Con Te Partiro)/Love On & On	1999	—	—	3.00
GEFFEN					
❑ 27939	Fascination/All Systems Go	1988	—	2.00	4.00
❑ 28165	Only the Fool Survives/Love Shock	1987	—	2.00	4.00
—A-side with Mickey Thomas					
❑ 28165 [PS]	Only the Fool Survives/Love Shock	1987	—	2.00	4.00
—A-side with Mickey Thomas					
❑ 28418	Dinner with Gershwin/(Instrumental)	1987	—	2.00	4.00
❑ 28418 [PS]	Dinner with Gershwin/(Instrumental)	1987	—	2.00	4.00
❑ 29142	Supernatural Love/Face the Music	1984	—	2.00	4.00
❑ 29142 [PS]	Supernatural Love/Face the Music	1984	—	2.00	4.00
❑ 29291	There Goes My Baby/Maybe It's Over	1984	—	2.00	4.00
❑ 29291 [PS]	There Goes My Baby/Maybe It's Over	1984	—	2.00	4.00
❑ 29805	The Woman in Me/Livin' in America	1982	—	2.00	4.00
❑ 29805 [PS]	The Woman in Me/Livin' in America	1982	—	2.00	4.00
❑ 29895	State of Independence/Love Is Just a Breath Away	1982	—	2.00	4.00
❑ 29895 [PS]	State of Independence/Love Is Just a Breath Away	1982	—	2.00	4.00
❑ 29982	Love Is In Control (Finger on the Trigger)/Sometimes Like Butterflies	1982	—	2.00	4.00
❑ 29982 [PS]	Love Is In Control (Finger on the Trigger)/Sometimes Like Butterflies	1982	—	2.50	5.00
❑ 49563	The Wanderer/Stop Me	1980	—	2.00	4.00
—Second pressings have WB logo replaced by Geffen logo					
❑ 49563 [PS]	The Wanderer/Stop Me	1980	—	2.50	5.00
❑ 49634	Cold Love/Grand Illusion	1980	—	2.00	4.00
❑ 49634 [PS]	Cold Love/Grand Illusion	1980	—	2.50	5.00
❑ 49664	Who Do You Think You're Foolin'/Runnin' for Cover	1981	—	2.00	4.00
MERCURY					
❑ 812370-7	She Works Hard for the Money/I Do Believe (I'll Fall in Love)	1983	—	2.00	4.00
❑ 812370-7 [PS]	She Works Hard for the Money/I Do Believe (I'll Fall in Love)	1983	—	2.50	5.00
❑ 814088-7	Unconditional Love/Woman	1983	—	2.00	4.00
❑ 814088-7 [PS]	Unconditional Love/Woman	1983	—	2.50	5.00
❑ 814922-7	Love Has a Mind of Its Own/Stop, Look and Listen	1983	—	2.00	4.00
—A-side with Matthew Ward					
OASIS					
❑ 401 A /B	Love to Love You Baby/Need-A-Man Blues	1975	3.00	6.00	12.00
—"Love to Love You Baby" has a radically different mix on the above first pressing					
❑ 401 AA/BB	Love to Love You Baby (4:55)/Love to Love You Baby (3:24)	1975	—	3.00	6.00
—Both sides are remixed compared to the original 45 mix					
❑ 405	Could It Be Magic/Whispering Waves	1976	—	3.00	6.00
❑ 406	Try Me, I Know We Can Make It/Wasted	1976	—	3.00	6.00
❑ 406 [PS]	Try Me, I Know We Can Make It/Wasted	1976	2.00	4.00	8.00
WARNER BROS./GEFFEN					
❑ 49563	The Wanderer/Stop Me	1980	—	3.00	6.00
—Original pressings have a WB logo on the left side and "Geffen Records" in a box at the top of the label					

Albums

Number	Title	Yr	VG	VG+	NM
ATLANTIC					
❑ 81987	Another Place and Time	1989	3.00	6.00	12.00
CASABLANCA					
❑ NBLP 7038	Four Seasons of Love	1976	2.50	5.00	10.00
❑ NBLP 7056	I Remember Yesterday	1977	2.50	5.00	10.00
❑ NBLP 7078 [(2)]	Once Upon a Time...	1977	3.00	6.00	12.00
❑ NBLP 7119 [(2)]	Live and More	1978	3.00	6.00	12.00
❑ NBPIX 7119 [PD]	The Best of Live and More	1979	5.00	10.00	20.00
❑ NBLP 7150 [(2)]	Bad Girls	1979	3.00	6.00	12.00
❑ NBLP 7191 [(2)]	On the Radio — Greatest Hits Vols. 1 and 2	1979	3.00	6.00	12.00
❑ NBLP 7201	Greatest Hits, Vol. 1	1979	2.00	4.00	8.00
❑ NBLP 7202	Greatest Hits, Vol. 2	1979	2.00	4.00	8.00
❑ NBLP 7244	Walk Away — Collector's Edition (The Best of 1977-1980)	1980	2.50	5.00	10.00
❑ 811123-1 [(2)]	Live and More	1985	2.50	5.00	10.00
❑ 822557-1 [(2)]	Bad Girls	1984	2.50	5.00	10.00
❑ 822558-1 [(2)]	On the Radio — Greatest Hits Vols. 1 and 2	1984	2.50	5.00	10.00
❑ 822559-1	Greatest Hits, Vol. 2	1984	2.00	4.00	8.00
❑ 822560-1	Walk Away	1984	2.00	4.00	8.00
EPIC					
❑ E2 69910 [(2)]	Live and More Encore	1999	3.75	7.50	15.00
GEFFEN					
❑ GHS 2000	The Wanderer	1980	2.50	5.00	10.00

Number	Title (A Side/B Side)	Yr	VG	VG+	NM
❏ GHS 2005	Donna Summer	1982	2.50	5.00	10.00
❏ GHS 24040	Cats Without Claws	1984	2.50	5.00	10.00
❏ GHS 24040 [DJ]	Cats Without Claws	1984	3.75	7.50	15.00
—Promo only on Quiex II vinyl					
❏ GHS 24102	All Systems Go	1987	2.50	5.00	10.00
MERCURY					
❏ 812265-1	She Works Hard for the Money	1983	2.50	5.00	10.00
❏ 826144-1	The Summer Collection	1985	2.50	5.00	10.00
OASIS					
❏ OCLP 5003	Love to Love You Baby	1975	3.00	6.00	12.00
—Add 50% if poster is included					
❏ OCLP 5004	A Love Trilogy	1976	3.00	6.00	12.00
❏ 822792-1	Love to Love You Baby	1985	2.00	4.00	8.00

SUMMITS, THE
45s
TIMES SQUARE

Number	Title (A Side/B Side)	Yr	VG	VG+	NM
❏ 422	Go Back Where You Came From/(B-side unknown)	1961	6.25	12.50	25.00

SUNBEAMS, THE (1)
45s
ACME

Number	Title (A Side/B Side)	Yr	VG	VG+	NM
❏ 109	Please Say You'll Be Mine/You've Got to Rock and Roll	1957	750.00	1500.	3000.
HERALD					
❏ 451	Tell Me Why/Come Back Baby	1955	75.00	150.00	300.00

SUPER NATURE
See SALT-N-PEPA.

SUPERIORS, THE (1)
45s
ATCO

Number	Title (A Side/B Side)	Yr	VG	VG+	NM
❏ 6106	Lost Love/Don't Say Goodbye	1957	17.50	35.00	70.00
MAIN LINE					
❏ 104	Lost Love/Don't Say Goodbye	1958	150.00	300.00	600.00
—With Fairmount Ave., Philadelphia street address on label					
❏ 104	Lost Love/Don't Say Goodbye	1962	10.00	20.00	40.00
—No address on label or only "Philadelphia, Pennsylvania" address on label					

SUPERIORS, THE (2)
45s
FAL

Number	Title (A Side/B Side)	Yr	VG	VG+	NM
❏ 301	What Is Love/Flee the Scene	1961	20.00	40.00	80.00
FEDERAL					
❏ 12436	I'm Sorry Baby (I Didn't Mean to Do You Wrong)/Dance of Love	1961	7.50	15.00	30.00

SUPREMES, THE
Motown girl group. Also see FLORENCE BALLARD; THE PRIMETTES; DIANA ROSS.

12-Inch Singles
MOTOWN

Number	Title (A Side/B Side)	Yr	VG	VG+	NM
❏ 37463 1157 1 [DJ]	Someday We'll Be Together (Sound Factory Mix 6:57) (Def Mix 8:42) (Radio Edit Mix 3:03)	1994	3.75	7.50	15.00
—As "Diana Ross and the Supremes"; remixes of the 1969 hit					

45s
EEOC

Number	Title (A Side/B Side)	Yr	VG	VG+	NM
❏ SL4M-3114 [DJ]	Things Are Changing (same on both sides)	1965	37.50	75.00	150.00
❏ SL4M-3114 [PS]	Things Are Changing (same on both sides)	1965	37.50	75.00	150.00
—Promotional item for the Equal Employment Opportunity Commission (number not on sleeve)					
GEORGE ALEXANDER INC.					
❏ 1079 [DJ]	The Only Time I'm Happy/Supremes Interview	1965	15.00	30.00	60.00
MOTOWN					
❏ 1008	I Want a Guy/Never Again	1961	75.00	150.00	300.00
❏ 1027	Your Heart Belongs to Me/(He's) Seventeen	1962	6.25	12.50	25.00
❏ 1027 [PS]	Your Heart Belongs to Me/(He's) Seventeen	1962	100.00	200.00	400.00
❏ 1034	Let Me Go the Right Way/Time Changes Things	1962	12.50	25.00	50.00
❏ 1040	My Heart Can't Take It No More/You Bring Back Memories	1963	10.00	20.00	40.00
❏ 1044	A Breath Taking, First Sight Soul Shaking, One Night Love Making, Next Day Heart Breaking Guy/Rock and Roll Banjo Band	1963	25.00	50.00	100.00
—Original pressing with long title. This does exist on stock copies as well as on promos.					
❏ 1044	A Breath Taking Guy/Rock and Roll Banjo Band	1963	6.25	12.50	25.00
❏ 1051	When the Lovelight Starts Shining Through His Eyes/Standing at the Crossroads of Love	1963	5.00	10.00	20.00
❏ 1054	Run, Run, Run/I'm Giving You Your Freedom	1964	6.25	12.50	25.00
❏ 1060	Where Did Our Love Go/He Means the World to Me	1964	5.00	10.00	20.00
❏ 1060 [PS]	Where Did Our Love Go/He Means the World to Me	1964	7.50	15.00	30.00
❏ 1066	Baby Love/Ask Any Girl	1964	5.00	10.00	20.00
❏ 1066 [PS]	Baby Love/Ask Any Girl	1964	7.50	15.00	30.00
❏ 1068	Come See About Me/Always in My Heart	1964	5.00	10.00	20.00
❏ 1074	Stop! In the Name of Love/I'm in Love Again	1965	3.75	7.50	15.00
❏ 1074 [PS]	Stop! In the Name of Love/I'm in Love Again	1965	7.50	15.00	30.00
❏ 1075	Back in My Arms Again/Whisper You Love Me Boy	1965	3.75	7.50	15.00
❏ 1075 [PS]	Back in My Arms Again/Whisper You Love Me Boy	1965	7.50	15.00	30.00
❏ 1080	Nothing But Heartaches/He Holds His Own	1965	3.75	7.50	15.00
❏ 1080 [PS]	Nothing But Heartaches/He Holds His Own	1965	7.50	15.00	30.00

Number	Title (A Side/B Side)	Yr	VG	VG+	NM
❏ 1083	I Hear a Symphony/Who Could Ever Doubt My Love	1965	3.75	7.50	15.00
❏ 1085	Children's Christmas Song/Twinkle, Twinkle Little Me	1965	5.00	10.00	20.00
❏ 1085 [DJ]	Children's Christmas Song/Twinkle, Twinkle Little Me	1965	6.25	12.50	25.00
—Promo only on red vinyl					
❏ 1085 [PS]	Children's Christmas Song/Twinkle, Twinkle Little Me	1965	8.75	17.50	35.00
❏ 1089	My World Is Empty Without You/Everything Is Good About You	1966	3.75	7.50	15.00
❏ 1094	Love Is Like an Itching in My Heart/He's All I Got	1966	3.75	7.50	15.00
❏ 1097	You Can't Hurry Love/Put Yourself in My Place	1966	3.75	7.50	15.00
❏ 1097 [PS]	You Can't Hurry Love/Put Yourself in My Place	1966	7.50	15.00	30.00
❏ 1101	You Keep Me Hangin' On/Remove This Doubt	1966	3.75	7.50	15.00
❏ 1101 [PS]	You Keep Me Hangin' On/Remove This Doubt	1966	7.50	15.00	30.00
❏ 1103	Love Is Here and Now You're Gone/There's No Stopping Us Now	1967	3.00	6.00	12.00
❏ 1107	The Happening/All I Know About You	1967	3.00	6.00	12.00
❏ 1111	Reflections/Going Down for the Third Time	1967	2.00	4.00	8.00
—Starting here, through 1156, as "Diana Ross and the Supremes"					
❏ 1116	In and Out of Love/I Guess I'll Always Love You	1967	2.00	4.00	8.00
❏ 1122	Forever Came Today/Time Changes Things	1968	2.00	4.00	8.00
❏ 1125	What the World Needs Now/Your Kiss of Fire	1968	—	—	—
—Unreleased					
❏ 1126	Some Things You Never Get Used To/You've Been So Wonderful to Me	1968	2.00	4.00	8.00
❏ 1135	Love Child/Will This Be the Day	1968	2.00	4.00	8.00
❏ 1139	I'm Livin' in Shame/I'm So Glad I Got Somebody	1969	2.00	4.00	8.00
❏ 1146	The Composer/The Beginning of the End	1969	2.00	4.00	8.00
❏ 1148	No Matter What Sign You Are/The Young Folks	1969	2.00	4.00	8.00
❏ 1156	Someday We'll Be Together/He's My Sunny Boy	1969	2.00	4.00	8.00
❏ 1162	Up the Ladder to the Roof/Bill, When Are You Coming Home	1970	—	3.00	6.00
—Starting here, name reverts to "The Supremes" (unless noted)					
❏ 1167	Everybody's Got the Right to Love/But I Love You More	1970	—	3.00	6.00
❏ 1172	Stoned Love/Shine on Me	1970	—	3.00	6.00
❏ 1182	Nathan Jones/Happy (Is a Bumpy Road)	1971	—	3.00	6.00
❏ 1190	Touch/It's So Hard for Me to Say Goodbye	1971	—	3.00	6.00
❏ 1195	Floy Joy/This Is the Story	1972	—	2.50	5.00
❏ 1200	Automatically Sunshine/Precious Little Things	1972	—	2.50	5.00
❏ 1206	Your Wonderful, Sweet Sweet Love/The Wisdom of Time	1972	—	2.50	5.00
❏ 1213	I Guess I'll Miss the Man/Over and Over	1972	—	2.50	5.00
❏ 1225	Bad Weather/Oh Be My Love	1973	—	2.50	5.00
❏ 1350	It's All Been Said Before/(B-side unassigned)	1975	—	—	—
—Unreleased					
❏ 1357	He's My Man/Give Out But Don't Give Up	1975	—	2.50	5.00
❏ 1374	Where Do I Go from Here/Give Out But Don't Give Up	1975	—	2.50	5.00
❏ 1391	I'm Gonna Let My Heart Do the Walking/Early Morning Love	1976	—	2.50	5.00
❏ 1407	You're My Driving Wheel/You're What's Missing in My Life	1976	—	2.50	5.00
❏ 1415	Let Yourself Go/You Are the Heart of Me	1977	—	2.50	5.00
❏ 1488	Medley of Hits/Where Did We Go Wrong	1980	—	2.00	4.00
—As "Diana Ross and the Supremes"					
❏ 1523	Medley of Hits/Where Did We Go Wrong	1981	—	2.00	4.00
—As "Diana Ross and the Supremes"					
TAMLA					
❏ 54038	I Want a Guy/Never Again	1961	31.25	62.50	125.00
—Lines label					
❏ 54038	I Want a Guy/Never Again	1961	15.00	30.00	60.00
—Globes label					
❏ 54045	Buttered Popcorn/Who's Lovin' You	1961	15.00	30.00	60.00
—Globes label					
❏ 54045	Buttered Popcorn/Who's Lovin' You	1961	31.25	62.50	125.00
—Lines label					
TOPPS/MOTOWN					
❏ 1	Baby Love	1967	18.75	37.50	75.00
—Cardboard record					
❏ 2	Stop in the Name of Love	1967	18.75	37.50	75.00
—Cardboard record					
❏ 3	Where Did Our Love Go	1967	18.75	37.50	75.00
—Cardboard record					
❏ 15	Come See About Me	1967	18.75	37.50	75.00
—Cardboard record					
❏ 16	My World Is Empty Without You	1967	18.75	37.50	75.00
—Cardboard record					

7-Inch Extended Plays
MOTOWN

Number	Title (A Side/B Side)	Yr	VG	VG+	NM
❏ S 621 [PS]	Where Did Our Love Go	1965	6.25	12.50	25.00
❏ S 621 [S]	He Means the World to Me/Baby Love/Ask Any Girl/Where Did Our Love Go/Come See About Me/Run, Run, Run	1965	6.25	12.50	25.00
—33 1/3 rpm, small hole					

Albums
DORAL

Number	Title (A Side/B Side)	Yr	VG	VG+	NM
❏ DRL 104	Doral Presents Diana Ross and the Supremes	1971	12.50	25.00	50.00
—Available through Doral cigarettes					
MOTOWN					
❏ M5-101V1	Superstar Series, Vol. 1	1981	3.00	6.00	12.00
—By "Diana Ross and the Supremes"					
❏ PR-102 [DJ]	Touch Interview	1971	6.25	12.50	25.00

Number	Title (A Side/B Side)	Yr	VG	VG+	NM
❏ M5-138V1	The Supremes A' Go-Go	1981	3.00	6.00	12.00
—Reissue of Motown 649					
❏ M5-147V1	I Hear a Symphony	1981	3.00	6.00	12.00
—Reissue of Motown 643					
❏ M5-158V1	The Supremes Sing Country Western and Pop	1981	2.00	4.00	8.00
—Reissue of Motown 625					
❏ M5-162V1	The Supremes at the Copa	1981	3.00	6.00	12.00
—Reissue of Motown 636					
❏ M5-182V1	The Supremes Sing Holland-Dozier-Holland	1981	3.00	6.00	12.00
—Reissue of Motown 650					
❏ M5-203V1	Diana Ross and the Supremes Greatest Hits, Volume 3	1981	3.00	6.00	12.00
—Reissue of Motown 702					
❏ M5-223V1	Meet the Supremes	1982	2.00	4.00	8.00
—Reissue of Motown 606					
❏ M5-237V1	Greatest Hits	1982	2.50	5.00	10.00
—Reissue (unknown if it's the complete 2-record set or an edited version)					
❏ M 606 [M]	Meet the Supremes	1963	225.00	450.00	900.00
—With group sitting on stools					
❏ M 606 [M]	Meet the Supremes	1963	7.50	15.00	30.00
—With close-up of group's faces					
❏ MS 606 [S]	Meet the Supremes	1964	10.00	20.00	40.00
—With close-up of group's faces					
❏ MT/MS 610	The Supremes Sing Ballads and Blues	1963	—	—	—
—Unreleased					
❏ M 621 [M]	Where Did Our Love Go	1964	7.50	15.00	30.00
❏ MS 621 [S]	Where Did Our Love Go	1964	10.00	20.00	40.00
❏ M 623 [M]	A Bit of Liverpool	1964	10.00	20.00	40.00
❏ MS 623 [S]	A Bit of Liverpool	1964	12.50	25.00	50.00
❏ M 625 [M]	The Supremes Sing Country Western & Pop	1965	6.25	12.50	25.00
❏ MS 625 [S]	The Supremes Sing Country Western & Pop	1965	7.50	15.00	30.00
❏ MT/MS 626	The Supremes Live! Live! Live!	1965	—	—	—
—Unreleased					
❏ M 627 [M]	More Hits by the Supremes	1965	6.25	12.50	25.00
❏ MS 627 [S]	More Hits by the Supremes	1965	7.50	15.00	30.00
❏ MT/MS 628	There's a Place for Us	1965	—	—	—
—Unreleased					
❏ M 629 [M]	We Remember Sam Cooke	1965	6.25	12.50	25.00
❏ MS 629 [S]	We Remember Sam Cooke	1965	7.50	15.00	30.00
—The above LP came out before Motown 627					
❏ M 636 [M]	The Supremes at the Copa	1965	6.25	12.50	25.00
❏ MS 636 [S]	The Supremes at the Copa	1965	7.50	15.00	30.00
❏ MT/MS 637	A Tribute to the Girls	1965	—	—	—
—Unreleased					
❏ MS 638 [S]	Merry Christmas	1965	10.00	20.00	40.00
—Same as above, but in stereo					
❏ MT 638 [M]	Merry Christmas	1965	7.50	15.00	30.00
❏ M 643 [M]	I Hear a Symphony	1966	6.25	12.50	25.00
❏ MS 643 [S]	I Hear a Symphony	1966	7.50	15.00	30.00
❏ MTMS 648	Pure Gold	1966	—	—	—
—Unreleased					
❏ M 649 [M]	The Supremes A' Go-Go	1966	6.25	12.50	25.00
❏ MS 649 [S]	The Supremes A' Go-Go	1966	7.50	15.00	30.00
❏ M 650 [M]	The Supremes Sing Holland-Dozier-Holland	1967	6.25	12.50	25.00
❏ MS 650 [S]	The Supremes Sing Holland-Dozier-Holland	1967	7.50	15.00	30.00
❏ M 659 [M]	The Supremes Sing Rodgers & Hart	1967	6.25	12.50	25.00
❏ MS 659 [S]	The Supremes Sing Rodgers & Hart	1967	7.50	15.00	30.00
❏ M 663 [(2) M]	Diana Ross and the Supremes Greatest Hits	1967	7.50	15.00	30.00
❏ MS 663 [(2) S]	Diana Ross and the Supremes Greatest Hits	1967	10.00	20.00	40.00
❏ MT/MS 663	Diana Ross and the Supremes Greatest Hits Poster	1967	2.50	5.00	10.00
❏ M 665 [M]	Reflections	1968	7.50	15.00	30.00
❏ MS 665 [S]	Reflections	1968	5.00	10.00	20.00
❏ MS 670	Love Child	1968	5.00	10.00	20.00
❏ M 672 [M]	Funny Girl	1968	7.50	15.00	30.00
—Mono appears to be promo only					
❏ MS 672 [S]	Funny Girl	1968	5.00	10.00	20.00
—The above LP came out before Motown 670					
❏ M 676 [M]	Live at London's Talk of the Town	1968	7.50	51.00	30.00
—Mono is promo only					
❏ MS 676 [S]	Live at London's Talk of the Town	1968	5.00	10.00	20.00
—The above LP came out before Motown 670 and 672					
❏ MS 689	Let the Sunshine In	1969	5.00	10.00	20.00
❏ MS 694	Cream of the Crop	1969	5.00	10.00	20.00
❏ MS 702	Diana Ross and the Supremes Greatest Hits, Volume 3	1970	5.00	10.00	20.00
❏ MS 705	Right On	1970	3.75	7.50	15.00
—By "The Supremes"; the first LP after Diana Ross left					
❏ MS 708 [(2)]	Farewell	1970	6.25	12.50	25.00
—By "Diana Ross and the Supremes"					
❏ MS 720	New Ways But Love Stays	1970	3.75	7.50	15.00
❏ MS 737	Touch	1971	3.75	7.50	15.00
❏ MS 746	Promises Kept	1972	—	—	—
—Unreleased					
❏ M 751L	Floy Joy	1972	3.75	7.50	15.00
❏ M 756L	The Supremes	1972	3.75	7.50	15.00
❏ M9-794L3 [(3)]	Anthology (1962-1969)	1974	6.25	12.50	25.00
—By "Diana Ross and the Supremes"					
❏ M6-828	The Supremes	1975	3.75	7.50	15.00
❏ M6-863S1	High Energy	1976	3.75	7.50	15.00
❏ M6-873S1	Mary, Scherrie and Susaye	1976	3.75	7.50	15.00
❏ M7-904R1	The Supremes at Their Best	1978	3.75	7.50	15.00
❏ 5245 ML	Love Child	1982	2.00	4.00	8.00
—Reissue of MS 670					
❏ 5252 ML	Merry Christmas	1982	2.50	5.00	10.00
—Reissue of MS 638					

Number	Title (A Side/B Side)	Yr	VG	VG+	NM
❏ 5270 ML	Where Did Our Love Go	1982	2.00	4.00	8.00
—Reissue of MS 621					
❏ 5278 ML	Captured Live on Stage	1982	2.00	4.00	8.00
—Reissue?					
❏ 5305 ML	Let the Sunshine In	1983	2.00	4.00	8.00
—Reissue of MS 689					
❏ 5313 ML	Great Songs and Performances That Inspired the Motown 25th Anniversary TV Special	1983	2.50	5.00	10.00
❏ 5361 ML	Motown Legends	1985	2.50	5.00	10.00
❏ 5371 ML	Diana Ross and the Supremes Sing Motown	1985	2.50	5.00	10.00
❏ 5381 ML3 [(3)]	25th Anniversary	1986	5.00	10.00	20.00
—By "Diana Ross and the Supremes"					

NATURAL RESOURCES

Number	Title (A Side/B Side)	Yr	VG	VG+	NM
❏ NR 4006T1	Where Did Our Love Go	1978	3.00	6.00	12.00
—Reissue of Motown 621					
❏ NR 4010	Merry Christmas	1978	3.00	6.00	12.00
—Reissue of Motown 638					

PICKWICK

Number	Title (A Side/B Side)	Yr	VG	VG+	NM
❏ SPC-3383	Baby Love	197?	3.00	6.00	12.00
—Edited reissue of Motown 621					

SUPREMES, THE, AND THE FOUR TOPS
Also see each artist's individual listings.
45s
MOTOWN

Number	Title (A Side/B Side)	Yr	VG	VG+	NM
❏ 1173	River Deep-Mountain High/Together We Can Make Such Sweet Music	1970	—	3.00	6.00
❏ 1181	You Gotta Have Love in Your Heart/I'm Glad About It	1971	—	3.00	6.00

Albums
MOTOWN

Number	Title (A Side/B Side)	Yr	VG	VG+	NM
❏ M5-123V1A	The Magnificent Seven	1981	3.00	6.00	12.00
—Reissue of Motown 717					
❏ MS 717	The Magnificent Seven	1970	3.75	7.50	15.00
❏ MS 736	The Return of the Magnificent Seven	1971	3.75	7.50	15.00
❏ MS 745	Dynamite	1971	3.75	7.50	15.00

SUPREMES, THE, DIANA ROSS AND, AND THE TEMPTATIONS
Also see each artist's individual listings.
45s
MOTOWN

Number	Title (A Side/B Side)	Yr	VG	VG+	NM
❏ 1137	I'm Gonna Make You Love Me/A Place in the Sun	1968	—	3.50	7.00
❏ 1137 [PS]	I'm Gonna Make You Love Me/A Place in the Sun	1968	5.00	10.00	20.00
❏ 1142	I'll Try Something New/The Way You Do the Things You Do	1969	—	3.50	7.00
❏ 1150	Stubborn Kind of Fellow/Try It Baby	1969	—	3.50	7.00
❏ 1153	The Weight/For Better or Worse	1969	—	3.50	7.00

Albums
MOTOWN

Number	Title (A Side/B Side)	Yr	VG	VG+	NM
❏ M5-139V1	Diana Ross and the Supremes Join the Temptations	1981	3.00	6.00	12.00
—Reissue of Motown 679					
❏ M5-171V1	TCB	1981	3.00	6.00	12.00
—Reissue of Motown 682					
❏ M 679 [M]	Diana Ross and the Supremes Join the Temptations	1968	7.50	15.00	30.00
❏ MS 679 [S]	Diana Ross and the Supremes Join the Temptations	1968	5.00	10.00	20.00
❏ MS 682	TCB	1968	5.00	10.00	20.00
❏ MS 692	Together	1969	5.00	10.00	20.00
❏ MS 699	On Broadway	1969	5.00	10.00	20.00

SURE!, AL B.
12-Inch Singles
WARNER BROS.

Number	Title (A Side/B Side)	Yr	VG	VG+	NM
❏ PRO-A-4423 [DJ]	Missunderstanding (Edit) (LP Version)	1990	—	3.00	6.00
❏ PRO-A-4609 [DJ]	Missunderstanding (7 versions)	1990	—	3.00	6.00
❏ PRO-A-4627 [DJ]	No Matter What You Do (Lasts So Long Radio Edit) (same on both sides)	1990	—	3.00	6.00
—With Diana Ross					
❏ 20782	Night and Day (3 versions)/Nuit et Jour (3 versions)	1988	2.50	5.00	10.00
❏ 20952	Off on Your Own (Girl) (4 versions)/Noche Y Dia	1988	—	3.00	6.00
❏ 21843	No Matter What You Do (3 versions)//Al'l Justify Your Love/Justi Muzak/Missunderstanding	1990	2.00	4.00	8.00
—A-side with Diana Ross					
❏ 40085	Had Enuf? (5 versions)	1991	—	3.50	7.00
❏ 40525	Right Now (Remix) (Remix Instrumental) (Remix Edit) (LP Version) (LP Instrumental) (LP Edit)	1992	—	3.00	6.00
❏ 40712	Natalie (12" R&B Remix) (7" R&B Remix) (Acoustic 12" Remix) (Acoustic 7" R&B Remix) (R&B Remix Instrumental) (Rock 12" Remix) (Rock 7" Remix) (LP Version) (Radio Edit) (Acoustic Remix Instrumental)	1992	—	3.00	6.00
❏ 40748	I Don't Wanna Cry (Remix) (Remix Instrumental) (Mount Vernon Mix) (7" Radio Remix) (Jeep It) (LP Version)	1993	—	3.00	6.00

45s
WARNER BROS.

Number	Title (A Side/B Side)	Yr	VG	VG+	NM
❏ 7-19455	No Matter What You Do/Al'l Justify Your Love	1990	—	2.00	4.00
—A-side with Diana Ross					
❏ 7-19590	Missunderstanding/Missunderstanding (Radio Edit)	1990	—	2.00	4.00
❏ 7-27556	If I'm Not Your Lover/If I'm Not Your Lover (Remix)	1989	—	—	3.00
❏ 7-27762	Rescue Me/(Instrumental)	1988	—	—	3.00

S

Number	Title (A Side/B Side)	Yr	VG	VG+	NM
❑ 7-27762 [PS]	Rescue Me/(Instrumental)	1988	—	—	3.00
❑ 7-27772	Killing Me Softly/(Instrumental)	1988	—	—	3.00
❑ 7-27772 [PS]	Killing Me Softly/(Instrumental)	1988	—	—	3.00
❑ 7-27870	Off on Your Own (Girl)/Nocha Y Dia	1988	—	—	3.00
❑ 7-27870 [PS]	Off on Your Own (Girl)/Nocha Y Dia	1988	—	—	3.00
❑ 7-28192	Nite and Day/Nuit Et Jour	1988	—	—	3.00
❑ 7-28192 [PS]	Nite and Day/Nuit Et Jour	1988	—	—	3.00

Albums

WARNER BROS.

❑ 25662	In Effect Mode	1988	2.00	4.00	8.00
❑ 26005	Private Times...And the Whole 9!	1990	3.00	6.00	12.00

SWALLOWS, THE
45s
AFTER HOURS

❑ 104	My Baby/Good Time Girls	1954	800.00	1600.	2400.

FEDERAL

❑ 12319	Oh Lonesome Me/Angel Baby	1958	10.00	20.00	40.00
❑ 12328	We Want to Rock/Rock-a-Bye-Baby Rock	1958	10.00	20.00	40.00
❑ 12329	Beside You/Laughing Boy	1958	10.00	20.00	40.00
❑ 12333	Itchy Twitchy Feeling/Who Knows, Do You?	1958	10.00	20.00	40.00

KING

❑ 4458	Will You Be Mine/Dearest	1951	500.00	1000.	1500.
❑ 4466	Since You've Been Away/Wishing for You	1951	—	—	—
—Unconfirmed on 45 rpm					
❑ 4501	Eternally/It Ain't the Meat	1952	200.00	400.00	800.00
—Black vinyl					
❑ 4501	Eternally/It Ain't the Meat	1952	625.00	1250.	2500.
—Blue vinyl					
❑ 4501	Eternally/It Ain't the Meat	1952	625.00	1250.	2500.
—Green vinyl					
❑ 4515	Tell Me Why/Roll, Roll, Pretty Baby	1952	1000.	1500.	2000.
❑ 4525	Beside You/You Left Me	1952	100.00	200.00	400.00
❑ 4533	You Walked In/I Only Have Eyes for You	1952	200.00	400.00	800.00
❑ 4579	Where Do I Go from Here/Please, Baby, Please	1952	200.00	400.00	800.00
❑ 4612	Laugh (Though You Want to Cry)/Our Love Is Dying	1953	125.00	250.00	500.00
❑ 4632	Nobody's Lovin' Me/Bicycle Tillie	1953	125.00	250.00	500.00
❑ 4656	Trust Me/Pleading Blues	1953	100.00	200.00	400.00
❑ 4676	I'll Be Waiting/It Feels So Good	1953	100.00	200.00	400.00

SWANS, THE (1)
45s
BALLAD

❑ 1003/6	It's a Must/Night Train	1954	150.00	300.00	600.00
❑ 1007	Happy/The Santa Claus Boogie	1955	150.00	300.00	600.00

FORTUNE

❑ 822	I'll Forever Love You/Mister Cool Breeze	1955	200.00	400.00	800.00

RAINBOW

❑ 233	No More/My True Love	1954	375.00	750.00	1500.
—Red vinyl					

STEAMBOAT

❑ 101	Believe in Me/In the Morning	1956	625.00	1250.	2500.

SWEAT, KEITH
12-Inch Singles
ELEKTRA

❑ ED 5588 [DJ]	Keep It Comin' (5 versions)	1991	3.75	7.50	15.00
❑ ED 5869 [DJ]	Just a Touch/Nobody (Ghetto Love Remix)	1997	3.00	6.00	12.00
❑ ED 5894 [DJ]	Nobody (6 versions)	1996	3.00	6.00	12.00
❑ ED 6025 [DJ]	Come with Me (Album Version) (same on both sides)	1997	2.50	5.00	10.00
—With Ronald Isley					
❑ ED 6026 [DJ]	Just a Touch (4 versions)	1997	3.75	7.50	15.00
❑ ED 6106 [DJ]	Come and Get with Me (5 versions)	1998	3.75	7.50	15.00
—With Snoop Dogg					
❑ ED 6115 [DJ]	Come and Go with Me (2 versions)	1998	3.75	7.50	15.00
—With Snoop Dogg					
❑ ED 6133 [DJ]	I'm Not Ready (3 versions) (same on both sides)	1999	3.75	7.50	15.00
❑ ED 6254 [DJ]	I'll Trade (A Million Bucks) (Remix) (Remix International)/(Album Version) (Instrumental) (Acappella)	2000	5.00	10.00	20.00
—With Lil' Mo					
❑ 63851	Come and Get with Me (Original Version) (Instrumental) (Clarkworld Remix Featuring Noreaga) (Acappella)	1998	2.50	5.00	10.00
—With Snoop Dogg					
❑ 63945	Come with Me (Album Version)/Just a Touch/Chocolate Girl/Just a Touch (Stevie J Bad Boy Remix) (Stevie J Bad Boy Remix w/o Rap) (Stevie J Bad Boy Remix Acappella)	1997	3.00	6.00	12.00
—With Ronald Isley					
❑ 66190	Get Up On It (LP Version) (Get It Up Mix) (Get In On Mix) (Do You Mix)	1994	2.50	5.00	10.00
❑ 66475	Keep It Comin' (5 versions)	1991	2.50	5.00	10.00

VINTERTAINMENT

❑ ED 5265 [DJ]	I Want Her (5 versions)	1987	3.75	7.50	15.00
❑ ED 5281 [DJ]	I Want Her (Dance Till Ya Sweat Mix) (same on both sides)	1987	3.75	7.50	15.00
❑ ED 5287 [DJ]	Something Just Ain't Right (Edit of LP Version) (Extended Version)/(LP Version) (Acapella Beat)	1988	3.75	7.50	15.00
❑ ED 5338 [DJ]	Don't Stop Your Love (5 versions)	1988	3.00	6.00	12.00
❑ ED 5404 [DJ]	Make You Sweat (5 versions)	1990	2.50	5.00	10.00
❑ ED 5478 [DJ]	Make You Sweat (4 versions)	1990	2.50	5.00	10.00

Number	Title (A Side/B Side)	Yr	VG	VG+	NM
❑ ED 5505 [DJ]	Your Love (Radio Version) (Club Version)/(Extended Version) (Acappella Version) (Instrumental)	1990	3.00	6.00	12.00
❑ ED 5506 [DJ]	I'll Give All My Love to You (4:29) (5:36)	1990	2.50	5.00	10.00
❑ 66563	Your Love — Part 2 (Edit of Remix) (Club Remix)/(LP Version) (Accapella)/Tell Me It's Me You Want	1991	3.75	7.50	15.00
❑ 66683	Make You Sweat (Edit of LP Version) (Extended Version)/(Sweat Beat) (Club Beat) (Instrumental)	1990	2.50	5.00	10.00
❑ 66776	Something Just Ain't Right (Extended Version) (Acapella Beat)/(Beat Version) (Instrumental)	1988	3.00	6.00	12.00
❑ 66788	I Want Her (Extended Version) (Acappella Dub Beat)/(Instrumental) (LP Version)	1987	3.75	7.50	15.00

45s
ELEKTRA

❑ 64245	Nobody/In the Mood	1996	—	2.00	4.00
❑ 64282	Twisted/Excerpts: Chocolate Girl/Funky Dope Lovin'/Just a Touch	1996	—	2.00	4.00

ELEKTRA SPUN GOLD

❑ 65923	I'll Give All My Love to You/Why Me Baby (Part 2)	1993	—	2.00	4.00
❑ 65963	I Want Her/Something Just Ain't Right	199?	—	—	3.00

VINTERTAINMENT

❑ 64894	Your Love — Part 2/Tell Me It's Me You Want	1991	—	2.00	4.00
❑ 64937	Merry Go Round/Make You Sweat	1990	—	2.00	4.00
❑ 64961	Make You Sweat/(The Love Pass)	1990	—	2.00	4.00
❑ 69359	Don't Stop Your Love/(Acapella Groove)	1988	—	—	3.00
❑ 69386	Make It Last Forever/(Vocal Beat)	1988	—	—	3.00
—With Jacci McGhee					
❑ 69411	Something Just Ain't Right (Long)/(Short)	1988	—	—	3.00
❑ 69431	I Want Her/(Part 2)	1987	—	—	3.00
❑ 69431 [PS]	I Want Her/(Part 2)	1987	—	2.00	4.00

Albums

ELEKTRA

❑ ED 5872 [DJ]	Keith Sweat	1996	3.75	7.50	15.00
—Promo-only sampler from LP of the same name					
❑ 61707	Keith Sweat	1996	3.00	6.00	12.00

VINTERTAINMENT

❑ 60763	Make It Last Forever	1987	2.00	4.00	8.00
❑ 60861	I'll Give All My Love to You	1990	3.00	6.00	12.00

SWEET INSPIRATIONS, THE
Also see CISSY HOUSTON.
12-Inch Singles
CARIBOU

❑ ASD 333 [DJ]	Black Sunday Parts 1 and 2 (same on both sides)	1977	3.75	7.50	15.00

RSO

❑ 304 [DJ]	Love Is On the Way (6:10)/(Instrumental)	1979	3.00	6.00	12.00

45s
ATLANTIC

❑ 2410	Why (Am I Treated So Bad)/I Don't Want to Go On Without You	1967	2.00	4.00	8.00
❑ 2418	Let It Be Me/When Something Is Wrong with My Baby	1967	2.00	4.00	8.00
❑ 2436	I've Been Loving You Too Long (To Stop Now)/That's How Strong My Love Is	1967	2.00	4.00	8.00
❑ 2449	O' What a Fool I've Been/Don't Fight It	1967	2.00	4.00	8.00
❑ 2465	Reach Out for Me/Do Right Woman — Do Right Man	1967	2.00	4.00	8.00
❑ 2476	Sweet Inspiration/I'm Blue	1968	2.00	4.00	8.00
❑ 2529	To Love Somebody/Where Did It Go	1968	2.00	4.00	8.00
❑ 2551	Unchained Melody/Am I Ever Gonna See My Baby Again	1968	2.00	4.00	8.00
❑ 2571	What the World Needs Now Is Love/You Really Didn't Mean It	1968	2.00	4.00	8.00
❑ 2620	Crying in the Rain/Everyday WIll Be Like a Holiday	1969	2.00	4.00	8.00
❑ 2638	Sweets for My Sweet/Get a Little Order	1969	2.00	4.00	8.00
❑ 2653	Don't Go/Chained	1969	2.00	4.00	8.00
❑ 2686	(Gotta Find) A Brand New Lover — Part I/(Gotta Find) A Brand New Lover — Part II	1969	2.00	4.00	8.00
❑ 2720	At Last I Found a Love/That's the Way My Baby Is	1970	—	3.00	6.00
❑ 2732	Them Boys/Flash in the Pan	1970	—	3.00	6.00
❑ 2750	This World/A Light Sings	1970	—	3.00	6.00
❑ 2779	Evidence/Change Me Not	1970	—	3.00	6.00

CARIBOU

❑ 9022	Black Sunday/(Instrumental)	1977	—	2.00	4.00

RSO

❑ 932	Love Is On the Way/(Instrumental)	1979	—	2.50	5.00
❑ 1013	Love Is On the Way/(Instrumental)	1979	—	2.00	4.00

STAX

❑ 0178	Emercury/Slipped and Tripped	1973	—	2.50	5.00
❑ 0203	Try a Little Tenderness/Dirty Tricks	1974	—	2.50	5.00

Albums

ATLANTIC

❑ SD 8155	The Sweet Inspirations	1968	5.00	10.00	20.00
❑ SD 8182	Songs of Faith and Inspiration	1968	5.00	10.00	20.00
❑ SD 8201	What the World Needs Now Is Love	1969	5.00	10.00	20.00
❑ SD 8225	Sweets for My Sweet	1969	5.00	10.00	20.00
❑ SD 8253	Sweet, Sweet Soul	1970	5.00	10.00	20.00

RSO

❑ RS-1-3058	Hot Butterfly	1979	2.50	5.00	10.00

STAX

❑ STS-3017	Estelle, Myrna and Sylvia	1973	5.00	10.00	20.00

Some years after his hits, Huey Smith was still going strong in New Orleans. *For Dancing*, his second LP, came out in 1961.

Goodnite, It's Time to Go was a compilation of Spaniels tracks issued on LP in 1958. This is the original cover, with the group's picture on the front.

Early in their recording career, the Spinners were on the Tri-Phi label. This is one of the singles they released, "I've Been Hurt," which was not the same song that was later a hit for Bill Deal and the Rhondels.

Meet the Supremes was the Motown group's first album. This is the sought-after original cover, with the three women sitting on stools.

One of the Supremes' biggest pop hits, "Stop! In the Name of Love," actually got stuck at #2 for four weeks on the R&B chart. Here is its picture sleeve.

Foster Sylvers had a hit in 1973 with "Misdemeanor," when he was 11 years old. He also was a member of the family group The Sylvers for many years. Years later, in 1990, he released this obscure solo 45 on A&M.

Number	Title (A Side/B Side)	Yr	VG	VG+	NM

SWITCH
45s
GORDY

Number	Title (A Side/B Side)	Yr	VG	VG+	NM
❏ 7159	There'll Never Be/You Pulled a Switch	1978	—	2.00	4.00
❏ 7163	I Wanna Be Closer/Somebody's Watching You	1979	—	2.00	4.00
❏ 7168	Best Beat in Town/It's So Real	1979	—	2.00	4.00
❏ 7175	I Call Your Name/Best Beat in Town	1979	—	2.00	4.00
❏ 7181	Don't Take My Love Away (Part 1)/Don't Take My Love Away (Part 2)	1980	—	2.00	4.00
❏ 7190	Next to You/My Friend in the Sky	1980	—	2.00	4.00
❏ 7193	Keep Movin' On/Love Over and Over Again	1980	—	2.00	4.00
❏ 7199	Get Back with You/You and I	1981	—	2.00	4.00
❏ 7214	I Do Love You/Without You in My Life	1981	—	2.00	4.00

Albums
GORDY

Number	Title	Yr	VG	VG+	NM
❏ G7-980R1	Switch	1978	3.00	6.00	12.00
❏ G7-988R1	Switch II	1979	3.00	6.00	12.00
❏ G8-993M1	Reaching for Tomorrow	1980	3.00	6.00	12.00
❏ G8-999M1	This Is My Dream	1980	3.00	6.00	12.00
❏ G8-1007M1	Switch V	1981	3.00	6.00	12.00

TOTAL EXPERIENCE

Number	Title	Yr	VG	VG+	NM
❏ TEL-8-5701	Am I Still Your Boyfriend?	1984	2.50	5.00	10.00

SYLVERS, FOSTER
Also see THE SYLVERS.
45s
A&M

Number	Title (A Side/B Side)	Yr	VG	VG+	NM
❏ 1480	I'll Do It/Pretty Baby	1990	—	2.50	5.00

—As "Foster Sylvers & Hy-Tech"
CAPITOL

Number	Title (A Side/B Side)	Yr	VG	VG+	NM
❏ 4553	Don't Let Me Go for Someone Else/Super Scoop	1978	—	2.00	4.00

MGM

Number	Title (A Side/B Side)	Yr	VG	VG+	NM
❏ 14580	Misdemeanor/So Close	1973	—	2.50	5.00
❏ 14630	Hey Little Girl/I'll Get You in the End	1973	—	2.50	5.00

PRIDE

Number	Title (A Side/B Side)	Yr	VG	VG+	NM
❏ 1031	Misdemeanor/So Close	1973	2.50	5.00	10.00

Albums
PRIDE

Number	Title	Yr	VG	VG+	NM
❏ 0027	Foster Sylvers	1973	3.00	6.00	12.00

SYLVERS, THE
Also see FOSTER SYLVERS.
12-Inch Singles
GEFFEN

Number	Title (A Side/B Side)	Yr	VG	VG+	NM
❏ 20258	In One Love and Out the Other (Extended)/(Instrumental)	1984	—	3.00	6.00

45s
CAPITOL

Number	Title (A Side/B Side)	Yr	VG	VG+	NM
❏ 4179	Boogie Fever/Free Style	1975	—	2.00	4.00
❏ 4255	Cotton Candy/I Can Be for Real	1976	—	2.00	4.00
❏ 4336	Hot Line/That's What Love Is Made Of	1976	—	2.00	4.00
❏ 4405	High School Dance/Lovin' You Is Like Lovin' the Wind	1977	—	2.00	4.00
❏ 4493	Any Way You Want Me/Lovin' Me Back	1977	—	2.00	4.00
❏ 4532	New Horizon/Charisma	1978	—	2.00	4.00

CASABLANCA

Number	Title (A Side/B Side)	Yr	VG	VG+	NM
❏ 938	Don't Stop, Get Off/Love Won't Let Me Go	1978	—	2.00	4.00
❏ 953	Forever Yours/Diamonds Are Rare	1978	—	2.00	4.00
❏ 992	I Feel So Good Tonight/Hoochie Coochie Dancin'	1979	—	2.00	4.00
❏ 2207	I Feels So Good Tonight/Mahogany	1979	—	2.00	4.00

GEFFEN

Number	Title (A Side/B Side)	Yr	VG	VG+	NM
❏ 29061	Falling for Your Love/(Instrumental)	1985	—	—	3.00
❏ 29293	In One Love and Out the Other/Falling for Your Love	1984	—	—	3.00
❏ 29293 [PS]	In One Love and Out the Other/Falling for Your Love	1984	—	—	3.00

MGM

Number	Title (A Side/B Side)	Yr	VG	VG+	NM
❏ 14352	You Got What It Takes/Time to Ride	1972	—	3.00	6.00
❏ 14579	Stay Away from Me/I'll Never Be Ashamed	1973	—	3.00	6.00
❏ 14678	Through the Love in My Heart/Cry of a Dreamer	1973	—	2.00	4.00
❏ 14698	Hang On Sloopy/Na Na Hey Hey Kiss Him Goodbye	1974	—	2.00	4.00

—As "Foster, Pat & Angie Sylvers"

Number	Title (A Side/B Side)	Yr	VG	VG+	NM
❏ 14721	I Aim to Please/Wish You Were Here	1974	—	2.00	4.00

PRIDE

Number	Title (A Side/B Side)	Yr	VG	VG+	NM
❏ 1001	Fool's Paradise/I'm Truly Happy	1972	—	2.50	5.00
❏ 1019	Wish That I Could Talk to You/How Love Hurts	1972	—	2.50	5.00
❏ 1029	Stay Away from Me/I'll Never Be Ashamed	1973	—	2.50	5.00
❏ 1029 [PS]	Stay Away from Me/I'll Never Be Ashamed	1973	—	3.00	6.00

SOLAR

Number	Title (A Side/B Side)	Yr	VG	VG+	NM
❏ 47949	Come Back, Lover, Come Back/There's a Place	1981	—	2.00	4.00
❏ 48002	Take It to the Top/I'm Getting Over	1982	—	2.00	4.00

VERVE

Number	Title (A Side/B Side)	Yr	VG	VG+	NM
❏ 10664	Come On Give Me a Chance/I'm Just a Lonely Soul	1971	2.50	5.00	10.00

Albums
CAPITOL

Number	Title	Yr	VG	VG+	NM
❏ ST-11465	Showcase	1976	2.50	5.00	10.00
❏ ST-11580	Something Special	1976	2.50	5.00	10.00
❏ ST-11705	New Horizons	1977	2.50	5.00	10.00
❏ ST-11868	Best of the Sylvers	1978	2.50	5.00	10.00

CASABLANCA

Number	Title	Yr	VG	VG+	NM
❏ NBLP 7103	Forever Yours	1978	2.50	5.00	10.00
❏ NBLP 7151	Disco Fever	1979	2.50	5.00	10.00

GEFFEN

Number	Title	Yr	VG	VG+	NM
❏ GHS 24039	Bizarre	1984	2.50	5.00	10.00

MGM

Number	Title	Yr	VG	VG+	NM
❏ SE-4930	The Sylvers III	1974	2.50	5.00	10.00

PRIDE

Number	Title	Yr	VG	VG+	NM
❏ 0007	The Sylvers	1972	3.00	6.00	12.00
❏ 0026	The Sylvers II	1973	3.00	6.00	12.00

SOLAR

Number	Title	Yr	VG	VG+	NM
❏ 22	Concept	1981	2.50	5.00	10.00

SYLVIA, MARGO
See TUNE WEAVERS.

SYLVIA (1)
R&B singer and record company mogul (All Platinum/Stang/Vibration, Sugar Hill). Also see MICKEY AND SYLVIA.
45s
ALL PLATINUM

Number	Title (A Side/B Side)	Yr	VG	VG+	NM
❏ 2303	I Can't Help It/It's a Good Life	1969	2.00	4.00	8.00
❏ 2350	Sho Nuff Boogie (Part 1)/Sho Nuff Boogie (Part 2)	1974	—	2.50	5.00

—With the Moments
JUBILEE

Number	Title (A Side/B Side)	Yr	VG	VG+	NM
❏ 5093	Drive, Daddy, Drive/I Found Somebody to Love	1952	12.50	25.00	50.00

—As "Little Sylvia"
STANG

Number	Title (A Side/B Side)	Yr	VG	VG+	NM
❏ 5015	Have You Had Any Lately/Anytime	1970	—	3.00	6.00

SUGAR HILL

Number	Title (A Side/B Side)	Yr	VG	VG+	NM
❏ 781	It's Good to Be the Queen/(B-side unknown)	1982	—	2.00	4.00

VIBRATION

Number	Title (A Side/B Side)	Yr	VG	VG+	NM
❏ 512	Next Time I See You/Gimme a Little Action	1972	—	3.00	6.00
❏ 521	Pillow Talk/My Thing	1973	—	3.00	6.00
❏ 524	Didn't I/Had Any Lately	1973	—	2.50	5.00
❏ 525	Soul Je T'Aime/Sunday	1973	—	2.50	5.00

—With Ralfi Pagan

Number	Title (A Side/B Side)	Yr	VG	VG+	NM
❏ 527	Alfredo/Lay It On Me	1973	—	2.50	5.00
❏ 528	Private Performance/If You Get the Notion	1974	—	2.50	5.00
❏ 529	Sweet Stuff/Had Any Lately	1974	—	2.50	5.00
❏ 530	Easy Evil/Give It Up in Vain	1974	—	2.50	5.00
❏ 536	Pussy Cat (Part 1)/Pussy Cat (Part 2)	1975	—	2.50	5.00
❏ 567	L.A. Sunshine/Taxi	1976	—	2.50	5.00
❏ 570	Lay It On Me (Vocal)/(Instrumental)	1977	—	2.50	5.00
❏ 572	Lollipop Man/Lay It On Me	1977	—	2.50	5.00
❏ 576	Automatic Lover/Stop Boy	1978	—	2.50	5.00

Albums
STANG

Number	Title	Yr	VG	VG+	NM
❏ 1010	Sylvia	197?	5.00	10.00	20.00

SUGAR HILL

Number	Title	Yr	VG	VG+	NM
❏ 258	Sylvia I	1981	2.50	5.00	10.00

VIBRATION

Number	Title	Yr	VG	VG+	NM
❏ 126	Pillow Talk	1973	3.75	7.50	15.00
❏ 131	Lay It On Me	1977	3.00	6.00	12.00
❏ 143	Brand New Funk	197?	3.00	6.00	12.00

SYMPHONICS, THE (2)
This Symphonics features FREDDIE SCOTT.
45s
ENRICA

Number	Title (A Side/B Side)	Yr	VG	VG+	NM
❏ 1002	Come On Honey/A Blessing to You	1959	5.00	10.00	20.00

SYREETA
Also see BILLY PRESTON AND SYREETA.
12-Inch Singles
MOTOWN

Number	Title (A Side/B Side)	Yr	VG	VG+	NM
❏ PR 90 [DJ]	Quick Slick/Out of the Box	1981	2.50	5.00	10.00

45s
MOTOWN

Number	Title (A Side/B Side)	Yr	VG	VG+	NM
❏ 1297	Come and Get This Stuff/Black Maybe	1974	—	2.50	5.00
❏ 1317	I'm Goin' Left/Heavy day	1974	—	2.50	5.00
❏ 1328	Your Kiss Is Sweeter/Spinnin' and Spinnin'	1975	—	2.50	5.00
❏ 1353	Harmour Love/Cause We've Ended As Lovers	1975	—	2.50	5.00
❏ 1353 [DJ]	Harmour Love (same on both sides?)	1975	2.50	5.00	10.00

—Promo only on red vinyl
MOWEST

Number	Title (A Side/B Side)	Yr	VG	VG+	NM
❏ 5016	I Love Every Little Thing About You/Black Maybe	1972	—	3.00	6.00
❏ 5021	Happiness/To Know You Is to Love You	1972	—	3.00	6.00

TAMLA

Number	Title (A Side/B Side)	Yr	VG	VG+	NM
❏ 1610	I Must Be in Love/Wish Upon a Star	1982	—	2.00	4.00
❏ 1675	Forever Is Not Enough/She's Leaving Home	1983	—	2.00	4.00
❏ 54333	Quick Slick/I Don't Know	1981	—	2.00	4.00

Albums
MOTOWN

Number	Title	Yr	VG	VG+	NM
❏ M6-808	Stevie Wonder Presents Syreeta	1974	2.50	5.00	10.00
❏ M6-891	Rich Love, Poor Love	1977	2.50	5.00	10.00

—With G.C. Cameron
MOWEST

Number	Title	Yr	VG	VG+	NM
❏	Syreeta	1972	3.00	6.00	12.00

TAMLA

Number	Title	Yr	VG	VG+	NM
❏ T6-349	One	1977	2.50	5.00	10.00
❏ T7-372	Syreeta	1980	2.50	5.00	10.00
❏ T8-376	Set My Love in Motion	1981	2.50	5.00	10.00
❏ 6039 TF	The Spell	1983	2.50	5.00	10.00

T

T.S.U. TORONADOES, THE

45s

ATLANTIC

Number	Title (A Side/B Side)	Yr	VG	VG+	NM
❑ 2579	Getting the Corners/What Good Am I!	1968	2.00	4.00	8.00
❑ 2614	Got to Get Through to You/The Goose	1969	2.00	4.00	8.00

VOLT

Number	Title (A Side/B Side)	Yr	VG	VG+	NM
❑ 4030	My Thing Is a Moving Thing/Still Love You	1969	—	3.00	6.00
❑ 4038	One Flight Too Many/Play the Music Toronadoes	1970	—	3.00	6.00

TAMPA RED

45s

RCA VICTOR

Number	Title (A Side/B Side)	Yr	VG	VG+	NM
❑ 47-4275	Boogie Woogie Women/I Won't Let Her Do It	1951	12.50	25.00	50.00
❑ 47-4399	She's a Cool Operator/Green and Lucky Blues	1951	12.50	25.00	50.00
❑ 47-4722	But I Forgive You/I'm Gonna Put You Down	1952	12.50	25.00	50.00
❑ 47-4898	True Love/Look-a There, Look-a There	1952	12.50	25.00	50.00
❑ 47-5134	All Mixed Up Over You/Too Late Too Long	1953	10.00	20.00	40.00
❑ 47-5273	I'll Never Let You Go/Got a Mind to Leave This Town	1953	10.00	20.00	40.00
❑ 47-5523	So Craazy About You Baby/So Much Trouble	1953	10.00	20.00	40.00
❑ 47-5594	If She Don't Come Back/Big Stars Falling	1954	10.00	20.00	40.00
❑ 50-0002	If You Ever Change Your Ways/Chicago Breakdown	1949	30.00	60.00	120.00
—Gray label, orange vinyl; With Big Maceo					
❑ 50-0019	Come On If You're Coming/When Things Go Wrong with You	1950	30.00	60.00	120.00
—Gray label, orange vinyl					
❑ 50-0027	It's a Brand New Boogie/Put Your Money Where Your Mouth Is	1950	30.00	60.00	120.00
—Gray label, orange vinyl					
❑ 50-0041	I'll Find My Way/That's Her Own Business	1950	30.00	60.00	120.00
—Gray label, orange vinyl					
❑ 50-0071	It's Too Late Now/Please Try to See It My Way	1950	25.00	50.00	100.00
—Gray label, orange vinyl					
❑ 50-0084	1950 Blues/Love Her with a Feelin'	1950	25.00	50.00	100.00
—Gray label, orange vinyl					
❑ 50-0094	It's Good Like That/New Deal Blues	1950	25.00	50.00	100.00
—Gray label, orange vinyl					
❑ 50-0107	Sweet Little Angel/Don't Blame Shorty for That	1951	20.00	40.00	80.00
❑ 50-0112	Midnight Boogie/I Miss My Lovin' Blues	1951	20.00	40.00	80.00
❑ 50-0123	She's Dynamite/Early in the Morning	1951	20.00	40.00	80.00
❑ 50-0136	Pretty Baby Blues/Since My Baby's Been Gone	1951	20.00	40.00	80.00

Albums

BLUEBIRD

Number	Title (A Side/B Side)	Yr	VG	VG+	NM
❑ AXM2-5501 [(2)]	Guitar Wizard	1975	3.75	7.50	15.00

BLUES CLASSICS

Number	Title (A Side/B Side)	Yr	VG	VG+	NM
❑ 25	Guitar Wizard (1935-53)	197?	3.00	6.00	12.00

BLUESVILLE

Number	Title (A Side/B Side)	Yr	VG	VG+	NM
❑ BVLP-1030 [M]	Don't Tampa with the Blues	1961	30.00	60.00	120.00
—Blue label, silver print					
❑ BVLP-1030 [M]	Don't Tampa with the Blues	1963	7.50	15.00	30.00
—Blue label, trident logo at right					
❑ BVLP-1043 [M]	Don't Jive Me	1962	30.00	60.00	120.00
—Blue label, silver print					
❑ BVLP-1043 [M]	Don't Jive Me	1963	7.50	15.00	30.00
—Blue label, trident logo at right					

FANTASY

Number	Title (A Side/B Side)	Yr	VG	VG+	NM
❑ OBC-516	Don't Tampa with the Blues	198?	2.50	5.00	10.00

YAZOO

Number	Title (A Side/B Side)	Yr	VG	VG+	NM
❑ 1039	Bottleneck Guitar	197?	3.00	6.00	12.00

TAMS, THE

45s

1-2-3

Number	Title (A Side/B Side)	Yr	VG	VG+	NM
❑ 1726	How Long Love/Too Much Foolin' Around	1970	—	3.00	6.00

ABC

Number	Title (A Side/B Side)	Yr	VG	VG+	NM
❑ 10825	Holding On/Is It Better to Have Loved a Little	1966	2.00	4.00	8.00
❑ 10885	Shelter/Get Away (Leave Me Alone)	1966	2.00	4.00	8.00
❑ 10929	Breaking Up/How 'Bout It	1967	2.00	4.00	8.00
❑ 10956	Everything Else Is Gone/Mary, Mary, Row Your Boat	1967	2.00	4.00	8.00
❑ 11019	All My Heard Times/A Little More Soul	1967	2.00	4.00	8.00
❑ 11066	Be Young, Be Foolish, Be Happy/That Same Old Song	1968	2.00	4.00	8.00
❑ 11128	Laugh at the World/Trouble Maker	1968	2.00	4.00	8.00
❑ 11183	Sunshine, Rainbow, Blue Sky, Brown Eyed Girl/There's a Great Big Change in Me	1969	2.00	4.00	8.00
❑ 11228	Be Young, Be Foolish, Be Happy/Love, Love, Love	1969	2.00	4.00	8.00
❑ 11358	Don't You Just Know It/Making Music	1973	—	2.50	5.00

ABC-PARAMOUNT

Number	Title (A Side/B Side)	Yr	VG	VG+	NM
❑ 10502	What Kind of Fool (Do You Think I Am)/Laugh It Off	1963	3.75	7.50	15.00
❑ 10533	It's All Right (You're Just in Love)/You Lied to Your Daddy	1964	3.00	6.00	12.00
❑ 10573	Hey Girl Don't Bother Me/Take Away	1964	3.00	6.00	12.00
❑ 10601	Silly Little Girl/Weep Little Girl	1964	3.00	6.00	12.00
❑ 10614	The Truth Hurts/Why Did My Little Girl Cry	1965	2.50	5.00	10.00
❑ 10635	What Do You Do/Unlove You	1965	2.50	5.00	10.00
❑ 10702	Concrete Jungle/Till the End of Time	1965	2.50	5.00	10.00
❑ 10741	Carryin' On/I've Been Hurt	1965	2.50	5.00	10.00
❑ 10779	Got to Get Used to a Broken Heart/Riding for a Fall	1966	2.50	5.00	10.00

ABC DUNHILL

Number	Title (A Side/B Side)	Yr	VG	VG+	NM
❑ 4290	Hey Girl Don't Bother Me/Weep Little Girl	1971	—	3.00	6.00
❑ 4290 [PS]	Hey Girl Don't Bother Me/Weep Little Girl	1971	2.50	5.00	10.00
—Title sleeve with "#1 in England"					

APT

Number	Title (A Side/B Side)	Yr	VG	VG+	NM
❑ 26010	Long Distance Operator/Numbers	1970	—	3.00	6.00

ARLEN

Number	Title (A Side/B Side)	Yr	VG	VG+	NM
❑ 711	Untie Me/Disillusioned	1962	3.00	6.00	12.00
❑ 717	Deep Inside Me/If You're So Smart (Why Do You Have a Broken Heart)	1962	3.00	6.00	12.00
❑ 720	You'll Never Know/Blue Shadows	1963	3.00	6.00	12.00
❑ 729	Don't Ever Go/Find Another Love	1963	3.00	6.00	12.00

CAPITOL

Number	Title (A Side/B Side)	Yr	VG	VG+	NM
❑ 3050	The Tams Medley/Wire Help	1971	—	3.00	6.00

COMPLEAT

Number	Title (A Side/B Side)	Yr	VG	VG+	NM
❑ 109	My Baby Sure Can Shag/Making True Love	1983	—	2.00	4.00

GENERAL AMERICAN

Number	Title (A Side/B Side)	Yr	VG	VG+	NM
❑ 714	My Baby Loves Me/Find Another Love	1962	3.75	7.50	15.00

HERITAGE

Number	Title (A Side/B Side)	Yr	VG	VG+	NM
❑ 101	Vacation Time/If Love Were Like Rivers	1961	75.00	150.00	300.00

KING

Number	Title (A Side/B Side)	Yr	VG	VG+	NM
❑ 6012	Untie Me/Find Another Love	1965	2.50	5.00	10.00

SWAN

Number	Title (A Side/B Side)	Yr	VG	VG+	NM
❑ 4055	Sorry/Valley of Love	1960	3.75	7.50	15.00

Albums

1-2-3

Number	Title (A Side/B Side)	Yr	VG	VG+	NM
❑ ST-567	The Best of the Tams	1970	5.00	10.00	20.00

ABC

Number	Title (A Side/B Side)	Yr	VG	VG+	NM
❑ ABCS-481 [R]	Presenting the Tams	1968	5.00	10.00	20.00
—Reissue of ABC-Paramount 481					
❑ ABCS-499 [S]	Hey Girl, Don't Bother Me	1964	5.00	10.00	20.00
—Reissue of ABC-Paramount 499					
❑ ABC-596 [M]	Time for the Tams	1967	7.50	15.00	30.00
❑ ABCS-596 [S]	Time for the Tams	1967	7.50	15.00	30.00
❑ ABCS-627	A Little More Soul	1968	6.25	12.50	25.00
❑ ABCS-673	A Portrait of the Tams	1969	6.25	12.50	25.00

ABC-PARAMOUNT

Number	Title (A Side/B Side)	Yr	VG	VG+	NM
❑ ABC-481 [M]	Presenting the Tams	1964	12.50	25.00	50.00
❑ ABCS-481 [R]	Presenting the Tams	1964	7.50	15.00	30.00
❑ ABC-499 [M]	Hey Girl, Don't Bother Me	1964	7.50	15.00	30.00
❑ ABCS-499 [S]	Hey Girl, Don't Bother Me	1964	10.00	20.00	40.00

CAPITOL

Number	Title (A Side/B Side)	Yr	VG	VG+	NM
❑ SM-11839	The Best of the Tams	1979	3.00	6.00	12.00

COMPLEAT

Number	Title (A Side/B Side)	Yr	VG	VG+	NM
❑ CMLP-5001 [EP]	Beach Music from the Tams	198?	2.00	4.00	8.00

SOUNDS SOUTH

Number	Title (A Side/B Side)	Yr	VG	VG+	NM
❑ SO-16010	The Mighty, Mighty Tams	1977	3.75	7.50	15.00

TASTE OF HONEY, A

45s

CAPITOL

Number	Title (A Side/B Side)	Yr	VG	VG+	NM
❑ 4565	Boogie Oogie Oogie/World Spin	1978	—	2.00	4.00
❑ 4565 [PS]	Boogie Oogie Oogie/World Spin	1978	—	2.50	5.00
❑ 4655	Distant/You're in Good Hands	1978	—	2.00	4.00
❑ 4668	Disco Dancin'/Sky High	1978	—	2.00	4.00
❑ 4744	Do It Good/I Love You	1979	—	2.00	4.00
❑ 4776	Let's Begin/Race	1979	—	2.00	4.00
❑ 4888	Rescue Me/Say That You'll Stay	1980	—	2.00	4.00
❑ 4932	I'm Talkin' 'Bout You/Don't You Lead Me On	1980	—	2.00	4.00
❑ 4953	Sukiyaki/Don't You Lead Me On	1980	—	2.00	4.00
❑ 4953 [PS]	Sukiyaki/Don't You Lead Me On	1980	—	2.50	5.00
❑ B-5099	I'll Try Something New/Good-Bye Baby	1982	—	2.00	4.00
❑ B-5099 [PS]	I'll Try Something New/Good-Bye Baby	1982	—	2.50	5.00
❑ B-5132	We've Got the Groove/This Love of Ours	1982	—	2.00	4.00

Albums

CAPITOL

Number	Title (A Side/B Side)	Yr	VG	VG+	NM
❑ ST-11754	A Taste of Honey	1978	2.50	5.00	10.00
❑ SOO-11951	Another Taste	1979	3.00	6.00	12.00
❑ ST-12089	Twice as Sweet	1980	3.00	6.00	12.00
❑ ST-12173	Ladies of the Eighties	1982	3.00	6.00	12.00

TAVARES

Also see CHUBBY AND THE TURNPIKES.

12-Inch Singles

CAPITOL

Number	Title (A Side/B Side)	Yr	VG	VG+	NM
❑ SPRO-9087 [DJ]	Straight from the Heart (7:23) (same on both sides)	1979	3.00	6.00	12.00

JDC

Number	Title (A Side/B Side)	Yr	VG	VG+	NM
❑ 002	C'est La Vie/Good 'n' Plenty/On My Mind Tonight	198?	—	3.00	6.00
❑ 003	She Freaks Out on the Floor (4 versions)	198?	—	3.00	6.00

RCA

Number	Title (A Side/B Side)	Yr	VG	VG+	NM
❑ PD-13434	Got to Find My Way Back to You/I Hope You Will Be Very Unhappy Without Me	1983	2.00	4.00	8.00
❑ PD-13612	Deeper in Love/I Really Miss You Baby	1983	2.00	4.00	8.00

45s

CAPITOL

Number	Title (A Side/B Side)	Yr	VG	VG+	NM
❑ 3674	Check It Out/The Judgment Day	1973	—	2.50	5.00
❑ 3794	That's the Sound That Lonely Makes/Little Girl	1973	—	2.50	5.00
❑ 3882	Too Late/Leave It Up to the Lady	1974	—	2.50	5.00
❑ 3957	She's Gone/To Love You	1974	—	2.50	5.00
❑ 4010	Remember What I Told You to Forget/My Ship	1974	—	2.50	5.00

T

Number	Title (A Side/B Side)	Yr	VG	VG+	NM
❏ 4111	It Only Takes a Minute/I Hope She Chooses Me	1975	—	2.50	5.00
❏ 4184	Free Ride/In the Eyes of Love	1975	—	2.50	5.00
❏ 4221	The Love I Never Had/In the City	1976	—	2.50	5.00
❏ 4270	Heaven Must Be Missing An Angel (Part 1)/Heaven Must Be Missing An Angel (Part 2)	1976	—	2.50	5.00
❏ 4348	Don't Take Away the Music/Guiding Star	1976	—	2.50	5.00
❏ 4398	Whodunit/Fool of the Year	1977	—	2.50	5.00
❏ 4453	Goodnight My Love/Watchin' the Woman's Movement	1977	—	2.50	5.00
❏ 4500	More Than a Woman/Keep in Touch	1977	—	2.00	4.00
❏ 4544	The Ghost of Love (Part 1)/The Ghost of Love (Part 2)	1978	—	2.00	4.00
❏ 4583	Timber/Feel So Good	1978	—	2.00	4.00
❏ 4658	Never Had a Love Like This Before/Positive Forces	1978	—	2.00	4.00
❏ 4703	Straight from the Heart/I'm Back for Me	1979	—	2.00	4.00
❏ 4738	One Telephone Call Away/Let Me Heal the Bruises	1979	—	2.00	4.00
❏ 4781	Hard Core Poetry/Stabilize	1979	—	2.00	4.00
❏ 4811	Bad Times/Got to Have Your Love	1979	—	2.00	4.00
❏ 4846	I Can't Go On Living Without You/Why Can't We Fall in Love	1980	—	2.00	4.00
❏ 4880	I Don't Want You Anymore/Paradise	1980	—	2.00	4.00
❏ 4933	Love Uprising/Not Love	1980	—	2.00	4.00
❏ 4969	Loneliness/Break Down for Love	1981	—	2.00	4.00
❏ A-5019	Turn Out the Nightlight/House of Music	1981	—	2.00	4.00
❏ A-5043	Loveline/Right On Time	1981	—	2.00	4.00
RCA					
❏ PB-13292	A Penny for Your Thoughts/The Skin You're In	1982	—	2.00	4.00
❏ PB-13433	Got to Find My Way Back to You/I Hope You Will Be Very Unhappy Without Me	1983	—	2.00	4.00
❏ PB-13530	Abra-Ca-Dabra Love You Too/Mystery Lady	1983	—	2.00	4.00
❏ PB-13611	Deeper in Love/I Really Miss You Baby	1983	—	2.00	4.00
❏ PB-13684	Words and Music/I'll Send Love (We Go Together)	1983	—	2.00	4.00
❏ GB-13799	A Penny for Your Thoughts/Got to Find My Way Back to You	1984	—	—	3.00
—Gold Standard Series					
Albums					
CAPITOL					
❏ ST-11258	Check It Out	1973	2.50	5.00	10.00
❏ ST-11316	Hard Core Poetry	1974	2.50	5.00	10.00
❏ ST-11396	In the City	1975	2.50	5.00	10.00
❏ ST-11533	Sky-High!	1976	2.50	5.00	10.00
❏ ST-11628	Love Storm	1977	2.50	5.00	10.00
❏ ST-11701	The Best of Tavares	1977	2.50	5.00	10.00
❏ SW-11719	Future Bound	1978	2.50	5.00	10.00
❏ SW-11874	Madam Butterfly	1979	2.50	5.00	10.00
❏ ST-12026	Supercharged	1980	2.50	5.00	10.00
❏ ST-12117	Love Uprising	1981	2.50	5.00	10.00
❏ ST-12167	Loveline	1982	2.50	5.00	10.00
❏ SN-16206	Love Storm	1981	2.00	4.00	8.00
—Budget-line reissue					
❏ SN-16207	Future Bound	1981	2.00	4.00	8.00
—Budget-line reissue					
RCA VICTOR					
❏ AFL1-4357	New Directions	1982	2.50	5.00	10.00
❏ AFL1-4700	Words and Music	1983	2.50	5.00	10.00

TAYLOR, BILL, AND SMOKEY JO
45s
FLIP

Number	Title (A Side/B Side)	Yr	VG	VG+	NM
❏ 502	Split Personality/Lonely Sweetheart	1955	375.00	750.00	1500.

TAYLOR, BILLY
45s
CITATION

Number	Title (A Side/B Side)	Yr	VG	VG+	NM
❏ 5002	Income Taxes and You/Lullaby to Carolyn	1962	3.75	7.50	15.00
FAME					
❏ 502	Little Jewel/Study Hall Romance	196?	75.00	150.00	300.00
FELCO					
❏ 101	Wombie Zombie/I'm Young	1959	5.00	10.00	20.00
FELSTED					
❏ 8564	Bandstand Baby/Cat with No Future	1959	5.00	10.00	20.00
TOWER					
❏ 421	Sunny/I Wish I Knew How I Would Feel to Be Free	1968	2.00	4.00	8.00

TAYLOR, BOBBY, AND THE VANCOUVERS
45s
GORDY

Number	Title (A Side/B Side)	Yr	VG	VG+	NM
❏ 7069	Does Your Mama Know About Me/Fading Away	1968	5.00	10.00	20.00
❏ 7073	I Am Your Man/If You Love Her	1968	5.00	10.00	20.00
❏ 7079	Malinda/It's Growing	1968	5.00	10.00	20.00
❏ 7088	Oh I've Been Blessed/It Should Have Been Me Loving Her	1969	150.00	300.00	600.00
❏ 7092	My Girl Is Gone/It Should Have Been Me Loving Her	1969	5.00	10.00	20.00
INTEGRA					
❏ 103	This Is My Woman/(B-side unknown)	1968	25.00	50.00	100.00
MOWEST					
❏ 5006	Hey Lordy/Just a Little Bit Closer	1971	3.75	7.50	15.00
PLAYBOY					
❏ 6046	Why Play Games/Don't Wonder Why	1975	—	2.50	5.00

Number	Title (A Side/B Side)	Yr	VG	VG+	NM
SUNFLOWER					
❏ 126	There Are Roses Somewhere in the World/It Was a Good Time	1972	6.25	12.50	25.00
V.I.P.					
❏ 25053	Oh I've Been Blessed/Blackmail	1969	6.25	12.50	25.00
Albums					
GORDY					
❏ G-930 [M]	Bobby Taylor and the Vancouvers	1968	20.00	40.00	80.00
—Mono is promo only					
❏ GS-930 [S]	Bobby Taylor and the Vancouvers	1968	15.00	30.00	60.00
❏ GS-942	Taylor Made Soul	1969	15.00	30.00	60.00

TAYLOR, CARMEN
45s
APOLLO

Number	Title (A Side/B Side)	Yr	VG	VG+	NM
❏ 489	Oh Please/Teen Age Ball	1956	15.00	30.00	60.00
ATLANTIC					
❏ 1002	Lovin' Daddy/Ding Dong	1953	12.50	25.00	50.00
❏ 1015	Big Mamou Daddy/Mamma Me and Johnny Free	1953	12.50	25.00	50.00
❏ 1041	Freddie/Ooh I	1954	30.00	60.00	120.00
GUYDEN					
❏ 100	Let Me Go Lover/No More, No Less	1954	10.00	20.00	40.00
KAMA SUTRA					
❏ 206	My Son/You're Puttin' Me On	1966	3.00	6.00	12.00
KING					
❏ 5085	So What/Why Did You Leave Me Alone	1957	12.50	25.00	50.00

TAYLOR, EDDIE
45s
VEE JAY

Number	Title (A Side/B Side)	Yr	VG	VG+	NM
❏ 149	Bad Boy/E.T. Blues	1955	30.00	60.00	120.00
❏ 185	Big Town Playboy/Ride 'Em On Down	1956	20.00	40.00	80.00
❏ 206	You'll Always Have a Home/Don't Knock at My Door	1956	15.00	30.00	60.00
❏ 267	I'm Gonna Love You/Looking for Trouble	1958	10.00	20.00	40.00
VIVID					
❏ 104	I'm Sitting Here/Do You Want Me to Cry	1964	5.00	10.00	20.00

TAYLOR, JOHNNIE
12-Inch Singles
BEVERLY GLEN

Number	Title (A Side/B Side)	Yr	VG	VG+	NM
❏ BG 2002	What About My Love/Reaganomics	1982	2.50	5.00	10.00

45s
BEVERLY GLEN

Number	Title (A Side/B Side)	Yr	VG	VG+	NM
❏ 2003	What About My Love/Reaganomics	1982	—	2.00	4.00
❏ 2004	I'm So Proud/I Need a Freak	1982	—	2.00	4.00
❏ 2007	Just Ain't Good Enough/Don't Wait	1983	—	2.00	4.00
❏ 2016	Seconds of Your Love/Shoot for the Stars	1983	—	2.00	4.00
COLUMBIA					
❏ AE7 1153 [DJ]	God Is Standing By/God Is Amazing	1977	2.00	4.00	8.00
—B-side by Deniece Williams; promo with "Suggested Christmas Programming" on label					
❏ 10281	Disco Lady/You're the Best in the World	1976	—	2.50	5.00
❏ 10334	Somebody's Gettin' It/Please Don't Stop (That Song from Playing)	1976	—	2.50	5.00
❏ 10478	Love Is Better in the A.M. (Part 1)/Love Is Better in the A.M. (Part 2)	1977	—	2.50	5.00
❏ 10541	Your Love Is Rated X/Here I Go (Through These Chains Again)	1977	—	2.50	5.00
❏ 10610	Disco 9000/Right Now	1977	—	2.00	4.00
❏ 10709	Keep On Dancing/I Love to Make Love When It's Raining	1978	—	2.00	4.00
❏ 10776	Give Me My Baby/Ever Ready	1978	—	2.00	4.00
❏ 11084	(Ooh-Wee) She's Killing Me/Play Something Pretty	1979	—	2.00	4.00
❏ 11315	I Got This Thing for Your Love/Signing Off with Love	1980	—	2.00	4.00
❏ 11373	I Wanna Get Into You/Baby Don't Hesitate	1980	—	2.00	4.00
DERBY					
❏ 101	Shine, Shine, Shine/Dance What You Wanna	1963	3.75	7.50	15.00
❏ 1006	Baby, We've Got Love/In Love with You	1963	3.75	7.50	15.00
❏ 1010	I Need Lots of Love/Getting Married Soon	1964	3.75	7.50	15.00
MALACO					
❏ 2107	Lady, My Whole World Is You/L-O-V-E	1984	—	—	3.00
❏ 2111	Good with My Hips/This Is Your Night	1985	—	—	3.00
❏ 2118	Still Called the Blues/She's Cheatin' on Me	1985	—	—	3.00
❏ 2125	Wall to Wall/(B-side unknown)	1986	—	—	3.00
❏ 2128	Can I Love You/There's Nothing I Wouldn't Do	1986	—	—	3.00
❏ 2132	Just Because/When She Stops Asking	1987	—	—	3.00
❏ 2135	Don't Make Me Late/Happy Time	1987	—	—	3.00
❏ 2140	If I Lose Your Love/Something Is Going Wrong	1987	—	—	3.00
❏ 2143	Everything's Out in the Open/Got to Leave This Woman	1988	—	—	3.00
❏ 2153	In Control/I Found a Love	1989	—	—	3.00
❏ 2159	Still Crazy for You/(B-side unknown)	1989	—	—	3.00
RCA					
❏ PB-11137	I Want You Back Again/Heaven Bless This Home	1977	—	2.50	5.00
SAR					
❏ 114	A Whole Lotta Woman/Why Oh Why	1961	5.00	10.00	20.00
❏ 131	Never Never/Rome (Wasn't Built in a Day)	1962	10.00	20.00	40.00
❏ 156	Oh, How I Love You/Run, But You Can't Hide	1964	3.75	7.50	15.00
STAX					
❏ 0009	Who's Making Love/I'm Trying	1968	2.00	4.00	8.00
❏ 0023	Take Care of Your Homework/Hold On This Time	1969	2.00	4.00	8.00

Number	Title (A Side/B Side)	Yr	VG	VG+	NM
❏ 0033	Testify (I Wanna)/I Had a Fight with Love	1969	2.00	4.00	8.00
❏ 0042	Just Keep On Loving Me/My Life	1969	2.00	4.00	8.00
—With Carla Thomas					
❏ 0046	I Could Never Be President/It's Amazing	1969	2.00	4.00	8.00
❏ 0055	Love Bones/Mr. Nobody Is Somebody	1969	2.00	4.00	8.00
❏ 0068	Steal Away/Friday Night	1970	—	3.00	6.00
❏ 0078	I Am Somebody (Part 1)/I Am Somebody (Part 2)	1970	—	3.00	6.00
❏ 0085	Jody's Got Your Girl and Gone/A Fool Like Me	1970	—	3.00	6.00
❏ 0089	I Don't Wanna Lose You/Party Life	1971	—	3.00	6.00
❏ 0096	Hijackin' Love/Love in the Streets	1971	—	3.00	6.00
❏ 0114	Standing In for Jody/Shackin' Up	1972	—	3.00	6.00
❏ 0122	Doing My Own Thing (Part 1)/Doing My Own Thing (Part 2)	1972	—	3.00	6.00
❏ 0142	Stop Doggin' Me/Stop Teasin' Me	1972	—	3.00	6.00
❏ 0155	Don't You Fool with My Soul (Part 1)/Don't You Fool with My Soul (Part 2)	1973	—	3.00	6.00
❏ 0161	I Believe in You (You Believe in Me)/Love Depression	1973	—	3.00	6.00
—With A-side time listed at 4:37					
❏ 0161	I Believe in You (You Believe in Me)/Love Depression	1973	—	3.00	6.00
—With A-side time listed at 3:58					
❏ 0176	Cheaper to Keep Her/I Can Read Between the Lines	1973	—	3.00	6.00
❏ 186	I Had a Dream/Changes	1966	2.50	5.00	10.00
❏ 193	I Got to Love Somebody's Baby/Just the One I've Been Looking For	1966	2.50	5.00	10.00
❏ 0193	We're Getting Careless with Our Love/Poor Make Believer	1974	—	3.00	6.00
❏ 202	Little Bluebird/Toe Hold	1967	2.50	5.00	10.00
❏ 0208	I've Been Born Again/At Night Time	1974	—	3.00	6.00
❏ 209	Ain't That Loving You/Outside Love	1967	2.50	5.00	10.00
❏ 226	If I Had It to Do Over/You Can't Get Away from It	1967	2.50	5.00	10.00
❏ 0226	It's September/Just One Moment	1974	—	3.00	6.00
❏ 235	Somebody's Sleeping in My Bed/Strange Thing	1967	2.50	5.00	10.00
❏ 0241	Try Me Tonight/Free	1975	—	3.00	6.00
❏ 247	Next Time/Sundown	1968	2.50	5.00	10.00
❏ 253	I Ain't Particular/Where There's Smoke There's Fire	1968	2.50	5.00	10.00
❏ 3201	It Don't Pay to Get Up in the Mornin'/Just Keep On Loving Me	1977	—	2.50	5.00

Albums

BEVERLY GLEN
❏ 10001	Just Ain't Good Enough	1982	3.00	6.00	12.00

COLUMBIA
❏ PC 33951	Eargasm	1976	3.00	6.00	12.00
—Originals have no bar code					
❏ PC 33951	Eargasm	1986	2.00	4.00	8.00
—Budget-line reissue with bar code					
❏ PCQ 33951 [Q]	Eargasm	1976	5.00	10.00	20.00
❏ PC 34401	Rated Extraordinaire	1977	3.00	6.00	12.00
❏ PCQ 34401 [Q]	Rated Extraordinaire	1977	5.00	10.00	20.00
❏ JC 35340	Ever Ready	1978	3.00	6.00	12.00
❏ JC 36061	She's Killing Me	1979	3.00	6.00	12.00
❏ JC 36548	A New Day	1980	3.00	6.00	12.00
❏ JC 37127	The Best of Johnnie Taylor	1981	3.00	6.00	12.00

ICHIBAN
❏ ICH-1022	Stuck in the Mud	198?	2.50	5.00	10.00
❏ ICH-1042	Ugly Man	198?	2.50	5.00	10.00

MALACO
❏ MAL-7421	This Is Your Night	198?	2.50	5.00	10.00
❏ MAL-7431	Wall to Wall	198?	2.50	5.00	10.00
❏ MAL-7440	Lover Boy	198?	2.50	5.00	10.00
❏ MAL-7446	In Control	198?	2.50	5.00	10.00
❏ MAL-7452	Crazy 'Bout You	1989	2.50	5.00	10.00
❏ MAL-7460	Just Can't Do Right	1991	2.50	5.00	10.00
❏ MAL-7463	The Best of Johnnie Taylor on Malaco, Vol. 1	1992	2.50	5.00	10.00

STAX
❏ ST-715 [M]	Wanted: One Soul Singer	1967	12.50	25.00	50.00
❏ STS-715 [S]	Wanted: One Soul Singer	1967	15.00	30.00	60.00
❏ STS-2005	Who's Making Love	1968	10.00	20.00	40.00
❏ STS-2008	Raw Blues	1969	6.25	12.50	25.00
❏ STS-2012	Rare Stamps	1969	6.25	12.50	25.00
❏ STS-2023	The Johnnie Taylor Philosophy Continues	1969	6.25	12.50	25.00
❏ STS-2030	One Step Beyond	1971	6.25	12.50	25.00
❏ STS-2032	Johnnie Taylor's Greatest Hits	1970	6.25	12.50	25.00
❏ STS-3014	Taylored in Silk	1973	5.00	10.00	20.00
❏ STX-4115	Who's Making Love	198?	2.50	5.00	10.00
—Reissue of 2005					
❏ STS-5509	Super Taylor	1974	5.00	10.00	20.00
❏ STS-5521	The Best of Johnnie Taylor	1975	5.00	10.00	20.00
❏ MPS-8508	Raw Blues	1982	2.50	5.00	10.00
❏ MPS-8520	Super Hits	1983	2.50	5.00	10.00
❏ MPS-8537	Taylored in Silk	1987	2.50	5.00	10.00
—Reissue of 3014					
❏ MPS-8558	Little Bluebird	1988	2.50	5.00	10.00
❏ 88001 [(2)]	Chronicle	1977	5.00	10.00	20.00

TAYLOR, KOKO
45s

ALLIGATOR
❏ 795	I'd Rather Go Blind/Something Strange Going On	1981	—	2.00	4.00

Albums

ALLIGATOR
❏ 4706	I Got What It Takes	1976	3.00	6.00	12.00

Number	Title (A Side/B Side)	Yr	VG	VG+	NM
CHESS					
❏ LPS-1532	Koko Taylor	1969	7.50	15.00	30.00
❏ CH-50018	Basic Soul	1972	6.25	12.50	25.00

TAYLOR, LITTLE JOHNNY
45s

GALAXY
❏ 718	You'll Need Another Favor/What You Need Is a Ball	1963	3.00	6.00	12.00
❏ 722	Part Time Love/Somewhere Down the Line	1963	5.00	10.00	20.00
❏ 725	Since I Found a New Love/My Heart Is Filled with Pain	1963	3.00	6.00	12.00
❏ 729	First Class Love/If You Love Me	1964	2.50	5.00	10.00
❏ 731	You Win, I Lose/Nightingale Melody	1964	2.50	5.00	10.00
❏ 733	True Love/I Smell Trouble	1964	2.50	5.00	10.00
❏ 735	For Your Precious Love/I've Never Had a Woman Like You Before	1965	2.00	4.00	8.00
❏ 736	Help Yourself/Somebody's Got to Pay	1965	2.00	4.00	8.00
❏ 739	One More Chance/Looking at the Future	1965	2.00	4.00	8.00
❏ 743	Please Come Home For Christmas/Miracle Maker	1965	2.00	4.00	8.00
❏ 745	My Love Is Real/All I Want Is You	1966	2.00	4.00	8.00
❏ 748	Zig Zag Lightning/The Things I Used to Do	1966	2.00	4.00	8.00
❏ 752	I Know You Hear Me Calling/Big Blue Diamonds	1967	2.00	4.00	8.00
❏ 756	Driving Wheel/Darling Believe in Me	1967	2.00	4.00	8.00
❏ 764	Double or Nothing/Sometimey Woman	1968	2.00	4.00	8.00

ICHIBAN
❏ 169	Christmas Is Here Again/Ugly Man	1988	—	3.00	6.00
❏ 174	Christmas Is Here Again/I Enjoy You	1989	—	3.00	6.00

RONN
❏ 43	Make Love to Me Baby/Sweet Soul Woman	1970	—	3.00	6.00
❏ 48	How Can a Broke Man Survive/Make Love to Me Baby	1970	—	3.00	6.00
❏ 51	How Are You Fixed for Love/Keep On Keepin' On	1971	—	3.00	6.00
❏ 55	Everybody Knows About My Good Thing Pt. 1/Pt. 2	1971	—	3.00	6.00
❏ 59	It's My Fault Darling/There Is Something On Your Mind	1972	—	3.00	6.00
❏ 64	Open House at My House (Part 1)/Open House at My House (Part 2)	1972	—	3.00	6.00
❏ 66	As Long As I Don't See You/Strange Bed with a Bad Head	1972	—	3.00	6.00
❏ 69	I'll Make It Worth Your While/You're Not the Only One	1973	—	3.00	6.00
❏ 73	My Special Rose/A Thousand Miles Away	1973	—	3.00	6.00
❏ 78	You're Savin' Your Best Lovin' for Me/What Would I Do Without You	1974	—	3.00	6.00
❏ 83	I Don't Want It All/I Can't See Myself As a One-Woman Man	1974	—	3.00	6.00
❏ 85	Found a New Love/Oh, How I Love My Baby	1975	—	3.00	6.00
❏ 87	True Love/When Are You Coming Home	1975	—	3.00	6.00
❏ 88	A Hard Head Makes a Sore Behind/The Future	1976	—	3.00	6.00
❏ 92	L.J.T./I Should Have Known	197?	—	3.00	6.00
❏ 98	Just One More Chance/New Song	197?	—	3.00	6.00

Albums

FANTASY
❏ MPF-4510	Little Johnny Taylor's Greatest Hits	1982	2.50	5.00	10.00

GALAXY
❏ 203 [M]	Little Johnny Taylor	1963	25.00	50.00	100.00
❏ 207 [M]	Little Johnny Taylor's Greatest Hits	1964	25.00	50.00	100.00
❏ 8203 [S]	Little Johnny Taylor	1963	37.50	75.00	150.00
❏ 8207 [S]	Little Johnny Taylor's Greatest Hits	1964	37.50	75.00	150.00

RONN
❏ LPS-7530	Everybody Knows About My Good Thing	1972	6.25	12.50	25.00
❏ LSP-7532	Open House at My House	1973	6.25	12.50	25.00
❏ LSP-7535	L.J.T.	1975	5.00	10.00	20.00

TAYLOR, LITTLE JOHNNY, AND TED TAYLOR
45s

RONN
❏ 75	Walking the Floor/Cry It Out Baby	1973	—	3.00	6.00
❏ 89	Pretending Love/Funky Ghetto	1976	—	3.00	6.00

Albums

RONN
❏ LSP-7533	The Super Taylors	1973	5.00	10.00	20.00

TAYLOR, R. DEAN
45s

20TH CENTURY
❏ 2510	Let's Talk It Over/Add Up the Score	1981	—	2.00	4.00

AUDIO MASTER
❏ 1	At the High School Dance/How Wrong Can You Be?	1960	50.00	100.00	200.00

FARR
❏ 001	We'll Show Them All/Magdalena	1976	—	2.50	5.00

MALA
❏ 444	I'll Remember/It's a Long Way to St. Louis	1962	25.00	50.00	100.00

RARE EARTH
❏ 5013	Indiana Wants Me/Love's Your Name	1970	—	3.00	6.00
❏ 5023	Ain't It a Sad Thing/Back Street	1970	—	2.50	5.00
❏ 5023 [PS]	Ain't It a Sad Thing/Back Street	1970	2.50	5.00	10.00
❏ 5026	Gotta See Jane/Back Street	1971	—	2.50	5.00
❏ 5030	Candy Apple Red/Woman Alive	1971	—	2.50	5.00
❏ 5041	Taos New Mexico/Shadow	1972	—	2.50	5.00

T

Number	Title (A Side/B Side)	Yr	VG	VG+	NM
STRUMMER					
❏ 3748	Let's Talk It Over/(B-side unknown)	1982	—	3.00	6.00
V.I.P.					
❏ 25027	Let's Go Somewhere/Poor Girl	1965	6.25	12.50	25.00
❏ 25042	Don't Fool Around/There's a Ghost in My House	1966	6.25	12.50	25.00
❏ 25045	Gotta See Jane/Don't Fool Around	1967	6.25	12.50	25.00
Albums					
RARE EARTH					
❏ RS-522	I Think, Therefore I Am	1971	3.75	7.50	15.00

TEARDROPS, THE (3)
45s

Number	Title (A Side/B Side)	Yr	VG	VG+	NM
JOSIE					
❏ 766	The Stars Are Out Tonight/Oh Stop It	1954	75.00	150.00	300.00
❏ 771	My Heart/Ooh Baby	1954	125.00	250.00	500.00
PORT					
❏ 70019	The Stars Are Out Tonight/Oh Stop It	1960	6.25	12.50	25.00

TEARDROPS, THE (4)
Even though on the same label as group (3), this is a different group.
45s

Number	Title (A Side/B Side)	Yr	VG	VG+	NM
JOSIE					
❏ 856	We Won't Tell/Al Chiar Di Luna (Porto Fortuna)	1959	6.25	12.50	25.00
❏ 862	Cry No More/You're My Hollywood Star	1959	6.25	12.50	25.00
❏ 873	Daddy's Little Girl/Always You	1960	6.25	12.50	25,00

TEARDROPS, THE (5)
45s

Number	Title (A Side/B Side)	Yr	VG	VG+	NM
KING					
❏ 5004	My Inspiration/I Prayed for Love	1956	6.25	12.50	25.00
❏ 5037	After School/Don't Be Afraid to Love	1957	6.25	12.50	25.00

TEASERS, THE
45s

Number	Title (A Side/B Side)	Yr	VG	VG+	NM
CHECKER					
❏ 800	I Was a Fool to Love You/How Could You Hurt One So	1954	150.00	300.00	600.00
❏ 800	I Was a Fool to Love You/How Could You Hurt One So	1954	300.00	600.00	1200.
—Red vinyl					

TECHNICS, THE
45s

Number	Title (A Side/B Side)	Yr	VG	VG+	NM
CHEX					
❏ 1010	Has He Told You/Workout With a Pretty Girl	1963	7.50	15.00	30.00
—As "Tony and the Technics"					
❏ 1012	Because I Really Love You/A Man's Confusion	1963	7.50	15.00	30.00
❏ 1013	Hey Girl Don't Leave Me/I Met Her on the First of September	1963	10.00	20.00	40.00

TECHNIQUES, THE (1)
45s

Number	Title (A Side/B Side)	Yr	VG	VG+	NM
ROULETTE					
❏ 4030	Hey! Little Girl/In a Round-About Way	1957	6.25	12.50	25.00
❏ 4048	(Why Did I Ever) Let Her Go/Marindy	1958	6.25	12.50	25.00
❏ 4097	The Wisest Man You Know/Moon Tan	1958	6.25	12.50	25.00
STARS					
❏ 551	Hey Little Girl/In a Round-About Way	1957	10.00	20.00	40.00

TEDDY AND HIS PATCHES
45s

Number	Title (A Side/B Side)	Yr	VG	VG+	NM
CHANCE					
❏ 100	Suzy Creamcheese/From Day to Day	1967	25.00	50.00	100.00
❏ 668	Suzy Creamcheese/It Ain't Nothin'	1967	25.00	50.00	100.00
❏ 669	Haight Ashbury/It Ain't Nothin'	1967	25.00	50.00	100.00

TEDDY AND THE CONTINENTALS
45s

Number	Title (A Side/B Side)	Yr	VG	VG+	NM
PIK					
❏ 235	Tick Tick Tock/Everybody Pony	1961	6.25	12.50	25.00
RAGO					
❏ 201	Tick Tick Tock/Wild Christening Party	1962	6.25	12.50	25.00
—B-side by the Teen Kings					
RICHIE					
❏ 445	Do You/Tighten Up	1961	25.00	50.00	100.00
—With no mention of Roulette distribution on label					
❏ 445	Do You/Tighten Up	1961	10.00	20.00	40.00
—With Roulette Records distribution mentioned on label					
❏ 453	Crying Over You/Crossfire With Me Baby	1963	12.50	25.00	50.00
❏ 1001	Tick Tick Tock/Everybody Pony	1961	15.00	30.00	60.00

TEDDY AND THE TWILIGHTS
45s

Number	Title (A Side/B Side)	Yr	VG	VG+	NM
SWAN					
❏ 4102	Woman Is a Man's Best Friend/Goodbye to Love	1962	6.25	12.50	25.00
❏ 4115	You Gotta Be Alone to Cry/Running Around	1962	5.00	10.00	20.00
❏ 4126	I'm Just Your Clown/Bimini Bimbo	1962	5.00	10.00	20.00

TEDDY BEARS, THE
With PHIL SPECTOR and Annette Kleinbard (a.k.a. Carol Connors).
45s

Number	Title (A Side/B Side)	Yr	VG	VG+	NM
DORE					
❏ 503	To Know Him, Is to Love Him/Don't You Worry My Little Pet	1958	7.50	15.00	30.00
❏ 520	Wonderful Loveable You/Till You'll Be Mine	1959	5.00	10.00	20.00
IMPERIAL					
❏ 5562	Oh Why/I Don't Need You Anymore	1959	7.50	15.00	30.00
❏ 5581	You Said Goodbye/If You Only Knew	1959	7.50	15.00	30.00
❏ 5594	Seven Lonely Days/Don't Go Away	1959	7.50	15.00	30.00
Albums					
IMPERIAL					
❏ LP-9067 [M]	The Teddy Bears Sing!	1959	75.00	150.00	300.00
❏ LP-12010 [S]	The Teddy Bears Sing!	1959	300.00	600.00	1200.

TEEN-KINGS, THE
45s

Number	Title (A Side/B Side)	Yr	VG	VG+	NM
BEE					
❏ 1114/5	That's a Teen-Age Love/Tell Me If You Know	1959	500.00	1000.	1500.
—Legitimate original copies are on black vinyl					
WILLETT					
❏ 118	Don't Just Stand There/My Greatest Wish	1959	62.50	125.00	250.00

TEEN QUEENS, THE
45s

Number	Title (A Side/B Side)	Yr	VG	VG+	NM
ANTLER					
❏ 4014	There's Nothing on My Mind (Part 1)/There's Nothing on My Mind (Part 2)	1959	3.75	7.50	15.00
❏ 4015	Politician/I'm a Fool	1959	3.75	7.50	15.00
❏ 4016	Donny (Part 1)/Donny (Part 2)	1960	3.75	7.50	15.00
❏ 4017	I Hear Violins/Magoo Can See	1960	3.75	7.50	15.00
KENT					
❏ 359	Eddie My Love/Just Goofed	1961	3.00	6.00	12.00
RCA VICTOR					
❏ 47-7206	Dear Tommy/You Good Boy-You Get Cookie	1958	4.00	8.00	16.00
❏ 47-7396	Movie Star/First Crush	1958	4.00	8.00	16.00
RPM					
❏ 453	Eddie My Love/Just Goofed	1956	7.50	15.00	30.00
—Black label					
❏ 453	Eddie My Love/Just Goofed	1956	30.00	60.00	120.00
—Red label					
❏ 460	So All Alone/Baby Mine	1956	6.25	12.50	25.00
❏ 464	Billy Boy/Until the Day I Die	1956	6.25	12.50	25.00
❏ 470	Red Top/Love Sweet Love	1956	6.25	12.50	25.00
❏ 480	My First Love/(B-side unknown)	1956	6.25	12.50	25.00
❏ 484	Rock Everybody/My Heart's Desire	1957	5.00	10.00	20.00
❏ 500	I Miss You/Two Loves and Two Lives	1957	5.00	10.00	20.00
Albums					
CROWN					
❏ CST-373 [R]	The Teen Queens	1963	7.50	15.00	30.00
❏ CLP-5022 [M]	Eddie My Love	1956	62.50	125.00	250.00
—Black label, all silver print					
❏ CLP-5022 [M]	Eddie My Love	196?	25.00	50.00	100.00
—Black label, "CROWN" in alternating colored letters					
❏ CLP-5373 [M]	The Teen Queens	1963	12.50	25.00	50.00
RPM					
❏ LRP-3007 [M]	Eddie My Love	1956	—	—	—
—Canceled					

TEEN TONES, THE
More than one group. Some may be listed as "Teen-Tones."
45s

Number	Title (A Side/B Side)	Yr	VG	VG+	NM
DANDY DAN					
❏ 2	Darling I Love You/My Sweet	1958	20.00	40.00	80.00
DECCA					
❏ 30895	Don't Call Me Baby, I'll Call You/Yes You May	1959	7.50	15.00	30.00
GONE					
❏ 5061	The Rockin' Rumble/Latino Part 2	1959	7.50	15.00	30.00
SWAN					
❏ 4040	My Little Baby/Head Strong Baby	1959	7.50	15.00	30.00
TRI-DISC					
❏ 102	I'm So Happy/Shoutin' Twist	1961	3.75	7.50	15.00
WYNNE					
❏ 107	Faded Love/Gypsy Boogie	1958	6.25	12.50	25.00

TEENA MARIE
12-Inch Singles

Number	Title (A Side/B Side)	Yr	VG	VG+	NM
EPIC					
❏ EAS 1533 [DJ]	Bad Boy (same on both sides)	1989	3.00	6.00	12.00
❏ EAS 1589 [DJ]	Bad Boy (Jack Swing Club Thing 8:00) (7" Radio Edit 4:10) (House Arrest Mix 7:55) +2	1989	2.50	5.00	10.00
❏ EAS 2094 [DJ]	Out on a Limb (same on both sides?)	1985	2.00	4.00	8.00
❏ EAS 2206 [DJ]	Here's Looking at You (New 12" Mix)/(7" Edit) (New Instrumental)	1990	3.00	6.00	12.00
❏ 49-04125	Fix It (Vocal 6:30) (Instrumental 8:16)	1983	2.00	4.00	8.00
❏ 49-04275	Midnight Magnet (2 versions)	1983	3.00	6.00	12.00
❏ 49-05100	Lovergirl (Dance Mix) (Instrumental)	1984	—	3.50	7.00
❏ 49-05148	Jammin' (3 versions)	1985	2.00	4.00	8.00
❏ 49-05227	Out on a Limb/Starchild	1985	2.00	4.00	8.00
❏ 49-05269	14K (Extended Version) (Dance Mix Instrumental)	1985	—	3.50	7.00
❏ 49-05376	Lips to Find You/(Instrumental)	1986	—	3.50	7.00

Number	Title (A Side/B Side)	Yr	VG	VG+	NM
❑ 49H-06907	Lovergirl (Special Dance Mix)Feels Like I'm in Love (6:23)	1986	2.00	4.00	8.00
—"Mixed Masters" reissue					
❑ 49-07574	Ooo La La La (unknown versions)	1988	2.00	4.00	8.00
❑ 49-07814	Work It (Special 12" Mix) (LP Version) (Instrumental) (Acappella)	1988	2.50	5.00	10.00
❑ 49-07897	Surrealistic Pillow (Extended Remix Featuring Cheba) (Sexy Pillow Remix) (Instrumental) (Bonus Beats)	1988	2.00	4.00	8.00
❑ 49-73495	Here's Looking at You (12" Club) (12" Underground) (Dub)/(LP Version) (Club Radio) (Instrumental Dub)	1990	2.50	5.00	10.00
MOTOWN					
❑ M 00024	I'm a Sucker for Your Love (5:59) (Instrumental)	1979	2.50	5.00	10.00
45s					
COLUMBIA					
❑ 34-06535	Lead Me On/(Instrumental)	1986	—	—	3.00
❑ 34-06535 [PS]	Lead Me On/(Instrumental)	1986	—	2.00	4.00
EPIC					
❑ 34-04124	Fix It (Part 1)/(Part 2)	1983	—	—	3.00
❑ 34-04124 [PS]	Fix It (Part 1)/(Part 2)	1983	—	2.00	4.00
❑ 34-04271	Midnight Magnet/(Instrumental)	1983	—	—	3.00
❑ 34-04415	Dear Lover/Playboy	1984	—	—	3.00
❑ 34-04619	Lovergirl/(Instrumental)	1984	—	—	3.00
❑ 34-04619 [PS]	Lovergirl/(Instrumental)	1984	—	3.00	6.00
❑ 34-04738	Jammin'/(Instrumental)	1985	—	—	3.00
❑ 34-04738 [PS]	Jammin'/(Instrumental)	1985	—	2.00	4.00
❑ 34-04943	Out on a Limb/Starchild	1985	—	—	3.00
❑ 34-04943 [PS]	Out on a Limb/Starchild	1985	—	—	3.00
❑ 34-05599	14K/(Instrumental)	1985	—	—	3.00
❑ 34-05599 [PS]	14K/(Instrumental)	1985	—	—	3.00
❑ 34-05872	Lips to Find You/(Instrumental)	1986	—	—	3.00
❑ 34-05872 [PS]	Lips to Find You/(Instrumental)	1986	—	—	3.00
❑ 34-06292	Love Me Down Easy/(Instrumental)	1986	—	—	3.00
❑ 34-06292 [PS]	Love Me Down Easy/(Instrumental)	1986	—	—	3.00
❑ 15-06449	Lovergirl/Out on a Limb	1986	—	—	3.00
—Reissue					
❑ 34-07708	Ooh La La La/Sing One to Your Love	1988	—	—	3.00
❑ 34-07708 [PS]	Ooh La La La/Sing One to Your Love	1988	—	—	3.00
❑ 34-07902	Work It/(Instrumental)	1988	—	—	3.00
❑ 34-07902 [PS]	Work It/(Instrumental)	1988	—	—	3.00
❑ 34-08040	Surrealistic Pillow/(Instrumental)	1988	—	—	3.00
❑ 15-08444	Lovergirl/Out on a Limb	1988	—	—	3.00
—Reissue					
❑ 34-68591	Bad Boy/Trick Bag	1989	—	—	3.00
GORDY					
❑ 7169	I'm a Sucker for Your Love/Deja Vu (I've Been There Before)	1979	—	2.00	4.00
❑ 7173	Don't Look Back/I'm Gonna Have My Cake (And Eat It Too)	1979	—	2.00	4.00
❑ 7180	Can It Be Love/Too Many Colors	1980	—	2.00	4.00
❑ 7184	Behind the Groove/You're All the Boogie I Need	1980	—	2.00	4.00
❑ 7189	I Need Your Lovin'/Irons in the Fire	1980	—	2.00	4.00
❑ 7194	First Class Love/Young Love	1981	—	2.00	4.00
❑ 7202	Square Biz/Opus III (Does Anybody Care)	1981	—	2.00	4.00
❑ 7212	It Must Be Magic/Yes I Need	1981	—	2.00	4.00
❑ 7216	Portuguese Love/The Ballad of Cradle Rob and Me	1981	—	2.00	4.00
Albums					
EPIC					
❑ FE 38882	Robbery	1983	2.50	5.00	10.00
❑ FE 39528	Starchild	1984	2.50	5.00	10.00
❑ FE 40318	Emerald City	1986	2.50	5.00	10.00
❑ FE 40318 [DJ]	Emerald City	1986	5.00	10.00	20.00
—Promo only on green vinyl					
❑ FE 40872	Naked to the World	1988	2.50	5.00	10.00
GORDY					
❑ G7-986R1	Wild and Peaceful	1979	3.00	6.00	12.00
❑ G7- 992R1	Lady T.	1980	3.00	6.00	12.00
❑ G8-997M1	Irons in the Fire	1980	3.00	6.00	12.00
❑ G8-1004M1	It Must Be Magic	1981	3.00	6.00	12.00
MOTOWN					
❑ 5370ML	Greatest Hits	1985	2.50	5.00	10.00

TEENAGERS, THE

These are records by the original group without FRANKIE LYMON. Also see FRANKIE LYMON AND THE TEENAGERS.

45s

Number	Title (A Side/B Side)	Yr	VG	VG+	NM
END					
❑ 1071	Crying/Tonight's the Night	1960	15.00	30.00	60.00
❑ 1076	Can You Tell Me/A Little Wiser Now	1960	10.00	20.00	40.00
GEE					
❑ 1046	Flip Flop/Everything to Me	1957	7.50	15.00	30.00
ROULETTE					
❑ 4086	My Broken Heart/Momma Wanna Rock	1958	20.00	40.00	80.00

TEENETTES, THE

45s

Number	Title (A Side/B Side)	Yr	VG	VG+	NM
BRUNSWICK					
❑ 55125	I Want a Boy with a Hi-Fi Supersonic Stereophonic Bloop Bleep/From the Word Go	1959	6.25	12.50	25.00
JOSIE					
❑ 830	My Lucky Star/Too Young to Fall in Love	1958	15.00	30.00	60.00

TEMPO-TONES, THE

45s

Number	Title (A Side/B Side)	Yr	VG	VG+	NM
ACME					
❑ 713	Get Yourself Another Fool/Ride Along	1957	37.50	75.00	150.00
❑ 715	In My Dreams/My Boy Sleep Pete	1957	125.00	250.00	500.00
❑ 718	Come Into My Heart/Somewhere There Is Sunshine	1957	125.00	250.00	500.00
❑ 722	The Day I Met You/Wishing All the Time	1957	100.00	200.00	400.00

TEMPOS, THE

Probably more than one group.

45s

Number	Title (A Side/B Side)	Yr	VG	VG+	NM
ASCOT					
❑ 2167	When You Loved Me/My Barbara Ann	1965	6.25	12.50	25.00
❑ 2173	I Wish It Were Summer/My Barbara Ann	1965	6.25	12.50	25.00
CANTERBURY					
❑ 504	Here I Come (Countdown) Part 1/Here I Come (Countdown) Part 2	1967	3.75	7.50	15.00
CLIMAX					
❑ 102	See You in September/Bless You My Love	1959	5.00	10.00	20.00
❑ 105	The Crossroads of Love/Whatever Happens	1959	5.00	10.00	20.00
FAIRMOUNT					
❑ 611	Oh Play That Thing/Monkey Doo	1963	3.00	6.00	12.00
HI-Q					
❑ 100	It's Tough/Sham-Rock	1959	10.00	20.00	40.00
KAPP					
❑ 178	Kingdom of Love/That's What You Do to Me	1957	6.25	12.50	25.00
❑ 199	Prettiest Girl in School/Never You Mind	1957	6.25	12.50	25.00
❑ 213	I Got a Job/Strollin' with My Baby	1958	6.25	12.50	25.00
MONTEL					
❑ 955	I Gotta Make a Move/It Was You	1966	3.75	7.50	15.00
PARIS					
❑ 550	Look Homeward, Angel/Under Ten Flags	1960	5.00	10.00	20.00
RHYTHM					
❑ 121	Promise Me/Never Let Me Go	1958	125.00	250.00	500.00
RILEY'S					
❑ 8781	Don't Leave Me/I Need You	1966	7.50	15.00	30.00
U.S.A.					
❑ 810	Why Don't You Write Me/A Thief in the Night	1965	6.25	12.50	25.00
Albums					
JUSTICE					
❑ JLP-104	Speaking of the Tempos	1966	125.00	250.00	500.00

TEMPREES

45s

Number	Title (A Side/B Side)	Yr	VG	VG+	NM
EPIC					
❑ 50192	I Found Love on a Disco Floor/There Ain't a Dream Been Dreamed	1976	—	2.50	5.00
WE PRODUCE					
❑ 1801	I'm for You, You for Me/Rules and Regulations	1971	2.00	4.00	8.00
❑ 1803	(Girl) I Love You/I Love You, You Love Me	1971	2.00	4.00	8.00
❑ 1805	My Baby Love/If I Could Say What's On My Mind	1972	2.00	4.00	8.00
❑ 1807	Explain It to Her Mama/Love Can Be So Wonderful	1972	2.00	4.00	8.00
❑ 1808	Dedicated to the One I Love/I Love You, You Love Me	1972	2.00	4.00	8.00
❑ 1810	A Thousand Miles Away/Chalk It Up to Experience	1973	2.00	4.00	8.00
❑ 1811	Love's Maze/Wrap Me in Love	1973	2.00	4.00	8.00
❑ 1812	At Last/Love Can Be So Wonderful	1974	—	3.50	7.00
❑ 1813	You Make Me Love You/You Make the Sunshine	1974	—	3.50	7.00
❑ 1814	Mr. Cool That Ain't Cool/Lovin' You Is So Easy	1974	—	3.50	7.00
❑ 1815	I Love, I Love/Your Love	1975	—	3.50	7.00
❑ 1816	Come and Get Your Love/I'll Live Her Life	1975	—	3.50	7.00
Albums					
WE PRODUCE					
❑ 1901	Love Men	1972	15.00	30.00	60.00
❑ 1903	Love Maze	1973	15.00	30.00	60.00
❑ 1905	Temprees 3	1974	15.00	30.00	60.00

TEMPTATIONS, THE

The famous Detroit/Motown male vocal group. Also see EDDIE KENDRICKS; DAVID RUFFIN; THE SUPREMES AND THE TEMPTATIONS.

12-Inch Singles

Number	Title (A Side/B Side)	Yr	VG	VG+	NM
GORDY					
❑ PR-68 [DJ]	Power (6:06)/Behind the Groove (6:04)	1980	6.25	12.50	25.00
—B-side by Teena Marie					
❑ PR-131 [DJ]	Miss Busy Body (Get Your Body Busy) (5:28) (Instrumental Part 2 5:32)	1983	2.50	5.00	10.00
—No label name mentioned; listed here as the 45 was on Gordy					
❑ PR-163 [DJ]	Treat Her Like a Lady (Club Reprise 3:45)/Let It All Blow (Club Mix 6:10) (Blowy's Reprise Instrumental 4:48) (Radio Edit of Club Mix 3:40)	1984	7.50	15.00	30.00
—B-side by Dazz Band; it also may have a "Motown" promo label					
❑ 4550GG	Do You Really Love Your Baby (Club Mix 6:36) (Radio Edit of Club Mix 4:17) (Dub Mix 5:04)/I'll Keep My Light in Your Window	1985	2.00	4.00	8.00
MOTOWN					
❑ PR-180 [DJ]	A Fine Mess (same on both sides)	1986	2.00	4.00	8.00
❑ 37463 1025 1 [DJ]	Hoops on Fire (3 versions)	1992	2.00	4.00	8.00
❑ 1132 [DJ]	Get Ready 1990 (4 versions)	1990	2.50	5.00	10.00
❑ 1604 [DJ]	The Jones' (4 versions)	1991	2.50	5.00	10.00

Number	Title (A Side/B Side)	Yr	VG	VG+	NM
❏ 4590MG	Papa Was a Rollin' Stone (Vocal 8:57) (Instrumental 7:15)	1987	—	—	—
—Canceled					
❏ 4598MG	Look What You Started (12-Inch Vocal 7:00) (Radio Edit 4:40)//(12-Inch Piano Dub 7:03) (12-Inch Beat Acapella 4:35)/More Love, Your Love	1987	2.50	5.00	10.00
❏ MOT-4649	All I Want from You/(Instrumental)	1989	2.00	4.00	8.00
❏ MOT-4679	Special/O.A.O. Lover	1989	2.00	4.00	8.00
❏ MOT-4698	Soul to Soul (unknown versions)	1990	2.00	4.00	8.00
❏ L33-17880 [DJ]	All I Want from You (Club Mix)/(Debbie Favorite Mix)	1989	2.00	4.00	8.00
❏ L33-18149 [DJ]	Soul to Soul (3 versions)	1990	2.50	5.00	10.00
❏ L33-18206 [DJ]	One Step at a Time (3 versions)	1990	2.50	5.00	10.00
❏ 20073 [DJ]	I'm Here (Radio Edit) (Instrumental) (LP Version) (Acappella)	2000	3.75	7.50	15.00
❏ 53954	Get Ready 1990 (4 versions)	1990	2.50	5.00	10.00

45s

ATLANTIC

Number	Title (A Side/B Side)	Yr	VG	VG+	NM
❏ 3436	In a Lifetime/I Could Never Stop Loving You	1977	—	2.00	4.00
❏ 3461	Think for Yourself/Let's Live in Peace	1978	—	2.00	4.00
❏ 3517	Bare Back/I See My Child	1978	—	2.00	4.00
❏ 3538	Ever Ready Love/Touch Me Again	1978	—	2.00	4.00
❏ 3567	Mystic Woman/I Just Don't Know How to Let You Go	1979	—	2.00	4.00

GORDY

Number	Title (A Side/B Side)	Yr	VG	VG+	NM
❏ 1616	Standing on the Top-Part 1/Part 2	1982	—	2.00	4.00
—With Rick James					
❏ 1631	More on the Inside/Money's Hard to Get	1982	—	2.00	4.00
❏ 1654	Silent Night/Everything for Christmas	1982	—	3.00	6.00
❏ 1666	Love on My Mind Tonight/Bring Your Body Here	1983	—	2.00	4.00
❏ 1683	Made in America/Surface Thrills	1983	—	2.00	4.00
❏ 1707	Miss Busy Body (Get Your Body Busy)/(Instrumental)	1983	—	2.00	4.00
❏ 1713	Silent Night/Everything for Christmas	1983	—	2.50	5.00
❏ 1720	Sail Away/Isn't the Night Fantastic	1984	—	2.00	4.00
❏ 1765	Treat Her Like a Lady/Isn't the Night Fantastic	1984	—	2.00	4.00
❏ 1781	My Love Is True (Truly for You)/Set Your Love Right	1985	—	2.00	4.00
❏ 1789	How Can You Say That It's Over/I'll Keep My Light in My Window	1985	—	2.00	4.00
❏ 1818	Do You Really Love Your Baby/I'll Keep My Light in My Window	1985	—	2.00	4.00
❏ 1834	Touch Me/Set Your Love Right	1986	—	2.00	4.00
❏ 1856	Lady Soul/Put Us Together Again	1986	—	2.00	4.00
❏ 1871	To Be Continued/You're the One	1986	—	2.00	4.00
❏ 1871 [PS]	To Be Continued/You're the One	1986	—	3.00	6.00
❏ 1881	Someone/Love Me Right	1987	—	2.00	4.00
❏ 7001	Dream Come True/Isn't She Pretty	1962	10.00	20.00	40.00
❏ 7010	Paradise/Slow Down Heart	1962	7.50	15.00	30.00
❏ 7015	I Want a Love I Can See/The Further You Look, The Less You See	1963	6.25	12.50	25.00
❏ 7020	May I Have This Dance?/Farewell, My Love	1963	6.25	12.50	25.00
❏ 7028	The Way You Do the Things You Do/Just Let Me Know	1964	3.75	7.50	15.00
❏ 7032	I'll Be in Trouble/The Girl's Alright with Me	1964	3.75	7.50	15.00
❏ 7035	Girl (Why You Wanna Make Me Blue)/Baby, Baby I Need You	1964	3.75	7.50	15.00
❏ 7038	My Girl/Nobody But My Baby	1965	3.75	7.50	15.00
❏ 7038 [PS]	My Girl/Nobody But My Baby	1965	30.00	60.00	120.00
❏ 7040	It's Growing/What Love Has Joined Together	1965	3.75	7.50	15.00
❏ 7043	Since I Lost My Baby/You've Got to Earn It	1965	3.75	7.50	15.00
❏ 7047	My Baby/Don't Look Back	1965	3.75	7.50	15.00
❏ 7049	Get Ready/Fading Away	1966	3.75	7.50	15.00
❏ 7054	Ain't Too Proud to Beg/You'll Lose a Precious Love	1966	3.75	7.50	15.00
❏ 7055	Beauty Is Only Skin Deep/You're Not an Ordinary Girl	1966	3.75	7.50	15.00
❏ 7055 [PS]	Beauty Is Only Skin Deep/You're Not an Ordinary Girl	1966	10.00	20.00	40.00
❏ 7057	(I Know) I'm Losing You/I Couldn't Cry If I Wanted To	1966	3.75	7.50	15.00
❏ 7061	All I Need/Sorry Is a Sorry Word	1967	2.50	5.00	10.00
❏ 7063	You're My Everything/I've Been Good to You	1967	2.50	5.00	10.00
—"Gordy" on left					
❏ 7063	You're My Everything/I've Been Good to You	1967	3.75	7.50	15.00
—"Gordy" on top					
❏ 7065	(Loneliness Made Me Realize) It's You That I Need/Don't Send Me Away	1967	2.50	5.00	10.00
❏ 7068	I Wish It Would Rain/I Truly, Truly Believe	1967	2.50	5.00	10.00
❏ 7072	I Could Never Love Another (After Loving You)/Gonna Give Her All the Love I've Got	1968	2.50	5.00	10.00
❏ 7074	Please Return Your Love to Me/How Can I Forget	1968	2.50	5.00	10.00
❏ 7081	Cloud Nine/Why Did She Have to Leave Me	1968	2.00	4.00	8.00
❏ 7082	Silent Night/Rudolph, the Red-Nosed Reindeer	1968	3.00	6.00	12.00
❏ 7084	Run Away Child, Running Wild/I Need Your Love	1969	2.00	4.00	8.00
❏ 7086	Don't Let the Joneses Get You Down/Since I've Lost You	1969	2.00	4.00	8.00
❏ 7093	I Can't Get Next to You/Running Away (Ain't Gonna Help You)	1969	2.00	4.00	8.00
❏ 7096	Psychedelic Shack/That's the Way Love Is	1970	—	3.00	6.00
❏ 7099	Ball of Confusion (That's What the World Is Today)/It's Summer	1970	—	3.00	6.00
❏ 7099 [PS]	Ball of Confusion (That's What the World Is Today)/It's Summer	1970	5.00	10.00	20.00
❏ 7102	Ungena Za Ulimwengu (Unite the World)/Hum Along and Dance	1970	—	3.00	6.00

Number	Title (A Side/B Side)	Yr	VG	VG+	NM
❏ 7105	Just My Imagination (Running Away with Me)/You Make Your Own Heaven and Hell Right Here on Earth	1971	—	3.00	6.00
❏ 7109	It's Summer/I'm the Exception to the Rule	1971	—	3.00	6.00
❏ 7111	Superstar (Remember How You Got Where You Are)/Gonna Keep On Tryin' Till I Win Your Love	1971	—	3.00	6.00
❏ 7115	Take a Look Around/Smooth Sailing (From Now On)	1972	—	3.00	6.00
❏ 7119	Mother Nature/Funky Music Sho Nuff Turns Me On	1972	—	3.00	6.00
❏ 7121	Papa Was a Rollin' Stone/(Instrumental)	1972	—	3.00	6.00
❏ 7126	Masterpiece/(Instrumental)	1973	—	3.00	6.00
❏ 7129	Plastic Man/Hurry Tomorrow	1973	—	3.00	6.00
❏ 7131	Hey Girl (I Like Your Style)/Ma	1973	—	3.00	6.00
❏ 7133	Let Your Hair Down/Ain't No Justice	1973	—	3.00	6.00
❏ 7135	Heavenly/Zoom	1974	—	3.00	6.00
❏ 7136	You've Got My Soul on Fire/I Need You	1974	—	3.00	6.00
❏ 7138	Happy People/(Instrumental)	1974	—	3.00	6.00
❏ 7142	Shakey Ground/I'm a Bachelor	1975	—	3.00	6.00
❏ 7144	Glasshouse/The Prophet	1975	—	3.00	6.00
❏ 7146	Keep Holding On/What You Need Most (I Do Best of All)	1975	—	3.00	6.00
❏ 7150	Up the Creek (Without a Paddle)/Darling Stand By Me (Song for a Woman)	1976	—	3.00	6.00
❏ 7151	Who Are You (And What Are You Doing the Rest of Your Life)/Darling Stand By Me (Song for a Woman)	1976	—	—	—
—Unreleased					
❏ 7152	Let Me Count the Ways (I Love You)/Who Are You (And What Are You Doing the Rest of Your Life)	1976	—	3.00	6.00
❏ 7183	Power/Power (Part 2)	1980	—	2.00	4.00
❏ 7183 [DJ]	Power (same on both sides)	1980	5.00	10.00	20.00
—Promo only on red vinyl					
❏ 7188	Struck by Lightning Twice/I'm Coming Home	1980	—	2.00	4.00
❏ 7208	Aiming at Your Heart/Life of a Cowboy	1981	—	2.00	4.00
❏ 7213	Oh What a Night/Isn't the Night Fantastic	1981	—	2.00	4.00

MIRACLE

Number	Title (A Side/B Side)	Yr	VG	VG+	NM
❏ 5	Oh, Mother of Mine/Romance Without Finance	1961	25.00	50.00	100.00
❏ 12	Check Yourself/Your Wonderful Love	1961	25.00	50.00	100.00

MOTOWN

Number	Title (A Side/B Side)	Yr	VG	VG+	NM
❏ 903	One Step at a Time/(Instrumental)	1990	—	2.00	4.00
❏ 1501	Take Me Away/There's More Where That Came From	1980	—	2.00	4.00
❏ 1837	A Fine Mess/Wishful Thinking	1986	—	2.00	4.00
❏ 1837 [PS]	A Fine Mess/Wishful Thinking	1986	—	3.00	6.00
❏ 1908	I Wonder Who She's Seeing Now/Girls (They Like It)	1987	—	—	3.00
❏ 1908 [PS]	I Wonder Who She's Seeing Now/Girls (They Like It)	1987	—	2.00	4.00
❏ 1920	Look What You Started/More Love, Your Love	1987	—	—	3.00
❏ 1933	Do You Wanna Go with Me/Put Your Foot Down	1988	—	—	3.00
❏ 1974	All I Want from You/(Instrumental)	1989	—	—	3.00
❏ 2004	Special/O.A.O. Lover	1989	—	2.00	4.00
❏ 2023	Soul to Soul (same on both sides?)	1990	—	2.00	4.00
❏ 860862-7	Stay/My Girl	1998	—	—	3.00

MOTOWN YESTERYEAR

Number	Title (A Side/B Side)	Yr	VG	VG+	NM
❏ 690	Silent Night/Everything For Christmas	198?	—	2.00	4.00

TOPPS/MOTOWN

Number	Title (A Side/B Side)	Yr	VG	VG+	NM
❏ 4	My Girl	1967	18.75	37.50	75.00
—Cardboard record					
❏ 13	The Way You Do the Things You Do	1967	18.75	37.50	75.00
—Cardboard record					

Albums

ATLANTIC

Number	Title (A Side/B Side)	Yr	VG	VG+	NM
❏ SD 19143	Hear to Tempt You	1977	3.00	6.00	12.00
❏ SD 19188	Bare Back	1978	3.00	6.00	12.00

GORDY

Number	Title (A Side/B Side)	Yr	VG	VG+	NM
❏ G 911 [M]	Meet the Temptations	1964	7.50	15.00	30.00
❏ GS 911 [S]	Meet the Temptations	1964	10.00	20.00	40.00
—Script "Gordy" at top of label					
❏ GS 911 [S]	Meet the Temptations	1967	5.00	10.00	20.00
—Block "GORDY" inside "G" on left of label					
❏ G 912 [M]	The Temptations Sing Smokey	1965	7.50	15.00	30.00
❏ GS 912 [S]	The Temptations Sing Smokey	1965	10.00	20.00	40.00
—Script "Gordy" at top of label					
❏ GS 912 [S]	The Temptations Sing Smokey	1967	5.00	10.00	20.00
—Block "GORDY" inside "G" on left of label					
❏ G 914 [M]	Temptin' Temptations	1965	6.25	12.50	25.00
❏ GS 914 [S]	Temptin' Temptations	1965	7.50	15.00	30.00
—Script "Gordy" at top of label					
❏ GS 914 [S]	Temptin' Temptations	1967	5.00	10.00	20.00
—Block "GORDY" inside "G" on left of label					
❏ G 918 [M]	Gettin' Ready	1966	6.25	12.50	25.00
❏ GS 918 [S]	Gettin' Ready	1966	7.50	15.00	30.00
—Script "Gordy" at top of label					
❏ GS 918 [S]	Gettin' Ready	1967	5.00	10.00	20.00
—Block "GORDY" inside "G" on left of label					
❏ G 919 [M]	The Temptations' Greatest Hits	1966	6.25	12.50	25.00
❏ GS 919 [S]	The Temptations' Greatest Hits	1966	7.50	15.00	30.00
—Script "Gordy" at top of label					
❏ GS 919 [S]	The Temptations' Greatest Hits	1967	5.00	10.00	20.00
—Block "GORDY" inside "G" on left of label					
❏ G 921 [M]	Temptations Live!	1967	6.25	12.50	25.00
❏ GS 921 [S]	Temptations Live!	1967	7.50	15.00	30.00
—Script "Gordy" at top of label					

Number	Title (A Side/B Side)	Yr	VG	VG+	NM
❑ GS 921 [S]	Temptations Live!	1967	5.00	10.00	20.00
—Block "GORDY" inside "G" on left of label					
❑ G 922 [M]	With a Lot o' Soul	1967	6.25	12.50	25.00
❑ GS 922 [S]	With a Lot o' Soul	1967	6.25	12.50	25.00
—Script "Gordy" at top of label					
❑ GS 922 [S]	With a Lot o' Soul	1967	5.00	10.00	20.00
—Block "GORDY" inside "G" on left of label					
❑ G 924 [M]	The Temptations in a Mellow Mood	1967	6.25	12.50	25.00
❑ GS 924 [S]	The Temptations in a Mellow Mood	1967	6.25	12.50	25.00
❑ G 927 [M]	The Temptations Wish It Would Rain	1968	10.00	20.00	40.00
—Mono is white-label promo only					
❑ GS 927 [S]	The Temptations Wish It Would Rain	1968	5.00	10.00	20.00
❑ GS 933	The Temptations Show	1969	5.00	10.00	20.00
❑ GS 938	Live at the Copa	1968	5.00	10.00	20.00
❑ GS 939	Cloud Nine	1969	5.00	10.00	20.00
❑ GS 947	Psychedelic Shack	1970	5.00	10.00	20.00
❑ GS 949	Puzzle People	1969	5.00	10.00	20.00
❑ GS 951	The Temptations' Christmas Card	1969	6.25	12.50	25.00
❑ GS 953	Live at London's Talk of the Town	1970	5.00	10.00	20.00
❑ GS 954	Temptations Greatest Hits II	1970	5.00	10.00	20.00
❑ GS 957	Sky's the Limit	1971	5.00	10.00	20.00
❑ G 961L	Solid Rock	1972	5.00	10.00	20.00
❑ G 962L	All Directions	1972	5.00	10.00	20.00
❑ G 965L	Masterpiece	1973	5.00	10.00	20.00
❑ G 966V1	1990	1973	3.75	7.50	15.00
❑ G6-969S1	A Song for You	1975	3.75	7.50	15.00
❑ G6-971S1	Wings of Love	1976	3.75	7.50	15.00
❑ G6-973S1	House Party	1975	3.75	7.50	15.00
❑ G7-975S1	The Temptations Do the Temptations	1976	3.75	7.50	15.00
❑ G8-994M1	Power	1980	3.00	6.00	12.00
❑ G8-998M1	Give Love at Christmas	1980	3.75	7.50	15.00
❑ G8-1006M1	The Temptations	1981	3.00	6.00	12.00
❑ 6008 GL	Reunion	1982	3.00	6.00	12.00
❑ 6032 GL	Surface Thrills	1983	3.00	6.00	12.00
❑ 6085 GL	Back to Basics	1984	3.00	6.00	12.00
❑ 6119 GL	Truly for You	1984	3.00	6.00	12.00
❑ 6164 GL	Touch Me	1986	3.00	6.00	12.00
❑ 6207 GL	To Be Continued	1986	3.00	6.00	12.00
MOTOWN					
❑ M5-140V1	Meet the Temptations	1981	3.00	6.00	12.00
—Reissue of Gordy 911					
❑ M5-144V1	Masterpiece	1981	3.00	6.00	12.00
—Reissue of Gordy 965					
❑ M5-159V1	Cloud Nine	1981	3.00	6.00	12.00
—Reissue of Gordy 939					
❑ M5-164V1	Psychedelic Shack	1981	3.00	6.00	12.00
—Reissue of Gordy 947					
❑ M5-172V1	Puzzle People	1981	3.00	6.00	12.00
—Reissue of Gordy 949					
❑ M5-205V1	The Temptations Sing Smokey	1981	3.00	6.00	12.00
—Reissue of Gordy 912					
❑ M5-212V1	All the Million Sellers	1982	3.00	6.00	12.00
❑ M 782 [(3)]	Anthology	1973	6.25	12.50	25.00
❑ 5251 ML	The Temptations Christmas Card	1982	2.50	5.00	10.00
—Reissue of Gordy 951					
❑ 5279 ML	Give Love at Christmas	1983	2.50	5.00	10.00
—Reissue of Gordy 998					
❑ 5389 ML [(2)]	25th Anniversary	1986	3.75	7.50	15.00
❑ 6246 ML	Together Again	1987	3.00	6.00	12.00
❑ MOT-6275	Special	1989	3.00	6.00	12.00
NATURAL RESOURCES					
❑ NR 4005T1	The Temptations in a Mellow Mood	1978	3.00	6.00	12.00
—Reissue of Gordy 924					
PICKWICK					
❑ SPC-3540	Psychedelic Shack	197?	3.00	6.00	12.00
—Reissue of Gordy 947					

TEMPTATIONS, THE (2)

White doo-wop group.

45s

GOLDISC

❑ 3001	Barbara/Someday	1960	7.50	15.00	30.00
—All-black label					
❑ 3001	Barbara/Someday	1960	5.00	10.00	20.00
—Multicolor (black, red, gold) label					
❑ 3007	Letter of Devotion/Fickle Little Girl	1960	6.25	12.50	25.00

TEMPTATIONS, THE (3)

45s

KING

❑ 5118	Standing Alone/Roaches Rock	1958	75.00	150.00	300.00

TEMPTATIONS, THE (4)

45s

PARKWAY

❑ 803	Temptations/Birds N' Bees	1959	7.50	15.00	30.00

TEMPTATIONS, THE (5)

45s

P&L

❑ 1001	Blue Surf/Egyptian Surf	1963	15.00	30.00	60.00

TEMPTATIONS, THE (6)

45s

SAVOY

❑ 1532	Mister Juke Box/Mad at Love	1958	5.00	10.00	20.00
❑ 1550	I Love You/Don't You Know	1958	5.00	10.00	20.00

TEMPTONES, THE

DARYL HALL was in this group.

45s

ARCTIC

❑ 130	Girl, I Love You/Good-Bye	1967	10.00	20.00	40.00
❑ 136	Say These Words of Love/This Could Be the Start of Something Good	1967	10.00	20.00	40.00

TENDERFOOTS, THE

45s

FEDERAL

❑ 12214	Kissing Bug/Watussi Wussi Wo	1955	15.00	30.00	60.00
❑ 12219	My Confession/Save Me Some Kisses	1955	15.00	30.00	60.00
❑ 12225	Those Golden Bells/I'm Yours Anyhow	1955	20.00	40.00	80.00
❑ 12228	Sindy/Sugar Ways	1955	30.00	60.00	120.00

TERRELL, ERNIE

45s

ARGO

❑ 5511	Dear Abbie/I Can't Wait	1965	3.00	6.00	12.00

TERRELL, TAMMI

Also see MARVIN GAYE AND TAMMI TERRELL; TAMMY MONTGOMERY.

45s

MOTOWN

❑ 1086	I Can't Believe You Love Me/Hold Me Oh My Darling	1965	2.50	5.00	10.00
❑ 1095	Come On and See Me/Baby Don'tcha Worry	1966	2.50	5.00	10.00
❑ 1115	What a Good Man He Is/There Are Things	1967	2.50	5.00	10.00
❑ 1138	This Old Heart of Mine (Is Weak for You)/Just Too Much to Hope For	1968	2.50	5.00	10.00
Albums					
MOTOWN					
❑ M5-231V1	Irresistible Tammi	1982	2.50	5.00	10.00
❑ MS-652	Irresistible Tammi	1969	12.50	25.00	50.00

TERRI AND THE KITTENS

45s

IMPERIAL

❑ 5728	Wedding Bells/You Cheated	1961	5.00	10.00	20.00

TERRI AND THE VELVETEENS

45s

KERWOOD

❑ 711	Bells of Love/You've Broken My Heart	1962	10.00	20.00	40.00

TERRI-TONES, THE

45s

CORTLAND

❑ 105	Go/The Sinner	1962	12.50	25.00	50.00
REGENCY					
❑ 929	Go/The Sinner	1962	7.50	15.00	30.00

TERRY, DOSSIE

45s

KING

❑ 5072	Thunderbird/I Got a Watch Dog	1957	12.50	25.00	50.00
❑ 5890	Thunderbird/Be-Bop Wino	1964	3.75	7.50	15.00
—B-side by the Lamplighters					
RCA VICTOR					
❑ 47-4474	Didn't Satisfy You/24 Years	1952	15.00	30.00	60.00
❑ 47-4648	When I Hit the Number/My Love Is Gone	1952	15.00	30.00	60.00
❑ 47-4864	Lost My Head/Sad, Sad Affair	1952	15.00	30.00	60.00

TERRY, SONNY

45s

CAPITOL

❑ F931	Telephone Blues/Dirty Mistreater Don't You Know	1950	30.00	60.00	120.00
CHESS					
❑ 1860	Dangerous Woman/Hootenanny Blues	1963	5.00	10.00	20.00
CHOICE					
❑ 15	Hootin'/Dupre	1961	5.00	10.00	20.00
GOTHAM					
❑ 517	Baby Let's Have Some Fun/Four O'Clock Blues	1951	10.00	20.00	40.00
❑ 518	Harmonica Rhumba/Lonesome Room	1951	10.00	20.00	40.00
GRAMERCY					
❑ 1004	Hootin' Blues/(B-side unknown)	1952	12.50	25.00	50.00
—Black vinyl					
❑ 1004	Hootin' Blues/(B-side unknown)	1952	25.00	50.00	100.00
—Colored vinyl					
GROOVE					
❑ 0015	Lost Jawbone/Louise	1954	7.50	15.00	30.00
❑ 0135	Ride and Roll/Hootin' Blues #2	1956	7.50	15.00	30.00
HARLEM					
❑ 2327	Dangerous Woman/I Love You Baby	1954	75.00	150.00	300.00

T

Number	Title (A Side/B Side)	Yr	VG	VG+	NM
JAX					
❑ 305	I Don't Worry (Sittin' on Top of the World)/Man Ain't Nothin' But a Fool	195?	100.00	200.00	400.00
—Colored vinyl					
OLD TOWN					
❑ 1023	Uncle Bud/Climbing on Top of the Hill	1956	6.25	12.50	25.00
RCA VICTOR					
❑ 47-5492	Hootin' and Jumpin'/Hooray, Hooray	1953	25.00	50.00	100.00
❑ 47-5577	Sonny Is Drinking/I'm Gonna Rock My Wig	1954	25.00	50.00	100.00
RED ROBIN					
❑ 110	Harmonica Hop/Doggin' My Heart Around	1952	75.00	150.00	300.00
Albums					
ALLIGATOR					
❑ AL-4734	Whoopin'	198?	3.00	6.00	12.00
—With Johnny Winter, Willie Dixon and others					
BLUE LABOR					
❑ 101	Robbin' the Grave	197?	3.00	6.00	12.00
BLUESVILLE					
❑ BVLP-1025 [M]Sonny's Story		1961	20.00	40.00	80.00
—Bright blue label, no trident logo					
❑ BVLP-1025 [M]Sonny's Story		1964	6.25	12.50	25.00
—Blue label with trident logo on right					
❑ BVLP-1069 [M]Sonny Is King		1963	20.00	40.00	80.00
—Bright blue label, no trident logo					
❑ BVLP-1069 [M]Sonny Is King		1964	6.25	12.50	25.00
—Blue label with trident logo on right					
COLLECTABLES					
❑ COL-5195	Chain Gang Blues	198?	2.50	5.00	10.00
❑ COL-5307	Sonny Terry	198?	2.50	5.00	10.00
ELEKTRA					
❑ EKL-14 [10]	Folk Blues	1954	37.50	75.00	150.00
❑ EKL-15 [10]	City Blues	1954	37.50	75.00	150.00
—With Alec Stewart					
FANTASY					
❑ OBC-521	Sonny Is King	198?	2.50	5.00	10.00
FOLKWAYS					
❑ FP-35 [10]	Harmonica and Vocal Solos	1952	37.50	75.00	150.00
❑ FA-2006 [10]	Sonny Terry's Washboard Band	195?	25.00	50.00	100.00
—Black and white cover (reissue)					
❑ FP-2006 [10]	Sonny Terry's Washboard Band	1950	37.50	75.00	150.00
—Blue and white cover					
❑ FA-2035 [10]	Harmonica and Vocal Solos	1952	25.00	50.00	100.00
❑ FS-2369	On the Road	196?	3.75	7.50	15.00
❑ 3821	A New Sound	198?	3.00	6.00	12.00
PRESTIGE					
❑ PRST-7802	Sonny Is King	1970	3.75	7.50	15.00
RIVERSIDE					
❑ RLP-644 [M]	Sonny Terry and His Mouth Harp	195?	20.00	40.00	80.00
STINSON					
❑ 55	Sonny Terry and His Mouth Harp	197?	3.00	6.00	12.00
—Reissue of 10-inch LP					
❑ SLP-55 [10]	Sonny Terry and His Mouth Harp	1950	37.50	75.00	150.00

TERRY, SONNY, AND BROWNIE MCGHEE

Also see each artist's individual listings.

Number	Title (A Side/B Side)	Yr	VG	VG+	NM
45s					
BLUESVILLE					
❑ 802	Let Me Be Your Big Dig/Stranger Here	196?	5.00	10.00	20.00
❑ 809	Pawnshop/Too Nicey Mama	196?	5.00	10.00	20.00
❑ 818	Freight Train/Beggin' and Tryin'	196?	5.00	10.00	20.00
CHOICE					
❑ 1	John Henry/Oh Lawdy Pick a Bale of Cotton	196?	5.00	10.00	20.00
—As "Brownie & Sonny"					
❑ 7	Study War No More/I'm Gonna Tell God	196?	5.00	10.00	20.00
—As "Brownie & Sonny"					
Albums					
ARCHIVE OF FOLK MUSIC					
❑ 242	Brownie & Sonny	198?	3.00	6.00	12.00
A&M					
❑ SP-4379	Sonny & Brownie	1973	3.00	6.00	12.00
BLUESVILLE					
❑ BVLP-1002 [M]Down Home Blues		1960	20.00	40.00	80.00
—Bright blue label, no trident logo					
❑ BVLP-1002 [M]Down Home Blues		1964	6.25	12.50	25.00
—Blue label with trident logo on right					
❑ BVLP-1005 [M]Blues and Folk		1960	20.00	40.00	80.00
—Bright blue label, no trident logo					
❑ BVLP-1005 [M]Blues and Folk		1964	6.25	12.50	25.00
—Blue label with trident logo on right					
❑ BVLP-1020 [M]Blues All Around My Head		1961	20.00	40.00	80.00
—Bright blue label, no trident logo					
❑ BVLP-1020 [M]Blues All Around My Head		1964	6.25	12.50	25.00
—Blue label with trident logo on right					
❑ BVLP-1033 [M]Blues in My Soul		1961	20.00	40.00	80.00
—Bright blue label, no trident logo					
❑ BVLP-1033 [M]Blues in My Soul		1964	6.25	12.50	25.00
—Blue label with trident logo on right					
❑ BVLP-1058 [M]Live at the Second Fret		1962	20.00	40.00	80.00
—Bright blue label, no trident logo					
❑ BVLP-1058 [M]Live at the Second Fret		1964	6.25	12.50	25.00
—Blue label with trident logo on right					
BLUESWAY					
❑ BLS-6028	Long Way from Home	1969	3.75	7.50	15.00
❑ BLS-6059	Couldn't Believe My Eyes	1970	3.75	7.50	15.00

Number	Title (A Side/B Side)	Yr	VG	VG+	NM
COLLECTABLES					
❑ COL-5198	Golden Classics: Blowin' the Fuses	198?	2.50	5.00	10.00
EVEREST					
❑ 206	Sonny Terry	1968	6.25	12.50	25.00
❑ 242	Brownie McGhee and Sonny Terry	1969	6.25	12.50	25.00
FANTASY					
❑ OBC-503	Sonny's Story	1984	2.50	5.00	10.00
❑ OBC-505	Brownie's Blues	1984	2.50	5.00	10.00
❑ F-3254 [M]	Sonny Terry & Brownie McGhee	1961	37.50	75.00	150.00
—Red vinyl					
❑ F-3254 [M]	Sonny Terry & Brownie McGhee	1961	10.00	20.00	40.00
—Black vinyl					
❑ F-3296 [M]	Just a Closer Walk with Thee	1962	37.50	75.00	150.00
—Red vinyl					
❑ F-3296 [M]	Just a Closer Walk with Thee	1962	10.00	20.00	40.00
—Black vinyl					
❑ F-3317 [M]	Blues and Shouts	1962	37.50	75.00	150.00
—Red vinyl					
❑ F-3317 [M]	Blues and Shouts	1962	10.00	20.00	40.00
—Black vinyl					
❑ F-3340 [M]	Sonny and Brownie at Sugar Hill	1962	37.50	75.00	150.00
—Red vinyl					
❑ F-3340 [M]	Sonny and Brownie at Sugar Hill	1962	10.00	20.00	40.00
—Black vinyl					
❑ FS-8091 [S]	Sonny and Brownie at Sugar Hill	1962	37.50	75.00	150.00
—Blue vinyl					
❑ FS-8091 [S]	Sonny and Brownie at Sugar Hill	1962	10.00	20.00	40.00
—Black vinyl					
❑ 24708 [(2)]	Back to New Orleans	1972	3.75	7.50	15.00
❑ 24721 [(2)]	Midnight Special	1977	3.75	7.50	15.00
❑ 24723 [(2)]	California Blues	1981	3.75	7.50	15.00
FOLKLORE					
❑ FRLP-14013 [M]Down Home Blues		1964	10.00	20.00	40.00
❑ FRST-14013 [S]Down Home Blues		1964	12.50	25.00	50.00
FOLKWAYS					
❑ FA-2327 [M]	Blues and Folk Songs	1960	7.50	15.00	30.00
❑ F-2421 [M]	Traditional Blues, Volume 1	1961	7.50	15.00	30.00
❑ FS-2421 [S]	Traditional Blues, Volume 1	1961	10.00	20.00	40.00
❑ F-2422 [M]	Traditional Blues, Volume 2	1961	7.50	15.00	30.00
❑ FS-2422 [S]	Traditional Blues, Volume 2	1961	10.00	20.00	40.00
FONTANA					
❑ SGF-67599	Where the Blues Begin	1969	6.25	12.50	25.00
KIMBERLEY					
❑ 2017 [M]	Southern Meetin'	1963	5.00	10.00	20.00
❑ 11017 [S]	Southern Meetin'	1963	6.25	12.50	25.00
MAINSTREAM					
❑ M-6049 [M]	Hometown Blues	1966	5.00	10.00	20.00
❑ MS-6049 [S]	Hometown Blues	1966	6.25	12.50	25.00
MOBILE FIDELITY					
❑ 1-233	Sonny and Brownie	1996	5.00	10.00	20.00
—Audiophile vinyl					
MUSE					
❑ 5117	Hootin'	198?	3.00	6.00	12.00
❑ 5131	You Hear Me Talkin'	198?	3.00	6.00	12.00
OLYMPIC					
❑ 7108	Hootin' & Hollerin'	1972	3.00	6.00	12.00
PRESTIGE					
❑ PRLP-7715	Best of Sonny Terry and Brownie McGhee	1969	3.75	7.50	15.00
❑ PRLP-7803	Live at the Second Fret	1970	3.75	7.50	15.00
ROULETTE					
❑ R-25074 [M]	The Folk Songs of Sonny & Brownie	1959	12.50	25.00	50.00
❑ RS-25074 [S]	The Folk Songs of Sonny & Brownie	1959	20.00	40.00	80.00
SAVOY					
❑ SJL-1137	Climbin' Up	1984	2.50	5.00	10.00
❑ 12218	Down Home Blues	1973	3.00	6.00	12.00
SHARP					
❑ 2003 [M]	Down Home Blues	195?	37.50	75.00	150.00
SMASH					
❑ MGS-27067 [M]Brownie McGhee at the Bunkhouse		1965	7.50	15.00	30.00
❑ SRS-67067 [S]Brownie McGhee at the Bunkhouse		1965	10.00	20.00	40.00
SMITHSONIAN/FOLKWAYS					
❑ SF-40011	Sing	198?	2.50	5.00	10.00
STORYVILLE					
❑ 4007	Brownie & Sonny	1972	3.00	6.00	12.00
TOPIC					
❑ T-29 [M]	Songs	1958	12.50	25.00	50.00
VEE JAY					
❑ VJLP-1138	Coffee House Blues	198?	2.50	5.00	10.00
—With Lightnin' Hopkins					
VERVE					
❑ MGV 3008 [M]Blues Is My Companion		1961	20.00	40.00	80.00
VERVE FOLKWAYS					
❑ FV 9010 [M]	Get Together	1965	6.25	12.50	25.00
❑ FVS 9010 [S]	Get Together	1965	7.50	15.00	30.00
❑ FV 9019 [M]	Guitar Highway	1965	6.25	12.50	25.00
❑ FVS 9019 [S]	Guitar Highway	1965	7.50	15.00	30.00
WASHINGTON					
❑ W-702 [M]	Talkin' 'Bout the Blues	1961	12.50	25.00	50.00
WORLD PACIFIC					
❑ ST-1294 [S]	Blues Is a Story	1960	20.00	40.00	80.00
❑ WP-1294 [M]	Blues Is a Story	1960	12.50	25.00	50.00
❑ ST-1296 [S]	Down South Summit Meetin'	1960	20.00	40.00	80.00
❑ WP-1296 [M]	Down South Summit Meetin'	1960	12.50	25.00	50.00

Number	Title (A Side/B Side)	Yr	VG	VG+	NM

TERRY AND THE PIRATES
45s
CHESS

Number	Title (A Side/B Side)	Yr	VG	VG+	NM
❑ 1696	Talk About the Girl/What Did He Say	1958	10.00	20.00	40.00

TEX, JOE
12-Inch Singles
EPIC

❑ 50352	Ain't Gonna Bump No More (With No Big Fat Woman)/Be Cool (Willie Is Dancing with a Sissy)	1977	5.00	10.00	20.00

45s
ACE

❑ 544	Cut It Out/Just for You and Me	1958	15.00	30.00	60.00
❑ 550	Mother's Advice/You Little Baby Face Thing	1958	20.00	40.00	80.00
❑ 559	Charlie Brown Got Expelled/Blessed Are These Tears	1959	15.00	30.00	60.00
❑ 572	Don't Hold It Against Me/Yum, Yum, Yum	1959	15.00	30.00	60.00
❑ 591	Boys Will Be Boys/Grannie Stole the Show	1960	10.00	20.00	40.00
❑ 674	Boys Will Be Boys/Baby You're Right	1963	3.75	7.50	15.00

ANNA

❑ 1119	All I Could Do Was Cry (Part 1)/All I Could Do Was Cry (Part 2)	1960	10.00	20.00	40.00
❑ 1124	I'll Never Break Your Heart (Part 1)/I'll Never Break Your Heart (Part 2)	1960	10.00	20.00	40.00
❑ 1128	Baby, You're Right/Ain't It a Mess	1961	10.00	20.00	40.00

ATLANTIC

❑ 2874	I'll Never Fall in Love Again (Part 1)/I'll Never Fall in Love Again (Part 2)	1972	—	3.00	6.00

CHECKER

❑ 1104	Baby, You're Right/All I Could Do Was Cry (Part 2)	1965	3.00	6.00	12.00

DIAL

❑ 1001	Bad Feet/I Know Him	1971	—	3.00	6.00
❑ 1003	Papa's Dream/I'm Comin' Home	1971	—	3.00	6.00
❑ 1006 [DJ]	King Thaddeus (mono/stereo)	1971	—	3.50	7.00
—May be promo only					
❑ 1008	Give the Baby Anything the Baby Wants/Takin' a Chance	1971	—	3.00	6.00
❑ 1010	I Gotcha/A Mother's Prayer	1972	—	3.00	6.00
❑ 1012	You Said a Bad Word/It Ain't Gonna Work Baby	1972	—	3.00	6.00
❑ 1018	Rain Go Away/King Thaddeus	1973	—	3.00	6.00
❑ 1020	Woman Stealer/Cat's Got Her Tongue	1973	—	3.00	6.00
❑ 1020 [PS]	Woman Stealer/Cat's Got Her Tongue	1973	2.00	4.00	8.00
❑ 1021	All the Heaven a Man Really Needs/Let's Go Somewhere and Talk	1973	—	3.00	6.00
❑ 1024	Trying to Win Your Love/I've Seen Enough	1973	—	3.00	6.00
❑ 1154	Sassy Sexy Wiggle/Under Your Powerful Love	1975	—	3.00	6.00
❑ 1155	I'm Goin' Back Again/My Body Wants You	1975	—	3.00	6.00
❑ 1156	Baby, It's Rainin'/Have You Ever	1975	—	3.00	6.00
❑ 1157	Mama Red/Love Shortage	1975	—	3.00	6.00
❑ 2800	Loose Caboose/Music Ain't Got No Color	1979	—	2.50	5.00
❑ 2801	Who Gave Birth to the Funk/If You Don't Want the Man	1979	—	2.50	5.00
❑ 2802	Discomania/Fat People	1979	—	2.50	5.00
❑ 3000	What Should I Do/The Only Girl I've Ever Loved	1961	3.00	6.00	12.00
❑ 3002	One Giant Step/The Rib	1961	3.00	6.00	12.00
❑ 3003	Popeye Johnny/Hand Shakin', Love Makin', Girl Talkin', Son-of-a-Gun From Next Door	1962	3.00	6.00	12.00
❑ 3007	Meet in Church/Be Your Own Judge	1962	3.00	6.00	12.00
❑ 3009	I Let Her Get Away/The Peck	1963	3.00	6.00	12.00
❑ 3013	Someone to Take Your Place/I Should Have Kissed You More	1963	3.00	6.00	12.00
❑ 3016	I Wanna Be Free/Blood's Thicker Than Water	1963	3.00	6.00	12.00
❑ 3019	Looking for My Pig/Say Thank You	1964	3.00	6.00	12.00
❑ 3020	I'd Rather Have You/Old Time Lover	1964	3.00	6.00	12.00
❑ 3023	I Had a Good Thing But I Left (Part 1)/I Had a Good Thing But I Left (Part 2)	1964	3.00	6.00	12.00
❑ 4001	Hold What You've Got/Fresh Out of Tears	1964	3.75	7.50	15.00
❑ 4003	You Better Get It/You Got What It Takes	1965	2.50	5.00	10.00
❑ 4006	A Woman Can Change a Man/Don't Let Your Left Hand Know	1965	2.50	5.00	10.00
❑ 4011	One Monkey Don't Stop No Show/Build Your Love on a Solid Foundation	1965	2.50	5.00	10.00
❑ 4016	I Want To (Do Everything For You)/Funny Bone	1965	2.50	5.00	10.00
❑ 4022	A Sweet Woman Like You/Close the Door	1965	2.50	5.00	10.00
❑ 4026	The Love You Save (May Be Your Own)/If Sugar Was As Sweet As You	1966	2.50	5.00	10.00
❑ 4028	S.Y.S.L.J.F.M. (Letter Song)/I'm a Man	1966	2.50	5.00	10.00
❑ 4033	I Believe I'm Gonna Make It/Better Believe It, Baby	1966	2.50	5.00	10.00
❑ 4045	I've Got to Do a Little Bit Better/What in the World	1966	2.50	5.00	10.00
❑ 4051	Papa Was Too/Truest Woman in the World	1966	2.50	5.00	10.00
❑ 4055	Show Me/A Woman Sees a Hard Time (When Her Man Is Gone)	1967	2.00	4.00	8.00
❑ 4059	Woman Like That, Yeah/I'm Going and Get It	1967	2.00	4.00	8.00
❑ 4061	A Woman's Hands/See See Rider	1967	2.00	4.00	8.00
❑ 4063	Skinny Legs and All/Watch the One	1967	2.50	5.00	10.00
❑ 4068	I'll Make Every Day Christmas (For My Woman)/Don't Give Up	1967	3.00	6.00	12.00
❑ 4069	Men Are Gettin' Scarce/You're Gonna Thank Me, Woman	1968	2.00	4.00	8.00
❑ 4076	I'll Never Do You Wrong/Wooden Spoon	1968	2.00	4.00	8.00
❑ 4079	Chocolate Cherry/Betwixt and Between	1968	2.00	4.00	8.00
❑ 4083	Keep the One You Got/Go Home and Do It	1968	2.00	4.00	8.00
❑ 4086	You Need Me, Baby/Baby, Be Good	1968	2.00	4.00	8.00
❑ 4089	That's Your Baby/Sweet, Sweet Woman	1968	2.00	4.00	8.00

Number	Title (A Side/B Side)	Yr	VG	VG+	NM
❑ 4090	Buying a Book/Chicken Crazy	1969	2.00	4.00	8.00
❑ 4093	That's the Way/Anything You Wanna Know	1969	2.00	4.00	8.00
❑ 4094	We Can't Sit Down Now/It Ain't Sanitary	1969	2.00	4.00	8.00
❑ 4095	I Can't See You No More (When Johnny Comes Marching Home Again)/Sure Is Good	1969	2.00	4.00	8.00
❑ 4096	Everything Happens on Time/You're Right, Ray Charles	1970	2.00	4.00	8.00
❑ 4098	I'll Never Fall in Love Again/The Only Way I Know to Love You	1970	2.00	4.00	8.00

EPIC

❑ 50313	Ain't Gonna Bump No More (With No Big Fat Woman)/I Mess Up Everything I Get My Hands On	1976	—	2.50	5.00
❑ 50426	Hungry for Your Love/I Almost Got to Heaven Once	1977	—	2.50	5.00
❑ 50494	Rub Down/Be Kind to Old People	1977	—	2.50	5.00
❑ 50530	Get Back, Leroy/You Can Be My Star	1978	—	2.50	5.00

HANDSHAKE

❑ 02565	Don't Do Da Do/Here Comes No. 34 (Do the Earl Campbell)	1981	—	2.00	4.00

KING

❑ 4840	Come In This House/Baby, You Upset My Home	1955	15.00	30.00	60.00
❑ 4884	My Biggest Mistake/Right Back to My Arms	1956	12.50	25.00	50.00
❑ 4911	She's Mine/I Had to Come Back to You	1956	12.50	25.00	50.00
❑ 4980	Get Way Back/Pneumonia	1956	12.50	25.00	50.00
❑ 5064	I Want to Have a Talk with You/Ain't Nobody's Business	1957	12.50	25.00	50.00
❑ 5981	Come In This House/I Want to Have a Talk with You	1965	2.50	5.00	10.00

Albums
ACCORD

❑ SN-7174	J.T.'s Funk	1982	2.50	5.00	10.00

ATLANTIC

❑ 8106 [M]	Hold What You've Got	1965	10.00	20.00	40.00
❑ SD 8106 [P]	Hold What You've Got	1965	12.50	25.00	50.00
❑ 8115 [M]	The New Boss	1965	10.00	20.00	40.00
❑ SD 8115 [S]	The New Boss	1965	12.50	25.00	50.00
❑ 8124 [M]	The Love You Save	1966	10.00	20.00	40.00
❑ SD 8124 [S]	The Love You Save	1966	12.50	25.00	50.00
❑ 8133 [M]	I've Got to Do a Little Better	1966	10.00	20.00	40.00
❑ SD 8133 [S]	I've Got to Do a Little Better	1966	12.50	25.00	50.00
❑ 8144 [M]	The Best of Joe Tex	1967	5.00	10.00	20.00
❑ SD 8144 [P]	The Best of Joe Tex	1967	6.25	12.50	25.00
❑ SD 8156	Live and Lively	1968	5.00	10.00	20.00
❑ SD 8187	Soul Country	1968	5.00	10.00	20.00
❑ SD 8211	Happy Soul	1969	5.00	10.00	20.00
❑ SD 8231	Buying a Book	1969	5.00	10.00	20.00
❑ SD 8254	Joe Tex Sings with Strings and Things	1970	3.75	7.50	15.00
❑ SD 8292	From the Roots Came the Rapper	1972	3.75	7.50	15.00
❑ 81278	The Best of Joe Tex	1985	2.50	5.00	10.00

CHECKER

❑ LP-2993 [M]	Hold On	1965	37.50	75.00	150.00

DIAL

❑ DL 6002	I Gotcha	1972	3.75	7.50	15.00
❑ DL 6004	Joe Tex Spills the Beans	1973	3.75	7.50	15.00
❑ DL 6100	He Who Is Without Funk Cast the First Stone	1979	2.50	5.00	10.00

EPIC

❑ PE 34666	Bumps and Bruises	1977	3.00	6.00	12.00

KING

❑ 935 [M]	The Best of Joe Tex	1965	25.00	50.00	100.00
❑ KS-935 [R]	The Best of Joe Tex	1965	18.75	37.50	75.00

LONDON

❑ LC-50017	Super Soul	1977	2.50	5.00	10.00

PARROT

❑ PA 61002 [M]	The Best of Joe Tex	1965	12.50	25.00	50.00
❑ PAS 71002 [R]	The Best of Joe Tex	1965	7.50	15.00	30.00

PRIDE

❑ PRD-0020	The History of Joe Tex	1973	2.50	5.00	10.00

RHINO

❑ RNLP-70191	I Believe I'm Gonna Make It: The Best of Joe Tex 1964-1972	1988	2.50	5.00	10.00

TEX AND THE CHEX
45s
20TH FOX

❑ 411	Beach Party/Now (Love Me)	1963	7.50	15.00	30.00

ATLANTIC

❑ 2116	I Do Love You/My Love	1961	15.00	30.00	60.00

NEWTOWN

❑ 5010	Watching Willie Wobble/Be on the Lookout for My Girl	1963	5.00	10.00	20.00

TEXAS SLIM
See JOHN LEE HOOKER.

TEXAS TESSIE
See MEMPHIS MINNIE.

THOMAS, CARLA
Also see OTIS AND CARLA; RUFUS AND CARLA.
45s
ATLANTIC

❑ 2086	Gee Whiz (Look at His Eyes)/For You	1960	3.75	7.50	15.00
❑ 2101	A Love of My Own/Promises	1961	3.00	6.00	12.00

T

Number	Title (A Side/B Side)	Yr	VG	VG+	NM
❏ 2113	Wish Me Good Luck/In Your Spare Time	1961	3.00	6.00	12.00
❏ 2132	The Masquerade Is Over/I Kinda Think He Does	1962	3.00	6.00	12.00
❏ 2163	I'll Bring It On Home to You/I Can't Take It	1962	3.00	6.00	12.00
❏ 2189	What a Fool I've Been/The Life I Live	1963	3.00	6.00	12.00
❏ 2212	Gee Whiz, It's Christmas/All I Want for Christmas Is You	1963	3.75	7.50	15.00
❏ 2238	I've Got No Time to Lose/A Boy Named Tom	1964	3.00	6.00	12.00
❏ 2258	A Woman's Love/Don't Let the Love Light Leave	1964	3.00	6.00	12.00
❏ 2272	How Do You Quit (Someone You Love)/The Puppet	1965	3.00	6.00	12.00

GUSTO

Number	Title (A Side/B Side)	Yr	VG	VG+	NM
❏ 816	All I Want For Christmas Is You/Gee Whiz, It's Christmas	1979	2.50	5.00	10.00

—A Canadian import ($5) from 1986 exists on King

SATELLITE

Number	Title (A Side/B Side)	Yr	VG	VG+	NM
❏ 104	Gee Whiz (Look at His Eyes)/For You	1960	125.00	250.00	500.00

STAX

Number	Title (A Side/B Side)	Yr	VG	VG+	NM
❏ 0011	I've Fallen in Love/Where Do I Go	1968	2.00	4.00	8.00
❏ 0024	I Like What You're Doing (To Me)/Strung Out	1969	2.00	4.00	8.00
❏ 0042	Just Keep On Loving Me/My Love	1969	2.00	4.00	8.00

—With Johnnie Taylor

| ❏ 0044 | I Can't Stop/I Need You Woman | 1969 | — | 2.50 | 5.00 |

—With William Bell

❏ 0056	Guide Me Well/Some Other Man (Is Beating Your Time)	1970	2.00	4.00	8.00
❏ 0061	The Time for Love Is Anytime/Living in the City	1970	—	3.00	6.00
❏ 0067	All I Have to Do Is Dream/Leave the Girl Alone	1970	—	2.50	5.00

—With William Bell

❏ 0080	Hi De Ho (That Old Sweet Roll)/I Loved You Like I Love My Very Life	1970	—	3.00	6.00
❏ 0113	You've Got a Cushion to Fall On/Love Means (You Never Have to Say You're Sorry)	1972	—	3.00	6.00
❏ 0133	Sugar/You've Got a Cushion to Fall On	1972	—	3.00	6.00
❏ 0149	I May Not Be All You Want/Sugar	1972	—	3.00	6.00
❏ 172	Stop! Look What You're Doing/Every Ounce of Strength	1965	3.00	6.00	12.00
❏ 0173	I Have a God Who Loves/Love Among People	1973	—	3.00	6.00
❏ 183	Comfort Me/I'm for You	1966	3.00	6.00	12.00
❏ 188	Let Me Be Good to You/Another Night Without My Man	1966	3.00	6.00	12.00
❏ 188 [PS]	Let Me Be Good to You/Another Night Without My Man	1966	25.00	50.00	100.00
❏ 195	B-A-B-Y/What Have You Got to Offer Me	1966	3.75	7.50	15.00
❏ 206	All I Want for Christmas Is You/Winter Snow	1966	3.00	6.00	12.00
❏ 207	Something Good (Is Going to Happen to You)/It's Starting to Grow	1967	2.50	5.00	10.00
❏ 214	Unchanging Love/When Tomorrow Comes	1967	2.50	5.00	10.00
❏ 222	I'll Always Have Faith in You/Stop Thief	1967	2.50	5.00	10.00
❏ 239	Pick Up the Pieces/Separation	1967	2.50	5.00	10.00
❏ 251	A Dime a Dozen/I Want You Back	1968	2.50	5.00	10.00

Albums

ATLANTIC

Number	Title	Yr	VG	VG+	NM
❏ 8057 [M]	Gee Whiz	1961	25.00	50.00	100.00

—With white "fan" logo

| ❏ 8057 [M] | Gee Whiz | 1963 | 10.00 | 20.00 | 40.00 |

—With black "fan" logo

| ❏ SD 8057 [S] | Gee Whiz | 1961 | 37.50 | 75.00 | 150.00 |

—With white "fan" logo

| ❏ SD 8057 [S] | Gee Whiz | 1963 | 12.50 | 25.00 | 50.00 |

—With black "fan" logo

| ❏ SD 8232 | The Best of Carla Thomas | 1969 | 6.25 | 12.50 | 25.00 |

STAX

❏ 706 [M]	Comfort Me	1966	8.75	17.50	35.00
❏ 706 [P]	Comfort Me	1966	12.50	25.00	50.00
❏ 709 [M]	Carla	1966	8.75	17.50	35.00
❏ 709 [S]	Carla	1966	12.50	25.00	50.00
❏ 718 [M]	The Queen Alone	1967	8.75	17.50	35.00
❏ 718 [S]	The Queen Alone	1967	12.50	25.00	50.00
❏ STS-2019	Memphis Queen	1969	8.75	17.50	35.00
❏ STS-2044	Love Means Carla Thomas	1971	8.75	17.50	35.00
❏ MPS-8538	Memphis Queen	1987	2.50	5.00	10.00

—Budget-line reissue

THOMAS, CARLA, AND RUFUS THOMAS
See RUFUS AND CARLA.

THOMAS, IRMA
45s

CANYON

Number	Title (A Side/B Side)	Yr	VG	VG+	NM
❏ 21	Save a Little Bit for Me/That's How I Feel About You	1970	—	3.00	6.00
❏ 31	I'll Do It All Over You/We Won't Be In Your Way Anymore	1970	—	3.00	6.00

CHESS

❏ 2010	Cheater Man/Somewhere Crying	1967	2.00	4.00	8.00
❏ 2017	A Woman Will Do Wrong/I Gave You Everything	1967	2.00	4.00	8.00
❏ 2036	Good to Me/We Got Something Good	1968	2.00	4.00	8.00

COTILLION

| ❏ 44144 | Full Time Woman/She's Taken My Part | 1972 | — | 3.00 | 6.00 |

IMPERIAL

❏ 66013	Wish Someone Would Care/Break-A-Way	1964	3.00	6.00	12.00
❏ 66041	Time Is On My Side/Anyone Who Knows What Love Is (Will Understand)	1964	3.00	6.00	12.00
❏ 66069	Times Have Changed/Moments to Remember	1964	2.50	5.00	10.00
❏ 66080	He's My Guy/(I Want a) True, True Love	1964	2.50	5.00	10.00

Number	Title (A Side/B Side)	Yr	VG	VG+	NM
❏ 66095	Some Things You Better Get Used To/You Don't Miss a Good Thing	1965	2.50	5.00	10.00
❏ 66106	Nobody Wants to Hear Nobody's Troubles/I'm Gonna Cry Till My Tears Run Dry	1965	2.50	5.00	10.00
❏ 66120	Hurts All Over/It's Starting to Get Me Now	1965	2.50	5.00	10.00
❏ 66137	Take a Look/What Are You Trying to Do	1965	2.50	5.00	10.00
❏ 66178	It's a Man-Woman's World (Part 1)/It's a Man-Woman's World (Part 2)	1966	2.50	5.00	10.00

MINIT

❏ 625	Cry On/Girl Needs Boy	1961	3.00	6.00	12.00
❏ 633	It's Too Soon to Know/That's All I Ask	1961	3.00	6.00	12.00
❏ 642	Gone/Done Got Over It	1962	3.00	6.00	12.00
❏ 653	It's Raining/I Did My Part	1962	3.00	6.00	12.00
❏ 660	Somebody Told Me/Two Winters Long	1963	3.00	6.00	12.00
❏ 666	Ruler of My Heart/Hitting on Nothing	1963	3.00	6.00	12.00

RON

| ❏ 328 | Don't Mess with My Man/Set Me Free | 1960 | 3.75 | 7.50 | 15.00 |
| ❏ 330 | Good Man/I May Be Wrong | 1960 | 3.75 | 7.50 | 15.00 |

UNITED ARTISTS

| ❏ 0088 | Wish Someone Would Care/Take a Look | 1973 | — | 2.00 | 4.00 |

—"Silver Spotlight Series" reissue

Albums

BANDY

Number	Title	Yr	VG	VG+	NM
❏ 70003	Irma Thomas Sings	197?	7.50	15.00	30.00

FUNGUS

| ❏ FB-25150 | In Between Tears | 1973 | 10.00 | 20.00 | 40.00 |

IMPERIAL

❏ LP-9266 [M]	Wish Someone Would Care	1964	12.50	25.00	50.00
❏ LP-9302 [M]	Take a Look	1966	12.50	25.00	50.00
❏ LP-12266 [S]	Wish Someone Would Care	1964	15.00	30.00	60.00
❏ LP-12302 [S]	Take a Look	1966	15.00	30.00	60.00

RCS

| ❏ 1004 | Safe with Me | 1980 | 7.50 | 15.00 | 30.00 |

THOMAS, RUFUS
Also see RUFUS AND CARLA.

12-Inch Singles

ICHIBAN

Number	Title	Yr	VG	VG+	NM
❏ 12-103	Rappin' Rufus (3 versions)	1985	2.00	4.00	8.00

45s

ARTISTS OF AMERICA

| ❏ 126 | If There Were No Music/Blues in the Basement | 1976 | — | 2.50 | 5.00 |

AVI

| ❏ 149 | Who's Makin' Love to Your Old Lady/Hot Grits | 1977 | — | 2.00 | 4.00 |
| ❏ 178 | I Ain't Gettin' Older, I'm Gettin' Better (Part 1)/I Ain't Gettin' Older, I'm Gettin' Better (Part 2) | 1977 | — | 2.00 | 4.00 |

HI

| ❏ 78520 | Fried Chicken/I Ain't Got Time | 1978 | — | 2.00 | 4.00 |

HIGH STACKS

| ❏ 9801 | Hey Rufus!/Body Fine | 1999 | — | — | 3.00 |

—B-side by the Barkays

ICHIBAN

| ❏ 85-103 | Rappin' Rufus/(Instrumental) | 1985 | — | 2.00 | 4.00 |

METEOR

| ❏ 5039 | I'm Steady Holdin' On/The Easy Livin' Plan | 1956 | 37.50 | 75.00 | 150.00 |

STAX

❏ 0010	Funky Mississippi/So Hard to Get Along With	1968	—	3.00	6.00
❏ 0022	Funky Way/I Want to Hold You	1969	—	3.00	6.00
❏ 0059	Do the Funky Chicken/Turn Your Damper Down	1969	—	3.00	6.00
❏ 0071	Sixty Minute Man/The Preacher and the Bear	1970	—	3.00	6.00
❏ 0079	(Do the) Push and Pull Part I/(Do the) Push and Pull Part II	1970	—	3.00	6.00
❏ 0090	The World Is Round/(I Love You) For Sentimental Reasons	1971	—	3.00	6.00
❏ 0098	The Breakdown (Part 1)/The Breakdown (Part 2)	1971	—	3.00	6.00
❏ 0112	Do the Funky Penguin (Part 1)/Do the Funky Penguin (Part 2)	1971	—	3.00	6.00
❏ 126	It's Aw-Rite/Can't Ever Let You Go	1962	3.75	7.50	15.00
❏ 0129	Love Trap/6-3-8	1972	—	3.00	6.00
❏ 130	The Dog/Did You Ever Love a Woman	1963	3.75	7.50	15.00
❏ 140	Walking the Dog/You Said	1963	3.00	6.00	12.00
❏ 140	Walking the Dog/Fine and Mellow	1963	7.50	15.00	30.00
❏ 0140	Itch and Scratch (Part 1)/Itch and Scratch (Part 2)	1972	—	3.00	6.00
❏ 144	Can Your Monkey Do the Dog/I Want to Get Married	1964	3.00	6.00	12.00
❏ 149	Somebody Stole My Dog/I Want to Be Loved	1964	3.00	6.00	12.00
❏ 0153	Funky Robot (Part 1)/Funky Robot (Part 2)	1973	—	3.00	6.00
❏ 157	Jump Back/All Night Worker	1964	3.00	6.00	12.00
❏ 167	Baby Walk/Little Sally Walker	1965	2.00	4.00	8.00
❏ 173	Willy Nilly/Sho' Gonna Mess Him Up	1965	2.00	4.00	8.00
❏ 0177	I Know You Don't Want Me No More/I'm Still in Love with You	1973	—	3.00	6.00
❏ 178	Chicken Scratch/The World Is Round	1965	2.00	4.00	8.00
❏ 0187	I'll Be Your Santa Baby/That Makes Christmas Day	1973	—	3.00	6.00
❏ 0192	The Funky Bird/Steal a Little	1973	—	3.00	6.00
❏ 200	Talkin' 'Bout True Love/Sister's Got a Boyfriend	1967	2.00	4.00	8.00
❏ 0219	Boogie Ain't Nothin' (But Gettin' Down) (Part 1)/Boogie Ain't Nothin' (But Gettin' Down) (Part 2)	1974	—	3.00	6.00
❏ 221	Sophisticated Sissy/Grasy Spoon	1967	2.00	4.00	8.00
❏ 0236	Do the Double Bump/Do the Double Bump	1975	—	3.00	6.00
❏ 240	Down Ta My House/Steady Holding On	1974	2.00	4.00	8.00
❏ 250	The Memphis Train/I Think I Made a Boo-Boo	1968	2.00	4.00	8.00
❏ 0254	Jump Back '75 (Part 1)/Jump Back '75 (Part 2)	1975	—	3.00	6.00

Number	Title (A Side/B Side)	Yr	VG	VG+	NM
❏ 1073	I'll Be Your Santa Claus/Christmas Comes Once A Year	197?	—	2.50	5.00

—B-side by Albert King; reissue

SUN

❏ 181	Bear Cat (The Answer to Hound Dog)/Walking in the Rain	1953	87.50	175.00	350.00

—With subtitle on A-side

❏ 181	Bear Cat/Walking in the Rain	1953	50.00	100.00	200.00

—No subtitle on A-side

❏ 188	Tiger Man (King of the Jungle)/Save Your Money	1953	125.00	250.00	500.00

78s

CHESS

❏ 1466	Night Walkin' Blues/Why Did You Dee Gee	1951	7.50	15.00	30.00
❏ 1492	No More Doggin' Around/Crazy 'Bout You Baby	1952	7.50	15.00	30.00
❏ 1517	Juanita/Decorate the Counter	1952	7.50	15.00	30.00

STAR TALENT

❏ 807	I'm So Worried/(B-side unknown)	1950	25.00	50.00	100.00

SUN

❏ 181	Bear Cat (The Answer to Hound Dog)/Walking in the Rain	1953	30.00	60.00	120.00

—With subtitle on A-side

❏ 181	Bear Cat/Walking in the Rain	1953	20.00	40.00	80.00

—No subtitle on A-side

❏ 188	Tiger Man (King of the Jungle)/Save Your Money	1953	50.00	100.00	200.00

Albums

ALLIGATOR

❏ AV-4769	That Woman Is Poison	1988	2.50	5.00	10.00

A.V.I.

❏ 6015	If There Were No Music	1977	3.75	7.50	15.00
❏ 6046	I Ain't Gettin' Older, I'm Gettin' Better	1978	3.75	7.50	15.00

GUSTO

❏ 0064	Rufus Thomas	1980	2.50	5.00	10.00

STAX

❏ ST-704 [M]	Walking the Dog	1963	37.50	75.00	150.00
❏ STS-2028	Do the Funky Chicken	1970	6.25	12.50	25.00
❏ STS-2039	Rufus Thomas Live/Doing the Push and Pull at P.J.'s	1971	6.25	12.50	25.00
❏ STS-3004	Did You Hear Me	1972	6.25	12.50	25.00
❏ STS-3008	Crown Prince of Dance	1973	6.25	12.50	25.00

THOMAS, TIMMY

12-Inch Singles

GOLD MOUNTAIN

❏ 81203	Gotta Give a Little Love/Gotta Give a Little Love (Dub)	1984	—	3.00	6.00
❏ 81203 [DJ]	Gotta Give a Little Love (5:26) (4:35)	1984	2.00	4.00	8.00

45s

GLADES

❏ 1703	Why Can't We Live Together/Funky Me	1972	—	3.00	6.00
❏ 1709	People Are Changin'/Rainbow Power	1973	—	3.00	6.00
❏ 1712	Let Me Be Your Eyes/Cold Cold People	1973	—	3.00	6.00
❏ 1717	What Can I Tell Her/Opportunity	1973	—	3.00	6.00
❏ 1719	One Brief Moment/Rio Girl	1974	—	3.00	6.00
❏ 1721	Deep in You/Spread Us Around	1974	—	2.50	5.00
❏ 1723	I've Got to See You Tonight/You're the Song (I've Always Wanted to Sing)	1974	—	2.50	5.00
❏ 1727	Sexy Woman/Sweet Brown Sugar	1975	—	2.50	5.00
❏ 1730	Ebony Affair/It's What They Can't See	1975	—	2.50	5.00
❏ 1735	Love Shine/Running Out of Time	1976	—	2.50	5.00
❏ 1740	Stone to the Bone/Watch It! Watch It!	1977	—	2.50	5.00
❏ 1748	Touch to Touch/When a House Got Music	1978	—	2.50	5.00
❏ 1749	Freak In, Freak Out/Say Love, Can You Chase	1978	—	2.50	5.00
❏ 1758	Drown in My Own Tears (Part 1)/Drown in My Own Tears (Part 2)	1980	—	2.50	5.00

GOLD MOUNTAIN

❏ 82004	Gotta Give a Little Love (Ten Years After)/Same Old Song	1984	—	2.00	4.00
❏ 82008	Love Is Never Too Late/Let It Flow	1984	—	2.00	4.00

GOLDWAX

❏ 320	Have Some Boogaloo/Liquid Mood	1967	3.75	7.50	15.00
❏ 327	It's My Life/Whole Lotta Shakin' Goin' On	1967	3.75	7.50	15.00

MARLIN

❏ 3348	Are You Crazy??? (Pt. 1)/Are You Crazy??? (Pt. 2)	1981	—	2.00	4.00

Albums

GLADES

❏ 33-6501	Why Can't We Live Together	1973	3.75	7.50	15.00

GOLD MOUNTAIN

❏ GM-80006	Gotta Give a Little Love	1984	2.50	5.00	10.00

THORNTON, BIG MAMA

45s

ARHOOLIE

❏ 512	Swing It On Home/My Heavy Load	1968	2.00	4.00	8.00
❏ 520	Ball and Chain/Wade in the Water	1968	2.00	4.00	8.00

BAYTONE

❏ 107	You Did Me Wrong/Big Mama's Blues	1961	3.75	7.50	15.00

GALAXY

❏ 749	Life Goes On/Because It's Love	1966	2.50	5.00	10.00

KENT

❏ 424	Before Day/Me and My Chauffeur	1965	2.50	5.00	10.00

MERCURY

❏ 72981	Hound Dog/Let's Go Get Started	1969	2.00	4.00	8.00

Number	Title (A Side/B Side)	Yr	VG	VG+	NM
PEACOCK					
❏ 1603	Everytime I Think of You/Mischievous Boogie	1952	25.00	50.00	100.00
❏ 1612	Hound Dog/Rock-a-Bye Baby	1953	50.00	100.00	200.00
❏ 1612	Hound Dog/Nightmare	1953	45.00	90.00	180.00
❏ 1621	They Call Me Big Mama/Cotton Pickin' Blues	1953	25.00	50.00	100.00
❏ 1626	Big Change/I Ain't No Fool Either	1953	25.00	50.00	100.00
❏ 1632	I've Searched the Whole World/I Smell a Rat	1954	15.00	30.00	60.00
❏ 1642	Stop Hoppin' on Me/Story of My Blues	1954	15.00	30.00	60.00
❏ 1647	Walking Blues/Rock-a-Bye Baby	1955	15.00	30.00	60.00
❏ 1650	The Fish/Laugh, Laugh, Laugh	1955	15.00	30.00	60.00
❏ 1681	Just Like a Dog/My Man Called Me	1957	10.00	20.00	40.00
SOTOPLAY					
❏ SO-0033/34	Summer Time/The Truth'll Come to the Light	1965	3.75	7.50	15.00
Albums					
ARHOOLIE					
❏ F-1028 [M]	Big Mama Thornton in Europe	1966	7.50	15.00	30.00
❏ F-1032 [M]	Chicago Blues: The Queen at Monterey	1967	7.50	15.00	30.00
❏ F-1039 [M]	Ball and Chain	1968	7.50	15.00	30.00
BACK BEAT					
❏ BLP-68	She's Back	1970	6.25	12.50	25.00
MERCURY					
❏ SR-61225	Stronger Than Dirt	1969	6.25	12.50	25.00
❏ SR-61249	The Way It Is	1970	6.25	12.50	25.00
PENTAGRAM					
❏ PE-10005	Saved	1971	5.00	10.00	20.00
VANGUARD					
❏ VSD-79351	Jail	1974	3.75	7.50	15.00
❏ VSD-79354	Sassy Mama	1975	3.75	7.50	15.00

THREE CHUCKLES, THE

45s

BOULEVARD

❏ 100	Runaround/At Last You Understand	1954	20.00	40.00	80.00

VIK

❏ 0186	Anyway/The Funny Little Things We Used to Do	1956	5.00	10.00	20.00
❏ 0194	Tell Me/And the Angels Sing	1956	5.00	10.00	20.00
❏ 0216	Gypsy in My Soul/We're Still Holding Hands	1956	5.00	10.00	20.00
❏ 0232	Fallen Out of Love/Midnight 'Til Dawn	1956	5.00	10.00	20.00
❏ 0244	Won't You Give Me a Chance/We're Gonna Rock Tonight	1956	5.00	10.00	20.00

"X"

❏ 0066	Runaround/At Last You Understand	1954	6.25	12.50	25.00
❏ 0095	Foolishly/If I Should Love Again	1955	6.25	12.50	25.00
❏ 0134	So Long/You Should Have Told Me	1955	6.25	12.50	25.00
❏ 0150	Blue Lover/Realize	1955	6.25	12.50	25.00
❏ 0162	Times Two, I Love You/Still Thinking of You	1955	6.25	12.50	25.00
❏ 0186	Anyway/The Funny Little Things We Used to Do	1956	6.25	12.50	25.00
❏ 0194	Tell Me/And the Angels Sing	1956	6.25	12.50	25.00
❏ 0216	Gypsy in My Soul/We're Still Holding Hands	1956	6.25	12.50	25.00

7-Inch Extended Plays

"X"

❏ EXA-192	(contents unknown)	1955	10.00	20.00	40.00
❏ EXA-192 [PS]	The Three Chuckles (Vol. 1)	1955	10.00	20.00	40.00
❏ EXA-193	(contents unknown)	1955	10.00	20.00	40.00
❏ EXA-193 [PS]	The Three Chuckles (Vol. 2)	1955	10.00	20.00	40.00
❏ EXA-194	(contents unknown)	1955	10.00	20.00	40.00
❏ EXA-194 [PS]	The Three Chuckles (Vol. 3)	1955	10.00	20.00	40.00

Albums

VIK

❏ LX-1067 [M]	The Three Chuckles	1956	62.50	125.00	250.00

THREE D'S, THE (1)

45s

BRUNSWICK

❏ 55152	Nothing to Wear/The Happiest Boy and Girl	1959	6.25	12.50	25.00

PARIS

❏ 503	Little Billy Boy/Let Me Know	1957	5.00	10.00	20.00
❏ 508	Never Let You Go/Birth of An Angel	1957	5.00	10.00	20.00
❏ 511	Baby Doll/Crazy Little Woman	1958	5.00	10.00	20.00
❏ 514	Jumpin' Jack/I Never Saw My Pretty Little Baby Alone	1958	5.00	10.00	20.00

PILGRIM

❏ 719	Broken Dreams/Tell Me That You Love Me	1956	6.25	12.50	25.00

SQUARE

❏ 502	Squeeze/Graveyard Cha-Cha	1959	20.00	40.00	80.00

THREE DEGREES, THE

45s

ARIOLA AMERICA

❏ 801	My Simple Heart/Hot Summer Night	1980	—	2.00	4.00
❏ 7721	Giving Up, Giving In/Woman in Love	1978	—	2.00	4.00
❏ 7742	Woman in Love/Out of Love Again	1979	—	2.00	4.00
❏ 7746	The Runner/Out of Love Again	1979	—	2.00	4.00

EPIC

❏ 50283	What I Did for Love/Macaronie Man	1976	—	2.00	4.00
❏ 50330	In Love We Grow/Standing Up for Love	1977	—	2.00	4.00

ICHIBAN

❏ 89-167	Tie U Up/(B-side unknown)	1989	—	2.50	5.00

METROMEDIA

❏ 109	Down in the Boondocks/Warm Weather Music	1969	2.00	4.00	8.00
❏ 128	Feeling of Love/Warm Weather Music	1969	2.00	4.00	8.00

NEPTUNE

❏ 23	Reflections of Yesterday/What I See	1970	—	3.00	6.00

Number	Title (A Side/B Side)	Yr	VG	VG+	NM

PHILADELPHIA INT'L.

Number	Title (A Side/B Side)	Yr	VG	VG+	NM
❑ 3534	Dirty Ol Man/Can't You See What You're Doing to Me	1973	—	3.00	6.00
❑ 3539	Year of Decision/A Woman Needs a Good Man	1974	—	2.50	5.00
❑ 3550	When Will I See You Again/Year of Decision	1974	—	2.50	5.00
❑ 3561	I Didn't Know/Dirty Ol Man	1975	—	2.50	5.00
❑ 3568	Take Good Care of Yourself/Here I Am	1975	—	2.50	5.00
❑ 3585	Free Ride/Loving Cup	1976	—	2.50	5.00

ROULETTE

Number	Title (A Side/B Side)	Yr	VG	VG+	NM
❑ 7072	Melting Pot/The Grass Will Sing for You	1970	—	3.00	6.00
❑ 7079	Maybe/Collage	1970	—	3.00	6.00
❑ 7088	I Do Take You/You're the Fool	1970	—	3.00	6.00
❑ 7097	You're the One/Stardust	1971	—	3.00	6.00
❑ 7102	There's So Much Love All Around/Yours	1971	—	3.00	6.00
❑ 7105	Ebb Tide/Low Down	1971	—	3.00	6.00
❑ 7117	Trade Winds/I Turn to You	1972	—	3.00	6.00
❑ 7125	Find My Way/I Wanna Be Your Baby	1972	—	3.00	6.00
❑ 7137	I Won't Let You Go/Through Misty Eyes	1972	—	3.00	6.00

SWAN

Number	Title (A Side/B Side)	Yr	VG	VG+	NM
❑ 4197	Gee Baby (I'm Sorry)/Do What You're Supposed to Do	1965	3.00	6.00	12.00
❑ 4214	I'm Gonna Need You/Just Right for Love	1965	3.00	6.00	12.00
❑ 4224	Close Your Eyes/Gotta Draw the Line	1965	3.00	6.00	12.00
❑ 4235	Look in My Eyes/Drivin' Me Mad	1965	3.00	6.00	12.00
❑ 4245	Maybe/Yours	1966	3.00	6.00	12.00
❑ 4253	I Wanna Be Your Baby/Tales Are True	1966	3.00	6.00	12.00
❑ 4267	Love of My Life/Are You Satisfied	1967	3.00	6.00	12.00

WARNER BROS.

Number	Title (A Side/B Side)	Yr	VG	VG+	NM
❑ 7198	Contact/Oh No Not Again	1968	2.50	5.00	10.00

Albums

ARIOLA AMERICA

Number	Title (A Side/B Side)	Yr	VG	VG+	NM
❑ OL 1501	Three D	1980	2.50	5.00	10.00
❑ SW-50044	New Dimensions	1978	2.50	5.00	10.00

EPIC

Number	Title (A Side/B Side)	Yr	VG	VG+	NM
❑ PE 34385	Standing Up for Love	1977	3.00	6.00	12.00

ICHIBAN

Number	Title (A Side/B Side)	Yr	VG	VG+	NM
❑ ICH-1041	Three Degrees...And Holding	198?	2.50	5.00	10.00

PHILADELPHIA INT'L.

Number	Title (A Side/B Side)	Yr	VG	VG+	NM
❑ KZ 32406	The Three Degrees	1974	3.00	6.00	12.00
❑ KZ 33162	International	1975	3.00	6.00	12.00
❑ PZ 33840	The Three Degrees Live	1975	3.00	6.00	12.00

ROULETTE

Number	Title (A Side/B Side)	Yr	VG	VG+	NM
❑ 3015	So Much Love	1975	2.50	5.00	10.00
❑ SR-42050	Maybe	1970	10.00	20.00	40.00

THREE DOTS AND A DASH
With JESSE BELVIN.
45s
IMPERIAL

Number	Title (A Side/B Side)	Yr	VG	VG+	NM
❑ 5164	I'll Never Love Again/Let's Do It	1951	125.00	250.00	500.00

THREE FRIENDS, THE (1)
45s
CAL-GOLD

Number	Title (A Side/B Side)	Yr	VG	VG+	NM
❑ 169	Walkin' Shoes/Blue Ribbon Baby	1961	50.00	100.00	200.00

IMPERIAL

Number	Title (A Side/B Side)	Yr	VG	VG+	NM
❑ 5763	Dedicated (To the Songs I Love)/Happy as a Man Can Be	1961	7.50	15.00	30.00
❑ 5773	You're a Square/Go On to School	1961	5.00	10.00	20.00

THREE FRIENDS, THE (2)
45s
BRUNSWICK

Number	Title (A Side/B Side)	Yr	VG	VG+	NM
❑ 55032	Jinx/Chinese Tearoom	1957	7.50	15.00	30.00

LIDO

Number	Title (A Side/B Side)	Yr	VG	VG+	NM
❑ 500	Baby I'll Cry/Blanche	1956	15.00	30.00	60.00
—Gray label					
❑ 500	Baby I'll Cry/Blanche	1956	10.00	20.00	40.00
—Blue label					
❑ 502	I'm Only a Boy/Jinx	1957	12.50	25.00	50.00
❑ 504	Now That You've Gone/Chinese Tea Room	1957	12.50	25.00	50.00

THREE SOULS, THE
45s
ARGO

Number	Title (A Side/B Side)	Yr	VG	VG+	NM
❑ 5369	The Horse/Madisonville	1960	5.00	10.00	20.00
❑ 5472	Hi-Heel Sneakers/Dangerous Dan Express	1964	3.75	7.50	15.00
❑ 5514	You're No Good/Chitterlins Con Carne	1965	3.00	6.00	12.00

NOTE

Number	Title (A Side/B Side)	Yr	VG	VG+	NM
❑ 10015	Night Time/Smorgasbord	1959	5.00	10.00	20.00

THREETEENS, THE
45s
REV

Number	Title (A Side/B Side)	Yr	VG	VG+	NM
❑ 3516	Dear 53310761/Doowaddie	1958	10.00	20.00	40.00
❑ 3522	X + Y = Z/For the Love of Mike	1959	6.25	12.50	25.00

TODD

Number	Title (A Side/B Side)	Yr	VG	VG+	NM
❑ 1021	X + Y = Z/For the Love of Mike	1959	5.00	10.00	20.00

THRILLERS, THE (1)
45s
BIG TOWN

Number	Title (A Side/B Side)	Yr	VG	VG+	NM
❑ 109	The Drunkard/Mattie, Leave Me Alone	1953	100.00	200.00	400.00

HERALD

Number	Title (A Side/B Side)	Yr	VG	VG+	NM
❑ 432	Lizabeth/Please Talk to Me	1954	100.00	200.00	400.00

THRILLER

Number	Title (A Side/B Side)	Yr	VG	VG+	NM
❑ 3530	Lessie Mae/I'm Going to Live My Life Alone	1953	250.00	500.00	1000.

THRILLERS, THE (2)
45s
UPTOWN

Number	Title (A Side/B Side)	Yr	VG	VG+	NM
❑ 715	Come What May/This I Know Little Girl	1965	3.00	6.00	12.00

TIFFANYS, THE
Probably not all the same group.
45s
ARCTIC

Number	Title (A Side/B Side)	Yr	VG	VG+	NM
❑ 101	Love Me/Happiest Girl in the World	1964	5.00	10.00	20.00

ATLANTIC

Number	Title (A Side/B Side)	Yr	VG	VG+	NM
❑ 2240	Please Tell Me/Gossip	1964	5.00	10.00	20.00

JOSIE

Number	Title (A Side/B Side)	Yr	VG	VG+	NM
❑ 942	I Feel the Same Way Too/I Just Wanna Be a Girl	1965	3.00	6.00	12.00
❑ 952	Heaven on Earth/Take Another Look at Me	1966	3.00	6.00	12.00

KR

Number	Title (A Side/B Side)	Yr	VG	VG+	NM
❑ 120	He's Good for Me/It's Got to Be a Great Song	1967	5.00	10.00	20.00
—As "The Tiffanies"					

MRS

Number	Title (A Side/B Side)	Yr	VG	VG+	NM
❑ 777	Please Tell Me/Gossip	1964	20.00	40.00	80.00

RKO

Number	Title (A Side/B Side)	Yr	VG	VG+	NM
❑ 120	He's Good for Me/It's Got to Be a Great Song	1967	2.50	5.00	10.00
—Are the KR and RKO releases one and the same? We don't know					

ROCKIN' ROBIN

Number	Title (A Side/B Side)	Yr	VG	VG+	NM
❑ 1	I've Got a Girl/I Don't Dig Western Movies	1963	75.00	150.00	300.00

SWAN

Number	Title (A Side/B Side)	Yr	VG	VG+	NM
❑ 4104	Atlanta/The Pleasure of Love	1962	5.00	10.00	20.00

TIL, SONNY
Also see THE ORIOLES.
45s
JUBILEE

Number	Title (A Side/B Side)	Yr	VG	VG+	NM
❑ 5060	I Never Knew (I Could Love Anybody)/My Prayer	1951	75.00	150.00	300.00
❑ 5066	Fool's World/For All We Know	1951	75.00	150.00	300.00
—Black vinyl					
❑ 5066	Fool's World/For All We Know	1951	200.00	400.00	800.00
—Red vinyl					
❑ 5090	Once in Awhile/I Only Have Eyes for You	1952	12.50	25.00	50.00
—With Edna McGriff					
❑ 5099	Good/Picadilly	1952	20.00	40.00	80.00
—With Edna McGriff					
❑ 5112	Have You Heard/Lonely Wine	1953	50.00	100.00	200.00
❑ 5118	(Danger) Soft Shoulders/Congratulations to Someone	1953	50.00	100.00	200.00
❑ 5394	Night and Day/Shimmy Time	1960	5.00	10.00	20.00

RCA VICTOR

Number	Title (A Side/B Side)	Yr	VG	VG+	NM
❑ 47-9733	You're All I Need/After You	1969	2.00	4.00	8.00
❑ 47-9759	Tears and Misery/I Better Leave Love Alone	1969	2.00	4.00	8.00
❑ 74-0390	Don't Feel No Pain/One Big Happy Family	1970	2.00	4.00	8.00
❑ 74-0432	Colours/Love Is What It's All About	1971	2.00	4.00	8.00
❑ 74-0529	'Til Then/Love or Desire	1971	2.00	4.00	8.00
❑ 74-0606	Crying in the Chapel/What Are You Doing New Year's Eve	1971	2.00	4.00	8.00

ROULETTE

Number	Title (A Side/B Side)	Yr	VG	VG+	NM
❑ 4079	Shy/First Blush	1958	5.00	10.00	20.00

Albums

DOBRE

Number	Title (A Side/B Side)	Yr	VG	VG+	NM
❑ 1026	Back to the Chapel	1978	3.00	6.00	12.00

RCA VICTOR

Number	Title (A Side/B Side)	Yr	VG	VG+	NM
❑ LSP-4451	Sonny Til Returns	1970	5.00	10.00	20.00
❑ LSP-4538	Old Gold/New Gold	1971	3.75	7.50	15.00

TIMETONES, THE
45s
ATCO

Number	Title (A Side/B Side)	Yr	VG	VG+	NM
❑ 6201	I've Got a Feeling/Pretty Pretty Girl	1961	6.25	12.50	25.00

LOST-NITE

Number	Title (A Side/B Side)	Yr	VG	VG+	NM
❑ 406	I've Got a Feeling/Pretty Pretty Girl	197?	2.00	4.00	8.00

RELIC

Number	Title (A Side/B Side)	Yr	VG	VG+	NM
❑ 526	The House Where Lovers Dream/Get a Hold of Yourself	1985	2.50	5.00	10.00
❑ 538	In My Heart/My Love	198?	2.50	5.00	10.00
❑ 539	I've Got a Feeling/Pretty Pretty Girl	198?	2.50	5.00	10.00
❑ 543	A Sunday Kind of Love/Angels in the Sky	198?	2.50	5.00	10.00

TIMES SQUARE

Number	Title (A Side/B Side)	Yr	VG	VG+	NM
❑ 26	A Sunday Kind of Love/Angels in the Sky	1964	6.25	12.50	25.00
❑ 34	The House Where Lovers Dream/Get a Hold of Yourself	1964	7.50	15.00	30.00
❑ 421	Here in My Heart/My Love	1961	7.50	15.00	30.00
❑ 421	In My Heart/My Love	1961	5.00	10.00	20.00

TINDLEY, GEORGE
45s
EMBER

Number	Title (A Side/B Side)	Yr	VG	VG+	NM
❑ 1058	The Gypsy/I Wish	1960	3.75	7.50	15.00
❑ 1060	Wedding Bells/No Lonely Nights	1960	3.75	7.50	15.00

HERALD

Number	Title (A Side/B Side)	Yr	VG	VG+	NM
❑ 558	Close Your Eyes/Heart of Gold	1961	3.00	6.00	12.00

Number	Title (A Side/B Side)	Yr	VG	VG+	NM
PARKWAY					
❏ 834	Fairy Tales/Just For You	1962	3.00	6.00	12.00
WAND					
❏ 11205	Ain't That Peculiar/It's All Over But the Shouting	1969	2.00	4.00	8.00
❏ 11208	Honky Tonk Women/So Help Me Woman	1969	2.00	4.00	8.00
❏ 11215	Wan-Tu-Wah-Zuree/Pity the Poor Man	1970	2.00	4.00	8.00

TIPTON, LESTER
45s
LA BEAT

Number	Title (A Side/B Side)	Yr	VG	VG+	NM
❏ P 6607	This Won't Change/Go On	196?	1000.	2000.	4000.

TITONES, THE
45s
SCEPTER

Number	Title (A Side/B Side)	Yr	VG	VG+	NM
❏ 1206	Symbol of Love/The Movies	1960	12.50	25.00	50.00
—White label					
❏ 1206	Symbol of Love/The Movies	1960	6.25	12.50	25.00
—Red label					
WAND					
❏ 105	Symbol of Love/My Movie Queen	1960	5.00	10.00	20.00

TLC
12-Inch Singles
EPIC

Number	Title (A Side/B Side)	Yr	VG	VG+	NM
❏ 49-77073	Get It Up (Remix) (Hip Hop Remix) (Radio Edit)/(LP Version) (Hip Hop Radio Mix) (Quiet Storm Mix)	1993	3.75	7.50	15.00
LAFACE					
❏ LFDP 4044 [DJ]	Hat 2 Da Back (Extended Remix)/(Album Version) (Remix Instrumental)	1993	3.00	6.00	12.00
❏ LFDP 4059 [DJ]	Sleigh Ride (same on both sides?)	1993	2.00	4.00	8.00
❏ LFDP 4354 [DJ]	No Scrubs (4 versions)	1999	2.00	4.00	8.00
❏ LFDP 4368 [DJ]	Silly Ho (Clean Version) (Album Version)/(Instrumental) (Acappella)	1998	3.75	7.50	15.00
❏ LFDP 4383 [DJ]	No Scrubs (Clean With Rap) (Main With Rap)	1999	2.00	4.00	8.00
❏ LFDP 4390 [DJ]	I'm Good at Being Bad (Dirty Version) (Clean Version) (Instrumental)/(B-side same)	1999	3.00	6.00	12.00
❏ LFDP 4391 [DJ]	Unpretty (Album Version) (Acappella) (Instrumental)	1999	2.50	5.00	10.00
❏ LFDP 4406 [DJ]	Unpretty (5 versions)	1999	3.00	6.00	12.00
❏ LFDP 4439 [DJ]	My Life (Clean Version 4:02) (Instrumental 4:02) (Acappella 4:02)	1999	3.00	6.00	12.00
❏ 24009	Ain't 2 Proud 2 Beg (Smoothed Down Extended Mix) (Album Version)/(Dallas Dirt Mix) (Left Eye's 3 Minutes and Counting) (Rap Version) (Instrumental)	1992	2.50	5.00	10.00
❏ 24032	Baby-Baby-Baby (unknown versions)	1992	2.50	5.00	10.00
❏ 24033	What About Your Friends (Extended Remix) (Jazz Remix)/(Album Version) (Air Remix Long) (Album Version Instrumental)	1992	2.50	5.00	10.00
❏ 24046	Hat 2 Da Back (Extended Remix) (Remix Radio Edit)/(Album Version) (Remix Instrumental)	1993	2.50	5.00	10.00
❏ 24088	Creep (LP Version) (Jermaine's Jeep Mix) (Instrumental LP Version) (Jermaine's Acappella Mix)	1994	3.75	7.50	15.00
❏ 24093	Creep (Untouchables Mix) (Darp Mix)/(Untouchables TV Mix) (Smooth Mix) (Untouchables Instrumental)	1994	2.50	5.00	10.00
❏ 24099	Red Light Special (LA's Flava Mix) (Album Version) (Gerald Hall's Remix)//(Acappella) (Instrumental)/My Secret Enemy	1995	2.50	5.00	10.00
❏ 24108	Waterfalls (Single Edit) (Darp Remix) (Album Instrumental)/(ONP Remix) (ONP Remix Instrumental) (Acappella)	1995	2.50	5.00	10.00
❏ 24386	No Scrubs (Album Version) (Album Version With Rap) (Instrumental)/Silly Ho (Album Version) (Instrumental)	1999	2.00	4.00	8.00
❏ 24425	Unpretty (Album Version) (Don't Look Any Further Remix) (Acappella) (Remix With Rap) (Pumpin' Dolls Club Mix)	1999	2.00	4.00	8.00

45s
LAFACE

Number	Title (A Side/B Side)	Yr	VG	VG+	NM
❏ 24097	Red Light Special/(Instrumental)	1995	—	2.00	4.00
❏ 24107	Waterfalls/(Instrumental)	1995	—	—	3.00
❏ 24107 [PS]	Waterfalls/(Instrumental)	1995	—	—	3.00

Albums
LAFACE

Number	Title (A Side/B Side)	Yr	VG	VG+	NM
❏ LFL 6155 [(2) DJ]	Fanmail	1999	3.75	7.50	15.00
—Promo-only "clean version" in company sleeve					
❏ 26055 [(2)]	Fanmail	1999	3.00	6.00	12.00

TOM AND JERRIO
45s
ABC-PARAMOUNT

Number	Title (A Side/B Side)	Yr	VG	VG+	NM
❏ 10638	Boo-Ga-Loo/Boomerang	1965	3.00	6.00	12.00
❏ 10704	Great Goo-Ga Moo-Ga/Come On and Love Me	1965	3.00	6.00	12.00
❏ 10787	Oolya-Coo/Bacardi	1966	3.00	6.00	12.00

TOMS, GARY, EMPIRE
45s
MCA

Number	Title (A Side/B Side)	Yr	VG	VG+	NM
❏ 40770	Turn It Out (Tear This Building Down)/Hurricane	1977	—	2.00	4.00

Number	Title (A Side/B Side)	Yr	VG	VG+	NM
MERCURY					
❏ 74012	1-2-3-4/Feelin' Good Again	1978	—	2.00	4.00
❏ 74023	Welcome to Harlem/(B-side unknown)	1978	—	2.00	4.00
P.I.P.					
❏ 6504	7-6-5-4-3-2-1 (Blow Your Whistle)/7-6-5-4-3-2-1 (Blow Your Whistle) (Long Version)	1975	—	2.50	5.00
❏ 6509	Drive My Car/The New Empire	1975	—	2.50	5.00
❏ 6517	Love Me Right (Short Version)/Love Me Right (Long Version)	1976	—	2.50	5.00
❏ 6524	Stand Up and Shout/Party Hardy	1976	—	2.50	5.00

Albums
MCA

Number	Title (A Side/B Side)	Yr	VG	VG+	NM
❏ 2289	Turn It Out	1977	2.50	5.00	10.00
MERCURY					
❏ SRM-1-3731	Do It Again	1978	2.50	5.00	10.00
P.I.P.					
❏ 6814	7-6-5-4-3-2-1 Blow Your Whistle	1975	2.50	5.00	10.00

TONETTES, THE
Two different groups?
45s
ABC-PARAMOUNT

Number	Title (A Side/B Side)	Yr	VG	VG+	NM
❏ 9905	Oh What a Baby/Howie	1958	5.00	10.00	20.00
DOE					
❏ 101	Oh What a Baby/Howie	1958	20.00	40.00	80.00
❏ 103	Uh Oh/He Loves Me, He Loves Me Not	1958	15.00	30.00	60.00
MODERN					
❏ 997	Tonight You Belong to Me/Don't Fall in Love Too Soon	1956	6.25	12.50	25.00
VOLT					
❏ 101	Please Don't Go/No Tears	1962	5.00	10.00	20.00
❏ 104	Stolen Angel/Teardrop Sea	1963	5.00	10.00	20.00

TONEY, OSCAR, JR.
45s
BELL

Number	Title (A Side/B Side)	Yr	VG	VG+	NM
❏ 672	For Your Precious Love/Ain't That True Love	1967	2.50	5.00	10.00
❏ 681	Turn On Your Love Light/Any Day Now	1967	2.50	5.00	10.00
❏ 688	Unlucky Guy/You Can Lead Your Woman to the Altar	1967	2.50	5.00	10.00
❏ 699	Without Love (There Is Nothing)/Love That Never Grows Old	1968	2.50	5.00	10.00
❏ 714	Never Get Enough of Your Love/Love That Never Grows Old	1968	2.50	5.00	10.00
CAPRICORN					
❏ 0005	I Do What You Wish/Thank You, Honey Chile	1972	—	3.00	6.00
❏ 8005	Down on My Knees/Seven Days Tomorrow	1970	2.00	4.00	8.00
❏ 8010	I Wouldn't Be a Poor Boy/Person to Person	1970	2.00	4.00	8.00
❏ 8018	Workin' Together/Baby Is Mine	1971	2.00	4.00	8.00
KING					
❏ 5906	Can It All Be Love/You Are Going to Need Me	1964	5.00	10.00	20.00
❏ 6108	Keep On Loving Me/I've Found a True Love	1967	3.00	6.00	12.00

Albums
BELL

Number	Title (A Side/B Side)	Yr	VG	VG+	NM
❏ 6006 [M]	For Your Precious Love	1967	6.25	12.50	25.00
❏ S-6006 [S]	For Your Precious Love	1967	7.50	15.00	30.00

TONY AND THE DAYDREAMS
45s
PLANET

Number	Title (A Side/B Side)	Yr	VG	VG+	NM
❏ 1008	Why Don't You Be Nice/I'll Never Tell	1958	25.00	50.00	100.00
❏ 1054	Christmas Lullaby/Handin' Hand	1961	50.00	100.00	200.00

TONY AND THE HOLIDAYS
45s
ABC-PARAMOUNT

Number	Title (A Side/B Side)	Yr	VG	VG+	NM
❏ 10295	There Goes My Heart Again/My Love Is Real	1962	50.00	100.00	200.00

TONY AND THE MASQUINS
45s
RUTHIE

Number	Title (A Side/B Side)	Yr	VG	VG+	NM
❏ 1000	My Angel Eyes/Fugi Womma	1961	25.00	50.00	100.00

TONY AND THE RAINDROPS
45s
CHESAPEKE

Number	Title (A Side/B Side)	Yr	VG	VG+	NM
❏ 609	While Walking/Our Love Is Over	1961	15.00	30.00	60.00
CROSLEY					
❏ 340	Tina/My Heart Cried	1962	50.00	100.00	200.00

TONY AND THE TWILIGHTERS
Early version of ANTHONY AND THE SOPHOMORES.
45s
JALYNNE

Number	Title (A Side/B Side)	Yr	VG	VG+	NM
❏ 106	Be My Girl/Did You Make Up Your Mind	1960	20.00	40.00	80.00
RED TOP					
❏ 127	Key to My Heart/Yes or No	1960	50.00	100.00	200.00

TONY AND TYRONE
45s
ATLANTIC

Number	Title (A Side/B Side)	Yr	VG	VG+	NM
❏ 2458	Please Operator/Apple of My Eye	1967	7.50	15.00	30.00

T

Number	Title (A Side/B Side)	Yr	VG	VG+	NM
COLUMBIA					
❑ 43432	Turn It On/Talkin' About the People	1965	3.75	7.50	15.00

TONY TONI TONE
12-Inch Singles

Number	Title (A Side/B Side)	Yr	VG	VG+	NM
MACOLA					
❑ (# unknown)	One Night Stand (Extended Dance Version 6:29) (Radio Mix 4:15) (Dub Version 6:58) (East Oakland Version 6:12)	1987	6.25	12.50	25.00
MCA					
❑ L33-1562 [DJ]	House Party II (I Don't Know What You Come to Do) (Extended Club Version) (Accapella) (Drum Beat)/(Radio Edit) (Instrumental) (Dub)	1991	2.50	5.00	10.00
❑ 54171	House Party II (I Don't Know What You Come to Do) (Extended Club Mix 6:51) (Instrumental 6:48) (Percussapella 6:51)	1991	3.00	6.00	12.00
MERCURY					
❑ MELP 128 [DJ]	Let's Get Down (Fitch Brothers Club Mix) (Dip Dub Beats) (Fitch Dip Dub-Rockin' Da Pink Stuf) (Fitch Brothers Radio Edit)	1997	3.75	7.50	15.00
❑ MELP 135 [DJ]	Thinking of You (5 versions?)	1997	—	3.50	7.00
❑ 574383-1	Thinking of You (Club Remix) (TV Mix) (LP Version)/Let's Get Down (Fitch Brothers Club Radio Edit)	1997	—	3.50	7.00
WING					
❑ 859057-1	If I Had No Loot (Extended Version) (Album Version) (Radio Edit)	1993	2.00	4.00	8.00
❑ 871109-1	Baby Doll (8 versions)	1988	—	3.50	7.00
❑ 871935-1	For the Love of You (Extended Mix) (Dub)/(Radio Edit) (Radio Edit 2 with Scream) (Album Version)	1989	2.00	4.00	8.00
❑ 873995-1	The Blues (The Mix) (The Other The Mix) (Extended Mix) (T.T.T. Mix) (The Dusted Mix)	1990	—	3.50	7.00
❑ 877437-1	Feels Good (12" Party Mix 8:30) (Extended Version 6:56) (Edit Version 4:33) (LP Version 4:56)	1990	3.00	6.00	12.00
❑ 879069-1	It Never Rains (In Southern California) (All the Way Live Version 6:32) (Raphael's Rap 5:36) (LP Version) (Mo' Guitar Version 4:47)	1990	5.00	10.00	20.00
❑ 879591-1	Whatever You Want (4 versions)	1991	2.50	5.00	10.00
❑ 887385-1	Little Walter (2 Tuff Radio Mix) (B.B. Mix) (Extended Dance Mix) (Serious Groove Mix)	1988	—	3.50	7.00
❑ 887680-1	Born Not to Know (Start Here Mix) (Now Bust This Mix) (So You Want More Huh Mix) (Still Ain't Had Enuff Mix)	1988	2.00	4.00	8.00

45s

Number	Title (A Side/B Side)	Yr	VG	VG+	NM
COLLECTABLES					
❑ COL 4939	My Christmas/Feels Good (House Mix)	1994	—	—	3.00
❑ COL 4948	Feels Good/Little Walter	199?	—	—	3.00
MERCURY					
❑ 574226-7	Let's Get Down/Thinking of You	1997	—	—	3.00
WING					
❑ 855762-7	Leavin' (same on both sides)	1994	—	—	3.00
❑ 858260-7	(Lay Your Heard on My) Pillow (same on both sides)	1993	—	2.00	4.00
❑ 859056-7	If I Had No Loot (same on both sides)	1993	—	—	3.00
❑ 859566-7	Anniversary (same on both sides)	1993	—	—	3.00
❑ 871108-7	Baby Doll (Teddy's Edit)/(Edit of Album Version)	1988	—	—	3.00
❑ 871108-7 [PS]	Baby Doll (Teddy's Edit)/(Edit of Album Version)	1988	—	—	3.00
❑ 871934-7	For the Love of You/Catch My Breath	1989	—	—	3.00
❑ 871934-7 [PS]	For the Love of You/Catch My Breath	1989	—	—	3.00
❑ 873994-7	The Blues/Jo-Jo	1990	—	2.00	4.00
❑ 877436-7	Feels Good/(Instrumental)	1990	—	2.00	4.00
❑ 879068-7	It Never Rains (In Southern California)/Jo-Jo	1990	—	—	3.00
❑ 879590-7	Whatever You Want/(Instrumental)	1991	—	—	3.00
❑ 887385-7	Little Walter/(Instrumental)	1988	—	—	3.00
❑ 887385-7 [PS]	Little Walter/(Instrumental)	1988	—	—	3.00
❑ 887680-7	Born Not to Know/Catch My Breath	1988	—	—	3.00
❑ 887680-7 [PS]	Born Not to Know/Catch My Breath	1988	—	—	3.00

Albums

Number	Title (A Side/B Side)	Yr	VG	VG+	NM
WING					
❑ 835549-1	Who?	1988	3.00	6.00	12.00
❑ 841902-1	Revival	1990	5.00	10.00	20.00

TOP NOTES, THE
45s

Number	Title (A Side/B Side)	Yr	VG	VG+	NM
ABC-PARAMOUNT					
❑ 10399	I Love You So Much/It's Alright	1963	2.50	5.00	10.00
ATLANTIC					
❑ 2066	A Wonderful Time/Walkin' with Love	1960	3.75	7.50	15.00
❑ 2080	Say Man/Warm Your Heart	1960	3.75	7.50	15.00
❑ 2097	Hearts of Stone/The Basic Things	1961	3.75	7.50	15.00
❑ 2115	Twist and Shout/Always Late (Why Lead Me On)	1961	6.25	12.50	25.00

TOPPS, THE
45s

Number	Title (A Side/B Side)	Yr	VG	VG+	NM
RED ROBIN					
❑ 126	What Do You Do (To Make Me Love You So)/Tippin'	1954	75.00	150.00	300.00
❑ 131	I've Got a Feeling/Won't You Come Home Baby	1954	75.00	150.00	300.00

TOPS, THE
45s

Number	Title (A Side/B Side)	Yr	VG	VG+	NM
SINGULAR					
❑ 712	An Innocent Kiss/Walkin' with My Baby	1957	30.00	60.00	120.00

TOPSIDERS, THE
45s

Number	Title (A Side/B Side)	Yr	VG	VG+	NM
JOSIE					
❑ 907	Heartbreak Hotel/Let the Good Times Roll	1963	3.00	6.00	12.00

TOUSAN, AL
See ALLEN TOUSSAINT.

TOUSSAINT, ALLEN
45s

Number	Title (A Side/B Side)	Yr	VG	VG+	NM
ALON					
❑ 9021	Go Back Home/Poor Boy, Got to Move	1965	2.50	5.00	10.00
BELL					
❑ 732	Get Out of My Life, Woman/Gotta Travel On	1968	2.00	4.00	8.00
❑ 748	Hans Christian Anderson/I've Got That Feeling Now	1968	2.00	4.00	8.00
❑ 782	Tequila/We the People	1969	2.00	4.00	8.00
RCA VICTOR					
❑ 47-7192	Whirlaway/Happy Times	1958	6.25	12.50	25.00
—As "Al Tousan"					
REPRISE					
❑ 1109	Soul Sister/She Once Belonged to Me	1972	—	2.50	5.00
❑ 1132	Am I Expecting Too Much/Out of the City	1972	—	2.50	5.00
❑ 1334	Country John/When the Party's Over	1975	—	2.00	4.00
SCEPTER					
❑ 12317	From a Whisper to a Scream/Secret Touch of Love	1971	—	3.00	6.00
❑ 12334	Working in a Coal Mine/What Is Success	1971	—	3.00	6.00
SEVILLE					
❑ 103	Chico/Sweetie-Pie	1960	3.75	7.50	15.00
—All Seville releases as "Al Tousan"					
❑ 110	Back Home in Indiana/Naomi	1960	3.75	7.50	15.00
❑ 113	A Blue Mood/Moo Moo	1961	3.75	7.50	15.00
❑ 124	Twenty Years Later/Real Churchy	1962	3.75	7.50	15.00
WARNER BROS.					
❑ 8561	Night People/Optimism Blues	1978	—	2.00	4.00
❑ 8609	Happiness/Lover of Love	1978	—	2.00	4.00

Albums

Number	Title (A Side/B Side)	Yr	VG	VG+	NM
RCA VICTOR					
❑ LPM-1767 [M]	The Wild Sounds of New Orleans	1958	75.00	150.00	300.00
—As "Al Tousan"					
REPRISE					
❑ MS 2062	Life, Love and Faith	1972	6.25	12.50	25.00
SCEPTER					
❑ 24003	Toussaint	1971	6.25	12.50	25.00
WARNER BROS.					
❑ BSK 3142	Motion	1978	3.00	6.00	12.00

TOWNSEND, ED
45s

Number	Title (A Side/B Side)	Yr	VG	VG+	NM
ALADDIN					
❑ 3373	Every Night/Love Never Dies	1957	6.25	12.50	25.00
CAPITOL					
❑ F3926	For Your Love/Over and Over Again	1958	3.75	7.50	15.00
❑ F3994	What Shall I Do/Please Never Change	1958	3.00	6.00	12.00
❑ F4048	When I Grow Too Old to Dream/You Are My Everything	1958	3.00	6.00	12.00
❑ F4104	Richer Than I/Getting By Without You	1958	3.00	6.00	12.00
❑ F4171	Don't Ever Leave Me/Lover Come Back to Me	1959	3.00	6.00	12.00
❑ F4240	This Little Love of Mine/Hold On	1959	3.00	6.00	12.00
❑ 4314	Be My Love/With No One to Love	1959	3.00	6.00	12.00
CHALLENGE					
❑ 9118	Ed Townsend's Boogie Woogie (Part 1)/Ed Townsend's Boogie Woogie (Part 2)	1961	3.00	6.00	12.00
❑ 9129	And Then Came Love/Little Bitty Dave	1961	3.00	6.00	12.00
❑ 9144	You Walked In/I Love to Hear That Best	1962	3.00	6.00	12.00
DOT					
❑ 15596	Tall Grows the Sycamore/My Need for You	1957	5.00	10.00	20.00
LIBERTY					
❑ 55516	Tell Her/Down Home	1962	3.00	6.00	12.00
❑ 55516	Tell Her/Hard Way to Go	1962	3.00	6.00	12.00
❑ 55542	That's What I Get for Loving You/There's No End	1963	3.00	6.00	12.00
MAXX					
❑ 325	I Love You/I Might Like It	1964	2.50	5.00	10.00
MGM					
❑ 13784	Mommy's Never Comin' Back Again/Who Would Deny Me	1967	2.50	5.00	10.00
POLYDOR					
❑ 14021	No/Color Me Human	1970	—	3.00	6.00
WARNER BROS.					
❑ 5174	Stay with Me/I Love Everything About You	1960	3.00	6.00	12.00
❑ 5200	Cherrigale/Dream World	1961	3.00	6.00	12.00

Albums

Number	Title (A Side/B Side)	Yr	VG	VG+	NM
CAPITOL					
❑ ST 1140 [S]	New in Town	1959	7.50	15.00	30.00
❑ T 1140 [M]	New in Town	1959	6.25	12.50	25.00
❑ ST 1214 [S]	Glad to Be Here	1959	7.50	15.00	30.00
❑ T 1214 [M]	Glad to Be Here	1959	6.25	12.50	25.00
CURTOM					
❑ 5006	Ed Townsend Now	1976	3.00	6.00	12.00

Number	Title (A Side/B Side)	Yr	VG	VG+	NM
TOWNSMEN, THE					
45s					
CARDINAL					
❏ 1022	Pretty Patricia/(B-side unknown)	195?	3.75	7.50	15.00
COLUMBIA					
❏ 43207	Please Don't Say Goodbye/Gotta Get Moving	1965	2.50	5.00	10.00
HERALD					
❏ 585	Is It All Over/Just a Little Bit	1963	3.75	7.50	15.00
JOEY					
❏ 6202	Moonlight Was Made for Lovers/I'm in the Mood for Love	1963	6.25	12.50	25.00
PJ					
❏ 1341	That's All I'll Ever Need/I Can't Let Go	1963	50.00	100.00	200.00
VANITY					
❏ 579/80	It's Time/Little Jeanie	1960	5.00	10.00	20.00
WARNER BROS.					
❏ 5190	You're Having the Last Dance with Me/Gloria's Theme from "Butterfield-8"	1960	3.00	6.00	12.00
TOYS, THE					
45s					
DYNO VOICE					
❏ 209	A Lover's Concerto/This Night	1965	3.00	6.00	12.00
❏ 214	Attack/See How They Run	1965	2.50	5.00	10.00
❏ 218	My My Heart Be Cast Into Stone/On Backstreet	1966	2.50	5.00	10.00
❏ 219	Can't Get Enough of You Baby/Silver Spoon	1966	2.50	5.00	10.00
❏ 222	Baby Toys/Happy Birthday Broken Heart	1966	2.50	5.00	10.00
DYNO VOX					
❏ 209	A Lover's Concerto/This Night	1965	6.25	12.50	25.00
MUSICOR					
❏ 1300	You Got It Baby/You've Got to Give Her Love	1968	2.00	4.00	8.00
❏ 1319	Sealed with a Kiss/I Got My Heart Set on You	1968	2.00	4.00	8.00
PHILIPS					
❏ 40432	Ciao Baby/I Got Carried Away	1967	2.50	5.00	10.00
❏ 40456	My Love Sonata/I Close My Eyes	1967	2.50	5.00	10.00
Albums					
DYNOVOICE					
❏ 9002 [M]	The Toys Sing "A Lover's Concerto" and "Attack!"	1966	10.00	20.00	40.00
❏ S-9002 [P]	The Toys Sing "A Lover's Concerto" and "Attack!"	1966	12.50	25.00	50.00
TRAITS, THE					
Also see ROY HEAD.					
45s					
ASCOT					
❏ 2108	Linda Lou/Little Mama	1962	7.50	15.00	30.00
PACEMAKER					
❏ 254	Too Good to Be True/Gotta Keep Cool	1967	5.00	10.00	20.00
RENNER					
❏ 221	Linda Lou/Little Mama	1962	10.00	20.00	40.00
❏ 229	Got My Mojo Working/Woe Woe	1962	6.25	12.50	25.00
—Black vinyl					
❏ 229 [DJ]	Got My Mojo Working/Woe Woe	1962	10.00	20.00	40.00
—Promo only on colored vinyl					
SCEPTER					
❏ 12169	Harlem Shuffle/Somewhere	1966	2.50	5.00	10.00
❏ 12169	Harlem Shuffle/Strange Lips Start Old Memories	1966	2.00	4.00	8.00
TNT					
❏ 164	One More Time/Don't Be Blue	1959	5.00	10.00	20.00
—Later reissued on TNT 194 credited to "Roy Head"					
❏ 175	Live It Up/Yes I Do	1960	5.00	10.00	20.00
❏ 177	My Baby's Fine/Here I Am in Love Again	1960	5.00	10.00	20.00
❏ 181	Summer Time Love/Your Turn to Cry	1960	5.00	10.00	20.00
❏ 185	Night Time Blues/Walking All Day	1961	5.00	10.00	20.00
UNIVERSAL					
❏ 30494	Harlem Shuffle/Somewhere	1966	7.50	15.00	30.00
TRAMMPS, THE					
Also see THE VOLCANOS.					
12-Inch Singles					
ATLANTIC					
❏ PR 102 [DJ]	The Night the Lights Went Out (same on both sides)	1977	3.00	6.00	12.00
❏ PR 139 [DJ]	Soul Bones/Love Magnet	1978	3.00	6.00	12.00
❏ PR 170 [DJ]	Teaser/Life Insurance Policy	1979	3.00	6.00	12.00
❏ DSKO 173	The Night the Lights Went Out (7:06)/Hooked for Life (4:40)	1977	3.75	7.50	15.00
❏ PR 224 [DJ]	Hard Rock and Disco (same on both sides)	1980	3.00	6.00	12.00
❏ PR 251 [DJ]	Looking for You/Mellow Out	1980	3.00	6.00	12.00
VENTURE					
❏ 5024	Up on the Hill (Mt. U)	1983	—	3.50	7.00
45s					
ATLANTIC					
❏ 3286	Hooked for Life/I'm Alright	1975	—	2.50	5.00
❏ 3306	That's Where the Happy People Go (Short)/That's Where the Happy People Go (Long)	1975	—	2.50	5.00
❏ 3345	Soul Searchin' Time/Love Is a Funky Thing	1976	—	2.50	5.00
❏ 3365	Ninety-Nine and a Half (Won't Do)/Can We Come Together	1976	—	2.50	5.00
❏ 3389	Disco Inferno/You Touch My Hot Line	1977	—	3.00	6.00
❏ 3389	Disco Inferno/That's Where the Happy People Go	1978	—	2.50	5.00
—Reissue in conjunction with the success of "Saturday Night Fever"					
❏ 3389 [PS]	Disco Inferno/You Touch My Hot Line	1977	2.00	4.00	8.00

Number	Title (A Side/B Side)	Yr	VG	VG+	NM
❏ 3403	I Feel Like I've Been Livin' (On the Dark Side of the Moon)/Don't Burn Bridges	1977	—	2.50	5.00
❏ 3442	The Night the Lights Went Out/I'm So Glad You Came Along	1977	—	2.50	5.00
❏ 3460	Seasons for Girls/Love Ain't Been Easy	1978	—	2.50	5.00
❏ 3460	Seasons for Girls/Body Contact Contract	1978	—	2.50	5.00
❏ 3537	Soul Bones/Love Magnet	1978	—	2.50	5.00
❏ 3573	More Good Times to Remember/Teaser	1979	—	2.50	5.00
❏ 3654	Dance Contest/Hard Rock and Disco	1980	—	2.00	4.00
❏ 3669	Music Freek/V.I.P.	1980	—	2.00	4.00
❏ 3777	Mellow Out/Looking for You	1980	—	2.00	4.00
❏ 3797	I Don't Want to Ever Lose Your Love/Breathtaking View	1981	—	2.00	4.00
BUDDAH					
❏ 306	Zing Went the Strings of My Heart/Penguin at the Big Apple	1972	2.50	5.00	10.00
—As "Tramps"					
❏ 306	Zing Went the Strings of My Heart/Penguin at the Big Apple	1972	—	3.00	6.00
—As "Trammps"					
❏ 321	Sixty Minute Man/Scrub Board	1972	—	3.00	6.00
❏ 339	Rubber Band/Pray All You Sinners	1973	—	3.00	6.00
❏ 507	Hold Back the Night/Tom's Song	1975	—	2.50	5.00
GOLDEN FLEECE					
❏ 3251	Love Epidemic/I Know That Feeling	1973	—	3.00	6.00
❏ 3253	Where Do We Go from Here/Shout	1974	—	3.00	6.00
❏ 3255	Trusting Heart/Down These Dark Streets	1974	—	3.00	6.00
Albums					
ATLANTIC					
❏ SD 18172	Where the Happy People Go	1976	2.50	5.00	10.00
❏ SD 18211	Disco Inferno	1977	2.50	5.00	10.00
❏ SD 19148	The Trammps III	1977	2.50	5.00	10.00
❏ SD 19194	The Best of the Trammps	1978	2.50	5.00	10.00
❏ SD 19210	The Whole World's Dancing	1979	2.50	5.00	10.00
❏ SD 19267	Mixin' It Up	1980	2.50	5.00	10.00
❏ SD 19290	Slipping Out	1981	2.50	5.00	10.00
BUDDAH					
❏ BDS-5641	The Legendary Zing Album Featuring the Fabulous Trammps	1975	3.00	6.00	12.00
GOLDEN FLEECE					
❏ KZ 33163	Trammps	1975	2.50	5.00	10.00
PHILADELPHIA INT'L.					
❏ PZ 33163	Disco Champs	1977	2.00	4.00	8.00
—Reissue of Golden Fleece LP					
TREBELAIRES, THE					
45s					
NESTOR					
❏ 16	There Goes That Train/I Gotta	1954	25.00	50.00	100.00
TREMAINES, THE					
45s					
CASH					
❏ 100/1	Jingle, Jingle/Moon Shining Bright	1958	100.00	200.00	400.00
KANE					
❏ 008	Heavenly/Wonderful, Marvelous	1959	12.50	25.00	50.00
OLD TOWN					
❏ 1051	Jingle, Jingle/Moon Shining Bright	1958	12.50	25.00	50.00
V-TONE					
❏ 507	Heavenly/Wonderful, Marvelous	1959	6.25	12.50	25.00
VAL					
❏ 100/1	Jingle, Jingle/Moon Shining Bright	1958	62.50	125.00	250.00
TREN-DELLS, THE					
45s					
CAPITOL					
❏ 4852	Nite Owl/Hully Gully Jones	1962	3.00	6.00	12.00
JAM					
❏ 101	Nite Owl/Hully Gully Jones	1962	6.25	12.50	25.00
❏ 111	Hey Da-Da Dow/Tough Little Buggy	1962	6.25	12.50	25.00
SOUND STAGE 7					
❏ 2508	Mr. Doughnut Man/Ain't That Funny	1963	3.00	6.00	12.00
TILT					
❏ 779	I'm So Young/Don't You Hear Me Calling Baby	1961	7.50	15.00	30.00
—As "The Trend-Els"					
❏ 788	Moments Like This/I Miss You So	1962	7.50	15.00	30.00
TREN-TEENS, THE					
45s					
CARNIVAL					
❏ 501	My Baby's Gone/Your Yah Yah Is Gone	1964	25.00	50.00	100.00
TRENDS, THE (1)					
45s					
ABC					
❏ 10817	A Night for Love/Gonna Have to Show You	1966	6.25	12.50	25.00
❏ 10881	No One There/That's How I Like It	1966	6.25	12.50	25.00
❏ 10944	Check My Tears/Don't Drop Out of School	1967	5.00	10.00	20.00
❏ 10993	Thanks for a Little Lovin'/I Never Knew How Good I Had It	1967	5.00	10.00	20.00
❏ 11091	Soul Clap/Big Parade	1967	5.00	10.00	20.00
❏ 11150	Not Another Day/You Sure Know How to Hurt a Guy	1968	10.00	20.00	40.00

T

Number	Title (A Side/B Side)	Yr	VG	VG+	NM

ABC-PARAMOUNT
| ❏ 10731 | Not Too Old to Cry/If You Don't Dig the Blues | 1965 | 10.00 | 20.00 | 40.00 |

SMASH
| ❏ 1914 | Dance with My Baby/To Be Happy Enough | 1964 | 6.25 | 12.50 | 25.00 |
| ❏ 1933 | Get Something Going/That's the Way the Story Goes | 1964 | 6.25 | 12.50 | 25.00 |

TRENDS, THE (2)
45s

ARGO
| ❏ 5341 | I'll Be True/Class Ring | 1959 | 7.50 | 15.00 | 30.00 |

SCOPE
| ❏ 102 | Gone Again/Silly Grin | 1959 | 20.00 | 40.00 | 80.00 |

TRENDS, THE (U)
Definitely not group (1), but it may not be group (2), either.
45s

RCA VICTOR
| ❏ 47-7733 | The Beard/Chug-a-Lug | 1960 | 3.75 | 7.50 | 15.00 |

TRESVANT, RALPH
Also see NEW EDITION.
12-Inch Singles

MCA
❏ L33-1190 [DJ] Sensitivity (5 versions)		1990	2.50	5.00	10.00
❏ L33-1296 [DJ] Do What I Gotta Do (6 versions)		1991	2.00	4.00	8.00
❏ L33-1311 [DJ] Stone Cold Gentleman (4 versions)		1991	2.00	4.00	8.00
❏ L33-1524 [DJ] Rated R (3 versions)		1991	2.00	4.00	8.00
❏ L33-1549 [DJ] Rated R (6 versions)		1991	2.00	4.00	8.00
❏ L33-1560 [DJ] Yo, Baby, Yo! (Extended Vocal) (Percussapella) (Radio Edit) (Instrumental) (Dub)		1991	2.00	4.00	8.00
❏ MCA8P-2878 [DJ]Who's the Mack (Radio) (LP Version) (Instrumental)		1993	2.00	4.00	8.00
❏ MCA8P-2966 [DJ]When I Need Somebody (unknown versions)		1994	2.50	5.00	10.00
❏ 53933	Sensitivity (Extended Version) (7" Radio Edit) (Ralph's Rap)	1990	2.50	5.00	10.00
❏ 54037	Do What I Gotta Do (unknown versions)	1991	2.00	4.00	8.00
❏ 54045	Stone Cold Gentleman (Extended Club Version) (Bonus Beats) (Radio Version) (Instrumental) (Club Dub)	1991	2.00	4.00	8.00
❏ 54148	Rated R (unknown versions)	1991	2.00	4.00	8.00
❏ 54169	Yo, Baby, Yo! (Extended Vocal Version) (Instrumental)	1991	2.50	5.00	10.00

Albums

MCA
| ❏ 10116 | Ralph Tresvant | 1990 | 3.00 | 6.00 | 12.00 |

TROY, DORIS
45s

APPLE
| ❏ 1820 | Ain't That Cute/Vaya Con Dios | 1970 | 2.00 | 4.00 | 8.00 |
| ❏ 1824 | Jacob's Ladder/Get Back | 1970 | 2.00 | 4.00 | 8.00 |

ATLANTIC
❏ 2188	Just One Look/Bossa Nova Blues	1963	5.00	10.00	20.00
❏ 2206	Tomorrow Is Another Day/What'cha Gonna Do About It	1963	3.00	6.00	12.00
❏ 2222	One More Chance/Please Little Angel	1964	3.00	6.00	12.00
❏ 2269	Hurry/He Don't Belong to Me	1965	3.00	6.00	12.00

CALLA
| ❏ 114 | Heartaches/I'll Do Anything | 1966 | 5.00 | 10.00 | 20.00 |

CAPITOL
| ❏ 2043 | Face Up to the Truth/He's Qualified | 1967 | 2.00 | 4.00 | 8.00 |

MIDLAND INT'L.
| ❏ MB-10806 | Lyin' Eyes/Give God Glory | 1976 | — | 2.50 | 5.00 |
| ❏ MB-11082 | Can't Hold On/Another Look | 1977 | — | 2.50 | 5.00 |

Albums

APPLE
| ❏ ST-3371 | Doris Troy | 1970 | 6.25 | 12.50 | 25.00 |

ATLANTIC
| ❏ 8088 [M] | Just One Look | 1964 | 7.50 | 15.00 | 30.00 |
| ❏ SD 8088 [P] | Just One Look | 1964 | 12.50 | 25.00 | 50.00 |
| —The title song is rechanneled |

TRU-TONES, THE
45s

CHART
| ❏ 634 | Tears in My Eyes/Magic | 1957 | 200.00 | 400.00 | 800.00 |

DEN RIC
| ❏ 4527 | I'm the Guy/(B-side unknown) | 196? | 10.00 | 20.00 | 40.00 |

KEB
| ❏ 6037 | Soldier's Last Letter/(B-side unknown) | 196? | 10.00 | 20.00 | 40.00 |

TUCKER, TOMMY
45s

CHECKER
❏ 1067	Hi-Heel Sneakers/I Don't Want 'Cha	1964	6.25	12.50	25.00
❏ 1075	Long Tall Shorty/Mo' Shorty	1964	3.75	7.50	15.00
❏ 1112	Alimony/All About Melanie	1965	3.75	7.50	15.00
❏ 1133	Chewing Gun/I've Been a Fool	1966	2.50	5.00	10.00
❏ 1178	I'm Shorty/Sitting Home Alone	1967	2.00	4.00	8.00
❏ 1186	A Whole Lot of Fun Before the Weekend Is Done/ Real True Love	1967	2.00	4.00	8.00

HI
| ❏ 2014 | Loving Lil/A Man in Love | 1959 | 7.50 | 15.00 | 30.00 |
| ❏ 2020 | Miller's Cave/The Strangers | 1960 | 6.25 | 12.50 | 25.00 |

RCA VICTOR
| ❏ 37-7838 | The Return of the Teenage Queen/Since You Have Gone | 1961 | 6.25 | 12.50 | 25.00 |
| —"Compact Single 33" (small hole, plays at LP speed) |
| ❏ 47-7838 | The Return of the Teenage Queen/Since You Have Gone | 1961 | 3.75 | 7.50 | 15.00 |
| ❏ 68-7838 | The Return of the Teenage Queen/Since You Have Gone | 1961 | 7.50 | 15.00 | 30.00 |
| —"Compact Single 33" in "Living Stereo" |

SUNBEAM
| ❏ 128 | My Blue Heaven/That Man Comes Around | 1959 | 3.75 | 7.50 | 15.00 |

Albums

CHECKER
| ❏ LP-2990 [M] | Hi-Heel Sneakers | 1964 | 62.50 | 125.00 | 250.00 |
| —Black label |
| ❏ LP-2990 [M] | Hi-Heel Sneakers | 1965 | 30.00 | 60.00 | 120.00 |
| —Blue label with checkers |

TULSA RED
See LOWELL FULSON.

TUNE WEAVERS, THE
45s

CASA GRANDE
❏ 101	Little Boy/Look Down That Lonesome Road	1959	10.00	20.00	40.00
❏ 3038	My Congratulations Baby/This Can't Be Love	1960	7.50	15.00	30.00
❏ 4037	Happy, Happy Birthday Baby/Ol' Man River	1957	37.50	75.00	150.00
❏ 4038	I Remember Dear/Pamela Jean	1957	7.50	15.00	30.00
❏ 4040	There Stands My Love/I'm Cold	1958	10.00	20.00	40.00

CHECKER
| ❏ 872 | Happy, Happy Birthday Baby/Ol' Man River | 1957 | 6.25 | 12.50 | 25.00 |
| ❏ 872 | Happy, Happy Birthday Baby/Yo Yo Walk | 1957 | 6.25 | 12.50 | 25.00 |
| —B-side by Paul Gayten |
| ❏ 880 | Ol' Man River/Tough Enough | 1957 | 6.25 | 12.50 | 25.00 |
| —B-side by Paul Gayten |
| ❏ 1007 | Congratulations on Your Wedding/Your Skies of Blue | 1962 | 6.25 | 12.50 | 25.00 |

CLASSIC ARTISTS
| ❏ 104 | Come Back to Me/I've Tried | 1988 | — | 2.00 | 4.00 |
| —As "Margo Sylvia and Tune Weavers" |
| ❏ 107 | Merry, Merry Christmas Baby/What Are You Doing New Year's Eve | 1988 | — | 2.00 | 4.00 |
| —As "Margo Sylvia and Tune Weavers" |

TUNEDROPS, THE
45s

GONE
| ❏ 5003 | Rosie Lee/Speak for Yourself | 1957 | 10.00 | 20.00 | 40.00 |
| ❏ 5072 | Smoothie/Jumpin' Jellybeans | 1959 | 6.25 | 12.50 | 25.00 |

METRO
| ❏ 20028 | Smoothie/Jumpin' Jelly Beans | 1959 | 10.00 | 20.00 | 40.00 |

TUNEMASTERS, THE
45s

MARK
| ❏ 7002 | Sending This Letter/It's All Over | 1957 | 75.00 | 150.00 | 300.00 |

TURBANS, THE
Also see THE TURKS/THE TURBANS.
45s

HERALD
| ❏ 458 | When You Dance/Let Me Show You (Around My Heart) | 1955 | 12.50 | 25.00 | 50.00 |
| —Yellow label, script print inside flag |
| ❏ 458 | When You Dance/Let Me Show You (Around My Heart) | 195? | 5.00 | 10.00 | 20.00 |
| —Yellow label, block print inside flag |
❏ 469	Sister Sookey/I'll Always Watch Over You	1956	7.50	15.00	30.00
❏ 478	B-I-N-G-O (Bingo)/I'm Nobody's	1956	7.50	15.00	30.00
❏ 486	It Was a Nite Like This/All of My Love	1956	7.50	15.00	30.00
❏ 495	Valley of Love/Bye and Bye	1957	7.50	15.00	30.00
❏ 510	Congratulations/The Wadda-Do	1957	6.25	12.50	25.00

IMPERIAL
❏ 5807	Six Questions/The Lament of Silver Gulch	1962	10.00	20.00	40.00
❏ 5828	This Is My Story/Clicky Clicky Clack	1962	6.25	12.50	25.00
❏ 5847	I Wonder (I Wanna Know)/The Damage Is Done	1962	5.00	10.00	20.00

MONEY
| ❏ 209 | Tick Tock Awoo/No No Cherry | 1955 | 50.00 | 100.00 | 200.00 |
| ❏ 209 | Tick Tock Awoo/Nest Is Warm | 1955 | 50.00 | 100.00 | 200.00 |

PARKWAY
| ❏ 820 | When You Dance/Golden Rings | 1961 | 6.25 | 12.50 | 25.00 |

RED TOP
| ❏ 115 | I Promise You Love/Curfew Time | 1959 | 12.50 | 25.00 | 50.00 |

ROULETTE
| ❏ 4281 | Diamonds and Pearls/Bad Man | 1960 | 5.00 | 10.00 | 20.00 |
| ❏ 4326 | Three Friends (Two Lovers)/I'm Not Your Fool Anymore | 1961 | 5.00 | 10.00 | 20.00 |

Albums

HERALD
| ❏ 5009 | Presenting the Turbans | 197? | 5.00 | 10.00 | 20.00 |
| —No such album was released in the 1950s; this is a bootleg that has some collector value. |

Number	Title (A Side/B Side)	Yr	VG	VG+	NM
LOST-NITE					
❏ LLP-25 [10]	The Turbans	1981	2.50	5.00	10.00
—Red vinyl					
RELIC					
❏ 5009	The Turbans' Greatest Hits	198?	3.00	6.00	12.00

TURBINES, THE
45s
CENCO

| ❏ 116 | We Got to Start Over/(B-side unknown) | 196? | 300.00 | 600.00 | 1200. |

TURKS, THE
More than one group.
45s
BALLY

❏ 1017	This Heart of Mine/Why Did You	1956	7.50	15.00	30.00
CASH					
❏ 1042	It Can't Be True/Wagon Wheels	1956	7.50	15.00	30.00
—As "The Original Turks"					
CLASS					
❏ 256	Hully Gully/Rockville U.S.A.	1959	5.00	10.00	20.00
IMPERIAL					
❏ 5783	I'm a Fool/It Can't Be True	1961	3.00	6.00	12.00
KEEN					
❏ 3-4016	Father Time/Okay	1958	5.00	10.00	20.00
KNIGHT					
❏ 2005	I'm a Fool/It Can't Be True	1958	5.00	10.00	20.00
MONEY					
❏ 215	I'm a Fool/I've Been Accused	1956	10.00	20.00	40.00
P.B.D.					
❏ 112	Baja/Dianne	196?	7.50	15.00	30.00
❏ 113	Wipeout/Hideaway	196?	7.50	15.00	30.00

TURKS, THE / THE TURBANS
Also see each artist's individual listings.
45s
MONEY

| ❏ 211 | Emily/When I Return | 1955 | 15.00 | 30.00 | 60.00 |

TURNER, IKE
Also see IKE AND TINA TURNER.
45s
ARTISTIC

❏ 1504	(I Know) You Don't Love Me/Down and Out	1958	7.50	15.00	30.00
COBRA					
❏ 5033	Box Top/Walking Down the Aisle	1959	7.50	15.00	30.00
FEDERAL					
❏ 12297	Do You Mean It/She Made My Blood Run Cold	1957	25.00	50.00	100.00
❏ 12304	Rock a Bucket/The Big Question	1957	12.50	25.00	50.00
❏ 12307	You've Changed My Love/Trail Blazer	1957	10.00	20.00	40.00
FLAIR					
❏ 1040	Cubano Jump/Loosely	1954	15.00	30.00	60.00
❏ 1059	Cuban Getaway/Go To It	1955	15.00	30.00	60.00
KING					
❏ 5553	The Big Question/She Made My Blood Run Cold	1961	3.75	7.50	15.00
LIBERTY					
❏ 56194	Takin' Back My Name/Love Is a Game	1970	—	2.50	5.00
RPM					
❏ 356	You're Driving Me Insane/Trouble and Heartaches	1952	100.00	200.00	400.00
❏ 362	My Heart Belongs to You/Lookin' for My Baby	1952	15.00	30.00	60.00
—As "Bonnie and Ike Turner"					
❏ 446	As Long As I Have You/I Wanna Make Love to You	1955	10.00	20.00	40.00
SUE					
❏ 722	My Love/That's All I Need	1959	5.00	10.00	20.00
UNITED ARTISTS					
❏ XW460	Take My Hand, Precious Lord/Father Alone	1974	—	2.50	5.00
❏ 50865	River Deep Mountain High/Na Na	1971	—	2.50	5.00
❏ 50900	Right On/Tacks in My Shoes	1972	—	2.50	5.00
❏ 50930	Lawdy Miss Clawdy/Tacks in My Shoes	1972	—	2.50	5.00
❏ 51102	Dust My Broom/You Won't Let Me Go	1973	—	2.50	5.00
78s					
CHESS					
❏ 1459	I'm Lonesome, Baby/Heartbroken and Worried	1951	12.50	25.00	50.00
FEDERAL					
❏ 12297	Do You Mean It/She Made My Blood Run Cold	1957	25.00	50.00	100.00
❏ 12304	Rock a Bucket/The Big Question	1957	12.50	25.00	50.00
❏ 12307	You've Changed My Love/Trail Blazer	1957	10.00	20.00	40.00
FLAIR					
❏ 1040	Cubano Jump/Loosely	1954	10.00	20.00	40.00
❏ 1059	Cuban Getaway/Go To It	1955	10.00	20.00	40.00
RPM					
❏ 356	You're Driving Me Insane/Trouble and Heartaches	1952	37.50	75.00	150.00
❏ 362	My Heart Belongs to You/Lookin' for My Baby	1952	7.50	15.00	30.00
—As "Bonnie and Ike Turner"					
❏ 446	As Long As I Have You/I Wanna Make Love to You	1955	7.50	15.00	30.00
Albums					
CROWN					
❏ CST-367 [R]	Ike Turner Rocks the Blues	1963	25.00	50.00	100.00
❏ CLP-5367 [M]	Ike Turner Rocks the Blues	1963	50.00	100.00	200.00
FANTASY					
❏ F-9597	The Edge	1980	2.50	5.00	10.00
POMPEII					
❏ SD 6003	A Black Man's Soul	1969	3.75	7.50	15.00
UNITED ARTISTS					
❏ UA-LA087-F	Bad Dreams	1973	3.75	7.50	15.00
❏ UAS-5576	Blues Roots	1972	3.75	7.50	15.00

TURNER, IKE AND TINA
Also see IKE TURNER; TINA TURNER.
12-Inch Singles
STRIPED HORSE

❏ 1201	Living for the City (5:02)/Bootsy Whitelaw (4:01)	1985	3.75	7.50	15.00
45s					
A&M					
❏ 1118	River Deep, Mountain High/I'll Keep You Happy	1969	2.50	5.00	10.00
❏ 1170	A Love Like Yours/Save the Last Dance for Me	1970	2.50	5.00	10.00
BLUE THUMB					
❏ 101	I've Been Loving You Too Long/Grumbling	1969	—	3.00	6.00
❏ 102	The Hunter/Crazy 'Bout You Baby	1969	—	3.00	6.00
❏ 104	Bold Soul Sister/I Know	1969	—	3.00	6.00
❏ 202	I've Been Loving You Too Long/Crazy 'Bout You Baby	1971	—	2.50	5.00
CENCO					
❏ 112	Get It-Get It/You Weren't Ready (For My Love)	1967	3.75	7.50	15.00
INNIS					
❏ 6666	Betcha Can't Kiss Me/Don't Lie to Me	1968	2.50	5.00	10.00
❏ 6667	So Fine/So Blue Over You	1968	2.50	5.00	10.00
KENT					
❏ 402	I Can't Believe What You Say (For Seeing What You Do)/My Baby Now	1964	2.50	5.00	10.00
❏ 409	Am I a Fool in Love/Please, Please, Please	1964	2.50	5.00	10.00
❏ 418	Chicken Shack/He's the One	1965	2.50	5.00	10.00
❏ 4514	Plaese, Please, Please (Part 1)/Please, Please, Please (Part 2)	1970	—	3.00	6.00
LIBERTY					
❏ 56177	I Want to Take You Higher/Contact High	1970	—	3.00	6.00
❏ 56207	Workin' Together/The Way You Love Me	1970	—	3.00	6.00
❏ 56216	Proud Mary/Funkier Than a Mosquito's Tweeter	1970	—	3.00	6.00
LOMA					
❏ 2011	I'm Thru with Love/Tell Her I'm Not Home	1965	2.50	5.00	10.00
❏ 2015	Somebody Needs You/Just to Be with You	1965	2.50	5.00	10.00
MINIT					
❏ 32060	I'm Gonna Do All I Can (To Do Right By My Man)/You've Got Too Many Ties That Bind	1969	—	3.00	6.00
❏ 32068	I Wish It Would Rain/With a Little Help from My Friends	1969	—	3.00	6.00
❏ 32077	I Wanna Jump/Treating Us Funky	1969	—	3.00	6.00
❏ 32087	Come Together/Honky Tonk Women	1970	—	3.00	6.00
MODERN					
❏ 1007	Good Bye, So Long/Hurt Is All You Gave Me	1965	2.50	5.00	10.00
❏ 1012	I Don't Need/Gonna Have Fun	1965	2.50	5.00	10.00
PHILLES					
❏ 131	River Deep — Mountain High/I'll Keep You Happy	1966	5.00	10.00	20.00
❏ 134	Two to Tango/A Man Is a Man Is a Man	1966	3.75	7.50	15.00
❏ 135	I'll Never Need More Love Than This/The Cash Box Blues Or (Oops We Printed the Wrong Story Again)	1967	3.75	7.50	15.00
❏ 136	I Idolize You/A Love Like Yours	1967	3.75	7.50	15.00
POMPEII					
❏ 7003	Betcha Can't Kiss Me/Cussin', Cryin', and Carryin' On	1969	2.00	4.00	8.00
❏ 66675	It Sho' Ain't Me/We Need An Understanding	1968	2.00	4.00	8.00
❏ 66700	Shake a Tail Feather/Cussin', Cryin', and Carryin' On	1969	2.00	4.00	8.00
SONJA					
❏ 2001	If I Can't Be First/I'm Going Back Home	1968	3.00	6.00	12.00
❏ 2005	You Can't Miss Nothing That You Never Had/God Gave Me You	1968	3.00	6.00	12.00
SUE					
❏ 135	Two Is a Couple/Tin Top House	1965	3.75	7.50	15.00
❏ 138	The New Breed (Part 1)/The New Breed (Part 2)	1965	3.75	7.50	15.00
❏ 139	Stagger Lee and Billy/Can't Chance a Breakup	1965	3.75	7.50	15.00
❏ 146	Dear John/I Made a Promise Up Above	1966	3.00	6.00	12.00
❏ 730	A Fool in Love/The Way You Love Me	1960	7.50	15.00	30.00
❏ 734	You're My Baby/A Fool Too Long	1960	6.25	12.50	25.00
❏ 735	I Idolize You/Letter from Tina	1960	6.25	12.50	25.00
❏ 740	I'm Jealous/You're My Baby	1961	6.25	12.50	25.00
❏ 749	It's Gonna Work Out Fine/Won't You Forgive Me	1961	7.50	15.00	30.00
❏ 753	Poor Fool/You Can't Blame Me	1961	5.00	10.00	20.00
❏ 757	Tra La La La La/Puppy Love	1962	3.75	7.50	15.00
❏ 760	Prancing/It's Gonna Work Out Fine	1962	3.75	7.50	15.00
❏ 765	You Shoulda Treated Me Right/Sleepless	1962	3.75	7.50	15.00
❏ 768	Tina's Dilemma/I Idolize You	1962	3.75	7.50	15.00
❏ 772	The Argument/Mind in a Whirl	1962	3.75	7.50	15.00
❏ 774	Please Don't Hurt Me/Worried and Hurtin' Inside	1962	3.75	7.50	15.00
❏ 784	Don't Play Me Cheap/Wake Up	1963	3.75	7.50	15.00
TANGERINE					
❏ 963	Beauty Is Only Skin Deep/Anything You Wasn't Born With	1966	2.50	5.00	10.00
❏ 967	Dust My Broom/I'm Hooked	1966	2.50	5.00	10.00

T

Number	Title (A Side/B Side)	Yr	VG	VG+	NM
UNITED ARTISTS					
❑ SP-48 [DJ]	I Want to Take You Higher/Ooh Poo Pah Doo	1971	2.50	5.00	10.00
❑ 0119	A Fool in Love/I Idolize You	1973	—	2.00	4.00
❑ 0120	It's Gonna Work Out Fine/Poor Fool	1973	—	2.00	4.00
❑ 0121	I Want to Take You Higher/Come Together	1973	—	2.00	4.00
❑ 0122	Proud Mary/Tra La La La La	1973	—	2.00	4.00
—0119 through 0122 are "Silver Spotlight Series" reissues					
❑ XW174	With a Little Help from My Friends/Early One Morning	1973	—	2.50	5.00
❑ XW257	Work On Me/Born Free	1973	—	2.50	5.00
❑ XW298	Nutbosh City Limits/Help Him	1973	—	3.00	6.00
❑ XW409	Get it Out of Your Mind/Sweet Rhode Island Red	1974	—	2.50	5.00
❑ XW524	Nutbush City Limits/Ooh Poo Pah Doo	1974	—	2.00	4.00
—Reissue					
❑ XW528	Sexy Ida (Part 1)/Sexy Ida (Part 2)	1974	—	2.50	5.00
❑ XW598X	Baby, Get It On/Baby, Get It On (Disco Version)	1975	—	2.50	5.00
❑ 50782	Ooh Poo Pah Doo/I Wanna Jump	1971	—	2.50	5.00
❑ 50837	I'm Yours/Doin' It	1971	—	2.50	5.00
❑ 50881	Do Wah Ditty (Got to Get Ya)/Up in Heah	1972	—	2.50	5.00
❑ 50913	Outrageous/Feel Good	1972	—	2.50	5.00
❑ 50939	Games People Play/Pick Me Up	1972	—	2.50	5.00
❑ 50955	Let Me Touch Your Mind/Chopper	1972	—	2.50	5.00
WARNER BROS.					
❑ 5433	A Fool for a Fool/No Tears to Cry	1964	3.00	6.00	12.00
❑ 5433 [PS]	A Fool for a Fool/No Tears to Cry	1964	10.00	20.00	40.00
❑ 5461	It's All Over/Finger Poppin'	1964	3.00	6.00	12.00
❑ 5493	Ooh Poop A Doo/Merry Christmas Baby	1964	3.00	6.00	12.00
Albums					
ABC					
❑ 4014	16 Great Performances	1975	3.00	6.00	12.00
ACCORD					
❑ SN-7147	Hot and Sassy	1981	2.50	5.00	10.00
A&M					
❑ SP-3179	River Deep — Mountain High	1982	2.50	5.00	10.00
—Budget-line reissue					
❑ SP-4178	River Deep — Mountain High	1969	6.25	12.50	25.00
—Official release of Philles 4011					
BLUE THUMB					
❑ BTS 5	Outta Season	1968	3.75	7.50	15.00
❑ BTS 11	The Hunter	1969	3.75	7.50	15.00
❑ BTS 49	The Best of Ike & Tina Turner	1973	3.00	6.00	12.00
❑ BTS-8805	Outta Season	1971	3.00	6.00	12.00
—Early reissue of Blue Thumb 5					
CAPITOL					
❑ ST-571	Her Man, His Woman	1971	3.75	7.50	15.00
COLLECTABLES					
❑ COL-5107	Golden Classics	198?	2.50	5.00	10.00
❑ COL-5137	It's Gonna Work Out Fine	198?	2.50	5.00	10.00
EMI AMERICA					
❑ ST-17212	It's Gonna Work Out Fine	1986	2.50	5.00	10.00
❑ SQ-17216	Workin' Together	1986	2.50	5.00	10.00
HARMONY					
❑ HS 11360	Ooh Poo Pah Doo	1969	3.75	7.50	15.00
❑ H 30567	Something's Got a Hold on Me	1971	3.75	7.50	15.00
KENT					
❑ KST-514 [S]	The Ike and Tina Turner Revue Live	1964	10.00	20.00	40.00
❑ KST-519 [S]	The Soul of Ike and Tina	1966	10.00	20.00	40.00
❑ KST-538	Festival of Live Performances	1969	7.50	15.00	30.00
❑ KST-550	Please Please Please	1971	7.50	15.00	30.00
❑ K-5014 [M]	The Ike and Tina Turner Revue Live	1964	7.50	15.00	30.00
❑ K-5019 [M]	The Soul of Ike and Tina	1966	7.50	15.00	30.00
LIBERTY					
❑ LT-917	Airwaves	1981	2.00	4.00	8.00
❑ LST-7637	Come Together	1970	3.75	7.50	15.00
❑ LST-7650	Workin' Together	1970	3.75	7.50	15.00
❑ LO-51156	Get Back!	1985	2.50	5.00	10.00
LOMA					
❑ L 5904 [M]	Live! The Ike & Tina Turner Show Vol. 2	1966	6.25	12.50	25.00
❑ LS 5904 [S]	Live! The Ike & Tina Turner Show, Vol. 2	1966	7.50	15.00	30.00
—Reissue of Warner Bros. 1579?					
MINIT					
❑ 24018	In Person	1969	5.00	10.00	20.00
PHILLES					
❑ PHLP 4011 [M]	River Deep — Mountain High	1967	2000.	4000.	8000.
—Value is for record alone; covers were not printed					
PICKWICK					
❑ SPC-3284	Too Hot to Hold	197?	2.50	5.00	10.00
POMPEII					
❑ SD 6000	So Fine	1968	6.25	12.50	25.00
❑ SD 6004	Cussin', Cryin' and Carryin' On	1969	6.25	12.50	25.00
❑ SD 6006	Get It Together	1969	6.25	12.50	25.00
STRIPED HORSE					
❑ SHL-2001	Golden Empire	1986	2.50	5.00	10.00
SUE					
❑ LP 1038 [M]	The Greatest Hits of Ike and Tina Turner	1965	75.00	150.00	300.00
❑ LP 2001 [M]	The Soul of Ike and Tina Turner	1961	100.00	200.00	400.00
❑ LP 2003 [M]	Ike and Tina Turner's Kings of Rhythm Dance	1962	100.00	200.00	400.00
—Despite the title, this is an all-instrumental album (Tina's vocals do not appear)					
❑ LP 2004 [M]	Dynamite	1963	100.00	200.00	400.00
❑ LP 2005 [M]	Don't Play Me Cheap	1963	100.00	200.00	400.00
❑ LP 2007 [M]	It's Gonna Work Out Fine	1963	100.00	200.00	400.00
SUNSET					
❑ SUS-5265	The Fantastic Ike & Tina Turner	1969	3.75	7.50	15.00
❑ SUS-5286	Ike & Tima Turner's Greatest Hits	1969	3.75	7.50	15.00
UNART					
❑ S 21021	Greatest Hits	197?	2.50	5.00	10.00
UNITED ARTISTS					
❑ UA-LA064-G [(2)]	The World of Ike & Tina Live	1973	3.75	7.50	15.00
❑ UA-LA180-F	Nutbush City Limits	1973	3.00	6.00	12.00
❑ UA-LA203-G	The Gospel According to Ike & Tina Turner	1974	3.00	6.00	12.00
❑ UA-LA312-G	Sweet Rhode Island Red	1974	3.00	6.00	12.00
❑ UA-LA592-G	Greatest Hits	1976	3.00	6.00	12.00
❑ UA-LA707-G	Delilah's Power	1977	3.00	6.00	12.00
❑ UA-LA917-H	Airwaves	1978	3.00	6.00	12.00
❑ UAS-5530	'Nuff Said	1971	3.00	6.00	12.00
❑ UAS-5598	Feel Good	1972	3.00	6.00	12.00
❑ UAS-5660	Let Me Touch Your Mind	1972	3.00	6.00	12.00
❑ UAS-5667	Ike & Tina Turner's Greatest Hits	1972	3.00	6.00	12.00
❑ UAS-9953 [(2)]	Live at Carnegie Hall/What You Hear Is What You Get	1971	3.75	7.50	15.00
WARNER BROS.					
❑ W 1579 [M]	Live! The Ike & Tina Turner Show	1965	7.50	15.00	30.00
❑ WS 1579 [S]	Live! The Ike & Tina Turner Show	1965	10.00	20.00	40.00
❑ WS 1810	Ike & Tina Turner's Greatest Hits	1969	6.25	12.50	25.00

TURNER, JOE

Also known as "Big Joe Turner," these are by the R&B and blues singer.

Number	Title (A Side/B Side)	Yr	VG	VG+	NM
45s					
ATLANTIC					
❑ 939	Chains of Love/After My Laughter Came Tears	1951	125.00	250.00	500.00
❑ 949	The Chill Is On/Bump Miss Suzie	1951	200.00	400.00	800.00
❑ 960	Sweet Sixteen/I'll Never Stop Loving You	1952	30.00	60.00	120.00
❑ 970	Don't You Cry/Poor Lover's Blues	1952	25.00	50.00	100.00
❑ 982	Still in Love/Baby I Still Want You	1953	25.00	50.00	100.00
❑ 1001	Honey Hush/Crawdad Hole	1953	50.00	100.00	200.00
❑ 1016	TV Mama/Oke-She-Moke-She-Pop	1954	30.00	60.00	120.00
❑ 1026	Shake, Rattle, and Roll/You Know I Love You	1954	20.00	40.00	80.00
❑ 1040	Well All Right/Married Woman	1954	17.50	35.00	70.00
❑ 1053	Flip, Flop, and Fly/Ti-Ri-Lee	1955	12.50	25.00	50.00
❑ 1069	Hide and Seek/Midnight Cannonball	1955	12.50	25.00	50.00
❑ 1080	Morning, Noon and Night/The Chicken and the Hawk	1956	12.50	25.00	50.00
❑ 1088	Corinne, Corinna/Boogie Woogie Country Girl	1956	7.50	15.00	30.00
❑ 1100	Rock a While/Lipstick, Powder, and Paint	1956	7.50	15.00	30.00
❑ 1122	Midnight Special Train/Feeling Happy	1957	7.50	15.00	30.00
❑ 1131	Red Sails in the Sunset/After a While	1957	7.50	15.00	30.00
❑ 1146	Love Roller Coaster/A World of Trouble	1957	7.50	15.00	30.00
❑ 1155	I Need a Girl/Trouble in Mind	1957	7.50	15.00	30.00
❑ 1167	Teen-Age Letter/Wee Baby Blues	1957	7.50	15.00	30.00
❑ 1184	Blues in the Night/Jump for Joy	1958	7.50	15.00	30.00
❑ 2034	Got You On My Mind/Love, Oh Careless Love	1959	5.00	10.00	20.00
❑ 2044	Tomorrow Night/Honey Hush	1959	5.00	10.00	20.00
❑ 2054	Chains of Love/My Little Honey Dripper	1960	5.00	10.00	20.00
❑ 2072	My Reason for Living/Sweet Sue	1960	5.00	10.00	20.00
BAYOU					
❑ 015	The Blues Jumped the Rabbit/The Sun Is Shining	1951	75.00	150.00	300.00
BLUESTIME					
❑ 45001	Two Loves Have I/Shake, Rattle and Roll	195?	10.00	20.00	40.00
BLUESWAY					
❑ 61009	Big Wheel/Bluer Than Blue	1967	2.00	4.00	8.00
CORAL					
❑ 62408	I Walk a Lonely Mile/I'm Packin' Up	1964	3.75	7.50	15.00
❑ 62429	Shake, Rattle and Roll/There'll Be Some Tears Falling	1964	3.75	7.50	15.00
DECCA					
❑ 29711	Piney Brown Blues/I Got a Gal for Every Day of the Week	1955	10.00	20.00	40.00
❑ 29924	Corrine, Corrina/It's the Same Old Story	1956	10.00	20.00	40.00
KENT					
❑ 512	Love Ain't Nothin'/10-20-25-30	1969	—	3.00	6.00
❑ 4561	Chains of Love/Battle Hymn of the Republic	1971	—	3.00	6.00
❑ 4569	One Hour in Your Garden/You've Been Squeezin' My Lemons	1972	—	3.00	6.00
MGM					
❑ 10719	Moody Baby/Feeling So Sad	1951	75.00	150.00	300.00
OKEH					
❑ 6829	Cherry Red/Joe Turner Blues	1951	50.00	100.00	200.00
RONN					
❑ 28	Up on the Mountain/I Love You Baby	1969	—	3.00	6.00
❑ 35	Morning Glory/Night-Time Is the Right Time	1969	—	3.00	6.00
RPM					
❑ 345	Riding Blues/Playful Baby	1952	50.00	100.00	200.00
—With Pete Johnson					
78s					
ALADDIN					
❑ 3013	Morning Glory/Low Down Yog	1949	37.50	75.00	150.00
❑ 3070	Back Breaking Baby/Empty Pocket Blues	1950	30.00	60.00	120.00
ATLANTIC					
❑ 939	Chains of Love/After My Laughter Came Tears	1951	25.00	50.00	100.00
❑ 949	The Chill Is On/Bump Miss Suzie	1951	37.50	75.00	150.00
❑ 960	Sweet Sixteen/I'll Never Stop Loving You	1952	12.50	25.00	50.00
❑ 970	Don't You Cry/Poor Lover's Blues	1952	10.00	20.00	40.00
❑ 982	Still in Love/Baby I Still Want You	1953	10.00	20.00	40.00
❑ 1001	Honey Hush/Crawdad Hole	1953	12.50	25.00	50.00
❑ 1016	TV Mama/Oke-She-Moke-She-Pop	1954	12.50	25.00	50.00
❑ 1026	Shake, Rattle, and Roll/You Know I Love You	1954	10.00	20.00	40.00

Number	Title (A Side/B Side)	Yr	VG	VG+	NM
❑ 1040	Well All Right/Married Woman	1954	7.50	15.00	30.00
❑ 1053	Flip, Flop, and Fly/Ti-Ri-Lee	1955	7.50	15.00	30.00
❑ 1069	Hide and Seek/Midnight Cannonball	1955	6.25	12.50	25.00
❑ 1080	Morning, Noon and Night/The Chicken and the Hawk	1956	7.50	15.00	30.00
❑ 1088	Corinne, Corinna/Boogie Woogie Country Girl	1956	7.50	15.00	30.00
❑ 1100	Rock a While/Lipstick, Powder, and Paint	1956	7.50	15.00	30.00
❑ 1122	Midnight Special Train/Feeling Happy	1957	10.00	20.00	40.00
❑ 1131	Red Sails in the Sunset/After a While	1957	10.00	20.00	40.00
❑ 1146	Love Roller Coaster/A World of Trouble	1957	10.00	20.00	40.00
❑ 1155	I Need a Girl/Trouble in Mind	1957	10.00	20.00	40.00
❑ 1167	Teen-Age Letter/Wee Baby Blues	1957	10.00	20.00	40.00
❑ 1184	Blues in the Night/Jump for Joy	1958	12.50	25.00	50.00

BAYOU

❑ 015	The Blues Jumped the Rabbit/The Sun Is Shining	1951	7.50	15.00	30.00

COLONY

❑ 108	Little Bitty Baby/Midnight Rocking	1952	7.50	15.00	30.00

CORAL

❑ 65004	Blues on Central Avenue/Sun Risin' Blues	1948	6.25	12.50	25.00
—Reissue of Decca 7889					

DECCA

❑ 4093	Rocks in My Bed/Goin' to Chicago Blues	1942	7.50	15.00	30.00
❑ 7824	Doggin' the Dog/Rainy Day Blues	1941	10.00	20.00	40.00
❑ 7827	Jumpin' Down Blues/Careless Love	1941	10.00	20.00	40.00
❑ 7856	Somebody's Got to Go/Ice Man	1941	10.00	20.00	40.00
❑ 7868	Nobody in Mind/Chewed Up Grass	1941	10.00	20.00	40.00
❑ 7885	Blues in the Night/Cry Baby Blues	1942	7.50	15.00	30.00
❑ 7889	Blues on Central Avenue/Sun Risin' Blues	1942	7.50	15.00	30.00
❑ 48042	I Got a Gal for Every Day in the Week/Little Bitty Gal's Blues	1947	6.25	12.50	25.00

DOOTONE

❑ 305	I Love Ya, I Love Ya, I Love Ya/Richmond Blues	1952	30.00	60.00	120.00
—B-side by Betty Hall Jones Combo					

DOWN BEAT

❑ 151	Trouble Blues/Radar Blues	194?	7.50	15.00	30.00
—With Pete Johnson and His Orchestra					
❑ 152	Wine-O-Baby Boogie/B&O Boogie	194?	7.50	15.00	30.00
—With Pete Johnson and His Orchestra					
❑ 153	Christmas Date Boogie/Tell Me, Pretty Baby	194?	7.50	15.00	30.00
—With Pete Johnson and His Orchestra					
❑ 154	Old Piney Brown Is Gone/Baby Won't You Marry Me	194?	7.50	15.00	30.00
—With Pete Johnson and His Orchestra					
❑ 168	Skid Row Boogie/Half Tight Boogie	194?	7.50	15.00	30.00
—With Pete Johnson and His Orchestra					
❑ 175	Wrinkle Head Boogie/Roadhouse Boogie	194?	7.50	15.00	30.00
—With Pete Johnson and His Orchestra					

FIDELITY

❑ 3000	Life Is a Card Game/When the Rooster Crows	1951	7.50	15.00	30.00
❑ 3007	After Awhile You'll Be Sorry/Just a Travelin' Man	1952	7.50	15.00	30.00

FREEDOM

❑ 1531	Still in the Dark/(B-side unknown)	1950	7.50	15.00	30.00

IMPERIAL

❑ 5090	Story to Tell/Sumpin' Tonight	1950	7.50	15.00	30.00
❑ 5093	Lucille/Love My Baby	1950	7.50	15.00	30.00

MGM

❑ 10274	Mardi Gras Boogie/My Heart Belongs to You	1948	7.50	15.00	30.00
❑ 10321	Messin' Around/So Many Women Blues	1948	7.50	15.00	30.00
❑ 10397	Rainy Weather Blues/I Don't Dig It	1949	7.50	15.00	30.00
❑ 10719	Moody Baby/Feeling So Sad	1951	7.50	15.00	30.00

NATIONAL

❑ 4002	My Gal's a Jockey/I Got Love for Sale	1946	7.50	15.00	30.00
❑ 4009	Sunday Morning Blues/Mad Blues	1946	7.50	15.00	30.00
❑ 4011	Miss Brown Blues/I'm in Sharp When I Hit the Coast	194?	7.50	15.00	30.00
❑ 4016	Sally Zu-Zazz/Rock of Gibraltar	194?	7.50	15.00	30.00
❑ 4017	That's When It Really Hurts/Whistle Stop Blues	194?	7.50	15.00	30.00
❑ 9010	S.K.'s Blues - Part 1/Part 2	1945	7.50	15.00	30.00
❑ 9011	Johnson and Turner Blues/Watch That Jive	1945	7.50	15.00	30.00
❑ 9099	It's a Lowdown Dirty Shame/Nobody in Mind	1950	6.25	12.50	25.00
❑ 9100	Ooh Wee Baby Blues/Hollywood Bed	1950	6.25	12.50	25.00
❑ 9106	My Gal's a Jockey/I'm Still in the Dark	1950	6.25	12.50	25.00
❑ 9144	Rocks in My Bed/Howlin' Wind	1951	7.50	15.00	30.00

OKEH

❑ 6829	Cherry Red/Joe Turner Blues	1951	5.00	10.00	20.00

RPM

❑ 345	Riding Blues/Playful Baby	1952	15.00	30.00	60.00
—With Pete Johnson					

SWING TIME

❑ 269	Christmas Date Boogie/How Do You Want Your Rollin' Done	1951	6.25	12.50	25.00

VOCALION

❑ 04607	Goin' Away Blues/Roll Away Pete	1939	7.50	15.00	30.00
—With Pete Johnson					

7-Inch Extended Plays

ATLANTIC

❑ EP 536	(contents unknown)	1955	37.50	75.00	150.00
❑ EP 536 [PS]	Joe Turner Sings	1955	37.50	75.00	150.00
❑ EP 565	(contents unknown)	1956	37.50	75.00	150.00
❑ EP 565 [PS]	Joe Turner Sings	1956	37.50	75.00	150.00
❑ EP 586	*Corrine Corrina/The Chicken and the Hawk/ Feeling Happy/Hide and Seek	195?	37.50	75.00	150.00
❑ EP 586 [PS]	Joe Turner	195?	37.50	75.00	150.00

Number	Title (A Side/B Side)	Yr	VG	VG+	NM
❑ EP 606	*Crawdad Hole/The Chicken and the Hawk/ Boogie Woogie Country Girl/Midnight Special Train	195?	30.00	60.00	120.00
❑ EP 606 [PS]	Rock with Joe Turner	195?	30.00	60.00	120.00

EMARCY

❑ EP-1-6132	(contents unknown)	195?	25.00	50.00	100.00
❑ EP-1-6132 [PS]	Joe Turner	195?	25.00	50.00	100.00

Albums

ATCO

❑ SD 33-376	Joe Turner — His Greatest Recordings	1971	3.75	7.50	15.00

ATLANTIC

❑ 1234 [M]	The Boss of the Blues	1956	30.00	60.00	120.00
—Black label					
❑ 1234 [M]	The Boss of the Blues	1960	25.00	50.00	100.00
—White "bullseye" label					
❑ 1234 [M]	The Boss of the Blues	1961	10.00	20.00	40.00
—White "fan" logo on label					
❑ 1234 [M]	The Boss of the Blues	1963	3.75	7.50	15.00
—Black "fan" logo on label					
❑ SD 1234 [S]	The Boss of the Blues	1959	45.00	90.00	180.00
—Green label					
❑ SD 1234 [S]	The Boss of the Blues	1960	37.50	75.00	150.00
—White "bullseye" label					
❑ SD 1234 [S]	The Boss of the Blues	1961	12.50	25.00	50.00
—White "fan" logo on label					
❑ SD 1234 [S]	The Boss of the Blues	1963	5.00	10.00	20.00
—Black "fan" logo on label					
❑ 1332 [M]	Big Joe Rides Again	1959	37.50	75.00	150.00
—Black label					
❑ 1332 [M]	Big Joe Rides Again	1960	10.00	20.00	40.00
—White "fan" logo on label					
❑ 1332 [M]	Big Joe Rides Again	1963	3.75	7.50	15.00
—Black "fan" logo on label					
❑ SD 1332 [S]	Big Joe Rides Again	1959	50.00	100.00	200.00
—Green label					
❑ SD 1332 [S]	Big Joe Rides Again	1960	12.50	25.00	50.00
—White "fan" logo on label					
❑ SD 1332 [S]	Big Joe Rides Again	1963	5.00	10.00	20.00
—Black "fan" logo on label					
❑ 8005 [M]	Joe Turner	1957	37.50	75.00	150.00
—Black label					
❑ 8005 [M]	Joe Turner	1961	10.00	20.00	40.00
—White "fan" logo on label					
❑ 8005 [M]	Joe Turner	1963	3.75	7.50	15.00
—Black "fan" logo on label					
❑ 8023 [M]	Rockin' the Blues	1958	30.00	60.00	120.00
—Black label					
❑ 8023 [M]	Rockin' the Blues	1960	10.00	20.00	40.00
—White "fan" logo on label					
❑ 8023 [M]	Rockin' the Blues	1963	3.75	7.50	15.00
—Black "fan" logo on label					
❑ 8033 [M]	Big Joe Is Here	1959	30.00	60.00	120.00
—Black label					
❑ 8033 [M]	Big Joe Is Here	1960	25.00	50.00	100.00
—White "bullseye" label					
❑ 8033 [M]	Big Joe Is Here	1960	10.00	20.00	40.00
—White "fan" logo on label					
❑ 8033 [M]	Big Joe Is Here	1963	3.75	7.50	15.00
—Black "fan" logo on label					
❑ 8081 [M]	The Best of Joe Turner	1963	12.50	25.00	50.00
❑ SD 8812	Boss of the Blues	1981	2.50	5.00	10.00
—Reissue of 1234					
❑ 81752	Greatest Hits	1987	2.50	5.00	10.00

BLUES SPECTRUM

❑ BS-104	Great Rhythm and Blues Oldies Vol. 4	197?	3.75	7.50	15.00

BLUESTIME

❑ 9002 [M]	The Real Boss of the Blues	196?	10.00	20.00	40.00
❑ 29002 [S]	The Real Boss of the Blues	196?	7.50	15.00	30.00

BLUESWAY

❑ BL 6006 [M]	Singing the Blues	1967	5.00	10.00	20.00
❑ BLS-6006 [S]	Singing the Blues	1967	6.25	12.50	25.00
❑ S-6060	Roll 'Em	1973	3.75	7.50	15.00

DECCA

❑ DL 8044 [M]	Joe Turner Sings Kansas City Jazz	1953	62.50	125.00	250.00

FANTASY

❑ OJC-497	Trumpet Kings Meet Joe Turner	1991	3.00	6.00	12.00

INTERMEDIA

❑ QS-5008	Rock This Joint	198?	2.50	5.00	10.00
❑ QS-5026	The Very Best of Joe Turner — Live	198?	2.50	5.00	10.00
❑ QS-5030	The Blues Boss — Live	198?	2.50	5.00	10.00
❑ QS-5036	Everyday I Have the Blues	198?	2.50	5.00	10.00
❑ QS-5043	Roll Me Baby	198?	2.50	5.00	10.00

KENT

❑ KST-542	Joe Turner Turns On the Blues	1973	3.75	7.50	15.00

MCA

❑ 1325	Early Big Joe	198?	2.50	5.00	10.00

MUSE

❑ MR-5293	Blues Train	198?	2.50	5.00	10.00
—With Roomful of Blues and Dr. John					

PABLO

❑ 2310717	Trumpet Kings Meet Joe Turner	197?	3.00	6.00	12.00
❑ 2310760	Nobody in Mind	197?	3.00	6.00	12.00
❑ 2310776	In the Evening	197?	3.00	6.00	12.00
❑ 2310800	Things That I Used to Do	197?	3.00	6.00	12.00
❑ 2310818	Every Day I Have the Blues	198?	3.00	6.00	12.00

T

TURNER, JOE (2)

Number	Title (A Side/B Side)	Yr	VG	VG+	NM
❏ 2310848	The Best of Joe Turner	1980	3.00	6.00	12.00
❏ 2310863	Have No Fear, Joe Turner Is Here	1983	3.00	6.00	12.00
❏ 2310883	Singing the Same, Sad, Happy, Forever Blues	1983	3.00	6.00	12.00
❏ 2310913	Patcha, Patcha, All Night Long	198?	3.00	6.00	12.00
❏ 2310937	Flip, Flop and Fly	1989	3.00	6.00	12.00
❏ 2405404	The Best of "Big" Joe Turner	198?	3.00	6.00	12.00
SAVOY					
❏ MG-14012 [M]	Blues'll Make You Happy	1958	37.50	75.00	150.00
❏ MG-14106 [M]	Careless Love	1963	20.00	40.00	80.00
SAVOY JAZZ					
❏ SJC-406	Blues'll Make You Happy	1985	2.50	5.00	10.00
—Reissue of Savoy 14012					
❏ SJL-2223 [(2)]	Have No Fear	197?	3.75	7.50	15.00

TURNER, JOE (2)

Frequently confused with the above Joe Turner, this is the stride pianist.

Albums

Number	Title (A Side/B Side)	Yr	VG	VG+	NM
CHIAROSCURO					
❏ 147	King of Stride	1976	3.75	7.50	15.00
CLASSIC JAZZ					
❏ 138	Effervescent	1976	3.75	7.50	15.00
PABLO					
❏ 2310763	Another Epoch Stride Piano	197?	3.00	6.00	12.00

TURNER, SPYDER

45s

Number	Title (A Side/B Side)	Yr	VG	VG+	NM
KWANZA					
❏ 7688	Since I Don't Have You/Happy Days	1973	—	3.00	6.00
MGM					
❏ 13617	Stand By Me/You're Good Enough for Me	1966	2.50	5.00	10.00
❏ 13692	Don't Hold Back/I Can't Take It Anymore	1967	2.00	4.00	8.00
❏ 13739	For Your Precious Love/I Can't Wait to See My Baby's Face	1967	2.00	4.00	8.00
❏ 14263	I Can't Make It Anymore/I'm Alive with a Lovin' Feeling	1971	—	3.00	6.00
WHITFIELD					
❏ 8526	I've Been Waiting/Tomorrow's Only Yesterday	1978	—	2.00	4.00
❏ 8596	Get Down/Is It Love You're After	1978	—	2.00	4.00
❏ 49190	You're So Fine/Only Love	1980	—	2.00	4.00

Albums

Number	Title (A Side/B Side)	Yr	VG	VG+	NM
MGM					
❏ E-4450 [M]	Stand By Me	1967	6.25	12.50	25.00
❏ SE-4450 [S]	Stand By Me	1967	7.50	15.00	30.00
WHITFIELD					
❏ BSK 3124	Music Web	1978	2.50	5.00	10.00
❏ BSK 3397	Only Love	1979	2.50	5.00	10.00

TURNER, TINA

Also see IKE AND TINA TURNER.

12-Inch Singles

Number	Title (A Side/B Side)	Yr	VG	VG+	NM
CAPITOL					
❏ V-8579	Let's Stay Together (5:14)/I Wrote a Letter	1983	2.00	4.00	8.00
❏ V-8597	What's Love Got to Do with It/Rock 'n' Roll Widow	1984	2.00	4.00	8.00
❏ V-8609	Better Be Good to Me (7:40)/When I Was Young	1984	2.00	4.00	8.00
❏ V-8620	Private Dancer/Nutbush City Limits	1985	2.50	5.00	10.00
❏ V-8635	Show Some Respect (Remix 5:42)/Let's Pretend We're Married	1985	2.00	4.00	8.00
❏ V-8655	We Don't Need Another Hero/(Instrumental)	1985	2.00	4.00	8.00
❏ SPRO-9140 [DJ]	I Might Have Been Queen/Better Be Good to Me//Steel Claw/Private Dancer	1984	3.75	7.50	15.00
—With "legs" cover					
❏ SPRO-9146 [DJ]	What's Love Got to Do with It (LP Version 3:49) (same on both sides)	1984	3.00	6.00	12.00
❏ SPRO-9196 [DJ]	What's Love Got to Do with It (Extended) (same on both sides)	1984	3.00	6.00	12.00
❏ SPRO-9224/34 [DJ]	Better Be Good to Me (LP Version) (Single Version)	1985	2.50	5.00	10.00
❏ SPRO-9238 [DJ]	Better Be Good to Me (3 versions)	1985	2.50	5.00	10.00
❏ SPRO-9264 [DJ]	Better Be Good to Me (Live) (same on both sides)	1984	2.50	5.00	10.00
❏ SPRO-9425/6 [DJ]	We Don't Need Another Hero (Remix) (Instrumental)	1985	—	3.00	6.00
❏ SPRO-9493/4 [DJ]	One of the Living (Club Version) (Single Version)	1985	2.50	5.00	10.00
❏ SPRO-9826 [DJ]	Back Where You Started (same on both sides)	1986	2.00	4.00	8.00
❏ SPRO-9867 [DJ]	Overnight Sensation (same on both sides)	1987	2.50	5.00	10.00
❏ V-15205	One of the Living (Special Club Version) (Dub) (Instrumental)	1985	2.00	4.00	8.00
❏ V-15249	Typical Male (Dance Mix) (Single Version) (Dub Mix)/Don't Turn Around	1986	2.00	4.00	8.00
❏ V-15261	Two People (Dance Mix) (Dub Mix) (Single Mix)/Havin' a Party	1986	2.00	4.00	8.00
❏ V-15273	What You Get Is What You See (4 versions)	1987	2.00	4.00	8.00
❏ V-15296	Break Every Rule (3 versions)/Take Me to the River	1987	2.00	4.00	8.00
❏ V-15349	Afterglow (12" Vocal Dance Mix) (7" Mix) (Glowing Dub) (Tina's House Mix)	1987	—	3.50	7.00
❏ V-15543	Steamy Windows (Vocal Mix) (House Mix) (12" Dub Mix) (12" House Dub Mix)	1989	—	3.50	7.00
❏ SPRO-79168/92 [DJ]	Afterglow (4 versions)	1987	2.00	4.00	8.00
FANTASY					
❏ D-161	Party Vibes (8:11)/Shame, Shame, Shame (5:06)	1980	3.00	6.00	12.00

Number	Title (A Side/B Side)	Yr	VG	VG+	NM
VIRGIN					
❏ SPRO 11056 [DJ]	Goldeneye (Morales Club Mix 10:00) (LP Version 4:47)/(Morales 007 Dub 9:37) (Morales Dub of Bond 5:36)	1995	—	3.50	7.00
❏ SPRO-12716 [DJ]	On Silent Wings (Soul Solutions' Club Mix) (Instrumental) (Percappella) (Radio Edit)	1996	3.75	7.50	15.00
❏ SPRO 14918 [DJ]	When the Heartache Is Over (Hex Hector 12" Vocal Mix 8:45) (Hex Hector 7" Vocal Mix 3:30) (Hex Hector 12" Just Drums Mix 5:01)	1999	3.00	6.00	12.00
❏ SPRO 14951 [(2) DJ]	When the Heartache Is Over (Hex Hector 12" Vocal Mix 8:45) (Hex Hector 7" Vocal Mix 3:30) (Hex Hector 12" Instrumental 8:45) (Hex Hector Acapella 4:02) (Metro Mix 5:45) (7th District Mix 5:11) (Hex Hector 12" Just Drums Mix 5:01) (LP Version 3:46)	1999	5.00	10.00	20.00
❏ SPRO 14964 [DJ]	When the Heartache Is Over (Superchumbo Mix) (same on both sides)	1999	10.00	20.00	40.00
❏ Y-38578	In Your Wildest Dreams (Pink Noise Club Mix) (Deep Dish Paradise Mix) (Pleasant Instrumental) (Joe Extended Remix) (Antonio Banderas Crossover Mix) (Crossover Dub)	1996	2.50	5.00	10.00
—With Barry White					
❏ Y-38691	When the Heartache Is Over (Hex Hector 12" Vocal Mix 8:45) (Hex Hector 7" Vocal Mix 3:30) (Hex Hector 12" Instrumental 8:45) (Metro Mix 5:45) (7th District Mix 5:11) (Hex Hector Acapella 4:02)	1999	2.00	4.00	8.00

45s

Number	Title (A Side/B Side)	Yr	VG	VG+	NM
CAPITOL					
❏ B-5322	Let's Stay Together/I Wrote a Letter	1984	—	—	3.00
❏ B-5322 [PS]	Let's Stay Together/I Wrote a Letter	1984	—	2.50	5.00
❏ B-5354	What's Love Got to Do with It/Rock 'N' Roll Widow	1984	—	—	3.00
❏ B-5354 [PS]	What's Love Got to Do with It/Rock 'N' Roll Widow	1984	—	2.00	4.00
❏ B-5387	Better Be Good to Me/When I Was Young	1984	—	—	3.00
❏ B-5387 [PS]	Better Be Good to Me/When I Was Young	1984	—	2.00	4.00
❏ B-5433	Private Dancer/Nutbush City Limits	1984	—	—	3.00
❏ B-5433 [PS]	Private Dancer/Nutbush City Limits	1984	—	2.00	4.00
❏ B-5461	Show Some Respect/Let's Pretend We're Married	1985	—	—	3.00
❏ B-5461 [PS]	Show Some Respect/Let's Pretend We're Married	1985	—	2.00	4.00
❏ B-5491	We Don't Need Another Hero (Thunderdome)/(Instrumental)	1985	—	—	3.00
❏ B-5491 [PS]	We Don't Need Another Hero (Thunderdome)/(Instrumental)	1985	—	2.00	4.00
❏ B-5518	One of the Living/One of the Living (Dub)	1985	—	—	3.00
❏ B-5518 [PS]	One of the Living/One of the Living (Dub)	1985	—	2.00	4.00
❏ B-5615	Typical Male/Don't Turn Around	1986	—	—	3.00
❏ B-5615 [PS]	Typical Male/Don't Turn Around	1986	—	—	3.00
❏ B-5644	Two People/Havin' a Party	1986	—	—	3.00
❏ B-5644 [PS]	Two People/Havin' a Party	1986	—	—	3.00
❏ B-5668	What You Get Is What You See/What You Get Is What You See (Live)	1987	—	—	3.00
❏ B-5668 [PS]	What You Get Is What You See/What You Get Is What You See (Live)	1987	—	—	3.00
❏ B-44003	Break Every Rule/Take Me to the River	1987	—	—	3.00
❏ B-44003 [PS]	Break Every Rule/Take Me to the River	1987	—	—	3.00
❏ B-44111	Afterglow/(B-side unknown)	1987	—	2.00	4.00
❏ B-44442	The Best/Undercover Agent for the Blues	1989	—	—	3.00
❏ B-44442 [PS]	The Best/Undercover Agent for the Blues	1989	—	—	3.00
❏ B-44473	Steamy Windows/The Best	1989	—	—	3.00
❏ B-44473 [PS]	Steamy Windows/The Best	1989	—	—	3.00
❏ NR-44510	Look Me in the Heart/Stronger Than the Wind	1990	—	—	3.00
❏ S7-57702	Way of the World/You Know Who	1992	—	—	3.00
FANTASY					
❏ 948	Lean On Me/Shame, Shame, Shame	1984	—	2.00	4.00
POLYDOR					
❏ PRO-002 [DJ]	Acid Queen/Pinball Wizard	1975	10.00	20.00	40.00
—B-side by Elton John; promo-only					
POMPEII					
❏ 66682	Too Hot to Hold/You Got What You Wanted	1968	2.50	5.00	10.00
UNITED ARTISTS					
❏ XW 724	Whole Lotta Love/Rockin' 'N' Rollin'	1975	—	3.00	6.00
❏ XW 730	Delilah's Power/That's My Power	1975	—	3.00	6.00
❏ XW 920	Come Together/I Want to Take You Higher	1977	—	3.00	6.00
❏ XW 1265	Fire Down Below/Viva La Money	1979	—	2.50	5.00
VIRGIN					
❏ S7-17401	I Don't Wanna Fight/Tina's Wish	1993	—	—	3.00
❏ S7-17498	Why Must We Wait Until Tonight/Shake a Tail Feather	1993	—	—	3.00
❏ S7-18047	Proud Mary (Edit Live Version)/The Best (Live)	1994	—	2.50	5.00
—Red vinyl					
❏ S7-19217	Missing You/Do Something	1996	—	—	3.00
❏ 38691	When the Heartache Is Over/On Silent Wings	2000	—	—	3.00

Albums

Number	Title (A Side/B Side)	Yr	VG	VG+	NM
CAPITOL					
❏ 1P 8192 [(2)]	Simply the Best	1991	5.00	10.00	20.00
—Columbia House edition (only US vinyl version)					
❏ ST-12330	Private Dancer	1984	2.00	4.00	8.00
❏ PJ-12530	Break Every Rule	1986	2.00	4.00	8.00
❏ C1-90126 [(2)]	Tina Live in Europe	1988	3.00	6.00	12.00
❏ C1-91873	Foreign Affair	1989	2.00	4.00	8.00
FANTASY					
❏ MFP-4520 [EP]	Mini	1984	2.00	4.00	8.00

Number	Title (A Side/B Side)	Yr	VG	VG+	NM
SPRINGBOARD					
❏ SPB-4033	The Queen	1972	2.50	5.00	10.00
UNITED ARTISTS					
❏ UA-LA200-F	Tina Turns the Country On	1973	3.75	7.50	15.00
❏ UA-LA495-G	Acid Queen	1975	3.00	6.00	12.00
❏ UA-LA919-G	Rough	1978	3.00	6.00	12.00
WAGNER					
❏ 14108	Good Hearted Woman	1979	3.00	6.00	12.00

TURNER, TITUS
45s
Number	Title (A Side/B Side)	Yr	VG	VG+	NM
ATCO					
❏ 6310	Baby Girl (Part 1)/Baby Girl (Part 2)	1964	2.00	4.00	8.00
ATLANTIC					
❏ 1127	A-Knockin' at My Baby's Door/Hungry Man	1957	5.00	10.00	20.00
COLUMBIA					
❏ 42873	Young Wings Can Fly/Goodbye Rose	1963	2.50	5.00	10.00
❏ 42947	Make Someone Love You/I'm a Fool About My Mama	1964	2.50	5.00	10.00
ENJOY					
❏ 1005	People Sure Act Funny/My Darkest Hour	1962	2.50	5.00	10.00
❏ 1015	Soulville/My Darkest Hour	1963	2.50	5.00	10.00
❏ 2010	Bow Wow/I Love You Baby	1963	2.50	5.00	10.00
GLOVER					
❏ 201	We Told You Not to Marry/Taking Care of Business	1959	6.25	12.50	25.00
❏ 202	When the Sergeant Comes Marching Home/(B-side unknown)	1960	6.25	12.50	25.00
JAMIE					
❏ 1174	Sound-Off/Me and My Lonely Telephone	1960	3.75	7.50	15.00
❏ 1177	Pony Train/Bla, Bla, Cha Cha Cha	1961	3.00	6.00	12.00
❏ 1184	Hey Doll Baby/I Want a Steady Girl	1961	3.00	6.00	12.00
❏ 1189	Horsin' Around/Chances Go Around	1961	3.00	6.00	12.00
❏ 1202	Shake the Hand of a Fool/Beautiful Stranger	1961	3.00	6.00	12.00
❏ 1213	Walk on the Wild Twist/Twistin' Train	1962	2.50	5.00	10.00
JOSIE					
❏ 990	I Just Can't Keep It to Myself/People Sure Are Funny	1968	—	3.00	6.00
❏ 1012	His Funeral, My Trial/Do You Dig It	1969	—	3.00	6.00
KING					
❏ 5067	Have Mercy Baby/You Turned Lamps Too	1957	3.00	6.00	12.00
❏ 5095	Hold Your Loving/Stop the Rain	1957	3.00	6.00	12.00
❏ 5129	Follow Me/Way Down Yonder	1958	3.00	6.00	12.00
❏ 5140	Coralee/Tears of Joy Fill My Eyes	1958	3.00	6.00	12.00
❏ 5186	The Return of Staggolee/Answer Me	1959	3.00	6.00	12.00
❏ 5213 [M]	Tarzan/Fall Guy	1959	3.00	6.00	12.00
❏ S-5213 [S]	Tarzan/Fall Guy	1959	7.50	15.00	30.00
❏ 5243	Bonnie Baby/Miss Rubberneck Jones	1959	3.00	6.00	12.00
❏ 5465	Way Down Yonder/Miss Rubberneck Jones	1961	2.50	5.00	10.00
MURBO					
❏ 1001	Huckle Buckle Beanstalk/Hoop Hoop Hoop a Hoopa Doo	1965	2.00	4.00	8.00
OKEH					
❏ 6844	Same Old Feeling/Don't Take Everybody to Be Your Friend	1951	7.50	15.00	30.00
❏ 6883	What'cha Gonna Do for Me/Got So Much Trouble	1952	6.25	12.50	25.00
❏ 6907	Jambalaya/Please Baby	1952	6.25	12.50	25.00
❏ 6929	Christmas Morning/Be Sure You Know	1952	7.50	15.00	30.00
❏ 6938	My Plea/It's Too Late Now	1953	6.25	12.50	25.00
❏ 6961	Big Mary's/Living in Misery	1953	6.25	12.50	25.00
❏ 7027	Over the Rainbow/My Lonely Room	1954	6.25	12.50	25.00
❏ 7038	Hello Stranger/Devilish Woman	1954	6.25	12.50	25.00
❏ 7244	Eye to Eye/What Kinda Deal Is This	1966	2.00	4.00	8.00
PHILIPS					
❏ 40445	(I'm Afraid the) Masquerade Is Over/Mary Mack	1967	2.00	4.00	8.00
WING					
❏ 90006	All Around the World/Do You Know	1955	5.00	10.00	20.00
❏ 90033	Sweet and Low/Big John	1955	5.00	10.00	20.00
❏ 90058	Get on the Right Track, Baby/I'll Wait Forever	1956	5.00	10.00	20.00
Albums					
JAMIE					
❏ JLP-3018 [M]	Sound Off	1961	5.00	10.00	20.00
❏ JLPS-3018 [S]	Sound Off	1961	7.50	15.00	30.00

TWILIGHTERS, THE (1)
45s
Number	Title (A Side/B Side)	Yr	VG	VG+	NM
BELL					
❏ 624	Be Faithful/Thumper	1965	5.00	10.00	20.00

TWILIGHTERS, THE (2)
45s
Number	Title (A Side/B Side)	Yr	VG	VG+	NM
BUBBLE					
❏ 1334	My Silent Prayer/Little Bitty Bed Bug	1962	10.00	20.00	40.00
CHESS					
❏ 1803	Scratchin'/Tears	1961	6.25	12.50	25.00
CHOLLY					
❏ 712	Let There Be Love/Eternally	1957	250.00	500.00	1000.
DOT					
❏ 15526	Eternally/I Believe	1957	10.00	20.00	40.00
EBB					
❏ 117	Pride and Joy/Live Like a King	1957	10.00	20.00	40.00
ELDO					
❏ 115	Nothin'/Do You Believe	1961	6.25	12.50	25.00

Number	Title (A Side/B Side)	Yr	VG	VG+	NM
IMPERIAL					
❏ 66201	Shake a Tail Feather/Road to Fortune	1966	3.00	6.00	12.00
❏ 66238	I Still Love You/Meat Ball	1967	3.00	6.00	12.00
JVB					
❏ 83	How Many Times/Water-Water	1957	200.00	400.00	800.00
MGM					
❏ 55011	Little Did I Dream/Gotta Get On the Train	1955	75.00	150.00	300.00
❏ 55014	Lovely Lady/Half Angel	1955	100.00	200.00	400.00
PICO					
❏ 2801	Eternally/I Believe	1957	20.00	40.00	80.00

TWILIGHTERS, THE (3)
45s
Number	Title (A Side/B Side)	Yr	VG	VG+	NM
CADDY					
❏ 103	Eternally/I Believe	1955	62.50	125.00	250.00

TWILIGHTERS, THE (4)
45s
Number	Title (A Side/B Side)	Yr	VG	VG+	NM
FRATERNITY					
❏ 889	To Love in Vain/The Beginning of Love	1961	6.25	12.50	25.00
—As "The Twi-Lighters"					

TWILIGHTERS, THE (5)
45s
Number	Title (A Side/B Side)	Yr	VG	VG+	NM
MARSHALL					
❏ 702	Please Tell Me You're Mine/Wondering	1953	50.00	100.00	200.00
—Black vinyl					
❏ 702	Please Tell Me You're Mine/Wondering	1953	250.00	500.00	1000.
—Red vinyl					

TWILIGHTERS, THE (6)
45s
Number	Title (A Side/B Side)	Yr	VG	VG+	NM
SPECIALTY					
❏ 548	It's True/Wha-Bop-Sh-Wah	1955	15.00	30.00	60.00

TWILIGHTERS, THE (7)
45s
Number	Title (A Side/B Side)	Yr	VG	VG+	NM
SPIN					
❏ 0001	Yes You Are/A Possibility	1960	50.00	100.00	200.00

TWILIGHTERS, THE (U)
45s
Number	Title (A Side/B Side)	Yr	VG	VG+	NM
GROOVE					
❏ 0154	Sittin' in a Corner/It's a Cold, Cold, Rainy Day	1956	15.00	30.00	60.00
—As "The Twi-Lighters"					
RICKI					
❏ 907	Help Me/Rockin' Mule	1961	10.00	20.00	40.00
SARA					
❏ 1048	Restless Love/Can't You Stay a Little Longer	1961	15.00	30.00	60.00
VANCO					
❏ 204	Out of My Mind/I Need Your Lovin'	1968	2.50	5.00	10.00

TWISTERS, THE
45s
Number	Title (A Side/B Side)	Yr	VG	VG+	NM
APT					
❏ 25045	Come Go with Me/Pretty Little Girl Next Door	1960	5.00	10.00	20.00
CAMPUS					
❏ 125	Elvis Leaves Sorrento/Street Dance	1961	7.50	15.00	30.00
CAPITOL					
❏ 4451	Turn the Page/Dancing Little Clown	1960	5.00	10.00	20.00
DUAL					
❏ 502	Silly Chilli/Peppermint Twist Time	1962	3.00	6.00	12.00
FELCO					
❏ 103	Count Down 1-2-3/Speed Limit	1959	6.25	12.50	25.00
SUN-SET					
❏ 501	Please Come Back/This Is the End	1961	150.00	300.00	600.00

TWISTIN' KINGS
45s
Number	Title (A Side/B Side)	Yr	VG	VG+	NM
MOTOWN					
❏ 1022	Xmas Twist/White House Twist	1961	10.00	20.00	40.00
❏ 1023	Congo (Part 1)/Congo (Part 2)	1962	10.00	20.00	40.00
Albums					
MOTOWN					
❏ M-601 [M]	Twistin' the World Around	1961	75.00	150.00	300.00

2 LIVE CREW, THE
Includes "Luke Featuring The 2 Live Crew" and "The New 2 Live Crew." Also see LUKE.
12-Inch Singles
Number	Title (A Side/B Side)	Yr	VG	VG+	NM
FRESH BEAT					
❏ FBR-001	The Revelation/2 Live "It's Gotta Be Fresh!"	1985	12.50	25.00	50.00
❏ FBR-002	What I Like (unknown versions)	1985	12.50	25.00	50.00
LIL' JOE					
❏ LJR 890	Shake a Lil' Somethin' (4 versions)	1996	—	3.50	7.00
❏ LJRX 891	Shake a Lil' Somethin' (7 versions)	1996	2.50	5.00	10.00
❏ LJR 893	Do the Wild Thing (4 versions)/(same on both sides)	1997	—	3.00	6.00
❏ LJR 893	Do the Damn Thing (4 versions)/You Should Be Dancing (Clean)/Puff Puff Give (Clean)/Stallion Strip (Clean)	1997	—	3.00	6.00

T

Number	Title (A Side/B Side)	Yr	VG	VG+	NM
❑ LJR 895	Be My Private Dancer (Radio Version) (Album Version (Accapella For You Mix) (Instrumental)/ Table Dance (Radio Version) (Album Version) (Accapella For You Mix) (Instrumental)	1997	2.00	4.00	8.00
❑ LJR 897	2 Live Party (7 versions)	1998	—	3.00	6.00
❑ LJR 899	The Real One (Explicit Version) (Clean Remix) (Extra Clean Version) (Instrumental)/ Shake Your Pants (Explicit) (Clean) (Instrumental)/ Album Snippets	1998	—	3.00	6.00
—As "The 2 Live Crew Featuring Ice-T"					
❑ LJR 902	2 Live Is Here (4 versions)/Ay Papi (4 versions)	1999	2.50	5.00	10.00
LUKE					
❑ GR 462	We Like to Chill (2 versions)/Greatest Hits Megamix	1993	—	3.00	6.00
❑ GR 476	Yeah, Yeah (4 versions)/Hell, Yeah (4 versions)	1994	—	3.50	7.00
—As "The New 2 Live Crew"					
❑ GR 481	You Go, Girl (10 versions)	1994	2.50	5.00	10.00
—As "The New 2 Live Crew"					
❑ GR 483	2 Live Freestyle (4 versions)	1994	—	3.00	6.00
—As "The New 2 Live Crew"					
❑ DMD 1671 [DJ]	Hangin' with the Homeboys and Dr. Feelgood (2 versions)/Vacate the Premises	1991	—	3.00	6.00
—As "2 Live Crew & Triple XXX"; with Vince Neil					
❑ DMD 1716 [DJ]	Pop That Pussy (4 versions)	1991	—	3.50	7.00
❑ DMD 1773 [DJ]	Who's Doin' Who (Clean Version) (X Rated Version)/The Caper	1991	2.50	5.00	10.00
❑ PR 3484 [DJ]	Banned in the U.S.A. (Radio Mix) (Radio Instrumental) (Black Mix) (Percapella)	1990	2.00	4.00	8.00
—As "Luke Featuring the 2 Live Crew"					
❑ PR 4389 [DJ]	Who's Doin' Who (same on both sides?)	1991	2.50	5.00	10.00
—As "Luke Featuring the 2 Live Crew"					
❑ 96216	Who's Doin' Who (2 versions)/The Caper	1991	2.50	5.00	10.00
❑ 96291	Pop That Pussy (LP Version Explicit)/Pop That Coochie (Clean) (Remix)/Mega Mix V	1991	—	3.00	6.00
❑ 96398	Do the Bart (Clean LP) (Clean Remix) (Explicit)/ Face Down A— Up/Face Down A—Up (Live in Concert)	1990	2.50	5.00	10.00
—As "Luke Featuring The 2 Live Crew"					
❑ 96416	Mama Juanita (5 versions)	1990	2.50	5.00	10.00
—As "Luke Featuring The 2 Live Crew"					
❑ 96440	Banned in the U.S.A. (Radio Mix) (Radio Instrumental) (Black Mix) (Percapella)	1990	2.50	5.00	10.00
—As "Luke Featuring The 2 Live Crew"					
LUKE SKYYWALKER					
❑ GR 105	Get It Girl (2 versions)/Cut It Up	1988	3.75	7.50	15.00
❑ GR 112	Move Somethin' (Clean Version) (XXX-Rated Mix)	1988	3.75	7.50	15.00
❑ GR 113	We Want Some P*ssy (3 versions)	1988	3.75	7.50	15.00
❑ GR 117	Do Wah Diddy (Remix Radio)/I Can't Go for That	1988	2.00	4.00	8.00
❑ GR 125	The Bomb Has Dropped/One and One	1989	3.00	6.00	12.00
—With Trouble Funk					
❑ GR 127	Me So Horny (Clean Version) (Nasty Version)/ Get the F**k Out of My House (Nasty Acid Mix) (Nasty Piano Mix) (Nasty LP Version)	1989	3.00	6.00	12.00
❑ GR 133	We Want Some Pussy ('89 House Mix 6:34) (Classic Dance Mix 2:53) (Liberty City Long Hard Mix 6:40) (Live In Concert Version 3:00)	1990	3.75	7.50	15.00
MACOLA					
❑ MRC-1014	The Revelation/What I Like	1985	7.50	15.00	30.00
SKYYWALKER					
❑ GR 137	C'mon Babe (Radio Mix) (Extended Bass Mix) (Doodoo Brown Mix)/If You Believe In Having Sex	1990	2.50	5.00	10.00
❑ GR 144	European Ultimix (10:32)/The Funk Shop (Radio)/The F*ck Shop (Nasty)	1990	3.00	6.00	12.00
WTG					
❑ PAS 1462 [DJ]	Yakety Yak (Dirty House Mix) (7" Radio Mix) (House Version) (Street Mix) (Bass Mix) (Bonus Beats)	1988	2.00	4.00	8.00
❑ 45-68168	Yakety Yak (Bass Mix) (Dirty House Mix) (House Version) (7" Radio Mix)	1988	2.50	5.00	10.00
45s					
LUKE					
❑ 98915	Banned in the U.S.A./(Instrumental)	1990	—	2.50	5.00
—As "Luke Featuring The 2 Live Crew"					
LUKE SKYYWALKER					
❑ LS-104 [DJ]	Move Somethin'/(Dirty Version)	1988	2.50	5.00	10.00
❑ LS-110 [DJ]	The Bomb Has Dropped (same on both sides)	1989	2.50	5.00	10.00
❑ LS-113 [DJ]	Me So Horny (same on both sides)	1989	3.75	7.50	15.00
WTG					
❑ 31-68491	Yakety Yak/(B-side unknown)	1988	—	2.00	4.00
Albums					
EFFECT					
❑ E 3003	Live in Concert	1990	2.50	5.00	10.00
LIL' JOE					
❑ XR-215 [(2)]	Shake a Lil' Somethin'	1996	3.75	7.50	15.00
❑ XR-227 [(2)]	The 2 Live Crew Goes to the Movies — A Decade of Hits	1997	3.00	6.00	12.00
❑ XR-231 [(2)]	The Real One	1998	3.00	6.00	12.00
❑ XR-238 [(2)]	Greatest Hits Vol. 2	1999	3.75	7.50	15.00
❑ XR- 239 [(2)]	Greatest Hits Vol. 2/Edit	1999	3.75	7.50	15.00
❑ 264 [(2)]	Private Personal Parts	2000	3.00	6.00	12.00
❑ 286 [(2)]	Essential DJ 12" and Mega Mixes	2002	2.50	5.00	10.00
LUKE					
❑ 122 [(2)]	Greatest Hits	1992	5.00	10.00	20.00

Number	Title (A Side/B Side)	Yr	VG	VG+	NM
❑ 123 [(2)]	Greatest Hits/Edit	1992	5.00	10.00	20.00
❑ 207 [(2)]	Back at Your Ass for the Nine-4	1994	5.00	10.00	20.00
—As "The New 2 Live Crew"					
❑ 208 [(2)]	Back At You for '94	1994	5.00	10.00	20.00
—As "The New 2 Live Crew"; edited version					
❑ DMD 1760 [(2)]	Sports Weekend (As Nasty As They Wanna Be Part II)	1991	3.75	7.50	15.00
—Promo-only vinyl issue in generic black cardboard sleeve					
❑ 91424	Banned in the U.S.A.	1990	3.75	7.50	15.00
—As "Luke Featuring The 2 Live Crew"					
LUKE SKYYWALKER					
❑ XR-100	The 2 Live Crew "Is What We Are"	1987	3.75	7.50	15.00
❑ XR-101	Move Somethin'	1988	3.00	6.00	12.00
❑ XR-107 [(2)]	As Nasty As They Wanna Be	1989	3.75	7.50	15.00
❑ XR- 108	As Clean As They Wanna Be	1989	3.75	7.50	15.00

2PAC

The below features a highly incomplete list of his 12-inch singles; more information is appreciated!

Number	Title (A Side/B Side)	Yr	VG	VG+	NM
12-Inch Singles					
INTERSCOPE					
❑ INT8P-6489 [DJ]	Changes (unknown versions)	1998	2.00	4.00	8.00
❑ INT8P-6508 [DJ]	God Bless the Dead (LP Version)/Troublesome '96 (LP Version)//God Bless the Dead (Clean Version)/Troublesome '96 (Clean Version)	1999	2.50	5.00	10.00
Albums					
AMARU/JIVE					
❑ 41628 [(3)]	R U Still Down? (Remember Me)	1997	6.25	12.50	25.00
DEATH ROW					
❑ 63008 [(4)]	All Eyez on Me	2001	5.00	10.00	20.00
—Reissue					
❑ 63012 [(2)]	The Don Killuminati — The 7 Day Theory	2001	3.75	7.50	15.00
—As "Makaveli"; reissue					
DEATH ROW/INTERSCOPE					
❑ INT2-90039 [(2)]	The Don Killuminati — The 7 Day Theory	1996	3.75	7.50	15.00
—As "Makaveli"					
❑ INT4-90301 [(4)]	Greatest Hits	1998	7.50	15.00	30.00
❑ 490413-1 [(2)]	Still I Rise	1999	3.75	7.50	15.00
—As "2Pac + Outlawz"					
❑ 490840-1 [(4)]	Until the End of Time	2001	7.50	15.00	30.00
❑ 524204-1 [(4)]	All Eyez on Me	1996	7.50	15.00	30.00
INTERSCOPE					
❑ 91767	2Pacalypse Now	1991	3.75	7.50	15.00
❑ 92399 [(2)]	Me Against the World	1995	5.00	10.00	20.00
RESTLESS					
❑ 72737 [(2)]	Strictly 4 My N.I.G.G.A.Z.	1998	3.75	7.50	15.00
—Vinyl reissue of 1993 album (we can't prove or disprove the existence of the original Interscope edition on vinyl)					

TYLER, WILLIE, AND LESTER

Number	Title (A Side/B Side)	Yr	VG	VG+	NM
Albums					
TAMLA					
❑ TM-265 [M]	Hello Dummy	1965	50.00	100.00	200.00

TYMES, THE

Number	Title (A Side/B Side)	Yr	VG	VG+	NM
12-Inch Singles					
RCA					
❑ PD-11068	How Am I to Know/I'll Take You There	1977	3.00	6.00	12.00
45s					
CAPITOL					
❑ 3440	When I Look Around Me/Smile a Tender Smile	1972	—	3.00	6.00
COLUMBIA					
❑ 44630	People/For Love of Ivy	1968	2.00	4.00	8.00
❑ 44799	God Bless the Child/The Love That You're Looking For	1969	—	3.00	6.00
❑ 44917	Find My Way/If You Love Me Baby	1969	—	3.00	6.00
❑ 45078	Love Child/Most Beautiful Married Lady	1970	—	3.00	6.00
❑ 45336	She's Gone/Someone to Watch Over Me	1971	—	3.00	6.00
MGM					
❑ 13536	Pretend/Street Talk	1966	5.00	10.00	20.00
❑ 13631	(Touch of) Baby/What Would I Do	1966	5.00	10.00	20.00
PARKWAY					
❑ 871	So in Love/Roscoe James McClain	1963	6.25	12.50	25.00
—Original title of A-side					
❑ 871	So Much in Love/Roscoe James McClain	1963	3.75	7.50	15.00
❑ 871 [PS]	So Much in Love/Roscoe James McClain	1963	7.50	15.00	30.00
❑ 884	Wonderful! Wonderful!/Come with Me to the Sea	1963	3.75	7.50	15.00
❑ 884 [PS]	Wonderful! Wonderful!/Come with Me to the Sea	1963	6.25	12.50	25.00
❑ 891	Somewhere/View from My Window	1963	3.75	7.50	15.00
❑ 891 [PS]	Somewhere/View from My Window	1963	6.25	12.50	25.00
❑ 908	To Each His Own/Wonderland By Night	1964	3.75	7.50	15.00
❑ 908 [PS]	To Each His Own/Wonderland By Night	1964	6.25	12.50	25.00
❑ 919	The Magic of Our Summer Love/With All My Heart	1964	3.75	7.50	15.00
❑ 919 [PS]	The Magic of Our Summer Love/With All My Heart	1964	6.25	12.50	25.00
❑ 924	Here She Comes/Malibu	1964	3.75	7.50	15.00
❑ 924 [PS]	Here She Comes/Malibu	1964	6.25	12.50	25.00
❑ 933	The Twelfth of Never/Here She Comes	1964	3.75	7.50	15.00
❑ 7039	Isle of Love/I'm Always Chasing Rainbows	1964	3.75	7.50	15.00
—Included as a bonus with album 7039					
RCA					
❑ PB-10862	Love's Illusion/Savannah Sunny Sunday	1976	—	2.00	4.00
❑ PB-11136	I'll Take You There/How Am I to Know (The Things a Girl in Love Should Know)	1977	—	2.00	4.00
❑ GB-12082	You Little Trustmaker/Ms. Grace	1980	—	—	—
—Unreleased?					

Carla Thomas' first hit, "Gee Whiz," was a hit on Atlantic. But it originally was issued on Satellite, which at the time had poor distribution outside Memphis. Satellite would later become known as Stax.

Rufus Thomas, father of Carla, had his first R&B hit in 1953 with "Bear Cat." This is one of the two variations of this rare Sun 45; other copies loudly proclaim this to be "The Answer to 'Hound Dog'."

"This Won't Change," a very obscure record by Lester Tipton, is highly sought after by collectors of Northern Soul and fetches high prices when it does come up for sale, which is not very often.

When it was first issued, the Toys' hit single "A Lover's Concerto" appeared on the DynoVox label. The name was quickly changed to DynoVoice.

This is one of the highly collectible early albums by Ike and Tina Turner on the Sue label. This album contains several of their biggest early hits, including "A Fool in Love" and "It's Gonna Work Out Fine."

Here's something you don't see too often – a copy of the Tymes' Parkway album *Somewhere* with the bonus 45 still with the package.

Number	Title (A Side/B Side)	Yr	VG	VG+	NM

RCA VICTOR

Number	Title (A Side/B Side)	Yr	VG	VG+	NM
❏ PB-10022	You Little Trustmaker/The North Hills	1974	—	2.50	5.00
❏ PB-10128	Ms. Grace/The Crutch	1974	—	2.00	4.00
❏ PB-10244	Interloop/Someday, Somehow I'm Keeping You	1975	—	2.00	4.00
❏ PB-10422	God's Gonna Punish You/If I Can't Make You Smile	1975	—	2.00	4.00
❏ GB-10493	You Little Trustmaker/The North Hills	1975	—	2.00	4.00

—Gold Standard Series

Number	Title (A Side/B Side)	Yr	VG	VG+	NM
❏ PB-10561	Good Morning Dear Lord/It's Cool	1976	—	2.00	4.00
❏ PB-10713	Goin' Through the Motions/Only Your Love	1976	—	2.00	4.00

WINCHESTER

Number	Title (A Side/B Side)	Yr	VG	VG+	NM
❏ 1002	These Foolish Things (Remind Me of You)/This Time It's Love	1967	2.50	5.00	10.00

Albums

ABKCO

Number	Title (A Side/B Side)	Yr	VG	VG+	NM
❏ 4228	The Best of Tymes	1973	3.00	6.00	12.00

COLUMBIA

Number	Title (A Side/B Side)	Yr	VG	VG+	NM
❏ CS 9778	People	1969	3.75	7.50	15.00

PARKWAY

Number	Title (A Side/B Side)	Yr	VG	VG+	NM
❏ P 7032 [M]	So Much in Love	1963	10.00	20.00	40.00

—With group standing in front-cover photo

Number	Title (A Side/B Side)	Yr	VG	VG+	NM
❏ P 7032 [M]	So Much in Love	1963	50.00	100.00	200.00

—With head-and-shoulders group photo on front cover

Number	Title (A Side/B Side)	Yr	VG	VG+	NM
❏ P 7038 [M]	The Sound of the Wonderful Tymes	1963	10.00	20.00	40.00
❏ SP 7038 [S]	The Sound of the Wonderful Tymes	1963	12.50	25.00	50.00
❏ P 7039 [M]	Somewhere	1964	12.50	25.00	50.00

—Includes bonus single 7039 (deduct 20 percent if missing)

Number	Title (A Side/B Side)	Yr	VG	VG+	NM
❏ P 7049 [M]	18 Greatest Hits	1964	10.00	20.00	40.00

RCA VICTOR

Number	Title (A Side/B Side)	Yr	VG	VG+	NM
❏ APL1-0727	Trustmaker	1974	3.00	6.00	12.00
❏ APL1-1835	Turning Point	1976	3.00	6.00	12.00
❏ APL1-2406	Diggin' Their Roots	1977	3.00	6.00	12.00

TYRELL, DANNY, AND THE CLEESHAYS
45s

EASTMAN

Number	Title (A Side/B Side)	Yr	VG	VG+	NM
❏ 784	You're Only Seventeen/Let's Walk, Let's Talk	1958	10.00	20.00	40.00

TYSON, ROY
45s

DOUBLE L

Number	Title (A Side/B Side)	Yr	VG	VG+	NM
❏ 723	Oh What a Night for Love/Not Too Young	1963	20.00	40.00	80.00
❏ 733	The Girl I Love/I Want to Be Your Boyfriend	1964	25.00	50.00	100.00

Number	Title (A Side/B Side)	Yr	VG	VG+	NM

U

U-KREW, THE
12-Inch Singles

ENIGMA

Number	Title (A Side/B Side)	Yr	VG	VG+	NM
❏ 75521	If U Were Mine (Extended) (Radio Edit) (Bonus Beats)/Rock That Shit	1989	2.00	4.00	8.00
❏ 75541	Let Me Be Your Lover (6 versions)	1990	2.00	4.00	8.00

Albums

ENIGMA

Number	Title (A Side/B Side)	Yr	VG	VG+	NM
❏ 7 73524 1	The U-Krew	1990	3.75	7.50	15.00

U.N.V.
12-Inch Singles

MAVERICK

Number	Title (A Side/B Side)	Yr	VG	VG+	NM
❏ PRO-A-6071 [DJ]	Something's Goin' On (Album Version) (Radio Edit)	1993	3.75	7.50	15.00

45s

MAVERICK

Number	Title (A Side/B Side)	Yr	VG	VG+	NM
❏ 7-18353	Straight from My Heart/Something's Goin' On	1993	—	2.00	4.00
❏ 7-18564	Something's Goin' On/Flipside	1993	—	2.00	4.00

ULTRAMAGNETIC MC'S, THE
12-Inch Singles

MERCURY

Number	Title (A Side/B Side)	Yr	VG	VG+	NM
❏ 866131-1	Make It Happen/(Instrumental)//A Chorus Line Pt 2/Make It Happen (Remix)	1991	5.00	10.00	20.00
❏ 866733-1	Poppa Large (East Coast Mix) (East Coast Instrumental) (West Coast Mix) (West Coast Instrumental) (East Coast Acappella)	1992	5.00	10.00	20.00

NEXT PLATEAU

Number	Title (A Side/B Side)	Yr	VG	VG+	NM
❏ 50051	Ego Trippin'/Ego Bits//Funky Potion/Funky Extension	1986	12.50	25.00	50.00
❏ 50058	Traveling at the Speed of Thought/Traveling Dub//M.C.'s Ultra (Part II)/B-Boy Bonus Break	1987	10.00	20.00	40.00
❏ 50069	Mentally Mad (Vocal) (Instrumental)/Funky (Vocal) (Instrumental)	1987	10.00	20.00	40.00
❏ 50079	Watch Me Now (Vocal) (Instrumental)/Feelin' It (Vocal) (Instrumental)	1988	7.50	15.00	30.00
❏ 50087	Ease Back (Vocal) (Instrumental)/Kool Keith Housing Things (Vocal) (Instrumental)	1988	7.50	15.00	30.00
❏ 50091	Give the Drummer Some (Vocal Remix) (LP Version) (Bonus Beats)/Moe Love's Theme (Vocal Remix) (LP Version) (Bonus Beats)	1989	6.25	12.50	25.00
❏ 50103	Traveling at the Speed of Thought (Hip-House Club Mix) (Radio) (Hip-House Instrumental) (Radio Instrumental)/A Chorus Line (Vocal) (Instrumental)/Traveling at the Speed of Thought (LP Version)	1989	6.25	12.50	25.00

TUFF CITY

Number	Title (A Side/B Side)	Yr	VG	VG+	NM
❏ 8083	I'm F**kin' Flippin'/New York What Is Funky/Ya Not That Large	1994	2.50	5.00	10.00
❏ 8088	Watch Your Back//Message/Delta Force	1996	2.50	5.00	10.00

WILD PITCH

Number	Title (A Side/B Side)	Yr	VG	VG+	NM
❏ V-56277	Two Brothers with Checks (San Francisco, Harvey) (LP Version) (Radio Version) (Instrumental)/One Two, One Two (LP Version) (Instrumental)	1993	7.50	15.00	30.00
❏ Y-58056	Raise It Up (LP Version) (Remix) (Instrumental)/The Saga of Dandy, the Devil and Day (Remix) (LP Version) (Instrumental) (Acappella)	1993	10.00	20.00	40.00

Albums

MERCURY

Number	Title (A Side/B Side)	Yr	VG	VG+	NM
❏ 510893-1	Funk Your Head Up	1991	5.00	10.00	20.00

NEXT PLATEAU

Number	Title (A Side/B Side)	Yr	VG	VG+	NM
❏ 1013 [(2)]	Critical Beatdown	1988	6.25	12.50	25.00
❏ 5482 [(2)]	B-Sides Companion	1997	3.75	7.50	15.00
❏ 5496 [(2)]	Critical Beatdown	199?	3.00	6.00	12.00

—Reissue

TUFF CITY

Number	Title (A Side/B Side)	Yr	VG	VG+	NM
❏ 618	The Basement Tapes 1984-1990	1994	3.75	7.50	15.00

—Compilation of older material

Number	Title (A Side/B Side)	Yr	VG	VG+	NM
❏ 624	Smack My Bitch Up	1998	5.00	10.00	20.00

—Compilation of older material

Number	Title (A Side/B Side)	Yr	VG	VG+	NM
❏ 4021	New York What Is Funky	1996	3.75	7.50	15.00

—Compilation of older material

Number	Title (A Side/B Side)	Yr	VG	VG+	NM
❏ 4023	Mo Love's Basement Tapes	1996	3.75	7.50	15.00

—Compilation of older material

WILD PITCH

Number	Title (A Side/B Side)	Yr	VG	VG+	NM
❏ WP 2010 [(2)]	The Four Horsemen	199?	3.75	7.50	15.00

—Reissue

Number	Title (A Side/B Side)	Yr	VG	VG+	NM
❏ E1-89917 [(2)]	The Four Horsemen	1993	5.00	10.00	20.00

UNDERGROUND KINGZ
12-Inch Singles

JIVE

Number	Title (A Side/B Side)	Yr	VG	VG+	NM
❏ 42096	Something Good (unknown versions)	1992	2.50	5.00	10.00
❏ 42121	Use Me Up (LP Version) (Extended Remix)/Ghetto Jeep (Remix) (Hip Hoip Remix) (LP Instrumental)	1992	2.50	5.00	10.00
❏ 42224	It's Supposed to Bubble (4 versions)	1994	3.00	6.00	12.00

Number	Title (A Side/B Side)	Yr	VG	VG+	NM
❑ 42582	Take It Off (LP Version) (Clean Radio) (Instrumental)/The Corrupter's Execution Master	1999	3.00	6.00	12.00
❑ 42639	Pimpin' Ain't No Illusion (2 versions)/Belts to Match (2 versions)	1999	2.50	5.00	10.00
❑ 42894	Let Me See It (unknown versions)	2001	—	3.00	6.00

Albums
JIVE

❑ 41502	Too Hard to Swallow	1992	3.75	7.50	15.00

—*Issued in generic black cover*

UNDERWOOD, VERONICA
12-Inch Singles
PHILLY WORLD

❑ DMD 860 [DJ]	Victim of Desire (Vocal) (Instrumental)	1985	3.00	6.00	12.00
❑ 96869	Victim of Desire (2 versions)	1985	2.50	5.00	10.00

45s
PHILLY WORLD

❑ 99632	Victim of Desire/(Instrumental)	1985	—	2.00	4.00

Albums
PHILLY WORLD

❑ 90297	Veronica Underwood	1985	2.50	5.00	10.00

UNDISPUTED TRUTH, THE
12-Inch Singles
WHITFIELD

❑ 8306	Let's Go Down to the Disco (9:10)/You + Me = Love	1976	5.00	10.00	20.00
❑ 8783	Show Time (8:59)/Misunderstood	1979	3.75	7.50	15.00

45s
GORDY

❑ 7106	Save My Love for a Rainy Day/Since I've Lost You	1971	2.00	4.00	8.00
❑ 7108	Smiling Faces Sometimes/You Got the Love I Need	1971	—	3.00	6.00
❑ 7112	You Make Your Own Heaven and Hell Right Here on Earth/Ball of Confusion (That's What the World Is Today)	1971	—	3.00	6.00
❑ 7114	What It Is/California Soul	1972	—	3.00	6.00
❑ 7117	Papa Was a Rollin' Stone/Friendship Train	1972	—	3.00	6.00
❑ 7122	With a Little Help from My Friends/Girl You're Alright	1972	—	3.00	6.00
❑ 7124	Mama I Got a Brand New Thing (Don't Say No)/Gonna Keep On Tryin' Till I Win Your Love	1973	—	3.00	6.00
❑ 7130	Law of the Land/Just My Imagination (Running Away with Me)	1973	—	3.00	6.00
❑ 7134	Help Yourself/What's Going On	1974	—	3.00	6.00
❑ 7139	I'm a Fool for You/Girl's Alright with Me	1974	—	3.00	6.00
❑ 7140	Big John Is My Name/L'il Red Ridin' Hood	1974	—	3.00	6.00
❑ 7141	Earthquake Shake/Spaced Out	1975	—	—	—

—*Unreleased*

❑ 7143	UFO's/Got to Get My Hands on Some Lovin'	1975	—	3.00	6.00
❑ 7145	Higher Than High/Spaced Out	1975	—	3.00	6.00
❑ 7147	Boogie Bump Boogie/I Saw Her When You Met Her	1975	—	3.00	6.00

WHITFIELD

❑ 8231	You + Me = Love/(Instrumental)	1976	—	3.00	6.00
❑ 8295	Let's Get Down to the Disco/Loose	1977	—	3.00	6.00
❑ 8362	Hole in the Wall/Sunshine	1977	—	3.00	6.00
❑ 8781	Show Time (Part 1)/(Part 2)	1979	—	3.00	6.00
❑ 8873	I Can't Get Enough of Your Love/Misunderstood	1979	—	3.00	6.00

Albums
GORDY

❑ G 955L	The Undisputed Truth	1971	6.25	12.50	25.00
❑ G5-959	Face to Face with the Truth	1972	5.00	10.00	20.00
❑ G5-963	Law of the Land	1973	5.00	10.00	20.00
❑ G6-968	Down to Earth	1974	5.00	10.00	20.00
❑ G6-970	Cosmic Truth	1975	5.00	10.00	20.00
❑ G6-972	Higher Than High	1975	5.00	10.00	20.00

WHITFIELD

❑ BS 2967	Method to the Madness	1977	5.00	10.00	20.00
❑ BSK 3202	Smokin'	1979	3.75	7.50	15.00

UNIFICS, THE
45s
KAPP

❑ 935	Court of Love/Which One Should I Choose	1968	3.00	6.00	12.00
❑ 957	The Beginning of My End/Sentimental Man	1968	3.00	6.00	12.00
❑ 957 [PS]	The Beginning of My End/Sentimental Man	1968	3.75	7.50	15.00
❑ 985	It's a Groovy World!/Memories	1969	3.00	6.00	12.00
❑ 985 [PS]	It's a Groovy World!/Memories	1969	3.75	7.50	15.00
❑ 2026	Toshisumasu/It's All Over	1969	3.00	6.00	12.00
❑ 2058	Got to Get You/Memories	1969	3.00	6.00	12.00

Albums
KAPP

❑ KS-3582	Sittin' In at the Court of Love	1968	6.25	12.50	25.00

UNIVERSALS, THE
Probably more than one group.
45s
ASCOT

❑ 2124	Dear Ruth/Gotta Little Girl	1963	15.00	30.00	60.00

CORA-LEE

❑ 501	The Picture/He's So Right	1958	10.00	20.00	40.00

FESTIVAL

❑ 1601	Dreaming/Love Bound	1961	15.00	30.00	60.00

—*No subtitle on A-side*

❑ 25001	Dreaming/Love Bound	1961	6.25	12.50	25.00

MARK-X

❑ 7004	Teenage Love/Again	1957	50.00	100.00	200.00

MODERN

❑ 1057	New Lease on Life/Without Friends	1968	2.50	5.00	10.00

SHEPHERD

❑ 2200	A Love Only You Can Give/I'm in Love	1962	12.50	25.00	50.00

SOUTHERN

❑ 102	Dear Ruth/Prayer of Love	1963	12.50	25.00	50.00

Albums
RELIC

❑ 5006	Acapella Showcase	197?	2.50	5.00	10.00

UNLIMITED TOUCH
12-Inch Singles
PRELUDE

❑ 410	Reach Out (Everlasting Lover) (2 versions)	1984	5.00	10.00	20.00
❑ 521	Searching to Find the One (unknown versions)	1981	5.00	10.00	20.00
❑ 577	No One Can Love Me (unknown versions)	1983	5.00	10.00	20.00
❑ 605	I Hear Music in the Streets (unknown versions)	1980	5.00	10.00	20.00
❑ 653	No One Can Love Me (unknown versions)	1983	5.00	10.00	20.00
❑ 683	Reach Out (Everlasting Lover) (2 versions)	1984	5.00	10.00	20.00

45s
PRELUDE

❑ 8023	I Hear Music in the Streets/In the Middle	1980	—	2.50	5.00
❑ 8029	Searching to Find the One (Remix Version)/ (Edited Album Version)	1981	—	2.50	5.00

UPBEATS, THE
45s
JOY

❑ 223	Oh What It Seemed to Be/The Night We Both Said Goodbye	1958	6.25	12.50	25.00
❑ 227	Keep Cool Crazy Heart/You're the One I Care For	1959	6.25	12.50	25.00
❑ 229	Satin Shoes/Teenie Weenie Bikini	1959	6.25	12.50	25.00
❑ 233	To Me You're a Song/Unbelievable Love	1959	6.25	12.50	25.00

PREP

❑ 119	Never in My Life/I Don't Know	1957	7.50	15.00	30.00
❑ 131	Will You Be Mine?/My Last Frontier	1958	7.50	15.00	30.00

SWAN

❑ 4010	Just Like in the Movies/My Foolish Heart	1958	6.25	12.50	25.00

UPFRONTS, THE
45s
LUMMTONE

❑ 103	It Took Time/Betty Lou and the Lions	1960	12.50	25.00	50.00
❑ 104	Too Far to Turn Around/Married Jive	1960	10.00	20.00	40.00
❑ 106	Why You Kiss Me/Little Girl	1961	12.50	25.00	50.00
❑ 107	Send Me Someone to Love Who Will Love Me/ Baby For Your Love	1961	12.50	25.00	50.00

—*White label*

❑ 107	Send Me Someone to Love Who Will Love Me/ Baby For Your Love	1961	7.50	15.00	30.00

—*Black label*

❑ 108	It Took Time/Baby For Your Love	1962	6.25	12.50	25.00
❑ 114	Do the Beetle/Most of the Pretty Girls	1964	15.00	30.00	60.00

UPTONES, THE
45s
LUTE

❑ 6225	No More/I'll Be There	1962	7.50	15.00	30.00

—*Black label*

❑ 6225	No More/I'll Be There	1962	5.00	10.00	20.00

—*Multicolor label*

❑ 6229	Be Mine/Dreamin'	1962	10.00	20.00	40.00

MAGNUM

❑ 714	Dreaming/Wear My Ring	1963	5.00	10.00	20.00

WATTS

❑ 1080	Dreaming/Wear My Ring	1963	7.50	15.00	30.00

URBAN DANCE SQUAD
12-Inch Singles
ARISTA

❑ AD 2072	Deeper Shade of Soul (Freak Mix) (Single Mix) (Dance Mix)	1990	2.00	4.00	8.00
❑ ADP 2210	Fastlane (4 versions)	1991	3.75	7.50	15.00

45s
ARISTA

❑ 2026	Deeper Shade of Soul/(Live Version)	1990	—	2.00	4.00

Albums
ARISTA

❑ ADP 2099 [DJ]	Hollywood Live July 24, 1990/Pinkpop Live June 4, 1990	1990	3.75	7.50	15.00
❑ AL 8640	Mental Floss for the Globe	1990	3.75	7.50	15.00

US3
12-Inch Singles
BLUE NOTE

❑ V-15892	Cantaloop (Radio Edit) (Flip Fantasia Mix) (Groovy Mix)/(Slain Pass Mix) (Instrumental)	1993	2.50	5.00	10.00

Number	Title (A Side/B Side)	Yr	VG	VG+	NM
❏ Y-58139	Tukka Yoot's Riddim (5 versions)	1994	2.00	4.00	8.00
❏ Y-58662	I'm Thinking About Your Body (unknown versions)	1997	—	3.00	6.00

45s
BLUE NOTE

Number	Title (A Side/B Side)	Yr	VG	VG+	NM
❏ S7-17707	Cantaloop (Flip Fantasia)/It's Like That	1994	—	2.50	5.00
❏ S7-17967	Tukka Yoot's Riddim/I Go to Work	1994	—	2.00	4.00

Albums
BLUE NOTE

Number	Title (A Side/B Side)	Yr	VG	VG+	NM
❏ B1-30027 [(2)]	Broadway & 52nd	1997	3.75	7.50	15.00
❏ B1-80883	Hand on the Torch	1993	3.75	7.50	15.00

USA FOR AFRICA
12-Inch Singles
COLUMBIA

Number	Title (A Side/B Side)	Yr	VG	VG+	NM
❏ US2-05179	We Are the World/Grace	1985	2.00	4.00	8.00

—*B-side by Quincy Jones*

45s
COLUMBIA

Number	Title (A Side/B Side)	Yr	VG	VG+	NM
❏ US7-04839	We Are the World/Grace	1985	—	—	3.00

—*B-side by Quincy Jones*

Number	Title (A Side/B Side)	Yr	VG	VG+	NM
❏ US7-04839 [PS]	We Are the World/Grace	1985	—	2.00	4.00

Albums
COLUMBIA

Number	Title (A Side/B Side)	Yr	VG	VG+	NM
❏ USA 40043	We Are the World	1985	3.00	6.00	12.00

—*Actually a various-artists LP, but listed here because it was credited to "USA For Africa"*

USHER
12-Inch Singles
ARISTA

Number	Title (A Side/B Side)	Yr	VG	VG+	NM
❏ ARDP-3984 [DJ]	U Remind Me (Radio Edit) (Instrumental) (LP Version) (Acappella)	2001	2.50	5.00	10.00
❏ ARDP-5040 [DJ]	U Got It Bad (Soulpower Radio Mix 4:07) (Soulpower Radio Mix Alternate Intro 4:20) (Soulpower Club Mix 5:28) (Soulpower Instrumental 4:06)	2001	3.00	6.00	12.00
❏ ARDP-5056 [DJ]	U Got It Bad (Tee's Latin Mix) (Tee's UK R&B Radio Mix) (Tee's In-House Club Mix) (Tee's Dub)	2001	2.00	4.00	8.00
❏ 15024	U Remind Me (Illicit Club Mix) (Illicit Acappella) (Pete & Vincent's Club Mix) (Pete & Vincent's Dub Mix)	2001	2.50	5.00	10.00
❏ 15036	U Got It Bad (unknown versions)	2001	2.00	4.00	8.00
❏ 15107	U Don't Have to Call — R&B Mixes (unknown versions)	2002	—	3.50	7.00
❏ 15125	U Don't Have to Call — Remixes (unknown versions)	2002	—	3.50	7.00

LAFACE

Number	Title (A Side/B Side)	Yr	VG	VG+	NM
❏ LFDP 4076 [DJ]	Can U Get Wit It (unknown versions)	1994	2.50	5.00	10.00
❏ LFDP 4259 [DJ]	You Make Me Wanna... (LP Version) (LP Instrumental) (Acappella) (Extended Version)	1997	3.00	6.00	12.00
❏ LFDP 4269 [DJ]	You Make Me Wanna... (JD Remix) (Acappella) (Lil' Jon's Eastside Remix) (Lil' Jon's Eastside Instrumental) (Timbaland Remix)	1997	3.75	7.50	15.00
❏ LFDP 4307 [DJ]	Nice & Slow (Live Mix) (B-Rock's Vasement Mix) (Album Version)/You Make Me Wanna ... (T and J Classic Garage Mix)	1998	2.50	5.00	10.00
❏ LFDP 4323 [DJ]	My Way (Remix w/JD) (Remix Instrumental) (Remix Acappella)/(Album Version) (Instrumental) (Acappella)	1998	2.50	5.00	10.00
❏ LFDP 4355 [DJ]	One Day You'll Be Mine (LP Version) (Instrumental) (Acappella)	1998	2.50	5.00	10.00
❏ LFDP 4360 [DJ]	One Day You'll Be Mine (With JD) (Instrumental) (Without JD) (Acappella)	1998	2.50	5.00	10.00
❏ LFDP 4486 [DJ]	Pop Ya Colla (Radio Mix) (Instrumental) (Radio Mix) (Acappella)	2000	2.50	5.00	10.00
❏ LFDP 4541 [DJ]	I Don't Know (Clean) (Instrumental) (Dirty) (Acappella)	2001	2.50	5.00	10.00
❏ 24052	Call Me a Mack (Vincent's 48 Hr. Mix) (Xtra Bits)/(Album Version) (CrazyCool Mix) (Percussamental)	1993	3.00	6.00	12.00
❏ 24077	Can U Get Wit It (4 versions)	1994	2.00	4.00	8.00
❏ 24106	The Many Ways (Album Version) (Album Instrumental)	1995	2.50	5.00	10.00
❏ 24131	Comin' For X-Mas (Santa's Main Mix) (Santa-Mental) (Elfapella)	1995	3.00	6.00	12.00
❏ 24269	You Make Me Wanna... (Album Version) (JD Remix) (Lil' Jon's Eastside Remix)/(Timbaland Remix) (Acappella) (Album Instrumental)	1997	2.00	4.00	8.00
❏ 24307	Nice & Slow (Live Mix) (B-Rock's Vasement Mix) (Album Version)/You Make Me Wanna ... (T and J Classic Garage Mix)	1997	2.00	4.00	8.00
❏ 24327	My Way (unknown versions)	1998	2.00	4.00	8.00
❏ 24545	I Don't Know (unknown versions)	2001	—	3.00	6.00

Albums
ARISTA

Number	Title (A Side/B Side)	Yr	VG	VG+	NM
❏ 14715 [(2)]	8701	2001	3.75	7.50	15.00

LAFACE

Number	Title (A Side/B Side)	Yr	VG	VG+	NM
❏ LFPL 6043 [DJ]	My Way	1997	3.75	7.50	15.00

—*Promo-only "clean" version*

Number	Title (A Side/B Side)	Yr	VG	VG+	NM
❏ 26008	Usher	1994	3.00	6.00	12.00
❏ 26082 [(2)]	All About U	2000	—	—	—

—*Canceled*

UTFO
12-Inch Singles
JIVE

Number	Title (A Side/B Side)	Yr	VG	VG+	NM
❏ 1402-1-JD	If You Don't Wanna Get Pregnant (LP Version) (Slammin' Remix) (Clean Version)/Hoein'	1990	5.00	10.00	20.00

SELECT

Number	Title (A Side/B Side)	Yr	VG	VG+	NM
❏ 62241	Beats and Rhymes (unknown versions)	1984	7.50	15.00	30.00
❏ 62254	Roxanne, Roxanne (Vocal) (Instrumental)/Hanging Out (Vocal) (Instrumental)	1984	7.50	15.00	30.00

—*"Roxanne, Roxanne" was the B-side but it became a rap phenomenon, totally eclipsing the original A-side*

Number	Title (A Side/B Side)	Yr	VG	VG+	NM
❏ 62256	The Real Roxanne/Roxanne's Back Side (Scratch It)	1985	5.00	10.00	20.00

—*By "Roxanne with UTFO"*

Number	Title (A Side/B Side)	Yr	VG	VG+	NM
❏ 62259	Leader of the Pack/(Instrumental)	1985	5.00	10.00	20.00
❏ 62263	Bite It (3 versions)	1985	5.00	10.00	20.00
❏ 62272	We Work Hard (5:21)/Kangol and Doc (5:52)	1986	6.25	12.50	25.00
❏ 62276	Split Personality (Remix) (Remix Dub)	1986	3.75	7.50	15.00
❏ 62293	Ya Cold Wanna Be with Me (5:15) (Radio Edit) (Radio Dub)	1987	5.00	10.00	20.00
❏ 62305	Lethal/S.W.A.T. (Get Down)	1987	2.50	5.00	10.00
❏ 62310	Let's Get It On (4 versions)	1988	3.75	7.50	15.00
❏ 62333	Wanna Rock (LP Version) (Forceful Mix) (Radio Edit)/(Extended Version) (Omar's Dub)	1989	3.75	7.50	15.00
❏ 62353	Rough and Rugged (3 versions)/My Cut's Correct	1989	3.75	7.50	15.00

45s
SELECT

Number	Title (A Side/B Side)	Yr	VG	VG+	NM
❏ 1182	The Real Roxanne/Roxanne, Roxanne	1985	2.00	4.00	8.00

—*A-side by "Roxanne with UTFO"*

Number	Title (A Side/B Side)	Yr	VG	VG+	NM
❏ 1186	Fairytale Lover/Hanging Out	1985	—	3.00	6.00
❏ 1190	Split Personality//(B-side unknown)	1986	—	3.00	6.00

Albums
JIVE

Number	Title (A Side/B Side)	Yr	VG	VG+	NM
❏ 1326	Bag It and Bone It	1991	5.00	10.00	20.00

SELECT

Number	Title (A Side/B Side)	Yr	VG	VG+	NM
❏ 21614	UTFO	1985	6.25	12.50	25.00
❏ 21616	Skeezer Pleezer	1986	3.00	6.00	12.00
❏ 21619	Lethal	1987	3.00	6.00	12.00
❏ 21629	Doin' It!	1989	3.00	6.00	12.00

UTMOSTS, THE
45s
PAN-OR

Number	Title (A Side/B Side)	Yr	VG	VG+	NM
❏ 1123	I Need You/Big Man	1962	30.00	60.00	120.00

UTOPIANS, THE
45s
IMPERIAL

Number	Title (A Side/B Side)	Yr	VG	VG+	NM
❏ 5861	Dutch Treat/Ain't No Such Thing	1962	7.50	15.00	30.00
❏ 5876	Along My Lonely Way/Hurry to Your Date	1962	100.00	200.00	400.00
❏ 5921	Let Love Come Later/Opera vs. the Blues	1963	6.25	12.50	25.00

UTOPIAS, THE
45s
LASALLE

Number	Title (A Side/B Side)	Yr	VG	VG+	NM
❏ 0072	Girls Are Against Me/(B-side unknown)	196?	300.00	600.00	1200.

UZI $ BROS.
12-Inch Singles
CAPITOL

Number	Title (A Side/B Side)	Yr	VG	VG+	NM
❏ V-15622	There's a Riot Jumpin' Off (Remix) (LP Version)/Cheeba Cheeba (Remix) (LP Version)	1990	2.00	4.00	8.00

—*B-side by Tone Loc*

ORIGINAL SOUND

Number	Title (A Side/B Side)	Yr	VG	VG+	NM
❏ 1290	Nothin' But a Gangster/We Got Mo' Soul/People Make the World Go Round (3 versions)	1989	5.00	10.00	20.00
❏ 1291	People Get Funny, When It Comes to Money/Gangster Grip	1990	5.00	10.00	20.00

Number	Title (A Side/B Side)	Yr	VG	VG+	NM

V

V.I.P.'S
45s
BIG TOP

Number	Title (A Side/B Side)	Yr	VG	VG+	NM
❏ 100	Don't Pass Me By/You Ain't Good for Nothing	1965	3.00	6.00	12.00
❏ 518	You Pulled a Fast One/Flashback	1964	3.00	6.00	12.00
❏ 521	I'm On to You Baby/If He Wants Me	1964	3.00	6.00	12.00

CONGRESS
| ❏ 211 | My Girl Cried/Strange Little Girl | 1964 | 3.75 | 7.50 | 15.00 |

VAL-CHORDS, THE
45s
GAME TIME

| ❏ 104 | Candy Store Love/You're Laughing at Me | 1957 | 75.00 | 150.00 | 300.00 |
—With no sword logo
| ❏ 104 | Candy Store Love/You're Laughing at Me | 1957 | 25.00 | 50.00 | 100.00 |
—With sword logo

VAL-TONES, THE
45s
DELUXE
| ❏ 6084 | Tender Darling/Siam Sam | 1955 | 37.50 | 75.00 | 150.00 |

VALADIERS, THE
45s
GORDY
| ❏ 7003 | While I'm Away/Because I Love Her | 1962 | 15.00 | 30.00 | 60.00 |
| ❏ 7013 | I Found a Girl/You'll Be Sorry Someday | 1963 | 15.00 | 30.00 | 60.00 |
MIRACLE
| ❏ 6 | Greetings/Take a Chance | 1961 | 20.00 | 40.00 | 80.00 |
—With no subtitle on A-side and 2:23 version of B-side
| ❏ 6 | Greeting (This Is Uncle Sam)/Take a Chance | 1961 | 12.50 | 25.00 | 50.00 |
—With subtitle on A-side and 2:15 version of B-side

VALAQUONS, THE
45s
LAGUNA
| ❏ 102 | Teardrops/Madeleine | 1964 | 50.00 | 100.00 | 200.00 |
RAYCO
| ❏ 516 | Jolly Green Giant/Diddy Bop | 1965 | 7.50 | 15.00 | 30.00 |
TANGERINE
| ❏ 951 | I Wanna Woman/Window Shopping on Girl's Avenue | 1965 | 6.25 | 12.50 | 25.00 |

VALENTINES, THE (1)
45s
BETHLEHEM
| ❏ 3055 | I'll Forget You/Yes, You Made It That Way | 1962 | 6.25 | 12.50 | 25.00 |
KING
❏ 5338	Please Don't Leave, Please Don't Go/That's It Man	1960	6.25	12.50	25.00
❏ 5433	That's How I Feel/Hey Ruby	1960	6.25	12.50	25.00
❏ 5830	I Have Two Loves/Camping Out	1963	5.00	10.00	20.00
UNITED ARTISTS
❏ 764	Alone in the Night/Mink Coats and Sneakers	1964	3.75	7.50	15.00

VALENTINES, THE (2)
45s
OLD TOWN
| ❏ 1009 | Tonight Kathleen/Summer Love | 1954 | 200.00 | 400.00 | 800.00 |
RAMA
| ❏ 171 | Lily Maebelle/Falling for You | 1955 | 50.00 | 100.00 | 200.00 |
—Blue label
| ❏ 171 | Lily Maebelle/Falling for You | 1955 | 12.50 | 25.00 | 50.00 |
—Red label
| ❏ 181 | I Love You Darling/Hand Me Down Love | 1955 | 37.50 | 75.00 | 150.00 |
| ❏ 186 | Christmas Prayer/K-I-S-S Me | 1955 | 125.00 | 250.00 | 500.00 |
—Blue label
| ❏ 186 | Christmas Prayer/K-I-S-S Me | 1955 | 12.50 | 25.00 | 50.00 |
—Red label
| ❏ 196 | Why/The Woo Woo Train | 1956 | 25.00 | 50.00 | 100.00 |
—Blue label
| ❏ 196 | Why/The Woo Woo Train | 1956 | 12.50 | 25.00 | 50.00 |
—Red label
❏ 201	Twenty Minutes (Before the Hour)/I'll Never Let You Go	1956	25.00	50.00	100.00
❏ 208	Nature's Creation/My Story of Love	1956	25.00	50.00	100.00
❏ 228	Don't Say Goodnight/I Cried Oh, Oh	1957	50.00	100.00	200.00
ROULETTE
❏ 58	Christmas Prayer/Nature's Creation	196?	2.50	5.00	10.00
—"Golden Goodies Series"

VALENTINES, THE (3)
45s
SOUND STAGE 7
| ❏ 2646 | I'm Alright Now/Gotta Get Yourself Together | 1969 | 3.75 | 7.50 | 15.00 |
| ❏ 2663 | If You Love Me/Breakaway | 1970 | 3.00 | 6.00 | 12.00 |

VALENTINES, THE (U)
45s
IONA
| ❏ 1003 | The Sock/Sixteen Senoritas | 196? | 3.75 | 7.50 | 15.00 |
LUDIX
| ❏ 102 | Johnny One Heart/Mama I Have Come Home | 1962 | 5.00 | 10.00 | 20.00 |

VALENTINOS, THE
Also see BOBBY WOMACK.
45s
ABKCO
| ❏ 4044 | It's All Over Now/Lookin' for a Love | 197? | 2.00 | 4.00 | 8.00 |
ASTRA
| ❏ 1026 | Lookin' for a Love/Somewhere There's a Girl | 196? | 2.50 | 5.00 | 10.00 |
—Reissue of Sar 132
CHESS
| ❏ 1952 | Do It Right/What About Me | 1966 | 3.00 | 6.00 | 12.00 |
| ❏ 1977 | Let's Get Together/Sweeter Than the Day Before | 1966 | 3.00 | 6.00 | 12.00 |
JUBILEE
| ❏ 5636 | Death of Love/Tired of Being Nobody | 1968 | 2.50 | 5.00 | 10.00 |
| ❏ 5650 | Two Lovers' History/You've Got the Kind of Love That's for Real | 1969 | 2.50 | 5.00 | 10.00 |
SAR
❏ 132	Lookin' for a Love/Somewhere There's a Girl	1962	5.00	10.00	20.00
❏ 137	I'll Make It Alright/Darling Come Back Home	1963	5.00	10.00	20.00
❏ 144	Baby, Lots of Luck/She's So Good to Me	1963	5.00	10.00	20.00
❏ 152	It's All Over Now/Tired of Living in the Country	1964	5.00	10.00	20.00
❏ 155	Bitter Dreams/Everybody Wants to Fall in Love	1964	3.75	7.50	15.00

VALIANTS, THE (1)
45s
ANDEX
| ❏ 4026 | Please Wait My Love/Freida, Freida | 1958 | 30.00 | 60.00 | 120.00 |
—Some copies were pressed with this label in error (Keen 4026 is the "correct" issue)
KEEN
❏ 4008	Temptation of My Heart/Freida, Freida	1958	12.50	25.00	50.00
❏ 4026	Please Wait My Love/Freida, Freida	1958	15.00	30.00	60.00
❏ 34004	This Is the Nite/Good Golly Miss Molly	1957	10.00	20.00	40.00
❏ 34007	Lover Lover/Walkin' Girl	1958	10.00	20.00	40.00
❏ 82120	This Is the Nite/Walkin' Girl	1960	5.00	10.00	20.00
SHAR-DEE
❏ 703	Dear Cindy/Surprise	1959	30.00	60.00	120.00
—No mention of London distribution on label
| ❏ 703 | Dear Cindy/Surprise | 1959 | 10.00 | 20.00 | 40.00 |
—With London distribution credit on label

VALQUINS, THE
45s
GAITY
| ❏ 161/2 | My Dear/Falling Star | 1959 | 200.00 | 400.00 | 800.00 |
| ❏ 161/2 | My Dear/Falling Star | 1959 | 500.00 | 1000. | 1500. |
—Red vinyl

VALTONES, THE
45s
GEE
| ❏ 1004 | You Belong to My Heart/Have You Ever Met an Angel | 1956 | 75.00 | 150.00 | 300.00 |

VAN DYKE, EARL, AND THE SOUL BROTHERS
45s
RENAISSANCE
| ❏ 5000 | September Song/(B-side unknown) | 196? | 18.75 | 37.50 | 75.00 |
SOUL
❏ 35006	Soul Stomp/Hot 'N' Tot	1964	5.00	10.00	20.00
❏ 35009	All for You/Too Many Fish in the Sea	1965	200.00	400.00	800.00
❏ 35014	I Can't Help Myself/How Sweet It Is To Be Loved By You	1965	5.00	10.00	20.00
❏ 35018	The Flick (Part 1)/The Flick (Part 2)	1966	5.00	10.00	20.00
❏ 35028	6 x 6/There Is No Greater Love	1967	5.00	10.00	20.00
—By Earl Van Dyke and the Motown Brass
| ❏ 35059 | Runaway Child, Running Wild/Gonna Give Her All the Love I've Got | 1969 | 5.00 | 10.00 | 20.00 |

Albums
MOTOWN
| ❏ M-631 [M] | The Motown Sound | 1965 | 10.00 | 20.00 | 40.00 |
| ❏ MS-631 [S] | The Motown Sound | 1965 | 12.50 | 25.00 | 50.00 |
SOUL
| ❏ SS-715 | The Earl of Funk | 1970 | 10.00 | 20.00 | 40.00 |

VAN DYKES, THE (1)
45s
DELUXE
| ❏ 6193 | The Bells Are Ringing/The Meaning of Love | 1960 | 6.25 | 12.50 | 25.00 |
DONNA
| ❏ 1333 | Gift of Love/Guardian Angel | 1961 | 10.00 | 20.00 | 40.00 |
FELSTED
| ❏ 8565 | Once Upon a Dream/Dame Tu Corazon | 1959 | 6.25 | 12.50 | 25.00 |
KING
| ❏ 5158 | The Bells Are Ringing/The Meaning of Love | 1958 | 17.50 | 35.00 | 70.00 |
SPRING
| ❏ 1113 | Gift of Love/Guardian Angel | 1961 | 30.00 | 60.00 | 120.00 |

VANDROSS, LUTHER

12-Inch Singles

ATLANTIC

Number	Title (A Side/B Side)	Yr	VG	VG+	NM
❑ DSKO 78 [DJ]	At Christmas Time (6:02)/May Christmas Bring You Happiness (4:24)	1976	3.75	7.50	15.00
—As "Luther"					

EPIC

Number	Title (A Side/B Side)	Yr	VG	VG+	NM
❑ EAS 1271 [DJ]	Any Love (3 versions)	1988	—	3.50	7.00
❑ EAS 1529 [DJ]	For You to Love (Vocal) (Instrumental)	1989	2.00	4.00	8.00
❑ AS 1547 [DJ]	Bad Boy/Having a Party (5:12) (3:57)	1982	2.00	4.00	8.00
❑ EAS 2244 [DJ]	If Only for One Night/Other Side of the World	1985	2.00	4.00	8.00
❑ EAS 4052 [DJ]	Power of Love/Love Power (4 versions)	1991	2.50	5.00	10.00
❑ EAS 4052 [DJ]	Power of Love/Love Power (4 versions)	1991	2.50	5.00	10.00
❑ 49-04232	I'll Let You Slide (5:18)/(Instrumental)	1983	2.00	4.00	8.00
❑ 49-04969	Superstar/Until You Come Back to Me (That's What I'm Gonna Do)/I Wanted Your Love	1984	2.00	4.00	8.00
❑ 49-05159	'Til My Baby Comes Home (Dance Version) (LP Version)	1985	—	3.00	6.00
❑ 49-05228	It's Over Now (Dance Version) (Instrumental)	1985	—	3.00	6.00
❑ 49-05980	Stop to Love (Extended Version) (Instrumental)	1986	2.00	4.00	8.00
❑ 49-06865	I Really Didn't Mean It (12" Mix 6:35) (7" Mix 3:59)/(Dub Mix 6:00) (Acapella Mix 5:22)	1987	—	3.00	6.00
❑ EAS 7659 [DJ]	The Mistletoe Jam (D-Man Club) (Lord G-Man Dub) (D-Man Jam Mix) (D-Man's Beats)	1995	2.00	4.00	8.00
❑ 49-08178	She Won't Talk to Me (12" Extended Mix) (7" Club Mix) (Acid House Dub) (Percapella)	1988	—	3.00	6.00
❑ EAS 9202 [DJ]	I Can Make It Better (Soulshock & Karlin Remix) (Charles Roane Remix) (Acappella) (Soulshock & Karlin Remix Instrumental)	1996	—	3.50	7.00
❑ EAS 9939 [DJ]	Love Don't Love You Anymore (TM's Main 12" Mix) (TM's Main Dub) (TM's Urban Mix) (TM's Urban Instrumental)	1997	3.00	6.00	12.00
❑ 49-73141	Never Too Much (4 versions)	1990	2.50	5.00	10.00
❑ 49-73379	Power of Love/Love Power (Powerful Mix) (Radio Edit) (Love Dub)	1991	2.00	4.00	8.00
❑ 49-73905	Don't Want to Be a Fool (LP Version) (Instrumental)	1991	2.50	5.00	10.00
❑ 49-74048	The Rush (Morales Radio Mix) (Morales 12" Mix)/(Morales Rush Dub) (Rush Vibe Dub)	1991	2.00	4.00	8.00
❑ 49-77105	Heaven Knows (6 versions)	1993	2.00	4.00	8.00
❑ 49-77755	Going in Circles (Radio Edit) (Album Version) (Instrumental)/Love the One You're With (Edit) (Cory's Main Mix) (Remix Edit)	1995	2.00	4.00	8.00

J

Number	Title (A Side/B Side)	Yr	VG	VG+	NM
❑ J1PV-21094 [(2)]	Take You Out (6 versions)	2001	3.75	7.50	15.00
❑ 21095	Take You Out (Allstars Remix) (Radio Edit) (Instrumental)/(same on both sides)	2001	2.50	5.00	10.00
❑ 21115	Can Heaven Wait (unknown versions)	2001	2.50	5.00	10.00
❑ 21134	Can Heaven Wait (unknown versions)	2001	2.50	5.00	10.00

45s

ATLANTIC

Number	Title (A Side/B Side)	Yr	VG	VG+	NM
❑ 89593	At Christmas Time/Santa's Rap	1984	—	2.50	5.00
—As "Luther"; B-side by the Treacherous Three					

COTILLION

Number	Title (A Side/B Side)	Yr	VG	VG+	NM
❑ 44200	It's Good for the Soul — Pt. 1/Pt. 2	1976	—	3.00	6.00
—As "Luther"					
❑ 44205	Funky Music (Is a Part of Me)/The 2nd Time Around	1976	—	3.00	6.00
—As "Luther"					
❑ 44216	This Close to You/Don't Wanna Be a Fool	1977	—	3.00	6.00
—As "Luther"					

EPIC

Number	Title (A Side/B Side)	Yr	VG	VG+	NM
❑ 14-02409	Never Too Much/You Stopped Loving Me	1981	—	2.00	4.00
❑ 14-02658	Don't You Know That?/I've Been Working	1981	—	2.00	4.00
❑ 14-02842	Sugar and Spice (I Found Me a Girl)/She's a Super Lady	1982	—	2.00	4.00
❑ 14-03205	Bad Boy/Having a Party//Once You Know How	1982	—	2.00	4.00
❑ ENR-03263	Bad Boy/Having a Party//(B-side blank)	1982	—	3.00	6.00
—One-sided budget release					
❑ 34-03487	Since I Lost My Baby/You're the Sweetest One	1982	—	2.00	4.00
❑ 34-03804	Promise Me/Better Love	1983	—	2.00	4.00
❑ 34-04231	I'll Let You Slide/(Instrumental)	1983	—	2.00	4.00
❑ 34-04231 [PS]	I'll Let You Slide/(Instrumental)	1983	—	2.00	4.00
❑ 34-04441	Superstar/I Wanted Your Love	1984	—	2.00	4.00
❑ 34-04494	Make Me a Believer/Busy Body	1984	—	2.00	4.00
❑ 34-04760	'Til My Baby Comes Home/(Instrumental)	1985	—	2.00	4.00
❑ 34-04760 [PS]	'Til My Baby Comes Home/(Instrumental)	1985	—	2.00	4.00
❑ 34-04944	It's Over Now/(Instrumental)	1985	—	2.00	4.00
❑ 34-04944 [PS]	It's Over Now/(Instrumental)	1985	—	2.00	4.00
❑ 34-05610	Wait for Love/My Sensitivity (Gets in the Way)	1985	—	2.00	4.00
❑ 34-05751	If Only for One Night/Other Side of the World	1986	—	2.00	4.00
❑ 34-06129	Give Me the Reason/Don't You Want My Love	1986	—	—	3.00
❑ 34-06129 [PS]	Give Me the Reason/Don't You Want My Love	1986	—	2.00	4.00
❑ 34-06523	Stop to Love/(Instrumental)	1986	—	—	3.00
❑ 34-06523 [PS]	Stop to Love/(Instrumental)	1986	—	—	3.00
❑ 34-06978	There's Nothing Better Than Love/(Instrumental)	1987	—	—	3.00
—A-side with Gregory Hines					
❑ 34-06978 [PS]	There's Nothing Better Than Love/(Instrumental)	1987	—	—	3.00
❑ 34-07201	I Really Didn't Mean It/(Instrumental)	1987	—	—	3.00
❑ 34-07434	So Amazing/(Instrumental)	1987	—	—	3.00
❑ 34-08047	Any Love/(Instrumental)	1988	—	—	3.00
❑ 13-08429	Stop to Love/So Amazing	1988	—	—	3.00
—Reissue					
❑ 13-08432	Give Me the Reason/Other Side of the World	1988	—	—	3.00
—Reissue					
❑ 34-08513	She Won't Talk to Me/(Instrumental)	1988	—	—	3.00
❑ 34-68742	For You to Love/(Instrumental)	1989	—	—	3.00
❑ 34-73029	Here and Now/Come Back	1989	—	3.00	6.00
❑ 34-73258	Treat You Right/I Know You Want To	1990	—	2.00	4.00
❑ 34-73778	Power of Love/Love Power//(Instrumental)	1991	—	2.00	4.00
❑ 34-73879	Don't Want to Be a Fool//Power of Love/Love Power	1991	—	2.00	4.00
❑ 34-74945	Little Miracles (Happen Every Day)/I'm Gonna Start Today	1993	—	2.00	4.00
❑ 34-74996	Heaven Knows/I Want the Night to Stay	1993	—	2.00	4.00
❑ 34-77209	Never Let Me Go/Can't Beat Doin' That Now	1993	—	2.00	4.00
❑ 34-77735	Always and Forever//Power of Love/Love Power	1994	—	2.00	4.00
❑ 34-77754	Love the One You're With/Going in Circles	1995	—	2.00	4.00
❑ 34-78400	Your Secret Love//Power of Love/Love Power	1996	—	2.00	4.00
❑ 34-78466	I Can Make It Better/A Kiss for Christmas	1996	—	—	3.00

J

Number	Title (A Side/B Side)	Yr	VG	VG+	NM
❑ 21077	Take You Out/(Instrumental)	2001	—	2.00	4.00
❑ 21137	Can Heaven Wait/Bring Your Heart to Mine	2001	—	—	3.00
❑ 21171	I'd Rather/Grown Thangs	2002	—	—	3.00

PERSPECTIVE

Number	Title (A Side/B Side)	Yr	VG	VG+	NM
❑ 28968 0010 7	The Best Things in Life Are Free (2 versions)	1992	—	2.00	4.00
—As "Luther Vandross and Janet Jackson with BBD and Ralph Tresvant"					

Albums

EPIC

Number	Title (A Side/B Side)	Yr	VG	VG+	NM
❑ FE 37451	Never Too Much	1981	2.50	5.00	10.00
❑ FE 38235	Forever, For Always, For Love	1982	2.50	5.00	10.00
❑ FE 39196	Busy Body	1983	2.50	5.00	10.00
❑ FE 39882	The Night I Fell in Love	1985	2.00	4.00	8.00
❑ FE 40415	Give Me the Reason	1986	2.00	4.00	8.00
❑ FE 44308	Any Love	1988	2.00	4.00	8.00
❑ E2 45320 [(2)]	The Best of Luther Vandross... The Best of Love	1989	3.00	6.00	12.00
❑ E 46789	Power of Love	1991	3.00	6.00	12.00
❑ HE 47451	Never Too Much	198?	7.50	15.00	30.00
—Half-speed mastered edition					
❑ E 57775	Songs	1994	3.75	7.50	15.00
❑ E 57795	This Is Christmas	1995	3.00	6.00	12.00
❑ E 67553	Your Secret Love	1996	3.00	6.00	12.00

VANGUARDS, THE (1)

45s

LAMP

Number	Title (A Side/B Side)	Yr	VG	VG+	NM
❑ 652	It's To Late for Love/The Thought of Losing Your Love	1970	3.00	6.00	12.00
—Yes, the label misspelled the A-side					
❑ 653	Girl Go Away/Man Without Knowledge	1970	3.00	6.00	12.00

WHIZ

Number	Title (A Side/B Side)	Yr	VG	VG+	NM
❑ 612	Somebody Please/I Can't Use You Girl	1969	2.50	5.00	10.00

VAUGHAN, SARAH

45s

ATLANTIC

Number	Title (A Side/B Side)	Yr	VG	VG+	NM
❑ 1012	It Might As Well Be Spring/You Go to My Head	1953	25.00	50.00	100.00
❑ 3835	Fool on the Hill/Get Back	1981	—	2.50	5.00

COLUMBIA

Number	Title (A Side/B Side)	Yr	VG	VG+	NM
❑ 1-199	Black Coffee/As You Desire Me	1949	10.00	20.00	40.00
—Microgroove 33 1/3 rpm single					
❑ 1-258 (?)	Tonight I Shall Sleep (With a Smile on My Face)/While You're Gone	1949	10.00	20.00	40.00
—Microgroove 33 1/3 rpm single					
❑ 1-321	That Lucky Old Sun (Just Rolls Around Heaven All Day)/Make Believe (You Are Glad When You're Sorry)	1949	10.00	20.00	40.00
—Microgroove 33 1/3 rpm single					
❑ 1-385 (?)	Fool's Paradise/Lonely Girl	1949	10.00	20.00	40.00
—Microgroove 33 1/3 rpm single					
❑ 1-395 (?)	I Cried for You/You Say You Care	1950	10.00	20.00	40.00
—Microgroove 33 1/3 rpm single					
❑ 1-485	I'm Crazy to Love You/Summertime	1950	10.00	20.00	40.00
—Microgroove 33 1/3 rpm single					
❑ 1-625 (?)	Just Friends/You Taught Me to Love Again	1950	10.00	20.00	40.00
—Microgroove 33 1/3 rpm single					
❑ 1-679	Our Very Own/Don't Be Afraid	1950	10.00	20.00	40.00
—Microgroove 33 1/3 rpm single					
❑ 1-757 (?)	(I Love the Girl) I Love the Guy/Thinking of You	1950	10.00	20.00	40.00
—Microgroove 33 1/3 rpm single					
❑ 6-757 (?)	(I Love the Girl) I Love the Guy/Thinking of You	1950	7.50	15.00	30.00
❑ 1-830 (?)	Perdido/Whippa Whippa Woo	1950	10.00	20.00	40.00
—Microgroove 33 1/3 rpm single					
❑ 6-830 (?)	Perdido/Whippa Whippa Woo	1950	7.50	15.00	30.00
❑ 1-926	The Nearness of You/You're Mine You	1950	10.00	20.00	40.00
—Microgroove 33 1/3 rpm single					
❑ 6-926	The Nearness of You/You're Mine You	1950	7.50	15.00	30.00
❑ 4-38925	(I Love the Girl) I Love the Guy/Thinking of You	1950	6.25	12.50	25.00
❑ 4-39001	Perdido/Whippa Whippa Woo	1950	6.25	12.50	25.00
❑ 4-39071	The Nearness of You/You're Mine You	1950	6.25	12.50	25.00
❑ 4-39124	I'll Know/Gas Pipe Leaking	1950	6.25	12.50	25.00
❑ 4-39207	Ave Maria/A City Called Heaven	1951	6.25	12.50	25.00
❑ 4-39370	These Things I Offer You (For a Lifetime)/Deep Purple	1951	6.25	12.50	25.00
❑ 4-39446	Vanity/My Reverie	1951	6.25	12.50	25.00
❑ 4-39494	After Hours/Out of Breath	1951	6.25	12.50	25.00
❑ 4-39576	I Ran All the Way Home/Just a Moment More	1951	6.25	12.50	25.00
❑ 4-39634	Pinky/A Miracle Happened	1952	5.00	10.00	20.00
❑ 4-39719	If Someone Had Told Me/Corner to Corner	1952	5.00	10.00	20.00
❑ 4-39789	Time to Go/Street of Dreams	1952	5.00	10.00	20.00

Number	Title (A Side/B Side)	Yr	VG	VG+	NM
❑ 4-39839	Say You'll Wait for Me/My Tormented Heart	1952	5.00	10.00	20.00
❑ 4-39873	Sinner or Saint/Mighty Lonesome Feeling	1952	5.00	10.00	20.00
❑ 4-39932	Lovers' Quarrel/I Confess	1953	5.00	10.00	20.00
❑ 4-39963	Spring Will Be a Little Late This Year/A Blues Serenade	1953	5.00	10.00	20.00
❑ 4-40041	Time/Linger Awhile	1953	5.00	10.00	20.00

MAINSTREAM

Number	Title (A Side/B Side)	Yr	VG	VG+	NM
❑ 5517	Imagine/Sweet Gingerbread Man	1971	—	2.50	5.00
❑ 5521	Pieces of Dreams/Once You've Been in Love	1972	—	2.50	5.00
❑ 5522	What Are You Doing the Rest of Your Life/The Summer Knows	1972	—	2.50	5.00
❑ 5523	Summer Me, Winter Me/The Story of a Frasier	1972	—	2.50	5.00
❑ 5527	And the Feeling's Good/Deep in the Night	1972	—	2.50	5.00
❑ 5533	Rainy Days and Mondays/Just a Little Lovin'	1973	—	2.50	5.00
❑ 5541	Send In the Clowns/(B-side unknown)	1973	—	2.50	5.00
❑ 5544	Alone Again (Naturally)/Run to Me	1973	—	2.50	5.00
❑ 5553	Do Away with April/I Need You More	1974	—	2.50	5.00

MERCURY

Number	Title (A Side/B Side)	Yr	VG	VG+	NM
❑ 10020 [S]	Smooth Operator/Maybe It's Because (I Love You Too Much)	1959	5.00	10.00	20.00
❑ 70423x45	Ol' Devil Moon/Saturday	1954	3.75	7.50	15.00
❑ 70469x45	Make Yourself Comfortable/Idle Gossip	1954	3.75	7.50	15.00
❑ 70534x45	How Important Can It Be/Waltzing Down the Aisle	1955	3.75	7.50	15.00
❑ 70595x45	Whatever Lola Wants/Oh Yeah	1955	3.75	7.50	15.00
❑ 70646x45	Experience Unnecessary/Slowly, With Feeling	1955	3.75	7.50	15.00
❑ 70693x45	Johnny, Be Smart/Hey Naughty Papa	1955	3.75	7.50	15.00
❑ 70727x45	C'est La Vie/Never	1955	3.75	7.50	15.00
❑ 70777x45	Mr. Wonderful/You Ought to Have a Wife	1956	3.00	6.00	12.00
❑ 70846x45	Hot and Cold Running Tears/That's Not the Kind of Love I Want	1956	3.00	6.00	12.00
❑ 70885x45	Fabulous Character/The Other Woman	1956	3.00	6.00	12.00
❑ 70947x45	It Happened Again/I Wanna Play House	1956	3.00	6.00	12.00
❑ 71020x45	The Banana Boat Song/I've Got a New Heartache	1956	3.00	6.00	12.00
❑ 71030x45	Leave It to Love/The Bashful Matador	1957	3.00	6.00	12.00
❑ 71085x45	Poor Butterfly/April Give Me One More Day	1957	3.00	6.00	12.00
❑ 71157x45	Band of Angels/Please Mr. Brown	1957	3.00	6.00	12.00
❑ 71235x45	Gone Train/Next Time Around	1957	3.00	6.00	12.00
❑ 71303	Padre/Spin the Bottle	1958	3.00	6.00	12.00
❑ 71326	What's So Bad About It/Too Much Too Soon	1958	3.00	6.00	12.00
❑ 71380	I Ain't Hurtin'/Everything I Do	1958	3.00	6.00	12.00
❑ 71407	Are You Certain/Cool Baby	1959	3.00	6.00	12.00
❑ 71433	Separate Ways/Careless	1959	3.00	6.00	12.00
❑ 71477	Broken-Hearted Melody/Misty	1959	3.00	6.00	12.00
❑ 71519 [M]	Smooth Operator/Maybe It's Because (I Love You Too Much)	1959	3.00	6.00	12.00
❑ 71562	Eternally/You're My Baby	1960	3.00	6.00	12.00
❑ 71610	Some Other Spring/Our Waltz	1960	3.00	6.00	12.00
❑ 71642	Maybe You'll Be There/Doodlin'	1960	3.00	6.00	12.00
❑ 71669	For All We Know/The Rough Years	1960	3.00	6.00	12.00
❑ 71702	Close to You/Out of This World	1960	3.00	6.00	12.00
❑ 71742	If You Are But a Dream/Mary Contrary	1960	3.00	6.00	12.00
❑ 72510	Darling/I'll Never Be Lonely Again	1965	2.00	4.00	8.00
❑ 72543	A Lover's Concerto/First Thing Every Morning	1966	2.00	4.00	8.00
❑ 72588	Everybody Loves Somebody/1-2-3	1966	2.00	4.00	8.00

MGM

Number	Title (A Side/B Side)	Yr	VG	VG+	NM
❑ K10705	Tenderly/I'll Wait and Pray	1950	7.50	15.00	30.00
❑ K10762	What a Difference A Day Made/I Can't Get Started	1950	7.50	15.00	30.00
❑ K10819	I Cover the Waterfront/Don't Worry 'Bout Me	1950	7.50	15.00	30.00
❑ K10890	I'm Gonna Sit Right Down and Write Myself a Letter/I'm Through with Love	1951	6.25	12.50	25.00
❑ K11068	Don't Blame Me/If You Could See Me Now	1951	6.25	12.50	25.00

ROULETTE

Number	Title (A Side/B Side)	Yr	VG	VG+	NM
❑ 4285	Serenata/Let's	1960	2.50	5.00	10.00
❑ 4325	True Believer/What's the Use	1961	2.50	5.00	10.00
❑ 4359	April/Oh Lover	1961	2.50	5.00	10.00
❑ 4378	Untouchable/The Hills of Assisi	1961	2.50	5.00	10.00
❑ 4397	If Love Is Good to Me/A Great Day	1961	2.50	5.00	10.00
❑ 4413	One Mint Julep/Mama (He Treats Your Daughter Mean)	1962	2.50	5.00	10.00
❑ 4482	Call Me Irresponsible/There'll Be Other Times	1963	2.00	4.00	8.00
❑ 4497	Once Upon a Summertime/Snowbound	1963	2.00	4.00	8.00
❑ 4516	What'll I Do/I Believe in You	1963	2.00	4.00	8.00
❑ 4547	The Wallflower Waltz/Only	1964	2.00	4.00	8.00
❑ 4604	A Taste of Honey/The Good Life	1965	2.00	4.00	8.00
❑ SSR-33-8047 [S]	When Your Lover Has Gone/I'm Gonna Laugh You Out of My Life	196?	3.75	7.50	15.00

—Small hole, plays at 33 1/3 rpm

WARNER BROS.

Number	Title (A Side/B Side)	Yr	VG	VG+	NM
❑ 49890	Theme from "Sharkey's Machine"/Sharkey's Theme	1981	—	2.00	4.00

—B-side by Eddie Harris

78s

ATLANTIC

Number	Title (A Side/B Side)	Yr	VG	VG+	NM
❑ 1012	It Might As Well Be Spring/You Go to My Head	1953	12.50	25.00	50.00

COLUMBIA

Number	Title (A Side/B Side)	Yr	VG	VG+	NM
❑ 38461	Bianca/Too Darn Hot	1949	3.00	6.00	12.00

—B-side by Lorenzo Fuller

Number	Title (A Side/B Side)	Yr	VG	VG+	NM
❑ 38462	Black Coffee/As You Desire Me	1949	3.00	6.00	12.00
❑ 38512	Tonight I Shall Sleep (With a Smile on My Face)/While You're Gone	1949	3.00	6.00	12.00
❑ 38559	That Lucky Old Sun (Just Rolls Around Heaven All Day)/Make Believe (You Are Glad When You're Sorry)	1949	3.00	6.00	12.00
❑ 38617	Fool's Paradise/Lonely Girl	1949	3.00	6.00	12.00
❑ 38630	I Cried for You/You Say You Care	1950	3.00	6.00	12.00
❑ 38701	I'm Crazy to Love You/Summertime	1950	3.00	6.00	12.00
❑ 38810	Just Friends/You Taught Me to Love Again	1950	3.00	6.00	12.00
❑ 38925	(I Love the Girl) I Love the Guy/Thinking of You	1950	2.50	5.00	10.00
❑ 39001	Perdido/Whippa Whippa Woo	1950	2.50	5.00	10.00
❑ 39071	The Nearness of You/You're Mine You	1950	2.50	5.00	10.00
❑ 39124	I'll Know/Gas Pipe Leaking	1950	2.50	5.00	10.00
❑ 39207	Ave Maria/A City Called Heaven	1951	2.50	5.00	10.00
❑ 39370	These Things I Offer You (For a Lifetime)/Deep Purple	1951	2.50	5.00	10.00
❑ 39446	Vanity/My Reverie	1951	2.50	5.00	10.00
❑ 39494	After Hours/Out of Breath	1951	2.50	5.00	10.00
❑ 39576	I Ran All the Way Home/Just a Moment More	1951	2.50	5.00	10.00
❑ 39634	Pinky/A Miracle Happened	1952	2.50	5.00	10.00
❑ 39719	If Someone Had Told Me/Corner to Corner	1952	2.50	5.00	10.00
❑ 39789	Time to Go/Street of Dreams	1952	2.50	5.00	10.00
❑ 39839	Say You'll Wait for Me/My Tormented Heart	1952	2.50	5.00	10.00
❑ 39873	Sinner or Saint/Mighty Lonesome Feeling	1952	2.50	5.00	10.00
❑ 39932	Lovers' Quarrel/I Confess	1953	2.50	5.00	10.00
❑ 39963	Spring Will Be a Little Late This Year/A Blues Serenade	1953	2.50	5.00	10.00
❑ 40041	Time/Linger Awhile	1953	2.50	5.00	10.00

CONTINENTAL

Number	Title (A Side/B Side)	Yr	VG	VG+	NM
❑ 6008	What More Can a Woman Do?/I'd Rather Have a Memory Than a Dream	1945	5.00	10.00	20.00
❑ 6024	Signing Off/Mean to Me	1945	5.00	10.00	20.00
❑ 6031	East of the Sun/Interlude	1945	5.00	10.00	20.00
❑ 6061	No Smokes Blues/(B-side unknown)	194?	5.00	10.00	20.00

MERCURY

Number	Title (A Side/B Side)	Yr	VG	VG+	NM
❑ 70423	Ol' Devil Moon/Saturday	1954	2.50	5.00	10.00
❑ 70469	Make Yourself Comfortable/Idle Gossip	1954	2.50	5.00	10.00
❑ 70534	How Important Can It Be/Waltzing Down the Aisle	1955	2.50	5.00	10.00
❑ 70595	Whatever Lola Wants/Oh Yeah	1955	2.50	5.00	10.00
❑ 70646	Experience Unnecessary/Slowly, With Feeling	1955	2.50	5.00	10.00
❑ 70693	Johnny, Be Smart/Hey Naughty Papa	1955	2.50	5.00	10.00
❑ 70727	C'est La Vie/Never	1955	2.50	5.00	10.00
❑ 70777	Mr. Wonderful/You Ought to Have a Wife	1956	3.00	6.00	12.00
❑ 70846	Hot and Cold Running Tears/That's Not the Kind of Love I Want	1956	3.00	6.00	12.00
❑ 70885	Fabulous Character/The Other Woman	1956	3.00	6.00	12.00
❑ 70947	It Happened Again/I Wanna Play House	1956	3.00	6.00	12.00
❑ 71020	The Banana Boat Song/I've Got a New Heartache	1956	3.00	6.00	12.00
❑ 71030	Leave It to Love/The Bashful Matador	1957	3.00	6.00	12.00
❑ 71085	Poor Butterfly/April Give Me One More Day	1957	3.00	6.00	12.00
❑ 71157	Band of Angels/Please Mr. Brown	1957	3.00	6.00	12.00
❑ 71235	Gone Train/Next Time Around	1957	3.00	6.00	12.00

MGM

Number	Title (A Side/B Side)	Yr	VG	VG+	NM
❑ 10549	The Man I Love/Once in a While	1949	3.00	6.00	12.00

—Both sides recorded for Musicraft but previously unissued

Number	Title (A Side/B Side)	Yr	VG	VG+	NM
❑ 10705	Tenderly/I'll Wait and Pray	1950	2.50	5.00	10.00

—Originally issued on Musicraft 504 and 586, respectively

Number	Title (A Side/B Side)	Yr	VG	VG+	NM
❑ 10762	What a Difference A Day Made/I Can't Get Started	1950	2.50	5.00	10.00

—A-side originally issued on Musicraft 552; B-side recorded for Musicraft but previously unissued

Number	Title (A Side/B Side)	Yr	VG	VG+	NM
❑ 10819	I Cover the Waterfront/Don't Worry 'Bout Me	1950	2.50	5.00	10.00

—Originally issued on Musicraft 503 and 500, respectively

Number	Title (A Side/B Side)	Yr	VG	VG+	NM
❑ 10890	I'm Gonna Sit Right Down and Write Myself a Letter/I'm Through with Love	1951	2.50	5.00	10.00

—A-side recorded for Musicraft but previously unissued; B-side originally issued on Musicraft 499

Number	Title (A Side/B Side)	Yr	VG	VG+	NM
❑ 11068	Don't Blame Me/If You Could See Me Now	1951	2.50	5.00	10.00

—Originally issued on Musicraft 504 and 380, respectively

MUSICRAFT

Number	Title (A Side/B Side)	Yr	VG	VG+	NM
❑ 380	If You Could See Me Now/You're Not the Kind	1946	3.75	7.50	15.00
❑ 398	I Could Make You Love Me/My Kinda Love	1946	3.75	7.50	15.00
❑ 494	Body and Soul/Everything I Have Is Yours	1947	3.75	7.50	15.00
❑ 499	I'm Through with Love/Lover Man	1947	3.75	7.50	15.00
❑ 500	Don't Worry 'Bout Me/September Song	1947	3.75	7.50	15.00

—These sides had been issued earlier credited to Teddy Wilson most prominently

Number	Title (A Side/B Side)	Yr	VG	VG+	NM
❑ 503	I Cover the Waterfront/I Don't Stand a Ghost of a Chance with You	1947	3.75	7.50	15.00
❑ 504	Tenderly/Don't Blame Me	1947	3.75	7.50	15.00
❑ 505	Penthouse Serenade/I've Got a Crush on You	1947	3.75	7.50	15.00
❑ 525	The Lord's Prayer/Sometimes I Feel Like a Motherless Child	1948	3.75	7.50	15.00
❑ 533	I Feel So Smoochie/Trouble Is a Man	1948	3.75	7.50	15.00
❑ 539	Gentleman Friend/Love Me or Leave Me	1948	3.75	7.50	15.00
❑ 552	What a Difference a Day Made/The One I Love Belongs to Somebody	1948	3.75	7.50	15.00
❑ 557	It's Magic/It's You or No One	1948	3.75	7.50	15.00
❑ 567	Nature Boy/I'm Glad There Is You	1948	3.75	7.50	15.00
❑ 586	I Get a Kick Out of You/I'll Wait and Pray	1948	3.75	7.50	15.00
❑ 593	Button Up Your Overcoat/(B-side unknown)	1949	3.75	7.50	15.00

7-Inch Extended Plays

COLUMBIA

Number	Title (A Side/B Side)	Yr	VG	VG+	NM
❑ B-2551	*Deep Purple/You're Mine, You/Street of Dreams/The Nearness of You	195?	5.00	10.00	20.00
❑ B-2551 [PS]	Sarah Vaughan (Hall of Fame Series)	195?	5.00	10.00	20.00
❑ B-2588	*Perdido/Linger Awhile/Time/Corner to Corner	1959	5.00	10.00	20.00
❑ B-2588 [PS]	Sarah Vaughan (Hall of Fame Series)	1959	5.00	10.00	20.00
❑ B-7452	Come Rain or Come Shine/Mean to Me//It Might As Well Be Spring/Can't Get Out of This Mood	195?	6.25	12.50	25.00
❑ B-7452 [PS]	Sarah Vaughan in Hi-Fi	195?	6.25	12.50	25.00

MERCURY

Number	Title (A Side/B Side)	Yr	VG	VG+	NM
❑ EP-1-3305	I'm in the Mood for Love/I Don't Know Why//Honey/Let's Put Out the Lights	195?	3.00	6.00	12.00
❑ EP-1-3305 [PS]	Songs by Sarah Vaughan	195?	3.00	6.00	12.00

Number	Title (A Side/B Side)	Yr	VG	VG+	NM
MGM					
❑ X1019	(contents unknown)	1953	3.75	7.50	15.00
❑ X1019 [PS]	I've Got a Crush on You	1953	3.75	7.50	15.00
❑ X1020	The Man I Love/Body and Soul//I Can Make You Love Me/Once in a While	1953	3.75	7.50	15.00
❑ X1020 [PS]	The Man I Love	1953	3.75	7.50	15.00
Albums					
ACCORD					
❑ SN-7195	Simply Divine	1981	2.50	5.00	10.00
ALLEGRO					
❑ 1592 [M]	Sarah Vaughan	1955	12.50	25.00	50.00
❑ 1608 [M]	Sarah Vaughan	1955	12.50	25.00	50.00
❑ 3080 [10]	Early Sarah	195?	20.00	40.00	80.00
ALLEGRO ELITE					
❑ 4106 [10]	Sarah Vaughan Sings	195?	7.50	15.00	30.00
ARCHIVE OF FOLK AND JAZZ					
❑ 250	Sarah Vaughan	197?	2.50	5.00	10.00
❑ 271	Sarah Vaughan, Volume 2	197?	2.50	5.00	10.00
❑ 325	Sarah Vaughan, Volume 3	197?	2.50	5.00	10.00
ATLANTIC					
❑ SD 16037	Songs of the Beatles	1981	3.00	6.00	12.00
BRYLEN					
❑ BN 4411	Desires	198?	2.50	5.00	10.00
—Last name is misspelled "Vaughn"					
CBS MASTERWORKS					
❑ FM 37277	Gershwin Live!	1982	2.50	5.00	10.00
—With the Los Angeles Philharmonic Orchestra					
❑ FM 42519	Brazilian Romance	1987	2.50	5.00	10.00
COLUMBIA					
❑ CL 660 [M]	After Hours with Sarah Vaughan	1955	12.50	25.00	50.00
❑ CL 745 [M]	Sarah Vaughan in Hi-Fi	1956	12.50	25.00	50.00
❑ CL 914 [M]	Linger Awhile	1956	12.50	25.00	50.00
❑ CL 6133 [10]	Sarah Vaughan	1950	30.00	60.00	120.00
COLUMBIA SPECIAL PRODUCTS					
❑ P 13084	Sarah Vaughan in Hi-Fi	1976	2.50	5.00	10.00
—Reissue of Columbia 745					
❑ P 14364	Linger Awhile	1978	2.50	5.00	10.00
—Reissue of Columbia 914					
CONCORD					
❑ 3018 [M]	Sarah Vaughan Concert	1957	7.50	15.00	30.00
CORONET					
❑ 277	Sarah Vaughan Belts the Hits	196?	3.75	7.50	15.00
EMARCY					
❑ EMS-2-412 [(2)]	Sarah Vaughan Live	197?	3.00	6.00	12.00
❑ MG-26005 [10]	Images	1954	20.00	40.00	80.00
❑ MG-36004 [M]	Sarah Vaughan	1955	20.00	40.00	80.00
❑ MG-36058 [M]	In the Land of Hi-Fi	1956	20.00	40.00	80.00
❑ MG-36089 [M]	Sassy	1956	12.50	25.00	50.00
❑ MG-36109 [M]	Swingin' Easy	1957	12.50	25.00	50.00
❑ 814187-1 [(2)]	The George Gershwin Songbook	1983	3.00	6.00	12.00
❑ 824864-1	The Rodgers & Hart Songbook	1985	2.50	5.00	10.00
❑ 826454-1	In the Land of Hi-Fi	1986	2.50	5.00	10.00
—Reissue of 36058					
FORUM					
❑ F-9034 [M]	Dreamy	196?	3.00	6.00	12.00
❑ SF-9034 [S]	Dreamy	196?	3.75	7.50	15.00
HARMONY					
❑ HL 7158 [M]	The Great Sarah Vaughan	196?	3.00	6.00	12.00
LION					
❑ L 70052 [M]	Tenderly	1958	6.25	12.50	25.00
MAINSTREAM					
❑ MRL 340	Time in My Life	1972	3.75	7.50	15.00
❑ MRL 361	Sarah Vaughan/Michel Legrand	1972	3.75	7.50	15.00
❑ MRL 379	Feelin' Good	1973	3.75	7.50	15.00
❑ MRL 404	Sarah Vaughan and the Jimmy Rowles Quintet	1974	3.75	7.50	15.00
❑ MRL 419	More Sarah Vaughan from Japan	1974	3.75	7.50	15.00
MASTERSEAL					
❑ MS-55 [M]	Sarah Vaughan Sings	195?	6.25	12.50	25.00
MERCURY					
❑ MGP-2-100 [(2) M]	Great Songs from Hit Shows	1957	15.00	30.00	60.00
❑ MGP-2-101 [(2) M]	Sarah Vaughan Sings George Gershwin	1957	15.00	30.00	60.00
❑ MG-20094 [M]	Sarah Vaughan at the Blue Note	1956	10.00	20.00	40.00
❑ MG-20219 [M]	Wonderful Sarah	1957	10.00	20.00	40.00
❑ MG-20223 [M]	In a Romantic Mood	1957	10.00	20.00	40.00
❑ MG-20244 [M]	Great Songs from Hit Shows, Vol. 1	1958	7.50	15.00	30.00
❑ MG-20245 [M]	Great Songs from Hit Shows, Vol. 2	1958	7.50	15.00	30.00
❑ MG-20310 [M]	Sarah Vaughan Sings George Gershwin, Vol. 1	1958	7.50	15.00	30.00
❑ MG-20311 [M]	Sarah Vaughan Sings George Gershwin, Vol. 2	1958	7.50	15.00	30.00
❑ MG-20326 [M]	Sarah Vaughan and Her Trio at Mr. Kelly's	1958	10.00	20.00	40.00
❑ MG-20370 [M]	Vaughan and Violins	1958	10.00	20.00	40.00
❑ MG-20383 [M]	After Hours at the London House	1958	10.00	20.00	40.00
❑ MG-20438 [M]	The Magic of Sarah Vaughan	1959	7.50	15.00	30.00
❑ MG-20441 [M]	No 'Count Sarah	1959	7.50	15.00	30.00
❑ MG-20540 [M]	The Divine Sarah Vaughan	1960	6.25	12.50	25.00
❑ MG-20580 [M]	Close to You	1960	6.25	12.50	25.00
❑ MG-20617 [M]	My Heart Sings	1961	6.25	12.50	25.00
❑ MG-20645 [M]	Sarah Vaughan's Golden Hits	1961	5.00	10.00	20.00
❑ MG-20831 [M]	Sassy Swings the Tivoli	1962	5.00	10.00	20.00
❑ MG-20882 [M]	Vaughan with Voices	1963	5.00	10.00	20.00
❑ MG-20941 [M]	Viva Vaughan	1964	3.75	7.50	
❑ MG-21009 [M]	Sarah Vaughan Sings the Mancini Songbook	1965	3.75	7.50	15.00
❑ MG-21069 [M]	Pop Artistry	1966	3.75	7.50	15.00
❑ MG-21079 [M]	The New Scene	1966	3.75	7.50	15.00
❑ MG-21116 [M]	Sassy Swings Again	1967	3.75	7.50	15.00
❑ MG-21122 [M]	It's a Man's World	1967	3.75	7.50	15.00
❑ MG-25188 [10]	Divine Sarah	1955	25.00	50.00	100.00
❑ SR-60020 [S]	After Hours at the London House	1959	10.00	20.00	40.00
❑ SR-60038 [S]	Vaughan and Violins	1959	10.00	20.00	40.00
❑ SR-60041 [S]	Great Songs from Hit Shows, Vol. 1	1959	10.00	20.00	40.00
❑ SR-60045 [S]	Sarah Vaughan Sings George Gershwin, Vol. 1	1959	10.00	20.00	40.00
❑ SR-60046 [S]	Sarah Vaughan Sings George Gershwin, Vol. 2	1959	10.00	20.00	40.00
❑ SR-60078 [S]	Great Songs from Hit Shows, Vol. 2	1959	10.00	20.00	40.00
❑ SR-60110 [S]	The Magic of Sarah Vaughan	1959	10.00	20.00	40.00
❑ SR-60116 [S]	No 'Count Sarah	1959	10.00	20.00	40.00
❑ SR-60240 [S]	Close to You	1960	7.50	15.00	30.00
❑ SR-60255 [S]	The Divine Sarah Vaughan	1960	7.50	15.00	30.00
❑ SR-60617 [S]	My Heart Sings	1961	7.50	15.00	30.00
❑ SR-60645 [S]	Sarah Vaughan's Golden Hits	1961	6.25	12.50	25.00
—Original black label version					
❑ SR-60645 [S]	Sarah Vaughan's Golden Hits	1965	3.75	7.50	15.00
—Red label version with white "MERCURY" alone at top					
❑ SR-60645 [S]	Sarah Vaughan's Golden Hits	1968	3.00	6.00	12.00
—Red label with multiple Mercury logos along the label edge					
❑ SR-60831 [S]	Sassy Swings the Tivoli	1962	6.25	12.50	25.00
❑ SR-60882 [S]	Vaughan with Voices	1963	6.25	12.50	25.00
❑ SR-60941 [S]	Viva Vaughan	1964	5.00	10.00	20.00
❑ SR-61009 [S]	Sarah Vaughan Sings the Mancini Songbook	1965	5.00	10.00	20.00
❑ SR-61069 [S]	Pop Artistry	1966	5.00	10.00	20.00
❑ SR-61079 [S]	The New Scene	1966	5.00	10.00	20.00
❑ SR-61116 [S]	Sassy Swings Again	1967	5.00	10.00	20.00
❑ SR-61122 [S]	It's a Man's World	1967	5.00	10.00	20.00
❑ 826320-1 [(6)]	The Complete Sarah Vaughan on Mercury Vol. 1: Great Jazz years (1954-56)	1986	10.00	20.00	40.00
❑ 826327-1 [(5)]	The Complete Sarah Vaughan on Mercury Vol. 2: Great American Songs (1956-57)	1986	10.00	20.00	40.00
❑ 826333-1 [(6)]	The Complete Sarah Vaughan on Mercury Vol. 3: Great Show on Stage (1954-56)	1986	10.00	20.00	40.00
❑ 830721-1 [(4)]	The Complete Sarah Vaughan on Mercury Vol. 4 Part 1: Live in Europe (1963-64)	1987	10.00	20.00	40.00
❑ 830726-1 [(5)]	The Complete Sarah Vaughan on Mercury Vol. 4 Part 2: Sassy Swings Again	1987	10.00	20.00	40.00
METRO					
❑ M-539 [M]	Tenderly	1965	3.00	6.00	12.00
❑ MS-539 [S]	Tenderly	1965	3.75	7.50	15.00
MGM					
❑ E-165 [10]	Tenderly	1950	30.00	60.00	120.00
❑ E-544 [10]	Sarah Vaughan Sings	1951	30.00	60.00	120.00
❑ E-3274 [M]	My Kinda Love	1955	12.50	25.00	50.00
—Combination of two 10-inch LPs on one 12-inch LP					
MUSICRAFT					
❑ 504	Divine Sarah	197?	2.50	5.00	10.00
❑ MVS-2002	The Man I Love	1986	2.50	5.00	10.00
❑ MVS-2006	Lover Man	1986	2.50	5.00	10.00
PABLO					
❑ 2310821	How Long	1978	2.50	5.00	10.00
❑ 2310885	The Best of Sarah Vaughan	1983	2.50	5.00	10.00
❑ 2312101	I Love Brazil	1978	2.50	5.00	10.00
❑ 2312111	The Duke Ellington Songbook One	1979	2.50	5.00	10.00
❑ 2312116	The Duke Ellington Songbook Two	1980	2.50	5.00	10.00
❑ 2312125	Copacabana	1981	2.50	5.00	10.00
❑ 2405416	The Best of Sarah Vaughan	1990	2.50	5.00	10.00
PABLO TODAY					
❑ 2312137	Crazy and Mixed Up	1982	2.50	5.00	10.00
PALACE					
❑ 5191 [M]	Sarah Vaughan Sings	195?	6.25	12.50	25.00
PICKWICK					
❑ PCS-3035	Fabulous Sarah Vaughan	197?	2.50	5.00	10.00
REMINGTON					
❑ RLP-1024 [10]	Hot Jazz	1953	50.00	100.00	200.00
RIVERSIDE					
❑ RLP 2511 [10]	Sarah Vaughan Sings with John Kirby	1955	25.00	50.00	100.00
RONDO-LETTE					
❑ A-35 [M]	Songs of Broadway	1958	6.25	12.50	25.00
❑ A-53 [M]	Sarah Vaughan Sings	1959	6.25	12.50	25.00
ROULETTE					
❑ RE-103 [(2)]	Echoes of An Era	197?	3.00	6.00	12.00
❑ K-105 [(2) M]	The Sarah Vaughan Years	196?	5.00	10.00	20.00
❑ K-105 [(2)]	The Sarah Vaughan Years	196?	5.00	10.00	20.00
❑ SK-105 [(2) S]	The Sarah Vaughan Years	196?	7.50	15.00	30.00
❑ R 52046 [M]	Dreamy	1960	7.50	15.00	30.00
❑ SR 52046 [S]	Dreamy	1960	10.00	20.00	40.00
❑ R 52060 [M]	Divine One	1960	6.25	12.50	25.00
❑ SR 52060 [S]	Divine One	1960	7.50	15.00	30.00
❑ R 52070 [M]	After Hours	1961	6.25	12.50	25.00
❑ SR 52070 [S]	After Hours	1961	7.50	15.00	30.00
❑ R 52082 [M]	You're Mine	1962	6.25	12.50	25.00
❑ SR 52082 [S]	You're Mine	1962	7.50	15.00	30.00
—Black vinyl					
❑ SR 52082 [S]	You're Mine	1962	15.00	30.00	60.00
—Red vinyl					
❑ R 52091 [M]	Snowbound	1962	5.00	10.00	20.00
❑ SR 52091 [S]	Snowbound	1962	6.25	12.50	25.00
❑ R 52092 [M]	The Explosive Side of Sarah	1962	5.00	10.00	20.00
❑ SR 52092 [S]	The Explosive Side of Sarah	1962	6.25	12.50	25.00
❑ R 52100 [M]	Star Eyes	1963	3.75	7.50	15.00
❑ SR 52100 [S]	Star Eyes	1963	5.00	10.00	20.00
❑ R 52104 [M]	Lonely Hours	1963	3.75	7.50	15.00

Number	Title (A Side/B Side)	Yr	VG	VG+	NM
❏ SR 52104 [S]	Lonely Hours	1963	5.00	10.00	20.00
❏ R 52109 [M]	The World of Sarah Vaughan	1964	3.75	7.50	15.00
❏ SR 52109 [S]	The World of Sarah Vaughan	1964	5.00	10.00	20.00
❏ R 52112 [M]	Sweet 'N Sassy	1964	3.75	7.50	15.00
❏ SR 52112 [S]	Sweet 'N Sassy	1964	5.00	10.00	20.00
❏ R 52116 [M]	Sarah Sings Soulfully	1965	3.75	7.50	15.00
❏ SR 52116 [S]	Sarah Sings Soulfully	1965	5.00	10.00	20.00
❏ R 52118 [M]	Sarah Plus Two	1965	3.75	7.50	15.00
❏ SR 52118 [S]	Sarah Plus Two	1965	5.00	10.00	20.00
❏ R 52123 [M]	Sarah Slightly Classical	1966	3.75	7.50	15.00
❏ SR 52123 [S]	Sarah Slightly Classical	1966	5.00	10.00	20.00

SCEPTER

Number	Title (A Side/B Side)	Yr	VG	VG+	NM
❏ CTN-18029	The Best of Sarah Vaughan	1972	3.00	6.00	12.00

SPIN-O-RAMA

Number	Title (A Side/B Side)	Yr	VG	VG+	NM
❏ 73 [M]	Sweet, Sultry and Swinging	196?	10.00	20.00	40.00
❏ S-73 [S]	Sweet, Sultry and Swinging	196?	12.50	25.00	50.00
❏ 114 [M]	The Divine Sarah Vaughan	196?	10.00	20.00	40.00
❏ S-114 [S]	The Divine Sarah Vaughan	196?	12.50	25.00	50.00

TRIP

Number	Title (A Side/B Side)	Yr	VG	VG+	NM
❏ 5501	Sarah Vaughan	197?	2.50	5.00	10.00
❏ 5517	Sassy	197?	2.50	5.00	10.00
❏ 5523	In the Land of Hi-Fi	197?	2.50	5.00	10.00
❏ 5551	Swingin' Easy	197?	2.50	5.00	10.00

WING

Number	Title (A Side/B Side)	Yr	VG	VG+	NM
❏ MGW-12123 [M]	All Time Favorites	1963	3.00	6.00	12.00
❏ MGW-12280 [M]	The Magic of Sarah Vaughan	1964	3.00	6.00	12.00
❏ SRW-16123 [S]	All Time Favorites	1963	3.75	7.50	15.00
❏ SRW-16123 [S]	The Magic of Sarah Vaughan	1964	3.75	7.50	15.00

VAUGHAN, SARAH, AND COUNT BASIE
Albums
PABLO

Number	Title (A Side/B Side)	Yr	VG	VG+	NM
❏ 2312130	Send In the Clowns	1980	2.50	5.00	10.00

ROULETTE

Number	Title (A Side/B Side)	Yr	VG	VG+	NM
❏ SR 42018	Count Basie and Sarah Vaughan	1968	3.75	7.50	15.00
❏ R 52061 [M]	Count Basie and Sarah Vaughan	1960	6.25	12.50	25.00
❏ SR 52061 [S]	Count Basie and Sarah Vaughan	1960	7.50	15.00	30.00

VAUGHAN, SARAH, AND BILLY ECKSTINE
Also see each artist's individual listings.
45s
MERCURY

Number	Title (A Side/B Side)	Yr	VG	VG+	NM
❏ 71122	Passing Strangers/The Door Is Open	1957	3.00	6.00	12.00
❏ 71393	Alexander's Ragtime Band/No Limit	1959	3.00	6.00	12.00

7-Inch Extended Plays
MGM

Number	Title (A Side/B Side)	Yr	VG	VG+	NM
❏ X1002	Dedicated to You/You're All I Need//Ev'ry Day/I Love You	195?	5.00	10.00	20.00
❏ X1002 [PS]	Dedicated to You	195?	5.00	10.00	20.00

Albums
EMARCY

Number	Title (A Side/B Side)	Yr	VG	VG+	NM
❏ 822526-1	The Irving Berlin Songbook	1984	2.50	5.00	10.00

LION

Number	Title (A Side/B Side)	Yr	VG	VG+	NM
❏ L-70088 [M]	Billy and Sarah	195?	6.25	12.50	25.00

MERCURY

Number	Title (A Side/B Side)	Yr	VG	VG+	NM
❏ MG-20316 [M]	Sarah Vaughan and Billy Eckstine Sing the Best of Irving Berlin	1959	7.50	15.00	30.00
❏ SR-60002 [S]	Sarah Vaughan and Billy Eckstine Sing the Best of Irving Berlin	1959	10.00	20.00	40.00

VAUGHAN, SARAH; DINAH WASHINGTON; JOE WILLIAMS
Albums
ROULETTE

Number	Title (A Side/B Side)	Yr	VG	VG+	NM
❏ R 52108 [M]	We Three	1964	3.75	7.50	15.00
❏ SR 52108 [S]	We Three	1964	5.00	10.00	20.00

VEL-TONES, THE
More than one group.
45s
COY

Number	Title (A Side/B Side)	Yr	VG	VG+	NM
❏ 101	Cal's Tune/Playboy	1959	1000.	1500.	2000.

GOLDWAX

Number	Title (A Side/B Side)	Yr	VG	VG+	NM
❏ 301	Darling/I Do	1966	3.75	7.50	15.00

JIN

Number	Title (A Side/B Side)	Yr	VG	VG+	NM
❏ 107	Lover Blues/Take a Ride	1959	10.00	20.00	40.00
❏ 115	Jailbird/I'm Yours Now	1959	10.00	20.00	40.00

KAPP

Number	Title (A Side/B Side)	Yr	VG	VG+	NM
❏ 268	Cal's Tune/Playboy	1959	25.00	50.00	100.00

LOST-NITE

Number	Title (A Side/B Side)	Yr	VG	VG+	NM
❏ 103	Now/I Need You So	1961	25.00	50.00	100.00

MERCURY

Number	Title (A Side/B Side)	Yr	VG	VG+	NM
❏ 71526	Fool in Love/Someday	1959	7.50	15.00	30.00

SATELLITE

Number	Title (A Side/B Side)	Yr	VG	VG+	NM
❏ 100	Fool in Love/Someday	1959	25.00	50.00	100.00

VEL

Number	Title (A Side/B Side)	Yr	VG	VG+	NM
❏ 9178	Broken Heart/Please Say You'll Be True	1960	375.00	750.00	1500.

WEDGE

Number	Title (A Side/B Side)	Yr	VG	VG+	NM
❏ 1013	My Dear/I Want to Know	1964	50.00	100.00	200.00

ZARA

Number	Title (A Side/B Side)	Yr	VG	VG+	NM
❏ 901	Now/I Need You So	1960	20.00	40.00	80.00

VELLS, THE
Later recorded as MARTHA AND THE VANDELLAS.
45s
MEL-O-DY

Number	Title (A Side/B Side)	Yr	VG	VG+	NM
❏ 103	There He Is At My Door/You'll Never Cherish a Love So True	1962	25.00	50.00	100.00

VELOURS, THE
45s
CLIFTON

Number	Title (A Side/B Side)	Yr	VG	VG+	NM
❏ 1987	Old Fashion Christmas/I Wish You Love	19??	—	3.00	6.00

CUB

Number	Title (A Side/B Side)	Yr	VG	VG+	NM
❏ 9014	Crazy Love/I'll Never Smile Again	1958	6.25	12.50	25.00
❏ 9029	Blue Velvet/Tired of Your Rock and Rollin'	1959	6.25	12.50	25.00

END

Number	Title (A Side/B Side)	Yr	VG	VG+	NM
❏ 1090	Lover Come Back/The Lonely One	1961	5.00	10.00	20.00

GOLDISC

Number	Title (A Side/B Side)	Yr	VG	VG+	NM
❏ 3012	Daddy Warbucks/Sweet Sixteen	1960	6.25	12.50	25.00

GONE

Number	Title (A Side/B Side)	Yr	VG	VG+	NM
❏ 5092	Can I Come Over Tonight/Where There's a Will (There's a Way)	1960	5.00	10.00	20.00

MGM

Number	Title (A Side/B Side)	Yr	VG	VG+	NM
❏ 13780	Don't Pity Me/I'm Gonna Change	1967	7.50	15.00	30.00

ONYX

Number	Title (A Side/B Side)	Yr	VG	VG+	NM
❏ 501	My Love Come Back/Honey Drop	1956	50.00	100.00	200.00
❏ 508	What You Do to Me/Romeo	1957	200.00	400.00	800.00
❏ 512	Can I Come Over Tonight/Where There's a Will (There's a Way)	1957	50.00	100.00	200.00
❏ 515	This Could Be the Night/Hands Across the Table	1957	30.00	60.00	120.00
❏ 520	Remember/Can I Walk You Home	1958	15.00	30.00	60.00

ORBIT

Number	Title (A Side/B Side)	Yr	VG	VG+	NM
❏ 9001	Remember/Can I Walk You Home	1958	12.50	25.00	50.00

RONA

Number	Title (A Side/B Side)	Yr	VG	VG+	NM
❏ 010	Woman for Me/(B-side unknown)	1966	6.25	12.50	25.00

STUDO

Number	Title (A Side/B Side)	Yr	VG	VG+	NM
❏ 9902	I Promise/Little Sweetheart	1959	12.50	25.00	50.00

VELVATONES, THE
45s
METEOR

Number	Title (A Side/B Side)	Yr	VG	VG+	NM
❏ 5042	Real Gone Baby/Feeling Kinda Lonely	1957	50.00	100.00	200.00

NU KAT

Number	Title (A Side/B Side)	Yr	VG	VG+	NM
❏ 110	Impossible/I'm Leaving Home	1959	12.50	25.00	50.00

VELVELETTES, THE
45s
I.P.G.

Number	Title (A Side/B Side)	Yr	VG	VG+	NM
❏ 1002	There He Goes/That's the Reason Why	1963	25.00	50.00	100.00

SOUL

Number	Title (A Side/B Side)	Yr	VG	VG+	NM
❏ 35025	These Things Will Keep Me Loving You/Since You've Been Loving Me	1966	5.00	10.00	20.00

V.I.P.

Number	Title (A Side/B Side)	Yr	VG	VG+	NM
❏ 25007	Needle in a Haystack/Should I Tell Them	1964	6.25	12.50	25.00
❏ 25013	He Was Realy Sayin' Somethin'/Throw a Farewell Kiss	1965	6.25	12.50	25.00
❏ 25017	I'm the Exception to the Rule/Lonely, Lonely Girl Am I	1965	5.00	10.00	20.00
❏ 25021	A Bird in the Hand (Is Worth Two in the Bush)/(B-side unknown)	1965	200.00	400.00	800.00
❏ 25030	A Bird in the Hand (Is Worth Two in the Bush)/Since You've Been Loving Me	1965	5.00	10.00	20.00
❏ 25034	These Things Will Keep Me Loving You/Since You've Been Loving Me	1966	7.50	15.00	30.00

VELVET KEYS, THE
45s
KING

Number	Title (A Side/B Side)	Yr	VG	VG+	NM
❏ 5090	My Baby's Gone/Let's Stay After School	1957	20.00	40.00	80.00
❏ 5109	Don't Take My Picture, Take Me/The Truth About Youth	1958	20.00	40.00	80.00

VELVET SOUNDS, THE
45s
COSMOPOLITAN

Number	Title (A Side/B Side)	Yr	VG	VG+	NM
❏ 100/101	Silver Star/The Devil and the Stocker	1953	150.00	300.00	600.00
❏ 105/106	Pretty Darling/Who'll Take My Place	1953	100.00	200.00	400.00
❏ 530/531	Hanging Up Christmas Stockings/Sing A Song Of Christmas Cheer	1953	125.00	250.00	500.00

VELVETEENS, THE
45s
GOLDEN ARTISTS

Number	Title (A Side/B Side)	Yr	VG	VG+	NM
❏ 614	I Feel Sorry for You Baby/Ching Bam Bah	1965	2.50	5.00	10.00

LAURIE

Number	Title (A Side/B Side)	Yr	VG	VG+	NM
❏ 3126	I Thank You/Meant to Be	1962	3.75	7.50	15.00

STARK

Number	Title (A Side/B Side)	Yr	VG	VG+	NM
❏ 101	Please Holy Father/Baby Baby	1961	12.50	25.00	50.00

—*Original title of A-side*

Number	Title (A Side/B Side)	Yr	VG	VG+	NM
❏ 101	The Teen Prayer/Baby Baby	1961	7.50	15.00	30.00

—*New A-side title*

Number	Title (A Side/B Side)	Yr	VG	VG+	NM
❏ 101	Teen Prayer/Baby Baby	1961	5.00	10.00	20.00

—*Slightly altered A-side title*

Number	Title (A Side/B Side)	Yr	VG	VG+	NM
❏ 105	I Thank You/Meant to Be	1962	6.25	12.50	25.00

Number	Title (A Side/B Side)	Yr	VG	VG+	NM

VELVETEERS, THE
45s
SPITFIRE

Number	Title (A Side/B Side)	Yr	VG	VG+	NM
❑ 15	Tell Me You're Mine/Boo Wacka Boo	1956	2000.	3000.	4000.

VELVETIERS, THE
45s
RIC

❑ 958	Oh Baby/Feelin' Right Saturday Night	1958	75.00	150.00	300.00

VELVETONES, THE (1)
45s
ALADDIN

❑ 3372	Glory of Love/I Love Her So	1957	50.00	100.00	200.00
❑ 3391	I Found My Love/Melody of Love	1957	50.00	100.00	200.00
❑ 3463	My Every Thought/Little Girl I Love You So	1960	75.00	150.00	300.00

D

❑ 1049	Come Back/Penalty of Love	1959	37.50	75.00	150.00
❑ 1072	Worried Over You/Space Man	1959	25.00	50.00	100.00

DEB

❑ 1008	Stars of Wonder/Who Took My Girl	1959	37.50	75.00	150.00

IMPERIAL

❑ 5878	The Glory of Love/I Love Her So	1962	7.50	15.00	30.00
❑ 66020	The Glory of Love/I Found My Love	1964	3.75	7.50	15.00

VELVETS, THE (1)
45s
MONUMENT

❑ 435	That Lucky Old Sun/Time and Again	1961	7.50	15.00	30.00
❑ 441	Tonight (Could Be the Night)/Spring Fever	1961	7.50	15.00	30.00
❑ 448	Lana/Laugh	1961	7.50	15.00	30.00
❑ 458	The Love Express/Don't Let Him Take My Baby	1962	6.25	12.50	25.00
❑ 464	Let the Good Times Roll/The Lights Go On, The Lights Go Off	1962	6.25	12.50	25.00
❑ 810	Crying in the Chapel/Dawn	1963	5.00	10.00	20.00
❑ 836	Nightmare/Here Comes That Song Again	1964	5.00	10.00	20.00
❑ 861	If/Let the Fool Kiss You	1964	5.00	10.00	20.00
❑ 961	Baby the Magic Is Gone/Let the Fool Kiss You	1966	3.75	7.50	15.00
❑ 8917	Tonight (Could Be the Night)/That Lucky Old Sun (Just Rolls Around Heaven)	197?	—	2.50	5.00

—"Golden Series" reissue

VELVETS, THE (2)
45s
EVENT

❑ 4285	I/At Last	197?	2.00	4.00	8.00

FURY

❑ 1012	I-I-I (Love You So-So-So)/Dance Honey Dance	1958	12.50	25.00	50.00

PILGRIM

❑ 706	I/At Last	1956	12.50	25.00	50.00
❑ 710	Tell Her/I Cried	1956	12.50	25.00	50.00

RED ROBIN

❑ 120	They Tried/She's Gotta Grin	1953	50.00	100.00	200.00
❑ 122	I/At Last	1953	37.50	75.00	150.00
❑ 127	Tell Her/I Cried	1954	37.50	75.00	150.00

VELVETS, THE (U)
These could be by group (1).
45s
20TH FOX

❑ 165	Happy Days Are Here Again/If I Could Be with You	1959	6.25	12.50	25.00

PLAID

❑ 101	Everybody Knows/Hand Jivin' Baby	1959	20.00	40.00	80.00

VENEERS, THE
45s
PRINCETON

❑ 102	Believe Me (My Angel)/I	1960	10.00	20.00	40.00

TREYCO

❑ 402	With All My Love/Recipe of Love	1963	3.75	7.50	15.00

VERONICA
Also see THE RONETTES; RONNIE SPECTOR.
45s
PHIL SPECTOR

❑ 1	So Young/Larry L	1964	50.00	100.00	200.00
❑ 2	Why Can't They Let Us Fall in Love/Chubby Danny D	1964	150.00	300.00	600.00

—Note slightly different A-side title

❑ 2	Why Don't They Let Us Fall in Love/Chubby Danny D	1964	50.00	100.00	200.00

VERSATILES, THE
More than one group.
45s
ATLANTIC

❑ 2004	Passing By/Crying	1958	10.00	20.00	40.00

PEACOCK

❑ 1910	White Cliffs of Dover/Just Words	1963	7.50	15.00	30.00

RAMCO

❑ 3717	Blue Feeling/Just Pretending	1962	50.00	100.00	200.00

RO-CAL

❑ 1002	I'll Whisper in Your ear/Lundee Dundee	1960	25.00	50.00	100.00

SEA CREST

❑ 6001	Lonely Boy/Moon Dawg	1964	6.25	12.50	25.00

VERSATONES, THE
Probably more than one group.
45s
ALL STAR

❑ 501	Tight Skirt and Sweater/Bila	1958	10.00	20.00	40.00

ATLANTIC

❑ 2211	Tight Skirt and Sweater/Bila	1963	5.00	10.00	20.00

FENWAY

❑ 7001	Tight Skirt and Sweater/Bila	1960	6.25	12.50	25.00

RCA VICTOR

❑ 47-6917	Wait for Me/De Obeah Man	1957	3.75	7.50	15.00
❑ 47-6976	Lovely Teenage Girl/Bikini Baby	1957	3.75	7.50	15.00

VIBES, THE (1)
45s
ABC-PARAMOUNT

❑ 9810	Darling/Come Back Baby	1957	12.50	25.00	50.00

VIBES, THE (2)
45s
AFTER HOURS

❑ 105	Stop Torturing Me/Stop Jibing, Baby	1954	500.00	1000.	2000.

CHARIOT

❑ 105	Stop Torturing Me/Stop Jibing, Baby	1954	375.00	750.00	1500.

VIBES, THE (3)
45s
ALLIED

❑ 10006	What's Her Name/You Are	1958	15.00	30.00	60.00
❑ 10007	Misunderstood/Let the Old Folks Talk	1959	10.00	20.00	40.00

VIBES, THE (4)
45s
PERSPECTIVE

❑ 5858	Pretty Baby (I Saw You Last Night)/Crying for You	1960	25.00	50.00	100.00

VIBES, THE (5)
45s
RAYNA

❑ 103	You Got Me Crying/A Killer Came to Town	196?	10.00	20.00	40.00

VIBRANAIRES, THE
Probably the same group as THE VIBES (2).
45s
AFTER HOURS

❑ 103	Doll Face/Ooh, I Feel So Good	1954	625.00	1250.	2500.

CHARIOT

❑ 103	Doll Face/Ooh, I Feel So Good	1954	500.00	1000.	2000.

VIBRATIONS, THE
Also see THE JAYHAWKS; THE MARATHONS (1).
45s
ATLANTIC

❑ 2204	Between Hello and Goodbye/Lonesome Little Lonely Girl	1963	3.00	6.00	12.00
❑ 2221	My Girl Sloopy/Daddy Woo-Woo	1964	3.00	6.00	12.00

BET

❑ 1	So Blue/Love Me Like You Should	1960	25.00	50.00	100.00

CHECKER

❑ 954	So Blue/Love Me Like You Should	1960	7.50	15.00	30.00
❑ 961	Feel So Bad/Cave Man	1960	5.00	10.00	20.00
❑ 967	Doing the Slop/So Little Time	1961	5.00	10.00	20.00
❑ 969	The Watusi/Wallflower	1961	5.00	10.00	20.00
❑ 974	The Continental/The Junkeroo	1961	5.00	10.00	20.00
❑ 982	Don't Say Goodbye/Stranded in the Jungle	1961	5.00	10.00	20.00
❑ 987	All My Love Belongs to You/Stop Right Now	1961	10.00	20.00	40.00
❑ 990	Let's Pony Again/What Made You Change Your Mind	1961	5.00	10.00	20.00
❑ 1002	Over the Rainbow/Oh, Cindy	1962	3.75	7.50	15.00
❑ 1011	The New Hully Gully/Anytime	1962	3.75	7.50	15.00
❑ 1022	Hamburgers on a Bun/If He Don't	1962	3.75	7.50	15.00
❑ 1038	Since I Fell for You/May the Best Man Win	1963	3.75	7.50	15.00
❑ 1061	Dancing Danny/(Instrumental)	1963	3.75	7.50	15.00

CHESS

❑ 2151	Shake It Up/Make It Last	1974	—	3.00	6.00

EPIC

❑ 10418	I Took an Overdose/Because You're Mine	1968	5.00	10.00	20.00

MANDALA

❑ 2511	Ain't No Greens in Harlem/Wind-Up Toy	1972	—	3.00	6.00
❑ 2514	Man Overboard/(B-side unknown)	1972	—	3.00	6.00

NEPTUNE

❑ 19	Expressway to Your Heart/Who's Gonna Help Me Now	1969	2.00	4.00	8.00
❑ 21	Smoke Signals/Who's Gonna Help Me Now	1970	2.00	4.00	8.00
❑ 28	Right On Brothers, Right On/Surprise Party for Baby	1970	2.00	4.00	8.00

OKEH

❑ 7205	Sloop Dance/Watusi Time	1964	3.00	6.00	12.00
❑ 7212	Hello Happiness/Keep On Keeping On	1965	3.00	6.00	12.00
❑ 7220	End Up Crying/Ain't Love That Way	1965	3.00	6.00	12.00

Number	Title (A Side/B Side)	Yr	VG	VG+	NM
❑ 7228	Talkin' 'Bout Love/If You Only Knew	1965	3.00	6.00	12.00
❑ 7230	Misty/Finding Out the Hard Way	1965	3.00	6.00	12.00
❑ 7238	Gina/The Story of a Starry Night	1966	—	—	—
—Unreleased					
❑ 7241	Canadian Sunset/The Story of a Starry Night	1966	2.50	5.00	10.00
❑ 7249	Forgive and Forget/Gonna Get Along Without You Now	1966	2.50	5.00	10.00
❑ 7257	And I Love Her/Soul a-Go-Go	1966	2.50	5.00	10.00
❑ 7276	Pick Me/You Better Beware	1967	2.50	5.00	10.00
❑ 7297	Together/Come To Yourself	1967	2.50	5.00	10.00
❑ 7311	Love in Them There Hills/Remember the Rain	1968	2.50	5.00	10.00

Albums

Number	Title (A Side/B Side)	Yr	VG	VG+	NM
CHECKER					
❑ LP-2978 [M]	The Watusi	1961	50.00	100.00	200.00
MANDALA					
❑ 3006	Taking a New Step	1972	5.00	10.00	20.00
OKEH					
❑ OKM-12111 [M]	Shout	1965	7.50	15.00	30.00
❑ OKM-12112 [M]	Misty	1966	7.50	15.00	30.00
❑ OKM-12114 [M]	New Vibrations	1967	7.50	15.00	30.00
❑ OKS-14111 [S]	Shout	1965	10.00	20.00	40.00
❑ OKS-14112 [S]	Misty	1966	10.00	20.00	40.00
❑ OKS-14114 [S]	New Vibrations	1967	10.00	20.00	40.00
❑ OKS-14129	The Vibrations' Greatest Hits	1969	7.50	15.00	30.00

VICEROYS, THE (1)
45s

Number	Title (A Side/B Side)	Yr	VG	VG+	NM
ALADDIN					
❑ 3273	Please, Baby, Please/I'm Yours As Long As I Live	1955	100.00	200.00	400.00

VICEROYS, THE (2)
45s

Number	Title (A Side/B Side)	Yr	VG	VG+	NM
BETHLEHEM					
❑ 3045	Seagrams/Moasin'	1962	6.25	12.50	25.00
—Original A-side title					
❑ 3045	Sea Green/Moasin'	1962	5.00	10.00	20.00
❑ 3070	The Fox/Buzz Bomb	1963	6.25	12.50	25.00
—Original A-side title					
❑ 3070	Joshin'/Buzz Bomb	1963	5.00	10.00	20.00
❑ 3088	Not Too Much Twist/Tears on My Pillow	1965	5.00	10.00	20.00

VICTORIALS, THE
45s

Number	Title (A Side/B Side)	Yr	VG	VG+	NM
IMPERIAL					
❑ 5398	I Get That Feeling/The Prettiest Girl in the World	1956	12.50	25.00	50.00

VICTORIANS, THE
45s

Number	Title (A Side/B Side)	Yr	VG	VG+	NM
ARNOLD					
❑ 571	Move In a Little Closer/Lovin'	1963	5.00	10.00	20.00
BANG					
❑ 550	Merry-Go-Round/Wasn't the Summer Short	1967	3.75	7.50	15.00
LIBERTY					
❑ 55574	Climb Every Mountain/What Makes Little Girls Cry	1963	5.00	10.00	20.00
❑ 55656	The Monkey Stroll/You're Invited to a Party	1964	3.75	7.50	15.00
❑ 55693	Happy Birthday Blues/Oh What a Night for Love	1964	3.75	7.50	15.00
❑ 55728	If I Loved You/The Monkey Stroll	1964	3.75	7.50	15.00
REPRISE					
❑ 0434	I Saw My Girl/Baby Toys	1965	3.75	7.50	15.00
SAXONY					
❑ 103	Heartbreaking Moon/I'm Rollin'	1956	125.00	250.00	500.00
SELMA					
❑ 1002	Wedding Bells/Please Say You Do	1956	75.00	150.00	300.00

VICTORY FIVE, THE
45s

Number	Title (A Side/B Side)	Yr	VG	VG+	NM
TERP					
❑ 101	I Never Knew/Swing Low	1958	150.00	300.00	600.00
—All copies on colored vinyl					

VIDALTONES, THE
45s

Number	Title (A Side/B Side)	Yr	VG	VG+	NM
JOSIE					
❑ 900	Forever/Someone to Love	1962	10.00	20.00	40.00

VIDELS, THE
45s

Number	Title (A Side/B Side)	Yr	VG	VG+	NM
EARLY					
❑ 702	I Wish/Blow, Winds, Blow	1960	100.00	200.00	400.00
JDS					
❑ 5004	Mr. Lonely/I'll Forget You	1960	7.50	15.00	30.00
—Gray label					
❑ 5004	Mr. Lonely/I'll Forget You	1960	5.00	10.00	20.00
—Multicolor label					
❑ 5005	She's Not Coming Home/Now That Summer Is Here	1960	7.50	15.00	30.00
—Gray label					
❑ 5005	She's Not Coming Home/Now That Summer Is Here	1960	5.00	10.00	20.00
—Multicolor label					
KAPP					
❑ 361	Streets of Love/I'll Keep On Waiting	1960	5.00	10.00	20.00

Number	Title (A Side/B Side)	Yr	VG	VG+	NM
❑ 405	A Letter from Ann/This Year's Mister New	1961	10.00	20.00	40.00
MEDIEVAL					
❑ 203	Be My Girl/A Place in Your Heart	1961	3.75	7.50	15.00
MUSICNOTE					
❑ 117	We Belong Together/It's All Over	1963	12.50	25.00	50.00
RHODY					
❑ 2000	Be My Girl/A Place in Your Heart	1959	12.50	25.00	50.00
TIC TAC TOE					
❑ 5005	She's Not Coming Home/Now That Summer Is Here	1962	12.50	25.00	50.00

VIDEOS, THE
45s

Number	Title (A Side/B Side)	Yr	VG	VG+	NM
CASINO					
❑ 102	Trickle, Trickle/Moonglow You Know	1958	12.50	25.00	50.00
—"Casino" in shadow print; no mention of distribution by Gone					
❑ 102	Trickle, Trickle/Moonglow You Know	1958	5.00	10.00	20.00
—With playing cards on label					
❑ 102	Trickle, Trickle/Moonglow You Know	1958	7.50	15.00	30.00
—"Casino" in normal print; no playing cards; no mention of distribution by Gone					
❑ 102	Trickle, Trickle/Moonglow You Know	1961	6.25	12.50	25.00
—No playing cards; with distribution by Gone					
❑ 105	Love or Infatuation/Shoo-Be-Doo-Be Cha Cha Cha	1959	75.00	150.00	300.00

VILLAGE PEOPLE
45s

Number	Title (A Side/B Side)	Yr	VG	VG+	NM
CASABLANCA					
❑ 896	San Francisco (You've Got Me)/Village People	1977	—	3.00	6.00
❑ 922	Macho Man/Key West	1978	—	2.50	5.00
❑ 945	Y.M.C.A./The Women	1978	—	2.50	5.00
❑ 973	In the Navy/Manhattan Woman	1979	—	2.50	5.00
❑ 973 [PS]	In the Navy/Manhattan Woman	1979	5.00	10.00	20.00
—Picture sleeve is promo only					
❑ 984	Go West/Citizens of the World	1979	—	2.50	5.00
❑ 2213	Sleazy/Save Me (Uptempo)	1979	—	2.00	4.00
❑ 2220	Ready for the 80's/Sleazy	1980	—	2.00	4.00
❑ 2261	Can't Stop the Music/Milkshake	1980	—	2.00	4.00
❑ 2261 [PS]	Can't Stop the Music/Milkshake	1980	2.00	4.00	8.00
❑ 2291	Magic Night/I Love You to Death	1980	—	2.00	4.00
RCA					
❑ PB-12258	5 O'Clock in the Morning/Food Fight	1981	—	2.00	4.00
❑ PB-12258 [PS]	5 O'Clock in the Morning/Food Fight	1981	—	2.50	5.00
❑ PB-12331	Jungle City/Action Man	1981	—	2.00	4.00

Albums

Number	Title (A Side/B Side)	Yr	VG	VG+	NM
CASABLANCA					
❑ NBLP-7064	Village People	1977	2.50	5.00	10.00
❑ NBPIX-7064 [PD]	Village People	1978	5.00	10.00	20.00
❑ NBLP-7096	Macho Man	1978	2.50	5.00	10.00
❑ NBPIX-7096 [PD]	Macho Man	1978	5.00	10.00	20.00
❑ NBLP-7118	Cruisin'	1978	2.50	5.00	10.00
❑ NBPIX-7118 [PD]	Cruisin'	1978	5.00	10.00	20.00
❑ NBLP-7144	Go West	1979	2.50	5.00	10.00
❑ NBLP-7183 [(2)]	Live and Sleazy	1979	3.00	6.00	12.00
RCA VICTOR					
❑ AFL1-4105	Renaissance	1981	2.50	5.00	10.00
RHINO					
❑ R1-70167	Greatest Hits	1988	2.50	5.00	10.00

VINSON, EDDIE "CLEANHEAD"
45s

Number	Title (A Side/B Side)	Yr	VG	VG+	NM
BETHLEHEM					
❑ 11097	Cherry Red/Kidney Stew	1961	5.00	10.00	20.00
BLUESWAY					
❑ 61005	Cadillac Blues/Old Maid Got Married	1967	3.00	6.00	12.00
KING					
❑ 4563	Good Bread Alley/I Need You Tonight	1952	15.00	30.00	60.00
❑ 4582	Lonesome Train/Person to Person	1952	15.00	30.00	60.00
❑ 6305	Person to Person/Cherry Red Blues	1970	—	3.00	6.00
MERCURY					
❑ 70334	Old Man Boogie/You Can't Have My Love No More	1954	50.00	100.00	200.00
❑ 70525	Anxious Heart/Suffer Fool	1954	30.00	60.00	120.00
❑ 70621	Tomorrow May Never Come/Big Chief Rain in the Face	1955	25.00	50.00	100.00
RIVERSIDE					
❑ 4512	Back Door Blues/Hold It	1962	5.00	10.00	20.00

Albums

Number	Title (A Side/B Side)	Yr	VG	VG+	NM
AAMCO					
❑ 312 [M]	Cleanhead's Back in Town	196?	10.00	20.00	40.00
BETHLEHEM					
❑ BCP-5005 [M]	Eddie "Cleanhead" Vinson Sings	1957	25.00	50.00	100.00
❑ BCP-6036	Back in Town	1978	3.75	7.50	15.00
BLUESWAY					
❑ BL-6007 [M]	Cherry Red	1967	6.25	12.50	25.00
❑ BLS-6007 [S]	Cherry Red	1967	6.25	12.50	25.00
CIRCLE					
❑ CLP-57	Kidney Stew	1983	3.00	6.00	12.00
DELMARK					
❑ 631	Old Kidney Stew Is Fine	1980	3.00	6.00	12.00
FLYING DUTCHMAN					
❑ 31-1012	You Can't Make Love Alone	197?	3.75	7.50	15.00

Number	Title (A Side/B Side)	Yr	VG	VG+	NM

KING
| ❏ KS-1087 | Cherry Red | 1969 | 6.25 | 12.50 | 25.00 |

MUSE
❏ MR-5116	The Clean Machine	1978	3.75	7.50	15.00
❏ MR-5208	Eddie "Cleanhead" Vinson and the Muse All-Stars: Live at Sandy's	1979	3.00	6.00	12.00
❏ MR-5243	Eddie "Cleanhead" Vinson and the Muse All-Stars: Hold It Right There	198?	3.00	6.00	12.00
❏ MR-5282	Cleanhead and Roomful of Blues	1982	3.00	6.00	12.00
❏ MR-5310	Eddie "Cleanhead" Vinson Sings the Blues	198?	3.00	6.00	12.00

PABLO
| ❏ 2310866 | I Want a Little Girl | 198? | 3.00 | 6.00 | 12.00 |

REGGIES
| ❏ 1000 | Rollin' Over the Devil | 1981 | 3.00 | 6.00 | 12.00 |

RIVERSIDE
| ❏ RLP-502 [M] | Back Door Blues | 1965 | 10.00 | 20.00 | 40.00 |
| ❏ RLS-9502 [S] | Back Door Blues | 1965 | 10.00 | 20.00 | 40.00 |

VINSON, EDDIE "CLEANHEAD"/JIMMY WITHERSPOON
Also see each artist's individual listings.
Albums
KING
| ❏ 634 [M] | Battle of the Blues, Volume 3 | 1960 | 375.00 | 750.00 | 1500. |

VISCAYNES, THE
Sylvester Stewart [Sly Stone] was a member.
45s
TROPO
| ❏ 101 | I Guess I'll Be/Stop What You're Doing | 1958 | 37.50 | 75.00 | 150.00 |
VPM
| ❏ 1006 | Yellow Moon/Heavenly Angel | 1961 | 10.00 | 20.00 | 40.00 |

VISITORS, THE (1)
45s
DAKAR
| ❏ 603 | I'm in Danger/Until You Came Along | 1969 | 2.00 | 4.00 | 8.00 |
| ❏ 613 | I'm Gonna Stay/Lonely One, Only Son | 1969 | 2.00 | 4.00 | 8.00 |
TANGERINE
| ❏ 1003 | My Love Is Ready and Waiting/What About Me | 1970 | 2.00 | 4.00 | 8.00 |
| ❏ 1010 | Anytime Is the Right Time/Nevertheless | 1970 | 2.00 | 4.00 | 8.00 |

VITO AND THE SALUTATIONS
45s
APT
| ❏ 25079 | High Noon/Walkin' | 1965 | 12.50 | 25.00 | 50.00 |
BOOM
| ❏ 60020 | Bring Back Yesterday/I Want You to Be My Baby | 1966 | 5.00 | 10.00 | 20.00 |
CRYSTAL BALL
| ❏ 105 | Unchained Melody/So Much | 1978 | — | 2.50 | 5.00 |
HERALD
| ❏ 583 | Unchained Melody/Hey Hey Baby | 1963 | 7.50 | 15.00 | 30.00 |
| ❏ 586 | Eenie Meenie/Extraordinary Girl | 1964 | 6.25 | 12.50 | 25.00 |
KRAM
| ❏ 5002 | Your Way/Hey, Hey Baby | 1962 | 12.50 | 25.00 | 50.00 |
RAYNA
| ❏ 5009 | Gloria/Let's Untwist the Twist | 1962 | 12.50 | 25.00 | 50.00 |
RED BOY
| ❏ 1001 | So Wonderful (My Love)/I'd Best Be Going | 1966 | 6.25 | 12.50 | 25.00 |
| ❏ 5009 | Gloria/Let's Untwist the Twist | 1962 | 7.50 | 15.00 | 30.00 |
REGINA
| ❏ 1320 | Get a Job/Girls I Know | 1964 | 7.50 | 15.00 | 30.00 |
RUST
| ❏ 5106 | Can I Depend on You/Hello Dolly | 1966 | 5.00 | 10.00 | 20.00 |
SANDBAG
| ❏ 103 | So Wonderful (My Love)/I'd Best Be Going | 1966 | 5.00 | 10.00 | 20.00 |
WELLS
❏ 1008	Can I Depend on You/Liverpool Bound	1964	12.50	25.00	50.00
—Yellow vinyl					
❏ 1008	Can I Depend on You/Liverpool Bound	1964	6.25	12.50	25.00
❏ 1010	The Banana Boat Song (Day-O)/Don't Count on Me	1964	6.25	12.50	25.00

VOCALEERS, THE
Possibly more than one group.
45s
OLD TOWN
| ❏ 1089 | This Is the Night/Love and Devotion | 1960 | 6.25 | 12.50 | 25.00 |
PARADISE
| ❏ 113 | I Need Your Love So Bad/Have You Ever Loved Someone | 1959 | 10.00 | 20.00 | 40.00 |
RED ROBIN
❏ 113	Be True/Oh! Where	1953	150.00	300.00	600.00
❏ 114	Is It a Dream/Hurry Home	1953	75.00	150.00	300.00
❏ 119	I Walk Alone/How Soon	1953	100.00	200.00	400.00
❏ 125	Will You Be True/Love You	1954	75.00	150.00	300.00
❏ 132	Angel Face/Lovin' Baby	1954	75.00	150.00	300.00
TWISTIME
| ❏ 11 | Cootie Snap/A Golden Tear | 1962 | 7.50 | 15.00 | 30.00 |
VEST
| ❏ 832 | Hear My Plea/The Night Is Quiet | 1960 | 20.00 | 40.00 | 80.00 |

VOICE MASTERS, THE
LAMONT DOZIER and DAVID RUFFIN were originally in this group, though they did not appear on the later sides.
45s
ANNA
| ❏ 101 | Hope and Pray/Oop's I'm Sorry | 1959 | 50.00 | 100.00 | 200.00 |
| ❏ 102 | Needed/Needed (For Lovers Only) | 1959 | 50.00 | 100.00 | 200.00 |
BAMBOO
❏ 103	You've Hurt Me Baby/If a Woman Catches a Fool	1968	6.25	12.50	25.00
❏ 105	Never Gonna Leave You/If a Woman Catches a Fool	1969	3.75	7.50	15.00
❏ 113	Dance Right Into My Heart/If a Woman Catches a Fool	1970	3.75	7.50	15.00
FRISCO
| ❏ 15235 | In Love in Vain/Two Lovers | 196? | 25.00 | 50.00 | 100.00 |

VOICES, THE
45s
CASH
❏ 1011	Why/Two Things I Love	1955	15.00	30.00	60.00
❏ 1014	Hey Now/My Love Grows Stronger	1955	15.00	30.00	60.00
❏ 1015	I Want to Be Ready/Takes Two to Make a Home	1955	15.00	30.00	60.00
❏ 1016	Santa Claus Boogie/Santa Claus Baby	1955	20.00	40.00	80.00
❏ 1016	Santa Claus Boogie/Santa Claus Baby	197?	—	2.50	5.00
—Reproduction					
SPECIALTY
| ❏ 754 | Santa Claus Boogie/Santa Claus Baby | 197? | 3.75 | 7.50 | 15.00 |
| —Red vinyl | | | | | |

VOICES OF EAST HARLEM, THE
45s
ELEKTRA
| ❏ 45753 | Sit Yourself Down/Oxford Town | 1971 | — | 3.00 | 6.00 |
| ❏ 45775 | Angry/New York Lightning | 1972 | — | 3.00 | 6.00 |
JUST SUNSHINE
❏ 504	Giving Love/New Vibrations	1973	—	2.50	5.00
❏ 510	I Like Having You Around/Cashing In	1973	—	2.50	5.00
❏ 517	Can You Feel It/Wanted Dead or Alive	1974	—	2.50	5.00
Albums
ELEKTRA
| ❏ EKS-74080 | Right On Be Free | 1970 | 2.50 | 5.00 | 10.00 |
JUST SUNSHINE
| ❏ 7 | Voices of East Harlem | 1973 | 2.50 | 5.00 | 10.00 |
| ❏ 3504 | Can You Feel It? | 1974 | 2.50 | 5.00 | 10.00 |

VOLCANOS, THE
Early version of THE TRAMMPS.
45s
ARCTIC
❏ 103	Make Your Move/Baby	1965	3.00	6.00	12.00
❏ 106	Storm Warning/Baby	1965	3.00	6.00	12.00
❏ 111	Help Wanted/Make Your Move	1965	3.00	6.00	12.00
❏ 115	(It's Against the) Laws of Love/(Instrumental)	1965	3.00	6.00	12.00
❏ 125	Lady's Man/Help Wanted	1966	2.50	5.00	10.00
❏ 128	You're Number 1/Make Your Move	1967	2.50	5.00	10.00

VOLUMES, THE
45s
AMERICAN ARTS
| ❏ 6 | Gotta Give Her Love/I Can't Live Without You | 1964 | 7.50 | 15.00 | 30.00 |
| ❏ 18 | I Just Can't Help Myself/One Way Lover | 1965 | 7.50 | 15.00 | 30.00 |
CHEX
❏ 1002	I Love You/Dreams	1962	75.00	150.00	300.00
—With typographical error crediting "The Valumes"					
❏ 1002	I Love You/Dreams	1962	10.00	20.00	40.00
—With no reference to Jay-Gee Records on label					
❏ 1002	I Love You/Dreams	1962	6.25	12.50	25.00
—With "Nationally Dist. by Jay-Gee Rec. Co. Inc." on label					
❏ 1005	Come Back Into My Heart/The Bell	1962	10.00	20.00	40.00
IMPACT
| ❏ 1017 | That Same Old Feeling/The Trouble I've Seen | 1966 | 12.50 | 25.00 | 50.00 |
INFERNO
❏ 2001	A Way to Love You/You Got It Baby	1967	5.00	10.00	20.00
❏ 2004	My Road Is the Right Road/My Kind of Girl	1967	5.00	10.00	20.00
❏ 5001	Ain't That Lovin' You/I Love You Baby	1968	5.00	10.00	20.00
JUBILEE
| ❏ 5446 | Sandra/Teenage Paradise | 1963 | 5.00 | 10.00 | 20.00 |
| ❏ 5454 | Our Song/Oh My Mother-in-Law | 1963 | 5.00 | 10.00 | 20.00 |
KAREN
| ❏ 1551 | Am I Losing You/Ain't Gonna Give You Up | 1970 | 2.00 | 4.00 | 8.00 |
OLD TOWN
| ❏ 1154 | Why/Monkey Hop | 1964 | 6.25 | 12.50 | 25.00 |

VOWS, THE
45s
MARKAY
❏ 103	I Wanna Chance/Have You Heard	1962	10.00	20.00	40.00
—Black label					
❏ 103	I Wanna Chance/Have You Heard	1962	100.00	200.00	400.00
—Orange label					
RAN-DEE
| ❏ 112 | Girl in Red/Born with the Rhythm | 196? | 15.00 | 30.00 | 60.00 |

Number	Title (A Side/B Side)	Yr	VG	VG+	NM
STA-SET					
❑ 402	Say You'll Be Mine/When a Boy Loves a Girl	1963	15.00	30.00	60.00
TAMARA					
❑ 506	The Things You Do to Me/Dottie	1963	10.00	20.00	40.00
❑ 760	Say You'll Be Mine/When a Boy Loves a Girl	1964	6.25	12.50	25.00
V.I.P.					
❑ 25016	Buttered Popcorn/Tell Me	1965	10.00	20.00	40.00

VOXPOPPERS, THE
45s

Number	Title (A Side/B Side)	Yr	VG	VG+	NM
AMP 3					
❑ 1004	Wishing for Your Love/The Last Drag	1958	10.00	20.00	40.00
MERCURY					
❑ 71282	Wishing for Your Love/The Last Drag	1958	5.00	10.00	20.00
❑ 71315	Pony Tail/Ping Pong Baby	1958	5.00	10.00	20.00
POPLAR					
❑ 107	Come Back Little Girl/A Love to Last a Lifetime	1959	5.00	10.00	20.00
VERSAILLES					
❑ 200	Can't Understand It/A Blessing After All	1959	7.50	15.00	30.00
WARWICK					
❑ 589	Lonely for You/Helen Isn't Tellin'	1960	3.00	6.00	12.00

—As "Freddie and the Voxpoppers"

7-Inch Extended Plays

Number	Title (A Side/B Side)	Yr	VG	VG+	NM
MERCURY					
❑ EP 1-3391	Wishing for Your Love/The Last Drag//Stroll Roll/ Guitar Stroll	1958	25.00	50.00	100.00
❑ EP 1-3391 [PS]	The Voxpoppers	1958	25.00	50.00	100.00

VY-DELLS, THE
45s

Number	Title (A Side/B Side)	Yr	VG	VG+	NM
GARNET					
❑ 101	What I'm Gonna Do/Unknown	196?	25.00	50.00	100.00

W

WALKER, JR., AND THE ALL STARS
45s

Number	Title (A Side/B Side)	Yr	VG	VG+	NM
HARVEY					
❑ 113	Willie's Blues/Twist Lackawanna	1962	6.25	12.50	25.00
❑ 117	Cleo's Mood/Brain Washer	1963	5.00	10.00	20.00
❑ 119	Good Rockin'/Brain Washer	1963	5.00	10.00	20.00
MOTOWN					
❑ 1352	Country Boy/What Does It Take (To Win Your Love)	1975	—	2.50	5.00
❑ 1380	I'm So Glad/Hot Shot	1976	—	—	—
—Unreleased					
❑ 1689	Blow the House Down/Ball Baby	1983	—	2.00	4.00
SOUL					
❑ 35003	Monkey Jump/Satan's Blues	1964	3.75	7.50	15.00
❑ 35008	Shotgun/Hot Cha	1965	3.75	7.50	15.00
❑ 35008	Shot Gun/Hot Cha	1965	25.00	50.00	100.00

—Not only is the A-side title listed as two words, but the record is credited to "Jr. Walker and All The Stars"!

Number	Title (A Side/B Side)	Yr	VG	VG+	NM
❑ 35008 [PS]	Shotgun/Hot Cha	1965	6.25	12.50	25.00
❑ 35012	Do the Boomerang/Tune Up	1965	2.50	5.00	10.00
❑ 35013	Shake and Fingerpop/Cleo's Back	1965	2.50	5.00	10.00
❑ 35015	(I'm a) Road Runner/Shoot Your Shot	1965	2.50	5.00	10.00
❑ 35017	Cleo's Mood/Baby You Know It Ain't Right	1966	2.00	4.00	8.00
❑ 35024	How Sweet It Is (To Be Loved By You)/Nothing But Soul	1966	2.00	4.00	8.00
❑ 35024 [PS]	How Sweet It Is (To Be Loved By You)/Nothing But Soul	1966	5.00	10.00	20.00
❑ 35026	Money (That's What I Want) Part I/Money (That's What I Want) Part II	1966	2.00	4.00	8.00
❑ 35030	Pucker Up Buttercup/Anyway You Wanna	1967	2.00	4.00	8.00
❑ 35036	Shoot Your Shot/Ain't That the Truth	1967	2.00	4.00	8.00
❑ 35041	Come See About Me/Sweet Soul	1967	2.00	4.00	8.00
❑ 35048	Hip City — Part 1/Hip City — Part 2	1968	2.00	4.00	8.00
❑ 35055	Home Cookin'/Mutiny	1969	2.00	4.00	8.00
❑ 35062	What Does It Take (To Win Your Love)/ Brainwasher — Part 1	1969	2.00	4.00	8.00
❑ 35067	These Eyes/Got to Find a Way to Win Maria Back	1969	—	3.00	6.00
❑ 35070	Gotta Hold On to This Feeling/Clinging to the Theory That She's Coming Back	1970	—	3.00	6.00
❑ 35073	Do You See My Love (For You Growing)/Groove and More	1970	—	3.00	6.00
❑ 35081	Holly Holy/Carry Your Own Load	1970	—	3.00	6.00
❑ 35084	Take Me Girl, I'm Ready/Right On Brothers and Sisters	1971	—	3.00	6.00
❑ 35090	Way Back Home/(Instrumental)	1971	—	3.00	6.00
❑ 35095	Walk in the Night/I Don't Want to Do Wrong	1972	—	3.00	6.00
❑ 35097	Groove Thang/Me and My Family	1972	—	3.00	6.00
❑ 35104	Gimme That Beat (Part 1)/Gimme That Beat (Part 2)	1973	—	3.00	6.00
❑ 35106	I Don't Need No Reason/Country Boy	1973	—	3.00	6.00
❑ 35108	Peace and Understanding (Is Hard to Find)/Soul Clappin'	1973	—	3.00	6.00
❑ 35110	Dancing Like They Do on Soul Train/I Ain't That Easy to Love	1973	—	3.00	6.00
❑ 35114 [DJ]	You Are the Sunshine of My Life/Until You Come Back to Me	1974	—	—	—
—Unreleased					
❑ 35116	I'm So Glad/Soul Clappin'	1975	—	2.50	5.00
❑ 35118	Hot Shot/You're No Ordinary Woman	1976	—	2.50	5.00
❑ 35122	Whopper Bopper Show Stopper/Hard Love	1977	—	2.50	5.00
WHITFIELD					
❑ 8861	Back Street Boogie/Don't Let Me Go Away	1979	—	2.00	4.00
❑ 49052	Wishing on a Star/Hole in the Wall	1979	—	2.00	4.00
Albums					
MOTOWN					
❑ M5-105V1	Motown Superstar Series, Vol. 5	1981	2.50	5.00	10.00
❑ M5-141V1	Shotgun	1981	2.50	5.00	10.00
—Reissue of Soul 701					
❑ M5-208V1	Greatest Hits	1981	2.50	5.00	10.00
—Reissue of Soul 718					
❑ M7-786 [(2)]	Anthology	1974	5.00	10.00	20.00
❑ 5297 ML	All the Great Hits of Jr. Walker and the All Stars	1984	2.50	5.00	10.00
❑ 6053 ML	Blow the House Down	1983	2.50	5.00	10.00
PICKWICK					
❑ SPC-3391	Shotgun	197?	3.00	6.00	12.00
SOUL					
❑ 701 [M]	Shotgun	1965	15.00	30.00	60.00
—Mostly white label with vertical "Soul" at left					
❑ 701 [M]	Shotgun	1965	5.00	10.00	20.00
—Purple swirl label with "Soul" at top					
❑ SS-701 [S]	Shotgun	1965	7.50	15.00	30.00
❑ 702 [M]	Soul Session	1966	15.00	30.00	60.00
—Mostly white label with vertical "Soul" at left					
❑ 702 [M]	Soul Session	1966	5.00	10.00	20.00
—Purple swirl label with "Soul" at top					
❑ SS-702 [S]	Soul Session	1966	7.50	15.00	30.00
❑ 703 [M]	Road Runner	1966	5.00	10.00	20.00
❑ SS-703 [S]	Road Runner	1966	7.50	15.00	30.00
❑ 705 [M]	"Live"	1967	5.00	10.00	20.00
❑ SS-705 [S]	"Live"	1967	7.50	15.00	30.00
❑ SS-710	Home Cookin'	1969	5.00	10.00	20.00

Number	Title (A Side/B Side)	Yr	VG	VG+	NM
❏ SS-718	Greatest Hits	1969	5.00	10.00	20.00
❏ SS-721	Gotta Hold on to This Feeling	1969	6.25	12.50	25.00
❏ SS-721	What Does It Take to Win Your Love	1970	5.00	10.00	20.00
—Retitled version of above					
❏ SS-726	A Gasssss	1970	3.75	7.50	15.00
❏ SS-732	Rainbow Funk	1971	3.75	7.50	15.00
❏ SS-733	Moody Jr.	1971	3.75	7.50	15.00
❏ SS-738	Peace and Understanding Is Hard to Find	1973	3.75	7.50	15.00
❏ S6-742	Jr. Walker and the All Stars	1973	—	—	—
—Canceled					
❏ S6-745	Hot Shot	1976	3.75	7.50	15.00
❏ S6-747	Sax Appeal	1976	3.75	7.50	15.00
❏ S6-748	Whopper Bopper Show Stopper	1977	3.75	7.50	15.00
❏ S7-750	Smooth	1978	3.75	7.50	15.00
WHITFIELD					
❏ WHK 3331	Back Street Boogie	1980	3.00	6.00	12.00

WALKER, T-BONE
45s
ATLANTIC

Number	Title (A Side/B Side)	Yr	VG	VG+	NM
❏ 1045	Papa Ain't Salty/T-Bone Shuffle	1955	12.50	25.00	50.00
❏ 1074	Why Not/Play On Little Girl	1955	10.00	20.00	40.00
BLUESWAY					
❏ 61008	Confusion Blues/Every Night I Have to Cry	1967	2.00	4.00	8.00
CAPITOL					
❏ F799	Go Back to the One You Love/On Your Way Blues	1950	37.50	75.00	150.00
❏ F944	Too Much Trouble Blues/She's My Old Time Used to Be	1950	37.50	75.00	150.00
IMPERIAL					
❏ 5202	Street Walkin' Woman/The Blues Is a Woman	1952	100.00	200.00	400.00
—Note: T-Bone Walker records on Imperial before 5202 are unconfirmed on 45 rpm.					
❏ 5216	Blue Mood/Got No Use for You	1953	50.00	100.00	200.00
❏ 5228	Railroad Station Blues/Long Distance Blues	1953	50.00	100.00	200.00
❏ 5239	Party Girl/You're Here in the Dark	1953	75.00	150.00	300.00
❏ 5247	Everytime/Tell Me What's the Reason	1953	37.50	75.00	150.00
❏ 5261	I'm About to Lose My Mind/I Miss You Baby	1954	25.00	50.00	100.00
❏ 5264	Pony Tail/When the Sun Goes Down	1954	20.00	40.00	80.00
❏ 5274	Vida Lee/My Baby Is Now on My Mind	1954	20.00	40.00	80.00
❏ 5284	Bye Bye Baby/Wanderin' Heart	1954	20.00	40.00	80.00
❏ 5299	Teenage Baby/Strugglin' Blues	1954	20.00	40.00	80.00
❏ 5311	Love Is Just a Gamble/High Society	1954	20.00	40.00	80.00
❏ 5330	I'll Understand/The Hard Way	1955	12.50	25.00	50.00
❏ 5384	You Don't Understand/Say! Pretty Baby	1956	12.50	25.00	50.00
❏ 5695	Travelin' Blues/Strollin' with Bones	1960	3.75	7.50	15.00
❏ 5832	Evil Hearted Woman/Life Is Too Short	1962	3.75	7.50	15.00
❏ 5962	Doin' Time/Cold, Cold Water	1963	3.00	6.00	12.00
JETSTREAM					
❏ 726	Reconsider Baby/I'm Not Your Fool Anymore	1966	2.50	5.00	10.00
❏ 730	T-Bone's Back/She's a Hit	1967	2.50	5.00	10.00
MODERN					
❏ 1004	Should I Let Her Go/Hey Hey Baby	1965	2.50	5.00	10.00
POST					
❏ 2002	I Get So Weary/Tell Me What's the Reason	1955	15.00	30.00	60.00

78s
ATLANTIC

Number	Title (A Side/B Side)	Yr	VG	VG+	NM
❏ 1045	Papa Ain't Salty/T-Bone Shuffle	1955	10.00	20.00	40.00
❏ 1074	Why Not/Play On Little Girl	1955	10.00	20.00	40.00
BLACK & WHITE					
❏ 110	Bobby Sox Blues/I'm Gonna Find My Baby	1946	10.00	20.00	40.00
❏ 111	No Worry Blues/Don't Leave Me Baby	1947	10.00	20.00	40.00
❏ 115	It's a Low Down Dirty Deal/Don't Give Me the Runaround	1947	10.00	20.00	40.00
❏ 121	I'm in an Awful Mood/Hard Pain Blues	1947	10.00	20.00	40.00
❏ 122	Call It Stormy Monday (But Tuesday Is Just As Bad)/I Know Your Wig Is Gone	1947	15.00	30.00	60.00
❏ 123	Long Skirt Baby Blues/Goodbye Blues	1948	10.00	20.00	40.00
❏ 125	T-Bone Jumps Again/I Want a Little Girl	1948	10.00	20.00	40.00
❏ 126	I'm Waiting for Your Call/That's Better for Me	1948	10.00	20.00	40.00
❏ 127	Midnight Blues/Plain Old Down Home Blues	1948	10.00	20.00	40.00
CAPITOL					
❏ 799	Go Back to the One You Love/On Your Way Blues	1950	6.25	12.50	25.00
❏ 944	Too Much Trouble Blues/She's My Old Time Used to Be	1950	6.25	12.50	25.00
❏ 10033	Mean Old World/I Got a Break, Baby	1942	12.50	25.00	50.00
❏ 70012	Vacation Blues/Prison Blues	1949	7.50	15.00	30.00
❏ 70014	Call It Stormy Monday (But Tuesday Is Just As Bad)/I Know Your Wig Is Gone	1949	7.50	15.00	30.00
—Reissue of Black & White 122					
❏ 70023	Long Lost Lover Blues/You're My Best Poker Hand	1949	7.50	15.00	30.00
❏ 70025	Hypin' Woman Blues/Born to Be No Good	1949	7.50	15.00	30.00
❏ 70042	T-Bone Shuffle/First Love Blues	1949	7.50	15.00	30.00
—Reissue of Comet 53					
COLUMBIA					
❏ 14064-D	Trinity River Blues/Wichita Falls Blues	1930	125.00	250.00	500.00
—As "Oak Cliff T-Bone"; his first recordings					
COMET					
❏ 50	West Side Baby/Lonesome Woman Blues	1948	7.50	15.00	30.00
❏ 51	I'm Still in Love with You/Inspiration Blues	1949	7.50	15.00	30.00
❏ 52	Description Blues/That Old Feeling Is Gone	1949	7.50	15.00	30.00
❏ 53	T-Bone Shuffle/First Love Blues	1949	15.00	30.00	60.00
IMPERIAL					
❏ 5071	Glamour Girl/Strollin' with Bones	1950	6.25	12.50	25.00
❏ 5081	The Hustle Is On/Baby Broke My Heart	1950	6.25	12.50	25.00

Number	Title (A Side/B Side)	Yr	VG	VG+	NM
❏ 5089	The Sun Went Down/You Don't Love Me	1950	6.25	12.50	25.00
❏ 5094	Travelin' Blues/Evil Hearted Woman	1950	6.25	12.50	25.00
❏ 5103	I Walked Away/Too Lazy	1950	6.25	12.50	25.00
❏ 5116	No Reason/Look Me in the Eye	1951	6.25	12.50	25.00
❏ 5147	You Don't Understand/Welcome Home Blues	1951	6.25	12.50	25.00
❏ 5153	Alimony Blues/Life Is Too Short	1951	6.25	12.50	25.00
❏ 5161	I Get So Weary/You Just Want to Use Me	1952	6.25	12.50	25.00
❏ 5171	Cold, Cold Feeling/News for My Baby	1952	6.25	12.50	25.00
❏ 5181	Get These Blues Off Me/I Got the Blues Again	1952	6.25	12.50	25.00
❏ 5193	Lillie Lou/I Got the Blues	1952	6.25	12.50	25.00
❏ 5202	Street Walkin' Woman/The Blues Is a Woman	1952	12.50	25.00	50.00
❏ 5216	Blue Mood/Got No Use for You	1953	10.00	20.00	40.00
❏ 5228	Railroad Station Blues/Long Distance Blues	1953	10.00	20.00	40.00
❏ 5239	Party Girl/You're Here in the Dark	1953	12.50	25.00	50.00
❏ 5247	Everytime/Tell Me What's the Reason	1953	10.00	20.00	40.00
❏ 5261	I'm About to Lose My Mind/I Miss You Baby	1954	10.00	20.00	40.00
❏ 5264	Pony Tail/When the Sun Goes Down	1954	7.50	15.00	30.00
❏ 5274	Vida Lee/My Baby Is Now on My Mind	1954	7.50	15.00	30.00
❏ 5284	Bye Bye Baby/Wanderin' Heart	1954	7.50	15.00	30.00
❏ 5299	Teenage Baby/Strugglin' Blues	1954	7.50	15.00	30.00
❏ 5311	Love Is Just a Gamble/High Society	1954	7.50	15.00	30.00
❏ 5330	I'll Understand/The Hard Way	1955	7.50	15.00	30.00
❏ 5384	You Don't Understand/Say! Pretty Baby	1956	10.00	20.00	40.00
MERCURY					
❏ 8016	My Baby Left Me/Come Back to Me Baby Blues	1946	12.50	25.00	50.00
RHUMBOOGIE					
❏ 4000	I'm Still in Love with You/Sail On Boogie	1946	10.00	20.00	40.00
❏ 4002	T-Bone Boogie/Evening	1946	10.00	20.00	40.00
❏ 4003	You Don't Love Me Blues/Mean Old World Blues	1946	10.00	20.00	40.00

7-Inch Extended Plays
CAPITOL

Number	Title (A Side/B Side)	Yr	VG	VG+	NM
❏ EAP 1-370	(contents unknown)	1953	50.00	100.00	200.00
❏ EAP 1-370 [PS]	Classics in Jazz	1953	50.00	100.00	200.00

Albums
ATLANTIC

Number	Title (A Side/B Side)	Yr	VG	VG+	NM
❏ 8020 [M]	T-Bone Blues	1959	55.00	110.00	220.00
—Black label					
❏ 8020 [M]	T-Bone Blues	1960	17.50	35.00	70.00
—Red and purple label					
❏ SD 8256	T-Bone Blues	1970	5.00	10.00	20.00
BLUE NOTE					
❏ BN-LA533-H2 [(2)]	Classics	1975	5.00	10.00	20.00
BLUESTIME					
❏ 29004	Everyday I Have the Blues	1968	7.50	15.00	30.00
❏ 29010	Blue Rocks	1969	7.50	15.00	30.00
BLUESWAY					
❏ BLS-6008	Stormy Monday Blues	1968	7.50	15.00	30.00
—Reissue of Wet Soul LP?					
❏ BLS-6014	Funky Town	1968	7.50	15.00	30.00
❏ BLS-6058	Dirty Mistreater	1973	3.75	7.50	15.00
BRUNSWICK					
❏ BL 754126	The Truth	1968	7.50	15.00	30.00
CAPITOL					
❏ H 370 [10]	Classics in Jazz	1953	250.00	500.00	1000.
❏ T 370 [M]	Classics in Jazz	1953	75.00	150.00	300.00
❏ T 1958 [M]	Great Blues Vocal and Guitar	1963	37.50	75.00	150.00
—Black "The Star Line" label (existence of black colorband label not confirmed)					
DELMARK					
❏ D-633 [M]	I Want a Little Girl	1967	10.00	20.00	40.00
❏ DS-633 [S]	I Want a Little Girl	1967	12.50	25.00	50.00
IMPERIAL					
❏ LP-9098 [M]	T-Bone Walker Sings the Blues	1959	75.00	150.00	300.00
❏ LP-9116 [M]	Singing the Blues	1960	62.50	125.00	250.00
❏ LP-9146 [M]	I Get So Weary	1961	75.00	150.00	300.00
MOSAIC					
❏ M9-130 [(9)]	The Complete Recordings of T-Bone Walker 1940-1954	199?	62.50	125.00	250.00
POLYDOR					
❏ 24-4502	Good Feelin'	1972	3.75	7.50	15.00
❏ PD-5521	Fly Walker Airlines	1973	3.75	7.50	15.00
REPRISE					
❏ 2RS 6483 [(2)]	Very Rare	1973	5.00	10.00	20.00
WET SOUL					
❏ 1002	Stormy Monday Blues	1967	12.50	25.00	50.00

WANDERERS, THE (1)
45s
CUB

Number	Title (A Side/B Side)	Yr	VG	VG+	NM
❏ 9003	A Teenage Quarrel/My Shining Hour	1958	7.50	15.00	30.00
❏ 9019	Collecting Hearts/Two Hearts on a Window Pane	1958	10.00	20.00	40.00
❏ 9023	Please/Shadrack, Meshack, and Abednego	1959	7.50	15.00	30.00
❏ 9035	Only When You're Lonely/I'm Not Ashamed	1959	7.50	15.00	30.00
❏ 9054	I Walked Through a Forest/I'm Waiting for Green Pastures	1959	7.50	15.00	30.00
❏ 9075	I Need You More/I Could Make You Mine	1960	7.50	15.00	30.00
❏ 9089	For Your Love/Sally Goodheart	1961	7.50	15.00	30.00
❏ 9094	I'll Never Smile Again/A Little Too Long	1961	7.50	15.00	30.00
❏ 9099	She Wears My Ring/Somebody Else's Sweetheart	1961	12.50	25.00	50.00
❏ 9109	There Is No Greater Love/As Time Goes By	1962	7.50	15.00	30.00
MGM					
❏ 13082	There Is No Greater Love/As Time Goes By	1962	5.00	10.00	20.00
ONYX					
❏ 518	Thinking of You/Great Jumpin' Catfish	1957	15.00	30.00	60.00

Number	Title (A Side/B Side)	Yr	VG	VG+	NM
ORBIT					
❑ 9003	A Teenage Quarrel/My Shining Hour	1958	15.00	30.00	60.00
SAVOY					
❑ 1109	We Could Find Happiness/Holy Mae Ethel	1953	125.00	250.00	500.00
UNITED ARTISTS					
❑ 570	After He Breaks Your Heart/Run, Run Senorita	1963	3.75	7.50	15.00
❑ 648	I'll Know/You Can't Run Away from Me	1963	7.50	15.00	30.00

WANDERERS, THE (2)
45s

Number	Title (A Side/B Side)	Yr	VG	VG+	NM
PANAMA					
❑ 3900	Quiet Night/One Look	1960	3.75	7.50	15.00

WANDERERS, THE (U)
May be by group (1).
45s

Number	Title (A Side/B Side)	Yr	VG	VG+	NM
GONE					
❑ 5005	Mask Off/My Lady Chocaonine	1957	7.50	15.00	30.00

WAR
12-Inch Singles

Number	Title (A Side/B Side)	Yr	VG	VG+	NM
AVENUE					
❑ 76028	Da Roof (3 versions)	1994	2.00	4.00	8.00
LAX					
❑ 02122	Cinco de Mayo (7:29) (3:59)	1981	2.50	5.00	10.00
PRIORITY					
❑ VL-9364	Low Rider '87 (Extended Version 7:45) (Radio Edit) (Instrumental)	1987	3.75	7.50	15.00
❑ VL-9502	Livin' in the Red (versions unknown)	1987	3.00	6.00	12.00
RCA					
❑ PD-13062	You Got the Power/Cinco de Mayo	1982	2.50	5.00	10.00
❑ PD-13239	Outlaw/I'm About Somebody	1982	2.50	5.00	10.00
❑ JD-13323 [DJ]	Just Because (same on both sides)	1982	2.00	4.00	8.00
❑ PD-13323	Just Because (Long Version)/The Jungle (Medley)	1982	2.50	5.00	10.00
SISAPA					
❑ 76707	Truth Be Known (4 versions)	1991	2.00	4.00	8.00
UNITED ARTISTS					
❑ SP-184 [DJ]	Youngblood (Livin' in the Streets) (9:07)/Keep On Doin'	1978	3.75	7.50	15.00

45s

Number	Title (A Side/B Side)	Yr	VG	VG+	NM
BLUE NOTE					
❑ 1009	L.A. Sunshine/Slowly We Walk Together	1977	—	2.50	5.00
COCO PLUM					
❑ 2002	Groovin'/(Instrumental)	1985	—	2.00	4.00
LAX					
❑ 02120	Cinco de Mayo/Don't Let No One Get You Down	1981	—	2.50	5.00
MCA					
❑ 40820	Galaxy (Part 1)/Galaxy (Part 2)	1977	—	2.50	5.00
❑ 40820 [PS]	Galaxy (Part 1)/Galaxy (Part 2)	1977	—	3.00	6.00
❑ 40883	Hey Senorita/Sweet Fighting Lady	1978	—	2.50	5.00
❑ 40995	Good, Good Feelin'/Baby Face (She Said Do Do Do Do)	1979	—	2.50	5.00
❑ 41061	I'm the One Who Understands/Corns & Callouses	1979	—	2.50	5.00
❑ 41158	Don't Take It Away/The Music Band 2 (We Are the Music Band)	1979	—	2.50	5.00
❑ 41209	I'll Be Around/The Music Band 2 (We Are the Music Band)	1980	—	2.50	5.00
RCA					
❑ PB-13061	You Got the Power/Cinco de Mayo	1982	—	2.00	4.00
❑ PB-13239	Outlaw/I'm About Somebody	1982	—	2.00	4.00
❑ PB-13322	Just Because/The Jungle (Medley)	1982	—	2.00	4.00
❑ JH-13426 [DJ]	Baby, It's Cold Outside (same on both sides)	1982	—	2.50	5.00
❑ PB-13544	Life (Is So Strange)/W.W. III	1983	—	2.00	4.00
UNITED ARTISTS					
❑ XW163	The Cisco Kid/Beetles in the Bog	1973	—	2.50	5.00
❑ XW281	Gypsy Man/Deliver the Word	1973	—	2.50	5.00
❑ XW350	Me and Baby Brother/In Your Eyes	1973	—	2.50	5.00
❑ XW432	Ballero/Slippin' Into Darkness	1974	—	2.50	5.00
❑ XW629	Why Can't We Be Friends?/In Mazatlin	1975	—	2.50	5.00
❑ XW629 [PS]	Why Can't We Be Friends?/In Mazatlin	1975	—	3.00	6.00
❑ XW706	Low Rider/So	1975	—	2.50	5.00
❑ XW706 [PS]	Low Rider/So	1975	—	3.00	6.00
❑ XW834	Summer/All Day Music	1976	—	2.50	5.00
❑ XW1213	Youngblood/(Instrumental)	1978	—	2.50	5.00
❑ XW1247	Sing a Happy Song/This Funky Music Makes You Feel Good	1978	—	2.50	5.00
❑ 50746	Lonely Feelin'/Sun Oh Sun	1971	2.00	4.00	8.00
❑ 50746 [PS]	Lonely Feelin'/Sun Oh Sun	1971	3.00	6.00	12.00
❑ 50815	All Day Music/Get Down	1971	2.00	4.00	8.00
❑ 50867	Slippin' Into Darkness/Happy Head	1971	—	3.00	6.00
❑ 50975	The World Is a Ghetto/Four Cornered Room	1972	—	3.00	6.00

7-Inch Extended Plays

Number	Title (A Side/B Side)	Yr	VG	VG+	NM
UNITED ARTISTS					
❑ SP-92 [DJ]	Where Was You At/City, Country, City//Beetles in the Bog/Four Cornered Room	1972	2.50	5.00	10.00
❑ SP-92 [PS]	Edited Versions from The World Is a Ghetto	1972	2.50	5.00	10.00

Albums

Number	Title (A Side/B Side)	Yr	VG	VG+	NM
AVENUE					
❑ R1 71706	Peace Sign	1994	3.75	7.50	15.00
BLUE NOTE					
❑ BN-LA690-G [(2)]	Platinum Jazz	1977	3.00	6.00	12.00

Number	Title (A Side/B Side)	Yr	VG	VG+	NM
LAX					
❑ PW 37111	All Day Music	1981	2.50	5.00	10.00
—Reissue of United Artists 5546					
❑ PW 37112	The World Is a Ghetto	1981	2.50	5.00	10.00
—Reissue of United Artists 5652					
❑ PW 37113	Why Can't We Be Friends?	1981	2.50	5.00	10.00
—Reissue of United Artists 441					
MCA					
❑ 745	Galaxy	1983	2.00	4.00	8.00
—Reissue of MCA 3030					
❑ 747	The Music Band	1983	2.00	4.00	8.00
—Reissue of MCA 3085					
❑ 751	The Music Band 2	1983	2.00	4.00	8.00
—Reissue of MCA 3193					
❑ 3030	Galaxy	1977	2.50	5.00	10.00
❑ 3085	The Music Band	1979	2.50	5.00	10.00
❑ 3193	The Music Band 2	1979	2.50	5.00	10.00
❑ 5156	The Music Band Live	1980	2.50	5.00	10.00
❑ 5362	Best of the Music Band	1982	2.50	5.00	10.00
❑ 5411	Music Band Jazz	1983	2.50	5.00	10.00
PRIORITY					
❑ SL 9467	The Best of War…And More	1987	2.50	5.00	10.00
RCA VICTOR					
❑ AFL1-4208	Outlaw	1982	2.50	5.00	10.00
❑ AFL1-4598	Life (Is So Strange)	1983	2.50	5.00	10.00
UNITED ARTISTS					
❑ SP-103 [DJ]	Radio Free War	1974	6.25	12.50	25.00
—Promo only on blue vinyl					
❑ UA-LA128-F	Deliver the Word	1973	3.00	6.00	12.00
❑ UA-LA193-J [(2)]	War Live!	1974	3.75	7.50	15.00
❑ UA-LA441-G	Why Can't We Be Friends?	1975	2.50	5.00	10.00
❑ UA-LA648-G	Greatest Hits	1976	2.50	5.00	10.00
❑ UAS-5508	War	1971	3.75	7.50	15.00
❑ UAS-5546	All Day Music	1971	3.75	7.50	15.00
❑ UAS-5652	The World Is a Ghetto	1972	3.00	6.00	12.00

WARD, BILLY, AND THE DOMINOES
Also includes "The Dominoes."
45s

Number	Title (A Side/B Side)	Yr	VG	VG+	NM
ABC-PARAMOUNT					
❑ 10128	You're Mine/The World Is Waiting for the Sunrise	1960	5.00	10.00	20.00
❑ 10156	You/Gypsy	1960	5.00	10.00	20.00
DECCA					
❑ 29933	St. Therese of the Roses/Home Is Where You Hang Your Hat	1956	7.50	15.00	30.00
❑ 30043	Come On, Shake, Let's Crawl/Will You Remember	1956	7.50	15.00	30.00
❑ 30149	Half a Love (Is Better Than None)/Evermore	1956	7.50	15.00	30.00
❑ 30199	Rock, Plymouth Rock/Till Kingdom Come	1957	7.50	15.00	30.00
❑ 30420	To Each His Own/I Don't Stand a Ghost of a Chance	1957	7.50	15.00	30.00
❑ 30514	September Song/When the Saints Go Marching In	1957	7.50	15.00	30.00
FEDERAL					
❑ 12001	Do Something For Me/Chicken Blues	1951	200.00	400.00	800.00
—Note: Federal 12010 and 12016 were issued only on 78s					
❑ 12022AA	Sixty Minute Man/I Can't Escape from You	1951	125.00	250.00	500.00
❑ 12036	Heart to Heart/Looking for a Man to Satisfy My Soul	1951	125.00	250.00	500.00
—With Little Esther					
❑ 12039	I Am with You/Weeping Willow Blues	1951	100.00	200.00	400.00
❑ 12059	That's What You're Doing to Me/When the Swallows Come Back to Capistrano	1952	100.00	200.00	400.00
❑ 12068AA	Have Mercy Baby/Deep Sea Blues	1952	62.50	125.00	250.00
❑ 12072	Love, Love, Love/That's What You're Doing to Me	1952	50.00	100.00	200.00
❑ 12105	I'd Be Satisfied/No Room	1952	45.00	90.00	180.00
❑ 12106	I'm Lonely/Yours Forever	1952	45.00	90.00	180.00
❑ 12114	The Bells/Pedal Pushin' Papa	1952	50.00	100.00	200.00
❑ 12129	These Foolish Things Remind Me of You/Don't Leave Me This Way	1953	75.00	150.00	300.00
—Green label, gold top					
❑ 12129	These Foolish Things Remind Me of You/Don't Leave Me This Way	1954	25.00	50.00	100.00
—Green label, silver top					
❑ 12129	These Foolish Things Remind Me of You/Don't Leave Me This Way	1955	7.50	15.00	30.00
—All-green label					
❑ 12139	You Can't Keep a Good Man Down/Where Now Little Heart	1953	25.00	50.00	100.00
❑ 12162	Until the Real Thing Comes Along/My Baby's 3 D	1954	25.00	50.00	100.00
❑ 12178	Tootsie Roll/Move to the Outskirts of Town	1954	25.00	50.00	100.00
❑ 12184	Handwriting on the Wall/One Moment with You	1954	50.00	100.00	200.00
❑ 12193	Above Jacob's Ladder/Little Black Train	1954	12.50	25.00	50.00
❑ 12209	Can't Do Sixty No More/If I Never Get to Heaven	1955	25.00	50.00	100.00
❑ 12218	Love Me Now or Let Me Go/Cave Man	1955	12.50	25.00	50.00
❑ 12263	Bobby Sox Baby/How Long, How Long Blues	1956	12.50	25.00	50.00
❑ 12301	St. Louis Blues/One Moment with You	1957	12.50	25.00	50.00
❑ 12308	Have Mercy Baby/Love, Love, Love	1957	10.00	20.00	40.00
JUBLIEE					
❑ 5163	Gimme, Gimme, Gimme/Come to Me, Baby	1954	7.50	15.00	30.00
❑ 5213	Sweethearts on Parade/Take Me Back to Heaven	1955	7.50	15.00	30.00
KING					
❑ 1280	Rags to Riches/Don't Ask Me	1953	12.50	25.00	50.00
❑ 1281	Christmas in Heaven/Ringing In a Brand New Year	1953	25.00	50.00	100.00

Left Column

Number	Title (A Side/B Side)	Yr	VG	VG+	NM
❏ 1342	Tenderly/Little Lie	1954	12.50	25.00	50.00
❏ 1364	Three Coins in the Fountain/Lonesome Road	1954	12.50	25.00	50.00
❏ 1368	Little Things Mean a Lot/I Really Don't Want to Know	1954	10.00	20.00	40.00
❏ 1492	Learnin' the Blues/May I Never Love	1955	10.00	20.00	40.00
❏ 1502	Over the Rainbow/Give Me You	1955	10.00	20.00	40.00
❏ 5322	Sixty Minute Man/Have Mercy Baby	1960	5.00	10.00	20.00
❏ 5463	Lay It on the Line/That's How You Know You're Growing Old	1961	5.00	10.00	20.00
❏ 6002	I'm Walking Behind You/This Love of Mine	1965	5.00	10.00	20.00
❏ 6016	O Holy Night/What Are You Doin' New Year's Eve	1965	5.00	10.00	20.00

LIBERTY

Number	Title (A Side/B Side)	Yr	VG	VG+	NM
❏ 55071	Star Dust/Lucinda	1957	6.25	12.50	25.00
❏ 55071 [PS]	Star Dust/Lucinda	1957	25.00	50.00	100.00
❏ 55099	Deep Purple/Do It Again	1957	6.25	12.50	25.00
❏ 55111	My Proudest Possession/Someone Greater Than I	1957	6.25	12.50	25.00
❏ 55126	Solitude/You Grow Sweeter As the Years Go By	1958	6.25	12.50	25.00
❏ 55136	Jennie Lee/Music, Maestro, Please	1958	6.25	12.50	25.00
❏ 55181	Please Don't Say No/Behave, Hula Girl	1959	6.25	12.50	25.00

RO-ZAN

Number	Title (A Side/B Side)	Yr	VG	VG+	NM
❏ 10001	Man in the Stain Glass Window/My Fair Weather Friend	1961	5.00	10.00	20.00

UNITED ARTISTS

Number	Title (A Side/B Side)	Yr	VG	VG+	NM
❏ 0017	Stardust/These Foolish Things	1973	—	2.50	5.00

—"Silver Spotlight Series" reissue

7-Inch Extended Plays
DECCA

Number	Title (A Side/B Side)	Yr	VG	VG+	NM
❏ ED 2549	(contents unknown)	1958	50.00	100.00	200.00
❏ ED 2549 [PS]	Billy Ward and His Dominoes	1958	50.00	100.00	200.00

FEDERAL

Number	Title (A Side/B Side)	Yr	VG	VG+	NM
❏ 212	Sixty Minute Man/Do Something for Me//Have Mercy Baby/Don't Leave Me This Way	1956	100.00	200.00	400.00

—Green label, silver top

Number	Title (A Side/B Side)	Yr	VG	VG+	NM
❏ 212	Sixty Minute Man/Do Something for Me//Have Mercy Baby/Don't Leave Me This Way	1956	25.00	50.00	100.00

—All-green label

Number	Title (A Side/B Side)	Yr	VG	VG+	NM
❏ 212 [PS]	Billy Ward and His Dominoes, Vol. 1	1956	25.00	50.00	100.00
❏ 262	*The Bells/Pedal Pushin' Papa/I'd Be Satisfied/That's What You're Doing to Me	1957	100.00	200.00	400.00

—Green label, silver top

Number	Title (A Side/B Side)	Yr	VG	VG+	NM
❏ 262	*The Bells/Pedal Pushin' Papa/I'd Be Satisfied/That's What You're Doing to Me	1957	25.00	50.00	100.00

—All-green label

Number	Title (A Side/B Side)	Yr	VG	VG+	NM
❏ 262 [PS]	Billy Ward and His Dominoes, Vol. 2	1957	25.00	50.00	100.00
❏ 269	*These Foolish Things Remind Me of You/Rags to Riches/When the Swallows Come Back to Capistrano/Harbor Lights	1957	100.00	200.00	400.00

—Green label, silver top

Number	Title (A Side/B Side)	Yr	VG	VG+	NM
❏ 269	*These Foolish Things Remind Me of You/Rags to Riches/When the Swallows Come Back to Capistrano/Harbor Lights	1957	25.00	50.00	100.00

—All-green label

Number	Title (A Side/B Side)	Yr	VG	VG+	NM
❏ 269 [PS]	Billy Ward and His Dominoes Singing the All Time Hit Standards	1957	25.00	50.00	100.00

LIBERTY

Number	Title (A Side/B Side)	Yr	VG	VG+	NM
❏ LEP-1-3056	(contents unknown)	1959	25.00	50.00	100.00
❏ LEP-1-3056 [PS]	Sea of Glass (Part One)	1959	25.00	50.00	100.00
❏ LEP-2-3056	Deep River/By and By//The House of the Lord/The Lullaby Divine	1959	25.00	50.00	100.00
❏ LEP-2-3056 [PS]	Sea of Glass (Part 2)	1959	25.00	50.00	100.00
❏ LEP-3-3056	(contents unknown)	1959	25.00	50.00	100.00
❏ LEP-3-3056 [PS]	Sea of Glass (Part 3)	1959	25.00	50.00	100.00
❏ LEP-1-3083	Stardust/Eatin' and Sleepin'//Music, Maestro, Please/I'll Never Ask for More Than This	1959	25.00	50.00	100.00
❏ LEP-1-3083 [PS]	Yours Forever (Part One)	1959	25.00	50.00	100.00
❏ LEP-2-3083	(contents unknown)	1959	25.00	50.00	100.00
❏ LEP-2-3083 [PS]	Yours Forever (Part 2)	1959	25.00	50.00	100.00
❏ LEP-3-3083	Smoke Gets in Your Eyes/Do It Again//If You Please/Yours Forever	1959	25.00	50.00	100.00
❏ LEP-3-3083 [PS]	Yours Forever (Part 3)	1959	25.00	50.00	100.00

Albums
DECCA

Number	Title (A Side/B Side)	Yr	VG	VG+	NM
❏ DL 8621 [M]	Billy Ward and the Dominoes	1958	50.00	100.00	200.00

FEDERAL

Number	Title (A Side/B Side)	Yr	VG	VG+	NM
❏ 295-94 [10]	Billy Ward and His Dominoes	1955	6000.	9500.	13000.
❏ 548 [M]	Billy Ward and His Dominoes	1958	375.00	750.00	1500.
❏ 559 [M]	Clyde McPhatter with Billy Ward and His Dominoes	1958	300.00	600.00	1200.

KING

Number	Title (A Side/B Side)	Yr	VG	VG+	NM
❏ 548 [M]	Billy Ward and His Dominoes	1958	—	—	—

—Unknown

Number	Title (A Side/B Side)	Yr	VG	VG+	NM
❏ 559 [M]	Clyde McPhatter with Billy Ward and His Dominoes	1958	150.00	300.00	600.00

—Yellow cover

Number	Title (A Side/B Side)	Yr	VG	VG+	NM
❏ 559 [M]	Clyde McPhatter with Billy Ward and His Dominoes	196?	75.00	150.00	300.00

—Pink cover

Number	Title (A Side/B Side)	Yr	VG	VG+	NM
❏ 733 [M]	Billy Ward and His Dominoes Featuring Clyde McPhatter and Jackie Wilson	1961	150.00	300.00	600.00
❏ 952 [M]	24 Songs	1966	12.50	25.00	50.00
❏ 5005	14 Hits	197?	3.00	6.00	12.00
❏ 5008	21 Hits	197?	3.00	6.00	12.00

LIBERTY

Number	Title (A Side/B Side)	Yr	VG	VG+	NM
❏ LRP-3056 [M]	Sea of Glass	1957	15.00	30.00	60.00

Right Column

Number	Title (A Side/B Side)	Yr	VG	VG+	NM
❏ LRP-3083 [M]	Yours Forever	1958	15.00	30.00	60.00
❏ LRP-3113 [M]	Pagan Love Song	1959	15.00	30.00	60.00
❏ LST-7113 [S]	Pagan Love Song	1959	25.00	50.00	100.00

WARD, SINGIN' SAMMY
45s
MOTOWN

Number	Title (A Side/B Side)	Yr	VG	VG+	NM
❏ 1004	Lover/That's Why I Love You So Much	1960	10.00	20.00	40.00

—With Sherri Taylor

SOUL

Number	Title (A Side/B Side)	Yr	VG	VG+	NM
❏ 35004	Bread Winner/You've Got to Change	1964	12.50	25.00	50.00

TAMLA

Number	Title (A Side/B Side)	Yr	VG	VG+	NM
❏ 54030	What Makes You Love Him/The Child Is Really Wild	1960	50.00	100.00	200.00

—With lines label

Number	Title (A Side/B Side)	Yr	VG	VG+	NM
❏ 54030	What Makes You Love Him/The Child Is Really Wild	1960	18.75	37.50	75.00

—With globe label

Number	Title (A Side/B Side)	Yr	VG	VG+	NM
❏ 54049	What Makes You Love Him/Don't Take It Away	1961	12.50	25.00	50.00
❏ 54057	Everybody Knew It/Big Joe Moe	1962	12.50	25.00	50.00
❏ 54071	Part Time Love/Someday Pretty Baby	1962	12.50	25.00	50.00

WARWICK, DEE DEE
45s
ATCO

Number	Title (A Side/B Side)	Yr	VG	VG+	NM
❏ 6754	Make Love to Me/She Didn't Know (She Kept On Talkin')	1970	—	3.00	6.00
❏ 6769	I'm Only Human/If This Was the Last Song	1970	—	3.00	6.00
❏ 6796	Cold Night in Georgia/Searchin'	1971	—	3.00	6.00
❏ 6810	Suspicious Minds/I'm Glad I'm a Woman	1971	—	3.00	6.00
❏ 6840	Everybody's Got to Believe in Somebody/Signed, Dee Dee	1971	—	3.00	6.00

BLUE ROCK

Number	Title (A Side/B Side)	Yr	VG	VG+	NM
❏ 4008	Do It with All Your Heart/Happiness	1965	2.50	5.00	10.00
❏ 4027	We're Doing Fine/I Want to Be with You	1965	2.50	5.00	10.00
❏ 4032	Baby I'm Yours/Gotta Get a Hold of Myself	1965	2.50	5.00	10.00

JUBILEE

Number	Title (A Side/B Side)	Yr	VG	VG+	NM
❏ 5459	You're No Good/Don't Call Me	1963	3.00	6.00	12.00

MERCURY

Number	Title (A Side/B Side)	Yr	VG	VG+	NM
❏ 72584	I Want to Be with You/Lover's Chant	1966	2.00	4.00	8.00
❏ 72638	I'm Gonna Make You Love Me/Yours Until Tomorrow	1966	2.00	4.00	8.00
❏ 72667	When Love Slips Away/House of Gold	1967	2.00	4.00	8.00
❏ 72710	Locked in Your Love/Alfie	1967	2.00	4.00	8.00
❏ 72738	Don't You Ever Give Up on Me/We've Got Everything Going for Us	1967	2.00	4.00	8.00
❏ 72788	Girls Need Love/It's Not Fair	1968	2.00	4.00	8.00
❏ 72834	I'll Be Better Off (Without You)/Monday, Monday	1968	2.00	4.00	8.00
❏ 72880	Foolish Fool/Thank You Girl	1969	2.00	4.00	8.00
❏ 72927	That's Not Love/It's Not Fair	1969	2.00	4.00	8.00
❏ 72940	Next Time (You Fall in Love)/Ring of Bright Water	1969	2.00	4.00	8.00
❏ 72966	I (Who Have Nothing)/Where Is That Rainbow	1969	2.00	4.00	8.00

PRIVATE STOCK

Number	Title (A Side/B Side)	Yr	VG	VG+	NM
❏ 45011	Get Out of My Life/Funny How We Change Places	1975	—	2.50	5.00
❏ 45033	This Time May Be My Last/Funny How We Change Places	1975	—	2.50	5.00

SUTRA

Number	Title (A Side/B Side)	Yr	VG	VG+	NM
❏ 134	Move with the World/The Way We Used to Be	1984	—	2.00	4.00
❏ 134 [PS]	Move with the World/The Way We Used to Be	1984	—	2.00	4.00

Albums
ATCO

Number	Title (A Side/B Side)	Yr	VG	VG+	NM
❏ SD 33-337	Turnin' Around	1970	6.25	12.50	25.00

MERCURY

Number	Title (A Side/B Side)	Yr	VG	VG+	NM
❏ MG-21100 [M]	I Want to Be with You	1967	6.25	12.50	25.00
❏ SR-61100 [S]	I Want to Be with You	1967	6.25	12.50	25.00
❏ SR-61221	Foolish Fool	1968	6.25	12.50	25.00

WARWICK, DIONNE
Includes records as "Dionne Warwicke." Also see DIONNE AND FRIENDS.
12-Inch Singles
ARISTA

Number	Title (A Side/B Side)	Yr	VG	VG+	NM
❏ ADP 9145 [DJ]	Got a Date (7:04) (4:07)	1983	2.00	4.00	8.00

RIVER NORTH

Number	Title (A Side/B Side)	Yr	VG	VG+	NM
❏ 51416 4686 1	What the World Needs Now Is Love (6 versions)	1998	2.50	5.00	10.00

—With the Hip-Hop Nation United

45s
ARISTA

Number	Title (A Side/B Side)	Yr	VG	VG+	NM
❏ 0419	I'll Never Love This Way Again/In Your Eyes	1979	—	2.00	4.00
❏ 0459	Deja Vu/All the Time	1979	—	2.00	4.00
❏ 0498	After You/Out of My Hands	1980	—	2.00	4.00
❏ 0527	No Night So Long/Reaching for the Sky	1980	—	2.00	4.00
❏ 0572	Easy Love/You Never Said Goodbye	1980	—	2.00	4.00
❏ 0602	Some Changes Are For Good/This Time Is Ours	1981	—	2.00	4.00
❏ 0630	There's a Long Road Ahead of Me/Medley of Hits	1981	—	2.00	4.00
❏ 0673	Friends in Love/What Is This	1982	—	2.00	4.00

—A-side with Johnny Mathis

Number	Title (A Side/B Side)	Yr	VG	VG+	NM
❏ 0701	For You/What Is This	1982	—	2.00	4.00
❏ 1015	Heartbreaker/I Can't See Anything But You	1982	—	2.00	4.00
❏ 1040	Take the Short Way Home/Just One More Night	1983	—	2.00	4.00
❏ 1067	All the Love in the World/You Are My Love	1983	—	—	—

—Unreleased?

Number	Title (A Side/B Side)	Yr	VG	VG+	NM
❏ 9032	All the Love in the World/You Are My Love	1983	—	2.00	4.00

Number	Title (A Side/B Side)	Yr	VG	VG+	NM
❑ 9073	How Many Times Can We Say Goodbye/What Can a Miracle Do	1983	—	2.00	4.00
—With Luther Vandross
❑ 9145	Got a Date/Two Ships Passing in the Night	1984	—	2.00	4.00
❑ 9281	Finder of Lost Loves/It's Love	1984	—	2.00	4.00
—A-side with Glen Jones
❑ 9341	Run to Me/No Love in Sight	1985	—	—	3.00
—A-side with Barry Manilow
❑ 9460	Whisper in the Dark/Extravagant Gestures	1986	—	—	3.00
❑ 9460 [PS]	Whisper in the Dark/Extravagant Gestures	1986	—	—	3.00
❑ 9567	Love Power/In a World Such As This	1987	—	—	3.00
—A-side with Jeffrey Osborne
❑ 9567 [PS]	Love Power/In a World Such As This	1987	—	—	3.00
❑ 9638	Reservations for Two/For Everything You Are	1987	—	—	3.00
—A-side with Kashif
❑ 9638 [PS]	Reservations for Two/For Everything You Are	1987	—	—	3.00
❑ 9652	Another Chance for Love/Cry on Me	1987	—	—	3.00
—A-side with Howard Hewett
❑ 9652 [PS]	Another Chance for Love/Cry on Me	1987	—	—	3.00
❑ 9901	Take Good Care of You and Me/Heartbreak of Love	1989	—	—	3.00
—A-side with Jeffrey Osborne; B-side with June Pointer
❑ 9940	I Don't Need Another Love/Hertbreaker	1990	—	—	3.00
—A-side with the Spinners
❑ 9940 [PS]	I Don't Need Another Love/Hertbreaker	1990	—	—	3.00
ATLANTIC
❑ 3029	Then Came You/Just As Long As We Have Love	1974	—	3.00	6.00
—With the Spinners
❑ 3202	Then Came You/Just As Long As We Have Love	1974	—	2.50	5.00
—With the Spinners
MUSICOR
❑ 6303	If I Ruled the World/Only Love Can Break a Heart	1977	—	2.50	5.00
RIVER NORTH
❑ 163024-7	What the World Needs Now Is Love (same on both sides)	1998	—	2.00	4.00
—With the Hip-Hop Nation United
SCEPTER
❑ 1239	Don't Make Me Over/I Smiled Yesterday	1962	3.00	6.00	12.00
❑ 1247	This Empty Place/Wishin' and Hopin'	1963	3.00	6.00	12.00
❑ 1247 [PS]	This Empty Place/Wishin' and Hopin'	1963	5.00	10.00	20.00
❑ 1253	Make the Music Play/Please Make Him Love Me	1963	3.00	6.00	12.00
❑ 1262	Anyone Who Had a Heart/The Love of a Boy	1963	3.00	6.00	12.00
❑ 1274	Walk On By/Any Old Time of Day	1964	3.00	6.00	12.00
❑ 1282	You'll Never Get to Heaven (If You Break My Heart)/A House Is Not a Home	1964	2.50	5.00	10.00
❑ 1285	Reach Out for Me/How Many Days of Sadness	1964	2.50	5.00	10.00
❑ 1294	You Can Have Him/Is There Another Way to Love Him	1965	2.50	5.00	10.00
❑ 1298	Who Can I Turn To/Don't Say I Didn't Tell You Something	1965	2.50	5.00	10.00
❑ 12104	Here I Am/They Long to Be Close to You	1965	2.50	5.00	10.00
❑ 12111	Looking with My Eyes/Only the Strong, Only the Brave	1965	2.50	5.00	10.00
❑ 12122	Are You There (With Another Girl)/If I Ever Make You Cry	1965	2.50	5.00	10.00
❑ 12133	Message to Michael/Here Where There Is Love	1966	2.00	4.00	8.00
❑ 12153	Trains and Boats and Planes/Don't Go Breaking My Heart	1966	2.00	4.00	8.00
❑ 12167	I Just Don't Know What to Do with Myself/In Between the Heartaches	1966	2.00	4.00	8.00
❑ 12181	Another Night/Go with Love	1966	2.00	4.00	8.00
❑ 12187	Alfie/The Beginning of Loneliness	1967	2.00	4.00	8.00
❑ 12196	The Windows of the World/Walk Little Dolly	1967	2.00	4.00	8.00
❑ 12203	I Say a Little Prayer/(Theme from) Valley of the Dolls	1967	2.00	4.00	8.00
❑ 12216	Do You Know the Way to San Jose?/Let Me Be Lonely	1968	2.00	4.00	8.00
❑ 12226	Who Is Gonna Love Me?/(There's) Always Something There to Remind Me	1968	2.00	4.00	8.00
❑ 12231	Promises, Promises/Whoever You Are, I Love You	1968	—	3.50	7.00
❑ 12241	This Girl's In Love with You/Dream Sweet Dreamer	1969	—	3.50	7.00
❑ 12249	The April Fools/Slaves	1969	—	3.50	7.00
❑ 12256	Odds and Ends/As Long As There's an Apple Tree	1969	—	3.50	7.00
❑ 12262	You've Lost That Lovin' Feeling/Window Wishing	1969	—	3.50	7.00
❑ 12273	I'll Never Fall in Love Again/What the World Needs Now Is Love	1970	—	3.50	7.00
❑ 12276	Let Me Go to Him/Loneliness Remembers What Happiness Forgets	1970	—	3.00	6.00
❑ 12285	Paper Mache/The Wine Is Young	1970	—	3.00	6.00
❑ 12294	Make It Easy on Yourself/Knowing When to Leave	1970	—	3.00	6.00
❑ 12300	The Green Grass Starts to Grow/They Don't Give Medals to Yesterday's Heroes	1970	—	3.00	6.00
❑ 12309	Who Gets the Guy/Walk the Way You Talk	1971	—	3.00	6.00
❑ 12326	Amanda/He's Moving On	1971	—	3.00	6.00
❑ 12336	The Love of My Man/Hurts So Bad	1971	—	3.00	6.00
❑ 12346	Raindrops Keep Falling on My Head/Is There Another Way to Love You	1972	—	3.00	6.00
❑ 12352	I'm Your Puppet/Don't Make Me Over	1972	—	3.00	6.00
❑ 12383	Medley: Reach Out to Touch (Somebody's Hand)-All Kinds of People/The Good Life	1973	—	3.00	6.00
WARNER BROS.
❑ 7560	If We Only Have Love/Close to You	1972	—	2.50	5.00

Number	Title (A Side/B Side)	Yr	VG	VG+	NM
❑ 7669	Don't Let My Teardrops Bother TYou/I Think You Need Love	1973	—	2.50	5.00
❑ 7693	(I'm) Just Being Myself/You're Gonna Need Me	1973	—	2.50	5.00
❑ 8026	Sure Thing/Who Knows	1974	—	2.50	5.00
❑ 8088	Take it from Me/It's Magic	1975	—	2.50	5.00
❑ 8154	Once You Hit the Road/World of My Dreams	1975	—	2.50	5.00
❑ 8183	His House and Me/Ronnie Lee	1976	—	2.50	5.00
❑ 8280	I Didn't Mean to Love You/He's Not for You	1976	—	2.50	5.00
❑ 8419	Do You Believe in Love at First Sight/Do I Have to Cry	1977	—	2.50	5.00
❑ 8501	Keepin' My Head Above Water/Livin' It Up Is Startin' to Get Me Down	1977	—	2.50	5.00
❑ 8530	Don't Ever Take Your Love Away/Do I Have to Cry	1978	—	2.00	4.00
7-Inch Extended Plays
SCEPTER
❑ SGS 565	Don't Make Me Over/Anyone Who Had a Heart/Wishin' and Hopin'//This Empty Place/(There's) Always Something There to Remind Me/Any Old Time of Day	1968	3.00	6.00	12.00
—Jukebox issue; small hole, plays at 33 1/3 rpm
❑ SGS 565 [PS]	Dionne Warwick's Golden Hits, Part One	1968	3.00	6.00	12.00
❑ SGS 568	Do You Know the Way to San Jose/Let Me Be Lonely/As Long As There's an Apple Tree//(Theme from) Valley of the Dolls/Up, Up and Away/Where Would I Go	1968	3.00	6.00	12.00
—Jukebox issue; small hole, plays at 33 1/3 rpm
❑ SGS 568 [PS]	Valley of the Dolls	1968	3.00	6.00	12.00
Albums
ARISTA
❑ AB 4230	Dionne	1979	2.50	5.00	10.00
❑ AL 8104	How Many Times Can We Say Goodbye	1983	2.50	5.00	10.00
❑ A2L 8111 [(2)]	Hot! Live and Otherwise	1983	2.50	5.00	10.00
—Budget-line reissue
❑ AL 8262	Finder of Lost Loves	1985	2.50	5.00	10.00
❑ AL 8295	Dionne	1985	2.00	4.00	8.00
—Budget-line reissue
❑ AL 8338	Heartbreaker	1985	2.00	4.00	8.00
—Budget-line reissue
❑ AL 8358	Friends in Love	1985	2.00	4.00	8.00
—Budget-line reissue
❑ AL 8398	Friends	1985	2.50	5.00	10.00
❑ AL 8446	Reservations for Two	1987	2.50	5.00	10.00
❑ AL 8540	Greatest Hits 1979-1990	1989	3.00	6.00	12.00
❑ AL 8573	Dionne Warwick Sings Cole Porter	1990	3.00	6.00	12.00
❑ A2L 8605 [(2)]	Hot! Live and Otherwise	1981	3.00	6.00	12.00
❑ AL 9526	No Night So Long	1980	2.50	5.00	10.00
❑ AL 9585	Friends in Love	1982	2.50	5.00	10.00
❑ AL 9609	Heartbreaker	1982	2.50	5.00	10.00
EVEREST
❑ 4103	Dionne Warwick	1981	2.50	5.00	10.00
MOBILE FIDELITY
❑ 2-098 [(2)]	Hot! Live and Otherwise	1982	7.50	15.00	30.00
—Audiophile vinyl
MUSICOR
❑ 2501	Only Love Can Break a Heart	1977	3.00	6.00	12.00
PAIR
❑ PDL2-1043 [(2)]	The Dynamic Dionne Warwick	1986	3.00	6.00	12.00
❑ PDL2-1098 [(2)]	Masterpieces	1986	3.00	6.00	12.00
PICKWICK
❑ PTP-2056 [(2)]	Alfie	1973	3.00	6.00	12.00
—As "Dionne Warwicke"
RHINO
❑ RNDA-1100 [(2)]	Anthology 1962-1971	1985	3.75	7.50	15.00
SCEPTER
❑ S-508 [M]	Presenting Dionne Warwick	1963	3.75	7.50	15.00
❑ SS-508 [S]	Presenting Dionne Warwick	1963	5.00	10.00	20.00
❑ S-517 [M]	Anyone Who Had a Heart	1964	3.75	7.50	15.00
❑ SS-517 [S]	Anyone Who Had a Heart	1964	5.00	10.00	20.00
❑ LP-523 [M]	Make Way for Dionne Warwick	1964	3.75	7.50	15.00
❑ SPS-523 [S]	Make Way for Dionne Warwick	1964	5.00	10.00	20.00
❑ LP-528 [M]	The Sensitive Sound of Dionne Warwick	1965	3.75	7.50	15.00
❑ SPS-528 [S]	The Sensitive Sound of Dionne Warwick	1965	5.00	10.00	20.00
❑ SPS-531 [S]	Here I Am	1965	5.00	10.00	20.00
❑ SRM-531 [M]	Here I Am	1965	3.75	7.50	15.00
❑ SPS-534 [S]	Dionne Warwick in Paris	1966	3.75	7.50	15.00
❑ SRM-534 [M]	Dionne Warwick in Paris	1966	3.00	6.00	12.00
❑ SPS-555 [S]	Here Where There Is Love	1966	3.75	7.50	15.00
❑ SRM-555 [M]	Here Where There Is Love	1966	3.00	6.00	12.00
❑ SPS-559 [S]	On Stage and in the Movies	1967	3.75	7.50	15.00
❑ SRM-559 [M]	On Stage and in the Movies	1967	3.00	6.00	12.00
❑ SPS-563 [S]	The Windows of the World	1967	3.75	7.50	15.00
❑ SRM-563 [M]	The Windows of the World	1967	3.00	6.00	12.00
❑ SPS-565 [S]	Dionne Warwick's Golden Hits, Part One	1967	3.75	7.50	15.00
❑ SRM-565 [M]	Dionne Warwick's Golden Hits, Part One	1967	5.00	10.00	20.00
❑ SPS-567 [S]	The Magic of Believing	1968	5.00	10.00	20.00
❑ SRM-567 [M]	The Magic of Believing	1968	7.50	15.00	30.00
❑ SPS-568 [S]	Valley of the Dolls	1968	3.75	7.50	15.00
❑ SRM-568 [M]	Valley of the Dolls	1968	12.50	25.00	50.00
—May only exist as a white label promo
❑ SPS-571	Promises, Promises	1968	3.75	7.50	15.00
❑ SPS-573	Soulful	1969	3.75	7.50	15.00
❑ SPS-575	Dionne Warwick's Greatest Motion Picture Hits	1969	3.75	7.50	15.00
❑ SPS-577	Dionne Warwick's Golden Hits, Part 2	1969	3.75	7.50	15.00
❑ SPS-581	I'll Never Fall in Love Again	1970	3.75	7.50	15.00
❑ SPS-587	Very Dionne	1970	3.75	7.50	15.00

Number	Title (A Side/B Side)	Yr	VG	VG+	NM
❑ SPS 2-596 [(2)]	The Dionne Warwicke Story	1971	5.00	10.00	20.00
—As "Dionne Warwicke"					
❑ SPS-598 [(2)]	From Within	1972	5.00	10.00	20.00
—As "Dionne Warwicke"					
SPRINGBOARD					
❑ SPS-4001	The Golden Voice of Dionne Warwicke	1972	2.50	5.00	10.00
—As "Dionne Warwicke"					
❑ SPS-4002	Dionne Warwicke Sings Her Very Best	1972	2.50	5.00	10.00
—As "Dionne Warwicke"					
❑ SPS-4003	One Hit After Another	1972	2.50	5.00	10.00
—As "Dionne Warwicke"					
❑ SPS-4032	Greatest Hits, Vol. 2	197?	2.50	5.00	10.00
UNITED ARTISTS					
❑ UA-LA337-G	The Very Best of Dionne Warwicke	1974	3.00	6.00	12.00
—As "Dionne Warwicke"					
WARNER BROS.					
❑ BS 2585	Dionne	1971	3.00	6.00	12.00
—As "Dionne Warwicke"					
❑ BS 2658	Just Being Myself	1973	3.00	6.00	12.00
—As "Dionne Warwicke"					
❑ BS 2846	Then Came You	1975	3.00	6.00	12.00
—As "Dionne Warwicke"					
❑ BS4 2846 [Q]	Then Came You	1975	5.00	10.00	20.00
—As "Dionne Warwicke"					
❑ BS 2893	Track of the Cat	1975	3.00	6.00	12.00
❑ BS 3119	Love at First Sight	1976	3.00	6.00	12.00

WASHINGTON, BABY

Also includes records as "Justine Washington."

45s

ABC-PARAMOUNT

Number	Title (A Side/B Side)	Yr	VG	VG+	NM
❑ 10223	My Time to Cry/Let Love Go By	1961	3.75	7.50	15.00
—As Jeanette "Baby" Washington					
❑ 10245	There You Go Again/Don't Cry, Foolish Heart	1961	3.75	7.50	15.00
AVI					
❑ 253	I Wanna Dance/I Can't Get Over Losing You	1978	—	2.50	5.00
—As Jeanette "Baby" Washington					
CHECKER					
❑ 918	I Hate to See You Go/Knock Yourself Out	1959	6.25	12.50	25.00
CHESS					
❑ 2099	Happy Birthday/Is It Worth It	1970	—	3.00	6.00
COTILLION					
❑ 44047	I Don't Know/I Can't Afford to Lose Him	1969	—	3.00	6.00
❑ 44065	Let Them Talk/I Love You Brother	1970	—	3.00	6.00
❑ 44086	Don't Let Me Lose This Dream/I'm Good Enough for You	1970	—	3.00	6.00
J&S					
❑ 1604	There Must Be a Reason/Congratulations Honey	1957	12.50	25.00	50.00
❑ 1632	I Hate to See You Go/Knock Yourself Out	1958	7.50	15.00	30.00
❑ 1656	Every Day/Smitty's Rock	1961	15.00	30.00	60.00
LIBERTY					
❑ 1393	Silent Night/Merry Christmas Baby	1980	—	2.50	5.00
—B-side by Charles Brown					
MASTER 5					
❑ 3500	Can't Get Over Losing You/(B-side unknown)	1974	—	3.00	6.00
❑ 9103	Forever/(B-side unknown)	1973	—	3.00	6.00
—With Don Gardner					
❑ 9104	Just Can't Get You Out of My Mind/(B-side unknown)	1973	—	3.00	6.00
❑ 9107	I've Got to Break Away/(B-side unknown)	1973	—	3.00	6.00
NEPTUNE					
❑ 101	The Time/You Never Could Be Mine	1959	7.50	15.00	30.00
❑ 104	The Bells (On Our Wedding Day)/(B-side unknown)	1959	7.50	15.00	30.00
❑ 107	Work Out/Let's Love in the Midnight	1960	7.50	15.00	30.00
❑ 120	Medicine Man/Tears Fall	1961	6.25	12.50	25.00
—As "Jeanette B. Washington"					
❑ 122	Nobody Cares (About Me)/(B-side unknown)	1961	6.25	12.50	25.00
—As "Jeanette (Baby) Washington"					
SUE					
❑ 104	The Clock/Standing on the Pier	1964	2.00	4.00	8.00
❑ 114	It'll Never Be Over for Me/Move On Drifter	1964	2.00	4.00	8.00
❑ 119	Your Fool/Run My Heart	1965	2.00	4.00	8.00
❑ 124	I Can't Wait Until I See My Baby/Who's Going to Take Care of Me	1965	2.00	4.00	8.00
—As Justine Washington					
❑ 129	Only Those in Love/The Ballad of Bobby Dawn	1965	2.00	4.00	8.00
❑ 149	Silent Night/White Christmas	1967	5.00	10.00	20.00
❑ 150	Either You're With Me (Or Either You're Not)/You Are What You Are	1967	3.75	7.50	15.00
❑ 764	Hey Lonely One/No Tears	1962	3.00	6.00	12.00
❑ 767	Handful of Memories/Careless Hands	1962	2.50	5.00	10.00
❑ 769	Hush Heart/I've Got a Feeling	1962	2.50	5.00	10.00
❑ 783	That's How Heartaches Are Made/There He Is	1963	2.50	5.00	10.00
❑ 790	Leave Me Alone/You and the Night and the Music	1963	2.50	5.00	10.00
❑ 794	Hey Lonely One/Doodlin'	1963	2.50	5.00	10.00
❑ 797	I Can't Wait Until I See My Baby/Who's Going to Take Care of Me	1964	2.50	5.00	10.00
—As Justine Washington					
UNITED ARTISTS					
❑ 0143	That's How Heartaches Are Made/Leave Me Alone	1973	—	2.50	5.00
—"Silver Spotlight Series" reissue					

Number	Title (A Side/B Side)	Yr	VG	VG+	NM
VEEP					
❑ 1274	Silent Night/White Christmas	1967	5.00	10.00	20.00
❑ 1297	Think About the Good Times/Hold Back the Dawn	1969	2.00	4.00	8.00
Albums					
AVI					
❑ 6038	I Wanna Dance	1978	2.50	5.00	10.00
COLLECTABLES					
❑ COL-5040	The Best of Baby Washington	198?	2.50	5.00	10.00
❑ COL-5108	Only Those in Love	198?	2.50	5.00	10.00
❑ COL-5124	That's How Heartaches Are Made	198?	2.50	5.00	10.00
SUE					
❑ LP-1014 [M]	That's How Heartaches Are Made	1963	37.50	75.00	150.00
❑ LP-1042 [M]	Only Those in Love	1965	37.50	75.00	150.00
❑ LPS-1042 [S]	Only Those in Love	1965	75.00	150.00	300.00
TRIP					
❑ 8009	The One and Only Baby Washington	1971	3.75	7.50	15.00
VEEP					
❑ VPS-16528	With You in Mind	1968	6.25	12.50	25.00

WASHINGTON, DINAH

45s

MERCURY

Number	Title (A Side/B Side)	Yr	VG	VG+	NM
❑ 5488	Harbor Lights/I Cross My Fingers	1950	6.25	12.50	25.00
❑ 5503	Time Out for Tears/Only a Moment Ago	1950	6.25	12.50	25.00
❑ 5510	How Deep Is the Ocean/Harbor Lights	1950	6.25	12.50	25.00
❑ 5665	I'm a Fool/If You Don't Believe I'm Leaving	1951	6.25	12.50	25.00
❑ 5728	Cold, Cold Heart/Mixed Emotions	1951	6.25	12.50	25.00
❑ 5736	Just One More Chance/Baby Did You Hear	1951	6.25	12.50	25.00
❑ 5804	No Time for Blues/(B-side unknown)	1952	6.25	12.50	25.00
❑ 5842	I Can't Face the Music/Mad About the Boy	1952	6.25	12.50	25.00
❑ 5906	Stormy Weather/Make Believe Dreams	1952	6.25	12.50	25.00
❑ 8181	I Wanna Be Loved/Love with Misery	1950	10.00	20.00	40.00
—Note: Earlier Dinah Washington 45s in the Mercury 8000 series may exist					
❑ 8187	I'll Never Be Free/Big Deal	1950	6.25	12.50	25.00
❑ 8192	How Deep Is the Ocean/Why Don't You Think Things Over	1950	6.25	12.50	25.00
❑ 8194	My Kind of Man/I Wanna Be Loved by You	1950	6.25	12.50	25.00
❑ 8195	It Isn't Fair/I'll Never Be Free	1950	6.25	12.50	25.00
❑ 8206	If I Loved You/My Kind of Man	1950	6.25	12.50	25.00
❑ 8207	Fast Movin' Mama/Juice Head Man of Mine	1950	6.25	12.50	25.00
❑ 8209	My Heart Cries for You/I Apologize	1951	6.25	12.50	25.00
❑ 8211	I Won't Cry Anymore/Don't Say You're Sorry Again	1951	6.25	12.50	25.00
❑ 8231	Ain't Nobody's Bizness If I Do/Please Send Me Someone to Love	1951	6.25	12.50	25.00
❑ 8232	I'm So Lonely I Could Cry/Fine Fine Daddy	1951	6.25	12.50	25.00
❑ 8249	Saturday Night/Be Fair to Me	1951	6.25	12.50	25.00
❑ 8257	Hey Good Lookin'/Out in the Cold Again	1951	20.00	40.00	80.00
—With The Ravens					
❑ 8267	Wheel of Fortune/Tell Me Why	1952	6.25	12.50	25.00
❑ 8269	Trouble in Mind/New Blowtop Blues	1952	6.25	12.50	25.00
❑ 8292	Pillow Blues/Double Dealin' Daddy	1952	6.25	12.50	25.00
❑ 8294	My Song/Half As Much	1952	6.25	12.50	25.00
❑ 10008 [S]	What a Diff'rence a Day Made/Come On Home	1959	6.25	12.50	25.00
—The A-side title is listed differently on the stereo 45 than on the mono 45 (71435)					
❑ 70046	I Cried for You/Gambler's Blues	1953	6.25	12.50	25.00
❑ 70125	Ain't Nothing Good/You Let My Love Grow Old	1953	6.25	12.50	25.00
❑ 70175	My Lean Baby/Never Never	1953	6.25	12.50	25.00
❑ 70214	TV Is the Thing (This Year)/Fat Daddy	1953	6.25	12.50	25.00
❑ 70263	Silent Night/The Lord's Prayer	1953	6.25	12.50	25.00
❑ 70284	Since My Man Has Gone and Went/My Man's an Undertaker	1953	6.25	12.50	25.00
❑ 70329	Short John/Feel Like I Wanna Cry	1954	5.00	10.00	20.00
❑ 70336	Such a Night/Until Sunrise	1954	5.00	10.00	20.00
❑ 70392	(No, No, No) You Can't Love Two/Big Long Slidin' Thing	1954	10.00	20.00	40.00
❑ 70439	I Don't Hurt Anymore/Dream	1954	5.00	10.00	20.00
❑ 70497	Teach Me Tonight/Wishing Well	1954	5.00	10.00	20.00
❑ 70537	That's All I Want from You/You Stay on My Mind	1955	5.00	10.00	20.00
❑ 70600	If It's the Last Thing I Do/I Diddie	1955	5.00	10.00	20.00
❑ 70653	I Hear Those Bells/The Cheat	1955	5.00	10.00	20.00
❑ 70694	I Concentrate on You/Not Without You	1955	5.00	10.00	20.00
❑ 70728	I'm Lost Without You Tonight/You Might Have Told Me	1955	5.00	10.00	20.00
❑ 70776	The Show Must Go On/I Just Couldn't Stand It No More	1956	3.75	7.50	15.00
❑ 70833	Let's Get Busy Too/Let's Go Around Together	1956	3.75	7.50	15.00
❑ 70868	Cat on a Hot Tin Roof/The First Time	1956	3.75	7.50	15.00
❑ 70906	Soft Winds/Tears to Burn	1956	3.75	7.50	15.00
❑ 70968	Relax, Max/The Kissing Way Home	1956	3.75	7.50	15.00
❑ 71018	All Because of You/To Love and Be Loved	1956	3.75	7.50	15.00
❑ 71043	You Let My Love Grow Old/I Know	1957	3.75	7.50	15.00
❑ 71087	Ain't Nobody Home/I'm Gonna Keep My Eyes on You	1957	3.75	7.50	15.00
❑ 71220	Everybody Loves My Baby/Blues Down Home	1957	3.75	7.50	15.00
❑ 71317	Ring-a My Phone/Never Again	1958	3.75	7.50	15.00
❑ 71377	Make Me a Present of You/All of Me	1958	3.75	7.50	15.00
❑ 71435	What a Diff'rence a Day Makes/Come On Home	1959	3.75	7.50	15.00
❑ 71508	Unforgettable/Nothing in the World	1959	2.50	5.00	10.00
❑ 71557	Ol' Santa/The Light	1959	3.00	6.00	12.00
❑ 71560	It Could Happen to You/Age of Miracles	1960	2.50	5.00	10.00
❑ 71635	This Bitter Earth/I Understand	1960	2.50	5.00	10.00
❑ 71696	Love Walked In/I'm in Heaven Tonight	1960	2.50	5.00	10.00
❑ 71744	We Have Love/Looking Back	1960	2.50	5.00	10.00

Number	Title (A Side/B Side)	Yr	VG	VG+	NM
❑ 71744 [PS]	We Have Love/Looking Back	1960	3.75	7.50	15.00
❑ 71778	Early Every Morning (Early Every Evening Too)/ Do You Want It That Way	1961	2.50	5.00	10.00
❑ 71778 [PS]	Early Every Morning (Early Every Evening Too)/ Do You Want It That Way	1961	3.75	7.50	15.00
❑ 71812	Our Love Is Here to Stay/Congratulations to Someone	1961	2.50	5.00	10.00
❑ 71812 [PS]	Our Love Is Here to Stay/Congratulations to Someone	1961	3.75	7.50	15.00
❑ 71876	September in the Rain/Wake the Town and Tell the People	1961	2.50	5.00	10.00
❑ 71876 [PS]	September in the Rain/Wake the Town and Tell the People	1961	3.75	7.50	15.00
❑ 71922	Tears and Laughter/If I Should Lose You	1962	2.50	5.00	10.00
❑ 71922 [PS]	Tears and Laughter/If I Should Lose You	1962	3.75	7.50	15.00
❑ 71958	Dream/Such a Night	1962	2.50	5.00	10.00
❑ 71958 [PS]	Dream/Such a Night	1962	3.75	7.50	15.00
❑ 72015	I Want to Be Loved/Am I Blue	1962	2.00	4.00	8.00
❑ 72015 [PS]	I Want to Be Loved/Am I Blue	1962	3.75	7.50	15.00
❑ 72040	Cold, Cold Heart/I Don't Hurt Anymore	1962	2.00	4.00	8.00
❑ 72040 [PS]	Cold, Cold Heart/I Don't Hurt Anymore	1962	3.75	7.50	15.00
ROULETTE					
❑ 4424	Where Are You/You're Nobody 'Til Somebody Loves You	1962	2.00	4.00	8.00
❑ 4444	For All We Know/I Wouldn't Know (What to Do)	1962	2.00	4.00	8.00
❑ 4455	You're a Sweetheart/It's a Mean Old Man's World	1962	2.00	4.00	8.00
❑ 4476	Romance in the Dark/No Hard Feelings	1963	2.00	4.00	8.00
❑ 4490	Soulsville/Let Me Be the First to Know	1963	2.00	4.00	8.00
❑ 4520	The Show Must Go On/I'll Drown in My Own Tears	1963	2.00	4.00	8.00
❑ 4534	That Sunday (That Summer)/A Stranger on Earth	1963	2.00	4.00	8.00
❑ 4538	Call Me Irresponsible/Funny Thing	1963	2.00	4.00	8.00
78s					
APOLLO					
❑ 368	Wise Woman Blues/No Voot — No Boot	1946	7.50	15.00	30.00
❑ 371	My Lovin' Papa/Mellow Mama Blues	1946	7.50	15.00	30.00
❑ 374	Rich Man's Blues/Walking Blues	1946	7.50	15.00	30.00
❑ 388	Blues for a Day/My Voot Is Really Vout	1947	7.50	15.00	30.00
❑ 396	Pacific Coast Blues/Chewin' Mama Blues	1948	7.50	15.00	30.00
KEYNOTE					
❑ 605	Evil Gal Blues/Homeward Bound	1944	10.00	20.00	40.00
—As "Sextet with Dinah Washington"					
❑ 606	Salty Papa Blues/I Know How to Do It	1944	10.00	20.00	40.00
—As "Sextet with Dinah Washington"					
MERCURY					
❑ 5488	Harbor Lights/I Cross My Fingers	1950	3.00	6.00	12.00
❑ 5503	Time Out for Tears/Only a Moment Ago	1950	3.00	6.00	12.00
❑ 5510	How Deep Is the Ocean/Harbor Lights	1950	3.00	6.00	12.00
❑ 5665	I'm a Fool/If You Don't Believe I'm Leaving	1951	3.00	6.00	12.00
❑ 5728	Cold, Cold Heart/Mixed Emotions	1951	3.00	6.00	12.00
❑ 5736	Just One More Chance/Baby Did You Hear	1951	3.00	6.00	12.00
❑ 5804	No Time for Blues/(B-side unknown)	1952	3.00	6.00	12.00
❑ 5842	I Can't Face the Music/Mad About the Boy	1952	3.00	6.00	12.00
❑ 5906	Stormy Weather/Make Believe Dreams	1952	3.00	6.00	12.00
❑ 8010	When a Woman Loves a Man/Oo-Wee Walkie Talkie	1946	5.00	10.00	20.00
❑ 8024	A Slick Chick (On the Mellow Side)/Postman Blues	1946	5.00	10.00	20.00
❑ 8030	Embraceable You/That's Why a Woman Loves a Heel	1946	5.00	10.00	20.00
❑ 8035	Stairway to the Stars/I Want to Be Loved	1947	5.00	10.00	20.00
❑ 8043	Evil Gal Blues/Homeward Bound	1947	5.00	10.00	20.00
—Reissue of Keynote 605					
❑ 8044	Salty Papa Blues/I Know How to Do It	1947	5.00	10.00	20.00
—Reissue of Keynote 606					
❑ 8050	Fool That I Am/Mean and Evil Blues	1947	5.00	10.00	20.00
❑ 8057	Since I Fell for You/You Can Depend on Me	1947	5.00	10.00	20.00
❑ 8061	There's Got to Be a Change/Early in the Morning	1947	5.00	10.00	20.00
❑ 8065	I Love You, Yes I Do/Don't Knock at My Door	1947	5.00	10.00	20.00
❑ 8072	Ain't Misbehavin'/No More Pretty Gal Blues	1948	3.75	7.50	15.00
❑ 8079	West Side Baby/Walkin' and Talkin' (And Cryin' My Blues Away)	1948	3.75	7.50	15.00
❑ 8082	I Want to Cry/Resolution Blues	1948	3.75	7.50	15.00
❑ 8085	Am I Asking Too Much/I Sold My Heart to the Junk Man	1948	3.75	7.50	15.00
❑ 8094	Tell Me So/In the Rain	1948	3.75	7.50	15.00
❑ 8102	You Satisfy/Laughing Boy	1948	3.75	7.50	15.00
❑ 8107	It's Too Soon to Know/I'll Wait	1948	3.75	7.50	15.00
❑ 8114	Why Can't You Behave/It's Funny	1949	3.75	7.50	15.00
❑ 8133	What Can I Say After I Say I'm Sorry/Pete	1949	3.75	7.50	15.00
❑ 8148	Baby Get Lost/Long John Blues	1949	3.75	7.50	15.00
❑ 8154	Good Daddy Blues/Richest Man in the Graveyard	1949	3.75	7.50	15.00
❑ 8163	I Only Know/New York, Chicago and L.A.	1950	3.75	7.50	15.00
❑ 8169	It Isn't Fair/Journey's End	1950	3.75	7.50	15.00
❑ 8181	I Wanna Be Loved/Love with Misery	1950	3.75	7.50	15.00
❑ 8187	I'll Never Be Free/Big Deal	1950	3.00	6.00	12.00
❑ 8192	How Deep Is the Ocean/Why Don't You Think Things Over	1950	3.00	6.00	12.00
❑ 8194	My Kind of Man/I Wanna Be Loved by You	1950	3.00	6.00	12.00
❑ 8195	It Isn't Fair/I'll Never Be Free	1950	3.00	6.00	12.00
❑ 8206	If I Loved You/My Kind of Man	1950	3.00	6.00	12.00
❑ 8207	Fast Movin' Mama/Juice Head Man of Mine	1950	3.00	6.00	12.00
❑ 8209	My Heart Cries for You/I Apologize	1951	3.00	6.00	12.00
❑ 8211	I Won't Cry Anymore/Don't Say You're Sorry Again	1951	3.00	6.00	12.00

Number	Title (A Side/B Side)	Yr	VG	VG+	NM
❑ 8231	Ain't Nobody's Bizness If I Do/Please Send Me Someone to Love	1951	3.00	6.00	12.00
❑ 8232	I'm So Lonely I Could Cry/Fine Fine Daddy	1951	3.00	6.00	12.00
❑ 8249	Saturday Night/Be Fair to Me	1951	3.00	6.00	12.00
❑ 8257	Hey Good Lookin'/Out in the Cold Again	1951	6.25	12.50	25.00
—With The Ravens					
❑ 8267	Wheel of Fortune/Tell Me Why	1952	3.00	6.00	12.00
❑ 8269	Trouble in Mind/New Blowtop Blues	1952	3.00	6.00	12.00
❑ 8292	Pillow Blues/Double Dealin' Daddy	1952	3.00	6.00	12.00
❑ 8294	My Song/Half As Much	1952	3.00	6.00	12.00
❑ 70046	I Cried for You/Gambler's Blues	1953	3.00	6.00	12.00
❑ 70125	Ain't Nothing Good/You Let My Love Grow Old	1953	3.00	6.00	12.00
❑ 70175	My Lean Baby/Never Never	1953	3.00	6.00	12.00
❑ 70214	TV Is the Thing (This Year)/Fat Daddy	1953	3.00	6.00	12.00
❑ 70263	Silent Night/The Lord's Prayer	1953	3.00	6.00	12.00
❑ 70284	Since My Man Has Gone and Went/My Man's an Undertaker	1953	3.00	6.00	12.00
❑ 70329	Short John/Feel Like I Wanna Cry	1954	3.00	6.00	12.00
❑ 70336	Such a Night/Until Sunrise	1954	3.00	6.00	12.00
❑ 70392	(No, No, No) You Can't Love Two/Big Long Slidin' Thing	1954	5.00	10.00	20.00
❑ 70439	I Don't Hurt Anymore/Dream	1954	3.00	6.00	12.00
❑ 70497	Teach Me Tonight/Wishing Well	1954	3.00	6.00	12.00
❑ 70537	That's All I Want from You/You Stay on My Mind	1955	3.00	6.00	12.00
❑ 70600	If It's the Last Thing I Do/I Diddie	1955	3.00	6.00	12.00
❑ 70653	I Hear Those Bells/The Cheat	1955	3.75	7.50	15.00
❑ 70694	I Concentrate on You/Not Without You	1955	3.75	7.50	15.00
❑ 70728	I'm Lost Without You Tonight/You Might Have Told Me	1955	3.75	7.50	15.00
❑ 70776	The Show Must Go On/I Just Couldn't Stand It No More	1956	3.75	7.50	15.00
❑ 70833	Let's Get Busy Too/Let's Go Around Together	1956	3.75	7.50	15.00
❑ 70868	Cat on a Hot Tin Roof/The First Time	1956	3.75	7.50	15.00
❑ 70906	Soft Winds/Tears to Burn	1956	3.75	7.50	15.00
❑ 70968	Relax, Max/The Kissing Way Home	1956	3.75	7.50	15.00
❑ 71018	All Because of You/To Love and Be Loved	1956	3.75	7.50	15.00
❑ 71043	You Let My Love Grow Old/I Know	1957	5.00	10.00	20.00
❑ 71087	Ain't Nobody Home/I'm Gonna Keep My Eyes on You	1957	5.00	10.00	20.00
❑ 71220	Everybody Loves My Baby/Blues Down Home	1957	5.00	10.00	20.00
7-Inch Extended Plays					
EMARCY					
❑ EP 1-6054	(contents unknown)	195?	6.25	12.50	25.00
❑ EP 1-6054 [PS]	After Hours with Miss "D"	195?	6.25	12.50	25.00
❑ EP-1-6080	*Lover Come Back to Me/I've Got You Under My Skin/There Is No Greater Love	1955	6.25	12.50	25.00
❑ EP-1-6080 [PS]	Dinah Jams	1955	6.25	12.50	25.00
❑ EP-1-6082	You Go to My Head (Beginning)/(Conclusion)	1955	6.25	12.50	25.00
❑ EP-1-6082 [PS]	Jammin' with Dinah	1955	6.25	12.50	25.00
MERCURY					
❑ EP 1-3395	(contents unknown)	195?	5.00	10.00	20.00
❑ EP 1-3395 [PS]	Dinah Washington	195?	5.00	10.00	20.00
❑ EP 1-4035	(contents unknown)	195?	5.00	10.00	20.00
❑ EP 1-4035 [PS]	Dinah Washington	195?	5.00	10.00	20.00
❑ EP 1-4041	(contents unknown)	195?	5.00	10.00	20.00
❑ EP 1-4041 [PS]	For Lonely Lovers	195?	5.00	10.00	20.00
ROULETTE					
❑ SBG 269 [PS]	Dinah Washington	196?	3.75	7.50	15.00
❑ SBG 269 [S]	What's New/Somebody Else Is Taking My Place/ I'll Never Stop Loving You//He's My Guy/To Forget About You/That Old Feeling	196?	3.75	7.50	15.00
—Jukebox issue; smal hole, plays at 33 1/3 rpm					
Albums					
ACCORD					
❑ SN-7207	Retrospective	1982	2.50	5.00	10.00
ARCHIVE OF FOLK AND JAZZ					
❑ 297	Dinah Washington	197?	3.00	6.00	12.00
COLLECTABLES					
❑ COL-5200	Golden Classics	1989	2.50	5.00	10.00
DELMARK					
❑ DL-451	Mellow Mama	1992	5.00	10.00	20.00
EMARCY					
❑ EMS-2-401 [(2)]	Jazz Sides	197?	3.75	7.50	15.00
❑ MG-26032 [10]	After Hours with Miss D	1954	30.00	60.00	120.00
❑ MG-36000 [M]	Dinah Jams	1955	12.50	25.00	50.00
❑ MG-36011 [M]	For Those in Love	1955	12.50	25.00	50.00
❑ MG-36028 [M]	After Hours with Miss D	1955	12.50	25.00	50.00
—Reissue of 26032					
❑ MG-36065 [M]	Dinah	1956	12.50	25.00	50.00
❑ MG-36073 [M]	In the Land of Hi-Fi	1956	12.50	25.00	50.00
❑ MG-36104 [M]	The Swingin' Miss "D"	1956	12.50	25.00	50.00
❑ MG-36119 [M]	Dinah Washington Sings Fats Waller	1957	12.50	25.00	50.00
❑ MG-36130 [M]	Dinah Washington Sings Bessie Smith	1957	12.50	25.00	50.00
❑ MG-36141 [M]	Newport '58	1958	10.00	20.00	40.00
❑ 814184-1 [(2)]	Slick Chick (On the Mellow Side)	1983	3.00	6.00	12.00
❑ 824883-1 [(2)]	Jazz Sides	198?	3.00	6.00	12.00
—Reissue of 401					
❑ 826453-1	In the Land of Hi-Fi	1986	2.50	5.00	10.00
GRAND AWARD					
❑ GA 33-318 [M]	Dinah Washington Sings the Blues	1955	12.50	25.00	50.00
—Add 50% if removable wrap-around cover is still there					
HARLEM HIT PARADE					
❑ 8002	Finer Dinah	197?	2.50	5.00	10.00

Number	Title (A Side/B Side)	Yr	VG	VG+	NM
MERCURY					
❑ MGP-2-103 [(2) M]	This Is My Story	1963	6.25	12.50	25.00
—Combines 20788 and 20789 in one package					
❑ MGP-2-603 [(2) S]	This Is My Story	1963	7.50	15.00	30.00
—Combines 60788 and 60789 in one package					
❑ MG-20119 [M]	Music for a First Love	1957	12.50	25.00	50.00
❑ MG-20120 [M]	Music for Late Hours	1957	12.50	25.00	50.00
❑ MG-20247 [M]	The Best in Blues	1958	12.50	25.00	50.00
❑ MG-20439 [M]	The Queen	1959	7.50	15.00	30.00
❑ MG-20479 [M]	What a Diff'rence a Day Makes!	1960	7.50	15.00	30.00
❑ MG-20523 [M]	Newport '58	1960	7.50	15.00	30.00
—Reissue of EmArcy 36141					
❑ MG-20525 [M]	Dinah Washington Sings Fats Waller	1960	7.50	15.00	30.00
—Reissue of EmArcy 36119					
❑ MG-20572 [M]	Unforgettable	1961	6.25	12.50	25.00
❑ MG-20604 [M]	I Concentrate on You	1961	6.25	12.50	25.00
❑ MG-20614 [M]	For Lonely Lovers	1961	6.25	12.50	25.00
❑ MG-20638 [M]	September in the Rain	1961	6.25	12.50	25.00
❑ MG-20661 [M]	Tears and Laughter	1962	6.25	12.50	25.00
❑ MG-20729 [M]	I Wanna Be Loved	1962	6.25	12.50	25.00
❑ MG-20788 [M]	This Is My Story — Dinah Washington's Golden Hits, Volume 1	1963	3.75	7.50	15.00
❑ MG-20789 [M]	This Is My Story — Dinah Washington's Golden Hits, Volume 2	1963	3.75	7.50	15.00
❑ MG-20829 [M]	The Good Old Days	1963	3.75	7.50	15.00
❑ MG-20928 [M]	The Queen and Quincy	1965	3.75	7.50	15.00
❑ MG-21119 [M]	Dinah Discovered	1967	5.00	10.00	20.00
❑ MG-25060 [10]	Dinah Washington	1950	30.00	60.00	120.00
❑ MG-25138 [10]	Dynamic Dinah	1952	30.00	60.00	120.00
❑ MG-25140 [10]	Blazing Ballads	1952	30.00	60.00	120.00
❑ SR-60111 [S]	The Queen	1959	10.00	20.00	40.00
❑ SR-60158 [S]	What a Diff'rence a Day Makes!	1960	10.00	20.00	40.00
❑ SR-60200 [S]	Newport '58	1960	10.00	20.00	40.00
❑ SR-60202 [S]	Dinah Washington Sings Fats Waller	1960	10.00	20.00	40.00
❑ SR-60232 [S]	Unforgettable	1961	7.50	15.00	30.00
❑ SR-60604 [S]	I Concentrate on You	1961	7.50	15.00	30.00
❑ SR-60614 [S]	For Lonely Lovers	1961	7.50	15.00	30.00
❑ SR-60638 [S]	September in the Rain	1961	7.50	15.00	30.00
❑ SR-60661 [S]	Tears and Laughter	1962	7.50	15.00	30.00
❑ SR-60729 [S]	I Wanna Be Loved	1962	7.50	15.00	30.00
❑ SR-60788 [S]	This Is My Story — Dinah Washington's Golden Hits, Volume 1	1963	5.00	10.00	20.00
❑ SR-60789 [S]	This Is My Story — Dinah Washington's Golden Hits, Volume 2	1963	5.00	10.00	20.00
❑ SR-60829 [S]	The Good Old Days	1963	5.00	10.00	20.00
❑ SR-60928 [S]	The Queen and Quincy	1965	5.00	10.00	20.00
❑ SR-61119 [S]	Dinah Discovered	1967	3.75	7.50	15.00
❑ 818815-1	What a Diff'rence a Day Makes!	198?	2.00	4.00	8.00
—Reissue					
❑ 822867-1	This Is My Story — Dinah Washington's Golden Hits, Volume 1	1985	2.00	4.00	8.00
—Reissue					
PICKWICK					
❑ SPC-3043	Dinah Washington	196?	2.50	5.00	10.00
❑ SPC-3230	I Don't Hurt Anymore	197?	2.50	5.00	10.00
❑ SPC-3536	Greatest Hits	197?	2.50	5.00	10.00
ROULETTE					
❑ RE 104 [(2)]	Echoes of An Era	196?	3.75	7.50	15.00
❑ RE 117 [(2)]	Queen of the Blues	1971	3.75	7.50	15.00
❑ RE 125 [(2)]	The Immortal Dinah Washington	1973	3.75	7.50	15.00
❑ R 25170 [M]	Dinah '62	1962	3.75	7.50	15.00
❑ SR 25170 [S]	Dinah '62	1962	5.00	10.00	20.00
❑ R 25180 [M]	In Love	1962	3.75	7.50	15.00
❑ SR 25180 [S]	In Love	1962	5.00	10.00	20.00
❑ R 25183 [M]	Drinking Again	1962	3.75	7.50	15.00
❑ SR 25183 [S]	Drinking Again	1962	5.00	10.00	20.00
❑ R 25189 [M]	Back to the Blues	1963	3.75	7.50	15.00
❑ SR 25189 [S]	Back to the Blues	1963	5.00	10.00	20.00
❑ R 25220 [M]	Dinah '63	1963	3.75	7.50	15.00
❑ SR 25220 [S]	Dinah '63	1963	5.00	10.00	20.00
❑ R 25244 [M]	In Tribute	1963	3.75	7.50	15.00
❑ SR 25244 [S]	In Tribute	1963	5.00	10.00	20.00
❑ R 25253 [M]	A Stranger on Earth	1964	3.75	7.50	15.00
❑ SR 25253 [S]	A Stranger on Earth	1964	5.00	10.00	20.00
❑ R 25269 [M]	Dinah Washington	1964	3.75	7.50	15.00
❑ SR 25269 [S]	Dinah Washington	1964	5.00	10.00	20.00
❑ R 25289 [M]	The Best of Dinah Washington	1965	3.75	7.50	15.00
❑ SR 25289 [S]	The Best of Dinah Washington	1965	5.00	10.00	20.00
❑ 42014	The Best of Dinah Washington	1968	3.00	6.00	12.00
—Reissue of 25289					
TRIP					
❑ 5500	Dinah Jams	1973	2.50	5.00	10.00
❑ 5516	After Hours	1973	2.50	5.00	10.00
❑ 5524	Tears and Laughter	1974	2.50	5.00	10.00
❑ 5556	Dinah Washington Sings Bessie Smith	197?	2.50	5.00	10.00
❑ 5565	The Swingin' Miss D	197?	2.50	5.00	10.00
❑ TLX 9505 [(2)]	Sad Songs — Blue Songs	197?	3.00	6.00	12.00
VERVE					
❑ 818930-1	The Fats Waller Songbook	1984	2.50	5.00	10.00
WING					
❑ PKW-2-121 [(2)]	The Original Queen of Soul	1969	5.00	10.00	20.00
❑ MGW-12140 [M]	The Late Late Show	1963	3.00	6.00	12.00
❑ MGW-12271 [M]	Dinah Washington Sings Fats Waller	1964	3.00	6.00	12.00
❑ SRW-16140 [S]	The Late Late Show	1963	3.00	6.00	12.00
❑ SRW-16271 [S]	Dinah Washington Sings Fats Waller	1964	3.00	6.00	12.00
❑ SRW-16386	The Original Soul Sister	196?	3.00	6.00	12.00

Number	Title (A Side/B Side)	Yr	VG	VG+	NM
WASHINGTON, DINAH, AND BROOK BENTON					
Also see each artist's individual listings.					
45s					
MERCURY					
❑ 71565	Baby (You Got What It Takes)/I Do	1960	3.75	7.50	15.00
❑ 71629	A Rockin' Good Way (To Mess Around and Fall in Love)/I Believe	1960	3.75	7.50	15.00
❑ 71629 [PS]	A Rockin' Good Way (To Mess Around and Fall in Love)/I Believe	1960	6.25	12.50	25.00
Albums					
MERCURY					
❑ MG-20588 [M]	The Two of Us	1960	6.25	12.50	25.00
❑ SR-60244 [S]	The Two of Us	1960	7.50	15.00	30.00
❑ 824823-1	The Two of Us	1985	2.00	4.00	8.00
—Reissue					
WASHINGTON, GINO					
45s					
ATAC					
❑ 101	Doin' the Popcorn/(B-side unknown)	1969	7.50	15.00	30.00
❑ 102	I'll Be Around/(B-side unknown)	1969	10.00	20.00	40.00
❑ 2830	Rat Race/(B-side unknown)	1969	7.50	15.00	30.00
❑ 7823	Like My Baby/(B-side unknown)	1969	10.00	20.00	40.00
CONGRESS					
❑ 269	Understanding/Water	1966	3.00	6.00	12.00
❑ 273	Beach Bash/Hi Hi Hazel	1966	3.00	6.00	12.00
CORREC-TONE					
❑ 503	Gino Is a Coward/Puppet on a String	1962	15.00	30.00	60.00
DJM					
❑ 1011	You Lovely Witch/Love Me, Love Me	1976	—	3.00	6.00
KAPP					
❑ 796	All I Need/Whatever Will Be, Will Be	1966	2.50	5.00	10.00
MALA					
❑ 12029	Like My Baby/I'll Be Around When You Want Me	1968	10.00	20.00	40.00
RIC-TIC					
❑ 100	Gino Is a Coward/Puppet on a String	1964	5.00	10.00	20.00
SIDRA					
❑ 9005	Romeo/Now You're Lonely	196?	6.25	12.50	25.00
SONBERT					
❑ 3770	Gino Is a Coward/Puppet on a String	1963	6.25	12.50	25.00
WAND					
❑ 147	Out of This World/Come Monkey with Me	1964	5.00	10.00	20.00
7-Inch Extended Plays					
NORTON					
❑ EP-080	Out of This World/Come Monkey with Me//Heartburn/Monkey Tree	1999	—	—	2.00
❑ EP-080 [PS]	Come Monkey with Gino Washington and the Atlantics	1999	—	—	2.00
Albums					
ATAC					
❑ 2730	Gino Washington's Golden Hits	1969	7.50	15.00	30.00
KAPP					
❑ KL-1415 [M]	Gino Washington's Ram Jam Band	1967	5.00	10.00	20.00
❑ KS-3415 [S]	Gino Washington's Ram Jam Band	1967	6.25	12.50	25.00
WASHINGTON, GROVER, JR.					
45s					
COLUMBIA					
❑ 07240	Summer Nights/Strawberry Moon	1987	—	—	3.00
❑ 07621	The Look of Love/Shwaree Ride	1987	—	—	3.00
❑ 73040	Jamaica/Split Second (Act II, The Bar Scene)	1989	—	2.00	4.00
ELEKTRA					
❑ 46060	Tell Me About It Now/Feel It Comin'	1979	—	2.00	4.00
❑ 47071	Let It Flow (For Dr. J.)/Winelight	1980	—	2.00	4.00
❑ 47103	Just the Two of Us/Make Me a Memory (Sad Samba)	1981	—	2.00	4.00
—Bill Withers sings on A-side, but is not credited on the record					
❑ 47103 [PS]	Just the Two of Us/Make Me a Memory (Sad Samba)	1981	—	2.50	5.00
❑ 47140	Let It Flow (For Dr. J.)/Winelight	1981	—	2.00	4.00
❑ 47246	Be Mine (Tonight)/Reaching Out	1981	—	2.00	4.00
❑ 47246 [PS]	Be Mine (Tonight)/Reaching Out	1981	—	2.50	5.00
❑ 47425	Jamming/East River Drive	1982	—	2.00	4.00
❑ 69680	When I Look at You/Secret Sounds	1984	—	2.00	4.00
❑ 69708	Inside Moves/Sassy Stew	1984	—	2.00	4.00
❑ 69834	I'll Be with You/Brazilian Memories	1983	—	2.00	4.00
❑ 69887	The Best Is Yet to Come/Bye Bye Love	1982	—	2.00	4.00
—With Patti LaBelle					
KUDU					
❑ 902	Inner City Blues/Ain't No Sunshine	1972	—	3.00	6.00
❑ 903	Mercy Mercy Me (Part 1)/Mercy Mercy Me (Part 2)	1972	—	3.00	6.00
❑ 909	No Tears in the End/Body and Soul	1972	—	3.00	6.00
❑ 912	Where Is the Love (Part 1)/Where Is the Love (Part 2)	1973	—	3.00	6.00
❑ 916	Masterpiece (Part 1)/Masterpiece (Part 2)	1973	—	3.00	6.00
❑ 924	Mister Magic/Black Frost	1975	—	2.50	5.00
❑ 930	Knuckle Head (Part 1)/Knuckle Head (Part 2)	1976	—	2.50	5.00
❑ 937	A Secret Place (Part 1)/A Secret Place (Part 2)	1977	—	2.50	5.00
❑ 942	Summer Song/Juffere	1978	—	2.50	5.00
MOTOWN					
❑ 1454	Do Dat/Reed Seed (This Tune)	1978	—	2.00	4.00
❑ 1486	Snake Eyes/Love	1979	—	2.00	4.00

Number	Title (A Side/B Side)	Yr	VG	VG+	NM
Albums					
COLUMBIA					
❑ FC 40510	Strawberry Moon	1987	2.50	5.00	10.00
❑ OC 44256	Then and Now	1988	2.50	5.00	10.00
❑ OC 45253	Time Out of Mind	1989	2.50	5.00	10.00
❑ C 48530	Next Exit	1992	5.00	10.00	20.00
ELEKTRA					
❑ 6E-182	Paradise	1979	2.50	5.00	10.00
❑ 6E-305	Winelight	1980	2.50	5.00	10.00
❑ 5E-562	Come Morning	1981	2.50	5.00	10.00
❑ 60215	The Best Is Yet to Come	1982	2.50	5.00	10.00
❑ 60318	Inside Moves	1984	2.50	5.00	10.00
❑ 60415	Anthology of Grover Washington, Jr.	1985	2.50	5.00	10.00
KUDU					
❑ KS-03	Inner City Blues	1971	3.00	6.00	12.00
❑ KS-07	All the King's Horses	1972	3.00	6.00	12.00
❑ KS-20	Mister Magic	1975	3.00	6.00	12.00
❑ KS-24	Feels So Good	1975	3.00	6.00	12.00
❑ KS-32	A Secret Place	1976	3.00	6.00	12.00
❑ KSQX-1213 [(2) Q]	Soul Box	1973	6.25	12.50	25.00
❑ KSX-1213 [(2)]	Soul Box	1973	3.75	7.50	15.00
❑ KSX-3637 [(2)]	Live at the Bijou	1977	3.75	7.50	15.00
MOTOWN					
❑ M5-165V1	A Secret Place	1981	2.00	4.00	8.00
—Reissue of Kudu 32					
❑ M5-175V1	Mister Magic	1981	2.00	4.00	8.00
—Reissue of Kudu 20					
❑ M5-177V1	Feels So Good	1981	2.00	4.00	8.00
—Reissue of Kudu 24					
❑ M5-184V1	Soul Box Vol. 1	1981	2.00	4.00	8.00
—Reissue of half of Kudu 1213					
❑ M5-186V1	All the King's Horses	1981	2.00	4.00	8.00
—Reissue of Kudu 07					
❑ M5-187V1	Soul Box Vol. 2	1981	2.00	4.00	8.00
—Reissue of half of Kudu 1213					
❑ M5-189V1	Inner City Blues	1981	2.00	4.00	8.00
—Reissue of Kudu 03					
❑ M7-910	Reed Seed	1978	2.50	5.00	10.00
❑ M7-933	Skylarkin'	1980	2.50	5.00	10.00
❑ M9-940 [(2)]	Baddest	1980	3.00	6.00	12.00
❑ M9-961 [(2)]	Anthology	1981	3.00	6.00	12.00
❑ 5232 ML	Skylarkin'	1982	2.00	4.00	8.00
—Reissue of 933					
❑ 5236 ML	Reed Seed	1982	2.00	4.00	8.00
—Reissue of 910					
❑ 5307 ML	Greatest Performances	198?	2.50	5.00	10.00
❑ 6126 ML	Grover Washington Jr. at His Best	198?	2.50	5.00	10.00
❑ 8239 ML2 [(2)]	Live at the Bijou	198?	3.00	6.00	12.00
NAUTILUS					
❑ NR-39	Winelight	1981	12.50	25.00	50.00
—Audiophile vinyl					

WATERS, CRYSTAL

Number	Title (A Side/B Side)	Yr	VG	VG+	NM
12-Inch Singles					
HOLLYWOOD					
❑ 66409	You Turn Me On (Vocal Mix) (Hump Mix) (Dub Mix) (Radio Edit) (LP Version)	1992	2.00	4.00	8.00
MERCURY					
❑ MELP 124 [DJ]	Say...If You Feel Alright (95 North Club Mix 8:12) (Henry Street Dub Mix 6:25) (Acapella 3:42) (X-Mix Club Mix 5:07) (95 North Hard Dub Mix 8:08) (Jam & Lewis Club Mix 5:24)	1997	2.50	5.00	10.00
❑ MELP 142 [DJ]	Just a Freak (Hex Hector Club Mix) (Soul Solution Club Mix) (95 'n' Sleazy Dub) (Soul Solution Dub)	1997	2.50	5.00	10.00
—With Dennis Rodman					
❑ MELP 196 [DJ]	In De Ghetto/Gypsy Woman '98	1998	—	3.00	6.00
❑ PRO 1122 [DJ]	100% Pure Love (Trance Vox) (Trance Dub) (PG Tips Anthem Mix) (EFX's Tribal Pump Mix)	1994	2.00	4.00	8.00
❑ 574061-1	Say...If You Feel Alright (6 versions)	1997	—	3.50	7.00
❑ 574433-1	Just a Freak (Hex Hector Club Mix) (Soul Solution Club Mix) (95 'n' Sleazy Dub) (Soul Solution Dub)	1997	2.00	4.00	8.00
—With Dennis Rodman					
❑ 578943-1	Say...If You Feel Alright (6 versions)	1997	2.00	4.00	8.00
❑ 852061-1	Relax (4 versions)	1995	2.50	5.00	10.00
❑ 858927-1	What I Need (Club Mix) (Hump Mix) (B.Y.C. Mix) (LP Version)	1994	2.50	5.00	10.00
❑ 866175-1	Surprise (The Surprise Mix 7:37) (Naughty Boy Hump 7:24) (Open Your Eyes Mix 7:50) (Rhythm & Black Club Mix 5:55)	1991	2.50	5.00	10.00
❑ 868209-1	Gypsy Woman (She's Homeless) (Red Bone Club Mix) (Radio Mix) (Basement Boy Strip to the Bone Mix) (Hump Instrumental Mix)	1991	2.50	5.00	10.00
❑ 868763-1	Makin' Happy (Basement Boys Happy Club Mix 7:52) (Basement Boys Happy Hump 6:14) (Hurley's Happy House Mix 6:23) (Hurleys's Insane Mix 6:24)	1991	2.50	5.00	10.00
45s					
MERCURY					
❑ 574228-7	Say...If You Feel Alright/You Bring the Sunshine	1997	—	—	3.00
—B-side by Gina Thompson					
❑ 868208-7	Gypsy Woman (She's Homeless) (Radio Mix)/(Basement Boy Strip to the Bone Mix)	1991	—	2.50	5.00
Albums					
MERCURY					
❑ 848894-1	Surprise	1991	3.00	6.00	12.00

WATERS, MUDDY

Number	Title (A Side/B Side)	Yr	VG	VG+	NM
45s					
CHESS					
❑ 1509	All Night Long/Country Boy	1952	625.00	1250.	2500.
—Note: Muddy Waters records on Chess before 1509 are unconfirmed on 45 rpm					
❑ 1514	Please Have Mercy/Looking for My Baby	1952	200.00	400.00	800.00
❑ 1526	Standing Around Crying/Gone to Main St.	1952	175.00	350.00	700.00
❑ 1537	She's All Right/Sad, Sad Day	1953	100.00	200.00	400.00
❑ 1542	Who's Gonna Be Your Sweet Man/Turn the Lamp Down Low	1953	75.00	150.00	300.00
❑ 1550	Mad Love/Blow, Wind, Blow	1953	30.00	60.00	120.00
❑ 1560	I'm Your Hoochie Coochie Man/You're So Pretty	1954	25.00	50.00	100.00
❑ 1571	Just Make Love to Me/Oh Yeh!	1954	15.00	30.00	60.00
❑ 1579	I'm Ready/I Don't Know Why	1954	15.00	30.00	60.00
❑ 1585	Lovin' Man/I'm a Natural Born Lover	1955	12.50	25.00	50.00
❑ 1596	I Want to Be Loved/My Eyes Keep Me in Trouble	1955	12.50	25.00	50.00
❑ 1602	Manish Boy/Young Fashion Ways	1955	17.50	35.00	70.00
❑ 1612	Trouble, No More/Sugar Sweet	1955	20.00	40.00	80.00
❑ 1620	Forty Days and Forty Nights/All Aboard	1956	10.00	20.00	40.00
❑ 1630	Don't Go No Farther/Diamonds at Your Feet	1956	12.50	25.00	50.00
❑ 1644	I Got to Find My Baby/Just to Be with You	1956	10.00	20.00	40.00
❑ 1652	Got My Mojo Working/Rock Me	1957	12.50	25.00	50.00
❑ 1667	Good News/Come Home Baby	1957	7.50	15.00	30.00
❑ 1680	I Live the Life I Love/Evil	1958	7.50	15.00	30.00
❑ 1692	I Won't Go/She's Got It	1958	7.50	15.00	30.00
❑ 1704	Close to You/She's Nineteen Years Old	1958	7.50	15.00	30.00
❑ 1718	Mean Mistreater/Walking Thru the Park	1959	6.25	12.50	25.00
❑ 1724	Ooh Wee/Clouds in My Heart	1959	6.25	12.50	25.00
❑ 1733	Take the Bitter with the Sweet/She's Into Somethin'	1959	6.25	12.50	25.00
❑ 1739	Recipe for Love/Tell Me Baby	1959	6.25	12.50	25.00
❑ 1748	I Feel So Good/When I Get to Thinking	1960	6.25	12.50	25.00
❑ 1752	I'm Your Doctor/Ready Way Back	1960	6.25	12.50	25.00
❑ 1758	Love Affair/Look What You've Done	1960	6.25	12.50	25.00
❑ 1765	Tiger in Your Tank/Meanest Woman	1960	6.25	12.50	25.00
❑ 1774	Got My Mojo Working/Woman Wanted	1960	6.25	12.50	25.00
❑ 1796	Messin' with the Man/Lonesome Room Blues	1961	5.00	10.00	20.00
❑ 1819	Going Home/Tough Times	1962	5.00	10.00	20.00
❑ 1827	Muddy Waters Twist/You Shook Me	1962	6.25	12.50	25.00
❑ 1839	You Need Love/Little Brown Bird	1962	6.25	12.50	25.00
❑ 1862	Five Long Years/Twenty-Four Hours	1963	3.75	7.50	15.00
❑ 1895	The Same Thing/You Can't Lose What You Never Had	1964	3.75	7.50	15.00
❑ 1914	Short Dress Woman/My John the Conqueror	1964	3.75	7.50	15.00
❑ 1921	Put Me in Your Lay-A-Way/Still a Fool	1965	3.00	6.00	12.00
❑ 1937	My Dog Can't Bark/I Got a Rich Man's Woman	1965	3.00	6.00	12.00
❑ 1973	I'm Your Hoochie Coochie Man/Corrina, Corrina	1966	3.00	6.00	12.00
❑ 2018	When the Eagle Flies/Birdnest on the Ground	1967	2.50	5.00	10.00
❑ 2085	Going Home/I Feel So Good	1970	2.00	4.00	8.00
❑ 2107	Making Friends/Two Steps Forward	1971	2.00	4.00	8.00
❑ 2143	Garbage Man/Can't Get No Grindin'	1973	—	3.00	6.00
78s					
ARISTOCRAT					
❑ 406	Screamin' and Cryin'/Where's My Woman	1950	75.00	150.00	300.00
❑ 412	Rollin' and Tumblin' - Pt. 1/Pt. 2	1950	250.00	500.00	1000.
❑ 1302	Gypsy Woman/Little Anna Mae	1948	62.50	125.00	250.00
❑ 1305	I Can't Be Satisfied/I Feel Like Going Home	1948	50.00	100.00	200.00
❑ 1307	Mean Red Spider/You're Gonna Miss Me	1948	50.00	100.00	200.00
❑ 1310	Streamline Woman/Muddy Jumps One	1949	50.00	100.00	200.00
CHESS					
❑ 1426	Rollin' Stone/Walkin' Blues	1950	75.00	150.00	300.00
❑ 1434	You're Gonna Need My Help/Sad Letter Blues	1950	50.00	100.00	200.00
❑ 1441	Louisiana Blues/Evans Shuffle	1950	37.50	75.00	150.00
❑ 1452	Long Distance Call/Too Young to Know	1951	37.50	75.00	150.00
❑ 1468	Honey Bee/Appealing Blues	1951	30.00	60.00	120.00
❑ 1480	My Fault/Still a Fool	1951	30.00	60.00	120.00
❑ 1490	Early Morning Blues/She Moves Me	1951	30.00	60.00	120.00
❑ 1509	All Night Long/Country Boy	1952	25.00	50.00	100.00
❑ 1514	Please Have Mercy/Looking for My Baby	1952	25.00	50.00	100.00
❑ 1526	Standing Around Crying/Gone to Main St.	1952	25.00	50.00	100.00
❑ 1537	She's All Right/Sad, Sad Day	1953	20.00	40.00	80.00
❑ 1542	Who's Gonna Be Your Sweet Man/Turn the Lamp Down Low	1953	20.00	40.00	80.00
❑ 1550	Mad Love/Blow, Wind, Blow	1953	12.50	25.00	50.00
❑ 1560	I'm Your Hoochie Coochie Man/You're So Pretty	1954	15.00	30.00	60.00
❑ 1571	Just Make Love to Me/Oh Yeh!	1954	12.50	25.00	50.00
❑ 1579	I'm Ready/I Don't Know Why	1954	12.50	25.00	50.00
❑ 1585	Lovin' Man/I'm a Natural Born Lover	1955	12.50	25.00	50.00
❑ 1596	I Want to Be Loved/My Eyes Keep Me in Trouble	1955	12.50	25.00	50.00
❑ 1602	Manish Boy/Young Fashion Ways	1955	17.50	35.00	70.00
❑ 1612	Trouble, No More/Sugar Sweet	1955	15.00	30.00	60.00
❑ 1620	Forty Days and Forty Nights/All Aboard	1956	12.50	25.00	50.00
❑ 1630	Don't Go No Farther/Diamonds at Your Feet	1956	12.50	25.00	50.00
❑ 1644	I Got to Find My Baby/Just to Be with You	1956	12.50	25.00	50.00
❑ 1652	Got My Mojo Working/Rock Me	1957	15.00	30.00	60.00
❑ 1667	Good News/Come Home Baby	1957	10.00	20.00	40.00
❑ 1680	I Live the Life I Love/Evil	1958	12.50	25.00	50.00
❑ 1692	I Won't Go/She's Got It	1958	12.50	25.00	50.00
❑ 1704	Close to You/She's Nineteen Years Old	1958	15.00	30.00	60.00
Albums					
BLUE SKY					
❑ PZ 34449	Hard Again	1977	3.00	6.00	12.00
—No bar code on cover					
❑ PZ 34449	Hard Again	198?	2.00	4.00	8.00
—Budget-line reissue with bar code					

Number	Title (A Side/B Side)	Yr	VG	VG+	NM
❏ JZ 34928	I'm Ready	1978	3.00	6.00	12.00
❏ PZ 34928	I'm Ready	198?	2.00	4.00	8.00
—Budget-line reissue					
❏ JZ 35712	Muddy "Missisiippi" Waters Live	1980	3.00	6.00	12.00
❏ PZ 35712	Muddy "Missisiippi" Waters Live	198?	2.00	4.00	8.00
—Budget-line reissue					
❏ JZ 37064	King Bee	1981	3.00	6.00	12.00
❏ PZ 37064	King Bee	198?	2.00	4.00	8.00
—Budget-line reissue					
CADET CONCEPT					
❏ CS-314	Electric Mud	1968	6.25	12.50	25.00
❏ CS-320	After the Rain	1969	6.25	12.50	25.00
CHESS					
❏ 127 [(2)]	Fathers and Sons	1969	6.25	12.50	25.00
❏ LP-1427 [DJ]	The Best of Muddy Waters	1957	500.00	1000.	1500.
—White label promo					
❏ LP-1427 [M]	The Best of Muddy Waters	1957	125.00	250.00	500.00
—Black label					
❏ LPS-1427 [R]	The Best of Muddy Waters	196?	3.00	6.00	12.00
—Black label					
❏ LP-1444 [DJ]	Muddy Waters Sings Big Bill	1960	250.00	500.00	1000.
—White label promo					
❏ LP-1444 [M]	Muddy Waters Sings Big Bill	1960	75.00	150.00	300.00
❏ LPS-1444 [R]	Muddy Waters Sings Big Bill	196?	3.75	7.50	15.00
—Rechanneled stereo reissue					
❏ LP-1449 [M]	Muddy Waters at Newport	1962	30.00	60.00	120.00
❏ LP-1483 [M]	Folk Singer	1964	30.00	60.00	120.00
❏ LP-1501 [M]	The Real Folk Blues of Muddy Waters	1965	15.00	30.00	60.00
❏ LP-1507 [M]	Muddy, Brass and Blues	1966	10.00	20.00	40.00
❏ LPS-1507 [S]	Muddy, Brass and Blues	1966	12.50	25.00	50.00
❏ LP-1511 [M]	More Real Folk Blues	1967	12.50	25.00	50.00
❏ LPS-1511 [S]	More Real Folk Blues	1967	10.00	20.00	40.00
❏ LP-1533 [M]	Blues from Big Bill's Copacabana	1968	12.50	25.00	50.00
❏ LPS-1539	Sail On	1969	6.25	12.50	25.00
❏ LPS-1553	They Call Me Muddy Waters	1971	5.00	10.00	20.00
❏ CH-9101	Rolling Stone	1985	3.00	6.00	12.00
❏ CH-9180	Rare and Unissued	1986	3.00	6.00	12.00
❏ CH-9197	Muddy Waters Sings Big Bill	1986	2.50	5.00	10.00
—Reissue of 1444					
❏ CH-9198	Muddy Waters at Newport	1986	2.50	5.00	10.00
—Reissue of 1449					
❏ CH-9255	The Best of Muddy Waters	1987	2.50	5.00	10.00
—Reissue of 1427					
❏ CH-9261	Folk Singer	1987	2.50	5.00	10.00
—Reissue of 1483					
❏ CH-9274	The Real Folk Blues of Muddy Waters	1987	2.50	5.00	10.00
—Reissue of 1501					
❏ CH-9278	More Real Folk Blues	1988	2.50	5.00	10.00
—Reissue of 1511					
❏ CH-9286	Muddy, Brass and the Blues	1989	2.50	5.00	10.00
—Reissue of 1507					
❏ CH-9291	Trouble No More: Singles 1955-1959	1989	3.00	6.00	12.00
❏ CH-9298	The London Muddy Waters Sessions	1989	2.50	5.00	10.00
—Reissue of 60013					
❏ CH-9299	They Call Me Muddy Waters	1989	2.50	5.00	10.00
—Reissue of 1553					
❏ CH-9319	Can't Get No Grindin'	1990	2.50	5.00	10.00
—Reissue of 50023					
❏ CH-50012	Muddy Waters Live	1972	5.00	10.00	20.00
❏ CH-50023	Can't Get No Grindin'	1973	5.00	10.00	20.00
❏ 2CH-50033 [(2)]	Fathers and Sons	1974	5.00	10.00	20.00
—Reissue of 127					
❏ CH-50035	The Muddy Waters Woodstock Album	1976	3.75	7.50	15.00
❏ 2CH-60006 [(2)]	McKinley Morganfield, A.K.A. Muddy Waters	1971	6.25	12.50	25.00
❏ CH-60013	The London Muddy Waters Sessions	1972	5.00	10.00	20.00
❏ CH-60026	London Revisited	1974	3.75	7.50	15.00
❏ CH-60031	"Unk" in Funk	1975	3.75	7.50	15.00
❏ CH6-80002 [(6)]	The Chess Box	1990	12.50	25.00	50.00
INTERMEDIA					
❏ QS-5071	Sweet Home Chicago	198?	2.50	5.00	10.00
MOBILE FIDELITY					
❏ 1-201	Folk Singer	1994	6.25	12.50	25.00
—Audiophile vinyl					
MUSE					
❏ MR-5008	Mud in Your Ear	198?	3.00	6.00	12.00
TESTAMENT					
❏ 2210	Stovall's Plantation	197?	3.00	6.00	12.00

WATERS, MUDDY, AND HOWLIN' WOLF

Also see each artist's individual listings.

Albums

Number	Title (A Side/B Side)	Yr	VG	VG+	NM
CHESS					
❏ CH-9100	Muddy and The Wolf	1985	3.00	6.00	12.00

WATKINS, LOVELACE

45s

Number	Title (A Side/B Side)	Yr	VG	VG+	NM
GROOVE					
❏ 58-0016	Tender Love/Ma Cherie Au Revoir	1963	7.50	15.00	30.00
❏ 58-0016 [PS]	Tender Love/Ma Cherie Au Revoir	1963	20.00	40.00	80.00
❏ 58-0023	I Won't Believe It/He'[s Lookin' Out for the World	1963	7.50	15.00	30.00
MGM					
❏ 12875	Hello Young Lovers/When I Fall in Love	1960	3.75	7.50	15.00
SUE					
❏ 10-003	Who Am I/Dreams	1968	3.00	6.00	12.00

Number	Title (A Side/B Side)	Yr	VG	VG+	NM
UNI					
❏ 55211	Fool on the Hill/Je Vous Aime Beaucoup	1970	3.00	6.00	12.00

WATLEY, JODY

Also see SHALAMAR.

12-Inch Singles

Number	Title (A Side/B Side)	Yr	VG	VG+	NM
ATLANTIC					
❏ DMD 2450 [(2)] DJ	Off the Hook (Maw Mix) (Maw Beats) (Soul Solution Club Mix) (LP Version)//(Kenlou Mix) (Kenlou Dub) (Soul Solution Dub) (Maw Dub)	1998	2.50	5.00	10.00
❏ DMD 2470 [(2)] DJ	If I'm Not in Love (Lenny Bertoldo Club Mix) (Pull KHZ Remix) (Roc & Presta Club Mix) (Pull Bass Dub)//(95 North Club Mix) (Pull Extended Mix) (Dano & BK Remix) (Lenny's DL Dub)	1998	3.75	7.50	15.00
❏ 84070 [(2)]	Off the Hook (Maw Mix) (Maw Beats) (Soul Solution Club Mix) (LP Version)//(Kenlou Mix) (Kenlou Dub) (Soul Solution Dub) (Maw Dub)	1998	3.00	6.00	12.00
AVITONE					
❏ 74506	Affection (Vocal) (Instrumental)/(same on both sides)	1995	—	3.00	6.00
MCA					
❏ L33-1505 [DJ]	I Want You (Single Version) (Instrumental) (Suite)	1991	2.00	4.00	8.00
❏ L33-2032 [DJ]	I Want You (Funk You Up Extended) (Funk You Up Radio Edit) (Funkstrumental) (Funkapella) (Ultimate Love Letter Mix) (Ultimate Love Letter Radio Edit) (Ultimate Love Letter Percussapella) (Ultimate Love Letter Accapella)	1991	—	3.50	7.00
❏ L33-2047 [DJ]	I'm the One You Need (Vocal) (Instrumental)	1992	—	3.00	6.00
❏ L33-2066 [DJ]	I Want You (In My House Version) (Houseapella) (Housin' Radio Version) (Housestrumental) (House Suite)	1991	—	3.00	6.00
❏ MCA8P-2160 [DJ]	I'm the One You Need (Extended) (Edit) (Dead Zone Version) (Def Dub)	1992	2.00	4.00	8.00
❏ MCA8P-2161 [DJ]	I'm the One You Need (Funky Chicken Version) (Funky Chicken Edit) (Chickstrumental) (Drize Bone Club Version)	1992	—	3.50	7.00
❏ MCA8P-2225 [DJ]	It All Begins with You (LP Version) (Instrumental) (Suite)	1992	—	3.50	7.00
❏ MCA8P-2866 [DJ]	Your Love Keeps Working on Me (Remix) (Instrumental Remix) (Radio Edit) (Original Version) (Instrumental)	1993	2.00	4.00	8.00
❏ MCA8P-2881 [DJ]	Your Love Keeps Working on Me (Extended MK Mix 5:43) (MK Instrumental Mix 4:46) (MK Brooklyn Mix 7:18) (MK's Working Dub 7:10)	1993	2.00	4.00	8.00
❏ MCA8P-2924 [DJ]	When a Man Loves a Woman (Edit) (LP Version) (Instrumental)/(same on both sides)	1993	—	3.50	7.00
❏ MCA8P-2940 [DJ]	When a Man Loves a Woman (7 versions)	1994	2.50	5.00	10.00
❏ MCA8P-2976 [DJ]	When a Man Loves a Woman (DJ's Club Mix 7:33) (DJ's Bentley Mix 6:07) (DJ's Dub Mix 4:59) (DJ's Other Dub Mix 5:33)	1994	2.00	4.00	8.00
❏ MCA8P-2987 [DJ]	When a Man Loves a Woman (Remix Radio Edit 4:30) (Remix Version 5:39) (Acapella Version 5:03) (Instrumental 5:37)	1994	2.00	4.00	8.00
❏ MCA8P-3024 [DJ]	When a Man Loves a Woman (Man/Man Version) (Woman/Woman Version) (More Man/Man Version) (More Woman/Woman Version) (Instrumental Version)	1994	—	3.50	7.00
❏ L33-17311 [DJ]	Still a Thrill (same on both sides)	1987	—	3.00	6.00
❏ L33-17448 [DJ]	Some Kind of Lover (Extended 7:18) (Radio Edit 5:30) (Instrumental 7:18) (Dub 4:18) (Bonus Beats 4:18)	1987	—	3.50	7.00
❏ L33-17792 [DJ]	Real Love (5 versions)	1989	2.00	4.00	8.00
❏ L33-17857 [DJ]	Friends (same on both sides)	1989	2.00	4.00	8.00
❏ L33-17991 [DJ]	Everything (same on both sides?)	1989	2.00	4.00	8.00
❏ L33-18164 [DJ]	Precious Love (same on both sides)	1990	—	3.00	6.00
❏ L33-18194 [DJ]	Precious Love (Tongue in Groove Mix 6:48) (Dub Instrumental 5:00) (LP Version 5:14) (Instrumental 4:45)	1990	2.00	4.00	8.00
❏ 23689	Looking for a New Love (Extended Club Version) (Radio Version) (Instrumental) (A Cappella) (Bonus Beats)	1987	2.00	4.00	8.00
❏ 23747	Still a Thrill (Extended Version 8:39) (Radio Edit) (Instrumental) (A Cappella) (Bonus Beats)	1987	—	3.00	6.00
❏ 23785	Don't You Want Me (4 versions)	1987	2.00	4.00	8.00
❏ 23816	Some Kind of Lover (3 versions)	1987	2.00	4.00	8.00
❏ 23825	Most of All (Remix) (7" Version) (Dub)	1988	—	3.00	6.00
❏ 23928	Real Love (Extended Version) (Extended Instrumental) (Dub Version) (Bassapella)	1989	2.00	4.00	8.00
❏ 23956	Friends (2 versions)/Private Life	1989	—	3.50	7.00
❏ 24010	Precious Love (Tongue in Groove Mix) (Dub)	1990	—	3.00	6.00
❏ 54138	I Want You (The Funk You Up Mix) (The Ultimate Love Letter Mix) (In My House Version)	1991	2.00	4.00	8.00
❏ 54278	I'm the One You Need (Extended) (Def Dub)	1992	2.00	4.00	8.00
❏ 54785	Your Love Keeps Working on Me (3 versions)	1993	2.50	5.00	10.00
❏ 54802	When a Man Loves a Woman (3 versions)	1994	2.00	4.00	8.00

45s

Number	Title (A Side/B Side)	Yr	VG	VG+	NM
ATLANTIC					
❏ 84071	Off the Hook (Single Edit)/(Instrumental)	1998	—	—	3.00
MCA					
❏ S45-17291 [DJ]	Looking for a New Love (same on both sides)	1987	—	2.50	5.00
❏ S45-17291 [PS]	Looking for a New Love (same on both sides)	1987	2.50	5.00	10.00
—Fold-out poster sleeve (not used on stock copies)					
❏ 52956	Looking for a New Love/Looking for a New Love (Acapella)	1987	—	—	3.00
❏ 52956 [PS]	Looking for a New Love/Looking for a New Love (Acapella)	1987	—	—	3.00

T-Bone Walker briefly recorded for Capitol around 1950. Two singles came out, both of which exist as hard-to-find 45s. This is the first, "Go Back to the One You Love."

One of the all-time early R&B classics is "Sixty Minute Man" by the Dominoes. It spent 14 weeks at #1 on the R&B charts and even got to the top 20 on the pop charts in 1951. But a near-mint 45 on the original Federal label is very hard to find.

Jeanette "Baby" Washington had 17 R&B hits spanning a 21-year period. Her biggest R&B hit, "That's How Heartaches Are Made," is the title song of this Sue LP.

One of the more interesting Dinah Washington 45s is this Mercury stereo issue of her biggest pop hit. Curiously, it uses the old title, "What a Diff'rence a Day Made," and the mono version used "What a Diff'rence a Day Makes."

The Best of Muddy Waters was the first long-player Chess released of the important blues man's work. At that point, he'd already been making records for about 10 years.

Later known as Johnny "Guitar" Watson, his early 45s on the Federal label called him "Young John Watson."

Number	Title (A Side/B Side)	Yr	VG	VG+	NM
❏ 53081	Still a Thrill/Looking for a New Love	1987	—	—	3.00
❏ 53081 [PS]	Still a Thrill/Looking for a New Love	1987	—	—	3.00
❏ 53162	Don't You Want Me/(Instrumental)	1987	—	—	3.00
❏ 53162 [PS]	Don't You Want Me/(Instrumental)	1987	—	—	3.00
❏ 53235	Some Kind of Lover/(Instrumental)	1988	—	—	3.00
❏ 53235 [PS]	Some Kind of Lover/(Instrumental)	1988	—	—	3.00
❏ 53258	Most of All/(Instrumental)	1988	—	—	3.00
❏ 53258 [PS]	Most of All/(Instrumental)	1988	—	—	3.00
❏ 53484	Real Love/(Instrumental)	1988	—	—	3.00
❏ 53484 [PS]	Real Love/(Instrumental)	1988	—	—	3.00
❏ 53660	Friends/Private Life	1989	—	—	3.00
❏ 53714	Everything/(Instrumental)	1989	—	—	3.00
❏ 53790	Precious Love/(Instrumental)	1990	—	—	3.00

Albums

ATLANTIC

Number	Title	Yr	VG	VG+	NM
❏ 83087	Flower	1998	3.75	7.50	15.00

MCA

❏ 5898	Jody Watley	1987	2.50	5.00	10.00
❏ 6276	Larger Than Life	1989	2.50	5.00	10.00
❏ 6343	You Wanna Dance with Me?	1989	3.00	6.00	12.00
❏ 10355	Affairs of the Heart	1991	3.00	6.00	12.00

SOLAR

| ❏ D1-72561 | Beginnings | 1988 | 2.50 | 5.00 | 10.00 |

WATSON, JOHNNY "GUITAR"

45s

ARVEE

Number	Title (A Side/B Side)	Yr	VG	VG+	NM
❏ 5016	Untouchable/Johnny Guitar	1960	6.25	12.50	25.00

—As "Johnny Watson"

A&M

| ❏ 2383 | Planet Funk/First Timothy Six | 1981 | — | 2.00 | 4.00 |
| ❏ 2398 | That's What Time It Is/First Timothy Six | 1982 | — | 2.00 | 4.00 |

CACTUS

| ❏ 118 | Let's Rock/(B-side unknown) | 1959 | 37.50 | 75.00 | 150.00 |

CLASS

| ❏ 246 | The Bear/One More Kiss | 1959 | 7.50 | 15.00 | 30.00 |

—As "Johnny Watson"

DJM

❏ 1013	I Need It/Since I Met You Baby	1976	—	2.50	5.00
❏ 1019	Superman Lover/We're No Exception	1976	—	2.50	5.00
❏ 1020	Ain't That a Bitch/Won't You Forgive Me Baby	1977	—	3.00	6.00
❏ 1020 [PS]	Ain't That a Bitch/Won't You Forgive Me Baby	1977	2.00	4.00	8.00
❏ 1024	A Real Mother for Ya/Nothing Left to Be Desired	1977	—	2.50	5.00
❏ 1029	Lover Jones/Tarzan	1977	—	2.50	5.00
❏ 1034	Love That Will Not Die/A Damn Shame	1978	—	2.50	5.00
❏ 1100	Virginia's Pretty Funky/The Institute	1978	—	2.50	5.00

—As "Watsonian Institute"

❏ 1101	Gangster of Love/Guitar Disco	1978	—	2.50	5.00
❏ 1106	What the Hell Is This?/Can You Handle It	1979	—	2.50	5.00
❏ 1304	Love Jones/(B-side unknown)	1980	—	2.50	5.00
❏ 1305	Telephone Bill/(B-side unknown)	1980	—	2.50	5.00

FANTASY

❏ 721	Like I'm Not Your Man/You Bring Love	1974	—	3.00	6.00
❏ 739	I Don't Want to Be a Lone Ranger/You Can Stay But the Noise Must Go	1975	—	3.00	6.00
❏ 752	It's Too Late/Tripping	1975	—	3.00	6.00

FEDERAL

❏ 12120	Highway 60/No I Can't	1953	37.50	75.00	150.00
❏ 12131	Motor Head Baby/Sad Fool	1953	37.50	75.00	150.00
❏ 12143	I Got Eyes/Walkin' to My Baby	1953	37.50	75.00	150.00
❏ 12157	What's Going On/Thinking	1953	37.50	75.00	150.00
❏ 12175	Half Pint of Whiskey/Space Guitar	1954	62.50	125.00	250.00
❏ 12183	Gettin' Drunk/You Can't Take It With You	1954	50.00	100.00	200.00

—All Federal 45s as "Young John Watson"

KEEN

| ❏ 3-4005 | Gangster of Love/One Room Country Shack | 1957 | 7.50 | 15.00 | 30.00 |
| ❏ 3-4023 | Deana Baby/Honey | 1957 | 7.50 | 15.00 | 30.00 |

KENT

| ❏ 328 | Those Lonely, Lonely Nights/(B-side unknown) | 1959 | 5.00 | 10.00 | 20.00 |

KING

❏ 5536	Posin'/Embraceable You	1961	5.00	10.00	20.00
❏ 5579	Broke and Lonely/Cuttin' In	1961	6.25	12.50	25.00
❏ 5607	The Nearness of You/I Just Want Me Some Love	1962	3.75	7.50	15.00
❏ 5666	What You Do to Me/Sweet Lovin' Mama	1962	3.75	7.50	15.00
❏ 5716	Cold, Cold Heart/That's the Chance You've Got to Take	1963	3.75	7.50	15.00
❏ 5774	Gangster of Love/In the Evening	1963	3.75	7.50	15.00
❏ 5833	I Say, I Love You/You Better Love Me	1964	3.75	7.50	15.00

OKEH

| ❏ 7263 | Keep On Lovin' You/South Like West | 1966 | 3.00 | 6.00 | 12.00 |
| ❏ 7270 | Hold On, I'm Comin'/Wolfman | 1967 | 3.00 | 6.00 | 12.00 |

RPM

❏ 423	Hot Little Mama/I Love to Love You	1955	12.50	25.00	50.00
❏ 431	Too Tired/Don't Touch Me	1955	12.50	25.00	50.00
❏ 436	Those Lonely, Lonely Nights/Someone Cares for Me	1955	10.00	20.00	40.00
❏ 447	Oh Baby/Give a Little	1955	10.00	20.00	40.00
❏ 455	Three Hours Past Midnight/Ruben	1956	10.00	20.00	40.00
❏ 471	She Moves Me/Love Me Baby	1956	10.00	20.00	40.00

VALLEY VUE

| ❏ 769 | Strike On Computers/(B-side unknown) | 1984 | — | 2.50 | 5.00 |

78s

FEDERAL

Number	Title (A Side/B Side)	Yr	VG	VG+	NM
❏ 12120	Highway 60/No I Can't	1953	15.00	30.00	60.00
❏ 12131	Motor Head Baby/Sad Fool	1953	15.00	30.00	60.00
❏ 12143	I Got Eyes/Walkin' to My Baby	1953	15.00	30.00	60.00
❏ 12157	What's Going On/Thinking	1953	15.00	30.00	60.00
❏ 12175	Half Pint of Whiskey/Space Guitar	1954	20.00	40.00	80.00
❏ 12183	Gettin' Drunk/You Can't Take It With You	1954	20.00	40.00	80.00

—All Federal 78s as "Young John Watson"

KEEN

| ❏ 4-4005 | Gangster of Love/One Room Country Shack | 1957 | 10.00 | 20.00 | 40.00 |
| ❏ 4-4023 | Deana Baby/Honey | 1957 | 10.00 | 20.00 | 40.00 |

RPM

❏ 423	Hot Little Mama/I Love to Love You	1955	10.00	20.00	40.00
❏ 431	Too Tired/Don't Touch Me	1955	10.00	20.00	40.00
❏ 436	Those Lonely, Lonely Nights/Someone Cares for Me	1955	10.00	20.00	40.00
❏ 447	Oh Baby/Give a Little	1955	10.00	20.00	40.00
❏ 455	Three Hours Past Midnight/Ruben	1956	10.00	20.00	40.00
❏ 471	She Moves Me/Love Me Baby	1956	10.00	20.00	40.00

Albums

A&M

| ❏ SP-4880 | That's What Time It Is | 1981 | 2.50 | 5.00 | 10.00 |

CADET

| ❏ LP-4056 [M] | I Cried for You | 1967 | 6.25 | 12.50 | 25.00 |
| ❏ LPS-4056 [S] | I Cried for You | 1967 | 7.50 | 15.00 | 30.00 |

CHESS

| ❏ LP-1490 [M] | Blues Soul | 1965 | 17.50 | 35.00 | 70.00 |
| ❏ LPS-1490 [S] | Blues Soul | 1965 | 20.00 | 40.00 | 80.00 |

DJM

❏ 3	Ain't That a Bitch	1976	2.50	5.00	10.00
❏ 7	A Real Mother for Ya	1977	2.50	5.00	10.00
❏ 13	Master Funk	1978	2.50	5.00	10.00

—As "Watsonian Institute"

❏ 19	Giant	1978	2.50	5.00	10.00
❏ 24	What the Hell Is This?	1979	2.50	5.00	10.00
❏ 27	E.D.P. Extra Disco Perception	1979	2.50	5.00	10.00

—As "Watsonian Institute"

❏ 31	Love Jones	1980	2.50	5.00	10.00
❏ 501	Johnny "Guitar" Watson and the Family Clone	1981	2.50	5.00	10.00
❏ 714	Funk Beyond the Call of Duty	1977	2.50	5.00	10.00

FANTASY

❏ MPF-4503	Greatest Hits	1981	2.50	5.00	10.00
❏ 9437	Listen	1973	3.00	6.00	12.00
❏ 9484	I Don't Want to Be Alone Stranger	1975	3.00	6.00	12.00

KING

| ❏ 857 [M] | Johnny Guitar Watson | 1963 | 100.00 | 200.00 | 400.00 |

MCA

| ❏ 5273 | The Very Best of Johnny "Guitar" Watson | 1981 | 2.50 | 5.00 | 10.00 |

OKEH

❏ OKM 12118 [M]	Bad	1967	7.50	15.00	30.00
❏ OKM 12124 [M]	In the Fats Bag	1967	7.50	15.00	30.00
❏ OKS 14118 [S]	Bad	1967	10.00	20.00	40.00
❏ OKS 14124 [S]	In the Fats Bag	1967	10.00	20.00	40.00

POWER PAK

| ❏ 306 | Gangster of Love | 1978 | 2.50 | 5.00 | 10.00 |

WATSON, JOHNNY "GUITAR", AND LARRY WILLIAMS

Also see each artist's individual listings.

45s

OKEH

Number	Title (A Side/B Side)	Yr	VG	VG+	NM
❏ 7274	Mercy, Mercy, Mercy/A Quitter Never Wins	1967	2.50	5.00	10.00
❏ 7281	Two for the Price of One/Too Late	1967	2.50	5.00	10.00
❏ 7281 [PS]	Two for the Price of One/Too Late	1967	6.25	12.50	25.00
❏ 7300	Find Yourself Someone to Love/Nobody	1967	6.25	12.50	25.00

—Backed by Kaleidoscope

Albums

OKEH

| ❏ OKM 12122 [M] | Two for the Price of One | 1967 | 10.00 | 20.00 | 40.00 |
| ❏ OKS 14122 [S] | Two for the Price of One | 1967 | 15.00 | 30.00 | 60.00 |

WATSONIAN INSTITUTE

See JOHNNY "GUITAR" WATSON.

WATTS, NOBLE

45s

BATON

Number	Title (A Side/B Side)	Yr	VG	VG+	NM
❏ 246	Easy Going (Part 1)/Easy Going (Part 2)	1957	6.25	12.50	25.00
❏ 249	The Slop/Midnite Flight	1957	6.25	12.50	25.00
❏ 249	Hard Times (The Slop)/Midnite Flight	1957	3.75	7.50	15.00
❏ 251	Rickey Tick/Blast Off	1958	3.75	7.50	15.00
❏ 254	The Slide/Shakin'	1958	3.75	7.50	15.00
❏ 257	Great Times/The Creep	1958	3.75	7.50	15.00
❏ 266	Flap Jack/Hot Tamales	1959	3.75	7.50	15.00

BRUNSWICK

| ❏ 55382 | Thingamajig/F.L.A. | 1968 | 2.00 | 4.00 | 8.00 |

CUB

| ❏ 9078 | The Beaver/Frog Hop | 1960 | 3.00 | 6.00 | 12.00 |

DELUXE

| ❏ 6066 | Mashing Potatoes/Pig Ears and Rice | 1954 | 7.50 | 15.00 | 30.00 |

ENJOY

| ❏ 1008 | Jookin'/What Ya Gonna Do | 1963 | 3.00 | 6.00 | 12.00 |

Number	Title (A Side/B Side)	Yr	VG	VG+	NM
SIR					
❏ 273	Boogie Woogie/Mashed Potatoes	1959	3.75	7.50	15.00

WATTS 103RD STREET RHYTHM BAND, THE
See CHARLES WRIGHT AND THE WATTS 103RD STREET RHYTHM BAND.

WELLS, MARY
Also see MARVIN GAYE AND MARY WELLS.

45s

Number	Title (A Side/B Side)	Yr	VG	VG+	NM
20TH CENTURY FOX					
❏ 544	Ain't It the Truth/Stop Takin' Me for Granted	1964	3.75	7.50	15.00
❏ 555	Use Your Head/Everlovin' Boy	1965	3.75	7.50	15.00
❏ 570	Never, Never Leave Me?Why Don't You Let Yourself Go	1965	3.75	7.50	15.00
❏ 590	He's a Lover/I'm Learnin'	1965	3.75	7.50	15.00
❏ 590 [PS]	He's a Lover/I'm Learnin'	1965	7.50	15.00	30.00
❏ 6606	Me Without You/I'm Sorry	1965	3.75	7.50	15.00
❏ 6619	I Should Have Known Better/Please Please Me	1965	5.00	10.00	20.00
ATCO					
❏ 6392	Dear Lover/Can't You See	1965	3.00	6.00	12.00
❏ 6423	Keep Me in Suspense/Such a Sweet Thing	1966	3.00	6.00	12.00
❏ 6436	Fancy Free/Me and My Baby	1966	3.00	6.00	12.00
❏ 6469	Coming Home/Hey You Set My Soul on Fire	1967	3.00	6.00	12.00
EPIC					
❏ 02664	Gigolo/I'm Changing My Ways	1982	—	2.00	4.00
❏ 02855	These Arms/Spend the Night With Me	1982	—	2.00	4.00
JUBILEE					
❏ 5621	The Doctor/Two Lovers' History	1968	3.75	7.50	15.00
❏ 5629	Can't Get Away From Your Love/A Woman in Love	1968	3.75	7.50	15.00
❏ 5639	Don't Look Back/500 Miles	1968	3.75	7.50	15.00
❏ 5676	Mind Reader/Never Give a Man the World	1969	3.00	6.00	12.00
❏ 5684	Dig the Way I Feel/Love Shooting Bandit	1969	3.00	6.00	12.00
❏ 5695	Sweet Love/It Must Be	1970	3.00	6.00	12.00
❏ 5718	Mr. Tough/Never Give a Man the World	1971	3.00	6.00	12.00
MOTOWN					
❏ 1003	Bye Bye Baby/Please Forgive Me	1960	12.50	25.00	50.00
❏ 1011	I Don't Want to Take a Chance/I'm Sorry	1961	7.50	15.00	30.00
—Pink "lines" label					
❏ 1011	I Don't Want to Take a Chance/I'm Sorry	1961	5.00	10.00	20.00
—Blue "map" label					
❏ 1011 [PS]	I Don't Want to Take a Chance/I'm Sorry	1961	20.00	40.00	80.00
❏ 1016	Strange Love/Come to Me	1961	5.00	10.00	20.00
❏ 1016 [PS]	Strange Love/Come to Me	1961	20.00	40.00	80.00
❏ 1024	The One Who Really Loves You/I'm Gonna Stay	1962	5.00	10.00	20.00
❏ 1024 [PS]	The One Who Really Loves You/I'm Gonna Stay	1962	20.00	40.00	80.00
❏ 1032	You Beat Me to the Punch/Old Love (Let's Try It Again)	1962	5.00	10.00	20.00
❏ 1032 [PS]	You Beat Me to the Punch/Old Love (Let's Try It Again)	1962	30.00	60.00	120.00
❏ 1035	Two Lovers/Operator	1962	5.00	10.00	20.00
❏ 1039	Laughing Boy/Two Wrongs Don't Make a Right	1963	5.00	10.00	20.00
❏ 1042	Your Old Stand By/What Love Has Joined Together	1963	5.00	10.00	20.00
❏ 1048	You Lost the Sweetest Boy/What's Easy for Two Is So Hard for One	1963	5.00	10.00	20.00
❏ 1056	My Guy/Oh Little Boy (What Did You Do to Me)	1964	5.00	10.00	20.00
❏ 1061	When I'm Gone/Guarantee for a Lifetime	1964	150.00	300.00	600.00
❏ 1065	Whisper You Love Me/I'll Be Available	1964	—	—	—
—Unreleased?					
REPRISE					
❏ 1031	I Found What I Wanted/I See a Future in You	1971	2.50	5.00	10.00
❏ 1308	If You Can't Give Her Love (Give Her Up)/Cancel My Subscription	1974	2.50	5.00	10.00

Albums

Number	Title (A Side/B Side)	Yr	VG	VG+	NM
20TH FOX					
❏ TFM 3171 [M]	Mary Wells	1965	10.00	20.00	40.00
❏ TFM 3178 [M]	Love Songs to the Beatles	1965	20.00	40.00	80.00
❏ TFS 4171 [S]	Mary Wells	1965	15.00	30.00	60.00
❏ TFS 4178 [S]	Love Songs to the Beatles	1965	25.00	50.00	100.00
❏ ST-90790 [S]	Love Songs to the Beatles	1965	37.50	75.00	150.00
—Capitol Record Club edition					
ALLEGIANCE					
❏ AV-444	The Old, the New, and the Best of Mary Wells	1984	2.50	5.00	10.00
ATCO					
❏ 33-199 [M]	Two Sides of Mary Wells	1966	6.25	12.50	25.00
❏ SD 33-199 [S]	Two Sides of Mary Wells	1966	7.50	15.00	30.00
EPIC					
❏ ARE 37540	In and Out of Love	1981	3.75	7.50	15.00
JUBILEE					
❏ JGS-8018	Servin' Up Some Soul	1968	6.25	12.50	25.00
MOTOWN					
❏ M5-161V1	Bye Bye Baby/I Don't Want to Take a Chance	1981	2.50	5.00	10.00
❏ M5-167V1	Mary Wells Sings My Guy	1981	2.50	5.00	10.00
❏ M5-221V1	Two Lovers	1981	2.50	5.00	10.00
❏ MLP-600 [M]	Bye Bye Baby/I Don't Want to Take a Chance	1961	75.00	150.00	300.00
—White label stock copy					
❏ MLP-600 [M]	Bye Bye Baby/I Don't Want to Take a Chance	1962	62.50	125.00	250.00
—With map; label address above the center hole					
❏ M 605 [M]	The One Who Really Loves You	1962	40.00	80.00	160.00
—With map; label address above the center hole					
❏ M 605 [M]	The One Who Really Loves You	1964	10.00	20.00	40.00
—With map; label address around lower part of label					
❏ M 607 [M]	Two Lovers and Other Great Hits	1963	30.00	60.00	120.00
—With map; label address above the center hole					
❏ M 607 [M]	Two Lovers and Other Great Hits	1964	10.00	20.00	40.00
—With map; label address around lower part of label					
❏ M 611 [M]	Recorded Live on Stage	1963	30.00	60.00	120.00
—With map; label address above the center hole					
❏ M 611 [M]	Recorded Live on Stage	1964	10.00	20.00	40.00
—With map; label address around lower part of label					
❏ M 612	Second Time Around	1963	—	—	—
—Canceled					
❏ M 616 [M]	Greatest Hits	1964	10.00	20.00	40.00
❏ MS 616 [S]	Greatest Hits	1964	10.00	20.00	40.00
❏ M 617 [M]	Mary Wells Sings My Guy	1964	12.50	25.00	50.00
❏ M 653 [M]	Vintage Stock	1967	12.50	25.00	50.00
❏ MS 653 [S]	Vintage Stock	1967	12.50	25.00	50.00
❏ 5233 ML	Greatest Hits	1982	2.50	5.00	10.00
MOVIETONE					
❏ 71010 [M]	Ooh	1966	6.25	12.50	25.00
❏ 72010 [S]	Ooh	1966	7.50	15.00	30.00

WESLEY, FRED
Also includes the J.B.'s.

45s

Number	Title (A Side/B Side)	Yr	VG	VG+	NM
ATLANTIC					
❏ 3408	Up for the Down Stroke/When In Doubt	1977	—	2.50	5.00
KING					
❏ 6317	The Grunt (Part 1)/The Grunt (Part 2)	1970	2.50	5.00	10.00
—As "The J.B.'s"					
❏ 6333	These Are the J.B.'s (Part 1)/These Are the J.B.'s (Part 2)	1970	2.50	5.00	10.00
—As "The J.B.'s"					
PEOPLE					
❏ 602	Gimme Some More/The Rabbit Got the Gun	1972	—	3.00	6.00
—As "The J.B.'s"					
❏ 607	Pass the Peas/Hot Pants Road	1972	—	3.00	6.00
—As "The J.B.'s"					
❏ 610	Givin' Up Food for Funk (Part 1)/Givin' Up Food for Funk (Part 2)	1972	—	3.00	6.00
—As "The J.B.'s"					
❏ 614	Backstabbers/J.B. Shout	1972	—	3.00	6.00
❏ 616	If You Don't Get It the First Time/You Can Have Her Boogie	1973	—	3.00	6.00
❏ 617	Alone Again (Naturally)/Watermelon Man	1973	—	3.00	6.00
❏ 619	Sportin' Life/Dirty Harri	1973	—	3.00	6.00
❏ 621	Doing It to Death/Everybody Got Soul	1973	—	3.00	6.00
❏ 627	If You Don't Get It the First Time, Back Up and Try It Again, Party/You Can Have Watergate, Just Give Me Some Bucks and I'll Be Straight	1973	—	3.00	6.00
❏ 632	Same Beat - Part 1/Same Beat - Part 2	1974	—	3.00	6.00
❏ 638	Damn Right I Am Somebody-Part 1/Damn Right I Am Somebody-Part 2	1974	—	3.00	6.00
❏ 643	Rockin' Funky Watergate (Part 1)/Rockin' Funky Watergate (Part 2)	1974	—	3.00	6.00
❏ 646	Little Boy Black/Rockin' Funky Watergate (Part 2)	1974	—	3.00	6.00
❏ 648	Breakin' Bread/Funky Music Is My Style	1974	—	2.50	5.00
❏ 651	Makin' Love/Rice and Ribs	1975	—	2.50	5.00
❏ 654	Thank You for Lettin' Me Be Myself and Be Yours (Part 1)/Thank You for Lettin' Me Be Myself and Be Yours (Part 2)	1975	—	2.50	5.00
❏ 655	(It's Not the Express) It's the J.B.'s Monaurail, Part 1/(It's Not the Express) It's the J.B.'s Monaurail, Part 2	1975	—	2.50	5.00
❏ 660	Thank You for Lettin' Me Be Myself (Part 1)/Thank You for Lettin' Me Be Myself (Part 2)	1975	—	2.50	5.00
❏ 663	All Aboard the Funky Soul Train/Thank You for Lettin' Me Be Myself and You Be Yourself	1976	—	2.50	5.00
❏ 2502	My Brother (Part 1)/My Brother (Part 2)	1971	—	3.00	6.00
—As "The J.B.'s"					
RSO/CURTOM					
❏ 1037	House Party/I Make Music	1980	—	2.00	4.00

Albums

Number	Title (A Side/B Side)	Yr	VG	VG+	NM
ATLANTIC					
❏ SD 18214	A Blow for Me, A Toot to You	1977	3.00	6.00	12.00
❏ SD 19254	Say Blow by Blow Backwards	1979	3.00	6.00	12.00
PEOPLE					
❏ PE-5601	Food for Thought	1972	20.00	40.00	80.00
❏ PE-5603	Doing It to Death	1973	20.00	40.00	80.00
❏ PE-6602	Damn Right I Am Somebody	1974	5.00	10.00	20.00
❏ PE-6604	Breakin' Bread	1974	5.00	10.00	20.00

WESTON, KIM
Also see MARVIN GAYE AND KIM WESTON.

45s

Number	Title (A Side/B Side)	Yr	VG	VG+	NM
ENTERPRISE					
❏ 9101	Beautiful People/Goodness Gracious	1974	—	2.50	5.00
GORDY					
❏ 7041	I'll Never See My Love Again/A Thrill a Moment	1965	5.00	10.00	20.00
❏ 7046	Take Me in Your Arms (Rock Me a Little While)/Don't Compare Me to Her	1965	5.00	10.00	20.00
❏ 7050	Helpless/A Love Like Yours (Don't Come Knocking Every Day)	1966	5.00	10.00	20.00
MGM					
❏ 13720	I Got What You Need/Someone Like You	1967	5.00	10.00	20.00
❏ 13804	That's Groovy/Land of Tomorrow	1967	5.00	10.00	20.00

Number	Title (A Side/B Side)	Yr	VG	VG+	NM
❏ 13881	Nobody/You're Just the Kind of Guy	1967	5.00	10.00	20.00
❏ 13927	Lift Every Voice and Sing/This Is America	1968	5.00	10.00	20.00
❏ 13928	The Impossible Dream/When Johnny Comes Marching Home	1968	3.75	7.50	15.00
❏ 13992	I Will Understand/Thankful	1968	3.75	7.50	15.00

PEOPLE

❏ 1001	Danger, Heartbreak Ahead/I'll Be Thinkin'	1970	2.50	5.00	10.00

PRIDE

❏ 1	Lift Every Voice and Sing/This Is America	1970	2.50	5.00	10.00

TAMLA

❏ 54076	It Should Have Been Me/Love Me All the Way	1963	12.50	25.00	50.00
❏ 54085	Just Loving You/Another Train Coming	1963	12.50	25.00	50.00
❏ 54100	Looking for the Right Guy/Feel Alright Tonight	1964	12.50	25.00	50.00
❏ 54106	A Little More Love/Go Ahead and Laugh	1964	25.00	50.00	100.00
❏ 54110	I'm Still Loving You/Go Ahead and Laugh	1964	15.00	30.00	60.00

VOLT

❏ 1502	If I Had My Way/Gonna Be Alright	1971	3.75	7.50	15.00
❏ 1503	Little By Little, Bit By Bit/(B-side unknown)	1971	3.75	7.50	15.00

Albums

MGM

❏ E-4477 [M]	For the First Time	1967	7.50	15.00	30.00
❏ SE-4477 [S]	For the First Time	1967	10.00	20.00	40.00
❏ SE-4561	This Is America	1968	10.00	20.00	40.00

VOLT

❏ VOS-6014	Kim, Kim, Kim	1971	6.25	12.50	25.00

WHIPPOORWILLS, THE

45s

JOSIE

❏ 892	Deep Within/Going to a Party	1961	15.00	30.00	60.00

VITA

❏ 1005	Blue Raindrops/I Must Have Holes in My Head	195?	25.00	50.00	100.00

WHIPS, THE

More than one group.

45s

DORE

❏ 502	Yes, Master/Rosie's Blues	1958	5.00	10.00	20.00

FLAIR

❏ 1025	Pleadin' Heart/She Done Me Wrong	1954	200.00	400.00	800.00

MGM

❏ 13401	Whip It on Me, Baby/First Dance Fear	1965	3.00	6.00	12.00

WHIRLERS, THE

45s

PORT

❏ 70025	Tonight and Forever/Magic Mirror	1961	5.00	10.00	20.00

WHIRLIN' DISC

❏ 108	Tonight and Forever/Magic Mirror	1956	20.00	40.00	80.00

WHIRLWINDS, THE

45s

GUYDEN

❏ 2052	Angel Love/The Mountain	1961	7.50	15.00	30.00

PHILIPS

❏ 40139	Heartbeat/At the Party	1963	31.25	62.50	125.00

WHISPERS, THE

Well-known male R&B vocal group.

12-Inch Singles

CAPITOL

❏ SPRO 10230 [DJ]	Come On Home (Album Version) (Heavy D Remix)	1995	2.00	4.00	8.00
❏ V-15598	Innocent (Extended Mix) (Heat of the Heat Mix) (Midnight & You Mix) (Instrumental) (Whispers Groove)	1990	—	3.50	7.00
❏ V-15637	Is It Good to You (Fel the Heat Remix) (Feel the Heat Instrumental) (Midnight and You Remix) (Midnight and You Dub) (Whispers Jazzy Remix)	1990	—	3.50	7.00
❏ SPRO-79803 [DJ]	I Want 2B the 14U (same on both sides)	1991	2.00	4.00	8.00

SOLAR

❏ ED 5017 [DJ]	Contagious (LP Version) (Edit Version)/Keep Your Love Around	1984	2.00	4.00	8.00
❏ ED 5036 [DJ]	Some Kinda Lover (same on both sides)	1984	2.00	4.00	8.00
❏ ED 5055 [DJ]	Don't Keep Me Waiting (4:08) (4:36)	1985	2.50	5.00	10.00
❏ AS-11565 [DJ]	Emergency (4:18 stereo/4:18 mono)	1982	3.00	6.00	12.00
❏ YD-11591	Can't Do Without Love (5:22) (same on both sides?)	1979	3.00	6.00	12.00
❏ YD-11895	And the Beat Goes On (7:30)/Can You Do the Boogie (6:07)	1979	5.00	10.00	20.00
❏ YD-12052	Out the Box/Welcome Into My Dream	1980	3.00	6.00	12.00
❏ YD-12155	It's a Love Thing (unknown versions)	1980	3.75	7.50	15.00
❏ YD-12233	I Can Make It Better/Say You (Would Love for Me Too)	1980	3.00	6.00	12.00
❏ YD-12299	This Kind of Lovin'/What Will I Do	1981	3.00	6.00	12.00
❏ 67930	Tonight (6:10)/Small Talkin' (4:06)	1983	2.50	5.00	10.00
❏ 67980	Love Is Where You Find It (5:20)/Say Yes	1982	2.50	5.00	10.00
❏ V-71153	Rock Steady (Vocal) (Instrumental)/Are You Going My Way	1987	2.00	4.00	8.00
❏ V-71163	No Pain No Gain (7 versions)	1988	2.00	4.00	8.00

SOUL TRAIN

❏ SD-10997	Make It with You/You Are Number One	1977	3.75	7.50	15.00

Number	Title (A Side/B Side)	Yr	VG	VG+	NM

45s

CANADIAN AMERICAN

❏ 179	It's Rainin', It's Pourin'/Tomorrow's On Your Side	1964	7.50	15.00	30.00

CAPITOL

❏ S7-18394	Make Sweet Love to Me/My Funny Valentine	1995	—	—	3.00
❏ S7-18727	Come On Home/Better Watch Your Heart	1995	—	—	3.00
❏ 7PRO-79170/215	Innocent (7" Edit)/(Club Edit)	1990	2.00	4.00	8.00

—Vinyl is promo only

DORE

❏ 724	It Only Hurts for a Little While/The Happy One	1964	6.25	12.50	25.00
❏ 729	Slow Jerk/Never Again	1965	5.00	10.00	20.00
❏ 735	The Dip/Weirdo	1965	5.00	10.00	20.00
❏ 740	As I Sit Here/Shake It, Shake It	1965	5.00	10.00	20.00
❏ 751	Doctor Love/Lonely Avenue	1966	5.00	10.00	20.00
❏ 758	Walkin' the Fat Man/I Was Born When You Kissed Me	1966	5.00	10.00	20.00
❏ 768	Take a Lesson from the Teacher/Claire De Looney	1966	5.00	10.00	20.00
❏ 792	You Got a Man on Your Hands/You Can't Fight What's Right	1967	3.75	7.50	15.00
❏ 794	Needle in a Haystack/Waltz for You	1967	3.75	7.50	15.00
❏ 833	Never Again/I Was Born When You Kissed Me	1969	3.00	6.00	12.00
❏ 842	The Dip/It Only Hurts for a Little While	1970	2.50	5.00	10.00

FONTANA

❏ 1564	My Long and Sleepless Night/Knowin'	1966	5.00	10.00	20.00

JANUS

❏ 140	There's a Love for Everyone/It Sure Ain't Pretty	1970	—	3.00	6.00
❏ 150	Your Love Is So Doggone Good/Cracker Jack	1971	—	3.00	6.00
❏ 174	Can't Help But Love You/A Hopeless Situation	1971	—	3.00	6.00
❏ 184	I Only Meant to Wet My Feet/You Fill My Life with Music	1972	—	3.00	6.00
❏ 200	Somebody Loves You/Can We Love Forever	1972	—	3.00	6.00
❏ 212	POW-MIA/Does She Care	1973	—	3.00	6.00
❏ 222	Feel Like Comin' Home/I Love the Way You Make Me Feel	1973	—	3.00	6.00
❏ 231	A Mother for My Children/What More Can a Girl Ask For	1973	—	3.00	6.00
❏ 238	Bingo/Once More with Feeling	1974	—	3.00	6.00
❏ 244	What More Can a Girl Ask For/Broken Home	1974	—	3.00	6.00
❏ 247	All I Ever Do (Is Dream of You)/Here Comes Tomorrow	1975	—	3.00	6.00
❏ 253	You're What's Been Missing in My Life/Given a Little Love	1975	—	3.00	6.00

SOLAR

❏ YB-11246	(Let's Go) All the Way/Chocolate Girl	1978	—	2.00	4.00
❏ GB-11328	Living Together (In Sin)/One for the Money	1978	—	—	3.00

—Gold Standard Series

❏ YB-11353	(Olivia) Lost and Turned Out/Try and Make It Better	1978	—	2.00	4.00
❏ YB-11449	Happy Holidays to You/Try and Make It Better	1978	—	3.00	6.00
❏ YB-11590	Can't Do Without Love/Headlights	1979	—	2.00	4.00
❏ YB-11685	Homemade Lovin'/You'll Never Get Away	1979	—	2.00	4.00
❏ YB-11739	A Song for Donny/(Instrumental)	1979	—	2.00	4.00
❏ YB-11739 [PS]	A Song for Donny/(Instrumental)	1979	—	3.00	6.00
❏ YB-11894	And the Beat Goes On/Can You Do the Boogie	1980	—	2.00	4.00
❏ YB-11928	Lady/I Love You	1980	—	2.00	4.00
❏ GB-11977	(Let's Go) All the Way/Lost and Turned Out	1980	—	—	3.00

—Gold Standard Series

❏ YB-12050	Out the Box/Welcome Into My Dream	1980	—	2.00	4.00
❏ YB-12154	It's a Love Thing/Girl I Need You	1981	—	2.00	4.00
❏ GB-12230	And the Beat Goes On/Lady	1981	—	—	3.00

—Gold Standard Series

❏ YB-12232	I Can Make It Better/Say You (Would Love for Me Too)	1981	—	2.00	4.00
❏ YB-12295	This Kind of Lovin'/What Will I Do	1981	—	2.00	4.00
❏ YB-13005	I'm the One for You/I'm Gonna Love You More	1981	—	2.00	4.00
❏ GB-13486	It's a Love Thing/Make That Move	1983	—	—	3.00

—Gold Standard Series; B-side by Shalamar

❏ 47961	In the Raw/Small Talkin'	1982	—	2.00	4.00
❏ 48008	Emergency/Only You	1982	—	2.00	4.00
❏ 48008 [PS]	Emergency/Only You	1982	—	3.00	6.00
❏ 69639	Don't Keep Me Waiting/Suddenly	1985	—	2.00	4.00
❏ 69658	Some Kinda Lover/Never Too Late	1985	—	2.00	4.00
❏ 69683	Contagious/(B-side unknown)	1984	—	2.00	4.00
❏ 69809	This Time/Love for Real	1983	—	2.00	4.00
❏ 69827	Keep On Lovin' Me/Try It Again	1983	—	2.00	4.00
❏ 69842	Tonight/Small Talkin'	1983	—	2.00	4.00
❏ 69965	Love Is Where You Find It/Say Yes	1982	—	2.00	4.00
❏ B-70006	Rock Steady/Are You Going My Way	1987	—	—	3.00
❏ B-70012	Just Gets Better with Time/Say Yes	1987	—	—	3.00
❏ B-70017	In the Mood/(Instrumental)	1987	—	—	3.00
❏ B-70020	No Pain, No Gain/(Instrumental)	1988	—	—	3.00

SOUL CLOCK

❏ 104	Great Day/I Can't See Myself Leaving	1969	2.50	5.00	10.00
❏ 107	The Time Will Come/Flying High	1969	2.50	5.00	10.00
❏ 109	What Will I Do/Remember	1969	2.50	5.00	10.00
❏ 1001	I Can Remember/Planets of Life	1970	2.00	4.00	8.00
❏ 1004	Seems Like I Gotta Do Wrong/Needle in a Haystack	1970	2.00	4.00	8.00
❏ 1005	I'm the One/You Must Be Doing All Right	1970	2.00	4.00	8.00

SOUL TRAIN

❏ SB-10430	In Love Forever/Fairytale	1975	—	2.50	5.00
❏ SB-10628	(You're a) Special Part of My Life/Grove Street	1976	—	2.50	5.00
❏ SB-10700	One for the Money (Part 1)/One for the Money (Part 2)	1976	—	2.50	5.00

Number	Title (A Side/B Side)	Yr	VG	VG+	NM
❏ SB-10773	Living Together (In Sin)/I've Got a Feeling	1976	—	2.50	5.00
❏ SB-10878	You're Only As Good As You Think You Are/ Sounds Like a Love Song	1977	—	2.50	5.00
❏ SB-10996	Make It with You/You Are Number One	1977	—	2.50	5.00
❏ SB-11139	I'm Gonna Make You My Wife/You Never Miss Your Water	1977		2.50	5.00

Albums
ACCORD

❏ SN-7100	I Can Remember	1981	2.50	5.00	10.00

ALLEGIANCE

❏ AV-5004	Excellence	1985	2.50	5.00	10.00

CAPITOL

❏ C1-92957	More of the Night	1990	3.00	6.00	12.00

DORE

❏ 338	Shhh	197?	3.00	6.00	12.00

INTERMEDIA

❏ QS-5075	Doctor Love	198?	2.50	5.00	10.00

JANUS

❏ JLS-3041	The Whispers' Love Story	1972	12.50	25.00	50.00
❏ JLS-3046	Life and Breath	1973	10.00	20.00	40.00
❏ 7006	Bingo	1974	10.00	20.00	40.00
❏ 7013	Greatest Hits	1975	7.50	15.00	30.00

SOLAR

❏ S-27	Love Is Where You Find It	1982	2.50	5.00	10.00
❏ BXL1-2270	Open Up Your Love	1978	3.00	6.00	12.00
—Reissue of Soul Train 2270					
❏ BXL1-2774	Headlights	1978	3.00	6.00	12.00
❏ BXL1-3105	Whisper in Your Ear	1979	3.00	6.00	12.00
❏ BXL1-3521	The Whspers	1979	3.00	6.00	12.00
❏ BXL1-3578	Imagination	1980	3.00	6.00	12.00
❏ AYL1-3839	Open Up Your Love	1981	2.00	4.00	8.00
—"Best Buy Series" reissue					
❏ BXL1-3976	This Kind of Lovin'	1981	3.00	6.00	12.00
❏ BXL1-4242	The Best of the Whispers	1982	3.00	6.00	12.00
❏ 60216	Love for Love	1983	2.50	5.00	10.00
❏ 60356	So Good	1984	2.50	5.00	10.00
❏ 60451	Happy Holidays to You	1985	3.00	6.00	12.00
❏ ST-72554	Just Gets Better with Time	1987	2.50	5.00	10.00
❏ PZ 75306	Vintage Whispers	1989	3.00	6.00	12.00

SOUL CLOCK

❏ 22001	Planets of Life	1969	25.00	50.00	100.00

SOUL TRAIN

❏ BVL1-1450	One for the Money	1976	3.75	7.50	15.00
❏ BVL1-2270	Open Up Your Love	1977	3.75	7.50	15.00

WHISPERS, THE (2)
45s
GOTHAM

❏ 309	Fool Heart/Don't Fool with Lizzie	1953	62.50	125.00	250.00
❏ 312	Are You Sorry/We're Getting Married	1953	375.00	750.00	1500.

WHITE, BARRY
12-Inch Singles
20TH CENTURY

❏ TCD-88	I Love to Sing the Songs I Sing/(B-side unknown)	1979	3.00	6.00	12.00
❏ TCD-102	How Did You Know It Was Me?/(B-side unknown)	1979	3.00	6.00	12.00

A&M

❏ 31458 1027 1	Come On (6 versions)	1995	2.00	4.00	8.00
❏ 31458 8375 1 [DJ]	Practice What You Preach (7 versions)	1994	2.00	4.00	8.00
❏ SP-12237	Sho You Right (Remix) (Instrumental)	1987	—	3.00	6.00
—Black vinyl					
❏ SP-12237 [DJ]	Sho You Right (Remix) (Instrumental)	1987	3.00	6.00	12.00
—White vinyl					
❏ SP-12317	Super Lover (3 versions)	1989	—	3.00	6.00
❏ SP-12327	I Wanna Do It Good to Ya (3 versions)	1989	2.00	4.00	8.00
❏ 18026 [DJ]	I Wanna Do It Good to Ya (5 versions)	1989	—	3.00	6.00

UNLIMITED GOLD

❏ AS 864 [DJ]	I Believe in Love (3:26) (8:01)	1980	2.50	5.00	10.00
❏ 1403	It Ain't Love, Baby (Until You Give It)/Hung Up in Your Love	1979	3.00	6.00	12.00
❏ AS 1509 [DJ]	Change (4:22) (7:04)	1982	2.50	5.00	10.00
❏ 02429	Louie Louie/Ghetto Letto	1981	2.50	5.00	10.00
❏ 03051	Change/I Like You, You Like Me	1982	2.50	5.00	10.00
❏ 03381	Passion (Long)/Passion (Short)	1982	2.50	5.00	10.00
❏ 03958	America/Life	1983	2.50	5.00	10.00
❏ 04099	Don't Let 'Em Blow Your Mind/Dreams	1983	2.50	5.00	10.00
❏ 70075	Mi Nueva Cancion (Love Makin' Music)/Ella Es Todo Para Mi (She's Everything to Me)	1981	5.00	10.00	20.00

45s
20TH CENTURY

❏ (no #) [PS]	"With Love from Barry White"	1975	5.00	10.00	20.00
—Pink and white sleeve issued with some stock copies of "What Am I Gonna Do with You"					
❏ 2018	I'm Gonna Love You Just a Little More Baby/Just a Little More Baby	1973	—	2.50	5.00
❏ 2042	I've Got So Much to Give/I've Got So Much to Give	1973		2.50	5.00
❏ 2058	Never Never Gonna Give Ya Up/No, I'm Never Gonna Give Ya Up	1973		2.50	5.00
❏ 2077	Honey Please Can't You See/Honey Please Can't You See	1974	—	2.50	5.00
❏ 2120	Can't Get Enough of Your Love, Babe/Just Not Enough	1974	—	2.50	5.00
❏ 2133	You're the First, the Last, My Everything/More Than Anything, You're My Everything	1974		2.50	5.00

Number	Title (A Side/B Side)	Yr	VG	VG+	NM
❏ 2177	What Am I Gonna Do with You/What Am I Gonna Do with You, Baby	1975	—	2.50	5.00
❏ 2208	I'll Do for You Anything You Want Me To/Anything You Want Me To	1975	—	2.50	5.00
❏ 2265	Let the Music Play/(Instrumental)	1975	—	2.50	5.00
❏ 2277	You See the Trouble with Me/I'm So Blue When You Are Too	1976	—	2.50	5.00
❏ 2298	Baby, We Better Try to Get It Together/If You Know, Won't You Tell Me	1976	—	2.50	5.00
❏ 2309	Don't Make Me Wait Too Long/Can't You See It's Only You I Want	1976	—	2.50	5.00
❏ 2328	I'm Qualified to Satisfy You/(Instrumental)	1977	—	2.50	5.00
❏ 2350	It's Ecstasy When You Lay Down Next to Me/I Never Thought I'd Fall in Love with You	1977	—	2.50	5.00
❏ 2361	Playing Your Game, Baby/Of All the Guys in the World	1977	—	2.50	5.00
❏ 2365	Oh What a Night for Dancing/You're So Good You're Bad	1978	—	2.50	5.00
❏ 2380	Your Sweetness Is My Weakness/It's Only Love Doing Its Thing	1978	—	2.50	5.00
❏ 2395	Just the Way You Are/Now I'm Gonna Make Love to You	1979	—	2.50	5.00
❏ 2416	I Love to Sing the Songs I Sing/Oh Me Oh My	1979	—	2.50	5.00
❏ 2433	How Did You Know It Was Me?/Oh Me Oh My	1979	—	2.50	5.00

A&M

❏ 31458 0924 7	Practice What You Preach/Come On	1995	—	—	3.00
—Second pressing indeed contains these two songs					
❏ 31458 0924 7	Practice What You Preach/Come On	1995	—	2.50	5.00
—First pressing actually contains Lo-Key?'s "I Got a Thang 4 Ya!"/"Sweet On U," which are otherwise unavailable on 45. Can be identified without playing by checking the trail-off vinyl for a different number than that on the record.					
❏ 1203	Right Night/There's a Place (Where Love Never Ends)	1988	—	—	3.00
❏ 1459	Super Lover/I Wanna Do It Good to Ya	1989	—	—	3.00
❏ 75021 1511 7	When Will I See You Again/Goodnight My Love	1990	—	—	3.00
❏ 2943	Sho' You Right/You're What's On My Mind	1987	—	—	3.00
❏ 2943 [PS]	Sho' You Right/You're What's On My Mind	1987	—	—	3.00
❏ 3000	For Your Love (I'd Do Most Anything)/I'm Ready for Love	1987	—	—	3.00
❏ 3000 [PS]	For Your Love (I'd Do Most Anything)/I'm Ready for Love	1987	—	—	3.00

FARO

❏ 613	Tracy/Flame of Love	1964	3.75	7.50	15.00
—B-side by the Atlantics					

UNLIMITED GOLD

❏ 1401	Any Fool Could See (You Were Meant for Me)/ You're the One I Need	1979	—	2.00	4.00
❏ 1404	It Ain't Love, Babe (Until You Give It)/Hung Up in Your Love	1979	—	2.00	4.00
❏ 1411	Love Ain't Easy/I Found Love	1980	—	2.00	4.00
❏ 1415	Sheet Music/(Instrumental)	1980	—	2.00	4.00
❏ 1418	Love Makin' Music/Ella Es Todo Mi (She's Everything to Me)	1980	—	2.00	4.00
❏ 1420	I Believe in Love/You're the One I Need	1980	—	2.00	4.00
❏ 02425	Louie Louie/Ghetto Letto	1981	—	2.00	4.00
❏ 02580	Beware/Tell Me Who Do You Love	1981	—	2.00	4.00
❏ 02956	Change/I Like You, You Like Me	1982	—	2.00	4.00
❏ 03379	Passion/It's All About Love	1982	—	2.00	4.00
❏ 03957	America/Life	1983	—	2.00	4.00
❏ 04098	Don't Let 'Em Blow Your Mind/Dreams	1983	—	2.00	4.00

Albums
20TH CENTURY

❏ T-407	I've Got So Much to Give	1973	2.50	5.00	10.00
❏ T-423	Stone Gon'	1973	2.50	5.00	10.00
❏ T-444	Can't Get Enough	1974	2.50	5.00	10.00
❏ T-466	Just Another Way to Say I Love You	1975	2.50	5.00	10.00
❏ T-493	Barry White's Greatest Hits	1975	2.50	5.00	10.00
❏ T-502	Let the Music Play	1976	2.50	5.00	10.00
❏ T-516	Is This Whatcha Wont?	1976	2.50	5.00	10.00
❏ T-543	Barry White Sings for Someone You Love	1977	2.50	5.00	10.00
❏ T-571	Barry White The Man	1978	2.50	5.00	10.00
❏ T-590	I Love to Sing the Songs I Sing	1979	2.50	5.00	10.00
❏ T-599	Barry White's Greatest Hits, Volume 2	1981	2.50	5.00	10.00

A&M

❏ SP-5154	The Right Night and Barry White	1987	2.50	5.00	10.00
❏ SP-5256	The Man Is Back!	1990	2.50	5.00	10.00
❏ 75021 5377 1	Put Me in Your Mix	1991	3.00	6.00	12.00

CASABLANCA

❏ 822782-1	Barry White's Greatest Hits	1984	2.00	4.00	8.00
❏ 822783-1	Barry White's Greatest Hits, Volume 2	1984	2.00	4.00	8.00

SUPREMACY

❏ SUP-8002	No Limit on Love	1974	3.00	6.00	12.00
—Compilation of older material					

UNLIMITED GOLD

❏ JZ 35763	The Message Is Love	1979	2.50	5.00	10.00
❏ FZ 36208	Barry White's Sheet Music	1980	2.50	5.00	10.00
❏ Z2X 36957 [(2)]	The Best of Our Love	1981	3.00	6.00	12.00
❏ FZ 37176	Beware	1982	2.50	5.00	10.00
❏ FZ 38048	Change	1982	2.50	5.00	10.00
❏ FZ 38711	Dedicated	1983	2.50	5.00	10.00

WHITE, BARRY AND GLODEAN
45s
UNLIMITED GOLD

❏ 02087	I Want You/Our Theme (Part 1)	1981	—	2.00	4.00

Number	Title (A Side/B Side)	Yr	VG	VG+	NM
❑ 02419	You're the Only One for Me/This Love	1981	—	2.00	4.00
❑ 70064	Didn't We Make It Happen, Baby/Our Theme (Part 2)	1981	—	2.00	4.00

Albums
UNLIMITED GOLD

Number	Title (A Side/B Side)	Yr	VG	VG+	NM
❑ FZ 37054	Barry and Glodean White	1981	2.50	5.00	10.00

WHITE, MAURICE
Also see EARTH, WIND & FIRE.
12-Inch Singles
COLUMBIA

Number	Title (A Side/B Side)	Yr	VG	VG+	NM
❑ 44-05262	Stand By Me (Extended Dance Mix) (Instrumental)	1985	2.00	4.00	8.00

45s
COLUMBIA

Number	Title (A Side/B Side)	Yr	VG	VG+	NM
❑ 38-05571	Stand By Me/Can't Stop Love	1985	—	2.00	4.00
❑ 38-05571 [PS]	Stand By Me/Can't Stop Love	1985	—	2.00	4.00
❑ 38-05726	I Need You/Believe in Magic	1985	—	2.00	4.00
❑ 38-05726 [PS]	I Need You/Believe in Magic	1985	—	2.00	4.00
❑ 38-05836	Love Is Love/Invitation	1986	—	2.00	4.00

Albums
COLUMBIA

Number	Title (A Side/B Side)	Yr	VG	VG+	NM
❑ FC 39883	Maurice White	1985	2.50	5.00	10.00

WILDWOODS, THE
Actually THE FIVE SATINS.
45s
CAPRICE

Number	Title (A Side/B Side)	Yr	VG	VG+	NM
❑ 101	When the Swallows Come Back to Capistrano/Heart of Mine	1961	37.50	75.00	150.00

MAY

Number	Title (A Side/B Side)	Yr	VG	VG+	NM
❑ 106	Golden Sunset/Here Comes Big Ed	1961	7.50	15.00	30.00

WILLIAMS, ANDRE
45s
AVIN

Number	Title (A Side/B Side)	Yr	VG	VG+	NM
❑ 103	Rib Tips (Part 1)/Rib Tips (Part 2)	1965	3.00	6.00	12.00

CHECKER

Number	Title (A Side/B Side)	Yr	VG	VG+	NM
❑ 1187	The Stroke/Humpin' Bumpin' and Trumpin'	1967	3.00	6.00	12.00
❑ 1205	Cadillac Jack/Mrs. Mother USA	1968	3.00	6.00	12.00
❑ 1214	Do the Popcorn/It's Gonna Be Fine in '69	1969	3.00	6.00	12.00
❑ 1219	Girdle Up/(Instrumental)	1969	3.00	6.00	12.00

EPIC

Number	Title (A Side/B Side)	Yr	VG	VG+	NM
❑ 9196	Bacon Fat/Just Because of a Kiss	1956	6.25	12.50	25.00

FORTUNE

Number	Title (A Side/B Side)	Yr	VG	VG+	NM
❑ 824	Pulling Time/Going Down to Tia-Juana	1955	20.00	40.00	80.00
❑ 827	Mozelle/Just Want a Little Lovin'	1956	10.00	20.00	40.00
❑ 828	Bobby Jean/It's All Over	1956	10.00	20.00	40.00
❑ 831	Bacon Fat/Just Because of a Kiss	1956	7.50	15.00	30.00
❑ 834	Mean Jean/You Are My Sunshine	1957	7.50	15.00	30.00
❑ 837	Jail Bait/My Tears	1957	20.00	40.00	80.00
❑ 839	Come On Baby/The Greasy Chicken	1957	7.50	15.00	30.00
—With Gino Park					
❑ 839	Don't Touch/Please Pass the Biscuits	1957	20.00	40.00	80.00
—With Gino Park					
❑ 839	The Greasy Chicken/Please Pass the Biscuits	1957	15.00	30.00	60.00
—With Gino Park					
❑ 842	My Last Dance with You/Hey! Country Girl	1958	7.50	15.00	30.00
❑ 847	Put a Chain on It/I'm All For You	1959	7.50	15.00	30.00
❑ 851	(Georgia May Is) Movin'/(Mmmm — Andre Williams Is) Movin'	1960	15.00	30.00	60.00
—With Gino Park					
❑ 856	Jail House Blues/I Still Love You	1960	7.50	15.00	30.00

MIRACLE

Number	Title (A Side/B Side)	Yr	VG	VG+	NM
❑ 4	Rosa Lee/Shoo Shoo	1960	300.00	600.00	1200.

NORTON

Number	Title (A Side/B Side)	Yr	VG	VG+	NM
❑ 45-069	Poor Mr. Santa (N-N-Naughty!)/Poor Mr. Santa (N-n-nice!)	1997	—	—	2.00
❑ 45-069 [PS]	Poor Mr. Santa (N-N-Naughty!)/Poor Mr. Santa (N-n-nice!)	1997	—	—	2.00

RIC-TIC

Number	Title (A Side/B Side)	Yr	VG	VG+	NM
❑ 124	You Got It And I Want It/I Can't Stop Crying	1967	6.25	12.50	25.00

RONALD

Number	Title (A Side/B Side)	Yr	VG	VG+	NM
❑ 1001	Please Give Me a Chance/(B-side unknown)	196?	6.25	12.50	25.00

SPORT

Number	Title (A Side/B Side)	Yr	VG	VG+	NM
❑ 105	Pearl Time/Soul Groove	1967	6.25	12.50	25.00

WINGATE

Number	Title (A Side/B Side)	Yr	VG	VG+	NM
❑ 014	Loose Juice/Sweet Little Pussycat	1966	3.75	7.50	15.00
❑ 021	Do It! (Part 1)/Do It! (Part 2)	1966	5.00	10.00	20.00

Albums
SDEG

Number	Title (A Side/B Side)	Yr	VG	VG+	NM
❑ 4020	Directly from the Streets	198?	2.50	5.00	10.00

WILLIAMS, BILLY
Also see THE CHARIOTEERS.
45s
CORAL

Number	Title (A Side/B Side)	Yr	VG	VG+	NM
❑ 61212	Sh-Boom (Life Could Be a Dream)/Whenever Wherever	1954	3.00	6.00	12.00
❑ 61264	Love Me/The Honeydripper	1954	3.00	6.00	12.00
❑ 1346	Fools Rush In/He Follows She	1955	3.00	6.00	12.00
❑ 6462	Glory of Love/Wonderful, Wonderful One	1955	3.00	6.00	12.00
❑ 6???	Just a Little Bit More/Learning to Love	1955	3.00	6.00	12.00

Number	Title (A Side/B Side)	Yr	VG	VG+	NM
❑ 61576	Cry Baby/A Crazy Little Place	1956	2.50	5.00	10.00
❑ 61639	Pray/You'll Reach Your Star	1956	2.50	5.00	10.00
❑ 61684	This Planet Earth/I Guess I'll Be On My Way	1956	2.50	5.00	10.00
❑ 61730	Shame, Shame, Shame/Don't Cry on My Shoulder	1956	2.50	5.00	10.00
❑ 61751	Stormy/Follow Me	1956	2.50	5.00	10.00
❑ 61795	Butterfly/The Pied Piper	1957	2.50	5.00	10.00
❑ 61830	I'm Gonna Sit Right Down and Write Myself a Letter/Date with the Blues	1957	3.00	6.00	12.00
❑ 61886	Got a Date with an Angel/The Lord Will Understand	1957	2.50	5.00	10.00
❑ 61932	Don't Let Go/Baby, Baby	1958	2.50	5.00	10.00
❑ 61961	There! I've Said It Again/Steppin' Out Tonight	1958	2.50	5.00	10.00
❑ 61999	I'll Get By/It's Prayin' Time	1958	2.50	5.00	10.00
❑ 62029	It Hurts So Much/So Long	1958	2.50	5.00	10.00
❑ 62069	Nola/Tied to the Strings of Your Heart	1959	2.50	5.00	10.00
❑ 62101	Goodnight Irene/Red Hot Love	1959	2.50	5.00	10.00
❑ 62131	Go to Sleep, Go to Sleep, Go to Sleep/Telephone Conversation	1959	2.00	4.00	8.00
—With Barbara McNair					
❑ 62140	Smack Dab in the Middle/I Wonder	1959	2.00	4.00	8.00
❑ 62218	I Cried for You/The Lover of All Lovers	1960	2.00	4.00	8.00
❑ 62230	Begin the Beguine/For You	1960	2.00	4.00	8.00
❑ 62438	Why Do I Love You So/Raise Your Hand	1964	—	3.00	6.00
❑ 62438	Why Do I Love You So/The Honeydripper	1964	—	3.00	6.00

MERCURY

Number	Title (A Side/B Side)	Yr	VG	VG+	NM
❑ 5866	Stay/Azure-Te (Paris Blues)	1952	3.75	7.50	15.00
❑ 5884	Who Knows/It's Best We Say Goodbye	1952	3.75	7.50	15.00
❑ 5902	That's What I'm Here For/Some Folks Do, Some Folks Don't	1952	3.75	7.50	15.00
❑ 70012	I Don't Know Why/Mad About 'Cha	1952	3.75	7.50	15.00
❑ 70094	Pour Me a Glass of Teardrops/It's a Miracle	1953	3.75	7.50	15.00
❑ 70180	This Side of Heaven/You're the One for Me	1953	3.75	7.50	15.00
❑ 70210	Why Do You Have to Go?/Cattle Call	1953	3.75	7.50	15.00
❑ 70271	If I Ever Get to Heaven/Ask Me No Questions	1953	3.75	7.50	15.00
❑ 70324	Invitation to Dance/I'll Close My Eyes	1954	3.75	7.50	15.00
❑ 70376	Go Home, Joe/You're the Only One I Adore	1954	3.75	7.50	15.00

MGM

Number	Title (A Side/B Side)	Yr	VG	VG+	NM
❑ 10764	Longing/I Didn't Slip	1950	5.00	10.00	20.00
❑ 10857	The Room I'm Sleeping In/Music by Angels	1950	5.00	10.00	20.00
❑ 10928	Gaucho Serenade/I Won't Cry Anymore	1951	3.75	7.50	15.00
❑ 10967	Pretty Eyed Baby/You Made Me Love You	1951	3.75	7.50	15.00
❑ 10998	Shang-Hai/A Wondrous Word	1951	3.75	7.50	15.00
❑ 11066	Sin/It's Over	1951	3.75	7.50	15.00
❑ 11117	I'll Never Find You/Busy Line	1951	3.75	7.50	15.00
❑ 11145	No Other Love/Callaway Went That-A-Way	1952	3.75	7.50	15.00
❑ 11172	Wheel of Fortune/What Can I Say	1952	3.75	7.50	15.00
❑ 11184	Confetti/Don't Grieve	1952	3.75	7.50	15.00
❑ 12537	Shang-Hai/Gaucho Serenade	1957	2.50	5.00	10.00

7-Inch Extended Plays
CORAL

Number	Title (A Side/B Side)	Yr	VG	VG+	NM
❑ EC 81164	*I'm Gonna Sit Right Down and Write Myself A Letter/Lucy Lou/The❑ Lord Will Understand (And Say "Well Done")/The Honeydripper	1957	3.00	6.00	12.00
❑ EC 81164 [PS]	(title unknown)	1957	3.00	6.00	12.00

Albums
CORAL

Number	Title (A Side/B Side)	Yr	VG	VG+	NM
❑ CRL 57184 [M]	Billy Williams	1957	15.00	30.00	60.00
❑ CRL 57251 [M]	Half Sweet, Half Beat	1959	12.50	25.00	50.00
❑ CRL 57343 [M]	The Billy Williams Revue	1960	12.50	25.00	50.00
❑ CRL 757251 [S]	Half Sweet, Half Beat	1959	20.00	40.00	80.00
❑ CRL 757343 [S]	The Billy Williams Revue	1960	15.00	30.00	60.00

MERCURY

Number	Title (A Side/B Side)	Yr	VG	VG+	NM
❑ MG 20317 [M]	Oh Yeah!	1958	15.00	30.00	60.00

MGM

Number	Title (A Side/B Side)	Yr	VG	VG+	NM
❑ E-3400 [M]	The Billy Williams Quartet	1957	15.00	30.00	60.00

WING

Number	Title (A Side/B Side)	Yr	VG	VG+	NM
❑ MGW-12131 [M]	Vote for Billy Williams	1959	10.00	20.00	40.00

WILLIAMS, BILLY DEE
Albums
PRESTIGE LIVELY ARTS

Number	Title (A Side/B Side)	Yr	VG	VG+	NM
❑ 30001 [M]	Let's Misbehave	1962	10.00	20.00	40.00

WILLIAMS, DENIECE
Also see JOHNNY MATHIS AND DENIECE WILLIAMS.
12-Inch Singles
ARC

Number	Title (A Side/B Side)	Yr	VG	VG+	NM
❑ 10991	I've Got the Next Dance/When Love Comes Calling	1979	3.00	6.00	12.00
❑ 11141	I Found Love/Are You Thinking?	1979	3.00	6.00	12.00
❑ 60504	What Two Can Do/Suspicious	1981	—	2.00	4.00

COLUMBIA

Number	Title (A Side/B Side)	Yr	VG	VG+	NM
❑ AS 1838 [DJ]	Let's Hear It for the Boy (6:00) (3:34)	1984	3.75	7.50	15.00
❑ CAS 2688 [DJ]	Never Say Never (3 versions)	1987	—	3.00	6.00
❑ 04988	Let's Hear It for the Boy (6:00) (4:13)	1984	2.00	4.00	8.00
❑ 05043	Next Love (7:07)/(Instrumental)	1984	2.00	4.00	8.00
❑ 05918	Wiser and Weaker (6:15) (5:50 Instrumental)	1986	2.00	4.00	8.00
❑ 06929	I Confess (3 versions)	1987	—	3.00	6.00
❑ 10513	Free/It's Important to Me	1977	3.75	7.50	15.00

45s
ARC

Number	Title (A Side/B Side)	Yr	VG	VG+	NM
❑ 02108	It's Your Conscience/Sweet Surrender	1981	—	2.00	4.00
❑ 02406	Silly/My Melody	1981	—	2.00	4.00

Number	Title (A Side/B Side)	Yr	VG	VG+	NM
❑ 02812	It's Gonna Take a Miracle/Part of Love	1982	—	2.00	4.00
❑ 03015	Waiting by the Hotline/Love Notes	1982	—	2.00	4.00
❑ 03242	It's Gonna Take a Miracle/Silly	1982	—	—	3.00
—Reissue					
❑ 03261	Waiting/How Does It Feel	1982	—	2.00	4.00
❑ 10971	I've Got the Next Dance/When Love Comes Calling	1979	—	2.00	4.00
❑ 11063	I Found Love/Are You Thinking?	1979	—	2.00	4.00
COLUMBIA					
❑ AE7 1153 [DJ]	God Is Amazing/God Is Standing By	1977	2.00	4.00	8.00
—B-side by Johnnie Taylor; promo with "Suggested Christmas Programming" on label					
❑ 03807	Do What You Feel/Love, Peace and Unity	1983	—	2.00	4.00
❑ 03807 [PS]	Do What You Feel/Love, Peace and Unity	1983	—	2.00	4.00
❑ 04037	I'm So Proud/It's Okay	1983	—	2.00	4.00
❑ 04218	Heaven in Your Eyes/Love, Peace and Unity	1983	—	2.00	4.00
❑ 38-04417	Let's Hear It for the Boy/(Instrumental)	1984	—	—	3.00
❑ 38-04417 [PS]	Let's Hear It for the Boy/(Instrumental)	1984	—	2.00	4.00
❑ 04537	Next Love/Picking Up the Pieces	1984	—	—	3.00
❑ 04537 [PS]	Next Love/Picking Up the Pieces	1984	—	2.00	4.00
❑ 04641	Black Butterfly/Blind Dating	1984	—	—	3.00
❑ 06157	Wiser and Weaker/(Instrumental)	1986	—	—	3.00
❑ 06157 [PS]	Wiser and Weaker/(Instrumental)	1986	—	—	3.00
❑ 06318	Healing/I Feel the Night	1986	—	—	3.00
❑ 07021	Never Say Never/Love Finds You	1987	—	—	3.00
❑ 07021 [PS]	Never Say Never/Love Finds You	1987	—	—	3.00
❑ 07357	I Confess/(Instrumental)	1987	—	—	3.00
❑ 07633	Water Under the Bridge/Love Finds You	1987	—	—	3.00
❑ 07704	I Believe in You/(Instrumental)	1988	—	—	3.00
❑ 08014	I Can't Wait/(Instrumental)	1988	—	—	3.00
❑ 08014 [PS]	I Can't Wait/(Instrumental)	1988	—	—	3.00
❑ 08425	Let's Hear It for the Boy/(Instrumental)	1988	—	—	3.00
—Reissue					
❑ 08507	This Is As Good As It Gets/Don't Stop the Love	1988	—	—	3.00
❑ 10429	Free/Cause You Love Me Baby	1976	—	2.50	5.00
❑ 10556	That's What Friends Are For/It's Important to Me	1977	—	2.50	5.00
❑ 10648	Baby, Baby My Love's All for You/Be Good to Me	1977	—	2.50	5.00
MCA					
❑ 53707	Every Moment/Do You Hear What I Hear?	1989	—	—	3.00
SPARROW					
❑ S7-18215	Do You Hear What I Hear/Silent Night	1994	—	2.50	5.00
—B-side by Bebe and Cece Winans; green vinyl					
TODDLIN' TOWN					
❑ 107	Love Is Tears/I'm Walkin' Away	1968	2.50	5.00	10.00
—As "Deniece Chandler"					
❑ 113	Hey Baby/Glorious Feeling	1968	2.50	5.00	10.00
—As "Deniece Chandler"; with Lee Sain					
❑ 118	I Don't Wanna Cry/Goodbye Cruel World	1969	2.50	5.00	10.00
—As "Deniece Chandler"					
❑ 127	Shy Boy/(B-side unknown)	1969	2.50	5.00	10.00
—As "Deniece Chandler"					
Albums					
ARC					
❑ AS 1432 [DJ]	Niecy	1982	6.25	12.50	25.00
—Promo-only picture disc					
❑ JC 35568	When Love Comes Calling	1979	2.50	5.00	10.00
❑ FC 37048	My Melody	1981	2.50	5.00	10.00
❑ PC 37048	My Melody	198?	2.00	4.00	8.00
—Budget-line reissue					
❑ FC 37952	Niecy	1982	2.50	5.00	10.00
❑ PC 37952	Niecy	198?	2.00	4.00	8.00
—Budget-line reissue					
❑ HC 47952	Niecy	1983	12.50	25.00	50.00
—Half-speed mastered edition					
COLUMBIA					
❑ PC 34242	This Is Niecy	1976	2.50	5.00	10.00
—No bar code on cover					
❑ PC 34242	This Is Niecy	198?	2.00	4.00	8.00
—Reissue with bar code on cover					
❑ JC 34911	Song Bird	1977	2.50	5.00	10.00
❑ PC 34911	Song Bird	198?	2.00	4.00	8.00
—Budget-line reissue					
❑ FC 38622	I'm So Proud	1983	2.50	5.00	10.00
❑ PC 38622	I'm So Proud	198?	2.00	4.00	8.00
—Budget-line reissue					
❑ FC 39366	Let's Hear It for the Boy	1984	2.50	5.00	10.00
❑ FC 40084	Hot on the Trail	1986	2.50	5.00	10.00
❑ FC 44322	As Good As It Gets	1989	2.50	5.00	10.00
MCA					
❑ 6338	Special Love	1989	2.50	5.00	10.00
SPARROW					
❑ SPR-1256	From the Beginning	1990	3.00	6.00	12.00
❑ ST-41039	So Glad I Know	1986	3.00	6.00	12.00

WILLIAMS, JOHNNY
See JOHN LEE HOOKER.

WILLIAMS, LARRY
Also see JOHNNY "GUITAR" WATSON AND LARRY WILLIAMS.
45s
BELL

Number	Title (A Side/B Side)	Yr	VG	VG+	NM
❑ 813	I Could Love You Baby/Can't Find No Substitute for Love	1969	2.50	5.00	10.00
—With Johnny Watson					
CHESS					
❑ 1736	My Baby's Got Soul/Every Day I Wonder	1959	5.00	10.00	20.00

Number	Title (A Side/B Side)	Yr	VG	VG+	NM
❑ 1745	Get Ready/Baby, Baby	1959	5.00	10.00	20.00
❑ 1761	I Wanna Know/Like a Gentle Man	1960	5.00	10.00	20.00
❑ 1764	Oh Baby/I Hear My Baby	1960	5.00	10.00	20.00
❑ 1805	Lawdy Mama/Fresh Out of Tears	1961	5.00	10.00	20.00
EL BAM					
❑ 69	Call on Me/Boss Lovin'	1965	3.00	6.00	12.00
FANTASY					
❑ 806	Doing the Best I Can (With What I Got)/Gimme Some	1977	—	2.50	5.00
❑ 810	One Thing or the Other (Part 1)/One Thing or the Other (Part 2)	1977	—	2.50	5.00
❑ 841	The Resurrection of Funk/(B-side unknown)	1978	—	2.50	5.00
MERCURY					
❑ 72147	Woman/Can't Help Myself	1963	3.75	7.50	15.00
OKEH					
❑ 7259	This Old Heart (Is So Lonely)/I'd Rather Fight Than Switch	1966	2.50	5.00	10.00
❑ 7280	I Am the One/You Ask for One Good Reason	1967	2.50	5.00	10.00
❑ 7294	Just Because/Boss Lovin'	1967	2.50	5.00	10.00
SMASH					
❑ 2035	Call on Me/Boss Lovin'	1966	3.00	6.00	12.00
SPECIALTY					
❑ 597	Just Because/Let Me Tell You Baby	1957	7.50	15.00	30.00
❑ 608	Short Fat Fannie/High School Dance	1957	10.00	20.00	40.00
❑ 608	Short Fat Fannie/High School Dance	1984	—	2.00	4.00
—Gold vinyl					
❑ 615	Bony Moronie/You Bug Me, Baby	1957	10.00	20.00	40.00
❑ 615	Bony Moronie/You Bug Me, Baby	1984	—	2.00	4.00
—Red vinyl					
❑ 626	Dizzy, Miss Lizzy/Slow Down	1958	10.00	20.00	40.00
❑ 626	Dizzy, Miss Lizzy/Slow Down	1984	—	2.00	4.00
—Blue vinyl					
❑ 626 [PS]	Dizzy, Miss Lizzy/Slow Down	1958	20.00	40.00	80.00
❑ 634	Hootchy-Koo/The Dummy	1958	6.25	12.50	25.00
❑ 634	Hootchy-Koo/The Dummy	1984	—	2.00	4.00
—Green vinyl					
❑ 647	I Was a Fool/Peaches and Cream	1958	6.25	12.50	25.00
❑ 658	Bad Boy/She Said "Yeah"	1959	7.50	15.00	30.00
❑ 658	Bad Boy/She Said "Yeah"	1984	—	2.00	4.00
—Orange vinyl					
❑ 665	Steal a Little Kiss/I Can't Stop Loving You	1959	6.25	12.50	25.00
❑ 677	Give Me Your Love/Teardrops	1959	6.25	12.50	25.00
❑ 682	Ting-a-Ling/Little Schoolgirl	1960	6.25	12.50	25.00
❑ 682	Ting-a-Ling/Little Schoolgirl	1984	—	2.00	4.00
—Gold vinyl					
VENTURE					
❑ 622	Shake Your Body Girl/Love I Can't Seem to Find It	1968	2.50	5.00	10.00
❑ 627	Wake Up (Nothing Comes to a Sleeper But a Dream)/Love I Can't Seem to Find It	1968	2.50	5.00	10.00
Albums					
CHESS					
❑ LP-1457 [M]	Larry Williams	1961	50.00	100.00	200.00
OKEH					
❑ OKM-12123 [M]	Larry Williams' Greatest Hits	1967	7.50	15.00	30.00
❑ OKS-14123 [S]	Larry Williams' Greatest Hits	1967	10.00	20.00	40.00
SPECIALTY					
❑ SP-2109 [M]	Here's Larry Williams	1959	50.00	100.00	200.00
—Original pressing on thick vinyl with no copyright information on back cover					
❑ SP-2109 [M]	Here's Larry Williams	198?	2.50	5.00	10.00
—Reissue with thinner vinyl and copyright information on back					
❑ SP-7002 [(2)]	Bad Boy	1990	5.00	10.00	20.00

WILLIAMS, LESTER
45s
DUKE

Number	Title (A Side/B Side)	Yr	VG	VG+	NM
❑ 123	Let's Do It/Good Lovin' Baby	1954	12.50	25.00	50.00
❑ 131	Crazy 'Bout You Baby/Don't Take Your Love from Me	1954	10.00	20.00	40.00
IMPERIAL					
❑ 5402	McDonald's Daughter/Daddy Loves You	1956	12.50	25.00	50.00
SPECIALTY					
❑ 422	I Can't Lose with the Stuff I Use/My Home Ain't Here	1952	25.00	50.00	100.00
❑ 431	Let Me Tell You a Thing or Two/Tryin' to Forget	1952	37.50	75.00	150.00
❑ 437	Sweet Lovin' Daddy/Lost Gal	1952	37.50	75.00	150.00
❑ 450	Brand New Baby/If I Knew How Much I Loved You	1953	25.00	50.00	100.00

WILLIAMS, MAURICE, AND THE ZODIACS
Also see THE GLADIOLAS.
45s
ATLANTIC

Number	Title (A Side/B Side)	Yr	VG	VG+	NM
❑ 2199	Funny/Loneliness	1963	3.75	7.50	15.00
—As "The Zodiacs"					
❑ 2741	Sweetness/Whirlpool	1970	—	2.50	5.00
COLE					
❑ 100	Golly Gee/"I" Town	1959	12.50	25.00	50.00
❑ 101	Lover (Where Are You)/She's Mine	1959	10.00	20.00	40.00
DEESU					
❑ 302	Baby Baby/Being Without You	1967	5.00	10.00	20.00
❑ 304	May I/This Feeling	1967	5.00	10.00	20.00
❑ 307	Ooh Poo Pa Doo (Part 1)/Ooh Poo Pa Doo (Part 2)	1967	5.00	10.00	20.00
❑ 309	Don't Ever Leave Me/Surely	1967	5.00	10.00	20.00
❑ 311	Don't Be Half Safe/How to Pick a Winner	1967	5.00	10.00	20.00

Number	Title (A Side/B Side)	Yr	VG	VG+	NM
❏ 318	Stay '68 (Live Version)/Dance, Dance, Dance	1968	3.75	7.50	15.00
HERALD					
❏ 552	Stay/Do You Believe	1960	5.00	10.00	20.00
❏ 556	Always/I Remember	1961	3.75	7.50	15.00
❏ 559	Do I/Come Along	1961	3.75	7.50	15.00
❏ 563	Someday/Come and Get It	1961	3.75	7.50	15.00
❏ 565	Please/High Blood Pressure	1961	3.75	7.50	15.00
❏ 572	It's Alright/Here I Stand	1962	3.75	7.50	15.00
RCA					
❏ 5363-7-R	Stay/She's Like the Wind	1987	—	—	3.00
—B-side by Patrick Swayze					
SCEPTER					
❏ 12113	Nobody Knows/I Know	1965	3.75	7.50	15.00
SEA HORN					
❏ 503	My Baby's Gone/Return	1964	3.75	7.50	15.00
SELWYN					
❏ 5121	Say Yeah/College Girl	1959	12.50	25.00	50.00
SPHERE SOUND					
❏ 707	So Fine/The Winds	1965	3.00	6.00	12.00
VEE JAY					
❏ 678	May I/Lollipop	1965	5.00	10.00	20.00
VEEP					
❏ 1294	My Reason for Living/The Four Corners	1969	2.00	4.00	8.00
Albums					
COLLECTABLES					
❏ COL-5021	The Best of Maurice Williams and the Zodiacs	198?	2.50	5.00	10.00
HERALD					
❏ HLP-1014 [M]	Stay	1961	125.00	250.00	500.00
RELIC					
❏ 5017	Greatest Hits	197?	3.75	7.50	15.00
SNYDER					
❏ 5586 [M]	At the Beach	196?	25.00	50.00	100.00
SPHERE SOUND					
❏ SR-7007 [M]	Stay	1965	30.00	60.00	120.00
❏ SSR-7007 [R]	Stay	1965	20.00	40.00	80.00

WILLIAMS, OTIS, AND HIS CHARMS

Also see THE CHARMS.

45s

Number	Title (A Side/B Side)	Yr	VG	VG+	NM
DELUXE					
❏ 6088	Miss the Love/Tell Me Now	1955	7.50	15.00	30.00
—As "Otis Williams and His New Group"					
❏ 6090	Gum Drop/Save Me, Save Me	1955	7.50	15.00	30.00
—As "Otis Williams and His New Group"					
❏ 6091	That's Your Mistake/Too Late I Learned	1955	7.50	15.00	30.00
❏ 6092	Rolling Home/Do Be You	1956	7.50	15.00	30.00
❏ 6093	Ivory Tower/In Paradise	1956	7.50	15.00	30.00
❏ 6095	One Night Only/It's All Over	1956	7.50	15.00	30.00
❏ 6097	I'd Like to Thank You Mr. D.J./Whirlwind	1956	7.50	15.00	30.00
❏ 6098	Gypsy Lady/I'll Remember You	1956	7.50	15.00	30.00
❏ 6105	Blues Stay Away from Me/Pardon Me	1957	6.25	12.50	25.00
❏ 6115	Walkin' After Midnight/I'm Waiting Just for You	1957	6.25	12.50	25.00
❏ 6130	Nowhere on Earth/No Got De Woman	1957	6.25	12.50	25.00
❏ 6137	Talking to Myself/One Kind Word from You	1957	6.25	12.50	25.00
❏ 6138	United/Don't Deny Me	1957	6.25	12.50	25.00
❏ 6149	Dynamite Darling/Well Oh Well	1957	6.25	12.50	25.00
❏ 6158	Could This Be Magic/Oh Julie	1958	6.25	12.50	25.00
❏ 6160	Let Some Love in Your Heart/Baby-O	1958	6.25	12.50	25.00
❏ 6165	Burnin' Lips/Red Hot Love (Do This Love)	1958	6.25	12.50	25.00
❏ 6174	Don't Wake Up the Kids/You'll Remain Forever	1958	6.25	12.50	25.00
❏ 6178	My Friends/The Secret	1958	6.25	12.50	25.00
❏ 6181	Pretty Little Things Called Girls/Welcome Home	1959	6.25	12.50	25.00
❏ 6183	My Prayer Tonight/Watch Dog	1959	6.25	12.50	25.00
❏ 6185	I Knew It All the Time/Tears of Happiness	1959	6.25	12.50	25.00
❏ 6186	In Paradise/Who Knows	1959	6.25	12.50	25.00
❏ 6187	Blues Stay Away from Me/Funny What True Love Can Do	1959	6.25	12.50	25.00
KING					
❏ 5323	Chief Um (Take It Easy)/It's a Treat	1960	5.00	10.00	20.00
❏ 5332	Silver Star/Rickety Rickshaw Man	1960	5.00	10.00	20.00
❏ 5372	Image of a Girl/Wait a Minute Baby	1960	12.50	25.00	50.00
❏ 5389	The First Sign of Love/So Be It	1960	5.00	10.00	20.00
❏ 5421	Wait/And Take My Love	1960	5.00	10.00	20.00
❏ 5455	Little Turtle Dove/So Can I	1961	5.00	10.00	20.00
❏ 5497	Just Forget About Me/You Know How Much I Care	1961	5.00	10.00	20.00
❏ 5527	Pardon Me/Panic	1961	5.00	10.00	20.00
❏ 5558	Two Hearts/The Secret	1961	5.00	10.00	20.00
❏ 5682	When We Get Together/Only Young Once	1962	3.75	7.50	15.00
❏ 5816	It Just Ain't Right/It'll Never Happen Again	1963	3.75	7.50	15.00
❏ 5880	Unchain My Heart/Friends Call Me a Fool	1964	3.75	7.50	15.00
❏ 6034	Bye Bye Baby/Please Believe in Me	1966	3.75	7.50	15.00
OKEH					
❏ 7225	Baby, You Turn Me On/Love Don't Grow on Trees	1965	3.75	7.50	15.00
❏ 7235	I Fall to Pieces/Gotta Get Myself Together	1965	3.75	7.50	15.00
❏ 7248	I Got Loving/Welcome Home	1966	3.75	7.50	15.00
❏ 7261	Ain't Gonna Walk Your Dog No More/Your Sweet Love (Rained Over Me)	1966	3.75	7.50	15.00
SCEPTER					
❏ 12376	Here Lie the Bones of Nellie Jones/When You Turn On the Love	1973	2.00	4.00	8.00
STOP					
❏ 301	Begging to You//(B-side unknown)	1968	2.50	5.00	10.00

Number	Title (A Side/B Side)	Yr	VG	VG+	NM
❏ 306	Begging to You/Everybody's Got a Song But Me	1968	2.50	5.00	10.00
❏ 346	Jesus Is a Soul Man/Make a Woman Feel Like a Woman	1969	2.50	5.00	10.00
❏ 360	Ling, Ting, Tong/For the Love	1970	2.50	5.00	10.00
❏ 388	I Wanna Go Country/Rocky Top	1971	2.00	4.00	8.00
—As "Otis Williams and the Midnight Cowboys"					
7-Inch Extended Plays					
DELUXE					
❏ EP-385	*That's Your Mistake/Too Late I Learned/Miss the Love/Gum Drop	1956	75.00	150.00	300.00
❏ EP-385	Otis Williams and His Charms	1956	75.00	150.00	300.00
Albums					
DELUXE					
❏ 570 [M]	Their All Time Hits	1957	250.00	500.00	1000.
KING					
❏ 570 [M]	Their All Time Hits	1957	150.00	300.00	600.00
❏ 614 [M]	This Is Otis Williams and His Charms	1959	100.00	200.00	400.00
STOP					
❏ STLP-1022	Otis Williams and the Midnight Cowboys	1971	6.25	12.50	25.00

WILLIAMS, TONY

Also see THE PLATTERS.

45s

Number	Title (A Side/B Side)	Yr	VG	VG+	NM
DOT					
❏ 16806	Endless Street/Smoke, Drink, Play 21	1965	2.00	4.00	8.00
MERCURY					
❏ 71158	Let's Start All Over Again/When You Return	1957	5.00	10.00	20.00
❏ 71532	Charmaine/Peg o' My Heart	1959	5.00	10.00	20.00
PHILIPS					
❏ 40069	Chloe/Second Best	1962	2.50	5.00	10.00
❏ 40123	Twenty-Four Lonely Hours/Save Me	1963	2.50	5.00	10.00
❏ 40141	How Come/When I Had You	1963	2.50	5.00	10.00
REPRISE					
❏ 20019	Sleepless Nights/Movin' In	1961	3.75	7.50	15.00
❏ 20030	Miracle/My Prayer	1961	3.75	7.50	15.00
❏ 20056	It's So Easy to Surrender/That's More Like It	1962	10.00	20.00	40.00
—Released only in Italy					
❏ 20067	Come Along Now/That's More Like It	1962	3.75	7.50	15.00
❏ 20073	Sing, Lover, Sing/Mandalino	1962	10.00	20.00	40.00
—Released only in Hong Kong					
❏ 20136	Dream/Loving You	1963	10.00	20.00	40.00
—Released only in Italy					
Albums					
MERCURY					
❏ MG-20454 [M]	A Girl Is a Girl Is a Girl	1959	10.00	20.00	40.00
❏ SR-60138 [S]	A Girl Is a Girl Is a Girl	1959	12.50	25.00	50.00
PHILIPS					
❏ PHM 200051 [M]	The Magic Touch of Tony	1962	6.25	12.50	25.00
❏ PHS 600051 [S]	The Magic Touch of Tony	1962	7.50	15.00	30.00
REPRISE					
❏ R-6006 [M]	His Greatest Hits	1961	6.25	12.50	25.00
❏ R9-6006 [S]	His Greatest Hits	1961	7.50	15.00	30.00

WILLIAMSON, SONNY BOY (2)

Really Aleck Ford, also known as Alex "Rice" Miller, before taking the name of his predecessor.

45s

Number	Title (A Side/B Side)	Yr	VG	VG+	NM
ACE					
❏ 511	Boppin' with Sonny/No Nights By Myself	1955	30.00	60.00	120.00
CHECKER					
❏ 824	Don't Start Me Talkin'/All My Love In Vain	1955	25.00	50.00	100.00
❏ 834	Let Me Explain/Your Imagination	1956	15.00	30.00	60.00
❏ 847	Keep It To Yourself/The Key to Your Door	1956	12.50	25.00	50.00
❏ 864	I Don't Know/Fattening Frogs for Snakes	1957	12.50	25.00	50.00
❏ 883	Born Blind/Ninety-Nine	1958	10.00	20.00	40.00
❏ 894	Your Funeral & My Trial/Wake Up, Baby	1958	10.00	20.00	40.00
❏ 910	Cross My Heart/Dissatisfied	1958	10.00	20.00	40.00
❏ 927	Let Your Conscience Be Your Guide/Unseeing Eye	1959	10.00	20.00	40.00
❏ 943	The Goat/It's Sad to Be Alone	1960	7.50	15.00	30.00
❏ 956	Temperature 110/Lonesome Cabin	1960	7.50	15.00	30.00
❏ 963	Trust Me Baby/Too Close Together	1960	7.50	15.00	30.00
❏ 975	The Hurt/Stop Right Now	1961	7.50	15.00	30.00
❏ 1003	One Way Out/Nine Below Zero	1962	7.50	15.00	30.00
❏ 1036	Bye Bye Bird/Help Me	1963	7.50	15.00	30.00
❏ 1065	Trying to Get Back on My Feet/Decoration Day	1963	7.50	15.00	30.00
❏ 1080	My Younger Days/I Want You Close to Me	1964	7.50	15.00	30.00
❏ 1134	Bring It On Home/Down Child	1966	6.25	12.50	25.00
TRUMPET					
❏ 144	West Memphis Blues/I Cross My Heart	1951	25.00	50.00	100.00
❏ 145	Sonny Boy's Christmas Blues/Pontiac Blues	195?	30.00	60.00	120.00
❏ 166	Nine Below Zero/Mighty Long Time	1952	25.00	50.00	100.00
❏ 167	Too Close Together/She Brought Life Back to the Dead	1952	—	—	—
—Unreleased					
❏ 168	Stop Now Baby/Mr. Downchild	1952	25.00	50.00	100.00
❏ 212	Cat Hop/Too Close Together	1952	20.00	40.00	80.00
❏ 215	Gettin' Out of Time/She Brought Life Back to the Dead	1952	20.00	40.00	80.00
❏ 216	Red Hot Kisses/Going in Your Direction	1952	20.00	40.00	80.00
❏ 228	From the Bottom/Empty Bedroom	1953	17.50	35.00	70.00
78s					
ACE					
❏ 511	Boppin' with Sonny/No Nights By Myself	1955	17.50	35.00	70.00

Number	Title (A Side/B Side)	Yr	VG	VG+	NM
CHECKER					
❏ 824	Don't Start Me Talkin'/All My Love In Vain	1955	12.50	25.00	50.00
❏ 834	Let Me Explain/Your Imagination	1956	12.50	25.00	50.00
❏ 847	Keep It To Yourself/The Key to Your Door	1956	12.50	25.00	50.00
❏ 864	I Don't Know/Fattening Frogs for Snakes	1957	12.50	25.00	50.00
❏ 883	Born Blind/Ninety-Nine	1958	12.50	25.00	50.00
❏ 894	Your Funeral & My Trial/Wake Up, Baby	1958	15.00	30.00	60.00
TRUMPET					
❏ 129	Eyesight to the Blind/Crazy About You Baby	1951	17.50	35.00	70.00
❏ 139	Do It If You Wanta/Cool Cool Blues	1951	15.00	30.00	60.00
❏ 140	Come On Back Home/Stop Crying	1951	15.00	30.00	60.00
❏ 144	West Memphis Blues/I Cross My Heart	1951	15.00	30.00	60.00
❏ 145	Sonny Boy's Christmas Blues/Pontiac Blues	1951	15.00	30.00	60.00
❏ 166	Nine Below Zero/Mighty Long Time	1952	15.00	30.00	60.00
❏ 167	Too Close Together/She Brought Life Back to the Dead	1952	—	—	—
—Unreleased					
❏ 168	Stop Now Baby/Mr. Downchild	1952	12.50	25.00	50.00
❏ 212	Cat Hop/Too Close Together	1952	12.50	25.00	50.00
❏ 215	Gettin' Out of Time/She Brought Life Back to the Dead	1952	12.50	25.00	50.00
❏ 216	Red Hot Kisses/Going in Your Direction	1952	12.50	25.00	50.00
❏ 228	From the Bottom/Empty Bedroom	1953	12.50	25.00	50.00
Albums					
ALLIGATOR					
❏ AL-4787	Keep It To Ourselves	1990	3.00	6.00	12.00
ARHOOLIE					
❏ 2020	King Biscuit Time	197?	3.00	6.00	12.00
CHECKER					
❏ LP-1437 [M]	Down and Out Blues	1959	80.00	160.00	320.00
CHESS					
❏ 2ACMB-206 [(2)]	Sonny Boy Williamson	1976	5.00	10.00	20.00
—Reissue of 50027					
❏ CHV-417	One Way Out	1975	3.75	7.50	15.00
❏ LP-1503 [M]	The Real Folk Blues	1966	20.00	40.00	80.00
❏ LP-1509 [M]	More Real Folk Blues	1966	20.00	40.00	80.00
❏ LPS-1536	Bummer Road	1969	6.25	12.50	25.00
❏ CH-9116	One Way Out	198?	2.50	5.00	10.00
❏ CH-9257	Down and Out Blues	1988	2.50	5.00	10.00
❏ CH-9272	The Real Folk Blues	1988	2.50	5.00	10.00
❏ CH-9277	More Real Folk Blues	1988	2.50	5.00	10.00
❏ 2CH-50027 [(2)]	This Is My Story	1972	6.25	12.50	25.00
GNP CRESCENDO					
❏ GNPS-10003	Sonny Boy Williamson in Chicago	198?	2.50	5.00	10.00
STORYVILLE					
❏ 4016	A Portrait in Blues	197?	3.00	6.00	12.00
❏ 4062	The Blues of Sonny Boy Williamson	197?	3.00	6.00	12.00

WILLIAMSON, SONNY BOY (2), AND THE YARDBIRDS
Albums

Number	Title (A Side/B Side)	Yr	VG	VG+	NM
MERCURY					
❏ MG-21071 [M]	Sonny Boy Williamson and the Yardbirds	1965	20.00	40.00	80.00
❏ SR-61071 [R]	Sonny Boy Williamson and the Yardbirds	1965	12.50	25.00	50.00
—First cover with a picture of the bluesman and the band					
❏ SR-61071 [R]	Sonny Boy Williamson and the Yardbirds	196?	6.25	12.50	25.00
—Later cover with cartoon artwork on the cover					

WILLIS, CHUCK
Also see THE ROYALS (2).
45s

Number	Title (A Side/B Side)	Yr	VG	VG+	NM
ATLANTIC					
❏ 1098	It's Too Late/Kansas City Woman	1956	6.25	12.50	25.00
❏ 1112	Juanita/Whatcha' Gonna Do When Your Baby Leaves You	1956	6.25	12.50	25.00
❏ 1130	C.C. Rider/Ease the Pain	1957	6.25	12.50	25.00
❏ 1148	Love Me, Cherry/That Train Has Gone	1957	6.25	12.50	25.00
❏ 1168	Betty and Dupree/My Crying Eyes	1958	6.25	12.50	25.00
❏ 1179	What Am I Living For/Hang Up My Rock And Roll Shoes	1958	7.50	15.00	30.00
❏ 1192	Thunder and Lightning/My Life	1958	5.00	10.00	20.00
❏ 2005	You'll Be My Love/Keep a-Driving	1958	5.00	10.00	20.00
❏ 2029	My Baby/Just One Kiss	1959	5.00	10.00	20.00
OKEH					
❏ 6810	I Tried/I Rule My House	1951	25.00	50.00	100.00
❏ 6841	Let's Jump Tonight/It's Too Late Baby	1951	20.00	40.00	80.00
❏ 6873	Lud Mouth Lucy/Here I Come	1952	20.00	40.00	80.00
❏ 6905	My Story/Caldonia	1952	12.50	25.00	50.00
❏ 6930	Salty Tears/Wrong Lake to Catch a Fish	1953	12.50	25.00	50.00
❏ 6952	Going to the River/Baby Has Left Me Again	1953	12.50	25.00	50.00
❏ 6985	Don't Deceive Me/I've Been Treated Wrong Too Long	1953	12.50	25.00	50.00
❏ 7004	My Baby's Coming Home/When My Day Is Over	1953	12.50	25.00	50.00
❏ 7015	You're Still My Baby/What's Your Name	1954	12.50	25.00	50.00
❏ 7029	I Feel So Bad/Need One More Chance	1954	15.00	30.00	60.00
❏ 7041	Change My Mind/My Heart's Been Broke Again	1954	10.00	20.00	40.00
❏ 7048	Give and Take/I've Been Away Too Long	1954	10.00	20.00	40.00
❏ 7051	Lawdy Miss Mary/Love-Struck	1955	10.00	20.00	40.00
❏ 7055	I Can Tell/One More Break	1955	10.00	20.00	40.00
❏ 7062	Search My Heart/Ring-Ding-Doo	1955	10.00	20.00	40.00
❏ 7067	Come On Home/It Were You	1956	10.00	20.00	40.00
❏ 7070	Two Spoons of Tears/Charged with Cheating	1956	10.00	20.00	40.00

Number	Title (A Side/B Side)	Yr	VG	VG+	NM
7-Inch Extended Plays					
ATLANTIC					
❏ EP 591	Juanita/Whatcha' Gonna Do When Your Baby Leaves You//Kansas City Woman/It's Too Late	1957	50.00	100.00	200.00
❏ EP 591 [PS]	Chuck Willis	1957	50.00	100.00	200.00
❏ EP 609	C.C. Rider/Ease the Pain//That Train Has Gone/Love Me, Cherry	1958	30.00	60.00	120.00
❏ EP 609 [PS]	Rock with Chuck Willis	1958	30.00	60.00	120.00
❏ EP 612	What Am I Living For/Hang Up My Rock and Roll Shoes//Betty and Dupree/My Crying Eyes	1958	37.50	75.00	150.00
❏ EP 612 [PS]	What Am I Living For	1958	50.00	100.00	200.00
EPIC					
❏ 7070	(contents unknown)	1956	50.00	100.00	200.00
❏ 7070 [PS]	Chuck Willis Sings the Blues	1956	50.00	100.00	200.00
Albums					
ATLANTIC					
❏ 8018 [M]	The King of the Stroll	1958	75.00	150.00	300.00
—Black label					
❏ 8018 [M]	The King of the Stroll	1960	37.50	75.00	150.00
—Purple and orange label					
❏ 8079 [M]	I Remember Chuck Willis	1963	37.50	75.00	150.00
❏ SD 8079 [P]	I Remember Chuck Willis	1963	50.00	100.00	200.00
EPIC					
❏ LN 3425 [M]	Chuck Willis Wails the Blues	1958	125.00	250.00	500.00
❏ LN 3728 [M]	A Tribute to Chuck Willis	1960	75.00	150.00	300.00

WILLOWS, THE (1)
Also see TONY MIDDLETON.
45s

Number	Title (A Side/B Side)	Yr	VG	VG+	NM
MELBA					
❏ 102	Church Bells Are Ringing/Beby Tell Me	1956	75.00	150.00	300.00
—Original A-side title					
❏ 102	Church Bells May Ring/Baby Tell Me	1956	25.00	50.00	100.00
❏ 106	Do You Love Me/My Angel	1956	15.00	30.00	60.00
❏ 115	Little Darlin'/My Angel	1957	20.00	40.00	80.00

WILLOWS, THE (2)
45s

Number	Title (A Side/B Side)	Yr	VG	VG+	NM
4-STAR					
❏ 1753	There's a Dance Goin' On/Now That I Have You	1961	75.00	150.00	300.00

WILLOWS, THE (3)
45s

Number	Title (A Side/B Side)	Yr	VG	VG+	NM
HEIDI					
❏ 103	It's Such a Shame/Tears in Your Eyes	1964	3.75	7.50	15.00
❏ 107	Sit by the Fire/Such a Night	1965	3.75	7.50	15.00

WILLOWS, THE (4)
45s

Number	Title (A Side/B Side)	Yr	VG	VG+	NM
MGM					
❏ 13484	Hurtin' All Over/My Kinda Guy	1966	3.00	6.00	12.00
❏ 13714	Snow Song/Outside the City	1967	3.00	6.00	12.00

WILMER AND THE DUKES
45s

Number	Title (A Side/B Side)	Yr	VG	VG+	NM
APHRODISIAC					
❏ 260	Give Me One More Chance/Git It	1968	2.00	4.00	8.00
❏ 261	Heavy Time/I'm Free	1969	2.00	4.00	8.00
❏ 261 [PS]	Heavy Time/I'm Free	1969	3.00	6.00	12.00
❏ 262	Living in the U.S.A./Count on Me	1969	2.00	4.00	8.00
❏ 263	Get Out of My Life, Women/I Do Love You	1969	2.50	5.00	10.00

WILSON, AL
45s

Number	Title (A Side/B Side)	Yr	VG	VG+	NM
BELL					
❏ 867	Mississippi Woman/Sometimes a Man Must Cry	1970	—	3.50	7.00
❏ 909	You Do the Right Thing/Bachelor Man	1970	—	3.50	7.00
CAROUSEL					
❏ 30051	I Hear You Knocking/Sugar Cane Girl	1971	—	3.00	6.00
❏ 30052	Falling/Bachelor Man	1971	—	3.00	6.00
PLAYBOY					
❏ 6062	I've Got a Feeling (We'll Be Seeing Each Other Again)/Be Concerned	1976	—	2.50	5.00
❏ 6076	Baby I Want Your Body/Stay with Me	1976	—	2.50	5.00
❏ 6076 [PS]	Baby I Want Your Body/Stay with Me	1976	—	3.00	6.00
❏ 6085	You Did It for Me/Differently	1976	—	2.50	5.00
ROADSHOW					
❏ PB-11583	Count the Days/Is This the End	1979	—	2.00	4.00
❏ PB-11714	Earthquake/You Got It	1979	—	2.00	4.00
ROCKY ROAD					
❏ 30060	Heavy Church/(B-side unknown)	1972	—	3.00	6.00
❏ 30067	Born on the Bayou/(B-side unknown)	1972	—	3.00	6.00
❏ 30073	Show and Tell/Listen to Me	1973	—	3.00	6.00
❏ 30076	Touch and Go/Settle Me Down	1974	—	3.00	6.00
❏ 30200	La La Peace Song/Keep On Loving You	1974	—	3.00	6.00
❏ 30202	I Won't Last a Day Without You-Let Me Be the One/Willoughbry Brook Road	1974	—	3.00	6.00
SOUL CITY					
❏ 759	When You Love, You're Loved Too/Who Could Be Lovin' You	1967	2.50	5.00	10.00
❏ 761	Do What You Gotta Do/Now I Know What Love Is	1968	2.00	4.00	8.00
❏ 767	The Snake/Getting Ready for Tomorrow	1968	2.00	4.00	8.00
❏ 771	Poor Side of Town/The Dolphins	1969	2.00	4.00	8.00

Number	Title (A Side/B Side)	Yr	VG	VG+	NM
❑ 773	I Stand Accused/Shake Me, Wake Me	1969	2.00	4.00	8.00
❑ 775	Lodi/By the Time I Get to Phoenix	1969	2.00	4.00	8.00
WAND					
❑ 1135	Help Me/(Instrumental)	1966	7.50	15.00	30.00
Albums					
PLAYBOY					
❑ PB 410	I've Got a Feeling	1976	3.00	6.00	12.00
❑ JZ 34744	I've Got a Feeling	1977	2.50	5.00	10.00
—Reissue of 410					
ROCKY ROAD					
❑ RR-3600	Weighing In	1973	3.75	7.50	15.00
❑ RR-3601	Show and Tell	1973	3.75	7.50	15.00
❑ 3700	La La Peace Song	1974	3.75	7.50	15.00
SOUL CITY					
❑ SCS-92006	Searching for the Dolphins	1969	6.25	12.50	25.00

WILSON, FLIP

45s

Number	Title (A Side/B Side)	Yr	VG	VG+	NM
LITTLE DAVID					
❑ 721	Don't Fight the Feeling/Geraldine-Killer	1972	—	2.50	5.00
❑ 730	There Oughta Be a Law/Berries in Salinas	1975	—	2.50	5.00
❑ 8113	There Oughta Be a Law/Berries in Salinas	1975	—	2.00	4.00
Albums					
ATLANTIC					
❑ 8149 [M]	Cowboys and Colored People	1967	6.25	12.50	25.00
❑ SD 8149 [S]	Cowboys and Colored People	1967	3.75	7.50	15.00
—Green and blue label					
❑ SD 8149 [S]	Cowboys and Colored People	1969	3.00	6.00	12.00
—Red and green label					
❑ SD 8179	You Devil You	1968	3.75	7.50	15.00
—Green and blue label					
❑ SD 8179	You Devil You	1969	3.00	6.00	12.00
—Red and green label					
IMPERIAL					
❑ LP-9155 [M]	Flippin'	1961	6.25	12.50	25.00
LITTLE DAVID					
❑ LD 1000	The Devil Made Me Buy This Dress	1970	3.00	6.00	12.00
❑ LD 1001 [M]	Geraldine/Don't Fight the Feeling	1972	6.25	12.50	25.00
—White label promo only; sticker on cover says "Promotional DJ Copy Monaural Not for Sale"					
❑ LD 1001 [S]	Geraldine/Don't Fight the Feeling	1972	3.00	6.00	12.00
❑ LD 2000	The Flip Wilson Show	1970	3.00	6.00	12.00
MINIT					
❑ 24012	Flippin'	1968	3.75	7.50	15.00
—Reissue of Imperial LP					
SCEPTER					
❑ S-520	Flip Wilson's Pot Luck	1964	5.00	10.00	20.00
SPRINGBOARD					
❑ SPB-4004	Funny and Live at the Village Gate	1972	3.00	6.00	12.00
—Reissue of Scepter LP					
SUNSET					
❑ SUS-5297	Flipped Out	1970	3.00	6.00	12.00
—Reissue of Minit LP					

WILSON, JACKIE

Also see THE DOMINOES.

45s

Number	Title (A Side/B Side)	Yr	VG	VG+	NM
BRUNSWICK					
❑ 9-55024	Reet Petite (The Finest Girl You Ever Want to Meet)/By the Light of the Silvery Moon	1957	7.50	15.00	30.00
❑ 9-55052	To Be Loved/Come Back to Me	1958	6.25	12.50	25.00
❑ 9-55070	As Long As I Live/I'm Wanderin'	1958	6.25	12.50	25.00
❑ 9-55086	We Have Love/Singing a Song	1958	6.25	12.50	25.00
❑ 9-55105	Lonely Teardrops/In the Blue of Evening	1958	7.50	15.00	30.00
❑ 55121	That's Why (I Love You So)/Love Is All	1959	6.25	12.50	25.00
❑ 55121 [PS]	That's Why (I Love You So)/Love Is All	1959	15.00	30.00	60.00
❑ 55136	I'll Be Satisfied/Ask	1959	6.25	12.50	25.00
❑ 55149	You Better Know It/Never Go Away	1959	5.00	10.00	20.00
❑ 55165	Talk That Talk/Only You, Only Me	1959	5.00	10.00	20.00
❑ 55165 [PS]	Talk That Talk/Only You, Only Me	1959	15.00	30.00	60.00
❑ 55166	Night/Doggin' Around	1960	10.00	20.00	40.00
—Maroon label (scarce original)					
❑ 55166	Night/Doggin' Around	1960	3.75	7.50	15.00
—Orange label (standard pressing)					
❑ 55166	Night/Doggin' Around	196?	2.50	5.00	10.00
—Black label, color-bar arrow (reissue pressing)					
❑ 55166 [PS]	Night/Doggin' Around	1960	12.50	25.00	50.00
❑ 55167	(You Were Made for) All My Love/A Woman, A Lover, A Friend	1960	5.00	10.00	20.00
❑ 55170	Alone at Last/Am I the Man	1960	5.00	10.00	20.00
❑ 55170 [PS]	Alone at Last/Am I the Man	1960	12.50	25.00	50.00
❑ 55201	My Empty Arms/The Tear of the Year	1961	3.75	7.50	15.00
❑ 55201 [PS]	My Empty Arms/The Tear of the Year	1961	10.00	20.00	40.00
❑ 55208	Please Tell Me Why/Your One and Only Love	1961	3.75	7.50	15.00
❑ 55216	I'm Comin' On Back to You/Lonely Life	1961	3.75	7.50	15.00
❑ 55219	Years from Now/You Don't Know What It Means	1961	3.75	7.50	15.00
❑ 55220	The Way I Am/My Heart Belongs to Only You	1961	3.75	7.50	15.00
❑ 55220 [PS]	The Way I Am/My Heart Belongs to Only You	1961	10.00	20.00	40.00
❑ 55221	The Greatest Hurt/There'll Be No Next Time	1962	3.75	7.50	15.00
❑ 55221 [PS]	The Greatest Hurt/There'll Be No Next Time	1962	10.00	20.00	40.00
❑ 55224	I Found Love/There's Nothing Like Love	1962	3.00	6.00	12.00
—With Linda Hopkins					
❑ 55225	Hearts/Sing (And Tell the Blues So Long)	1962	3.75	7.50	15.00
❑ 55229	I Just Can't Help It/My Tale of Woe	1962	3.75	7.50	15.00
❑ 55233	Forever and a Day/Baby That's All	1962	3.75	7.50	15.00
❑ 55236	What Good Am I Without You/A Girl Named Tamiko	1962	3.75	7.50	15.00
❑ 55236 [PS]	What Good Am I Without You/A Girl Named Tamiko	1962	7.50	15.00	30.00
❑ 55239	Baby Workout/I'm Going Crazy	1963	5.00	10.00	20.00
❑ 55243	Shake a Hand/Say I Do	1963	3.00	6.00	12.00
—With Linda Hopkins					
❑ 55246	Shake! Shake! Shake!/He's a Fool	1963	3.00	6.00	12.00
❑ 55250	Baby Get It (And Don't Quit It)/The New Breed	1963	3.00	6.00	12.00
❑ 55254	Silent Night/Oh Holy Night	1963	3.75	7.50	15.00
❑ 55260	Haunted House/I'm Travelin' On	1964	2.50	5.00	10.00
❑ 55263	Call Her Up/The Kickapoo	1964	2.50	5.00	10.00
❑ 55266	Big Boss Line/Be My Girl	1964	2.50	5.00	10.00
❑ 55269	Squeeze Her-Tease Her (But Love Her)/Give Me Back My Heart	1964	2.50	5.00	10.00
❑ 55273	Watch Out/She's All Right	1964	2.50	5.00	10.00
❑ 55277	Danny Boy/Soul Time	1965	2.00	4.00	8.00
❑ 55278	Yes Indeed/When the Saints Go Marching In	1965	2.00	4.00	8.00
—With Linda Hopkins					
❑ 55280	No Pity (In the Naked City)/I'm So Lonely	1965	2.00	4.00	8.00
❑ 55283	I Believe I'll Love On/Lonely Teardrops	1965	2.00	4.00	8.00
❑ 55287	Think Twice/Please Don't Hurt Me	1965	2.00	4.00	8.00
—With LaVern Baker					
❑ 55289	I've Got to Get Back/3 Days, 1 Hour, 30 Minutes	1966	2.00	4.00	8.00
❑ 55290	Soul Galore/Brand New Things	1966	2.00	4.00	8.00
❑ 55294	I Believe/Be My Love	1966	2.00	4.00	8.00
❑ 55300	Whispers (Gettin' Louder)/The Fairest of Them All	1966	2.00	4.00	8.00
❑ 55309	I Don't Want to Lose You/Just Be Sincere	1967	2.00	4.00	8.00
❑ 55321	I've Lost You/Those Heartaches	1967	2.00	4.00	8.00
❑ 55336	(Your Love Keeps Lifting Me) Higher and Higher/I'm the One to Do It	1967	2.50	5.00	10.00
❑ 55354	Since You Showed Me How to Be Happy/The Who Who Song	1967	2.00	4.00	8.00
❑ 55365	For Your Precious Love/Uptight	1968	2.00	4.00	8.00
❑ 55373	Chain Gang/Funky Broadway	1968	2.00	4.00	8.00
❑ 55381	I Get the Sweetest Feeling/Nothing But Heartaches	1968	2.00	4.00	8.00
❑ 55392	For Once in My Life/You Brought About a Change in Me	1968	2.00	4.00	8.00
❑ 55402	I Still Love You/Hum De Dum De Do	1969	2.00	4.00	8.00
❑ 55418	Helpless/Do It the Right Way	1969	2.00	4.00	8.00
❑ 55423	With These Hands/Why Don't You (Do Your Thing)	1969	2.00	4.00	8.00
❑ 55435	Let This Be a Letter (To My Baby)/Didn't I	1970	—	3.00	6.00
❑ 55435 [PS]	Let This Be a Letter (To My Baby)/Didn't I	1970	3.00	6.00	12.00
❑ 55443	(I Can Feel Those Vibrations) This Love Is Real/Love Uprising	1970	—	3.00	6.00
❑ 55449	This Guy's in Love with You/Say You Will	1971	—	3.00	6.00
❑ 55454	Say You Will/(B-side unknown)	1971	—	3.00	6.00
❑ 55461	Love Is Funny That Way/Try It Again	1971	—	3.00	6.00
❑ 55467	You Got Me Walking/The Mountain	1972	—	3.00	6.00
❑ 55475	The Girl Turned Me On/Forever and a Day	1972	—	3.00	6.00
❑ 55480	What a Lovely Way/You Left the Fire Burning	1972	—	3.00	6.00
❑ 55490	Beautiful Day/What 'Cha Gonna Do About Love	1973	—	3.00	6.00
❑ 55495	Because of You/Go Away	1973	—	3.00	6.00
❑ 55499	Sing a Little Song/No More Goodbyes	1973	—	3.00	6.00
❑ 55504	It's All Over/Shake a Leg	1973	—	3.00	6.00
❑ 55522	Don't Burn No Bridges/(Instrumental)	1975	—	3.00	6.00
—With the Chi-Lites					
❑ 55536	Nobody But You/I've Learned About Life	1977	—	3.00	6.00
❑ 7-78002 [S]	(You Were Made) For All My Love/One Kiss	196?	10.00	20.00	40.00
—Jukebox issue; small hole, plays at 33 1/3 rpm					
COLUMBIA					
❑ 38-07329	Reet Petite/You Better Know It	1987	—	2.50	5.00
❑ 38-07329 [PS]	Reet Petite/You Better Know It	1987	—	2.50	5.00
78s					
BRUNSWICK					
❑ 55024	Reet Petite (The Finest Girl You Ever Want to Meet)/By the Light of the Silvery Moon	1957	10.00	20.00	40.00
❑ 55052	To Be Loved/Come Back to Me	1958	10.00	20.00	40.00
❑ 55070	As Long As I Live/I'm Wanderin'	1958	12.50	25.00	50.00
❑ 55086	We Have Love/Singing a Song	1958	12.50	25.00	50.00
❑ 55105	Lonely Teardrops/In the Blue of Evening	1958	50.00	100.00	200.00
7-Inch Extended Plays					
BRUNSWICK					
❑ EB 71040	To Be Loved/Reet Petite//Danny Boy/As Long As I Live	1959	15.00	30.00	60.00
❑ EB 71040 [PS]	The Versatile Jackie Wilson	1959	15.00	30.00	60.00
❑ EB 71042	Lonely Teardrops/It's Too Bad We Had to Say Goodbye//Someone to Need Me/Joke	1960	15.00	30.00	60.00
❑ EB 71042 [PS]	Jumpin' Jack	1960	15.00	30.00	60.00
❑ EB 71045 [M]	That's Why/Love Is All//You Better Know It/Each Time	1960	15.00	30.00	60.00
❑ EB 71045 [PS]	That's Why (I Love You So)	1960	15.00	30.00	60.00
❑ EB 71046	Talk That Talk/Ask//I'll Be Satisfied/Wishing Well	1960	15.00	30.00	60.00
❑ EB 71046 [PS]	Talk That Talk	1960	15.00	30.00	60.00
❑ EB 71047	(contents unknown)	1960	15.00	30.00	60.00
❑ EB 71047 [PS]	Mr. Excitement	1960	15.00	30.00	60.00
❑ EB 71048	So Much/Only You, Only Me//Happiness/Magic of Love	1960	15.00	30.00	60.00
❑ EB 71048 [PS]	Jackie Wilson	1960	15.00	30.00	60.00
❑ EB 71049	Night/Doggin' Around//All My Love/A Woman, a Lover, a Friend	1960	15.00	30.00	60.00
❑ EB 71049 [PS]	Jackie Wilson	1960	15.00	30.00	60.00

Number	Title (A Side/B Side)	Yr	VG	VG+	NM
❑ EB 71101	The Greatest Hurt/I Don't Know You Anymore//Tear of the Year/There'll Be No Next Time	1962	15.00	30.00	60.00
❑ EB 71101 [PS]	Jackie Wilson	1962	15.00	30.00	60.00
❑ EB 71102	I Just Can't Help It/My Tale of Woe//Bad News Travels Fast/You Ought to Be Ashamed	1962	15.00	30.00	60.00
❑ EB 71102 [PS]	Jackie Wilson	1962	15.00	30.00	60.00
❑ EB 71103	Baby Workout/Say You Will//Kickapoo/Yeah Yeah Yeah	1963	15.00	30.00	60.00
❑ EB 71103 [PS]	Baby Workout	1963	15.00	30.00	60.00
❑ EB 71104	(contents unknown)	1963	15.00	30.00	60.00
❑ EB 71104 [PS]	Shake a Hand	1963	15.00	30.00	60.00
❑ 7-78009	No Pity (In the Naked City)/Mama of My Song/Soul Time//Danny Boy/She's All Right/No Time Out	196?	12.50	25.00	50.00
—Jukebox issue; small hole, plays at 33 1/3 rpm					
❑ 7-78009 [PS]	Soul Time	196?	12.50	25.00	50.00
❑ EB 771045	That's Why/Love Is All//You Better Know It/Each Time	1960	20.00	40.00	80.00
❑ EB 771045 [PS]	That's Why (I Love You So)	1960	20.00	40.00	80.00

Albums

BRUNSWICK

Number	Title (A Side/B Side)	Yr	VG	VG+	NM
❑ BL 54042 [M]	He's So Fine	1959	30.00	60.00	120.00
—All-black label					
❑ BL 54042 [M]	He's So Fine	1964	6.25	12.50	25.00
—Black label with color bars					
❑ BL 54045 [M]	Lonely Teardrops	1959	37.50	75.00	150.00
—All-black label					
❑ BL 54045 [M]	Lonely Teardrops	1964	6.25	12.50	25.00
—Black label with color bars					
❑ BL 54050 [M]	So Much	1960	25.00	50.00	100.00
—All-black label					
❑ BL 54050 [M]	So Much	1964	5.00	10.00	20.00
—Black label with color bars					
❑ BL 54055 [M]	Jackie Sings the Blues	1960	37.50	75.00	150.00
—All-black label					
❑ BL 54055 [M]	Jackie Sings the Blues	1964	5.00	10.00	20.00
—Black label with color bars					
❑ BL 54058 [M]	My Golden Favorites	1960	15.00	30.00	60.00
—All-black label					
❑ BL 54058 [M]	My Golden Favorites	1964	6.25	12.50	25.00
—Black label with color bars					
❑ BL 54059 [M]	A Woman, a Lover, a Friend	1961	12.50	25.00	50.00
—All-black label					
❑ BL 54059 [M]	A Woman, a Lover, a Friend	1964	5.00	10.00	20.00
—Black label with color bars					
❑ BL 54100 [M]	You Ain't Heard Nothin' Yet	1961	12.50	25.00	50.00
—All-black label					
❑ BL 54100 [M]	You Ain't Heard Nothin' Yet	1964	5.00	10.00	20.00
—Black label with color bars					
❑ BL 54101 [M]	By Special Request	1961	12.50	25.00	50.00
—All-black label					
❑ BL 54101 [M]	By Special Request	1964	5.00	10.00	20.00
—Black label with color bars					
❑ BL 54105 [M]	Body and Soul	1962	12.50	25.00	50.00
—All-black label					
❑ BL 54105 [M]	Body and Soul	1964	5.00	10.00	20.00
—Black label with color bars					
❑ BL 54106 [M]	The World's Greatest Melodies	1962	12.50	25.00	50.00
—All-black label					
❑ BL 54106 [M]	The World's Greatest Melodies	1964	5.00	10.00	20.00
—All-black label					
❑ BL 54108 [M]	Jackie Wilson at the Copa	1962	12.50	25.00	50.00
—All-black label					
❑ BL 54108 [M]	Jackie Wilson at the Copa	1964	5.00	10.00	20.00
—Black label with color bars					
❑ BL 54110 [M]	Baby Workout	1963	12.50	25.00	50.00
—All-black label					
❑ BL 54110 [M]	Baby Workout	1963	5.00	10.00	20.00
—Black label with color bars					
❑ BL 54112 [M]	Merry Christmas from Jackie Wilson	1963	7.50	15.00	30.00
❑ BL 54113 [M]	Shake a Hand	1964	6.25	12.50	25.00
❑ BL 54115 [M]	My Golden Favorites, Volume 2	1964	6.25	12.50	25.00
❑ BL 54117 [M]	Somethin' Else	1964	6.25	12.50	25.00
❑ BL 54118 [M]	Soul Time	1965	6.25	12.50	25.00
❑ BL 54119 [M]	Spotlight on Jackie	1965	6.25	12.50	25.00
❑ BL 54120 [M]	Soul Galore	1966	6.25	12.50	25.00
❑ BL 54122 [M]	Whispers	1966	6.25	12.50	25.00
❑ BL 54130 [M]	Higher and Higher	1967	6.25	12.50	25.00
❑ BL 54134 [M]	Manufacturers of Soul	1968	12.50	25.00	50.00
—With Count Basie					
❑ BL 54138 [M]	I Get the Sweetest Feeling	1968	25.00	50.00	100.00
—Yellow label promo only; "Monaural" sticker over the word "Stereo" on cover					
❑ BL 754050 [S]	So Much	1960	37.50	75.00	150.00
—All-black label					
❑ BL 754050 [S]	So Much	1964	6.25	12.50	25.00
—Black label with color bars					
❑ BL 754055 [S]	Jackie Sings the Blues	1960	50.00	100.00	200.00
—All-black label					
❑ BL 754055 [S]	Jackie Sings the Blues	1964	6.25	12.50	25.00
—Black label with color bars					
❑ BL 754059 [S]	A Woman, a Lover, a Friend	1961	20.00	40.00	80.00
—All-black label					
❑ BL 754059 [S]	A Woman, a Lover, a Friend	1964	6.25	12.50	25.00
—Black label with color bars					
❑ BL 754100 [S]	You Ain't Heard Nothin' Yet	1961	20.00	40.00	80.00
—All-black label					

Number	Title (A Side/B Side)	Yr	VG	VG+	NM
❑ BL 754100 [S]	You Ain't Heard Nothin' Yet	1964	6.25	12.50	25.00
—Black label with color bars					
❑ BL 754101 [S]	By Special Request	1961	20.00	40.00	80.00
—All-black label					
❑ BL 754101 [S]	By Special Request	1964	6.25	12.50	25.00
—Black label with color bars					
❑ BL 754105 [S]	Body and Soul	1962	20.00	40.00	80.00
—All-black label					
❑ BL 754105 [S]	Body and Soul	1964	6.25	12.50	25.00
—Black label with color bars					
❑ BL 754106 [S]	The World's Greatest Melodies	1962	20.00	40.00	80.00
—All-black label					
❑ BL 754106 [S]	The World's Greatest Melodies	1964	6.25	12.50	25.00
—Black label with color bars					
❑ BL 754108 [S]	Jackie Wilson at the Copa	1962	20.00	40.00	80.00
—All-black label					
❑ BL 754108 [S]	Jackie Wilson at the Copa	1964	6.25	12.50	25.00
—Black label with color bars					
❑ BL 754110 [S]	Baby Workout	1963	20.00	40.00	80.00
—All-black label					
❑ BL 754110 [S]	Baby Workout	1963	6.25	12.50	25.00
—Black label with color bars					
❑ BL 754112 [S]	Merry Christmas from Jackie Wilson	1963	10.00	20.00	40.00
❑ BL 754113 [S]	Shake a Hand	1964	7.50	15.00	30.00
❑ BL 754115 [S]	My Golden Favorites, Volume 2	1964	7.50	15.00	30.00
❑ BL 754117 [S]	Somethin' Else	1964	7.50	15.00	30.00
❑ BL 754118 [S]	Soul Time	1965	7.50	15.00	30.00
❑ BL 754119 [S]	Spotlight on Jackie	1965	7.50	15.00	30.00
❑ BL 754120 [S]	Soul Galore	1966	7.50	15.00	30.00
❑ BL 754122 [S]	Whispers	1966	7.50	15.00	30.00
❑ BL 754130 [S]	Higher and Higher	1967	7.50	15.00	30.00
❑ BL 754134 [S]	Manufacturers of Soul	1968	5.00	10.00	20.00
—With Count Basie					
❑ BL 754138 [S]	I Get the Sweetest Feeling	1968	5.00	10.00	20.00
❑ BL 754140	Jackie Wilson's Greatest Hits	1969	5.00	10.00	20.00
❑ BL 754154	Do Your Thing	1969	5.00	10.00	20.00
❑ BL 754158	It's All a Part of Love	1970	5.00	10.00	20.00
❑ BL 754167	This Love Is Real	1971	5.00	10.00	20.00
❑ BL 754172	You Got Me Walking	1971	5.00	10.00	20.00
❑ BL 754185	Beautiful Day	1972	3.75	7.50	15.00
❑ BL 754199	Nowstalgia	1974	3.75	7.50	15.00
❑ BL 754212	Nobody But You	1977	3.75	7.50	15.00

COLUMBIA

Number	Title (A Side/B Side)	Yr	VG	VG+	NM
❑ FC 40866	Reet Petite: The Best of Jackie Wilson	1987	3.00	6.00	12.00

EPIC

Number	Title (A Side/B Side)	Yr	VG	VG+	NM
❑ EG 38623 [(2)]	The Jackie Wilson Story	1983	5.00	10.00	20.00
❑ FE 39408	The Jackie Wilson Story, Vol. 2	1985	3.00	6.00	12.00
❑ PE 39408	The Jackie Wilson Story, Vol. 2	198?	2.00	4.00	8.00
—Budget-line reissue					

RHINO

Number	Title (A Side/B Side)	Yr	VG	VG+	NM
❑ RNLP-70230	Through the Years: A Collection of Rare Album Tracks and Single Sides	1987	3.00	6.00	12.00

WILSON, PEANUTS

45s

BRUNSWICK

Number	Title (A Side/B Side)	Yr	VG	VG+	NM
❑ 55039	Cast Iron Arm/You've Got Love	1957	37.50	75.00	150.00

WINSTONS, THE

45s

METROMEDIA

Number	Title (A Side/B Side)	Yr	VG	VG+	NM
❑ 117	Color Him Father/Amen, Brother	1969	2.00	4.00	8.00
❑ 142	Love of the Common People/Wheel of Fortune	1969	—	3.00	6.00
❑ 151	Birds of a Feather/The Greatest Love	1969	—	3.00	6.00

Albums

METROMEDIA

Number	Title (A Side/B Side)	Yr	VG	VG+	NM
❑ MD-1010	Color Him Father	1969	12.50	25.00	50.00

WITHERS, BILL

12-Inch Singles

COLUMBIA

Number	Title (A Side/B Side)	Yr	VG	VG+	NM
❑ CAS 2112 [DJ]	Something That Turns You On (same on both sides)	1985	2.00	4.00	8.00

45s

COLUMBIA

Number	Title (A Side/B Side)	Yr	VG	VG+	NM
❑ 02071	I Want to Spend the Night/Memories Are That Way	1981	—	2.00	4.00
❑ 02651	USA/Paint Your Pretty Picture	1981	—	2.00	4.00
❑ 02651 [PS]	USA/Paint Your Pretty Picture	1981	—	2.50	5.00
❑ 04841	Oh Yeah!/Just Like the First Time	1985	—	2.00	4.00
❑ 05424	Something That Turns You On/You Tried to Find a Love	1985	—	2.00	4.00
❑ 05424 [PS]	Something That Turns You On/You Tried to Find a Love	1985	—	2.00	4.00
❑ 05675	We Could Be Sweet Lovers/You Just Can't Smile It Away	1985	—	2.00	4.00
❑ 10255	Make Love to Your Mind/I Love You Dawn	1975	—	2.50	5.00
❑ 10308	I Wish You Well/She's Lonely	1976	—	2.50	5.00
❑ 10357	Family Table/Hello Like Before	1976	—	2.50	5.00
❑ 10420	If I Didn't Mean You Well/My Imagination	1976	—	2.50	5.00
❑ 10459	Close to Me/I'll Be with You	1976	—	2.50	5.00
❑ 10627	Lovely Day/It Ain't Because of Me Baby	1977	—	2.50	5.00
❑ 10702	Lovely Night for Dancing/I Want to Spend the Night	1978	—	2.50	5.00
❑ 10892	Don't It Make It Better/Love Is	1979	—	2.00	4.00

Number	Title (A Side/B Side)	Yr	VG	VG+	NM
❑ 10958	You Got the Stuff/Look to Each Other for Love	1979	—	2.00	4.00
SUSSEX					
❑ 219	Ain't No Sunshine/Harlem	1971	—	3.00	6.00
❑ 227	Grandma's Hands/Sweet Wanomi	1971	—	2.50	5.00
❑ 235	Lean On Me/Better Off Dead	1972	—	3.00	6.00
❑ 241	Use Me/Let Me In Your Life	1972	—	2.50	5.00
❑ 247	Let Us Love/The Gift of Giving	1972	—	2.50	5.00
❑ 247 [PS]	Let Us Love/The Gift of Giving	1972	2.00	4.00	8.00
❑ 250	Kissing My Love/I Don't Know	1973	—	2.50	5.00
❑ 257	Friend of Mine/Lonely Town, Lonely Street	1973	—	2.50	5.00
❑ 513	The Same Love That Made Me Laugh/Make a Smile for Me	1974	—	2.50	5.00
❑ 518	You/Stories	1974	—	2.50	5.00
❑ 629	Heartbreak Road/Ruby Lee	1974	—	2.50	5.00
❑ 638	Who Is He (And What Is He to You)/Harlem	1975	—	2.50	5.00
Albums					
COLUMBIA					
❑ PC 33704	Making Music	1975	2.50	5.00	10.00
❑ PC 34327	Naked and Warm	1976	2.50	5.00	10.00
❑ JC 34903	Menagerie	1977	2.50	5.00	10.00
❑ JC 35596	'Bout Love	1979	2.50	5.00	10.00
❑ JC 36877	The Best of Bill Withers	1981	—	—	—
—Canceled?					
❑ FC 37199	Bill Withers' Greatest Hits	1981	2.50	5.00	10.00
—Re-release of 36877 with "Just the Two of Us" added					
❑ FC 39887	Watching You Watching Me	1985	2.50	5.00	10.00
❑ PC 40177	Still Bill	1985	2.00	4.00	8.00
—Reissue of Sussex 7014					
❑ PC 40178	Just As I Am	1985	2.00	4.00	8.00
—Reissue of Sussex 7006					
SUSSEX					
❑ SXBS-7006	Just As I Am	1971	5.00	10.00	20.00
❑ SXBS-7014	Still Bill	1972	5.00	10.00	20.00
❑ SXBS-7025-2	[(2)]Bill Withers Live at Carnegie Hall	1973	5.00	10.00	20.00
❑ SUX-8032	+'Justments	1974	3.75	7.50	15.00
❑ SUX-8037	The Best of Bill Withers	1975	3.75	7.50	15.00

WITHERSPOON, JIMMY
45s

Number	Title (A Side/B Side)	Yr	VG	VG+	NM
ABC					
❑ 11288	Handbags and Gladrags/Stay with Me Baby	1971	—	3.00	6.00
BLUE NOTE					
❑ XW716	Pearly Whites/Sign on the Building	1975	—	2.50	5.00
BLUESWAY					
❑ 61028	Just a Dream/I Don't Know	1969	—	3.00	6.00
CAPITOL					
❑ 3998	Love Is a Five Letter Word/Other Side of Love	1974	—	2.50	5.00
CHECKER					
❑ 798	Big Daddy/When the Lights Go Out	1954	7.50	15.00	30.00
❑ 810	Time Brings About a Change/Waiting for Your Return	1955	7.50	15.00	30.00
❑ 826	It Ain't No Secret/Why Do I Love You Like I Do	1955	7.50	15.00	30.00
FEDERAL					
❑ 12095	Foolish Prayer/Two Little Girls	1952	7.50	15.00	30.00
❑ 12099	Lucille/Blues in Trouble	1952	7.50	15.00	30.00
❑ 12107	Don't Tell Me Now/Corn Whiskey	1952	7.50	15.00	30.00
❑ 12118	Jay's Blues (Part 1)/Jay's Blues (Part 2)	1953	7.50	15.00	30.00
❑ 12128	One Fine Gal/Back Home	1953	7.50	15.00	30.00
❑ 12138	Back Door Blues/Last Mile	1953	7.50	15.00	30.00
❑ 12155	Fast Women and Sloe Gin/Miss Mistreater	1953	7.50	15.00	30.00
❑ 12156	Sad Life/Move Me Baby	1953	12.50	25.00	50.00
—With the Lamplighters					
❑ 12173	24 Sad Hours/Just for You	1954	7.50	15.00	30.00
❑ 12180	It/Highway to Happiness	1954	7.50	15.00	30.00
❑ 12189	Oh Boy/I Done Told You	1954	7.50	15.00	30.00
GNP CRESCENDO					
❑ 156	Ain't Nobody's Business/No Rollin' Blues	1959	3.00	6.00	12.00
HIFI					
❑ 594	Everytime I Feel the Spirit/Oh Mary Don't You Weep	1960	3.00	6.00	12.00
KENT					
❑ 4551	Ain't Nobody's Business (Part 1)/Ain't Nobody's Business (Part 2)	1971	—	3.00	6.00
KING					
❑ 5997	Foolish Prayer/Two Little Girls	1965	2.50	5.00	10.00
MODERN					
❑ 857	The Wind Is Blowin'/My Baby Make a Change	1952	10.00	20.00	40.00
—Note: Earlier Jimmy Witherspoon 45s on Modern are not known to exist					
❑ 877	Love My Baby/Daddy Pinocchio	1952	10.00	20.00	40.00
❑ 895	Baby Baby/Slow Your Speed	1953	10.00	20.00	40.00
❑ 903	Each Step of the Way/Let Jesus Fix It for You	1953	10.00	20.00	40.00
❑ 909	Oh Mother, Dear Mother/I'll Be Right On Down	1953	10.00	20.00	40.00
PACIFIC JAZZ					
❑ 327	Ain't Nobody's Business/Times Have Changed	1961	2.50	5.00	10.00
PRESTIGE					
❑ 266	One Scotch, One Bourbon, One Beer/Baby, Baby, Baby	196?	2.50	5.00	10.00
❑ 274	Mean Ole Frisco/Sail On Little Girl	196?	2.50	5.00	10.00
❑ 291	Goin' to Chicago Blues/You Made Me Love You	196?	2.50	5.00	10.00
❑ 298	I Had a Dream/S.K. Blues	1963	2.50	5.00	10.00
❑ 307	Money's Gettin' Cheaper/Ever In	1963	2.50	5.00	10.00
❑ 340	I Never Will Marry/Happy Blues	1964	2.50	5.00	10.00
❑ 341	Some of My Best Friends Are the Blues/You're Next	1964	2.50	5.00	10.00

Number	Title (A Side/B Side)	Yr	VG	VG+	NM
❑ 358	Come On and Walk with Me/Two Hearts Are Better Than One	196?	2.00	4.00	8.00
❑ 378	Love Me Right/Make This Heart of Mine Smile Again	196?	2.00	4.00	8.00
❑ 402	I Never Thought I'd See the Day/If There Wasn't Any You	196?	2.00	4.00	8.00
RCA VICTOR					
❑ 47-6977	Ain't Nobody's Business/Who Baby Who	1957	5.00	10.00	20.00
❑ 47-7377	Confessin' the Blues/Ooo Wee, Then the Lights Go Out	1958	5.00	10.00	20.00
REPRISE					
❑ 0275	Key to the Highway/I'd Rather Drink Muddy Water	1964	2.00	4.00	8.00
❑ 20013	The Masquerade Is Over/I Don't Know	1961	2.50	5.00	10.00
❑ 20029	Warm Your Heart/Hey Mrs. Jones	1961	2.50	5.00	10.00
VEE JAY					
❑ 322	Everything But You/I Know, I Know	1959	3.00	6.00	12.00
VERVE					
❑ 10439	It's All Over But the Crying/My Blue Tears	1966	2.00	4.00	8.00
❑ 10495	Fast Forty Blues/My Baby Quit Me	1967	2.00	4.00	8.00
WORLD PACIFIC					
❑ 814	Ain't Nobody's Business/There's Good Rockin' Tonight	1960	3.00	6.00	12.00
Albums					
ABC					
❑ 717	Handbags and Gladrags	1970	6.25	12.50	25.00
ANALOGUE PRODUCTIONS					
❑ APR 3008	Evenin' Blues	199?	3.75	7.50	15.00
BLUE NOTE					
❑ BN-LA534-G	Spoonful	1976	3.00	6.00	12.00
BLUESWAY					
❑ BLS-6026	Blues Singer	1969	6.25	12.50	25.00
❑ BLS-6040	Hunh	1970	6.25	12.50	25.00
❑ BLS-6051	The Best of Jimmy Witherspoon	1970	6.25	12.50	25.00
CAPITOL					
❑ ST-11360	Love Is a Five Letter Word	1975	3.00	6.00	12.00
CHESS					
❑ CH-93003	Spoon So Easy: The Chess Years	1990	3.00	6.00	12.00
CONSTELLATION					
❑ CM 1422 [M]	Take This Hammer	1964	12.50	25.00	50.00
❑ CMS 1422 [R]	Take This Hammer	1964	7.50	15.00	30.00
CROWN					
❑ CST-215 [S]	Jimmy Witherspoon Sings the Blues	1961	37.50	75.00	150.00
—Red vinyl; contrary to prior reports, this album -- at least the red vinyl version -- is in true stereo!					
❑ CST-215 [S]	Jimmy Witherspoon Sings the Blues	1961	25.00	50.00	100.00
—Black vinyl; this value assumes that this is in true stereo, as the red vinyl version is, but this has not been confirmed					
❑ CLP-5156 [M]	Jimmy Witherspoon	1959	20.00	40.00	80.00
—Black label, silver print					
❑ CLP-5156 [M]	Jimmy Witherspoon	1961	6.25	12.50	25.00
—Gray label, black print					
❑ CLP-5192 [M]	Jimmy Witherspoon Sings the Blues	1959	20.00	40.00	80.00
—Black label, silver print					
❑ CLP-5192 [M]	Jimmy Witherspoon Sings the Blues	1961	6.25	12.50	25.00
—Gray label, black print					
FANTASY					
❑ OBC-511	Evenin' Blues	1988	3.00	6.00	12.00
—Reissue of Prestige 7300					
❑ OBC-527	Baby, Baby, Baby	1990	3.00	6.00	12.00
—Reissue of Prestige 7290					
❑ 9660	Rockin' L.A.	1989	3.00	6.00	12.00
❑ 24701 [(2)]	The 'Spoon Concerts	1972	5.00	10.00	20.00
HIFI					
❑ R-421 [M]	At the Monterey Jazz Festival	1959	25.00	50.00	100.00
❑ SR-421 [S]	At the Monterey Jazz Festival	1959	15.00	30.00	60.00
❑ R-422 [M]	Feelin' the Spirit	1959	25.00	50.00	100.00
❑ SR-422 [S]	Feelin' the Spirit	1959	15.00	30.00	60.00
❑ R-426 [M]	Jimmy Witherspoon at the Renaissance	1959	25.00	50.00	100.00
❑ SR-426 [S]	Jimmy Witherspoon at the Renaissance	1959	15.00	30.00	60.00
JAZZ MAN					
❑ 5013	Jimmy Witherspoon Sings the Blues	1980	3.00	6.00	12.00
LAX					
❑ PW 37115	Love Is a Five Letter Word	1981	2.50	5.00	10.00
—Reissue of Capitol LP					
MUSE					
❑ MR-5288	Jimmy Witherspoon Sings the Blues	1983	2.50	5.00	10.00
❑ MR-5327	Midnight Lady Called the Blues	1986	2.50	5.00	10.00
PRESTIGE					
❑ PRLP-7290 [M]	Baby, Baby, Baby	1963	10.00	20.00	40.00
❑ PRST-7290 [S]	Baby, Baby, Baby	1963	10.00	20.00	40.00
❑ PRLP-7300 [M]	Evenin' Blues	1964	10.00	20.00	40.00
❑ PRST-7300 [S]	Evenin' Blues	1964	10.00	20.00	40.00
❑ PRLP-7314 [M]	Blues Around the Clock	1964	10.00	20.00	40.00
❑ PRST-7314 [S]	Blues Around the Clock	1964	10.00	20.00	40.00
❑ PRLP-7327 [M]	Blue Spoon	1964	10.00	20.00	40.00
❑ PRST-7327 [S]	Blue Spoon	1964	10.00	20.00	40.00
❑ PRLP-7356 [M]	Some of My Best Friends Are the Blues	1965	6.25	12.50	25.00
❑ PRST-7356 [S]	Some of My Best Friends Are the Blues	1965	6.25	12.50	25.00
❑ PRLP-7418 [M]	Spoon in London	1966	6.25	12.50	25.00
❑ PRST-7418 [S]	Spoon in London	1966	6.25	12.50	25.00
❑ PRLP-7475 [M]	Blues for Easy Livers	1967	6.25	12.50	25.00
❑ PRST-7475 [S]	Blues for Easy Livers	1967	5.00	10.00	20.00
❑ PRST-7713	The Best of Jimmy Witherspoon	1969	5.00	10.00	20.00
❑ 7855	Mean Old Frisco	1974	3.75	7.50	15.00

Number	Title (A Side/B Side)	Yr	VG	VG+	NM
RCA VICTOR					
❑ ANL1-1048	Goin' to Kansas City Blues	1976	2.50	5.00	10.00
—Reissue					
❑ LPM-1639 [M]	Goin' to Kansas City Blues	1957	25.00	50.00	100.00
REPRISE					
❑ R-2008 [M]	Spoon	1961	10.00	20.00	40.00
❑ R9-2008 [S]	Spoon	1961	15.00	30.00	60.00
❑ R-6012 [M]	Hey, Mrs. Jones	1961	10.00	20.00	40.00
❑ R9-6012 [S]	Hey, Mrs. Jones	1961	15.00	30.00	60.00
❑ R-6059 [M]	Roots	1962	10.00	20.00	40.00
❑ R9-6059 [S]	Roots	1962	15.00	30.00	60.00
UNITED					
❑ 7715	A Spoonful of Blues	197?	3.00	6.00	12.00
VERVE					
❑ V-5007 [M]	Blue Point of View	1966	5.00	10.00	20.00
❑ V6-5007 [S]	Blue Point of View	1966	6.25	12.50	25.00
❑ V-5030 [M]	Blues Is Now	1967	6.25	12.50	25.00
❑ V6-5030 [S]	Blues Is Now	1967	5.00	10.00	20.00
❑ V-5050 [M]	A Spoonful of Soul	1968	7.50	15.00	30.00
❑ V6-5050 [S]	A Spoonful of Soul	1968	5.00	10.00	20.00
WORLD PACIFIC					
❑ WP-1267 [M]	Singin' the Blues	1959	25.00	50.00	100.00
❑ WP-1402 [M]	There's Good Rockin' Tonight	1961	15.00	30.00	60.00
—Reissue of 1267					

WITHERSPOON, JIMMY, AND RICHARD "GROOVE" HOLMES
Albums

Number	Title (A Side/B Side)	Yr	VG	VG+	NM
OLYMPIC GOLD MEDAL					
❑ 7107	Groovin' and Spoonin'	1974	3.00	6.00	12.00
SURREY					
❑ S-1106 [M]	Blues for Spoon and Groove	1965	6.25	12.50	25.00
❑ SS-1106 [S]	Blues for Spoon and Groove	1965	7.50	15.00	30.00

WITHERSPOON, JIMMY, AND GERRY MULLIGAN
Albums

Number	Title (A Side/B Side)	Yr	VG	VG+	NM
ARCHIVE OF FOLK AND JAZZ					
❑ 264	Jimmy Witherspoon and Gerry Mulligan	197?	3.00	6.00	12.00

WITHERSPOON, JIMMY, AND BEN WEBSTER
Albums

Number	Title (A Side/B Side)	Yr	VG	VG+	NM
VERVE					
❑ V6-8835	Previously Unreleased Recordings	197?	3.75	7.50	15.00

WOMACK, BOBBY
Also see THE VALENTINOS.

12-Inch Singles

Number	Title (A Side/B Side)	Yr	VG	VG+	NM
MCA					
❑ L33-17104 [DJ]	Gypsy Woman/Whatever Happened to the Times? (2 versions)	1986	2.00	4.00	8.00
❑ 23688	(I Wanna) Make Love to You/Whatever Happened to the Times?	1986	2.00	4.00	8.00
❑ 23795	Living in a Box (3 versions)	1987	—	3.00	6.00
❑ 23827	Outside Myself (3 versions)	1988	—	3.00	6.00
SOLAR					
❑ ZAS 1923 [DJ]	Save the Children (3 versions)	1989	2.00	4.00	8.00

45s

Number	Title (A Side/B Side)	Yr	VG	VG+	NM
ARISTA					
❑ 0421	How Could You Break My Heart/I Honestly Love You	1979	—	2.00	4.00
❑ 0446	The Roads of Life/Give It Up	1979	—	2.00	4.00
ATLANTIC					
❑ 2388	Night Train/It's Karate Time	1967	2.50	5.00	10.00
BEVERLY GLEN					
❑ 2000	If You Think You're Lonely Now/Secrets	1981	—	2.00	4.00
❑ 2001	Where Do We Go from Here/Just My Imagination	1982	—	2.00	4.00
❑ 2012	Love Has Finally Come at Last/American Dream	1984	—	2.00	4.00
—With Patti LaBelle					
❑ 2014	Tell Me Why/Through the Eyes of a Child	1984	—	2.00	4.00
—B-side with Patti LaBelle					
❑ 2018	It Takes a Lot of Strength to Say Goodbye/Who's Foolin' Who	1984	—	2.00	4.00
—A-side with Patti LaBelle					
❑ 2021	Someday We'll All Be Free/I Wish I Had Someone to Go Home To	1985	—	2.00	4.00
❑ 2023	I'm So Proud/Searching for My Love	1985	—	2.00	4.00
CHECKER					
❑ 1122	Lonesome Man/I Found a True Love	1965	3.75	7.50	15.00
COLUMBIA					
❑ 10437	Home Is Where the Heart Is/We've Only Just Begun	1976	—	2.50	5.00
❑ 10493	Standing in the Safety Zone/A Change Is Gonna Come	1977	—	2.50	5.00
❑ 10672	Trust Your Heart/When Love Begins, Friendship Ends	1978	—	2.50	5.00
❑ 10732	Wind It Up/Stop Before We Start	1978	—	2.50	5.00
LIBERTY					
❑ 56186	I'm Gonna Forget About You/Don't Look Back	1970	2.00	4.00	8.00
❑ 56206	Something/Everybody's Talkin'	1970	2.00	4.00	8.00
MCA					
❑ 52624	I Wish He Didn't Trust Me So Much/Got to Be with You Tonight	1985	—	2.00	4.00

Number	Title (A Side/B Side)	Yr	VG	VG+	NM
❑ 52624 [PS]	I Wish He Didn't Trust Me So Much/Got to Be with You Tonight	1985	—	2.00	4.00
❑ 52709	Let Me Kiss It Where It Hurts/Check It Out	1985	—	2.00	4.00
❑ 52793	Gypsy Woman/What Evert Happened to the Times	1986	—	—	3.00
❑ 52955	(I Wanna) Make Love to You/The Launch	1986	—	—	3.00
❑ 52955 [PS]	(I Wanna) Make Love to You/The Launch	1986	—	—	3.00
❑ 53190	Living in a Box/I Can't Stay Mad	1987	—	—	3.00
❑ 53263	Outside Myself/A Woman Likes to Hear Than	1988	—	—	3.00
MINIT					
❑ 32024	Baby, I Can't Stand It/Trust Me	1967	2.50	5.00	10.00
❑ 32030	Somebody Special/Broadway Walk	1967	2.50	5.00	10.00
❑ 32037	What Is This/What You Gonna Do (When Your Love Is Gone)	1968	2.50	5.00	10.00
❑ 32048	Fly to the Moon/Take Me	1968	2.50	5.00	10.00
❑ 32055	California Dreamin'/Baby, You Oughta Think It Over	1968	2.50	5.00	10.00
❑ 32059	I Left My Heart in San Francisco/Love, The Time Is Now	1969	2.00	4.00	8.00
❑ 32071	It's Gonna Rain/Thank You	1969	2.00	4.00	8.00
❑ 32081	How I Miss You Baby/Tried and Convicted	1969	2.00	4.00	8.00
❑ 32093	More Than I Can Stand/Arkansas State Prison	1970	2.00	4.00	8.00
SOLAR					
❑ 74006	Save the Children/(Instrumental)	1989	—	—	3.00
THE RIGHT STUFF					
❑ 58815	Dear Santa Claus/Dear Santa Claus (Kids Version)	1999	—	—	3.00
UNITED ARTISTS					
❑ 0123	That's the Way I Feel About Cha/Woman's Gotta Have It	1973	—	2.00	4.00
—"Silver Spotlight Series" reissue					
❑ XW196	Across 110th Street/Hang On In There	1973	—	2.50	5.00
❑ XW255	Nobody Wants You When You're Down and Out/I'm Thru Trying to Prove My Love	1973	—	2.50	5.00
❑ XW375	Lookin' for a Love/Let It Hang Out	1973	—	2.50	5.00
❑ XW439	You're Welcome, Stop On By/I Don't Want to Be Hurt	1974	—	2.50	5.00
❑ XW525	Lookin' for a Love/Nobody Wants You When You're Down and Out	1974	—	2.00	4.00
—Reissue					
❑ XW526	Harry Hippie/Sweet Caroline	1974	—	2.00	4.00
—Reissue					
❑ XW527	California Dreamin'/Fly Me to the Moon	1974	—	2.50	5.00
❑ XW561	I Don't Know/Yes, Jesus Loves Me	1974	—	2.50	5.00
❑ XW621	Check It Out/Interlude No. 2	1975	—	2.50	5.00
❑ XW674	It's All Over Now/Git It	1975	—	2.50	5.00
❑ XW735	Where There's a Will, There's a Way/Everything's Gonna Be Alright	1975	—	2.50	5.00
❑ XW763	Daylight/Trust Me	1976	—	2.50	5.00
❑ XW804	I Feel a Groove Comin' On/Trust Me	1976	—	2.50	5.00
❑ 50773	The Preacher/More Than I Can Stand	1971	—	3.00	6.00
❑ 50816	Communication/Fire and Rain	1971	—	3.00	6.00
❑ 50847	That's the Way I Feel About 'Cha/Come L'Amore	1971	—	3.00	6.00
❑ 50902	Woman's Gotta Have It/Give It Back	1972	—	3.00	6.00
❑ 50946	Harry Hippie/Sweet Caroline (Good Times Never Seemed So Good)	1972	—	3.00	6.00
❑ 50988 [DJ]	Harry Hippie (mono/stereo)	1972	2.00	4.00	8.00
—Apparently, no stock copy exists					

Albums

Number	Title (A Side/B Side)	Yr	VG	VG+	NM
ARISTA					
❑ AB 4222	Roads of Life	1979	2.50	5.00	10.00
BEVERLY GLEN					
❑ 10000	The Poet	1981	2.50	5.00	10.00
❑ 10003	The Poet II	1984	2.50	5.00	10.00
COLUMBIA					
❑ PC 34384	Home Is Where the Heart Is	1977	2.50	5.00	10.00
❑ JC 35083	Pieces	1978	2.50	5.00	10.00
LIBERTY					
❑ LST-7645	The Womack "Live"	1971	3.00	6.00	12.00
❑ LN-10171	Bobby Womack's Greatest Hits	198?	2.00	4.00	8.00
—Budget-line reissue of United Artists 346					
MCA					
❑ 5617	So Many Rivers	1985	2.00	4.00	8.00
MINIT					
❑ 24014	Fly Me to the Moon	1968	7.50	15.00	30.00
❑ 24027	My Prescription	1969	7.50	15.00	30.00
UNITED ARTISTS					
❑ UA-LA043-F	Facts of Life	1973	3.00	6.00	12.00
❑ UA-LA199-G	Lookin' for a Love Again	1974	3.00	6.00	12.00
❑ UA-LA346-G	Bobby Womack's Greatest Hits	1974	3.00	6.00	12.00
❑ UA-LA353-G	I Don't Know What the World Is Coming To	1975	3.00	6.00	12.00
❑ UA-LA544-G	Safety Zone	1975	3.00	6.00	12.00
❑ UA-LA638-G	B.W. Goes C and W	1976	3.00	6.00	12.00
❑ LM-1002	Understanding	1980	2.00	4.00	8.00
—Reissue of 5577					
❑ UAS-5225	Across 110th Street	1972	3.00	6.00	12.00
❑ UAS-5539	Communication	1971	3.00	6.00	12.00
❑ UAS-5577	Understanding	1972	3.00	6.00	12.00

WONDER, STEVIE

Also see PAUL McCARTNEY AND STEVIE WONDER.

12-Inch Singles

MOTOWN

Number	Title (A Side/B Side)	Yr	VG	VG+	NM
❑ PR 161 [DJ]	Love Light in Flight (Special 12" Version 6:30) (Instrumental 7:38)	1984	2.50	5.00	10.00
❑ L33-1065 [DJ]	Keep Our Love Alive/(Instrumental)	1990	2.00	4.00	8.00
❑ L33-1093 [DJ]	Gotta Have You (3 versions)	1991	2.50	5.00	10.00
❑ 37463 1215 1 [DJ]	Tomorrow Robins Will Sing (7 versions)	1995	2.50	5.00	10.00
❑ 37463 1261 1 [DJ]	For Your Love (Single Version) (LP Version) (Instrumental) (A Cappella)	1995	2.50	5.00	10.00
❑ 37463 1482 1 [DJ]	Kiss Lonely Goodbye (6 versions)	1996	3.75	7.50	15.00
❑ L33-1602 [DJ]	Fun Day (Edit) (LP) (Instrumental)	1991	2.50	5.00	10.00
❑ L33-1690 [DJ]	Fun Day (8 versions)	1991	3.00	6.00	12.00
❑ 4517 MG	Happy Birthday/Martin Luther King: Excerpts from His Speeches	1984	20.00	40.00	80.00
❑ 4527 MG	Don't Drive Drunk (12" Version 8:18) (Instrumental 8:27)/Did I Hear You Say You Love Me (8:27)	1984	2.00	4.00	8.00
❑ 4593 MG	Skeletons (6:43)/(Instrumental)	1987	2.00	4.00	8.00
❑ MOT-4616	My Eyes Don't Cry (Extended Version 6:30) (Radio Edit 5:18) (Dub Mix 7:21)	1988	2.00	4.00	8.00
❑ MOT-4626	With Each Beat of My Heart (LP) (Edit) (Instrumental)	1988	2.00	4.00	8.00
❑ MOT12-4665	Keep Our Love Alive/(Instrumental)	1990	2.00	4.00	8.00
❑ MOT12-4759	Gotta Have You (3 versions)/Feeding Off the Love of the Land	1991	2.50	5.00	10.00
❑ L33-17755 [DJ]	With Each Beat of My Heart (LP) (Edit) (Instrumental)	1987	2.00	4.00	8.00

TAMLA

Number	Title (A Side/B Side)	Yr	VG	VG+	NM
❑ PR 61 [DJ]	A Seed's a Star-Tree Medley/Power Flower//Black Orchid/Outside My Window	1979	5.00	10.00	20.00
—Promo-only sampler for "Journey Through the Secret Life of Plants"					
❑ PR 76 [DJ]	Master Blaster (Jammin') (6:11)/Master Blaster (Dub) (6:27)	1980	17.50	35.00	70.00
❑ PR 77 [DJ]	I Ain't Gonna Stand For It//All I Do/Did I Hear You Say You Love Me	1980	15.00	30.00	60.00
—Promo-only sampler for "Hotter Than July"					
❑ PR 98/99 [(2) DJ]	Do I Do (10:27) (Instrumental 10:27)//Front Line (6:01) (Instrumental 6:01)	1982	6.25	12.50	25.00
—Two-record promo set					
❑ PR 186 [DJ]	Land of La La (8:40)/(Instrumental)	1986	2.00	4.00	8.00
❑ 4548 TG	Part Time Lover (12-Inch Vocal Version 8:20) (12-Inch Instrumental 8:20)	1985	2.50	5.00	10.00
❑ 4553 TG	Go Home (12" Version 9:22)/(Radio Edit of 12" Version 6:26) (Instrumental 8:36)	1985	2.50	5.00	10.00

45s

GORDY

Number	Title (A Side/B Side)	Yr	VG	VG+	NM
❑ 7076	Alfie/More Than a Dream	1968	6.25	12.50	25.00
—As "Eivets Rednow" (read it backwards)					

MOTOWN

Number	Title (A Side/B Side)	Yr	VG	VG+	NM
❑ 1745	I Just Called to Say I Love You/(Instrumental)	1984	—	—	3.00
❑ 1745 [PS]	I Just Called to Say I Love You/(Instrumental)	1984	10.00	20.00	40.00
—Sleeve is labeled promo only, though it has been found on the (very) occasional stock copy					
❑ 1769	Love Light in Flight/It's More Than You	1984	—	—	3.00
❑ 1769 [PS]	Love Light in Flight/It's More Than You	1984	—	2.00	4.00
❑ 1907	Skeletons/(Instrumental)	1987	—	—	3.00
❑ 1907 [PS]	Skeletons/(Instrumental)	1987	—	2.00	4.00
❑ 1919	You Will Know/(Instrumental)	1988	—	—	3.00
❑ 1919 [DJ]	You Will Know/You Will Know-Stevie Wonder Interview	1988	—	3.00	6.00
—Promo-only release					
❑ 1919 [PS]	You Will Know/(Instrumental)	1988	—	2.00	4.00
❑ 1919 [PS]	You Will Know/You Will Know-Stevie Wonder Interview	1988	—	3.00	6.00
—Only the promo sleeve mentions the interview					
❑ 1946	My Eyes Don't Cry/(Instrumental)	1988	—	—	3.00
❑ 1946 [PS]	My Eyes Don't Cry/(Instrumental)	1988	—	—	3.00
❑ 1953	With Each Beat of My Heart/(Instrumental)	1989	—	—	3.00
❑ 1990	Keep Our Love Alive/(Instrumental)	1990	—	2.50	5.00
❑ 2081	Gotta Have You/Feeding Off the Love of the Land	1991	—	2.00	4.00
❑ 2127	Fun Day/(Instrumental)	1991	—	2.00	4.00
❑ 2143	These Three Words (same on both sides)	1991	—	2.00	4.00
❑ 860310-7	For Your Love/(Instrumental)	1995	—	2.00	4.00
❑ 860418-7	Tomorrow Robins Will Sing/For Your Love	1995	—	2.00	4.00

MOTOWN YESTERYEAR

Number	Title (A Side/B Side)	Yr	VG	VG+	NM
❑ Y 620F	I Wish/Sir Duke	1978	—	—	3.00
—Reissue					
❑ Y 621F	Another Star/As	1978	—	—	3.00
—Reissue					
❑ Y 646F	Master Blaster (Jammin')/Master Blaster (Dub)	1982	—	—	3.00
—Reissue					
❑ Y 647F	I Ain't Gonna Stand For It/Lately	1982	—	—	3.00
—Reissue					
❑ Y 657F	That Girl/Do I Do	1983	—	—	3.00
—Reissue					
❑ Y 684F	I Just Called to Say I Love You/Love Light in Flight	1985	—	—	3.00
—Reissue					
❑ Y 685F	Don't Drive Drunk/(Instrumental)	1985	—	—	3.00
—First U.S. edition of this song on 45					

TAMLA

Number	Title (A Side/B Side)	Yr	VG	VG+	NM
❑ 1602	That Girl/All I Do	1982	—	2.00	4.00
❑ 1612	Do I Do/Rocket Love	1982	—	2.00	4.00
❑ 1639	Ribbon in the Sky/Black Orchid	1982	—	2.00	4.00
❑ 1639 [PS]	Ribbon in the Sky/Black Orchid	1982	—	2.00	4.00
❑ 1808	Part-Time Lover/(Instrumental)	1985	—	—	3.00
❑ 1808 [PS]	Part-Time Lover/(Instrumental)	1985	—	2.00	4.00
❑ 1817	Go Home/(Instrumental)	1985	—	—	3.00
❑ 1817 [PS]	Go Home/(Instrumental)	1985	—	2.00	4.00
❑ 1832	Overjoyed/(Instrumental)	1986	—	—	3.00
❑ 1832 [PS]	Overjoyed/(Instrumental)	1986	—	2.00	4.00
❑ 1846	Land of La La/(Instrumental)	1986	—	—	3.00
❑ 1846 [PS]	Land of La La/(Instrumental)	1986	—	2.00	4.00
❑ 54061	I Call It Pretty Music But The Old People Call It the Blues (Part 1)/I Call It Pretty Music But The Old People Call It the Blues (Part 2)	1962	7.50	15.00	30.00
❑ 54061 [PS]	I Call It Pretty Music But The Old People Call It the Blues (Part 1)/I Call It Pretty Music But The Old People Call It the Blues (Part 2)	1962	20.00	40.00	80.00
❑ 54070	Little Water Boy/La La La La La	1962	6.25	12.50	25.00
❑ 54074	Contract on Love/Sunset	1963	6.25	12.50	25.00
❑ 54080	Fingertips — Pt. 2/Fingertips — Pt. 1	1963	5.00	10.00	20.00
❑ 54080 [PS]	Fingertips — Pt. 2/Fingertips — Pt. 1	1963	12.50	25.00	50.00
❑ 54086	Workout Stevie, Workout/Monkey Talk	1963	3.75	7.50	15.00
❑ 54090	Castles in the Sand/Thank You (For Loving Me All the Way)	1964	3.75	7.50	15.00
—Up to and including this, as "Little Stevie Wonder"					
❑ 54096	Hey Harmonica Man/This Little Girl	1964	3.75	7.50	15.00
❑ 54096 [PS]	Hey Harmonica Man/This Little Girl	1964	10.00	20.00	40.00
❑ 54103	Sad Boy/Happy Street	1964	5.00	10.00	20.00
❑ 54108	Pretty Little Angel/Tears in Vain	1964	—	—	—
—Unreleased					
❑ 54114	Kiss Me Baby/Tears in Vain	1965	3.00	6.00	12.00
❑ 54119	High Heel Sneakers/Music Talk	1965	3.00	6.00	12.00
❑ 54119	High Heel Sneakers/Funny How Time Slips Away	1965	5.00	10.00	20.00
❑ 54124	Uptight (Everything's Alright)/Purple Rain Drops	1965	3.75	7.50	15.00
❑ 54130	Nothing's Too Good for My Baby/With a Child's Heart	1966	3.00	6.00	12.00
❑ 54136	Blowin' in the Wind/Ain't That Asking for Trouble	1966	3.00	6.00	12.00
❑ 54136 [PS]	Blowin' in the Wind/Ain't That Asking for Trouble	1966	6.25	12.50	25.00
❑ 54139	A Place in the Sun/Sylvia	1966	3.00	6.00	12.00
❑ 54139 [PS]	A Place in the Sun/Sylvia	1966	6.25	12.50	25.00
❑ 54142	Some Day at Christmas/The Miracles of Christmas	1966	3.75	7.50	15.00
❑ 54147	Travlin' Man/Hey Love	1967	2.50	5.00	10.00
❑ 54151	I Was Made to Love Her/Hold Me	1967	2.50	5.00	10.00
❑ 54157	I'm Wondering/Every Time I See You I Go Wild	1967	2.50	5.00	10.00
❑ 54165	Shoo-Be-Doo-Be-Doo-Da-Day/Why Don't You Lead Me to Love	1968	2.00	4.00	8.00
❑ 54168	You Met Your Match/My Girl	1968	2.00	4.00	8.00
❑ 54174	For Once in My Life/Angie Girl	1968	2.00	4.00	8.00
❑ 54180	My Cherie Amour/Don't Know Why I Love You	1969	2.00	4.00	8.00
—Re-release with A and B side switched and new title on B-side					
❑ 54180	I Don't Know Why/My Cherie Amour	1969	2.50	5.00	10.00
❑ 54188	Yester-Me, Yester-You, Yesterday/I'd Be a Fool Right Now	1969	2.00	4.00	8.00
❑ 54191	Never Had a Dream Come True/Somebody Knows, Somebody Cares	1970	—	3.00	6.00
❑ 54196	Signed, Sealed, Delivered, I'm Yours/I'm More Than Happy	1970	—	3.00	6.00
❑ 54200	Heaven Help Us All/I Gotta Have a Song	1970	—	3.00	6.00
❑ 54202	We Can Work It Out/Never Dreamed You'd Leave in Summer	1971	—	3.00	6.00
❑ 54208	If You Really Love Me/Think of Me As Your Soldier	1971	—	3.00	6.00
❑ 54214	What Christmas Means to Me/Bedtime for Toys	1971	—	3.00	6.00
❑ 54216	Superwoman (Where Were You When I Needed You)/I Love Every Little Thing About You	1972	—	3.00	6.00
❑ 54223	Keep On Running/Evil	1972	—	3.00	6.00
❑ 54226	Superstition/You've Got It Bad Girl	1972	—	2.50	5.00
❑ 54232	You Are the Sunshine of My Life/Tuesday Heartbreak	1973	—	2.50	5.00
❑ 54235	Higher Ground/Too High	1973	—	2.50	5.00
❑ 54242	Living for the City/Visions	1973	—	2.50	5.00
❑ 54245	Don't You Worry 'Bout a Thing/Blame It on the Sun	1974	—	2.50	5.00
❑ 54252	You Haven't Done Nothin'/Big Brother	1974	—	2.50	5.00
❑ 54254	Boogie On Raggae Woman/Seems So Long	1974	—	3.00	6.00
—With incorrect spelling of A-side					
❑ 54254	Boogie On Reggae Woman/Seems So Long	1974	—	2.50	5.00
—With correct spelling of A-side					
❑ 54274	I Wish/You and I	1976	—	2.50	5.00
❑ 54281	Sir Duke/He's Misstra Know-It-All	1977	—	2.50	5.00
❑ 54281 [PS]	Sir Duke/He's Misstra Know-It-All	1977	2.50	5.00	10.00
❑ 54286	Another Star/Creepin'	1977	—	2.50	5.00
❑ 54291	As/Contusion	1977	—	2.50	5.00
❑ 54303	Send One Your Love/(Instrumental)	1979	—	2.00	4.00
❑ 54303 [PS]	Send One Your Love/(Instrumental)	1979	—	3.00	6.00
❑ 54308	Outside My Window/Same Old Story	1980	—	2.00	4.00
❑ 54308 [PS]	Outside My Window/Same Old Story	1980	—	3.00	6.00
❑ 54317	Master Blaster (Jammin')/(Instrumental)	1980	—	2.00	4.00
❑ 54317 [PS]	Master Blaster (Jammin')/(Instrumental)	1980	—	3.00	6.00
❑ 54320	I Ain't Gonna Stand For It/Knocks Me Off My Feet	1980	—	2.00	4.00
❑ 54323	Lately/If It's Magic	1981	—	2.00	4.00
❑ 54328	Did I Hear You Say You Love Me/As If You Read My Mind	1981	—	2.00	4.00
❑ 54331	Happy Birthday/(Instrumental)	1981	—	—	—
—Canceled					

TOPPS/MOTOWN

Number	Title (A Side/B Side)	Yr	VG	VG+	NM
❑ 8	Fingertips Part 2	1967	18.75	37.50	75.00
—Cardboard record					

Mary Wells continued to record after she left Motown, but with nowhere near the success. In 1968, she issued *Servin' Up Some Soul* on the Jubilee label, which also failed to sell.

Featuring most of his early hits, *Here's Larry Williams* came out on Specialty in 1959.

This highly collectible album was issued in the wake of Maurice Williams and the Zodiacs' biggest hit, "Stay."

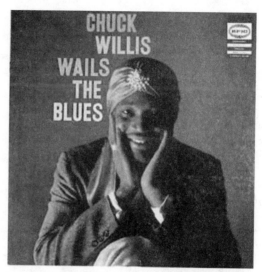

Issued shortly after his death in 1958, *Chuck Willis Wails the Blues* compiles singles he recorded before his hit days at Atlantic. As such, it's very hard to find today.

Jackie Wilson had a prodigious though uneven output in his career. Roughly a dozen EPs of his material were issued; the most sought after is the stereo version of *That's Why.*

In 1970, Stevie Wonder made the Tamla LP *Signed, Sealed and Delivered.* A year later, he had gained a large amount of creative control over his future work.

Number	Title (A Side/B Side)	Yr	VG	VG+	NM
☐ 10	Uptight (Everything's Alright)	1967	18.75	37.50	75.00

—Cardboard record

7-Inch Extended Plays

TAMLA

Number	Title (A Side/B Side)	Yr	VG	VG+	NM
☐ T 340EP	Saturn/Ebony Eyes//All Day Sucker/Easy Goin' Evening	1976	—	2.00	4.00

—Called "A Something's Extra for Songs in the Key of Life," this was issued with the 2-LP set of the same name and is sometimes found separately, though it was never sold separately; not issued with picture sleeve

Albums

GORDY

Number	Title (A Side/B Side)	Yr	VG	VG+	NM
☐ GS 932	Eivets Rednow	1968	7.50	15.00	30.00

—As "Eivets Rednow"

JOBETE

Number	Title (A Side/B Side)	Yr	VG	VG+	NM
☐ JSA-6253 [DJ]	The Wonder of Stevie	1988	5.00	10.00	20.00

—Publisher's demo with excerpts of 105 (!) Stevie Wonder songs

MOTOWN

Number	Title (A Side/B Side)	Yr	VG	VG+	NM
☐ M5-131V1	Recorded Live/Little Stevie Wonder/The 12 Year Old Genius	1981	3.00	6.00	12.00
—Reissue of Tamla 240					
☐ M5-150V1	With a Song in My Heart	1981	3.00	6.00	12.00
—Reissue of Tamla 250					
☐ M5-166V1	Down to Earth	1981	3.00	6.00	12.00
—Reissue of Tamla 272					
☐ M5-173V1	Tribute to Uncle Ray	1981	3.00	6.00	12.00
—Reissue of Tamla 232					
☐ M5-176V1	Signed, Sealed and Delivered	1981	3.00	6.00	12.00
—Reissue of Tamla 304					
☐ M5-179V1	My Cherie Amour	1981	3.00	6.00	12.00
—Reissue of Tamla 296					
☐ M5-183V1	Up-Tight Everything's Alright	1981	3.00	6.00	12.00
—Reissue of Tamla 268					
☐ M5-219V1	The Jazz Soul of Little Stevie	1981	3.00	6.00	12.00
—Reissue of Tamla 233					
☐ 31453 0238-1 [(2) DJ]	Conversation Peace	1995	6.25	12.50	25.00
—Vinyl is promo only; white cover with custom sticker					
☐ M9-804A3 [(3)]	Looking Back	1977	6.25	12.50	25.00
—Withdrawn after Stevie Wonder objected to its release					
☐ 5255 ML	Someday at Christmas	1982	2.50	5.00	10.00
—Reissue of Tamla 281					
☐ 6108 ML	The Woman in Red	1984	3.00	6.00	12.00
—With no sticker proclaiming "New Stevie Wonder Album"					
☐ 6108 ML	The Woman in Red	1984	2.50	5.00	10.00
—With sticker at top proclaiming "New Stevie Wonder Album"					
☐ 6248 ML	Characters	1987	2.50	5.00	10.00
☐ 6291 ML	Music from the Movie Jungle Fever	1991	5.00	10.00	20.00

TAMLA

Number	Title (A Side/B Side)	Yr	VG	VG+	NM
☐ T 232 [M]	Tribute to Uncle Ray	1962	37.50	75.00	150.00
☐ T 233 [M]	The Jazz Soul of Little Stevie	1962	37.50	75.00	150.00
☐ T 240 [M]	Recorded Live/Little Stevie Wonder/The 12 Year Old Genius	1963	30.00	60.00	120.00
—The above three LPs as "Little Stevie Wonder"					
☐ T 248 [M]	Workout Stevie, Workout	1963	250.00	500.00	1000.
—Canceled; test pressings or acetates may exist					
☐ T 250 [M]	With a Song in My Heart	1964	20.00	40.00	80.00
☐ T 255 [M]	Stevie at the Beach	1964	20.00	40.00	80.00
☐ T 268 [M]	Up-Tight Everything's Alright	1966	6.25	12.50	25.00
☐ TS 268 [S]	Up-Tight Everything's Alright	1966	7.50	15.00	30.00
☐ T 272 [M]	Down to Earth	1966	5.00	10.00	20.00
☐ TS 272 [S]	Down to Earth	1966	6.25	12.50	25.00
☐ T 279 [M]	I Was Made to Love Her	1967	5.00	10.00	20.00
☐ TS 279 [S]	I Was Made to Love Her	1967	6.25	12.50	25.00
☐ T 281 [M]	Someday at Christmas	1967	7.50	15.00	30.00
☐ TS 281 [S]	Someday at Christmas	1967	10.00	20.00	40.00
☐ T 282 [M]	Greatest Hits	1968	7.50	15.00	30.00
☐ TS 282 [S]	Greatest Hits	1968	5.00	10.00	20.00
☐ TS 291	For Once in My Life	1968	5.00	10.00	20.00
☐ TS 296	My Cherie Amour	1969	5.00	10.00	20.00
☐ TS 298	Stevie Wonder Live	1970	5.00	10.00	20.00
☐ TS 304	Signed Sealed and Delivered	1970	5.00	10.00	20.00
☐ TS 308	Where I'm Coming From	1971	5.00	10.00	20.00
☐ T 313L	Stevie Wonder's Greatest Hits Vol. 2	1971	5.00	10.00	20.00
—Some, if not all, LP covers have the title mis-punctuated as "Stevie Wonders' Greatest Hits Vol. 2"					
☐ T 314L	Music of My Mind	1972	5.00	10.00	20.00
☐ T 319L	Talking Book	1972	3.75	7.50	15.00
—Original pressings have a braille note on cover					
☐ T 319L	Talking Book	1973	2.50	5.00	10.00
—No braille note on cover					
☐ T 326L	Innervisions	1973	3.75	7.50	15.00
☐ T6-332S1	Fulfillingness' First Finale	1974	3.75	7.50	15.00
☐ T13-340C2 [(2)]	Songs in the Key of Life	1976	5.00	10.00	20.00
—With booklet and bonus 7-inch EP (deduct 25% if missing)					
☐ T7-362R1	Someday at Christmas	1978	5.00	10.00	20.00
—Unusual reissue of 281					
☐ T13-371C2 [(2)]	Journey Through the Secret Life of Plants	1979	3.75	7.50	15.00
☐ T8-373S1	Hotter Than July	1980	3.00	6.00	12.00
☐ 6002 TL2 [(2)]	Stevie Wonder's Original Musiquarium I	1982	3.75	7.50	15.00
☐ 6134 TL	In Square Circle	1985	2.50	5.00	10.00

WONDER, STEVIE, AND MICHAEL JACKSON

Also see each artist's individual listings.

12-Inch Singles

MOTOWN

Number	Title (A Side/B Side)	Yr	VG	VG+	NM
☐ 4606 MG	Get It (6:44) (Instrumental 6:47)	1988	2.00	4.00	8.00

45s

MOTOWN

Number	Title (A Side/B Side)	Yr	VG	VG+	NM
☐ 1930	Get It/(Instrumental)	1988	—	—	3.00
☐ 1930 [PS]	Get It/(Instrumental)	1988	—	—	3.00

WONDERETTES, THE

45s

ENTERPRISE

Number	Title (A Side/B Side)	Yr	VG	VG+	NM
☐ 5025	Love's Got a Hold on Me/Work Out Fine	1964	6.25	12.50	25.00

RUBY

Number	Title (A Side/B Side)	Yr	VG	VG+	NM
☐ 5065	I Feel Strange/Wait Until Tonight	1965	10.00	20.00	40.00

UNITED ARTISTS

Number	Title (A Side/B Side)	Yr	VG	VG+	NM
☐ 944	I Feel Strange/Wait Until Tonight	1965	6.25	12.50	25.00
☐ 997	Mend My Broken Heart/And If I Had My Way	1966	5.00	10.00	20.00

—By "Rose St. John and the Wonderettes"

VEEP

Number	Title (A Side/B Side)	Yr	VG	VG+	NM
☐ 1231	Fool Don't Laugh/I Know the Meeting	1966	6.25	12.50	25.00

—As "Rose St. John and the Wonderettes"

WOODS, MICKEY

45s

TAMLA

Number	Title (A Side/B Side)	Yr	VG	VG+	NM
☐ 54039	They Rode Through the Valley/Poor Sam Jones	1961	12.50	25.00	50.00
☐ 54052	Please Mr. Kennedy/(They Call Me) Cupid	1962	10.00	20.00	40.00

WRENS, THE

45s

RAMA

Number	Title (A Side/B Side)	Yr	VG	VG+	NM
☐ 53	Love's Something That's Made for Two/Beggin' for Love	1955	375.00	750.00	1500.
☐ 65	Come Back My Love/Beggin' for Love	1955	37.50	75.00	150.00
☐ 65	Come Back My Love/Eleven Roses	1955	100.00	200.00	400.00
☐ 110	Love's Something That's Made for Two/Eleven Roses	1955	75.00	150.00	300.00
☐ 174	Hey Girl/Serenade of the Bells	1955	100.00	200.00	400.00
☐ 184	I Won't Come to Your Wedding/What Makes You Do the Things That You Do	1956	100.00	200.00	400.00
☐ 194	C'est La Vie/C'est La Vie	1956	100.00	200.00	400.00

—B-side by Jimmy Wright and His Orchestra

WRIGHT, BETTY

12-Inch Singles

FIRST STRING

Number	Title (A Side/B Side)	Yr	VG	VG+	NM
☐ 268	I Can (2 versions)/Music Street	1986	2.50	5.00	10.00

JAMAICA

Number	Title (A Side/B Side)	Yr	VG	VG+	NM
☐ 9002	One Step Up, Two Steps Back (9:52) (7:57 Dub)	1984	2.00	4.00	8.00
☐ 9004	Sinderella (6:30) (5:28)	1985	2.00	4.00	8.00

MS. B.

Number	Title (A Side/B Side)	Yr	VG	VG+	NM
☐ 1217	From Pain to Joy (Project Mix)/From Pain to Joy (Project Mix with Rap)	1989	2.00	4.00	8.00
☐ 1230	We Down (5 versions)	1989	2.00	4.00	8.00

T.K. DISCO

Number	Title (A Side/B Side)	Yr	VG	VG+	NM
☐ 125	Lovin' Is Really My Game (2 versions)	1979	3.00	6.00	12.00

VISION

Number	Title (A Side/B Side)	Yr	VG	VG+	NM
☐ 7005	After the Pain (6:56)/After the Pain (Project Mix)	1988	2.00	4.00	8.00

45s

ALSTON

Number	Title (A Side/B Side)	Yr	VG	VG+	NM
☐ 3711	Shoorah! Shoorah!/Tonight Is the Night	1974	—	2.50	5.00
☐ 3713	Where Is the Love/My Baby Ain't My Baby Anymore	1975	—	2.50	5.00
☐ 3715	Ooola La/To Love and Be Loved	1975	—	2.50	5.00
☐ 3718	Slip and Do It/I Think I Better Think About It	1975	—	2.50	5.00
☐ 3719	Everybody Was Rockin'/Show Your Girl	1976	—	2.50	5.00
☐ 3722	If I Ever Do Wrong/Rock On Baby, Rock On	1976	—	2.50	5.00
☐ 3725	Life/If I Was a Kid	1976	—	2.50	5.00
☐ 3734	You Can't See for Lookin'/Sometime Kind of Thing	1977	—	2.50	5.00
☐ 3736	Man of Mine/Sweet	1978	—	2.50	5.00
☐ 3740	Tonight Is the Night (Part 1)/Tonight Is the Night (Part 2)	1978	—	2.50	5.00
☐ 3745	Lovin' Is Really My Game/A Song for You	1979	—	2.50	5.00
☐ 3747	My Love Is/I Believe It's Love	1979	—	2.50	5.00
☐ 3749	Thank You for the Many Things You've Done/ Child of the Man	1979	—	2.50	5.00
☐ 4569	Girls Can't Do What the Guys Do/Sweet Lovin' Daddy	1968	2.00	4.00	8.00
☐ 4571	He's Bad Bad Bad/Watch Out, Love	1968	2.00	4.00	8.00
☐ 4573	The Best Girls Don't Always Win/Circle of Heartbreaks	1969	2.00	4.00	8.00
☐ 4575	The Wrong Girl/The Joy of Becoming a Woman	1969	2.00	4.00	8.00
☐ 4580	I'm Not Free Hearted/A Woman Was Made for One Man	1969	2.00	4.00	8.00
☐ 4581	Soldier Boy/A Woman Was Made for One Man	1969	2.00	4.00	8.00
☐ 4587	Pure Love/If You Ain't Got It	1970	—	3.50	7.00
☐ 4589	I Found That Guy/If You Love Like I Love You	1970	—	3.50	7.00
☐ 4594	I Love the Way You Love/When We Get Together Again	1971	—	3.50	7.00
☐ 4601	Clean Up Woman/I'll Love You Forever	1971	—	3.00	6.00
☐ 4609	If You Love Me Like You Say You Love Me/I'm Gettin' Tired Baby	1972	—	3.00	6.00
☐ 4611	Is It You Girl/Crying in My Sleep	1972	—	3.00	6.00
☐ 4614	Baby Sitter/Outside Woman	1972	—	3.00	6.00
☐ 4617	It's Hard to Stop (Doing Something When It's Good to You)/Who'll Be the Fool	1973	—	3.00	6.00

Number	Title (A Side/B Side)	Yr	VG	VG+	NM
❑ 4619	Let Me Be Your Lovemaker/Jealous Man	1973	—	3.00	6.00
❑ 4620	It's Bad for Me to See You/One Thing Leads to Another	1974	—	3.00	6.00
❑ 4622	Secretary/Value Your Love	1974	—	3.00	6.00

EPIC

Number	Title (A Side/B Side)	Yr	VG	VG+	NM
❑ 02143	I Like Your Loving/Body Slang	1981	—	2.00	4.00
❑ 02521	Goodbye Him Hello You/Make Me Love the Rain	1981	—	2.00	4.00
❑ 03523	He's Older Now/Special Love	1983	—	2.00	4.00
❑ 03954	Burning Desire/Show Me	1983	—	2.00	4.00
❑ 51009	What Are We Gonna Do About It/I Believe in You	1981	—	2.00	4.00

FIRST STRING

Number	Title (A Side/B Side)	Yr	VG	VG+	NM
❑ 965	Pain/(B-side unknown)	1985	—	2.00	4.00
❑ 968	The Sun Don't Shine/Music Street	1986	—	2.00	4.00

JAMAICA

Number	Title (A Side/B Side)	Yr	VG	VG+	NM
❑ 3	One Step Up, Two Steps Back/(B-side unknown)	1984	—	2.00	4.00

MS. B.

Number	Title (A Side/B Side)	Yr	VG	VG+	NM
❑ 4501	No Pain, No Gain/(Instrumental)	1988	—	2.00	4.00
❑ 4503	After the Pain/Love Days	1988	—	2.00	4.00
❑ 4504	A Christmas To Remember/2nd Chapter Of The Book Of Mathew	1988	—	—	3.00
❑ 4505	From Pain to Joy/From Pain to Joy (The Project Mix)	1989	—	2.00	4.00
❑ 4508	Quiet Storm/We Down	1989	—	2.00	4.00

Albums

ALSTON

Number	Title (A Side/B Side)	Yr	VG	VG+	NM
❑ SD 33-388	I Love the Way You Love	1972	3.75	7.50	15.00
❑ 4400	Danger High Voltage	1974	3.00	6.00	12.00
❑ 4406	This Time for Real	1977	3.00	6.00	12.00
❑ 4408	Betty Wright Live	1978	3.00	6.00	12.00
❑ 4410	Betty Travelin' in the Wright Circle	1979	3.00	6.00	12.00
❑ SD 7026	Hard to Stop	1973	3.75	7.50	15.00

ATCO

Number	Title (A Side/B Side)	Yr	VG	VG+	NM
❑ SD 33-260	My First Time Around	1968	6.25	12.50	25.00

COLLECTABLES

Number	Title (A Side/B Side)	Yr	VG	VG+	NM
❑ COL-5118	Golden Classics	198?	2.50	5.00	10.00

EPIC

Number	Title (A Side/B Side)	Yr	VG	VG+	NM
❑ JE 36879	Betty Wright	1981	2.50	5.00	10.00
❑ FE 38558	Wright Back at You	1983	2.50	5.00	10.00

FANTASY

Number	Title (A Side/B Side)	Yr	VG	VG+	NM
❑ 9644	Sevens	1986	2.50	5.00	10.00

MS. B.

Number	Title (A Side/B Side)	Yr	VG	VG+	NM
❑ 3301	Mother Wit	1988	2.50	5.00	10.00
❑ 3318	Passion and Compassion	198?	3.75	7.50	15.00

WRIGHT, CHARLES, AND THE WATTS 103RD STREET RHYTHM BAND

45s

ABC

Number	Title (A Side/B Side)	Yr	VG	VG+	NM
❑ 12127	Is It Real/One Lie	1975	—	2.00	4.00

—*Charles Wright solo*

ABC DUNHILL

Number	Title (A Side/B Side)	Yr	VG	VG+	NM
❑ 4363	Liberated Lady/You Threw It All Away	1973	—	2.00	4.00
❑ 4364	(Well I'm) Doing What Cums Naturally Part 1/Part 2	1973	—	2.00	4.00
❑ 4381	The Weight of Hate/You Threw It All Away	1974	—	2.00	4.00
❑ 15027	Don't Rush Tomorrow/Is It Real	1974	—	2.00	4.00

KEYMEN

Number	Title (A Side/B Side)	Yr	VG	VG+	NM
❑ 108	Spreadin' Honey/Charlie	1967	2.50	5.00	10.00

—*As "The Watts 103rd Street Rhythm Band"*

WARNER BROS.

Number	Title (A Side/B Side)	Yr	VG	VG+	NM
❑ 7175	Brown Sugar/Caesar's Palace	1968	2.50	5.00	10.00

—*Through 7298, as "The Watts 103rd Street Rhythm Band"*

Number	Title (A Side/B Side)	Yr	VG	VG+	NM
❑ 7222	Bottomless/65 Bars and a Taste of Soul	1968	2.50	5.00	10.00
❑ 7250	Do Your Thing/A Dance, a Kiss, and a Song	1969	2.00	4.00	8.00
❑ 7298	Till You Get Enough/Light My Fire	1969	2.00	4.00	8.00
❑ 7338	Must Be Your Thing/Comment	1969	—	3.00	6.00
❑ 7365	Love Land/Sorry Charlie	1970	—	3.00	6.00
❑ 7417	Express Yourself/Living on Borrowed Time	1970	—	3.00	6.00
❑ 7475	Your Love (Means Everything to Me)/What Can You Bring Me	1971	—	2.50	5.00
❑ 7504	Nobody/Wine	1971	—	2.50	5.00
❑ 7577	I've Got Love/Let's Make Love — Not War	1972	—	2.50	5.00
❑ 7600	Soul Train/Run Judy Run	1972	—	2.50	5.00
❑ 7630	Here Comes the Sun/You Gotta Know Whatcha Doin'	1972	—	2.50	5.00

Albums

ABC

Number	Title (A Side/B Side)	Yr	VG	VG+	NM
❑ D-887	Lil' Encouragement	1975	3.00	6.00	12.00

ABC DUNHILL

Number	Title (A Side/B Side)	Yr	VG	VG+	NM
❑ DS-50162	[(2)]Doin' What Comes Naturally	1973	3.75	7.50	15.00
❑ DS-50187	Ninety Day Cycle People	1974	3.00	6.00	12.00

WARNER BROS.

Number	Title (A Side/B Side)	Yr	VG	VG+	NM
❑ WS 1741	The Watts 103rd Street Rhythm Band	1968	5.00	10.00	20.00

—*Green label with "W7" logo*

Number	Title (A Side/B Side)	Yr	VG	VG+	NM
❑ WS 1761	Together	1969	5.00	10.00	20.00

—*Green label with "W7" logo*

Number	Title (A Side/B Side)	Yr	VG	VG+	NM
❑ WS 1761	Together	1970	3.75	7.50	15.00

—*Green label with "WB" logo*

Number	Title (A Side/B Side)	Yr	VG	VG+	NM
❑ WS 1801	In the Jungle, Babe	1969	5.00	10.00	20.00

—*Green label with "W7" logo*

Number	Title (A Side/B Side)	Yr	VG	VG+	NM
❑ WS 1801	In the Jungle, Babe	1970	3.75	7.50	15.00

—*Green label with "WB" logo*

Number	Title (A Side/B Side)	Yr	VG	VG+	NM
❑ WS 1864	Express Yourself	1970	3.75	7.50	15.00

Number	Title (A Side/B Side)	Yr	VG	VG+	NM
❑ WS 1904	You're So Beautiful	1971	3.75	7.50	15.00
❑ BS 2620	Rhythm and Poetry	1972	3.75	7.50	15.00

—*Green label with "WB" logo*

Number	Title (A Side/B Side)	Yr	VG	VG+	NM
❑ BS 2620	Rhythm and Poetry	1973	3.00	6.00	12.00

—*"Burbank" palm-trees logo*

WRIGHT, O.V.

45s

ABC

Number	Title (A Side/B Side)	Yr	VG	VG+	NM
❑ 12119	What More Can I Do (To Prove My Love to You)/Henpecked Man	1975	—	3.00	6.00
❑ 12154	Nobody But You/Slow and Easy	1976	—	3.00	6.00

BACK BEAT

Number	Title (A Side/B Side)	Yr	VG	VG+	NM
❑ 544	Don't Want to Sit Down/Can't Find True Love	1965	2.50	5.00	10.00
❑ 548	You're Gonna Make Me Cry/Monkey Dog	1965	2.50	5.00	10.00
❑ 551	I'm In Your Corner/Poor Boy	1965	2.50	5.00	10.00
❑ 558	Gone for Good/How Long Baby	1966	2.50	5.00	10.00
❑ 580	Eight Men, Four Women/Fed Up with the Blues	1967	2.00	4.00	8.00
❑ 583	Heartaches-Heartaches/Treasured Moments	1967	2.00	4.00	8.00
❑ 586	What About You/What Did You Tell This Girl of Mine	1967	2.00	4.00	8.00
❑ 591	Oh Baby Mine/Working Your Game	1968	2.00	4.00	8.00
❑ 597	I Want Everyone to Know/I'm Gonna Forget About You	1968	2.00	4.00	8.00
❑ 604	Missing You/This Must Be Real	1969	2.00	4.00	8.00
❑ 607	I'll Take Care of You/Why Not Give Me a Chance	1969	2.00	4.00	8.00
❑ 611	Love the Way You Love/Blowin' in the Wind	1970	2.00	4.00	8.00
❑ 615	Ace of Spade/Afflicted	1970	2.00	4.00	8.00
❑ 620	When You Took Your Love from Me/I Was Born All Over	1971	—	3.00	6.00
❑ 622	A Nickel and a Nail/Pledging My Love	1971	—	3.00	6.00
❑ 625	He Made Woman for Man/Don't Let My Baby Ride	1972	—	3.00	6.00
❑ 626	Drowning on Dry Land/I'm Gonna Forget About You	1973	—	3.00	6.00
❑ 628	I'd Rather Be (Blind, Cripple and Crazy)/Please Forgive Me	1973	—	3.00	6.00
❑ 631	I've Been Searching/I'm Going Home	1974	—	3.00	6.00
❑ 5103	I'm In Your Corner/Poor Boy	1974	—	3.00	6.00

GOLDWAX

Number	Title (A Side/B Side)	Yr	VG	VG+	NM
❑ 106	That's How Strong My Love Is/There Goes My Used to Be	1964	3.00	6.00	12.00

HI

Number	Title (A Side/B Side)	Yr	VG	VG+	NM
❑ 2315	Rhymes/Without You	1976	—	3.00	6.00
❑ 77501	Into Something (Can't Shake Loose)/The Time We Have	1977	—	3.00	6.00
❑ 77506	Precious, Precious/You Gotta Have Love	1977	—	3.00	6.00
❑ 78514	I Don't Do Windows/I Feel Love Growin'	1978	—	3.00	6.00
❑ 78521	No Easy Way to Say Goodbye/Bottom Line	1978	—	3.00	6.00
❑ 79531	We're Still Together/I Don't Know Why	1979	—	3.00	6.00

Albums

BACK BEAT

Number	Title (A Side/B Side)	Yr	VG	VG+	NM
❑ 61 [M]	If It's Only for Tonight	1965	25.00	50.00	100.00
❑ S-61 [S]	If It's Only for Tonight	1965	37.50	75.00	150.00
❑ 66	Eight Men, Four Women	1968	15.00	30.00	60.00
❑ 67	Nucleus of Soul	1969	15.00	30.00	60.00
❑ 70	A Nickel and a Nail and Ace of Spade	1971	15.00	30.00	60.00
❑ 72	Memphis Unlimited	1973	12.50	25.00	50.00

HI

Number	Title (A Side/B Side)	Yr	VG	VG+	NM
❑ 6001	Into Something	1977	6.25	12.50	25.00
❑ 6008	Bottom Line	1978	6.25	12.50	25.00
❑ 6011	We're Still Together	1979	6.25	12.50	25.00

WRIGHT, RITA

Later recorded as SYREETA.

45s

GORDY

Number	Title (A Side/B Side)	Yr	VG	VG+	NM
❑ 7064	I Can't Give Back the Love I Feel for You/Something on My Mind	1967	2.50	5.00	10.00

Number	Title (A Side/B Side)	Yr	VG	VG+	NM

X

XSCAPE
12-Inch Singles
LAFACE
| ❏ 4284 | Let's Do It Again (LP Version) (LP Instrumental) (Acappella) | 1997 | 2.50 | 5.00 | 10.00 |

SO SO DEF
❏ CAS 7228 [DJ]	Feels So Good (4 versions)	1995	2.50	5.00	10.00
❏ CAS 7360 [DJ]	Do You Want To (4 versions)	1995	2.50	5.00	10.00
❏ 44-77120	Just Kickin' It (Extended Remix) (Remix Instrumental) (Radio Edit) (Radio Edit Instrumental)/WSS Deez Nuts	1993	2.00	4.00	8.00
❏ 44-77408	Love on My Mind (6 versions)	1994	2.00	4.00	8.00
❏ 44-77920	Feels So Good (Untouchables Flava Remix) (So So Def Remix) (LP Version)/(Untouchables Remix) (So So Def Remix Instrumental) (A Cappella)	1995	2.50	5.00	10.00
❏ 44-78052	Do You Want To (5 versions)/Who Can I Run To	1995	2.50	5.00	10.00
❏ 44-79044	My Little Secret (5 versions)	1998	2.50	5.00	10.00

45s
COLUMBIA
| ❏ 38-77341 | Understanding/Just Kickin' It | 1993 | — | — | 3.00 |

—Small "So So Def" logo on Columbia label

| ❏ 38-77438 | Love on My Mind (LP Version)/(With Rap) | 1994 | — | — | 3.00 |

—Small "So So Def" logo on Columbia label

SO SO DEF
| ❏ 38-78788 | The Arms of the One Who Loves You/ (Instrumental) | 1998 | — | — | 3.00 |
| ❏ 38-79078 | Softest Place on Earth/My Little Secret | 1998 | — | — | 3.00 |

Albums
SO SO DEF
| ❏ C 57107 | Hummin' Comin' At Cha | 1993 | 3.00 | 6.00 | 12.00 |
| ❏ C 67022 | Off the Hook | 1995 | 3.00 | 6.00 | 12.00 |

XYMOX
12-Inch Singles
WING
❏ PRO 711-1 [DJ]	Obsession (Edit) (LP Version)/In a City	1989	3.00	6.00	12.00
❏ PRO 787-1 [DJ]	Blind Hearts (unknown versions)	1989	2.50	5.00	10.00
❏ PRO 950-1 [DJ]	Phoenix of My Heart (unknown versions)	1991	3.00	6.00	12.00
❏ 867321-1	At the End of the Day (Endless Day Mix) (7" Remix) (Hutchinson Remix) (Hutchinson Dub)/ Dream House	1991	2.50	5.00	10.00
❏ 868133-1	Phoenix of My Heart (3 versions)/Love Thy Neighbor	1991	3.00	6.00	12.00
❏ 871707-1	Obsession (Club Mix) (Edit)/Hitchhiker's Dance Guide	1989	2.50	5.00	10.00
❏ 873001-1	Imagination (3 versions)/Obsession (Club Mix)	1990	3.75	7.50	15.00
❏ 889633-1	Blind Hearts (2 versions)/Shame	1989	2.00	4.00	8.00

45s
WING
| ❏ 871707-7 | Obsession/(B-side unknown) | 1989 | — | 2.50 | 5.00 |

Albums
RELATIVITY
| ❏ EMC 8037 | The Clan of Xymox | 1985 | 6.25 | 12.50 | 25.00 |

WING
| ❏ 839233-1 | Twist of Shadows | 1989 | 3.00 | 6.00 | 12.00 |
| ❏ 848516-1 | Phoenix | 1991 | 3.00 | 6.00 | 12.00 |

XZIBIT
12-Inch Singles
INTERSCOPE
| ❏ INT8P-6549 [DJ] | 25 to Life (at least 5 versions) | 1999 | 5.00 | 10.00 | 20.00 |

—With Juvenile, Nature, Ja Rule and Reptile

LOUD
❏ 1968	X (Radio Edit) (Album Version) (Instrumental)/ (same on both sides)	2001	2.50	5.00	10.00
❏ 1997	Front 2 Back (Album Version) (Radio Version) (Instrumental)/Alkaholik (Album Version) (Instrumental)	2001	2.50	5.00	10.00
❏ RPROLP 4351	Year 2000 (Explicit Version) (Clean Version) (Instrumental) (Acapella)/(same on both sides)	2000	3.00	6.00	12.00
❏ RPROLP 4504	Front 2 Back (Rado Version) (Album Version) (Instrumental)/(same on both sides)	2001	5.00	10.00	20.00
❏ 44-79368	Year 2000 (Explicit Version) (Clean Version) (Instrumental) (Acapella)/(same on both sides)	2000	3.00	6.00	12.00

LOUD/RCA
| ❏ 64631 | Eyes May Shine (Radio Edit) (Album Version) (Instrumental) (Acapella) | 1996 | 2.00 | 4.00 | 8.00 |
| ❏ 65466 | 3 Card Molly (4 versions) | 1998 | 3.00 | 6.00 | 12.00 |

—Featuring Rass Kass and Saafir

| ❏ 65506 | What U See Is What U Get (3 versions?)/3 Card Molly | 1998 | 3.00 | 6.00 | 12.00 |
| ❏ 65522 | What U See Is What U Get (4 versions) | 1998 | 3.00 | 6.00 | 12.00 |

Albums
LOUD
| ❏ 1885 [(2)] | Restless | 2001 | 3.75 | 7.50 | 15.00 |

LOUD/RCA
| ❏ 66816-1 [(2)] | At the Speed of Life | 1996 | 3.75 | 7.50 | 15.00 |
| ❏ 67578 | 40 Dayz & 40 Nightz | 1998 | 3.75 | 7.50 | 15.00 |

Number	Title (A Side/B Side)	Yr	VG	VG+	NM

Y

YOUNG, ELDEE
Also see RAMSEY LEWIS; YOUNG-HOLT UNLIMITED.
Albums
ARGO
❏ LP-699 [M]	Just for Kicks	1962	3.75	7.50	15.00
❏ LPS-699 [S]	Just for Kicks	1962	5.00	10.00	20.00
❏ LP-1003 [M]	Eldee Young and Company	1962	5.00	10.00	20.00
❏ LPS-1003 [S]	Eldee Young and Company	1962	6.25	12.50	25.00

YOUNG, KATHY, AND THE INNOCENTS
Also see THE INNOCENTS.
45s
INDIGO
❏ 108	A Thousand Stars/Eddie My Darling	1960	7.50	15.00	30.00
❏ 115	Happy Birthday Blues/Someone to Love	1961	5.00	10.00	20.00
❏ 115 [PS]	Happy Birthday Blues/Someone to Love	1961	12.50	25.00	50.00
❏ 121	Our Parents Talked It Over/Just As Though You Were Here	1961	5.00	10.00	20.00
❏ 125	Magic Is the Night/Du Du'nt Du	1961	5.00	10.00	20.00
❏ 125 [PS]	Magic Is the Night/Du Du'nt Du	1961	12.50	25.00	50.00
❏ 137	Baby, Oh Baby/The Great Pretender	1961	5.00	10.00	20.00
❏ 141	Time/Dee Dee Di Oh	1962	5.00	10.00	20.00
❏ 146	Lonely Blue Nights/I'll Hang My Letters Out to Dry	1962	5.00	10.00	20.00
❏ 147	Send Her Away/Dream Awhile	1962	5.00	10.00	20.00

MONOGRAM
| ❏ 506 | Dreamboy/I'll Love That Man | 1962 | 5.00 | 10.00 | 20.00 |

PORT
| ❏ 3025 | A Thousand Stars/Eddie My Darling | 196? | — | 2.50 | 5.00 |

STARFIRE
| ❏ 112 | Sparkle and Shine/Please Love Me Forever | 1979 | — | 2.50 | 5.00 |

7-Inch Extended Plays
INDIGO
| ❏ 1001 | Sparkle and Shine/Eddie My Darling//Happy Birthday Blues/Angel on My Shoulder | 1961 | 50.00 | 100.00 | 200.00 |
| ❏ 1001 [PS] | Kathy Young | 1961 | 50.00 | 100.00 | 200.00 |

YOUNG-HOLT UNLIMITED
Also see ELDEE YOUNG.
45s
BRUNSWICK
| ❏ 55305 | Wack Wack/This Little Light of Mine | 1966 | 2.00 | 4.00 | 8.00 |

—As "The Young-Holt Trio"

| ❏ 55317 | Ain't There Something Money Can't Buy/Mellow Yellow | 1967 | 2.00 | 4.00 | 8.00 |

—As "The Young-Holt Trio"

| ❏ 55338 | The Beat Goes On/Doin' the Thing | 1967 | 2.00 | 4.00 | 8.00 |

—As "The Young-Holt Trio"

❏ 55356	Dig Her Walk/You Gimmie Thum	1967	2.00	4.00	8.00
❏ 55374	Soul Sister/Give It Up	1968	2.00	4.00	8.00
❏ 55391	Soulful Strut/Country Slicker Joe	1968	2.00	4.00	8.00
❏ 55400	Who's Making Love/Just Ain't No Love	1969	—	3.00	6.00
❏ 55410	Just a Melody/Young and Holtful	1969	—	3.00	6.00
❏ 55417	Straight Ahead/California Montage	1969	—	3.00	6.00
❏ 55420	Soulful Samba/Horoscope	1969	—	3.00	6.00

COTILLION
❏ 44092	Mellow Dreaming/Got to Get My Baby Back Home	1970	—	2.50	5.00
❏ 44111	Luv Bugg/Wah Wah Man	1971	—	2.50	5.00
❏ 44120	Hot Pants/I'll Be There	1971	—	2.50	5.00

PAULA
| ❏ 380 | Superfly/Give Me Your Love | 1973 | — | 2.50 | 5.00 |
| ❏ 382 | Could It Be I'm Falling in Love/HeyPancho | 1973 | — | 2.50 | 5.00 |

Albums
ATLANTIC
| ❏ SD 1634 | Oh Girl | 1973 | 3.00 | 6.00 | 12.00 |

BRUNSWICK
| ❏ BL 54121 [M] | Wack-Wack | 1966 | 5.00 | 10.00 | 20.00 |

—As "Young-Holt Trio"

| ❏ BL 54125 [M] | On Stage | 1967 | 5.00 | 10.00 | 20.00 |

—As "Young-Holt Trio"

| ❏ BL 54128 [M] | The Beat Goes On | 1967 | 7.50 | 15.00 | 30.00 |
| ❏ BL 754121 [S] | Wack-Wack | 1966 | 5.00 | 10.00 | 20.00 |

—As "Young-Holt Trio"

| ❏ BL 754125 [S] | On Stage | 1967 | 5.00 | 10.00 | 20.00 |

—As "Young-Holt Trio"

❏ BL 754128 [S]	The Beat Goes On	1967	5.00	10.00	20.00
❏ BL 754141	Funky But!	1968	5.00	10.00	20.00
❏ BL 754144	Soulful Strut	1968	3.75	7.50	15.00
❏ BL 754150	Just a Melody	1969	3.75	7.50	15.00

CADET
| ❏ LP-791 [M] | Feature Spot | 1967 | 7.50 | 15.00 | 30.00 |
| ❏ LPS-791 [S] | Feature Spot | 1967 | 5.00 | 10.00 | 20.00 |

—As "Eldee Young and Red Holt (of the Ramsey Lewis Trio)"

COTILLION
| ❏ SD 18001 | Mellow Dreamin' | 1971 | 3.00 | 6.00 | 12.00 |
| ❏ SD 18004 | Born Again | 1972 | 3.00 | 6.00 | 12.00 |

PAULA
| ❏ LPS-4002 | Super Fly | 1973 | 5.00 | 10.00 | 20.00 |

YOUNG RASCALS, THE
See THE RASCALS.

Number	Title (A Side/B Side)	Yr	VG	VG+	NM

Z

Z'LOOKE
12-Inch Singles
ORPHEUS

Number	Title (A Side/B Side)	Yr	VG	VG+	NM
❏ V-72300	Girl Danz with Me (4 versions)	1990	2.00	4.00	8.00
❏ V-72651	Lovesick (The Cure) (6 versions)	1989	—	3.00	6.00
❏ V-72655	Can U Read My Lips (4 versions)	1988	—	3.00	6.00
❏ V-72685	Gitchi U (6 versions)	1989	2.00	4.00	8.00

45s
ORPHEUS

Number	Title (A Side/B Side)	Yr	VG	VG+	NM
❏ B-72650	Lovesick (The Cure)/(Doctor's Groove)	1989	—	2.00	4.00
❏ B-72654	Can U Read My Lips/(Remix)	1988	—	2.00	4.00
❏ B-72678	Gitchi U/Take Away the Heartache	1989	—	2.00	4.00

Albums
ORPHEUS

Number	Title (A Side/B Side)	Yr	VG	VG+	NM
❏ D1-75600	Take U Back to My Place	1988	3.00	6.00	12.00

ZAGER, MICHAEL
12-Inch Singles
BANG

Number	Title (A Side/B Side)	Yr	VG	VG+	NM
❏ B 737 D	Do It with Feeling/This Is the Life	1978	2.00	4.00	8.00

—As "Michael Zager's Moon Band"; PEABO BRYSON appears on this record

CBS ASSOCIATED

Number	Title (A Side/B Side)	Yr	VG	VG+	NM
❏ 4Z9-05046	Shot in the Dark (6:56) (Breakdown Mix)	1984	2.00	4.00	8.00

COLUMBIA

Number	Title (A Side/B Side)	Yr	VG	VG+	NM
❏ AS 787 [DJ]	Don't Sneak on Me (4:54) (same on both sides)	1980	2.50	5.00	10.00

MOSAIC

Number	Title (A Side/B Side)	Yr	VG	VG+	NM
❏ 4Z9-05371	Like a Tiger (New York Mix) (Uptown Mix) (Bonus Beats) (Downtown Mix)	1985	2.00	4.00	8.00

—As "Michael Zager from ABC Funfit"

PRIVATE STOCK

Number	Title (A Side/B Side)	Yr	VG	VG+	NM
❏ PS 5104	Let's All Chant/Love Express	1978	2.00	4.00	8.00
❏ PS 5107	Music Fever/Freak	1978	2.00	4.00	8.00

45s
BANG

Number	Title (A Side/B Side)	Yr	VG	VG+	NM
❏ 720	Do It with Feeling/This Is the Life	1976	—	3.50	7.00

—As "Michael Zager's Moon Band"; PEABO BRYSON appears on this record

CBS ASSOCIATED

Number	Title (A Side/B Side)	Yr	VG	VG+	NM
❏ ZS4-04546	Shot in the Dark/(Instrumental)	1984	—	2.00	4.00

COLUMBIA

Number	Title (A Side/B Side)	Yr	VG	VG+	NM
❏ 1-11080	You Don't Know a Good Thing/Still Not Over	1979	—	2.50	5.00
❏ 1-11273	Don't Sneak on Me/Bring Me Love	1980	—	2.00	4.00

PRIVATE STOCK

Number	Title (A Side/B Side)	Yr	VG	VG+	NM
❏ 45,184	Let's All Chant/Love Express	1978	—	2.50	5.00
❏ 45,202	Soul to Soul/Freak	1978	—	2.50	5.00

Albums
COLUMBIA

Number	Title (A Side/B Side)	Yr	VG	VG+	NM
❏ JC 35771	Life's a Party	1979	2.50	5.00	10.00
❏ JC 36348	Zager	1980	2.50	5.00	10.00

PRIVATE STOCK

Number	Title (A Side/B Side)	Yr	VG	VG+	NM
❏ PS 7013	Let's All Chant	1978	2.50	5.00	10.00

ZAPP
12-Inch Singles
REPRISE

Number	Title (A Side/B Side)	Yr	VG	VG+	NM
❏ PRO-A-6596 [DJ]	Slow and Easy (Edit) (LP Version)	1993	3.00	6.00	12.00

—As "Zapp & Roger"

Number	Title (A Side/B Side)	Yr	VG	VG+	NM
❏ PRO-A-8418 [DJ]	Living for the City (Radio Edit) (LP Version) (Instrumental) (Acapella)	1996	2.50	5.00	10.00

—As "Roger & Zapp"

Number	Title (A Side/B Side)	Yr	VG	VG+	NM
❏ PRO-A-8496 [DJ]	Living for the City (8 versions)	1996	3.75	7.50	15.00

—As "Roger & Zapp"

Number	Title (A Side/B Side)	Yr	VG	VG+	NM
❏ 21298	Ooh Baby Baby (12" Version)/(LP Version) (Instrumental)	1989	2.00	4.00	8.00
❏ 21407	I Play the Talk Box (Radio Edit) (LP Version) (Extended Version) (Jake Mix) (Dub Mix)	1989	2.00	4.00	8.00
❏ 21743	Fire (4 versions)/Jake E. Stanstill	1990	3.00	6.00	12.00
❏ 40982	Mega Medley (Mega Fresh Mix) (With Bonus Beats)/I Want to Be Your Man	1993	2.50	5.00	10.00

—As "Zapp and Roger"

WARNER BROS.

Number	Title (A Side/B Side)	Yr	VG	VG+	NM
❏ PRO-A-2402 [DJ]	It Doesn't Really Matter/Ja Ready to Rock	1985	3.00	6.00	12.00
❏ 20140	I Can Make You Dance (8:21) (3:59)	1983	12.50	25.00	50.00

45s
REPRISE

Number	Title (A Side/B Side)	Yr	VG	VG+	NM
❏ 17510	Living for the City/(Instrumental)	1996	—	—	3.00

—As "Roger & Zapp"

Number	Title (A Side/B Side)	Yr	VG	VG+	NM
❏ 22849	Ooh Baby Baby/(Instrumental)	1989	—	—	3.00
❏ 22849 [PS]	Ooh Baby Baby/(Instrumental)	1989	—	2.50	5.00

WARNER BROS.

Number	Title (A Side/B Side)	Yr	VG	VG+	NM
❏ 28608	Radio People/Tut-Tut Jazz	1986	—	2.00	4.00
❏ 28719	Itchin' for Your Twitchin'/(Long Version)	1986	—	2.00	4.00
❏ 28805	Computer Love Part I/Part II	1985	—	2.00	4.00
❏ 28879	It Doesn't Really Matter/Make Me Feel Good	1985	—	2.50	5.00
❏ 29380	Spend My Whole Life/Play Some Blues	1984	—	2.50	5.00
❏ 29462	Heartbreaker (Part I)/(Part II)	1983	—	2.50	5.00
❏ 29553	I Can Make You Dance (Part I)/(Part II)	1983	—	2.50	5.00
❏ 29779	Do You Really Want an Answer?/Playin' Kind of Ruff	1983	—	2.50	5.00
❏ 29891	Doo Wa Ditty (Blow That Thing)/Come On	1982	—	2.50	5.00

Number	Title (A Side/B Side)	Yr	VG	VG+	NM
❏ 29961	Dance Floor (Part I)/(Part II)	1982	—	2.50	5.00
❏ 49534	More Bounce to the Ounce Part I/Part II	1980	—	3.00	6.00
❏ 49623	Be Alright — Part I/Part II	1980	—	2.50	5.00

Albums
REPRISE

Number	Title (A Side/B Side)	Yr	VG	VG+	NM
❏ 25807	Zapp V (Vibe)	1989	3.00	6.00	12.00

WARNER BROS.

Number	Title (A Side/B Side)	Yr	VG	VG+	NM
❏ BSK 3463	Zapp	1980	2.50	5.00	10.00
❏ 23583	Zapp II	1982	2.50	5.00	10.00
❏ 23875	Zapp III	1983	2.50	5.00	10.00
❏ 25327	The New Zapp IV U	1985	2.00	4.00	8.00

ZHANE
12-Inch Singles
EPIC/FLAVOR UNIT

Number	Title (A Side/B Side)	Yr	VG	VG+	NM
❏ 49-77121	Hey Mr. D.J. (Maurice's Club Mix) (Maurice's Club Mix Without Rap) (Original Mix)/(Mo's Hey D.J. Work This Dub) (UBQ's Underground Dub) (Morapella)	1993	2.50	5.00	10.00

ILLTOWN

Number	Title (A Side/B Side)	Yr	VG	VG+	NM
❏ 37463 1217 1	Vibe (4 versions?)	1994	2.50	5.00	10.00
❏ 37463 2024 1	Request Line (Extended) (Instrumental) (Acapella)/(Radio Edit) (LP Version) (Pretty Pella)	1997	3.00	6.00	12.00
❏ 37463 2041 1	Request Line (Fitch Bros. in a Low Rider Mix) (Fitch Bros. Floor Filler Mix) (Nitebreed's Got You on Hold Mix) (Nitebreed's Northface Killa Dub)	1997	3.75	7.50	15.00
❏ 37463 2050 1	Crush (LP Version) (Instrumental) (Acappella)/ Saturday Night (Radio Edit) (LP Version) (Full Version with No Rap)	1997	3.00	6.00	12.00
❏ 37463 4854 1	Sending My Love (unknown versions)	1994	3.00	6.00	12.00
❏ 37463 4862 1	Vibe (unknown versions)	1994	3.00	6.00	12.00
❏ 860615-1	Request Line (6 versions)	1997	3.00	6.00	12.00
❏ 860625-1	Request Line (unknown versions)	1997	2.50	5.00	10.00
❏ 860641-1	Crush (LP Version) (Instrumental)/Saturday Night (LP Version) (Instrumental) (Rap Intro)	1997	3.00	6.00	12.00
❏ 860643-1	Request Line (unknown versions)	1997	3.00	6.00	12.00

MOTOWN

Number	Title (A Side/B Side)	Yr	VG	VG+	NM
❏ 37463 1141-1	Groove Thang (unknown versions)	1993	3.75	7.50	15.00
❏ 37463 1150 1	Groove Thang (unknown versions)	1994	3.75	7.50	15.00
❏ 37463 4848 1	Groove Thang (unknown versions)	1993	3.00	6.00	12.00

ZULEMA
12-Inch Singles
LEJOINT

Number	Title (A Side/B Side)	Yr	VG	VG+	NM
❏ 3012	Change (7:34)/Hanging On to a Memory	1978	2.00	4.00	8.00

45s
LEJOINT

Number	Title (A Side/B Side)	Yr	VG	VG+	NM
❏ 5N-34001	Change/Hanging On to a Memory	1978	—	2.50	5.00
❏ 5N-34002	I'm Not Dreaming/(B-side unknown)	1979	—	2.50	5.00

RCA

Number	Title (A Side/B Side)	Yr	VG	VG+	NM
❏ PB-10815	Hungry for Your Love/Suddenly There Was You	1976	—	2.50	5.00

RCA VICTOR

Number	Title (A Side/B Side)	Yr	VG	VG+	NM
❏ PB-10116	Wanna Be Where You Are/No Time Next Time	1974	—	2.50	5.00
❏ PB-10246	Standing in the Back Row of Your Heart/Hail, Hail America	1975	—	2.50	5.00
❏ PB-10406	Just Look What You've Done/Your Love Has Put Me in Jeopardy	1975	—	2.50	5.00
❏ PB-10541	Half of Your Heart/What Kind of Person Are You	1976	—	2.50	5.00
❏ PB-10704	Pity for the Children/I Love You Baby	1976	—	2.50	5.00

SUSSEX

Number	Title (A Side/B Side)	Yr	VG	VG+	NM
❏ 242	This Child of Mine/Don't Be Afraid	1972	—	3.00	6.00
❏ 504	Telling the World Good-Bye (Try to Find Yourself)/Tree	1973	—	2.50	5.00

Albums
LEJOINT

Number	Title (A Side/B Side)	Yr	VG	VG+	NM
❏ LEJ 17000	Z-Licious	1978	3.75	7.50	15.00

RCA VICTOR

Number	Title (A Side/B Side)	Yr	VG	VG+	NM
❏ APL1-0819	Zulema	1975	3.75	7.50	15.00
❏ APL1-1152	R.S.V.P.	1975	3.75	7.50	15.00
❏ APL1-1423	Suddenly There Was You	1976	3.75	7.50	15.00

SUSSEX

Number	Title (A Side/B Side)	Yr	VG	VG+	NM
❏ SXBS 7015	Zulema	1972	3.75	7.50	15.00
❏ SRA 8029	Ms. Z.	1973	3.75	7.50	15.00

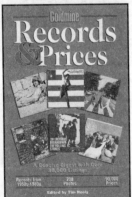

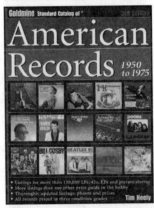